Handbook of Jig and Fixture Design

Second Edition

William E. Boyes
Editor

Ramon Bakerjian
Staff Editor

Edited from
Handbook of Fixture Design

First Edition

Frank W. White,
Editor-in-Chief

John M. Holt, Jr.,
Associate Editor

Handbook of Jig and Fixture Design

ISBN No. 0-87263-365-9

Library of Congress Catalog No. 89-62218

Society of Manufacturing Engineers (SME)

Copyright© 1989 by Society of Manufacturing Engineers,
One SME Drive, P.O. Box 930, Dearborn, Michigan 48121

First edition published in 1962 by McGraw-Hill Book Co. in cooperation with SME under earlier Society name, American Society of Tool Engineers (ASTE), and under title *Handbook of Fixture Design*.

Printed in the United States of America.

Thanks to Gary Price and Graphis 6 Inc.

PREFACE

This book is based on the Volume, *Handbook of Fixture Design* (1962), by the Society of Manufacturing Engineers. Chapters have been expanded and updated, and entirely new subjects and technologies introduced.

The purpose of this book is to supply student and professional tool and gage designers with generally accepted procedures for designing a jig or fixture, or adapting a commercially available workholding device to hold a workpiece during machining, assembly, or inspection.

In addition, specific examples of successful solutions to many workholding problems have been included to provide the designer with ideas that can be adapted to his or her particular problem.

Chapters 1 through 4 cover the general steps necessary to provide economical and efficient tooling for today's expanding and competitive manufacturing industry. These steps include predesign analysis, locating, supporting, clamping, positions, and the design of bodies for workholding devices.

Chapter 5 is a new chapter dealing with tooling for Numerical Control (NC).

Chapter 6 is also new and is included to provide the tool designer with a basic understanding of Geometric Dimensioning and Tolerancing (GD&T).

Chapters 7 through 13 provide more specific information regarding the design of jigs and fixtures for the various machining operations such as: milling, drilling, reaming, turning, boring, grinding, sawing, broaching, planing, shaping, and slotting.

Chapter 14 is another new chapter on tooling for Flexible Manufacturing Systems (FMSs).

Chapters 15 and 16 cover tooling for assembly and inspection respectively.

I would like to extend my gratitude to the many machine, tooling, and component manufacturers who furnished materials, photographs, and advice.

Finally, my thanks to the publications development staff at SME.

William E. Boyes

ABOUT THE EDITOR

William E. Boyes retired as Section Manager of the Metrology and Quality Control Engineering Departments of Mack Trucks, Incorporated, Powertrain Division, Hagerstown, Maryland, where he worked in various quality control positions for over 20 years.

Mr. Boyes is both a Certified Manufacturing Engineer and a Registered Professional Engineer. Prior to his retirement, he was an active member of many engineering societies and associations including the American Society of Quality Control, the Precision Measurements Association, the American Society for Non-destructive Testing, and the American Defense Preparedness Association. Mr. Boyes was also a member delegate to the National Conference of Standards Laboratories and the Mack Trucks representative to GIDEP (Government-Industry Data Exchange Program).

An SME member since 1958, Mr. Boyes has served on SME's Tool Engineering Council in many capacities. He was chairman of the council from 1974 to 1978 and prior to that served as Chairman of its Gage Division. Mr. Boyes is editor of the Manufacturing Update Series book, *Jigs and Fixtures* (1982). He is also the editor of the book, *Low-cost Jigs, Fixtures and Gages for Limited Production* (1986).

LIST OF CONTRIBUTORS TO THE FIRST EDITION *

Frederic N. Abel, *Tool Designer, Universal Engineering Corporation, Cedar Rapids, IA*
Edwin A. Aldous, *Sales Engineer, Cincinnati Churchill, Ltd., Windsor, Ontario, Canada*
John G. Anderson, *Engineer, Square D Company, Cedar Rapids, IA*
Robert Arva, *Industrial Engineer, AMP, Inc., Harrisburg, PA*
Thomas Atkins, *Safety Engineer, Ford Motor Company of Canada, Windsor, Ontario, Canada*
James W. Barlow, *Tool Designer, Kelsey Wheel, Windsor, Ontario, Canada*
Isaac Barsky, *Methods Engineer, Ford Motor Company of Canada, Windsor, Ontario, Canada*
A. G. Baumgartner, *Sales Manager, The Cincinnati Shaper Company, Cincinnati, OH*
Joseph Benedict, *Production Tooling Engineer, DoALL Company, Des Plaines, IL*
Walter D. Bristow, *Tool Designer, Caterpillar Tractor Company, Peoria, IL*
E. Cairelli, *Tool Engineer, Wilson-Jones Company, Chicago, IL*
Edmond E. Canfield, *Toolmaker, Hyster Company, Peoria, IL*
Robert F. Carbrey, *President, Valley Engineering Company, Binghamton, NY*
Walter Fischbacher, *Chief Tool Engineer, LeTourneau-Westinghouse Company, Peoria, IL*
Donald Frantz, *Tool Designer, Caterpillar Tractor Company, Peoria, IL*
Eleonora Freeman, *Tool Designer, General Electric Company, Johnson City, NY*
Gunter K. Gersbach, *Staff Engineer, Caterpillar Tractor Company, Peoria, IL*
James F. Goodall, *Industrial Engineer, Collins Radio Company, Cedar Rapids, IA*
Otto E. Gunthner, *Tool Design Supervisor, Caterpillar Tractor Company Peoria, IL*
Kendall W. Hamlin, *Mechanical Engineering Dept., State University of Iowa, Iowa City, IA*
J. Nelson Harris, *Chief Tool Engineer, New Holland Machine Company, New Holland, PA*
Harold J. Hartlieb, *Sales Engineer, Precision Metals Div., Hamilton Watch Company, Lancaster, PA*
George Heindel, *Tool Engineer, York Div., Borg-Warner Corporation, York, PA*
E. C. Helmke, *Chief Engineer, Gisholt Machine Company, Madison WI*
Norman E. Hinkel, *Tool Designer, Square D Company, Cedar Rapids, IA*
Carl A. Holmer, *Chief Tool Designer, Caterpillar Tractor Company, Peoria, IL*
Graham Jones, *Senior Tool Designer, Ford Motor Company of Canada, Windsor, Ontario, Canada*
Joseph I. Karash, *Corporate Staff, Manufacturing Engineer, Reliance Electric & Engineering Company, Cleveland, OH*
Stephan A. Konz, *Instructor, Dept. of Mechanical Engineering, University of Illinois, Urbana, IL*
Robert L. Kristufek, *Assistant Head Quality Control, Borg-Beck Div., Borg-Warner Corporation, Chicago, IL*
Barry Krumeich, *Tool Designer, IBM, Owego, NY*
Orin E. Lillie, *Tool Analyst, IBM, Owego, NY*
Robert A. Lubbock, *Tool Designer, Universal Engineering, Cedar Rapids, IA*
James. E. Lynch, *Process Engineer, AMP, Inc., Harrisburg, PA*
Mario Martellotti, *Development Engineer, Cincinnati Milling Machine Company, Cincinnati, OH*
William S. Mazar, *Chief Tool Engineer, Link Div., General Precision, Inc., Binghamton, NY*
Robert W. Newton, *Associate Engineer, IBM, Owego, NY*

* At the time the first edition was published

Gerald H. Ohrt, *Tool Designer, Caterpillar Tractor Company, Chillicothe, IL*
Paul E. Orr, *Plant Engineer, Electroline Manufacturing Company, Windsor, Ontario, Canada*
David E. Ostergaard, *Proprietor, Chief Engineer, Ostergaard Company, Park Ridge, IL*
Walter J. Peters, *Tool and Die Designer, Caterpillar Tractor Company, Peoria, IL*
Howard Poland, *Tool Design Supervisor, LeTourneau-Westinghouse Company, Peoria, IL*
Richard Poultney, *Process Supervisor, Ford Motor Company of Canada, Windsor, Ontario, Canada*
Robert J. Quilici, *Design Section Leader, Scully-Jones and Company, Chicago, IL*
Ira L. Rabourn, *Tool Engineer, Square D Company, Cedar Rapids, IA*
W. Stanley Rice, *Tool Engineer, Chrysler Corporation of Canada, Windsor, Ontario, Canada*
Michael A. Romano, *Chief Tool Engineer, Craft Manufacturing Company, North Chicago, IL*
John Sepanek, *Chief Engineer, Speed-O-Print Corporation, Chicago, IL*
Ludwig G. Schlappner, *Chief Tool Designer, Mack Trucks, Inc. Plainfield, NJ*
George H. Sheppard, *Director of Research, The DoALL Company, Des Plaines, IL*
Stanley J. Snorek, *Dept. Chief, Tool Design, Western Electric Company, Inc., Chicago, IL*
Richard C. Spoor, *Tool Engineer, Linde Company, Div. Union Carbide, Indianapolis, IN*
Kenneth E. Starr, *Manufacturing Development, Caterpillar Tractor Company, Inc., Peoria, IL*
E.T. Swenson, *Tool Design Supervisor, Western Electric Company, Inc., Chicago, IL*
Gordon Way, *Tool Engineer, Chrysler Corporation of Canada, Windsor, Ontario, Canada*
James C. Wilson, *Chief Tool Designer, Universal Instruments Corporation, Binghamton, NY*
Leslie B. Wilson, *Tool Designer, Caterpillar Tractor Company, Peoria, IL*
Allen I. Young, *Tool Engineer, Collins Radio Company, Cedar Rapids, IA*

INTRODUCTION

This book deals primarily with the design and application of locating and workholding devices that are used to accurately position, support, and hold a workpiece during a machining, assembly, inspection, or related operation. Those devices are known as *fixtures*. Also covered are devices which provide additional guidance to the cutting tool. Those devices are known as *jigs*.

In this book, jigs and fixtures will be known collectively as fixtures.

Fixtures are usually classified by the type of operation using the fixture (for example, grinding fixture, milling fixture, assembly fixture, inspection fixture).

Jigs are mainly used for drilling, boring, tapping, and related operations. Sometimes they are named by the operation they perform, but usually they are referred to according to their method of construction. Some of the jigs that will be discussed in this book include template drill jigs (flat plate, circular, and nesting), plate jigs (open, table, and sandwich), universal or pump jigs (regular and cross-hole), leaf jigs, channel jigs, and tumble box jigs.

The term *gage* in this book refers to a device placed onto or into a workpiece to determine whether or not a workpiece is within specification limits. Fixed functional gages, such as plug gages, thread gages, and snap gages are named because of their shape or form. Other gages, which are more specialized, are usually named for the characteristic that they are used to check (for example, length gages, depth gages, width gages). If an indicator is added to the gage to permit actual measurements to be taken, the gage is usually further referred to as a dial or indicating type gage (for example, dial depth gage, indicating length gage). Whenever it is necessary to place the workpiece into a gaging device to permit inspection of the workpiece, the gaging device is usually referred to as an *inspection fixture*. Jigs, fixtures, and other workpiece locating, clamping, and indicating equipment will be collectively referred to as *tooling*.

Cutting tool design, which is a closely related but separate branch of tool design, is covered in this book only to the extent that it directly applies to the design of a jig or a fixture, that is, cutter material, size and configuration, chip control, and cutting forces.

The design of forming equipment used in the production of sheet metal parts, extrusions, forgings, castings, and other formed parts is not covered.

A NOTE ON METRICATION

In some cases (particularly Figures and Tables) in this book the numerical values listed are only in the english system. If you wish to use an appropriate metric value in its place (or convert from metric to english), the following conversion factors are listed below.

Multiply	by	To get
inches	25.4	millimeters
millimeters	0.039	inches
in.-lbf	0.113	newton-meter (N·m)
newton-meter (N·m)	8.851	in.-lbf
lbf	4.448	newton (N)
newton (N)	0.225	lbf
psi	6.895×10^3	pascal (P)
pascal (P)	1.450×10^{-4}	psi
ft-lb	1.285×10^{-3}	Btu
Btu	778.26	ft-lb

The reader will notice that metrication was not performed for either diameters and radiuses or for tolerances. There are English standard diameters which do not have direct metric equivalents, so to be consistent (and keep the reader from trying to second-guess metric equivalents), metrication was not performed on diameters and radiuses.

In the case of tolerancing, the reader may choose from two methods put forth in ASTM Standard E 380-1989, page 247, paragraph 4.5.1. It is reproduced here courtesy of ASTM. The standard states that there are two methods for converting toleranced dimensions from english to metric: Method A, where rounding is done to values *nearest* to each limit, and Method B, where rounding is performed to values always *inside* the limits.

4.5.1 *General*—The number of decimal places given in Table 9 for rounding converted toleranced dimensions relates the degree of accuracy to the size of the tolerances specified. Two methods of using Table 9 are given: Method A, which rounds to values nearest to each limit, and Method B, which rounds to values always inside the limits.

In Method A, rounding is effected to the nearest rounded value of the limit, so that, on the average, the converted tolerances remain statistically identical with the original tolerances. The limits converted by this method, where acceptable for interchangeability, serve as a basis for inspection.

In Method B, rounding is done systematically *toward the interior* of the tolerance zone so that the converted tolerances are never larger than the original tolerances. This method must be employed when the original limits have to be respected absolutely, in particular, when components made to converted limits are to be inspected by means of original gages.

Method A—The use of this method ensures that even in the most unfavorable cases neither of the two original limits will be changed by more than 5% of the value of the tolerance. Proceed as follows:

(*a*) Calculate the maximum and minimum limits in inches.

(*b*) Convert the corresponding two values exactly into millimetres by means of the conversion factor 1 in. = 25.4 mm.

(*c*) Round the results obtained to the nearest rounded value as indicated in Table 9, depending on the original tolerance in inches, that is, on the difference between the two limits in inches.

Method B—This method must be employed when the original limits may not be violated, for instance, certain critical mating parts. In extreme cases, this method may increase the lower limit a maximum of 10% of the tolerance and decrease the upper limit a maximum of 10% of the tolerance.

(*a*) Proceed as in Method A step (*a*).

TABLE 9 Rounding Tolerances Inches to Millimetres

Original Tolerance, inches		Fineness of Rounding,
at lease	less than	mm
0.000 04	0.000 4	0.0001
0.000 4	0.004	0.001
0.004	0.04	0.01
0.04	0.4	0.1
0.4		1

(*b*) Proceed as in Method A step (*b*).

(*c*) Round each limit toward the interior of the tolerance, that is, to the next lower value for the upper limit and to the next higher value for the lower limit.[8]

Examples:

A dimension is expressed in inches as	1.950 ±0.016
The limits are	1.934 and 1.966
Conversion of the two limits into millimetres gives	49.1236 and 49.9364

Method A—The tolerance equals 0.032 in. and thus lies between 0.004 and 0.04 in. (see Table 9). Rounding these values to the nearest 0.01 mm, the values in millimetres to be employed for these two limits are . . . . .   49.12 and 49.94

Method B—Rounding toward the interior of the tolerance, millimetre values for these two limits are . . . .   49.13 and 49.93

This reduces the tolerance to 0.80 instead of 0.82 mm given by Method A.

4.5.2 *Special Method for Dimensions with Plus and Minus Deviations*—In order to avoid accumulation of rounding errors, the two limits of size normally are converted separately: thus, they must first be calculated if the dimension consists of a basic size and two deviations. However (except when Method B is specified) as an alternative, the basic size may be converted to the nearest rounded value and each of the deviations

---

[8] If the digits to be rounded are zeros, the retained digits remain unchanged.

converted toward the interior of the tolerance. This method, which sometimes makes conversion easier, gives the same maximum guarantee of accuracy as Method A, but usually results in smaller converted tolerances.

4.5.3 *Special Methods for Limitation Imposed by Accuracy of Measurements*—If the increment of rounding for the tolerances given in Table 9 is too small for the available accuracy of measurement, limits that are acceptable for interchangeability must be determined separately for the dimensions. For example, where accuracy of measurement is limited to 0.001 mm, study shows that values converted from 1.0000 ±0.0005 in can be rounded to 25.413 and 25.387 mm instead of 25.4127 and 25.3873 mm with little disadvantage, since neither of the two original limits is exceeded by more than 1.2% of the tolerance.

4.5.4 *Positional Tolerance*—If the dimensioning consists solely of a positional tolerance around a point defined by a nontoleranced basic dimension, the basic dimension must be converted to the nearest rounded value and the positional variation (radius) separately converted by rounding downward.

CONTENTS

CHAPTER 1
PREDESIGN ANALYSIS AND FIXTURE-DESIGN PROCEDURE

Jigs and fixtures are not mainly designed on the drawing board. While the details of a design are developed as drafting proceeds, its main features will have been conceived in the designer's mind before he or she started sketches and working drawings.

The tool designer's responsibility is to recommend and design tooling that will consistently, expeditiously, and safely produce a part or product that meets all requirements at the lowest possible cost.

A successful fixture design is the result of the designer's ability to analyze all information and conditions which are in any way pertinent to a given manufacturing operation and to incorporate design features that offset or eliminate all difficulties or problems associated with the operations.

If a fixture fails, it is either because of a faulty analysis or because an analysis, substantially correct throughout, was followed by a fixture design that did not overcome the problems and difficulties clearly shown by the analysis.

Nonhomogeneous strip or sheet stock, irregular workpieces, such as castings or forgings, or workpieces having variations in size, properties, etc., can be a main cause of improper functioning of a fixture. The characteristics and properties of the workpiece are known at the outset of fixture planning; therefore all possible non-uniformities and variations in a work material will have to be considered in its analysis as a basis for subsequent decisions in planning the fixture as a whole, as well as its details.

The main concern of this section is with procedures for tool designers to follow in analyzing and assessing all conditions which can influence, to any degree, the design of a fixture.

Of necessity, all tool designers conduct some form of analysis when confronted with a tool-design problem. A systematic analytical approach, consisting of a procedure in a certain chronological order presented in written form, may help the beginner or improve the experienced designer's method.

It is found desirable in design practice to consistently follow a chronological analytical pattern, because each phase of the analysis is dependent upon or influenced by preceding phases, as are design decisions made during each phase.

There is no infallible procedure that can be applied to any design problem and that, on being compared to all variables found in checklists and questions, will automatically ensure the conception of a perfect or nearly perfect design of a tool. There is no formula in which the fixture designer can insert values and variables associated with the five major phases of design (see Fig. 1-1) and similarly evolve perfection in the design of a fixture.

It is not to be inferred that the outlined approach to and suggested procedure for designing are unique or error-proof. There are many capable and experienced designers who may desire to start planning by first considering machine and equipment characteristics

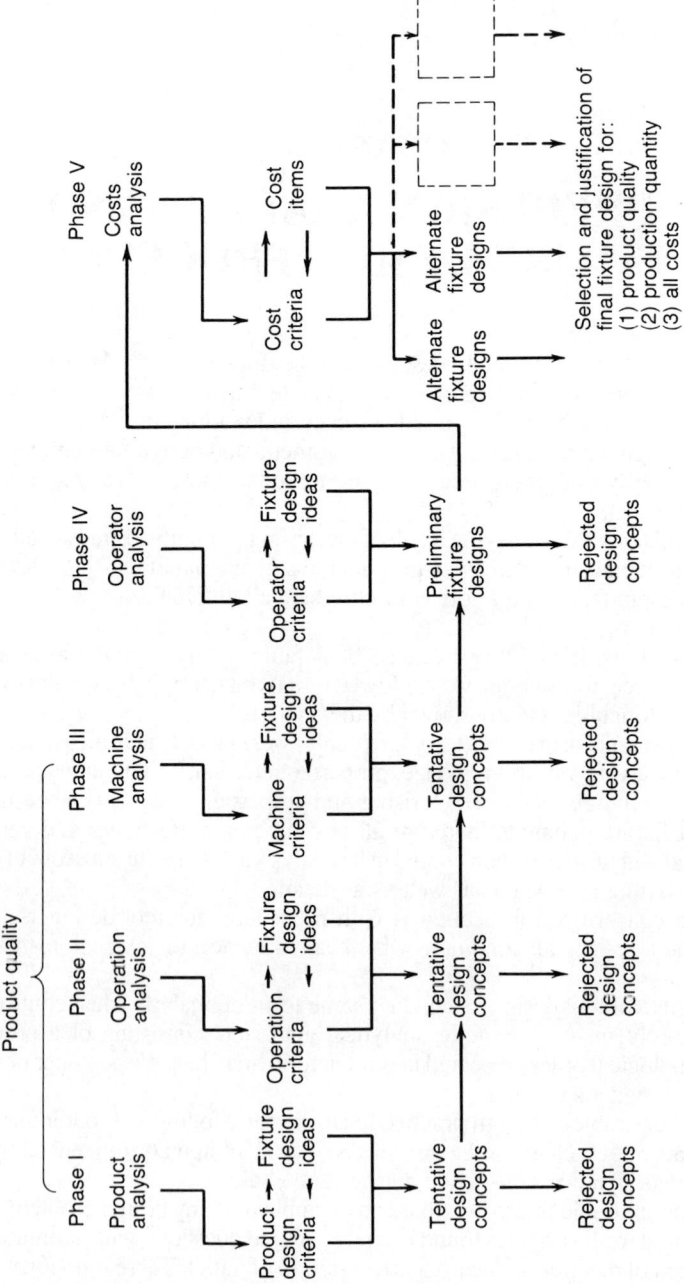

Fig. 1-1 Dependent flow of analytic design criteria, idea, and concept variables.

(Phase III, Fig. 1-1). There is no problem with this attitude and action, since all the many variables relating to the five phases are not entirely independent. Major decisions are not always final; and since later considerations may affect earlier decisions, some steps in the procedure may have to be retraced and previous decisions reevaluated. It is logical to start design planning with Phase I, because the quality of the product, as specified by the product designer, is considered during this phase.

PREDESIGN CHECKLISTS

Checklists (Tables 1-1 thru 1-3) are included to provide the tool designer with a list of variables to consider in the combinations recognized during the predesign analysis and fixture design procedure. The designer must also estimate their effect on the fixture design considerations listed in Table 1-4. These, or similar checklists are suitable for almost all products requiring machining, assembly, or inspection operations.

DESIGN PROCEDURE

A systematic and orderly procedure for jig and fixture design consists of five major phases or steps (see Fig. 1-1):

First Phase—Product Analysis. Few tool designers can change the specifications of a product (or workpiece), and since the fixture must ensure that the specifications are met, an examination of the product can be the first order of business for the designer. An examination of the product, Phase I, is an analysis, based upon certain criteria which suggests fixture design ideas (see Table 1-1). Some of these ideas and concepts are immediately rejected;

TABLE 1-1
Product Analysis Criteria for Fixture Predesign (Phase I)

PROPERTIES	GEOMETRY
1. Conductivity (thermal)	1. Combined shapes
2. Durability	2. Conical
3. Hardness	3. Cylindrical
4. Machinability	4. Flat
5. Resistance (electrical)	*a.* Circular
6. Rigidity	*b.* Rectangular
7. Strength	*c.* Irregular
8. Weight	5. Pyramidal
a. Amount	6. Spherical
b. Distribution (c.g.)	7. Trapezoidal

TYPE	SPECIFICATIONS (holes, bosses, surfaces, etc.)
1. Bar stock	
2. Casting	1. Form characteristics
3. Components	2. Locations
4. Forging	3. Numbers
5. Preformed stock	4. Position characteristics
6. Stamping	5. Sizes
7. Other	6. Surface conditions
	7. Other

MATERIAL

1. Ferrous
2. Nonferrous
3. Nonmetallic

others will be rejected during the first four phases of the procedures; while the other remaining fixture ideas and designs will survive the analyses and tests by the designer as one or more of the finalized and justified designs.

Examination of product (workpiece) blueprints and specifications from Product Engineering provides the tool designer with the rough and finished workpiece dimensions, metallurgical or nonmetallic properties, and any specialized treatment required.

Second Phase—Operation Analysis. This phase examines the operations to be performed (see Table 1-2). The information is usually provided by the Manufacturing Engineering Department on process sheets. Analysis of the specified operations provides the tool

TABLE 1-2
Operation Analysis Criteria for Fixture Predesign (Phase II)

MACHINING OPERATIONS

1. Boring
2. Broaching
3. Brushing
4. Counterboring
5. Countersinking
6. Cutoff
7. Deburring
8. Drilling
9. Gear finishing
   a. Grinding
   b. Honing
   c. Lapping
   d. Rolling
   e. Shaving
10. Gear and spline
   a. Bevel
   b. Broaching
   c. G-TRAC
   d. Hobbing
   e. Milling
   f. Rolling
   g. Shaping
11. Grinding
   a. Abrasive belt
   b. Center hole
   c. Cylindrical
   d. Jig
   e. Surface
12. Honing
13. Lapping
14. Manual
15. Milling
16. Multifunction
17. Nontraditional
18. Planing
19. Polishing
20. Reaming
21. Sawing
   a. Band
   b. Circular
   c. Hack
22. Shaping
23. Slotting
24. Spotfacing
25. Threading
   a. Chasing
   b. Grinding
   c. Milling
   d. Rolling
   e. Single point
   f. Tapping
26. Turning
27. Other

ASSEMBLY OPERATIONS

1. Adhesive joining
2. Brazing
3. Eyelet installation
4. Fastener-spec. purpose
5. Injected metal
6. Pinning
7. Pressing
8. Retaining ring installation
9. Riveting
10. Seal and gasket
11. Shrink and expansion fit
12. Soldering
13. Staking
14. Stapling
15. Stitching
16. Tab-bending
17. Threaded fastener
   a. Bolts
   b. Inserts
   c. Screws
   d. Special
18. Welding
19. Other

TABLE 1-2 *(continued)*

INSPECTION OPERATIONS

1. Balance
2. Geometrics
3. Leak testing
4. Linear dimensions

5. Mechanical testing
6. Nondestructive testing
7. Surface conditions
8. Other

MISCELLANEOUS OPERATIONS

1. Cooling of plastic parts
2. Foundry
3. Heat treatment

4. Painting (masks)
5. Plating
6. Other

NUMBER AND ORDER OF OPERATIONS

A. SINGLE **B. MULTIPLE—SEQUENTIAL** **C. MULTIPLE—SIMULTANEOUS**

designer with in-process dimensions and the type, distribution, direction, and amount of machining, or other forces, required to complete the operation. For some assembly operations, such as welding, the analysis includes considerations of heat and electricity.

Third Phase—Machine Analysis. Machine Analysis is usually performed jointly with Operation Analysis because of their mutual influence (see Table 1-3).

TABLE 1-3
Machine and Equipment Analysis Criteria for Fixture Predesign (Phase III)

MACHINING EQUIPMENT

1. Abrasive belt
2. Abrasive cutoff
3. Bevel gear cutting
4. Bevel gear grinding
5. Boring type (vertical, etc.)
6. Broaching type (surface, etc.)
7. Brushing
8. Deburring
9. Drilling type (radial, etc.)
10. Gear finishing
    a. Grinding
    b. Honing
    c. Lapping
    d. Rolling
    e. Shaving
11. Grinding type (surface, etc.)
12. Honing
13. Lapping
14. Lathe
15. Milling type (universal, etc.)
16. Multifunction
    a. Center drill and facing
    b. Chucking
    c. Headchanging
    d. Horizontal boring
    e. Machining center
    f. Multiple-spindle
       auto. bar and chuck

g. Multi-spindle vert. automatic
h. Single spindle automatic lathe
i. Single spindle automatic screw
j. Turret lathe
k. Swiss automatic screw
l. Vertical boring
17. Nontraditional
    a. Chemical
    b. Electrical
    c. Mechanical
    d. Thermal
    e. Other
18. Planing
19. Polishing
20. Sawing type (band, etc.)
21. Spline/Gear
    a. Broaching
    b. G-TRAC
    c. Hobbing
    d. Milling
    e. Rolling
    f. Shaping
22. Shaping type
23. Tapping type (vertical, etc.)
24. Thread grinding
25. Thread milling
26. Thread rolling

TABLE 1-3 *(continued)*

ASSEMBLY EQUIPMENT

1. Adhesive joining
2. Brazing type (induction, etc.)
3. Eyelet
4. Injected metal
5. Pinning
6. Pressing
7. Retaining ring
8. Riveting
9. Seal and gasket installation
10. Shrink and expansion
11. Soldering type
    (conduction, etc.)
12. Staking
13. Stapling
14. Stitching
15. Tab-bending
16. Threaded fasteners
    a. Bolts
    b. Inserts
    c. Screws
    d. Special
17. Welding type (arc, etc.)

INSPECTION EQUIPMENT

1. Angle measurement
2. Balancing
3. Coordinate measuring machine
4. Direct measuring
    (micrometers, etc.)
5. Fixed functional gages
    (plug gages, etc.)
6. Gage blocks
7. Gear and spline measuring
8. Hardness testing (Brinell, etc.)
9. Indicating gages
10. In-process gaging
11. Laser devices
12. Machine vision
13. Nondestructive
    (ultrasonic, etc.)
14. Optical comparators
15. Optical instruments
    (borescopes, etc.)
16. Overlay templates
17. Robotic systems
18. Special fixtures
19. Surface plate equipment
    (angle irons, etc.)
20. Surface texture
21. Thread measurement

MISCELLANEOUS EQUIPMENT

1. Foundry operation
2. Heat treating
3. Painting
4. Peening
5. Plating
6. Other

This phase examines the machine and equipment assigned to perform the operation. This information is also usually provided by the Manufacturing Engineering Department on process sheets.

Analysis of this material usually provides the tool designer with the actual machine and/or equipment assigned to perform the operation, along with information regarding machine capacity, production rates, handling equipment, etc. For material removal operations it also provides speeds and feeds, cutting tool information, cooling facilities, stroke, shuttle travel, and other machine-related information.

During the second and third phase, some of the design concepts tentatively proposed and based exclusively on the product analysis are eliminated. Those which are retained are subject to decisions that are wholly dependent upon operation criteria (as they affect fixture design) unique to (1) the type of operation, (2) the sequence of operations, and (3) specific machine characteristics (bed size, tooling areas, etc.), as listed in Table 1-3.

Generally, decisions to design either a single fixture or a number of fixtures, based upon operation and machine considerations and characteristics, result in tentative alternate fixture-design concepts which may appear in preliminary rough sketches.

The proposed alternate designs are further modified according to the assigned production quantity and rate.

Product quality for required production has now been established by these tentative design concepts that have been retained in the designer's mind and perhaps illustrated by rough sketches.

Fourth Phase—Operator Analysis. This phase examines the alternative design concepts and their possible change because of operator considerations, which consists of the elements of time, fatigue, and safety. These elements, as fixture-design criteria, are directly related to the loading, clamping, and unloading of the workpiece, as well as to the cleaning of the proposed fixture(s), as listed in Table 1-4. When this has been completed, preliminary jig or fixture designs suitable for cost estimates should be prepared.

TABLE 1-4
Fixture Design Considerations (as determined or affected by Product, Operation, and Machine Analyses)

I. Locating considerations
  A. Angularity
  B. Datums
    1. Axis
    2. Feature
    3. Line
    4. Plane
    5. Point
    6. Surface
    7. Target
  C. Concentric
  D. Feature dimensioning
    1. Coordinates
      a. Radial
      b. Rectangular
    2. LMC - least material condition
    3. MMC - maximum material condition
    4. RFS - regardless of feature size
    5. True position
  E. Parallelism
  F. Perpendicularity
  G. Symmetric
  H. Other

II. Chip considerations
  A. Accumulation
  B. Disposal

III. Positioning considerations (relation to tool and orientation in the fixture)
  A. Indexing
    1. Circular
    2. Linear
  B. Rotating
  C. Sliding
  D. Tilting

IV. Clamping considerations
  A. Actuation
    1. Manual
    2. Power
  B. Amount of clamping forces
  C. Direction of clamping forces
  D. Rapidity

V. Supporting considerations
  A. Relation to clamping pressure
  B. Relation to thin walls, sections of workpiece
  C. Relation to tool forces

VI. Loading considerations (including manual lifting and sliding, hoisting, unloading chutes, magazines)
  A. Ease
  B. Rapidity
  C. Safety

VII. Coolant considerations
  A. Direction

Fifth Phase—Cost Analysis. This final phase is the evaluation of the preliminary design(s) for lowest fixturing cost per part, which includes tool design and fabrication costs, costs of fixture operation, amortization, and all other costs that are applicable wholly or in part to the design(s).

It is certainly true that the tool design must provide the necessary quality, safety, production rates, so that up to this point in the design, their effect on costs is not considered. The initial design should fulfill these necessary requirements and then its estimated cost should be compared with that allowed. Should this design cost be less than allowed, the designer might consider further design improvements if they can be justified on the basis of additional savings.

There are many methods of determining whether or not the expenditure is justifiable. The following formula is recommended because of its relative simplicity:

$$S \geq \text{(equals or is greater than) } KT + (T \div N) \tag{1}$$

where:

S = gross annual savings before expenses.

K = return expected on the investment after tax.

T = estimated tool cost.

N = estimated life of the tooling (set by constant—company policy).

If the above condition is fulfilled, then the expenditure would provide at least the specified return on the investment after tax.

Example 1:

S = $750.00

K = 15%

T = $1200.00

N = 2 years

Calculation:

$$S \geq \text{(equals or is greater than) } KT + (T \div N) \tag{1}$$

$$\$750.00 \geq (0.15 \times \$1200.00) + (\$1200.00 \div 2)$$

$$\$750.00 \geq \$180.00 + \$600.00$$

$$\$750.00 \geq \$780.00$$

Since $750.00 is neither greater than or equal to $780.00, the expenditure would not provide 15% return on the investment and therefore should not be undertaken.

APPLICATIONS OF PREDESIGN ANALYSIS AND PROCEDURE

Example 2: Design a fixture to assemble (press-fit) the two components shown in Fig. 1-2.

Product Data

The machined components (A and B) were made from SAE 32510 malleable iron castings and weigh approximately 2 lb (0.9 kg) each.

Surface X is flat and 90° to the bore axis; mating diameters are chamfered.

Quality requirements are as follows:
1. Radial relationship of the large holes to the small hole and mating diameters (press-fit) to be as shown in Figs. 1-2 and 1-3.
2. Concentricity of ID (diameter S) of both parts to be held within 0.005 in. full indicator movement (FIM) to OD (diameter T) of both parts after assembly (see Fig. 1-4).
3. Joint faces to be tight after assembly (see Fig. 1-2).

Quantity requirements:
    50 assemblies per hour, net
    8000 assemblies per year; 3 year period

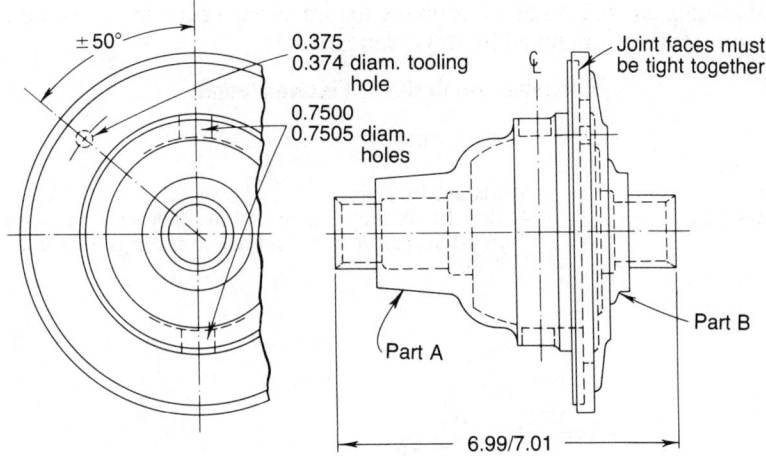

Fig. 1-2 Components to be assembled (press-fit) in the fixture of Fig. 1-9.

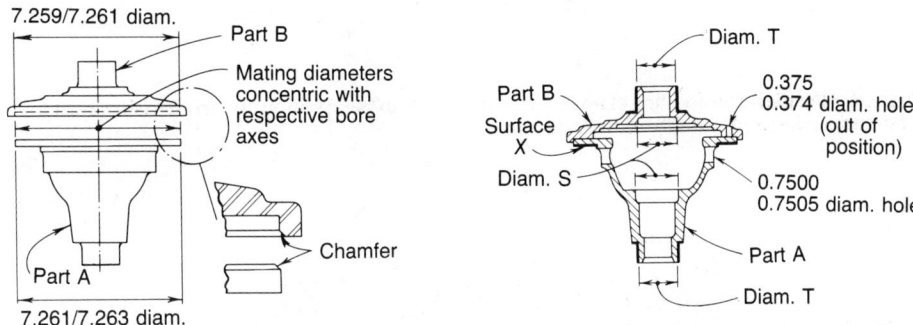

Fig. 1-3 Mating diameters, parts of Fig. 1-2.

Fig. 1-4 After assembly, diameters _T_ and _S_ to be concentric within 0.005 in. FIM.

Operation Data

Press-fit thrust of 500 lbf (2.2 kN) is specified for interference fit.

Machine Data

The arbor press, air-operated and of 1,000 lbf (4.4 kN) capacity specified by the process engineer, has T-slots and a tapped hole in its arbor. Bed area; closed and open height are shown in Fig. 1-5.

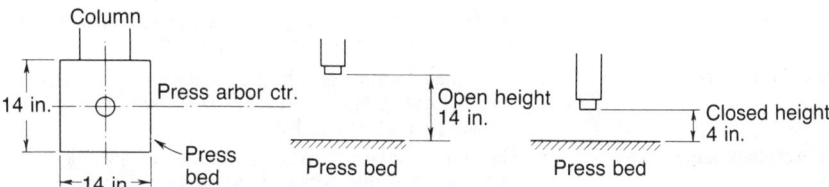

Fig. 1-5 Press data.

Operator Data

Manual loading and unloading of assembly fixture during operator's idle time allowed from another operation is required by work standards.

I. Product Analysis for Fixture Design

Criteria	*Design Decision*
Size, fairly small	
Weight, light	5* Manual handling.
Distribution (c.g.)	1, 4 Part *A* to be supported for stability with small end down in fixture, part *B* with small end up (see Figs. 1-6a and 1-7).

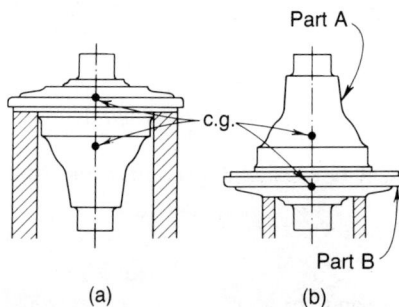

(a)   (b)

Fig. 1-6 Alternative positioning of assembly components in the assembly fixture; decision: as at (*a*) for best supporting and stability of both parts.

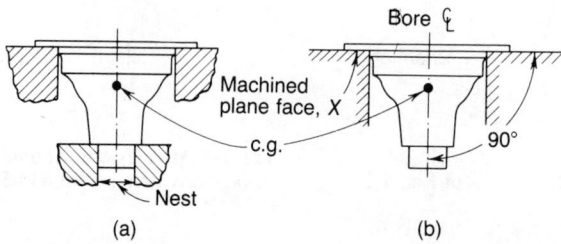

(a)   (b)

Fig. 1-7 Supporting decisions: at (*a*) a lower nest is not needed, since at (*b*) the part is adequately supported on its flanged surface *X*, which is also maintained at 90° to the bore axis.

Surface *X* (part *A*)	1, 4 Placement of part *A* with small end down provides for its best support and ensures verticality (see Fig. 1-7b).
Surface *Y* (part *B*)	3 Uneven, unmachined surface unsuitable for applying pressure (see Fig. 1-8); therefore not used.
Surface *Z* (part *B*)	3 Machined surface satisfactory for pressure to be applied by pressure ring (see Fig. 1-8).
Surface of bore *U* (part *B*)	1 Incorporate locating plug held in pressure ring to engage bore *U*, locating part *B* vertically before pressure ring contacts part *B* (see Fig. 1-8).
Outside surface of flange (part *B*)	1 This surface to be approximately located by a spring-loaded locating ring, which allows slight movement of part *B* to facilitate entry of locating plug into bore *U* (see Fig. 1-8).

* Numbers correspond to design considerations, Table 1-4

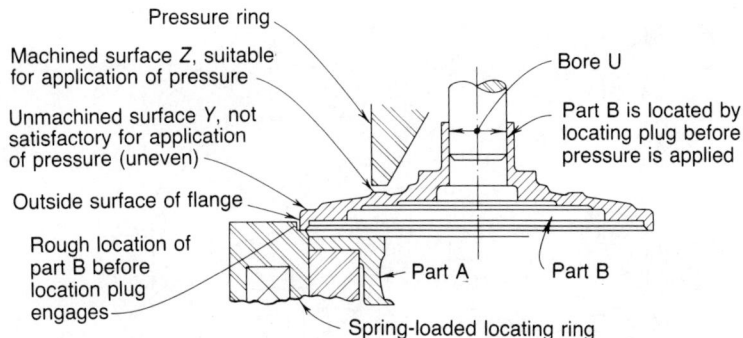

Fig. 1-8 Surface considerations for pressure application, part *B*.

Chamfer on inside flange (part *B*)	2	Facilitates alignment and force fit of parts (see Fig. 1-3).
Chamfer on OD (part *A*)	2	Facilitates alignment and force fit of parts (see Fig. 1-3).
50° angle between axes of 0.375-in. hole in part *B* and the 0.750-in. hole in part *A*	1	Provides retractable spring-loaded swing locating pin (1) and removable locating pin (2) to establish required angle (see Fig. 1-9).

II. Operation Analysis for Fixture Design

Criteria

Design Decision

Vertical press-filling force directed downward with no torque or vibratory components

2 Fixture to be open at top for pressure ring's unobstructed contact with part *B*.
4 Moderate unidirectional force requires fixture construction to withstand fairly low stresses.

III. Machine Analysis for Fixture Design

Criteria

Design Decision

Tooling area

Does not affect fixture design; adequate for fixture accommodation.

Open and closed height

(see Fig. 1-5)

Capacity

Adequate per-process specification.

Mounting

Fixture key to be included.

IV. Operator Analysis for Fixture Design

Criteria

Design Decision

Loading and unloading

5 Height of fixture allows space between pressure tool and top of fixture for parts insertion and removal.

Ease of locator operation

5 Provided by swinging locator and removable locating pin both having knurled handles; latter slides in slots rather than holes.

Operator safety

No hazards to be reflected in fixture design.

V. Cost Analysis for Fixture Design

Criteria

Design Decision

Total costs per assembly with desired product quality

Fixture costs justified by amortization for production quantity.

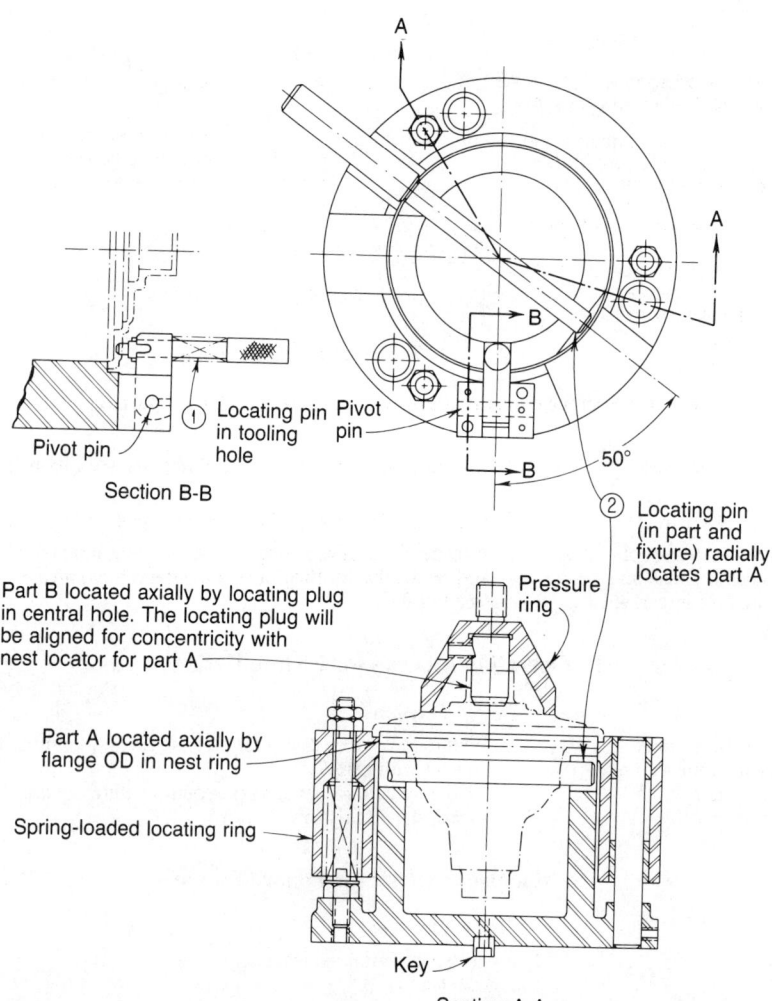

A

A

B

B

50°

Pivot pin

Locating pin in tooling hole

Pivot pin

① Locating pin in tooling hole

Section B-B

② Locating pin (in part and fixture) radially locates part A

Part B located axially by locating plug in central hole. The locating plug will be aligned for concentricity with nest locator for part A

Part A located axially by flange OD in nest ring

Spring-loaded locating ring

Pressure ring

Key

Section A-A

Fig. 1-9 A fixture for assembling parts *A* and *B*.

Example 3: Design a fixture to drill and ream a connecting rod cap.

Product Data

The connecting-rod cap shown in Fig. 1-10 was made from an SAE 1041 steel forging; surfaces *A*, *B*, *C*, and *D* are finish machined.

Weight, 4 oz (113 g).

Quality requirements (see Fig. 1-10)

   1. Hole size, 0.3760 ±0.0005 in.

   2. Hole location, 0.512 ±0.002 in.

   3. Interhole distance, 3.2675 ±0.0025 in.; from center line, ±0.0025 in.

Quantity requirements:

    400 parts per hour, net

    800,000 parts per year; 3 year period

Operation Data

Drill, ream, chamfer (2) holes, counterbore (1) hole, according to quality requirements (above).

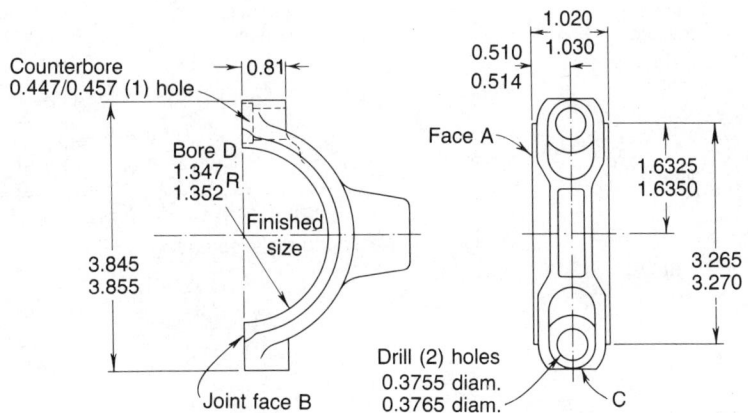

Fig. 1-10 Manufacturing drawing of workpiece (connecting-rod cap) to be drilled, reamed, and counterbored.

Machine Data

Greenlee horizontal one-way-indexing drill machine time:

Index	3 sec
Rapid advance	2
Drill	34
Dwell	1
Rapid return	2
	42 sec

Index table to be drilled for bolting fixtures to it.

I. Product Analysis for Fixture Design

Criteria	*Design Decision*
Weight	5 Manual handling.
Hole location from face *A*	1 Locate against face *A*(1).
Interhole location (1.6325/1.6350 in.)	1 Locate from broached bore.
Perpendicularity of holes with parting face	1 Locate on joint face *B* (2).
	1, 3 The tentative design decisions (1) and (2) necessitate a clamping force with consequent distortion (see Fig. 1-11*a*). A preliminary locating design concept (see Fig. 1-11*b*, *c*, and *d*) retains design decisions (1) and (2) and prevents distortion, without the need of clamping forces in more that one direction.

Its depth will be nearly as thick as the edge of the part for maximum surface contact with it. Inside edges will be chamfered for ease of loading.

It was concluded that the incorporation of a nest in the fixture would necessitate changes in product dimensions (length and width). The changes *A* and *B* listed below will not affect the function of the workpiece as discussed.

Proposed Product Changes (see Fig. 1-12).

A. Considerations for holding the 0.510/0.514 in. dimension and to arrive at a new part width, as well as nest dimensions are:
   1. The mean part width is 1.024 in. (2 × 0.512 in.).
   2. Part-width tolerance, 0.002 in.
   3. Minimum clearance between part and nest to prevent difficult locating, 0.002 in.

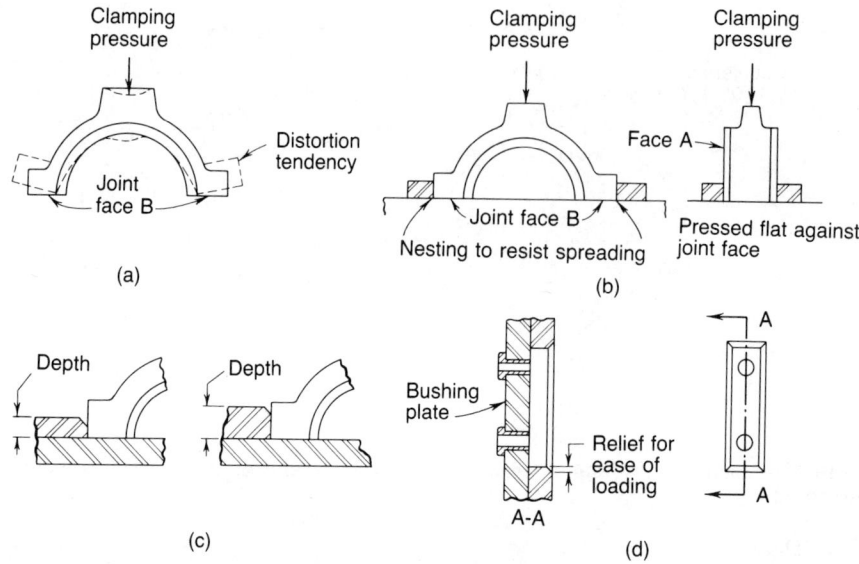

Fig. 1-11 Distortion considerations and their effect on tentative locating design.

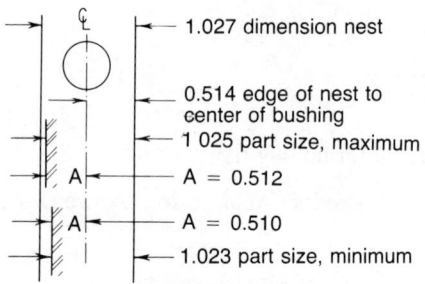

Fig. 1-12 Proposed dimensional part redesign for fixture planning.

4. Part width, determined by (1) and (2), 1.023/1.025 in.
5. Nest width, determined by (3) and (4), 1.027 in.

The establishment of a part width of 1.025 in. with drill bushings at 0.510 in. from the nest face will also establish a distance of 0.512/0.514 in. and from hole centers to face A. A part width of 1.023 in. will permit a variation of 0.510 to 0.514 in. The 1.6325/1.6350 in. dimension will be maintained indirectly since the hole location will not be taken from the center of the bore radius.

B. Considerations for holding the part to a mean length of 3.8515 in.
   1. Part-length tolerance of 0.003 in. for machining.
   2. Minimum clearance between part and nest, 0.002 in.
   3. The part length, determined by mean length and tolerance (1), is 3.850/3.853 in. The distance from the center of the bearing radius to the end of the part is 1.9265/1.9250 in.
   4. The next length, based on (2) and (3), is 3.855 in.
   5. The bushings are spaced 3.2670 in. center-to-center and 0.294 in. from the nest edges.
   6. The hole in the longer part (3.853 in.) will be from 1.631 to 1.633 in. from the center of the bore radius (see Fig. 1-13a, b).
   7. The hole in the shorter part (3.850 in.) will be from 1.6325 to 1.6375 in. from the center of the bore radius (see Fig. 1-13c, d).
   8. The nest location and dimensions (with the bushings spaced at 3.2670 in.) will consistently produce parts within tolerances if clamping forces do not distort it or disturb its location.

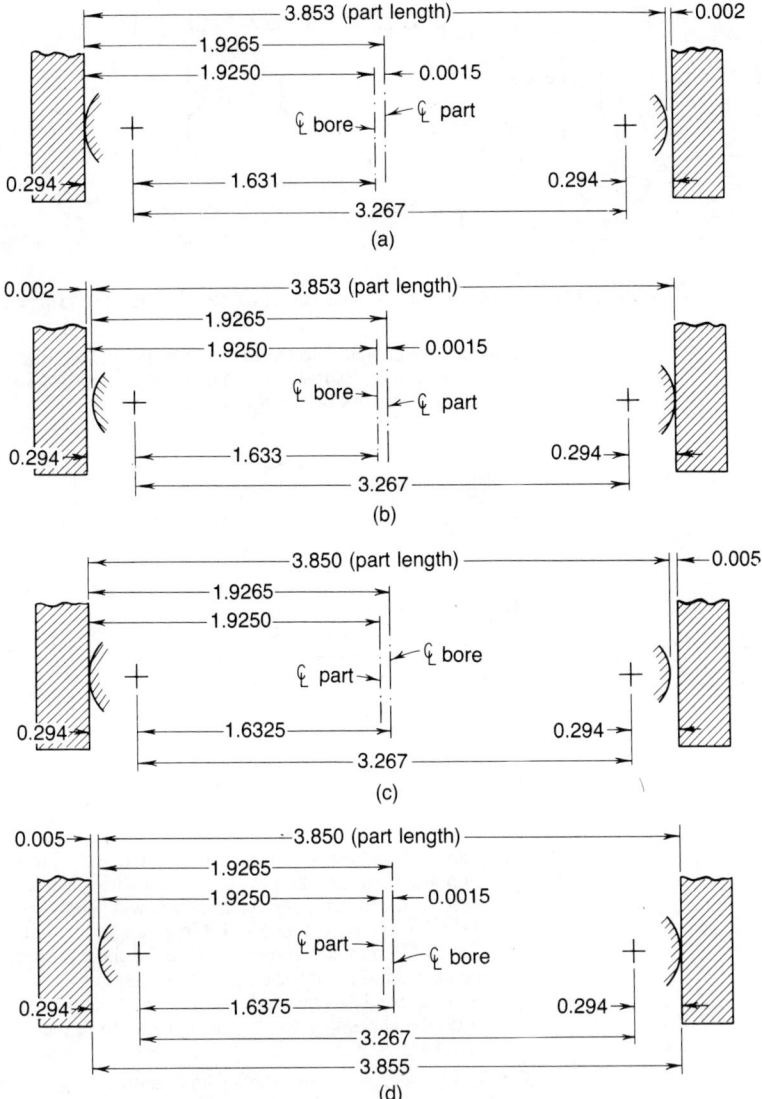

Fig. 1-13 Hole center to bore center variation.

I. Product Analysis for Fixture Design

Criteria	Design Decision
Face *A* Face *B*	3 A single clamping force against these faces is not desirable and can cause tilting of the part (no particular squareness held in previous operation) and loss of accuracy in the 0.510-0.514 in. dimension and perpendicularity of the holes (see Fig. 1-14*a*). Two clamping forces (see Fig. 1-14*b*) are not desirable because perpendicularity of the holes will not be ensured.

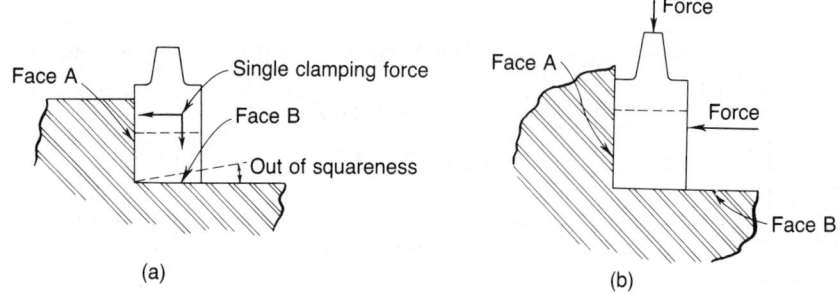

Fig. 1-14 Clamping force considerations: (*a*) one force; (*b*) two independent forces.

Clamping points	3, 4 Boss faces were selected as clamping points (see Fig. 15*b*) for more positive part support than a single force (see Fig. 1-15*a*); there is less risk of part distortion.

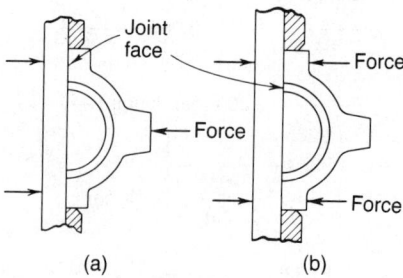

Fig. 1-15 Clamping force selection.

Boss faces	3 Variations in boss thickness (not more than 0.005 in.) can result in nonuniform clamping with a nonequalizing clamp (see Fig. 1-16*a*). A compensating clamp design will be used (see Fig. 1-16*b*).The type seen in Fig. 1-17*a* is simpler than that of Fig. 1-17*b*, although it must withstand drilling pressure. Final design decisions: three clamps each to clamp two workpieces, each actuated by one toggle-clamp (for speed and locking action) and clamp yokes having a groove to restrict its swing (see Figs. 1-18 and 1-19).
Quantity Cycle time	3, 5 Cycle time, including indexing time, confirms clamp design (above) for rapid clamping and suggests fixture mounting arrangements (see Fig. 1-20) to drill 12 holes. Arrangement 3 (see Figs. 1-20 and 1-21) will be used since it allows adequate room for each fixture and clamp, and for loading and unloading the workpieces.

II. Operation Analysis for Fixture Design

Criteria	*Design Decision*
Simultaneous drilling of 12 holes with a horizontal spindle and 12 drills	4 Fixture must withstand drilling pressure of 200 lbf (890 N) per drill.
Coolant application	6 Coolant pipes on multiple-head side of index table direct coolant to bushings.
Chip removal means	7 Not a part of fixture; air blast directed by operator into nests.

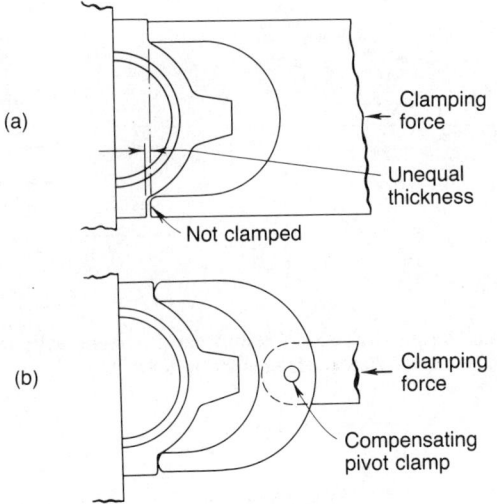

(a)

Clamping
force

Unequal
thickness

Not clamped

(b)

Clamping
force

Compensating
pivot clamp

Fig. 1-16 Boss thickness considerations for clamp design.

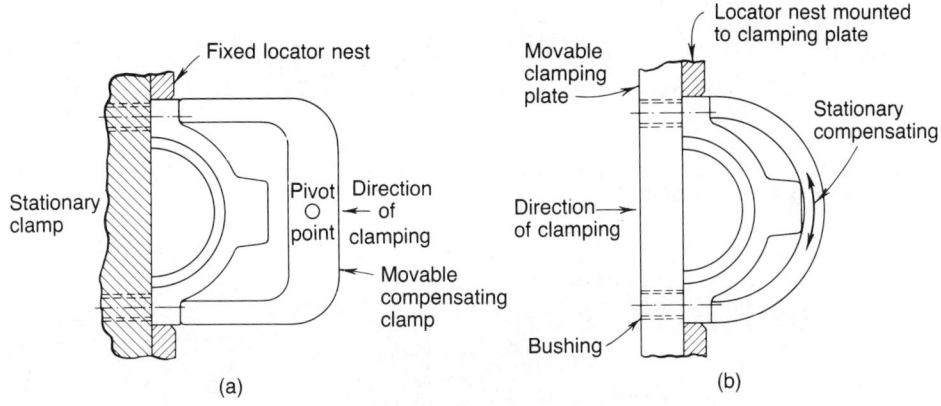

Fixed locator nest

Stationary
clamp

Pivot
point

Direction
of
clamping

Movable
compensating
clamp

(a)

Movable
clamping
plate

Locator nest mounted
to clamping plate

Stationary
compensating

Direction
of clamping

Bushing

(b)

Fig. 1-17 Equalizing-clamp design.

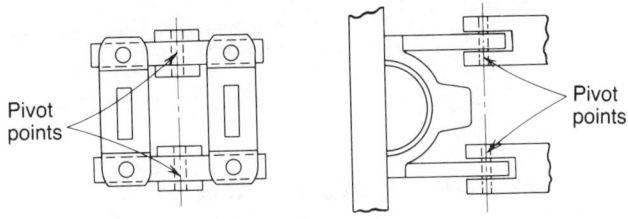

Pivot
points

Pivot
points

Fig. 1-18 Compensating (equalizing) clamp to hold two workpieces.

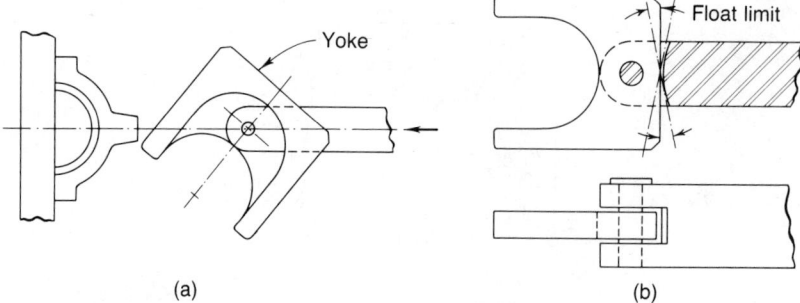

Fig. 1-19 Equalizing-clamp design details: (*a*) clamp can interfere with workpiece; (*b*) radial movement (float) is limited to ensure clamp engagement at boss faces.

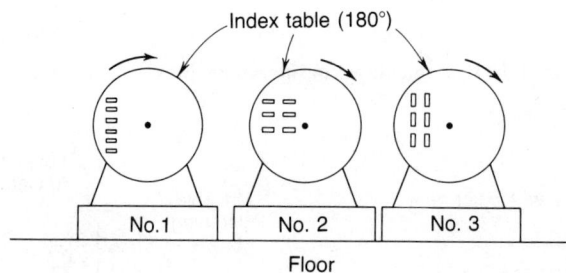

Fig. 1-20 Fixture arrangements on index plate at load-unload station for six workpieces (working stations are duplicates, oriented 180°).

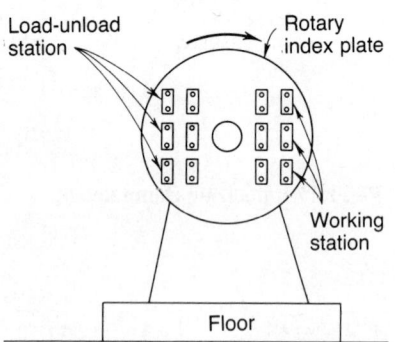

Fig. 1-21 Design decision for fixture placement on index plate (arrangement 3, Fig. 1-20).

III. Machine Analysis for Fixture Design

Criteria	*Design Decision*	
Tooling area	2	Adequate for mounting fixtures on index plate, which is to be drilled for mounting holes.
Clearance	2	Adequate between fixture and drill points.

IV. Operator Analysis for Fixture Design

Criteria	Design Decision
Ease and rapidity of loading, clamping, unclamping, and unloading	5 Design decisions for locating nests and clamps permit easy fixture operation. An ejector, similar to that of Fig. 1-22 will be incorporated.
Safety	5 Fixture guards unnecessary since drills approach from side of index plate opposite to that of fixture. Spacing of clamps allows their manipulation without hazard to operator's hands.

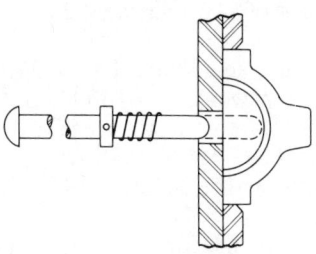

Fig. 1-22 Ejector-pin design.

V. Cost Analysis for Fixture Design

Criteria	Design Decision
Total costs per workpiece with desired product quality	Fixture costs justified by amortization for production quantity.

MANUFACTURING COSTS

Manufacturing costs are classified as indirect and direct costs. *Indirect costs* are costs that cannot be directly identified with the production of a specific item and are not covered in this book.

Direct costs. Direct costs can be charged directly to each part produced. Direct costs include:

1. Investment charges on tooling for the actual costs incurred for tooling.
2. Costs for labor plus fringe benefits for the personnel directly involved in the production operations.
3. Costs of the workpiece material. This cost does not usually concern the tool designer since the material has almost always been decided before tooling decisions are made.

Tool Costs versus Labor Costs. The amount of money that can be spent on tooling and labor to manufacture a part is usually decided before the tool engineer is involved.

It becomes the tool designer's responsibility to recommend the right combination of tooling and labor cost. First of all, labor costs can almost always be reduced by using jigs and fixtures. Conversely, undertooling can increase labor costs. This relationship can be seen in the following example:

A thousand (1000) parts must be produced at a cost of $4.50 per part for a total of $4500. This can be spent in many combinations such as $1500 for labor and $3000 for tooling, or the other way around—$1500 for tooling and $3000 for labor.

Decisions regarding the total expenditure for tooling are affected by the following:

1. Number of parts to be produced.
2. Variations in tooling cost.
3. Level of labor skill used.

Number of Parts to be Produced. The initial and total number of parts to be produced has a decided affect on tooling costs. For example, a manufacturer agrees to produce 500 parts at a total cost of $3750 based on the estimate that a skilled machinist without special tooling could manufacture 2 parts per hour at an hourly rate (including burden and labor) of $15.00/hr (that is, 500 parts/2 parts per hour × $15.00/hr). A profit could be made by increasing the production rate with special tooling operated by less skilled operators.

If special tooling can be provided that will produce 20 parts/hour allow using skilled operators who will be paid $12.00/hr (including labor and burden), the 500 parts could be produced in 25 hours at a labor cost of $300 (25 hours × $12.00/hr). This would allow $3450 ($3750 - $300) for special tooling and profit. If this tooling could be made for $2000, the 500 parts will be produced for a total expenditure of $2300 ($2000 + $300) resulting in a break-even manufacturing cost of $4.60 per part ($2300/500 parts) and a profit of $1450 ($3750 - $2300).

If it is decided later to produce an additional lot of 250 parts, requiring 12.5 hours of labor, the labor costs on this run would be $150 (12.5 × $12.00/hr). If there were no additional costs for tooling, the total cost to produce the two lots would be $2450 ($2000 + $300 + $150) or a cost per part of $3.27 ($2450/750 parts). If the tooling had to be replaced to complete the run, total costs would be $4450 ($2000 + $2000 + $300 + $150) or a cost per part of $5.93 ($4450/750 parts).

Variations in Tooling Costs. When labor is charged on a hourly basis, the labor cost per part decreases as the production rate increases. It is a generally accepted fact that more expensive tooling will permit faster parts production than cheaper tooling, thereby lowering labor costs. If this is not the case, the additional cost is not justified unless some other advantage, such as improved accuracy, is desired. Conversely, cheap tooling increases labor costs if it adds time to the operation.

Level of Labor Skills. As mentioned previously, one of the main advantages of jigs and fixtures is that it reduces chances for human error and permits operations to be performed by less-skilled operators without jeopardizing the quality of the finished product. Obviously, the use of less-skilled operators reduces the labor costs.

Presenting the Tool Estimate. Jigs and fixtures are often looked upon by management as costly, but necessary evils. Just getting them to accept a proposal is often frustrating to the tool designer. Consequently, the tool designer should realize that management must consider each tooling problem from a profit or loss standpoint, and that proposals to management should include tooling estimates that are structured around cost savings and profit potential. He or she must also be prepared to justify the proposed expenditures. The minimum a proposal should include are the following:

1. Design and build cost of the proposed tooling.
2. Estimated hourly production rate using the proposed tooling.
3. Projected profit or savings using the proposed tooling.

Once production rates and the proposed tooling costs are estimated, projected profit or savings can be calculated using the following formulas:

$$A = \frac{C}{D} \times F \tag{2}$$

$$B = \frac{C}{E} \times G \tag{3}$$

$$H = \frac{A}{C} \tag{4}$$

$$J = \frac{B + K}{C} \tag{5}$$

$$L = C(H - J) \tag{6}$$

$$M = \frac{K}{H - J} \tag{7}$$

where:

A = estimated cost of labor with existing tooling.
B = estimated cost of labor with special tooling.
C = lot size.
D = estimated hourly production rate with existing tooling.
E = estimated hourly production rate with special tooling.
F = hourly wage rate (including fringe benefits) with existing tooling.
G = hourly wage rate (including fringe benefits) with special tooling.
H = estimated cost per part using existing tooling.
J = estimated cost per part using special tooling.
K = estimated special tooling costs.
L = estimated total savings with special tooling.
M = break-even point (minimum lot size necessary to justify special tooling).

Example 4: There are 500 parts to be drilled. The estimated production rate with existing tooling is 5 parts/hr with a labor cost of $16.00/hr. A specially designed drill jig costing $500 is proposed that will increase the production rate to 100 parts/hr using labor costing only $12.00/hr.

1. What is the estimated cost of labor using existing tooling?
2. What is the estimated cost of labor using the jig?
3. What is the estimated cost per part using existing tooling?
4. What is the estimated cost per part using the jig?
5. What are the estimated total savings that can be realized using the special jig?
6. What is the break-even point that will justify the special jig?

The calculations for labor costs A and B are:

$$A = \frac{C}{D} \times F \tag{2}$$

$$= \frac{500 \text{ parts}}{5 \text{ parts/hr}} \times \$16.00/\text{hr}$$

$$= 100 \times \$16$$

$$= \$1600 \text{ Estimated cost of labor with existing tooling}$$

$$B = \frac{C}{E} \times G \tag{3}$$

$$= \frac{500 \text{ parts}}{100 \text{ parts/hr}} \times \$12.00/\text{hr}$$

$$= 5 \times \$12$$

$$= \$60 \text{ Estimated cost of labor with special tooling}$$

The calculations for cost per part H and J are:

$$H = \frac{A}{C} \tag{4}$$

$$= \frac{\$1600}{500 \text{ parts}}$$

= \$3.20 Estimated cost per part using existing tooling

$$J = \frac{B + K}{C} \tag{5}$$

$$= \frac{\$60 + \$500}{500 \text{ parts}}$$

$$= \frac{\$560}{500}$$

= \$1.12 Estimated cost per part using special tooling

The calculation for tool savings is:

$$L = C(H - J) \tag{6}$$

$$= 500 \, (\$3.20 - \$1.12)$$

$$= 500 \times \$2.08$$

= \$1040 Estimated savings with special tooling

The calculation for the break-even point is:

$$M = \frac{K}{H - J} \tag{7}$$

$$= \frac{\$500}{\$3.20 - \$1.12}$$

$$= \frac{\$500}{\$2.08}$$

= 241 Break-even point (minimum lot size necessary to justify special tooling).

Many times the tool designer will have to consider a number of different methods for machining a fixed quantity of parts. In this case, he or she might find it useful to make a special cost analysis such as the one shown in Table 1-5 for a lot size of 300 fittings. It can be immediately seen from the table that if time is not a factor, method 2 is the most economical method for 300 parts. This information can then be transferred to a graph such as the one shown in Fig. 1-23. For example, the graph shows that the use of existing tooling (method 1) would be the most economical for lot sizes up to 247 pieces. For lot sizes between 248 and 393 pieces, the simplified fixture (method 2) would be more economical, and for lot sizes 394 pieces and over, the more costly conventional fixture (method 3) would be the most economical.

Occasionally the cost analysis will find an operation that does not warrant a special jig or fixture, especially on low volume parts for which tooling costs cannot be justified. In this case, the tool designer might recommend some other way to process the part without affecting the accuracy or interchangeability of the part. Three methods that could be recommended are the machine set-up system, the master part system and the limited-production group system.

Machine Set-up System. This method uses machine set-ups with conventional tooling and equipment. To avoid confusion, drawings by process engineers, such as the one shown in Fig. 1-24, are usually provided for the operation involved.

TABLE 1-5
Cost Analysis of Three Machining Methods

METHOD	Time min/unit	Units per hr.	Total hours	Labor cost ($16/hr.)	Tool cost	Total cost (Labor + Tooling)
EXISTING TOOLING (Method 1)	10	6	50	$800	—	$800
SPECIAL FIXTURE (SIMPLIFIED) (Method 2)	5	12	25	$400	$330	$730
SPECIAL FIXTURE (CONVENTIONAL) (Method 3)	3	20	15	$240	$540	$780

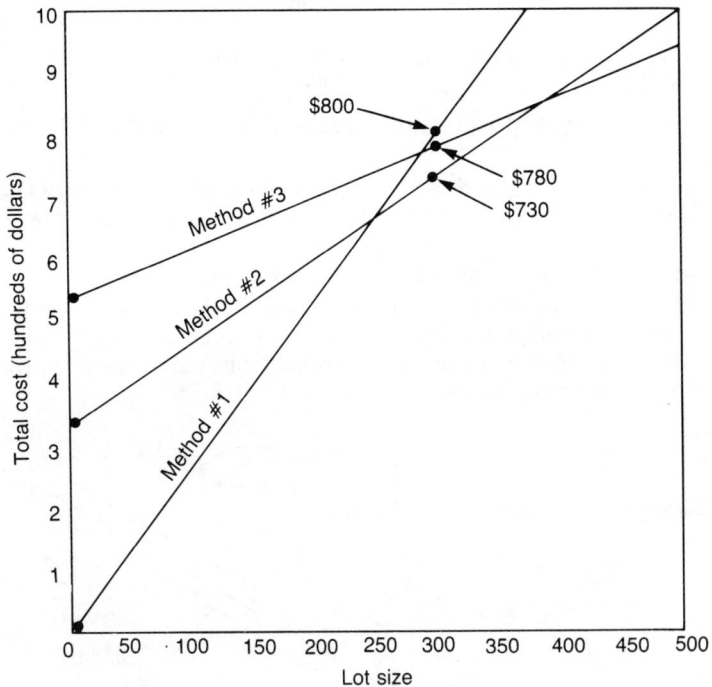

Fig. 1-23 Graphic tooling analysis of three machining methods.

1-23

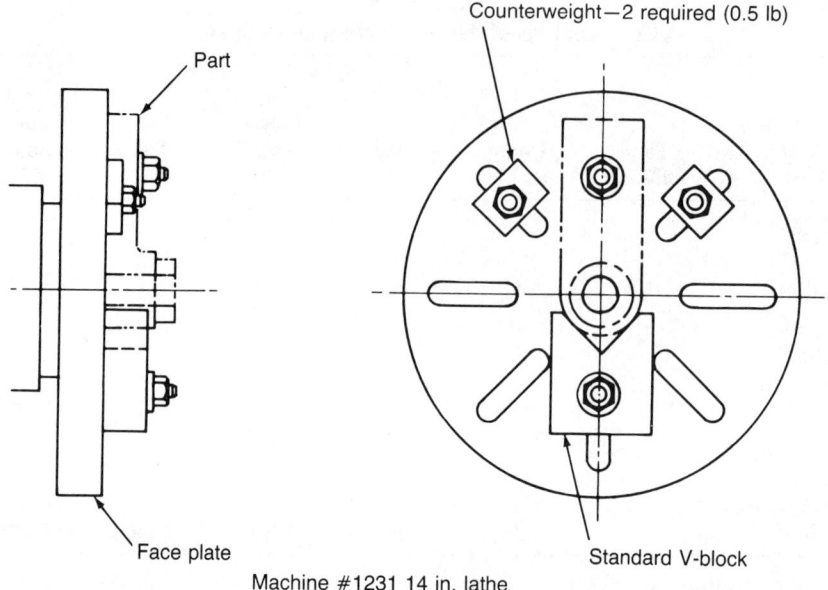

Counterweight—2 required (0.5 lb)

Part

Face plate

Standard V-block

Machine #1231 14 in. lathe

Operation 10: Turn 0.750 diameter and
Bore 0.500 diameter hole

Fig. 1-24 Typical machine setup sketch for a lathe.

Master Part System. Simulated or actual parts which have been fabricated to closer tolerances than the actual part tolerances (master parts) are used as a template or jig. Figure 1-25 shows a master part being used for locating holes. In this case, the master and workpiece are clamped together and the hole locations transferred from the master to the part with a punch. Sometimes hardened bushings are inserted into the master part, increasing its life and accuracy and permitting it to be used as a regular template drill jig. Master parts are also used to set cutters on machines by simply substituting them for workpieces in the holding device and setting the cutter as shown in Fig. 1-26.

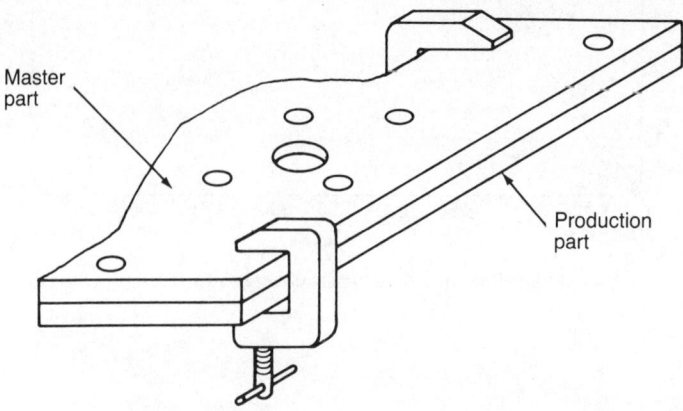

Master part

Production part

Fig. 1-25 Master part method of transferring hole locations.

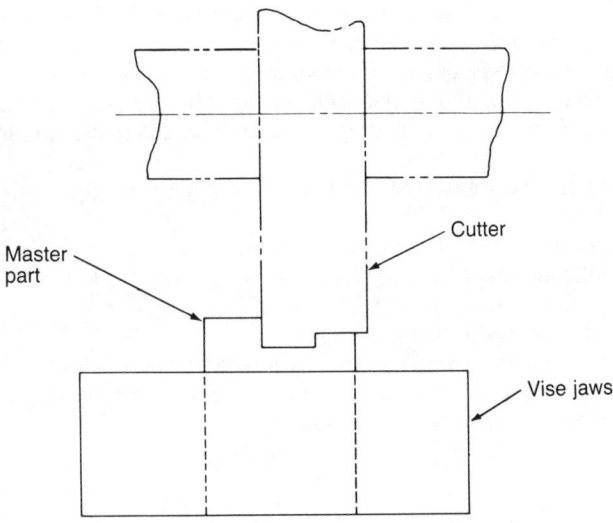

Fig. 1-26 Master part used to reduce machine tool setup time.

Limited-Production Group System. Sometimes parts must be manufactured with the equipment and tooling that is available. This however, requires highly skilled operators. Some companies process the parts through their tool fabrication section, while other companies have a separate small department which is provided with versatile NC and CNC equipped machines and machining centers just for this purpose.

MULTIPURPOSE JIGS AND FIXTURES

Sometimes the tool designer will simply not be able to justify spending money to provide a jig or fixture for a particular operation. In these cases, the tool designer should consider combining the features of two or more jigs or fixtures into a single jig or fixture. Tools designed to be used for multiple operations or multiple parts are called *multipurpose jigs or fixtures*. Multipurpose tooling should be seriously considered whenever similar parts or similar operations are scheduled to be run, and when permitted by production scheduling.

At the outset of any new project, parts and operations should be carefully reviewed by the tool designer for similarity. Any similar operations or parts should be examined jointly to determine design features that could be incorporated into a single jig or fixture. If this is possible, production requirements should be thoroughly investigated to see if multipurpose tooling would be compatible with time schedules and quantity requirements. Multipurpose jigs and fixtures should be considered only when workpieces are required on a part-time basis, not when they must be run continuously or at the same time.

Consider the case of two similar workpieces, part A and part B. A lot quantity of 80 of each is required. A multipurpose jig is being proposed that would require 1 hour machining time for part A and 0.8 hours machining time for part B. Therefore, the lot quantity for part A would require 80 hours to complete and the lot quantity for part B would require 64 hours to complete using the multipurpose jig. However, if only 80 hours are available to machine both parts, then part A will have to be run continuously leaving no time to machine part B. In a case like this, a multipurpose jig should not be considered unless a new design can be developed which will handle both parts in the allotted time.

On the other hand, if total production time is not limited, a multipurpose jig could be used to produce all of part A followed by all of part B. Other production requirements, such as providing 50 of each part on a monthly basis over a period of years, would require that lots be produced alternately A-B-A-B, etc. This way production time to machine both parts would total 144 hours plus the amount of time required to convert the jig from part A operations to part B operations and back if necessary. This changing back and forth from A to B is called a *changeover* and the time required is called *changeover time*. Changeover time is important when estimating a multipurpose jig or fixture since the costs of these change-overs may cancel out any gains. A simple cost study should be made before proceeding with their design.

Estimating for Multipurpose Tooling. A multipurpose jig or fixture cost estimate requires the following:

1. Design and build cost of the jig or fixture.
2. The total design and build costs of all of the single-purpose tooling that the multipurpose tooling will replace.
3. Estimated changeover time.
4. Number of changeovers required by production schedules.
5. The hourly labor and burden rate for changeover personnel.

The formulas to be used in the estimate are:

$$A = BC \tag{8}$$

$$D = AE \tag{9}$$

$$F = G - (H + D) \tag{10}$$

$$J = \frac{G - H}{A} \tag{11}$$

where:

A = estimated cost of each changeover.
B = estimated changeover time.
C = hourly labor and burden rate for changeover personnel.
D = estimated total cost of changeovers to complete the order.
E = number of changeovers necessary to complete the order.
F = estimated savings using the multipurpose tools.
G = total design and build costs of all replaced single-purpose tooling.
H = total design and build cost of the multipurpose jig or fixture.
J = maximum number of changeovers up to the break-even point. (If the number of changeovers is greater than J, then single purpose tools should be used).

Example 5: For a certain machining operation on two similar parts, two separate drill jigs can be designed and fabricated at a cost of $600 for one and $500 for the other—a total of $1100. A multipurpose drill jig for both parts can be designed and built for an estimated $800. Production schedules call for five lots to be produced of each part. Five lots of two parts each will require 10 operations and nine tooling changeovers. Changeover time is estimated at 0.6 hours with a cost of $16.00/hr (labor and burden). Consider the following questions:

1. What is the estimated cost of each changeover?
2. What is the estimated total cost for changeovers?
3. What are the estimated savings using the multipurpose tool?
4. What is the maximum number of changeovers up to the break-even point?

The estimated cost of each changeover is:

$$A = BC \tag{8}$$

$$= 0.6 \times \$16.00$$

$$= \$9.60$$

The estimated total cost for changeovers is:

$$D = AE \tag{9}$$
$$= \$9.60 \times 9$$
$$= \$86.40$$

The estimated savings using the multipurpose tool is:

$$F = G - (H + D) \tag{10}$$
$$= \$1100 - (\$800 + \$86.40)$$
$$= \$1100 - \$886.40$$
$$= \$213.60$$

The maximum number of changeovers up to the breakeven point is:

$$J = \frac{G - H}{A} \tag{11}$$

$$= \frac{\$1100 - \$800}{\$9.60}$$

$$= \frac{\$300}{\$9.60}$$

$$= 31.25 \text{ or } 31$$

The results of this cost analysis indicate an estimated savings of $213.60 in favor of the multipurpose drill jig. If 32 or more changeovers were necessary however, the advantage of lower cost would be with the two separate, single-purpose jigs.

Knowing the changeover breakeven point before deciding on the type of tooling to be used is very important since production schedules can often be adjusted to permit fewer changeovers.

Designing Multipurpose Tooling. Two separate applications of multipurpose tooling are described in the following section. One fixture is used to perform different operations on a single workpiece, while the drill jig is used to drill similar, but different workpieces.

Combining Operations. The motor bracket shown in Fig. 1-27 was considered a good candidate for multipurpose tooling because both milling and drilling operations could be performed without affecting schedules.

The combination milling fixture and drill jig designed to perform these operations is shown in Fig. 1-28. It consists of a base with holes reamed in two planes to suit two removable reamed-hole keys which can be mounted in either plane. Holes in the two planes are also provided to accommodate the installation of a T-nut assembly to attach the fixture to the machine table. A press-fitted dowel is used to locate the part and four standard hook clamps are used to clamp the part for machining. A detachable bushing plate is used to guide the drill.

For the flat milling operation, the bushing plate is removed and a workpiece that has been cut to the finish length is mounted in the fixture, and the fixture mounted on a milling machine. The flats are then gang-milled as shown in Fig. 1-29. To mill the other slots, the reamed-hole keys and the T-nut assembly are relocated in the alternate pair of holes as shown in Fig. 1-30. The slots are then gang-milled on one side, the workpiece reversed in the fixture, and the slots on the other side gang-milled.

To drill the four 0.125 in. diameter holes, the fixture is converted into a drill jig by attaching the bushing plate and removing the reamed-hole keys and T-nut assembly as shown in Fig. 1-31. Two holes are then drilled, the workpiece is reversed, and the other two holes drilled.

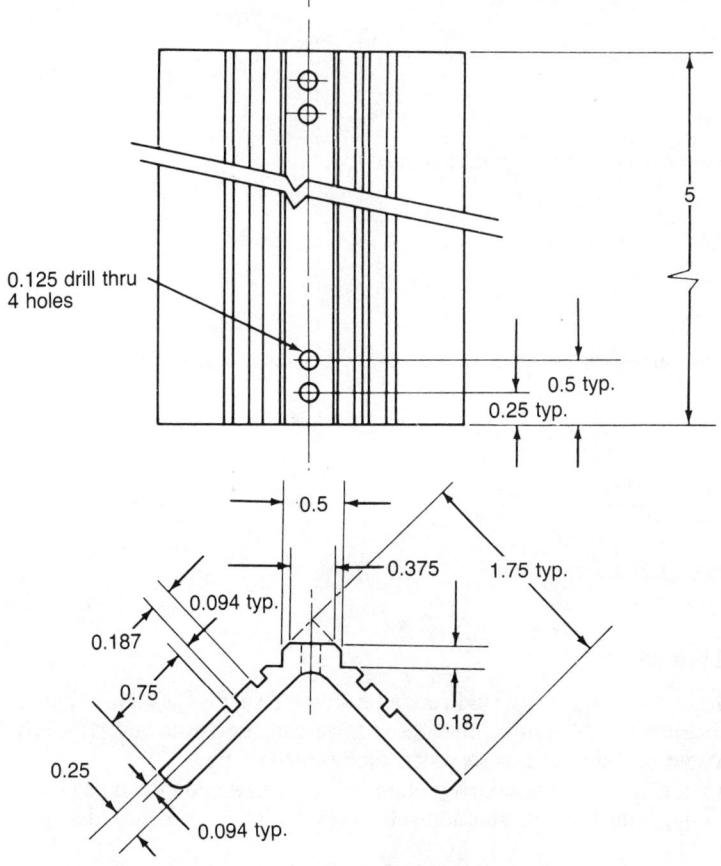

0.125 drill thru
4 holes

5

0.5 typ.

0.25 typ.

0.5

0.375 1.75 typ.

0.094 typ.

0.187

0.75

0.187

0.25

0.094 typ.

Fig. 1-27 Motor bracket made of 304 stainless steel structural angle.

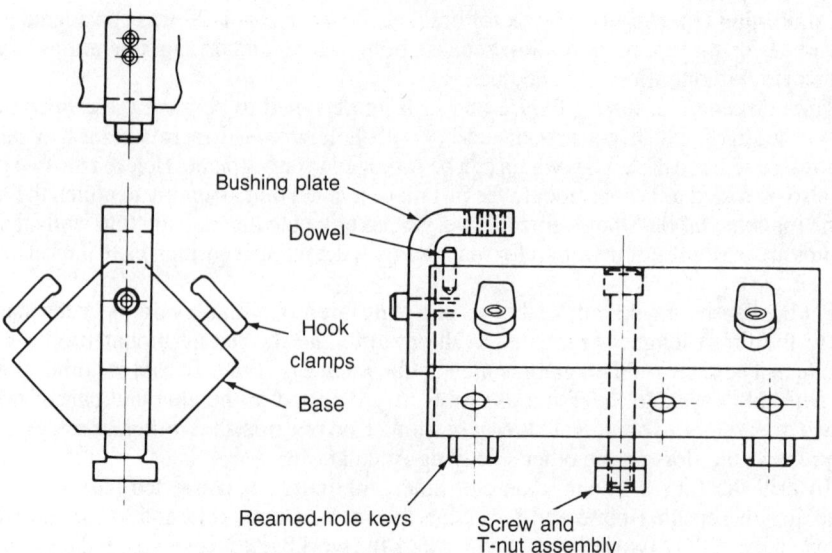

Bushing plate

Dowel

Hook
clamps

Base

Reamed-hole keys

Screw and
T-nut assembly

Fig. 1-28 Multipurpose fixture designed for milling and drilling the motor bracket in Fig. 1-27.

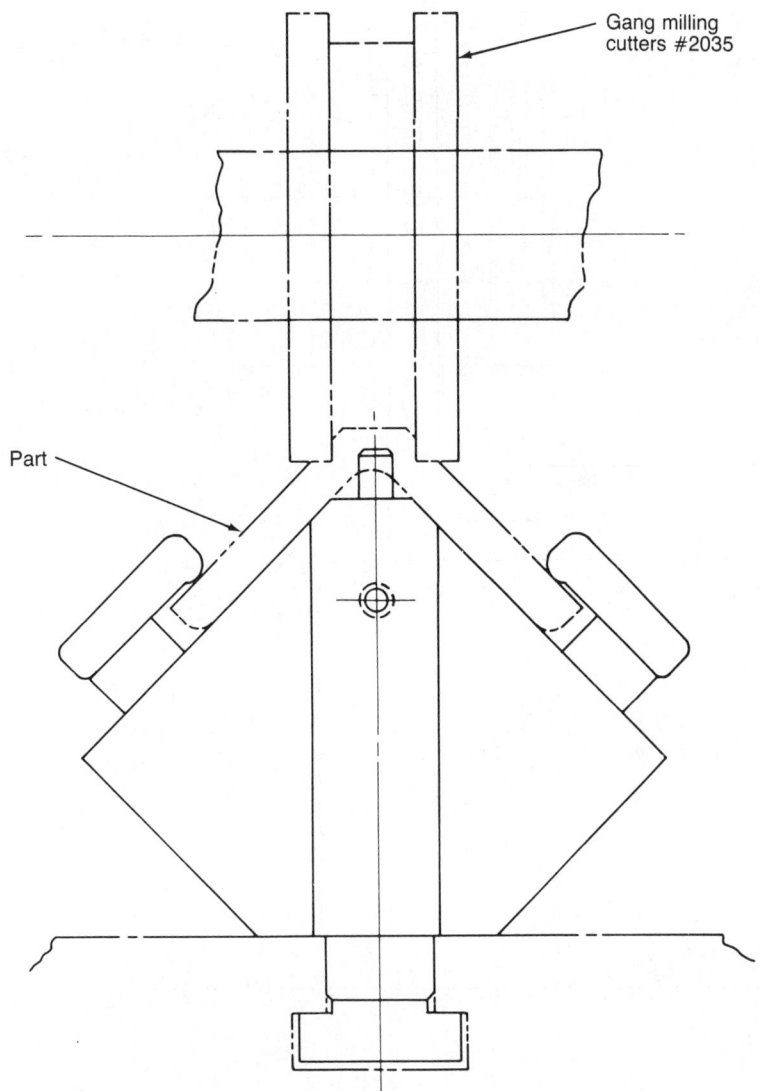

Fig. 1-29 Setup for milling the flats on the motor bracket.

Combining Similar Parts. The three links shown in Fig. 1-32 were considered good candidates for multipurpose tooling because of their similarity and common hole size. The multipurpose drill jig used to drill these workpieces is shown in Fig. 1-33. The drill jig was designed with a dowel-located, removable bushing plate which can be moved as required to accommodate all three links. Interchangeable 0.5 in. and 0.25 in. spacers are fastened to the bushing plate to allow for the 1.0 in. and 1.5 in. wide links. No spacer is needed for the 2.0 in. wide link. Since the holes in the ends of all of the links have the same pattern, no change in the jig is necessary when changing over from one link to another. The workpieces are held in place for drilling with two socket set screws. To drill these holes, the jig is tumbled to rest on its end surface.

Reducing Jig and Fixture Costs. It is the tool designer's responsibility to reduce tooling costs to the absolute minimum and at the same time provide a jig or fixture that fulfills the basic requirements of locating, supporting, and clamping the workpiece, and in the case of

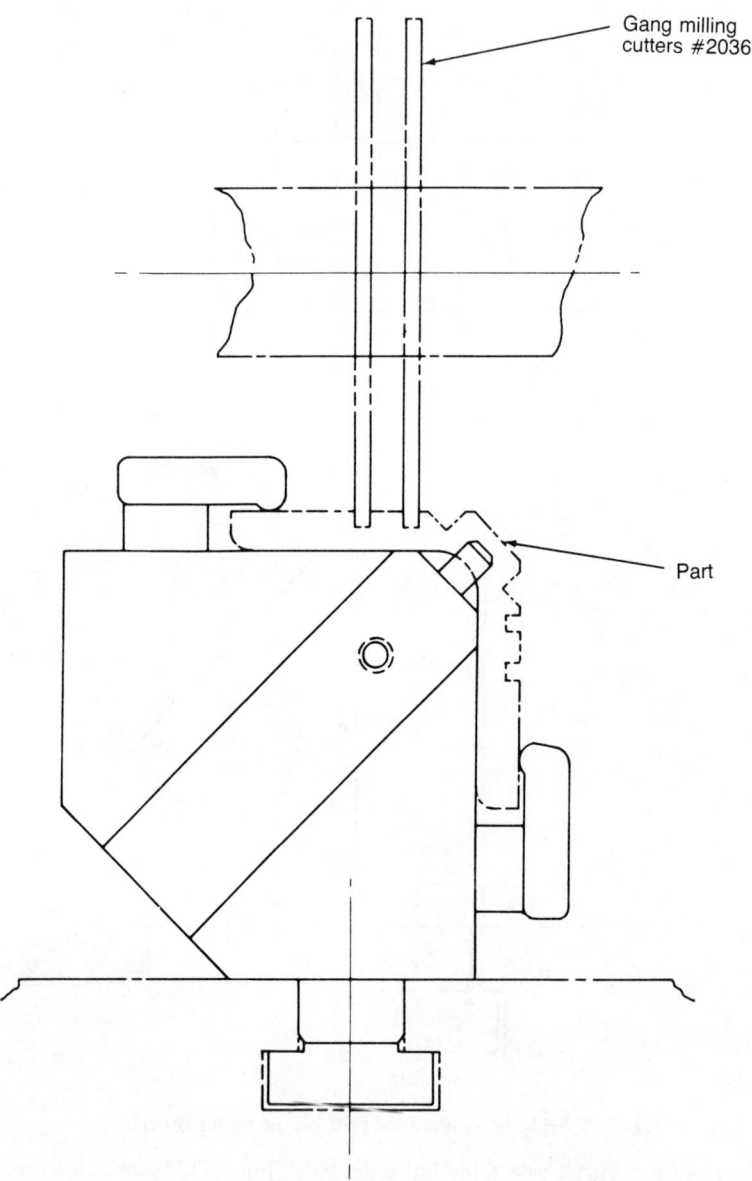

Gang milling
cutters #2036

Part

Fig. 1-30 Setup for milling the slots of the motor bracket.

jigs, guiding the tool. This is especially important when tooling for limited production. Some methods of doing this are discussed in the following section:

- Use wider tolerances—Tooling costs are greatly affected by the tolerances applied to the tool drawing. The tool designer should carefully select the tolerance necessary to satisfy the accuracy requirements of the workpiece. In general, tooling tolerances are between 33% and 50% of the corresponding workpiece tolerances. (For inspection fixtures, tolerances are held to 10% of the corresponding workpiece tolerance). Studies have shown that it costs approximately 30% more to machine to tolerances of 0.0005 in. than to machine to 0.001 in. Two drill jigs are shown in Fig. 1-34. Both are designed to perform the same operation. The conventional drill jig locates the part

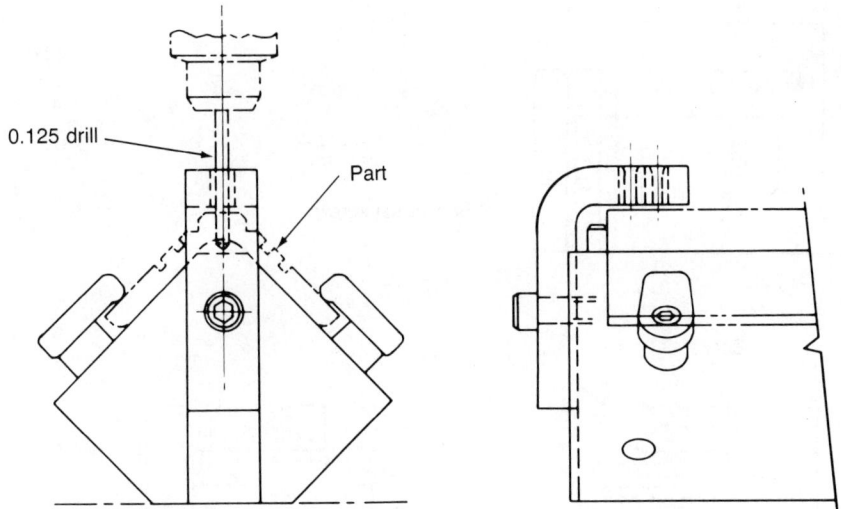

Fig. 1-31 Multipurpose fixture converted into a drill jig.

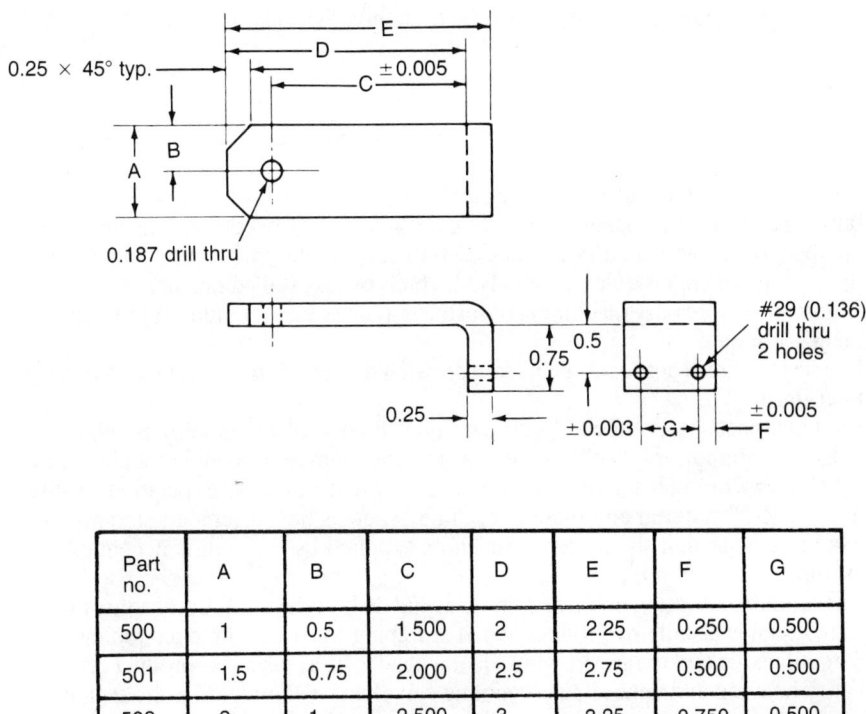

Part no.	A	B	C	D	E	F	G
500	1	0.5	1.500	2	2.25	0.250	0.500
501	1.5	0.75	2.000	2.5	2.75	0.500	0.500
502	2	1	2.500	3	3.25	0.750	0.500

Link—material 1020 Steel

Fig. 1-32 Drawing for three steel links.

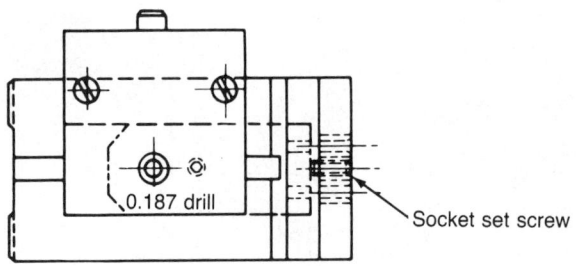

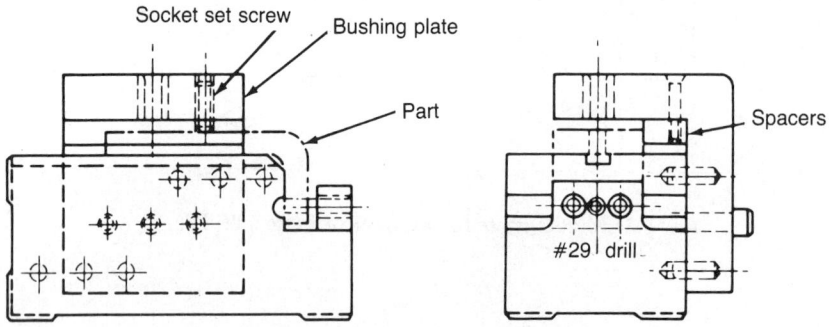

Fig. 1-33 Multipurpose drill jig for drilling all three links shown in Fig. 1-32.

with three solid rest buttons which requires that the bushing be located accurately. This accuracy is not required, however, in the economical jig since the three locating screws used to locate the workpiece can be adjusted as necessary to position the drill bushing at the proper location for drilling the hole in the workpiece. Adjusting screws are then locked with a jam nut and sealed to prevent their movement and minimize tampering. The adjustable jig can also be built by less skilled personnel.

- Eliminate unnecessary machining of surfaces that have no relation to the accuracy of the jig or fixture.
- Use surface finish notations on the tool drawing to indicate those surfaces requiring a finer finish.
- Use notations such as "stock", "saw-cut", and "flame cut" for dimensions when exact sizes are unimportant. Without these words, the toolmaker would probably use the next larger size stock and finish machine it close to the exact size specified, resulting in a waste of material and machining time, whereas the aforementioned notations would indicate that the material finish as supplied by the mill is acceptable. An example is shown in Fig. 1-35.
- Use simplified drafting practices. The fact that 30% of the total cost of a jig or fixture is in design is usually overlooked when searching for ways to reduce tooling costs. Sometimes, jig and fixture drawings do not need to be as formal as product drawings. Fancy lettering and unnecessary detailing can often be eliminated without causing a break in communications between the tool designer and tool builder. Figure 1-36 compares conventional and simplified methods of drawing screw and dowel locations. With the simplified method it is only necessary to show the centerlines and use letters D and S to distinguish dowels from screws. When many holes of various sizes are involved, a method such as that shown in Fig. 1-37 is quite satisfactory.

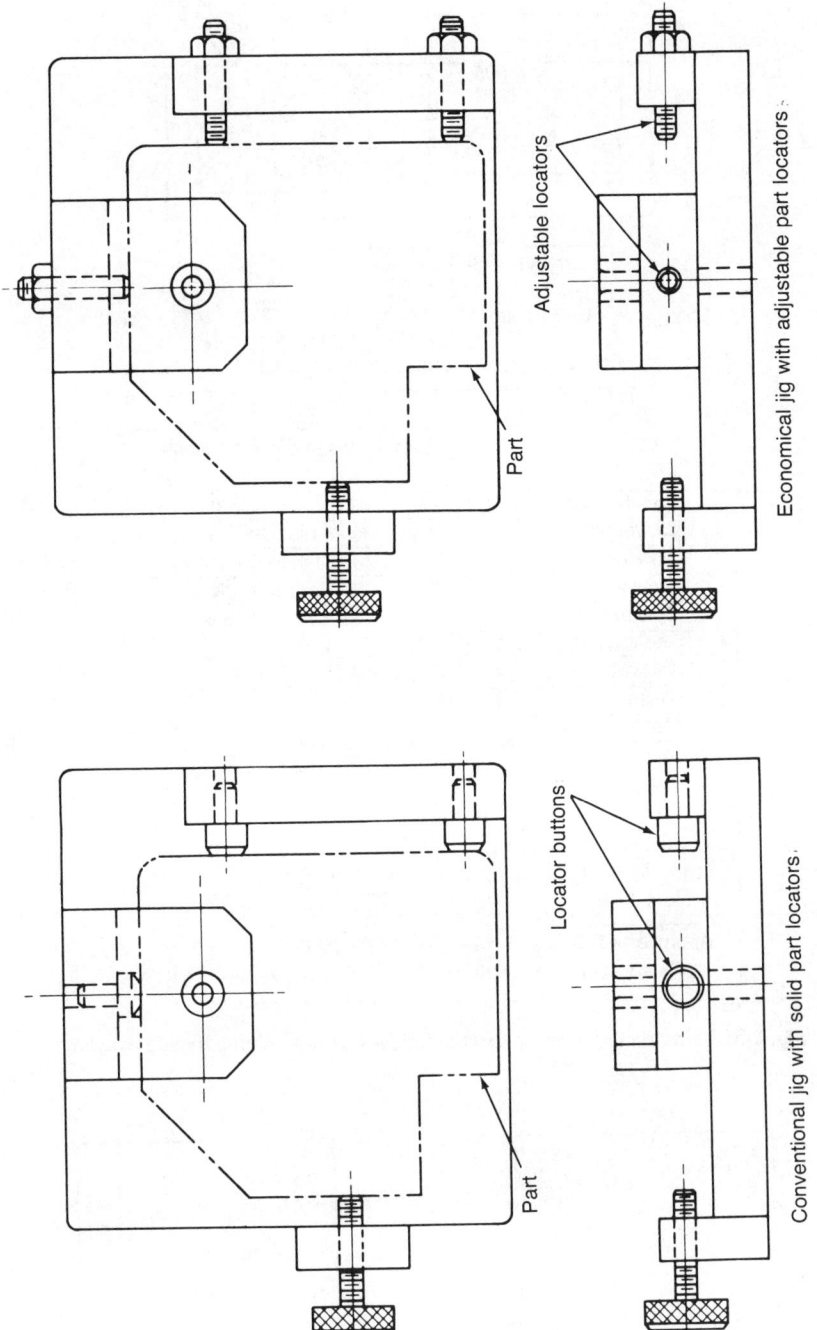

Adjustable locators

Part

Economical jig with adjustable part locators.

Locator buttons

Part

Conventional jig with solid part locators.

Fig. 1-34 Two methods of jig design.

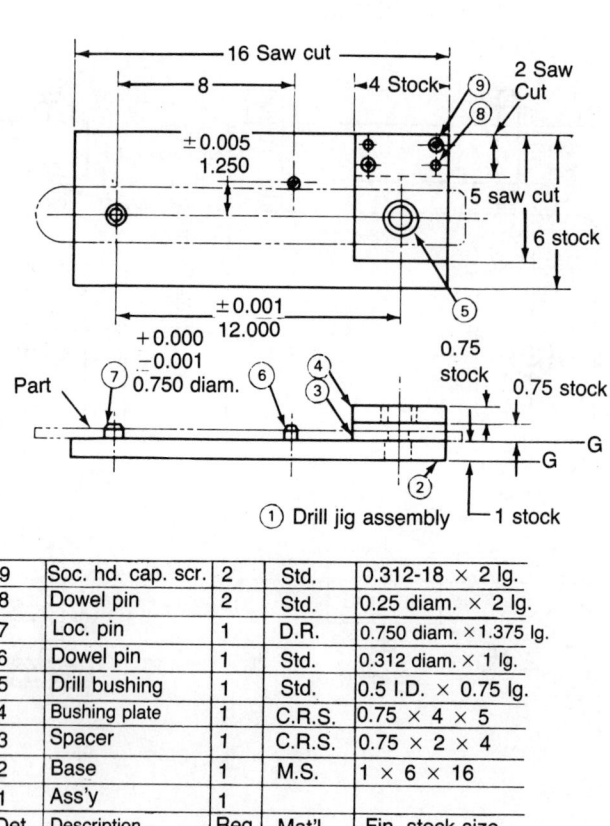

9	Soc. hd. cap. scr.	2	Std.	0.312-18 × 2 lg.
8	Dowel pin	2	Std.	0.25 diam. × 2 lg.
7	Loc. pin	1	D.R.	0.750 diam. ×1.375 lg.
6	Dowel pin	1	Std.	0.312 diam. × 1 lg.
5	Drill bushing	1	Std.	0.5 I.D. × 0.75 lg.
4	Bushing plate	1	C.R.S.	0.75 × 4 × 5
3	Spacer	1	C.R.S.	0.75 × 2 × 4
2	Base	1	M.S.	1 × 6 × 16
1	Ass'y	1		
Det.	Description	Req.	Mat'l.	Fin. stock size

Drill jig

Drawn by—C.D.D. Date 4-15-85	Drawing no.
Approved—F.S. Date 4-19-85	N—2232

Fig. 1-35 Method of specifying surface finishes on low-volume tooling drawings.

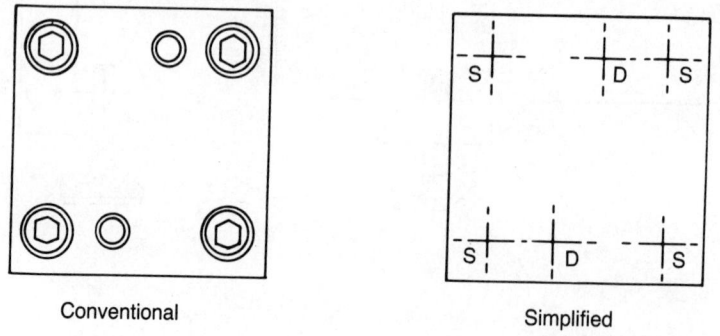

Conventional   Simplified

Fig. 1-36 Methods of drawing screw and dowel locations.

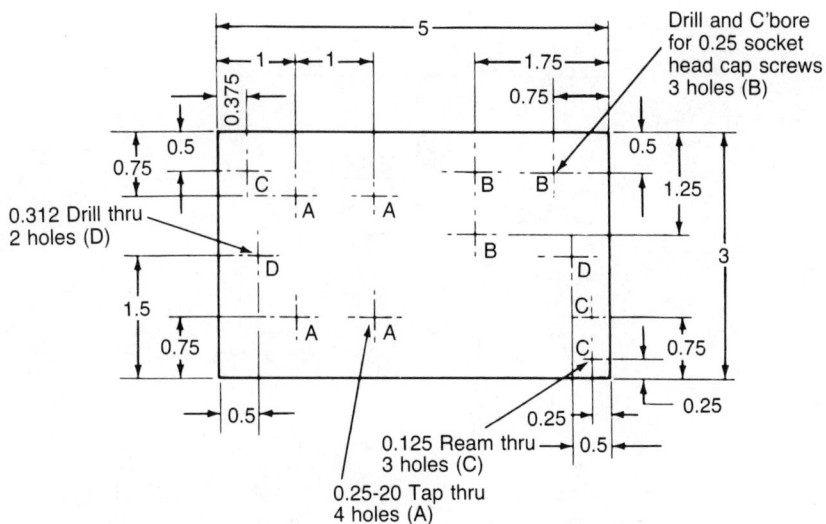

Fig. 1-37 Simplified method of drawing hole locations.

The tool builder is highly skilled and often works with a minimum of information. In many cases an assembly drawing with the necessary detail dimensions is sufficient. If the precise location of a component such as a dowel or screw is unimportant, the tool builder can scale the location directly from the drawing. For further savings, the tool designer may locate standard components as shown in Fig. 1-38 instead of drawing

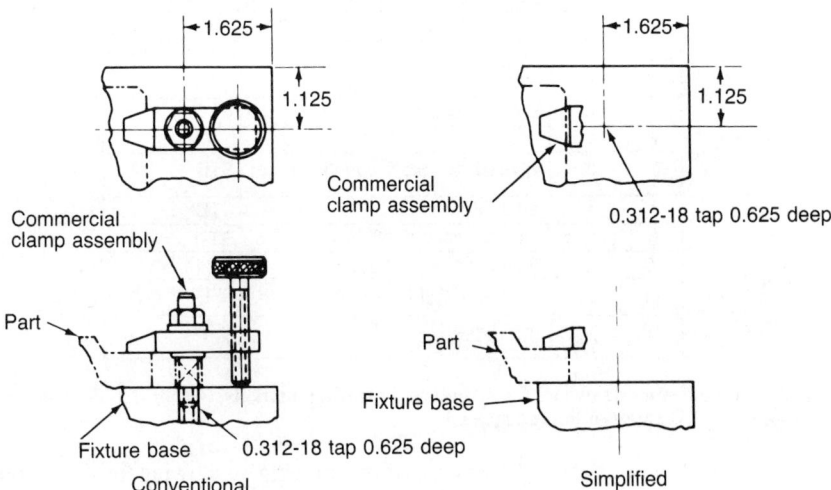

Fig. 1-38 Methods of drawing commercial parts.

them the conventional way. The drawings shown in Figs. 1-39 and 1-40 illustrate conventional and simplified methods for designing a milling fixture. The conventional method took about four hours to draw, while the simplified took less than three hours. The shortcuts leading to the shorter design time were as follows:
1. Elimination of detail drawings by adding pertinent directions to the assembly views.

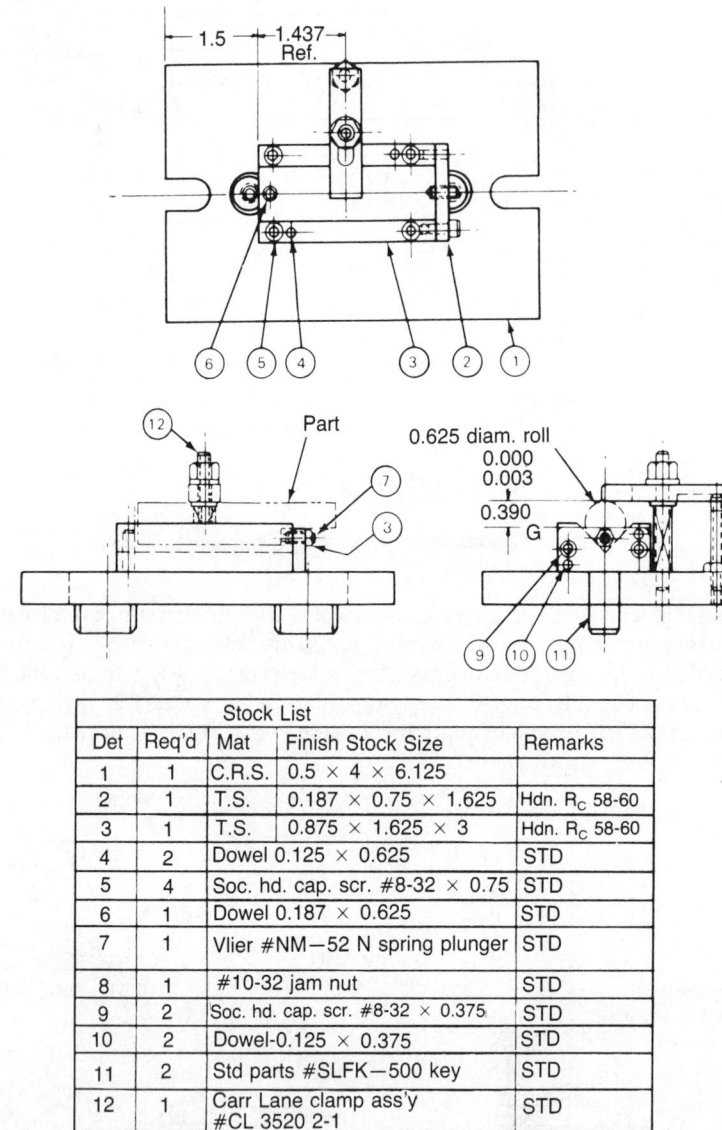

Stock List				
Det	Req'd	Mat	Finish Stock Size	Remarks
1	1	C.R.S.	0.5 × 4 × 6.125	
2	1	T.S.	0.187 × 0.75 × 1.625	Hdn. R_C 58-60
3	1	T.S.	0.875 × 1.625 × 3	Hdn. R_C 58-60
4	2	Dowel 0.125 × 0.625		STD
5	4	Soc. hd. cap. scr. #8-32 × 0.75		STD
6	1	Dowel 0.187 × 0.625		STD
7	1	Vlier #NM—52 N spring plunger		STD
8	1	#10-32 jam nut		STD
9	2	Soc. hd. cap. scr. #8-32 × 0.375		STD
10	2	Dowel-0.125 × 0.375		STD
11	2	Std parts #SLFK—500 key		STD
12	1	Carr Lane clamp ass'y #CL 3520 2-1		STD

Fig. 1-39 Milling fixture drawn with conventional drafting methods. (Other details of this drawing have been deleted because of limited space.)

2. Elimination of some dimensions on the drawing by showing finished detail sizes in the stock list.
3. Provision of notes for the tool builder.

- Specify prefinished material, such as ground flat stock, drill rod, and low carbon plate, on the bill of material. An example of a low-production milling fixture constructed entirely from prefinished stock is shown in Fig. 1-41.
- Don't recess cap screws unless absolutely necessary.
- Substitute cap screw heads for jig feet or rest buttons on low-production jigs and fixtures as shown in Fig. 1-42.
- Use spring pins and grooved pins instead of dowels when location tolerances permit.

1-36

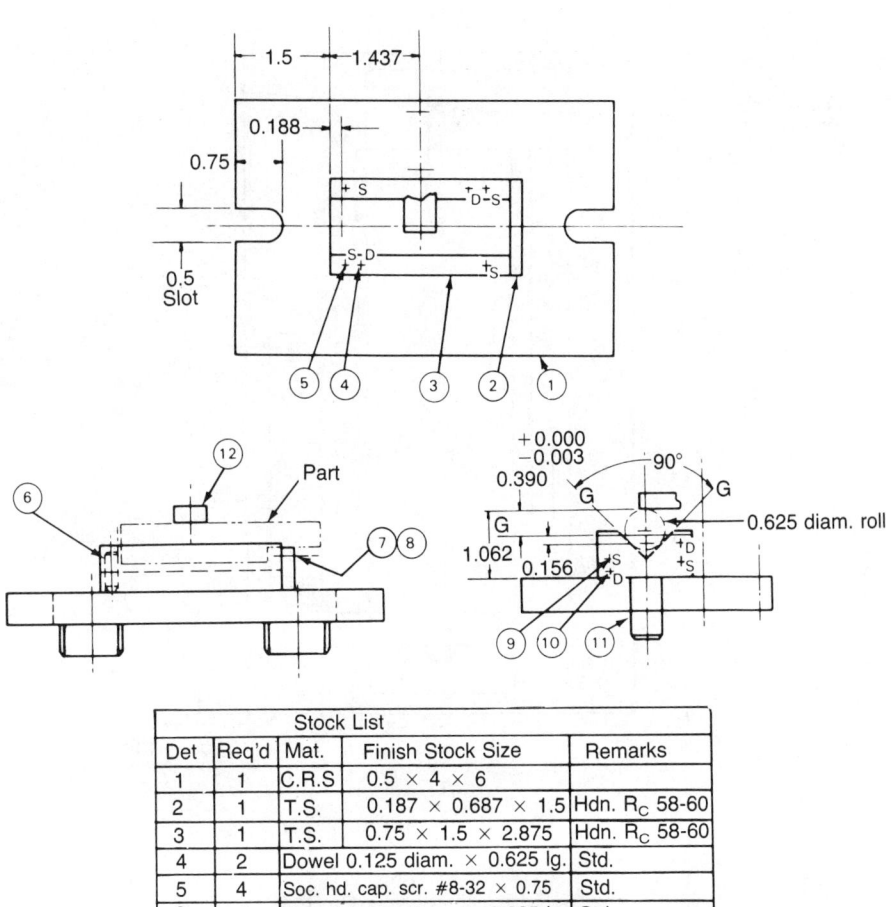

Stock List				
Det	Req'd	Mat.	Finish Stock Size	Remarks
1	1	C.R.S	0.5 × 4 × 6	
2	1	T.S.	0.187 × 0.687 × 1.5	Hdn. R_C 58-60
3	1	T.S.	0.75 × 1.5 × 2.875	Hdn. R_C 58-60
4	2	Dowel 0.125 diam. × 0.625 lg.		Std.
5	4	Soc. hd. cap. scr. #8-32 × 0.75		Std.
6	1	Dowel 0.187 diam. × 0.625 lg.		Std.
7	1	Vlier #NM—52 N spring G plunger		Std.
8	1	#10-32 jam nut		Std.
9	2	Soc. hd. cap. scr. #8-32 × 0.375		Std.
10	2	Dowel 0.125 diam. × 0.375 lg.		Std.
11	2	Std. parts #SLFK—500 key		Std.
12	1	Carr Lane clamp ass'y #CL-3520—2-1		Std.

Notes
1. Scale all dimensions not shown.
2. For information not shown, work to toolmaker's standard practice.
3. Unless otherwise specified, locate all screws and dowels to suit stock list.

Fig. 1-40 Milling fixture drawn with simplified, economical drafting methods.

They can be installed in a drilled hole, thereby eliminating the need for reaming or lapping.
• Eliminate slotting or grooving operations to install fixture keys. Figure 1-43 shows the conventional method along with alternatives. With the conventional method, keys are usually set into a machined slot or groove in the fixture base and secured by screws. In the simplified method, a reamed hole with a diameter the same as the

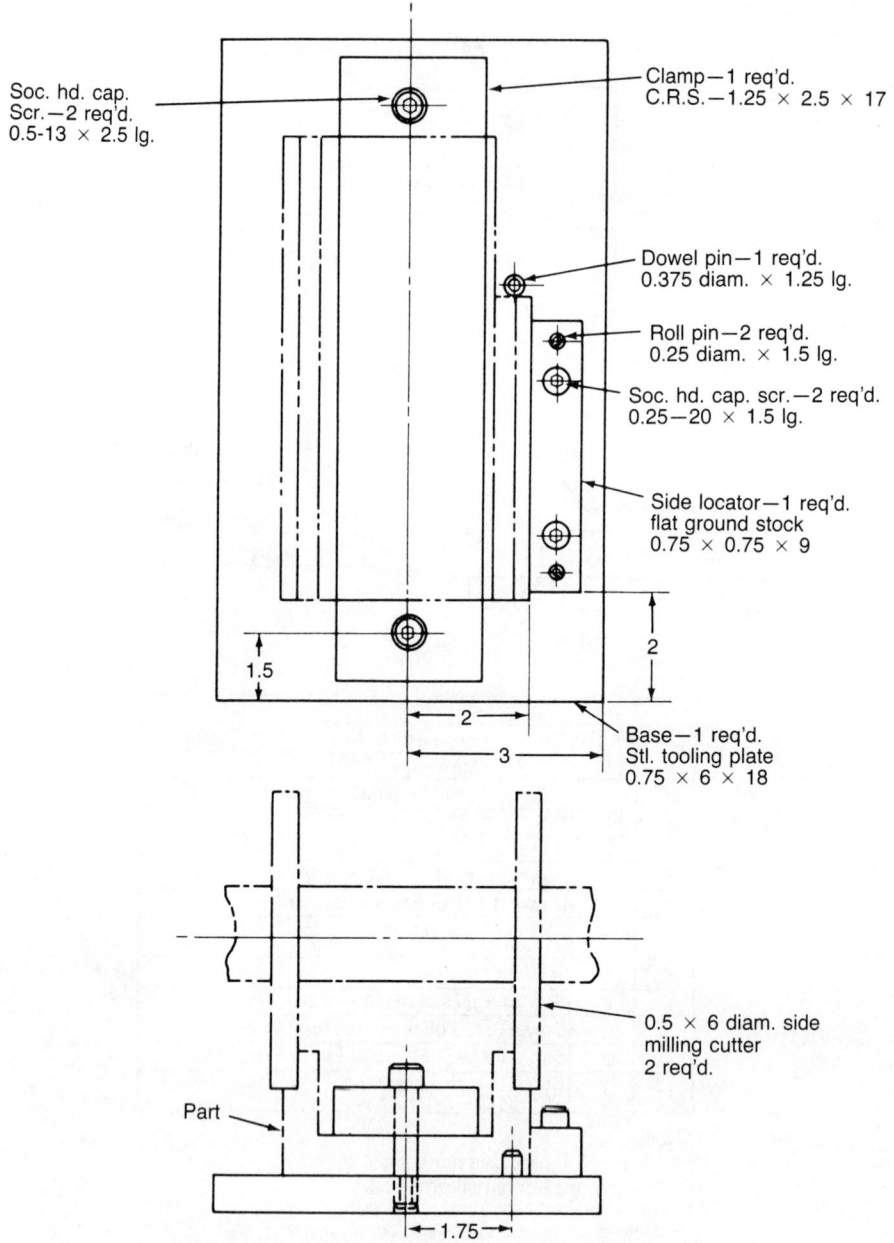

Soc. hd. cap.
Scr.—2 req'd.
0.5-13 × 2.5 lg.

Clamp—1 req'd.
C.R.S.—1.25 × 2.5 × 17

Dowel pin—1 req'd.
0.375 diam. × 1.25 lg.

Roll pin—2 req'd.
0.25 diam. × 1.5 lg.

Soc. hd. cap. scr.—2 req'd.
0.25—20 × 1.5 lg.

Side locator—1 req'd.
flat ground stock
0.75 × 0.75 × 9

1.5

2

2

3

Base—1 req'd.
Stl. tooling plate
0.75 × 6 × 18

0.5 × 6 diam. side
milling cutter
2 req'd.

Part

1.75

Fig. 1-41 Milling fixture constructed from prefinished material.

keyway or T-slot of the machine base is machined into the base of the fixture and a dowel or stud is pressed into it. With the method shown in *c*, a 0.6250 in. diameter reamed hole is machined into the base of the fixture and the fixture key is mounted as shown.

- Use standard components such as clamps, locators, and rest buttons. It is more economical to buy than to fabricate similar parts. In many cases standard components can be modified to suit a special application.
- Use premachined section forms and bases such as those shown in Fig. 1-44. These

Locator block

Base

G

Jig feet—standard
socket head cap screw

Grind at assemble

Fig. 1-42 Screw heads substituted for jig feet.

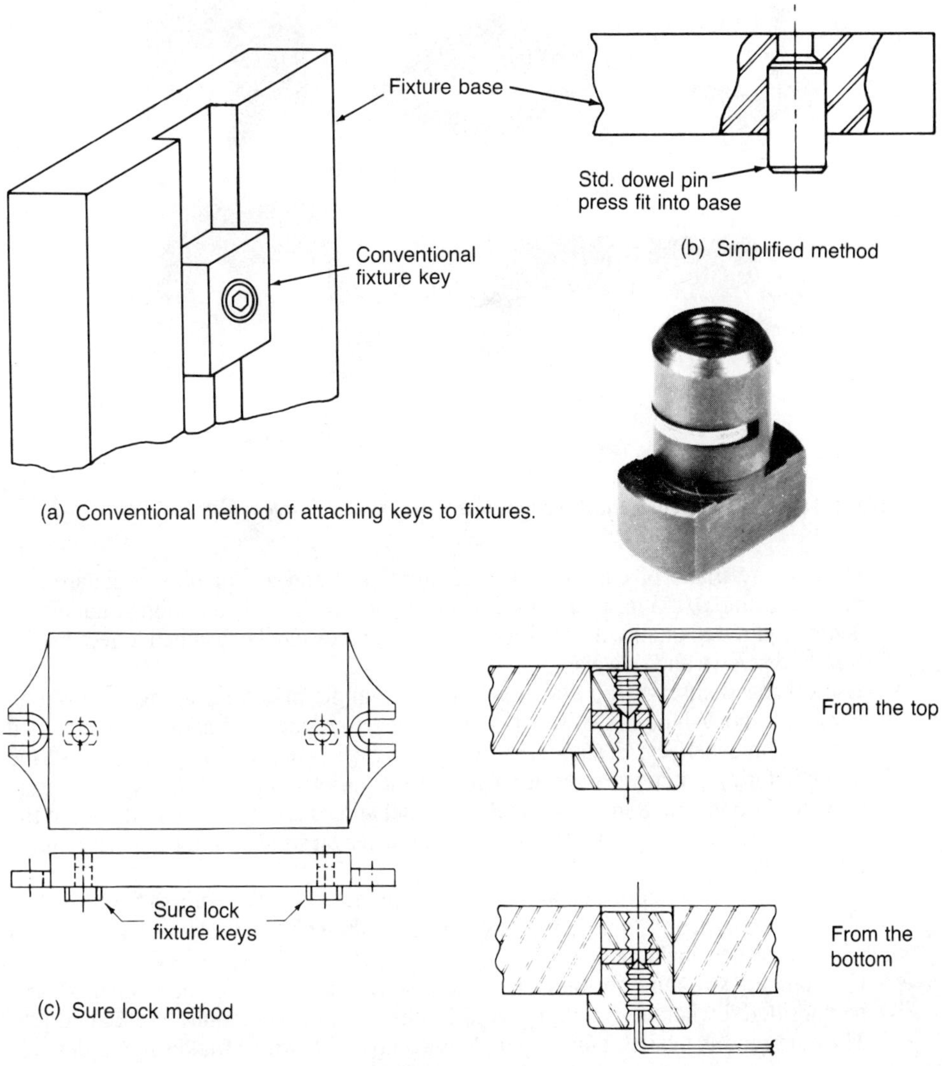

Fixture base

Std. dowel pin
press fit into base

(b) Simplified method

Conventional
fixture key

(a) Conventional method of attaching keys to fixtures.

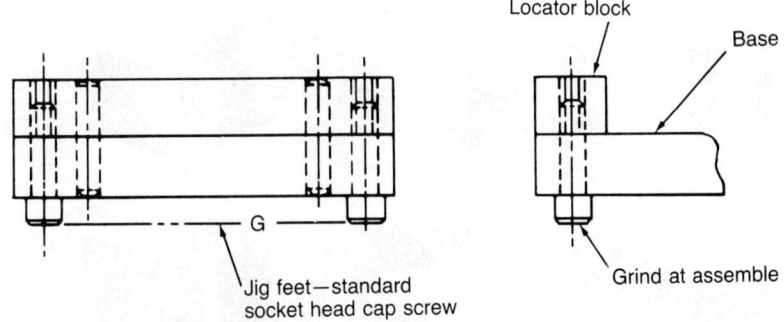

Sure lock
fixture keys

From the top

From the
bottom

(c) Sure lock method

Fig. 1-43 Fixture keys. (*Sure-Loc method, (c), courtesy Carr Lane Mfg. Co.*)

Fig. 1-44 Standard premachined section forms and bases. (*Courtesy Carr Lane Mfg. Co.*)

sections are made of cast iron or cast aluminum and are machined square and parallel within 0.005 in./ft on all sides except the end. Usually additional machining is not required to qualify the finished surface and they can be fastened together with standard screws and dowels.

- Use off-the shelf cast iron and cast aluminum angle plates, right angle irons, box parallels, and V-block (see Fig. 1-45) for the same purposes as the premachined sections, but where closer squareness and parallelism is required. Figure 1-46 lists the manufacturing practices and tolerances for the various angles and blocks. V-block surfaces of 6 in. and 8 in. are typically parallel and square with each other, and the Vee centrally located within 0.0005 in. Tolerances on smaller V-blocks are proportionately less.
- Use section components such as those shown in Fig. 1-47. They can save considerable time and expense since they are available off-the-shelf and generally can be used without further machining.
- Use standard structural forms such as those shown in Fig. 1-48. These forms should be considered when designing jigs and fixtures that do not require great accuracy. They are readily available in varying lengths up to 5 ft which makes them ideal for large tooling. A combination drill jig and milling fixture made from this material is shown in Fig. 1-49.

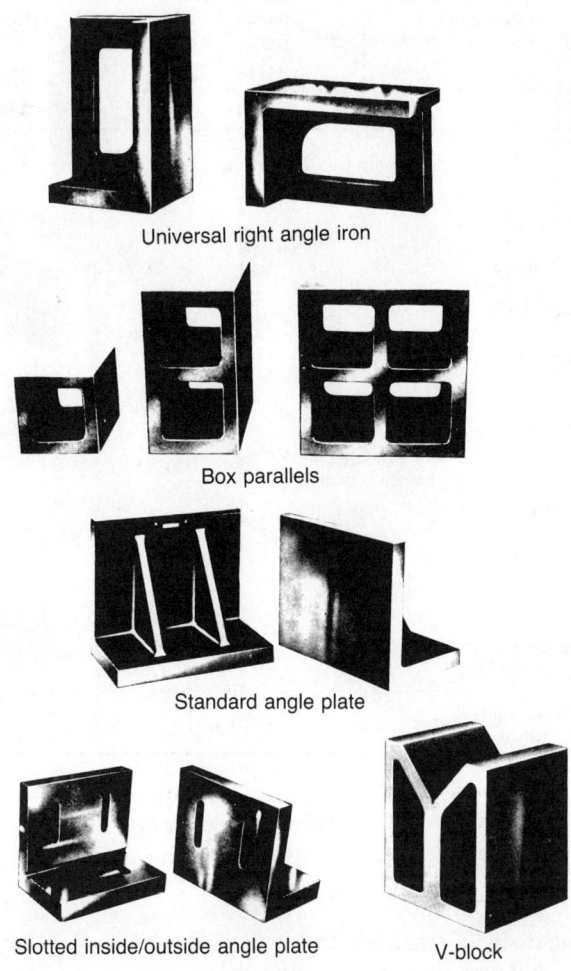

Universal right angle iron

Box parallels

Standard angle plate

Slotted inside/outside angle plate   V-block

Fig. 1-45 Precision surface equipment. (*Courtesy The Challenge Machinery Co.*)

- Consider building the jig or fixture from magnesium or aluminum. Table 1-6 shows the properties of the different alloys and compares them with cast iron and steel. Magnesium and aluminum are both much lighter than cast iron or steel. For example, a cubic foot (28,317 cm³) of magnesium weighs only about 112 lb (51 kg) compared to 165 lb (74.8 kg) for the same volume of aluminum and nearly 500 lb (227 kg) for steel. Both magnesium and aluminum can be machined at higher speeds and feeds resulting in lower labor and overhead costs. Another advantage is the greater tool life which also results in lower labor costs as well as lower tool costs and less downtime for tool changing. Aluminum and magnesium extrusions and tooling plates are readily available in a wide range of mill standard sizes. Magnesium and aluminum both cost considerably more than steel but the savings resulting from their better machining characteristics can often make up the difference.
- Consider making the jig or fixture from wood. Wood can often be substituted for steel when building jigs and fixtures that do not require great accuracy, or where heavy use or abuse is not expected. Some of the advantages of using wood are as follows:
    1. It can be formed easily with ordinary woodworking tools by relatively unskilled personnel.

1-41

Manufacturing practices and tolerances (standards)				Maximum grinding height Capacity = 28 in.			Ground finish unless otherwise specified	
		Name	Flat	Square	Parallel		Size	
							Working	Nonworking
ELL Shapes / Angles	◣	Tool maker's knees	Within 0.00025 in. up to 8 in.				0.30 in.	±0.030 in.
		Standard angle	Within 0.0005 in. up to 6 in. and graduated to 0.0001 per inch over 6 in.		Non applicable			
		Slotted angle						
		T-slotted angle						
		Inside-outside angle		0.00025 in 6 in.			±0.30 in.	
		Universal angle iron					±0.010 in.	Non applicable
Box Shapes / Box (Blocks)	▦	Universal box angle					±0.005 in.	
		Box parallel						
		Height blocks						
		Parallel straight edge		0.0005 in 72 in.			± 0.30 in.	±0.30 in.
		Stacked box angle mach. finish	0.002 in.	0.001 in 12 in.				

Fig. 1-46 Manufacturing practices and tolerances.
(Courtesy The Challenge Machinery Co.)

2. It can be easily fastened together with nails, screws, and glue.
3. It has a very high compression strength.
4. Expansion and contraction is negligible.
5. Wood absorbs shocks and dampens vibrations better than most materials.
2. Wood does not rust.

Wood, however, has the following disadvantages:
1. It has a tendency to warp, shrink, and swell as humidity changes.
2. It cannot be subjected to extreme heat.
3. It cannot be formed into another shape.
4. The hardness of wood is limited and cannot be changed without changing its character.

Designing wood tooling is generally the same as designing for equivalent conventional tooling. However, the tool designer must thoroughly understand the aforementioned advantages and disadvantages in order to provide a jig or fixture that will meet service requirements and avoid any distortion of it from warping and fabrication stresses. The tool designer should:
1. Select the proper wood.
2. Understand basic wood construction methods, joinery, and special hardware.
3. Provide for protection of the completed jig or fixture.

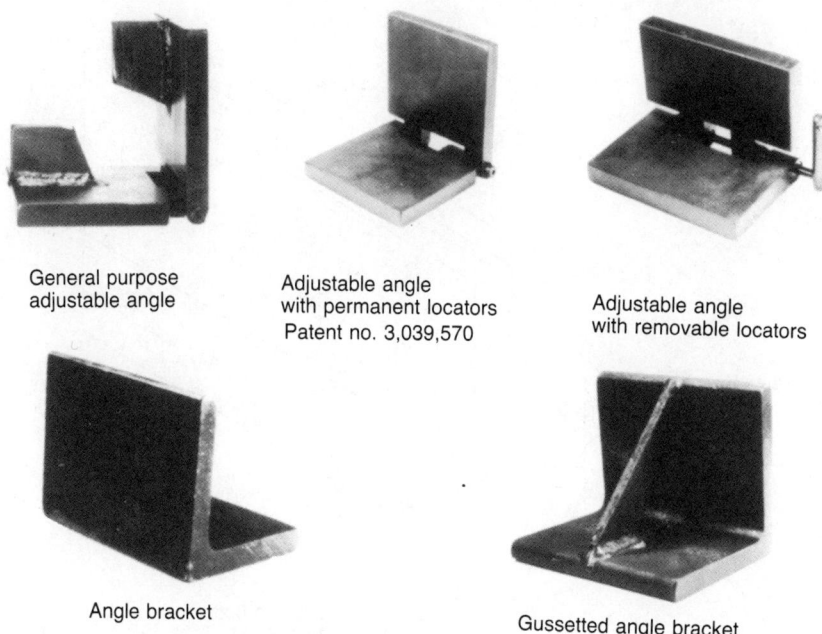

General purpose
adjustable angle

Adjustable angle
with permanent locators
Patent no. 3,039,570

Adjustable angle
with removable locators

Angle bracket

Gussetted angle bracket

Fig. 1-47 Section components. (*Courtesy Carr Lane Mfg. Co.*)

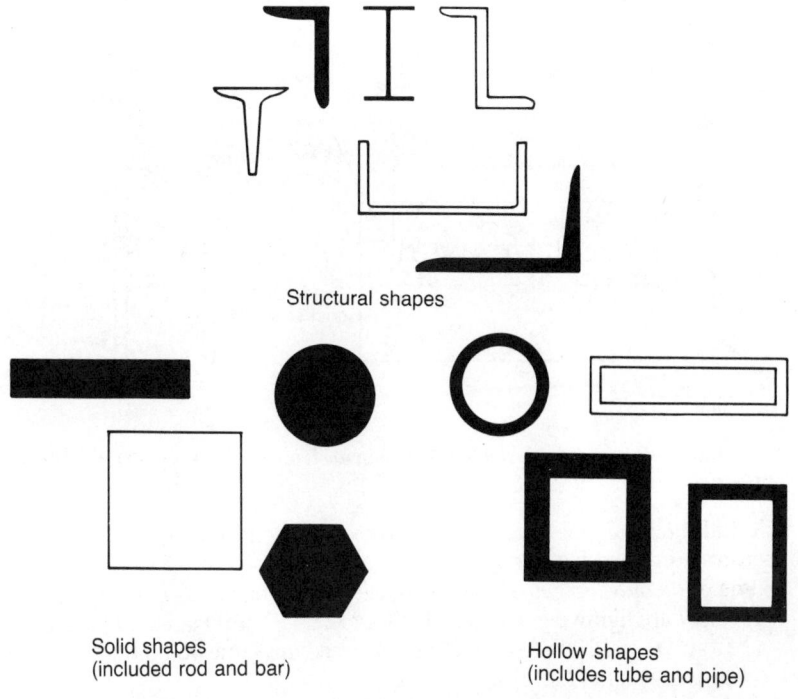

Structural shapes

Solid shapes
(included rod and bar)

Hollow shapes
(includes tube and pipe)

Fig. 1-48 Structural shapes, solid shapes, and hollow shapes.

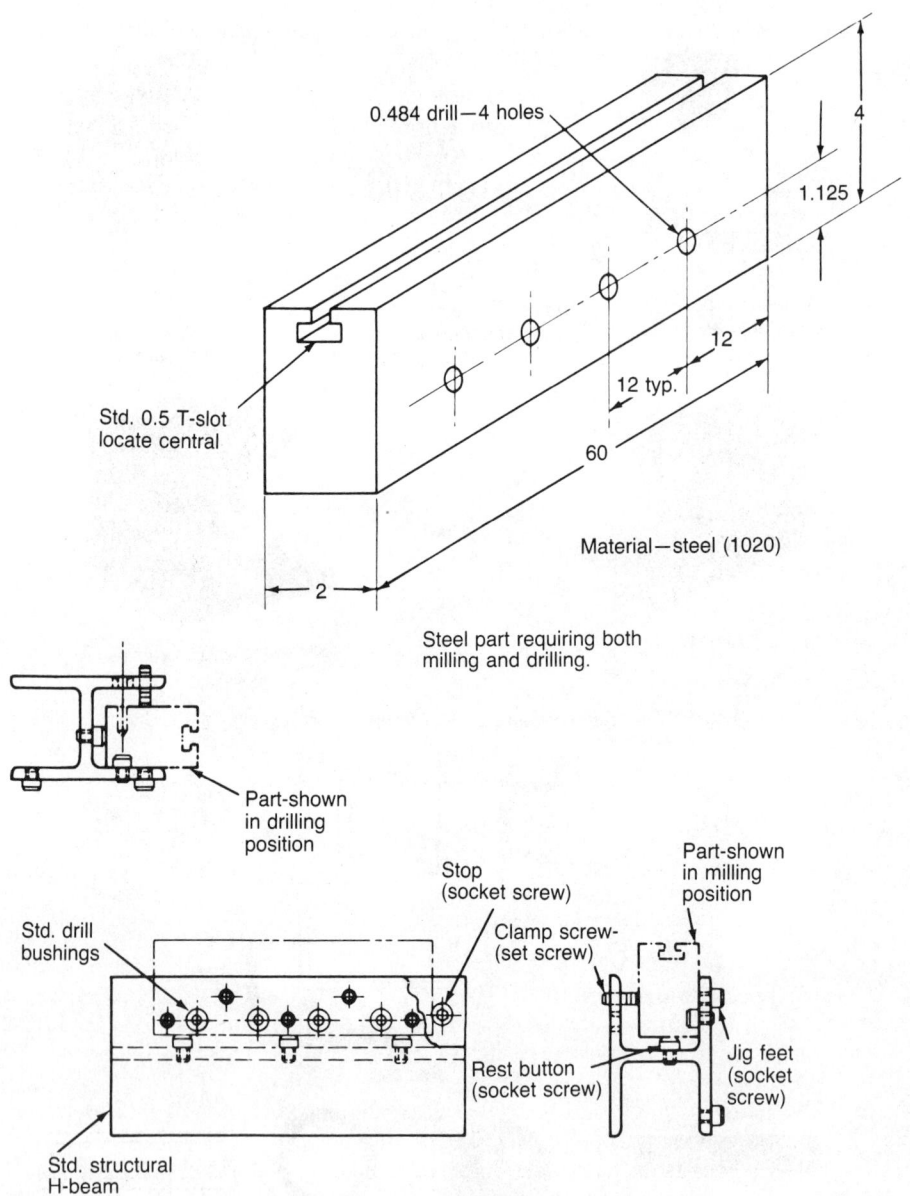

0.484 drill—4 holes

Std. 0.5 T-slot
locate central

4

1.125

12

12 typ.

60

2

Material—steel (1020)

Steel part requiring both
milling and drilling.

2.5

Part-shown
in drilling
position

Part-shown
in milling
position

Stop
(socket screw)

Clamp screw-
(set screw)

Std. drill
bushings

2.5

Jig feet
(socket
screw)

Rest button
(socket screw)

Std. structural
H-beam

Fig. 1-49 Combination drill jig and milling fixture made from structural material (H-beam) for the part shown.

- Consider plastic tool construction—Epoxy resins are the principle plastics used to construct jigs and fixtures.
  Some of the advantages of using epoxies for tooling are as follows:
  1. They are lightweight. One cubic foot (28,317 cm³) of cured plastic will weigh from 70 to 120 lb (32 to 54 kg) whereas the same volume of steel will weigh nearly 500 lb (227 kg).
  2. Lead time is usually short because epoxy tools can be easily formed to the desired shape without machining.

TABLE 1-6
Properties of Magnesium Alloys Compared with Aluminum, Cast Iron, and Steel

Alloy	Specific Gravity	Tensile Strength (typ.), ksi (MPa)	Yield Strength (typ.), ksi (MPa)	Elongation in 2 in. (50.8 mm) %	Brinell Hardness
Magnesium tooling plate AZ31B	1.77	38 (262)	28 (193)	14	49
Magnesium shapes AZ61A (as extruded)	1.80	46 (317)	33 (228)	17	60
Magnesium shapes ZK60A (artificially aged)	1.83	49 (338)	38 (262)	14	75
Cast aluminum tooling plate, alca plus	2.80	26 (179)	15 (104)	7	65
Wrought aluminum tooling plate 6061 T-651	2.70	45 (311)	40 (276)	12	64
Aluminum shapes 6063T5	2.70	27 (186)	21 (145)	12	73
Cast iron ASTM 40	7.20	40 (276)	—	—	210
Hot rolled steel 1018	7.80	58 (400)	32 (221)	25	116

3. Epoxies are easily formed to complex shapes by laminating or casting around a master pattern, such as a prototype part, a production part, or a scale model made of wood, plastic, plaster, or metal.
4. Epoxies are resistant to corrosion, grease, and oil.
5. Epoxy tooling can be modified and repaired quickly and easily.

Plastics, however, have the following disadvantages:

1. Epoxies do not have the strength, durability, and stability of other materials, and mechanical properties deteriorate with heat. Plastic tools should not be considered when temperatures are expected to exceed 180°F (82.2°C).
2. Since machining is seldom required on plastic tooling, the accuracy cast into the tool will be the accuracy transferred to the workpiece. Therefore, the master pattern on which the tooling is laminated or cast must be the same accuracy as that required of the tooling.
3. Many of the plastics used today can cause health problems. Suppliers of these materials are using better packaging to minimize these problems and furnish complete instructions which point out the dangers and offer methods to avoid them. They should be closely followed.

Designing Epoxy Tools. Although epoxy tooling designs differ considerably from conventional designs, they are not usually any more difficult to design, and their formability provides the ingenious tool designer with unlimited possibilities.

When designing epoxy tooling, the tool designer must understand the various construction methods, along with the advantages and disadvantages of each method. Basically, there are four plastic tooling methods: laminate, surface cast, mass cast, and paste. These methods can be used singly or in any combination.

Before undertaking a jig or fixture design, the tool designer must decide which of the construction methods is best suited for the application in mind. To determine this, seven factors should be considered: dimensional stability, shrinkage, weight, labor cost, material cost, strength, and durability. Table 1-7 lists these seven factors for each of the four construction methods. The table is a general guide only, since conditions for a particular application can cause them to change.

TABLE 1-7
Plastic Tooling Construction Methods

	Dimensional Stability	Shrinkage (during cure)	Low Weight	Labor Cost
Laminate	Excellent	Excellent	Excellent	Poor
Surface cast (metal core)	Fair	Fair	Poor	Fair
Mass cast	Poor	Poor	Fair	Excellent
Paste	Satisfactory	Satisfactory	Satisfactory	Satisfactory

	Material Cost (per lb)	Strength	Toughness
Laminate	Poor	Excellent	Excellent
Surface cast (metal core)	Fair	Satisfactory	Satisfactory
Mass cast	Excellent	Fair	Poor
Paste	Satisfactory	Poor	Fair

(Courtesy Ciba-Geigy Tooling Systems)

The next step is the selection of the epoxy material. This should be done very carefully since there are just about as many grades of epoxies as there are applications. The epoxy formulator can furnish comprehensive material selection charts to help the designer make the proper choice. In complex cases, the epoxy formulator should always be consulted.

Epoxy jigs and fixtures can usually be fabricated from sketches. Nevertheless, permanent records showing the source and grade of the epoxy used should be kept in case the jig or fixture needs to be repaired or modified.

Note: Because of the difference in thermal expansion rates between plastics and metals, epoxy cast tooling should be designed to avoid the bonding or fastening of long lengths of metal. Additionally, any metal weldments should be normalized before attachment to the tooling.

In cast tooling, metal components such as studs, plates, and drill bushings are easily cast into the face of the tooling. In laminated tooling, a hole is drilled that is slightly larger than the component and epoxy paste is used to hold the component in place. Metal components must be shaped or drilled to provide a strong bond. Figure 1-50 illustrates some methods of interlocking the parts in the epoxy. Metal components can also be mechanically attached.

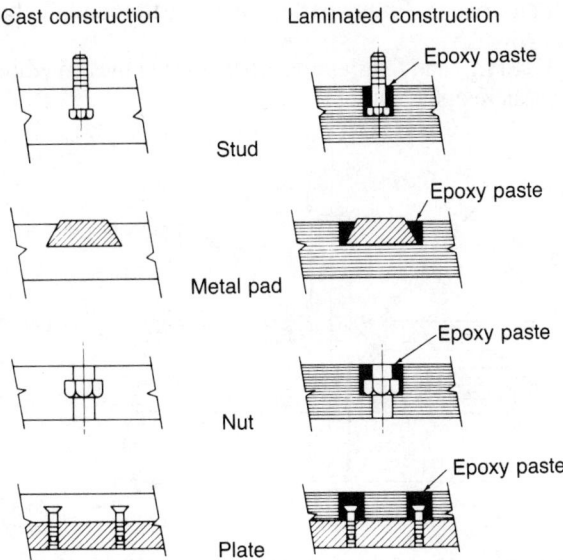

Fig. 1-50 Methods of attaching metal parts to epoxy tooling.

Conventional drill jig bushings should not be used in plastic tooling. Special bushings designed for this purpose are readily available.

Methods for inserting bushings in plastic tooling differs from the conventional method. When using a casting method of construction, the drill bushing must be positioned in the correct position before pouring the liquid epoxy. This positioning is usually done using a model or sample part as shown in Fig. 1-51. The locating pins should have snug fits to assure accurate placement. Normal casting procedures are then followed.

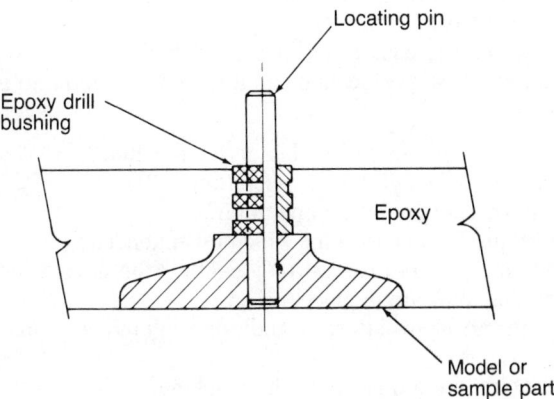

Fig. 1-51 Method of locating and bonding drill bushings in cast epoxy.

For laminated construction, the normal laminating procedure is followed and the tool allowed to cool before removing it from the model. Pilot holes to locate the drill bushings are then drilled using the model or sample part as a jig. The laminated tooling is then removed from the model or sample part and the holes redrilled to a diameter that is 0.0625 in. greater than the OD of the bushings. Next the laminated tooling is replaced on the model or sample part, snug fitting locating pins are inserted through the oversized drilled bushing holes and into the holes in the model or sample part. Bushings are then placed over the pins and into the oversized holes in the tooling. Epoxy paste is then cast around the bushing as shown in Fig. 1-52.

Typical examples of jigs and fixtures constructed using these methods are shown in the following chapters where applicable.

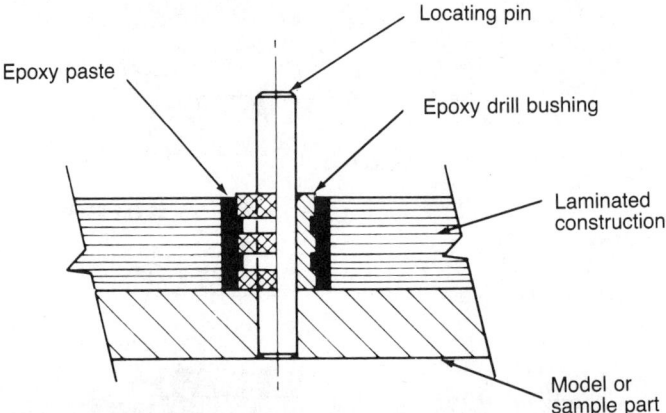

Fig. 1-52 Method of locating and bonding drill bushings in laminated epoxy.

FIXTURE DESIGN QUESTIONS[1]

The tool designer might find the following list of fixture design questions useful to ask as a final review of a design before fabrication, or during a phase of the design procedure as they apply to that particular phase.

0. Setting Up the Jig or Fixture

0.1. *Shop Layout*

Is there any obstruction in the shop layout which will affect setting up the fixture, e.g., are building columns in the way?

Are the necessary services, such as air lines, available?

If a hoist is required, is it available; and can it be maneuvered into place?

0.2. *Machine*

Are the correct speeds and feeds available on the machine?

Is the machine accurate enough for the operation?

Is the machine sturdy enough for the operation?

Will the fixture fit into the machine for which it is intended?

Has the machine sufficient room and stroke length of the slide to perform the operation when the jig and cutting tools are in place?

Is there sufficient throat depth between spindle and column of the machine to accommodate the jig?

Is the weight of the fixture too great for the machine?

Do the T-slots in the table line up with the clamping holes or slots in the fixture?

Is there enough clearance in these holes or slots to permit adjustment of the jig under the machine spindle?

Will the fixture overhang the end of the table when it is in place?

Are the register blocks in the fixture base the correct size for the machine, and are they correctly located?

Is there any projection, boss, bolthead, or other machine part which will foul the jig or fixture?

Will any operating handle of the machine strike on the fixture or be prevented from moving by the fixture?

Will the jig interfere with any other jig or fixture next to it on a multispindle machine?

Are jig-hole spacings within the range of adjustment of the spindles when a multispindle head is used?

0.3. *Cutters*

Can the setup man see whether the cutter or drill is correctly set?

Can cutting tools be adjusted when the fixture is in place?

Can cutters be readily removed for sharpening without disturbing the fixture?

0.4. *Setting Aids*

Can setting blocks, bushings, stops, or collars be used in setting up the cutting tools?

If dial indicators are required for the setup, are there suitable places for mounting them on the cutters or fixture?

Have suitable locating plugs been provided for setting up?

Is the accuracy of the part such that built-in adjustments are required in the fixture to compensate for machine misalignment?

Will an accurate sample part be useful as a setting master?

0.5. *Operator*

Does the setup man need more than one size of wrench? If so, can the number of sizes be reduced?

Are the hold-down bolts awkwardly placed, making their insertion or tightening difficult?

Is the setup man required to handle excessively heavy or awkward equipment?

1. Loading and Location of Part

1.1. *Shop Layout*

Is there any obstruction in the shop layout which will hinder the loading of the part into the fixture?

Is the jig design correctly related to the flow line of the process?

Is the fixture to be used in conjunction with material-handling aids, such as hoists, hoppers, or conveyors?

If so, is the design correctly related to such equipment?

1.2. *Nature of the Part*

How will allowable variations in the shape of the part affect its location in the jig or fixture?

Is there enough clearance in the jig to allow for all lumps, fins, lugs, burrs, or protrusions on the part for all normal variations in size and shape? (Castings and forgings often vary from the drawings.)

Will a profile plate on the jig base or sighting holes in the jig plate be useful in locating parts which are not consistent in shape or size?

If no previous operations have been done on the part, are there suitable datum faces or points from which to locate?

Can such points be properly related to the results required from this operation?

If the shape of the part makes location difficult, is it possible to have it modified to assist in locating it?

If the completed shape cannot be changed, can some temporary lug or other helpful feature be provided which can be machined off when its purpose has been fulfilled?

If the component is heavy, can arrangements be made to slide rather than lift it into place?

Where only one end of a long component has to be loaded into a fixture, has a suitable support or outrigger been provided to carry the free end?

Have V-locators been placed in the correct plane so that variations in the locating diameters will not affect the accuracy of this operation?

Are the locating points as widely spaced as possible?

Are the locators affected by the material from which the part is made?

Is the component material so abrasive as to warrant the use of carbide locators?

Are the locating points those from which the result of this operation is dimensioned on the part drawing?

If the part is a rough casting, can a three-point location scheme be used?

If not, can a suitable jack pin or adjustable locator be used to provide the fourth point?

Should any other locators be adjustable to allow for casting variations?

Are centralizing devices required to compensate for part variations?

Are all locators on the same side of the parting line of a casting or of the flash of a forging?

If not, what effect on the location will mismatching have?

Is it possible to have all the locators on the bushing plate of a drill jig, thus ensuring correct relationship between locators and holes?

Where several parts are located in the tool, should each one have its own locators, or will the accumulation of errors caused by parts resting on one another be acceptable?

1.3. *Previous Operations*

Do previous operations provide suitable datum and location points?

Is the tolerance on the locating points sufficiently close to obtain the accuracy required from this operation?

Can all subsequent operations be located from the same points?

If so, can the locators in all these fixtures be made identical in size and shape?

Have locators been relieved to accommodate burr thrown up by previous operations?

Have locating surfaces on the jig been kept as small in area as practicable?

Where they locate on a machine surface, do the rest pads come well within the boundaries of the machined area?

Are they well above chip-collecting surfaces?

Are they easy to keep clean?

Does the required accuracy demand expanding pins when locating from previously machined holes?

In boring fixtures where more than one hole is to be finish-bored after rough or intermediate boring, has the part been located from the smallest bore in order to minimize deflection of the slender boring bar with an eccentric cut?

Where location is from accurately machined or fine-finished surfaces, have steps been taken to avoid scratching or distortion of the part by locators?

1.4. *Cutters*

Are locators safe from damage by cutters overrunning or being set too deep?

Do any cutters, such as long drills, interfere with loading or location of the part? This sometimes happens when drilling on different levels with a multispindle head.

1.5. *Operator*

Can the jig be made easier to load and unload?

Is there plenty of room for the operator's hands when loading and locating the part?

Are the clamps well out of the way when loading and unloading?

Are the locating points easily visible to the operator?

Have locating pins been reduced to their shortest practicable length and smallest permissible diameter?

Have they been provided with effective bullet noses?

Where two locating pins are used, has one been relieved to a diamond shape and is one shorter than the other to make loading easier?

Is there enough clearance for the part to be easily lifted over or into locating and centering devices?

If the part is heavy and is to be located from previously drilled holes, is it possible to provide disappearing location pins which can be raised when the part has been slid into its approximate located position?

Can one end of a heavy part be rested in its approximate position while the operator loads and locates the opposite end?

Have sliding pins and other hand-operated locators been provided with comfortable handles, allowing a good grip?

Has it been considered that knurled knobs or screws, used continuously, will make the operator's fingers very sore?

Can all movable locators or jack pins be operated with one handle or one movement by the operator?

Can locators or jack pins be locked by the act of clamping the part in the jig?

Are all movable locators and adjustments on the side of the fixture nearest to the operator?

Should duplicate holding devices be provided so that one may be loaded during the machine cycle?

If the fixture is designed for several parts, can they be prepositioned during the machine cycle in some form of magazine or loading rack?

Is it possible to load the jig with one hand while the other hand is discarding the completed part?

Is there a fouling device to prevent the part from being loaded incorrectly?

Do the burrs thrown up by this operation interfere with unloading?

Is it desirable to provide an ejector?

If so, can it be operated automatically when the work is unclamped?

Can the finished part be ejected by loading the new part?

2. Clamping and Supporting the Part

2.1. *Kind of Operation*

Is the cutting force heavy or light in this operation?

If it is light, is it possible to avoid clamping the part in the fixture?

If heavy, is the part rigidly supported and clamped in a manner best suited to resist the cutting forces?

Is the part supported as close as possible to the point where the load is applied?

Is the cutting force resisted by a solid support rather than by the clamp?

Will the cutting load distort or bend the part or the jig because of inadequate support?

Will the operation tend to tip or tilt the part in the jig?

Will it upset or twist the jig on the machine table?

Can the cutting force be used to help locate and secure the part in the jig?

Is the clamp strong enough to provide the necessary holding force?

If the fixture rotates, will centrifugal force tend to loosen the clamp?

2.2. *Nature of the Part*

Will the clamping force bend, crush, or mar the work?

Should a torque-limiting screw, or similar safety device, be built into the clamp in order to prevent overstraining of the frail parts?

Should brass, leather, or fiber faces be used on the clamps to avoid spoiling the surface finish of the work?

Has the clamp enough range to take care of allowable variations in the workpiece?

When more than one part is to be clamped, have suitable equalizing devices been included in the clamp to cover their variations in size?

If there is more than one clamping point on the part, are the points as widely spaced as practicable?

Is the work supported directly under the clamping points?

Will the clamping force distort the part enough to allow the surface machined in this operation to spring out of true when the clamp is released?

Will the clamping force bend the jig plate or other part of the tool and cause inaccurate work?

2.3. *Machine*

Can the movement of the machine table or quill be used to operate the clamp?

If an air-operated clamp is used, can the control valve be worked by the engagement of the machine feed lever?

Can a hydraulic clamping device be built into the circuit of the machine?

Does the clamping mechanism place any undue strain on the machine?

When the clamp is thrown or dropped open, can it do any damage to the machine?

2.4. *Cutters*

Will the cutter be struck by the clamp when it is being opened or closed?

Will the cutter strike the supporting surfaces when it passes through the work?

Will cutter vibration or chatter tend to loosen the clamp?

2.5. *Operator*

Can the clamping be done easily and quickly?

Can all clamping devices be operated from the side of the fixture nearest to the operator?

Does the operator need a special wrench to clamp the work? Is more than one needed?

If so, is it possible to arrange for one standard wrench to tighten all the clamps?

Better still, can all clamps be self-contained, thus avoiding loose wrenches?

Can C-washers or clamp plates be made captive by hinges or pins in order to do away with loose parts?

Can all clamping arrangements be combined so as to operate with the movement of one handle?

Would the clamp be easier to lift or move if a handle is attached?

Does the operator need a fixed handle, or similar grip, in order to hold the jig firmly while operating the clamp with his or her other hand?

Does clamping require much exertion by the operator?

Does the size of the work or the required clamping force warrant the use of compressed air or hydraulically-operated clamps?

Can the clamping be speeded up by means of compressed-air, cam-operated, or quick-action toggle clamps?

Is possible to clamp the jig with one hand, while the other is engaging the feed lever?

Has provision been made to prevent clamps from twisting or turning when tightened?

Have clamps been provided with springs or other means of lifting them clear of the part when loosened?

3. Positioning Tool to Cutter

3.1. *Tool Features*

Have headed bushings been provided so that they project above the chips and coolant lying on the jig plate?

Are the jig feet large enough to span the T-slots in the table?

Are the feet high enough to allow the drill to pass through the component without striking or injuring the machine table?

Have roll-over curves been provided to assist in turning the jig over?

Can the jig be clamped directly under the machine spindle?

If not, is it light enough to position easily under the spindle?

3.2. *Special Equipment*

Could the jig be more effectively presented to the cutters by mounting it on a rotary or indexing table or on trunnion mountings?

Would it be advantageous to rest the jig in an angle block clamped under the machine spindle when drilling holes on an angle?

3.3. *Machine*

When used on a multispindle machine, can the jig be nested into suitable table stops under each spindle as it is moved from one position to another?

Can suitable fences, or table stops, be used to prevent the jig from rotating with the cutter?

3.4. *Cutters*

Has the fixture been designed to keep the amount of cutter travel to a minimum?

Is it possible to design the jig so that all holes of the same size can be drilled to their correct depths with one setting of the cutter spindle?

Is the jig light enough to enable it to be pulled into place by a slender drill if it is not quite correctly positioned?

3.5. *Operator*

Can the operator see clearly all the bushings or cutter guides when positioning the jig?

Does the jig need a handle to allow the operator to control it easily and to resist its tendency to twist?

If the fixture is to index, can the index pin be withdrawn easily?

Can the index pin be unlocked and withdrawn by the one movement?

Will the index pin locate quickly and accurately when engaged?

Will a handle or handwheel assist the operator to index the fixture?

4. Cutter Guiding

4.1. *Nature of Operation*

Do the cutters need guiding for this operation?

If so, are the guide bushings long enough to give adequate support to the cutting tool?

Are the bushings too long, thus giving excessive rubbing surface and restricting the escape of chips?

Is the required accuracy such that the bushings need to touch, or almost touch, the surface of the work?

Is the surface of the work contoured or on an angle so that the drill cannot enter squarely?

If so, does the end of the bushing need to follow the contour of the part in order to guide the drill effectively?

Would a bushing supported on ball bearings be an advantage for piloting a slender boring bar?

4.2. *Second Operations*

Do the tools need guiding for a second operation, such as countersinking or reaming?

If not, would a hinged or latch-type jig plate swinging out of the way after the first operation be better than removing slip bushings?

Is it possible to avoid slip bushings by using stepped drills for combining the drilling and counterboring operations?

If a stepped drill is used, has the largest diameter entered the bushing—and is it adequately guided—before the smaller leading end begins to cut?

If slip bushings are required, have hardened liner bushings been provided to locate them?

4.3. *Coolant*

Is the machine equipped with a coolant pump and tank?

Can the coolant reach the cutting edges of the tool?

Would suitable funnels or channels be an advantage to carry the coolant where it is required?

Are fences or guides necessary to prevent the used coolant from running to waste?

Is a guard required to protect the operator from coolant spray?

4.4. *Cutters*

Have chip flutes been provided in the pilots of counterbores, etc., to prevent them from binding in the guide holes?

When the cutters have been shortened by sharpening, will any part of the chuck, collet, or arbor foul on the jig or fixture body?

Can the heads of bushings be used as depth stops by allowing hardened collars on the cutter stems to contact them?

Have the bushings an adequate lead-in chamfer for the drills?

If a drill strikes a headless bushing hard and drives it a little way through the jig plate, will this affect the accuracy of the operation? Perhaps heading bushings would be better.

Long slender drills tend to whip when running at high speed. Is there any disadvantage to having them guided in the bushings all the time, even when the jig is being loaded and unloaded?

4.5. *Operator*

Has the bushing plate been correctly marked near the bushings with the drill sizes to be used in the respective holes?

Have slip bushings been marked "drill" or "ream" according to their function?

If slip bushings cannot be avoided, are the heads large enough and fluted (not knurled) to allow the operator to grip and turn them easily?

Is there room for finger tips under the heads of the slip bushings?

Would it be an advantage to provide handles for extracting slip bushings?

Have the slip bushings been provided with an effective means of locking them in place?

When taking slip bushings out, can the operator turn them to a stop before lifting them, thus making it unnecessary to feel for the right place?

5. Chip Control

5.1. *Nature of the Part*

Is the material of the part such that it will produce continuous chips (as in steel) or discontinuous powdery chips (as in cast iron)?

Will the accuracy of the part allow enough space between the drill bushing and the work to allow discontinuous chips to escape without having to pass through the bushing?

When drilling materials which produce stringy continuous chips, has the clearance between the bushing and the work been reduced to zero to enable chips to pass up through the bushing, thus avoiding chip tangles within the jig?

5.2. *Tool Features*

Do all supporting pads and pins stand well clear of chip-collecting surfaces?

Have all locating pins with rest shoulders been relieved in the corners to provide chip and burr clearances?

Have locating and supporting surfaces been kept as small in area as practicable?

Has chip and burr clearance been provided in V-locators?

Have chip-collecting pockets and corners been eliminated as far as possible?

Have openings and ramps been provided to allow chips to escape from the jig?

Can channels or races be provided to allow the coolant to wash the chips away in a desirable direction?

Have suitable guards or shields been provided to prevent chips from fouling and wearing jack pins, index plates, and plungers?

Will chips foul the clamp lifting springs?

Have the jig feet been kept in as small an area as possible, consistent with their ability to bridge the T-slots of the machine table?

Can the jig feet be secured to the jig from their top surfaces, thus avoiding holes in the bearing faces where chips may collect?

5.3. *Machines*

Is it desirable to fit chip-removal equipment to the machine?

Are chip tangles likely to interfere with operation of the machine?

Is an air blast desirable for cleaning out the fixture before reloading it?

5.4. *Cutters*

Has ample chip clearance been provided in flutes of the cutters?

Has the fixture been designed so that the cutter flutes are not prevented from discharging chips when covered up?

5.5. *Operator*

Are all locators and supports easy for the operator to see and keep clean?

If the operator cleans the chips out by knocking the jig on a bench or on the edge of the machine table, can suitable bumpers of fiber, hardwood, or Neoprene be provided to minimize damage to both jig and machine?

Should the operator be provided with a chip rake or cleaning probe?

6. Measurement of Part

6.1. *Cleaning*

Is it necessary to measure the part while it is still in the fixture?

If so, is it possible to clean it sufficiently for this to be done?

Will burrs prevent the accurate measurement of the part?

6.2. *Clearance*

Is there enough clearance between the tools and the part to admit the necessary scales, gages, or calipers?

Will the cutter be in the way?

6.3. *Nature of Measurement*

Is the nature of the measurement such that the whole jig, complete with part clamped in it, should be presented to the measuring device?

If so, has the tool been designed to suit the gaging device?

6.4. *Datum Face*

Is it desirable to provide measuring blocks, a datum surface, etc., from which to check?

6.5. *Operator*

Can the operator easily see the surface to be measured?

Can the gage or scale be seen in the measuring position?

7. Safe Working

7.1. *Part*

Have all necessary steps been taken to prevent the parts from being damaged during the operation or in the handling to and from it?

7.2. *Tool*

Is the tool sturdy enough to prevent it from being damaged or broken during normal use and abuse?

Can it be damaged or rendered inaccurate through parts being inserted incorrectly?

7.3. *Machine*

Is the machine likely to be damaged by accidental breakage of part, tool, or cutter?

If the fixture rotates, has it been balanced to minimize machine vibration?

7.4. *Cutters*

Is it necessary for the operator to have his or her hands near the cutter while it is in motion?

If so, is the cutter properly guarded?

Could the cutter be damaged by striking the jig or fixture?

7.5. *Operator*

Can the operator see clearly what is going on at all times?

Have all unnecessary sharp edges and corners been removed from the fixture to avoid cutting or bruising the operator's hand?

Have screw heads been let into counterbores wherever possible?

Are there any sharp or awkwardly placed levers or handles to catch in clothing?

Is there ample clearance for fingers and knuckles around all handles, knobs, and slip bushings?

Is any leaf, cover, or clamp likely to fall on the operator's fingers?

Is the operator protected from flying chips or coolant spray?

If the clamp failed, could the part fly out of the jig and injure someone?

If the clamp is air- or hydraulically-operated, should the mechanism contain a positive interlock so that if the air pressure failed, the clamp would not become loose?

Have suitable safety stops or guards been employed on air- or hydraulically-operated clamps to avoid crushing the operator's fingers?

Should the tool be marked with a warning notice to caution the operator against improper or dangerous practice?

8. Handling and Storage

8.1. *Lifting Aids*

Have lifting lugs, eyebolts, or chain slots been provided for slinging heavy tools?

Have lifting handles been attached to all awkward or heavy loose parts of the fixture?

8.2. *Loose Parts*

If loose parts such as spacing pieces, wrenches, or locating pins are unavoidable, can they be attached to the fixture with keeper screws or light chains to prevent loss in storage?

8.3. *Fragile Parts*

Is there any fragile part of the jig which needs a protective cover in storage?

Is the tool so delicate or highly finished as to require a special case, cover, or box to protect it in storage?

8.4. *Identification*

Has the tool, and all loose items belonging to it, been marked clearly with identification numbers or symbols?

8.5. *Storage Aids*

Can the tool be stowed safely without danger of tipping over?

Is a special storage stand or rack desirable for safe and convenient storage?

9. Manufacture and Maintenance

9.1. *Cost*

Has the cost of the tool been properly related to the quantity and accuracy of the part to be produced?

Is it too expensive for low-volume production?

Are the production requirements high enough to warrant a better class of tool?

9.2. *Standards*

Have standard, or readily purchasable, parts been specified wherever practicable?

Have all parts been designed for manufacture from stock-size materials with a minimum amount of machining?

If the material is not carried in stock, is the right kind and size readily available?

9.3. *Manufacturing Facilities*

Can the tool be made with the available toolmaking labor and equipment?

Are the tool dimensional tolerances as wide as possible?

Has the design included suitable datum surfaces for toolmaking operations?

Is it easy to set up the fixture for grinding locators or supports which have to be sized in assembly?

If so, is there plenty of clearance for the grinding wheel and spindle?

Has provision been made for easy alignment and starting of pressed-in parts which need accurate location?

Have blind holes been avoided wherever possible?

Would it help the heat-treater to drill a small hole in each part, which normally has no holes in it, so that it may be suspended it in a salt bath by a wire threaded through the hole?

9.4. *Design Points*

Are all parts well designed to take the loads imposed on them in service?

Is the tool sturdy enough to stand considerable abuse?

Is the fixture amply proportioned to damp out vibration and chatter? This applies especially to milling fixtures.

Is the design of all parts and mechanisms as simple as possible?

Have cylindrical plungers and holes been used in preference to square or polygonal ones?

Have holes for headed pressed-in parts (such as for accurate location of rest pins) been countersunk to allow any excess press lubricant to collect in the countersink (allowing the rest pin to vibrate slightly in service) instead of gradually squeezing out under the head?

Have spring pocket holes been countersunk on their open ends?

Are the dowel pins in each part as widely spaced as practicable?

Where detachable parts need very accurate location, have register keys or pins been used instead of dowels?

Is the accuracy of the operation such that the base of the fixture should be scraped to fit the machine table?

Have breather holes been drilled to allow air to escape from close-fitting plunger holes?

Is it possible to forecast any part design changes and to make allowance for them in the design of the fixture?

9.5. *Provision for Maintenance*

Has provision been made for lubricating the tool mechanisms?

Have all wearing parts been hardened?

Are these parts easily made and replaced?

Have correct materials and heat-treatment been specified?

Has provision been made for easy removal or pressed-in parts?

Can vulnerable parts be removed and replaced quickly without disturbing the setup of the fixture on the machine?

Table 1-8 lists the factors that are related to each function of a jig or fixture. It is designed to direct the tool engineer to the group number and section number where the pertinent questions can be found.

TABLE 1-8
Checking Factors for Fixture Design[1]

Group number	Function of jig or fixture	Related factors and section numbers				
0.	Setting up	0.1. Shop layout	0.2. Machine	0.3. Cutters	0.4 Setting aids	0.5 Operator
1.	Loading and location of part	1.1 Shop layout	1.2. Nature of part	1.3 Previous operations	1.4 Cutters	1.5 Operator

TABLE 1-8 (*continued*)

2.	Clamping and support of part	2.1 Kind of operation	2.2 Nature of part	2.3 Machine	2.4 Cutters	2.5 Operator
3.	Positioning tool to cutters	3.1 Tool features	3.2 Special equipment	3.3 Machine	3.4 Cutters	3.5 Operator
4.	Cutter guiding	4.1 Nature of operation	4.2 Second operation	4.3 Coolant	4.4 Cutters	4.5 Operator
5.	Chip control	5.1 Nature of part	5.2 Tool features	5.3 Machine	5.4 Cutters	5.5 Operator
6.	Measurement of part	6.1 Cleaning	6.2 Clearance	6.3 Nature of measurements	6.4 Datum faces	6.5 Operator
7.	Safe working	7.1 Part	7.2 Tool	7.3 Machine	7.4 Cutters	7.5 Operator
8.	Handling and storage	8.1 Lifting aids	8.2 Loose parts	8.3 Fragile parts	8.4 Identification	8.5 Storage aids
9.	Manufacture and maintenance	9.1 Cost	9.2 Standards	9.3 Manufacturing facilities	9.4 Design features	9.5 Provision for maintenance

References

1. G.R. Tindale, "Checklist for Jig and Fixture Design, " *American Machinist*, (Sept. 12, 26, 1955).

CHAPTER 2
PRINCIPLES OF LOCATING AND SUPPORTING

Once the decision has been made to build a fixture to perform a particular operation on a workpiece, the tool designer must finalize the proposed design in the form of a tool drawing which contains all the information necessary to build the fixture.

The steps in this procedure are as follows:

1. Locating the workpiece.
2. Adding intermediate or auxiliary supports, if required.
3. Clamping the workpiece.
4. Guiding the cutting tool.
5. Providing the fixture body to contain the above elements.

The first two steps, locating and supporting the workpiece will be the subject of this chapter.

GENERAL CONSIDERATIONS

The first and most important step—locating the workpiece—requires the constant and full attention of the tool designer. He or she must never forget that the main purpose of a fixture is to accurately and expeditiously locate, support, and hold a workpiece so that it, and all other workpieces produced with the fixture, will be alike within specified limits.

Serious consideration should be given to the following points when establishing the locating and supporting surfaces for a workpiece:

- Before designing a new fixture, check for off-the-shelf holding devices that might work as is or be modified to work.
- Before designing a new fixture, check in-house for something that might work as is or be modified to work.
- Design fixtures around standard components.
- Choose locating surfaces carefully, using datum surfaces when specified. Where locating surfaces are not specified on the part drawing, locate from the surfaces used to dimension the part.
- Locate from machine surfaces whenever possible.
- Don't locate from parting lines, gates, overflows, etc.
- Use the same locating surfaces for all machining operations, thereby eliminating errors that can accumulate when changing locating surfaces.
- Provide a clear view of the locating surfaces for a visual check on locating.
- Support points should be as far apart as practical to provide maximum stability.
- When more than three points of support are needed, the additional supports should be the manually adjustable or self-registering types.

- Support points of contact should be as small as possible without permitting damage to the workpiece from the tool or clamping forces.
- Supports should be equally placed from the center of gravity of the workpiece.
- Supports and locators should be easily replaceable.
- Avoid duplicate locators.
- When using two locating pins, one of the pins should be relieved.
- Properly orient V-locators so that variations in the workpiece locating diameter will not affect the accuracy of the operation.
- Keep locators well above chip-collecting surfaces and provide relief around locating surfaces for the escape of unwanted chips and foreign matter.
- Locators should provide for quick and easy loading and unloading of the workpiece.
- Locators should be placed to permit proper loading of workpieces without interference due to rough part variation.
- Make locators strong enough to resist cutting forces.
- Provide expanding locators for datum locating holes when RFS is specified.
- Locators should be safe from damage by cutters overrunning or being set too deep.
- Provide a method for sliding heavy workpieces into the fixture instead of having to lift them into place. This may require retractable locating pins which can be raised when the part has been slid into place.
- Use carbide locators with abrasive workpieces.
- Use realistic tolerances. Fixture tolerances generally should be 30 to 50% of the workpiece tolerance. (For inspection fixtures the tolerance should be 10% of the workpiece tolerance.)
- The fixture should be as foolproof as possible. Some method should be provided to prohibit insertion of the workpiece in the wrong position.
- Use centralizers to compensate for workpiece variations.
- Provide for easy removal of chips and foreign matter.
- Provide for coolant drainage.
- Eliminate jamming.
- Provide for safe operation.

LOCATING PRINCIPLES

Relationship Between Workpiece Locating and Clamping. The definition of workpiece locating may be further refined by clarifying what it is not. Locating and clamping are different, though related, subjects (problems). In the performance of a manufacturing operation, it is generally necessary to provide some kind of a clamping mechanism to maintain the workpiece in a desired position and to resist the effects of gravity and/or operational forces. Very often the workpiece locating and clamping may be simultaneously accomplished by the same mechanism.

The proper solution of the workpiece-locating problem requires certain points (or surfaces) of contact between the workpiece and the workpiece-holding device, and may also require a definition of direction and degree of holding force. In this sense, locating and clamping are related; but whether the clamp mechanism is actuated by a screw, wedge, cam, toggle, power cylinder, or some other method, selection of the proper actuation is a problem in itself and is a separate consideration from the fundamental problem of workpiece locating.

Failure to recognize or to appreciate the fact that locating and clamping are separate problems can cause considerable indecision and design rework. Care must be taken that the logical method of workpiece locating is incorporated into the initial design of a clamping device for a specific fixture. This will ensure that later workpiece considerations do not cause problems with the initial design. These problems could cause a clamp to act in the wrong direction or with improper force, or to interfere with loading or unloading the workpiece.

The proper initial decision is to resolve the problems of workpiece locating; their solution will define a direction and degree of required clamping force. A suitable clamping mechanism can then be devised, thus completing a compatible locating and clamping scheme.

Tangible and Intangible Factors of Workpiece Locating. Both the manufacturing engineer and tool designer are constantly confronted with many conflicting objectives. Due to intermittent economic fluctuations and technological evolutions, these conflicting objectives have patterns that seem logical and orderly, but they are, in fact, always changing and different. Some of these conflicting objectives are as follows:

- Capital equipment cost.
- Tooling costs; tool-design time, toolmaking time.
- Tool material cost.
- Manufacturing cost: setup time, per-piece operation time.
- Required productive capacity.
- Required workpiece accuracy.

All these objectives are related and interdependent. All can be affected directly or indirectly, favorably or adversely, by the selected method of workpiece locating.

To illustrate some of the tangible and intangible factors involved, required workpiece accuracy will be analyzed, as normally recorded on the product drawing, in terms of dimensions and tolerances. A tolerance is the permissible dimensional variance. Thus, dimensional tolerance is a goal, whereas actual dimensional variances are the results of operations. If a dimensional variance is not within the dimensional tolerance of a particular standard, then the product is not made according to the drawing and must be scrapped or reworked.

Drawings sometimes do not, and for practical and economic reasons cannot, show all possible dimensional interrelationships. To illustrate this, an extremely simple geometric form, such as a gage block or a paving brick (a parallelepiped), is considered. Normal product configurations are far more complex than such a simple six-sided body but it will serve for purposes of discussion.

This oblong body is made up of 6 faces, 24 angles, and 12 edges. A product drawing which recorded a dimension and a tolerance for every possible dimensional interrelationship, from any face to any face, any edge to any edge, any angle to any angle, and any face to any edge to any angle, would be fantastically complicated, expensive, and in a practical sense, incomprehensible in the shop.

Because of the astronomical number of possible dimensional interrelationships, product drawings tend to show only the essential information related to the problems of product design (those dimensions which control product appearance and its mating to other parts).

Typical product drawings carry a footnote such as "Unless otherwise stated all dimensions to be held to plus or minus 0.010 in." or some similar generalization. In actual practice, these footnotes enjoy or endure a considerable amount of interpretation and, like other generalizations, may sometimes result in some fantastic interpretations or misinterpretations.

It is evident that the manufacturing engineer must have knowledge of certain, and sometimes considerable, supplementary data (in addition to that shown on the product drawing), such as intimate knowledge of the end use of the product.

Some of the common causes of dimensional variance in the finished product are:

1. Raw material dimensional variances (for example, castings, forgings, weldments, bar stock, etc., will vary within drawing or mill specifications).

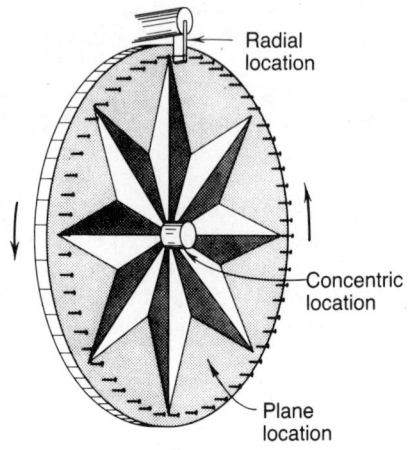

Fig. 2-1 Plane, concentric, and radial locating.

2. The record could be true with respect to plane locating (the plane does not wobble), but at the same time it could be off concentrically if the center pin of the turntable does not coincide with the center of rotation of the turntable; the record would then rotate eccentrically.
3. For the wheel of chance, the radial location either could be true (the one winning number) or it could be off (any losing number) regardless of whether (within reasonable limits) the plane of the wheel is wobbling or whether the wheel is rotating eccentrically.

The logical analysis of a workpiece-locating problem will be resolved into some combination or multiple of these three different locating requirements: (1) plane locating, (2) concentric locating, and (3) radial locating.

So far, only combinations have been illustrated. To illustrate multiple locating, consider a common paving brick, made up of six faces, and located from one face and two edges (lengthwise and crosswise), thus locating it in three plane axes. Since it does not have a diametrical surface, there can be no concentric locating, and because radial locating is a supplement to concentric locating, there can be no radial locating.

Another example would be a cylindrical shaft that has been center-drilled in both ends and is located between the centers of a lathe. The shaft would be located internally concentrically on each end. The driving dog would normally not be considered a radial locator.

Analysis of Workpiece Surfaces. Before consideration of workpiece locating (and the subsequent problem of clamping), the workpiece must first be analyzed to very clearly identify the essential workpiece-locating surfaces.

A workpiece may be made up of any conceivable number or variety of elementary surfaces, but for any one locating problem, often only a very few such surfaces can be used. To help identify these few key workpiece surfaces, a general pattern of questions follows:

1. Are the datums specified on the part drawing?
2. What is the end use of the product?
3. What work is to be accomplished in the proposed operation?
4. What are the dimensional interrelationships between the surfaces to be machined and the other workpiece surfaces?

The answer to these and other necessary questions will usually lead to the identification of the workpiece-locating surfaces.

Workpiece-locating surfaces are those surfaces which are to be the basis of alignment for workpiece locating.

Pure (Individual) Locating Problems. The manufacturing engineer or tool designer seldom, if ever, encounters a workpiece-locating problem that is so simple it can be solved by locating to only one single surface, point, or axis of the workpiece. Almost invariably, some combination of plane, concentric, and radial locating surfaces that have to be considered in the design of locators is present.

This analysis should provide the tool designer with the information necessary to design a fixture which, when correctly positioned on the machine, will consistently establish the desired relationship between the workpiece and the cutting tool. Locating should be such that each successive workpiece, when properly loaded and clamped, occupies the exact same position in the fixture.

Degrees of Freedom. An unrestrained workpiece is free to move in any direction. It can move in either direction along the three mutually perpendicular axes and can also rotate in either direction around these axes. Each of these movements is considered one degree of freedom for a total of twelve degrees of freedom as shown in Fig. 2-2. To completely immobilize a part would require restriction of movement in all of the twelve degrees of freedom. This however, is not always necessary and depends on conditions such as the direction of tool thrust and weight of the workpiece (gravity). Degrees of freedom are normally restricted by using a combination of locators and clamps.

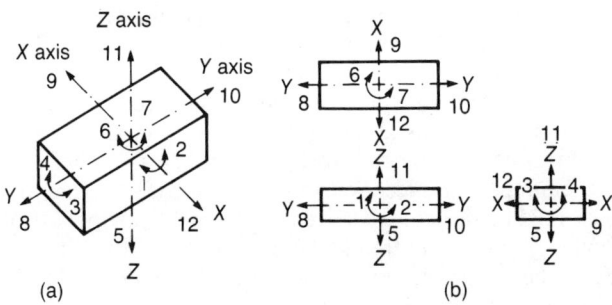

Fig. 2-2 Twelve degrees of freedom.

The Basic Method of Locating. The basic method of locating a workpiece is the 3-2-1 method, also called the six-point method. With this method, the position of the vertical Z axis is established by locating the workpiece on three pins as shown in Fig. 2-3. These three pins also restrict rotation around the X and Y axes resulting in a restriction of five of the twelve degrees of freedom. The addition of two more pins as shown in Fig. 2-4 establishes the position of one of the horizontal axes (X or Y) and restricts rotation around the vertical X axis resulting in a restriction of eight of the twelve degrees of freedom. The addition of one more pin in the remaining horizontal axis as shown in Fig. 2-5 establishes the position along that axis resulting in a restriction of nine of the twelve degrees of freedom. Since the addition of three more pins to completely restrict movement of the workpiece would make it impossible to load and unload the workpiece, the three remaining degrees of freedom can be restricted with clamps if necessary.

2. Workpiece-locating dimensional variance (chucking or fixturing positioning variance).
3. Workpiece-relocating dimensional variance (most products are not made in one operation but in a series of consecutive operations to most effectively utilize the skills of men or machines).
4. Workpiece-clamping distortion which may not be apparent until the machined workpiece is released. While clamped it may be of desired size and to shape, but when released distortion may occur.
5. Workpiece warpage, due to release of internal strains by cutting away material.
6. Basic-machine dimensional inaccuracy (machines have acceptable or unacceptable inherent dimensional error).

Manufacturing engineers and tool designers have no standard reference tables to determine dimensional variances. If dimensional variances are known, there is the added problem that they act in cumulative (additive) and differential (subtractive) combinations.

The purpose of describing the general problems of dimensional tolerance and dimensional variance is not to criticize existing drawing conventions (for no better system is proposed) nor to overemphasize shop problems, but to discuss the causes and effects of dimensional tolerances and variances.

Problem-Solving Procedure for Workpiece Locating. The procedure that the manufacturing engineer uses to resolve workpiece-locating problems can be compared to the technique used by a chemist.

The skilled chemist assumes that the test specimen is made up of some combination of known basic chemical elements. The chemist has systematic procedures for establishing the presence or absence of any of these basic chemical elements.

Similarly, the manufacturing engineer analyzes the workpiece to see whether or not it is made up of some combination of familiar elemental workpiece surfaces. Since it is known how to locate to these elemental workpiece surfaces, the manufacturing engineer extends and implements this know-how to solve workpiece problems related to the particular combination of elemental workpiece surfaces.

Language of the Shop. Workpiece-locating problems (the mating of the workpiece and the workpiece-holding device) are solved by the practical application of the principles of conventional geometry. There can be considerable difficulty in reconciling the classical Euclidean theorems with the language of the trade as it is commonly used when discussing workpiece-locating problems.

Shop talk was coined and is commonly used for aptly stating certain specialized or certain combinations of geometric terms, which include words and phrases which may have no single direct counterpart in classical geometry.

Since it is impractical or impossible to convert the manufacturing industry to the use of pure Euclidean expressions, the prevailing idioms that are indigenous to the trade are explained.

Elemental Workpiece Surfaces. For the purpose of workpiece-locating analysis, the four basic kinds of workpiece surfaces (which in various combinations make up the total configuration of any workpiece) are as follows:

1. Flat surface.
2. Inside diameter (ID).
3. Outside diameter (OD).
4. Irregular surface.

The definition of an flat surface is considered to be self-evident. In the shop, flat surfaces are also referred to by a variety of different names all meaning some specialized variation of this elemental surface (for example, face, shoulder, flange, plane, wall, etc.), but they are all flat surfaces.

An example of an inside diameter (ID) is the inside (concave) face of a drilled or bored hole.

An example of an outside diameter (OD) is the outer (convex) face of a turned cylinder.

An irregular surface is any surface which is neither a flat, an inside diameter, nor an outside diameter. A simple example of an irregular surface is that of a vane of a ship's propeller.

Inasmuch as the definition of an irregular surface is defined by exception (not a flat, an OD, or an ID) and is all-inclusive, any one individual workpiece surface can be classified as belonging to one, and only one, of the four elemental workpiece surfaces.

Degree of Workpiece-Surface Smoothness and/or Dimensional Variance. Any one of the previously described four elemental workpiece surfaces can individually have any conceivable degree of smoothness and/or dimensional variance. However, for the purposes of this book, terms shall apply to only two contrasting workpiece surfaces: (1) rough or (2) finished.

Thus, a flat workpiece surface may be rough or finished. An ID surface may be rough or finished. An OD surface may be rough or finished. An irregular surface may be rough or finished.

The term "rough" is intended to designate a workpiece surface common to raw materials such as castings, weldments, forgings, hot-rolled bar stock, boiler plate, etc. A rough surface by definition has inherent dimensional variance to the degree that it cannot be ignored in considering workpiece locating.

The term "finished" is intended to mean a smooth machined surface (this section is limited to the metal-cutting industries). For the purpose of discussion, a finished surface has negligible dimensional variance unless otherwise specifically stated.

A typical shop workpiece can be, for example, a casting which is made up of some combination of the four elemental surfaces, (flat, ID, OD, and irregular surfaces), and each of these elemental workpiece surfaces may be either rough or finished.

The tooling most practical to locate to rough surfaces may have to be different from tooling to locate to finished surfaces. This difference in tooling may not be merely one of degree, but rather one of a more basic difference.

Locating Nomenclature. In locating to the four previously defined elemental workpiece surfaces (and their rough and finished surface variations), certain specialized descriptive words and phrases are commonly used by manufacturing personnel. For example:

Locating to a flat workpiece surface is usually referred to as plane locating.

Locating to an outside diameter or inside diameter is ordinarily referred to as concentric locating.

After a workpiece has been concentrically located, there may be a supplementary locating requirement which is called radial locating. There are only two locating considerations involved in placing an ordinary phonograph disk on a record-player turntable. The small center hole in the record is engaged downward over the mating pin in the center of the turntable. The record is now internally concentrically located. When the face of the record and the face of the turntable are in contact, the record is now properly concentrically and plane located. The direction of clamping force (gravity) is down. In this example, there is no requirement for radial locating.

When a wheel of chance has similarly been properly located, plane and concentrically (see Fig. 2-1), and if it stops with the ratchet finger pointing to a desired number, the wheel can be said to be properly located radially. These three criteria for locating are independent, which the following various combinations of conditions of locating demonstrate.

1. The record could be true concentrically while simultaneously off-plane, since the plane of the record could wobble when rotating.

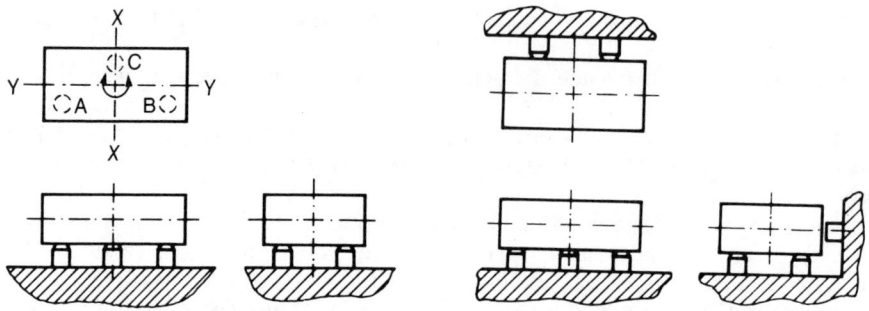

Fig. 2-3 Three pins restrict five degrees of freedom. Part is single defined.

Fig. 2-4 Five pins restrict eight degrees of freedom. Part is double defined.

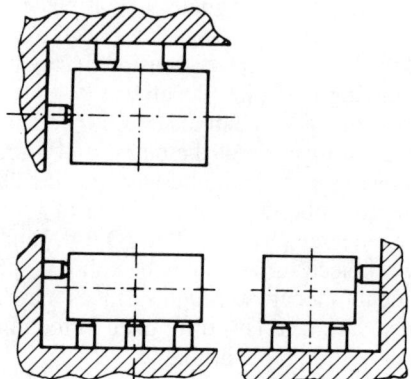

Fig. 2-5 Six pins restrict nine degrees of freedom. Part is fully defined.

Locating planes should be perpendicular to each other whenever possible to avoid any wedging action which tends to lift the workpiece, or, to prevent any magnification of any error caused by dirt or chips on the locating surface as shown in Fig. 2-6. The total error when locating against an inclined plane is equal to the thickness of the dirt or chips times the cosecant of angle $\propto$.

Concentric and Radial Methods of Locating. When locating a workpiece concentrically as shown in Fig. 2-7, the base restricts rotation around the X and Y axes and establishes the position of the X axis. The centrally located pin establishes the position of the X and Y axes resulting in the restriction of nine degrees of freedom. The addition of a radial locator as seen in Fig. 2-8 prevents rotation around the X axis resulting in the restriction of eleven of the twelve degrees of freedom. The remaining degree of freedom (vertical movement in the Z axis) can be restricted by clamping.

Locating from a Vee. When locating a workpiece in a Vee as shown in Fig. 2-9, the base plane establishes the position of the Y axis and restricts rotation around the X axis resulting in a restriction of three degrees of freedom. The vertical locating plane establishes the position of the X axis and restricts the rotation around the Y axis resulting in a restriction of six degrees of freedom. The addition of the pin establishes the position of the Z axis resulting in a restriction of seven degrees of freedom. The cylinder is still

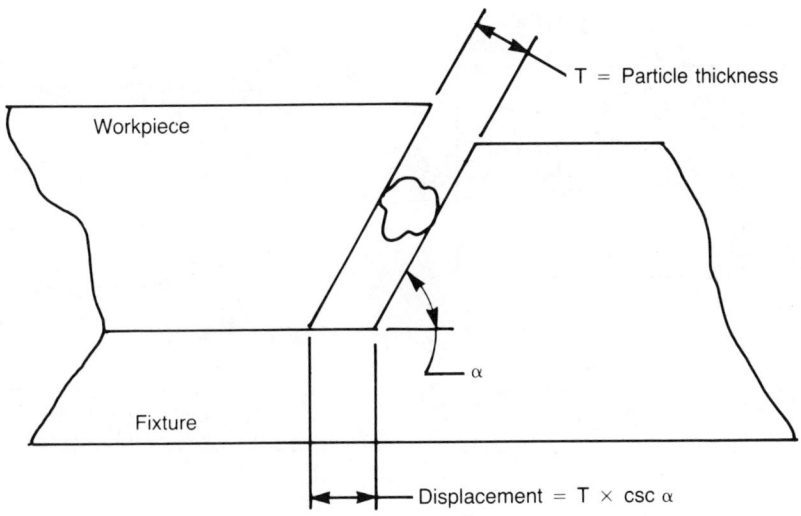

Fig. 2-6 The effect of locating against an inclined plane.

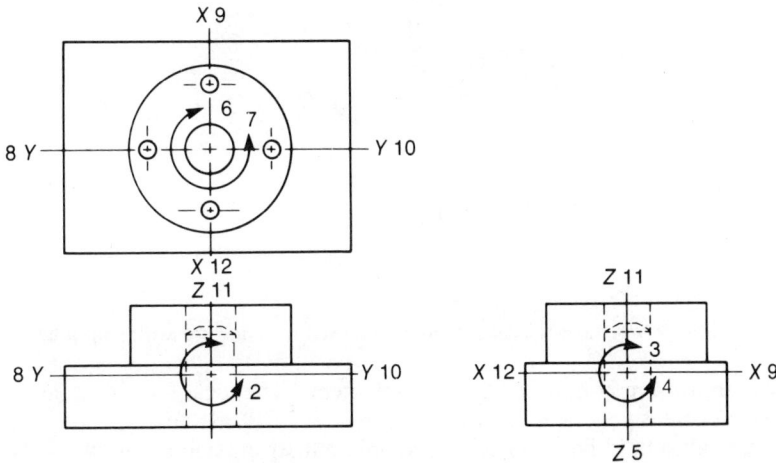

Fig. 2-7 Base and center pin restrict nine degrees of freedom.

free to move in one direction in each axis and rotate in either direction around the Z axis.

These five degrees of freedom can be restricted by clamping. However, it must be realized that clamping in the direction of the Vee does not truly locate the workpiece radially around the Z axis.

LOCATING METHODS

Locating From A Plane. When the locating surfaces of a workpiece are finished, the workpiece is often located with solid locators such as those shown in Fig. 2-10. The solid locator, *a*, is integral to the body of the jig or fixture. It is probably the least used method since it requires extra machining and is not easily repaired if worn or damaged. The assembled locator, *b*, also requires extra machining, but is replaceable. The rest

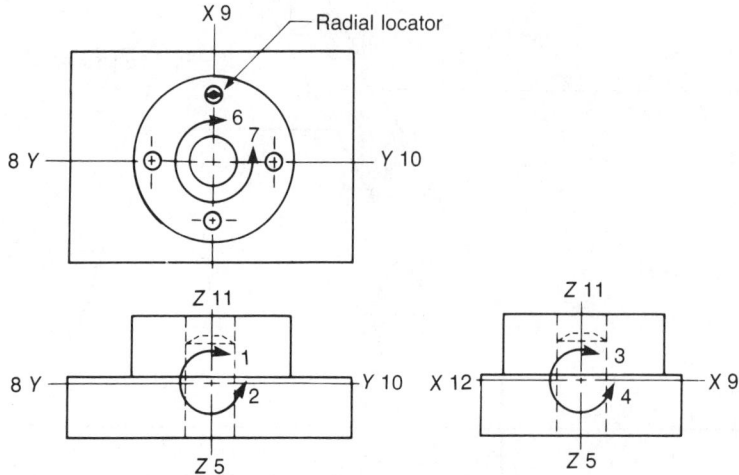

Fig. 2-8 Base, center pin, and radial locator restrict eleven degrees of freedom.

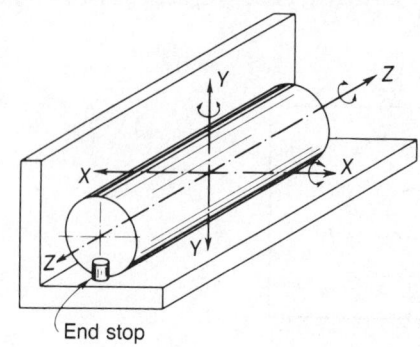

Fig. 2-9 Seven degrees of freedom restricted by V-locator with stop pin.

buttons, *c*, shown are commercially available items. The location and number of locators in each plane is generally determined using the 3-2-1 method.

The locators should be as small as possible but strong enough to resist the cutting forces. They should be positioned as far apart as practical and form a triangle in the base that surrounds the cutting area to ensure stability and accuracy during the machining process. Locating surfaces should be chosen carefully. Use datums when specified. When they are not specifically indicated, use surfaces that are used to dimension the workpiece. Use the same locating surfaces for all operations, thereby eliminating any accumulation of errors caused by changing locations. Locators should be positioned or relieved to avoid chips and foreign matter. Avoid overdefining as shown in Fig. 2-11, and make sure that the locators will not interfere with, nor cause unnecessary delays loading or unloading a workpiece from the jig or fixture.

When the locating surface of a workpiece is rough or uneven, as is found on castings or forgings, adjustable supports and equalizing supports are often used in conjunction with solid supports to compensate for part irregularities. Adjustable supports and equalizing supports are also used as auxiliary supports between fixed locators to eliminate deflection caused by tool forces. Adjustable locators are sometimes needed to locate rough or irregular surfaces in the other planes.

Locating from an Internal Diameter (ID). Internal locating of a workpiece which

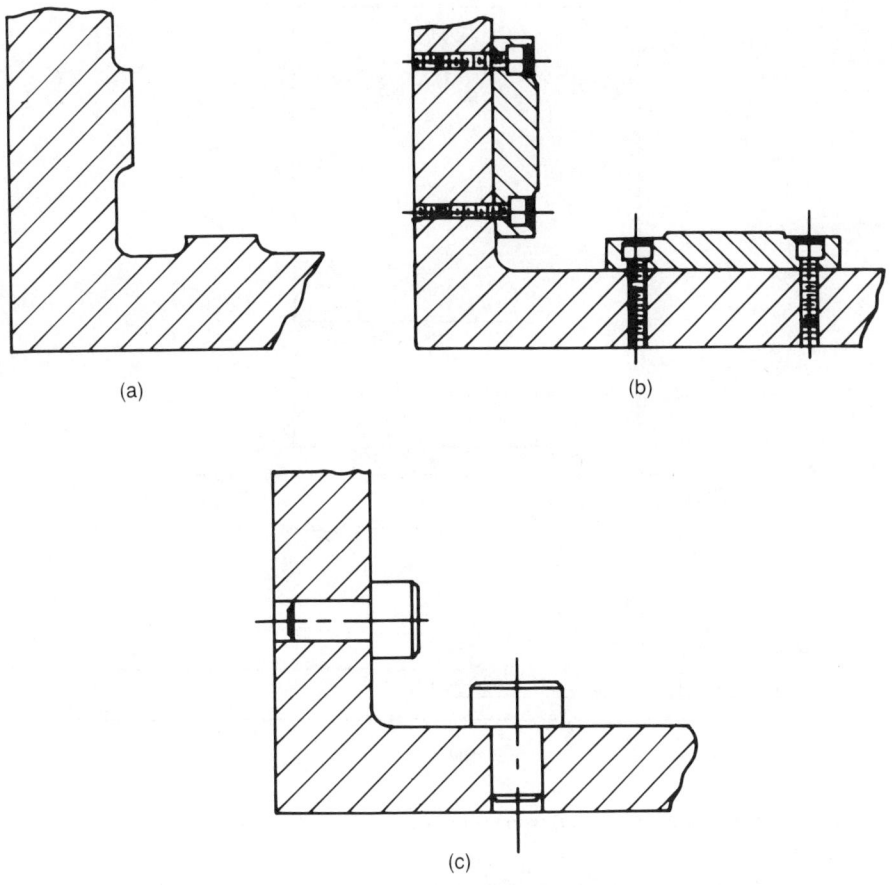

Fig. 2-10 Solid locators: (*a*) **integral;** (*b*) **assembled;** (*c*) **rest buttons.**

has been previously bored and faced is shown in Fig. 2-12. A hole is to be drilled a specific distance from the center of the bored hole. The arrangement shown will establish plane and concentric locating.

Workpieces with flat machined surfaces on one face can also be located from a hole pattern using locating pins. A simple example of this is shown in Fig. 2-13. The workpiece is placed over the two pins—usually one diamond pin and one round pin—with the machined surface of the workpiece resting on the base locating surface. This is a variation of concentric and radial location. The only possible movement of the workpiece is upwards. This can be prevented by clamping if necessary.

Locating From an Outside Diameter (OD). External locating of a workpiece which has been previously turned and faced is shown in Fig. 2-14. A hole is to be drilled a specific distance from the centerline of the workpiece. The arrangement shown will establish plane and concentric loading.

Locating From an Irregular Surface. Irregular surfaces are usually located by nesting. This can be done in many ways. The method shown in Fig. 2-15 uses a cavity the same size as the workpiece to contain and locate the workpiece. Being restrained this way, the only way the workpiece can move is upward, and this can be prevented by clamping if necessary.

Locating Rough Workpieces. The most practical methods for concentrically locating rough workpieces may differ basically from the methods used for concentrically locat-

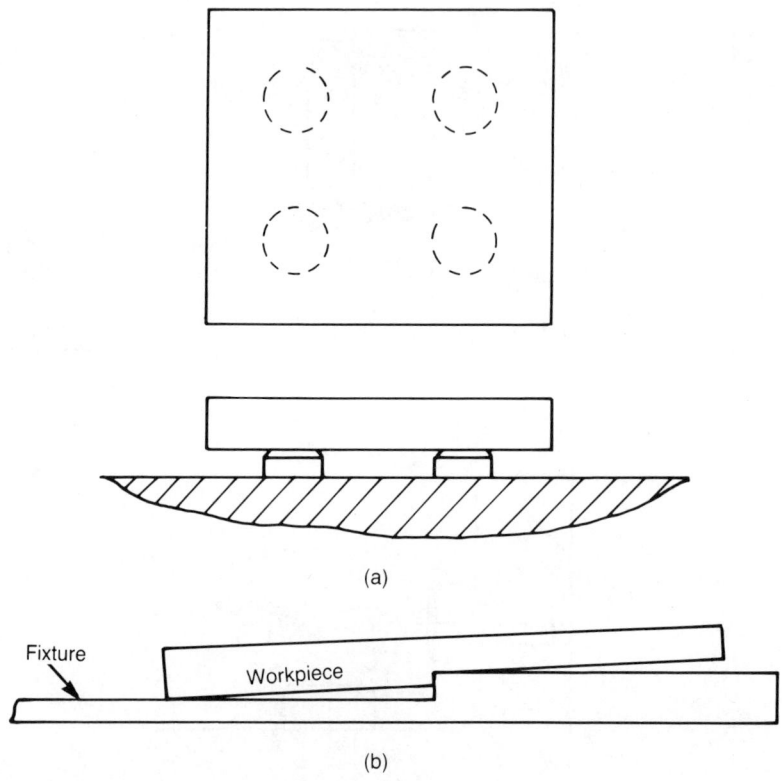

(a)

(b)

Fig. 2-11 Overdefining a plane: (a) using four rest buttons; (b) using two plane surfaces.

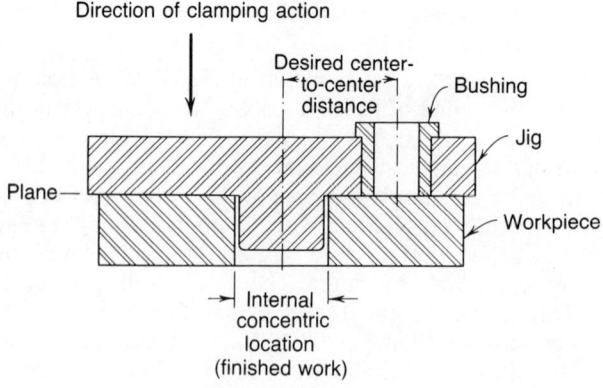

Fig. 2-12 Internal concentric locating.

ing finished workpieces. For example (see Fig. 2-16a), if the locator can enter the smallest cored hole, including surface roughness, etc., the locating method is inaccurate when the same locator engages a casting having the largest cored hole with fairly smooth surfaces. The potential locating error is equivalent to the difference between minimum and maximum casting variations; this holds true of external concentric locators as shown in Fig. 2-16b.

2-12

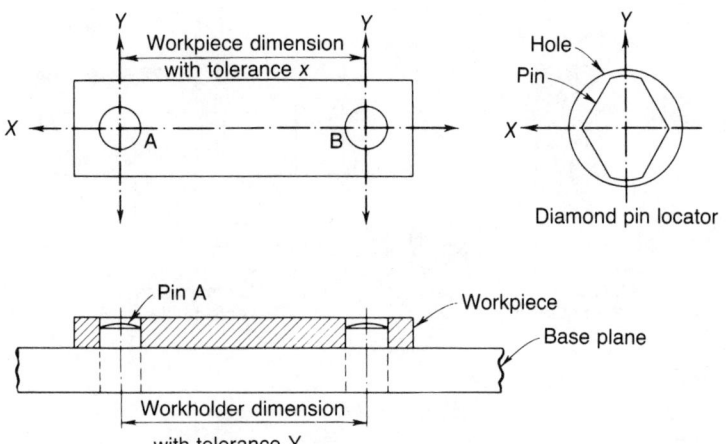

Fig. 2-13 Concentric and radial location using locating pins.

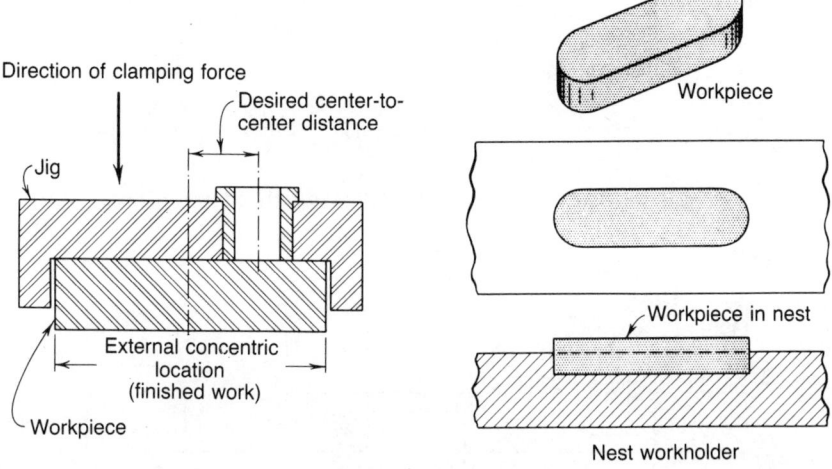

Fig. 2-14 External concentric locating.   Fig. 2-15 Nest-type workholder.

Averaging Method for Locating Rough Workpieces. Internal concentric averaging locating, as shown in Fig. 2-17a, is achieved by an internal locator which is a truncated cone that will center itself into any diameter within its capacity. The casting variation, reflected in spacing variation between the bushing plate and the workpiece support, coincides with the center line of the drill and does not change the correct relation of drill and workpiece. The jig must be constructed to maintain the bushing plate and workpiece support parallel for all positions of the bushing plate. The locating cone should be long enough for a lead to readily enter the workpiece. An internal concentric averaging locator can be inverted (see Fig. 2-17b).

External Concentric Averaging Locating. The principles for concentric internal locating apply to concentric external locating, as illustrated by Fig. 2-18a and b.

Figure 2-19a shows the workpiece located in a Vee; the workpiece size variation results in its incorrect locating to the drill bushing. Shown in Fig. 2-19b is an example of a correct averaging locator for the same workpiece. This effect will be covered in greater detail later in the chapter.

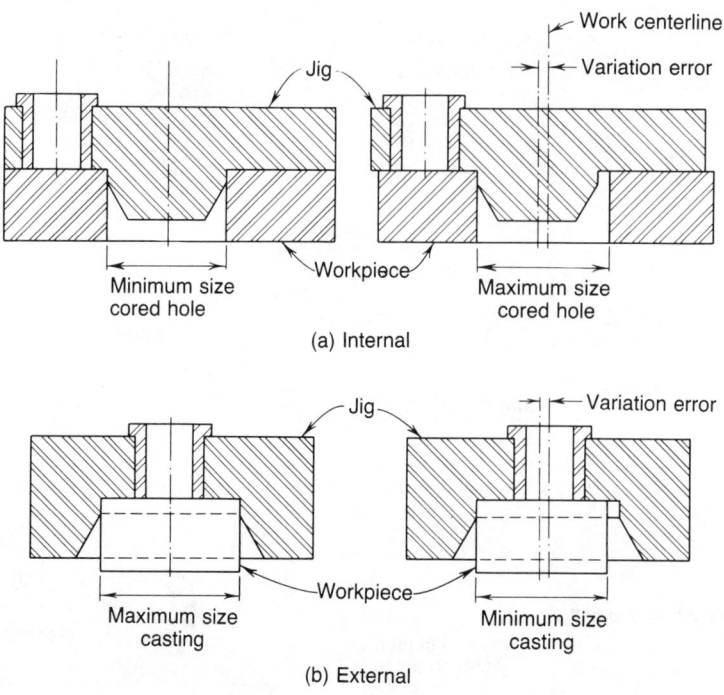

(a) Internal

(b) External

Fig. 2-16 Concentric averaging locating of finished workpieces.

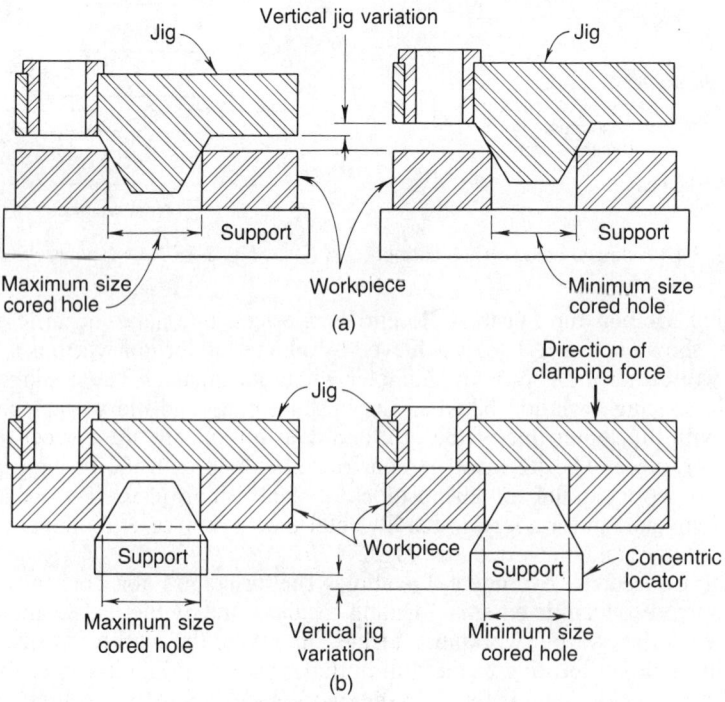

(a)

(b)

Fig. 2-17 Internal concentric averaging locating of rough workpieces.

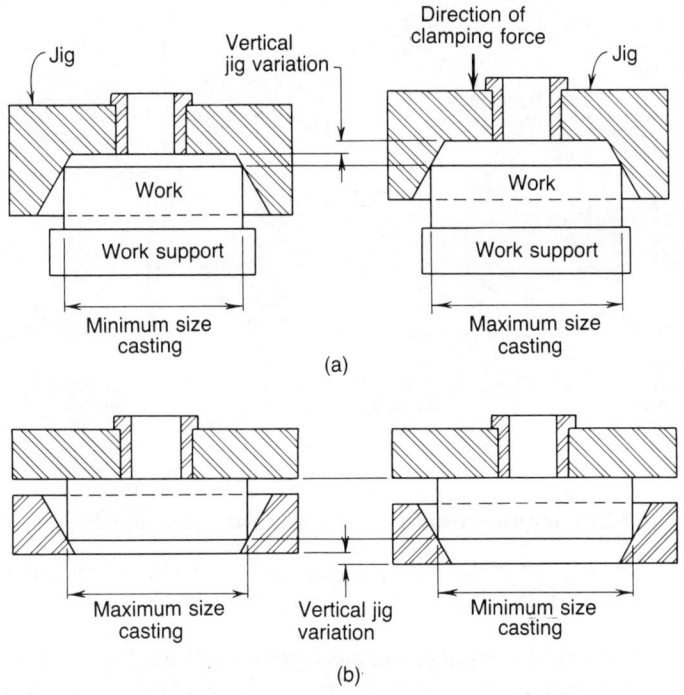

Fig. 2-18 Concentric averaging locating of rough workpieces.

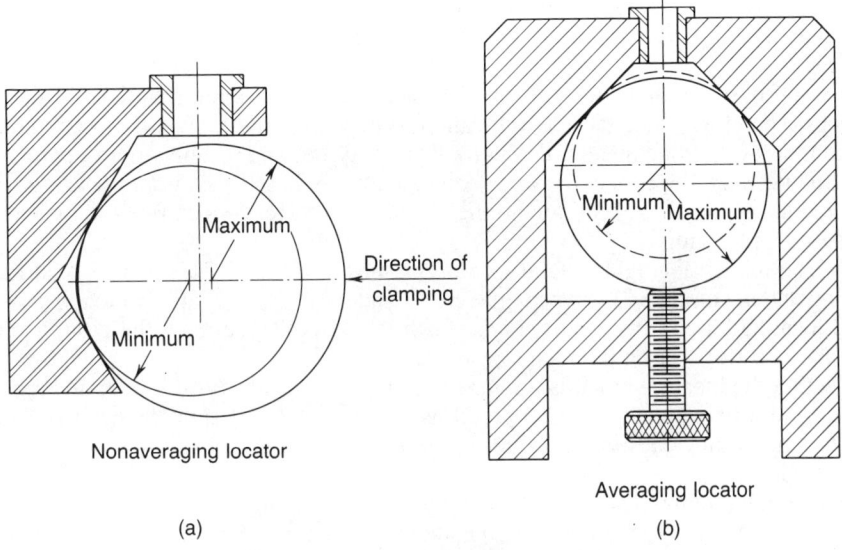

Fig. 2-19 External concentric averaging locating of a cylindrical workpiece.

An irregular-shaped workpiece that requires both concentric and radial location is shown in Fig. 2-20a. The workpiece, finished all over, will not only have to be located concentrically but will also require a radial locator, as shown, to establish radial alignment between its irregular shape and the drill bushing. If it were not for the radial locating block, the workpiece could be turned about the concentric locator and drilled

2-15

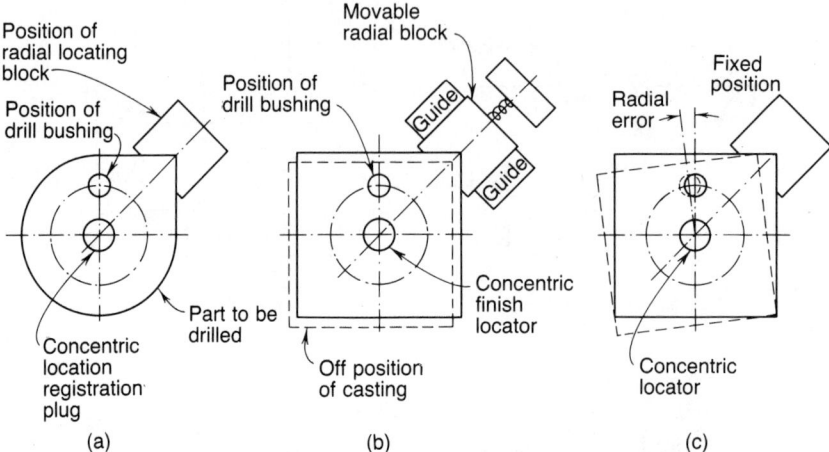

Fig. 2-20 Workpieces requiring concentric and radial locating.

in the correct concentric but in the wrong radial position. There is only one correct spot for the hole to be drilled, and that is at the intersection of the concentric and vertical center lines.

Concentric and Radial Locating of Second-Operation Work. The drilling of a rough casting having a machined bore frequently presents problems in location to its rough and smooth surfaces.

Concentric locating to the rough casting body cannot be accurate; it will have to be accomplished in relation to the machined surface.

Radial locating, if required, generally must be true to the irregular, rough-cast surfaces.

One jig must simultaneously locate a workpiece with different relations to the two surfaces. Therefore, since these two locations (concentric and radial) are often made to different surfaces (machined and rough), there may be (and usually is) an appreciable variation between the concentric and radial locating points. This variation can be compensated for by locating accurately to the machined surface (concentric) and by averaging the radial locating.

An example of averaging radial locating is shown in Fig. 2-20b. A V-shaped radial locating block, mounted between guides, is under spring pressure which keeps the radial locating block in constant contact with the workpiece even if the casting variations are on the low or on the high side.

Whether the locating block is forward or retracted, it is always in true radial relation to the central pivot point. Any proposed averaging-locator design should be checked with this important question in mind: Is the locator true in both the forward and the retracted position?

An averaging radial locator need not necessarily be spring operated as shown.

A radial locator is fundamentally intended for locating only and not for clamping. If there is no established central locator to prevent the workpiece from shifting, a locator of this type will not average-locate but will force the workpiece out of true concentric position. It correctly functions only when acting against another locator that holds the workpiece in a true central position.

If a nonaveraging radial locator is used (see Fig. 2-20c), it is necessary to set the radial locator back far enough to clear maximum chucking and casting variation; otherwise, the parts will jam between the concentric and radial locators. If the fixed radial locator is set back far enough to clear the maximum position, the smallest casting would be able to rotate appreciably and thus vary the radial location of the hole to be drilled. It is ordinarily best to use an extreme edge of workpiece for radial registration for maximum radial locating accuracy.

DESIGN OF LOCATING COMPONENTS

Sighting. Perhaps the simplest method of locating a flat workpiece is by sighting to lines on the jig or fixture, such as shown in Fig. 2-21a, or by sighting through holes and slots as shown in Fig. 2-21b. This method is often used when dimensions are not critical. The use of opposing adjusting screws and clamps makes alignment and clamping easier.

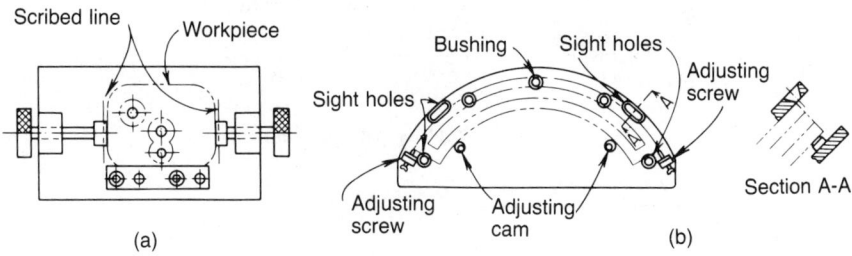

Fig. 2-21 Sight locators: (a) by scribed lines; (b) by sighting holes.

Nesting. The nesting method of locating is ideal for locating workpieces having complex irregular two-dimensional and three-dimensional surfaces as well as for flat surfaces. A nesting type jig of the simplest form has already been shown in Fig. 2-15. Some disadvantages of nesting the workpiece one above the other can readily be seen from this simple illustration:

1. The part could be difficult to remove from the nest.
2. The burrs on the workpiece caused by the machining operation tend to lock the workpiece in the nest.
3. It is difficult to remove chips from the nest which could interfere with the loading of the next workpiece.
4. They could be expensive. Obviously, the more detailed the cavity is, the more expensive the workholder will be.

The first two disadvantages could be overcome with the addition of ejectors, however this makes the workholder more expensive and adds processing time to the operation.

Partial nests, such as that shown in Fig. 2-22, can eliminate many of these disadvantages for the following reasons:

1. Less machining time is required with resulting savings in build costs.
2. Space has been provided for the operator's fingers to grip the workpiece for insertion and removal, eliminating the need for an ejector.
3. Chips are easier to remove.

A simpler and less expensive method of nesting is shown in Fig. 2-23. It was designed to contain the part with five dowel pins pressed into the jig as shown. Many standard components such as rest buttons and adjustable locators work equally well for this purpose.

To provide for easy chip and foreign matter removal, burr grooves and/or undercut pins are usually provided.

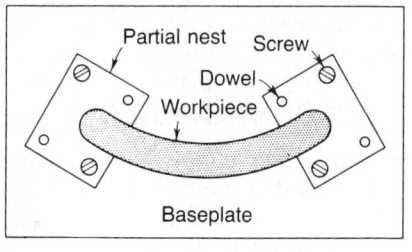

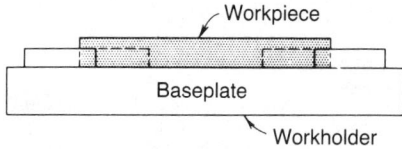

Fig. 2-22 Workholder with partial nests.

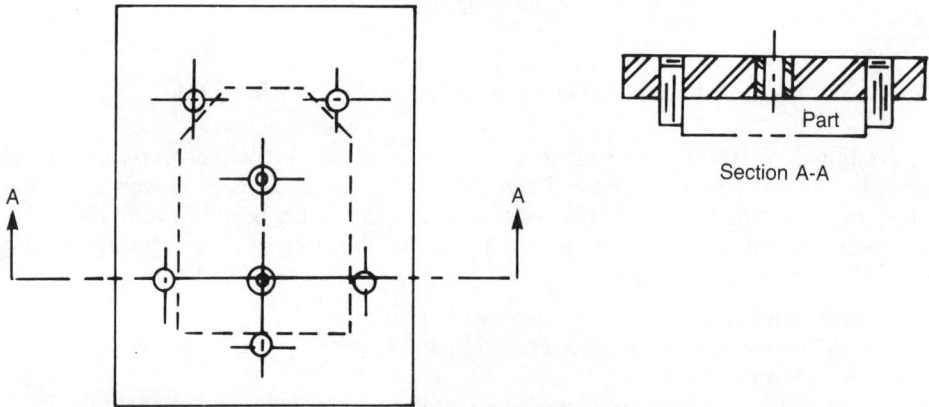

Fig. 2-23 Nesting type drill jig using dowel pins.

Nesting type jigs and fixtures for locating complex three-dimensional workpieces, such as shown in Fig. 2-24, are usually made by casting with epoxy, thermoplastic, or low-melt alloys. Nests are formed by pouring the casting material around a workpiece, or pattern of the workpiece while it is suspended in a box-like container in the position desired. Grooves and/or recesses are often cast or machined in the cast surface to provide for chip clearance, easy removal, and wider tolerances.

Locating Pads. Locating pads can be integral to the jig or fixture (see Fig. 2-25) or assembled (see Fig. 2-26). They are mainly used where a large support area is needed to properly support the workpiece. With cast fixtures, the pads are cast with the rest of the fixture. With a welded fixture they are welded in place. Commercial rest pads, such as shown in Fig. 2-27, can be added to the fixture by assembly with screws.

All rest pads require machining on the fixture body. The cast and welded pads are least preferred since they cannot easily be repaired if worn or damaged, whereas the assembled type is easily replaceable. Large pads should be grooved to provide better control over chips and foreign matter, and to facilitate coolant drainage. A good rule of thumb in providing sufficient support, while minimizing wear, would be to allow one square inch (645 mm^2) support for each 25 lb (11.3 kg) requiring support.

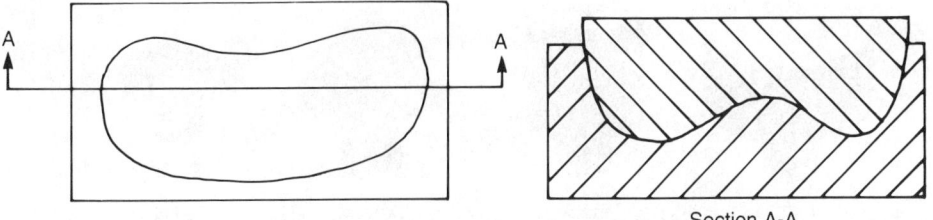

Fig. 2-24 Three-dimensional nest.

Section A-A

Fig. 2-25 Integral locators.

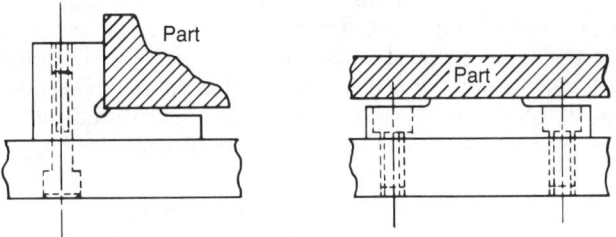

Part

Part

Fig. 2-26 Assembled locators.

Fig. 2-27 Rest pads. (*Courtesy Jergens, Inc.*)

Buttons. Commercial buttons are readily available in various sizes and styles, such as shown in Fig. 2-28. The flat buttons are used against machined surfaces, the crowned (spherical) buttons mainly against rough surfaces, and the conical buttons to support and locate a workpiece at a single point. Other buttons shown are equipped with self-aligning balls, V-locators, and edge positioners. Buttons are available with ground shanks for press fitting or installation in liner bushings with a lock screw or with a threaded shank. When buttons are used to support the workpiece, they are called rest buttons.

| Flat | Stack | Conical | Radial |

| Self-aligning | Edge | Vee |

Fig. 2-28 Commercial buttons. (*Courtesy QU-CO*)

Pins. Dowel pins, such as shown in Fig. 2-29, are used to assure precise location of assembled components, such as in built-up fixture bodies. In principle, two dowel pins are required to locate a component. They are placed as far apart as practical. The components are assembled and clamped in their correct position. Holes are then drilled through the components and reamed to size. Cylindrical (straight) dowel pins are usually press-fitted through both components unless future disassembly is expected. In those cases the dowel pin is press-fit through one component and slip-fit into the other component. The tapered dowel pin also works well for locating components which are frequently disassembled. Figure 2-30 shows some typical uses of buttons and pins as locators.

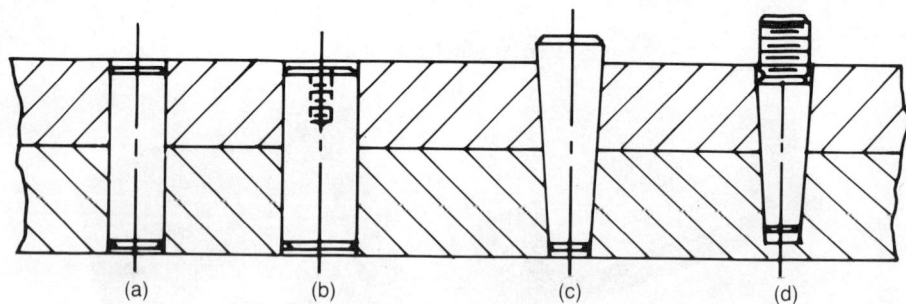

| (a) | (b) | (c) | (d) |

Fig. 2-29 Dowel pins: (*a*) straight; (*b*) straight pull type; (*c*) tapered; (*d*) tapered pull type.

Spring Locating Pins. Another locating pin that could be useful in some instances is the patented spring locating pin shown in Fig. 2-31 along with a matching eccentric liner. The tapered pin is anchored in a spring base and operates as illustrated in Fig. 2-32 along with pertinent application data.

Concentric Locators. Internal locators are used to locate workpieces from an ID such as a bored hole. They include machined internal locators, such as shown in Fig. 2-33, round and diamond locating pins, male conical locators, mechanical and hydraulic expanding ID chucks, arbors, collets, and mandrels.

When locating from an ID, avoid overdefining, as seen in Fig. 2-34. Trying to locate from more than one diameter will likely make it impossible to load the piece. In the event that it can be loaded it probably will tip the piece away from the base.

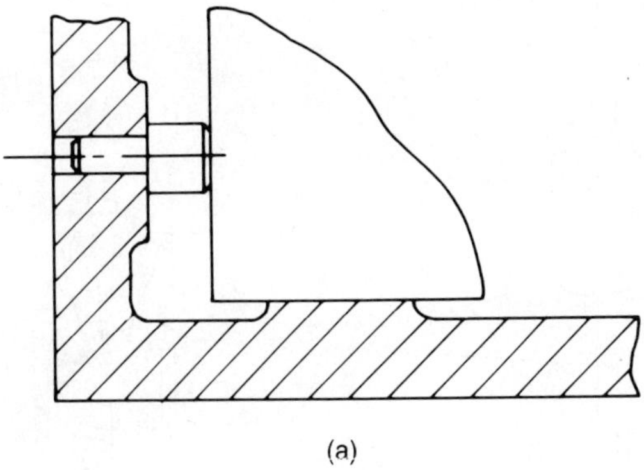

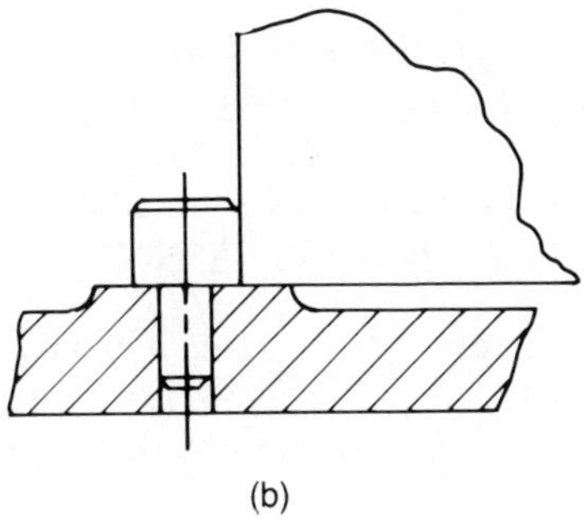

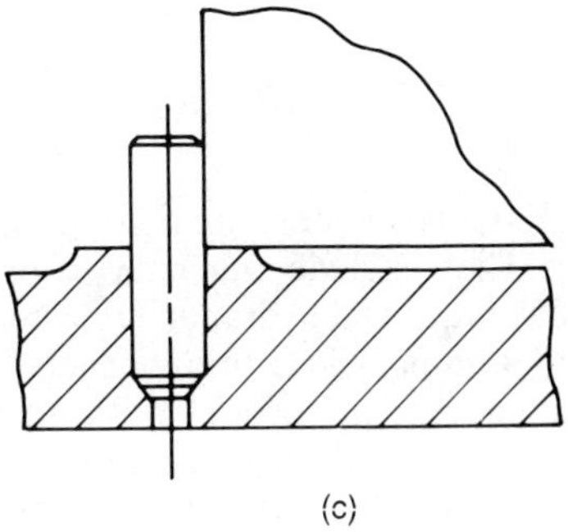

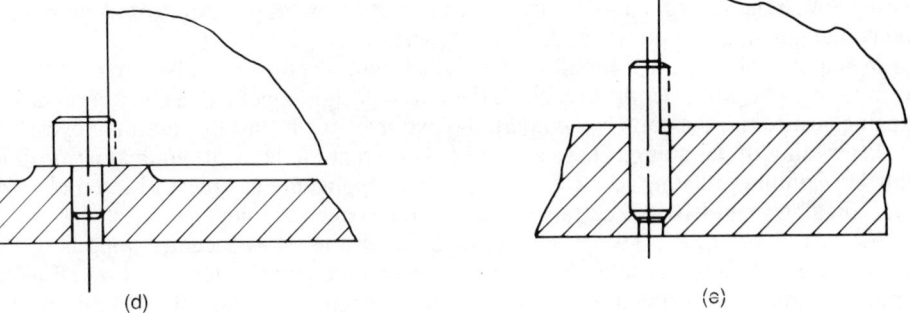

Fig. 2-30 Buttons and pins used as locators: (*a*) rest button used as a stop button; (*b*) rest button used as a side locator; (*c*) dowel pin used as a side locator; (*d*) and (*e*) rest button and dowel pin with ground flat for use as side locators.

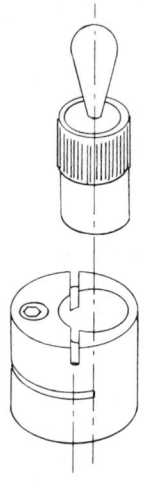

Fig. 2-31 Spring locating pin and liner.
(Courtesy Carr Lane Mfg. Co.)

External locators are used to locate workpieces from an OD such as a turned diameter. They include machine external locators (shown in Fig. 2-35), V-blocks, and mechanical and hydraulic OD chucks.

Jamming. Close-fitting concentric locators, whether internal or external, may have a tendency to jam or lock with the work. Jamming, illustrated in Fig. 2-36, is exaggerated to show the basic condition of engaging two close-fitting concentric parts regardless of which is the locator and which is the work.

The diameter of the male part is smaller than any diagonal, such as that shown by the arrows. This diagonal is the hypotenuse of a right triangle. The two parts cannot engage in skewed position but will jam. The application of force may only cause the two to jam more tightly.

If an attempt is made to disengage the two after they have been hopelessly jammed, instead of straightening out and retracting, the parts may tilt past the perfect alignment point and jam in the opposite relation, as shown in Fig. 2-36.

When the two parts are engaged beyond jamming depth side-wall contact will prevent tilting. Once this depth is reached, the two will slide together easily; but on disengaging, just before the parts come apart, the two may again start the jamming cycle.

Prevention of Jamming. There are several different methods of eliminating or minimizing jamming relating to clearance, length of engagement, spherical internal locators, aligning shoulders, and cutting the side of the concentric plug.

Clearance Allowance. The closer the fit between the two concentric members, the greater the inclination to lock. The situation can sometimes be remedied by allowing ample clearance as dictated by work tolerance. This practice, however, should not be carried to excess; beyond a certain point, increased clearance will merely contribute to a poor fit.

The closeness of fit has a direct relation to the size of the parts being engaged. The entrance of a 0.246 in. diameter plug into a 0.250 in. diameter hole allows 0.004 diameter clearance. The two parts should show almost no tendency to jam; in fact, they should enter so readily as to feel excessively loose. On the other hand, if a 15.996 in. diameter plug is entered into a 16.000 in. diameter hole, which also has 0.004 diameter clearance, the parts will have a decided tendency to lock if slightly misaligned. Thus the amount of clearance in itself will not necessarily determine the ease of engaging, for

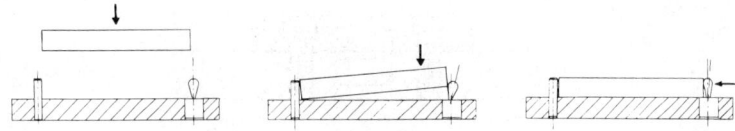

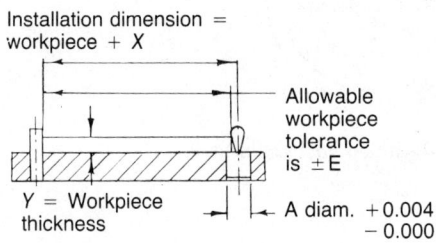

Installation dimension =
workpiece + X

Allowable
workpiece
tolerance
is ±E

Y = Workpiece
thickness

A diam. +0.004
          −0.000

Spring locating pin

A nominal diam.

B diam. +0.000
          −0.004

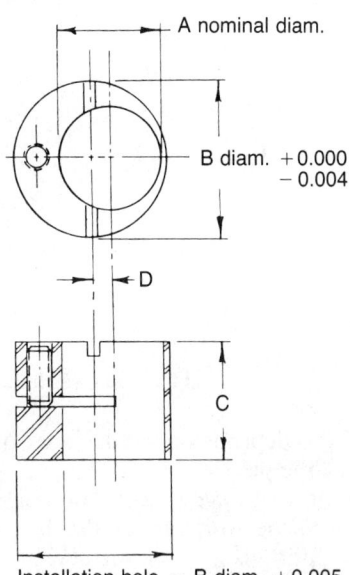

D

C

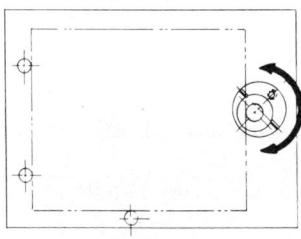

Provides additional adjustment for
workpieces with looser tolerances.

Installation hole = B diam. +0.005
                              −0.000

Liner

Dimensions–Inch

A	B	C	D	E*
0.25	0.500	0.390	0.079	0.020
0.38	0.625	0.469	0.079	0.031
0.44	0.688	0.469	0.079	0.039
0.50	0.750	0.547	0.079	0.051
0.63	1.000	0.705	0.118	0.063

E* Allowable workpiece tolerance

Fig. 2-32 Application of spring locating pins and liners. (*Courtesy Carr Lane Mfg. Co.*)

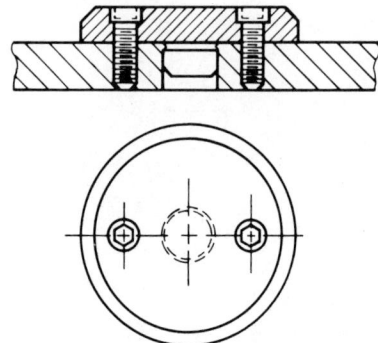

Fig. 2-33 Machined internal locator.

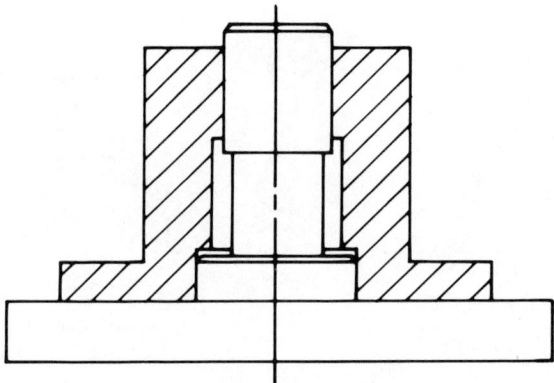

Fig. 2-34 Overdefining using two diameters and a plane.

this also depends on the diameter of the members. Small pieces require less clearance than large pieces.

Length of Engagement. The relative length of engagement (axial length of contact between the workpieces) also has an important bearing on the ease with which the close fitting concentric members can be engaged. Length of engagement is shown in Fig. 2-37.

There are three fundamental conditions that occur as the length of engagement is increased to the point where the parts are engaged deep enough to be unable to jam:

1. If the length of engagement is short enough, the parts will be unable to jam.
2. There is a critical point at which maximum jamming action is reached.
3. Beyond this depth, the parts engage freely.

For a very short distance, the two parts can be engaged without any possibility of jamming; this is illustrated in Fig. 2-38.

If all the other factors (amount of clearance, size and work, etc.) are made constant, all jamming action may usually be eliminated by sufficiently shortening the length of engagement.

In using short lengths of engagement, preliminary engagement is greatly facilitated by providing a lead on one member (see Fig. 2-39).

It is not the lead itself which eliminates jamming; the lead merely assists preliminary

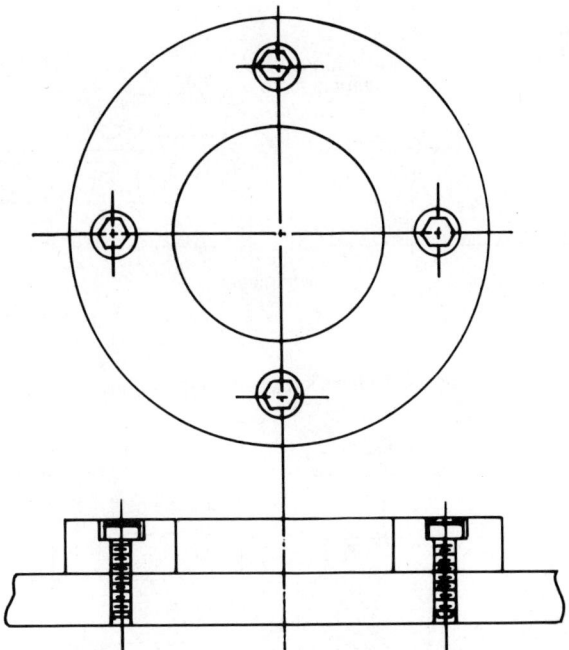

Fig. 2-35 Machined external locator.

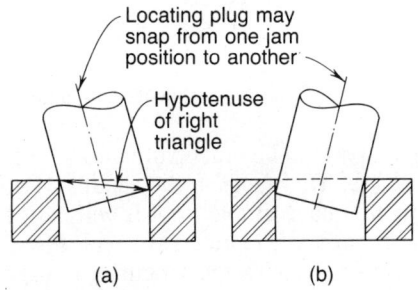

Locating plug may snap from one jam position to another

Hypotenuse of right triangle

(a)   (b)

Fig. 2-36 Jamming or sticking of locators.

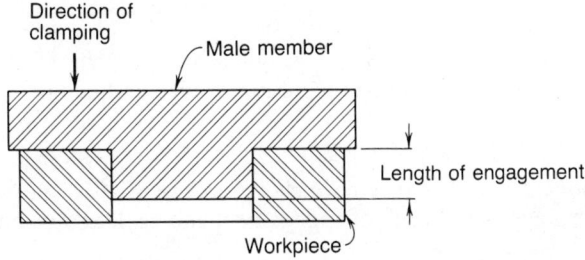

Direction of clamping

Male member

Length of engagement

Workpiece

Fig. 2-37 Length of engagement.

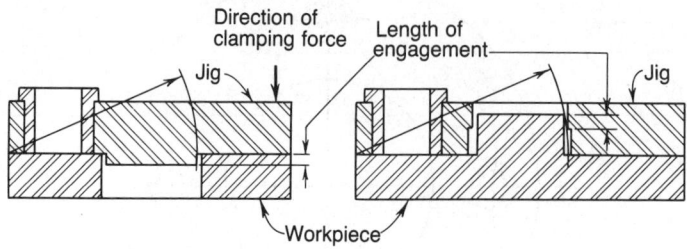

Fig. 2-38 Short length of engagement.

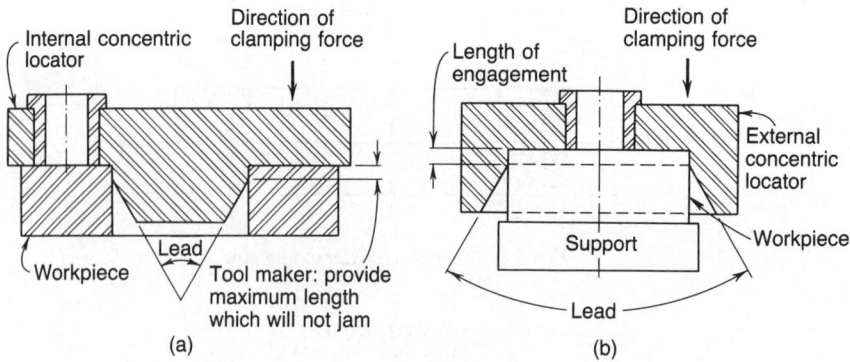

Fig. 2-39 Lead on locators for ease of engagement.

positioning, allowing the parts to be practically thrown together rather than being carefully positioned to engage. This fact can be readily verified by engaging two close-fitting concentric parts that have ample lead. It will be found that, although the length of engagement is long enough, the mating parts will show a strong tendency to jam in a slightly misaligned position. Besides the length of engagement, the size of work and amount of clearance will also determine the critical depth before jamming begins.

The length of engagement may be determined with the following formula:

$$A = \sqrt{2(2B + C)(C - D)} \qquad (1)$$

where:

A = length of engagement (height of locating plug)
B = distance from pivot point to the edge of the hole
C = diameter of the hole
D = diameter of the plug

Example 1: For the workpiece shown in Fig. 2-40, if the workpiece is pivoted around the long edge, the length of engagement can be determined as follows:

For:

B = 2.000
C = 2.000
D = 1.995

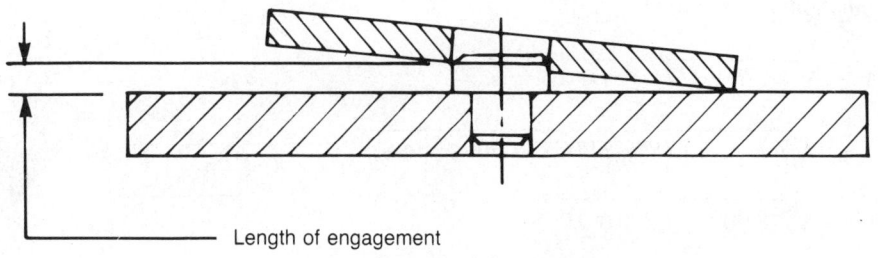

Length of engagement

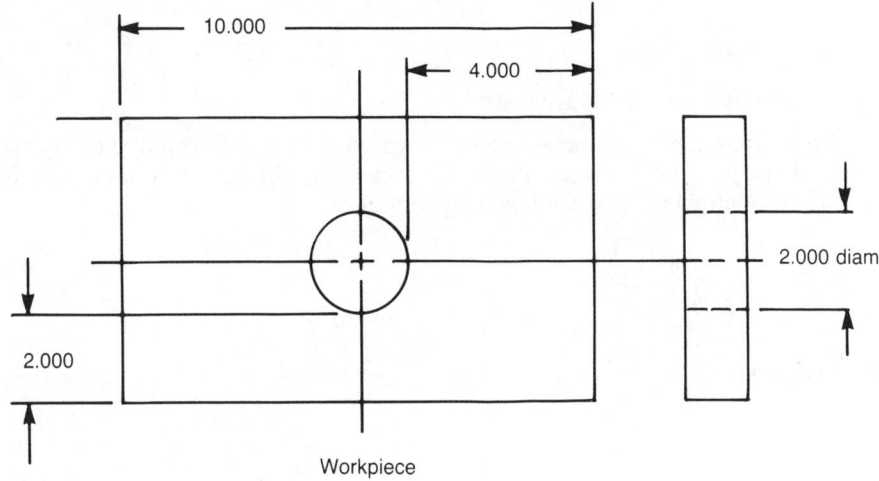

Workpiece

Fig. 2-40 Determining length of engagement.

Calculation:

$$A = \sqrt{2(2B + C)(C - D)} \qquad (1)$$

$$= \sqrt{2(2 \times 2.000 + 2.000)(2.000 - 1.995)}$$

$$= \sqrt{2(4.000 + 2.000)(0.005)}$$

$$= \sqrt{2(6.000)(0.005)}$$

$$= \sqrt{0.06}$$

$$= 0.245 \text{ length of engagement}$$

For the same workpiece shown in Fig. 2-40, if the workpiece is pivoted around the short edge:

For:

B = 4.000
C = 2.000
D = 1.995

Calculation:

$$A = \sqrt{2(2B + C)(C - D)} \tag{1}$$

$$= \sqrt{2(2 \times 4.000 + 2.000)(2.000 - 1.995)}$$

$$= \sqrt{2(8.000 + 2.000)(0.005)}$$

$$= \sqrt{2(10.000)(0.005)}$$

$$= \sqrt{0.10}$$

$$= 0.316 \text{ length of engagement}$$

The maximum plug diameter can be increased if the 0.245 length of engagement is retained and the part is pivoted around the long edge. The new maximum plug diameter can be determined using the following formula:

$$D = C - \frac{A^2}{2(2B + C)} \tag{2}$$

Example 2:

For:

$$B = 4.000$$
$$C = 2.000$$
$$A = 0.245$$

Calculation:

$$D = C - \frac{A^2}{2(2B + C)} \tag{2}$$

$$= 2.000 - \frac{(0.245)^2}{2(2 \times 4.000 + 2.000)}$$

$$= 2.000 - \frac{0.0600}{20.000}$$

$$= 2.000 - 0.003$$

$$= 1.997 \text{ diameter of plug}$$

It can be seen that by shortening the length of engagement from 0.316 to 0.245 and pivoting around the short edge, that the locating plug could be increased from 1.995 diameter to 1.997 diameter resulting in more accurate location.

If the workpiece hole is chamfered, the length of engagement can be increased. The following formula can be used to determine the new length of engagement:

$$A = E + \sqrt{(2B + C)(C - D)} \tag{3}$$

where:

E = depth of chamfer

Example 3:

For:

B = 4.000
C = 2.000
D = 1.995
E = 0.150

Calculation:

$$A = E + \sqrt{(2B + C)(C - D)} \qquad (3)$$

$$= 0.150 + \sqrt{(2 \times 4.000 + 2.000)(2.000 - 1.995)}$$

$$= 0.150 + \sqrt{(8.000 + 2.000)(0.005)}$$

$$= 0.150 + \sqrt{(10.000)(0.005)}$$

$$= 0.150 + \sqrt{.05}$$

$$= 0.150 + 0.224$$

$$= 0.374 \text{ new length of engagement}$$

From this it can be seen that the addition of the 0.150 chamfer permitted the length of engagement to be increased by 0.058 (0.374 - 0.316). On the other hand, the maximum plug diameter can be increased if the 0.316 length of engagement is retained. The new maximum plug diameter can now be determined using the following formula:

$$D = C - \frac{(A - E)^2}{2B + C} \qquad (4)$$

Example 4:

For:

A = 0.316
B = 4.000
C = 2.000
E = 0.150

Calculation:

$$D = C - \frac{(A - E)^2}{2B + C} \qquad (4)$$

$$= 2.000 - \frac{(0.316 - 0.150)^2}{(2 \times 4.000) + 2.000}$$

$$= 2.000 - \frac{(0.166)^2}{8.000 + 2.000}$$

$$= 2.000 - \frac{0.0276}{10.000}$$

$$= 2.000 - 0.0028$$

$$= 1.9972 \text{ new plug diameter}$$

Spherical Internal Locators. A spherical internal locator, if properly proportioned, will not jam because of misalignment.

A sphere has only one dimension, and so, no matter in which direction it is turned, it has no dimension larger or smaller than its diameter and therefore cannot generate a jamming action.

Figure 2-41a shows an example of a simple spherical internal locator incorporated in a drill jig. No matter how misaligned the work and concentric locator, the two will always engage and disengage freely. This type of locator acts as lead for preliminary engagement.

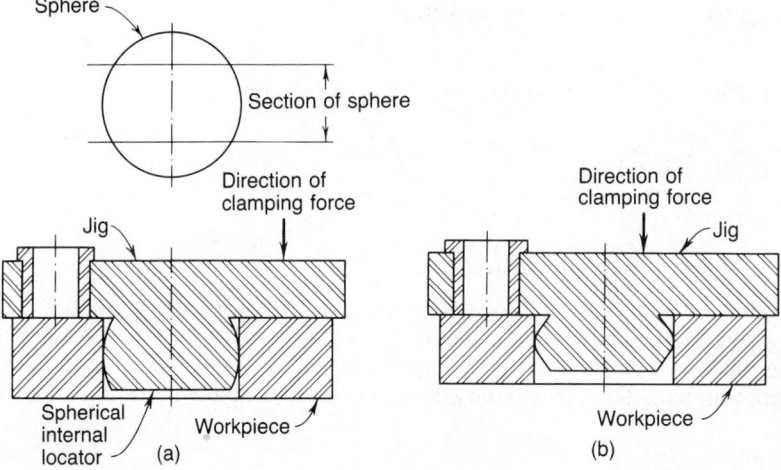

Fig. 2-41 Spherical locators.

Locators of smaller radius (less wearing surface) can also be used as nonlocking locators, as shown in Fig. 2-41b. Instead of being spherical, the locator can be of any shape containable in a sphere.

Such locators will not jam. The essential difference between these and the spherical type is the wearing surface, or life. Inasmuch as it is rather difficult to machine a spherical surface, this second type will probably cost a little less.

Aligning Grooves. Aligning grooves provide a simple and practical method of minimizing locking action when a close-fitting, internal concentric locator is used. The method consists in machining a small groove near the end of the internal locator, as shown in Fig. 2-42.

When the plug has entered into the hole in a misaligned position as shown, it can travel only a very short distance before the work edge of the hole strikes the shoulder of the plug. To meet the shoulder, the work edge must enter slightly into the locator shoulder groove. This allows the plug to move slightly sideways, and it is thus possible for the opposite edge of the plug to enter into the hole deep enough to pass the critical point at which jamming ordinarily occurs. Once the plug has entered below the depth of this critical point, no jamming can occur and the two members engage freely. On

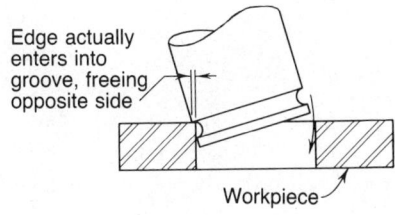

Edge actually enters into groove, freeing opposite side

Workpiece

Fig. 2-42 Aligning grooves.

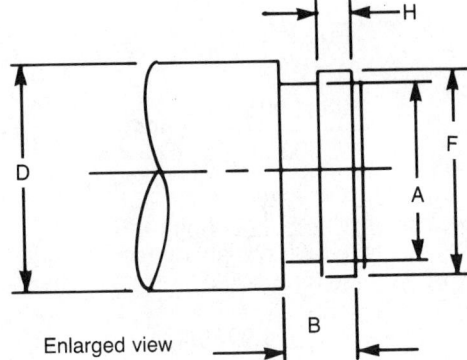

Enlarged view

retracting the plug from the hole, the reverse process takes place, allowing the members to disengage freely.

The following formulas can be used to determine pilot dimensions:

$$A = 0.95D \tag{5}$$

$$B = CD \tag{6}$$

$$F = \frac{2D^2}{E} - D \tag{7}$$

$$G = E - F \tag{8}$$

$$H = \sqrt{2FG} \tag{9}$$

where:

A = groove diameter
B = minimum length of pilot and grooves
C = coefficient of friction between plug and workpiece
D = plug diameter
E = hole diameter
F = pilot diameter
G = clearance
H = pilot length

Example 5:

For:

C = 0.20
D = 1.995
E = 2.000

Calculations:

$$A = 0.95D \tag{5}$$
$$= 0.95 \times 1.995$$
$$= 1.895 \text{ groove diameter}$$

$$B = CD \tag{6}$$
$$= 0.20 \times 1.995$$
$$= 0.40 \text{ min. length of pilot and groove}$$

$$F = \frac{2D^2}{E} - D \qquad\qquad (7)$$

$$= \frac{2 \times (1.995)^2}{2.000} - 1.995$$

$$= \frac{2 \times 3.980}{2.000} - 1.995$$

$$= \frac{7.960}{2.000} - 1.995$$

$$= 3.980 - 1.995$$

$$= 1.985 \text{ pilot diameter}$$

$$G = E - F \qquad\qquad (8)$$

$$= 2.000 - 1.985$$

$$= 0.015 \text{ clearance}$$

$$H = \sqrt{2FG} \qquad\qquad (9)$$

$$= \sqrt{2 \times 1.985 \times 0.015}$$

$$= \sqrt{0.060}$$

$$= 0.245 \text{ pilot length}$$

Similar results can be accomplished by a ball-end spherical portion, as shown in Fig. 2-43a, or any form of end that can be enclosed in the sphere.

Equilateral Diamond Locators. While not as accurate, jamming can also be minimized by cutting away three sides of the male locator, leaving three circular 30° lands, 120° apart, as shown in Fig. 2-43b. The locator has no two engaging points opposite each other; thus, the jamming is lessened though not entirely eliminated.

The following formulas can be used to determine the dimensions of an equilateral diamond locator:

$$A = 0.35B \qquad\qquad (10)$$

$$C = A + \frac{B}{2} \qquad\qquad (11)$$

$$D = 2.4(2E + 0.85B)(F - B) \qquad\qquad (12)$$

$$G = 0.207(F - B) \qquad\qquad (13)$$

where:

A = distance from flat to plug centerline
B = plug diameter
C = distance from flat to opposite bearing surface
D = length of engagement
E = distance from pivot to edge of hole

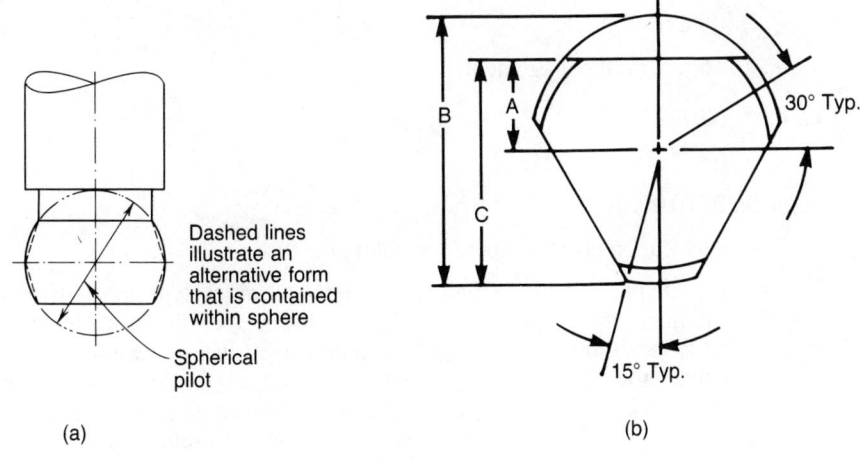

(a)   (b)

Dashed lines
illustrate an
alternative form
that is contained
within sphere

Spherical
pilot

30° Typ.

15° Typ.

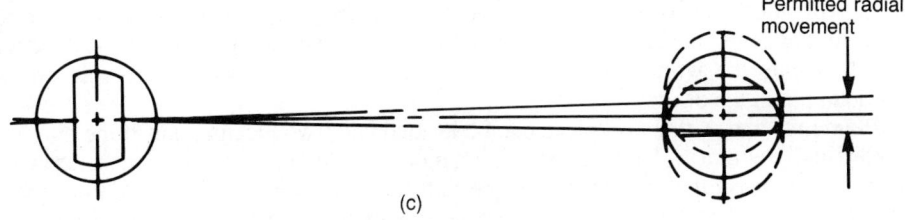

Permitted radial
movement

(c)

Fig. 2-43 Locator modification.

F = hole diameter
G = location error compared to solid plug

For:

B = 1.995
E = 4.000
F = 2.000

Calculations:

$$A = 0.35B \tag{10}$$
$$= 0.35 \times 1.995$$
$$= 0.698 \text{ distance from flat to centerline of plug}$$

$$C = A + \frac{B}{2} \tag{11}$$

$$= 0.698 + \frac{1.995}{2}$$

$$= 0.698 + 0.9975$$

$$= 1.6955 \text{ distance from flat to opposite bearing surface}$$

$$D = 2.4(2E + 0.85B)(F - B) \tag{12}$$

$$= 2.4 (2 \times 4.000 + 0.85 \times 1.995)(2.000 - 1.995)$$

$\quad = 2.4\ (8.000\ +\ 1.696)(0.005)$

$\quad = 2.4\ (9.696)(0.005)$

$\quad = 0.116\ \text{length of engagement}$

$G = 0.207(F\ -\ B)$ \hfill (13)

$\quad = 0.207\ (2.000\ -\ 1.995)$

$\quad = 0.207\ (0.005)$

$\quad = 0.001\ \text{location error compared to solid plug}$

The same principle can be applied to instances in which two concentric engagements must be made into the same part. Such a case is also illustrated in Fig. 2-43c. The engaging locators are cut away so that each establishes a location that does not conflict with the other locator engagement. For example, the left-hand engagement establishes the vertical relationship, and the right-hand engagement establishes the horizontal relationship. The purpose of such a scheme is to relieve the jamming that would be caused by very small-dimensional location variation between the holes in the work. This method is often recommended and used by some designers, but it must be realized that some movement can still take place as shown by the dotted lines. A better way to locate the workpiece would be to use a full pin to locate one hole and a diamond pin in the other.

Diamond Pins. A flat workpiece can be located with two locating pins if the pins are made small enough to handle any combination of hole sizes and centerdistance variance that is permitted by the workpiece and tool drawing specifications. Pins small enough to do this, however, allow a workpiece with holes spaced closer or farther than nominal to fit snug and seem to be properly located, while nominally spaced holes allow the workpiece to locate loosely in a wide variety of positions—an unsatisfactory condition for many applications. The diamond pin solves these problems by using a full round pin to locate one hole about which the workpiece can rotate. A relieved pin (diamond pin) is used in the other hole to restrain the workpiece radially.

The proper orientation of a diamond pin when used with a full round pin is shown in Fig. 2-44a. The use of one diamond pin in combination with a flat is shown in Fig. 2-44b. Typical dimensions of a diamond locating pin are shown in Fig. 2-45.

With diamond pins the smaller that the area of contact with the workpiece is, the larger the pin diameter can be and visa versa. The pin diameter should be as large as possible to provide locating accuracy, but is limited by the smallest contact width that will wear satisfactorily. The recommended contact width should not be less than one-eighth the diameter of the hole located by the diamond pin, and never less than 0.031 in.

However, it can be seen from Fig. 2-45 that the contact width must be short enough to provide a clearance of $C/2$ where C is equal to the sum of tolerances between the centers of the pins and centers of the holes.

Formulas for designing special pins are as follows:

$$A = \frac{B}{8}$$ \hfill (14)

$$C = D + E$$ \hfill (15)

$$G = \frac{B}{C}\ (B\ -\ F)\ -\ \frac{C}{2}$$ \hfill (16)

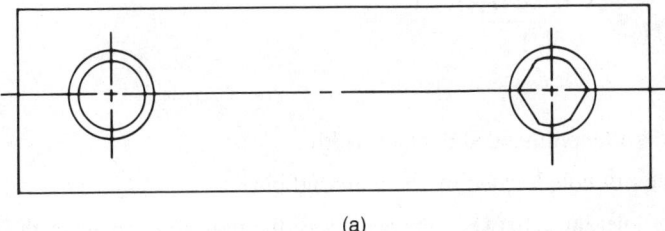

(a)

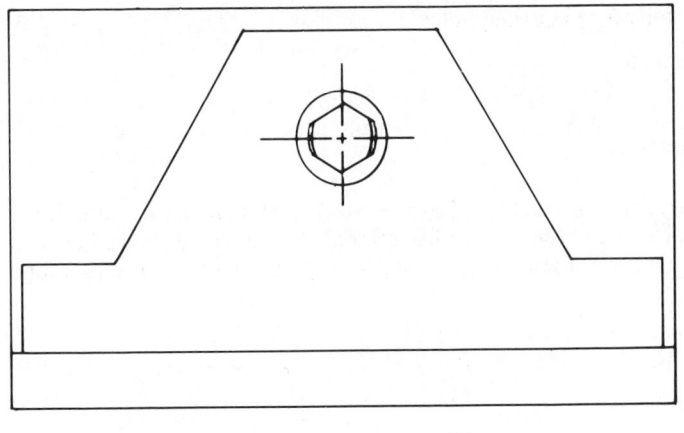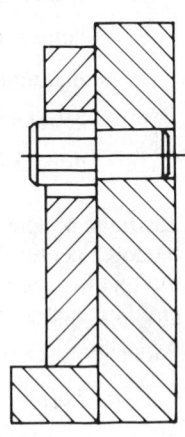

(b)

Fig. 2-44 Diamond pin orientation.

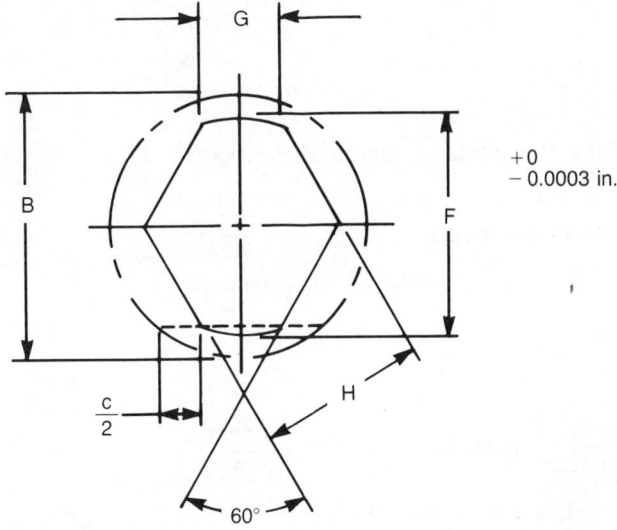

Fig. 2-45 Diamond locator.

2-35

$$H = 0.866G + \frac{\sqrt{B^2 - G^2}}{2} \qquad (17)$$

where:

    A = minimum recommended contact width

    B = diameter of hole located by the diamond pin

    C = sum of tolerances between the centers of the pins and centers of the holes

    D = center-distance tolerance between pins

    E = center-distance tolerance between holes

    F = diamond pin diameter

    G = contact width

    H = dimension across flats

Example 6: The workpiece shown in Fig. 2-46*a* has two 2.000 diameter locating holes having a center-distance between them of 12.000 ±0.002. The center-distance between the locating pins on the fixture shown in Fig. 2-46*b* is 12.000 ±0.0002. The diamond pin diameter is 1.9990.

For:

    B = 2.0000

    D = ±0.0002

    E = ±0.002

    F = 1.9990

Calculations:

$$A = \frac{B}{8} \qquad (14)$$

$$= \frac{2.0000}{8}$$

= 0.250 minimum recommended contact width

$$C = D + E \qquad (15)$$

= 0.0004 + 0.004

= 0.0044 sum of center-distance tolerances

$$G = \frac{B}{C}(B - F) - \frac{C}{2} \qquad (16)$$

$$= \frac{2.0000}{0.0044}(2.0000 - 1.9990) - \frac{0.0044}{2}$$

= 454.54 × 0.0010 - 0.0022

= 0.4545 - 0.0022

= 0.4523 maximum contact width for a 1.9990 diameter pin

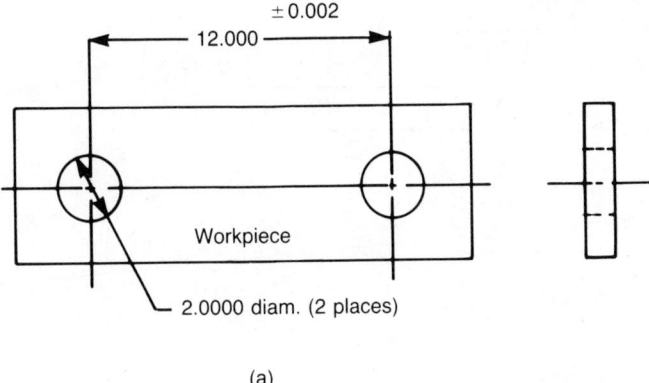

(a)

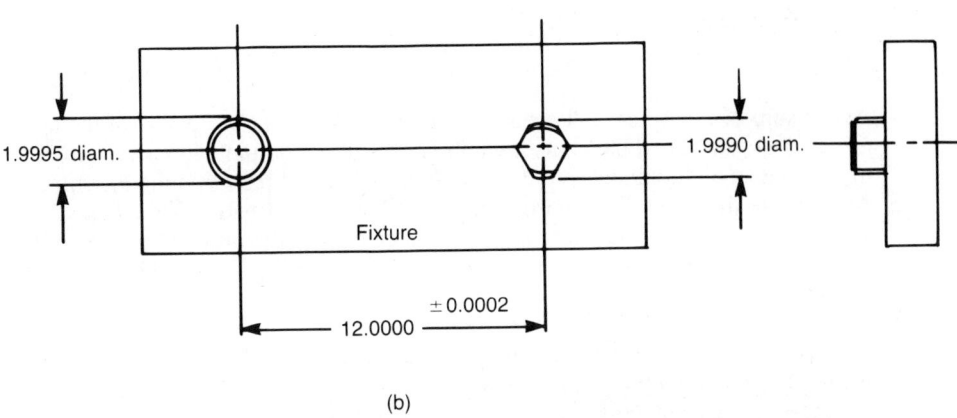

(b)

Fig. 2-46 Workpiece and fixture for determining diamond pin dimensions.

This width is well above the minimum recommended. If the pin diameter was increased to 1.9995, the contact width would be as follows:

$$G = \frac{B}{C}(B - F) - \frac{C}{2} \tag{16}$$

$$= \frac{2.0000}{0.0044}(2.0000 - 1.9990) - \frac{0.0044}{2}$$

$$= 454.54 \times 0.0005 - 0.0022$$

$$= 0.2273 - 0.0022$$

$$= 0.2251 \text{ maximum contact width for 1.9995 diameter pin}$$

This width is less than the minimum recommended and would suggest that the clearance between the diamond pin and the hole be increased.

For: $G = 0.250$

$$H = 0.866G + \frac{\sqrt{B^2 - G^2}}{2} \qquad (17)$$

$$= 0.866 \times 0.250 + \frac{\sqrt{(2.0000)^2 - (0.250)^2}}{2}$$

$$= 0.216 + \frac{\sqrt{4.0000 - 0.0625}}{2}$$

$$= 0.216 + \frac{\sqrt{3.9375}}{2}$$

$$= 0.216 + \frac{1.984}{2}$$

$$= 0.216 + 0.992$$

$$= 1.208 \text{ dimension across flats}$$

In summary:

1. As the sum of tolerances between the centers of the pins and centers of the holes C increases, the allowable contact width G on a diamond pin will lessen, provided the diameters and tolerances of the hole B and diamond pin F remain the same.
2. As the hole diameter B increases, the allowable contact width G increases; provided the sum of the tolerances between the centers of the pins and centers of the the hole C and the clearance $(B - F)$ between the diamond pin and hole remains the same.
3. If the contact width G is less than the minimum recommended contact width A, the clearance between the diamond pin and the hole $(B - F)$ should be increased slightly if possible to provide better wear.

The contact width G for commercial diamond pins has been standardized at one-third the pin diameter.

Diamond Pin Substitutes. Figure 2-47 shows a floating pin locator bushing which can be used in place of a diamond pin for many applications. Installation instructions are also shown. Slotted hole locator bushings, such as shown in Fig. 2-48, can also be used in place of diamond pins. They are usually used with the L-pins and T-pins shown in the same figure. For use with plastic tooling, these bushings are available with a knurled OD.

The floating pin and slotted hole locator bushings can provide good radial location in cases where the centerdistance between the holes varies over a wide range. For best results they are used with a close fitting full pin in the other hole.

Centralizing Locators. Conical locators, as previously shown in Fig. 2-17, are used primarily as centralizing locators for rough workpieces such as castings that have wide variations in hole size to locate the workpiece for first operation machining. The methods shown in the figures requires that the jig be constructed to maintain parallelism between the drill bushing plate and the workpiece. A better alternative would be to use a spring loaded cone as is shown in Fig. 2-49 which would provide centering and permit the workpiece to be solidly supported by the rest buttons and eliminate the need for bushing plate guidance. Precision cone locators (centers), such as shown in Fig. 2-50, are widely used to locate and/or support workpieces with machined female centers. They are mainly used for lathe and related machining operations.

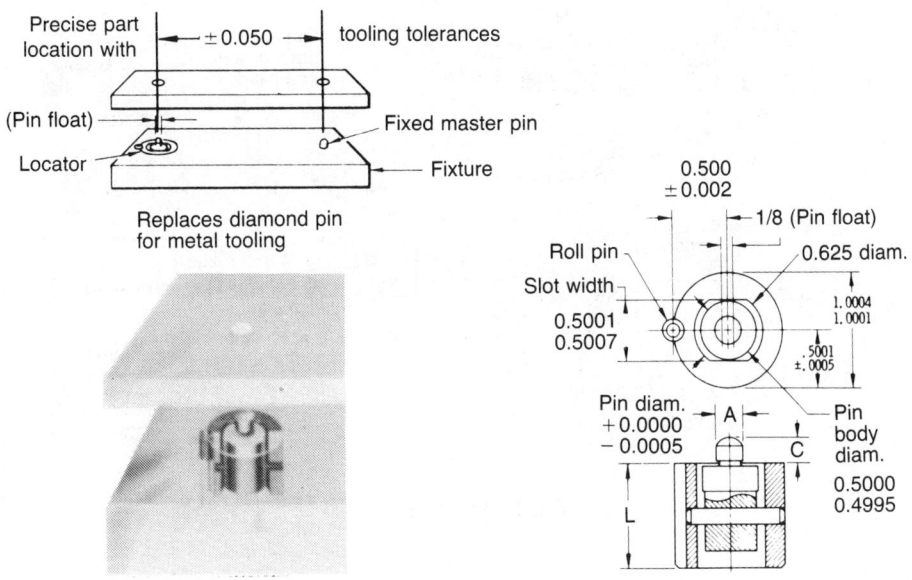

Precise part location with — ±0.050 — tooling tolerances

(Pin float)

Fixed master pin

Locator

Fixture

Replaces diamond pin for metal tooling

0.500
±0.002

1/8 (Pin float)

Roll pin

0.625 diam.

Slot width

0.5001
0.5007

1.0004
1.0001

.5001
±.0005

Pin diam.
+0.0000
−0.0005

A

C

Pin body diam.

0.5000
0.4995

L

Fig. 2-47 Floating pin locator bushing. (*Courtesy American Drill Bushing Co.*)

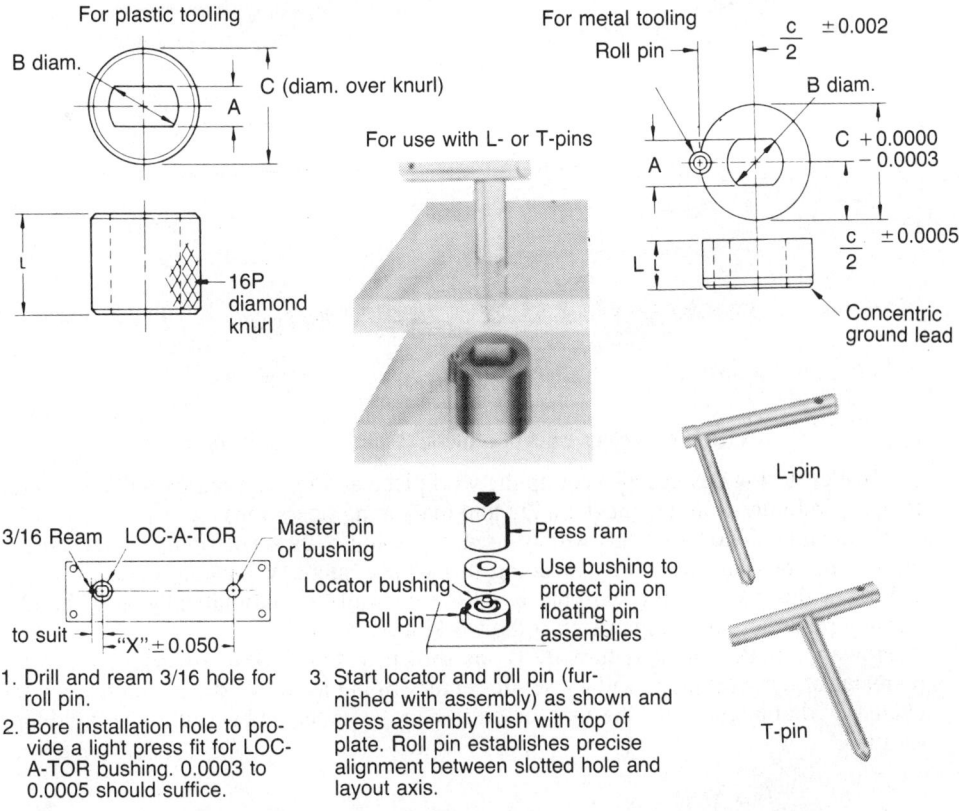

For plastic tooling

B diam.

C (diam. over knurl)

A

L

16P diamond knurl

For use with L- or T-pins

For metal tooling

Roll pin

$\frac{c}{2}$ ±0.002

B diam.

C +0.0000
−0.0003

A

L

$\frac{c}{2}$ ±0.0005

Concentric ground lead

L-pin

T-pin

3/16 Ream   LOC-A-TOR   Master pin or bushing

Press ram

Locator bushing

Use bushing to protect pin on floating pin assemblies

Roll pin

to suit — "X" ±0.050

1. Drill and ream 3/16 hole for roll pin.
2. Bore installation hole to provide a light press fit for LOC-A-TOR bushing. 0.0003 to 0.0005 should suffice.

3. Start locator and roll pin (furnished with assembly) as shown and press assembly flush with top of plate. Roll pin establishes precise alignment between slotted hole and layout axis.

Fig. 2-48 Slotted hole locator bushing. (*Loc-A-Tor Bushing, courtesy American Drill Bushing Co.*)

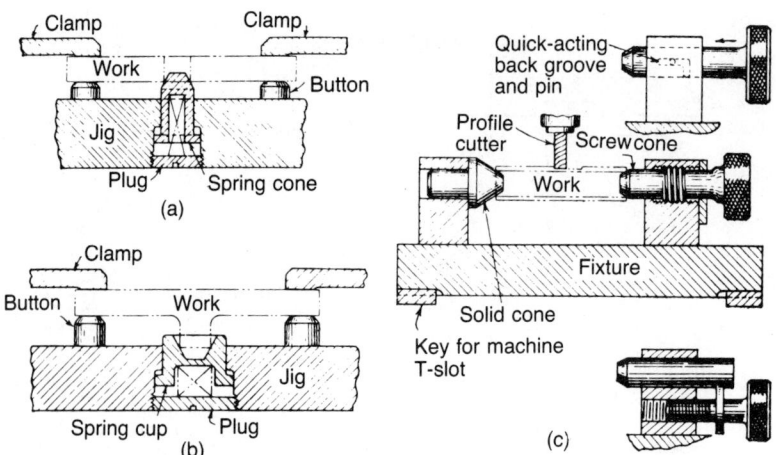

Fig. 2-49 Conical locators.

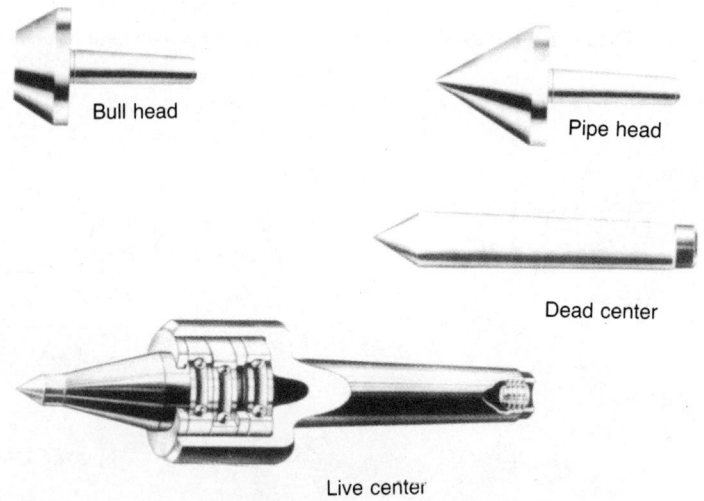

Fig. 2-50 Various types of centers. (*Courtesy Royal Products*)

Most centering devices also clamp the workpiece and for that reason will be covered in detail in future chapters on clamping and machining operations.

V-Locators. V-locators are widely used to establish the centerplane of cylindrical work. The most accurate way of doing this with a single V-locator is shown in Fig. 2-51a. In this position the workpiece will be centralized automatically with the drill bushing regardless of the diameter of the workpiece.

However, if the block is turned 90° as shown in Fig. 2-51b, any variation in the diameter of the workpiece will cause off-center drilling as the workpiece shifts with the changing diameters. The amount of shift can be determined using the following formula:

$$A = \text{Csc} \left(\frac{a}{2}\right)\left(\frac{B - C}{4}\right) \qquad (18)$$

2-40

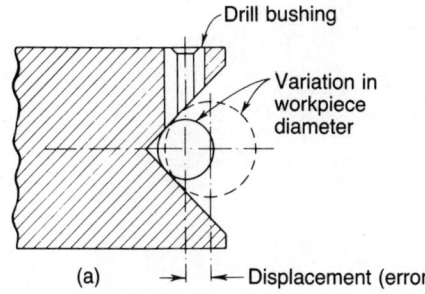

Drill bushing

Variation in workpiece diameter

(a) Displacement (error)

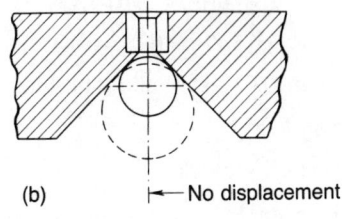

(b) No displacement

Fig. 2-51 Minimizing error by proper placement of a V-locator.

where:

A = shift about bushing centerplane

B = maximum diameter

C = minimum diameter

a = included angle of Vee

For:

B = 2.020

C = 1.980

a = 90°

Calculation:

$$A = \operatorname{Csc}\left(\frac{a}{2}\right)\left(\frac{B - C}{4}\right) \tag{18}$$

$$= \operatorname{Csc}\left(\frac{90°}{2}\right)\left(\frac{2.020 - 1.980}{4}\right)$$

$$= \operatorname{Csc} 45° \frac{0.040}{4}$$

$$= \operatorname{Csc} 45° \times 0.01$$

$$= 1.4142 \times 0.01$$

$$= 0.014 \text{ Shift about bushing centerplane (90° V-block)}$$

Example 7:

For a 120° V-block:

a = 120°

Calculation:

$$A = \operatorname{Csc}\left(\frac{120°}{2}\right)\left(\frac{2.020 - 1.980}{4}\right) \tag{18}$$

$$= \operatorname{Csc} 60°\left(\frac{0.040}{4}\right)$$

$$= \text{Csc } 60° \times 0.01$$

$$= 1.1547 \times 0.01$$

$$= 0.012 \text{ shift about bushing centerplane } (120° \text{ V-block})$$

Example 8:

For a 60° V-block:

$$a = 60°$$

Calculation:

$$A = \text{Csc } \left(\frac{60°}{2}\right)\left(\frac{2.020 - 1.980}{4}\right) \tag{18}$$

$$= \text{Csc } 30° \left(\frac{0.040}{4}\right)$$

$$= \text{Csc } 30° \times 0.01$$

$$= 2.0000 \times 0.01$$

$$= 0.02 \text{ shift about bushing centerplane } (60° \text{ V-block})$$

From the examples above, it can be seen that the 120° V-block is less sensitive to diameter variances than the 60° V-block. However, as the included angle increases, the Vee will not locate the workpiece as securely. Most off-the-shelf V-blocks have an included angle of 90°.

Some V-block applications are shown in Fig. 2-52.

Adjustable Locators. As previously noted, adjustable locators that are used to locate a horizontal plane surface are commonly called adjustable supports.

Spring type adjustable locators, such as shown in Fig. 2-53, are normally used in conjunction with fixed locators to provide extra support of the workpiece during machining. Spring pressures are kept low enough to prevent them from lifting the workpiece from the main fixed locators. They are actuated to register on the workpiece and locked with the same hand knob, and compensate automatically for workpiece irregularities. They are often referred to as jackpins or spring jack locks.

The threaded adjustable locators shown in Fig. 2-54 are used in a similar manner but are adjusted by hand to register with the workpiece. They are also used in place of fixed supports and locators to provide for adjustment for wear, or those cases where a rough workpiece surface such as a casting varies from piece to piece or from lot to lot. When used for this purpose they are locked in position with a jamnut before machining. When they are used as supports, they are often referred to as jackscrews.

Some additional applications of adjustable locators are shown in Fig. 2-55.

Equalizing locators as shown in Fig. 2-56 are used to provide support to rough or uneven surfaces.

Index Plungers. Index plungers and bushings, such as shown in Fig. 2-57, are used mainly for indexing a jig or fixture to permit an operation to be repeated at intervals along (linear indexing) or around (radial indexing) a workpiece. Figures 2-58 and 2-59 show examples of jigs using these components.

Centerline Ball Arbors and Chucks. When precise locations from an ID or OD, which is often necessary on inspection fixturing, centerline ball arbors and chucks (see Fig. 2-60) can often solve the problem. These arbors and chucks are built with a circle of precision balls in one or more raceways which are free to move radially and contact the workpiece as they are forced outward. Each row of balls moves independently so that the workpiece moves easily into place and can be rotated freely on the balls. Axes can be located within 0.00005 in.

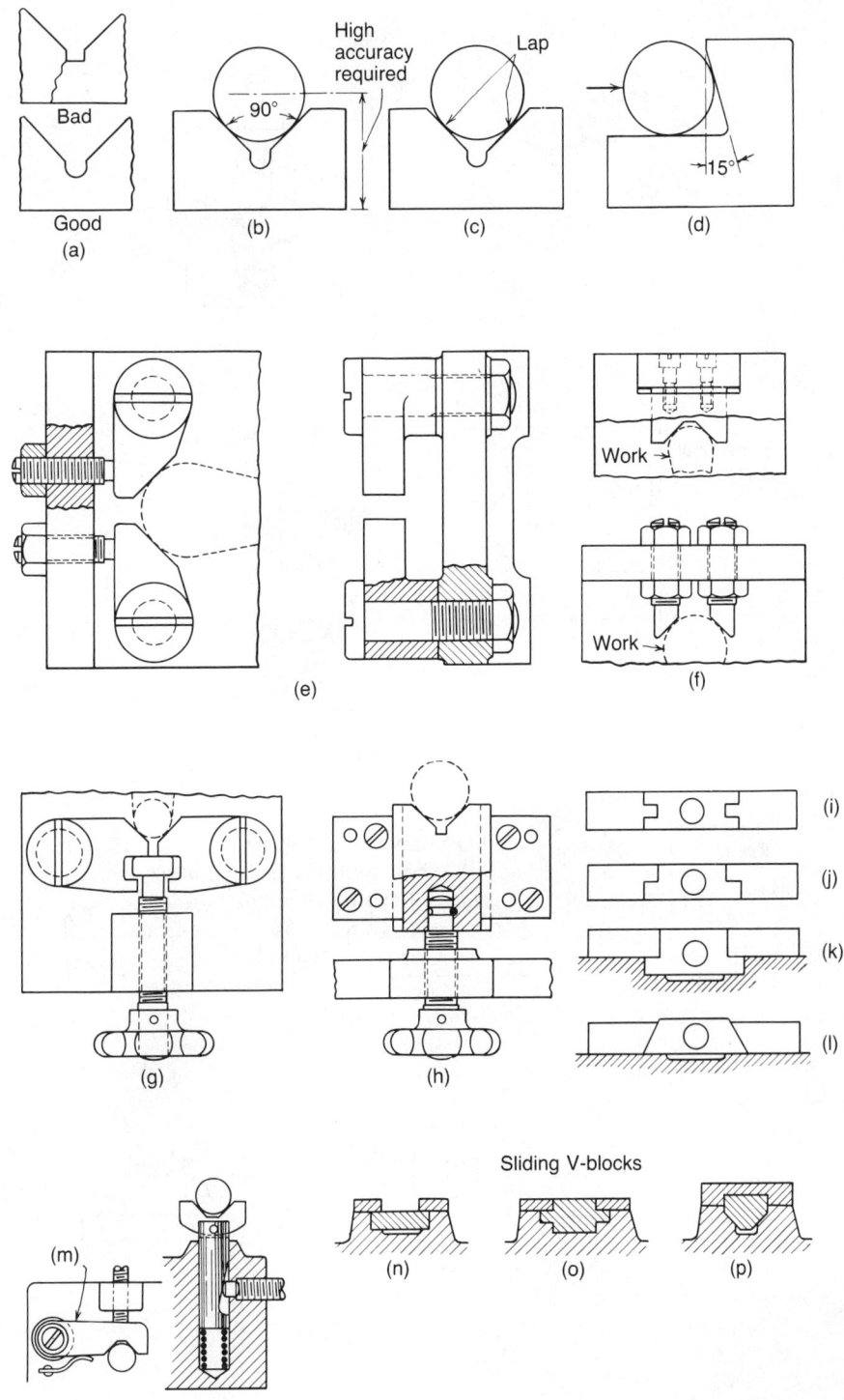

Fig. 2-52 A variety of V-block applications.[1]

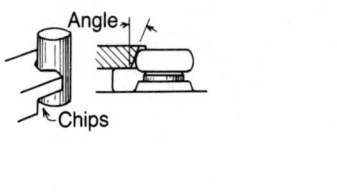

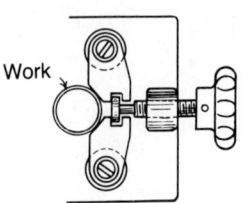

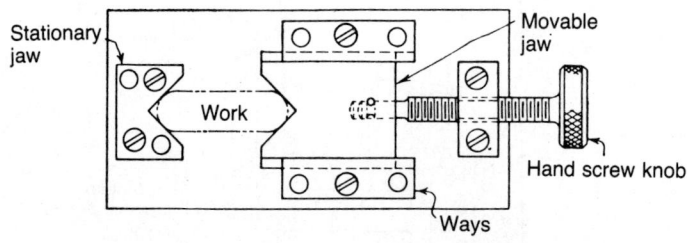

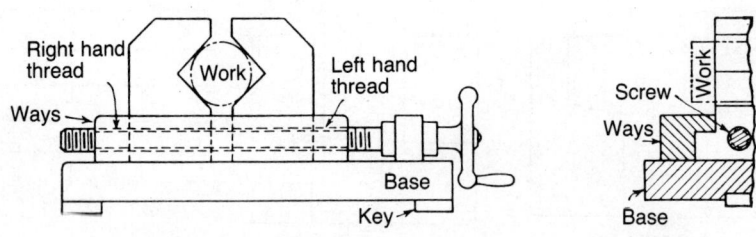

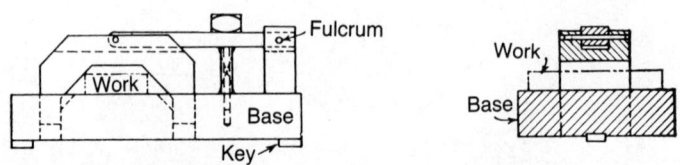

Fig. 2-52 *(continued)*

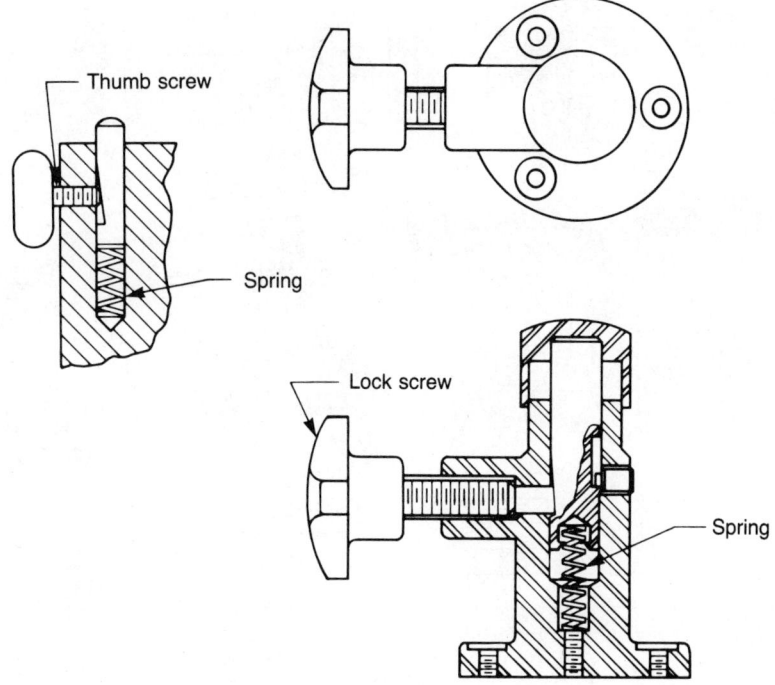

Fig. 2-53 Spring type adjustable locators (supports).

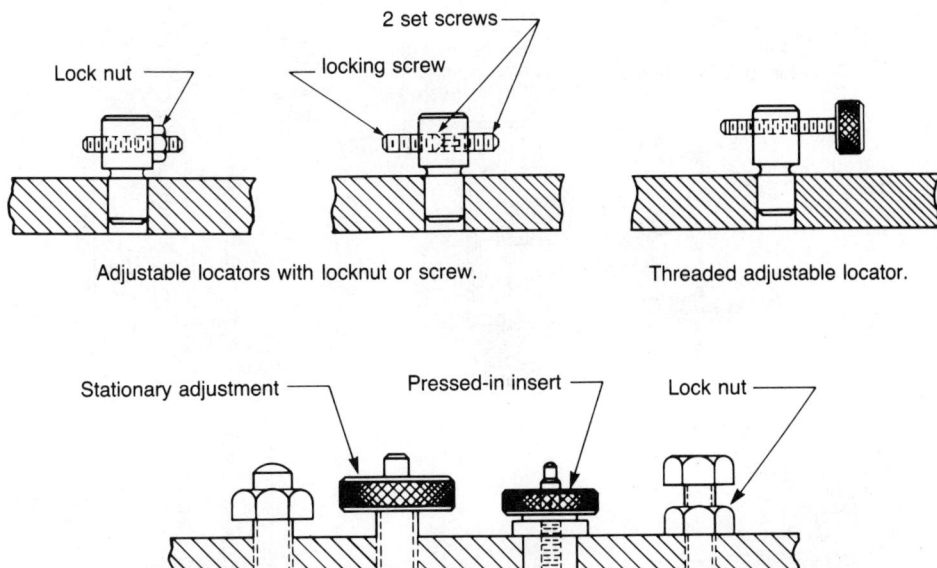

Adjustable locators with locknut or screw.

Threaded adjustable locator.

Threaded type adjustable supports.

Fig. 2-54 Threaded type adjustable supports and locators.

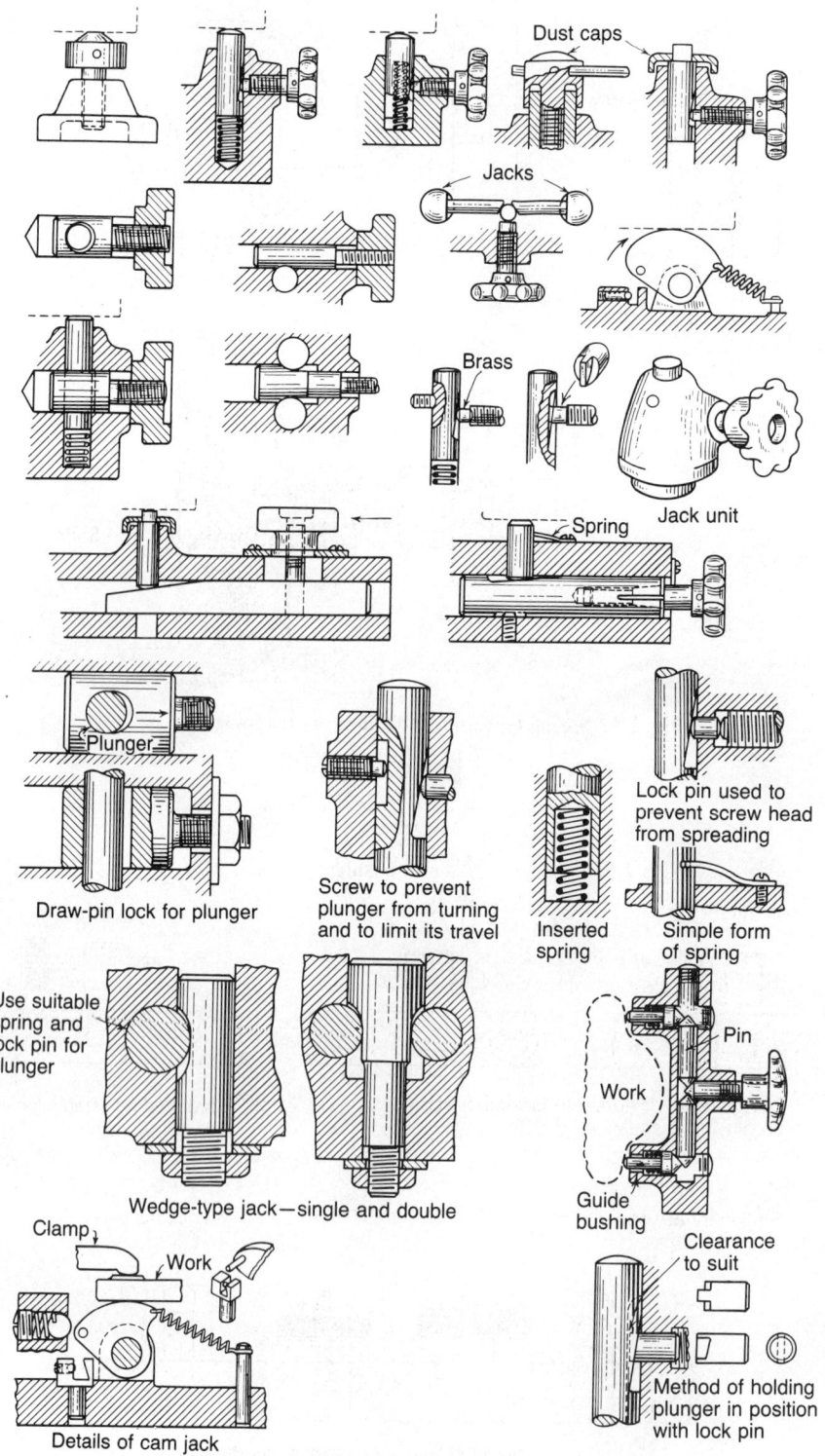

Fig. 2-55 Application of adjustable locators.[2]

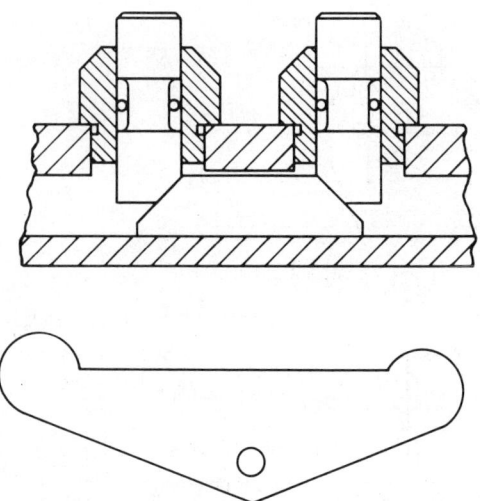

Fig. 2-56 Equalizing type adjustable locators (supports).

Fig. 2-57 Index plungers and bushings. (*Courtesy TE-CO*)

Expanding Arbors and Chucks. Also useful for precision locating are the wide variety of mechanical and hydraulic expanding arbors and chucks. They are very useful for establishing axes and planes on workpieces in those cases where the axis or plane must be precisely located regardless of the feature size. Since these devices usually hold the workpiece as well as locate it, they will be covered in future chapters on clamping and machining.

Power operated locators, supporters, and indexers are readily available for many of the applications discussed in this chapter. However, since they too are mainly used in conjunction with the power workholding systems, they will also be covered later along with pneumatic and hydraulic power workholding systems in the chapters on clamping, modular tooling, and NC tooling.

Burrs and Chips. This chapter would not be complete without a discussion about burrs and chips.

Figure 2-61 shows the formation of burrs around a drilled hole. The burr raised at the point of entry of the drill is called the *minor* or *secondary burr* while the burr as the drill exits the part is called the *major* or *primary burr*. Either of these burrs can make it difficult to remove a workpiece from a jig depending on the method that is used to load and unload the workpiece. If the workpiece can be lifted from the jig, there is no tendency to shear the burrs; however, if the workpiece must be slid across the burr, sticking would hinder removal. This can be avoided by providing suitable clearance grooves or slots in the jig.

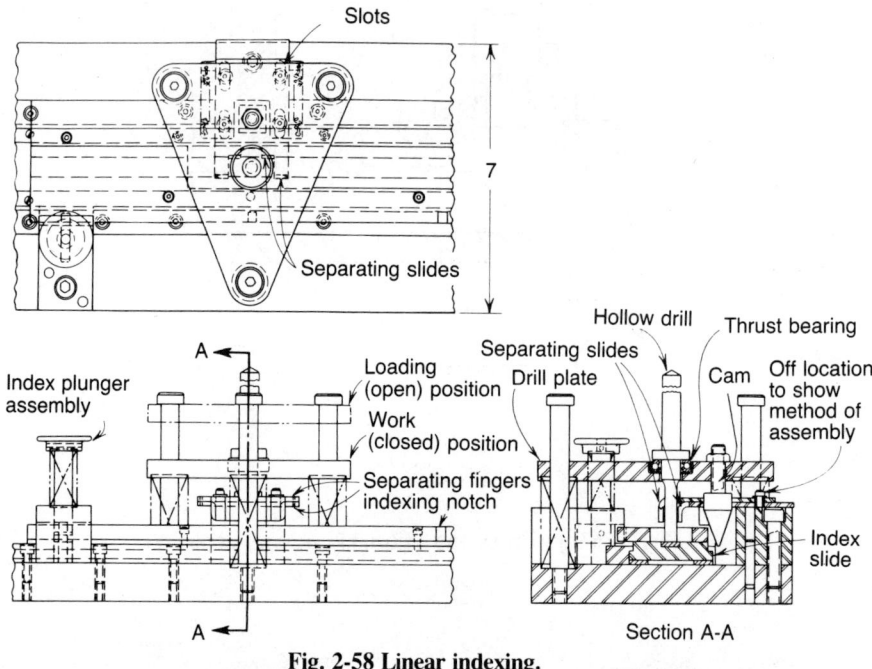

Fig. 2-58 Linear indexing.

Chips and foreign matter on locating surfaces causes wear as well as incorrect locating. Methods should be provided to keep these surfaces clean. Some of the possible methods of doing this include:

- Making the locators as small as practical without permitting damage to the workpiece from tool or clamping forces.
- Providing for a clear view of the locating surfaces for a visual check of the surfaces and proper locating of the workpiece.
- Raising the workpiece supports, as shown in Fig. 2-62, so that chips fall off or can be swept off easily.
- Eliminating pockets in the jig or fixture that could collect chips and foreign matter.
- Providing self-cleaning locators that scrape chips and foreign matter off workpiece surfaces as they slide across them.
- Using fixed wipers to push chips along as a fixture is traversed on the machine tool table.
- Providing a means to flush the chips away with the coolant.
- Using compressed air to blow the dirt and chips away, providing proper safety equipment is available.
- Designing the jig or fixture so that the locating surfaces are entirely covered by the workpiece when loaded.
- Providing protection for indexing mechanisms, adjustable supports, and other sliding mechanisms.

Examples of proper chip clearance around locating pins and blocks is shown in Fig. 2-63. Figure 2-64a shows a drill jig equipped to automatically clean the locating surfaces. In use, when the bushing plate is fully opened, an air blast is turned on and is directed at the locators. When the bushing is lowered, the air blast is shut off until the next cycle. An air blast in front of the cutter in view (b) is used to remove chips in a milling operation.

2-48

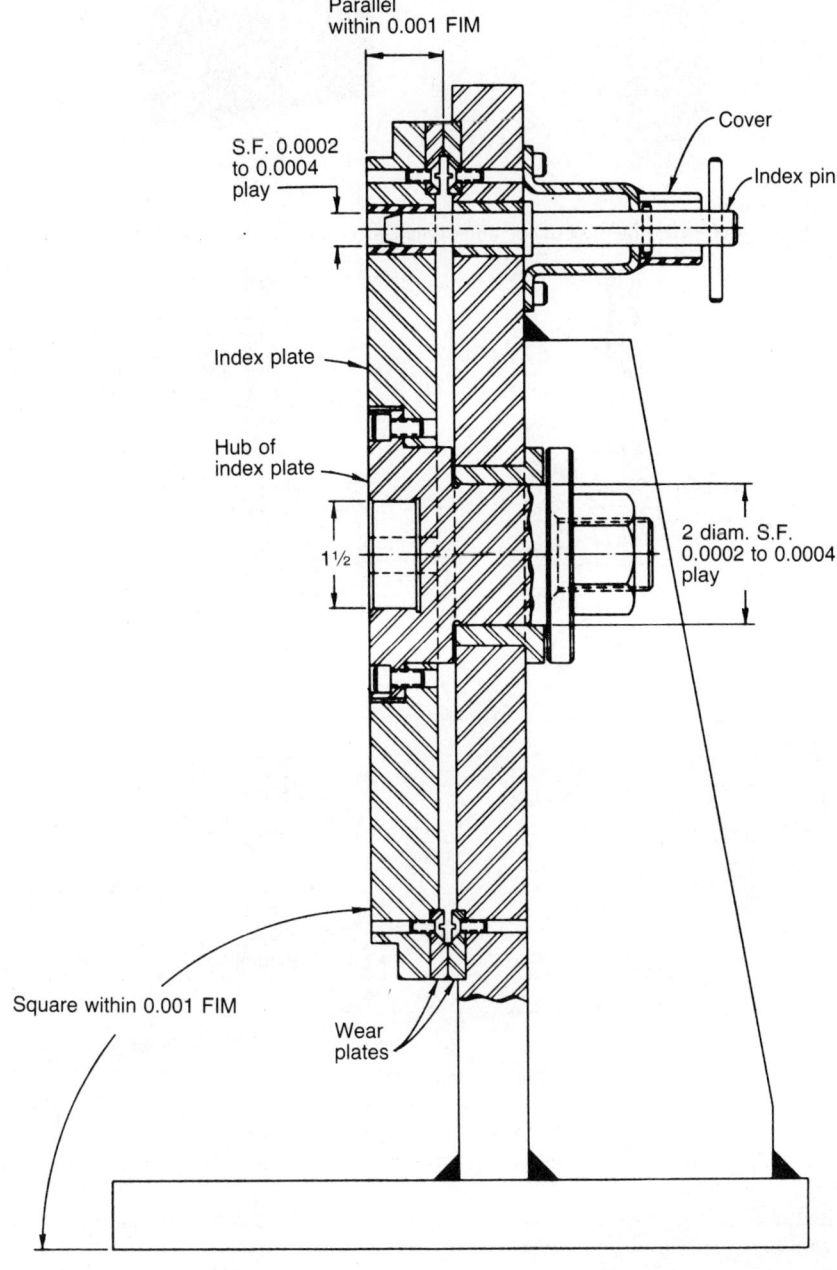

Parallel
within 0.001 FIM

Cover

S.F. 0.0002
to 0.0004
play

Index pin

Index plate

Hub of
index plate

1½

2 diam. S.F.
0.0002 to 0.0004
play

Square within 0.001 FIM

Wear
plates

Fig. 2-59 Radial indexing.

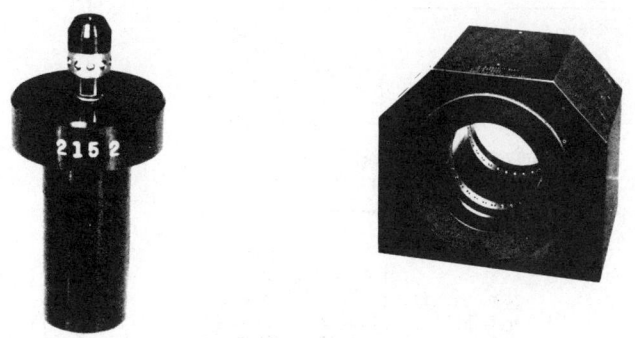

Fig. 2-60 Center line ball arbor and chuck. (*Courtesy Precision Devices, Inc.*)

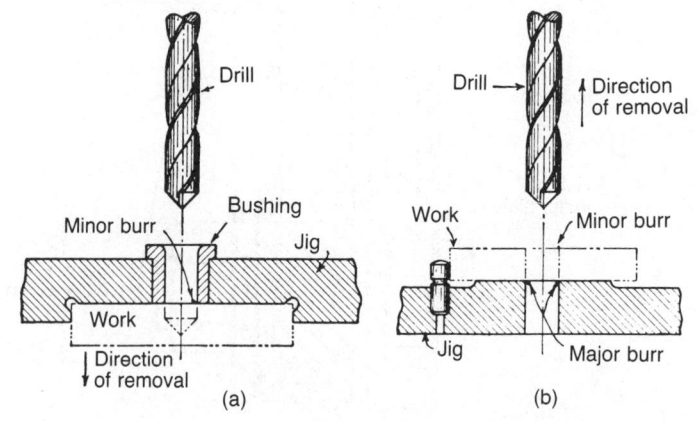

Fig. 2-61 Burrs.

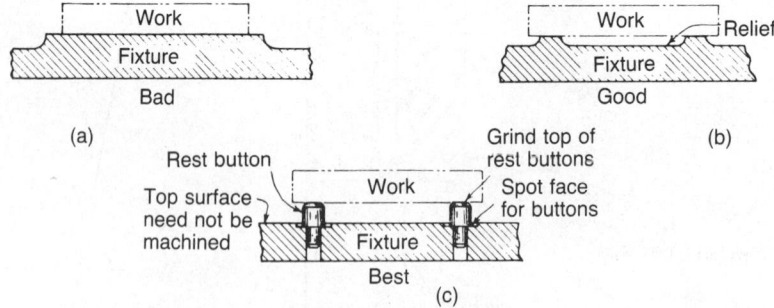

Fig. 2-62 Raised workpiece supports.

Suction is another means of removing light, discontinuous chips from the locating areas, particularly when dry grinding or milling nonmetallic materials, such as the phenolics.

Control of Locator Wear.[3] There are several types of wear a manufacturing engineer or tool designer should be aware of:

1. *Rubbing wear.* Normally, metallic surfaces are coated with a thin film of corrosion. With this coating or when lubricated, contact wear (atomic pickup from one surface to another) is minimal for bearing pressures less than 25 psi (172 kPa). Above this pressure the wear rate rises rapidly in proportion to pressure and

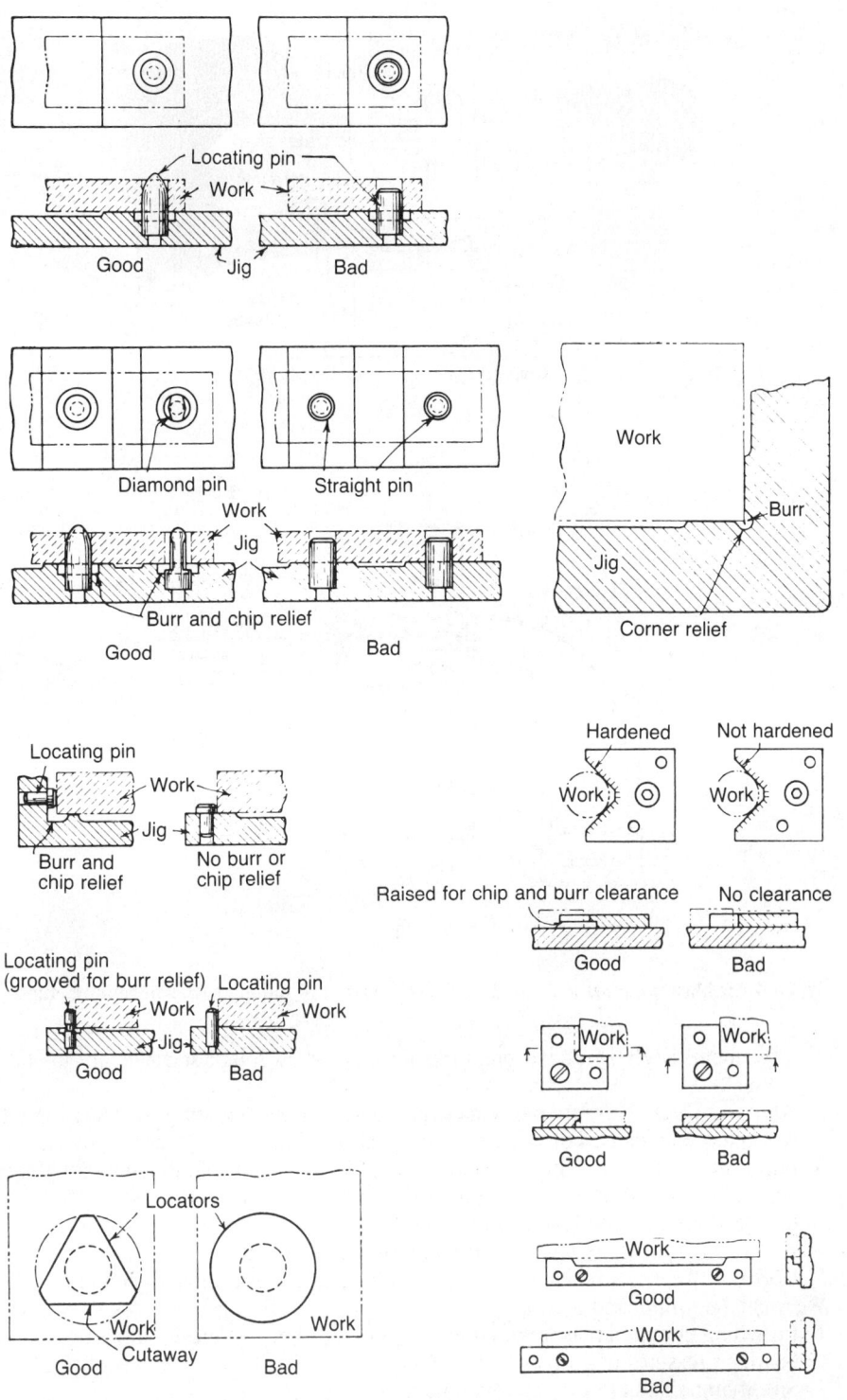

Fig. 2-63 Examples of proper chip clearance around locating pins and blocks.

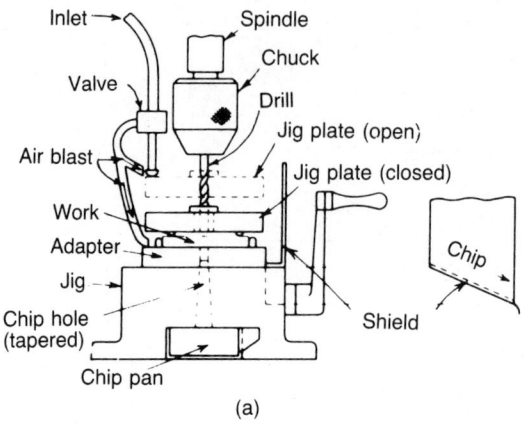

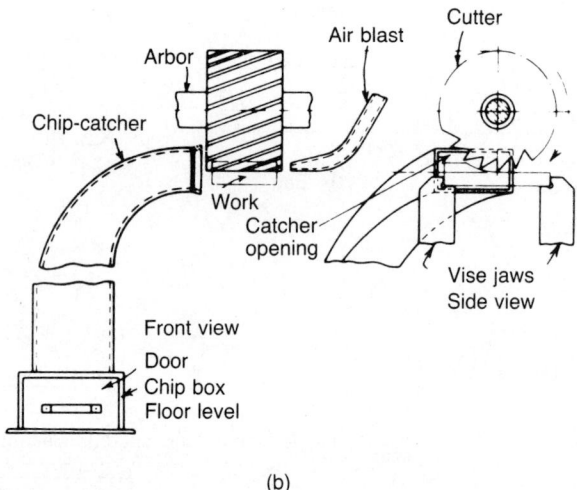

Fig. 2-64 Air blast used: (a) to clean drill jig; (b) in front of milling cutter to remove chips.

movement. High, localized pressures develop when rough surfaces are in sliding contact.

2. *Abrasive wear.* Foreign particles lying between the locating surfaces and the workpiece can cause considerable wear by abrasion.

3. *Impressive wear.* This kind of wear takes place between rolling, contacting surfaces and causes peening or chipping of the surfaces if the compressive stresses on localized areas exceed the proportional limit of the material.

4. *Erosive wear.* Erosive wear is caused by fluid movement.

5. *Corrosive wear.* Corrosive wear is caused by chemical action between materials.

Wear can be minimized by:

1. Providing contact areas large enough to support the workpiece without exceeding bearing pressures of 25 psi (172 kPa).

2. Specifying adequate surface refinement.

3. Rolling the workpiece, instead of sliding it, when practical.

4. Providing adequate lubrication between the surfaces.

5. Hardening locating surfaces.
6. Protecting wear surfaces from dust, dirt, and corrosive substances.

References

1. Wilson, Frank W., ed., "Jigs and Fixtures," *Tool Engineers Handbook*, 2nd ed. (Dearborn, MI: Society of Manufacturing Engineers, 1959), pp. 91-12, 91-13.

2. *Ibid.*, p. 91-27

3. *Ibid.*, "Control of Locator Wear," p. 91-7

CHAPTER 3
CLAMPING AND POSITIONING

The function of any clamping device is that of applying and maintaining sufficient counteracting holding force to a workpiece to withstand all tooling forces.

Some of the mechanical means of doing this are shown in Fig. 3-1. They include the screw, *a*, which is a simple machine of the inclined plane type which transfers and magnifies the rotary motion into an axial movement; the cam, *b*, which redirects and magnifies the rotary motion of the handle into a linear motion by making use of the changing radial distance from the pivot point to the point of contact; the wedge, *c*, which magnifies and changes the direction of a linear force by means of an inclined plane; the toggle linkage, *d*, which magnifies and changes the direction of a linear force by utilizing the same kinematic principles as the eccentric cam; the lever, *e*, which transmits and usually magnifies a force by rotating a beam about a pivot point; and the rack-and pinion, *f*, which transfers and magnifies the rotary motion of a pinion gear into a linear motion of the rack. These methods are often combined as shown in Fig. 3-2.

Proper clamp design, based upon simplicity with utility, affects total tool and product costs and permits optimum production, surface finish, and tool life, if other process conditions are controlled.

Clamp selection is predicated upon analyses of the workpiece, the operation on it, and the quantity of parts to be produced. Clamp design considerations should include its location in the fixture to achieve the following purposes:

1. Direct clamping pressure to supported and/or rigid portions of the work so as not to distort the workpiece.
2. Facilitate easy and/or rapid loading and unloading.
3. Maintain required workpiece relation to locators, gages, and tools.
4. Provide minimum hazards to operator, workpiece, fixture, and tool before, during, and after the work cycle.
5. Allow its incorporation as an integral part of the fixture.

Clamping Forces in Various Operations. The type and amount of tooling forces in the various operations requiring clamping of the workpiece must be considered when designing clamps.

Since *milling operations* induce vibrations in the workpiece from components of cyclic forces as the cutter contacts and leaves the work, clamping arrangements must be designed to prevent the clamp from loosening under these forces. Large tooling forces are generally present in milling operations because of the large metal-removal rate; therefore, strong, carefully located clamps must be used to hold the workpiece without distorting it.

Planing and *shaping* tool forces are smaller but more uniform than forces present in milling, and clamping requirements are less exacting with respect to size and resistance to loosening.

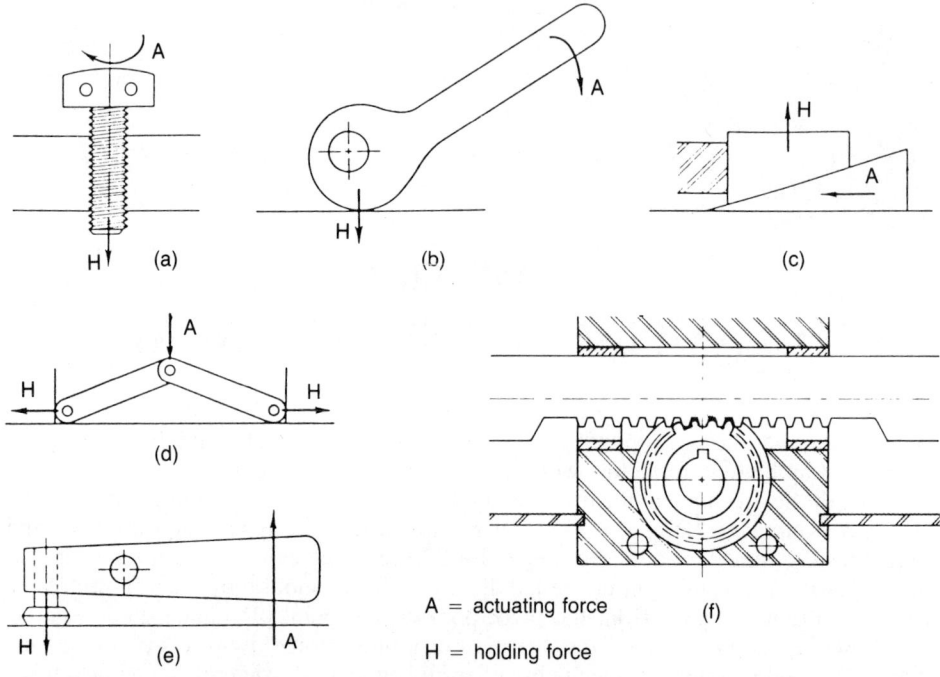

Fig. 3-1 Mechanical methods of transmitting and multiplying force.

A = actuating force
H = holding force

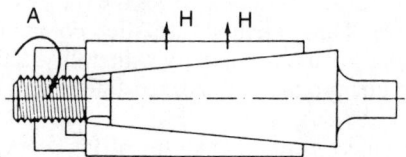

Fig. 3-2 Combined screw and wedge.

In *drilling* and *tapping*, the clamping force must exceed the torsional force of the drill or tap.

In *welding*, considerable stresses are created by thermal expansion and contraction of the workpiece and/or the fixture. Clamps must be designed to withstand these forces, with respect to both cross-section and material selection (high yield strength), to prevent excessive deflection or failure. Another consideration is that of the fit between the clamp and other members of the fixture to allow for uniform thermal expansion and contraction of the members. The thermal conductivity of the clamp material selected must also be considered when clamps, in addition to supplying a holding force, are required to dissipate (chill) or retain heat in an area adjacent to a welded joint. Since a clamp sometimes serves as an electrode, such as in flash butt welding, it must have good electrical conductivity. Application requirements influence clamp-material selection in regard to any tendency of the electrode material to weld to the workpiece.

In *soldering* fixtures, the forces of thermal expansion and contraction are smaller, since generally less mass and heat input are involved than in welded joints. This permits clamps to be reduced in size and strength.

In *chemical bonding* and *adhesive joining*, the amount of heat energy generated by chemical action, or otherwise concentrated in a fixture, is generally negligible; and little consideration to the thermal properties of the clamp material need given.

ESTIMATING CLAMPING FORCES

The accurate estimation of cutting forces that must be resisted by fixturing and clamping is often neglected when designing a fixture. This can result in a fixture that is either overdesigned (which, while capable of holding the workpiece securely in place, adds unnecessarily to the cost of the fixture) or weak and unsafe.

The procedure for estimating these forces is not that difficult or time-consuming. The tool designer is usually provided with a process sheet which specifies the machine and cutting tools to be used along with speeds, feeds, and depth of cut. With this information, he or she can easily determine the cutting force using formulas in subsequent chapters where applicable, or by consulting a source book such as the *Machinability Data Handbook*.[1]

Workpiece Considerations for Clamp Design. The *configuration* of the workpiece may require contoured clamps or product redesign to add bosses, lugs, etc., as clamp areas for adequate holding; or the workpiece may be held by magnetic, electrostatic, or vacuum devices instead of conventional clamps.

Equalizing clamps, or clamps with very long or short travel, or small but powerful pneumatic or hydraulic clamps may have to be used with workpieces of complex and/or asymmetrical contours.

For large workpieces, one of two clamping methods can be used: (1) a greater number of small clamps or (2) fewer, larger, and stronger clamps. The choice will depend upon which arrangement provides the best holding force combined with minimum clamp operation, design, and fabrication costs.

Surface finish of the workpiece may necessitate clamps incorporating soft or resilient faces of nylon, rubber, plastic, etc., to prevent the defacing of workpieces.

Surface variations, normal for some castings, may dictate equalizing-clamp design to compensate for these and similar irregularities. If surfaces of the clamps contacting the workpiece are subject to appreciable wear, such surfaces should be hardened or equipped with wear inserts.

These considerations and others that require close attention before making clamping decisions are included in the following checklist:

- Check for the possibility of machining the workpiece without clamping.
- Before designing a new jig or fixture, check in-house for something that might work as is or be modified to work. Also check for off-the-shelf clamping devices, such as vises, arbors, mandrels, collets, chucks, etc., that might work as is, or be modified to work.
- If in-house fixtures are not available use standard commercial clamps whenever possible.
- Check for possible use of a nonmechanical clamping method such as with magnetic, vacuum, and electrostatic chucks; jaws made from plastic and low-melt alloys; adhesive bonding; and others.
- Use pneumatic or hydraulic clamping when indicated. Operate with machine circuits whenever possible.
- With pneumatic and hydraulics, do not operate cylinders beyond their rated stroke length.
- Clamping should be clearly visible, easy to use, and be able to be operated from the operator's side of the machine in a safe and efficient manner.
- Foolproof clamping arrangements whenever possible.
- Whenever possible, locate clamps to direct their force toward rigid supporting surfaces of the jig or fixture. When this is not possible, auxiliary supports must be provided to prevent the part from bending or distorting.
- Provide clamps strong enough to hold the workpiece against the locators with sufficient force to resist all machining forces. Use the proper bolts to mount the

clamps and engage them for the full length of the thread.

- Make sure that clamping forces cannot distort the workpiece enough to allow the surface machined to spring out of specifications when the clamping is released. Use clamping that will not bend, crush, or mar the workpiece. Use torque limiting screws or other safety devices to prevent overstraining fragile parts.
- If the fixture rotates, make sure that centrifugal force will tend to tighten rather than loosen the clamp(s).
- Do not exceed clamping force ratings.
- Provide suitable equalizers to cover any size variance when clamping more than one workpiece with a single clamp, or when clamping a workpiece at more than one place with a single clamp.
- If more than one clamping point is used to hold a workpiece, they should be as far apart as practical.
- Provide clamps with sufficient range to handle part variations.
- Provide for clamps to completely clear the workpiece for loading and unloading.
- Make sure that the cutter will not be struck by the clamp when it is being opened or closed.
- Clamps should be provided with springs or other means to lift them clear of the workpiece when loosened.
- Clamps should be easily replaceable.
- Try to do all clamping with the least amount of handles and the least amount of movement.
- Use machine movement or machine levers to operate clamps if possible.
- Provide clamping that will not loosen from vibration.
- Make sure that clamping will not bend any part of the tooling, cause strain on the machine, or foul the machine in any position.
- Prevent clamps from twisting when tightened.
- Provide plastic, leather, brass shoes, etc., when necessary to avoid spoiling the surface finish of the workpiece.
- If wrenches are needed with clamping, try to keep to one size.
- Provide the stowage and cables for loose details.

TYPES OF CLAMPS

All clamps are variations of the following basic types: strap, screw, wedge, cam, toggle, or rack-and-pinion. Clamping forces can be transmitted by screws, cams, levers, or wedges and by rack-and-pinion, electrostatic, magnetic, or vacuum devices, alone or in combination. Actuation can be manual, for example, with a wrench, key, lever, crank, or it can be automatic, that is, by means of an air or hydraulic valve or a limit switch, which is tripped by movement of a member of the machine such as the table, ram, etc.

Strap Clamps. A strap clamp, one of the simplest forms of a clamp, is a rectangular beam and subject to the laws of applied mechanics, particularly to the laws of levers and strength of materials.

All strap clamps belong to one of the three classes of levers, as illustrated in Fig. 3-3, where F is the fulcrum or clamp rest, W is the force applied to the lever, and P is the clamping force on the workpiece.

In the arrangement shown in view a, the fulcrum or clamp rest should be as near as possible to the part. The distance L_2 between the workpiece and the fulcrum should not exceed the distance L_1 between the applied force and the fulcrum.

If the arrangement of view b is adopted, the part should be as near as possible to the clamp rest.

The class of lever shown in view c is the simplest and probably the most commonly used arrangement. Since this arrangement gives the smallest value for the clamping force,

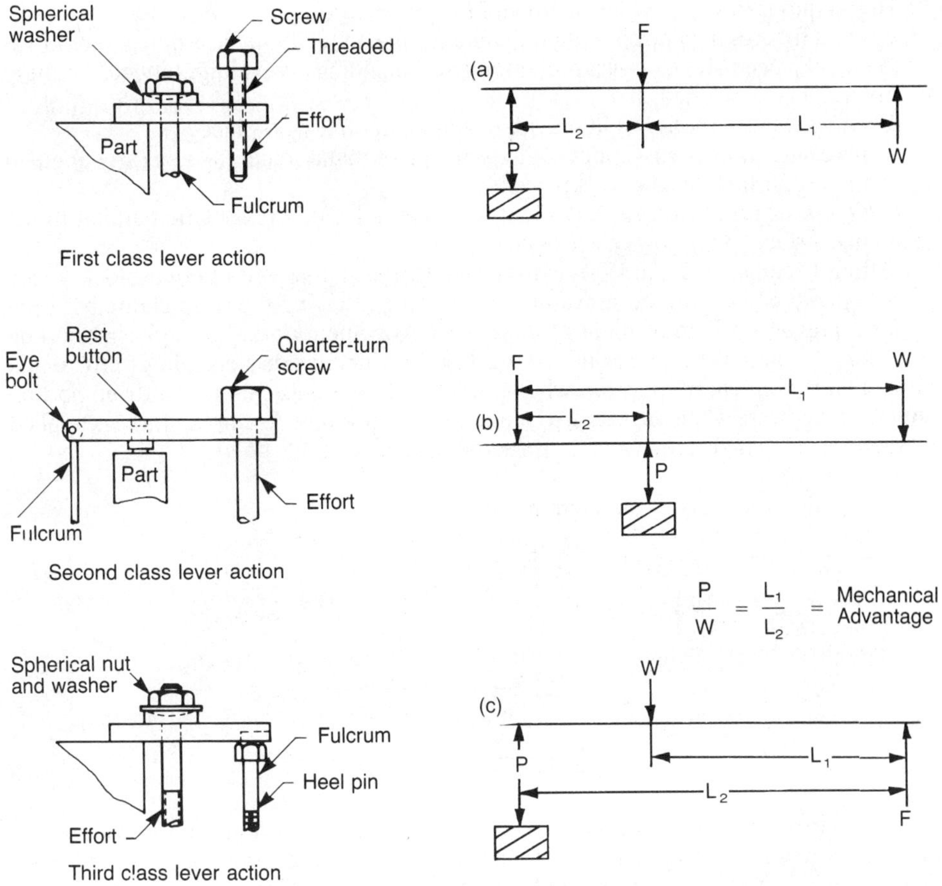

First class lever action

$$\frac{P}{W} = \frac{L_1}{L_2} = \text{Mechanical Advantage}$$

Second class lever action

Third class lever action

Fig. 3-3 Classes of levers and strap clamps.

the force W should act as close to the workpiece as possible.

The simplest of all strap-clamp designs is shown in Fig. 3-4a. The strap bears against the workpiece and a loose fulcrum block, and holding pressure is applied by a nut and a stud. A compression spring between the base and strap keeps the strap up when the nut is loosened. A suitable, integral nut-and-handle component, such as a wing nut, a bar handle, a knob, etc., would eliminate a wrench to turn the nut. The design of Fig. 3-4b reduces clamping time, since a separate fulcrum block and its positioning are eliminated. The height of the fulcrum block is fixed, while that of Fig. 3-4c is adjustable.

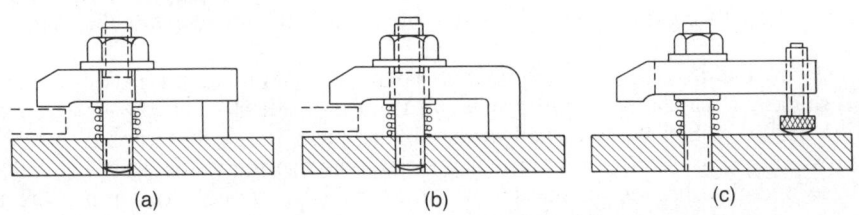

Fig. 3-4 Strap clamp design.[2]

3-5

This clamp is the class of lever shown in Fig. 3-3c.

Jigs and fixtures may necessitate movable clamps to facilitate insertion and removal of the workpiece. Movable strap clamps can be sliding, swiveling, hinged, or these motions can be combined.

A *sliding* clamp's motion is in one plane onto and off a workpiece.

A *swiveling* clamp moves about the axis of a pivot that is generally at a right angle to the clamping surfaces of the workpiece.

A *hinged* clamp moves about a pivot axis that is located in a plane parallel to the clamping surface of the workpiece.

Sliding Clamps. The clamp shown in Fig. 3-5a has a slotted fulcrum block which provides both constraint and movement to the strap. Placing the strap clamp between uprights prevents side movement of the strap; engagement of the strap pins in the side slots controls direction and amount of strap travel. Curved side slots allow vertical and horizontal movement of the strap when retracted. These slots can have a dwell portion to permit the strap, when retracted, to remain in that position. Clamping force is applied by the lever-actuated screw which also serves as a handle.

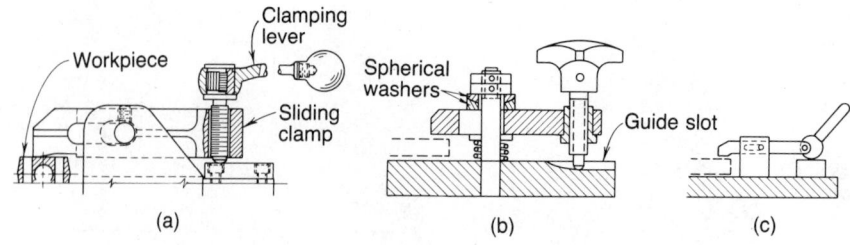

(a) (b) (c)

Fig. 3-5 Slide clamps.[2]

The slotted strap clamp of Fig. 3-5b is fastened to the base with a stud, two adjusting nuts, and a pair of mating spherical washers. A compression spring between the strap and the base keeps the assembly under tension. The hand screw assembly is aligned with the workpiece by the guide slot in the base.

A simple cam-actuated sliding clamp is shown in Fig. 3-5c. The design of cam clamps is discussed elsewhere in this section.

A commonly used simple sliding-clamp design is shown in Fig. 3-6 along with recommended dimensions.

Swing Clamps. The fixed-height swing clamp of Fig. 3-7a has a strap that bears against the workpiece, with the clamping force applied to the strap between the pivot post and workpiece. The swinging clamps shown in views b and c apply the clamping force at the center of the strap. One design is removable; the other is secured to the fixture.

The swing clamp of Fig. 3-7d is adjustable in height to accommodate workpieces of various thicknesses. It has no separate wrench or key to tighten the screw head, which is the handle for one-hand operation. The strap should be short and of a cross section large enough to resist deflection. The pivot must be large enough to resist the clamping forces.

The swing clamp of Fig. 3-7e is effective when space is limited. It is usually cylindrical in shape with an integral lug projecting from one side. Its outside surface is the bearing surface when it is inserted in the fixture base. It is counterbored to hold a compression spring. A cap screw fastens the clamp and spring to the base. The hole in the base and the threads on the screw should be long enough to compensate for variations in workpiece height. With the lug projecting over the workpiece, clamping pressure is applied by tightening the screw. When it is loosened, the spring raises the

Recommended Dimensions for Strap Clamps
inches

A	W	L	D	E	F	G
0.75	1.50	2.75	0.53	1.06	0.31	0.53
		3.50		1.69		
		4.50		2.31		
0.88	1.75	4.50	0.66	1.94	0.38	0.66
		5.00		2.44		
		6.50		3.19		
1.00	2.00	4.75	0.78	2.31	0.44	
		6.00		2.94		
		7.50		3.69		
1.50		8.00	1.03	3.63	0.50	0.78
		10.00		4.63		
		12.00		5.63		

Material: SAE 1112 steel, heat-treated.

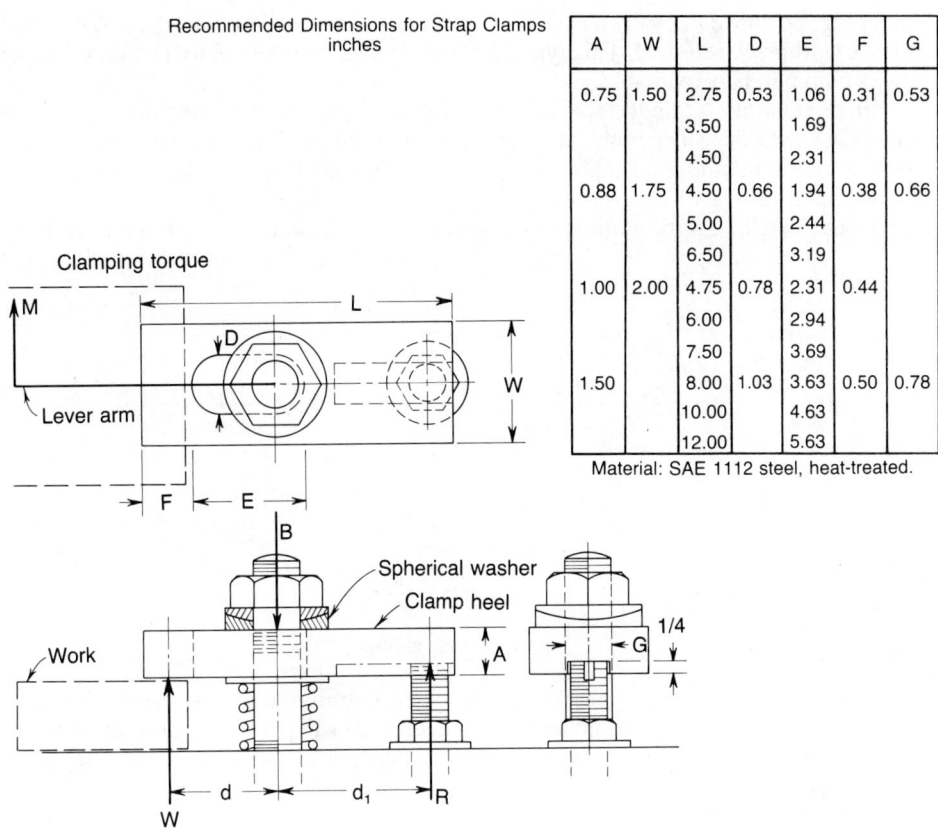

Fig. 3-6 **Sliding clamp design.** (*Courtesy Cincinnati Milacron*)

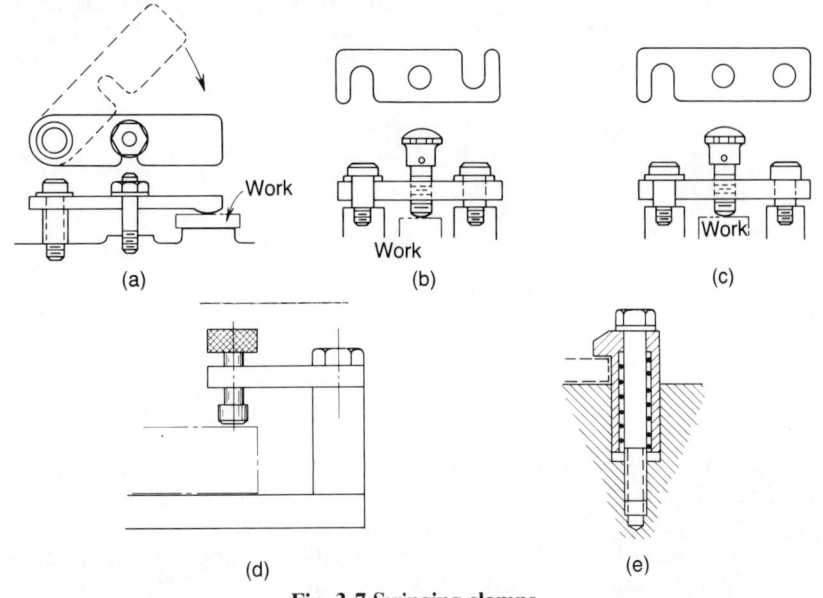

Fig. 3-7 **Swinging clamps.**

clamping lug above the workpiece. The clamp is then pivoted around the screw, which allows workpiece removal. This type of clamp is usually referred to as a hook clamp, and is commercially available.

Hinge Clamps. A hinge type of strap clamp, adjustable for workpiece height, is shown in Fig. 3-8a. Since both the strap and bolt are hinged, they can be rapidly swung to their clamping and load-unloading positions. By rounding the edge of the strap, as shown, less nut travel is required to clear it for the clamping position. A range of workpiece heights can be clamped by adjustment of the clamping stud in the strap.

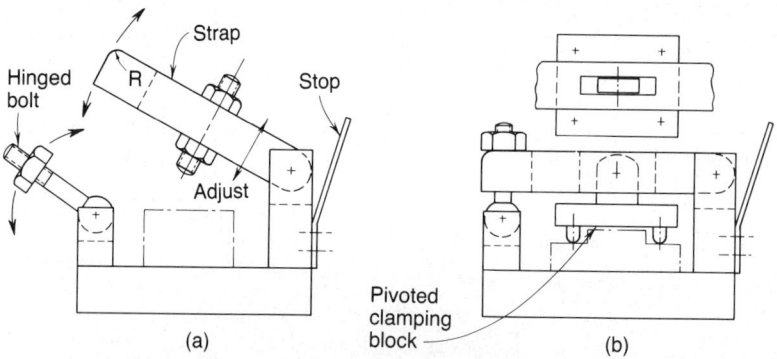

Fig. 3-8 Hinge clamps.

Figure 3-8b shows an equalizing-hinge type of strap clamp which incorporates a pivoted block in place of the adjustable stud shown in Fig. 3-8a. Clamping pressure, directed to four points on the workpiece, is equalized for slight variations in workpiece height.

A poor clamping condition can result from differences in workpieces and fulcrum-block heights. By interposing a pair (male-female) of spherical washers between the nut and the strap (see Fig. 3-9), full bearing surfaces are utilized despite the inclination of the stud caused by the difference in heights of the fulcrum block and workpiece. The angle of inclination that can be tolerated is limited by the clearance between the stud and the ID of the washers. The modification of the strap ends, that of raised and rounded toes, provides more effective clamping than a design having flat strap ends.

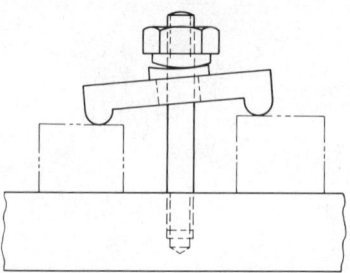

Fig. 3-9 Spherical washers for equalizing clamping forces.

The design of Fig. 3-10 includes a sliding strap clamp (section A-A) and a pair of equalizing pivoting strap clamps (section B-B). These clamps, incorporated in a milling fixture, are actuated by a clamping wheel and a clamping knob which are centrally located on the fixture. The pivoting clamp produces a clamping force which tends to seat the workpiece against the locating and supporting surfaces. The clamp is retracted from the workpiece when unclamped by pivoting on the fulcrum. A pivoting clamp

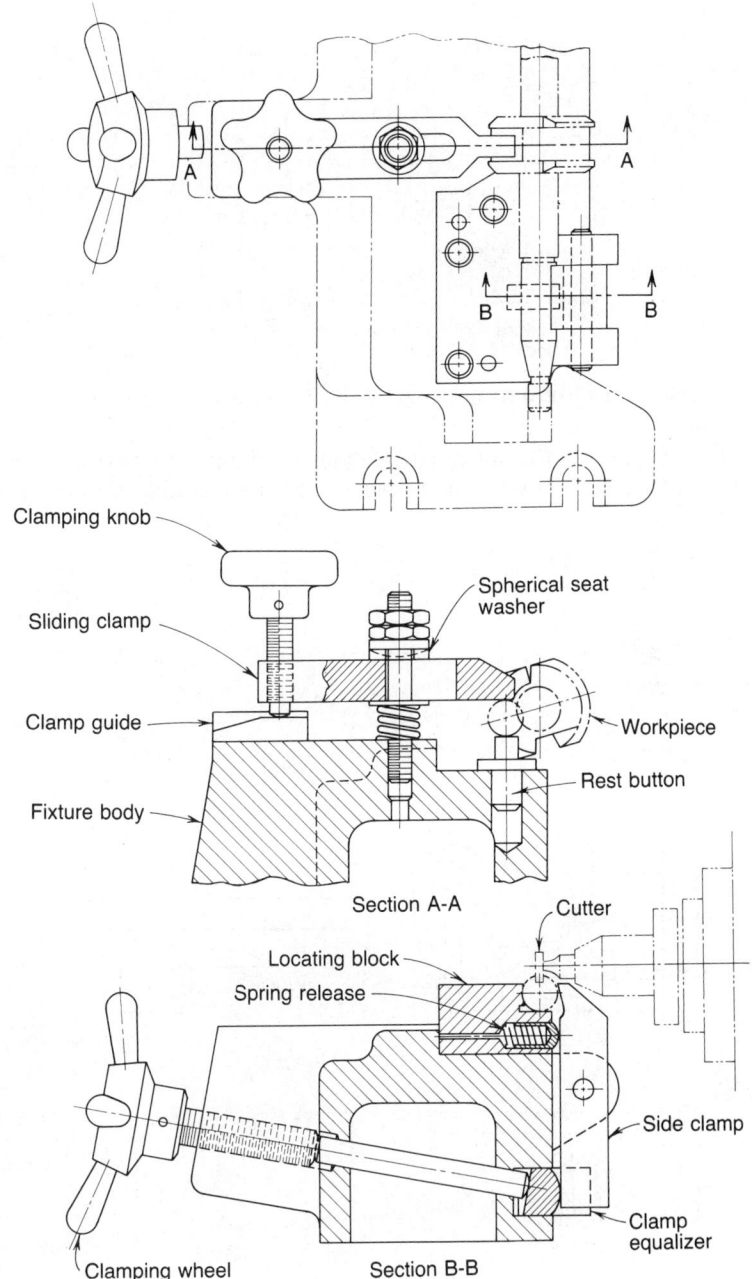

Fig. 3-10 Method of clamping a small crankshaft by use of a sliding clamp and equalizing pivoting clamps. (*Courtesy Cincinnati Milacron*)

takes less space than a sliding clamp. Figure 3-11 illustrates a pivoting clamp actuated by a setscrew.

Two-way or Multiple Clamps. An advantage of a two-way clamp is that all clamping actuation is done from one central position, usually adjacent to the fixture loading position. If separate clamps are used, the machine operator may be required to reach across the workpiece or travel to the other side of the machine to operate the clamps.

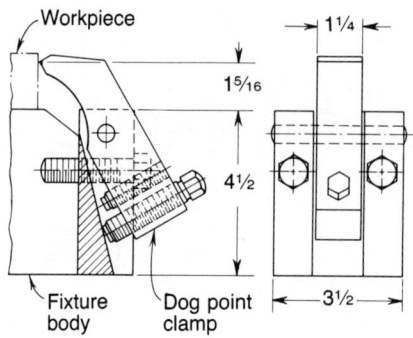

Fig. 3-11 Pivoted strap clamp. (*Courtesy Cincinnati Milacron*)

Figures 3-10, 3-12, and 3-13 illustrated methods of clamping workpieces at two or more points or of clamping two or more workpieces by centrally actuated clamping devices.

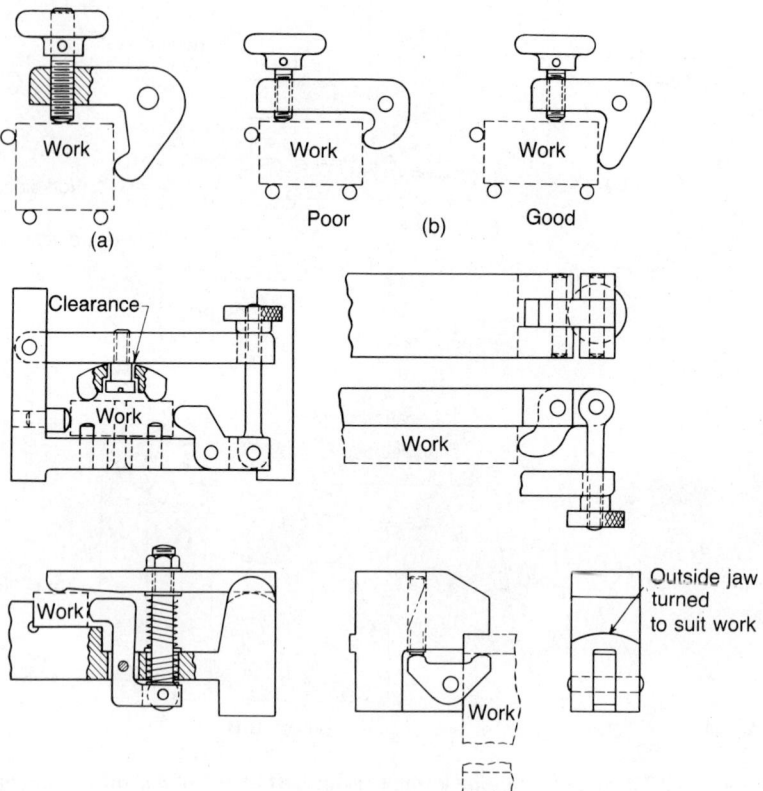

Fig. 3-12 Two-point clamping devices.

Dimensions of Strap Clamps.[3] Clamping force is generally applied by a screw or threaded rod (stud bolt) in tension or compression or by a pivot pin in double shear. The diameter of the screw and/or the pin and clamp dimensions should be proportioned so that each is of equal strength.

The five cases shown in Figs. 3-14 and 3-15 represent the usual variations of the bar

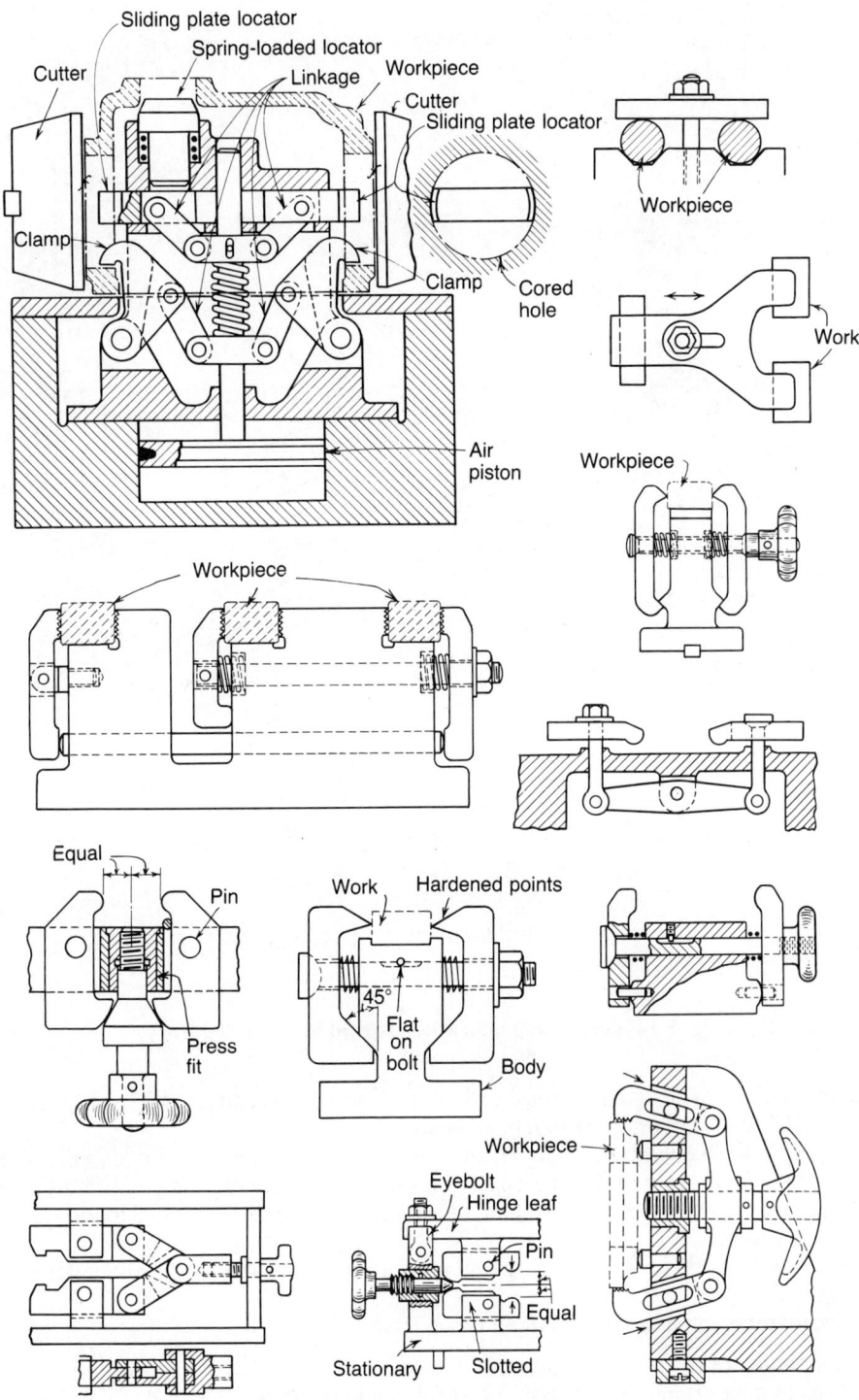

Fig. 3-13 Centrally actuated clamping devices.

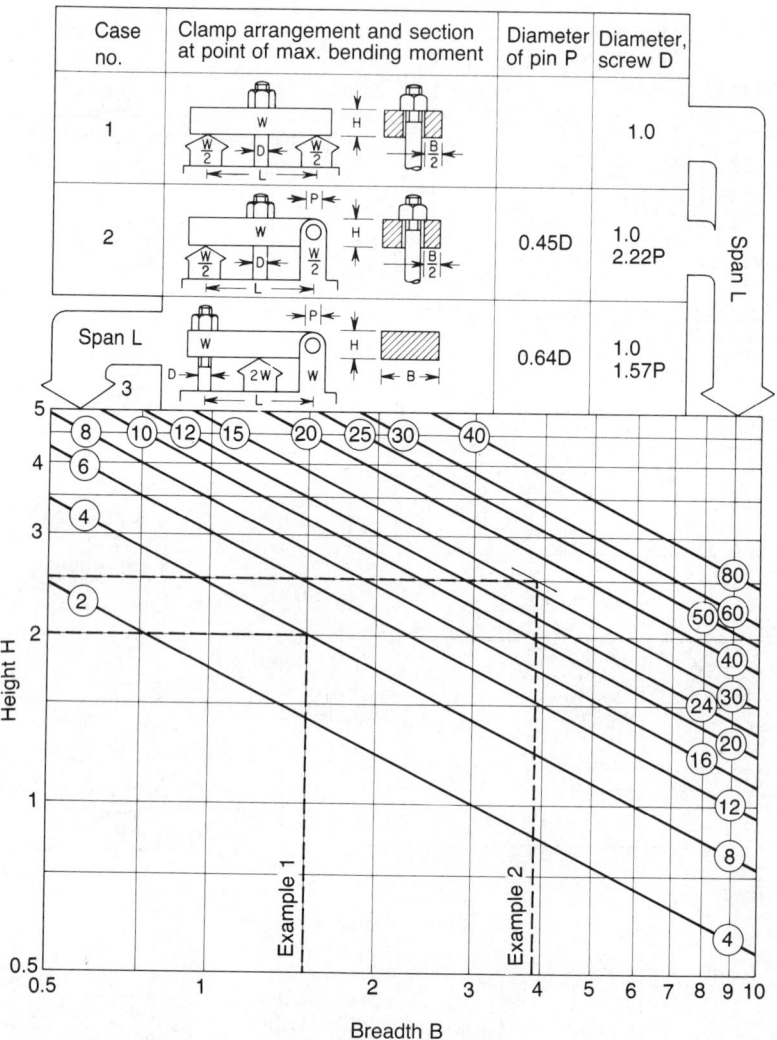

Fig. 3-14 Strap clamp dimensions related to screw diameter.[3]

clamp used in tool design. In cases 2 to 5, where both screws and pivot pins are used, the relationship between their diameters is shown.

In Fig. 3-14 the width B, height H, and span L of the clamps are related to the screw diameter D. In cases 1 and 2 the chart gives the effective width only. To find the full width of the clamp, the screw diameter, plus its clearance, must be added to the value of the nomograph.

In cases 4 and 5 (see Fig. 3-15), beam proportions are related to the diameter of the pivot pin P.

Nomograph values are based upon these assumptions:

1. Loading of the beam is central.
2. Root area of the screw is 65% of its full diameter area.
3. Pivot pin is in double shear.
4. Ultimate shear strength of the pivot pin is 80% of the ultimate tensile strength of the screw and clamp.

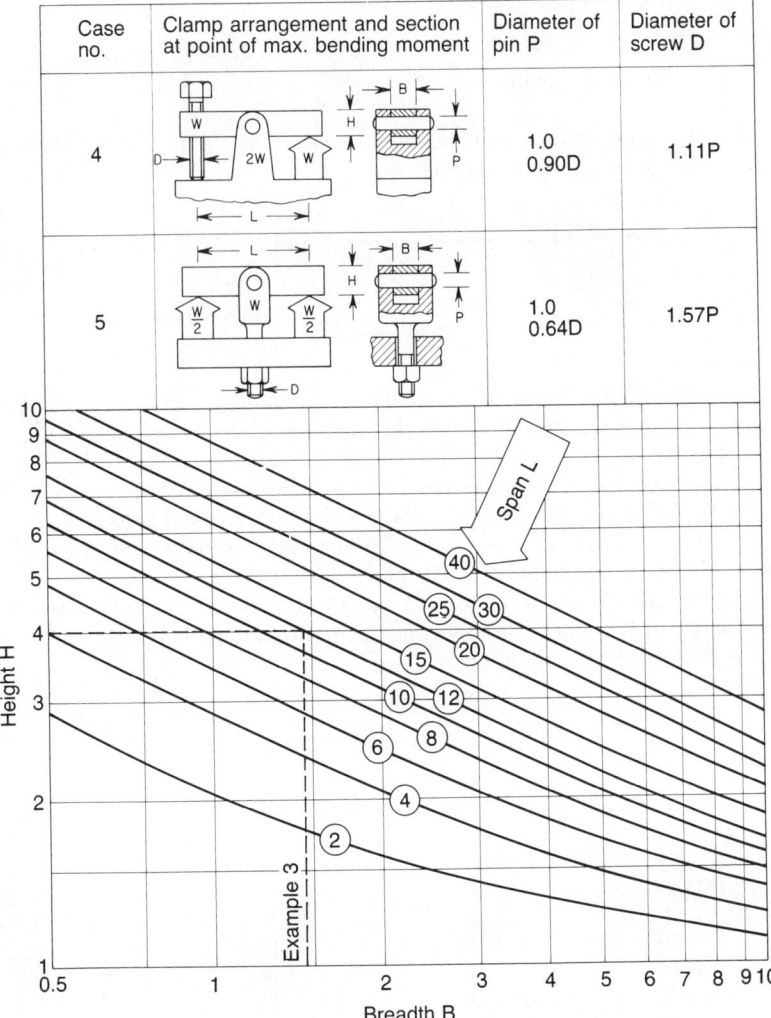

Case no.	Clamp arrangement and section at point of max. bending moment	Diameter of pin P	Diameter of screw D
4		1.0 0.90D	1.11P
5		1.0 0.64D	1.57P

Fig. 3-15 Strap clamp dimensions related to pin diameter.[3]

In cases 1, 2, and 3, given the clamping force required, the screw diameter D is easily determined; the span, effective width, and height of the clamp beam are found by multiplying their charted values by D.

Equations used in compiling Fig. 3-14 are:

$$\text{Stress in bolt} = \frac{2W}{D^2} \tag{1}$$

$$\text{Stress in beam: Cases 1 and 2} = \frac{WL}{4Z} \tag{2}$$

$$\text{Case 3} = \frac{WL}{2Z} \tag{3}$$

3-13

where W = clamping force exerted by screw

$$Z = \text{section modulus of beam} = \frac{BH^2}{6}$$

By equating the stress in beam and screw and assuming value of 1 for D, the relationship between D, B, H, and L is established:

$$L = \frac{4BH^2}{3} \text{ in cases 1 and 2} \tag{4}$$

$$L = \frac{2BH^2}{3} \text{ in case 3} \tag{5}$$

Example 1: Assume that a bar clamp, arranged as in case 1 or case 2 (see Fig. 3-14), has a span L of 6 in. (152 mm), and that it is used to clamp a workpiece with force $W/2$ of 2,000 lbf (8.9 kN).

The material used is machinery steel having an ultimate tensile strength of 60,000 psi (414 MPa). With a factor of safety of 4, the design stress is 15,000 psi (103.4 MPa). In this case, the screw must exert a force W twice the clamping load or 4,000 lbf (17.8 kN). Root area of the screw must be 4,000/15,000 = 0.267 in.²

Since the root area of the screw is 65% of its full diameter, the full area of the bolt is 0.267 in.² × 100/65 = 0.411 in.² By comparing this area with Table 3-1, it can be seen that a ¾ in. bolt fulfills the requirements.

TABLE 3-1
Full Sectional Area of Bolts (A = πr^2)

Bolt Diameter (in.)		Area (in.²)	Bolt Diameter (mm)	Area (mm²)
3/16	0.1875	0.0276	6	28.274
1/4	0.2500	0.0491	8	50.265
5/16	0.3125	0.0767	10	78.540
3/8	0.3750	0.1104	12	113.097
7/16	0.4375	0.1503	14	153.938
1/2	0.5000	0.1963	16	201.062
9/16	0.5625	0.2485	18	254.469
5/8	0.6250	0.3068	20	314.159
3/4	0.7500	0.4418	22	380.133
7/8	0.8750	0.6013	24	452.389
1	1.0000	0.7854	27	572.555
1 1/8	1.1250	0.9940	30	706.858
1 1/4	1.2500	1.2272	33	855.299
1 3/8	1.3750	1.4849	36	1017.876
1 1/2	1.5000	1.7671	39	1194.591

The ratio of the span to the bolt diameter must now be determined by dividing the span L by the bolt diameter D. In this case, L = 6 in./0.750 in. = 8.

Turn now to the nomograph in Fig. 3-14 and follow the right-hand arrow down to the curve for span = 8; then move along the curve to select suitable height and width factors—say 2 in. high by 1½ in. wide. Multiply these factors by the diameter of bolt D, giving a height of 1½ in. and an effective width of 1⅛ in. If a 13/16 in. screw hole has been drilled in the bar, this amount is added to the effective width, making the full width 1⅛ in. + 13/16 in. = 1-15/16, or say 2 in.

The height and width of the beam, therefore, are 1½ × 2 in. at the center.

Example 2: Consider now an arrangement, as in case 3 (see Fig. 3-14), having a span L of 6 in. (152 mm), and a clamping force $2W$ at the workpiece of 2,000 lbf (8.9 kN), as before. The allowable design stress is again 15,000 psi (103.5 MPa). In this case, the screw must exert a force of half the clamping load, or 1,000 lbf (4.4 kN).

The full sectional area of the bolt will be $(1,000 \times 100)/(15,000 \times 65) = 0.103$ in.^{2} Comparing this with Table 3-1 shows that a $\frac{3}{8}$ in. screw will suffice.

Dividing the span of 6 in. by 0.375 in. shows the span factor is 16.

This time follow the left-hand arrow down, and interpolate between the curves for 15 and 20. Choose suitable proportions, such as $2\frac{1}{2} \times 4$, approximately, for height and width.

These factors multiplied by the diameter of the $\frac{3}{8}$ in. bolt gives proportions of 15/16 in. $\times$ $1\frac{1}{2}$ in. Because there is no hole in the center of this beam, no addition will have to be made to the width of the strap. Rounded out, the strap would be dimensioned with a height of 1 in. and width of $1\frac{1}{2}$ in.

In Fig. 3-15, the proportions of the beam in both cases 4 and 5 are related to the pin diameter. In the diagram, the pin in case 4 carries twice the load of that in case 5; and when related to screw diameter, D, it has twice the cross-sectional area of the pin in case 5.

To proportion the beam, the pin diameter in both cases is taken as 1, and the load carried by the pin is assumed to be W.

$$\text{Stress in pin} = 0.8S$$

where S = allowable stress in beam,

$$\text{Stress in beam } S = \frac{WL}{4Z}$$

$$\text{When section modulus } Z = \frac{BH^3 - BP^3}{6H}$$

$$S = \frac{6WLH}{4(BH^3 - BP^3)} \tag{6}$$

By equating stress in beam and pin and assuming a value of 1 for P,

$$L = 0.53B \left(H^2 - \frac{1}{H} \right) \tag{7}$$

It follows that, when the pin diameter has been calculated from the known clamping load and the span of the clamp has been established, division of the latter by the former will give the chart value of span L. Then decide upon suitable chart values of B and H, and these multiplied by the actual pin diameter will give the required dimensions for the beam.

Example 3: A beam is loaded, as in case 4 or 5 (see Fig. 3-15), with the beam proportions related to the diameter of the pivot pin P.

As before, span L is 6 in. (152 mm), and the clamping load at the workpiece is 2,000 lbf (8.9 kN). The force exerted at the pivot pin is $2,000 \times 2 = 4,000$ lbf (17.8 kN), and this load is carried by a pin in double shear with a design stress of 12,000 psi (82.7 MPa).

The cross section of the pin is 4,000 lbf/$(12,000 \times 2) = 0.167$ in.^{2}, and its diameter is 0.46 or $\frac{1}{2}$ in.

The span factor is 6 divided by $\frac{1}{2} = 12$.

Follow the curve for span 12 on Fig. 3-15, and select height and width factors, for example, $4 \times 1\frac{1}{2}$.

These factors multiplied by the pin diameter give a beam 2 in. deep by ¾ in. wide.

No addition to the height is required to take account of the pivot-pin hole, because this has been included in the nomographs.

Dimensions of Clamp Screws. Clamping forces, commonly transmitted and applied by fixture members having screw threads, such as commercially available bolts, nuts, wheels, etc., have the largest mechanical advantage of all simple machines.

By definition, a screw thread is a circular inclined plane (wedge). References in this section to screw threads are restricted to the Unified thread form.

To induce a clamping force by means of screw threads, one member, either the nut or the screw, must not revolve, while the other member must be free to rotate. Clamping force parallel to the axis of the threads is generated by rotation of one of the members. The amount of axial movement in one revolution is equal to the pitch or lead of a screw or nut having a single thread.

When torque (force × lever arm) is applied, axial movement occurs; but, since both threaded members are in intimate contact, frictional resistance must be overcome by the applied torque, as well as tension resistance of the thread assembly. The clamping force applied to the workpiece must withstand the total tooling forces.

Lengthy formulas for computing screw torque are not exact, since the value of the coefficient of friction cannot be predicted accurately. The values found with the following formula [Eq.(8)] will be a close approximation of those calculated with more complicated formulas.

Computing Torque in Screws.[4] The torque T, required on a screw to obtain a clamping force W_{min}, is approximately

$$T = 0.2dW_{min} = FL \tag{8}$$

Rearranging terms, the length of the lever arm to apply this force is:

$$L = \frac{0.2dW}{F} = \frac{T}{F}$$

where:

T = torque, in.-lbf
d = nominal screw diam, in. (mm)
W = axial clamping force, lbf (N)
F = force at handle of wrench, lbf (N)
L = length of lever arm, in. (mm)

Example 4: Determine the torque required to give a clamping force of 1,000 lbf (4,448 N) on a 9/16-12 UNC bolt. Also determine the minimum lengths of handle required to apply this clamping force if the operator applies a force on the handle ranging between 30 and 90 lbf (134 to 400 N).

$$T = 0.2 \times 0.5625 \times 1,000 = 112.5 \text{ in.-lbf} \tag{8}$$

$$L_{min} = \frac{T}{F_{min}}$$

$$= \frac{112.5 \text{ in.-lbf}}{30 \text{ lbf}}$$

$$= 3.75 \text{ in. minimum length of lever arm}$$

To provide a grip for the operator, another 1½ to 2 in. should be added. A satisfactory handle length would be 5½ in.

While a handle of this length will assure a clamping force of 1,000 lbf (4,448 N), it must be realized that if the operator applies the maximum force of 90 lbf (400 N) the applied torque and clamping forces will be much higher.

For example:

$$T = F_{max} \times L$$

$$= 90 \text{ lbf} \times 3.75 \text{ in.}$$

$$= 337.5 \text{ in.-lbf}$$

Table 3-2 can be checked to see that T in the example does not exceed the maximum limit for a 9/16 in. bolt. In the examples it is well below the limit even with the maximum force being applied to the handle.

To withstand total stress in it the nominal diameter of a screw supplying a clamping force W_{min} is

$$d = 1.355 \frac{W_{min}}{S_t} \tag{9}$$

where S_t = total shear and tensile stresses, psi. (Pa)

To arrive at a working or allowable stress for the screw, the ultimate strength of the screw material may be divided by a safety factor of from 6 to 10.

The torque values listed in Table 3-2 are offered as a guide.

TABLE 3-2
General Torque Specifications

U. S. Standard

Grade of Bolt		S.A.E. 1 & 2	S.A.E. 5	S.A.E. 6	S.A.E 8		
Minimum Tensile Strength		64,000 P.S.I.	105,000 P.S.I.	133,000 P.S.I.	150,000 P.S.I.		
Grade Markings On Head						Socket or Wrench Size	
U.S. Standard			Torque (In Pound-Feet)			**U.S. Regular**	
Bolt Diameter	Dec. Equiv.					Bolt Head	Nut
1/4	0.250	5	7	10	10.5	3/8	7/16
5/16	0.3125	9	14	19	22	1/2	9/16
3/8	0.375	15	25	34	37	9/16	5/8
7/16	0.4375	24	40	55	60	5/8	3/4
1/2	0.500	37	60	85	92	3/4	13/16
9/16	0.5625	53	88	120	132	7/8	7/8
5/8	0.625	74	120	167	180	15/16	1
3/4	0.750	120	200	280	296	1-1/8	1-1/8
7/8	0.875	190	302	440	473	1-5/16	1-5/16
1	1.000	282	466	660	714	1-1/2	1-1/2

TABLE 3-2 (continued)
General Torque Specifications

Metric Standard

Grade of Bolt		5D	8G	10K	12K		
Minimum Tensile Strength		71,160 P.S.I.	113,000 P.S.I.	142,000 P.S.I.	170,674 P.S.I.		
Grade Markings On Head		5D	8G	10K	12L	Socket or Wrench Size	
Metric Bolt Diameter	Dec. Equiv.	Torque (In Pound-Feet)				Metric Bolt Head	Nut
6mm	0.2362	5	6	8	10	10mm	10mm
8mm	0.3150	10	16	22	27	14mm	14mm
10mm	0.3937	19	31	40	49	17mm	17mm
12mm	0.4720	34	54	70	86	19mm	19mm
14mm	0.5512	55	89	117	137	22mm	22mm
16mm	0.6299	83	132	175	208	24mm	24mm
18mm	0.709	111	182	236	283	27mm	27mm
22mm	.8661	182	284	394	464	32mm	32mm
24mm	0.945	261	419	570	689	36mm	36mm

(Sturtevant Richmont)

NOTE: To be used as reference only

The following rules apply to the chart:
1. Consult manufacturer's specific recommendations when available.
2. The chart may be used directly when any of the following lubricants are used:
   Never-Seez Compound, Molykote, Fel-Pro C-5, graphite and oil, or similiar mixtures.
3. Increase the torque by 20% when using engine oil or chassis grease as a lubricant.
   (These lubricants are not generally recommended for fasteners)
4. Reduce torque by 20% when cadmium plated bolts are used.
   CAUTION: Tightening into aluminum usually will require less torque.

The average torque required to turn a knob depends on the shape and size of the knob. For most commercial knobs, studies show this to average 50 in.-lbf (5.6 N·m). One practice is to reduce these forces by approximately 50% for calculating the operating clamping force, and increasing them approximately 50% for calculating maximum forces.

The length of the lever arm may be dictated by reasons of space, location, or other limitations. The lever arm must be long enough to utilize the minimum force and yet short enough to preclude failure of the clamping device if a large force is applied. The torque for a given-size bolt of any of the materials listed in Table 3-2 should not be exceeded. Hence the designer must consider such values in the table when determining the length of the lever arm.

Many threaded devices such as socket head cap screws, bolts, hand knob assemblies, thumb screws, threaded spring plungers, swivel screw clamps, etc., are used for direct screw clamping.

A good example of a direct screw clamp is the quick-acting screw clamp shown in Fig. 3-16. These clamps can save considerable loading and unloading time as shown in the same figure. Another example of a direct-acting screw clamp is the spring loaded

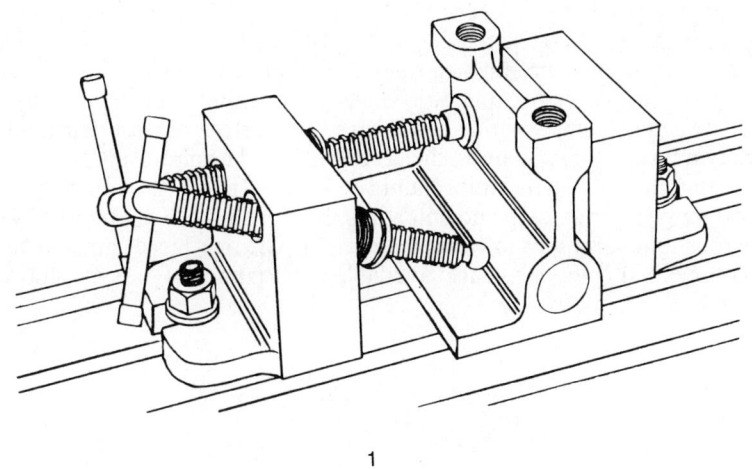

1

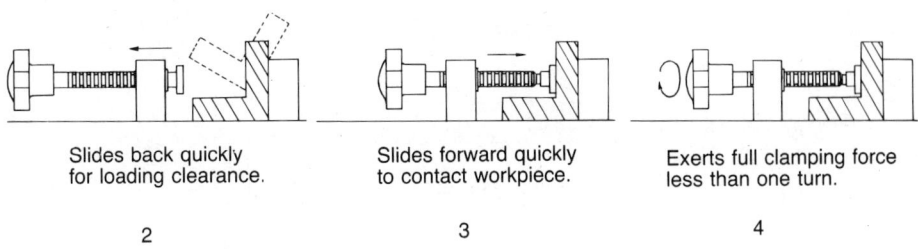

Slides back quickly
for loading clearance.

Slides forward quickly
to contact workpiece.

Exerts full clamping force
less than one turn.

2   3   4

Fig. 3-16 Quick-acting screw clamps. (*Courtesy Carr Lane Mfg. Co.*)

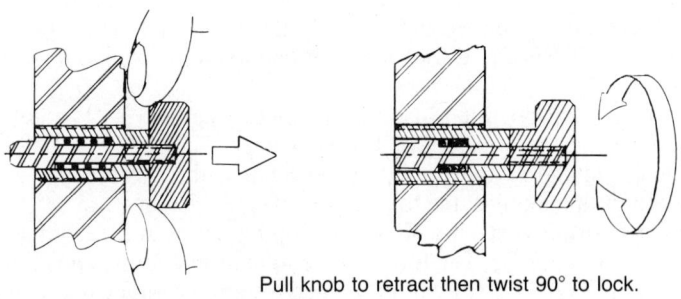

Pull knob to retract then twist 90° to lock.

Fig. 3-17 Retractable spring-loaded plunger. (*Courtesy Carr Lane Mfg. Co.*)

plunger shown in Fig. 3-17. It can also be manually retracted and locked with a 90° twist. They can be used with standard mounting blocks or mounted directly through a tapped hole.

Cam Clamps. Cam clamps provide rapid and effective clamping forces if properly designed and applied. They are available commercially as standard items.

The surfaces of cams and thrust plates are subject to wear, and most cam clamps tend to shift the thrust plate or workpiece during their clamping and unclamping. They may unclamp as the result of vibrations generated by tool forces. For those reasons, they require some attention by the operator for their proper working.

A cam clamp is a machine member having a curved surface which changes distance with respect to its pivot when rotated. Since the distance between the cam's pivot and the workpiece is fixed, the cam must be rotated to apply a clamping force, directly or indirectly, to the workpiece. A cam's resistance to loosening is dependent upon frictional force between its contact surface and that of the surface against which it bears.

There are two types of cam clamps, the eccentric and the spiral cam.

The swiveling cam-actuated strap clamp of Fig. 3-18 has a strap which pivots around the center post for loading and unloading the workpiece. The spherical washers compensate for slight variations in workpiece height. The one-piece cam and handle is a standard commercial component, also available in variations of the type shown.

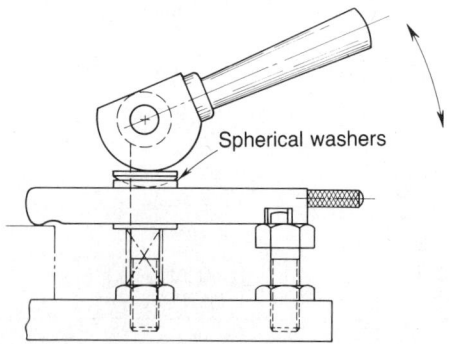

Spherical washers

Fig. 3-18 Swiveling cam-actuated strap clamp.

The design of Fig. 3-19a can also be swiveled about the eyebolt, but it utilizes a fork cam having two bearing surfaces. The guide rest (see Fig. 3-19b) allows the strap to be slid on and off the workpiece but prevents strap rotation. As the handle is turned, the strap clamp of Fig. 3-19c is retracted by pressure of a push pin against a dowel which is press-fit in the strap. The clamp is returned by the compression spring.

Two cams are each rotated by hydraulically-actuated, rack-and-pinion assemblies, as shown in Fig. 3-20. Return of the clamping and locating arms is assisted by return springs.

A sliding-wedge cam operated by an air cylinder (see Fig. 3-21) exerts downward pressure, through spherical washers, on the workpiece. The clamp is released when the air flow, reversed in the cylinder, is directed against the largest end of the piston, ensuring maximum unlocking force to overcome frictional force.

A cam-locking spring keeps the pivoted clamping levers in the clamped position in the design shown in Fig. 3-22. The levers move to their unclamped position only when oil under pressure is directed to the spring-loaded piston. Hydraulic pressure transmitted to the cam moves it against its spring and permits the pusher pins to move toward each other. The inward movement of the pins allows the two spring-actuated plungers to swing the levers around their hinge pins to their unclamped position. The clamped position is adjusted by the dog-point setscrews bearing against the pusher pins.

In the design of Fig. 3-23, pressure from a cam is transmitted to a sliding wedge (1) by a connecting link (2). The link is slotted to allow its impact on a pin (3) to aid in releasing the pivoted jaws (4) when the cam handle is rotated clockwise.

Rotation of the cams in the designs of Figs. 3-24 and 3-25 is around axes below the workpieces. The jaws shown in Fig. 3-24 are adapted for round and curved workpieces, while those of Fig. 3-25 hold two workpieces; equalization is secured by a slot in the cam.

The clamp of Fig. 3-26 secures positive release of the workpiece by means of the pin (1) bearing against the lower end of the slotted link (2) as the cam handle (3) is rotated

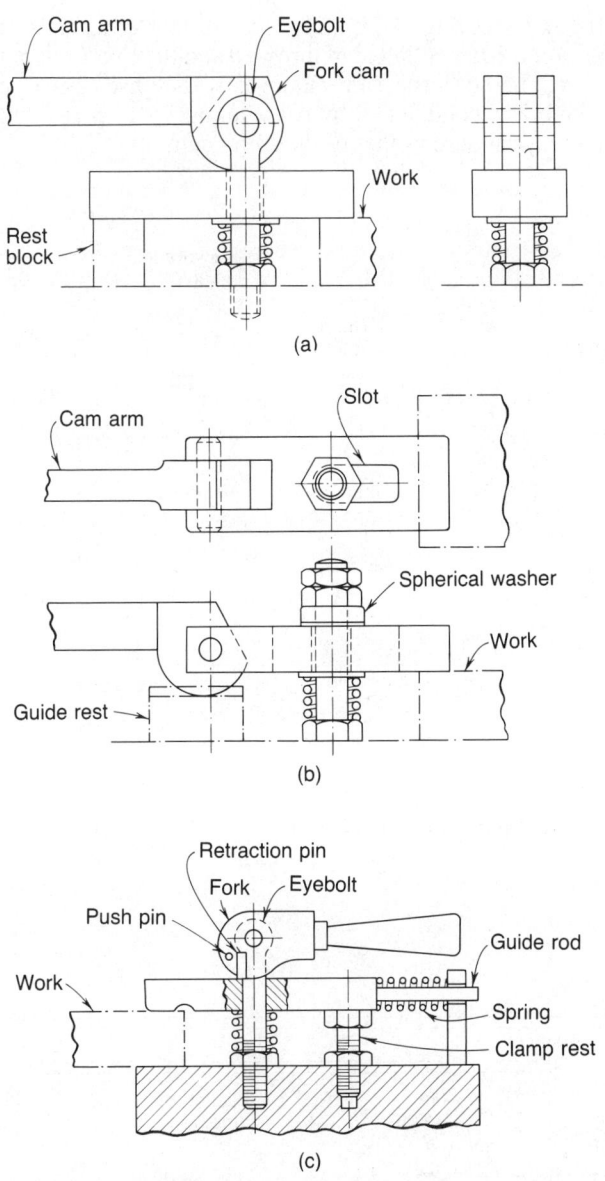

(a)

(b)

(c)

Fig. 3-19 Cam-actuated strap clamps. (*Courtesy Cincinnati Milacron*)

counterclockwise. As the cam is rotated, the equalizing bar (4) is raised, causing the clamps (5) to move upward and away from the workpiece.

Figures 3-27 and 3-28 illustrate some additional applications of cams in clamping arrangements.

Cam Design. Cams to suit almost any application are now available from many component suppliers, and should be considered before designing a new one from scratch.

However, for those cases where nothing suitable is available, the following computations should provide the designer with all of the information necessary to design a cam.

Eccentric Cam.[4] An eccentric cam consists of a circular-cam body which is turned about an eccentric axis (see Fig. 3-29). The eccentricity e depends upon the angle through which the cam is rotated (angle of throw) θ and the rise T but not upon the size of the cam radius R. The eccentric cam clamp is widely used because of its simple construction, although it is condemned by some authorities because its propensity to stay locked is not always as sure as that of the spiral cam.

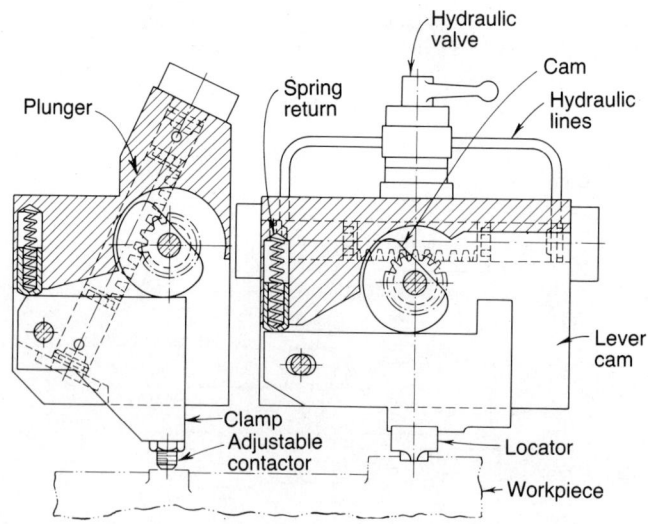

Fig. 3-20 Hydraulic cam actuation. (*Courtesy Cincinnati Milacron*)

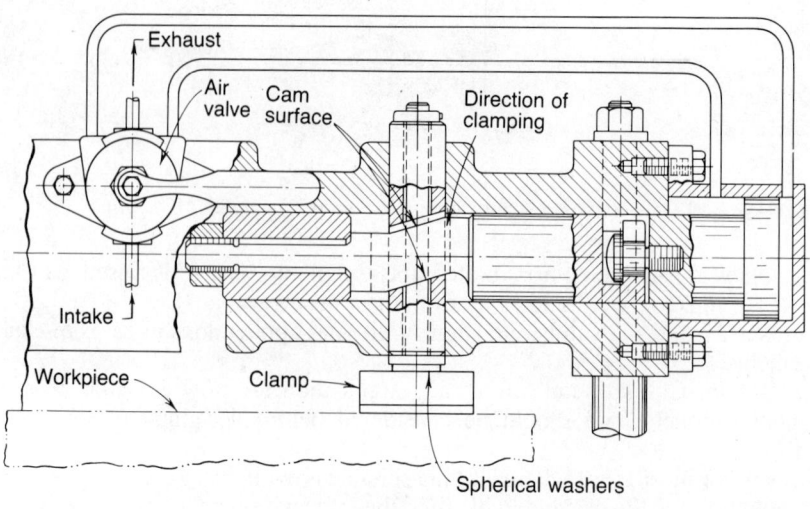

Fig. 3-21 Sliding-wedge cam actuation. (*Courtesy Cincinnati Milacron*)

Eccentricity may be calculated from the equation

$$e = \frac{T}{1 - \cos \theta} \tag{10}$$

and the radius determined by the equation

$$R = e \cos \theta + \frac{\sin \theta}{f} \tag{11}$$

where f = coefficient of friction for which a value of 0.10 is generally used.

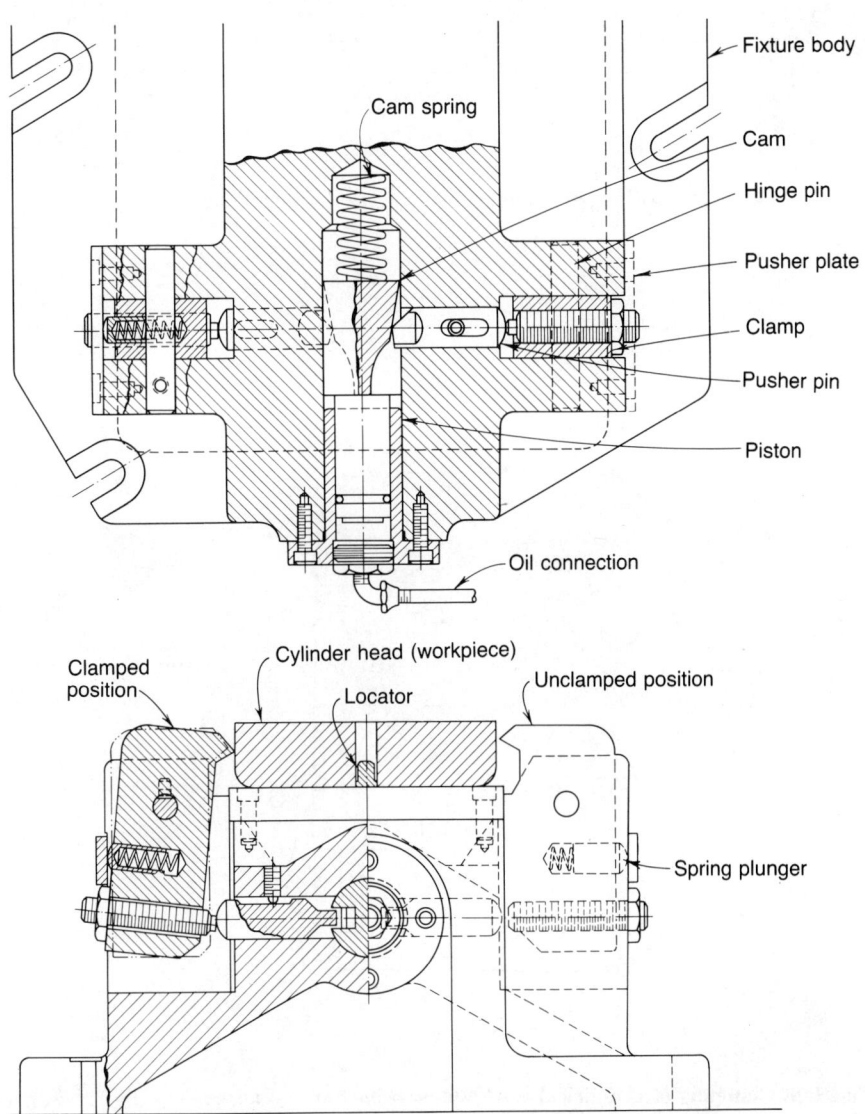

Fig. 3-22 Hydraulic cam releasing. (*Courtesy Cincinnati Milacron*)

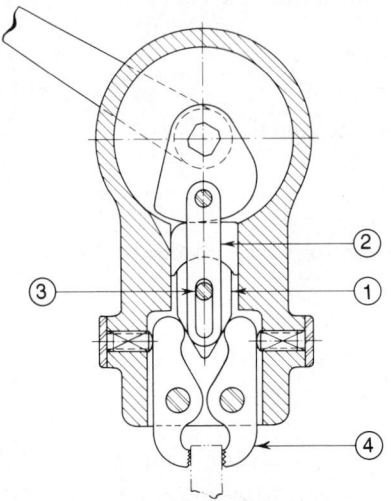

Fig. 3-23 Floating-jaw clamp. (*Courtesy Special Engineering Services, Inc.*)

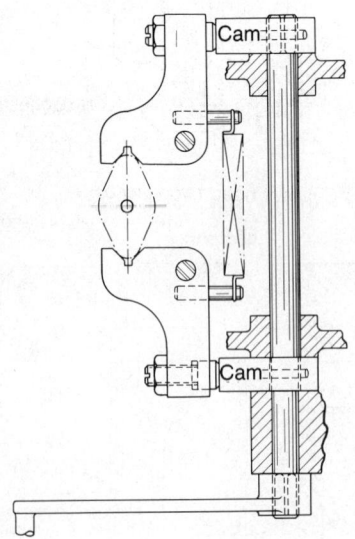

Fig. 3-24 Clamping of cylindrical workpieces. (*Courtesy Special Engineering Services, Inc.*)

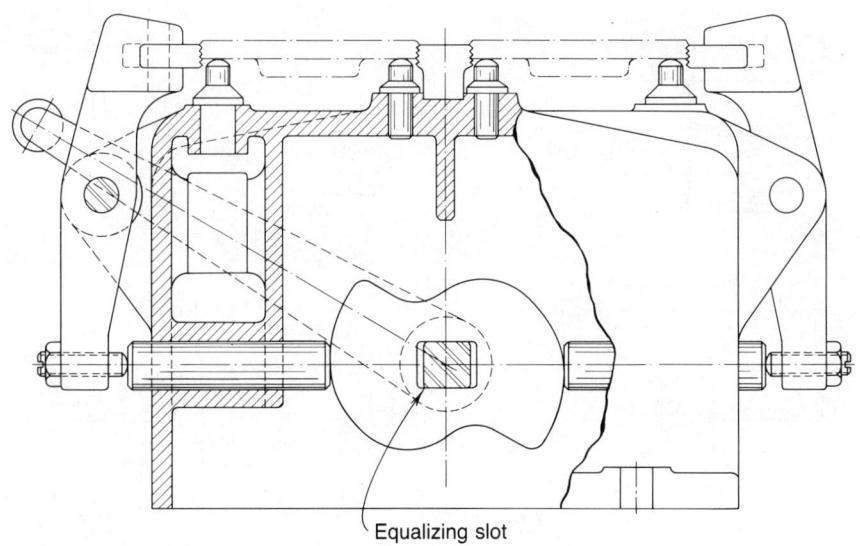

Fig. 3-25 Cam clamping of two workpieces. (*Courtesy Special Engineering Services, Inc.*)

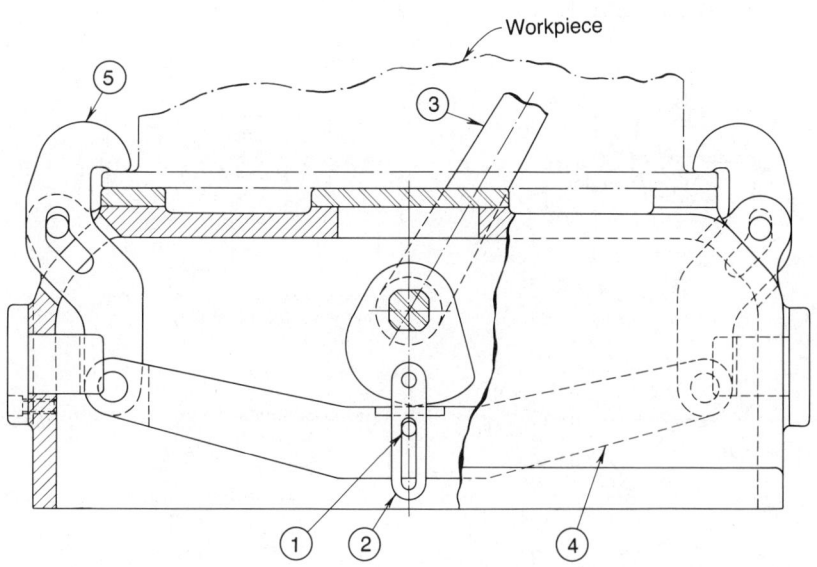

Fig. 3-26 Positive-release cam clamp. (*Courtesy Special Engineering Services, Inc.*)

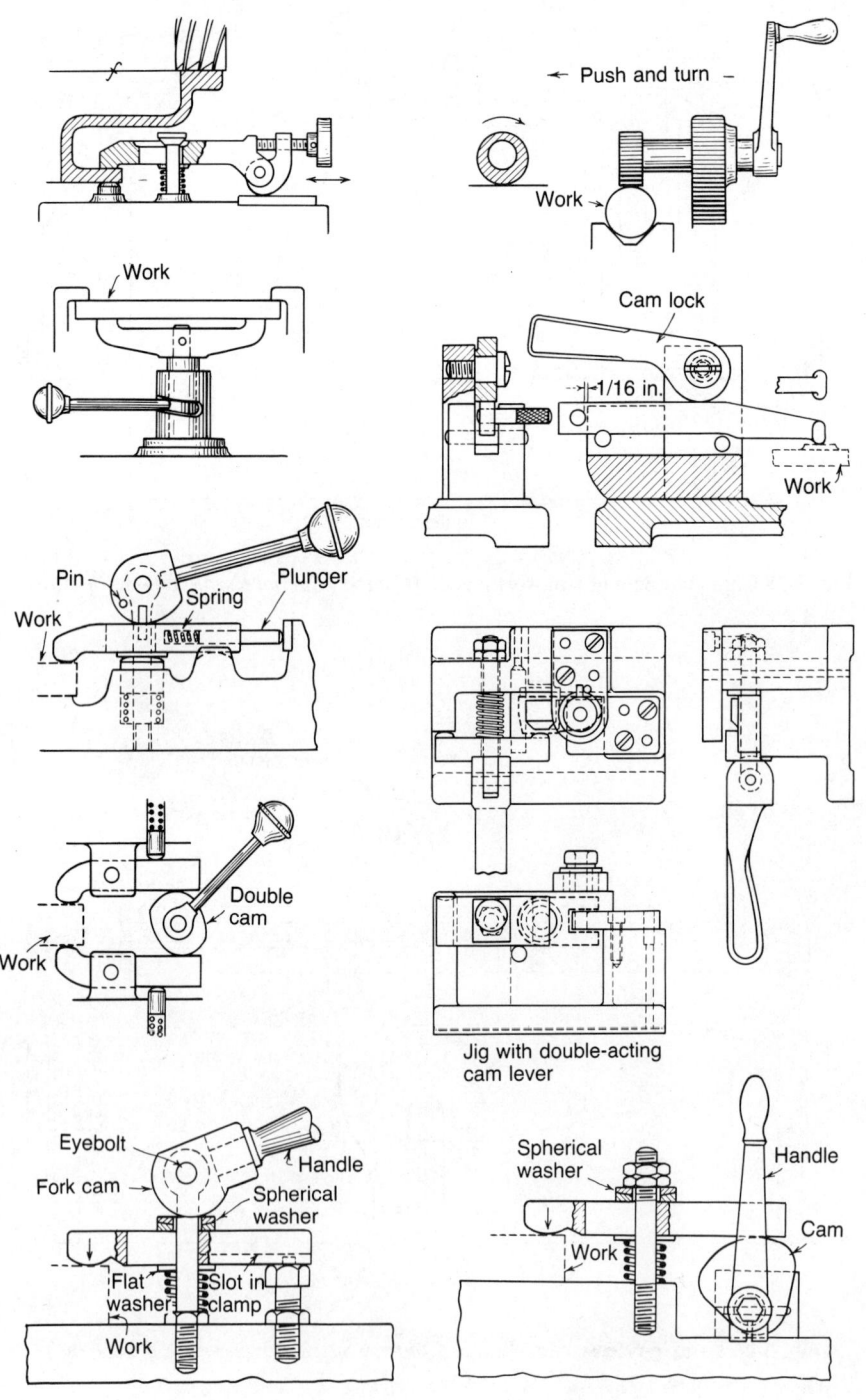

Fig. 3-27 Types of cam-actuated clamps.

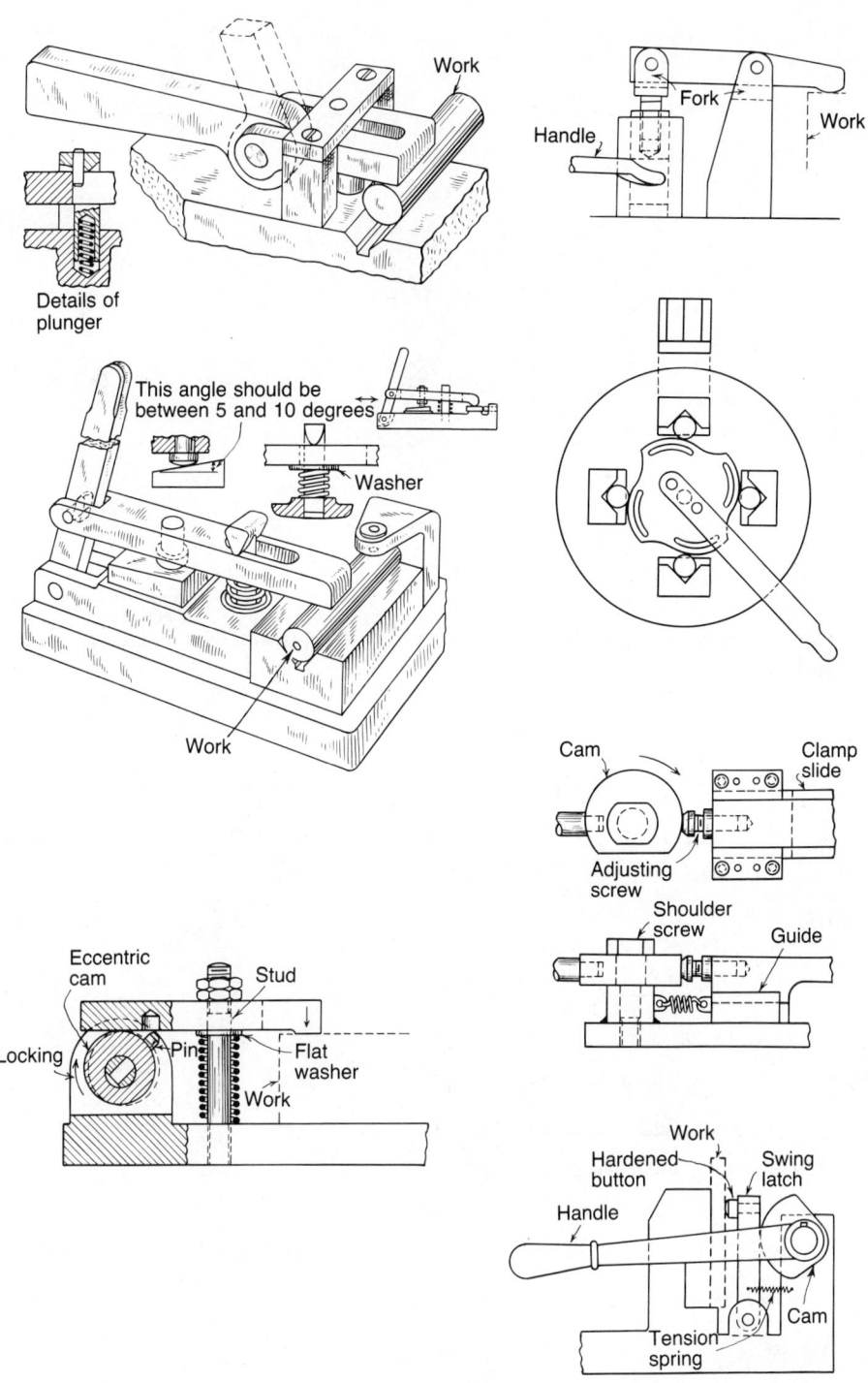

Details of plunger

Work

Handle — Fork — Work

This angle should be between 5 and 10 degrees

Washer

Work

Cam — Clamp slide

Adjusting screw

Shoulder screw — Guide

Eccentric cam — Stud

Locking — Pin — Flat washer

Work

Work

Hardened button — Swing latch

Handle

Cam

Tension spring

Fig. 3-28 Types of cam- and wedge-actuated clamps.

3-27

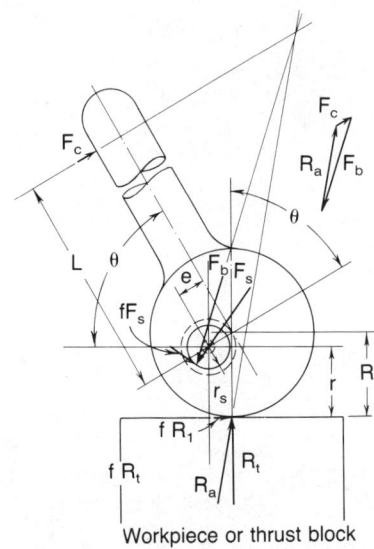

Fig. 3-29 Forces acting on an eccentric cam during engagement. (*The Tool and Manufacturing Engineer*)

The radius of the pivot pin, r_s, may be found from the equation:

$$r_s = 0.667 \sqrt{\frac{n}{S_s} \left(F_{c\,min} + R_t \right)} \tag{12}$$

where:

$$n = \frac{F_{c\,max}}{F_{c\,min}} = \frac{R_{t\,max}}{R_{t\,min}} \tag{13}$$

$F_{c\,max}$ = force applied to cam, lbf (N), max

$F_{c\,max}$ = force applied to cam, lbf (N), min

S_s = working shear stress of the pivot, psi

R_t = force imposed by the cam, lbf (N)

The length of the lever arm, L, of an eccentric cam can be found from the relationship

$$L = \frac{R_t [fR + e (\sin \theta - f \cos \theta)] + fr_s F_b}{F_c} \tag{14}$$

where $F_b = R_t + F_c$ approximately $\tag{15}$

Example 5: Compute the eccentricity, minimum radius, and lever arm of a cam for a throw angle of 90°, a rise of 0.125 in. (3.18 mm), to impose a force of 900 lbf (4 kN), with a force of 30 to 90 lbf (134 to 400 N) applied.

For: T = 0.125 in.

        θ = 90°

        f = 0.1

        $F_{c\,max}$ = 90

        $F_{c\,min}$ = 30

        $R_{t\,min}$ = 900

$$e = \frac{0.125}{1-0} = 0.125 \text{ in.} \quad \text{Eccentricity.} \tag{10}$$

$$R = 0.125\,(0 \times 1/0.1) = 1.25 \text{ in.} \quad \text{Cam radius.} \tag{11}$$

$$r_s = 0.667\sqrt{\frac{3}{10,000}}\,(30+900) = 0.35 \text{ in.} \quad \text{Pin radius.} \tag{12}$$

The pin's radius can be rounded to 0.375 in., making the pin diameter 0.750 in.

$$L = \frac{900\,[\,0.1 \times 1.25 + 0.125\,(1 - 0.1 \times 0)\,] + (0.1 \times 0.375 \times 930)}{30} \tag{14}$$

L = 8.66 in.   Length of lever arm.

To provide for operator's grasp, the handle should be made 10¼ in. long.

$$F_b = 900 + 30 = 930 \tag{15}$$

Spiral Cam.[4] The contour of a spiral cam is based on the spiral of Archimedes. Its locking action is better than that of an eccentric cam although it is somewhat more expensive to make. The forces acting on a spiral cam, shown in Fig. 3-30, are the reaction R_t from the workpiece normal to the cam surface; the friction force fR_t; the force F_c applied to the handle; the normal force F_s of the pivot pin on the cam; and its frictional force fF_s. The resultant force of R_t and fR_t is R_a. The resultant of F_s is fF_s is F_b, which is tangent to the friction circle having a radius for practical purposes of fr_s.

Example 6: Compute the size of the pin, the minimum radius and lead of the cam, and the length of the lever arm for a spiral cam which will exert 900 lbf. The handle will be rotated through 90° with a force of 30 lbf min and 90 lbf max. The rise of the steel cam, hardened to 400 Brinell, is 0.125 in. The allowable shear stress for the pin is 10,000 psi (689 MPa).

For the radius of the pivot pin from Eq.(12),

$$r_s = 0.667\sqrt{\frac{3}{10,000}}\,(30+900) = 0.35 \text{ in.} \quad \text{Pin radius.}$$

The pin's radius can be rounded out to 0.375 in., making the diameter 0.750 in.

The rise from the smallest radius r_1 to the largest radius r of the cam is the lead l of the cam, from the expression

$$r - r_1 = \frac{\theta l}{360}$$

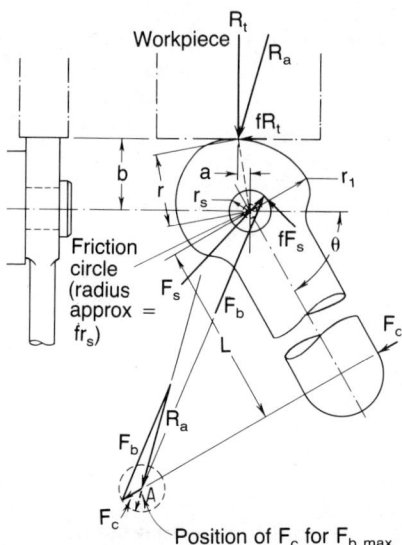

Fig. 3-30 Forces which act on a spiral cam during engagement. (*The Tool and Manufacturing Engineer*)

where θ is in degrees and l is the lead of the cam, in.

$$0.125 \text{ in. } = \frac{90}{360} \, l \tag{16}$$

$$l = 0.500 \text{ in.}$$

Since, for a self-locking spiral cam, the minimum radius r_1 is

$$r_1 = \frac{1}{2\pi f} \tag{17}$$

where:

$$f = 0.1$$

$$r_1 = \frac{0.5}{0.6283} = 0.796 \text{ in.}$$

Choose a minimum radius of 0.875 in. The maximum radius, r, would then equal 0.875 in. $+ (r - r_1)$ or $0.875 + 0.125 = 1.00$ in.

The projected area (cam thickness × pin diameter) of the bearing for the pivot pin must be large enough to limit the unit pressure to 3,000 psi (20.7 MPa), in keeping with accepted practice for bearings for slow speeds and intermittent loads.

The load on the bearing is

$$F_b = R_a + F_{c \text{ max}} \tag{18}$$

where:

$$R_a = \frac{nR_t}{\cos T}$$

Since $\quad n = \dfrac{F_{c\,max}}{F_{c\,min}} = \dfrac{90}{30} = 3$ (13)

and $\quad f = 0.1 = \tan T$

$$T = 5° 43'$$

$$\cos T = 0.995$$

$$F_{b\,max} = \frac{2,700}{0.995} + 90 = 2714 + 90 = 2,804 \text{ lbf}$$

Since the unit stress on this area should not exceed 3,000 psi,

$$t = \frac{2,804 \text{ lbf}}{3,000 \times \frac{3}{4}}$$

$$t = 1.25 \text{ in.}$$

From the following equation and Table 3-3, the minimum allowable length of the cam radius r_{min} can be computed:

$$r_{min} = \frac{1.1 R_t}{Kt}$$ (19)

where:

t = thickness of cam, in.

K = constant, selected from Table 3-3

$$r_{min} = \frac{1.1 \times 2,700}{5,530 \times 1.25}$$

$$= 0.43 \text{ in.}$$

TABLE 3-3
Values of Compressive Endurance Limit
$(S_e)_c$ and of k for Steel of Various Hardnesses

BHN	$(S_e)_c$ (ksi)	k
150	50	480
200	70	940
250	90	1550
300	110	2310
350	130	3230
400	170	5530
500	190	6900
600	230	10100

Since this is less than the chosen radius of 0.875 in., the 0.875 in. radius should be ample to withstand the compressive stress.

The expression for the length L of the lever arm is

$$L = \frac{R_t[\ (l/2\pi) + r_1 f\ ] + r_s\ f_s\ F_b}{F_c} \qquad (20)$$

where:

F_b is 900 lbf and

$$L = \frac{900[0.08 + (1.0 \times 0.1)] + (0.375 \times 0.1 \times 900)}{30}$$

$\quad = 6.53$ in.   Length of lever arm.

To provide for the operator's grasp, the handle should be $8\frac{1}{4}$ in. long.

Wedge Clamps. A wedge is a movable inclined plane which provides (and should maintain) the desired clamping force. The movement of the wedge should not require a large force for actuation. These requirements are controlled by the wedge angle (angle of inclination).

The Wedge Angle and Forces on It. The diagram of Fig. 3-31 shows the forces acting on a wedge at the instant removal begins. It is assumed that the wedge has previously been inserted to exert a clamping force F_2 on the workpiece with a reaction F_1 from the wedge block. F_1 and F_2 act normal to the bearing surfaces. The taper angle of the top of the wedge is α. Two friction forces F_3 and F_4 resist removal of the wedge by pull P. For a coefficient of friction designated by f,

$$F_3 = fF_1$$

and

$$F_4 = fF_2$$

Because the sum of the vertical forces equals zero,

$$F_2 = F_1 \cos \alpha + F_3 \sin \alpha$$
$$= F_1 (\cos \alpha + f \sin \alpha)$$

Also, since the horizontal forces must equal zero,

$$P = F_3 \cos \alpha + F_4 - F_1 \sin \alpha$$
$$= F_1 [\ 2f \cos \alpha + (f^2 - 1) \sin \alpha]$$

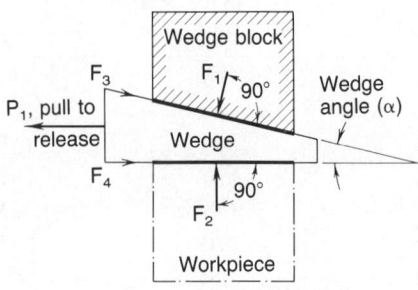

Fig. 3-31 Force diagram for a wedge.

Since f is small, f^2 is much smaller and may be neglected, so that

$$P = F_1 (2f \cos \alpha - \sin \alpha) \qquad (21)$$

For small values of α, $2f \cos \alpha$ is larger than $\sin \alpha$, and a positive effort is required to extract the wedge. As α is made larger, $\cos \alpha$ decreases and $\sin \alpha$ increases. An angle is reached where P becomes zero, and the wedge no longer stays in place of its own accord. For large angles, P has increasingly negative values, which means there is less and less inclination for the wedge to remain in place. If Eq.(21) is solved for $P = 0$, the result is

$$\tan \alpha = 2f \qquad (22)$$

Practical Wedge Angles. The angle α must have a tangent less than twice the value of the coefficient of friction if the wedge is to stay tight. If the angle is small, the wedge is inclined to stick, and the pull P to remove the wedge becomes very large.

For a coefficient of friction of 0.15, α by Eq.(21) is approximately 16°. It is almost certain that a taper angle of over 16° will not stay in place. But in the presence of oil and other slippery conditions, f may drop below 0.1, for which an angle less than 10° is required. A practical working angle for tapered keys is 7°.

The effectiveness of wedge clamping cannot be accurately predetermined, because the coefficient of friction is difficult to evaluate. It depends upon wedge-surface variables, such as the presence of oils or cutting fluids and the surface finish and hardness.

Larger wedge angles can be used if an auxiliary holding device, as shown in Fig. 3-32, is provided.

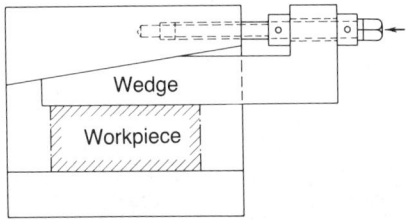

Fig. 3-32 A wedge clamp with an auxiliary holding device.

Examples of wedge clamps are shown in Fig. 3-33. In *a*, clamping action is provided by a wedge in the handle as shown in the section view of the cam face. As the handle is swung, it is forced up by the wedge action causing downward thrust on the workpiece. Figure 3-33*b* shows a wedge block type power chuck which is used for high speed turning. Jaws move in and out by the back and forth movement of the wedge bars. The wedge bars have rack-type teeth on the top which mesh with teeth on the bottom of the jaws. The wedge bars are moved back and forth by a rack-and-pinion action. Gripping forces greater than 36,000 lbf (160 kN) can be produced with a 12 in. chuck of this type. The wedge bars are semi-self-locking which helps to maintain the gripping force necessary for high-speed operations.

Another wedge operated chuck is shown in Fig. 3-33*c*. This patented wedge hook design uses wedges to convert axial movement to in-and-out movement of the jaws. The wedge is T-shaped and set at a 10° to 20° incline. Axial movement of the drawbar causes the T-section to slide on the puller ramp causing radial motion of the jaw.

The collet action of *d* and *e* is another form of wedge action. It is readily seen from the illustrations that the axial movement of a drawbar can be translated into a radial movement to grip an ID or OD.

Toggle Clamps. The toggle clamp provides heavy pressure, is quickly operated, and

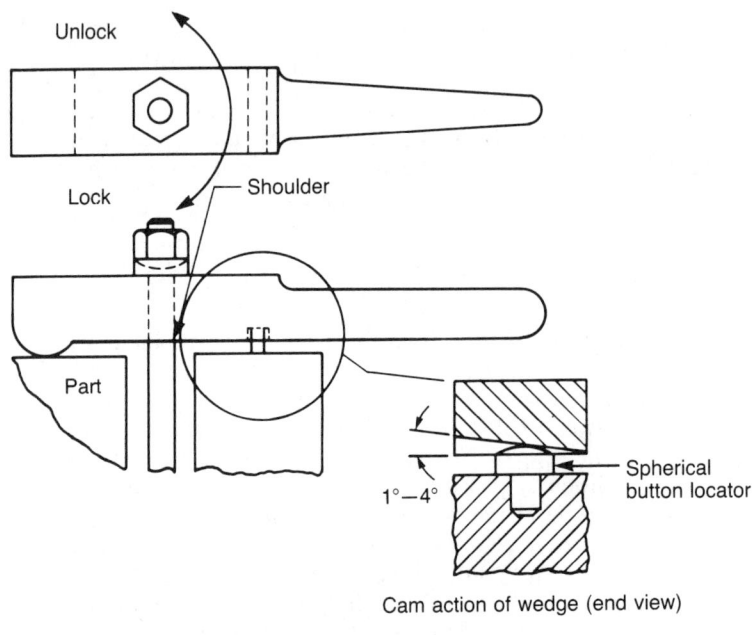

Unlock

Lock

Shoulder

Part

Spherical
button locator

1°—4°

Cam action of wedge (end view)

(a)

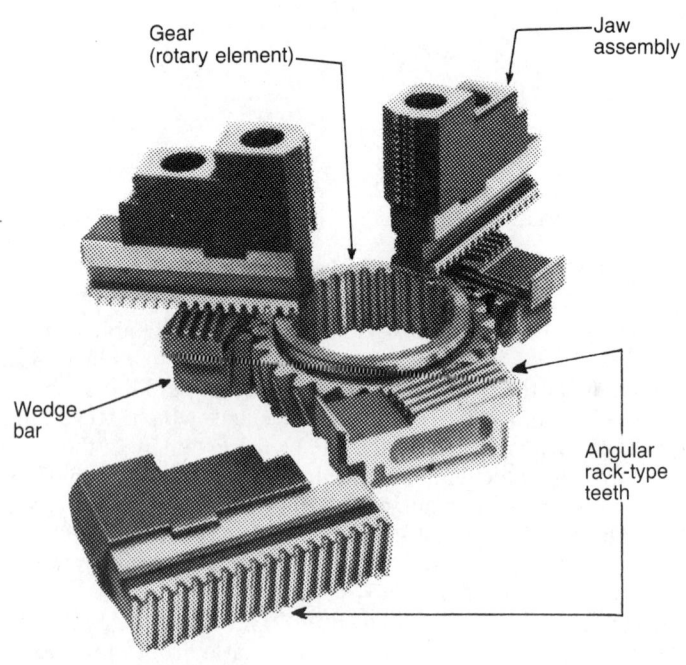

Gear
(rotary element)

Jaw
assembly

Wedge
bar

Angular
rack-type
teeth

(b)

Fig. 3-33 Wedge type clamps. (*Courtesy (b) Forkhardt, Inc.; (c) Universal Engineering Div.,
Houdaille Industries; (e) Rovi Products, Inc.*)

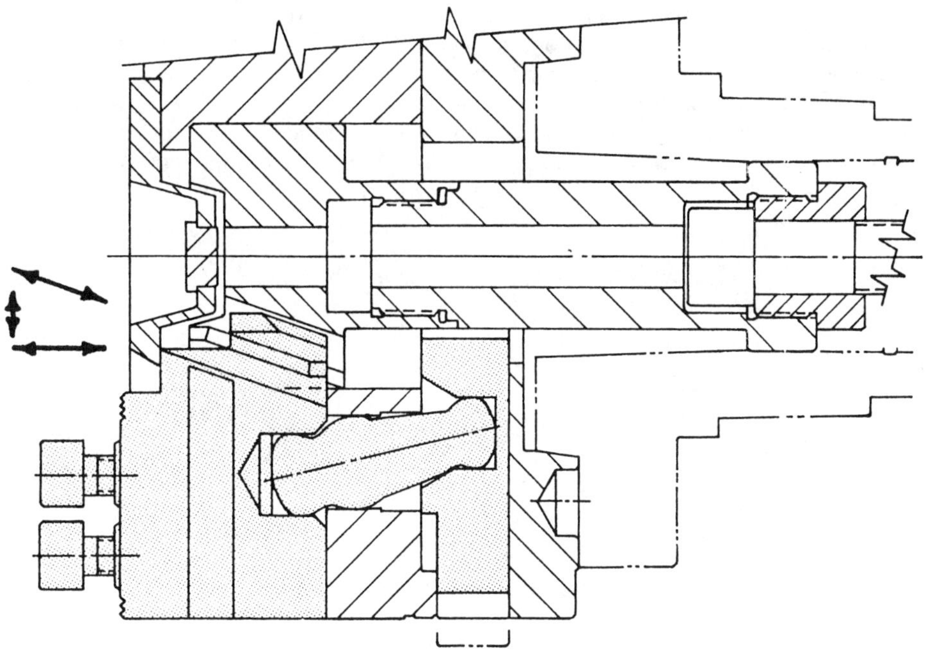

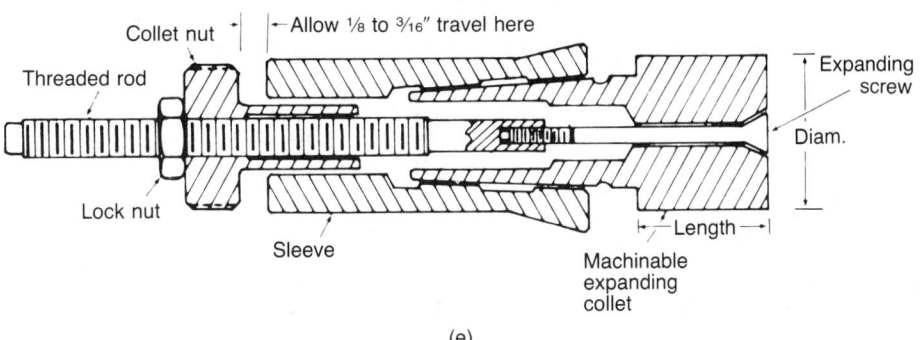

(c)

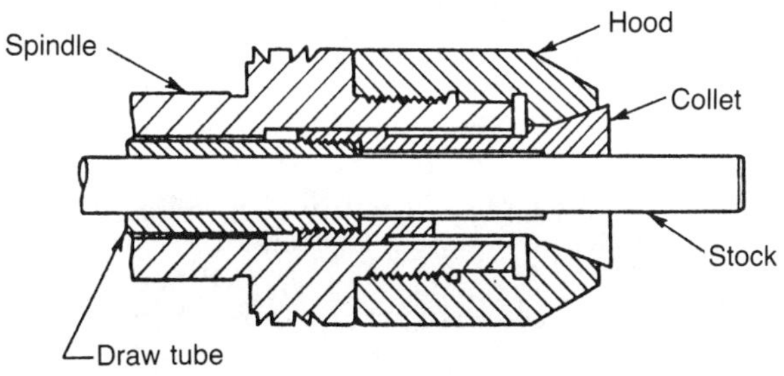

Spindle — Hood — Collet — Stock — Draw tube

(d)

Collet nut — Allow ⅛ to ³⁄₁₆″ travel here — Expanding screw — Threaded rod — Diam. — Lock nut — Length — Sleeve — Machinable expanding collet

(e)

Fig. 3-33 (Continued)

gives complete clearance for loading and unloading the fixture. This type of clamp can accommodate only minor variations in stock thickness and must therefore have a means of adjustment in the clamping end. A C-type toggle clamp is shown in Fig. 3-34a. An adjustment for stock thickness variations is provided by the setscrew in the clamping end. The handle end of the C-frame rests on another screw for adjustment of travel beyond dead center. A similar principle is applied on a pusher-type clamp shown in Fig. 3-34b.

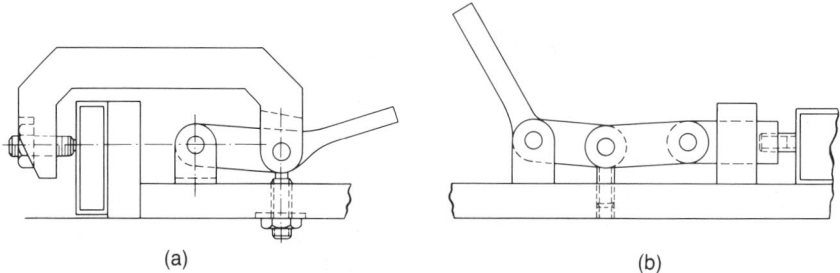

(a)   (b)

Fig. 3-34 Toggle clamps: (a) C-frame type, (b) pusher type.

The maximum clamping force developed in any toggle type clamp is attained when the three pivot points are in a straight line. However, in this position, vibration and intermittent load conditions that are found in most industrial applications could unlock the clamp. This can be eliminated by providing over-center travel, which is usually a few thousandths of an inch (one-tenth of a millimeter) at the hinge point in the clamping mechanism. The proper over-center travel to produce maximum holding power, and yet insure positive locking, is a carefully calculated and controlled dimension developed by years of experimentation and experience by toggle clamp manufacturers.

The toggle clamp manufacturers have also evaluated stresses, forces, safety factors, etc., for their designs, so that the ratings for applied and clamping forces in their catalogs preclude excessive deflection of the toggle members. For this reason, commercial toggle clamps should be used whenever possible.

Toggle clamp manufacturers rate the capability of their clamps by the load that they will contain when in the clamped position. This load is called the holding capacity and is the maximum amount of force that the clamp can withstand without damage to itself. Clamping pressure is the amount of force applied by the clamp to the workpiece, and is considerably less than the rated holding capacity. The maximum recommended clamping pressure for manually operated clamps is approximately 50% of the rated holding capacity. Toggle clamps are available with holding capacities ranging from 25 to 10,000 lbf (222 N to 44 kN).

Four basic toggle actions are shown in Figs. 3-35 thru 3-38. Figure 3-35a shows hold down action toggle clamps with vertical handles, b shows hold down clamps with horizontal handles, and c shows hold down clamps with pull-down handles.

Pull-action toggle clamps are shown in Fig. 3-36. Figure 3-36a shows latch-type clamps. With this type of clamp, one hand is used to engage or disengage the latch bar while the other hand moves the handle. Hook or U-bolt type latch clamps, b, operate in the same manner, but can be adjusted since the U-bolts are threaded.

Figure 3-37 illustrates two types of squeeze action toggle clamps. The clamps shown in a are the plier type, while those in b are called pull-down squeeze action clamps. Many squeeze action clamps have a trigger release to permit one-hand operation. These clamps are readily available in many different configurations.

3-36

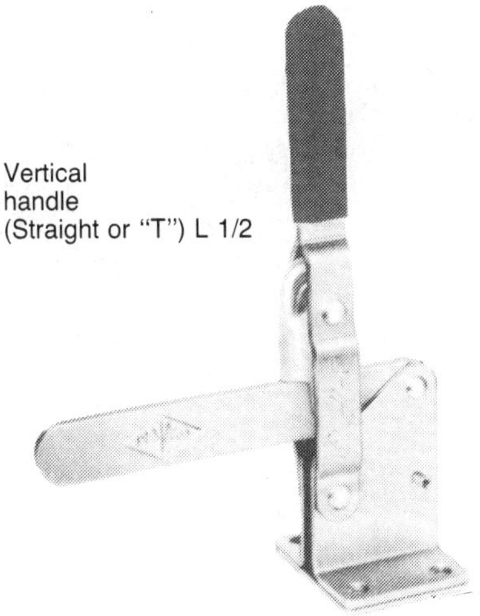

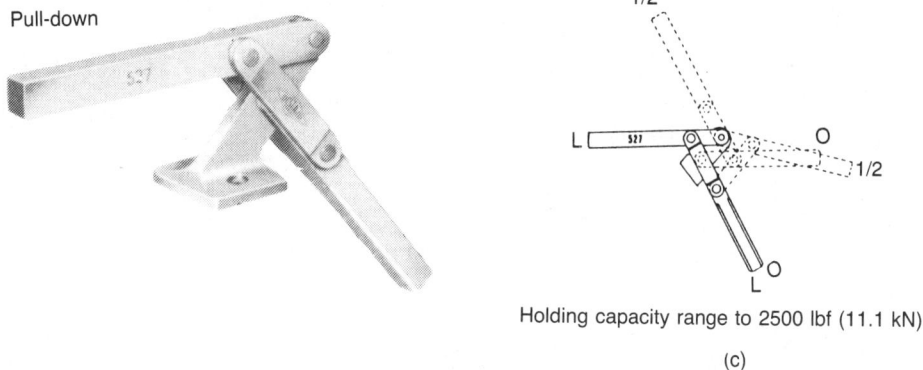

Vertical
handle
(Straight or "T") L 1/2

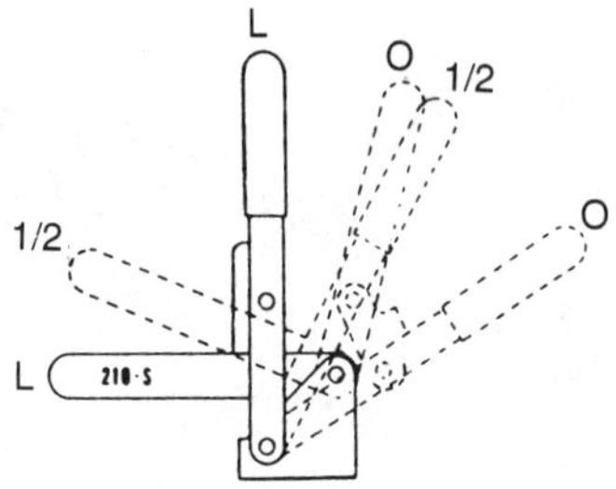

L
O
1/2
1/2
O
L
210-S

Holding capacity range to 6000 lbf (26.7 kN)

(a)

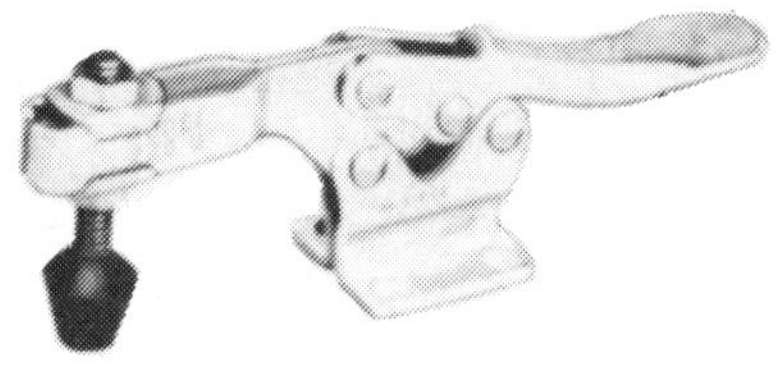

Horizontal
handle

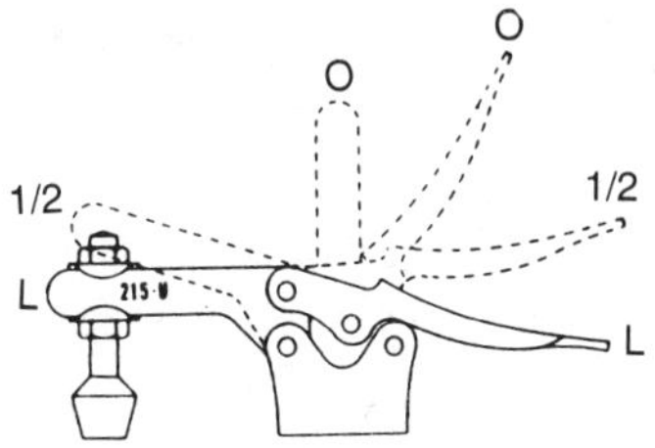

O
O
1/2
1/2
L
215-U
L

Holding capacity range to 1000 lbf (4.4 kN)

(b)

Pull-down
527

1/2
L
527
O
1/2
L
O

Holding capacity range to 2500 lbf (11.1 kN)

(c)

Fig. 3-35 Hold down action toggle clamps. (*Courtesy De-Sta-Co Div., A Dover Resources Company*)

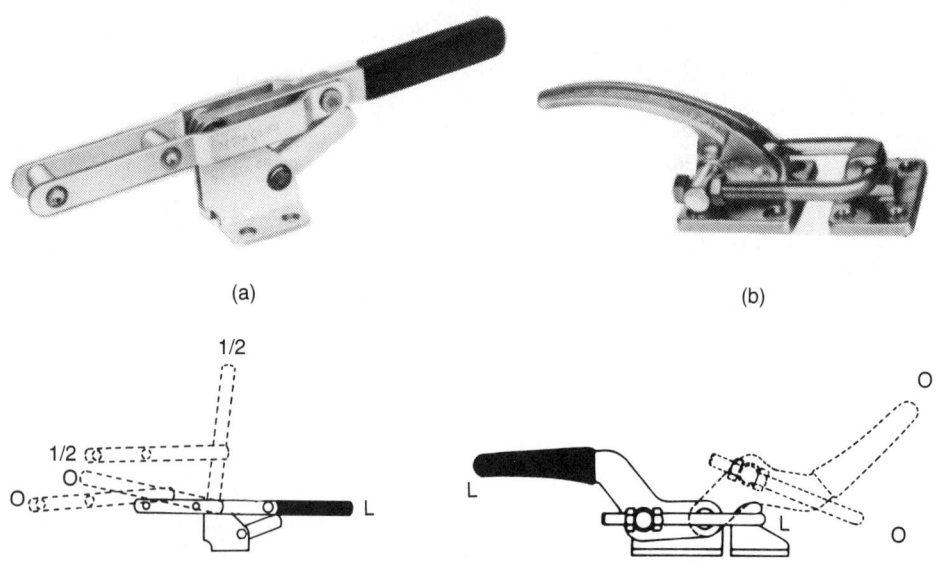

Fig. 3-36 Pull action toggle clamps. (*Courtesy De-Sta-Co Div., A Dover Resources Company*)

Plier   Pull-down

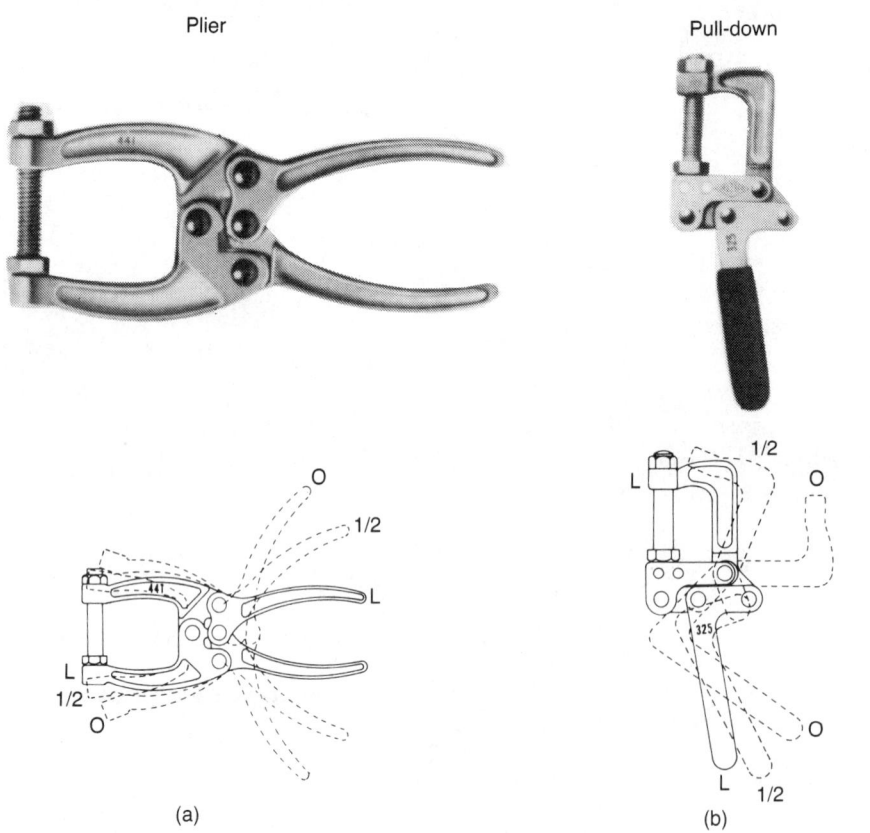

(a)   (b)

Fig. 3-37 Squeeze action toggle clamps. (*Courtesy De-Sta-Co Div., A Dover Resources Company*)

Straight action toggle clamps for push and pull clamping are shown in Fig. 3-38. Figure 3-38*a* shows regular straight line action clamps where the plunger moves forward and locks as the handle moves forward. The plunger also locks in the retracted position when the handle is moved backward. Figure 3-38*b* shows straight line action clamps with reverse handle movement; the plunger moves forward and locks as the handle is moved backward to horizontal position. The plunger retracts as the handle is moved forward, but does not lock in the retracted position.

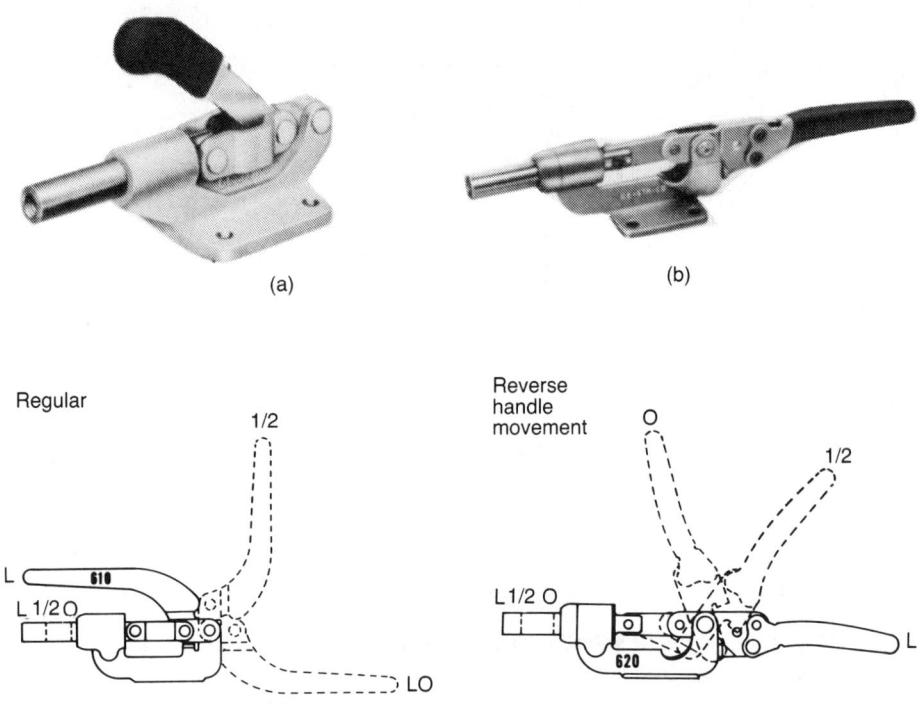

Fig. 3-38 Straight action toggle clamps. (*Courtesy De-Sta-Co Div., A Dover Resources Company*)

A patented toggle clamp is shown in Fig. 3-39 which automatically adjusts for different workpiece thicknesses and clamps with the same force anywhere within its adjustment range of 1¼ in. To set up, the contact spindle is adjusted to the average workpiece height and the desired clamping force is set by turning an adjustment screw in the handle with a screwdriver.

Air/hydraulic powered toggle clamps are shown in Fig. 3-40. Different types that are available include *a*, hold-down action with the clamping bar parallel to the cylinder; *b*, hold-down action with the bar at a right angle to the cylinder; and *c*, a straight-line (plunger) action type. These power clamps combine toggle action with air or oil cylinders.

In the unlikely event that a commercial toggle clamp is not available for a particular problem, the formulas in the following section may be useful.

Basic Toggles, Variations, and Limitations. The principle of the toggle joint is illustrated by the simple form of Fig. 3-41*a*. The two arms *AB* and *BC* are connected by a joint at *B*. At one end, *A*, a joint permits rotation only, and at the other end, *C*, lateral

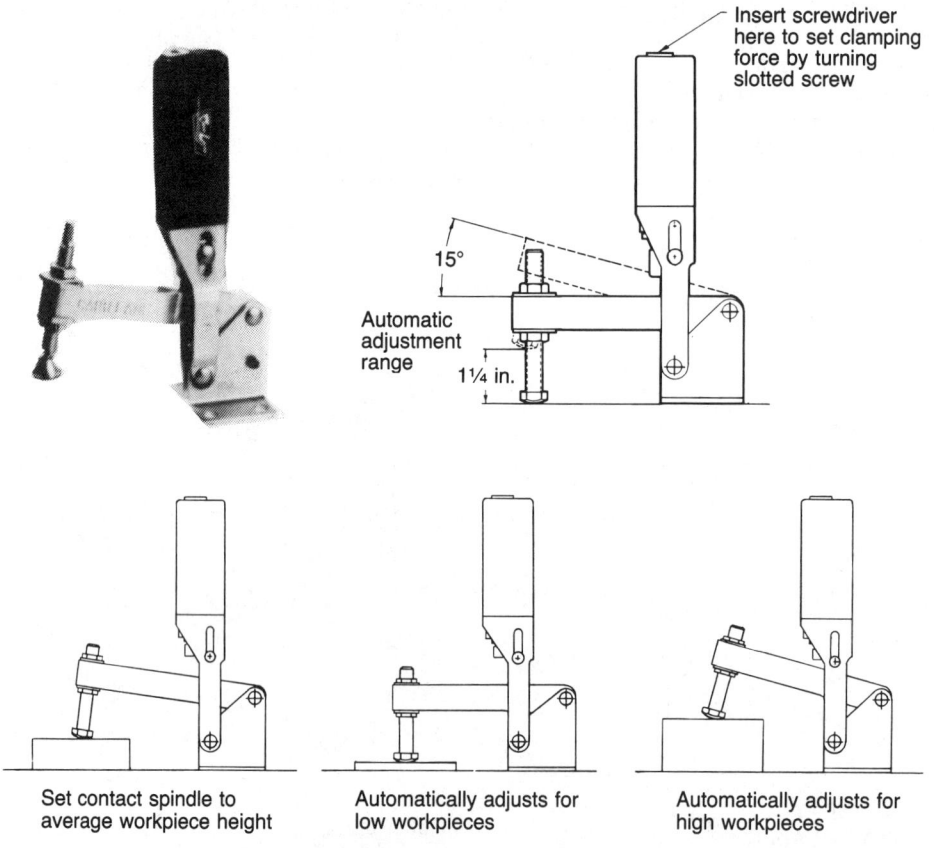

Insert screwdriver here to set clamping force by turning slotted screw

15°

Automatic adjustment range

1¼ in.

Set contact spindle to average workpiece height

Automatically adjusts for low workpieces

Automatically adjusts for high workpieces

Fig. 3-39 Automatic adjusting toggle clamp. (*Courtesy Carr Lane Mfg. Co.*)

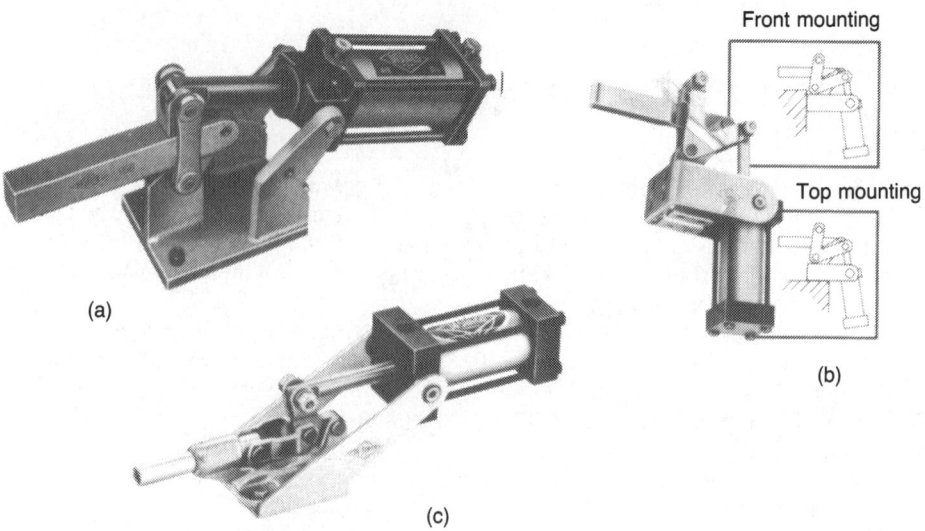

Front mounting

Top mounting

(a)

(b)

(c)

Fig. 3-40 Air/hydraulic powered toggle clamps. (*Courtesy De-Sta-Co Div., A Dover Resources Company*)

movement is possible. To oppose a force, F, applied at B, a reaction, R, at C is necessary. The force along the arm BC must have a vertical component, $F/2$, and a horizontal component, R, for equilibrium. From the force diagram,

$$\frac{R}{\dfrac{F}{2}} = \cot \alpha$$

and $\qquad R = \dfrac{F}{2} \cot \alpha$

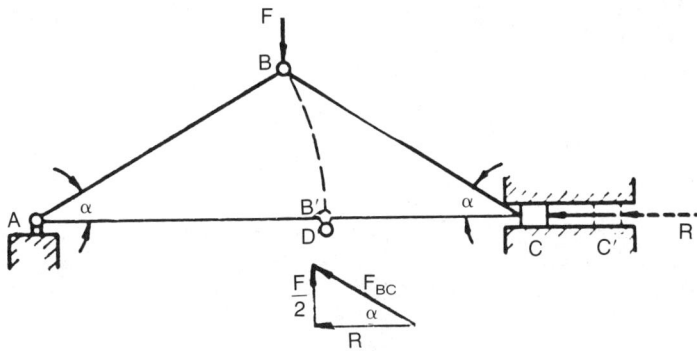

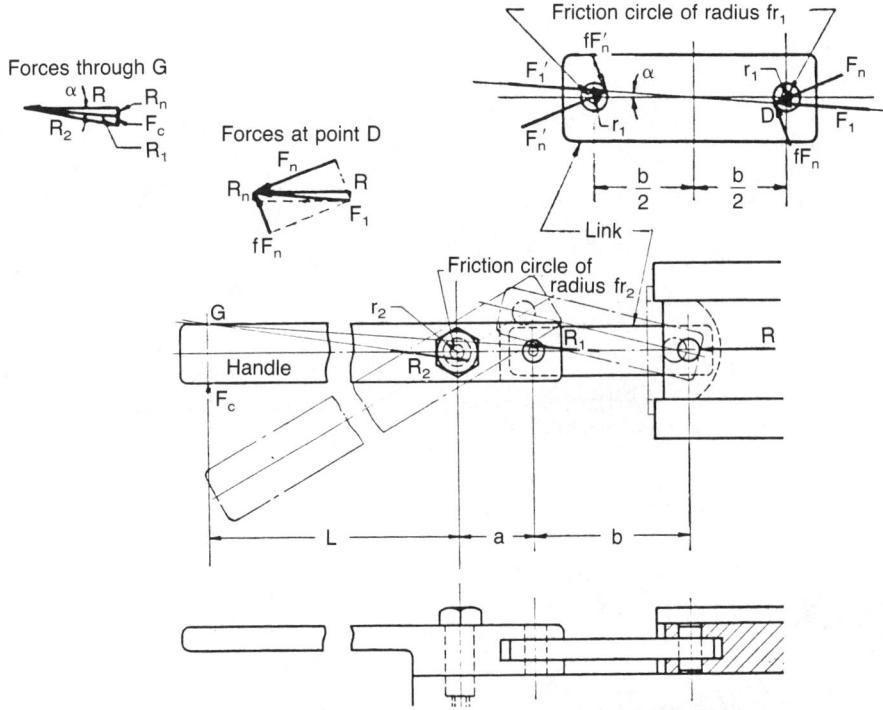

Fig. 3-41 Forces acting on a simple toggle clamp. (*The Tool and Manufacturing Engineer*)

3-41

As α decreases, cot α increases to infinity. Without friction, a force, F, of any magnitude would theoretically set up an infinite reaction, P, when α reaches 0. Actually this condition is never entirely realized in a toggle because of the friction in the joints which must be overcome by the applied force.

A number of variations of the toggle joint are utilized. The link connecting the handle and base furnishes the locking action when it is brought in line with the handle. When the handle is pulled back, it retracts the toggle bar.

A toggle linkage must be brought to a definite setting to be fully effective and locked. Variations must be taken up by flexure in the linkage.

Forces in a Toggle Clamp. The forces acting on a toggle clamp are shown in Fig. 3-41b. The clamp is actuated by a clamping force, F_c, at a lever arm distance, L, and meets a reaction, R, in the fully engaged position. At each of its pin connections, the link is subjected to a force, F_1. These forces act in the same line and are tangent to the friction circles around the centers of the pins. The angle at which the forces F_1 act from the line of centers is small so that

$$\sin \alpha = \tan \alpha = \frac{fr_1}{\dfrac{b}{2}} = \frac{2f\,r_1}{b}$$

The smaller r_1 is in comparison with b, the smaller are sin α and α, and the more closely R, F_1, and R_1 are alike.

The diagram of the forces acting on the handle is shown in Fig. 3-41b. From that diagram,

$$R_2{}^2 = R^2 + (F_c + R_n)^2$$

But R_n is quite small, so a close approximation is

$$R_2 = \sqrt{R^2 + F_c{}^2}$$

Formulas:

Since

$$\frac{F_{c\,max}}{F_{c\,min}} = \frac{R_{t\,max}}{R_{t\,min}}$$

$$R_{t\,max} = \frac{F_{c\,max} \times R_{T\,min}}{F_{c\,min}}$$

$$r_1 = 0.47 \frac{R_t}{S_s} \tag{23}$$

$$r_2 = \frac{0.67}{S_s} \times \sqrt[4]{R_{t\,max}^2 + F_{c\,max}^2} \tag{24}$$

$$L = \frac{fr_2\sqrt{R_t^2 + F_c^2} + \dfrac{2a + b}{b} \times fr_1 R_t}{F_c} \tag{25}$$

where:

r_1 = link pin radius (based on 0.2 coefficient of friction)

S_s = allowable shear stress

r_2 = pivot pin radius (based on 0.2 coefficient of friction

L = length of lower arm

f = coefficient of friction

a = pin centerdistance—pivot to link

b = pin centerdistance on link

$F_{c\,max}$ = max. input force

$F_{c\,min}$ = min. input force

R_{max} = max. clamping force

$R_{t\,min}$ = min. clamping force

Example 7: A fixture is closed by a toggle such as shown in Fig. 3-41*b*. The pin centerdistance of the link is 1 in. The pin centerdistance from the pivot to the link is 0.625 in. A minimum clamping force of 2,000 lbf (8.9 kN) is required on the workpiece. The handle should be designed to provide clamping with an applied force of 15 lbf (67 N). Linkage should be able to withstand an applied force of 90 lbf (400 N). The coefficient of friction is assumed to be 0.15 and the allowable shear stress on hardened alloy steel pins is 75,000 psi (517 MPa). Determine the diameter of the link and pivot pins, and the length of handle necessary to apply the minimum clamping force.

Calculations:

$$R_{t\,max} = \frac{F_{c\,max} \times R_{t\,min}}{F_{c\,min}} \tag{13}$$

$$= \frac{90 \times 2,000}{15}$$

$$= 12,000 \text{ lbf}$$

$$r_1 = 0.47 \left(\frac{12,000}{75,000} \right) \tag{23}$$

= 0.188 in. link pin radius. A ⅜ in. diameter link pin would suffice.

$$r_2 = \frac{0.67}{\sqrt{75,000}} \times \sqrt[4]{12,000^2 + 90^2} \tag{24}$$

$$= 0.00245 \times 109.55$$

= 0.268 in. pivot pin radius. This can be rounded out to a 9/16 in. diameter pivot pin.

$$L = \frac{0.15 \times 0.281 \sqrt{2,000^2 + 15^2} + \frac{2 \times 0.625 + 1}{1} (0.15 \times 0.188 \times 2,000)}{15} \tag{25}$$

3-43

= 14.06 in.   Length of lever arm

To provide for operator's grasp, the handle should be made 15½ in. long.

Rack-and-pinion Clamps. The Rack-and-pinion type clamp uses the motion of a rack to transmit a clamping force. The rack is moved axially by the pinion gear as it is rotated to either clamp or release a workpiece. Rack-and-pinion devices usually require a locking mechanism since motion through the system is reversible. They are often used in conjunction with other clamping devices such as cams and self-locking wedges.

One example of a rack-and-pinion system was already illustrated in Fig. 3-20, where it was used in conjunction with a cam. Some additional applications are shown in Fig. 3-42. Perhaps the most recognizable example is the arbor press, *a*. Figure 3-42*b* uses the translation of rotary action of the handle into a linear movement for use as fixture locks, jigs, etc. Holding power is provided by perfectly mated male and female cones. The male cones are on the pinion shaft, while the female cones are an integral part of the base. The rotary actuator, *c*, uses an air-operated rack to transmit a rotary force to the pinion gears to raise or lower a drill plate.

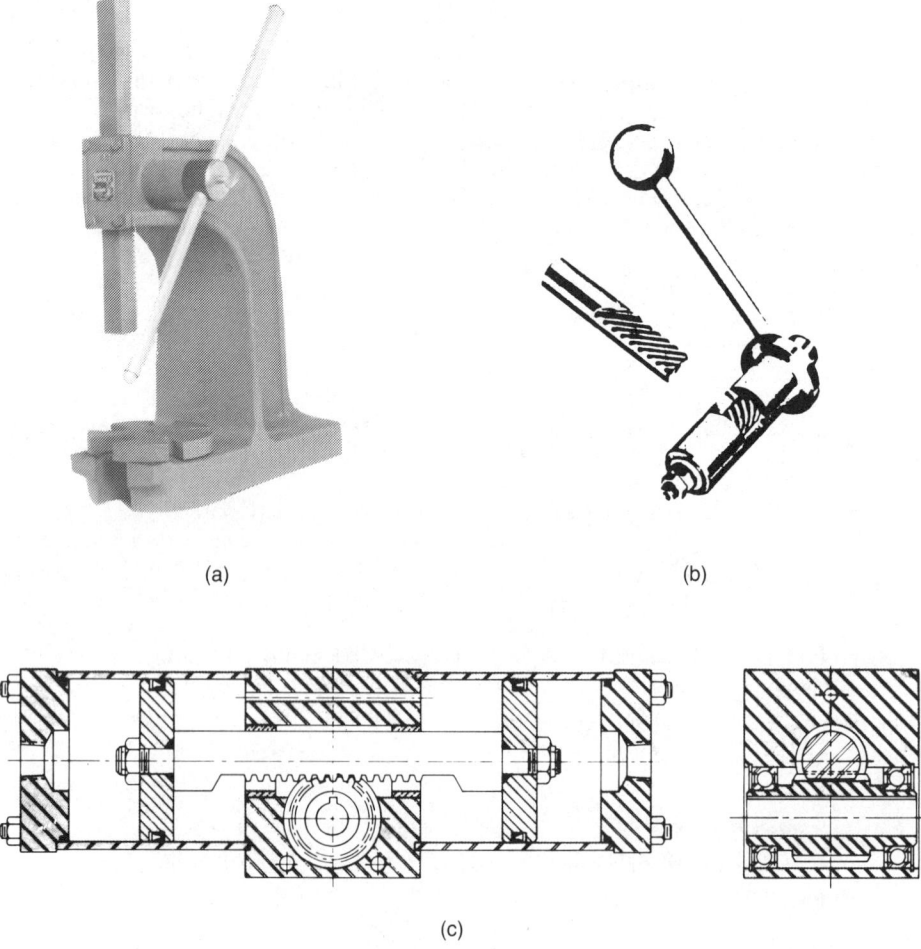

(a)   (b)

(c)

Fig. 3-42 Rack-and-pinion systems. (*Courtesy (a) Dake Div., JSJ Corp.*; (*c*) *Universal Vise and Tool Co.*)

Miscellaneous Clamps. The clamps mentioned in this chapter represent only a small portion of the commercial off-the-shelf varieties that are available. Any tool designer would find it well worth the effort to browse through as many component manufacturer's catalogs as possible.

Some of the more notable clamps not mentioned are included in the following pages. Others will be discussed in the future chapters, especially the chapters on NC milling and tooling.

For one-of-a-kind setups, many clamping arrangements are available. One of the most widely used is the step-clamp kit shown in Fig. 3-43 which consists of an assortment of various size step blocks, matching step clamps, studs, flange nuts, and T-nuts.

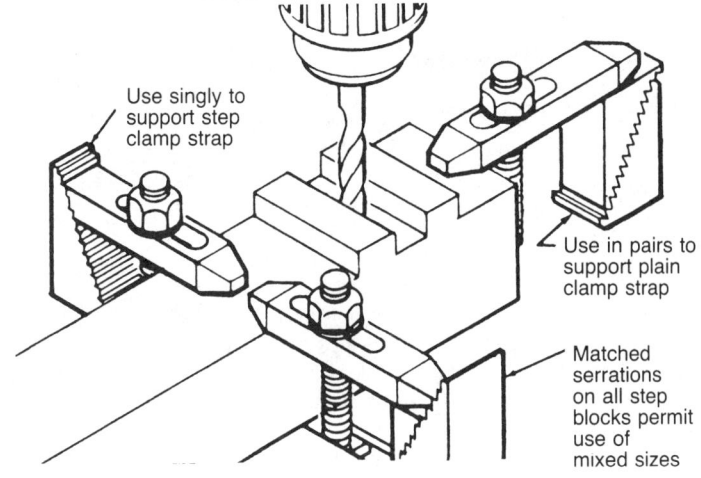

Use singly to support step clamp strap

Use in pairs to support plain clamp strap

Matched serrations on all step blocks permit use of mixed sizes

Fig. 3-43 Step blocks and clamp straps. (*Courtesy American Drill Bushing Co.*)

T-slot clamps (see Fig. 3-44) are an excellent alternative to conventional step clamps. Their one-piece construction provides the same flexibility as the step clamps, but without the need to assemble individual details. Clamp straps slide for loading clearance and can be rotated 180° for use as a straight or gooseneck strap.

Another series of clamps useful for clamping parts directly on the machine table are shown in Fig. 3-45. The machine clamps, *a*, provide a positive clamping action as the sliding jaw moves forward and downward to prevent the workpiece from lifting during machining. They can also be used to hold non-magnetic material on magnetic base plates.

The flat clamps, *b*, provide for low-profile edge clamping that leaves the top surface of the workpiece clear for machining. The slot clamps, *c*, can be used to clamp plates as thin as ⅛ in. since the portion of the clamping mechanism is located in the slot area. The swing machine clamps, *d*, use a hinge type clamping action to provide a forward and downward clamping force to hold the workpiece. These clamps can also be used to hold non-magnetic materials on magnetic base plates.

Still another kit of setup equipment for locating, clamping, holding, and supporting the workpiece directly to the machine table is shown in Fig. 3-46. Included are adjustable parallel support blocks, *a*; matched set up blocks, *b*, of various thicknesses; adjustable jacks, *c*, ranging in height from 2.75 to 23 in. (70 to 585 mm); leveling wedges, *d*; chuck jaw parallel blocks, *e*, which can be used either as a support unit or holding vise; pressure clamps, *f*; pipe jacks and pipes, *g*, ranging in length from 18 to 52 in. (560 to 1320 mm); pin hole thrust pins, *h*, for positioning various types and sizes of workpieces;

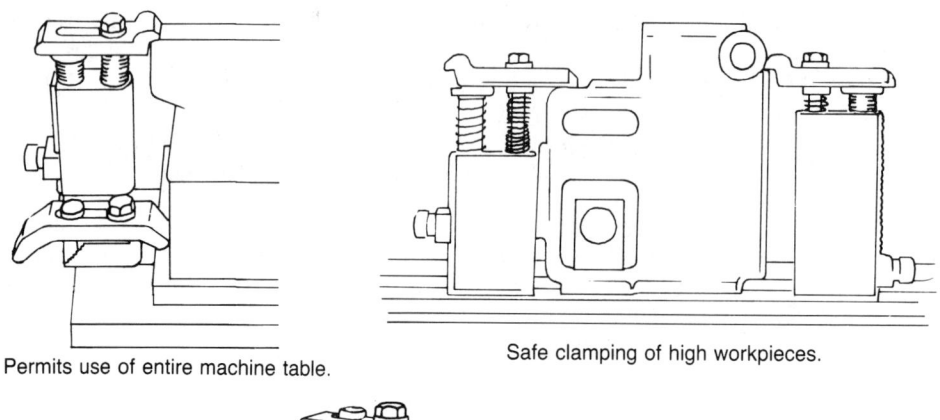

Permits use of entire machine table.

Safe clamping of high workpieces.

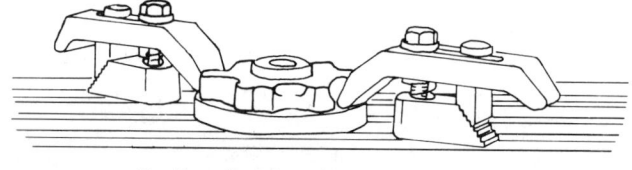

Positive clamping of low-profile work

Fig. 3-44 T-slot clamps. (*Courtesy Carr Lane Mfg. Co.*)

T-slot thrust blocks, *i*; and adjustable clamp posts, *j*, covering a range from 2 ⅞ to 68 in. (73 to 1727 mm). Also included are various size U-clamps, *k*; offset V-clamps, *l*; pin type V-clamps, *m*; and the necessary studs, T-bolts, and T-slot stud holders for attachment to the machine table.

The system shown in Fig. 3-47 consists of a variety of straps, jacks, bases, support tubes, and couplings along with a selection of T-slot nuts, threaded studs, coupling nuts, hexnuts, and washers which can be assembled in combinations to provide clamping from 0 to 60 in. (0 to 1524 mm). A milling machine T-square is often used with these clamping systems, sometimes by attaching the clamp directly to the T-square.

The clamps shown in Fig. 3-48 are self-contained, T-slot clamps capable of handling workpieces up to 18 in. high. Two or more heads can be combined on one base to position and hold down as well as support the workpiece. The clamps are designed to deliver 100% of the holding force onto the workpiece.

The edge grip clamps shown in Fig. 3-49 consist of two separate pieces which can be mounted to the T-slot table to hold any length workpiece that will fit on the table. Clamping action is both horizontal and downward to force, as well as clamp, the workpiece onto the table.

Figure 3-50 shows a self-adjusting universal hold down clamp suitable for clamping jigs and fixtures to the machine table or for holding parts directly on the table.

The hinge clamp shown in Fig. 3-51 can be swung completely clear of a workpiece when released to provide fast and free access to the workpiece.

Vises. Vises are among the most widely known and used workholders. They are available in a wide variety of styles, many of which are quite inexpensive. Figure 3-52 shows some of the universal type vises that are readily available. The machinist's vise, *a*, is a general purpose vise used mainly to hold a workpiece for hand operations. Machine vises, *b*, are generally set up on a machine for a particular operation. Once set up and properly secured to the machine, they are used to locate and clamp the workpiece against the fixed jaw with the same movement of the handle.

Once the vise has been set up on the machine, the accuracy of the machining operation depends on the ability of the vise to repeatedly locate and hold successive

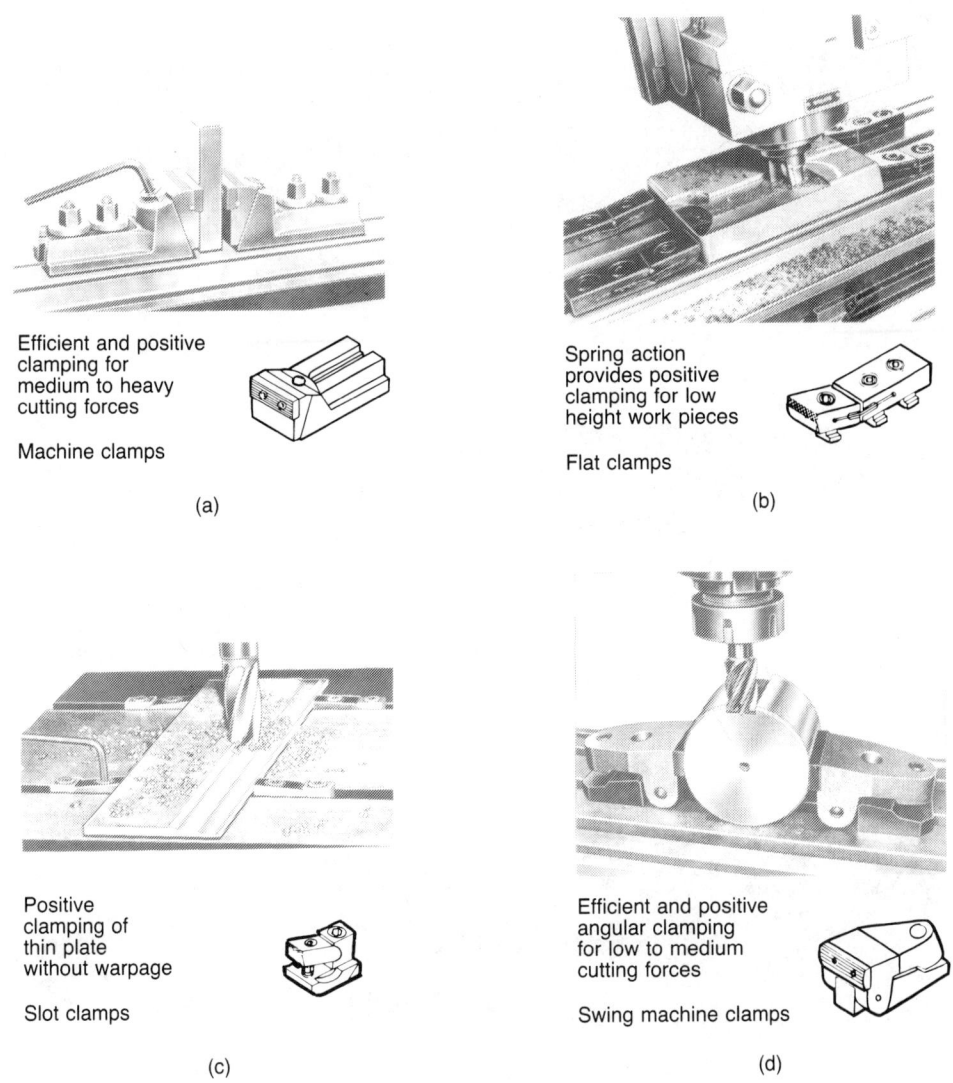

Efficient and positive clamping for medium to heavy cutting forces

Machine clamps

(a)

Spring action provides positive clamping for low height work pieces

Flat clamps

(b)

Positive clamping of thin plate without warpage

Slot clamps

(c)

Efficient and positive angular clamping for low to medium cutting forces

Swing machine clamps

(d)

Fig. 3-45 T-slot edge clamps. (*Courtesy James Morton, Inc.*)

workpieces in the same position within specifications. For this reason it is imperative that the vise selected to do the job be distortion-free and have the necessary repeatability.

Many operations require that the workpiece be precisely centered for machining. Self-centering vises are used for this purpose. The vise shown in Fig. 3-52c is an air-operated, self-centering vise capable of centering a workpiece within ±0.001 in. Self-centering vises are also available for mechanical or hydraulic operation. For angled operations, sine vises set with gage blocks and direct-reading angle vises are available. A simple sine vise is shown in *d*, while a vise for setting compound angles is shown in *e*. The direct-reading vise, *f*, is set with protractor and vernier dials. The vise jaws on this vise can also be swiveled in either direction. The direct-reading compound angle vise, *g*, uses accurate machine cut graduations for settings. This vise can also be swiveled to any angle since it can rotate 360°.

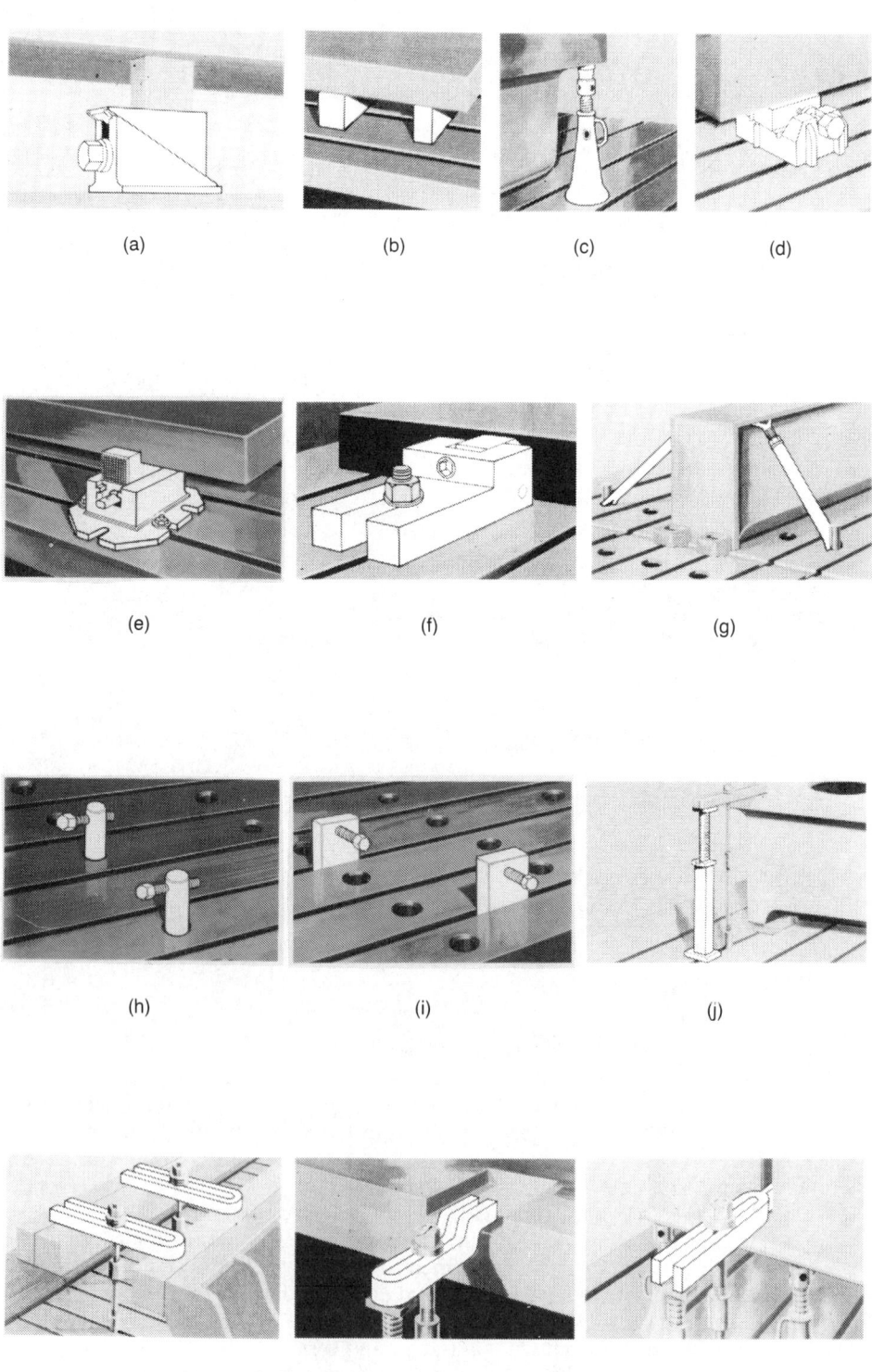

(a)   (b)   (c)   (d)

(e)   (f)   (g)

(h)   (i)   (j)

(k)   (l)   (m)

Fig. 3-46 Setup clamps and accessories. (*Courtesy Ingersoll Milling Machine Co.*)

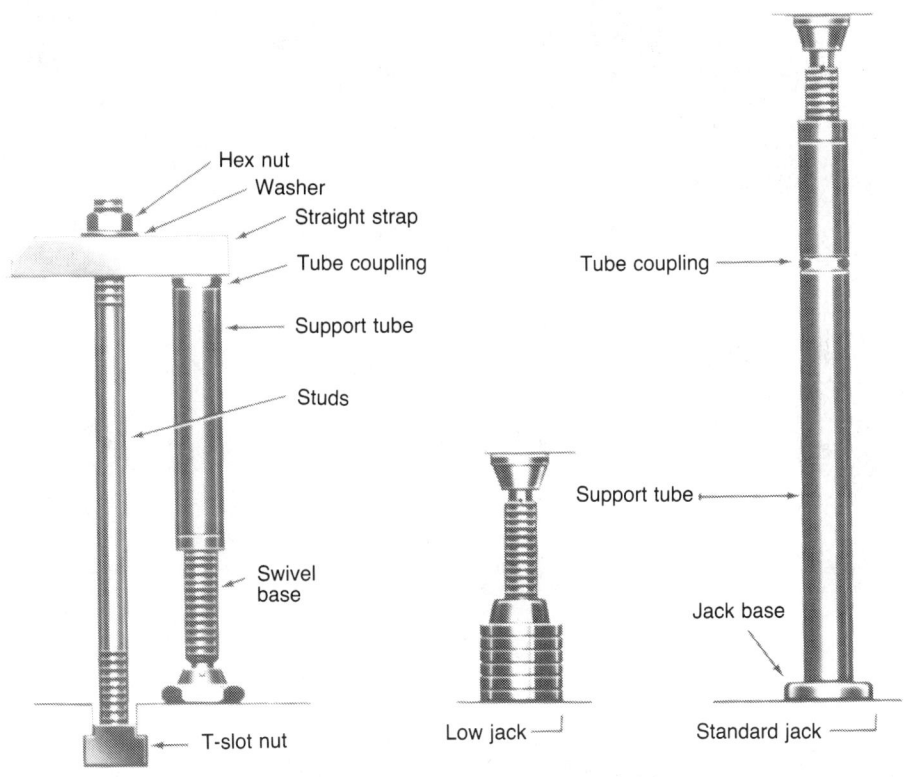

Hex nut
Washer
Straight strap
Tube coupling
Support tube
Studs
Swivel base
T-slot nut

Tube coupling
Support tube
Jack base

Low jack
Standard jack

Fig. 3-47 Clamping system. (*"Clamp-N-Jack" setup system, courtesy Universal Vise & Tool Co.*)

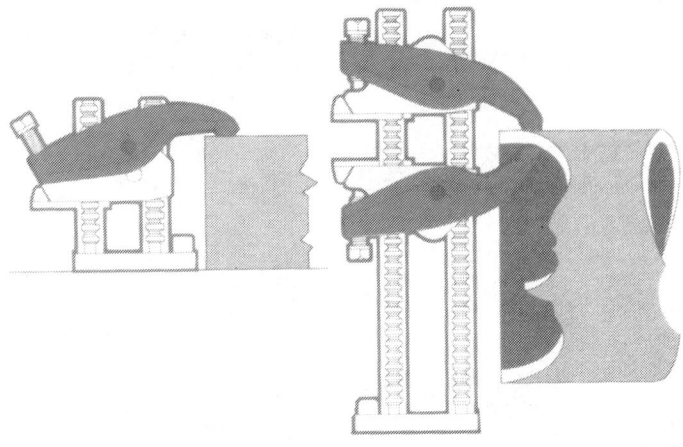

Fig. 3-48 Clamps. (*Carver clamps, courtesy De-Sta-Co Div., A Dover Resources Company*)

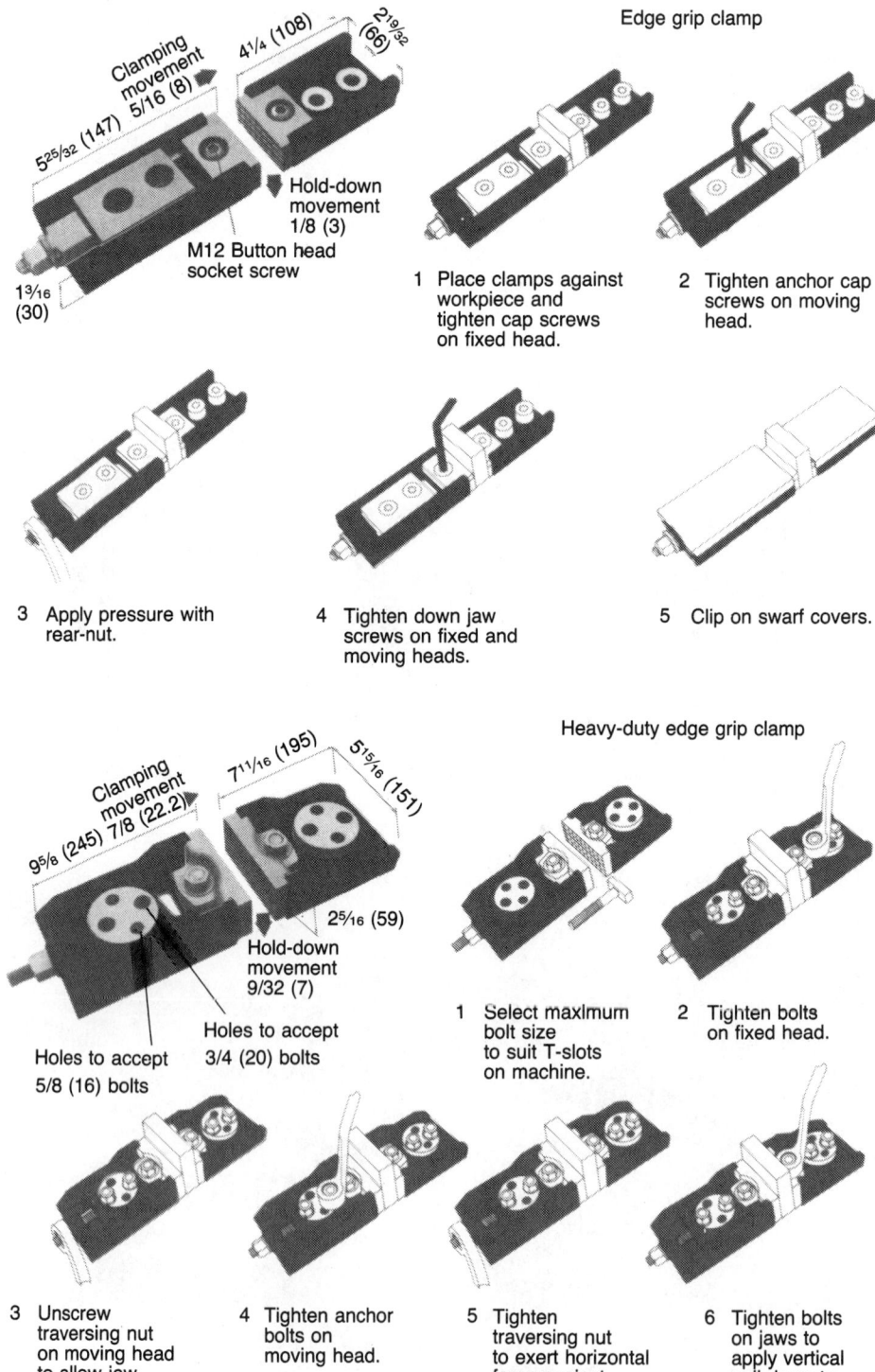

Edge grip clamp

Clamping movement 5/16 (8)
$5^{25}/_{32}$ (147)
$4^{1}/_4$ (108)
$2^{19}/_{32}$ (66)
Hold-down movement 1/8 (3)
M12 Button head socket screw
$1^{3}/_{16}$ (30)

1 Place clamps against workpiece and tighten cap screws on fixed head.

2 Tighten anchor cap screws on moving head.

3 Apply pressure with rear-nut.

4 Tighten down jaw screws on fixed and moving heads.

5 Clip on swarf covers.

Heavy-duty edge grip clamp

Clamping movement 7/8 (22.2)
$9^{5}/_8$ (245)
$7^{11}/_{16}$ (195)
$5^{15}/_{16}$ (151)
$2^{5}/_{16}$ (59)
Hold-down movement 9/32 (7)
Holes to accept 3/4 (20) bolts
Holes to accept 5/8 (16) bolts

1 Select maximum bolt size to suit T-slots on machine.

2 Tighten bolts on fixed head.

3 Unscrew traversing nut on moving head to allow jaw assembly to be moved forward.

4 Tighten anchor bolts on moving head.

5 Tighten traversing nut to exert horizontal force against workpiece.

6 Tighten bolts on jaws to apply vertical pull-down to machine bed.

Fig. 3-49 Edge grip clamps. (*Courtesy De-Sta-Co Div., A Dover Resources Company*)

3-50

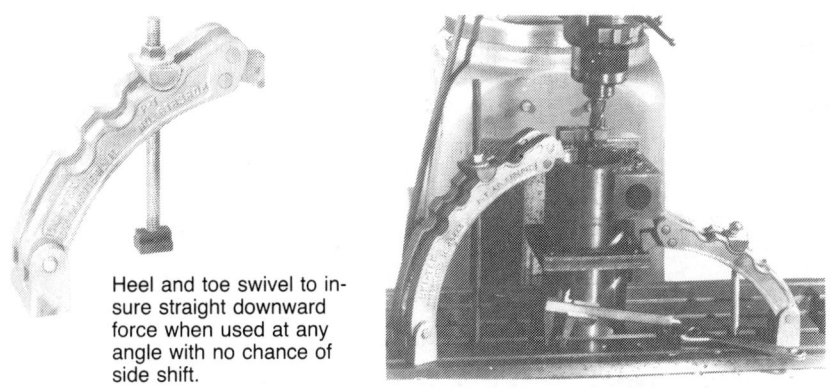

Heel and toe swivel to insure straight downward
force when used at any
angle with no chance of
side shift.

Fig. 3-50 Self-adjusting hold-down clamp. (*Courtesy Uni-Tek Mfg. Co.*)

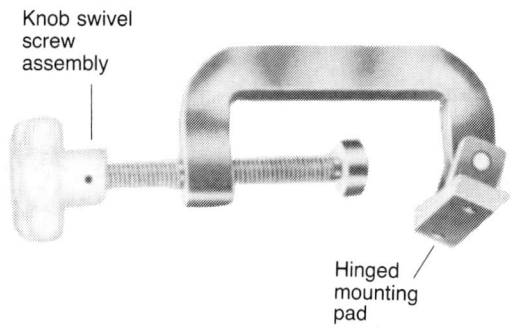

Knob swivel
screw
assembly

Hinged
mounting
pad

Fig. 3-51 Hinge clamp. (*Courtesy American Drill Bushing Co.*)

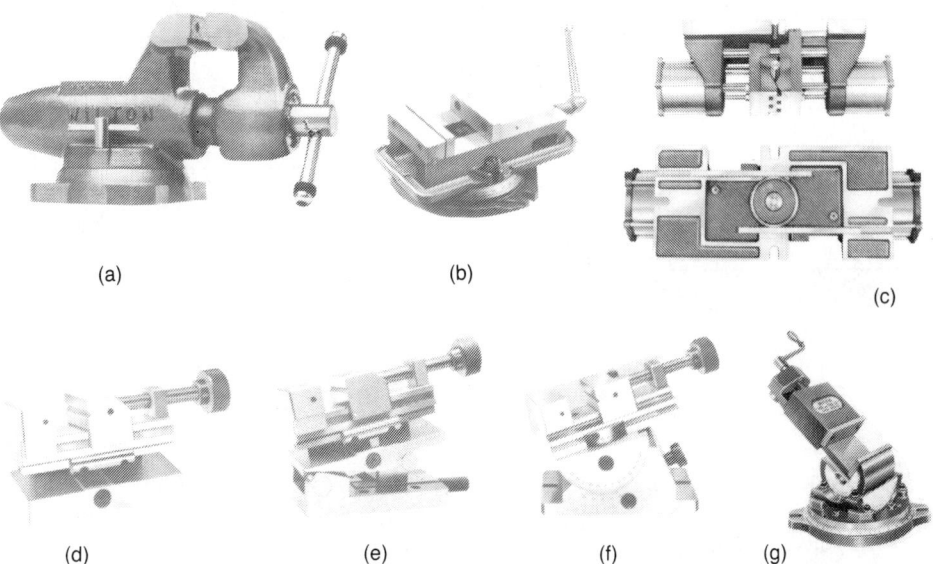

(a)

(b)

(c)

(d)

(e)

(f)

(g)

Fig. 3-52 Vises. (*Courtesy (a) and (b), Wilton; (c), Heinrich Tools, Inc.; (d) thru (f), Grinding Technology, Inc.; (g), Universal Vise & Tool Co.*)

Many other types of vises are available for machining operations. These will be discussed later in the various machining chapters.

Interchangeable jaws are available for most of the vises previously discussed. Some of these are shown in Fig. 3-53.

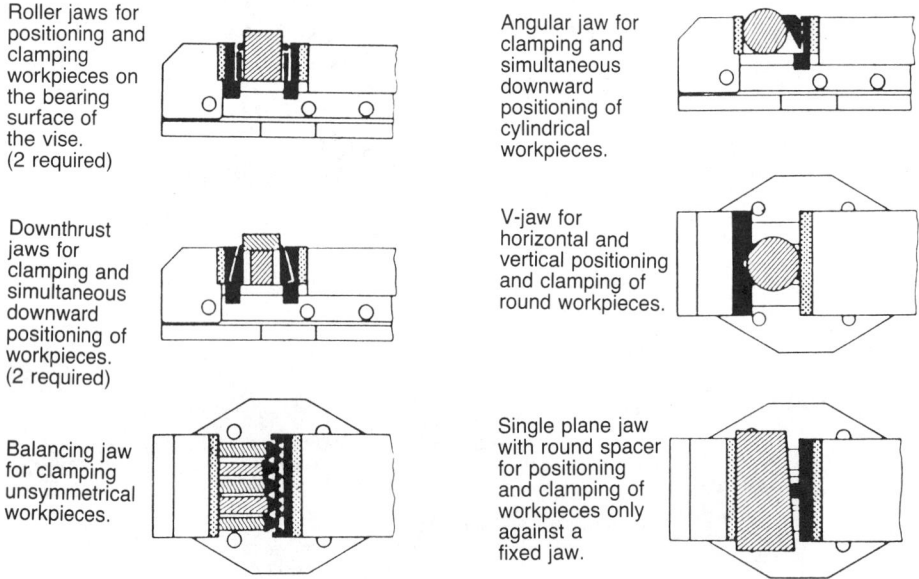

Roller jaws for positioning and clamping workpieces on the bearing surface of the vise. (2 required)

Angular jaw for clamping and simultaneous downward positioning of cylindrical workpieces.

Downthrust jaws for clamping and simultaneous downward positioning of workpieces. (2 required)

V-jaw for horizontal and vertical positioning and clamping of round workpieces.

Balancing jaw for clamping unsymmetrical workpieces.

Single plane jaw with round spacer for positioning and clamping of workpieces only against a fixed jaw.

Fig. 3-53 Interchangeable vise jaws. (*Courtesy Jergens, Inc.*)

The universal swivel blocks shown in Fig. 3-54 can be used with machining vises to securely clamp workpieces with irregular surfaces, tapers, or compound angles. It can eliminate the unreliable method of using shim stock to compensate for these irregularities. In extreme cases, two small units can be used with one larger unit by placing the two smaller units in line with the ball pads of the larger unit. Typical applications of universal swivel blocks are shown in Fig. 3-55.

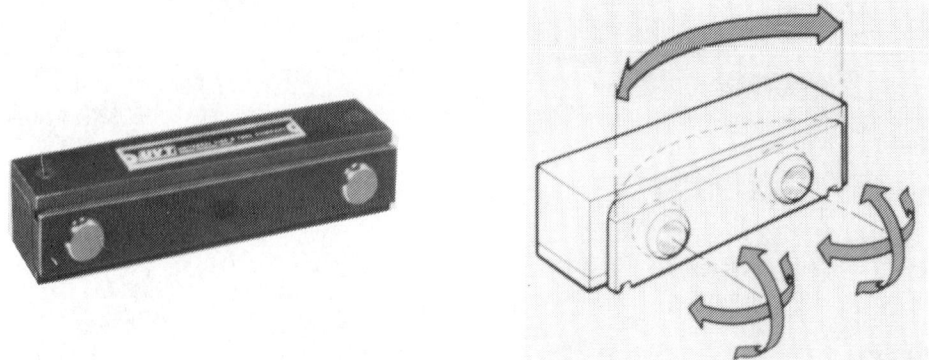

Fig. 3-54 Universal swivel block. (*Courtesy Precision Devices, Inc.*)

The self-adjusting, variable contour vise jaw, shown in Fig. 3-56, features multiple jaws each mounted to individual, hydraulically connected pistons. These pistons interact to the normal pressure applied when tightening the vise jaws, causing the jaws to adjust to the irregular contour of the workpiece and clamp it firmly in place.

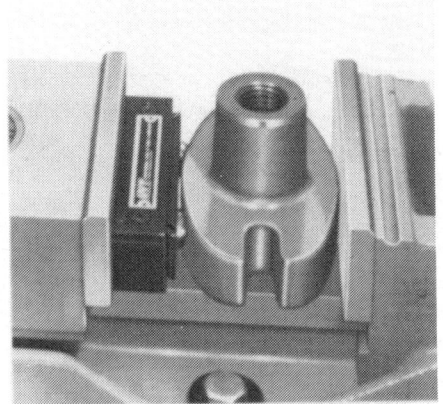

Fig. 3-55 Typical applications of universal swivel blocks. (*Courtesy Precision Devices, Inc.*)

Fig. 3-56 Self-adjusting variable contour vise jaw. (*Courtesy Hydra-Jaw Co.*)

Figure 3-57 shows a multi-purpose vise that can be quickly set up to hold an odd-shaped workpiece securely for machining. To set up, the jaw stacks are first arranged to the configuration of the workpiece to be held. The lower jaws of each stack are then pushed out at the required height for parallels and both cams are locked to hold the jaw stacks in position. Figure 3-58 illustrates some of the possible applications.

The versatile, self-centering vise shown in Fig. 3-59 can be used with special jaws designed with cavities into which a sample part can be placed and surrounded with an epoxy resin or paste to make a form fitting workholder in less than an hour. A sketch of the jaws and sizes that are available is shown in Fig. 3-60.

Often vises can be used alone, or with one of the off-the-shelf jaws that are commercially available. For example, any machine vise with V-locator jaws could be used to drill and tap a noncritical hole in the center of a production lot of short shafts. This is done by merely positioning and clamping the vise to a drill press table so that the V-locator on the vise is properly positioned on the center of the shaft beneath the tool. The vise could also be used to straddle-mill a tang on a production lot of relatively soft parts. This could be done by properly positioning and clamping the vise to the milling

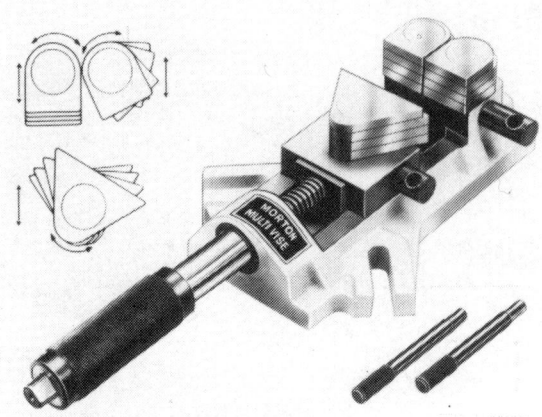

Fig. 3-57 Multi-purpose vise. (*Courtesy James Morton, Inc.*)

machine table, in the proper relationship to the reference surface that located the tang, and using a standard work stop such as shown in Fig. 3-61.

For even more versatility, vise jaws can be modified in many ways, such as shown in Fig. 3-62. From the figure it can be seen that:

1. Round parts can be held in various types of V-blocks.
2. Jaws can be extended horizontally or vertically to increase the capacity of the vise.
3. Guide pins and tongue and groove jaws can be used for accurate alignment for close tolerance work.
4. Jaws can be angled to hold workpieces requiring angular machining.
5. Equalizers can be added for multiple workpiece machining.
6. Auxiliary devices can be added to further locate and hold the workpiece.
7. Ejectors can even be added to simplify the removal of workpieces.

Pneumatic and hydraulic versions of many of the previously discussed vises are finding wide use in industry where clamping must be fast and uniform; especially when used in conjunction with other power workholding systems. Pneumatic and hydraulic systems work in much the same way, with the main difference being in the size of the cylinders since pneumatic systems work with pressures around 100 psi (690 kPa) while hydraulic systems work with pressures up to 10,000 psi (70 MPa).

Magnetic Workholding Devices. The most widely used magnetic workholding devices are the electromagnetic and permanent magnet versions of the chucks shown in Fig. 3-63, along with their accessories. Heavy duty models of electromagnetic chucks, *a*, provide sufficient power for heavy stock removal operation such as milling, planing, and grinding. The rotary chuck, *b*, with the radial pole design is recommended for holding circular workpieces, while the rotary chuck with the concentric gap design, *c*, is used for holding workpieces nested together. Magnetic parallels and V-blocks, *d*, are used with the chucks to hold workpieces which cannot easily be held directly on the chuck surface. The magnetic holding force is transmitted through them to the workpiece.

The patented hold-downs, *e*, can be used to hold any rigid nonmagnetic workpiece on a permanent magnet chuck by placing one member of the hold-down against the back plate of the chuck, then placing the workpiece on the chuck surface between, and in tight contact with, the other member. When the chuck is energized, the jaws of the

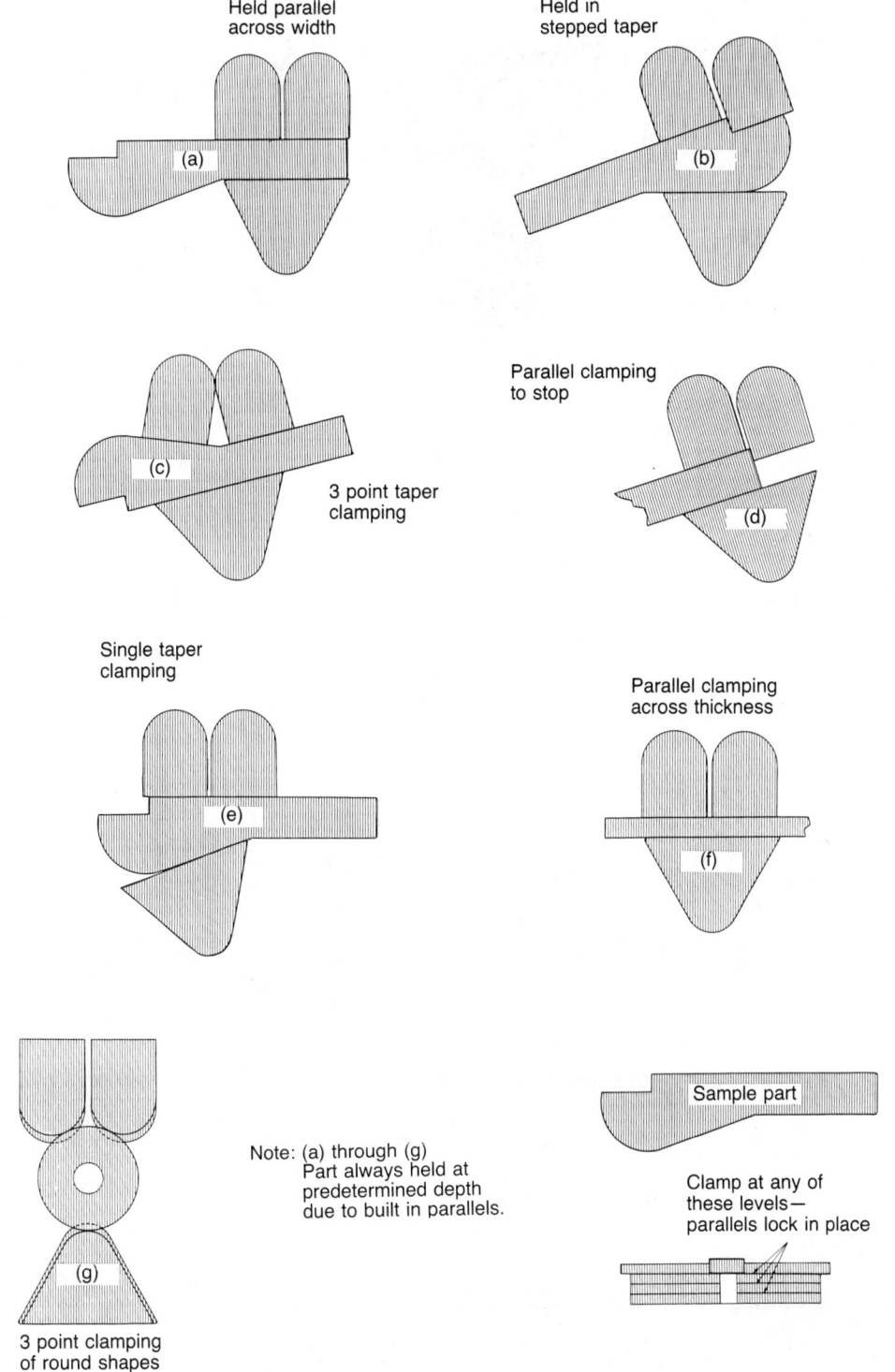

Held parallel
across width

(a)

Held in
stepped taper

(b)

(c)

3 point taper
clamping

Parallel clamping
to stop

(d)

Single taper
clamping

(e)

Parallel clamping
across thickness

(f)

(g)

3 point clamping
of round shapes

Note: (a) through (g)
Part always held at
predetermined depth
due to built in parallels.

Sample part

Clamp at any of
these levels—
parallels lock in place

Fig. 3-58 Applications using a multi-vise. (*Courtesy James Morton, Inc.*)

Fig. 3-59 Quick-tooled casting for drilling and tapping on a 6-in. vise. (*Sure Center vise, courtesy Schmitz Industries, Inc.*)

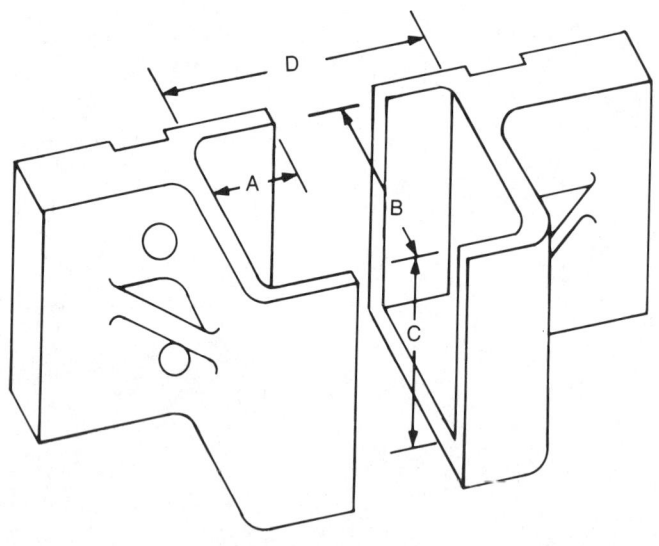

Code	A	Cavity Dim B	C	Maximum D	To Fit
6 qt (5.7 l)	0.6875 in. (17.5 mm)	1.625 in. (41.3 mm)	2.375 in. (60.3 mm)	3 in. (76.2 mm)	6 in. (152.4 mm) Vise
8 qt (7.6 l)	1 in. (25.4 mm)	2 in. (50.8 mm)	3.375 in. (85.7 mm)	4.5 in. (114.3 mm)	8 in. (203.2 mm) Vise
14 qt (13.2 l)	1.5 in. (38.1 mm)	3 in. (76.2 mm)	4.375 in. (111.1 mm)	9 in. (228.6 mm)	14 in. (355.6 mm) Vise

Fig. 3-60 Jaws for casting a form-fitted workholding device. (*Courtesy Schmitz Industries, Inc.*)

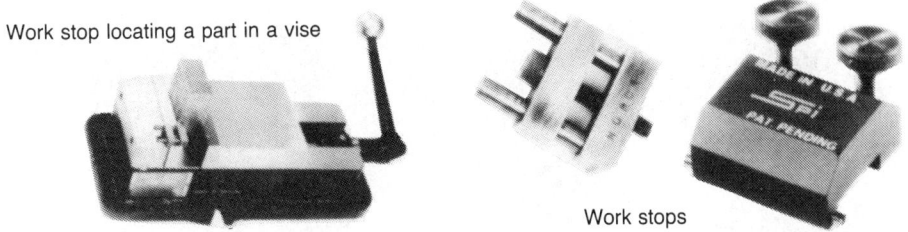

Work stop locating a part in a vise

Work stops

Fig. 3-61 Work stops for machine vises. (*Courtesy Swiss Precision Instruments, Inc.*)

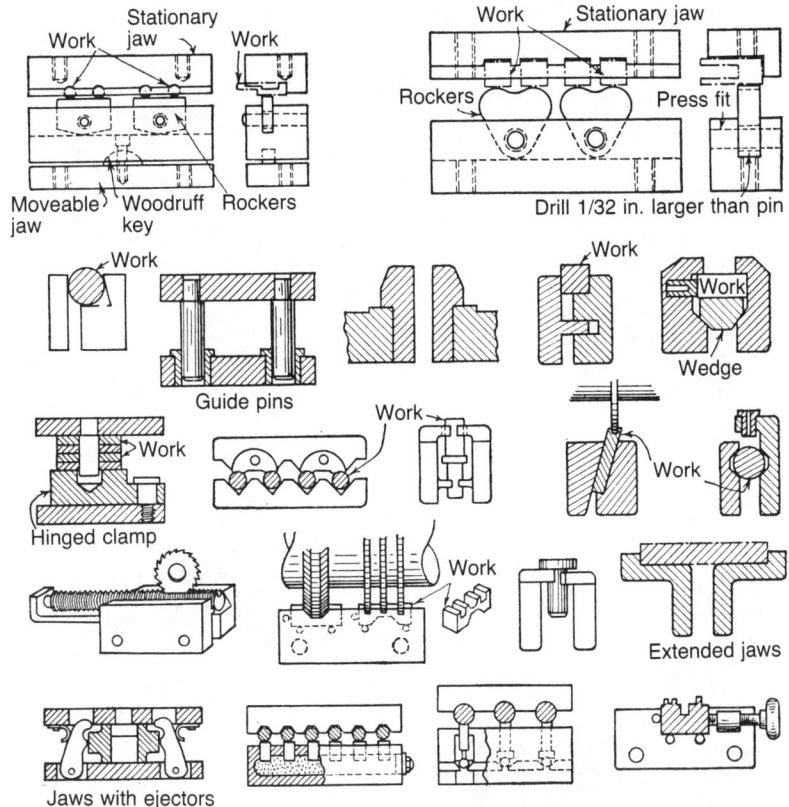

Fig. 3-62 Vise jaw modifications.

clamps are pulled toward the face of the chuck thereby wedging the workpiece securely in place against the face of the chuck.

Some other magnetic workholding devices are shown in Fig. 3-64. These permanent magnet devices perform some of the same functions as the accessories shown previously in Fig. 3-63d, but without the need of the chuck. They must however be used on a magnetically conductive surface. The block, a, V-block, b, and toolmaker's knee, c, are ideal for holding small workpieces for toolmaking, light machining, or inspection purposes.

The holding power of magnetic chucks, of either the permanent magnet or the electromagnet type, is dependent upon the attractive force of the magnets incorporated. The effective force holding the workpiece is dependent upon the amount, direction, and

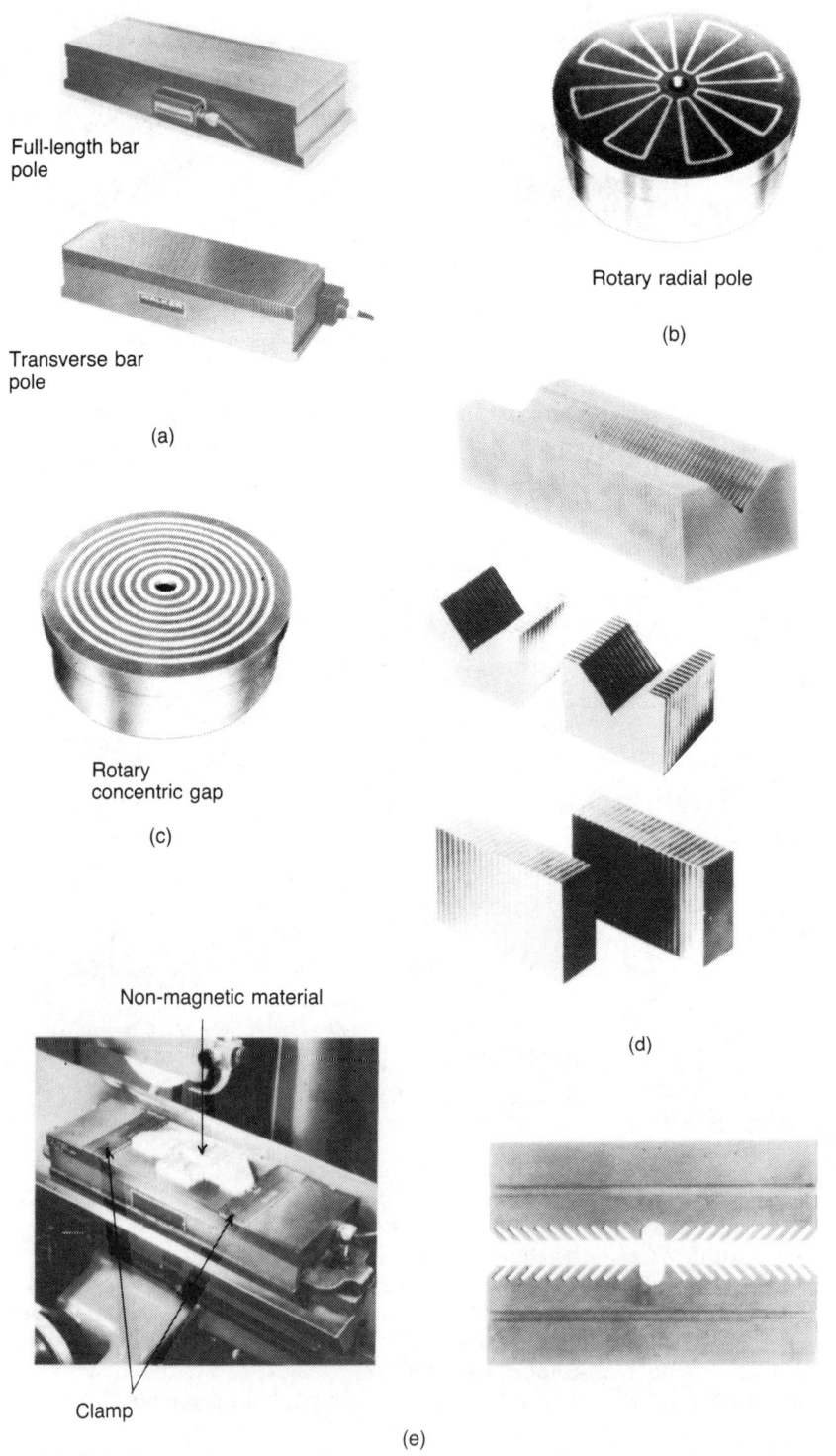

Full-length bar
pole

Transverse bar
pole

(a)

Rotary radial pole

(b)

Rotary
concentric gap

(c)

(d)

Non-magnetic material

Clamp

(e)

Fig. 3-63 Magnetic chucks and accessories. (*Courtesy (a) thru (c), O.S. Walker; (d) and (e), Brown and Sharpe Mfg. Co.*)

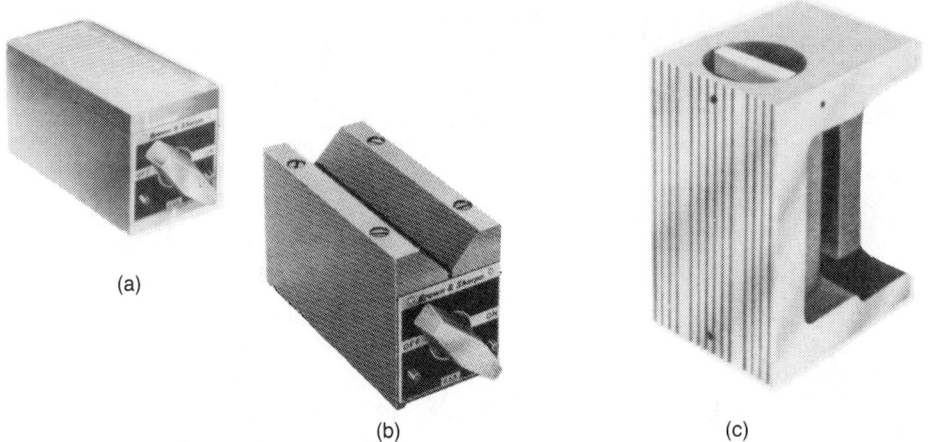

(a)

(b)   (c)

Fig. 3-64 Magnetic workholding devices. (*Courtesy Brown and Sharpe Mfg. Co.*)

concentration of such forces upon the workpiece. There is considerable variation in the responses of various ferromagnetic materials to a magnetizing force. Variations in holding power of a 36-watt, 6-volt chuck for different positions of steel test blocks on a 6×12 in. (152×305 mm) surface, as shown in Fig. 3-65, are listed in Table 3-4. For cast iron blocks of the same dimensions, the vertical pull required is approximately 60% of that listed for steel test bars.

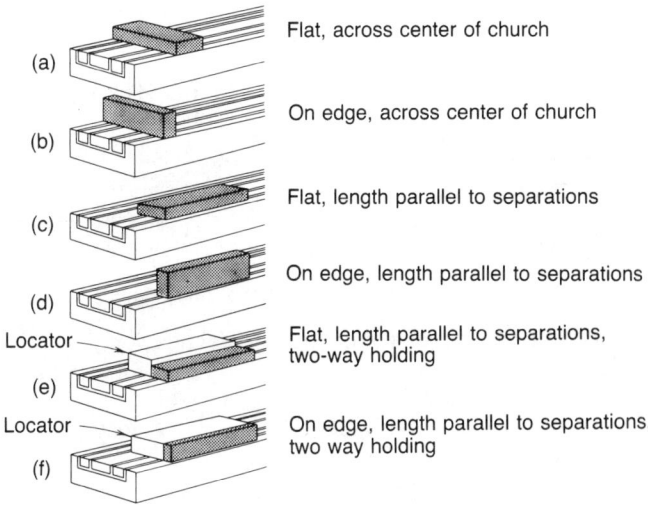

(a)   Flat, across center of church

(b)   On edge, across center of church

(c)   Flat, length parallel to separations

(d)   On edge, length parallel to separations

Locator   Flat, length parallel to separations, two-way holding

(e)

Locator   On edge, length parallel to separations, two way holding

(f)

Fig. 3-65 Test-block position for test data of Table 3-4.[5]

A chuck of the permanent magnet type incorporates a series of permanent magnets mounted on a sliding member underneath the working surface of the chuck. A lever, when moved to the ON position, allows the magnetic flux to complete its circuit through the workpiece on the working surface of the chuck, and the part is held by the magnetic force. At the OFF position, the magnets are aligned with a series of nonmagnetic separators, and the magnetic flux passes through the chuck's working surface but not through the workpiece, allowing it to be removed from the chuck.

TABLE 3-4
Vertical pull, lb, necessary to remove a 1½ in.× 6 in. steel
(SAE 1018) block from a 36-watt electromagnetic chuck[5]

Block position (See Fig. 3-65)	Block thickness, inches							
	1-1/2	1	3/4	1/2	3/8	1/4	1/8	1/16
A	1350	1125	900	450	300	150	50	15
B	1350	875	700	400	250	175	80	35
C	450	400	375	350	350	325	250	100
D	450	450	450	300	125	60	55	50
E	2050	1400	925	700	400	300	150	40
F	2050	1650	1300	825	600	400	200	100

Electromagnetic chucks activated by direct current are larger and more powerful than those of the permanent magnet type.

Flux dams, which are bars or plates of nonmagnetic metal, divert magnetic flux (see Fig. 3-66) with deep penetration, as shown at *b*, consequently with greater holding power.

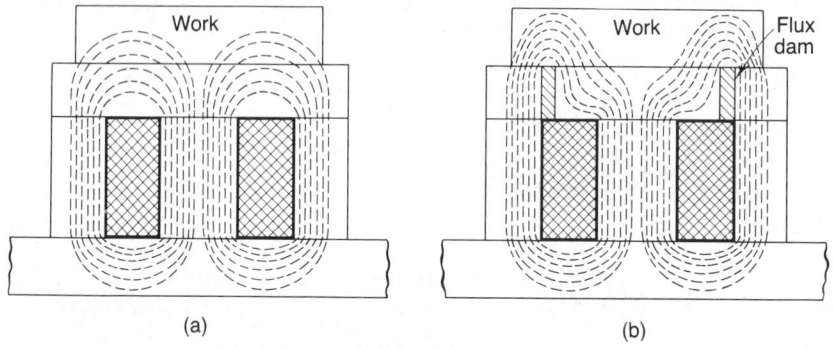

(a)   (b)

Fig. 3-66 Flux concentrations with flux dams.[6]

Thin, nonmagnetic workpieces can be clamped under heavier magnetic keeper plates, as shown in Fig. 3-67, for edge-finishing operation. Magnetic force holds the keeper plate against the magnetic locator plate.

The application and release of the holding force of an electromagnetic chuck are instantaneous with the opening and closing of its switch, and its amount may be varied with a rheostat. Auxiliary safety stops can be incorporated to prevent possible workpiece damage and operator injury in the event that the magnetic holding force is accidentally released.

Since workpieces of steel and other ferromagnetic metals and alloys tend to remain somewhat permanently magnetized after they have been held by a magnetic chuck, they may have to be demagnetized before other machining operations. Residual magnetism in the work piece may limit its function or tightly hold accumulated chips to it.

Vacuum Workholding Devices. Vacuum clamping is useful for holding a non-magnetic workpiece securely against a locating surface for various machining operations. A vacuum chuck works by creating a vacuum on the surface of the workpiece contacting the chuck faceplate, allowing the normal atmospheric pressure of approximately 15 psi

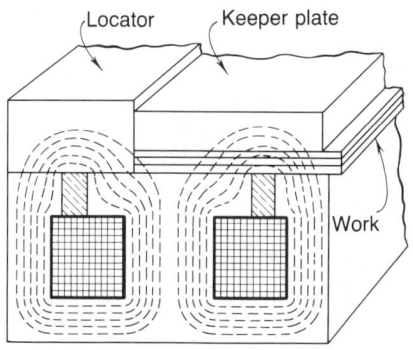

Locator   Keeper plate

Work

Fig. 3-67 Holding non-magnetic workpieces.[6]

(103 kPa) (or approximately 12 psi (83 kPa) effective, at maximum efficiency) against the rest of the workpiece to force the workpiece against the chuck face. This means that a 12 in. (305 mm) square plate would be held to the face of the chuck with a total force of 1728 lbf (7686 N). The method used to mount a workpiece varies according to the type of chuck face used. For example:

Pinhole vacuum chucks (see Fig. 3-68) have a faceplate that is drilled with closely spaced holes over the entire surface of the faceplate. With this type, a thin masking plate made of rubber, plastic sheet, or thin sheet metal cut to the same, but slightly smaller, shape as the workpiece is used to seal off the portion of the faceplate not covered by the workpiece thereby allowing the vacuum to form and clamp the workpiece.

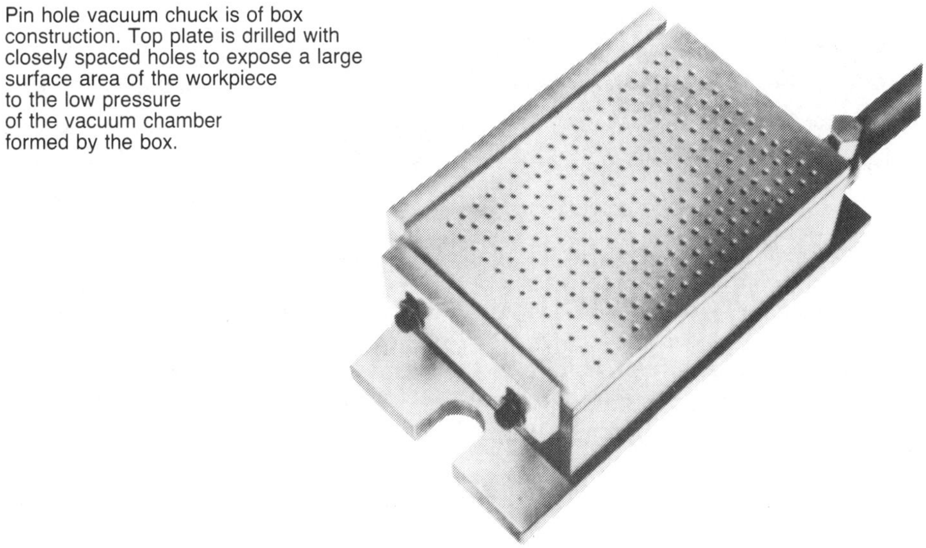

Pin hole vacuum chuck is of box construction. Top plate is drilled with closely spaced holes to expose a large surface area of the workpiece to the low pressure of the vacuum chamber formed by the box.

Fig. 3-68 Pinhole vacuum chuck. (*Courtesy Dunham Tool Co.*)

Grooved faceplate vacuum chucks (see Fig. 3-69) have concentric or equally spaced grooves that are machined into the faceplate and connected individually to a vacuum supply. Grooves which are not covered by the workpiece are either masked or blocked off if the port holes are tapped for set screws.

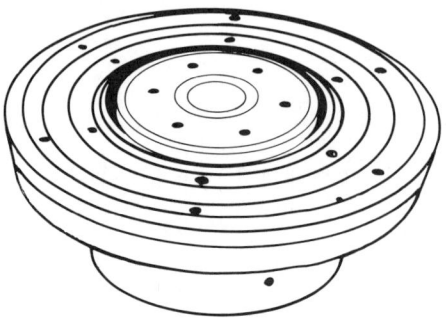

Fig. 3-69 Grooved face plate vacuum chuck. (*Courtesy Dunham Tool Co.*)

In cases where some leakage still occurs, or where the workpiece does not cover all of the parts or grooves, the outermost groove that is covered by the workpiece is sealed with an O-ring (or patented "Flapseal", as is shown in Fig. 3-70) that will seal as the vacuum is applied.

Flapseal for grooved chucks (plate warpage is exaggerated for illustration). Atmospheric pressure on the plate compresses the flapseal from above, while the same pressure into the flap seals it upward tightly against the plate to insure a good vacuum seal.

Fig. 3-70 Sealing grooved vacuum chucks. (*Courtesy Dunham Tool Co.*)

Universal vacuum top plates (see Fig. 3-71) are drilled, tapped, and counterbored over the entire surface to accept special port screws which when turned in all the way, seal off the air ports and make the chuck inoperative. Ports under the workpiece surface are then opened by backing out the screws several turns in a pattern matching the workpiece. These port screw holes can also be used to attach locating devices when required.

Porous ceramic plates (see Fig. 3-72) are used when the workpiece is so thin or fragile that the port holes or grooves will deform the workpiece. The complete area of the chuck not covered by the workpiece must be sealed to prevent leakage. This is done by masking.

All of these faceplates are available for rotary, as well as rectangular, chucks.

In using vacuum clamping, the tool designer must choose a holding surface that can be sealed without distorting the part. Vacuum chucking is not limited to workpiece material as long as it is not porous.

The special vacuum chuck shown in Fig. 3-73 was designed to hold a long, odd-shaped workpiece. Spiral grooves 0.001 in. deep in the locating surface of the fixture are used to distribute the vacuum over the lower surface of the workpiece. Rubber tubing in the outside grooves in the fixture is flattened by the weight of the workpiece and forms a seal between it and the fixture.

Universal top plate shown held on magnetic chuck of surface grinder. Recessed in the holes are vacuum port screws which seal off the evacuation holes. Side support plates are locked in place by button head screws turned into the port holes from which vacuum screws have been removed.

Fig. 3-71 Universal top plate. (*Courtesy Dunham Tool Co.*)

Porous top plates. These chucks are fitted with a top plate made of porous ceramic material. They extend the contact holding area to the full surface of the part. Their basic use is for thin parts which tend to be drawn into normal types of air evaluation ports, causing distortion. Rubber, metal, or plastic masks are used to block off portions of the face plate not covered by the part.

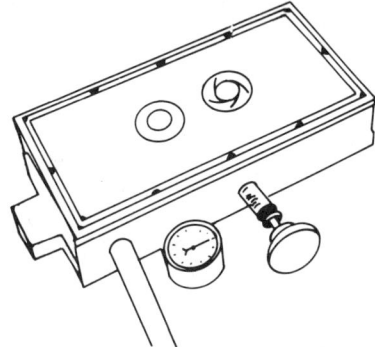

Fig. 3-72 Porous ceramic plate. (*Courtesy Dunham Tool Co.*)

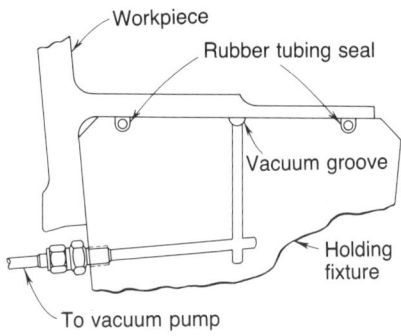

Fig. 3-73 Special vacuum chuck. (*The Tool and Manufacturing Engineer*)

To prevent any problems that might arise due to loss of vacuum, a safety system has been developed to use shop air pressure and a venturi system to create a vacuum that will continue to hold the workpiece until the machine can be stopped.

ID and OD Chucking. A wide variety of workholding devices are available for locating and clamping workpieces from the ID, OD, or other feature for machining operations. These include universal lathe chucks, collet chucks, arbors, and mandrels. These devices are used extensively for turning and boring operations and will be covered in detail in the chapter on Turning and Boring. This chapter will deal with their use as workholding devices for non-turning operations such as milling and grinding.

Universal Chucks. Universal chucks, such as the one shown in Fig. 3-74, can be used in any position to locate and clamp workpieces from an ID or OD. With different jaw arrangements, workpieces of just about any configuration can be located and held for machining operations such as milling, drilling, or grinding. They are also widely used with CNC machining centers. Chucks can be:

1. Independent chucks where each jaw can be moved separately without disturbing the position of the other jaws.
2. Self-centering chucks where all jaws move to or away from the workpiece and are maintained on one common center.
3. Combination chucks which combines the feature of both the independent and self-centering chucks.

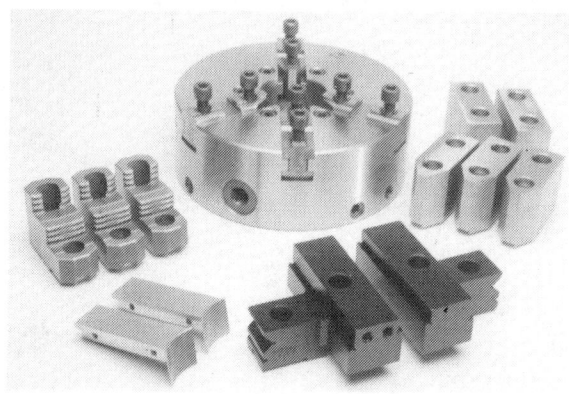

Fig. 3-74 Universal chuck. (*Courtesy Buck Chuck Co.*)

The workholding jaws may be moved collectively as in the self-centering chuck and/or individually adjusted as in an independent chuck. Chucks can be hand, air, or hydraulically operated.

Chucks can be fitted with compensating jaws to locate rough workpieces, cast plastic and low-alloy nests for odd-shaped workpieces, vacuum, magnetic, and electrostatic faceplates as well as specially designed fixtures.

Arbors and Mandrels. Plain mandrels, also referred to as lathe mandrels, are short, solid shafts usually having a taper of about 0.0005 in./in. They are used by forcing them into the workpiece, as shown in Fig. 3-75. They are generally suitable for low production only.

The split sleeve expanding mandrel shown in Fig. 3-76a has a tapered arbor which is used with a split sleeve having an internal taper matching that of the arbor. The sleeve is expanded to suit the workpiece by tapping the large end of the arbor with a mallet. A similar tap on the small end of the arbor releases the split sleeve from the workpiece. The mandrel in b is operated by a drawbar which pulls the sleeve along the taper, which

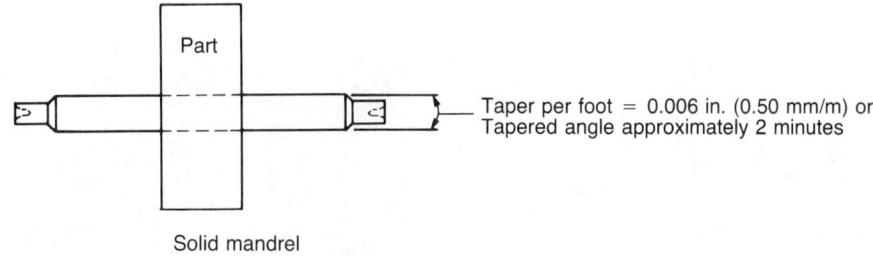

Taper per foot = 0.006 in. (0.50 mm/m) or
Tapered angle approximately 2 minutes

Solid mandrel

Fig. 3-75 Plain mandrel.

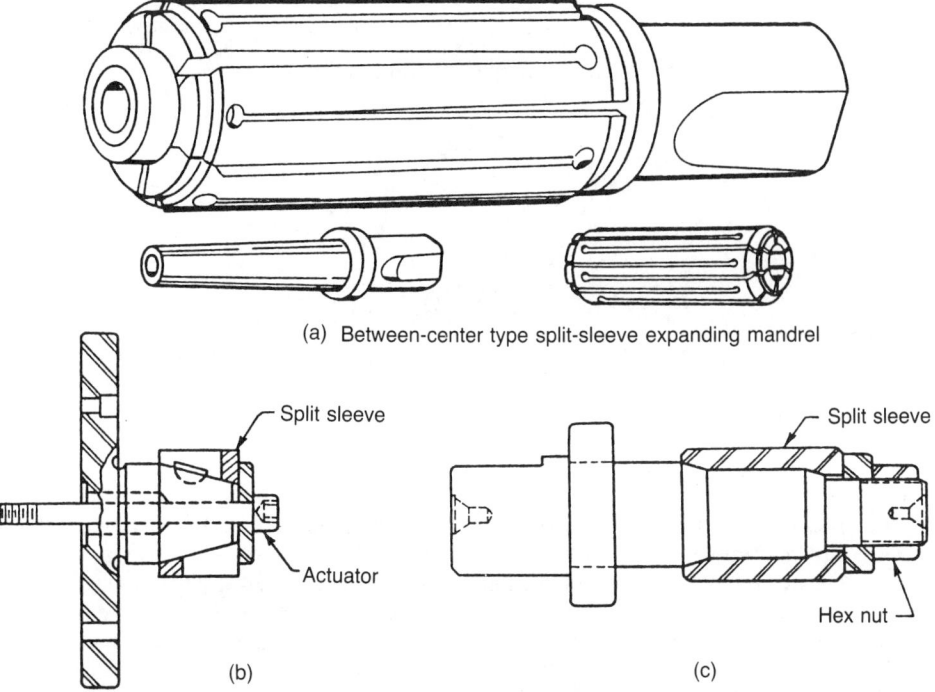

(a) Between-center type split-sleeve expanding mandrel

Split sleeve

Actuator

Split sleeve

Hex nut

(b)   (c)

Fig. 3-76 Split sleeve expanding mandrels. (*Courtesy (a), Western Tool & Mfg. Co., Inc., (b), Speedgrip Chuck, Inc.; (c), courtesy Erikson Tool Co.*)

expands to hold the workpiece on its inside surface. The mandrel in *c* has a taper at each end of the sleeve to expand the sleeve and hold the workpiece as a nut is tightened at the end of the arbor. Others are operated by drawbars. Each mandrel of this type will usually accept a broad range of sleeves (diameters) while maintaining accuracies of 0.0002-0.0005 in. FIM. Special sleeves can be manufactured to grip on square, hex, splined, or other irregular surfaces. Fixtures, such as shown in Fig. 3-77, are commercially available and can be adapted for use in a wide variety of operations, especially inspection.

Another mandrel finding wide use for inspection work is the push-on expanding mandrel shown in Fig. 3-78. These mandrels are ground slightly oversize and compress to size as they are inserted into the workpiece or as the workpiece is placed on them. They can be used with bench centers or used as locating plugs in fixtures. Since these mandrels are specially designed and built, accuracies of 0.0001 in. are possible.

Torq-loc fixture

Zero spindle and torq-loc combination

Fig. 3-77 Fixtures. (*Torq-Loc system, courtesy ITW Zero Systems*)

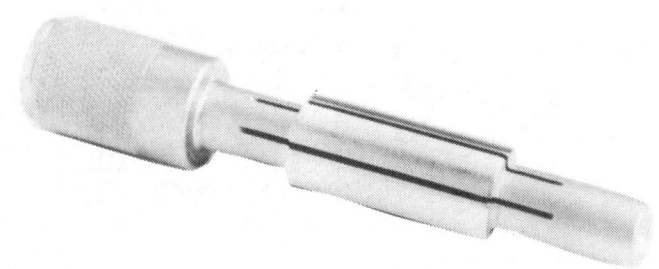

Fig. 3-78 Push-on expanding mandrel. (*Courtesy N. A. Woodworth Co.*)

A standard universal collet fixture along with available accessories is shown in Fig. 3-79. It can be used with 5C collets or any of the accessories shown to locate and hold a workpiece for many nonturning operations. In addition to the 24 division indexing and 360° graduations, it features adjustable stops and a pin with a sine arrangement for locating between indexes for precise positioning. A relatively low-cost 5C collet fixture for holding a workpiece in a vertical or horizontal position for machining is shown in Fig. 3-80a. Also shown are 5C collet blocks, b, which can be used to hold a workpiece for machining parallel, square, or hex shapes, as well as for cross drilling at 60°, 90°, or 120°.

Hydraulically Expanded Arbors and Chucks. Hydraulically expanded arbors and chucks, such as shown in Fig. 3-81, function on the principle of expanding or compressing metals within their elastic limits, under hydraulic pressure. They are self-contained and can be manually operated or power actuated. The same figure illustrates the basic principles upon which the devices function. The actuator screw is turned clockwise, advancing the piston which places the hydraulic system under high pressure. In the case of the chuck shown in a, the compression sleeve is compressed over the full chucking area between the hydraulic seals. With the arbor shown in b, the expansion sleeve is expanded over the full gripping area between the hydraulic sleeves.

There is no expansion of the gripping or chucking areas beyond the hydraulic seal area. The gripping or chucking area of the sleeves under equalized fluid pressure, expand or compress uniformly from their geometric centerline assuring extreme accuracy in workpiece positioning. The minimum chucking diameter of arbors is 0.250 in. For chucks, the minimum diameter is 0.06 in. The maximum chucking diameters for

Fig. 3-79 Universal collet fixture with accessories. (*Courtesy Harig Mfg. Corp.*)

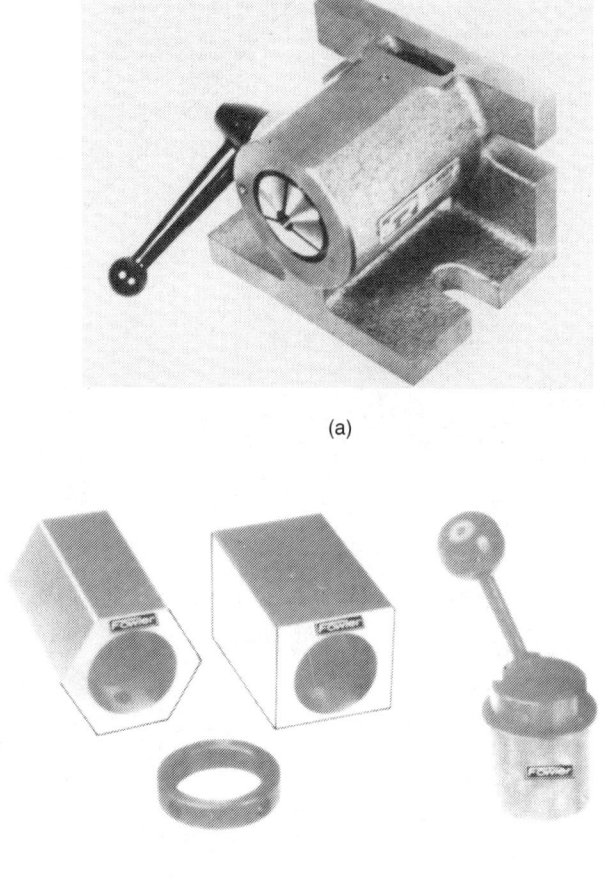

(a)

(b)

Fig. 3-80 Collet Fixture, (*a*) and collet blocks, (*b*). (*Courtesy (a), Ralmike's Tool -A-Rama; (b), Fred W. Fowler Co., Inc.*)

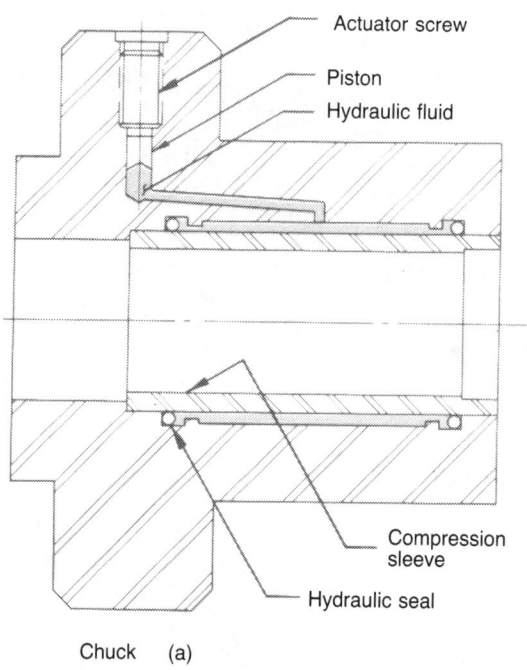

Actuator screw

Piston

Hydraulic fluid

Compression
sleeve

Hydraulic seal

Chuck   (a)

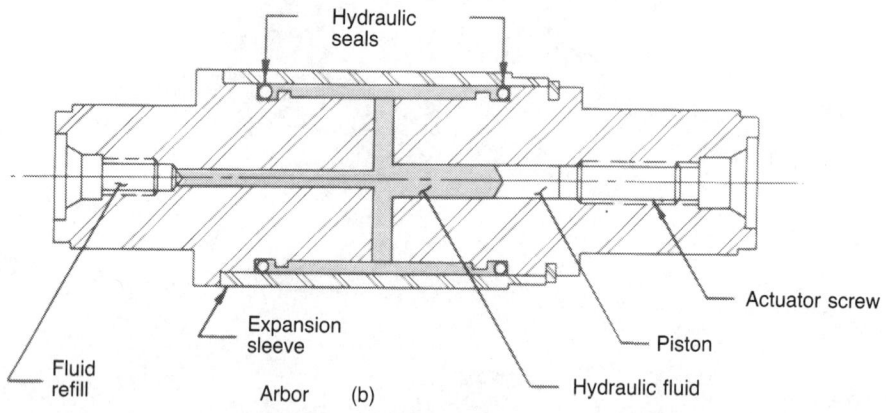

Hydraulic
seals

Actuator screw

Expansion
sleeve

Piston

Fluid
refill

Arbor   (b)

Hydraulic fluid

Fig. 3-81 Hydraulically expanded arbors and chucks. (*Courtesy A. G. Davis Gage & Engineering*)

both arbors and chucks are limited by part and tolerance variables. In general, standard expansion limits are 0.003 in. for the first inch of diameter, and 0.001 in. for each additional inch of diameter. Special expansions are available, but at the expense of accuracy and rigidity. The gripping force should be custom engineered for each application. It can range from only a few pounds per square inch (kilopascals) to several thousand pounds per square inch (Megapascals).

The location of the actuator mechanism in the arbor or chuck is very flexible, as seen in Fig. 3-82. It is determined by:

1. The method of actuating the self-contained hydraulic system—manually or by power.
2. The type of machine spindle, faceplate, special adapter, or fixture with which it is used. Figure 3-83 illustrates some of the possibilities.

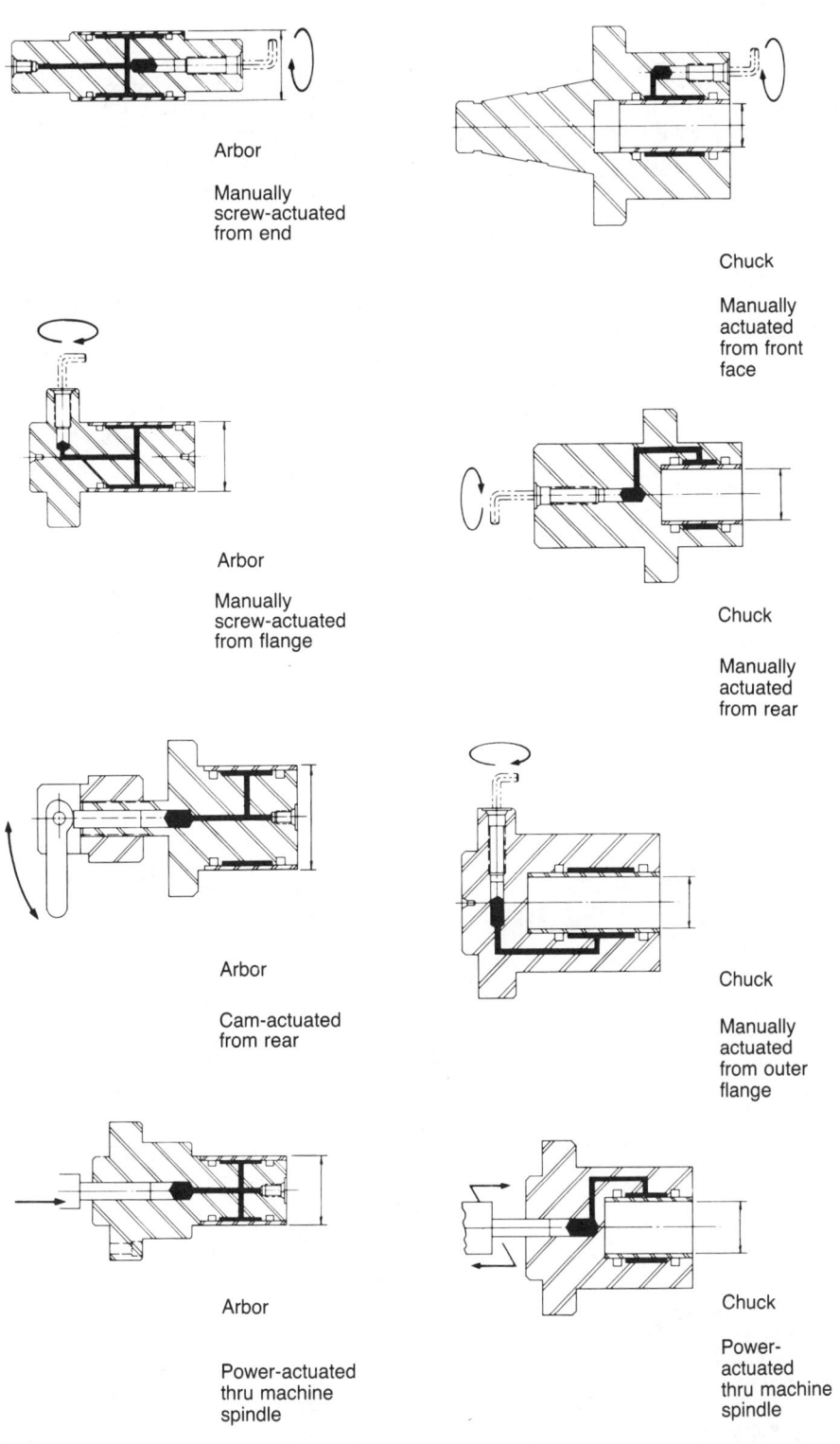

Arbor

Manually
screw-actuated
from end

Chuck

Manually
actuated
from front
face

Arbor

Manually
screw-actuated
from flange

Chuck

Manually
actuated
from rear

Arbor

Cam-actuated
from rear

Chuck

Manually
actuated
from outer
flange

Arbor

Power-actuated
thru machine
spindle

Chuck

Power-
actuated
thru machine
spindle

Fig. 3-82 Actuator mechanisms. (*Courtesy A. G. Davis Gage & Engineering*)

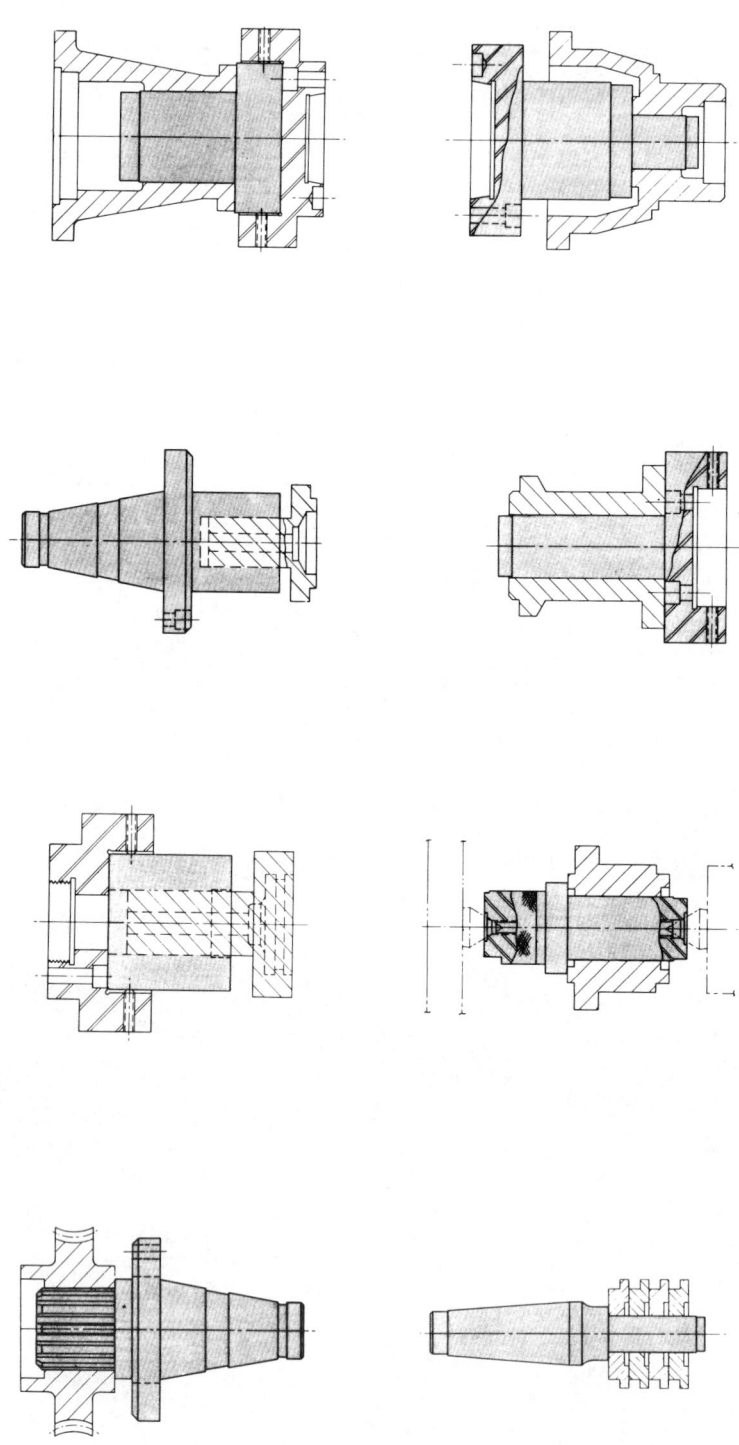

Fig. 3-83 Machine adaptability. (*Courtesy A. G. Davis Gage & Engineering*)

Figure 3-84 shows how the gripping surface of the hydraulically expanded arbors and chucks conform to the chucking surface of the workpiece thereby locating from the true centerline regardless of taper, *a*, bell-mouth, *b*, or out-of-roundness, *c*.

Hydraulically expanded arbors and chucks also find wide use for multiple part chucking, interrupted bore chucking, and two diameter chucking as seen in Fig. 3-85.

Split sleeve adapters make it possible to locate workpieces of different diameters with a single arbor or chuck as seen in Fig. 3-86*a*. Split sleeve adapters also make it possible to locate from two diameters that must be approached from different ends of the workpiece (see Fig. 3-86*b*).

Hydraulically expanded arbors are also widely used for accurately locating from the pitch, major or minor diameter of splines, gears, and serrations, as well as the pitch diameters of internal and external threads. They can be adapted for grinding, balancing, drilling, hobbing, shaving, honing, facing, turning, boring, inspection, and other similar operations.

Hydraulically Expanded Flats or Gibs. Another hydraulically expanded device that could be useful is the expanding flat or gib shown in Fig. 3-87. The application shown in the figure adjusts a workholding block to a very close tolerance sliding fit in the dove-tail way, or could be locked for a precise broaching operation.

Expanding flats or gibs can be used for critical sliding fits to eliminate the need for continuous adjustment, or for precise locking of workpieces in the working position on ways or slides.

Low-melt Chuck Jaws. Chuck jaws for holding irregular-shaped workpieces for machining operations can be made quickly, accurately, and economically using a low-temperature melting, bismuth alloy called Cerromatrix®.

Durable chuck jaws of the most intricate shapes can be made with this simple process of casting against the object to be held, with the end result being an accurate fitting pair of chuck jaws for a fraction of the usual cost (Cerromatrix® can be cast against metal parts, die castings, rubber, wood, and most plastic products without any danger of burning or warping the item used as a pattern. The hardness of the Cerromatrix® and the fact that it expands slightly upon solidifying, add to the advantages for this purpose). Experience has shown that chuck jaws made by this method can be used for long production runs, especially when workpieces are of uniform size.

Figure 3-88 shows a set of removable jaws that were made to hold a forged brass workpiece for a milling operation. The jaws fit into a machined cavity in a steel or brass holder so that they may be removed and replaced with cast jaws for other workpieces.

For heavier work, a more durable type of chuck is usually made by casting into a retaining shell of steel or brass as shown in Fig. 3-89.

Figure 3-89*a* shows the essential parts for making the chuck. They are: The two halves of the brass retaining shell, two wooden spacers, and the die casting which is to be held by the jaws. The spacers can be carved out of solid wood to match the contour of the die casting. A quicker and less expensive method is to nail two thin strips of wood to a thicker centerpiece, leaving a groove on the inside that is the length of the spacer. The thin side pieces are then sawed to fit the radial ridges on the die casting. The grooves are then filled with a babbiting clay (such as Babbitrite, made by Products Manufacturing and Sales Company), or similar material. The spacer is then pressed against the die casting to make the impression in the clay.

Figure 3-89*b* shows the die casting in place between the two spacers, which serve as separators during the pouring operation, and for supporting the die casting in the correct position relative to the walls of the retaining shell.

Figure 3-89*c* shows the two halves of the brass shell brought against the spacers and clamped in position. Everything is now ready for the pouring (the Cerromatrix® should be melted and stirred frequently, especially before pouring). Pouring temperatures should be between 300° and 350°F (149° and 177°C).

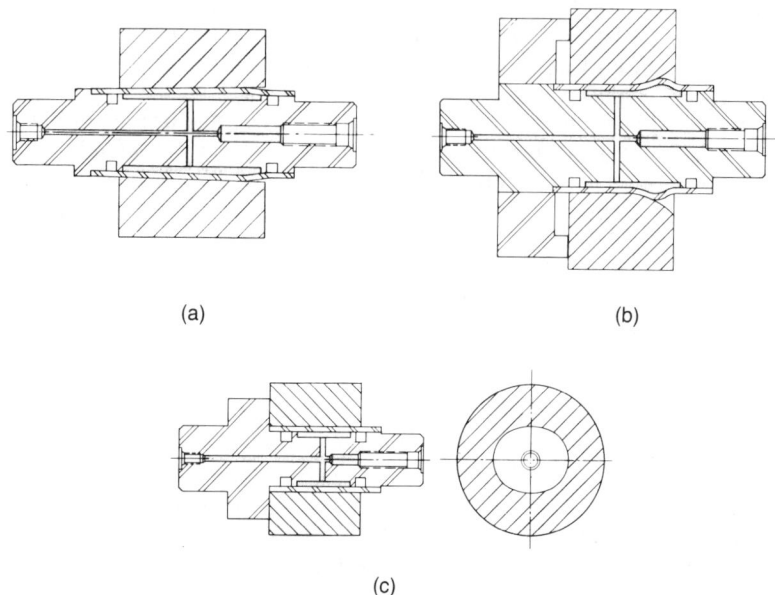

(a)

(b)

(c)

Fig. 3-84 Establishing true centerline. (*Courtesy A. G. Davis Gage & Engineering*)

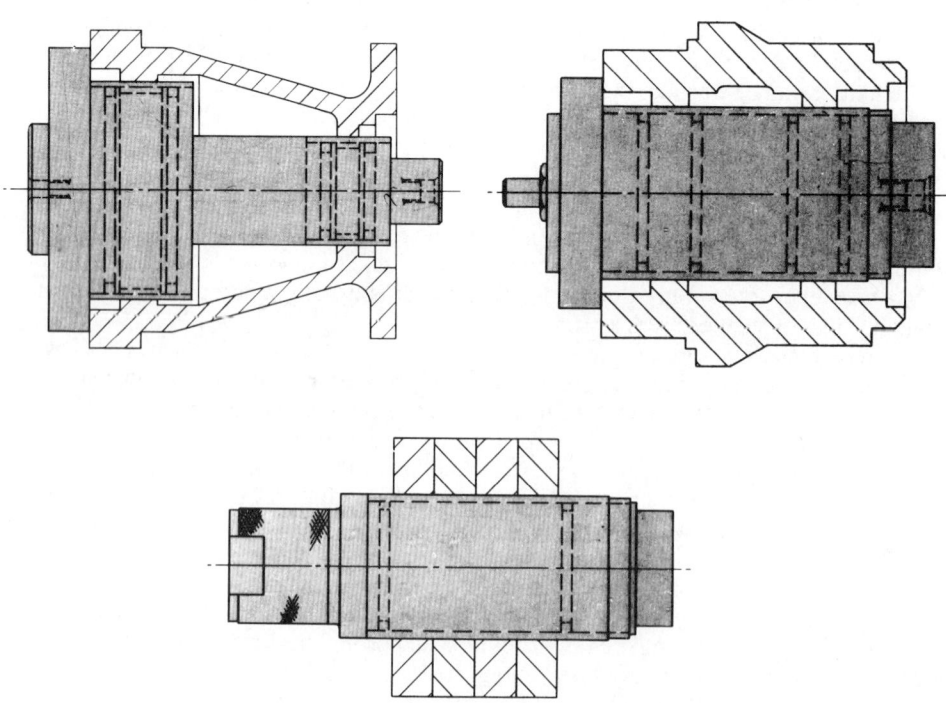

Fig. 3-85 Application of hydraulically expanded arbors and chucks. (*Courtesy A. G. Davis Gage & Engineering*)

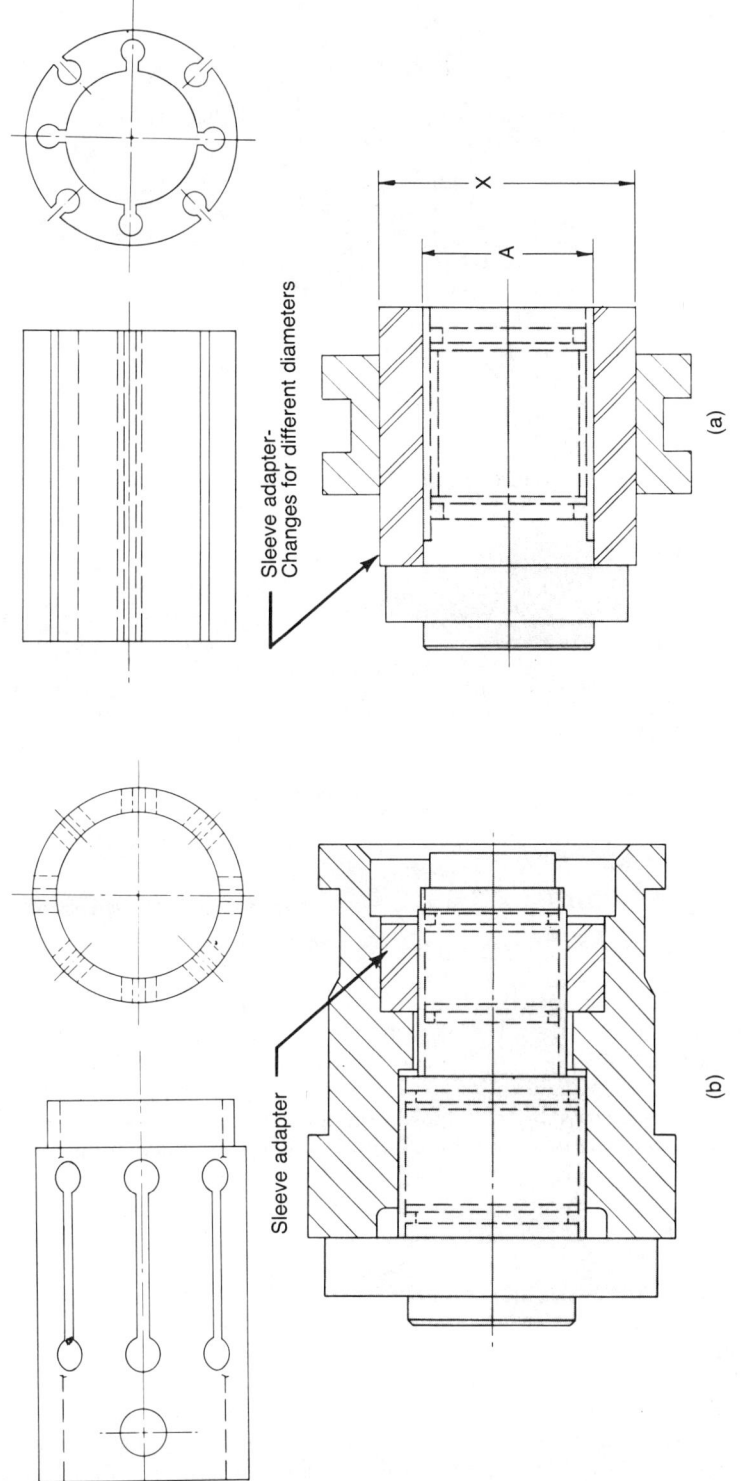

Sleeve adapter-
Changes for different diameters

X

A

(a)

Sleeve adapter

(b)

Fig. 3-86 Split sleeve adaptors. (*Courtesy A. G. Davis Gage & Engineering*)

Fig. 3-87 Hydraulically expanded flat. (*Courtesy The Gordon N. Cameron Co.*)

Fig. 3-88 Removable jaws. (*Cerromatrix®, courtesy Cerro Metal Products*)

When the Cerromatrix® has solidified, the clamps are removed completing the operation. The chuck jaws are shown in Fig. 3-89*d*. The wide spacers between the two halves during the pouring regulate the depth of the cavities to prevent them from becoming deeper than necessary to properly locate and clamp the workpiece for machining. Spacers should be thick enough for this purpose while keeping opening and closing movements to a minimum. Correct spacing is shown in Fig. 3-89*e*.

The life of a pair of chuck jaws can be materially increased if the cavity surrounding the workpiece is filled with hardened steel balls before casting the Cerromatrix®. The balls should be in a preheated range of 300° to 350°F (149° to 177°C) to prevent chilling of the alloy during the casting operation.

Note: The surface of the part used as a pattern should be smoked or coated with lamp black to permit easy parting and provide a slight clearance between the part and the cast alloy.

Many of the clamps, chucks, arbors, vises, and other workholding devices discussed throughout this chapter can be mounted directly on dividing heads, rotary tables, precision adjustable angle plates, indexing fixtures, and other positioning tables to make them more versatile. They are also used in matched sets for multiple workpiece set ups on CNC machining centers.

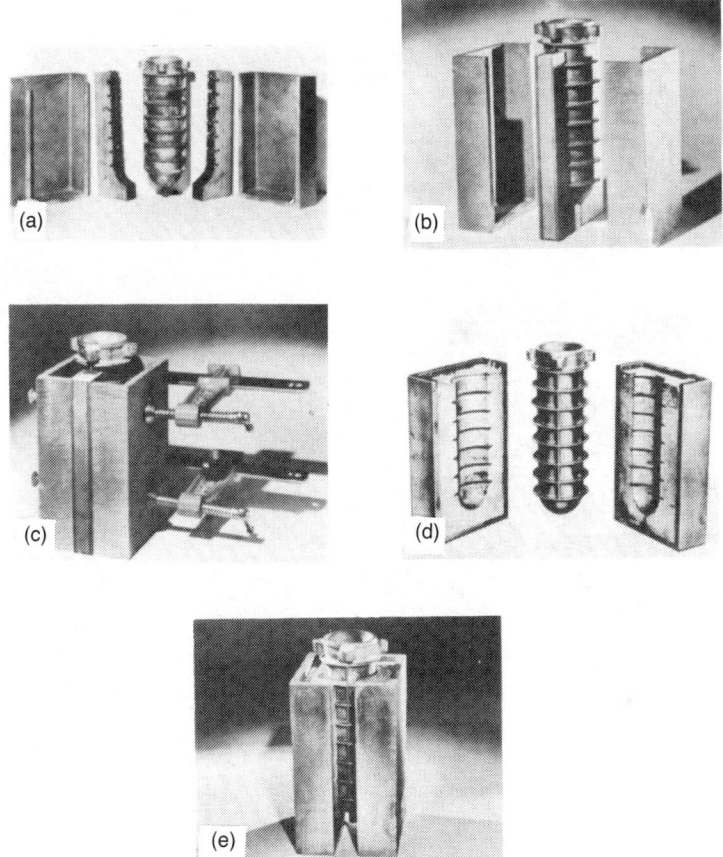

Fig. 3-89 An easy method of making chuck jaws. (*Cerromatrix®, courtesy Cerro Metal Products*)

Power Workholding. Many types of the clamps discussed in this chapter are available in pneumatic and hydraulic versions. They are mainly used where clamping must be fast and uniform.

All pneumatic and hydraulic powered components work in much the same way, with the main difference being in the size of the cylinder since pneumatic systems work with pressures around 100 psi (690 kPa), while hydraulic systems work with pressures up to 10,000 psi (70 MPa). Both systems permit close control of the forces applied to the workpiece.

The applied force will be equal to the air or oil pressure multiplied by the effective surface area. For example: If the oil supplied to the cylinder has a pressure of 5,000 psi (34.5 MPa) and the surface area of the plunger is 4 in.² (2580 mm²) the force would be determined using the following formula:

$$F = P \times A \tag{26}$$

where:

F = force

P = pressure = 5,000 psi (34.5 MPa)

A = surface area of the cylinder plunger = 4 in.² (2580 mm²)

Calculation:

$$F = P \times A$$
$$= 5,000 \text{ psi (34.5 MPa)} \times 4 \text{ in.}^2 \text{ (2580 mm}^2\text{)}$$
$$= 20,000 \text{ lbf (89 kN)}$$

The components that make up one hydraulic workholding system are shown in Figs. 3-90 thru 3-103 along with typical applications.

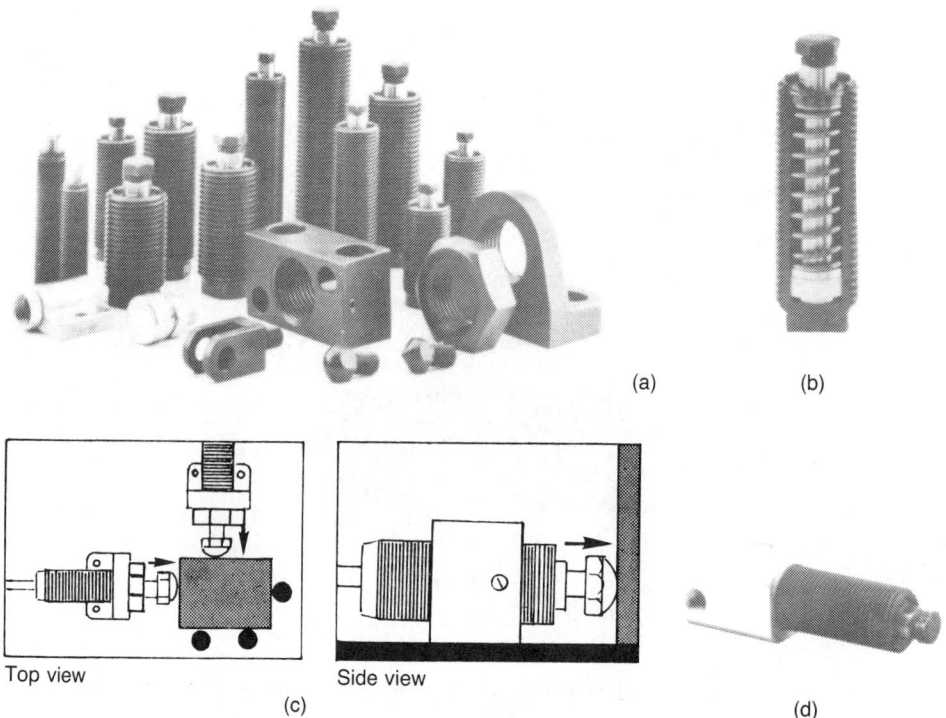

Fig. 3-90 Threaded cylinders. (*Courtesy Vlier Engineering*)

Threaded cylinders and their accessories, such as shown in Fig. 3-90a, provide a compact means of applying force to position and clamp workpieces. They can be mounted using the brackets shown in the figure or installed directly in the body of a fixture.

The cutaway view, b, shows the typical construction of a threaded cylinder. It can be seen that the plunger is extended by hydraulic pressure and retracted by the spring pressure. The step in the plunger diameter provides a positive stop and prevents solid compression of the spring.

A typical application using threaded cylinders to position a workpiece against locators is shown in c. The larger sizes with higher pressures can be used for clamping. Standard accessories include mounting brackets, flat, spherical, and conical buttons, toggle pads, and a clevis. View d shows a double acting threaded cylinder which is hydraulically powered in both the thrust and retract modes. It has sufficient power to push aside large metal chips or other obstructions on the return stroke. The threaded front end provides for easy installation on a fixture. The cylinder develops 1,200 lbf (5.3 kN) clamping force at 3,000 psi (20.7 MPa), has a 1.5 in. (38 mm) stroke, and a return force of 600 lbf (2.7 kN).

Standard cylinders and their accessories as shown in Fig. 3-91*a* are used for heavier duty applications and are more capable of resisting side loads. These cylinders can also be mounted using the bracket shown or mounted directly in a fixture. They are held in place with a retaining ring.

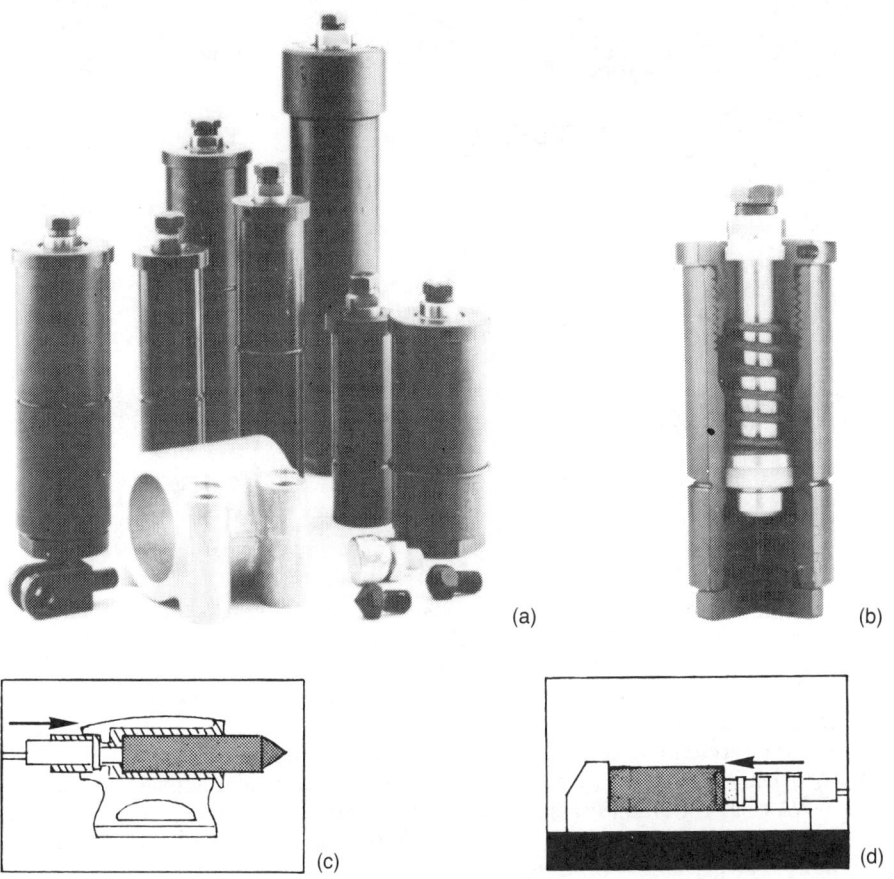

(a)

(b)

(c)

(d)

Fig. 3-91 Standard cylinders. (*Courtesy Vlier Engineering*)

The cutaway view, *b*, shows the internal construction and operation to be basically the same as for the threaded cylinder. A typical application using a cylinder to apply a constant force is shown in *c*. Another application, *d*, shows a custom made vise powered by a standard cylinder. Plungers are tapped with a 5/16-24 thread to accept a standard hex head capscrew, any of the accessories shown, or any other component with a matching male thread.

Hollow cylinders as shown in Fig. 3-92*a* have a hole through their center which is tapped to accept a stud from either end of the cylinder providing for its application in either a pulling or pushing mode. The cutaway views, *b*, show the internal construction of a hollow cylinder.

A typical application using the pushing action with a strap clamp is shown in *c*. In this case, a bolt was put through the cylinder to prevent the strap from turning. In *d*, a T-bolt is screwed directly into the cylinder to provide pulling action to hold a plate directly to a T-slotted machine table. The direct pushing action in *e* is used to clamp a workpiece. Accessories include the hardened pressure points and lock nuts shown in *a*.

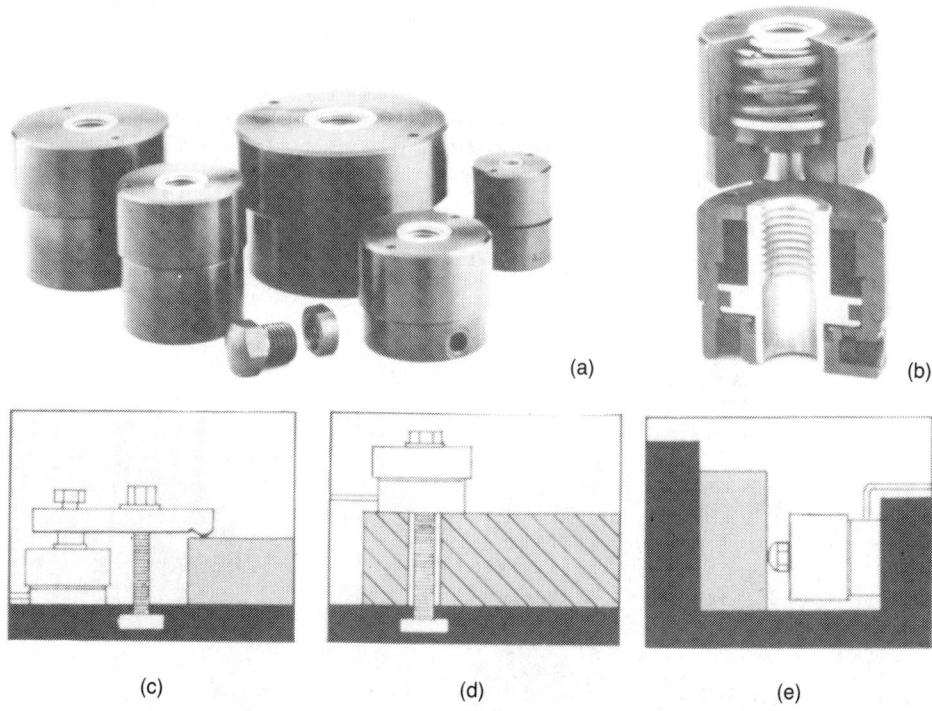

(a)

(b)

(c)

(d)

(e)

Fig. 3-92 Hollow cylinders. (*Courtesy Vlier Engineering*)

Swing cylinders as shown in Fig. 3-93*a* rotate 90° as they begin their stroke, then continue without rotation from final clamping. Swing cylinders are constructed as shown in the cutaway view, *b*, so that it is easy to adjust to push and/or pull (double-action) applications, or to change from the standard right-hand pivot to left-handed action (the left-hand track is hidden in the cutaway view). In *c*, the swing cylinder is used without the turning ball to serve as a double-acting cylinder. A double-clamping arm is used to distribute the load evenly between the two clamping points. Application *d* demonstrates a range of mounting options and clamp arms. The easiest mounting is to provide a clearance hole for the body and use the four mounting holes. Clamping arms reaching up to 6 in. (152 mm) off-center can be used.

Two types of retracting clamps are shown in Fig. 3-94. The retracting clamps in the center and left-hand of the figure have soft steel clamping arms to which custom clamping members can be welded. They are designed to be mounted horizontally, vertically, or above or beneath a work table.

The retracting clamp shown in the right hand of the figure permits 90° rotation of the clamp arm as one of the three hydraulic cylinders shown in *b* exerts a force upon the arm. This action permits clamping of flat, curved, or beveled workpieces whether thick or thin. The application *c* shows that the rounded, hardened nose of the clamp can be used equally well for clamping a workpiece on a vertical, sloping, or horizontal face. With a long stroke cylinder, the clamp can go from a retracting position, all the way to clamp sheet metal as shown in *d*. By welding an extension (dotted line) to the clamping arm as shown in *e*, any action around the pivot point can be created. In *f*, an extension (dotted line) is welded to the clamping arm to permit installation of the cylinder under the table.

Swing clamps (see Fig. 3-95) have a clamping arm that swings 90° to position itself over a workpiece. Then a vertical plunger exerts a force on the back end of a swing arm, which converts to a powerful downward pressure to clamp the workpiece. They can be adjusted to swivel either clockwise or counter-clockwise. The cutaway view, *b*, shows

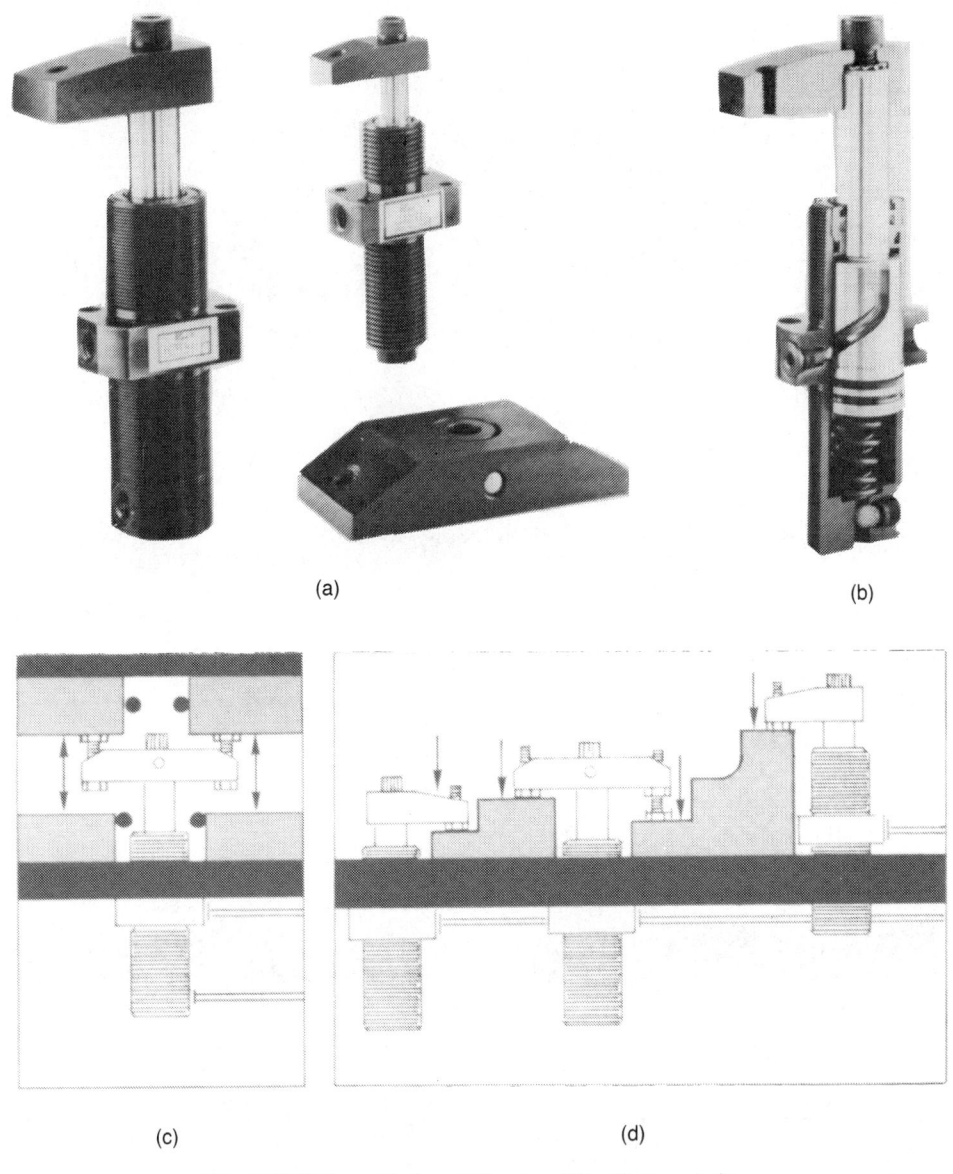

(a)

(b)

(c)

(d)

Fig. 3-93 Swing cylinders. (*Courtesy Vlier Engineering*)

the internal workings of the swing clamps components. First a horizontal plunger, visible in the cutaway portion on the right, exerts pressure on the vertical pivot shaft on the right, causing the clamping arm to turn into position. A sequence valve prevents fluid from reaching the vertical plunger seen in the left hand opening until pressure reaches 1,000 psi (6.9 MPa). Then the plunger extends upward producing the clamping action. The typical application shown in *c* is an actual in-plant operation depicting how edge milling of large helicopter blades requires many clamping points and individual control as cutters progress along the edges of a stack of blades. By converting to power workholding, this company realized an 800% productivity increase over previous stop-and-go manual clamping. The hydraulic controls were set up to release one pair of the clamps at a time to allow them to swing out of the way as the cutters pass as shown in *d*.

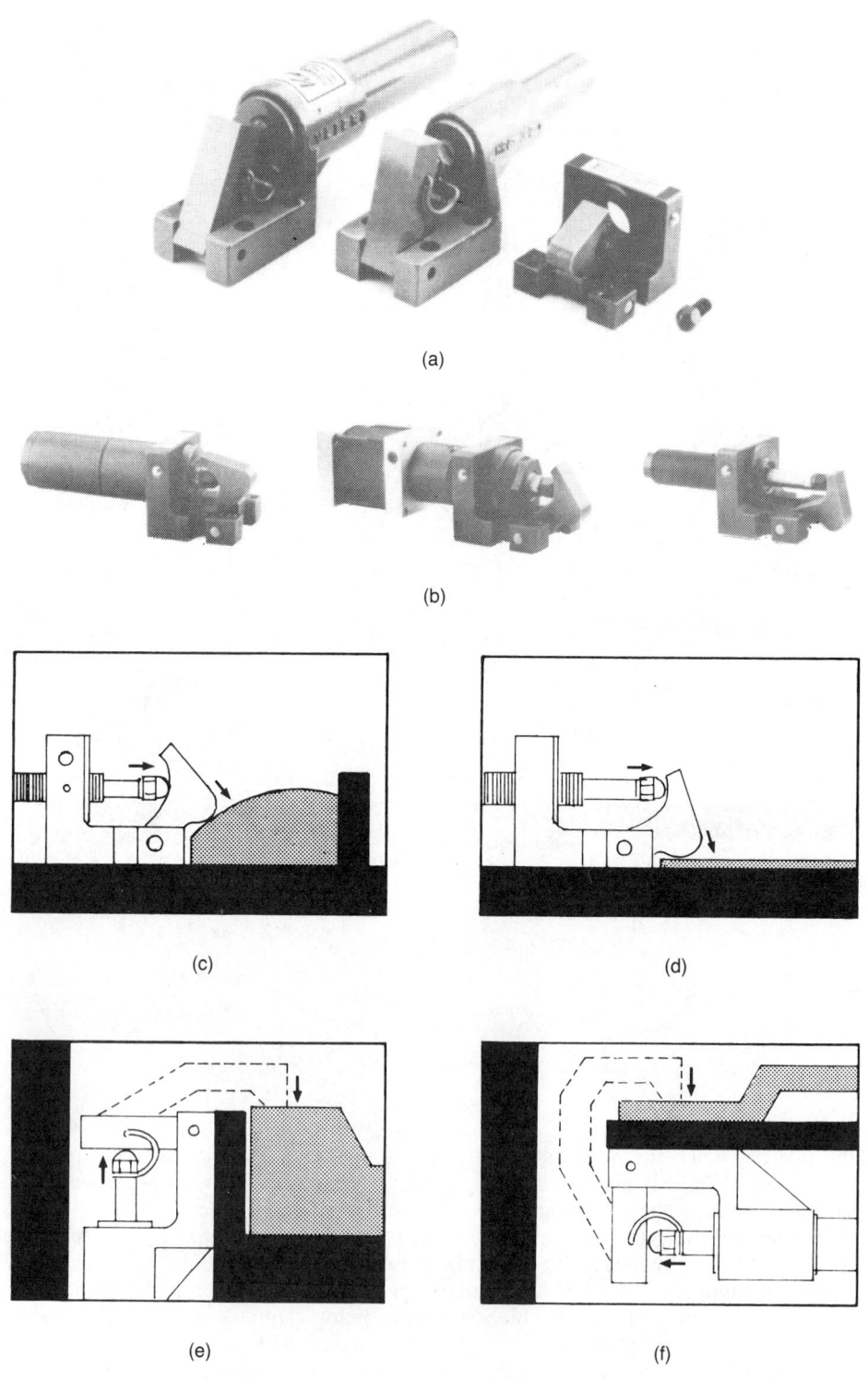

(a)

(b)

(c)

(d)

(e)

(f)

Fig. 3-94 Retracting clamps. (*Courtesy Vlier Engineering*)

(a)

(b)

(c)

Top view

Cutter

(d)

Fig. 3-95 Swing clamps. (*Courtesy Vlier Engineering*)

The air/hydraulic clamp shown in Fig. 3-96 is a self-contained, air/hydraulic cylinder which provides all of the advantages of reliable, precise, hydraulic clamping with the conveniences of shop air to power it. It requires no intensifier or hydraulic plumbing. It operates by turning compressed air on and off, while multiplying 100 psi (690 kPA) of ordinary shop pressure to 1,000 psi (6.9 MPa) of hydraulic force. A clear window in the air cavity displays a read panel whenever cylinder travel is excessive or a malfunction occurs.

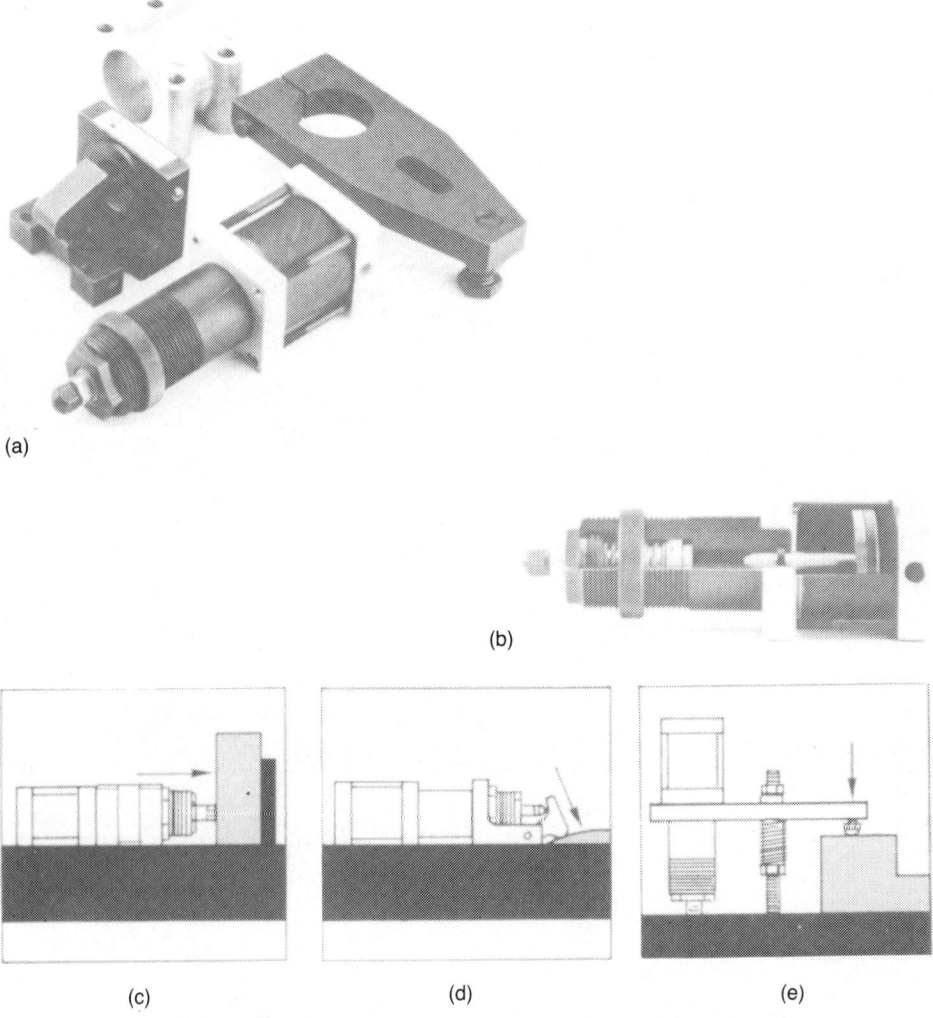

(a)

(b)

(c)   (d)   (e)

Fig. 3-96 Air/hydraulic clamp. (*Courtesy Vlier Engineering*)

The cutaway of the air/hydraulic clamp, *b*, consists of an intensifier, seen on the right, and a hydraulic cylinder, seen on the left. An oil cavity in the center is pressurized by the plunger entering from the right, exerting force on the clamp at the left. When air pressure is applied, the air piston moves. Air on the left side of the piston is vented through a hole that can be protected with a fitting (not shown) and hose to avoid ingestion of coolant or other foreign matter. If the piston reaches the end of its stroke, it becomes visible through a clear section of the air cylinder. Oil can be replenished as needed through a port leading directly to the oil cavity.

In application *c*, the clamp is used with the accessory bracket shown in *a* to provide direct clamping of a workpiece. In *d*, the clamp is used with a retracting clamp to clamp a sloping surface. It could even be used to clamp a thin, flat workpiece. However, the limited stroke of the air/hydraulic clamp will limit retraction of the clamp arm. The air/hydraulic clamp shown in *e* is used with the strap clamp accessory shown in *a*, along with a standard T-slot bolt or stud to provide a powerful, finger-tip control strap-clamp with a minimal investment.

Three different work supports for different applications are shown in Fig. 3-97. They vary in available stroke and support force. All three use friction plates which squeeze together at just the right height. This one-way support prevents any distortion of the workpiece during processing or machining.

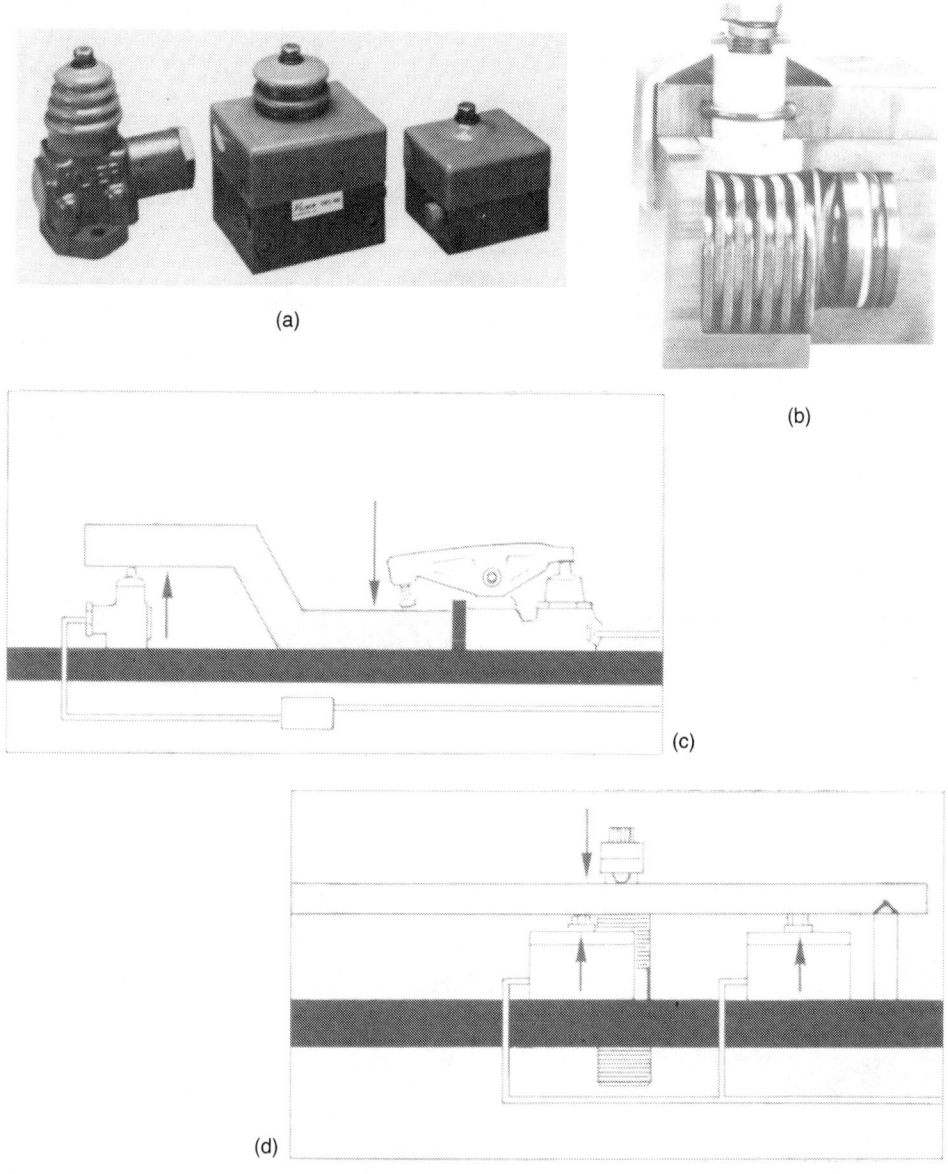

Fig. 3-97 Work supports. (*Courtesy Vlier Engineering*)

The cutaway view, *b*, shows the work support in a resting position. From this position, individual plate springs raise every other plate into direct contact with the plunger, forcing it out to its maximum stroke point. When a workpiece is positioned over the work support, its weight depresses the plunger to the proper height which varies depending on the particular workpiece's dimension. Hydraulic fluid entering on the right forces the plunger to the left, compressing a stack of friction plates and creating a very solid support.

When using work supports, the workpiece is usually clamped first to allow all surfaces to find their natural positions. A work support is then activated to an exposed section to prevent deflection or vibration during machining. In application *c*, the workpiece is first clamped with a swing clamp. The work support is then energized after being delayed by a sequence valve.

In application *d*, the workpiece is positioned first on a reference surface. Next, work supports which contact the workpiece in several places are energized and locked. Finally, swing cylinders which have been delayed by a sequence valve clamp the workpiece over the work supports.

Some workholding problems require one clamp or work support to operate before another. The adjustable sequence valve shown in Fig. 3-98 accomplishes this because it is designed for single line plumbing systems. The valve actuates at a predetermined pressure level so that sections not controlled by the valve operate first, followed by those connected after the sequence valve as shown in *b*.

Sometimes a workpiece must be held with different forces on different parts of the workpiece and choosing different size clamping cylinders will not always work. The pressure limiting valve shown in Fig. 3-99*a* allows precise control over pressures reaching specific clamps. The valve is designed for incorporation into straightforward plumbing runs. Pressure build-up to a preset level closes the valve, thus stabilizing pressure to that section of the fixture as shown in *b*.

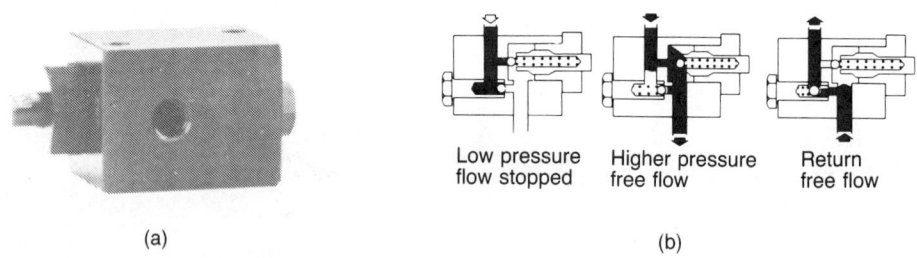

(a)   (b)

Fig. 3-98 Adjustable sequence valve. (*Courtesy Vlier Engineering*)

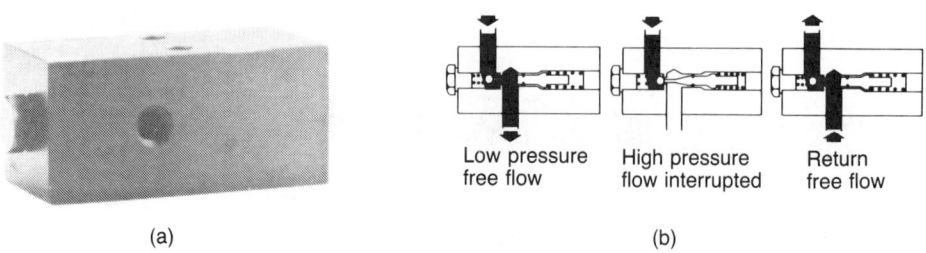

(a)   (b)

Fig. 3-99 Pressure limiting valve. (*Courtesy Vlier Engineering*)

The holding valves shown in Fig. 3-100*a* and *b* will trap or hold fluid under pressure in one section of a fixture even though the intensifier in another section is relieved of pressure, thus permitting independent control of different branches of the same fixture. Conversely, a holding valve can be used to prevent the flow of fluid into a section of a fixture until needed. Fluid flow is shown in *c*.

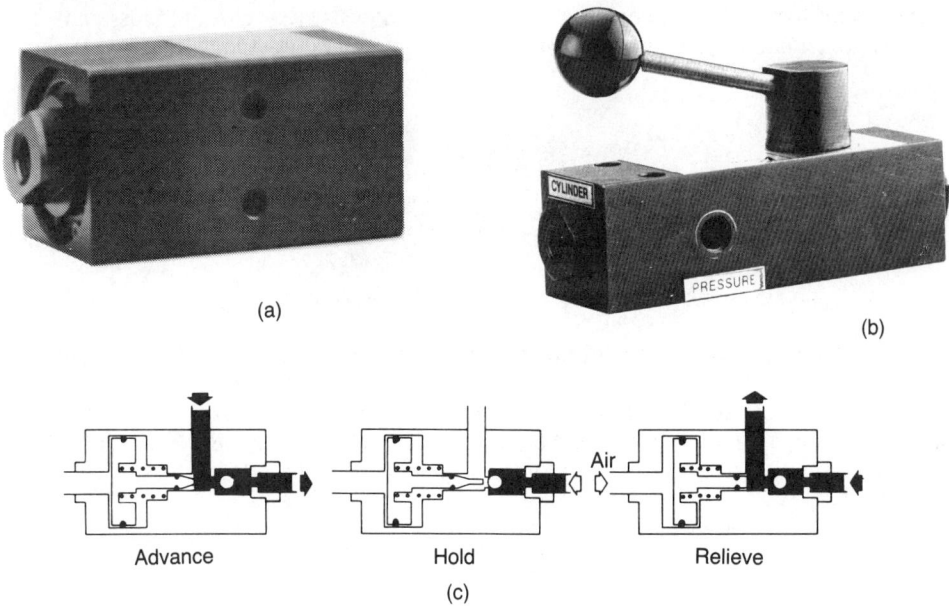

(a)

(b)

Advance   Hold   Relieve

(c)

Fig. 3-100 Holding valves. (*Courtesy Vlier Engineering*)

A remote control valve, which is intended for use with an air hydraulic pump to control the flow of pressurized fluid to and from a fixture, is shown in Fig. 3-101. Several valves can be used in parallel from the same pump. The valve is a four-way valve with a closed center position. It can be used to control two fixtures to be energized in alternating sequence. Fitted with a check valve on the incoming pressure port to prevent any return of pressurized fluid (vital when more than one valve is connected to the same power source), the valve is also used frequently as a three-way valve. The construction and operating diagram is shown in *b*.

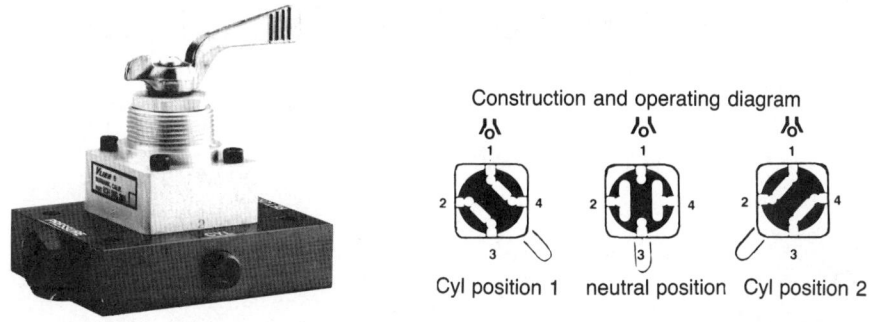

Construction and operating diagram

Cyl position 1   neutral position   Cyl position 2

Fig. 3-101 Remote control valve. (*Courtesy Vlier Engineering*)

The accumulator (see Fig. 3-102) maintains pressure in a fixture which has been disconnected from a hydraulic power source. With no attached power source, maintaining pressure in the fixture depends on leak-free plumbing which is not always the case. The accumulator compensates for slight leakage by maintaining pressure at the desired level. The accumulator, spring-actuated and adjustable for pressures ranging from 1,000 to 2,800 psi (6.9 to 19.3 MPa), is sufficient to maintain pressure in a reasonably tight system for weeks. The external warning rod shows any system fluid loss and can be used to actuate a microswitch to provide a light or sound warning signal.

Fig. 3-102 Accumulator. (*Courtesy Vlier Engineering*)

Five separate power sources for this system are shown in Fig. 3-103. The air/hydraulic pump, *a*, runs on shop air of 60 to 125 psi (414 to 862 kPa). It has a one gallon (3.78 L) reservoir, 4,500 psi (31 MPa) pressure rating, double outlets, on-off valve, air filter, and a pressure regulator to regulate the pressure level. The flow rate is 2.7 in.^{3}/s (44,245 mm^3/s). A smaller version delivers approximately 1.6 in^3/s (26,219 mm^3/s) at 2,615 psi (18 MPa).

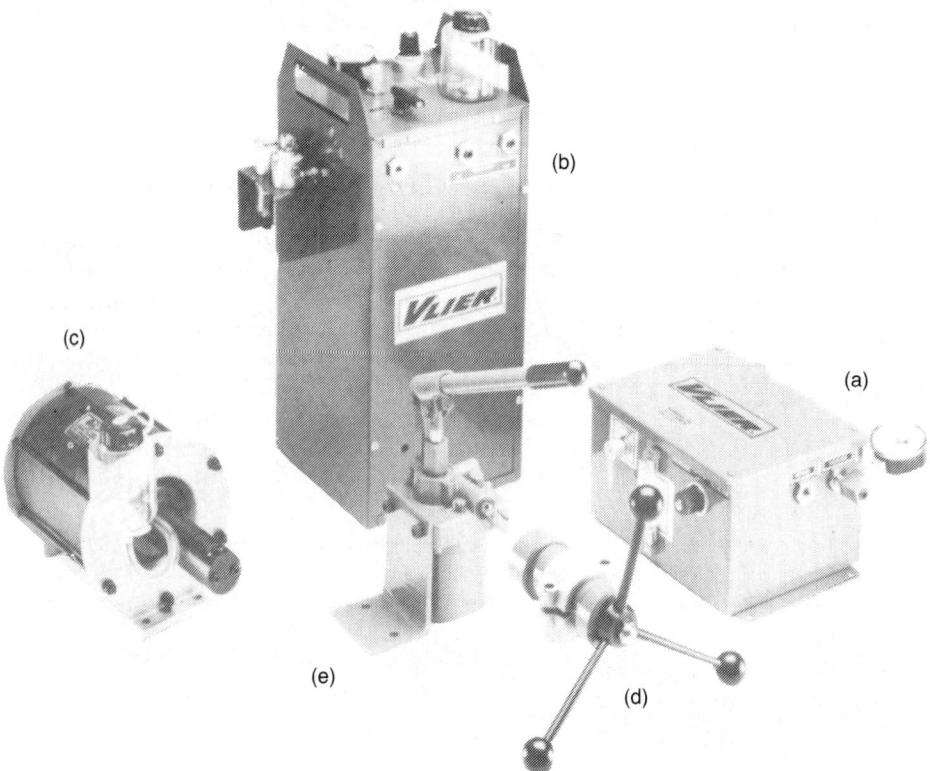

Fig. 3-103 Power sources. (*Courtesy Vlier Engineering*)

The intensifiers, *b* and *c*, are the most widely used power sources. The intensifier delivers its volume of fluid in one continuous motion which results in a speedy response time. Intensifiers are available with fluid capacities ranging from 2.5 to 10.0 in.^{3} (40,967 to 163,870 mm^3) and have a flow rate of 5 in.^{3}/s (81,935 mm^3/s). They can be installed close to the fixture or at a remote location. They operate with factory air ranging from 20 to 125 psi (138 to 862 kPa) and provide 22 times magnification of the air pressure supplied, up to the maximum of 2,750 psi (19 MPa).

The lever pump, *d*, is a hand-operated unit having a capacity of 22 in.^{3} (360,514 mm^3). An internal pressure relief valve can be set to either 2,500 or 5,000 psi (17.2 or 34.5 MPa).

The screw pump, *e*, is the most compact and simple pump available. It provides up to 6.2 in.^{3} (101,600 mm^3) of fluid at a 2,500 psi (17.2 MPa) rating.

Accessories used to complete the hydraulic working system are shown in Fig. 3-104. Their use has already been covered in the section under definitions.

Typical applications of hydraulic clamping are shown in Figs. 3-105 thru 3-107. Included are the following:

- An air/hydraulic pump system application (see Fig. 3-105). When the four-way hydraulic valve, *A*, is opened, a threaded cylinder, *B*, positions the workpiece against stops. The swing clamp, *C*, activates and then the work support, *D*, "freezes", having been delayed previously by a sequence valve, *E*. An optional pressure limiting valve, *F*, limits the force of the threaded cylinder which positions the workpiece, *H*. The power source is an air/hydraulic pump, *G*.

- A hydropneumatic intensifier system (see Fig. 3-106). Several swing cylinders, *A*, hold down a long workpiece for milling. The system is powered by shop air connected to a hydraulic intensifier, *B*. By using a manifold, *C*, to branch lines close to the clamps, multiple hydraulic lines from the hydraulic intensifier are eliminated.

  Other components include the filter/regulator/lubricator, *D*, to regulate air pressure and keep the air free of impurities; the safety check valve, *E*, to maintain air pressure in event of pressure loss in the shop; the three-way manual valve, *F*, which instantly opens and closes the air supply; the rapid exhaust valve, *G*, with a silencer, *H*, to facilitate quick, quiet unclamping when air pressure to the hydraulic intensifier is released.

- Hydraulic clamping for FMS operations (see Fig. 3-107). FMS machining is made more efficient and precise with the pallet and tombstone outfitted with a quick-disconnect, hydraulic clamping system. The threaded cylinder, *A*, and retracting clamp, *B*, powered with a standard cylinder, *C*, hold the workpiece against stops while work support, *D*, delayed by sequence valve, *E*, keeps the workpiece in the proper machining position. The entire system is powered by an air/hydraulic pump, *F*. Quick disconnect fittings, *G*, permit the pallet to be moved around the plant for machining after the clamping system is activated. The holding valve, *H*, keeps the hydraulic fluid under pressure in the pallet. The remote control valve, *I*, allows rapid injection of fluid into the pallet when connected, and pressure relief when re-connected. The accumulator, *J*, maintains hydraulic pressure in the pallet on a long term basis, even if the plumbing system has minor fluid leakage.

Standard drafting practices for fluid power diagrams can be found in ANSI Y14.17. Graphic symbols for fluid power diagrams can be found in ANSI Y32.10.

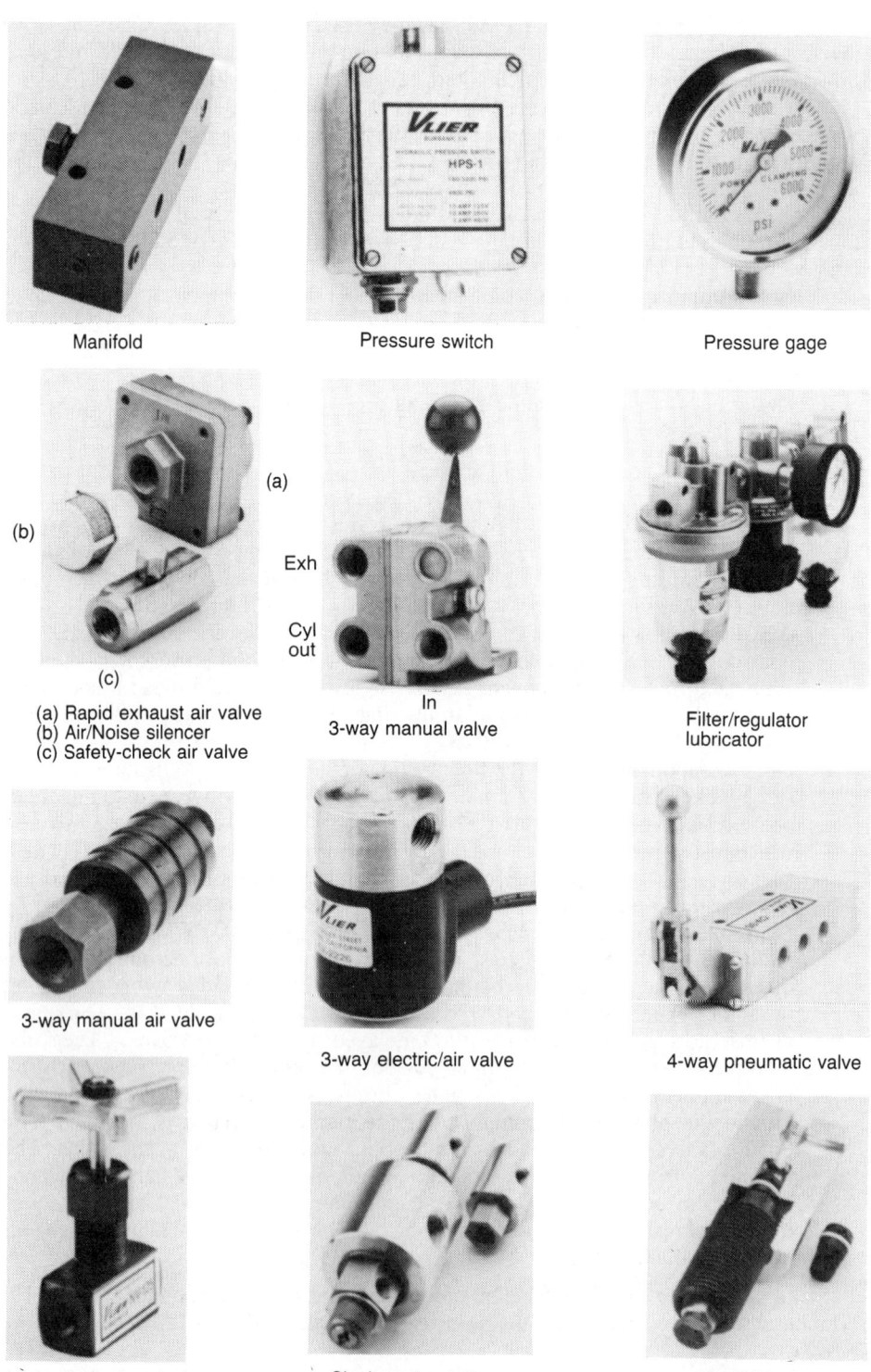

Manifold

Pressure switch

Pressure gage

(a)

(b)

Exh

Cyl
out

(c)

In

(a) Rapid exhaust air valve
(b) Air/Noise silencer
(c) Safety-check air valve

3-way manual valve

Filter/regulator
lubricator

3-way manual air valve

3-way electric/air valve

4-way pneumatic valve

Hydraulic flow control
needle valve

Single path rotating
union

Manifold adapter

Fig. 3-104 Hydraulic system accessories. (*Courtesy Vlier Engineering*)

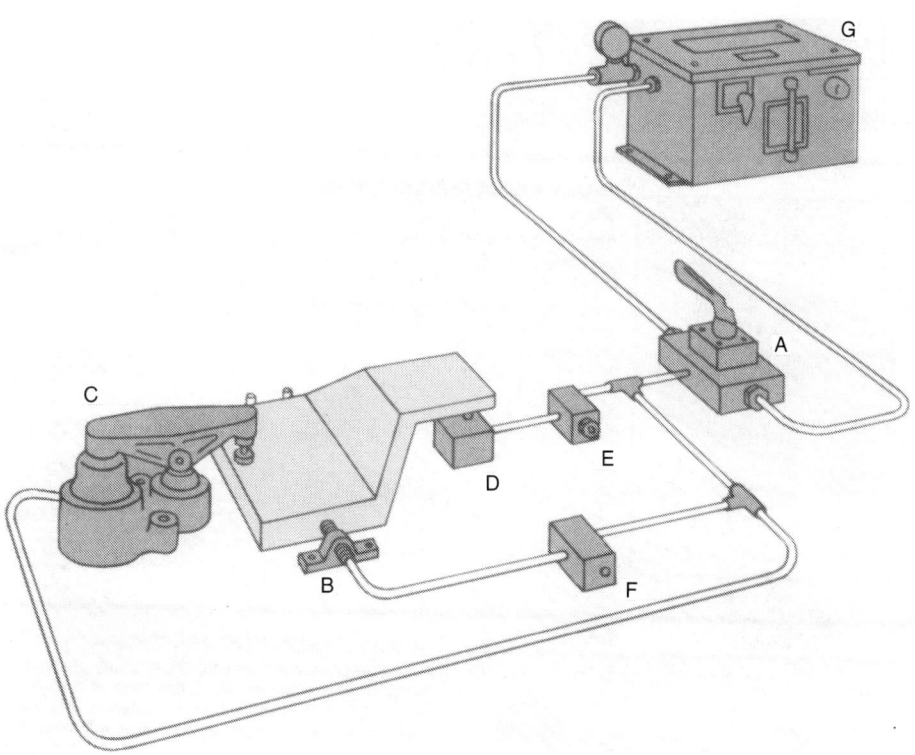

Fig. 3-105 Air/hydraulic pump system application data. (*Courtesy Vlier Engineering*)

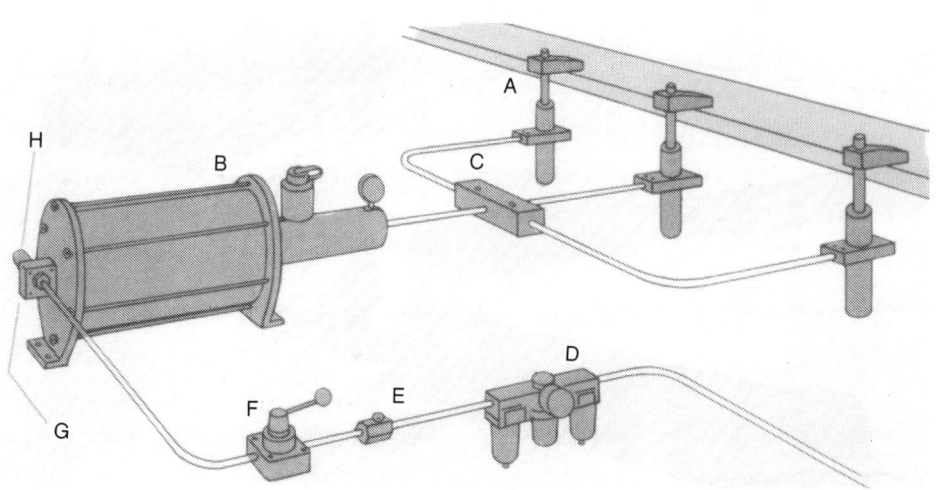

Fig. 3-106 Hydro-pneumatic intensifier system. (*Courtesy Vlier Engineering*)

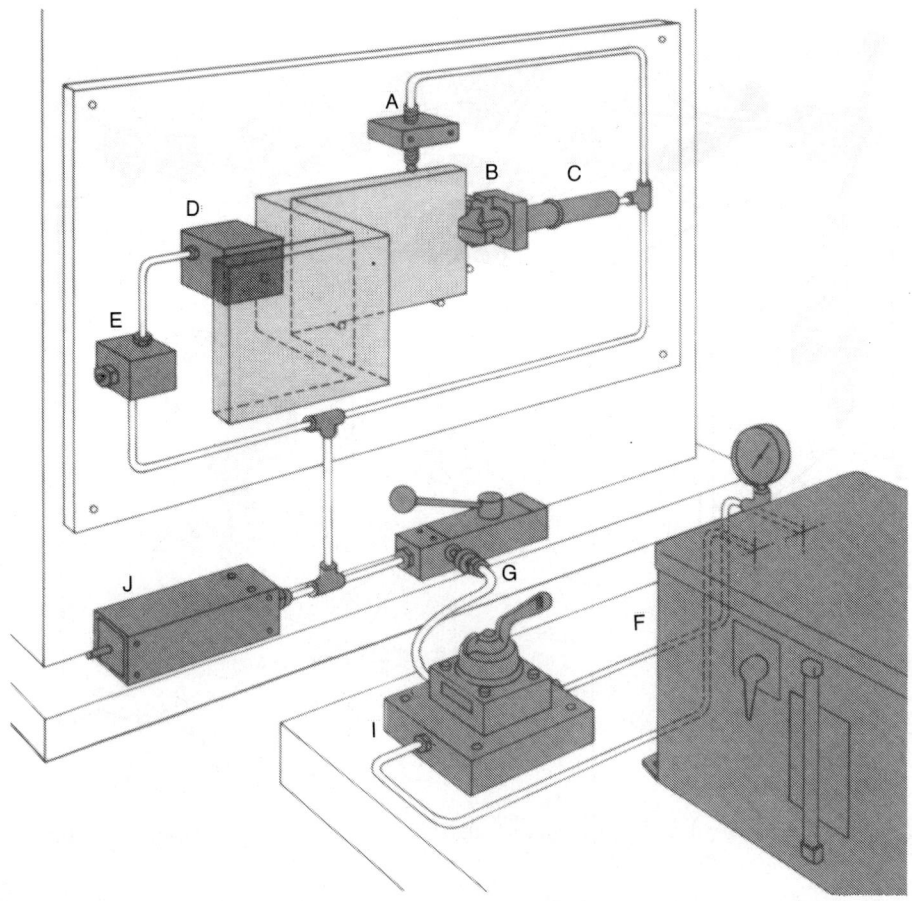

Fig. 3-107 Hydraulic clamping for FMS operations. (*Courtesy Vlier Engineering*)

CHAPTER 4
FIXTURE BODY DESIGN

The final step in the design of a jig or fixture is the design of the fixture body. Once the choice and placement of locating, clamping, and supporting details has been made and shown on a layout drawing, the designer can proceed to connect the details together to form a strong and rigid workholder. He or she must consider and provide for the following:

1. The fixture must fit onto the machine or pallet for which it is intended and not interfere with any of the machine parts.
2. The total weight of the fixture (and pallet if used) and the workpiece must be within the limits of the machine for which it is intended.
3. The fixture base must match the method of mounting on the machine or pallet, that is, T-slot, subplate, clamping directly on the table, etc. In some cases, a method for making slight adjustments must be provided to properly locate the fixture under the machine spindle.
4. The method of registering the fixture with the machine or pallet must be in agreement.
5. When using multiple fixtures, they must not interfere with each other.
6. Fixtures should be designed to permit the adjustment and changing of cutters, without disturbing the fixture, whenever possible.
7. The fixture should provide a clear view of the cutter's action.
8. Setting blocks, dial indicators, or some other suitable method must be provided for setting the cutter(s).
9. Lifting hooks or other provisions must be made to handle heavy or awkward fixtures.
10. Provide a method to establish "Program Zero" if required.
11. Provide sufficient clearance in the fixture to allow for any fins, burrs, or protrusions on the workpiece as well as normal variations in size and shape such as found on rough castings and forgings.
12. For heavy workpieces, make arrangements to slide them into the fixture rather than lifting them into place. Use retractable locating pins if necessary.
13. Provide an outrigger or some other suitable support for the free end of the workpiece when only one end of the workpiece is loaded into the fixture.
14. The operator must be able to load and unload the workpiece without interference by the machine or cutting tool(s).
15. Provide sufficient room for the operator's hands or fingers for loading and unloading the workpiece.
16. Locators must be protected from damage by cutters overrunning or being set too deep.

17. Provide sufficient clearance for the workpiece to be lifted over or into locating and centering devices.
18. Removable locating pins and adjusting devices should be located on the operator's side of the fixture.
19. Fixtures should be foolproofed to prevent a workpiece from being located incorrectly.
20. Provide ejectors for difficult-to-remove workpieces.
21. Provide a properly proportioned fixture with sufficient strength to resist cutting forces and damp out vibration and chatter.
22. Use universal commercial fixtures. Modify them to locate and clamp the workpiece as necessary.
23. Design fixtures around commercial indexing and angle setting equipment when practical.
24. Provide a fixture that is safe to use—protect the operator from the cutter.
25. Keep cutter travel to a minimum.
26. Provide adequate guides for cutting tools when required.
27. Provide stowage for loose details or attach them with a cable assembly.
28. Make sure that the coolant can reach the cutting edges of the tool.
29. Identify interchangeable and/or loose details, such as drill bushings and locating pins, with size and other pertinent information, such as "drill," "ream," etc.
30. Provide for easy chip removal.
31. Provide a channel to allow the coolant to wash chips away while draining from the fixture.
32. Use an air blast to clean the fixture before reloading when indicated.
33. Protect the operator from coolant spray, flying chips, and air blast.
34. Make provisions and necessary clearances to measure the workpiece, while mounted in the fixture, when indicated. Provide datum references on the fixture to measure from, if required.
35. Balance the fixture if it rotates.
36. Prevent the workpiece from flying out of the fixture if clamping fails.
37. Use interlocks to prevent clamps from loosening if air or hydraulic pressure fails.
38. Provide the operator with necessary instructions or warnings.
39. Provide a means of lubricating any tool mechanisms, if required.

Further considerations that apply mainly to drill jigs are covered in Chapter 8, Tooling for Drilling, Reaming and Related Processes.

TOOLING MATERIALS

The specific material selected for a particular tooling application is normally determined by the physical and mechanical properties necessary for the proper operation of the tool.

These properties include: weight, color, thermal and electrical conductivity, rate of thermal expansion, melting point, strength (tensile, compressive, shear, and yield), hardness (Rockwell and Brinell), wear resistance, toughness, brittleness, plasticity, ductility, malleability, and modulus of elasticity (bending and torsion).

These materials should be selected only after a careful study and evaluation of the function and requirements of the proposed tooling. In most applications, more than one type of material will be satisfactory, and a final choice will normally be governed by material availability and economic considerations.

The principal materials used for tooling can be divided into three major categories: ferrous materials, nonferrous materials, and nonmetallic materials. Ferrous tool materials have iron as a base metal and include tool steel, alloy steel, carbon steel, and cast iron. Nonferrous materials have a base metal other than iron, and include aluminum, magnesium, zinc, lead, bismuth, copper, and a variety of alloys. Nonmetallic materials are those materials such as woods, plastics, rubbers, and epoxy resins.

FERROUS TOOL MATERIALS

Many ferrous materials may be used in tool construction. Typically, materials such as carbon steel, alloy steel, tool steel, and cast iron are widely used for jigs, fixtures, dies, and similar special tools. These materials are supplied in several different forms. The most common types used for tools are hot rolled, cold rolled, and ground.

Carbon Steels. Carbon steels are used extensively in fixture construction. Carbon steels are those steels which only contain iron and carbon, and small amounts of other alloying elements. Carbon steels are the most common and least expensive type of steel used for tools. The three principal types of carbon steels used for tooling are low carbon, medium carbon, and high carbon steels. Low carbon steel contains between 0.05 and 0.30% carbon, medium carbon steel between 0.30 and 0.70% carbon, and high carbon steel between 0.70 and 1.50% carbon. As the carbon content is increased in carbon steel, the strength, toughness, and hardness also increase when the metal is heat treated (see Fig. 4-1).

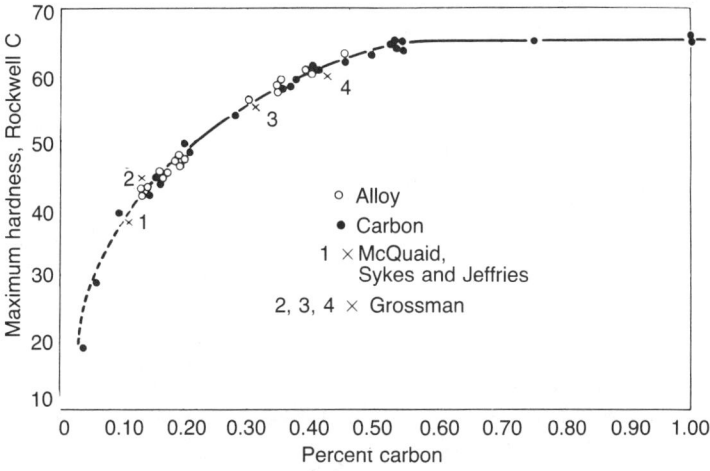

Fig. 4-1 Carbon content in relation to hardness possible.

Low Carbon Steels. Low carbon steels are soft, tough steels that are easily machined and welded. Due to their low carbon content, these steels cannot be hardened, except by case hardening. Low carbon steels are well suited for fixture bodies and similar situations where strength and wear resistance are not required. Low carbon steels are also easily welded.

Medium Carbon Steels. Medium carbon steels are used where greater strength and toughness is required. Since medium carbon steels have a higher carbon content they can be heat treated to make parts such as studs, pins, axles, and nuts. Steels in this group are more expensive, as well as more difficult to machine and weld than low carbon steels.

High Carbon Steels. High carbon steels are the most hardenable type of carbon steel and are used frequently for parts where wear resistance is an important factor. Other applications where high carbon steels are well suited include drill bushings, locators, and wear pads. Since the carbon content of these steels is so high, parts made from high carbon steel are normally difficult to machine and weld. Carbon steels are available in bars, strips, sheets, and special shapes.

Alloy Steels. Alloy steels are basically carbon steels with additional elements added to alter the characteristics and bring about a predictable change in the mechanical properties of the alloyed metal. Alloy steels are not normally used for most tools due to their increased cost, but some have found favor for special applications. The alloying elements used most often in steels are manganese, nickel, molybdenum, and chromium.

Another type of alloy steel frequently used for tooling applications is stainless steel. Stainless steel is a term used to describe high chromium and nickel-chromium steels. These steels are used for tools which must resist high temperatures and corrosive atmospheres. Some high chromium steels can be hardened by heat treatment and are used where resistance to wear, abrasion, and corrosion are required.

Tool Steels. Tool steels are alloy steels which are produced primarily for use in cutting tools, locators, and gages. Proper selection of tool steels is complicated by their many special properties. The five principal properties of tool steels are heat resistance, abrasion resistance, shock resistance, resistance to movement or distortion in hardening, and cutting ability.

Because no one steel can possess all of these properties to the optimum degree, hundreds of different tool steels have been developed to meet the total range of service demands.

Table 4-1 lists the basic characteristics of steels used for tooling purposes.

The general nature and application of the various standard tool steel classes are as follows:

W: Water-Hardening Tool Steels. This group includes plain carbon (W1) and carbon vanadium (W2). Carbon steels were the original tool steels. Because of their low cost, abrasion-resisting and shock-resisting qualities, ease of machinability, and ability to take a keen cutting edge, the carbon grades are widely applied. Both W1 and W2 steels are shallow-hardening and are readily available.

O: Oil-Hardening Tool Steels. Types O1 and O2 are manganese oil-hardening tool steels. They are readily available and inexpensive. These steels have less internal molecular movement than the water-hardening steels, and are of equal toughness with water-hardening steels when the latter are hardened throughout. Wear resistance is slightly better than that of water-hardening steels of equal carbon content. Steel O7 has greater wear resistance because of its increased carbon and tungsten content.

A: Air-Hardening Die Steels. Type A2 is the principal air-hardening tool steel. It has minimum movement in hardening and has higher toughness than the oil-hardening die steels, with equal or greater wear resistance. Steels A4, A5, and A6 can be hardened from lower temperatures, but have lower wear resistance and better distortional properties.

D: High-Carbon High-Chromium Die Steels. Type D2 is the principal steel in this class. It finds wide application for long-run dies. It is deep-hardening, fairly tough, and has good resistance to wear. Steels D3, D4, and D6, containing additional carbon, have very high wear resistance and lower toughness. Steels D2 and D4 are air-hardened.

S: Shock-Resisting Tool Steels. These steels contain less carbon and have higher toughness. They are applied where heavy cutting or forming operations are required and where breakage is a serious problem. Steels S1, S4, and S5 are readily available. Steels S4 and S5 are more economical than S1.

H: Hot-Work Die Steels. These steels combine red hardness with good wear resistance and shock resistance. They are air-hardening and on occasion are used for cold-work applications. They have relatively low carbon content and intermediate to high alloy content.

T and M: Tungsten and Molybdenum High Speed Steels. Steels T1 and M2 are equivalent in performance and have good red hardness and abrasion resistance. They have higher toughness than many of the other die steels. They may be hardened by conventional methods or carburized for cold-work applications. Steels M3, M4, and T15 have

TABLE 4-1
Comparison of Basic Characteristics of Steels Used For Tooling

AISI Steel No.	Non-deforming Properties	Safety in Hardening	Toughness	Resistance to Softening Effect of Heat	Wear Resistance	Machin-ability
W1	Poor	Fair	Good	Poor	Fair	Best
W2	Poor	Fair	Good	Poor	Fair	Best
01	Good	Good	Fair	Poor	Fair	Good
02	Good	Good	Fair	Poor	Fair	Good
07	Good	Good	Fair	Poor	Fair	Good
A2	Best	Best	Fair	Fair	Good	Fair
A4	Best	Best	Fair	Poor	Fair	Fair
A5	Best	Best	Fair	Poor	Fair	Fair
A6	Best	Best	Fair	Poor	Fair	Fair
D2	Best	Best	Fair	Fair	Good	Poor
D3	Good	Good	Poor	Fair	Best	Poor
D4	Best	Best	Poor	Fair	Best	Poor
D6	Good	Good	Poor	Fair	Best	Poor
S1	Fair	Good	Good	Fair	Fair	Fair
S2	Poor	Fair	Best	Fair	Fair	Fair
S4	Poor	Fair	Best	Fair	Fair	Fair
S5	Fair	Good	Best	Fair	Fair	Fair
H11	Best	Best	Best	Good	Fair	Fair
H12	Best	Best	Best	Good	Fair	Fair
H13	Best	Best	Best	Good	Fair	Fair
H21	Good	Good	Good	Good	Fair	Fair
H26	Good	Good	Good	Best	Good	Fair
T1	Good	Good	Fair	Best	Good	Fair
T15	Good	Fair	Poor	Best	Best	Poor
M2	Good	Fair	Fair	Best	Good	Fair
M3	Good	Fair	Fair	Best	Good	Fair
M4	Good	Fair	Fair	Best	Best	Poor
L2	Fair	Fair	Good	Poor	Fair	Fair
L3	Fair	Poor	Fair	Poor	Fair	Good
L6	Good	Good	Good	Poor	Fair	Fair
F2	Poor	Poor	Poor	Fair	Best	Fair

greater cutting ability and resistance to wear. They are more difficult to machine and grind because of their increased carbon and alloy contents.

L: Low-Alloy Tool-Steels. Steels L3 and L6 are used for special die applications. Other L steels find application where fatigue and toughness are important considerations, such as in coining or impression dies.

F: Finishing Steels. Steel F2 is of limited use but occasionally applied where extremely high wear resistance in a shallow-hardening steel is desired.

Cast Iron. Cast iron is essentially an alloy of iron and carbon, containing from 2 to 4% carbon, 0.5 to about 3.00% silicon, 0.4 to approximately 1% manganese, plus phosphorus and sulphur. Other alloys may be added depending on the properties desired.

The high compressive strength and ease of casting of the gray irons are utilized in large forming and drawing dies to produce such items as automobile panels, refrigerator cabinets, bath tubs, and other large articles. Conventional methods of hardening result in little distortion.

Alloying elements are added to contract graphitization, to improve mechanical properties, or to develop special characteristics.

NONFERROUS TOOL MATERIALS

In jig and fixture design some nonferrous materials are used extensively where magnetism or tool weight are important factors.

Aluminum. Aluminum is a nonferrous metal which has been used for special tooling for quite some time. The principal advantages in using aluminum are high strength-to-weight ration, non-magnetic properties, and relative ease in machining and forming. Pure aluminum is corrosion resistant, but not well suited for use as a tooling material except in very limited low strength applications. Aluminum alloys, while not as corrosion resistant as pure aluminum, are much stronger and are well suited for many special tooling applications. The alloys most frequently used for tooling applications are aluminum/copper (2000 series) and aluminum/zinc (7000 series). Depending on composition, some aluminum alloys are weldable and some can be heat treated. One form of aluminum alloy finding increased use today is aluminum tooling plate. This material is available in sheets and bars made to very close tolerances. Aluminum tooling plate is very useful for a wide variety of tooling applications. From supports and locators to base plates and tool bodies, aluminum tooling plate provides a lightweight alternative to steel. Other variations of aluminum frequently used for tooling are aluminum extrusions and cast bracket materials. In most cases, the materials can be used as is with little or no machining required.

Magnesium. Magnesium, like aluminum, is a lightweight yet strong tooling material. Magnesium is lighter than aluminum and has a very good strength-to-weight ratio. Magnesium is commercially available in sheets, bars, tooling plates, and extruded forms. The only disadvantage to using magnesium is its potential fire hazard. When specifying magnesium as a tooling material make sure those who are to make the various parts are well acquainted with the precautions which must be observed when machining this material.

The reader can refer to Table 1-6 for lists of the properties of the aluminum and magnesium alloys used for tooling and compares them with cast iron and steel.

Bismuth Alloys. Bismuth alloys have several different uses in special tools. One application of these alloys is for cast workholders. Here the material is melted and poured around the part and once cool, the part is removed and the cast nest is used to hold subsequent parts for machining.

One of the principal advantages of bismuth alloys is their very low melting temperature. Many alloy compositions will melt in boiling water. In addition to acting as a reusable nesting material, these low-melt alloys are also useful when machining parts with very thin cross sections, such as turbine blades. In these applications, the material is cast around the thin section and acts as a support during machining. Once the machining is complete, the material is melted off the part and can be reused.

Carbides. Carbides are a family of tooling materials made from the carbides of tungsten, titanium, tantalum or a combination of these elements. They are powder metals consisting of the carbide with a binder—usually cobalt—hot pressed or sintered to desired shapes. The most common carbide material used is tungsten carbide. All carbides are characterized by high hardness values and resistance to wear, making them an excellent choice for cutting tools and gages.

NONMETALLIC TOOLING MATERIALS

Nonmetallic tooling materials are chiefly used where the production of parts is limited and where the cost of using tool steels or similar materials would not be economically practical. The principal nonmetallic materials used for special tooling are wood, composition materials, plastics, epoxy resins, rubber, and urethane.

WOOD

Wood is divided into two general classes—hardwood and softwood. These terms are imprecise, for no definite degree of hardness divides hardwoods from softwoods. The terms are used in a general sense to indicate the type of tree—whether deciduous or evergreen—from which the wood is taken. Therefore, when wood is selected, its actual rated strength, and not the term by which it is known should be considered. A realistic classification of the properties of the most common species of trees used for construction is listed in Table 4-2.

TABLE 4-2
Properties of Wood

Wood	Strength	Shrinkage	Workability	Resistance to Shock	Resistance to Splitting
Softwood					
Cedar	Medium	Very Little	Excellent	Excellent	Good
Cypress	Medium	Moderate	Poor	Poor	Good
Fir, Douglas	Medium	Moderate	Poor	Poor	Poor
Pine, White	Low	Very Little	Excellent	Poor	Good
Spruce	Low	Moderate	Fair	Poor	Good
Hardwood					
Ash	High	Moderate	Good	Good	Fair
Beech	High	Considerable	Poor	Good	Fair
Birch	High	Considerable	Fair	Excellent	Fair
Cherry	High	Moderate	Fair	Good	Fair
Chestnut	Medium	Moderate	Good	Fair	Poor
Elm	Medium	Considerable	Poor	Excellent	Excellent
Maple, Hard	High	Moderate	Good	Good	Fair
Hickory	High	Considerable	Poor	Excellent	Poor
Oak	High	Considerable	Fair	Good	Poor
Walnut	High	Moderate	Good	Good	Fair

Strength. The cross-section of a log from any type of tree will show many concentric layers or rings. These layers are made up of millions of cells of wood fiber and are commonly known as growth rings, or annual rings, since a new layer appears each year that the tree continues to grow. The growth rings differ greatly in width and density among different species and among trees of the same species.

The quality of wood, particularly its density and strength, is directly related to the growth rings in all tree species. Wide-ringed wood generally indicates lumber of inferior quality. Not only is this type of wood weaker than normal wood, but it is also subject to high degrees of shrinkage and warpage. Wood of the best quality for tooling construction is usually produced when the growth rate results in more than six growth rings per inch.

The direction of the force or load in relation to the growth rings is also important to wood's maximum strength. Usually very little attention is paid to this factor, but experiments and tests have proven that greatest strength is obtained when the growth rings lie perpendicular to the load. When the rings lie parallel to the load, medium strength is obtained, but when the growth rings are at 45° to the load, the strength of the wood is considerably reduced.

Warpage. The main disadvantage of wood is its tendency to shrink or swell with changes in humidity. When such shrinkages or swellings occur across areas of different density in wood, warpage may result. Warpage is the change or variation from a flat or plane surface of a board.

The warpage of boards can be countered to some extent by laminated construction in which two or more boards are bonded together with an adhesive.

PROCESSED WOOD

Processed wood is wood that has been re-formed or altered by some type of manufacturing process. By the processes which the wood undergoes, some of its unfavorable properties—warpage, splitting, and limited hardness—are reduced, while some of its favorable properties—strength, limited expansion and contraction, and shock absorption—are improved. Three types of processed wood are especially useful for tool construction. They are plywood, metal-clad plywood, and compressed wood.

Plywood. Plywood is wood paneling composed of wood layers bonded together with moisture-resistant or moisture-proof glue. The layers are juxtapositioned so that their grains run in different directions, generally at right angles to each other, so the resultant plywood sheet is equally strong in all directions. Exterior plywood, bonded with moisture-proof glue, is best for tooling construction because it resists the processing coolants and oils better than interior plywood.

In addition to its added strength and resistance to warping, splitting, and checking, plywood will not expand or contract to the extent of regular wood because of its cross-grained construction.

For increased versatility as a tooling construction material, exterior panels of plywood can be soaked with water or steamed and bent to almost any curvature.

Metal-Clad Plywood. Metal-clad (or metal-faced) plywood is fabricated by bonding thin sheets of metal to one or both faces of a piece of plywood. The resulting product is equivalent in rigidity to a solid steel section four times its weight. Many different types of metal are used to face the panels, but the most common are Monel™ metal (Inco Alloys International, Inc.), galvanized steel, aluminum, and stainless steel.

The advantages of metal-clad plywood as a tooling material are:
- Good resistance to buckling and bending. Metal-clad plywood offers greater resistance to buckling and bending per unit weight, than any other construction material.
- Good wear resistance. Wear resistance characteristics are created by the metal facing.
- Resistance to damage by surface blows. Unless struck by sharp objects, this type of plywood is not vulnerable to damage from heavy use. The plywood core has a tendency to absorb the energy of a blow and distribute it over a large surface instead of buckling or breaking as a thin sheet of metal would do.
- Resistance to heat and fire. Metal-clad plywood, as compared with unclad plywood, has substantial advantages in this area.
- Ease in working. It can be cut easily with standard wood or metal-cutting tools.

In addition to the characteristics listed above, metal-clad plywood possesses certain other characteristics useful to the toolmaker. For example, the edges of the plywood may be protected by cutting back the plywood core and folding over either one or both of the exposed metal edges.

Finally, this material is easy to shape. Plywood with a metal facing on one side only may be bent or formed to create minor curves. In this process the metal must be on the outside of the curve. The material must be processed through bending rolls, as with sheet metal, to obtain more acute curves.

Compressed Wood. Compressed wood is a manufactured product composed of many layers or veneers of wood ranging in thickness from 0.01 to 0.08 in. (0.3 to 2.0 mm) and bonded with phenolic resin under high pressure and heat. The amount of pressure applied determines the density of the finished product.

Because of its favorable characteristics, compressed wood is being used more and more for the construction of jigs and fixtures for limited production. At present its two main applications are in the aircraft industry and in the fabrication of steel-rule dies.

Its main advantage is its excellent machinability. Compressed wood can be machined easily with standard woodworking tools at speeds and feeds comparable to those recommended for natural wood. These machinability characteristics produce man-hour-tool economies not possible with conventional materials.

COMPOSITION MATERIALS

Composition materials are materials normally made from a filler, or base material, and some type of resin acting as a binder. Two typical composition materials used for special tooling are phenolic and Bakelite. Both materials are used for the same applications as wood, but are more stable and less susceptible to moisture.

Plastics. Plastics are some of the newer tooling materials, and are used where the operations are not severe and the production run is short to medium. Plastics are resistant to chemicals, moisture, and temperature. They are inexpensive and facilitate tool repair and modification. In most cases, plastics can be machined with the same tools and equipment as metals and can be easily adapted to toolroom uses. Plastics have been recently developed to withstand high heat, abrasion, and some have a non-stick surface that makes an excellent sliding surface. Some newer "space-age" plastics have tensile and shear strength equal to steels. With constant research and development in the plastics industry, plastics will play an increasingly important role as a tool material.

Epoxy Resins. Epoxy resins are mainly used for casting and laminating. Castable resins are used for jig plates, workholders, silk screen fixtures, duplicating patterns, and for large forming dies. In addition to the resin, a filler material is added to the mixture to increase its strength and to provide better dimensional stability. Typical filler materials include glass beads, metal beads, and metal filings. Cast resins are strong and relatively lightweight. When properly cast, these resins require little or no machining. Laminated resins are used for large, stretch forming dies and checking fixtures. These materials are generally laminated over a wooden frame.

In either case, epoxy resins combine low cost, ease of modification, and shortened lead times into a single tooling material. They work well with intricate or complex part shapes, and depending on the filler material, will normally last a long time.

Rubber. Today, rubber is used less than it was in earlier times. This is due in large part to the newer and better materials which have been developed. But rubber is still used for specialized drawing, blanking, and bulging die operations as well as protective elements for other special tools.

Urethane. Urethane is a material that is becoming widely used for special tooling. It is available in solid bars that can be machined to suit a specific application or cast into almost any desired form. Urethane is noncompressive and acts as a liquid when force is applied. That is, when force is applied, urethane displaces the force equally in all directions. By containing and redirecting these displaced forces, urethane can be used to form complex shapes without marring the workpiece material. When used as a clamp pad, urethane transfers all the clamping forces without damaging the workpiece surfaces.

Urethane does not shrink an appreciable amount and can be used to duplicate parts exactly. Lack of shrinkage makes urethane ideal for nests for ultrasonic fixtures or molds for model parts.

HEAT TREATING

The purpose of heat treatment is to control the properties of a metal or alloy through the alteration of the structure of the metal or alloy by heating it to definite temperatures and cooling at various rates. This combination of heating and controlled cooling determines not only the nature and distribution of the microconstituents, which in turn determine the properties, but also the grain size.

Heat treating should improve the alloy or metal for the service intended. Some of the various purposes of heat treating are as follows:

1. To remove strains after cold working.
2. To remove internal stresses such as those produced by drawing, bending, or welding.
3. To increase the hardness of the material.
4. To improve machinability.
5. To improve the cutting capabilities of tools.
6. To increase wear-resisting properties.
7. To soften the material, as in annealing.
8. To improve or change properties of a material, such as corrosion resistance, heat resistance, magnetic properties, or others, as required.

TREATMENT OF FERROUS MATERIALS

Iron is the major constituent in the steels used in tooling, to which carbon is added in order that the steel may harden. Alloys are put into steel to enable it to develop properties not possessed by plain carbon steel, such as the ability to harden in oil or air, increased wear resistance, higher toughness, and greater safety in hardening.

Heat treatment of ferrous materials involves several important operations which are customarily referred to under various headings, such as normalizing, spheroidizing, stress relieving, annealing, hardening, tempering, and case hardening.

Normalizing. Normalizing involves heating the material to a temperature of about 100° to 200°F (55 to 110°C) above the critical range and cooling in still air. This is about 100°F (55° C) over the regular hardening temperature.

The purpose of normalizing is usually to refine grain structures that have been coarsened in forging.

High-alloy, air-hardened steels are never normalized, since to do so would cause them to harden and defeat the primary purpose.

Spheroidizing. Spheroidizing is a form of annealing which, in the process of heating and cooling steel, produces a rounded or globular form of carbide—the hard constituent in steel.

Tool steels are normally spheroidized to improve machinability. This is accomplished by heating to a temperature 1380 to 1400°F (749 to 760°C) for carbon steels and higher for many alloy tool steels, holding at heat one to four hours, and cooling slowly in the furnace.

Stress Relieving. This is a method of relieving the internal stresses set up in steel during forming, cold working, and cooling after welding or machining. It is the simplest heat treatment and is accomplished merely by heating to 1200 to 1350°F (649 to 732°C) followed by air or furnace cooling.

Welded sections often have locked-in stresses owing to a combination of differential heating and cooling cycles as well as to changes in cross section. Such stresses will cause considerable movement in machining operations.

Annealing. The process of annealing consists of heating the steel to an elevated temperature for a definite period of time and, usually, cooling it slowly. Annealing is done to produce homogenization and to establish normal equilibrium conditions, with corresponding characteristic properties.

Tool steel is generally purchased in the annealed condition. Sometimes it is necessary to rework a tool that has been hardened, and the tool must then be annealed. For this type of anneal, the steel is heated slightly above its critical range and then cooled very slowly.

Hardening. This is the process of heating to a temperature above the critical range, and cooling rapidly enough through the critical range to appreciably harden the steel.

Tempering. This is the process of heating quenched and hardened steels and alloys to some temperature below the lower critical temperature to reduce internal stresses setup in hardening. Thus, the hard martensite resulting from the quenching operation is changed in tempering in the direction of the equilibrium properties, the degree being dependent on the tempering temperature and rate of cooling.

Case Hardening. The addition of carbon to the surface of steel parts and the subsequent hardening operations are important phases in heat treating. The process may involve the use of molten sodium cyanide mixtures, pack carburizing, and dry cyaniding.

The carbon content of the surface is raised to 0.80 to 1.20% and the case depth can be closely controlled by the time, the temperature, and the carburizing medium used. Pack carburizing is generally done at 1700°F (927°C) for eight hours to produce a case depth of 1/16 in. (1.6 mm). Light cases up to 0.005 in. (0.13 mm), can be obtained in liquid cyanide baths, and case depths to 1/32 in. (0.8 mm) are economically practical in liquid carburizing baths.

Usually, low-carbon and low-carbon alloy steels are carburized. The normal carbon range is 0.10 to 0.30% carbon, though higher carbon-content steels may be carburized as well.

TREATMENT OF NONFERROUS MATERIALS

The heat treatment of nonferrous metals and alloys closely approximates that of steel except that the temperature ranges used are lower, and hardening is accomplished by the precipitation of hard metallic compounds or particles.

Nonferrous metals and alloys that are not heat-treatable harden by cold work only.

For the heat-treatable alloys of aluminum, hardening is accomplished by precipitation. When an alloy is water-quenched from the "hardening heat" it is very soft; this is known as the solution treatment. Hardness is accomplished by aging, which follows the quenching operation. The aging temperature for some aluminum alloys is room temperature; others may require an elevated temperature such as 290 to 360°F (143 to 182°C), depending on the alloy. As a rule, the lower the aging temperature, the longer the time required for the alloy to reach full hardness.

Beryllium copper is a precipitation-hardening alloy and is usually furnished by the manufacturer in the very soft solution-treated condition. It has excellent forming properties in this condition. Formed parts are hardened by aging at 560 to 620°F (293 to 327°C) for two hours at heat. A hardness of R_c 38 to 42 can be expected.

All other brass and bronze alloys are hardenable only by cold working and may be softened to various degrees by stress relieving or annealing.

COMMERCIAL FIXTURES AND ELEMENTS

Before proceeding with this final step in the design of a fixture, the designer must thoroughly investigate the possibility of using commercially available equipment and fixtures.

Commercially available fixtures, components, and hardware can reduce jig and fixture design time and cost. Many fixturing problems can be solved with vendor components and services. Constant research and development resulting in new offerings makes it impractical to provide a complete index of available vendor items.

Costs will be increased if every fixture component is designed and fully detailed. Standard items seldom need to be drawn other than in outline form on assembly drawings. Most vendors furnish templates for their products to allow outlines and other dimensional data to be easily and quickly traced onto an engineering drawing.

Many others have 2D and 3D tooling component libraries for computer-aided tool design.

A standard component will generally be of certified quality and structural adequacy, while original component design may include some analysis of probable load, which may result in overdesign to compensate for variables in workmanship and materials.

The purchase price of a mass-produced component is usually considerably less than the cost of its fabrication in the plant. Purchased components also reduce assembly labor costs because they are designed for ease of assembly. Fixture maintenance costs are reduced by standardization and off-the-shelf availability of components.

The designer often assumes responsibility for the decision to make or buy a fixture. He or she can survey the complete range of fixtures that are commercially available and consider the advantages of standardization, cost, and off-the-shelf availability, with or without minor in-plant rework. If a complete unit is unavailable, it may be fabricated from purchased major components. Standard hardware, such as bushings, clamps, buttons, straps, etc., should be considered even in the case of a complex fixture.

The make-or-buy decision will be further influenced by the availability of skilled manpower and facilities and by consideration of the probable work load at the proposed fabrication time. In the toolroom, the heavy work load accompanying product change will usually preclude doing major fixture work. At other times, fixture work might be a profitable way to use required stand-by technicians.

COMMERCIAL POSITIONING EQUIPMENT

Linear and rotary positioning equipment, such as shown in Fig. 4-2, can be used as is, or equipped with chucks or collet fixtures to hold workpieces for machining or inspection. They are widely used for prototype parts and small production lots where the cost of a special single purpose fixture would be prohibitive. Most equipment of this nature can be furnished with digital readout.

The rotary table, a, and the tilting-rotary table, b, provide indexing accuracy of 30 seconds and can be motorized and equipped with a preset indexer which permits use of a stepping motor-powered rotary table as an independent rotary positioning system or add-on 4th axis to be actuated by "M" functions on a 3-axis machining center. A dividing attachment such as shown in, c, is available for these tables.

The cross slide table, d, can be used for precision positioning on the X-Y axes, while the cross slide rotary table, e, can be used for precision rotary positioning as well as the X-Y axes positioning.

The universal indexing head shown in Fig. 4-3 is suitable for horizontal indexing of both cylindrical and tapered workpieces between centers. Universal indexing heads can be used for spiral milling and milling cam plates with archimedian spiral.

COMMERCIAL ANGLE SETTING AND CHECKING EQUIPMENT

Figure 4-4 shows some of the different types of heavy-duty angle setting equipment that are available commercially. All provide a fast means of positioning a workpiece for layout, machining, or inspection. T-slots are usually provided for clamping the workpiece, or attaching workholding devices or fixtures. Many are equipped with verniers to provide accurate setting to within 5 sec. For closer settings they are set with a sine bar which in some cases is integral to the fixture.

Sine plates and compound sine plates similar to those shown in Fig. 4-5 a and b are available in various sizes. Tapped holes are usually provided for clamping purposes.

Clamping for sine plates and compound sine plates, such as shown in c and d, is provided by a permanent magnet which is turned on and off by changing the alignment

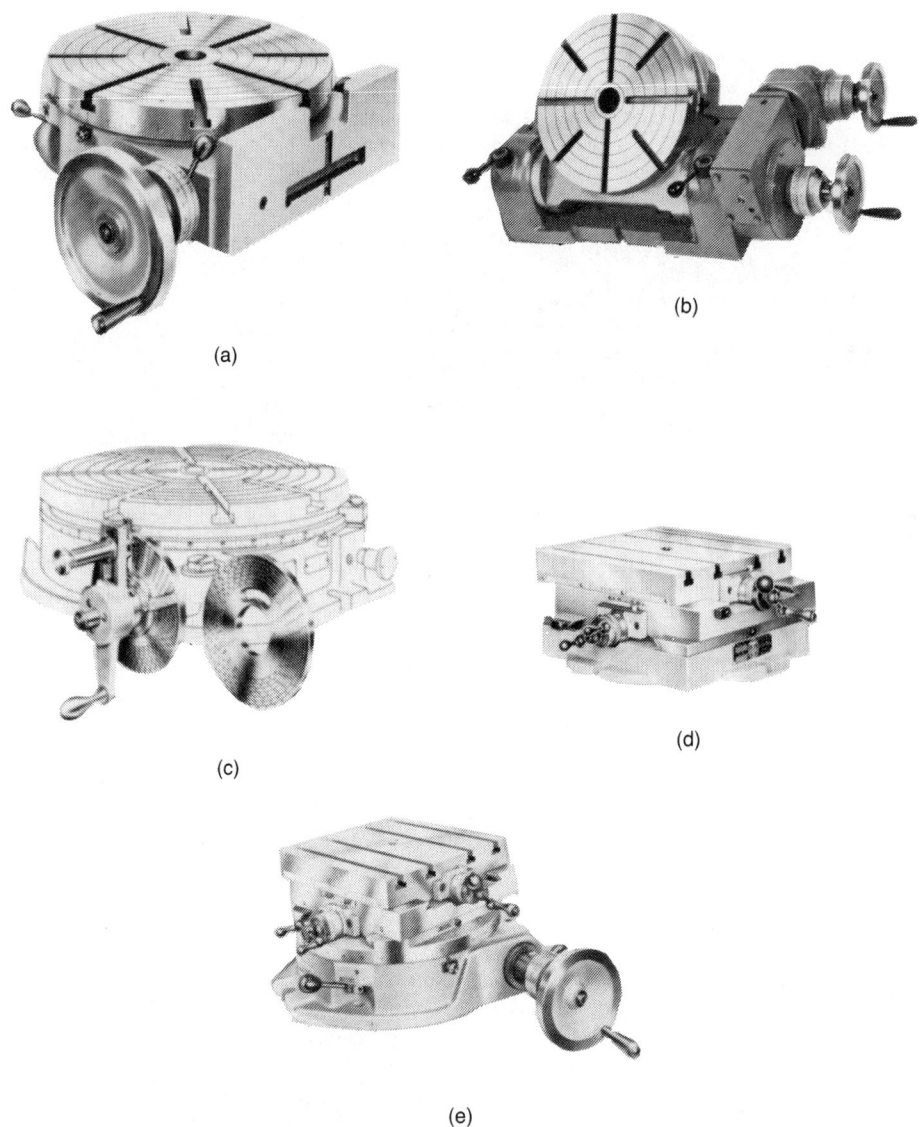

(a)

(b)

(c)

(d)

(e)

Fig. 4-2 Precision linear and rotary positioning equipment. (*Courtesy Troyke Mfg. Co.*)

of the internal magnets with a hex wrench or handle. Similar equipment (not shown) is available with electromagnetic chucking which is turned on and off by an electrical switch.

COMMERCIAL FIXTURES

The fixtures shown in Fig. 4-6 thru Fig. 4-10, with the addition of interchangeable jaws, locators, bushings, etc., are suitable for high-production drilling, tapping, threading, and milling operations on small parts.

The hand-operated vise fixture (see Fig. 4-6) incorporates self-centering horizontal master jaws that are held open by a spring and closed by turning the clamping screw.

Fig. 4-3 Universal indexing head. (*Courtesy Dapra Corp.*)

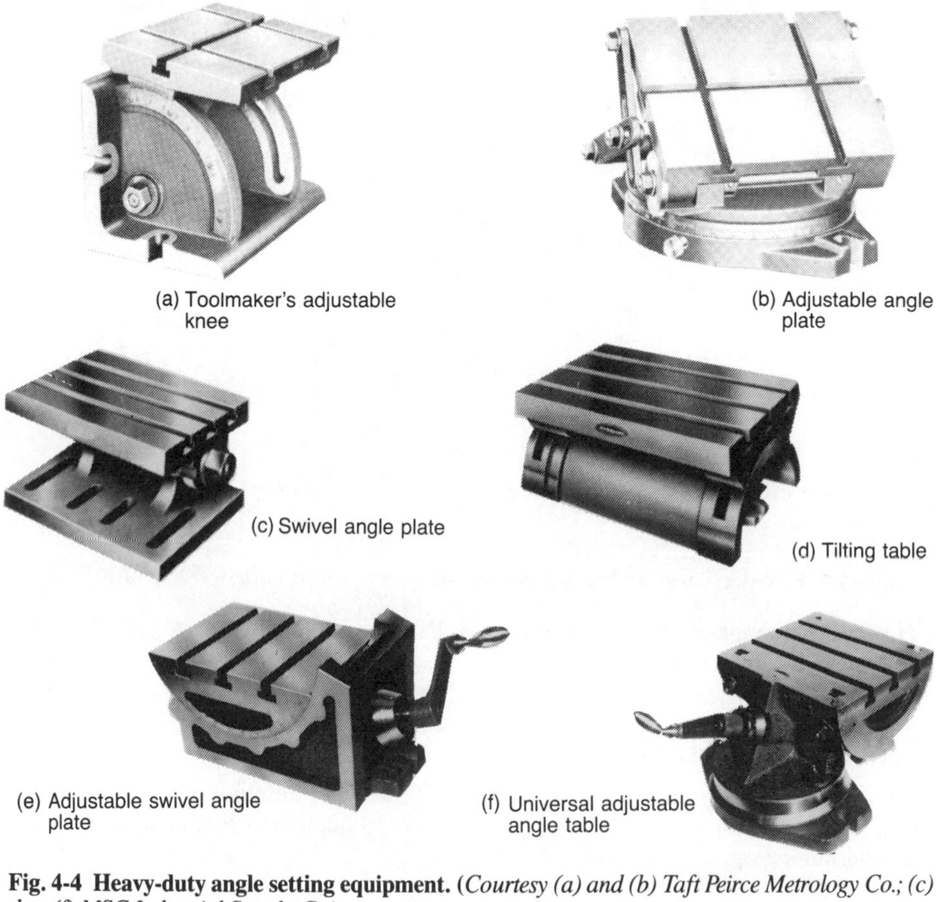

(a) Toolmaker's adjustable knee

(b) Adjustable angle plate

(c) Swivel angle plate

(d) Tilting table

(e) Adjustable swivel angle plate

(f) Universal adjustable angle table

Fig. 4-4 Heavy-duty angle setting equipment. (*Courtesy (a) and (b) Taft Peirce Metrology Co.; (c) thru (f) MSC Industrial Supply Co.*)

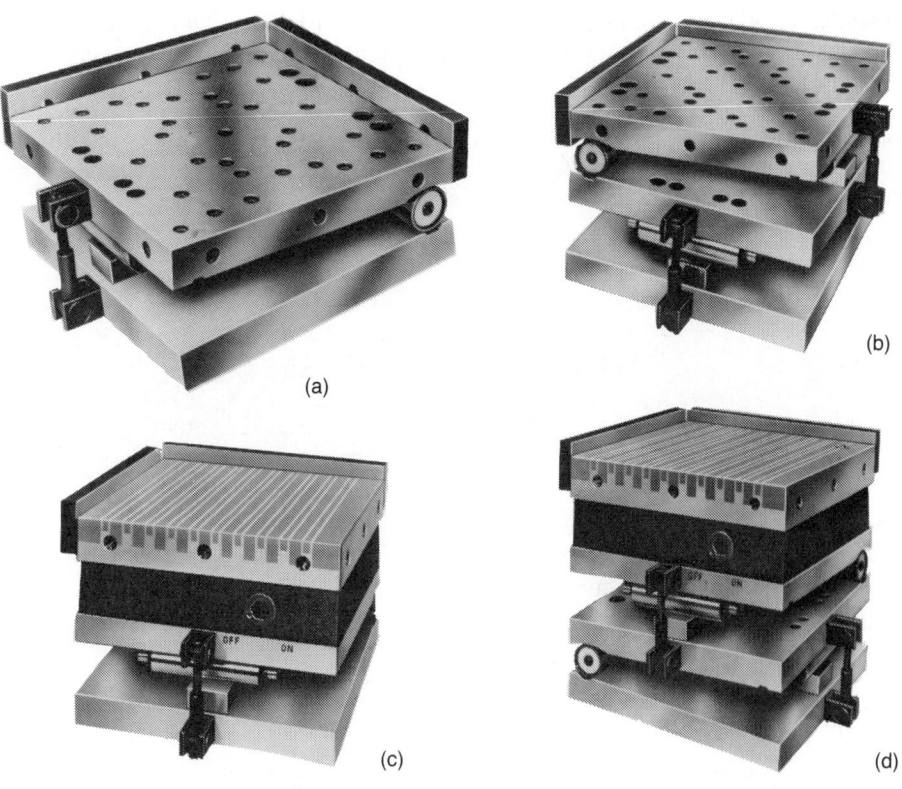

(a)

(b)

(c)

(d)

Fig. 4-5 Sine plates. (*Courtesy Herman Schmidt Co.*)

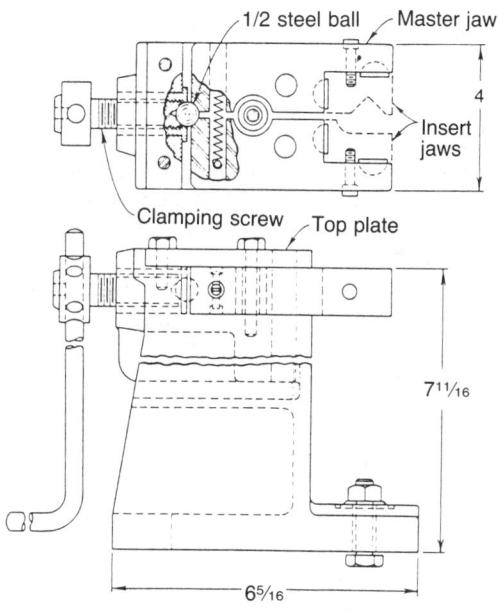

1/2 steel ball   Master jaw

Insert jaws

4

Clamping screw   Top plate

$7^{11}/_{16}$

$6^{5}/_{16}$

Fig. 4-6 Hand-operated vise fixture.

Interchangeable jaws hold small round parts (3/16 to 1 in. diam.) for vertical drilling or tapping. A support arm for drill bushings may be mounted to the top plate, and special jaws may be made to fit contoured parts.

The air-operated vise fixture (see Fig. 4-7) is suitable for drilling and tapping small parts (up to 1 ⅛ in. diam.). An air cylinder closes the jaws by moving a roller between them. The limit-switch lever, contacted by the workpiece or tripped by the operator, releases air pressure through a solenoid valve.

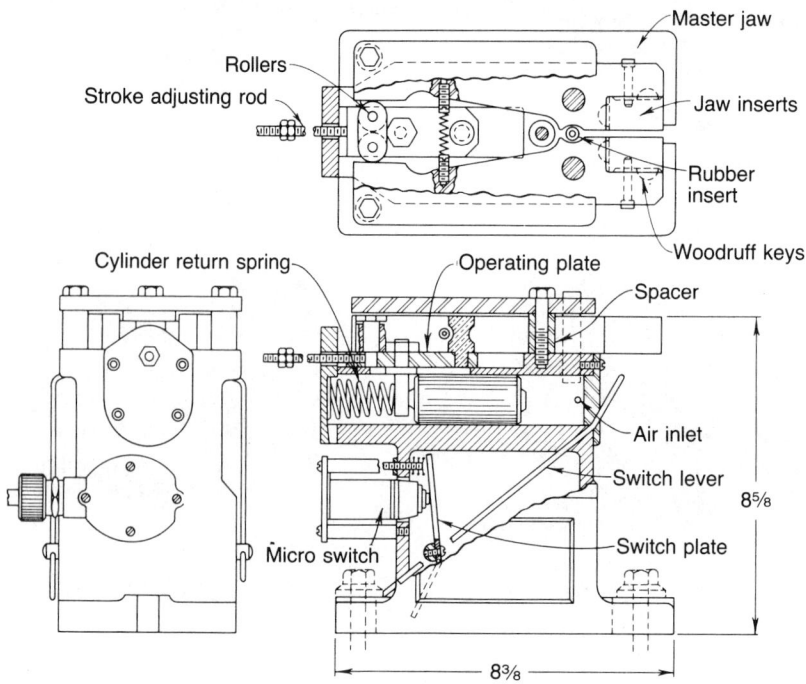

Fig. 4-7 Air-operated vise fixture.

Another fixture operated by air pressure (see Fig. 4-8) vertically clamps the workpiece and incorporates an automatic spring-loaded kick-out pin for part ejection. The clamp plate and work adapter can be modified, and the bushings are interchangeable for different workpieces and hole sizes. Insertion of the workpiece trips the limit switch which controls travel of the lift-clamping piston.

An air-operated, horizontal-indexing fixture (see Fig. 4-9) is particularly suited for die-head threading, drilling, or tapping. Brass fittings are threaded (⅛-27 NPT) at a net production rate of 2,800 pieces per hour with the die head operating at 1,250 rpm. The drum dial is automatically indexed by an air cylinder and valve interlocked with the machine cycle. Nests, located away from the rotating tool, are close to the operator for manual loading.

The dial type of air-operated fixture, as shown in Fig. 4-10 has a 7½ in. (190 mm) dial plate, which may have from 10 to 36 stations for drilling and allied operations on small parts. The air cylinder may be interlocked with the machine circuit for timing automatic indexing with the spindle cycle.

Pump jigs (see Fig. 4-11) are essentially quick-acting vises. They incorporate hand-lever actuation of either a rack and pinion or a cam mechanism to vertically move a top plate or a plunger. Lever movement clamps the workpiece between tooling attached to the plate and the moving member. Locking devices, built into the jig, control clamping

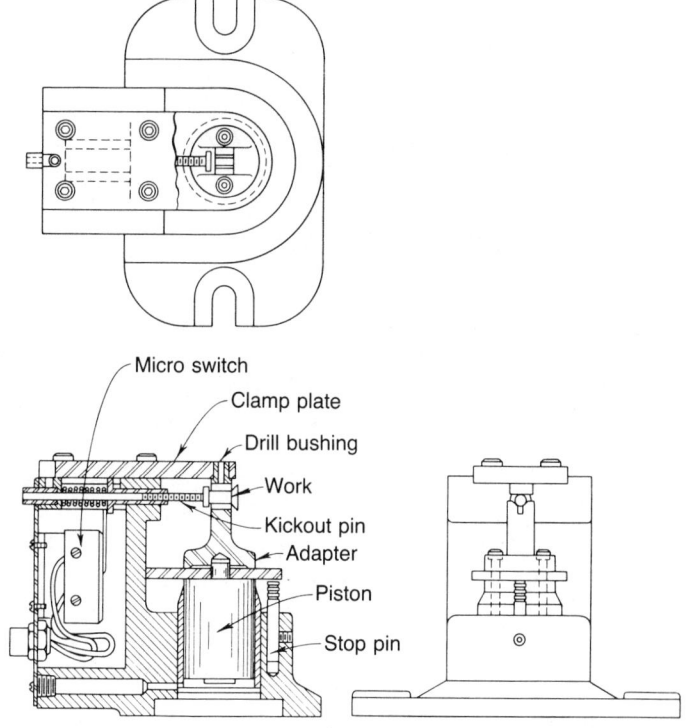

Fig. 4-8 Lift-clamping fixture.

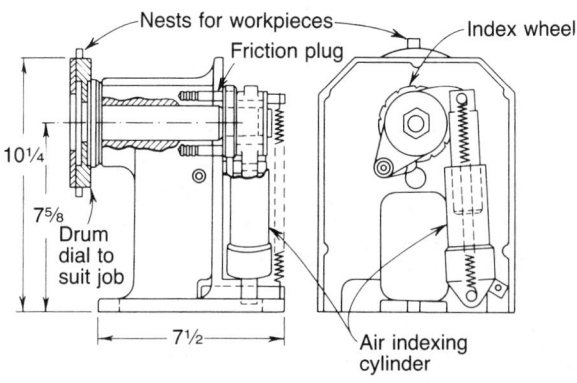

Fig. 4-9 Drum-type horizontal indexing fixture.

pressure. Pump jigs may be used for different parts and drill sizes by interchanging locators, plates, drill bushings, etc.

One type of fixture (see Fig. 4-11c) incorporates a swiveling top plate which facilitates loading and unloading. When equipped with a double-end top plate, multiple operations such as drilling and reaming are facilitated in a small area at the same location. This type of jig has two finished faces perpendicular to each other, permitting operations at right angles to the initial operation. On another type as shown in Fig. 4-11 d, the top plate tilts back for clear workpiece loading. Pump jigs are available in a variety of styles, sizes, and types.

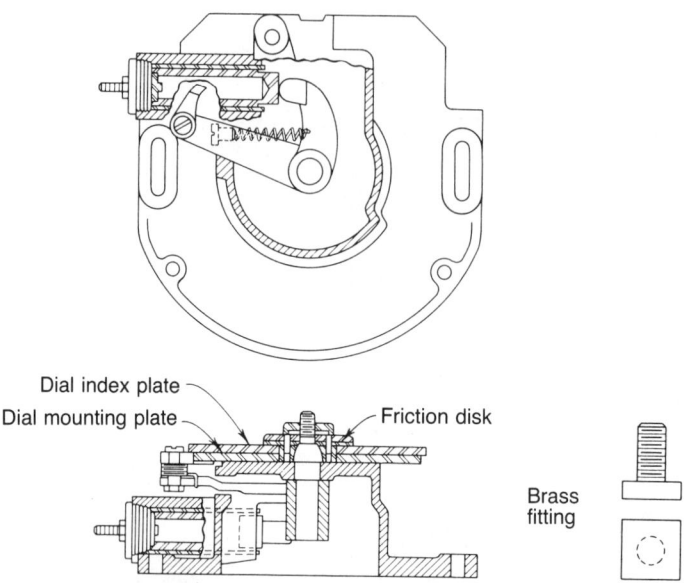

Fig. 4-10 Dial-type indexing fixture. (*Courtesy Snow Mfg. Co.*)

Figure 4-12 shows three possible applications of a universal drill jig. The jig is furnished complete with a V-block nest and a 5C collet fixture. It requires only a simple nest and drill bushings to put it on the job.

The equipment shown in Fig. 4-13 is for turning and related processes. Holding equipment for turning operations includes magnetic, conventional three-jaw and four-jaw mechanical chucks, and collet devices. The same devices with minor variations are available for fixtures which may be designed for indexing.

It is sometimes advantageous to enclose the workpiece, thereby retaining the desired relationship between operations performed in any of the surrounding planes. A tumble box jig is seen in Fig. 4-14*a*. These jigs are made of cast iron and are readily available in many sizes. Figure 4-14*b* shows a cast iron leaf jig which is also available in various sizes. A single box or tumble jig can be designed to hold the workpiece during a series of operations, thereby eliminating individual fixtures for each operation.

FIXTURE BODY CONSTRUCTION

The three basic methods used to construct the fixture body are the built-up type, the casting, and the weldment (see Fig. 4-15).

Built-up Fixture Bodies. This type of fixture body is built-up from a base to which upright sections are attached to support the locating and clamping elements as necessary. Some, like the box jig, have a top as well as uprights on four sides. The structure must be sufficiently rigid, strong, and stable enough to withstand machining forces and keep vibration and chatter to a minimum.

Bases for this type of construction are usually made from low to medium carbon steel, aluminum or magnesium plate, wood, epoxy materials, or one of the cast iron premachined sections previously shown in Fig. 1-44. Individual details and components are assembled by screw and dowel construction which consists of drilling, reaming, and pressfitting dowel pins thru the details to be assembled and using screws to hold the details together. Dowels must be located as far apart as possible, which is usually diagonally opposite from each other. Dowel pin diameters are generally slightly smaller than the assembly screws used. Dowel pin holes are drilled through whenever possible

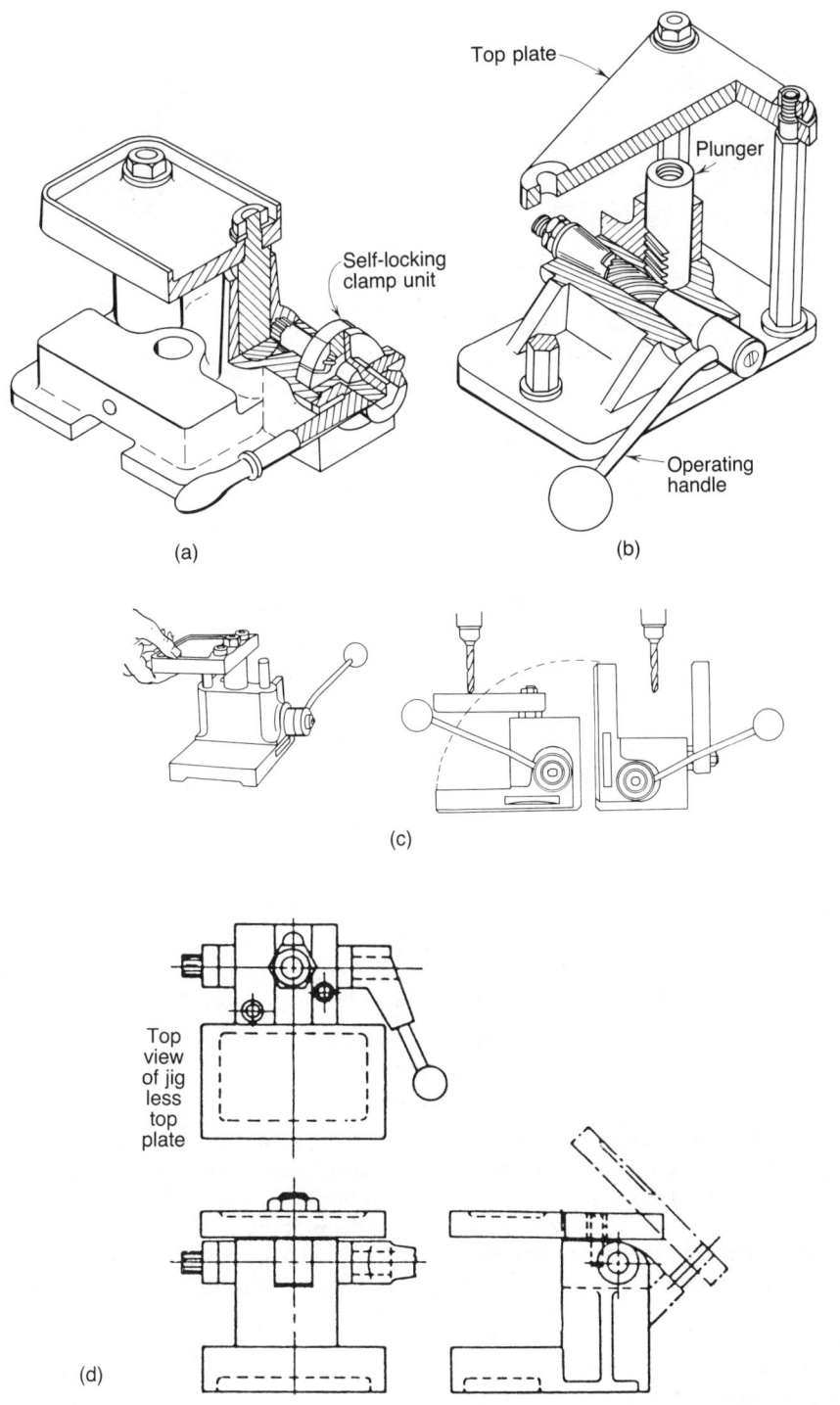

Fig. 4-11 Pump jigs: (*a*) typical rack-and-pinion type; (*b*) plunger-operated post type; (*c*) swiveling type; (*d*) lift type. (*Courtesy (a) thru (c) Accurate Bushing Co.; (d) Carr Lane Mfg. Co.*)

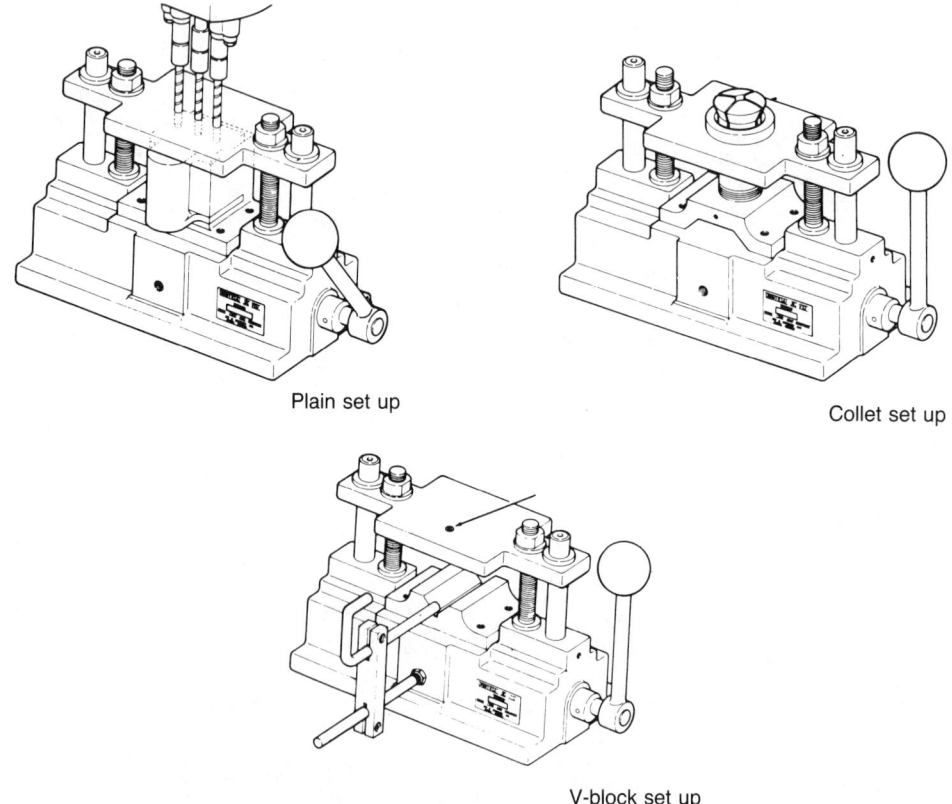

Plain set up

Collet set up

V-block set up

Fig. 4-12 Universal drill jig. (*Courtesy Ralmike's Tool-A-Rama*)

to permit easy removal if necessary at a later date. If this is not possible, the blind hole should be drilled deeper than usual with an undersize drill and then reamed to the depth required (usually 1½ to 2 times the diameter of the dowel). This will reduce any build-up of air pressure behind the dowel pin at the bottom of the hole. The minimum length of engagement of the screw thread should be as follows:

- Steel   1½ times the screw diameter
- Cast iron   2 times the screw diameter
- Aluminum   3 times the screw diameter

In those cases where a detail such as an interchangeable drill plate must be removed on a regular basis, bullet nose dowels or pins (usually one round and one relieved) are press fit into the fixture body and matching liner bushings are installed in the removable detail. Quarter turn screws are used to lock the detail in place.

Cast Fixture Bodies. Cast fixture bodies can be made of cast iron, cast aluminum, or cast epoxies. Being fully integral, they are usually quite rigid as compared with the built-up or welded types. One of the disadvantages of the cast fixture is the need for a pattern which adds both to the overall cost and to the procurement time.

Welded Fixture Bodies. Welded fixture bodies are generally made from section components (refer to Fig. 1-47), structural shapes (refer to Fig. 1-48), and other hot-rolled, low carbon steel materials which are electrically arc welded together into a finished fixture using a variety of weld joints. Welded fixtures can be made to just about any size.

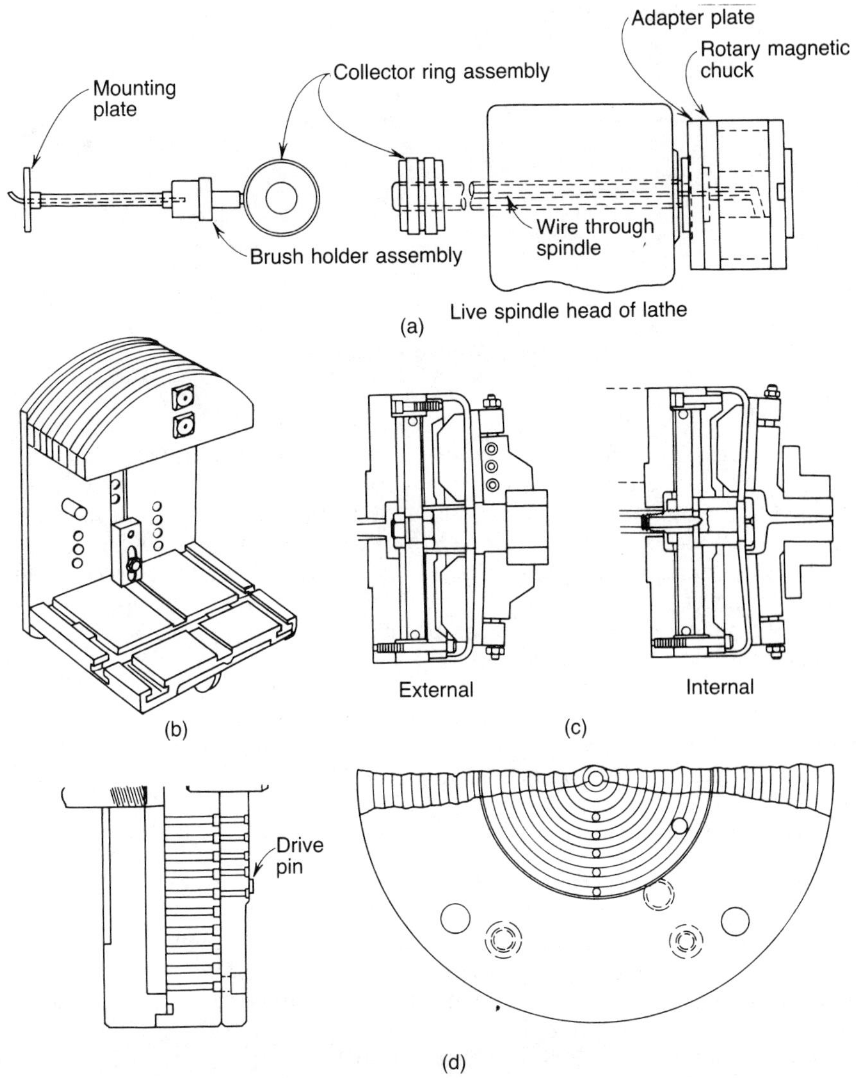

Mounting plate

Collector ring assembly

Adapter plate

Rotary magnetic chuck

Brush holder assembly

Wire through spindle

Live spindle head of lathe

(a)

External

Internal

(b)

(c)

Drive pin

(d)

Fig. 4-13 Commercial chucks: (*a*) rotary magnetic chuck; (*b*) adjustable lathe fixture; (*c*) diaphram chuck; (*d*) vacuum chuck. (*Courtesy (a) Magna-Lock Corp.; (b) Universal Vise & Tool Co.; (c) N. A. Woodworth Co.; (d) Cushman Chuck Co.*)

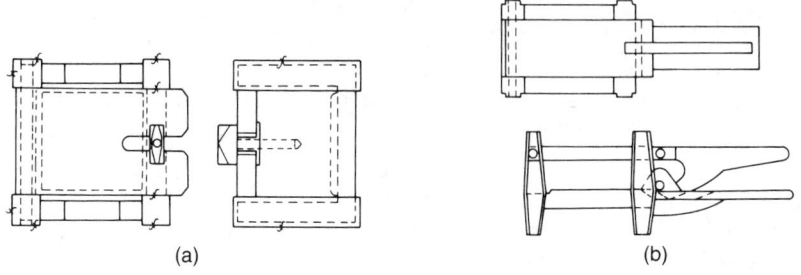

(a)

(b)

Fig. 4-14 Commercial jigs: (*a*) box jig, (*b*) lead jig. (*Courtesy West Point Mfg. Co.*)

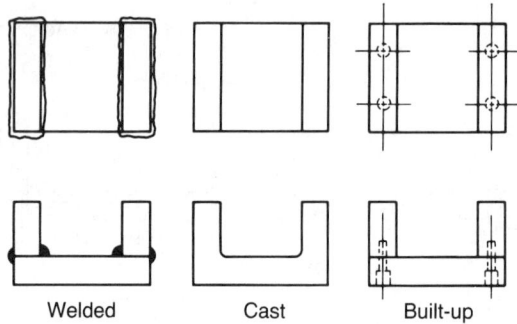

Welded   Cast   Built-up

Fig. 4-15 Three types of tool bodies.

EJECTORS

Often it is necessary to provide some means for ejecting the workpiece from the jig or fixture, especially in those cases where the workpiece is located on a stud or plug, or in some kind of a nest. Prying the workpiece out of the fixture is a poor practice that can damage the workpiece and/or the locator. This problem is one that can be eliminated very easily by providing the fixture with an ejector. An ejector can be either something as simple as a spring plunger or one of those shown in Fig. 4-16. The operation of an ejector can be made automatic and combined with the release of a clamp using mechanical, pneumatic, or hydraulic means.

Ejectors on fixtures are relatively inexpensive since they usually do not require precision machining. On the other hand, ejector systems used with automatic sorting and classifying equipment can be relatively expensive. Ejector systems of this sort will be discussed in Chapter 16, Inspection Fixtures and Gages.

FOOLPROOFING

Foolproofing is the incorporation of design features that makes it impossible to load a workpiece(s) into a jig or fixture in the wrong position.

A simple example is shown in Fig. 4-17. The most common methods use blocks or pins that will clear a correctly positioned workpiece, but interfere with an incorrectly positioned workpiece. Any feature that disturbs the symmetry of a workpiece can be used.

The tool designer must not be fooled by a workpiece that can be inserted in one way only when rotated, but can be incorrectly inserted easily when the workpiece is turned upside down.

Foolproofing can be integral to the fixture body, locators, or clamps. Occasionally a separate detail will be required.

COMMERCIAL ASSEMBLIES

Many complete assemblies for use in building a fixture are available as off-the shelf items. They are both cost effective and time saving, and should be considered for use with any of the aforementioned methods of construction. Examples include the following:

- Trunnions, such as shown in Fig. 4-18. Trunnions are precision bearing mounts for revolving fixtures. They are usually used in pairs with one of them being equipped with a locking device.
- Hinged bushing plate assemblies (see Fig. 4-19). Separate details are also available.

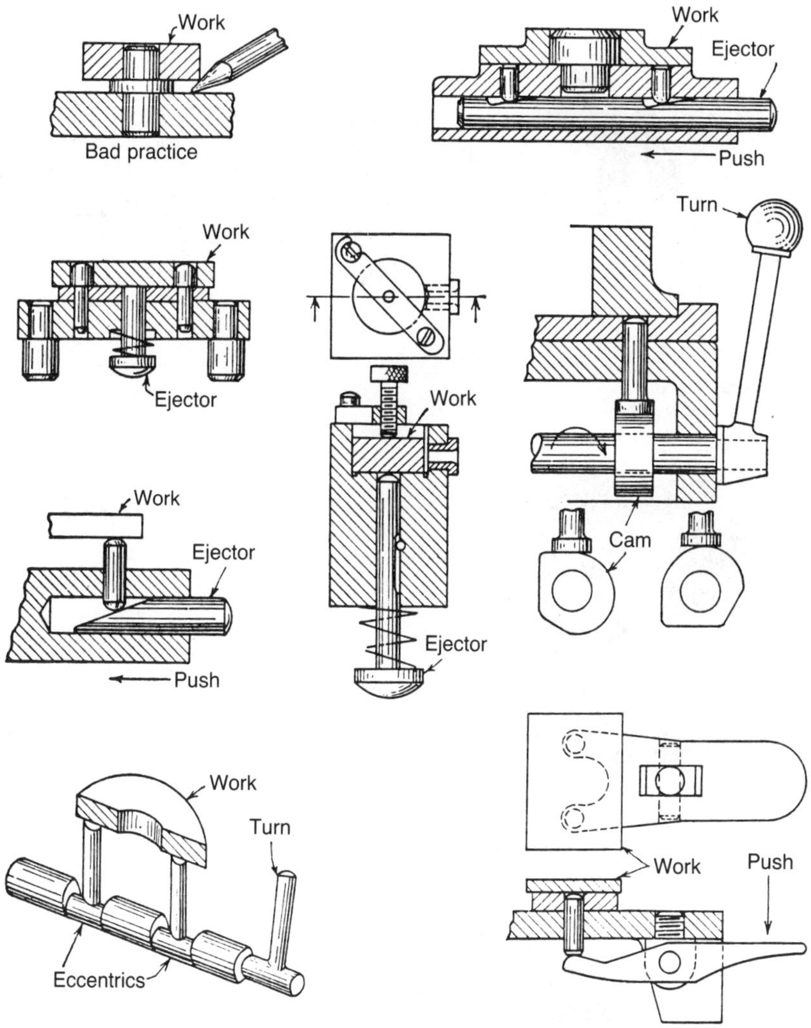

Work

Bad practice

Work

Work
Ejector

Push

Turn

Work
Ejector

Work

Cam

Work
Ejector

Push

Work
Ejector

Push

Work
Turn

Eccentrics

Work

Push

Fig. 4-16 Various types of ejectors commonly used in jig and fixture applications.

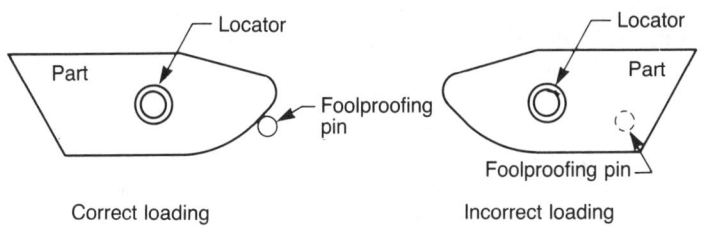

Locator
Part
Foolproofing pin

Correct loading

Locator
Part
Foolproofing pin

Incorrect loading

Fig. 4-17 Foolproofing.

4-23

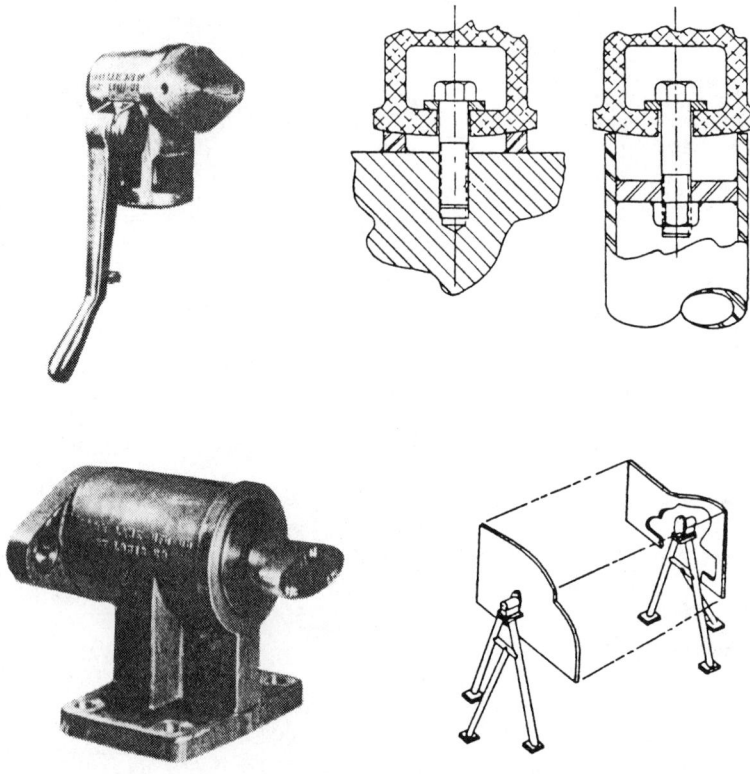

Fig. 4-18 Trunnions. (*Courtesy Carr Lane Mfg. Co.*)

Fig. 4-19 Hinged bushing plate assembly. (*Courtesy Atco Precision Tool Inc.*)

- Plug and retainer assemblies (see Fig. 4-20).
- A fixture lock, such as that shown in Fig. 4-21, can save considerable design and build time by eliminating the need for special locking details. Standard bar lengths of 9 in. and 10 in. (229 and 254 mm) are available off-the-shelf. Special bar lengths up to 24 in. (610 mm) can be provided. Three applications of fixture locks are shown in Fig. 4-22. In *a*, the problem was to step drill an 11/32 in. and No. F drill in a switch cover casting to make an opening for a push button. The solution was to use a fixture lock to butt the casting against the back of the fixture. Dowel pins were used to support the bottom of the casting for positioning before locking in position. The fixture in *b* was designed to mill stock from an aluminum casting. A fixture lock was used to hold the casting in place while three carbide-

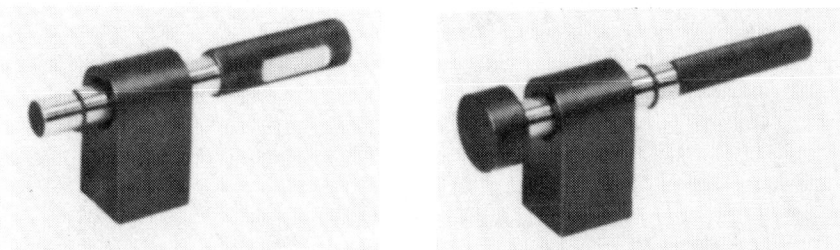

Fig. 4-20 Plug and retainer assembly. (*Courtesy Atco Precision Tool Inc.*)

Fig. 4-21 Fixture lock. (*Courtesy Heinrich Tools, Inc.*)

tipped milling cutters removed the approximately ⅛ in. (3.17 mm) stock from the casting. Tolerances were held to 0.002 in. The fixture shown in *c* was designed to tap (2) ¼-18 NPT holes 90° apart in the workpiece. One hole was tapped with the workpiece located as shown in the left hand figure. The clamp and part were then rotated 90° as shown in the right hand figure to permit tapping of the other hole. Turning of the clamp instead of the whole fixture was done to permit clamping of the fixture to the table at all times.

- Precision center assemblies, such as shown in Fig. 4-23, can be used to establish a precise axis parallel to the base within ±0.0001 in. The fixed center assembly (head stock) shown in *a*, the spring retractable center assembly (tail stock) shown in *b*, and a handle retractable center assembly (not shown), have centerline heights of 3.2500 in. (82.550 mm). Similar center assemblies including tailstocks operated by a handle or handwheel are available with a centerline height of 4.5000 in. (114.300 mm). All feature either a 0.5000 $^{+0.0002}_{-0.0000}$ in. or a 0.7500 $^{+0.0002}_{-0.0000}$ in. key slot.

- Ball and roller slides, such as shown in Fig. 4-24, are available in a wide range of sizes and load carrying capacities. Commercial slides similar to this are available with just about any degree of sophistication required, such as motor power, digital readout, etc.

Many other commercial assemblies are available for inspection fixtures and gages. These will covered later in Chapter 16, Inspection Fixtures and Gages.

MAJOR COMMERCIAL COMPONENTS

Major commercial components include the following:
- Mill fixture bases as shown in Fig. 1-44. These bases are made of ASTM class 40 cast iron which has been normalized and ground flat and parallel to the bottom surface within 0.002 in. FIM. They are also jig bored for two fixture keys, as

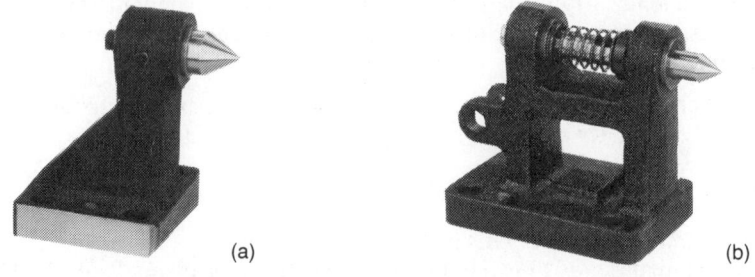

(a)

(b)

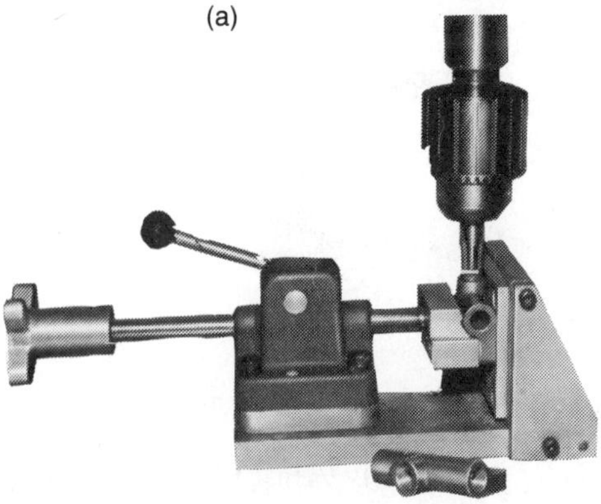

(c)

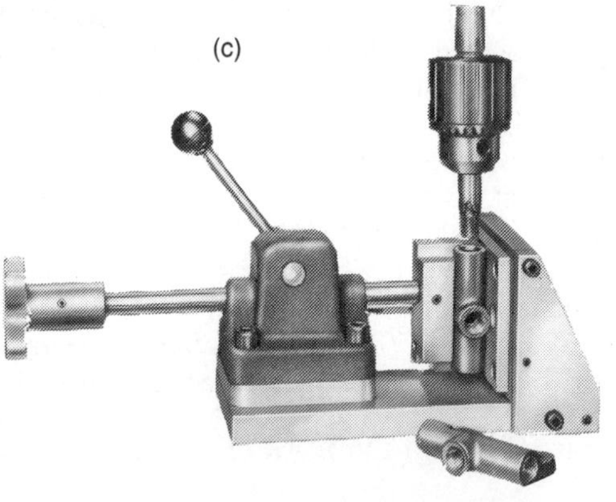

Fig. 4-22 Fixture lock applications. (*Courtesy Heinrich Tools, Inc.*)

(a)

(b)

Fig. 4-23 Center assemblies. (*Courtesy AA Gage, Inc.*)

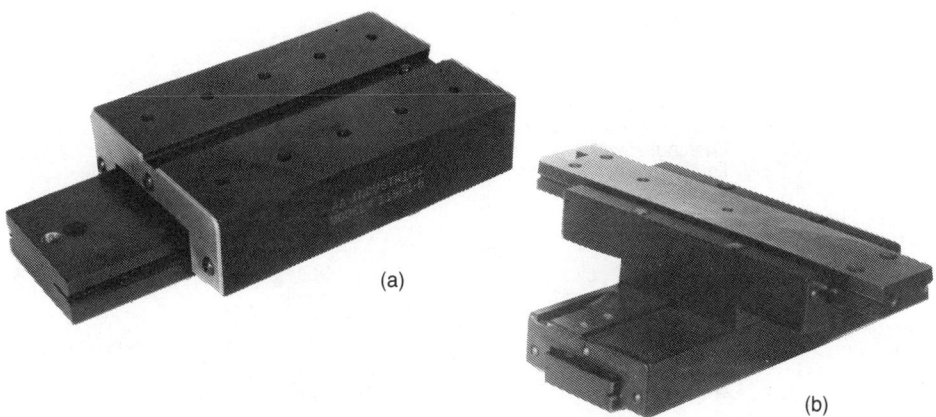

(a)

(b)

Fig. 4-24 Ball & roller slides: (*a*) **single axis,** (*b*) **double axis.** (*Courtesy AA Gage, Inc.*)

shown in Fig. 1-43. Sizes range from 6 × 9 in. (152 × 229 mm) to 12 × 18 in. (305 × 457 mm).

   Large fixtures are often constructed using a cored bench plate as the base. These plates range in size from 12 × 18 in. (305 × 457 mm) to 48 × 72 in. (1219 × 1829 mm).

- Adjustable angle brackets and gusseted angle brackets are shown in Fig. 1-47. The adjustable angles are made from 1020 steel and can be set to any angle required. They can then be either welded or bolted into place. The gusseted angle brackets are made of ASTM A36 steel and can usually be used without additional machining. Sizes range from 2 × 2½ × 1½ in. (51 × 63 × 38 mm) long to 6 × 6 × 6 in. (152 × 152 × 152 mm) long. Normalized, cast-iron T-angle plates (not shown) are also available that can be used for many applications, such as bases for milling or drilling fixtures. The addition of a few details can provide a complete fixture at a reasonable cost. T-angle plate are available in a wide range of sizes.
- Cast-iron and cast-aluminum angle plates, right-angle irons, box parallels, and V-blocks, as shown in Fig. 1-45, are used for the same purposes as the premachined sections, but where closer squareness and parallelism is required.
- The various types of index plungers and bushings available are shown in Fig. 4-25.
- Adjustable and fixed spring jack locks are shown in Fig. 4-26.

One currently available base features pneumatic support of the upper plate during its movement or rotation. By introducing air pressure, the base and plate are separated a few thousandths of an inch, the plate being supported by the column of air. In this position, the heaviest load can be repositioned by hand. With release of the air pressure, the plate seats on the base for subsequent machining operations. Pneumatic-type fixture plates are available in many sizes, including some plates that are capable of supporting over 28,000 lb (12,700 kg).

DESIGNING AND FABRICATING WOOD TOOLS

   It is often preferable to build wood tools in the pattern or woodworking shop. If the patternmaker is not familiar with metalworking, then it may be wise to combine the facilities of toolmaking and pattern rooms and allow metalworking and woodworking specialists to pool their knowledge. Companies that lack the proper facilities or personnel for wood tooling may find it to their economic benefit to subcontract all wooden jigs and fixtures to outside pattern or woodworking shops.

Straight index plunger and bushing

Straight index plunger and bushing, rotary cam flange mount

Straight index plunger and bushing, rotary cam, standard mount

Taper index plunger and bushing

Taper index plunger, rotary cam flange mount

Taper index plunger and bushing, rotary cam, standard mount

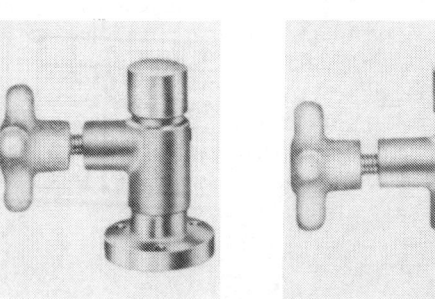

Fig. 4-25 Various types of index plungers and bushings. (*Courtesy American Drill Bushing Co.*)

Fixed spring pressure

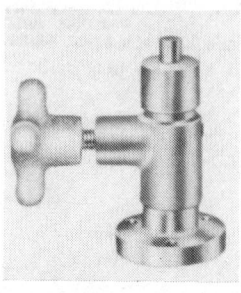

Flange base

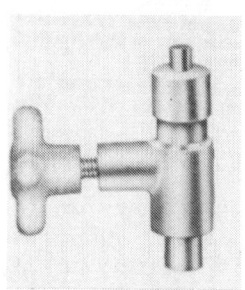

Press fit

Adjustable spring pressure

Flange base

Press fit

Fig. 4-26 Spring jack locks. (*Courtesy American Drill Bushing Co.*)

WOOD SELECTION

The hardwoods maple and birch are usually the best for heavy-duty tooling construction, for these two woods possess many favorable qualities. Any of the manufactured woods will also be a successful choice. But for jigs and fixture that are subjected to light duty, it is possible to use pine, a softwood that is light in weight, straight-grained, and easily worked and which will not warp, shrink, or check as readily as some other woods.

In case of uncertainty about the most desirable wood to use for a given tooling problem, refer to Table 4-2, Properties of Wood.

JOINING METHODS

Jigs and fixtures made of wood will almost always include one or more joints in their construction, and their details may be joined with glue or mechanical methods, such as nails. For increased strength in a joint, a combination of glue and one of the mechanical methods should be used. Although there are many types of joints that can be used for wood construction, some of them are simply variations or combination of a few basic types—butt, rabbet, dado, mortise-and-tenon, and miter.

Butt. The butt joint is the simplest and most popular of the woodworking joints. Unfortunately, it is the weakest joint when it is not reinforced. Figure 4-27 illustrates the end-to-end and end-to-side butt joints, respectively. The end-to-end joint is difficult to glue and rarely meets requirements of strength and durability because the glue is rapidly absorbed by the end grain. The lap and scarf joints are methods of joining the stock so that end-grain absorption is more or less avoided and more area of contact is provided for the glue. The end-to-side joint should be reinforced, as shown in Fig. 4-27, for maximum strength.

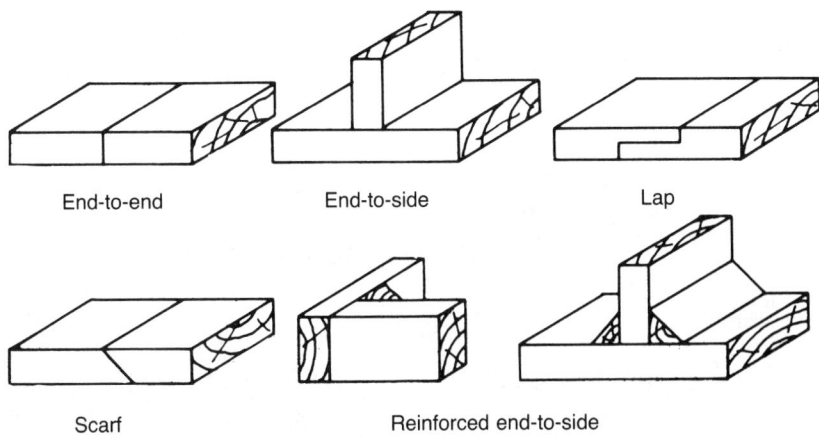

End-to-end   End-to-side   Lap

Scarf   Reinforced end-to-side

Fig. 4-27 Types of butt joint construction.

Rabbet and Dado. The rabbet and dado joints are very similar to each other in construction. For a rabbet joint, the wood pieces are joined at the ends, as in Fig. 4-28. The dado joint consists of a groove made across the grain of a piece of wood into which another member is fitted. The dado joint can be made even more rigid by cutting additional shoulders. The combination of dado and rabbet forms a highly satisfactory corner construction.

Mortise-and-Tenon. When great strength and rigidity are required, the mortise-and-tenon joint shown in Fig. 4-29 is used. The joining may be cut into the two members or

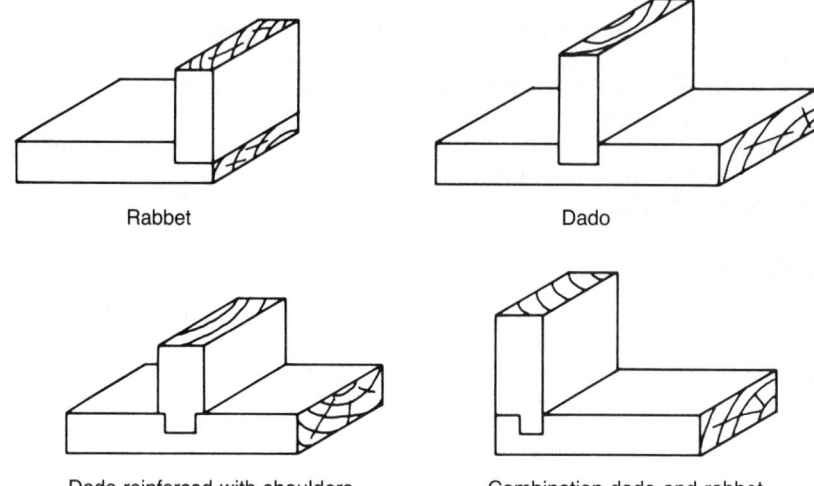

Rabbet

Dado

Dado reinforced with shoulders

Combination dado and rabbet

Fig. 4-28 Rabbet and dado joints.

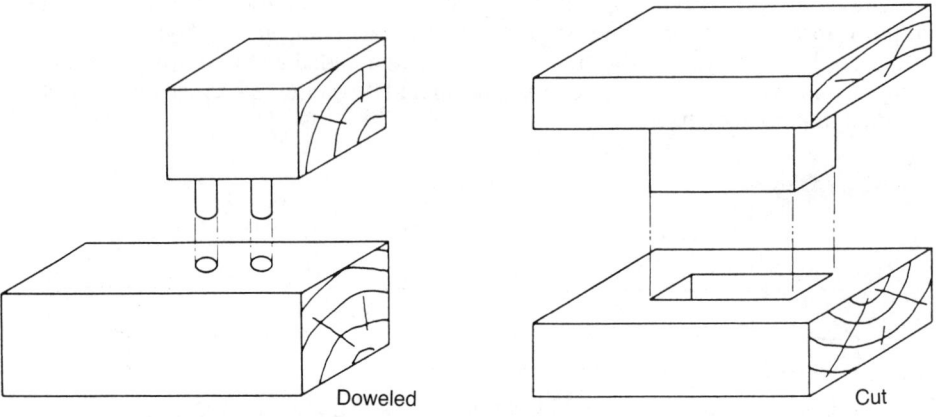

Doweled

Cut

Fig. 4-29 Mortise-and-tenon joints.

dowel pins may be used. The latter form is often referred to as a dowel joint. The mortise-and-tenon joint is difficult to make accurately and should be used only when a simpler method will not serve.

Miter. A miter joint should be used when the end grain must not be exposed. Figure 4-30 illustrates its construction. If it is not possible to use a corner reinforcement, the joint may be strengthened by the use of wood dowels or corrugated metal fasteners.

Mechanical Reinforcements. Mechanical reinforcements should be used for tools that may be subjected to hard use, because it is estimated that reinforced joints are 50% stronger.

HARDWARE FOR WOOD TOOLS

A jig or fixture will seldom be totally constructed of wood. Usually, metal components, such as locators, stops, wear plates, and conventional hardware, must be used to maintain part orientation and reduce wear. Many of these metal components are available commercially, and they should be used whenever economically feasible.

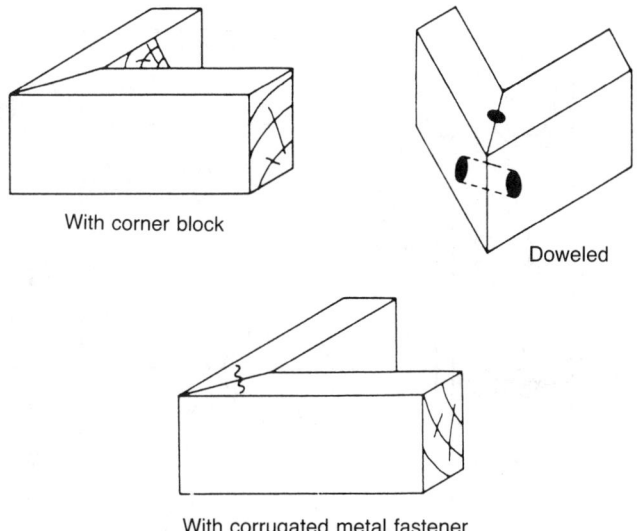

With corner block

Doweled

With corrugated metal fastener

Fig. 4-30 Reinforced miter joints.

Because tooling hardware for limited-production tools does not need to be hardened, as does that for mass-production tools, stops and locators for wood tools in limited production may consist merely of standard screws with nuts and washers. However, the ends or locating surfaces of the screws should be machined or ground after tightening to align them properly. Washers are necessary to prevent the screws and nuts from depressing the wood surface. If a larger locating area is desired, the screw and nut assembly can be replaced by a sheet metal plate bonded to the wood or fastened to it with flat-head wood screws.

Steel threaded inserts must be embedded into the wood if components such as studs and machine screws are to be attached. Inserts can be specially made, or standard commercial Allen-type socket nuts can be used. These nuts have been used in wood tool construction with outstanding results. They are knurled on their outer circumference, and when press fitted they lock into the wood to prevent rotation. For added strength, glue can be applied to the outside or knurled portion of the nut prior to assembly.

Wood tooling may occasionally require the use of dowel pins for alignment and other purposes. The standard cylindrical dowel pins frequently used for conventional tooling will not work in wood, however. Grooved or spring pins must be used instead.

A wood drill jig incorporating various tooling hardware is displayed in Fig. 4-31. The jig consists of a plywood base, a top bushing plate, and two wood side spacer rails. A sheet metal plate is bonded to the top of the wood base to reduce wear and depression as the part or work is clamped. The base, top, and side rails are joined with wood screws and the four screw assemblies which also serve as jig feet. A spring pin is used as an end stop. Side locators also consist of screw assemblies. A hand knob clamp and thumb screw are standard tooling components used with socket nuts as threaded inserts. Drill bushings are the standard type used for wood tooling.

WOOD PROTECTION

Protecting a wooden jig or fixture by coating it to seal its open cells or pores is an important step in its completion. The sealing will reduce swelling and warpage caused by the absorption of atmospheric moisture or the oil and coolants used in manufacturing.

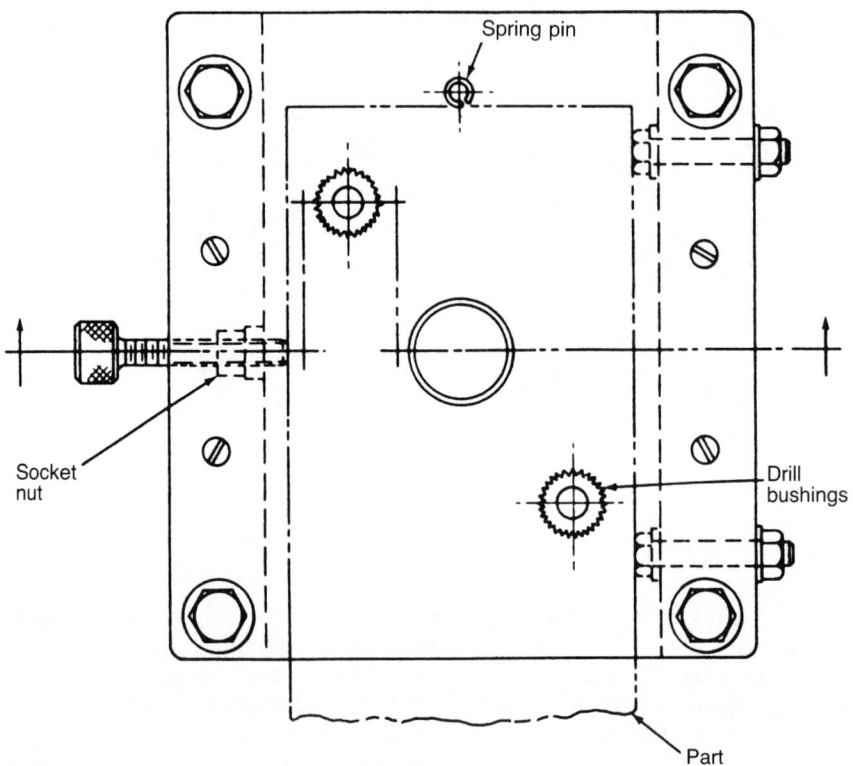

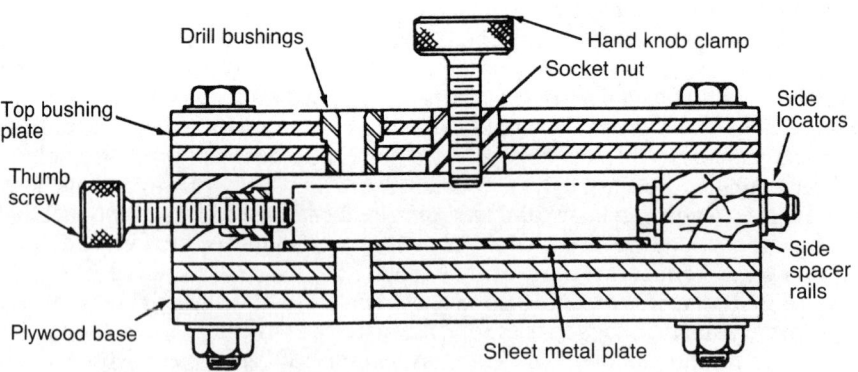

Fig. 4-31 Wooden drill jig incorporating standard tooling hardware.

FABRICATING EPOXY TOOLS

A *pattern* or *mold* must be built for any of the four construction methods previously mentioned in Chapter 1, Predesign Analysis and Fixture Design Procedures. The pattern may be wood, plaster, metal, or plastic. In some cases, a prototype or production part can be used.

All patterns must be properly prepared before they can be used. If the pattern is wood or plaster, it must be sealed with several coats of lacquer. This is not required with metal or plastic models. If the pattern is to be made on a flat base, wax must be used to seal between the model and the base. A high-quality mold release agent is then applied to all surfaces of the model base and sides that make up the pattern. When the release agent has thoroughly dried, lamination, casting, or molding of the tool may begin.

LAMINATION

In the laminating method of construction, alternate layers of glass cloth and epoxy are built up on a form until the desired thickness is obtained. The actual steps to making a laminated tool are shown in Fig. 4-32.

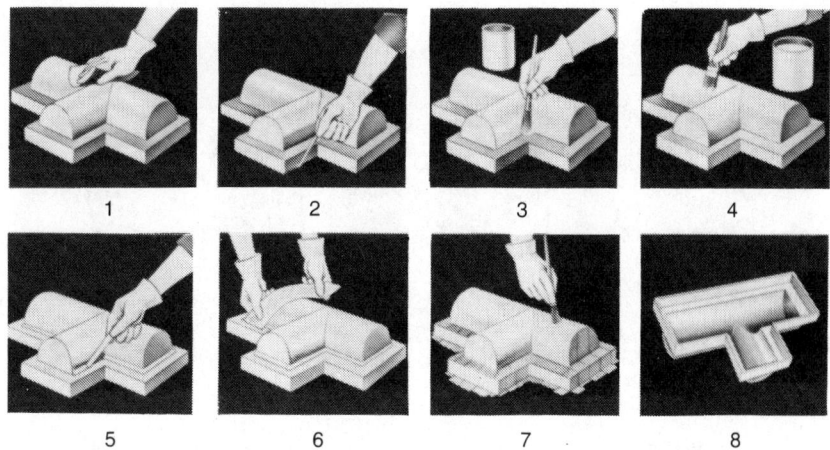

Fig. 4-32 Constructing a laminated tool. (*Courtesy Hysol Div., The Dexter Corp.*)

First, repair any imperfections in the surface to be reproduced. This can be accomplished by conventional methods, such as filling holes with hard wax or clay.

Second, seal the model with several coats of lacquer as previously noted. If the pattern is to be made on a flat base, use wax to seal between the model and the base.

Third, apply mold release to the entire model and base, if used. Be sure to brush well into corners. Cut the required number of layers of glass cloth to the desired shape (approximately 3 to 4 layers for every 0.0625 in., 1.588 mm of laminate thickness). Add the hardener to the surface coat and mix thoroughly. Mix only the amount that can be used in about thirty minutes.

Next, apply the mixed surface coat to the model with a stiff brush to a uniform coating of 0.0312 to 0.0625 in. (0.79 to 1.59 mm). Allow to cure until the surface is firm, but not hard. The viscosity of the surface coat is designed to give a film which will stay on a vertical surface without running off, and will reproduce the exact detail of the model.

Fifth, all sharp corners, edges, or projections should be blended into a radius with putty. A putty can be made by adding glass fibers or filler to the laminating mix.

Sixth, press the first layer of glass cloth into the firm surface coat. The coat should be firm enough to leave a finger imprint but not stick. If the surface coat has cured hard, sand the surface lightly and apply a coat of the prepared laminating mix. Place the first layer of glass cloth onto the wet surface. Proceed to work the laminating mix into the cloth with a brush. The cloth must contact all surfaces and lay smoothly or it will bridge and cause air pockets that will break through in service and cause unnecessary repairs. The cloth may have to be notched or tailored so that it will conform to contours of the surface. Joints should be lapped one inch (25 mm).

Next, add the hardener to the laminating resin and mix thoroughly. Mix only the amount that can be used in thirty minutes. Apply the prepared laminating mix to the cloth with a stiff brush so that it penetrates. Do not leave any excess, and work out trapped air. Excess resin between the layers of cloth may cause distortion, and the strength of the laminate will also be impaired.

Finally, proceed with additional layers of glass cloth in the same manner until the desired thickness is obtained. Six to eight layers of cloth are sufficient for most fixtures. Edge trimming, if required, can be done with a sharp knife before the laminate is completely hard, or trimmed with a band saw after hardening.

Reinforcement with Egg Crate Method. Figure 4-33 shows the proper method of reinforcing the complete laminate using the following egg crate method. First, make ribs to the contour of the tool and position as shown. Use materials such as masonite, plywood, or pressboard.

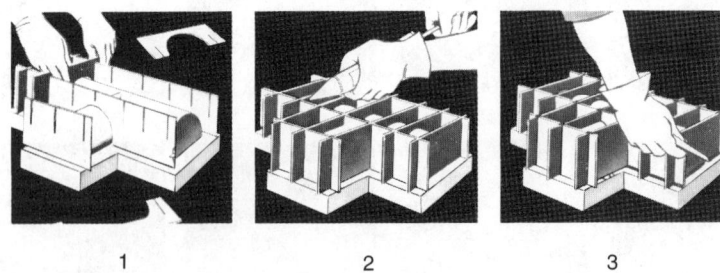

    1   2   3

Fig. 4-33 Egg crate method of reinforcement. (*Courtesy Hysol Div., The Dexter Corp.*)

Next, cement all corners with putty used as filleting where ribs join. This can be done rapidly with a caulking gun. Allow to cure.

After the structure has cured, cement it to the laminate with thin putty. Cement along both sides of all ribs. Allow to cure.

Reinforcement with Tubular Method. Figure 4-34 shows the proper method of reinforcing the laminate using the tubular method. First, make the reinforcement by cutting tubing to length and carefully fitting all joints for maximum contact. Use epoxy, aluminum, or similar tubing.

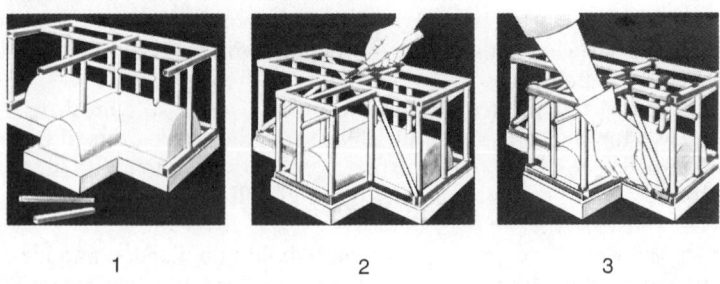

    1   2   3

Fig. 4-34 Tubular method of reinforcement. (*Courtesy Hysol Div., The Dexter Corp.*)

Second, cement the tubing together with putty. To strengthen joints, wrap with glass tape impregnated with laminating mix. Allow to cure.

Last, after the joints have cured, cement the structure to the laminate with putty. Impregnated glass tape can also be used here for additional strength. Cure at room temperature.

The laminate can be cut, machined, drilled, and tapped. Bushings can be inserted and cemented with the paste, as described in Chapter 1. Bushings can also be pressed into steel pads which are then cemented to the laminate. This method is usually used if the bushings require replacement since they can be easily pressed out and new ones inserted. The tubular method also permits drilling a hole into the laminate large enough to provide for chips and cooling of the bushing.

Vacuum Bag Method. A vacuum is sometimes applied to laminates to insure uniform contact and to force out excess resin after the laminate is completed. This procedure is shown in Fig. 4-35.

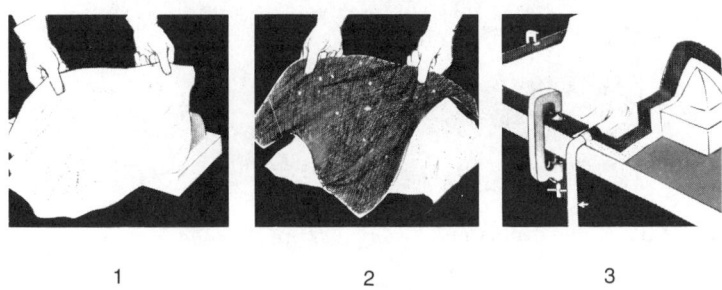

| 1 | 2 | 3 |

Fig. 4-35 Vacuum bag method. (*Courtesy Hysol Div., The Dexter Corp.*)

Before the curing process begins, the first step is to place the laminate on a table and cover it with a sheet of thin perforated (or random-slit) plastic film such as polyethylene, or PVA. Next, cover the film with several layers of absorbent material, such as burlap, to leave space for air to escape and absorb excess resin.

Finally, cover the absorbent material with a thin sheet of unperforated plastic which is sealed at the table or model. A vacuum is then drawn through the hose placed under the edges of the film. As the vacuum builds up, the film stretches and conforms to the contour of the laminate, exerting pressure and forcing out excess resin. The vacuum is held until the laminate is set. After setting, the plastic film is easily stripped off.

An alternate method is to place the entire tool in a plastic bag, seal the bag to the vacuum line, and draw a vacuum.

Cure. The curing of the laminate will usually be completed in three to five hours, but a longer time, or overnight is preferred. High temperature systems require heat cure. Refer to the product's bulletin for specific cure recommendations.

A finished fixture removed from the mold is shown in Fig. 4-36. This fixture could be used as a checking fixture, or if bushings were inserted, it could be converted into a drilling fixture.

Jigs and fixtures of laminated construction are hard to surpass when accuracy, low cost, low fabrication time, strength, and light weight are major considerations. Laminated tools possess the best dimensional stability of any of the plastic tooling types, and for this reason they are widely used in industry as gages and checking fixtures.

SURFACE CASTING

Surface-cast tooling is constructed by casting an epoxy face approximately 0.125 to 1.00 in. (3.18 to 25.4 mm) thick on a prefabricated core. The thickness depends on the size of the tool and the method surface casting. The core can be made of any suitable material.

Surface casting is widely employed for sheet metal forming dies and for numerous jig and fixture applications. The dimensional stability of surface-cast tools is somewhat less than that of laminated tools, but it is sufficient for most applications. A typical surface-cast form is shown in Fig. 4-37.

Fig. 4-36 Laminated fixture. (*Courtesy Hysol Div., The Dexter Corp.*)

Fig. 4-37 Typical surface-cast epoxy plastic form. (*Courtesy Ciba-Geigy Tooling Systems*)

There are three methods of surface casting—pour, squash, and pressure. The core for any of these methods, and especially for the squash method, should always be tried in the mold before the epoxy is added. This trial is to check for points at which air could be trapped by the core, thereby pushing the epoxy away from the core's face. If air might be trapped, vent holes can be drilled through the core, or the mold might be elevated slightly on one side to release the air. The core should always be placed above the form so air bubbles will not be formed on the working surface of the mold. Epoxy should be poured into the mold from one position and in one steady stream to prevent voids from being formed in the tool.

Pour Method. In this method, the core is suspended with ample clearance between it and the working face of the pattern. The edges of the space between the mold and the core are sealed, and epoxy is then poured through spouts or an open end of the mold into the space. This method is illustrated in Fig. 4-38.

Squash Method. A core is placed into the cavity of a pattern mold partially full of liquid or paste epoxy and allowed to settle to a predetermined position. The squash method is shown in Fig. 4-39.

Pressure Method. As in the pour method, the core for the pressure method is suspended over the mold and the edges between the mold and the core are sealed.

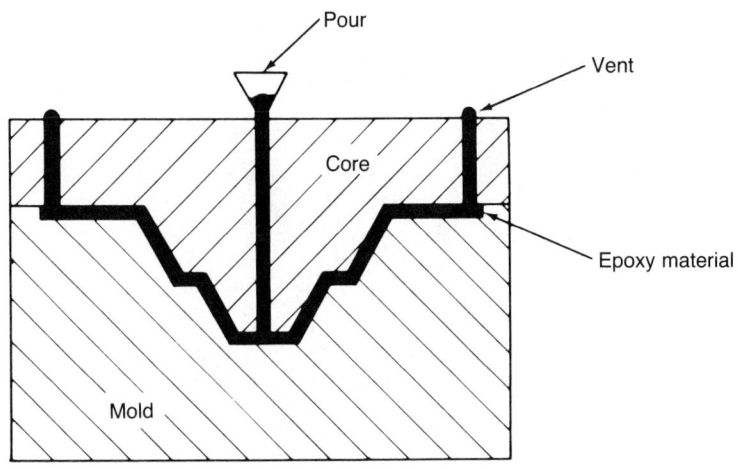

Fig. 4-38 Surface casting, pour method.

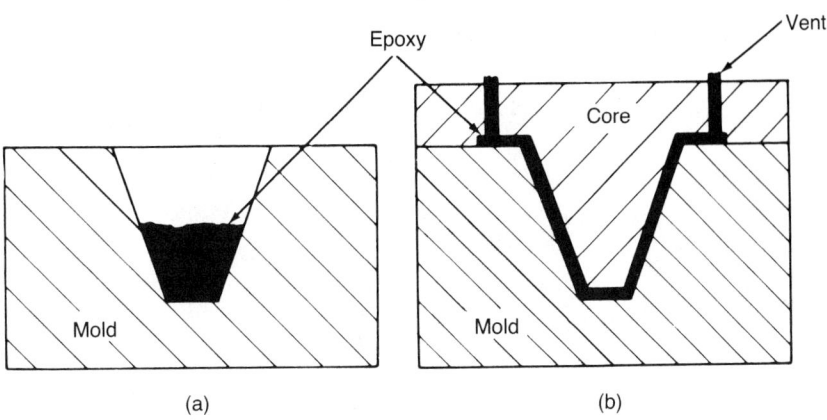

Fig. 4-39 Surface casting, squash method.

Liquid epoxy is then forced into the mold at a low point and is then allowed to vent at a high point (see Fig. 4-40). This method requires a pressure pot or other means of forcing the epoxy into the cavity. The pressure pot should be located close to the mold to eliminate an excessive amount of hose line, and the pressure pot and system must be thoroughly cleaned immediately after the epoxy has been pumped into the mold.

MASS CASTING

No core is used in mass casting—the construction method in which epoxy liquid is poured into a prepared mold (see Fig. 4-41). The liquid plastic must be poured slowly to avoid the development of air pockets, and when castings over 6 in. (152 mm) thick are poured, one of the previously listed fillers should be added to the epoxy to add strength and reduce shrinkage in the casting. The casting with filler will also require less epoxy and allow material costs to be reduced. The mass cast vacuum fixture in Fig. 4-42 is typical of the type of tool constructed by this method.

A step-by-step procedure for producing a production tool or mold with this method is illustrated in Fig. 4-43. The first step is too attach or place the model to a board or plate using any convenient method. Use wax to seal the model to the base.

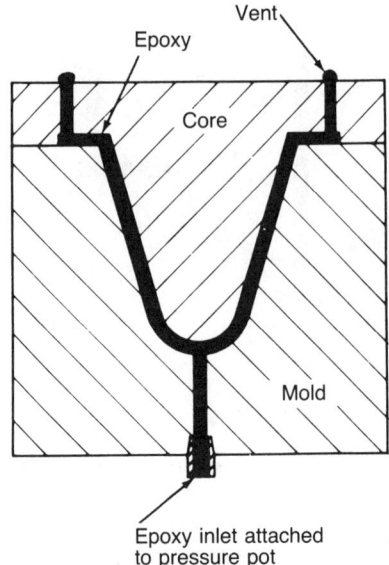

Fig. 4-40 Surface casting, pressure-pot method.

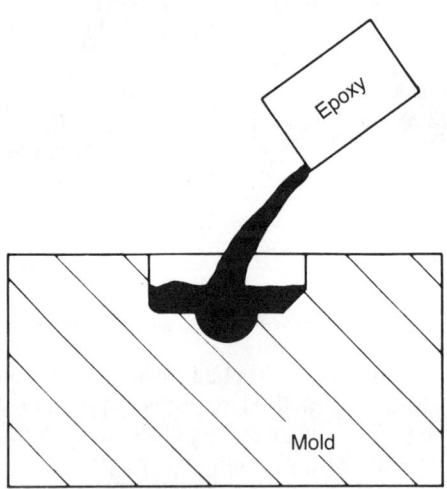

Fig. 4-41 Mass casting.

Second, using C-clamps and metal or plywood for the sides, construct a mold to the necessary size. If the model is wood or plaster, seal it with lacquer, as previously noted. Apply mold release to the entire model and the base and sides of the mold. Be sure to brush well into corners. Air dry for several minutes.

Next, select a casting compound to suit your requirements and apply a thick prime coat of the mixed material to the entire mold with a stiff brush. Use firm strokes to force the compound into sharp corners and to eliminate the trapping of small air bubbles on the surfaces.

The fourth step is to carefully pour the remainder of the mixed material into the mold from one point, allowing the compound to flow out and fill the mold to eliminate air bubbles.

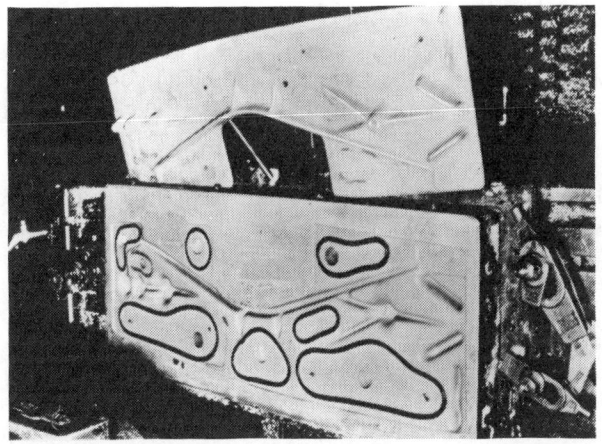

Fig. 4-42 Epoxy mass-cast vacuum fixture. (*Courtesy Ciba-Geigy Tooling Systems*)

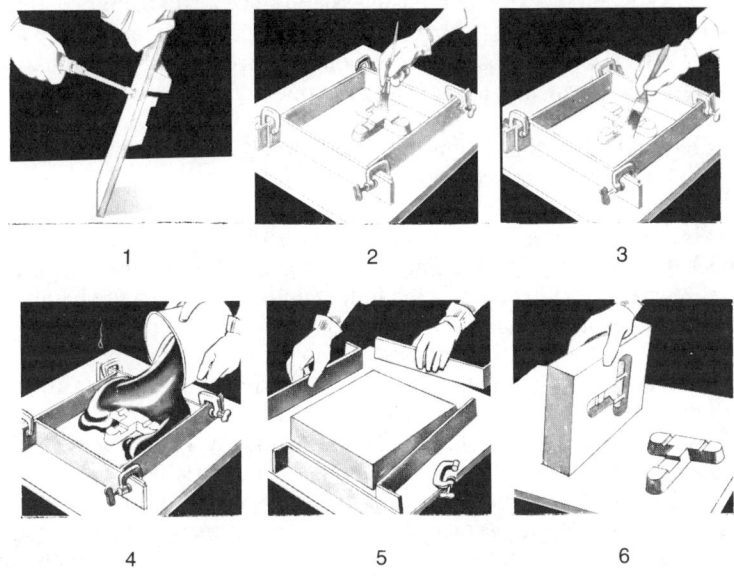

Fig. 4-43 Producing a production tool or mold using the cast method. (*Courtesy Hysol Div., The Dexter Corp.*)

Fifth, allow the casting to cure as specified in the product's bulletin. Dismantle the mold sides and remove the casting with wedges or knock-out pins. And finally, Fig. 4-43 shows the completed tool or mold, ready to be put to work, or used to cast duplicates of the original model.

Although the simplicty of the mass casting method implies the greatest savings in time and material of all the methods, this is often not the case. Mass casting does provides some savings, for it eliminates the cost of the core needed for surface casting.

The greatest limitation of mass cast tools is their low strength. High shrinkage in heavy castings because of heat generated in curing is another unfavorable characteristic of this method. Recent material developments improved these properties to a great extent, however, and fixture discoveries in this field may eliminate them and make epoxy mass casting a highly efficient toolmaking method.

THERMOPLASTICS IN TOOLING

One thermoplastic (Rigidax® tooling compound) used in tooling is a castable, thermoplastic compound for stabilizing, supporting, and holding hard-to-fixture, thin wall, odd-shaped, and nonmagnetic parts. It is melted to a fluid form and poured in and around the part. After machining, it is melted and reused.

It is primarily used in any of three ways. Single or multiple parts can be cast in Rigidax® through the use of a base plate and damming box for the first method. The cast parts are then machined as required.

Another option is to convert a part to a solid to eliminate chatter and vibration. Or thirdly, small electronic, ceramic, plastic honeycomb core, and nonmagnetic parts can be clamped for machining with a thin film of Rigidax®.

Rigidax® tooling compound is available in four basic grades. Type WS is water-soluble and should be used when the parts will be machined without coolants and where only hot water is available for cleaning. It should not be used with coolants.

Type WI-green is water-insoluble. It is the strongest, hardest, and has the lowest shrinkage factor and the best adhesion to parts and fixtures. It should be considered when high cutting tool pressures are required. Type WI-green is used when coolants are employed and hot solvent or vapor degreasing systems are available for cleaning parts.

Type WI-NMF is also water-insoluble. It has a lower pouring temperature and is not a strong as the WI-green, but has excellent holding capabilities. It also can be used when coolants are employed, and hot solvent or vapor degreasing systems are available for cleaning parts.

Type WI is basically the same as type WI-NMF, but has greater strength because of an aluminum powder filler in the compound.

Rigidax® tooling compound is compatible with grinding. No changes in types of grinding wheels are necessary. The compound does not load the wheels and no supplementary wheel dressing is required. The added stabilization of the supported parts tangibly increases wheel life because of the reduction in vibration and chatter.

The compound does not usually affect speeds and feeds. There will be cases when the speed and feed may, in fact, be increased due to the higher rigidity of the parts.

Handling Instructions. Complete handling and safety instructions, are available from the manufacturer and should be rigidly followed for best results.

Applications. Two separate machining problems that were solved with Rigidax® tooling compound are shown in Figs. 4-44 and 4-45. The first problem is with a part cast of 302 stainless steel with some titanium in it. Surface A must be faced off within ±0.001 in. and held parallel to surface B. Initially, three operations were required to finish the part—lathe, deburr, and finish grind. The machining cycle was one hour per part with a 65% reject rate. Figure 4-44 shows a solution to this problem. The second problem was with a tube made from 347 stainless which required facing off surafce A and the cutting of two grooves B. Chatter, vibration, and distortion prevented the delivery of parts. By filling the part with Rigidax® before machining as shown in Fig. 4-45, the problem was solved.

Another example showing how Rigidax® can be used to clamp small parts for high production operations is shown in Chapter 10, Grinding.

PASTE CONSTRUCTION

Paste construction is the method in which an epoxy paste made of epoxy resin, filler, and a hardening agent is applied to the tool pattern with a spatula, putty knife, or caulking gun. Figure 4-46 shows the procedure for preparing and applying epoxy paste.

Parts in Rigidax®

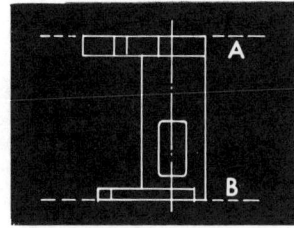

Rigidax® Solution

   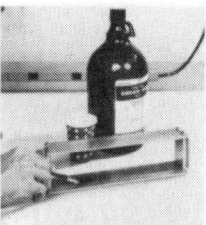

Base plate for multiple part fixture. Base plate is trued for proper location.

Parts are placed on base plate locator posts.

Allen screws locate the part on the base plate.

A damming box is used to hold melted Rigidax®. Sides are angled for easy release and shrinkage control. Tincture of green soap serves as release agent.

 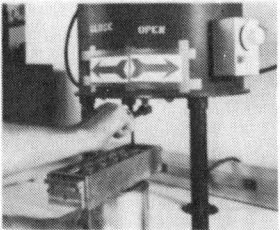 

Parts are preheated to 125°F (51.6°C) for better Rigidax® adherence.

Fixture is filled in 2.5 min. with a Rigidax® 5 gal (18.93 L) melter.

Plate locates against locator pins. Cast parts are down milled—12 finished parts per pass.

   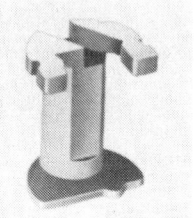

Completed parts.

Melt out takes place at 250°F (121°C).

Remaining thin film cleaned quickly and completely in vapor degreaser.

Finished part. Machining time. One min. per part. Reject rate zero.

Fig. 4-44 Parts in Rigidax®. (*Courtesy M. Argueso & Co., Inc.*)

Rigidax® in parts

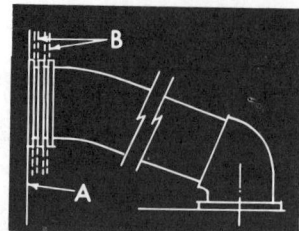

Rigidax® solution

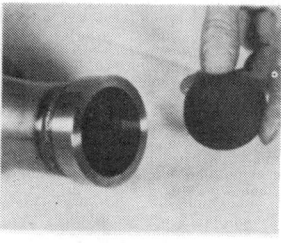

Neophrene plug holds molten Rigidax® in tube.

Plug is placed 2 in. into tube.

Preheat to 125°F (51.6° C).

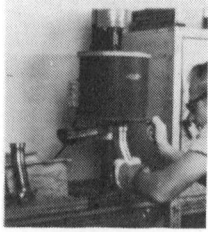

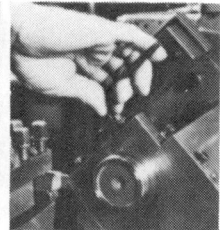

Fill to top from Rigidax® dispenser.

Place in rack for solidification.

Part is distorted from brazing and must be gaged to determine specific metal removal.

Part is bolted and clamped in box on lathe.

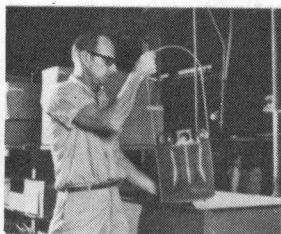

Melt out.

Degrease.

Finished part has 15 micro finish. Rejection rate is zero.

Fig. 4-45 Rigidax® in parts. (*Courtesy M. Argueso & Co., Inc.*)

For the first step, measure proper proportions of resin and hardener into two piles on a flat surface. Note the use of two putty knives.

Next, mix the resin and hardener thoroughly. Do not mix more than can be used in 25 to 30 minutes. Make sure that the surfaces to which the putty will be applied are clean (sanded preferred). To prevent adhesion to any surface, coat the particular surface with wax.

Third, apply the mixed paste with caulking gun. Most pastes can be applied up to 0.25 in. (6.4 mm) thick in one application. Or fourth, apply the paste with a spatula or

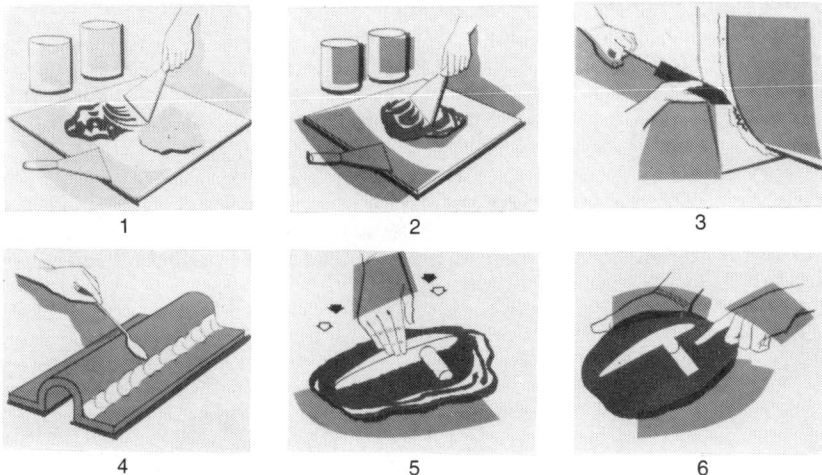

1 2 3

4 5 6

Fig. 4-46 Steps in preparation and application of epoxy paste. (*Courtesy Ciba-Geigy Tooling Systems*)

similar tool. For the fifth step, use the paste in a squash method to make an impression of any definite form.

Lastly, allow the paste to set up and remove the model, leaving the impression desired. Most pastes will set up in 60 to 90 minutes at room temperature.

Because epoxy paste is nonflowing, it does not have to be formed on a level surface as liquid epoxy does. It can be applied to vertical surfaces, and it generally does not have to be held in position with special equipment. As noted above, epoxy paste is also perfectly suited to the squash method of surface casting.

Epoxy paste has wide use in the metalworking industry, especially in tooling construction. One of its uses is in the construction of fixtures to locate or hold parts of complex or irregular contour. Figure 4-47 shows a dimensionally stable holding fixture

Fig. 4-47 Plastic steel holding fixture for an irregularly-shaped part. (*Courtesy Devcon Corp.*)

for an irregularly-shaped part, formed from an epoxy compound (Plastic Steel®). As a tooling material, Plastic Steel® makes dimensionally accurate forms that are durable and inexpensive. It cures quickly to a metallic mass that can be drilled, sanded, and machined. It cures as a result of a chemical reaction between the resin and hardener, not through the evaporation of a solvent; therefore Plastic Steel® does not shrink during cure.

HARDWARE ATTACHMENT

Methods for attaching metal parts to epoxy tooling have previously been covered in Chapter 1.

CHAPTER 5
TOOLING FOR NUMERICAL CONTROL

It has been known for a long time that to make money in the manufacturing business, machines must be producing parts as much of the time as possible. Over the years machine tool builders have responded with automatic and special-purpose machines, transfer machines, CNC machining centers, headchanging machines, and flexible manufacturing systems.

Dedicated special-purpose multifunction machines and fixturing work fine for producing large quantities of identical parts at high production rates. When combined with similar machines and connected by transfer devices to automatically transfer workpieces between them, they provide the ultimate in automation, because they permit the maximum number of operations to be performed at the same time.

Several methods have been used to adapt the transfer machine concept to handle lower volumes of similar workpieces, and even different workpieces, by providing a means for quick changeovers between production runs, the addition of idle stations, standardizing dimensions, mounting interchangeable fixtures on pallets integral to the machines, etc. This naturally led to flexible manufacturing systems (FMS). These use CNC machining centers or headchangers, or a combination of both, tied together by a material transport system and controlled by a central computer. They machine similar workpieces at mid-volume production rates based on actual assembly needs. With FMSs, all loading and unloading of workpieces is done while the machines are working, resulting in good machine utilization and complete flexibility. Fixturing for these systems usually consists of duplicate or near duplicate fixtures of the dedicated type, but with interchangeable locating and clamping components that can be quickly changed to handle the slight variations found in a family of parts.

For low-volume production, and the production of prototype parts for preproduction testing, the CNC controlled machining centers with automatic toolchangers, multiposition dial index tables, pallet shuttle systems, and automatic pallet changers are proving to be the most cost effective.

Prior to the introduction of CNC machining centers, efforts were mainly directed toward decreasing machining time, and little effort was given to reducing setup time. Once CNC was introduced however, the sharp reduction in machining time showed immediately that too much time was spent on setups.

The arrival of the CNC multi-pallet shuttle machine greatly reduced the time required to change workpieces, but the problem of initial setup still remained. Benefits of the multi-pallet CNC machines could only be realized after the initial setup was completed. The problem now became one of designing fixturing systems to decrease the time involved in initial setups.

The four main considerations in designing fixtures for the CNC machines are accessibility, accuracy, rigidity, and easy changing of the workpiece. To be effective, these fixtures must be able to:

- Mount quickly and precisely onto the machining center pallet with no loss in location accuracy when changed from one pallet to another.
- Locate the workpiece quickly and accurately, and ensure repeatability with multiple changes of the workpiece.
- Provide for easy clamping of the workpiece.
- Completely machine the workpiece in a single machine cycle, whenever possible.
- Eliminate the need for dedicated fixtures as much as possible.

SPECIAL DESIGN CONSIDERATIONS

Accessibility. Since CNC machining centers can perform many operations such as milling, drilling, tapping, turning, and boring, the fixtures must be designed for all of the operations. This requires cutter accessibility to all parts of the workpiece that need machining operations as shown in Fig. 5-1. It should also be kept in mind that the closer a clamp is placed to a machined feature, the more the machining operation is restricted. Clamping can affect the tool diameter, cycle time, finish, and accuracy.

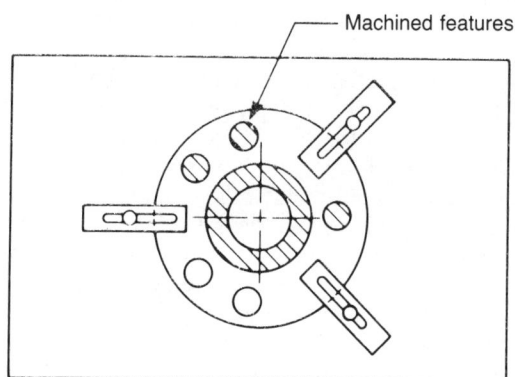

Fig. 5-1 Cutter accessibility.

Probably the most important objective is to keep the fixture and clamping to a low profile to prevent interference with the ideal programmed pattern for the cutting tool. The programmer must raise the tool above the clamp, move it over the clamp, and then drop it back down before resuming a cutting operation. Keeping the clamping as low as possible (see Fig. 5-2) reduces the amount of travel to jump over the clamp, which results in cycle time savings. It also permits the tool to be chucked as short as possible as seen in Fig. 5-3.

Accuracy. Most CNC machining centers are capable of holding extremely close tolerances, especially where all machining can be done with the same setup. For example, a machine may position to within 0.0005 in. of the programmed coordinates and return to the same position (repeatability) over and over within half that amount, or ±0.00025 in. Fixtures for CNC have an equal role in transferring this accuracy to the workpiece. While closer tolerances increase the cost of a fixture, they can also deliver a more accurate, consistent product.

Particular attention should be paid to flatness and parallelism when designing fixtures for CNC. Figure 5-4 illustrates the effect on an 18 in. workpiece when held between vise jaws that are misaligned a total of 0.003 in. If a slot were milled down the center, it would be out of parallel by 0.009 in. This could be enough to scrap the workpiece. The same is true of flatness as illustrated in Fig. 5-5.

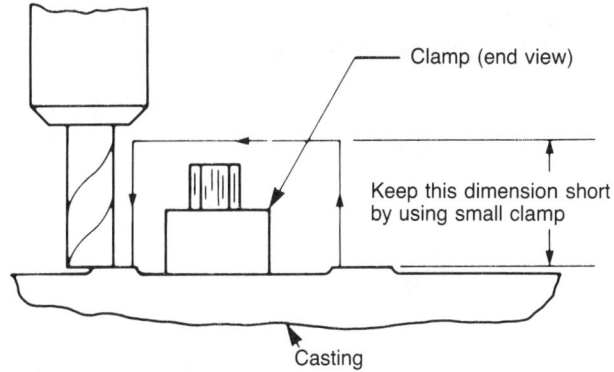

Fig. 5-2 Minimize tool travel time over clamp.

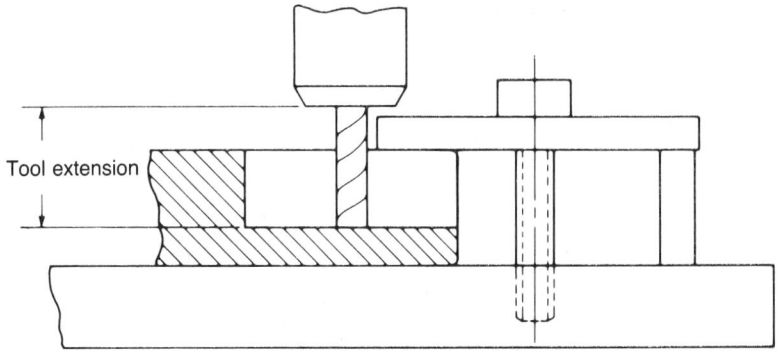

Fig. 5-3 Tool chucked as short as possible.

Rigidity. Accuracy, surface finish, and productivity are affected by rigidity. The cutting tools produce severe shock, pressure, and vibration on the workpiece which must be alleviated with good fixturing.

At least one or two solid surfaces should be designed into the fixture, as shown in Fig. 5-6, to take the shock of the cutting tool. Clamps should be strong enough to hold the workpiece securely without distorting it.

Speed and Ease of Workpiece Changing. The tool designer must also consider loading and unloading the workpiece. Usually the lot size and total quantity of parts to be machined will dictate the amount of money that can be spent on the fixture. Using standard off-the-shelf fixture components can lower the build cost substantially.

In many cases a simple clamp as seen in Fig. 5-7 will work fine. This type of clamp can be guided as shown in Fig. 5-8 when close positioning is required.

Many of the more sophisticated mechanical, pneumatic, and hydraulic clamping systems shown in previous chapters can also be used. These clamps move out of the way when released and permit easy removal of the workpiece. The fluid-operated systems provide the additional advantage of being activated jointly by a single lever, button, or programmed sequence.

Realizing and acting on these needs, however, may not eliminate two relatively serious problems:

1. How to supply the large number of individual fixtures for the many different workpieces in a timely manner.

2. Where to store the fixtures after completing the workpiece(s) that they were used to hold.

Dedicated fixtures for each workpiece are not feasible. The process and time involved to provide a dedicated fixture from inception to the time it is put on the job may be factors. Can it be done in-house or must it be "farmed out"?

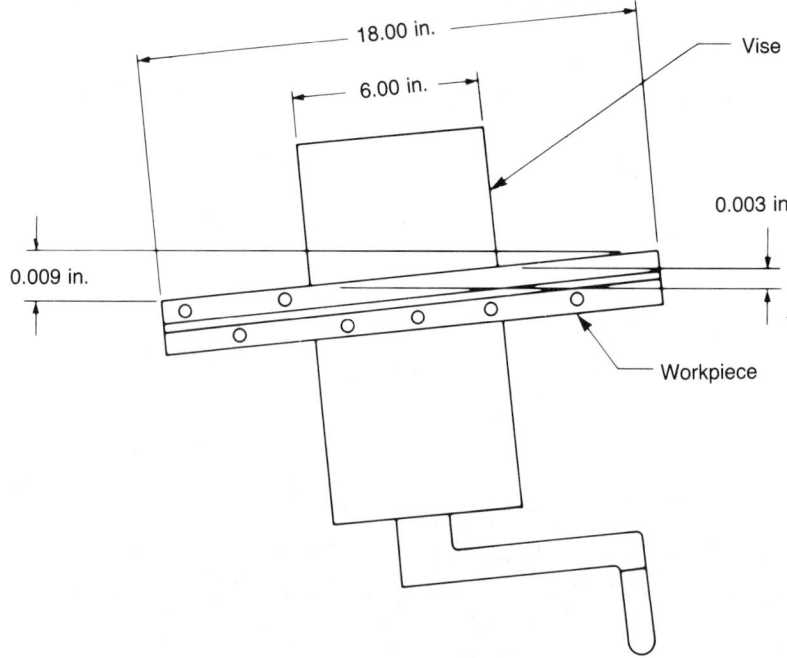

Fig. 5-4 Angular misalignment.

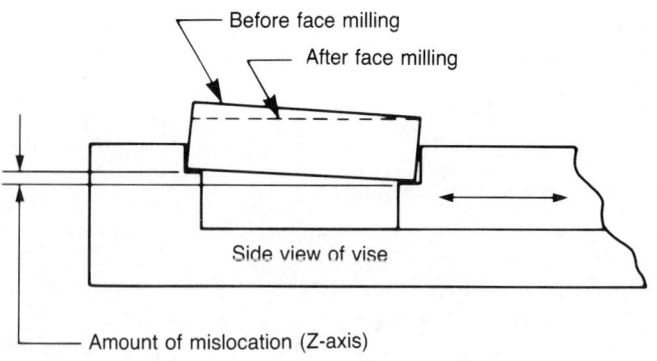

Fig. 5-5 Out of tolerance for flatness.

As for storing large quantities of dedicated fixtures for possible reuse in the future, there is no practical solution. Either they are scrapped out and new ones are built the next time they're needed, or they are stored in space that could be better utilized producing parts.

Modular tooling systems were designed to solve both of these problems at the same time. These systems are called by other names, but regardless of the name, they are all kits of tooling components which can be used together in various combinations to

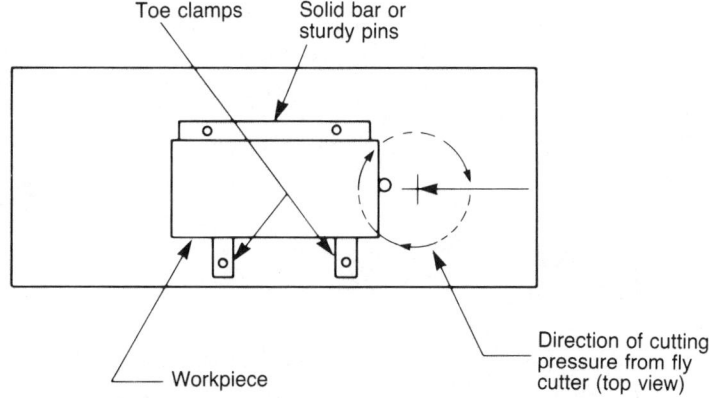

Toe clamps   Solid bar or
              sturdy pins

Direction of cutting
pressure from fly
cutter (top view)

Workpiece

Fig. 5-6 Rigidity in tool design.

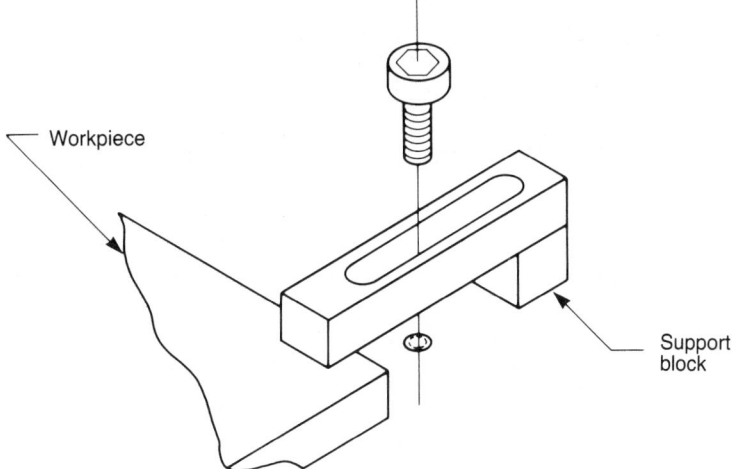

Workpiece

Support
block

Fig. 5-7 Simple clamp.

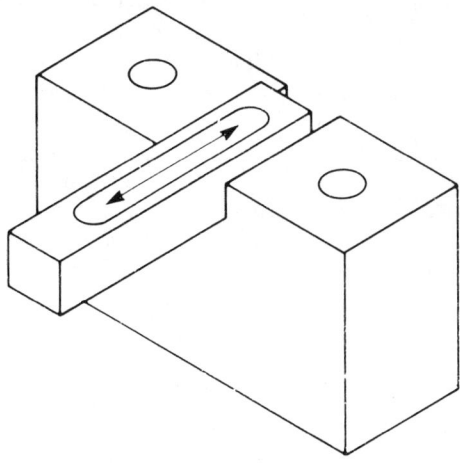

Fig. 5-8 Guided clamp.

locate and clamp workpieces for machining, assembly, and inspection operations.

The components of a typical starter kit are illustrated in Fig. 5-9. A kit consists of mounting plates, angle plates, locators, clamps, and mounting accessories. Adapter are also available to permit the use of many standard and power workholding devices. The method of assembling these components varies between systems and will be covered in detail later in the chapter.

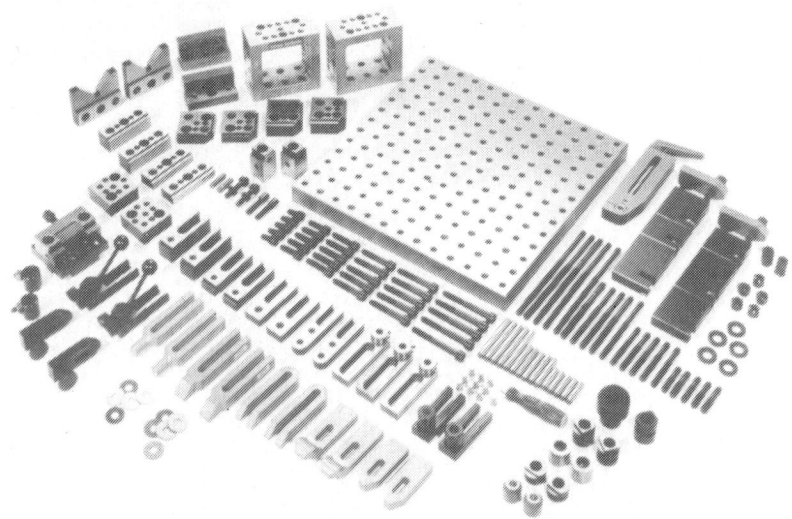

Fig. 5-9 Starter kit of modular fixturing components. (*Courtesy Fritz Werner Machine Tool Corp.*)

Fixtures made from modular tooling kits can also be used on standard machines and NC machines as well as CNC machining centers. They can also be positioned on U.S. or metric machine tables.

Modular tooling systems are invaluable when confronted with short lead time or small production quantities that do not warrant the design and build of a special jig or fixture.

The initial costs for these kits can be quite expensive. However, when one considers their availability, versatility, and accuracy, and the fact that they can be used over and over, these costs can usually be written off within a year's time.

According to one manufacturer of modular tooling systems, there are two different ways to use modular tooling to reduce tooling costs. These two methods are seen in Fig. 5-10. Method *a* was designed to cut setup time by using a dedicated fixture on modular components. This setup can be done in five minutes or less using a dedicated fixture made from a standard tooling plate, which is mounted on two narrow profile angle plates that have been located on a standard subplate. The same setup using conventional techniques on a T-slotted table or pallet would require 3.8 hours.

This approach should be considered under the following conditions:

- Repeat production runs of the workpiece are likely.
- Personnel capable of making setups using components as illustrated in method *b* are not available.
- Setup changes and workpiece changes are frequent, allowing insufficient time for setups using individual components such as illustrated in method *b*.

Method *b* was designed to eliminate tooling costs by setting up the fixture with reusable components. This setup would require about 3.6 hours.

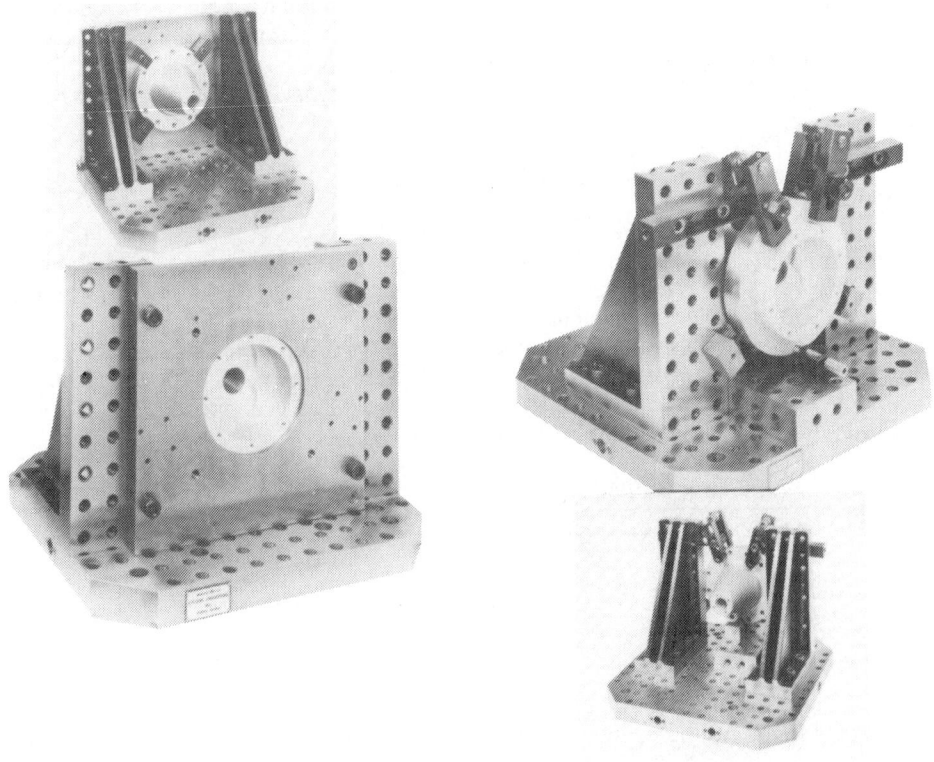

Fig. 5-10 Two ways of using modular tooling. (*Stevens Modular Tooling System, courtesy Stevens Engineering, Inc.*)

This approach should be considered under the following conditions:

- The workpiece is a preproduction part or a prototype part which will probably not be run again.
- The machine cycle time is sufficient enough to permit the machine operator to make setups between loading and unloading.
- Facilities for the design and build of dedicated fixtures are not readily available.
- Storage space for additional dedicated fixtures is not available.

Using the dedicated fixture approach (method *a*) the payout was determined as follows:

$$\text{Payout} = \frac{\text{Investment in modular tooling}}{\text{Savings in setup cost}} \qquad (1)$$

$$= \frac{\$3{,}776}{(3.8\text{-}0.1) \times \$45/\text{hr.}}$$

$$= \frac{\$3{,}776}{\$166}$$

$$= 22.6 \text{ setups}$$

It can be seen that if average savings per setup amounted to about $166, the invest-ment in modular tooling would be paid for after about 23 setups. If a change was made once a week, the investment would be paid for in less than 6 months.

On the other hand, if modular tooling setup components (method b) are used, then the payout would be:

$$\text{Payout} = \frac{\text{Investment in modular tooling}}{\text{Net savings in tooling expense}} \qquad (2)$$

The cost of a fixture to duplicate the setup shown in b was estimated to be about $1800. However, the net savings in tooling expense will be $1800 less the cost of setting up with modular components (3.6 hours × $45 = $162), or $1638.

The actual cost of the individual modular components used in this setup is $5234. However, an assortment of modular tooling with setup components offering reasonable flexibility in setting up parts in this size range would cost approximately $13,800. Accordingly, the payout is determined as follows:

$$\text{Payout} = \frac{\text{Investment in modular tooling}}{\text{Net savings for each setup}}$$

$$= \frac{\$13800}{\$1638}$$

$$= 8.42 \text{ setups}$$

These figures show that if $1638 will be saved for each setup the tooling package will be paid for after nine setups. The payout time will depend on how many fixtures are normally made in a specific time span.

Modular Fixture Design. Tool design is minimized with modular tooling. Most fixtures can be built directly from the information on tool data sheets (process sheets) and part drawings. This information must indicate the locating points, areas of the workpiece to be machined, and the machine assigned to the job. Supporting and clamp-ing the part then becomes the responsibility of the tool assembler.

A typical tool data sheet drawing, with the required information, is shown in Fig. 5-11. With this information and machine assignment, the tool assembler can easily and quickly construct a drill jig with tooling components from the modular tooling kit. When confronted with short lead time or the need for prototypes, freehand sketches will often suffice. After construction, and prior to placing a modular jig or fixture into production, photographs from all angles should be taken of it, and all of the components listed. The photographs and listings should be filed away for future reference. The components can usually be reassembled in half of the original assembly time with these records.

With modular tooling, engineering changes can be processed in a swift, efficient manner. Once the tool assembler is notified of the change, the jig or fixture can be modified to suit the change almost immediately—a response not possible with a con-ventional tooling program which requires the notification of the change to the tool engineer, revision of tool data sheets and tool drawings, and delivery of the revised tool drawing to the tool room where the necessary changes are made to the jig or fixture. The tool revision could be further delayed if the revision required the procurement of material or components not in stock.

The most effective means for modular fixturing design according to one supplier of modular tooling is the CAD/CAM approach (see Fig. 5-12). A database representing all elements of the modular fixturing system in either 2-D or 3-D is created by the user or delivered by the supplier. IGES is often the transfer means from one CAD system to

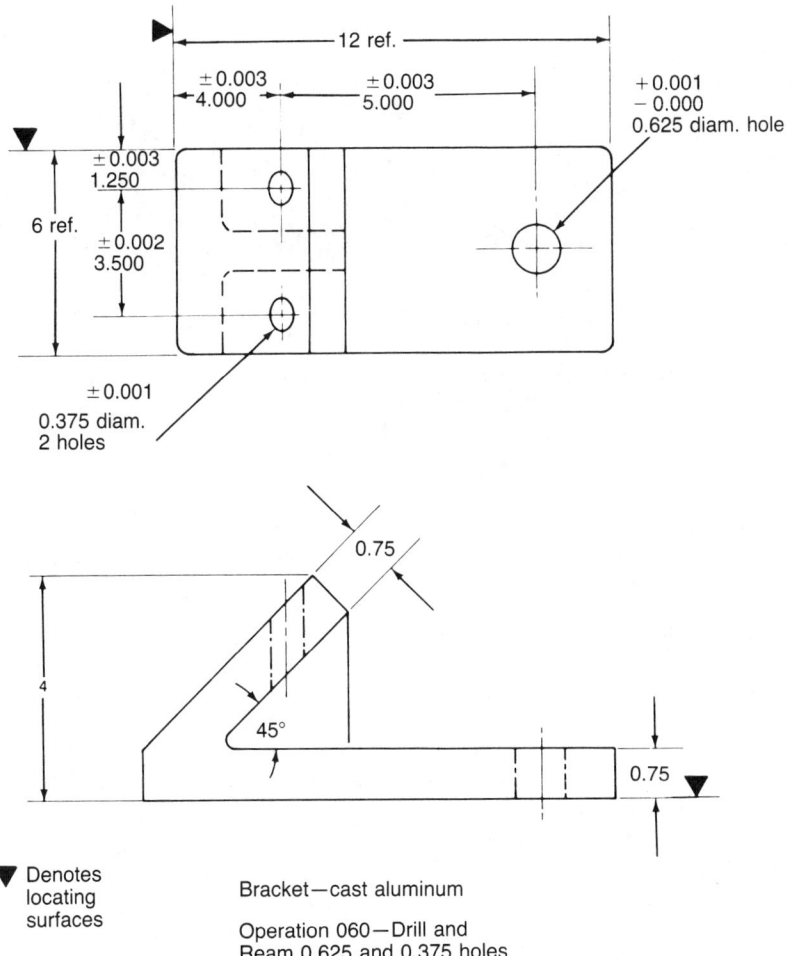

Fig. 5-11 Typical tool data sheet drawing for assembly of a jig using modular tooling.

another. Having access to the part geometry, it is a simple matter to assemble a fixture almost as if it were done in the shop with the actual part and its components. Once the fixture is complete on the terminal, a plotter completes the documentation for the assembler. Any changes in fixture concept, from design to actual construction, can easily be accommodated with the CAD system.

Coordination between the various functions within an organization is critical to the successful implementation of modular fixturing. One user has experienced such success in a very difficult manufacturing environment. They manufacture a standard machine with a large variety of interface hardware to suit a specific customer's requirements. This results in a work load that changes frequently with extremely low volumes. This is an ideal situation for CNC and a real serious problem for tool design and the NC programmer.

The solution is simple. These two functions can be integrated into a single department. Provided with CAD terminals connected to the company's mainframe computer, the programmer has access to the geometric data for released designs. Fixtures are created by selecting modular fixturing elements from the library. The NC program is written by the same person. Cutter paths are plotted and interferences noted for correction before the fixture is delivered to the machine.

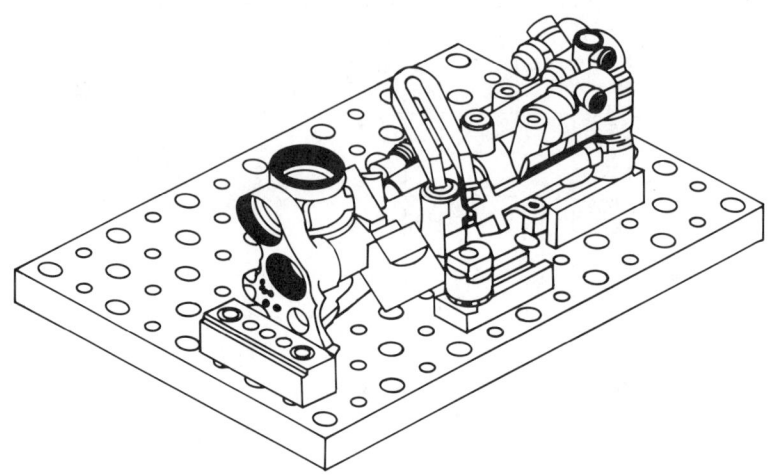

Fig. 5-12 CAD/CAM approach for modular fixture design. (*Courtesy Fritz Werner Machine Tool Corp.*)

The finished and tested program with documentation is delivered to the machine operator. Each machine is equipped with a full set of modular fixturing components and base plates (see Fig. 5-13). From the storage cabinets located next to each machine, the operator sets up the fixture required for the next part during machining of the first. Most of the machines are equipped with pallet changers allowing in-cycle changeover of the fixturing. Total rebuild time for a new fixture, documented by sketch, photo, or CAD drawing, averages 20 minutes.

Fig. 5-13 Modular fixturing components at the machine. (*Courtesy Fritz Werner Machine Tool Corp.*)

An interesting relationship develops between the programmers and the operators. The operators know that the programmers have debugged the fixturing process thru his or her CAD/CAM terminal and that interferences between cutter and "perishable" clamps have been eliminated. The operator builds the fixture exactly as it was conceived. The programmer is confident that the operator will build the fixture as designed and therefore is free to be creative in solving manufacturing problems. Because of this relationship, the company prospers while the machine tools are more effectively utilized.

Constructing Modular Tooling Fixtures. The first step in assembling a jig or fixture is to select a base large enough to handle the workpiece. Next, the main structure is constructed with riser blocks and reinforced with stop-thrust elements. Finally, the more specialized elements are added to properly locate and clamp the workpiece for machining.

An erector-set fixture is shown in Fig. 5-14 without a workpiece in place and in Fig. 5-15 with a workpiece in place. Machining is to be performed under the following conditions:

Fixture:	Assembled mounting plate size
	24.8 × 31.1 in. (630 × 790 mm)
Machine:	Horizontal boring and milling machine;
	face milling cutter 7.87 in. (200 mm) diameter,
	16 reversible carbide tips
Workpiece:	Spheroidal graphite iron
	Weight 1146 lbs (520 kg),
	Height 25.6 in. (650 mm)
Machining Data:	Spindle speed, 112 rpm
	Feed, 17 ipm (431 mm/min)
	Feed per cutter, 0.009 in. (0.23 mm)
	Cutter; Cutting depth, 0.2 in. (5 mm)
	Cutting speed, 233 fpm (1.18m/sec)

Construction with Sample Parts. An ideal method of constructing a jig or fixture with a modular tooling kit is to build it around a sample part. Simply place the sample part on the base and add locators and clamps as needed. This method reduces the construction time to a fraction of the time it would take to design and build a dedicated jig or fixture to do the same job. If the sample part is accurately machined, assembly can often be done without measuring instruments. For some complex jigs and fixtures, it becomes economical to fabricate a single, accurate part just for this purpose. The use of a sample part can also expedite frequent assembly and disassembly of jigs and fixtures.

Construction with a Template. When no sample part is available, a jig or fixture can be assembled around a template of the part. Templates are also useful to check for interference that could occur when loading or unloading a part.

Machining on Modular Fixtures. Jigs and fixtures assembled from modular tooling seldom need machining. Occasionally, limited machining may be required to produce a special component. Excessive machining, however, should always be avoided, since it will eliminate the economic advantages of the system. If, for some reason, the jig or fixture is impossible to construct without considerable machining, modular tooling should not be used.

The Tool Assembler. Even though modular tooling is easily assembled, the need for tooling knowledge and experience is not diminished. Jigs and fixtures constructed with modular tooling kits must be strong enough to withstand machining forces imposed on them, they must be built to utilize adjustable components, and must often be built to accommodate an in-process part. The tool assembler must have the imagination and experience to foresee and plan ahead. The selection of a tool assembler requires careful consideration.

Fig. 5-14 Erector-set fixture without a workpiece in place. (*Courtesy Flexible Fixturing Systems, Inc./Erwin Halder, Ltd.*)

Fig. 5-15 Erector-set fixture shown in Fig. 5-14 with a workpiece in place. (*Courtesy Flexible Fixturing Systems, Inc./Erwin Halder, Ltd.*)

ADVANTAGES OF MODULAR TOOLING

Reduced Lead Time. Reduced lead time is the major advantage of a modular tooling system. Jigs and fixtures can usually be assembled in a few hours time with components on hand, virtually eliminating lead time. The tooling can often be assembled in less time than it takes to prepare a tape for the part.

Adaptability. Tooling changes to accommodate new products or revisions to existing products are fast and easy with modular tooling. For companies experiencing frequent product changes, new products will not be held up waiting for tooling, since changes to existing tooling can be made immediately without interrupting production. Sometimes tool trials show the need for revisions that are difficult and time consuming to make on a dedicated fixture. These changes can be made easily and quickly with modular tooling.

Even when a dedicated fixture is planned, modular tooling can be used to establish the basic design and tool clearances.

Reusability. Although modular tooling kits are fairly expensive, they usually pay for themselves in a year or two. At the completion of a production run, the modular jig or fixture can be completely dismantled and the components returned to the kit for reuse, whereas conventional tooling is usually stripped of any reusable parts and then scrapped at a fraction of its original cost. An example of this is shown in Fig. 5-16. The fixture on the left will be useless at the end of the production run, whereas the modular fixture will be completely torn down and the components returned to the kit for reuse. Storage of the dedicated fixture for possible revision and reuse at a later date may be considered, but storage costs, where added to revision costs, usually makes this an expensive proposition.

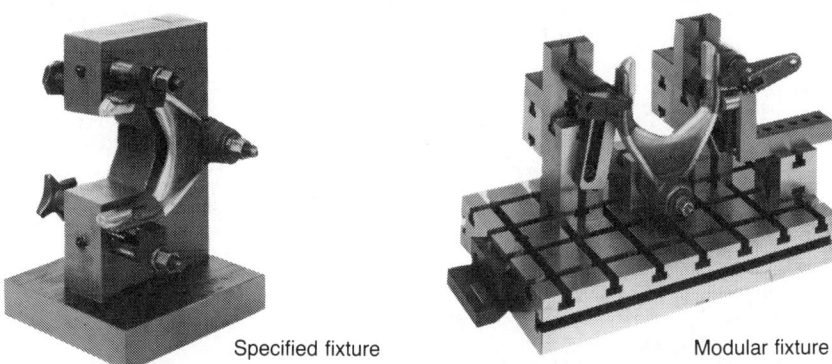

Specified fixture   Modular fixture

Fig. 5-16 Two methods of constructing a milling fixture. (*Courtesy Flexible Fixturing Systems, Inc./Erwin Halder, Ltd.*)

Backup Ability. Modular tooling can be swiftly assembled to temporarily replace a dedicated jig or fixture while it is being repaired, reworked, or revised. Just having backup tooling available for emergencies makes modular tooling well worth the investment.

MODULAR TOOLING SYSTEMS

All modular tooling systems include most of the major components listed in Fig. 5-17 thru 5-23. Typically, all of the major components of a modular tooling system feature a grid pattern of accurate locating holes or precision-spaced T-slots which are used to accurately position components to locate and clamp workpieces for machining. The major components include subplates, riser/tooling blocks, four-sided, six-sided and two-sided tooling blocks, angle plates, and tooling cubes.

Subplates. Subplates or tooling plates, such as shown in Fig. 5-17, are being used at an increasing rate by progressive job shop and production manufacturers to increase productivity while lowering tooling costs. Subplates are adaptable to any machine table or pallet system and greatly increase the number of locating and clamping points available on the table surface.

Subplates are simple in concept as well as design. They can greatly reduce setup time, provide for easy and accurate workpiece and fixture location, and usually eliminate the need for special fixtures.

Programmers save time by being able to program from qualified holes, edges, T-slot insertion points, etc. Operators save time by setting up more parts per cycle. Altogether, the combined reduction in setup, machining, and programing time can dramatically reduce the total manufacturing costs.

Subplates are machined for an exact fit to the customer's machining center or machine, and subplate sets are available for machines using shuttle tables. The use of matched sets greatly reduces the need to indicate individual tables, thereby increasing the production capacity of multi-pallet machines.

Fig. 5-17 Subplates. (*Courtesy Mid-State Machine Products*)

Riser/Tooling Blocks. Most machining centers have unusable dead space between the centerline of the spindle and the top of the machine table or pallet. This dead space varies between machines, but in each case it poses limitations on the machine.

To work around these limitations, operators will sometimes move the workpiece to the edge of the table to get more vertical quill movement. This arrangement, however, prevents machining the back of the workpiece without resetting the job, thereby eliminating the cost saving potential provided by the indexable pallet.

Another method used by operators is to elevate the workpiece on blocks which are high enough to eliminate the dead space. This method is costly in terms of setup time, particularly on high volume jobs where the same operations are performed repeatedly.

Additionally, these setups are often less than solid. Riser/tooling blocks, such as shown in Fig. 5-18, offer a workable alternative to the time-consuming double setups and eliminates the need for unstable parallels. The riser/tooling block is mounted squarely in the center of the machining center pallet. The dead space is eliminated by the additional height of the block, thereby allowing the operator to make full use of the machine's indexing capacity and to machine up to five sides of a workpiece in one setup. The riser/tooling block's heavy-duty construction, along with qualified dowel holes or T-slots, assures setups will be solid and repeatable.

Fig. 5-18 Riser/tooling blocks. (*Courtesy Mid-State Machine Products*)

Four-sided Tooling Blocks. Four-sided tooling blocks, such as shown in Fig. 5-19, are designed for use on horizontal machining centers and provide four identical surfaces for attaching workpieces or other components. When mounted on a rotary table or 4th axis they can be indexed 90° to present four work setups to the cutting tool in rapid succession. In some cases, even the top surface is used to locate the workpieces for machining.

Six-sided Tooling Blocks. Six-sided tooling blocks (see Fig. 5-20) are used in the same manner as the four-sided blocks, but with two additional identical mounting surfaces.

Two-sided Tooling Blocks. Two-sided tooling blocks (see Fig. 5-21) are setup on the machine table in the same way that the four-way blocks are setup, but provide for more

Z-axis travel. When mounted on a rotary table or 4th axis they can be indexed 180° to present two work setups to the cutting tool in rapid succession. Two-sided tooling blocks are the logical solution to mounting workpieces which are too large to clear the spindle or the coolant-chip shield if mounted on a column subplate. The open frame design provides an access opening so the spindle can reach the back of the workpiece after indexing. Operations can then be performed on the front and back of a workpiece using the same setup.

Fig. 5-19 Four-sided tooling blocks. (*Courtesy Mid-State Machine Products*)

Angle Plates. Angle plates, such as shown in Fig. 5-22, are ideal for machining operations where a four-sided tooling block is neither required nor economically feasible. They are ideal for applications that require the fixture be mounted near the front edge of the pallet, for extra thick workpieces that take up most of the pallet, and for workpieces that require their centerline to be on the centerline of the pallet.

Tooling Cubes. Tooling cubes, such as seen in Fig. 5-23, were designed for use on many of the newer machining centers that are equipped with pallet changers having limited weight capacities. The inside of the tooling cube is hollow and necked down at both ends to reduce weight while still providing sufficient rigidity to resist intense machining forces. Tooling cubes can be located quickly against edge stops with dowel pins or parallels. They are usually bolted to the pallet through the center with threaded alloy bolts using either standard straps or a made-to-fit cover.

Some systems consist only of major components, such as those shown in Fig. 5-17 thru 5-23. They do not include the locating or clamping components that are found in most systems. Workpieces are located and clamped using off-the-shelf jig and fixture components or special dedicated fixtures. Systems such as this are usually referred to as sub-plate systems. All of the components making up this particular system are provided in one-piece, stress-relieved Meehanite (or equivalent cast iron), or aluminum castings. Four styles are available as follows:

- Plain, with no holes.
- Blind tapped holes, any size, located within ±0.005 in.
- With precision T-slots which are held either to ±0.0008 in. for size and ±0.0015 in. for location, or ±0.010 in. for size and location.
- Made with multipurpose (bored at the top and tapped at the bottom) qualified holes on either a 1.0000 ±0.0005 in. or a 2.0000 ±0.0005 in. grid. Holes can be

Fig. 5-20 Six-sided tooling blocks. (*Courtesy Mid-State Machine Products*)

Fig. 5-21 Two-sided tooling blocks. (*Courtesy Mid-State Machine Products*)

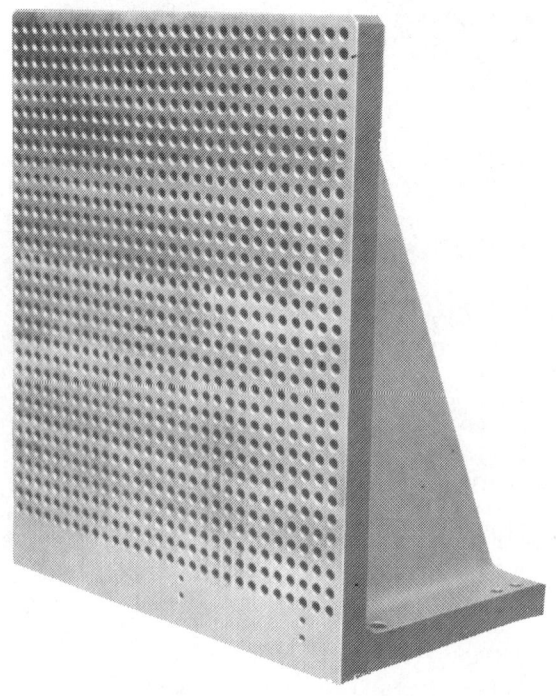

Fig. 5-22 Angle plates. (*Courtesy Mid-State Machine Products*)

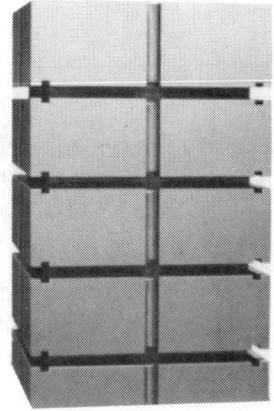 

Fig. 5-23 Tooling cubes. (*Courtesy Mid-State Machine Products*)

0.6250 ±0.0005 in. diameter with a 0.500-13 tapped hole below it, or 0.7500 ±0.0005 in. diameter with a 0.625-11 tapped hole below it, or 0.8750 ±0.0005 in. with a 0.750-10 tapped hole below it.

Major components are available in a wide range of sizes to suit most any application.

Applications using many of the major modular tooling components shown can be seen in Fig. 5-24.

The subplate system shown in Fig. 5-25 features plain versions of the same components as the previous system, to which tooling plates, made by the customer or to the customer's specifications, are assembled.

Another subplate system is made up of various sizes of cubes, T-blocks, and subplate surface configurations as shown in Fig. 5-26.

Type *A* features multipurpose 0.6254 ±0.0002 in. diameter locating bushings with 0.500-13 UN-2B tapped holes at the bottom which are located on 3.0000 ±0.0005 in. centers.

Type *B* features straight 0.6254 ±0.0005 in. wide horizontal and vertical slots equally spaced at 3.0000 ±0.0005 in. intervals from the base and true center with 0.500-13 UN-2B tapped holes located as shown.

Type *C* is the same as type *B* but without the tapped holes. Type P (not shown) is plain.

Standard specifications for all components are as follows:

- Flatness is held to 0.00025 in./ft.
- Parallelism is held to 0.0005 in./ft.
- Perpendicularity is held to 0.0005 in./ft.

A Modular, Dowel-Type Tooling System. The major components that make up another system are provided in a standard series which uses a grid pattern of 0.5011-0.5012 in. ID × 0.81 in. long hardened bushings precisely located at 5.0000 ±0.0002 in. intervals for use with 0.5006-0.5007 in. diameter pull dowels to permit quick and positive location of modular components and accessories. Provisions for ½-13 tapped holes at 1.250 in. intervals between the bushings permit assembly of the various components of the system with standard socket head capscrews as shown in Fig. 5-27. The system is also provided in a heavy-duty series which features a grid pattern of 0.7506-0.7507 in. ID × 1.29 in. long hardened bushings precisely located at 8.0000 ±0.0002 in. intervals for use with 0.7501-0.7502 in. diameter pull dowels, along with ¾-10 tapped holes located at 2.000 in. intervals.

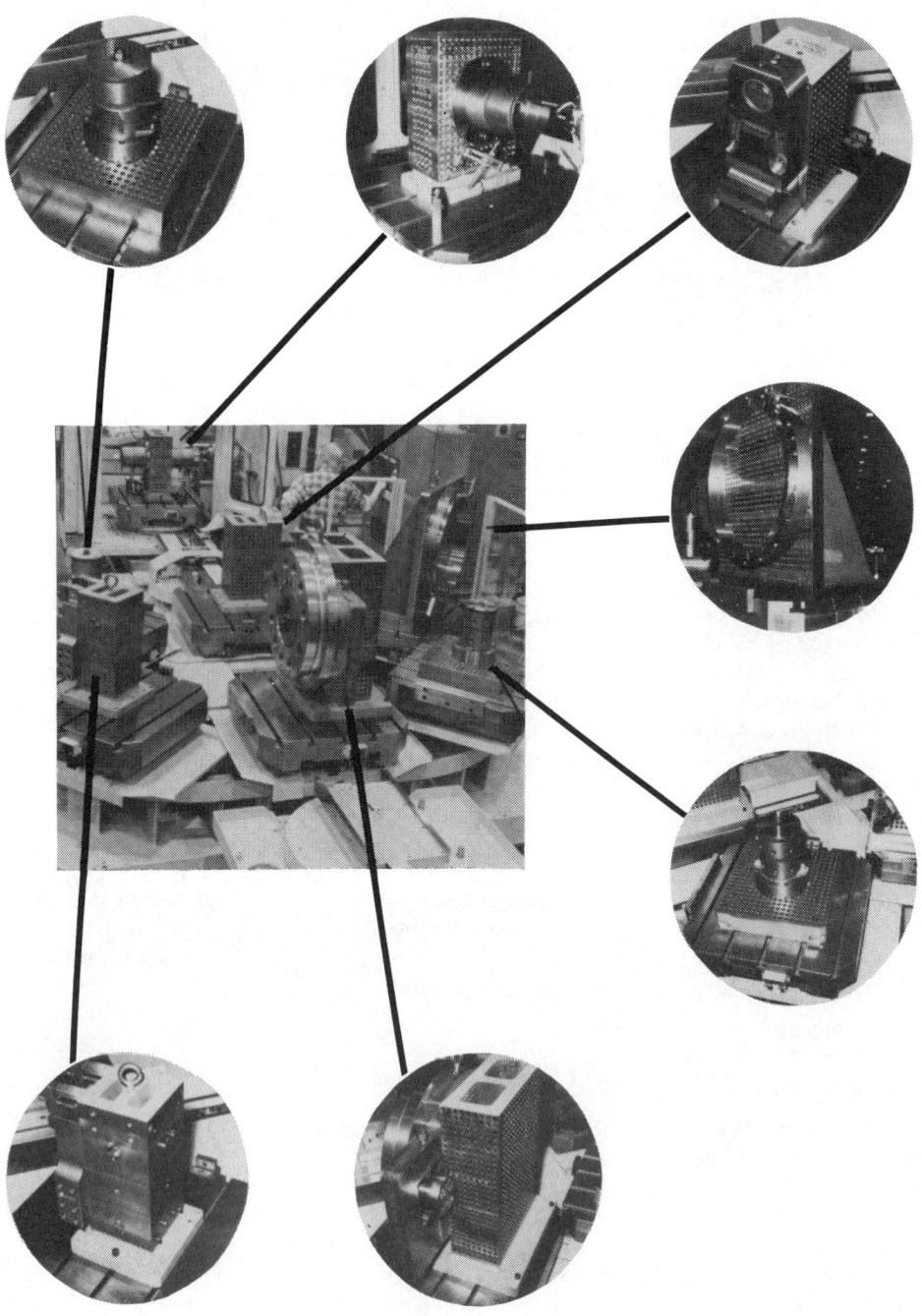

Fig. 5-24 Applications of major modular tooling components. (*Courtesy Mid-State Machine Products*)

Fig. 5-25 Cube system. (*Courtesy Viking Kube Systems*)

Fig. 5-26 Matrix positioning system components. (*MATRIX Positioning System, courtesy Midwest Specialties, Inc.*)

The major components of this modular tooling system include:

Subplates. Subplates for this system can be sized to fit any machine table. They are made from stabilized carbon steel ground to a flatness of 0.001 in./40 in. and parallelism of 0.0005 in. Subplates are fastened to the machine T-slots with T-nuts and cap screws which locate in counterbored holes in the subplate. Trough-type subplates are provided for machines in which the coolant must be returned to the setup through an opening in the top of the working surface of the machine table. Subplates without a trough are used with machines that are provided with a coolant trough surrounding the work area.

Column Subplates. Column subplates are provided with a wide variety of face plate mounting surfaces ranging from approximately 7.5 in. (190 mm) wide × 11 in. high to 28 in. wide × 50 in. (1270 mm) high. Plain finish ground columns are available for situations in which a dedicated four-sided fixture is desired or where a user wishes to

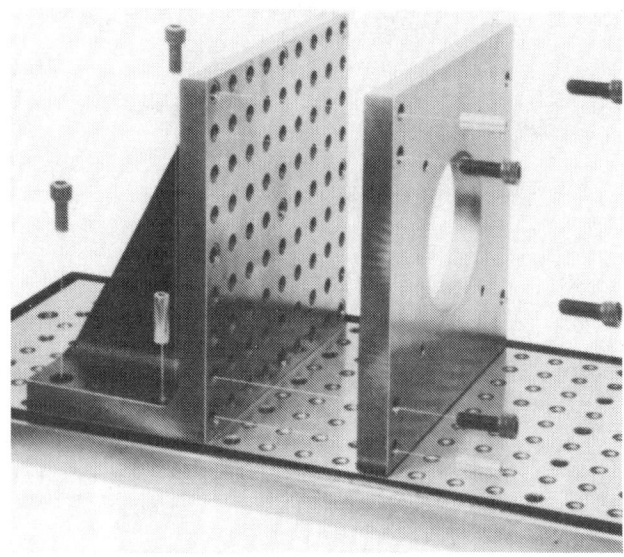

Fig. 5-27 Modular, dowel-type tooling system. (*Stevens Modular Tooling System, courtesy Stevens Engineering, Inc.*)

machine his or her own hole patterns. Plain columns are also available unground for the user who plans extensive machining on the vertical surfaces. Column subplates are perpendicular and flat within 0.0008 in./ft.

Column subplates are made of stabilized steel and feature detachable base plates which are furnished with hold-down patterns and sized to fit the machine table or pallet on which they are to be used.

Angle Plates. Angle plates are made from ductile iron and are ground to a flatness of 0.0005 in. Perpendicularity between the base and vertical surface is 0.0008 in./ft. Mounting surfaces range from approximately 6 in. to 24 in. square. Narrow angle plates measuring 3.75 × 11.25 in. (95 × 286 mm) and 6.00 × 18.00 in. (152 × 457 mm) are also provided.

Double Access Angle Plates. Double access angle plates are made from stabilized steel. Mounting surfaces are approximately 24 in. square and are ground perpendicular to the base within 0.0008 in./ft. The location of one face with respect to the other will be within 0.0015 in. A vertical subplate is available to cover the center opening when it is not needed.

This modular tooling system also provides many other components, some of which can be seen in Figs. 5-28 thru 5-34.

The series of four photos in Figs. 5-28 and 5-29 illustrates how a transfer case is set up in separate orientations for machining complete on a horizontal machining center. In the first operation (see Fig. 5-28) the large open end of the casting and the opposite end are fully machined.

The casting is located on two V-blocks (1 and 2) using V-block extenders of two different heights to locate the part horizontally. The extenders locate on the round portion of the casting avoiding cast bosses and ribs. The rear V-block is mounted on the high density subplate (3) which raises the workpiece and allows indexing of the V-block at close intervals. The secondary locator is a combination of an adjustable rest pad (4) a threaded hole riser, and a rest base. This combination is mounted on the vertical surface of the large utility block (5). The large utility block is mounted on a utility slide (6) and a double axis slide base (7). This allows for positioning the locator precisely where it is needed. The end locator is a rest pad base (8). A three-axis clamp (9) clamps the work

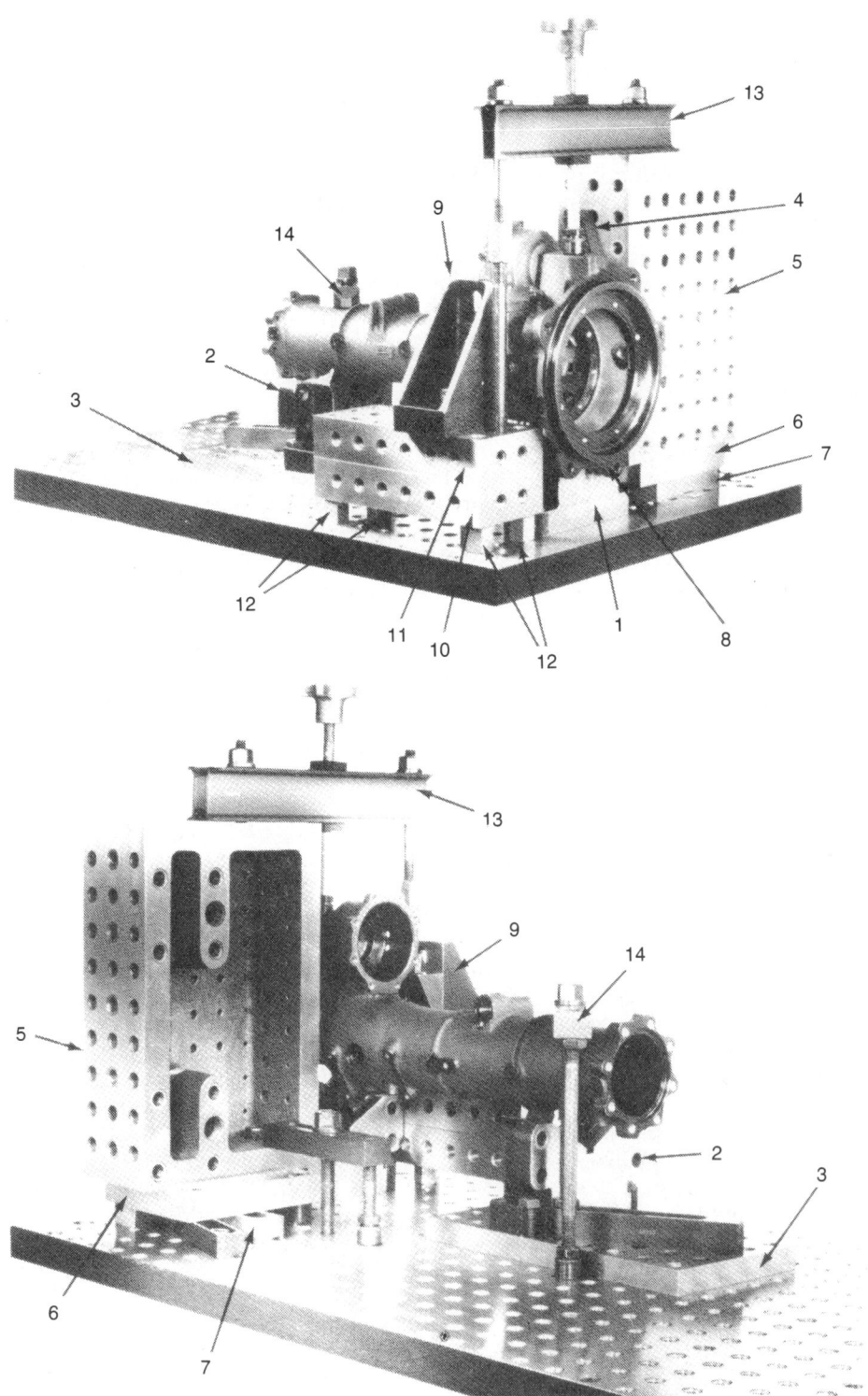

Fig. 5-28 Modular tooling setup for machining a transfer case—first operation. (*Stevens Modular Tooling System, courtesy Stevens Engineering, Inc.*)

against the secondary locator. The three-axis clamp is elevated on two small utility blocks (10 and 11) which rest on four threaded hole risers (12). A clamp beam (13) holds the casting down on V-block extenders. A bar clamp (14) near the opposite end holds the casting down on the rear V-block setup.

The third and fourth photos (see Fig. 5-29) show the second operation setup for machining all other features on the casting. The hole pattern machined on the large flange face in the first setup is used for locating the workpiece for the second setup. To do this, pins (one round (15) and one diamond (16)) sized to fit the holes are located precisely relative to machine zero using double axis slides. The locator pins are mounted in locator bases (17 and 18). These are locked into two single-axis slides (19 and 20). These slide on double-axis slide bases (21 and 22). After positioning the locating pins with gage blocks as shown in Fig. 5-30, the slides are secured with capscrews. The finished flange face rests on five small rest pads (23 thru 27). These are positioned where needed using adjustable rest pads (28 thru 32). The small rest pads are elevated to the proper height using shims. Five bar clamps placed directly over the rest pads complete the setup.

With this modular tooling system, all surfaces on all small utility blocks, large utility blocks, and high density subplates are ground to exact and matching dimensions. In addition, bushed hole locations relative to the edges on these components are also closely controlled and correspond exactly with bushed hole-to-edge dimensions on each of them, and various edge locators in the system. This allows them to be used individually, or in any combination with other components on which the same dimension is accurately held.

Single-axis slides can also be used to position a variety of locating elements in virtually any position along a single axis of travel. The double-axis slides perform the same function except that the double-axis slide offers accurate positioning of the bushed hole in two axes rather than one. The location of the bushed hole in the slides may be' positioned with greater accuracy using a round-edge locator and gage blocks as illustrated in Fig. 5-30.

Additional components of the system can be seen in Fig. 5-31 which shows how a workpiece requiring support under a thin, flexible member is setup for milling, drilling, and boring. V-locators (1 and 2) are screwed into T-nut slides (3 and 4) which are mounted on the face of an edge locator bracket (5). The Vees locate on round cast features on the workpiece. Two adjustable rest pads (6 and 7), support the casting underneath. One of these locators is built-up to the proper height by addition of shims (8) a rest pad base (9) and a rest pad (10). A spring jack (11) supports the thin leaf member of the workpiece under heavy cuts. When the workpiece is positioned in the fixture, the plunger (12), is depressed by the thin leaf member. The clamp screw (13) is tightened to secure the plunger. Two clamp bases (14 and 15) raise the spring jack to the approximate height needed. Two toggle screws (16 and 17) clamp the workpiece. They are mounted on two work supports (18 and 19).

The bridge fixture shown in Fig. 5-32 holds the workpiece for machining on a vertical mill. The fixture is made from a tooling plate (1) and two six-inch parallels (2 and 3). The parallels are doweled to the subplate and secured with capscrews. The tooling plate which has been machined and fitted with clamps to hold the workpiece, is screwed and doweled to the parallels. The tooling plate can be quickly removed and relocated on other modules for machining the part in other orientations.

The modular vises shown in Fig. 5-33 were designed for use on subplates, columns, and angle plates. The fixed and movable jaws are separate assemblies allowing them to be separated by any interval on the surface to which they are mounted. The jaw face may be oriented parallel to any machine axis. The jaw face and left edge of the jaw are qualified with respect to the bushed hole pattern which means that when several vises are mounted on the same subplate or module, the faces of the fixed jaws will be in the

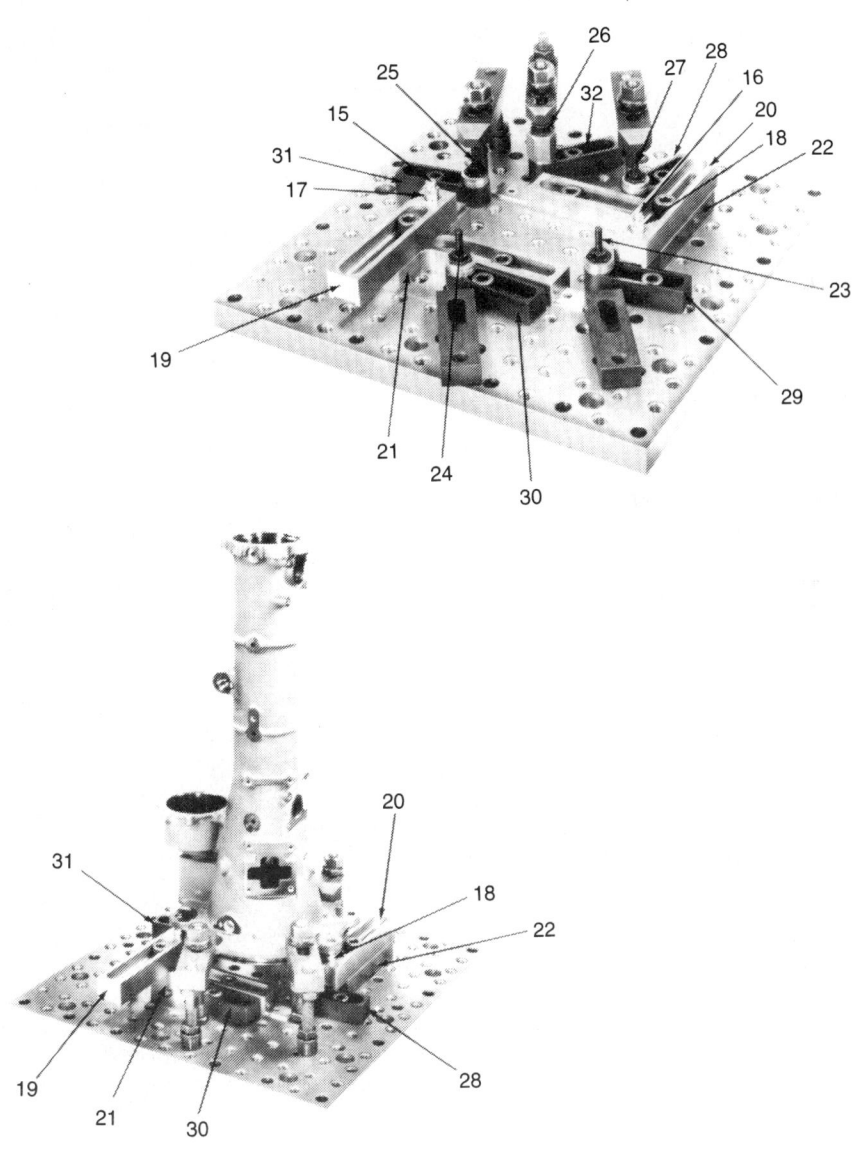

Fig. 5-29 Modular tooling setup for machining a transfer case—second operation. (*Stevens Modular Tooling System, courtesy Stevens Engineering, Inc.*)

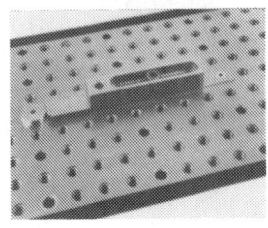

Fig. 5-30 Positioning with gage blocks: (*a*) **single axis slide,** (*b*) **double axis slide, and** (*c*) **utility slide.** (*Stevens Modular Tooling System, courtesy Stevens Engineering, Inc.*)

same exact plane.

Vise adapters can also be provided to mount many type of vises on primary components of the system such as subplates, column, and angle plates. Vises are mounted on vise adapters by aligning the fixed jaw plate with the bushing pattern and doweling the vise to the adapter.

Other components that make up the system are shown in Fig. 5-34. They include the following:

- The right angle slide, *a*, which can be used in combination with a special key to form a single directional slide. The key is placed in appropriately located bushed holes on any component. After the key is positioned, the center slot on the bottom surface is engaged with the key and the slide is secured in place with capscrews through the clearance slots once the desired position has been established. Various accessories such as the V-block, small utility block, locators, and clamps may then be positioned on either surface.
- The two axis clamp, *b*, is a low profile clamp which permits placement of the clamping force at any desired location within a single plane.
- The flat edge locator, *c*, and the edge locator bar, *d*, which are used to locate workpieces along with the round edge locators previously shown. Since the dimension from their centerlines to the edge is identical to the other edge locators, subplates, and utility blocks, they may be used in any combination, as their edges or points of tangency will lie in the same plane.
- The fixed work support, *e*, and the adjustable work support, *f*, can be inserted anywhere on the system. Threaded holes in the sides of the supports will accept a wide variety of members suitable for clamping.
- The bushing rise, *g*, is used to elevate a bushed location without loss of position accuracy.
- The clamp bracket, *h*, provides another method of elevating a tapped hole.
- The retracting locator base, *i*, enables the user to move the locating pins in and out of registration holes on the workpiece when positioning heavy or awkward workpieces.
- The risers, *j*, are designed for elevating clamping assemblies and other structures to any desired height. They are often used in combination with a riser base, *k*, which has a slot in the base to enable positioning precisely where the structure is needed.

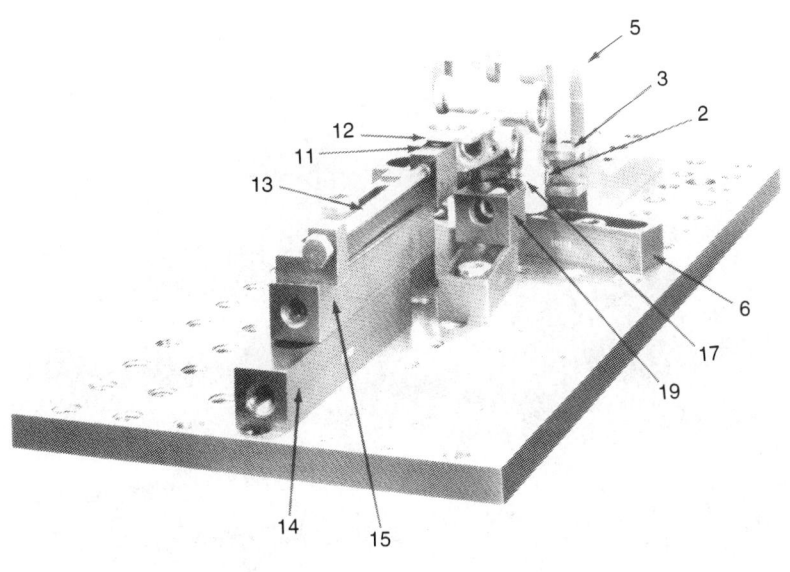

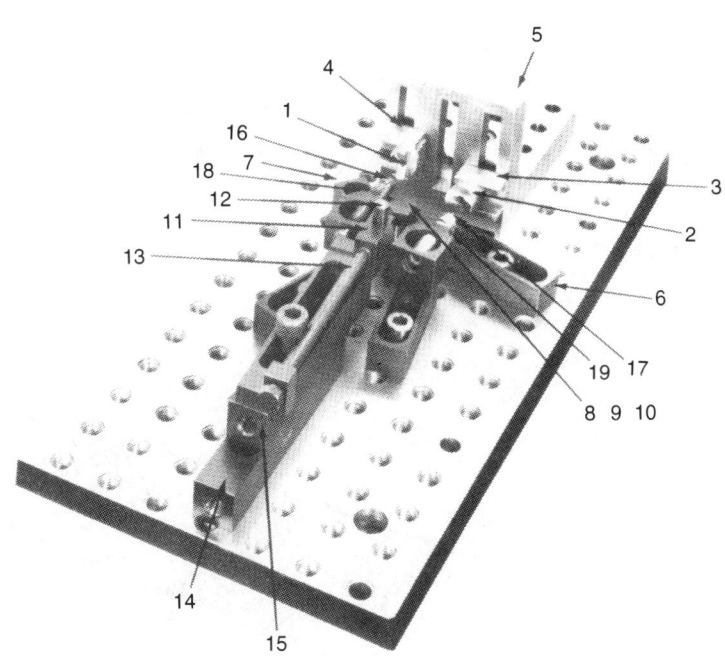

Fig. 5-31 Modular tooling setup for milling, drilling, and boring. (*Stevens Modular Tooling System, courtesy Stevens Engineering, Inc.*)

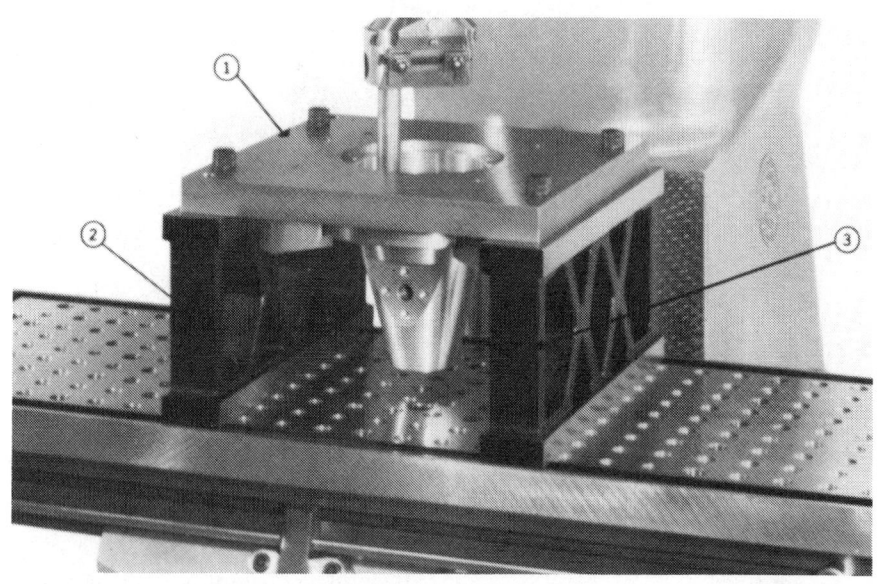

Fig. 5-32 Bridge fixture. (*Stevens Modular Tooling System, courtesy Stevens Engineering, Inc.*)

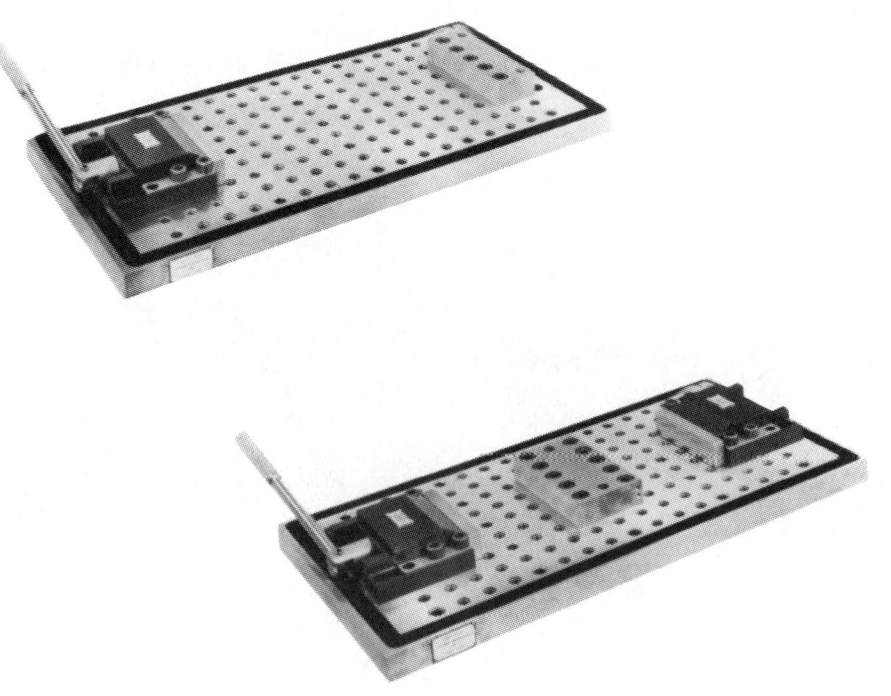

Fig. 5-33 Modular vises: (*a*) **standard,** (*b*) **duplex fixed jaw.** (*Stevens Modular Tooling System, courtesy Stevens Engineering, Inc.*)

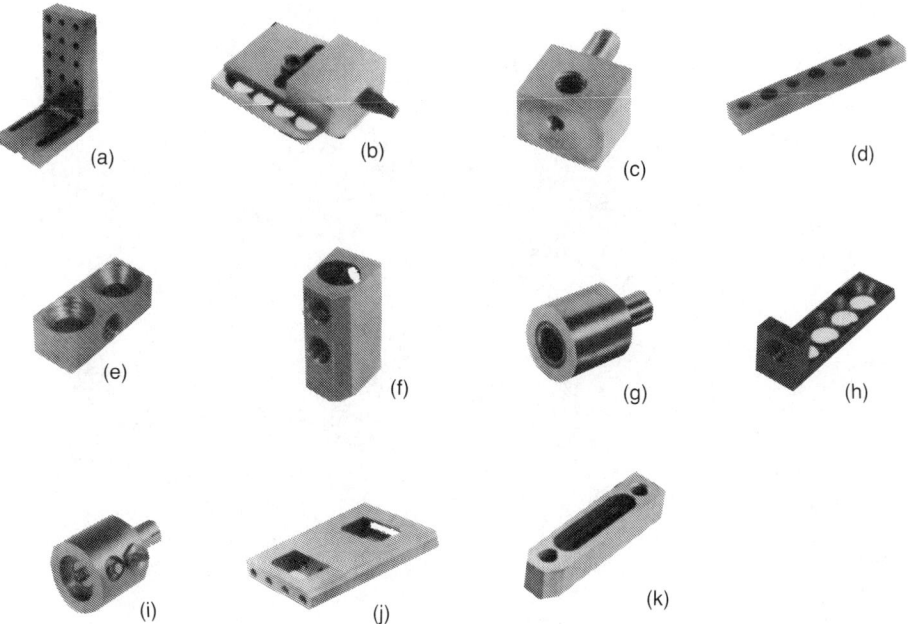

Fig. 5-34 Components of the modular, dowel-type tooling system. (*Stevens Modular Tooling System, courtesy Stevens Engineering, Inc.*)

Miscellaneous hardware such as washers, nuts, thrust and toggle screws, threaded hole adapters, toggle pads, chip plugs, studs, T-slot nuts, coupling nuts, U-straps, taper nose straps, tapped straps, toe clamps, and adjustable clamp heels completes the system.

A Modular, Dowel-Type Fixturing System. Another modular fixturing system is based on an alternating system of tapped holes and accurately spaced, hardened steel bushings, as shown in Fig. 5-35. The *system is dimensioned completely in metric* but should cause no problem since the parts within each system are completely compatible with one another.

Three grid patterns are provided as follows:

The small series has an alternating pattern of 10 mm diameter dowel holes and M10 tapped holes which are equally spaced on a 30 ±0.01 mm centerdistance.

The medium series has an alternating pattern of 12 mm diameter dowel holes and M12 tapped holes which are equally spaced on a 40 ±0.01 mm centerdistance.

The large series has an alternating pattern of 16 mm diameter dowel holes and M16 tapped holes which are equally space on a 50 ±0.01 mm centerdistance.

Components from one series are not interchangeable with components from the other two series. However, having three separate systems makes it possible to match the size of the modular tooling system with the size of the workpiece to be fixtured. In other words, small, medium, and large workpieces can be fixtured using components that relatively are small, medium, or large.

Other technical data for the system is as follows:

- Base plates and angles are made from high-grade cast iron.
- Plane parallelism on components of the system is held to 0.01 mm per 500 mm.
- All locating edges and surface towers are hardened to R_C 60.
- All V-block surfaces are case hardened.
- Locating surfaces dimensions on locating edges and towers are held to ±0.01 mm.

- Centerdistance accuracy between dowel holes in the X-Y plane is within 0.01 mm/500 mm.
- Squareness is held to 0.01 mm/300 mm.

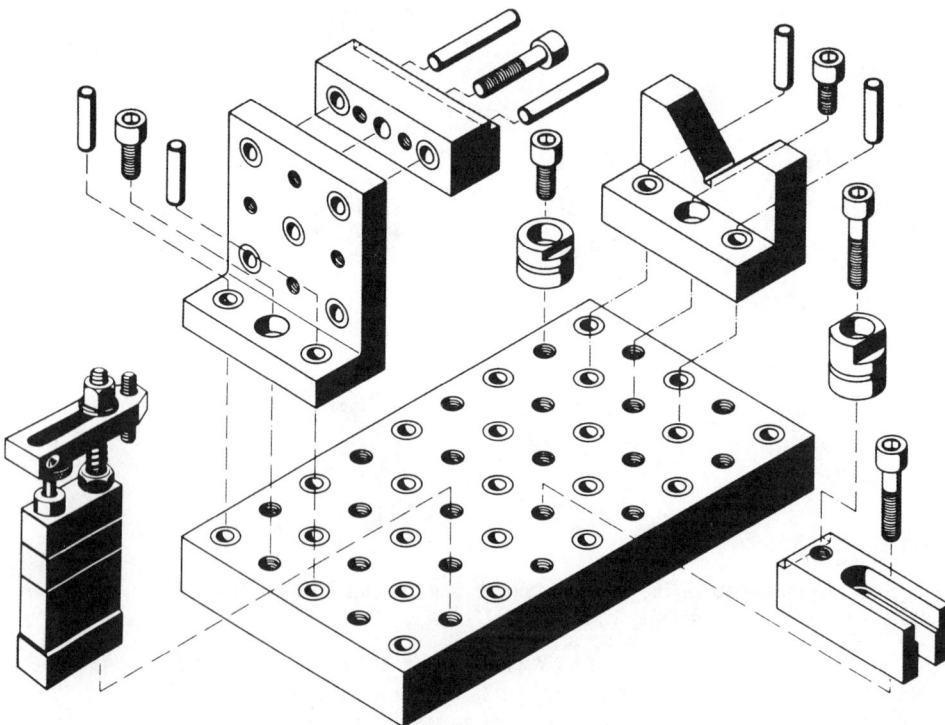

Fig. 5-35 Modular, dowel-type fixturing system. (*Bluco Technik System, courtesy Fritz Werner Machine Tool Corp.*)

Fixtures assembled with these modular fixturing components are shown in Fig. 5-36.
This system is made up of the following major components which are available in a wide range of sizes:

- Rectangular, round, and base plates. These base plates are often tailored to match the pallet or machine table on which they will be mounted. Examples of fixtures using round and rectangular base plates are shown in Fig. 5-36a and b.
- Double plate angle bases (see Fig. 5-36c) provide working surfaces on two sides. Cubes (see Fig. 5-36d) present four sides for mounting workpieces.
- Angle plates to provide vertical working surfaces. A typical setup using an angle block can be seen in Fig. 5-36e.
- Consoles which have an alternating pattern of bushings and tapped holes on two adjacent sides and bushings and clearance holes on the other two sides to provide the necessary clearances over the fixture base for the spindle, tool, and holder while maintaining the system's accuracies to vertical surfaces and to different levels. Fixtures using consoles are shown in Fig. 5-36b and f.
- Adjustable angle bases, such as shown in Fig. 5-37, feature a vernier scale that allows adjustment of angles to within a tenth of a degree. The base has bushings and clearance holes for mounting to a base plate. The adjustable top has similar bushings and tapped holes to interface with a second base plate.

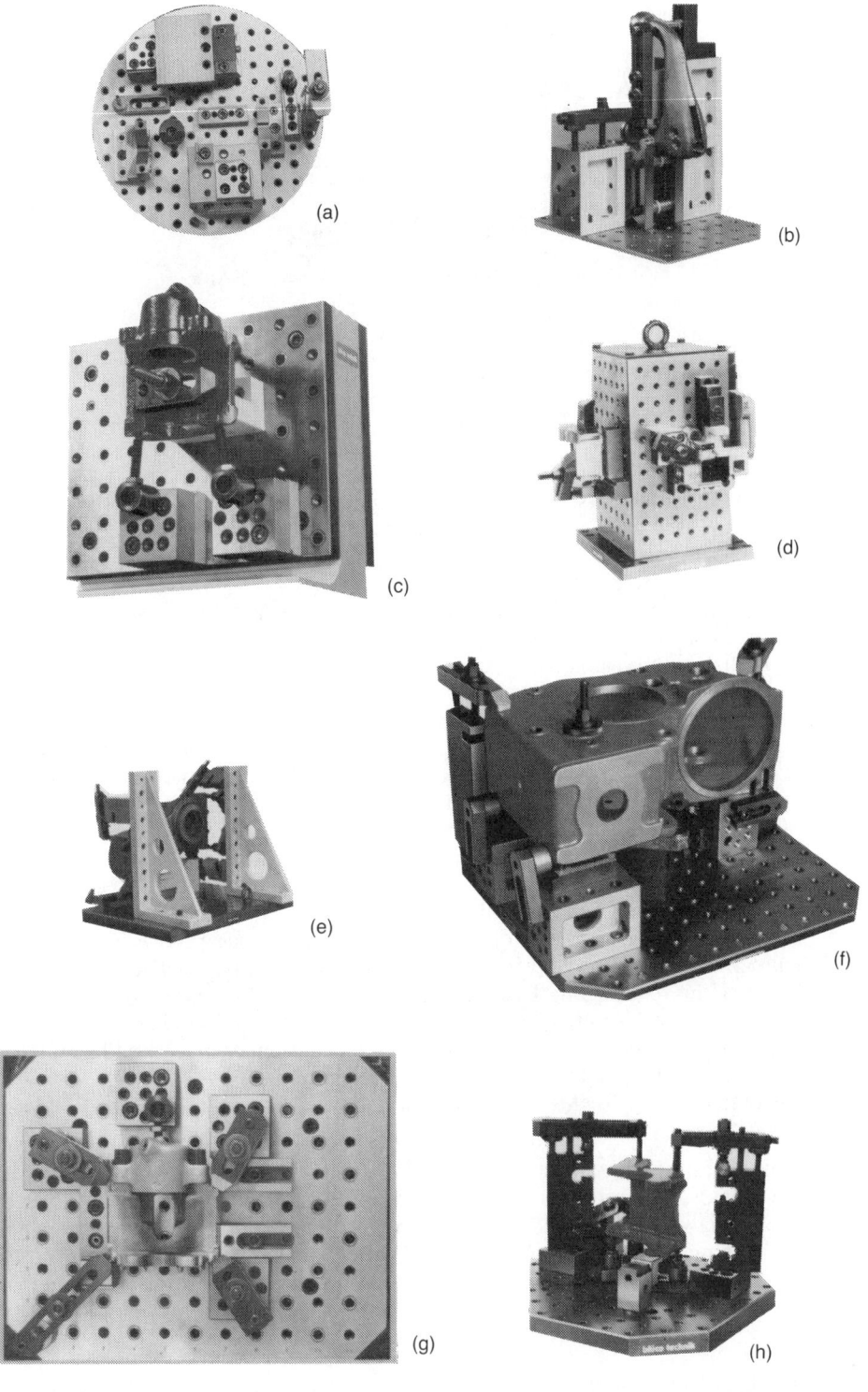

Fig. 5-36 Assembled fixtures. (*Bluco Technik System, courtesy Fritz Werner Machine Tool Corp.*)

Fig. 5-37 Adjustable angle base. (*Courtesy Fritz Werner Machine Tool Corp.*)

Locating elements of the system are shown in Fig. 5-38 and include:

- Surface and edge bars and dual surface and edge blocks (shown in Fig. 5-38*a*) which are used as risers and edge locators either individually or in combination with other components of the system having the same hole pattern. An application showing their use can be seen in Fig. 5-36*a*.
- Adjustable surface and locating bars, such as shown in Fig. 5-38*b*, which are required because most workpieces to be fixtured will not fall into the exact pattern of the fixturing system. These components have locating surfaces in one plane that are identical with the fixed locators, and adjustable positioning for another plane. Adjustable surface and locating bars are used in Fig. 5-36*g*.
- The coordinates support shown in Fig. 5-38*c* which provides close control of the height from the base plate while allowing adjustment in two planes for any component mounted on the top of the support.
- Various additional surface locators (towers), such as shown in Fig. 5-38*d*. They include multi-surface, adjustable surface, locating and magnetic, and angle towers. The ground spacers permit the precise establishment of in-between heights. Their use can be seen in Fig. 5-36*h*.
- V-locators, such as shown in Fig. 5-38*e*. Variations include 120° V-blocks, 150° V-blocks, adjustable V-towers, and V-bars. They can be used to locate from diameters up to 200 mm. Even larger diameters can be handled with the 150° V-pad and base. The use of V-locators can be seen in Fig. 5-36*a* and *b*.
- Other components shown in the same figure include center spacer, *f*, adapter bars, *g*, adapter blocks, *h*, adjustment stops, *i*, and support bars, *j*.
- Customizing bars, angles, and plates (not shown) are available for special user applications.

Clamping arrangements are shown in Fig. 5-39. They include the pressure clamp, *a*, ball screw clamps, *b*, serrated speed clamps, *c*, a speed clamp with an adjustable bar, *d*, adjustable vise jaws, *e*, and bridge clamps, *f*, along with the clamping supports shown in *g*. These clamping components are used with a variety of clamp screws, carbide inserts, clamping straps, and holders. Their use can be seen in some of the fixtures shown in Fig. 5-36.

The usual selection of studs, nuts, screws, dowels, hole plugs, etc., completes the system.

A Modular Fixturing System with an Alternating Grid Pattern of Dowel and Tapped Holes. One particular dowel pin system uses a grid pattern of alternating 0.5011-0.5012 in. diameter bushed dowel holes and ½-13 tapped holes which are

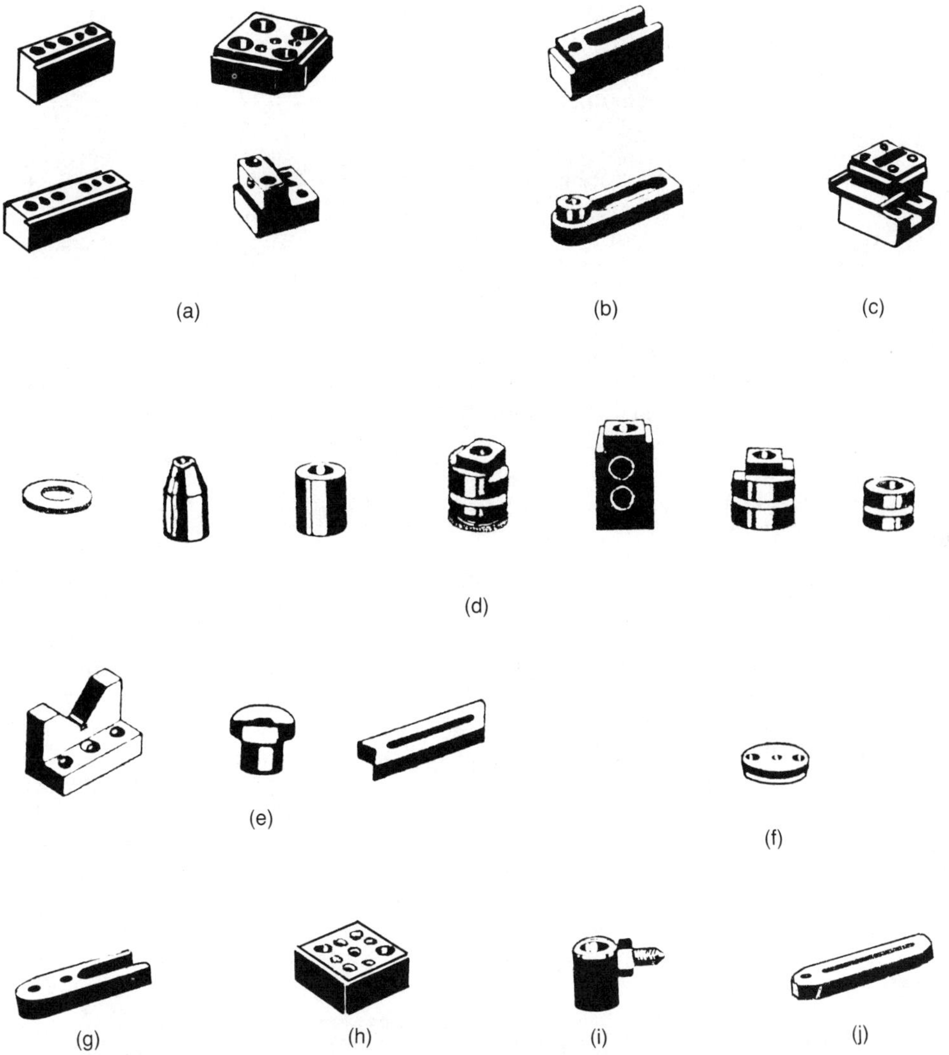

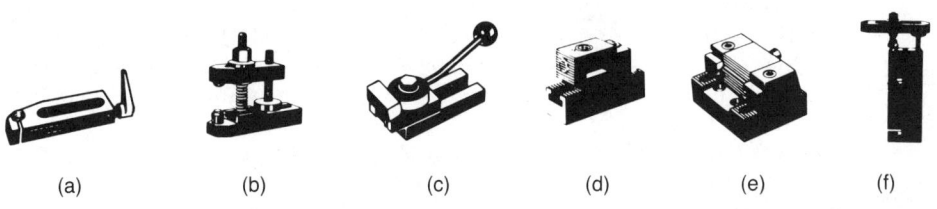

(a)   (b)   (c)

(d)

(e)   (f)

(g)   (h)   (i)   (j)

Fig. 5-38 Locating elements of the modular, dowel-type fixturing system. (*Bluco Technik System, courtesy Fritz Werner Machine Tool Corp.*)

(a)   (b)   (c)   (d)   (e)   (f)

Fig. 5-39 Clamping elements of the modular, dowel-type fixturing system. (*Bluco Technik System, courtesy Fritz Werner Machine Tool Corp.*)

located on 1.250 in. centers. Dowel hole locations are held to ±0.0002 in. while threaded hole locations are held to ±0.005 in. The system also features T-slot overlays to provide the system with some of the flexibility of a T-slot based modular system.

The major components making up this system include the following:

- Base plates for mounting on standard pallets and machine tables. Base plates can also be ganged in any combination. They are located and positioned relative to each other by use of gage bars or blocks which will ensure continuation of tolerance and grid pattern. Gage bars can be removed after the plates are secured to the machine table.
- Columns, which require assembly with column extenders and subplates as shown in Fig. 5-40. Various combinations of the components can be assembled to provide working surfaces up to 23.23 × 37.46 in.
- T-column bases, which are assembled in the same manner as the columns. Separate models are available for mounting on base plates or subplates. T-column bases for mounting on base plates can be assembled that provide working surfaces ranging from 19.75 to 31.50 in. square. T-columns for subplate mounting can be assembled in a wider variety of working surfaces ranging up to 23.23 × 24.98 in.
- Angle plates with working surfaces up to 12.48 × 14.75 in.

Application of the overlays that are available with this system are shown in Fig. 5-41. The multi-angle overlay is used to rotate the grid pattern of the system 15°, 30°, 45°, or 60° as shown in *a*, while the 45° T-slot overlay provides some of the flexibility of the T-slot systems as shown in *b*. Square T-slot and 90° overlays are also available.

Many of the remaining components of the system are shown in Fig. 5-42. Included for locating are all of the rest buttons (positioners) previously shown in Fig. 2-28. They are available with threaded shanks or with slip fit diameters for use with bushings. They can be mounted directly on the components or on adjustable positioners, rest pads, and spring jacks. Shim spacers are used as necessary for fine positioning.

Other locating components that can be seen in Fig. 5-42 include utility blocks, inside and outside corner edge blocks, edge bars, fixed and adjustable edge towers, rest bars, riser blocks, parallel bars, 120° Vees, 45° and 30°-60° half-Vees, 30°-60° half-Vee edge blocks, 30°, 60°, 30°-60° and 45° vertical half-Vees, and adjustable locator stops that are used with ½-13 bolts.

Also provided are:

- Fixed and slide block radius locators which are used as shown in Fig. 5-43. The radius locator provides the fixed location, and the slide block radius locator provides secondary location. A workpiece may be located directly on either locator's pin, or, radius locator spacers may be used in conjunction with the pin. Additional locating spacers, along with C-washers and ¼-20 cap screws may then be used to clamp the workpiece. The slide block is guided between two parallels to ensure that the pins are on a common centerline.
- Round stack locating pads as shown in Fig. 5-44 which can be used separately to locate a workpiece on the height of the pad, or on the diameter of the pad. Two pads may also be used together to form a single height and edge locator, as shown in the figures. Pads of various heights and diameters may be selected to form locators with different heights and edge sizes. Pads are held in position through the use of a tapered set screw lock. Fig. 5-44*a* illustrates their use along with a hex-locator stop to locate from an ID, while Fig. 5-44*b* shows their use along with nuzzler edge clamps to locate from an OD.
- Serrated locators with screw hole patterns that permit them to be assembled to components at angles of 90°, 45°, 30°, and 60° to the grid pattern.
- Round and flat knife edge locators for low profile single point location as shown

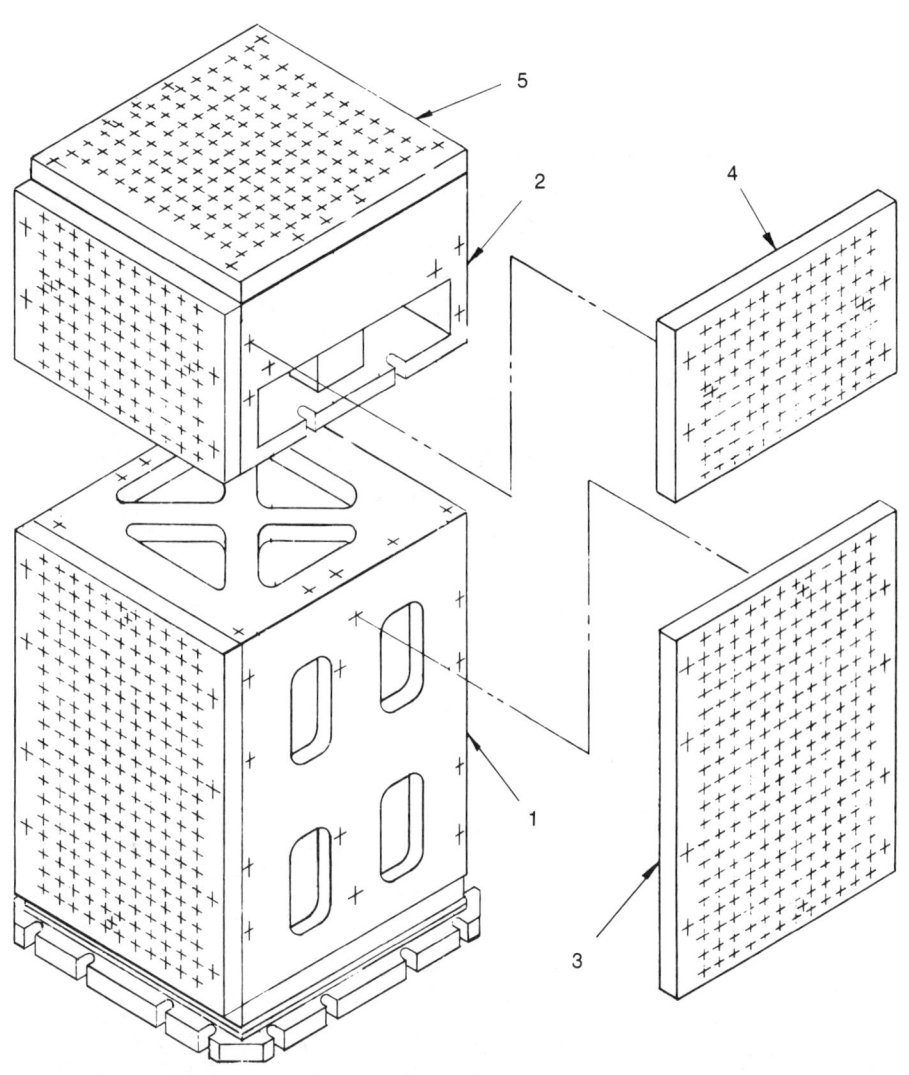

Column Assembly

Symbol	Description
1	Column
2	Column Extender
3	Subplate
4	Half Subplate
5	Top Subplate

Fig. 5-40 Base plate or subplate mounted onto column and column extender. (*Courtesy QU-CO*)

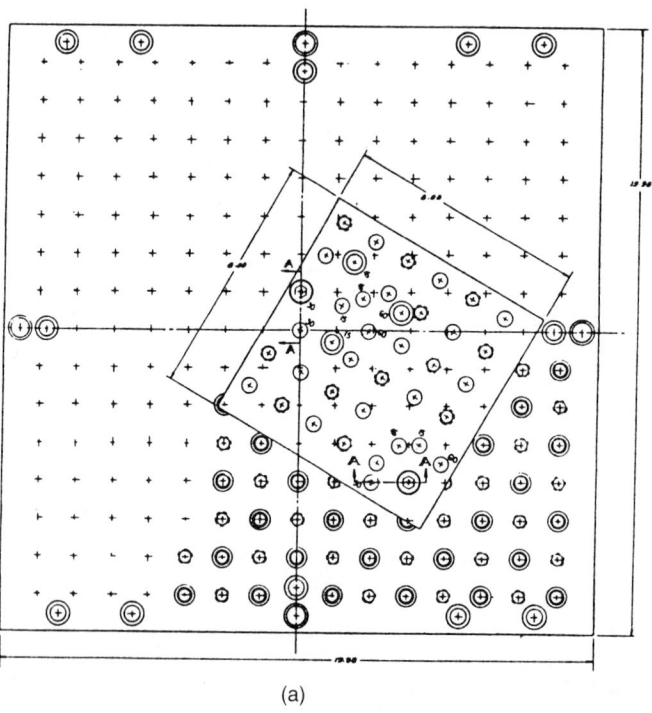

(a)

(b)

Fig. 5-41 Overlays: (*a*) multi-angle, (*b*) T-slot. (*Courtesy QU-CO*)

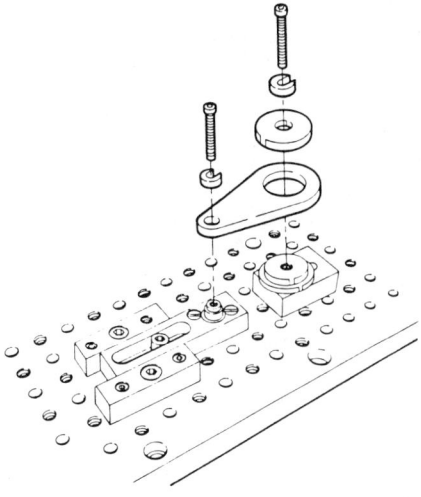

Fig. 5-42 Components of the modular fixturing system with alternating grid pattern of dowel and tapped holes. (*Courtesy QU-CO*)

Fig. 5-43 Slide block radius locator and radius locator. (*Courtesy QU-CO*)

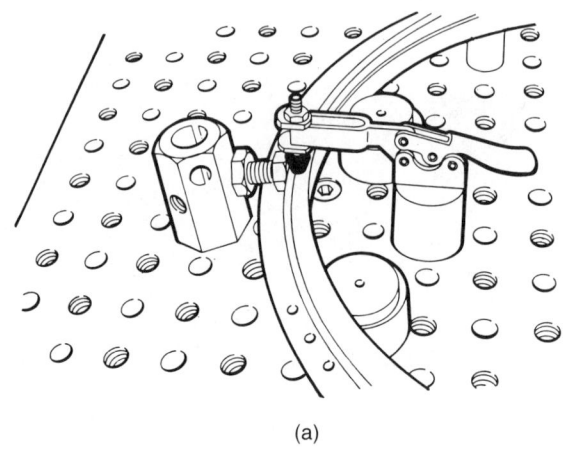

(a)

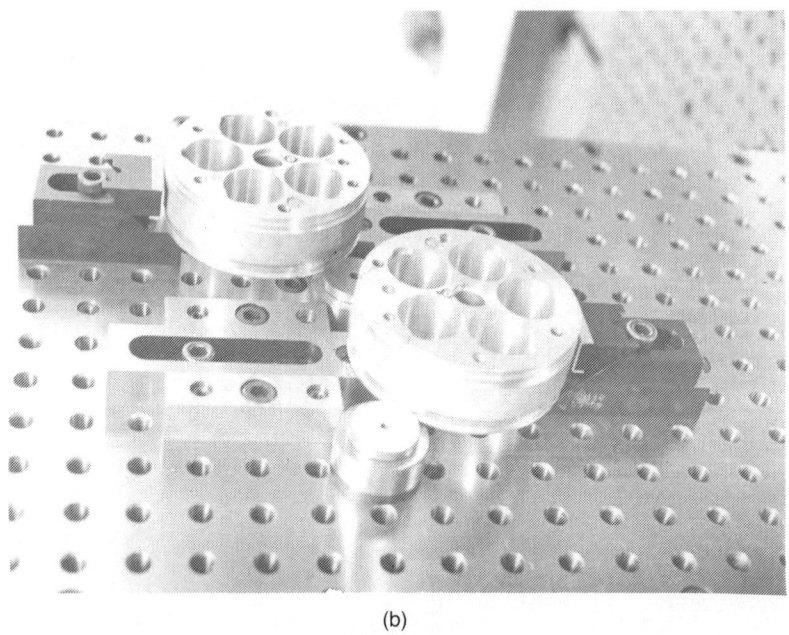

(b)

Fig. 5-44 Round stack locating pads. (*Courtesy QU-CO*)

in Fig. 5-45. Matching 0.250 in. and 0.500 in. elevating spacers are available for most of the locators.

Clamping units include the rotating toggle clamps, swing clamps, hook clamps, and step blocks shown in Fig. 5-42, all of which can be mounted directly to the components of the system or to the risers shown in the same figure.

Other clamps that are available are shown in Fig. 5-46. They include: the pinch clamp, *a*, with adjustable jaws and reversible thrust bolts to locate and hold irregular shapes; the adjustable locator clamp, *b*, which can be used to locate and hold rough castings; the beam clamp assembly, *c*, which is supported over the workpiece for downward clamping; single and multi-nosed edge clamps, *d*; double cam clamps, *e*; and

Fig. 5-45 Knife edge locators. (*Courtesy QU-CO*)

(a)

(b)

(c)

(d)

(e)

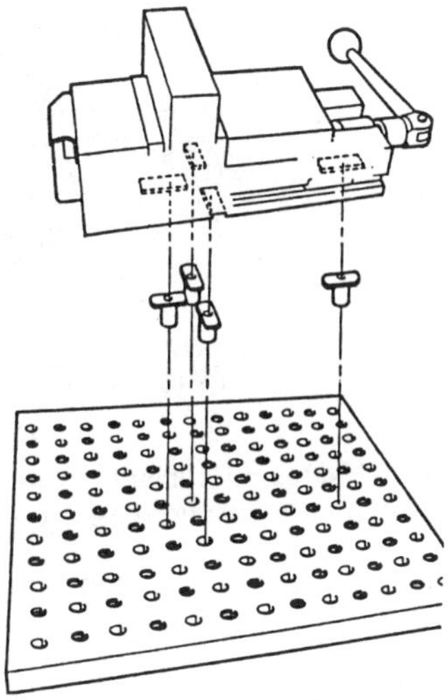

(f)

Fig. 5-46 Miscellaneous clamps for modular tooling. (*Courtesy QU-CO*)

the vises, *f*. They are shown along with the method of mounting them to the subplates.

The remaining components of this system are the usual variety of strap clamps, dowel pins, sine keys, round and diamond locating pins, nuts, bolts, and washers.

A Modular Fixturing System Using Multipurpose Positioning Holes. The components that make up this modular fixturing system are shown in Fig. 5-47. The system is a dowel pin type system which uses a grid pattern of multipurpose mounting holes every 2.0000 in. Each multipurpose positioning hole has a double construction which consists of a precision alignment bushing on top, with a threaded insert on the bottom. Two grid patterns are provided: Standard, with $0.5000 {\,}^{+\,0.0013}_{+\,0.0006}$ in. diameter alignment bushing and ½-13 threaded inserts; and heavy duty, with $0.6250 {\,}^{+\,0.0013}_{+\,0.0006}$ in. diameter alignment bushings and ⅝-11 threaded inserts.

All tooling plates and blocks in the system are made from cast or ductile iron. Positioning holes are located within 0.0008 in. of true position. Plate and block surfaces are machined flat to 0.0004 in. FIM per 6 in. square, parallel to 0.0016 in. FIM, and square to 0.0008 in. FIM per 12 in. For large workpieces, two or more tooling plates can be connected together with locating gages.

Components are assembled with $0.5000 {\,}^{-\,0.0006}_{-\,0.0013}$ in. diameter locating bolts with a ½-13 thread, and $0.6250 {\,}^{-\,0.0006}_{-\,0.0013}$ in. bolts with a ⅝-11 thread respectively. Locating diameters of components are held to $0.5000 {\,}^{+\,0.0007}_{-\,0.0000}$ in. and $0.6250 {\,}^{+\,0.0007}_{-\,0.0000}$ in. respectively.

Fig. 5-47 Modular fixturing system using multipurpose positioning holes. (*Carr Lane/Yuasa Modular Fixturing System, courtesy Carr Lane Mfg. Co.*)

Major mounting components include the following:

- Round tooling plates with working diameters ranging from approximately 16 to 24 in.
- Rectangular tooling plates with working surfaces ranging up to approximately 32 × 24 in.
- Thin tooling plates with working surfaces ranging up to approximately 20 × 24 in. which are for vertical use.

- Square tooling plates ranging in size from 15.748 to 31.496 in.
- Platform tooling plates ranging in size from 17.750 to 29.50 in. square which are used on horizontal machining centers to raise low workpieces for easier tool access.
- Two-sided tooling blocks that provide two working surfaces ranging up to approximately 22.5 in. square.
- Four-sided blocks that provide four working surfaces ranging up to approximately 15.5 × 22.5 in.
- Riser plates that provide working surfaces ranging up to 10.25 × 5.88 in.
- Angle plates that provide working surfaces ranging up to 6.68 × 19.68 in.

Locators for this system are shown in Fig. 5-48. Included are: the plain and shouldered support cylinders, *a*; edge supports, *b*; the extension supports, *c*, with a ground step for edge supporting and a tapped hole which is ideal for positioning components between grid holes; round and diamond locating pins, *d*; spring stop buttons and spring locating pins, *e*; adjustable stops, *f*; V-blocks, *g*, for locating cylindrical parts with diameters between 0.56 and 3.13 in.; riser blocks, *h*; riser cylinders, *i*; and the screw jacks, *j*, with radiused, conical, or V-shaped tips. The riser blocks and riser cylinders can be used individually or stacked to raise many of the components.

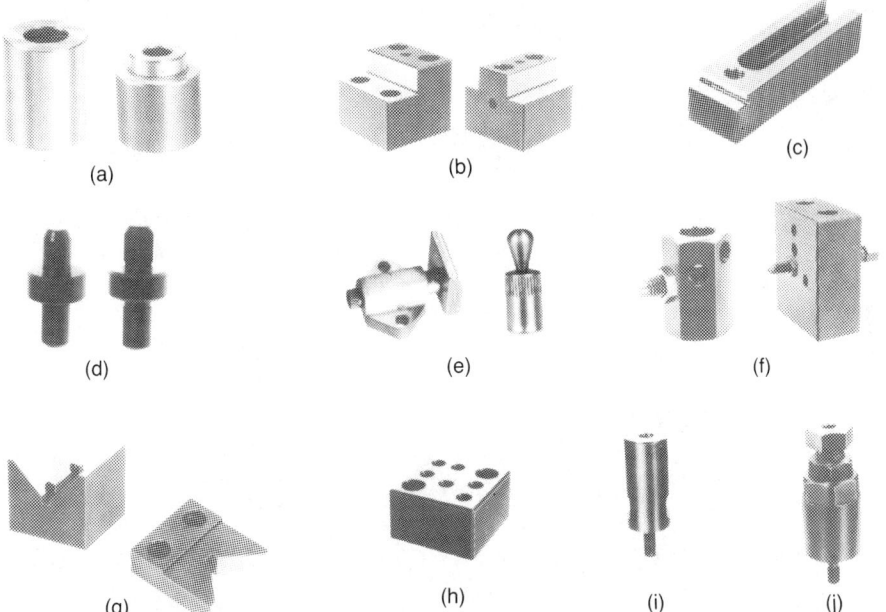

Fig. 5-48 Locators. (*Carr Lane/Yuasa Modular Fixturing System, courtesy Carr Lane Mfg. Co.*)

Downholding clamps for the system are shown in Fig. 5-49. They include high-rise clamps, *a*, clamp strap assemblies, *b*, hook clamps, *c*, swing clamp assemblies, *d*, and horizontal and vertical toggle clamps, *e*.

Side clamps are shown in Fig. 5-50 and include: pivoting edge clamps, *a*, screw edge clamps, *b*, adjustable screw clamps, *c*, serrated adjustable clamps, *d*, and toggle push clamps, *e*. Unground riser blocks are provided to raise clamping heights.

T-slot Type Modular Tooling System. This metric-dimensioned, T-slot type modular tooling system uses a grid pattern of precision T-slots which are spaced 70 ±0.01 mm apart and at exactly 90° from each other. The heart of the system is a patented clamping system shown in Fig. 5-51. The five different versions of T-clamping blocks shown in the figure are used to connect all of the components of the system to one

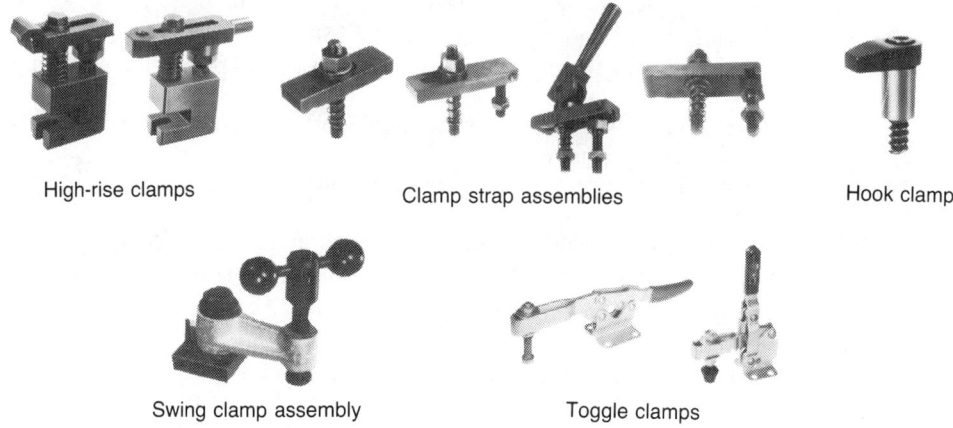

High-rise clamps   Clamp strap assemblies   Hook clamp

Swing clamp assembly   Toggle clamps

Fig. 5-49 Downholding clamps. (*Carr Lane/Yuasa Modular Fixturing System, Courtesy Carr Lane Mfg. Co.*)

Pivoting edge clamps   Screw edge clamps   Adjustable screw clamp

Serrated adjustable clamps   Toggle push clamp

Fig. 5-50 Side clamps. (*Carr Lane/Yuasa Modular Fixturing System, courtesy Carr Lane Mfg. Co.*)

another. This system allows clamping with both M12 and M16 threads.

Locating and clamping points can be accurately positioned along all axes without dependence on grid points, thereby permitting infinite adjustability for locating components anywhere in all three axes. Accurate and positive zero point positioning exists at every slot intersection.

The T-clamping blocks individually connect all components with matching T-slots, thereby providing both frictional and form clamping over the entire surface. The forces between the slot and T-clamping block take place in the following ways for each coordinate axis:

X axis—frictional and form locking.
Y axis—form locking.
Z axis—frictional locking.

Fixtures assembled with components from this system are shown in Fig. 5-52.

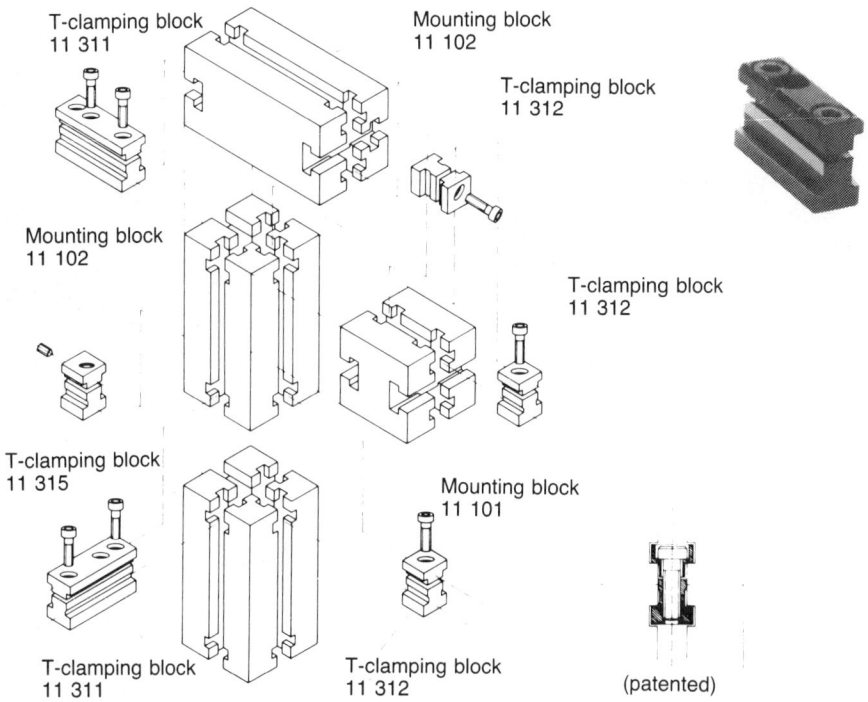

Fig. 5-51 Metric-dimensioned, T-slot type modular tooling system. (*Courtesy Flexible Fixturing Systems, Inc.*)

The mounting plates shown in Fig. 5-53 are the foundation of the system. The rectangular plates, *a*, are provided in three sizes ranging up to 630 × 370 mm and can be jointed together in any combination using a connecting element as shown in *b*.

The mounting plates, *c*, are provided for all standard pallets. Circular mounting plates, *d*, are provided with 300 and 400 mm diameters. Mounting plates and all other structural components are machined out of 5115 series case hardened steel (R_C 60).

Other structural components are shown in Fig. 5-54 and include: standard size pallets, *a*, which have a 70 mm grid pattern; *b*, which has a tapped hole pattern; and *c*, which has standard T-slots; pallet angle, *d*, angle plate, *e*, and 4-sided clamping block, *f*, to which 500 mm square mounting plates must be assembled; and the clamping angle, *g*, two of which can be assembled with a mounting plate to provide a vertical working surface of 630 × 370 mm.

The remainder of the components are shown in Figs. 5-55 and 5-56. The following components are shown in Fig. 5-55: mounting blocks, *a*, *b*, and *c*, which are used as shown in Fig. 5-52*a* thru *f*; slotted clamping angles, *d*, used as shown in Fig. 5-52*b* and *d*; intermediate elements, *e*, which are used to rotate the grid pattern either 15°, 30°, or 45°; clamping bars, *f*, which are used as shown in Fig. 5-52*e*; abutments, *g*, which are used as shown in Fig. 5-52*c*; thrust angles, *h* and *i*, which are used as shown in Fig. 5-52*c* and *f*; T-slot centering blocks which are chiefly used in conjunction with intermediate plates, *j*, and locating pins to locate a workpiece from tooling holes. T-slot centering blocks are frequently used as stops with a positioning pin screwed into one of the holes while using the remaining two holes to clamp the block in the T-slot. T-clamping blocks, *k*, and butt straps, *l*, are used for clamping mounting plates to the machine table. V-blocks, *m* and *n*, and locating segments, *o*, are used in pairs as shown in Fig. 5-52*b* to locate circular parts. They are located using T-blocks, *p*, as shown in the same figure; adjustable rotating elements, *q*, which rotate the grid pattern to any desired degree; and the positioning clamping bar, *r*, which enables the workpiece to be supported and clamped simultaneously.

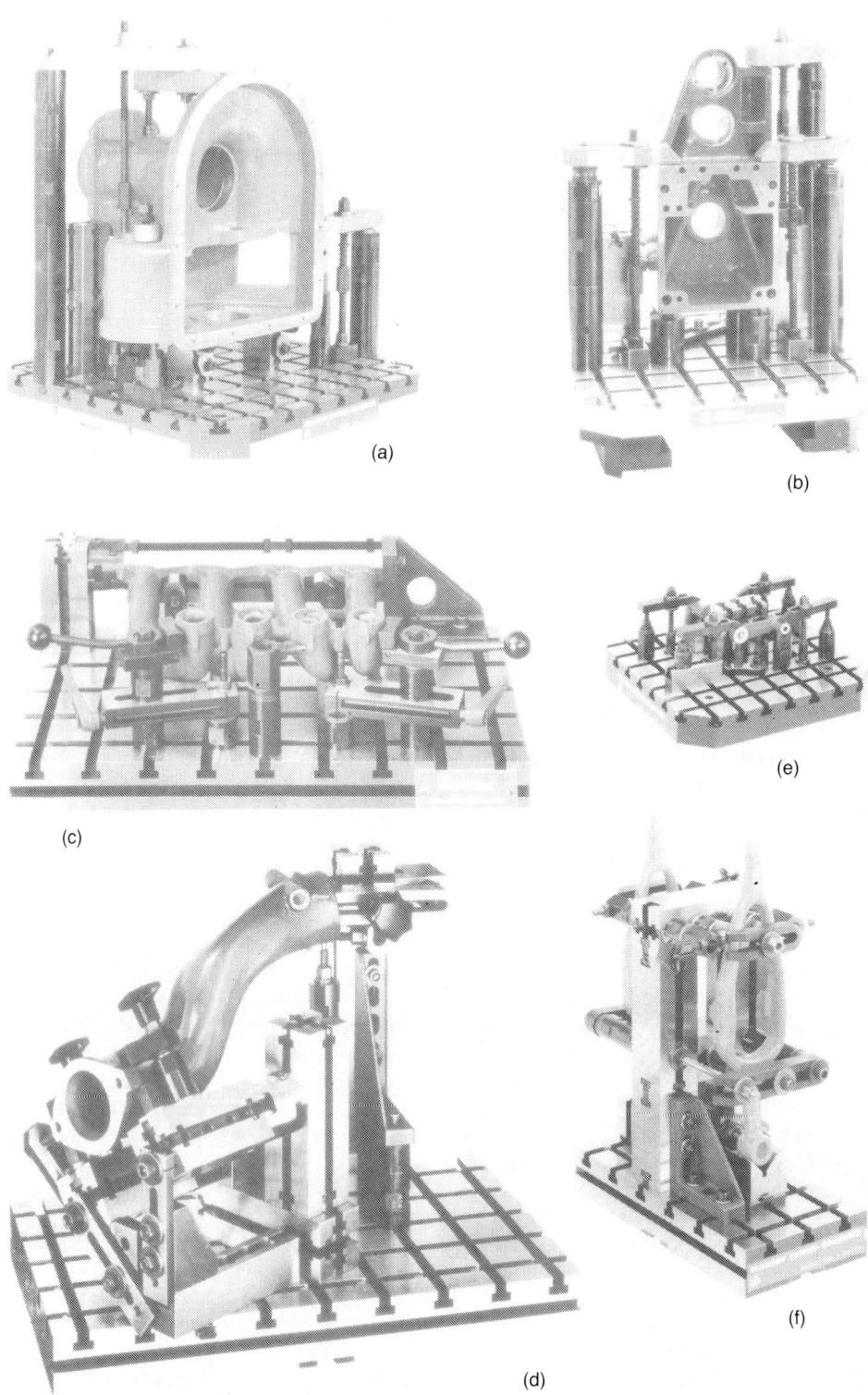

(a)

(b)

(c)

(d)

(e)

(f)

Fig. 5-52 Assembled fixtures. (*Halder Modular System, courtesy Flexible Fixturing Systems, Inc.*)

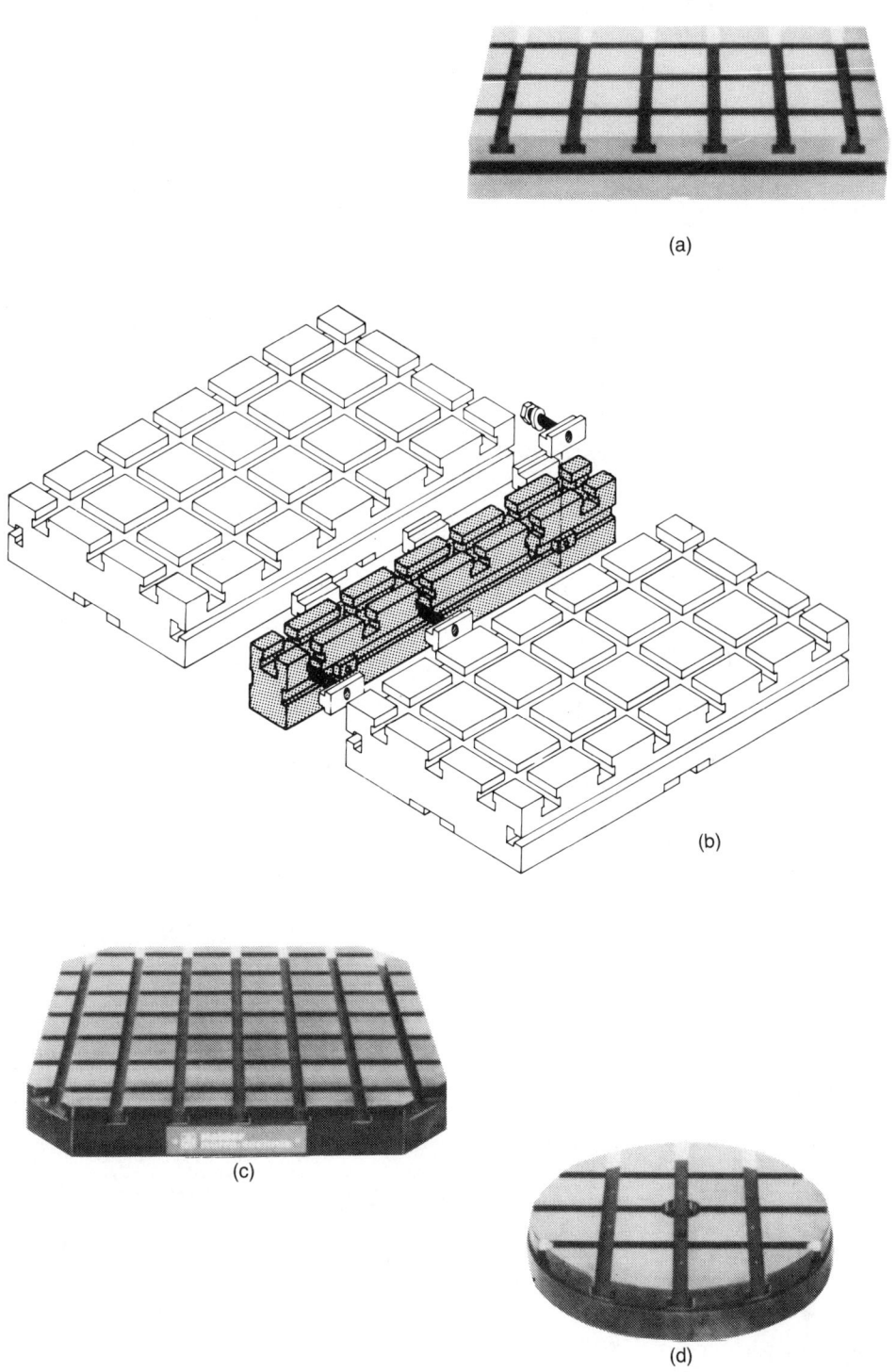

(a)

(b)

(c)

(d)

Fig. 5-53 Mounting plates. (*Halder Modular System, courtesy Flexible Fixturing Systems, Inc.*)

5-45

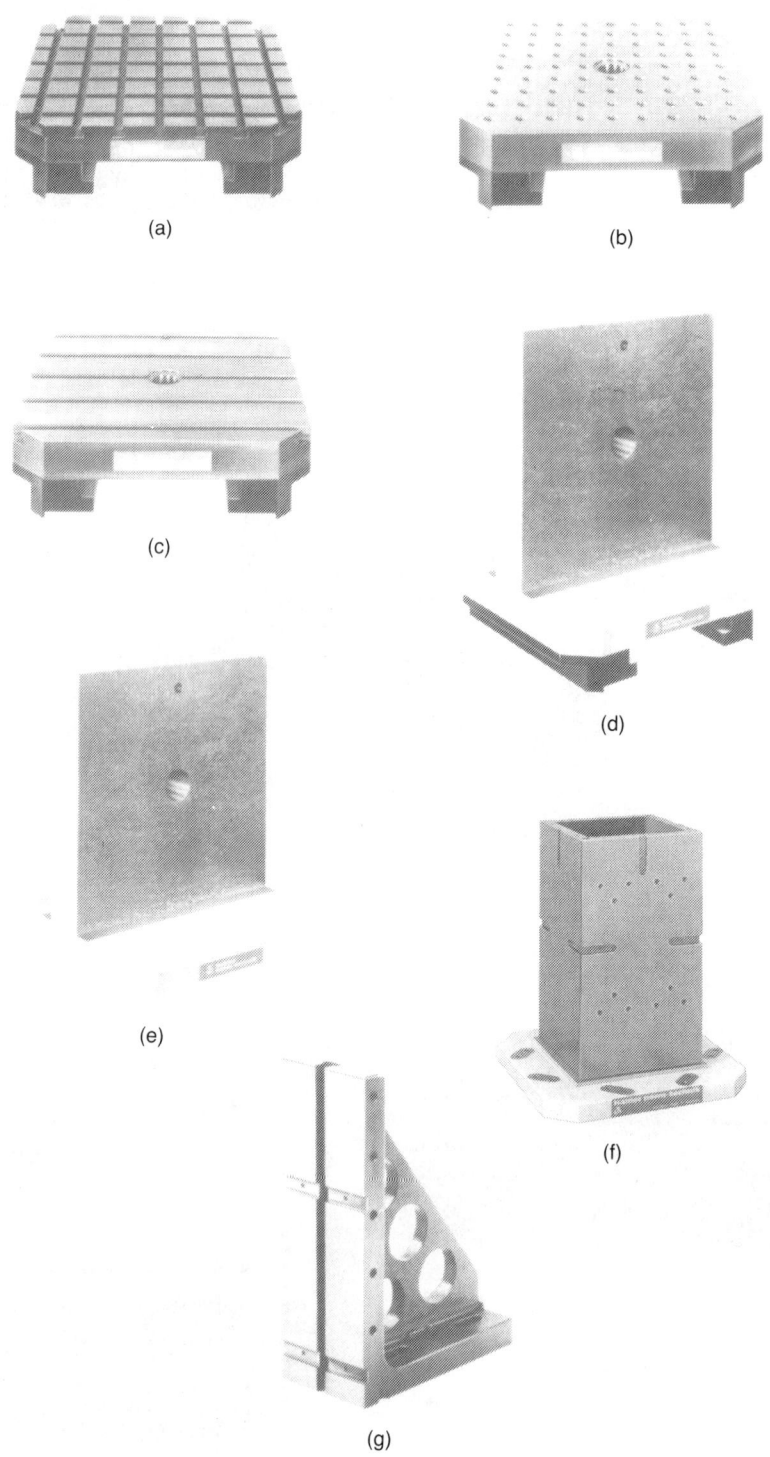

(a)

(b)

(c)

(d)

(e)

(f)

(g)

Fig. 5-54 Structural components. (*Halder Modular System, courtesy Flexible Fixturing Systems, Inc.*)

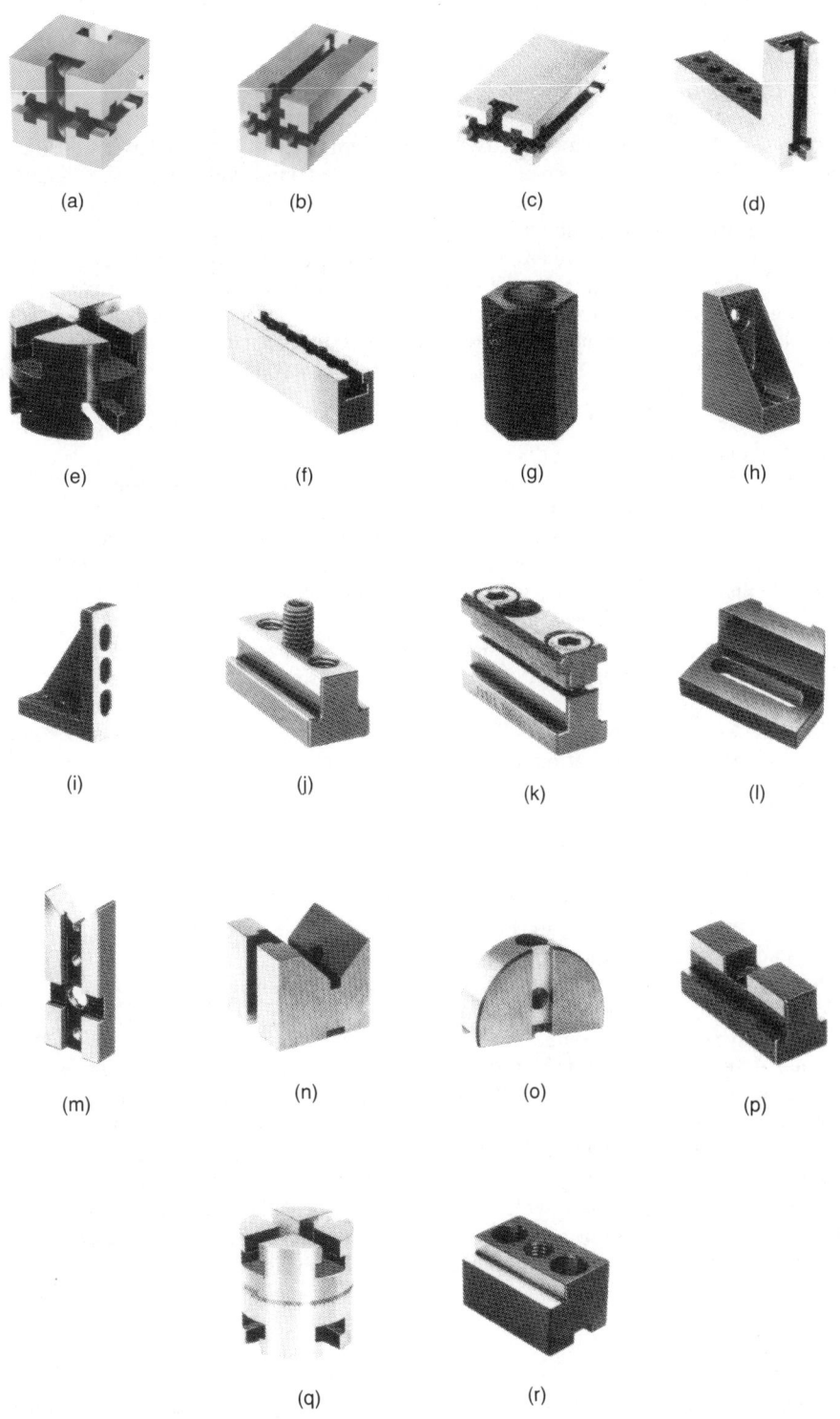

(a) (b) (c) (d)

(e) (f) (g) (h)

(i) (j) (k) (l)

(m) (n) (o) (p)

(q) (r)

Fig. 5-55 Components. (*Halder Modular System, courtesy Flexible Fixturing Systems, Inc.*)

5-47

The following components are shown in Fig. 5-56: Clamping heads, *a*, and clamping blocks, *b*, which are used to mount clamping studs as shown in Fig. 5-52*a* and *b*; down-hold clamps and grips, *c* thru *e*, which are used as shown in Fig. 5-52*c*; down thrust clamps, *f*, which can be used along with support elements, *g*, support clamping bars, *h*, and positioning rings, *i*, to ensure that clamping is always exactly at the same point; compensating seat elements, *j*, that compensate for any variation in height and can be locked in any position so that it is possible to clamp workpieces at more than three points without causing distortion; height adjusting cylinders, *k*, that provide for stepless adjustment of the clamping height of the down-thrust clamps as shown in Fig. 5-52*c*; up thrust clamps, *l*, which are used for clamping workpieces that have already been machined on one side and have to be further machined with that side as a datum; intermediate plates, *m* and *n*; cylindrical stops, *o*; supporting plates, *p*; bedding supports, *q*, which are used as shown in Fig. 5-52*c*; and screw jack holders and caps, *r*, which are used to provide extra support where needed.

This system also provides some components to assemble drill jigs for drilling operations. They are shown in Fig. 5-57.

Locating pins, thrust pads, spring plungers, rest buttons, T-nuts, studs, clamp straps, etc., complete the system.

There is another scaled-down version of this modular jig and fixture system which can handle workpieces ranging from 33,000 cubic millimeters (2 cubic inches) to 147,000 cubic millimeters (9 cubic inches). It was designed to fixture small workpieces for machining on machining centers. T-slots for this system are spaced 40 ±0.01 mm apart and can be adapted to the larger system with special T-clamping blocks. The larger system, however, can not be adapted to this system.

A comparison of the size of system 40 and system 70 details can be seen in Fig. 5-52*e* and *f*. The fixtures were photographed together with the system 40 fixture on the left and the system 70 fixture on the right.

Modular Tooling System with Self-Adjusting Fixturing Elements. The major components of this system include grid plates, pallets, consoles, tombstones, double angle plates, and angle plates in various sizes.

Mounting holes are multipurpose with 0.50 in. diameter bushings at the top, and ½-13 threaded inserts at the bottom, or with 0.63 in. diameter bushings at the top and ⅝-11 threaded inserts at the bottom. They are located on a grid pattern with either 2.0000 ±0.0006 in. or 2.0000 ±0.0004 in. spacing between centers. Components can be attached using dowel pins to locate them and bolts to clamp them with, or by using two shoulder bolts which both locate and clamp.

The system uses clamping elements which function as shown in Fig. 5-58.

With conventional clamping, castings and forgings—which are often badly warped—are usually clamped at three points using strap clamps. The warped undersurface locates unevenly at these points as shown in Fig. 5-58*a*. When clamping pressure is applied, severe strains are produced as shown in *b*. After machining, the machined surface will spring out of flat when the clamps are released as shown in *c*, resulting in scrap or rework.

With this system, the hardened steel elements "float" in their sockets to adjust to workpiece irregularities and surface profile as in shown *d*. The upper arms of the clamps adjust in the same manner during clamping as shown in *e* without causing distortion of the workpiece. When the workpiece is removed, the machine surface does not change.

To provide flexibility, components of this system are provided with ball diameters ranging from 0.31 to 1.57 in. to provide clamping pressures ranging from 1,350 to 4,000 lbf (6 to 18 kN). Hydraulic components provide clamping pressures up to 7,440 lbf (33 kN) at 5,000 psi (34.4 MPa).

Locating and supporting elements of the system are shown in Fig. 5-59, they include the following: V-blocks, *a*, for round parts ranging from 0.39 to 3.15 in. in diameter, and *b* which can be used in a clamping unit or in a clamping bar; adjustable locators, *c*, used for varying height and edge positioning; spacer block and locator, *d*; fixed locators, *e*, for locating

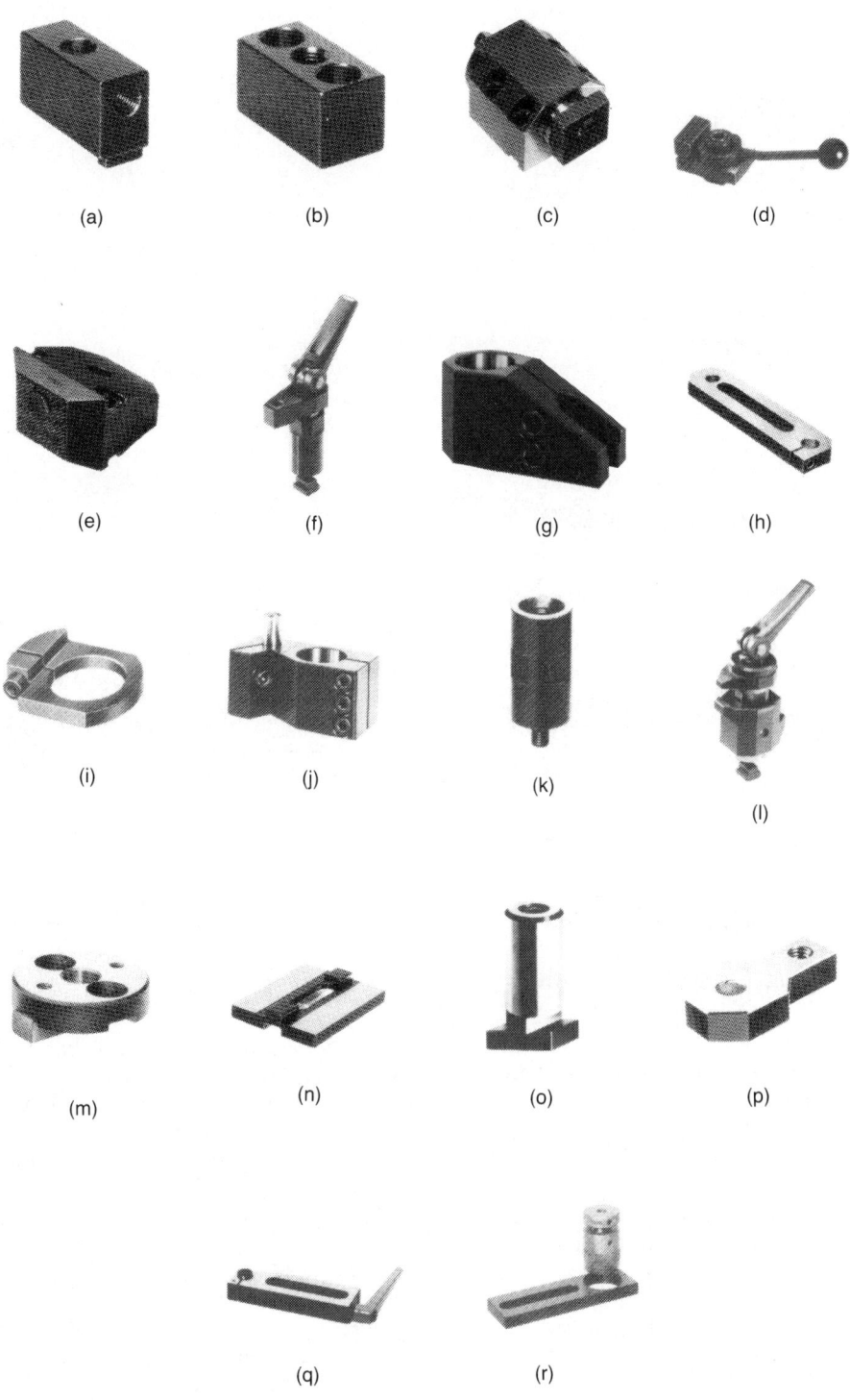

(a)   (b)   (c)   (d)

(e)   (f)   (g)   (h)

(i)   (j)   (k)   (l)

(m)   (n)   (o)   (p)

(q)   (r)

Fig. 5-56 Components. (*Halder Modular System, courtesy Flexible Fixturing Systems, Inc.*)

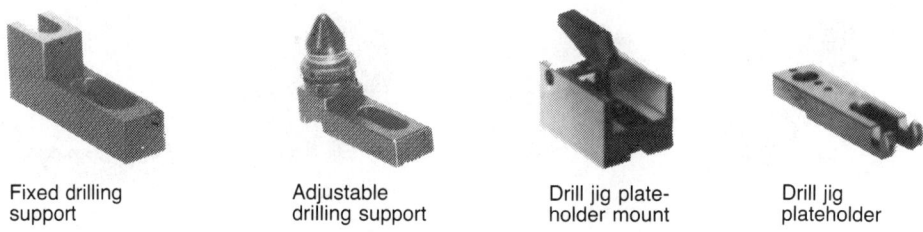

| Fixed drilling support | Adjustable drilling support | Drill jig plate-holder mount | Drill jig plateholder |

Fig. 5-57 Components for constructing drill jigs. (*Halder Modular System, courtesy Flexible Fixturing Systems, Inc.*)

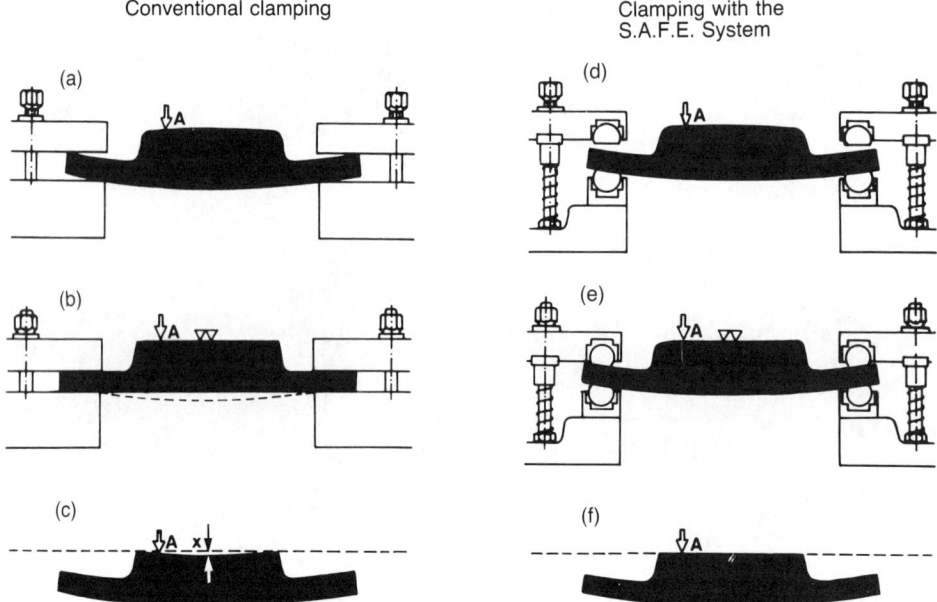

Fig. 5-58 Modular tooling system with self-adjusting fixturing elements. (*S.A.F.E. System, courtesy Enerpac Group, Applied Power, Inc.*)

workpieces when holes or flanges for clamping are unavailable; adapter V-bar, f, which can be used with a spacer plate or a flatted ball element; support and edge bars, g; support and edge towers h; adjustable support and edge tower, i; push-in and threaded support plugs, j thru l; spacer rings, m, which can be used as a fixed-height support, edge locator, or height extension; and the cube element, n, which is used to set "program zero" and tool lengths.

Horizontal positioning units are illustrated in Fig. 5-60. They include: a fixed positioning unit, a, and adjustable manual clamping unit, b, with a force capacity of 5,620 lbf (25 kN) at 27.6 ft-lbs (37.4 N·m), a hydraulic clamping unit, c, with a force capacity of 2,450 lbf (11 kN) at 5,000 psi (35 MPa), and the edge clamp, d.

Supporting units are shown in Fig. 5-61. Supporting unit a is mechanically clamped, b is spring loaded and mechanically clamped, c is provided either as an adjustable unit or fixed at 3.20 in. (81.3 mm), d is also provided either as an adjustable unit or fixed at 3.20 in. (81.3 mm), e is mechanically locked and self-adjusting for low heights, f is hydraulically operated and will support loads up to 5,200 lbs (2,360 kg) at 5,000 psi (35 MPa).

(a)   (b)   (c)   (d)

(e)   (f)   (g)   (h)

(i)   (j)   (k)   (l)

(m)   (n)

Fig. 5-59 Locating elements of self-adjusting fixturing elements system. (*S.A.F.E. System, cour-tesy Enerpac Group, Applied Power, Inc.*)

(a)

(b)

(c)

(d)

Fig. 5-60 Horizontal positioning units of self-adjusting fixturing elements system. (*S.A.F.E. System, courtesy Enerpac Group, Applied Power, Inc.*)

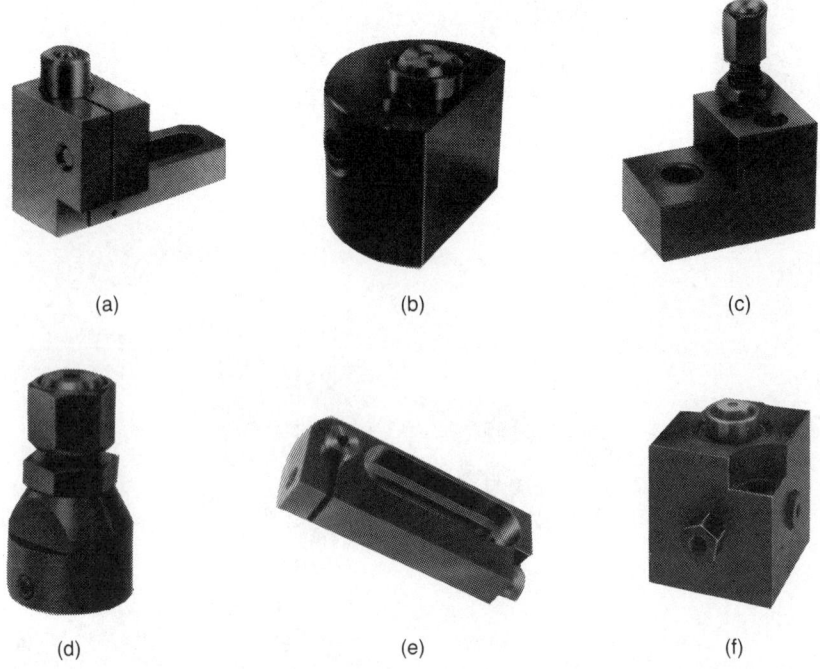

(a)

(b)

(c)

(d)

(e)

(f)

Fig. 5-61 Supporting elements of self-adjusting fixturing elements system. (*S.A.F.E. System, courtesy Enerpac Group, Applied Power, Inc.*)

Vertical positioning units with clamping screws are shown in Fig. 5-62. All of them feature flatted-ball elements and are designed to clamp workpieces that have a clamping lug or hole. Clamping this way permits complete access to the machining surface during machining operations. Included are the following:

1. Fixed units, *a* and *b*.
2. Adjustable ball element units, *c* and *d*.
3. Sliding ball elements; *e* with a longitudinal slide, and *f* with a transverse slide.
4. Grid adjuster, *g*.

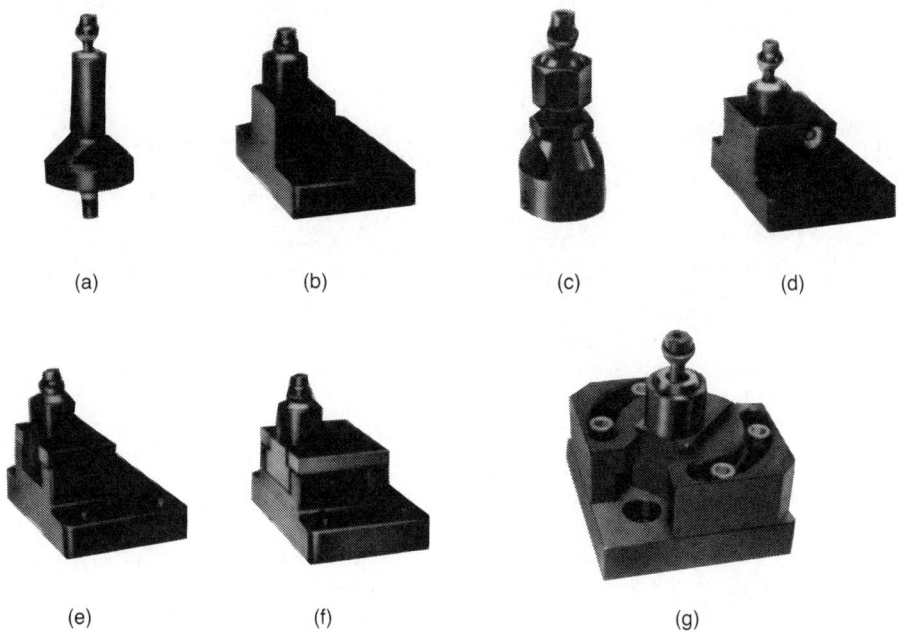

(a) (b) (c) (d)

(e) (f) (g)

Fig. 5-62 Vertical positioning units of self-adjusting fixturing elements system. (*S.A.F.E. System, courtesy Enerpac Group, Applied Power, Inc.*)

Positioning and clamping units are provided in a wide range of configurations and include units with edge locators, locating pins and swing clamps. The various types are shown in Fig. 5-63: Clamp *a* has a fixed support height, *b* has an adjustable support height, *c* is furnished with a support element and clamping bar, *d* has a clamping bar and locator, *e* has a clamping bar and locating pin, *f* is a swing clamp, *g* has a clamping bar with a longitudinal slide and locating pin, and *h* has a clamping bar with a transverse slide and locating pin. Force capacities of these clamps range from 1,124 lbf (5 kN) at 18.4 ft-lb (25 N·m) torque to 4,047 lbf (18 kN) at 73.7 ft-lb (100 N·m) torque. Spacer blocks are available in several heights to extend clamping ranges.

Many of the clamping units in Fig. 5-63 are also available in hydraulically operated versions.

Exploded views of fixtures assembled using this modular tooling system, along with a list of parts, are shown in Fig. 5-64. The views show how easily combined components can be used to construct fixtures to locate and clamp workpieces of various shapes and sizes.

A Universal Workholding System. The modular components of this system were developed to permit their assembly, with minimum machining, into workholders for the machining of a variety of workpieces on machining centers and turning machines (see Figs. 5-65 thru 5-67).

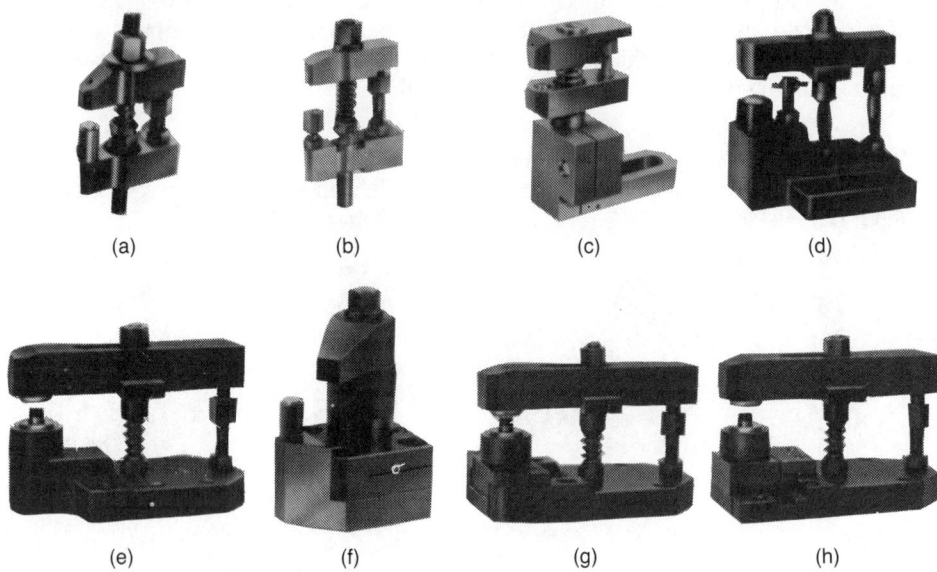

(a)   (b)   (c)   (d)

(e)   (f)   (g)   (h)

Fig. 5-63 Positioning and clamping units of self-adjusting fixturing elements system (*S.A.F.E. System, courtesy Enerpac Group, Applied Power, Inc.*).

The complete system which is shown in part in Fig. 5-68 is made up of round, square, and rectangular base plates, concentric, semi-finished base plate locators, radial locators, locating pin blocks, work stops, shims and clamp-paks.

Some fixtures constructed using this system are shown in Fig. 5-69.

Base plates are built with mild steel, stress-relieved, and ground flat and parallel within 0.0005 in./ft with a maximum variation of 0.001 in. Two precision locating key holes are provided for mounting to the machine with sine fixture keys.

Round base plates, such as used to construct the fixture in Fig. 5-69a, are provided with a 120° hole pattern as shown in Fig. 5-70, or with a straight grid of tapped holes, in diameters ranging from 8 to 30 in. Square and rectangular plates as shown in Fig. 5-69b are provided either blank, with a straight grid of tapped holes, or with a combination of straight grid and 120° pattern holes. Square plates range from 8 to 30 in. square and rectangular from 8 × 16 in. to 30 × 60 in. A 3.000 in., semi-finished base locator is provided to locate the base plates on the center of rotation of a pallet or fifth axis.

Semi-finished, plain and threaded insert-style workpiece locators, such as shown in Fig. 5-69c, are provided to locate workpieces from ID's ranging from 2.100 to 28.000 in. The threaded insert style locators permit the use of the threaded inserts, round clamps, swing C-washers, and the adapters shown in the same figure.

Workpiece locators are shown in Fig. 5-71. They include the following:

- The adjustable work stops, *a*, which are used to locate round, rectangular, or odd-shaped workpieces from surfaces normal to the grid pattern as shown in Fig. 5-69a and b.
- The adjustable work stop blocks, *b*, which are used to position and clamp round, rectangular, or odd-shaped workpieces from surfaces normal to the grid pattern as shown in Fig. 5-69a and b.
- The castle stop blocks, *c*, which allow work stops or clamp screws to be positioned at angles of 15°, 30°, and 45° to the grid hole pattern as shown in Fig. 5-69b.
- The combination round and diamond pin/rest button blocks, *d*, to locate from tooling holes.

5-54

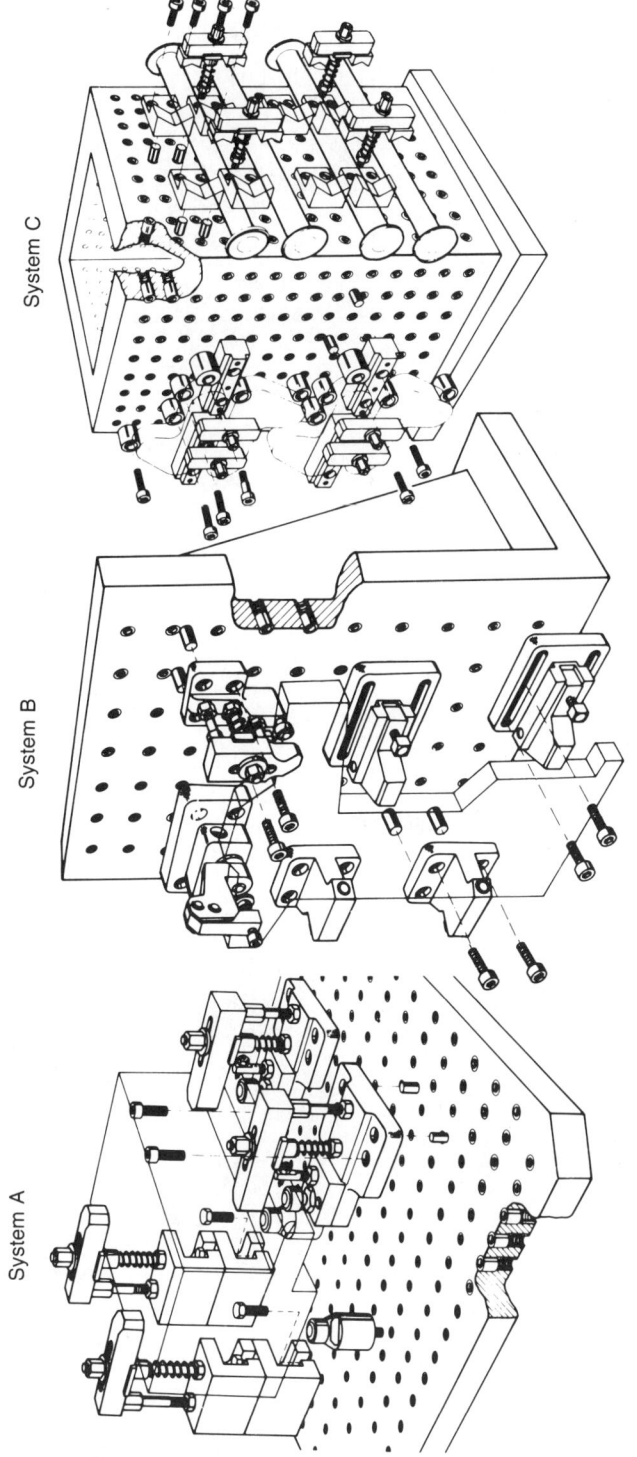

System C

System B

System A

Fig. 5-64 Exploded views of fixture assemblies. (*S.A.F.E. System, courtesy Enerpac Group, Applied Power, Inc.*)

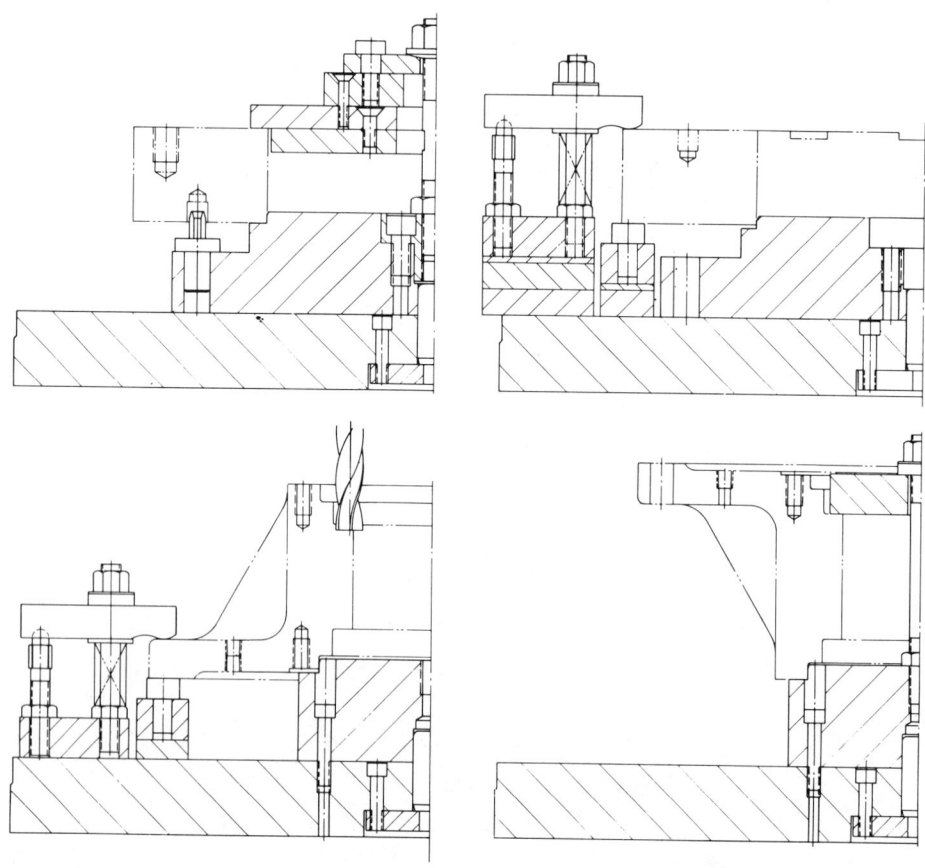

Fig. 5-65 Vertical machining center application. (*Tru-Positioning Workholding System, courtesy International CNC Machining, Inc.*)

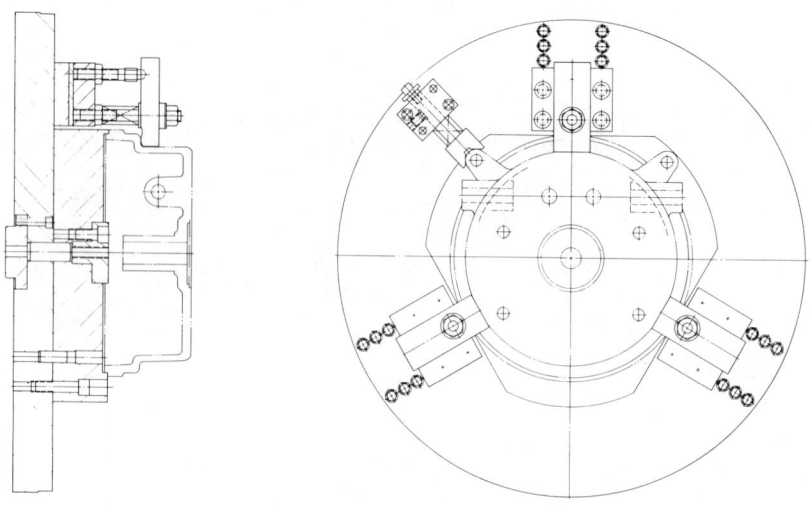

Fig. 5-66 Horizontal machining center application. (*Tru-Positioning Workholding System, courtesy International CNC Machining, Inc.*)

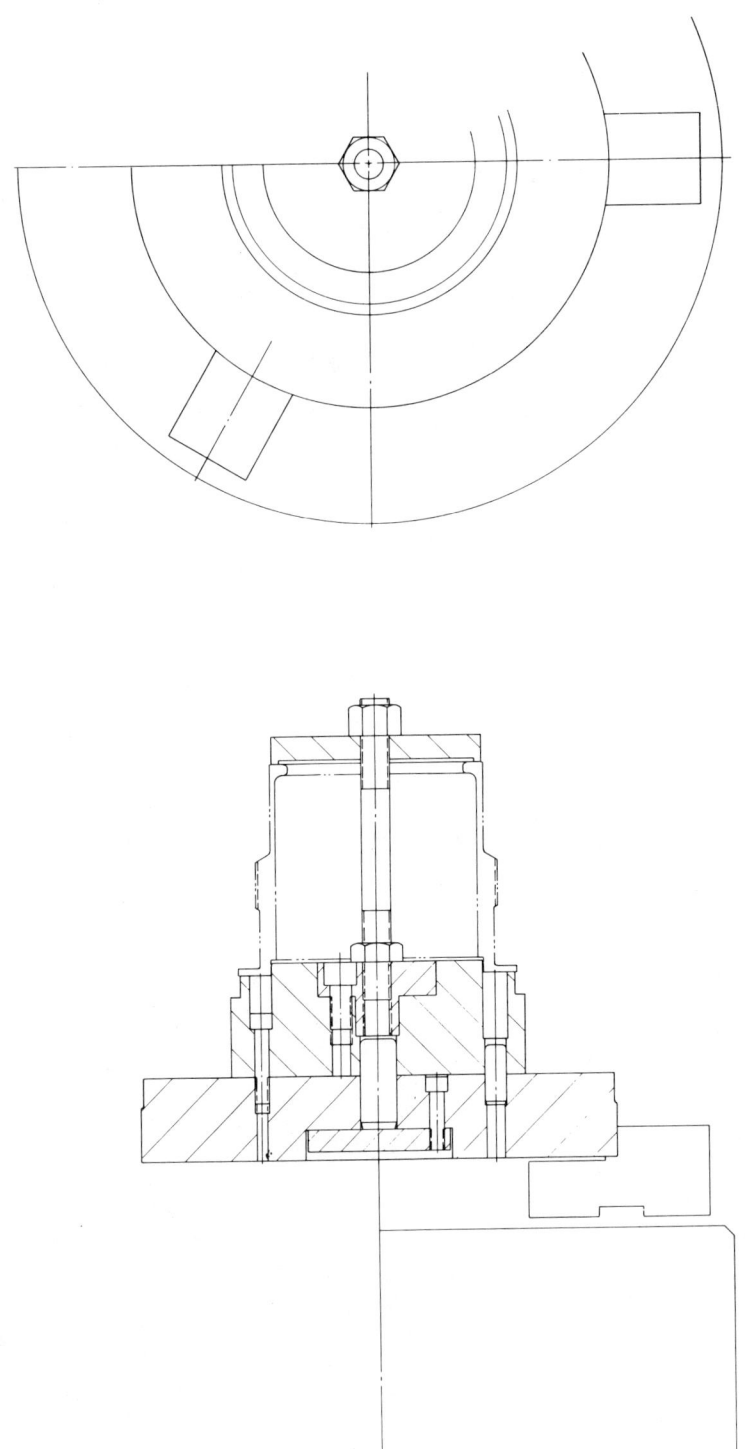

Fig. 5-67 Lathe face plate application. (*Tru-Positioning Workholding System, courtesy International CNC Machining, Inc.*)

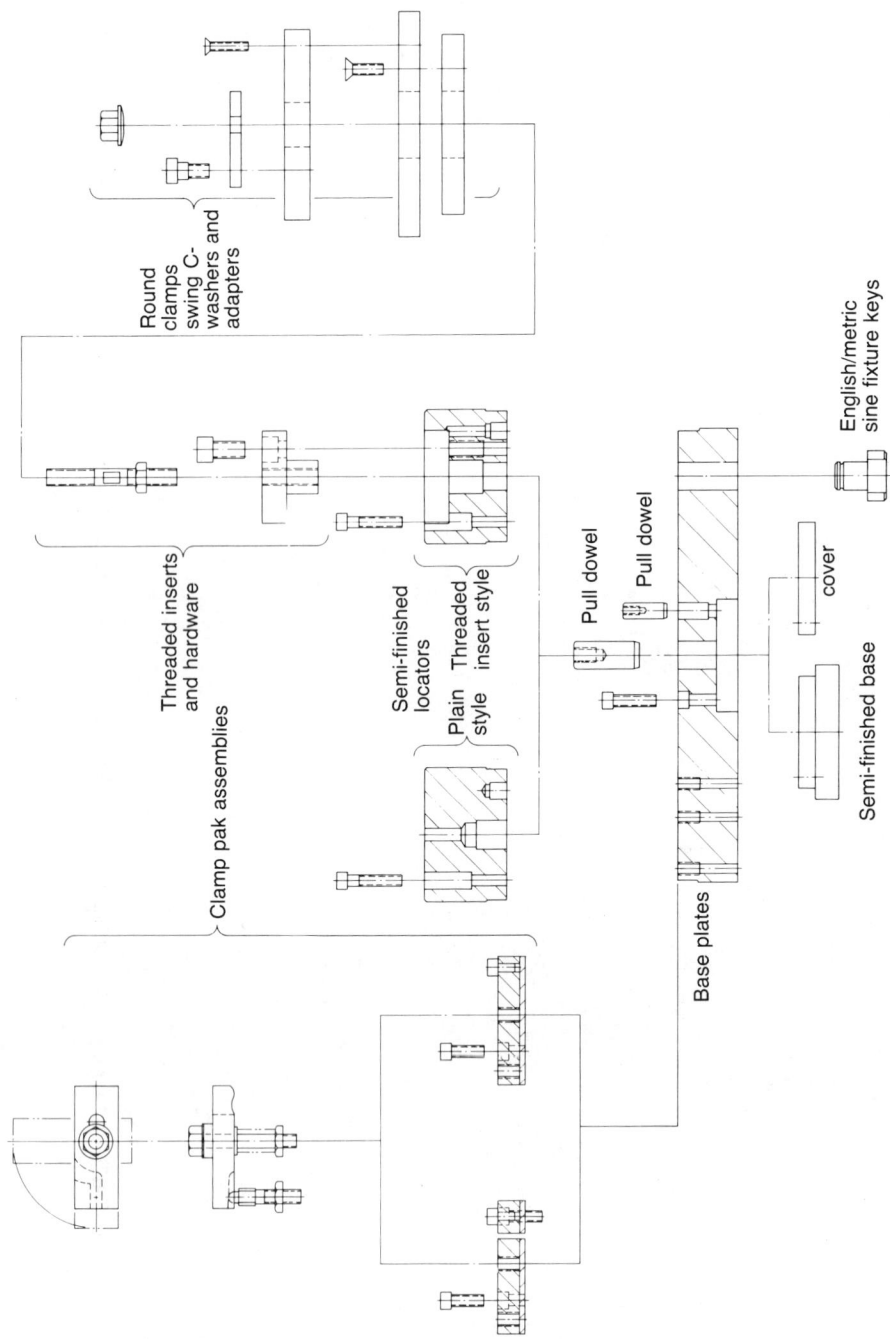

Fig. 5-68 Universal workholding system. (*Tru-Positioning Workholding System, courtesy International CNC Machining, Inc.*)

Round
clamps
swing C-
washers and
adapters

Threaded inserts
and hardware

Clamp pak assemblies

Semi-finished
locators

Plain Threaded
style insert style

Base plates

Pull dowel

Pull dowel

English/metric
sine fixture keys

cover

Semi-finished base

Fig. 5-69 Fixtures built with universal workholding system components. (*Tru-Positioning Workholding System, courtesy International CNC Machining, Inc.*)

- The clamp pak assemblies and rest button blocks, *e*, which are provided in five stud sizes ranging from ⅛ in. to ⅝ in. diameters for combined workpiece support and clamping as shown in 5-69*a*, *b*, and *c*.

Figure 5-72 shows some unique features:

1. There is radial travel at the end of the out stroke—in addition to the normal in-and-out travel—for maximum workpiece clearance.
2. The ramp angle on the strap for the heel rest helps to prevent any tendency for the strap to back off from the workpiece surface.
3. A true sphere of the heel bearing surface and mating clamp surface allows the clamp to float, and provides positive position on the workpiece surface, creating line contact with the true radius of the clamp toe.

MOUNTING MODULAR TOOLING

The major methods used to mount fixtures (including tooling plates and blocks) on a machine work table are:

- Banking the fixture against stops as shown in Fig. 5-73. This is commonly used on machines using a rotary table or having a fixed zero.
- Keying to T-slots as shown in Fig. 5-74. This method provides alignment and position in one axis only.
- Pinning to a subplate which has been attached to the machine table as shown in Fig. 5-75. The programmer has the option of calling out a specific location or having it placed wherever it is convenient for the operator.

Base Plate Dimensions – Inch

A Dia.	B	I	C-Hole-Base To Mach. Table No.	C-Hole-Base To Mach. Table Size	D-Riser Mtg. Holes No.	D-Riser Mtg. Holes Size	E Max	F Min	Increment	(3) Groups of G Clamp Pac Holes No.	(3) Groups of G Clamp Pac Holes Size	Locator In Mtg. Hole Size	J Radial PIN Locator
8.000	1.4000	0.6250	—	0.500	4	0.375	3.750	1.500	0.375	14	1/4-20		1.0000
10.000			2		4		4.750	1.750		18			2.0000
12.000			2		4		5.500	2.000		16		1/4-20	3.5000
16.000			2		4		7.625	2.625		22	3/8-16	3/8-16	1.0000 2.0000 3.5000 5.0000
20.000	1.6000		2	0.625	None		9.625	3.625	0.500	26		1/4-20	1.0000
24.000			2		None		11.625	4.125		32		3/8-16	2.0000
30.000			2		None		14.625	6.125		36		1/2-13	3.5000 5.0000 7.0000

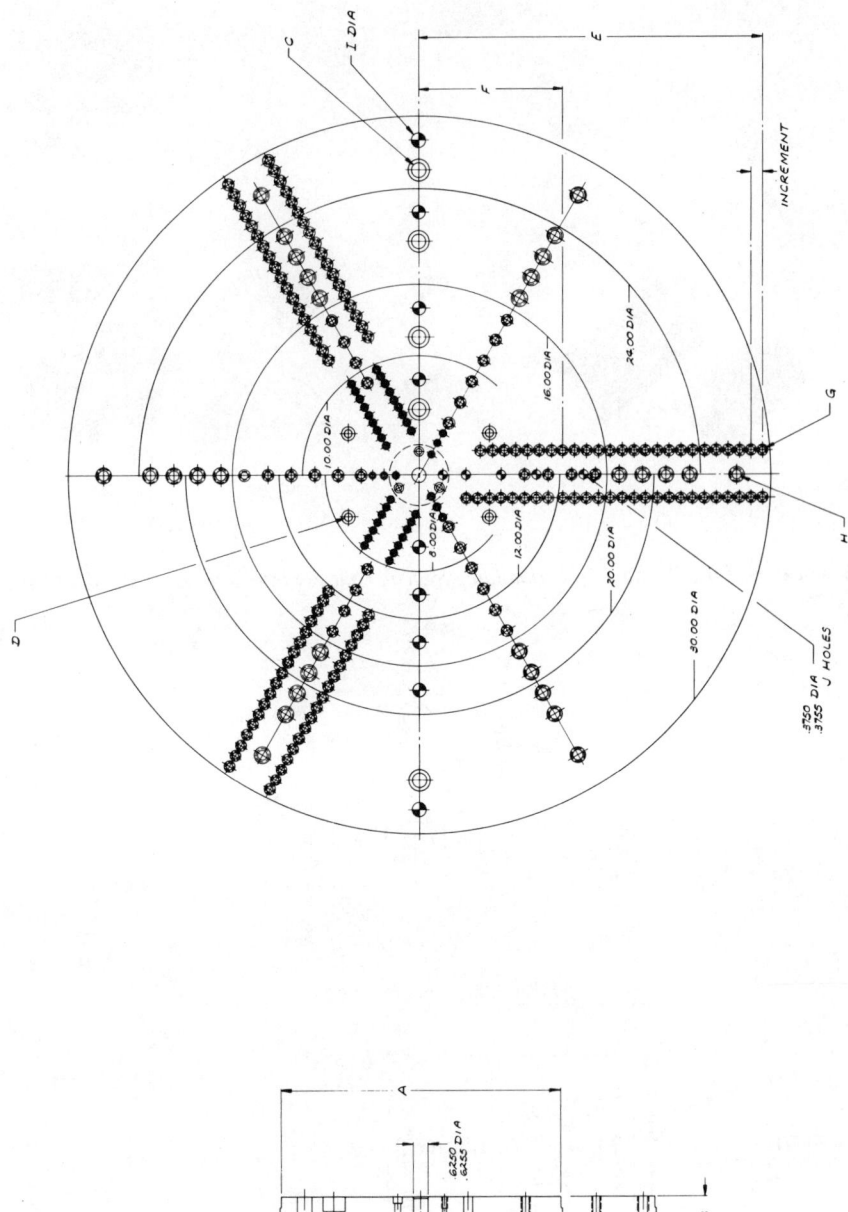

Fig. 5-70 Round base plates. (*Tru-Positioning Workholding System, courtesy International CNC Machining, Inc.*)

5-61

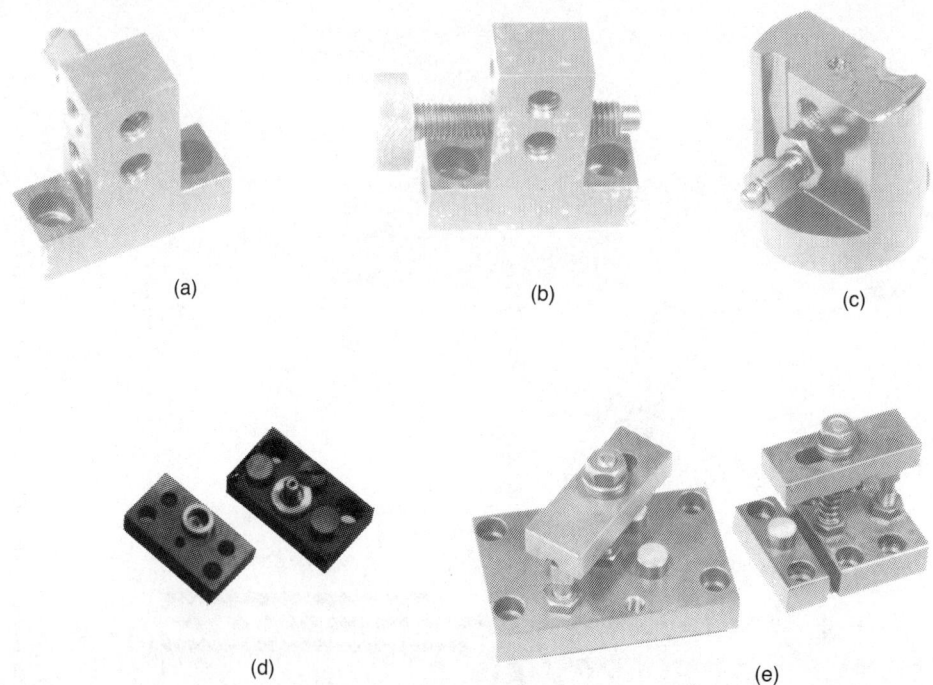

(a)   (b)   (c)

(d)   (e)

Fig. 5-71 Locators. (*Tru-Positioning Workholding System, courtesy International CNC Machining, Inc.*)

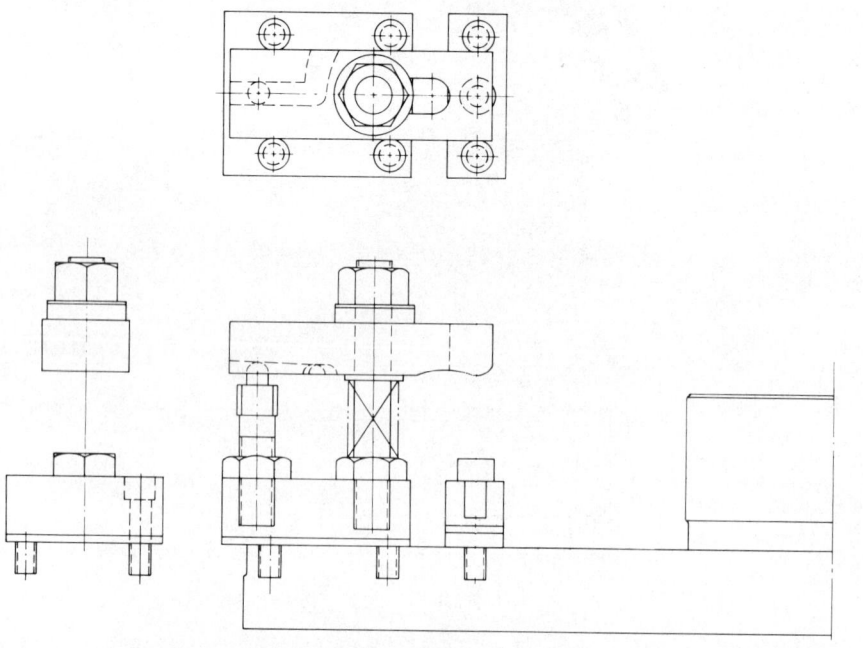

Fig. 5-72 Clamp details. (*Clamp-Pac details, Tru-Positioning Workholding System, courtesy International CNC Machining, Inc.*)

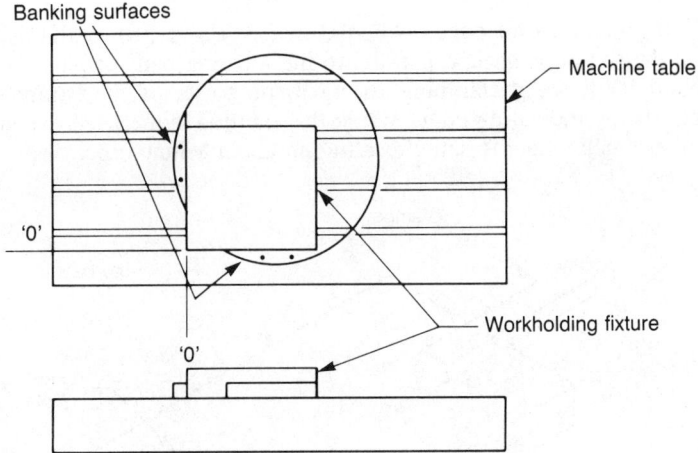

Banking surfaces

Machine table

'0'

Workholding fixture

'0'

Fig. 5-73 Banking a fixture against a stop.

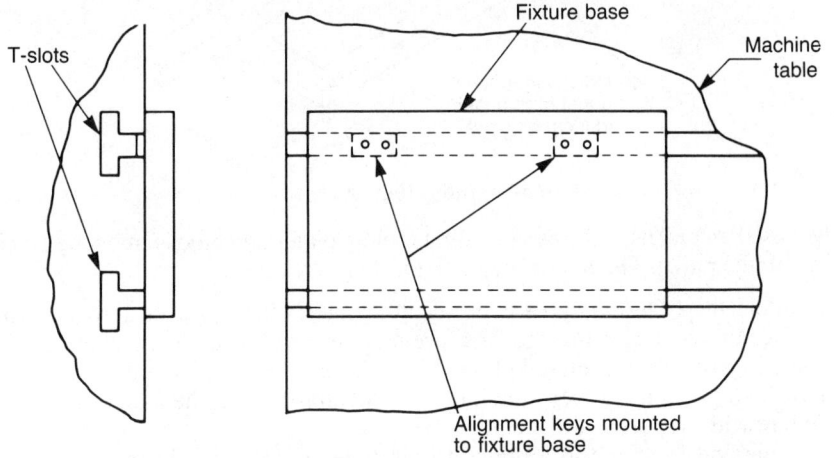

T-slots

Fixture base

Machine table

Alignment keys mounted to fixture base

Fig. 5-74 Keying to T-slots.

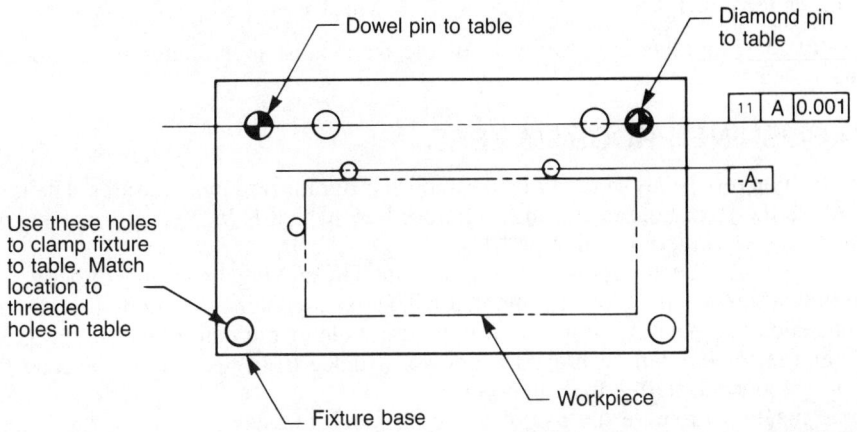

Dowel pin to table

Diamond pin to table

11 │ A │ 0.001

-A-

Use these holes to clamp fixture to table. Match location to threaded holes in table

Fixture base

Workpiece

Fig. 5-75 Pinning a worktable.

- Using an indicating edge on the fixture (see Fig. 5-76). With this system, an edge on the fixture is ground parallel to the locating pads or pins. The operator uses available holes or clamping arrangements to secure the fixture while tramming across the indicating edge. While this method is the least expensive to build, it takes much longer to setup resulting in idle machine time.

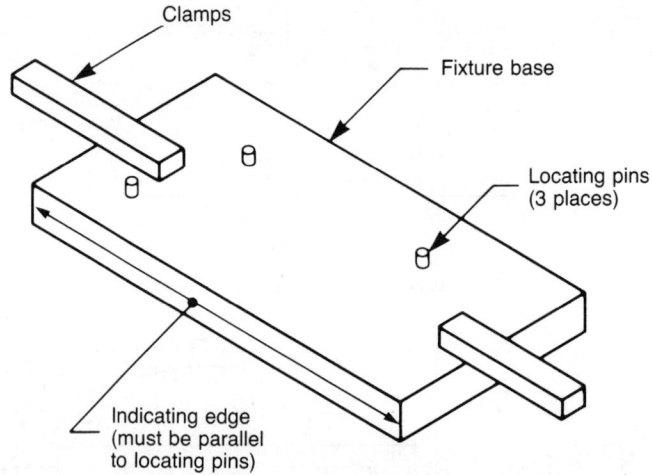

Clamps

Fixture base

Locating pins
(3 places)

Indicating edge
(must be parallel
to locating pins)

Fig. 5-76 Indicating on edge.

When used on pallets, fixtures (including tooling plates and blocks) must be precisely centered on the pallet. The major methods for doing this are:

- Banking the fixture against edge locator plates which project above the pallet surface on two adjacent edges that are precisely related to the machine axis.
- Matching precisely centered plugs and bushings on the pallet and fixture, respectively, along with one key which fits in a locating slot on the pallet to square the fixture with respect to the machine axes.
- Pinning and fastening to a previously installed subplate as discussed in the previous section.
- Using three fixture keys which engage two perpendicular locating slots in the slots in the the pallet.

Any of these options are readily available from most manufacturers of modular tooling systems.

ESTABLISHING PROGRAM ZERO

At one time provisions were made to establish program zero in all fixtures. The most common is the tram hole or pin in the fixture base which is located at some known distance from workpiece locating points.

To "zero in", the center of the hole or pin is found by moving the spindle directly over it and indicating it with a dial test indicator. The exact center is found by jogging the machine slides. Depending on programming, the hole or pin can either be "program zero", or the spindle can be moved a known distance from the hole or pin and the machining sequence started from that point.

Some machines require the use of a setting block to establish zero in the Z-axis. Gage blocks set to a specific height can do the same job. In any case, machine manuals should be checked and followed.

Today's machines use manual offset or probes to establish zero making the exact location of the fixture on the base plate irrelevant.

OTHER NC TOOLING

Pallet/Fixture Changers. Pallet/fixture changers provide another means of increasing the output of a vertical machining center.

The arrangement shown in Fig. 5-77 allows the machine operator to load and unload a vise pallet or T-slotted pallet/fixture while workpieces on another pallet/fixture are being machined as shown in the same figure. The pallet clamping fixture provides 0.0004 in. repeatability using round and diamond locators and clamping forces ranging from 4400 to 6600 lbf (19.6 to 29.4 kN).

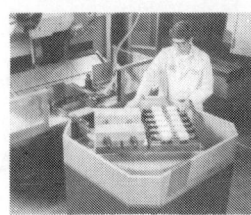
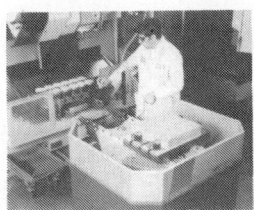
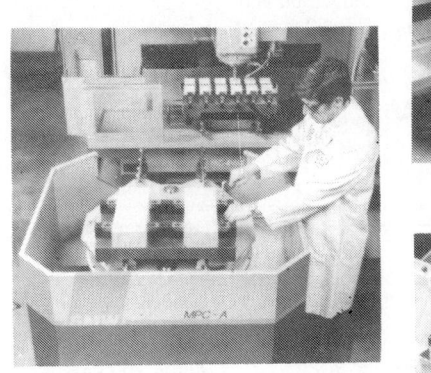
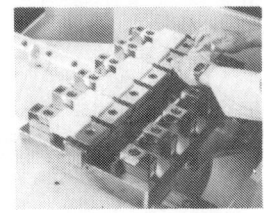
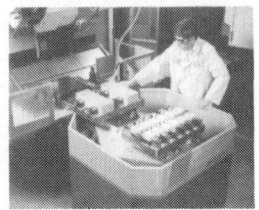

Fig. 5-77 Pallet fixture changer. (*Courtesy SMW Systems, Inc.*)

Vises. Some of the vises that are available for use on CNC machines have already been discussed previously along with modular tooling systems. Some other vise systems include:

- The CNC vises, which are shown in Fig. 5-78a and b, are provided in a range of sizes for clamping workpieces up to 23.5 in. (600 mm) long, depending on the position of the jaws, c. In use, the vise pulls the moveable jaw against the workpiece as it pulls and exerts pressure against the stationary jaw from each side, equalizing pressure and eliminating stationary jaw tilt. The vise permits holding of two equal or unequal size workpieces within its range as illustrated in d. Accessories include the speed handle, e, semi-adjustable workstop, f, and the adjustable workstop, g.
- The vises shown in Fig. 5-79 are designed especially for use with vertical machining centers. They are provided with up to 20 quick-acting clamps and a moveable guiderail that can be adjusted to suit a wide variety of workpiece sizes and arrangements. A typical changeover is shown in the same figure. In the case shown, twelve workpieces are setup for machining in two different positions by locating the workpieces against the center guiderail and repositioning the clamps. Changeover time is approximately two minutes. The guiderail provides a constant reference in both end and center positions.
- The machining center vises (MCVs) mounted back-to-back in Fig. 5-80. These vises were designed for multiple setups on CNC machines. The vise bodies are accurately ground on five sides and have three slots for alignment and attachment

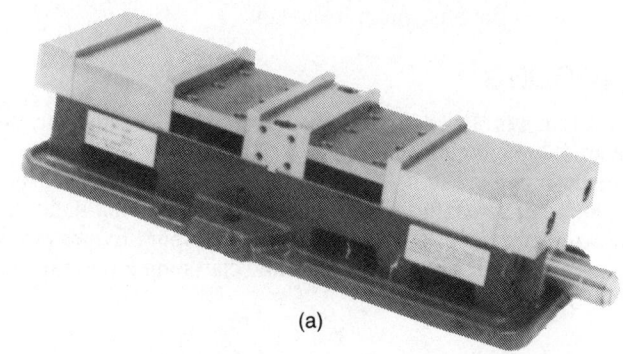

(a)

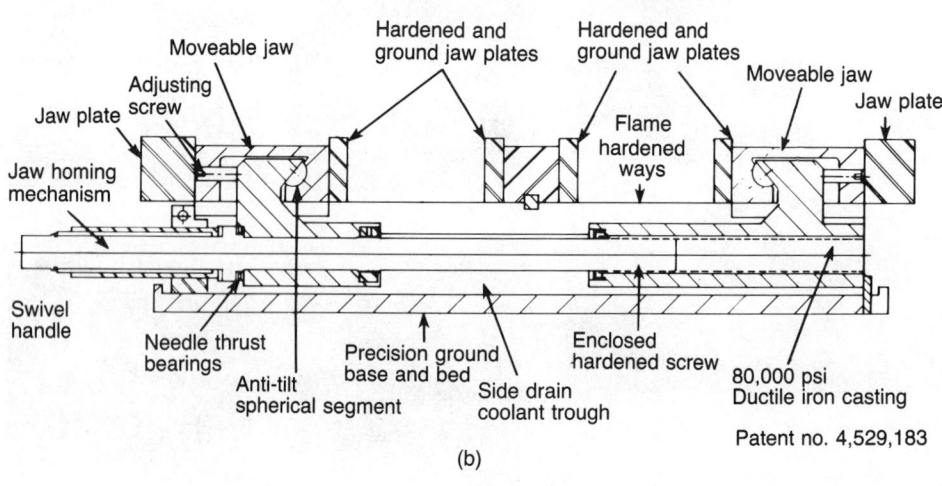

Moveable jaw

Adjusting screw

Jaw plate

Jaw homing mechanism

Swivel handle

Needle thrust bearings

Anti-tilt spherical segment

Hardened and ground jaw plates

Hardened and ground jaw plates

Moveable jaw

Jaw plate

Flame hardened ways

Precision ground base and bed

Side drain coolant trough

Enclosed hardened screw

80,000 psi Ductile iron casting

Patent no. 4,529,183

(b)

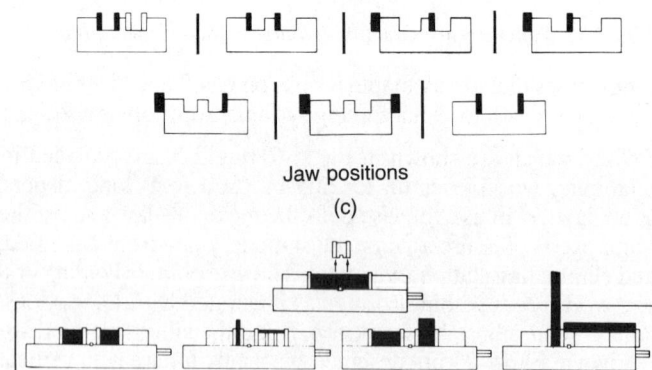

Jaw positions

(c)

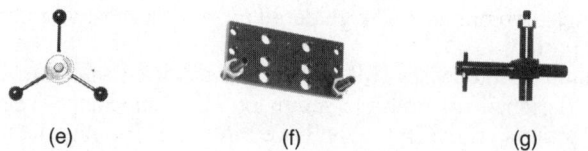

Clamping equal or unequal size workpieces

(d)

(e)   (f)   (g)

Fig. 5-78 CNC vise. (*Bi-Lok, courtesy Chick Machine Co., Inc.*)

Fig. 5-79 Vector vises. (*Courtesy SMW Systems, Inc.*)

with T-keys to machine and indexing tables or pallets. The MCVs shown are matched in sizes within 0.0008 in. Clamping pressures can be closely controlled and repeated, resulting in position repeatability within 0.0004 in. Two different fixed jaw positions provide for internal or external clamping. Vises and jaws can be provided in various sizes and configurations to permit external and internal clamping of workpieces. Footplates can be provided for use as risers or tooling plates for quick mounting to subplates, machine tables, or pallets.

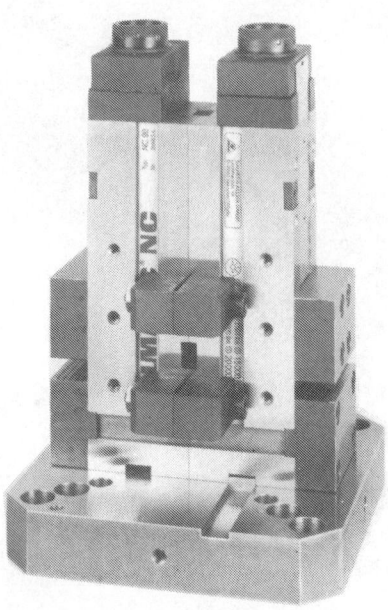

Fig. 5-80 Machining center vises. (*Courtesy Dapra Corp.*)

Some typical applications are shown in Fig. 5-81. In *a*, four MCVs are mounted in a back-to-back setup with special jaws to hold a round shaft for machining. In *b*, four MCVs are mounted on a single footplate to clamp four workpieces (either the same or different) for machining. A single MCV with the fixed jaw removed is used in *c* to vertically clamp a gear box directly to the subplate after aligning it on the subplate with dowel pins. In *d*, two MCVs are mounted back-to-back to clamp two workpieces (either the same or different) for multiple-sided machining operations.

- The pull type vise shown in Fig. 5-82*a*. These vises were designed for use either singly or in multiple setups for machining workpieces on CNC machines as well as manual equipment. They are provided with internal bolt holes for clamping to the machine table, thereby eliminating the need for external straps or toe clamps. Sides are ground flat and parallel to permit mounting either horizontally or vertically in both directions.

The twin machine vise fixture (refer to Fig. 5-82*b*) provides two vertical surfaces for mounting these vises or other 6 in. (152 mm) machine vises. The fixture is designed for mounting on a standard 11.81 in. (300 mm) pallet. The cast aluminum body is filled with an epoxy resin to absorb vibration and to reduce weight.

The fixtures shown in Fig. 5-83 combine four double vises with a rigid column to provide workholding for up to eight workpieces. In *a*, the fixture is mounted on the fourth axis of a CNC machining center. In *b*, a base plate has been added for mounting on a horizontal CNC machining center. Fixtures are also available that combine 6 and 8 double vises to provide workholding for 12 and 16 workpieces respectively.

Chucks. Stationary hydraulic/pneumatic chucks, such as shown in Fig. 5-84, can be provided singly or in matched sets to hold round and square parts for CNC machining.

Indexers. Figure 5-85 shows a setup using a large tailstock supported tombstone fixture which will permit machining three sides of sixteen workpieces on the one setup, thereby permitting long periods of unmanned machining during which the machine

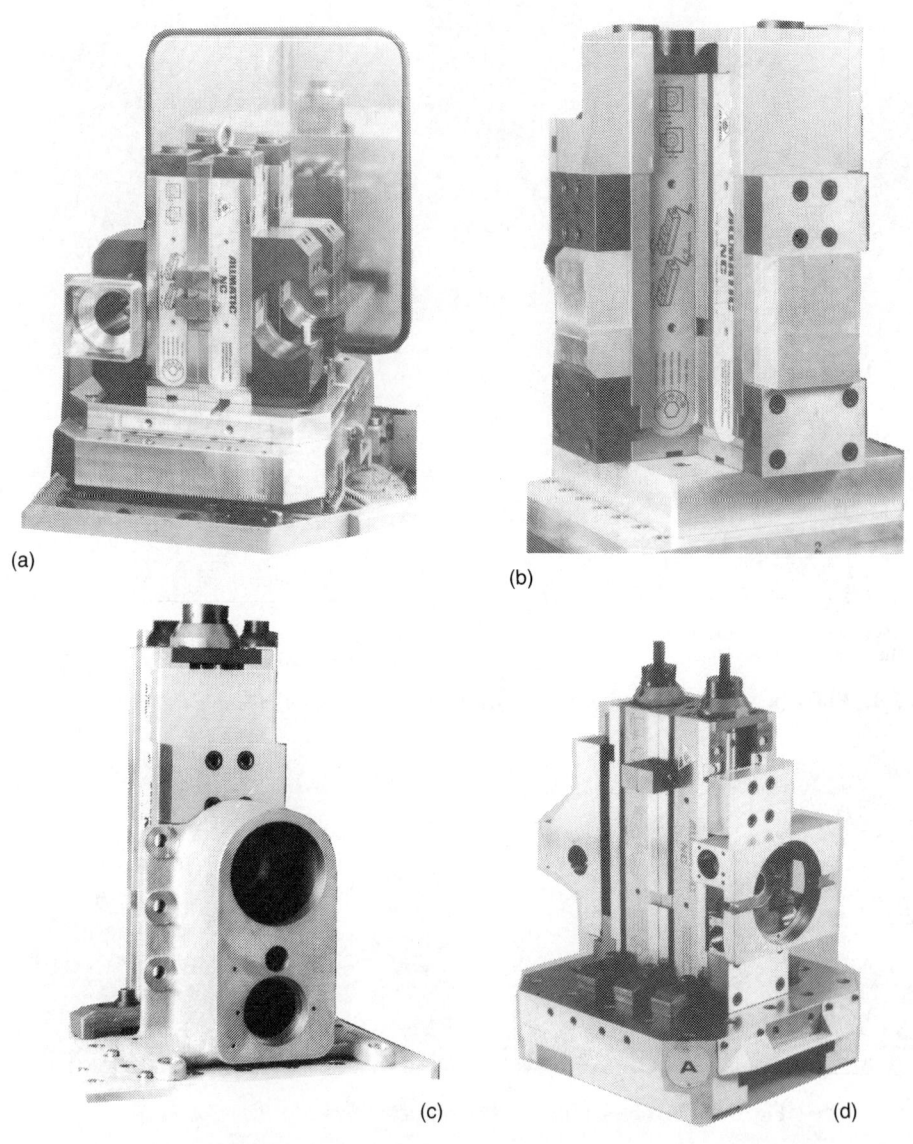

(a)

(b)

(c)

(d)

Fig. 5-81 Applications of machining center vises. (*Courtesy Dapra Corp.*)

operator can run additional machines or prepare for the next changeover. Changeover time with these fixtures can be reduced to a few minutes time using quick-change pallets as shown in Fig. 5-86.

The indexers shown in Fig. 5-87a and b along with standard accessories, c, can provide great flexibility to a vertical machining center. The indexers shown in a are provided with face plate diameters of 6.3, 7.9, and 12.4 in. All have 72.5° indexing positions with positioning accuracy of ±5 arc seconds, and repeatability of 2½ arc seconds. The indexer shown in b will provide 0.001° indexing increments (360,000 positions) having a cumulative positioning accuracy of 15 seconds and repeatability of 2 seconds.

5-69

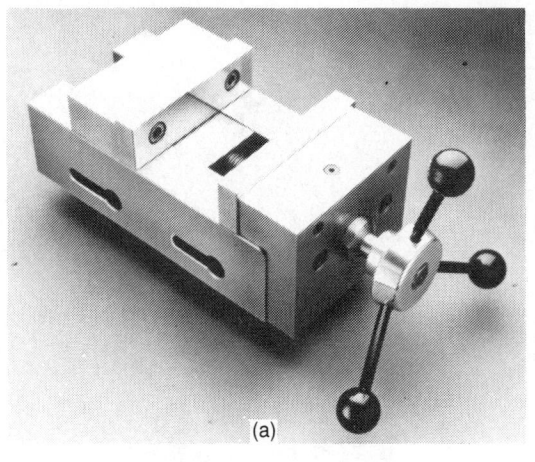
(a)

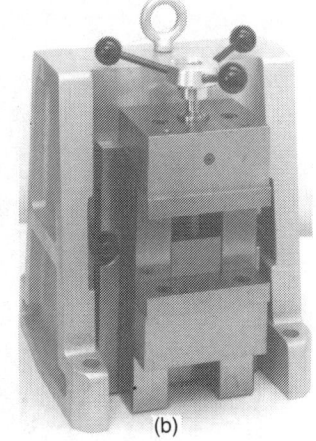
(b)

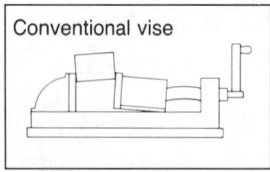
Conventional vise

Main screw buckles under pushing pressure, jaw lifts, and workpiece tilts.

Pull-type vise

Pulling action keeps main screw straight, jaw lift is reduced and workpiece is held accurately.

Fig. 5-82 Pull type vise and twin mounting fixture. (*Courtesy Huron Machine Products, Inc.*)

Fig. 5-83 Fixtures. (*Multi-Lok/8, courtesy Chick Machine Co., Inc.*)

In Fig. 5-88 the indexer is used along with a simple clamping arrangement to machine four sides of a single workpiece in one setup.

Figure 5-89 shows two separate setups using a tombstone-type mounting fixture. In *a* the workpieces are mounted in a manner that will permit machining on three sides of four workpieces, saving two setups. In *b* the workpieces are mounted in a manner that will permit machining on six sides on two workpieces saving four setups.

Another indexer for use with CNC machines is shown in Figure 5-90. This programmable 5C collet head, equipped with a servo motor provides for 144,000 different indexing positions with an accuracy of ± 15 seconds in one direction, repeatability within 10 seconds, and resolution of $0.0025°$. Standard accessories include air collet closers, tailstocks, and 5.25 in. lathe chucks. The spindle speed of this unit can be easily controlled for arc or spiral milling.

Fig. 5-84 Stationary chuck with accessories. (*Courtesy Buck Chuck Co.*)

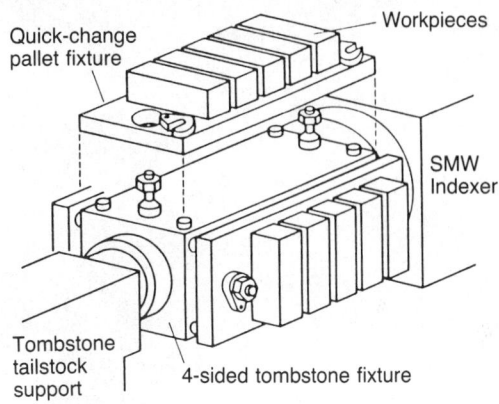

Fig. 5-85 Machining three sides of four workpieces. (*Courtesy SMW Systems, Inc.*)

Fig. 5-86 Quick change pallets. (*Courtesy SMW Systems, Inc.*)

Special designs combining indexing tables are shown in Figs. 5-91 and 5-92. The unit in Fig. 5-91 was designed to machine disk brake saddles. It features two axes, each with four NC-indexing devices with built-in clamping cylinders. The tilting motions are also NC controlled. The unit in Fig. 5-92 is a 31.5 in. (800 mm) planetary indexing table with nine stations. The vertical faces with 12.6 in. (320 mm) centerdistances accommodate nine 7.9 in. (200 mm) indexing tables. Indexing tables for applications such as this can be provided with indexing accuracies as fine as ±1.5 seconds with repeatability 10% of the accuracy. Tables can be provided for fixed indexing or equipped with positioning motors for setting any angular increment.

Other applications of these indexers can be seen in Fig. 5-93. For example, square and round workpieces can be held and indexed in chucks, *a*, and built-in collet closers can be used to hold a workpiece as shown in *b* and *c*. In *d*, a power-operated center/-clamp is used to hold a differential case for machining.

For heavy duty work, the servo rotary table shown in Fig. 5-94 can be mounted either horizontally or vertically, and interfaced to a CNC machine for use with 5C, 16C, and 3J collets, 8 or 10 in. chucks, and 8 or 11 in. (203 or 279 mm) faceplates. Indexing accuracy of this unit is ±10 seconds in one direction, repeatability is within 10 seconds, and resolution is 0.00133°.

Figure 5-95 shows an application requiring CNC control of tilt along with rotary indexing. For the unit shown, indexing accuracies of ±20 seconds or ± 5 seconds can be provided.

(a)

(b)

(c)

Fig. 5-87 Indexers. (*Courtesy SMW Systems, Inc.*)

Fig. 5-88 Machining four sides of a single workpiece in one setup. (*Courtesy SMW Systems, Inc.*)

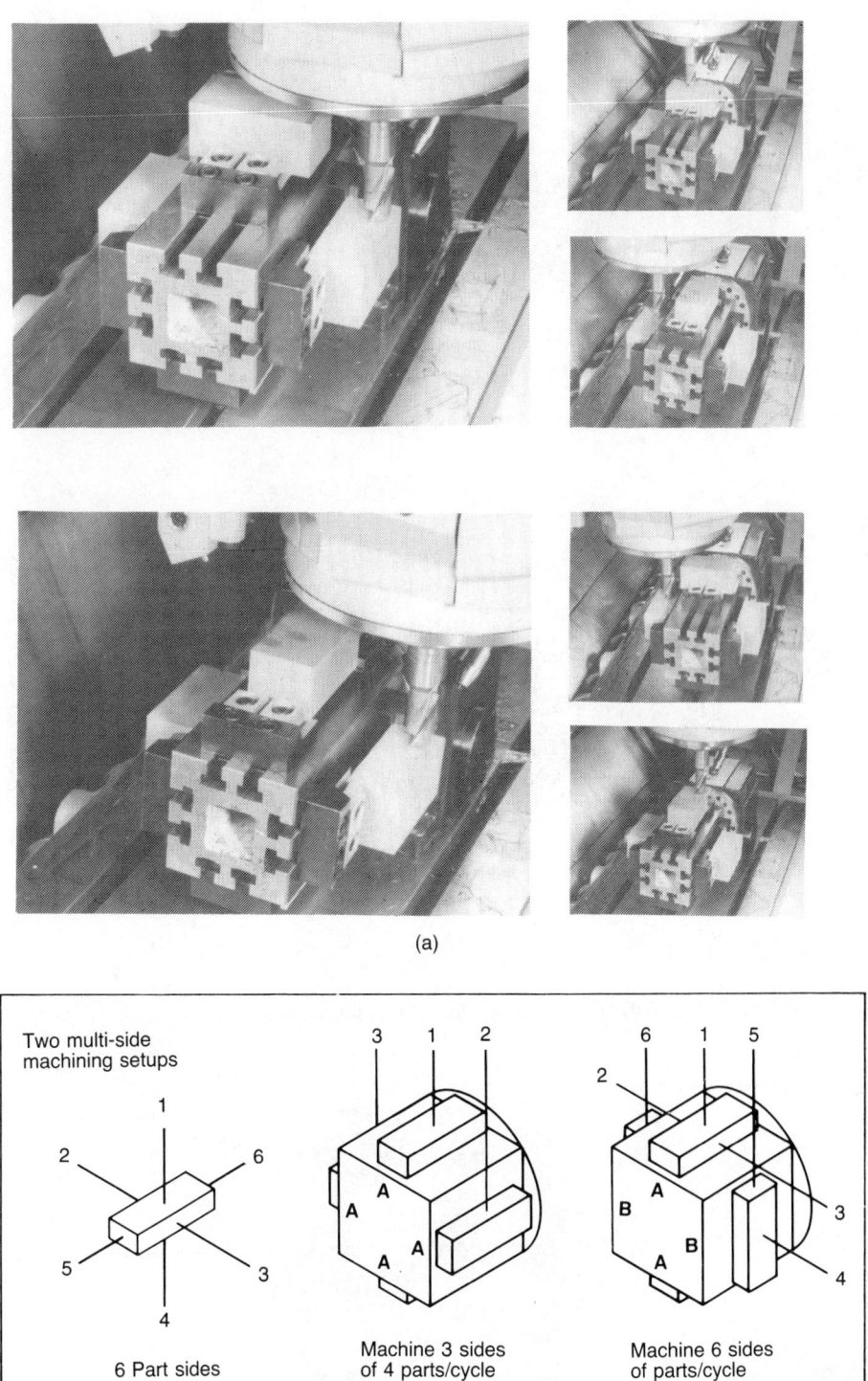

(a)

(b)

Fig. 5-89 Two different multi-side machining setups using a tombstone fixture. (*Courtesy SMW Systems, Inc.*)

Fig. 5-90 Programmable 5C collet head. (*Courtesy Haas Automation Inc.*)

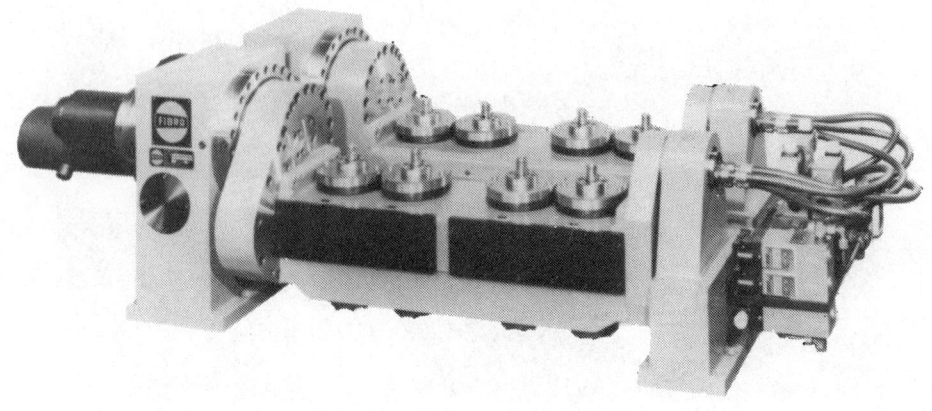

Fig. 5-91 Special design indexing table. (*Courtesy Fibro, Inc.*)

Fig. 5-92 Planetary indexing table. (*Courtesy Fibro, Inc.*)

Fig. 5-93 Indexer applications. (*Courtesy SMW Systems, Inc.*)

Fig. 5-94 Servo rotary table. (*Courtesy Haas Automation Inc.*)

Fig. 5-95 CNC control of tilt with rotary indexing. (*Rotary-Tilt module, courtesy Jones & Shipman, P.L.C.*)

CHAPTER 6

GEOMETRIC DIMENSIONING AND TOLERANCING

The intent of the product designer is visually expressed by means of a part drawing or blueprint. These drawings, along with specifications, must clearly define the composition, size, and shape of the part. In addition, since no two parts will be exactly alike in the absolute sense, the designer must provide a tolerance—either directly or indirectly—to every dimension or specification. This tolerance will represent the total allowable variation from a specific dimension or specification. In simple terms, the designer specifies an ideal, but unattainable, condition, along with a margin of error that can be tolerated.

To arrive at these tolerances, the product designer must consider a number of factors, such as the function of the product for which the tolerance must be compatible; the appearance of the product for aesthetic reasons; the capability of the machines that will produce the part; and finally the cost, since as tolerances become smaller, the cost of achieving them increases rapidly. Studies have shown that it costs about 30% more to machine to tolerances of 0.0005 in. than to 0.001 in., and when tolerances are further reduced from 0.001 in. to 0.00025 in. machining costs increase more than 50%. In cases where the fit between mating parts is held to very close tolerances for proper function as an assembly, it is often more economical to combine relaxed part tolerances with selective assembly.

Prior to Geometric Dimensioning and Tolerancing, the part was shown in a fixed relationship with mutually perpendicular reference planes. This method of dimensioning is called "Coordinate Dimensioning", and the location of each element of the part is defined by stating the desired distance from each of these reference planes along with any allowable variations. This is illustrated in Fig. 6-1 where the element so dimensioned can be located anywhere within the shaded rectangle formed by the minimum and maximum values of the X and Y dimensions established by the ±0.125 tolerances.

The product designer's intent can also be conveyed by stating the desired distance of the element from each plane and how far the element can vary from this position. This is illustrated in Fig. 6-2 where the element so dimensioned can be located anywhere within the shaded circle having a diameter of 0.250 and its center located at the desired X-Y position. This method of dimensioning is called "True Position Tolerancing" or more recently "Positional Tolerancing".

CONVERSION CHARTS

The chart shown in Fig. 6-3 can be used to determine the plus and minus variations allowed by a positional tolerance. To use the chart, the *diameter* of the positional tolerance is found on the vertical scale and followed back to the horizontal scale where

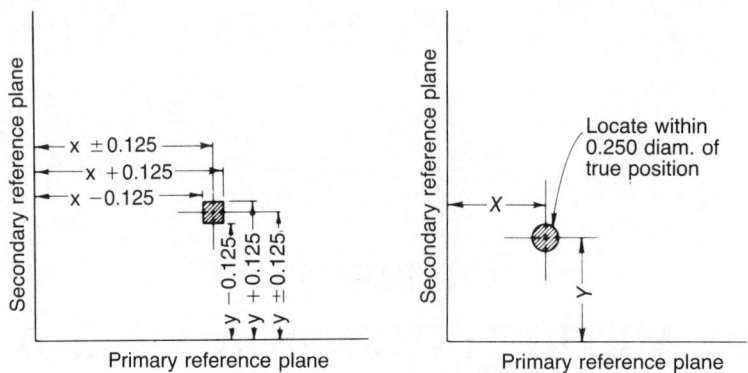

Fig. 6-1 Coordinate dimensioning. Fig. 6-2 Positional tolerancing.

it can be read directly as a bilateral tolerance in the coordinate system. This can also be approximated mathematically by multiplying the positional tolerance *diameter* by 0.7. For example:

0.010 diam. × 0.7 = 0.007 (±0.0035).

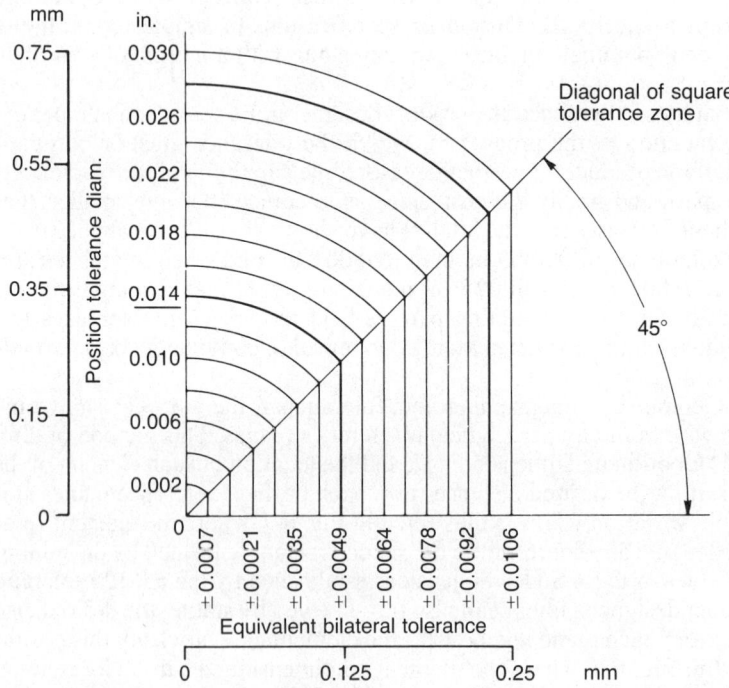

Fig. 6-3 Conversion chart: positional tolerance to bilateral. (*Courtesy The Sandia Corp.*)

Conversely, the chart shown in Fig. 6-4 can be used to determine whether the center of a machined hole is within the positional tolerance specified, and also determine the actual deviation (radius) from true position. For example: The deviation of the center of a hole from nominal is determined by coordinate measurements and it is desired to know whether or not the hole is within the positional tolerance specified on the drawing. To use the chart, the intersection of the X and Y coordinate differences is found on the

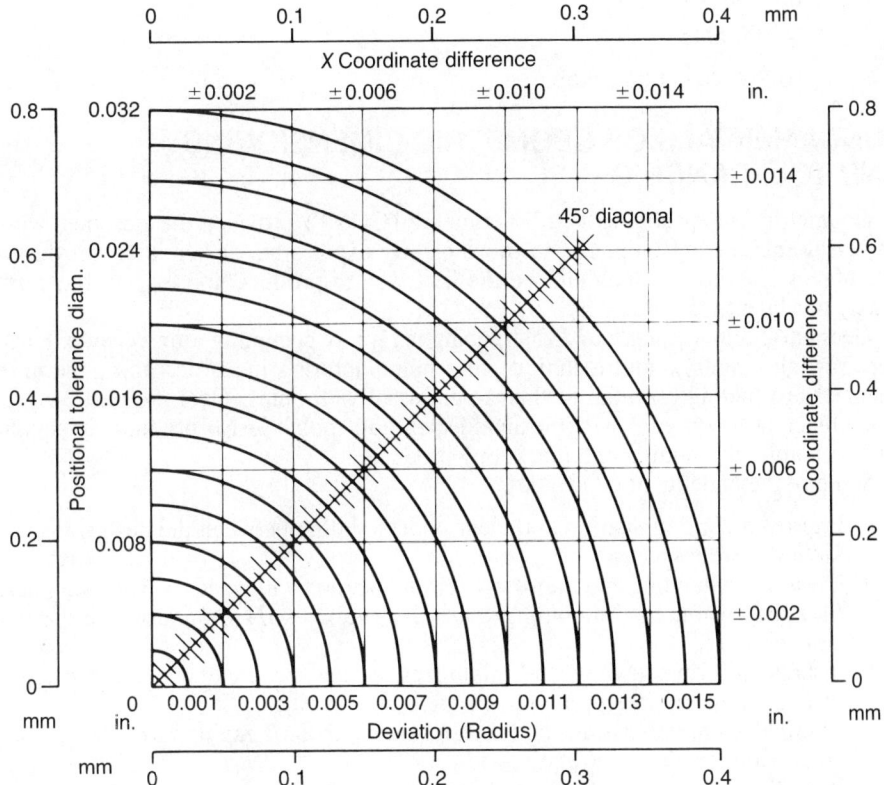

Fig. 6-4 Conversion chart: bilateral to positional tolerance. (*Courtesy The Sandia Corp.*)

chart using the values shown in the upper and right hand borders. A radius is then drawn through that point, intersecting the 45° diagonal line. The deviation can now be read from the scale on the 45° line using the values shown in the lower border. This can also be determined mathematically using the following formula:

$$D = \sqrt{X_d^2 + Y_d^2} \tag{1}$$

where:

D = Deviation (radius)

X_d = X coordinate deviation

Y_d = Y coordinate deviation

Example 1:

For:

X_d = + 0.003

Y_d = + 0.006

Calculations:

$$D = \sqrt{X_d^2 + Y_d^2}$$
$$= \sqrt{0.003^2 + 0.006^2}$$

$$= \sqrt{0.000009 + 0.000036}$$

$$= \sqrt{0.000045}$$

$$= 0.0067 \text{ Deviation (radius)}$$

FUNDAMENTALS OF GEOMETRIC DIMENSIONING AND TOLERANCING

Geometric Dimensioning and Tolerancing (GD&T) provides the designer with a universal engineering language to more clearly express his or her intent to the part manufacturer, who can then choose the best way to produce and inspect the part to satisfy this intent.

Geometric dimensioning and tolerancing is rapidly becoming a universal engineering drawing language and technique that manufacturing industries and government agencies are finding essential to their operational well-being. Over the past 30 years, this subject has matured to become an indispensable tool; it assists productivity, quality, and economies in building and marketing products.

Some of the benefits of GD&T are:

- Improved communication and clear understanding between the designer, manufacturer, and inspector.
- Clear understanding and improved communication with vendors (incoming material) and customers (outgoing products). Reinforces JIT programs and warranty policies.
- Insures uniform drawings and minimizes written specifications and instructions. Provides uniform interpretation.
- Eliminates implied datums and dictates the method of gaging rather than relying on an individual's interpretation.
- Provides a clear understanding of how the part functions.
- Identifies product problems early in the design stage.
- Provides greater tolerances for manufacturing in the design stage, and later in the form of "bonus tolerancing".
- Insures assembly of components.
- Provides savings in time and money.

In order to fully realize the advantages of GD&T, it is necessary to understand the fundamental concepts, rules, terms, and symbols associated with GD&T as endorsed by the American National Standards Institute (ANSI) and documented in ANSI Y14.5M, "Dimensioning and Tolerancing". Since many drawings presently in existance were dimensioned using previous ANSI Y14.5 revisions, differences from the present revision are noted and shown in italics.

SYMBOLS

The geometric characteristics and symbols endorsed by ANSI Y14.5M are shown in Fig. 6-5. Other endorsed symbols and their definitions are as follows:

Basic Dimension. A theoretical value used to describe the exact size or location of a feature. A tolerance is always required with a basic dimension to show the permissible variation. A basic dimension is symbolized by boxing. Example: $\boxed{2.000}$. *On older drawings basic dimensions were identified by adding the word BASIC or the abbreviation BSC next to the dimension.*

Datums. Points, lines, planes, and other features and surfaces which are considered to be exact for purposes of determining the location or form of other part features. Datum features and surfaces are actual part features and surfaces including all of their feature or surface inaccuracies. Datums provide a *guide* to the tool designer for fixturing the

Characteristic	Symbol	Type
Flatness	▱	Form
Straightness	—	
Roundness (Circularity)	○	
Cylindricity	⌀	
Profile of any line	⌒	Profile
Profile of any surface	⌓	
Perpendicularity (Squareness)	⊥	Orientation
Angularity	∠	
Parallelism	∥	
Runout (Circular)	↗	Runout
Runout (Total)	↗↗	
Position	⊕	Location
Concentricity	◎	

Fig. 6-5 Geometric characteristics and types.

workpiece, and should be given careful attention since conformance of the finished workpiece to the part drawing specifications *must* be verified to the datums. Datums are symbolized by boxing. For example: ⎸-A-⎹ . Each feature used as a datum is identified by a different letter. The letters I, O, & Q are not used to eliminate confusion. Double letter such as AA, BB, etc., are used when single letters have been used up.

To ensure correct drawing interpretation, three plane datum reference frames are used. For prismatic parts, parts are located for manufacturing and inspection from datum surfaces using the 3-2-1 principle (primary, secondary, tertiary respectively) as shown in Fig. 6-6. For cylindrical parts the primary datum is usually a flat base or surface; the secondary datum is the axis of the part; and the tertiary axis, if needed, is a feature, such as a hole, slot, tang, or pin, to locate the part radially as shown in Fig. 6-7.

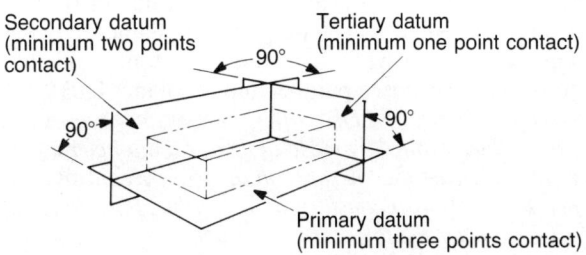

Fig. 6-6 Three plane datum reference frame for prismatic parts.

A common datum, such as the axis or centerplane, of a workpiece can be established by using two datum letters separated by a dash. For example:⎸A-B⎹. Datums will be covered in greater detail throughout the remainder of the chapter.

Feature Control Frame. A boxed expression containing the geometric characteristic symbol, the tolerance shape zone symbol where applicable, and the tolerance; plus any datum references and modifiers for the feature or datums. A typical example is shown in Fig. 6-8.

It can be seen from this figure that the feature control frame specifies the type, shape, and size of the tolerance zone, designates the datums and their order of precedence, and specifies any applicable material condition modifiers to the tolerance and datums in the following manner:

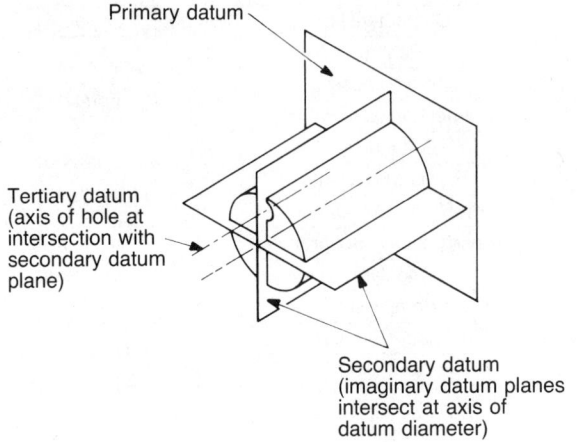

Primary datum

Tertiary datum
(axis of hole at
intersection with
secondary datum
plane)

Secondary datum
(imaginary datum planes
intersect at axis of
datum diameter)

Fig. 6-7 Three plane datum reference frame for cylindrical parts.

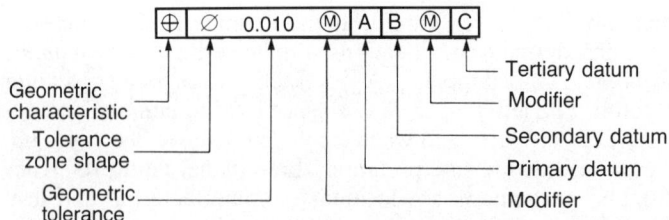

Geometric
characteristic

Tolerance
zone shape

Geometric
tolerance

Tertiary datum

Modifier

Secondary datum

Primary datum

Modifier

Fig. 6-8 Feature control frame.

- The first symbol $\oplus$ indicates that the tolerance that follows is a position tolerance.
- The next symbol $\varnothing$ and the following tolerance value of 0.010 indicates that the tolerance zone has a cylindrical shape 0.010 in diameter. In cases where the tolerance is not preceeded by a symbol, the tolerance zone would be considered to be the area contained between two parallel lines or planes 0.010 apart. *In the first revision of Y14.5, the abbreviation DIA after the tolerance was used instead of the symbol $\varnothing$ in the feature control frame to designate a diameter tolerance zone. The use of the abbreviation R after the tolerance in the feature control frame to designate a radius tolerance zone was also considered acceptable. For a total width tolerance zone, the word TOTAL after the tolerance was used.*
- The tolerance is followed by the modifier. In this case M which designates that the tolerance applies only when the feature is at its MMC size.
- The datums, including any modifiers, are shown last in order of importance. In this case the primary datum A, which requires a minimum of three points of contact is shown first. This is followed by the secondary datum B, which requires a minimum of two points of contact. Datum B is also followed by the material condition modifier (M) which in essence provides additional tolerance as datum B digresses from MMC. The tertiary datum C, which requires a minimum of one point of contact, is shown last. Listing datums by importance provides manufacturing and inspection personnel with the information needed to locate the work-piece for machining and/or inspection using the 3-2-1 method discussed in a previous chapter. *In the 1966 revision of Y14.5, datums were listed ahead of the tolerance in the feature control frame. In the 1973 revision, datums could be either before or after the tolerance.*

Feature Control Frames can be applied either to a feature or a feature of size by proper placement of the feature control frame as shown in Figs. 6-9 and 6-10. It can be seen from these figures that when a feature control frame applies to a feature, it is set apart from any feature of size and a leader is drawn from it to the feature; whereas when the feature control frame applies to a feature of size, it is placed directly below the dimension.

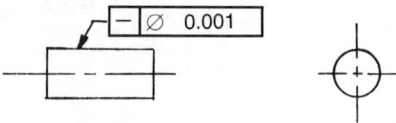

Fig. 6-9 Feature control frame applied to a feature RFS.

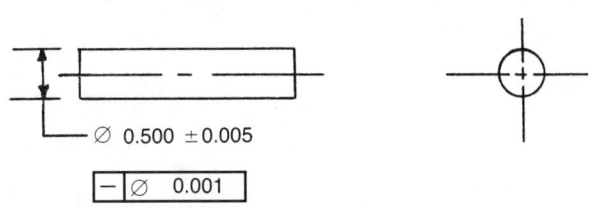

Fig. 6-10 Feature control frame applied to a feature of size RFS.

Datum Targets. Points, lines, or surfaces that are specified on the product drawing to specify the placement of locating points, lines, or surfaces on the tooling. Basic dimensions are used to locate datum targets as well as describe their shape and size. Target areas can be any shape and are identified on the part drawing by diagonal slash lines within a phantom outline of the area. Datum targets are identified on the part drawing by a datum target symbol. Examples of the previous symbol, the current symbol and its proper application are shown in Fig. 6-11.

Projected Tolerance Zone. A tolerance zone applied to a hole in which a projecting part, such as a pin, bolt, stud, etc., is to be inserted. The projected tolerance zone controls the perpendicularity of the hole to the extent necessary to assure assembly with a mating part. The projected tolerance zone extends beyond the surface of the part for a distance equal to the functional length of the pin, bolt, stud, etc. Projected tolerance zone is designated by the symbol Ⓟ .

MATERIAL CONDITION MODIFIERS

There are three types of material condition modifiers: Maximum Material Condition, Least Material Condition, and Regardless of Feature Size.

• Maximum Material Condition (MMC)—A material condition modifier in which a feature of size contains the maximum amount of material. For example, the minimum diameter of a hole or the maximum diameter of a shaft. MMC is designated by the symbol Ⓜ . When the MMC symbol is shown with the tolerance or a datum reference letter in the feature control frame, the tolerance applies only when the feature is at its MMC size.

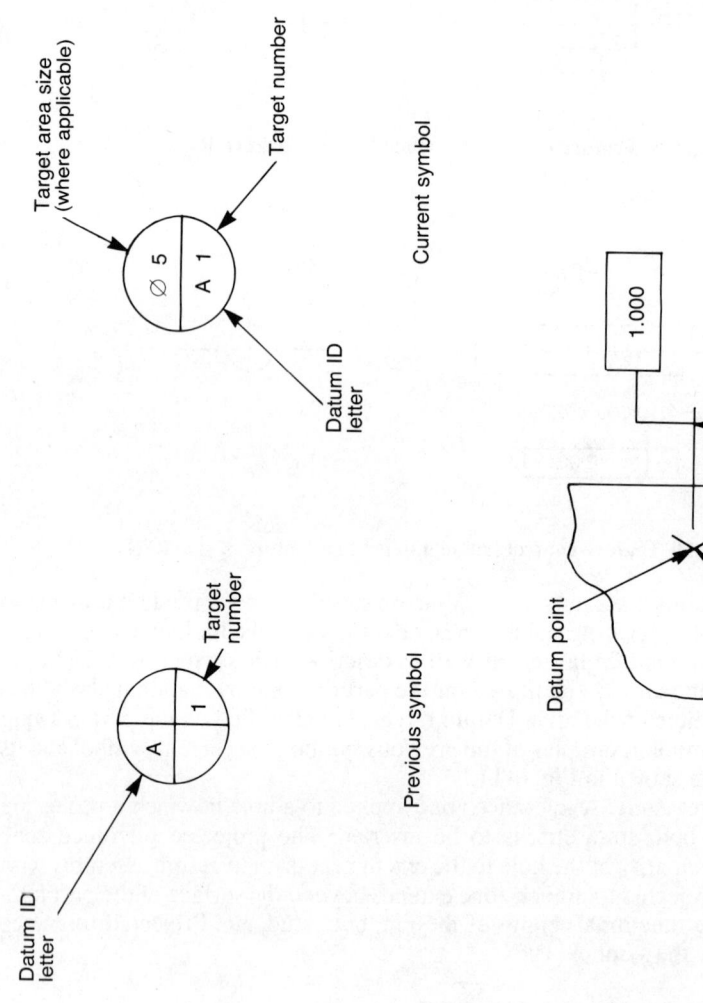

Target area size (where applicable)

Target number

Datum ID letter

Ø 5 | A 1

Current symbol

Datum ID letter

Target number

A | 1

Previous symbol

1.000

1.000

Datum point

Datum points

A 1

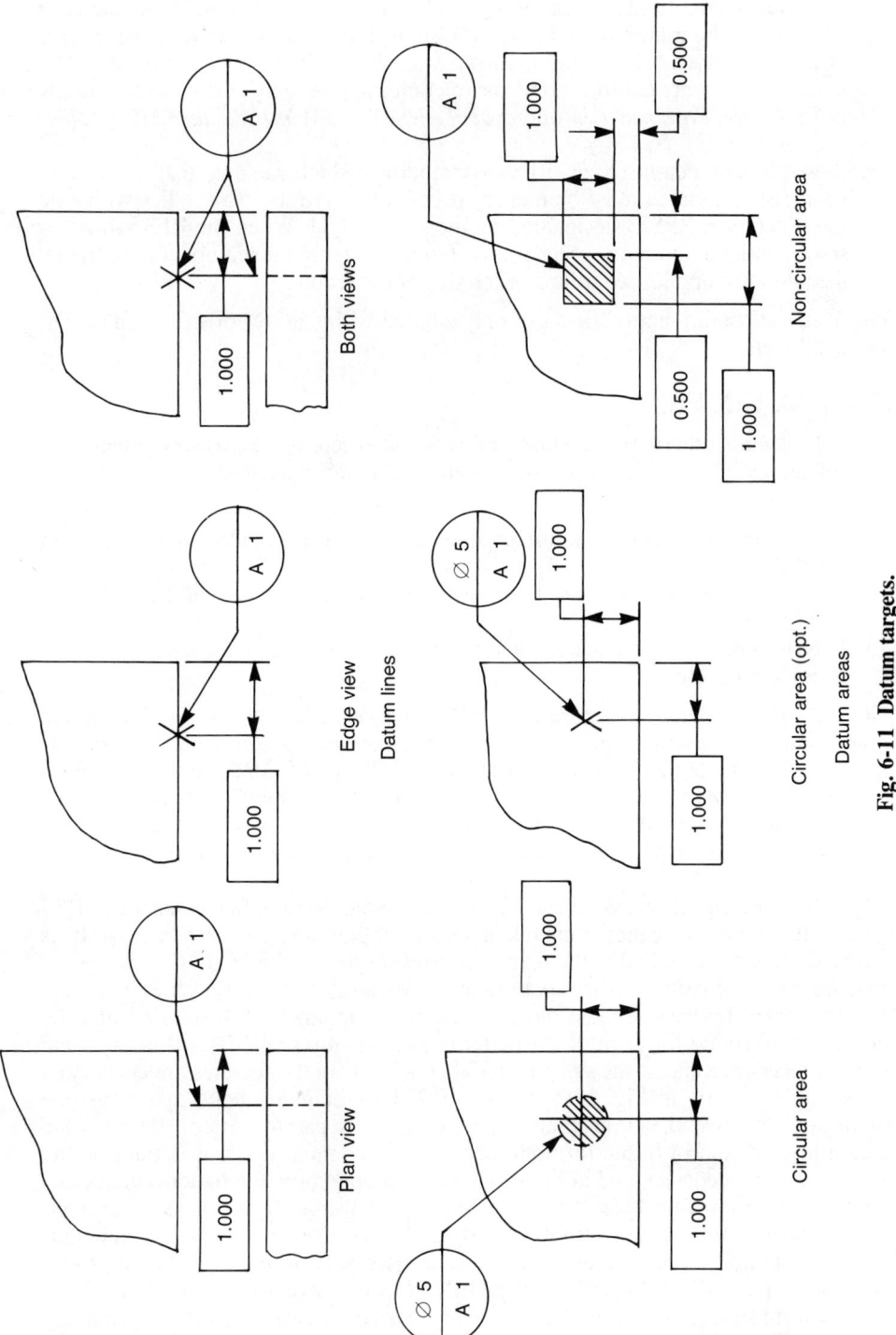

Fig. 6-11 Datum targets.

6-9

- Least Material Condition (LMC)—The opposite of MMC—in which a feature of size contains the least amount of material. For example, the maximum diameter of a hole or the minimum diameter of a shaft. LMC is designated by the symbol Ⓛ . When the LMC symbol is shown with the tolerance or a datum reference letter in the feature control frame, the tolerance applies only when the feature is at its LMC size. *Previous to the approval of ANSI Y14.5M in 1982, the LMC modifier was not used.*
- Regardless of Feature Size (RFS)—A modifier which requires that a specified geometric tolerance must be met regardless of where the feature lies within its size tolerance. RFS is designated by the symbol Ⓢ. When the RFS symbol is shown with the tolerance or a datum reference letter in the feature control frame, the tolerance applies regardless of the size of the feature.

Note: Material condition modifiers can only be used with features of size, such as IDs, ODs, widths, etc.

GENERAL RULES

Rule 1—Unless otherwise specified, and with the exception of axis straightness, the limits of an individual feature of size controls the form as well as the size (see Fig. 6-12).

1. No element of the actual feature shall extend beyond a boundary of perfect form at MMC.
2. The actual measured size at any cross section of the feature shall be within the LMC limit for size.
3. This rule does not apply to non-rigid parts or commercial stock, such as bar stock, plates, tubing, etc.

Rule 2—For a tolerance of position; MMC, RFS, or LMC *must* be specified in the feature control frame with respect to the individual tolerance and/or datum reference as applicable (see Fig. 6-13). *In previous revisions of ANSI Y14.5, MMC was implied for a tolerance of position in those cases where a material condition symbol was omitted from the feature control frame. An Ⓢ had to be specified in the feature control frame when it was required. ISO standards were just the opposite. When no symbol was used, RFS was implied.*

Rule 3—For other than tolerances of position, where *no* modifier is specified, RFS applies with respect to the individual tolerance and/or datum reference. Where MMC is required, it must be specified in the feature control frame (see Fig. 6-14).

Separate requirements—When more than one pattern of features such as holes and slots are located by basic dimensions from common datum features of size, and the feature control frame for each of the patterns contains the same datums in the same order of precedence and at the same material condition, all the features are considered as one single pattern. In Fig. 6-15, the two 0.221 in. diameter holes appear as one pattern, and the two 0.391 in. diameter holes are a separate pattern. Because the location feature control frame for both hole patterns contain the same datums, in the same order of precedence, and at the same material condition, the patterns are considered one pattern of four holes. The parts inspector must verify the dimensional conformance of both hole patterns simultaneously. If the designer had felt this interrelationship of the four holes was not required between the two patterns of features in Fig. 6-15, a notation such as SEPARATE REQUIREMENTS would have been placed beneath the feature control frames. This would allow each pattern of features to shift independently in relationship to the common datum system. The parts inspector would then verify each pattern of holes separately.

Screw thread specification—When GD&T is used to control a screw thread, or when

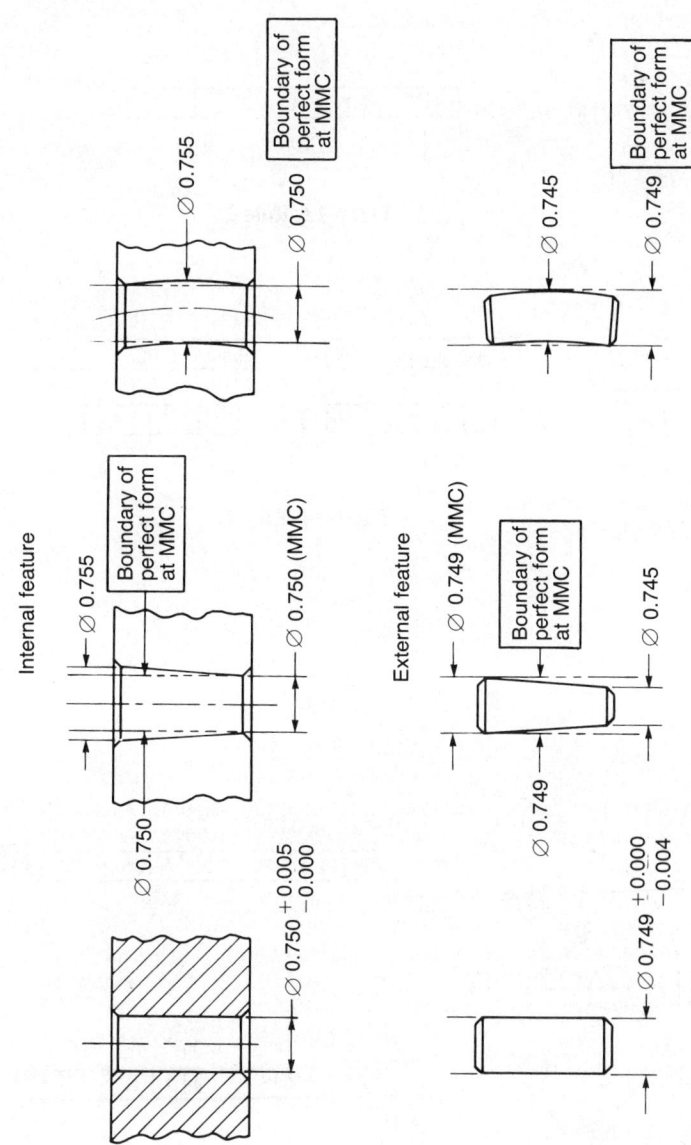

Fig. 6-12 Rule 1.

6-11

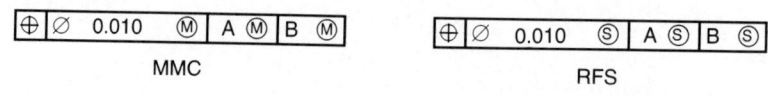

MMC

RFS

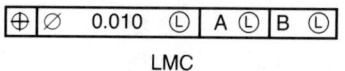

LMC

Fig. 6-13 Rule 2.

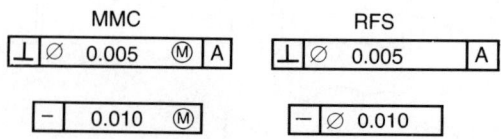

Fig. 6-14 Rule 3.

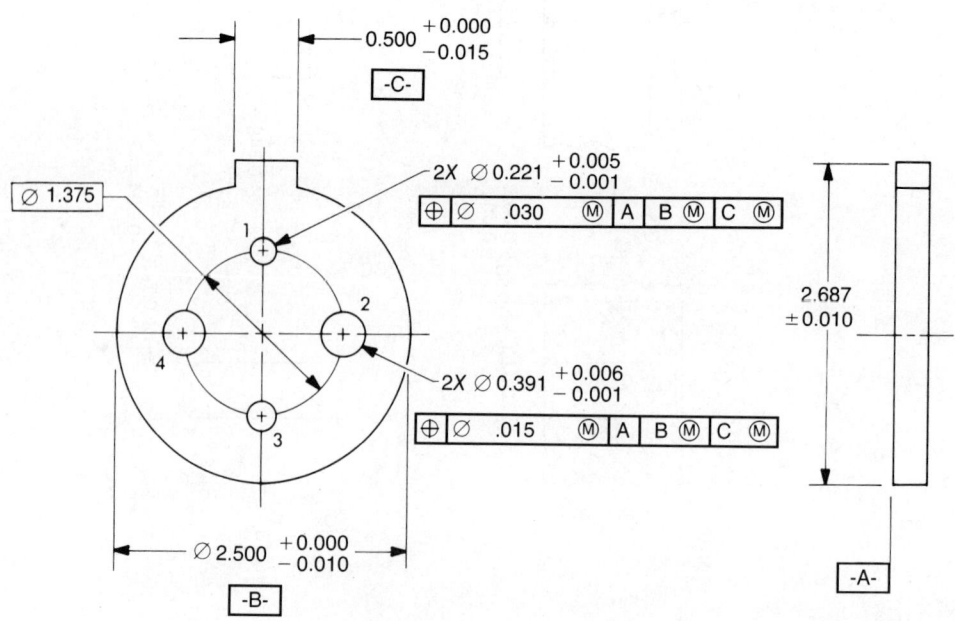

Fig. 6-15 Separate requirements.

a screw thread is designated as a datum, the application applies to the pitch cylinder. Where an exception to this is necessary, the notation MINOR DIA or MAJOR DIA must be added beneath the feature control frame or datum identification symbol (see Fig. 6-16).

Gear and spline specification—When GD&T is used to control a gear or spline, or when a gear or spline is designated as a datum, the notation MINOR DIA, MAJOR DIA, or PITCH DIA must be added beneath the feature control frame or datum identification symbol (see Fig. 6-17).

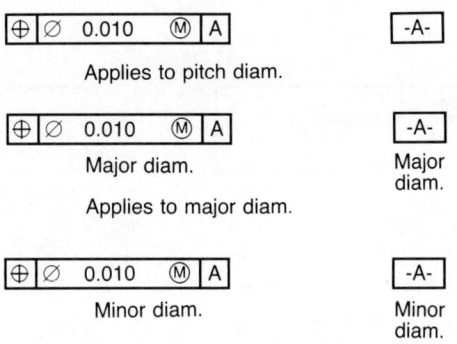

Fig. 6-16 Screw thread datums.

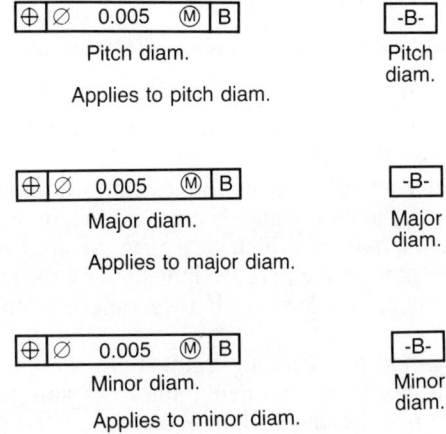

Fig. 6-17 Spline and gear datums.

FORM CONTROL TOLERANCES

The four form control symbols used with tolerances in the feature control frame to control form or shape are as follows:

1. Flatness ▱
2. Straightness ⎯
3. Circularity (Roundness) ○
4. Cylindricity ⌀

Note: Datums are not required or proper with form control tolerances.

Flatness. Flatness is having all elements of a surface in the same plane. The flatness tolerance stipulates a tolerance zone bordered by two parallel planes within which the entire surface must lie. When checking flatness, all elements of the concerned surface must also be within the specified limits of size and the boundary of perfect form at MMC. An example of flatness tolerance and its interpretation is shown in Fig. 6-18.

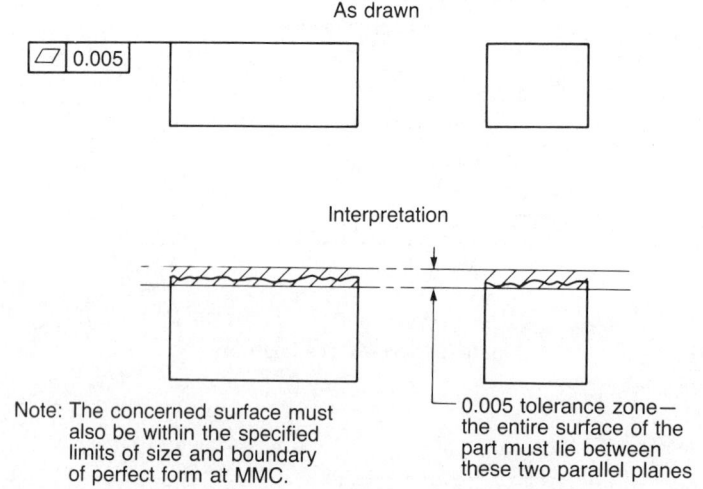

Fig. 6-18 Flatness tolerance and its meaning.

Gaging Methods for Checking Flatness. Various methods of checking flatness are available. Method selection depends on the accuracy required, the size of the part, and the time available to make the check.

One of the most widely used methods for checking flatness is the direct contact method. With this method, the part being checked is brought into direct contact with a reference plane of known flatness which has been covered with a thin coating of prussion blue. The high spots on the part are indicated by the transfer of the blue dye. This method, however, does not lend itself to geometrics since the results are not measurable.

Another common method for checking flatness is with an indicator, height stand, leveling device, and a surface plate of known flatness, as shown in Fig. 6-19.

If the bottom surface is to be checked, *a*, a theoretical flat plane is established by placing three equal length gage blocks on the surface plate to support the part surface to be checked. The entire underside surface is then explored with the test indicator to determine the full indicator movement (FIM), which is the measure of flatness.

If the top surface is to be checked, *b*, the high points of the surface are established by adjusting a leveling plate or leveling screws while exploring with the test indicator. The entire surface is then explored with the test indicator to determine the full indicator movement (FIM), which is the variation in flatness. Variations of this method (the Rahn Planekator Method) using a precision granite straight edge and a special indicator are used to check large areas, such as surface plates.

Figure 6-20 shows a relatively fast and accurate method for checking flatness pro-

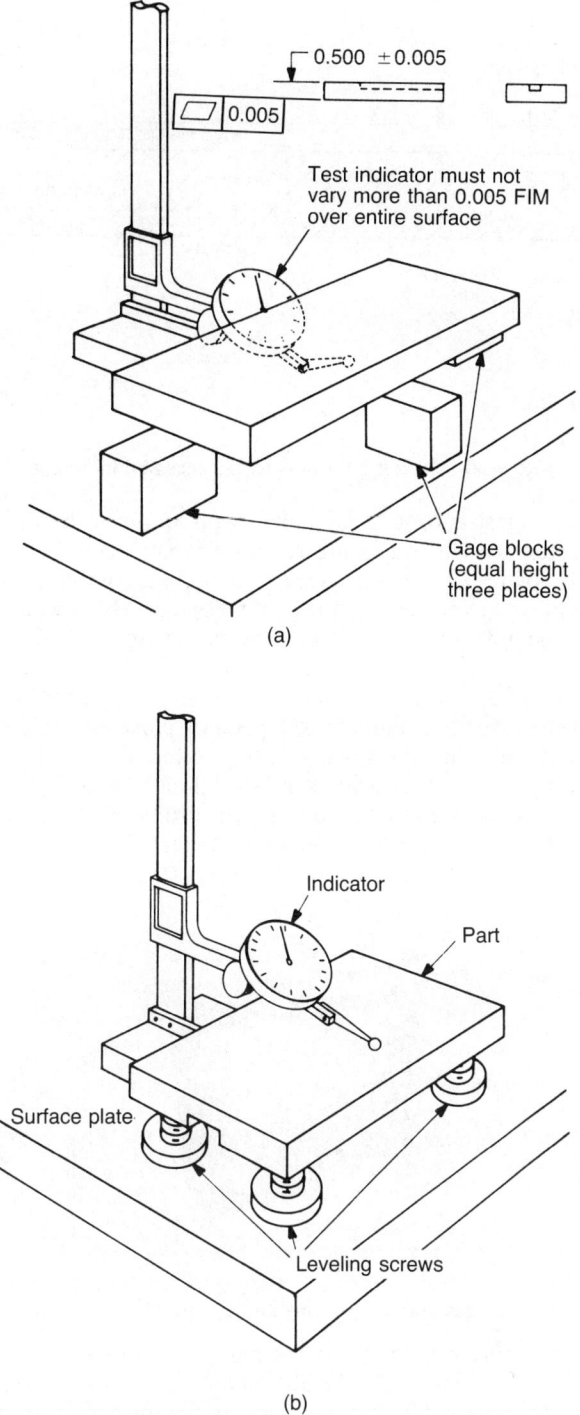

0.500 ±0.005

0.005

Test indicator must not
vary more than 0.005 FIM
over entire surface

Gage blocks
(equal height
three places)

(a)

Indicator

Part

Surface plate

Leveling screws

(b)

Fig. 6-19 Checking flatness: (a), checking the bottom surface; (b), checking the top surface.

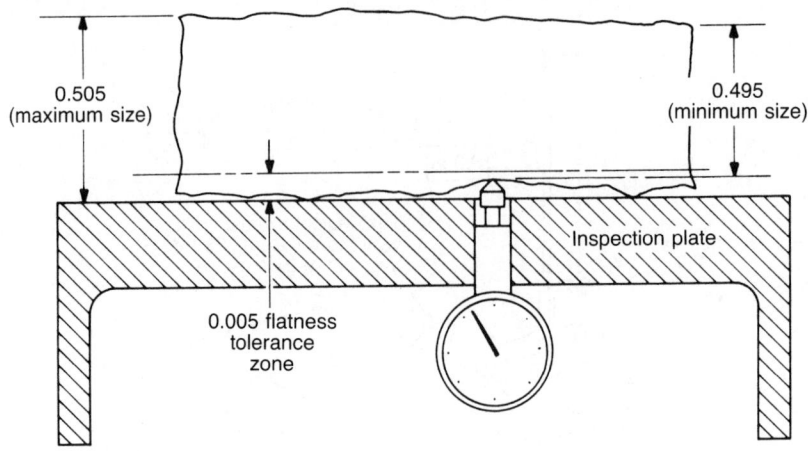

Fig. 6-20 Checking flatness with a recessed indicator.

ductively. The gage consists of a surface plate with an air probe, electronic probe, or mechanical indicator (shown) set into a recessed mount with the measuring contact projecting past the plate surface. To check flatness, the complete surface area to be measured is then passed over the extended contact point which measures and displays the differences of the individual elements on the surface to determine the full indicator movement (FIM).

The combination of an optical flat and a monochromatic light source as shown in Fig. 6-21, is used for checking flatness of lapped or polished surfaces on parts being produced on a production line. Differences from perfect flatness on the surface being checked cause differences in the parallelism, straightness, and spacing of the interference fringes, which are proportional to the flatness error when the optical flat is applied to the surface of the part under the monochromatic light. The phenomenon of interference bands is shown in Fig. 6-22. Different conditions and degrees of flatness error are shown in Fig. 6-23.

Fig. 6-21 Optical flats and a monochromatic light. (*Courtesy Van Keuren Co.*)

For large, accurate surfaces, the inspector must use a precision level or an autocollimator, such as shown in Fig. 6-24. While each of these instruments has a different principle of operation, the use of the instruments for the measurement of flatness is basically the same. In each case, the instrument is used to measure a change in angular rotation of a carriage resting on two feet as the carriage is moved along several tracks on the surface in equal distances. This rotation is changed into linear rise and fall and

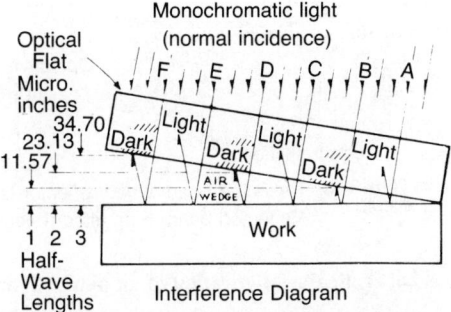

Certain rays, B, D, F, etc., fall where wedge thicknesses are just one, two, three, etc., half—wavelengths, and are reflected partly from the flat and partly from the work. At reflection each of these particular rays interferes with itself, in accordance with optical laws, thus cancelling its own light and appearing from above as a narrow dark band. Since each dark band is like a contour line, it defines a path across the wedge wherever its thickness is exactly uniform. The dark bands are thus useful for precise measurement of work flatness. Other rays, A, C, E, etc., reflect upward without interference and appear as wide alternate bright bands.

Fig. 6-22 The phenomenon of interference bands. (*Courtesy Van Keuren Co.*)

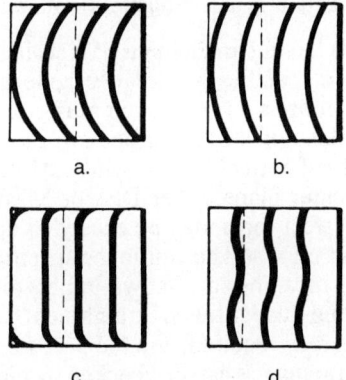

Different conditions and degrees of flatness error. The right edge of the work is in contact with the flat-explanation of patterns follows.

    a. Convex surface: side edges low 11.57 millionths.
    b. Convex surface: side edges low 5.78 millionths.
    c. Nearly flat: side edges low or rounded 5.78 millionths.
    d. Surface both convex and concave: hollow in center, higher each side of center and lower at side edges: error, 3 millionths.

Fig. 6-23 Different conditions and degrees of flatness. (*Courtesy Van Keuren Co.*)

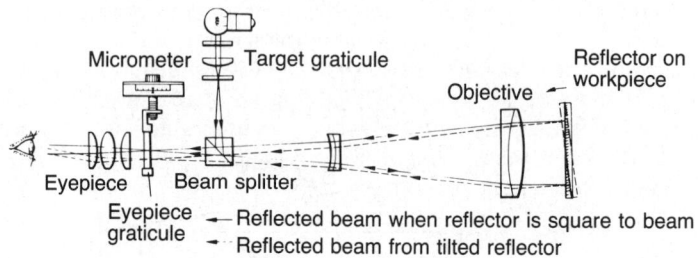

Fig. 6-24 Optical configuration of an autocollimator.

the tracks are related to one another as the surface area is mapped to indicate the changes from a reference plane.

The autocollimator can be used to check surface straightness in the same manner. Figure 6-25 illustrates the checking of flatness and straightness with an autocollimator.

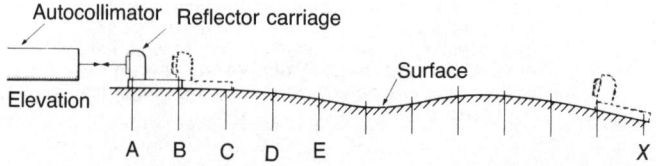

Fig. 6-25 Checking flatness and straightness with an autocollimator.

Straightness. Straightness is having an element of a surface or an axis in a straight line. The straightness tolerance specifies a tolerance zone bordered by two parallel straight lines within which the entire axis or element must lie. When checking straightness of a surface element, all elements of the surface must also be within the specified size tolerance and the boundary of perfect form at MMC. However, when checking the straightness of an axis or a center plane either RFS or MMC, and virtual condition results, and the boundary of perfect form may be exceeded up to the stated tolerance, but each cross sectional element must still be within the specified part size. Examples of straightness tolerance and their meanings are shown in Figs. 6-26 and 6-27.

Gaging Methods for Checking Straightness. Straightness can be checked by various methods depending on the accuracy required, and the part size.

For very small tolerances, straightness can be checked by placing a toolmaker's knife edge directly on the part as shown in Fig. 6-28. Differences in straightness are indicated by the presence and width of light gaps. Deciding straightness by this method, however, does not generally provide measurable results.

Another common method of checking straightness is with gage blocks and a surface plate of known straightness. With this method, the part to be checked is supported at two places equidistant from the surface plate, and the differences from parallel measured along its length with gage blocks or with a test indicator as shown in Fig. 6-29. Cylindrical parts and narrow surfaces are sometimes placed directly on the surface plate and the differences checked with thickness stock.

A more practical and accurate check can be made with a measuring machine or a precision slide. The tracking accuracy of these machines permits checking, with a high degree of resolution, the locations of many separate points along the surface and provides numerical information on any out-of-straight condition.

Figure 6-30 shows an arrangement for checking straightness where the part is mounted on the slide and passed under an indicating device which displays variations from a straight line. Figure 6-31 shows an arrangement where the part is held motionless while an indicating device mounted on a precision slide moves over the part. In both cases, the part must be aligned with the slide track to determine the full indicator movement, unless the equipment is equipped with an auto-level device, which eliminates the need. When these machines are equipped with computer-assist, precision setups are not needed and the condition can be displayed directly.

Large, accurate straightness measurements are made with precision levels, electronic levels, autocollimators, or alignment telescopes using the same methods described for checking flatness.

When straightness of a feature of size is specified MMC, it can be checked with a functional gage. A simple gage to check the straightness of an axis (MMC) on the cylindrical part shown in Fig. 6-26 is shown in Fig. 6-32. A gage to check the straightness of a centerplane (MMC) on the flat part shown in Fig. 6-26 would basically consist of two parallel surfaces 0.510 apart through which the part must pass to be acceptable.

Circularity (Roundness). With respect to a cylinder or cone, circularity is having all elements of the surface intersected by any plane at right angles to a common axis, equidistant from the axis.

With respect to a sphere, circularity is having all points of the surface intersected by any plane passing through a common center, equidistant from that center.

The circularity tolerance specifies a tolerance zone bounded by two concentric circles within which each circular element of the surface must lie. No datum is needed nor proper with a circularity tolerance. When checking circularity, all elements of the surface must also be within the specified size tolerance and boundary of perfect form at MMC to be acceptable. Examples of circularity tolerances and their meaning are shown in Fig. 6-33.

Gaging Methods for Checking Circularity. Although the common method for checking circularity is by indicating a part while it is being rotated in a V-block or between centers, it is not recommended in this text. The many possible sources of error, such as lobing, angle of V-block, center misalignment, etc., contribute to an inaccurate reading of the conditions. Circularity should be checked with a precision rotating spindle, rotating table, or circular tracing instrument, such as shown in Fig. 6-34. Measurement is made by centering the part to be measured on the table, establishing an axis, and placing a stylus in contact with the surface of the circular cross section. The stylus contacts the surface normal to the axis that is being examined to pick up, magnify, and display departures from roundness for determination of any out-of-round. These instruments can be equipped with auto-centering capability, eliminating the need to precisely align the part before checking. Properly equipped, these same instruments can also be used for the complete analysis of circular sections. Figure 6-35 shows a special roundness gage for checking crankshaft journals.

Along with any of the above checks, elements of the surface must be measured separately to assure that they are within the specified size tolerance and the boundary of perfect form at MMC.

Cylindricity. Cylindricity is having all elements on the surface of a cylinder equal distances from a common axis. Cylindricity tolerance specifies a tolerance zone bounded by two concentric cylinders within which the surface must lie. No datum is needed or proper with a cylindricity tolerance. When checking cylindricity, all elements of the concerned surface must also be within the specified size tolerance and the boundary of perfect form at MMC. An example of cylindricity tolerance and its meaning is shown in Fig. 6-36.

Gaging Methods for Checking Cylindricity. Cylindricity is checked with the same equipment that is used to check roundness, except that roundness readings must be

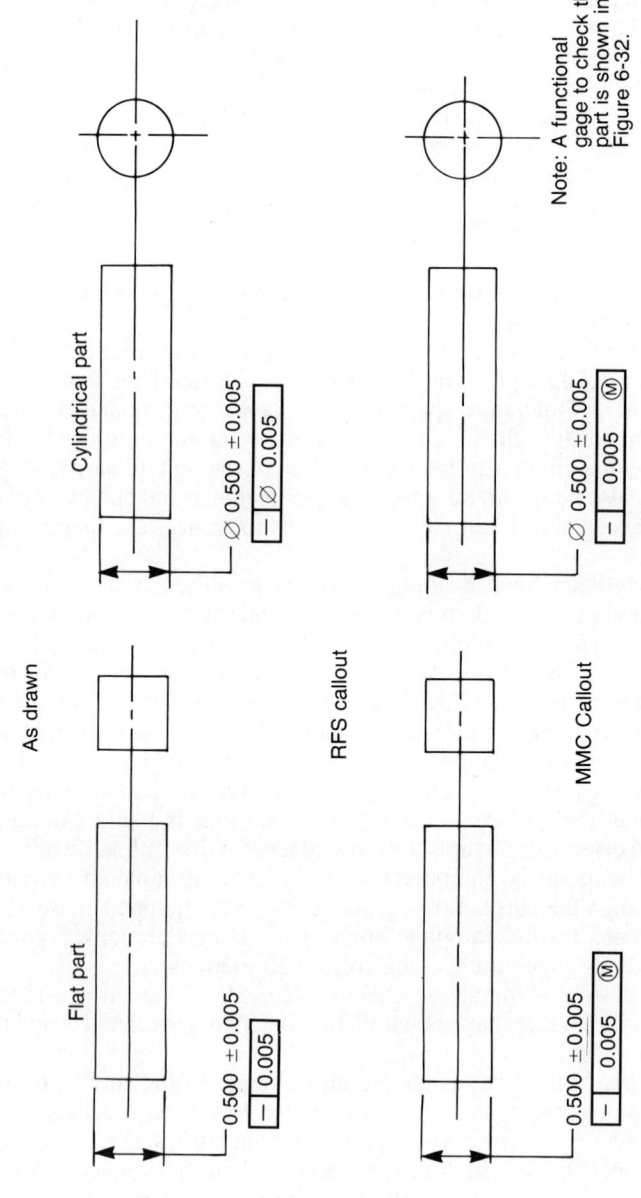

Flat part

As drawn

Cylindrical part

0.500 ± 0.005

| — | 0.005 |

Ø 0.500 ± 0.005

| — | ⌀ | 0.005 |

RFS callout

MMC Callout

0.500 ± 0.005

| — | 0.005 Ⓜ |

Ø 0.500 ± 0.005

| — | 0.005 Ⓜ |

Note: A functional gage to check this part is shown in Figure 6-32.

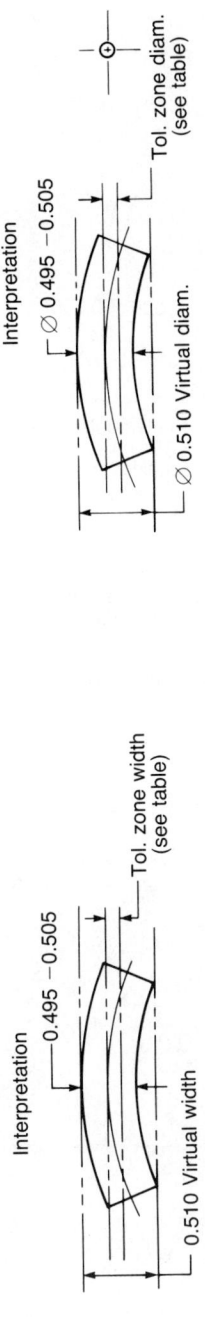

Interpretation

0.495 − 0.505

Tol. zone width
(see table)

0.510 Virtual width

Actual width	Bonus	Tolerance zone width	
		MMC	RFS
0.505 (MMC)	0.000	0.005	0.005
0.504	0.001	0.006	0.005
0.503	0.002	0.007	0.005
0.502	0.003	0.008	0.005
0.501	0.004	0.009	0.005
0.500	0.005	0.010	0.005
0.499	0.006	0.011	0.005
0.498	0.007	0.012	0.005
0.497	0.008	0.013	0.005
0.496	0.009	0.014	0.005
0.495 (LMC)	0.010	0.015	0.005

Interpretation

⌀ 0.495 − 0.505

Tol. zone diam.
(see table)

⌀ 0.510 Virtual diam.

Actual diameter	Bonus	Tolerance zone diameter	
0.505 (MMC)	0.000	0.005	0.005
0.504	0.001	0.006	0.005
0.503	0.002	0.007	0.005
0.502	0.003	0.008	0.005
0.501	0.004	0.009	0.005
0.500	0.005	0.010	0.005
0.499	0.006	0.011	0.005
0.498	0.007	0.012	0.005
0.497	0.008	0.013	0.005
0.496	0.009	0.014	0.005
0.495 (LMC)	0.010	0.015	0.005

Fig. 6-26 Straightness tolerance and its meaning—applied to a feature of size.

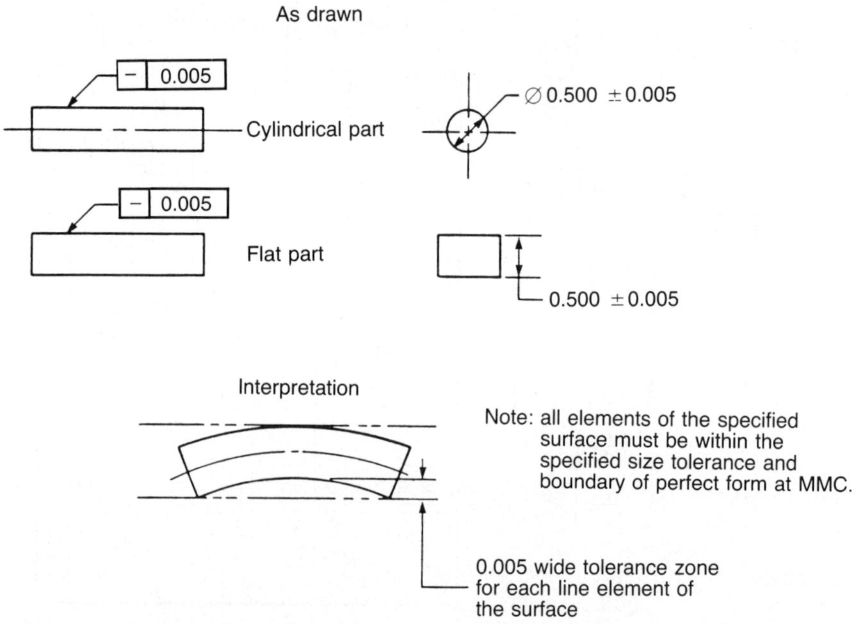

As drawn

-| 0.005

———————— Cylindrical part

⌀ 0.500 ±0.005

-| 0.005

Flat part

0.500 ±0.005

Interpretation

Note: all elements of the specified
surface must be within the
specified size tolerance and
boundary of perfect form at MMC.

0.005 wide tolerance zone
for each line element of
the surface

Fig. 6-27 Straightness tolerance and its meaning—applied to a feature.

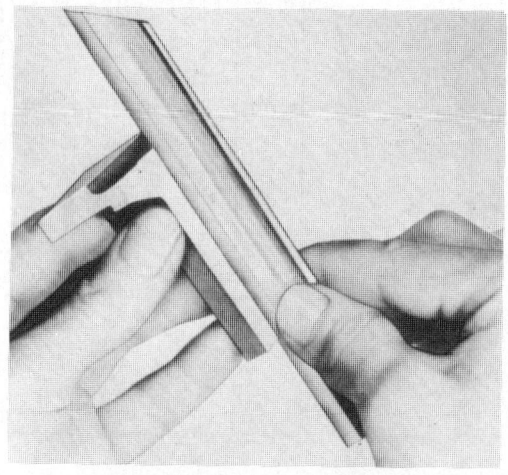

Fig. 6-28 Checking straightness with a toolmaker's straightedge.

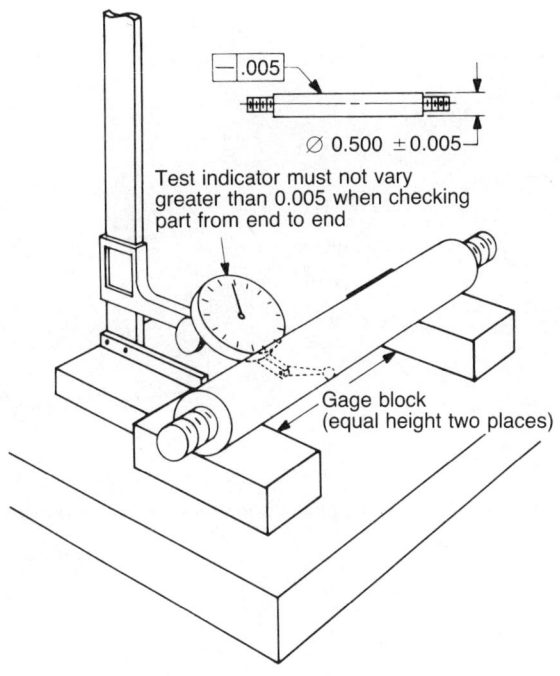

Test indicator must not vary greater than 0.005 when checking part from end to end

Gage block (equal height two places)

Fig. 6-29 Determining straightness on bottom of part surface.

Fig. 6-30 Checking straightness with a part mounted on a slide—indicator fixed. (*Courtesy Pneumo Precision, Inc.*)

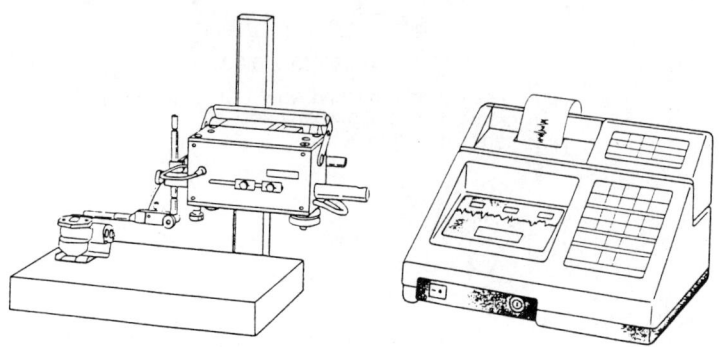

Fig. 6-31 Checking straightness with the part stationary—indicator moving. (*Courtesy Valmet, Inc.*)

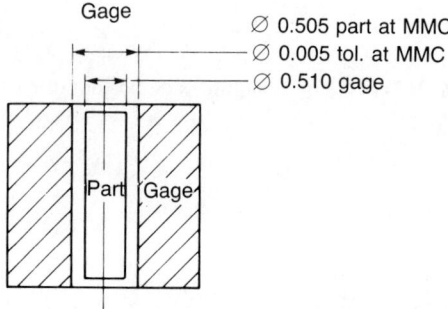

Gage

∅ 0.505 part at MMC
∅ 0.005 tol. at MMC
∅ 0.510 gage

Fig. 6-32 Functional gage to check straightness of an axis MMC—for part shown in Fig. 6-26.

taken at a number of sections along the entire length of the part and placed in order to establish a common axis from which a tolerance zone can be established and measurements made to determine whether or not they fall within the tolerance zone specified. As with the circularity checks, elements of the cylindrical surface must be measured separately to assure that they are within the specified size tolerance and boundary of perfect form at MMC.

PROFILE CONTROL TOLERANCES

The two profile control symbols used with tolerances in the feature control frame to control profile are:

1. Profile of a line ⌒
2. Profile of a surface ⌒

Profile tolerancing is used to specify an allowable deviation from a desired profile where other geometric controls cannot be used. The profile tolerance specifies a uniform boundary along the desired profile within which the elements of the line or surface must lie.

Roundness of a cylinder

As drawn

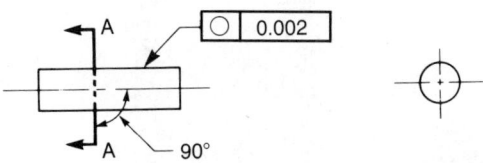

Roundness of a cone

As drawn

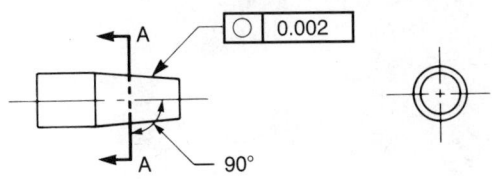

Interpretation

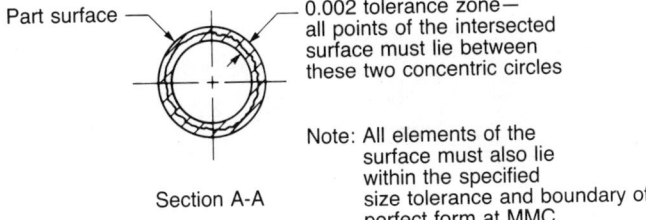

Part surface

0.002 tolerance zone—
all points of the intersected
surface must lie between
these two concentric circles

Note: All elements of the
surface must also lie
within the specified
size tolerance and boundary of
perfect form at MMC.

Section A-A

Fig. 6-33 Circularity tolerance and its meaning.

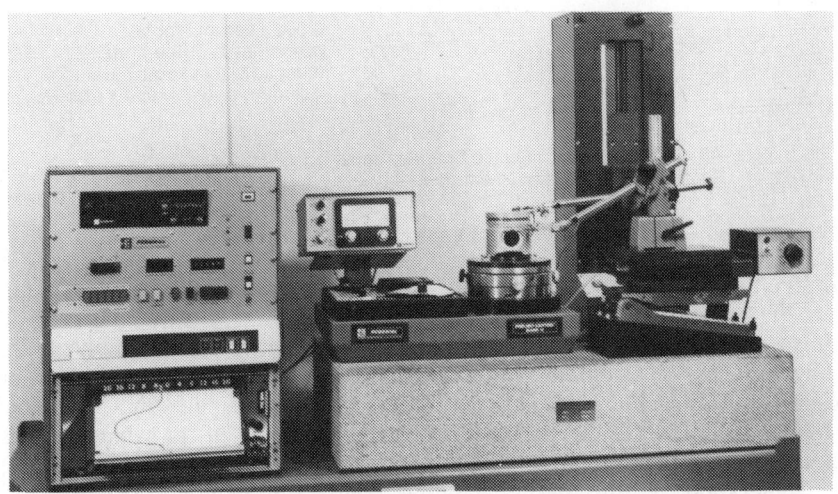

Fig. 6-34 Checking roundness and cylindricity. (*Courtesy Federal Products Corp.*)

Fig. 6-35 Roundness gage for checking crankshafts. (*Courtesy Federal Products Corp.*)

As drawn

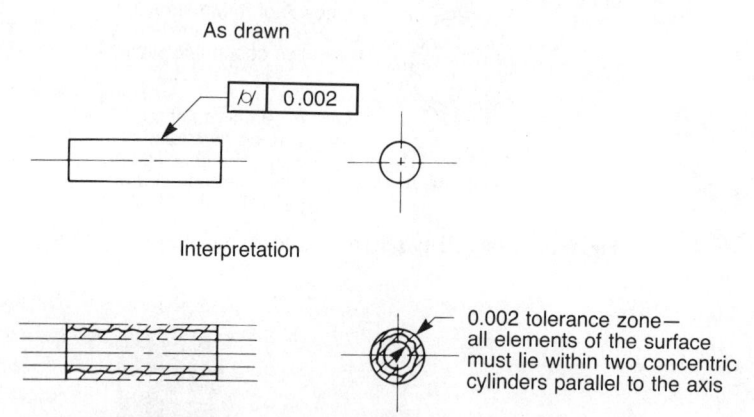

Interpretation

0.002 tolerance zone—
all elements of the surface
must lie within two concentric
cylinders parallel to the axis

Note: All elements of the specified surface must be within the
specified size tolerance and boundary of perfect form at MMC.

Fig. 6-36 Cylindricity tolerance and its meaning.

A profile tolerance can be applied either unilaterally or bilaterally by indicating the intent on the part drawing as shown in Fig. 6-37.

Datums may or may not be necessary to establish proper relationship of the profile to mounting surfaces for assembly purposes, etc. Most profiles are defined using basic dimensions, and as such are not covered by Rule 1, which requires that form control must be contained within the part size tolerance. However, if for whatever reason, conventional size dimensions and tolerances are associated with the profile tolerancing, Rule 1 would apply and the profile would be required to be within the specified size tolerance. Examples of profile tolerances and their meaning are shown in Fig. 6-38.

6-26

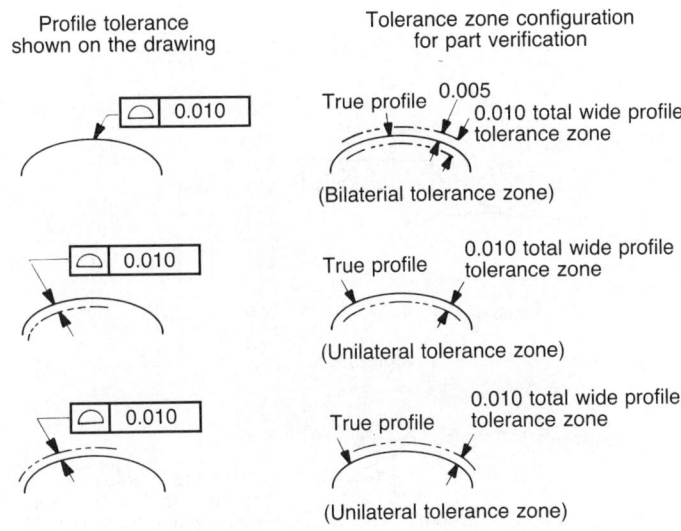

Profile tolerance
shown on the drawing

Tolerance zone configuration
for part verification

0.010

True profile   0.005
                 0.010 total wide profile
                 tolerance zone

(Bilateral tolerance zone)

0.010

True profile   0.010 total wide profile
                 tolerance zone

(Unilateral tolerance zone)

0.010

True profile   0.010 total wide profile
                 tolerance zone

(Unilateral tolerance zone)

Fig. 6-37 Profile tolerance zones.

Gaging Methods for Checking Profiles. Many profiles are checked with contour gages having the opposite form of the nominal contour of the part, as limit gages representing the go and no-go sizes of the part as determined by the maximum and minimum material conditions resulting from the compound effects of the form and size tolerances. Neither of these methods are suitable for GD&T.

One suitable method would be to compare the part with a master profile conforming exactly with the basic dimensions of the part. A method for doing this is shown in Fig. 6-39.

Figure 6-40 shows another generally accepted method which uses a fixture with several indicating devices mounted side-by-side in a plane which contains the profile to be inspected. The indicators must be set with a master representing the basic profile. Conformance of the part to specification is easily determined by reading any part variances directly from the indicators.

For many years small cams and other profiles which could be rotated were checked in a similar manner by having the indicator follow a master part as it and the part were rotated, and reading FIM direct from the indicator. While this method works fine, the cost of a master part is very expensive and usually can only be used to check one part. Modern technology, however, makes it possible to read these profiles directly as they are rotated with accurate long-range digital reading sensors, compare the readings with a perfect master in the memory of a microcomputer and print out any out-of-tolerance conditions along with their location. While machines of this type are fairly expensive, they are completely universal and the software to check a new part can be prepared in a short period of time.

Other methods include optical comparators, coordinate measuring machines, and image recognition systems.

The profile measuring instrument shown in Fig. 6-41 is useful for checking internal as well as external profiles involving small length displacements, such as found with threads. It works on the same principle as the instrument shown in Fig. 6-31, except on a larger scale. As the stylus moves across the profile of the part, the movement is magnified and traced on a timed chart which can be easily interpreted geometrically. For very fine displacements, the actual instrument shown in Fig. 6-31 for checking straightness is often used.

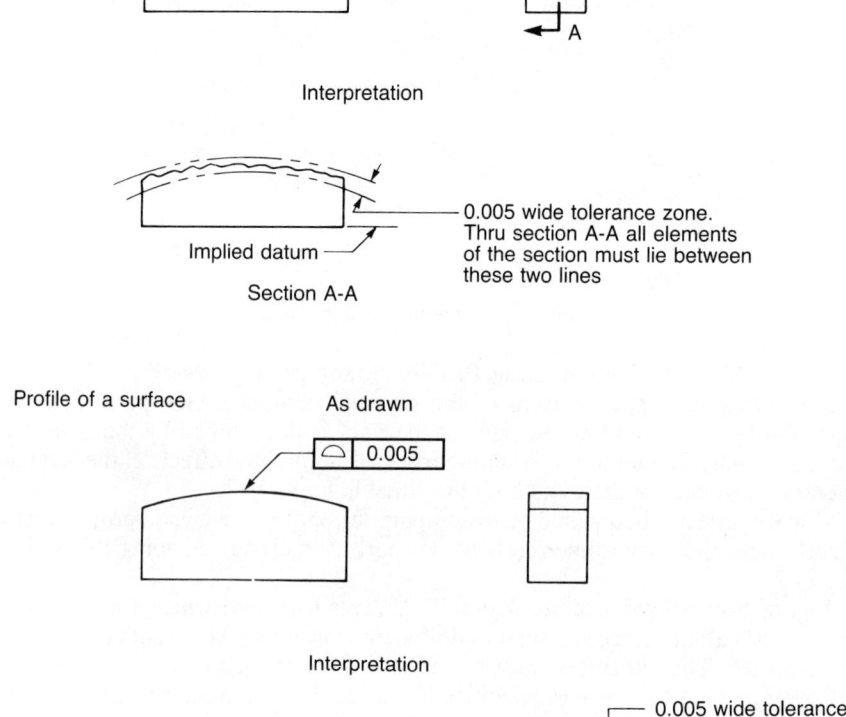

Fig. 6-38 Profile tolerances and their meanings.

ORIENTATION CONTROL TOLERANCES.

The three orientation control symbols used with tolerances in the feature control frame to control orientation are:

1. Perpendicularity ⊥
2. Angularity ∠
3. Parallelism ∥

Perpendicularity (Squareness). Perpendicularity is having all elements of a surface, median plane, or axis exactly 90° from a datum plane or datum axis. A perpendicularity tolerance always requires a datum and is specified by one of the following:

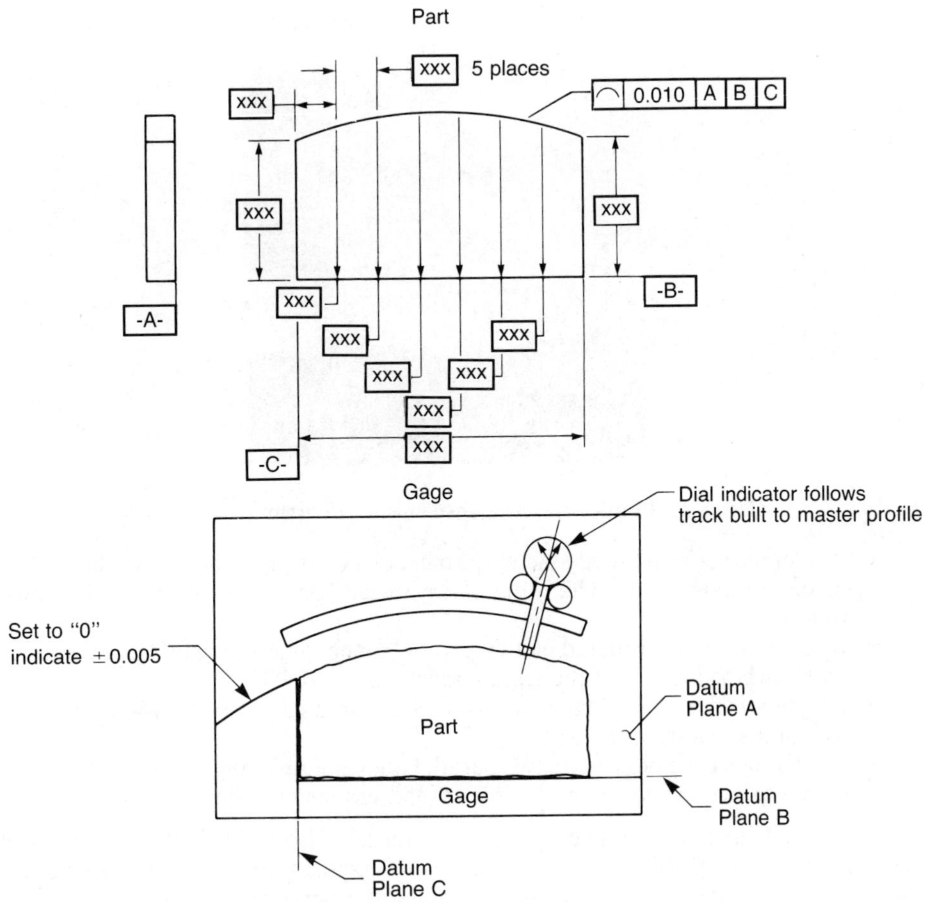

Part

xxx 5 places

⌒ 0.010 A B C

xxx

xxx

xxx

-B-

xxx

-A-

xxx

xxx

xxx

xxx

xxx

xxx

-C-

Gage

Dial indicator follows
track built to master profile

Set to "0"
indicate ± 0.005

Datum
Plane A

Part

Gage

Datum
Plane B

Datum
Plane C

Fig. 6-39 Checking profile—indicator following a master profile.

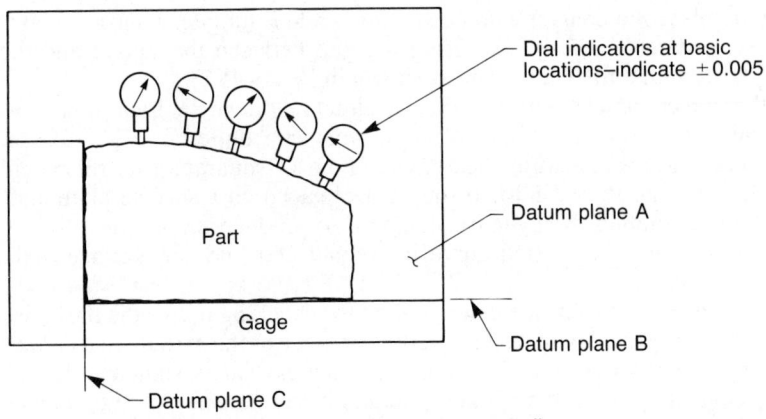

Dial indicators at basic
locations–indicate ± 0.005

Datum plane A

Part

Gage

Datum plane B

Datum plane C

Note: Dial indicators to be set to "0" with master part built
to basic DIMS.

Fig. 6-40 Checking profile—fixed indicators set to master part.

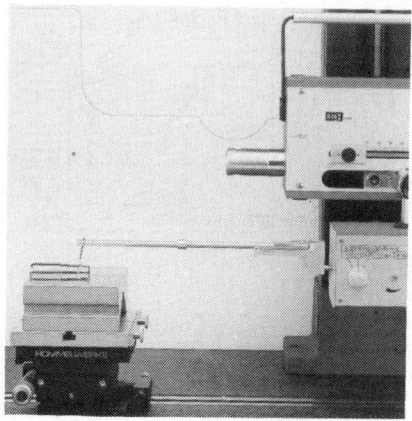

Fig. 6-41 Profile measuring instrument. (*Courtesy Valmet, Inc.*)

- A tolerance zone bordered by two parallel planes at a right angle to a datum plane or datum axis within which the entire surface or median plane of the feature must lie.
- A tolerance zone bordered by two parallel planes at a right angle to a datum axis within which the axis of the feature must lie.
- A cylindrical tolerance zone at a right angle to a datum plane within which the axis of the feature must lie.
- A tolerance zone defined by two parallel lines at a right angle to a datum plane or datum axis within which an element of the surface must lie.

A perpendicularity tolerance applied to a surface also controls the flatness of the surface to the extent of the stated tolerance and requires the surface to be within the stated limits of size. Examples of perpendicularity tolerances and their meanings are shown in Figs. 6-42 thru 6-44.

Gaging Methods for Checking Perpendicularity. The most common method of checking perpendicularity of surfaces (see Fig. 6-42) is by direct comparison with gages of known squareness, such as the precision square. To make this check, the square and the part are placed in contact with each other while resting on a surface plate. Out-of-squareness is determined by measuring the gap between the square and the part at several places with a thickness gage as shown in Fig. 6-45.

Another direct contact method utilizes a direct reading cylindrical square, which is a cylindrical square with one face off-angle and with dotted curves and graduations etched on the surface indicating the amount of out-of-squareness for the bounded area. In use, the part and the cylindrical square are placed on a surface plate and brought together while rotating the cylindrical square to produce the smallest light gap. The number of the top-most dotted curve in contact with the part surface indicates the squareness error.

Another widely used surface plate method for checking perpendicularity is to check whether two preselected points on the vertical surface of the part are in a common plane at right angles to the surface plate that the part and gage are resting on. Measurement is made by contacting the part with the spherical base of the comparator square and the probe of the indicator mounted in the stand as shown in Fig. 6-46. Before the measurement is made, the indicator is set to zero with the aid of a cylindrical square as shown in the same figure.

With this method, multiple checks must be made at varying heights to get an

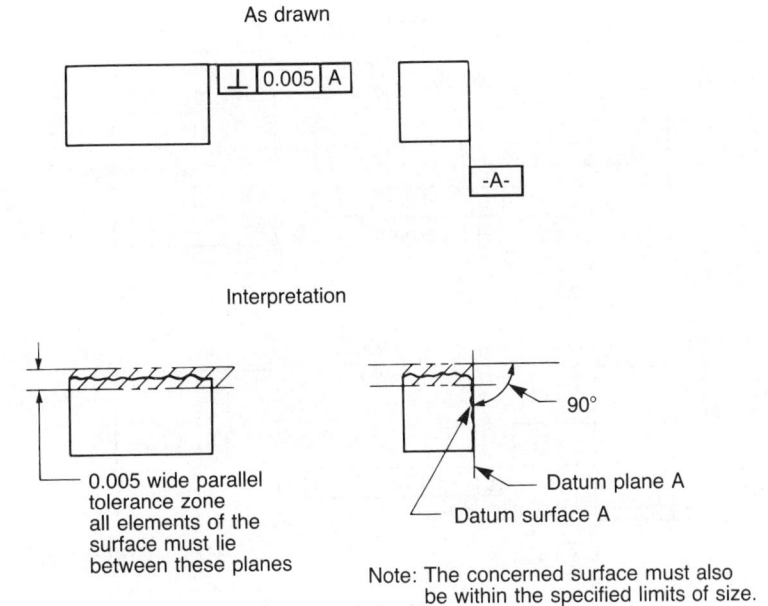

As drawn

⊥ | 0.005 | A

-A-

Interpretation

0.005 wide parallel
tolerance zone
all elements of the
surface must lie
between these planes

90°

Datum plane A

Datum surface A

Note: The concerned surface must also
be within the specified limits of size.

Fig. 6-42 Perpendicularity tolerance and its meaning—for a plane surface.

indication of the complete surface condition.

The squareness gage, shown with its master in Fig. 6-47, measures in a similar manner except that the part surface can be completely indicated in a vertical manner due to the precision guideways built into the gage. Accuracy is maintained by comparing and adjusting the squareness to the master gage.

Large, accurate perpendicular measurements are generally made with an autocollimator, optical square, and reflector stand using a setup as shown in Fig. 6-48.

Sometimes, special fixtures are used, such as those shown in Fig. 6-49, which permit the concerned feature to be searched with indicating depth gages.

None of the above methods, however, are applicable to checking the perpendicularity of a cylindrical feature such as shown in Fig. 6-43 or a non-cylindrical feature as shown in Fig. 6-44. The examples specifying perpendicularity, cylindrical size feature RFS, and noncylindrical feature RFS cannot be checked by functional gaging. They would also be difficult to check economically by other means, since a number of direct or differential measurements would have to be made, just to establish the location of the axis or median plane. For small quantities, the part could be checked by standard layout methods with the help of a simple staging fixture to quickly establish the datum plane at 90° to the surface plate so that the feature was parallel to the surface plate, and then exploring the entire surface with a height stand and indicator as shown in Fig. 6-50. For production quantities, fixtures are generally designed with air or electronic probes properly positioned and connected to determine the squareness of the axis or median plane to the datum surface.

The example specifying perpendicularity of the axis of a cylindrical feature of size MMC could be checked with a functional gage as shown in Fig. 6-51.

Angularity. Angularity is having all elements of a surface or axis at a specified angle (other than 90°) from a datum plane or datum axis. Angularity tolerance specifies a tolerance zone defined by two parallel planes at a specified basic angle from a datum plane or axis, within which the surface or axis of the feature must lie. A datum is always

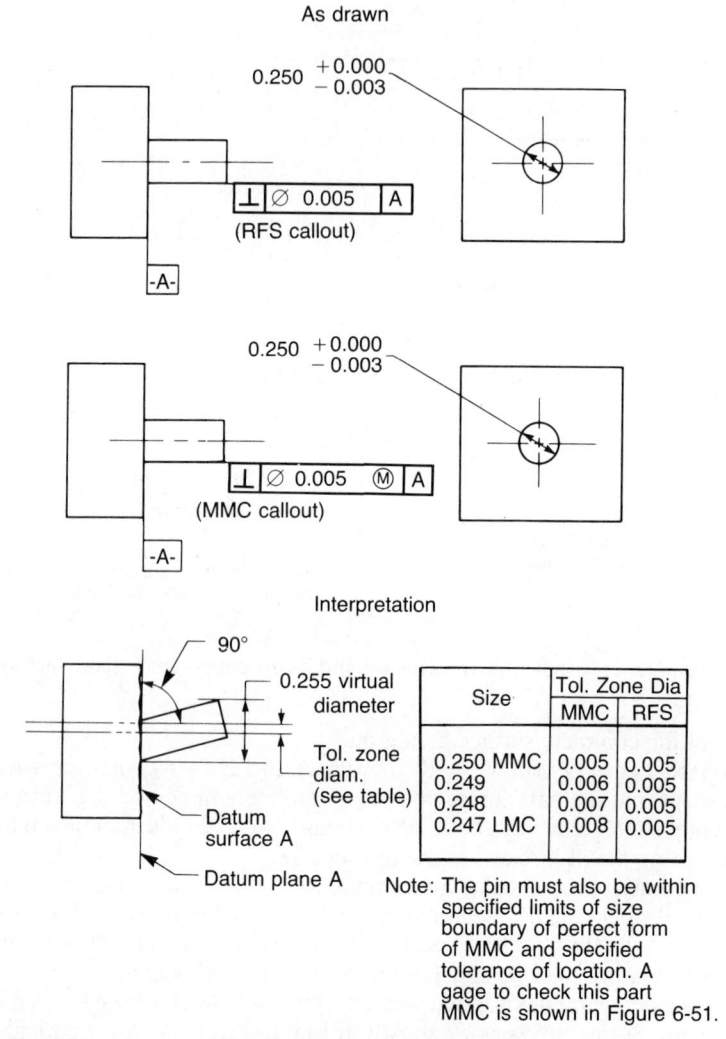

As drawn

$0.250 \begin{array}{c} +0.000 \\ -0.003 \end{array}$

| ⊥ | ⌀ 0.005 | A |

(RFS callout)

-A-

$0.250 \begin{array}{c} +0.000 \\ -0.003 \end{array}$

| ⊥ | ⌀ 0.005 | Ⓜ | A |

(MMC callout)

-A-

Interpretation

90°

0.255 virtual
diameter

Tol. zone
diam.
(see table)

Datum
surface A

Datum plane A

Size	Tol. Zone Dia	
	MMC	RFS
0.250 MMC	0.005	0.005
0.249	0.006	0.005
0.248	0.007	0.005
0.247 LMC	0.008	0.005

Note: The pin must also be within
specified limits of size
boundary of perfect form
of MMC and specified
tolerance of location. A
gage to check this part
MMC is shown in Figure 6-51.

Fig. 6-43 Perpendicularity tolerance and its meaning—for an axis.

required, and the desired angle is always shown as a basic angle. When checking angularity, all elements of the concerned feature must also be within the specified tolerance of location to be acceptable. On surfaces, the angularity includes a control of flatness to the extent of the angularity tolerance. Examples of angularity tolerances and their meaning are shown in Figs. 6-52 and 6-53.

Gaging Methods for Checking Angularity. Angularity tolerance is another RFS tolerance which cannot be checked with functional gaging.

Most short-run parts are checked for angularity with standard surface plate methods. Sine plates or simple staging fixtures are used to place the datum surface of the concerned feature in proper alignment with the surface plate. A height stand and test indicator then are used to check the surface as shown in Fig. 6-54.

For production quantities, fixtures are generally designed with specifically located and interrelated air or electronic probes which determine and then display any out-of-tolerance condition of the feature angle being checked.

As drawn

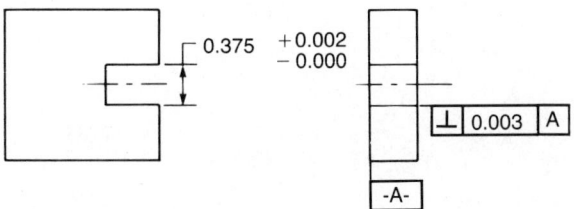

0.375 $\begin{array}{r}+0.002\\-0.000\end{array}$

| ⊥ | 0.003 | A |

-A-

Interpretation

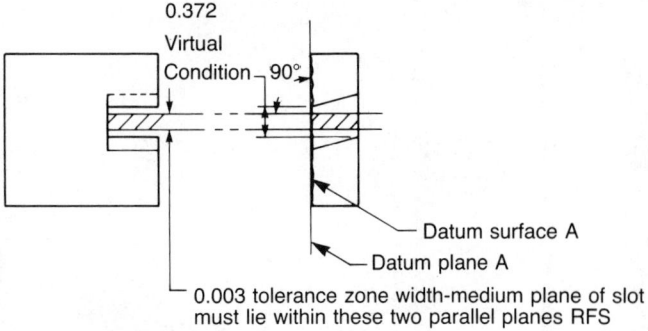

0.372
Virtual
Condition — 90°

— Datum surface A
— Datum plane A

0.003 tolerance zone width-medium plane of slot
must lie within these two parallel planes RFS

Note: Slot must also be within specified limits of size boundary of
perfect form at MMC and specified tolerance of location.

Fig. 6-44 Perpendicularity tolerance and its meaning—for a median plane.

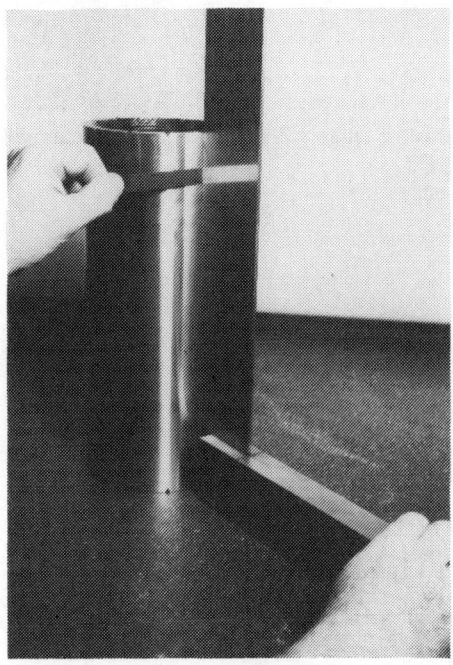

Fig. 6-45 Checking squareness with a square. (*Courtesy L.S. Starrett Co.*)

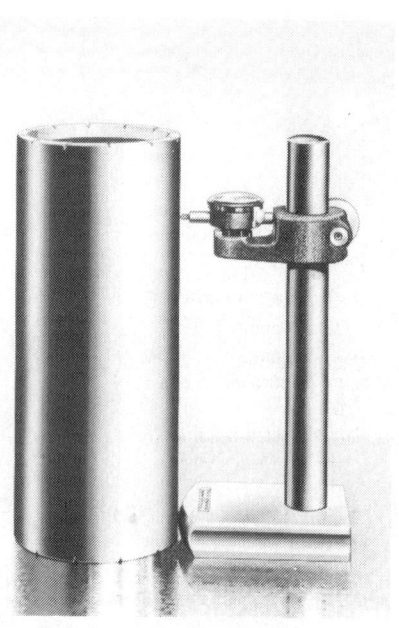

Fig. 6-46 Transfer inspection of squareness using cylindrical and comparator squares.
(*Courtesy Taft Peirce*)

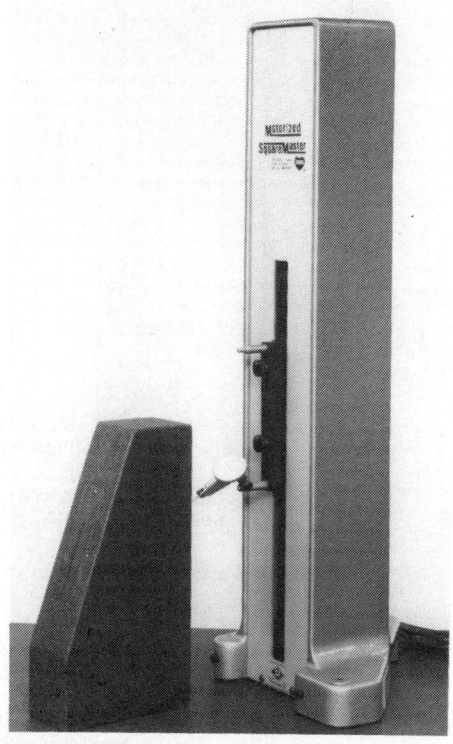

Fig. 6-47 Squareness gage and master.
(*Courtesy PMC Industries*)

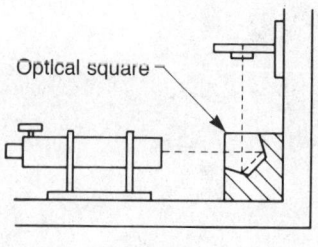

Optical square

Operation

Light beams from the autocollimator which is aligned with the datum plane are turned at an exact right angle with an optical square (pentaprism) which permits the measurement of perpendicularity by observing the reflection from a mirror moved along the second plane.

Fig. 6-48 Checking perpendicularity with an autocollimator.

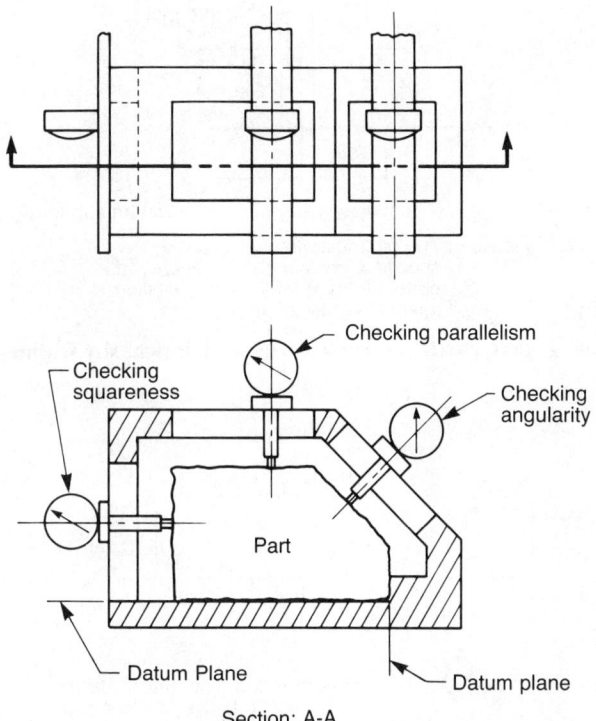

Checking parallelism

Checking squareness

Checking angularity

Part

Datum Plane

Datum plane

Section: A-A

Entire concerned part surface is searched by sliding indicating depth gage around qualified surface. Dimensions can also be checked at the same time by setting the depth gage to a proper master.

Fig. 6-49 Checking squareness, parallelism, and angularity with indicating depth gages.

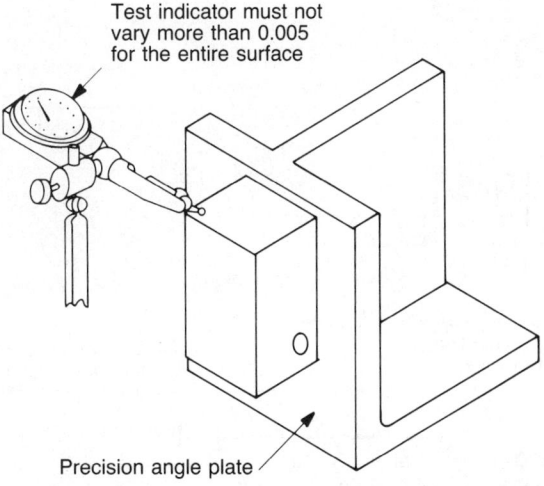

Test indicator must not vary more than 0.005 for the entire surface

Precision angle plate

Fig. 6-50 Checking perpendicularity using an angle plate, height stand, and test indicator.

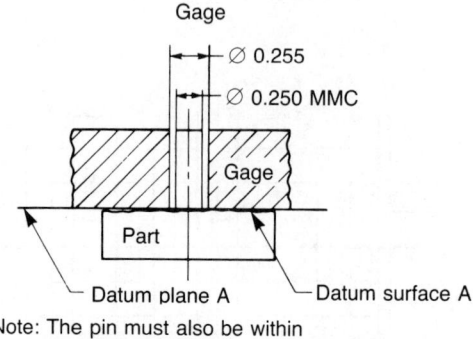

Note: The pin must also be within specified limits of size, boundary of perfect form at MMC, and specified tolerance of location

Fig. 6-51 Functional gage to check perpendicularity—cylindrical size feature, MMC for part shown in Fig. 6-43.

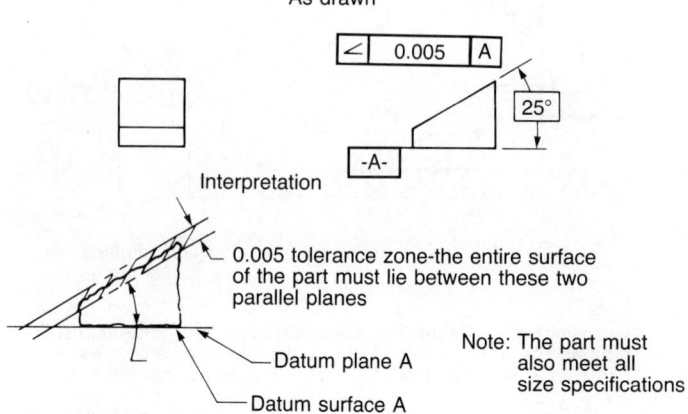

Note: The part must also meet all size specifications

Fig. 6-52 Angularity tolerance and its meaning—for a surface.

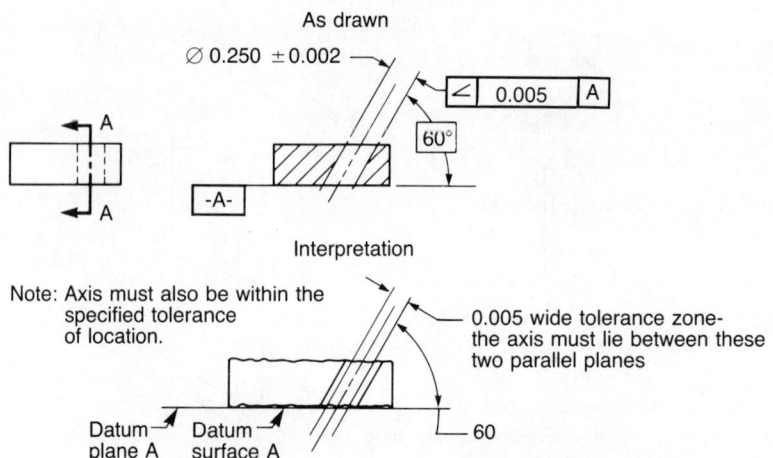

Fig. 6-53 Angularity tolerance and its meaning—for an axis.

6-36

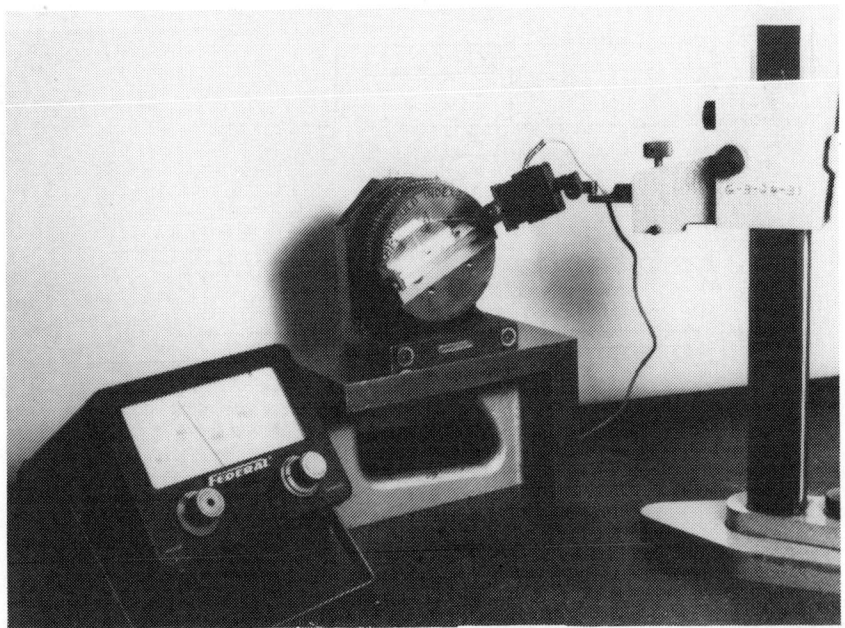

Fig. 6-54 Checking angularity with a height stand and indicator. (*Courtesy Federal Products Corp.*)

Large, accurate angularity measurements are generally made with an autocollimator or special fixtures and indicating depth gages in a manner similar to those shown for checking perpendicularity in Figs. 6-48 and 6-49.

Parallelism. Parallelism is having all elements of a surface, line, or axis equidistant from a datum plane or axis at all points. A parallelism tolerance always requires a datum and is specified by one of the following:

1. A tolerance zone bounded by two parallel planes or lines parallel to a datum plane or datum axis within which the elements of the surface or the axis of the feature must lie.
2. A cylindrical tolerance zone whose axis is parallel to a datum axis within which the axis of the feature must lie.

The parallelism tolerance applied to a surface also controls the flatness of a surface to the extent of the stated tolerance unless otherwise specified. It also requires the entire surface to be within the stated limits of size.

When specifying parallelism for an axis RFS, the axis must be within the stated tolerance of location and lie within a tolerance zone bounded by two parallel planes RFS which are parallel to the datum plane.

When specified MMC, the tolerance zone width increases as the feature of size approaches LMC.

When parallelism is specified as a cylindrical tolerance zone RFS, the axis must be within the stated tolerance of location and lie within a cylindrical tolerance diameter RFS which is parallel to the datum. When specified MMC the tolerance zone diameter increases as the feature of size approaches LMC.

Examples of parallelism tolerances and their meaning are shown in Figs. 6-55 and 6-56.

Gaging Methods for Checking Parallelism. Parallelism of a surface is generally checked by placing the datum of the part on a surface plate and searching for any

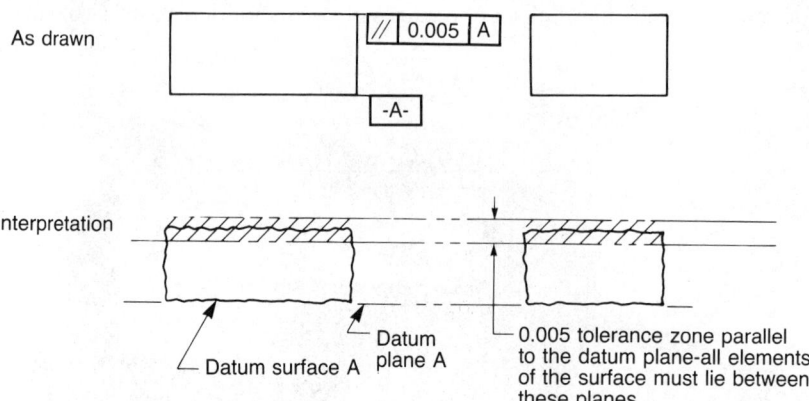

As drawn

// 0.005 A

-A-

Interpretation

Datum
plane A

Datum surface A

0.005 tolerance zone parallel
to the datum plane-all elements
of the surface must lie between
these planes

Note: All elements of the surface must also be within the
specified size limits

Fig. 6-55 Parallelism tolerance and its meaning—for a surface.

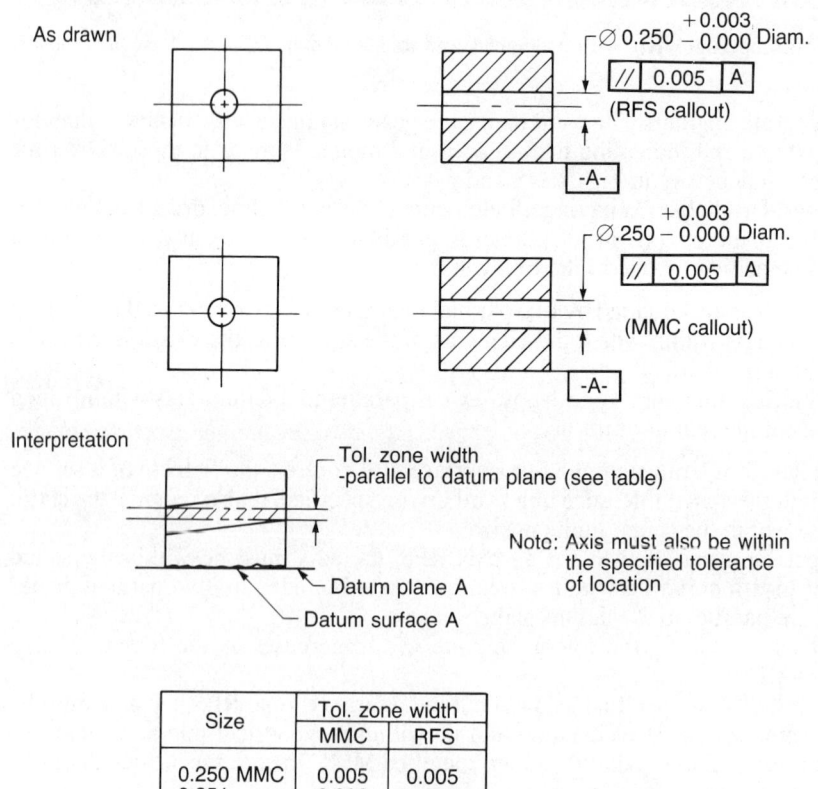

As drawn

$\varnothing\ 0.250\ {\substack{+0.003 \\ -0.000}}$ Diam.

// 0.005 A

(RFS callout)

-A-

$\varnothing.250\ {\substack{+0.003 \\ -0.000}}$ Diam.

// 0.005 A

(MMC callout)

-A-

Interpretation

Tol. zone width
-parallel to datum plane (see table)

Note: Axis must also be within
the specified tolerance
of location

Datum plane A

Datum surface A

Size	Tol. zone width	
	MMC	RFS
0.250 MMC	0.005	0.005
0.251	0.006	0.005
0.252	0.007	0.005
0.253 LMC	0.008	0.005

Fig. 6-56 Parallelism tolerance and its meaning—for an axis.

out-of-parallel conditions with a height stand and indicator as shown in Fig. 6-57. A surface plate setup to check parallelism of the axes of two cylindrical features of size is shown in Fig. 6-58.

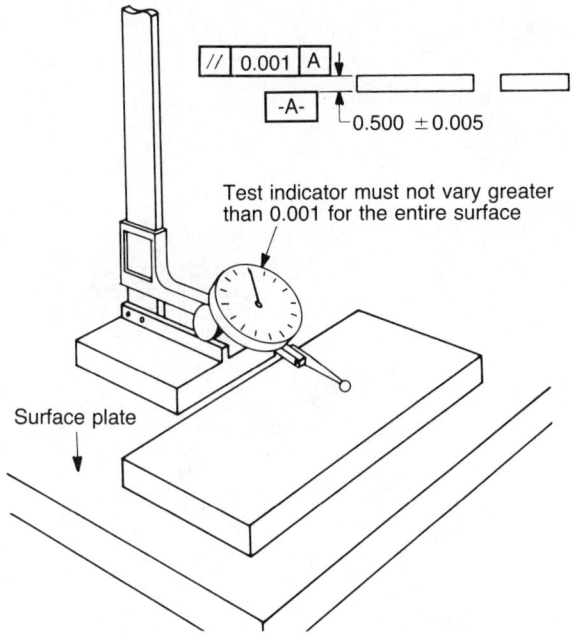

Fig. 6-57 Checking parallelism of a surface with a height stand and indicator.

Many times, a part must be placed in a special fixture to check perpendicularity, angularity, location, etc. In these cases, a check for parallelism is generally incorporated in the same fixture as shown in Fig. 6-49.

When parallelism concerns cylindrical size features of datums, the inspection becomes more difficult especially when the feature, datum, or both are RFS. Here again, standard layout methods using a surface plate, height stand, and indicator can be used for small quantities as long as the inspector understands the meaning expressed by the feature control symbol.

Figure 6-59 shows a design approach that can be used to check the parallelism of these cylindrical size features.

RUNOUT TOLERANCES

The two runout symbols used to control runout are as follows:

1. Circular runout ⟋
2. Total runout ⟋⟋

Runout is the composite deviation from the desired form of a part surface when the part is rotated 360° about a datum axis. The runout tolerance specifies the FIM allowed during the 360° rotation. Runout tolerance is always applied on an RFS basis and always requires a datum. It is used to maintain surface-to-axis control on a part.

Circular runout ⟋ controls only circular elements of a surface individually and independently from one another. Total runout ⟋⟋ provides composite control of all surface elements at the same time. When checking runout, all elements of the con-

6-39

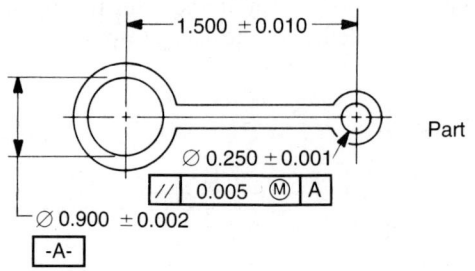

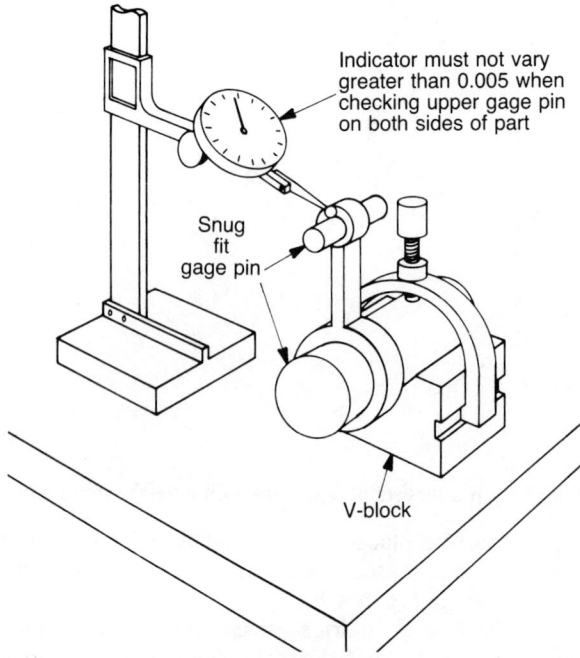

Fig. 6-58 Surface plate check of parallelism of two cylindrical features of size.

cerned surface must also be within the specified limits of size and the boundary of perfect form at MMC. Examples of runout tolerances and their meaning are shown in Fig. 6-60.

Gaging Methods for Checking Runout Tolerances. Checking runout on a part on which the datum axis is established by two centers in the part is relatively simple and easily understood. Low production parts are generally mounted between the centers of a bench center and rotated 360° with a test indicator in contact with the surface to be checked, as shown in Fig. 6-61. For high production, special fixtures using several air, electronic, or mechanical indicators, such as shown in Fig. 6-62 and 6-63, are generally more practical.

Parts where the datum axis is established by two functional IDs or ODs are generally checked in the same manner, except that the datum is established by expanding or closing in on the datum diameters with expanding arbors or chucks, as shown previously in Fig. 3-81, and taking a reading in the same manner as from centers.

Another method widely used with electronic gaging allows the part to be mounted in any suitable fashion while indicating the datums, as well as features, to be checked. The

Part

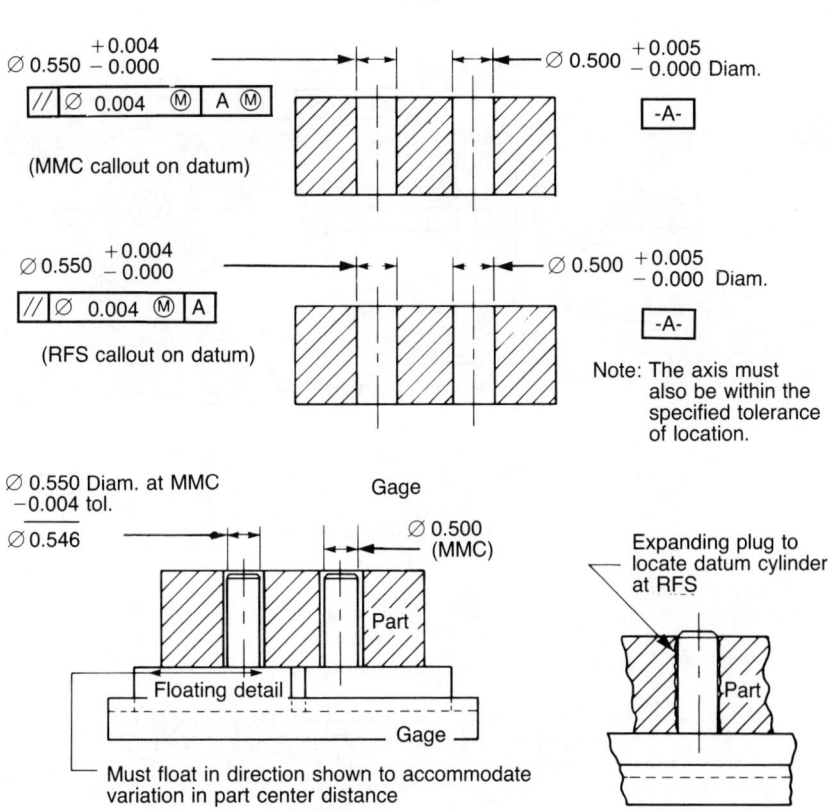

$\varnothing\ 0.550\ {}^{+0.004}_{-0.000}$

| // | $\varnothing$ 0.004 | Ⓜ | A | Ⓜ |

(MMC callout on datum)

$\varnothing$ 0.500 ${}^{+0.005}_{-0.000}$ Diam.

-A-

$\varnothing\ 0.550\ {}^{+0.004}_{-0.000}$

| // | $\varnothing$ 0.004 | Ⓜ | A |

(RFS callout on datum)

$\varnothing$ 0.500 ${}^{+0.005}_{-0.000}$ Diam.

-A-

Note: The axis must
also be within the
specified tolerance
of location.

$\varnothing$ 0.550 Diam. at MMC
−0.004 tol.
$\varnothing$ 0.546

Gage

$\varnothing$ 0.500
(MMC)

Part

Floating detail

Gage

Must float in direction shown to accommodate
variation in part center distance

Expanding plug to
locate datum cylinder
at RFS

Part

Gage shown is for datum at MMC (for datum at RFS, the 0.500 diam. pin
would be replace with an expanding plug as shown in inset)

Fig. 6-59 Gage for checking parallelism—cylindrical tolerance zones.

readings are then automatically adjusted electronically within the equipment and the runout displayed directly.

Methods of checking runout on parts where the datum is established from a diameter, or a combination of datum diameter and functional face, are shown in Figs. 6-64 thru 6-66. In all of these cases, the cylindrical datums must be established with expanding arbors or chucks, or established electronically as previously noted since runout is always RFS.

LOCATION TOLERANCES

The two location tolerance symbols used to control location are as follows:

1. Position $\oplus$
2. Concentricity ◎

Location tolerances are used to control:

- The location of a feature(s) of size from a datum(s)
- Centerdistance between features of size
- Concentricity of features of size (Coaxiality)
- Symmetry of features of size

6-41

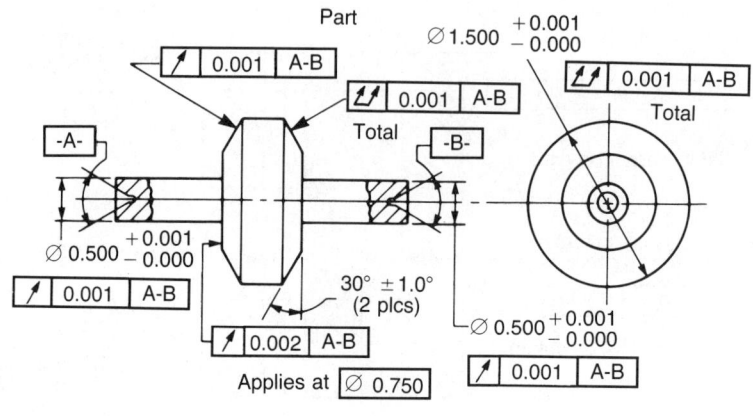

Part

Interpretation

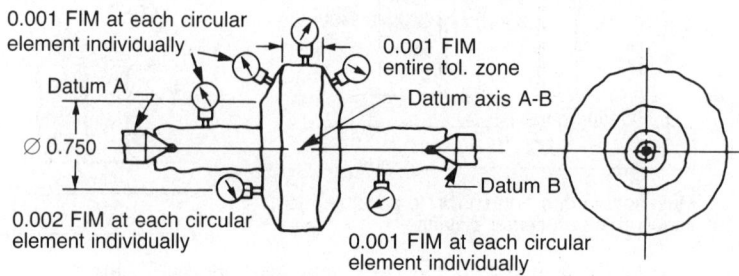

Rotate part 360° to check

0.001 FIM at each circular element individually

0.001 FIM entire tol. zone

Datum A

Datum axis A-B

∅ 0.750

Datum B

0.002 FIM at each circular element individually

0.001 FIM at each circular element individually

Nctes:
1. Indicators to be normal to surface being checked
2. All features concerned must be within their specified limits of size and boundary of perfect form at MMC.

Fig. 6-60 Runout tolerance and its meaning.

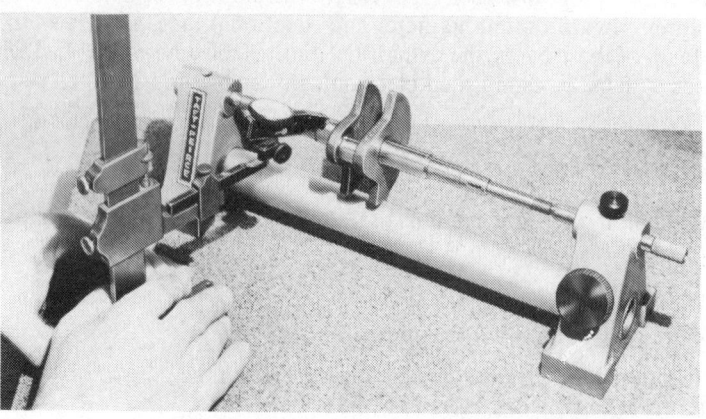

Fig. 6-61 Checking runout with standard inspection tools. (*Courtesy Taft Peirce*)

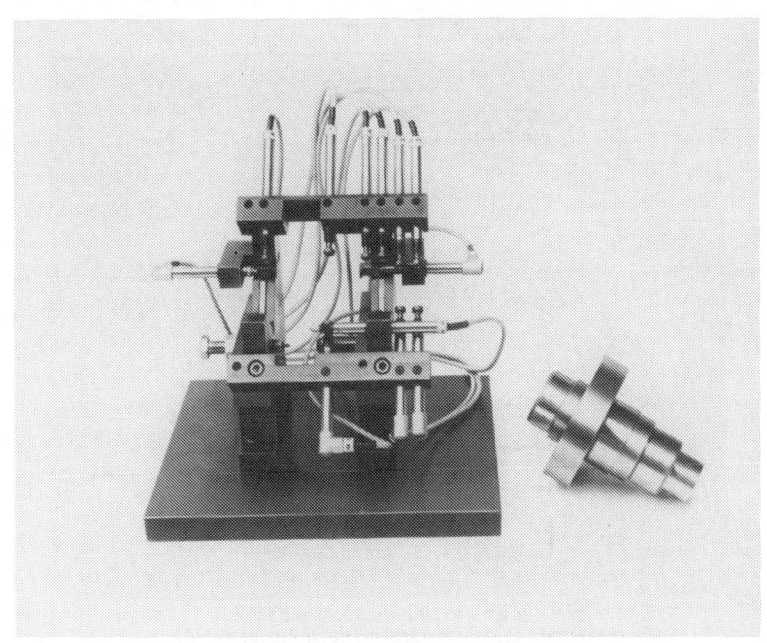

Fig. 6-62 Fixture for checking runout.

Fig. 6-63 Checking runout with non-contact gaging. (*Courtesy Dearborn Gage Co.*)

6-43

Part

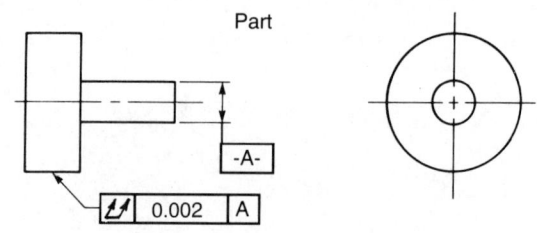

-A-

⟋⟍	0.002	A

Method of checking

0.002 FIM–entire cylindrical
tol. shown as part is rotated
360°

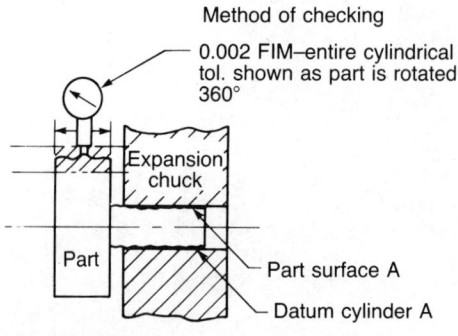

Expansion
chuck

Part

Part surface A

Datum cylinder A

Notes:
1. Datum cylinder axis must be established RFS.
2. All concerned features including datum must be within the
   specified limits of size and boundary of perfect form at MMC.

Fig. 6-64 Checking runout from an OD datum.

Location tolerances are applied only to a feature of size and one of the modifiers LMC, MMC, or RFS must be specified in the feature control frame with each tolerance and with any datum that is a feature of size. Datums are always required except when specifying the alignment of features of size which have already been located from a datum with another tolerance of position. Basic dimensions are used to describe the exact size or location of a feature of size.

Position. Position tolerance, formerly called true position tolerance, is a tolerance of location which is used to define a tolerance zone within which the center, axis, or centerplane of a feature of size may vary from the theoretically exact location (true position) shown on the part drawing. Positional tolerance interpretation and bonus tolerance is shown in Fig. 6-67.

Position tolerance is three-dimensional and extends over the length of the feature unless otherwise specified. The position tolerance for cylindrical parts is the diameter of a cylinder equal to the tolerance, within which the axis of the feature of size must lie, as shown in Fig. 6-68. This figure also shows how position tolerance indirectly controls orientation. For noncylindrical parts such a slots, tangs, etc., position tolerance is the width of a zone equal to the tolerance, within which the centerplane of the feature of size must lie.

Gaging Methods for Checking Position Tolerances. For short runs, position tolerance is usually checked with a height stand, test indicator, and surface plate equipment. With this method, parts are mounted from the specified datums and X-Y measurements taken and recorded. The X-Y results obtained from such an inspection can then be converted to position tolerances using conversion charts or the formulas shown earlier in the chapter.

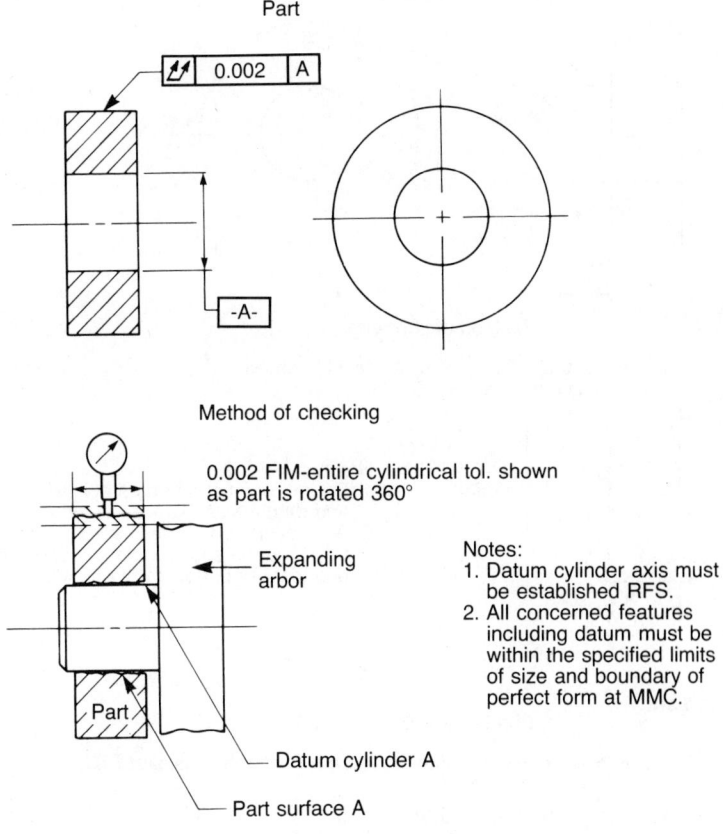

Part

0.002 A

-A-

Method of checking

0.002 FIM-entire cylindrical tol. shown
as part is rotated 360°

Expanding
arbor

Notes:
1. Datum cylinder axis must
   be established RFS.
2. All concerned features
   including datum must be
   within the specified limits
   of size and boundary of
   perfect form at MMC.

Part

Datum cylinder A

Part surface A

Fig. 6-65 Checking runout from an ID datum.

Another method of checking *X-Y* results for conformance to position tolerancing is by the use of graphical inspection analysis techniques wherein deviations from basic locations are plotted on graph paper and compared with a transparent overlay chart on which the position tolerance zone has been drawn.

When position tolerance is applied in an MMC basis, it allows functional gaging to be used. Some examples are shown in Fig. 6-69 thru 6-81.

Figure 6-69 shows two identical parts containing clearance holes and assembled with two 0.5 diameter bolts. Each part can be dimensioned and toleranced as shown, with MMC specified after the hole location tolerance. Also shown is a hole relation gage for checking the parts. Hole relation gages such as these check hole-to-hole relationship, not hole location to some other part feature. The gage could be made using fixed pins in place of the separate gage pins shown which fit tight into nominally located bushings in the gage.

Location and squareness are controlled by the actual difference in size between the gage pin and the clearance hole feature. Because feature size will vary from hole to hole, from part to part, and from process to process, the true tolerance is a variable ranging from 0.010 to 0.020 since the ⌀ 0.500 bolt or gage pin and the interchangeable design requirement remains a constant. The positional tolerance is ⌀ 0.010 only at MMC, which in this case is where the hole diameter is 0.510.

Substituting RFS for the MMC callout would make gaging difficult, since the gage pin must always be 0.010 smaller than the actual hole size. Eleven or more gage pins

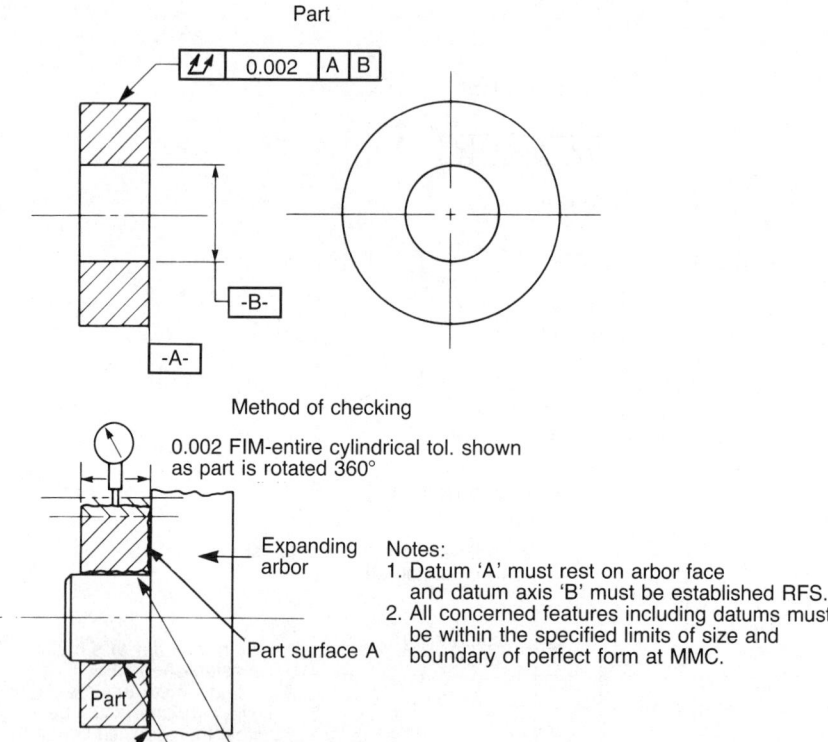

Fig. 6-66 Checking runout from a functional face and ID.

would be required for each hole $\varnothing 0.500$, $\varnothing 0.501$, $\varnothing 0.502$, etc., so that, if a particular hole measured $\varnothing 0.512$, the $\varnothing 0.502$ gage would be used, etc.

Figure 6-70 shows how the true tolerance varies with hole size. All tolerances greater than 0.010 diameter are bonus tolerances and are only available when the position tolerance is applied MMC.

Figure 6-71 shows the tolerances and gages for the manufacture and assembly of two different parts. One part contains clearance holes and the other part contains holes tapped for $\varnothing 0.500$ bolts. Gage thickness or bushing height on both gages must be at least the maximum thickness of the mating part to guarantee that the bolts will be properly located and square for assembly. Two GO thread gages simulate the bolts at assembly. The gage bushing size for the gage to check part 2 is determined by adding the $\varnothing 0.010$ positional tolerance to the $\varnothing 0.500$ bolt size. Stepped gage pins with GO threads may be used to take advantage of standard bushing size as long as a $\varnothing 0.010$ difference is maintained between the gage bushing and that portion of the gage pin that lies within the bushing.

Basic Design Rules for Positionally-Toleranced Parts. Two basic rules govern the design of gages for positionally toleranced parts. These principles apply regardless of the number of features that make up an interchangeable pattern.

1. For parts with internal features, the nominal gage feature size is directly determined by subtracting the total positional tolerance specified at MMC from the specified MMC size of the feature to be gaged for location.

2. For parts with external features, the nominal gage feature size is directly determined by adding the total positional tolerance specified at MMC to the specified MMC size of the feature to be gaged for location.

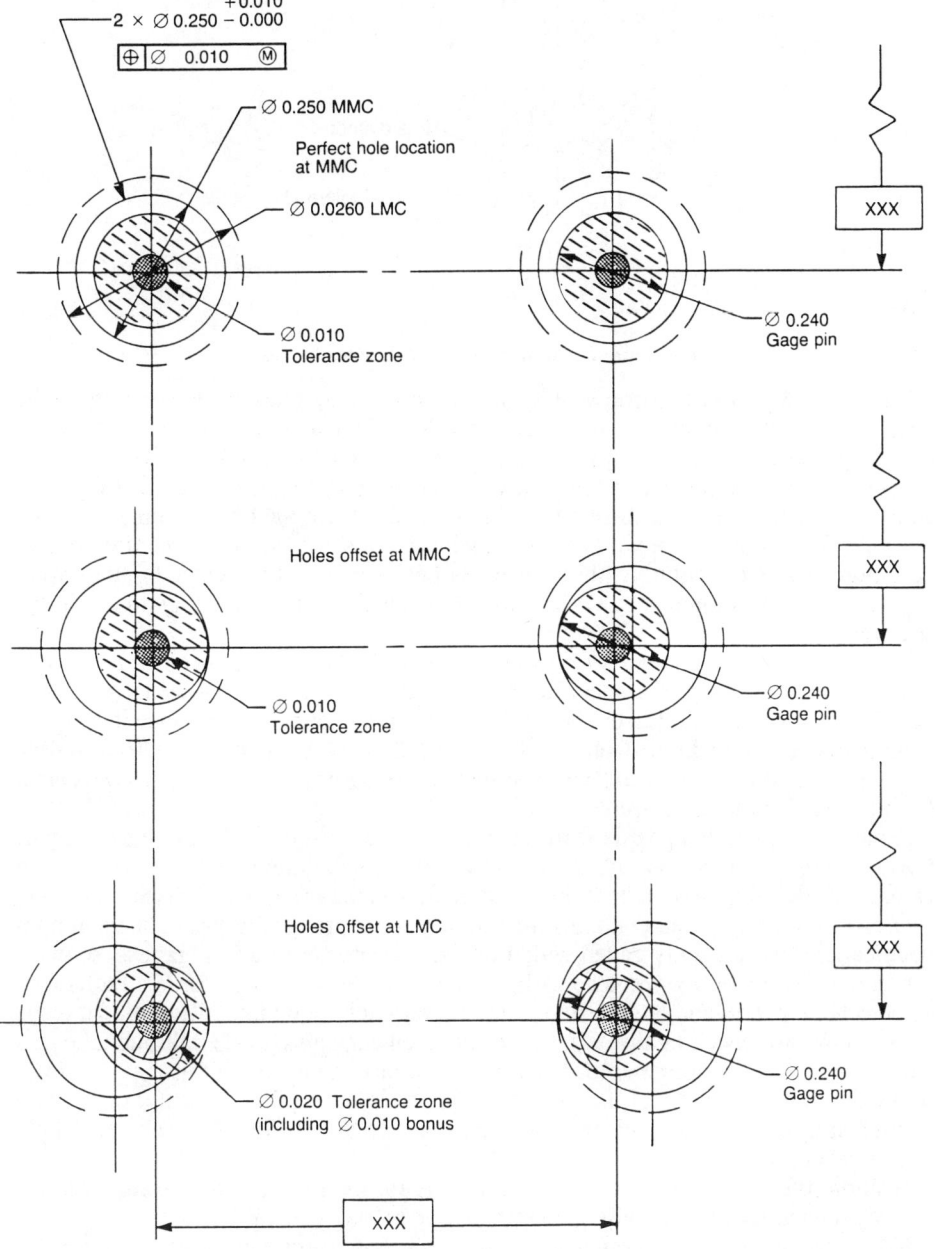

$2 \times \varnothing\, 0.250 \begin{smallmatrix} +0.010 \\ -0.000 \end{smallmatrix}$

| ⊕ | ∅ | 0.010 | Ⓜ |

∅ 0.250 MMC

Perfect hole location at MMC

∅ 0.0260 LMC

∅ 0.010 Tolerance zone

∅ 0.240 Gage pin

Holes offset at MMC

∅ 0.010 Tolerance zone

∅ 0.240 Gage pin

Holes offset at LMC

∅ 0.020 Tolerance zone (including ∅ 0.010 bonus

∅ 0.240 Gage pin

XXX

XXX

XXX

XXX

Fig. 6-67 Position tolerance interpretation and bonus tolerance.

6-47

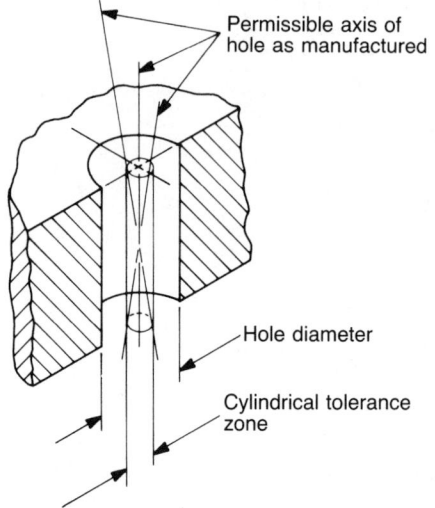

Fig. 6-68 Position tolerance cylindrical zone.

Figure 6-72 shows a workpiece with four holes that must be located from the specific center (datum) of the workpiece regardless of the actual workpiece size (RFS). The design specification drawing includes the exact pickup points so that the same center can be repeatedly found. Also shown is a hole relation gage which uses four dial indicators to determine and correctly position the datum for the hole gaging operation.

Figure 6-73 shows a similar workpiece with the less critical MMC requirement on the datum diameter requiring that the holes be located in the center of the datum diameter when the datum is at MMC. Also shown is the design of a gage to check the part functionally.

Figure 6-74 shows another workpiece in which the holes never need to be exactly located from the center of a specified datum feature. A gage fit allowance has been specified that is directly reflected in the size of the datum gage feature since the gage is 0.995 in diameter and differs from the MMC size of the part diameter (1.000) by 0.005. Quite a large allowance could be specified if the datum was merely a convenient starting place for manufacturing.

A pattern of interchangeable features (holes) is the most critical feature on the part shown in Fig. 6-75, but is not locationally critical in relation to any single datum feature. The 0.300 minimum breakout specification is the result of a stress analysis, and is an end-product requirement. No single datum is specified, and the 0.300 minimum specification can be readily gaged with a tubing micrometer or a fork gage as shown.

Figure 6-76 shows a workpiece with seven holes. The specified positional tolerance includes the location and angularity tolerances for each radial hole. Also shown is the gage required for checking the part. In use, all seven gage pins must go through the part at one time. In designating the datum, if RFS callouts had been used instead of MMC for the diameter and width of the slot, the gage would be required to center on the two datum features. As a result, one gage pin could be used to individually qualify each hole in reference to the datum.

Position tolerance is often used to control the location of coaxial mating part features, as shown in Fig. 6-77, along with the gages to check them.

Figure 6-78 shows the method used to check bore alignment functionally when specified MMC. Another common application of position tolerance MMC is on noncylindrical mating parts, such as shown in Fig. 6-79.

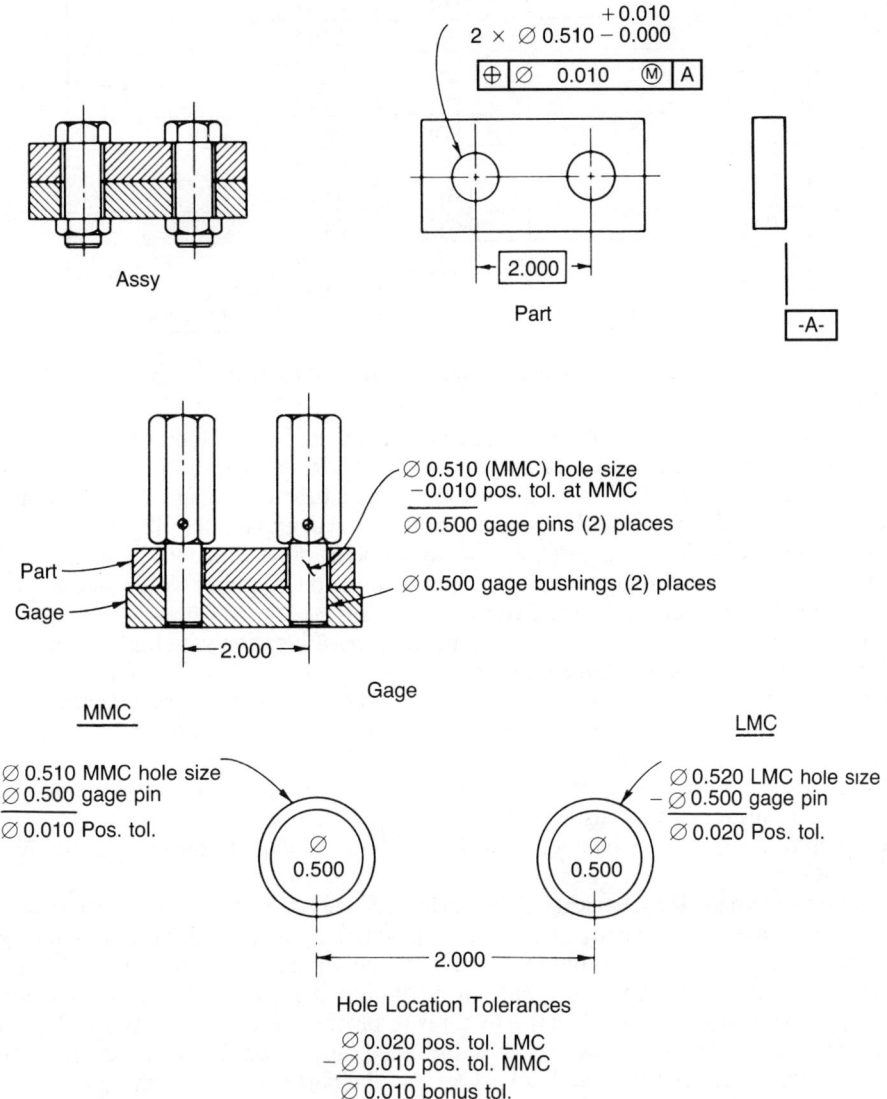

Fig. 6-69 Two parts with clearance holes, assembled with bolts.

Occasionally, a projected tolerance zone will be specified to prevent interference at assembly as shown in Fig. 6-80, along with its interpretation.

A case where it was desired to place all the usable size and location tolerances into the size limit by stating the position tolerance as zero (0.000) at MMC is shown in Fig. 6-81, along with the functional gage to check the part. It should be noted that the gage eliminates the need for a go-plug gage check.

Functional gaging generally becomes more expensive when position tolerance is

Feature diameter	Bonus tolerance	Positional and squareness tolerances diameter
0.510 (MMC or most critical size)	0.000	0.010 at MMC (tightest tolerance)
0.511	0.001	0.011
0.512	0.002	0.012
0.513	0.003	0.013
0.514	0.004	0.014
0.515	0.005	0.015
0.516	0.006	0.016
0.517	0.007	0.017
0.518	0.008	0.018
0.519	0.009	0.019
0.520 (LMC or least critical size)	0.010	0.020 at LMC (loosest tolerance)

Fig. 6-70 Variable tolerances allowed by MMC.

applied MMC and a datum feature of size is specified RFS, since the axis or centerplane of the datum must be exactly established prior to checking location MMC. Figure 6-82 shows a part with an RFS datum callout along with a functional gage to check it. In this case, the exact center of the datum is established by an expanding plug prior to trying the gage pins. Checks of this sort are now mainly being done with coordinate measuring machines equipped with tapered probes or electronic touch probes which automatically determine the exact center of the datum.

Concentricity. Concentricity is another tolerance of location which is used to maintain axis-to-axis control on an RFS basis. It is having two or more solid features of size, in any combination, sharing a common axis. A concentricity tolerance specifies the diameter of a cylindrical tolerance zone within which the axis of the feature or features must lie. The axis of the tolerance zone must coincide with the axis of the datum feature or features which are always required. When checking concentricity, all elements of the concerned surfaces must also be within the specified size limits of the part to be acceptable. An example of a concentricity tolerance and its meaning is shown in Fig. 6-83.

Gaging Methods for Checking Concentricity. Since concentricity tolerance is always on an RFS basis, it requires that the datum axis be established by expanding type devices which close onto or into the part, or by electronic means previously described under runout, which allows the part to be mounted in any suitable fashion while indicating the datums as well as the features to be checked. The results are electronically interpreted and any eccentricity is displayed directly on the readout. All features must also be measured separately to assure that the part conforms to the specified size tolerances.

Symmetry. Symmetry is being the same size, shape, and distance from a centerplane on both sides of a part. Symmetry is specified using the position tolerance symbol applied RFS. This callout specifies a tolerance zone bounded by two parallel planes equidistant from the centerplane of the datum feature of size, which is always required. When checking symmetry, all elements of the concerned feature of size must also be within the specified size limits of the part to be acceptable. An example of position tolerance being used to specify symmetry and its interpretation is shown in Fig. 6-84. The old method of specifying symmetry is shown in the figure for comparison.

Gaging Methods for Checking Symmetry. Symmetry is checked by placing the part on a surface plate and measuring and recording the distance from the surface plate to

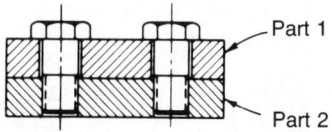

Part 1

Part 2

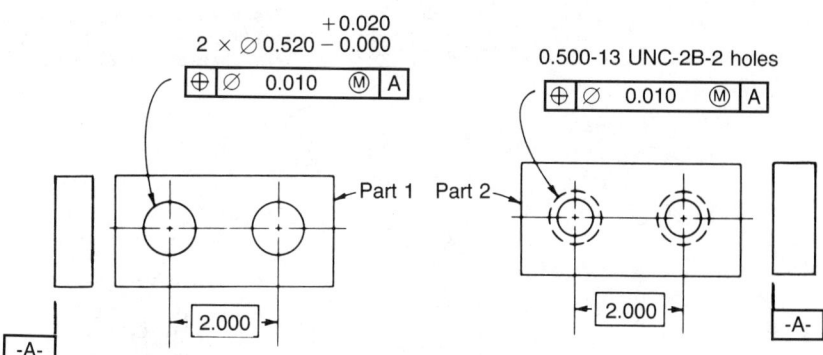

$2 \times \varnothing 0.520 \begin{smallmatrix} +0.020 \\ -0.000 \end{smallmatrix}$

| ⊕ | ⌀ | 0.010 | Ⓜ | A |

0.500-13 UNC-2B-2 holes

| ⊕ | ⌀ | 0.010 | Ⓜ | A |

Part 1   Part 2

2.000

2.000

-A-

-A-

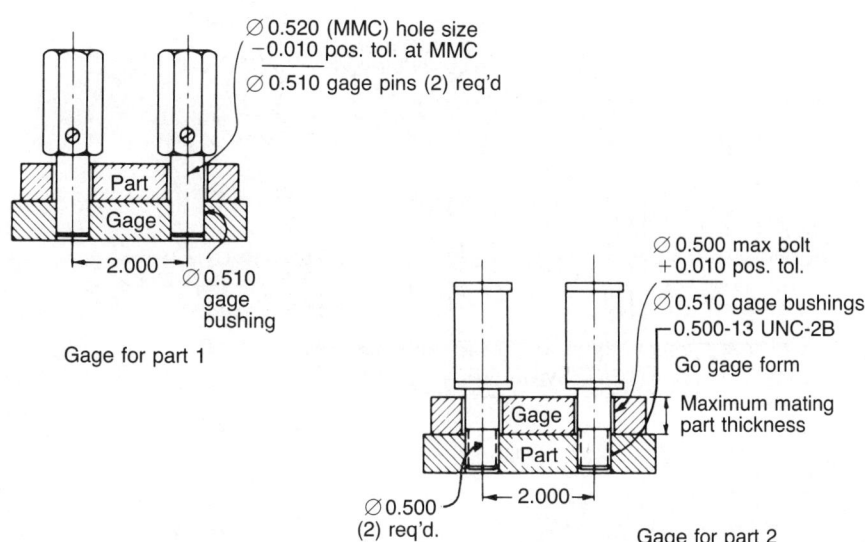

⌀ 0.520 (MMC) hole size
−0.010 pos. tol. at MMC

⌀ 0.510 gage pins (2) req'd

Part

Gage

2.000

⌀ 0.510
gage
bushing

Gage for part 1

⌀ 0.500 max bolt
+0.010 pos. tol.

⌀ 0.510 gage bushings
0.500-13 UNC-2B

Go gage form

Maximum mating
part thickness

Gage

Part

⌀ 0.500
(2) req'd.

2.000

Gage for part 2

Fig. 6-71 Tolerance and gages for the manufacture and assembly of two mating parts.

6-51

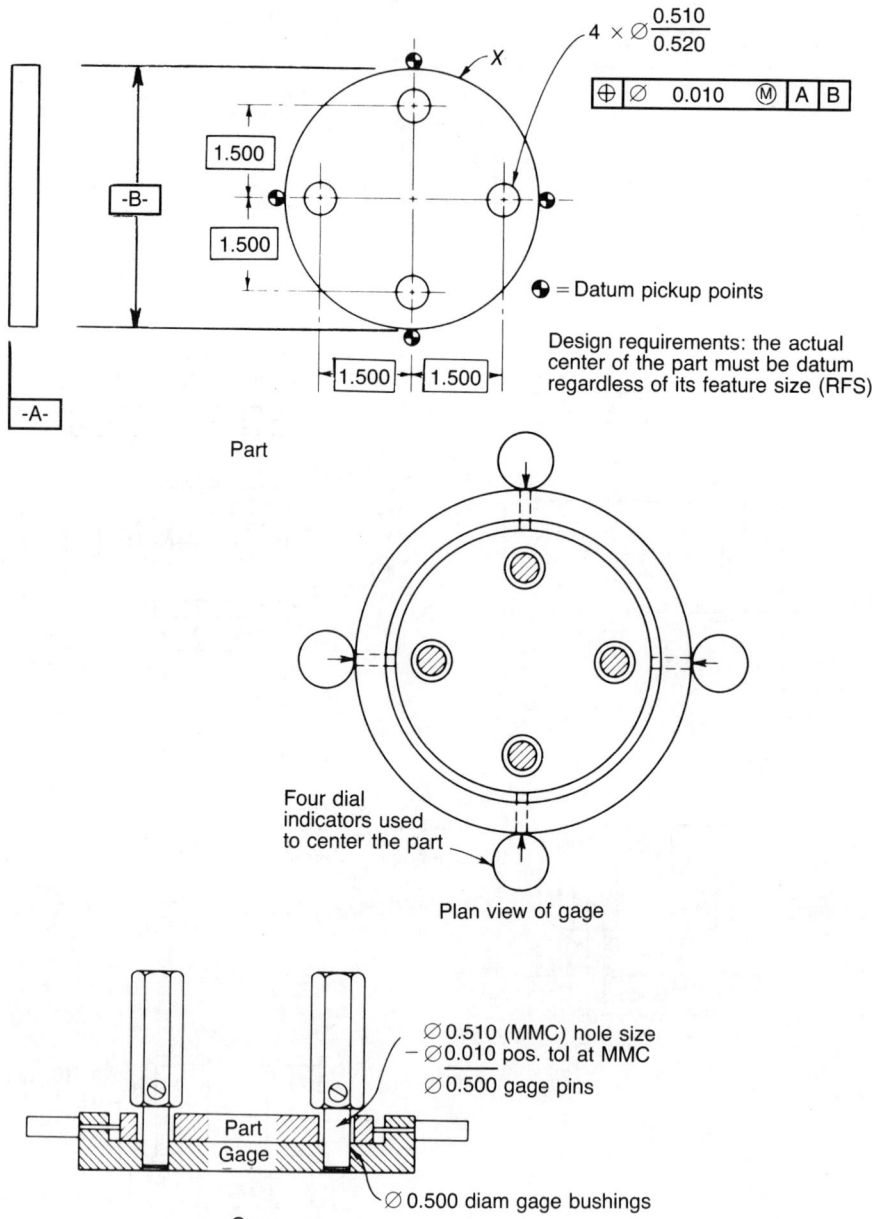

$4 \times \varnothing \dfrac{0.510}{0.520}$

| $\oplus$ | $\varnothing$ | 0.010 | Ⓜ | A | B |

1.500

-B-

1.500

1.500 1.500

-A-

🜨 = Datum pickup points

Design requirements: the actual
center of the part must be datum
regardless of its feature size (RFS)

Part

Four dial
indicators used
to center the part

Plan view of gage

$\varnothing\,0.510$ (MMC) hole size
$-\,\varnothing\underline{0.010}$ pos. tol at MMC
$\varnothing\,0.500$ gage pins

Part
Gage

$\varnothing\,0.500$ diam gage bushings

Gage

Fig. 6-72 Checking the location of four holes that are located from the exact center (RFS) of the part.

6-52

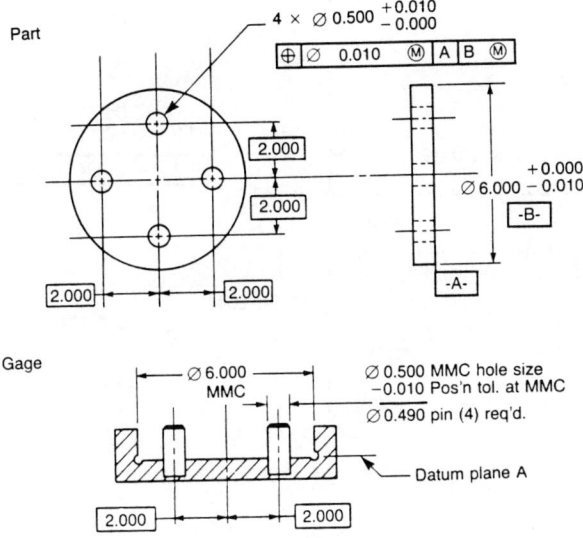

Fig. 6-73 "Shake" gage to check four holes that are located from an MMC datum OD.

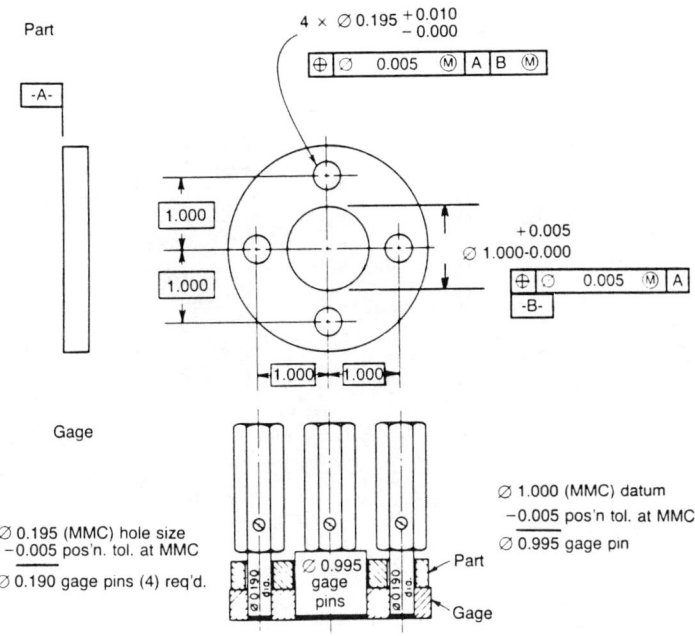

Fig. 6-74 Gaging the location of four holes that are located from an MMC datum ID.

6-53

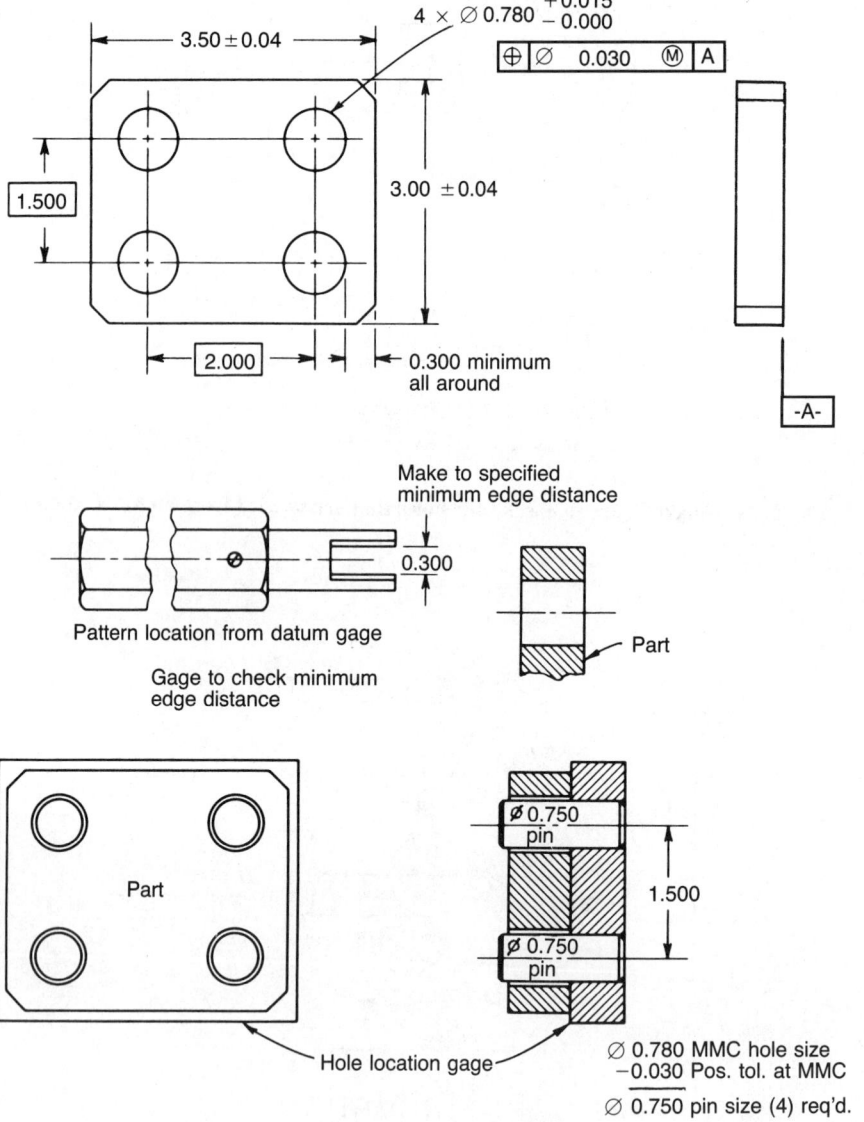

4 × Ø 0.780 +0.015 / −0.000

⊕ | Ø | 0.030 | Ⓜ | A

3.50 ± 0.04

1.500

3.00 ± 0.04

2.000

0.300 minimum
all around

-A-

Make to specified
minimum edge distance

0.300

Pattern location from datum gage

Gage to check minimum
edge distance

Part

Part

Ø 0.750
pin

1.500

Ø 0.750
pin

Hole location gage

Ø 0.780 MMC hole size
−0.030 Pos. tol. at MMC

Ø 0.750 pin size (4) req'd.

Fig. 6-75 Gaging a finished part.

6-54

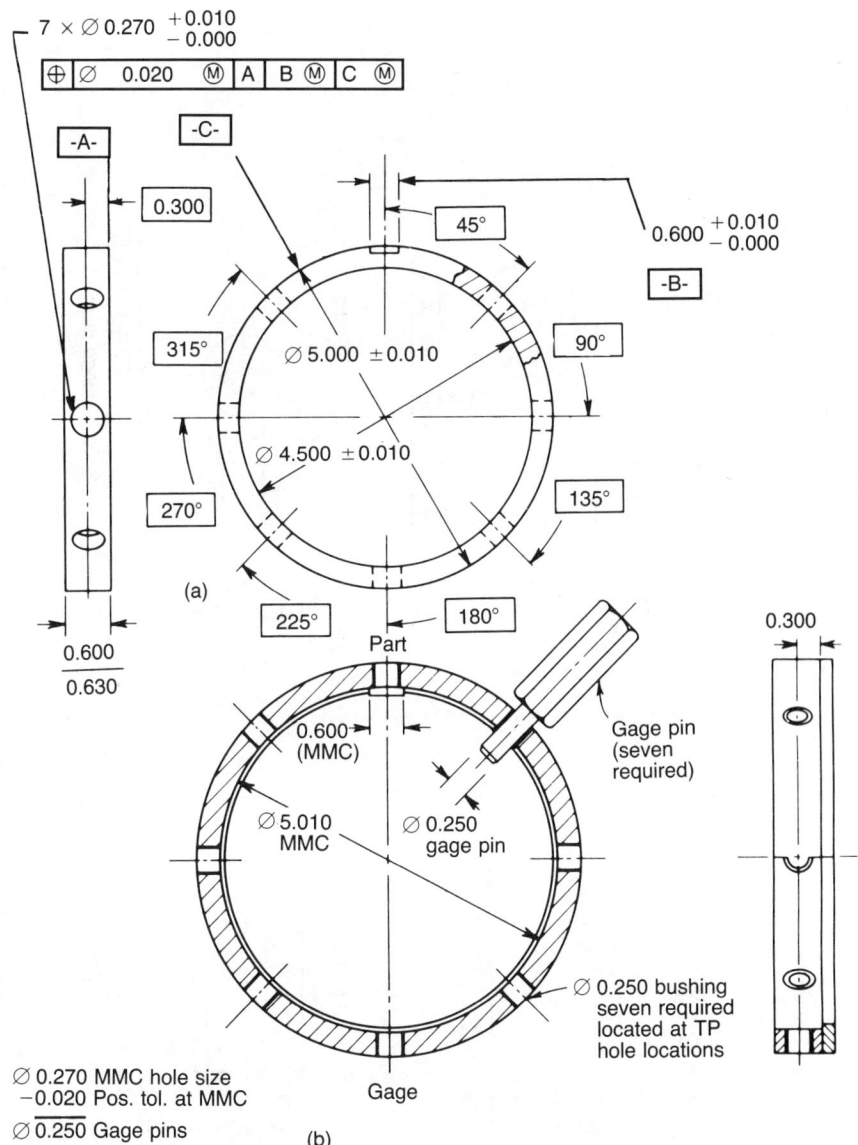

$7 \times \varnothing 0.270 \; ^{+0.010}_{-0.000}$

| ⊕ | ∅ | 0.020 | Ⓜ | A | B | Ⓜ | C | Ⓜ |

-A-

-C-

0.300

45°

$0.600 \; ^{+0.010}_{-0.000}$

-B-

315°

$\varnothing 5.000 \pm 0.010$

90°

$\varnothing 4.500 \pm 0.010$

270°

135°

(a)

225°

180°

Part

0.600
0.630

0.300

0.600 (MMC)

Gage pin (seven required)

$\varnothing 5.010$ MMC

$\varnothing 0.250$ gage pin

$\varnothing 0.250$ bushing seven required located at TP hole locations

$\varnothing 0.270$ MMC hole size
-0.020 Pos. tol. at MMC
$\varnothing \overline{0.250}$ Gage pins

Gage

(b)

Fig. 6-76 Gaging a radial hole pattern.

one side of the feature. The part is then rotated 180° and the distance from the surface plate to the opposite side of the feature is measured and recorded (see Fig. 6-85). The difference between these values is the measurement of symmetry and must be less than that specified in the feature control frame for the part to be acceptable.

Least Material Condition. Occasionally a situation arises where it is desired to relax the position tolerance as the feature of size approaches MMC, which is just the opposite of the MMC modifier that provides additional position tolerance as the feature of size approaches LMC. A good example would be to control wall thickness or edge distance. An interpretation of LMC is shown in Fig. 6-86.

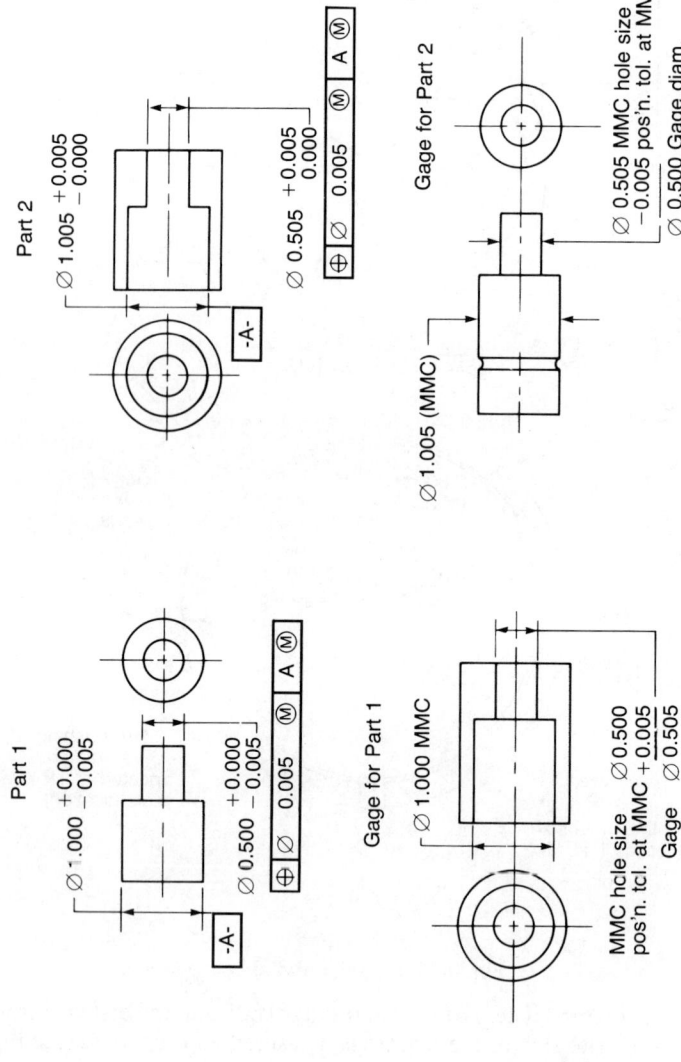

Fig. 6-77 Gaging coaxial mating parts at MMC.

6-56

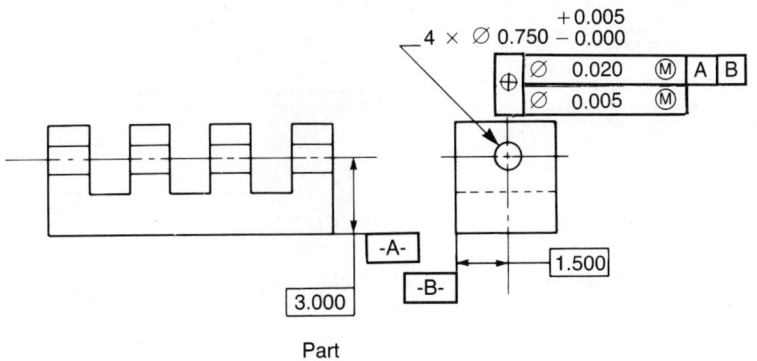

Part

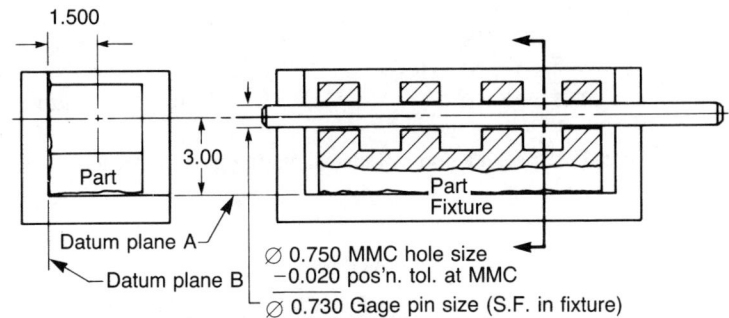

First Gage

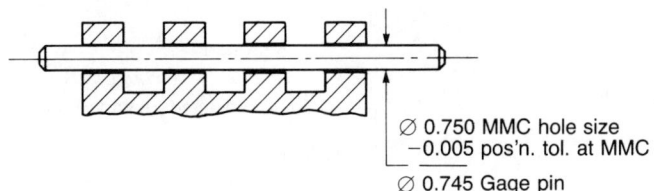

∅ 0.750 MMC hole size
−0.005 pos'n. tol. at MMC

∅ 0.745 Gage pin

Note: Part must accept both gages

Second Gage

Fig. 6-78 Checking bore alignment at MMC.

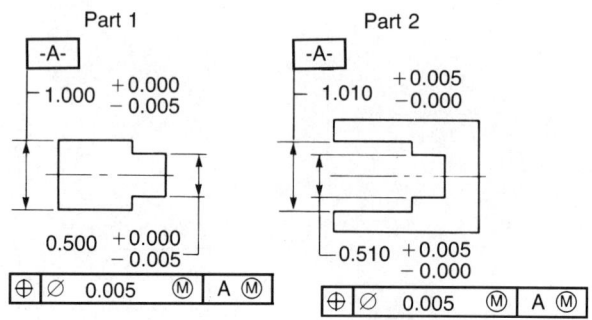

Fig. 6-79 Checking non-cylindrical mating parts at MMC.

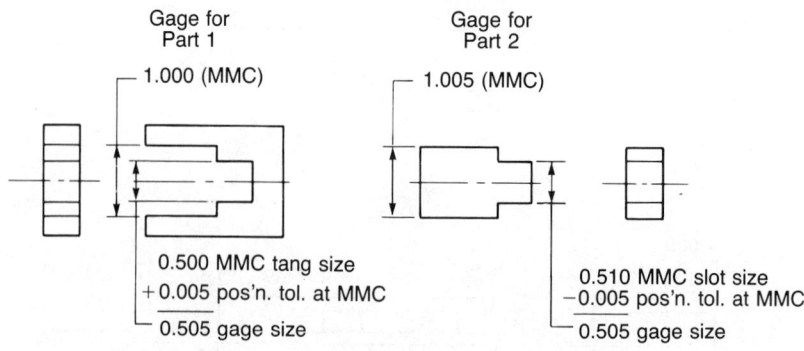

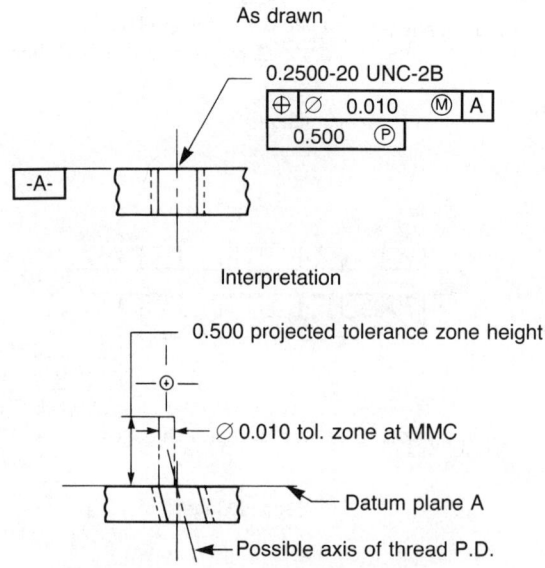

Fig. 6-80 Projected tolerance zone.

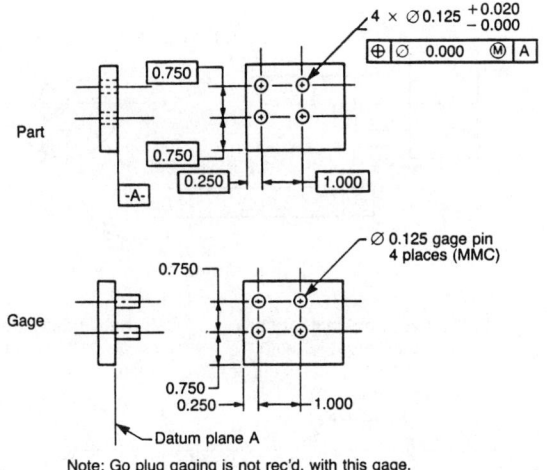

Note: Go plug gaging is not rec'd. with this gage.

Fig. 6-81 Position tolerance of zero at MMC.

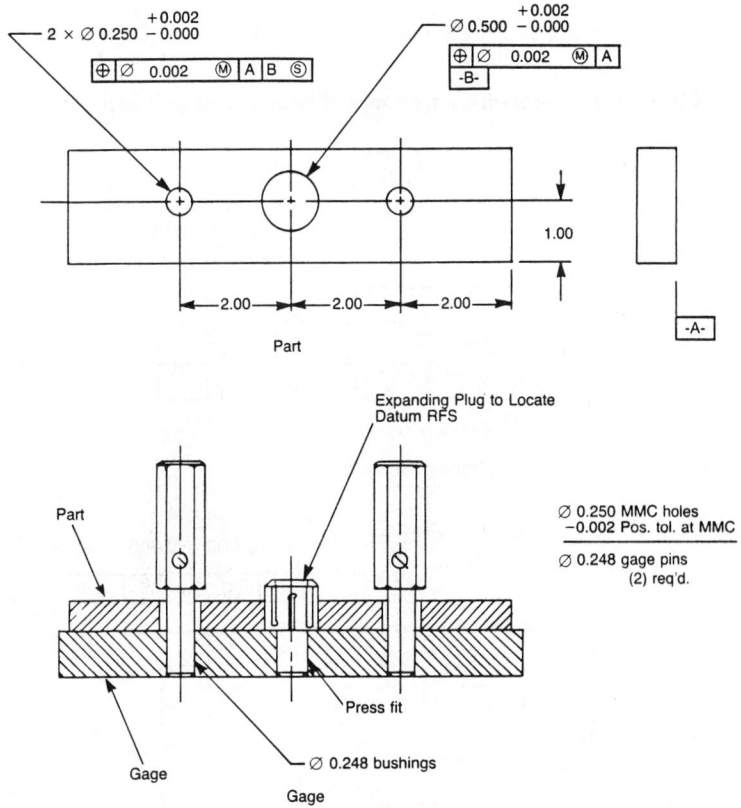

Fig. 6-82 Gaging a hole pattern MMC from an RFS datum.

6-59

As drawn

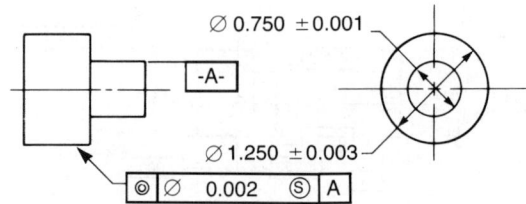

∅ 0.750 ±0.001

-A-

∅ 1.250 ±0.003

| ◎ | ∅ | 0.002 | Ⓢ | A |

Interpretation

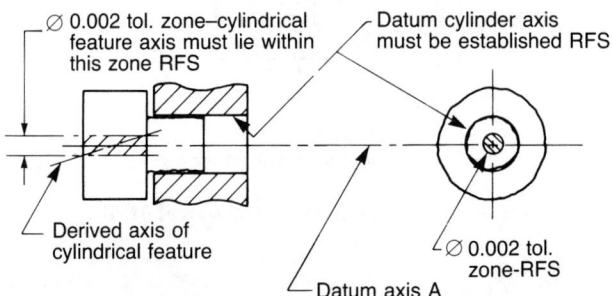

∅ 0.002 tol. zone–cylindrical
feature axis must lie within
this zone RFS

Datum cylinder axis
must be established RFS

Derived axis of
cylindrical feature

∅ 0.002 tol.
zone-RFS

Datum axis A

Note: Part must also be within specified limits of size.

Fig. 6-83 Concentricity: a tolerance of location and its interpretation.

As drawn

0.500 ± 0.005

| ⌰ | 0.020 | TOTAL | A |

-A-

1.500 ± 0.005

Previous Method

0.500 ±0.005

| ⊕ | 0.020 | Ⓢ | A | Ⓢ |

-A-

1.500 ±0.005

Current Method

Fig. 6-84 Symmetry: a tolerance of location and its interpretation.

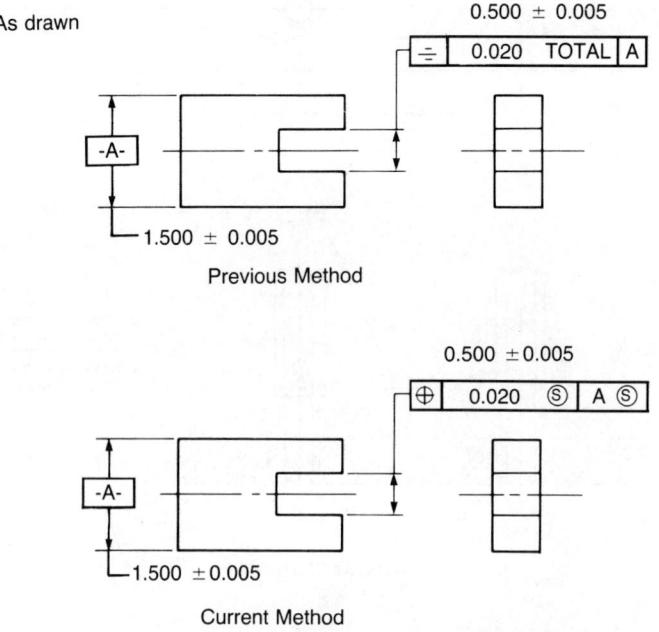

Interpretation

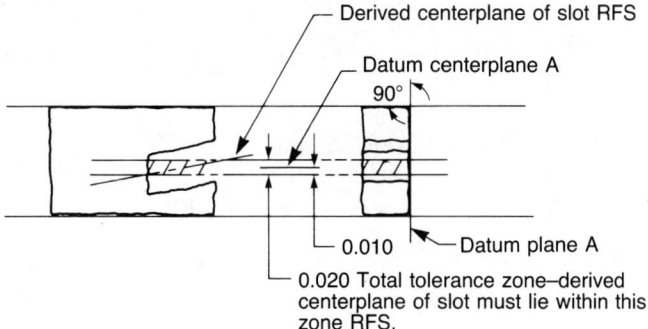

Derived centerplane of slot RFS

Datum centerplane A

90°

0.010

Datum plane A

0.020 Total tolerance zone–derived centerplane of slot must lie within this zone RFS.

Note: Part must also be within specified limits for size.

Fig. 6-84 (*Continued*)

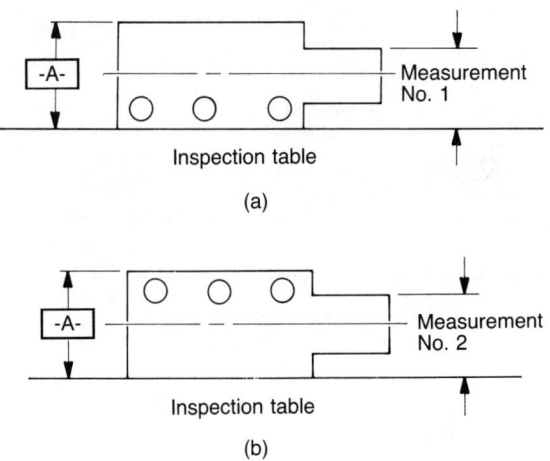

-A-

Measurement No. 1

Inspection table

(a)

-A-

Measurement No. 2

Inspection table

(b)

Fig. 6-85 Checking symmetry.

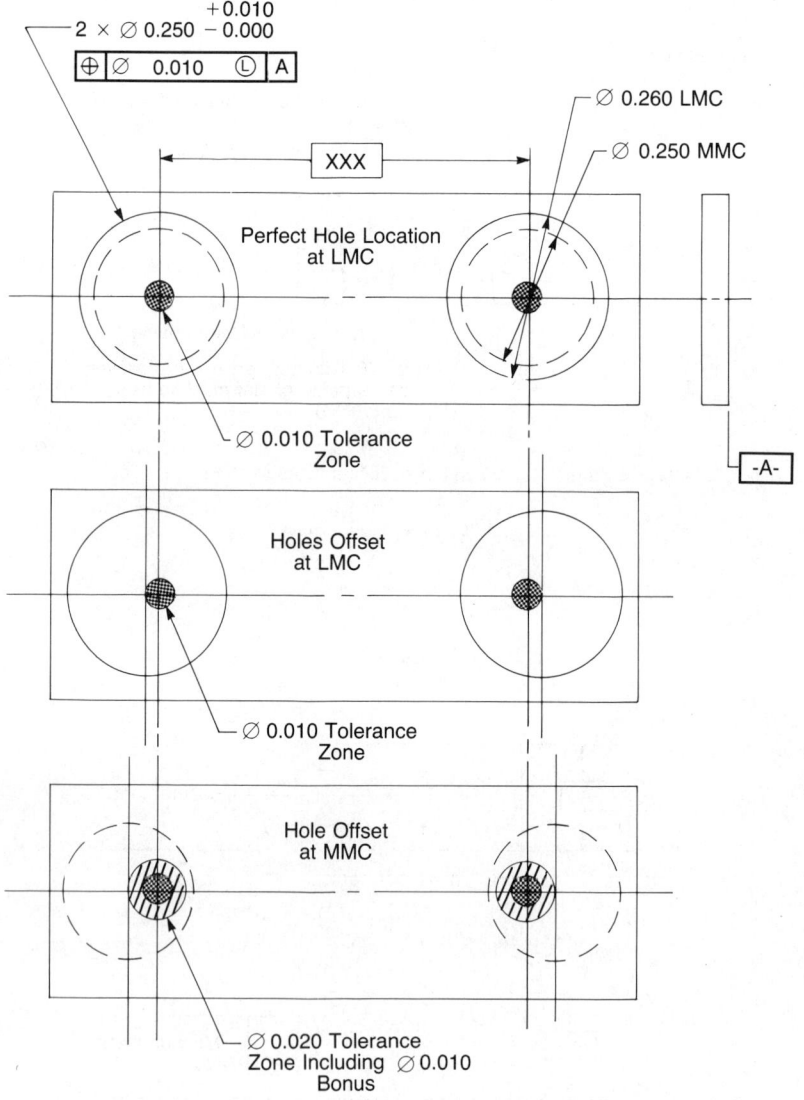

Fig. 6-86 Interpretation of LMC.

CHAPTER 7
MILLING FIXTURES

Milling is a machining process for removing material from a workpiece by relative motion between a rotating cutter having multiple cutting edges and the workpiece. In most cases, the workpiece is fed into a rotating milling cutter with a fixed cutter axis. In others, the workpiece is held stationary while the rotating cutter is moved past it, or both the workpiece and the cutter are advanced in relation to one another and in relation to the milling machine.

The basic milling processes are peripheral (slab) and face milling. In peripheral milling the surface being milled is parallel to the cutter axis, while in face milling the surface being milled is generally at a right angle to the cutter axis. Many milling processes, however, are referred to by the type of cutter used, such as end, side, straddle, and gang milling; or by the type of workpiece being machined, such as gear, thread, and cam milling.

The periphery milling processes can be further broken down into up milling and down milling. When performing up milling, metal is removed by rotating the cutter against the travel of the workpiece as shown in Fig. 7-1. With this method, the cutting tool tends to push the workpiece away from it and lift it from the fixture. Up milling is also referred to as conventional milling, out-cut milling, or "feeding against the cutter". When performing down milling, cutter rotation is in the direction of workpiece travel as shown in Fig. 7-2. With this method the cutting tool tends to pull the workpiece into the cutter. Down milling is also referred to as climb milling, in-cut milling, or "feeding with the cutter".

MILLING METHODS

Several different methods are used to stage work relative to the cutters. They are shown in Fig. 7-3 and include the following:

- Single piece milling, *a*—A single workpiece is clamped on the table or in a fixture mounted on the table and milled. The workpiece is then removed, replaced, and the cycle repeated.
- String milling, *b*—Two or more workpieces are clamped in a row on the table in a direction of feed and milled in consecutive order.
- Abreast milling, *c*—Two or more workpieces are clamped in a row on the table in a direction perpendicular to the direction of feed and milled simultaneously. String and abreast milling are often combined.
- Progressive milling, *d*—A method utilizing string and abreast milling to perform two or more operations on a workpiece, either consecutively or simultaneously.
- Reciprocal milling, *e*—Workpieces are clamped on both ends of the table to permit loading and unloading of one workpiece while the workpiece at the other end of the table is being milled.

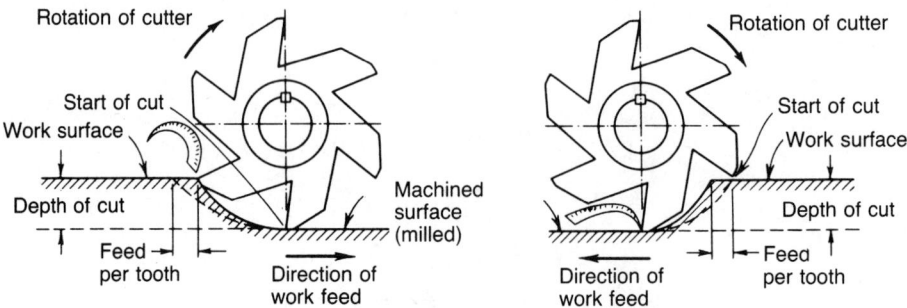

Fig. 7-1 Up or conventional milling.   **Fig. 7-2 Down or climb milling.**

- Transfer base milling, *f*—A method similar to reciprocal milling except that the workpieces are clamped 180° apart on a rotary indexing table or device to permit loading and unloading of one workpiece while the workpiece on the other side of the rotary table is being milled.
- Index milling, *g*—This method is used to perform multiple identical operations on one or more workpieces by indexing after each operation and repeating the operation.
- Rotary milling, *h*—Workpieces are clamped to a rotary table which may revolve continuously.
- Box milling, *i*—A method coordinating the longitudinal and cross slides to mill four sides of a square opening automatically.
- Profile milling, *j*—In this method the cutter is guided by a master template(s).

MILLING MACHINES

Horizontal Knee and Column-type Milling Machines. Horizontal knee and column-type milling machines have a horizontal spindle which is mounted at a fixed height in a stationary rear support column.

The worktable is mounted on a saddle member above a knee support member attached to the rear support column. The table can be moved in three directions: vertically by sliding the knee up and down on the rear support column; crosswise (in-and-out) by sliding the saddle member on the top of the knee; and longitudinally (right and left) by sliding the worktable on the top of the saddle member. All movements are mutually perpendicular.

Universal Milling Machines. Universal milling machines are horizontal knee and column-type milling machines with a swivel table added below the saddle to permit angular cuts without moving the workpiece.

Vertical Knee and Column-type Milling Machines. Vertical knee and column-type milling machines are also basically the same as the horizontal-type but with a vertically mounted spindle which slides up and down on the rear support column in place of the fixed horizontal spindle. Variations of this type include:

- Ram head machines which have a movable ram mounted on top of the rear column to move the spindle head. The spindle head is mounted on single or double swivels, which move in and out parallel to the saddle, allowing the spindle axis to be oriented horizontally, vertically, or at an angle.
- Turret ram machines on which the movable ram is mounted on a swivel base on top of the rear column.

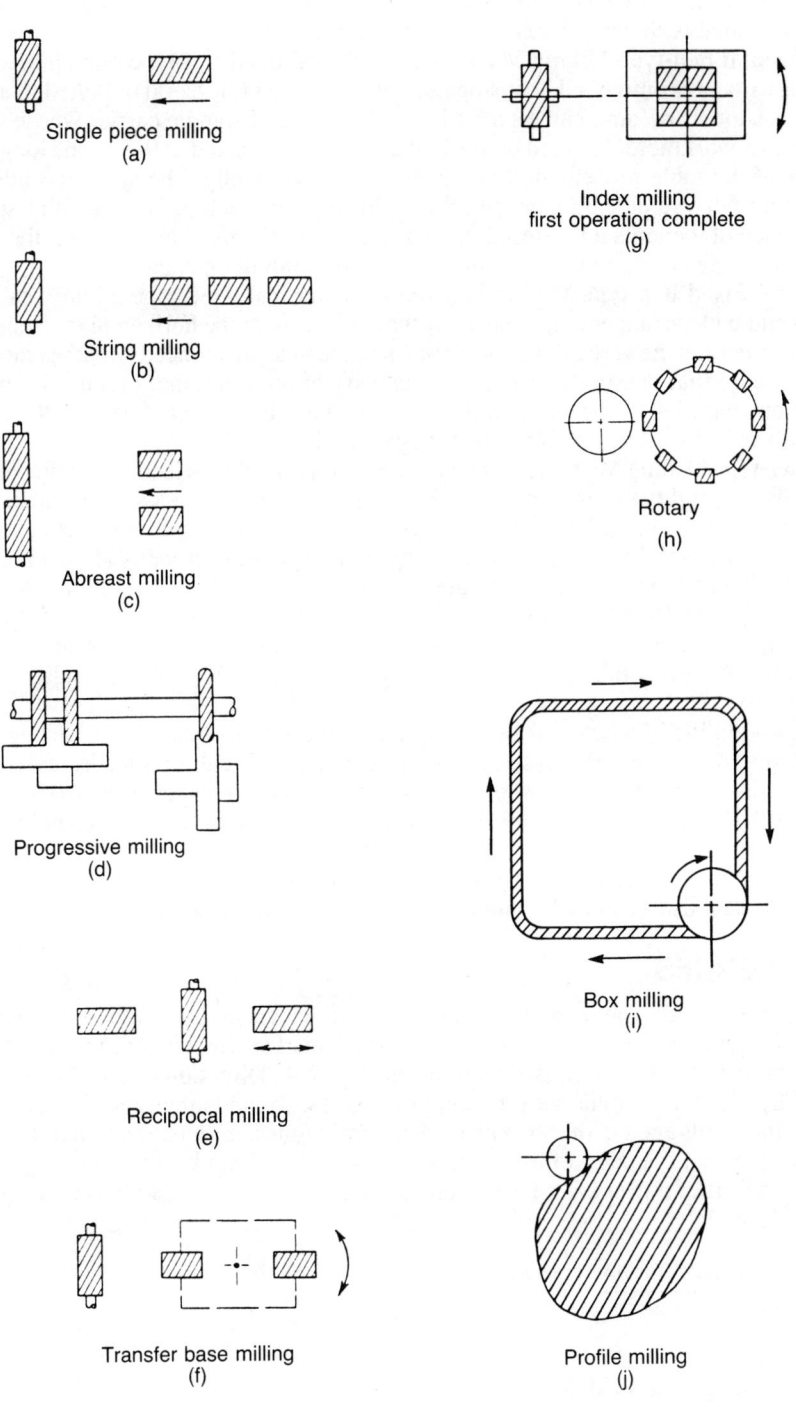

Single piece milling
(a)

String milling
(b)

Abreast milling
(c)

Progressive milling
(d)

Reciprocal milling
(e)

Transfer base milling
(f)

Index milling
first operation complete
(g)

Rotary
(h)

Box milling
(i)

Profile milling
(j)

Fig. 7-3 Milling methods

- Compound universal machines on which the knee ram also can be moved longitudinally and swiveled about a horizontal axis in addition to the movements associated with a regular compound machine.

Horizontal Bed-type Milling Machines. Horizontal fixed bed-type milling machines are built with a rear mounted headstock or column which is integral or bolted to a fixed bed. This support column carries a horizontally mounted spindle carrier whose axis is parallel to a worktable mounted on the bed of the machine, and at 90° to the longitudinal axis of the table movement and can be moved vertically. The spindle is adjusted axially through a spindle quill or ram. When this type of machine is built with a spindle on each side of the table it is referred to as a duplex milling machine, whereas the single spindle machine is referred to as a simplex or plain milling machine.

Vertical Fixed Bed-type Milling Machines. On vertical fixed-type milling machines the bed and table arrangement is basically the same as with the horizontal machine. The main difference is the vertical mounting of a spindle in a carrier head (which is mounted on a rear base that is usually attached to the bed), or on a ram that permits in-and-out adjustment parallel to the table and at 90° to the table travel. The spindle can be adjusted vertically along its own axis through a quill.

Planer-type Milling Machines. Planer-type milling machines feature a rigid crossrail mounted on uprights located on either side of the table to which a spindle carrier(s) is mounted on vertical and horizontal saddles to provide in-and-out and vertical movement. In some cases the entire crossrail is raised and lowered vertically along the Z-axis and/or horizontally in-and-out along the Y-axis.

Gantry-type Milling Machines. These machines are basically the same as the planer-type except that the entire gantry, which includes the crossrail, uprights, and saddles, can be moved horizontally parallel to the worktable while the table generally remains stationary.

Thread-Milling Machines. These are special universal machines for producing accurate internal or external threads. Conventional machines feature a leadscrew, master screw, or sine bar arrangement to permit milling of threads with leads from 0.031 to 60 in. (0.8 to 1524 mm) and a cutter head that can be swiveled to the required helix angle. In planetary thread-milling machines, the workpiece is held stationary while the cutter describes a planetary motion as it is fed radially into the workpiece.

Threads can also be milled on many NC/CNC machining centers.

TOOL FORCES

Tangential Load. The tangential load is a force which serves as a basis for making several design decisions in milling applications. This force is tangent to the effective cutting radius of the cutter, as illustrated in Fig. 7-4. Direction of the force can be derived by a simple graphic vector summation of the individual cutting forces of each tooth or insert engaged in the workpiece. For continuous cuts, the direction of force lies on a line between the point of tooth entry and the point of tooth exit.

Once the cutter power has been calculated, the tangential load can be derived from it with the formula:

$$T = \frac{126{,}000 \times hp}{D \times rpm} \tag{1}$$

where:

T = tangential load, lbf (N)
hp = horsepower required at the cutter
D = cutter diameter, in.
rpm = rotational speed of the cutter

This formula for tangential load assumes constant load on the cutter, which may not be the case.

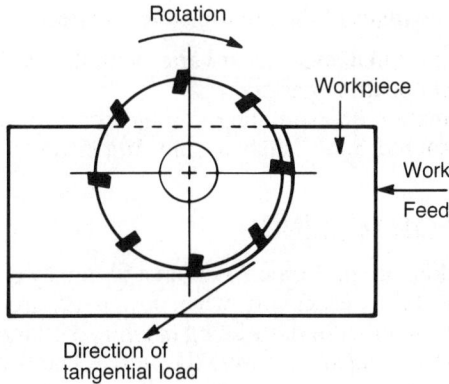

Rotation

Workpiece

Work
Feed

Direction of
tangential load

Fig. 7-4 Tangential load for face milling cutter.

Feed Force. The tangential load has a direct relationship to the force required to feed the work into the cutter or vice versa. The tangential load for a plain milling cutter used in a climb or down milling application tends to pull the workpiece into the cutter. This results in a small feed load. The action also produces a downward force which increases the load on the table ways of a horizontal milling machine. This increased frictional load, however, is usually minimal, and its effects are more than offset by the pulling action. For such applications, the force required to feed the work into the cutter can be low and may represent only that force necessary to overcome the weight of the work-piece, fixture, and table, plus the friction of the table ways and the feed drive trains. In some cases, the cutter may overcome the resistance and pull the workpiece into itself with possible disastrous results.

Conventional or up milling with a plain milling cutter tends to lift the workpiece off the table of a horizontal milling machine; the tangential load directly opposes the direction of table feed. For such applications, it is usually safe to assume that the force required to feed the table will not exceed the value of the tangential force created by the cutter, nor will it exceed any other allowances required for table and feed drive-train friction.

Face milling applications can be analyzed in much the same manner. Depending upon the direction of cutter rotation in relation to the direction of feed, as well as the location of the area being milled, such applications produce either positive or negative feed loads. However, since climb milling is almost always preferred, the tendency is to pull the work into the cutter. As is the case with the previously explained plain milling applications, this results in minimal or negative loads.

Resultant components of the tangential force can be calculated from the formulas:

$$A = T \tan \beta$$
$$B = T \cos \alpha$$
$$C = T \sin \alpha$$

where:

A = resultant force along axial axis, lbf (N)

B = resultant force along feed axis, lbf (N)

C = resultant force at 90° to feed axis, lbf (N)

T = tangential force produced by cutter, lbf (N)

α = angle between tangential force line and feed axis, degrees

β = helix angle of the flutes of the milling cutter, degrees

Angle α is difficult to estimate because it varies with the workpiece material, cutter design, cutting fluid, and operating parameters.

For additional information on estimating tooling forces in milling operations, it is recommended that a source book, such as the *Machinability Data Handbook*, be consulted.

WORKHOLDING FOR MILLING

Many milling operations are performed without a fixture by clamping the workpiece on the milling-machine table, especially when few parts are to be machined. For production jobs when the number of parts being machined is large enough to justify the cost, a fixture is used for holding and locating the work. Quantity alone however, is not the only criterion for determining the application of a fixture; workpiece accuracy and shape may dictate its use, although only a few parts may be machined.

A milling fixture, like any other piece of shop equipment, must justify its use by contributing to the reduction in the cost of a milling operation for which it was designed. Fixtures are sometimes very complicated and expensive units, but on the other hand they may be rather simple modifications of the familiar milling-machine vise.

Fixtures used in milling operations may be any of the following types or combinations:

- Milling-machine vises may be used for holding relatively small parts.
- Temporary fixtures may be built up with commercial parts such as clamps. T-bolts, locators and stops, and standard milling-machine attachments, using the table of the milling machine as the base of the fixture. Temporary set-ups are generally used in the toolroom or when few parts of a special nature are to be milled which would not justify the cost of a permanent fixture.
- Permanent fixtures are made when the number of parts in production is large enough to warrant the cost of the fixture.

Fixtures are sometimes classified in accordance with the type of operation performed on the work, such as slotting, straddle milling, face milling, form milling, etc. A more comprehensive classification identifies their design features, such as hand clamping, power clamping, automatic, center-type, pilot or stud-type, V-block, stationary, cradle-type, rotary, drum, indexing, oscillating, rise and fall, transfer, built in, universal contour or profile, etc.

The design of a fixture should not be started without necessary data concerning the type and configuration of the milling machine with which the fixture will be used, including capacity, the dimensions of the milling-machine table, center-to-center distance, and dimension of T-slots; the range of vertical, longitudinal, and transverse table travel; the power capacity and speed and feed ranges.

Other factors that must be considered are:

1. Size, strength, rigidity, and the locating surfaces of the part.
2. Operation to be performed, such as form milling, thread milling, facing, slotting, straddle milling, etc.
3. Required finish and accuracy of the milled surface.
4. Stock to be removed and machinability of the workpiece material.
5. Number of parts to be milled and rate of production.
6. Milling method.

7. Type and design of the fixture.
8. Cutter design and material.

The checklists in Chapters 1 thru 4 for locating, supporting, clamping, and general fixture design should be applied to the design of milling fixtures. Special attention should be given to the following:

- A fixture should be designed for as many milling operations as possible on a part.
- Gaging or setting surfaces are required for locating the cutter in relation to the work and the fixture and to ensure that the cut is within the specified tolerance limits.
- Clearance space should be provided to allow cutter change without disturbing the setup.
- The workpiece area to be milled should always be located within the area determined by the supporting points, or the supporting points should be under the area to be milled.
- Fixtures should be designed with a low profile.

MILLING TIME

In cases where the estimated milling time must be determined by the tool designer, the following formula can be used:

$$t = \frac{L + A + O_1 + O_2}{F} \qquad (2)$$

where:

t = time required to complete cut, min

L = length of surface to mill, in. (mm)

A = cutter approach, in. (mm)

O_1 = pretravel of cutter before engagement with workpiece, in. (mm)

O_2 = overtravel of cutter after engagement with workpiece, in. (mm)

F = feed rate, in. per min. (mm per min.)

Before this equation can be solved, the pretravel of the cutter before engaging the workpiece and the overtravel of the cutter after engagement with the workpiece must be determined as follows:

In peripheral milling (see Fig. 7-5), the cutter approach may be determined by

$$A = \sqrt{H(D - H)} \qquad (3)$$

In face milling, with cutter centered on the center line of the workpiece (see Fig. 7-6),

$$A = \frac{D}{2} - \frac{D}{2}\sqrt{1 - \frac{W^2}{D}} \qquad (4)$$

For a face-milling cutter off center on amount M, the cutter approach is

$$A = \frac{D}{2} - \frac{D}{2}\sqrt{1 - \frac{W + 2M^2}{D}} \qquad (5)$$

where:

H = depth of cut, in. (mm)

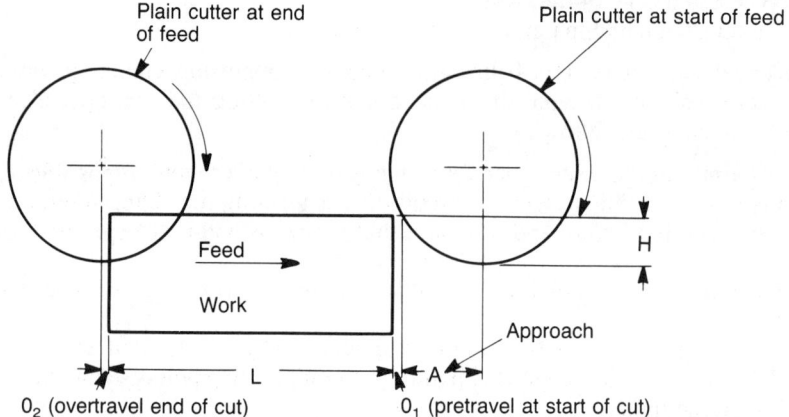

Fig. 7-5 Cutter approach, pretravel, and overtravel in peripheral milling.

D = diameter of cutter, in. (mm)

W = width of cut, in. (mm)

M = cutter offset from centerline of part, in. (mm)

The time for milling a group of pieces by the string method would be expressed as

$$t = \frac{nw + (n-1)s + A + O}{F} \tag{6}$$

where:

n = number of pieces in a row

w = length of milled surface of each piece, in. (mm)

s = space between two pieces, in. (mm)

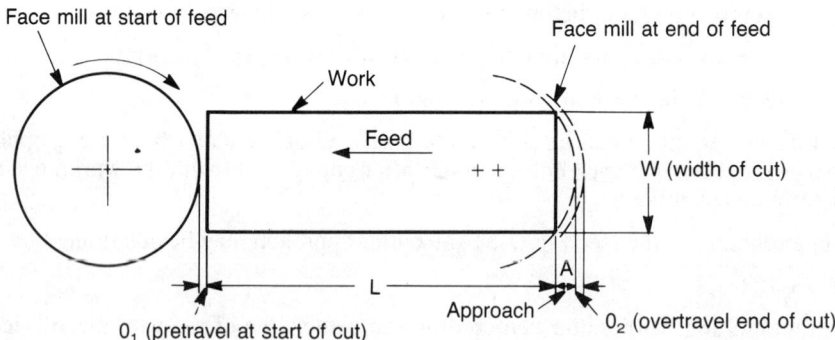

Fig. 7-6 Cutter approach, pretravel, and overtravel in face milling.

Milling time is at a minimum when the space between the parts is zero. If this cannot be arranged, the alternative is to make the space as narrow as possible. The increase in milling time resulting from spaced parts in a row can in part be minimized by adding rows abreast; this will decrease the milling time in inverse relation to the number of rows abreast.

In all cases, the idle machine time, including the time spent in placing the workpiece near the cutter, the time required to return the workpiece or cutter to the starting position after milling, and time spent in loading and unloading, must be added to the milling time to arrive at a cycle time.

MILLING-FIXTURE DESIGN

Fixtures consist of essential elements which may vary in shape and arrangement as required by the nature of the workpiece, but they are identical in the duty which they perform. The essential elements of a milling fixture are shown in Fig. 7-7.

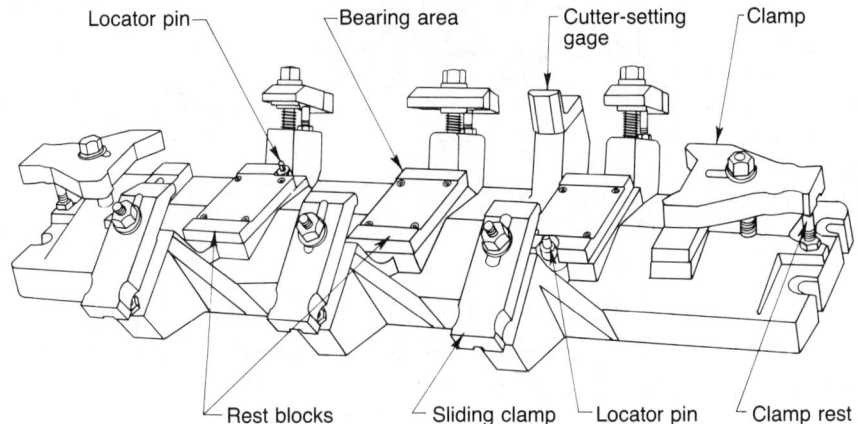

Fig. 7-7 **Essential elements of a milling fixture.** (*Courtesy Cincinnati Milacron*)

The relative position between the workpiece and cutters may be determined by means of a gage or properly located setting surfaces. The setting surfaces may be incorporated in the fixture and are either fixed or removable. When the setting surface is located so that it would be in the path of the cutter, provision is usually made either to remove the gage or to set it down or over a certain distance from the cutter to avoid interference. A feeler gage of proper thickness is then provided for gaging the position of the cutter.

Figure 7-8 illustrates the use of an 0.0625 in. (1.587 mm) feeler gage between the setup gage and cutter. The use of a straightedge to establish the relationship between cutter and setup gage is shown in Fig. 7-9. A removable setting gage is shown in Fig. 7-10. The gage is positioned by the central locating plug on the fixture and a small pin, which are the means of locating the workpiece on the fixture.

Vise Jaws. A commonly used workholding device for milling is the plain or universal vise (see Fig. 7-11). Provision is made for attaching special jaw inserts to the fixed and movable vise jaws.

Self-adjusting vise jaws for simultaneously holding three cylindrical workpieces are illustrated in Fig. 7-12. The fixed jaw (1) has three vertical 90° V-grooves. The movable jaw (2) has three horizontal plungers (3) opposite the V-grooves, and on closing the vise, each workpiece is clamped in one of the V-grooves by a plunger. The variation in part diameter is compensated for automatically by a lateral adjustment of the angle-faced plungers (4). Vertical pins (5) transmit motion from plunger to plunger.

Figure 7-13 illustrates three methods of holding round stock in vise jaws. View *a* shows a set of jaws with equalizers for holding four headed parts. Two spring-loaded equalizers (1) are in one jaw while four Vees are in the second jaw.

A set of jaws for holding two cylindrical parts while milling the circular grooves are shown in Fig. 7-13*b*. The part is positioned vertically and supported by the pin (2).

The jaws of view *c* are used to hold two ¼ in. diameter shafts while milling a slot in the end. The shafts are supported on a ledge of one jaw (3) and clamped by beveled surfaces (similar to a dovetail) in both jaws. An end stop block (5) locates and supports the parts while being milled.

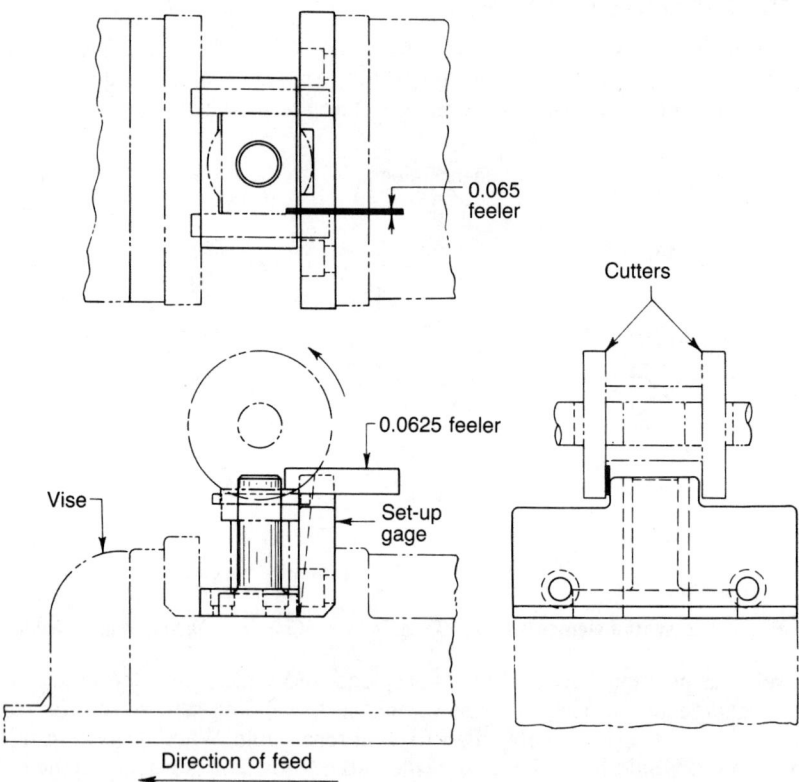

Fig. 7-8 Setup gage incorporated in a vise jaw. (*Courtesy Cincinnati Milacron*)

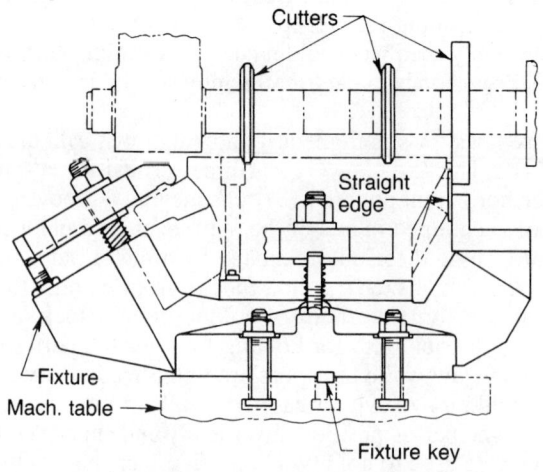

Fig. 7-9 Using a straightedge for setting fixture-cutter relationship. (*Courtesy Cincinnati Milacron*)

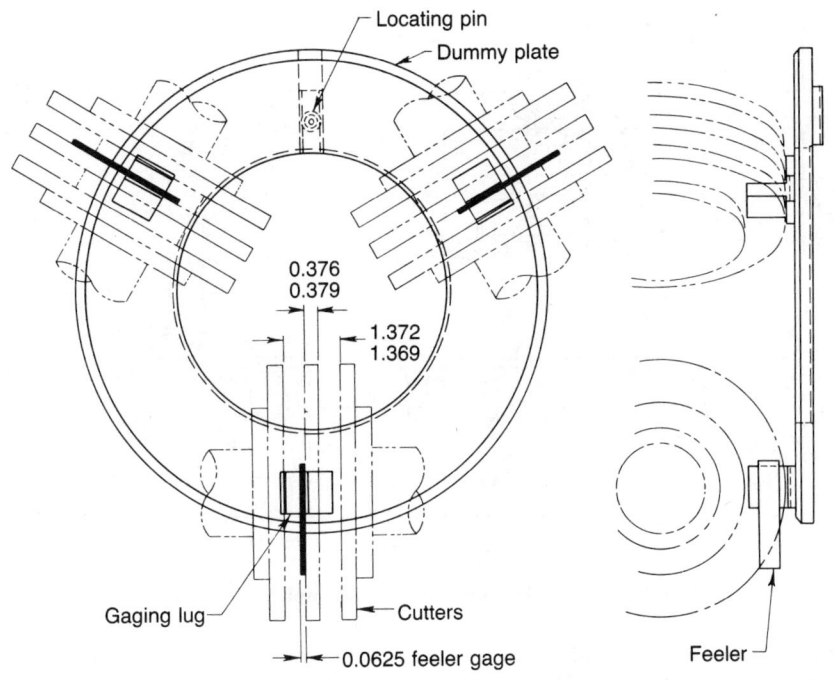

Fig. 7-10 Removable cutter-setting gage. (*Courtesy Cincinnati Milacron*)

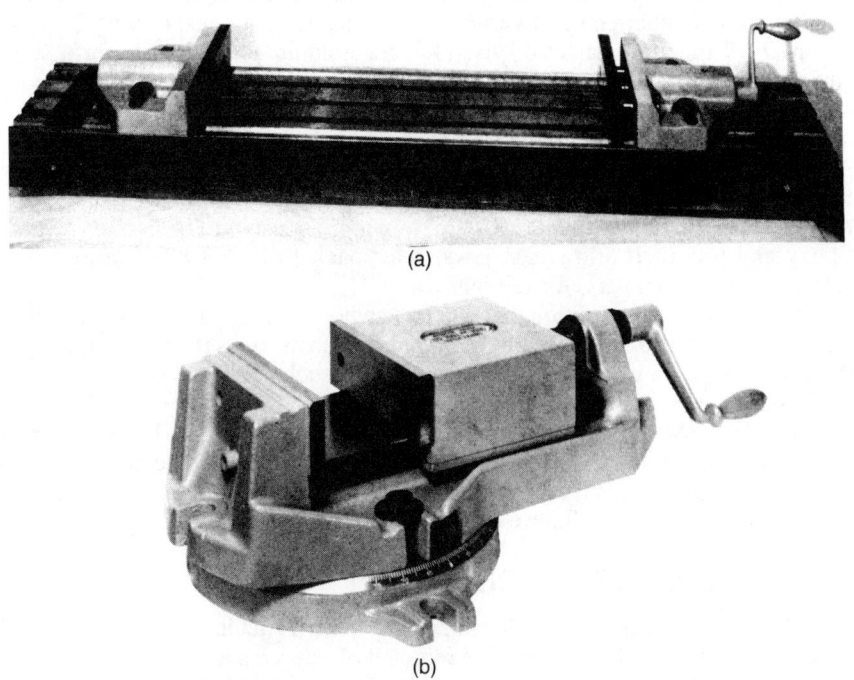

(a)

(b)

Fig. 7-11 Vises: (*a*) milling machine vise, and (*b*) swivel base vise. (*Courtesy Universal Vise & Tool Co.*)

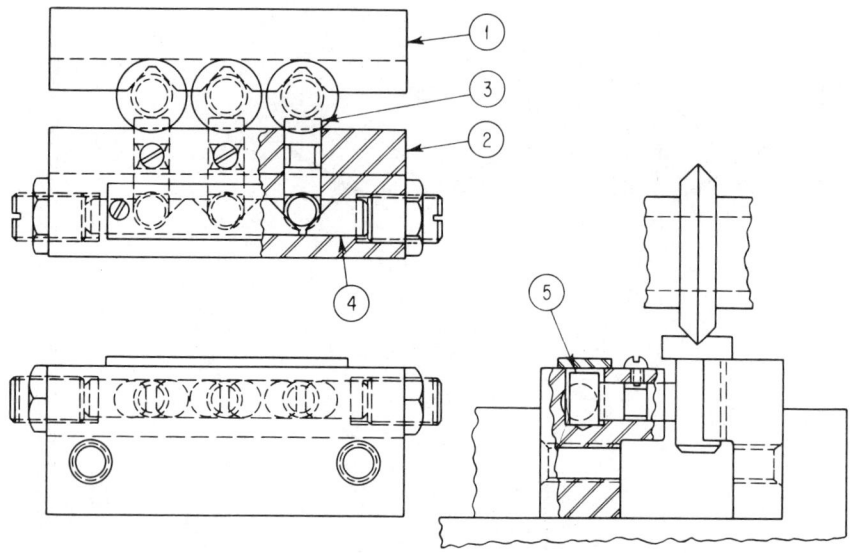

Fig. 7-12 Self-adjusting vise jaws for multiple parts.[1]

All of these jaws were made of tool steel, hardened and ground. For low-production items, the jaws may be made of low-carbon steel, either case-hardened or in the soft state.

Small castings and forgings may also be held in special vise jaws. Figure 7-14 shows a set of vise jaws having an equalizing bar (1) for holding a part in a horizontal V-slot at one end and at the other end in a vertical V-slot and against a rest button (2).

Figure 7-15 illustrates a set of vise jaws for holding a valve body for a straddle-milling operation on its hexagon-shaped portion. Since the surface being milled is off center of the gripping surface, the surface beneath the cut rests in a V-slot. A locator (1) is provided to locate the part to the cutters.

Another vise with special jaws is shown in Fig. 7-16. This one has a gaging surface which can be used with a feeler gage for setting the cutters.

Additional vise jaw modifications were shown previously in Fig. 3-62.

Epoxy and low melt allow cast jaws (refer back to Fig. 3-89) can also be used advantageously to hold parts for milling.

Figure 7-17 shows a condition that can arise when milling a deep slot in a workpiece held in a vise. Distortion is caused by the clamping pressure as the material is removed from the center of the workpiece. A simple fixture, such as shown in Fig. 7-18, should be used under these circumstances.

Figure 7-19 shows a fixture for holding a single bar for milling. The fixture consists of a subplate, rest pad bases, and four modular vises which have been mounted to the subplate. The fixed jaws have been doweled in position with their faces lying in the same plane. All parts of this fixture can be reused when it is no longer needed.

FIRST OPERATION FIXTURES

Irregular shaped castings and forgings are often difficult to hold firmly without distortion while milling. In addition, the removal of any substantial amount of material from a rough workpiece can either cause or relieve internal stress. To minimize this distortion, workpieces are usually premachined to provide a good working surface for future operations.

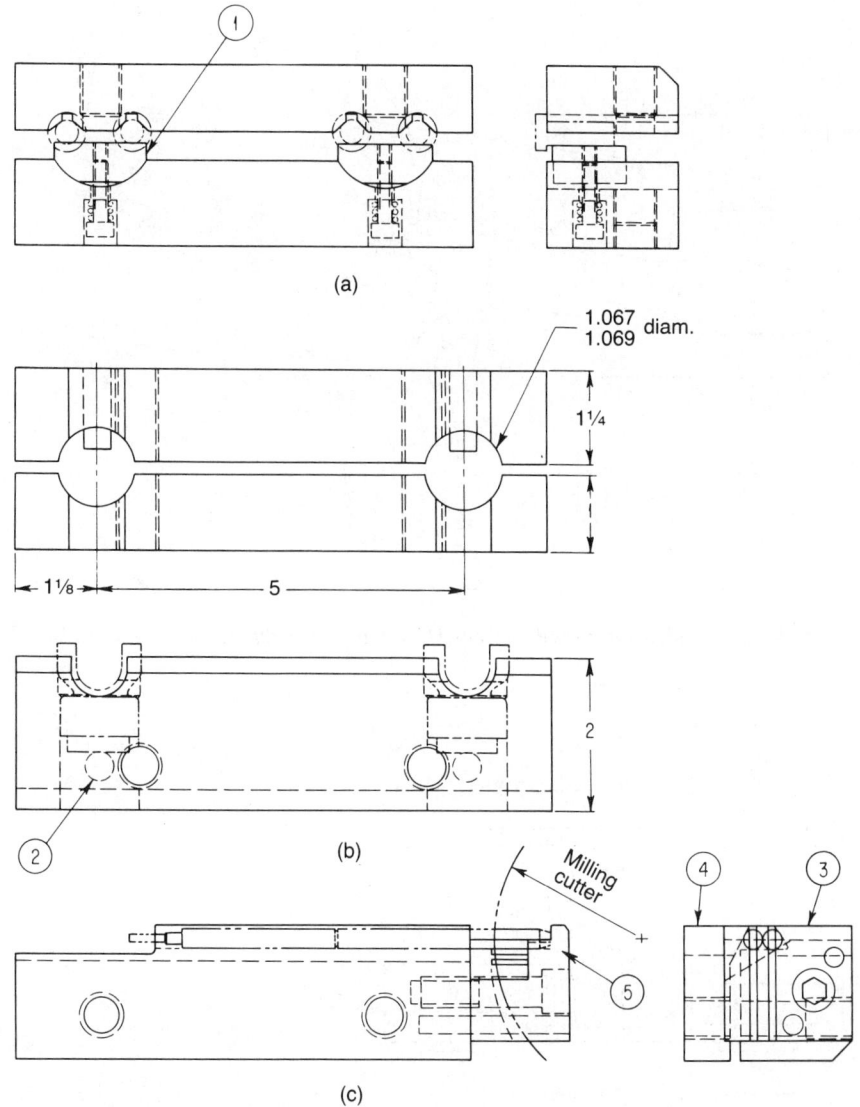

Fig. 7-13 **Vise jaws for holding round stock.** (*Courtesy American Standard Controls Div.*)

Poor fixturing and clamping practices can add greatly to the problem. The first milling cut must be made so that the machined surface will remain flat when removed from the fixture. To do this, the workpiece must be supported and clamped firmly in its "free" condition with the minimum force needed to overcome the cutting tool forces. (The S.A.F.E. system described in Chapter 5 and illustrated in Fig. 5-58 was designed especially to minimize this problem.)

Stresses, of course, can be caused by other factors such as dull cutters, insufficient cooling, excessive speeds and feeds, etc. These must be dealt with by following good machining practices.

First Operation Milling Fixture for an Aluminum Casting. Figure 7-20 shows a fixture for holding an aluminum casting for a first operation to mill three bottom pads on the casting smooth and flat. This finished surface is to be located 0.375 in. (9.53

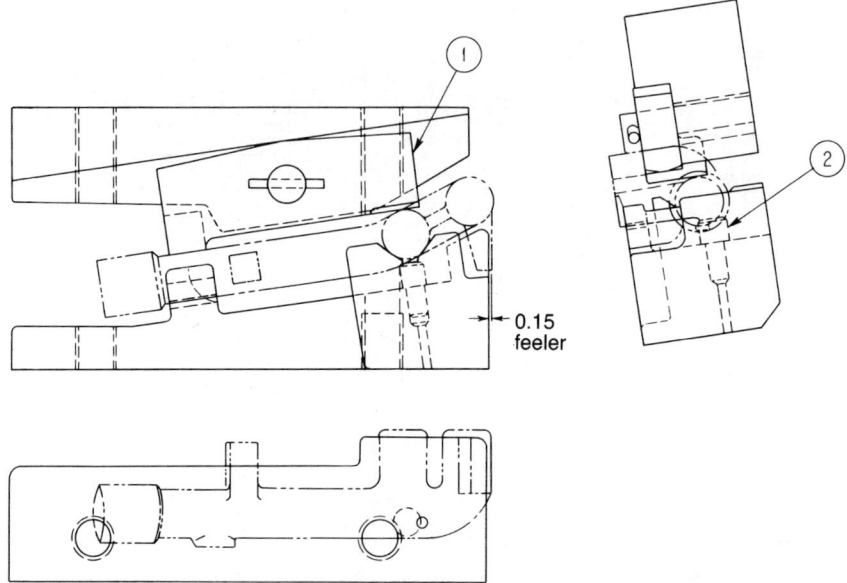

Fig. 7-14 Vise jaws for a small casting. (*Courtesy American Standard Controls Div.*)

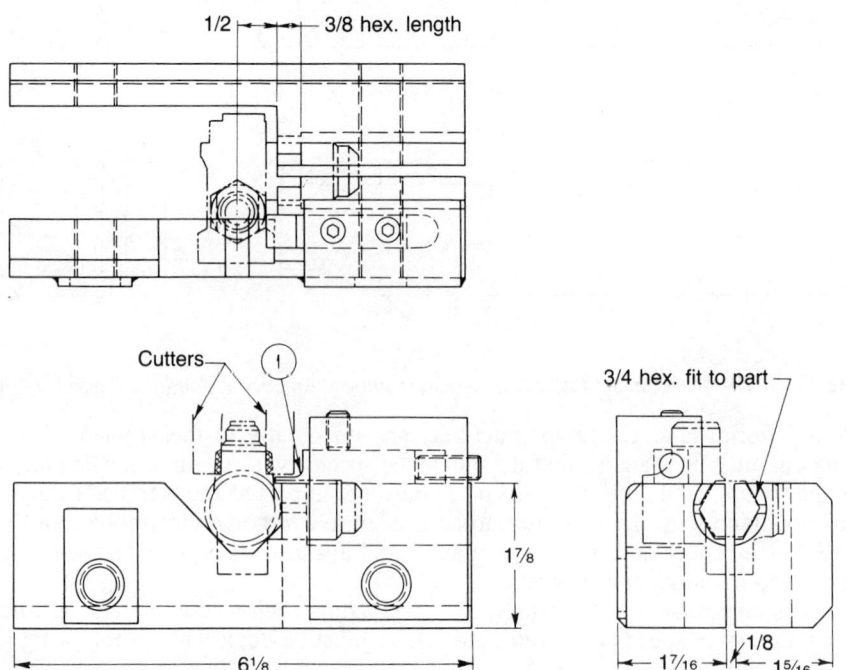

Fig. 7-15 Vise jaws for straddle-milling a valve body. (*Courtesy American Standard Controls Div.*)

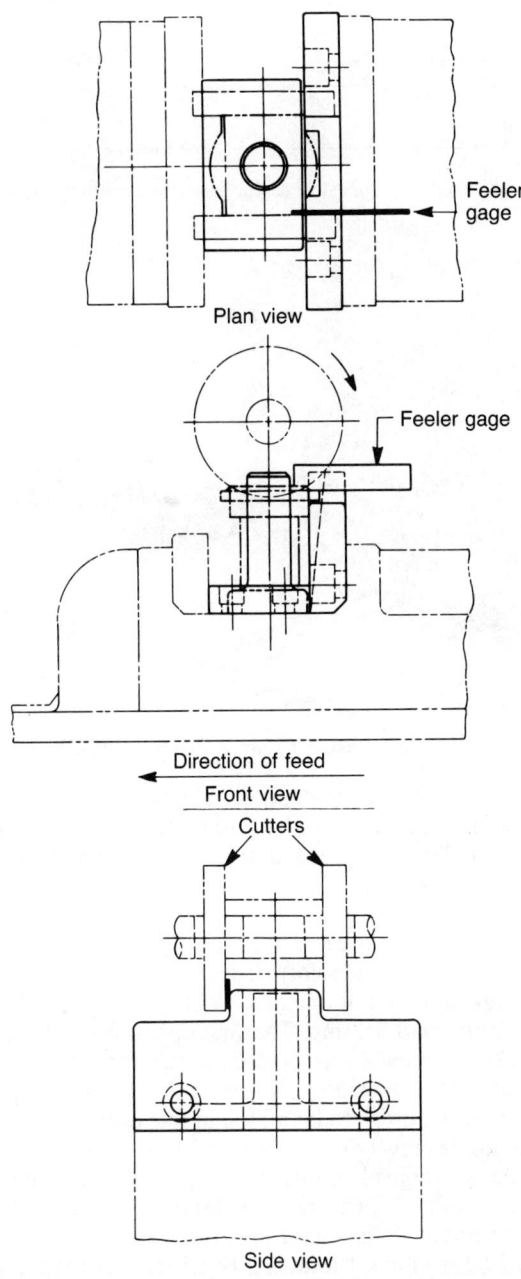

Plan view

Feeler gage

Feeler gage

Direction of feed

Front view

Cutters

Side view

Fig. 7-16 Vise with special jaws for clamping a workpiece—one jaw has a setting-gage surface for use with a feeler gage.

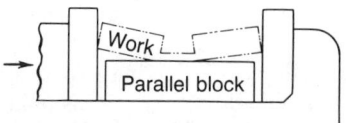

Work

Parallel block

Fig. 7-17 Distortion when milling a deep slot in a workpiece held between vise jaws.

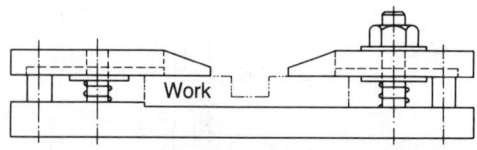

Fig. 7-18 Fixture to prevent distortion when milling a deep slot.

Fig. 7-19 Modular vises. (*Courtesy Stevens Engineering, Inc.*)

mm) from the inside wall of the casting and thereby becomes the reference surface for this operation. This surface is established by three jack pins against which three opposing clamping pins hold the workpiece during the milling operation. A set block mounted on the fixture is used with an 0.020 in. (0.51 mm) feeler gage to set the cutter for milling the pads to the 0.375 in. (9.53 mm) dimension.

Since the casting is supported near, but not at, the point the cutting forces will be applied, heavy cutting forces could possibly deflect the workpiece. To avoid this, a series of light cuts are to be taken in lieu of one heavy cut.

A Fixture for Mounting-pad Milling. The first operation in the machining of many parts is the milling of the reference surface used in subsequent operations. Figure 7-21 shows the fixture for the first operation on a small casting. One adjustable (2) and three fixed (1) rest pins support the areas to be milled in this fixture. The part is held against two locators (3) by a thumbscrew (4). The cutting force is opposed by the stop (5) while the clamp (6) holds the workpiece against the stop. Hold-down clamping is accomplished by the clamp assembly (7) bearing on a cutout in the center tongue. A cutter set block (8) is provided to establish the cutter position.

A First-operation Fixture for a Mounting Bracket. The fixture (see Fig. 7-22) for milling the mounting pads of a small casting uses a sight gage (1) to position the part prior to machining. Three adjustable jackscrews (2) position and support the workpiece. The spring-loaded support pin (3) is locked by the thumbscrew (4), thereby providing direct support beneath two of the milled surfaces. Downward clamping force is applied with the clamp plate (5).

Modular Tooling System with Self-Adjusting Fixturing Elements for First Operation. The first operation fixture shown in Fig. 7-23 is built up of the following components: (1) grid plate 24.80 × 19.69 × 2.00 in. (630 × 500 × 51 mm), (4) vertical adjustable supporting and clamping units and (3) adjustable locators.

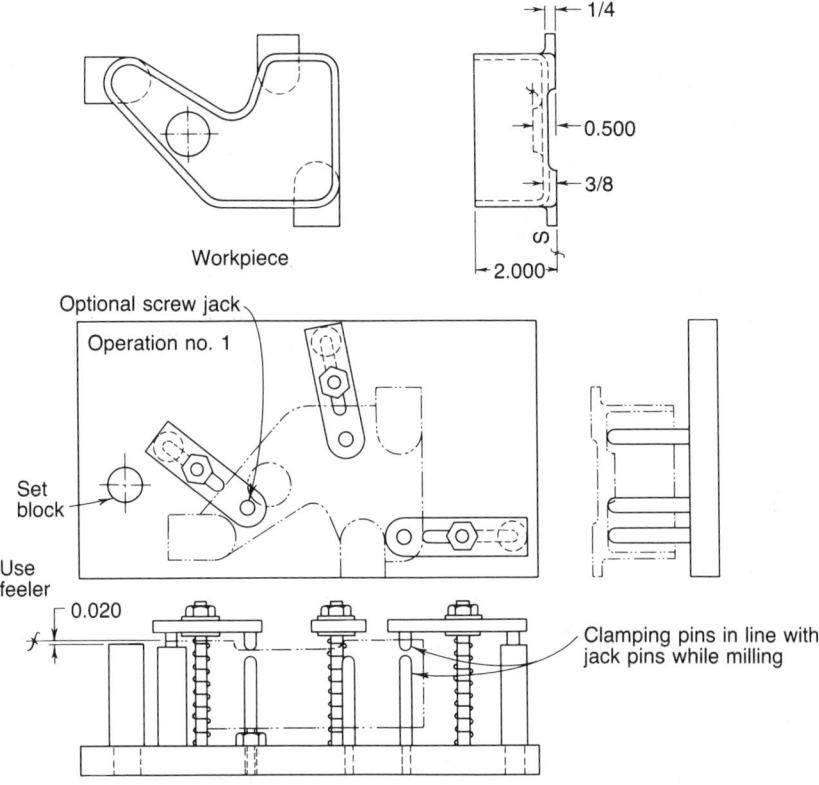

Fig. 7-20 Workpiece with first-operation milling fixture.

The "floating" balls in the vertical supporting and clamping units adjust to the irregularities of the "as cast" workpiece surface and profile, allowing the workpiece, when clamped to rest against the flat contact surface of the balls and be securely clamped in place without distortion. The workpiece is located in the other two planes by the three adjustable locators. One of the milled surfaces finished in this operation is used to locate the workpiece for second operation machining.

FIXTURES FOR SECOND AND SUBSEQUENT OPERATIONS

Fixtures for all operations after the first operation are generally designed to locate from the same previously machined surfaces, thereby eliminating errors that can accumulate when changing surfaces. An example of this is the fixture shown in Fig. 7-24 for the second milling operation on the workpiece shown in Fig. 7-20. The operation is to be performed on a vertical milling machine. The surface generated in the first operation is used to locate the workpiece for this operation. In use, the workpiece is clamped in place for milling with three strap clamps. Details of this are also shown in Fig. 7-24. A stepped set block is mounted on the fixture as shown for use with an 0.020 in. (0.51 mm) feeler gage to set the cutter for milling the 0.500 and 2.000 in. (12.7 and 51.8 mm) dimensions. Light cutting forces are used to minimize deflection. If no fixture is provided, this operation could be performed by clamping the workpiece directly to the machine table as shown in Fig. 7-25 and setting the cutter with gage blocks or setup blocks as shown in Fig. 7-26. Some additional methods of setting cutters with set blocks and feeler gages are shown in Fig. 7-27.

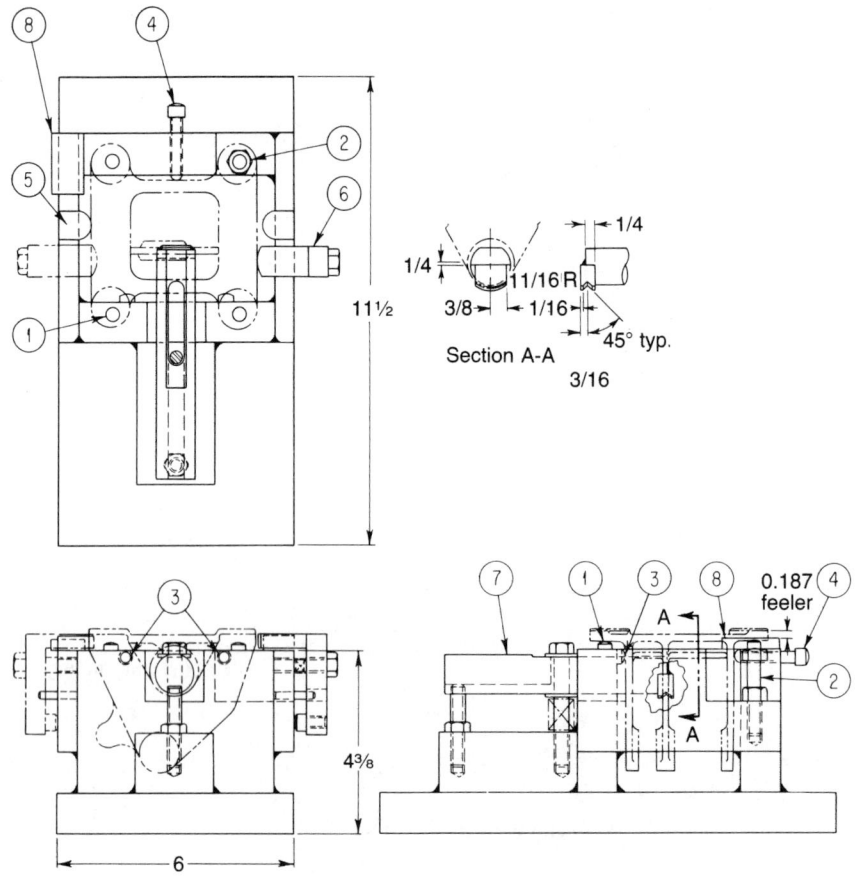

Fig. 7-21 First operation milling fixture for an aluminum casting.

Second Operation Fixture for Use on Several Machines. The fixture shown in Fig. 7-28 was designed to mill the 3.000 ±0.002 in. (76.20 ±0.05 mm) and 6.000 ±0.002 in. (152.4 ±0.05 mm) dimensions on the part shown in the same figure. The workpiece is located on the base and primary reference plane established at the first milling operation. In use, the workpiece is clamped to the fixture and indexed as necessary to present the four surfaces to the milling cutter(s). The three views show how the fixture could be used for fly cutting, side milling, or straddle milling.

Milling Slots in Shafts. Figure 7-29 illustrates how a slot can be milled in a workpiece using either a horizontal or vertical spindle machine. A simple fixture to hold a workpiece for milling a long thru slot on a vertical mill is shown in Fig. 7-30.

SINGLE PIECE MILLING FIXTURES

Milling a 0.315 in. (8.00 mm) Slot. Figure 7-31 illustrates a fixture for milling a 0.315 in. (8.00 mm) wide slot in an aluminum forging. The part is located by two flatted or diamond pins (1). These pins are held in place by a ball detent (2). A ⅛ in. diameter rod brazed to the strap clamp (3) fits in a groove to hold the part down during the milling operation. A set block (4) and a 0.050 in. (1.27 mm) feeler set the cutter to the workpiece. Two blocks (5) fastened to the base plate (6) position the workpiece.

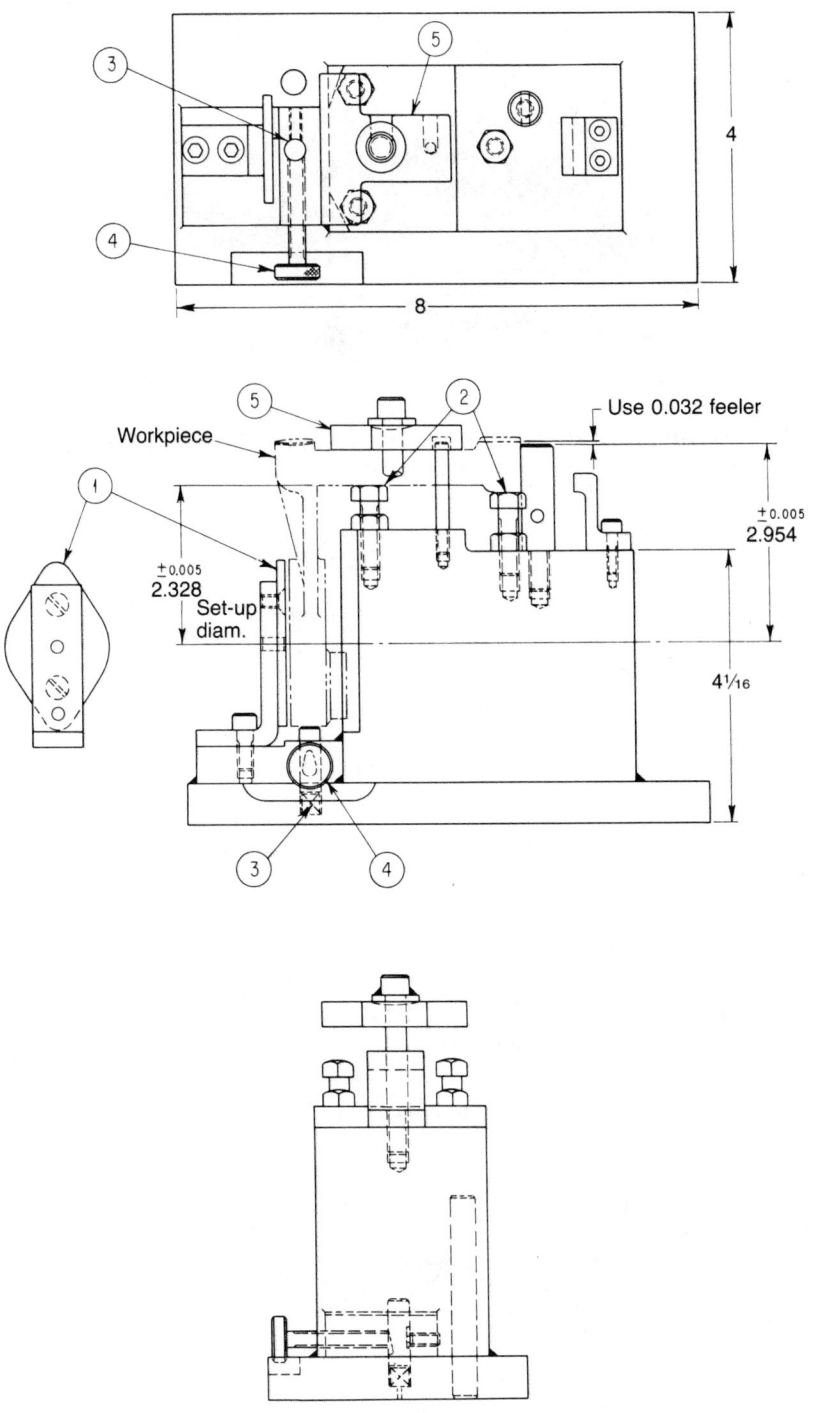

Fig. 7-22 Milling fixture for mounting bracket. (*Courtesy Koehler Aircraft Co.*)

Fig. 7-23 Self-adjusting fixturing elements system for first operation machining. (*S.A.F.E. System, courtesy Enerpac Group, Applied Power, Inc.*)

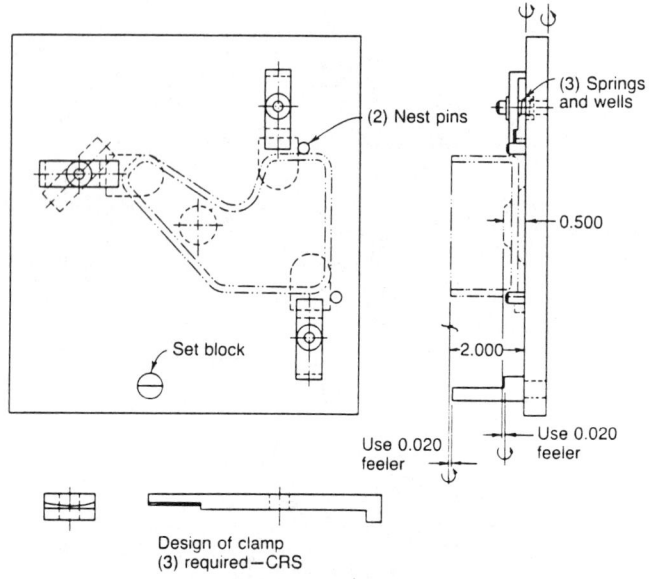

Fig. 7-24 Fixture for a vertical milling operation.

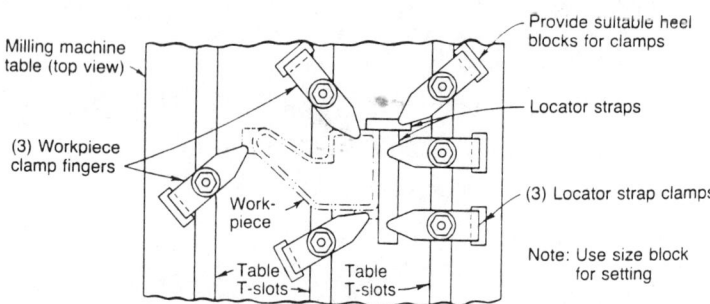

Fig. 7-25 Workpiece attached directly to machine table for vertical milling operation.

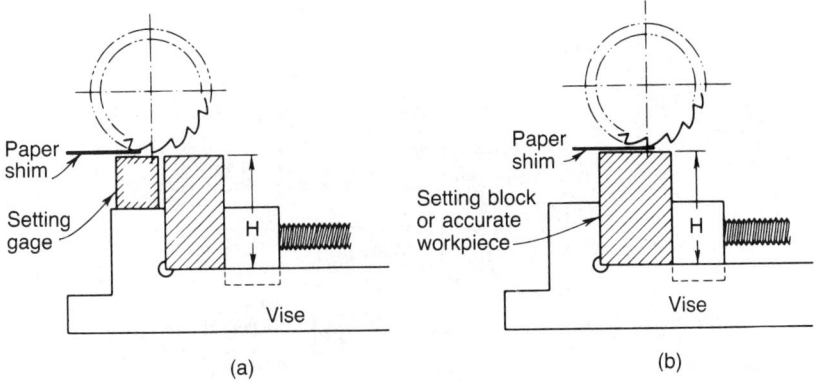

Paper shim

Setting gage

H

Vise

(a)

Paper shim

Setting block or accurate workpiece

H

Vise

(b)

Fig. 7-26 Use of a gage block in setting up a milling operation.

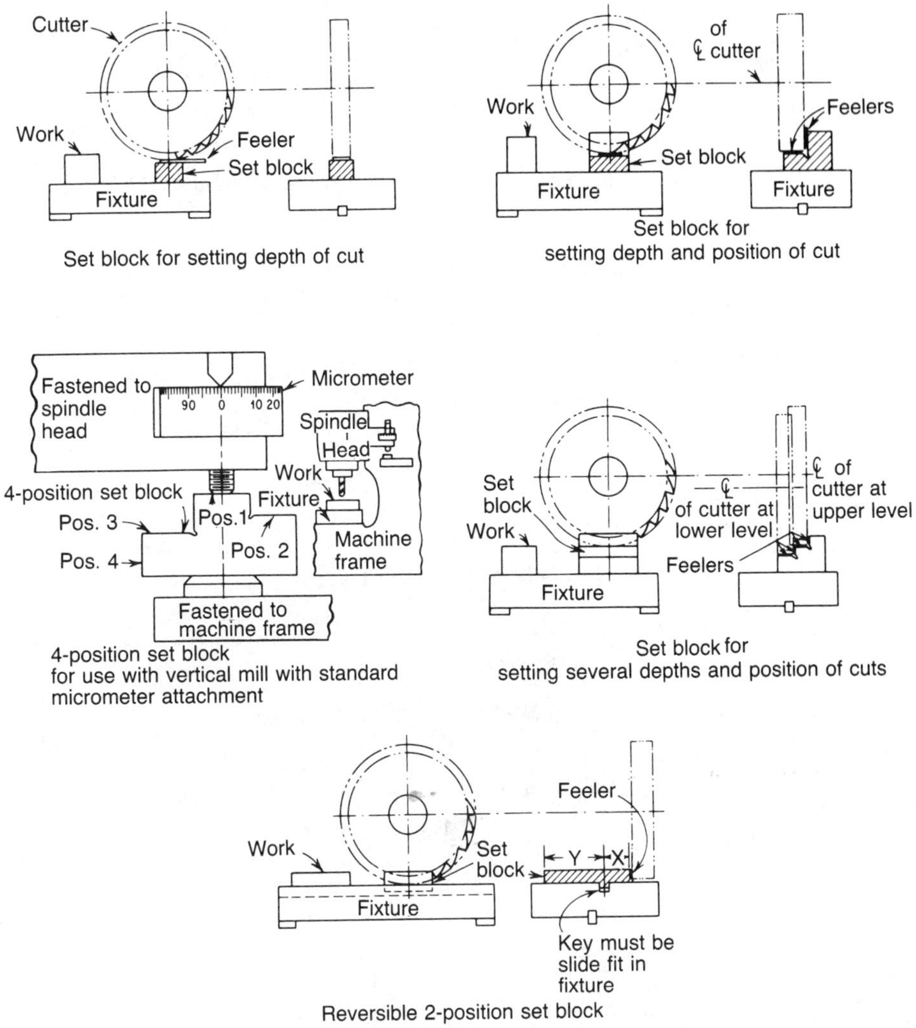

Cutter

Work

Feeler
Set block

Fixture

Set block for setting depth of cut

of ℄ cutter

Work

Feelers

Set block

Fixture

Fixture

Set block for
setting depth and position of cut

Fastened to spindle head

90 0   10 20

Micrometer

Spindle Head

4-position set block

Pos. 3

Pos. 4

Pos.1

Pos. 2

Work
Fixture

Machine frame

Fastened to
machine frame

4-position set block
for use with vertical mill with standard
micrometer attachment

Set block

Work

℄ of cutter at
lower level

℄ of
cutter at
upper level

Feelers

Fixture

Set block for
setting several depths and position of cuts

Feeler

Work

Set block

Y X

Fixture

Key must be
slide fit in
fixture

Reversible 2-position set block

Fig. 7-27 Cutter setting with set blocks and feelers.

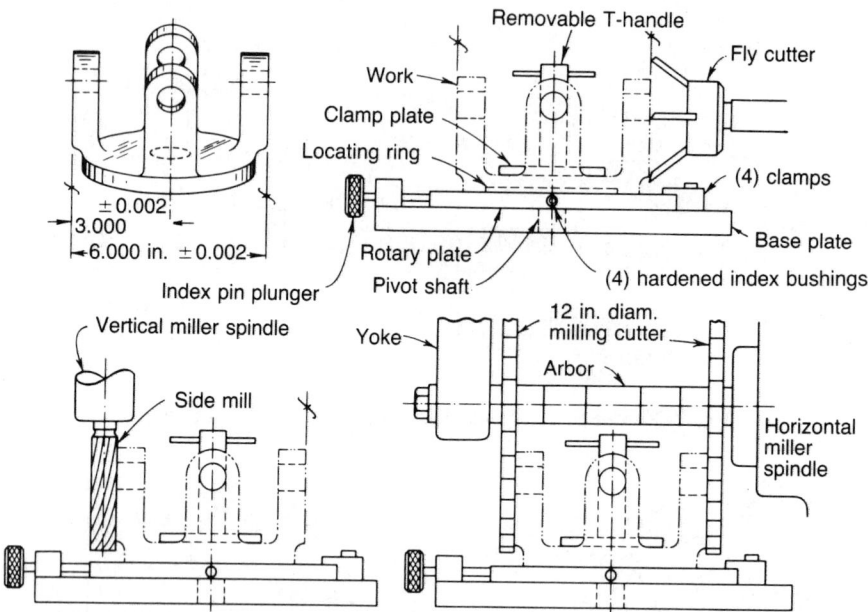

Fig. 7-28 Fixtured workpiece processed by several different methods.

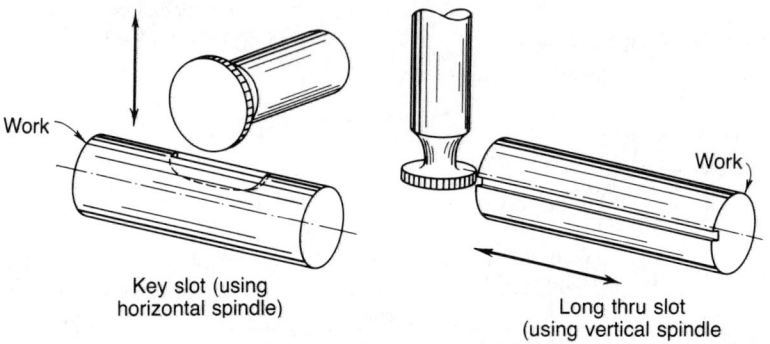

Fig. 7-29 Milling slots in shafts.

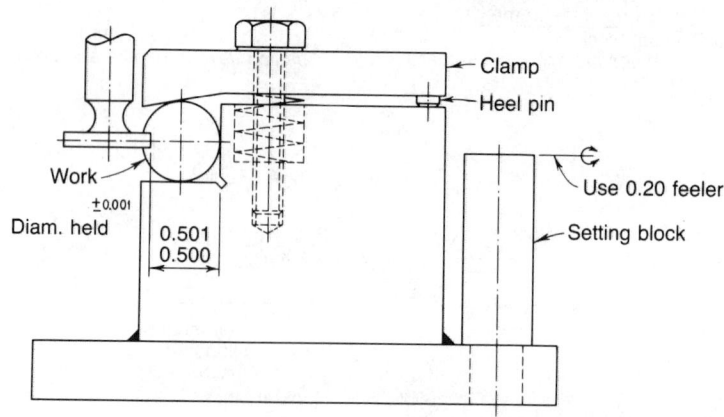

Fig. 7-30 Fixture for milling a long thru slot on a vertical mill.

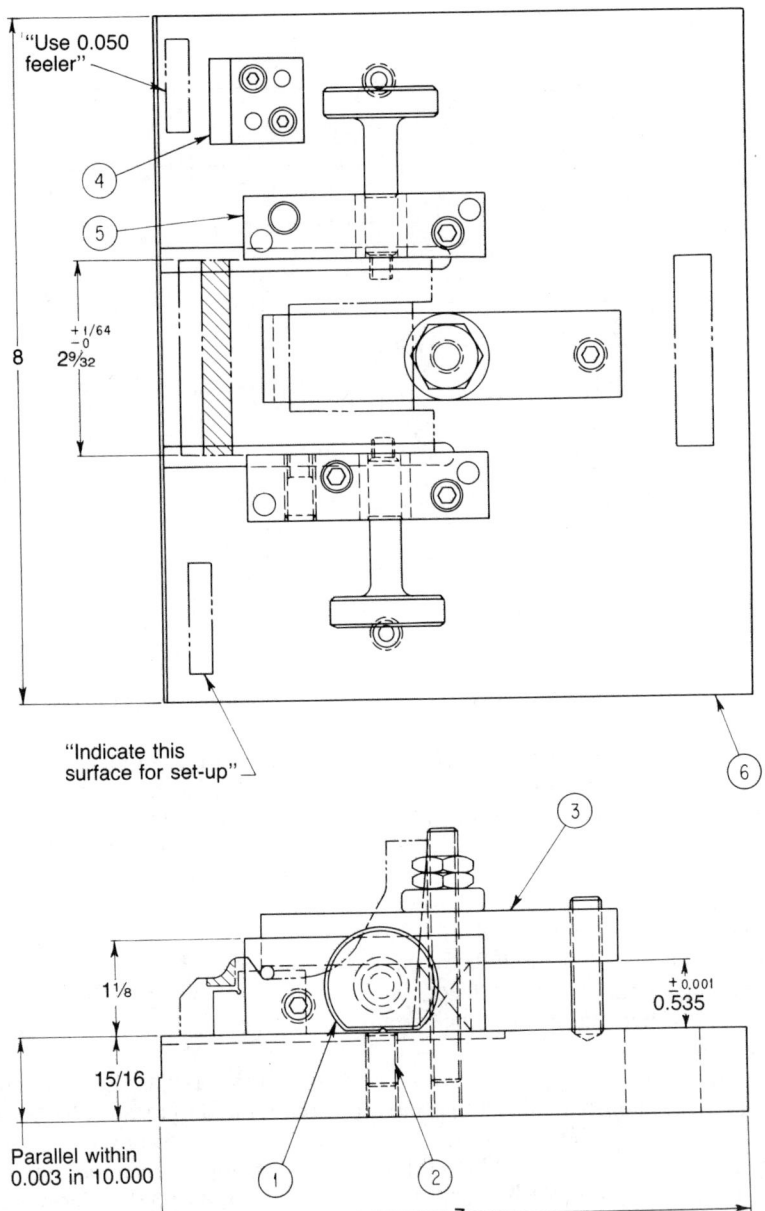

Fig. 7-31 Milling fixture for 0.315 in. (8.00 mm) wide slot. (*Courtesy The Emerson Electric Mfg. Co.*)

End Milling a Groove in an Aluminum Casting. The fixture of Fig. 7-32 is for end-milling a groove in an aluminum die-cast part. Since the cutting pressure is small, it is permissible to perform the operation against the clamp.

The part is placed over the locating pin (1) which is pressed into the base plate (2) and against the smaller pin (3). The clamp (4) is tightened against the part by a socket-head cap screw (5). A slot in the top plate (6) of the welded fixture base gives the milling cutter access to the work area.

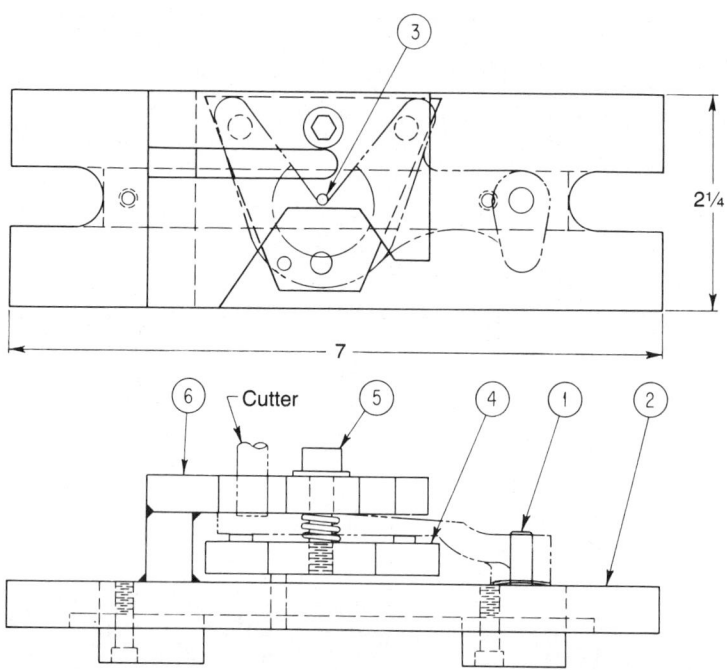

Fig. 7-32 End-milling a slot in an aluminum die casting. (*Courtesy Allen Gauge & Tool Co.*)

A Fixture for Milling a Compound Angle. The fixture of Fig. 7-33 is used in milling a compound angle on the end of a right-hand and left-hand bracket. The part is positioned sidewise by the two-point locator (1) and endwise by another locator (2). A tapered block (3) supports the end of the clamp (4) and forces it to hold the part against the side locator (1). An adjustable jackscrew (5) provides support for the milled surface.

For construction and inspection purposes, two 0.875 in. diameter holes and two 0.500 in. diameter construction balls (6) are incorporated in the fixture. The cutter is positioned by a set block (7) and a 0.050 in. (1.27 mm) feeler gage.

A Face-milling Fixture with Equalizer. The milling fixture of Fig. 7-34 incorporates equalizing supports and clamps which maintain location and rigid support necessary for the successful milling of the part.

The supports are of two types, the positive and the spring-actuated adjustable type. Since three points establish a plane, three supports are required to locate a workpiece in a plane parallel to, or on the flat surface of, a fixture. Positive location in one plane is achieved with two fixed supports (1) and two equalizing adjustable supports (2). The latter are connected by a pivot bar with the result that should one be depressed, the other must rise.

At the ends of the workpiece, adjustable spring-loaded supports (3) prevent the part from being distorted by tool pressure. After the part has been located and clamped, these supports are locked in position with hand screws (4).

The part is located centrally on the fixture by eight diamond-shaped locating pins (5) which enter holes in the part. These pins permit a small amount of mislocation in a longitudinal direction but little or no variation in crosswise hole spacing.

Two sets of equalizing clamps (6) on each side of the part are attached to clamping levers (7) by shoulder screws. Each pair of clamps is connected by a shaft having right-hand threads on one end and left-hand threads on the other, providing independent clamping.

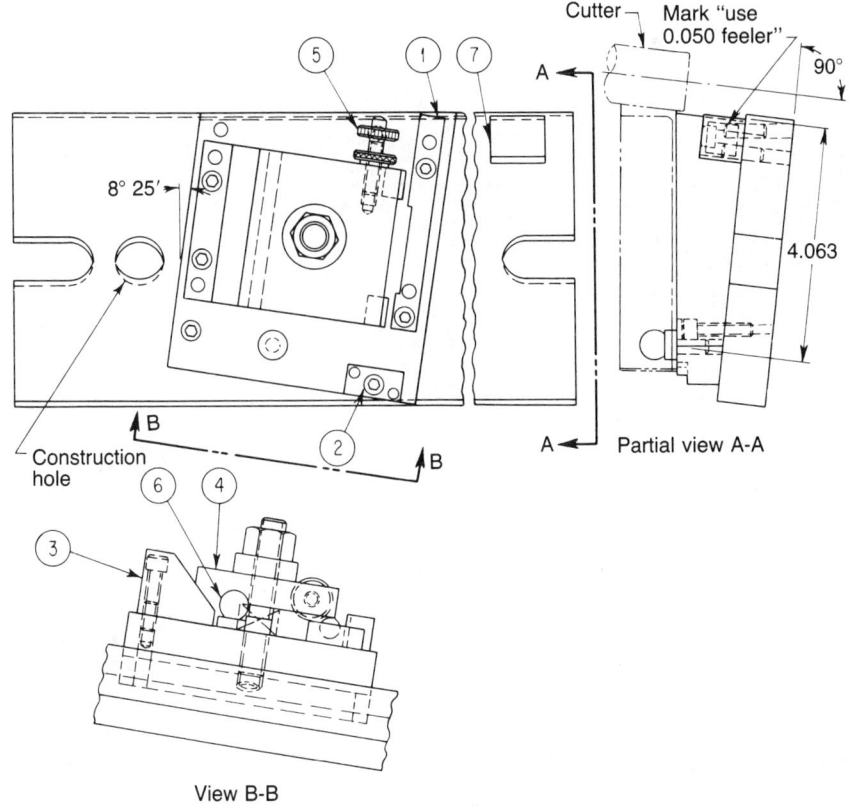

Fig. 7-33 **Milling fixture for compound angle.** (*Courtesy The Emerson Electric Mfg. Co.*)

A cutter set block (not shown) is incorporated in one block containing the end supports.

Fixture keys are provided for aligning the fixture on the machine table, as are slots for T-bolts to hold the fixture on the table.

Automatic Clamping-and-unloading Fixture. The fixture of Fig. 7-35 is of the automatic clamping-and-unloading type operated by hand. It consists of a base (1) and a trolley assembly (2) riding in guides within the fixture. One guide or gib (3) has a cam surface. The opposite gib (6) is wedge-shaped and can be moved to adjust the fit and to contact pressure of the rollers (4) mounted to the trolley. The trolley is in two parts hinged at *A* and separated at *B* by a compression spring (5) which opens the square opening between the two members of the trolley.

As the trolley travels from left to right, the part is clamped in the square opening for milling. When it is moved farther to the right, the two jaws formed by the trolley members are opened by the spring, releasing their grip on the part, which drops into the chute. Small variations in the diameter of the part are equalized by the spring.

The loading position of the trolley fixture is at the extreme left, where the distance between the gib surfaces for the rollers is greater than when it is in position for milling. As the trolley is moved toward the cutter to the right, this distance becomes smaller and finally remains constant through the travel of the trolley during the cutting stroke.

Movement of the trolley is controlled by a lever (6) which is under control of the operator. The milling-machine table is stationary and is used only to locate the fixture in proper position. Milling occurs during movement of the trolley.

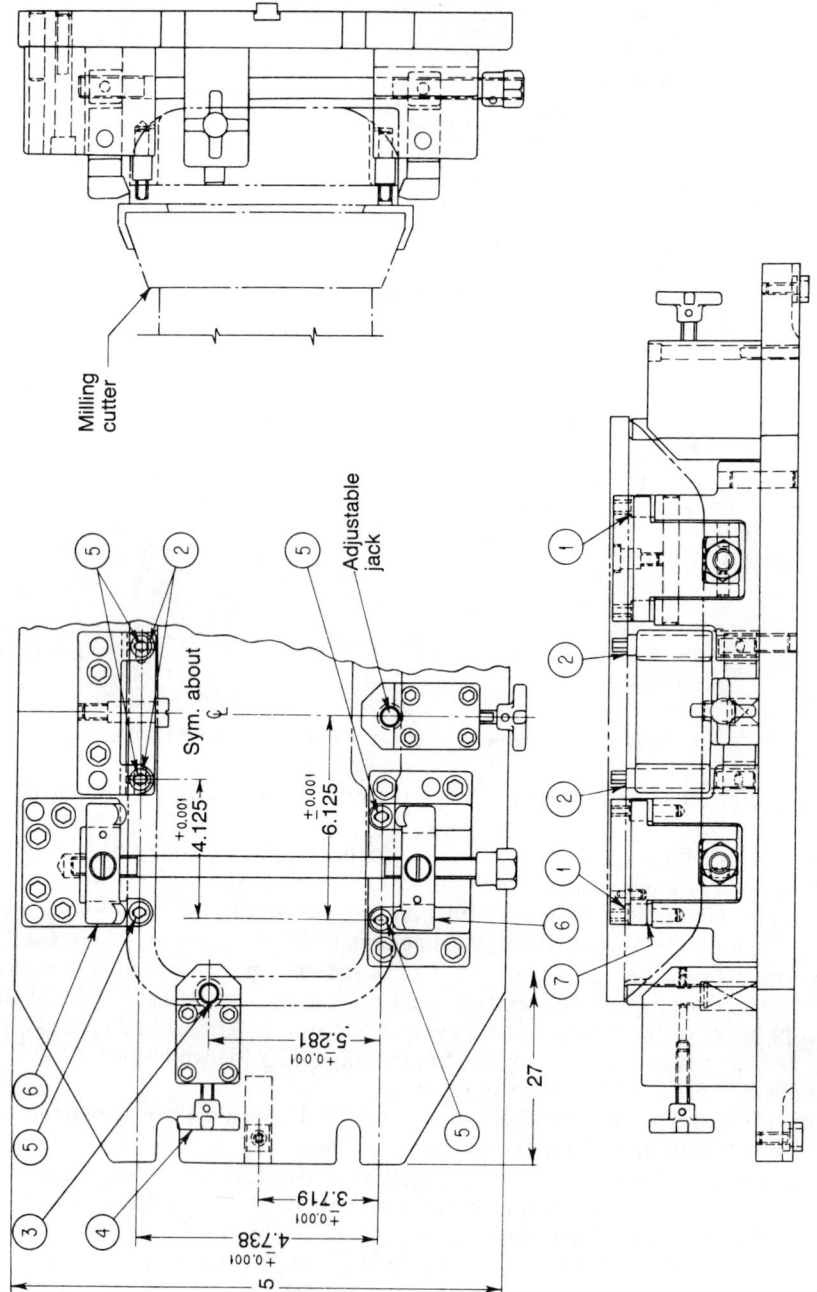

Fig. 7-34 Fixture for face milling an oil sump pan. (*Courtesy Allison Div., General Motors Corp.*)

Milling cutter

Adjustable jack

Sym. about ℄

$4.125 \pm^{+0.001}$

6.125 ± 0.001

5.281 ± 0.001

3.719 ± 0.001

4.738 ± 0.001

15

27

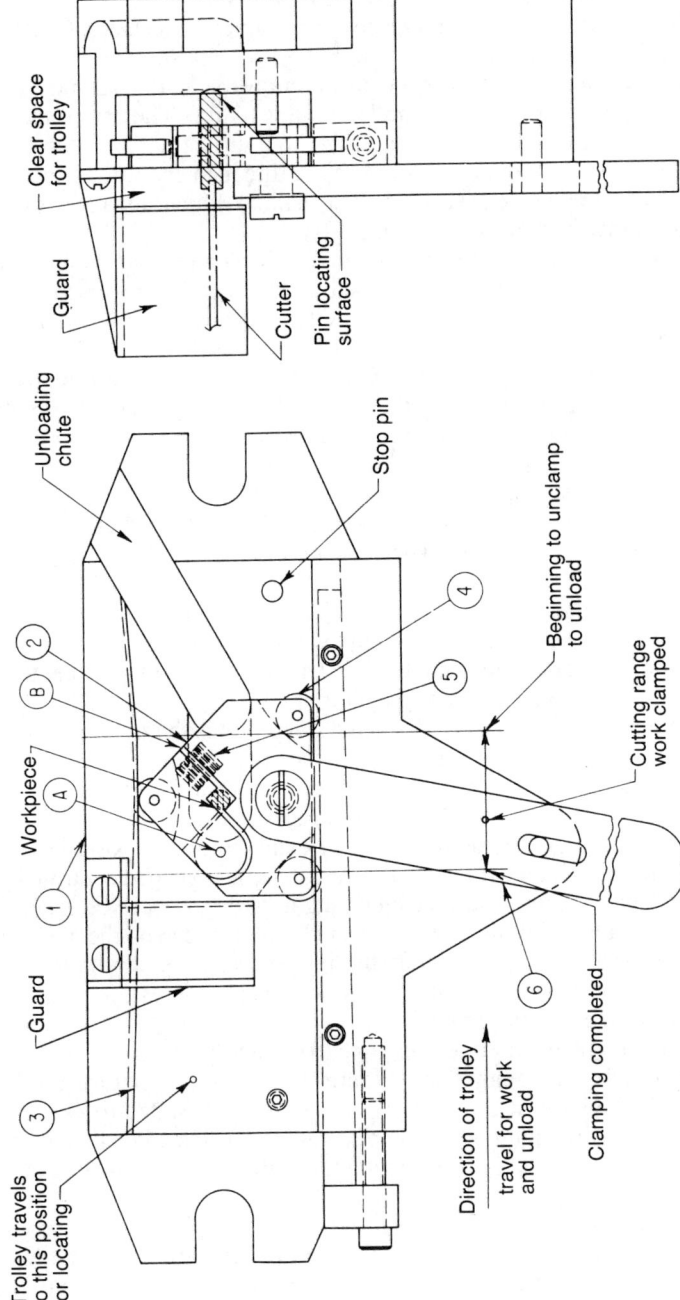

Fig. 7-35 Manually operated automatic clamping and unloading of part for milling. *(Courtesy Goodyear Tire & Rubber Co.)*

Another automatic locating and clamping fixture is shown in Fig. 7-36. This fixture was designed for use on a transfer line. The view in the figure is in the direction of the workpiece transfer.

Fixtures for Milling Plain and Micrometer Stop Bodies. The fixture of Fig. 7-37 has two female centers that locate one of two parts, a plain stop body or a micrometer stop body, from bosses while milling a V-groove and adjacent surfaces. One female center (1) is fixed and is press-fitted into the stand (2). The opposite end of this locator along with two ¼ in. diameter dowel pins locates a removable cutter-set gage (3) which sets the cutter for either of the two parts milled on this fixture. The end of the locator (1) is threaded to receive a standard hexagon nut to hold the set gage in place.

An adjustable female-center locator (4) has a threaded end which screws into a fixed nut (5). The center is rotated by a machine handle which advances or retracts it to accommodate either part between centers.

The parts are located laterally by a locator (6) which has two sloping surfaces. One surface is used to locate the plain stop body. The locator is reversed, positioning the other sloping surface for locating the micrometer stop body. A thumbscrew (7) holds the parts against this locator.

Since the V-groove is 15/16 in. (23.8 mm) from the center of the boss in the plain stop unit and 1⅛ in. (28.6 mm) from the center of the boss on the micrometer stop unit, the setting gage (3) is reversible on the fixture for setting the cutter for either part.

The subsequent milling operations on the two stop bodies are not similar; therefore different fixtures are required.

The second operation on the plain stop body finish-mills and chamfers one end at a time with the fixture of Fig. 7-38. The stop body is located from the surface milled in the first operation.

The cutter is guided in a liner bushing and a drill bushing (which functions as a stop collar). The vertical adjustment of the part is made by a dog-point setscrew (1). The cutting tool consists of a holder for a two-lip end mill which mills to center and for two brazed carbide tips for the chamfering operation.

The second operation on the micrometer stop body is the milling of the 1 in. (25.4 mm) wide slot. A fixture for this operation is shown in Fig. 7-39.

The part is located on an inverted V-rest surface (1) and a flat-rest surface (2) from the previously milled V-groove and adjacent flat surfaces. A hand screw (3) threaded into a hole in the part locates the piece sidewise and holds it in position.

A strap clamp (4) with a cutter-clearance slot has a V-shaped centralizing groove in the toe. Its heel has a sloping surface engaging a mating surface on a heel support (5) adjustable for height. A clamping wheel (6) pulls down and in on the workpiece, seating it on the V-rest and pressing it against the flat rest surface. Compression springs (7) support the clamp in the unclamped position. Another compression spring (8) holds the clamp away from the workpiece for loading and unloading.

A separately mounted cutter-setting gage (9) is incorporated.

Milling a Small Aluminum Part. Figure 7-40 shows a fixture used on a small horizontal mill. The base of the fixture (1) is keyed and bolted to the machine table. Four milling cutters are mounted on the machine arbor. The machine table is traversed parallel to the arbor to align the fixture with the cutters; then it is locked in place for the milling operation.

The workpiece shown in the same figure is a 0.170 in. (4.32 mm) cube with two slots milled in one face. Round-bar stock is clamped in the fixture and fed into a gang of three milling cutters. The two outer cutters straddle the bar to cut two parallel flats. The inner cutter produces a slot in the face of the workpiece midway between the flats. The workpiece is manually rotated 90° and again presented to the cutters. The second pass results in two parallel flats and a slot, all perpendicular to the cuts of the first pass. The fixture is again retracted from the cutting position, the upper element swiveled 90°, and

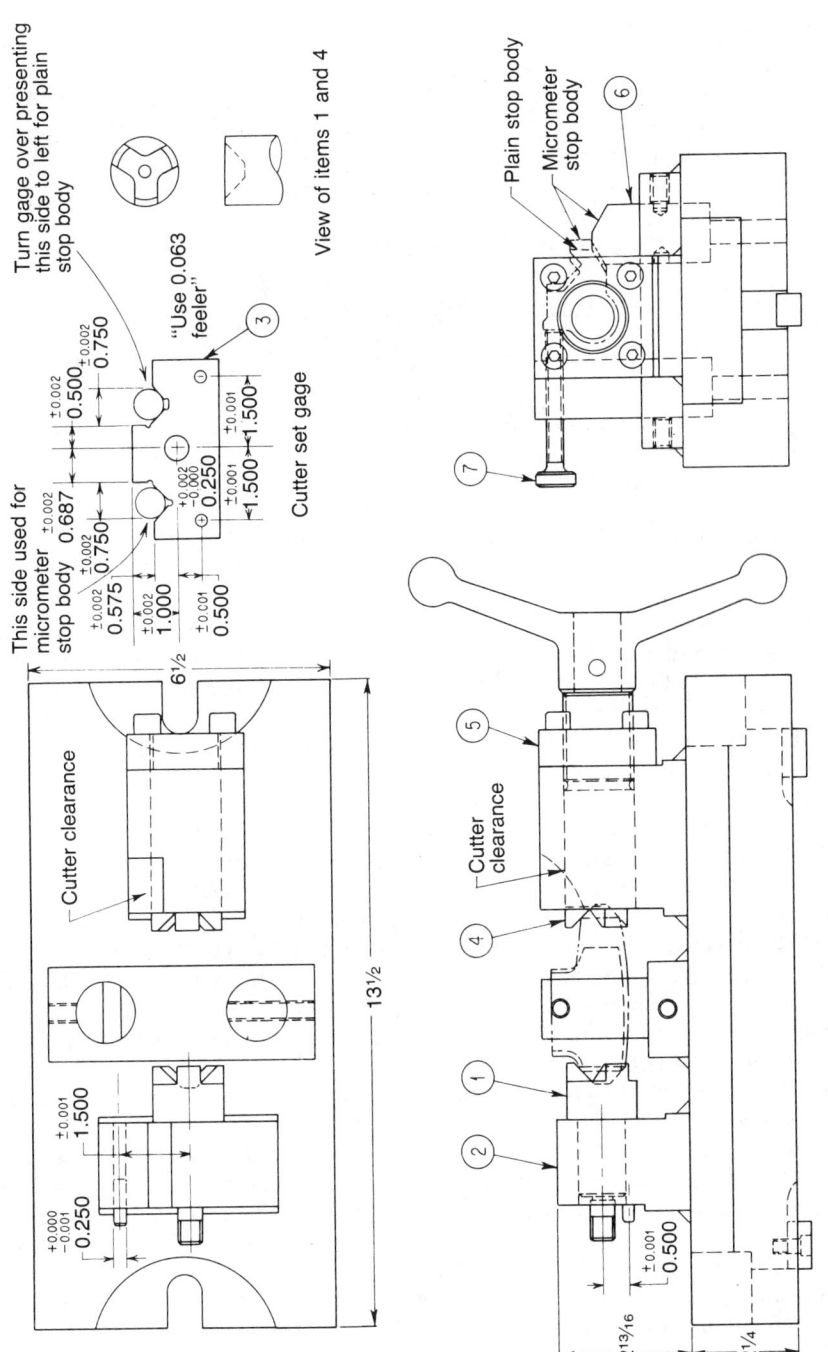

Fig. 7-36 V-groove milling fixture for stop bodies. (*Courtesy Rockwell Mfg. Co.*)

Turn gage over presenting this side to left for plain stop body

View of items 1 and 4

"Use 0.063 feeler"

This side used for micrometer stop body

Cutter set gage

Cutter clearance

Plain stop body

Micrometer stop body

Cutter clearance

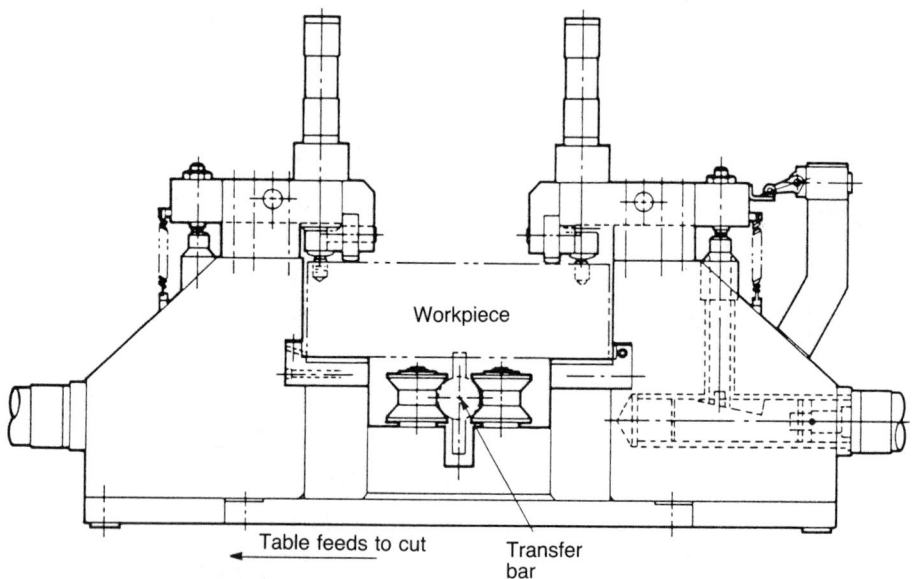

Workpiece

Table feeds to cut ◄——

Transfer
bar

Fig. 7-37 Fixture for use on a transfer line. (*Courtesy Cincinnati Milacron*)

the part cut off from the bar stock by a fourth milling cutter.

The fixture base (1) is a 1¼ in. (3.18 mm) low-carbon steel plate. A CRS locating plate (2) with a circular track is bolted and doweled to the base. A CRS swivel plate (3) is attached to the fixture base by a hex nut, washer, and stud around which the swivel plate pivots. A T-bolt fastened to the swivel plate rides in the machined circular track of the locating plate and limits the travel of the swivel plate to 90°. A pin (4) locks the swivel plate in position at either end of its travel. A feed track (5) bolted to the swivel plate provides for initial alignment of the bar stock. Actual alignment to the milling cutters is dependent on a base (6), a collet assembly (7), and key (8). The bar stock is fed through the collet until it encounters a stop block (9). The collet locknut (10) is tightened to grasp and center the stock. With the stopblock rotated out of the way, the machine table is traversed presenting the bar to the three milling cutters (11). The table is retracted, the key is pulled up, and the collet is rotated 90° where it is again engaged by the key for the second milling operation. The cutoff milling cutter (12) is used after the swivel plate has been indexed and locked in its second position.

A Milling Fixture for Four Operations To reduce tooling costs on low-production items, it is often desirable to use one fixture for more than one operation. The fixture shown in Fig. 7-41 is used for operations involving plain, straddle, and three face milling operations.

The fixture is designed for down milling in the first operation, with the thrust against the solid locator (1). The workpiece is located on two round locators (1 and 2) which fit the 1.024 in. diameter end holes. One of the locators (2) also serves as a clamp. Equalizing clamps (3) with a compression spring between them are guided by gibs (4) and are used for the first and second operations on the part.

When milling the 15° surface, the fixture is set crosswise on the machine table and is tilted to a 15° angle. It is aligned on the machine table T-slot with a fixture key. Tilting of the fixture allows side milling of the 15° surface in a plane normal to the machine table. The vertical setting of the milling cutter is done by using a 0.062 in. (1.57 mm) feeler on the surface provided. Lateral positioning is accomplished by using a 1 in. (25.4 mm) gage block and a straightedge.

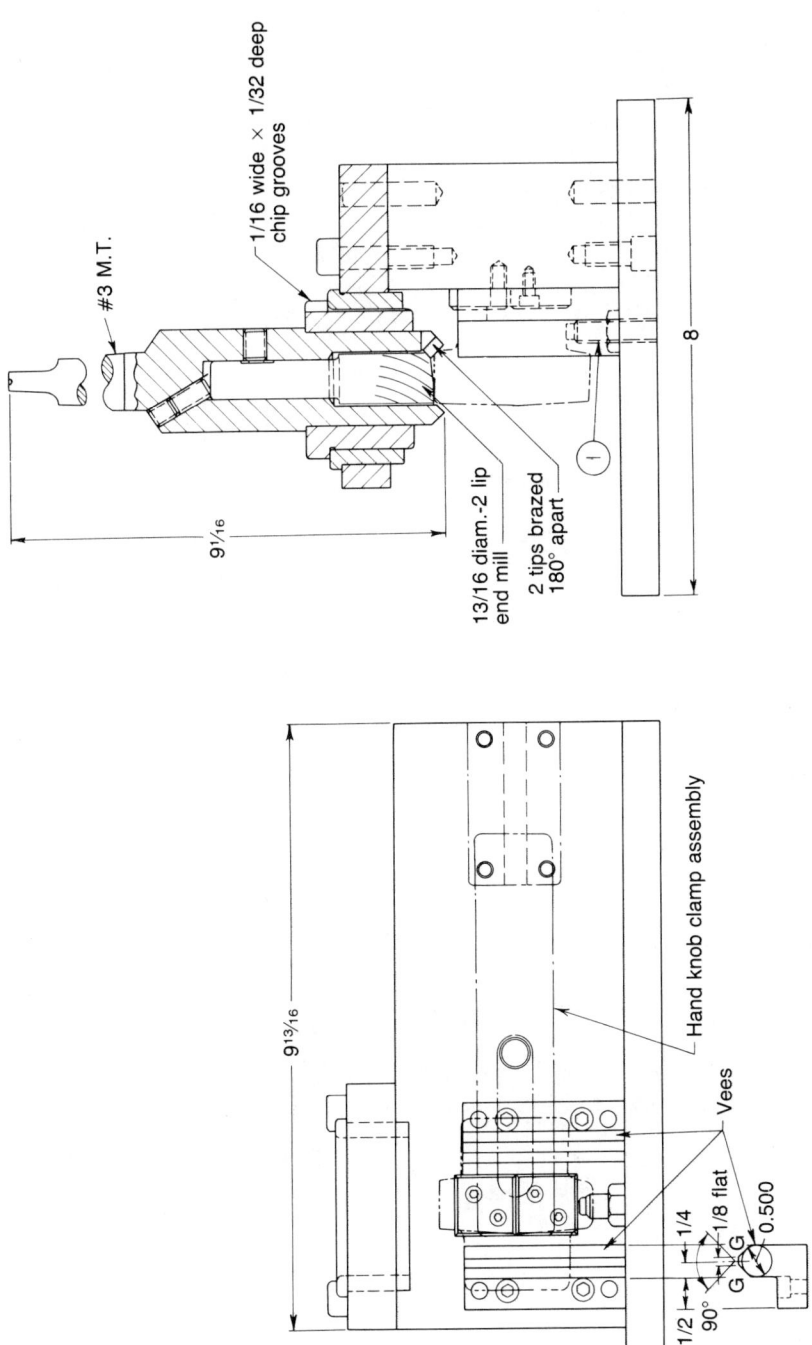

Fig. 7-38 Fixture for end-milling and chamfering plain stop bodies. (*Courtesy Rockwell Mfg. Co.*)

#3 M.T.

1/16 wide × 1/32 deep chip grooves

13/16 diam.-2 lip end mill

2 tips brazed 180° apart

9¹⁄₁₆

8

Hand knob clamp assembly

Vees

9¹³⁄₁₆

1/8 flat

0.500

1/4

1/2

90°

G G

G

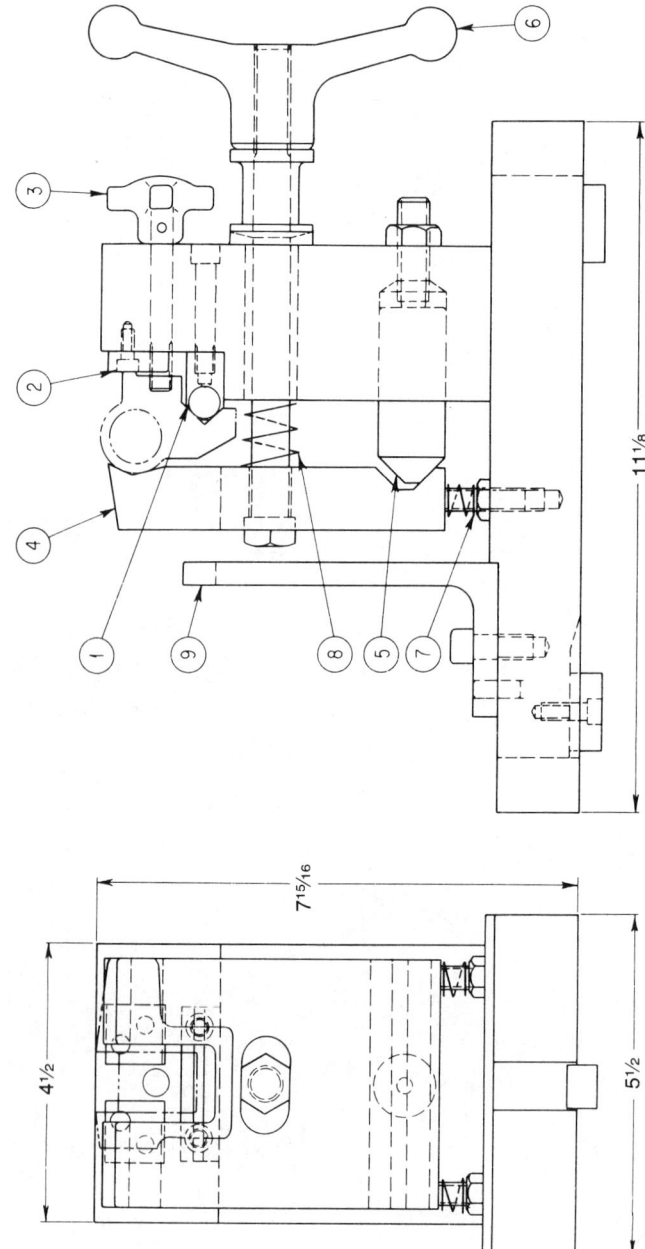

Fig. 7-39 Fixture for milling a 1 in. (25.4 mm) wide slot in micrometer stop bodies. (*Courtesy Rockwell Mfg. Co.*)

7-32

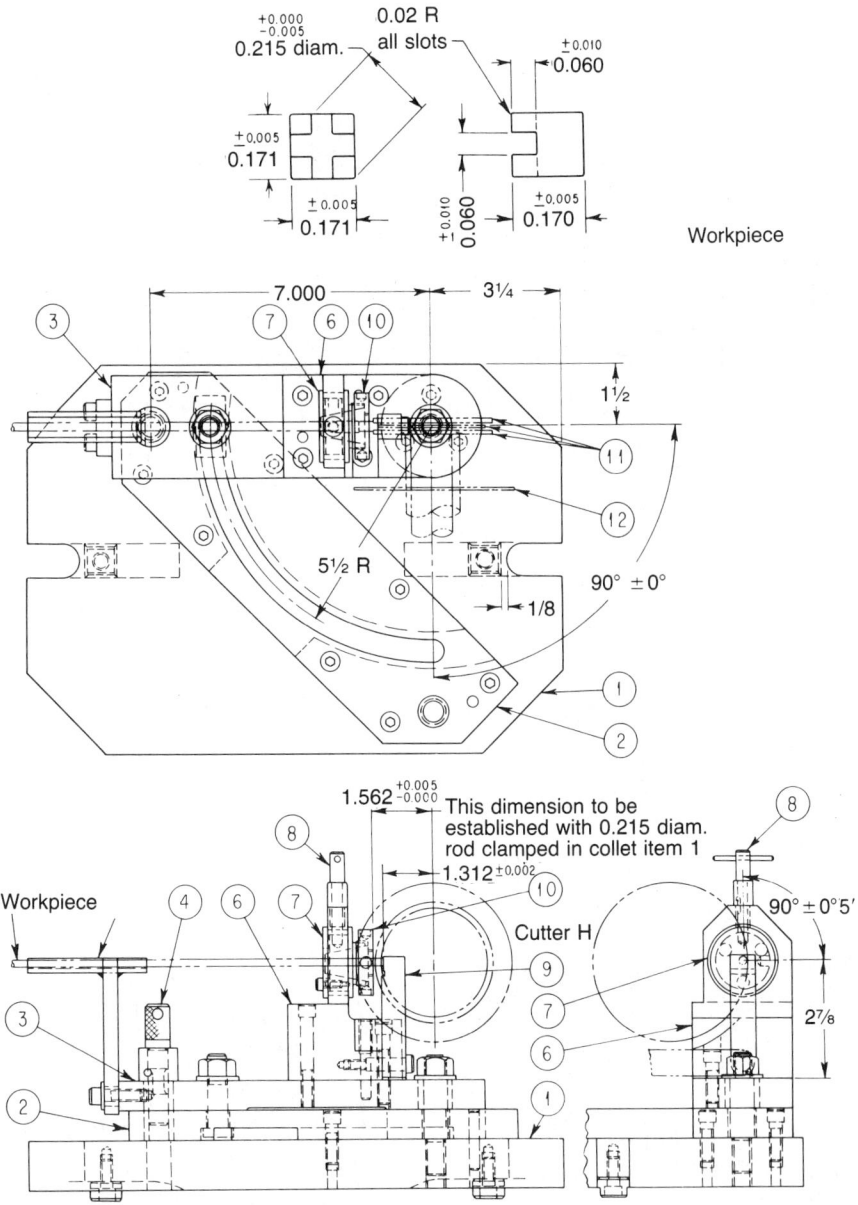

Fig. 7-40 Fixture for milling a small aluminum part. (*Courtesy U.S. Naval Gun Factory*)

For milling the 23° surface, a third position of the fixture is provided. The fixture rests on the surface of the main base crosswise on the machine table located by a fixture key. A second pair of jaws (5 and 6) replaces previously used jaws (3). This operation may be performed on a horizontal milling machine using an arbor-mounted side-milling cutter or with an end mill in a vertical machine.

Progressively Milling a Gearbox Casting. The five surfaces of a gearbox casting are machined on a planer-type milling machine, using a face-milling cutter in the fixture of Fig. 7-42. The five surfaces are machined in one machine cycle. The part is progressively moved from left to right by the operator during the machine cycle.

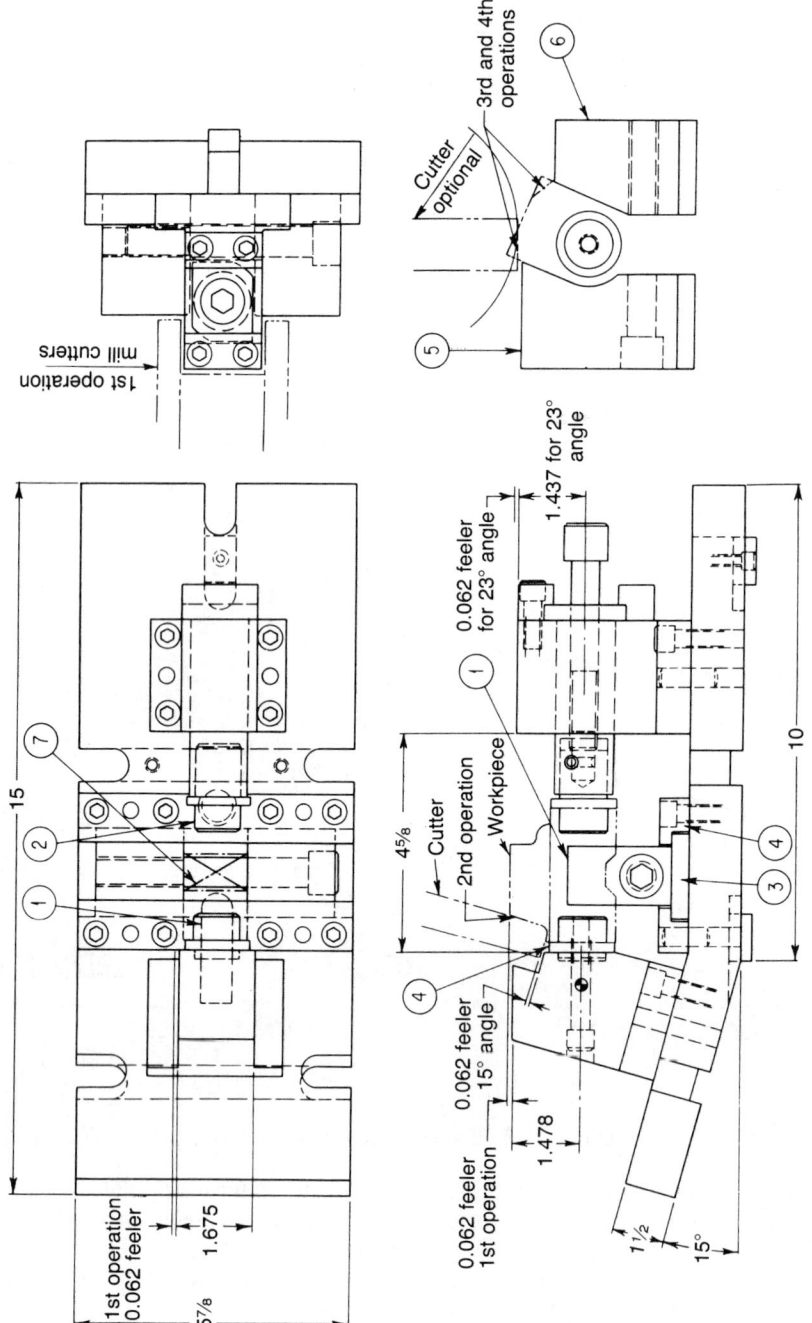

Fig. 7-41 Milling fixture for four operations. (*Courtesy Chiksan Co.*)

1st operation
mill cutters

3rd and 4th
operations

Cutter
optional

1.437 for 23°
angle

0.062 feeler
for 23° angle

10

4⅝

Cutter
2nd operation

Workpiece

0.062 feeler
15° angle

1.478

1.5

15°

0.062 feeler
1st operation

15

1.675

1st operation
0.062 feeler

5⅞

7-34

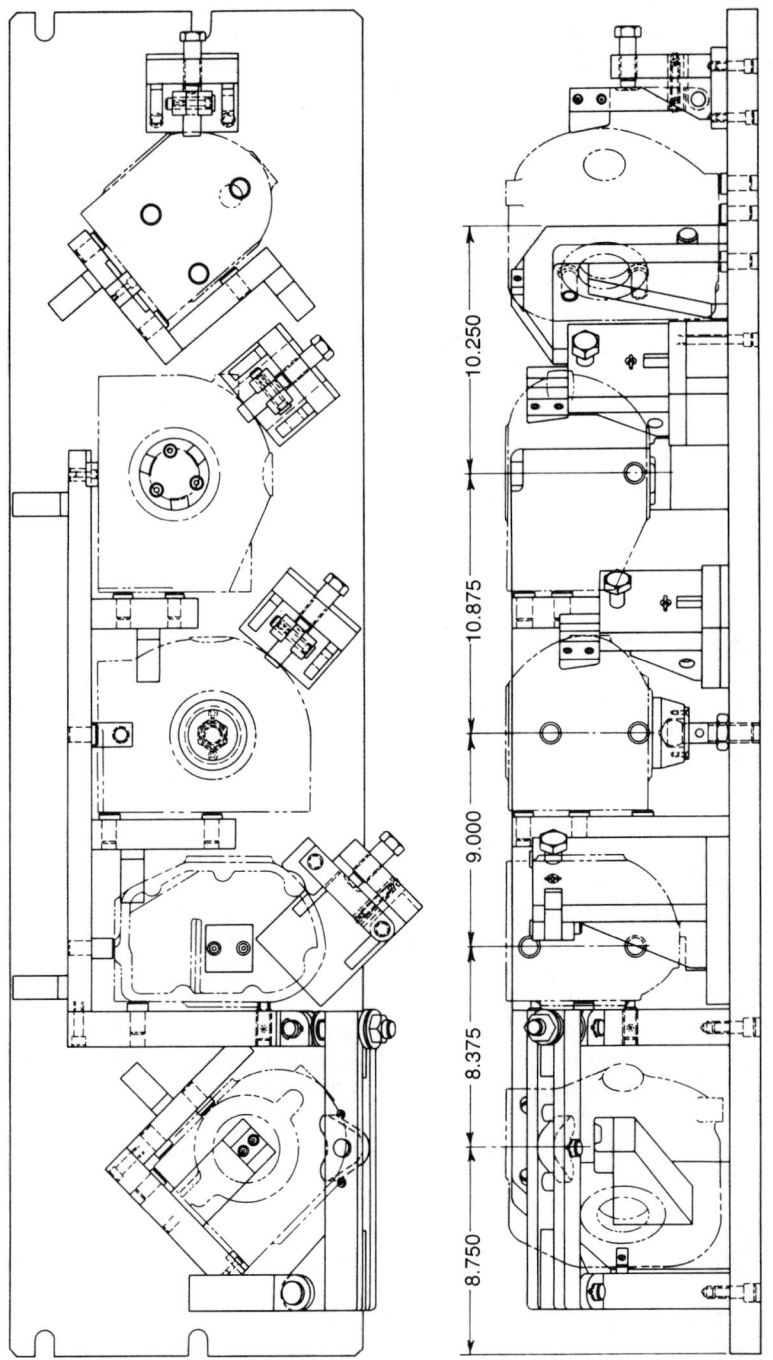

Fig. 7-42 Progressive milling of five surfaces of a gearbox casting. (*Courtesy New Holland Machine Div., Sperry Rand Corp.*)

10.250

10.875

9.000

8.375

8.750

The fixture base plate is hot-rolled steel $1\frac{1}{2} \times 15 \times 56\frac{1}{2}$ in. ($38 \times 381 \times 1435$ mm). The clamp assemblies and locators for each position of the workpiece are attached to the base plate with cap screws and dowels.

Milling a Contoured Slot. The workpieces were machined to the dimensions necessary for locating them in the fixture of Fig. 7-43. This includes the spline hole which locates on the straight locators (1), the 0.187 in. diameter hole for the diamond locators (2), and the surface which rests on the side of the fixture.

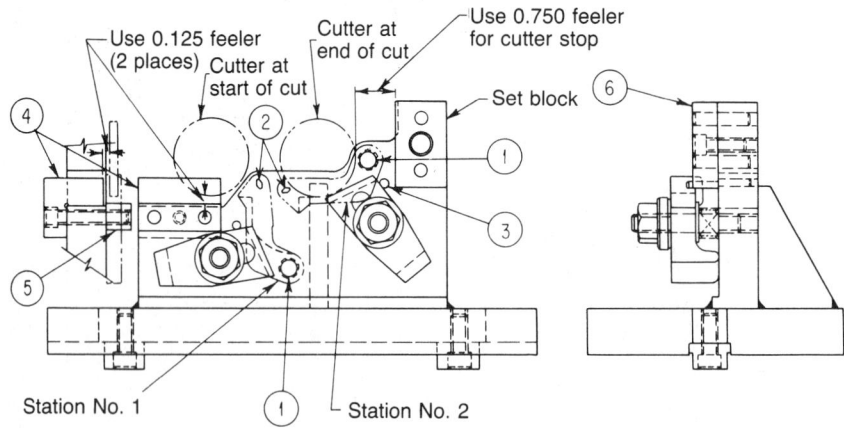

Fig. 7-43 Fixture for milling slots in an alloy steel arm. (*Courtesy U.S. Naval Ordnance Plant*)

The fixture, of welded construction and of extremely simple design, is very efficiently arranged so that the cutter cuts continuously from the beginning of the action in station 1 to its end in station 2. One workpiece is completed for each cutter cycle by this progressive-milling method.

Operation 1 mills a slot $0.187 \begin{smallmatrix} +0.005 \\ -0.000 \end{smallmatrix}$ in. wide while the workpiece is located in station 1.

Operation 2 mills the continuation of the slot cut in operation 1 with the workpiece located in station 2 from the same holes and surface used in locating it in station 1. This locating method ensures that the blended slotted surfaces will be cut with greater accuracy than would be possible by changing the locating points. Each part is clamped by a single retractable strap clamp with an integral heel support. Both clamps are kept in a slanting position and prevented from falling into a vertical position by guide pins (3). These pins hold the clamps in position when they are unclamped and retracted, thus minimizing clamp operation time. This method accomplishes the same result as the conventional design of a slot in the underside of a strap clamp engaging the heel support, and it costs less.

The setting of the cutter for height and side position is made by using a 0.125 in. (3.18 mm) feeler gage with set blocks (4 and 5) for the height and side or cross positions. Another set block (6) sets fixture longitudinal travel with a 0.750 in. (19.05 mm) feeler gage.

Abreast Milling Long Thin Parts. A simple but efficient fixture for abreast milling of two tool-steel strips is shown in Fig. 7-44.

An $11\frac{1}{2}°$ angular surface to be milled along the edge of the workpiece is suited to abreast milling.

The fixture is made up of few parts and is efficient because two pieces are milled at a

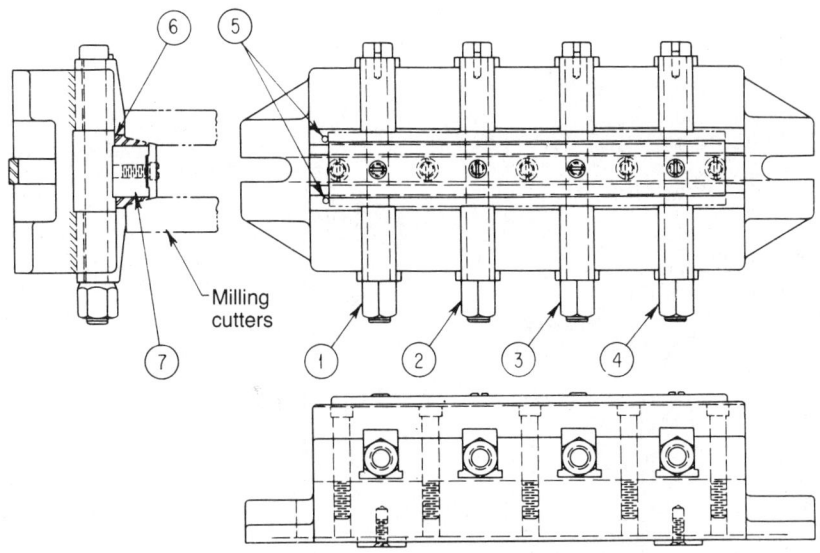

Fig. 7-44 Fixture for abreast milling of two strips. (*Courtesy The L.S. Starret Co.*)

time. The handling of two parts instead of one requires slightly more time, while clamping time remains the same.

The four clamping bolts (1 to 4), which are operated individually, could by a slight modification be tightened in pairs, thus reducing the clamping time. To further reduce clamping time, each bolt could be provided with an air cylinder for simultaneous clamping and unclamping.

The endwise location of the parts is accomplished by pushing the parts against the stop pins (5). The rest surfaces (6 and 7) extend the full length of the workpiece.

Milling a Small Triangular Part. The size and shape of the part shown in Fig. 7-45*a* presented difficult handling and machining problems. The stock for this part is 3/16 × ⅜ in. alloy-steel bars sawed into 12 in. (304 mm) lengths. These bars are ground on both sides to a thickness of 0.140 $^{+0.003}_{-0.001}$ in. and milled on one edge to a width of 0.337 in. (8.56 mm).

In the next operation, four bars are clamped into the fixture shown in Fig. 7-45*b* and machined to size while maintaining the 25° angle and the 0.140, 0.300, and 0.374 in. (3.56, 7.62, and 9.50 mm) dimensions.

A 5 × ½ × 1 in. (127 × 12.7 × 25.4 mm) side-milling cutter and a 6 × 1/16 × 1 in. (152 × 1.57 × 25.4 mm) metal slitting saw with side chip clearance are used for cutting the workpiece.

The workpieces are placed in four V-grooves in the block (1) and up against a locator (2). Two strap clamps (3) hold the part for milling and cutting off.

Six Station Hydraulic Slotting Fixture. Six arbor mounted milling cutters are used to mill slots in six workpieces at the same time by placing the six pieces side-by-side in the hydraulic fixture shown in Fig. 7-46.

Reciprocal Milling of Slots. Two fixtures of identical design are used for this operation (see Fig. 7-47). To speed up clamping and unclamping of the parts, the clamps are operated hydraulically. The fixture has a V-block (2) as rest and locating surfaces for the cylindrical shape of the workpiece. The workpiece is placed vertically in the fixture and rests in a nest pad (1). It is clamped against a V-block by a V-clamp (3) actuated by a crank (4). A crank is rotated by a push rod (5) which receives its motion through a

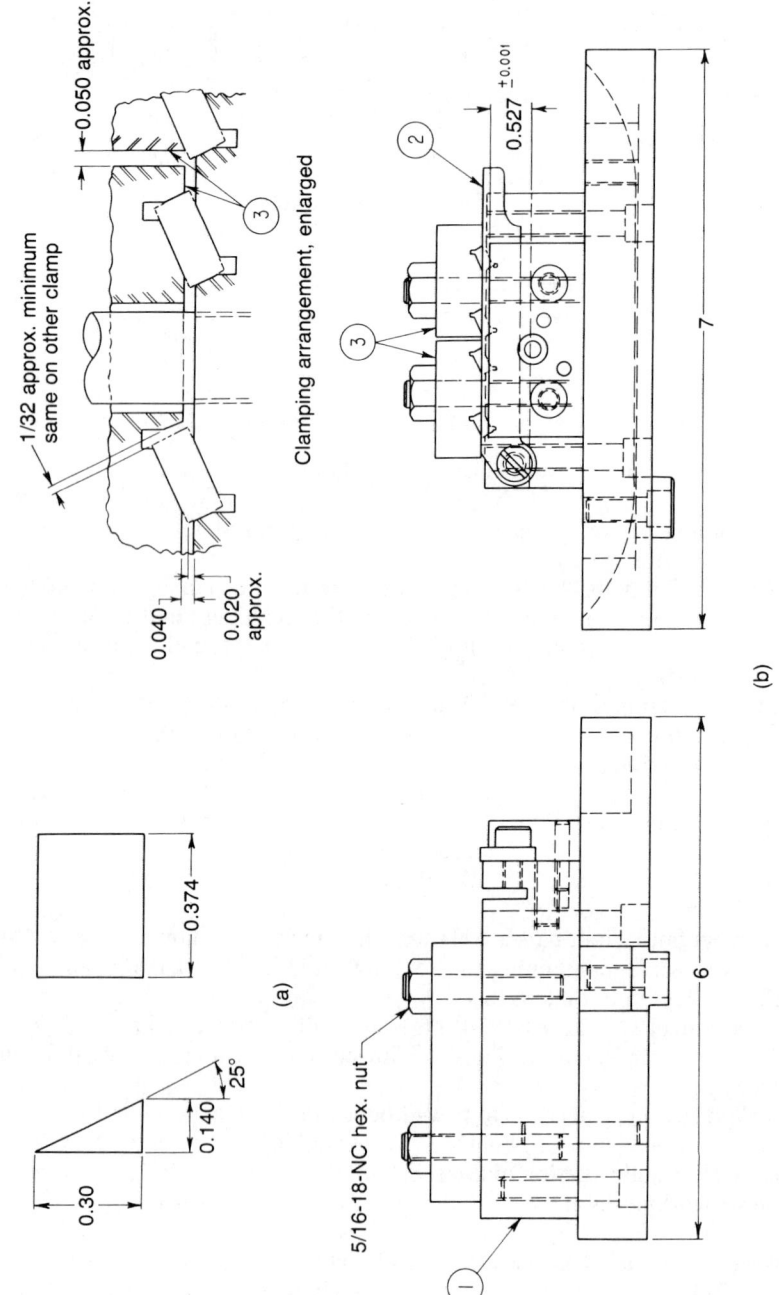

0.050 approx.

1/32 approx. minimum
same on other clamp

0.040

0.020
approx.

Clamping arrangement, enlarged

(a)

0.374

0.30

0.140

25°

5/16-18-NC hex. nut

6

7

0.527 ±0.001

(b)

Fig. 7-45 Milling fixture for a small triangular-shaped part. (*Courtesy U.S. Naval Gun Factory*)

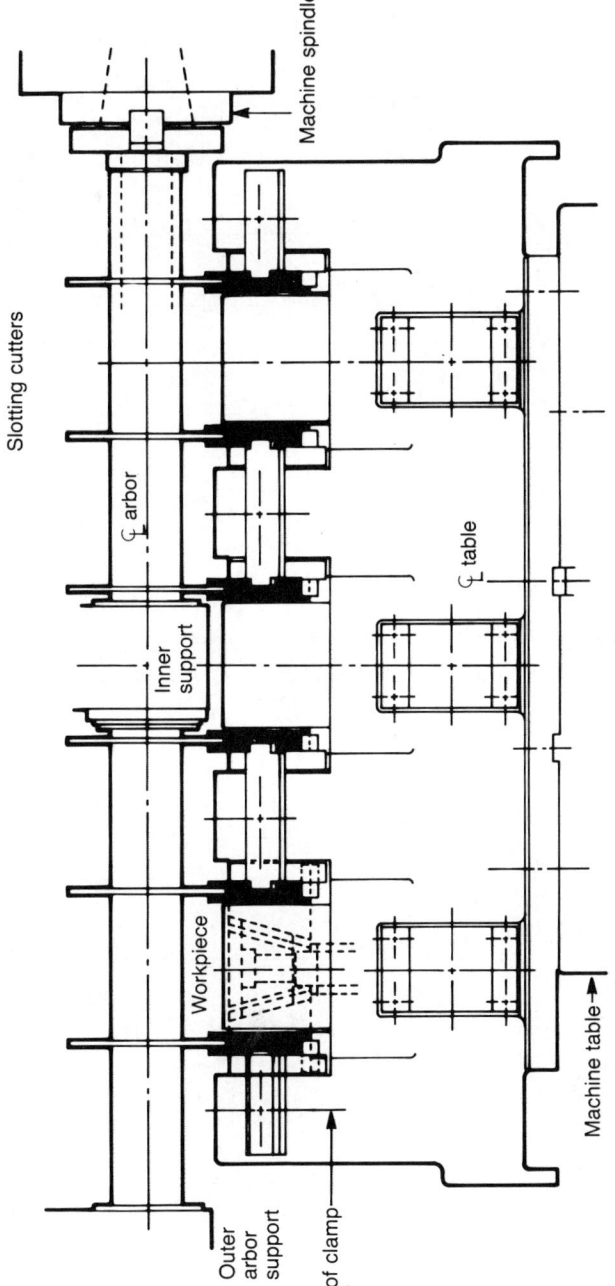

Fig. 7-46 End view of a hydraulic fixture for slotting six workpieces at the same time. (*Courtesy Cincinnati Milacron*)

7-39

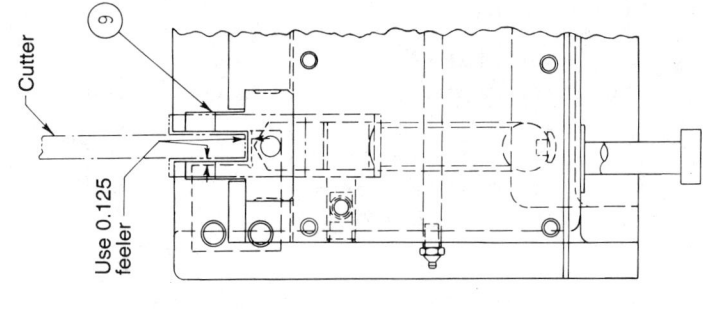

Cutter

Use 0.125
feeler

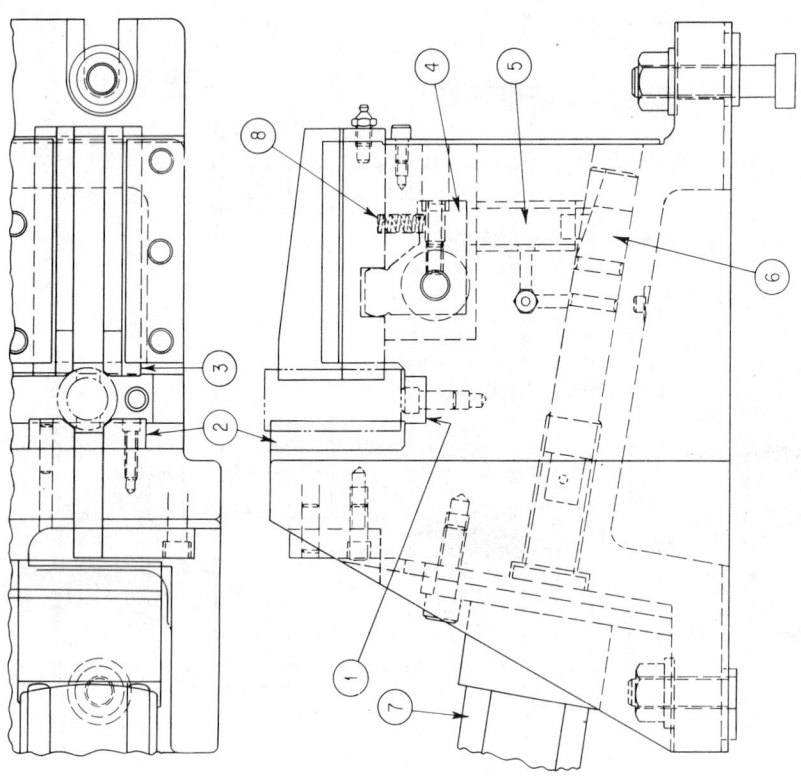

Fig. 7-47 Three-station abreast fixture for slot milling a cylindrical part. (*Courtesy Cincinnati Milacron*)

7-40

wedge cam (6) operated by a hydraulic cylinder (7). A spring (8) pushes on the crank and retracts it when the hydraulic pressure is released.

The wedge-type cam holds the clamp in position without the assistance of the hydraulic pressure, because its angle is smaller than the friction angle of the sliding surfaces of the push rod and the wedge cam. There are three identical stations abreast in each fixture.

The setting gage is shown at (9). Two gaging surfaces are used; the vertical surface is used for setting the cutter transversely and the horizontal surface is used for setting it vertically.

Straddle Milling a Lever Arm. Figure 7-48 illustrates the holding of an offset lever arm while straddle-milling one end. The part is located by a pin (1) and a stop plate (2). The part is held against the stop by a hand screw (3). A spring-loaded back-up pin (4) is locked during the milling operation by the hand screw (5). Two straps clamp the part to the fixture.

Straddle Milling Nonrigid Flanges. The fixture of Fig. 7-49 is designed to support the nonrigid flanges of an aluminum casting while straddle- and face-milling bosses on the flanges. Predrilled holes position the part which bears on surfaces milled in the fixture of Fig. 7-21.

Tapered slots in a plate (1) hold the flanges against screw clamps (2). The balanced cutting action of the straddle-milling cutters holds the center flange during the cutting. The wide clamps (3) with two bearing points hold the casting against the support pads (4). A cutter-set block (5) at the end of the fixture positions the cutters.

Straddle Milling a Block. In the fixture of Fig. 7-50 the width of the rest surface is slightly less than that of the workpiece. Two locators (1) of the wedge type easily locate the workpiece sidewise by approximately centering it on the rest surface.

In order not to interfere with the cutters that mill the top surface, the clamp (2) is of the bell-crank type. A square-head setscrew applies pressure to the clamp. A hardened rest button (3), placed beneath the setscrew, prevents indentation of the fixture base at that point. The fixture is located on the machine table by two fixture keys (4).

In setting up the operation, the fixture is centralized between the straddle-milling cutters. The depth of the groove in the top surface of the workpiece is set with the set block (5) and a feeler gage of appropriate thickness.

Straddle and Slot Milling Round Stock. Two different rods (see Fig. 7-51a and b) are held abreast in the fixture of Fig. 7-51c for milling a tang (straddle milling) in one rod, a, and a slot in the second rod, b. After milling the slot, workpiece b is located from the slot in another fixture (not shown) to mill the flat. The two fixtures are mounted on the table of the same milling machine and are located at the left and right of the spindle respectively. Thus three milling operations are performed progressively using abreast, single, and reciprocal methods of milling.

PROFILE-MILLING FIXTURES

Profile milling in two or three dimensions can be accurately done with relatively inexperienced operators whether the workpiece is flat, uniformly curved, cylindrical, spherical, or irregular in shape. Some of the machines can be used to reduce, enlarge, reverse, or invert the shape of the master at a part-to-master ratio of 1 to 1, or any other ratio within the limits of the machine.

In addition to a workholding fixture, profile milling requires a master or model which guides the cutter in its path through tracer-finger contact with the master or model. For short-run setups, inexpensive masters of wood, brass, aluminum, plastic, or even cardboard may be used. The accuracy of the finished part depends upon the precision of the master. In machines using a ratio of 1 to 1, the accuracy of the part depends directly upon the accuracy of the master. When a reduction ratio is used, that

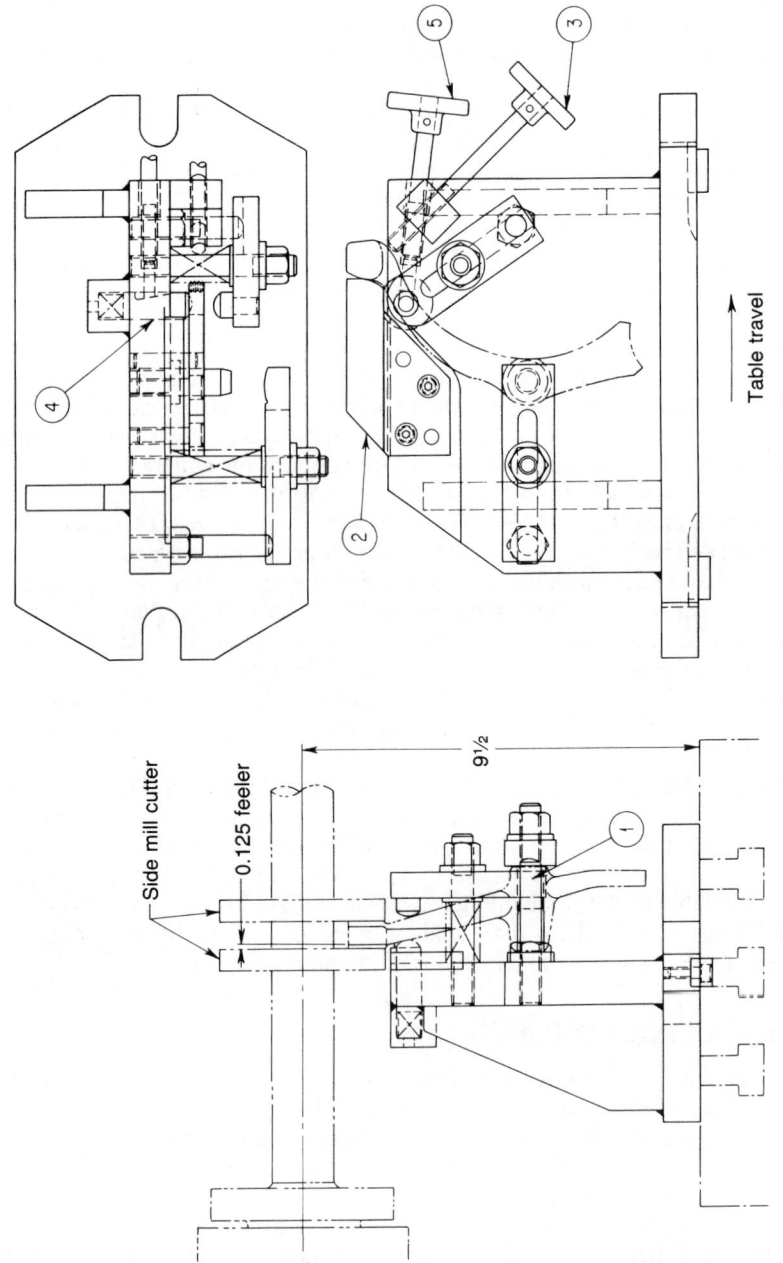

Fig. 7-48 Straddle milling fixture for a lever arm. (*Courtesy Fisher Body Div., General Motors Corp.*)

Table travel

Side mill cutter

0.125 feeler

9½

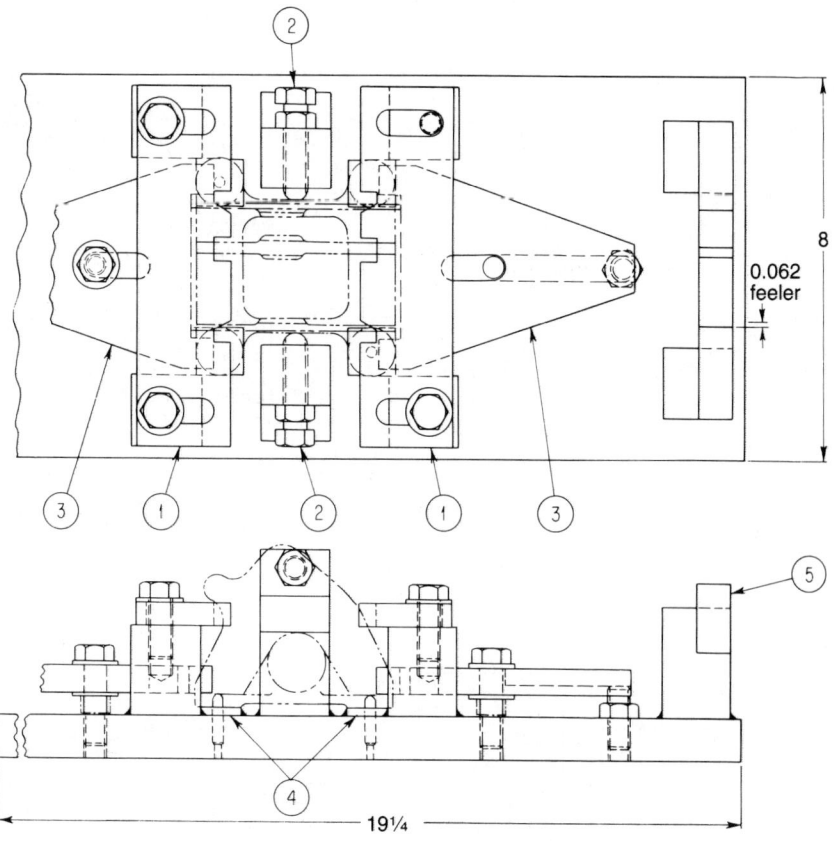

Fig. 7-49 Milling of non-rigid flanges on an aluminum casting.

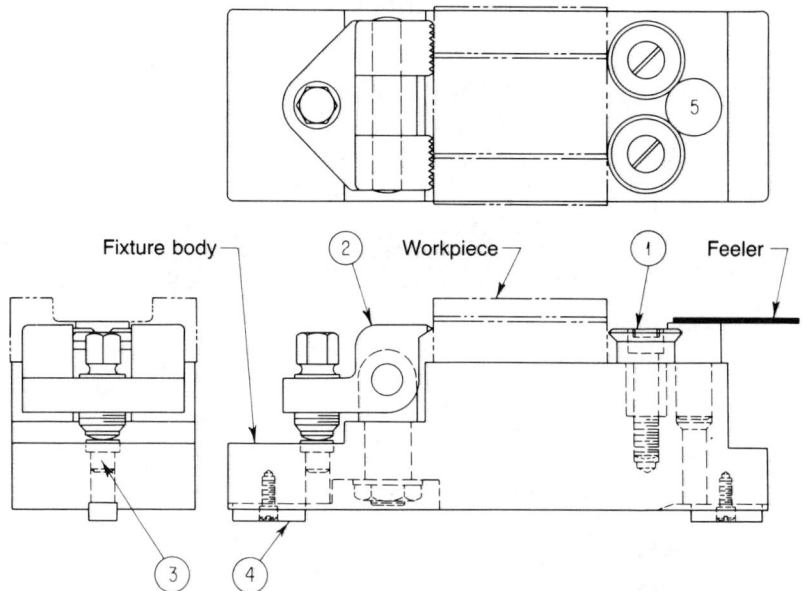

Fig. 7-50 Straddle-milling fixture. (*Courtesy Cincinnati Milacron*)

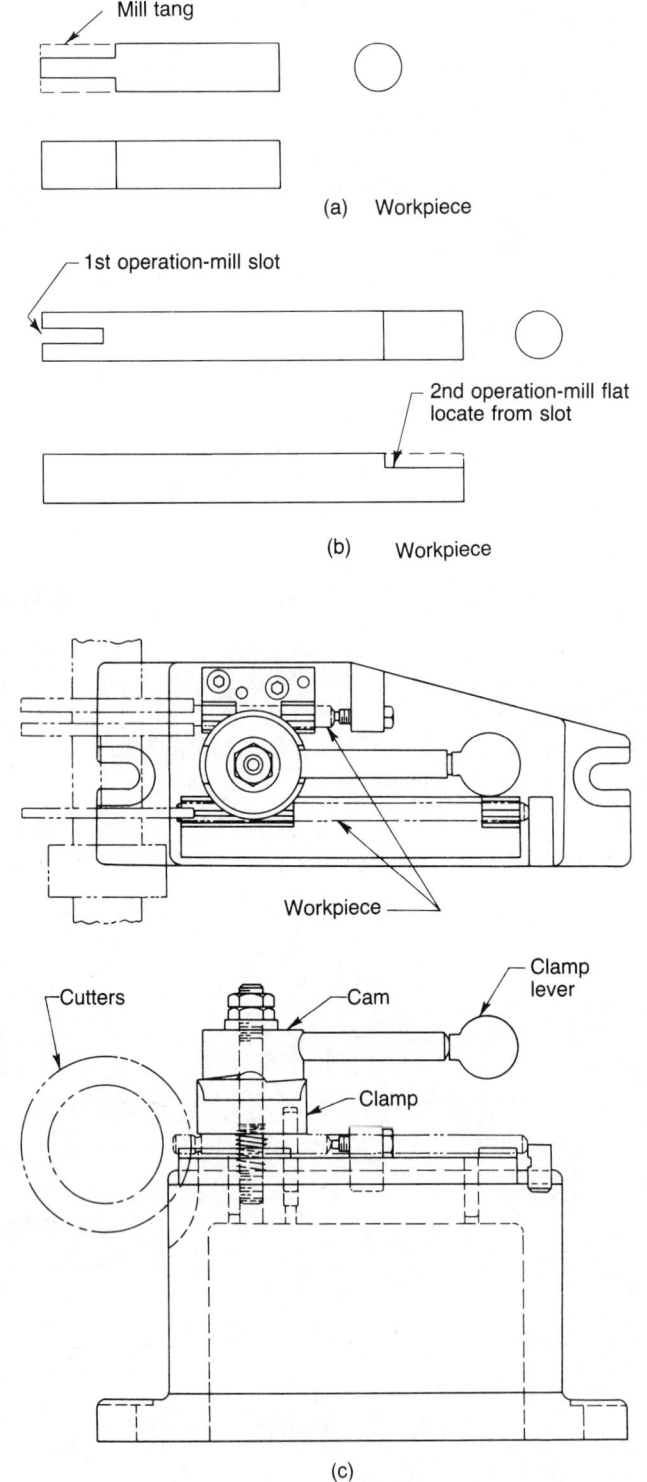

Mill tang

(a)   Workpiece

1st operation-mill slot

2nd operation-mill flat
locate from slot

(b)   Workpiece

Workpiece

Cutters

Cam

Clamp
lever

Clamp

(c)

Fig. 7-51 Straddle-milling and slot milling for round stock. (*Courtesy Cincinnati Milacron*)

is, the master is larger than the finished part, the accuracy or error is inversely proportional to the reduction ratio. For example, an error of 0.010 in. (0.25 mm) in the master would be reduced to 0.001 in. (0.03 mm) when employing a reduction ration of 10 to 1.

When designing profile-milling masters, the designer must remember that the center line of the cutter follows the path of the center line of the tracer stylus. Figure 7-52 illustrates a 1 in. diameter workpiece being machined with a ¼ in. diameter cutter on a machine having a 10 to 1 reduction ration. The path of the cutter center line describes a circle of 0.625 in. radius; therefore the stylus center line must follow a path having a radius of 6.25 in. The radius of the master depends upon the radius of the stylus. For a 1 in. diameter stylus, the radius of the master would be 6.25 - 0.50 or 5.75 in. (11.5 in. diameter). The tracing stylus can be oversize for rough or semifinish cuts, leaving a small amount of stock on the workpiece until the finish cut is taken with a true proportional size of stylus. The diameter of the cutter limits the size of inside diameters or fillet radii which can be cut. The radius of the cutter is the minimum fillet radius that may be milled.

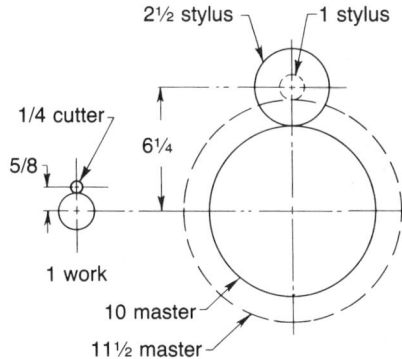

Fig. 7-52 Diagram showing relationship of cutter to stylus and work to master for profile milling.

A technique used to reduce setup time is to key the workholding fixture to a T-slot on the worktable and key the master fixture to a T-slot on the copy table so that the angular or parallel location, whichever the case may be, is correct. In addition, setup holes are incorporated in the fixture and in the master or its fixture so that the machine operator may install a tracing stylus in the chuck of the work spindle as well as in the tracing stylus position; then the operator moves the workholding fixture until the styli in the cutter spindle and tracing spindle are in the corresponding holes of the respective fixtures.

Workpieces of approximately the same size may be held in adapters in a universal fixture, such as that shown in Fig. 7-53. This base fixture is positioned on the machine table by fixture keys (1) and held down by T-bolts in the slots shown. Two cam-actuated clamps (2 and 3) hold the blank which is positioned against the stop pins (4) and centralized on the adapter plate (5). The stop pins are in the adapter plate and located to suit the particular part.

Figure 7-54 shows an adapter plate with the outline of the blank and finished part. The cam clamps of the base fixture hold the blank while holes for the clamp screws (1 and 2) and the locating pin (3) are drilled. Two holes are drilled with a No. 3 center drill as a target point for coordinating the profile master.

A fixture for locating the profile master on the copy table is shown in Fig. 7-55. The fixture keys (1) align the fixture with the table T-slots. The profile master is shown in Fig. 7-56. The master plate (1) is profiled to the shape of the workpiece and has holes

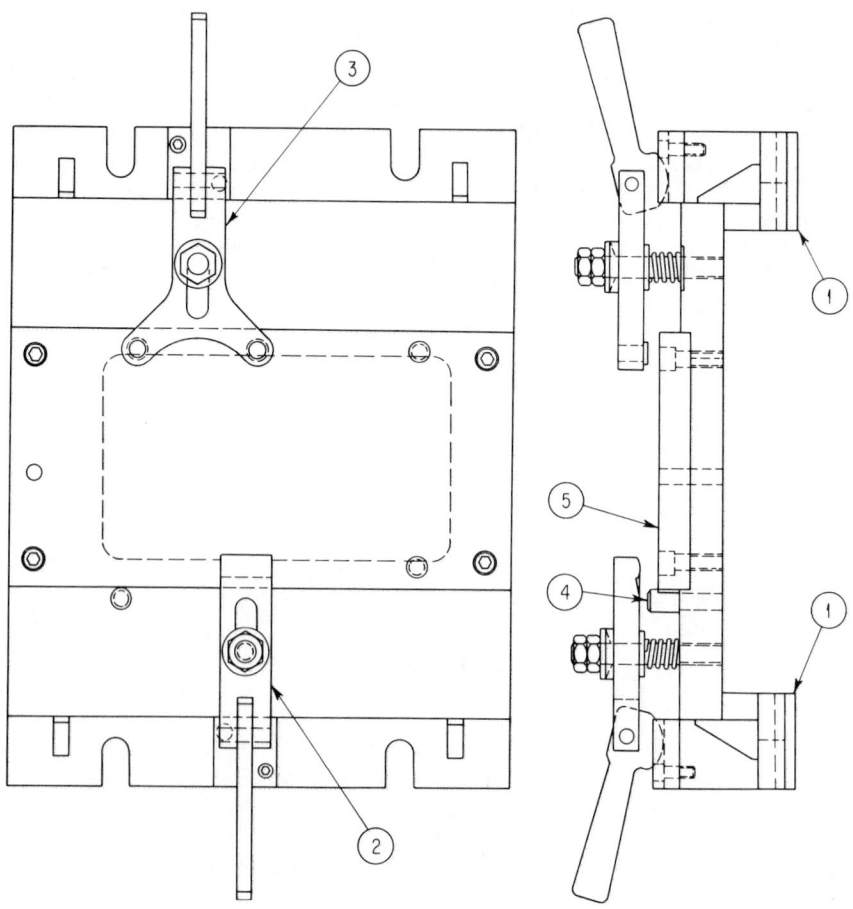

Fig. 7-53 Universal fixture for profile milling. (*Courtesy Geo. Gorton Machine Co.*)

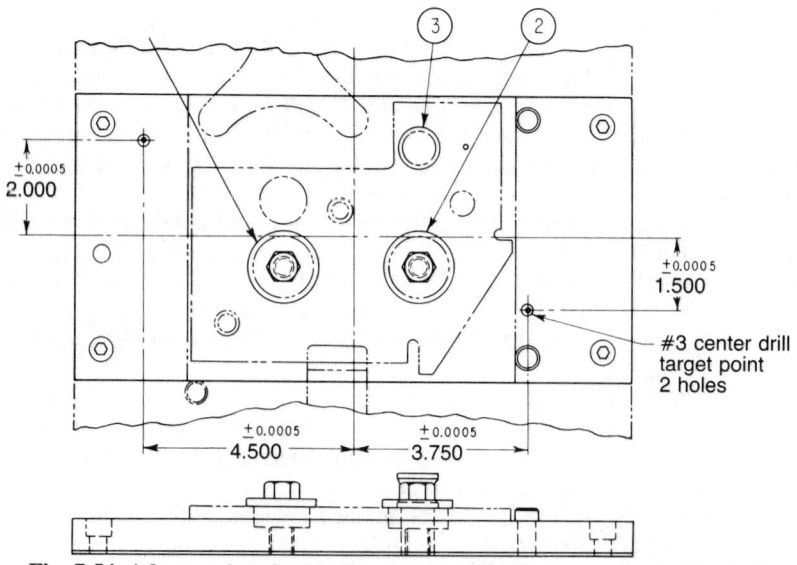

Fig. 7-54 Adapter plate for locating a part in the fixture shown in Fig. 7-53.

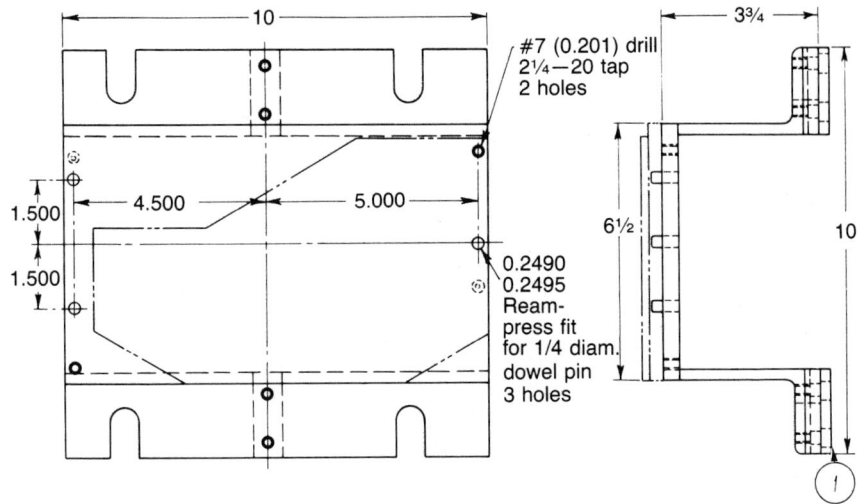

Fig. 7-55 **Fixture for holding a master profile template.** (*Courtesy Geo. Gorton Machine Co.*)

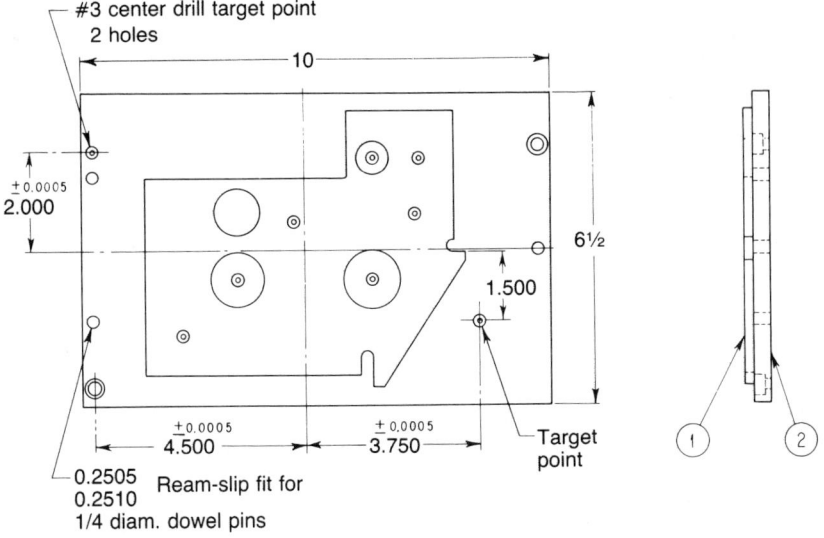

Fig. 7-56 **Profile master for use with the fixture shown in Fig. 7-53.** (*Courtesy Geo. Gorton Machine Co.*)

and center-drill points for locating internal cutouts. The base plate (2) has dowel and cap-screw holes for locating and attaching to the master fixture. Two target points in the same location as on the adapter plate in Fig. 7-54 are provided for positioning.

Milling an Outside Contour. A fixture for milling the outside contour of a belt-feed lever is shown in Fig. 7-57. The fixture base (1) is a semisteel casting. The part is centrally located by a shoulder screw (2), and each end is clamped against a rest button (3) by a sliding clamp (4). The fixture is located on the machine table by fixture keys (5). The cutter spindle is coordinated with the tracer spindle by placing the stylus in the hole for the shoulder screw. Since the rest buttons and the supporting surface at the center are hardened, they have been relieved to clear the profile cutter. Figure 7-58 illustrates the profile master.

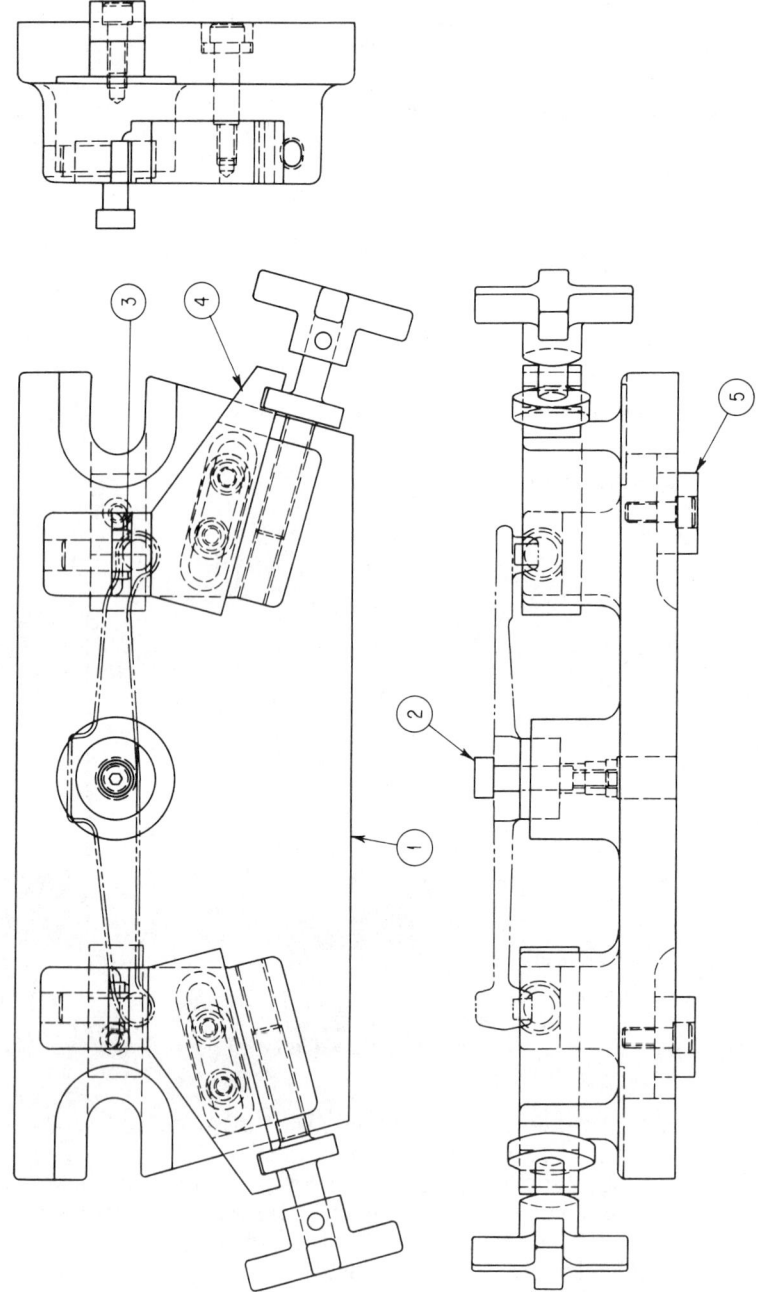

Fig. 7-57 Milling fixture to mill the outside contour of a belt-feed lever. (*Courtesy Geo. Gorton Machine Co.*)

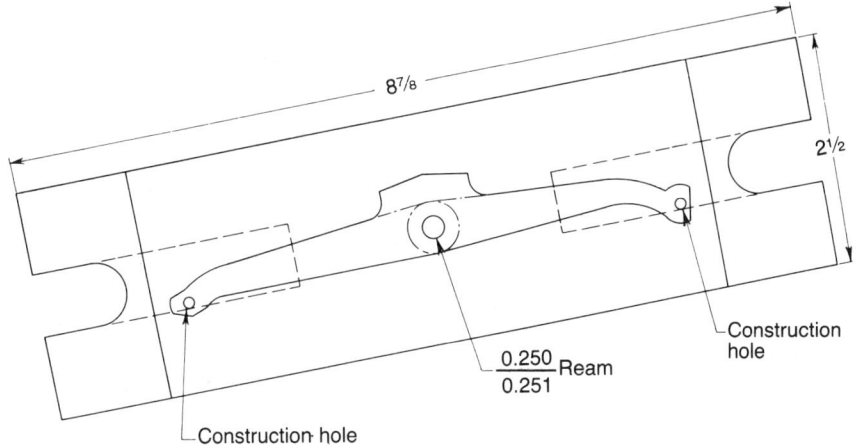

Fig. 7-58 Profile master.

Fixture for Milling the Outside Edges of Three Mounting Pads. The fixture shown in Fig. 7-59 was designed to mill the outside edges of the three mounting pads on the workpiece shown in Fig. 7-20. The top plate is hardened steel with ground edges which serve as a template and a mounting surface to which the workpiece can be clamped. The workpiece is located in the other two planes by stop pins so that the edges protrude into the path of the cutter. Clamping is kept as close as possible to the surface being machined. A follower (roller) on the cutter maintains a constant distance from the template. The follower diameter is 0.250 in. (6.35 mm) greater than the cutter diameter thereby causing the cutter path to be displaced 0.125 in. (3.17 mm) outward from the template. Figure 7-60 shows an alternate method of performing the same operation. In this case, the template is mounted separately to provide for the rapid loading and unloading of the workpiece. A pantograph-type machine coordinates the relative position between the cutter and follower. Also shown in this figure is the use of adjustable tapered (Design A) and non-adjustable straight (Design B) followers.

Profile Milling a Textile Machine Pawl. The parts are first located on the right-hand side of the fixture shown in Fig. 7-61 for milling clearance on the back side of the pawl.

The part is placed over the locating pin (1) and clamped with the hand screw (2) against the stop (3) until the top clamps are tightened. The hand screw is then loosened and revolved 120° to provide a clear path for the cutter. The thin cross section of the part does not provide enough rigidity, making two clamps necessary. To provide additional support, two spring-loaded pins (5) are located within each clamp (4). These support pins are locked by two vertical pins (6) through the thick washer (7) beneath the clamping nut (8).

After the parts are finished on the right-hand side of the fixture, they are placed over a pin (9) on the left-hand side to finish the cam side. A hand screw (10), which forces the part against a stop pin (11) provides temporary clamping until the top clamp (12) is tightened. The hand screw is rotated 90° to clear the cutter. The top clamp also has spring-loaded back-up pins to provide additional support.

The base of the fixture is cast iron, and the pawls rest on tool steel blocks, hardened and ground.

Profile Milling a Slot in a Bearing Half. The simple hand-operated fixture of Fig. 7-62 holds half a bronze bearing for the milling of a slot at an 80° angular distance.

The workpiece is located on its ID by a half-round locator, while round rest pads locate its edges and end.

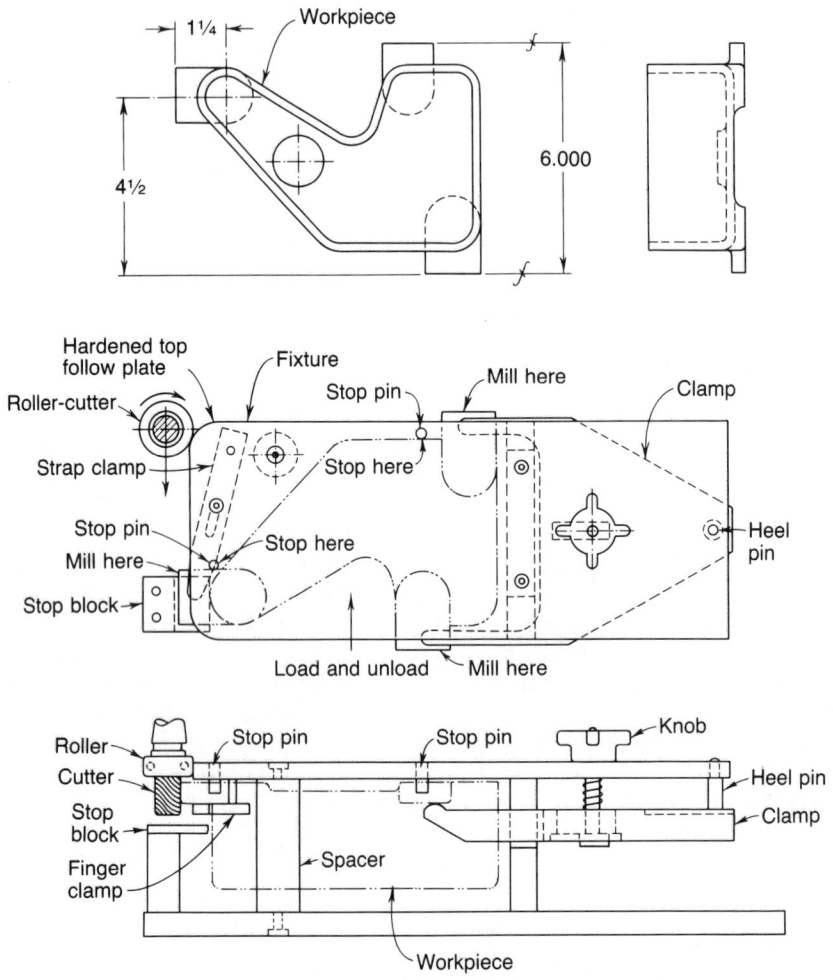

Fig. 7-59 Profile milling the workpiece shown in Fig. 7-20.

A hinged half-round clamp (6), made in two parts, clamps the workpiece at both ends. The space between the clamps, lined with nylon strips (5) to prevent damage to the workpiece, allows for milling-cutter travel. The strap clamp (7) applies pressure to the two lined clamps and, for loading and unloading, is rotated and retracted. It is held open by spring pressure.

A cam or template (1) attached to the fixture body (2) guides the milling cutter (3) by means of a roller follower (4) mounted on the spindle carrier of the machine.

The relations shown of the cutter, rollers, and fixture and the locating and clamping areas are good layout practice and check the final design and details.

Profile Milling of Propellers. Two propellers are milled simultaneously in the fixture of Fig. 7-63, thus halving the milling time.

Each propeller is held in a separate fixture for alignment of each fixture under its own milling-cutter spindle and of the master to the tracer finger. After alignment, the three fixtures are bolted together. Spacing washers of suitable thickness maintain alignment for this and recurrent setups.

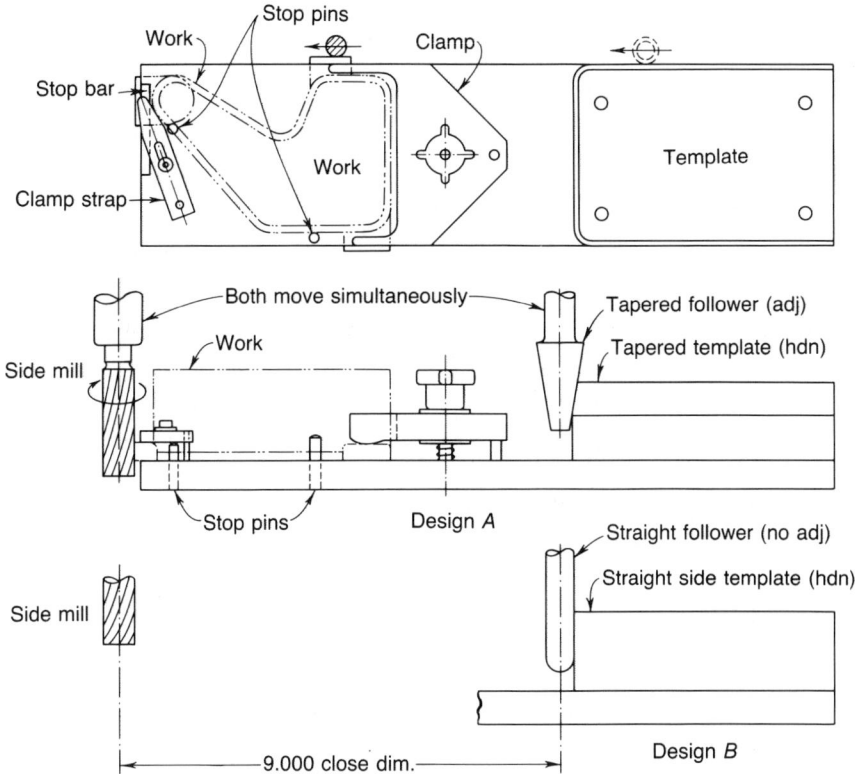

Fig. 7-60 Alternate method for milling the workpiece shown in Fig. 7-20.

The workpiece is located on its hub diameter and against a locating screw and a supporting jack for each blade to be milled. Each blade is located against a stop screw and a leaf support. Each blade is indexed in a special four-station indexing fixture that approximately locates it horizontally. To align each fixture vertically, transversely, and longitudinally with its corresponding machine spindle, setting surfaces are provided on the top of each fixture and the master bracket. An aligning bar and a special setup tracer finger of the same diameter as the aligning bar are inserted between the machine spindles and the tracer bracket.

If the milling operation is composed of a roughing and a finishing cut, a different tracer finger will be required for each type of cut. Corresponding sets of feeler gages will be required for the vertical setting but not for the transverse and longitudinal settings. These settings remain unaltered for either type of cut, because control of stock removal depends on the vertical relation of the cutter to the tracer finger.

To locate the propellers properly in the fixtures, a separate setup gage and a work adapter which fits both the setup gage and the fixture are required. The setup gage (see Fig. 7-64) consists of a base and a circular table that is positioned on the base by means of dowel pins at four different stations (1 to 4). The table is held in the selected station by hook clamps.

Stations 1 and 2 are used when milling the face and back of a forward propeller, and stations 3 and 4 are used when milling the face and back of an aft propeller.

Mounted on the base of the setup gage is a bracket which holds four different plug gages. Their probe ends conform to the required settings of the propeller. These gages

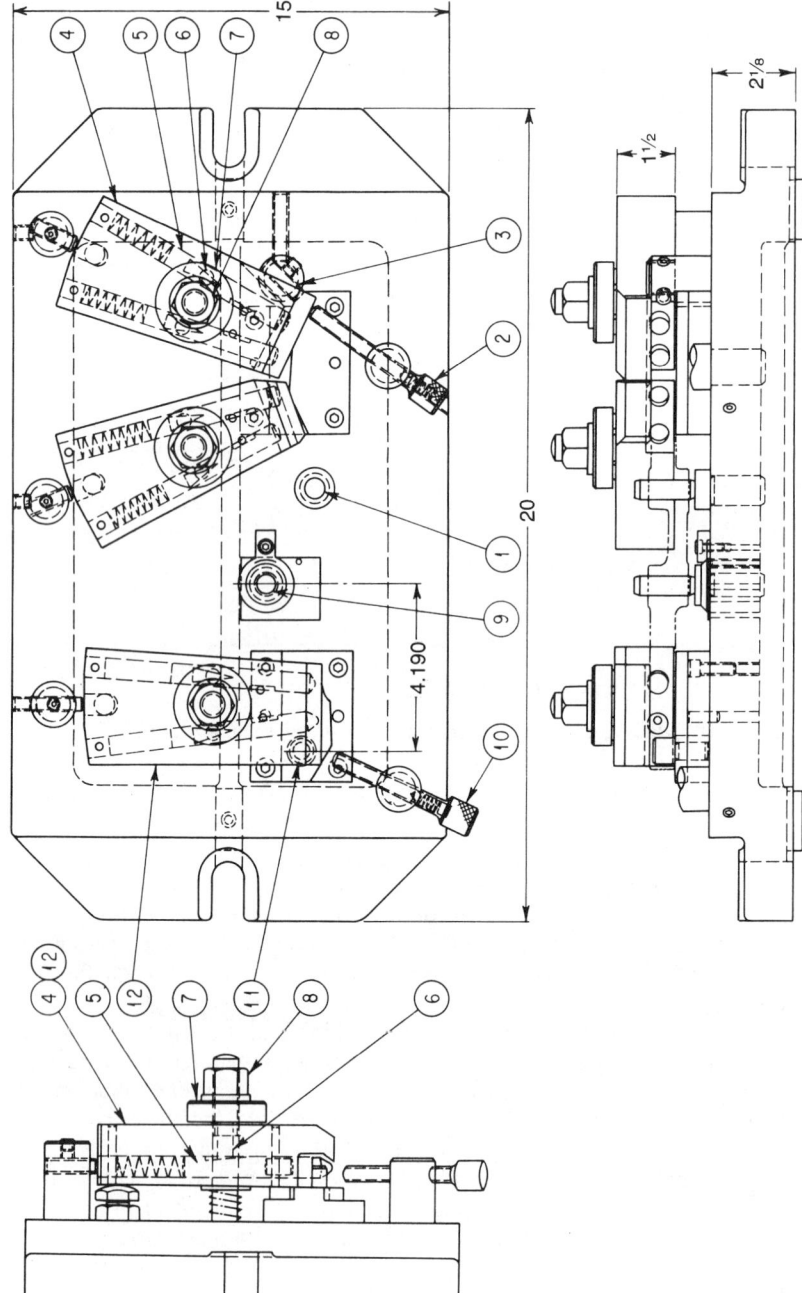

Fig. 7-61 Fixture for profile milling a textile machine pawl. (*Courtesy Textile Machine Works*)

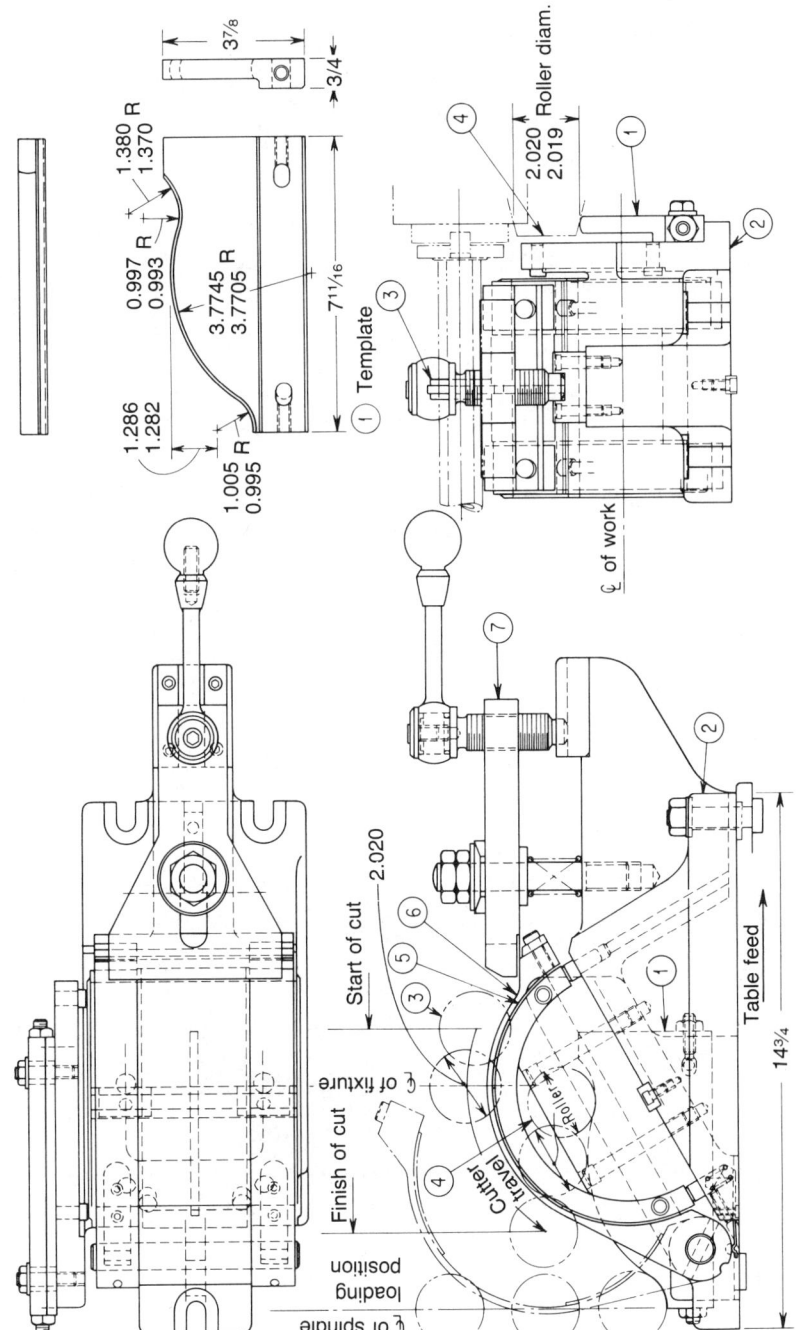

Fig. 7-62 Template-guided milling of a groove in a bronze bearing.

7-53

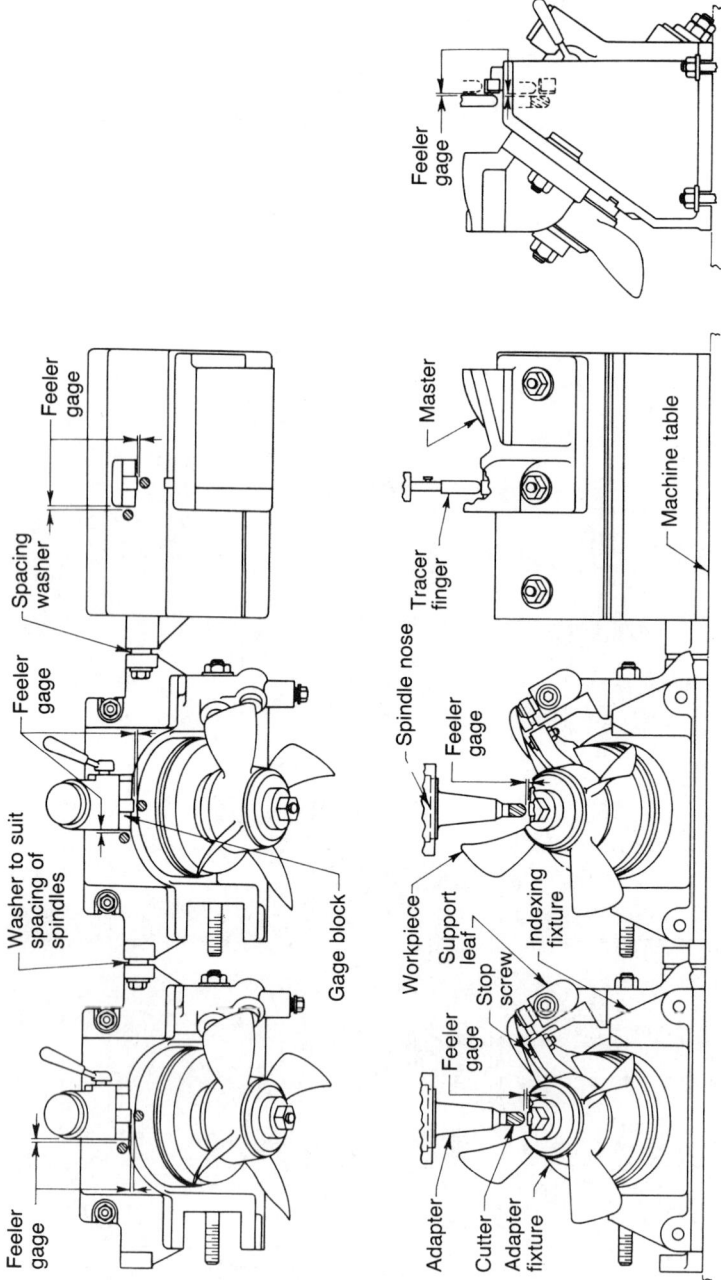

Fig. 7-63 Fixture for profile milling of propellers. (*Courtesy Cincinnati Milacron*)

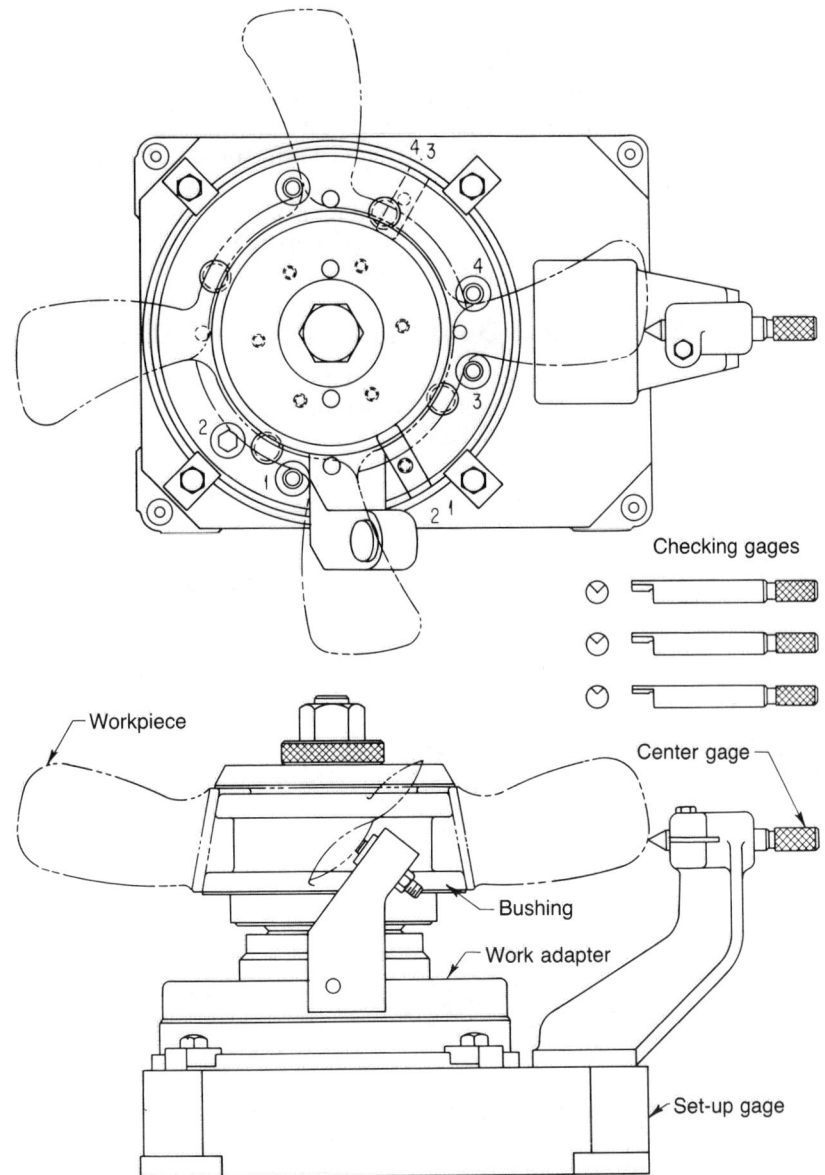

Checking gages

Workpiece

Center gage

Bushing

Work adapter

Set-up gage

Fig. 7-64 Setup gage for the fixture shown in Fig. 7-63. (*Courtesy Cincinnati Milacron*)

are characterized by the distance which the gaging point deviates from its center line. The center gage (shown in position in the fixture) sets the propeller. The others are checking gages which determine whether the stock removed from each blade is within the required limits.

The propellers are held on four work adapters required for roughing and finishing cuts on the aft and forward propellers. Each adapter has two bushings, one for roughing and the other for the finish-milling operation, and will fit in both the setup gage and the fixture.

After locating the selected adapter with the proper bushing in the setup gage, a propeller forging is placed in the adapter. The stop screw in the adapter is then adjusted until the tip of the propeller blade lines up with the gaging point in the setup gage and is then locked.

At this point the work adapter is transferred to the fixture. The propeller is repositioned in the adapter, relocated against the stop screw, and clamped in position by the large nut on the fixture stud. A leaf support is then swung into position (see Fig. 7-59) for additional support of the blade. The same procedure is followed for setting the work adapter in the second fixture.

Most complex profiling operations with milling machines are now being done on machines with NC/CNC and/or tracer control. Tracers can be operated mechanically, hydraulically, pneumatically, or in any combination of the three.

MISCELLANEOUS MILLING FIXTURES AND ACCESSORIES

Milling fixtures can be made from many standard commercial items such as premachined sections, forms and bases, angle irons, parallels, and V-blocks; section components; and standard structural forms. Examples of these can be seen in Figs. 1-41 and 1-49. Additional examples are as follows:

- Figure 7-65 shows a milling fixture made from standard L-section tooling material.

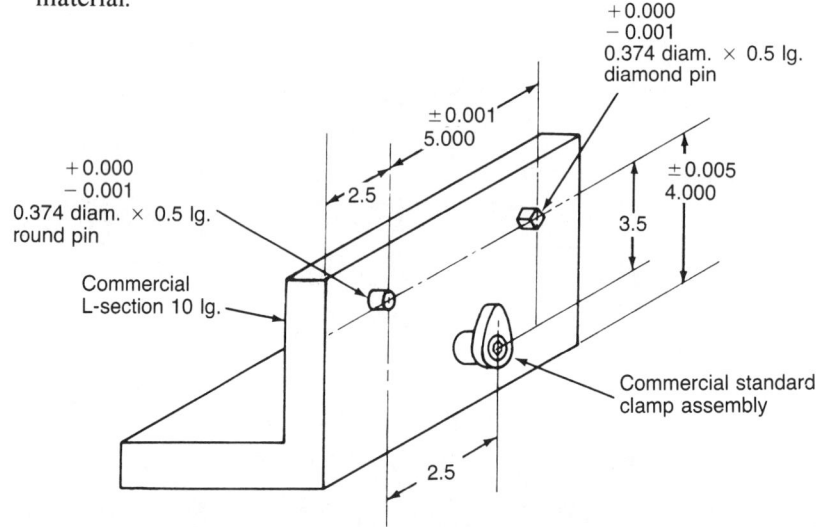

Fig. 7-65 Milling fixture made from standard L-section tooling material.

- Figure 7-66 shows a milling fixture made from flat tooling plate. Construction time was 3.5 hours.
- Figure 7-67 shows a combination milling fixture and drill jig made from structural material (H-beam) for the part shown in the same figure.

The modular tooling systems discussed in Chapter 5 are often used to provide tooling for milling machines. Especially when tooling is needed in a hurry, for milling prototype parts, and when manufacturing single lots. Some typical examples are:

- Figure 7-68 shows a milling fixture for a housing that was assembled on a 25 × 15 × 3 in. (630 × 370 × 70 mm) mounting plate in 2.5 hours.
- Figure 7-69 shows a milling fixture for face milling an angular aluminum workpiece. It was assembled in 2.0 hours on a 17 × 9 × 3 in. (420 × 230 × 70 mm) mounting plate.

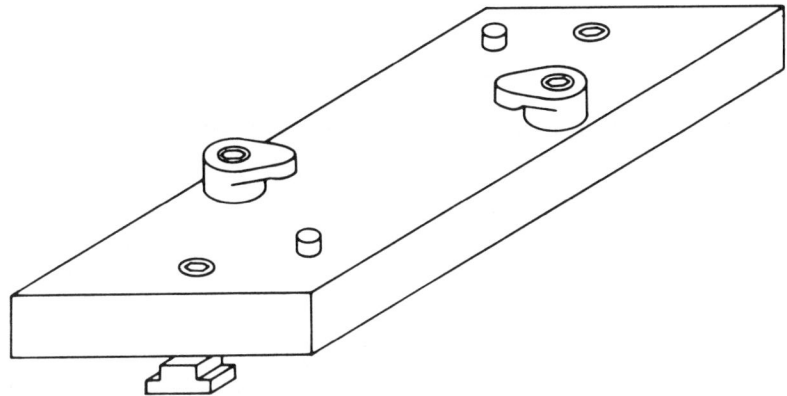

Fig. 7-66 Milling fixture made from flat tooling plate.

- Figure 7-70 shows a milling fixture that was assembled on a 25 × 15 × 3 in. (630 × 370 × 70 mm) mounting plate in 4 hours. It is used for both face milling and milling with side milling cutters.

The universal milling machine fixture shown in Fig. 7-71 can often be substituted for a more expensive fixture. It has two T-slot key positions at 90° to each other to permit accurate alignment with the machine table T-slots for use in either the horizontal or vertical position.

Many other workholding devices, such as hydraulic expanding arbors chucks and flats, vacuum chucks, magnetic devices, universal chucks, collet fixtures, etc., can be used to hold work for milling (see Chapter 3). Additionally, these devices can be mounted directly on dividing heads, rotary tables, tilt tables, adjustable angle plates, and other positioning tables to present a workpiece for milling (see Chapter 4).

A MODULAR TOE CLAMP SYSTEM FOR MILLING MACHINES

A complete toe clamp system for locating and holding an unusual workpiece is illustrated in Fig. 7-72. As seen in this illustration, the top surface is left completely free for machining. The system can be used on either conventional or NC milling machines. With it, workpieces from 0.156 (4 mm) to 8 in. (200 mm) can be quickly and securely clamped for profitable production.

Operation. Just how the system works can be described in conjunction with Fig. 7-73 as follows:

Situation 1. Here, the jaw has moved forward. The two outside, flexible fingers are longer than the center solid finger and have contacted the workpiece, while the solid finger is not yet touching.

Situation 2. Using a hex key, the rear screw is tightened two-thirds of a turn. The outer fingers bend and force the workpiece down. The center finger contacts the workpiece and completes the clamping action. It is only necessary to tighten from one side of the workpiece. The fingers, on the other side of the workpiece, automatically operate in the same manner. A two thirds turn of the screw gives a maximum 2000 lbf (8.9 kN) of holding force.

This 2000 lbf (8.9 kN) of holding force, transmitted through the center fingers of the jaws, translates to 17,000 psi (117 MPa) grip at that point. This holding force gives a secure hold on the workpiece and allows for heavy milling cuts, yet does not mar the workpiece. For delicate workpieces, less holding force can be used as long as the center finger contacts the part.

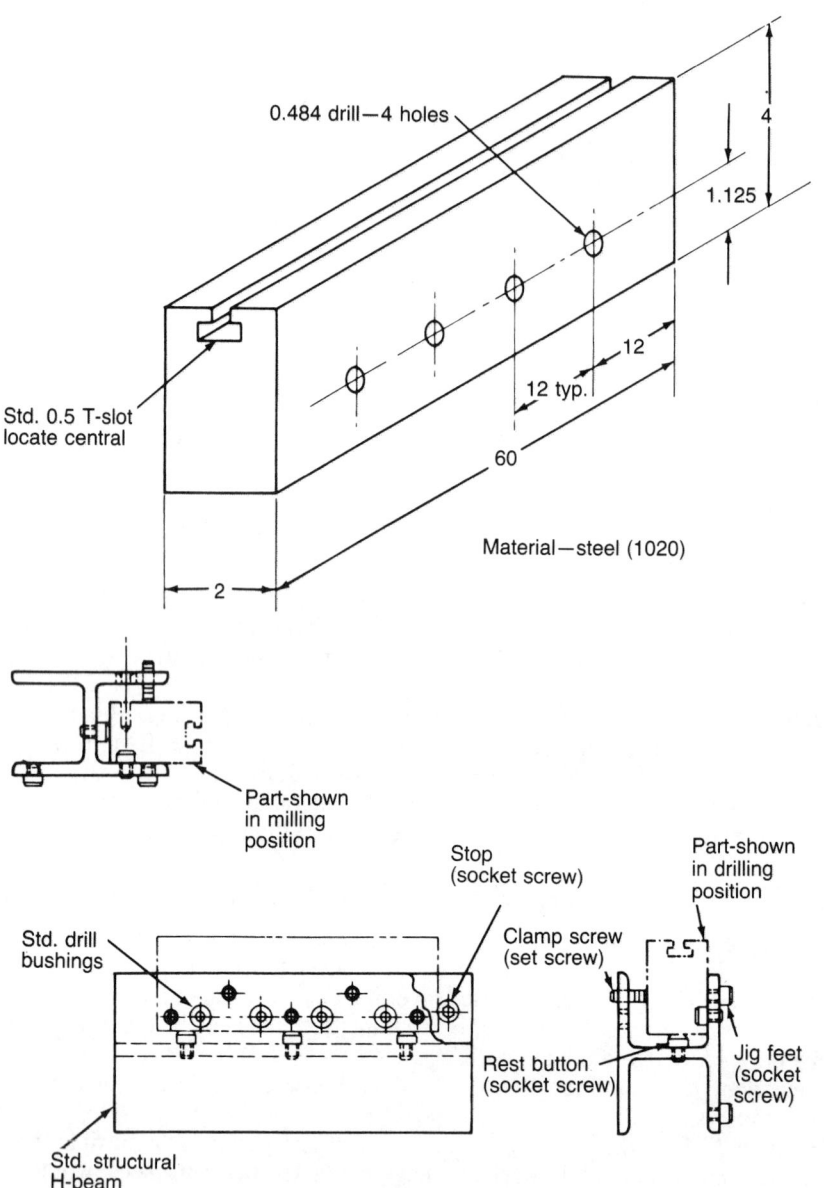

Fig. 7-67 Combination milling fixture and drill jig made from structural material. (*Courtesy H-beam*)

Components. Mounting elements and their functions are detailed in Fig. 7-74. The *mounting bar* is the basic element that is to be mounted to a milling table and to which the clamps/locators are in turn mounted in the proper position, to hold the workpiece. The mounting bar is made for T-slot distances from 1.75 to 6.25 in. (44 to 159 mm). The complete length of the bar is 18 in. (457 mm). The bar is ground to a thickness of 1.0938 $^{+0.0000}_{-0.0004}$ in. over its entire length. The mounting bars are fixed to the milling table with two cap screws and T-nuts. The bar can be mounted parallel or perpendicular to the T-slots, and in most cases two bars are required.

Fig. 7-68 Milling fixture for a housing. (*Courtesy Flexible Fixturing Systems, Inc./Erwin Halder, Ltd.*)

Fig. 7-69 Milling fixture for an angular aluminum workpiece. (*Courtesy Flexible Fixturing Systems, Inc./Erwin Halder, Ltd.*)

Fig. 7-70 Milling fixture for a lever. (*Courtesy Flexible Fixturing Systems, Inc./Erwin Halder, Ltd.*)

Fig. 7-71 Universal milling machine fixture. (*Courtesy Universal Vise and Tool Co.*)

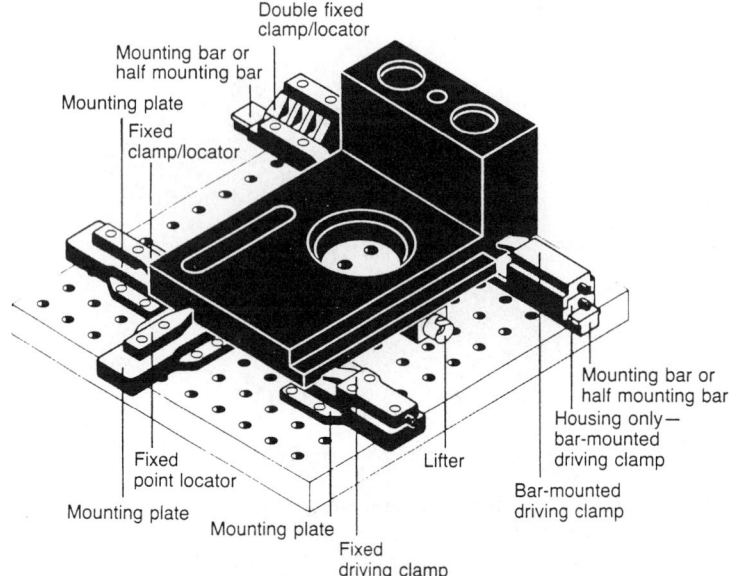

Fig. 7-72 Toe clamp system. (*Courtesy Royal Products*)

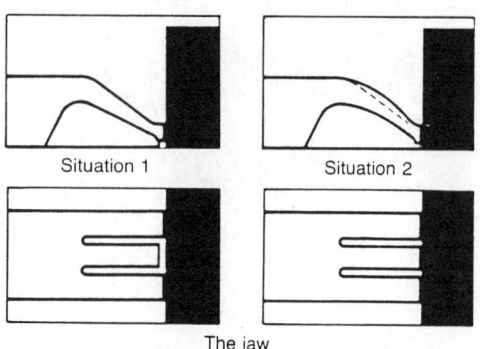

Fig. 7-73 How the toe clamp system works. (*Courtesy Royal Products*)

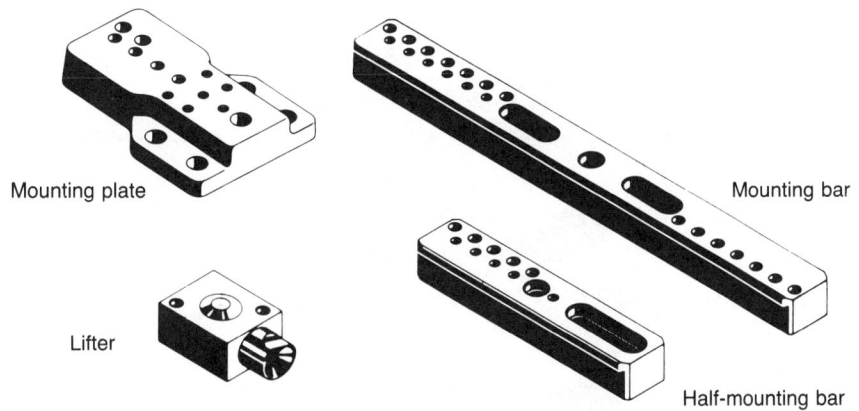

Fig. 7-74 **Mounting elements for a toe clamp system.** (*Courtesy Royal Products*)

The *half mounting bar* is made to the same specifications, but is used for T-slot distances from 1.5 to 4 in. (38 to 102 mm). The overall length of the half bar is 8.75 in. (222 mm).

The *mounting plate* is used on special fixtures, subplates, or any plate designed to mount on a milling machine. It can also be directly mounted to a milling table. Length is 6 in. (152 mm), maximum width is 4.25 in. (108 mm), and the thickness is the same as for the mounting bars.

The *lifter* is 3.125 in. (79 mm) long, 1.875 in. (48 mm) wide, and the same thickness as the mounting bars and plates. If necessary, it can be attached to the subplate by two cap screws. The piston in the lifter has a total travel of 0.093 in. (2.36 mm) and is raised by inserting a 6 mm hex key and turning clockwise until the piston touches the work and the key is removed. The screw can only turn clockwise, and once the piston touches the workpiece, the piece is fully supported. The lifter is used as an additional support to prevent bending or deflection of workpieces.

Driving clamps are shown in Fig. 7-75. The bar-mounted driving clamps can be quickly mounted to the bars and half bars. They can be easily positioned every 0.75 in. (19 mm) with the use of a bayonet pin in the housing, which fits into a mating hole on the mounting bars. Fixed driving clamps are used on the mounting plate or on specially designed fixtures. Three different types of jaws are available and interchangeable for each of the bar-mounted and fixed driving clamps, and therefore the specifications are the same.

The *fixed clamp/locators* shown in Fig. 7-76 can be used on mounting bars, mounting plates, or special tooling fixtures. With the exception of the fixed point locator, they can serve as both work locators and clamps. The regular fixed clamp/locators function in the manner of the driving clamps but are not adjustable. The fixed point locator is used only to locate a workpiece. It can be used on mounting bars, mounting plates, and special tooling fixtures. The double fixed clamp/locator #1 is used to hold material from 2.5 to 5 in. (64 to 127 mm) high. The two fixed clamp/locators guarantee that the workpiece is held securely and is forced down on the mounting bars or mounting plates to which they are attached. On the opposite side of the workpiece, the bar-mounted driving clamp is placed on the bar-mounted driving clamp housing only to raise it to the proper height. The double fixed clamp/locator is positioned by a locating pin 0.315 in. (8 mm) in diameter. The distance between the center of the dowel locator and the center figure is 3.846 ±0.0004 in. It is fixed to the bar by three cap screws.

The double fixed clamp/locator #2 (see Fig. 7-76) is used to hold workpieces from 5

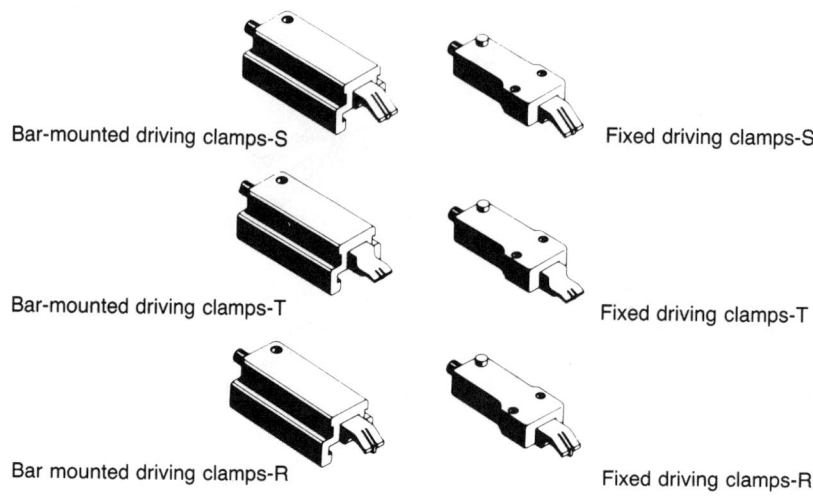

Bar-mounted driving clamps-S

Fixed driving clamps-S

Bar-mounted driving clamps-T

Fixed driving clamps-T

Bar mounted driving clamps-R

Fixed driving clamps-R

Fig. 7-75 Driving clamps for a toe clamp system. (*Courtesy Royal Products*)

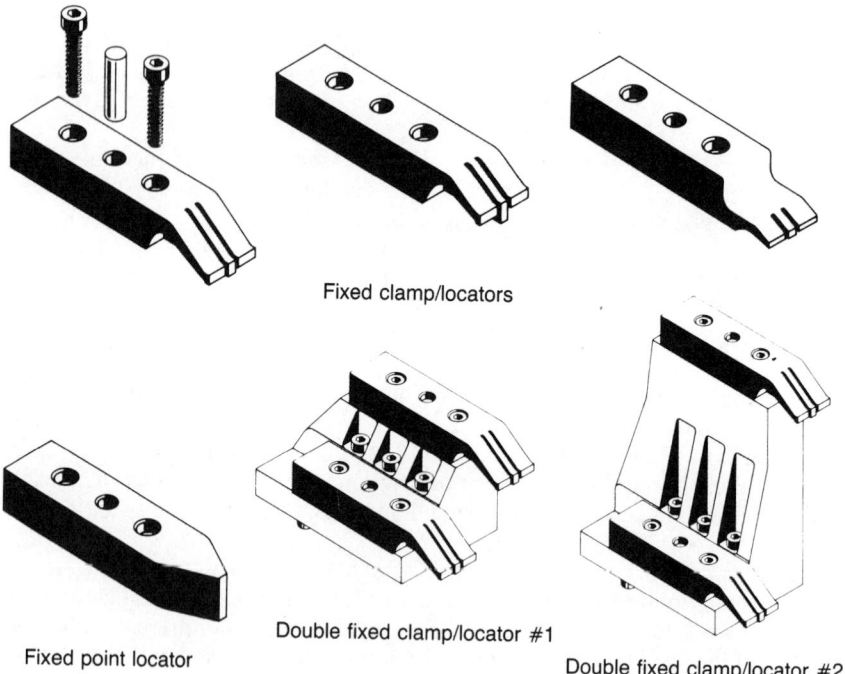

Fixed clamp/locators

Fixed point locator

Double fixed clamp/locator #1

Double fixed clamp/locator #2

Fig. 7-76 Clamp locators for a toe clamp system. (*Courtesy Royal Products*)

to 8 in. (127 to 203 mm) in height. Construction and operation are the same as with the #1 unit and it is used with the same accessories. On the opposite side of the workpiece, the bar-mounted driving clamp is placed on the riser block #2.

Riser blocks and *adapters* are shown in Fig. 7-77. The bar-mounted riser block #1 fits the mounting bars and is used as a riser for the bar-mounted driving clamp opposite the fixed double clamp/locator #1. The bar-mounted riser block #2 fits the mounting bars and is used as a riser for the bar-mounted driving clamp opposite the fixed double

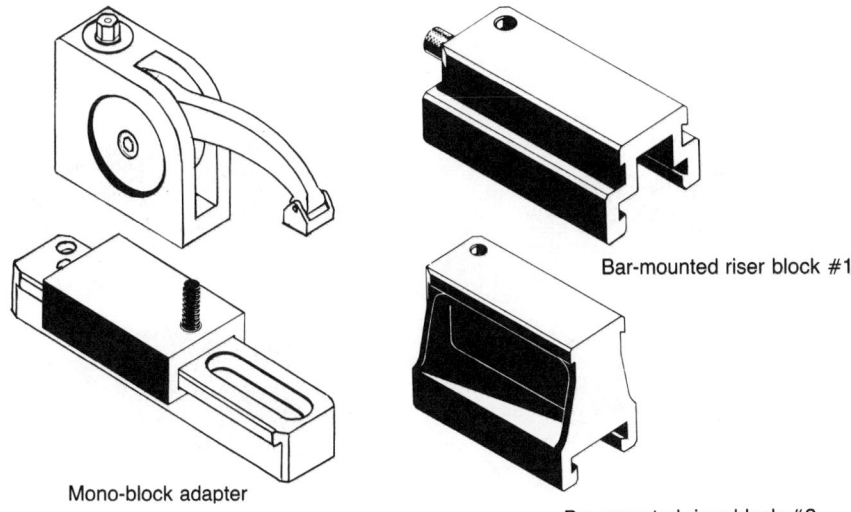

Bar-mounted riser block #1

Mono-block adapter

Bar-mounted riser block #2

Fig. 7-77 Riser blocks and adapters for a toe clamp system. (*Courtesy Royal Products*)

clamp/locator #2. The adapter adapts the vertical clamps (as shown in Fig. 7-87a) to the riser blocks. It also adapts to the riser block #2 and to the bar-mounted driving clamps.

Examples of this particular *toe clamp system* in use are shown in Figs. 7-78 and 7-79. They function as follows:

In Fig. 7-78, the mounting bar and two bar-mounted driving clamps, *a*, give a capacity of 0 to 8 in. (0 to 203 mm) in length. With a fixed clamp/locator on one side of the bar, the maximum capacity is increased to 8.875 in. (225 mm). Fingers with different thicknesses can be used so that very thin material or pieces with base radius or a chamfer can be held.

Two half mounting bars with two bar-mounted driving clamps, *b*, give a holding capacity of 0 to 20 in. (0 to 508 mm). One bar-mounted driving clamp can be replaced by a fixed clamp/locator. This allows for the same capacity. It is important to line up the half bars carefully. With short pieces, the full bars are easier to work with. Fingers with different thicknesses can also be used so that very thin material can be held, or pieces with base radius or chamfer can be held.

Two half mounting bars, *c*, are used with a double fixed clamp/locator #1 on one bar, and the bar-mounted driving clamp mounted on a bar-mounted riser block #1 on the other half bar. The workpiece can be 2.5 to 5 in. (63 to 127 mm) in height. To assure proper clamping in horizontal as well as down directions, the bar-mounted driving clamp must always be exactly between the double fixed clamp/locators.

Two half mounting bars, *d*, are used with a double fixed clamp/locator #2 mounted on one bar, and a bar-mounted driving clamp and a riser block #2 mounted on the other bar. This combination allows for a workpiece from 5 to 8 in. (127 to 203 mm) high in height.

Two mounting bars are used with a fixed clamp/locator and a bar-mounted driving clamp on one bar, and two bar-mounted driving clamps on the other bar, *e*. The workpiece is located off the fixed clamp/locator. Variations in the part dimension are compensated for by the bar-mounted driving clamp, located on the same side of the workpiece as the fixed clamp/locator. The workpiece is clamped by turning the hex head screw two-thirds of a turn on the two bar-mounted driving clamps on the opposite side.

7-63

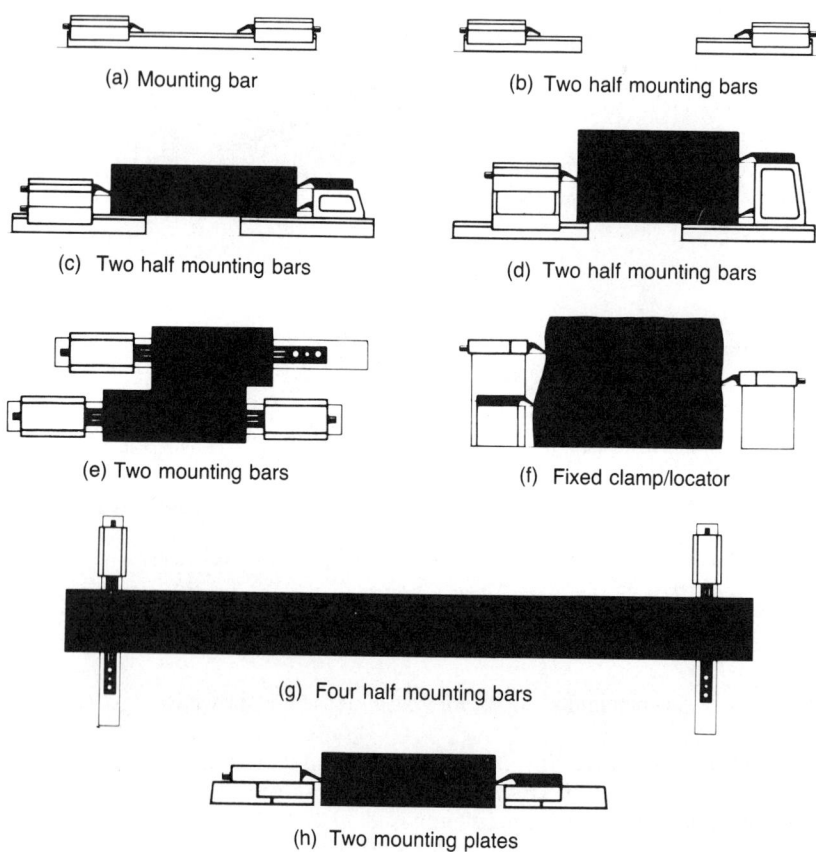

(a) Mounting bar

(b) Two half mounting bars

(c) Two half mounting bars

(d) Two half mounting bars

(e) Two mounting bars

(f) Fixed clamp/locator

(g) Four half mounting bars

(h) Two mounting plates

Fig. 7-78 Toe clamp system in use. (*Courtesy Royal Products*)

The fixed clamp/locator and two fixed driving clamps are mounted on a special holding fixture, *f*. The workpiece is located off the fixed clamp/locator. Variations in the forging or casting are compensated for by the fixed driving clamp, above the fixed clamp/locator. The part is clamped by the fixed driving clamp on the opposite side. For best results, the fixed driving clamp must be placed half way between the fixed clamp/locator and the fixed driving clamp on the opposite side.

Four half mounting bars are used with two fixed clamp/locators and two bar-mounted driving clamps, *g*. This gives a workpiece length of 40 in. (1.016 mm). This is an ideal application for the lifter. The lifter will support the workpiece and eliminate vibration and deflection during machining.

Two mounting plates can be used with a fixed clamp/locator mounted in fully extended position on one end side, and the fixed driving clamp also mounted in the fully extended position on the other mounting plate, *h*. The workpiece can be set directly on the table of the machine

By using the mounting plate in Fig. 7-79, along with a fixed clamp/locator or double fixed clamp/locator, a datum line is generated. This is used for workpiece location on conventional or NC milling machines. This process is described as follows:

A fixed clamp/locator is mounted on a mounting plate, *a*, thereby generating the datum line (and half of the clamping setup). On the opposite side is a half mounting bar with a bar-mounting driving clamp. Parts up to 2.5 in. (63 mm) high can be held.

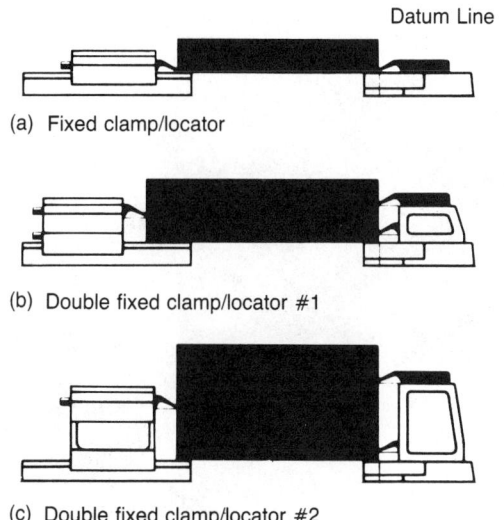

(a) Fixed clamp/locator

(b) Double fixed clamp/locator #1

(c) Double fixed clamp/locator #2

Fig. 7-79 Establishing a datum with a toe clamp system. (*Courtesy Royal Products*)

A double fixed clamp/locator #1 is mounted on a mounting plate, *b*, generating the datum line (and half of the clamping setup) for a workpiece from 2.5 to 5 in. (63 to 127 mm) thick. On the other side of the mounting plate is a half mounting bar with a bar-mounted driving clamp mounted on bar-mounted riser block #1.

A double fixed clamp/locator #2 is mounted on a mounting plate, *c*, and generates the datum line (and half of the clamping setup). In this case, the workpiece can be from 5 to 8 in. (127 to 203 mm) in height. On the opposite side is a half mounting bar with a bar-mounting driving clamp mounted on bar-mounted riser block #2.

POWER WORKHOLDING FOR MILLING

Power workholding is used extensively to hold parts for milling because clamping is fast, many clamps can be operated simultaneously, and clamping can be coordinated relatively easily to operate by machine movement, machine levers, machine circuits, and NC programs. Power workholding systems are readily available from many manufacturers. One such system is the hydraulic flexible clamping system for rectangular workpieces shown in Fig. 7-80. The fixture shown holds sixteen workpieces and was constructed entirely from the stock components shown in Fig. 7-81. Components include the following:

- Fixture bases, *a*, in four sizes ranging from 19½ × 15½ in. (495 × 394 mm) to 19½ × 39⅛ in. (495 × 994 mm) which permits clamping of up to 24 workpieces. Bases are ground flat and parallel within 0.0012 in. FIM. The mounting holes (with bushings) are located within 0.002 in.
- Locating backstops with side locators, *b*, in lengths to suit the fixture bases.
- Rest plate, *c*, on which the manifolds are fastened. Rest plates are precision ground to ±0.0004 in. and are available in four heights to suit the various bases.
- Manifold blocks, *d*, into which the threaded-body push clamps, *e* thru *g*, are installed. Manifolds can be provided with either 2, 4, 6, or 8 clamps installed depending on the length of the base.
- Miscellaneous components such as hydraulic bases, screws, T-nuts, pressure gages, etc.

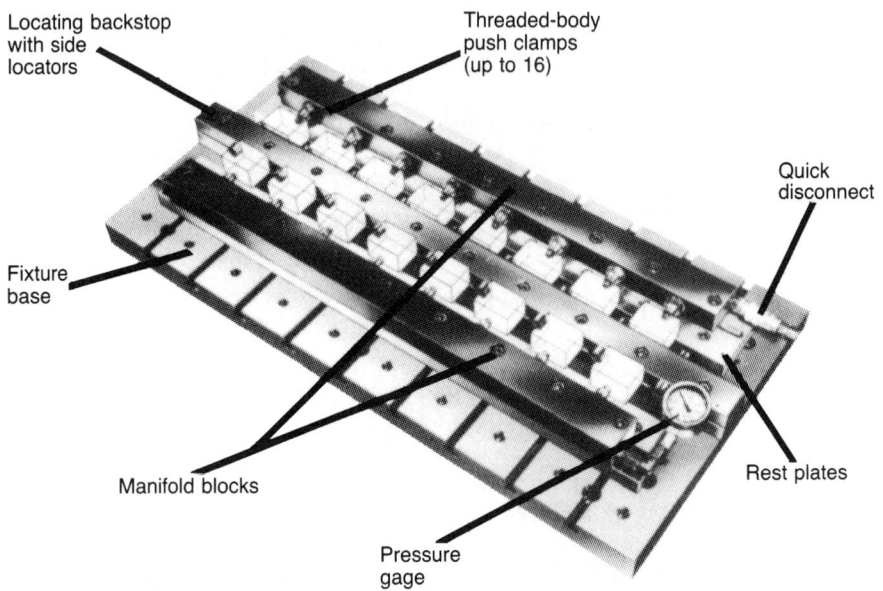

Locating backstop with side locators

Threaded-body push clamps (up to 16)

Quick disconnect

Fixture base

Manifold blocks

Rest plates

Pressure gage

Fig. 7-80 Flexible clamping system for rectangular workpieces. (*Courtesy Carr Lane Roemheld Mfg. Co.*)

Adjustment in the *Y*-axis is made by sliding the manifold block sideways in the rest plates T-nut slot.

Adjustment in the *X*-axis is by sliding the rest plates in and out along the T-nut slots in the base, carrying the manifolds along with them. Locating backstops can be mounted on any of the five rows of mounting holes in the base (see Fig. 7-82). By setting the two manifold blocks independently, workpieces can be clamped in different positions for performing two operations simultaneously. Adjustments in *X* and *Y* are illustrated in Fig. 8-83.

Fixtures assembled with one, two, and three manifolds are shown in Fig. 7-84. The system is designed for use with hydraulic pressure up to 4000 psi (28 MPa).

Most of the main types of hydraulic and pneumatic clamps have already been discussed in Chapter 3. However, to relate their use more directly to milling operations, some typical applications have been illustrated in Figs. 7-85 and 7-86.

ADDITIONAL TOOLING FOR MILLING

Clamps. The vertical clamping system shown in Fig. 7-87a can be mounted directly to the milling machine table as shown. The components consist of clamping units, riser blocks, and direct mount adapters for mounting to T-slots.

They are available for light duty, standard, and heavy duty. Specifications are as follows:

Light duty. Clamping force of 1,300 lb (5.782 kN) when tightened to 25.5 ft-lb (35 N·m) with the standard 2 in. (51 mm) clamping arm, and 580 lbf (2.580 kN) when tightened to 25.5 ft-lb (34.6 N·m) using 5½ in. (140 mm) extension arms. Clamping range with the standard clamping arm is 0 to 2¼ in. (0 to 57 mm) and 0 to 3 5/16 in. (0 to 84 mm) with the extension arm . Up to three riser blocks can be added to clamp parts up to 9½ in. (241 mm) high.

Standard duty. Clamping force of 3,200 lbf (14.233 kN) when tightened to 58 ft-lb (78.6 N·m) with the standard 1⅜ in. (35 mm) arm, and 1,500 lbf (6.672 kN) when tightened to 58 ft-lb (78.6 N·m) using 4¾ in. (121 mm) extension arms. Clamping

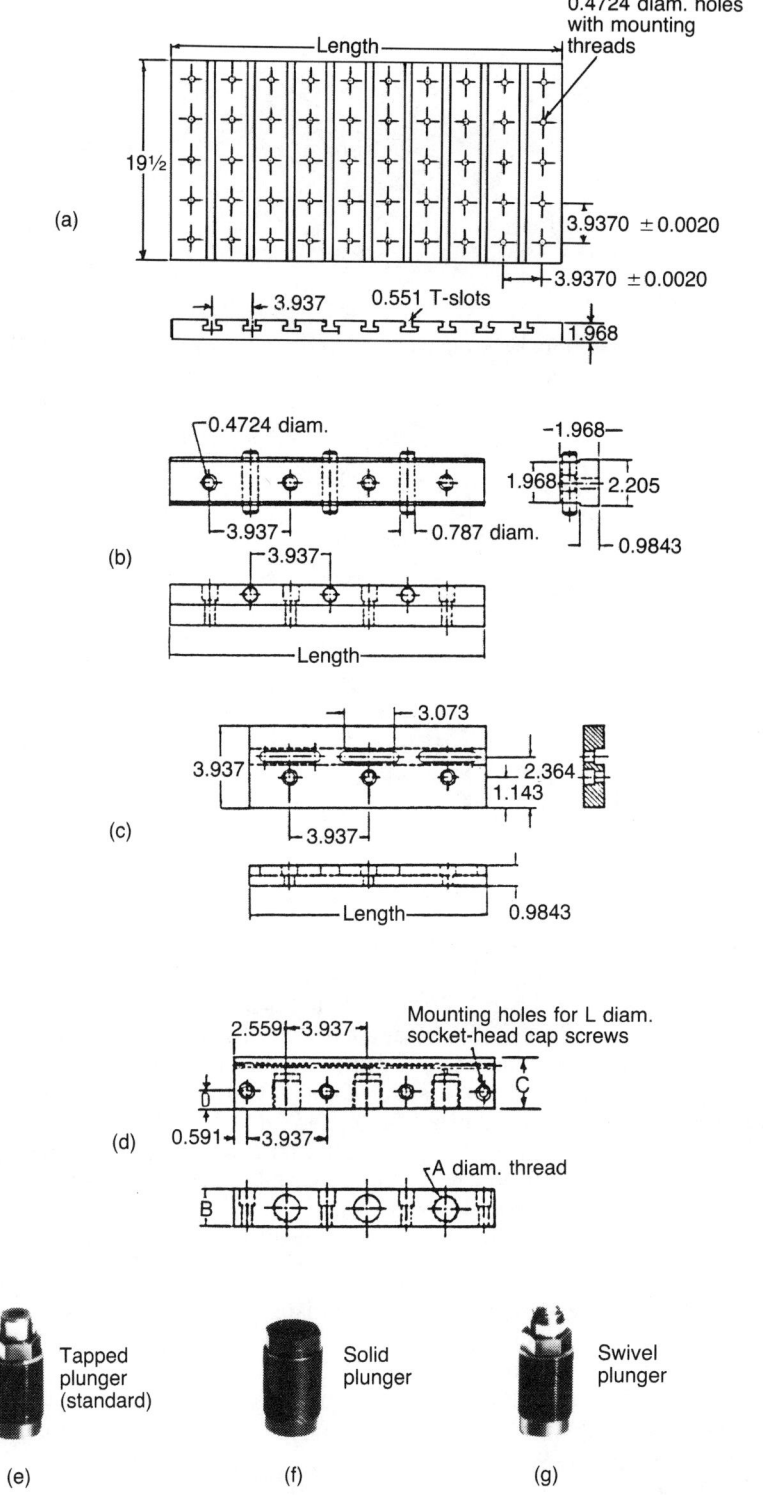

Fig. 7-81 Flexible clamping system components. (*Courtesy Carr Lane Roemheld Mfg. Co.*)

7-67

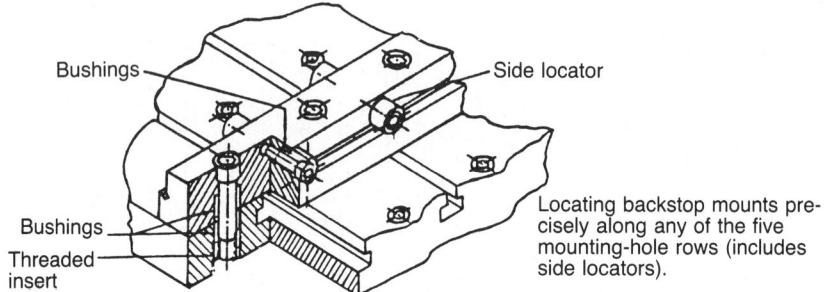

Fig. 7-82 Locating backstop mounts. (*Courtesy Carr Lane Roemheld Mfg. Co.*)

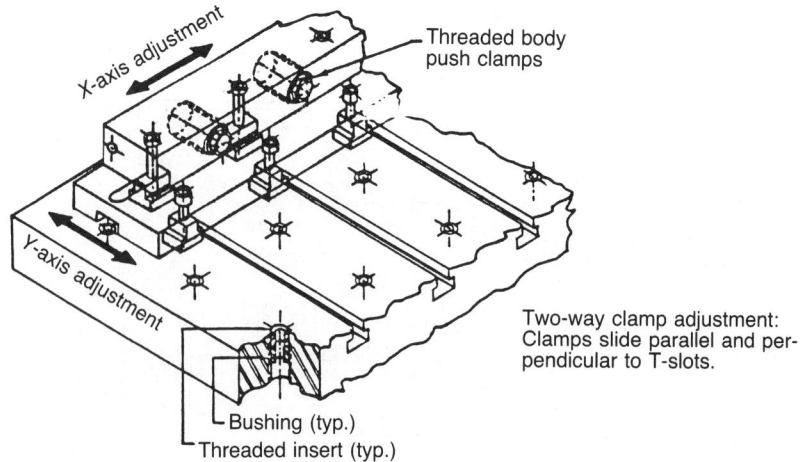

Fig. 7-83 Two-way clamp adjustment. (*Courtesy Carr Lane Roemheld Mfg. Co.*)

ranges are 0 to 3¼ in. (0 to 83 mm) and 0 to 4½ in. (0 to 114 mm) respectively. With a 2⅝ in. (67 mm) arm a clamping force of 2,400 lbf (10.675 kN) can be applied when tightened to 58 ft-lb (78.6 N·m). With a 5⅝ in. (143 mm) extension arm, a clamping force of 1,300 lbf (5.782 kN) can be applied when tightened to 58 ft-lb (78.6 N·m). Clamping ranges are 0 to 4 in. (0 to 102 mm), and 0 to 5½ in. (0-140 mm) respectively. Workpieces up to 12 in. (304 mm) can be clamped with the addition of riser blocks.

Heavy duty. Clamping force of 8,000 lbf (35.584 kN) when tightened to 51 ft-lb (69.2 N·m) with 2 in. (51 mm) arms, and 6,400 lbf (28.467 kN) when tightened to 51 ft-lb (69.2 N·m) with 3¾ in. (95 mm) arms. Clamping ranges are ⅝ to 3 in. (16 to 76 mm) and 0 to 4 in. (0 to 102 mm) respectively.

A diagram of "How they work" is shown in Fig. 7-87*b* thru *e*. The steps are as follows:

1. Slide the T-nut and screw into approximate position, *b*. Slide the riser block or clamping unit over the screw. Tighten the screw through the opening in the riser block with a T-wrench.
2. Slide the clamping unit over the screw on the riser block, *c*.
3. Tighten the screw on the riser block with a T-wrench through the clearance on the clamping unit, *d*.
4. Clamp the workpiece, *e*.

The clamps can also be used with the modular clamping system shown Fig. 7-72.

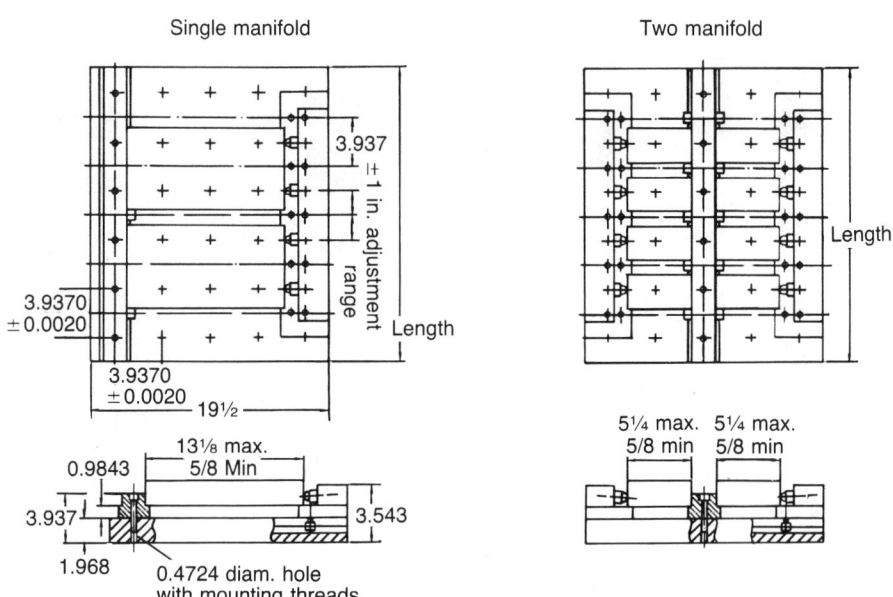

Single manifold

3.937
± 1 in. adjustment range

3.9370
±0.0020

3.9370
±0.0020

19½

Length

13⅛ max.
5/8 Min

0.9843

3.937

1.968

3.543

0.4724 diam. hole
with mounting threads

Two manifold

Length

5¼ max. 5¼ max.
5/8 min   5/8 min

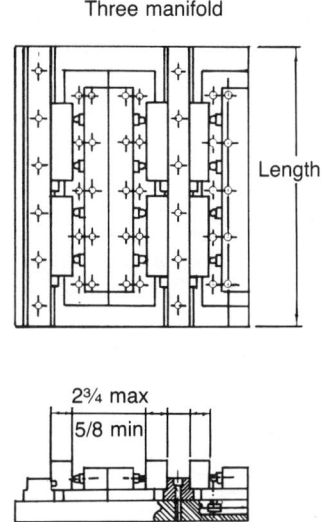

Three manifold

Length

2¾ max
5/8 min

Fig. 7-84 Fixtures assembled with one, two, and three manifolds. (*Courtesy Carr Lane Roemheld Mfg. Co.*)

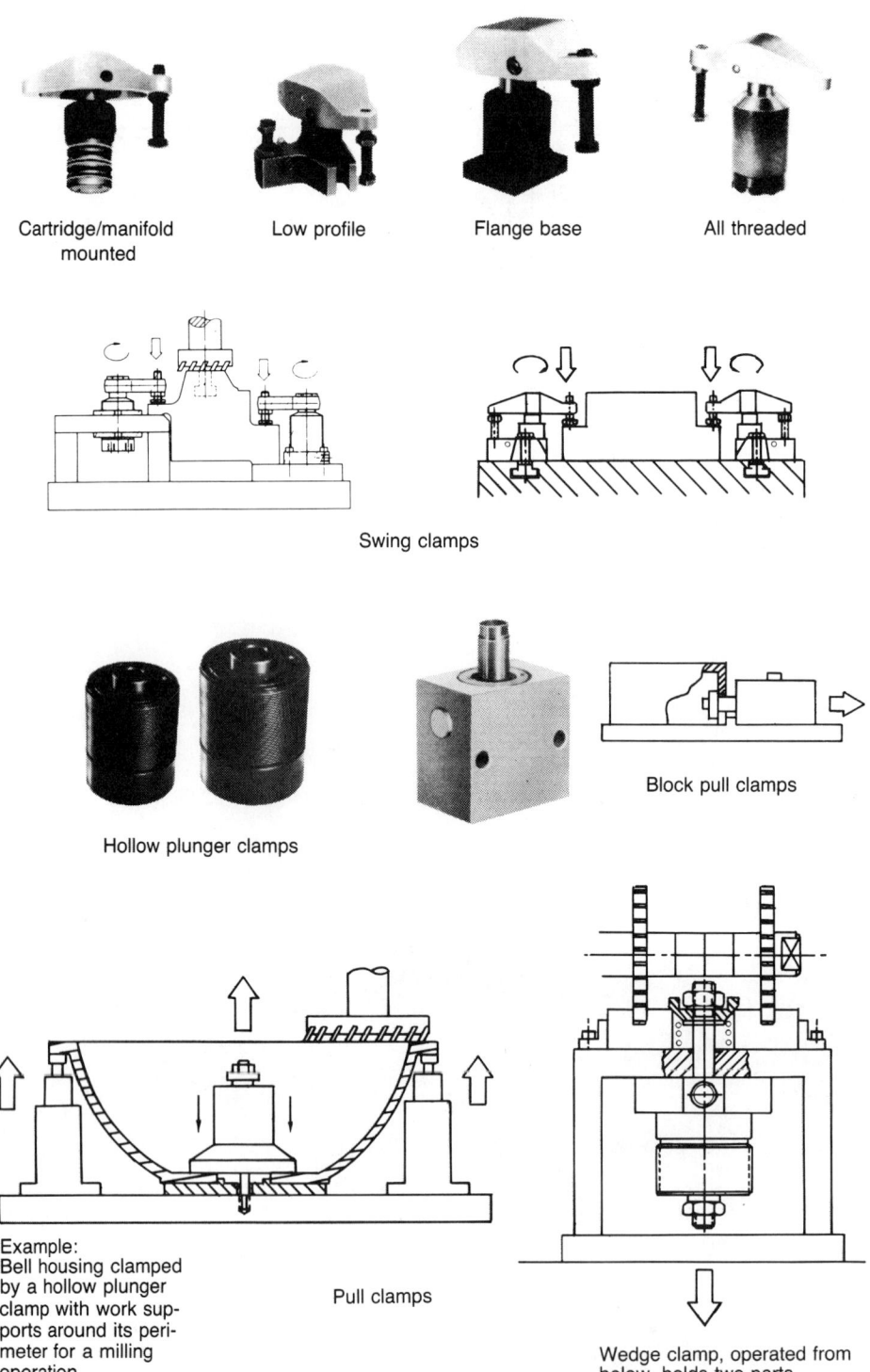

Cartridge/manifold
mounted

Low profile

Flange base

All threaded

Swing clamps

Hollow plunger clamps

Block pull clamps

Example:
Bell housing clamped
by a hollow plunger
clamp with work sup-
ports around its peri-
meter for a milling
operation.

Pull clamps

Wedge clamp, operated from
below, holds two parts.

**Fig. 7-85 Applications of hydraulic clamps for milling operations—swing clamps and pull
clamps.** (*Courtesy Carr Lane Roemheld Mfg. Co.*)

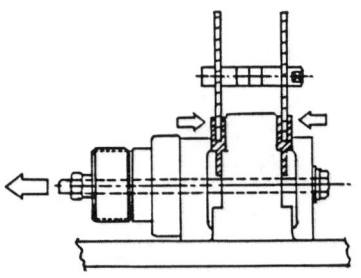

Two clamp straps squeeze parts against
a central locating block.

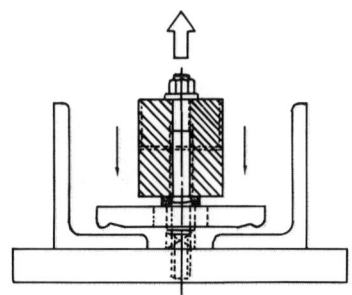

Clamp strap quickly converted
to power clamping.

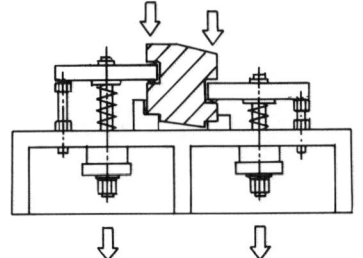

Clamp strap assemblies operated from
below to keep plumbing out
of work area

Fig. 7-85 *(Continued.)*

Block push clamps

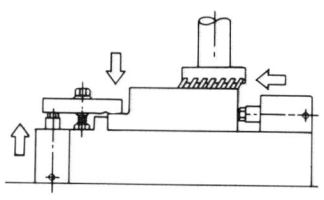

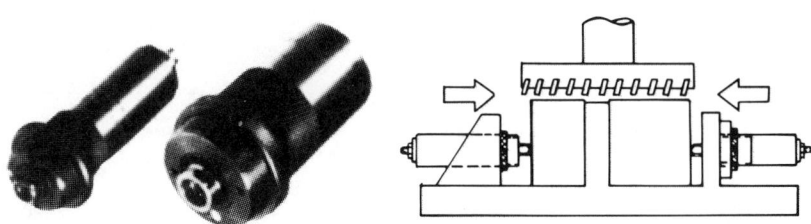

Threaded-collar push clamps

Fig. 7-86 **Applications of hydraulic clamps for milling operations edge clamps, push clamps,
and extending clamps.** *(Courtesy Carr Lane Roemheld Mfg. Co.)*

Threaded-body
push clamps

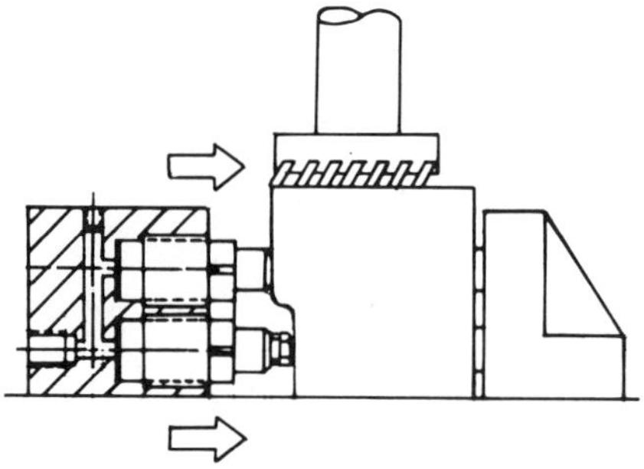

Edge clamps

Low block

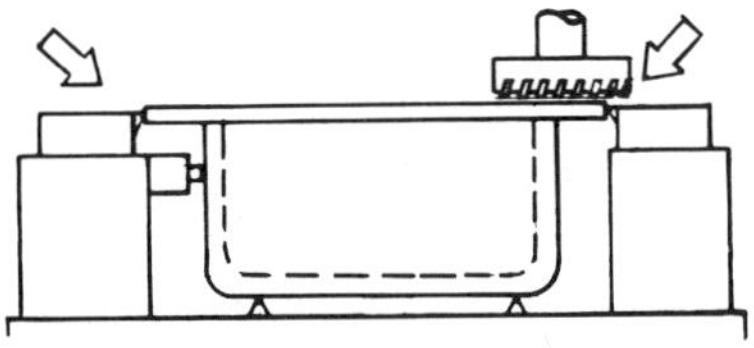

Clamping on a thin
flange just below
cutting plane

3° Inclined plunger

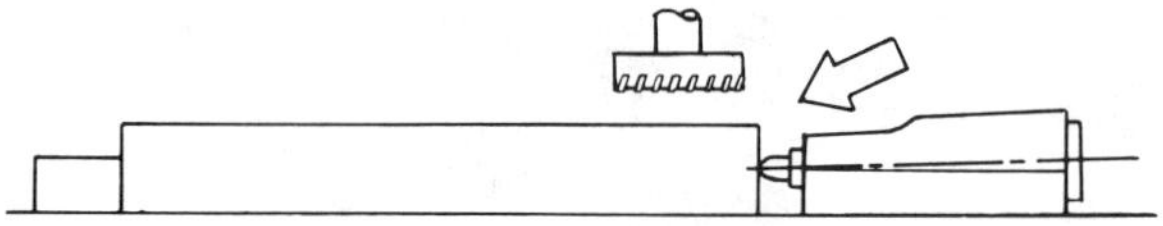

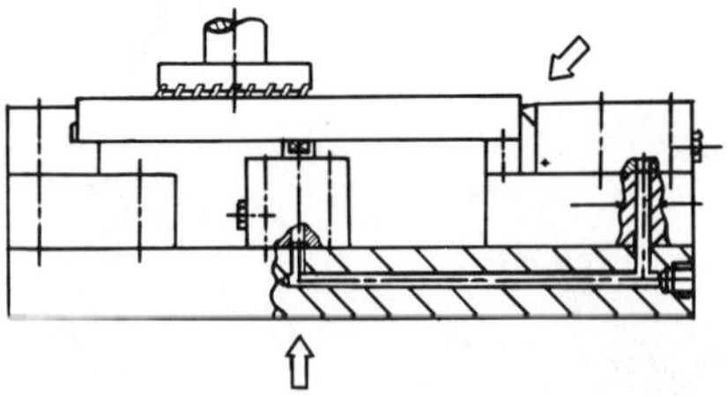

Edge clamp used
with a work support,
manifold mounted for
easy chip removal

Flush-retracting arm

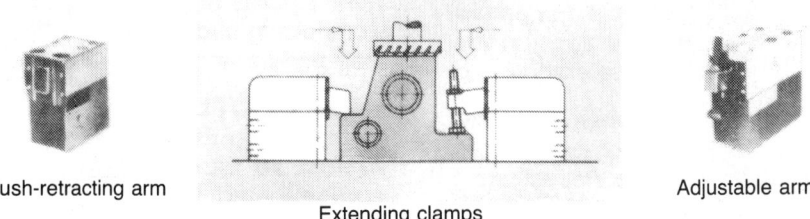

Extending clamps

Adjustable arm

Fig. 7-86 *(Continued)*

7-72

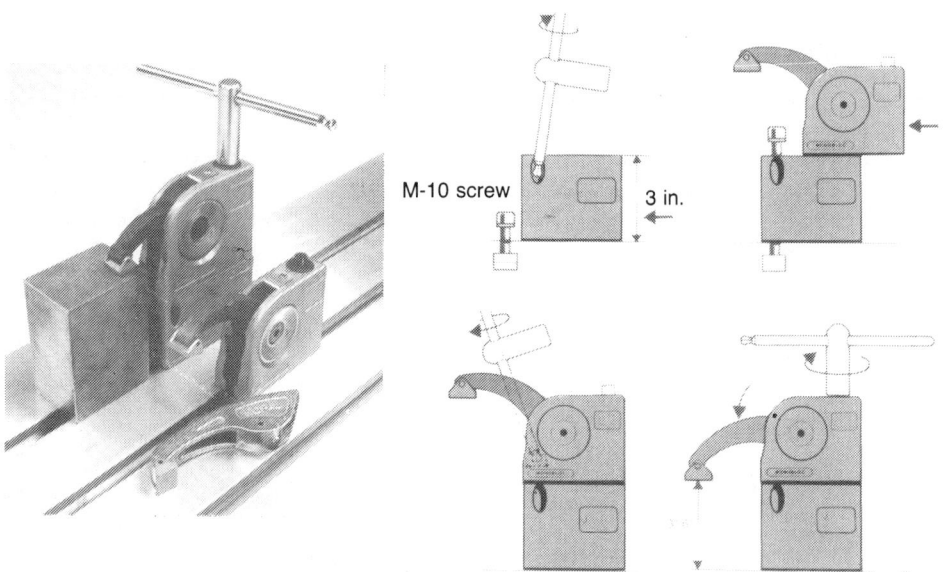

Fig. 7-87 **Vertical clamping system.** (*Courtesy Royal Products*)

A base for angled workpieces is shown in Fig. 7-88a. This component is designed to raise the workpiece above the surface of the machine table, and for workpieces with shapes that are not parallel.

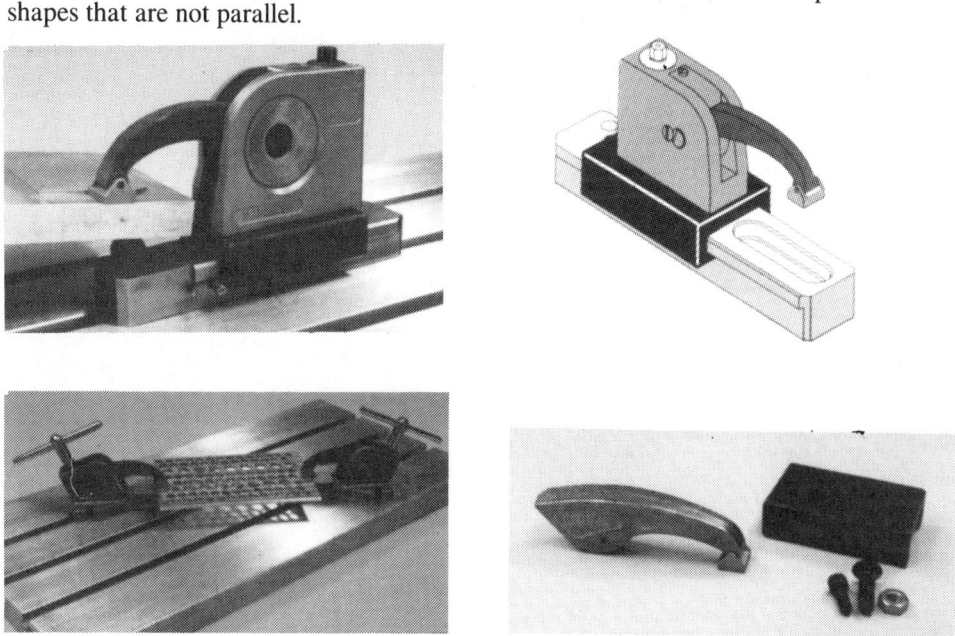

Fig. 7-88 **Accessories for the clamping system shown in Fig. 7-87.** (*Courtesy Royal Products*)

The platform blocks (see Fig. 7-88b) are also used to clamp or support workpieces in a raised position as shown.

The extension arm and mounting bar adapter shown in Fig. 7-88c allows either light-duty or standard-duty units to be mounted on bar and half-bar components of the modular toe clamp system shown in Fig. 7-72.

The retracting clamps shown in Fig. 7-89*a* are also used for clamping directly to the machine table. These clamps combine two automatic movements in one operation: A horizontal movement toward the workpiece being clamped, and a vertical movement bearing down on that workpiece. The clamping stroke is 5/32 in. (3.96 mm). Clamping capacity is ⅞ to 1-1/32 in. (22 to 26 mm), without risers. With risers, workpieces from ⅞ to 4½ in. (22 to 114 mm) high can be clamped. A 2,000 lbf (8.9 kN) force can be applied by tightening the handle to 15 ft-lb (20.3 N·m). Installation instructions are shown in Fig. 7-89*b*. They are as follows:

1. Install the attaching screw.
2. Insert the clamp.
3. Secure the clamp when in the correct position using a T-wrench inserted through the hole in the middle of the clamp.

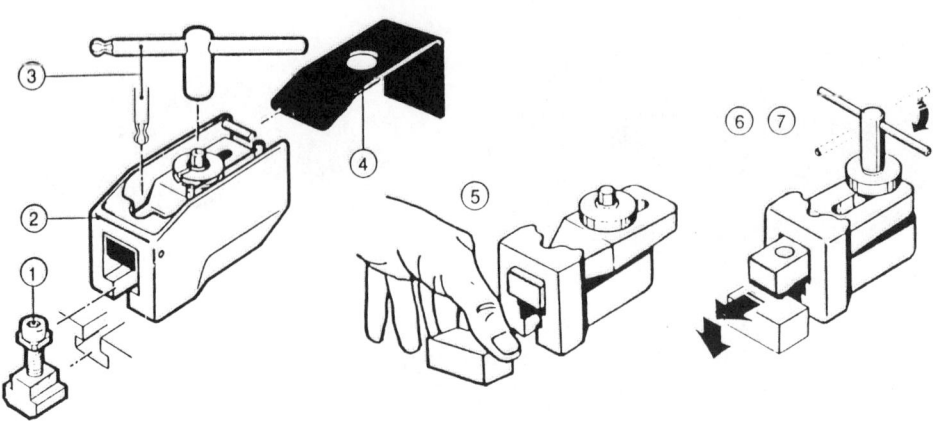

Fig. 7-89 Retracting clamps. (*Courtesy Royal Products*)

4. Clip the protective cover in place.
5. Place the workpiece in position.
6. Turn the handle ½ turn and the clamp arm will extend.
7. Turn the handle an additional ½ turn to clamp the workpiece.

The clamping system shown in Fig. 7-90a uses a simple cam action for fast, strong clamping for milling and drilling operations. The unique principle is based on two simple components: a hardened steel socket cap screw and a brass hexagonal washer. The screw head is offset to provide the cam action. As the screw is turned, the washer is moved in the direction of the cam, exerting a strong lateral force that can be applied in any direction. The system is available in multiple workpiece fixture clamp and table slot clamp versions, in a wide range of inch and metric sizes with holding forces ranging from 205 to 6,000 lbf (0.9 to 26.7 kN).

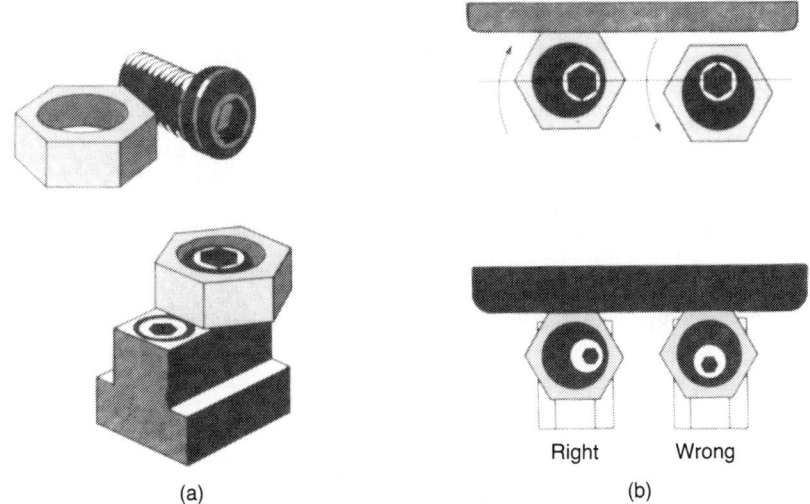

(a)   (b)

Fig. 7-90 Cam action clamping system. (*Courtesy Ossipee Precision Products Co.*)

Installation instructions when used as fixture clamps are as follows:

1. Drill and tap a hole on proper location.
2. Put screw in washer.
3. Screw in until tight, then back off 1 to 1 ½ turns.
4. Insert workpiece.
5. Tighten clamp.

For use with T-slots, install as follows:

1. Slide T-nut into T-slot of machine table.
2. Screw the clamp all the way down, then back off one turn.
3. Position the cam of the large screw as shown in Fig. 7-90b.
4. Move the clamp into position and tighten the set screw in the T-nut.
5. Insert the workpiece.
6. Tighten clamp.

Fixtures using this system are shown in Fig. 7-91.

Fig. 7-91 Fixtures using the cam action clamping system shown in Fig. 7-90. (*Courtesy Ossipee Precision Products Co.*)

The same cam action is used with the riser clamp shown in Fig. 7-92. This riser clamp consists of a base element with a T-nut for direct mounting on a machine table. The base element provides a 10° angle for the clamping element and establishes the mounting surface that holds the workpiece ½ in. (12.7 mm) off the table. One surface of the clamping element is smooth, the other is serrated for additional grip when required. The system also includes an 8 in. (203 mm) clamp bar to locate the opposite side of the workpiece. An adjustable end stop provides additional positioning as seen on the single and double workpiece setups shown in Fig. 7-93.

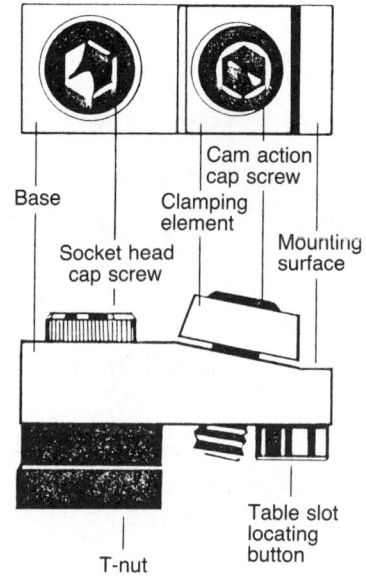

Fig. 7-92 Cam action riser clamps. (*Courtesy Ossipee Precision Products Co.*)

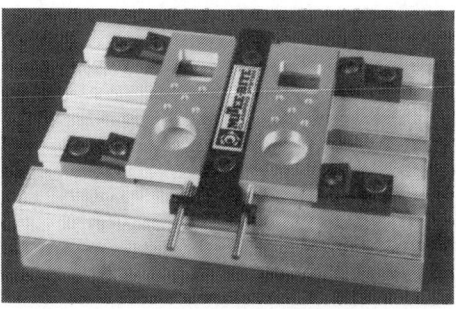 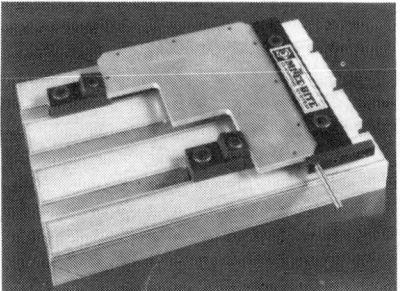

Fig. 7-93 **Setups using cam action riser clamps.** (*Courtesy Ossipee Precision Products Co.*)

The patented adjustable vise jaws shown in Fig. 7-94 are designed to allow a workpiece to be quickly positioned on top of parallels to provide a workpiece surface which is precisely parallel to the base of the vise for precision milling, drilling, slotting, and other operations. The jaws feature a cam-actuated lever movement which is spring-loaded to adjust the workpiece from 0.045 to 0.055 in. evenly at both ends of the jaw, eliminating the need to tap the workpiece while repeatly tightening the vise to achieve parallelism.

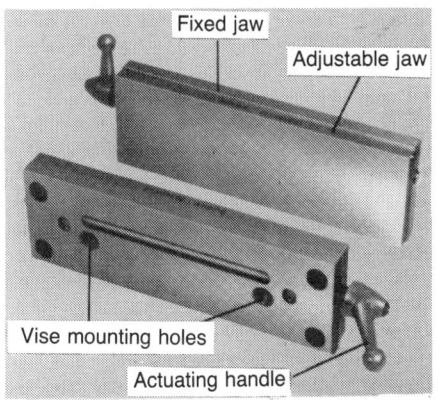 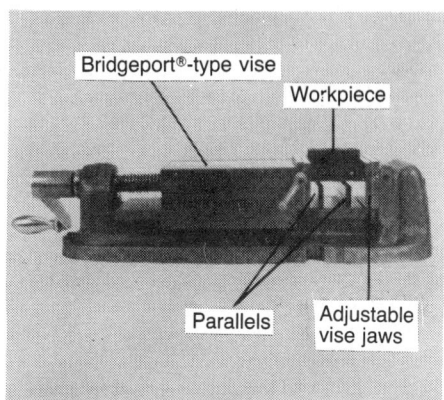

Fig. 7-94 **Patented adjustable vise jaws.** (*Courtesy The Dunham Tool Co., Inc.*)

The jaws can be either manually or air-actuated. On manual models, the cam assembly is removable to put the adjustment handle on either end of the jaw to keep hands away from the cutting area. Air-actuated models can be hand or foot operated to provide greater efficiency and less operator fatigue.

References

1. C. Andrews, "Vise Jaws Self-adjusting for Multiple Parts," *Machining* (October 1958).

CHAPTER 8

TOOLING FOR DRILLING, REAMING AND RELATED PROCESSES

Drilling generally refers to the production or enlarging of holes by the relative motion of a cutting tool known as a drill and the workpiece. The drill, workpiece, or both are rotated while being advanced axially.

Holes are produced using a wide variety of drilling machines, some of which are discussed later in the chapter. Drilling is also done on turning and boring machines, automatic screw machines, machining centers, and other multifunction machines.

Drilling machines usually require a precision workholding device known as a jig to hold, support, and locate a workpiece while accurately guiding the cutting tool as the operation is being performed.

Other operations that utilize drilling machines and jigs include:

Reaming—A machining process that uses a multi-edge, fluted cutting tool, known as a reamer, to enlarge, smooth, and/or accurately size an existing hole.

Counterboring—A machining process using an end-cutting tool to concentrically enlarge an existing hole to a limited depth. If the cut is shallow, leaving only a finished face around the original hole, it is called spotfacing.

Countersinking (also referred to as chamfering)—A machining process that uses an angled end-cutting tool to cut an angular opening at the end of an existing hole.

Tapping—A machining process for producing internal, helical threads using a tool called a tap, which has teeth on its periphery to cut threads in an existing hole.

DRILLING MACHINES

Since the design of a drill jig can be widely affected by the type of drilling machine, the various types which are specifically designed to perform drilling and related operations are briefly described in this section. They include the following:

Hand-fed Portable Drills. Hand-fed portable drills are primarily used when the workpiece cannot be taken to a drilling machine. Perhaps the most recognized portable drilling machines are the air and electric powered, heavy-duty industrial versions of the hand-fed portable drill found in most households. These units are widely used for drilling small holes in thin material where accuracy is not required. Sometimes these drills are attached to magnetic bases or other devices to position and clamp them in place for a particular operation.

Portable, Self-feeding Drill Motors. Portable, self-feeding drill motors are also used when the workpiece cannot be taken to a drilling machine. These units are equipped with self-locking nosepieces known as drill bushing tips, which along with the proper mounting accessories, effectively align and hold the units in position while absorbing the thrust and torque of the cutting tool (see Fig. 8-1).

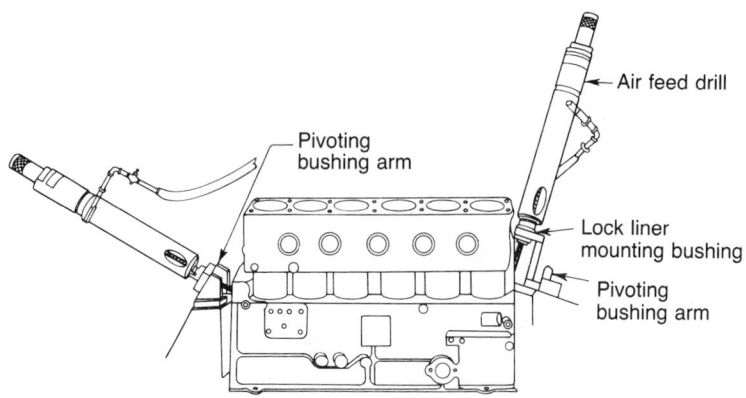

Fig. 8-1 Air drill setup for oil holes. (*Courtesy Keller Tool Div., Gardner-Denver Co.*)

In use, a threaded drill bushing tip is screwed into the nose of the drilling unit which can then be accurately located and mounted to a jig or fixture to perform the desired operation.

Portable units are primarily powered by air, with electrically and hydraulically powered units used to a lesser degree depending on availability of the power source.

Light-duty Sensitive Drilling Machines. Light-duty sensitive drilling machines (often referred to as drill presses), are single-spindle, general purpose machines which are most widely used for light drilling (up to about 1 in.) and other related operations. Most are hand-fed, but automatic feeds are available on some models. Fixtures used with the light-duty machines are mostly the hand-held type.

Heavy-duty Upright or Vertical Drilling Machines. Heavy-duty upright or vertical drilling machines are similar to the light-duty machines, but more massive for heavy-duty applications. These machines are generally equipped with power feed and square, T-slotted tables for clamping drilling fixtures or workpieces.

Either of the above non-portable drilling machines can also be equipped with multispindle heads to permit simultaneous machining operations thereby minimizing the need for toolchanging.

Layout Drilling Machines. Layout drilling machines are basically vertical drilling machines equipped with digital readout and precision slides for the saddle and table to permit more precise operation.

Gang Drilling Machines. Gang drilling machines consist of two or more of any of the aforementioned machines mounted on a common base or table. This arrangement permits higher production rates on workpieces which have different hole sizes or multiple operations that would require a change of tools on a single-spindle machine.

Multispindle Drilling Machines. Most multispindle machines are tooled-up for a specific part or family of parts which require multiple operations, multiple holes, or both. In some cases they are equipped with a shuttle table, a rotary indexing table, or a multi-position workholding fixture. Figure 8-2 shows a rectangular drill head and fixture installed in a multispindle drilling machine.

Turret Drilling Machines. Upright drilling machines discussed previously are available with indexing drums or turrets which permit performing a number of operations in a hole or group of holes without changing tools. These machines are also often equipped with shuttle tables, rotary indexing devices, or multi-position fixtures.

Radial Drilling Machines. The radial drilling machine consists of a horizontal arm supported by a vertical column. The entire arm can be raised, lowered, and rotated around the column axis while the drillhead, which is mounted on the arm, can be

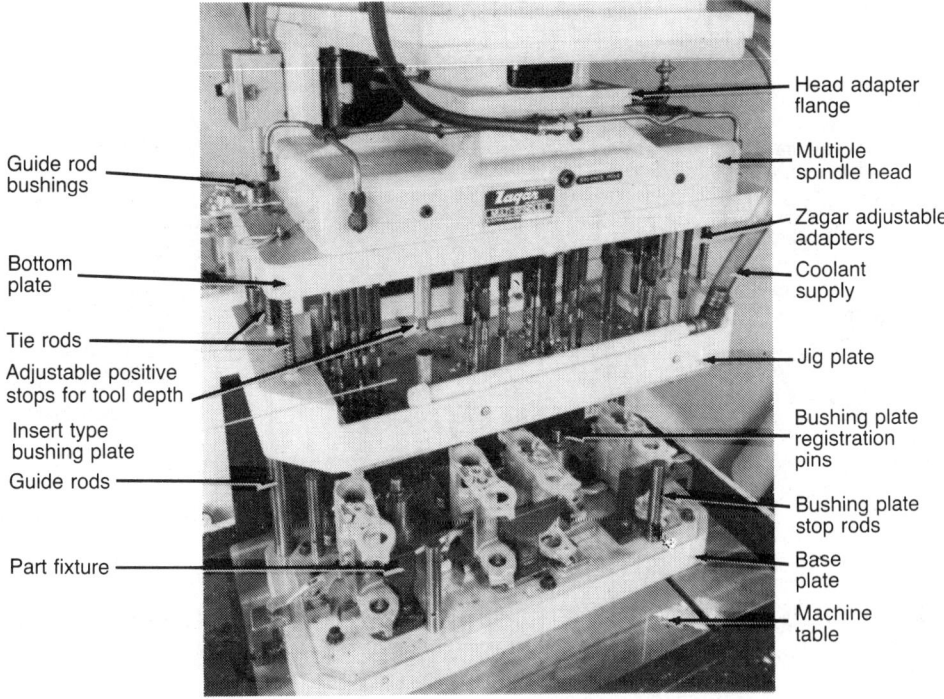

Guide rod bushings

Bottom plate

Tie rods

Adjustable positive stops for tool depth

Insert type bushing plate

Guide rods

Part fixture

Head adapter flange

Multiple spindle head

Zagar adjustable adapters

Coolant supply

Jig plate

Bushing plate registration pins

Bushing plate stop rods

Base plate

Machine table

Fig. 8-2 **Rectangular drill head and fixture assembly installed in a multispindle drilling machine.** (*Courtesy Zagar Inc.*)

repositioned along the arm and clamped in any desired position. This permits drilling and related operations to be done with the workpiece or fixture securely clamped in a fixed position. Some radial drilling machines have tilting drillheads to permit angular drilling.

Deep Hole Drilling Machines. Most deep hole drilling machines are specifically designed for deep hole drilling with gundrilling, gunboring, trepanning, or other self-guided tools. Some are designed to feed a rotating cutting tool into a stationary held workpiece; others rotate the workpiece while a non-rotating cutting tool is fed into it.

Special Purpose Drilling Machines. Many other drilling machines are built for special applications. Some examples are ultrasensitive drilling (for drilling close toleranced small holes shown in Fig. 8-3), shuttle transfer, dial index, ring index, trunnion index, and in-line transfer machines.

Automatic Self-feeding Drill Units. Automatic self-feeding drilling and precision lead screw tapping units, such as shown in Fig. 8-4, are self-contained units usually mounted to special fixtures designed to perform single or multiple drilling and/or related operations on a particular workpiece. Units can be mounted at various angles to perform these operations simultaneously in more than one plane. Once the parameters have been set, the machining operations are automatic.

Most of the related operations, that is, reaming, counterboring, countersinking, and tapping are done with the same machines that are used for drilling. In fact, many of these operations are done consecutively in the same jig. Nevertheless, special tapping machines and drilling and tapping machines are readily available. They are usually used for high speed operations.

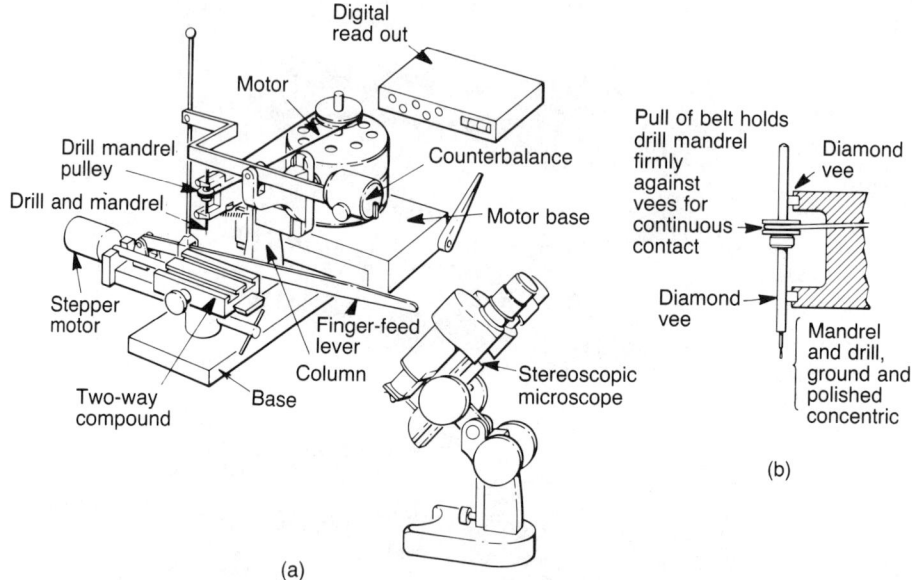

Fig. 8-3 Ultrasensitive drilling machine for producing small holes. It can be used with digital readout and/or a microscope. Tool breakage is minimized by the mounting shown in the view at right.

Fig. 8-4 Precision drilling and lead screw tapping units. (*Courtesy Snow Mfg. Co.*)

TOOL FORCES

In drilling and related operations, the forces generated by the cutting action of the tool are radial, due to torque, and downward, due to the thrust of the tool. Theoretically, two pins and a support beneath a workpiece as shown in Fig. 8-5 will resist these forces without the need to clamp the workpiece. However, once the drill breaks through the workpiece, an upward force is created which may cause the workpiece to climb up the drill. If this force is not restrained, the workpiece may rise above the pins and start to spin, thereby creating a dangerous condition.

An upward force could occur if the drill gets jammed in a workpiece and must be withdrawn. Also, if the spindle is reversed, to remove a tool or for some other reason, the workpiece would be free to turn in the same direction. These opposite forces are generally small compared to forces required to drill the hole, and are easily controlled by clamping.

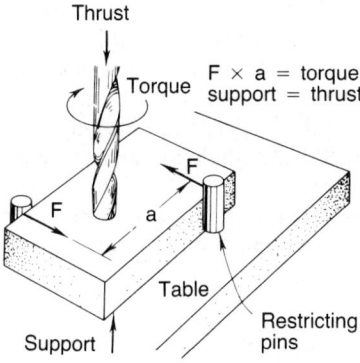

Thrust

Torque

F × a = torque
support = thrust

F

F

a

Support

Table

Restricting pins

Fig. 8-5 Pin-type drill fixture resisting torque and thrust.

In tapping, the workpiece must be restrained from turning in both directions and be held down to resist the lifting action of the tap. For leadscrew tapping, thrust and lifting actions are eliminated, but resistance to torque is still required. When tapping two or more holes simultaneously on a multi-spindle setup, each tap acts as a restraint to prevent workpiece rotation caused by the torque of the other taps. However, a hold down would still be required when tapping without a leadscrew. Tapping forces are illustrated in Fig. 8-6.

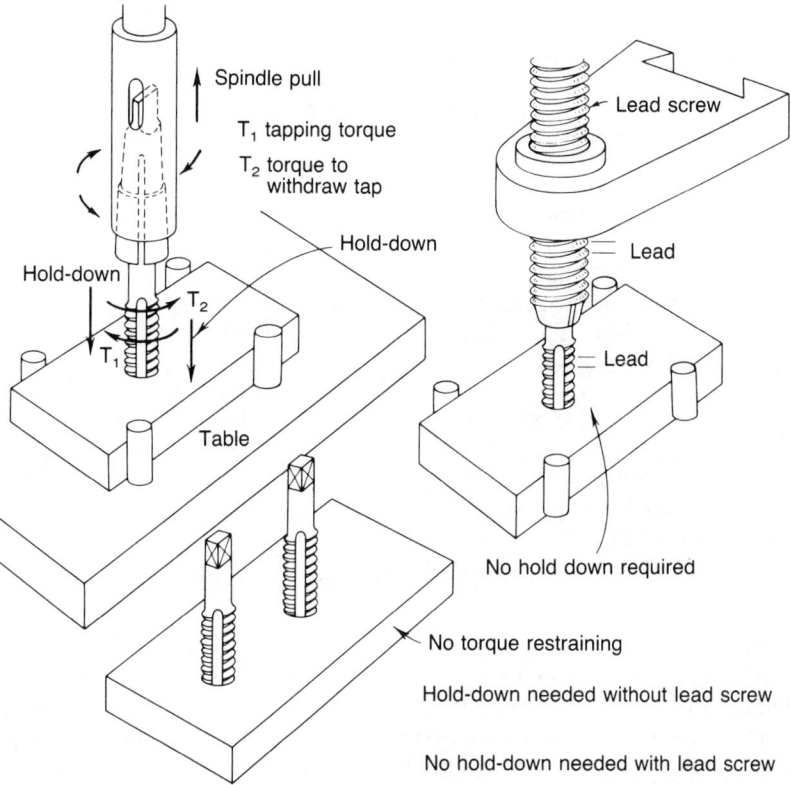

Spindle pull

T_1 tapping torque

T_2 torque to withdraw tap

Hold-down

Hold-down

T_2

T_1

Table

Lead screw

Lead

Lead

No hold down required

No torque restraining

Hold-down needed without lead screw

No hold-down needed with lead screw

Fig. 8-6 Workholder to resist torque and thrust in a tapping operation.

Estimating Drilling Forces. With twist drills, thrust force is very sensitive to variations in chisel edge length or web thickness.[1] Web thinning reduces thrust requirements, decreases the cutting temperature, increases drill life, and improves hole geometry.

Research and analysis indicate that drill torque and thrust are functions of the drill diameter, drill chisel edge length, feed per revolution, and workpiece material. The effects of cutting fluids and drill helix angle are relatively minor unless difficulty with chip ejection is encountered.

Reasonable estimates of torque and thrust requirements of sharp twist drills of various sizes and designs can be made from the following formulas:

For torque:

$$M = Kf^{0.8} d^{1.8} A \qquad (1)$$

For thrust:

$$T = 2Kf^{0.8} d^{1.8} B + Kd^2 E \qquad (2)$$

where:

M = torque, in.-lbf

T = thrust force, lbf (N)

K = work-material constant, (see Table 8-1)

f = drill feed, ipr

d = drill diameter, in.

A, B, E = Drill design constants (see the following text and Table 8-2).

TABLE 8-1
Work-Material Constants for
Calculating Torque and Thrust

Work Material	K
Steel, 200 Bhn	24,000
Steel, 300 Bhn	31,000
Steel, 400 Bhn	34,000
Most aluminum alloys	7,000
Most magnesium alloys	4,000
Most brasses	14,000
Leaded brass	7,000
Cast iron, 165 Bhn	15,000
Free-machining mild steel, resulfurized	18,000
Austenitic stainless steel (Type 316)	34,000

(Courtesy National Twist Drill, Div. of Regal-Beloit Corp.)

The most important drill design feature affecting torque and thrust is the ratio of the chisel edge length, c, to the drill diameter, d. The torque and thrust constants, A, B, and E, in Table 8-2 are based upon the ratio c/d. Because it is often easier to measure the web thickness at the point w, the table also includes approximate values of the ratio w/d. For drills of standard design, $c/d = 0.18$ can be used, and for drills with split points, $c/d = 0.03$ gives a reasonable estimate. To simplify raising the feed, f, and diameter, d, to the powers required in the formulas, values are given in Tables 8-3 and 8-4. If exact values

TABLE 8-2
Torque and Thrust Constants Based upon Ratios c/d or w/d

c/d	Approx. w/d	Torque constant A	Thrust constant B	Thrust constant E
0.03	0.025	1.000	1.100	0.001
0.05	0.045	1.005	1.140	0.003
0.08	0.070	1.015	1.200	0.006
0.10	0.085	1.020	1.235	0.010
0.13	0.110	1.040	1.270	0.017
0.15	0.130	1.080	1.310	0.022
0.18	0.155	1.085	1.355	0.030
0.20	0.175	1.105	1.380	0.040
0.25	0.220	1.155	1.445	0.065
0.30	0.260	1.235	1.500	0.090
0.35	0.300	1.310	1.575	0.120
0.40	0.350	1.395	1.620	0.160

(*Courtesy National Twist Drill, Div. of Regal-Beloit Corp.*)

* c = chisel edge length, in. (mm)
d = drill diameter, in. (mm)
w = web thickness, in. (mm)

TABLE 8-3
Torque and Thrust Terms Based upon Feed

Feed, f, ipr	$f^{0.8}$	Feed, f, ipr	$f^{0.8}$
0.0005	0.0025	0.012	0.030
0.001	0.004	0.015	0.035
0.002	0.007	0.020	0.045
0.003	0.010	0.025	0.055
0.004	0.012	0.030	0.060
0.005	0.014	0.035	0.070
0.006	0.017	0.040	0.075
0.008	0.020	0.050	0.090
0.010	0.025		

(*Courtesy National Twist Drill, Div. of Regal-Beloit Corp.*)

are not found in the tables, the use of the next larger value in the tables will give conservative results. Interpolation, however, gives more accurate results. The formulas yield torque and thrust requirements for sharp drills. An extra 30-50% should be provided to allow for dulling.

Complete english and metric unit tables for estimating drilling torque and thrust are readily available in publications such as the *Machinability Data Handbook*. Tables are based on material and hardness, feed per revolution, drill diameter, and the type of drill point.

Formulas for estimating torque and thrust in drilling are listed in Chapter 3.

TABLE 8-4
Torque and Thrust Terms Based upon Diameter

Diam, d, in.	$d^{0.8}$	$d^{1.8}$	d^2
0.063	0.110	0.007	0.004
0.094	0.150	0.014	0.009
0.125	0.190	0.025	0.016
0.156	0.225	0.035	0.025
0.188	0.260	0.050	0.035
0.218	0.295	0.065	0.050
0.250	0.330	0.082	0.065
0.281	0.365	0.105	0.080
0.313	0.395	0.125	0.105
0.344	0.425	0.145	0.120
0.375	0.455	0.170	0.140
0.438	0.515	0.225	0.190
0.500	0.575	0.285	0.250
0.563	0.630	0.355	0.315
0.625	0.685	0.430	0.390
0.688	0.740	0.510	0.470
0.750	0.795	0.595	0.565
0.875	0.900	0.785	0.765
1.000	1.000	1.000	1.000
1.125	1.010	1.235	1.270
1.250	1.195	1.495	1.565
1.375	1.290	1.775	1.890
1.500	1.385	2.075	2.250
1.625	1.475	2.400	2.640
1.750	1.565	2.740	3.060
1.875	1.655	3.100	3.520
2.000	1.740	3.480	4.000
2.250	1.915	4.300	5.070
2.500	2.080	5.200	6.250
2.750	2.250	6.190	7.560
3.000	2.410	7.240	9.000
3.500	2.720	9.500	12.250
4.000	3.030	12.100	16.000

(Courtesy National Twist Drill, Div. of Regal-Beloit Corp.)

ESTIMATING TAPPING TORQUE

Tapping torque is the effort required to rotate the tap to cut or form the internal thread in the workpiece.[2] It is a function of the volume of material to be moved or removed and is influenced by the effects of chip accumulation, the cutting fluid used, and other factors. On thin-walled large holes, excessive tapping torque can cause deformation of the workpiece, either by the tap or by necessarily high clamping forces. The volume of chips generated can be critical in deep holes or where thread finish is critical.

Three thread design factors affect tapping torque; thread diameter, thread pitch, and percentage of thread height. Tapping torque is almost directly proportional to thread diameter for any given thread pitch and thread height percentage. Increasing the thread height from 55-85% doubles the required torque.

Numerous controlled tests of threaded joint strength have shown that, for standard lengths of engagement, maximum strength is reached when the internal thread height is 55%. Standard nut engagement length is slightly less than one major (nominal) diameter. For engagement lengths of one full nominal diameter, maximum strength is reached at 33% thread height. Whether the joint is pulled in tension or pushed in compression and made of soft or hardened internal or external threads, there is no gain in failure strength by increasing the thread height above 55% with normal engagement lengths.

Tests also show that the torque required for tapping 55% thread height is only 60-70% of that required for 75% thread height. This torque difference directly relates to difficulty in tapping as evidenced by tap wear, breakage, and speed capability. In general, a tap drill size equivalent to 60-65% theoretical thread height provides an adequate factor of safety to allow for normal variations in drilled hole diameter and roundness and ensures full joint strength.

Thread pitch also has an effect on tapping torque. For example, a 6-pitch thread requires nearly seven times the tapping torque of the 18-pitch thread.

Tapping torque for producing leadscrew nut threads can often be a problem. If the leadscrew design is changed to one having multiple thread lead, tapping torque can be significantly reduced. For example, the tapping torque for a 1½—6 nut is 1450 in.-lbf. The torque for a double-lead 1½—12 nut is 850 in.-lbf. For a triple-lead 1½—18 nut, the tapping torque is only 650 in.-lbf. Multiple-thread leadscrews, however, are difficult to manufacture and should not be specified indiscriminately.

Tapping torque can be roughly estimated from the formula:

$$M = KC_T C_M \tag{3}$$

where:

M = estimated torque at the tap, in.-lbf

K = work material constant (see Table 8-5)

C_T = tapping condition constant (see Table 8-6)

C_m = tap torque factor (see Table 8-7)

Work material constant, K, gives the energy in inch-pounds required to remove one cubic inch of metal under normal metalcutting conditions. This formula often gives results that are lower than actual torque requirements, which can be as high as four times the values calculated.

TABLE 8-5
Constants, K, for Various Workpiece Materials
to be Used in Determining Tapping Torque

Work Material	K
Steel, 200 Bhn	350,000
Steel, 300 Bhn	450,000
Steel, 400 Bhn	500,000
Most aluminum alloys	100,000
Most magnesium alloys	60,000
Most brasses	200,000
Leaded brass	100,000

(Courtesy National Twist Drill, Div. of Regal-Beloit Corp.)

TABLE 8-6
Constants, C_T, for Determining Tapping Torque of Various Type Taps

| | C_T | |
Tap Type	Sharp	Dull
Chip driver (spiral point)	1.0	1.5
R. H. helical flutes	1.3	2.0
Straight flutes		
Shallow holes (taps over 1½ in. diam.)	1.3	2.0
Taps up to 1½ in. diam. and deep hole for larger taps	1.7	2.5

(Courtesy National Twist Drill, Div. of Regal-Beloit Corp.)

TABLE 8-7
Torque Constants, $C_M \times 10^6$, for UNC, NC, UNF, and NF Threads*

Tap Size	Thread Height				Tap Size	Thread Height			
	55%	65%	75%	85%		55%	65%	75%	85%
6—32	8	11	13	16	—18	300	400	500	600
—40	6	7	9	11	1 3/4— 5	3150	4150	5100	6200
8—32	10	13	16	19	— 8	1375	1800	2250	2700
—36	8	11	13	16	—12	675	875	1100	1350
10—24	20	25	31	37	—16	400	525	650	800
—32	12	15	19	23	1 7/8— 8	1475	1900	2400	2950
12—24	23	29	36	43	—12	725	925	1175	1450
—28	12	15	19	23	—16	425	550	700	875
1/4—20	36	46	57	68	2— 4 1/2	4400	5600	7050	8550
—28	20	26	32	39	— 8	1600	2050	2550	3150
5/8—11	270	350	430	520	—12	775	1000	1250	1550
—18	110	150	180	220	—16	450	600	750	925
3/4—10	390	500	620	750	2 1/4— 4 1/2	4950	6350	8000	9700
—16	170	220	270	340	— 8	1800	2300	2900	3550
7/8—9	540	700	870	1100	—12	875	1125	1400	1750
—14	250	320	410	500	—16	525	675	850	1050
1—8	770	990	1200	1500	2 1/2— 4	6800	8750	10900	13300
—12	380	490	610	740	— 8	2000	2550	3250	3950
1 1/4—7	1200	1600	2000	2400	—12	975	1250	1550	1950
—12	480	610	770	940	—16	575	750	950	1150
1 1/2— 6	2000	2500	3200	3800	5/16-18	55	70	88	110
— 8	1175	1500	1900	2300	—24	33	43	53	65
—12	575	750	925	1050	3/8—16	82	110	130	160
—16	350	450	575	700	—24	40	52	65	79
—18	275	375	475	575	7/16—14	120	160	190	230
1 5/8— 8	1275	1650	2050	2500	—20	65	84	110	130
—12	625	800	1000	1250	1/2—13	160	200	250	310
—16	375	475	600	750	—20	75	96	120	150

TABLE 8-7 *(continued)*

Torque Constants, $C_M \times 10^6$, for UNC, NC, UNF, and NF Threads*

Tap Size	Thread Height				Tap Size	Thread Height			
	55%	65%	75%	85%		55%	65%	75%	85%
9/16—12	210	260	330	400	— 8	3000	3900	4900	6000
—18	100	130	170	200	—12	1450	1900	2350	2900
					—16	875	1125	1425	1750
2 3/4— 4	7500	9650	12100	14800					
— 8	2200	2800	3550	4350	4— 4	11050	14300	17900	21900
—12	1050	1375	1750	2150	— 8	3200	4150	5250	6400
—16	650	825	1050	1275	—12	1550	2000	2550	3100
					—16	925	1200	1550	1850
3— 4	8200	10600	13200	16200					
— 8	2400	3100	3900	4750	4 1/2— 8	3600	4650	5900	7200
—12	1150	1500	1900	2350	—12	1750	2250	2850	3500
—16	700	900	1150	1400	—16	1050	1350	1700	2100
3 1/4— 4	8950	11500	14400	17600	5— 8	4000	5200	6550	8000
— 8	2600	3350	4200	5200	—12	1950	2500	3150	3900
—12	1250	1650	2050	2500	—16	1175	1500	1900	2350
—16	750	975	1250	1500	5 1/2— 8	4400	5700	7200	8850
3 1/2— 4	9650	12400	15600	19000	—12	2150	2750	3500	4300
— 8	2800	3600	4550	5600	—16	1275	1650	2100	2600
—12	1350	1750	2200	2700	6— 8	4800	6250	7900	9650
—16	825	1050	1325	1650	—12	2350	3000	3800	4700
3 3/4— 4	10350	13300	16700	20500	—16	1400	1800	2300	2800

(Courtesy National Twist Drill, Div. of Regal-Beloit Corp.)

* Actual torque constants are $\dfrac{1}{1,000,000}$ times the tabulated values. Thus 2500 in this table means 0.002500.

Tap torque can be converted to horsepower by the formula:

$$hp = \frac{MN}{63,025} \tag{4}$$

where:

hp = horsepower

M = torque, in.-lbf

N = rotational speed, rpm

Rotational speed, N, is calculated from the formula:

$$N = \frac{3.82V}{D} \tag{5}$$

where:

V = cutting speed, sfm

D = nominal tool diameter, in.

Example 1: Determine the torque for driving a short 3-in. diameter, 8-pitch tap with 75% thread height in 200 Bhn steel at 40 sfm. From Tables 8-5, 8-6, and 8-7, C_M =

0.003900, $K = 350,000$, and $C_T = 2.0$ (dull tap), therefore:

$$M = KC_TC_M \qquad (3)$$
$$= 350,000 \times 0.003900 \times 2$$
$$= 2730 \text{ in.-lbf}$$

$$N = \frac{3.82V}{D} = \frac{3.82 \times 40}{3} \qquad (5)$$
$$= 51 \text{ rpm}$$

$$hp = \frac{16\,M\,N}{1,000,000} \qquad (4)$$
$$= \frac{16 \times 2730 \times 51}{1,000,000} = 2.23$$

This is the shaft horsepower and torque at the machine spindle or work chuck. Since most machines have a transmission efficiency of about 85%, a drive motor of 3 hp should be adequate for this tapping job. Drive motor torque requirements must account for gear or pulley ratios.

DRILL JIGS

The workpiece, production rates, and machine availability normally determine the size, shape, and construction details of any jig. However, all jigs must conform to certain design principles which will provide for the efficient and productive manufacture of quality workpieces by providing a method to:

1. Correctly locate the workpiece with respect to the tool.
2. Securely clamp and rigidly support the workpiece during the operation.
3. Guide the tool.
4. Position and/or fasten the jig on a machine.

These features will insure interchangeability and accuracy of parts, plus provide the following advantages:

1. Minimize tool breakage.
2. Minimize the possibility of human error.
3. Permit the use of less skilled labor.
4. Reduce manufacturing time.
5. Eliminate retooling for repeat orders.

Jigs are often divided into two broad categories, open and closed. Open jigs are generally used when machining a single surface of a workpiece, whereas closed jigs are used when machining multiple surfaces. Examples of open and closed jigs are shown in Fig. 8-7.

More often, jig types are identified by the method used to construct the jig (for example: template, plate, leaf, channel, etc.). The main types are discussed in the following sections.

Template Drill Jigs. Template drill jigs are not actually true jigs because they do not incorporate a clamping device. However, they can be used on a wide variety of parts and are among the simplest and least expensive drill jigs to build. Template drill jigs are simply plates containing holes or bushings to guide a drill. They are usually placed and located directly on a feature of the part itself to permit the drilling of holes at the desired location. When this is impractical, they are located on the part by measurement or by sight lines scribed on the template.

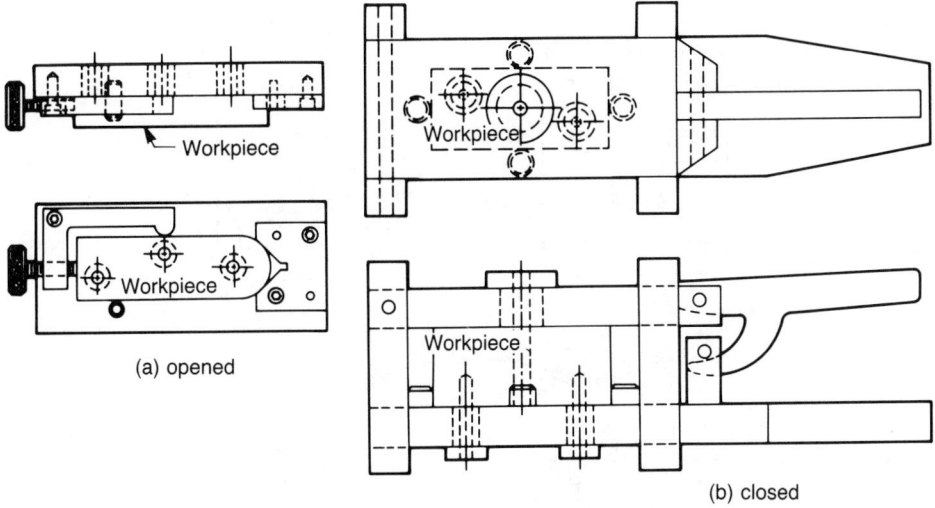

Fig. 8-7 Open and closed types of drill jigs.

Two flat plate template drill jigs are shown in Fig. 8-8. Both are designed to drill a hole through the center of the rounded end of a lever. The jig shown in *a* consists mainly of a drill guide plate and a locating V-block. The jig in *b* does the same job, but has been further simplified by using dowel pins to accomplish the same centralizing action as the V-block.

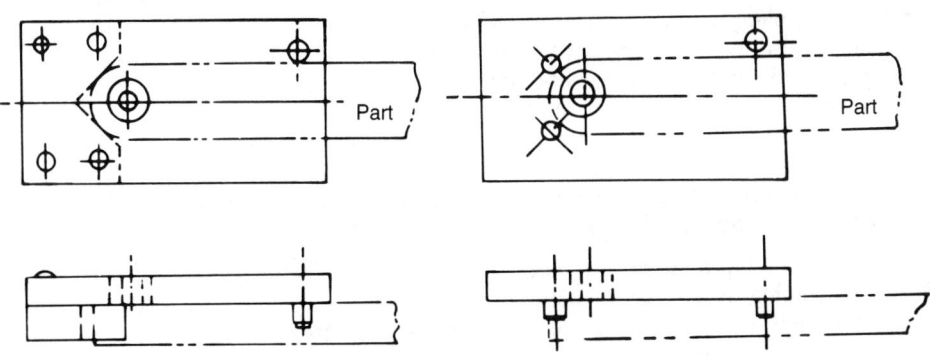

Fig. 8-8 Flat plate template drill jigs.

Another flat plate template drill jig is shown in Fig. 8-9. This jig was designed to drill a three-hole pattern into either a left or right hand version of a workpiece. This was made possible by having the pins protrude from both sides of the drill plate, thereby permitting it to be flip-flopped to suit the workpiece being drilled. A common practice with template drill jigs is to place a pin into the first hole drilled to prevent excessive movement of the jig while the remaining holes are drilled.

Three circular-type template drill jigs are shown in Fig. 8-10. All are designed to locate from the maximum material condition (MMC) of the part diameter. Jig *a* was designed to locate from the OD of a shaft, jig *b* from the ID of a part, and jig *c* from a boss diameter. In all cases, a pin of the proper size was placed into the first hole drilled to properly position the jig to drill the second hole.

8-13

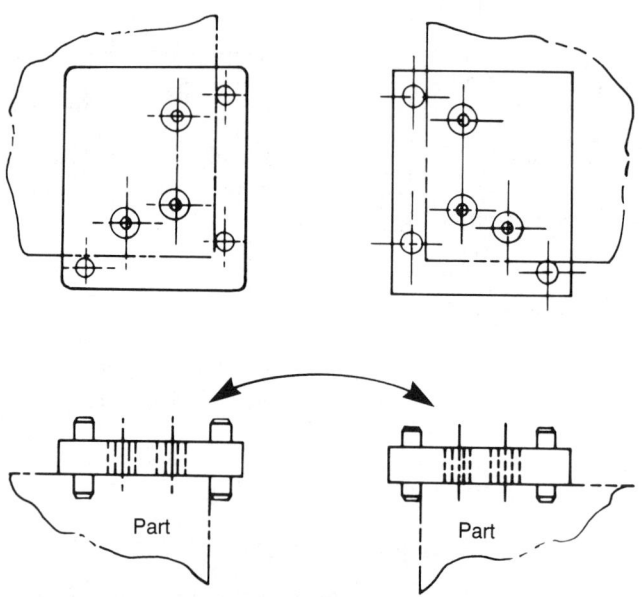

Fig. 8-9 Flat plate template drill jig—L/R hand.

Figure 8-11 illustrates two nesting type template drill jigs. Jig *a* is designed to locate a small sheet metal workpiece in a cavity, to permit drilling two holes which are located from the periphery of the workpiece. Jig *b* was designed to perform the same operation by using five dowel pins press-fitted into the jig in lieu of the cavity to locate the workpiece, reducing the cost to build the jig.

A template drill jig is often used to drill holes in one portion of a large workpiece where a conventional jig large enough to hold the entire part would be impractical and costly. Template jigs usually cost much less than conventional jigs, often making it more economical to use two or three template drill jigs in lieu of one large conventional jig.

Some of the main disadvantages of template jigs are:

- They are not as foolproof as most other types, which may result in inaccurate machining by a careless operator.
- Orientation of the hole pattern to workpiece datums may not be as accurate as with other types. However, the accuracy of the hole pattern within the template jig itself is comparable to that of any conventional jig.
- They are usually not practical when locating datums are dimensioned regardless of feature size (RFS).

Plate Jigs. Plate jigs are basically template jigs equipped with a workpiece clamping system. Initial construction costs are greater for plate jigs than for template jigs, but plate jigs are generally more accurate and last longer.

A plate jig incorporates a plate, which is generally the main structural member, that carries the drill or liner bushings. Slip bushings of various sizes can be used with liner bushings, allowing a series of drilling and related operations without the need to relocate or reclamp the workpiece.

The plate jig's open construction makes it easy to load and unload a workpiece and to get rid of chips.

Three different types of plate jigs are shown in Fig. 8-12. The open plate jig, *a*, is basically a template jig equipped with a means to clamp the workpiece, with work being supported by the drill press table. The table plate jig, *b*, consists of a drill plate,

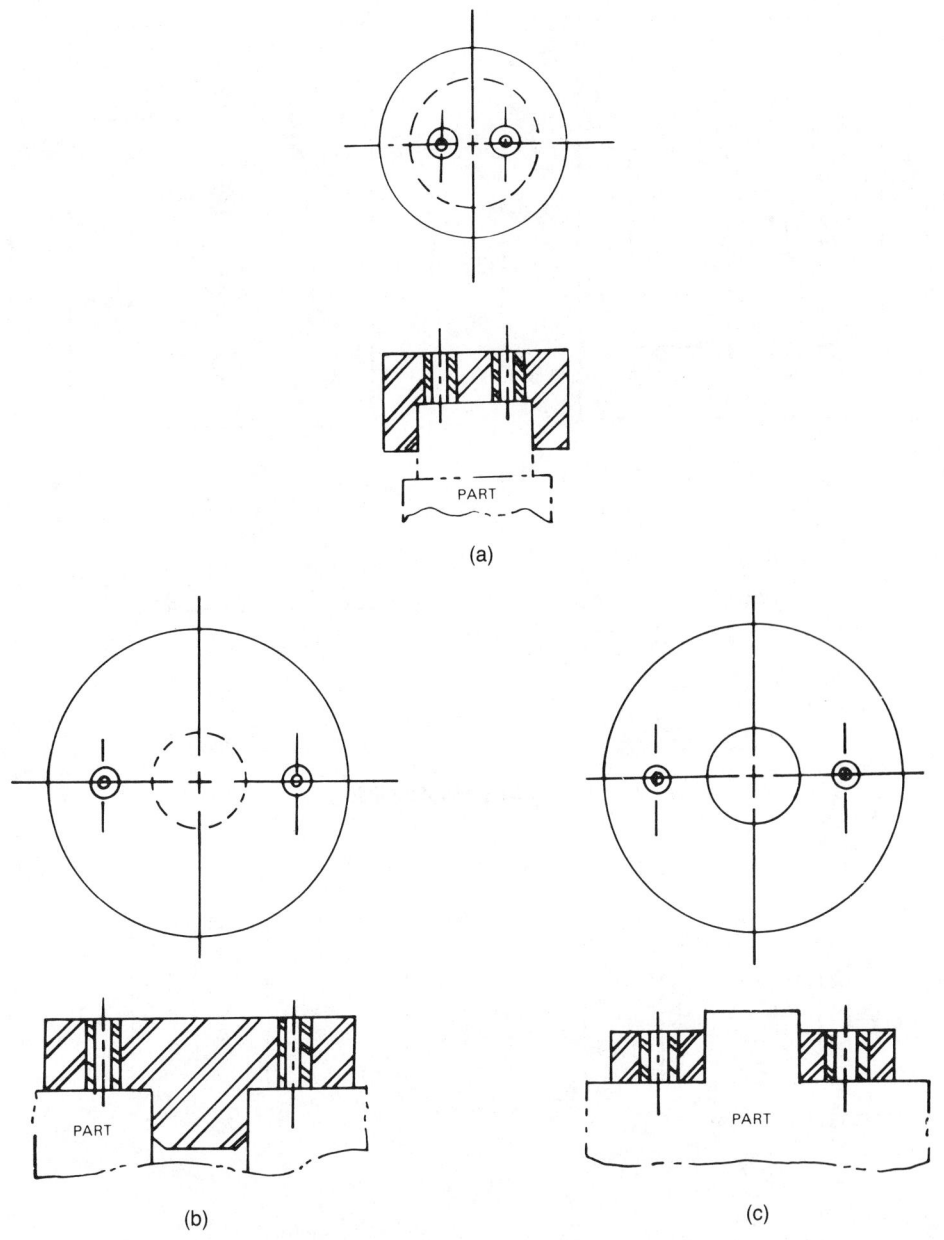

Fig. 8-10 Circular plate template drill jigs.

locating stud, and clamping screw, with standard screws being used as jig feet. This type
of jig is usually hand-held on the drill press table instead of being clamped to the table
so that it may be easily inverted for easy loading and unloading. Consequently, table
plate jigs are usually used for smaller parts. Especially note that tool thrust in this type
of jig is directed towards the clamps rather than the rigid portions of this jig. Therefore
it is imperative that the clamping method be strong enough to resist the thrust of the
drill.

For obvious reasons, the jig shown in Fig. 8-12c is called a sandwich plate jig. With

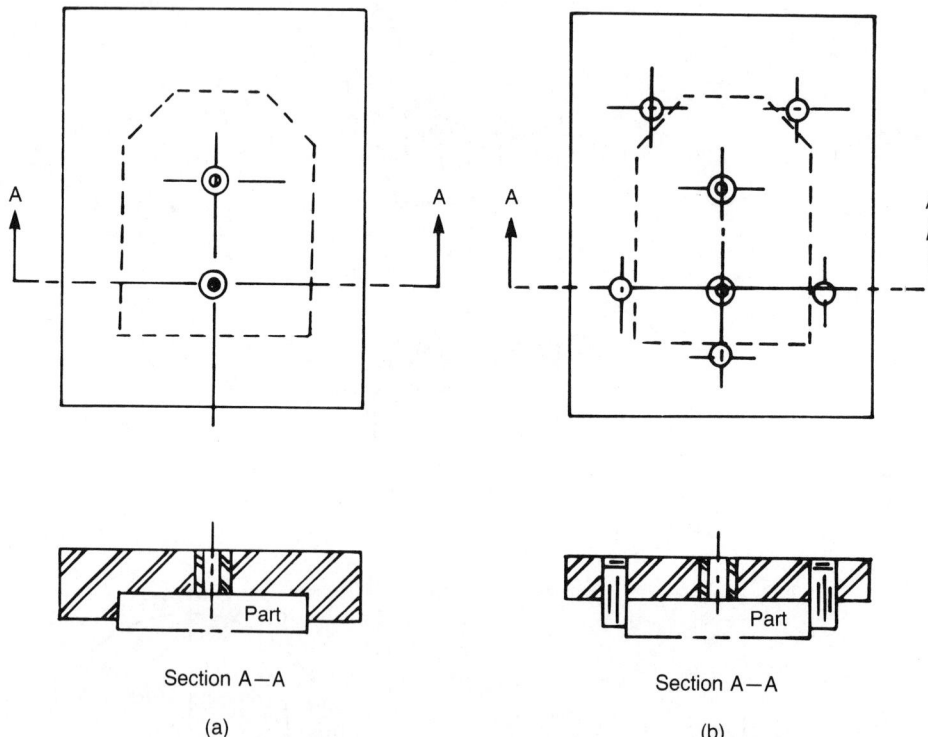

Fig. 8-11 Nesting template drill jigs.

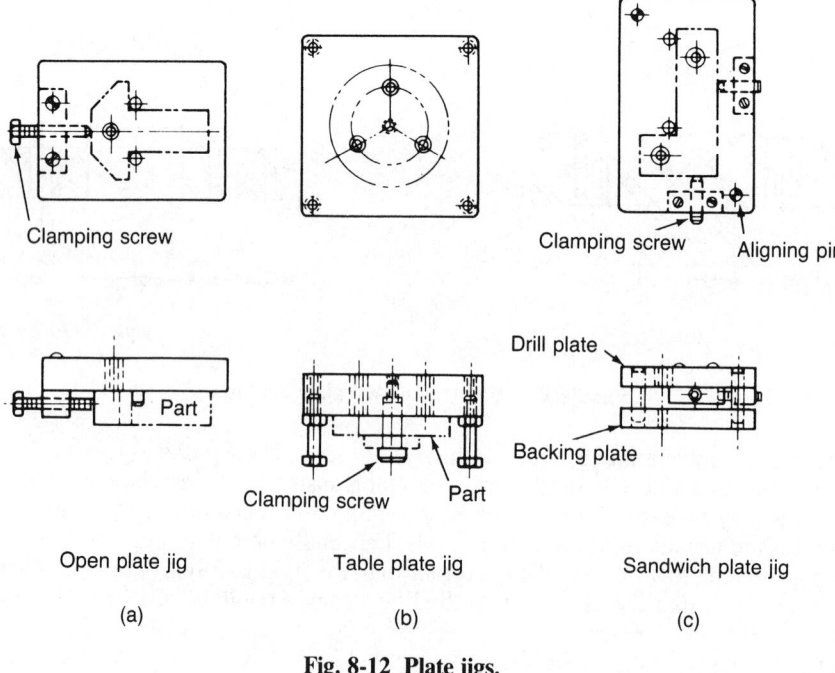

Fig. 8-12 Plate jigs.

this type of jig, the workpiece is positioned between two plates; a drill plate containing the drill jig bushings, locators and clamps, and a backup plate to provide support only. The backup plate has clearance holes for the drill and is aligned with the drill plate by two pins. The backup plate makes it ideal for drilling thin parts which would otherwise buckle from the thrust of the drill.

The angle plate jigs shown in Fig. 8-13 are primarily used to drill workpieces at an angle to the part locators. The plain angle plate jig, *a*, is designed to drill holes perpendicular to the locating surface, while the modified angle plate jig, *b*, is designed to drill holes at angles other than 90° to the locating surface.

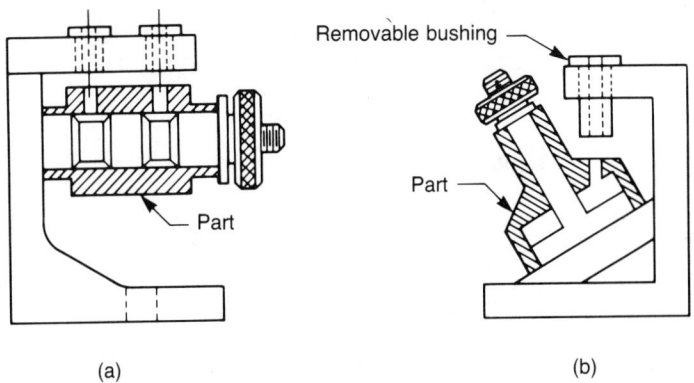

(a)   (b)

Fig. 8-13 Angle plate jigs.

Plate type jigs are usually moved around the table by hand. Therefore, special safety precautions should be provided to prevent the jig from whirling around the spindle whenever a cutting tool jams. The best way to prevent this is to build the jig with an extension handle long enough for the machine operator to overcome the torque of the jammed tool. When a plate jig is to be used with a radial drill, provision can often be made to clamp the drill jig or the workpiece to the machine table.

Other examples of plate jigs are shown in Figs. 8-14 thru 8-18.

The plate jig shown in Fig. 8-14 has three drill bushings (1) pressed into a plate (5) and two others in a locator block (4). The channel-shaped workpiece is also located by a dowel pin (2) and held by clamps (3).

The workpieces (locknuts) shown in Fig. 8-15 were formerly held in a jig designed for drilling three stacked locknuts at a time. However, since the flat faces of some of the locknuts were not parallel when stacked together in the jig, the holes could not be drilled perpendicular to the faces. The jig shown in the same figure was designed to drill one part at a time while eliminating the problem. In use, the fixture is fastened to the drill press table so that drill bushing *A* is directly under the drill spindle. The locknut is placed against the lower locating pins, and the cam handle is pushed down lowering the bushing plate and allowing the upper location pins to slide over and locate the locknut. The travel *X* of the slide on the base between the four guide pins is the interhole distance, limited by the stop pins. The stop screw prevents the bushing plate from rising when pressure is applied by the cam, while a spring keeps the plate up when the cam is released to permit loading. A hardened button is pressed into the base to provide a wear surface for the cam. After the first hole is drilled, the cam is released and the slide is pulled forward, centering the drill spindle over drill bushing *B*. Cam pressure is reapplied, and the second hole is drilled.

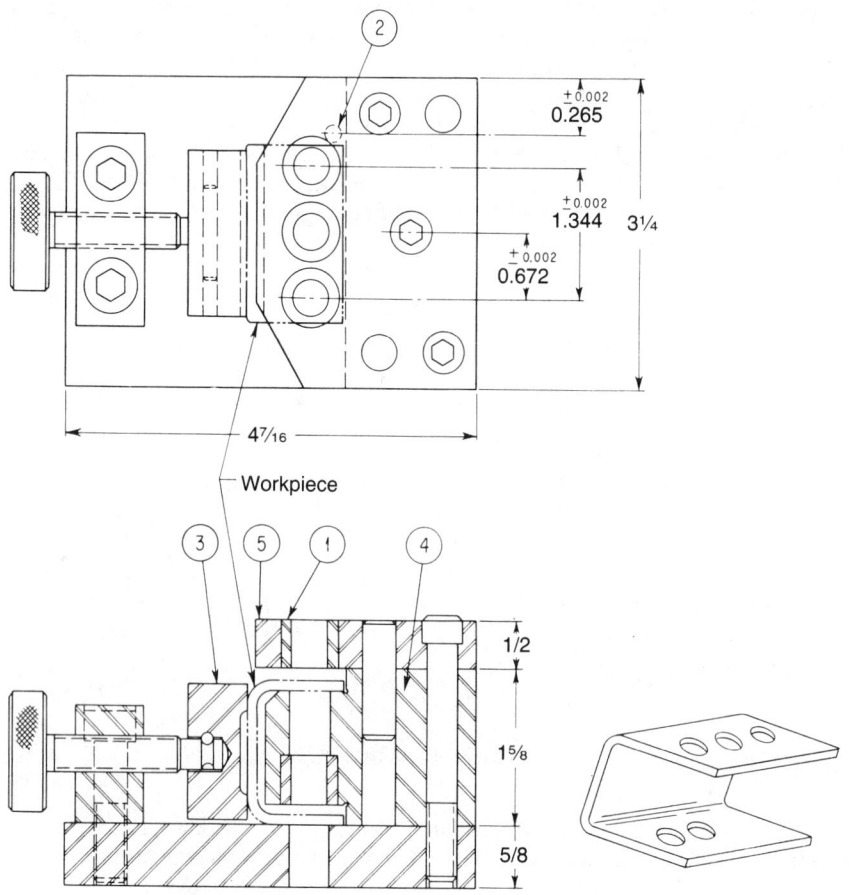

Fig. 8-14 Jig for drilling a channel. (*Courtesy Barth Corp.*)

The jig in Fig. 8-16 was designed for use with a three-spindle drill press to drill, countersink, and tap two holes in an irregular aluminum casting. It was designed to use standard, commercial jig legs. A diamond locator (5) and a round locator (1) are used to locate a casting which is clamped against four standard rest buttons (4). A swing-latch clamp (2) swings to the right for loading and unloading. A swivel pad (6) on the end of a knob and shoe assembly (3) compensates for variations in the bottom of the workpiece. Two drill bushings (7) are mounted in a changeable plug (8) which fits in a liner (9). For accurate drilling, the center line of the bushings and locators are parallel to each other and square to the ends of the jig legs and rest buttons within 0.001 in. FIM.

Forty-eight holes around the upper flange and eight around the lower flange of a tapered cylinder are drilled using the jig shown in Fig. 8-17. The flat base or plate (7) supports a center column (6). A bushing-assembly plate (8) carries the upper and lower drill bushings (3, 5) as well as an upper locating ring (1). The workpiece on a revolving locating ring (9) and a locating slide (10) is pushed into a locating notch in the workpiece. The bushing-assembly plate is located on a center plug (11) and is accurately oriented to the workpiece by the locating button (12) mounted on the bracket (13) as shown in the auxiliary view. The swinging C-clamp (4) holds the upper bushing-assembly plate to the center plug. The plate or base rests on, and is indexed by, a rotary table mounted on the table of a radial drill.

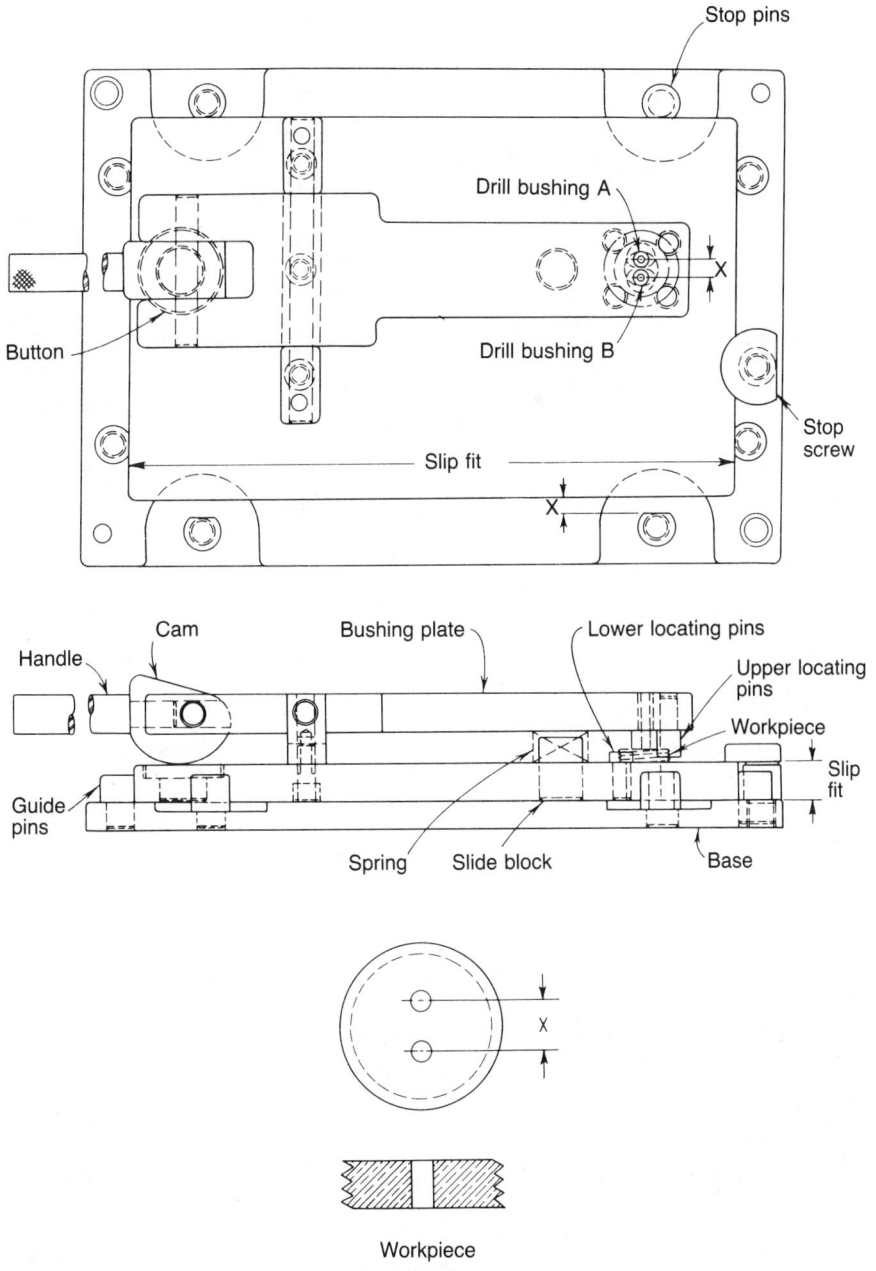

Fig. 8-15 Plate jig with quick-acting cam.[3]

The circular jig plate of Fig. 8-18 is inverted twice between four drilling operations, inverted before finish reaming and chamfering and inverted once more for unloading.

The upper and lower halves of the fixture are radially timed (properly located and oriented with each other) by a button locator (1). The halves are held together by six swing C-washers (2) equally spaced around their circumferences. Six sets of clamps (3, 4, and 5), equally spaced around the circular flanges of the workpiece, hold it to the upper and lower halves of the fixture.

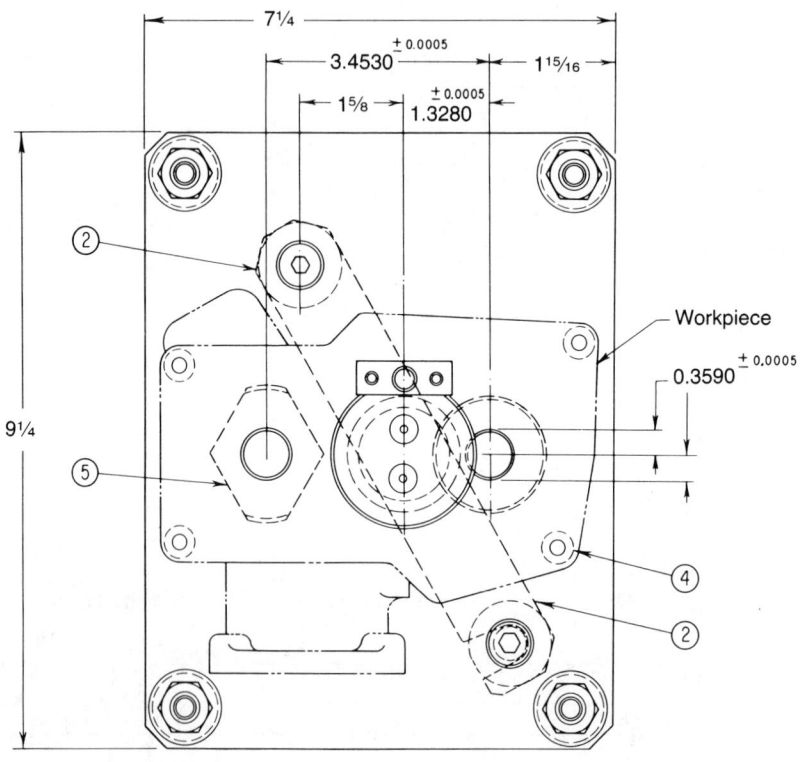

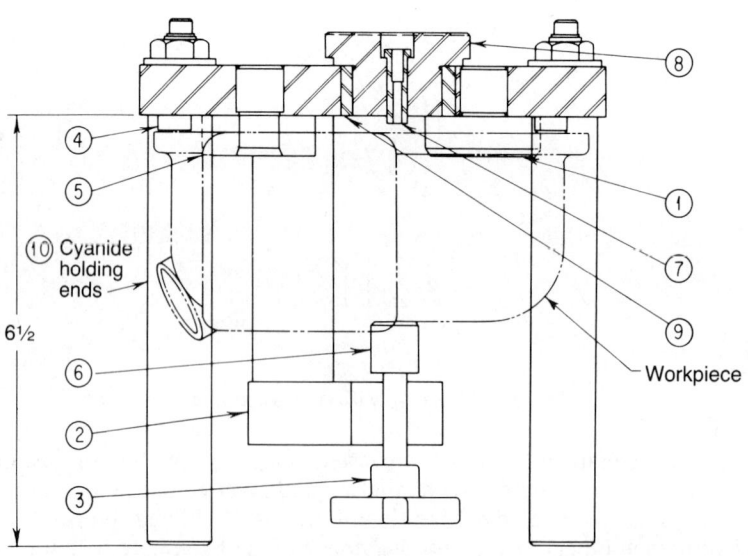

Fig. 8-16 Plate jig for an irregular aluminum casting. (*Courtesy Thompson Products, Inc.*)

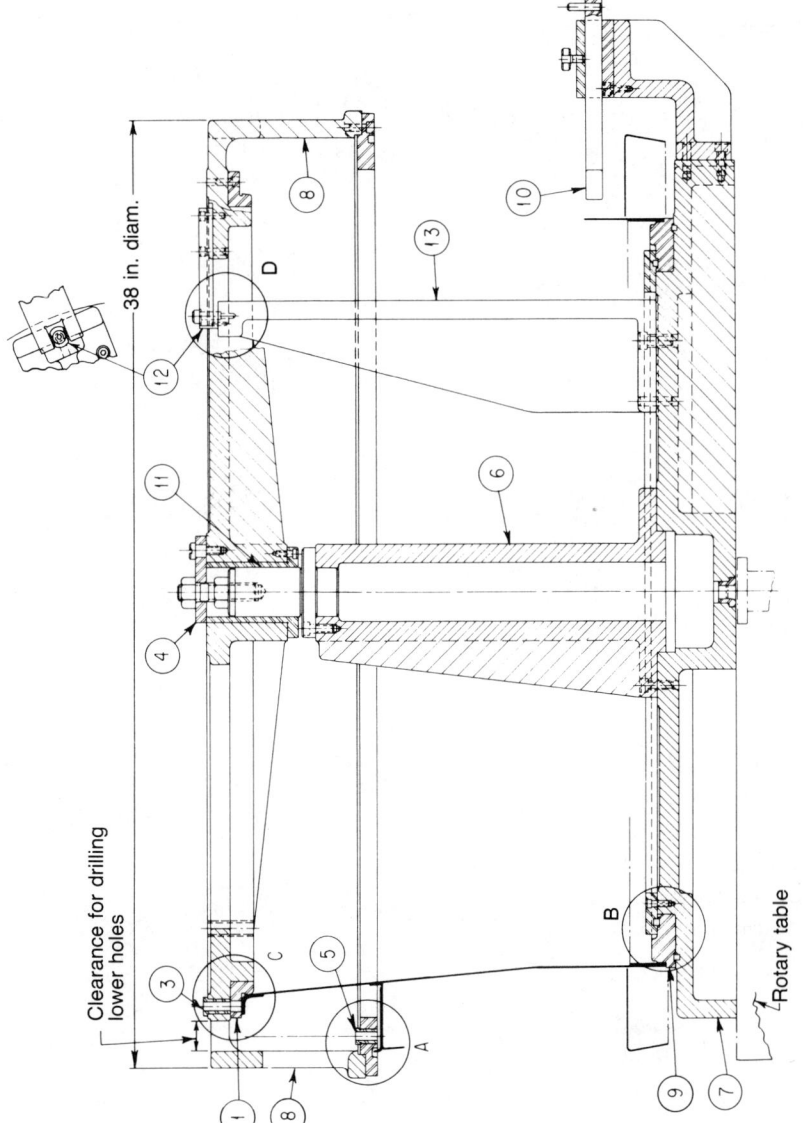

Clearance for drilling lower holes

38 in. diam.

Rotary table

Fig. 8-17 Plate jig with center column. (*Courtesy Pratt & Whitney Aircraft*)

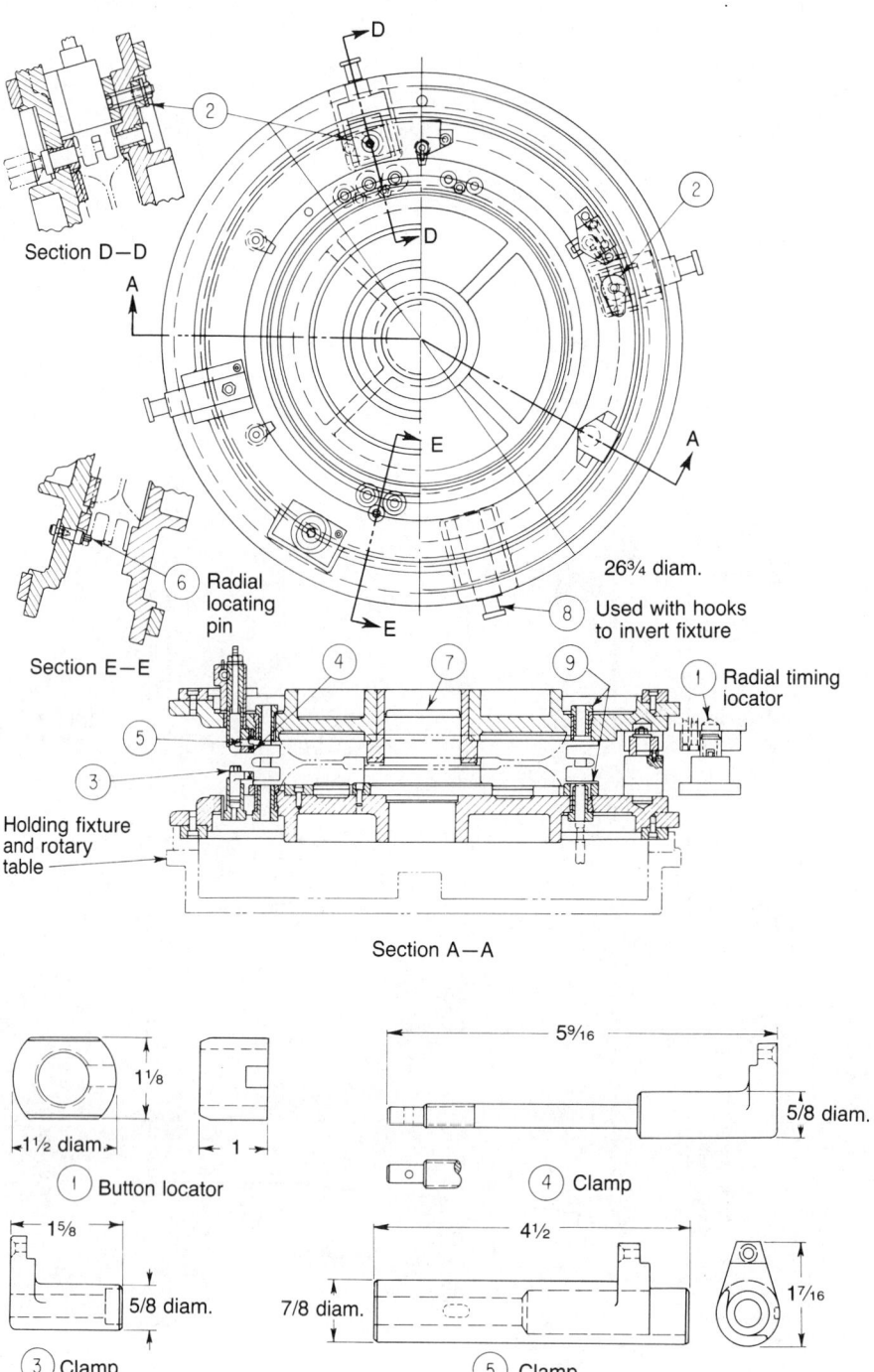

Section D—D

Section E—E

② Radial locating pin

② Radial timing locator

26¾ diam.

⑧ Used with hooks to invert fixture

Holding fixture and rotary table

Section A—A

1⅛
1½ diam.
1

① Button locator

5⁹⁄₁₆
5/8 diam.

④ Clamp

1⅝
5/8 diam.

③ Clamp

4½
7/8 diam.
1⁷⁄₁₆

⑤ Clamp

Fig. 8-18 Plate jig for multiple inversion. (*Courtesy Pratt & Whitney Aircraft*)

The part is located from a hole on one flange by a diamond locator (6) and from the large center hole by a locating plug (7). Thirty-eight holes equally spaced around the workpiece are drilled halfway through, then the fixture is turned over and the operation is repeated. This operational pattern is repeated for successive redrilling, reaming, and chamfering operations with changes of suitable bushings (9). Lugs (8) are used with hooks to invert the fixture.

Universal Jigs. Universal jigs (sometimes called pump jigs) utilize a handle connected to a cam or rack and pinion to move either a bushing plate or a nest plate, generally vertically, to clamp the workpiece. Parts held in universal jigs have surfaces adaptable to fitting against the surfaces of the bushing plate and nest.

Universal jigs are readily available in a wide variety of different styles and sizes similar to those shown in Fig. 8-19. Universal jigs are well designed, ruggedly built, and can be easily prepared to drill a specific part. Usually all that is required is to add part locators and drill jig bushings.

Air operated
4 poster

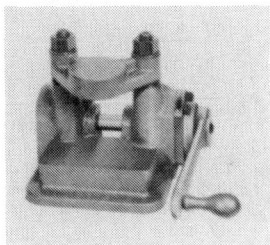

LO type fixtures

L type fixtures

LS (Spring type) fixtures

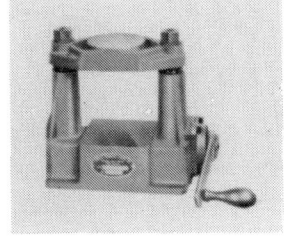

LL type fixtures

LH type fixtures

Air operation

Fig. 8-19 Universal jigs. (*Courtesy Swartz Fixture Div., Universal Vise & Tool Co.*)

Some typical applications are shown in Fig. 8-20. Jig *a* was set up to drill a hole through the center (RFS) of a small rod. It features a self-locating V-bushing liner, an adjustable end stop, and a riser block. This same operation could be accomplished with another type of universal jig called a cross-hole jig, *b*. In this type of jig, the drill is guided by a standard slip-fixed, renewable bushing which is fitted into the jig clamping plate and precisely centered above a hardened and ground V-block.

Either of these jigs could easily be adapted to drill a wide variety of parts, each having a different diameter or hole size merely by changing the renewable slip-fixed jig bushing and adjusting the end stop.

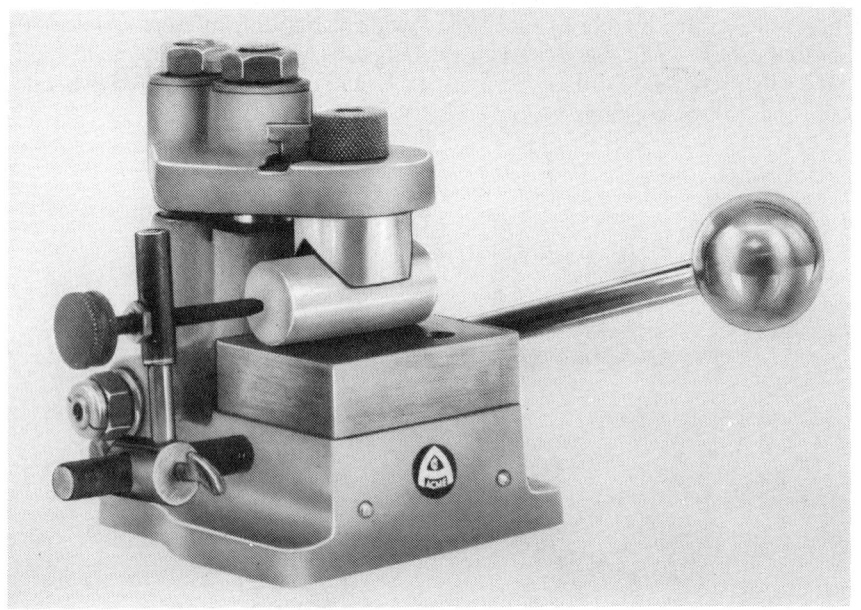

(a)

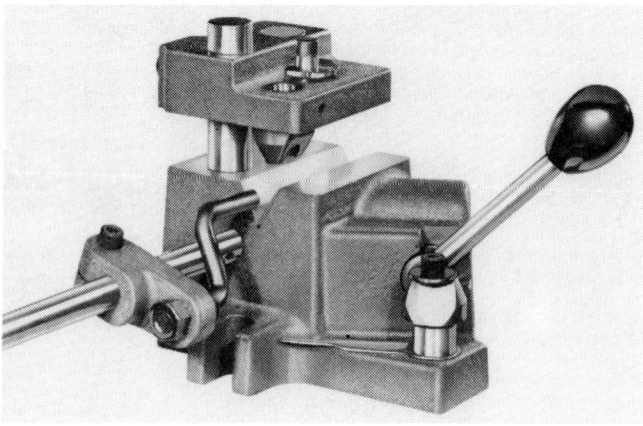

(b)

Fig. 8-20 (*a*) **Universal jig ready for production,** (*b*) **adjustable cross-hole drill jig.** (*Courtesy (a) Acme Industrial Company, (b) Heinrich Tools, Inc.*)

Compare these jigs with the plate jig shown in Fig. 8-21 which was specifically designed and built to perform a similar operation. Needless to say, the universal type jig could be put on the job in a fraction of the time and at a lower cost.

By utilizing the wide variety of standard drill bushings, liners, and tooling components, universal jigs can be adapted to drill a wide variety of parts. They are also reusable for other jobs, although it may require replacement of the drill plate, which, incidentally, is interchangeable and available separately from the manufacturer. Because of this versatility, universal jigs are ideal for limited production manufacturing. One manufacturer states that tooling costs can be reduced by one-third. With few exceptions, universal jigs can be designed and adapted to do a job in a fraction of the time required to design and build a conventional jig to perform the same function.

Applications of pump jigs are shown in Figs. 8-22 and 8-23. In Fig. 8-22, the pump jig has the bottom of the bushing cut away at an angle to allow the bushing to be brought down close to the workpiece for drilling a hole at a 60° angle.

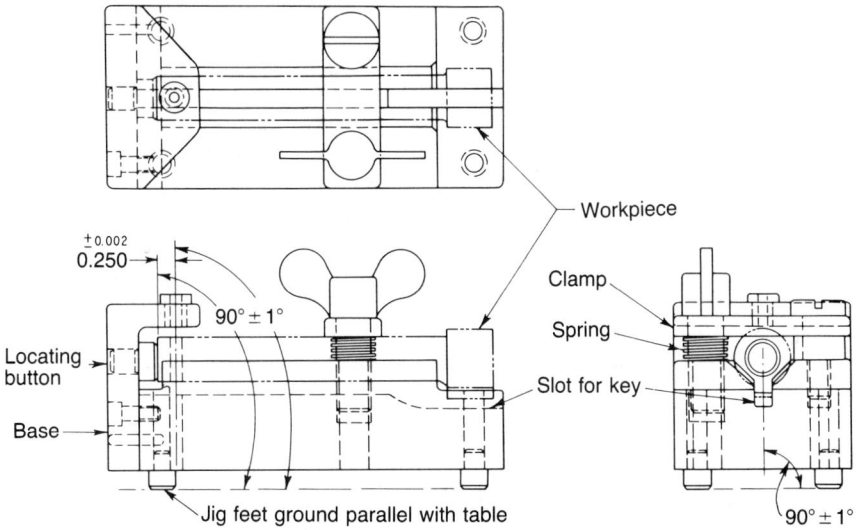

Fig. 8-21 Plate jig for cross-hole drilling. (*Courtesy SME Chapter 100*)

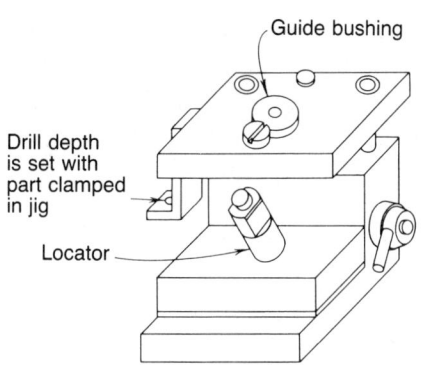

Fig. 8-22 Pump jig for drilling a hole at a 60° angle. (*Courtesy AMP Inc.*)

8-25

In Fig. 8-23, the nest plate (4) of the jig moves an equalizing spherical surface up to clamp the workpiece against the bushing plate. The workpiece is located by a center locating plug (1) and two locators (3). Correct alignment is provided by a foolproof pin (2) which will interfere with the lug of a workpiece that is incorrectly located. Four rest buttons (5) and six drill bushings (6 and 7) are press-fit in the bushing plate. A guard (8) protects the spherical surface and mating conical surfaces from chips and dirt.

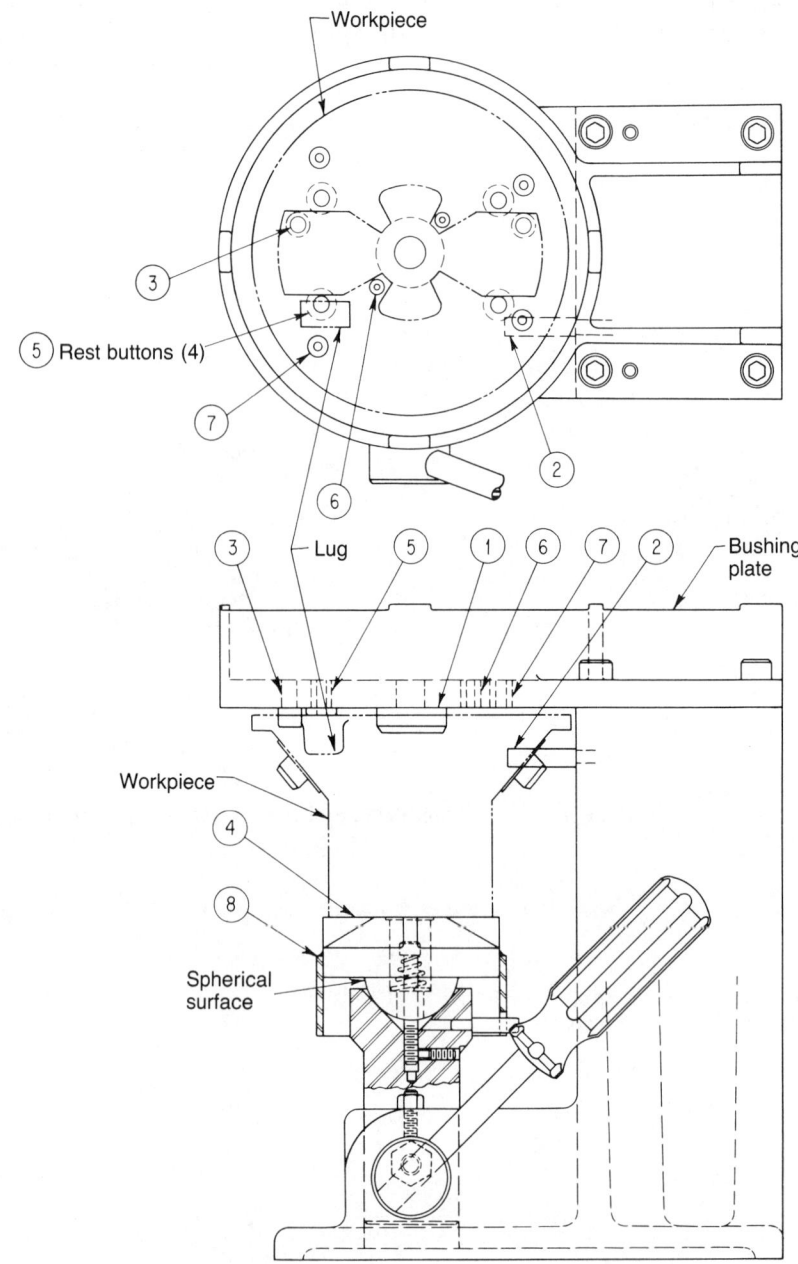

Fig. 8-23 Pump jig with a spherical nest surface for equalizing. (*Courtesy Millers Falls Paper Co.*)

Leaf Jigs. A leaf jig is generally a small jig incorporating a hinged leaf that carries the bushings, and through which clamping pressure is applied. Although the leaf jig can be used for large and cumbersome workpieces, most designs are limited in size and weight for easy handling. A leaf jig can be boxlike in shape, with four or more sides for drilling holes perpendicular to each side. Leaf jigs that are provided with additional feet to permit operations from more than one side are often called tumble jigs.

Off-the-shelf, tumble-type leaf jigs, such as those shown in Fig. 8-24, are available in a variety of sizes from many manufacturers. Construction consists of a drill plate (leaf) attached to the jig body with a precise fitting hinge at one end and a positive positioning clamp at the other end. As with universal jigs, all that is required to prepare it for use is to provide a means to locate the part and to add drill bushings. Lids swing up to provide easy loading from three sides. Occasionally, a side plate is attached to the lid or base to permit crossdrilling.

Fig. 8-24 Leaf jigs. (*Courtesy Carr Lane Manufacturing Company*)

The lead jig shown in Fig. 8-25 was specifically designed and built to drill two holes in a small connecting rod. The hinged drill plate contains the drill bushings and is precisely located at both ends by the slots in the body of the jig. The workpiece is located and clamped between two V-blocks, one fixed and the other movable. The V-blocks are tapered to force the workpiece down against the base of the jig body.

Another built-up leaf jig is shown in Fig. 8-26. The workpiece, which is shown in the same figure, is located from the inner holes of the workpiece with round and diamond locating pins. It is clamped on both sides by sliding wedge clamps. The workpiece, an assembly of two jaws, is held down by two pressure pads mounted on the leaf. Disk springs and a cam lever provide pressure to the pads while the central pivoting holes in the jaws are reamed. The heads of the pressure pads and the disk springs are contained in counterbored holes in the leaf to prevent chip entry and interference with the springs. The cam latch clamp shown in Fig. 8-27 is a standard design.

Two approaches to the same job are shown in Fig. 8-28. In *a*, separate, renewable slip fixed bushings in the top plate were used for drilling and reaming. In *b*, the installation of press fit bushings in the top plate for drilling and in the bottom plate for reaming make it a tumble type leaf jig.

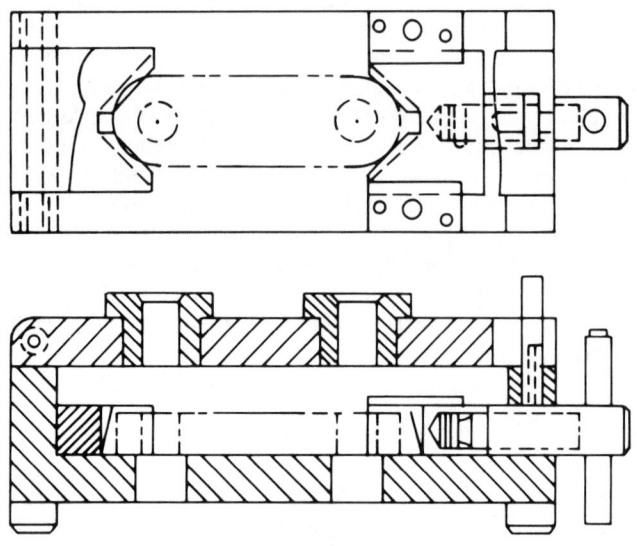

Fig. 8-25 Leaf jig for drilling two holes in a small connecting rod.

While these built-up jigs will certainly do the job intended, an off-the-shelf leaf jig could probably be adapted to do the same job in less time and at a fraction of the cost.

The double-leaf jig shown in Fig. 8-29 was designed to drill and ream holes in a workpiece with closely spaced holes which made it impractical to fit standard bushings in either leaf of the jig. Each leaf was therefore made of hardened steel with guide holes for the drill or reamer. The workpiece, clamped by thumbscrew pressure, has a center hole for locating on a stud. A pin locks either leaf in its working position under the spindle, while the other is swung out of the way.

The leaf jig shown in Fig. 8-30 was designed to drill two holes in a diestock. The workpiece is placed between locating studs and held in place by a spring-loaded plunger. An eyebolt is swung upward into the upper leaf, and the handknob is tightened to bring the locator assembly above the center hole in the diestock. The locator assem-

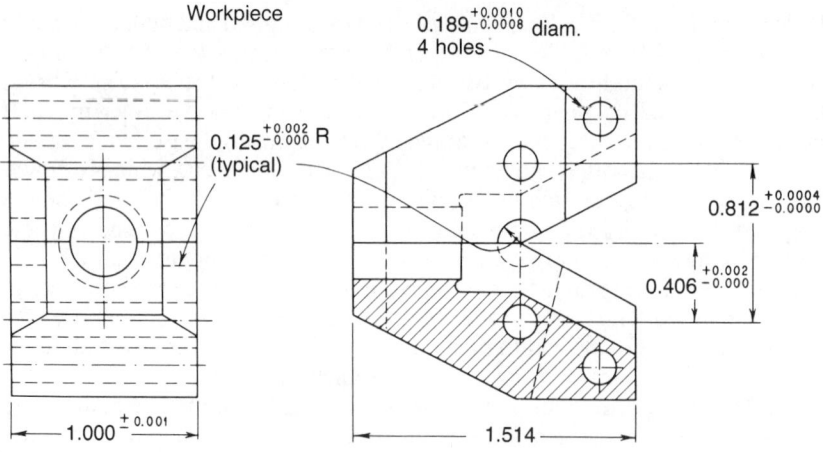

Fig. 8-26 Workpiece and leaf jig for workpiece-assembly drilling. (*Courtesy AMP, Inc.*)

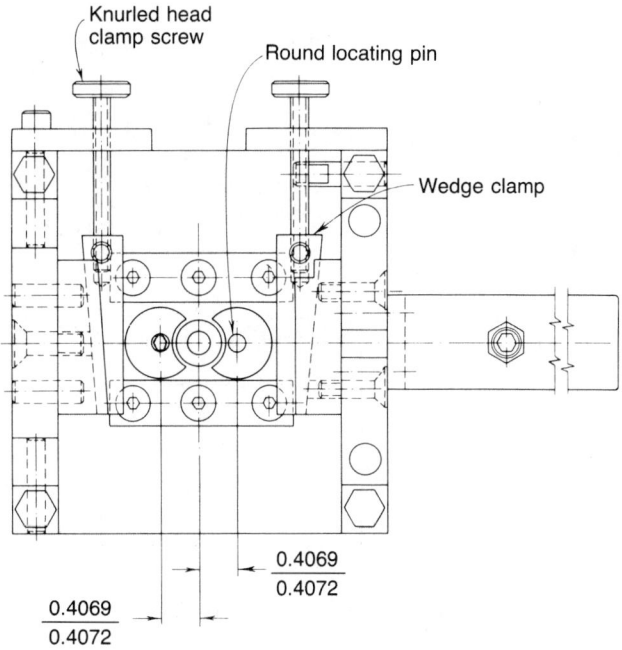

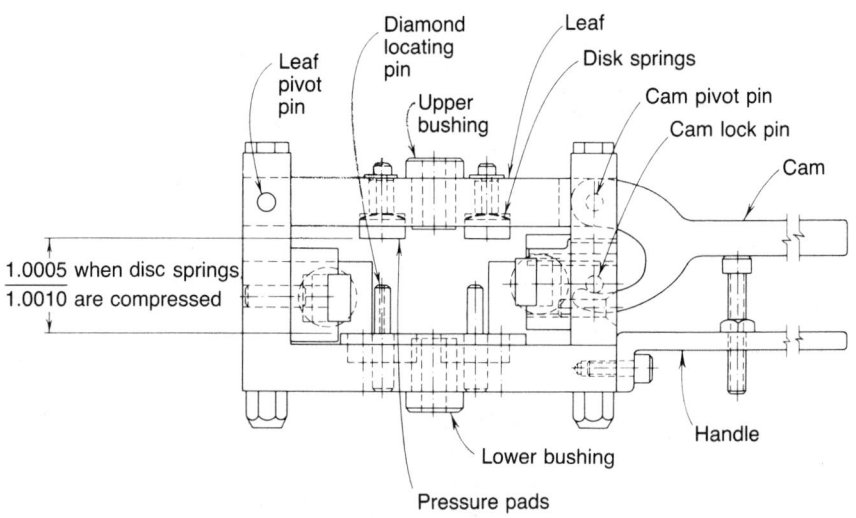

Knurled head
clamp screw

Round locating pin

Wedge clamp

0.4069
0.4072

0.4069
0.4072

Diamond
locating
pin

Leaf

Leaf
pivot
pin

Disk springs

Cam pivot pin

Upper
bushing

Cam lock pin

Cam

1.0005 when disc springs
1.0010 are compressed

Handle

Lower bushing

Pressure pads

Fig. 8-26 (*Continued*)

bly in the leaf enters the central hole in the diestock when the clamp-screw of the locator assembly is screwed in.

A special leaf jig for drilling snap gage frames is shown in Fig. 8-31. The frame is nested in the bed (6) of the jig. A clamp (8) is released with a knurled knob (7) which allows a plunger (9) to force the workpiece snugly into the nest. A clamp screw (2) is adjusted to bring a clamp (1) downward on the part. A knob (10) locks the leaf. The lock assembly has clutch-action teeth (3 and 4) which allow only predetermined, constant, spring-loaded pressure on the leaf for minimum distortion. After the *A* holes

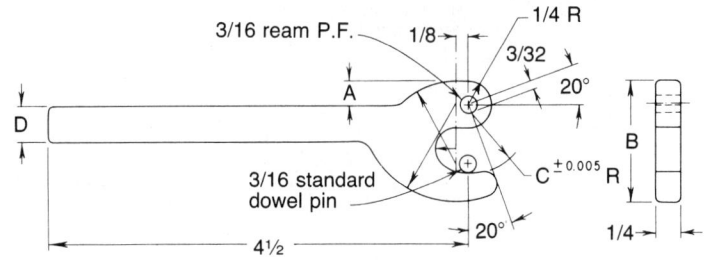

Dimensions-Inches

A	B	C	D
3/16	1 1/16	0.500	5/16
1/4	1 3/16	0.625	3/8
1/2	1 3/8	0.750	3/8
1/2	1 1/2	0.875	1/2

Fig. 8-27 Cam latch clamps.

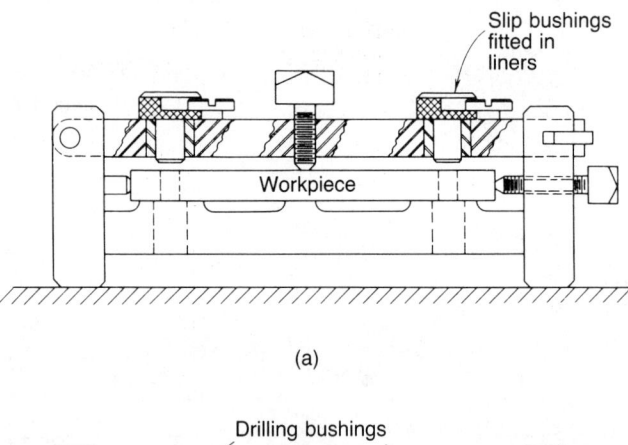

(a)

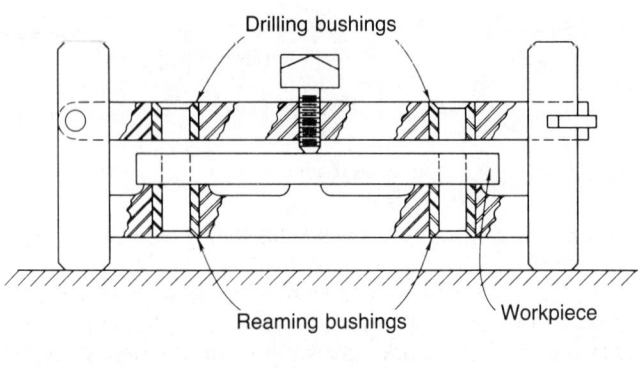

(b)

Fig. 8-28 Two approaches to the same job. (*Courtesy H. J. Gerber, SME member-at-large*)

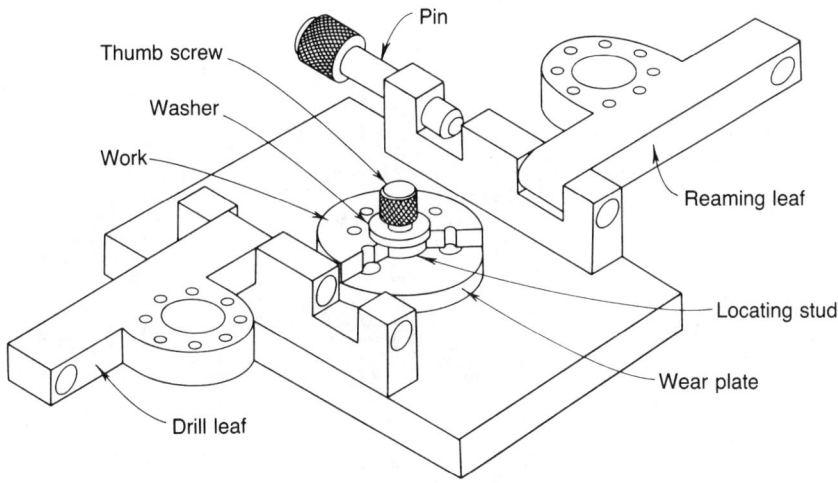

Fig. 8-29 Double leaf jig.[4]

are drilled, bushings (5) and locator pins are inserted in the holes to offset any side thrust produced during the drilling of four other holes. The drills are guided by two sets of bushings (11 and 12).

Figures 8-26, 8-28, and 8-31 are tumble type leaf jigs.

Channel and Tumble Box Jigs. Channel and tumble box jigs, such as those shown in Figs. 8-32 and 8-33, permit drilling into more than one surface of a workpiece without relocating the workpiece in the jig. This results in greater accuracy with less handling than required using several separate jigs. These jigs can be quite complicated and more expensive to build than several simpler types, but they can still be very cost-effective if properly designed.

The channel jig shown in Fig. 8-32 was designed to drill holes into three surfaces. A U-shaped channel was used as the main body along with press fit drill bushings, locators, and clamping details. The U-shaped channels used to construct this type of jig can be cast, built-up, or of welded construction. However, to keep building cost to a minimum, the designer should seriously consider using standard U-shaped sections discussed previously.

Tumble box jigs, such as the one shown in Fig. 8-33, permit drilling and similar operations from all six sides. The one in the figure is shown with the hinged top open to permit loading and unloading. Tumble box jigs are commercially available in a variety of sizes which can be prepared to machine a particular part by adding drill bushings and a means to locate and clamp the part. Because of this off-the-shelf availability, designers often choose a tumble box jig over a channel jig when machining only two or three sides of a workpiece.

Built-up Tumble Jigs. Some tumble jigs for unusual applications are shown in Figs. 8-34, 8-35, and 8-36.

One side of a tumble jig (see Fig. 8-34, opposite the drill bushing for hole A) is machined at a 90° angle to the axis of the bushing. This side serves as a base while machining hole A. During the drilling of holes B and C, the side opposite each is used as a base.

The jig is bored to a slip fit for a workpiece locating hole, and a hole (1) through one side provides clearance for the stud in the workpiece. This side is flatted on both sides of its center, providing openings (2 and 3) for the escape of chips. A bayonet-lock clamp fits into the enlarged locating hole. The slots (4) form cam surfaces which transmit

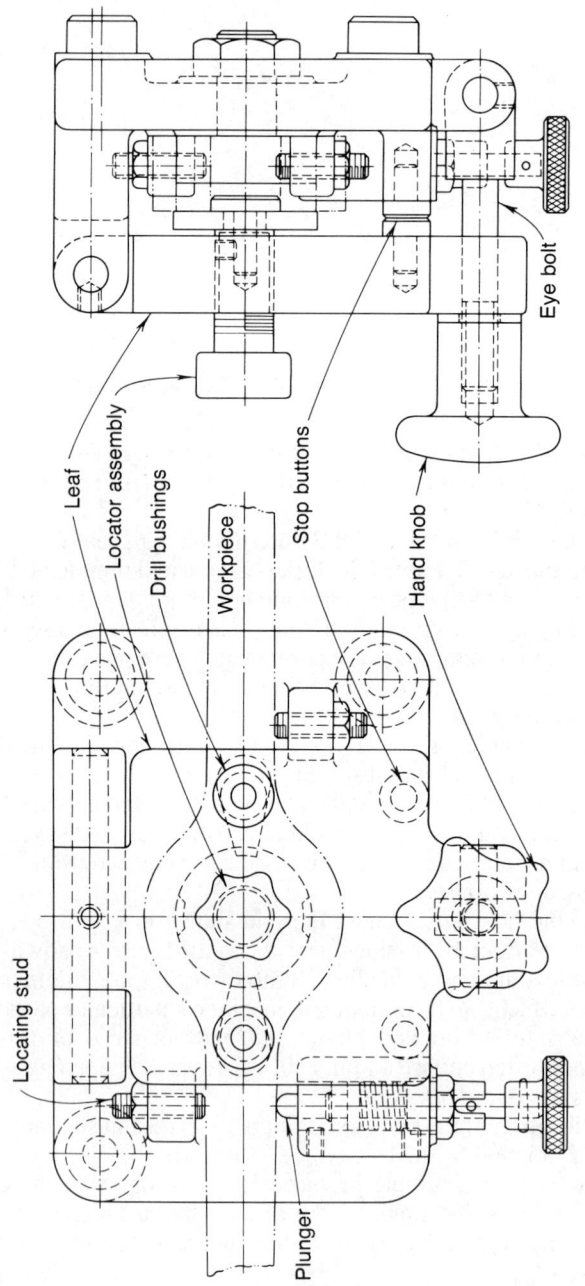

Fig. 8-30 Leaf jig for drilling a diestock. (*Courtesy SME Chapter 100*)

Locating stud

Leaf

Locator assembly

Drill bushings

Workpiece

Stop buttons

Hand knob

Plunger

Eye bolt

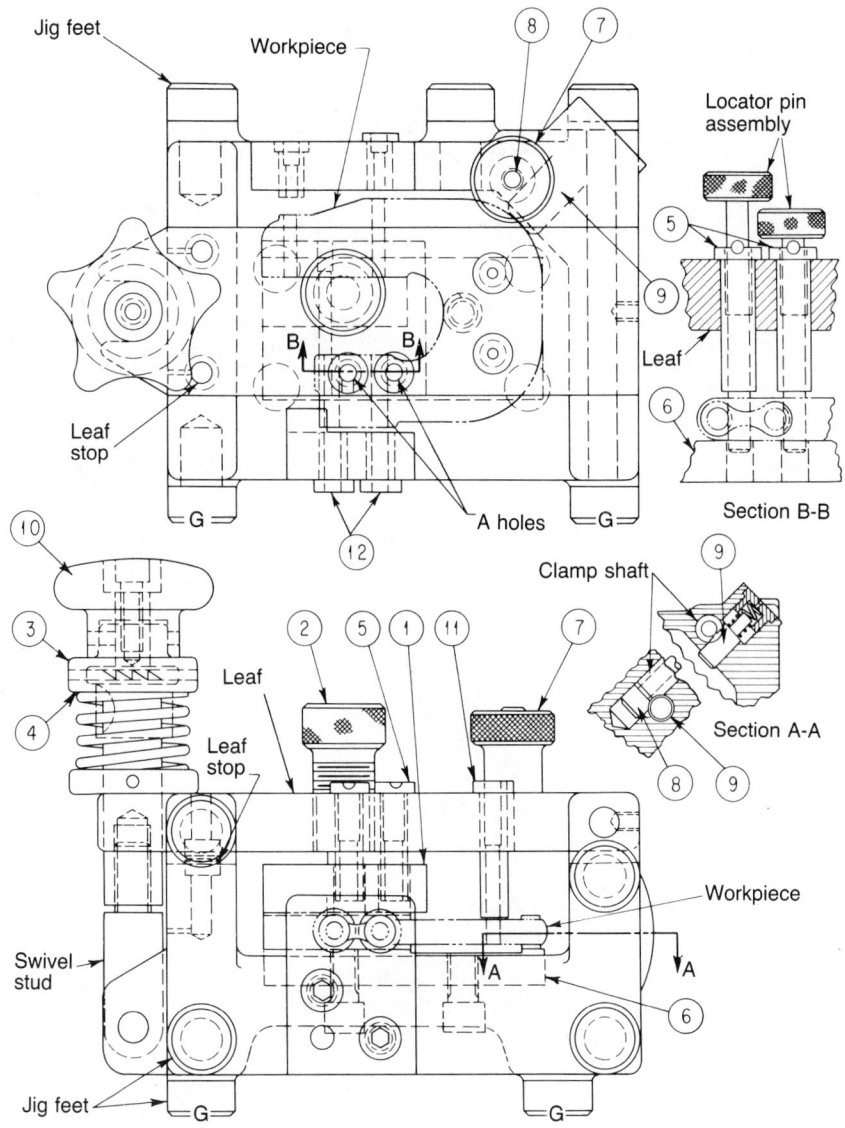

Fig. 8-31 Leaf jig having constant clamping pressure. (*Courtesy SME Chapter 100*)

clamping pressure to the workpiece when the hub is turned clockwise with an allen wrench. Reverse rotation of the hub releases clamping pressure for loading and unloading the jig.

The workpiece shown in Fig. 8-35, a cast pipe having a rectangular base, is located by a round and diamond locating pin. Two strap clamps (6) hold it against three rest blocks (5) secured to the bottom of the jig.

A removable bushing carrier plug assembly (1) is pushed through the square cutout in the fixture, and the rectangular end of the wedge rod is slipped into the base of the pipe. Rotation of a hex nut (7) on the outer end of a wedge rod (2) forces two clamp pins (3) and two steel balls (4) outward against the four flat surfaces of the base. A pin (12)

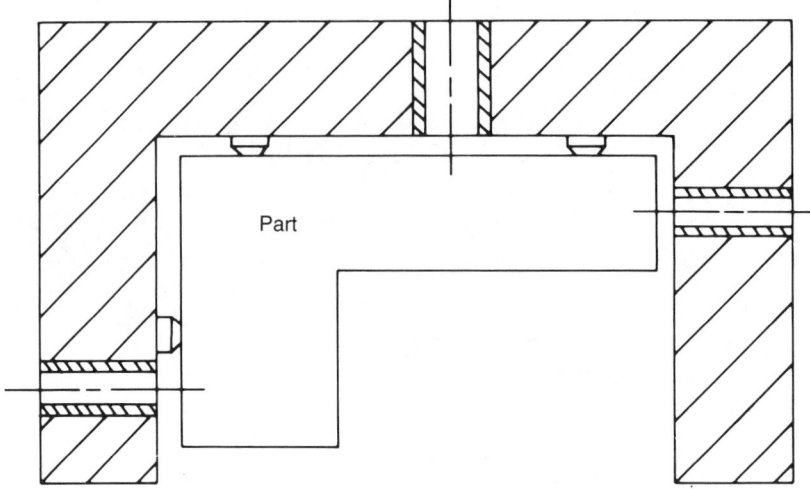

Fig. 8-32 Cross section of a typical channel jig (clamping details not shown).

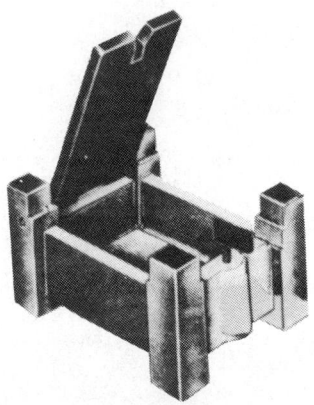

Fig. 8-33 Tumble box jig. (*Courtesy Carr Lane Mfg. Co.*)

pressed in the wedge rod prevents its rotation. The assembly is thus clamped firmly in the base of the pipe to position four guide bushings (8) for drilling four 0.1302 in. diameter holes in the flange of the workpiece. The tumble jig is turned for drilling and reaming a 0.046 in. diameter hole, as well as tapping, counterboring, and countersinking operations on the hole, using suitable removable slip-fixed bushings (10). Twelve rest buttons (11) function as jig feet.

The workpiece, a magnesium casting, is held by three clamps (1, 2), in the fixture shown in Fig. 8-36, during the drilling of three 0.187 in. diameter holes at 109° to the axis of another drilled and counterbored hole. Three locating studs (5, 9, and 10) are adjusted and located against ribs of the casting. Three thumbscrews (3 and 4) also apply clamping pressure against ribs and the end of the workpiece. The three small bushings (6) guide the 0.187 in. diameter pilot drill, and suitable bushings (7) guide a 0.250 in. diameter drill and a 0.750 in. diameter counterbore. For each of these operations, the jig rests on a a separate set of jig feet (8).

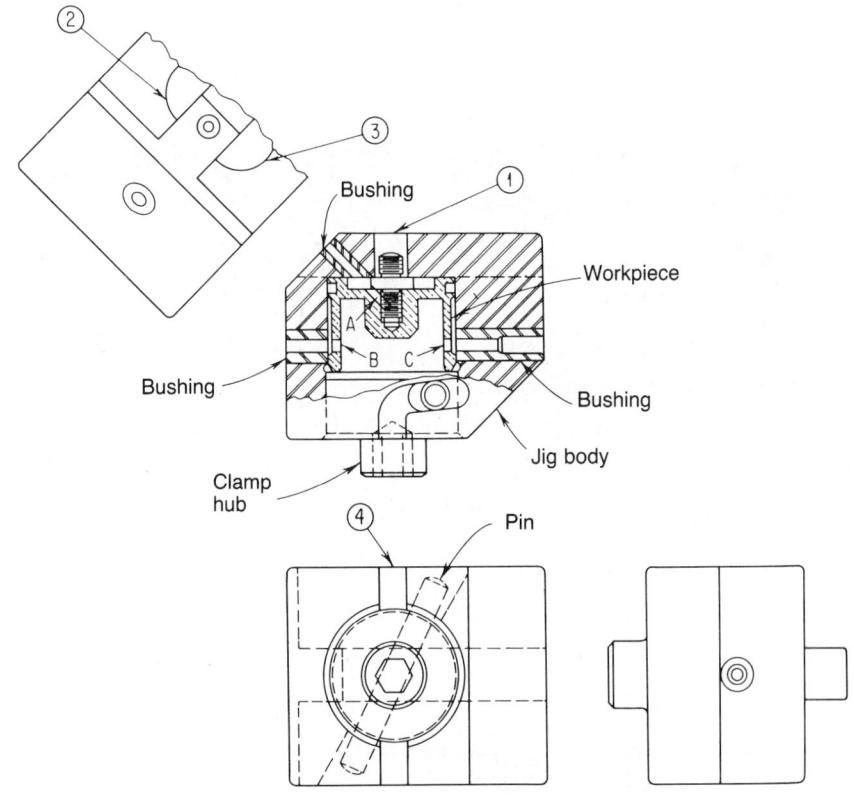

Fig. 8-34 Tumble jig with bayonet-lock clamp.[5]

Indexing Jigs. Indexing jigs are used to drill holes in a pattern, usually radial. Location for the holes is generally taken from the first hole drilled, a datum hole in the part, or from registry with an indexing device incorporated in the jig.

The simple jig shown Fig. 8-37 features a base made from a standard angle iron section into which a locating stud (2) has been placed to position a bored cylindrical workpiece (1) which is clamped on the stud with a C-washer (4) and a hex nut (3). A drill bushing (5) is press fit into the bushing plate (8). In use, the hex nut is loosened after the first hole is drilled the workpiece is revolved, the index pin (6) which is held in place with a flat spring (7), is pushed into the hole, and the second of four holes 90° apart, is drilled after the nut is tightened. Indexing is repeated until all four holes have been drilled.

Another indexing jig shown in Fig. 8-38 utilizes an angle plate of welded construction. A spindle pressed into the jig's pivot point is threaded on one end for the locking wheel. Clamping for the workpiece is not shown. The workpiece, bushing plate, and bushings are rotated for drilling holes at various angles which are determined by the location of the index holes in the jig and angle plate.

Figure 8-39 shows an indexing jig that is adaptable for drilling holes radially toward the center of pistons, cylinders, or shafts. The workpiece is held in a locator (6) by a cam-lock clamp (7). Movement of the indexing handle (1) controls the engagement of the index plunger (3) with the twelve bushings (2) which are equally spaced around an index plate (4). A renewable slip-fixed bushing (5) guides the drill. Indexing is accurate because the tapered index plunger and tapered index bushings eliminate any side thrust and movement of the workpiece.

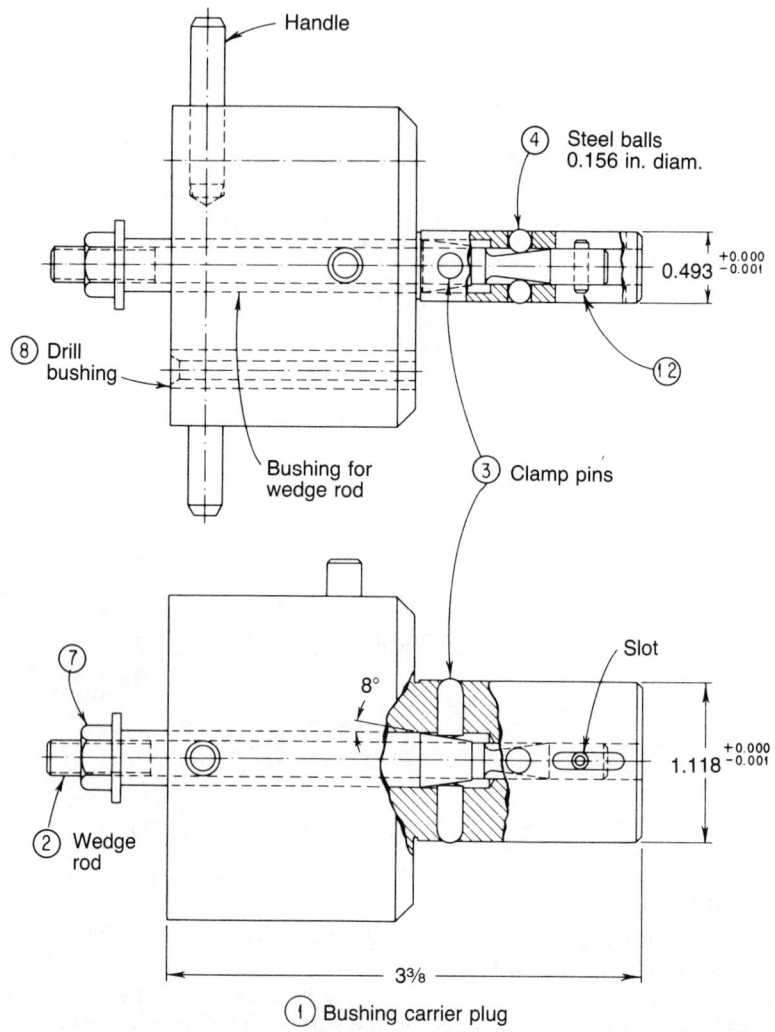

Fig. 8-35 Tumble jig for drilling a rectangular pipe. (*Courtesy Emerson Electric Mfg. Co.*)

The workpiece to be drilled with the fixture shown in Fig. 8-40 is located with a diamond locator (6) and a round locator (9). It is held by four clamps (7 and 8). Drill bushings (2, 3, and 5) guide the drills after the jig is mounted on the indexing angle plate (see Fig. 8-41) by inserting the 1½ in. diameter locating plug (1) of the jig into the 1½ in. diameter bore on the index plate of the angle iron and securing it with four socket and two strap clamps (not shown). A series of bushed holes around the index plate can be engaged by the index pin on the indexing angle plate to orient the workpiece for drilling at the desired angle. A cover is provided for the index pin to keep dirt out to maintain accuracy of ±0.0002 in.

The trunnion jig shown in Fig. 8-42 is another type of indexing jig. Trunnion jigs are usually used when it is necessary to drill holes into more than one plane of a large and/or heavy part, and for odd-shaped parts that are difficult and time-consuming to clamp. In use, a workpiece is located and clamped inside the boxlike structure, which is then positioned on the trunnion. Operations are then performed on each of the individual planes as the jig is indexed to present a new drill plate.

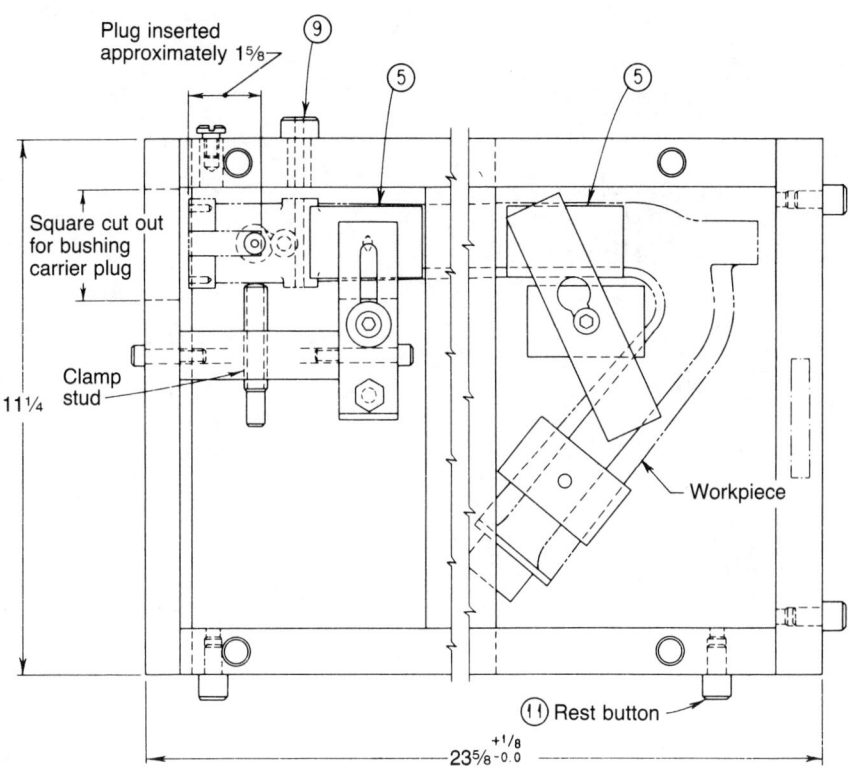

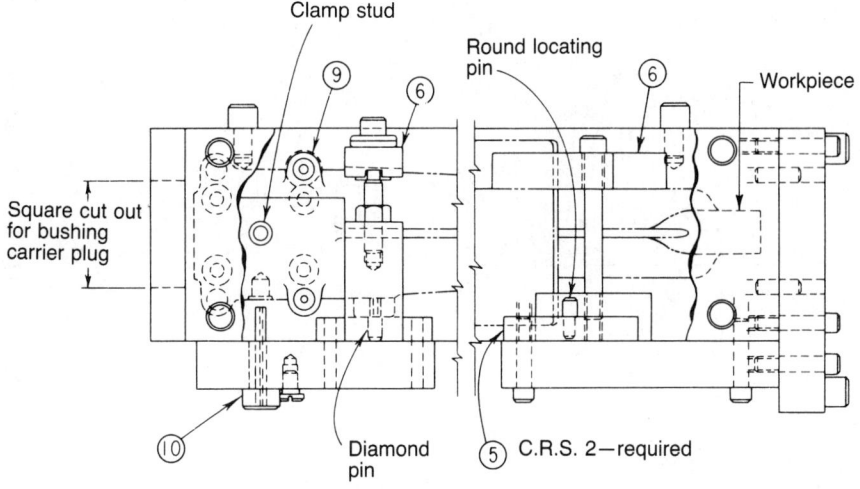

Fig. 8-35 (*Continued*)

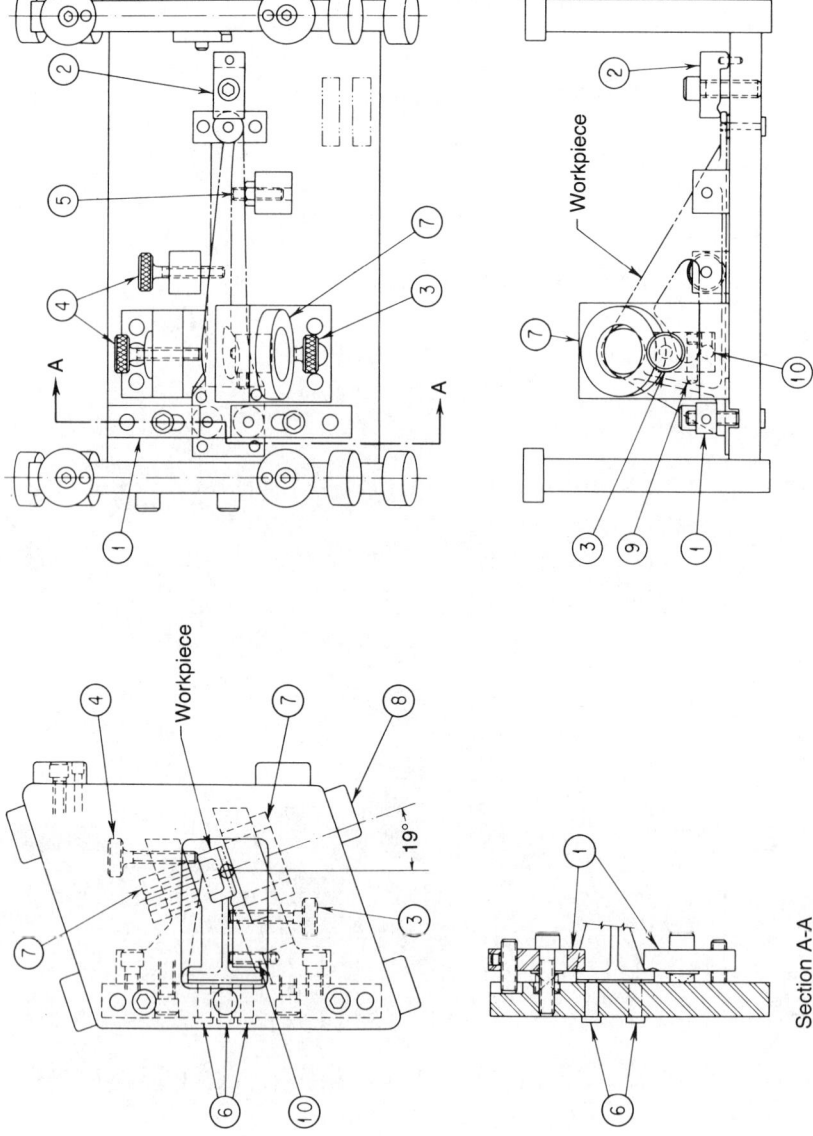

Workpiece

Workpiece

19°

A

A

Section A-A

Fig. 8-36 Tumble jig for drilling holes not at right angles to each other. (*Courtesy McDonnell Aircraft Corp.*)

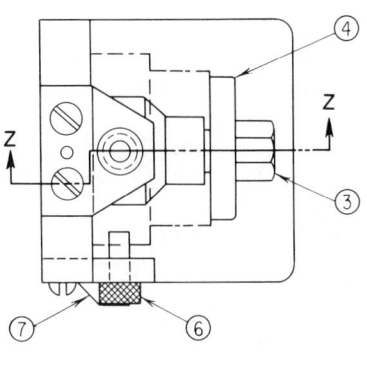

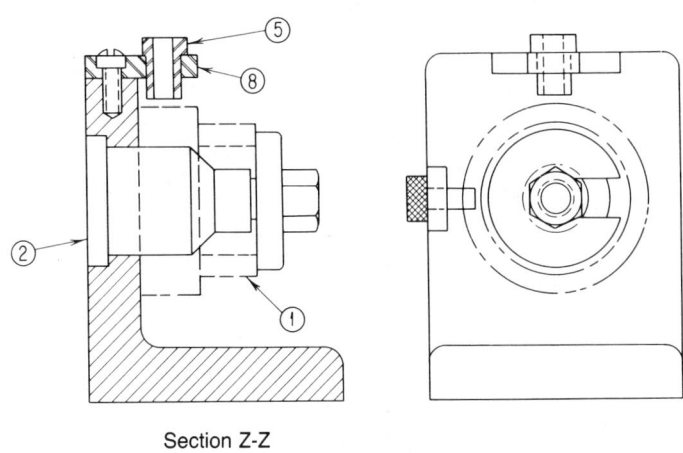

Section Z-Z

Fig. 8-37 Simple indexing jig with a base of standard angle iron.[6]

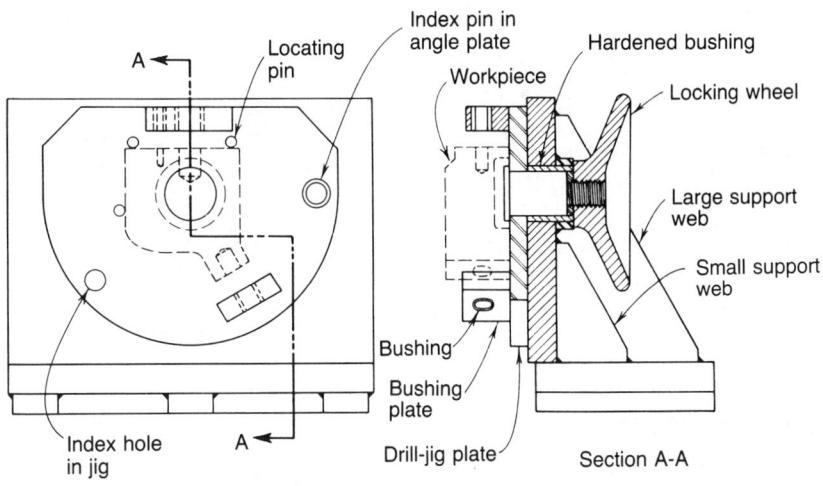

Index pin in angle plate

Locating pin

Workpiece

Hardened bushing

Locking wheel

A

Large support web

Small support web

Bushing

Bushing plate

Index hole in jig

A

Drill-jig plate

Section A-A

Fig. 8-38 Indexing jig of welded construction.[7]

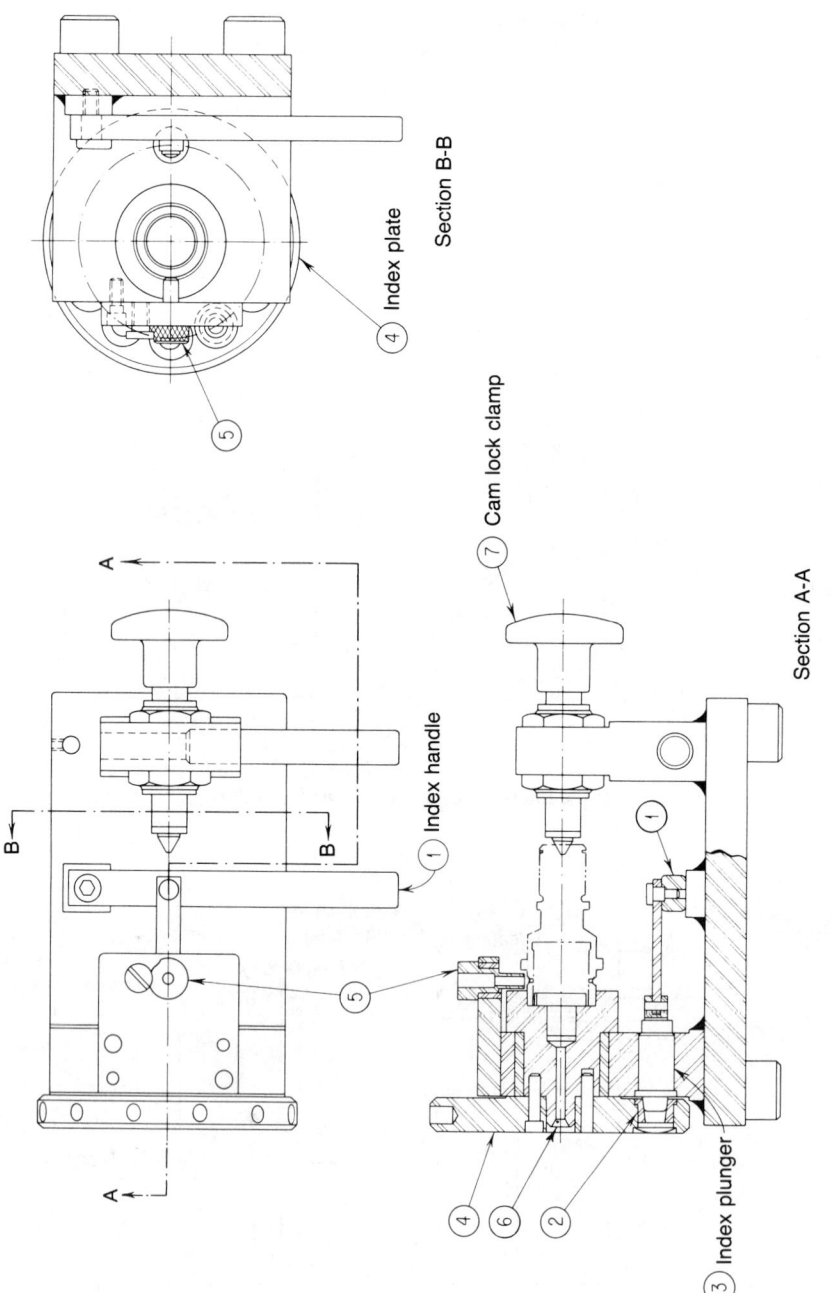

Section B-B

④ Index plate

⑤

Section A-A

① Index handle

⑦ Cam lock clamp

⑤

④ ⑥ ②

③ Index plunger

Fig. 8-39 Indexing jig for drilling twelve holes. (*Courtesy Thompson Products, Inc.*)

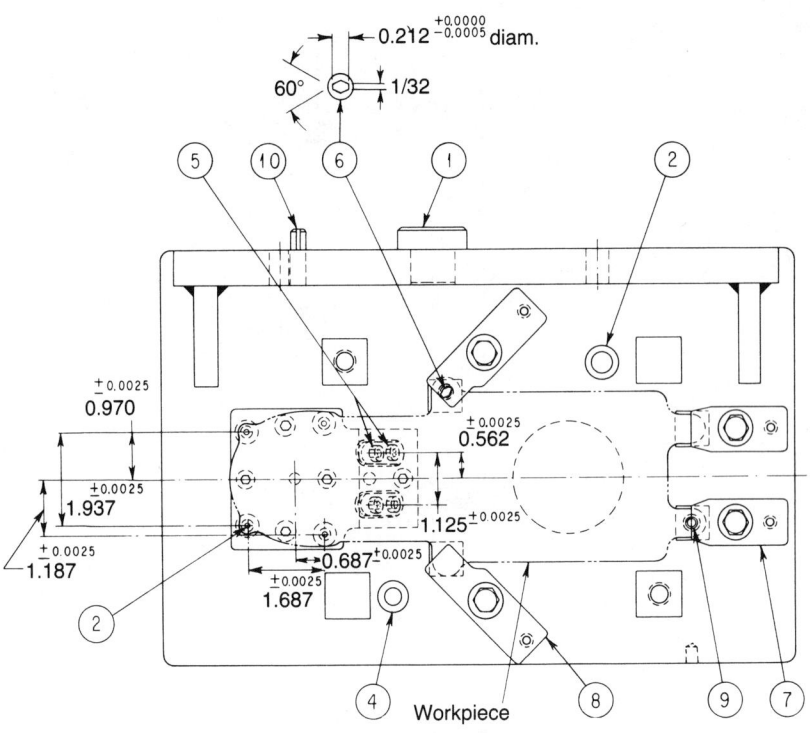

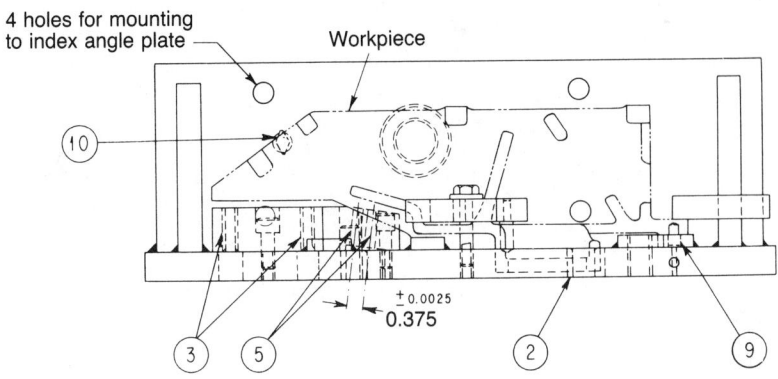

Fig. 8-40 Jig for use with the indexing angle plate shown in Fig. 8-41. (*Courtesy International Business Machines Corp.*)

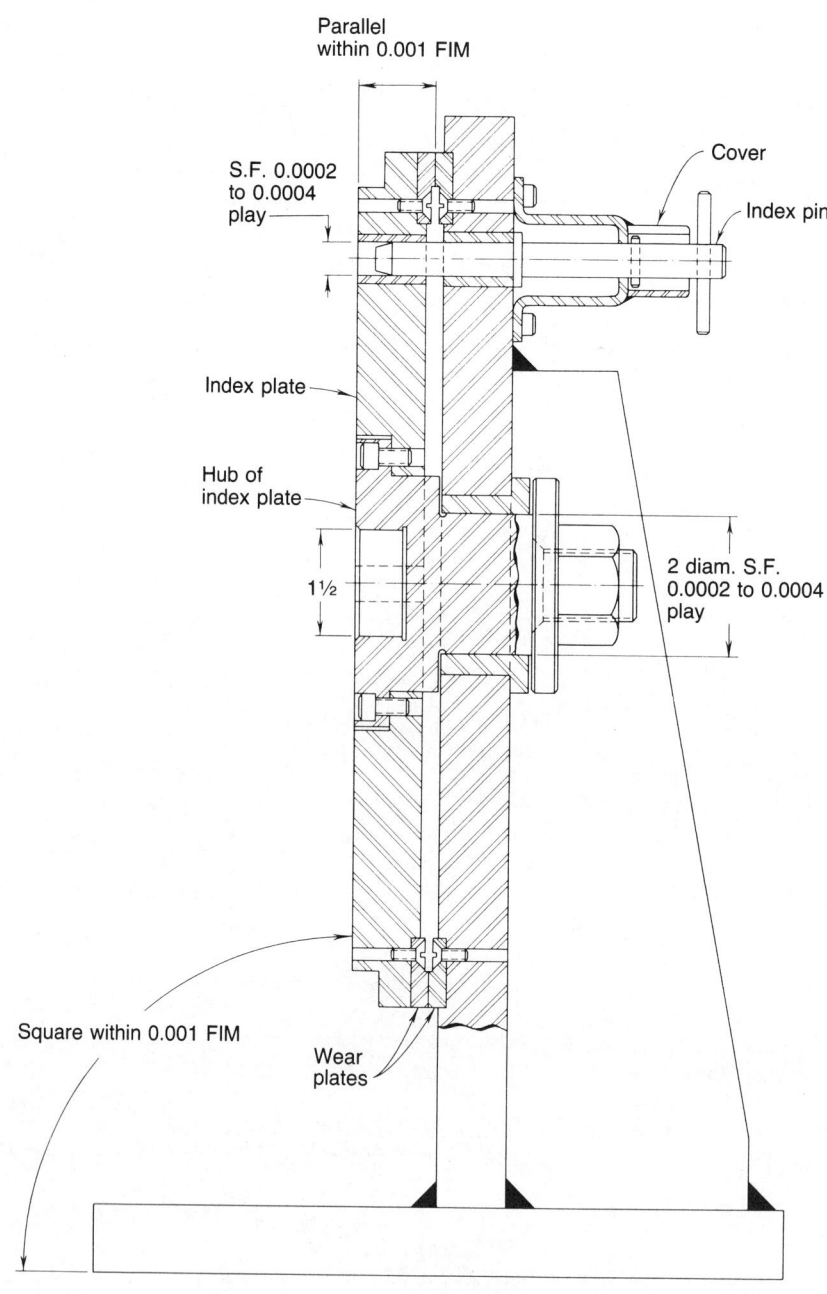

Fig. 8-41 Indexing plate to mount the drill fixture of Fig. 8-40. (*Courtesy International Business Machines Corp.*)

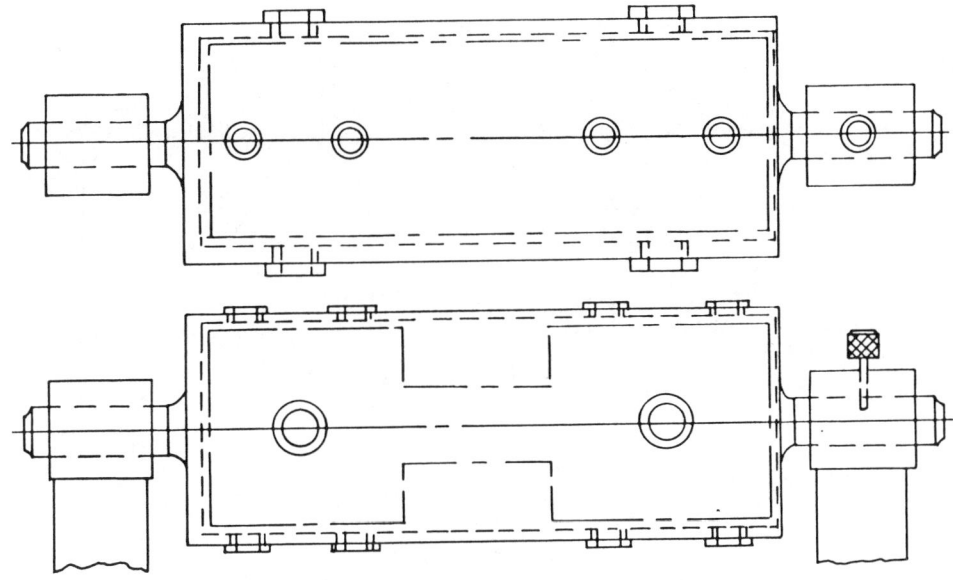

Fig. 8-42 Trunnion fixture.

JIGS FOR MULTIPLE-HOLE DRILLING

A problem that frequently confronts the tool or process engineer is the question of when to use multiple-spindle operations. Such operations should not be used unless the result is a definite saving.

The most important basis for multiple-spindle selection is the quantity of parts required. Estimate production requirements by week, day, and hour. If a part with 4 holes is required at 100 parts per hour, a single setup with a 4-spindle head and a quick-clamping fixture will do the job. For 300 parts per hour, the parts may be produced more economically with a 16-spindle head, 4 parts clamped at a time. But for 1000 parts per hour, a more elaborate setup would be required, probably with mechanized feed and ejection (see Fig. 8-43).

If a part requires more holes than is convenient with available equipment, the work might be fixtured on a slide and indexed across the table under a head that drills only one or two rows of holes at a time (see Fig. 8-44). However, gearless heads have been built for as many as several hundred spindles, so the total number of holes is not normally a critical problem. Complications more often develop because of too-close centerdistances, unequal hole sizes, and difficult hole patterns.

An analysis of present methods of producing similar parts may help in planning a new setup. If a single deep hole is to be drilled along with several shorter holes that take less cycle time, the deep hole can be split up between several spindles, each drill starting to cut where the previous drill left off (see Fig. 8-45). Production rate: 50 parts per hour.

When a large number of spindles is available, it is usually practical to operate as many of them as possible to allow the shortest cycle time.

For parts that must be drilled in several faces, the simplest kind of jig is a box or a tumble jig. It holds the part during several operations and keeps the drill bushings in constant alignment with the work. The jig may be simply shifted and tumbled on a long table, stopped by rails or pins, and positioned under a large multi-spindle head at several stations or under several separate heads, all mounted over the same table. Production rate: 25 parts per hour.

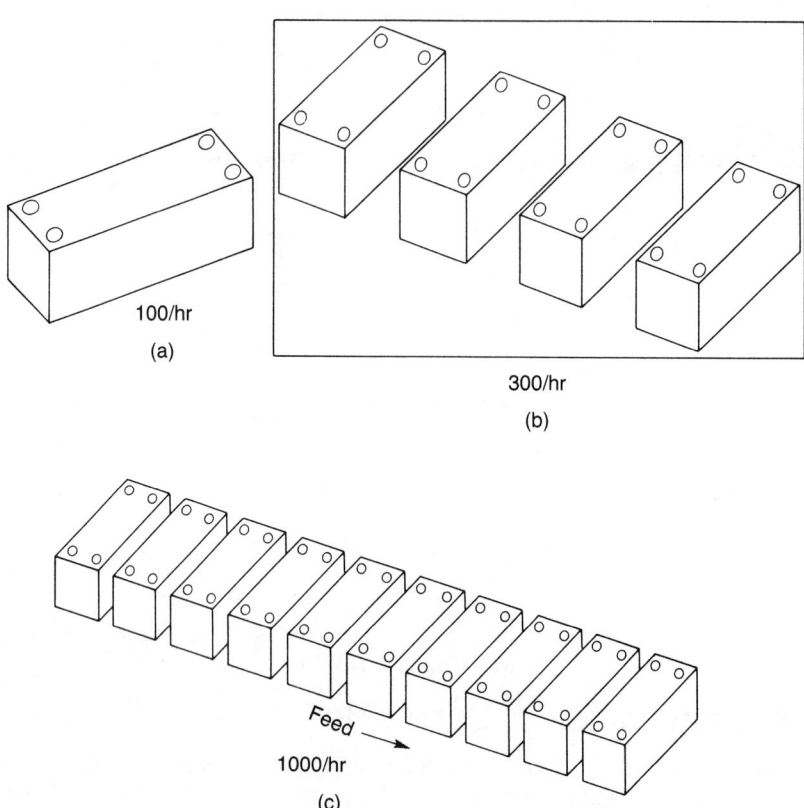

100/hr

(a)

300/hr

(b)

Feed ⟶

1000/hr

(c)

Fig. 8-43 Setups for drilling four holes at various rates.

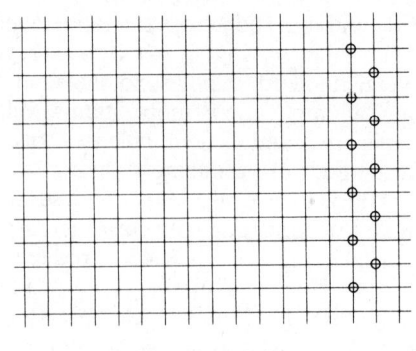

Part indexed

Fig. 8-44 Drilling one or two rows of holes at a time.

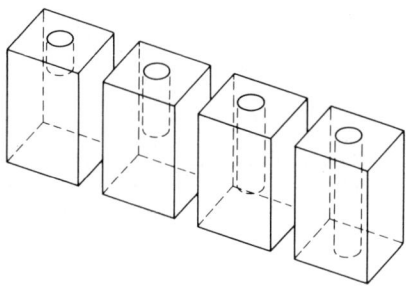

Fig. 8-45 Progressive drilling of five holes.

Assuming that the same number of spindles are set up to drill a limited number of holes, production can be roughly tripled by moving parts through a straight-line setup. A single large jig or several smaller ones can be aligned and clamped to the table to hold parts in several different positions. Parts progress through the jig from station to station, moved and clamped by hand. One completed part is produced at each machine cycle; however, there is lost time between cycles as the operator shifts parts from one location to the next.

Some of this lost time shifting parts could be eliminated by off-machine loading. By providing identical box jigs for each station, plus one additional, parts could be loaded and unloaded during the machine cycle. Between cycles, the jig from the final station would be removed from the machine, the other jigs tumbled and shifted to the next station, and a newly loaded jig placed in the first station. All jigs would be positioned and clamped as previously discussed. As the machine was recycled, the finish-machined part in the idle jig would be exchanged with an unmachined one.

The total number of spindles would be the same with a box jig, moving fixture setup, or with multiple box jigs; but with the last two arrangements, all spindles would be working at the same time (see Fig. 8-46). Production rate: 75 parts per hour.

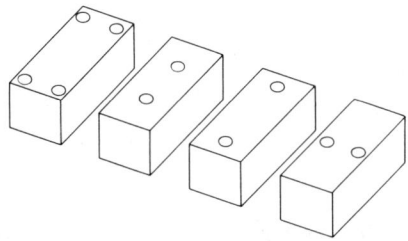

Fig. 8-46 Methods of drilling holes in several faces.

Trunnion fixtures also allow higher production rates and reduce the amount of parts handling. The part is clamped once, then indexed around to several stations. Several parts are in the fixture at one time, and a complete part is produced at each machine cycle. Only one clamping and unclamping is required (see Fig. 8-47). Production rates: 100 parts per hour.

Progressive operations such as drilling, counterboring, reaming, and, tapping can be set up on a straight-line arrangement under a single head or a number of heads. A single fixture may be moved along rails if all operations are on a single work face, or parts may be shifted progressively from one clamping fixture to the next. In either case, the workpiece must be located exactly at each station so the tools will come down on the

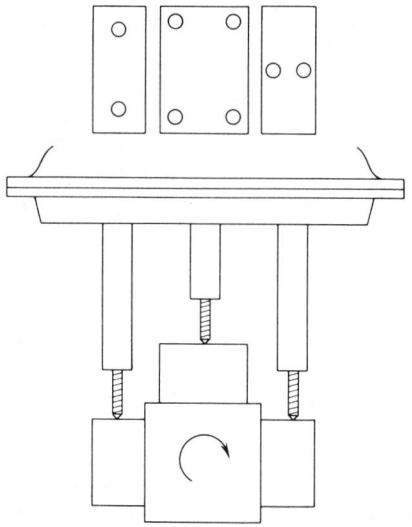

Fig. 8-47 Trunnion fixture.

center line common to each part. Work may be shifted by hand, but the machine arrangement may be as similar to a mechanized transfer machine as can be justified by the quantity of parts (see Fig. 8-48).

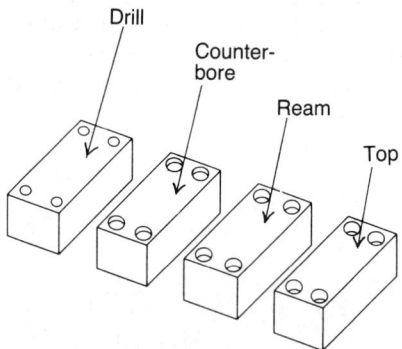

Fig. 8-48 Progressive operations: part and fixture moved to various working positions or stations.

Rotary indexing tables increase cycle rate and production output. Jigs are locked to a rotary table which indexes under power. Proper alignment requires careful setup, but this can be justified by a high output. The workpiece remains clamped until all operations are complete, and clamping and unclamping can be done while the machine is working (see Fig. 8-49). Production rates can be compared this way: assume that 50 parts per hour can be made with a manual straight-line arrangement for small parts; a rotary table that clamps 1 part each station can produce about 200 parts per hour and attain about 300 parts per hour with 4 parts clamped at each station.

Tooling for Multiple-Spindle Operations. A multiple-spindle jig is shown in Fig. 8-50. It incorporates a spring-loaded bushing carrier (1) which slides vertically on leader pins (2). As the drill head (3) moves down, upper locators (4) engage the

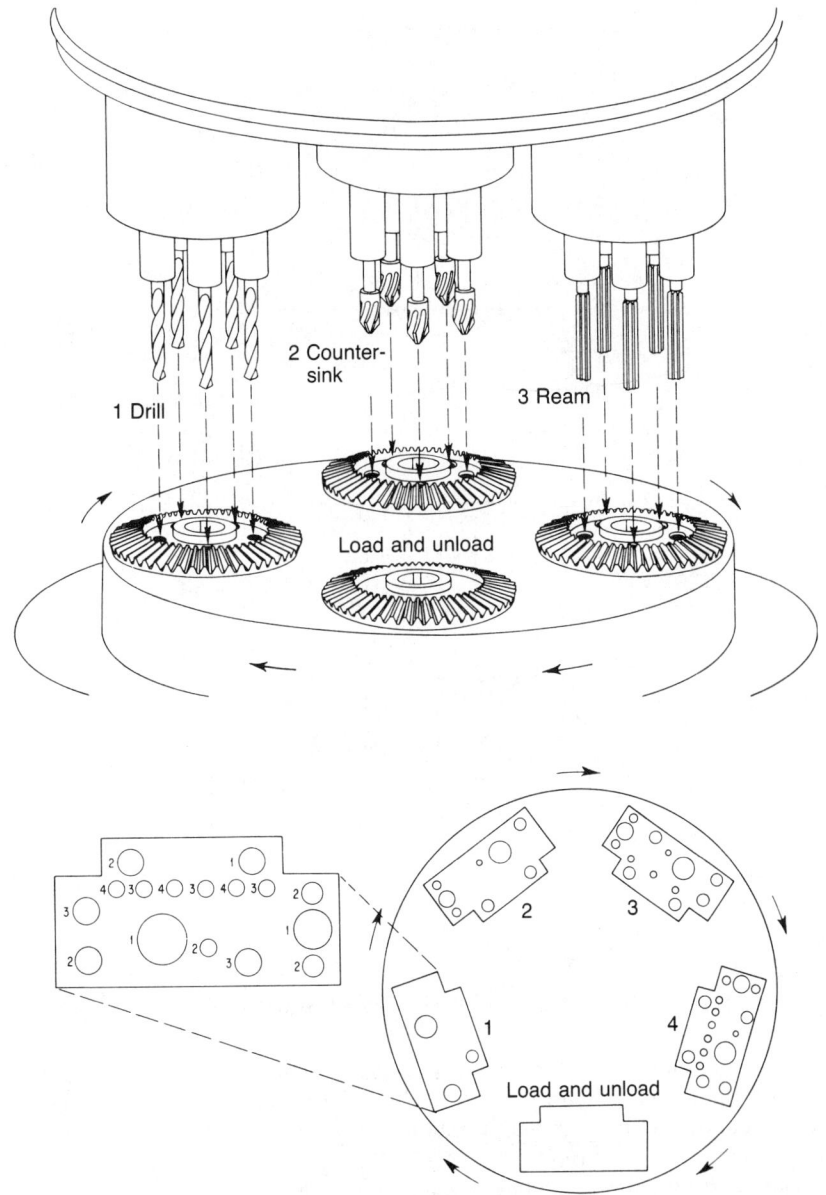

Fig. 8-49 Rotary indexing.

workpiece which had been approximately located by the lower locators (5). Spring plungers (6) clamp the workpiece. Stop pins (7) in the bushing carrier and in the jig base (8) limit travel of the bushing carrier and maintain it parallel to the top of the workpiece. Cross pins (9), inserted through holes in the holding pins (10), allow the bushing carrier to be lowered for drill changing and sharpening.

Note: When a bushing carrier supplies clamping pressure to irregular parts, it may cause cocking of the parts, necessitating the use of separate clamps mounted on the jig base.

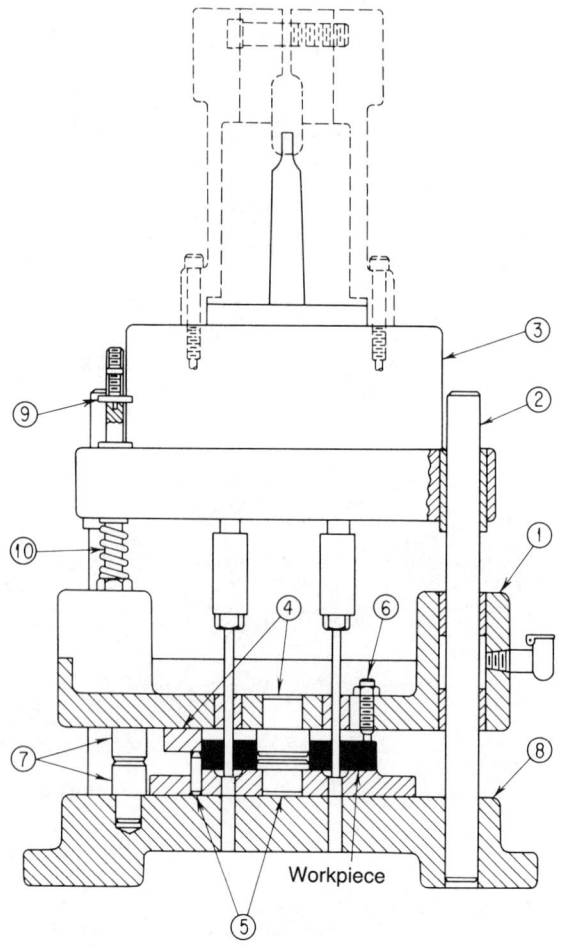

Fig. 8-50 Jig for multiple spindle drilling.

The jig shown in Fig. 8-51 is one of two identical jigs (except for guide bushings) mounted on the bases of hydraulic feed drills. The drilling of a 0.040 in. hole in the workpiece is done in the jig shown, while the hole is countersunk in the second jig. The workpiece is placed on a post (4) and against the Vee of a plunger (3). The descending drill spindle and jig plate (5) clamp the workpiece under a special guide bushing (1) having a spherical surface matching that of the workpiece. A stripper (2) allows the plunger to eject the workpiece after the rapid return of the spindle and jig plate. The pressure of the workpiece against the plunger, transmitted to the hydraulic actuating valve, starts the rapid descent of the spindle through a hydraulic circuit and slows its rate as the drill passes through the workpiece. The operator feeds both jigs, resulting in the production of 1,320 workpieces per hour.

In the jig shown in Fig. 8-52, the workpiece (a diestock) is located on a locating stud while its handle is located against a locating bracket. It is held on the stud by an air cylinder actuating a linked swinging clamp. A lower locating bracket, interchangeable drill bushings, and locating studs allow three holes to be drilled in diestocks of different sizes.

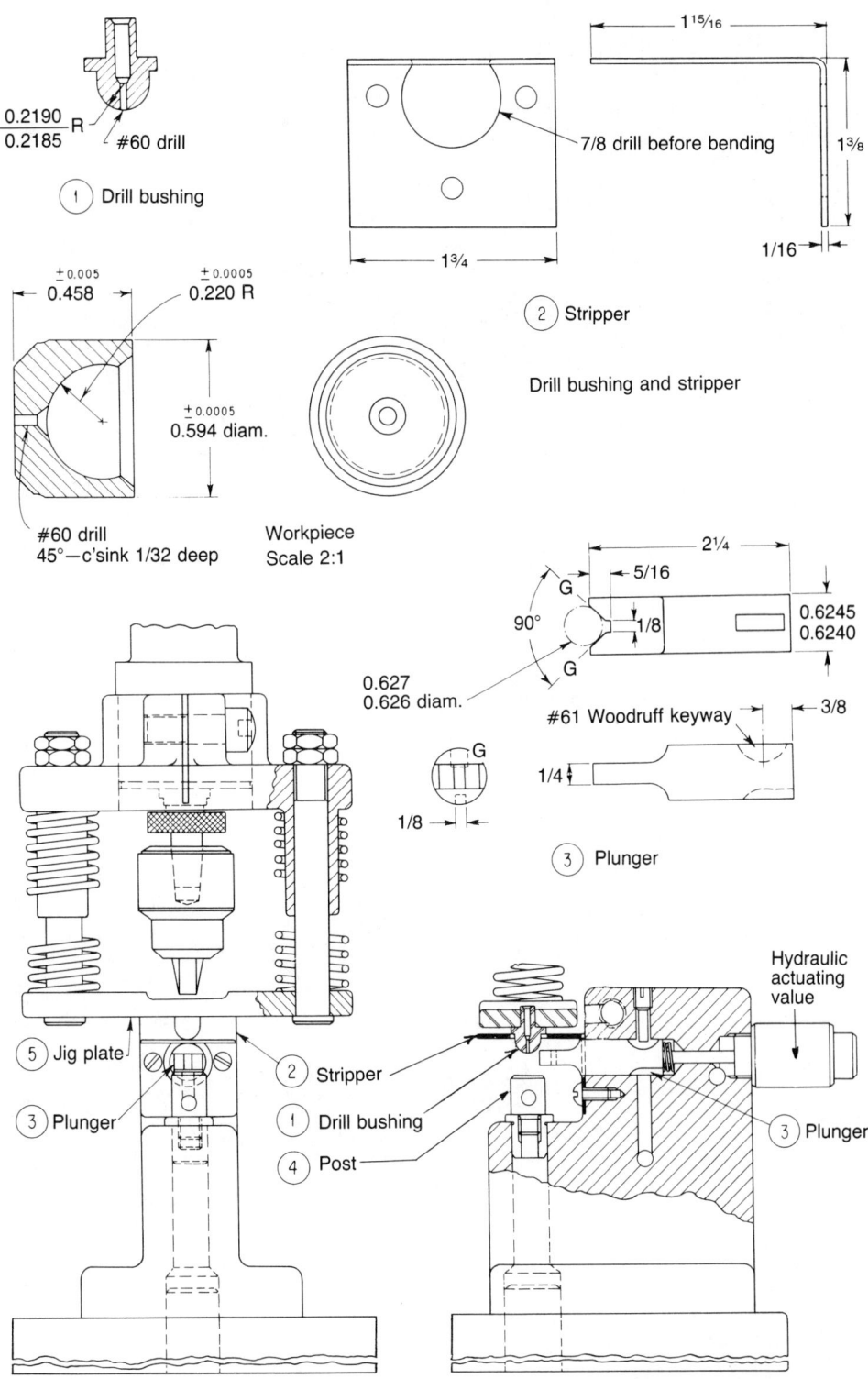

Fig. 8-51 Jig for two spindle operation. (*Courtesy Parts Mfg. Co.*)

8-49

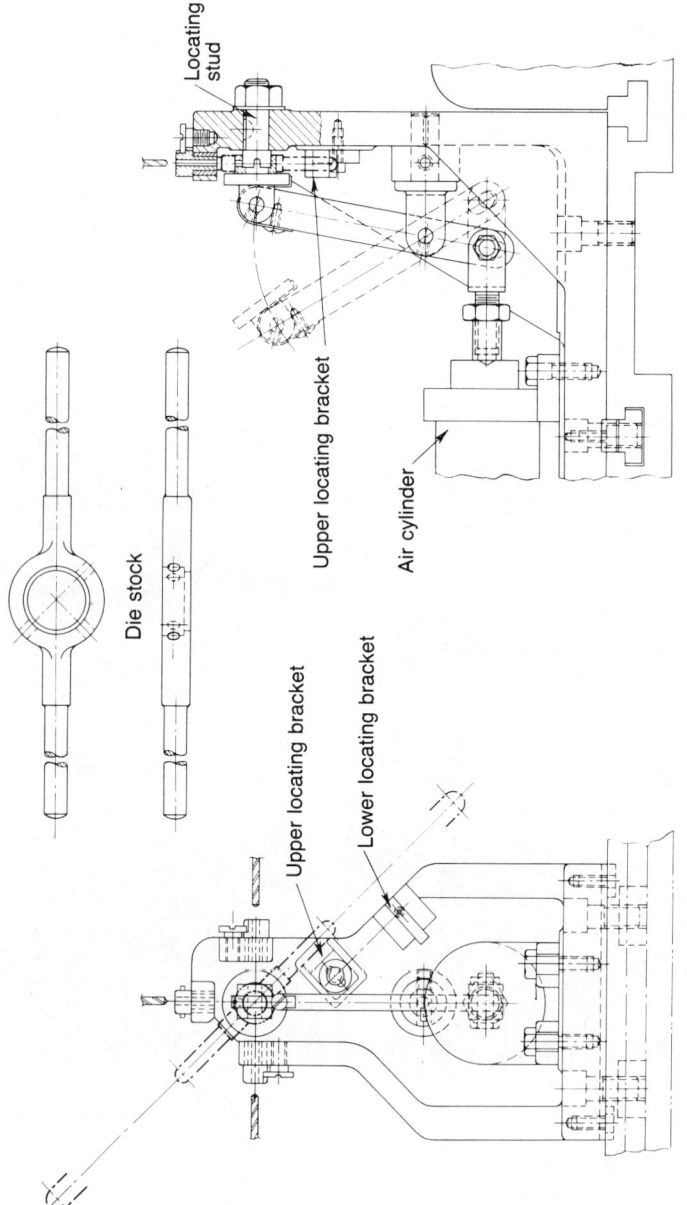

Fig. 8-52 Air-clamping for three-spindle drilling. (*Courtesy SME Chapter 100*)

Locating stud

Upper locating bracket

Air cylinder

Die stock

Upper locating bracket

Lower locating bracket

A fragile, thin-walled aluminum die casting is located in the tumble jig shown in Fig. 8-53 by a diamond locating pin (3) and a round locating pin (6) which engage bored holes in the casting. Rotation of the collar screw (5) forces the clamp leaf (9) and two rest buttons (4) down to clamp the casting against the rest block (7). Actuation of a hand knob (8) clamps the end of the workpiece. Two diamond locators (2) and two round locators (1) align the jig with a bushing plate shown in Fig. 8-54 attached to the drill head. These locators engage bushings (2) in the bushing plate to position the jig under a drill and two reamers guided by a drill bushing (6) and two reamer bushings (7).

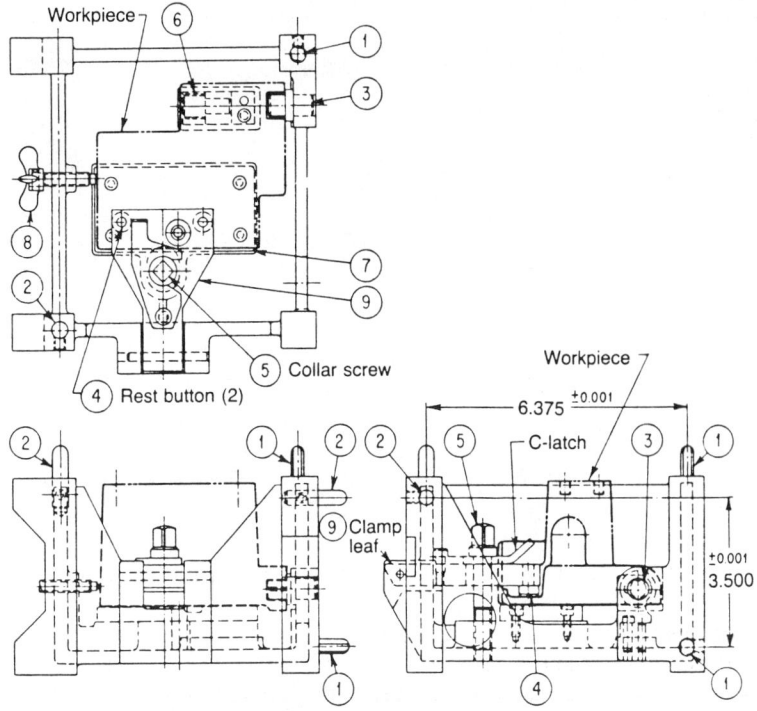

Fig. 8-53 Jig for spindle-to-spindle drilling with interchangeable bushing plates. (*Courtesy Universal Winding Co.*)

After drilling and reaming are completed, the jig is shifted to allow the locators to enter the right-hand bushings in the bushing plate, which positions three reamer bushings (8 and 9) under three reamers. Three other similar bushing plates allow the positioning of the tumble jig under three different sets of spindles for drilling, reaming, and tapping operations. The jig is rotated for some of these operations, which are at right angles to each other, and is positioned by the corresponding locators (1 and 2). Straight-line, spindle-to-spindle production output, using the four bushing plates with the tumble jig, is from 500 to 2,000 workpieces per month.

The shuttle-type jig of Fig. 8-55 incorporates four wheels which run on the rails of an auxiliary table clamped to the drill press table. The table is adjusted until the rails are parallel with the centers of the four spindles. With a handle the operator slides the fixture under the spindles for the sequence of operations shown.

The workpiece, a cast lever shown in the same figure, is located and clamped between two cones. Air pressure is applied to one cone for clamping the cored hole of the workpiece through a wedge cam, a clamping lever, and a clamp rod. An adjustable stop prevents rotation of the workpiece around the cones. The production rate is from 60 to 100 parts per hour.

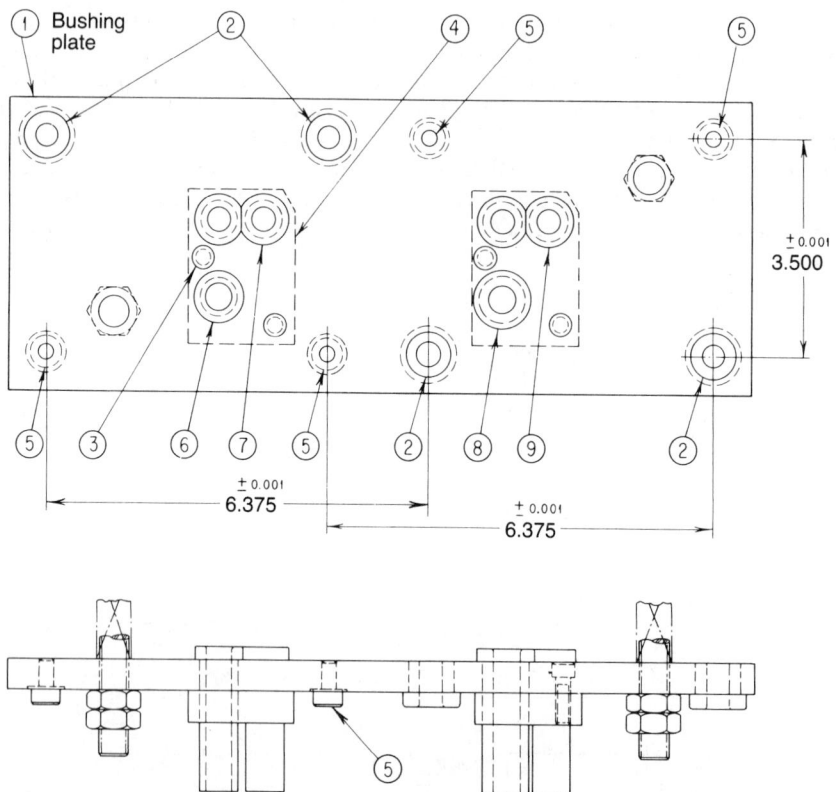

Fig. 8-54 Bushing plate attached to drill head for use with the jig shown in Fig. 8-53.

Miscellaneous Drill Jigs. Drill jigs can be made from many standard commercial items such as premachined section forms and bases (see Fig. 1-44); angle irons, parallels, and V-blocks (see Fig. 1-45); section components (see Fig. 1-47); and standard structural forms (see Fig. 1-48). Following are some examples of drill jigs constructed of these materials.

- Premachined sections were used to construct the drill jig shown in Fig. 8-56. The base was made from a standard commercial T-section to which a bushing plate made from a flat section was attached with screws and dowels. The addition of standard jig feet, drill bushings, and clamps completed the assembly.
- The drill jig shown in Fig. 8-57 was built from a U-shaped, premachined cast iron section and a flat section. It was built in 9.5 hours with a savings of 30% in build time.
- The drill jig shown in Fig. 8-58 was built from standard structural form materials. It consists of two pieces of angle iron welded to a channel iron to form a V-section. A larger angle iron was welded over the V-section to serve as a bushing plate and clamping mount. The addition of a standard thumb screw, a drill bushing, and a section of rod completed the assembly.

Wooden Drill Jigs. As noted in Chapter 1, wooden tooling is often overlooked. An example of its use for drilling is shown Fig. 8-59. The jig consists of a plywood base, two wood side spacer rails, and a plywood bushing plate joined together with wood screws, and four bolts which also serve as jig feet. To reduce wear and provide additional support, a sheet metal plate is bonded to the top of the base. The part is located

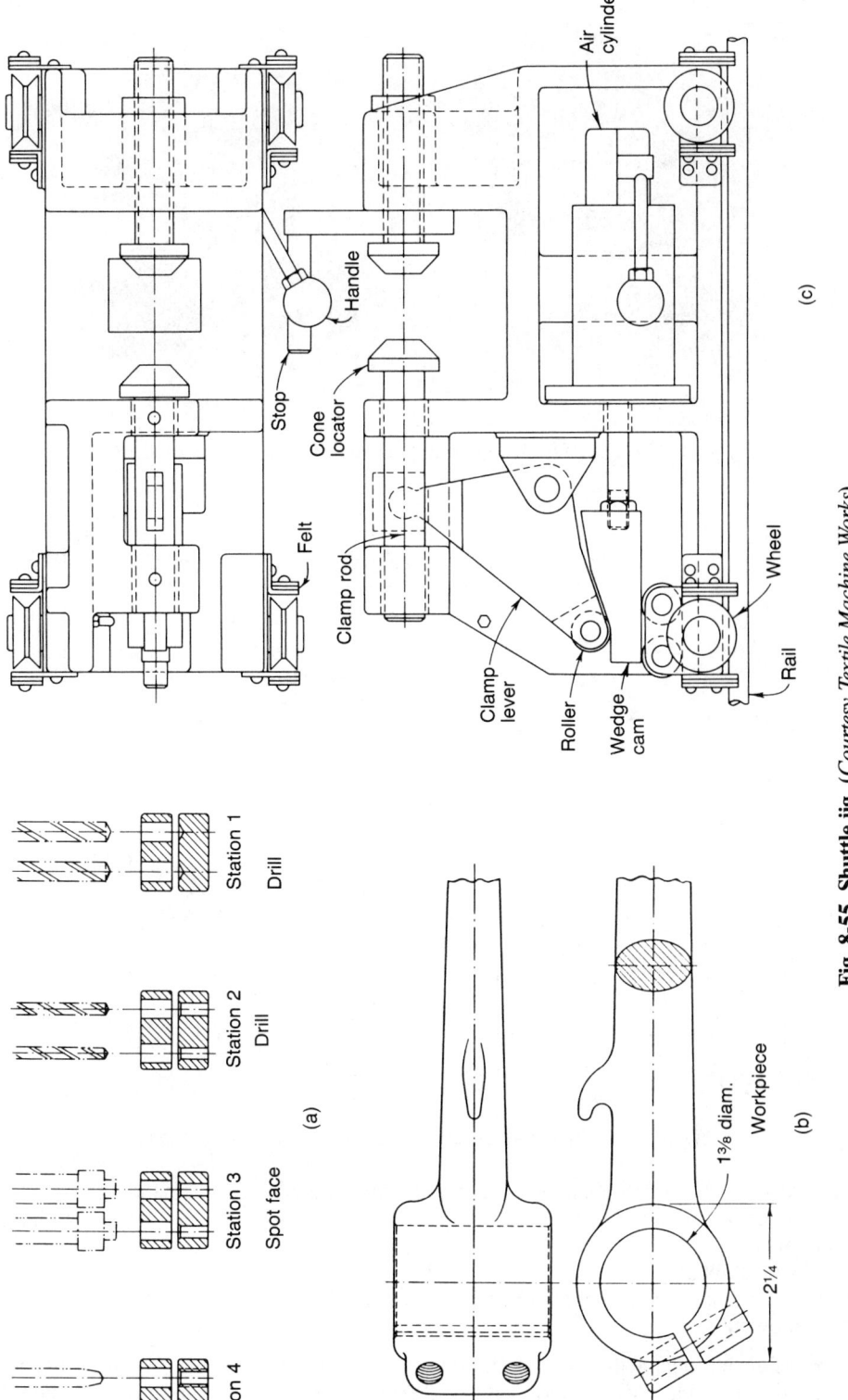

Fig. 8-55 Shuttle jig. (*Courtesy Textile Machine Works*)

Station 1
Drill

Station 2
Drill

Station 3
Spot face

Station 4
Tap

(a)

Air cylinder

Handle

Stop

Cone locator

Felt

Clamp rod

Clamp lever

Roller

Wedge cam

Wheel

Rail

(c)

Workpiece

1³⁄₈ diam.

2¹⁄₄

(b)

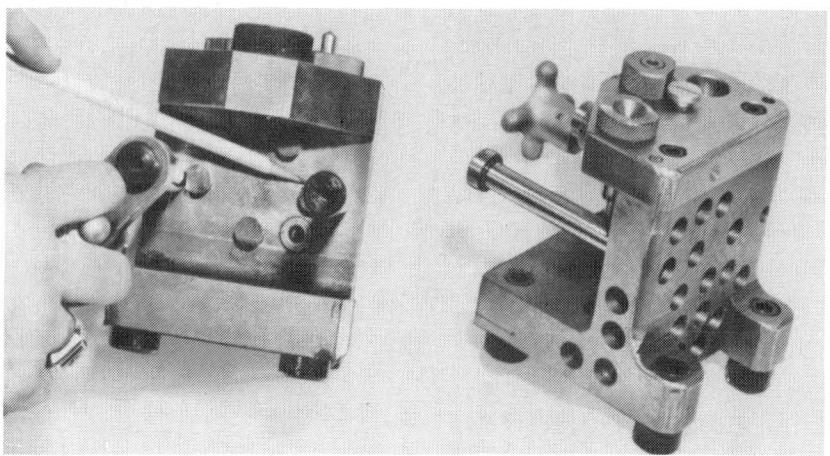

Fig. 8-56 Drill jig made from standard T-section. (*Courtesy Standard Parts Co.*)

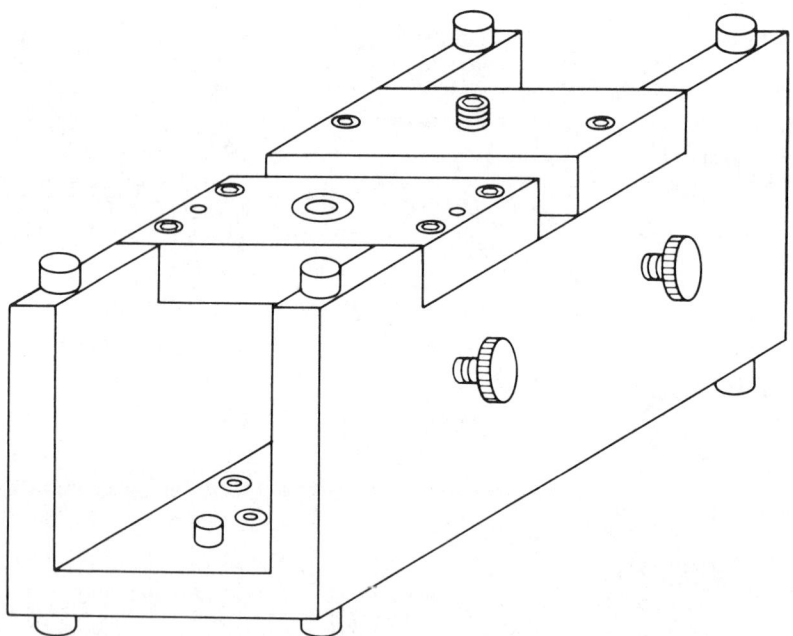

Fig. 8-57 Drill jig made from standard U-section tooling material.

against a pressed-in roll pin and two more bolts thru the side rail. The hand knob clamp, thumb screw, threaded socket, and serrated type bushings are all standard tooling components.

Plastic Drill Jigs. The use of plastics was also discussed in Chapter 1. Some of the things that require special consideration when using these materials for drill jigs include the following:

- Conventional drill bushings should not be used in this type of tooling. Castable drill bushings (seen later in Fig. 8-73*g*) are designed for this purpose and should be used.

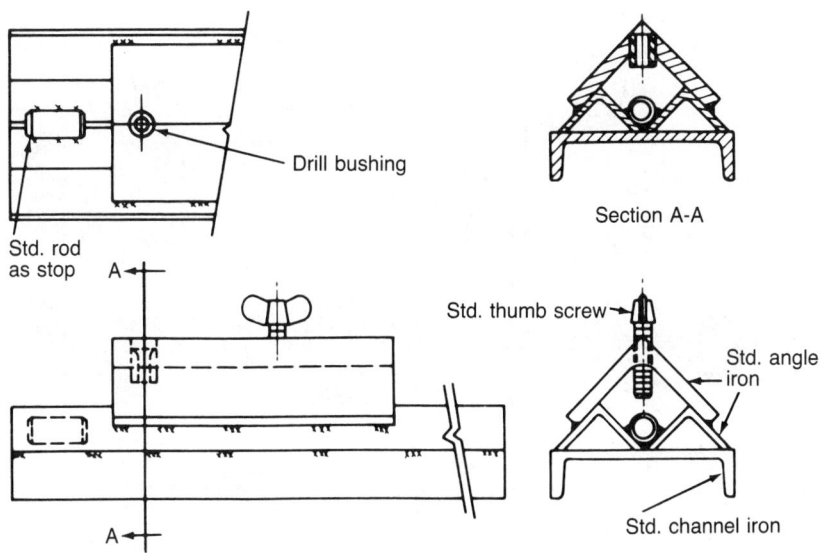

Fig. 8-58 Drill jig made from standard structural form material (channel and angle iron).

- Drill bushings must be positioned in the exact location before pouring the liquid epoxy, thermoplastic compound, or low-melt alloy. Methods for doing this were covered in Chapter 1.
- When designing epoxy tooling, the tool designer should understand the various construction methods, available along with the advantages and disadvantages of each method. He or she should also be familar with the many grades of epoxies, or seek help from the epoxy formulators, especially when designing complex tooling.

General construction of a cast epoxy drill jig is shown in Fig. 8-60. A drill jig constructed by the laminating method is shown in Fig. 8-61.

Modified Vises. The drill jigs shown in Fig. 8-62 along with their respective work-pieces, were all made by adding details to a commercially available vise. Jig *a* was designed to drill a locating hole in a sprocket shaft. Jig *b* was designed to both drill one 0.277 in. diameter hole and also to drill, countersink, and tap a 0.3125-24 hole in a pivot block. Jig *c* was designed to drill (1) No. 38 and (1) 3/32 in. diameter hole in a pivot pin. For positioning on the machine table, the vises are bolted to precision ground sub-bases and located against a rail and stop pins as shown in *d*.

Collet Fixtures. As shown in Fig. 8-63, 5C collet blocks and collet fixtures mounted vertically can be used to hold workpieces for drilling, tapping, and related operations. The collet fixture shown in the figure has been mounted on a sub-base to permit long workpieces to pass through the fixture. The torq-loc fixture previously shown in Fig. 3-77 can also be used for this purpose.

Self-centering Vises. The self-centering vise shown in Fig. 8-64 was fitted with false jaws to center and clamp a cast iron elbow for drilling and tapping. Form-fitting cast jaws perform a similar function as shown previously in Fig. 3-59.

Drilling Accessories. The safety quickacting drill vise shown in Fig. 8-65 features built-in recessed parallel jaw inserts to hold work square. A vertical V-groove in the jaw is provided to grip round workpieces. The same figure shows the method of mounting the vise to the table to prevent spinning or breaking loose from the table.

The quick dividing device shown mounted to an angle knee in Fig. 8-66 can speed up the drilling of equally spaced hole patterns of 2, 3, 4, 6, 8, 12, or 24 holes on a

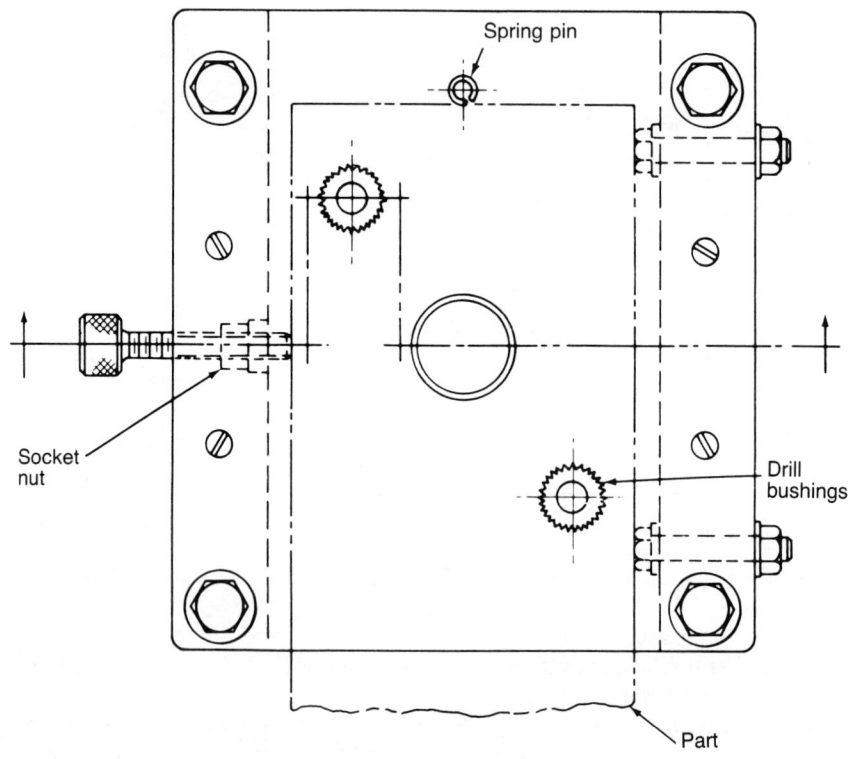

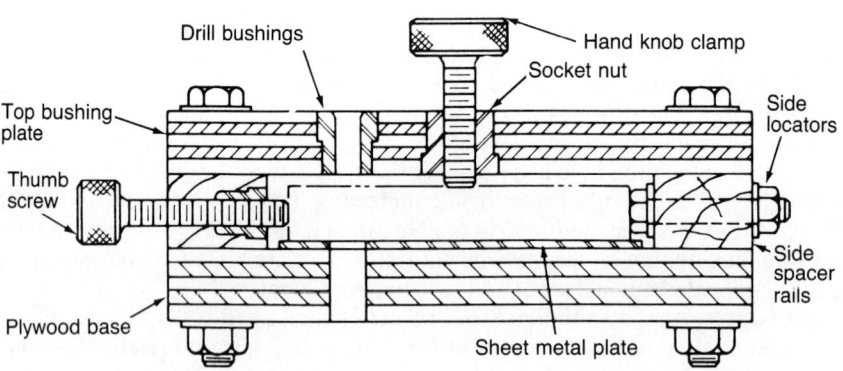

Fig. 8-59 Wooden drill jig incorporating standard tooling hardware.

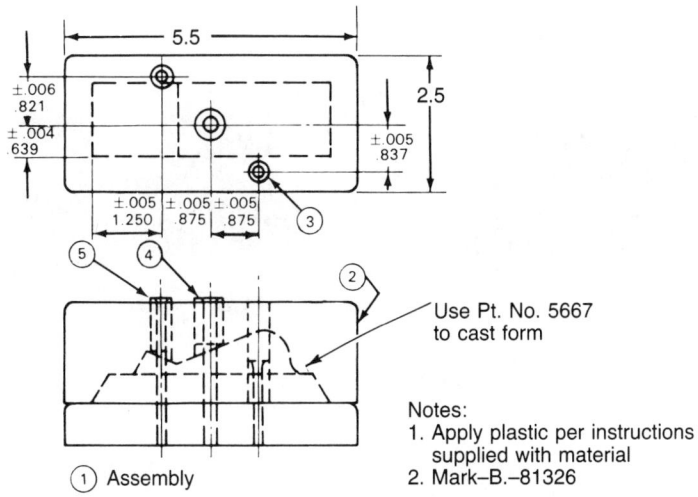

① Assembly

Use Pt. No. 5667
to cast form

Notes:
1. Apply plastic per instructions
   supplied with material
2. Mark–B.–81326

5	1	Drill Bushing (Plastic Type)	American Type DGV. 0.156 ID x 0.406 x 1 LG.	STD.
4	1	Drill Bushing (Plastic Type)	American Type DGV. 0.25 ID x 0.5 ID x 0.875 LG.	STD.
3	1	Drill Bushing (Plastic Type)	American Type DGV. 0.125 ID x 0.312 x 0.75 LG.	STD.
2	1	Body	REN Plastics Inc. #RP–3203–2	
1	1	Assembly		
Det. No.	No. Req'd	Name	Stock Size	Mat.
Stock List				
Drill Jig				
Drawn By – E. C. Key Date – 5-1-85			App. By – CD Date – 5-6-85	
			B–81236	Rev 1

Fig. 8-60 Drawing of an epoxy drill jig.

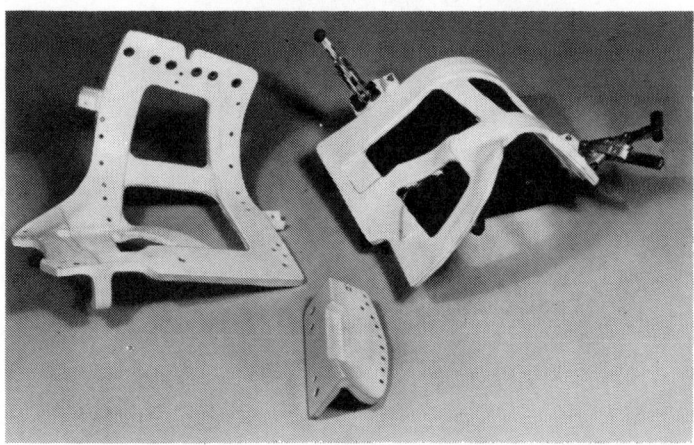

Fig. 8-61 Plastic drill jigs and scribe templates. (*Courtesy Ciba-Geigy Tooling Systems*)

8-57

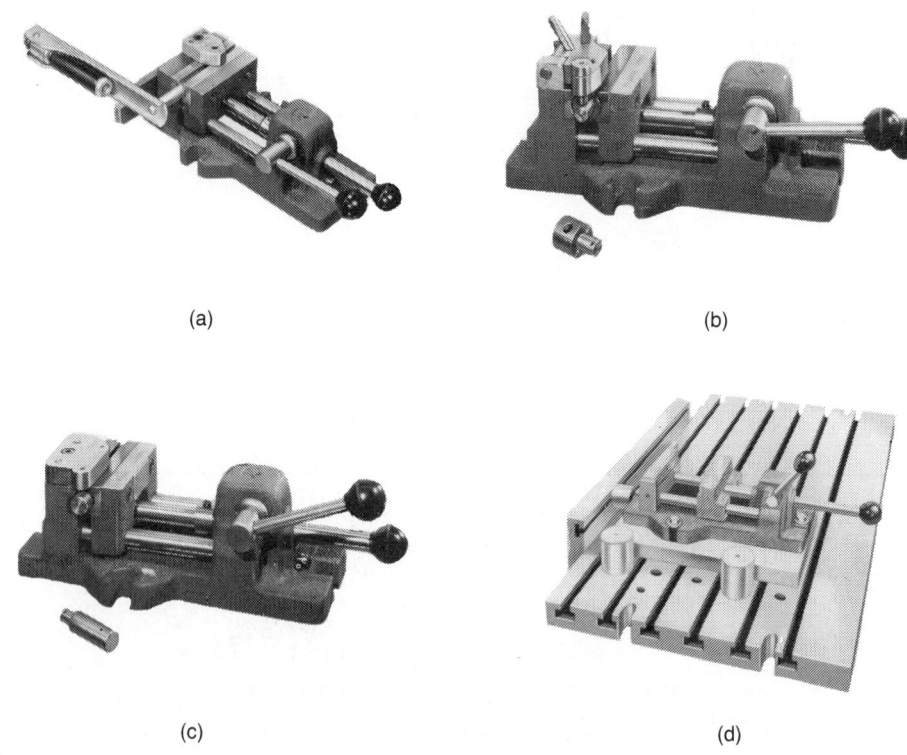

(a)

(b)

(c)

(d)

Fig. 8-62 Modified vises. (*Courtesy Heinrich Tools, Inc.*)

Fig. 8-63 Air collet fixture. (*Courtesy Heinrich Tools, Inc.*)

Fig. 8-64 Self-centering vise with false jaws. (*Courtesy Heinrich Tools, Inc.*)

Fig. 8-65 Safety drill vise. (*Courtesy Heinrich Tools, Inc.*)

Fig. 8-66 Quick divider. (*Courtesy Willis Machinery & Tools Co.*)

workpiece OD, or when used without the knee, for drilling equally spaced hole patterns on any bolt circle diameter desired on the face of the workpiece.

The universal drill jig shown in Fig. 8-67 can be readily adapted for drilling a wide variety of workpieces. It features a solid jaw with an adjustable end stop and several movable bushing carriers which can be oriented for the different workpieces.

Drilling applications using a multi-purpose vise are shown in Fig. 8-68. Some of the possible jaw configurations possible are shown in Fig. 3-58.

The mounting table (see Fig. 8-69) can be used for light drilling as well as electrical discharge machining (EDM), milling, boring, and jig grinding. The workpiece is located and held on the square ledges of the rails and a movable support block which permits the fixture to be used for a wide range of workpiece sizes. The application shown is a setup for an NC drill press.

A drill press clamp (two Hol-Down products are shown in Fig. 8-70a) can be very useful for clamping a workpiece directly on the drill press table. Standard clamping attachments are shown in Fig. 8-70b. The unit can also be used to guide a drill by replacing the clamp screw with a suitable drill bushing.

Many other devices shown in previous chapters can also be used to position workpieces for drilling and related operations.

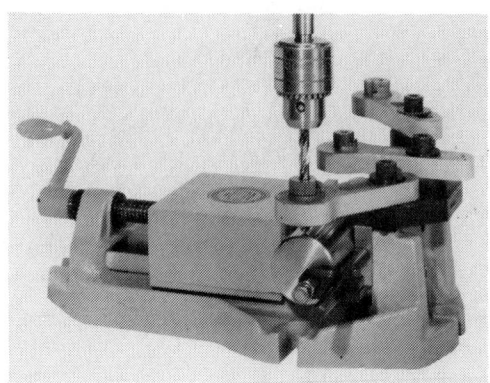

Fig. 8-67 Universal drill jig. (*Courtesy Universal Vise & Tool Co.*)

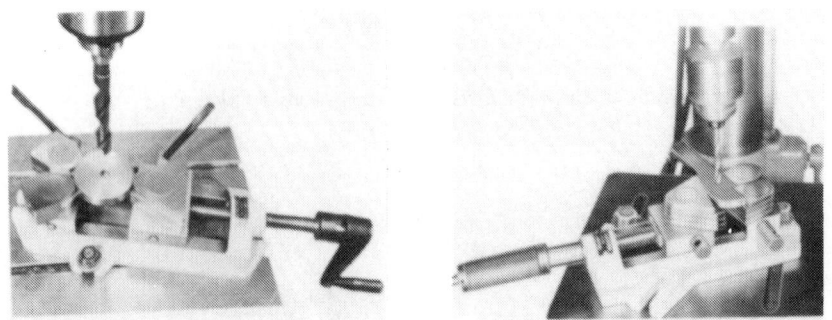

Fig. 8-68 Multi-purpose vise. (*Courtesy James Morton, Inc.*)

Fig. 8-69 Edge mounting table. (*Courtesy Harig Mfg. Co.*)

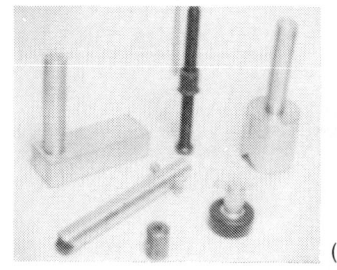

(b)

(a)

Fig. 8-70 Drill press clamps. (*Hol-down drill press clamp, Courtesy James Morton, Inc.*)

DRILL JIG BUSHINGS

Drill jig bushings are used to position and guide the tools that do the cutting. The basic styles are shown in Fig. 8-71. They are available in a wide range of styles and types to handle various applications. Most are readily available in hardened steel or carbide. Bushings made of other materials such as bronze, stainless steel, etc., are also available from the bushing manufacturers by special order. Most bushings and liners can be supplied with the OD ground to industry standards, or left unground (type U) for custom grinding.

Drill jig bushings and liners may be specified by either the individual manufacturer's identification system or by the universally accepted ANSI designation system which, regardless of the manufacturer, will insure delivery of the proper bushing. Specifying the type of cutting tool and its diameter will assure correct tool clearance.

Headless Press Fit Bushings. Headless press fit bushings, type P and PU, are the most popular and least expensive bushings. They are used for a single size cutting tool application where light axial loads are expected. Since they are permanently pressed into the jig plate, they are generally used where replacement is not anticipated during the expected life of the tool. They are ideal where the top of the bushing must be flush with the jig plate or where hole spacing is too close to use headed bushings.

Head Press Fit Bushings. Head press fit bushings, type H and HU, are also used for permanent installations requiring greater bearing area or where heavy axial loads that could force the bushing through the jig hole are anticipated. Since the bearing area extends beyond the jig plate, the thickness of the jig plate can often be reduced, thereby lightening the overall weight of the jig. Cases where the head must be flush with the jig plate require counterboring of the mounting hole in the jig plates.

Although designed for permanent installations, press fit bushings are easily replaced, but at the expense of losing some mounting hole accuracy with each replacement.

Slip Renewable and Slip-Fixed Renewable Bushings. Slip renewable bushings, type S, and slip-fixed renewable bushings, type SF, are used with a headless liner, type L, or a head liner, type HL, where multiple operations, such as drilling and reaming or drilling and tapping, are to be performed on the same hole; or, where long production runs require occasional changing of the bushing to maintain jig integrity. They are available for use with lock screws, type LS and TW; round clamps, type CL; round end clamps, type RE; or flat clamps, type FC, as shown in Fig. 8-72. Both diameters of the bushings and the ID of the liner are finish ground to industry standards, while the liners are available with the OD finish ground or unground.

Type P & PU
Headless
press fit

Type S
Slip
renewable

Type L
Headless
liner

Type H & HU
Head
press fit

Type SF
Slip
renewable

Type HL
Head
liner

Type UL
Un-a-lok liners

Oil groove
bushing

Fig. 8-71 Drill bushings and liners. (*Courtesy American Drill Bushing Co.*)

When used for multiple operations, the first operation bushing is installed and the hole drilled. The bushing is then replaced with the second operation bushing and the second operation performed. This process is repeated until the hole is completely machined. The first operation bushing is then reinstalled and procedure repeated on the next workpiece.

When slip-fixed renewable bushings are used on jigs to perform single operations on long production runs, they are usually secured in the fixed mode by a lock screw. When used to perform more than one operation on the same hole, they are secured in the slip mode for easy changing.

Type UL liners (such as UN-A-LOC) are used with ANSI slip renewable bushings. These special liners eliminate the need for a bushing locking device. In use, the bushing is locked tight in the liner by the torque of the drill bit. UN-A-LOC liners must be installed with an arbor press.

Oil Groove Bushings. Oil groove bushings are designed to provide complete lubrication between the cutting tool and the bushing when maximum cooling is required during a machining operation. Over two dozen separate groove patterns are available.

Drill Bushings for Special Applications. Some of the more common drill bushings for special applications are shown Fig. 8-73. When installing any of these bushings, the individual manufacturer's recommendations should be followed closely.

Bushings and Liners for Plastic, Castable, and Soft Material Tooling. Bushing types HGV, HGP, and DGV have serrated or grooved OD's for casting in-place with epoxy resins, thermoplastic tooling compounds, or low-melt alloys. Bushing type SGP is for press-in installation in soft materials such as aluminum, magnesium, wood, or masonite.

Lock screws

Type LS and TW

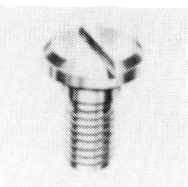

Used for locking renewable bushings in liners. Available for all styles of renewable bushings.

Round clamps

Type CL

Used instead of lock screws for locking ANSI and Extended Range fixed renewable bushings in liners.

Round end clamps

Type RE

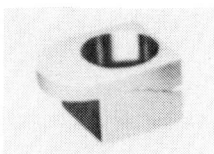

Used instead of lock screws for locking ANSI and Extended Range fixed or slip renewable bushings in liner. Available for applications requiring either flush or projected mounting of liners.

Flat clamps

Type FC

Used for locking ANSI and Extended Range Type FX fixed renewable bushings with heads milled for flat clamp mounting. Available for applications requiring either flush or projected mounting of liners.

Fig. 8-72 Accessories. (*Courtesy American Drill Bushing Co.*)

The liner type ULD serves the same function as the type UL, except that it is knurled for use in plastic tooling.

Template Bushings. Type TB bushings are used with thin template materials ranging from 1/16 to ⅜ in. (1.6 to 9.5 mm) thick to provide low cost tooling. Installation is shown in Fig. 8-74.

Rotary Bushings. Rotary bushings (not shown) feature precision tapered roller or ball bearings capable of handling high thrust and/or radial loads encountered in some jig applications, such as supporting a piloted cutting tool for extremely close machining.

Drill Bushing Tips and Accessories. Drill bushing tips (see Fig. 8-75) are used with automatic self-feed drill motors. Most are constructed by a two piece method consisting of a collar which contains the screw threads, alignment diameter, and the lock flange. It also contains a pressed-in shank which is a plain bushing with ID ground to guide and support the cutting tool, and the OD ground to suit the liner bushing mounted on the jig.

Mounting of Bushings. Jig mounting with a lock liner bushing and lock nut is the conventional method of mounting the drilling unit to a jig or fixture. To install, a hole is bored into the jig or fixture to suit the lock liner bushing, which is then assembled to the jig or fixture and then held in place with a lock nut. (The Taper-Loc liner bushing is a compact, one-piece version of the lock liner bushing.)

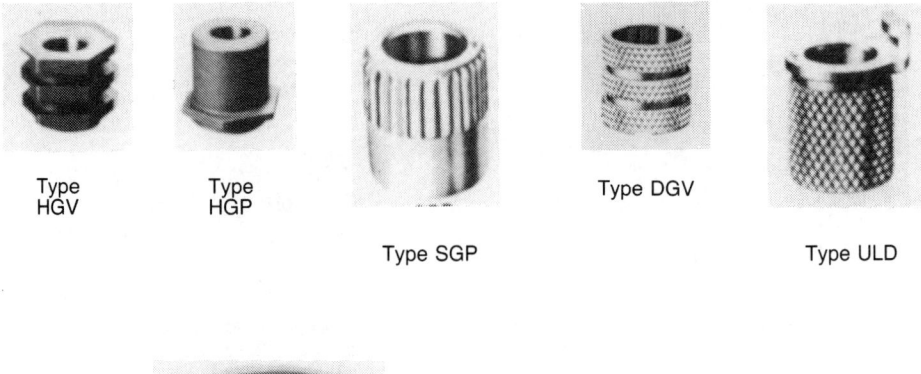

Type HGV   Type HGP   Type SGP   Type DGV   Type ULD

Type TB
template
bushing

Type TB
Lock
ring

Fig. 8-73 Special drill bushings. (*Courtesy American Drill Bushing Co.*)

Direct jig mounting is an alternate method used when holes are so closely spaced that lock liner bushings cannot be used. In this case, lock screws are mounted directly on the jig and a hardened, headless liner is pressed into the jig to accept the drill bushing tip shank.

Lock strip mounting is another mounting method for holes that are closely spaced. It features a lock strip along each side of a row of holes in the jig. A hardened, headless liner to accept the shank of the drill bushing tip is also pressed into the jig with this method.

INSTALLATION OF DRILL BUSHINGS

To assure accuracy in the workpiece, drill bushings must be properly located and installed using the following rules:

- Mounting holes should be round and properly sized to prevent bushing closure and jig plate distortion. For this reason it is recommended that the mounting holes be jig bored or reamed to size. Headless press fit and liner bushings are generally installed with a diametral interference of 0.0005 to 0.0008 in., while headed press fit bushings are generally installed with a diametral interference of 0.0003 to 0.0005 in. Interference greater than this may reduce the diameter of the bushing ID to the point where the tool may seize, or, in the case of liners, prevent insertion of a renewable bushing. On the other hand, too little interference will result in a loosely installed bushing which may spin or be forced out of place. Drill bushings for special applications should be installed in accordance with the individual manufacturer's recommendations.
- Sufficient chip clearance, as illustrated in Fig. 8-76, should be provided between the bushing and the workpiece to allow for chip removal, except in cases where extreme accuracy is required. In this case, the bushing should be in direct contact with the workpiece. In most cases, a clearance of 1 to 1½ times the bushing ID

① Lay out holes

Lay out holes observing hole spacing and edge distance minimums

Bushing OD	A Min. Hole Spacing	B Min. Edge Distance
0.375	0.60	0.250
0.500	0.73	0.312
0.750	0.98	0.438

Trim edge

② Ream

Bushing O.D.
Template

Ream bushing hole 0.001-0.003 in. Larger than bushing O.D.

③ Countersink

Lock ring to be flush with or a max. of 0.015 above bushing groove

Aluminum lock ring
Bushing
Bushing chamfer must seat here
Reamed hole   Template
Flush to 0.015
90°

Countersink reamed hole with 90° included angle countersink tool to permit bushing to seat flush to 0.015 inside surface of template. The countersink must be normal and concentric to the reamed hole and free of chatter. For best results, use micro stop countersink tool with piloted countersink cutter.

④ Install

Installation tool   Rivet gun
Bushing
Lock ring
Bucking tool

The Rivet Gun Method

Ram of arbor press
Installation tool
Bed of arbor press
Lock ring
Template

The Arbor Press Method

The arbor press method of installation is recommended whenever template size permits. The rivet gun method is used for large templates. Template Bushing Tool is threaded for adaptation to rivet gun. Use lowest impact pressure adjustment that will properly form the aluminum lock ring. Note that impact pressure will vary for bushings of different outside diameters. Excessive impact pressure will flatten lock ring causing insecure mounting of bushing.

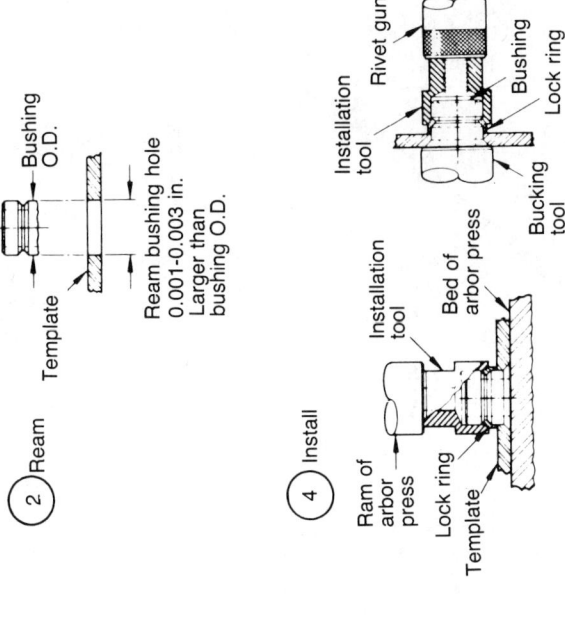

Fig. 8-74 Installing template bushings. (*Courtesy American Drill Bushing Co.*)

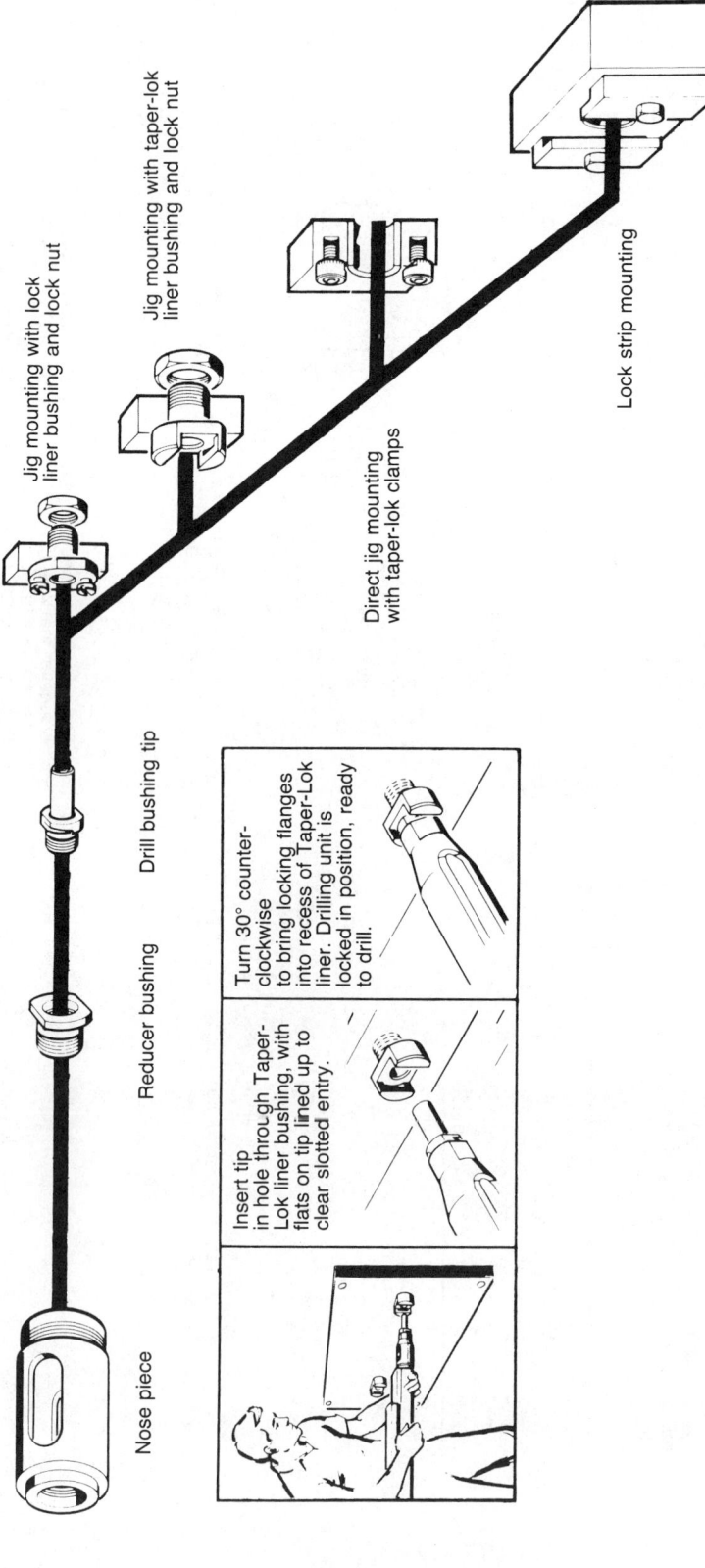

Jig mounting with lock
liner bushing and lock nut

Jig mounting with taper-lok
liner bushing and lock nut

Lock strip mounting

Direct jig mounting
with taper-lok clamps

Nose piece

Reducer bushing

Drill bushing tip

Insert tip in hole through Taper-Lok liner bushing, with flats on tip lined up to clear slotted entry.

Turn 30° counter-clockwise to bring locking flanges into recess of Taper-Lok liner. Drilling unit is locked in position, ready to drill.

Fig. 8-75 Drill bushing tips. (*Courtesy American Drill Bushing Co.*)

should be used when machining materials such as cold-rolled steel which produces long stringy chips, while a clearance of ½ times the bushing ID is recommended when machining materials such as cast iron, which produces small chips. Excessive chip clearance should be avoided because (1) most cutting tools are slightly larger at the cutting end due to back taper, and (2) excessive clearance will reduce the guiding effect of the bushing resulting in less accurate drilling.

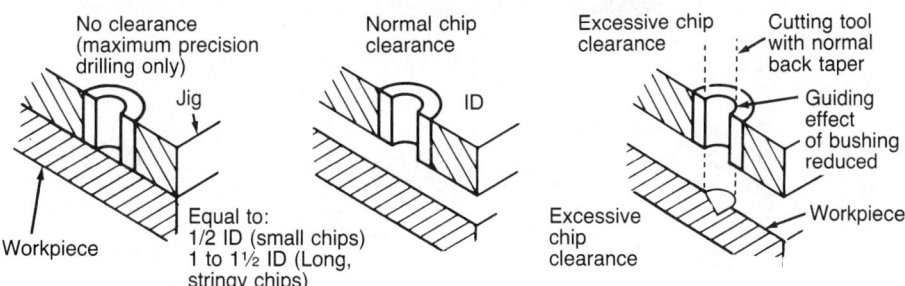

Fig. 8-76 Recommended clearance between workpiece and bushing. (*Courtesy American Drill Bushing Co.*)

Chip control should be closely monitored after the jig is put into production. As a general rule, if the chips have a tendency to lift the bushing, more clearance is needed. If the cutting tool wanders or bends, less clearance is needed.

When performing multiple operations such as drilling and reaming, slip renewable bushings of different lengths should be used to provide optimum chip clearance for each operation as shown in Fig. 8-77.

- Clearance between the bushing and the workpiece must also be provided when drilling wiry metals such as copper, which tends to produce secondary, or minor, burrs around the top of the drilled hole, as shown in Fig. 8-78. This in turn, causes the jig to lift from the workpiece or makes it difficult to remove the workpiece from side-loaded jigs. A burr clearance of ½ times the bushing ID is recommended. Provisions must also be made to the jig itself to provide clearance for the primary, or major, burrs that form as the tool exits the workpiece.

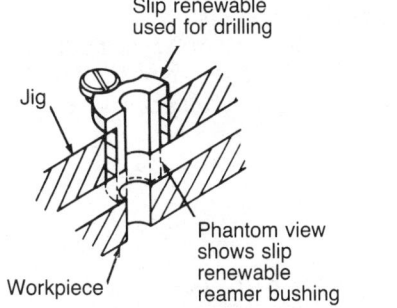

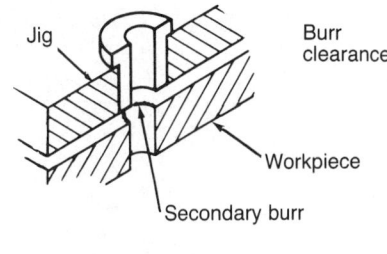

Fig. 8-77 Chip clearance for multiple operations. (*Courtesy American Drill Bushing Co.*)

Fig. 8-78 Burr clearance. (*Courtesy American Drill Bushing Co.*)

- In order to properly support and guide the cutting tool, the length of the drill bushing under normal circumstances should range between 1½ to 2½ times the diameter of the bushing ID and the jig plate supporting the bushing should be thick enough to sustain the bushing. Usually a thickness between 1 to 2 times the cutting tool will be sufficient.

- When drilling irregular work surfaces, the ends of the bushings should be formed to the contour of the workpieces as shown in Fig. 8-79. This will prevent the tool from pushing off center. The distance between the workpiece and the bushing should also be held to a minimum under these circumstances.

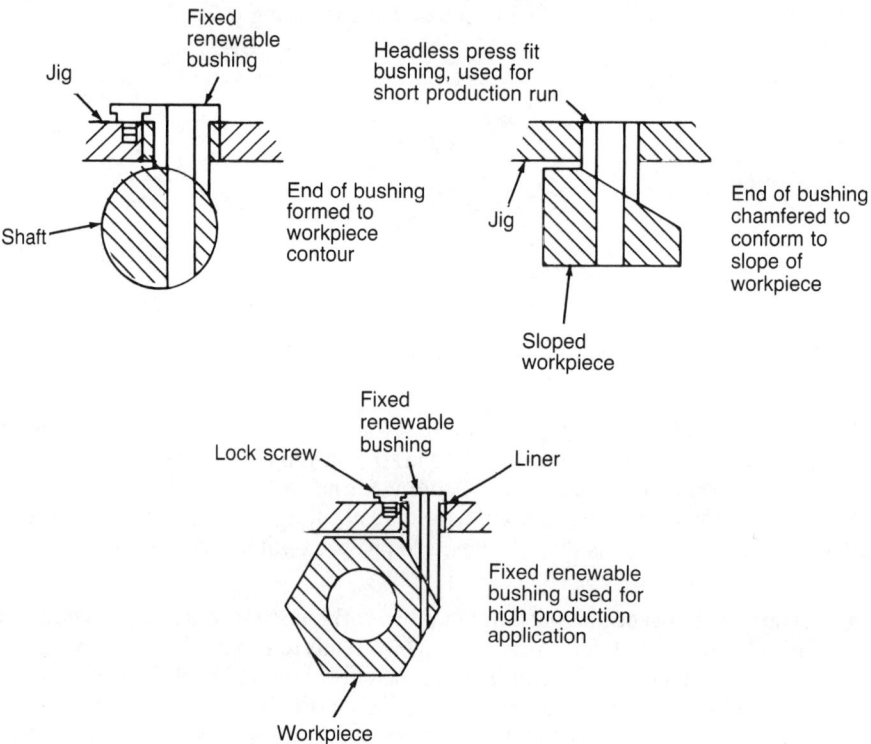

Fig. 8-79 Drilling irregular worksurfaces. (*Courtesy American Drill Bushing Co.*)

- Sometimes hole centerdistances are so close that there is not enough room for the bushings. In these cases, extra thinwall bushings, or, standard headed or headless bushings which have flats ground on them might work as shown in Fig. 8-80. Sometimes a single, hardened steel insert with two or more holes in it, such as shown in Fig. 8-81, must be used.

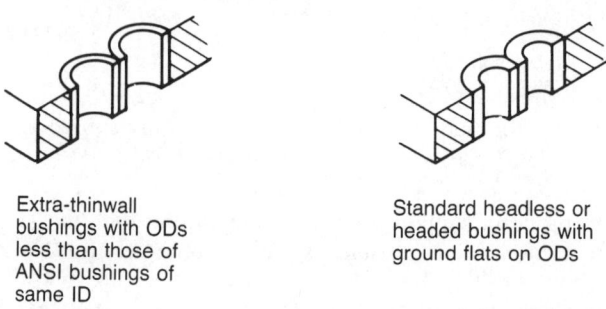

Extra-thinwall bushings with ODs less than those of ANSI bushings of same ID

Standard headless or headed bushings with ground flats on ODs

Fig. 8-80 Close hole patterns. (*Courtesy American Drill Bushing Co.*)

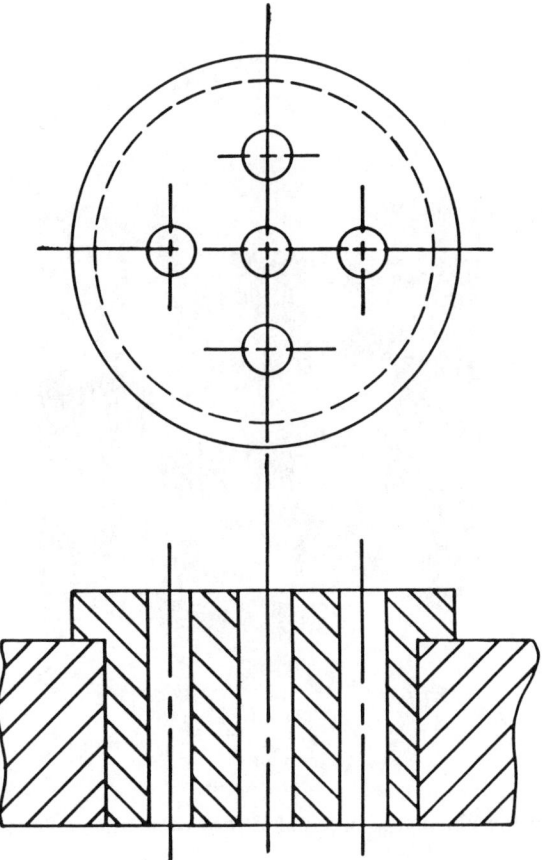

Fig. 8-81 Hardened steel insert.

TOOLING FOR MULTIPLE-SPINDLE OPERATIONS

Many multiple drilling, reaming, and tapping operations are performed using standard drill jigs and other workholding fixtures, such as shown in Fig. 8-82. Other arrangements use bushing plates which are built in much the same way that one would build a plate jig. Some are suspended from the drill head by guide rods as shown in Fig. 8-83. Bushing plates are spring loaded and clamp the workpiece automatically as the head descends. Other arrangements include that shown in Fig. 8-84 which was constructed using an off-the-shelf, self-clamping jig of the type shown in Fig. 8-85.

Figure 8-86 shows the arrangement used for multiple-spindle lead screw tapping.

FIXTURING COMPONENTS

Figure 8-87 shows several fixtures that can be used individually or in combinations to solve many drilling problems. Included are the following:

- The horizontal air clamping fixture, *a*, which can be used to end clamp or face clamp a workpiece.
- The vertical air clamping fixture, *b*, which can handle any type of workpiece requiring top clamping action.
- The self-centering air vise, *c*, which can hold any round, hex, or square workpiece for drilling, tapping, milling, or slotting operations.
- The indexing fixture which can be used in either a horizontal, *d*, or vertical position, *e*. The number of indexes is adjustable.

Fig. 8-82 Continuous production of precision drilled parts using a 4-station turntable index-ing fixture. (*Courtesy Zagar, Inc.*)

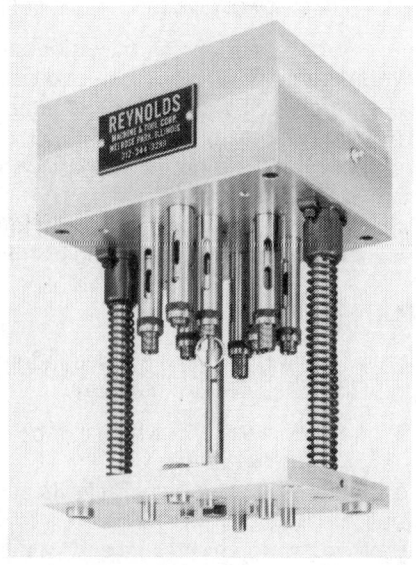

Fig. 8-83 Self-clamping spring loaded bushing plate suspended from drill head by guide rods. (*Courtesy Reynolds Machine & Tool Corp.*)

Fig. 8-84 Bushing plate mounted on self-clamping jig. (*Courtesy Zagar, Inc.*)

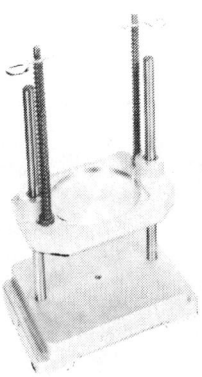

Fig. 8-85 Self-clamping jig blank assembly. (*Courtesy Zagar, Inc.*)

- The automatic parts loader with a self-centering fixture, *f*. The linear feed mechanism can transfer piece parts in 0.3 sec. Feed rails are adjustable for different workpiece sizes. The unit can be used with a magazine, hopper, or vibratory bowl.

In Fig. 8-88, a vertically mounted indexing fixture is combined with a horizontal clamping fixture to drill the workpiece shown.

In Fig. 8-89, a horizontally mounted indexing fixture is combined with a vertical clamping fixture for drilling with a multiple-spindle head.

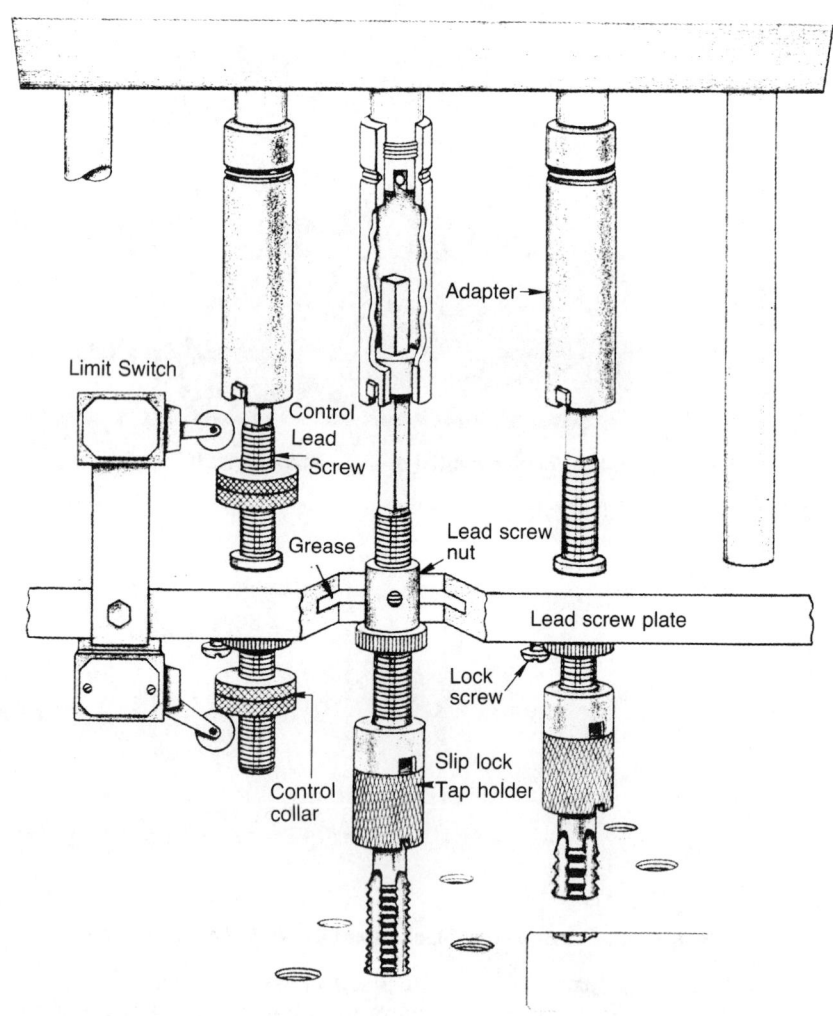

Fig. 8-86 Arrangement for multiple spindle lead screw tapping. (*Courtesy Zagar, Inc.*)

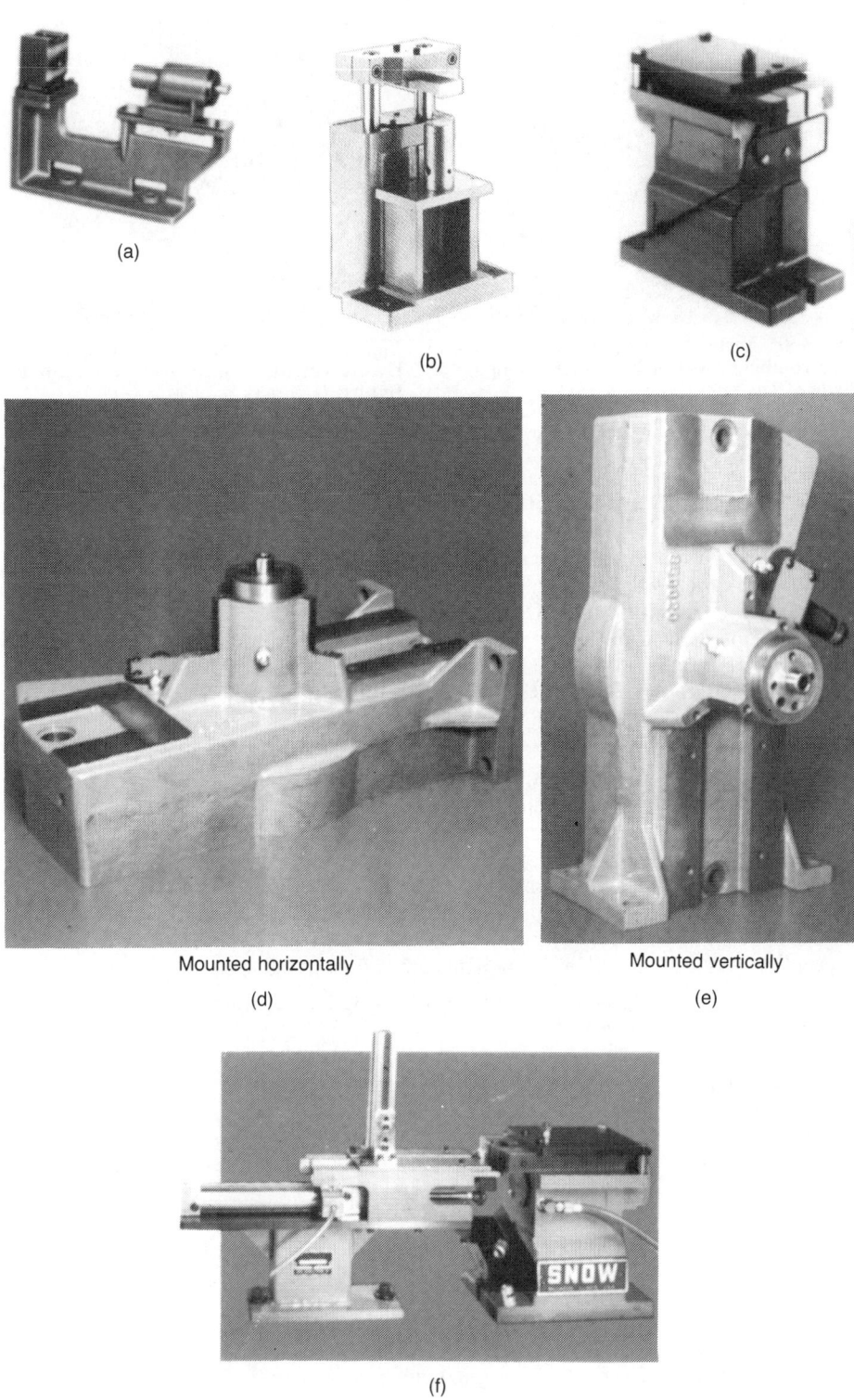

(a)

(b)

(c)

Mounted horizontally

(d)

Mounted vertically

(e)

(f)

Fig. 8-87 Fixturing components. (*Courtesy Snow Mfg. Co.*)

8-73

Fig. 8-88 Vertically mounted indexing fixture combined with a horizontal clamping fixture. (*Courtesy Snow Mfg. Co.*)

Fig. 8-89 Horizontally mounted indexing fixture combined with a vertical clamping fixture. (*Courtesy Snow Mfg. Co.*)

TOOLING FOR AUTOMATIC FEED SYSTEMS

Automatic feed drills (AFDs) and tappers (AFTs) as shown in Fig. 8-90 are available in a wide range of speeds with either air or electric motors up to 1 hp. They provide an effective and lower cost alternative to dedicated machines in production environments. The optimum feed drill, *e*, automatically adjust its feed rate during the drilling cycle, to maintain the drill spindle motor at its optimum power. It is ideally suited to drilling deep holes, sandwich material, and difficult materials.

An air-operated, peck-feed control is available for drilling deeper holes. After a preset drilling time period, the drill automatically retracts until it is clear of the hole. At this point, an automatic re-start signal recycles the drill so that it returns rapidly to the point of the previous drilled depth. The drill then slows down to the cutting feed rate and proceeds to drill to the next stage. This cycle is repeated until the drill reaches total hole depth at which point the drill retracts and discontinues action.

A dwell control unit is also available when it is desirable to allow the drill to dwell at the bottom of its stroke which may be necessary where extreme accuracy in depth control is required. It can also be used when it is necessary to remove a specific amount of material as in a balancing operation or to polish the bottom of a blind hole.

Other accessories include adjustable and fixed spindle multiheads and the mounting clamps shown in Fig. 8-91.

Applications utilizing these components are shown in the following figures:

Figure 8-92*a* was designed to drill the following holes in an aluminum die casting with a cycle time of 30 seconds:

4 holes - #17
4 holes - #26
2 holes - ⅛ in.
5 holes - 3.1 mm
3 holes - #40

A layout is shown in Fig. 8-92*b*. Its operations are as follows:

1. Manual load.
2. Press "Start"—the component is clamped pneumatically.
3. (10) holes are drilled by the AFDs marked *.
4. Cylinders *A* and *B* retract (1 ½ in. travel), moving AFDs marked *X* into position.
5. Holes marked *X* and 8 are drilled by AFDs.
6. Cylinders *A* and *B* return to original position.
7. Air clamps retract.
8. Component is unloaded.

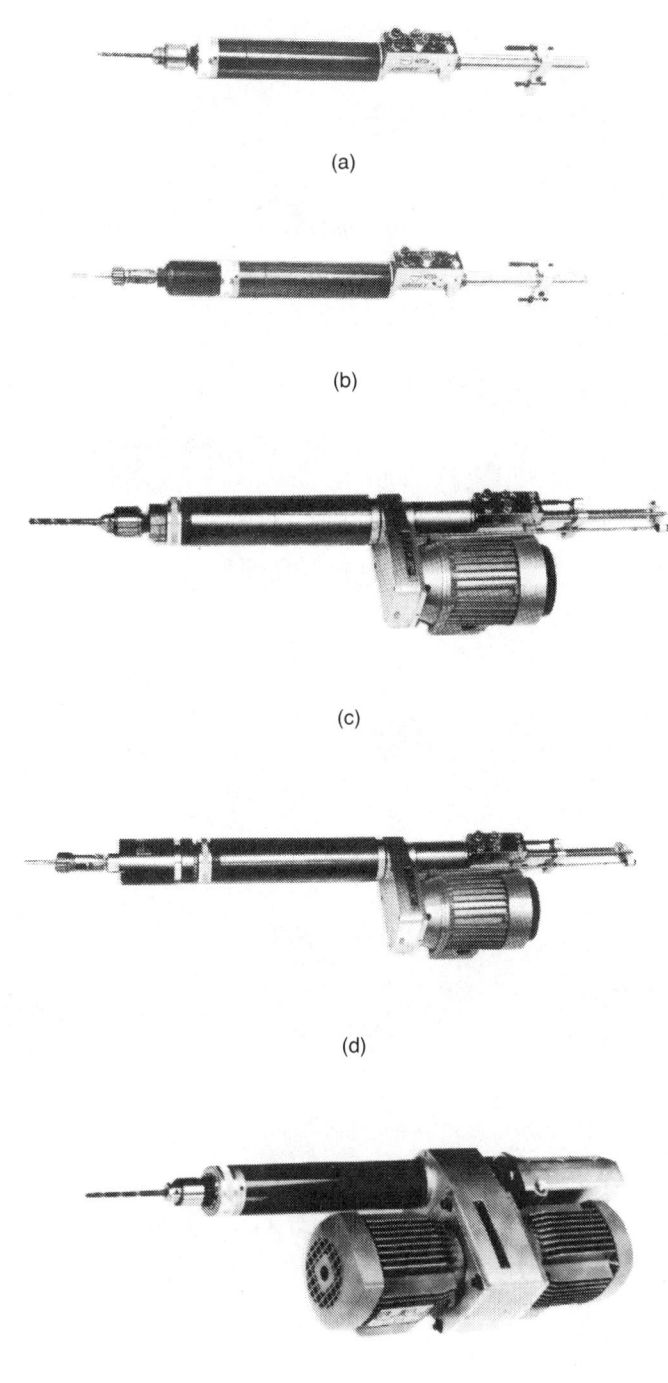

(a)

(b)

(c)

(d)

(e)

Fig. 8-90 Auto-feed drills and tappers: (*a*) **pneumatic drill;** (*b*) **pneumatic tapper;** (*c*) **electric drill;** (*d*) **electric tapper;** (*e*) **optimum feed drill.** (*Courtesy Desoutter Inc.*)

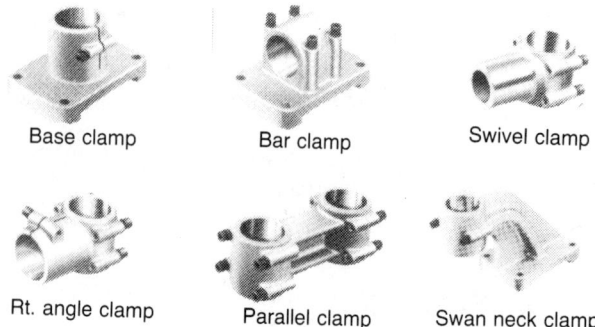

Base clamp   Bar clamp   Swivel clamp

Rt. angle clamp   Parallel clamp   Swan neck clamp

Fig. 8-91 Mounting clamps. (*Courtesy Desoutter, Inc.*)

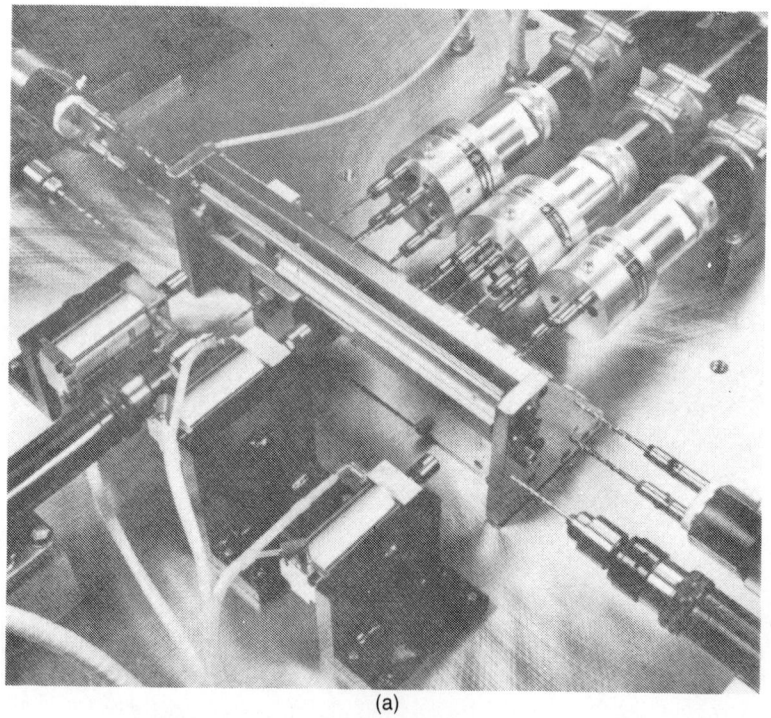

(a)

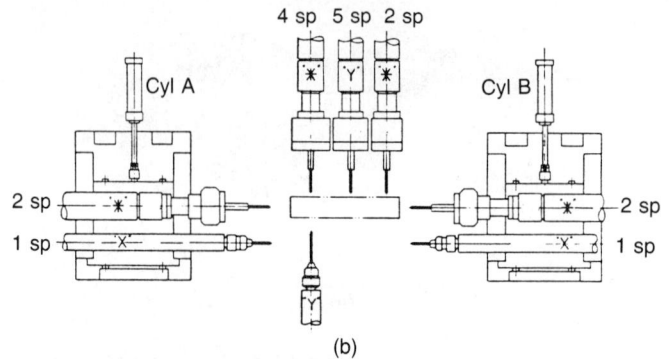

(b)

Fig. 8-92 Multiple drilling operation. (*Courtesy Desoutter, Inc.*)

Figure 8-93 was designed to drill 50 holes in the polypropylene interior skin of the side on a recreational vehicle. The machine uses 47 miniature drilling units similar to that shown in Fig. 8-90(a) and one standard size one equipped with a 3-spindle head. The minature drills each drill 5.0 mm diameter holes, and the larger drills three 4.8 mm diameter holes. The cycle time of the machine is 11 seconds. The cost of this machine was amortized in 90 days production.

Fig. 8-93 Drilling fifty holes in 11 seconds. (*Courtesy Desoutter, Inc.*)

REAMING

Jig design for reaming is basically the same as for drilling, which has been discussed throughout the chapter. The main difference is the need to hold closer tolerances on the jigs and bushings, and provide additional support to guide the reamer. For long holes it is essential to guide the reamer at both ends, as shown in Fig. 8-94*a*, using special piloted reamers designed for this purpose. Jigs should be designed so that the pilot enters the bushing before the reamer enters the workpiece, and remains piloted until the reaming operation is completed. For short holes the reamer is usually guided at one end only, as seen in Fig. 8-94*b*, with the bushing sized to fit the OD of the reamer. Additionally, bushings for reaming are generally longer than for drilling, usually 3 or 4 times the reamer diameter. Chip clearance is also generally less for reaming than for drilling, varying from one-fourth to one-half the tool diameter down to a maximum of ⅛ to ¼ in. regardless of the reamer diameter.

Bushing bores must be closely controlled. Bushings that are too small can cause tool seizure and breakage. Bushings that are too large will result in bellmouthed or out-of-round holes. The data in Table 8-8 can be used as a guide.

Carbide bushings should be considered for long production runs or where abrasive conditions are present. Roller or ball bearing, rotary-type bushings also provide maximum wear while maintaining close tolerances under high loads.

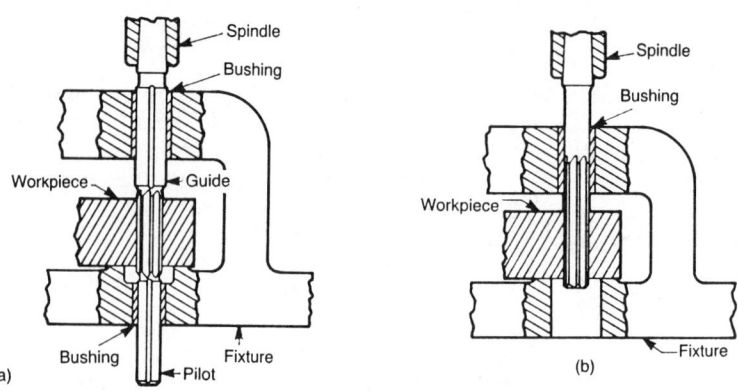

Fig. 8-94 Fixtures for guiding reamers.

TABLE 8-8
Tolerance Requirements for Reaming

Tolerance requirement for hole be reamed, in. (mm)	Tolerance		Remarks
	Reamer OD, in. (mm)	Bushing ID,* in. (mm)	
0.0005 (0.013)	0.0002-0.0003 (0.005-0.008) under high limit of hole	0.0002-0.0003 (0.005-0.008) under high	Carbide reamer and bushings necessary
0.001 (0.03)	0.0005-0.0006 (0.013-0.015) under high limit of hole	0.0003-0.0005 (0.005-0.013) under high limit of hole	Carbide reamers and bushings generally necessary
0.002 (0.05)	To mean tolerance of hole to be reamed	0.0005 (0.013) under high limit of hole	HSS reamers and bushings generally satisfactory

(Zagar, Inc.)

* Light lapping of bushing bore to a maximum of 0.0001 in. (0.003 mm) and selective matching with reamers to be used may be required.

References

1. Thomas J. Drozda and Charles Wick, eds., "Drilling, Reaming and Related Processes," *Tool and Manufacturing Engineers Handbook*, Vol. 1, 4th ed. (Dearborn, MI: Society of Manufacturing Engineers, 1983), pp. 9-78 to 9-80.
2. Thomas J. Drozda and Charles Wick, eds., "Threading," *Tool and Manufacturing Engineers Handbook*, Vol. 1, 4th ed. (Dearborn, MI: Society of Manufacturing Engineers, 1983), pp. 12-99 to 12-100.
3. R.W. Newton, "Jig for Drilling Spanner - Wrench Holes," *Machinery* (March 1951).
4. C.T. Bower, "Drop-leaf Fixture Helps Drill, Ream Closely Spaced Holes," *American Machinist (November 21, 1955).*
5. *R.W. Newton, "Jig Designed for Rapid Drilling of Air Valve Part," Machinery* (September 1950).
6. F.L. Rush, "Drill Jig for Uniformly Spaced Radial Holes," *Machinery* (September 1957).
7. H.G. Frommer, "Rotating Fixture on Angle Plate Indexes Parts for Drilling," *American Machinist* December 1, 1949).

CHAPTER 9
FIXTURES FOR TURNING AND BORING

TURNING[1]

Turning is a machining process in which a workpiece is held and rotated about its longitudinal axis on a machine tool called a lathe. Cutting tools mounted on the lathe are fed into the workpiece to remove material and thus produce the required shape. The principal surfaces machined are concentric with the longitudinal axis of the workpiece.

Turning operations are defined as the removal of material from external surfaces on rotating workpieces. Related operations on external surfaces, also performed on lathes, include facing, chamfering, grooving or necking, knurling, skiving, threading, and cutoff (parting).

Operations that can be performed on internal surfaces with a lathe include drilling, reaming, boring, threading, and recessing. Boring operations are also performed on special-purpose machines discussed later in this chapter, as well as on multifunction machines. Drilling and reaming operations are also performed on special-purpose machines and multifunction machines.

Lathes are one of the most versatile machine tools available. Most lathes have the capability for threading, and with attachments or NC, can cut tapered or contoured surfaces, both external and internal. Other operations that can be performed on some lathes include spinning, honing, polishing, and buffing.

Workpieces are held in a lathe between centers or by a chuck, collet, fixture, or faceplate. Rotation of the workpiece is accomplished by a spindle mounted in the lathe headstock. The spindle is sometimes driven directly by an electric motor, but the drive is usually through belts and/or a gear train.

Chucks or faceplates connected to the headstock spindle are used to hold short, large-diameter workpieces. Collets are used for short, small-diameter workpieces or workpieces machined on the end of a bar or tube that is fed through the spindle and parted from the stock when completed. Between-center holding is used for long workpieces and requires that center holes be previously drilled in each end of the workpiece.

For between-center turning, a center is provided on the spindle and a tailstock is mounted on the outboard end of the bedways. The tailstock is adjustable along the ways for various workpiece lengths and is equipped with a center. The center can be replaced by a drill or reamer when required for chucking operations. Steadyrests or follow rests are sometimes placed against the workpiece at positions between the centers to minimize deflection during machining.

LATHES

Many different types of lathes of varying complexity are available to suit specific applications. A number of these lathes are discussed in the next section of this chapter.

The basic requirements for any of these lathes are (1) means for holding and rotating the workpieces and (2) a means for holding and moving the cutting tools.

Lathes can be controlled manually, semi-automatically, or automatically. Major type of lathes include the following:

Engine Lathes. An engine lathe is usually classified as either a chucking type, on which workpieces are held in chucks or collets or on spindle mounted faceplates; or a center type, on which workpieces are supported between centers mounted in the head and tailstocks of the machine. Small workbench mounted engine lathes are usually referred to as bench lathes. They can usually handle parts up to 24 in. (610 mm) long and have a maximum swing ranging from 4 to 9 in. (102 to 228.6 mm).

Larger types, such as that shown in Fig. 9-1, are available with a wide range of swings and beds of any practical length. Precision lathes manufactured to very close tolerances are referred to as toolroom lathes.

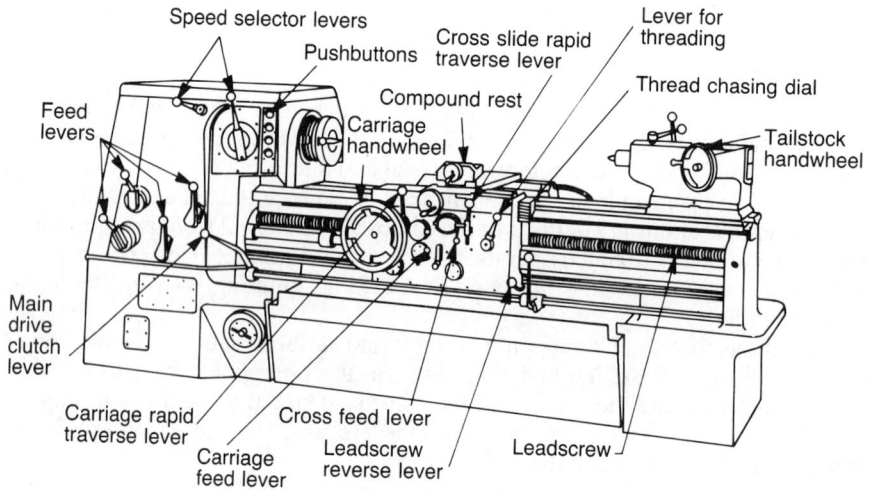

Fig. 9-1 Center-type engine lathe.

Special purpose engine lathes include:

- Gap lathes, which have a section cut out of the bed in front of the headstock to swing large diameter workpieces.
- Hollow spindle lathes, which feature enlarged, hollow headstock spindles to permit loading stock from the rear of the headstock.
- Right angle lathes (see Fig. 9-2), which feature a bed that is 90° to the axis of the spindle. These machines are also called T-lathes or facing lathes.
- Special purpose engine lathes which are built for special applications such as turning camshafts, brake drums, large rolls, etc.

Contouring Lathes. Contouring lathes are used to produce 3-D forms on workpieces by controlling the path of the cutting tool with a tracing attachment where a stylus moves over the surface of a flat template, master part, or model to control the movement of the cutting tool and thereby duplicate the required shape. Automatic tracer lathes are designed especially for this purpose. Most contour turning is now being done on NC lathes.

Horizontal Turret Lathes. The horizontal turret lathe differs from the engine lathe by the addition of a square turret mounted on the cross slide in place of the compound rest and a multisided turret mounted in place of the tailstock. These turrets can be rotated about vertical axes to bring different cutting tools into position for cutting.

Horizontal turret lathes can be hand operated, power-fed, automatic, or numerically controlled. Turret units are mainly the ram type, where the turret is mounted on a slide which moves longitudinally in a stationary saddle, and the saddle type, where the entire saddle moves along the ways. An automatic turret lathe, commonly called a single spindle automatic chucking machine is shown in Fig. 9-3. They are usually loaded and unloaded by hand with the machining cycle being completely automatic.

Single-Spindle Automatic Lathes. These machines (see Fig. 9-4) are used for high-speed production. Basically they are similar to the lathes previously discussed but permit a number of tools, which are mounted on several synchronized slides to cut simultaneously with automatic cycling.

Other turning-type machines include:

- Automatic screw machines which are designed for high production of parts from bar or coil stock.
- Multiple-spindle automatic bar and chucking machines (see Fig. 9-5) which in contrast to the single spindle machine where one turret face at a time is working on one spindle, the multiple-spindle machine has each turret or end-slide tool working on its respective spindle at the same time.
- Vertical turret lathes, which will be covered along with vertical boring machines.
- Multiple-spindle vertical automatic chucking machines (see Fig. 9-6) which feature six or eight separate vertically-mounted machining units, each of which is set up to perform a specific operation as the spindle is indexed into each station. Since all stations are working simultaneously on different operations, each spindle successively transfers a finished workpiece as it indexes through the loading station.

TOOL FORCES[2]

The following equations can be used to calculate the horsepower and power actually required by a single-point cutting tool to turn a specific material:

For U.S. customary units:

$$hp_c = (uhp)\, 12\, CV f d \tag{1}$$

For SI metric units:

$$P_c = U_p \times \frac{V}{60} \times Cfd \tag{2}$$

where:

hp_c = horsepower at the cutting tool, hp

P_c = power at the cutting tool, kW

uhp = unit horsepower

U_p = unit power

C = feed correction factor

V = cutting speed, sfm (m/min)

f = feed rate, ipr (mm/rev)

d = depth of cut, in (mm)

Unit Horsepower and Unit Power. For each different material to be machined, a measure of the power required is the unit horsepower (uhp) and its SI metric equivalent,

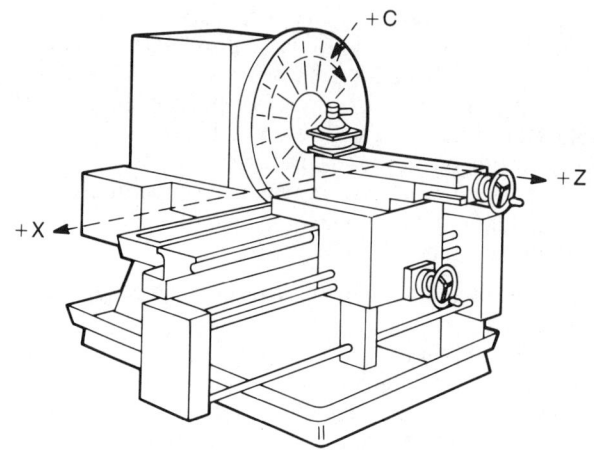

Fig. 9-2 Right-angle lathe.

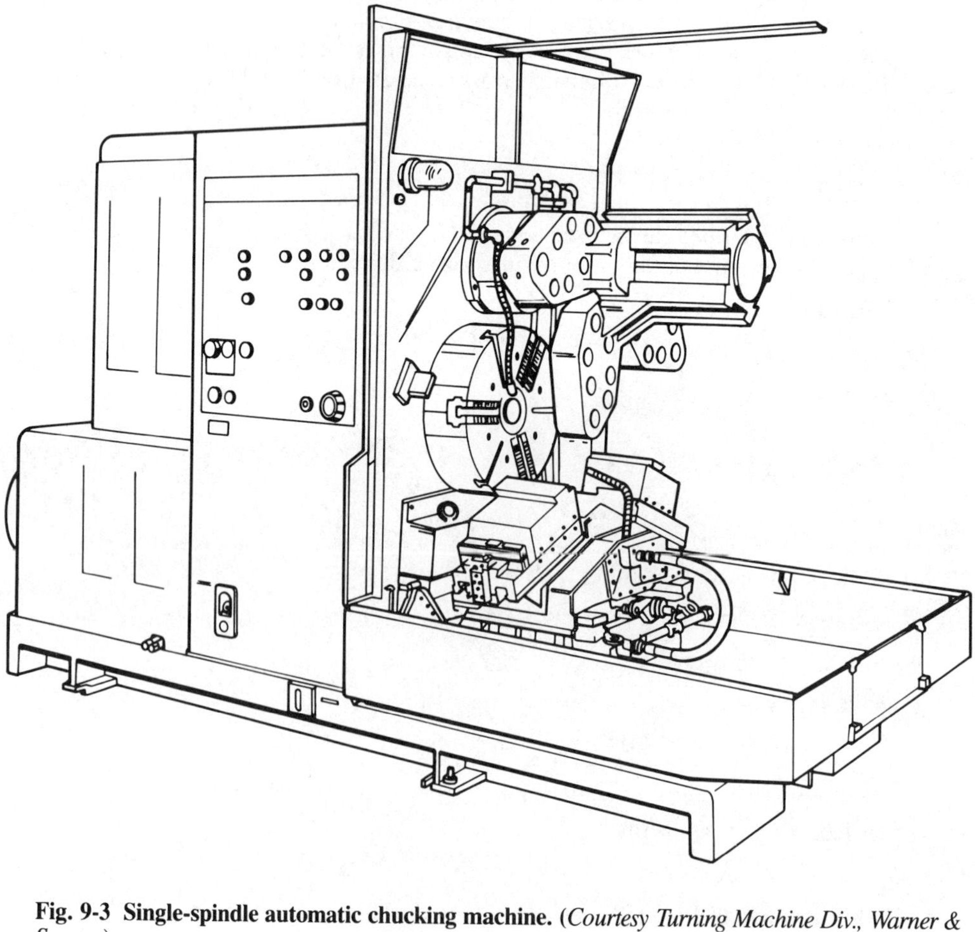

Fig. 9-3 Single-spindle automatic chucking machine. (*Courtesy Turning Machine Div., Warner & Swasey*)

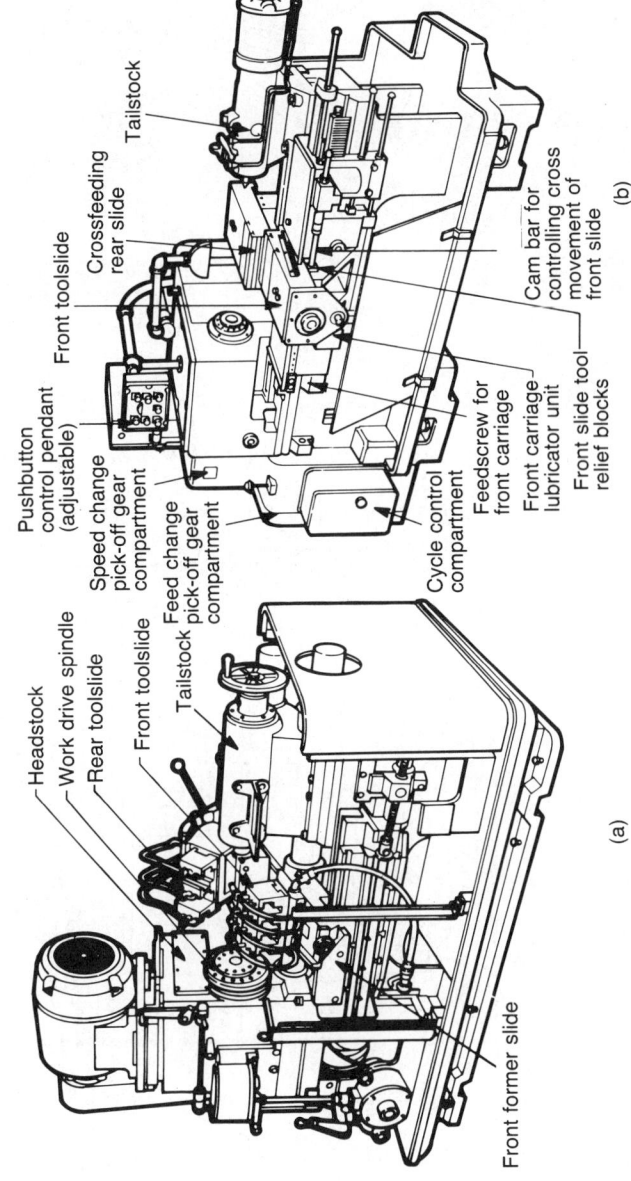

Fig. 9-4 Single-spindle automatic lathes: (a) cam feed for front slide and (b) leadscrew-fed front slide.

Headstock

Work drive spindle

Rear toolslide

Front toolslide

Tailstock Feed change pick-off gear compartment

Front former slide

(a)

Pushbutton control pendant (adjustable)

Speed change pick-off gear compartment

Cycle control compartment

Tailstock

Crossfeeding rear slide

Front toolslide

Cam bar for controlling cross movement of front slide

Feedscrew for front carriage

Front carriage lubricator unit

Front slide tool relief blocks

(b)

9-5

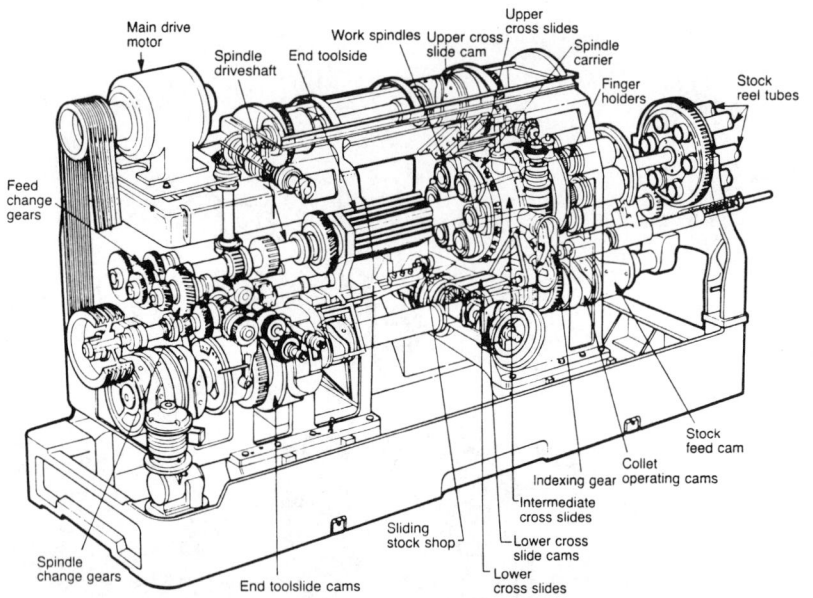

Fig. 9-5 **Six-spindle automatic bar machine.** (*Courtesy National Acme Co.*)

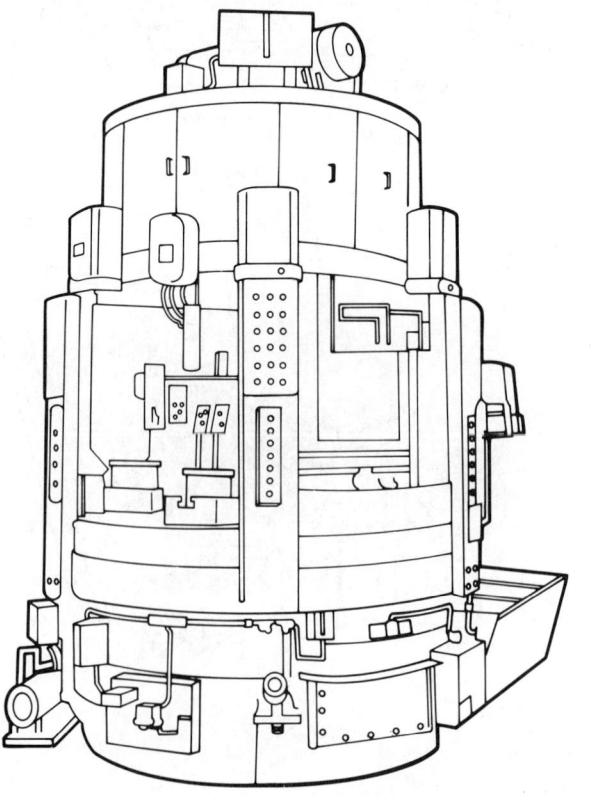

Fig. 9-6 **Multiple-spindle automatic chucker.** (*Courtesy DeVlieg-Sundstrand*)

the unit power (U_p). Unit horsepower, also called specific power consumption, is defined as the horsepower required to remove a material at a rate of one cubic inch per minute. Unit power is the power required to remove a material at a rate of 1,000 cubic millimeters, or one cubic centimeter, per second.

Values of both unit horsepower and unit power for single-point tools are determined experimentally be measuring cutting forces with dynamometers and applying the results to the following equations:

For U.S. customary inch units:

$$uhp = \frac{F_c}{396,000 \, f \, d} \qquad (3)$$

For SI metric units:

$$U_p = \frac{F_c}{f \, d} \qquad (4)$$

where:

$\quad F_c$ = cutting force, lbf (kN)

$\quad f$ = feed rate, ipr (mm/rev)

$\quad d$ = depth of cut, in (mm)

Representative values of unit horsepower and unit power for turning different materials with single-point tools can be found in source books such as the "Machinability Data Handbook". Values given are for cutting with sharp tools, and results obtained using the values should be increased to reflect the increased power needed for cutting with worn tools. The tool wear allowance should be about 10% for finishing cuts and 30% for most roughing cuts. When heavy roughing cuts are taken, such as in roll turning for which a large amount of wear is allowed before the tool is replaced, the power used may increase as much as 100% compared with the power required for sharp tools.

For multiple-tool operations, the power required by each tool must be calculated at the point in the cycle when the most power is needed. When tools are removing varying amounts of material and attachments are operating simultaneously, more than one calculation is necessary to determine the maximum power required.

Feed Rate Variations. The unit horsepower and unit power change with variations in the feed rate. Correction factors to compensate for this variation can also be found in the same source books.

Undeformed Chip Thickness. As the undeformed chip thickness is increased, horsepower required per unit of metal removal is reduced.[3] Increasing undeformed chip thickness by increasing the feed rate increases horsepower consumption, but the incremental increase in power is proportionally smaller than the incremental increase in metal removal rate. This is because extra power is required to deform the metal in the chip that passes over the tool. As chip thickness is increased, this extra power becomes smaller in comparison to the total power required.

Undeformed chip thickness depends upon the feed per revolution and the lead angle of the tool or toolholder. In a single-point tool operation with no lead angle, the undeformed chip thickness equals the feed rate. With a lead angle and a given feed, the undeformed chip thickness is reduced. When a lead angle is used, the undeformed chip thickness can be determined by the following formula:

$$t = f_r \cos c \qquad (5)$$

where:

t = undeformed chip thickness, in. (mm)

f_r = feed rate, ipr (mm/rev)

c = lead angle, degrees

Effect of Rake Angle. Within practical limits, the cutting speed, cutting tool material, and depth of cut can be considered to have little or no effect on the values of unit horsepower and unit power. Tool geometry, however, particularly the true rake angle, does affect these values. Increasing the rake angle in a positive direction results in a reduction of the unit horsepower and unit power by about 1% per degree of change. Conversely, decreasing the rake angle increases these values.

Utilization of a positive rake angle with positive or positive/negative-rake inserts can result in reductions to 10% of calculated power requirements. As the rake angle is increased, however, support for the cutting edge of the insert becomes weaker and the number of available cutting edges may be reduced. Molded-in chipbreakers on the inserts also tend to reduce power requirements. Coated inserts can also reduce cutting forces and horsepower consumption.

Mechanical Efficiency of Lathe. Additional power is required to overcome the resistance of the bearings, gears, slides, and other components of the lathe used. A measurement of this power requirement is called the mechanical efficiency—a ratio obtained by dividing the power delivered to the cutting tool by the power supplied to the machine. Most machine tool builders do not provide information on the mechanical efficiency of their machines. Estimates for single-point lathes are 90% or less for direct spindle drives, 85% or less for one-belt drives, and 70% or less for two-belt drives and geared heads.

CUTTING FORCE

Once all corrections to unit horsepower (*uhp*) or its SI metric equivalent, the unit power (U_p), have been made, the cutting force can be estimated using the following formulas:

For U.S. customary inch units:

$$F_c = 396,000\, f\, d\, uhp \tag{6}$$

For SI metric units:

$$F_c = U_p f d \tag{7}$$

where:

F_c = cutting force, lbf (kN)

f = feed rate, ipr (mm/rev)

d = depth of cut, in. (mm)

For additional information on estimating tooling forces in turning operations, it is recommended that a source book such as the "Machinability Data Handbook" be consulted.

WORKHOLDING FOR TURNING

Safe, fast, accurate, and rigid means of holding workpieces on lathes are critical requirements for successful turning. All the power required at the cutting tool must be transmitted through the workholding device to the workpiece. As a result, solid gripping of the workpiece is essential. This is especially important with the trend toward higher speed machining and the increased requirements for closer tolerances and smoother finishes.

Force requirements for safe workholding depend on many variables, including the geometry and overhand of the workpieces, workpiece materials and their properties, cutting tools used, speed and feed rates, and whether the workpiece must be kept free of marks and distortion. Formulas have been developed to calculate force requirements as they relate to safety factors, coefficients of friction, and other variables. A formula for force requirements that can be used with jaw-type chucks is presented later in this section.

The safe maximum speed for any rotary workholding device also depends on many factors. These include the workpiece size, shape, and finish; rigidity of the setup; the type and condition of the workholding device; the gripping force available at maximum speed; the type of operations performed; and the cutting tools used.

Major types of workholding devices are faceplates and fixtures, mandrels, jaw-type chucks, step chucks, collets, and occasionally, magnetic and vacuum chucks. The workpiece, lathe, and tooling used often dictate the type of workholding device that can be employed. In many cases, however, the use of several types is possible and judicious selection is required.

GRIPPING THE WORKPIECE

Regardless of the type used, the workpiece should be gripped on the largest diameter practical. This assures a favorable relationship between the gripping and cutting diameters to accommodate torque more easily. Workpieces should also be gripped as close to the faces of chucks as possible.

The moments of force (torque) around the center of these diameters are proportional to the length of their lever arms (radii) and can provide a mechanical advantage for the gripping member over the cutting tools.

The workpiece must be gripped on a section which must remain rigid during and after machining. An example of this is the fixturing of a multiple-grooved V-belt sheave shown in Fig. 9-7. The sheave was located on a stub mandrel and clamped with a draw rod (1), ring (2), and C-washer (3) against three support pads (4).

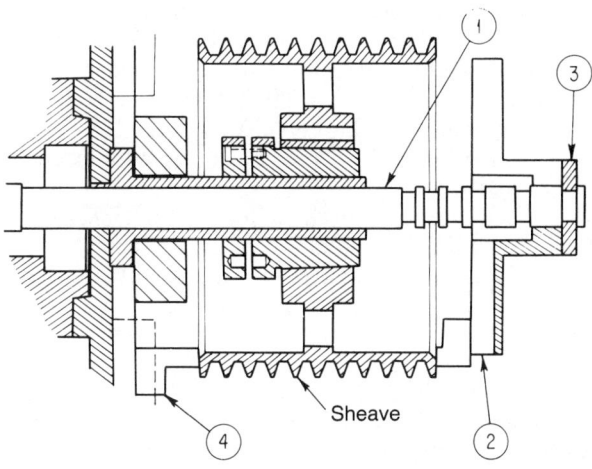

Fig. 9-7 Lathe fixture for turning OD and grooving operation.

Clamping the rim of the sheave between three support pads and a clamping ring normally should keep the workpiece securely gripped during the OD turning and grooving operation. However, the sheave slipped during the grooving operation, damaging the finished sides and frequently damaging the grooving tools.

Slipping did not occur until after at least three grooves had been cut; the rim of the sheave, which before grooving had formed a rigid gripping surface, became resilient after the cut. Larger air-clamping forces distorted the previously cut grooves. A solid pin locating in one of the cored holes in the web of the sheave provided a satisfactory driver for the sheave.

Magnetic and Vacuum Chucks.[4] While magnetic and vacuum chucks are more commonly used on machine tables for grinding and milling, they are also employed occasionally for light-duty turning operation. These operations are generally of the precision type and involve shallow cuts. Vacuum or magnetic chucks can be designed to hold many different odd-shaped parts and often eliminate problems of distortion when fragile thin-walled components are turned. A discussion of these chucks is included in Chapter 3.

Magnetic Chucks. Permanent magnetic and electromagnetic chucks are used on lathes. They are now available with higher holding-power ratings and the capability of providing gripping to all edges of the chucking surface. Controls to vary the holding power are available on some electromagnetic units.

Advantages of magnetic chucks include rapid loading and unloading, minimum distortion, no marking of the workpiece surfaces, and less chance of interference with the cutting tools. When required, demagnetizers are used to reverse the magnetic field and eliminate residual magnetism from the workpieces, tools, and machine components.

Vacuum Chucks. Rotating faceplate-type vacuum chucks usually require a rotating union to be installed in back of the chuck, extending through the machine spindle and connecting to an air exhaust line. In some cases, the connection can be made to a rotating union mounted through the face or faceplate of the chuck. The nondistorting, nondamaging holding force of such chucks makes them suitable for thin or fragile parts.

Clamping pressure available with vacuum chucks is generally about 12 psi (83 kPa). The chucks are built with porous, pin hole, or grooved plates. Portions of the chuck face not covered by the workpiece are masked or blocked to eliminate leakage. Cone-shaped or domed vacuum chucks have been built for secondary operations on spun parts or workpieces that have been contour machined.

Locating the Workpiece. Satisfactory lathe operations on the workpiece also require that the workpiece be suitably located. Often the location must be taken from a rough bore, and a spring-loaded tapered plug similar to that shown in Fig. 9-7 may be used. The plug is tapered and is free to move axially in the fixture body, thus compensating for variations in the rough hole. Standard or special chuck jaws, machined or ground, depending upon whether they are soft or hard, may be used for locating and gripping on a previously machined diameter.

Locating the workpiece axially in the chuck requires suitable supports which can be either adjustable or of a fixed height. In many instances, the locating surface can be a step on the chuck jaws. It is advisable to avoid the use of surfaces on the chuck jaws for locating the work axially, because these surfaces must move with the opening and closing of the jaws. If the location is to be taken from a rough surface, this jaw motion frequently causes undesirable axial motion of the workpiece while it is being chucked.

Location should be taken from three surfaces, and these surfaces should be kept as small as possible for minimum cleaning. On special fixtures using a ring for locating the workpiece axially, the ring should be relieved to reduce the contact area to three small areas, thereby providing three-point location in one plane and reducing the amount of surface requiring cleaning.

For ease of loading the workpiece, locating pins and studs should have tapered pilots and locating surfaces that are as short as possible. If two locating pins are required, one must be diamond shaped with its narrow width placed to accommodate allowable variations in the location of the two locating holes in the workpiece. To reduce handling time, ejectors may be incorporated to remove the workpiece from the locating pins.

Thin Workpieces. Fragile workpieces or sections under heavy cutting pressure require support. If locating is from a previously machined surface and support is required at particular points, adjustable supports may be provided in addition to the separate or critical locating and supporting surfaces.

Certain parts are so fragile that they can only be successfully located radially with the very lightest amount of pressure. These parts must be held with clamps designed to hold the workpiece in an unstressed position during machining.

Frail workpieces can present vibration problems due to cutting stress. Neoprene-lined dampening rings, pressure pads, or spring-actuated plungers can dampen induced vibrations.

Problems Induced by High Speeds. The new cutting materials and machine tools with higher spindle speeds present some problems to the fixture designer.

Vibration in the rotating assembly may originate in the machine itself, the chuck or fixture, the jaws, the bolts holding the chuck or fixture to the spindle, the bolts holding the jaws to the fixture bases, or the workpiece. Vibrations originating in the machine or chuck may be dampened or reduced by the machine-tool or chuck manufacturer or by the machine repair department.

The bolts that hold the chucks and fixtures to the machine spindle and the chuck jaws to the jaw bases may vary somewhat in weight and should be brought to the same weight to decrease or prevent vibratory forces, particularly when the chuck or fixture is frequently removed. Special chuck jaws should be of the same weight to minimize torsional vibrations therein.

Irregularly shaped workpieces must be counterweighted for the same reason. Size variations in a run of castings or forgings preclude exact imbalance correction for each workpiece with one counterweight.

Individual corrections should be made for each of the above named sources of vibration so that when a changeover is made from one holding device to another or from one workpiece to another, the source of any new vibration can be easily found.

Centrifugal forces may cause workpiece distortion and lowered chucking pressure in the ordinary lever-operated power chuck.

This loss of chucking force is not always serious since most pneumatic or hydraulic cylinders have more capacity than is actually required. However, when chucking a frail part, loss in chucking force with high spindle speed becomes important because the necessary increase in chucking pressure to overcome centrifugal force may distort the workpiece when it is not revolving. In cases of this kind, a power chuck having a self-locking type of operating mechanism is required.

BETWEEN-CENTER TURNING OPERATIONS[5]

Many workpieces, particularly shorter parts, are turned on chucking-type lathes without the use of centers. This is done with chucks, collets, or other workholding devices, or by bolting workpieces or fixtures directly to the faceplates of lathes. Some faceplates are equipped with jaws for rotating large-diameter workpieces. Many other workpieces, particularly longer ones, require support on one or two lathe centers with at least one steadyrest in between.

Turning on centers requires that conical center holes be drilled in the ends of the workpieces prior to the operation; these holes are often ground for precision operations. The end of the workpiece adjacent to the lathe tailstock is always supported by a center mounted in the tailstock. The opposite end of the workpiece can be gripped by a chuck or collet, or it can be supported by a center mounted in the headstock spindle.

Types of Centers. Some of the various centers, both live and dead types, used on lathes are illustrated in Fig. 2-50. Headstock centers always rotate with the lathe spindles and workpieces. Tailstock centers may be of the live type, rotating with the workpiece, or the dead type, stationary.

Rotating the Workpiece. Workpiece rotation by means of a headstock-mounted chuck or collet provides a rigid setup and minimizes any chance of chatter during machining. More precise results, however, can often be obtained by supporting the workpiece between two centers.

Rotation of a workpiece held between centers is accomplished with a slotted driver plate, such as the one shown in Fig. 9-8a, mounted on the spindle nose of the lathe. A lathe dog, several types of which are shown in Fig. 9-8b is secured to the workpiece, and the bent end (tail) of the dog is positioned in one of the slots in the driver plate. A compensating chuck, with either a solid or spring-loaded center, can also be used to rotate workpieces between centers.

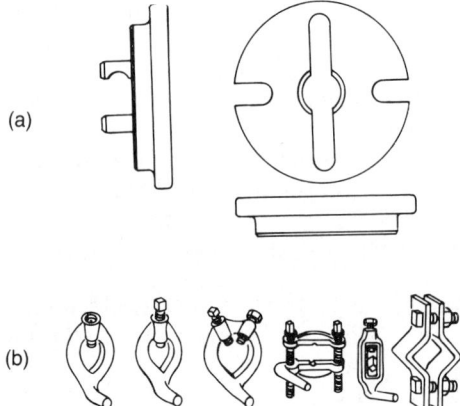

(a)

(b)

Fig. 9-8 (*a*) **typical driver plate and** (*b*) **various types of dogs used to rotate workpieces held between centers on a lathe.**

Face Drivers. When the design of the workpiece permits, exerting driving power on one face of the workpiece can increase productivity. Face drivers permit machining the entire OD of a part in one clamping, as well as turning at high speeds. A high degree of accuracy is maintained because the position of the workpiece does not have to be changed.

One type of face driver (see Fig. 9-9) consists of a driving head and a locating shank that fits on the spindle nose of a lathe. The driving head contains a spring-loaded center, drive pins, and a compensating device that permits each drive pin to adjust to irregularities on the face of the workpiece.

As the lathe tailstock applies axial force to the workpiece, the center of the driver retracts slightly against its spring pressure to allow the chisel-edged drive pins to bite into the end face of the workpiece. During cutting, torque is increased and the pins bite deeper into the face for positive clamping. Some workpiece faces have holes and the driving pins enter the holes.

MANDRELS

Mandrels, or arbors for holding work to be machined, are of two types, plain and expanding.

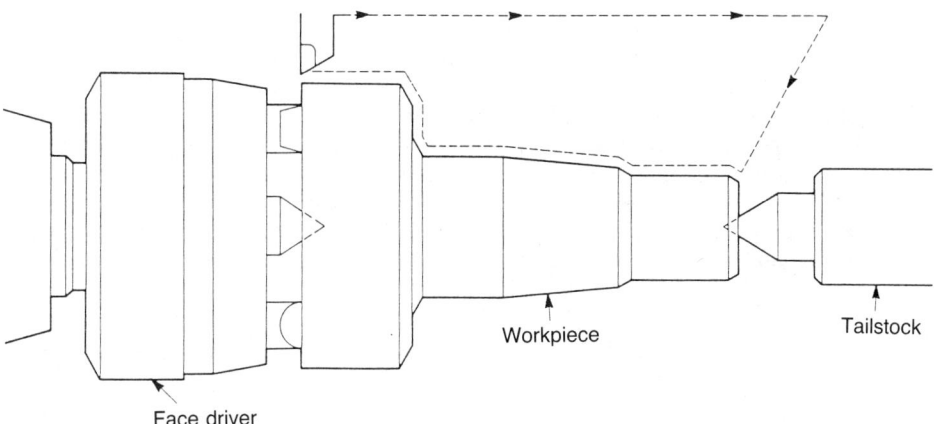

Workpiece

Tailstock

Face driver

Fig. 9-9 Face driver permits turning entire OD of workpiece mounted between centers in one clamping.

Plain mandrels (see Fig. 3-75) have a taper of about 0.006 in. per ft (0.5 mm/m) and are forced into the work. Because of possible wear when driving mandrels on and off workpieces, they are generally suitable for low production only.

Expanding mandrels for locating and in many cases for driving from the bore of a workpiece can be of many designs.

Wherever possible, expanding mandrels should be provided with a positive driver to help drive the workpiece. Locating shoulders and pins must be incorporated to locate the workpiece longitudinally in the machine.

Use of Mandrels.[6] Pin-type mandrels are used for gripping cast, forged, or rough bores. Three or six pins or shoes move outward to centralize and grip the parts. These pins are usually power operated through a drawbar that is attached to the mandrel to push the pins, by cam action, through openings in the body of the mandrel. Figure 9-10 illustrates an expanding mandrel with serrated shoes for gripping a 34 in. (864 mm) long workpiece.

Inner shank (rear)
Outer shank
Serrated shoes (front)
Draw bolt Inner shank (front)
Serrated shoes (rear)
Workpiece

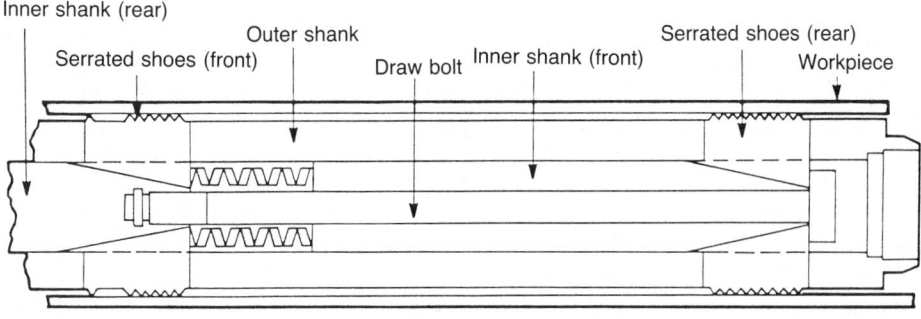

Fig. 9-10 Expanding mandrel and serrated shoes for gripping long, thin-walled workpieces. (*Courtesy Kennametal Inc.*)

Expanding bushing type mandrels are generally used in smooth or finished bores. They usually provide better concentricity (end-to-end) than solid plug mandrels because the bore tolerance does not affect the accuracy as expansion centralizes the workpiece. One type of expanding-bushing mandrel consists of a tapered shaft assembly, threaded on one end, over which various-sized slotted sleeves with a corresponding taper can be fitted to suit a number of workpieces. Rotation of a clamping bolt in the end of the shaft forces the sleeve up the tapered surface on the shaft to grip the workpiece. Drive can be a problem with this type of mandrel, and the use of a drive pin is suggested when possible if heavy cuts are to be taken.

Mandrels are not limited to workpieces having finished or smooth bores. If the ID is a rough cast surface having a dimensional variation wider than that which can be handled by an expanding sleeve, a segmented sleeve, such as the one shown in Fig. 9-11, is used. Segmented sleeves can handle ID variations of ⅛ in. or more; on large workpieces, variations up to ¾ in.. are possible. Segmented sleeves consist of three individual segments held together with spring bands. These sleeves may have serrated segments, or they can be used with end locators.

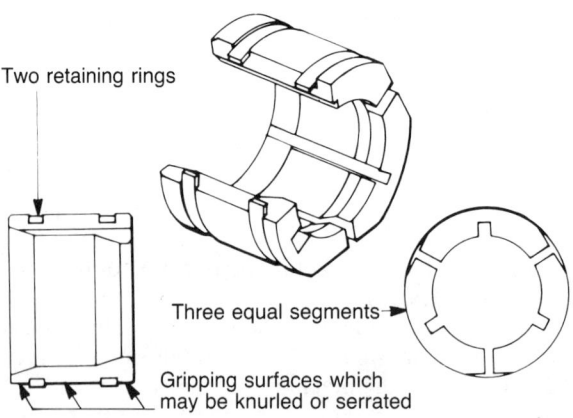

Two retaining rings

Three equal segments

Gripping surfaces which may be knurled or serrated

Fig. 9-11 Three-segment sleeve for handling ID variations. (*Courtesy Kennametal Inc.*)

If the end locating surfaces of workpieces have previously been machined square with the bores to be gripped, locators that are flat and square are used. If not, compensating locators must be used. The locators or end stops are sometimes serrated to increase the driving force.

When the ID is relatively small compared to the OD of a workpiece, expanding mandrels can be used with auxiliary clamp supports for increased rigidity. An expanding mandrel and a set of outboard clamps (see Fig. 9-12) is used for rigid holding and positive positioning of gear blanks. In the unit illustrated in Fig. 9-12, an inner threaded locknut forces the expanding sleeve up the mandrel. To simplify removal of the OD support for workpiece mounting, a plate with a swing-out C-clamp is employed. After the workpiece is mounted on the mandrel, the threaded locknut is tightened and locked and the end-clamps are applied.

The drawbar-operated expanding mandrels shown in Fig. 9-13 were designed to reduce changeover time in machining a family of 17 splined hubs which were being machined from 16 different steel forgings. Changeover time was reduced from one hour to approximately one minute with these mandrels by enabling all 17 parts to be held on the same mandrels; the parts are located so that the tooling does not have to be moved to run the various hubs.

Four mandrels with post locators (see Fig. 9-13*a*) for holding rough workpieces, and four with snap-on end locators for machined faces, *b*, are run on a New Britain 88-S 8-spindle chucker simultaneously. By using a double index on the machine, two dissimilar parts can be run at the same time.

The construction and functional principles of the clamping elements of one particular system (the Ringspann® system) are shown in Fig. 9-14. For better understanding of

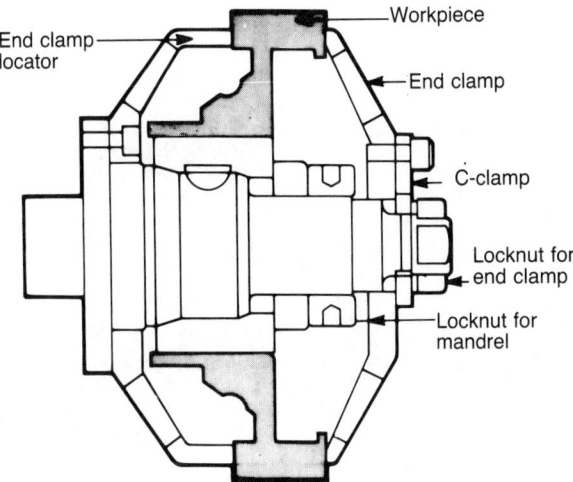

Fig. 9-12 Expanding mandrel and outboard clamps for holding a gear blank. (*Courtesy Kennametal Inc.*)

the overall system, the elements used for chucking are shown along with those used for mandrels. Included are the following elements:

- Discs, *a*, which are shallow-tapered rings of a special hardened spring steel, that are slotted alternately from inside and outside, making them highly flexible. The unique slotting system permits a wide range of flexibility in the taper angle and diameter which characterize the highly advantageous properties of this radial clamping element.
- The bonded disc assembly, *b*, which is made up of a number of discs that are carefully packed and bonded together by a highly resilient rubber compound. This produces a compact component which is easily fitted and impervious to the type of fouling normally encountered in machining work.
- The clamping mandrels with taper collets, *c*, which have a high rigidity especially for small diameters. The design of the collets assures perfect contact between the collet and component when in a clamped position. Even small diameter mandrels transmit high torques.
- The diaphragm elements, *d*, which create the clamping movement by the elastic deformation of the special material used to manufacture them. The workholding devices of the diaphragm type guarantee the highest level of repeatability and accuracy due to the solid one piece construction of the body and clamping element.
- The flat register chuck, *e*, where the inner diameter of the reinforced outer rim is reduced by an axial force. The workpiece is centered, radially clamped, and at the same time pulled against the true-running locating shoulder.
- The basket type chuck, *f*, functions on the same principle. It is employed where the workpiece has to protrude further into the chuck.
- The flat register arbor, *g*, functions in reverse to those of Fig. 9-14*e*. The outside diameter is increased by distortion. The workpiece is centered in its bore, radially clamped firmly and pulled against the true-running shoulder.
- The short clamping elements, *h*. The principle of these elements is similar to that shown in Fig. 9-14*g*. They offer the advantage of clamping into the shortest recesses and blind bores.

The true running accuracy of these elements can be below 0.0004 in. Workpieces are centered and aligned automatically by being clamped into position against the wobble

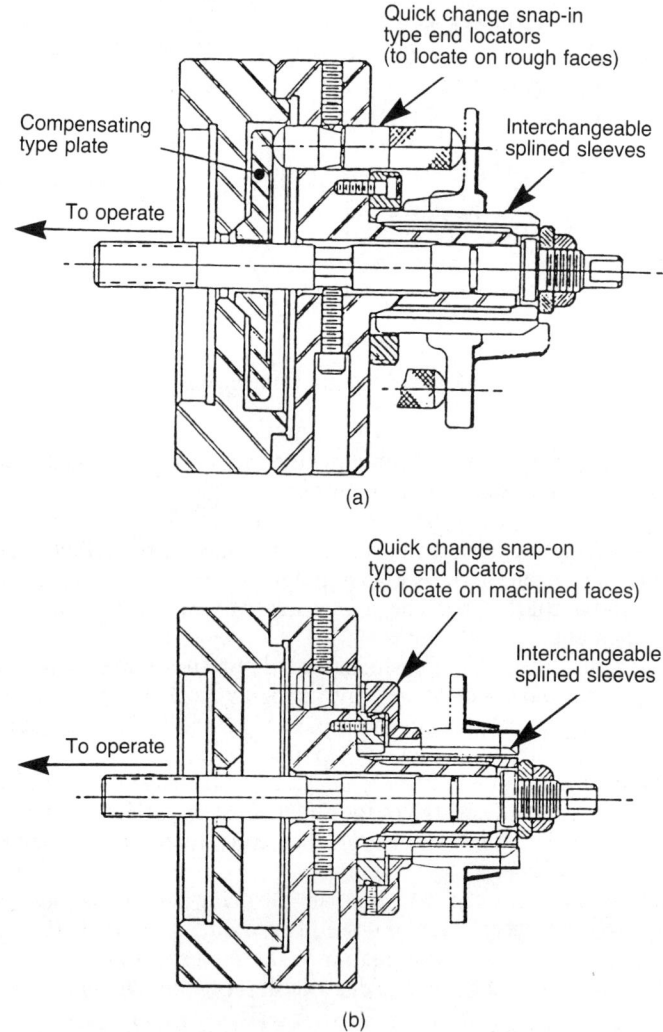

Quick change snap-in
type end locators
(to locate on rough faces)

Compensating
type plate

Interchangeable
splined sleeves

To operate

(a)

Quick change snap-on
type end locators
(to locate on machined faces)

Interchangeable
splined sleeves

To operate

(b)

Fig. 9-13 Flexible ID grip mandrels with quick-change locator posts. (*Courtesy Kennametal, Inc.*)

free locating surface by the clamping elements. Elements locate the entire circumference of the workpiece eliminating the risk of triangular or rectangular distortion at the clamping point with "positive pullback".

Mandrels using this system are shown in Figs. 9-15 and 9-16.

The mandrel shown in Fig. 9-15 can be used to hold a complete family of similar workpieces which vary in length and diameter by moving the right hand disc set and interchanging the slotted bushing.

The mandrel shown in Fig. 9-16 is used to center and clamp the two halves of a divided gear housing against each other for collective machining.

Threaded Mandrels. Threaded mandrels, both ring and plug types, provide means of locating from threads on workpieces. Holding is done by running the workpiece onto the threaded locator and against a stop. The stop can be made retractable to facilitate unloading. Threaded mandrels can be mounted to chuck faces, and the jaw movement used to position and retract the top.

Some additional mandrels are shown in Chapter 3 and in Figs. 9-17 thru 9-26. Included are the following:

A Roller-Actuated Expanding Sleeve Mandrel. This mandrel (see Fig. 9-17) is expanded by turning the actuating cone clockwise. The spiral motion of the rollers, held in a cage at an angle to the center line, forces the cone toward a positive stop as though it were threaded. A wedging action between the tapers expands the sleeve. This tool can be used for turning and similar operations on a lathe, as well as for grinding and inspection. The mandrel shown has a flange for faceplate mounting but can be designed to mount between centers on a lathe or grinder. Figure 9-18 shows the same type of construction for clamping on an external surface.

An Expanding Mandrel for Internal Gears. The mandrel shown in Fig. 9-19 will locate on or near the pitch diameter of an internal gear or spline. The splined part is slipped over the pins and rotated. The pins move along cam lobes gripping the part on or near the pitch diameter. The pins can also be moved outward, and they are accurately located on the periphery of the expanding sleeve. These mandrels can be designed for faceplate or between-centers mounting.

A Collet-type Mandrel. The mandrel of Fig. 9-20 is reversed collet, that is, a collet which grips the workpiece from the inside surfaces. It has all the advantages of a collet. It has one member which grips and releases the inside of the workpiece with the same action as a collet which grips and releases the outside of a part. When its stiff fingers are twisted half a turn between the taper and the mandrel portion, a reversal of the gripping motion occurs. Since the motion is now outward, the mandrel portion opens and grips the workpiece from the inside. The gripping force increases as the pull on the collet mandrel increases. Mandrels are ground to an accuracy of less than 0.001 in. runout.

In view *a*, the mandrel is collapsed. In view *b*, it is expanded to the same diameter as originally ground. View *c* shows the mandrel expanded to a diameter greater than that ground, which is not to exceed 1/32 in. At this position the high points run true.

This mandrel may be used on any lathe that uses a collet. Diameters may range from ½ to 4 in.

A Mandrel for Machining Cams. The machining of cams, throws, and other eccentric parts is facilitated by the mandrel shown in Fig. 9-21. Workpieces are reamed to fit the mandrel and have broached keyways to hold them in position. Centers are machined in the end of the mandrel and the end collar according to the eccentricity required. The parts are held on the mandrel by the lockout. The pins through the end collar are a close fit into the slot in the mandrel.

It is possible to machine parts of different eccentricity by changing to different centers, and the mandrel can be made long enough so that several cams can be machined at the same time.

A Precision Expanding Mandrel. To eliminate the need for an excessive number of similar tools, a mandrel with adjustable jaws, similar to that shown in Fig. 9-22, can be used to obtain a greater bore and bearing range.

Principal components of this mandrel are the three sliding jaws, the retaining springs, the tapered mandrel, and the sliding-lock sleeve. When the workpiece is located on the jaws, the sleeve and parallel jaws slide up inclined planes on the mandrel until the part is firmly retained. The sleeve is then locked by the setscrew to retain the jaws and part during the machining operation. The jaws slide in a groove in the arbor to keep them parallel.

A Mandrel for Large-diameter Rings. Precision between-center turning or cylindrical grinding of the OD of large-diameter rings can be done with the mandrel illustrated in Fig. 9-23.

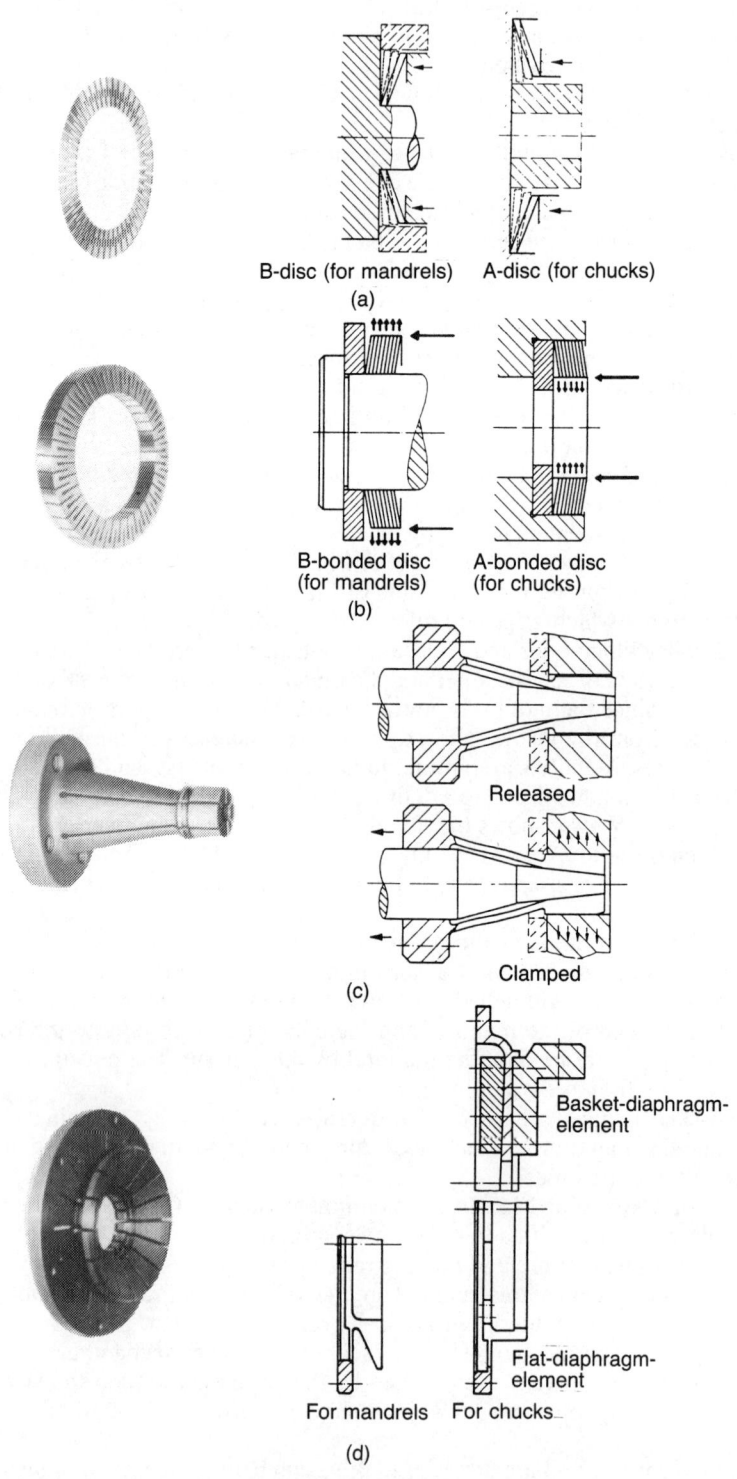

B-disc (for mandrels)   A-disc (for chucks)

(a)

B-bonded disc   A-bonded disc
(for mandrels)   (for chucks)

(b)

Released

Clamped

(c)

Basket-diaphragm-
element

Flat-diaphragm-
element

For mandrels   For chucks

(d)

Fig. 9-14 Clamping element construction and functional principles. (*Ringspann® Clamping Elements, courtesy Powerhold, Inc.*)

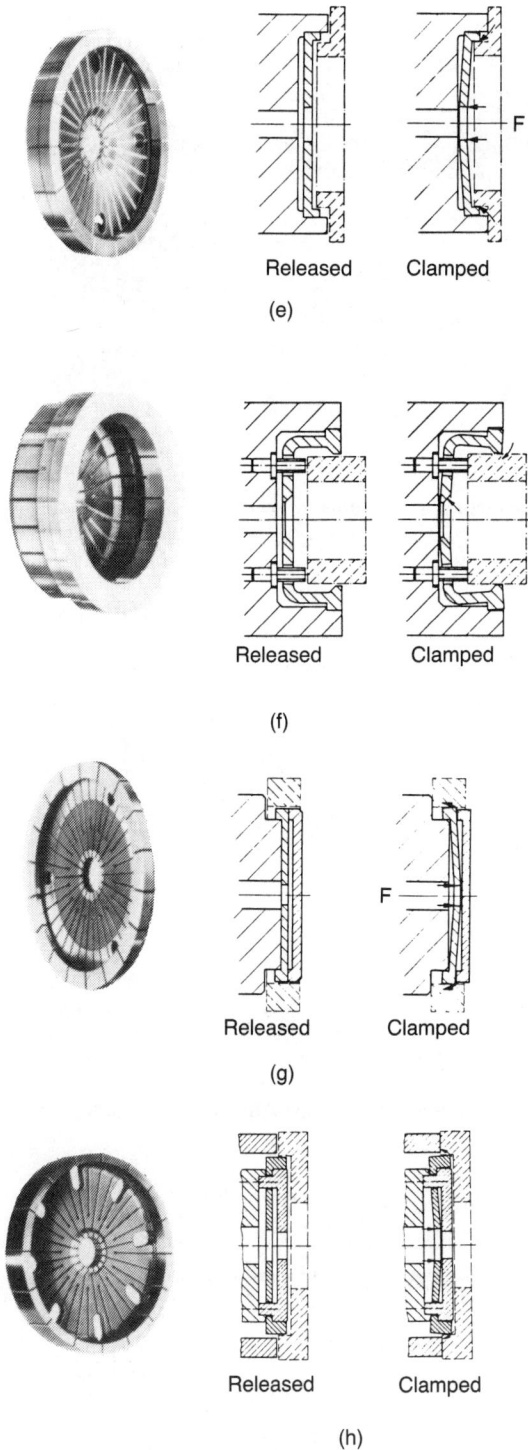

Released   Clamped

(e)

Released   Clamped

(f)

Released   Clamped

(g)

Released   Clamped

(h)

Fig. 9-14 (*Continued*)

9-19

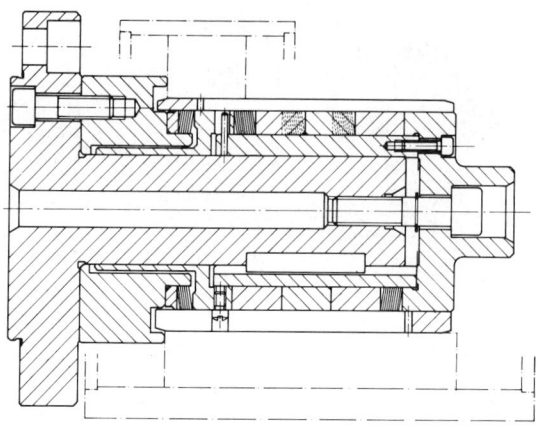

Fig. 9-15 Mandrel for clamping stators of various lengths. (*Ringspann® Mandrel, courtesy Powerhold, Inc.*)

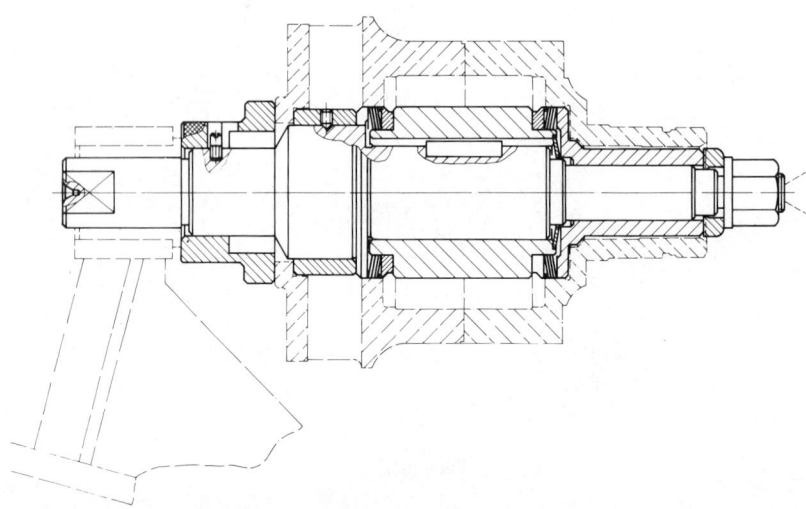

Fig. 9-16 Mandrel for clamping a divider gear housing for machining. (*Ringspann® Mandrel, courtesy Powerhold, Inc.*)

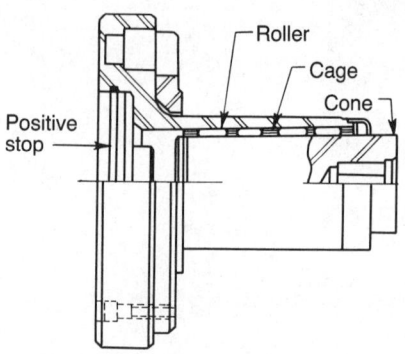

Fig. 9-17 Roller-actuated expanding-sleeve mandrel. (*Courtesy Schully-Jones & Co.*)

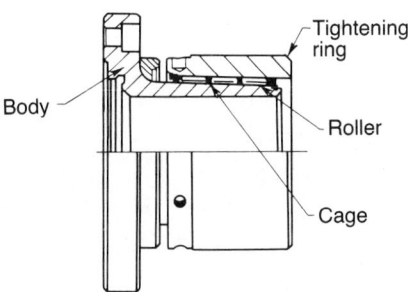

Fig. 9-18 Roller-actuated mandrel for clamping on the outside surface of a workpiece. (*Courtesy Schully-Jones & Co.*)

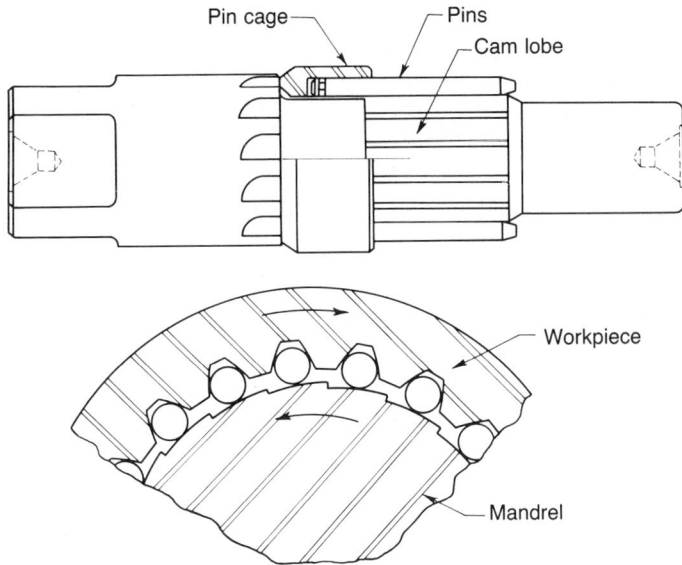

Fig. 9-19 Expanding mandrel for internal gears, splines, and serrations. (*Courtesy Schully-Jones & Co.*)

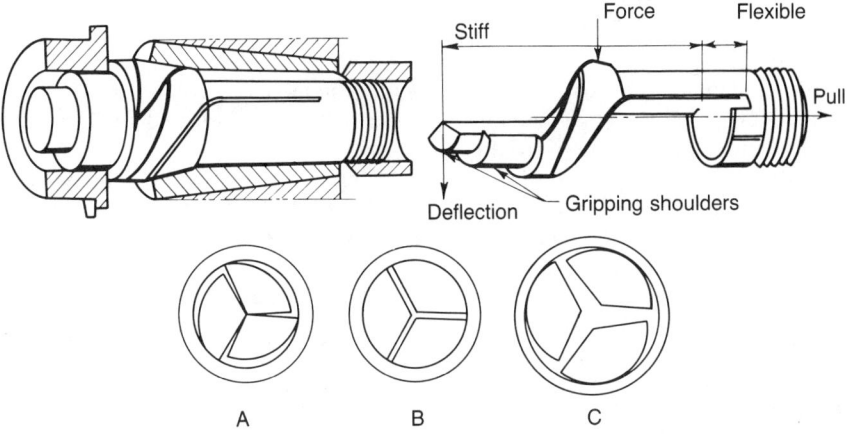

Fig. 9-20 Collet-type mandrel which grips on inside surfaces. (*Courtesy E. Westberg Corp.*)

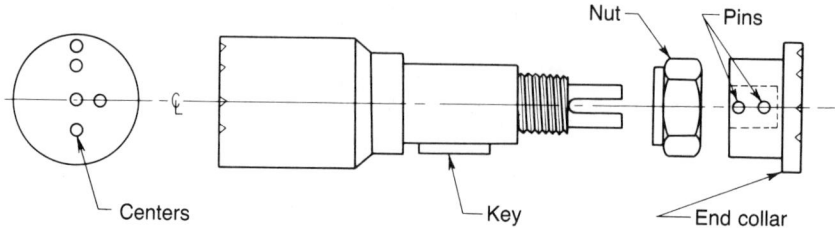

Fig. 9-21 Mandrel for machining cams.[7]

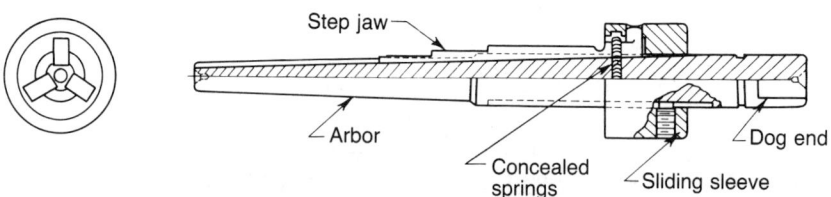

Fig. 9-22 Parallel sliding-jaw mandrel.[8]

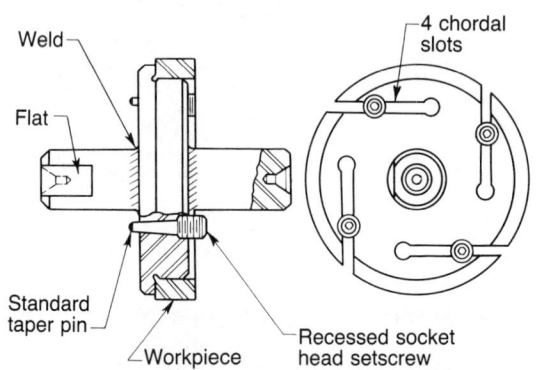

Fig. 9-23 Mandrel for large diameter rings.[9]

A round blank of the proper size is bored and fitted to a central shaft, and the two are welded together. After stress relieving, the weldment is center-drilled and finished to the required diameter for a snug fit in the workpiece.

The layout of the four chordal slots is made, but before they are machined, the holes for taper pins and setscrews are drilled, taper-reamed, and tapped. The setscrews should be located near the outer end of the slot for effective clamping.

When the setscrews are tightened against the standard taper pins in the tapered holes, the segments between the slots will expand outward and tightly grip the workpiece. To release the workpiece, the setscrews are backed off and the small end of the hardened taper pin rapped with a mallet.

On some jobs, the taper pins and setscrews may be replaced with standard taper-pipe plugs.

A Mandrel for Threaded Parts. One of the main problems in doing secondary work on internally threaded parts is to hold the work securely and concentric with the threads and to permit its easy removal from the work holder.

The surface of the OD of the part shown in Fig. 9-24 is polished and will not allow the use of a gripping device which might mar it. The mandrel is of soft tool steel and turned to fit the taper in the lathe spindle. It is finish-turned; its threads are chased; and a shoulder is faced, against which the workpiece bears after it is screwed on the mandrel. The threaded end is slit along the center line and a hole for a setscrew drilled and tapped through one side. A cup-point setscrew seats against a steel ball to open and close the mandrel.

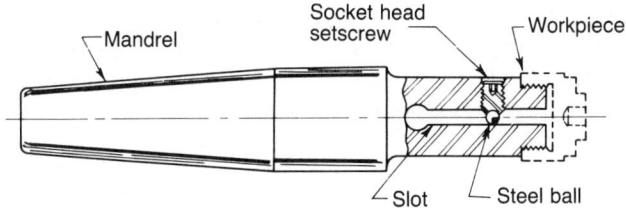

Fig. 9-24 Mandrel for threaded parts.[10]

A Differential Expanding Mandrel. When hollow castings having stepped bores are machined on the exterior, it is often essential that uniform wall thicknesses be maintained. One way of locating a casting internally with a differential expanding type of mandrel is illustrated in Fig. 9-25. Two sets of locating members contact the interior walls of the casting. They operate independently of one another and adjust themselves automatically to size variations and steps in the bore.

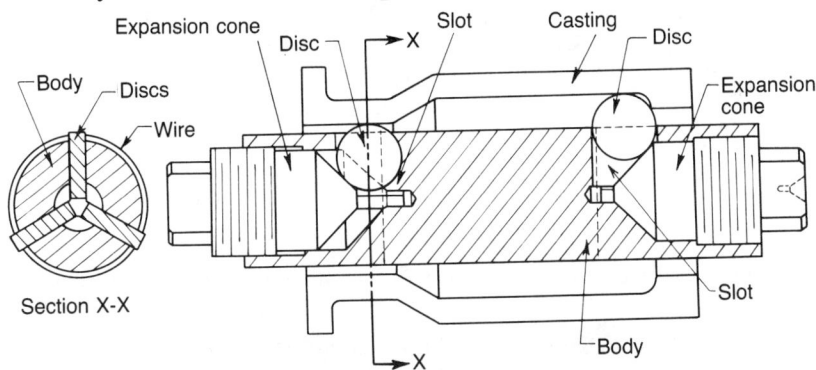

Fig. 9-25 Expanding mandrel for stepped bores.[11]

The mandrel body is a solid-steel cylinder with recesses bored in each end to accommodate expansion cones. Each cone has right-hand threads along about half of its straight length for engagement with a corresponding internal thread in the mandrel recess. A cylindrical guide portion on each cone ensures positive radial location. The cones are case-hardened, and their outer ends are center-drilled for mounting between lathe centers. Flats are machined on the projecting ends for engaging with a wrench.

Three hardened-steel discs form the expanding members which engage the interior walls of the component. The discs slide without clearance in radial slots machined in the mandrel body. They are pushed outward by the expansion cones. The discs are prevented from falling out of the slots when the mandrel is unloaded by a ring of spring wire which passes through a small hole drilled through each disc.

Disc-shaped locators have the advantage of ease in manufacture. Even in the maximum expansion position, they are adequately supported by the mandrel body. The grip of the discs on the work surface is sufficient to prevent the work from slipping under heavy turning cuts.

In use, the lathe driving dog is attached to one of the expansion cones. The rotary driving action will tend to tighten the cone and force out the locating members to press firmly on the interior walls of the castings. The drag of the tailstock center on the right-hand expansion cone has a similar tightening effect.

Since the gripping members expand independently, they adapt themselves readily to internal surfaces. When gripping such a workpiece, there is a tendency for heavy cutting-tool pressure to slide the workpiece axially. This effect can be minimized by providing some positive form of stop for the workpiece. This might be a sleeve slipped over the mandrel and bearing at the left-hand end on the driving dog.

A Ball Expanding Mandrel. A ball expanding mandrel (see Fig. 9-26) provides a positive centralizing method of registering accurately through the center of a part, regardless of variations in size or taper in its bore.

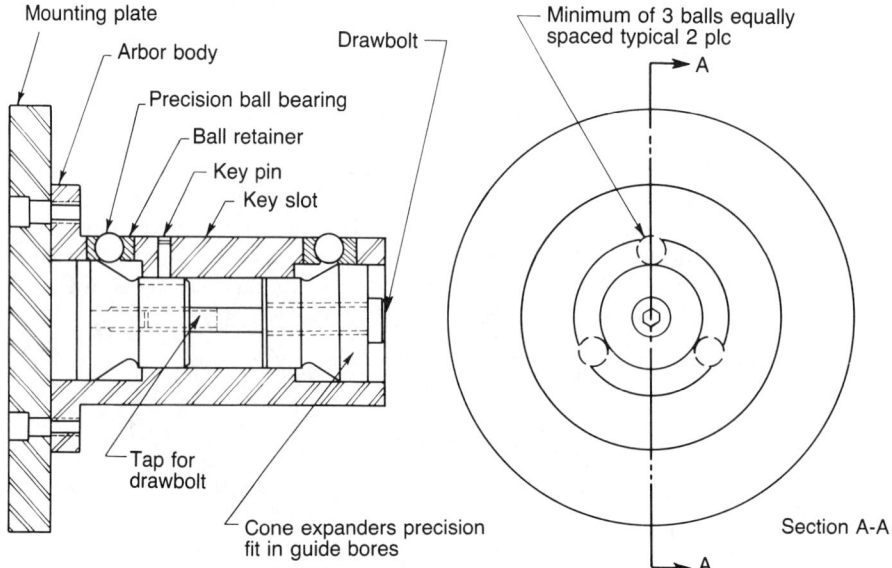

Fig. 9-26 Double expanding arbor compensates for variation in bore diameter. (*Courtesy Commercial Air Products, Inc.*)

It is well adapted for locating in two bores of different sizes, provided the space between bores can accommodate the cylindrical cones and that the diameters of the radially spaced balls and of one cylindrical cone correspond to those of the work-piece bores.

The cones have a register diameter at each end having a minimum diametrical clearance which allows a sliding fit. The precision balls are retained in cages that are located without any linear error.

As the cones are drawn together by the drawbolt, the balls are forced outward. As one set of balls engages the part, additional tightening moves the other set until they have engaged the part. The part is automatically centralized at both ends in relation to the center line of the bore(s) of the part. It is recommended that the ball cages and cylindrical cones be hardened to prevent indentation and wear.

Steadyrests and Follower Rests.[12] Long, slender workpieces are often supported for between-center turning by steadyrests or follower rests (see Fig. 9-27). When work is mounted between centers, a general rule-of-thumb is that any part having a length-to-diameter ratio of 10:1 or more requires some kind of support. More than one rest is frequently used for very long parts or precision operations. Steadyrests are also used to support the outer ends of chucked workpieces for facing, boring, and other operations.

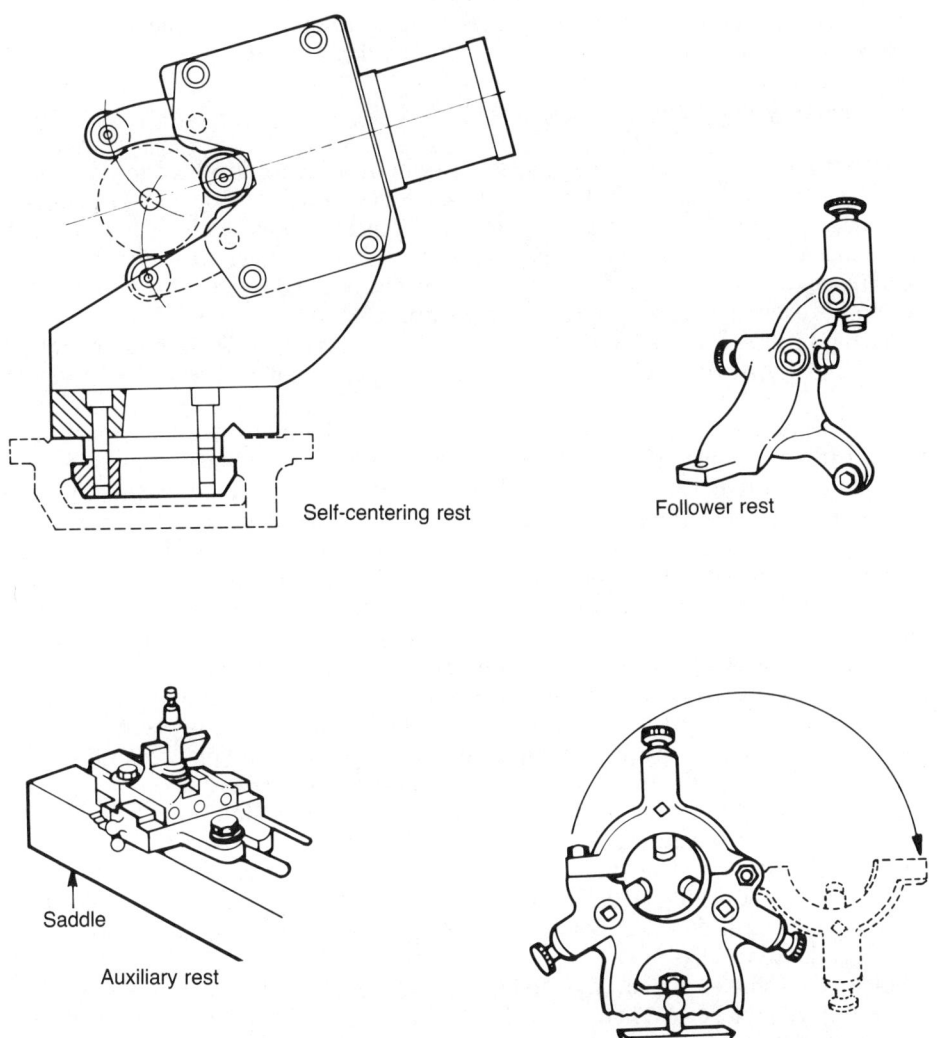

Self-centering rest

Follower rest

Saddle

Auxiliary rest

Steadyrest

Fig. 9-27 Typical steadyrest, auxiliary rest, and follower rest used to support long workpieces on lathes.

Steadyrests can be clamped to the lathe bed at any desired position along the workpiece length. Follower rests are attached to the carriages of lathes and support the workpieces at points opposite the cutting tools. Auxiliary or full-swing rests mount on the forward wings of lathe saddles for turning to the maximum diameter capacities of the machines.

Steadyrests can be the self-centering or independent-jaw type and can be hand or power operated. They generally consist of a frame containing adjustable or telescoping jaws or rollers to provide three-point bearing. The frame of a steadyrest is usually hinged on one side, allowing the upper half to swing open to facilitate loading and unloading workpieces. Some are designed to automatically open and close, thus permitting turning operations to pass the rest without interference.

Surfaces on which the rests are to ride should be smooth or machined prior to the lathe operation, before the jaws or rolls are brought to bear against the surfaces. On most NC lathes, the steadyrest can be controlled by the NC unit.

COLLETS FOR LATHES

Collets, also called collet or bar chucks, are workholding devices used to grip workpieces or stock—including cold-drawn and centerless ground bars having smooth or machined surfaces—on smaller size lathes and other machine tools. Advantages of collets include high holding power because of their large contact area with the stock, the absence of clamping marks normally left by chucks, and relatively low cost. Also they do not lose their gripping force due to centrifugal effects.

Standard collets are available with a concentricity of 0.001 in. (0.03 mm) measured 1 in. (25.4 mm) from the faces of the collets. Special collets are made to closer accuracies, with concentricities within 0.0002 in. (0.005 mm). Diameters machined on a workpiece held in a collet will be concentric with each other and as accurate as the full indicator movement of the machine spindle. Concentricity of the machined diameters with respect to the chucking diameter will equal that of the collet FIM.

A collet is usually seated directly in the spindle of a lathe. In operation, the collet opens under its own spring tension to allow bar stock to be fed through it or workpieces to be placed in it. The collet is then closed to securely grip the stock or workpiece.

Collets are hollow steel cylinders generally having slots extending along most of their length, with a tapered OD at the closing end and, in some cases, ID threads at one end for mounting stock stops, and OD threads at the opposite end for connecting to a draw bar. They are available in fractional, decimal, letter, number, and metric sizes for holding round, square, rectangular, hexagonal, and special-shaped stock. While most collets are made to hold stock on-center, they can be designed to hold stock off-center any desired distance, as is required for eccentric or odd-shaped workpieces.

Serrated, taper hole, step, plug chuck, and extended-nose collets provide additional means to grip stock. So-called emergency collets have a pilot hole that can be drilled or bored to required size. This design is useful for short production runs or when exact collet sizes are not readily available. The three basic collet styles used for metalcutting are stationary, push out, and draw in. These styles are illustrated in Fig. 9-28, the draw-in collet shown has interchangeable serrated pads.

Stationary Collets. Since these collets do not move longitudinally in the spindle, changes in workpiece lengths caused by variations in stock diameter are virtually eliminated. A typical stationary collet is shown mounted in a spindle in Fig. 9-29.

The collet seats directly against a spindle nose cap to prevent outward movement of the collet. Surrounding the collet is a sleeve that is threaded into a push bar. After the bar stock is fed through the spindle and open collet to the required length, or after a workpiece has been chucked, the sleeve is pushed outward against the mating tapered surface of the collet head by the push bar. This forces the collet to close and grip the stock.

Push-out Collets. These collets, such as the one illustrated in Fig. 9-30, can provide accurate control of part lengths if the bar stock is fed up to a turret-mounted stock stop as the collet closes. After the bar stock has been fed through the open collet, the push bar or plunger pushes the tapered nose of the collet against a mating tapered bore in the spindle nose cap. This action forces the collet to close around the bar stock and hold it in place for machining.

Draw-in Collets. With this design, the collet is pulled into the spindle by a drawbar. This action forces the tapered OD of the collet head to press against the tapered ID of the spindle nose cap, thus causing the collet to close and securely grip the stock.

For use in automatic screw machines a feed finger is threaded into a feed tube, as

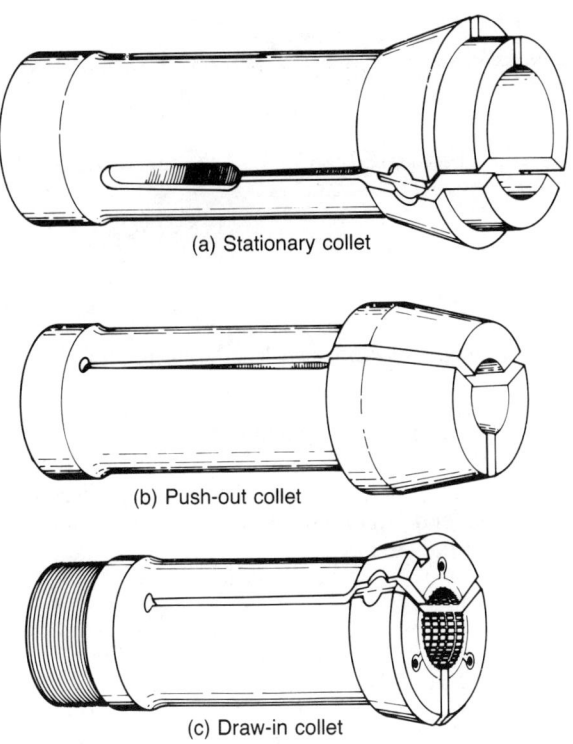

(a) Stationary collet

(b) Push-out collet

(c) Draw-in collet

Fig. 9-28 Three basic styles of collets are: (*a*) stationary, (*b*) push-out, and (*c*) draw-in.

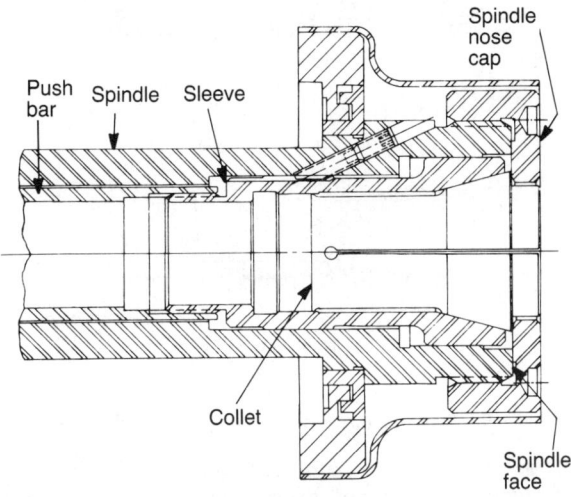

Spindle
nose
cap

Push
bar   Spindle   Sleeve

Collet

Spindle
face

Fig. 9-29 Typical stationary collet shown mounted in a spindle, minimizes changes in workpiece lengths.[6]

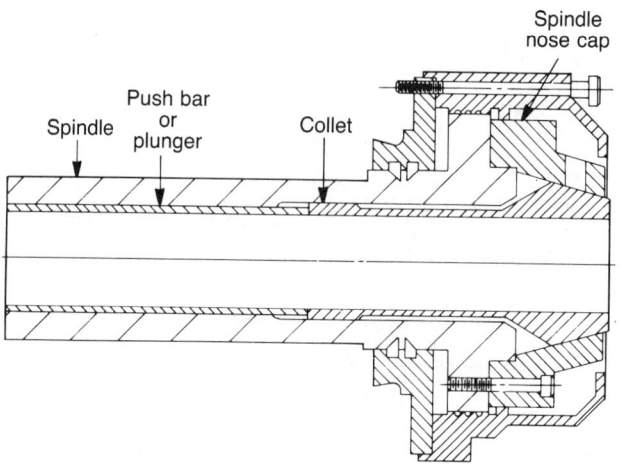

Fig. 9-30 Push-out style collet provides accurate length control because stock does not pull away from the stop.[6]

shown in Fig. 9-31. As the feed finger grips the bar stock, the feed tube pushes the feed finger, which in turn pushes the stock through the open collet to the required length. The collet is then drawn back into the spindle by the drawbar, forcing the collet to close. Both the feed tube and the feed finger automatically retract in the spindle, and the feed finger regrips the stock for the next cycle.

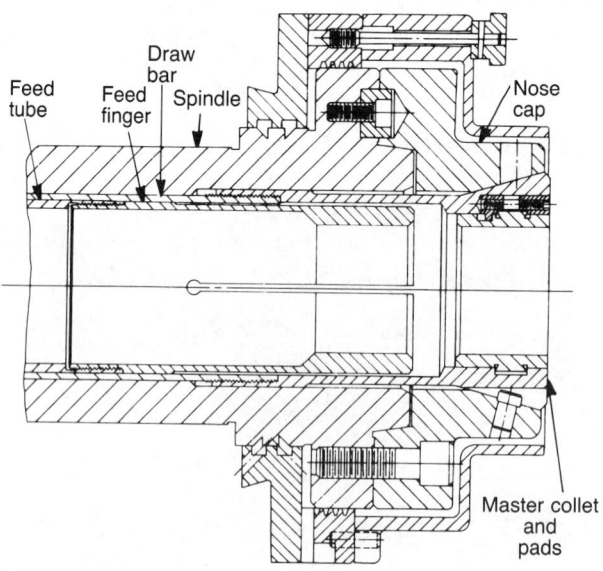

Fig. 9-31 Draw-in collet equipped with a feed finger threaded into a feed tube.[6]

Draw-in collets operate for other lathe-type machines by the same principle as for automatic screw machines. Instead of using a feed tube and feed finger, however, the collet is threaded into a drawbar that is connected to a collet closer. Opening and closing of the collet is either manually or pneumatically controlled by the machine operator. Bar stock can be automatically fed through the spindle by several types of bar feeding devices.

Minimizing Stock Pushback. When a draw-in collet is used, stock pushback can be caused by an oversized or worn collet; a collet with a scored or galled ID; bent, scored, or nicked bar stock; too deep a cut; too fast a feed rate; improper cutting tools; or incorrect collet closing pressure.

An excessively undersized collet (see Fig. 9-32a) will cause the collet to grip the stock at six points on the innermost gripping area of a three-split collet. An oversized collet (see Fig. 9-32b) will provide only three points of contact, toward the face of the collet. Both of these conditions will allow stock to push back and also result in bar whip.

Pushback may be corrected by using a collet having the same size as the stock to be machined, as shown in Fig. 9-32c. If the problem of pushback still persists, a serrated extra-spread collet, 0.003-0.005 in. under size, may provide a solution.

When performing secondary operations (chucking semi-finished workpieces), stock stops may be threaded into some draw-in collets to help prevent stock from pushing back into the collet. This method helps maintain closer length tolerances.

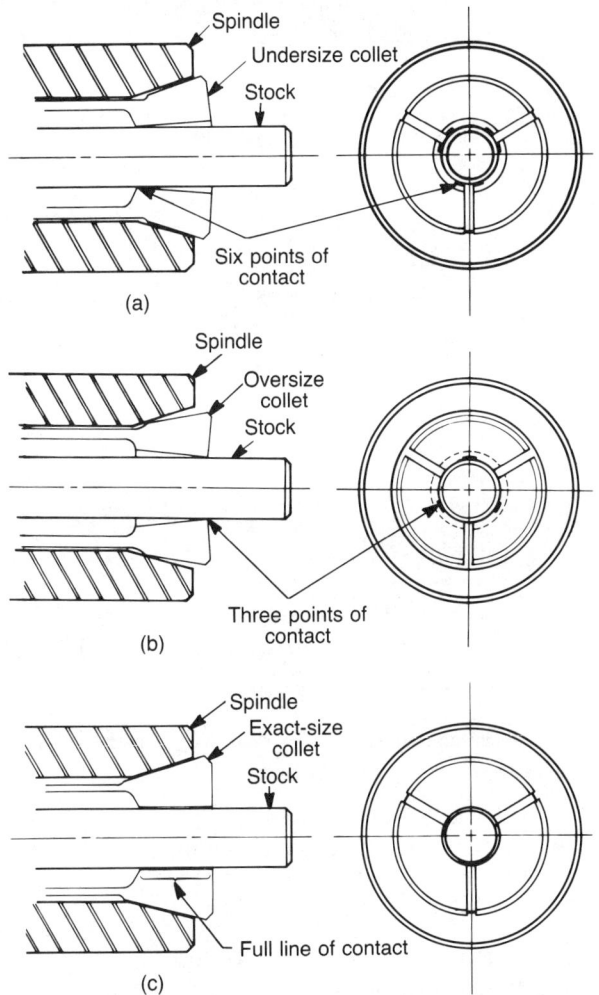

Fig. 9-32 Influence on clamping of (*a*) undersized collet, (*b*) oversized collet, and (*c*) exact-sized collet.

9-29

Minimizing Stock Pullback. Draw-in collets usually have a 1:3 ratio variation between part diameter and length. For example, if there is 0.001 in. variation in the OD of the stock, a 0.003 in. variation in workpiece length will result when the collet closes, even though the stock is located against a stop in the collet.

Workpiece lengths can be controlled to less than 0.001 in. for secondary operations on 5C spindle machines by using Dead-Length collets made by Hardinge Brothers, Inc. These collets allow shoulders and faces to be machined to precision length regardless of variations in the OD of the stock.

As illustrated in Fig. 9-33, the stop body of a Dead-Length collet is threaded into an inner collet which is spring-loaded into an outer collet. To maintain accurate location, the inner collet is keyed to the outer collet. As the collet assembly is mounted into the machine spindle, the inner collet becomes spring loaded against the spindle face to prevent the possibility of axial and end movements of the workpiece. Workpieces are loaded into the inner collet and located against a shoulder or adjustable solid stop.

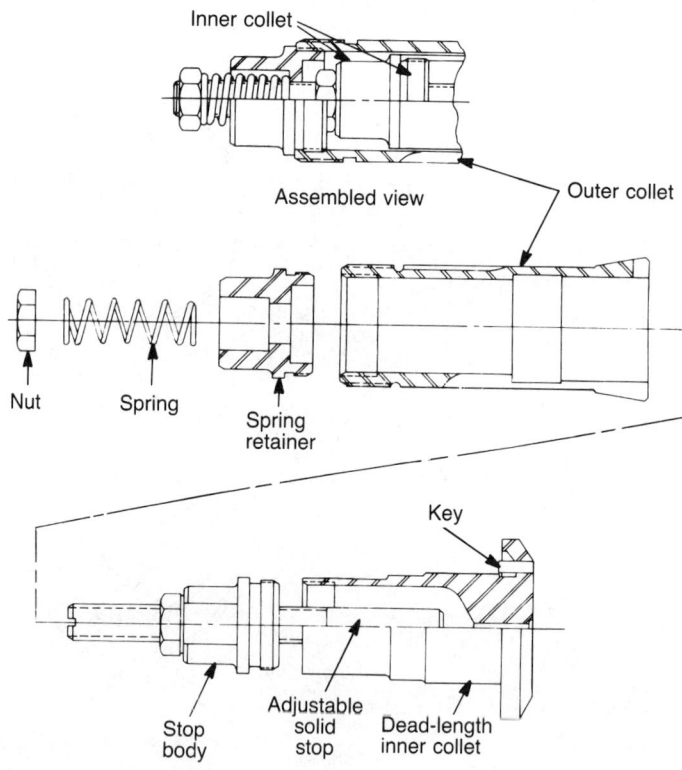

Fig. 9-33 Exploded and assembled views of a dead-length collet used for close control of workpiece length.[6]

Step Chucks. Step chucks are collets used on draw-in spindles to hold workpieces that are beyond the collet capacity of the chucking machine. The chucks are available in standard sizes in both regular and extra-depth capacities. Emergency step chucks, such as the one shown in Fig. 9-34, can be machined to the exact size required by the machine operator.

Closers are always used with step chucks. As the step chuck is drawn into the spindle, the tapered OD on the chuck presses against a corresponding taper in the bore of the closer to grip the workpiece.

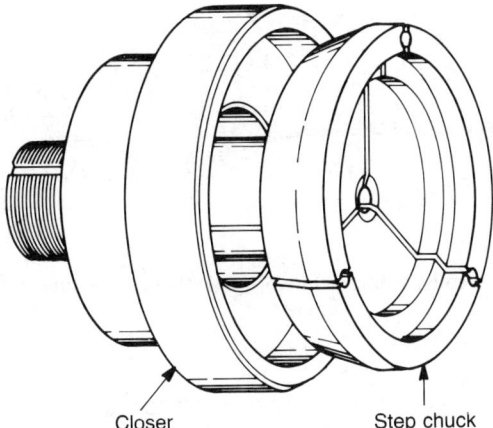

Closer   Step chuck

Fig. 9-34 Emergency step chuck for draw-in spindle can be machined to hold a large workpiece.

Built-in Air Actuation. Air-powered collet chucks are available that incorporate a chuck and air-actuating device in an integral unit mounted on the spindle nose of a lathe. No alterations to the machine are required. A double-acting air cylinder actuates a ball-cam mechanism to open and close the collet. Air is supplied through a standard filter-regulator-lubricator, and actuation can be automated or by a manually operated valve.

One air-actuated workholding device made by the Jacobs Manufacturing Co. uses Rubber-Flex collets consisting of hardened steel inserts molded in a synthetic rubber compound. Flexibility of the rubber matrix gives each collet a gripping range of ⅛ in. and only 11 collets can handle round bars ranging from 1/16 to 1⅜ in. When mounted on a true spindle, runout measured at the nose of the chuck does not exceed 0.0007 in. The chucks can be operated at speeds to 5,000 rpm.

Expanding Collets. These workholding devices provide internal gripping of workpieces requiring secondary machining operations. The shoulders, faces, and OD's of workpieces having previously machined bores can be machined concentric and square when the workpieces are held in this way. If an expanding collet is long in relation to its diameter, it may be necessary to support the outer end of the collet with a tailstock center or steadyrest.

Some expanding collets, such as the one illustrated in Fig. 9-35, are furnished with machinable pads that can be turned to required size in the machine spindle. This provides concentricity as accurate as the runout of the machine spindle. The shoulder faced on the pads locates the workpieces for length control when repetitive parts are machined to the same length.

Two expanding (OD) collets are used for the mandrel-type lathe fixture illustrated in Fig. 9-36. This fixture (made by Drewco Corp.) holds a cylindrical casting measuring about 5⅛ in. diam. × 10-5/16 in.(262 mm) long. Before the OD of the casting is machined and both ends are faced, the ID is finish bored in one setup while the casting is held on this fixture. The fixture is held at one end by engaging the spindle nose on the lathe and at the other end by the lathe tailstock engaging an insert in the end cap of the fixture.

Both collets in this fixture are keyed to a mandrel body to assure precise concentricity. Actuation is through the action of an expander cap threaded to the drawbar of the lathe. As the drawbar retracts, it forces the collets and a slider to the left. When the left-hand collet contacts a conical surface on the mandrel, both collets are expanded to

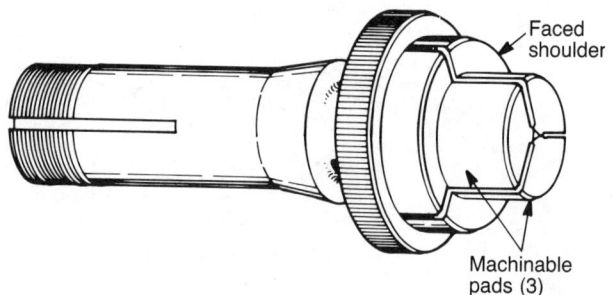

Fig. 9-35 Expanding collet with machinable pads that can be turned to required size.

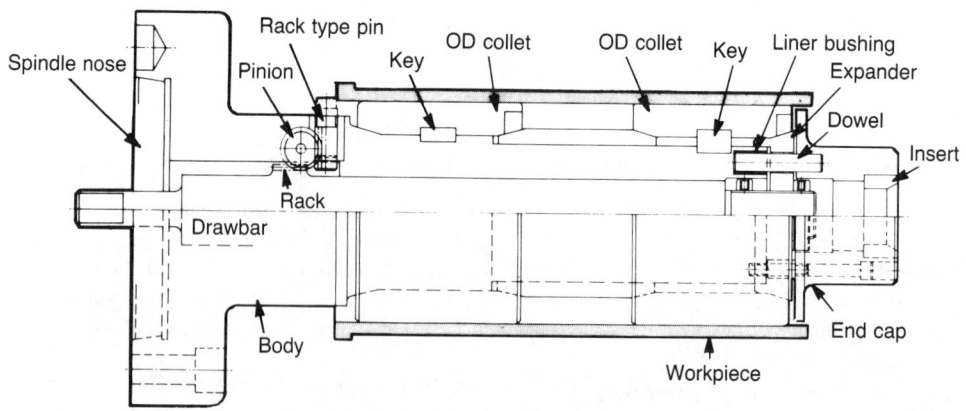

Fig. 9-36 Mandrel-type lathe fixture that has two expanding collets for holding castings between centers.

securely hold the workpiece.

A rack is machined on both the drawbar and the work locating pin of the fixture, and a pinion engages both racks. As the drawbar retracts to expand the collets, the rotating pinion withdraws the pin from contact with the workpiece, thus permitting facing of the locating surface.

Details of some additional collet applications for lathes are shown in Figs. 9-37 thru 9-46. Descriptions are as follows:

The collet chuck of Fig. 9-37a, available in a wide range of sizes, is an attachment fastened to the spindle of a lathe and holds a slotted spring collet. It is used primarily on toolroom lathes and for low production work. Tightening of the handwheel moves the operating sleeve back against the collet and closes it to grip the work. Collet chucks of the handwheel type are also available for use with Rubber-Flex chucks. A faster-operating version substitutes a hand lever for the handwheel. The lever moves a closing collar which actuates a series of cam levers that force the collet into the tapered closing ring. This collet can be closed and opened without stopping rotation of the machine spindle. A specialized version (see Fig. 9-37b) uses a steel spring collet with opposed closing tapers and with two sets of spring slots, each slotted from opposite ends. It is closed by a tapered sleeve moving toward the machine spindle and also forcing it against a companion sleeve. The sleeves, in closing the collet at both ends, provide a uniform and parallel action, ensuring close concentricity of work and spindle.

Extra-capacity collets grip workpieces of larger sizes than can be accommodated by standard collets. They are usually used only for second-operation work. Figure 9-38a shows a typical extra-capacity collet of the drawback type. The back end fits the spindle

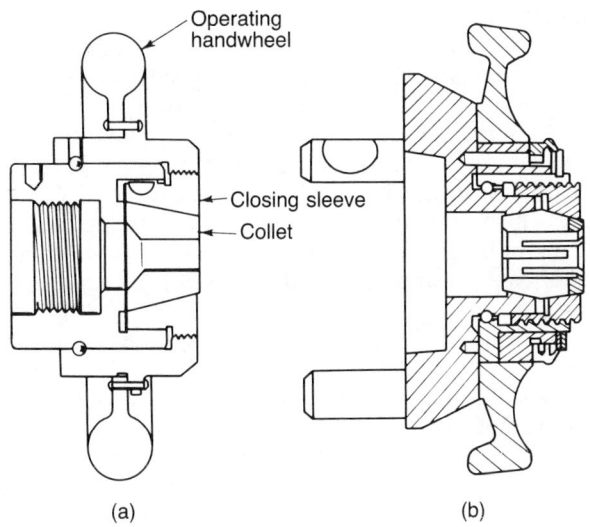

Fig. 9-37 Collet chucks for mounting on a lathe spindle nose.

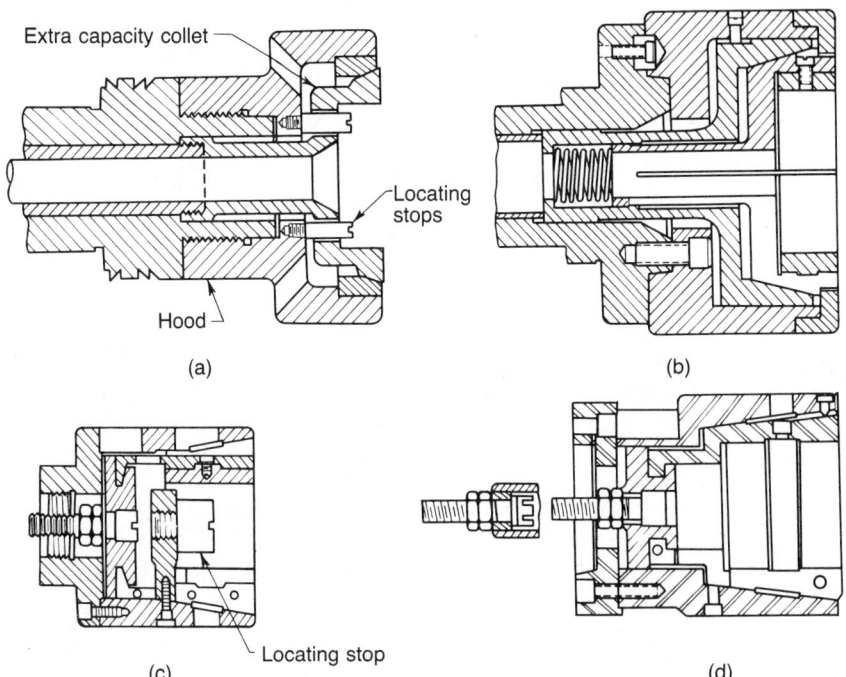

Fig. 9-38 Extra-capacity collet chucks.

of the machine and is threaded to receive the drawbar which retracts to close the collet. The oversize gripping portion has tapered closing surfaces that fit a mating taper in the closing ring pressed into its hood which is threaded on the machine spindle. Also illustrated are stationary locating stops for accurately locating the part longitudinally as the collet and work are drawn back during the closing operation.

Figure 9-38*b* shows an extra-capacity collet of the stationary type which is closed by the forward movement of a sleeve actuated by the push-out mechanism in the machine. The collet is similar to a master collet since it is arranged to hold interchangeable pads. Collet and closing sleeve are contained in a cylindrical retainer fastened to the spindle nose of the machine. To retain the collet, a ring-shaped hood is threaded to the forward end of the retainer.

Figure 9-38*c* shows a skeleton collet for second-operation work in turret lathes. It is a drawback type of three-sectional master collet mounted in a cylindrical housing which is threaded on the spindle and cored out for chip disposal. Closing is usually done by an air cylinder which permits a longer than usual closing stroke, and it is consequently suitable for holding rough work which varies considerably in diameter. As shown, this collet can be arranged with a fixed stop to locate the workpiece longitudinally.

Another type of collet chuck for turret lathes (see Fig. 9-38*d*) operates on the drawbar principle and incorporates a three-section split collet to which sets of pads are fastened with machine screws and accommodates various sizes of workpieces. It has a housing which holds the collet segments. The offset portion at the rear of the collet segments fits into the groove of a cylindrical yoke fastened to the drawtube. The matching tapers on the inside of the housing and outer periphery of the collet segments provide parallel closing action when the drawtube retracts. Coiled springs are used to separate the collet segments and to keep them from collapsing in the open position. The housing is fastened to an adapter ring that fits the spindle nose of the machine.

Figure 9-39 shows a spring-ejector stop collet designed specially to accommodate one particular workpiece. It requires no adjustment as do the adjustable general purpose stop collets available commercially, and its use for repetitive high-production work reduces machine setup time. The stop body is fastened to the back of the standard collet with two opposed pins. The body projects into the collet to allow its forward face to position the workpiece for the turning operation. With the workpiece loaded in the collet, the spring plunger recedes completely into the stop body. For effective ejection of the workpiece, the spring plunger normally travels within 1/32 in. (0.79 mm) of the face of the collet.

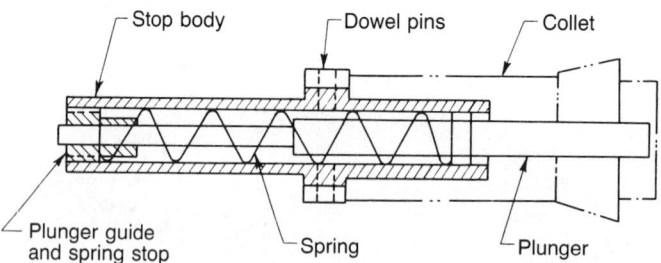

Fig. 9-39 Stop and ejector assembly for screw-machine collet. (*Courtesy Western Electric Co., Inc.*)

Figure 9-40 shows a stop collet for second-operation work on long parts when the portion of the part extending into the machine spindle is longer than the collet. It consists of a standard spring collet and a tubular body fastened to the collet with flat-head screws. A cylindrical plug fastened to the rear of the tubular body holds a setscrew that longitudinally positions the long workpiece. The diameter of the stop body is a close fit in the machine spindle near the collet and near the other end of the tube to reduce whipping of the collet and workpiece during the turning operation. To load this stop collet into a hand screw machine without removing the turret, the collet and body are disassembled; the body is loaded from the back of the spindle and then assembled to

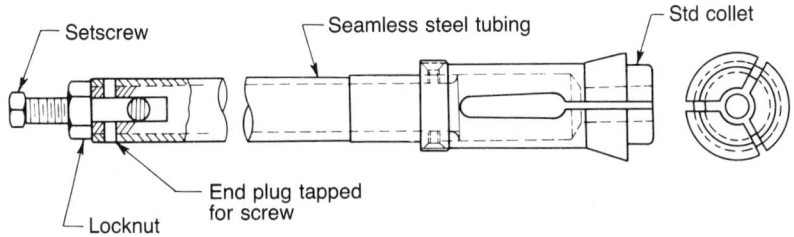

Setscrew   Seamless steel tubing   Std collet

End plug tapped
for screw

Locknut

Fig. 9-40 Spring collet and stop for long workpiece. (*Courtesy Western Electric Co., Inc.*)

the collet which is loaded from the front. The long workpieces are loaded through two diametrically opposed unused tool positions in the machine turret.

Gripping Small-headed Parts. A duplex collet arrangement for gripping the body (0.375 in. diam.) of a workpiece for turning its small end while the large (0.562 in. diam.) head at the opposite end is cleared within the collet is shown in Fig. 9-41. This special collet opens to permit automatic loading of the workpiece with the large head entering first. This collet is designed for use in a five-spindle machine.

In operation, the outer collet grips the inner collet which in turn grips the body diameter of the workpiece. The inner collet is bored to clear the large diameter of the workpiece. The outer collet is operated by the machine's drawback-collet closing mechanism and the inner collet by the stock-feed mechanism. When the outer collet is opened, the inner collet is fed out until its gripping end is completely outside the outer collet. In this position, the inner collet springs open to accept the workpiece, with its large-head end first, from a loading tool in the machine turret. The advancing workpiece contacts the spring ejector and stop, which move inward and reinsert the inner collet into the outer collet. The workpiece and loading tool maintain pressure until the drawback mechanism closes the outer collet to complete the clamping.

Three equally spaced slots in the inner collet provide the free, spring type of opening action required. The gripping end is a three-pronged spider which fits mating slots in the outer collet, permitting rotation of both collets as a unit.

The outer collet is similar to a conventional drawback type of spring collet. The gripping portion is slotted for the inner collet and also for a key which prevents rotation of the collets in the wear sleeve mounted in the machine spindle. The forward end of the outer collet tube is tapped to receive the outer collet. The inner end is fastened to the collet-tube ring which is actuated by the drawbar mechanism of the machine.

The inner collet tube is tapped to receive the inner collet, and the opposite end is mounted in a thrust bearing fastened to the stock-feeding mechanism.

The stock stop is screwed to an extension rod which bears against a spring-loaded ejector. The extension rod and the spring ejector have tungsten-carbide bearing surfaces to reduce wear.

A safety feature of the design is that which retracts the inner collet if a workpiece has been loaded into the machine. Without a workpiece to push the inner collet into the outer collet, the inner collet could be gripped while projecting beyond the spindle. To prevent this, a safety collar is threaded to the inner collet tube and secured with a locknut. During the backward movement of the drawbar mechanism which closes the outer collet, the collet-tube thrust ring contacts the safety collar, thus retracting the inner collet tube and moving the empty inner collet into the outer collet.

A Collet Bushing for Small-diameter Stock. Small sizes of nonmetallic bar stock, such as hard rubber, are usually difficult to load into production machines because of their tendency to bend or whip away from the hole in the collet. To overcome this, a collet and bushing assembly with a special feed finger (see Fig. 9-42) can be used. A bushing pressed into the rear of a standard collet guides the stock into the gripping

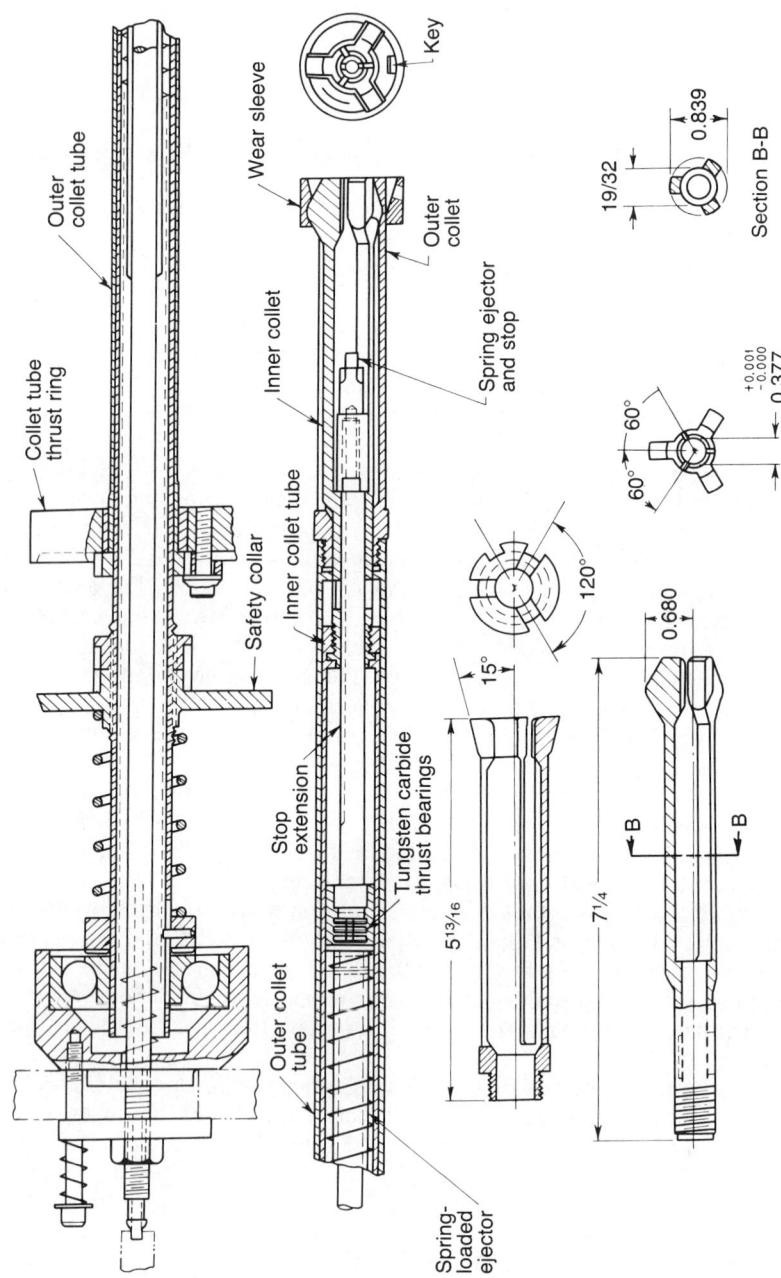

Key

Wear sleeve

Outer collet tube

Collet tube thrust ring

Outer collet

Inner collet

Safety collar

Inner collet tube

Spring ejector and stop

Stop extension

Tungsten carbide thrust bearings

Outer collet tube

Spring-loaded ejector

0.839

19/32

Section B-B

+0.001
−0.000
0.377

60°

60°

60°

120°

15°

5¹³/₁₆

0.680

7¼

B

B

Fig. 9-41 Duplex collet arrangement for gripping small-headed parts.

9-36

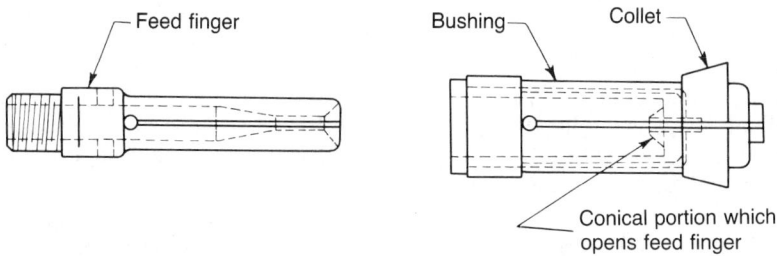

Fig. 9-42 **Collet bushing and feed finger for small-diameter stock.** (*Courtesy Western Electric Co., Inc.*)

portion of the collet. The long slotted feed finger carries the stock forward to the end of the bushing bore where a conical projection opens the feed finger, releases its grip, and permits the stock to continue feeding through the collet. The hole in the bushing is 0.0002 in. larger than the bar stock and must be concentric with the hole in the collet. The forward end of the feed finger is slotted to provide a spring action to grip the stock.

A Collet for Powdered Metal Parts. The special collet of Fig. 9-43 holds a fragile powdered metal ring while facing one end and chamfering the edges of both its ID and OD. It securely grips parts which vary 1/32 in. in diameter, without crushing those of maximum size. The nose is removed from the end of the spindle of an automatic screw machine, and the collet is positioned longitudinally by a tubular extension fastened to the collet.

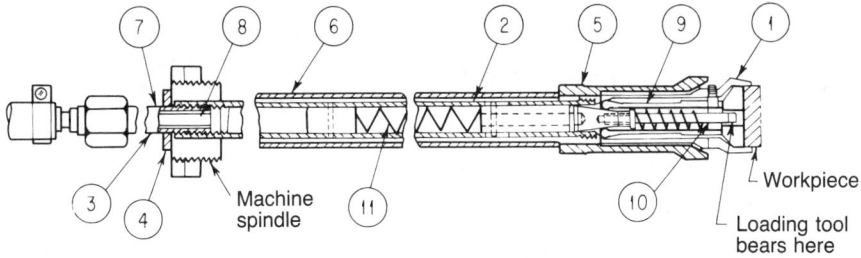

Fig. 9-43 **Collet assembly for holding a powdered metal part.** (*Courtesy Western Electric Co., Inc.*)

The collet (1) is a modified drawback type with ten equally spaced slots to provide a uniform gripping action around the entire periphery of the fragile workpiece. The back end is threaded to receive an extension tube (2) which has a threaded connection to another tubular extension (3). The body diameter of the extension is less than the threaded portion of the tube (2) and provides a shoulder which restricts longitudinal travel of a collar (4). This collar normally bears against the back end of the machine spindle to longitudinally position the collet. The collet is closed by moving the collet closing sleeve (5) forward to engage mating tapers on the inner bore of the sleeve and outer portion of the collet. The sleeve is actuated by the standard collet-closing tube (6) of the machine. To prevent crushing maximum-diameter workpieces, the collet can be moved slightly forward by the action of the closing sleeve against the pressure of a spring (7) behind the collar.

Also threaded into the back end of the extension is a tube (8) which has a hose connection permitting air to be blown through the spindle to clear the collet of chips. Located within the collet, but not fastened to it, is a stop (9) which keeps the workpiece from shifting longitudinally under pressure of the turning operation. The back end has four longitudinal slots similar to those in a collet to permit the stop to be locked in position by bearing against two tapered surfaces, one on the back of the bore of the collet and the other on the spring plunger (10). A spring (11) forces the plunger forward through a hole in the workpiece to complete the locking action. Positioning the workpiece is controlled by a loading tool which inserts it into the collet where it bears against the stop. Simultaneously the loading tool bears against the forward end of the plunger, locking the stop in position when the collet is closed. Variation in the longitudinal position of the collet due to variation in workpiece diameters is compensated by the spring.

An Oversize Collet for a Fragile Part. A special oversize collet for holding a fragile die-cast frame during a series of facing and turning operations in an automatic screw machine is illustrated in Fig. 9-44. The workpiece is manually placed into a loading tool which inserts it into the collet. This is a stationary collet closed by a sliding sleeve. To prevent crushing of the fragile workpiece, the closing action is controlled by a coupling spring between the sliding sleeve and the collet-closing mechanism of the machine. Upon reaching a predetermined gripping pressure, further advance of the closing mechanism is prevented by compression of the coupling spring.

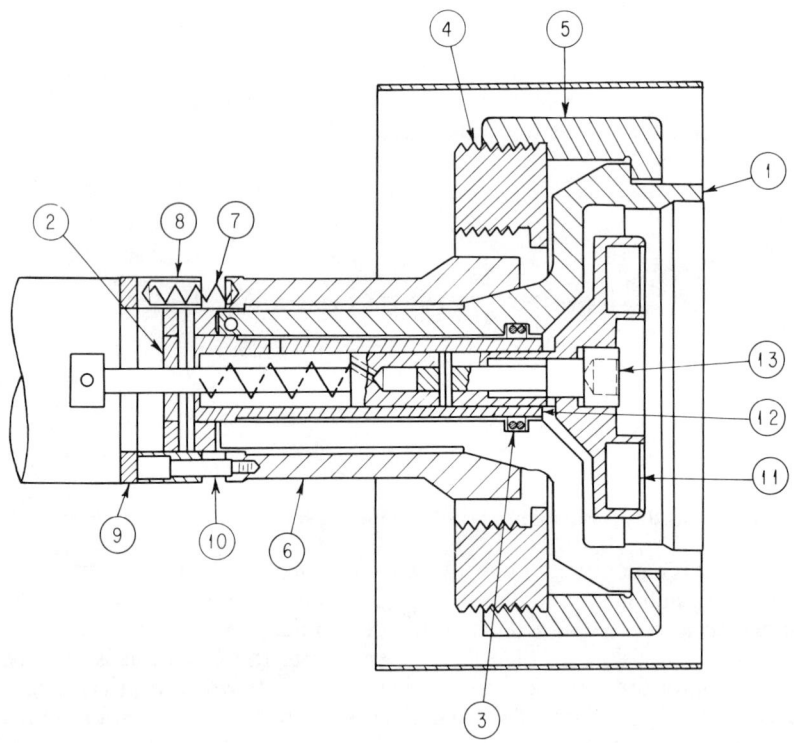

Fig. 9-44 Oversize collet for a fragile part. (*Courtesy Western Electric Co., Inc.*)

The collet is made of four individual pieces and does not follow conventional design. The gripping portion consists of three equal segments (1) pinned to a retaining yoke (2) which permits the segments to open and close for workpiece gripping and ejection. A torsion spring (3) prevents the collet sections from collapsing inwardly when empty. An adapter (4) and a hood (5) replace the standard machine hood and retain the collet in the spindle. The closing sleeve (6) closes the collet when moved forward by the collet-closing mechanism in the machine spindle. The coupling spring which controls the gripping pressure of the collet consists of twelve springs (7) mounted in a retainer (8). It is backed up by a wear plate (9). Both retainer and plate move forward as a unit to close the collet when actuated by the collet-closing tube in the machine spindle. Three retaining screws (10) fasten the retainer to the sleeve. The spring-actuated stop (11) is recessed to clear projecting lugs on the workpiece. The stop recedes into the collet as the loading tool inserts the workpiece and provides longitudinal positioning when it contacts the forward edge of the stop body (12). The body is pinned to the yoke (2) which also holds the collet segments. When the collet opens, the workpiece is partially ejected by a spring behind the stop. Final ejection is accomplished by an ejector (13) through the action of a compression spring moving the workpiece forward far enough to eject it from the recesses in the stop.

A Collet for Bottle Molds. A collet chuck used in an automatic turret lathe for turning ring-neck molds used in the bottle-mold industry is shown in Fig. 9-45. This collet is a large drawback type fastened to the face of the machine spindle and supported by an outboard bearing. The collet (1) is made in six equal sections which are threaded to a base plate (2) that is fastened to a drawbar (3). The collet assembly is contained in a housing (4) secured to the spindle and fitted to the spindle nose to ensure concentricity. A cylindrical sleeve (5) fits inside the collet and is fastened to a bumper plate (6); this assembly is used as an end stop for positioning the workpiece and is held in place by three screws in the studs (11) which are threaded into the housing. A felt ring (10) impregnated with graphite acts as a bearing between the stationary bumper plate and the collet. Support at the outer end of the collet chuck is provided by a bearing (7) fitted to the collet housing and supported in the saddle (8) which is mounted on the ways of the lathe. The saddle is supported at its upper end by the overhead bar in a bearing (9). The bearing is lubricated by a gravity oil line from the headstock oil reservoir.

A Hydraulically-actuated Collet Chuck. Figure 9-46 illustrates an externally operated hydraulic collet chuck designed to take full advantage of the bore size of the machine spindle. The collet consists of a pad adapter (1), the three sections of which are held apart by springs, and of three sectional pads (2), in sizes and shapes to suit the bar stock, that are fastened to the pad adapter. The pad adapter is retained in the hood (3) by a ring (4), and the entire mechanism is mounted in a body (5) fastened to the spindle nose of the machine. Collet closing and opening takes place through the action of three levers (5) pivoted in the body. The levers are operated by the tapered inner bore of a cylindrical slider wedge (6) fitted around the chuck body and which is arranged to move axially through the action of a pivoted fork (7) whose opposite end is actuated by a hydraulic cylinder (8). This is a single-action cylinder whose return stroke is actuated by a spring. The cylinder and fork are contained in a cast housing fastened to the head of the machine.

JAW-TYPE CHUCKS[13]

Chucks for use on engine, toolroom, turret, and automatic lathes are designed to fit the spindle noses specified in ANSI Standard B5.9-1967 (reaffirmed 1972). Dimensions of the chucks and jaws are listed, and classifications for different types of duty are specified in ANSI Standard B5.8-1972 (reaffirmed 1979). At present, however, this standard is incomplete in that it does not cover many chuck designs now available.

Chuck Selection. In selecting a chuck, a complete analysis of the requirements for the specific application should be made. Factors that must be considered include the size range of the workpieces to be machined, setup and tooling to be used, speed of the operation, production requirements, and jaw forces necessary to hold the workpieces rigidly.

Jaw forces required to drive a workpiece can be computed from the formula presented in Fig. 9-47. This formula is only recommended for relatively short or tailstock-supported workpieces and when the axial force is absorbed through a workpiece stop.

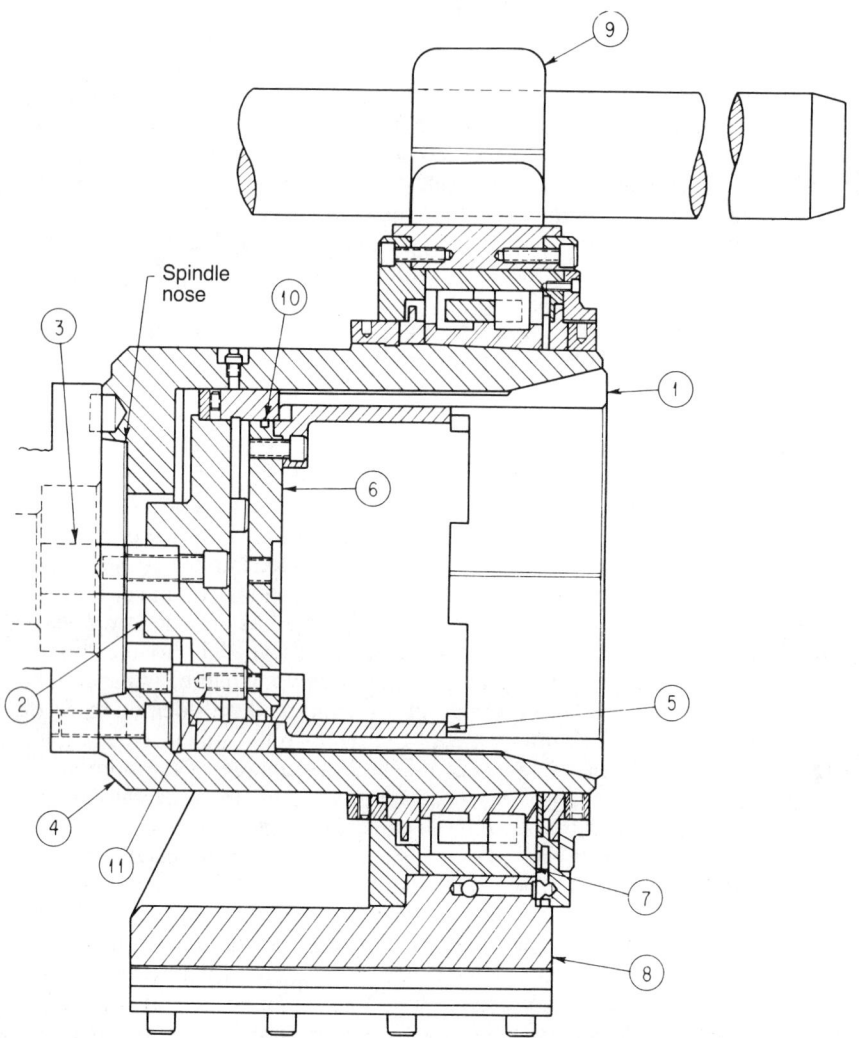

Fig. 9-45 Collet chuck for turning bottle molds in an automatic turret lathe. (*Courtesy Gisholt Machine Co.*)

Gripping forces vary widely, depending upon the size and design of the chuck. Typical gripping forces for a 10 in. diam. chuck are 5,000 to 8,500 lbf (22.2 to 37.8 kN) per jaw; for a 24 in diam. chuck, typical gripping forces are 10,000 to 22,000 lbf (44.5 to 97.9 kN). Chucks are generally guaranteed to maintain from 50 to 75% of their rated gripping force at maximum speed. Some are provided with internal jaw locks that maintain gripping force in case of power failure or stripped threads on the drawbar tube. Chucks are available for operation at speeds in the range 4,000 to 6,000 rpm or more.

Chucks with improved accuracy are now available to take full advantage of the improved accuracy of NC lathes. Accuracies of 0.001 in. FIM and repeatability of 0.0005 in. are not uncommon for chucks 15 in. or less in diameter.

Type of Chucks. Lathe chucks are available in a wide variety of types and designs, and are either manually or power actuated. Manually operated chucks are generally restricted to toolroom, maintenance, or limited production requirements because the time required for chucking may take longer than for machining. Power chucks cost

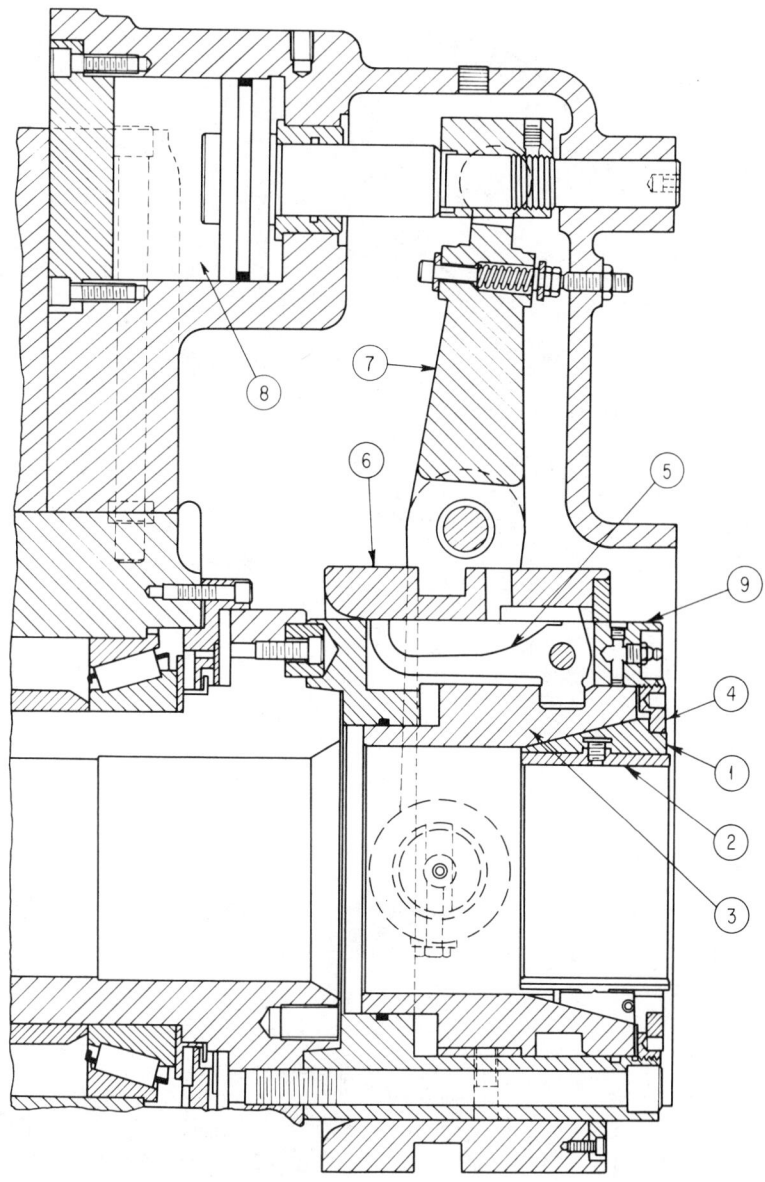

Fig. 9-46 Hydraulically actuated collet chuck. (*Courtesy Gisholt Machine Co.*)

more, but are faster and more productive. They also permit adjusting the gripping force to suit various requirements. Major types of chucks are independent and self-centering.

Independent Chucks. In an independent chuck, each individual workholding jaw can be moved toward or away from the workpiece without influencing the other jaws. They are widely used to grip square or irregular-shaped workpieces. Most independent chucks are constructed with four equally spaced jaws (see Fig. 9-48), but they are also available with two jaws for irregular-shaped castings and forgings that have to be trued up individually before machining.

Independent motion of the jaws on these chucks is accomplished by a screw beneath

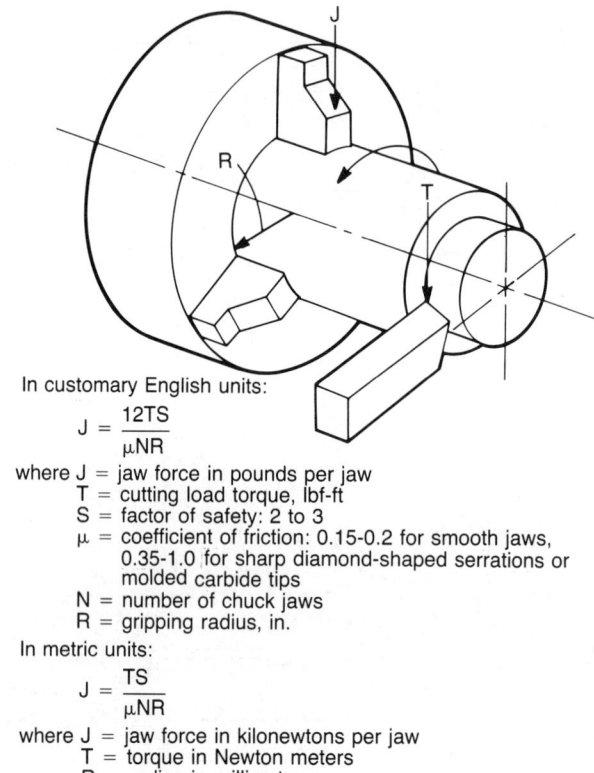

In customary English units:

$$J = \frac{12TS}{\mu NR}$$

where J = jaw force in pounds per jaw
 T = cutting load torque, lbf-ft
 S = factor of safety: 2 to 3
 μ = coefficient of friction: 0.15-0.2 for smooth jaws,
   0.35-1.0 for sharp diamond-shaped serrations or
   molded carbide tips
 N = number of chuck jaws
 R = gripping radius, in.

In metric units:

$$J = \frac{TS}{\mu NR}$$

where J = jaw force in kilonewtons per jaw
 T = torque in Newton meters
 R = radius in millimeters

Fig. 9-47 Formula for computing jaw force requirements to drive a workpiece on a lathe.

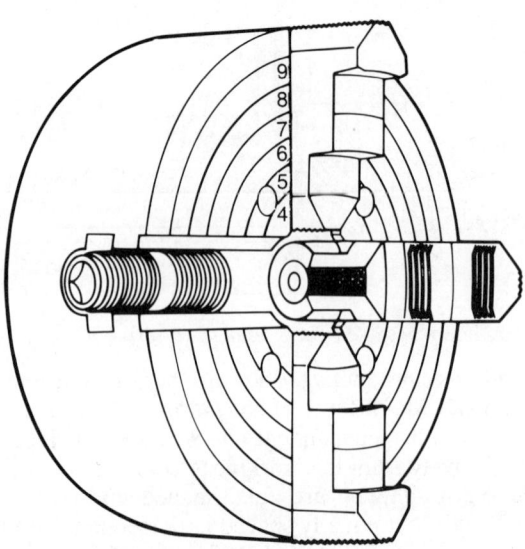

Fig. 9-48 Four-jaw independent chuck (shown with one jaw removed) for gripping irregular-shaped workpieces. (*Courtesy Cushman Industries, Inc.*)

each jaw which is fixed to the chuck body by a thrust ring. A mating screw thread is machined in the bottom of each jaw. When the operating screw is rotated by a wrench inserted in a socket in the end of the screw, the jaw moves inward or outward, depending upon the direction of screw rotation. With this design, high mechanical advantages are achieved, usually in a ratio of 30-40:1.

Independent chucks require more time to grip workpieces than self-centering and power types; they also require skill and care in setup. The jaws should be indicated to assure that their grip points are a constant distance from the center of rotation. This is necessary to minimize vibration and chatter.

Self-centering Chucks. This type of chuck is available in a wide variety of styles and configurations. One is the scroll, or geared-scroll, chuck which is still the most commonly used for general applications in holding round work. These chucks are particularly suitable for short-run requirements of a large variety of workpieces. Combination chucks are also available having both self-centering and independent jaw action.

A three-jaw, self centering chuck of geared-scroll design is shown in Fig. 9-49. In this design, a pinion is rotated by a manual or power operated drive which, in turn, rotates a gear mounted on a plate. On the reverse side of the gear plate is a face gear commonly referred to as a scroll. Teeth on the scroll engage similar teeth cut in the back of the master jaws.

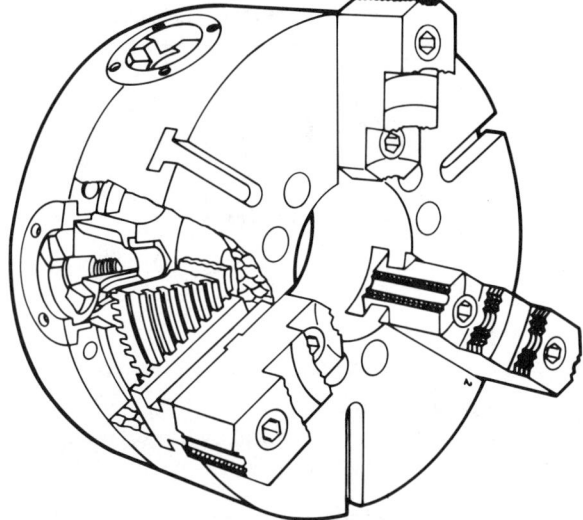

Fig. 9-49 Three jaw self-centering chuck of geared-scroll design. (*Courtesy Cushman Industries, Inc.*)

The set of three jaws on a geared-scroll chuck are matched with the proper offsets so that they move simultaneously toward the chuck center to engage the workpiece and hold it concentric with powerful gripping action. These chucks are made in light, medium, and heavy-duty series to suit various jobs to be performed. It is important that the proper chuck be selected for a specific application to assure accuracy and longevity of the mechanism.

For larger sized lathes, self-centering, geared-scroll chucks can be operated by a wrench that is powered electrically, hydraulically, or pneumatically. Power-wrench chucks provide a more powerful yet consistent gripping pressure and thereby relieve the operator of a strenuous task.

Power Chucks. Power chucks operated by a pneumatically or hydraulically powered drawbar or tube, or having a self-contained power actuating device, are better suited for medium-to-long, repetitive production runs. Many NC lathes are provided with chucks such as these.

Power chucks typically have a shorter jaw stroke than independent or geared-scroll chucks and generally must be equipped with top jaws suited to the workpieces to be machined. Most power chucks have a jaw movement limited to about ⅜ to ½ in. per jaw. This permits a variation of about 1 in. on the gripping diameter, but the contour of the top jaws does not permit the best gripping condition on all diameters within the range. It is therefore recommended that the variation be limited to about ¼ in. on diameters to be gripped with the same set of top jaws. Chucks jaws are discussed later in this section.

Many different designs of power chucks are available from various manufacturers. The higher speed capability of modern NC lathes has necessitated the development of improved power chucks to provide better retention of gripping force under increased centrifugal forces. Most power chucks are either wedge or lever type.

Wedge-type Power Chucks. These chucks consists of a body, wedge, and master jaws which slide radially within slots in the body. As the wedge is drawn to the rear of the chuck, the jaws are drawn radially inward. This type of chuck is available in wedge-hook and wedge-block designs, with the wedge-hook design being the most popular. The wedge-type power chuck illustrated in Fig. 9-50 has been modified for high-speed operation by the addition of levers and counterweight slides.

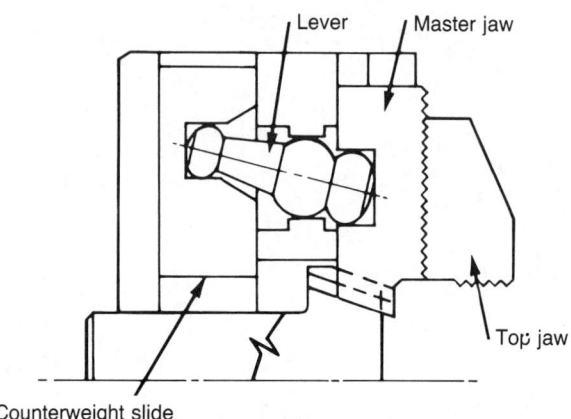

Fig. 9-50 Wedge-hook power chuck equipped with levers and counter-weight slides for high speed operation. (*Courtesy Universal Engineering Div., Stanwich Ind.*)

Many power chucks are actuated by an air or hydraulic cylinder mounted on the rear of the lathe spindle, with a drawbar or tube in the spindle connecting the cylinder to the chuck. Many modern NC lathes have spindle-ported hydraulic systems, and power chucks are available that contain a hydraulic cylinder within the chuck body. This eliminates the need for a rear-mounted cylinder and reduces space requirements. The spindle bore is also left open to accept maximum-size bar or tube stock.

Similar chuck designs are available for air operation. Figure 9-51 illustrates a wedge-hook chuck having a built-in air cylinder. This permits front mounting and eliminates the need for rear cylinder, drawbar, and coupling. Large through holes in these chucks permit bar work. The integral air piston operates the wedge-hook master jaws, with a shallow 10° wedge-lock angle to provide gripping force in the event that the trapped air is lost.

Wedge-type power chucks are available in the following styles:

1. Self-centering chucks with nonadjustable jaws for repetitive operations or dedicated machines for which jaw adjustment is not required.
2. Chucks with serrated master jaws for operations requiring a wide range of jaw

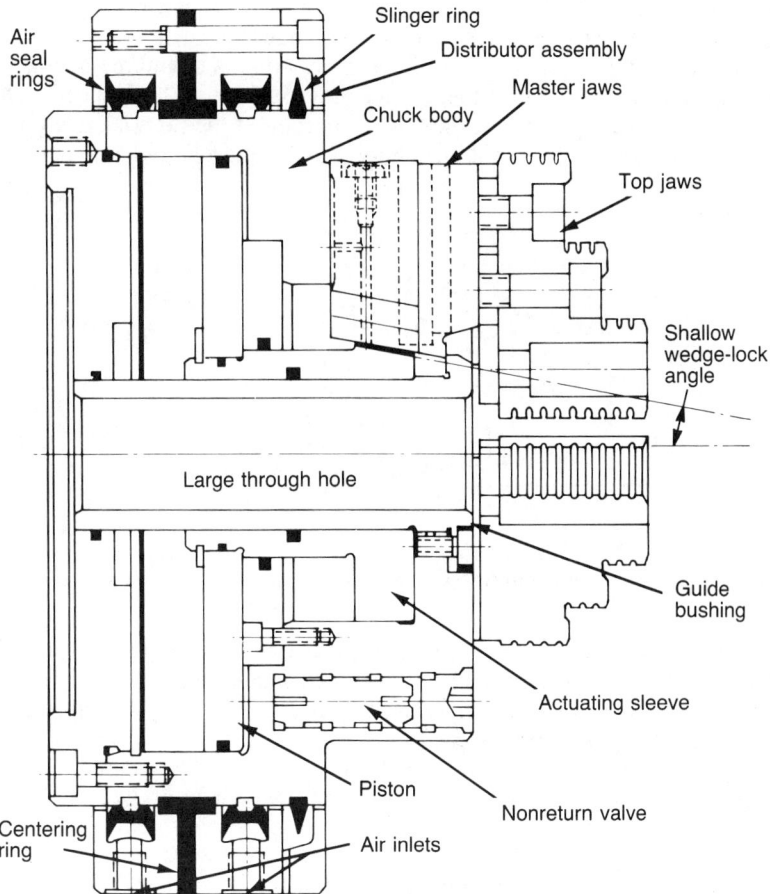

Fig. 9-51 **Front-mounted chuck which has a built-in air cylinder.** (*Courtesy SMW Systems, Inc.*)

capacities. Size changes are achieved by stepping the top jaws along the master jaws.

3. Chucks with independently adjustable jaws which are sometimes used for irregularly shaped workpieces.

Lever-type Power Chucks. These chucks are similar in appearance to wedge-type chucks; however, instead of having wedges, they have levers which transmit axial motion of the power cylinder into radial motion of the jaws. As the levers are pivoted, eccentrics on their thrust ends force the master jaws toward the centerline of the chuck and cause the top jaws to grip the workpiece.

One advantage of lever-type chucks is that a larger through hole, for performing either bar work or swallowing of workpieces, can be more readily achieved. These chucks may also be designed with master jaws that have a provision to affix collet pads. Lever chucks have a power advantage over wedge chucks in larger sizes because longer levers can be used for greater mechanical advantages. Wedge chucks, however, sometimes have greater repeatability and may be preferred when concentricity between the gripping diameter and the diameters to be machined is critical.

Another advantage of lever-type chucks is their ability to be shifted from high to low gripping pressures on-the-fly without the need for stopping the chuck and regripping the workpiece. This allows for high clamping forces during roughing cuts and a lighter grip during finishing, thus eliminating distortion of fragile workpieces.

In most instances, lever-type chucks are now of counterbalanced design. Counterweights are affixed to the rears of the levers, thus providing a counterbalancing effect on the centrifugal force exerted by the master and top jaws at high speeds. On the typical lever type shown in Fig. 9-52, the shaded portion at the rear of the lever is the mass that counterbalances the combined mass of the master and top jaws, bolts, and T-nuts.

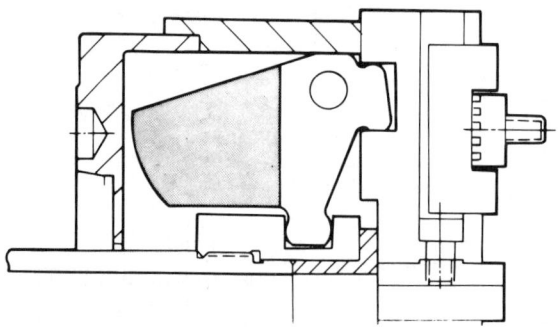

Fig. 9-52 Lever-type chuck with counterbalance weight (shaded area) attached to rear of lever. (*Courtesy The S-P Manufacturing Co.*)

At least one chuck manufacturer uses integral countercentrifugal lobes, with the counterweights and levers combined in one-piece elements. Another manufacturer of chucks offers a butterfly design. Each jaw has two counterweights pivoting in a milled pocket in the chuck body (see Fig. 9-53).

Chuck Jaws. With jaw-type chucks, workpieces are generally secured by replaceable jaws, referred to as top jaws, which attach to the master jaws of the chucks. Class I chucks (see ANSI Standard B5.8-1972, reaffirmed 1979) are for medium-duty use on engine lathes and for applications in which the service is not severe. Class II chucks are for heavy-duty use on turret lathes and for applications in which the service is severe.

Types of Master Jaws. Four types of master jaws in use today are illustrated in Fig. 9-54. With the fine serrated design, which is more widely used in Europe than the United States, both the master and top jaws have saw tooth serrations, either 1/16 in. (1.6 mm) or 3/32 in. (2.4 mm) pitch × 90°. The chuck jaws can be moved in multiples of either increment. With the American Standard square serrated design, the master jaw is serrated and the top jaw has a serrated key mounted in it. Adjustment is in ¼ in. (6.3 mm) increments or, by reversing the key, ⅛ in. (3.2 mm) increments. The square serrations are milled or broached.

Tongue-and-groove and Acme serrated jaws are the most popular designs in the United States. Jaws with the American Standard tongue-and-groove are nonadjustable but are widely used for high-production requirements for which the top jaws are machined to hold only one part. The American Standard Acme serrated design is similar to the square serrated design except that the teeth have a 29° taper. Adjustment is in ¼ in. (6.3 mm) increments or, by reversing the key, ⅛ in. (3.2 mm) increments.

Standard Top Jaws. Many standard top jaws are available from supplier stocks. Standard top jaws supplied with chucks are generally of single-step design and only available in sets. Work stops are recommended with these jaws. Some standard top jaws are also available with more than one step, but they have limitations with respect to gripping diameters.

Special Top Jaws. When top jaws are designed for special applications, many design features should be considered. For example, the location of the bolts that mount the top

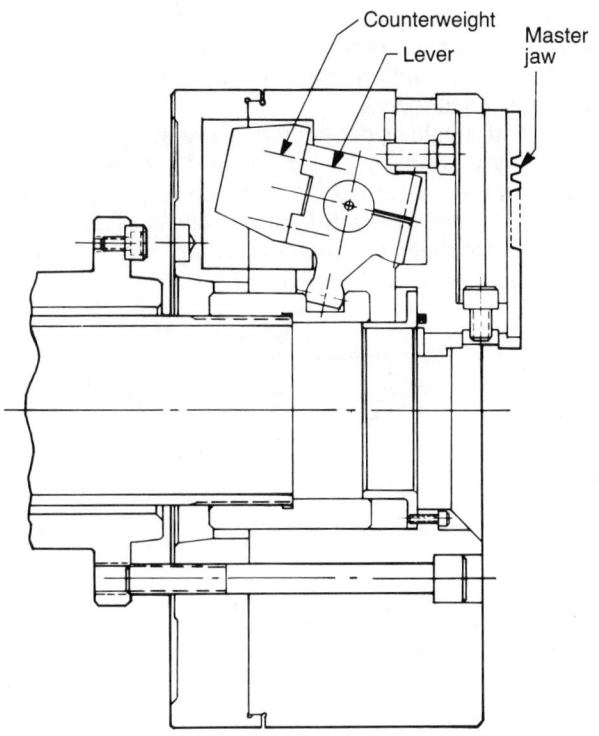

Fig. 9-53 Lever-type chuck with counterweights pivoting in milled pockets. (*Courtesy Cushman Industries, Inc.*)

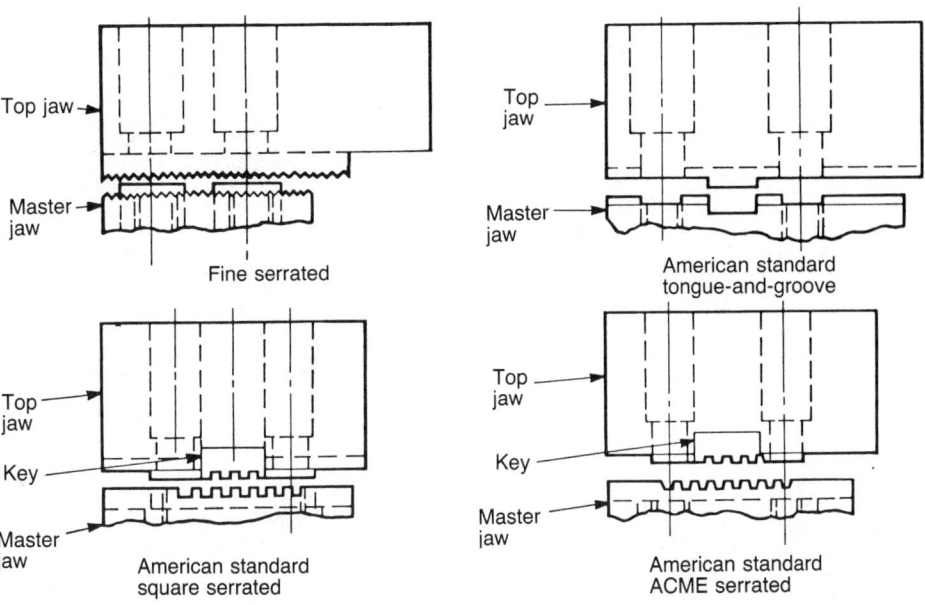

Fig. 9-54 Four types of master jaws currently in use. (*Courtesy Cushman Industries, Inc.*)

jaw to the master jaw should be planned so that one bolt is in a position to oppose the cantilever action of the clamping force on as long a momentum arm as possible. Jaws should be balanced, as lightweight as possible, and consistent with strength requirements to minimize centrifugal forces.

Some design rules that should be considered in designing special top jaws, as well as in selecting standard ones, are illustrated in Fig. 9-55. As shown in view *a*, top jaws should not exceed a 1:1 ratio with respect to length-to-height. Also, the height of the top jaw should not exceed the length of the master jaw. Chucking pressure should be reduced about 10% for each inch (25 mm) exceeding 3 in. (76 mm) of jaw height to prevent breaking master jaws, levers, or wedges.

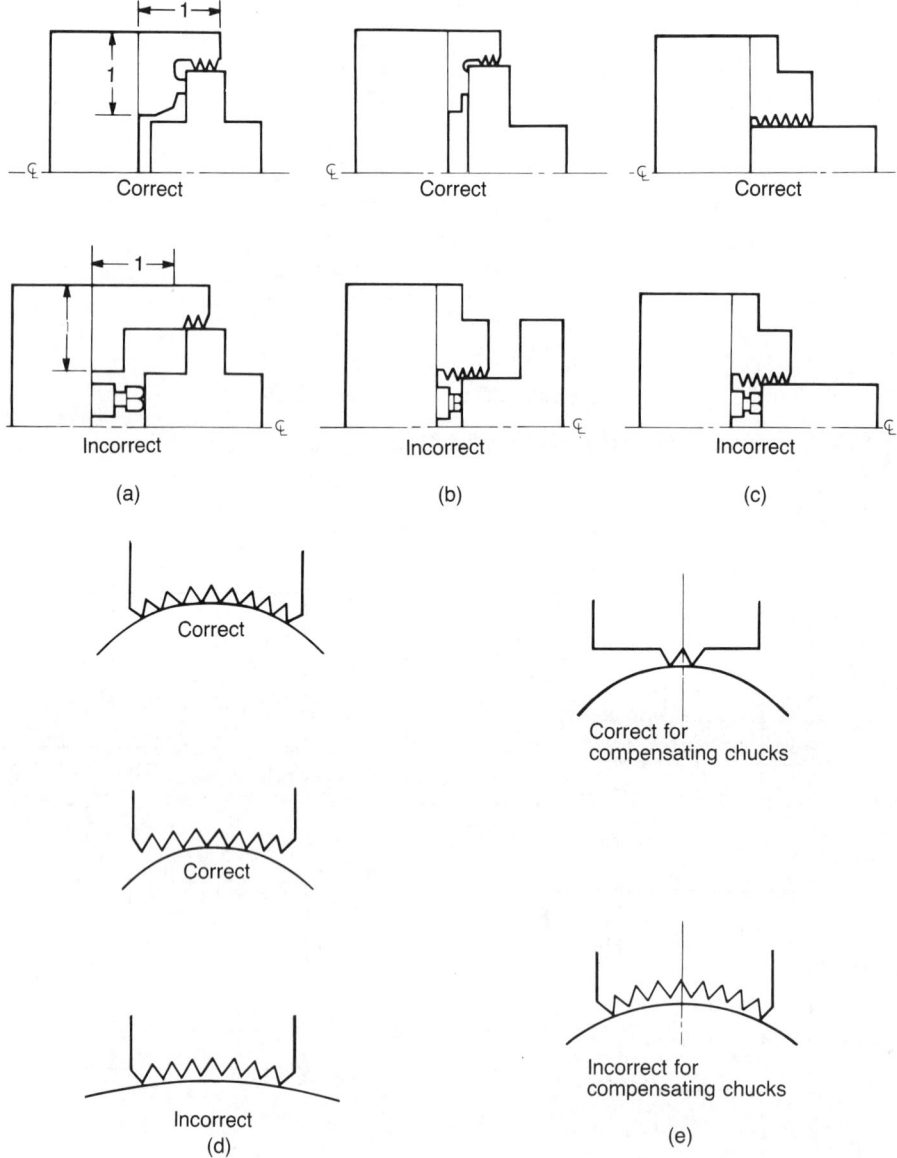

Fig. 9-55 **Correct and incorrect designs of top jaws.** (*Courtesy Cushman Industries, Inc.*)

The gripped diameter should be equal to or larger than the diameter being machined (see view *b*). If the workpiece has more than one diameter, the largest diameter should be used for chucking. When this is not possible, the feed rate and the depth of cut should be reduced. Workpieces should be gripped as close to the face of the chuck as possible (see view *c*), and special jaws with a longer grip should be used for larger, longer, or heavier workpieces.

For rough workpiece, the jaws of self-centering chucks should be designed, if possible, so that the gripping surfaces fully contact the workpieces (see Fig. 9-55*d*). Standard stepped top jaws, however, seldom achieve this goal, and it is desirable for the center serrations to bite into the workpiece first. On compensating chucks, the jaws should contact the workpiece as close to its centerline as possible (see view *e*); they should not wrap around the workpiece.

For gripping forgings, castings, or other workpieces having irregular or tapered surfaces, hardened jaws with inserted pins (see Fig. 9-56*a*) that can penetrate the material should be used. The points of pins generally extend about 1/16 in. (1.6 mm) beyond the serrations. Pivoted rocking-type jaws (view *b*) are also used for rough castings and forgings, as well as comparatively fragile parts. Wraparound-type jaws are often used on fragile or thin-walled workpieces to distribute the gripping pressure over a larger area and to minimize distortion. These chucks also provide greater drive friction and permit holding ID's to close tolerances with respect to OD's. Wraparound jaws, however, should not be used in compensating chucks for between-center operations.

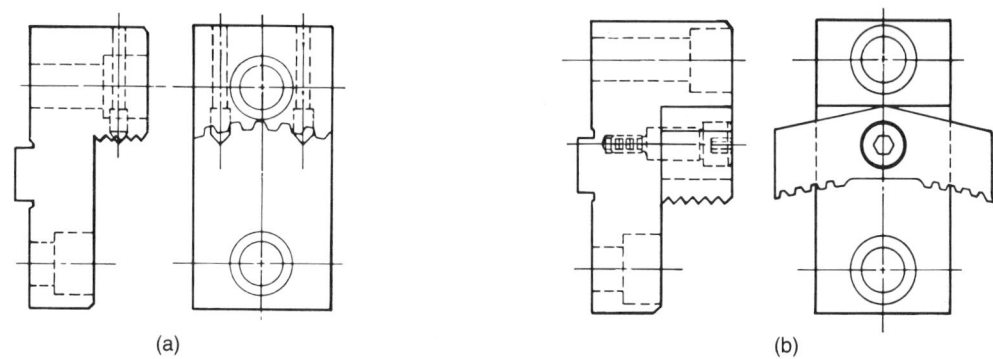

(a)   (b)

Fig. 9-56 Special chuck jaws: (*a*) hardened jaws with inserted pins and (*b*) rocking jaws.

Soft jaws should be qualified to the required size by boring with a ring or plug mounted under or in front of the top jaws, not under the master jaws. The ring or plug should be as far as possible from the face of the chuck. During boring, the same gripping pressure should be used as expected in production application of the chuck.

Carburized and hardened jaws are recommended for roughing operations. For rough surfaces, the jaws are often made from 8615 steel to obtain greater core strength and resist fracturing under heavy gripping pressures. For second operation work, jaws are generally made from a medium carbon steel or a chromium-molybdenum steel such as 4140 or 4150. To strengthen the jaws and resist chipping, the jaws are generally heat treated to a hardness of R_c28-30. When necessary for accuracy, they are ground.

Whenever possible (when the quality of the workpiece will not suffer) sharp pointed serrations should be provided on the jaws for maximum penetration of the workpiece. Serrations having a ⅛ in. (3.2 mm) pitch and 60° included angle are often used. Carbide gripping pads are sometimes used in the jaws to prevent workpiece slippage. Soft jaws or smooth hard jaws are commonly used on previously finished surfaces.

Top Jaw Applications. The application of special jaws can often result in reducing the number of chucking operations required with standard jaws. Figure 9-57a shows special jaws, designed to fit the draft angle of the hub, which provide a solid grip for removing stock from the large end of the workpiece. For the second operation, special soft jaws grip the circular surface, which is almost twice the diameter of the surface to be machined, and maintain a desirable relationship between the driving and cutting torques. Figure 9-57b illustrates the application of standard jaws requiring an additional chucking because they will not fit the draft angle of the hub.

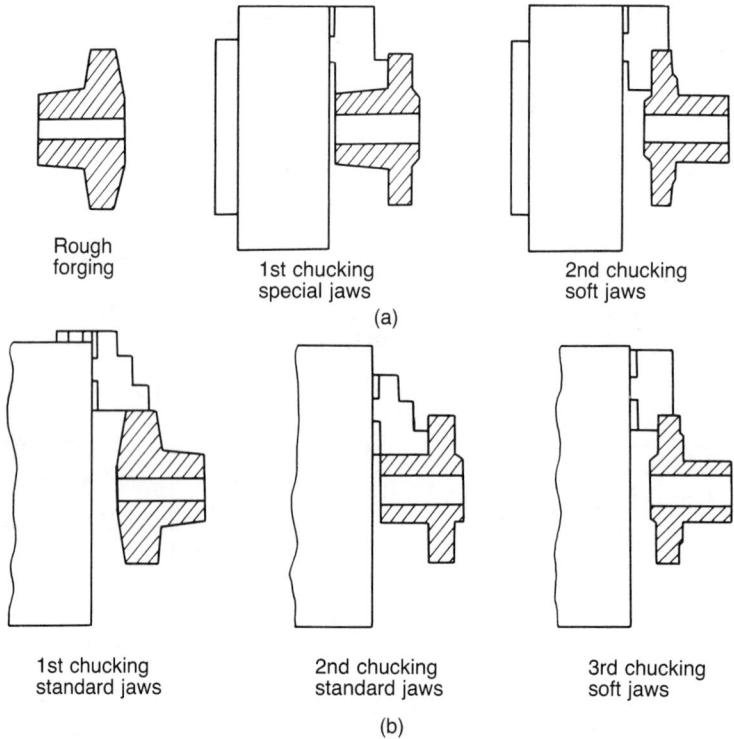

Rough
forging

1st chucking
special jaws

2nd chucking
soft jaws

(a)

1st chucking
standard jaws

2nd chucking
standard jaws

3rd chucking
soft jaws

(b)

Fig. 9-57 Application of chuck jaws: (a) special jaws and (b) standard jaws.

To produce screw-machine box-tool bodies, a manufacturer of such tools uses special top jaws for a 12-in. Class II power chuck to properly locate and turn the shanks and face the backs of the bodies in the lathe. The general contour of the box-tool body is suitable for gripping in a three-jaw rather than in a four-jaw chuck.

Figure 9-58 shows the chuck top jaws used for gripping and properly locating the shank in relation to the body contour. The jaws' lengths are measured from the tongue, and two of the jaws have construction holes for measuring and machining purposes.

The working face of jaw A makes a 15° angle with the sides of the jaw and has small straight serrations for better gripping, but it has no pad against which the workpiece can be rested. Jaw B has its working face square with the sides and incorporates serrations and a step against which the part rests. Jaw C has its serrated working face at an angle with the sides, and one end of its step is cut away to permit jaws A and B to come close together. The jaws are made of tool steel, hardened and ground.

Top Jaws with Inserts. For boring the inside and facing the outer faces of the flanges of ball bearing cages, an automatic lathe with an air-operated chuck holds and drives the cages. The top jaws (1) in Fig. 9-59 are machined to accommodate a set of

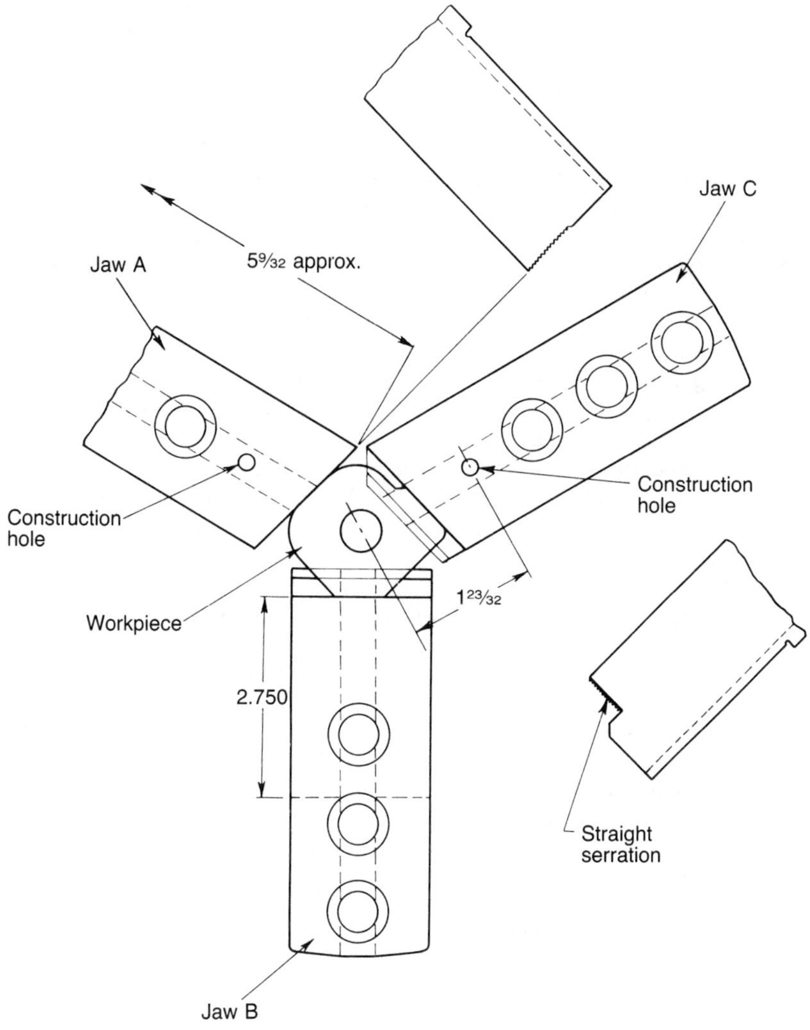

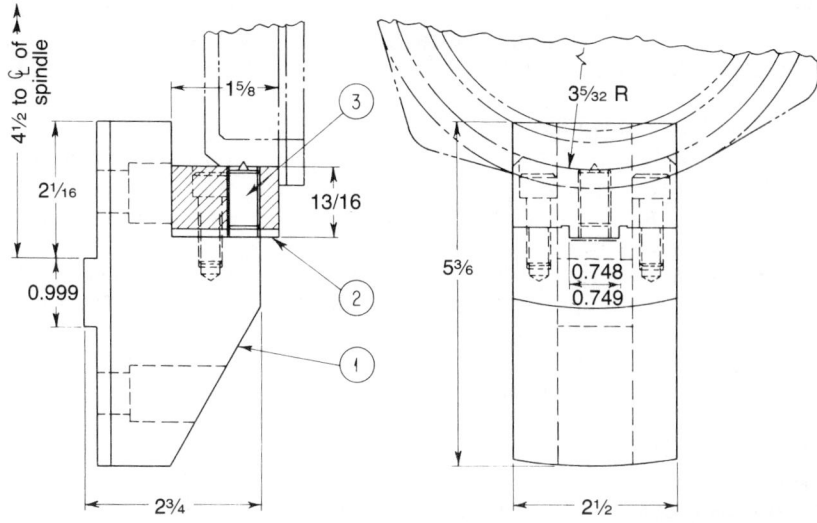

Fig. 9-58 Top jaws for gripping screw-machine box-tool body. (*Courtesy Boyar-Schultz Corp.*)

Jaw A

5⁹/₃₂ approx.

Jaw C

Construction hole

Construction hole

Workpiece

1²³/₃₂

2.750

Straight serration

Jaw B

4½ to ℄ of spindle

1⁵/₈

③

3⁵/₃₂ R

2¹/₁₆

13/16

5³/₆

0.999

②

①

0.748
0.749

2¾

2½

Fig. 9-59 Top jaw with hardened inserts. (*Courtesy International Harvester Co.*)

hardened-steel inserts (2) which can be replaced for similar parts of different dimensions. Cone-pointed setscrews (3) slightly penetrate the workpiece to ensure its driving, while the smooth-faced jaw inserts act only as a centering device. Air pressure to the chuck is reduced to avoid distortion of the thin-walled bearing cage. The small conical impressions in the workpiece are not objectionable.

When the design of the workpiece permits or the operation requires additional gripping pressure, the face of the inserts may be serrated with a square or diamond pattern.

Equalizing Top Jaws. The chuck jaws of Fig. 9-60 grip a tractor rear-wheel hub during turning, boring, and facing. These operations require that the large flanged end of the workpiece be nearest to the chuck face, with the smaller end extending toward the cutting tools, and that both ends be centered for concentricity. These locating requirements are met by providing a hinged block (1 and 2) on jaws A and B respectively, with the contact point below the center of the hinge pin on the block on jaw A and approximately centrally spaced about the hinge pin in the block of jaw B. When loading the workpiece into the chuck, the blocks are swung outward; but when in place, the gripping pressure holds them securely without any other locking means. The inserts have serrations on their working faces and are hardened and ground. The top jaws are also hardened and ground. A rotary pilot pushing (3) is mounted in the chuck to guide the boring bar.

An Adjustable-and-compensating Top Jaw. Figure 9-61 shows an adjustable-and-compensating jaw assembly for holding a very large, frail steel forging while the ID and one face of it are machined. This jaw was used on a special six-jaw 42-in. diam. chuck but can be used on three- or four-jaw chucks of smaller diameters as well.

The jaw consists of the faceplate (1) which is machined to fasten to the master jaw (2) of the chuck. Mounted to this faceplate are two separate pivoting sub-bases (3) to which two clamping or top jaws (4) are mounted and which pivot about the stud (5).

The pivoting action compensates for variations in the diameter of the forging, and once the forging is securely held in the jaws, the pivoting sub-base is locked in place with clamp screws (6). The top jaws are provided with circular inserts (7) threaded with a suitable right-hand thread to form serrations that grip the workpiece. Any tendency of the part to slip in the chuck causes it to be pulled inward and against the locating surface (8) of the top jaws by the serrations.

Three keyways (9) and a T-slot (10) are machined in the sub-base plate for each top jaw, so that workpieces of various diameters can be held with one set of jaws. To release the workpiece after machining, the locking screws (6) must first be loosened; and to limit the outward travel of each set of jaws, stops (11) are screwed to the chuck face which engage each end of the base plates (1) in the outward direction. For durability, almost all the parts are made of high-strength steels, heat-treated, and ground for accuracy.

To stabilize the top-jaw assembly, spacer plates (12) with two wear plates (13) are fastened to the chuck face.

Compensating Jaws as Work Drivers. Figure 9-62 shows a simple compensating-jaw design used with a standard three-jaw air chuck for gripping on the rough OD of the shank of special drill blanks. Since all work, including rough and finished machining and grinding of the drill blanks, must be done between centers, a system of compensating jaws is required to grip and drive the workpieces.

A conventional male center (1) is mounted in an adapter in the chuck body, and a female center (2) is mounted in the lathe tailstock.

Incorporated in the top jaw (3) is a pivoted insert (4). This method of clamping minimizes distortion in the workpiece and supports it near the work area.

Top Jaws for Centering Sheet-metal Part. Figure 9-63 shows a three-jaw chuck used to grip and drive a sheet-metal part while it is centered on a cone arbor fastened to

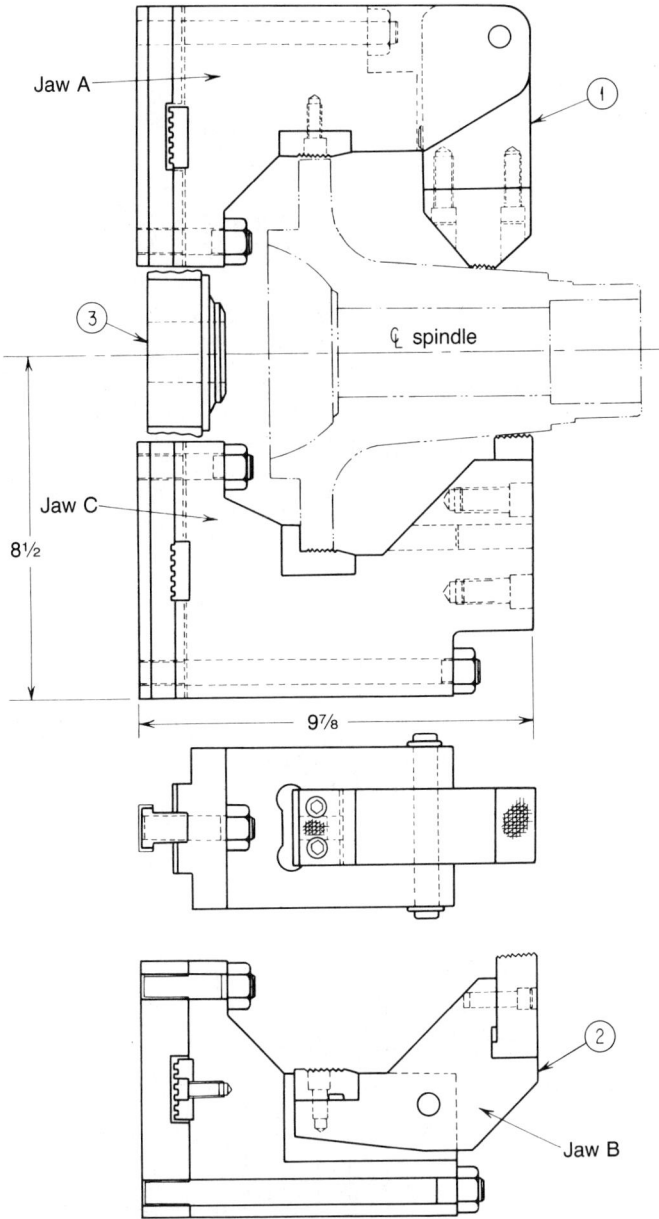

Fig. 9-60 Equalizing top jaws. (*Courtesy International Harvester Co.*)

the chuck face.

One-third of a circular plate (1) is fastened to the top jaws (2) to support the workpiece at its large end while turning and facing its flange. The outboard end of the part is centered and supported by a cone-arbor assembly (3) during the facing of the small end.

OTHER TYPES OF CHUCKS[14]

Many other types of chucks are used on lathes. These include diaphragm, spring-jaw,

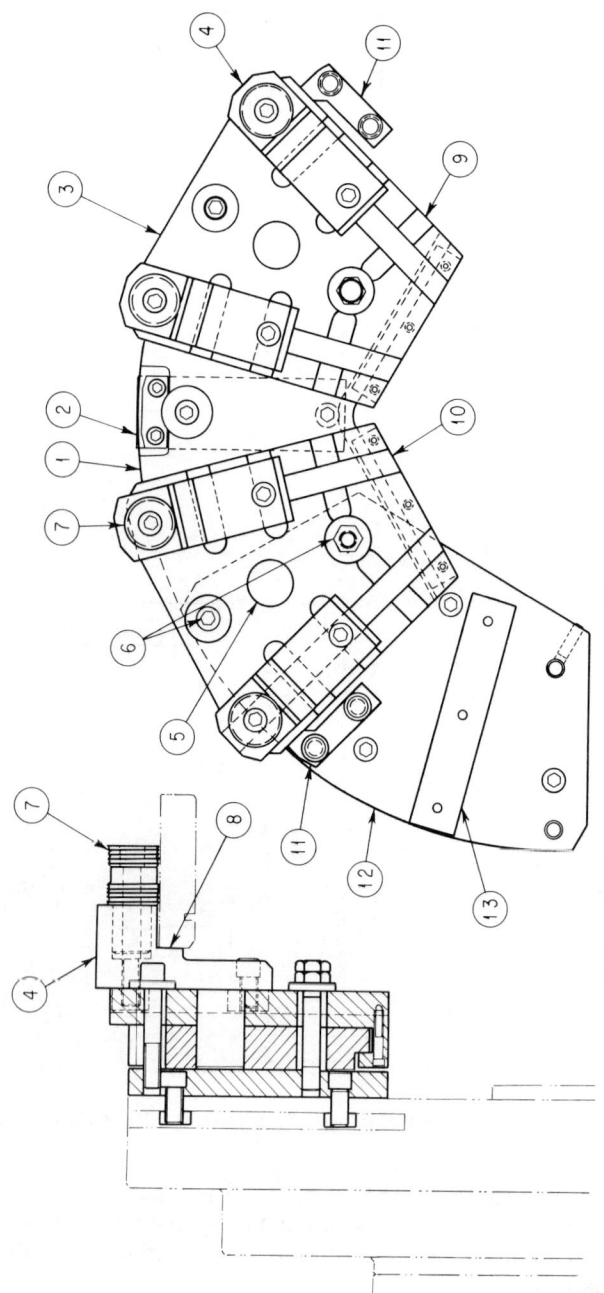

Fig. 9-61 Adjustable and compensating top jaws. (*Courtesy Gisholt Machine Co.*)

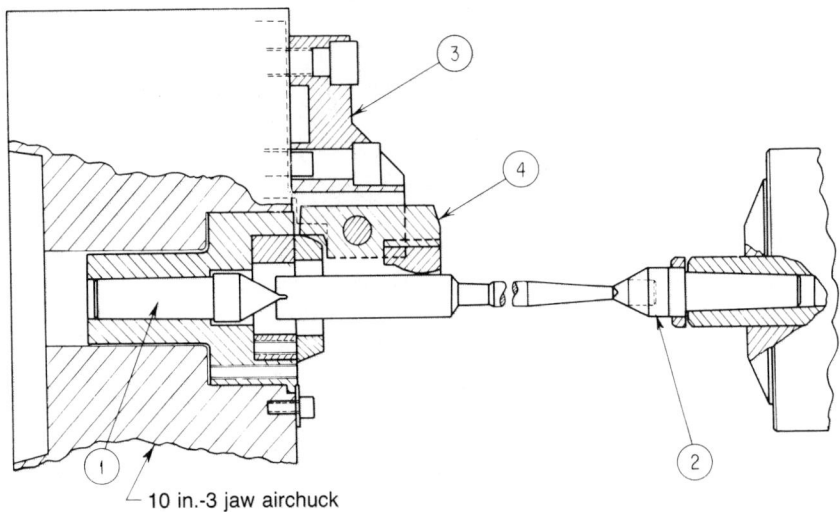

10 in.-3 jaw airchuck

Fig. 9-62 Compensating top jaws used as a work driver. (*Courtesy Gisholt Machine Co.*)

trunnion-type, indexing, pot, and oval chucks, as well as various proprietary devices. Drill chucks are discussed in Chapter 8.

Diaphragm Chucks. These workholding devices, more widely used for grinding operations (see Chapter 10) than for turning, have jaws mounted on a flexible thin-metal diaphragm. The diaphragm completely covers the chuck face and provides a seal over the actuating device. Jaws are generally mounted with dowels or welded to the face of the diaphragm. These chucks have limited jaw movement, and are more costly than most other lathe chucks. The double-diaphragm chuck shown in Fig. 9-64 holds a long workpiece in two places, helping to square the workpiece with the centerline of rotation.

A cutaway view of a diaphragm chuck is shown in Fig. 9-65.

For chucking gears, an interchangeable diaphragm assembly with master jaws can be used with gear cages, as illustrated in Fig. 9-66 The master jaws are ground to a nominal diameter; by changing cages which are designed for specific parts, any gear within the chuck's range can be processed. The gears, whether spur or helical, are located from the pitch diameter, assuring concentricity between the pitch circle and bore. For bevel gears, the chuck must incorporate fingers or clamps which pull the gears toward the chuck.

Spring-jaw Chucks.[15] These devices operate in much the same way that diaphragm chucks operate. An air or hydraulic cylinder pushes a bar to open the jaws. When pressure is released, spring pressure causes the jaws to grip the workpiece (see Fig. 9-67). These chucks are widely used to hold gears, because their jaws can be equipped with pins to locate on the pitch diameters of the gears.

The fixture of Fig. 9-68 is designed to locate and hold torque-converter housings in a multiple-station, vertical-index type of machine while turning and grinding the 1.9367- to 1.9380-in.-diam. hub concentric and square with the 12.855-in. diam. within 0.005 in. FIM, and while milling 0.690-in.-wide tangs equally spaced within 0.008 in. The fixture is actuated by spring pressure only, with air being used solely for unclamping; this is necessitated by the fact that the fixtures are mounted on an indexing work table.

At the loading station, a push bar (1) is actuated by a pneumatic cylinder located at this station to bear against a cam block (2) and a sleeve (3). At the top of its stroke, the push rod has opened or unclamped the fixture. The part is loaded onto the fixture or

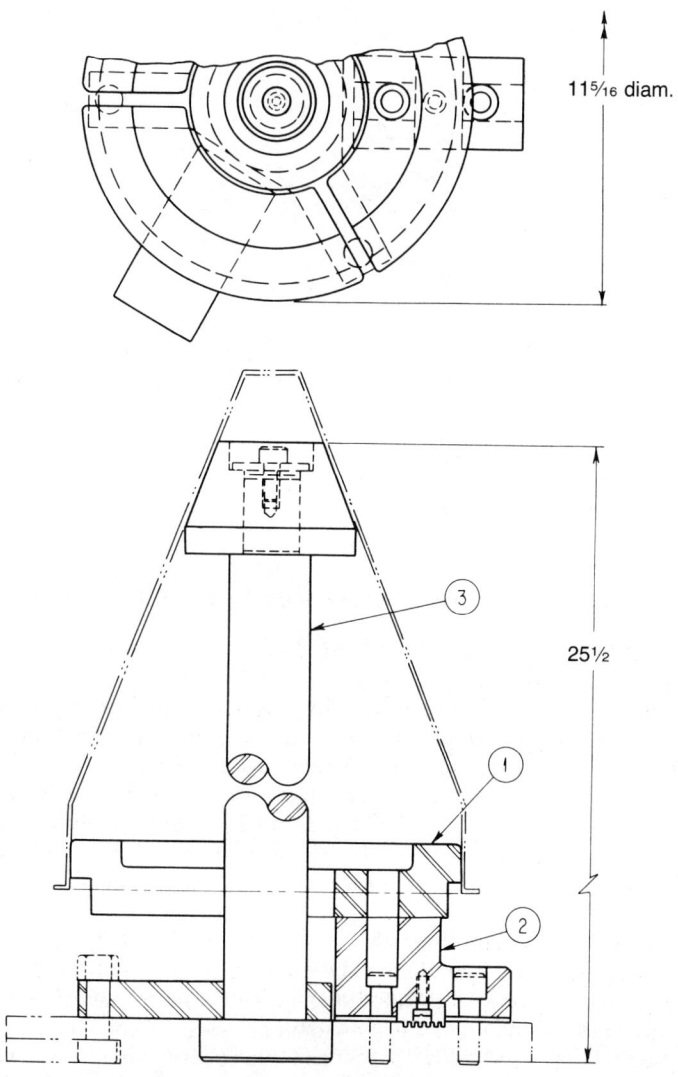

11⁵⁄₁₆ diam.

25½

③

①

②

Fig. 9-63 Top jaws for centering and gripping a sheet metal part. (*Courtesy Pratt & Whitney Aircraft*)

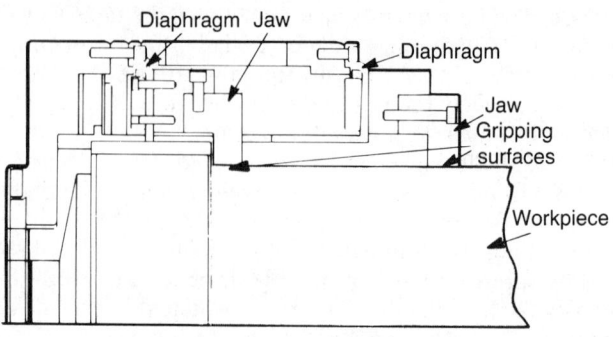

Diaphragm Jaw

Diaphragm

Jaw
Gripping
surfaces

Workpiece

Fig. 9-64 Diaphragm chuck with jaws mounted on a flexible thin-metal diaphragm.
(*Courtesy Kennametal Inc.*)

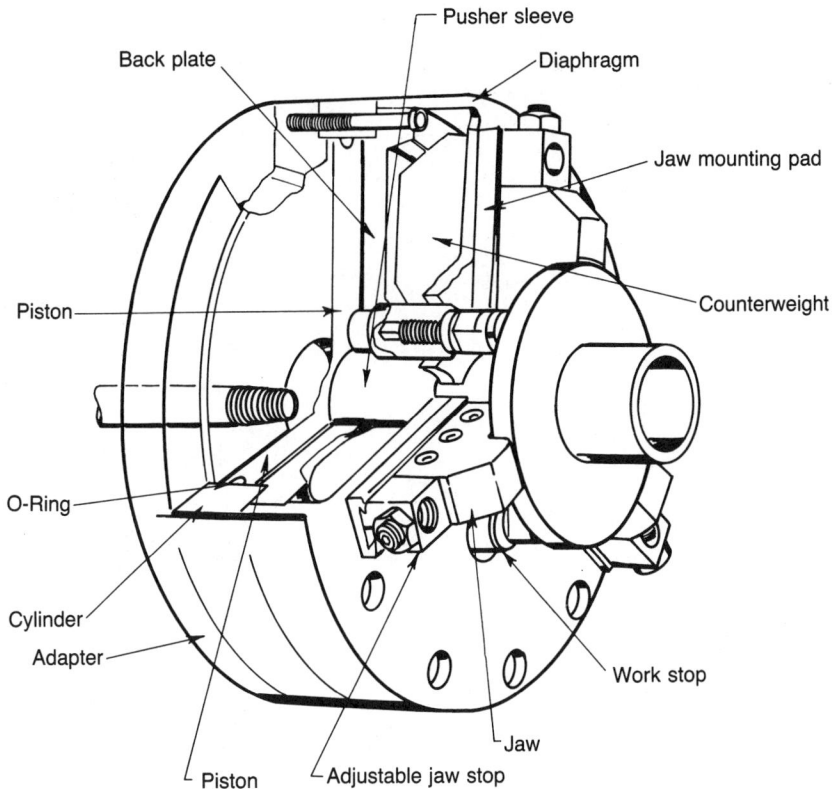

Back plate — Pusher sleeve — Diaphragm — Jaw mounting pad — Counterweight — Piston — O-Ring — Cylinder — Adapter — Piston — Adjustable jaw stop — Jaw — Work stop

Fig. 9-65 A diaphragm chuck. (*Courtesy N.A. Woodworth Co.*)

chuck, located from its 12.855-in. ID, and rested on the surface near its periphery. The push bar, working off the pneumatic cylinder, is retracted.

The following sequence of programmed motions then occurs: to locate, round out, dampen, and clamp the part prior to its indexing around to the work stations. Compression springs (4) exert a downward pressure on the cam block. As this block moves down, six pins (5) are expanded to centralize and round out the housing, engaging it at the 12.855-in. ID. Simultaneously, the drawbar (6), working off a spring (7), pulls down and expands the Neoprene washer (8) in the ID of the hub. This washer dampens or erases any vibrations which may result from the machining or grinding operations. As the pins (5) round out the housing and reach the end of their travel, the cam block likewise reaches the end of its travel. At this point six support pins (9) have been brought to bear and locked by means of a cam block (10), and fingers (11) below the housing support the area around the hub during machining.

The downward movement of the cam block (2) releases a linkage (12), allowing three jaw assemblies (13) to pivot about a fulcrum pin (14). With pressure exerted on the jaws by springs (15), the workpiece is clamped on the outside. The part has thus been located and clamped ready for machining. Pressure from a push rod and an air cylinder reverses the train of motions and releases or unclamps the chuck for unloading.

A Compensating Jaw Spring Chuck. The rectangular compensating-jaw spring chuck of Fig. 9-69 is used for boring and facing a vacuum-tube part of a turret lathe. The compensating feature distinguishes its design from that of other spring chucks. It is important that the part be bored centrally in relation to the four small drilled holes in the

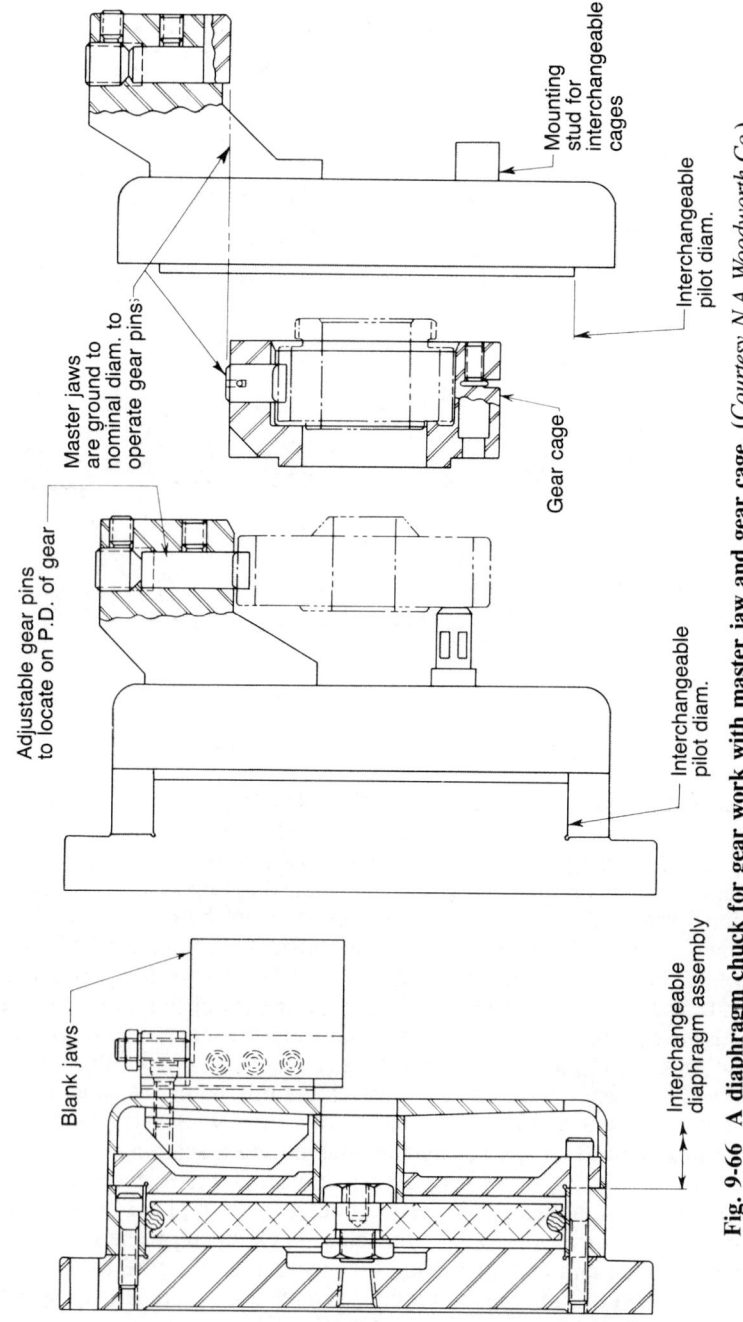

Mounting stud for interchangeable cages

Interchangeable pilot diam.

Gear cage

Master jaws are ground to nominal diam. to operate gear pins

Adjustable gear pins to locate on P.D. of gear

Interchangeable pilot diam.

Blank jaws

Interchangeable diaphragm assembly

Fig. 9-66 A diaphragm chuck for gear work with master jaw and gear cage. (*Courtesy N.A. Woodworth Co.*)

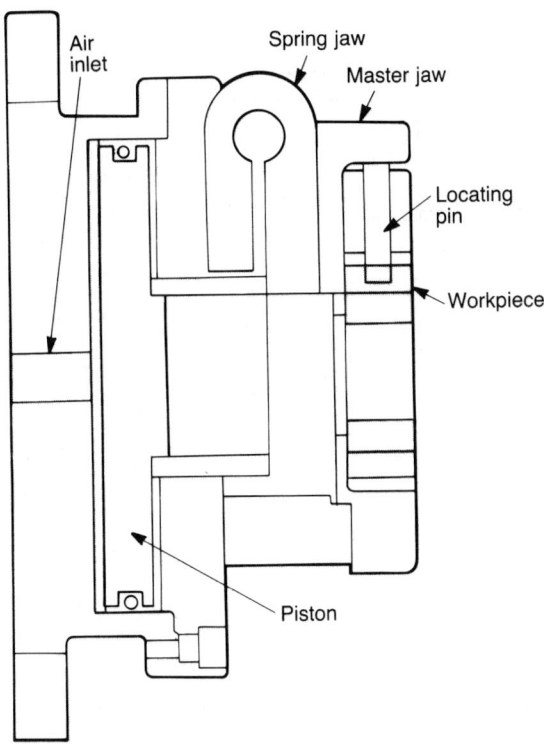

Fig. 9-67 Spring-jaw chuck operated by air pressure. (*Courtesy Kennametal Inc.*)

part. Since the location of these holes may vary in relation to the periphery of the part, the usual spring chuck, which centralizes the part in respect to its periphery, would not meet the requirements.

A chuck body (1) mounted on the spindle nose of the machine carries on its front end a spider (2) serving three purposes:

1. Driving the chuck by means of a key (3).
2. Acting as a rest plate, thereby positioning the part longitudinally.
3. By means of a round pin (4) and a diamond-shaped pin (5) locating the part laterally on two of the drilled holes with respect to the center of the work spindle.

The chuck closing sleeve (6) departs from the usual collet-chuck design in that the front end is allowed a predetermined amount of float in the chuck body, and the back end is tapered slightly to permit it to pivot inside the spindle. Within the closing sleeve, the spring chuck is carried in the usual manner, except that its four jaws project through openings in the spider to grip the part on its periphery. Variations in the positions of the locating holes in the part with respect to the four sides require the chuck and sleeve assembly to be slightly eccentric with the machine spindle at the gripping end and to pivot from the rear end of the chuck sleeve. The taper and float of the sleeve within the chuck cap permit this deviation from normal position. Nevertheless, since the part is resting on the spider, instead of being seated within the tilted chuck, it may be machined square and true.

After machining operations on the part have been completed, a heavy spring (7) between the spring chuck and the chuck closing sleeve moves the closing sleeve backward, permitting the chuck to open and release its grip on the part. The spring ejector, an adaptation of a standard ejector assembly, then removes the part.

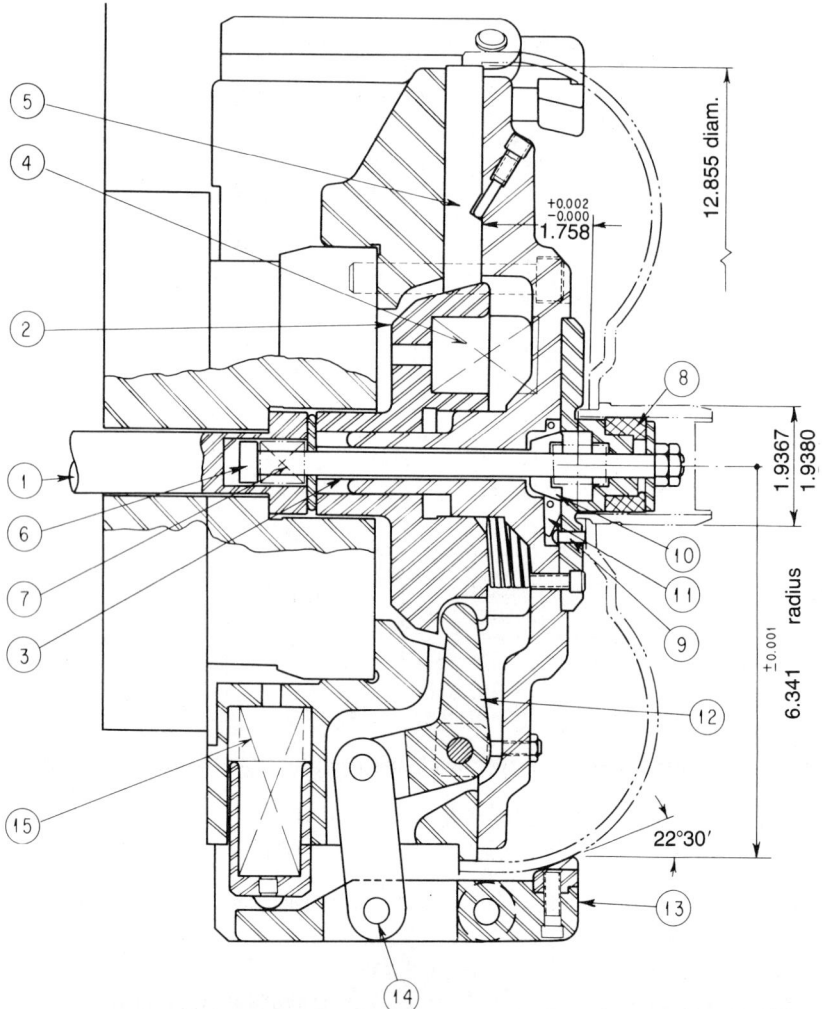

Fig. 9-68 Spring-actuated chuck for vertical multiple-station indexing machine. (*Courtesy Borg and Beck Div., Borg Warner Corp.*)

The next part to be processed is then loaded manually over the two locating pins and held flat against the spider by a pressure bar in the turret while the chuck is closed.

A Manually-actuated Spring Chuck. A simple chuck (see Fig. 9-70) for accurately chucking and maintaining concentricity in internal-boring or grinding and facing operations consists of a body (1), a split collet (2), and a closing screw (3). While the fixture illustrated was especially designed for the workpiece illustrated, the principle may be applied to other work which must be chucked on the OD and, at the same time, must be accurately positioned.

The body is made of machine steel which is pack-hardened and ground on the ID, back, and inside face. It may be machined for mounting on a faceplate or spindle-nose adapter. The collet is made of tool steel that is spring-tempered, with the OD and ID ground to fit respectively the ID of the body and the OD of the workpiece.

To operate, the part is placed in the collet and the screw is tightened, springing the collet against the work. While the part shown has a large center hole which permits

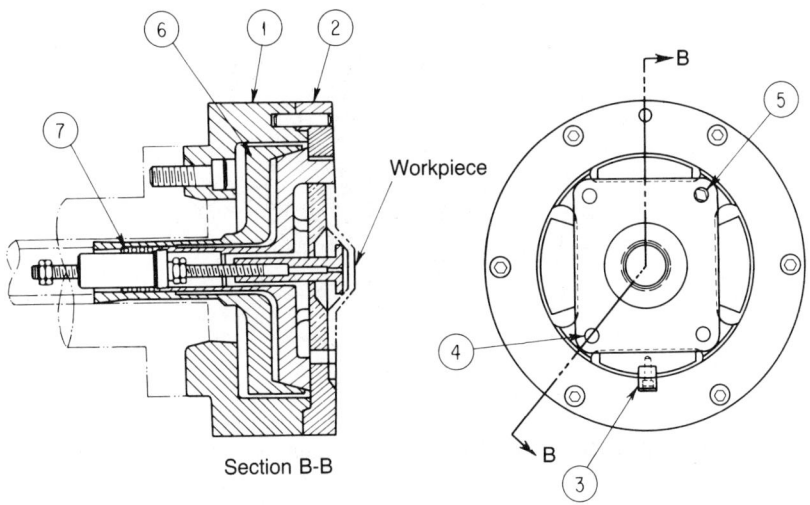

Fig. 9-69 Rectangular compensating-jaw spring chuck. (*Courtesy Western Electric Co., Inc.*)

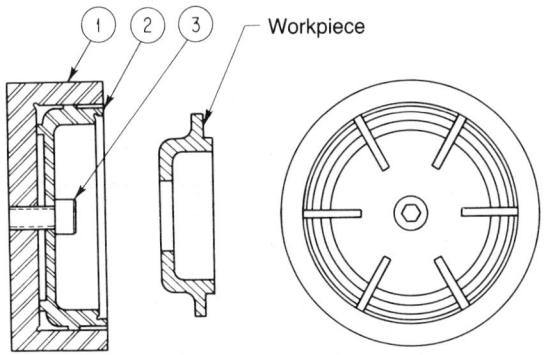

Fig. 9-70 Manually actuated spring chuck.

access to the screw for tightening with a wrench, the same effect can be obtained by using a drawbar through the spindle of the machine when chucking a part without a center hole.

Trunnion-type Chucks. These devices, also called Garrison chucks, are used extensively by the gear-producing industry. Gripping is achieved by a number of jaws that are rotated into and out of contact with the workpiece by an internal plate equipped with a ring gear (see Fig. 9-71). Jaws on these chucks have toothed segments that match the tooth forms on the gears to be held.

Indexing Chucks. These devices are used for workpieces, such as valve bodies, that have intersecting axes on which operations must be performed on two or more faces or bores (see Fig. 9-72). They enable several operations to be performed in one chucking. Air or hydraulic actuation of the indexing cycle can be controlled manually or automatically. Some indexing chucks are available with a proximity pickup sensor for electronic interfacing with the machine's NC unit for a positive interlock between the indexing and machining functions.

Self-contained Collet Chucks. The workholder shown in Fig. 9-73 features a built-in cylinder, single angle collet, and three positive end stops. It was designed to provide

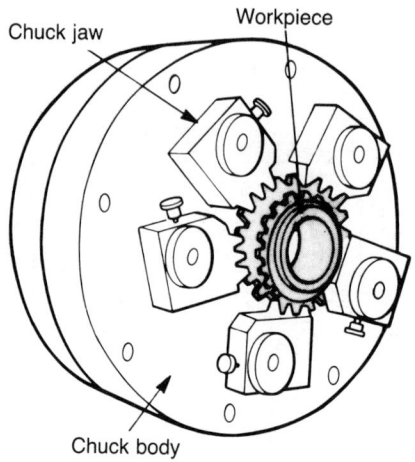

Chuck jaw

Workpiece

Chuck body

Fig. 9-71 Trunnion type chuck used extensively for holding gears. (*Courtesy Kennametal Inc.*)

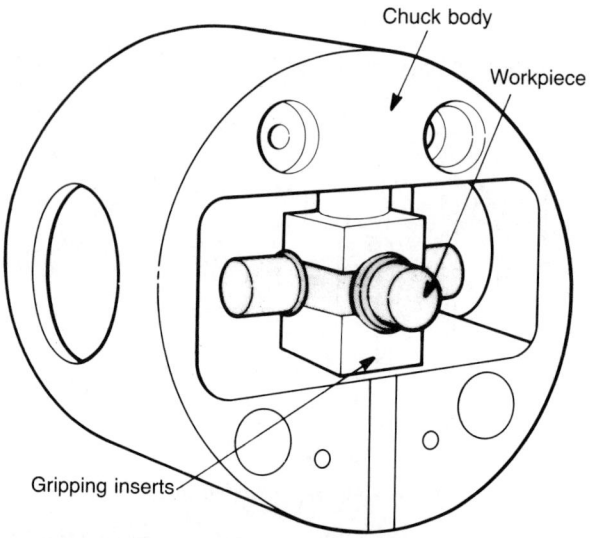

Chuck body

Workpiece

Gripping inserts

Fig. 9-72 Indexing-chuck permits performing several operations in one chucking. (*Courtesy Kennametal Inc.*)

360° support along with pullback action to positively seat a piston against the locating stops for processing.

Chuck and Collet Combination. Push and pull type power chuck and collet combinations, such as shown in Fig. 9-74, can be used for both chucking and collet work. These chucks are made with extra large center holes for chucking hex, round, or square bars. They are operated by air or hydraulic actuators which also have large through holes. To convert from chucking to bar work, the top jaws are removed and the master collet is inserted into the collet bushing. For push-type chucks, *a*, installation is completed by slipping the collet chuck body over the head of the master and bolting it to the face of the chuck. For pull-type chucks, *b*, top jaws are removed and the collet adapter is bolted to the face of the chuck. The master collet is then inserted into the collet bushing. Radial location of the master collet is maintained by the collet key. Conversion time from collet to chuck or vise versa is approximately 15 minutes.

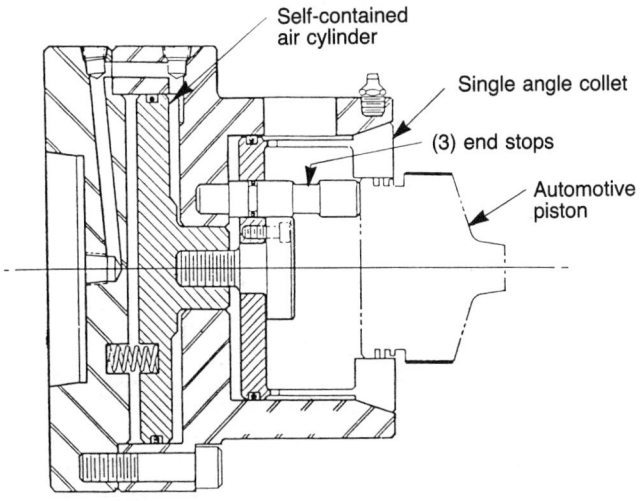

Fig. 9-73 Self-contained collet chuck. (*Courtesy Kennametal, Inc.*)

Self-centering and Compensating Chucks. A drawbar operated chuck of this type is shown in Fig. 9-75. The master jaws are moved by an eccentric cam mechanism. Pivot pins are provided for reaction at the rear of the master jaws. The pivot pins are tied together by a pivot ring that can either float (compensating mode) or be fixed in position (self-centering mode). The pivot ring is fixed in position by adjusting compensating blocks, using setscrews. In the compensating mode, the setscrews are backed out, and the compensating blocks retracted by means of capscrews.

The change from self-centering to compensating mode can be done with the chuck on the machine. For between-center turning, the chuck is equipped with a face mounted center and placed in compensating mode. With this arrangement, the jaws grip the OD of the workpiece without moving it off center, even if the OD is not concentric with the two centers.

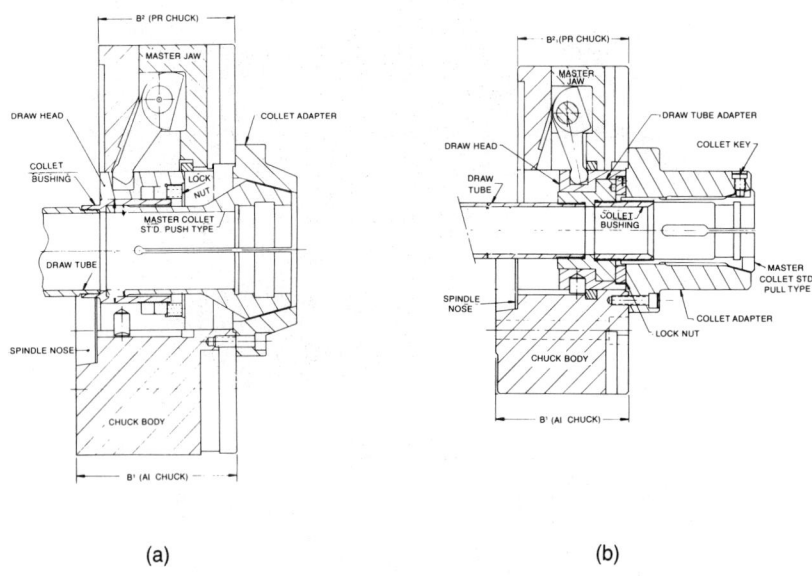

(a)   (b)

Fig. 9-74 Power chuck and collet combination. (*Courtesy Powerhold, Inc.*)

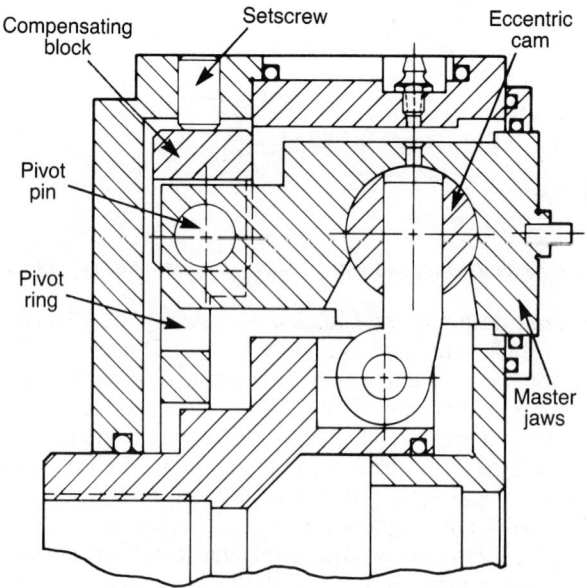

Fig. 9-75 Self-centering and compensating chuck. (*Courtesy Stace-Allen Chucks, Inc.*)

Ringspann® Chucks. The construction and functional principles of the clamping elements of this system were covered in the section on mandrels (refer to Fig. 9-14). Applications of the various elements for clamping with "positive pullback" can be seen in Figs. 9-76 thru 9-79.

The use of a bonded disc assembly (refer to Fig. 9-14*b*) can be seen in the differential chuck shown in Fig. 9-76 which was designed to clamp on two different diameters for boring and machining the front faces of the workpiece simultaneously from both sides. By interchanging the clamping elements (bonded discs, thrust ring, and guide bushings) a wide range of workpieces can be clamped for machining. The integral hydraulic cylinder is double acting.

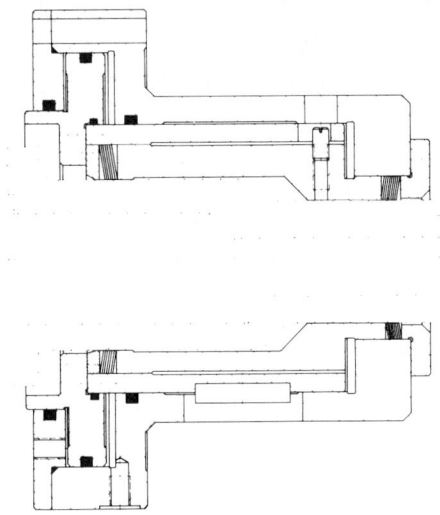

Fig. 9-76 Differential chuck for clamping on two different diameters. (*Ringspann®, courtesy Powerhold, Inc.*)

A basket type clamping element (refer to Fig. 9-14*f*) is used on the chuck shown in Fig. 9-77, which was designed to accommodate the extra long section of a differential half.

The flat register chuck (see Fig. 9-78) is used for checking workpieces of various sizes on a transfer line. Workpieces of various sizes can be clamped by interchanging the flat register element (see Fig. 9-14*e*), drawbolts, and locating pins.

A diaphragm element (see Fig. 9-14*d*) and a mandrel are combined in the fixture shown in Fig. 9-79 which is used for small batch turning or balancing operations on parts requiring minimum distortion when fixtured. The clamping element fitted into this fixture, can, simply by turning, be used for clamping either on an ID or OD.

Retractable Jaw Chuck. The power chuck shown in Fig. 9-80 features retractable jaws and a built-in face driver. Prior to machining, shaft components must be faced to length and center drilled on both ends. The workpiece is then loaded between the center built into the chuck and the tail stock center of the machine. The jaws, which are designed to compensate for the out-of-round found in castings or forgings, are actuated to clamp the workpiece for heavy cutting at high speeds. As the cutting tool approaches the jaws the spindle speed is reduced by the machine control system. The jaws, while still rotating at the lower speed, open and retract to a position below the face of the chuck where the rotational force necessary to finish turn the workpiece is supplied by the face driver built into the chuck.

Indexing Chuck. The hydraulically-operated indexing chuck shown in Fig. 9-81 was

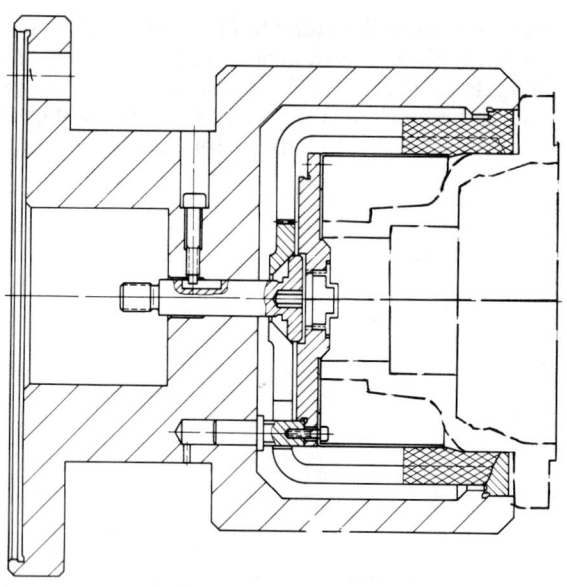

Fig. 9-77 Basket chuck for a differential housing. (*Ringspann®, courtesy Powerhold, Inc.*)

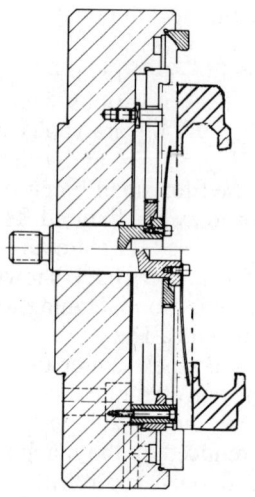

Fig. 9-78 Flat register chuck. (*Ringspann®, courtesy Powerhold, Inc.*)

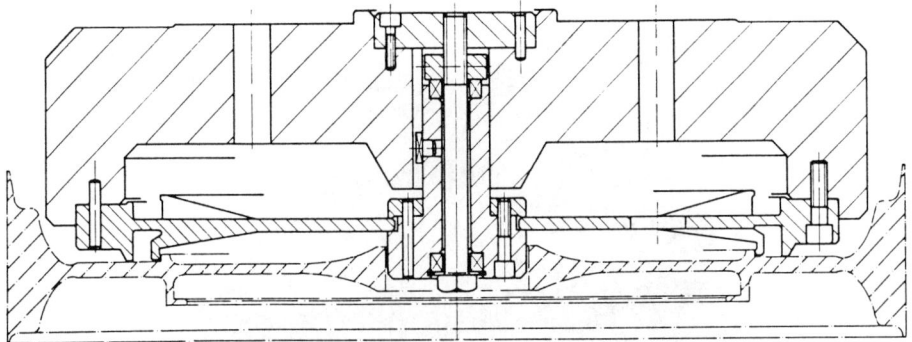

Fig. 9-79 Diaphragm chuck and mandrel combination. (*Ringspann®, courtesy Powerhold, Inc.*)

designed to machine components with intersecting center axes in one setup, eliminating the need for multiple chucking operations. Once a workpiece is hydraulically clamped in the chuck, it remains clamped for the entire machining process and is indexed while the machines spindle is rotating. Clamping, indexing, locking, and unclamping of the workpiece is managed by hydraulic pistons integral to the chuck. In use, the workpiece is nested in the lower jaw which is bolted to the indexing spindle, while the upper jaw which is bolted to the clamping piston hydraulically clamps the workpiece. An indexing mechanism rotates the indexing spindle and workpiece through the required indexes while, in most cases, the machine spindle is rotating at full speed.

Big Bore Sequencing Chucks. Chucks, such as shown in Fig. 9-82, are designed to save time locating and clamping workpieces requiring self-compensation. These chucks feature three self-centering arms which upon actuation protrude forward out of the chuck body (see Fig. 9-82*a*) and clamp in a centering mode. This holds the workpiece on center while an additional three jaws in the chuck close about the workpiece in the compensating mode. When the compensating jaws are totally closed, the centering jaws are opened and the arms retracted into the chuck body (see Fig. 9-82*b*). The lathe cycle can then be initiated.

Piggyback Chucks. The system shown in Fig. 9-83 consists of a master ID grip mandrel that stays on the machine and to which OD grip chucks are bolted as needed to machine three dissimilar clutch components on a W&S 3AC lathe as shown in the figure. It was designed to reduce changeover time from 90 minutes to 10 minutes in order to meet just-in-time quantities of the workpieces. Note that both rocker jaw and serrated jaw pull back design OD grip chucks have been provided.

Another workholder designed to reduce setup time is shown in Fig. 9-84. Before its development, eight hours were required to change the workholding setup from part to part in a seven member family of valve bodies. By providing seven quick-change swivel clamp fixtures that could be attached to self-contained air cylinders mounted to the rotating spindles of two indexers, changeover time was reduced to 10 minutes. The machine (a Chiron Vertical Machining Center) is no longer dedicated to one part for a long period of time. Loading and unloading of the workpiece is simplified, both by the swivel clamps and the safety part locators designed into them to prevent the workpieces from being loaded out of position.

Precision Air Chucks. The chuck shown in Fig. 9-85, along with supporting components, can be used for internal or external chucking, either vertical or horizontal, on grinders, boring, or milling machines, as well as lathes. Tolerances of 0.00001 in. for concentricity and end length can be provided. The air cylinder is integral to the chuck and the jaws can be actuated—either automatically or manually. The chucks can be mounted on standard adapter plates and moved from machine to machine in minutes.

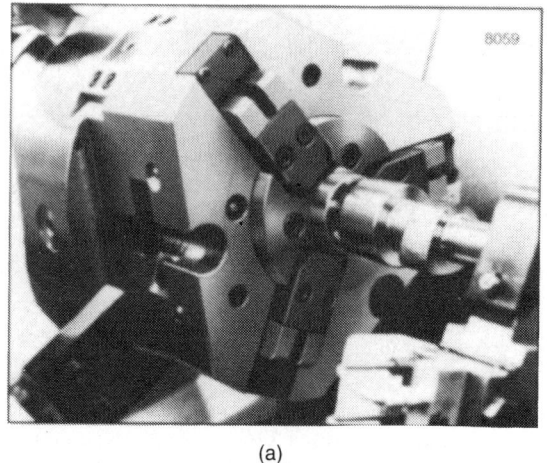

(a)

(b)

Fig. 9-80 Power chuck with retractable jaws. (*Courtesy Forkardt, Inc.*)

Quick Changing Jaws. Today's CNC lathes require a high degree of flexibility to reduce setup time. To provide this, chuck manufacturers have developed several methods which permit rapid changing of jaws to handle a wide variety of parts. With many of these systems, such as that shown in Fig. 9-86, the jaws can be changed in less than a minute with a positioning and repeatability accuracy within 0.001 in.

In the system shown, the locking and drive of the top jaws (1) is undertaken by engaging an accurately ground square serrated receiver (3) located in the master-jaw (2). The chuck is mounted directly on the spindle nose.

Release of the top jaws is only possible when the chuck is fully open with the drawhead (4) and the actuating cylinder piston in the full forward position. A special key (5) is supplied with the chuck to ensure jaw-by-jaw release.

With the handle of the key parallel to the face of the chuck (see Fig. 9-86a), radially introduce the key towards the center of the chuck. Push the key fully into its housing to lock the drawhead (6). The gripping system is thus rendered inoperative. The rotary

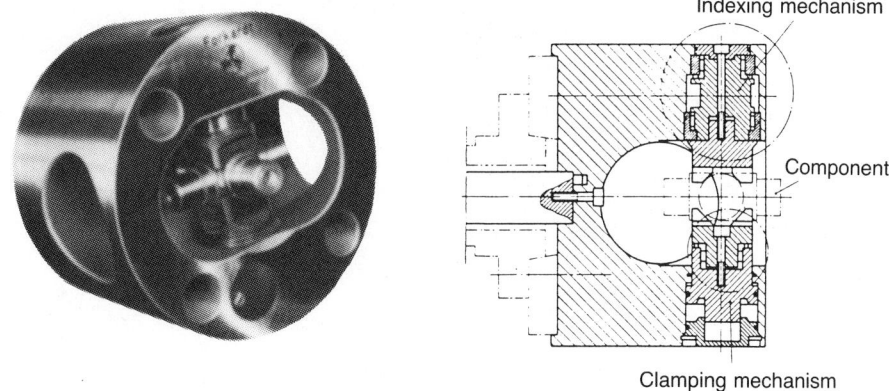

Indexing mechanism

Component

Clamping mechanism

Fig. 9-81 Hydraulically-operated indexing chuck. (*Courtesy Forkardt, Inc.*)

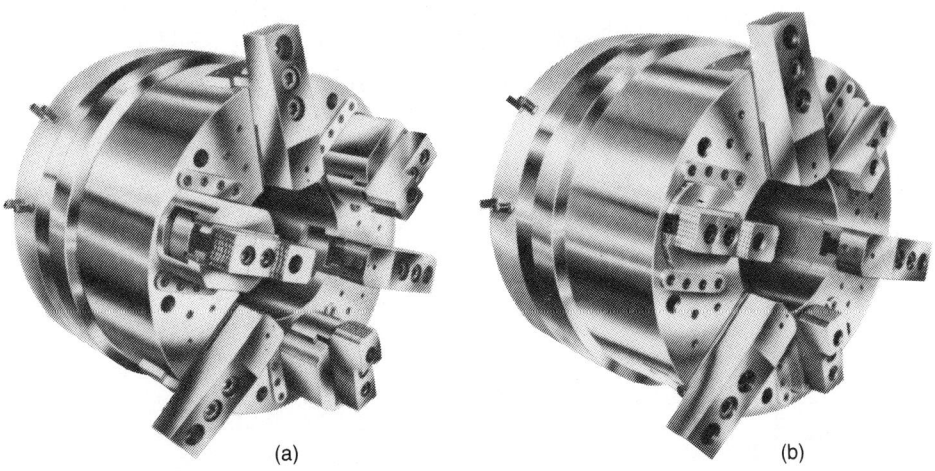

(a)   (b)

Fig. 9-82 Big bore sequencing chucks. (*Courtesy SMW Systems, Inc.*)

actuating cylinder equipped with a stroke control system will prevent the spindle from rotating even before the jaw is freed.

Turning the key 180° in a counterclockwise direction, *b*, acts on a system with an eccentric which causes the jaw locking serrations to retract. In this position the jaws can be moved, reversed, or changed.

The positioning of the jaws is facilitated by marks on both the jaws and the chuck body front face. In addition, a sensitive pushrod (7) enables the serrations of the jaw to be easily positioned in line with those of the master jaw.

The jaws are designed with non-serrated safety areas (8). In this way, the jaws are always engaged on all the teeth of the engagement piece.

Turning the key 180° in a clockwise direction (see Fig. 9-86*c*) causes engagement of the serrations which lock the jaw and the master jaw together. Returning the key to its original position guarantees that the jaw is correctly locked. The key can only be removed in this initial position thus freeing the control of the chuck. Safety locking of the drawhead, locking by means of an eccentric, and flats on jaws with straight

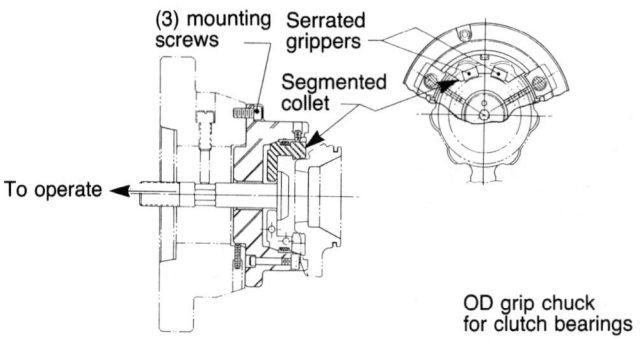

(3) mounting screws Serrated grippers

Segmented collet

To operate ◄

OD grip chuck
for clutch bearings

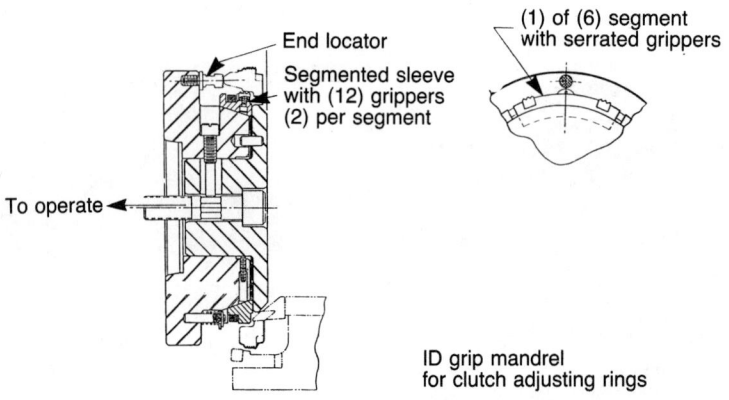

End locator

Segmented sleeve
with (12) grippers
(2) per segment

(1) of (6) segment
with serrated grippers

To operate ◄

ID grip mandrel
for clutch adjusting rings

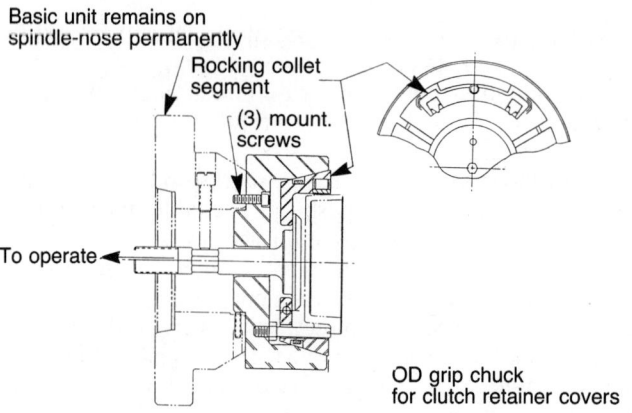

Basic unit remains on
spindle-nose permanently

Rocking collet
segment

(3) mount.
screws

To operate ◄

OD grip chuck
for clutch retainer covers

Fig. 9-83 A system of "piggyback chucks". (*Courtesy Kennametal, Inc.*)

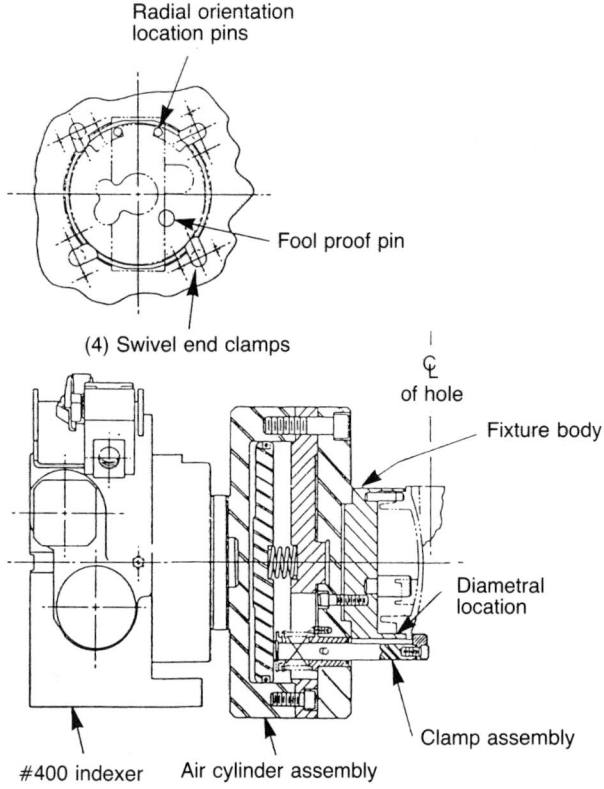

Radial orientation
location pins

Fool proof pin

(4) Swivel end clamps

$\mathcal{C}_L$
of hole

Fixture body

Diametral
location

Clamp assembly

#400 indexer   Air cylinder assembly

Fig. 9-84 Quick-change workholder. (*Kennametal, Inc.*)

serrations are patented by Gamet.

The two designs of wedge chucks with split master jaws shown in Fig. 9-87 show another manufacturer's approach to fast changing of chuck jaws. The positive cam-lock design, *a*, uses a lobed cam that locks the upper half of a split master jaw in place when engaged. To unlock, the cam is rotated 180° with a special wrench, which allows the lobe to clear a recess in the jaw permitting the jaw to be slid out of the chuck and replaced.

The cam is locked by rotating it to the locked position with the special wrench that is inserted into the cam and then pushed to disengage the locking detent. As a safety feature, the wrench cannot be removed unless the lobe cylinder is in the locked position and the locking detent is engaged.

With the multiple-position split master jaw design, *b*, a modified adjustment screw with the threads removed on one side can be rotated with a special wrench to disengage and engage the threads and perm.. the jaw to be quickly repositioned or replaced. When engaged, the screw threads lock the upper half of the split master jaw, which can be located and locked in several radial positions.

The manual quick-change system is shown in Fig. 9-88 and consists of a master jaw, key locator, lockscrew, and top jaws. The master jaw is integral with the actuator arm of the chuck and is fitted with the key locator. Top jaws, which are machined to mate with the key locator, are secured to the master jaw by hand tightening the lock screws. Loosening the lockscrews permits the top jaws to be replaced without removing the key locator.

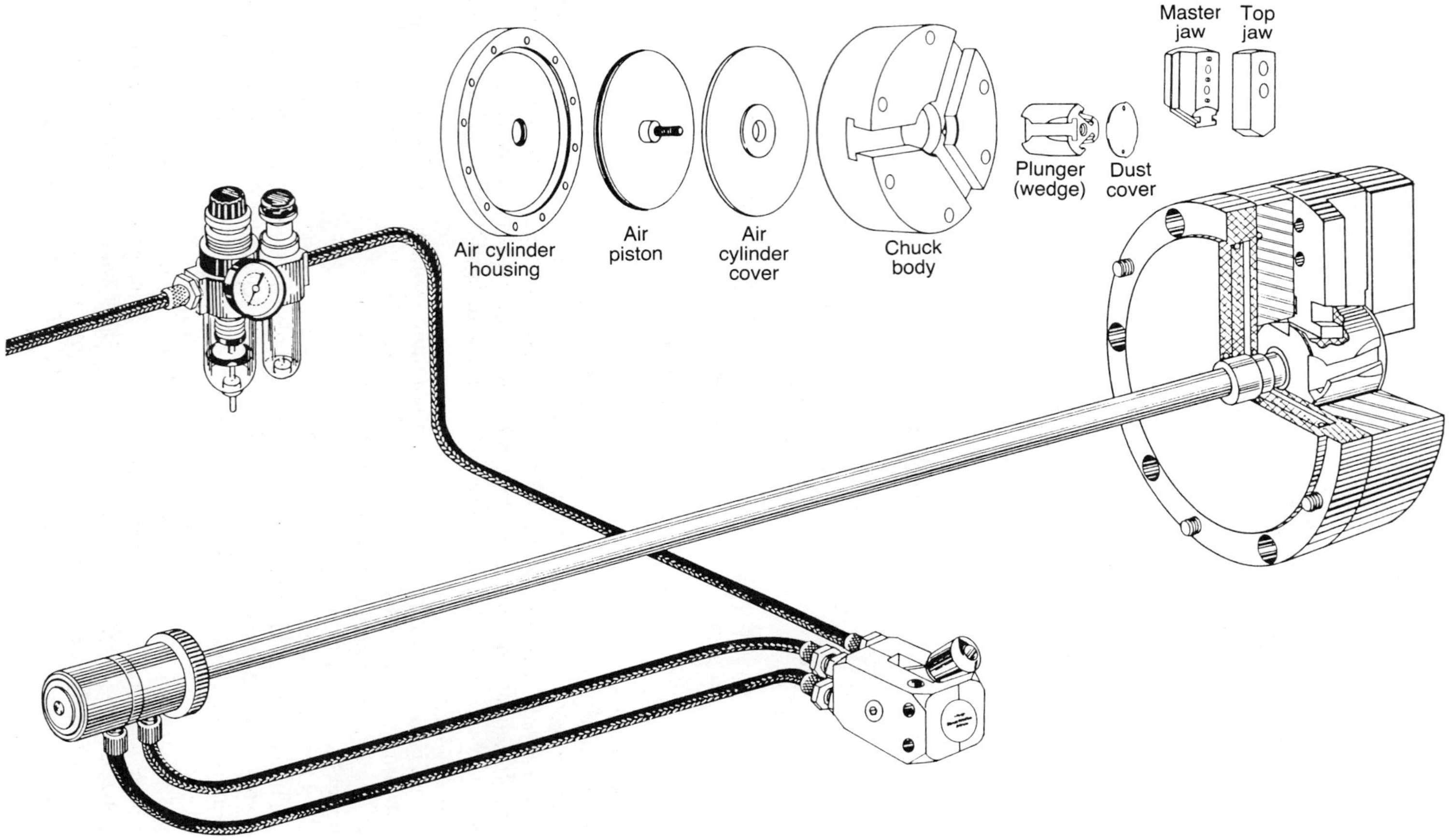

Fig. 9-85 Precision air chuck. (*Courtesy Northfield Precision Instrument Corp.*)

Top
jaw

Master
jaw

Dust
cover

Plunger
(wedge)

Chuck
body

Air
cylinder
cover

Air
piston

Air cylinder
housing

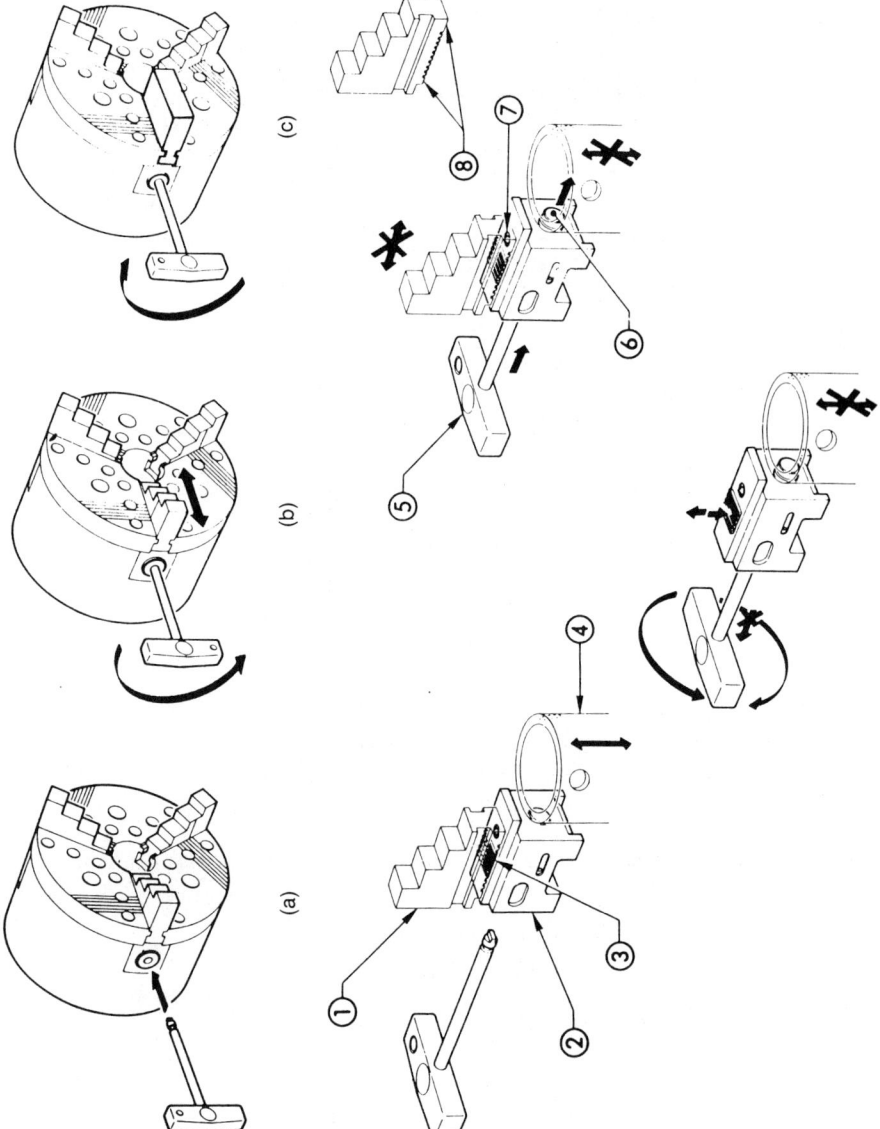

Fig. 9-86 Quick-change jaws. (*Gamet® jaws, courtesy Powerhold, Inc.*)

9-73

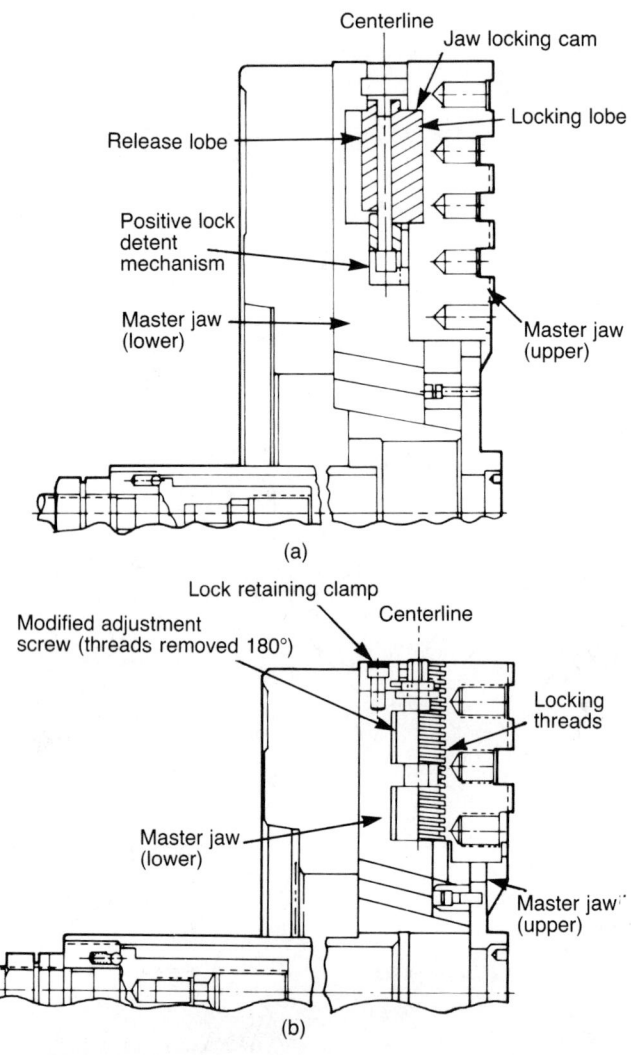

Fig. 9-87 **Two designs for quick-changing of chuck jaws.** (*Courtesy Cushman Industries*)

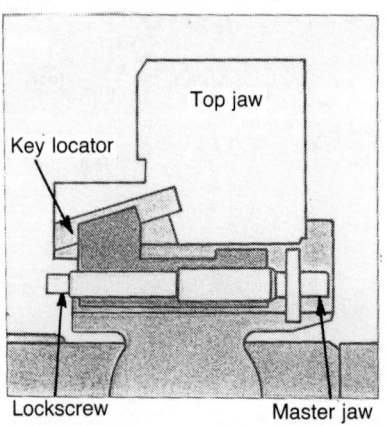

Fig. 9-88 **Manual quick-change design for changing top jaws.** (*Courtesy ITW Woodworth*)

In the power chuck shown in Fig. 9-89 the jaw locking mechanism is disengaged hydraulically to permit the top jaws to be removed from the chuck body to adjust the diameter, reverse the jaws, or exchange the jaws. Accidental operation of the machine spindle while the jaw locking mechanism is disengaged is prevented by mechanical and electrical interlocks from the actuator limit switch control.

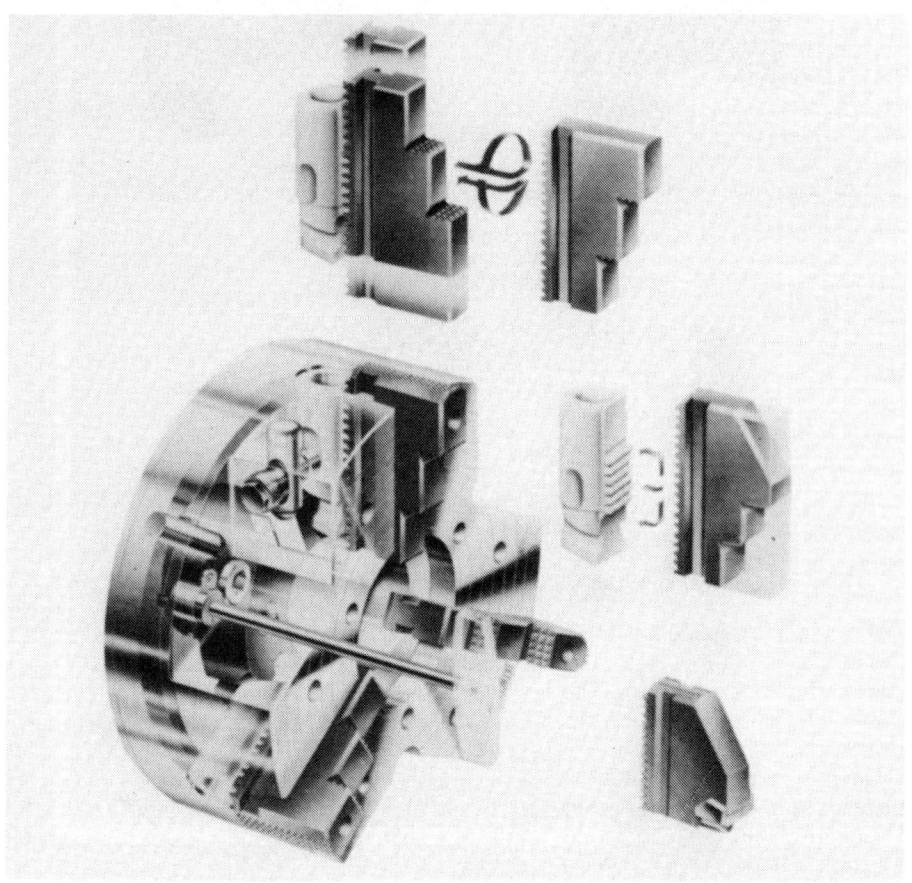

Fig. 9-89 Hydraulically-operated jaw locking mechanism. (*Courtesy Forkardt, Inc.*)

Figure 9-90 shows another quick-change system for OD clamping. The standard serrated-base jaws are replaced with an L-head shaped configuration. The top jaw slides onto the L-shaped base jaw and is secured without the use of additional tooling. For both OD and ID clamping, the serrated-base jaws are replaced by a T-head shaped base jaw with a built-in locking mechanism. The top jaws move sideways onto the T-heads, supported by a T-hook on the base jaw. A manually operated, spring-pin loading mechanism secures the top jaws in place and against lateral movement.

A quick-change system for drawtube-actuated collets and chucks is shown in Fig. 9-91. The system consists of a chuck body, clamping head, and changing tool. To accommodate workpieces having a different diameter, the clamping head is changed, while the chuck body remains in place on the machine. Clamping heads can be changed using a manually, pneumatically, or hydraulically operated tool. The unit can be easily adapted to automated handling or robotic systems.

All three top jaws can be changed simultaneously with the system shown in Fig. 9-92. The system consists of a handling system and double jaw carrier. When the

Fig. 9-90 Quick-change system for OD chucking. (*Courtesy Forkardt, Inc.*)

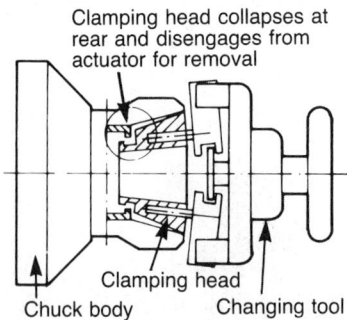

Clamping head collapses at
rear and disengages from
actuator for removal

Clamping head

Chuck body

Changing tool

Fig. 9-91 Quick changeover system for collet chucks. (*Courtesy Microcentric Corp.*)

machine spindle is indexed into position, the jaw carrier moves to the left and grips all jaws at the same time. Automatic depressing of unlocking pins disengages the cross-slides and unlocks the jaws. The jaw carrier disengages the jaws from their gearing, rotates 180°, engages the new set of jaws, locks automatically, and returns to its starting position.

The automatic jaw changer shown in Fig. 9-93 also replaces a set of three jaws in one operation. The changer is operated by either a workpiece loading gantry or a robot. In one movement to the machine spindle, the changer replaces the set of top jaws with new ones and returns the used set to the storage area.

Another automatic system for changing three top jaws of a power chuck is shown in Fig. 9-94. The system consists of a series of aluminum pallets, each of which stores a set of top jaws, and uses an automatic loading device such as a robot for loading and unloading the top jaws. To change jaws the loader grasps the hub on an empty pallet and places it over the chuck. The chuck releases the top jaws, which are simultaneously located and secured by the pallet. The pallet is then moved to storage and a pallet with the new jaws is placed over the chuck and released as they are located and clamped.

There are many applications where it becomes necessary to change the complete chuck in order to maximize the use of the machine(s). Systems for doing this will be covered in Chapter 14, Tooling for Flexible Machining Systems.

SPECIAL CHUCKS

Special chucks may be used when the gripping action of the jaws is not suitable, when additional clamping or locating features are required, when a smaller chuck is required, or when the distance from the spindle nose to the workpiece must be reduced.

A Centralizing Chuck for Pressure Plates. The chuck shown in Fig. 9-95 for machining pressure plates for automotive clutches centralizes and pulls the workpiece

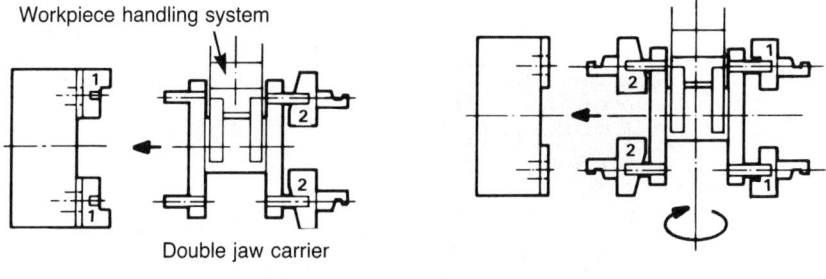

Workpiece handling system

Double jaw carrier

Fig. 9-92 System for changing all three jaws. (*Courtesy Rohm Products of America*)

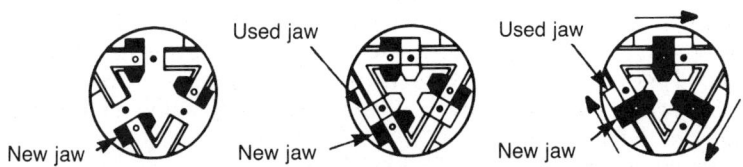

Used jaw

Used jaw

New jaw

New jaw

New jaw

Fig. 9-93 Three-jaw changer. (*Courtesy Forkardt, Inc.*)

back against rest buttons and then clamps the workpiece prior to its being faced, bored, and chamfered. The air-actuated chuck employs six jaws (1) to clamp the workpiece against three fixed adjustable rest buttons (2) to locate and support it in a parallel plane.

The workpiece has three lugs nesting into recesses in the chuck body which act as positive drivers.

Actuation of the air cylinder coupled to the chuck by the drawbar (3) starts the retraction of the jaw-carrier assembly (4). The jaws (1), on being retracted into the chuck, ride with their back edges on hardened cam blocks (5). The cam blocks direct the motions of the jaws to clamp on the OD of the workpiece while pulling it firmly against the rest buttons. The jaws are hard-faced, serrated, and ground to the same angle as the draft angle on the OD of the cast-iron workpiece.

The chuck can accommodate similar parts having different diameters and thicknesses by changing the jaws and by adjusting the stop pins. The chuck can also be adapted to clamp on the ID of parts to facilitate machining of the OD.

Fig. 9-94 Automatic jaw changing. (*SMW Systems, Inc.*)

Boring a Frail Workpiece. Figure 9-96 shows a chuck that locates and holds a very frail workpiece for the contour boring of its full inside contour.

A three-jaw universal chuck incorporates top jaws to center and drive the small end of the workpiece. To locate it longitudinally, a shoulder is provided in the jaws (1). To support the workpiece fully, a contoured ring, or a work support (2), is screwed onto a longitudinally adjustable carrier (3); this carrier compensates for slight variations in the outside contoured surface and over-all length of the workpiece. A carrier-ring housing (4), machined to bridge over the chuck jaws and to rigidly support and drive the work support, is screwed to the chuck face.

In operation, screws (5) are released, the workpiece is forced against the locating area (1) in the top jaws, and the jaws are tightened. In forcing the part forward, the work-supporting ring seats itself against the contour of the workpiece and moves along with it against the tension exerted by a spring (6) and is locked in this position by the screws.

A Chuck for Glass Parts. The chuck in Fig. 9-97 provides means for gripping and driving rectangular or elliptical objects of glass, such as the bulb of a cathode-ray tube, to maintain them centrally in relation to the axis of the lathe. With or without alterations, this chuck could be the answer to some holding and driving problems presented by metallic workpieces.

The chuck comprises a circular supporting plate or body (1) having a central opening enabling it to be secured over a dish-shaped hub (2) for attaching to the lathe spindle and for forming a vacuum chamber (3) for partially holding an object during chucking.

An annular recess of rectangular section in the chuck body nests three concentric rings (4, 5, and 6) which are free to rotate. The cover plate (7) encloses the rings and carries four slides (8) which move the chuck jaws (9).

The outer ring (4) and the inner ring (6) contain two arcuate eccentric slots, 180° apart, which extend a distance of 20° to 25° and have ample lead pitch to accommodate workpieces of different sizes.

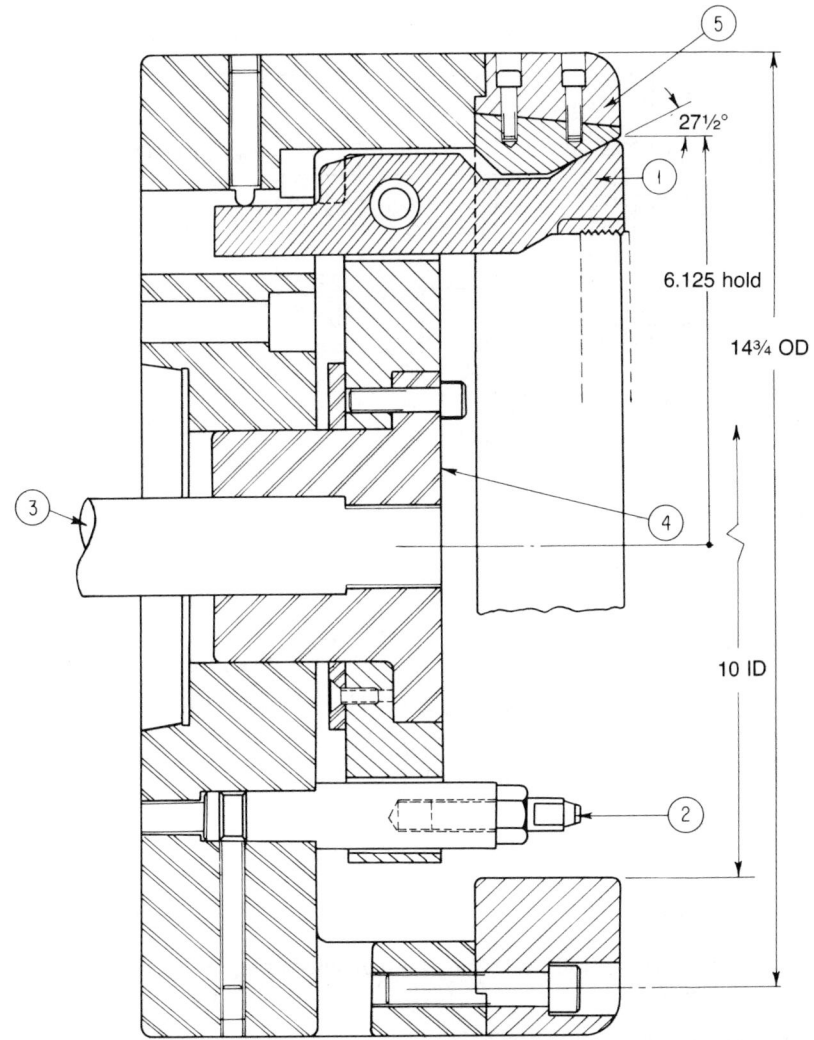

6.125 hold

14¾ OD

10 ID

27½°

Fig. 9-95 Special chucks for automotive-clutch pressure plates. (*Borg and Beck Div., Borg Warner Corp.*)

The outer and inner rings are connected and driven by the center ring (5) by means of toggle levers (10) which either pivot on a pin pressed into the center ring or are held in a circular recess in the ring. The extremities of the levers fit into circular recesses in the rings (4 and 6), having clearance to allow the levers to pivot through an angle of about 20°.

Each of the slides (8) supporting the jaws carries a pin which extends through radial slots in the cover plate (11) into and to follow the arcuate slots.

Attached to the underside of the driving ring (5) is a rack (12) which engages a pinion (13) keyed to a shaft (14) that is actuated by a knurled knob (15). Means are provided for locking the knob at any position of rest.

A Vacuum Chuck for Sheet Stock. The vacuum chuck of Fig. 9-98 holds sheet stock of various thicknesses for turning, facing, and counterboring. The unit has three components: the vacuum pump and motor, the rotary joint, and the chuck.

In operation, a workpiece is held against the chuck, and a vacuum is drawn behind the part. Assuming the efficiency of the device to be 75%, a 6-in.-diam. workpiece is

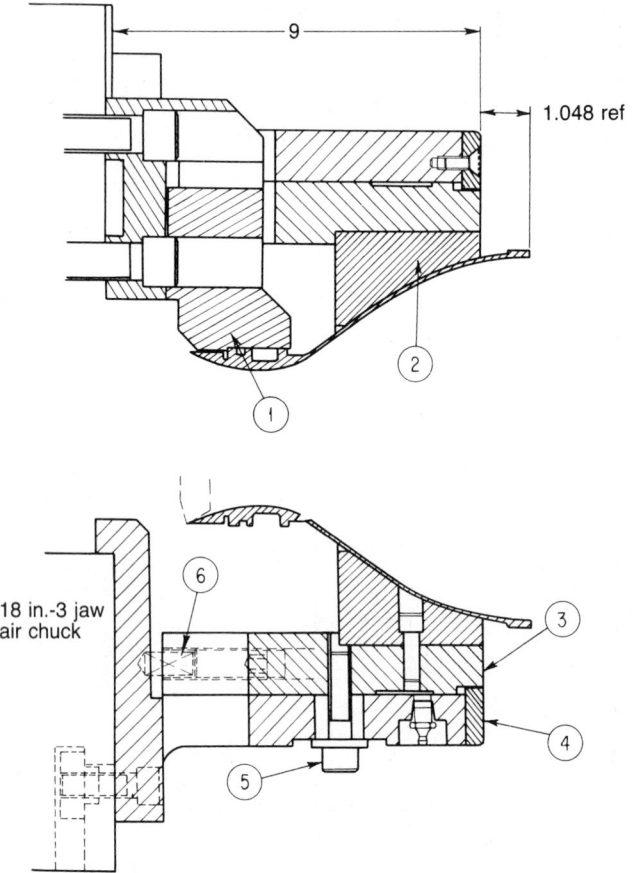

Fig. 9-96 Chuck for holding frail workpiece while contour-boring the entire internal surface. (*Courtesy Gisholt Machine Co.*)

held with a force of 300 lbf (1.3 kN). As the workpiece area increases, the holding force increases.

Materials as thin as 0.005 in. (0.13 mm) are held by using a flat disc for backup. Six to eight ¼-in.-diam. holes are drilled per square inch of the auxiliary disc area to expose the workpiece to the vacuum.

The chuck is machined from a linen-based, laminated phenolic plate 2 in. (51 mm) thick. It is bored and threaded to fit the lathe spindle. After mounting the plate, the chuck is finish-turned, faced, and grooved to receive rubber sealing rings. A hole is drilled from the outside to the inside diameter and sealed at the outer end. Holes connecting the single radial hole are drilled between each pair of sealing rings. Connecting holes are tapped so they can be sealed as necessary to ensure a vacuum behind the workpiece. Rubber rings are cemented in the grooves.

Machining of thin contoured parts may be accomplished with vacuum chucks made to fit the contour of the workpiece.

Rubber Expander-type Lathe Fixture. A rubber expander-type lathe fixture for holding parts easily distorted by chuck jaws is illustrated in Fig. 9-99. Clamping pressure is equalized by means of a floating shoe. With the design shown, the fixture is actuated by a hexagonal clamp nut; however, the fixture could be designed for drawbar actuation by means of an air or hydraulic cylinder.[17]

A
B
11
4
8
5
6
10
12
13,14,15
9
7
3
2
1
14
15
Section A-A
Section B-B

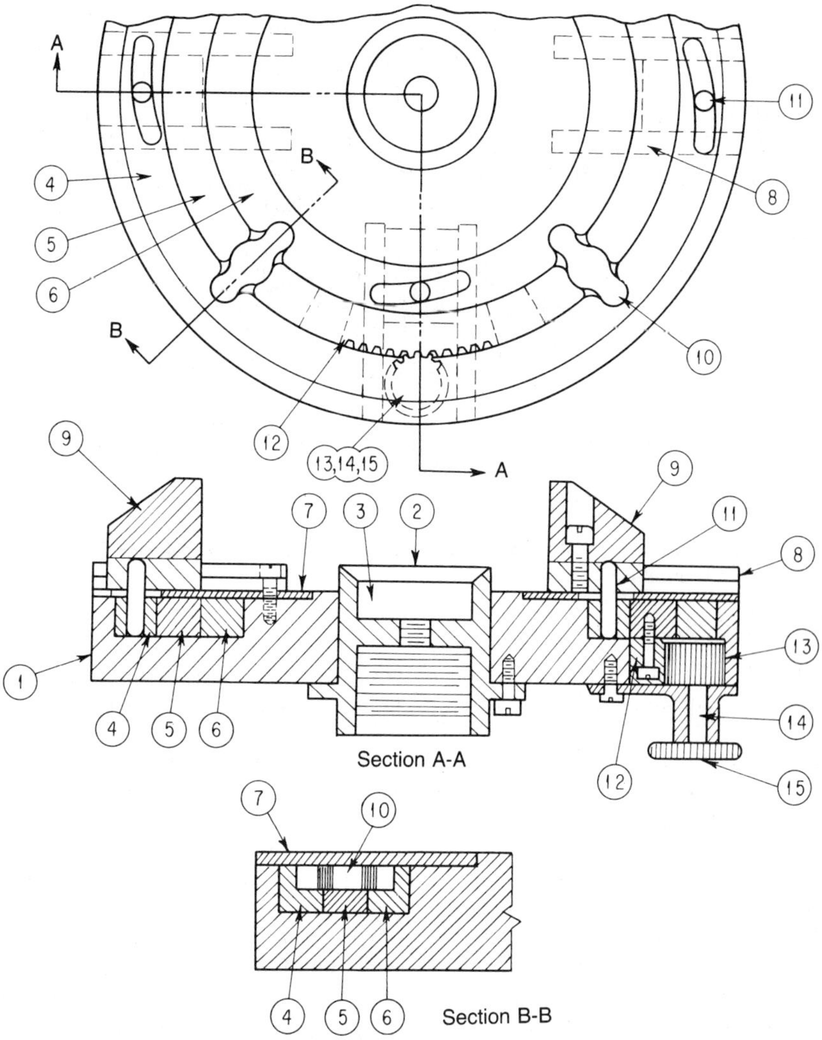

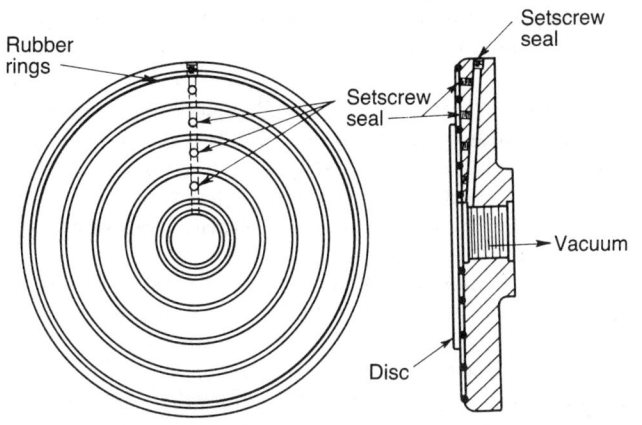

Fig. 9-97 Chuck for gripping objects of glass. (U.S. patent no. 2,780,570).

Rubber rings
Setscrew seal
Setscrew seal
Vacuum
Disc

Fig. 9-98 Vacuum chuck for sheet stock.[16]

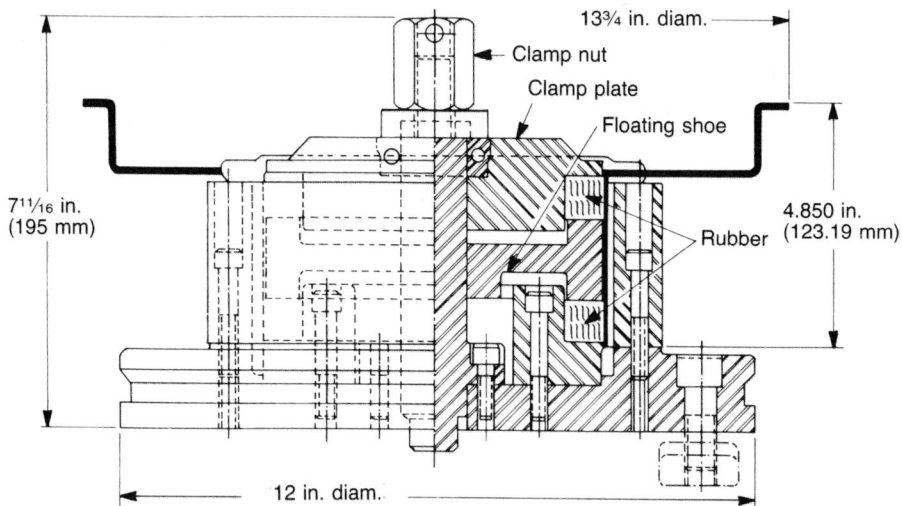

Fig. 9-99 Rubber expander-type lathe fixture for easily distorted workpieces has a floating shoe to equalize clamping pressure.

FACEPLATE FIXTURES

A lathe faceplate fixture, usually fastened to the lathe faceplate, incorporates conventional fixture-clamping and locating devices for holding a workpiece for lathe operations.

A shallow counterbore in the lathe faceplate receives a fixture back plug to locate the lathe fixture on the lathe-spindle center line. The fixture is secured to the faceplate by cap screws inserted through the fixture into tapped holes in the faceplate or by T-bolts inserted into T-slots in the faceplate. For more accurate positioning of the fixture on the lathe-spindle center line, circular-fixture base plates having indicating grooves or other accurately machined surfaces are used (see Figs. 9-102 and 9-106).

On high-speed lathes, the fixture, with a workpiece in place, should be dynamically balanced as accurately as possible. For low-speed operations, a reasonably exact static balancing is satisfactory. Balancing of the fixture with the workpiece in place helps to reduce vibration.

Faceplate Fixture to Produce a Radius. A faceplate fixture used to produce a 1.906 in. radius on a sector-shaped workpiece is shown in Fig. 9-100. A diamond pin and a plug that enters the bore of the workpiece are used for locating. A wedge-type clamp is used because of the difficulty of holding the workpiece while having the clamp clear the cutting tool.[18]

Commercial Faceplate Fixtures. Figure 9-101 illustrates a commercially available faceplate fixture for general use. The position of the worktable (1) is adjustable to suit workpiece requirements. The workpiece may be clamped to the table through the T-slots. Adjustable counterweights (2) are provided to ensure proper balance in operation. The base plate (3) is fastened to the lathe faceplate by cap screws inserted through the faceplate slots into tapped holes provided.

Faceplate Fixture for Threading and Boring. The fixture of Fig. 9-102 locates and internally holds a cylindrical part for turning the OD, which is then clamped on the outside while boring and threading the ID.

To eliminate the need of two fixtures, two clamping arrangements are supplied for one basic fixture. Each set of clamps is removed before the other set is used.

The 4.098-in.-diam. bore is used as an indicating surface to position the fixture accurately on the lathe-spindle center line.

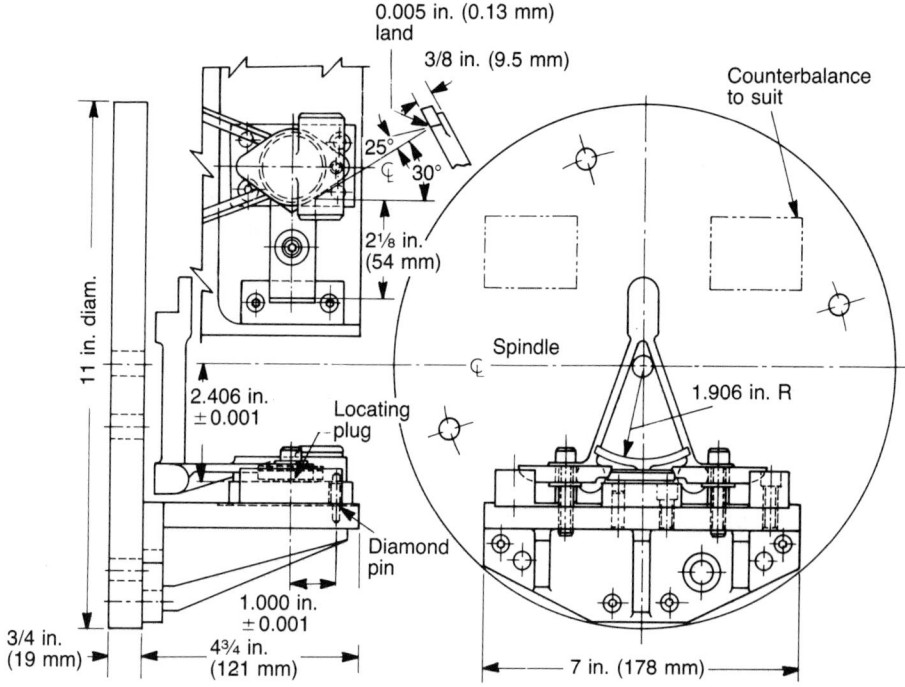

Fig. 9-100 Faceplate fixture with wedge-type clamp used to produce a radius on a sector-shaped workpiece.

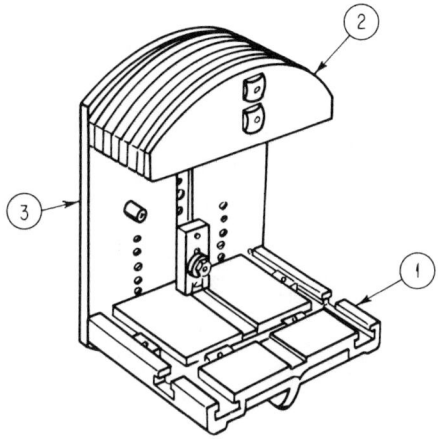

Fig. 9-101 Commercial-lathe faceplate fixture. (*Courtesy Universal Vise & Tool Co.*)

Boring Two Holes in Two Operations. The fixture shown in Fig. 9-103 locates and clamps a casting for accurately boring holes at two places by moving the holding part of the fixture to another spot on the faceplate. The casting is located on the sub-base plate (1) by a diamond pin (2) and a round pin (3). The sub-base plate is fastened to the base (4) by cap screws. As illustrated, the fixture is set up for boring hole *A* of the workpiece. To bore hole *B*, the sub-base plate containing the locating pins (5) pressed into the sub-base plate accurately position the plate by engaging bushed holes in the base plate.

9-83

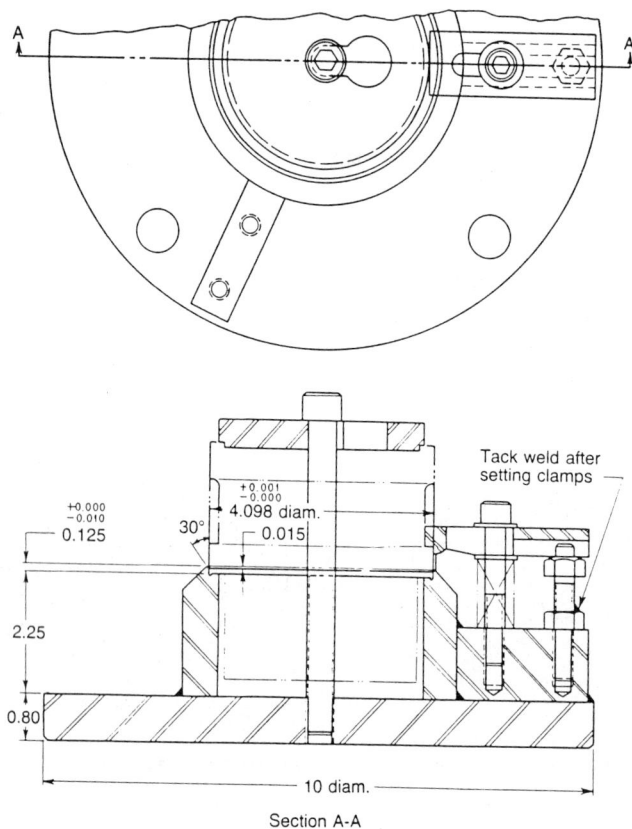

Section A-A

Fig. 9-102 Faceplate fixture to turn, bore, and tap a cylindrical part. (*Courtesy McDonnell Aircraft Co.*)

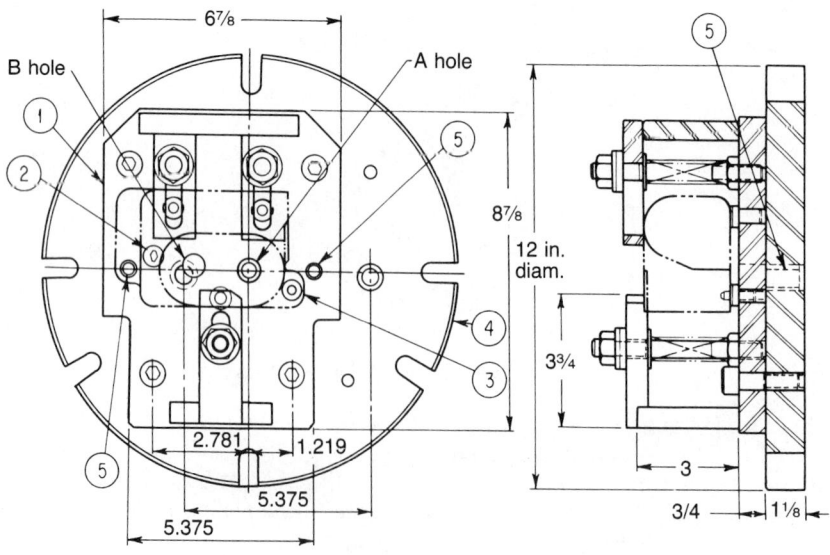

Fig. 9-103 Fixture for boring two holes in different locations in two operations. (*Courtesy Boyar-Schultz Corp.*)

A Right-angle Faceplate Fixture. The fixture of Fig. 9-104 is used for boring a hole in the end of the part of Fig. 9-103. Locating pins engaging the same workpiece holes utilized in the fixture of Fig. 9-103 are mounted in a right-angle bracket (1) which is fastened to a base plate (2). The part is supported on three rest buttons (3) and clamped by a strap clamp (4). Clamping pressure is applied within the triangular area described by the three supporting points.

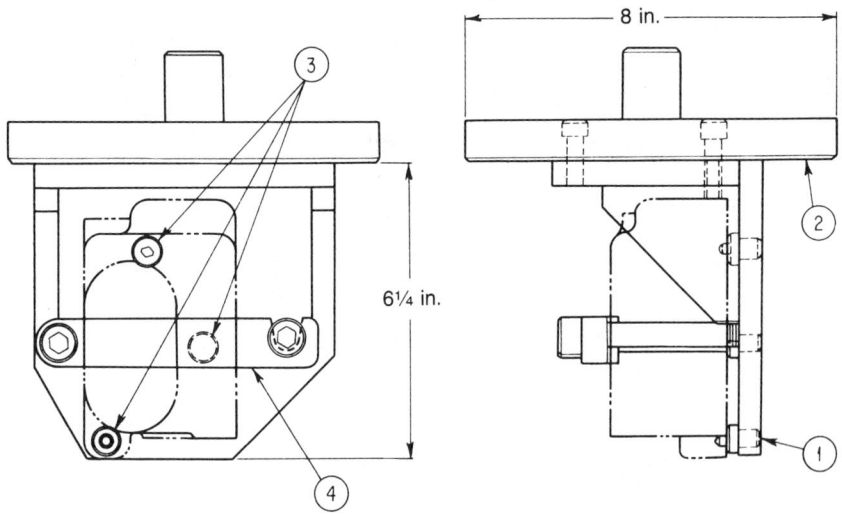

Fig. 9-104 Right-angle faceplate fixture. (*Courtesy Boyar-Schultz Corp.*)

Boring a Thin Part in a Lathe. Figure 9-105 illustrates a simple fixture for holding a part in a lathe while boring a hole at a 15° angle to the face of a flat plate 1-13/16 in. (46.04 mm) square and 1/16 in. (1.58 mm) thick.

The fixture is of welded construction using standard strap clamps to hold the part. Three dowel pins position the part and a fourth pin prevents rotation of the part if it slips under insufficient clamping pressure. A 15/16-in.-diam hole in the center of the fixture is used as an indicating surface to properly position the fixture on the spindle center line.

A Fixture for a Micrometer Stop Body. Figure 9-106a illustrates a fixture that holds and locates a workpiece while four operations are performed in a horizontal turret lathe. The workpiece shown in Fig. 9-106b is a small casting. Surfaces (1) to (5) were finished in a prior operation, and a hole (6) was previously drilled and tapped.

The fixture has a cast-iron faceplate (1) for mounting on the headstock of a turret lathe. A locator (2) made of CRS, machined, hardened, and ground, mates to workpiece surfaces (2, 3, and 5). A screw (5) engages the tapped hole (6) in the workpiece and draws the workpiece down to the nesting element. An upper block (3), also hardened and ground CRS, guides a profiled jaw (4) which clamps the top of the workpiece by rotation of a jackscrew (6). The fixture parts are attached to the faceplate with cap screws, and their location and alignment are ensured by dowels.

The nested workpiece is drilled, counterbored, tapped, and faced at the surfaces respectively numbered (7, 8, 9, and 10).

Chucking Threaded Workpieces. It is sometimes necessary or desirable to chuck a workpiece on a threaded portion of the part. If such a workpiece has a hexagonal or some other flat-sided surface, it can easily be unscrewed with a wrench at the conclusion of the operation. A wrench is generally necessary to break the seal formed between the work and the chuck face by the pressure of the cutting tools. If the part to be

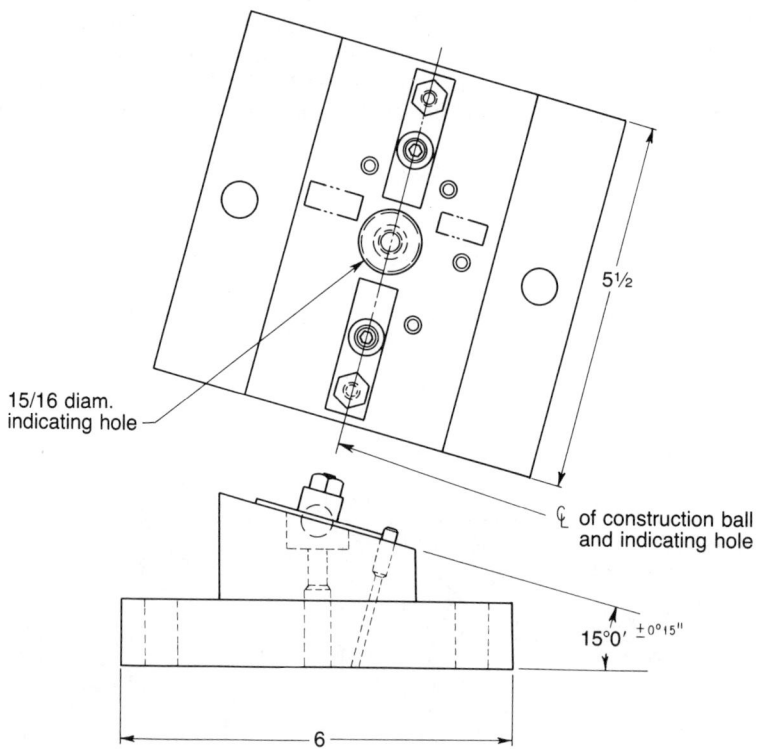

Fig. 9-105 Boring a thin part on a lathe. (*Courtesy The Emerson Electric Mfg. Co.*)

machined is round with no flat surfaces, or if the surfaces are not to be marked or damaged, the chuck must be designed so that this seal can be broken without using a wrench.

The chuck illustrated in Fig. 9-107*a* is used for holding a symmetrical piston by means of an internal thread while machining the opposite end of the part. The chuck seen in Fig. 9-107*b* is employed for holding a bushing by means of an external thread while finish-boring the work. An entirely different approach is necessary in designing chucks to hold workpieces by external threads than is required for those that hold by internal threads.

The chuck of view *a* consists of a body which is internally threaded to fit the spindle nose of a screw machine. A stud is threaded on one end to fit the workpiece and has a left-hand thread on the opposite end to fit a plate. The stud is a slip fit in a hardened bushing, which is pressed into the chuck body.

For better accuracy in locating the work, a hardened cover, which is screwed and doweled to the chuck body, is machined to fit the bead on the face of the piston. A handle, screwed into the plate, can be moved through an angle of 60° in a clearance slot provided in the chuck body. The handle is pushed against the forward end of the slot before a piece is screwed on the chuck; and after the machining operation is completed, it is pushed to the other end of the slot. This rotates the plate on the stud, thereby breaking the seal between the piston and the cover. A hole drilled radially in the periphery of the chuck body provides a means for mounting and removing the chuck from the machine spindle with a spanner wrench.

The chuck of view *b* consists of a body which is threaded to fit a master-chuck adapter. A nut, screwed on the chuck body, is internally threaded to fit the workpiece.

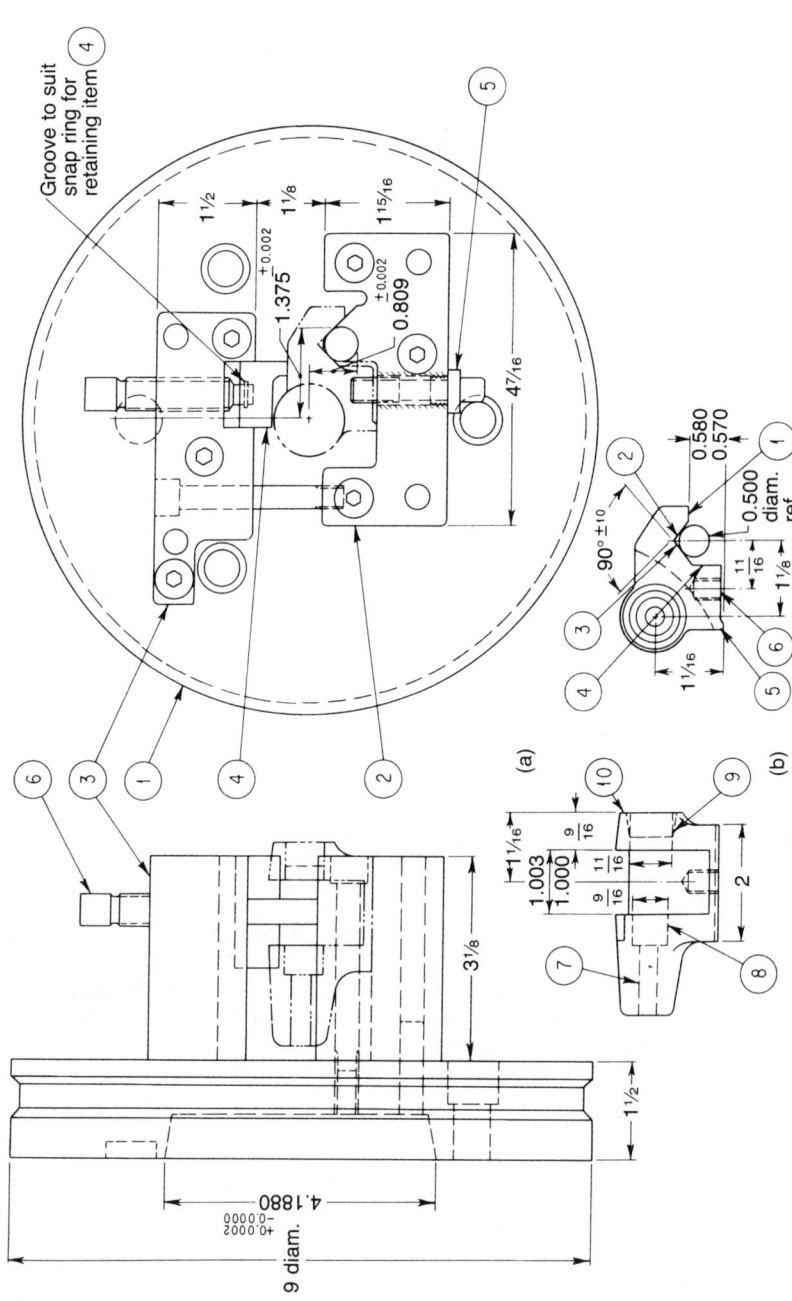

Groove to suit
snap ring for
retaining item (4)

(a)

(b)

Fig. 9-106 (a) Fixture for multiple operations in a horizontal turret lathe and (b) workpiece for fixture of (a). (*Courtesy Rockwell Mfg. Co.*)

9-87

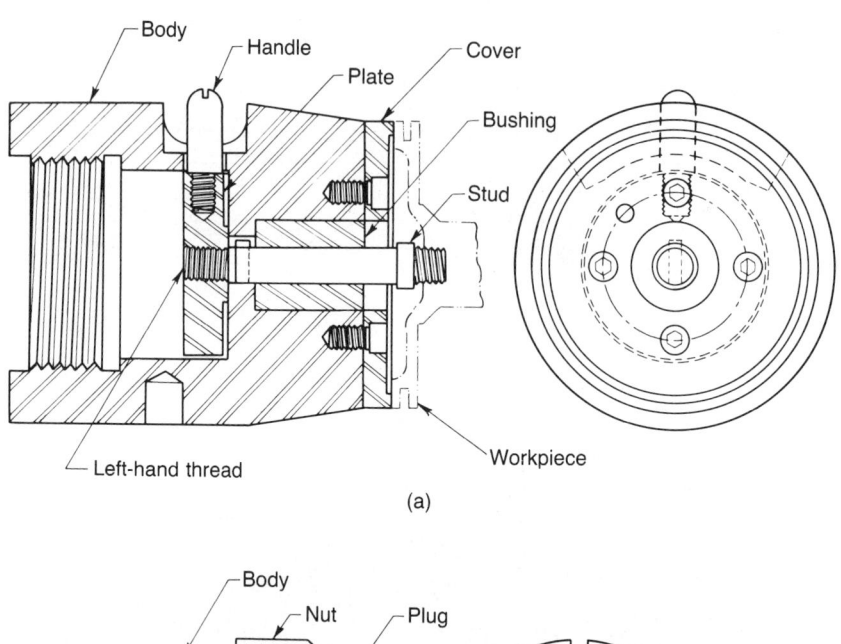

(a)

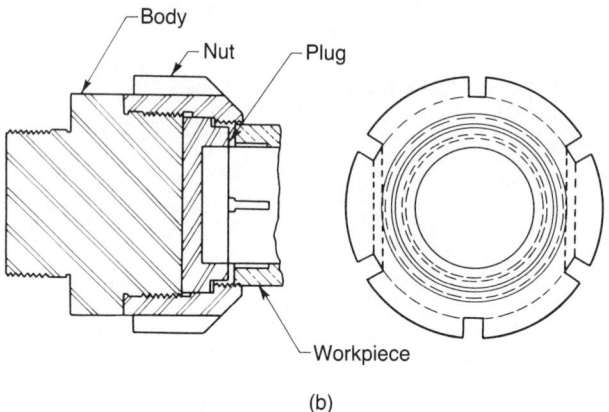

(b)

Fig. 9-107 Chucks for holding workpiece by threaded sections. (*Courtesy Machinery*)

The outside of the nut is slotted for a spanner wrench. A loose plug is a slip fit in the nut and rests against the face of the body. A recess is provided in the center of the plug to clear the boring tool.

In chucking, the work is screwed against this plug. After the machining operation, a slight turn of the nut will break the seal formed between the work and the plug. Flats, or pin-spanner wrench holes, are provided on the chuck body for wrenching it on or off the adapter.

These chucks can be designed to fit a large variety of workpieces and can be used on many types of machines. They are economical to make and yet provide a quick and accurate means to hold work.

A Pull-back Type of Clamp Fixture. A pull-back fixture (see Fig. 9-108), with air-operated clamps, clamps comparatively frail parts in a lathe after locating them radially on locating pins (1).

Six clamping fingers (2), each three of which are supported in a self-compensating manner in the two spiders shown (3 and 4), draw the workpiece firmly against the locating pads (5) to properly clamp it laterally. Compensation is accomplished by two Neoprene rings (6 and 7) at the centers of the spiders and by bronze spherical seats (8) on the clamping-finger pins (9).

9-88

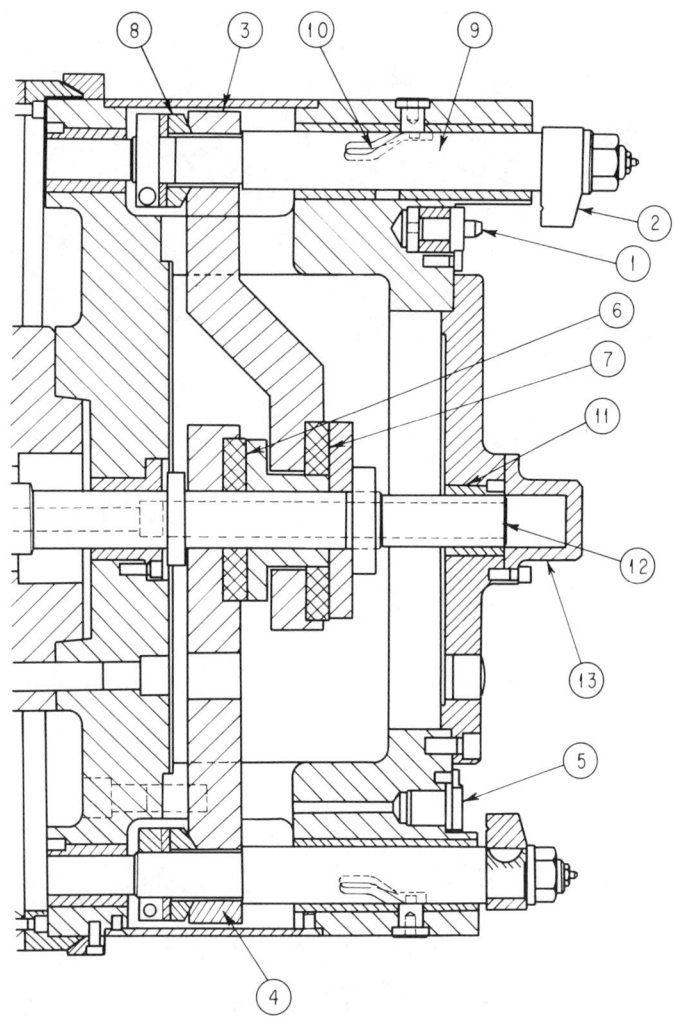

Fig. 9-108 Special air-clamping fixture with compensating clamps. (*Courtesy Gisholt Machine Co.*)

The cam tracks (10) in the pins rotate the clamping fingers out of position for loading and unloading the work. To keep the mechanism clean and to provide a bearing (11) for the end of the drawtube (12), a cover (13) is provided.

A Fixture with a Plastic Nest. Figure 9-109 illustrates a fixture incorporating a cast plastic workpiece nest. The fixture base (1), 13-in.-diam. by 1-in.-thick HRS, is tapped and drilled for mounting to the faceplate of a lathe. The cast-epoxy nest (2) is attached to the fixture base by a socket-head cap screw and three press-fit dowels. Two of the dowels (3) extend above the nest to serve as radial locators for the workpiece. Two clamps (4) slide in and are tightened to hold the workpiece in the nest. The smooth center hole in the fixture base is an indicating hole for centering during setup.

A Fixture with Reversible Clamps. Figure 9-110 illustrates a method of holding thin circular workpieces.

The base of the fixture (1) is a circular 16½-in.-diam. HRS plate. The base is machined for mounting to a lathe faceplate and has symmetrically located tapped holes for the mounting of the other fixture elements. A 1⅛ × 12-in.-diam. HRS plate (2),

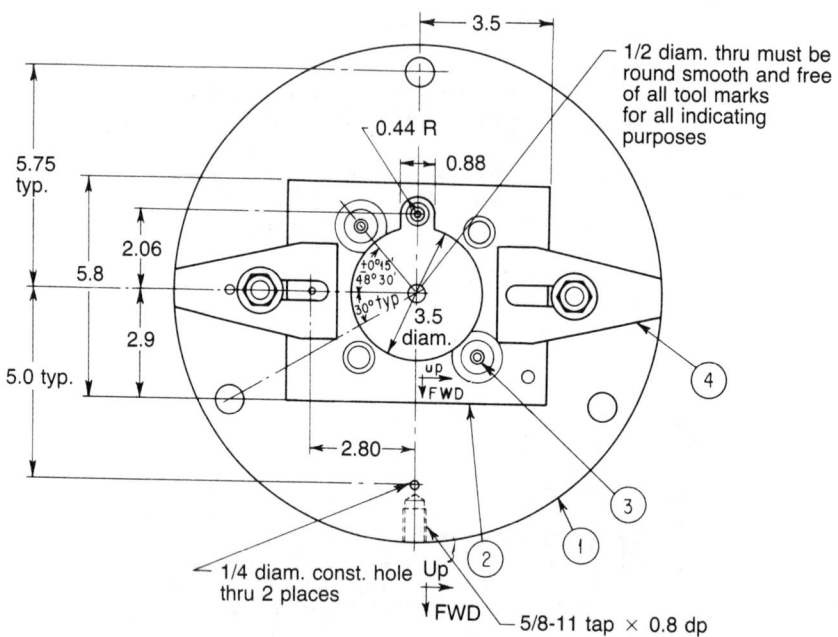

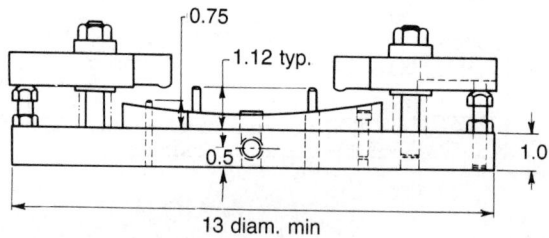

Fig. 9-109 Fixture with cast plastic nest. (*Courtesy McDonnell Aircraft Co.*)

profiled to the contour of the workpiece, is the workpiece nest. Four clamps (3) are located 90° apart around the perimeter of the base. The clamps have contoured pads (4) which mate to and bear on the nested workpiece. Two clamps can be mounted to bear on the workpiece from a location beyond the OD of the workpiece, as shown. In this position, the ID of the workpiece is accessible for finishing. With the clamps mounted in the inner set of holes, the OD of the workpiece is accessible.

A Faceplate Fixture for Turning an OD. Figure 9-111 illustrates a fixture of welded construction that holds a light workpiece for turning its OD.

The fixture base (1) is 1¼-in. (31.75 mm) thick HRS. Minor fixture elements (2 to 6), also of HRS, are machined and welded to the base, and the assembly is then normalized. The minor elements are tapped and drilled to receive threaded studs (7) which with jam nuts are used as adjustable workpiece locators. Three studs (8) with jam nuts are threaded into the base and also function as adjustable locators.

A triangular CRS plate (9) with three adjustable studs (10) is mounted on two pins (11 and 12) that are pressed into the fixture base. At both points of contact with the pins, the triangular plate is chamfered on both sides to leave a land of 1/16 in. (1.58 mm).

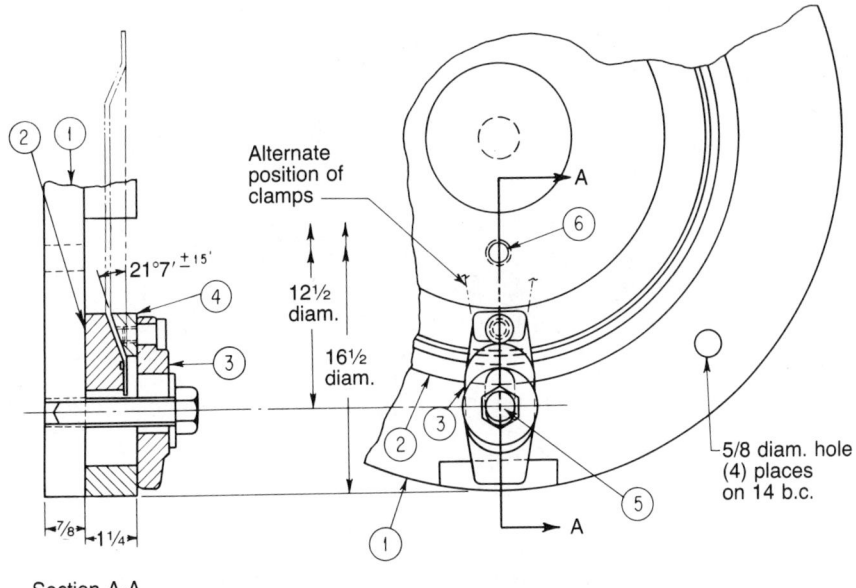

Section A-A

Fig. 9-110 **Fixture for alternately boring ID and OD of thin workpieces.** (*Courtesy The Martin Co.*)

The larger pin (12) protrudes approximately 2-1/16 in. (52.38 mm) farther from the base than the other pin (11). A CRS block (13) is placed on the large pin and is locked in that position by a drill-rod key (14). To prevent loss, the key is attached to the block with a flexible cable. An adjustable threaded stud (15) bears on the center of the triangular plate. The adjustable studs in the triangular plate bear on the workpiece at the points where it is supported by three locators (8).

The fixture base has a 1-in.-diam. indicating hole for centering the fixture on the lathe faceplate.

BORING

All or nearly all of the considerations in the design of jigs and fixtures used with machine tools for all types of metal-cutting operations must also be considered in the design of fixtures for boring operations.

Some considerations or conditions unique to boring-fixture design are:

1. Since some types of boring are performed on boring machines that allow the adjustment of the machine table or of the boring bar, it may be advantageous to provide indicating surfaces and holes in the fixture.
2. While master plates, measuring bars, or other devices for alignment and positioning of the bar with respect to the fixture and workpiece holes may or may not be integral with the fixture, they are frequently designed by the fixture designer.
3. Allowances should be made for bar travel and boring-tool adjustment without interference with the fixture.
4. When the fixture is designed to support the bar, hardened stationary bushings of frictionless bearings should be incorporated to minimize vibration and whip in the bar for best accuracy of hole size and location.
5. If the fixture designer is also responsible for bar design, the surfaces of the bar contacting the bearings in a fixture should be chrome-plated or hardened for minimum wear.

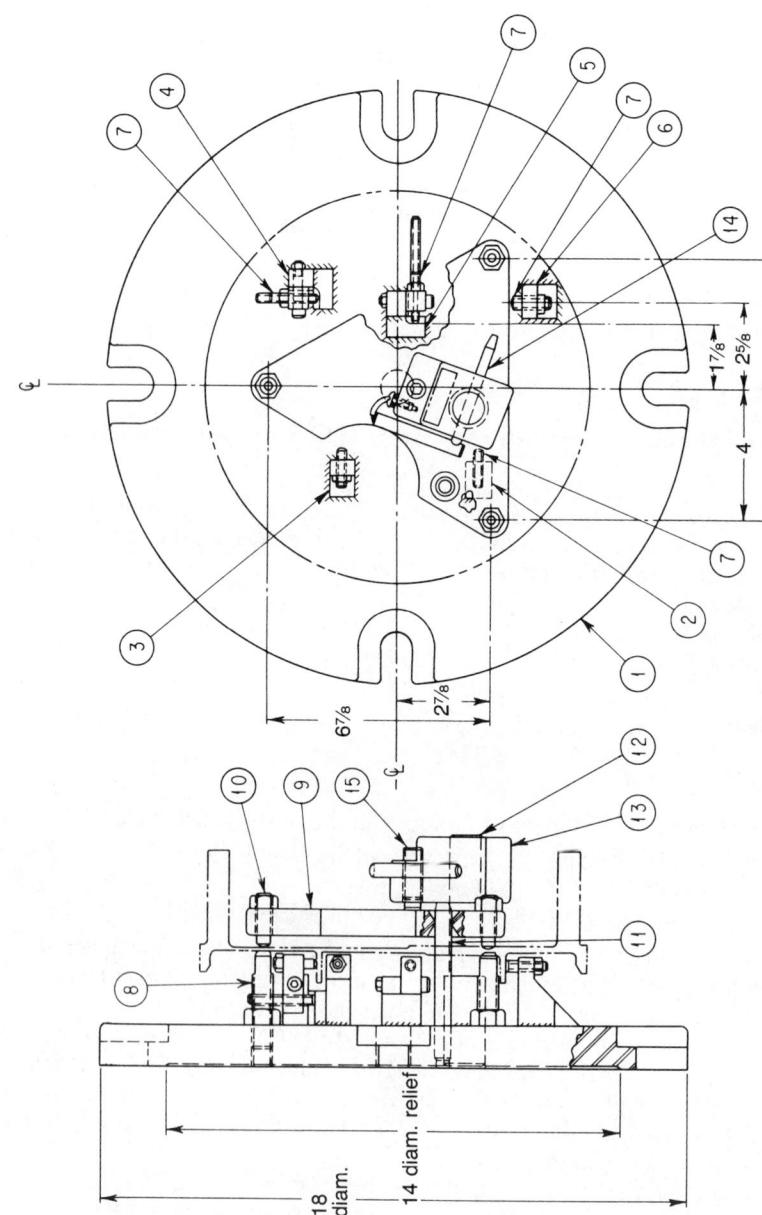

Fig. 9-111 Faceplate fixture for holding a drum while turning its OD. (*Courtesy The Emerson Electric Mfg. Co.*)

9-92

Boring is a precision machining process for generating internal cylindrical forms by removing metal with single-point tools or tools with multiple cutting edges.[19] This process is most commonly performed with the workpiece held stationary and the cutting tool both rotating and advancing into the work. Boring is also done, however, with the cutting tool stationary and the workpiece rotating.

Common applications for boring include the enlarging or finishing of cored, pierced, or drilled holes and contoured internal surfaces. Related operations sometimes performed simultaneously with boring include turning, facing, chamfering, grooving, and threading.

Boring can be done on horizontal, vertical, or angular machines as long as the machine design provides the inherent rigidity and accuracy to produce the tolerances required. It is also performed on some drilling machines, particularly radial drills, described in Chapter 8.

Applications of boring can be divided into heavy cutting and precision operations. Heavy boring is generally done on large horizontal and vertical boring machines, including vertical turret lathes and boring, drilling, and milling machines. These machines and other machines also used for boring include automatic lathes, multispindle bar and chucking machines, machining centers, and transfer machines.

Precision boring is performed on machines specifically designed for this purpose. These machines generally take relatively light cuts, maintain close tolerances, and are often capable of high production rates.

ACCURACY IN PRECISION BORING

Accuracies that can be maintained in precision boring operations depend upon many factors. These include the design and condition of the boring machine and spindles used, proper workholding equipment, the correct cutting tool material and geometry, and optimum cutting speeds and feed rates. The design of the machine tool is one of the most important factors in the economic achievement of desired results.

For very close tolerance requirements, temperature is an important factor. Heat generated during the cutting process may have to be dissipated by the flow of cutting fluid, and the fluid itself may have to be temperature controlled to obtain the necessary tolerances. In some cases, it may be necessary to use thermal-controlled machine components or to install the boring machine in a temperature-controlled room.

PRECISION-BORING MACHINES

Precision-boring machines are available in a wide variety of types to suit many different applications. Configurations include single or multiple spindles arranged horizontally, vertically, or at any required angle. Selection of the type to be used depends primarily upon the size and configuration of the workpieces, operations to be performed, and production requirements.

Cutting tool or workpiece rotation for precision boring depends upon the specific application and the size, shape, and balance of the workpiece. The ability to rotate workpieces or tooling makes it possible to perform many difficult operations simultaneously or in sequence. It also assures concentric diameters and square faces, which are difficult to obtain when a workpiece is relocated for separate operations. Irregularly shaped and/or unbalanced workpieces are generally bored with rotating tools. Rotating tools and multiple spindles are also often used when several holes have to be bored in the same workpiece. Rotation of the workpiece is sometimes preferred for more complex operations.

Many types of precision-boring machines are available. Major types include horizontal single and double-end machines, center-drive machines, vertical machines, way-type machines, and NC machines.

Since heat and vibration are major deterrents to the accuracies and finishes required in precision boring, heavy-duty rigid bases are required for the machines to minimize problems of chatter and vibration. Also, to isolate vibrations and avoid heat distortion of machine components, all electrical, hydraulic, and drive equipment is generally located external to the base.

Horizontal Single-end Machines. A typical horizontal precision-boring machine arranged for single-end operation is illustrated in Fig. 9-112. The single spindle is mounted on a bridge over the table at the left-hand end of this hydraulically operated machine. These single-end machines can be provided with two or more spindles depending upon the size of the workpiece, operation to be performed, and production requirements.

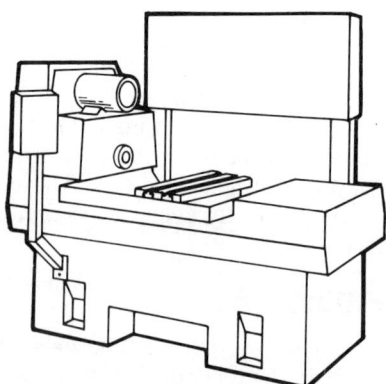

Fig. 9-112 Horizontal, single-spindle, precision-boring machine.

Single-end boring machines can be also be arranged with cross slides to provide either linear motion or feed motions in a direction at a right angle to the direction of slide travel. In addition, the cross slide can be fitted with a manual or automatically operated, indexing or rotary table for mounting workholding fixtures. Tailstocks can also be mounted on the machines for between-center operations.

Additional buildup can be made on this type of boring machine by adding a toolholding turret to an indexing table located on the cross slide. This configuration permits multiple turning and facing-type operations to be performed when the spindle(s) is equipped with a chuck for rotating the workpiece. The machines are also often arranged with automatic loading and unloading equipment to shorten the cycle time.

Double-end Machines. Horizontal precision-boring machines can also be arranged for double-end operation. This is accomplished by also mounting a bridge and spindle(s) at the right-hand end of the machine. One or more spindles can be provided at each end.

On double-end machines, an operator often loads workpieces on or unloads them from one end while parts on the other end are being machined, thereby saving what otherwise would be downtime for loading and unloading workpieces. As is the case with single-end machines, various attachments are available to improve production.

Workpieces are generally rotated by chucks or fixtures on the spindles for turning-type operations; tools are mounted on the cross slide. For boring, tools are mounted on the spindle quills and rotated, and the workpieces are mounted on the cross slide. Automatic cycling, tool-wear adjustment, gaging, and workpiece locating clamping are available.

Center-drive Machines. A double-end cam-controlled, center-drive boring and contouring machine is illustrated in Fig. 9-113. Contouring slides at each end of the

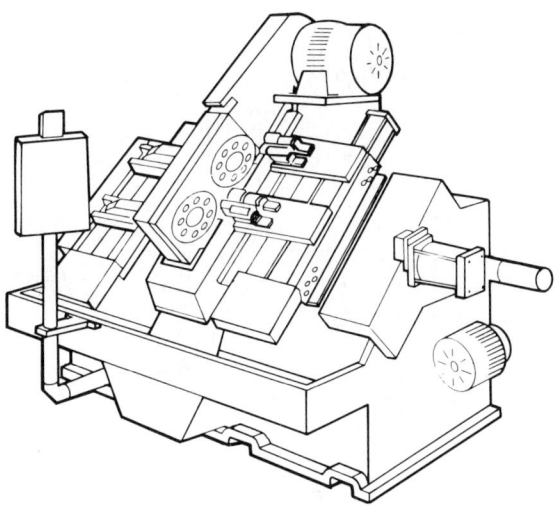

Fig. 9-113 Cam-operated, center-drive, precision-boring machine with two spindles.

center-driven spindles have cam-controlled strokes. Boring, facing, and contouring can be performed on both ends of the workpieces simultaneously, thus assuring concentricity of opposing bores.

On these center-drive machines, workpieces must be held on their outside surfaces by collet or diaphragm chucks mounted within hollow spindles shafts. The angular configuration of the frame on the machine shown in Fig. 9-113 is used to minimize the loading reach to the rear spindle and to provide adequate slope for chip disposal.

Vertical Machines. Precision-boring machines with vertical spindles and tools fed from above are often preferred for heavier workpieces. This design facilitates loading and unloading, makes it easier to adjust and change tools, and requires less floor space. Like most other precision-boring machines, these machines can be supplied for completely automatic cycling, controlled by hard-wired relay logic or a programmable controller.

A typical precision-boring machine arranged with two vertical spindles is shown in Fig. 9-114. Turning, facing, contouring, and boring-type operations are performed by means of a compound slide on which the cutting tools are mounted. The machine illustrated is cam operated, but a hydraulic machine would look essentially the same. The cylinder shown in Fig. 9-114 holds the cam followers against the cam and retracts the vertical slide to its uppermost position for easier loading and unloading.

Way-type Machines. A way-type precision-boring machine, in its simplest configuration, can be essentially the same as a single-end boring machine, with one exception. Instead of the spindle and motor being stationary on a bridge at one end of the machine, with a hydraulically operated table on a slide in the middle of the machine, the design is reversed. With a way-type machine, the table becomes the stationary section and the spindle and motor are mounted on a hydraulically operated table and slide unit, complete with a self-contained motor spindle drive system. This permits the self-contained spindle slide unit, with its spindle-mounted tool, to traverse toward the stationary machine table holding a fixture-mounted workpiece.

This same feature can be used by configuring the machine with two self-contained slide units adjacent to one another.

With this design, two parts can be machined at a time when the stationary table is equipped with two workholding fixtures. Another version, depending upon the type of

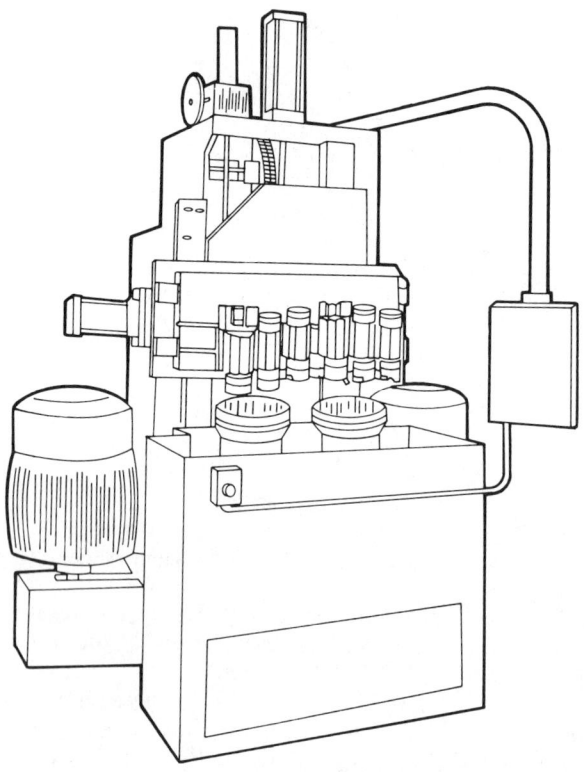

Fig. 9-114 Cam-operated precision-boring machine with two vertical spindles.

workpieces and production requirements, is an end-loading way-type machine with workholding fixture(s) at that same end and self-contained spindle-slide units traversing toward the operator and fixtures. These way-type machine tools are quite versatile, permitting spindle-slide units to operate individually, simultaneously, and/or sequentially.

Dial-type Machines. Precision-boring machines can also be set up as way-type machines. These concepts lead to dial-type configurations in which all the self-contained spindle-slide units are in a circle, mounted on slide wings, and simultaneously traversing toward the center. The center portion of these machines is usually equipped with a large indexing table and subplate containing several workholding chucks or fixtures. The indexing table automatically positions at each station (or wing) having a self-contained spindle-slide unit with its tooling.

Dial-type machines are fully automatic; the operator simply loads and unloads parts as the machine indexes and the slide units traverse in and out (see Fig. 9-115). These machines are usually designed for high production requirements. They can also be equipped with tool-mounted vertical slide units and/or hopper feeding for bushing or bearing insertions during the automatic cycle.

NC Boring Machines. One type of numerically controlled precision-boring machine is illustrated in Fig. 9-116. This horizontal, ballscrew-actuated, CNC machine has three spindles for high-volume production. These machines are also available with one, two, or four spindles and can operate at high metal removal rates with close tolerances capabilities. They also offer the flexibility necessary for high-volume production. Electric servo axes and variable-speed spindle drives allow infinitely programmable variations of spindle speeds, feed rates, and tooling-path control.

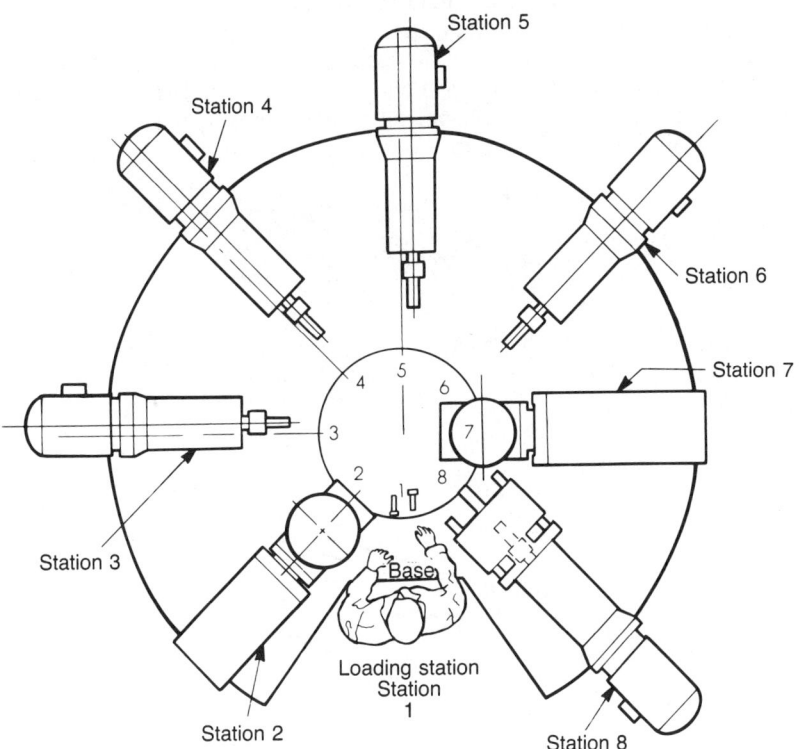

Fig. 9-115 Dial-type precision-boring machine having eight stations. (*Courtesy Wadell Machine & Tool Co.*)

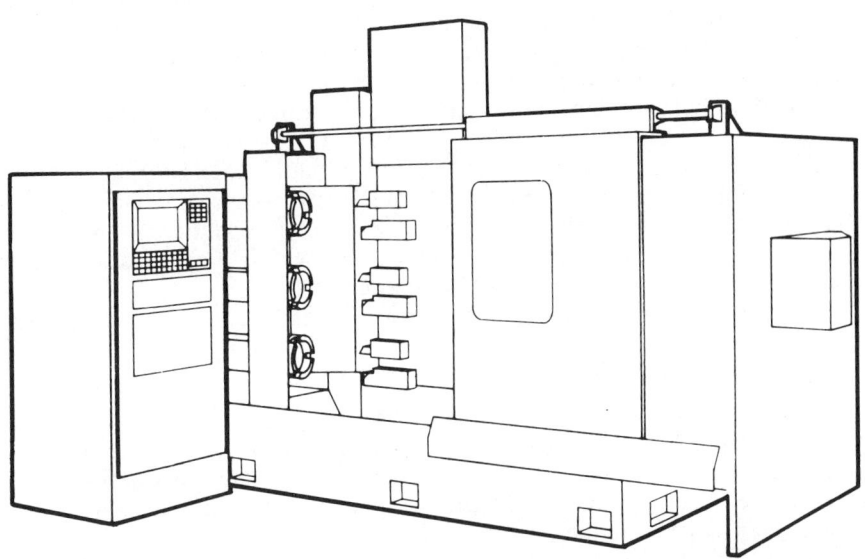

Fig. 9-116 CNC precision-boring machine having three spindles for high production. (*Courtesy The Olofsson Corp.*)

A versatile CNC boring machine (see Fig. 9-117) for machining odd-shaped work-pieces consists basically of a rotating head with a feed-out slide on which various tools can be mounted. The workpieces are held stationary. The machine has two axes of CNC motion. The first axis is the slide that moves radially on the rotating head to control bore sizes and facing feed rates. The second axis is the entire headstock moving relative to the workpieces or the workpiece moving relative to the tool. This provides axial motion for boring feed rates and controlling the depths on flanges, faces, etc. The combination of both motions can produce tapers or contours.

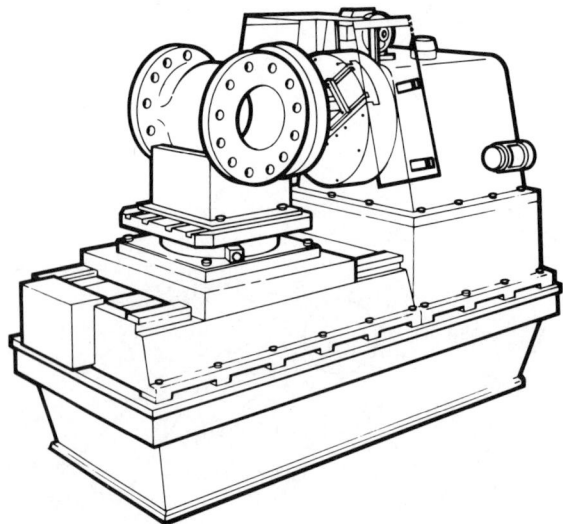

Fig. 9-117 CNC boring machine has two axes of motion: A slide that moves radially on the rotating head and the entire headstock. (*Courtesy Davis Tool Co.*)

Modular design allows the machine to be built with a stationary head and rotary table on a slide; the head movable on a slide and the rotary table stationary; the head movable on a slide and the rotary table mounted on a cross slide; dual head to machine both ends of a workpiece simultaneously; and other configurations.

Horizontal Boring Machines. Horizontal boring machines (HBMs) usually do many other operations besides boring, especially milling. As a result, they are often called horizontal boring mills or horizontal boring, milling, drilling, and tapping machines. These heavy-duty machines are employed extensively for large, complex castings, forgings, weldments, and similar workpieces. They perform different operations at various locations on the workpieces without the need for changing the basic setup, and they can maintain accurate relationships between the machined surfaces. These machines are not, however, high-production machines and are generally limited to low to medium size runs.

Characteristic features of HBMs include the following:

1. Horizontal spindles that rotate the cutting tools.
2. Horizontal surfaces on which workpieces are mounted.
3. Power feed of the spindle to advance cutting tools into the workpieces.
4. Power-fed relative motion between the spindle and workpiece in at least two axes perpendicular to the spindle axis.
5. Power saddle feed parallel to the spindle axis.
6. Outboard supports, on some machines, for the ends of line boring bars and arbor-mounted slotting cutters.

Horizontal boring machines are available in a wide range of capacities. The size of a machine is often identified by the diameter of its spindle, which generally varies from 3 to 10 in. Spindle rigidity is directly related to the fourth power of its diameter. As a result, considerable additional cutting power is obtainable with larger spindle diameters. Main drive motors range from 15 to 75 hp (11.2 to 56 kW) or more.

Various designs of horizontal boring machines are available. Three major designs are table, planer, and floor-type machines. They are also available in traveling-bar and traveling-head types. With respect to boring only (excluding milling and other operations), they can be classified as stub boring or line boring machines. Stub boring is done with a bar supported only by the spindle. Line boring is done with a bar that extends through the workpiece and is supported at one or more points in addition to the machine spindle. Cross-feed column machines are also available, providing the column with two axes of travel: one perpendicular to the spindle travel and the other parallel to the spindle travel.

Table-type Machines. In table-type machines (see Fig. 9-118), the table feeds horizontally on saddle ways both parallel and at right angles to the spindle axis. On machines having a long table travel perpendicular to the spindle support, additional outboard supports on runways are often provided. The headstock moves vertically on the column, and the spindle has a horizontal feed motion. This type of machine is well suited to general-purpose work for which other machining operations are required in addition to boring.

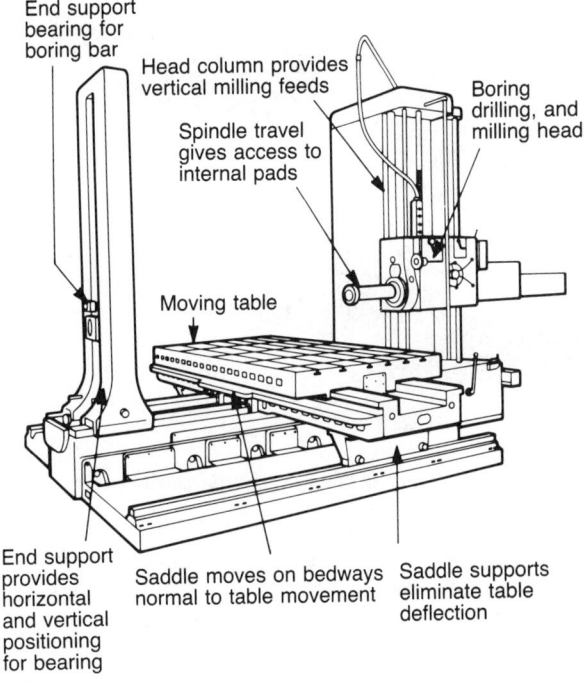

Fig. 9-118 Table-type horizontal boring, drilling, and milling machine with end support for line boring operations.

Planer-type Machines. These horizontal boring machines are similar to the table-type design except that they have no table-supporting saddle. The table travel is at right angles to the spindle along the base ways. Feed perpendicular to the table (parallel to the spindle) is obtained by feed motion of the spindle. Feed motion of the column along the base ways is used when exceptional rigidity is required to maintain accuracy in machining long and heavy work. A horizontal-spindle planer-type boring machine equipped with CNC and a rotary table is shown in Fig. 9-119.

Fig. 9-119 Planer-type horizontal boring machine equipped with rotary table. (*Courtesy Cincinnati Gilbert Machine Tool Co.*)

Floor-type, Traveling-column Machines. These machines (see Fig. 9-120) use a stationary floor plate equipped with T-slots instead of a table to hold the work. They are ordinarily used to handle large workpieces of a weight, size, or shape that would make it impractical to employ a reciprocating table. Horizontal feeds perpendicular to the spindle axis are obtained by movement of the column along the base ways rather than by table movement. The headstock moves vertically on the column, and the spindle has a horizontal feed motion. On some machines of this type, the column is mounted on a saddle providing an additional motion parallel to the spindle axis.

Portable Machines. This type of machine is used when it is more convenient to move the machine to the workpiece. Such machines are used inside large vessels and/or to repair assembled components of large mechanisms in place.

Traveling-bar Machines. Traveling-bar, heavy horizontal boring machines consist essentially of a headstock containing a motor and gear reduction unit giving rotary

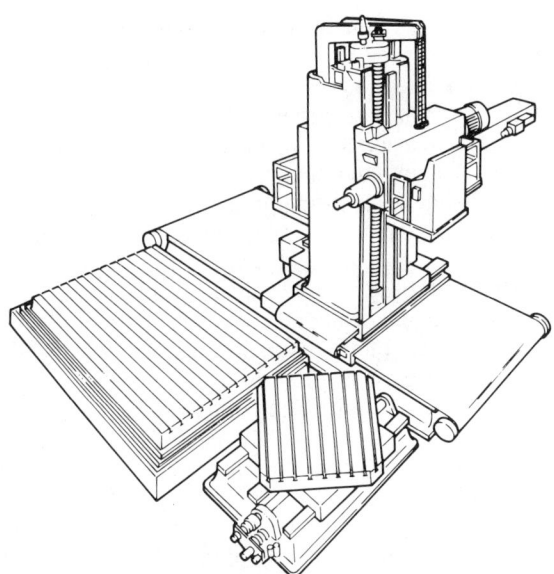

Fig. 9-120 Floor-type horizontal boring machine. (*Courtesy G. A. Gray Div., Kearney & Trecker Corp.*)

motion to the bar or spindle. A transmission unit is also included giving feed and rapid traverse motion, in and out, to the bar. An outboard support is used to support the bar after the bar has been positioned through the bore of the workpiece. A boring head is added and clamped securely to the bar; feeding motion is then given to the bar through means in the headstock. This type of heavy-duty horizontal boring machine has one disadvantage in that it must occupy floor space almost three times its own length because of the length of the boring bar.

Traveling-head Machines. Traveling-head machines are essentially the same as the traveling-bar machines except that the boring bar contains a screw attached by a nut to the boring head and derives its feed motion from a planetary-type gearbox attached to the outboard or inboard end of the boring bar. The headstock supplies power to rotate the bar while the feed mechanism on the bar imparts feed and rapid traverse to the boring head. For loading and unloading the workpiece, the boring head may be locked securely to the outboard support. An air motor is attached to a coupling on the outboard end of the screw; and with a rolling dolly to support the boring bar, the bar is traversed to a loading position and returned to operating position after work loading is completed.

When split workpieces such as some housings and casings are machined, the lower half of the workpiece is positioned on supports under the boring bar. The bar is then lowered onto pedestal supports and the upper half of the workpiece is bolted to its lower half, with the boring bar inside the workpiece.

This machine requires floor space twice its own length and then only when loading and unloading a workpiece. Constant sag is maintained in the boring bar between two supports because the boring head feeds over the bar. A traveling-support head may be used when long holes are to be bored to fairly close tolerances.

Toolchanging HBMs. Many builders of horizontal boring machines offer automatic toolchangers as an option. This places the machines in the class of machining centers.

MACHINE CONTROLS

Horizontal boring machines are still built for manual operation, but most are now supplied with manual data input (MDI) or CNC for relative positioning between the cutting tool and workpiece. Digital readout units are used extensively on manually controlled machines.

MDI Controls. Manual data input controllers provide a simple and more economical alternative to CNC for small-lot production. With these controllers, the machine operator places required dimensional, feed, and speed data into the control by means of dials or switches. Once the command data is entered, the operator pushes a button and the machine automatically moves to the commanded position in the prescribed manner. The next data is then entered, the button is pushed again, and so on until the workpiece is completed.

Controllers with MDI are now available with electronic, integrated memory systems. The control/memory unit automatically records each operating sequence instructed by the machine operator. Sequence numbers are automatically assigned to each operation. Program instructions can also be entered manually, viewed, and/or edited. In most cases, in order to retain maximum operator control, feed rates and spindle speeds are not stored.

In the automatic mode, a stored program operates the controller and machine. The controller operates block by block, stopping at the completion of each block. Information for the next block is displayed, so the operator can change feed rates and spindle speeds as required. Displayed programs can be modified without changing the stored programs. The stored programs can be transferred to any compatible storage medium, such as tape cassettes, punched paper tape, or hard copy. Prerecorded program tapes can be loaded into storage.

CNC Units. Horizontal boring machines equipped with CNC can produce slopes, circles, arcs, and complex shapes. Most HBMs have four motions under CNC. On table-type machines, the spindle, head, table, and saddle are controlled; on planer-type machines, the spindle, head, table and column are controlled; and on floor-type machines, the spindle, head, column, and on certain machines, the saddle.

Slide motions on horizontal boring machines with CNC are generally identified as follows:

- X-axis.....Table, horizontal.
- Y-axis.....Head, vertical.
- Z-axis.....Spindle.
- W-axis.....Saddle, column, or rotary table on slide.
- A-axis.....Rotary table tilt.
- B-axis.....Rotary table, horizontal.
- C-axis.....Rotary table, vertical.

Vertical Boring Machines. Vertical boring machines (VBMs), such as the one shown in Fig. 9-121 and vertical turret lathes (VTLs) (see Fig. 9-122) are turning machines that in many ways are similar to conventional lathes turned on end. Workpieces are mounted on a horizontal table or chuck rotating about a vertical axis. Cutting tools, which are generally nonrotating, are fed horizontally or vertically into the workpieces.

Operations performed on a VBM or VTL are similar to those done on conventional lathes. They include turning, facing, boring, grooving, generating threads, and contouring. These machines are commonly used to make round parts having short lengths in relation to their diameters and to make large, heavy, and cumbersome parts.

DIFFERENCES BETWEEN VBMs AND VTLs

Vertical boring machines (or mills) originally had one or two ram-type heads, while VTLs had a turret-type head. Since modern machines frequently combine the two types of heads and many ram heads now have indexable turrets, the historical distinction between the two machines has less validity than before. Also, the basic construction, tooling, workholding, controls, and operation of the machines are essentially the same.

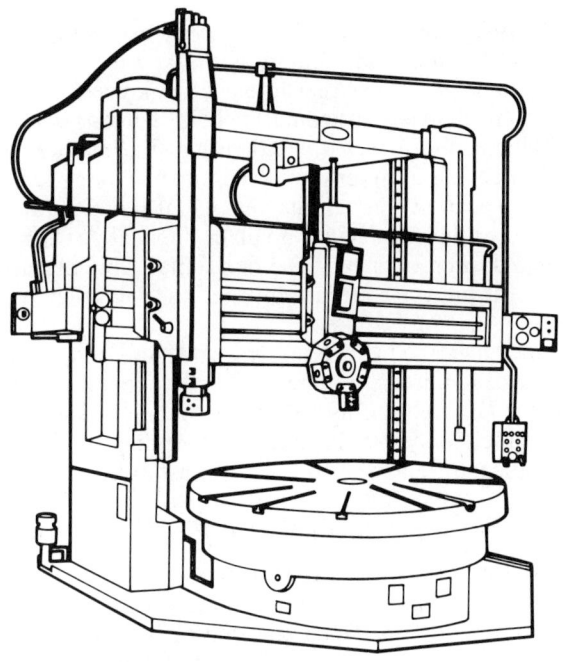

Fig. 9-121 Vertical boring machine. (*Courtesy DeVlieg-Sundstrand*)

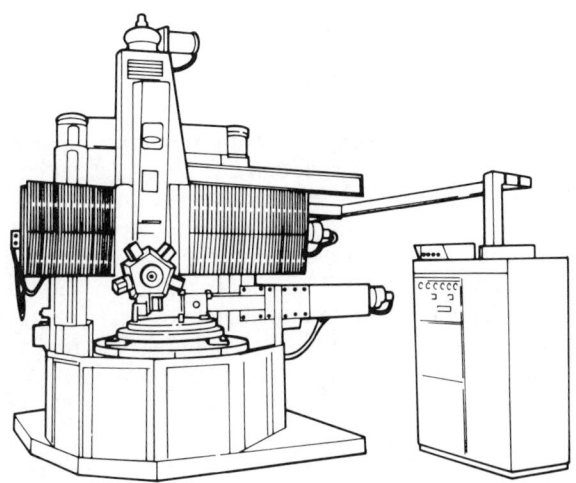

Fig. 9-122 Vertical turret lathe with CNC. (*Courtesy DeVlieg-Sundstrand*)

To avoid confusion, the term "vertical turning machine" is sometimes used for both machine types.

Some machine builders and users distinguish between a VBM and VTL based on machine size and, to a lesser extent, the volume of the production run. Loosely defined, a machine is called a VTL if it handles workpiece sizes to 100 in. diam.; for workpieces above that diameter, the machine is designated a VBM. To some extent, VBMs are often characterized by one-of-a-kind and small-lot production requirements; but they can be tooled for long production runs.

ADVANTAGES OF THE MACHINES

An important advantage of VBMs and VTLs is the ease with which large or heavy workpieces can be set up and held. Gravity is the key to the relative ease of work handling with these machines. It is easier to place workpieces on the horizontal table top than it is to mount them on horizontal-spindle machines. The weight of heavy workpieces is distributed uniformly downward through the bearings and absorbed in the massive bases of the machines. This ensures accurate machining, even at relatively high cutting speeds; reduces chatter; and permits high metal-removal rates.

Another advantage of these machines involves applications that require indicating for quality assurance during job setup. The horizontal table presents workers with a surface on which parts may be set up adjusted, and leveled without preliminary strapping.

Vertical boring machines and turret lathes provide increased workpiece accessibility and reduced floor-space requirements compared to horizontal-spindle lathes of similar machining capability. Through the use of counterbalances applied to the top of the worktable, they have the ability to easily balance irregular or off-center workloads and to eliminate excessive centrifugal force or radial thrust load.

WORKHOLDING FOR BORING

Many of the various types of chucks and collets discussed under turning in a preceding section of this chapter are also used for precision boring, as well as for combination machining operations. Fixtures are also used extensively for precision boring.

Fixturing of workpieces for precision-boring operations is an extremely important and critical matter. When the high degree of accuracy usually demanded of the operation performed by the machine is considered, holding the part during the operation demands careful consideration of the correct locating surfaces and clamping must minimize distortions, which influence accuracy. The compromise between adequate, rigid clamping and small distortions can present a challenge in ingenuity of fixture design.

Design of the part itself can be an extremely important factor. Special provisions for locating and clamping made during part design can often prevent many problems and reduce fixture cost considerably. Adequate preparation of the part in processing prior to precision boring can also help considerably in overcoming problems in fixturing.

Fixtures can be extremely simple or complex, depending upon various factors. Low production requirements may only justify a simple approach with manual clamping. However, some low-production fixtures may demand power clamping. High production may demand a highly sophisticated, automatic clamping fixture. Regardless, fixtures should be designed with ease of loading in mind, and always with careful attention given to proper clearance for the boring bar and the removal of the chips made by the process.

Fixtures can be divided into three main categories; stationary, indexing, and rotating.

Stationary Fixtures. Fixtures that do not index or revolve are considered to be stationary fixtures. The fixture may be mounted on the table of the machine so that it moves to the left or right to approach the tools for the operation, or it may be mounted fixed to the base of the machine so that operations are performed by spindles mounted on slides which approach the fixture. These fixtures may be of the load and reload type. This means that the part is loaded into one section of the fixture, a position at which certain operations are performed and after which the part is reloaded into another section for further operations. This can be a useful and economic device for approaching a part in different directions with only one motion of the table or spindle slide or for performing multiple machining operations involving different spindles without the need for an indexing mechanism.

With the need for accuracy, an inherent requirement of fixturing for precision boring, good fixture design is extremely important. Rigid structures must be employed, over-hangs must be reduced to an absolute minimum, and adequate non-distorting clamps should be used. The use of contact jacks, which support the part against the cutting forces of the tool without exerting distorting forces on the part, may often be required.

For heavy parts, it is often necessary to provide guide rails to support the part during the loading operation and also to have retracting locators for the part that will accu-rately locate the part from a rough position. For high-production work and when it is necessary to minimize operator attendance, the machine may be automatically loaded and unloaded. For heavy parts, power loading can also be employed to assist the operator.

Examples of simple manual-clamp fixtures are shown in Fig. 9-123. The fixture seen in view *a* is for precision boring a cast iron planet-pinion carrier. The fixture employs a gate-type clamp with a three-point equalizing clamp plate. The part is located by the two top pins, and the lower pin acts as a rough locator to facilitate loading. The simple fixture in view *b* is for boring the crank end of a connecting rod and is mounted on a standard universal fixture to facilitate setup. Shown in view *c* is a typical boring fixture that employes manual swing clamps.

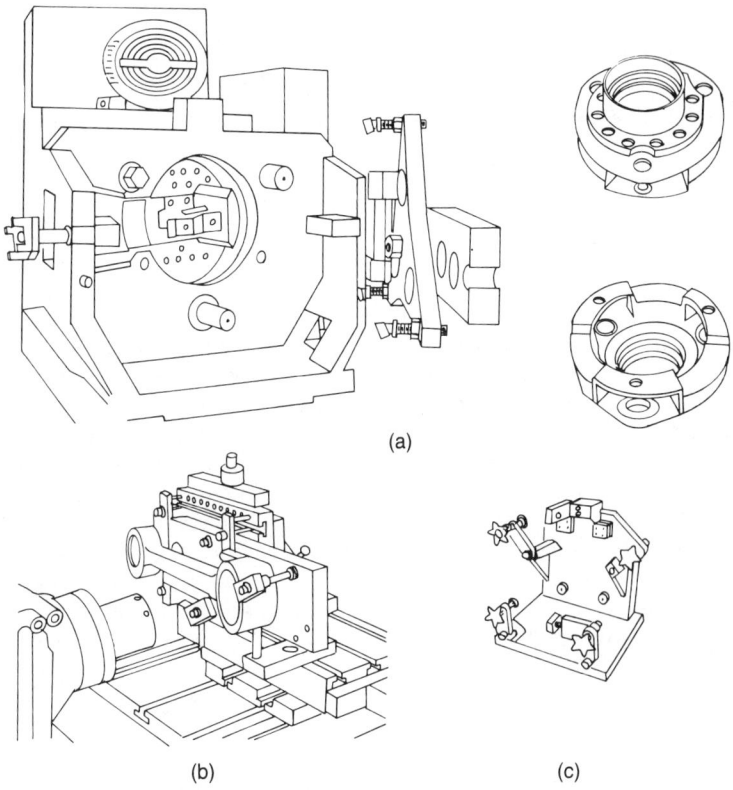

(a)

(b)   (c)

Fig. 9-123 Simple stationary, manually-clamped fixtures for precision boring. The fixture in (*a*) is for planet-pinion carriers; the fixture in (*b*) is for connecting rods; the fixture in (*c*) has swing clamps.

Accurate positioning of a stationary fixture is of prime importance for precise results since the part to be bored must be positioned accurately with reference to the boring-head spindle and the direction of table travel. Although the fixture base may be scraped to exact height, and positioning keys locating the table slots may also be scraped, precise corrections and adjustments are far more easily made when the fixture-locating plate is supplied with jackscrews, as illustrated in Fig. 9-124 to permit adjustment of the plate itself.

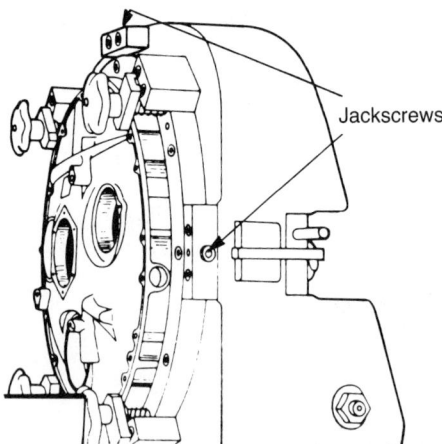

Fig. 9-124 Stationary fixture with jackscrew provision for easy adjustment.

Figure 9-125 shows a two-part fixture for loading and reloading a part. The part is first loaded in the front position, and then reloaded in the rear position so that operations can be performed on the part in another plane. Two parts are always in the machine during the machine cycle, and thus a finished part is obtained from the machine at each cycle.

Indexing Fixtures. An indexing fixture is necessary to move the part, while located and clamped, between two or more positions on the machine in order to complete all the operations to be performed. Indexing mechanisms may be part of the fixture itself, or fixtures may be mounted on standard indexing slides or rotary tables. A common type of index motion employed on precision-boring machines is a cross slide, which indexes the part at right angles to the table feed motion. An arrangement such as this permits operations to be performed on a bore by two or more spindles, sequentially. This allows a rough or semifinish boring operation to be made on the part immediately prior to the finish pass. An advantage of this arrangement from an accuracy standpoint is that consistent stock removal during finishing can be reasonably assured.

Rotary index tables can be employed to rotate the part so that it is presented at different angles to the spindles. They can also provide a means of moving between different spindles. In the case of way-type machines, spindles may be mounted around the table so that the part is approached at each index position.

A shuttle-type fixture is shown in Fig. 9-126. Two pump bodies are loaded in a pair of chuck-type fixtures in front of three equally spaced spindles. When the spindle slide moves in, the center spindle bores and counterbores the central hole in one casting. At the same time, one of the outer spindles trepans the groove eccentric to the central hole in the other casting. A lateral movement of the fixture then brings the two parts into a second position. When the spindle slide again moves in, the counterbore is formed in the part that was previously trepanned and the eccentric groove is trepanned in the part that was bored and counterbored.

A special indexing-type fixture is shown in Fig. 9-127. Here a number of bores are

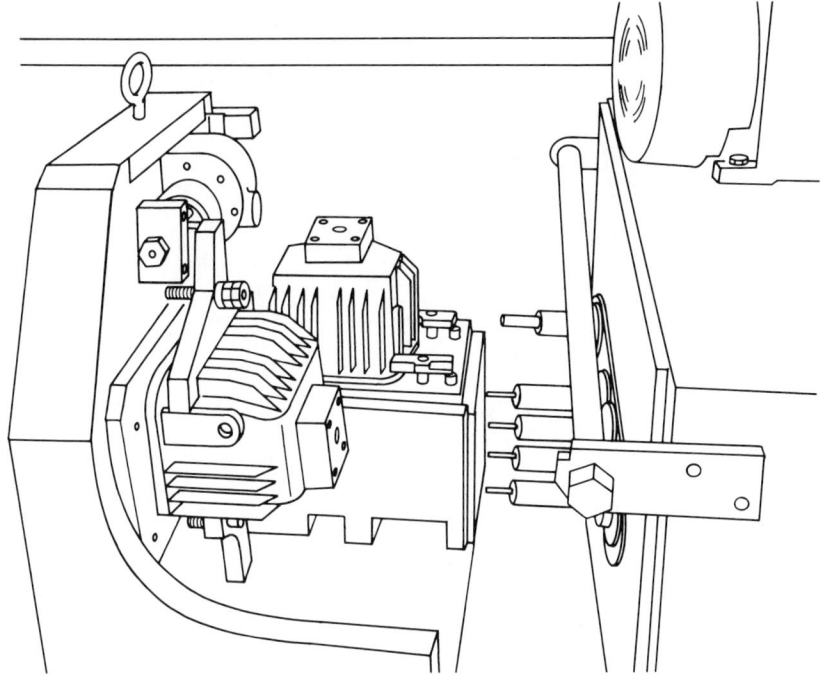

Fig. 9-125 Two-part fixture for loading and reloading workpieces.

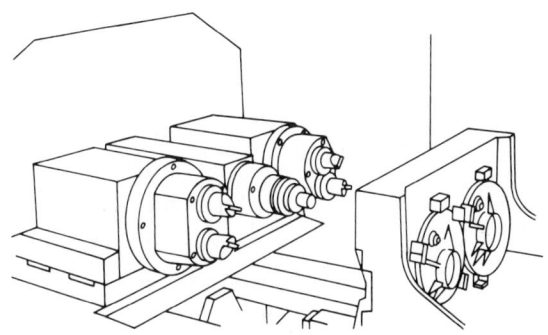

Fig. 9-126 Shuttle-type fixture for precision-boring operations.

produced on a part at an angle by indexing the part (held at an angle) between successive boring operations.

Rotating Fixtures. Fixtures or chucks that are mounted on spindles so that the part itself is rotated about the axis of the spindle are called rotating fixtures. Various surfaces of revolution can thus be generated by tools mounted on the feed slides. The most common is the standard chuck, such as a centralizing jaw or diaphragm type, discussed earlier in this chapter under the subject of chucks for turning. These are usually power operated by cylinders at the rear of the spindle, and the chucks are usually precision type to achieve the accuracy desired. Many special rotating fixtures and chucks are designed to suit a variety of applications.

One of the disadvantages of rotating the workpiece, particularly if the part is not symmetrical, is the out-of-balance forces that may be involved. It is extremely impor-

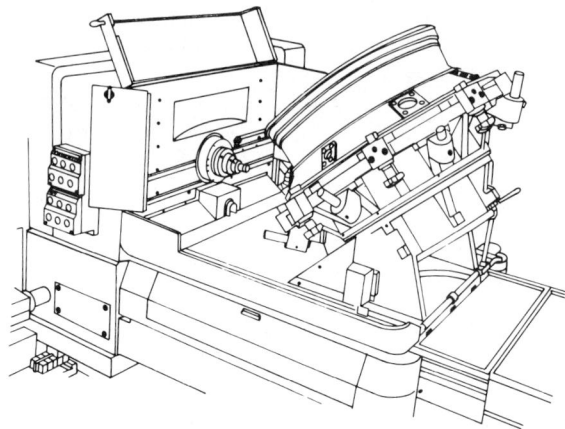

Fig. 9-127 Special indexing-type fixture for successive boring of holes at an angle.

tant, particularly when high rotational speeds are involved, that the rotating fixture or chuck be accurately balanced with the workpiece in place. Figure 9-128 shows two special rotating fixtures (or chucks) arranged to hold various size gears while a boring operation is performed on the ID of the part. The gears are located on the pitch diameter of their teeth to obtain concentricity.

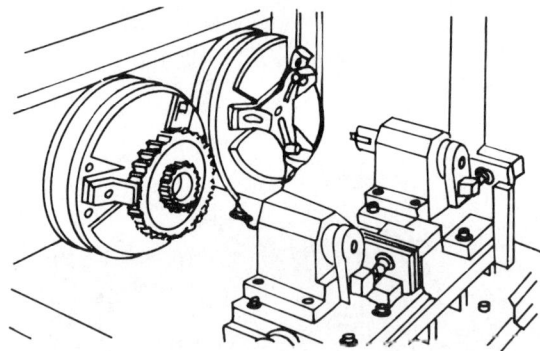

Fig. 9-128 Special gear chucks and retracting toolblocks for precision boring.

The fixture illustrated in Fig. 9-129 is designed to machine concentric bores in both ends of a cast workpiece on which there are no other concentric surfaces. Three clamping fingers (only one is shown) are mounted on the master jaws of a standard air-operated chuck. A floating ring equalizes the finger action compensating for casting distortion or mismatch.

Precision-boring machines, particularly those that also perform turning-type operations, are often fully automated by means of various types of loading and unloading mechanisms. Sometimes a finished part may be ejected automatically from the chuck and removed from the machine by a conveyor or gravity chute. At other times, it is more convenient mechanically to remove the part with an unloading device. Parts are usually loaded by some type of loading device that picks the part from a magazine in which it has been loaded, either by an operator or automatically from a conveyor. Figure 9-130 illustrates a slant-bed, two-spindle, cam-controlled, precision-boring

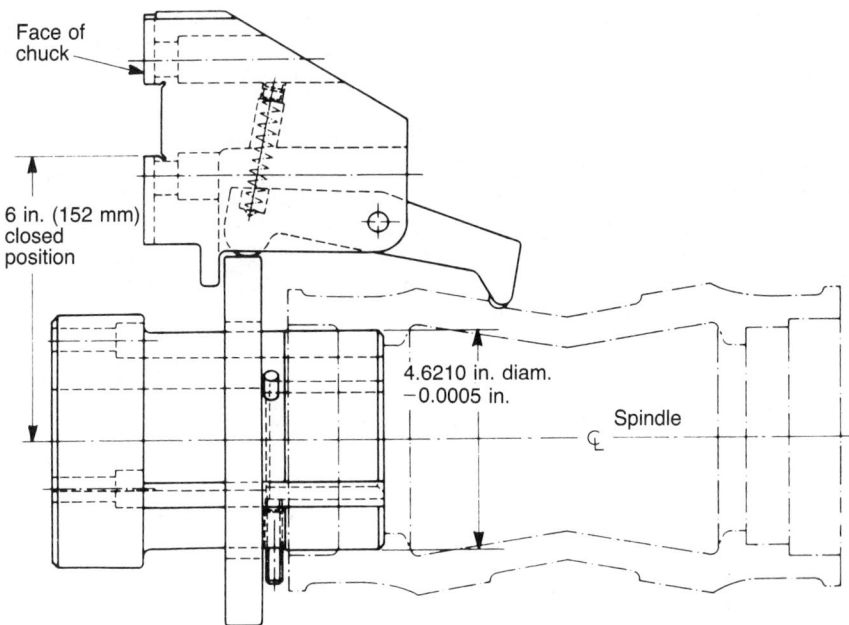

Face of chuck

6 in. (152 mm) closed position

4.6210 in. diam. −0.0005 in.

Spindle

Fig. 9-129 Special chuck fixture for machining bores concentric in both ends of castings.

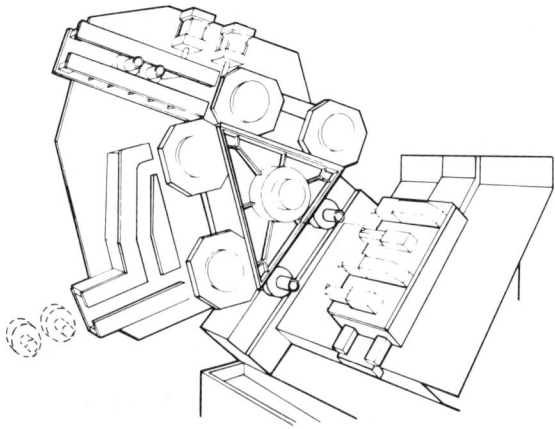

Fig. 9-130 Indexing-type loading and unloading mechanism on a two-spindle precision boring machine. (*Courtesy Olofsson Corp.*)

machine equipped with an indexing-type loading and unloading mechanism. Work changers and industrial robots are used to load and unload machines, as well as to transfer workpieces to other machines.

SETUP AND OPERATION OF HORIZONTAL BORING MACHINES

Rigid setups, with adequate bar support and proper fixtures, are critical to performing successful operations on horizontal boring machines. The most successful boring operations are performed when there is adequate rigidity in all elements, including the machine.

Bar Support. In horizontal boring machines, the workpieces are normally stationary during machining operations, but the workpieces are sometimes moved on rotary index tables. Cutting tools are mounted on various types of boring bars that transmit motion, and power is imparted to them from the machine spindle. The method of bar support varies to suit the length of bar required to reach the surface to be machined, the accessibility of the bore, and the degree of precision or finish required.

Stub bars are supported only at the spindle end and are used to bore holes that may be positioned comparatively close to the headstock. Blind holes do not permit extension of a line bar through the work to an end support, and ordinarily a stub bar must be employed. Line bars extend through the workpiece and require some form of support external to the spindle. Generally, an end support (see Fig. 9-131a) is used for this purpose, since it may be readily brought into alignment by a simple adjustment of its bearing block.

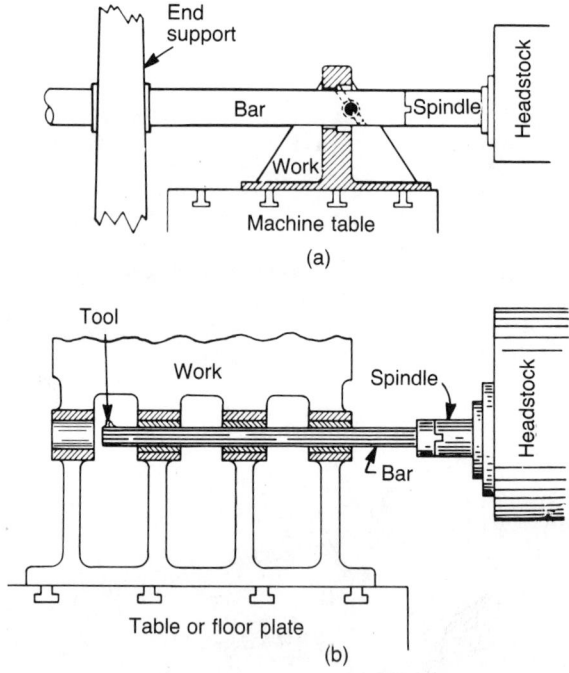

Fig. 9-131 Support of boring bar by: (a) end-support column and (b) workpiece.

The use of the workpiece for bar support (see Fig. 9-131b) may sometimes be preferable or necessary. In certain types of blind holes with lateral holes that permit inspection of the cutter, the finished bore behind the cutter may be bushed to bar size. This procedure is also used when some form of support between the machine spindle and the end column is required and when the workpiece obstructs the use of fixture bearings at points of necessary support. Although the use of the workpiece for bar support usually consumes more machining time and in most cases is not desirable, it may be preferable over a fixture when the cost of the latter is prohibitive.

When workpiece support of the bar is not possible, a back rotary-pilot support is sometimes used, especially for deep-hole boring. A stub tool can be employed to bore the starting hole and then replaced with a piloted boring bar. A better method is to use a stationary bushing, mounted on a machine underarm support or on its own support on the machine table, to guide the piloted boring tool.

Back-piloted boring bars (see Fig. 9-132) have a rotary pilot behind the cutting tools. The bars hold at least one rough-boring cutter, followed by a finishing cutter. The pilot is designed to remain stationary in relation to the workpiece, with the bar revolving in the pilot. Proper clearance between the pilot and workpiece is essential to prevent jamming. A supply of cutting fluid through the tool is necessary for extended tool life.

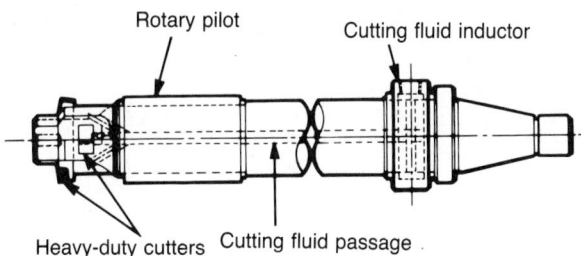

Fig. 9-132 Rotary-piloted boring bar. (*Courtesy Muskegon Tool Industries*)

Back-piloted bars for operation in blind holes are designed to permit chips to escape through the centers of the hollow bars. If the hole is large enough, this can be accomplished by providing a bronze roller pilot on which wear strips are mounted. Otherwise, wear pads are mounted directly on the bar and rotate on the ID of the bore instead of remaining stationary. High-pressure cutting fluid, forced over the bar, flushes chips back through the center of the hollow bar.

Boring Fixtures. When the need arises, boring fixtures are used to support and at the same time align the bar at the proper position preparatory to a boring operation. In general, they are used to increase the productivity of the machine when large quantities are involved. Best applications of fixtures simplify the setup and facilitate any subsequent shifting of the work on the table to a new position during the machining. Boring fixtures are of distinct advantage in producing work involving the duplication of center distances.

Most applications favor two bearing supports for every bar position in the fixture. Thus, the fixture is responsible for bar alignment and eliminates the need for close adjustments of the headstock. A floating adapter connection between bar and spindle is generally used to compensate for small differences in alignment between the axis of the fixture bearings and the spindle. The fixture bearings are usually the sleeve type, made of cast iron, hardened steel, bronze, or bearing alloy to suit the hardness of the bar and the probable length of service of the fixture. Antifriction bearings are to be preferred when center distances and first cost allow for this more expensive construction, or when high surface speeds tend to cause heat resulting from friction which may cause the bar to seize and score.

With NC machines, many line-boring operations are being performed by saddle feeding of the workpiece. This reduces the need for line bars or fixtures.

Combined Operations. Combined machining operations are typical on horizontal boring machines. Figure 9-133 shows the application of two continuous-feed facing and boring heads set up on a line bar, one head at each end of a workpiece. The use of two heads eliminates the need to turn the work after one end is machined and gives a common center. Such a tooling arrangement is warranted when large quantities are involved, since the machining is approximately half that required when only one head is used. This is a good example of boring, counter-boring, and facing operations being performed in one setup.

Some typical applications of special boring bars for performing combined operations are illustrated in Fig. 9-134.

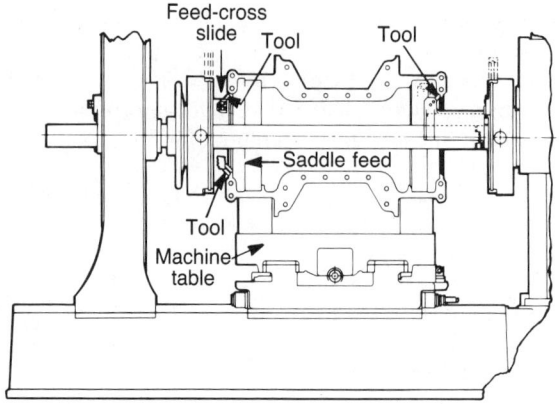

Fig. 9-133 Boring and facing both ends of axle housings using two continuous-feed heads.

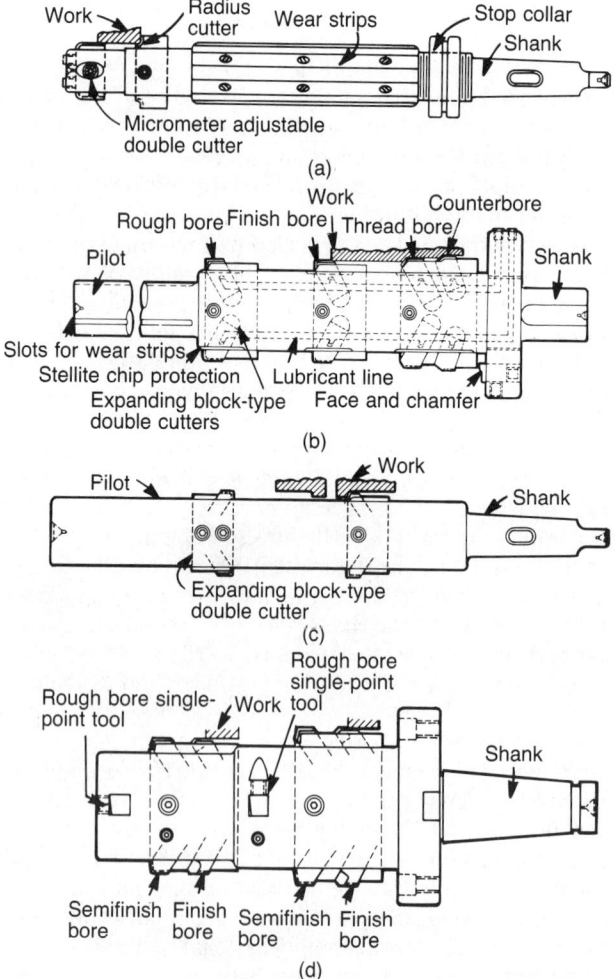

(a)

(b)

(c)

(d)

Fig. 9-134 Special boring bars for performing the following combination operations: (*a*) boring and forming radius; (*b*) boring, counterboring, facing, and chamfering; (*c*) boring and back boring; and (*d*) rough, semifinish, and finished boring two different diameters.

Additional boring fixtures are shown in Figs. 9-135 thru 9-145. They include the following:

A Double-purpose Fixture. The fixture of Fig. 9-135 is designed to hold a previously machined casting for additional boring operations on a jig mill; and for milling certain surfaces. Two cutter set blocks (4) are provided.

Tapered locating pins (1 and 2) are inserted in locating holes in the workpiece which is clamped against rest buttons (7) and rest plates (8 and 9) by clamps (3, 5, and 6).

The fixture is correctly positioned on the table of a jig mill by a straight key (11), an eccentric key (10), a locating pin (12), and an indicator properly contacting the ID of the indicating hole bushing (13).

A Fixture for Boring and Fly-cutting. Four locating blocks (2) of the fixture of Fig. 9-136b engage the central hole in the workpiece shown in Fig. 9-136a, while a diamond locating pin (1) engages a hole on the front surface of the casting. Two sliding strap clamps (3 and 4) hold the workpiece, a casting, on the relieved edges of the locating blocks. The location of all parts of the fixture is established from the central construction (reference) hole.

Boring with a Master Plate. The centering fixture of Fig. 9-137a is positioned with its locating plug and bolted to the table of a small, vertical boring machine. The boring fixture of Fig. 9-137b has a master plate with 30 holes for registration with the bayonet-type locating pin projecting upwards from the centering fixture. Moving the fixture and plate over the centering fixture is a fast method of exactly positioning the fixture and workpiece and permits the holes, which are held to a tolerance of 0.0005 in., to be bored at locations corresponding to the accurate hole layout of the master plate.

The workpiece is placed on four rest blocks (1) and is located by a round locating pin (3) and a diamond locating pin (2) which are pushed through holes in the workpiece and into bushings (5). Four strap clamps (4) hold the workpiece against the rest blocks.

A Fixture for Horizontal Boring. The workpiece, a casting to be bored in the fixture of Fig. 9-138, is located on two diamond pins (3 and 7) and by a spring-loaded pin (8). It rests on three rest buttons (2). A pin (5) and a rest button (6) press-fit in a swing-latch clamp (1) contact the top and bottom of the casting.

Clamping pressure is applied at these points by a collar screw (9) after a C-clamp is swung under it.

Two fixture keys (10) align the fixture on a riser plate fastened to the table of a double-end boring machine.

A Fixture for Boring, Countersinking, and Facing. The fixture of Fig. 9-139 incorporates locating pins (1) which engage three of the eight holes in the outer rim of the workpiece, a ribbed aluminum spider; the pins also establish concentricity of the hole to be bored (0.002 in.) with these holes.

The relieved end (4) of a cam-lock clamp assembly (6) clamps the hub against a locating plate (2). Distortion of the workpiece from thrust and torque of the boring tool is prevented by this clamp and also by three air-actuated clamps (3) which are aligned with the supporting pads.

The handle (7) of the air valve (11) controls three double-acting air cylinders (8) which, together with the hand clamp (6), permit rapid clamping and release of the work.

The rapidity and ease of clamping, loading, and unloading and the boring, countersinking, and facing by one pass of the boring quill permit fast and economical machining of large production quantities.

Fixture keys (9) align the fixture with the table of a boring machine, which is necessary to produce holes with a size tolerance of +0.000, -0.001 in.

The air valve with its Aro speed connector (5) and piping is mounted on the fixture to allow its easy removal as a unit from the boring-machine table.

A Leaf Boring Fixture. A leaf type of fixture (see Fig. 9-140) incorporates two independently sliding V-jaws (6) to compensate for casting variations in the workpiece.

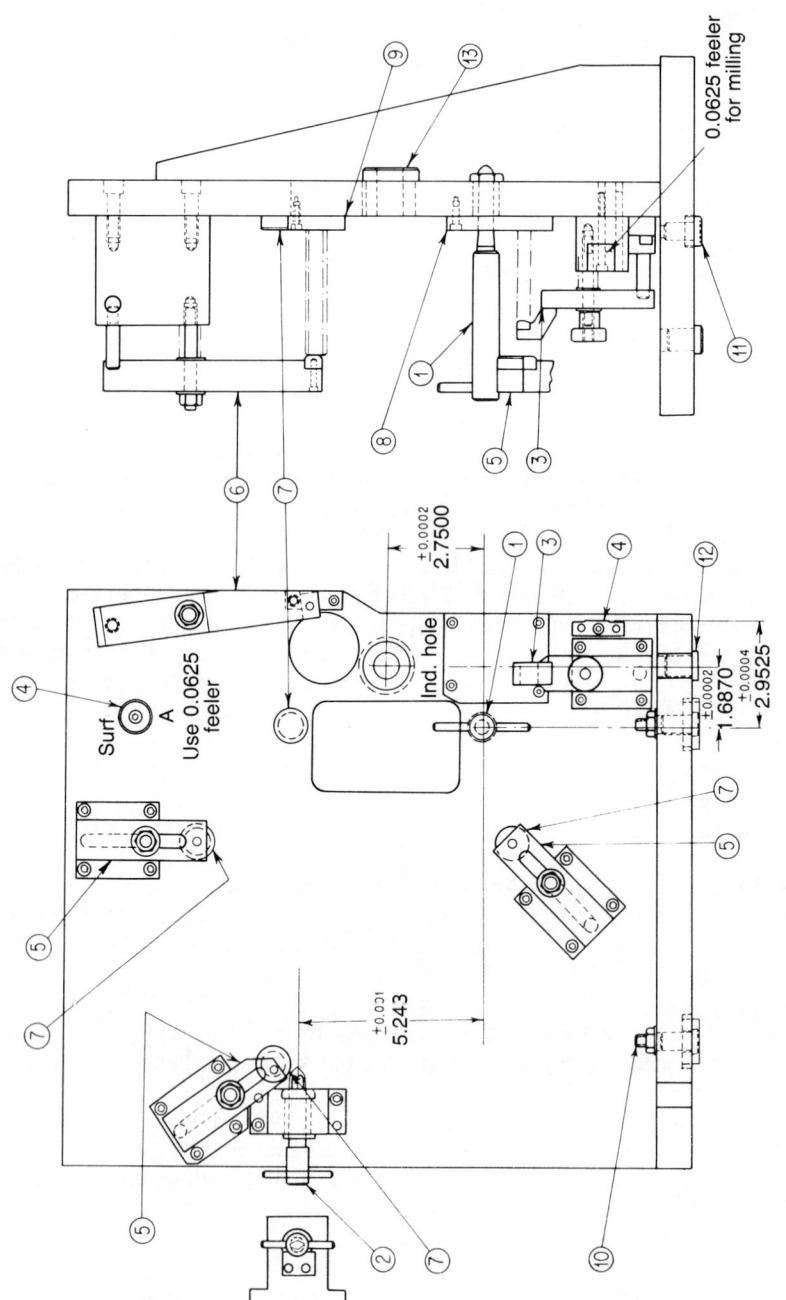

Fig. 9-135 Fixture for a jig mill. (*Courtesy IBM*)

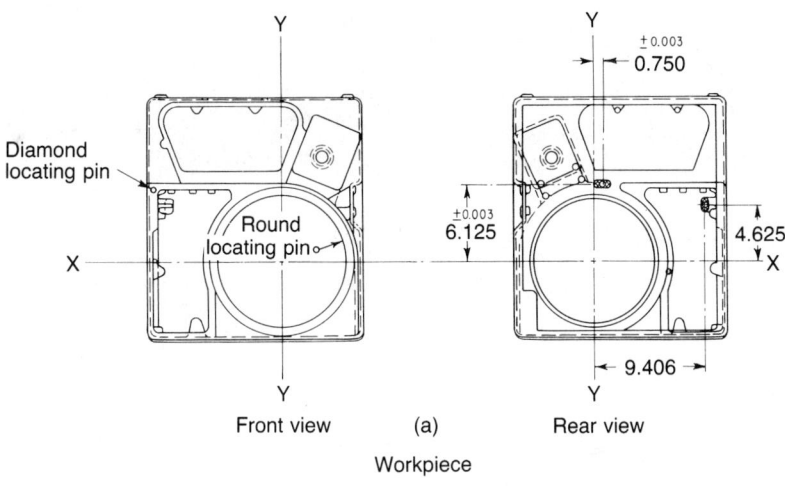

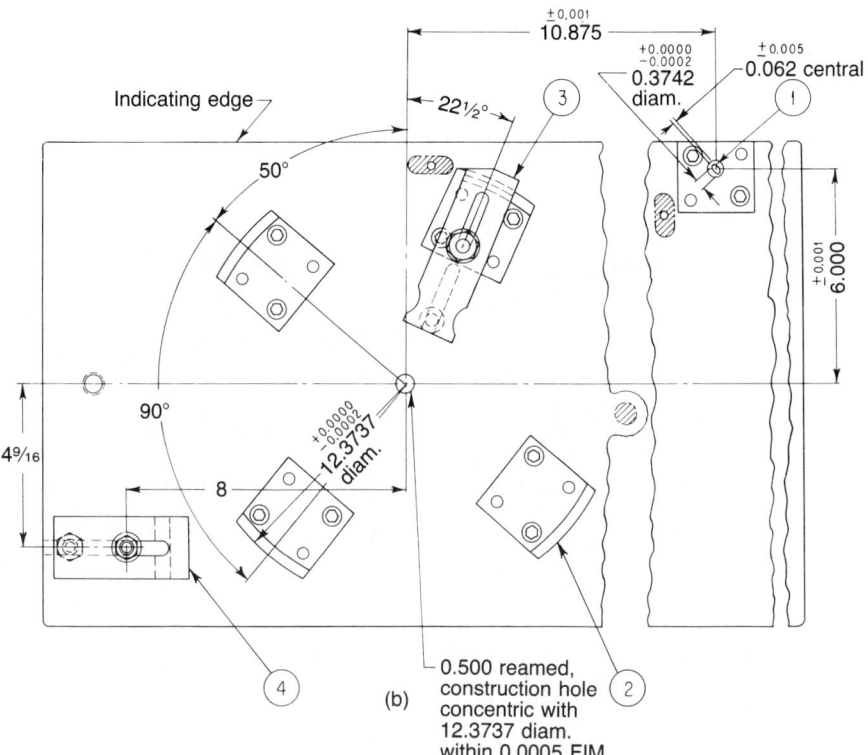

Fig. 9-136 Fixture for boring and fly-cutting five pads. (*Courtesy IBM*)

9-115

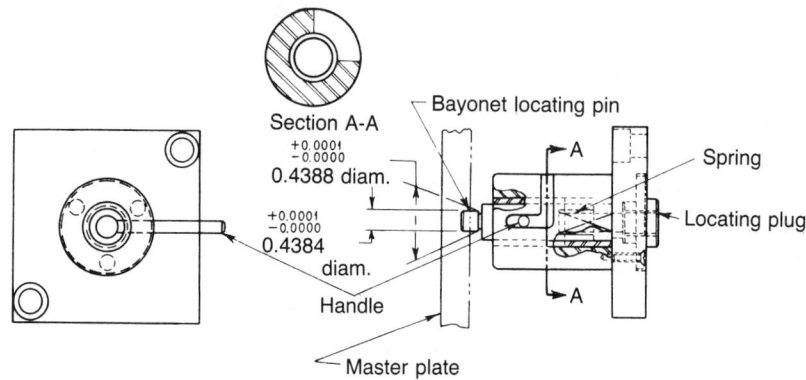

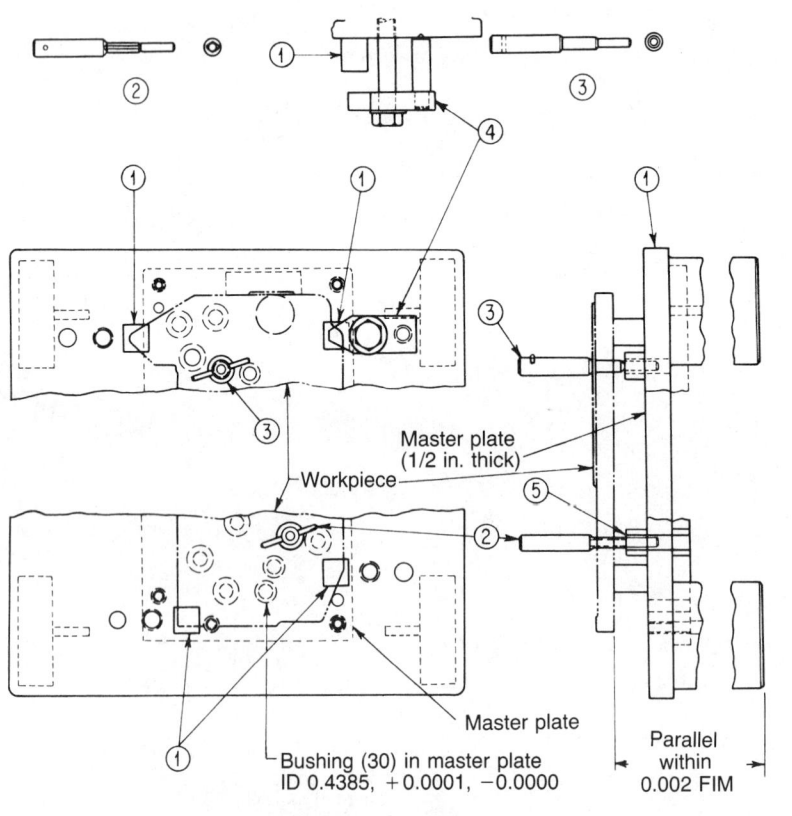

(a) Centering fixture for boring fixture (b)

(b) Fixture

Fig. 9-137 Boring fixture and master plate. (*Courtesy IBM*)

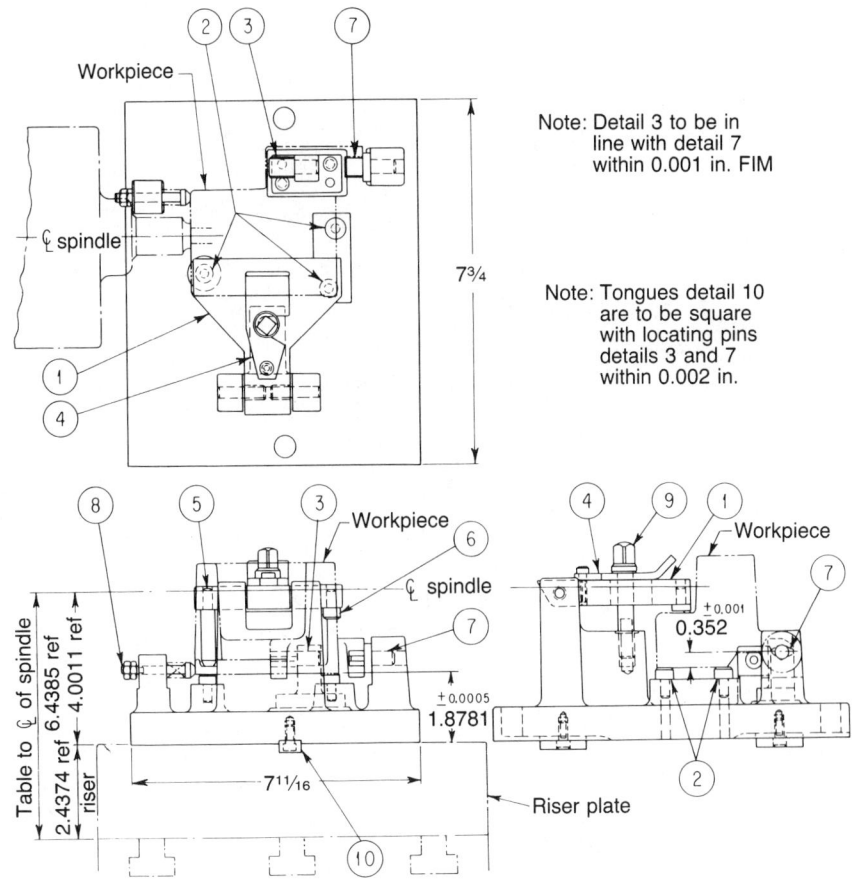

Fig. 9-138 Fixture for horizontal boring. (*Courtesy Universal Winding Co.*)

The leaf (3), carrying two drill bushings (11), applies no clamping pressure to the workpiece to force the bushings out of alignment. The workpiece is placed on a round locating pin (8) and a diamond pin (9) and is held by the sliding jaws, which are clamped by four thumbscrews (7).

A quarter-turn screw (4) holds the leaf against two clamps (2) which hold the workpiece. The heels of two spring-loaded strap clamps (2) rest on two clamp rests (5) and are held by socket-head cap screws.

Extra-long bushings (11 and 12) for piloting the reamers for boring two holes in the workpiece are jig-ground to size after they are in place in the fixture.

Two bushings (14) that are press-fit in the two uprights (13) and two others (15) press-fit in the leaf function as bearings for the leaf hinge pin (10).

Four small jig feet (1) function as rest buttons for the leaf.

It takes a drilling machine 12 minutes to bore the four holes.

A Fixture for Boring a Thin-walled Aluminum Casting. To avoid distortion of the thin walls of the aluminum workpiece of Fig. 9-141, clamping pressure is exerted on its exterior projecting portions rather than across its major diameter. The workpiece, a die casting, is located in a shaped block (1) and clamped by a bolt (2) and handwheel (3), as shown in Fig. 9-142. After positioning the casting, floating clamps (4, 5, 6, and 7) are tightened by rotating hand knobs (8). These two clamp assemblies, mounted on clamp posts (9 and 10) respectively, are free to move vertically, until air pressure is applied to the pistons of two air cylinders (14 and 15).

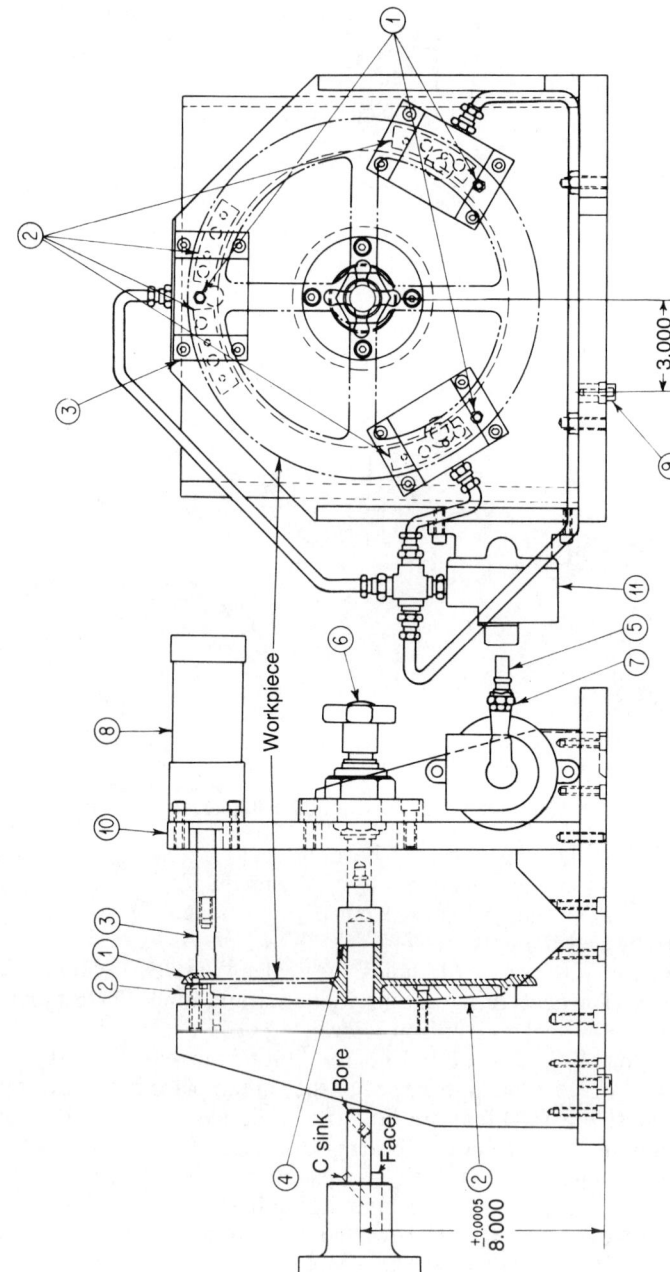

Fig. 9-139 Fixture for combined boring, facing and countersinking. (*Courtesy The Maytag Co.*)

9-118

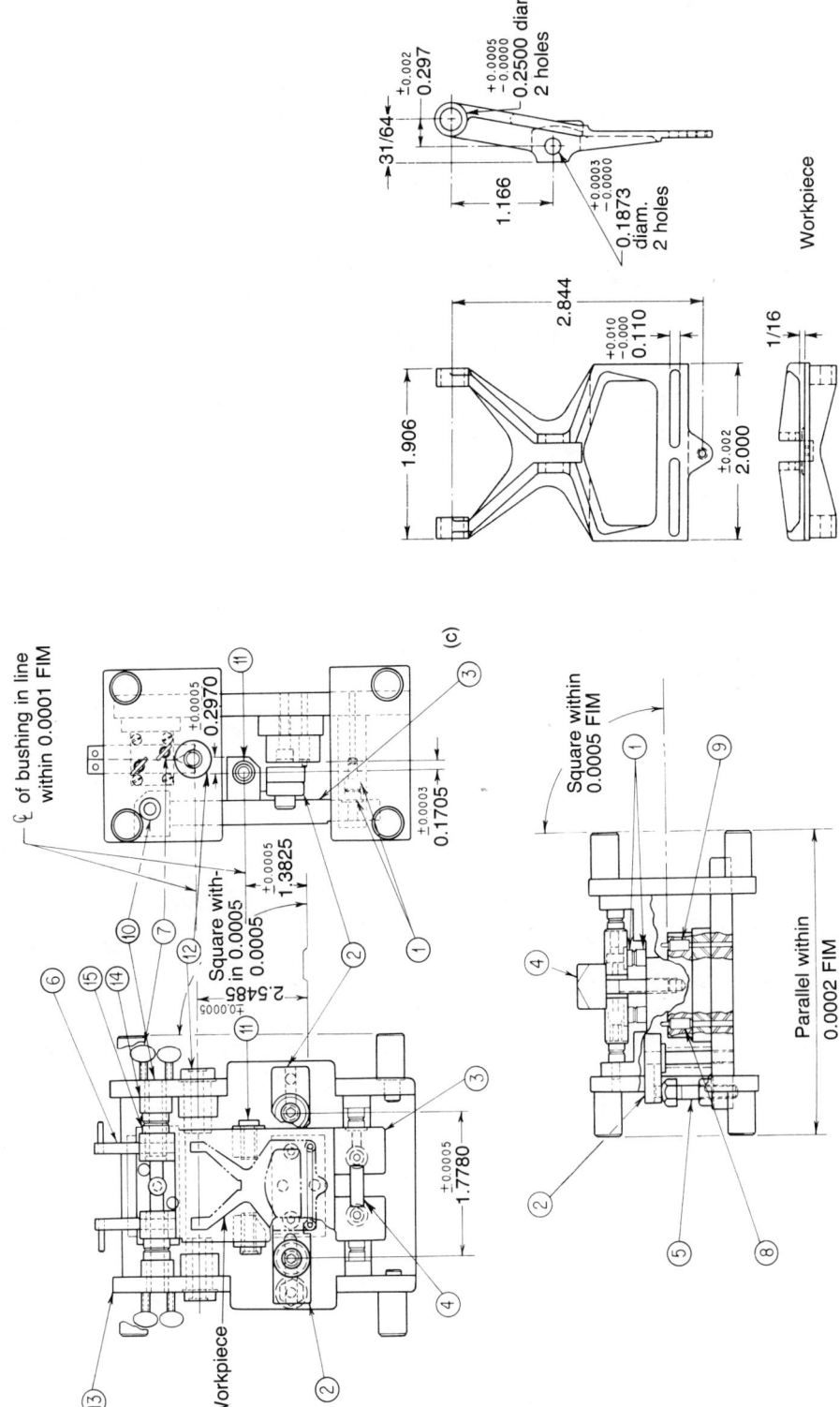

Fig. 9-140 Leaf-type boring fixture. (*Courtesy IBM*)

9-119

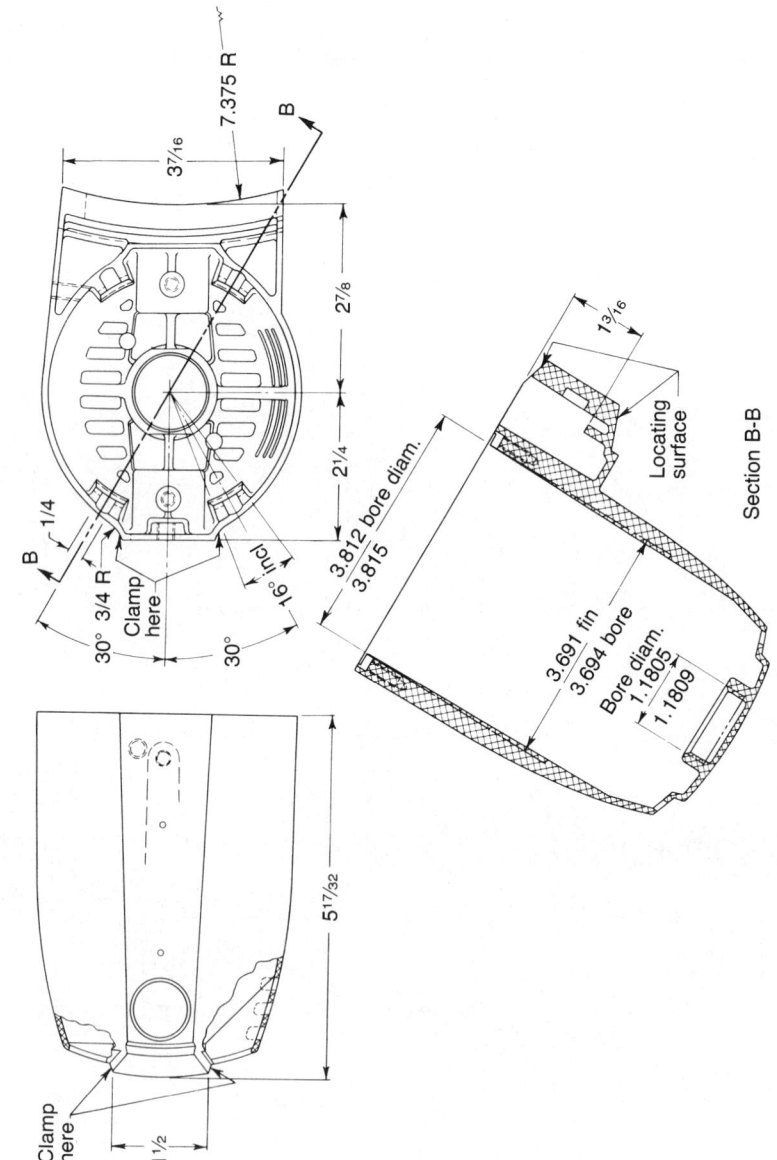

Fig. 9-141 Workpiece bored in fixture of Fig. 9-140.

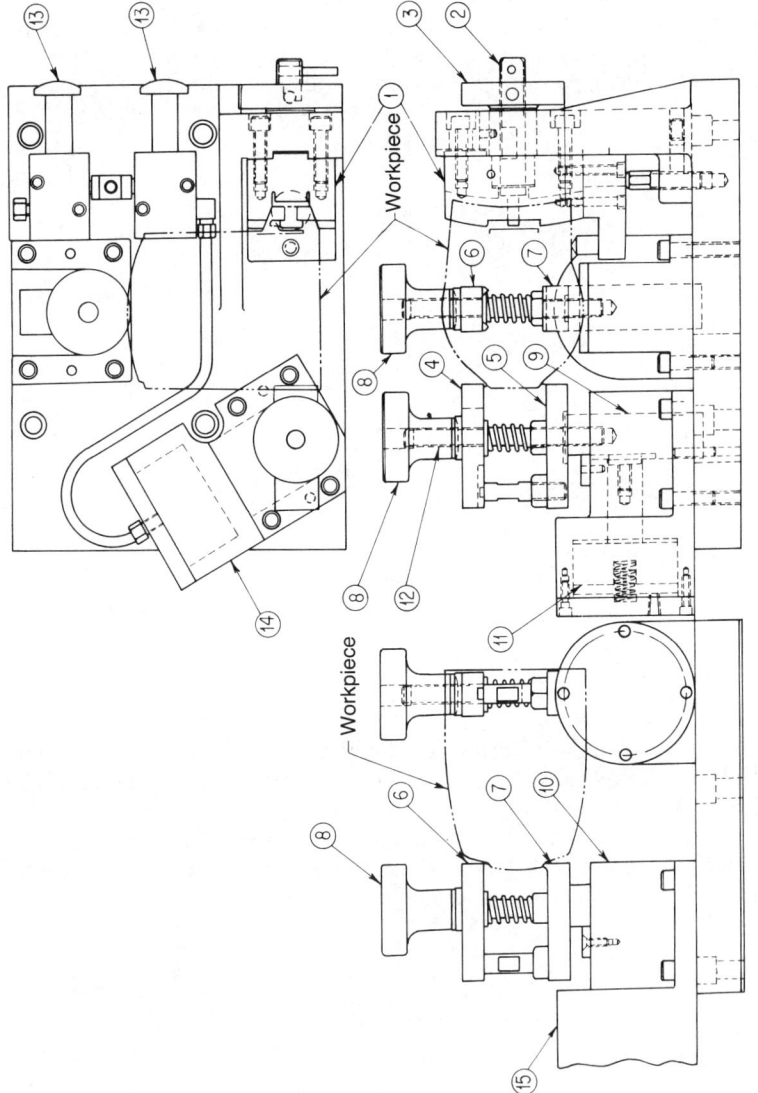

Fig. 9-142 Fixture for boring a thin-walled aluminum casting. (*Courtesy Millers Falls Co.*)

9-121

When push-pull air valves (13) are opened, the rod ends of the pistons (11) press against the clamp posts, providing solid support to the workpiece held in the clamp assemblies.

After boring is completed, the air valves are opened, and the floating clamps are loosened and rotated for unloading.

A Horizontal Bushed Boring Fixture. If the distance from the spindle face to the workpiece hole to be bored is more than five times the hole diameter, it is recommended that the end of the boring bar be piloted as shown in Fig. 9-143.

Two stop blocks and two diamond locating pins locate the workpiece on the fixture base. A leaf clamp holds it on the base, which is keyed to the machine table. A pilot bushing is mounted in an upright member which is held square to the face of the spindle.

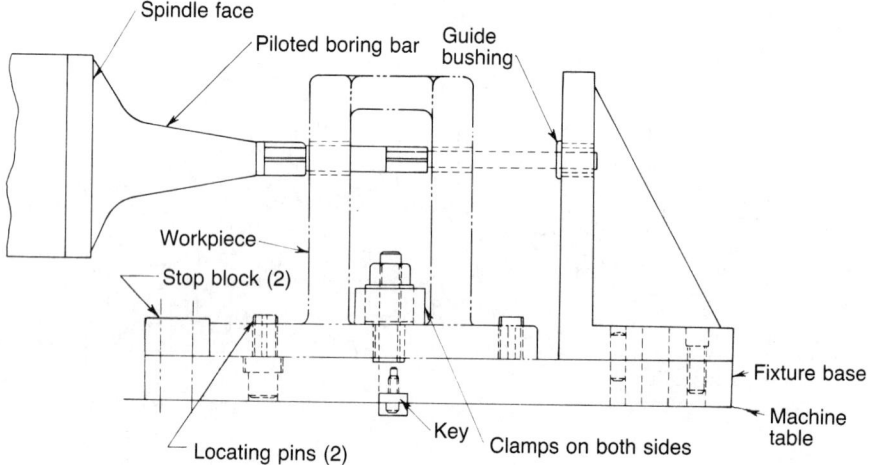

Fig. 9-143 A boring fixture with single-boring bar bushing. (*Courtesy Ex-cello Machinery Sales Co.*)

A Fixture with Two Split Bushings. The workpiece, made of 1035 steel tubing (see Fig. 9-144), is held by suitable clamps (not shown) on the locating pads. The chrome-plated boring bar rotates in two bushings tapered at each end but having a straight bore approximately 1½ in. (38.1 mm) long. The split halves of the bushings are squeezed around the bar by clamps fitted around the OD of each bushing, securing minimum bar runout and a bore finish of 125 microinches (3.175 mm).

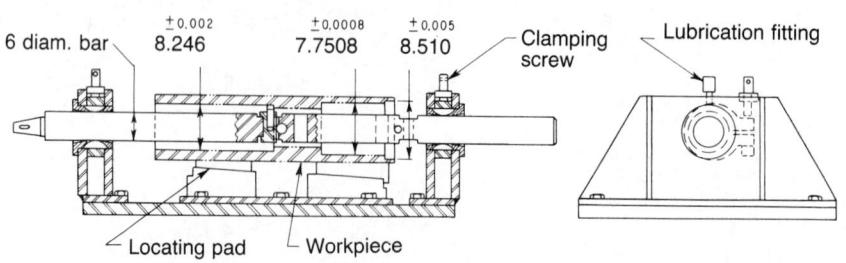

Fig. 9-144 A boring fixture with two split bushings. (*Courtesy LeTourneau-Westinghouse Co.*)

A Boring Fixture with Upper and Lower Pilot Bushings. The workpiece shown in Fig. 9-145 is located by a plug fitting on its splined end, and it is clamped against the vertical locating plate by the clamp screw and hand knob. A cam-lock clamp handle is rotated to hold the splined end of the workpiece up against the rest buttons.

The boring bar has hard bronze wear strips and is piloted in the upper bushing. The lower roller-bearing bushing accommodates and pilots the lower end of the boring bar.

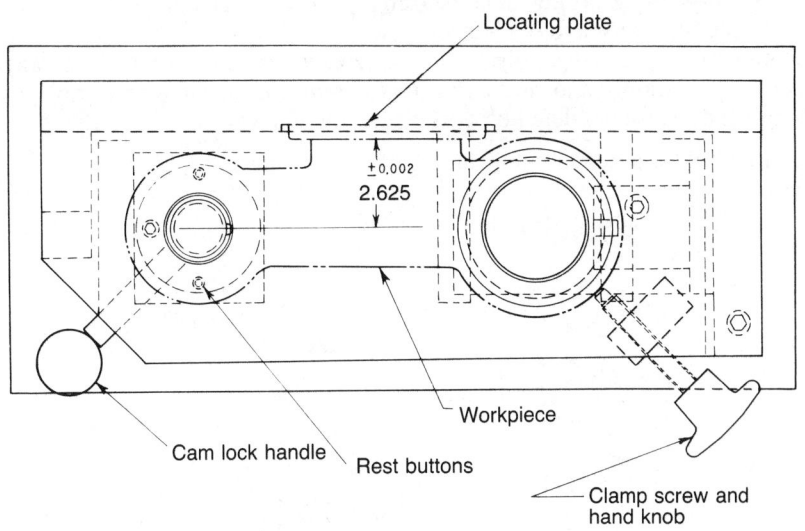

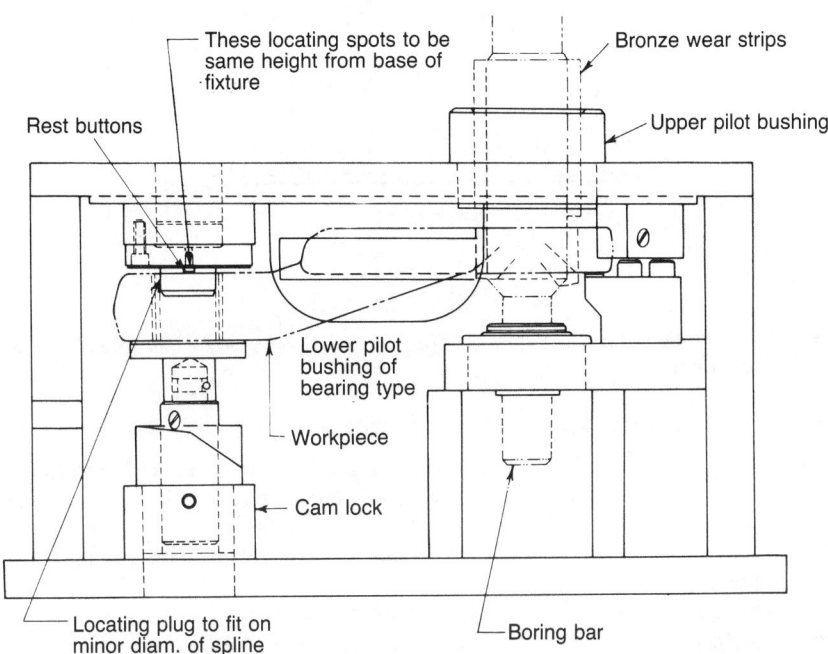

Fig. 9-145 A vertical-boring fixture with upper and lower pilot bushings. (*Courtesy W. D. Bristow*)

JIG BORING[20]

The term jig borer originally pertained to tool (jig and fixture) manufacturing, but the continually increasing demands for accuracy within many branches of metalworking has extended the application possibilities for jig-boring machines. The importance of the jig-boring machine in manufacturing has been firmly established. Without its aid, the present day state of the art in precision metalworking could never have been achieved. The modern jig-boring machine brings into close agreement the professional disciplines of the machinist and the metrologist.

Applications of Jig Boring. Jig-boring machines are used for a wide range of applications. The locating and measuring features of the machine are employed for establishing the dimensional detail of workpieces, including:

1. Jigs used for the production machining of multiple parts.
2. Press tools, such as the lamination die seen in Fig. 9-146.
3. Gages used to qualify parts produced on other machines.

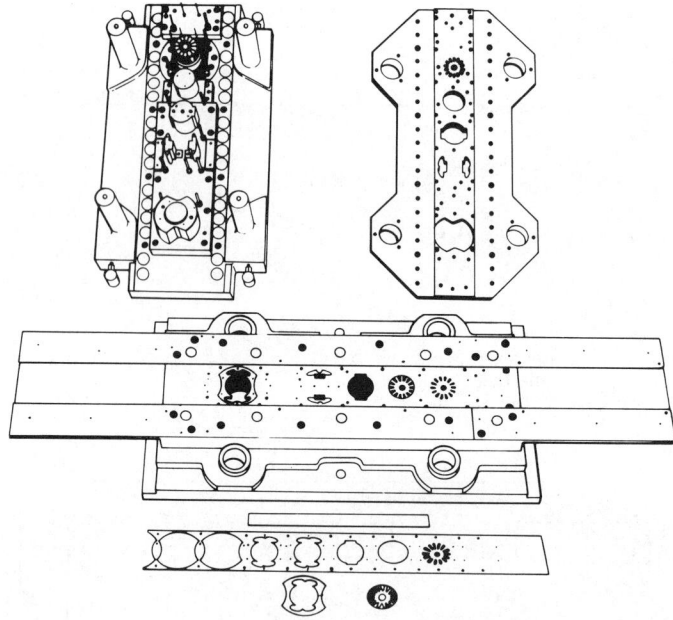

Fig. 9-146 Lamination die illustrates the precise requirements for locational accuracies afforded by the jig borer.

These machines are also used for the production of:

1. Prototype parts needed before custom tooling can be designed and manufactured.
2. Parts for which the required accuracy of hole location and surfaces, as well as the quality of the surface finish, cannot be otherwise obtained.
3. Parts calling for the ultimate in dimensional integrity, such as mating components in an assembly.
4. Delicate or complex parts with a minimum of distortion.
5. Parts, including die components, machined prior to hardening to allow for the more efficient application of jig grinding for finishing.

Jig-boring Machines. In general terms, the jig-boring machine employs a precision spindle to drive the cutting tool and a table to support the workpiece. The table and spindle are movable and are fitted with built-in measuring devices that provide means for establishing X, Y, Z, and A coordinate positions. The machine is designed to locate and bore holes and to generate surfaces to the highest level of accuracy. Three basic designs of jig-boring machines in common use are open-sided (C-frame), adjustable-rail, and fixed-bridge construction.

Open-sided Construction. Jig-boring machines of this C-frame design employ a single column for supporting the machine's vertical spindle and housing assembly (see Fig. 9-147). Guideways in the column control the perpendicular alignment of the spindle centerline throughout the full range of its adjustment along the Z-axis.

The machine table is supported on a compound slide and is movable along the X-axis. The compound itself is supported on the machine base and is movable along the Y-axis. Coordinate settings locating the table under the spindle's vertical centerline are controlled by the linear positioning system for each axis.

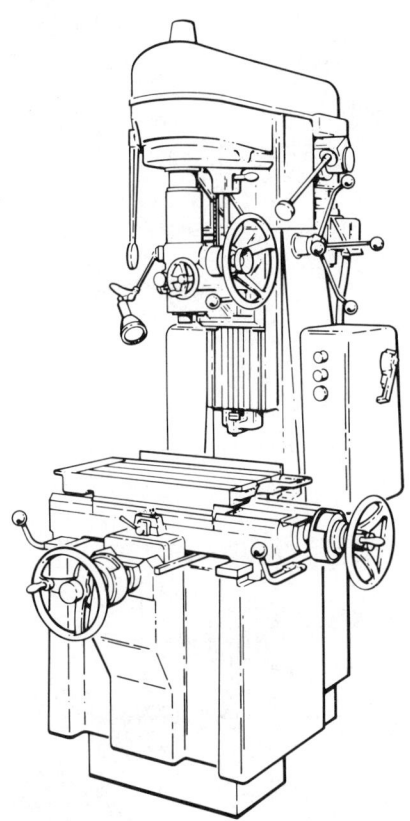

Fig. 9-147 Jig boring machine of open-sided construction.

Adjustable-rail Construction. On planer-type jig-boring machines (see Fig. 9-148), the crossrail is supported and adjusted vertically on two columns. The rail serves to carry the vertical spindle in its housing along the Y-axis. The table is supported on the base of the machine and is movable along the X-axis.

Fixed-bridge Construction. On jig-boring machines of this design, as illustrated in Fig. 9-149, the worktable is mounted on the base guideways and traverses in the longitudinal (X-axis) direction. The spindle is supported on the cross-slide carriage and

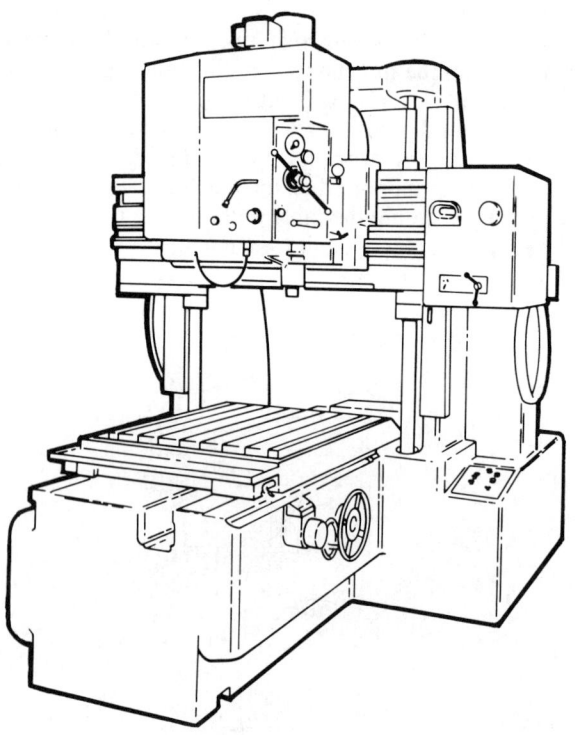

Fig. 9-148 Adjustable-rail or planer-type jig boring machine equipped with graduated-scale measuring system.

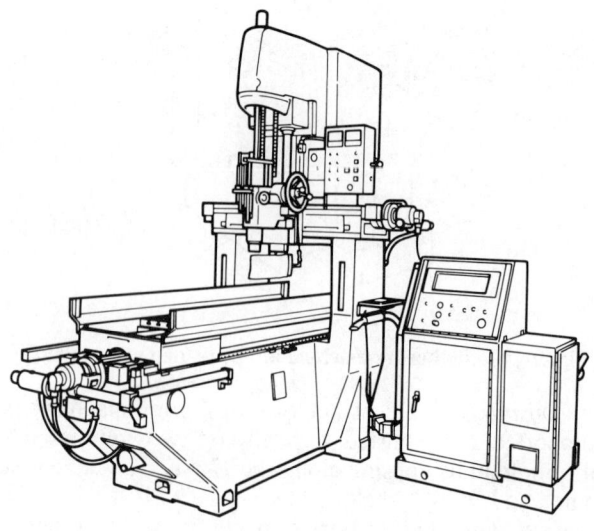

Fig. 9-149 Fixed-bridge design of jig-boring machine on which the worktable traverses in the longitudinal direction.

travels with it in the transverse (*Y*-axis) direction on the guideways of the fixed bridge. Vertical guideways, an integral part of the cross-slide carriage, support the spindle housing and guide its vertical adjustment.

NC/CNC Jig-boring Machines. Jig-boring machines equipped with numerical or computer numerical control systems (see Fig. 9-150) are effectively employed when the job process can be preplanned. Machine functions for coordinate positioning and contouring operations are automatically controlled, thus relieving the operator of the need to attend to the tedious, repetitive setting of machine dials and other control devices.

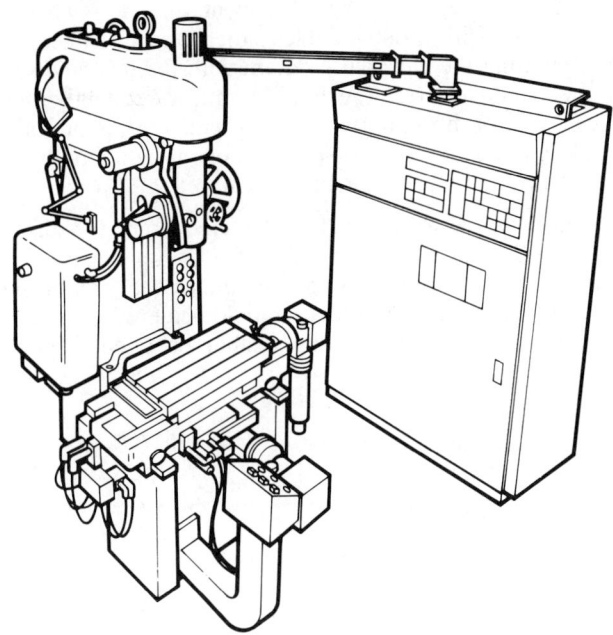

Fig. 9-150 Numerically-controlled jig-boring machine of the open-side type.

Production output of NC machines can be predicted with greater certainty since their operation is less dependent upon the operator. The precision machining of curvilinear details in cams, templates, and press tool components can be developed efficiently. Many jobs exist that would be impractical to process on a manually operated jig-boring machine. One job, for example, permits precise, irregularly curved forms to be generated on cams or master templates without operator involvement.

Measuring Systems. Three types of rectilinear coordinate measuring systems employed on jig-boring machines are end measures, graduated or Inductosyn scales, and micrometer leadscrews.

- End measures. These are accurate end standards used in combination with micrometers. The basic end standard measures in one inch or one centimeter increments, while the micrometer subdivides these increments. A selection of end measures and micrometer settings are used when establishing the datum and related coordinate positions.
- Graduated scales. The graduated scale employs an optical or electronic system for reading and establishing the measured position. Provisions are made for subdividing the graduated increment on the precision scale. Electro-optical or electronic feedback systems are used for machines equipped with a readout or automatic positioning control system using Inductosyn scales.

- Micrometer Leadscrews. The micrometer leadscrew provides the means for displacing the machine slide while establishing its coordinate position. The leadscrew measuring system is used directly with its micrometer dial or with an electronic feedback system for coordinate positioning control and/or display.

Machine Accessories. A wide selection of accessories are available for jig-boring machines, making them conveniently adaptable to a variety of precision machining operations. They fall into two groups: setup and spindle accessories.
- Setup Accessories. This group includes parallel setup blocks, precision vises, angle irons, microsine plates, rotary and rotary/tilting tables, and matching V-blocks. Their use is discussed in the subsequent section on workholding.
- Spindle Accessories. This group includes indicators, line finders, and microscopes for use in orientating the workpiece datum with the machine spindle centerline. The toolmaker's indicator (see Fig. 9-151) is most frequently used for picking up holes, edges, pins, or bosses, and when aligning reference surfaces with the machine slide motion. An electronic indicator may be employed for these purposes if higher accuracy for the pickup is required.

Line finders, consisting of an accurately centered point for aligning the spindle centerline with datum lines or points scribed on the workpiece, can be used when the detail to be machined does not require a precise dimensional relationship with existing features. The microscope with its reference reticle centered on the machine spindle centerline is used when the datum feature cannot be fixed using the toolmaker's indicator.

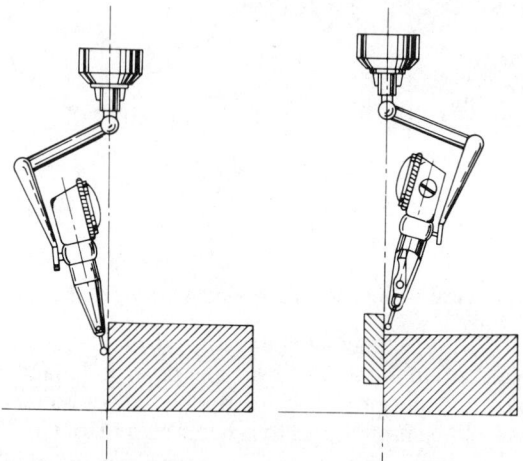

Fig. 9-151 Picking up edge with toolmaker's indicator. Indicator is set against edge of workpiece, raised, and rotated 180° to touch gage block held against edge.

Workholding Methods. A workpiece must be fixed to the machine table with its datum and geometric features related to the measuring system and the machine spindle centerline. If generating angular features or establishing details having angular dimensions is required, a precision rotary table is used. Angular inclination of the workpiece relative to the horizontal plane of the machine table may be necessary when setting up the workpiece. A microsine table (see Fig. 9-152) or an inclinable rotary table (see Fig. 9-153) can be used for this purpose.

To prevent the machine table itself from being cut, the workpiece is supported on parallel setup blocks or in a specially designed fixture. The setup blocks or fixture must be accurately made and arranged to provide adequate and stress-free support for the workpiece.

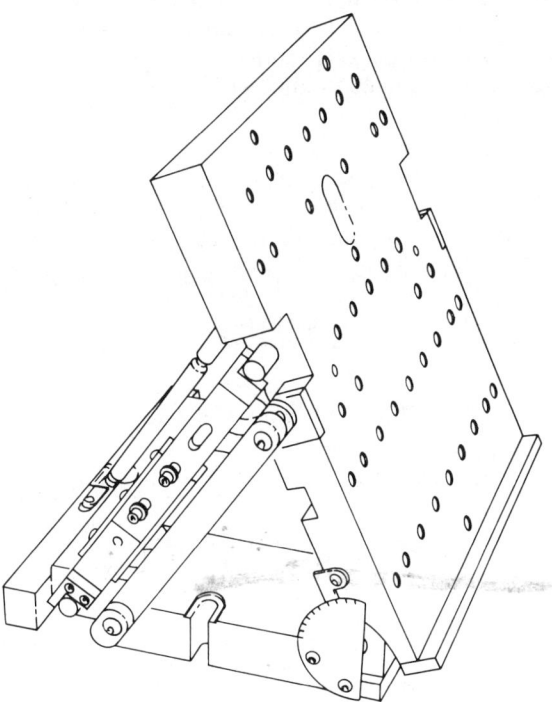

Fig. 9-152 Microsine plate on which angle is set by inserting gage blocks between the gage pins.

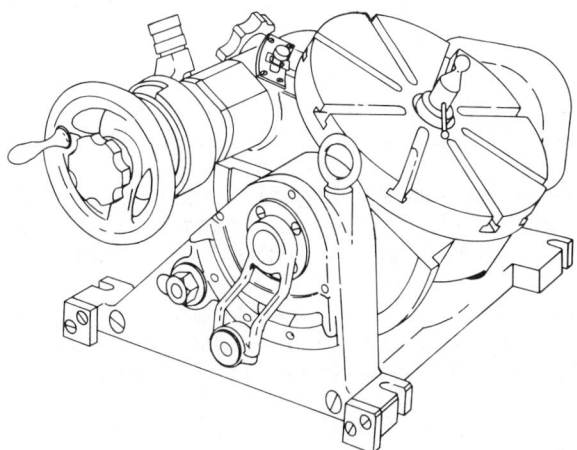

Fig. 9-153 Inclinable rotary table combines angular movement in two planes.

Preparation of the reference and/or mounting surfaces of the workpiece is critical. Flatness and the geometric relationship of these surfaces must be established to conform to the setup equipment. This should be done before the workpiece is fastened to the machine table so that these surfaces may, in turn, be related to the machine's rectilinear system. It may be necessary to machine, hand scrape, or lap these surfaces even though they are not functional.

Clamping arrangement and pressure applied must be sufficient to prevent any movement of the workpiece during machining. Clamping points should be as close as possible to the best supported areas of the workpiece to prevent distortion of the table, the workpiece, or both (see Fig. 9-154). For repetitive work, time may be saved by using simple nests assembled from parallel setup blocks and arranged to function as both supports and locators, as illustrated in Fig. 9-155.

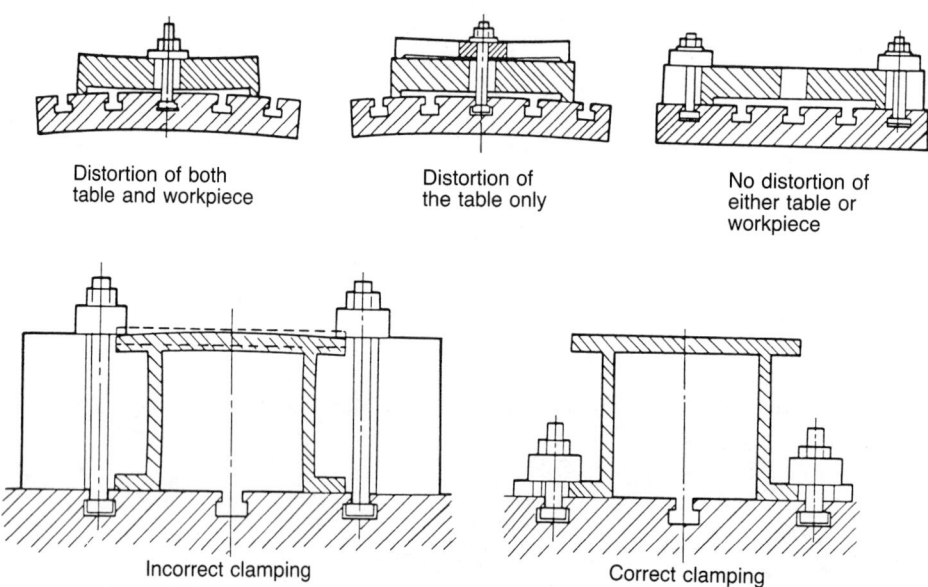

Distortion of both
table and workpiece

Distortion of
the table only

No distortion of
either table or
workpiece

Incorrect clamping

Correct clamping

Fig. 9-154 Improper arrangement of clamps and supports can result in nonparallel holes.

Alignment of the workpiece with the machine slides is set by positioning the workpiece against the machine's straightedge or a locator on the fixture. This parallel alignment can be confirmed by traversing the reference edge against an indicator probe. Adjustments are made by tapping the workpiece or fixture into aligned position before setting the clamps.

Cylindrical work is supported and aligned by using V-blocks or by mounting it between centers of an indexing device such as a rotary table. The rotary table is set up with its axis horizontal and arranged with a tailstock to support the outboard end of the workpiece (see Fig. 9-156).

Angular inclination of the workpiece relative to the X- and Y-axis slide motion is set up using a microsine plate and gage blocks or a rotary/tilting table. The horizontal tilt axis of the sine plate and the reference edge of the workpiece are aligned with the table travel.

Workpieces requiring the machining of compound angles can be accommodated using a rotary table mounted on a microsine plate (see Fig. 9-157) or an inclinable rotary table. Any compound angle can be attained by setting up the required angles using the rotary and tilt axes.

When machining a number of angularly spaced holes, the operator has the option of using rectangular coordinates (converted from angular values by trigonometry) or using polar coordinates for setting angular values with the rotary table directly.

JIG-BORING FIXTURES

A Vertical Jig-boring Fixture. The locating surfaces of the rest blocks (5) of the

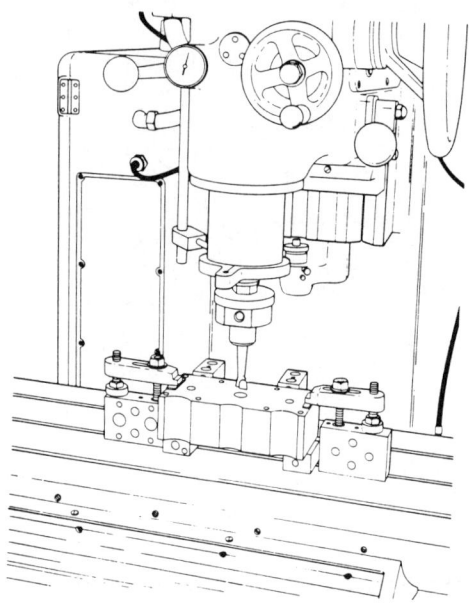

Fig. 9-155 Nests assembled from parallel blocks serve to support and locate workpieces.

fixture of Fig. 9-158 are ground parallel to and 0.812 ±0.0002 in. from the center of the indicating hole, which is 1.875 ±0.0002 in. from the center of the round locating pin.

The bottom of the indicating groove in the upright (6) is ground parallel to its outside edges within 0.0002 in. FIM and square to the bottom of the base (7) of the fixture within 0.0005 in. FIM.

The fixture is placed on a vertical jig borer; and with its probe in the indicating hole, the indicator is brought to zero. The fixture is also oriented on the jig-borer table with the probe bearing against the indicating edge of the fixture.

The workpiece is located by a round locating pin (1) and a diamond pin (2) which are spring-loaded for firm seating in workpiece holes and slide-in bushings (3). A keeper plate (4) bearing against a flat on the diamond pin prevents its rotation.

A clearance of 1/32 in. (0.79 mm) between the shoulder of the diamond pin and its bushing is allowed for variations in the locating holes in the part.

The left-hand clamp straddles the part to rigidly hold the workpiece, while the wide right-hand clamp exerts pressure directly over finished pads on the mounting surface.

A Fixture for Boring 15 Holes. Twelve 0.0928-in. holes (B-holes) and three 0.5000-in. holes (A, S1, and S2 holes) are bored in the workpiece, a casting, of Fig. 9-159. The workpiece is placed on rest plates (8, 9, and 10) in the fixture of Fig. 9-160, and a diamond locating pin (3) is pushed into the locating hole in the side of the casting.

A keeper plate (4) bears against a flat on the side of this pin to prevent its rotation in a bushing (6).

A tapered locating pin (1) is inserted through the S2 hole in the casting and into a bushing (5) in a post (13). Three cam clamps (7), pressing directly on three pads on the part, are tightened; the tapered pin is removed; and the S2 hole is finish-bored. This pin is replaced by a slightly larger one (2), and all other holes in the casting are bored. The

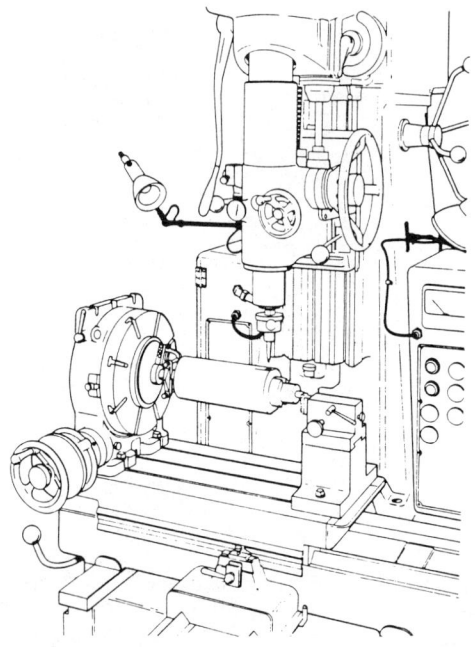

Fig. 9-156 Rotary table mounted with its axis of rotation horizontal and arranged with a tailstock center to support a long workpiece.

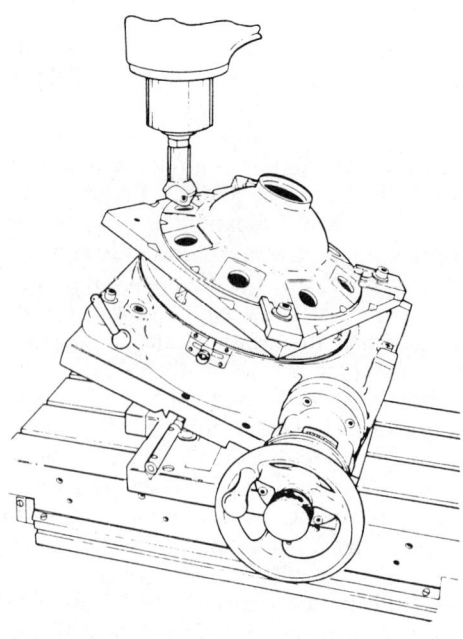

Fig. 9-157 Rotary table set up on a microsine table for machining compound angles.

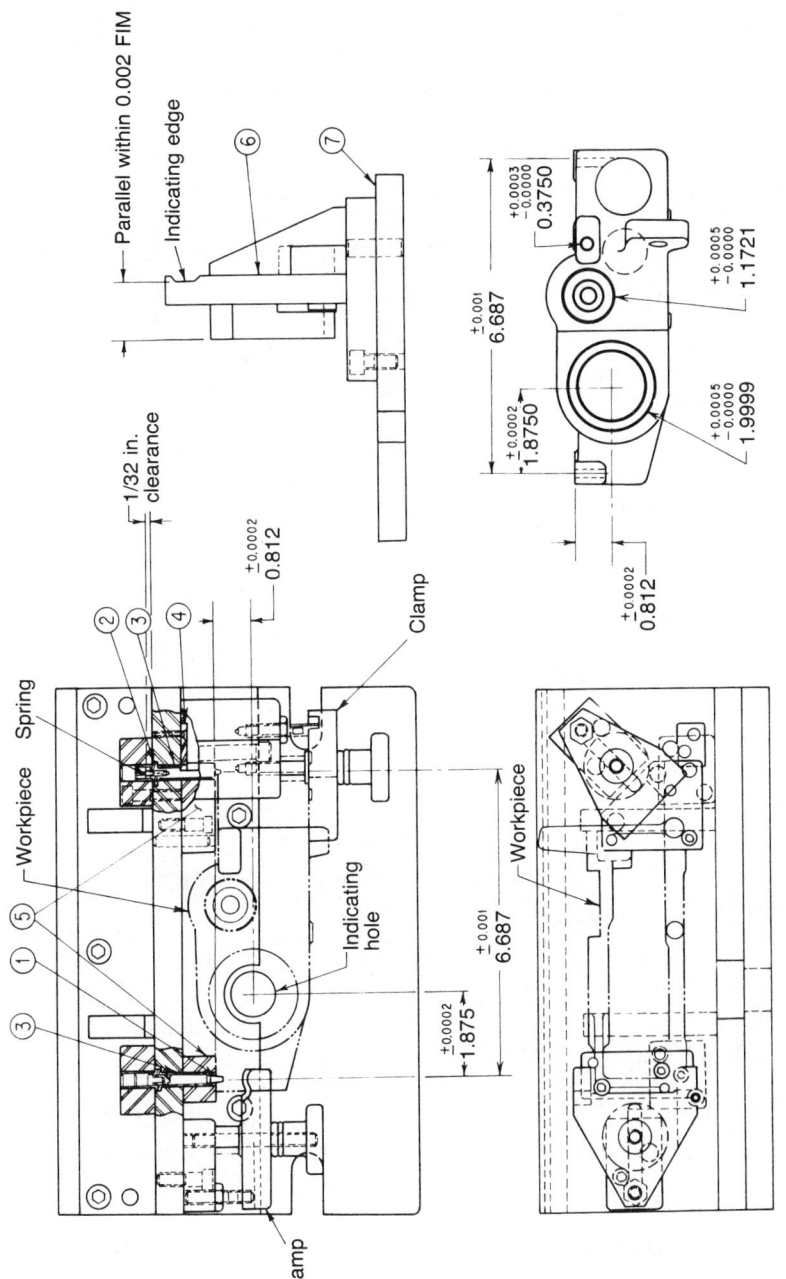

Fig. 9-158 Fixture for vertical jig boring. (*Courtesy IBM*)

9-133

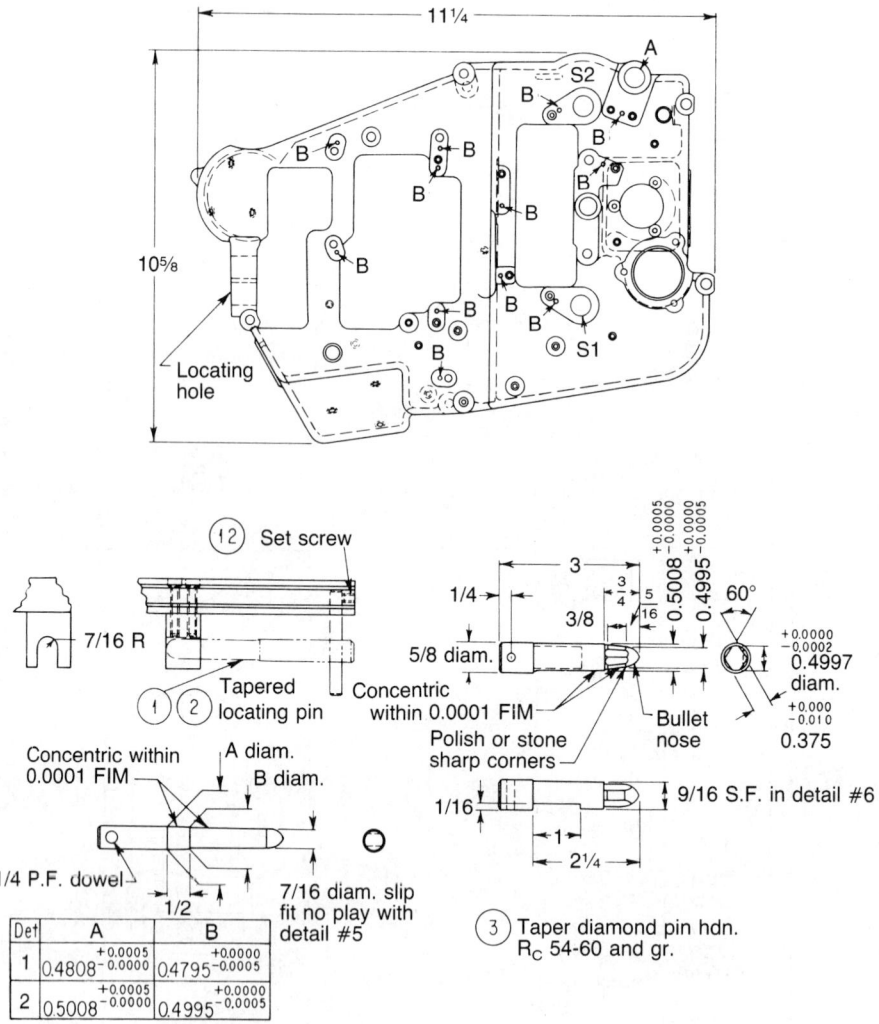

Fig. 9-159 Workpiece for and details of the fixture of Fig. 9-160.

tapered pins snugly fit the hole in the workpiece and accurately locate it.

An indicating edge is ground in the back of the base (11) for orientation of the fixture on the table of a jig borer.

For storage, one tapered pin is left in its bushing (5), and a setscrew (12) secures the other pin to the fixture.

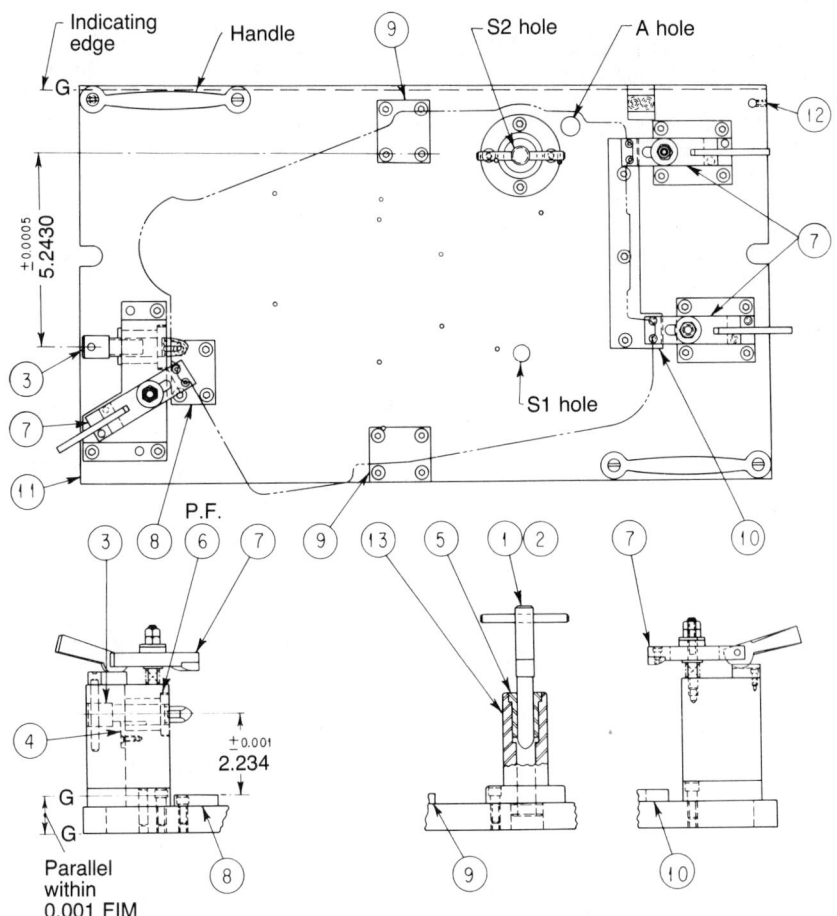

Fig. 9-160 Fixture for a jig borer. (*Courtesy IBM*)

References

1. Thomas J. Drozda and Charles Wick, eds., "Turning and Boring," *Tool and Manufacturing Engineers Handbook*, Volume 1, 4th ed. (Dearborn, MI: Society of Manufacturing Engineers, 1983), pp. 8-1, 8-47.
2. *Ibid.*, pp. 8-64 to 8-67.
3. Carboloy Systems Dept., *Turning Handbook of High-Efficiency Metal Cutting* (Detroit: General Electric Co., 1980).
4. Drozda and Wick, *op. cit.*, p. 8-62.
5. *Ibid.*, pp. 8-47 to 8-48.
6. *Ibid.*, pp. 8-48 to 8-49.
7. Charles Spicer, "Mandrel for Machining Cams," *The Tool Engineer* (January 1958).
8. "Precision Expanding Mandrels," *The Tool Engineer* (September 1958).
9. H.J. Gerber, "Precision Mandrel for Large Rings," *The Tool Engineer* (December 1954).
10. George W. Brown, "Mandrel for Threaded Parts," *The Tool Engineer* (August 1959).
11. C.T. Bower, "Differential Expanding Mandrel," *The Tool Engineer* (May 1956).
12. Drozda and Wick, *op. cit.*, pp. 8-49 to 8-53.

13. *Ibid.*, pp. 8-53 to 8-60.
14. *Ibid.*, p. 8-60.
15. *Ibid.*
16. "Vacuum Faceplate Holds Sheet Stock," *The Tool Engineer* (February 1955).
17. Drozda and Wick, *op. cit.*, p. 8-92.
18. *Ibid.*
19. *Ibid*, pp. 8-80 to 8-82, 15-42 to 15-44, 15-53 to 15-54, 8-95 to 8-98, 15-50 to 15-52.
20. *Ibid.*, pp. 8-101 to 8-106.

CHAPTER 10
GRINDING FIXTURES

Grinding is a process of removing material from a workpiece either with a grinding wheel or disc composed of abrasive grains held together by a bonding material, or with coated abrasives which consist of flexible or semi-rigid backings to which abrasive grains are bound by an adhesive.

Grinding processes include:

- Surface grinding, which produces a flat, high-quality surface on a workpiece.
- Cylindrical grinding, which is used to produce a high-quality surface on internal (ID) or external (OD) surfaces of a workpiece.
- Center hole grinding (plunge or generated) for producing a precise center hole in a workpiece.
- Jig grinding which is used to generate accurately sized and located holes in hardened material.
- Abrasive belt grinding which uses a continuous belt consisting of a flexible or semi-rigid backing to which abrasive grains are bonded by an adhesive.
- Abrasive cutoff, which uses thin, bonded abrasive wheels to cut up billets, bar-stock, castings, etc., for future processing. Because of the similarity to circular saw cutoff operations, abrasive cutoff is covered in Chapter 11, Sawing and Abrasive Cutoff Fixtures.
- Honing, which is an abrasive process using bonded adhesive stones to remove small amounts of material or to improve surface finish.
- Special grinding operations such as thread grinding, gear and spline grinding, tool and cutter grinding, cam grinding, crankshaft grinding, roll grinding, and so on.

Surface Grinding. Surface grinding can be further broken down into periphery grinding with either transverse or rotary workpiece motion (see Fig. 10-1); wheel-face grinding with either transverse or rotary workpiece motion (see Fig. 10-2); single and double disc grinding (see Fig. 10-3); and creep-feed grinding (see Fig. 10-4) where table speeds are low and the wheel is fed to full depth in one or two passes.

Cylindrical Grinding. External cylindrical grinding (OD grinding) usually falls into one of three self-defining types: (1) workpiece mounted between centers, (2) workpiece chuck mounted, and (3) centerless grinding. In the first two types, wheel travel can be either transverse or plunge as shown in Fig. 10-5.

With centerless grinding, three different methods are used to present the workpiece for grinding as follows:

1. Throughfeed grinding, where the workpiece is passed between the grinding wheel and the regulating wheel as shown in Fig. 10-6.
2. Infeed grinding, where the workpiece is placed on the work blade and regulating wheel, and against the end stop and advanced (plunged) into the grinding wheel

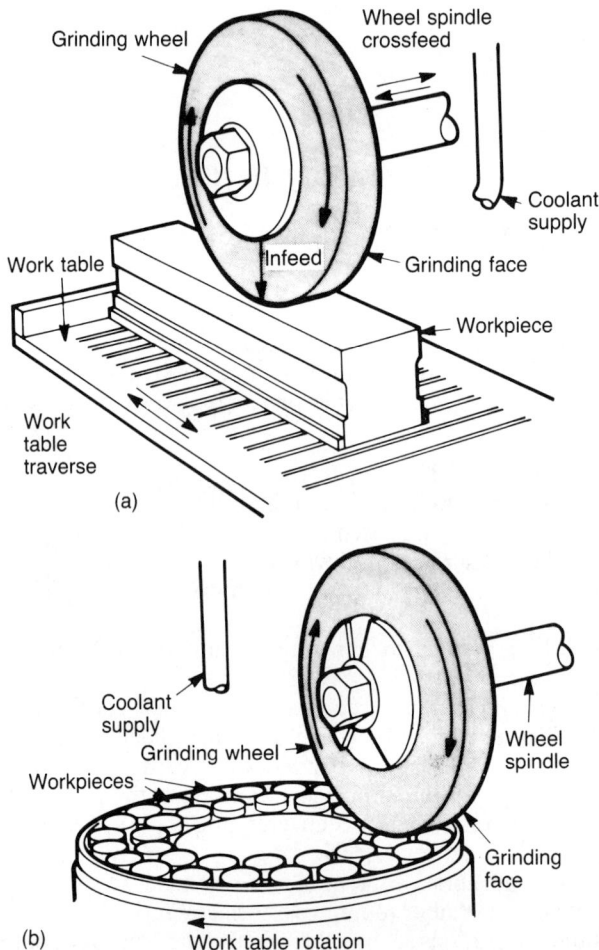

Grinding wheel

Wheel spindle
crossfeed

Coolant
supply

Work table

Infeed

Grinding face

Workpiece

Work
table
traverse

(a)

Coolant
supply

Grinding wheel

Workpieces

Wheel
spindle

Grinding
face

(b)

Work table rotation

Fig. 10-1 Periphery grinding: (a) transverse workpiece motion, (b) rotary workpiece motion.

as shown in Fig. 10-7. When grinding is completed, the regulating wheel is retracted and the part ejected.
3. Endfeed grinding, where the workpiece is fed axially between the grinding wheel and the regulating wheel to an end stop as shown in Fig. 10-8.

Internal cylindrical grinding also falls into three main types: (1) the conventional chuck type which rotates the workpiece as a rotating grinding wheel is fed in and out of the workpiece; (2) the planetary type where the workpiece is held stationary while the rotating grinding wheel describes a planetary motion and is fed radially into the workpiece while gradually increasing the orbiting diameter; and (3) centerless internal grinding.

Either IDs or ODs can be ground, with or without a shoulder, using plunge grinding in which the grinding is fed into the workpiece in a radial (XFEED), axial (ZFEED), or oblique direction (VECTOR FEED). Four methods of producing a cylindrical surface with an adjacent shoulder are shown in Fig. 10-9.

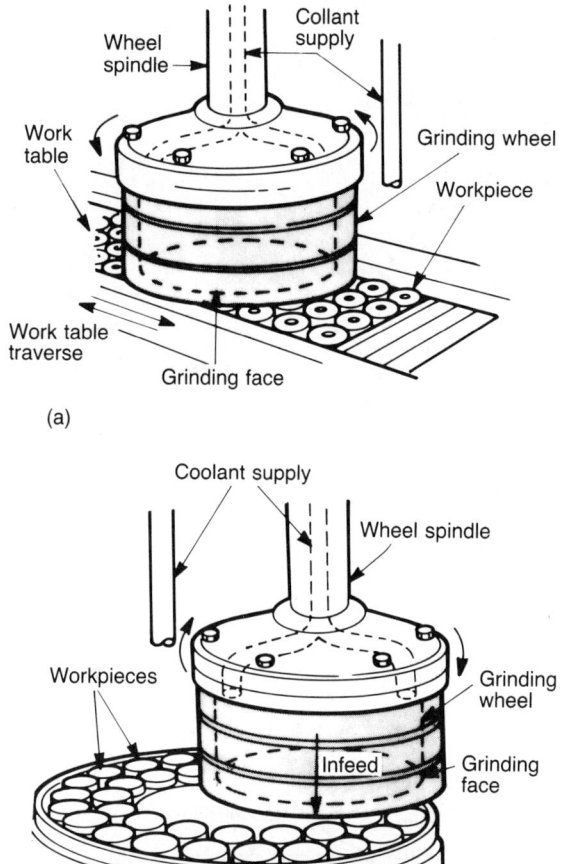

Fig. 10-2 Wheel-face grinding: (*a*) transverse workpiece motion, (*b*) rotary workpiece motion.

GRINDING MACHINES

Horizontal Spindle (Peripheral) Surface Grinders. As the name implies, these machines are built with a grinding wheel that is mounted on a horizontal spindle above the worktable as previously shown in Fig. 10-1. There are two main types: The traversing worktable type which has a reciprocating worktable, and the rotary worktable type which may be equipped with either a reciprocating ram or a reciprocating rotary table to effect traverse motion. Traversing types are widely used to grind flat parallel surfaces, flat tapered surfaces, flat surfaces at different angles, slotting, etc. Rotary types are useful for batched production or for grinding a concave or convex surface on thin round parts.

Vertical Spindle (Wheel Face) Surface Grinders. These machines are built with one or more grinding wheels (cup, cylinder, or segmented-shaped type) that are mounted on vertical spindles above the workpiece as shown in Fig. 10-2. The two main types are the same as for horizontal spindle machines, namely, traverse and rotary workpiece motion.

Vertical spindle surface grinders are self-dressing and produce a crosshatch pattern

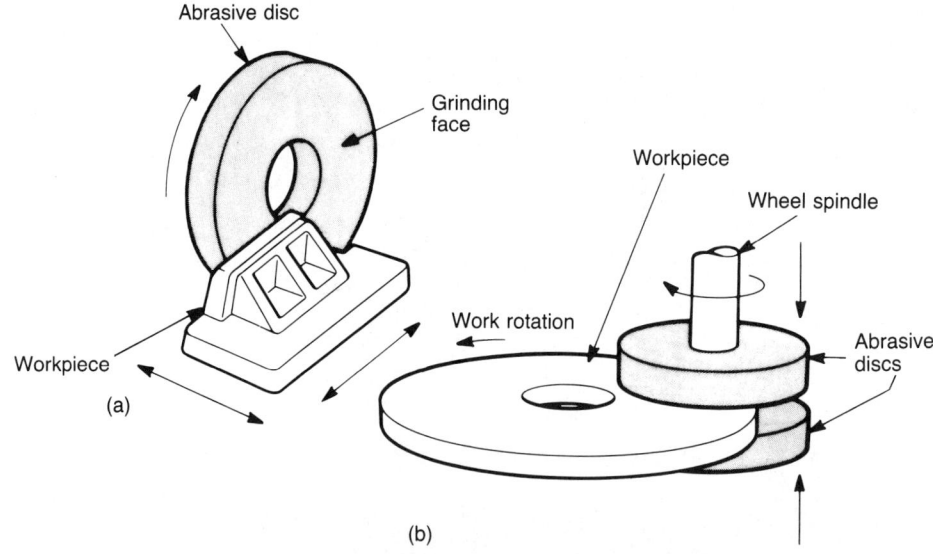

Fig. 10-3 Disc grinding: (a) single-disc, (b) double-disc.

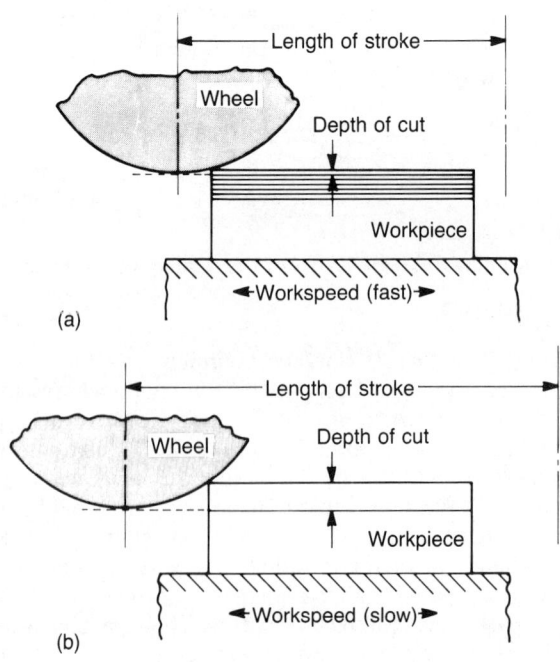

Fig. 10-4 Feed, length of stroke, and depth of cut for: (a) conventional surface grinding and (b) creep-feed grinding.

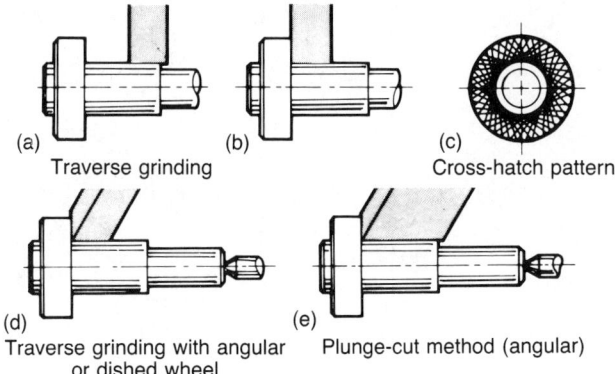

(a)   (b)   (c)
Traverse grinding   Cross-hatch pattern

(d)   (e)
Traverse grinding with angular   Plunge-cut method (angular)
or dished wheel

Fig. 10-5 Comparison of traverse and plunge grinding.

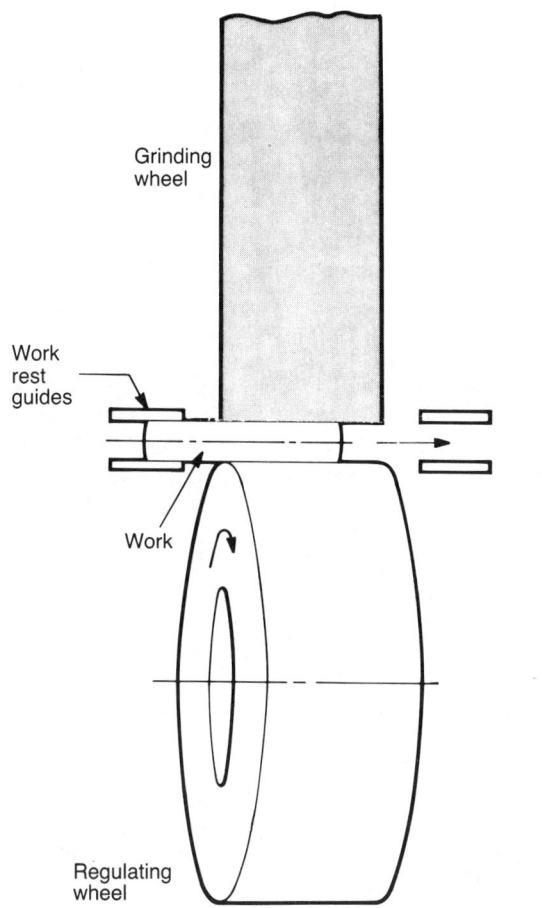

Grinding
wheel

Work
rest
guides

Work

Regulating
wheel

Fig. 10-6 Top view of throughfeed centerless grinding setup.

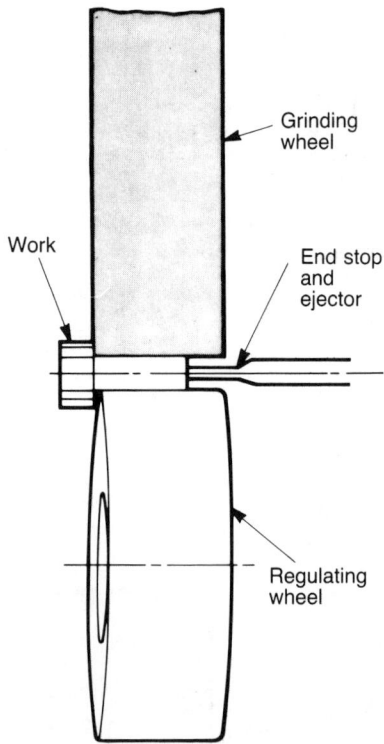

Fig. 10-7 Top view of infeed centerless grinding.

which makes them desirable for flat grinding of precision workpieces. Larger machines can remove up to ½ in. (13 mm) of cast iron in a single pass.

Surface grinders are available in various configurations and sizes with horsepower ratings up to 250-300 hp (186-224 kW).

Disc Grinders. Single and double disc grinders use the faces of abrasive discs to remove material. They are very efficient for producing close-toleranced flat surfaces at high production rates. Disc grinders are available with horizontally or vertically mounted spindles. Feeding principles are shown in Fig. 10-10.

OD Center-type Cylindrical Grinders. These machines are designed for plain cylindrical grinding of workpieces mounted between centers. The wheel slide and workhead are mounted at a right angle to the table travel. On the plain type OD center-type cylindrical grinder, neither the wheelslide or workhead can be swiveled, whereas, on the universal type OD center-type cylindrical grinder, the workhead can be swiveled about its base and adjusted to different positions along the table. Angular wheel slide and straight plunge type machines fall into this category.

Chucking-type Cylindrical Grinders. Chucking-type cylindrical grinders hold workpieces in a chuck or fixture mounted on a rotating spindle in the workhead. They are used for OD grinding of relatively short workpieces that lack center holes and/or a suitable method for driving the workpiece.

Production-type Centerless Grinders. In these machines, a grinding wheel drives the workpiece while a regulating wheel controls the work speed as previously illustrated in Fig. 10-6 thru 10-8. These machines are usually equipped with automatic loading and unloading, wheel dressing, and gaging.

Shoe-type Centerless Grinders. These grinders are special machines that work on the same principle as the production-type centerless grinders, but with the workpiece

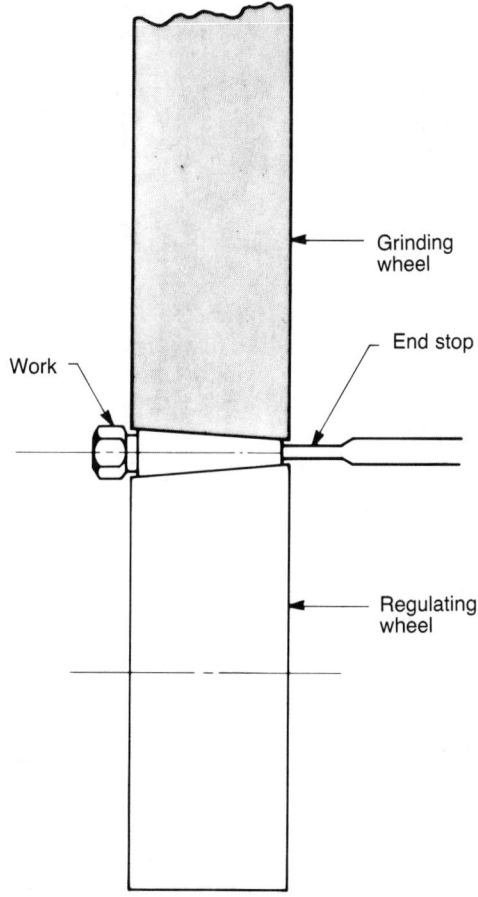

Fig. 10-8 Top view of endfeed centerless grinding.

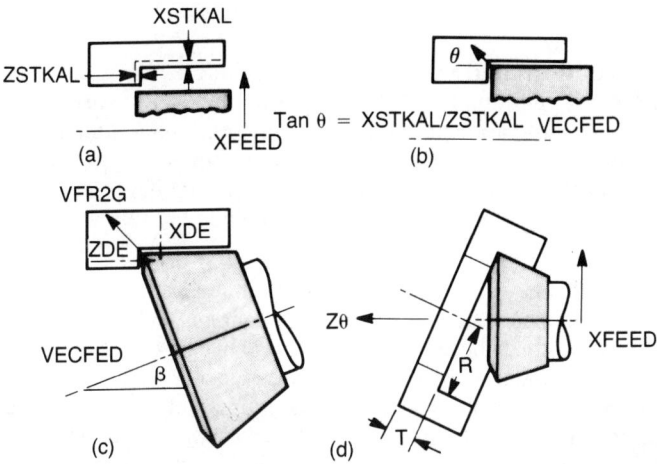

Fig. 10-9 Four methods of producing a cylindrical surface with an adjacent shoulder.

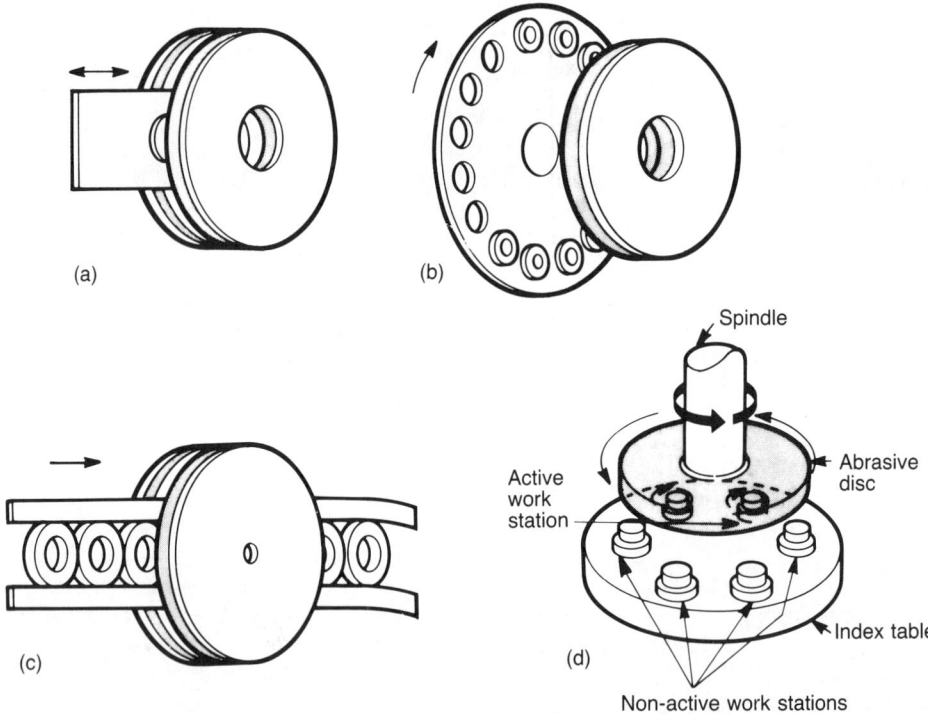

(a)   (b)

Spindle

Active
work
station

Abrasive
disc

Index table

(c)   (d)

Non-active work stations

Fig. 10-10 Feeding principles used in disc grinding as applied by: (*a*) reciprocating fixture, (*b*) rotary fixture, (*c*) throughfeed fixture, (*d*) indexing, rotating fixture. (*Courtesy Litton Industrial Automation Systems*)

being driven by a magnetic chuck while supported by two non-rotating work rests with attached wear pads called shoes. These machines consist mainly of a bed, tilting wheel-head, and a workhead for holding the workpieces for grinding.

Conventional-type Internal Grinders. These machines are built with a horizontal workhead spindle on one end of the machine to rotate the workpiece during the grinding operation. They also have a wheelhead which is mounted on longitudinal and cross slides on the other end to move the grinding wheel axially and radially with respect to the workpiece.

Production-type Horizontal Spindle Internal Grinders. These machines are some-times built with the longitudinal slide or cross slide under the workhead. Machines of this type are very versatile and can be used to grind external diameters, internal faces, and external faces in addition to straight and tapered bores.

Figure 10-11 illustrates some of the configurations available in a line of universal internal grinders featuring CNC. Configurations include the following:

1. Compound slide under the wheel, *a*.
2. Compound slide under the wheel with front facing attachment, *b*.
3. Compound slide under the wheel with rear facing attachment, *c*.
4. Compound slide under both bore and facing wheels (4 axes), *d*.
5. Compound slide under a two-spindle arrangement, *e*.
6. Compound slide under the wheel with a workhead cross slide (3 axes), *f*.
7. Longitudinal slide under the wheel and the cross slide under the workpiece, *g*.
8. Cross slide under the wheel and the longitudinal slide under the workpiece, *h*.
9. Compound slide under the workpiece, *j*.

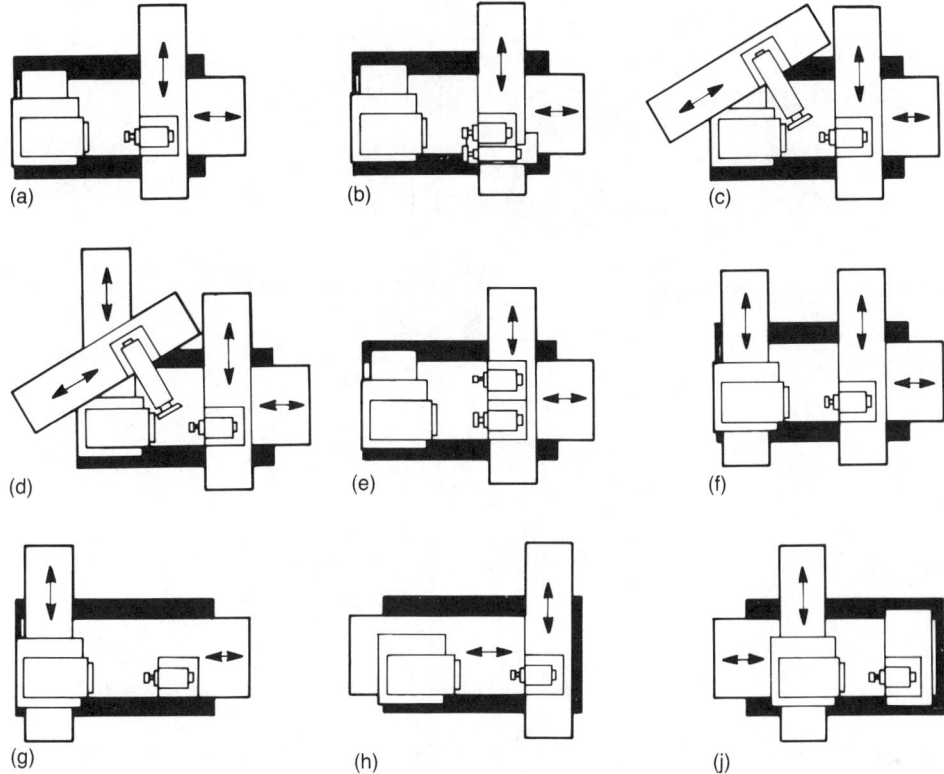

Fig. 10-11 Configurations of a universal CNC internal grinder featuring modular components. (*Courtesy Bryant Grinder Corp.*)

Vertical Internal Grinders. Vertical mounted spindle machines are used to perform the same operations as the horizontal spindle machines. In addition, they are capable of grinding contoured bores using simple, cam-operated fixtures. The horizontal work-tables on these machines makes them ideal for grinding heavy workpieces, since the weight of the workpiece adds to the holding power of the workholder.

Planetary Internal Grinders. On these machines, the workpiece is held stationary in a fixture at one end of the machine while the grinding wheel is fed radially into the workpiece while describing a planetary motion about the work axis. These machines are used when it is impractical to rotate the workpiece during grinding.

Center Hole Grinders. Center hole grinders (see Fig. 10-12) are built especially to generate precision center holes to locate workpieces for future operations.

Jig Grinding Machines. Jig grinding machines, such as shown in Figs. 10-13 and 10-14, were originally designed to grind holes accurately to size and to coordinate locations in hardened steel, as required for the manufacturing of press tools. These machines utilize the same principles of rectilinear-positioning control employed in jig borers. They are commonly used as companion machines to the jig borer. Modern jig borers can generate vertical surfaces in the X-Y plane as well as internal and external diameters.

Jig grinding machines differ from jig borers in that the machine spindle is replaced by a more complex unit offering the following capabilities:

1. Means for adjusting the radial offset of the grinding spindle to accommodate various diameters or radii.

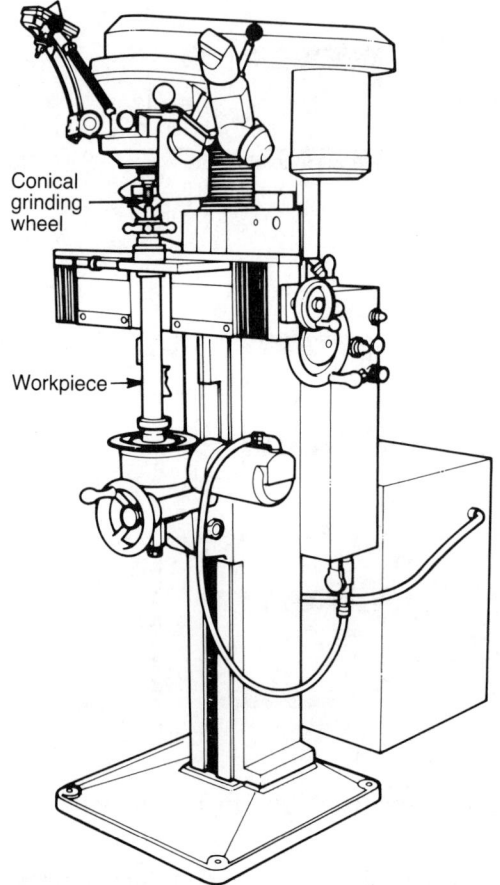

Conical
grinding
wheel

Workpiece→

Fig. 10-12 Center hole grinder for generating precision center holes. (*Courtesy Bryant Grinder Corp.*)

2. Provisions to drive the grinding spindle in a planetary orbit at controlled speeds.
3. Fine adjustment of the radial offset engineered to function while the main machine spindle is operating.
4. An automatic vertical reciprocating feed motion for the grinding spindle with provisions for control of its rate and traverse range.
5. Means for generating the vertical surfaces of workpiece at set angles, producing tapered diameters and contoured surfaces as required for clearance in press tools.
6. Provisions for controlling the angular direction of the planetary offset for the grinding spindle relative to the machine's slide motion.
7. An engineered system for transmitting and controlling power to the machine spindle and the grinding wheel, both simultaneously and independently.
8. Provisions for interchanging a variety of grinding spindles as required for universal application.

NC and CNC equipped jig grinding machines are designed to operate automatically, performing the functions for positioning control, spindle start and stop, vertical feed motion, and linear feed rates for contouring in the X-Y plane.

Abrasive Belt Machines. Abrasive belt machines are available in a wide variety of configurations to suit special applications, such as those shown in Fig. 10-15.

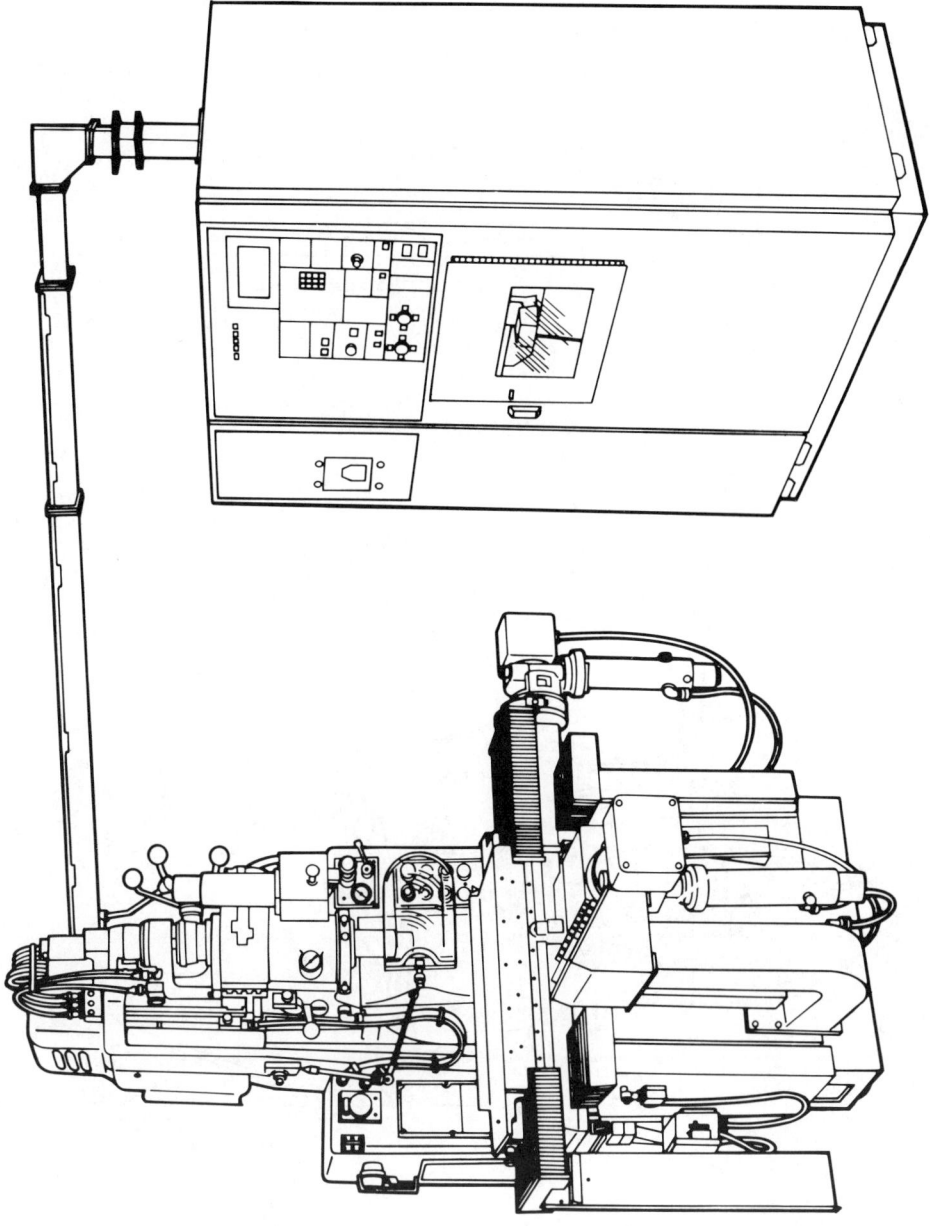

Fig. 10-13 Open side-type jig grinding machine, numerically controlled. (*Courtesy Moore Special Tool Co., Inc.*)

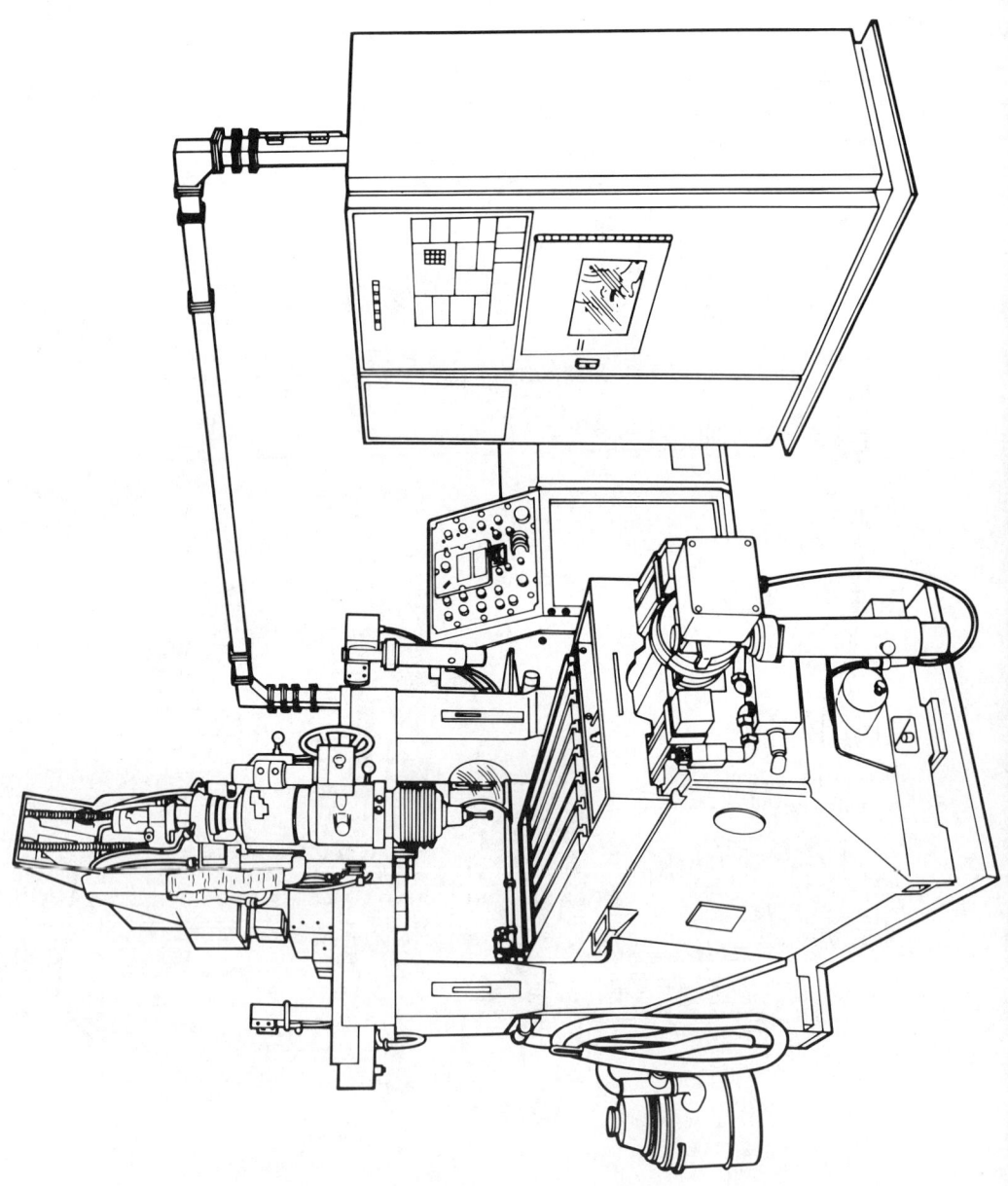

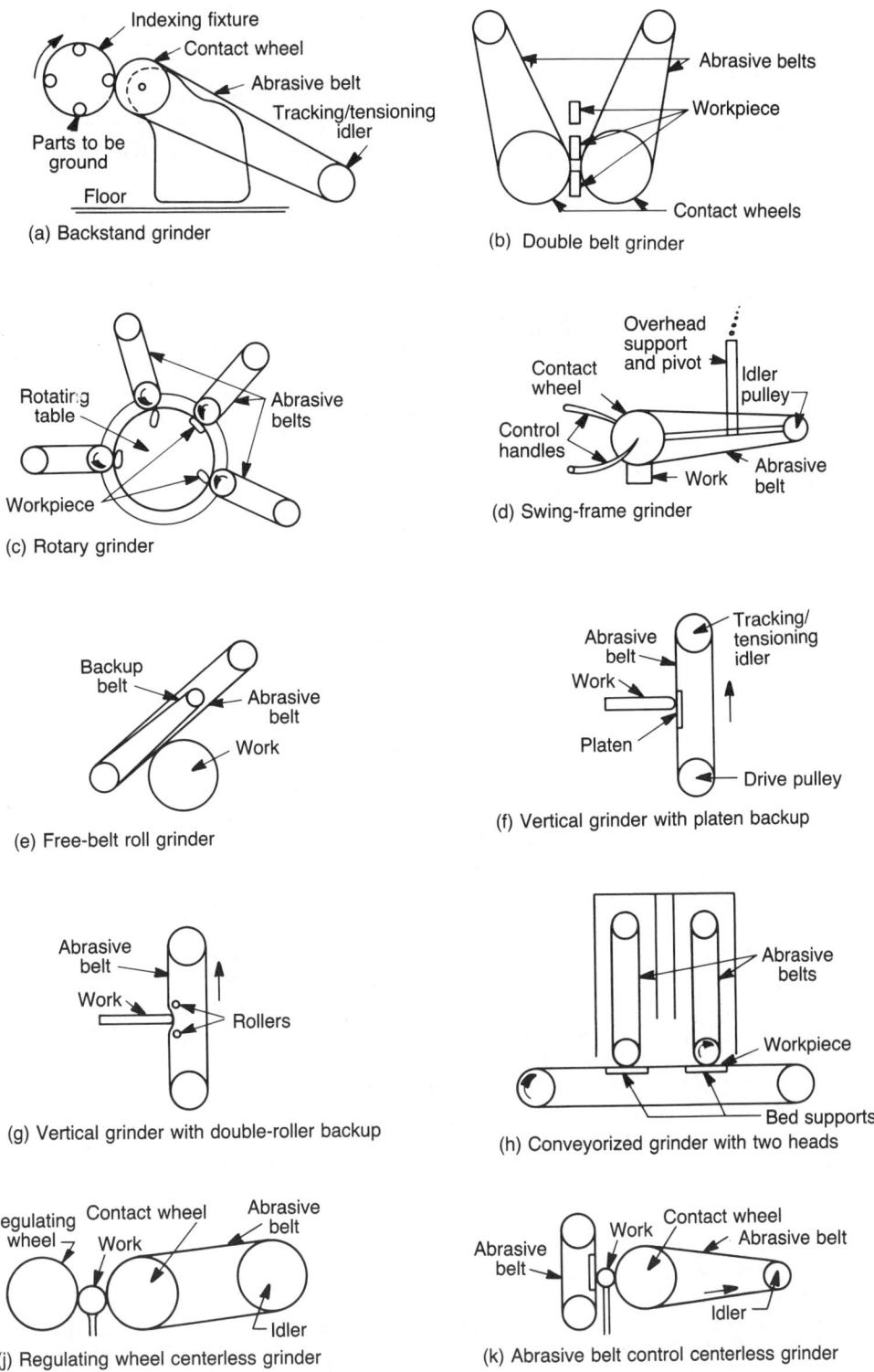

(a) Backstand grinder

(b) Double belt grinder

(c) Rotary grinder

(d) Swing-frame grinder

(e) Free-belt roll grinder

(f) Vertical grinder with platen backup

(g) Vertical grinder with double-roller backup

(h) Conveyorized grinder with two heads

(j) Regulating wheel centerless grinder

(k) Abrasive belt control centerless grinder

Fig. 10-15 Typical configurations and applications of abrasive belt machining.

Honing Machines. Basic honing machines (see Fig. 10-16) provide tool rotation but require the operator to supply the force needed to stroke the part back and forth over the honing tool, while with the power-stoked honing machine the operator loads the part, starts the cycle, and unloads the finished part when the cycle is finished. Automatic honing machines that gage the bore diameter while it is being honed, and stop the honing operation when size has been reached are also available. For heavy stock removal, vertical machines, such as that shown in Figure. 10-17, are used.

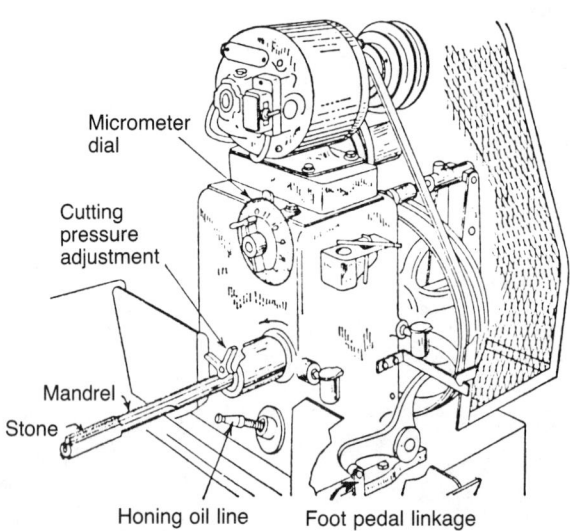

Micrometer dial

Cutting pressure adjustment

Mandrel

Stone

Honing oil line   Foot pedal linkage

Fig. 10-16 Bench-type honing machine. (*Courtesy Sunnen Products Co.*)

Thread Grinding Machines. Thread grinding machines, as shown in Fig. 10-18, are generally classified as internal, external, or universal machines which can be used to produce internal or external threads. They differ from other cylindrical-type grinders by the addition of a leadscrew or change gears to establish the correct pitch or lead, a means of inclining the plane of rotation of the grinding wheel to suit the helix angle being ground, and a means of dressing or truing the cutting wheel to the proper form. Grinding wheels can be single rib or multirib as shown in Fig. 10-19. Machines are available for locating the workpiece on centers for grinding, or for centerless grinding in a manner similar to that used in plain centerless cylindrical grinding.

Gear and Spline Grinding Machines. Gear and spline grinding machines basically fall into two types: intermittent-indexing form grinders and involute-generation types. The form grinding types remove material by plunge grinding with a wheel dressed to the proper contour. Tooth spacing is controlled by precise indexing.

The involute generation types are built in both intermittent-indexing and continuous indexing types: Both types use a grinding wheel(s) with a rack tooth profile to generate the involute form.

Tool and Cutter Grinders. These specialized machines are mainly used to recondition cutting tools. They include drill grinders, drill-point web-thinning machines, face-mill grinders, end-mill grinders, hob sharpeners, tap grinders, broach grinders, and others.

Tools to be sharpened or reconditioned are generally held either between centers, in a work spindle having a tapered female opening, or in collets actuated by a drawbar.

Cam Grinders. These special machines for grinding camshafts are similar to external cylindrical grinders except that workpieces are mounted and supported on a rocker

Fig. 10-17 Vertical honing machine. (*Courtesy Micromatic Hone Co.*)

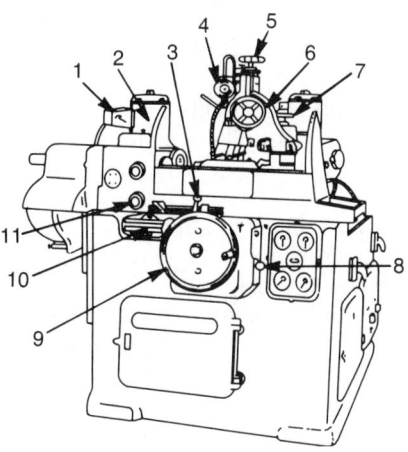

Fig. 10-18 External thread and form grinder: (1) High-low speed switch for workhead speed ranges; (2) workhead motor; (3) knob for automatic cycle release and power transverse of worktable to right or left; (4) crusher feed-motor and feed change gears; (5) crusher feed wheel for hand feed; (6) crusher positioning wheel; (7) wheel for helix-angle setting of wheelhead; (8) lever for wheelhead pull-in for plunge grinding; (9) wheel for positioning grinding wheel; (10) accessory for microvariations of thread lead; (11) knob for micropositioning of worktable. (*Courtesy Automation & Measurement Div., Bendix Corp.*)

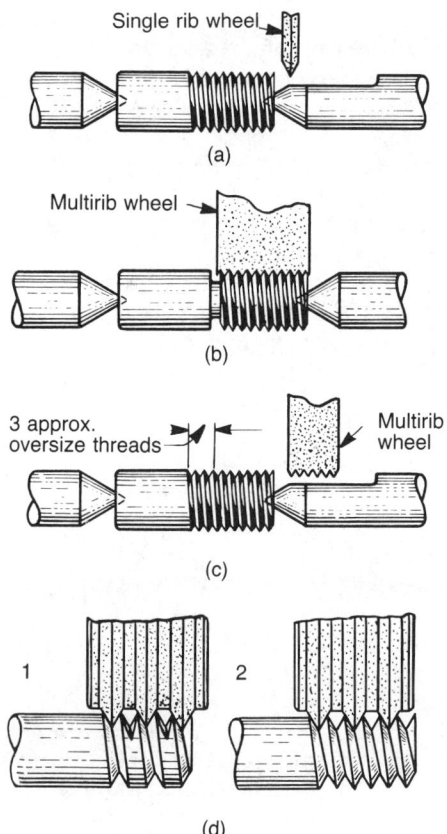

Single rib wheel

(a)

Multirib wheel

(b)

3 approx.
oversize threads

Multirib
wheel

(c)

1   2

(d)

Fig. 10-19 Use of ribbed wheels: (*a*) complete traverse grinding with single rib wheels, (*b*) partial traverse grinding with multirib wheel, (*c*) complete traverse grinding with multirib wheel, (*d*) multirib wheel with nib pitch twice the thread pitch–(1) at end of first revolution of the work; (2) at end of second revolution of the work.

bar mechanism that permits the workpiece to move toward and away from the grinding wheel as the workpiece is rotated. This rocking action, which is controlled by a cam follower rolling against a master cam in the workhead permits generation of the cam contour.

Other special grinding machines include multiple-wheel crankshaft grinders and roll grinders for external grinding and crowning of large workpieces, such as steel mill rolls.

The grinding fixtures shown and described in this section are classified according to the grinding process or the type of grinding machine with which they are used, since no standard or quasi-universal classification is presently in use. Although good design practice always applies, these are conditions unique to the grinding process or machine that must be considered in the design of a fixture.

Some of the parts and problems which may affect or be reflected in the design of grinding fixtures are:

1. Coolant nozzles, spray guards, part feeders, and other such devices.
2. Coolant escape or control.
   a. Coolant delivery through the fixture to the workpiece.
   b. Coolant and sludge escape from the fixture.
3. Mounting of wheel dressers on or close to the fixture.
4. Rotating fixtures and chucks generally require dynamic balancing.

WORKHOLDING FOR GRINDING

In grinding, the force of the tool acting on the workpiece is significantly smaller than in metalcutting operations used for comparable purposes.[6] This distinguishing condition beneficially affects the required workholding system. Consequently, the clamping force needed for ensuring dependable retention of the workpiece is lessened, resulting in substantially simplified methods and operation as well as reduced cost of workholding devices for grinding. A typical example is magnetic holding devices for workpieces carrying out either rotating or reciprocating movements. Magnetic chucks or plates are used widely on grinding machines. Equivalent metalcutting operations employ mechanical lathe chucks or other workholding devices that exert considerable clamping force. These workholding devices often are designed expressly for a particular type of workpiece. In other grinding machine operations, specifically in centerless grinding, no workholding device is needed; the grinding force acting on the workpiece is sufficient to ensure secure retention of the workpiece against a solid support element, the work blade.

Several specific advantages of grinding resulting from simplified workholding methods are:

- Faster loading and unloading of workpieces, thereby reducing total time of the operation.
- Simplified application of process automation.
- Workholding devices that are often less expensive to procure and operate than those for other processes.
- Delicate work handling permitted by light clamping force, which reduces the incidence of workpiece distortion and/or surface marring.
- Consistently accurate location of the workpiece held in grinding machines. The location is much less dependent on the skill of the operator than in metalcutting operations which require work clamping with considerable force that has a potential dislocating effect.

Surface Grinding. For many surface grinding operations, workpieces are simply held on magnetic chucks, vacuum chucks, or in precision vises, such as those covered in Chapter 3.

Workpieces made of steel or other magnetic materials can be held directly on magnetic chucks. Non-magnetic workpieces must be contained in place with steel blocks or parallels. Small magnetic workpieces are also often contained as a safeguard in case magnetism is lost. The patented hold-downs shown previously in Fig. 3-62e can be useful for holding non-magnetic workpieces on a magnetic chuck.

A modular workholding system combining these devices with interchangeable V-blocks, angle irons, etc., is shown in Fig. 10-20. Components include the following: sine plates, *a*; compound sine plates, *b*; permanent magnetic chucks, *c*; electromagnetic chucks, *d*; vacuum chucks, *e*; magnetic sine plates, *f*; magnetic compound sine plates, *g*; angle plates, *h*; V-blocks, *i*; precision vises, *j*; precision sine vises, *k*; and indexing and non-indexing whirl-gigs, *l*, which can be used for "spinning" a part to grind an angle or a form. All components can be bolted together in various ways without clamping and with little or no indicating. They can also be used individually.

For surface grinding on rotary chucks, small flat workpieces are usually arranged close together to form a complete circle between two steel rings having a thickness less than the finished length of the workpieces.

Cylindrical Grinding. For many cylindrical grinding operations, workpieces are simply held between centers or mounted on standard chucks, mandrels, expanding arbors, collets and faceplates, such as those covered in Chapters 3 and 9. On the other hand, some workpieces require special fixturing which may or may not be used in conjunction with these devices. Examples of these are shown in the following section.

(a)

(b)

Used as
parallel or
squaring chuck

(c)

Bolted to
Sine System Sine Plate

(d)

Bolted to
Sine System
Angle Plate

Bolted to
Sine System
Sine Plate

(e)

(f)

(g)

Fig. 10-20 A modular workholding system for grinding. (*Courtesy Swiss Precision Instruments, Inc.*)

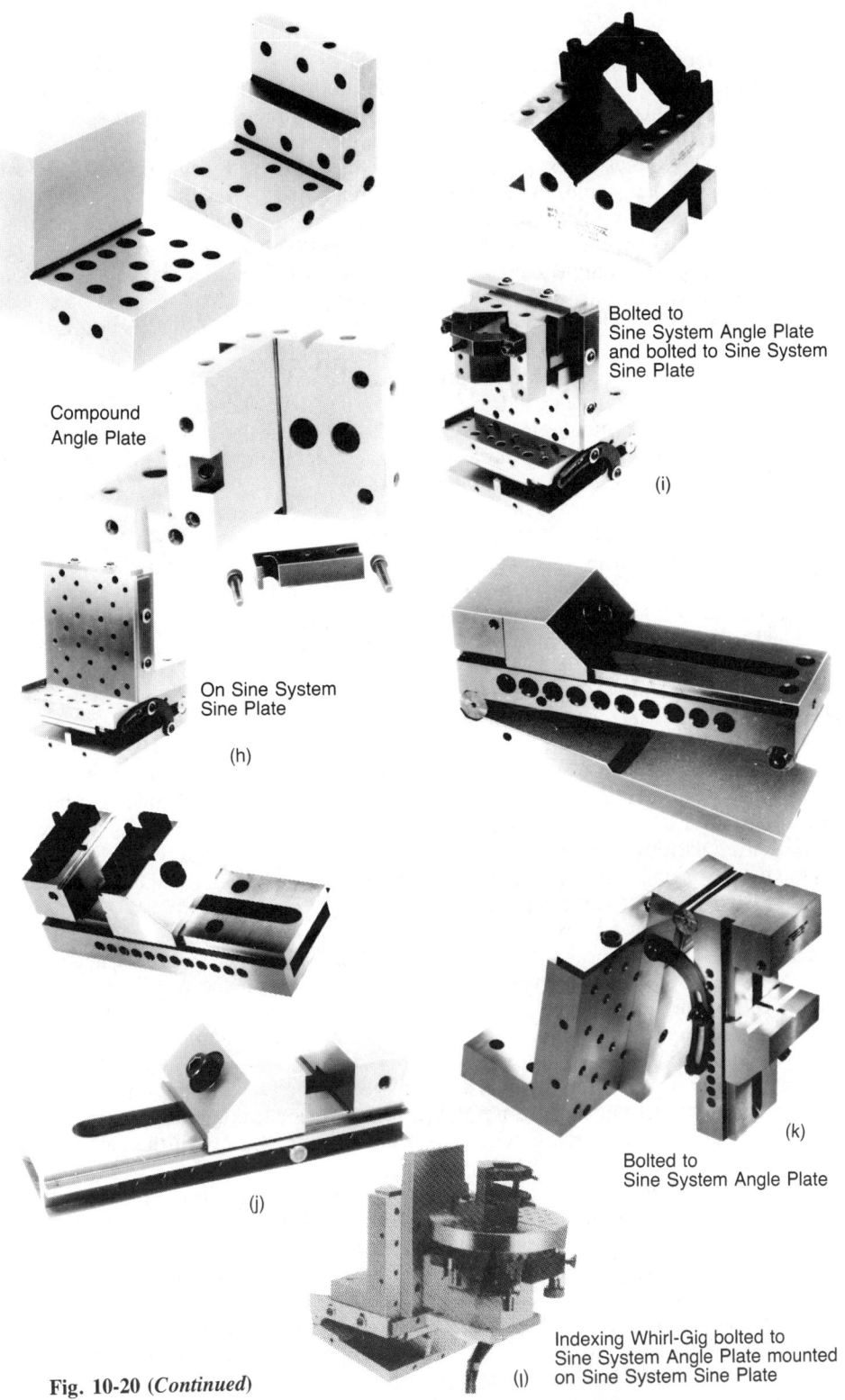

Compound
Angle Plate

Bolted to
Sine System Angle Plate
and bolted to Sine System
Sine Plate

(i)

On Sine System
Sine Plate

(h)

(j)

(k)

Bolted to
Sine System Angle Plate

Indexing Whirl-Gig bolted to
Sine System Angle Plate mounted
on Sine System Sine Plate

(l)

Fig. 10-20 (*Continued*)

FIXTURES FOR SURFACE GRINDERS

Wherever possible, magnetic or vacuum chucks should be incorporated into the design of the fixture to save the costs of elaborate fixturing that would otherwise be incurred. When this is not the case and mechanical clamping is required, special care must be taken to provide proper orientation between the fixture and the chuck.

Figure 10-21 shows an example of thin film clamping (with Rigidax® tooling compound which is a castable, thermoplastic compound for stabilizing, supporting, and holding hard to fixture, thin wall, odd-shaped and non-magnetic parts). To use, it is melted to a fluid form and poured in and around a part(s). After machining, it is melted and reused. (In the example shown, Rigidax® was used to hold a fragile Germanium crystal for dicing. The parts are very fragile and tinning is critical. The method could be used equally well to clamp other small electronic, ceramic, plastic, honeycomb, and non-magnetic parts for high production grinding operations.)

Surface grinder fixtures can be relatively simple and inexpensive, as shown in Fig. 10-22. This fixture was designed to confine, rather than clamp the workpieces. The fixture is used with a magnetic chuck so that both it and the workpieces are held in place by the chuck during the grinding operation. Lateral movement of the workpieces is prevented by the packing action of the fixture.

A variation of this fixture is shown in Fig. 10-23 which was designed with individual holes for the workpieces.

A similar fixture for use with reciprocating-table grinder is shown in Fig. 10-24.

Another simple surface grinding fixture is shown in Fig. 10-25. This fixture was made of T-section tooling material and required only four hours construction time.

Figure 10-26 shows a clamping fixture made from standard angle iron or L-section tooling material, threaded stock, and nuts. It was designed to grind the edges of the rough stock perpendicular to their sides. The fixture is capable of holding twenty-five parts at a time. In use, four identical fixtures are mounted on a rotary-table type grinder for grinding 100 parts per setup.

The fixture shown in Fig. 10-27 was designed to grind the two top surfaces of a workpiece—four at a time. Workpieces are forced together by the main clamp at the end of the fixture. The other clamp, which uses a nylon pad to compensate for minor surface irregularities in the workpieces, holds the workpieces against the upright section of the fixture to ensure squareness. In use, the smaller surface is ground first. The larger surface is ground next along with the shoulder.

Figure 10-28 shows a vise jaw fixture designed to locate and hold four cylindrical workpieces for angular grinding. The flatted sides of the workpieces are located against the solid block (3) assembled to the movable jaw (1) and the rest directly on the extended portion of the jaw.

Four self-equalizing plungers (4) located and moving within the stationary jaws (2) compensate for diameter variations in the parts.

The medium for the equalizing system can be oil or any other high-viscosity material, but the plungers must be a tight slip fit to prevent leakage of the medium. To prevent cocking of the parts, blocks (5) are machined to closely fit the parts without gripping them.

The universal grinding fixture shown in Fig. 10-29a was designed for grinding various angles on a multitude of small flat parts. The fixture consists of a commercial premachined cast-iron T-section into which fifteen holes have been drilled and tapped to mount three eccentric-headed bolts (2) for locating the workpiece using the 3-2-1 principle.

Four typical examples are shown in Fig. 10-29b thru e. Angle setups with this fixture are virtually limitless. A toggle clamp (3) or a clamp similar to the one shown holds the workpiece against the face of the fixture.

Thin Film Clamping

Tinned germanium crystal

Dicing pattern

Rigidax® solution

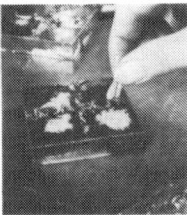

Aluminum fixturing block on hot plate. Rigidax® being applied.

Part placed on fixture block against locator pins.

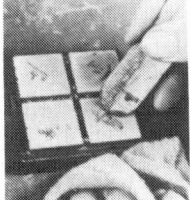

Moved to water-cooled plate where final location takes place just before solidification.

First cut to be made on Brown & Sharpe grinder with 12 diamond cutters on mandrel.

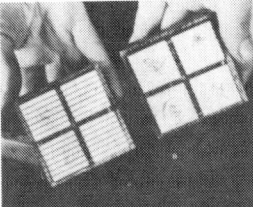

First cut is compared with uncut waffers. Gaps in first cut must be filled to prevent pop out during second cut.

Gaps are filled with Rigidax® from secondary hot plate.

Load 5 up for final cut.

Dicing completed.

Melt out on hot plate.

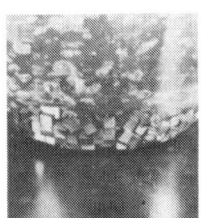

Cleaning.

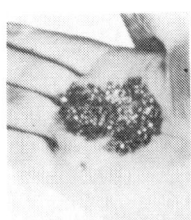

Finished parts—negligible loss of materials. Entire dicing handled by one operator.

Fig. 10-21 Thin film clamping. (*with Rigidax®, courtesy Argueso & Co., Inc.*)

Figure 10-30 shows a trunnion type fixture designed for angular grinding. The fixture incorporates a plate (2) which swings on two stripper bolts (3) and a base (1) held on the machine table. The plate is drilled and tapped to receive the bolts of hold-down clamps (not shown) for clamping the work on it. The plate can be fixed at any desired angle by tightening the stripper bolts with a hexagon key.

A vise fixture for grinding flats on a shaft is shown in Fig. 10-31. Flats are to be ground parallel to each other and to the axis of a hole in the shaft which was previously ground between centers. Hardened centers are pressed into angle-iron brackets which

10-21

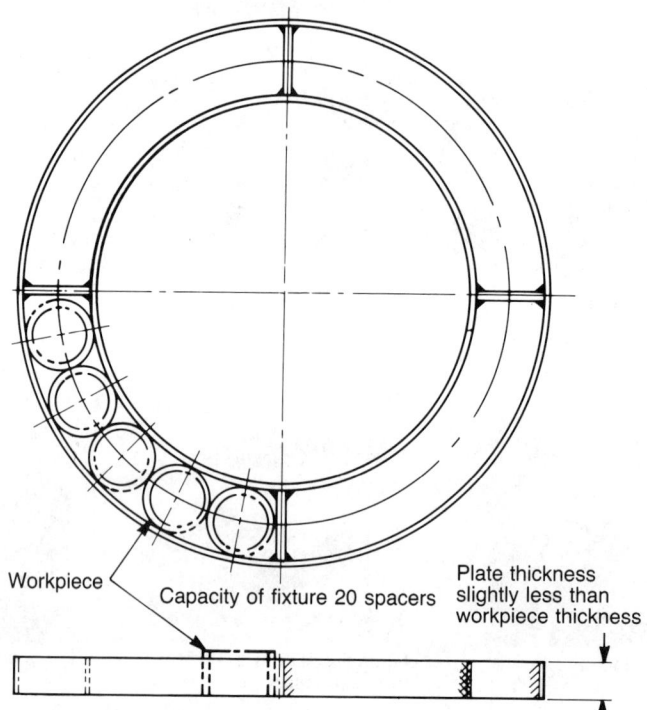

Workpiece   Capacity of fixture 20 spacers   Plate thickness slightly less than workpiece thickness

Fig. 10-22 Simple retaining fixture for a rotary table surface grinder.

Holes bored to suit workpiece size

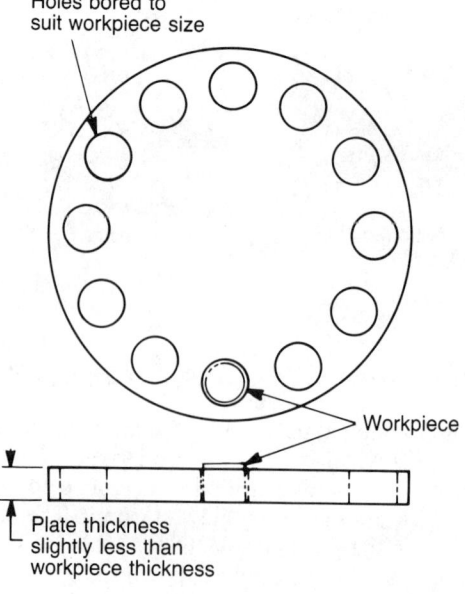

Workpiece

Plate thickness slightly less than workpiece thickness

Fig. 10-23 Retaining fixture for a rotary table surface grinder designed to prevent lateral movement of workpieces during grinding.

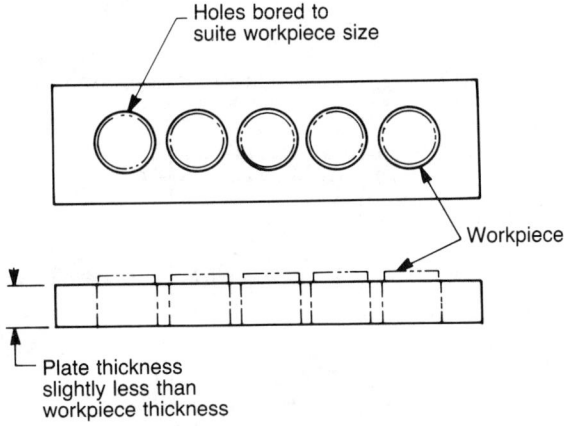

Fig. 10-24 Retaining fixture for a reciprocating-table surface grinder.

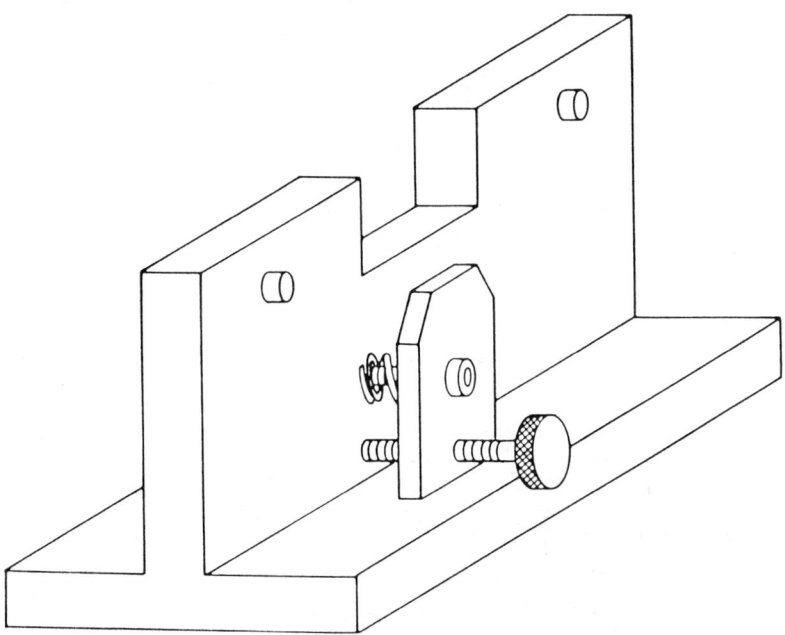

Fig. 10-25 Grinding fixture made from T-section tooling material.

are drilled and pinned to the jaws of a grinding vise. The yoke has reamed through holes for the indexing pin. The pin is inserted through the yoke and shaft, and the leg of the yoke is located in an elongated hole in the left-hand bracket. The shaft is placed between the centers as the vise is tightened. One flat is ground on one side of the shaft; and then the shaft is turned, indexed, and held for grinding the opposite flat.

A more sophisticated fixture for grinding flats is shown in Fig.10-32. It features a standard indexing head mounted on a bench center type base with a matching tailstock that can be moved axially to accommodate workpieces of different lengths within its range. The 24-hole indexing plate permits grinding of flats at 15° intervals. For greater versatility the standard indexing head could be replaced with an indexer that would permit grinding flats at virtually any angle around the periphery.

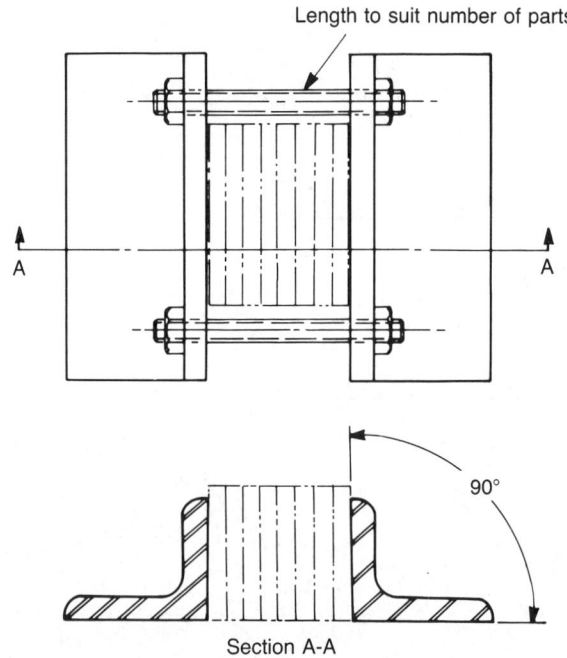

Length to suit number of parts

A ← → A

90°

Section A-A

Fig. 10-26 Clamping fixture to hold 25 workpieces.

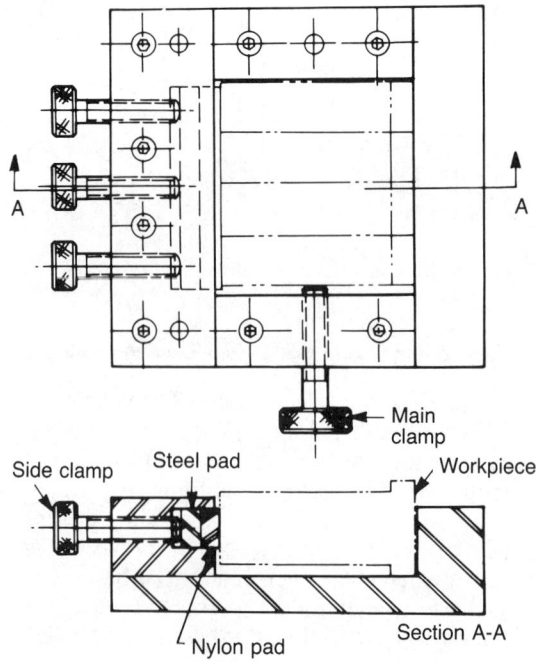

A ← → A

Main clamp

Side clamp Steel pad Workpiece

Nylon pad Section A-A

Fig. 10-27 Clamping fixture ensures squareness between locating and work surfaces.

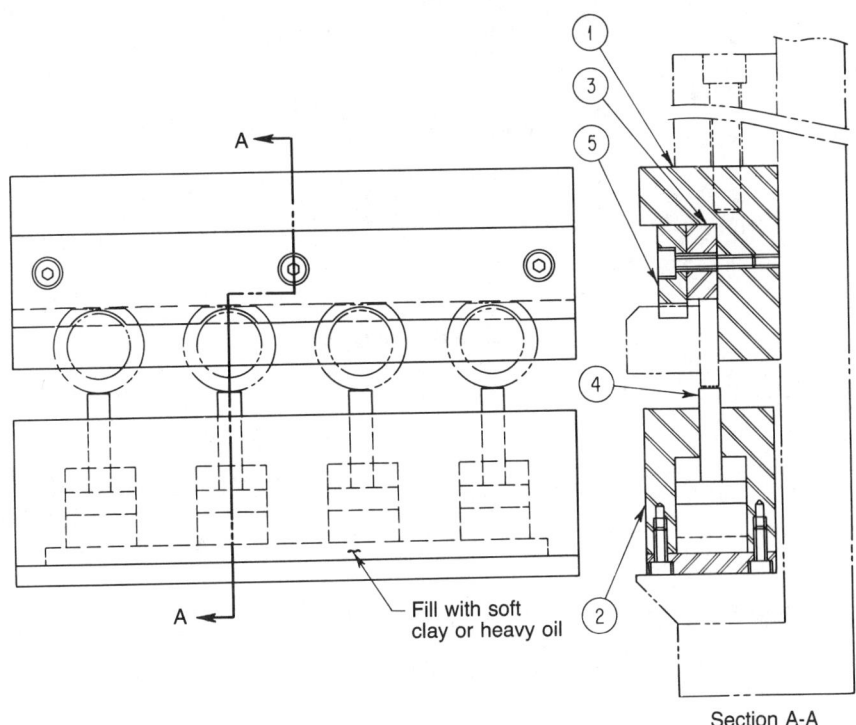

Fig. 10-28 Self-equalizing grinding fixture for multiple parts.

Section A-A

Fill with soft
clay or heavy oil

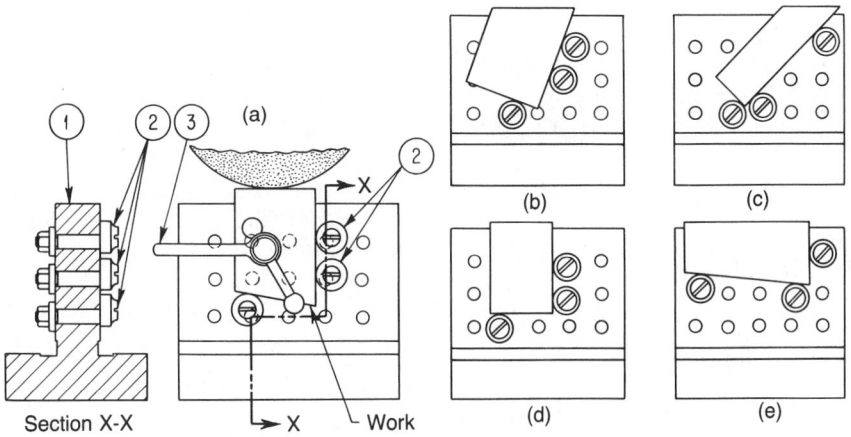

Section X-X

Work

Fig. 10-29 Universal grinding fixture for holding flat workpieces at various angles.[1]

The fixture shown in Fig. 10-33 is for grinding a steel try square.

The cast-iron body (1) of the fixture can be mounted on any surface grinder for grinding the outer long edge of the workpiece.

A pin (8) having a press fit in the spring-loaded plunger (2) holds the edge of the workpiece against the locating block (3) until it is clamped. The workpiece is placed against, and located vertically by, a pin (6) and is held down by hook clamps (4) which

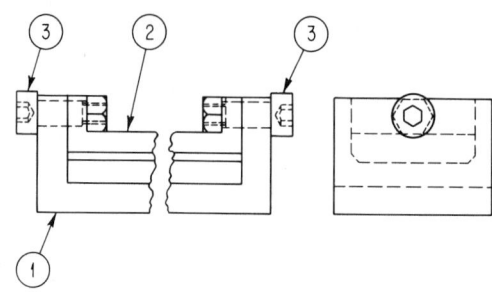

Fig. 10-30 Trunnion-type adjustable grinding fixture.[2]

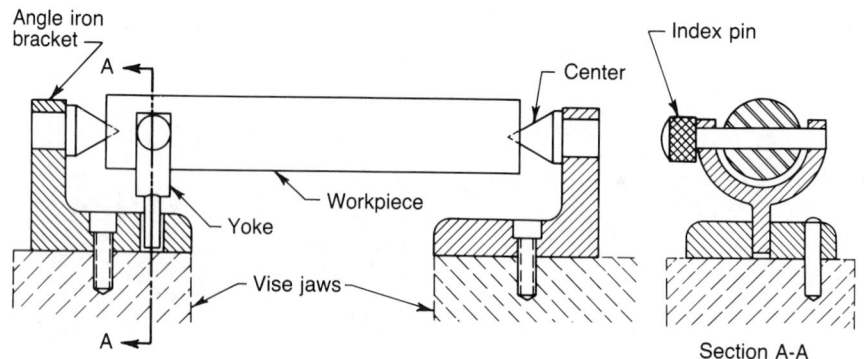

Fig. 10-31 Vise fixture for grinding flats on a shaft.[3]

are tightened by two wing nuts (5). The locating block is adjusted to a master square with an adjusting screw (7).

The simple angle-plate fixture of Fig. 10-34 was designed for grinding the outside surface of the small stamping shown in the same figure to 0.0522 ±0.001 in. from the center of the 0.156 in. diameter hole and square within 0.003 in. per inch to the inside surface of the part.

The body (1) of the fixture is a cast-iron angle plate to which is fastened a mounting block (7) for the toggle clamp (8). In another block (2) are mounted a locating pin (3), a rest pin (4), a finger jack (5), and its locking thumbscrew (6).

The workpiece is located against the rest pin and on the locating pin engaging the 0.156 in. diameter hole. The finger jack, moved up to support the part, is locked in place by the thumbscrew, which does not change squareness and dimensional relationships of the part. Production is approximately 65 parts per hour.

All sides of an octagonal cam are ground in the fixture shown in Fig. 10-35. The mandrel has splines that provide a sliding fit in the broached hole in the cam, which is held in place on the mandrel by a C-washer and nut. The mandrel is held in the spindle by a drawbolt (6). An index ring (1) is held in contact with the spindle by a setscrew (2). A spacer is fitted between the ring and the rear bearing. A locknut (4) holds the rear bearing in place. An indexing assembly, consisting of an index plunger (9), a plunger housing (8), a spring (10), and a dog-point setscrew (11) (to prevent plunger rotation), is mounted on the top of the fixture body.

Retraction of the plunger and turning of the handwheel (5) successively bring the notches of the index ring under the plunger. The plunger slides through a bushing (7),

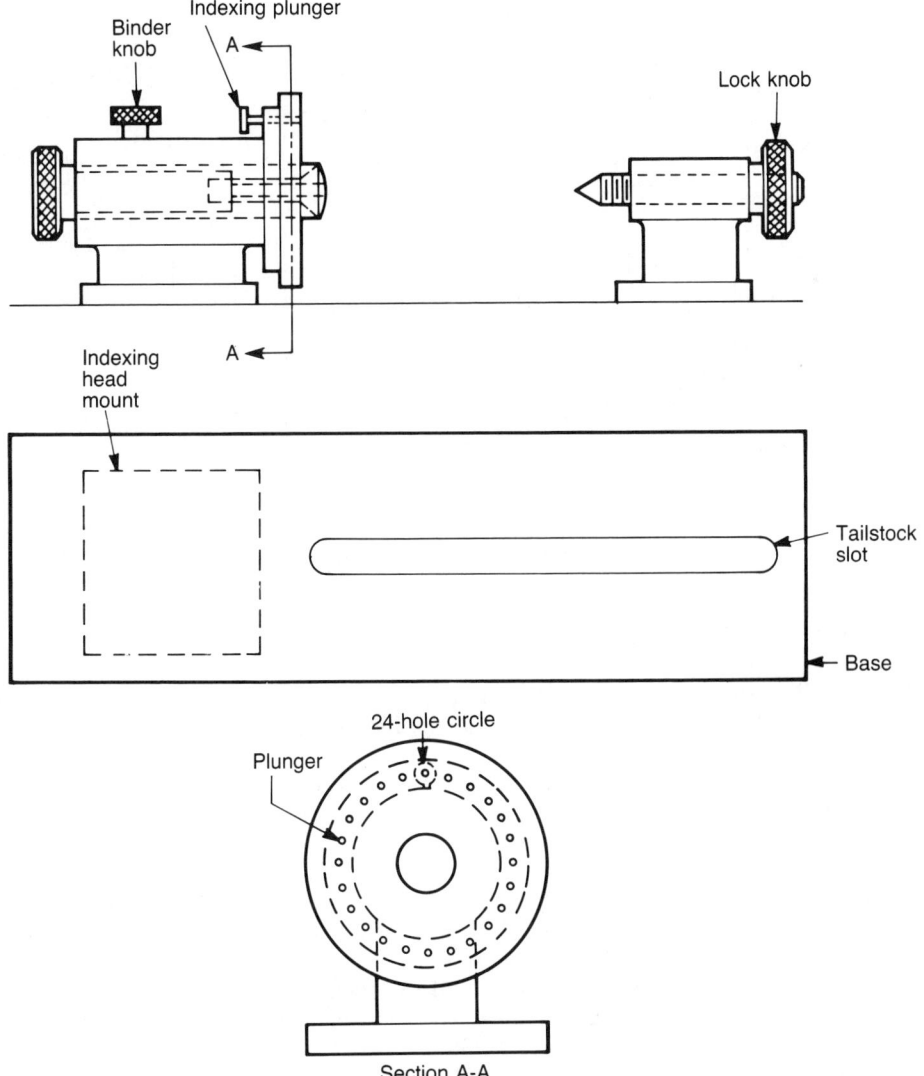

Fig. 10-32 Universal indexing fixture for grinding flats at 15° intervals around the periphery of a cylindrical workpiece.

engages the notches, and locks the part for grinding each of the eight flat surfaces. The fixture fits over the V-ways of grinding machine and is held in position by keys and T-bolts.

Twenty workpieces (small pump pistons) are vertically placed in the fixture of Fig. 10-36 with their spherical ends on locating pins (1) for grinding the other ends to establish piston lengths of 1.237 to 1.239 in. (31.42 to 31.47 mm). Rotation of the hand knob (2) clamps all of the pistons between the double V-block (4) and two clamping bars (3). Rubber inserts are incorporated in the bars to compensate for variations in diameters of the pistons. Four guide pins (5) set at an angle, as shown, direct a downward component of the clamping force to seat the spherical surfaces of the pistons on the locating pins. A dowel (9) driven through a hole in the head of the clamping stud (6) and into the rear clamping bar prevents the stud from rotating with the hand knob.

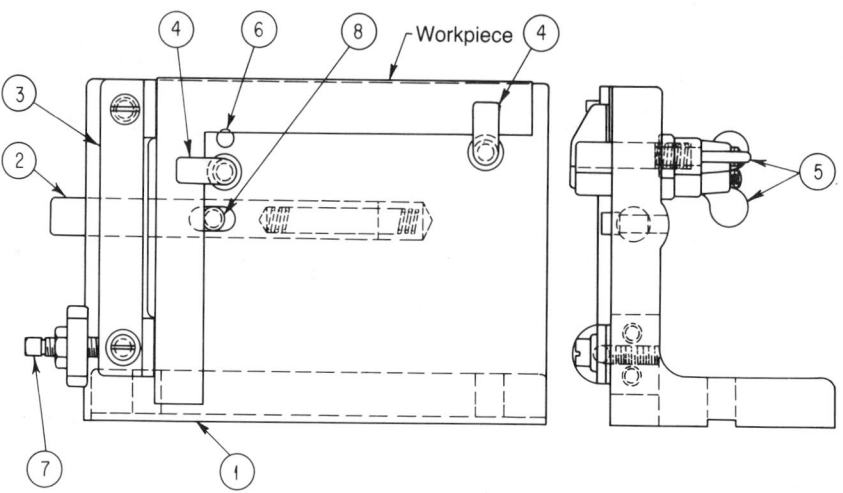

Fig. 10-33 Fixture for grinding a steel try square. (*Courtesy L. S. Starrett Co.*)

After the pistons have been lightly clamped, they are tapped with a rubber mallet to seat them firmly against the locating pins. Further turning of the hand knob sets up full clamping forces.

Each of the six workpieces held in the fixture of Fig. 10-37 is composed of thin, magnetically soft (Mumetal) laminations which have been stacked to form a small magnetic-core assembly.

The long inside edge of each stacked core rests against two 1/16 in. diameter locating pins (2) presenting surface *A* of the edges of the laminations to the grinding wheel. A knurled, tapered pusher pin (3), which is a slip fit in the fixture body (1), contacts the opposite edge of the core and holds the part snugly against the locating pins. Socket-head cap screws (5) and light steel clamps (4) hold the cores against the vertical surface of the fixture body.

The top surface of the body is ground to establish a distance of 0.060 $^{+0.000}_{-0.001}$ in. between it and the upper edges of the twelve locating pins for setup and for grinding the width of the laminations to 0.061 $^{+0.000}_{-0.001}$ in.

After surface *A* is ground, each core is removed and reversed in the fixture (with surface *B* up) for grinding surface *B*.

The fixture shown in Fig. 10-38 was designed to grind the 0.093 $^{+0.000}_{-0.003}$ in. dimension on the electrical core assembly shown in the same figure.

Each workpiece is located by a pin (3) engaging the 0.022 in. diameter hole. The workpiece is positioned by this pin and a dowel (4) which bears against the outside of the core. A socket-head screw (5) and a small strap clamp (2) hold the assembly against the vertical face of the fixture body (1). Since the fixture holds six workpieces, the distance between the six locating pins and top surface of the body is established at 0.090 $^{+0.0002}_{-0.0000}$ in. by grinding the top of the body and accurately fitting the pins for setup and true location of each workpiece.

A brass insert (6) between the body and the base (1) concentrates magnetic lines of force in the base (which rests upon a magnetic chuck).

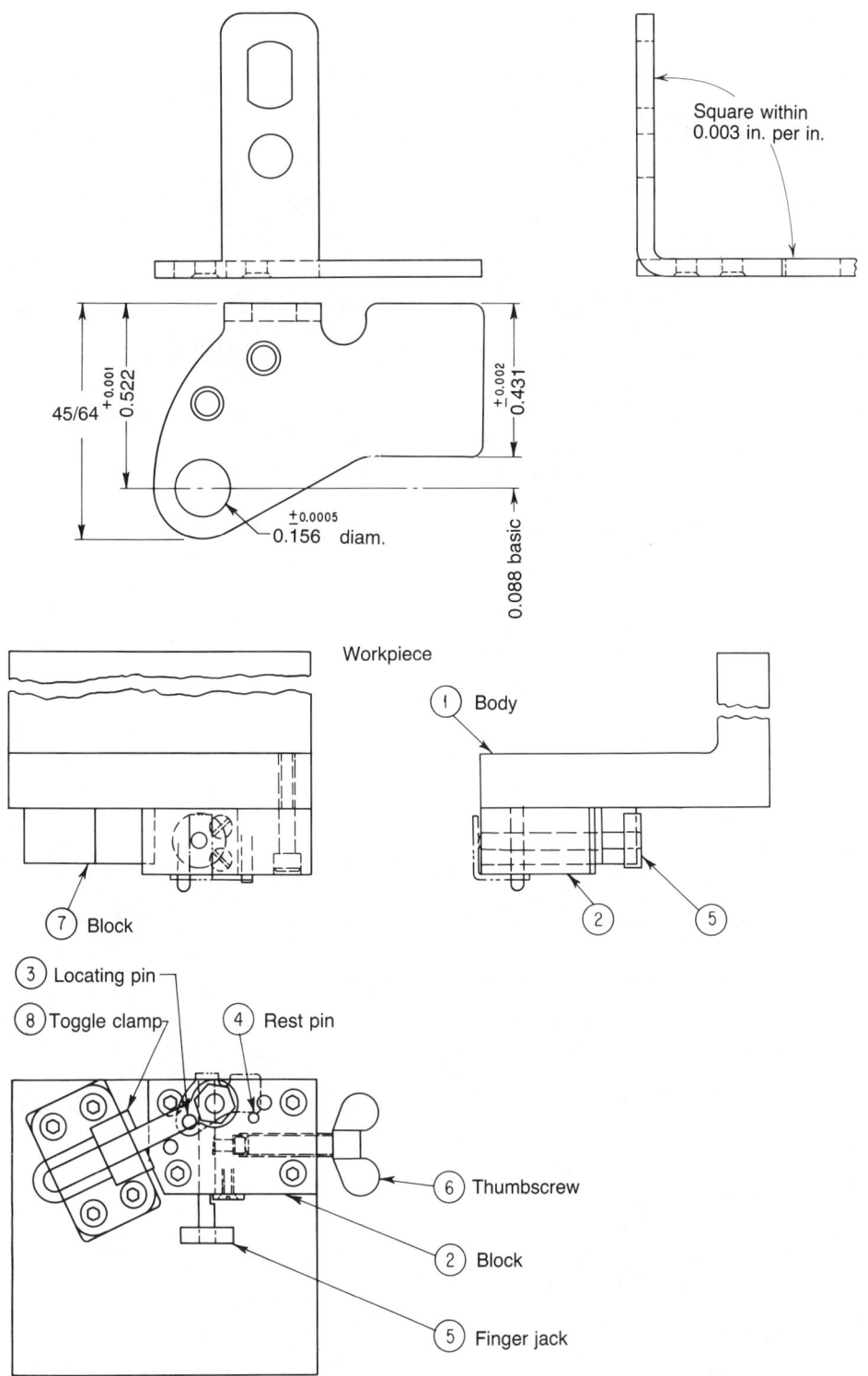

Square within
0.003 in. per in.

45/64

$0.522^{+0.001}_{-}$

$0.431^{+0.002}_{-}$

$0.156^{+0.0005}_{-}$ diam.

0.088 basic

Workpiece

① Body

⑦ Block

③ Locating pin

⑧ Toggle clamp

④ Rest pin

② Block

⑤ Finger jack

⑥ Thumbscrew

② Block

⑤ Finger jack

Fig. 10-34 Angle plate surface grinding fixture. (*Courtesy Unisys Corp.*)

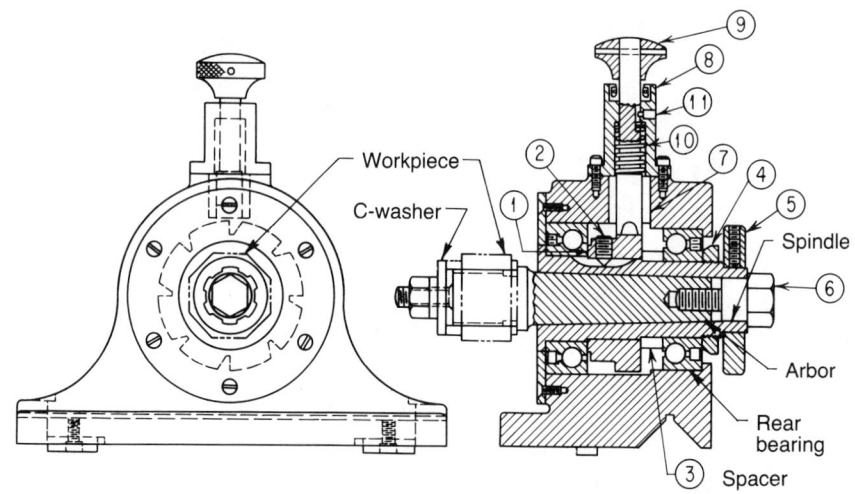

Fig. 10-35 Indexing fixture for an octagonal cam.[4]

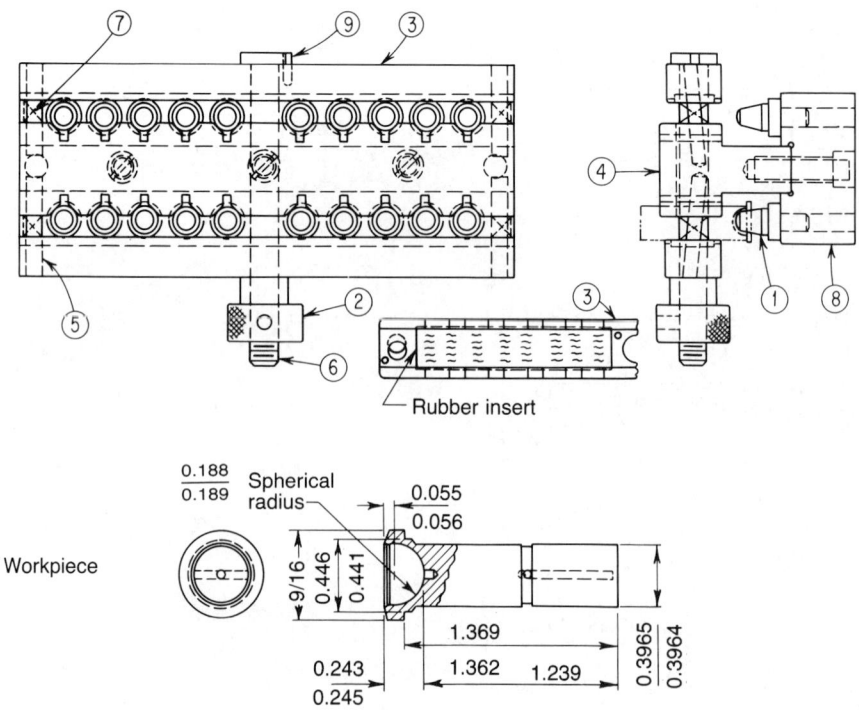

Fig. 10-36 Fixture for grinding small pistons—twenty at a time.[5]

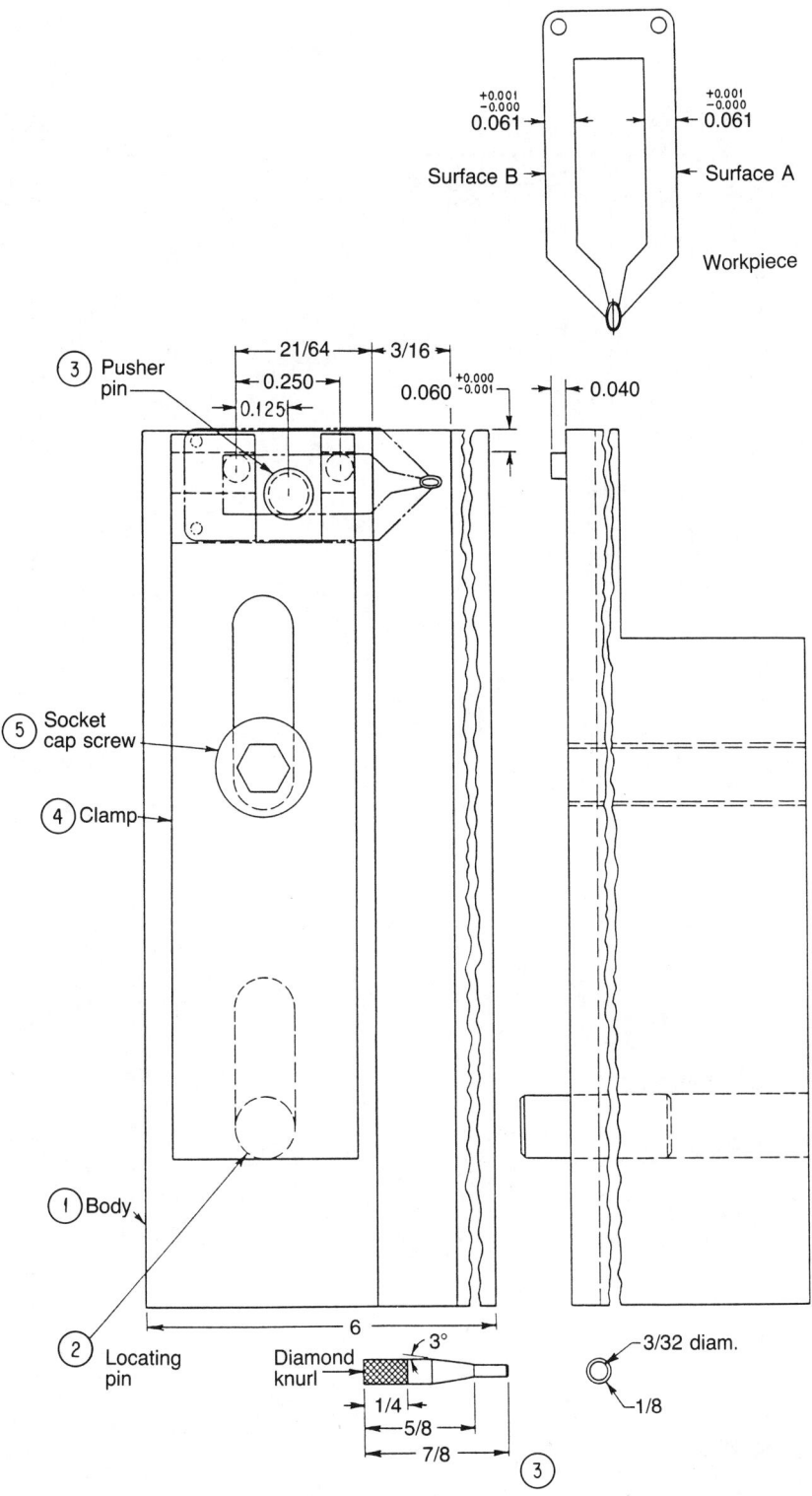

Fig. 10-37 Fixture for grinding small electromagnet cores—six at a time.

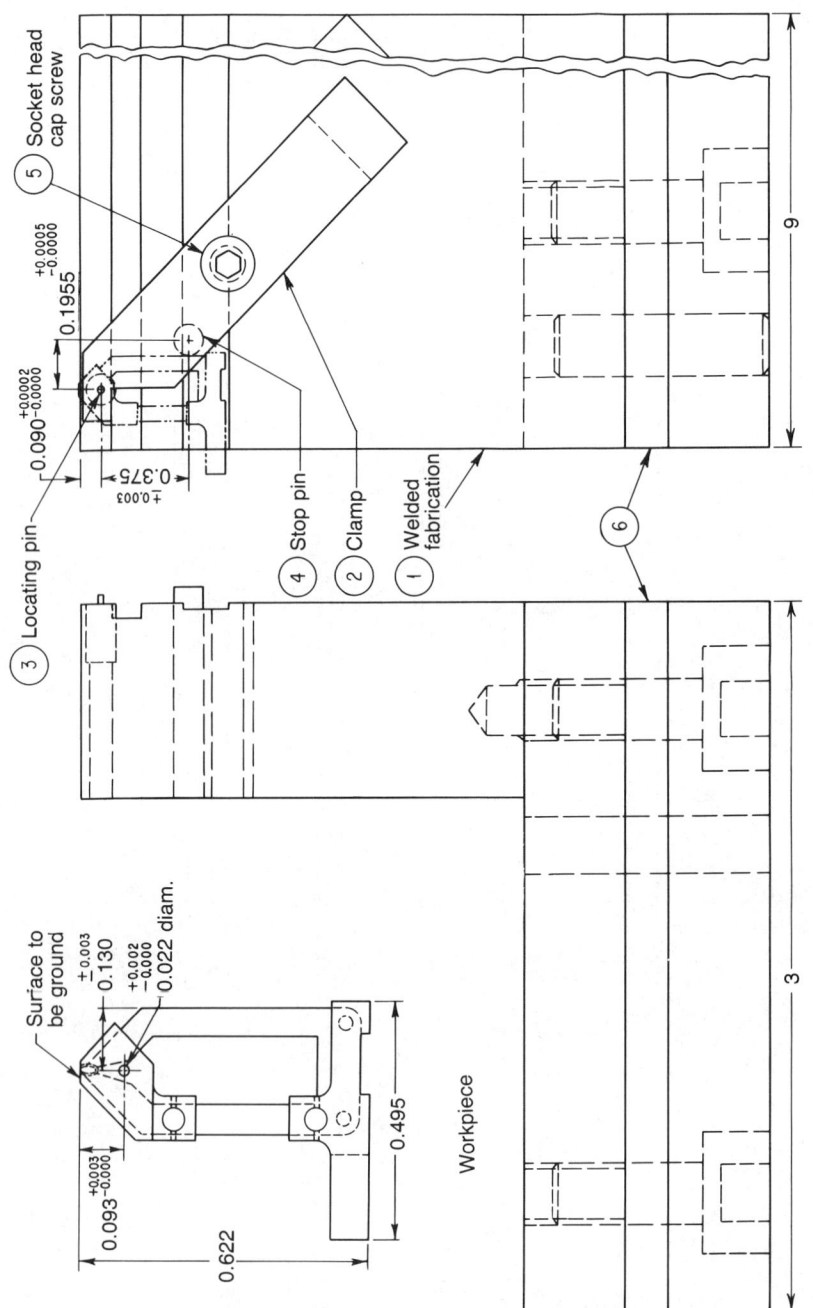

Fig. 10-38 Fixture for grinding core assemblies. (*Courtesy IBM*)

10-32

The tip of a firing-pin body is ground by a crush-formed grinding wheel in the fixture of Fig. 10-39. The crush-form roll holder is placed in the adapter (1) to crush-form the grinding wheel. The roll holder is removed and replaced by the workholding assembly. A shoulder on the workpiece is placed against a shoulder on the fixture and held in the groove by a hinged clamp.

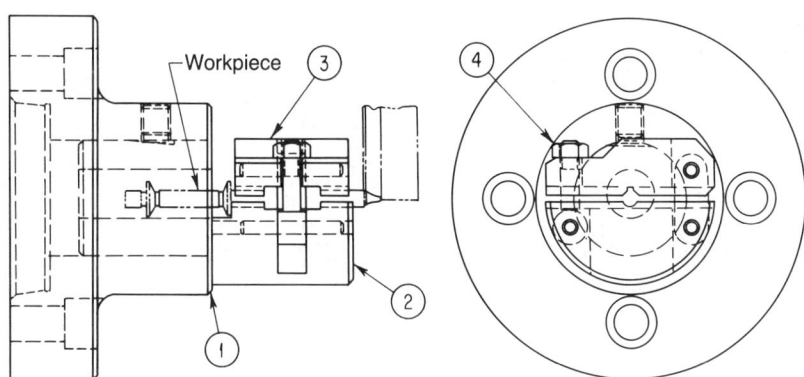

Fig. 10-39 Fixture for crush-form grinding. (*Courtesy U.S. Naval Ordnance Plant*)

The fixture consists of a body (2), a hinged clamp (3), and a clamp bolt (4).

The V-grooves in a roll-formed strip are ground in the fixture of Fig. 10-40 by a four-wheel form grinder.

A filler block, held by T-bolts to the base of the grinding machine, supports the fixture and the magnetic chuck and aligns the Vees in the sides of the strip with the wheels and crusher rolls.

The magnetic chuck is energized, and four strips are placed in the locating blocks (2) and magnetically held against the vertical faces of the blocks. Their V-grooves are located on removable pins (3) and their ends against four stop blocks (1). Four more parts are placed in the locating blocks with their ends butted against the ends of the parts in the fixture. All parts are then rapped with a mallet to force them to be correctly located and seated.

When the Vees on one side of the strips are ground, the magnetic-chuck circuit is opened for removal and cleaning of the strips and of the pins. The fixture is cleaned and another set of larger pins, which compensates for stock ground from the Vees, is inserted. The strips are reversed in the fixture for grinding the other Vees.

The fixture shown in Fig. 10-41 is a typical fixture for use with a double-disc grinder.

The fixture is a thin metal plate. It can be of cast iron or machine steel with a cutout (1) in which the workpiece is placed. The fixture and workpiece are fed manually or by power between the grinding areas of two double disks for the grinding of two parallel surfaces simultaneously. Other plates, identical except for cutout dimensions, accommodate workpieces of various sizes. Another fixture for double-disk grinders is the rotary carrier, which is a round plate with cutouts around its perimeter. It is mounted on the machine and rotated to successively position each cutout and part between the abrasive disks.

FIXTURES FOR CYLINDRICAL GRINDERS

The most commonly used workholding devices for general-purpose cylindrical grinding are centers, chucks, mandrels, collets, and faceplates.[7]

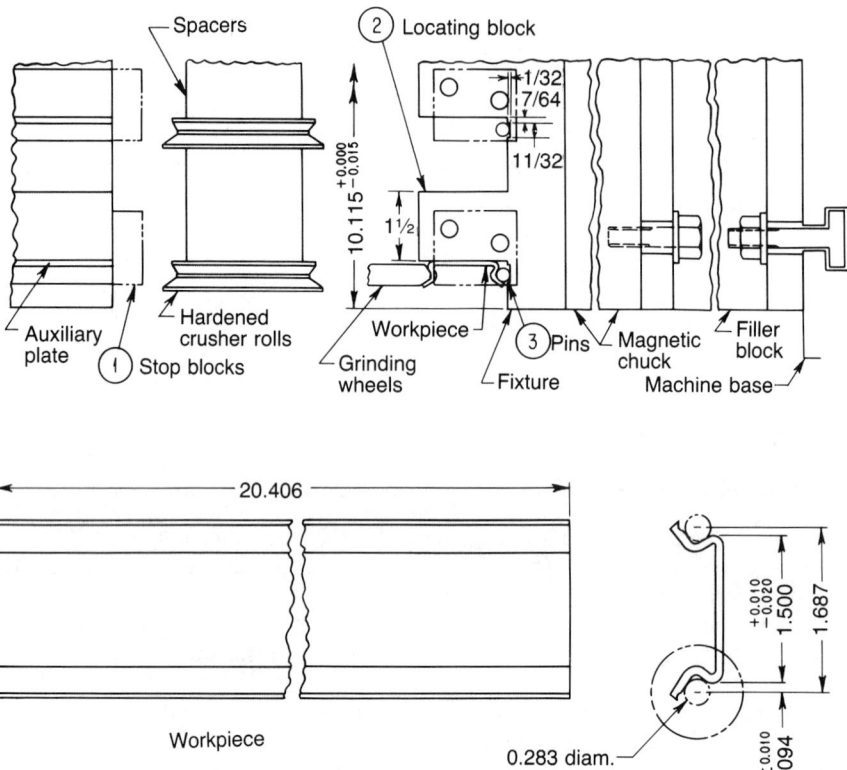

Fig. 10-40 Magnetic chuck and fixture for multiple-form grinding. (*Courtesy IBM*)

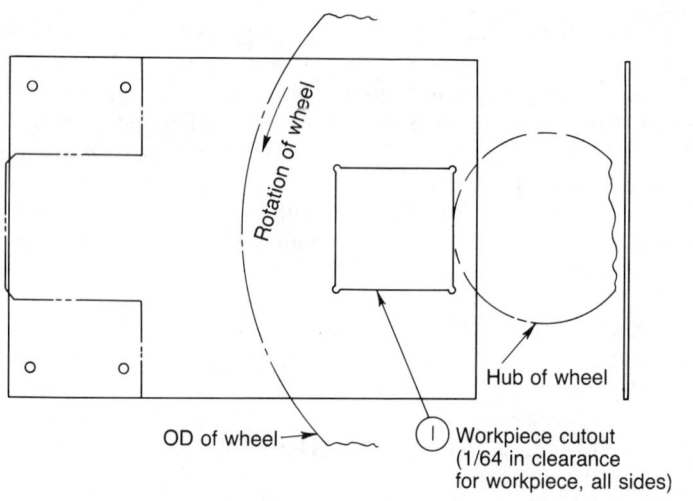

Fig. 10-41 Fixture for a double disc grinder. (*Courtesy IBM*)

Cylindrical grinding fixtures are similar in design to lathe turning fixtures (see Chapter 3, Fixtures for Turning and Boring). There are, however, several unique features of grinding that must be considered when designing a cylindrical grinding fixture. These considerations include the following:

1. Since grinding is essentially a finishing operation when dimensions are held to very close tolerances, accuracy of the fixture is a prime concern.
2. In most cases only a relatively small amount of material is removed; consequently, grinding fixtures do not require the bulk characteristics of machining fixtures.
3. Locating parts properly is very important. However, since most parts to be ground have already been machined, a relatively accurate surface should be available to hold and locate the part.
4. Thin workpieces cannot be permitted to deflect during grinding. If necessary, auxiliary work supports (steady rests, etc.) must sometimes be used in addition to the fixture to prevent distortion.
5. Heat build-up should be controlled with a proper application of fluid.
6. Grinding fluid nozzles should be selected to deliver a large volume of fluid with minimum pressure. The contact line between wheel and work must be well flooded with fluid.
7. Fixtures must be designed to permit easy removal of fluid and sludge. All pockets in which these materials can accumulate must be eliminated or the balance of the fixture could easily be affected.
8. Fluid nozzles should never inhibit the movement or operation of the fixture.
9. Wheel dressing and trueing should be performed without removing the fixture or without seriously reducing the grinding time.
10. Fixtures that are intended to rotate must be balanced. If the fixture cannot be balanced internally, an auxiliary counterweight must be selected and positioned to ensure dynamic balance.

Fixtures used for cylindrical grinding are normally classified by the grinding process they perform or by the type of grinding machine with which they are used. In addition, fixtures may also be classified by their basic construction characteristics. For the purpose of this discussion, the latter method of identification is used to distinguish these fixtures.

CENTERS

The most common type of workholding device used on cylindrical grinding machines is the center. In practice, the work is actually mounted between centers on the center points. Centers generally have a 60° point on the workholding end and a taper on the other end which goes into the footstock or headstock. Points on these centers may be either high-speed steel or tungsten carbide. High-speed steel or carbide grinding centers should have some type of lubrication between the center and the workpiece. In some cases, special centers are used in the headstock for driving the workpiece as well as for holding it in position. This can be done only when a live-spindle headstock has been supplied with the machine. This technique eliminates the need for driving dogs or pins.

On all center-type grinding machines, the workpiece and wheel have a negative contact between one another. Viewing the workpiece and grinding wheel from the headstock end of the machine, both the workpiece and wheel would be revolving in a clockwise direction. At the point of contact between the workpiece and wheel, the workpiece would be traveling in one direction and the grinding wheel in the opposite direction. These directions of rotation are maintained to provide solid contact between the dog clamped on the workpiece and the driving pin which sticks out of the headstock. If the headstock rotates in the opposite direction, it would act as a break to stop the workpiece from rotating. These directions of rotation are useful when grinding is done between centers, since the work is simply supported by the centers (without being actually clamped in place). They are all that gives the work positive drive with the headstock.

CHUCKS, COLLETS AND FACEPLATES

Chucks, collets, and faceplates are workholding devices which are sometimes used for fixturing parts that must be cylindrically ground. In most cases the fixtures designed to be used in these workholders are very similar to turning fixtures (see Chapter 9, "Fixtures for Turning and Boring). The principle difference between these fixtures and turning fixtures is their closer attention to tolerance and balance.

Before chucks can be used in grinding, a live-spindle headstock (workhead) is needed. This means that chucks can be used only on universal center-type grinders or plain grinders with live-spindle headstocks. A four-jaw independent chuck is useful when odd-shaped work must be ground and there are no center holes. When this type of chuck is used, the work must be indicated and each jaw adjusted separately so that the surface to be ground rotates concentrically with the axis of rotation of the headstock spindle. When using a chuck to grind work, the runout in the headstock spindle must also be taken into consideration. As a matter of fact, anytime a live spindle is used, the runout in the headstock spindle determines the roundness of the workpiece.

Illustrated in Fig. 10-42 is an example of a fixture designed to be used in either a four-jaw chuck or collet. With this fixture, the part is designed to be mounted between the tailstock center and the center in the fixture. The three set screws are then tightened to provide a positive drive. Fixtures like this are frequently used to hold parts that have only one center hole.

Another fixture of similar design used to hold a punch is shown in Fig. 10-43. Here the part is held on the diameter below the head. This diameter is the critical size. The diameter of the head is relatively unimportant and has a tolerance of ±0.010 in. When mounting the part, the upper cap is removed and the punch inserted. The cap is then reinstalled and tightened. The positive drive is accomplished by inserting the punch locator in the fixture.

MANDRELS

Mandrels are commonly used for locating and driving workpieces in grinding operations. In addition to providing excellent fixturing, mandrels also provide an accurate method to ensure concentricity between the OD and ID of the workpiece. The principle variations of mandrels commonly used for fixturing are: solid mandrels, expansion mandrels, nut mandrels, and special-purpose mandrels.

Solid Mandrels. Solid mandrels are generally used for close tolerance concentric grinding. These mandrels are normally made of tool steel and are hardened and ground with lapped center holes. The gripping area of these mandrels generally has a taper ground to match the tolerance of the part. In cases in which the OD must be concentric to the ID and square to the sides, a fixture, such as that shown in Fig. 10-44, can be used. Here the mandrel is used to mount and drive the part. The sliding sleeve is used to ensure the squareness of the part on the mandrel.

Expansion Mandrels. Expansion mandrels are normally used for parts that have a larger tolerance on the ID of the workpiece or for parts that do not have an extremely close concentricity tolerance. Expansion mandrels are capable of tolerances in the range of 0.0003-0.001 in. FIM. As shown in Fig. 10-45, expansion mandrels are rather simple in design. In Fig. 10-45, the fixture body is made of tool steel and is hardened and ground with lapped center holes. In use, the part is mounted and the set screw is

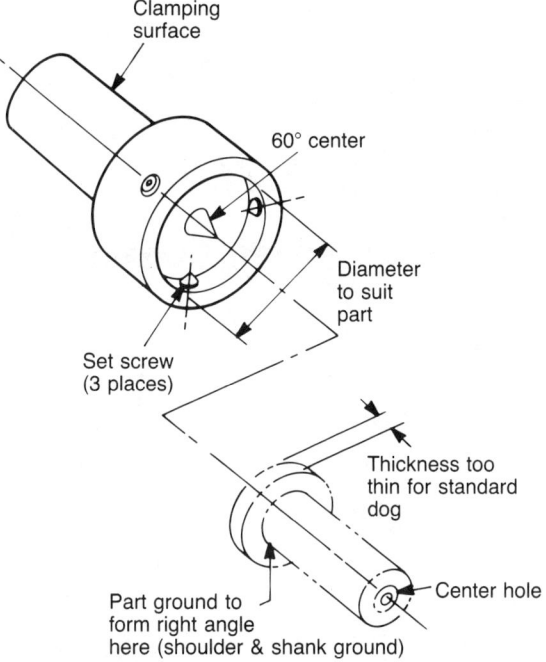

Clamping
surface

60° center

Diameter
to suit
part

Set screw
(3 places)

Thickness too
thin for standard
dog

Part ground to
form right angle
here (shoulder & shank ground)

Center hole

Fig. 10-42 Grinding fixture for parts to be mounted between the workhead center and the center in the fixture.

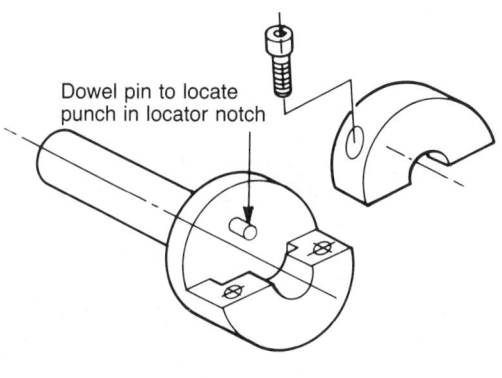

Dowel pin to locate
punch in locator notch

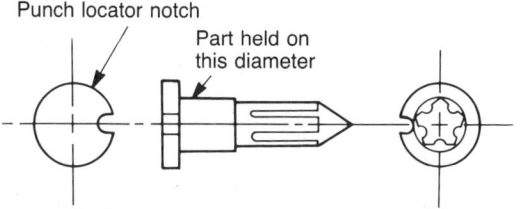

Punch locator notch

Part held on
this diameter

Fig. 10-43 Grinding fixtures—cap is removed, the part is installed, and the cap is replaced and tightened to provide location and to drive the workpiece.

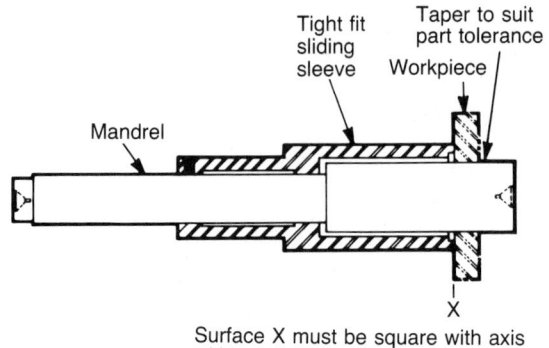

Surface X must be square with axis
within 0.0002 in. FIM

Fig. 10-44 Solid mandrel.

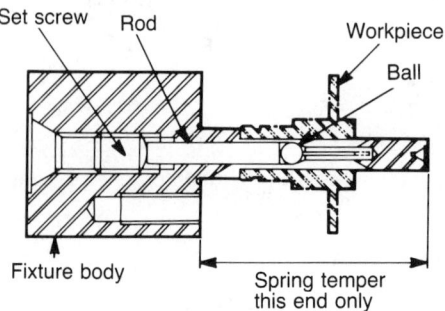

Fig. 10-45 Expanding mandrel.

tightened against the rod which exerts pressure against the ball, expanding the mandrel.

Another variation of this principle is shown in Fig. 10-46. The mandrel in Fig. 10-46 is activated by a set screw which applies pressure against wedge rods to expand the mandrel. This type of expanding mandrel is normally mounted on a faceplate or in a chuck. In this application the fixture is not removed from the machine to change parts.

Another form of expansion mandrel is shown in Fig. 10-47. This type of expansion mandrel is designed to be used in either a chuck or a collet. To use this type of expansion mandrel, the mandrel OD is first machined to a size slightly larger than the part. The mandrel is mounted in the grinder and expanded. Then the mandrel OD is ground to approximately 0.001 in. greater than the workpiece ID. The expansion screw is loosened, and the part is mounted. The screw is then tightened to the proper tension. The principle advantage to using this type of expansion mandrel is cost. These mandrels are made to be thrown away after a single job or are machined to fit a workpiece with a smaller ID.

Nut Mandrels. Nut mandrels are similar in design to solid mandrels, the principle difference being the method used to secure the part. Nut mandrels use pressure from either a screw or nut rather than wedge action of a taper, to secure the part to the mandrel. As shown in Fig. 10-48, the basic nut mandrel holds a workpiece by simply applying force to one end of the part and binding it against the opposite side of the mandrel.

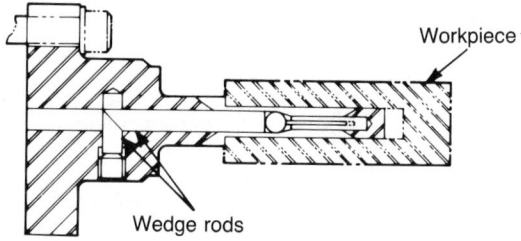

Fig. 10-46 Faceplate expansion mandrel.

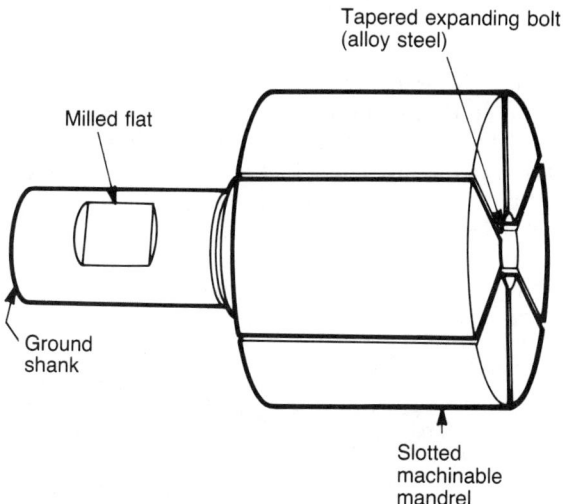

Fig. 10-47 Expansion mandrel for use in either a chuck or collet.

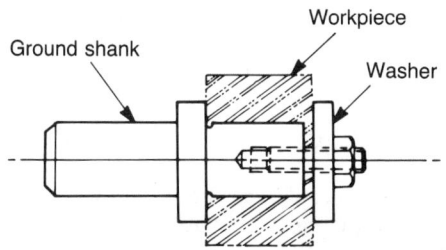

Fig. 10-48 Nut mandrel.

A variation of this principle is shown in Fig. 10-49. Here the part is thin walled and could bend or distort from end pressure. In this case a Neoprene bushing is used to hold the part by being compressed by a socket-head cap screw. The important points to remember here are that the bearing surface must be long enough to ensure accurate seating and the washer must be smaller than the ID of the part.

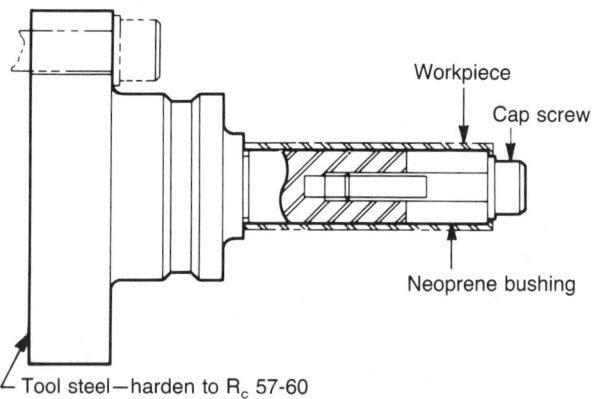

Fig. 10-49 Nut mandrel for thin-walled workpieces.

Another form of nut mandrel is shown in Fig. 10-50. Here the workpiece OD must be held concentric to the ID to within 0.00025 in. FIM. The surface Y is previously ground square to the bore and is used to establish the required squareness. The ground and lapped center holes in the mandrel ensure the concentricity of the mandrel. The sleeve is pressed on the mandrel and has three equally spaced pins that maintain the squareness of the part by contacting surface Y. The spring loaded centralizer establishes the position of the center hole and is held in place by the cover. The clamping pressure is applied by a spherically seated hand knob which forces the washer against the part.

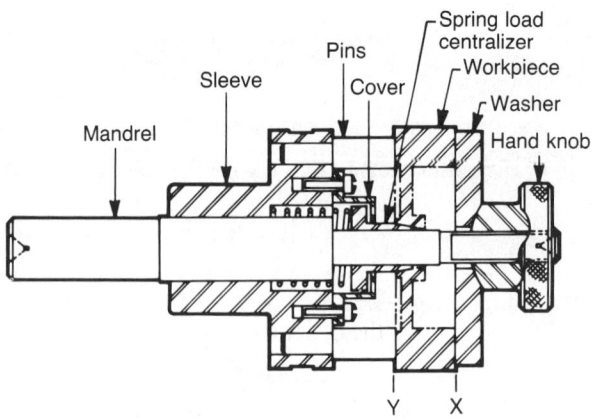

Fig. 10-50 Nut mandrel for parts requiring close concentricity between OD and ID.

Special Mandrels. Special mandrels are those that are not easily classified by any standard term. These mandrels include those designed to hold parts with odd, or irregular, internal details or those that combine features of the standard form of mandrels. The mandrel shown in Fig. 10-51 is specially designed to hold the part shown. With this mandrel, the bearing surface has a pentagonal form to match the internal detail of the die insert. These inserts must be ground concentric to the pentagon to within 0.0005 in. FIM. To accomplish this, the mandrel is made to a size that permits a slight interference-fit in the broached inserts. The washer and the socket-head cap screw are included to prevent lateral movement of the workpiece during grinding. The concentricity of the mandrel is ensured by ground and lapped center holes in the hardened-tool-steel mandrel body.

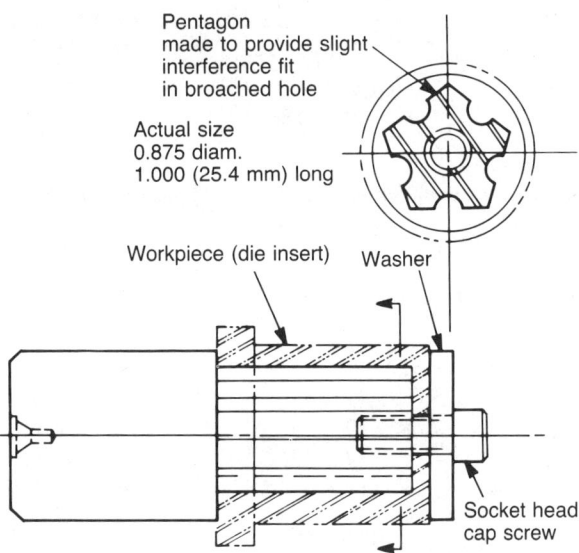

Fig. 10-51 Special mandrel for grinding a die insert.

Another type of special mandrel is shown in Fig. 10-52. This mandrel is used for mounting threaded parts that must be ground concentric to the threaded ID. The mandrel shown is made of hardened and ground tool steel with ground and lapped center holes. The area of the mandrel where the part is mounted is cut to the diameter and pitch of the required thread, and the second thread is cut larger and left hand. This second thread is used to lock the part on the mandrel. When the mounting threads of the part are cut, great care must be used to ensure that the pitch diameter is correct. When parts like this must be concentric to a thread, both the part and mandrel pitch diameters must be closely controlled.

The fixture of Fig. 10-53, a spring collet, holds the workpiece shown in the same figure during the grinding of its tapered OD. A spring chuck is threaded to fit the headstock of a Norton cylindrical grinder, and its other end is a slip fit in the center hole of the slotted and spring-tempered collet. A drawbar inserted through the grinder headstock and chuck is fastened to the collet with a flat-head cap screw. A compression spring between the headstock and the special hexagon head screw on the drawbar holds the collet in its expanded (workholding) position. The drawbar is mounted on the grinder headstock. Movement of the draw barhandle releases the workpiece from the collet, which fits the ID on the workpiece.

FIXTURES FOR INTERNAL GRINDING

The split collet fixture in Fig. 10-54 was designed to grind a counterbore in a gear. The adapter plate (3) of the fixture of fits the spindle of a Bryant internal grinder for

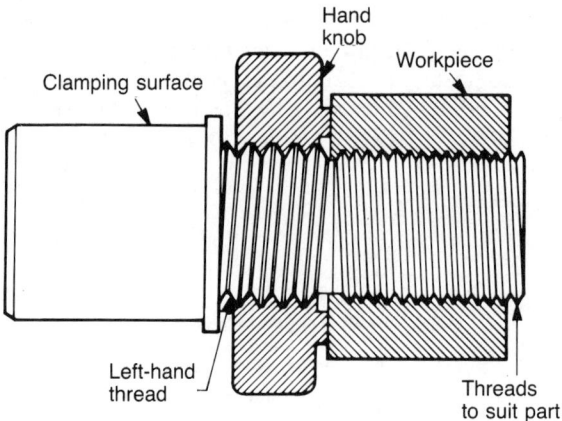

Fig. 10-52 Special mandrel for mounting threaded workpieces that must be ground concentric to the threaded ID.

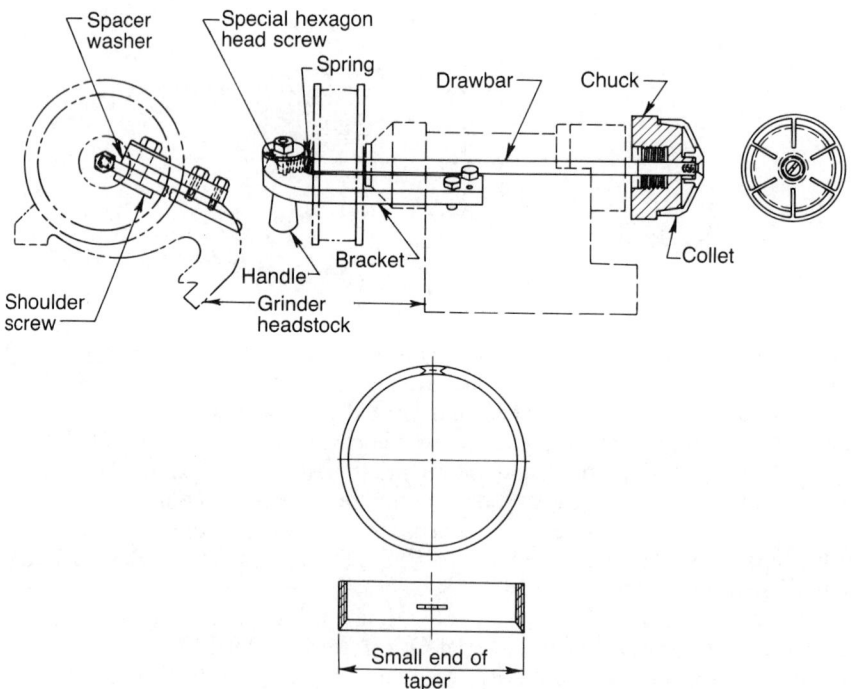

Fig. 10-53 Spring chuck for cylindrical grinding a plastic bushing.[8]

grinding a counterbore in a gear. A hardened and spring-tempered split collet (1) fits on a flanged shaft (2) which is bolted to the adapter plate.

The workpiece, a gear, squares up against the ground face of a stop collar (4) when the gear is clamped. An expansion plug (5) is threaded on a pull bar (6) which exerts a 1,200 lb (5.3 KN) force on the plug. The expansion plug is adjusted so that it will not interfere with the wheel grinding the counterbore (according to reference dimension, 0.688 to 0.692 in.). A collet OD of 1.250 to 1.251 in., to fit the ID of the gear without distorting it, is also secured by this adjustment.

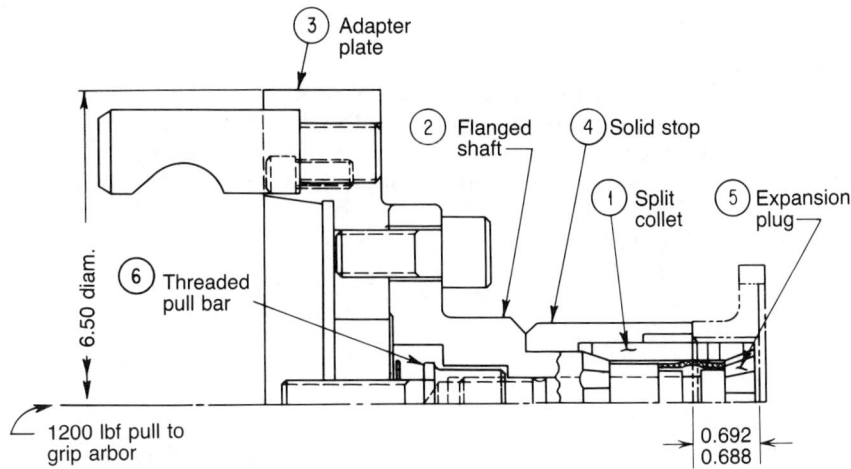

Fig. 10-54 Split collet to grind a counterbore. (*Courtesy N. A. Woodworth Co.*)

In the fixture of Fig. 10-55, a chamfer is ground in the hub of a casting. After one chamfer is ground, the part is reversed in the fixture for the grinding of a chamfer in the opposite end of the bore. Locating from the pitch diameter of the splined hub allows the chamfers to be ground concentric with that diameter.

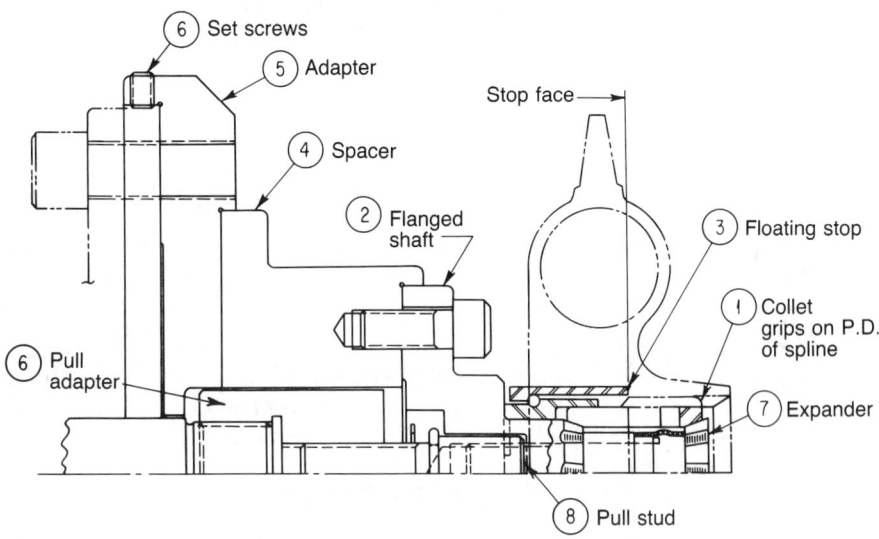

Fig. 10-55 Collet for grinding chamfers concentric with pitch diameter of a splined hub. (*Courtesy N. A. Woodworth Co.*)

The adapter (5) of the fixture is mounted on a Heald internal grinder and is adjusted by setscrews (6) when the entire fixture is mounted on the grinder.

A flanged shaft (2) is bolted to a spacer (4) which in turn is mounted on the adapter. A spring-tempered collet (1) fits the internal splines in the hub of the workpiece. The collet and a floating stop (3) are mounted on the shaft.

A collet expander (7) is fastened to a pull stud (8). The stud is connected to the drawbar of the grinder by a pull adapter (9). With the pull stud in the forward position, the expander is adjusted until the OD of the collet is 1.915 in. (for adequate clamping of the part's hub without distorting it).

The cylindrical aluminum part (1) shown in the fixture of Fig. 10-56 is preloaded in a V-bottom carrier against a stop plate (2) for grinding the ID. After the bore on one end of the part is ground, the carrier is unclamped and reversed for grinding the bore on the opposite end. Spare carriers are preloaded for insertion in the fixture to replace carriers with finished parts. The carrier is ground to a close slip fit for the OD of the part, which is held in the carrier by a screw (3).

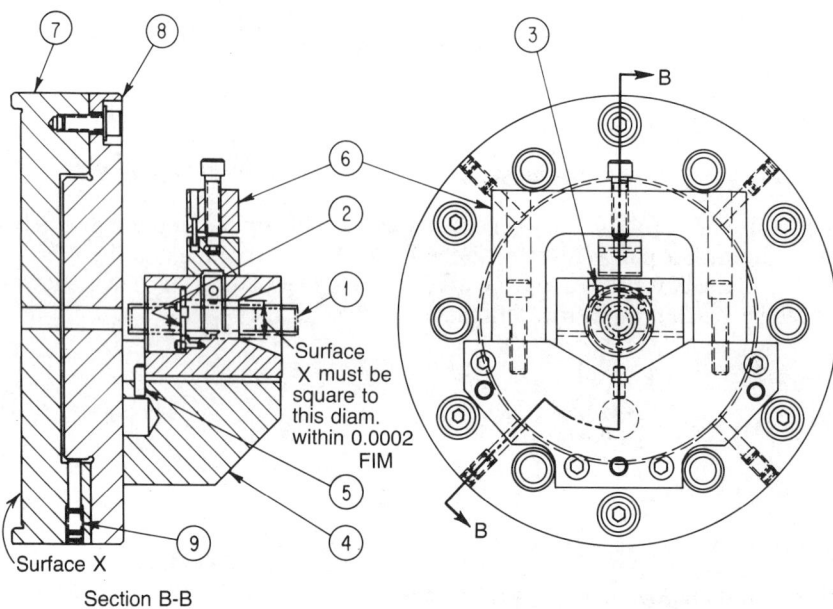

Fig. 10-56 Faceplate fixture for grinding two opposite bores concentrically. (*Courtesy Thompson Products, Inc.*)

The carrier is placed in the V-ways of a block (4) against a stop pin (5) and is clamped against the V-ways with a yoke-clamp assembly (6). The faceplate assembly (7), the block, and a subplate (8) are mounted on a Heald grinder. The entire fixture is adjusted to be perfectly concentric with the spindle center line by four setscrews (9). Such a fixture should always be balanced with the part in place.

FIXTURES FOR TOOL AND CUTTER GRINDING

Universal type fixtures are widely used for tool and cutter grinding. Some of these are shown in Fig. 10-57. They include the following:

1. Spade drill sharpener, *a*.
2. End mill fixture for grinding primary and secondary relief on the end teeth, *b*.
3. Flute grinding fixture, *c*.
4. Flip type tool bit fixture for sharpening turning tool bits, *d*.
5. Side milling cutter grinding fixture, *e*.
6. Woodruff cutter grinding fixture, *f*.

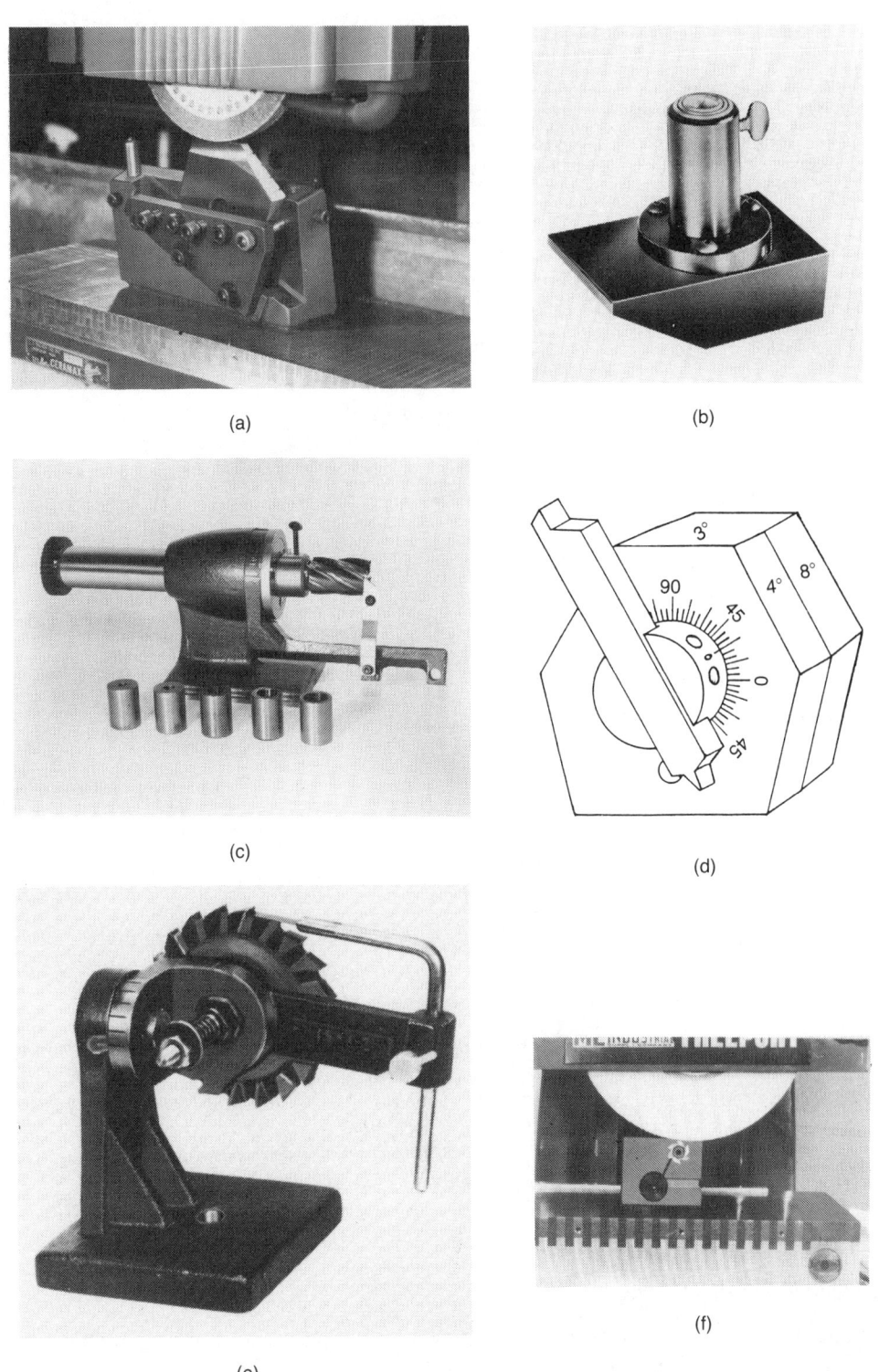

(a)

(b)

(c)

(d)

(e)

(f)

Fig. 10-57 Universal fixtures for tool and cutter grinding. (*Courtesy Ralmike's Tool-A-Rama*)

Special fixtures for tool and cutter grinding are shown in Figs. 10-58 thru 10-62.

The fixture of Fig. 10-58 consists three cold-rolled-steel plates welded together and then ground to size. The spacing of the tapped holes for the clamp screws permits various sizes of shear blades and similar workpieces to be ground.

Six single-point tools are clamped in the body (1) of fixture of Fig. 10-59 by socket-head screws (2). A hydraulic surface grinder sharpens the cutting angles on from 28 to 33 tools per hour.

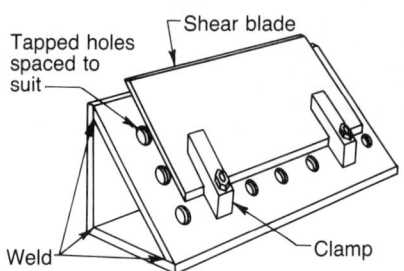

Fig. 10-58 Fixture for grinding shear blade edges. (*Tool & Manufacturing Engineer*)

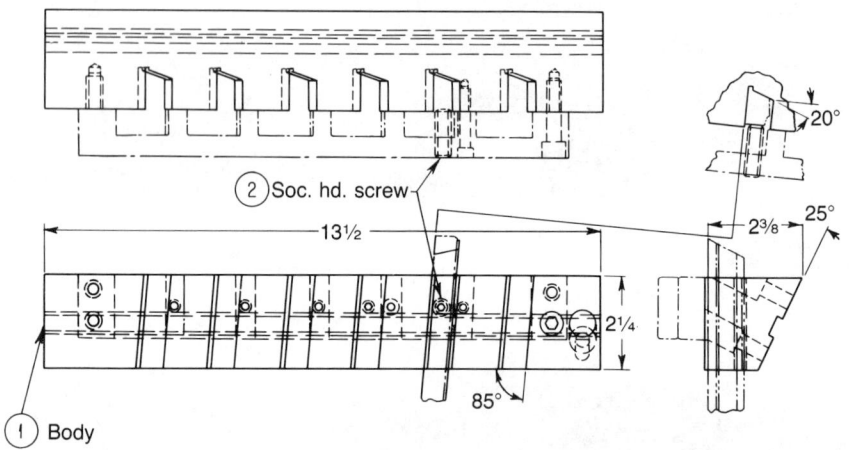

Fig. 10-59 Fixture for grinding single point tools. (*Tool & Manufacturing Engineer*)

The swinging fixture of Fig. 10-60 consists of two center heads which are adjustable along slots in the base for holding mandrels of different lengths between the centers. A slot across the back of each head at an angle of 45° to the horizontal contains an adjustable slide which is supported by the table center of the grinding machine.

The workpiece (a thin cutter or saw) and a hardened index wheel are clamped on a mandrel which is mounted between the fixture centers.

An adjustable mount holds a two-fingered, spring-steel indexing catch which allows the grinding of a cutter having twice as many teeth as the index wheel.

The stop plate can be adjusted to allow the fixture to swing about the table centers and to bring the workpiece only to full cutter depth against the wheel.

The fixture of Fig. 10-61 for grinding lathe and grinder centers has front and rear supports which slide between rails to accommodate tapered centers of different lengths. A hardened and ground tail center supports the small end of the center. Setscrews in a gripping ring attached to a retainer plate securely lock the small end of the workpiece against the tail center.

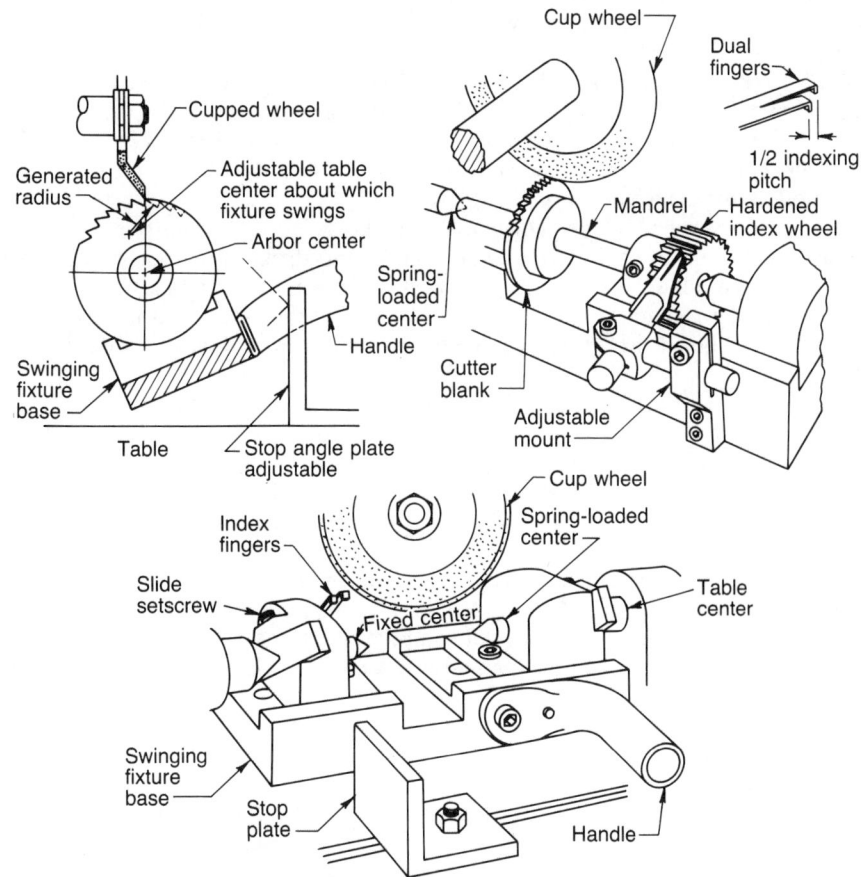

Fig. 10-60 Fixture for grinding cutters and saws.[9]

Labels for Fig. 10-60:
- Cupped wheel
- Generated radius
- Adjustable table center about which fixture swings
- Arbor center
- Swinging fixture base
- Handle
- Table
- Stop angle plate adjustable
- Cup wheel
- Dual fingers
- 1/2 indexing pitch
- Mandrel
- Hardened index wheel
- Spring-loaded center
- Cutter blank
- Adjustable mount
- Cup wheel
- Index fingers
- Spring-loaded center
- Slide setscrew
- Fixed center
- Table center
- Swinging fixture base
- Stop plate
- Handle

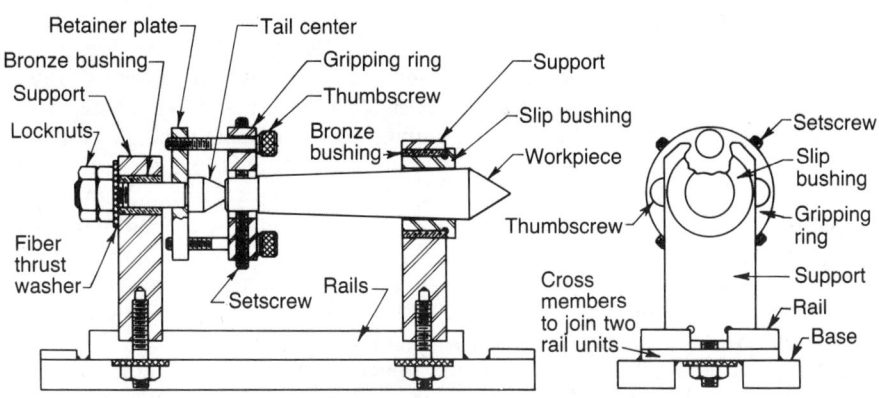

Fig. 10-61 Lathe center grinding fixture.

Labels for Fig. 10-61:
- Retainer plate
- Tail center
- Bronze bushing
- Gripping ring
- Support
- Support
- Thumbscrew
- Slip bushing
- Locknuts
- Bronze bushing
- Setscrew
- Workpiece
- Slip bushing
- Fiber thrust washer
- Thumbscrew
- Gripping ring
- Setscrew
- Rails
- Cross members to join two rail units
- Support
- Rail
- Base

The large end of a workpiece is adequately supported (for the light grinding pressures involved) by the front edge of the ID of the slip bushing. When changing from one size taper to another, the bushing is interchanged for one of the correct diameter. Rotation of the workpiece is manual.

The fixture may be used on any cutter-grinding machine without the use of a set of accurate tapered adapter sleeves.

The workpiece of Fig. 10-62, a swaging die, is placed on two rest plates and clamped against two relieved locating blocks, which are fastened to a cradle of the fixture.

The turning of the handle positions the cradle, through rotation of the worm gear (2) and wheel (1), to align the outside edge of the conical surface of the die cavity with the direction of grinding-wheel travel.

As the grinding-machine table moves back and forth, a cam-operated air valve, tripped at the end of each stroke, synchronizes the stroke of the air cylinder with the reversal of the table. The cylinder piston, through a ratchet and pawl and worm-gear reduction, intermittently revolves the crank pin and the cradle. During each stroke of the machine table, a narrow band along the conical surface of the die cavity is presented to the edge of the wheel.

After each 180° rotation of the crank pin, the pawls are repositioned to produce intermittent rotation in the opposite direction, and the grinding wheel is lowered to remove more die material.

CONTROL GAGING FOR GRINDING OPERATIONS[10]

Machine control gaging can be used to automate and simplify the operation of almost any grinding process. These gaging systems can vary from complex microprocessor-based systems, which can be programmed to control the execution of an exact taper grind, to a simple comparator stand checking parts after they have been produced.

The greatest returns on a gaging investment are seen on machines that are designed for rapid and continuous production. Among these are the centerless, internal, single-disc, double-disc, and center-type grinders. The end results of fitting one of these machines with the proper control gaging system include reduction of scrap, reduction of cost, improved quality, increased abrasive life, and dramatic increases in overall production.

When more "intelligence" is built into the basic grinding machine, the machine operator is able to make more efficient use of his time. Operator skill and attention requirements are reduced. Most effective gaging systems have the ability to control the entire grinding process. In the bearing industry, in which the use of automatic gaging is quite prevalent, it is common to see one person operating as many as four machines. These machines incorporate control gaging to monitor part size, position grinding wheels when size corrections are necessary, dress grinding wheel, automatically and shut down the machining process in the event of an emergency. These capabilities reduce operator requirements extensively, making proper machine and gage setup the operator's primary function. As with most manufacturing aids, gaging can do more harm than good if it is not maintained or if it is set up incorrectly. If an incorrect gage setup is made and not noticed, and entire production run could be ground to the wrong size.

Most new high-production grinders are equipped with some type of control gaging system installed as original equipment. Gaging can also be easily retrofitted to older machines that were originally designed for manual operation. It may be more cost effective to increase productivity on an older machine than it would be to purchase a new machine to do the same job. Careful consideration must be placed upon tolerance requirements and the overall condition and capability of the existing grinder before this

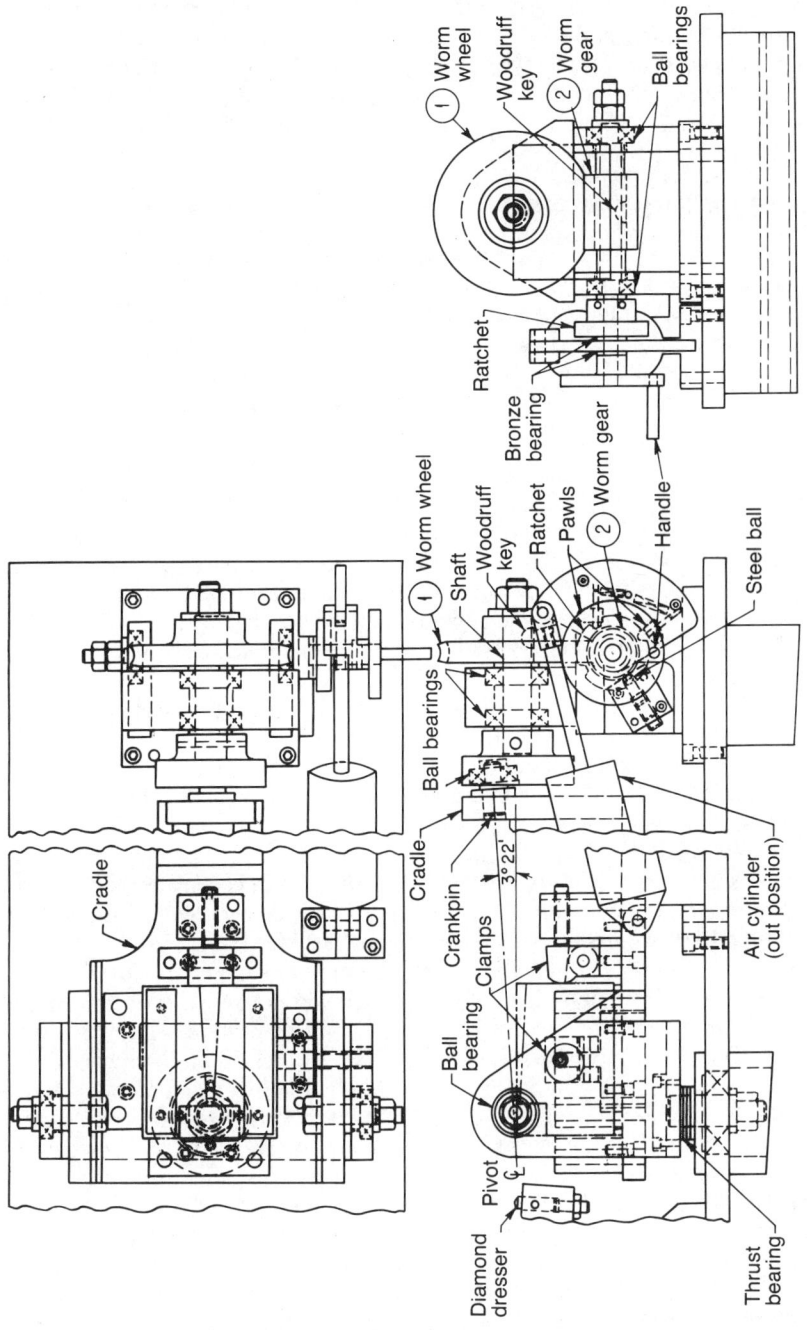

Fig. 10-62 Fixture for grinding a swaging die. (*Courtesy Navistar International, Inc.*)

decision can be made. As a general rule of thumb, if a skilled operator can maintain proper size manually and if the machine has the necessary rigidity and accuracy, the machine can be controlled with a gaging system.

There are four categories that control gaging systems fall into when applied to abrasive operations. These are referred to as pre-process gaging, in-process gaging, post-process gaging, and match gaging. The first three are widely used, with each having its own distinct advantages and disadvantages that should be given proper attention when a decision is made as to which type would best suit a particular grinding process. The fourth, match gaging, is more specialized and only used in limited applications.

PRE-PROCESS GAGING

Pre-process gaging is used when overall work size must be consistent before entering a manufacturing process. It is commonly used when finishing parts on throughfeed centerless grinders or lappers. Better tolerances on size and surface finish can be maintained on these machines when the parts entering them are consistent.

This type of gaging is also useful when off-sized workpieces entering a process may cause extensive damage to a machine or may destroy an elaborate setup. These workpieces can be detected and segregated from the work flow.

IN-PROCESS GAGING

In-process gaging is the most common type of machine control and can be applied to most grinding operations. This technique monitors the part size while machining is taking place. On center-type or internal grinders, an in-process gaging system controls the complete grinding cycle. The gage tells the wheelhead when to rapid infeed, when to initiate the wheel dressing, when to slow infeed, when to spark out, and when desired size is achieved.

When using in-process gaging on center-type or centerless infeed grinders, the response time of the control becomes critical. Parts will be ground undersize if the gage does not keep up with the infeed rate of the wheel.

When positive-stop, OD grinding is used, final size is directly related to the condition of the grinding wheel. When freshly dressed, a wheel is free cutting and lower forces are required to remove the same amount of stock. As the wheel becomes glazed or loaded, these forces become higher, and since the grinding cycle is constant, more deflection is built up in the machine and part. This causes a greater oversize condition than would occur with a freshly dressed wheel. When the wheel breaks down, giving a freer cutting condition, part size will constantly become larger unless manual compensation is made on the machine. When the machine is controlled with a gage, this oversize trend duc to wheel breakdown can be eliminated. The gage, if properly designed, will retract the wheelhead when the part comes to size, regardless of wheel breakdown.

Taper is a machine alignment and deflection function and cannot be eliminated by a gage. In some applications, however, it can be controlled so that a part with one end ground undersized does not have to be scrapped. This is accomplished by putting a gage on both ends of the part; whichever gage indicates size first will retract the wheelhead. If taper exists, the small end will be to size and the other end will be oversize.

Roundness is a direct function of workholding conditions, such as center holes and rate of feed per revolution of the workpiece, at wheelhead retraction. If the feed rate is 0.00005 ipr (0.0013 mm/rev) at finish size, it is unlikely the part will be better than 0.00005 in. (0.0013 mm) roundness. The roundness can be improved by introducing a dwell or spark-out near finish size, which essentially represents an extra-fine feed. This will greatly affect size on a machine that is not gage controlled, because of the unequal cutting forces due to the wheel condition. However, on a machine that is gage controlled an electrical contact in the control unit can be set to block the feed rate a few ten-thousandths of an inch (about 0.007 mm) from size. This will provide a controlled dwell until the part reaches the size limit on the gage. It also gives an extra-fine feed rate that is not based on time, thus providing roundness and size control.

Time to reach final size is often variable depending upon the deflection force present at the time feed is stopped. Some controls allow for the restoring of feed after a set time interval.

Surface finish produced is controlled entirely by a combination of wheel grading, wheel condition, feed rate or force at finish size, and cleanliness of the cutting fluid. A gage may help in achieving the proper finish during production runs by introducing a controlled dwell to more or less burnish the workpiece to size.

TREND GAGING

Trend gaging is a form of in-process gaging that is normally used for continuous applications such as throughfeed centerless grinding. On this type of operation, the part size remains fairly consistent from one piece to the next. They are so consistent, in fact, that some systems are unable to detect any differences at all. This enables the gage to maintain tolerance requirements without having to check every piece. Circuit designs let the gage overlook sporadic readings that may be caused by dirt or sludge.

On some applications in which the parts to be gaged are subjected to extreme contamination or vibration, sensing the position of the wheel may be more advantageous than actually gaging the part during machining. This is a method of in-process gaging that is used successfully on infeed centerless grinding. Because of the ease of setup, wheel position gaging is often used when one machine is employed to grind a variety of different parts.

POST-PROCESS GAGING

Post-process gaging is used to measure part size after machining has been completed and parts have left the machine. The gaging area can be located some distance from the operation; however, for best results as a machine control, the part should be gaged as quickly as possible. This enables size corrections to be made on the machine before the desired tolerance is exceeded.

This type of gaging interfaces well with CNC equipment, such as the type used to grind multiple diameters with a single grinding wheel. After being ground, the part goes to an inspection station, which analyzes all dimensions and sends information back to the controller so that any size corrections can be made on the next piece.

With the coming of age of microprocessor technology, some post-process gages feed information back to the in-process gage to determine the final-size kick-out point on a grinder. For instance, it is an easy task for the post-process gage with a computer to perform a running statistical analysis of any desired parameter on parts exiting a grinding machine. Using this information, a normal curve can be constructed. The center of distribution of this curve can be determined, limits set for its drift, and the information used to control the final-size point on the in-process gage which will keep the distribution within the predetermined limits. The computer can also automatically compare the statistical distribution with the norm and indicate when the machine is going out of control.

Optical gages are also used in a post-process mode to monitor the surface finish condition enabling the operator to determine if dressing the wheel is necessary.

MATCH GAGING

Match gaging is a system which enables an operator to grind pieces to size, using a previously manufactured part as the gaging standard. Clearance between the mating parts can be set in the gaging system and maintained regardless of the variations in the previously machined part. This type of gaging is most frequently used in applications in which a cylindrical part is inserted in a bore, such as a valve body and spool configuration.

CONTACT GAGING

All types of control gaging must sense the size of the parts either directly or indirectly. Gaging systems that make mechanical contact with the workpiece tend to be the most accurate and are used when tight tolerance requirements are to be maintained. Gage contacts must be made of high wear-resistant material, such as diamond or carbide, and arms and holders must be rigid enough not to deflect or distort when part contact is made. Thermal deflection of gage elements is an important consideration.

When using contact gaging for in-process systems, it is important to electrically or mechanically overlook false part-size readings, which may be caused by dirt or sludge passing between the piece and the gage tip. This is when trend gaging becomes most beneficial.

Contacting-gages have the ability to snap on a workpiece, even when considerable stock has to be removed. In most cases, this overtravel can be in excess of 0.080 in. (2.03 mm). This type of gage also has the ability to span interrupted work, such as a keyway or even a spline. A contacting-type gage can be used in conjunction with an air or electronic cartridge, which is easily calibrated without the need for minimum or maximum setting masters. It is usually easy to design in adjustability to cover an even wider range of part sizes.

Contacting gages do, however, have a few characteristics that could be troublesome, but most of these can be overcome by good design. Wear on the contact points is constantly present, but this condition can be tolerated by manual adjustment of the gage box. Proper selection of materials, such as ceramics, epoxy, or the proper grade of carbide contact tips, can minimize this wear.

For automated installations, a post-process gage located in a more suitable atmosphere can be used to check the finished parts and feed back any size variation to the in-process gage. Contact-type gages, with their moving parts, are more susceptable to contamination present during grinding, and dirt and grit can easily jam the moving parts. To avoid these problems, the pivot joints and fragile air cartridges can be encased in their housings and pressurized to ensure cleanliness.

New design concepts in contact gage fixtures and improved electronic controllers have reduced the actual pressure exerted on the piece part from the gage to about 1.7 oz. (50 g). This light contact pressure is essential on throughfeed centerless machines, because any back pressure can affect finish and final size of parts.

NONCONTACT GAGING

Although contact gaging systems are by far the most common, they may not be practical on some processes. When this happens, the use of a noncontact type of gaging system may be necessary. The most widely used form of noncontact gaging is employed with pneumatics. The biggest advantage that air gaging has over the other forms of noncontact gaging is that it can be used in highly contaminated environments due to the emission of air blowing contamination away from the surface during gaging.

Noncontacting or open-orifice gages have no wear characteristics to speak of. There are no moving parts; therefore, dirt is of no major concern to their reliability. Also, they cannot cause chatter or burnish marks on the workpiece, because of the absence of physical contact. However, large stock removal cannot be tolerated because of the fixed gap between the gage orifice and finished workpieces.

The limitation caused by excessive stock removal can be overcome by spring loading the orifices against a fixed stop. When an oversized piece comes between the orifices, they are opened to allow the piece through and then closed against the fixed stops. By using an air-to-electronic pressure transducer and the proper electronic circuit, air gaging can be used to check parts that have interrupted surfaces.

If the metallic structure of the parts being ground remains constant and tolerance requirements are not excessively tight, systems using capacitance or inductive pick-up heads can be used.

Other forms of noncontact gaging incorporate electronic proximity sensors, and still others use scanning lasers against photosensitive backgrounds.

New designs in scanning lasers have resolutions down to 10 millionths of an inch (0.25 μm) and can check a number of parameters on the same piece. Accuracy of laser gaging is greatly dependent upon a clean environment. This, along with its bulky components, makes it impractical in most in-process gaging applications.

GAGE CONTROL UNITS

There are three different ways a control system can interpret information from a sensing unit. It can interpret using all electronics, all pneumatics, or a combination of the two. The all electronics and combination types are by far the most widely used in industry today. When using pneumatic control, an open orifice or air cartridge, whichever is used in the gage tooling, sends a signal to the control unit in the form of either an increasing or decreasing back pressure. This back pressure is used in two ways. It is fed into a pressure dial, which is calibrated in inches or millimeters rather than pounds per square inch, or Pascals, to offer a visual indication of how far the part is from the finished size. It is also simultaneously fed into a number of pneumatic pressure switches that are preset to actuate at a specific pressure, which in turn represent a definite part size. The resulting electrical signals are used to control the machine, such as reducing the feed rate or retracting the wheelhead when finished size is reached.

For most in-process applications, linearity and amplification are not too important. The most important thing is a consistent firing point when finished size is reached. However, for throughfeed centerless or matched-hole gaging, amplification, linearity, and the absence of hysteresis are of prime importance.

In the combination of an air and electronic gage system, the back pressure from the air orifice being used is changed to an analog electronic signal before it reaches the control console. This signal is then processed electronically and displayed on a meter. With this system, one achieves the advantages of a self-cleaning air gage and the accuracy, versatility, and dependability of an electronic control console.

An all-electronic gage system is the most accurate and simplest type to use and maintain. As with the air-electronic system, the control console is all solid state and can be made without any moving or mechanical parts. This is done through the use of LED displays and solid state relay outputs.

SELECTING A GAGING SYSTEM

With all these different varieties of machine control gaging systems available, it becomes necessary to consider some important points when choosing which system would best suit a particular process. These are maintenance, ease of setup, stability, accuracy required, and the condition of the machine.

Any initial gains in machine efficiency achieved through the use of gaging can easily be lost at a later date if the system cannot easily be maintained. Simplicity and quick replacement of primary components are important design features. Production can also be lost if the gage set-up procedure is difficult or takes a great amount of time to execute properly. A system of this type would be extremely impractical for shorter production runs.

Overall stability in any type of gaging system is essential. Gage fixtures must be well designed and free from mechanical hysteresis or twist; electronic controls must be accurate and consistent. Rapid heat buildup can adversely affect the performance of a gaging system. A brief warm-up period of the machine may be necessary in order for the process to thermally stabilize.

The condition of the grinding machine must be taken into account when it is being considered for use with a gaging system. Any machine condition which produces erratic or uncontrollable situations will make it more difficult to maintain tolerances regardless of the gaging system being used. It is important for the machine slides to be free to move. Spindles and spindle bearings must be in good shape, and lead screws should be free of backlash.

Every good machine control gaging system should come complete with protection circuitry to shut down gage function in the event of failure. For example, when a machine is dependent upon a signal from a gage before executing a different function and that signal never arrives, extensive machine damage could result. These fail-safe control features can be incorporated through the use of load meters, which sense how hard the grinding wheel motors are working, or through the use of timers, which can automatically shut the machine down if a proper signal is not sensed within a reasonable amount of time. The same features can be used to provide better process control over variables.

Fail-safe features should also be designed into the mechanical tooling of the gage fixtures themselves. For instance, as a machine process begins and a gage is improperly adjusted, it would be more economical to shear off a gage contact than to freeze up a precision machine slide. It also protects the more complicated inner tooling of the gages if the contacts are the first component to break. It usually requires very little down time to replace broken contact arms.

Progressive gaging companies are expanding their product lines to include special grinding fixtures that are used to upgrade old, worn-out grinders to match or better the performance of a new machine. For example, an old centerless grinder with worn slides can be used as a precision infeed grinder providing the spindles are still good. This is done with the use of a fixture to convert the machine from normal operation to a tangential grind.

GAGING FOR INTERNAL GRINDING

For the toolroom or for low-production internal operations, holes are generally gaged manually. This done by manually interrupting the finish grind or spark-out cycle and checking the hole with a go-no-go plug, dial-bore, gage, air gage, or electronic gage. On high-production internal grinders, gaging is generally automatic. The most common and least costly approach is the diamond sizing method shown in Fig. 10-63. Here the dressing tool (diamond) serves as a reference point. After the wheel is dressed, it is fed a constant amount (0.001 in., 0.03 mm is typical). The bore radius will be equal to the fixed distance, D, that the diamond is set from the center of the work, plus the amount, F, that the wheel is fed after dressing. With this method, sizing accuracy is 0.001-0.003 in. depending upon variation in wheel wear after dressing, diamond wear, slide repeatability, system deflection, and thermal drift.

To maintain closer bore tolerances (0.0001-0.0004 in.) on high-production internal grinders, and to eliminate the effect of OD size variation in centerless grinding, in-process gaging is used. A solid or spidered plug gage is urged against the back of the bore whenever the reciprocating wheel is withdrawn, as shown in Fig. 10-64. When the plug enters the hole, a switch is made in the plug gaging mechanism, thus signaling the machine that final size is reached. Plug sizing is limited to straight bores, and sizing accuracy is influenced by variations of chamfer on the end of the bore, wear of the plug,

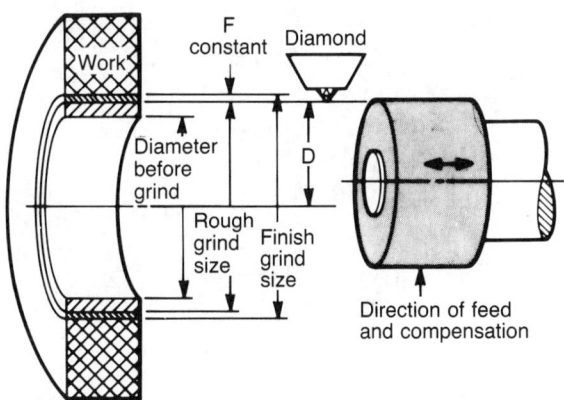

Fig. 10-63 Diamond sizing method of automatically gaging internal grinding operations.

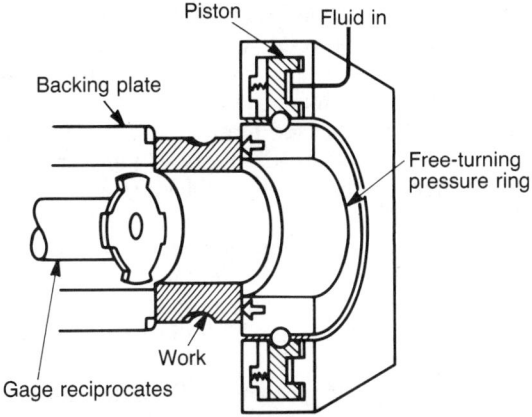

Fig. 10-64 Reciprocating plug for in-process gaging on high production internal grinders.

and rate of stock removal per wheel reciprocation.

In contrast to plug gaging (which is intermittent) continuous gaging uses one or two probes (fingers or forks), which continually measure the hole being ground. The finger may be a diamond-tipped stylus operating an electronic transducer or an air jet operating a pneumatic amplifier, as shown in Fig. 10-65. Continuous in-process gaging produces close hole-size tolerances and is influenced more by thermal distortion of the gage mechanism, stylus wear, and grinding-rate variation (coupled with machine response time) than by gage transducer resolution or amplifier drift.

Modern automatic internal grinders not only use in-process gages to signal final size and retract the wheel, but they also can change feed forces or feed rates as the hole approaches final size, initiate dressing, and detect and correct for diamond wear and thermal drift. This will keep either amount of finishing time, finishing stock, or size point for gage release within preselected limits. These gages may also be used as post-process gages when holes are too small or unsuitably shaped for in-process gaging. By measuring the workpiece after it is ground, a post-process gage will improve the accuracy of a diamond sizing unit by detecting thermal drift or diamond wear, and feed corrections to the feed stop or diamond position.

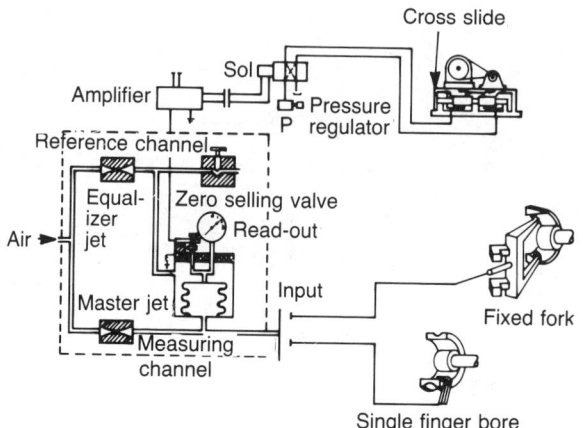

Fig. 10-65 Continuous in-process gaging of internal grinding operations.

HONING

Honing differs from grinding in that honing stones have a relatively large area of abrasive in contract with the work at relatively slow speeds and low pressure. Surface temperature is low and there is no surface damage. Grinding, on the other hand, has a relatively high pressure and a line contact between abrasive and bore, and runs at high speeds. Extremely high localized surface temperature is developed and the surface structure of the bore may be permanently damaged. Honing produces greater accuracy and a finer surface finish than grinding, and provides a stress-free base metal surface in the bore.

In internal grinding, support for the grinding wheel is outside the bore, in the spindle bearing. With honing, the part being honed is stabilized on the honing unit itself. Thus there is no deflection between the honing unit and the bore, nor any change in the bore's axis; high accuracy is achieved. This is especially important in long bores with small diameters.

Honing stones are self-sharpening because abrasive grains dislodge when they become dull, allowing sharp new grains to contact the work surface. The honing operation produces geometrically perfect bores with a cross-hatched base-metal finish having thousands of microscopic pockets that are ideal for supporting a uniform lubrication film.

Lapping, on the other hand, is a slow, tedious process requiring considerable skill. It employs a tool of soft metal which must be frequently "charged" with a lapping compound. Lapping can produce extreme accuracy but the loose abrasive may cause washouts at ports, lands, and at the ends of the bore.

Honing Forces. Honing applies three forces to the workpiece being hones, as illustrated in Fig. 10-66:

1. Outward as the expansion of the stone forces abrasives against the wall of the workpiece.
2. The torque caused by the rotation of the honing tool.
3. The axial force caused by stroking the workpiece, which in combination with the rotation of the honing tool, removes material and provides the high degree of accuracy in roundness and straightness required.

Workholding for Honing. There are ten common bore errors associated with machining, heat treating, and chucking (see Fig. 10-67). Honing can correct all of these with the least possible amount of material removal when properly applied.

10-56

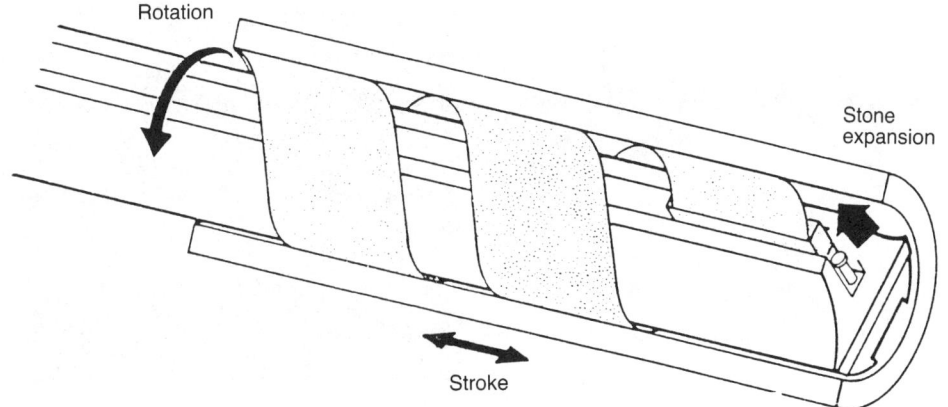

Fig. 10-66 Honing forces. (*Courtesy Sunnen Products Company*)

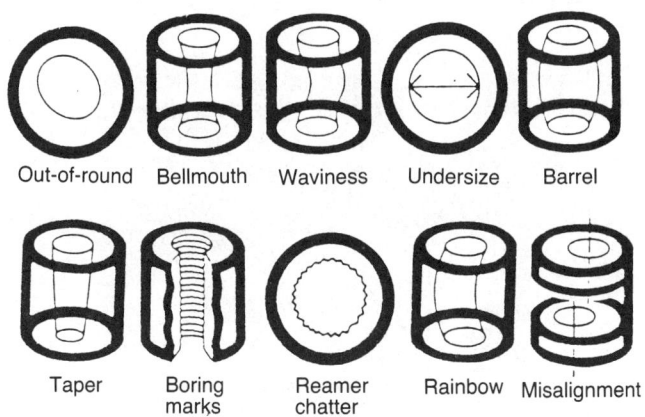

Out-of-round Bellmouth Waviness Undersize Barrel

Taper Boring marks Reamer chatter Rainbow Misalignment

Fig. 10-67 Ten common bore errors. (*Courtesy Sunnen Products Company*)

The primary design considerations when fixturing for honing are:

1. The fixture must absorb the honing torque.
2. The bore must be free to align itself with the mandrel.
3. The fixture must not distort the part.
4. The fixture should permit quick, easy loading and unloading.

Universal Fixturing. Figures 10-68 thru 10-74 show standard off-the-shelf fixturing items for use with the honing machines shown in Fig. 10-16. Included are the following:

Loop-grip Workholders, such as shown in Fig. 10-68, use emery cloth to hold the part securely without distortion. They can be used to hold a great variety of shapes and sizes such as thin-wall tubes, glass barrels, small parts with smooth surfaces, and parts with sharp projections such as gears and milling cutters. As the work attempts to rotate with the tool, leverage locks the loop tightly on the work, preventing it from turning. The operator does not grasp the handle but holds and strokes the work itself. The handle take the honing torque as it slides along the bar. The loop-grip holder often saves the trouble of making a special holder for a short run job.

The *Part Support Fixture* (see Fig. 10-69) which is designed to support a workpiece which is too heavy to be supported by the mandrel being used. A small contact rest is used for workpieces with a flat or irregular face. A large rest used is for workpieces with a curved OD.

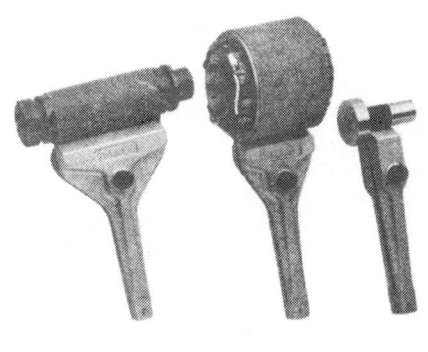

(a)   (b)

Fig. 10-68 Loop grip workholders holding various workpieces (a); honing a workpiece (b). (*Courtesy Sunnen Products Company*)

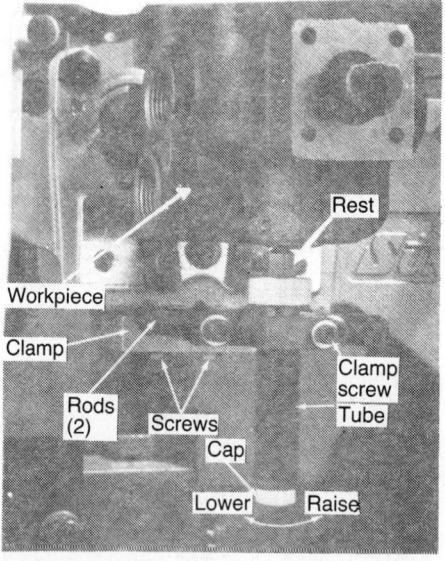

Fig. 10-69 Part support fixture. (*Courtesy Sunnen Products Company*)

The *Right Angle Face Plate Fixture* for honing extremely short bores (see Fig. 10-70) that must be honed one-at-a-time instead of stacking to assure that the bore is at an absolute right angle to the parallel faces of the workpiece.

Gimbal Fixtures, such as shown in Fig. 10-71, which are designed to connect the workholder to the stroking arm of power-stroked honing machines. Gimbal fixtures allow the workpiece to float freely on the mandrel and provide ease in loading and unloading the workpiece.

Universal Honing Fixtures, such as that shown in Fig. 10-72, are designed to absorb the end thrust from stroking on heavy stock removal operations. Universal honing fixtures can be set up for internal honing as shown in Fig. 10-72a or for external honing, as shown in Fig. 10-72b. They are used with the power stroking machines previously shown in Fig. 10-16b.

Face plate

Bolt
keeps
work
from
turning

Short
workpiece
held against
face and
stroked with
fixture

Hex key
attached
to face plate

KKN-100
stroking arm

Adjustable
stroke length
stops

Fig. 10-70 Right angle face plate honing fixture. (*Courtesy Sunnen Products Company*)

Fig. 10-71 Gimbal fixture. (*Courtesy Sunnen Products Company*)

The *Adjustable Finger Fixture*, as shown in Fig. 10-73, which is also designed for use with power stroking machines to absorb end thrust from stroking on light honing operations.

The *Universal Tube Honing Fixture* (see Fig. 10-74) which is designed for use on the horizontal/vertical honing machine shown in Fig. 10-75 to hold parts up to 10 in. diameter. The fixtures can be used in pairs for horizontal holding, as shown in Fig. 10-74*a*, or singly for vertical workholding, as shown in Fig. 10-74*b*. The machine shown in Fig. 10-75 was designed primarily for honing cylinder bores and main bearing bores on 4 and 6 cylinder and V-6 and V-8 cylinder blocks. However, it can be used on a wide variety of tubular parts up to 46 in. (1,168 mm) long.

10-59

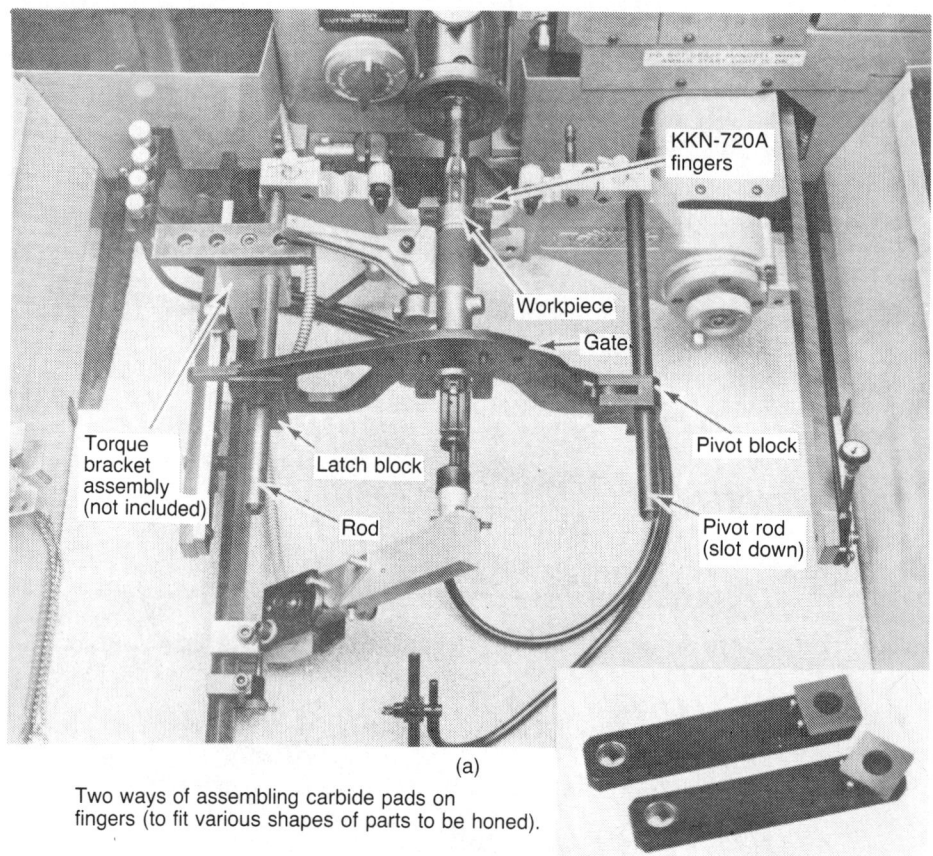

KKN-720A fingers

Workpiece

Gate

Torque bracket assembly (not included)

Latch block

Pivot block

Rod

Pivot rod (slot down)

(a)

Two ways of assembling carbide pads on fingers (to fit various shapes of parts to be honed).

Fig. 10-72 Universal honing fixture set up for internal honing (*a*); Universal honing fixture set up for external honing (*b*). (*Courtesy Sunnen Products Company*)

Workholders for Manual Honing. In almost every case, a workholding fixture makes manual honing much easier and allows the operator to get the work out faster.

While the operator must still provide the "push" or thrust required to stroke the piece back and forth over the mandrel, a properly designed workholding fixture relieves him or her of holding the piece against honing torque. This eliminates a big part of the effort required in manual honing.

Workpieces with irregular surfaces often have a projection that can "ride" on the work support. No work dog or clamp is needed. Where the workpieces have no external projections to overhang a work support, then a simple clamp dog, such as shown in Fig. 10-76, is usually sufficient. The clamp in the figure will hold either round or odd-shaped workpieces over a wide range of sizes. The clamp handle slides along the work support which absorbs all torque. Tubular-shaped workpieces with thin walls should not be clamped like this; for such work, use the loop-grip workholders shown in Fig. 10-68.

Thin-wall, tubular-shaped workpieces that might deform under radical clamping should be stacked and clamped endwise, as shown in Fig. 10-77. In this case, inner races of miniature ball bearings are first lined up by their bores on an expanding mandrel, eleven to a stack, then clamped endwise in a holder. A handle (not shown) is screwed into the holder to absorb torque. The cross-section view shows the workpieces in position for honing.

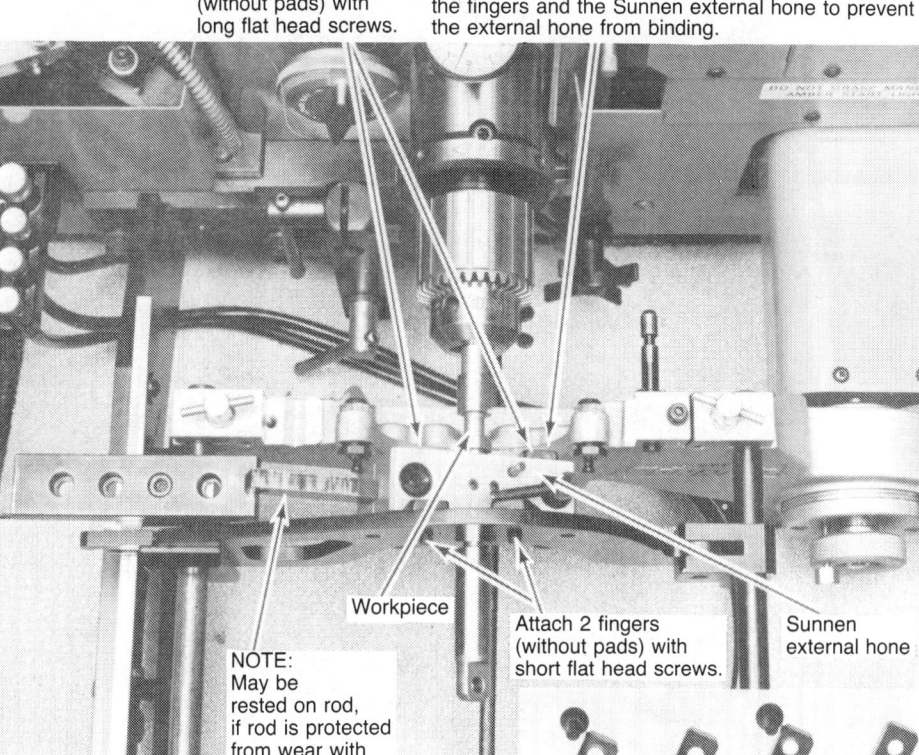

Attach 2 fingers (without pads) with long flat head screws.

NOTE: There must be a slight clearance between the fingers and the Sunnen external hone to prevent the external hone from binding.

Workpiece

NOTE: May be rested on rod, if rod is protected from wear with plastic tube.

(b)

Attach 2 fingers (without pads) with short flat head screws.

Sunnen external hone

Fingers (without pads) used for external honing.

Fig. 10-72 (*Continued*)

Odd-shaped parts such as bevel gears with spherical ends call for a special but very simple holder. Since the gears were not suitable for stacking but were difficult to hold free-hand, the simple holder shown in Fig. 10-78 was devised to absorb torque and make holding easier. The workpiece is not clamped in the holder, but is held in place by light thumb pressure.

Some workpieces have such short lengths that they must be lined up and clamped in a stack for axial stability and honed as one long bore. (This also increases production greatly.) A cross-section of a holding fixture for this purpose is shown in Fig. 10-79. When using this method, workpieces with varying inside diameters should be sorted before stacking. This permits centering of the rough bores within close limits and prevents misalignment in the holder. In addition, the inside diameter of the holding fixture must be larger than the outside diameter of the workpieces to provide sufficient clearance inside the holder to permit lining up of the IDs with an expanding mandrel.

If there is considerable stock to be removed by honing and no close concentricity to be maintained, the bores can be centered roughly on a solid plug. Figure 10-80 shows a method of aligning the workpieces using the honing tool. With this method the honing tool is used as an expanding mandrel. The holding cup is slipped over the tool first, then the stack of parts followed by the jam nut. The stone is expanded, the cap slipped over

Fig. 10-73 Adjustable finger fixture. (*Courtesy Sunnen Products Company*)

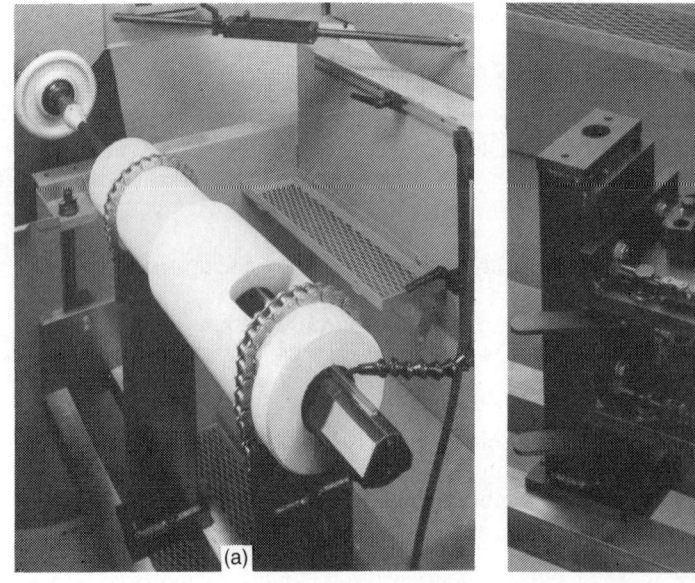

Fig. 10-74 Universal tube holding fixture. (*Courtesy Sunnen Products Company*)

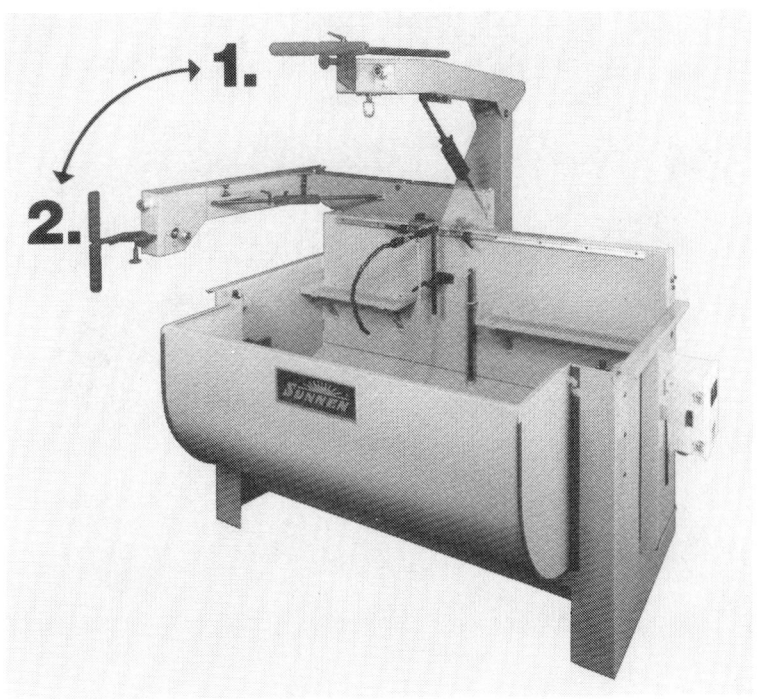

Fig. 10-75 Horizontal/vertical honing machine. (*Courtesy Sunnen Products Company*)

Fig. 10-76 A universal clamp dog. (*Courtesy Sunnen Products Company*)

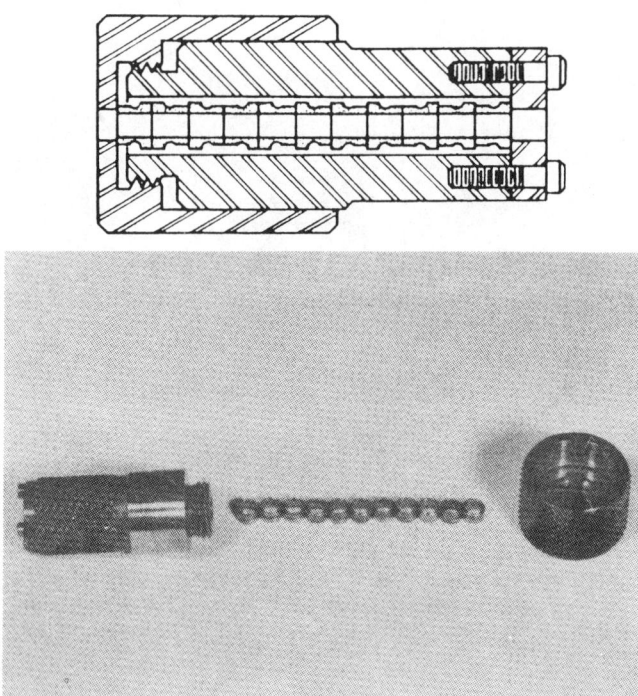

Fig. 10-77 Stacking small thinwall parts for honing. (*Courtesy Sunnen Products Company*)

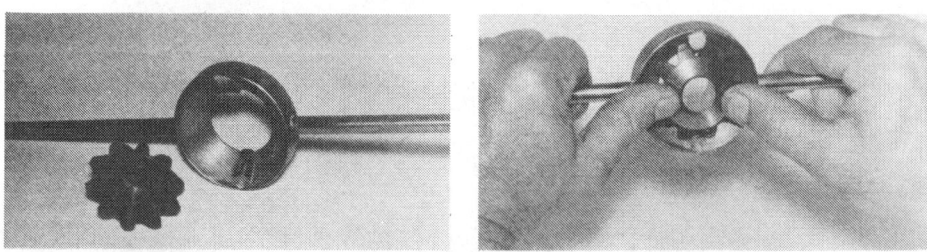

Fig. 10-78 Holder for a bevel gear. (*Courtesy Sunnen Products Company*)

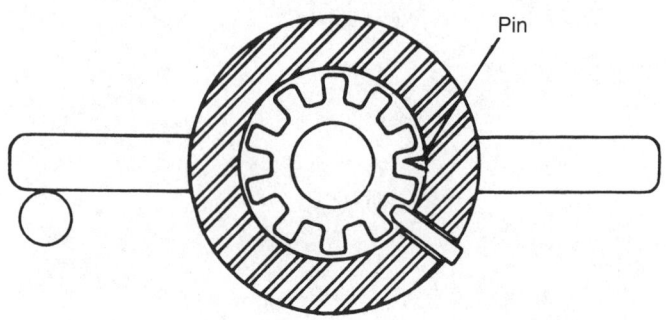

Pin

Fig. 10-79 Stacking short parts for honing. (*Courtesy Sunnen Products Company*)

Fig. 10-80 Using the honing tool for precise bore alignment. (*Courtesy Sunnen Products Company*)

the stack and the jam nut tightened sufficiently to prevent the workpieces from slipping. The complete assembly is then removed from the honing tool and tightened securely before honing.

NOTE: Any misalignment due to size variations will result in loss of concentricity after honing. If concentricity must be maintained, use the loose stacking technique previously described.

When stacked work has sufficient length, a double handle, such as shown in Fig. 10-81, can be used. The operator can use both hands for stroking when the ratio of bore length to diameter is great enough to provide stability and resist "cocking" from uneven thrust forces in stroking. Turn the holder upside down to reverse the work. Note that this handle assembly pivots top and bottom on the cup, acting like a universal joint; it allows the work bore to be self aligning on the honing tool.

Fig. 10-81 Using a double handle.
(*Courtesy Sunnen Products Company*)

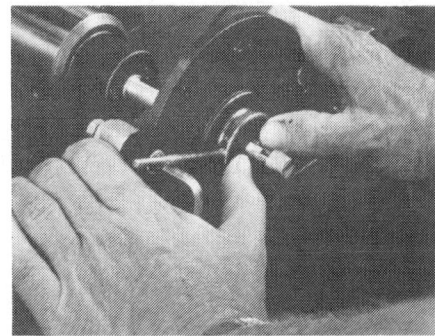

Fig. 10-82 Stroking with a right angle face plate. (*Courtesy Sunnen Products Company*)

There are extremely short bores that, although they may have parallel end surfaces and could be stacked, have tolerance specifications so close that they are best honed one part at a time while being held and stroked with a right angle face plate, such as shown in Fig. 10-82.

While the majority of parts that call for a holder can be held in very simple "universal" type holders, there are times when it pays to make up a special fixture having quick-loading and unloading features to save time on a production run job. See Figs. 10-83 and 10-84.

Figure 10-83 was designed to hold gears, with teeth that would tear up the emery cloth on the the loop-grip holder. Additionally, production quantities required fast loading and unloading. Twisting the handle of this hose clamp fixture quickly clamps or releases the workpiece, the handle slides along the work support during stroking, and absorbs the honing torque.

Fig. 10-83 Special holder for honing gears. (*Courtesy Sunnen Products Company*)

Figure 10-84 shows a fast-operating, self-locking fixture for holding a short-length cam roller. Note that for rapid locking and unlocking, the right end of the fixture is inserted in a stationary holder for leverage.

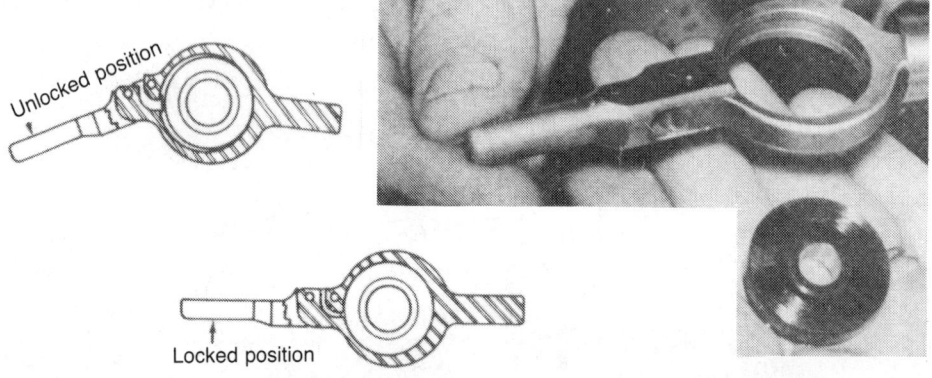

Fig. 10-84 Fast-operating, self-locking fixture. (*Courtesy Sunnen Products Company*)

Workholders for Power Stroking. For heavy stock removal on workpieces which have a round outer surface and a substantial wall thickness, the setup previously shown in Fig. 10-72a could be used. On light honing operations, an adjustable finger fixture (see Fig. 10-73) could be used.

On parts with thin walls, a loop-grip workholder would be used to keep the workpiece from turning. This type of holder is essential to prevent distortion. End caps must be fabricated and put over the ends, as shown in Fig. 10-85, to give the fingers or faceplate a surface to bear upon.

Parts with projections on the outer surface usually require no workholder and are set up as shown in Fig. 10-86. To keep a workpiece with a hole in the outer surface from turning, merely stick a rod in the hole and set up in the same manner as the workpiece with the projection on the outer surface.

The best method of holding a workpiece with an irregular outer surface is to find a flat, a protrusion, a slot, or an indentation on the OD and fabricate a wrench type holder, as shown in Fig. 10-73, to engage the workpiece to keep it from turning.

Fig. 10-85 Setup for power stroking parts with thin walls. (*Courtesy Sunnen Products Company*)

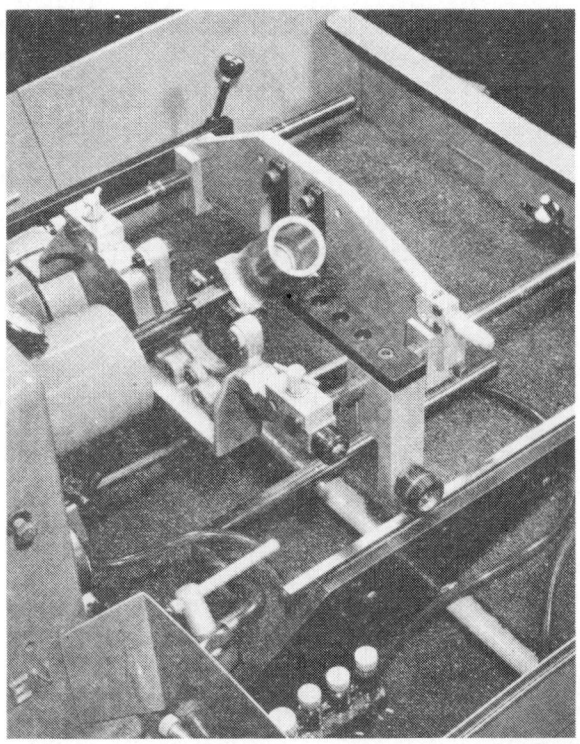

Fig. 10-86 Power stroking parts with projections on the outer surface. (*Courtesy Sunnen Products Company*)

For workpieces which are too short to be honed one-at-a-time, a pot fixture (see Fig. 10-87) should be made to accommodate as many parts as can be efficiently honed with the mandrel you will use. A combined part length equal to or longer than stone length is a good place to start. The pot fixture must be open at both ends and should have a screw cap, bayonet, or clamp to contain the parts. A rod is used to keep the pot fixture from turning.

CAUTION: End faces of parts must be flat, parallel, and reasonably square with the bore. The ID of the parts should be lined up as closely as possible with a plug or expanding mandrel. (A long mandrel of the same diameter as being honed with would be ideal.) Part-to-part variation of rough size should be minimized.

Fig. 10-87 Pot fixture for power stroking stacked parts. (*Courtesy Sunnen Products Company*)

If the parts are shaped so that a convenient way can be found to keep each part from turning individually, lining up and clamping is not necessary. But the stroke must be adjusted so no more than ½ the length of the end parts extends beyond the end of the stone at each extreme position of the stroke.

When the diameter of a bore is more than three times its length, and the workpiece has a flat face, power stroking can create or maintain squareness between the bore and the face. In some cases, this can even be achieved when the diameter of the bore is only twice its length.

Use a face plate to absorb forward stroke end thrust while keeping the bore square to the face. Configuration of the workpiece will dictate the method to use to keep it from turning.

End thrust on the back stroke can be absorbed with a universal honing fixture, as shown in Fig. 10-88, or with an adjustable finger fixture (see Fig. 10-73). The important thing is that the workpiece must be held flat against the face plate in order to create or maintain squareness. Flex pads can often be used to hold the workpiece flat against the face plate as shown; pads should exert pressure on the workpiece.

The method shown in Fig. 10-89 is used to hone workpieces having blind holes. If at all possible, provide a relief (undercut) at the closed end of the hole to permit the stone to over-stroke the honed surface. The relief does not have to be more than a few thousandths deep and can actually blend in with the bore when finish honed, but it should be as long as possible, preferably 1/3 the length of the stone. In honing blind

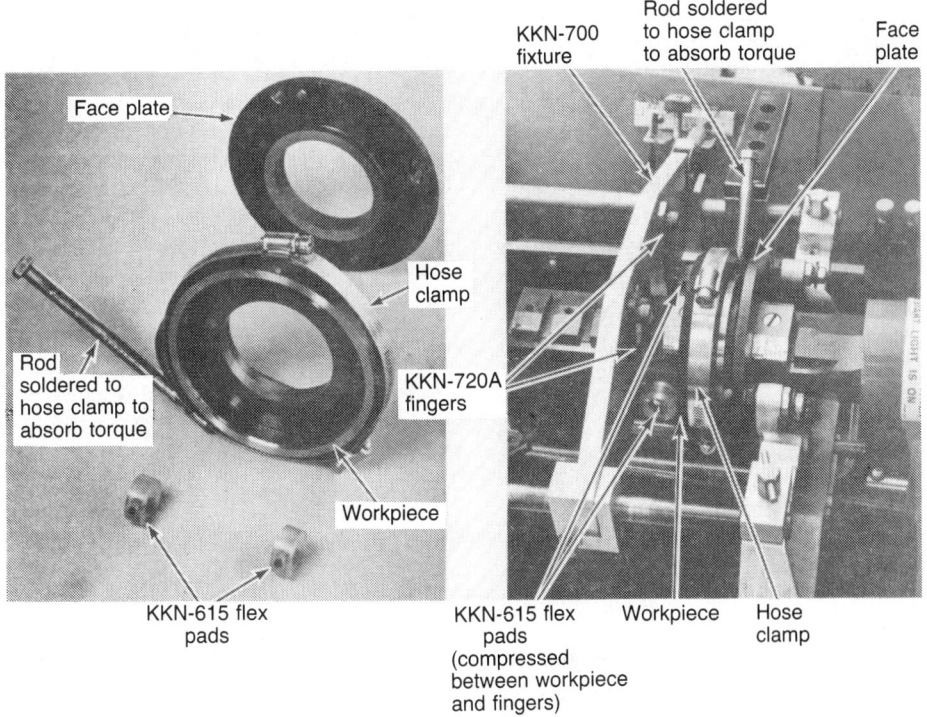

Fig. 10-88 Setup for power stroking parts with short bores that must be held square to the face. (*Courtesy Sunnen Products Company*)

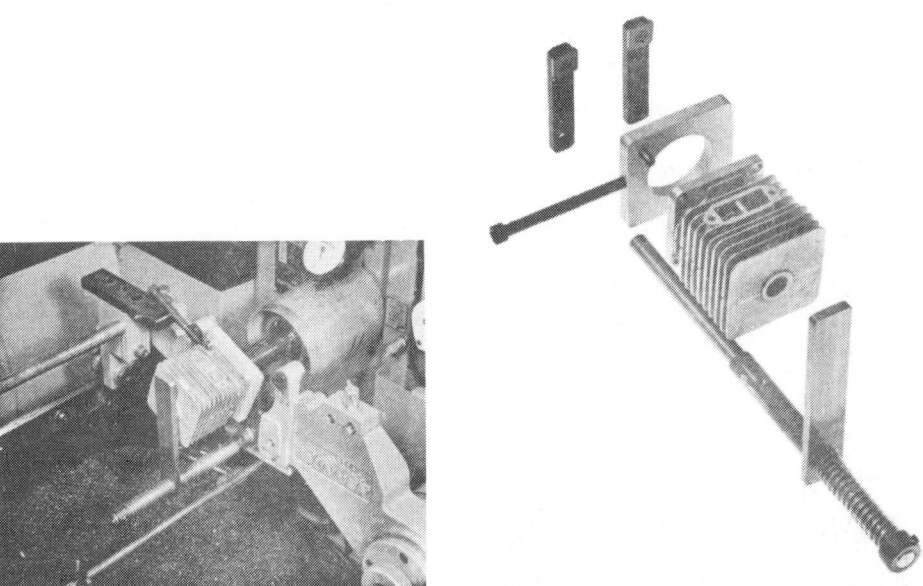

Fig. 10-89 Honing workpieces with blind holes. (*Courtesy Sunnen Products Company*)

holes, it is necessary for the stone and guide shoes to extend flush with the tip of the honing unit. On some mandrels the tip must be cut off, as shown in Fig. 10-90a. In honing blind holes, the stone and guide shoe length should be 2/3 to ¾ of the blind hole length (including relief length). This is necessary to provide for proper stroking. When alteration of the stone and shoe length is necessary, remove material from the back end only as shown. To maintain stability of the stone in the mandrel, it is important that 50% of the stone be behind the forward wedge contact on the stoneholder. Otherwise the stone could rock, causing bore inaccuracies as the work is stroked over the honing unit. To avoid any chance for the stoneholder to "rock" when honing extremely shallow or short blind holes, b, it may be necessary to cut back the stoneholder (as well as the abrasive), mandrel, shoes, and wedge tip so that only 1/16 in. (1.58 mm) extends from the front wedge contact. Pressure from the wedge is then applied evenly to the stoneholder.

The most important thing to remember in fixturing blind-hole parts for power stroking is that *the stroke must be longer than the travel of the stone.* This sounds incongruous at first, but is accomplished by using a spring in the fixturing. The spring permits the stroker arm to continue moving for a short distance after the mandrel has bottomed out in the bore. During this period, the bottom of the bore receives extra honing, called "dwell".

It is necessary to dwell in order to minimize the tightness that results from the inability to over-stroke the part at the blind end. Note especially the spring in Fig. 10-89. It is the one element that must always be present for successful blind-hole honing.

When alteration of the standard abrasive honing stone is necessary, cut through the abrasive with an old hacksaw blade and break the unwanted section of the stone from the stone holder with a pair of pliers. Do not cut into the die cast stoneholder (except as described under blind hole alteration). Superabrasive stones are best ordered in the required special length, in order to not waste money by cutting away expensive abrasive. Use a file or bench grinder to shorten the guiding surfaces of the shoe. Both stone and guide shoe should be altered identically and in the same relative position.

Alterations for Tandem Holes. Honing units can be used to size two or more "in-line" or tandem bores in perfect alignment. Stone and guide shoes must be of the proper length so that the entire stone surface will contact one or the other of the bores at some time during the honing stroke. To keep the honing unit true during the operation, the stones and guide shoe length must be at least twice the center-to-center tandem distance of the bores, as shown in Fig. 10-90c. When the honing unit meets this requirement, alteration is not required. It may be necessary to reverse the part end-for-end on the honing unit to obtain identical sizes. Never stroke either of the tandem bores completely off the stone and guide shoes.

Should the stone and guide shoe length be less than twice the tandem distance, the center area of the stone and guide shoe will not wear and a resulting "hump" in the honing unit will bellmouth the inside ends of both bores of the tandem. In some tandem applications, it is necessary to alter the honing unit by cutting away the area of stone and guide shoe that would become the "hump" (see Fig. 10-90d). Remove from the center of both the stone and guide shoe, an amount equal to the amount that the stone (and guide shoe) is short of being twice the tandem distance. For example, a part having a 2¾ in. (69.8 mm) tandem spacing would require a 5½ in. (139.7 mm) stone and guide shoe, but the honing unit has a stone and guide length of only 4½ in. (114.3 mm). This honing unit can be used by removing 1 in. (25.4 mm) from the center of the 4½ in. (114.3 mm) stone and guide shoe length. Multiple-stone honing units can sometimes be used by setting up the honing unit to leave out the center stones and shoes.

Special tandem type mandrels can generally be supplied for those applications which have too long a tandem distance for honing with the altered honing units.

Alterations for Short Bores using Automatic Size Control. Always consider the possibility of stacking parts with short bores so that they may be honed as one long bore using standard honing units. For precision sizing of open holes, the stone and guide shoe length should be between 2/3 and 1½ times the bore length to be honed, as shwon in Fig. 10-90e.

Alterations for Short Open Holes. Always consider the possibility of stacking parts with short bores so that they may be honed as one long bore using standard honing units. Individual parts (if they have at least one flat face) with bore lengths of ¼ the diameter, or less, can also be honed by holding the parts flat against the face plate of the square honing fixture. For precision sizing of short open holes, the stone and guide shoe length should be between 2/3 and 1½ times the bore length to be honed. (see Fig. 10-90f.)

When alteration is necessary, both the stone and guide shoe must be shortened by the same amount. Any alteration of this type should shorten the stone and shoe equally from both ends so that the honing area remaining is centered over the wedge contacts on the stoneholder. If greater accuracy is required than is obtained after the alteration, refer to the honing unit manufacturer.

Long parts which have a short land to be honed on one end must be supported so they don't sag or whip.

The supporting fixtures illustrated in Fig. 10-91 are designed to clamp onto one of the rods on the finger fixture. If the finger fixture is not used a rod can be inserted into the clamp on the bottom of the stroking arm. The enclosed-type supporting fixture, *a*, is designed for a particular part. It is recommended for production honing, or for high-speed honing where there is a chance for the part to whip.

The open-type supporting fixture, *b*, is more versatile, accommodating many different ODs. It is very useful for toolroom use, or where ever short runs of various parts is the rule. Dimensions on the drawings are for typical fixtures; they can be varied as needed to suit a particular job. A setup using an enclosed type supporting fixture is shown in Fig. 10-92.

Sometimes, a part cannot be held by any of the preceding methods. The reasons could be varied. In the case illustrated in Fig. 10-93, the bevel gear to be honed seems to defy any attempt to hold it. This particular fixturing problem was solved by cutting both ends out of an empty tuna fish can and using it as a mold to make a fixture with Devcon Plastic Steel.® A rod was inserted through a slot in the side of the can and into the fixture before it hardened; the rod to be used to keep the part from turning during honing.

Workpieces to be externally honed are held in adapter chucks, as shown in Fig. 10-72b. The workpiece is rotated as the external hone is stroked.

Fixtures for Vertical Honing. Cylindrical, thick-walled workpieces with ODs over 6 in. can be held with toe clamps, as shown in Fig. 10-94. The different length towers allow the toe clamps to be positioned at various heights. The part elevators must be made long enough to accommodate overstroke and any cradle height adjustment that may be necessary. To reverse the workpiece, it must be removed from the fixture.

For thick-walled workpieces with ODs of 6 in. or less, and end clamping fixture, such as shown in Fig. 10-95, can be used.

The Chuck Fixture, shown in Fig. 10-96, can be used to hold long, cylindrical, thick-walled workpieces that have small ODs. The chuck is mounted on channel iron as shown. A lathe chuck was used for this particular fixture. Note that the hole through the chuck must be larger than the outside diameter of the workpiece.

Workpieces should be loaded in the fixture to the same height to reduce the amount of cradle height adjustment required. Height indicators have been attached to the fixture for this purpose.

An *Air Bag Fixture*, such as shown in Fig. 10-97, can be used to hold cylindrical,

Alteration for extremely short blind holes

3/4 bore length

Note that at least half of stone length is behind front wedge contact

Front wedge contact

1/16 in. (1.5 mm)

(b)

Alteration for tandem bores

Center to center tandem distance

If stone and guide shoe length is less than twice tandem distance, alteration is required.

Remove

Remove

(d)

Alteration for blind holes

2/3-3/4 bore length

Alteration of integral shoe mandrel

(a)

Tooling for tandem bores

Center to center tandem distance

If stone and guide shoe length is equal to at least twice tandem distance, alteration is not required.

(c)

10-72

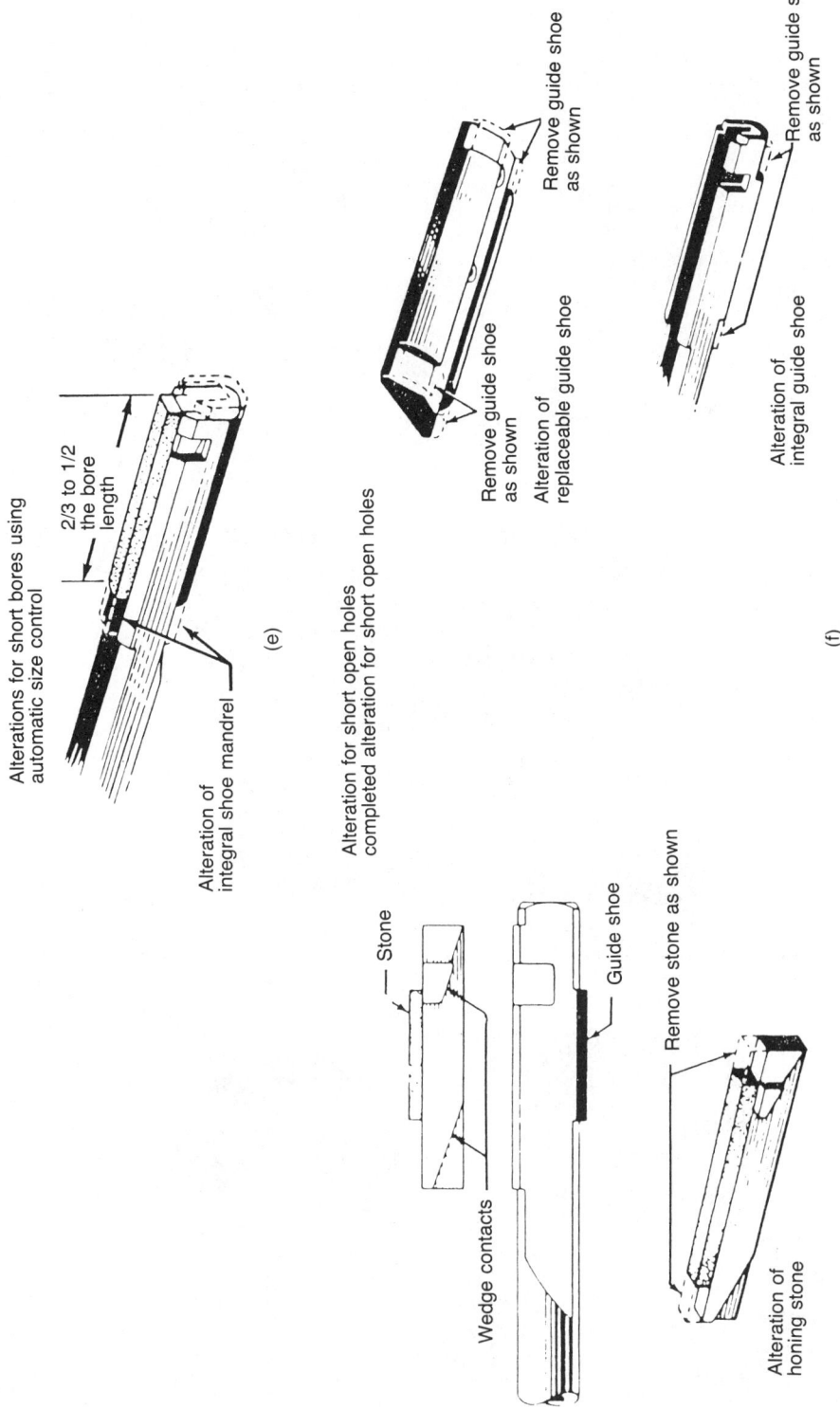

Alterations for short bores using automatic size control

2/3 to 1/2 the bore length

Alteration of integral shoe mandrel

(e)

Alteration for short open holes completed alteration for short open holes

Remove guide shoe as shown

Remove guide shoe as shown

Alteration of replaceable guide shoe

Remove guide shoe as shown

Alteration of integral guide shoe

(f)

Stone

Wedge contacts

Guide shoe

Remove stone as shown

Alteration of honing stone

Fig. 10-90 Alterations to honing units. (*Courtesy Sunnen Products Company*)

Fig. 10-91 Supporting fixtures. (*Courtesy Sunnen Products Company*)

Fig. 10-92 Setup using enclosed type supporting fixture. (*Courtesy Sunnen Products Company*)

Fig. 10-93 Plastic steel honing fixture. (*Courtesy Sunnen Products Company*)

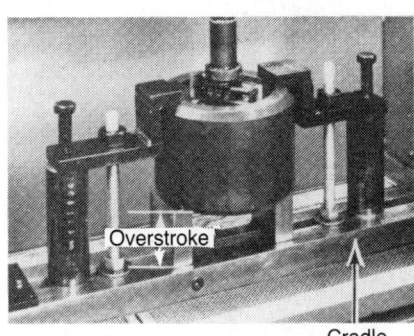
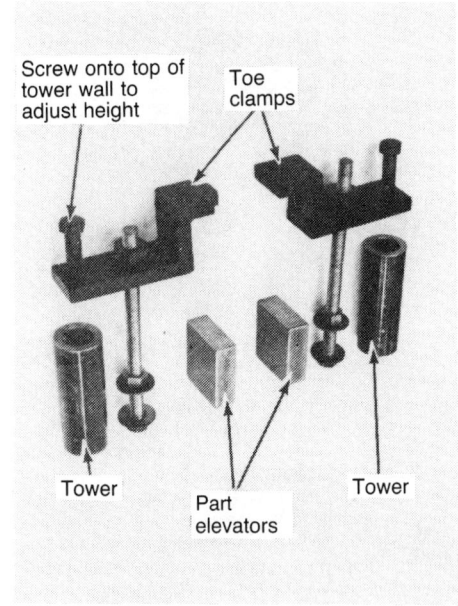

Fig. 10-94 Toe clamping fixture. (*Courtesy Sunnen Products Company*)

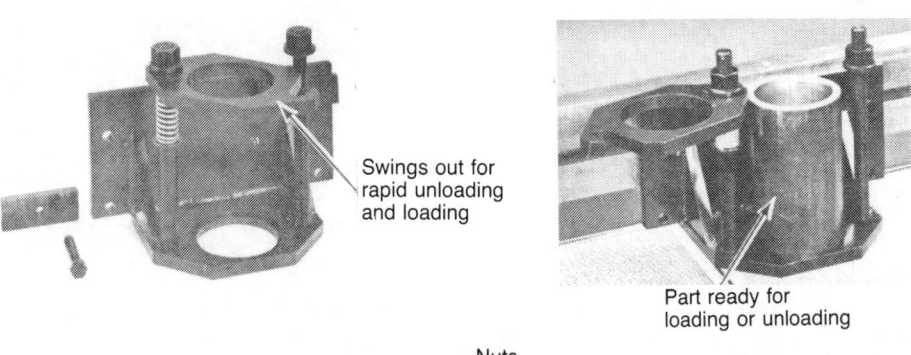

Fig. 10-95 End clamping fixture. (*Courtesy Sunnen Products Company*)

Cradle   Height indicators

Fig. 10-96 Chuck fixture. (*Courtesy Sunnen Products Company*)

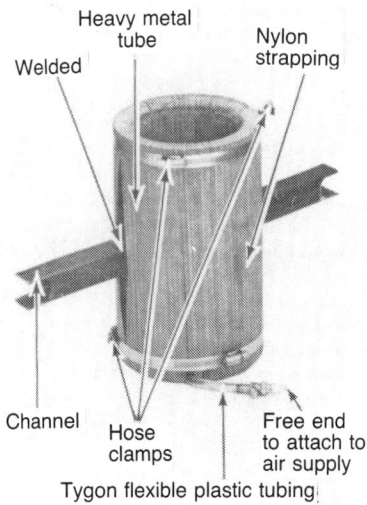

Heavy metal tube

Welded

Nylon strapping

Channel   Hose clamps   Free end to attach to air supply

Tygon flexible plastic tubing

Cradle

Fig. 10-97 Air bag fixture. (*Courtesy Sunnen Products Company*)

thin-walled workpieces that distort under clamping pressure. The air bag consists of Tygon Flexible Plastic Tubing coiled around the inside diameter of a heavy metal tube. Nylon strapping is wrapped around the plastic tubing with one end of the plastic tubing allowed to hang out. The nylon strapping is held in place with hose clamps. The thin wall part is inserted into the fixture and the plastic tubing is inflated with compressed air until the part is held fast in the fixture. Generally 5 to 10 psi (34.4 to 68.9 KPa) of pressure is required to hold the part. Any cylindrical part with a thin wall can be honed in this type of fixture.

CAUTION: Honing oil causes most plastic tubing to harden. Be sure the brand that is used (such as Tygon brand), will not be affected by honing oil.

The *Tunnel Fixture,* shown in Fig. 10-98, can be used to hold workpieces whose overall shape is rectangular. A 0.05 to 0.10 in. (1.27 to 2.54 mm) clearance on the height and width between tunnel and workpiece should be provided to permit easy loading and unloading. The clamp is used to keep the workpiece located in the fixture, and not absorb honing forces.

The *Square Base Fixture* (see Fig. 10-99) is an end clamping fixture that has been modified for a workpiece with a square base. The distinctive feature of the square base

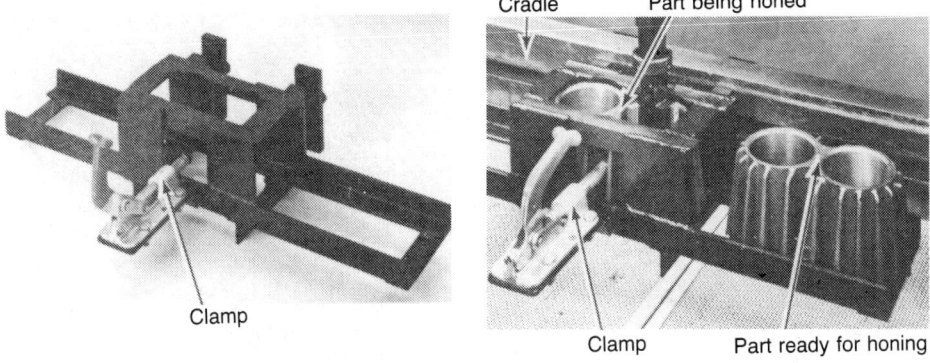

Fig. 10-98 **Tunnel fixture.** (*Courtesy Sunnen Products Company*)

Fig. 10-99 **Square base fixture.** (*Courtesy Sunnen Products Company*)

fixture is that it enables honing torque to be absorbed by the square base of the workpiece, rather than end clamping pressure. Therefore, workpieces that would deform under end clamping pressure can sometimes be successfully honed using this fixture. To use this fixture with different size parts, make the hole in the seat large and use adapters to hold the part at the top.

Air compressor cylinders are typical of parts that can be fixtured using tunnel fixtures and square base fixtures. Parts which are to be mounted when in use should be fixtured using the mounting provisions when feasible.

The *Pin and Clamp Fixture* (see Fig. 10-100) used for light parts, consists of pins to locate the part and simple clamps to hold the part.

The *Back Plate Fixture* (see Fig. 10-101), used for heavy parts, consists of two back plates mounted to the cradle and mounting bolts (to mount the parts on the ing conditions:

1. Parts must have flat, parallel end surfaces.
2. Parts must not deform under end clamping pressure.

Bore size variation prior to honing and out-of-squareness (bore to end surfaces) require additional stock removal. Concentricity can be maintained only when all bores have the same diameter prior to honing. The fixture should be made to clamp as close

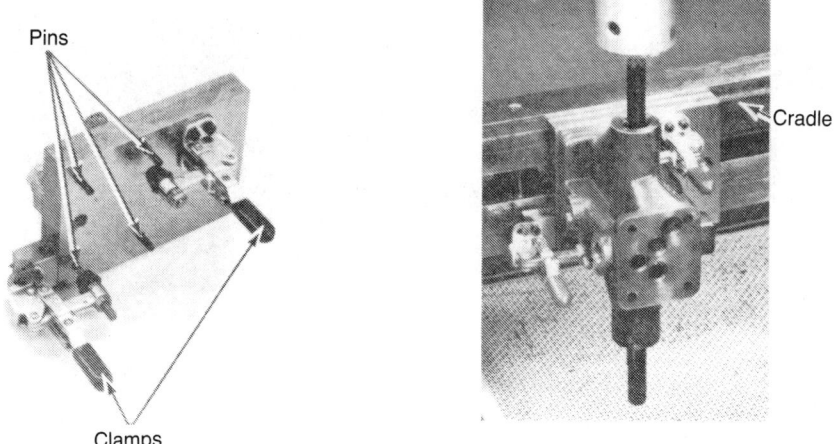

Fig. 10-100 Pin and clamp fixture. (*Courtesy Sunnen Products Company*)

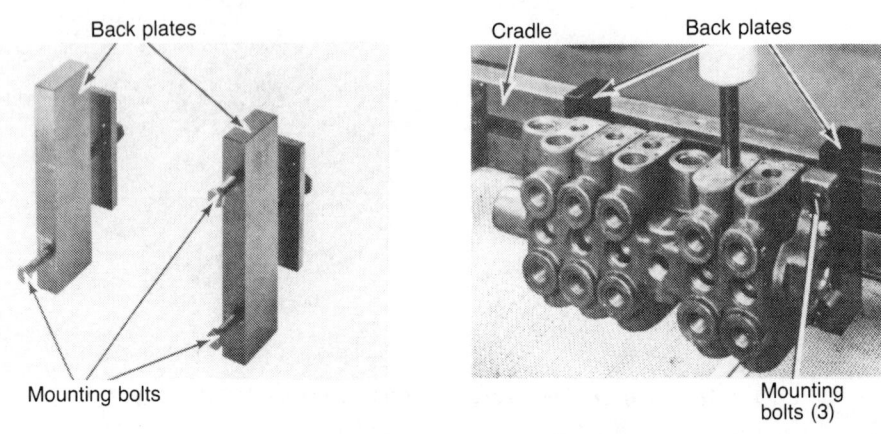

Fig. 10-101 Back plate fixture. (*Courtesy Sunnen Products Company*)

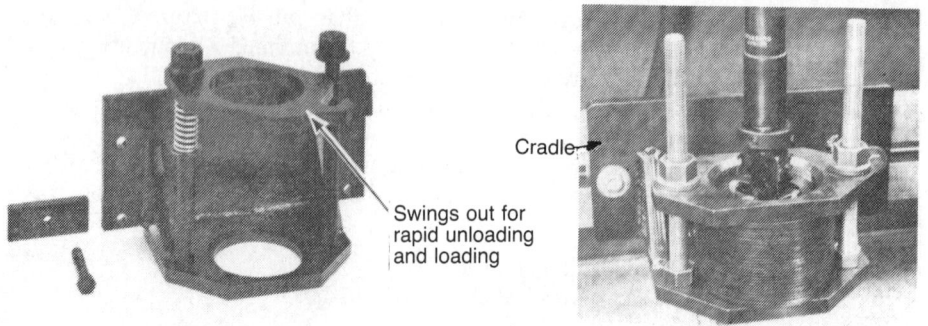

Fig. 10-102 End clamping fixture. (*Courtesy Sunnen Products Company*)

as practical to the bore diameter to help avoid deforming parts during clamping. The height of the stack of parts must be less than the stone length. Align the bores by expanding the honing tool in the loose stack, and then tighten the end clamping fixture. The stack can now be honed as one long bore.

The fixtures, in Figs. 10-95, 10-96, and 10-98 through 10-102, enable the workpieces to be easily reversed (essential for extreme accuracy) by rotating the cradle 180°. Overstroking is not obstructed by the fixture or the cradle.

References

1. J. Sobkowiak, "Grinding Fixture for Holding Work at Any Angle," *Machinery* (March 1953).
2. R. Minser, "Grinding Fixture Has Adjustable-angle Feature", *Machinery* (October 1979).
3. F.L. Rush, "Flat-grinding Fixture on Vise," *American Machinist* (December 3, 1956).
4. R. Mawson, "Fixture Speeds Critical Grinding," *Iron Age* (February 1950).
5. C.S. Ricker, "Universal Grinding Fixture Positions Thin Cutters and Saws," *American Machinist* (June 25, 1951).
6. Thomas J. Drozda and Charles Wick, eds., "Grinding," *Tool and Manufacturing Engineers Handbook*, 4th ed., Vol.I (Dearborn, MI: Society of Manufacturing Engineers, 1983), p.3.
7. *Ibid.*, pp. 11-87 to 11-90.
8. R.W. Newton, "Spring Chuck and Fixture for Grinding a Molded Plastic Bushing," *Machinery* (December 1951).
9. Ricker, *op. cit.*
10. Drozda and Wick, *op. cit.*, pp. 11-105 to 11-109.

CHAPTER 11
SAWING AND ABRASIVE CUTOFF FIXTURES

Sawing is a machining process which uses straight, continuous band, or circular blades which have many cutting teeth along their edges to cut the workpiece or material.

Abrasive cutoff machines are used to perform operations that are basically the same as those performed using circular cutoff saws, except cutting is done with a thin, bonded abrasive wheel. Because of this similarity and the fact that workholding for both of these machining methods is also similar, they are being covered together in this chapter.

SAWING MACHINES

Sawing machines fall into three main categories:

Hacksaws—which cut by the back and forth action of a short, straight blade with cutting teeth.

Bandsaws—which cut by continuous action of a long, endless driven band having many cutting teeth along one edge of the band.

Circular saws—which cut by the action of a power-driven blade having cutting teeth around its periphery.

The choice of a particular saw depends on many factors such as: Stock size, physical properties of the material to be cut, accuracy and finish requirements, and most of all, the cost to produce a slug or cut that meets all specifications. The various types include:

Horizontal Power Hacksaws. A horizontal power hacksaw consists of a base to support the work and either a column or hinge mounted support to carry the reciprocating mechanism and saw blade which is fed downward to saw the material or workpiece.

Vertical Power Hacksaws. Vertical power hacksaws have the support carrying the reciprocating mechanism and saw blade mounted to the rear of a machine base in a vertical position which is fed toward the front of the machine to saw the material.

Power hacksaws are relatively slow-cutting, but can handle most materials over a wide range of sizes.

Vertical Bandsawing Machines. Vertical contour-type bandsaws feature a horizontal mounting table through which the continuous saw band passes while cutting the workpiece. Fixed-table models are usually hand-fed and used for short run sawing. For higher production, tables are hydraulically or air powered to move the work through the band. For sawing angles, most tables can be tilted 10° above to 45° below their normal horizontal position. Contouring devices are available which rotate the piece while it is being cut.

Horizontal Bandsawing Machines. Horizontal bandsaws, sometimes called cutoff saws, consist of a workpiece mounting table, above which the continuous sawband and its driving mechanism, which together is called the sawing head, is mounted on columns or a hinge. Cutting occurs as the saw band is fed downward. On the hinge mounted types, the sawing head can be swung from the 90° cutoff position to any angle up to 45°. Angle cutting with these machines is inconvenient, therefore most production cutting of angles is done on a tilt-frame universal machine.

Tilt-frame Universal Bandsawing Machines. On tilt-frame universal bandsawing machines, the sawing head is mounted with pivot bearings onto a moving carriage which cuts when fed toward the workpiece that is positioned and clamped on the table. The pivoted frame can be set to cut any angle up to 45° to the right or left of vertical.

The use of power bandsaws is not limited to the operations shown later in Fig. 11-3. They are also used for the following operations:

- Band filing for light stock removal.
- Band polishing to remove burrs and improve surface finish.
- Abrasive-wire bandsawing for machining hard and complex workpieces such as dies, cams, etc. Mainly used with CNC contour type bandsawing machines.
- Friction sawing for high speed cutting.
- Spiral edge bandsawing for cutting intricate patterns without rotating the workpiece.
- Diamond bandsawing for cutting abrasive materials or workpieces that are easily crumbled.
- Scallop-edge cutting with wavy, knifelike bands for machining materials that tend to tear easily.

Pivot-arm Circular Sawing Machines. A vertical pivot arm circular saw, sometimes called a chopstroke saw, consists of a mounting base with a mounting table to clamp the workpiece. A circular saw head is hinged (pivoted) at the rear of the mounting base. Cutting occurs as the sawblade moves downward as the saw head is rotated about the hinge.

Vertical Column Circular Sawing Machines. On vertical column machines the saw head is mounted between columns directly above the work table. Parts or materials are positioned and clamped below the centerline of the saw blade. To cut, the sawhead is fed straight downward.

Horizontal Travel Circular Sawing Machines. On horizontal travel machines the saw head is mounted on a horizontal slide and the material or a workpiece is clamped to a table. The saw is fed into the workpiece from the side.

One variation of a horizontal travel machine is called a circular plate saw. It features a long table and equally long guideways to carry the blade for cutting long lengths of nonferrous material.

ABRASIVE CUTOFF MACHINES

The four basic types of cutoff machines are shown in Fig. 11-1. Each of these types is available for semi-automatic and automatic operations as well as for manual operations. They include:

Chopstroke Cutoff Machines. A chopstroke abrasive cutoff machine, *a*, consists of a mounting base with mounting table to clamp the barstock or workpiece and an abrasive cutoff wheel which is mounted on an arm that is hinged (pivoted) at the rear of the base. In operation, workpieces are clamped on the machine mounting table in a fixed position and the cutoff wheel cuts down through the work as it is rotated about the hinge.

Chopstroke abrasive cutoff machines are mainly—but not exclusively—used for cutting bar stock up to 4 in. (100 mm) thick and tubing up to 6 in. in diameter.

Oscillating Abrasive Cutoff Machines. An oscillating abrasive cutoff machine, *b*, is built in the same manner as the chopstroke cutoff machine except that the abrasive cutoff wheel is also oscillated back and forth in a manner similar to a hacksawing operation as it cuts down through the work which is clamped in a fixed position on the machine mounting table. Oscillating type cutoff machines can handle stock or workpieces up to 12 in. (300 mm) thick.

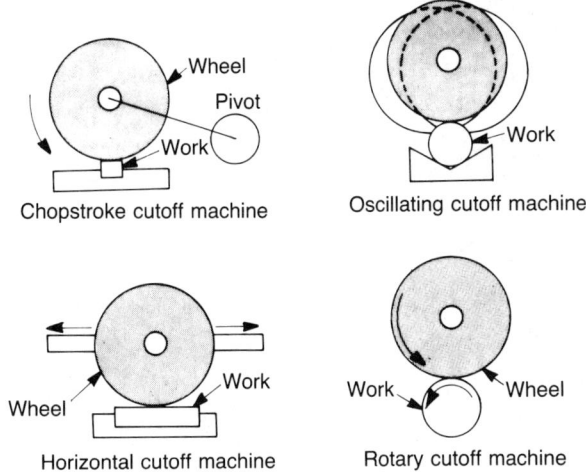

Fig. 11-1 The four basic types of abrasive cutoff machines.

Horizontal Cutoff Machines. Horizontal cutoff machines, *c*, are built in two different configurations. In one, plates or workpieces are clamped in a fixed position on the worktable and the abrasive cutoff wheel is moved horizontally through the work. This type is mainly used for cutting plates up to 3 in. (75 mm) thick. In the other configuration, the work is moved horizontally into the abrasive cutoff wheel which is mounted on a fixed spindle. This type is mainly used to cut non-metallic materials such as tile and glass.

Rotary Abrasive Cutoff Machines. With rotary abrasive cutoff machines, *d*, both the abrasive cut-off wheel and the workpieces are rotated during the cutting action permitting the cutoff of stock twice the diameter that could be cut off if the work was held stationary making it the machine of choice for work over 8 in. (200 mm) in diameter. Some of these machines provide oscillation and controlled vibration of the wheel to improve chip clearance and wheel cooling.

WORKHOLDING FOR POWER HACKSAWING

Workholders used with power hacksaws are mainly heavy-duty machine vises, some of which are integral to the machine, and others that are attached to the workpiece mounting surface. Most have interchangeable jaws which can be altered to fit the profile or shape of any barstock or workpiece. For obvious economic reasons, it is important to cut as many pieces as possible with each setup. Some recommendations for nesting parts to accomplish this are shown in Fig. 11-2.

Other recommendations for clamping barstock and workpieces are as follows:
- Thin strips should lie flat and be clamped so that most of the teeth on the blade are in contact with the workpieces.
- To provide proper clamping and accuracy, cut short sections of stock one at a time.
- Use an overhead guide bar when clamping workpieces for multiple cutoffs whenever possible. This will insure clamping from four sides.
- Whenever possible, clamp the workpiece in a manner that eliminates starting the cut on a sharp corner of the work. If unavoidable, recommend a fine-toothed blade.

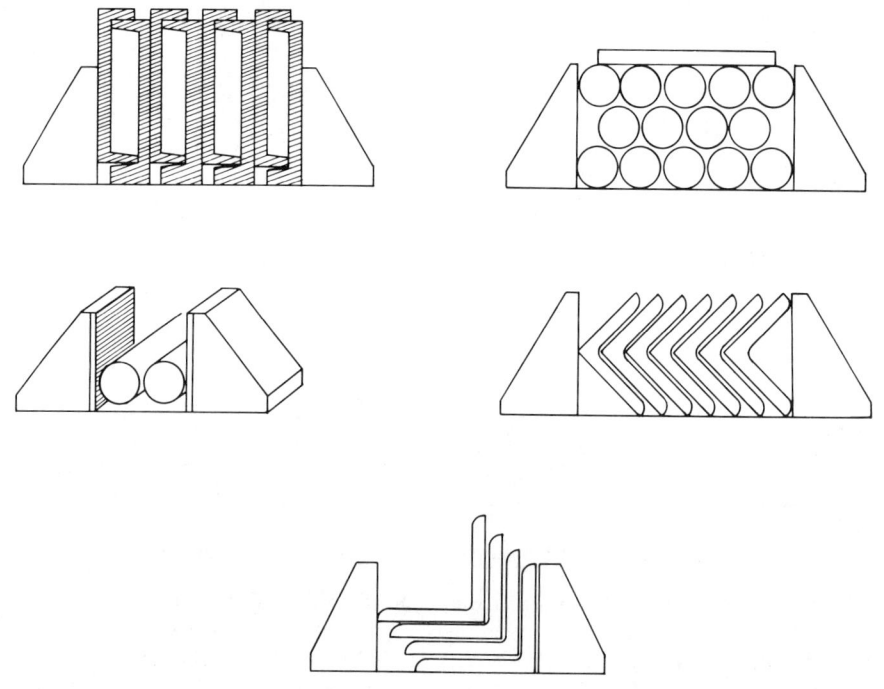

Fig. 11-2 Clamping multiple parts on a power hacksaw.

WORKHOLDING FOR BANDSAWING

In contemplating the fixturing of any bandsawing machine, the tool designer should understand some of the basic principles embodied in the design of the basic bandsawing machine.

The basic bandsawing operations are shown in Fig. 11-3. Almost all bandsawing applications include one or more of these operations.

Figure 11-4 illustrates the holding forces created by the downward thrust of the saw band and the inward forces of the table feed. In many operations, this eliminates the need for clamps. The long continuous band of cutting teeth provides a uniform force which holds the workpiece down on the table.

In any exploratory survey considering the use of tooling, the following factors should be thoroughly investigated prior to adapting the tooling to the bandsaw:
- Type of material being cut.
- Size, shape, hardness, and weight of the workpiece.
- Suitable locating surfaces or tooling holes to locate the workpiece.
- Proper band width for minimum radius to be cut. (see Fig. 11-5).
- Thorough check of the product to see whether standard bandsaw fixturing can be used or if special fixturing should be considered.

If a product is to be fed manually into the machine, tooling can be of a simple design and easy to build. This type of tooling with the bandsaw has successfully proved its worth on extensive production runs. In mass production where automation is required, fixturing would be comparable to any of the standard automatic machining or workpiece-feeding mechanisms.

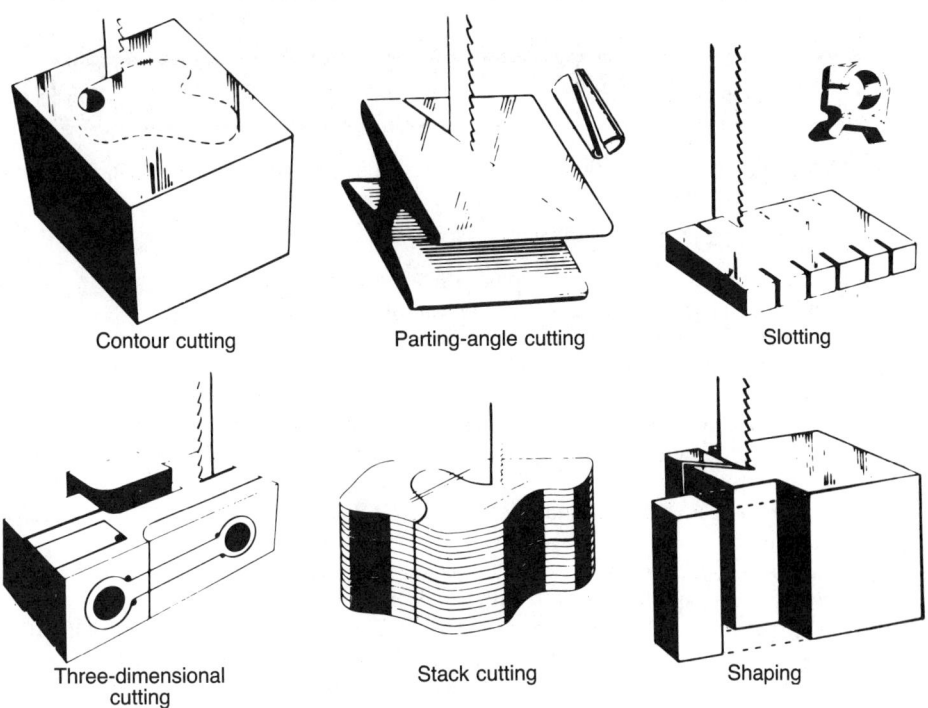

Contour cutting Parting-angle cutting Slotting

Three-dimensional cutting Stack cutting Shaping

Fig. 11-3 Basic bandsawing operations. (*Courtesy The DoALL Co.*)

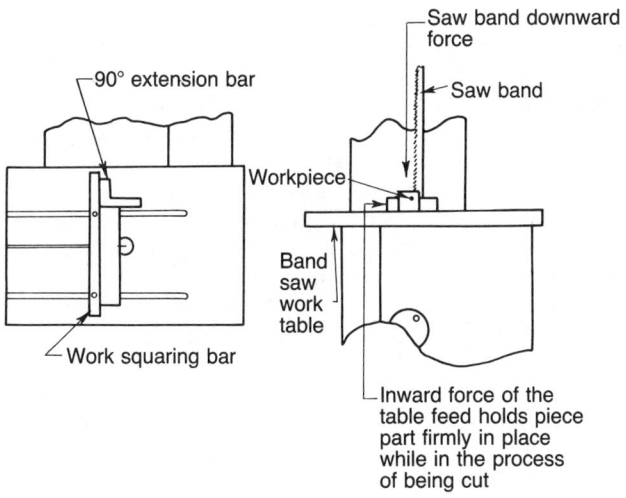

90° extension bar

Saw band downward force

Saw band

Workpiece

Band saw work table

Work squaring bar

Inward force of the table feed holds piece part firmly in place while in the process of being cut

Fig. 11-4 Forces on a vertical bandsaw. (*Courtesy The DoALL Co.*)

Width of saw band in.	2	1½	1¼	1	3/4	5/8	1/2	3/8	1/4	3/16	1/8	3/32	1/16
Radius that can be sawed in.	28	21	12	7¼	5⁷/₁₆	3¾	2½	1⁷/₁₆	5/8	5/16	1/8	1/16	SQ.

Fig. 11-5 Approximate radii dimensions that can be sawed with bands of different widths. (*Courtesy The DoALL Co.*)

VERTICAL BANDSAW FIXTURES

Standard vises and attachments, such as shown in Fig. 11-6, can be adapted to maintain good production rates on both straight and contoured cuts.

Standard attachments include the following:

- The calibrated work fixture, *a*, for accurate dimensional sawing of workpieces. It can be used for straight cutoff work and angles up to 45°.
- The contouring workholder, *b*, for contouring work on a sliding table.
- The miter gage with pusher, *c*, which attaches to the front T-slot of a fixed table for precision miter cuts.
- The miter gage, *d*, which attaches to the front T-slot of a sliding table for precision miter cuts.
- The rack and pinion pusher, *e*, which attaches to the front T-slot of a fixed table for precision miter or straight cuts with mechanical feed.
- The rip fence, *f*, which attaches to the front T-slot and is equipped with lateral fine adjustment, allowing straight and accurate cuts.
- The universal workholders, *g* and *h*, which are used with a sliding table to hold a wide variety of workpieces for sawing.
- The circle cutting attachments, *i* and *j*, for cutting discs or arcs having a radius ranging from 1½ in. to 15 in. or 30 in. discs.

Sometimes special fixtures may be necessary for any or all of the following reasons:
1. To automate and/or speed up an operation.
2. Reduce operator fatigue.
3. Improve workpiece accuracy and repeatability.
4. Support odd-shaped and/or fragile stock and workpieces.
5. Locate the workpiece from datum surfaces and/or tooling holes.
6. Provide workpiece interchangeability.

In many applications, fixtures can be manufactured of steel or aluminum. There are applications in which a wood or plastic fixture base plate is suitable to supply the necessary holding power or the support required while cutting the product. Clamps are unnecessary on most fixtures because of the downward force of the band. If the operation involves stack cutting, it is advisable to clamp the stacked workpieces to the fixture base plate. Adjustable jackscrews can be used when the workpiece requires outboard support. Many variations of clamping can be adapted, depending on the stock that is to be cut. Quick-action toggle clamps are usually preferred, but for some fixtures cam locks are more suitable. Each fixture design should be determined from the stock's characteristics and the volume of production.

The holding of cylindrical and similar-shaped workpieces is shown in Fig. 11-7. The workpiece rests on the machine table while being positioned by bevel-edged blocks. Strap clamps and long hold-down bolts are used to clamp the workpiece to the table.

Figure 11-8 illustrates a simple, quick-loading fixture for making a saw cut through the lug of a bronze casting. The base plate is made of low-carbon steel. The locator could be

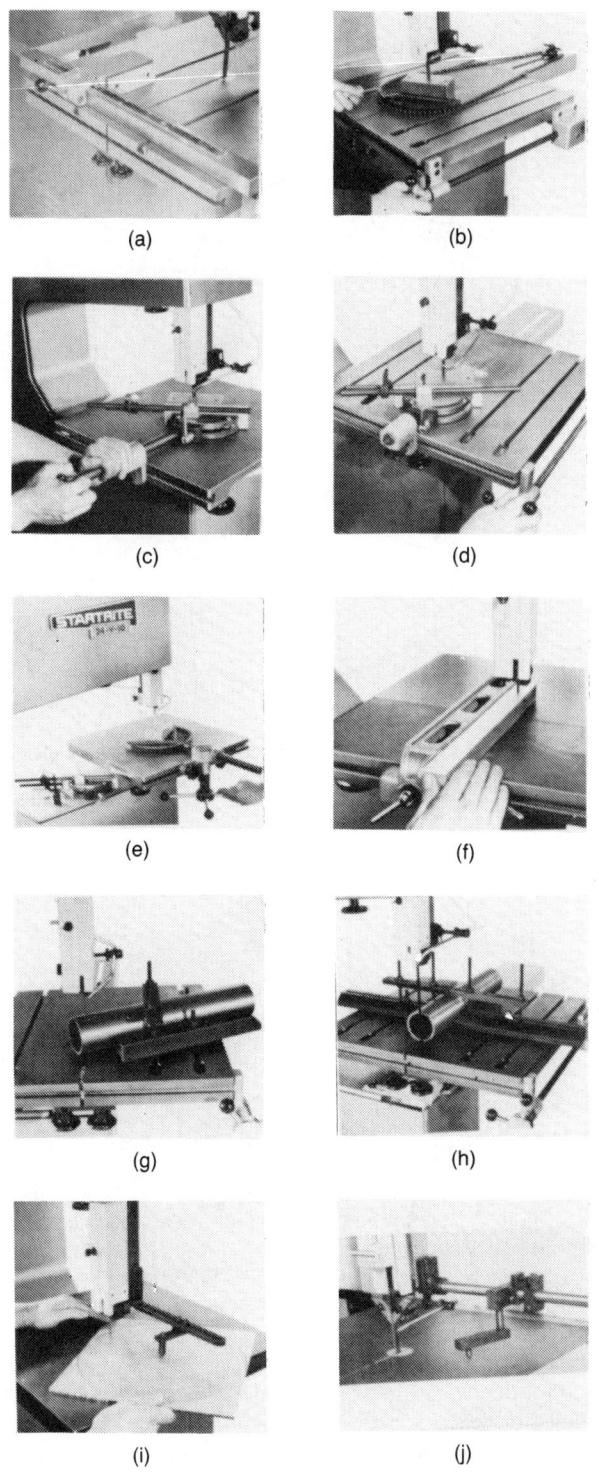

Fig. 11-6 Standard attachments. (*Courtesy Startrite Inc.*)

11-7

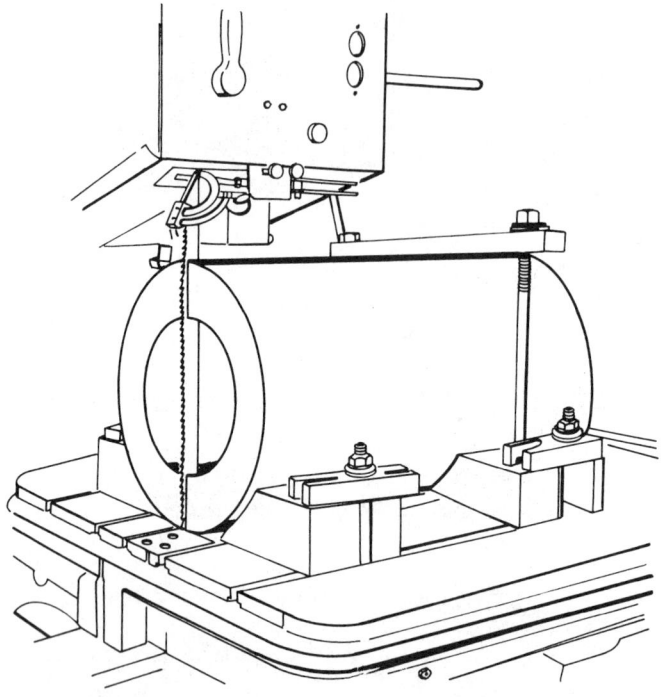

Fig. 11-7 Holding cylindrical workpieces. (*Courtesy The DoALL Co.*)

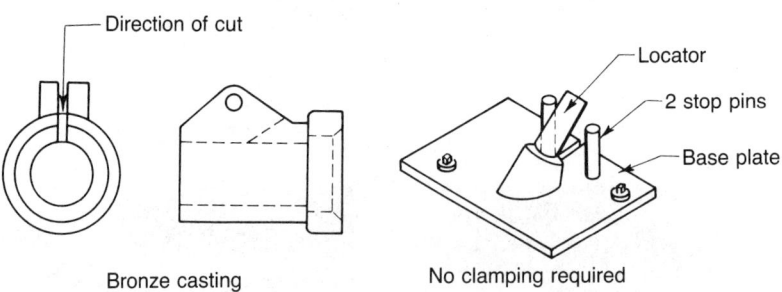

Direction of cut

Locator

2 stop pins

Base plate

Bronze casting

No clamping required

Fig. 11-8 Fixture for sawing a bronze casting. (*Courtesy The DoALL Co.*)

made of low-carbon steel and left soft, or carburized and hardened; or it could be made of tool steel and heat-treated; depending upon production requirements. The two stop pins could be made of cold-rolled steel or drill rod and pressed into the base plate. Standard T-bolts can be used to secure the fixture to the machine table.

A simple indexing fixture, such as that shown in Fig. 11-9, may be used for applications when equally spaced slots are needed around the periphery of a product. The fixture consists of a base plate, a locator and pivot post, and an index pin. Any suitable material can be used for the base plate. The locator is made of drill rod. The index pin can be either spring-loaded or screw-actuated. In operation, the workpiece is placed over the locator and the first cut made. The workpiece is then rotated to the second slot position, the index pin inserted into the first slot, and the second slotting operation performed. The process is repeated for cutting the remaining slots. Depending upon the thickness of the workpiece, more than one part can be cut at one time.

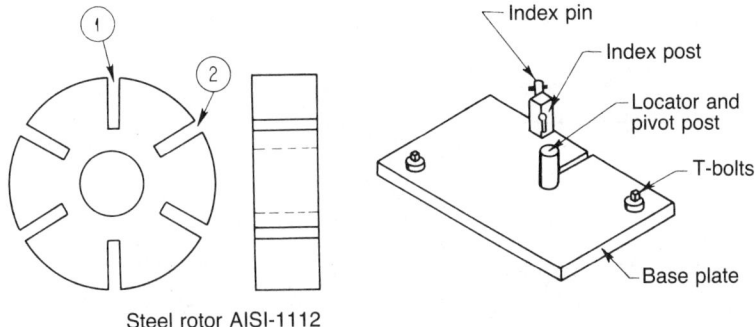

Steel rotor AISI-1112

Fig. 11-9 Manually indexed sawing fixture. (*Courtesy The DoALL Co.*)

An indexing fixture for cutting a cylindrical workpiece into equal segments is shown in Fig. 11-10. A center post (2) is screwed into a tapped hole in the base plate (1). The locating sleeve (3) is held to the center post by a shoulder screw (4). For ease of rotation, a bronze sleeve bearing and a ball thrust bearing are used in the assembly. The base of the sleeve has four chamfered holes positioned 90° apart around the periphery and serves as an index plate. A spring-loaded pin locator (5) enters the holes in the index plate to correctly position the workpiece to the saw blade. A square cavity in the top of the locating sleeve provides a flat clamping surface. A toggle clamp (6) holds the workpiece to the fixture while the cuts are made.

Sawing operations may be performed using automatically indexed and fed fixtures. These units can be independently operated or synchronized with the machine's hydraulic power unit. If an air actuated cylinder is the source of power for the fixture, an electrical cycle control can be designed and timed with the hydraulic power unit. The table feed would operate alternately with any fixture mechanism. With an 80 psi (552 kPa) air supply, a 2 or 3 inch (51 or 75 mm) cylinder usually will supply enough force to energize the index or transfer mechanisms. Figure 11-11 illustrates an air-operated indexing fixture whose action is coordinated with the machine table movement. With this and similar fixturing, loading and unloading systems are incorporated to achieve automatic operation.

A fixture for a series of four cutting operations on a workpiece with minimum handling is shown in Fig. 11-12. The fixture consists of a base plate, a transfer plate, and an index plate. The part locator also serves as a pivot pin for the index plate. A keyway in the workpiece locates it radially. The transfer plate is located and guided by a gib and is positioned by a pin. The travel of the transfer plate is determined by the distance of the saw cuts from each other. The index plate and pin position the workpiece radially.

A fixture for holding a workpiece while making three cuts in a workpiece without removing it from the fixture is shown in Fig. 11-13. The fixture consists of a base plate, a round locator, a positive stop, a clamping device, and a spacer block. In operation, the universal calibrated work fixture of Fig. 11-6a is placed on the base against the extension bar. The spacer bar is placed between the fixture and extension bar for cut #1. Cut #2 is made with the space bar removed. The fixture is rotated 180° and located against the extension bar, and the third cut is made. The fixture is designed so that the distance from cut #2 to the edge of the fixture is the same as from cut #3 to the opposite edge; thus the position of the extension bar need not be changed.

Figure 11-14 illustrates the use of power feed in generating a contoured slot. The fixture is mounted on a saw table with automatic infeed and retraction. Two cuts are required in the production sequence. A shuttle plate moves the workpiece to the starting position of each cut. A pivoting plate rotates the workpiece during the second cut. The cold rolled steel base plate is profiled, drilled, and tapped as required. A shuttle plate (2)

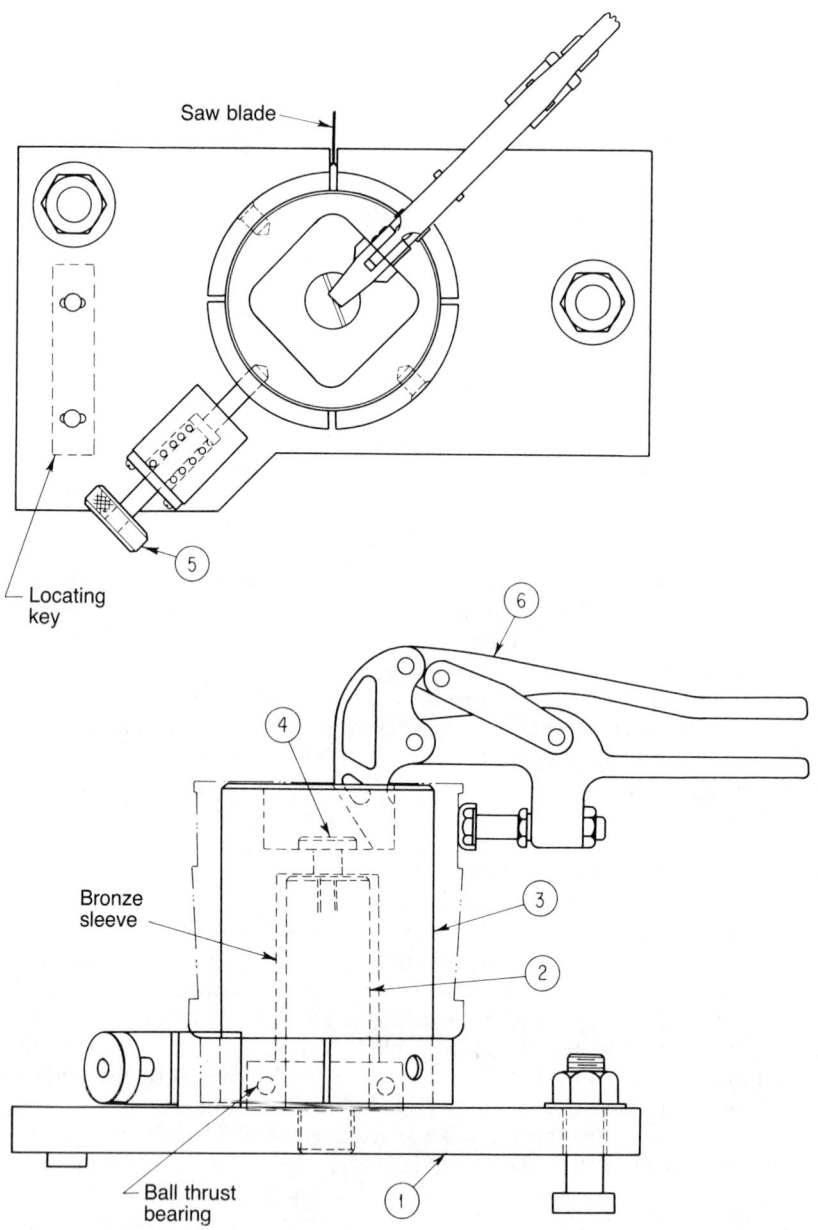

Saw blade

Locating
key

Bronze
sleeve

Ball thrust
bearing

Fig. 11-10 Fixture for sawing a cylinder into circular segments. (*Courtesy The DoALL Co.*)

secured to a pivot plate (3) by gibs (4) is moved to the saw blade by an air cylinder. A locating block (5) and a nest (6) support the workpiece against the pressure of two clamping cylinders (7). The pivot plate (3) is revolved by the pivoting cylinder (9) about the axis, which is fixed by the pivot shoulder screw (8). Adjustable stops (10) limit shuttle and pivoting motion. The saw table cycles in and out during the straight cut. The shuttle plate moves the workpiece to the starting point of the second cut. The infeed and retraction cycle for the second cut is coordinated with the rotation of the pivoted plate to cut to the required contour.

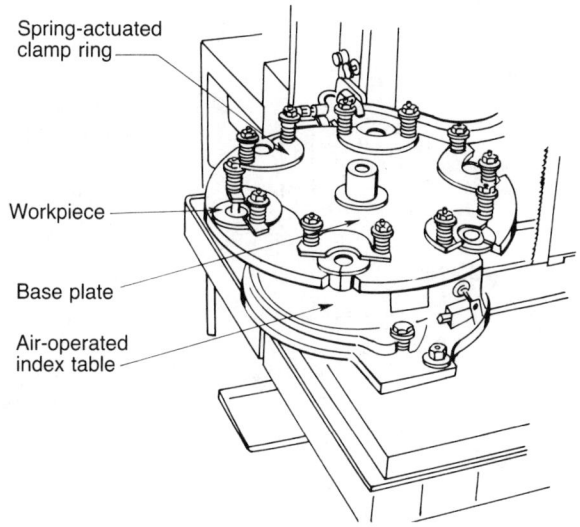

Spring-actuated clamp ring

Workpiece

Base plate

Air-operated index table

Fig. 11-11 Air-operated indexing fixture. (*Courtesy The DoALL Co.*)

The air-actuated fixture of Fig. 11-15 was designed to obtain a maximum production rate with minimum operator attention. This fixture is completely automatic in operation, except for the loading of each stack of five bars. The air cylinder actuating the stock-feeding mechanism is synchronized with the table feed by solenoid controlled valves. In operation, the bar stock is pushed into the fixture with the index table in the forward position. The air-actuated clamps and vise are closed for the first cut. The clamps are released, the index table is moved back, and the clamp on the table closes while the air actuated vise releases its grip on the bars. The clamp ahead of the saw does not close until the index table returns to the forward position. This allows the cutoff pieces to be pushed ahead by the advancing bar stock.

The principle of the circle cutting attachments of Fig. 11-6*i* and *j* is used in the fixture of Fig. 11-16. Two pivot points are provided. With the pivot plate on the 2⅛ in. radius point, the workpiece edge is partially cut. The workpiece is then inverted, and the opposite edge is partially cut to the same radius. The pivot plate is moved to the 1 in. radius point, and the workpiece is again inverted. The resultant 1 in. radius cut blends into the partial 2⅛ in. radius cut. One last inversion of the workpiece permits finishing of the opposite edge. The fixture base plate (1) is drilled for mounting to a saw table and has two bored holes fixing the pivot points. The pivot plate (2) has two locating pins (3 and 4) which fix the location of the workpiece. A handfeed bar (5) permits manual operation, and an optional pull bar (6) is provided for hydraulic actuation. The 2⅛ in radius pivot pin is pressed into the base plate. A dowel pin is inserted into the 1 in. radius point for the second portion of the production sequence and is removed when the pivot plate is returned to the 2⅛ in. (54 mm) pivot point. The locating pins can be replaced with longer pins to permit the stacking of parts during the operation.

The geometry of a product and the production rate are two of the factors to consider in designing contour-cutting fixtures for the bandsaw. Another important factor is that the position of the pivot point controls the contour of the part. The centerline of the fixture's pivot point must be at 90° or parallel to the leading edge of the band's cutting edge. Any variation from this location will result in an undesired workpiece contour. It will also cause binding and scoring of the bandsaw. Figure 11-6*i* and *j* illustrates the cutting of circles with cylindrical sides at 90° angles to the base and with the pivot point at a 90° angle to the bandsaw. If the sides were to be tapered, the part would be pivoted along and

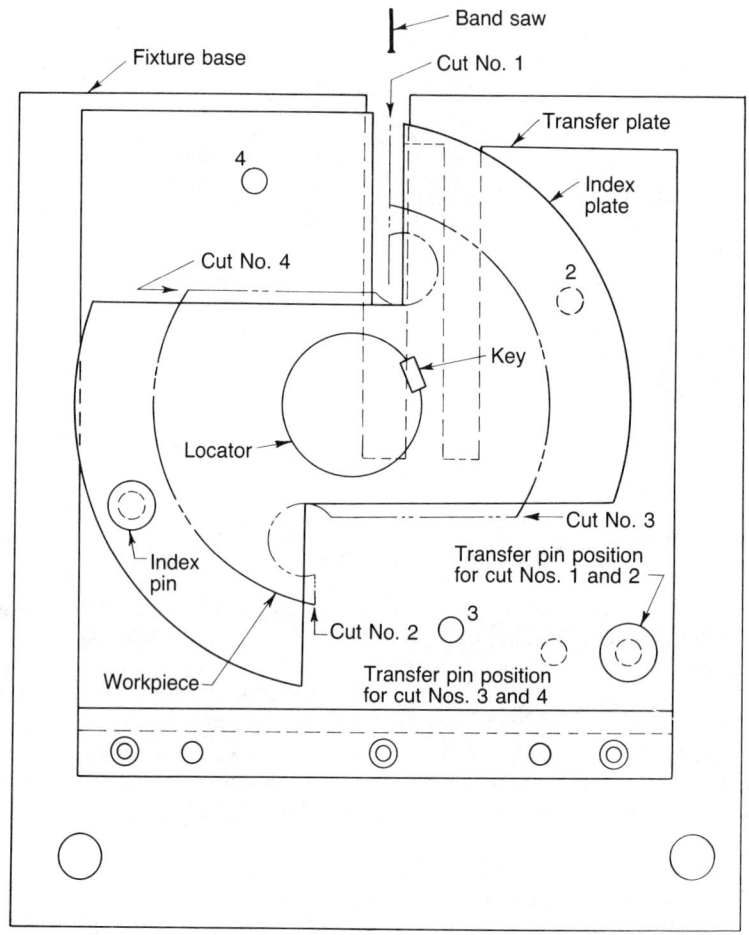

Fig. 11-12 Index plate and transfer plate for making four saw cuts. (*Courtesy The DoALL Co.*)

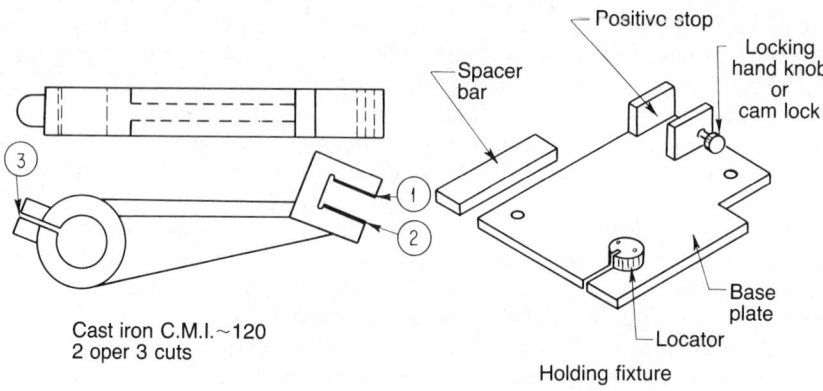

Fig. 11-13 Fixture for making three saw cuts with one setup. (*Courtesy The DoALL Co.*)

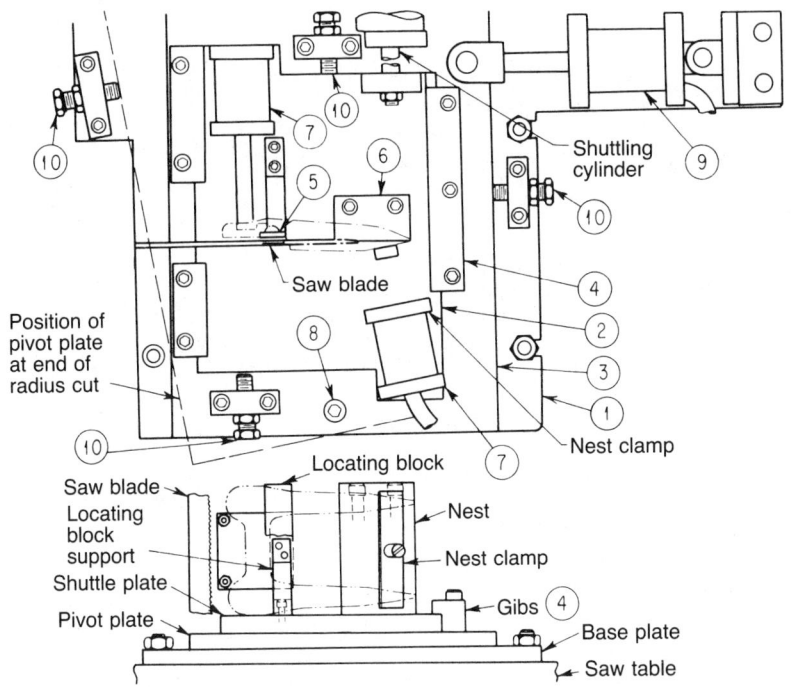

Position of
pivot plate
at end of
radius cut

Shuttling
cylinder

Saw blade

Nest clamp

Saw blade
Locating
block
support
Shuttle plate
Pivot plate

Locating block

Nest

Nest clamp

Gibs ④

Base plate

Saw table

Fig. 11-14 Slotting fixture. (*Courtesy The DoALL Co.*)

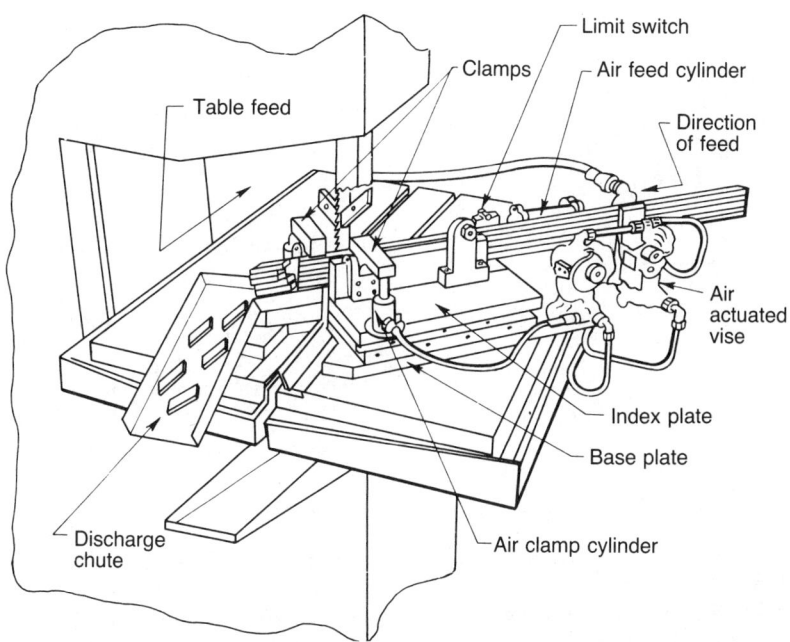

Limit switch

Clamps

Air feed cylinder

Table feed

Direction
of feed

Air
actuated
vise

Index plate

Base plate

Discharge
chute

Air clamp cylinder

Fig. 11-15 Air-operated feeding and clamping devices on a bar-stock sawing fixture.
(*Courtesy The DoALL Co.*)

11-13

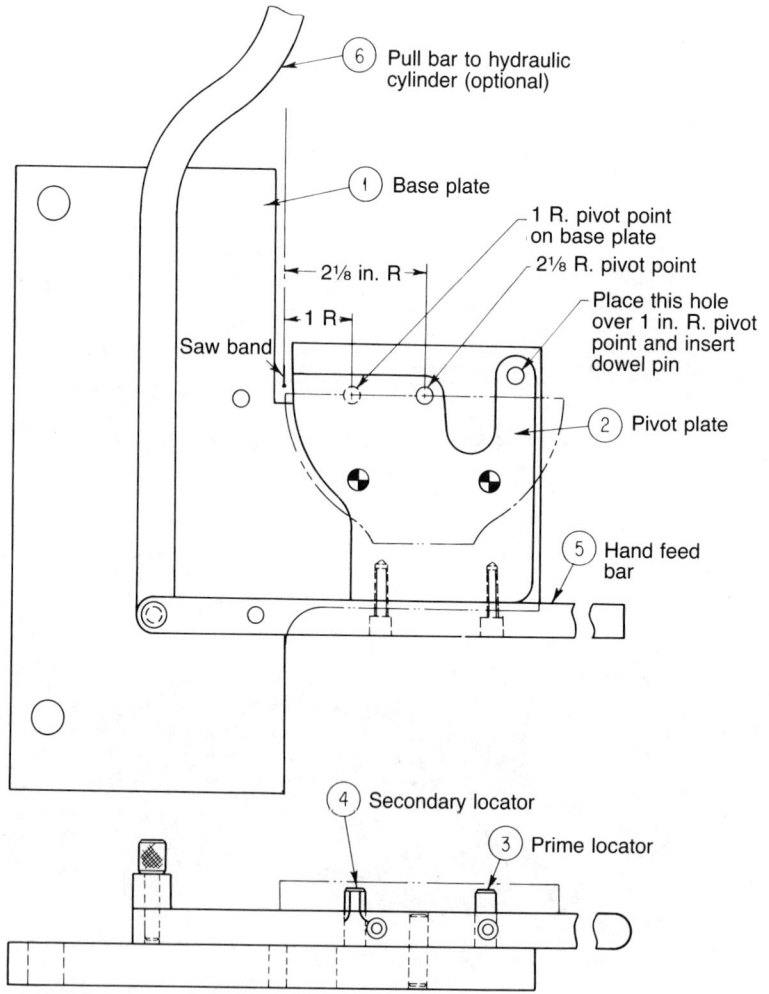

Fig. 11-16 Fixture for cutting blended radii. (*Courtesy The DoALL Co.*)

parallel to the bandsaw, as well as having a pivot point at a 90° angle to the band. The fixture of Fig. 11-17 produces a spiral surface with a bandsaw. A hinged pivot point is located on the true center line of the saw. The vertex of the tilting plane is always on the center line of the hinge pin. A vertical plate cam rotates the tilting plate a specified number of degrees for each inch of forward movement; this action produces the desired spiral.

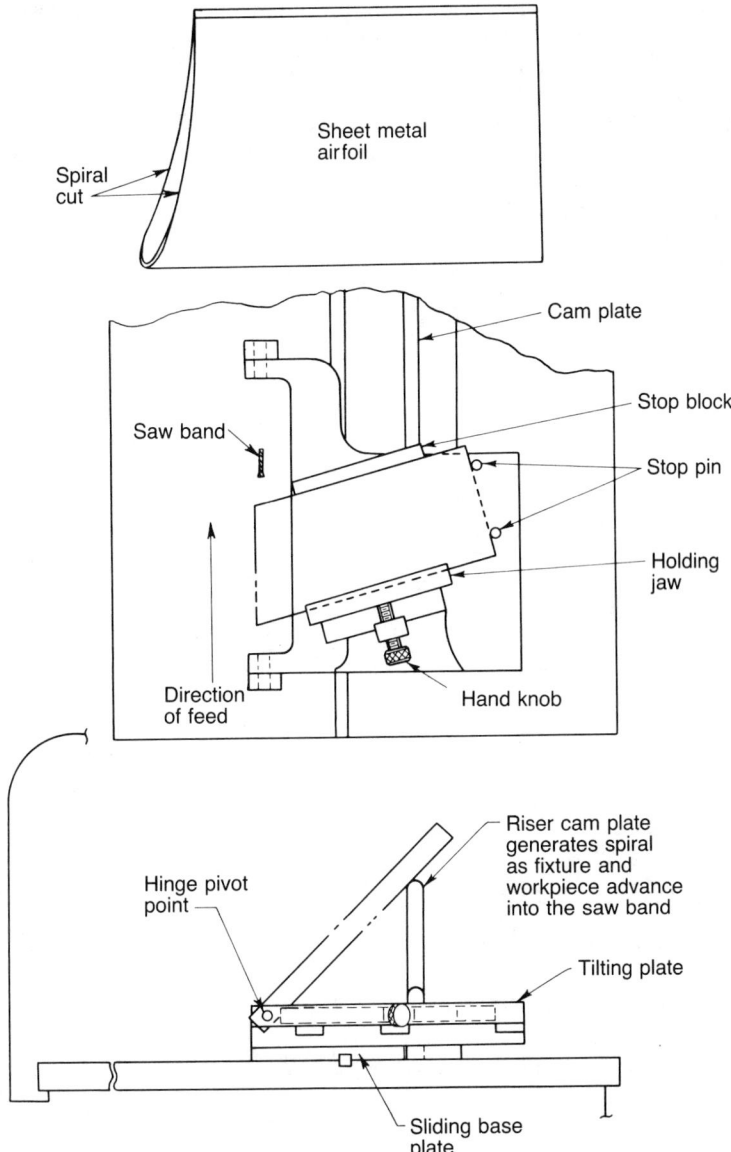

Fig. 11-17 Pivoting-plate fixture cuts spiral surface on an airfoil. (*Courtesy The DoALL Co.*)

HORIZONTAL BANDSAW FIXTURES

The fixturing of the horizontal bandsaw is usually limited to straight cuts on mill or structural shapes. Although many variations of straight cuts can be obtained, a standard vise is used for most applications. Fixtures and other holding devices may be designed to accommodate special conditions. Special jaws may be used on the standard vises to firmly grip round, hexagonal, or irregularly shaped bar stock. Should the workpiece be other than a mill shape, such as a forging or casting, automatic feeding and transfer fixtures can be designed.

Figure 11-18 illustrates a horizontal bandsawing machine with an automatic stock-feeding device. The workpiece is gripped by the rear vise which moves forward to the cutting position. Both vises grip the work at this position and during the cutting operation. Roller supports assist in feeding the work.

The clamping of round or tubular stock is shown in Fig. 11-19. An air cylinder pressing on the top of the stock holds it securely between the vise jaws.

In Fig. 11-20 connecting rods are manually loaded into two vertical loading chutes. The automatic fixture moves two pieces per stroke into the cutting position, where the ends of the two workpieces are split by the saw. The workpieces are held down by air cylinders during the sawing operation.

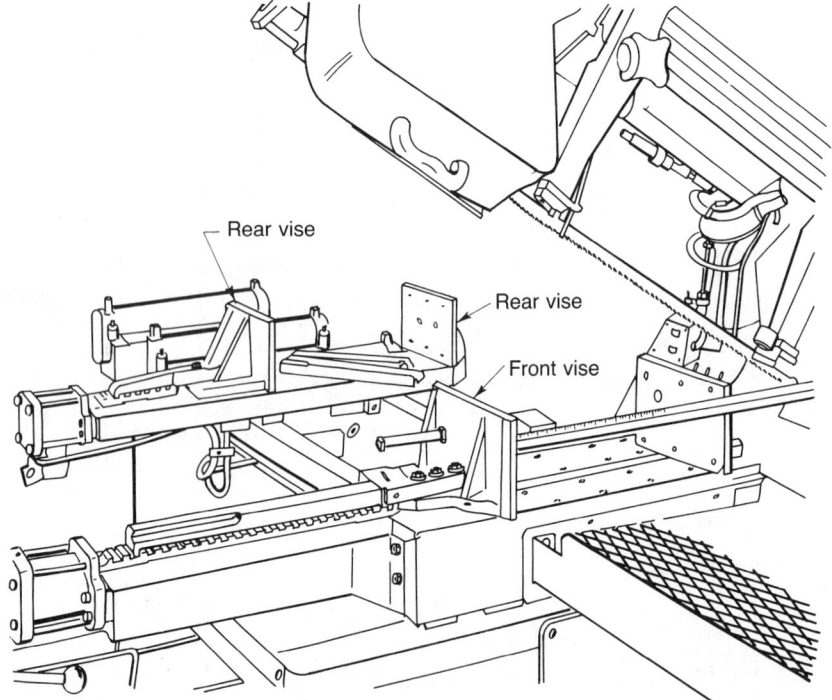

Fig. 11-18 Clamping arrangement on a horizontal bandsaw. (*Courtesy The DoALL Co.*)

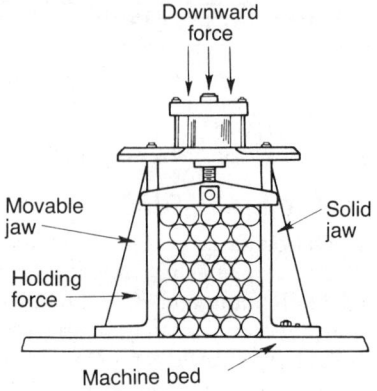

Fig. 11-19 Horizontal bandsaw fixture for stacking bar-stock. (*Courtesy The DoALL Co.*)

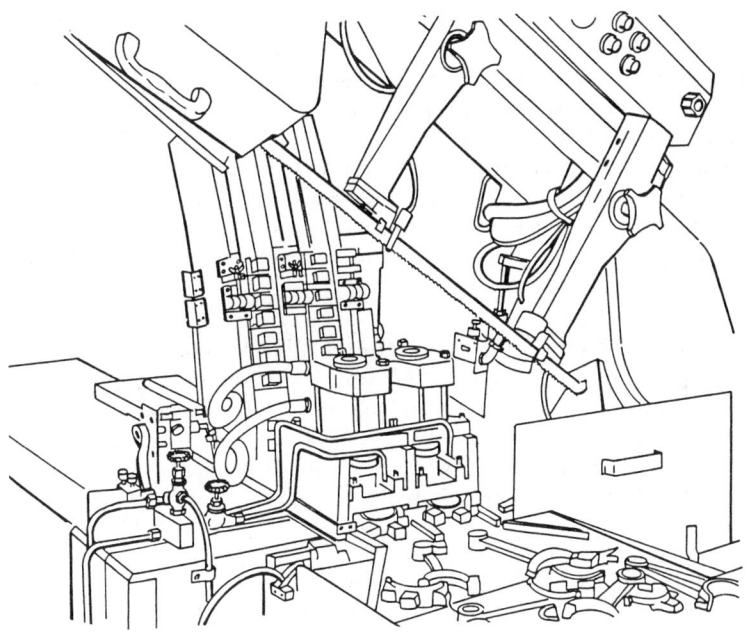

Fig. 11-20 Automatic splitting of connecting rods on a horizontal handsaw. (*Courtesy The DoALL Co.*)

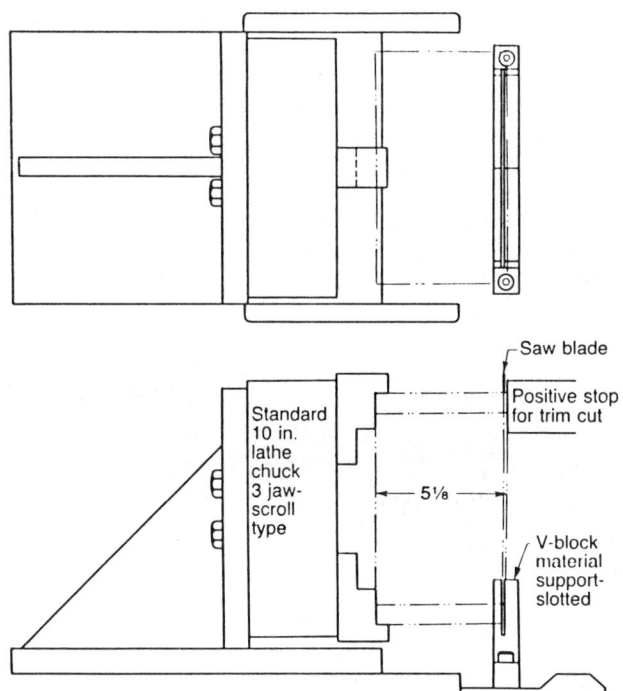

Saw blade

Positive stop
for trim cut

Standard
10 in.
lathe
chuck
3 jaw-
scroll
type

5⅛

V-block
material
support-
slotted

Fig. 11-21 Sawing fixture incorporating a standard lathe chuck. (*Courtesy The DoALL Co.*)

A standard three-jaw lathe chuck to hold 9 in. diameter tubing for slicing off sections is shown in Fig. 11-21. The chuck is mounted on an angle plate. The stock is brought to the machine in pieces 5⅛ in. (130 mm) long, clamped by the chuck jaws, and the fixture is manually advanced to a positive stop. The machine makes a trim cut to finish the rough end of the raw stock, retracts the saw blade, advances the fixture 0.945 in. (24.00 mm) and then cuts through the stock, repeating the cycle until five pieces are cut. The 0.045 in. (1.14 mm) saw kerf will result in pieces approximately 0.900 in. (22.86 mm) wide. The stock remaining in the chuck is manually reversed and the final cut made. A V-block slotted to clear the saw blade supports the stock against the downward force of the saw blade.

WORKHOLDING FOR CIRCULAR SAWING FIXTURES

Circular sawing is mainly used for straight, miter, and compound miter cuts on ferrous and non-ferrous extrusions, bar stock, and tubing. With manually operated machines most clamping is done one piece at a time with V-blocks, such as shown in Fig. 11-22, and standard machine or built-in vises. However, to increase production, workpieces can be gang-cut using the clamping methods shown in Fig. 11-23. For higher production rates, most machines are equipped with automatic feeding, clamping, and discharging systems, such as that shown in Fig. 11-24. In operation, the released infeed clamps are traversed back along the billet for a distance equal to the preset length to be cut, while the holding clamps hold the billet. Discharge clamps at this point are also open. Once the infeed clamps reach the preset length, they close and grip the billet. The holding clamps are then released and the billet is fed across the sawline until the infeed clamp is stopped by the holding clamp. At this point, all clamps are closed and grip the workpiece during cutoff. When cutting is complete, the infeed clamps are released and the holding clamps back the uncut portion of the billet away from the saw to prevent damage to the blade as the pivoting saw head retracts. Simultaneously, the discharge clamps release and discharge the slug onto a roller conveyor. The cycle is then repeated.

Automatic operations such as this often require magazines to deliver a steady supply of material to the machine feed and indexing unit. Three different systems are shown in Fig. 11-25. They include:

- The slanting magazine, *a*, which is used for automatic input of round, square, and flat bars.
- The chain magazine for automatic input of material with just about any profile.
- The bundle magazine for automatic input of tubes.

Combined automatic systems such as just described are almost always controlled by a

Fig. 11-22 V-block fixture for large diameters. (*Courtesy Western Tool and Manufacturing Co., Inc.*)

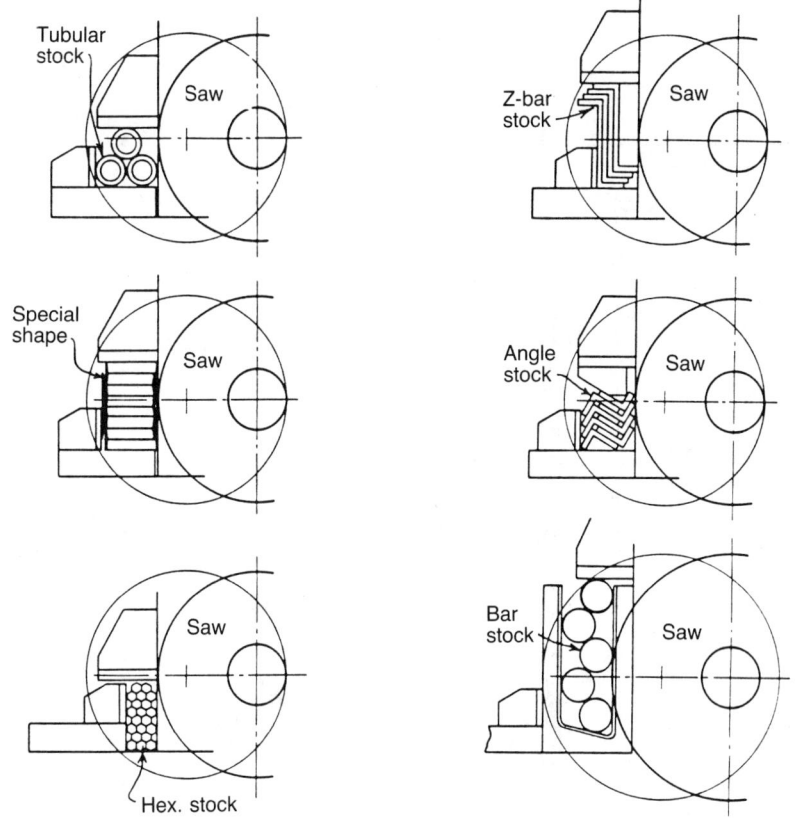

Fig. 11-23 Various methods of clamping different shaped material for cutting several parts in a single pass.

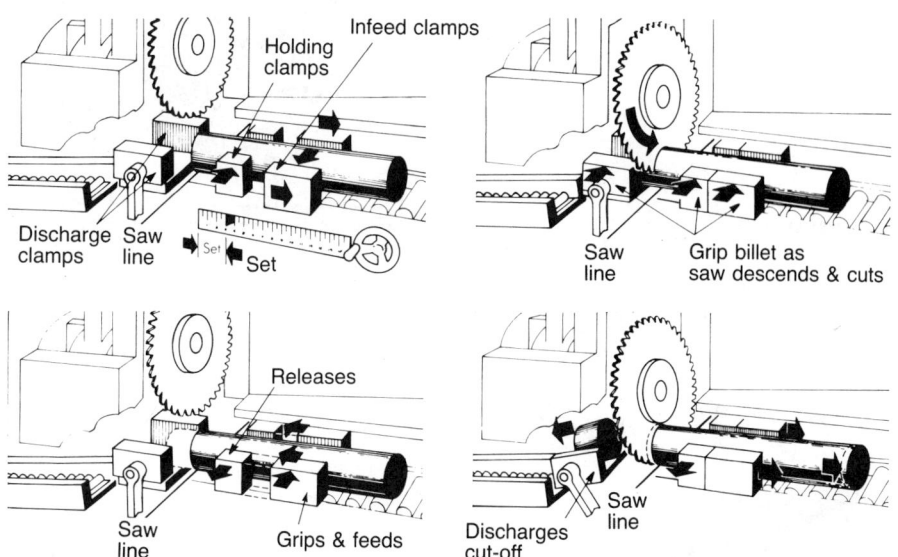

Fig. 11-24 Feeding, clamping, and discharging arrangement on a circular sawing system. (*Courtesy The Hill Acme Co.*)

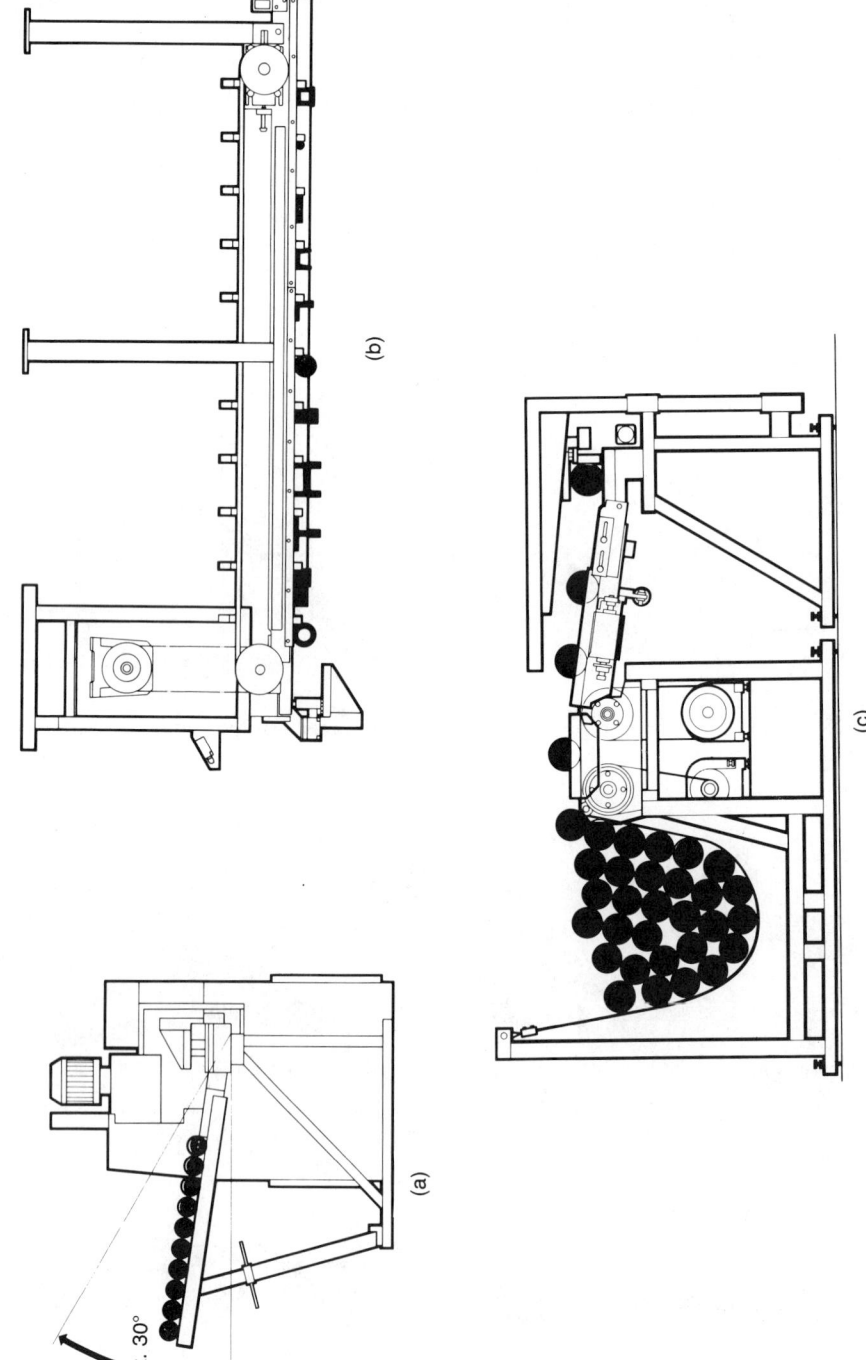

Fig. 11-25 Magazines for automatic input of material. (*Courtesy Eisele*)

CNC unit, which automatically controls all phases of the operation from the transference of the material (from the storage magazine to the feed and indexing unit), cutting to length, ejecting remnant pieces, and discharging the cut slugs into containers. The schematic for a CNC circular sawing system is shown in Fig. 11-26.

Other applications of circular sawing machines are shown in Figs. 11-27 thru 11-30. They include:

- Sawing with a circular sawing machine of odd-shaped workpieces held in simple fixtures, such as shown in Fig. 11-27.
- Combined cutting and milling operations as shown in Fig. 11-28.
- Sawing of fragile tubing and special shapes by holding them with form jaws (such as shown in Fig. 11-29) or special clamping jaws (shown in Fig. 11-30).
- Friction sawing.

WORKHOLDING FOR ABRASIVE CUTOFF MACHINES

With the exception of the rotary cutoff machine, bar stock, billets, and workpieces could be held in the same manner that would be used to hold them for comparable circular saw operations. With the rotary cutoff machine, workpieces would have to be held in a manner that would permit their rotation during the cutting operation.

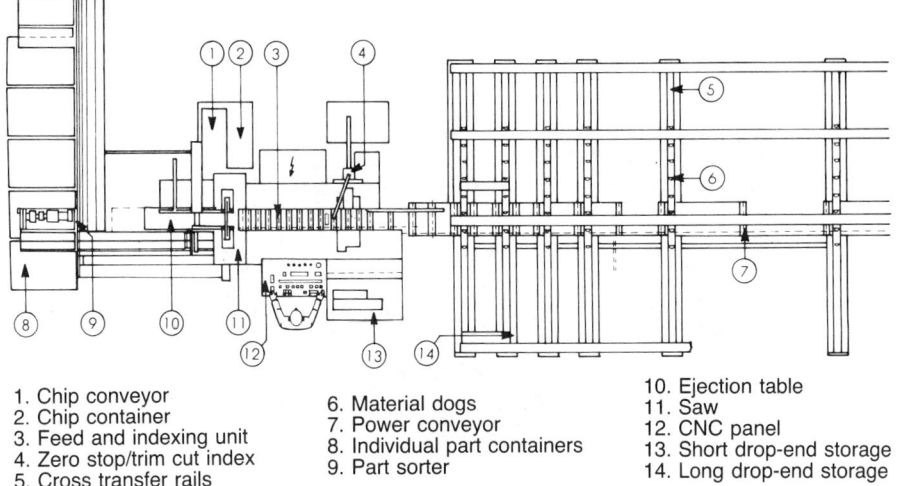

1. Chip conveyor
2. Chip container
3. Feed and indexing unit
4. Zero stop/trim cut index
5. Cross transfer rails
6. Material dogs
7. Power conveyor
8. Individual part containers
9. Part sorter
10. Ejection table
11. Saw
12. CNC panel
13. Short drop-end storage
14. Long drop-end storage

Fig. 11-26 CNC circular sawing system. (*Courtesy Kaltenback, Inc.*)

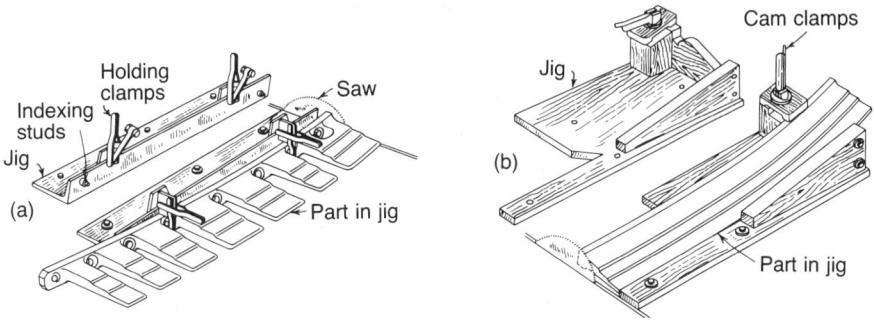

Fig. 11-27 Two special fixtures for sawing irregular shapes. (*Courtesy Northrop Aircraft, Inc.*)

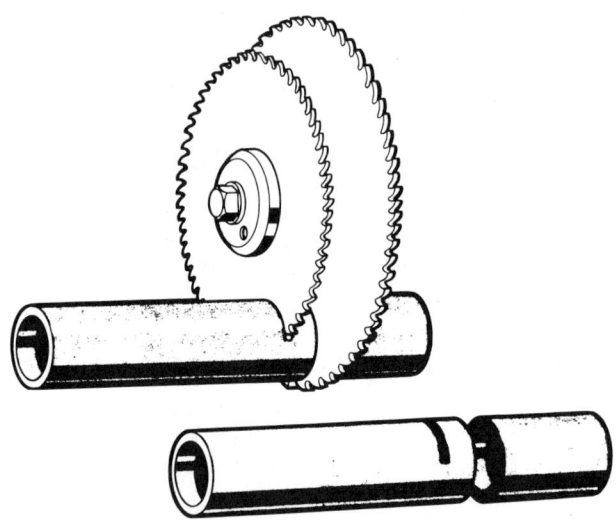

Fig. 11-28 Combined cutting-milling operation. (*Courtesy Eisele*)

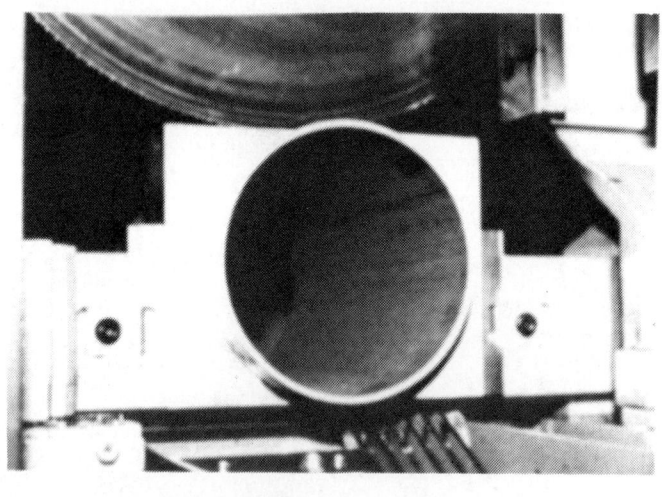

Fig. 11-29 Form jaws. (*Courtesy Eisele*)

Fig. 11-30 Special clamping jaws. (*Courtesy Eisele*)

CHAPTER 12
BROACHING FIXTURES

BROACHING[1]

Broaching is a process for internal or external machining of flat, round, or contoured surfaces. Machines of different types are used to push or pull a multitooth cutting tool or the workpiece in relation to each other to remove material. Each tooth on the cutting tool (broach) is generally higher than the preceding tooth. As a result, the depth of the cut increases as the operation progresses.

Generally, broaching machines differ from other machine tools in that they provide only cutting speed and force—the feed is built into the broach. Infeed, however, is provided by the workholding fixture for some applications. Another exception is helical broaching in which the machine provides rotary motion.

Broaching also differs from other machining processes in that roughing, semifinishing, and finishing teeth are often positioned along the axis of a single tool. This permits completing an operation in a single pass. Several types of broaches are sometimes used in combination to cut different surfaces on the workpiece simultaneously.

Broaching applications are of two major types: external (surface) broaching and internal broaching. Both types are used for machining configurations ranging from flat surfaces to complex contours on or in workpieces varying from small precision components to very ' .ge parts made from many different materials. For some applications both external and internal broaching are combined in one operation. While broaching is generally not considered to be a heavy stock removal operation, there are applications of surface broaching in which 1/2 in. (12.7 mm) or more of stock is removed in a single pass.

Workpieces with internal surfaces to be broached require a starting hole for insertion of the tool. Surfaces to be broached must be parallel to the direction of tool or work travel, but uniformly rotating sections such as helical gear teeth can be broached by rotating the tool or work as each moves in relation to the other. No obstructions such as protuberances on or in the workpieces can block the passage of the broach, but blind holes may be broached by limiting the travel of a series of short push-type broaches. A recess, however, larger in diameter than the hole to be broached must be provided at the bottom of the blind hole for chip space.

Surface broaching applications are practically unlimited. Any external form can be produced as long as the surfaces are in a straight line and unobstructed. Such forms include slots and keyways, flat and contoured surfaces, rack and gear teeth, and serrations.

An infinite number of forms can also be produced by internal broaching. In addition to machining round, square, rectangular, and other shaped holes, the process is used to cut contoured surfaces, keyways, splines, serrations, and gear teeth. This method is also used to rifle the bores of gun barrels. Starting holes for internal broaching are generally produced by casting, forging, punching, drilling, or boring.

VERTICAL SURFACE BROACHING MACHINES

Single-ram Broaching Machines. Standard vertical surface broaching machines with a single ram and downward cutting stroke are available in sizes from 1 ton (8.9 kN), 18 in. (457 mm) stroke to 50 ton (445 kN), 120 in. (3048 mm) stroke, and larger size machines are available on special order. Most are equipped with an in-and-out motion shuttle table or a tilting-type table that allows the operator to unload and reload during the return (upward) stroke of the machine ram. Vertical surface broaching machines are usually adaptable to automatic workpiece handling and most have power take-off or an auxiliary power supply for clamping and fixture motion. Machines equipped with wide rams can sometimes hold two or more sets of broaching tools to machine several workpieces simultaneously.

Dual-ram Broaching Machines. Dual-ram machines, such as the one shown in Fig. 12-1, operate like two single-ram vertical surface broaching machines mounted side by side in a common frame, with the two rams moving alternately upward and downward. These machines are preferable to single-ram machines for high production requirements because they permit one operator to load and unload in front of one ram on its return stroke while broaches on the other ram are in the cutting mode.

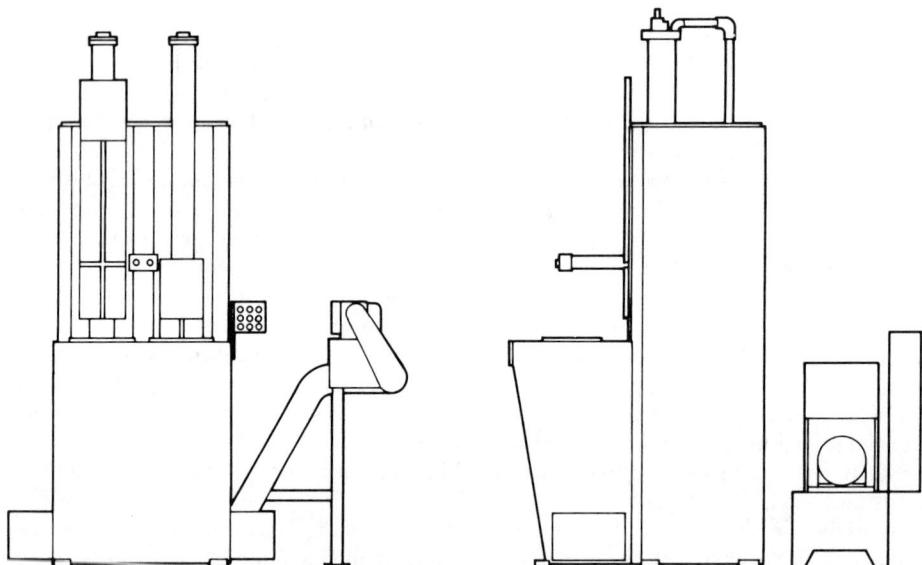

Fig. 12-1 Dual-ram vertical surface broaching machine with hydraulic drive. (*Courtesy Colonial Broach*)

VERTICAL INTERNAL BROACHING MACHINES

Standard vertical internal broaching machines are available in sizes from 2 ton (17.8 kN), 12 in. (305 mm) stroke to 75 ton (667 kN), 120 in. (3048 mm) stroke and are made in various styles for different applications and production requirements. The length of the broach tool to be used in relation to its cross section may determine whether it must be pulled or pushed through the workpiece because the tool is stronger in tension than compression.

Pushdown Broaching. Vertical internal broaching machines of the pushdown type are basically presses, most of which are of C-frame construction and hydraulically powered. In some cases, the broach is attached to the machine ram and is pushed downward and pulled upward through the workpiece—a process called strip broaching. For most applications, however, the broach drops into a catcher tray after being pushed through the workpiece or a lower powered slide is provided to lift the broach for retrieval.

Pushdown vertical internal broaching is normally used only for low-volume production or for applications requiring manual alignment of the broach with respect to the workpieces. Some high-volume applications exist, however, primarily for burnishing-type jobs. In all cases, stock removal is usually minimal.

Pullup Broaching. The pullup method was the original one used on vertical machines for internal broaching. Workpieces are manually or automatically placed in alignment with the broach pull-shank, and the broach is raised through both the workpiece and a thrust plate called a platen until the upper end of the broach engages an automatic broach puller. The upward pulling motion of the broach lifts the workpiece until it contacts a bushing fixture mounted on the platen. Cutting force holds the workpiece against the bushing face until the broach is pulled through, after which the workpiece drops onto a sloping surface for gravity ejection from the machine.

Standard pullup vertical machines for internal broaching are available in sizes from 6 ton (53.4 kN), 24 in. (610 mm) stroke to 50 ton (445 kN), 72 in. (1829 mm) stroke. Practically all of these machines are hydraulically powered and generally tooled to pull from one to six broaches simultaneously. Problems with chip disposal, cutting fluid application, and the handling of large and heavy workpieces, however, make them undesirable for some applications, and they are now specified less frequently.

Pulldown Broaching. The pulldown method of broaching is by far the most commonly used on vertical internal broaching machines. Pulldown broaching is often preferred to the pullup method because large workpieces can be handled more easily and because gravity helps the cutting fluid reach the cutting teeth and facilitates chip removal. Progressive work, in which several broaches are used in succession, is easier to perform, and the machines lend themselves well to automatic loading and unloading.

The construction of vertical internal broaching machines of the pulldown type varies to suit different applications. Small table-top machines often rely on the operator for manual handling of the workpieces and broaches and have one or two stations. High-speed machines usually range in size from 5 ton (44.5 kN), 24 in. (610 mm) stroke to 20 ton (178 kN), 48 in. (1219 mm) stroke and are available with one to four stations and cutting speeds of about 120 fpm (36.6 m/min).

Machines with a way-type main slide and a movable, upper broach-handling slide are the most common. The broach-handling slide travels in unison with the main slide throughout the cutting stroke for maximum broach support and alignment. Pulldown slide-type vertical internal broaching machines generally range in size from 4 ton (35.6 kN), 24 in. (610 mm) stroke to 75 ton (667 kN), 120 in. (3048 mm) stroke, with one to six stations and cutting speeds to 100 fpm (30.5 m/min). Most are hydraulically powered, and a few have electro-mechanical drives.

Pulldown slide-type and high-speed vertical internal broaching machines are usually equipped with shuttle tables that move in and out or with automatic loading/unloading fixtures. Floor pits or operator platforms are required for machines having strokes longer than 24 in. (610 mm).

VERTICAL COMBINATION BROACHING MACHINES

Vertical combination (universal) broaching machines feature a swing-away or detachable toolhandling slide for internal broaching and a machined slide face for surface broach tooling. On three-way machines the broach can be pushed down for broaching external surfaces or pushed or pulled down for cutting internal surfaces.

These machines are of the slide type, and most are hydraulically powered. They are generally available in sizes from 4 ton (35.6 kN), 18 in. (457 mm) stroke to 15 ton (133.4 kN), 36 in. (914 mm) stroke, with cutting speeds to 50 fpm (15.2 m/min). The combination machines are usually employed for job shop or multiple operation requirements.

HORIZONTAL INTERNAL BROACHING MACHINES

At one time, horizontal machines were the predominant type used for internal broaching. Today, however, with the high cost of floor space and a generally lower productivity rate compared to vertical machines, they represent less than 10% of the broaching machines purchased. They are still used where ceiling heights prohibit vertical machines, for large and heavy broaching tools that require in-line pulling, for small tools that require manual handling, for some special low-profile equipment that is adaptable to automated transfer lines, and for short-run job shop applications.

Horizontal internal broaching machines have a box-type framework with a platen on one end. The platen is equipped with a clearance hole to allow the broaches to be pulled through the stationary workpieces in a horizontal direction. A pulling head rides on ways within the machine frame and is aligned with the hole in the platen. Most modern machines have optional outboard and inboard broach supports. They can be supplied with automatic equipment for broach handling and workpiece loading and unloading.

Sizes of horizontal machines for internal broaching generally range from 1 ton (8.9 kN), 18 in. (457 mm) stroke to 100 ton (89 kN), 120 in. (3048 mm) stroke. The first machines of this type were screw driven; however, this type drive is now obsolete. Most machines are now hydraulically powered. The hydraulic cylinder is mounted on the machine frame, at the opposite end from the platen, and aligned with the pulling hole and head to provide in-line pulling force. Some machines are electro-mechanically driven.

HORIZONTAL SURFACE BROACHING MACHINES

In a class by themselves, large horizontal machines for broaching external surfaces are used extensively by the automotive industry for heavy stock removal. Surfaces are machined on large parts such as cast engine blocks, cylinder heads, manifolds, and bearing clusters, with stock removals of 1/4 in. (6.4 mm) or more using carbide broach inserts. Close tolerances are maintained and smooth surface finishes produced, and the machines have proven to be reliable and efficient with little downtime for toolchanging and maintenance.

One-way and Two-way Broaching Machines. These horizontal surface broaching machines are made in single-station, one-way models that cut in one direction only and in two-way models that are capable of cutting in both directions. Workpieces are cradled in swing-up fixtures. On two-way machines for V-type and in-line engine blocks, the pan-rail, half-bore, and bearing-lock surfaces are broached as the machine ram moves in one direction. Then an automatic transfer mechanism moves the block to a rollover fixture that rotates the casting 180°. The head joint face or both bank faces on the block are broached on the return stroke of the ram.

Horizontal surface broaching machines were originally powered hydraulically and available in sizes to 30 ton (267 kN), 120 in. (3048 mm) stroke, with cutting speeds from 30 to 100 fpm (9 to 30.5 m/min). Most machines today are driven electro-mechanically and are available in sizes over 100 tons (890 kN), with strokes to 30 ft (9 m) and speeds to 200 fpm (61 m/min) for cast iron or 300 fpm (91 m/min) for aluminum.

Continuous Broaching Machines. Continuous chain-type surface broaching machines consist of a horizontal framework having a drive sprocket mounted at one end and an idler sprocket at the opposite end. These sprockets support and power a pair of parallel, continuous chains which move workholding fixture carriers suspended between them. The carriers are guided by a set of ways within the machine frame, and the broaching tools are mounted in a tunnel on top of the machine (see Fig. 12-2).

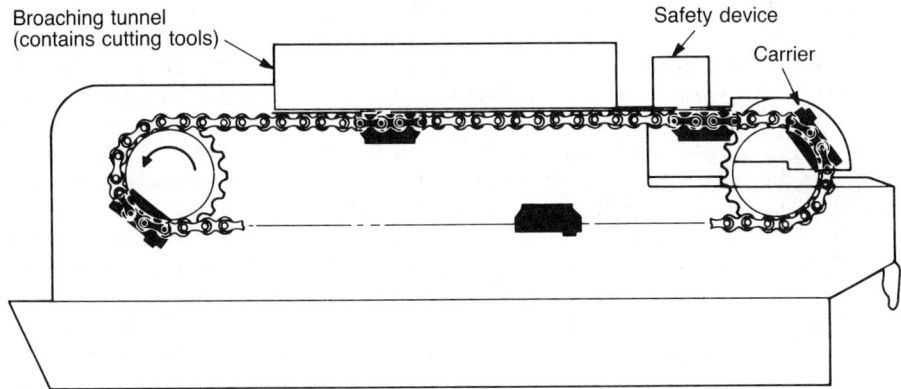

Fig. 12-2 Schematic of a continuous surface broaching machine. Workpieces are loaded on chain-driven carriers that move them through the broaching tunnel.

Workpieces to be broached are manually or automatically placed in the moving fixtures at one end of the machine. Clamping of the workpieces in the fixtures is generally done automatically, and safety devices can be provided to automatically stop the machine if misaligned workpieces or workpieces with excessive stock are detected before they enter the broaching tunnel.

Properly aligned workpieces with the correct amount of stock are pulled through the stationary broachholder assembly (tunnel) to complete the broaching operation. The workpieces are automatically unclamped and ejected from the fixtures by gravity at the other end of the machine.

Production rates from continuous broaching machines are high, usually from four to ten times that of vertical surface broaching machines. This is because of the continuous cutting action and elimination of the noncutting portion of other broaching machine cycles. Productivity from these machines can also be varied by changing the speed of the chain or increasing or decreasing the number of fixtures used; the maximum number of fixtures is limited by the length and tonnage capacity of the machine.

High production requirements are necessary, however, to justify the high cost of these machines. Their use is also usually restricted to workpieces small enough to pass through the tunnel and sturdy enough to permit gravity ejection without damage. Automatic loading and unloading equipment is available for most workpieces.

While stationary tooling is most common on these continuous machines, one variation, used for heavy stock removal, is to mount the broaches on the chain-driven carriers to cut a stationary workpiece. This adaptation has been used with the chains operating horizontally (over, under, or alongside the stationary workpiece) and vertically, with the chains making one complete revolution each cycle. Chain lengths up to 480 in. (12 to 192 mm) are possible. Continuous broaching machines designed for this modified method are generally restricted to special applications because of the high cost of the equipment.

Conventional continuous machines are generally available with ratings from 2.5 to 60 tons (22.2 to 533.8 kN) and broach tunnels from 18 to 250 in. (457 to 6350 mm) long. Cutting speeds are usually adjustable through change gears from 12 to 60 sfm (3.7 to 18.3 m/min); some continuous machines have d-c motor drives that provide infinitely adjustable speeds within a given range. One manufacturer offers machines with hydrostatic hydraulic drive that permits variable speeds and constant torque.

SPECIAL MACHINES

Pot Broaching Machines. Pot broaching derives its name from the hollow surface-type broaching tool assembly, called the pot, which is used to surround a workpiece for broaching external contours, such as gear teeth, splines, slots, and cam surfaces, in a single pass.

One of the older methods of pot broaching consists of mounting the workpiece on a post-type fixture and pushing the pot broach assembly, which is mounted on the ram of a vertical surface broaching machine, downward to cut the part. With this method, work unloading is automatic but loading is done manually and can slow the operation.

Modern machines designed specifically for pot broaching have a stationary pot assembly. Three types of machines are available: pushdown, pushup, and pullup. Pushup pot broaching, in which workpieces are pushed up through the stationary pot, offers advantages of chips falling, by gravity, away from the tool and workpiece; simple work feeding; easy loading and unloading; and simplified toolchanging.

Pullup pot broaching, in which workpieces are pulled up through a stationary tooling pot with a pull head, permits broaching of parts having deeper teeth and wider faces by using longer tools. These machines, however, must be higher than pushup machines because the upper end of the pull rod has to be retracted below the workpiece with a retriever and the lower end has to be pulled up past the top of the pot for unloading.

Most pot broaching machines are hydraulically powered and generally range in size from 1 ton (8.9 kN), 12 in. (305 mm) stroke to 50 tons (445 kN), 48 in. (1219 mm) stroke. Cutting speeds usually vary from 30 to 120 fpm (9.1 to 36.6 m/min), but special machines are available with speeds to 240 fpm (73.2 m/min).

Other Special Broaching Machines. Many other types of broaching machines are available for specific applications. One example is short-stroke vertical broaching machines with dial index tables for cutting internal or external shapes on workpieces having interference surfaces that prevent passing conventional broaches completely over or through the workpieces. Tooling stations on the index table hold a series of broaches, either punch or ring-type, and the workpiece is retained in a fixture attached to the machine ram. As each broach station is indexed under the workpiece, the ram strokes downward to cut and upward to strip the workpiece from the tool. This cycle is repeated until the last broach has completed the operation.

Most machines of this type are hydraulically powered, with ratings of 4 to 30 tons (35.6 to 267 kN) and strokes of about 6 in. (152 mm). The machines can generally be furnished with automatic loaders and unloaders and lend themselves well to in-line automation. They are particularly suitable for broaching splines or serrations not more than 0.070 in. (1.78 mm) deep in thin tubular parts. It is claimed that one broaching machine with fully automatic work handling can replace four to nine gear shapers.

Rotary Broaching Machines. Machines for rotary broaching are considered special (except for the revacycle machines made by the Gleason Works). The automatic Revacycle machines are classified as gear-cutting machines, but actually perform broaching operations. They are widely used in the production of straight bevel gears.

Some special rotary broaching machines have the broaches rotating on a faceplate and the workpiece held stationary in a fixture. A few double-ended machines have been built for higher production with a faceplate holding broaches mounted on each end of the machine spindle. The broaches on one plate are staggered 180° with respect to those on the other plate so that cutting can be done at one end of the machine while the other end is being unloaded and reloaded. Another variation for rotary broaching consists of mounting workpieces on the periphery of a rotating disc to carry them past stationary broaches.

Portable and Other Special Machines. Some smaller broaching machines are available mounted on wheels for moving to various jobs. Hand-held, portable broaching units are used in the marine, construction, and aircraft industries to enlarge, relieve stresses, and improve the accuracy of previously drilled holes in large assemblies that cannot be brought to broaching machines. Spiral and rifling-type broaching machines are also available.

TOOLING FORCES

Broaching force requirements, which determine the tonnage ratings of the machines needed for specific applications, depend on many variables. These include the composition, hardness, and condition of the material to be broached; the amount of stock to be removed; the stroke length and cut per tooth; the broach strength and design (pitch, chip space, gullet geometry, and use of chipbreakers and shear angles); the sharpness of the broach; and the cutting fluid used.

Since the cut per tooth and the material to be broached are the major variables affecting force requirements, the minimum force needed can be approximated by using the following formulas and the values for the broaching constant presented in Table 12-1. The safety factors used in calculating broach strengths are generally sufficient to compensate for variations in actual force requirements.

For surface broaches:

$$F = WNRC \tag{1}$$

For round-hole internal broaches:

$$F = 3.14\ DNRC \tag{2}$$

For splined-hole broaches:

$$F = NSWRC \tag{3}$$

where:

F = minimum pulling or pushing force required, lbf (kgf, kilogram-force)
W = width of cut per tooth or spline, in. (mm)
N = maximum number of broach teeth engaged in workpiece
R = rise or cut per tooth, in. (mm)
C = broaching constant from Table 12-1 (Note: To conserve space, values for C in Table 12-1 are given in ksi and kgf/mm^2. When working in the U.S. customary system of units, values of C given in ksi should be converted to psi for use in the formula 1 ksi = 1000 psi. When working in the metric system, values of C given in kgf/mm^2 can be used in the formula as given.)
D = hole diameter before broaching, in. (mm)
S = the number of splines (for splined holes)

WORKHOLDING FOR BROACHING

Properly designed workholding fixtures are necessary for successful broaching. They must be rigid enough to prevent movement of the workpieces and minimize deflection under high forces. The cutting forces in broaching are generally higher than for other machining processes because of the number of cutting edges simultaneously in contact with the workpiece. Insufficient rigidity will result in vibration and tool chatter, causing poor surface finishes, inaccuracies, and possible tool breakage or short life.

Good fixture design can provide substantial cost savings by reducing work handling time and labor costs. Other benefits include improved product quality (closer tolerances and smoother finishes), longer tool life, and improved operator safety.

Principal functions of fixtures are to accurately locate and rigidly hold workpieces during broaching. Other functions include facilitating loading and unloading; providing means for chip clearance and disposal; allowing free access of cutting fluid to the broach teeth; and for some applications, guiding broaches.

TABLE 12-1
Typical Values for Broaching Constant C Used to Calculate Minimum Forces
Needed to Broach Various Materials

Cut Per Tooth in. (mm)	C, ksi (kgf/mm²) Material to be Broached							
	Mild Steels	Alloy Steels	Cast Irons	Malleable Irons	Aluminum	Brass	Bronze	Diecastings
0.0005 (0.013)	900 (633)	1100 (773)	816 (574)	726 (510)	375 (264)	250 (176)	412 (290)	320 (225)
0.001 (0.03)	655 (460)	890 (626)	610 (429)	522 (367)	275 (193)	208 (146)	333 (234)	248 (174)
0.0015 (0.038)	552 (388)	770 (541)	510 (359)	445 (313)	262 (184)	196 (138)	288 (203)	234 (164)
0.002 (0.05)	490 (344)	680 (478)	445 (313)	390 (274)	231 (162)	180 (127)	250 (176)	221 (155)
0.0025 (0.063)	422 (311)	617 (434)	404 (284)	361 (254)	210 (148)	168 (118)	227 (160)	200 (141)
0.003 (0.08)	390 (274)	565 (397)	361 (254)	313 (220)	192 (135)	159 (112)	212 (149)	194 (136)
0.004 (0.10)	361 (254)	532 (374)	336 (236)	290 (204)	181 (127)	150 (105)	198 (139)	190 (124)
0.005 (0.13)	340 (239)	500 (351)	313 (220)	270 (190)	170 (120)	141 (99)	183 (129)	186 (131)
0.0075 (0.190)	330 (232)	460 (323)	280 (197)	250 (176)	156 (110)	133 (94)	168 (118)	181 (127)
0.010 (0.25)	315 (221)	440 (309)	270 (190)	240 (169)	150 (105)	127 (89)	160 (112)	176 (124)
0.0125 (0.317)	313 (220)	422 (297)	261 (184)	236 (166)	143 (101)	123 (86)	154 (108)	172 (121)
0.015-0.020 (0.38-0.51)	294 (207)	413 (290)	261 (184)	236 (166)	140 (98)	120 (84)	150 (105)	172 (121)

(General Broach and Engineering Co.)

12-8

For successful broaching, all elements of the broached surface must remain parallel with the broach axis; there must be no obstructions in the plane of the broached surfaces; and the walls of the part being broached must be sufficiently heavy or adequately supported to withstand the pressures of the operations. Compliance with these prerequisites makes broaching-fixture design more exacting and difficult than the design of many other types of fixtures.

The broaching-fixture designer should have a layout of each broaching machine in his or her plant. Over this layout, the designer can make a sketch showing the important parts of the fixture, the workpiece, the broach bar, the machine elements related to the setup, and the necessary accessories such as pullers, broach-bar ends, retrievers, etc. From this layout, the fixture designer can determine the clearances necessary for the broach bar or broach-bar holder.

Because of the high pressures involved in the broaching operation, the workpiece should be supported by fixed stops (positive locking cams or wedges with locking angles), never directly by air or hydraulic pressure. Pneumatic or hydraulic cylinders or machine-table devices should be used only to move clamps or back-up devices into position.

TYPES OF FIXTURES[2]

Fixtures for broaching can vary from simple locating plates or bushings to complex devices. The major types of fixtures include fixed (stationary), shuttle, swivel, tilt, indexing, and universal. Fixtures must be of equalizing design when square bearing surfaces are not available on the workpieces. Broaching fixtures can be operated manually, by power with manual control, or automatically, interlocked with the operation of the machine ram.

Universal or multipurpose fixtures can be a major factor in reducing broaching costs. They are especially desirable for short-run production requirements of families of similar parts. In some cases, only interchangeable jaws, collets, clamps, or locator nests have to be changed to broach different parts. In other applications, subassemblies may have to be replaced. For cylindrical parts, a V-shaped locating nest can accommodate a range of different diameters.

To meet high production requirements, automatic fixtures are often used in conjunction with automatic loading and unloading equipment. Automation devices commonly employed include magazine loaders, vibratory hoppers, workpiece ejectors, and industrial robots.

FIXTURE COMPONENTS

Whenever possible, broaching fixtures should be designed so that the cutting forces are aligned with the machine ram. In addition, all fixture components should have smooth internal surfaces without holes, corners, or pockets that might trap chips. The fixtures should nest the workpieces as deeply as possible so that only the areas to be broached are exposed.

Locating pads, blocks, or pins should be directly opposite the surfaces to be broached; support pads or jacks should be as close as possible to the surfaces to be broached and should be easily adjustable and replaceable. Previously machined surfaces on the workpieces should be used for locating and support purposes. If this is not possible, some means of adjustment must be provided to compensate for irregularities.

Wear surfaces of the fixture should be hardened and replaceable, and adjustability is often desirable. Workholding clamps for the fixtures should be simple and foolproof; they should be designed for easy operation and should provide room for easy loading and unloading. The clamps are generally of cam, screw, toggle, or wedge design, with manual or power operation.

FIXTURES FOR SURFACE BROACHING

The fixtures used for broaching external surfaces are generally subjected to higher forces than those used for internal broaching. Forces are exerted both parallel and perpendicular to the stroke, and if shear-angled teeth are used on the broach, in a direction transverse to the tool stroke.

In most cases, except when the broach is stripped back over the broached surface, a major requirement for surface broaching fixtures is removal or retraction of the workpiece from the broach path after the operation to allow the broach to return to its starting position. Many vertical surface broaching machines are equipped with automatic table retraction, which is interlocked with operation of the machine ram. If not, however, a fixed, tilting, shuttling, swiveling, or indexing fixture must be used.

Vise-type fixed (stationary) fixtures are manually unclamped, unloaded, and reloaded after the machine ram returns to its starting position. Manually operated, stationary fixtures are slower than other types but are suitable for short-run application. They are not used extensively, however, because the need for the operator to place his or her hands in the cutting zone can be unsafe.

Tilting, trunnion, or tip-up fixtures, as well as shuttling or swiveling fixtures, permit faster production because workpieces can be loaded and unloaded while the machine ram is returning. Such fixtures can be operated manually, semiautomatically, or automatically, with air or hydraulic power.

For deep surface cuts, which normally require a long-stroke broaching machine, it may be more economical to make multiple passes with a shorter stroke broaching machine at high speeds. This is done with a reciprocating infeed table, synchronized with the machine ram operation, that can be programmed to automatically move the workpiece in and out of the broach path for the preset number of roughing passes required. Then a longer stroke finishing pass can bring the cut to the required depth. To widen the same cut, a crossfeed can be used to shift the fixture sideways and the infeed cycle can be repeated. To produce several slots in the same workpiece, an indexing fixture can be used. Cuts to about 1½ in. (38 mm) deep and 12 in. (305 mm) wide can be broached in this way with standard equipment.

Rotary indexing fixtures permit the continuous cycling of single-ram machines. Some stations on such fixtures can be unloaded and reloaded while a workpiece held at another station is being broached. Rotary indexing fixtures can be used in conjunction with in-out shuttle fixtures for additional clearance.

FIXTURES FOR INTERNAL BROACHING

Forces exerted on fixtures used for internal broaching are generally less complex than those exerted on fixtures used for surface broaching. The major forces are usually in the direction of broach travel. The broach often locates itself, and the workpiece absorbs most of the force, which is directly transferred to the broaching fixture and machine platen.

Simple internal broaching operations can often be performed without a fixture and with no workpiece clamping. A shouldered bushing is sometimes placed in the central hole in a faceplate. The workpiece bears against the face of the bushing and is held firmly in place by the cutting pressure, thereby eliminating the need for clamping. The pilot on the broach centers the workpiece.

For round workpieces, a rough-locating counterbore can be provided near the faceplate bushing for easier positioning. If the end surface of the workpiece that will bear against the bushing face or the counterbore in the bushing is not square, a spherical swiveling washer can be provided in the bushing.

STANDARD INTERCHANGEABLE FIXTURES[3]

The general-purpose workholding and handling systems (modular broach tooling) shown in Figs. 12-4 thru 12-19 can be used with a machine such as that shown in Fig.

12-3. The fixtures are available in different sizes to accommodate the different ranges of similar work requirements. These standard, interchangeable broach and fixture modules can be quickly combined and assembled for routine broaching on many different parts. Individual workholding collets, jaws, adaptors, or locator nests only are required for each workpiece, and these can usually be fabricated with ordinary toolroom equipment. Broaching and workholding operations can be manual, semi-automatic or fully automatic.

In addition, when using any of the manual or automatic modular tooling systems with a broaching machine such as that shown in Fig. 12-3, an air/hydraulic system automatically interlocks the ram motion with the fixture clamping/unclamping and work positioning functions. In most cases, automatic part ejection can be provided using a pneumatic cylinder with a push rod which is activated automatically after the unclamping function occurs.

The fast changeover time—and consequent reduction in machine downtime—afforded by modular broach tooling makes them ideal for ''just-in-time'' (JIT) manufacturing.

Fixtures for External Broaching. The basic broaching tooling modules for external broaching include:

Vise Fixtures. Manually-operated, fixed-position units, such as shown in Fig. 12-4, can be used for broaching simple flats or side slots on a variety of parts. Very often, when broaching the sides or ends of shafts, a single V-nest can accommodate a wide range of diameters up to 2½ in. A universal orientation device can be provided for this fixture to precisely position the workpiece for a second adjacent cut. Vise fixturing can be mounted on shuttle tables.

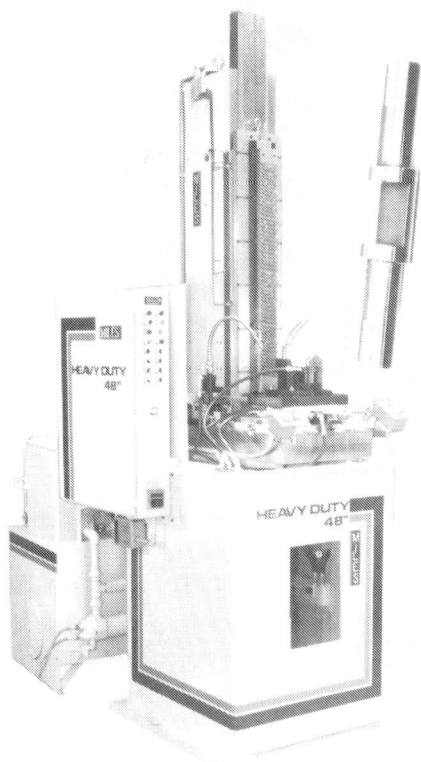

Fig. 12-3 Heavy duty broach. *(Courtesy Ty Miles, Inc.)*

12-11

Front-load Fixtures. These fixtures provide easier access for reloading (see Fig. 12-5). They can be mounted on shuttle tables to provide simple and easy loading/unloading for slot or straddle broaching. When equipped with a V nest, they also can accommodate a wide range of part diameters.

Manual Tilt Tables. These tables (see Fig. 12-6) are designed for use with a vise or collet index fixture to permit easy loading and unloading of the workpiece away from the path of the broach while the broach is returning to its start position—with a resultant reduction in cycle time. This fixture is ideal for slab broaching flats and slots, plus straddle broaching (making parallel cuts on adjacent or opposite sides of a workpiece).

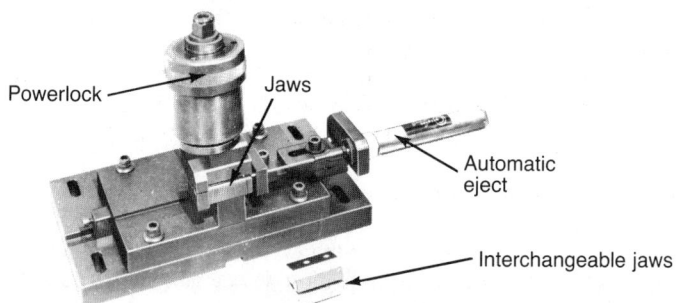

Fig. 12-4 Vise fixtures. *(Courtesy Ty Miles, Inc.)*

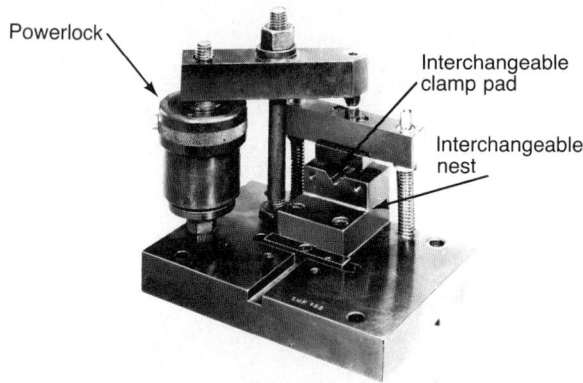

Fig. 12-5 Front-load fixture. *(Courtesy Ty Miles, Inc.)*

Fig. 12-6 Manual tilt table. *(Courtesy Ty Miles, Inc.)*

No. "1" Manual Collet Index Fixtures. The fixture shown in Fig. 12-7 is used to expedite indexing or ordinary workpiece holding. In the figure, it is shown mounted on a manual tilt table. Interchangeable index plates permit manual indexing of the workpiece to the desired position for each cut. An interchangeable anvil can be provided to support the workpiece. Long workpieces can be fed through from the back of the fixture, making the tilt table unnecessary. The standard 1 in. diameter size uses a 5C fixed-position collet arranged to prevent axial movement of the workpiece during the broach stroke. Other collets can be adapted to the fixture.

Manual Universal Shuttle Tables. These tables (see Fig. 12-8) can be used with various fixtures as shown to permit fast easy loading and unloading of the workpiece while the machine ram is returning to its start position. A thumb switch built into the toggle handle permits the operator to manually position the slide and activate the ram with one hand. For safety, his other hand must be on the machine palm button. In this way, the synchronized workpiece clamping and ram travel sequence occurs while the operator's hands are away from the pinch area.

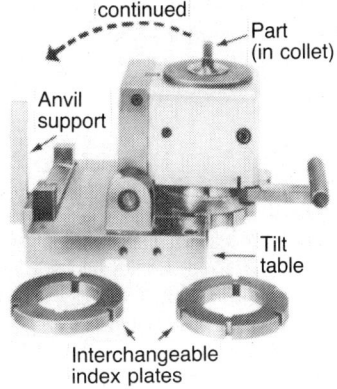

continued
Part (in collet)
Anvil support
Tilt table
Interchangeable index plates

Fig. 12-7 Manual collet index fixture. *(Courtesy Ty Miles, Inc.)*

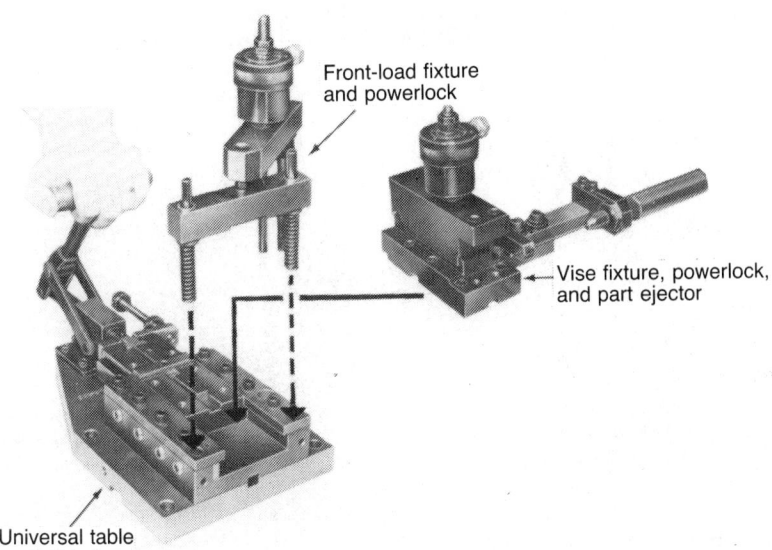

Front-load fixture and powerlock
Vise fixture, powerlock, and part ejector
Universal table

Fig. 12-8 Manual universal shuttle table. *(Courtesy Ty Miles, Inc.)*

Broach-Rolls. The unit shown in Fig. 12-9 is used for threading, knurling, or serration operations using standard flat dies. In the figure, tooling for a threading operation is shown mounted on a 12 in. stroke machine. In operation, a movable die mounted on the machine ram engages and rolls the workpiece against a stationary die mounted on the fixture. Knurling and serration operations are performed in the same manner. Cycle time is about one second. With manual loading and unloading, production rates are about 1000 per hour. This process can be automated.

Automatic Shuttle Tables. Tables, such as shown in Fig. 12-10, are used for mounting various manual or automatic fixtures so that workpieces can be loaded and automatically "shuttled" into a precise broaching position, broached, and then shuttled back for unloading and reloading while the ram is returning. A heavy duty vise fixture is shown.

Reciprocating In-feed Tables. These tables (see Fig. 12-11) are used to produce extremely deep cuts automatically by advancing the workpiece incrementally, as many times as necessary using the roughing teeth of the broach to reach depth; then a final full finishing stroke is taken using the rest of the teeth. This technique of combining multiple broach strokes with precisely controlled feeding is referred to as "peckering". In effect, it extends a short-stroke machine into a long-stroke machine. When not used for in-feed operations, the table can serve as a shuttle slide for one-pass jobs to permit loading/ unloading away from the pinch area. Standard and special fixtures for a wide variety of workpieces can be easily mounted to the table.

Automatic Tilt Tables. Figure 12-12 shows a tilt table that uses the same angled workpiece feeding principle as the manual tilt fixture shown in Fig. 12-7, except that operation is automatic. Various fixed position fixtures can be mounted on the tilt table.

Automatic Rotary Dial Tables. Rotary tables, such as shown in Fig. 12-13, can serve as multi-station systems for non-stop broaching of flats, slots, or straddle cuts since the workpiece can be unloaded and reloaded at the second station while the workpiece in the first station is being broached. The table is interlocked with the machine ram operation for completely automatic sequencing. Whether manual or automatic loading/unloading is used depends upon the workpiece configuration. This system is normally mounted on a shuttle table to provide clearance for broach return. Up to four fixtures can be mounted on this table.

Automatic In-feed/Cross-feed Tables. This unit (see Fig. 12-14) is used for "peckering" deep and wide flats using multiple strokes and economical short broaches. Automatic in-feed combined with full broach strokes produce successively deeper cuts

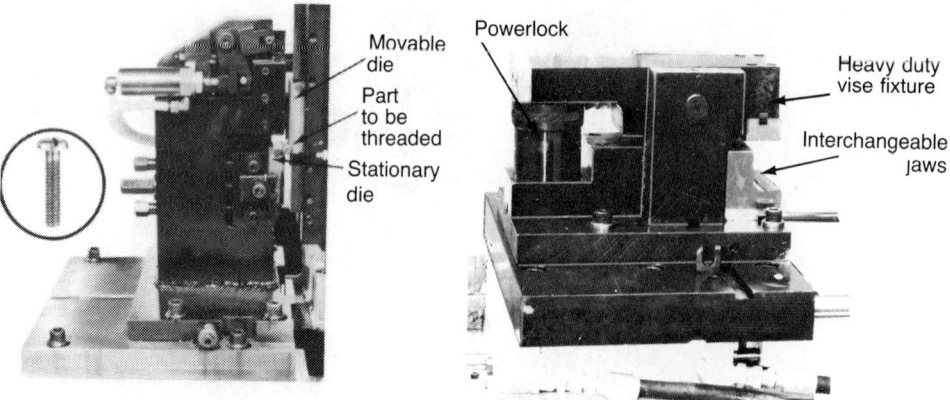

Fig. 12-9 "Broach-roll" for threading, knurling, and serration operations.
(Courtesy Ty Miles, Inc.)

Fig. 12-10 Automatic shuttle table.
(Courtesy Ty Miles, Inc.)

Fig. 12-11 Reciprocating in-feed table. *(Courtesy Ty Miles, Inc.)*

Fig. 12-12 Automatic tilt table. *(Courtesy Ty Miles, Inc.)*

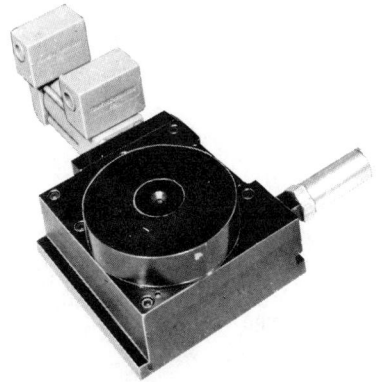

Fig. 12-13 Automatic rotary dial table. *(Courtesy Ty Miles, Inc.)*

until the desired dimension is reached. At this point, the workpiece is automatically shifted sideways a preset distance and the in-feed cycle resumes to widen the preceeding cut.

Automatic Rotary Collet Index Fixtures. These fixtures (see Fig. 12-15) function in a manner similar to the manual collet index fixture shown in Fig. 12-7, except that operation is automatically air-operated.

Magazine Fixtures. Fixtures, such as shown in Fig. 12-16, are used for high production broaching of shafts. Non-stop operation is provided by interlock with the ram motion of a vertical broaching machine, plus automatic parts ejection. The operator's only function is to keep the magazine filled with workpieces. Production rates normally exceed 1000 parts per hour. Flats, slots, or straddle cuts—even at opposite ends of long shafts—can be

Fig. 12-14 Automatic in-feed/cross-feed table. *(Courtesy Ty Miles, Inc.)*

Workpiece
(fed through
fixture)

Part
(in collet)

Interchangeable
anvil work
support

Fig. 12-15 Automatic rotary collet index fixture. *(Courtesy Ty Miles, Inc.)*

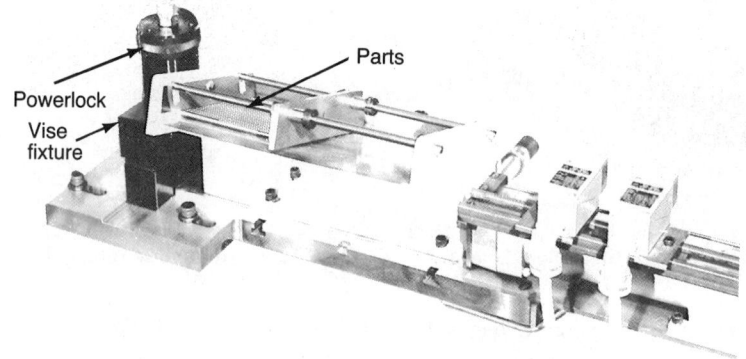

Parts

Powerlock

Vise
fixture

Fig. 12-16 Magazine fixture. *(Courtesy Ty Miles, Inc.)*

cut in one stroke. The application shown in this figure is for broaching a 1/8 in. (3.2 mm) deep flat, about 15/16 in. (23.8 mm) long on the side of 4 in. (101.6 mm) long shafts. The magazine is adjustable and can handle shafts up to 10 in. (254 mm) long and 3/4 in. diameter.

Another automatic magazine loader is shown in Fig. 12-17. The application shown is to cut a 7/8 in. (22.2 mm) long flat on a 303 stainless steel shaft. Production is 1200 parts per hour. A built-in magnetic sensor warns the operator when the magazine needs

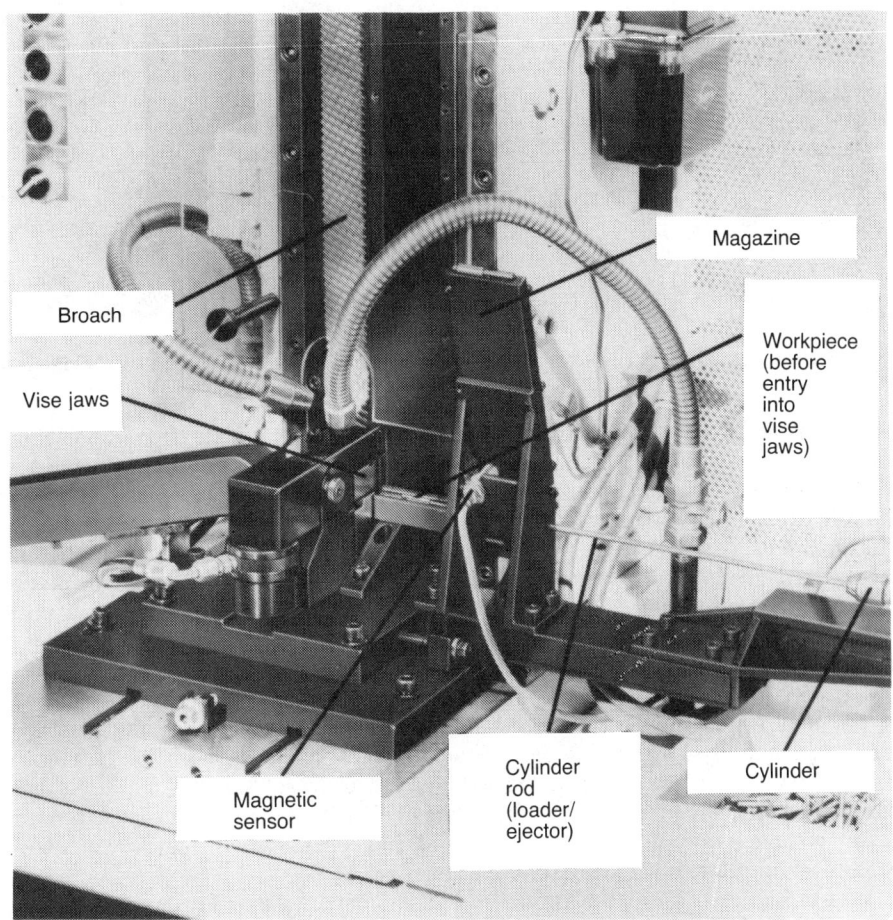

Fig. 12-17 Automatic magazine loader. *(Courtesy Ty Miles, Inc.)*

refilling. In operation, a hydraulic cylinder rod pushes the lowermost workpiece from the magazine along a trough and against a stop in the vise fixture—where the jaws clamp the workpiece. Next, the broach descends to cut the flat. After broaching, the cylinder rod advances again to eject the part and retracts again, ready to push the next workpiece into the fixture.

Fixtures for Internal Broaching. The basic broaching tooling modules for internal broaching include:

Bridge Fixtures. Bridge fixtures, such as shown in Fig. 12-18, quickly convert a broaching machine, like that shown in Fig. 12-3, for internal pull-down broaching. The automatic broach puller shown in the figure is sized to the shank diameter of the internal broach being pulled. The puller block shown in the figure is fastened to the machine ram. Workholding nests for various workpieces can be easily fabricated by the user. These fixtures can be provided with a shuttle slide for loading and unloading workpieces away from the pinch area while the broach returns to its start position.

Automatic Shuttle Bridge Tables. The table shown in Fig. 12-19 is an automatic version of the manual bridge fixture shown in Fig. 12-18. A shuttle function moves the workpiece in and out of the broach path. Loading/unloading is done in the retract position during the time the broach is returning to the start position. Simple workholding nests for use with these fixtures can be easily fabricated by the user. In the operation shown, the

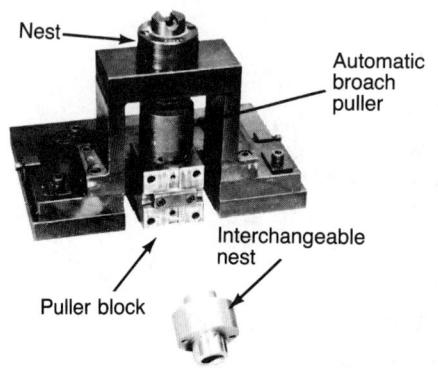

Nest

Automatic broach puller

Interchangeable nest

Puller block

Fig. 12-18 Bridge fixture. *(Courtesy Ty Miles, Inc.)*

Fig. 12-19 Automatic shuttle bridge table. *(Courtesy Ty Miles, Inc.)*

operator is replacing a broached part with a new workpiece for single pass broaching of precision splines. The operation is as follows: After the operator reloads and depresses the dual palm buttons, the automatic shuttle table moves the fixtured workpiece precisely into the path of the broach. The broach then descends a preset amount to engage an automatic broach puller inside the fixture. The machine ram is then activated, pulling the broach rapidly through the workpiece, cutting the splines. After the broach reaches the bottom of its stroke, the shuttle table automatically returns the fixture and part to its original position for reloading, while a retriever descends and returns the broach to its start position. The overall cycle time is 7 seconds.

Machine Programming. Simple machine programming capability (dial-in controls) can be provided which completely automates the previously mentioned multipass "peckering" technique used for cutting deep slots with short broaches (see Fig. 12-11). Three separate motions are programmed: the down/up broach travel (number and stroke length), the in/out part feed function, and the rotary indexing function. No matter how many passes are programmed, there is just one loading operation. In high production, this permits an operator to handle several machines.

If quantities justify, small parts can be fed automatically to many of the basic fixtures with vibratory hoppers.

Combining Operations. To also machine a hole during a broaching cycle, an automated drill can be mounted on the machine ram adjacent to the broach(es). The drill operates automatically at the bottom of the broach stroke. In addition to combining the broaching/drilling operations, this arrangement maintains an accurate dimensional relationship between broached surface(s) and drilled hole.

If it is desired to drill the hole in a different plane from the broached surfaces, simply mount the drill elsewhere on the machine. Even a second drill can be positioned to automatically cut another hole in the same or a different plane.

FIXTURE DESIGN FOR BROACHING KEYWAYS

Keyways are successfully broached on both horizontal and vertical machines. The horizontal machine uses a conventional broach bar requiring one or two passes to complete the keyway. Some of the vertical machines use a special cutter bar which is automatically reciprocated and fed into the required keyway depth. The complexity of the fixtures required to hold the part usually reflect the intricacy of the part.

A fixture for cutting keyways is often a simple plate, plug, or horn which establishes the correct position of the workpiece in relation to the broach bar and machine faceplate.

Keyway Broaching Fixture Layout. A layout related to the machine, broach bar, fixture, and workpiece is shown in Fig. 12-20. Table 12-2 gives the dimensions for standard keyway broaches.

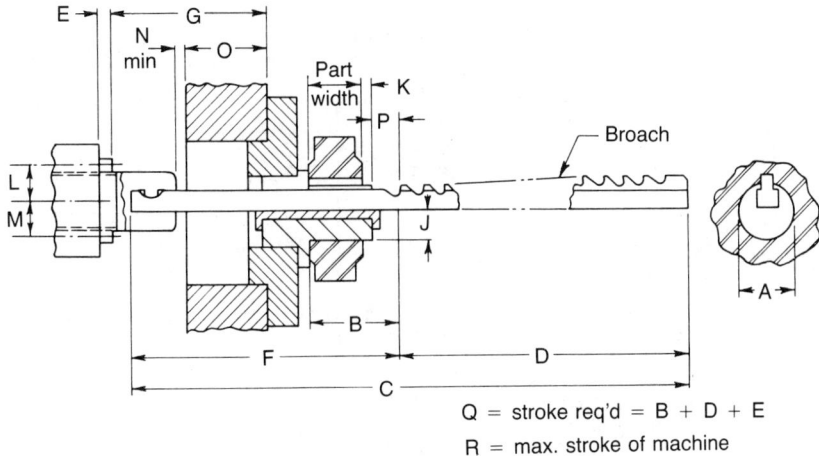

$$Q = \text{stroke req'd} = B + D + E$$
$$R = \text{max. stroke of machine}$$

Fig. 12-20 Layout for keyway-broaching machine.

Dimensions G, L, M, O, and R are obtained from the machine or machine specifications. Dimension E, the amount of stroke lost by the setup or the distance the forward stop is set back from its maximum forward position, will vary according to broach shank length, part thickness, fixture thickness, etc.

Dimension P depends upon the method of loading the part of the fixture. If the part is slipped over the broach, P must be not less than the part width. If the broach shank is fed through the part after it is on the fixture, then P is 1/2 in. (12.7 mm) minimum. If the broach has a loading step, dimension P may be a minimum of 1/2 in. (12.7 mm).

Dimension L-M is the adjustment of the sliding head on the ram face above and below the ram center line. This feature reduces the need for the center line of the horn to be below the center line of the ram or faceplate mounting hole.

The required stroke Q of the machine equals $B + D + E$, which should equal not more than the maximum machine stroke minus 1 in. (25.4 mm).

The minimum hole size given in Table 12-2 allows the part to pass over the last tooth on the broach bar. If the hole in the workpiece is smaller than this dimension, the plug will be fragile and difficult to make.

If the keyway must be broached in more than one pass, a shim or a thicker wear strip is placed under the broach, and the pull head is adjusted upwards to level the broach bar.

Keyway Broaching Horns. The broaching of keyways and other internal shapes commonly requires the use of horns to hold the broach in correct relationship to the work. Since the hole through the machine faceplate has a large diameter, the fixture horns are mounted to a faceplate adapter. This adapter has an extension on one side to fit the hole in the machine faceplate and a through hole to accommodate the fixture plug. The adapter is cap-screwed and dowel-pinned to the machine but easily removed for other adapters.

Figure 12-21 illustrates the design of fixture horns for broaching keyways. To minimize wear on the broach bar and to adjust the depth of the keyway after broach sharpening, a wear strip is used. This wear strip may be of heat-treated steel for maximum wear resistance or of a hard bronze, although chips may become embedded in the bronze strip making it unsatisfactory. View a of Fig. 12-21 shows the design of wear strips over 1/8 in. thick and view b of those under 1/8 in. (3.2 mm) thick. The minimum thickness of a wear strip is about 0.050 in. (1.27 mm). A wear strip is not used when the slot would make the plug too thin.

The best material for fixture plugs is a nondeforming tool steel. The guide slot is machined to size before hardening, necessitating grinding only on diameters and the faces of the mounting flange.

TABLE 12-2. Dimensions for Standard Keyway Broaches*

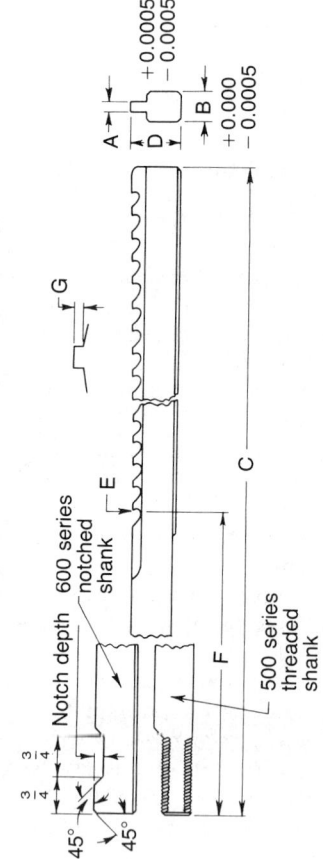

Broach number†	Min. hole size	Min. length cut	Max. length cut	A‡ Nom. dim.	A‡ Dec. dim.	B, width of back	C, total length	D, height last tooth	E, height starting tooth	F, length of shank	G, keyway depth¶	No. of cuts	Thread size, 500 series	Notch depth, 600 series
01	3/8	3/8	1 1/4	1/16	0.0635	0.1552	20	0.313	0.271	7 13/16	0.042	1	1/4-20	1/16
02	7/16	1/2	1 1/2	3/32	0.0948	0.1865	24	0.367	0.309	8 1/4	0.058	1	5/16-18	1/16
03	5/8	5/8	2 1/2	3/32	0.0948	0.249	33	0.491	0.433	10	0.058	1	3/8-16	1/16
04	1/2	1/2	1 1/2	1/8	0.126	0.249	30	0.438	0.364	9	0.074	1	3/8-16	1/16
05	7/8	5/8	2 1/2	1/8	0.126	0.3115	36	0.594	0.520	10	0.074	1	1/2-13	1/8
06	19/32	1/2	1 1/2	5/32	0.1572	0.249	30	0.525	0.436	9	0.089	1	3/8-16	1/8
07	23/32	5/8	2 1/2	5/32	0.1572	0.3115	33	0.625	0.536	10	0.089	1	1/2-13	1/8
08	11/16	5/8	2 1/2	3/16	0.1885	0.374	36	0.581	0.476	10	0.105	1	1/2-13	1/8
09	15/16	11/16	3 1/2	3/16	0.1885	0.374	36	0.796	0.691	10 11/16	0.105	1	1/2-13	1/8
10	11/16	5/8	2 1/2	7/32	0.2198	0.374	33	0.557	0.437	10	0.120	1	1/2-13	1/8
11	15/16	11/16	3 1/2	7/32	0.2198	0.374	42	0.813	0.693	11 1/16	0.120	1	1/2-13	1/8
12	11/16	5/8	2 1/2	1/4	0.251	0.374	36	0.612	0.476	10	0.136	1	1/2-13	1/8
13	1	11/16	4	1/4	0.251	0.499	45	0.877	0.741	11 13/16	0.136	1	5/8-11	1/8
14	1 7/16	7/8	6	1/4	0.251	0.624	51	1.250	1.114	13 1/2	0.136	1	3/4-10	7/32

12-20

Broach number†	Min. hole size	Min. length cut	Max. length cut	A‡ Nom. dim.	A‡ Dec. dim.	*B*, width of back	*C*, total length	*D*, height last tooth	*E*, height starting tooth	*F*, length of shank	*G*, key-way depth¶	No. of cuts	Thread size, 500 series	Notch depth, 600 series
15	7/8	11/16	4	9/32	0.2828	0.499	42	0.716	0.564	11 5/8	0.152	1	5/8-11	1/8
16	1 1/4	7/8	6	9/32	0.2828	0.499	51	1.093	0.941	13 1/2	0.152	1	5/8-11	3/16
17	1	11/16	4	5/16	0.314	0.499	45	0.908	0.741	11 13/16	0.167	1	5/8-11	1/8
18	1 5/16	7/8	6	5/16	0.314	0.499	51	1.158	0.991	13 1/2	0.167	1	5/8-11	3/16
19	1 1/16	11/16	4	3/8	0.3765	0.499	45	0.938	0.739	11 13/16	0.199	1	5/8-11	1/8
20	1 5/16	7/8	6	3/8	0.3765	0.499	54	1.189	0.990	13 1/2	0.199	1	5/8-11	3/16
21	1 9/16	11/16	4	7/16	0.439	0.624	48	1.390	1.160	12	0.230	1	3/4-10	7/32
22	2	1	8	7/16	0.439	0.624	48	1.611	1.496	15 5/8	0.230	2	3/4-10	7/32
23	1 1/2	11/16	4	1/2	0.5015	0.624	48	1.312	1.051	12	0.261	1	3/4-10	7/32
24	1 1/2	1	8	1/2	0.5015	0.624	48	1.377	1.246	16 1/2	0.261	2	3/4-10	7/32
25	1 3/4	11/16	4	9/16	0.5645	0.6865	54	1.438	1.146	11 13/16	0.292	1	1-8	7/32
26	1 5/8	1	8	9/16	0.5645	0.6865	51	1.391	1.245	16	0.292	2	1-8	7/32
27	2 1/4	1 1/8	12	9/16	0.5645	0.874	60	1.641	1.495	20	0.292	2	1-8	7/32
28	1 7/8	11/16	4	5/8	0.627	0.749	60	1.625	1.301	12 3/16	0.324	1	1-8	7/32
29	2 1/2	1	8	5/8	0.627	0.874	54	1.657	1.495	16 3/8	0.324	2	1-8	7/32
30	2 1/4	1 1/8	12	5/8	0.627	0.874	57	1.657	1.495	20	0.324	2	1-8	7/32
31	1 7/8	11/16	4	3/4	0.752	0.874	60	1.625	1.239	12 3/16	0.386	1	1-8	7/32
32	2	1	8	3/4	0.752	0.999	60	1.688	1.495	16 1/4	0.386	2	1 1/4-7	7/32
33	2 1/4	1 1/8	12	3/4	0.752	0.999	57	1.688	1.560	20	0.386	3	1 1/4-7	7/32
34	2 1/4	11/16	4	7/8	0.877	1.124	63	1.875	1.426	12 3/8	0.449	1	1 1/4-7	7/32
35	2 1/4	1	8	7/8	0.877	1.124	63	1.719	1.494	15 3/4	0.449	2	1 1/4-7	7/32
36	2 1/4	1 1/8	12	7/8	0.877	1.124	63	1.719	1.569	20	0.449	3	1 1/4-7	7/32
37	2 1/4	5/8	2 1/2	1	1.002	1.249	63	1.750	1.239	10 1/2	0.511	1	1 1/2-6	7/32
38	2 1/4	7/8	6	1	1.002	1.249	63	1.750	1.494	14 1/4	0.511	2	1 1/2-6	7/32
39	2 1/4	1 1/8	12	1	1.002	1.249	60	1.750	1.580	20	0.511	3	1 1/2-6	7/32

*All dimensions are in inches.
†Add prefix 5 for threaded shank and 6 for notched shank.
‡Tolerance is ±0.0002 in. for numbers 01 to 24 inclusive, ±0.0003 in. for the remainder.
¶Keyway depth at side of slot is indicated.

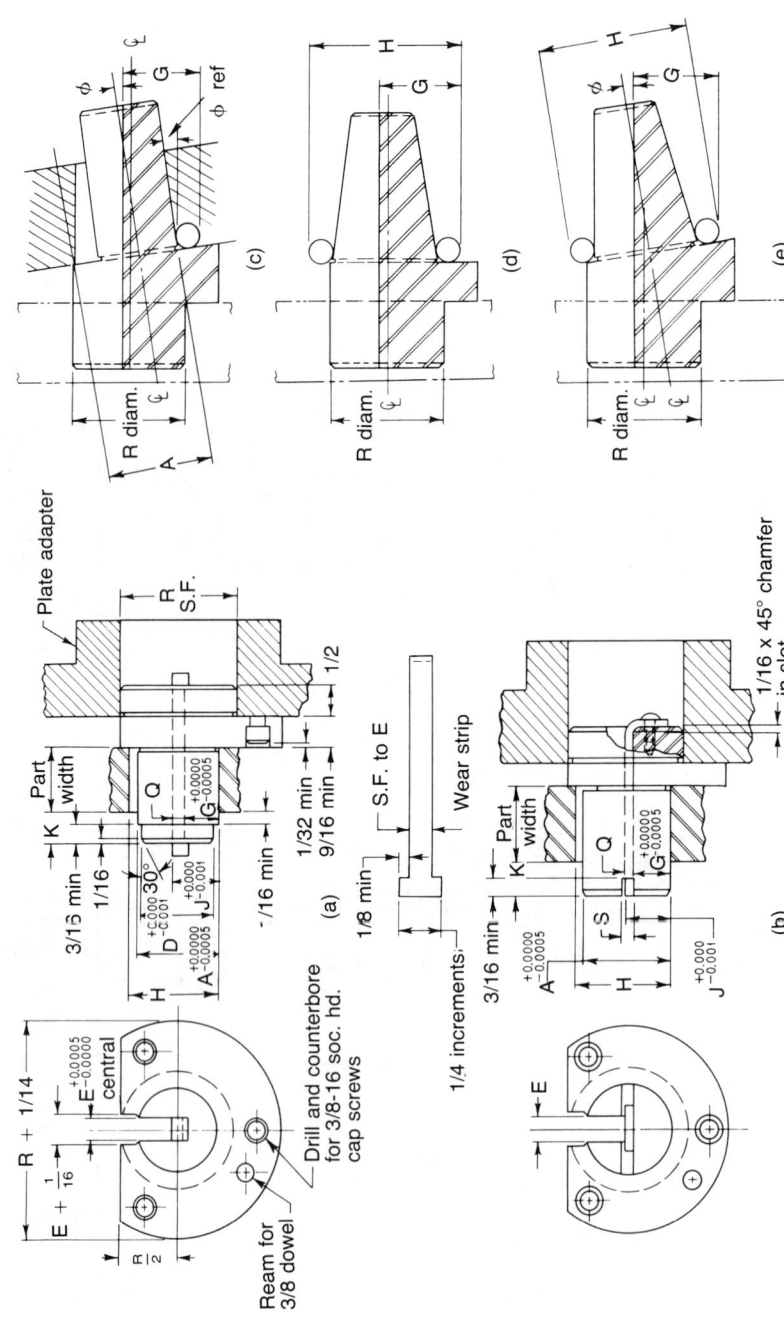

Fig. 12-21 Keyway broaching horns: (*a*) horn design with wear strips over 1/8 in. (3.18 mm) thick; (*b*) horn design with wear strips under 1/8 in. (3.18 mm) thick; (*c*) horn for angular keyway; (*d*) horn for keyway parallel to center line in tapered hole; (*e*) horn for keyway parallel to taper in tapered hole.

Recommended dimensions and specifications for the design of Fig. 12-21 are:

A = low limit of part

H = height of keyway on part (see Fig. 12-22 and Table 12-3)

D = $A-0.003$ (do not use lead when tolerance on hole is over 0.001 in.)

E = 0.001 in. over high limit of broach-bar width

F = 1.5 $(A-J)$ or 1/4 in. min when A is under 1 in., 1/2 in. min when A is 1 to 2 in., 3/4 in. min when A is over 2 in.

G = $J-Q$

J = H minus height of last tooth (D of Table 12-2) minus 0.002 in.

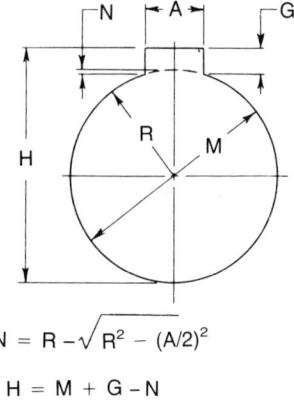

$$N = R - \sqrt{R^2 - (A/2)^2}$$

$$H = M + G - N$$

Fig. 12-22 Calculating keyway height.

TABLE 12-3. Chord Rise N for Calculating Keyway Depths*†

M diameter	Key width A												
	1/16	3/32	1/8	5/32	3/16	7/32	1/4	5/16	3/8	7/16	1/2	5/8	3/4
1/4	0.004	0.009	0.016										
3/8	0.003	0.006	0.011	0.017	0.025								
1/2	0.002	0.004	0.008	0.013	0.018	0.025	0.032						
5/8	0.001	0.003	0.006	0.010	0.014	0.019	0.025	0.041					
3/4	0.001	0.003	0.005	0.008	0.012	0.016	0.022	0.034	0.051				
7/8	0.001	0.002	0.004	0.007	0.010	0.014	0.017	0.028	0.042	0.058			
1	0.001	0.002	0.004	0.006	0.009	0.012	0.015	0.024	0.036	0.050	0.067		
1 1/8	.....	0.002	0.003	0.005	0.008	0.011	0.013	0.021	0.032	0.044	0.058	0.095	
1 1/4	.....	0.002	0.003	0.005	0.007	0.010	0.012	0.019	0.029	0.039	0.052	0.084	0.125
1 1/2	.....	0.001	0.002	0.004	0.006	0.008	0.011	0.016	0.024	0.032	0.042	0.068	0.100
1 3/4	.....	0.001	0.002	0.003	0.005	0.007	0.009	0.014	0.020	0.027	0.038	0.059	0.084
2	.....	0.001	0.002	0.003	0.004	0.006	0.008	0.012	0.017	0.024	0.031	0.050	0.073
2 1/4	.....	.....	0.002	0.003	0.004	0.005	0.007	0.010	0.015	0.021	0.028	0.044	0.065
2 1/2	.....	.....	0.002	0.003	0.004	0.005	0.006	0.009	0.014	0.019	0.025	0.040	0.057
2 3/4	.....	.....	.....	0.002	0.003	0.004	0.005	0.008	0.013	0.017	0.023	0.036	0.052
3	.....	.....	.....	0.002	0.003	0.004	0.005	0.008	0.011	0.016	0.021	0.033	0.046
3 1/4	.....	.....	.....	0.001	0.002	0.003	0.004	0.007	0.011	0.014	0.019	0.030	0.044
3 1/2	.....	.....	.....	.....	0.002	0.003	0.004	0.007	0.010	0.013	0.018	0.027	0.041
3 3/4	.....	.....	.....	.....	0.001	0.002	0.004	0.006	0.009	0.012	0.016	0.026	0.037
4	.....	.....	.....	.....	.....	0.002	0.004	0.006	0.009	0.012	0.016	0.025	0.035

*All dimensions are in inches.

†See Fig. 12-22

Q = 1/8 in. min, 1/4 when possible
R = snug-fit in hole in faceplate adapter
S = next fraction over wear-strip thickness
U = No. 8-32 screw or larger when possible

Horns for Keyways in Angular and Tapered Holes. Keyway broaching horns may be required for keyways not parallel to the part center line or in parts having tapered bores. Figure 12-21c illustrates a horn for an angular keyway in a straight hole. View *d* shows a horn for a keyway parallel to the center line of a tapered hole. View *e* shows a horn for broaching a keyway parallel to the side of a tapered hole.

To eliminate the difficulties in making a horn of the type shown in Fig. 12-21c and *e*, the angle of inclination can be incorporated in the adapter plate (see Fig. 12-23a).

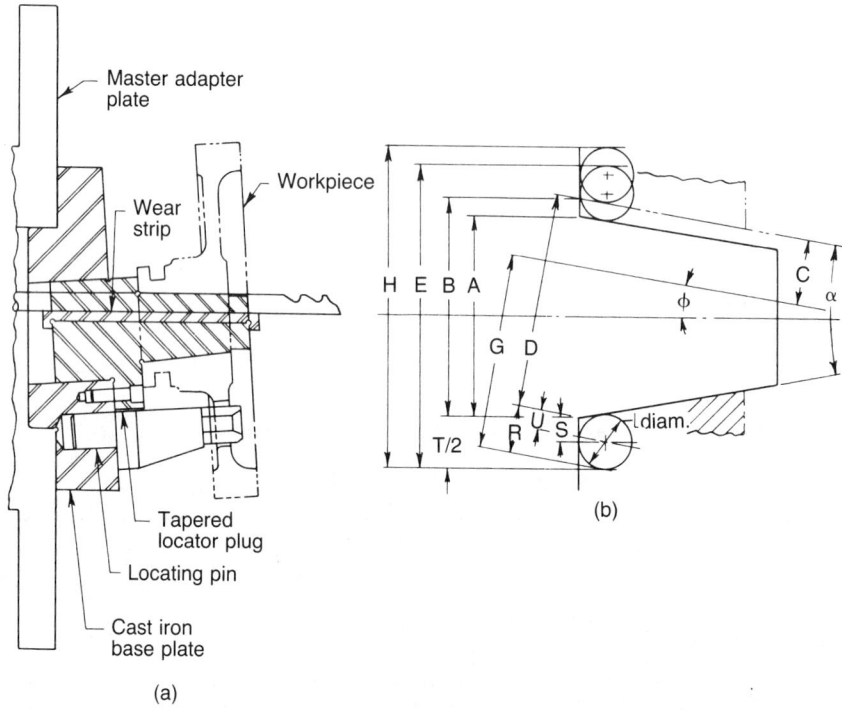

(a)

(b)

Fig. 12-23 (*a*) adapter for angular keyway broaching; (*b*) dimensions for tapered horns.

Dimensions for tapered plugs can be calculated from the following equations (see Fig. 12-23b):

$$H = B + T \tag{4}$$
$$E = A + T \tag{5}$$
$$T = 2S + L \tag{6}$$
$$S = \frac{L}{2} \tan \frac{90-\phi}{2} \tag{7}$$
$$C + G = D + R \tag{8}$$
$$D = B \cos \phi \tag{9}$$
$$S = \frac{L}{2} + S \cos \phi - \frac{L}{2} \sin \phi \tag{10}$$

Where α = included angle for a given taper per foot (TPF)
$\phi = \alpha/2$; $\tan \phi$ = TPF/24
H = dimensions over pins at large end of taper, in. (mm)

B = dimension from bottom of taper to top of keyway at large end, high limit, in. (mm)
A = diameter of taper at large end, in. (mm)
L = diameter of gage pins, in. (mm)
E = dimension over pins for large end of taper, in. (mm)
C = height of broach bar plus wear-strip thickness, in. (mm)
G = height over lower pin to bottom of broach-guide slot, in. (mm)

Off-center Locating Horns. Horns (see Fig. 12-24) are used for broaching keyways in large holes having radii greater than the outward adjustment of the broach in the sliding head on the machine ram. The horn serves to orient the workpiece so that the keyway is approximately at the ram center line.

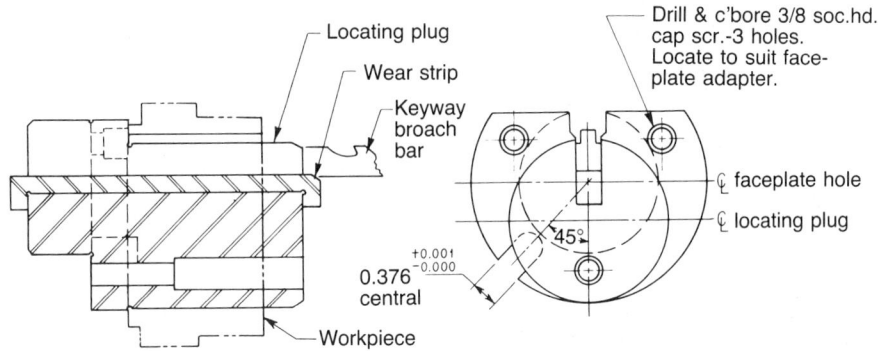

Fig. 12-24 Off-center keyway-fixture horn.

The diameter of the mounting flange should be large enough for adequate support of the workpiece during broaching.

Both the locating plug and wear strip should be made of tool steel, hardened for toughness and wear resistance.

Broaching Keyways in Thin Parts. Parts with a thickness of less than the minimum required for a keyway broach bar may be stacked on a plug to obtain the required thickness. To prevent the loading of more parts on the plug than originally planned, the K dimension of Fig. 12-21a and b may be increased approximately 1/4 in. (6.35 mm) and tapered.

The tolerances on the bores of the thin parts should be ± 0.001 in., or less, to minimize part movement.

Universal Keyway Broaching Fixture. A broaching fixture with radial location accurate to 1/2° is shown in Fig. 12-25. This fixture was designed for low-production runs of special equipment levers having keyway location tolerances of $\pm 1°$.

Setscrews (1) in the locating block (2) are adjustable to suit the thickness of the levers. The blocks holding the screws are adjusted away from the faceplate and the locating plug to suit lever width and length.

A removable locating pin (3) is provided for parts having a hole suitable for radial location of the keyway.

The locating plugs used in this fixture are similar to those shown in Figs. 12-21 and 12-25.

Broaching and Marking a Timing Gear. Figure 12-26 shows a fixture for broaching a keyway in a gear with previously cut teeth and also for marking the gear in line with the keyway and at a 90° angle to the keyway.

The fixture base is cast iron with a pilot diameter to suit the machine faceplate. The center hole is bored for a fixture plug similar to those shown in Fig. 12-21. An adjustable

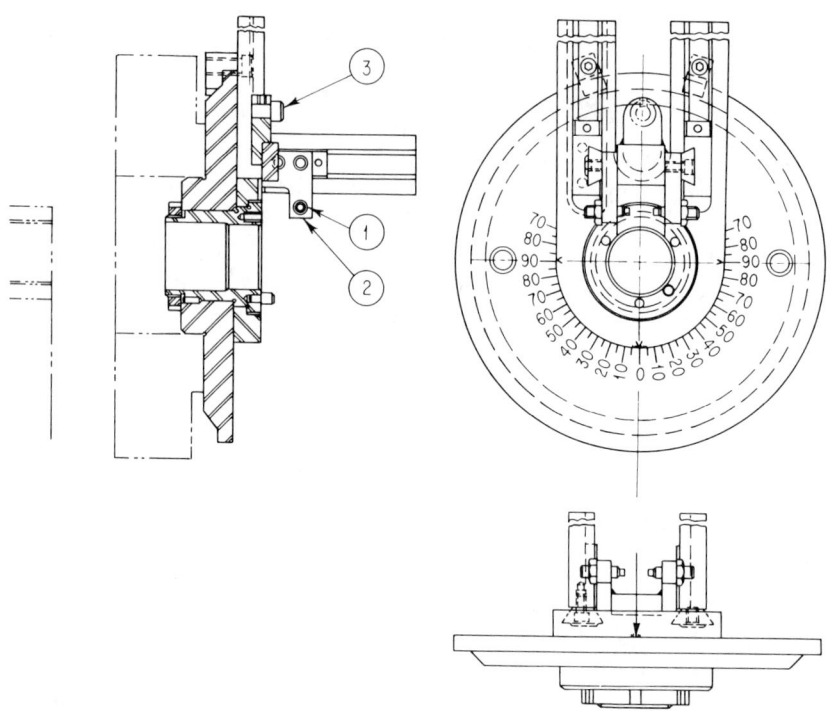

Fig. 12-25 Universal keyway-broaching fixture.

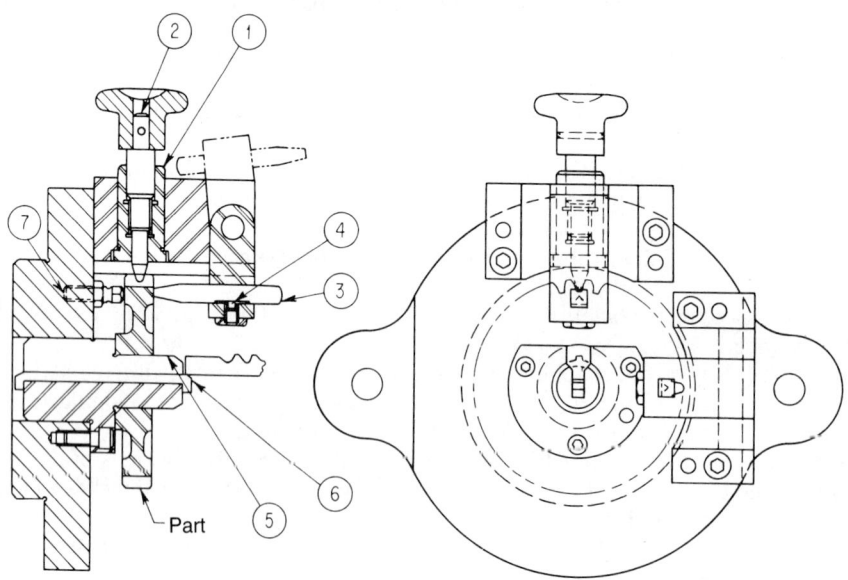

Fig. 12-26 Broaching a keyway in a timing gear.

stop (7) supports the gear opposite each marking device (3), which is a standard steel stamp mounted in a swinging holder and held by a dog-point setscrew (4).

The locating pin (2), made of hardened and ground SAE 8645 steel, is piloted on each end in a bushing (1) to advance and lock it in position during the broaching operation. The fixture plug (5) incorporates a wear strip (6).

Indexing Fixture for Broaching Serrations. Figure 12-27 illustrates a fixture for broaching splines, serrations, etc., in a straight hole. This fixture is probably not practical for small-diameter holes if a machine with capacity for pulling full round spline-broach bars is available.

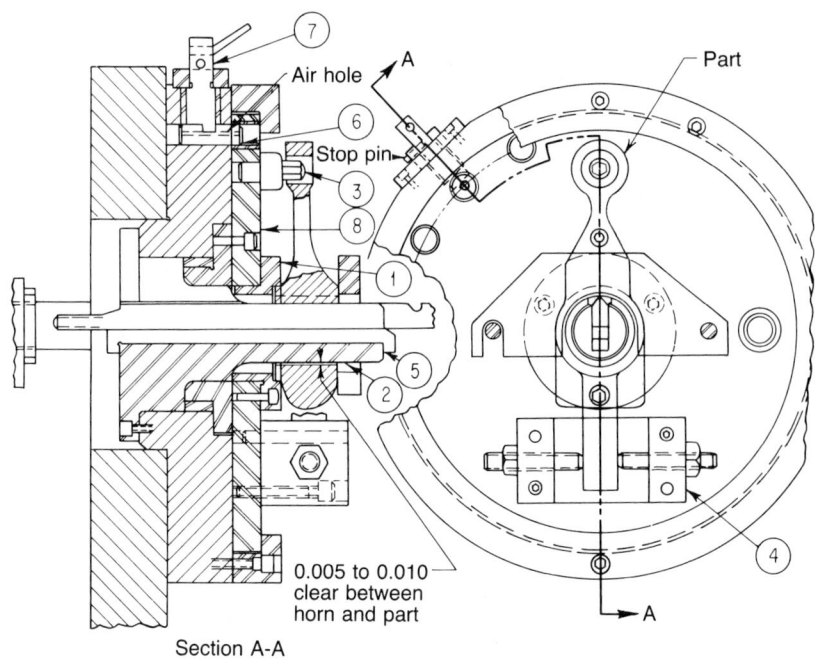

Section A-A

Fig. 12-27 Hand-indexing fixture for broaching splines and serrations.

The fixture has a locator (1), a broach guide (2), and a small locating pin (3) for locating the workpiece from previously machined holes. Adjustable stops may be used instead of the locating pin to position the part from a lever arm. The index plate detent pin (6) is actuated by a hand-operated eccentric pin (7).

The broach guide, the index plate (8), and the locating plate may be changed for broaching other parts.

The external locating diameter is specified, since a clearance of 0.010 to 0.020 in. is required between the broach guide and bore of the workpiece.

Tilting Table Fixture with Indexing. Figure 12-28 shows a tilting-table fixture, incorporating an indexing mechanism for use on a vertical keyseating machine. The fixture is mounted on the horizontal table (1) of the machine and clears the machine vertical column (2). The column supports and guides the arm (3) to which the cutting tool (4) is attached.

With a workpiece bearing directly on the table, the tool path and resultant cut are perpendicular to the bearing surface. The tilting table (5) permits generation of splines, gear teeth, etc., at an angle to the bearing surface. The index plate (6) establishes the position of the generated characteristic on the ID of the workpiece. The support column (7) must be of sufficient cross-sectional area to withstand operation pressures without deflection. Extra index plates are provided for various workpieces.

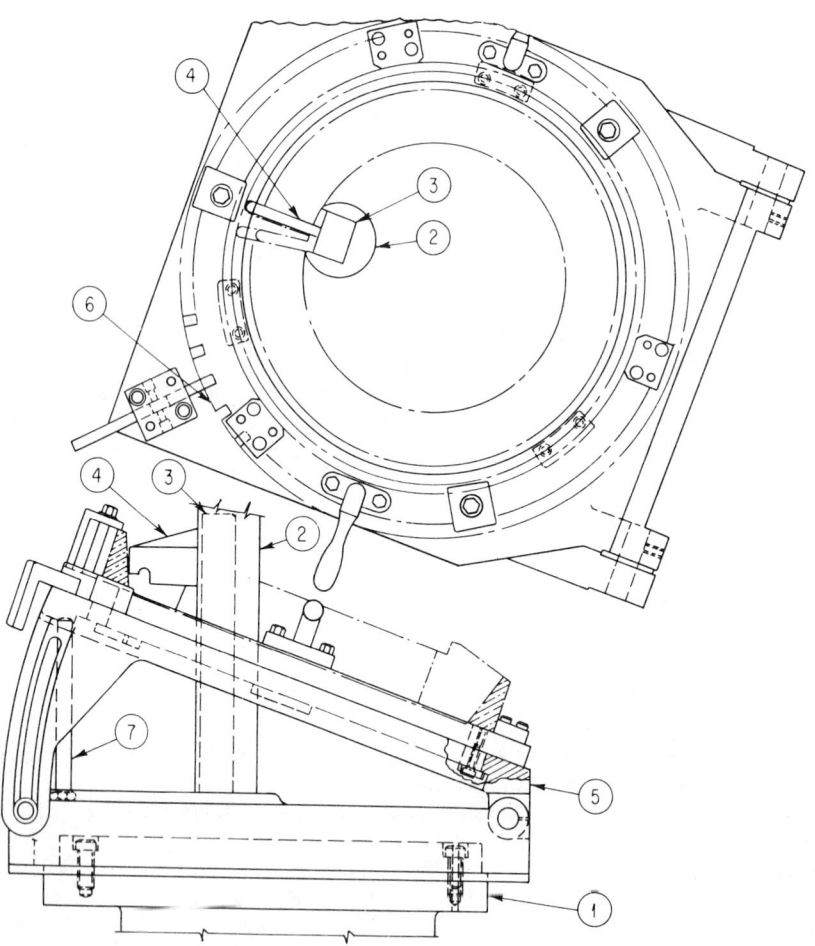

Fig. 12-28 Tilting-table fixture with indexing arrangements. *(Courtesy Mitts and Merrill)*

In-line Indexing Fixture. Figure 12-29 illustrates a fixture for broaching one keyway in two holes and two wide keyways in four holes in a workpiece. The workpiece is located on two horns, one fixed (1) and the other (2) pivoted to allow for variation in the distance between the holes. The fixture is mounted on rollers (3) for indexing between each of the six stations. The fixture moves on an overhead rail from station to station and is held on the bottom by keeper plates (4). The index plunger (5) is held in indexing slots by a weighted handle (6). Felt wipers (7) remove dirt and chips from the overhead rail.

12-28

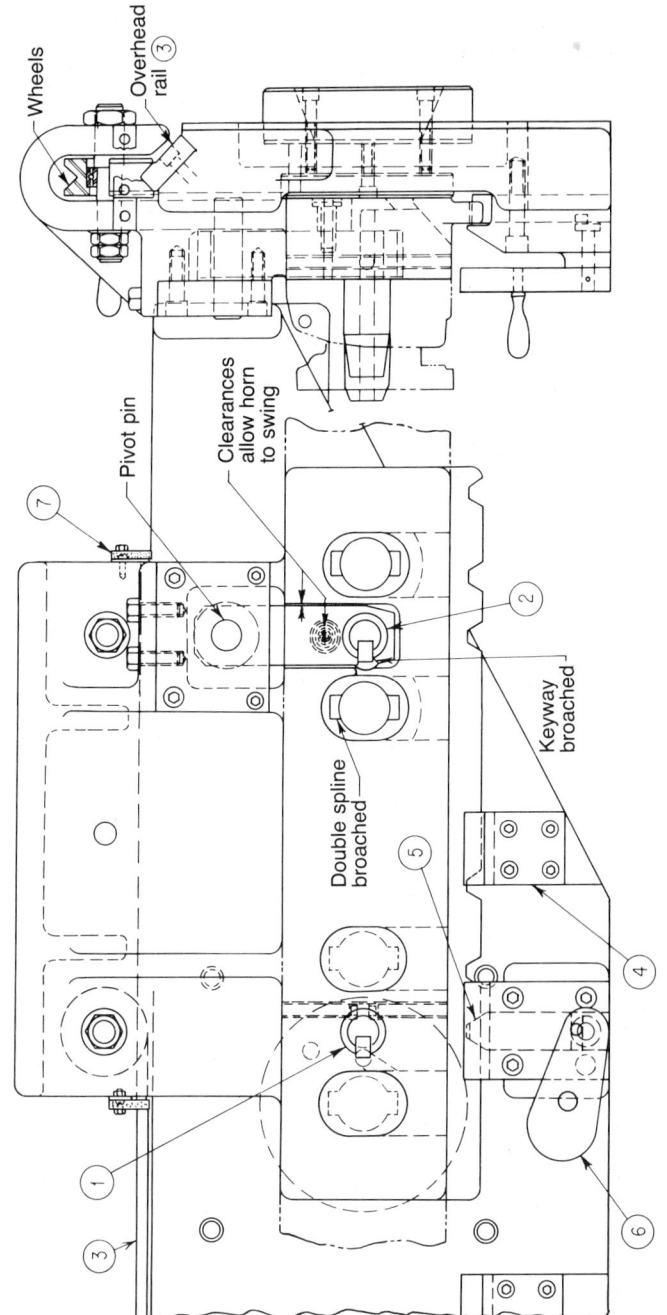

Fig. 12-29 Trolley-type fixture for broaching keyways. (*Courtesy Continental Tool Works Div. of Ex-Cell-O Corp.*)

Wheels

Overhead rail ③

Pivot pin

Clearances allow horn to swing

Double spline broached

Keyway broached

12-29

BROACHING INTERNAL FORMS

This type of broaching is similar to keyway broaching inasmuch as the broach bar is guided by a slot in the fixture.

Broaching an Irregular Hole. The fixture of Fig. 12-30 is used to broach four internal surfaces in an irregular hole in a forging. The broach bar is guided by two keys to produce broached surfaces concentric to the finish-turned diameters of the workpiece. A close fit between the counterbore of the workpiece and the fixture plug holds the workpiece concentric with the axis of the bar.

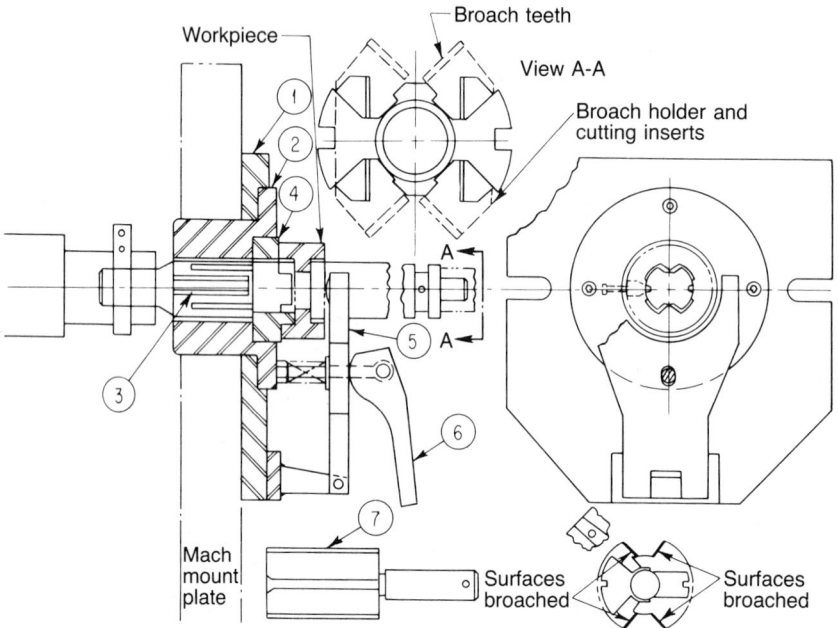

Fig. 12-30 Horizontal broaching fixture with keys to guide the broach bar.

Guide keys in this type of fixture have a sliding fit in the grooves of the broach bar. The guide keys assure alignment of the broach bar and pull head and guide the bar to offset the drift experienced in horizontal internal broaching. A similar application would be that of symmetrically elongating a hole on each side of its center line.

Because of an unequal amount of stock on each surface, it was necessary to clamp the workpiece securely before broaching. A positioning gage (7) is used to equalize the stock removal as much as possible.

The fixture consists of a base plate (1), a large hollow plug (2) with guide strips (3), a workpiece locator (4), a straddle clamp (5), and a cam (6) to actuate the straddle clamp.

Surface Broaching Internal Pads. Figure 12-31 shows a fixture for broaching three pads on a casting in three passes. The workpiece is supported on a mandrel and positioned by an index pin (2) through holes in its periphery. A back-up cam (3) presses the part against the index pin to dampen any tendency to chatter, and a cam-actuated bottom-support pin (4) takes up any clearance between the part bore and the mandrel.

The broach bar is guided and supported by two hardened and ground steel guides (5). Since the broach bar is not supported beneath the cut, the bar must be thick enough to resist deflection between the front and rear guides.

The fixture is made of two castings with press-fit bushings for the workpiece, support mandrel, and index pin.

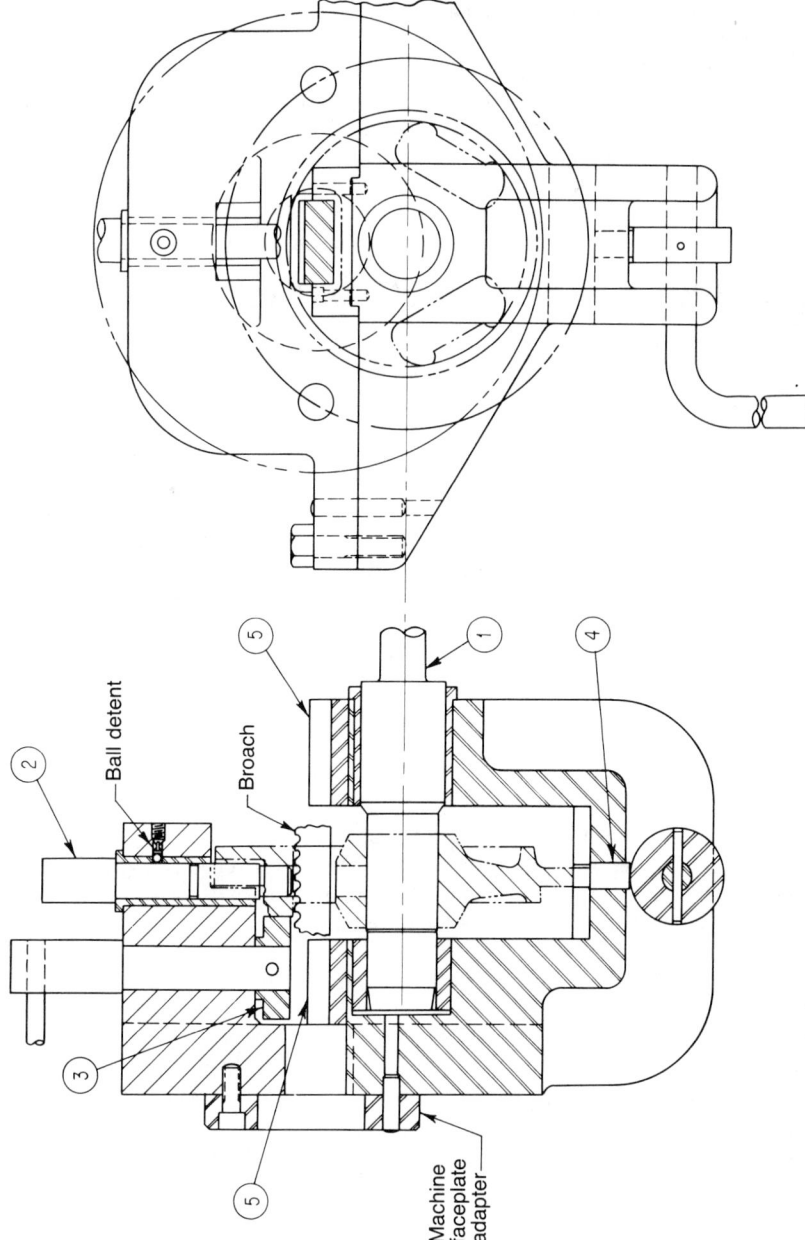

Fig. 12-31 Fixture for broaching three internal pads. *(Courtesy National Broach and Machine Co.)*

Ball detent

Broach

Machine
faceplate
adapter

12-31

A Cam-locking Fixture for Internal Broaching. Figure 12-32 illustrates a fixture for broaching a door-closing cylinder. The cylinder is approximately 4⅛ in. (104.8 mm) long, 1⅞ in. diam., with the slot 3¼ (82.6 mm) by 1 in. (25.4 mm). Three surfaces of the slot are broached. One side becomes a rack, and each end is finished to size. The rack is broached first; then ribs on the broach bar engage the rack teeth to act as a guide while the top and bottom surfaces are finished.

The workpiece is placed in the fixture through a slot at the top; it rests, for endwise location, on a swinging locator. A small flat on each side of the slot bears against hardened locators which also serve as broach guides. A cam-actuated clamp holds the part against these locators. The part is centrally located by a pair of V-blocks, one of which is actuated by a cam for clamping purposes. Weights are incorporated in the operating handles of these cams to assist in keeping them in locked position.

When the broaching is complete, the clamps are released; and the end locator swings aside, allowing the part to fall out of the bottom of the fixture.

SURFACE BROACHING ON A HORIZONTAL BROACHING MACHINE

With proper fixturing and broach support, surface as well as internal broaching may be done on a horizontal machine.

Indexing Fixture for Dovetails. Figure 12-33 illustrates a fixture which holds and guides the broach-bar holder with a dovetail guide. The workpiece is located by a round pin (1) and a diamond-shaped pin (2); it is clamped by four hook pins (3) pulled through the base of the part nest (4) by a plate and central screw assembly (5) with a handwheel. The operation on the part is the broaching of two sets of dovetailed grooves whose bottom surfaces are at an included angle of 152°. The broaching is done in two passes of the broach bar.

The fixture pivots through 28° and is held in each position by a pin (6) nesting in a grooved, spring-loaded latch bar (7). Back-up bars (8) swing in and out of position for each pass. Bottom- and side-adjusting screws move the broach-bar guide for initial adjustments.

The broach-insert holder (see Fig. 12-34) is made of SAE 8645 steel. The inserts are of high-speed steel, hardened and ground. The positioning of the finishing teeth is accomplished by an adjusting wedge. The roughing and semifinishing inserts are positioned by placing shim stock between them and the holder.

Double Station Corner Broaching Fixture. The part broached in the fixture of Fig. 12-35 is a small casting requiring the inside of each corner to be finished. The fixture has two slots for identical broach-insert holders pulled by a two-station pull head for broaching two parts at each pass.

Two cams (1) clamp the piece through the plunger assemblies (2) and a V-block (3). The plunger-assembly retainer is cap-screwed and keyed with vertical and horizontal keys to the base casting.

The broach holder is guided by a slotted bar which has been hardened and ground for a minimum clearance of 0.001 in. between the broach holder and slot. Top guide strips (5) are used as a part nest, as well as to retain the broach holder (6) in the guide slots. Broach inserts (4) are fastened to the broach holder.

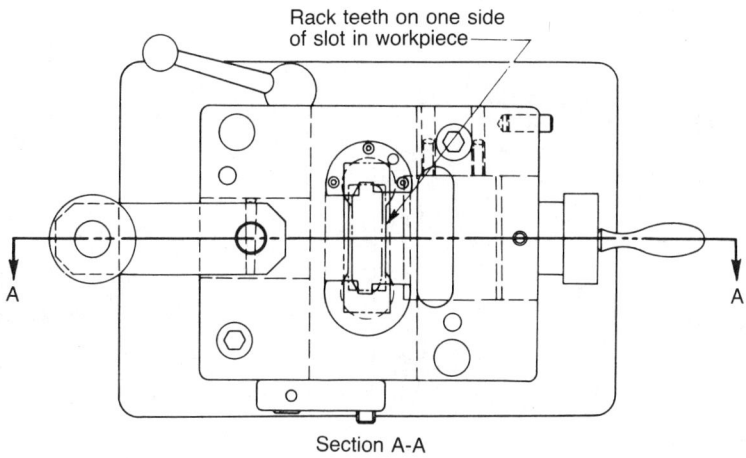

Rack teeth on one side
of slot in workpiece

A ─────────────────────── A

Section A-A

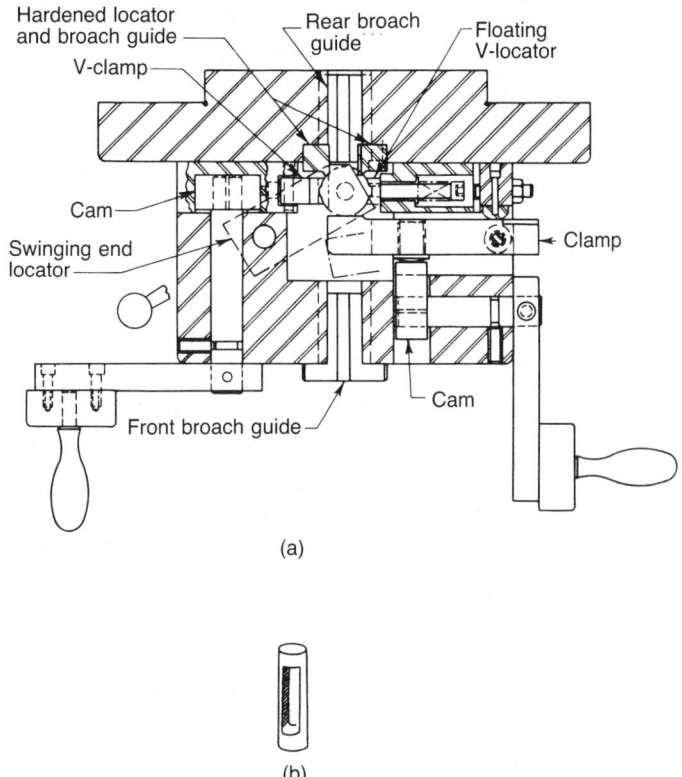

Hardened locator
and broach guide

Rear broach
guide

Floating
V-locator

V-clamp

Cam

Clamp

Swinging end
locator

Front broach guide

Cam

(a)

(b)

Fig. 12-32 (*a*) **Fixture for broaching part with internal gear rack;** (*b*) **internal gear rack broached.** *(Courtesy National Broach and Machine Co.)*

12-33

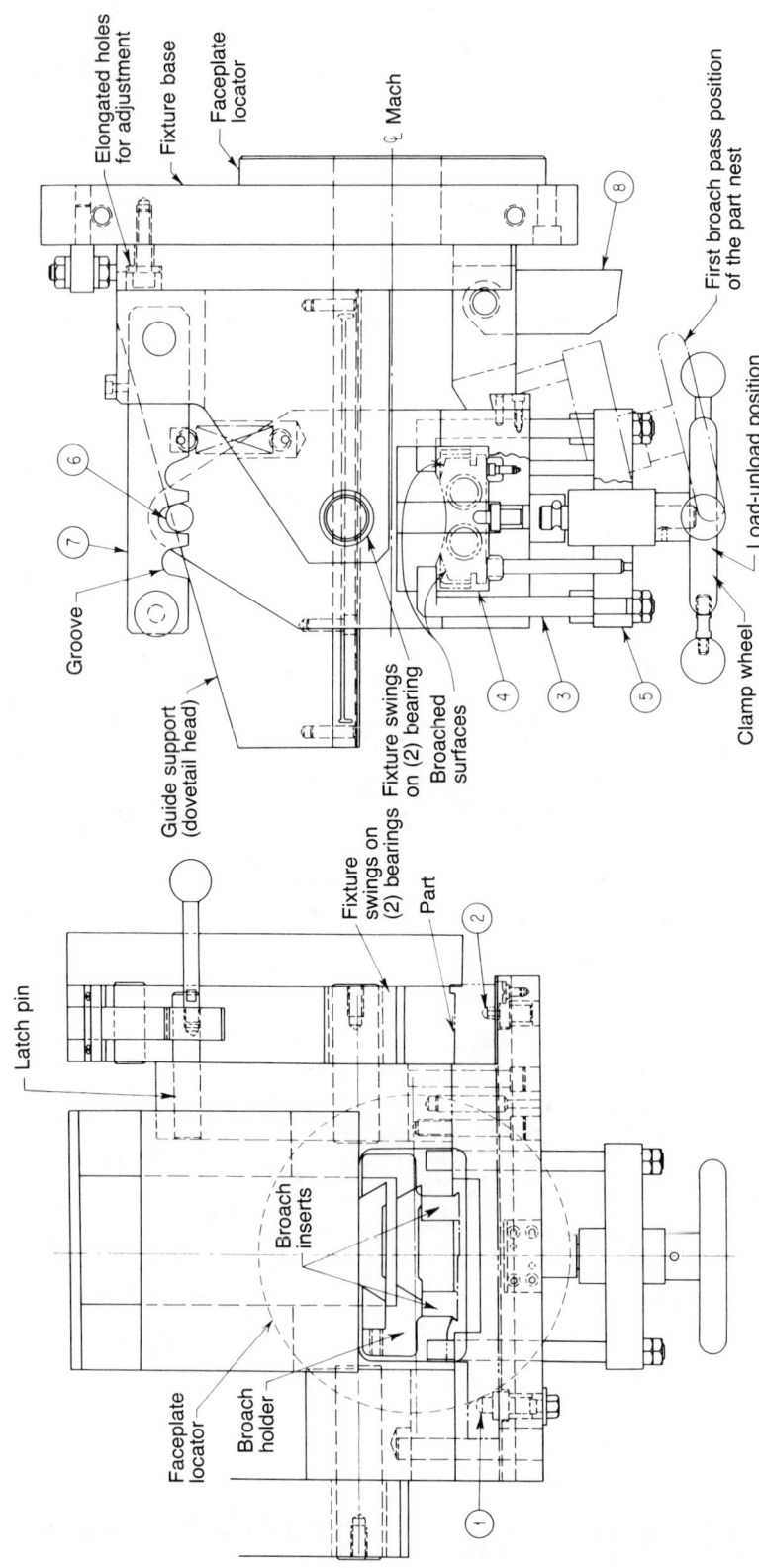

Fig. 12-33 Indexing broaching fixture for dovetail grooves. *(Courtesy National Broach and Machine Co.)*

Latch pin

Faceplate locator

Broach holder

Broach inserts

Fixture swings on (2) bearings

Part

Elongated holes for adjustment

Fixture base

Faceplate locator

℄ Mach

First broach pass position of the part nest

Load-unload position of part nest

Clamp wheel

Groove

Guide support (dovetail head)

Fixture swings on (2) bearing

Broached surfaces

12-34

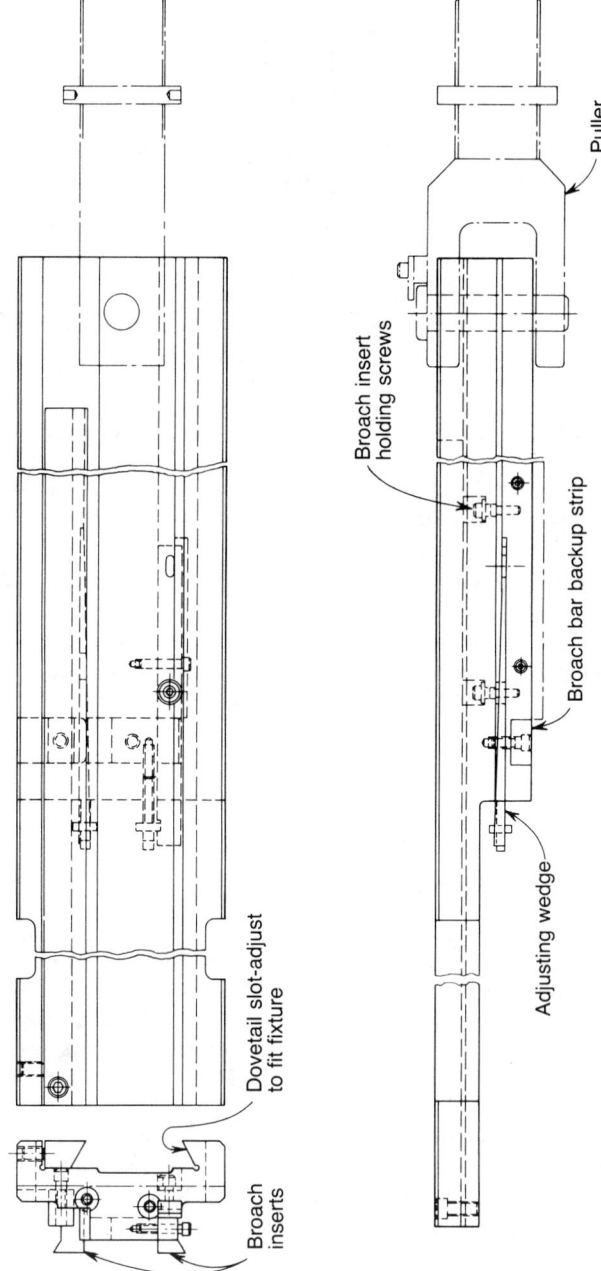

Broach inserts

Dovetail slot-adjust to fit fixture

Broach insert holding screws

Broach bar backup strip

Adjusting wedge

Puller

Fig. 12-34 Broach holder used with the fixture of Fig. 12-33. *(Courtesy National Broach and Machine Co.)*

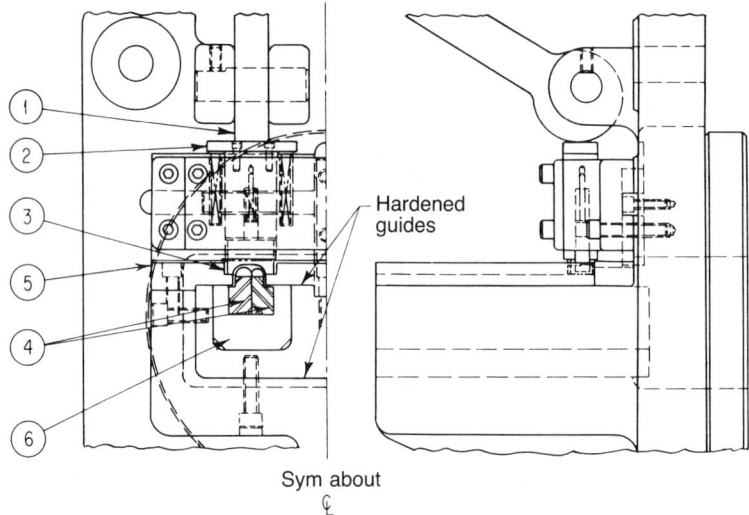

Fig. 12-35 Double-station fixture for broaching inside corners. *(Courtesy Ex-Cell-O Corp.)*

HORIZONTAL BROACHING OF ROUNDS, SPLINES AND SIMILAR FORMS

In this type of broaching, the broach bar is not usually guided or supported by the fixture. For support it must depend upon the pull head, the workpiece, or the rear carrier if the machine is equipped with one. Rear carriers were originally added to broaching machines to support the finish-tooth ends of heavy broach bars but can be used to great advantage to support light bars for better alignment. A rear carrier will not eliminate all the sag of a broach bar due to the weight of the bar or workpiece.

For machines without a rear carrier, it is preferable to design fixtures with workpiece supports or centering devices. Supported or centered parts are usually started on the broaching operation in better alignment than can be accomplished by depending on the operator to level the bar by eye.

Universal Fixtures for Round or Spline Broaching. When parts of various sizes are to be broached by one broach machine, it is often desirable to have a minimum number of faceplate adapters with replaceable bronze bushings and hardened pressure plates similar to those shown in Fig. 12-36. The faceplate adapter may be of cast iron or low-carbon steel with a pilot turned to fit the hole in the machine faceplate. Holes are drilled and counterbored for attaching this plate to the machine.

A hole is bored in the center of the faceplate adapter, as shown in the illustration, to receive the bronze bushing. The number of adapters made will depend upon the maximum desirable wall thickness of the bushing. Holes are tapped in the adapter plate for mounting the pressure plate.

The pressure plate, usually hardened and ground, holds the bushing in place and acts as a bearing surface for the workpiece. The hole through the pressure plate should be from 1/16 to 1/8 in. (1.59 to 3.17 mm) larger than the hole to be broached.

The hole through the bronze bushing should only be a few thousandths of an inch larger than the broached hole. This bushing is always soft to prevent damage to the broach teeth in case they accidentally contact it or if the broach bar is returned through the bushing.

Pot Type of Fixture for Locating on OD of Part. The fixture shown in Fig. 12-37 centers the part and supports the broach bar while the hole is being broached. This type of fixture may be used for more than one part if the individual parts are too short to be broached separately.

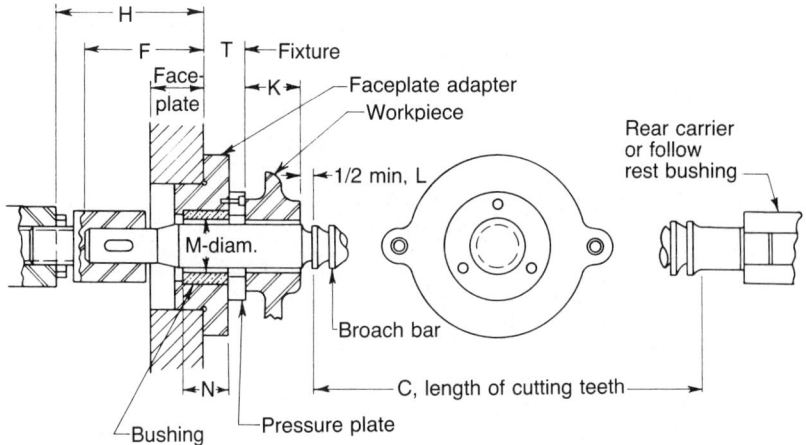

Fig. 12-36 Universal fixture for round or spline broaching.

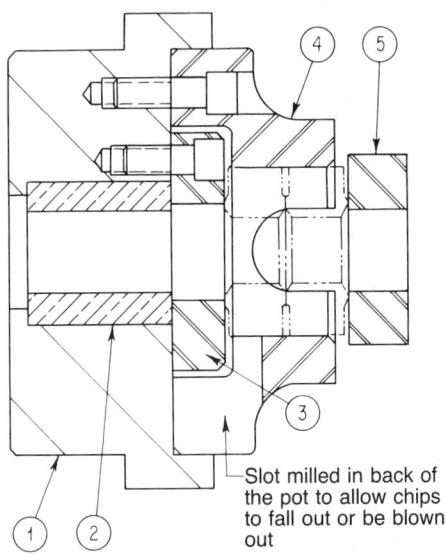

Fig. 12-37 Pot-type internal-broaching fixture.

This fixture consists of a base plate (1), a bushing (2), a pressure plate (3), a locating ring (4), and if necessary, a clamp assembly (5). The parts (2, 3, and 4) are interchangeable as a group or individually, depending upon the part requirements.

Thin parts must be securely clamped to prevent chips from lodging between them, a cause of faulty parts. It has been found that a series of 1/8-in. (3.18 mm)-thick parts moved so much when not clamped that a spline broach produced a nearly round hole in the parts.

Fixture for Broaching 0.156-in. (3.96 mm)-thick Parts. This type of broaching requires that the combined height of stacked parts broached at one time be not less than twice the pitch of the broach-bar teeth plus 1/16 in. (1.59 mm). Locating of the parts by their periphery is preferred, but they can be located by the front pilot section of the broach bar and clamped securely before the broaching cycle starts.

The fixture shown in Fig. 12-38 holds nine parts 0.156 in. (3.96 mm) thick and 6.062 in. diam. while broaching an internal spline. The parts rest in a semicircular locator and are held in position by air-actuated clamps.

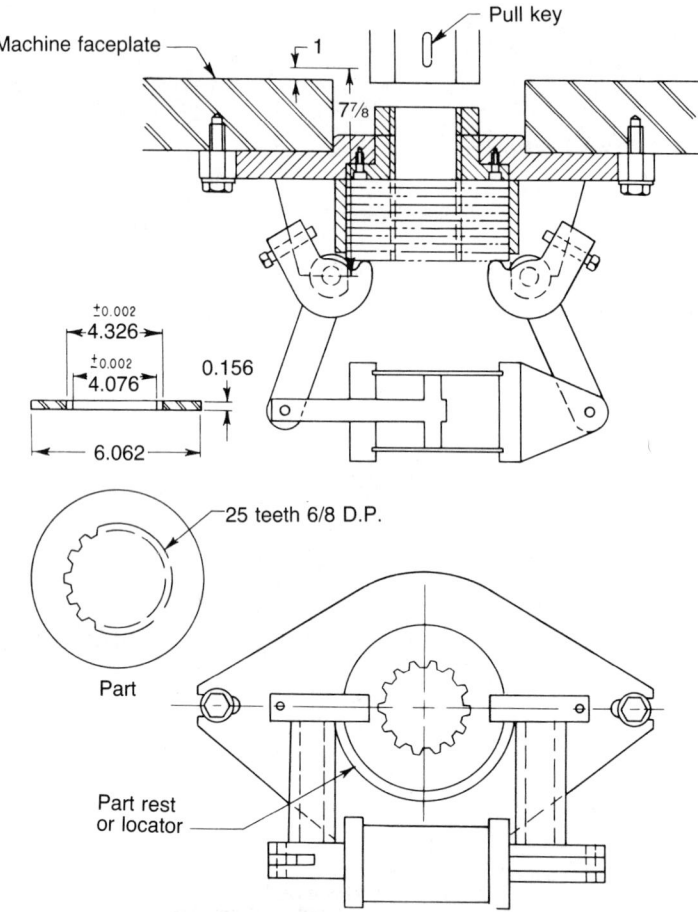

Fig. 12-38 Fixture for clamping thin parts with an air cylinder. *(Courtesy Le Tourneau-Westinghouse Co.)*

Positioning Type of Spline Broaching Fixture. Figure 12-39 illustrates a horizontal broaching fixture for broaching a splined hole with a specified relationship to a reference point, in this case a hole in the web of the part.

The basic fixture is similar to that shown in Fig. 12-36, but with the addition of a diamond-shaped locating pin and two blocks used to position the broach pull head. The broach bar was designed for correct relationship between the flats on the pull end and one spline. The pull head has flats ground on the outer sleeve which establish its proper relationship with the inside locator. It is not necessary for the pull head to reenter the positioning blocks after each stroke, but only occasionally to recheck its position.

To operate the fixture successfully, it was necessary to hold the distance between the faces of the hub and flange to 0.250 in. (+0.004, −0.000 in.). Rest buttons under the flange hold the gear-face runout to a minimum. Because of broach-bar drift, the part should be finish-turned and the gear teeth cut after broaching.

Spline Broaching Fixture with Lead Bar. Figure 12-40 illustrates the layout of a spiral or helical spline-broaching fixture with a lead bar. In broaching internal spiral or helical splines, the arrangement of the teeth on the broach, when brought to bear on a smooth bore, causes a turning moment. For helix angles of less than 5°, a ball-bearing fixture bushing which permits the workpiece to rotate as the broach passes through is satisfactory. An alternate method uses a swivel-type puller permitting the broach to rotate as it is pulled through the workpiece. Although the turning moment exists at larger helix angles, better quality can be achieved by controlling the rotation of the broach as it is pulled through the workpiece.

The lead bar (1) has a spiral groove machined at the required helix angle. As the broach (2) is pulled through the workpiece (3) by the piston rod (4), the gearbox (5) moves on

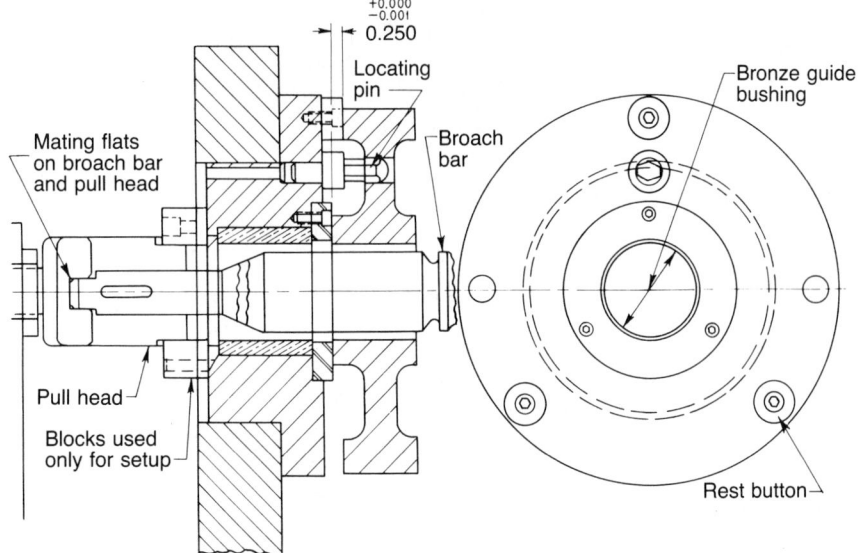

Fig. 12-39 Horizontal broaching fixture with positive workpiece positioning to a tooth of a spline.

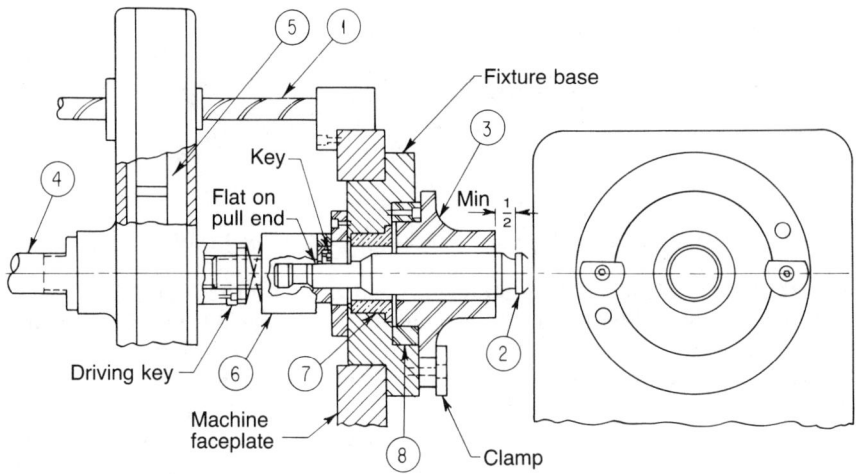

Fig. 12-40 Layout of spiral broaching fixture showing lead-bar attachment.

12-39

the stationary lead bar, causing rotation of the gear train which is keyed to the spiral groove. The gear keyed to the lead bar rotates a mating gear on a shaft keyed to the broach puller (6). The broach has a machined flat which mates with the puller. Broach rotation is, therefore, a positive duplication of the lead-bar groove.

The machined fixture base has a bronze bushing (7) to prevent contact with and possible damage to the broach. An expendable ring (8) serves as a workpiece nest and as a thrust plate.

Automatic Spline Broaching. Figure 12-41 illustrates the fixturing of a horizontal broaching machine which automatically cuts internal splines in gear blanks.

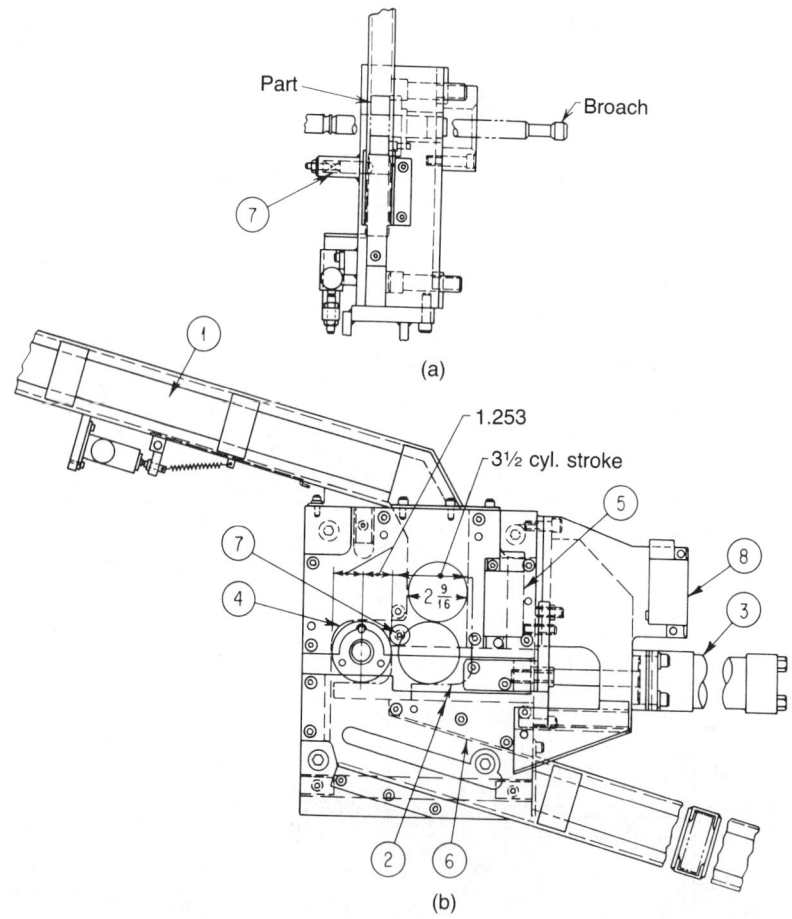

Fig. 12-41 Automatic spline broaching of gear blanks. *(Courtesy Detroit Broach Co.)*

The workpiece, 0.840 in. (21.34 mm) wide and having an OD of 2%16 in. with a concentric 15/16-in.-diam. bore, rolls down an inclined loading chute (1) and drops to the loading platform (2). A hydraulic cylinder (3) moves the platform to the broaching position and clamps the workpiece between the platform and the broaching nest (4). The platform, at the completion of the loading stroke, actuates a limit switch (5) which starts the broaching cycle. An automatic toolholder advances the broach through the bore to engage the broach puller, and the broach is pulled through the part. The loading platform returns to its initial position under the chute while the finished part drops to and rolls down the disposal chute (6).

A workpiece dropping to the loading platform is kept from prematurely entering the nest or disposal chute by a spring detent (7).

The platform on completing its retraction contacts a second limit switch (8) to initiate the return of the broach from the pulling head to the tool-handling mechanism. An interlock prevents platform motion during broach return.

The machine cycle, including loading, broaching, part disposal, and return of the broach, is completed in eight seconds.

The loading and unloading chutes and the fixture-mounting brackets are weldments. Working surfaces, including the loading platform and workpiece nest, are hardened tool steel.

VERTICAL BROACHING

Vertical broaching can be divided into three general categories: pull down, push down, and pull up, depending upon the method of holding the broach and direction of applied force. Both internal and external, or surface, broaching operations are performed on vertical machines.

The machine layout will provide the fixture designer with dimensions necessary to develop the size of the fixture elements. The travel of the machine elements is of particular significance, in that the broach length must be specified therefrom. The broach must clear the workpiece at the extreme upward and downward positions, and the first broach tooth must clear the workpiece before the stroke begins.

Pull Down Internal Broaching Fixtures. A general arrangement and some of the design considerations involved in pull-down broaching are shown in Fig. 12-42. The fixture has a loading table (1) which is manually alternated between the load and work positions.

The loaded table is placed in the work position, and the shank of the broach (2) is passed through the workpiece. The puller (3) engages the broach and pulls it through and clear of the workpiece. With the loading table returned to the outward position, the puller travels upward to return the broach to the retriever (4). The upward travel of the broach puller causes a release ring (5) to contact a ring (6) which releases the broach to the retriever head.

Although a spring-detent type of retriever head is shown, the use of this type with heavy broach bars is not advised.

When designing fixtures for vertical pull-down internal-broaching operations, the designer must make sure that the first broach tooth clears the workpiece with the puller engaged.

Vertical Broaching with a Fixture Guided Broach Bar. Figure 12-43 illustrates a pull-down type of broaching fixture for generating internal helical splines.

The workpiece is a flanged, circular member with a number of concentric internal and external diameters. The flange face is machined perpendicular to the center line of the diameters. Short helical splines, broached in the inside of the workpiece, are concentric with the various diameters and perpendicular to the machined face of the flange.

An alternate method of first broaching the spline and then machining the diameters and face was considered and rejected because of the relative shortness of the splines.

A machined circular collar (1) and three bushings (2, 3, and 4) hold the workpiece. Correct radial location is assured by locating from mounting holes in the flange of the workpiece with pin locators (5).

The broach bar is guided by three bushings (6), one above and two below the workpiece. The lower bushings also absorb part of the thrust load. Each bushing has eight equally spaced identical broach-guide inserts (7). The inserts are ground after assembly in the bushings.

Surface Broaching a Universal Joint Yoke. A vertical pull down broaching fixture for holding a universal-joint yoke while finishing the inner faces is shown in Fig. 12-44.

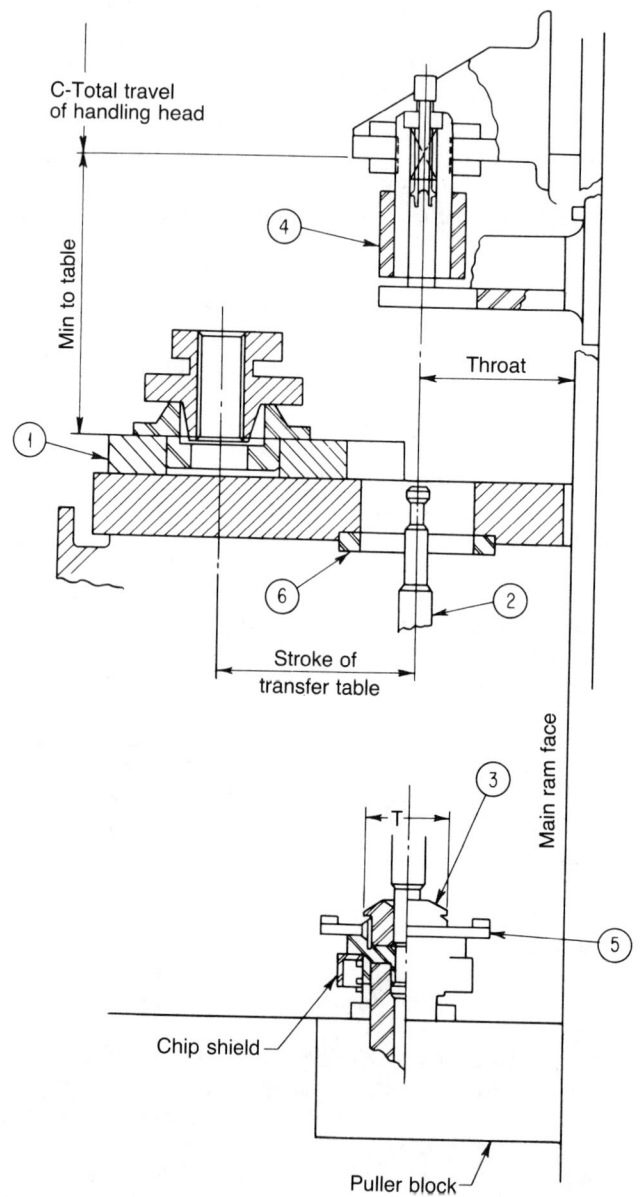

Fig. 12-42 Transfer-type pull-down broaching fixture.

The workpiece is placed over the loading pin (1) while in the vertical position, then rotated to the horizontal position. The lower portion of the pin is threaded to receive a stop collar (2) and locknut (3). The threads provide an adjustment for positioning the yoke. Different lengths of stop collars may be used for different yokes.

Two air cylinders (4), through levers (5), move plunger assemblies (6) which support and back up the workpiece. Locating pins (7) have a taper fit in each plunger to facilitate interchangeability. The slightly tapered face of the locating pin facilitates guiding it into the hole in the yoke. Two other air cylinders (8) move wedges (9) which lock the plunger assemblies, thus preventing their movement during the broaching operation.

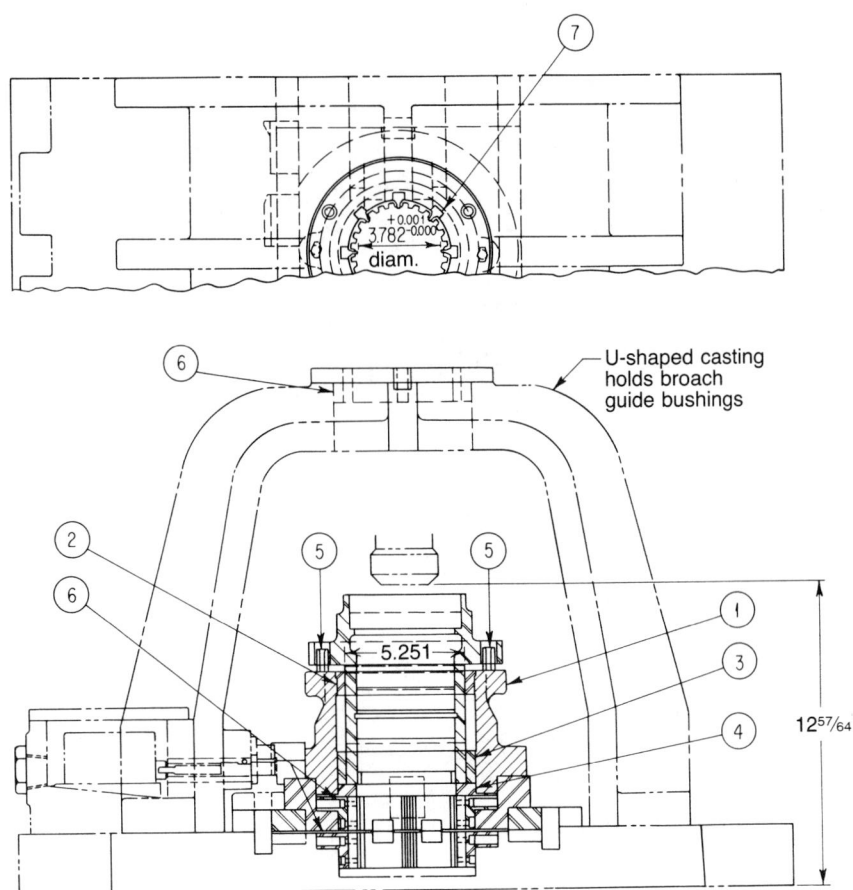

Fig. 12-43 Pull-down type of fixture with fixture-guided broach bar. *(Courtesy Colonial Broach Co.)*

In the broach holder, not shown, are two roughing broaches with shear-type teeth, two finishing broaches with straight teeth, and two broach inserts for finishing the fillet and adjoining surface.

Vertical Surface Broaching Fixture with Air Clamping. Figure 12-45 illustrates a vertical pull-down broaching fixture with air-actuated locating and clamping.

The workpiece, a fork-shaped wheel spindle, has two inside faces that are surface-broached. The spindle is placed in a circular nest (1). An air cylinder (2) moves two pivoted arms (3) to insert two locating pins (4) into two holes in the arms of the workpiece. Two air cylinders move lever arms (5) to rotate cams (6) which contact the workpiece for support during broaching.

An air cylinder (7) actuates a rack (8) which revolves a gear (9) and cam (10). This cam has three pins pressed into it which fit in three holes in the clamp bar (11). The initial movement of the cam moves the clamp bar over the workpiece. Continued cam rotation applies pressure to the underside of the pivoted clamp bar which clamps the workpiece in the nest.

A vertical passage through the center of the fixture contains the broach bars (12), the broach holder (13), and two fixture-mounted bar guides (14).

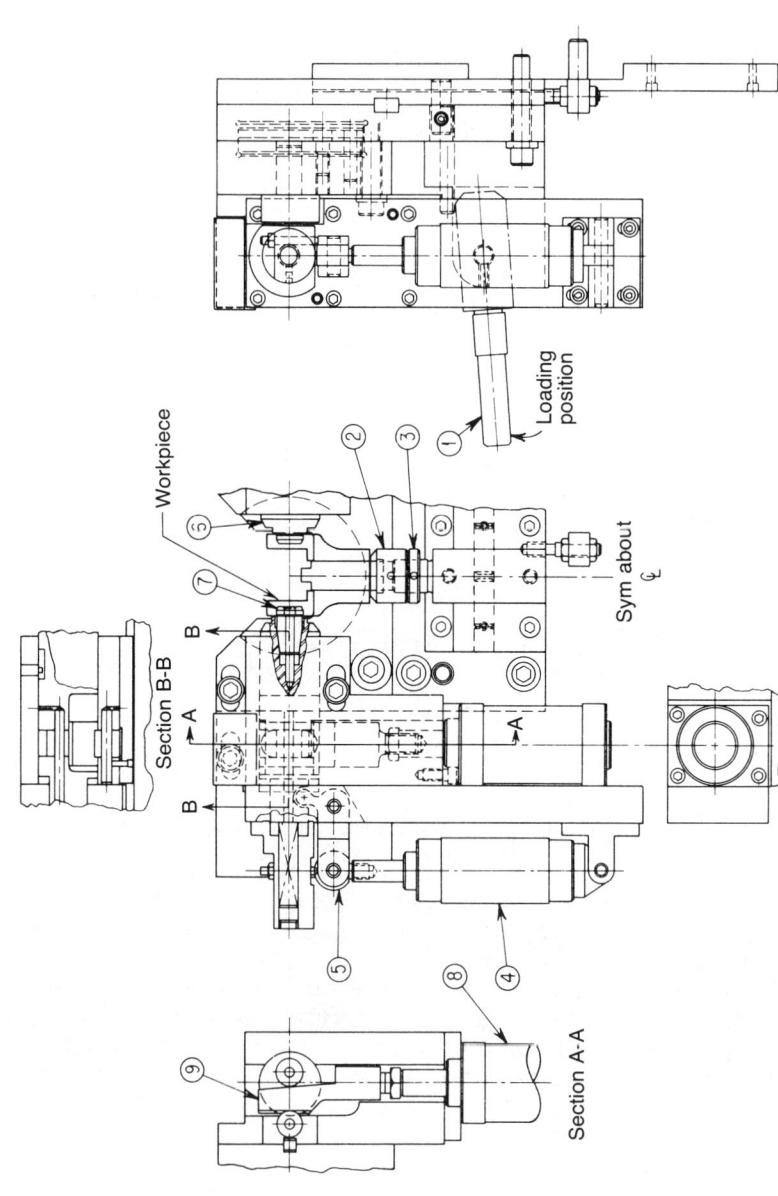

Fig. 12-44 Pull-down broaching fixture for inside faces of universal-joint yokes. (*Courtesy National Broach and Machine Co.*)

Workpiece

Loading position

Sym about ℄

Section B-B

Section A-A

Vertical Broaching Fixture with Automatic Clamping. Figure 12-46 illustrates a fixture for broaching to length the legs of spider-shaped forgings.

Two workpieces are placed on round locators (1) with the legs of the workpieces resting in V-blocks (2). The V-blocks are movable to compensate for variations in the forgings. Clamps (3) are manually pushed forward over the workpieces. At the forward position of the clamps, a limit switch is actuated to start the machine cycle. As the machine table on which the fixture is mounted moves from the loading position to the broaching position, cam levers (4) are rotated by actuating stops (5), causing cams (6) to bear on the underside of the pivoted clamps, which in turn bear down on the workpieces. The actuating stops mounted on the machine frame are adjustable and spring-loaded to compensate for overtravel of the fixture and ensure clamping action.

The broach holder (7) retains and orients four broach bars (8), ensuring their perpendicularity to the broached surfaces of the workpieces. The outward travel of the machine table after the broaching cycle again causes rotation of the cam levers, allowing manual retraction of the clamps for workpiece removal or reorientation. Two machinery cycles are required to complete two workpieces.

Two Station Rotary Indexing Vertical Push Broaching Fixture. Figure 12-47 illustrates a two-station rotary-index vertical broaching fixture. Five workpieces are manually loaded in slots (1); then the fixture is manually indexed, placing the workpieces in the broaching position. A stationary block (2) attached to the machine frame ensures proper positioning and support of the workpieces during the broaching operation. The second station of the fixture is loaded during the first-station broaching operation. As the fixture is again manually indexed, ejectors (3) strip the finished workpieces from the slots. During the broaching cycle, the fixture is locked in position by a spring-loaded plunger (4). The plunger is manually retracted to permit rotation of the fixture dial but must engage and enter the fixture to trip an adjacent limit switch which completes the circuit initiating the broaching cycle.

Vertical Push Broaching Fixture for Concave Slots. A vertical fixture for broaching curved slots around the perimeter of an adapter nozzle is illustrated in Fig. 12-48.

The saucer-shaped workpiece is placed in a counterbored locator (1). A manually actuated cam clamp (2) with a swiveling plate (3) holds the workpiece. After the slot is broached, the workpiece is rotated to align the slot with a manually actuated index plunger (4), and the next slot is broached.

The fixture is mounted on a dovetail subplate (5) for adjustment with the machine throat and is centered with the broach bar by adjustment of a stud (6). Fixture-base mounting holes (7) are drilled oversize to permit adjustment.

The fixture base and subplate are made of machine steel. The locator (1) and the index-plunger housing (6) are made of SAE 6145 steel. The index plunger is of hardened and ground oil-hardening tool steel.

Vertical Straddle Broaching Fixture. Figure 12-49 illustrates a two-station fixture for straddle broaching the crank and pin bosses of a connecting rod. The workpiece (1) is held and centered by fixture members (2) that bear on the sides of the web section. Web clamping is accomplished by positioning the workpiece and then turning the handwheel jackscrew (3). Clamping in the vertical plane is accomplished by turning the handle (4) to revolve the cam (5) which presses the pivoted clamp bar (6) down on the workpiece. A weight on the handle helps hold the clamp locked.

The broach bars (7) straddle the parallel faces of the crank end of the workpiece. Wedges (8) under the broach bars allow their centered 0.679-in. (17.25 mm) spacing.

In the second station, fixture pads (9) center the workpiece parallel to the faces broached in the first station. Vertical clamping is achieved by the method described above. Broach bars (10) mounted on wedges (11) provide centering and adjustment.

The fixture base is cast iron. Hardened inserts are provided at wear points. Working members are hardened and ground tool steel. Bronze bushings are provided for working shafts.

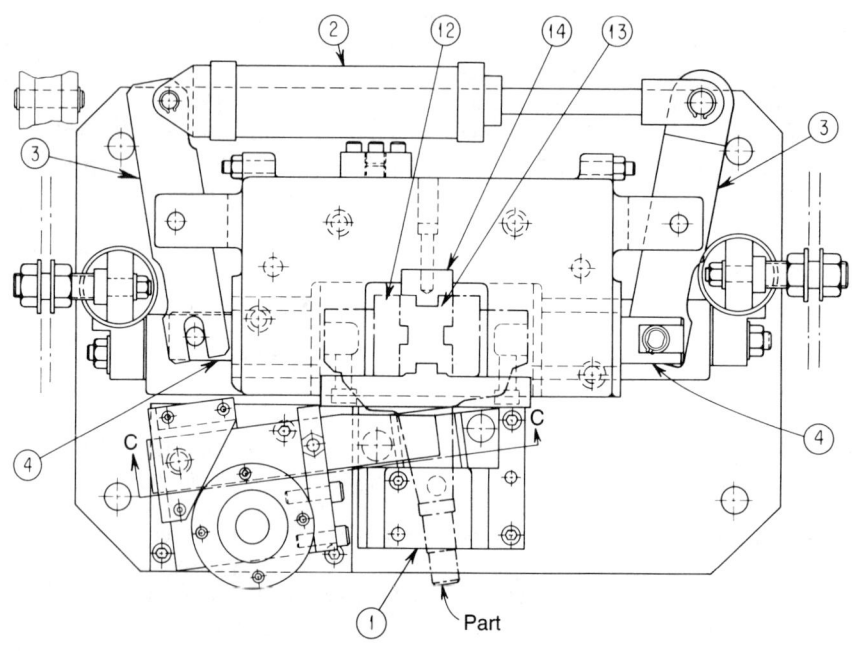

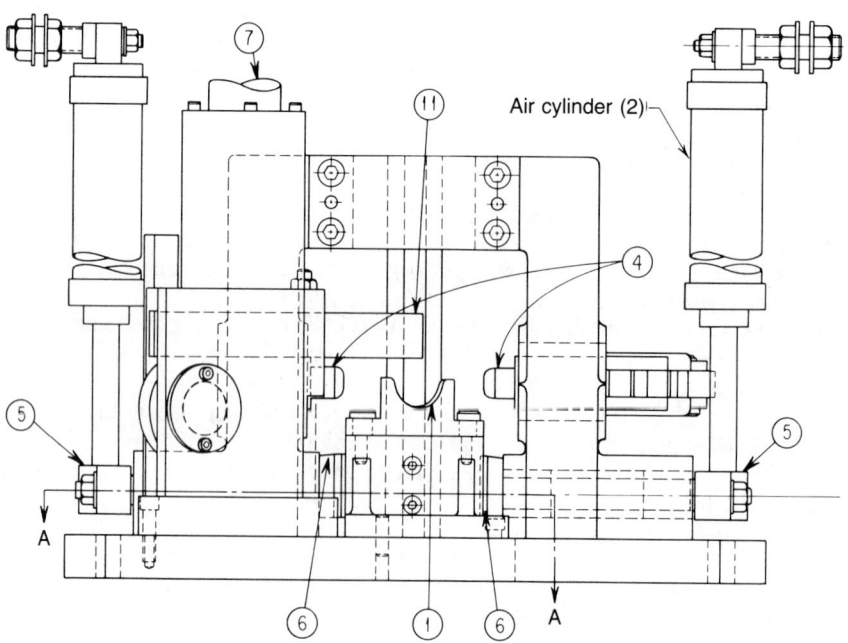

Fig. 12-45 Air cylinder locating and clamping fixture. *(Courtesy National Broach and Machine Co.)*

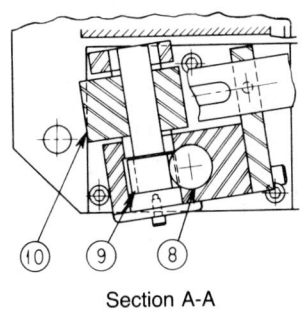

Section A-A

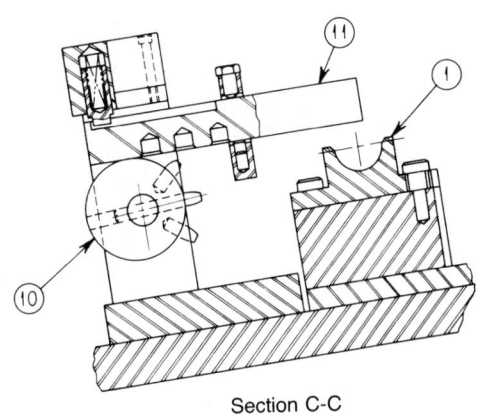

Section C-C

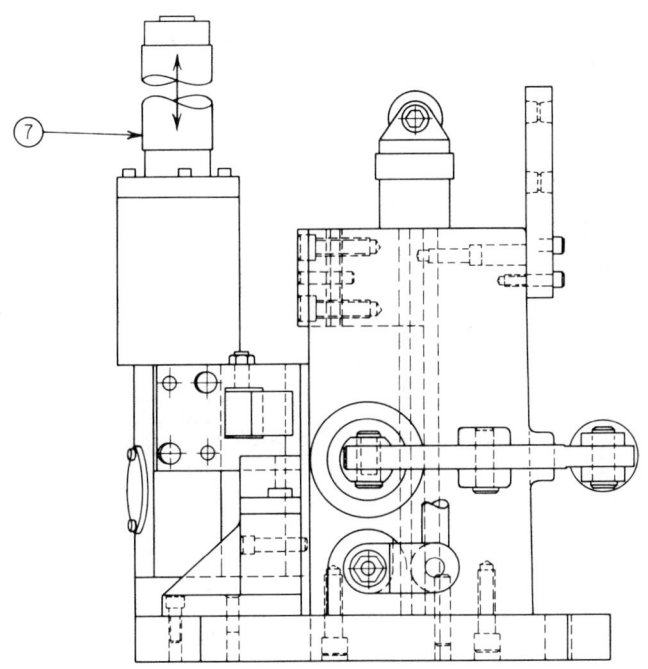

Fig. 12-45 *(Continued)*

12-47

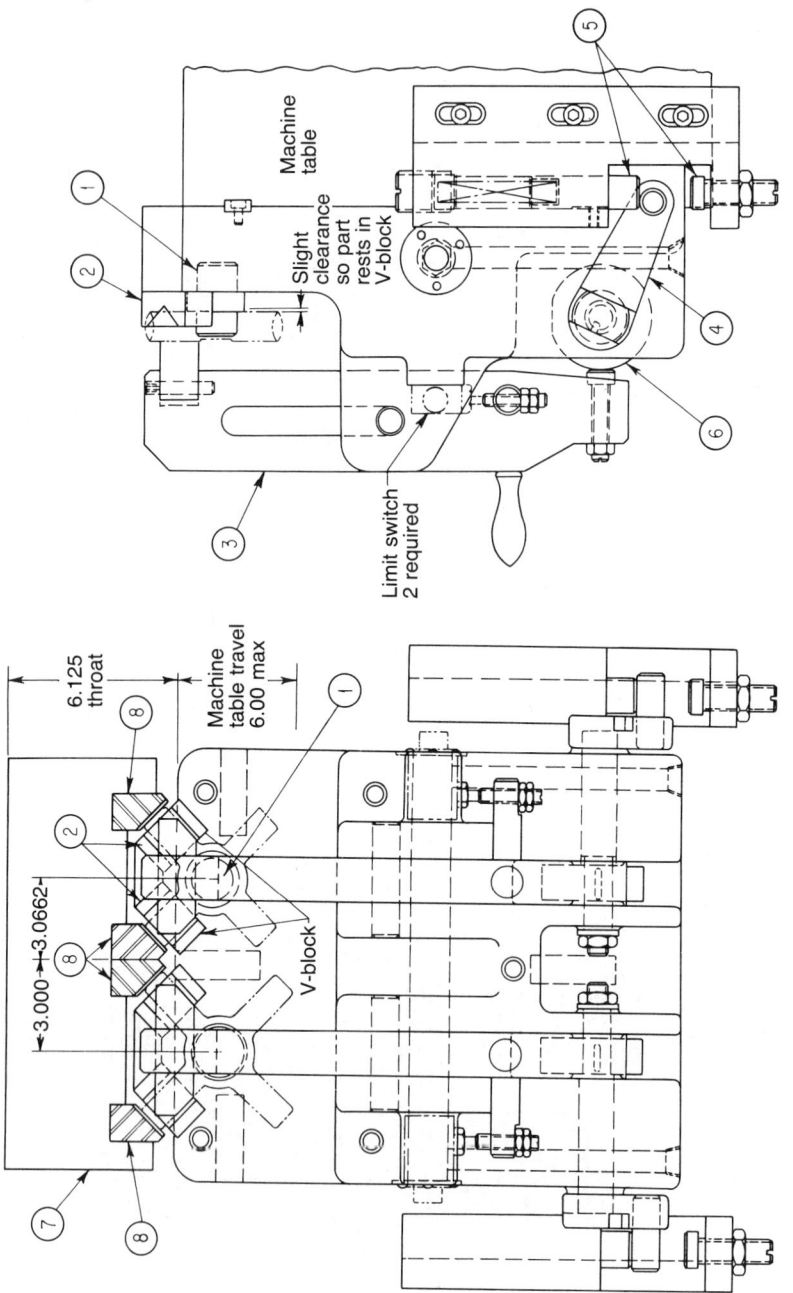

Fig. 12-46 Vertical broach fixture with transfer table clamping. *(Courtesy Ford Motor Co.)*

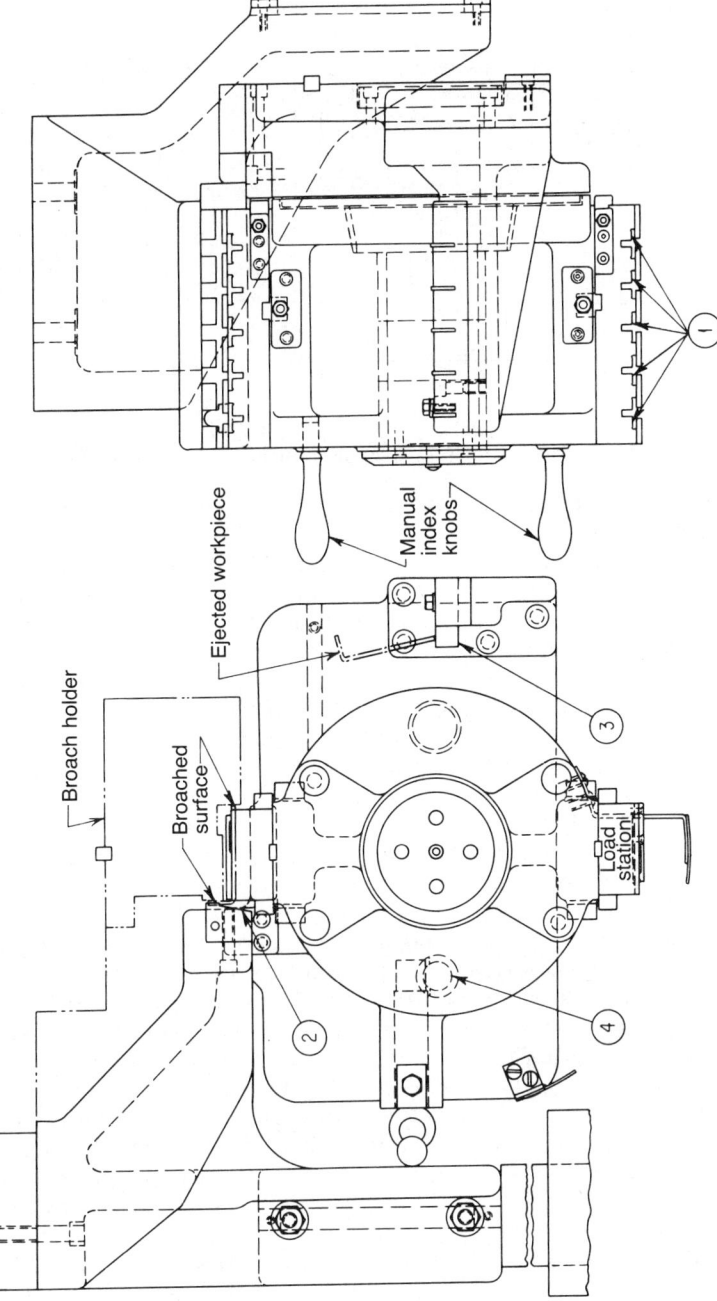

Broach holder

Broached
surface

Ejected workpiece

Manual
index
knobs

Load
station

Fig. 12-47 Two-station rotary-indexing vertical broach fixture. *(Courtesy Ex-Cell-O Corp.)*

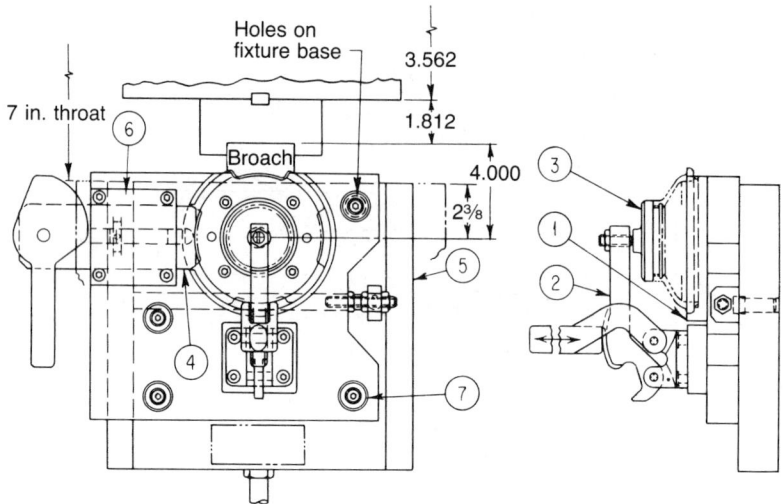

Fig. 12-48 Vertical form broaching fixture. *(Courtesy Apex Broach Co., Inc.)*

Piloted Push Broach Layout. A layout for a push broaching with the broach bar guided by a pilot in the fixture is shown in Fig. 12-50.

The workpiece (1) is placed on the bushing (2) which acts as a thrust plate. The pilot (3), an integral part of the broach-bar holder, enters and is centered by a guide bushing (5) before the shell-type broach bar (4) engages the workpiece. A conical surface on the broach bar permits the workpiece to center itself.

At the completion of its stroke, the broach puller (6) with pushing pin (7) strikes the releasing plate (8) and is disengaged from the broach. The lower retriever slide (9) takes the broach below the level of the workpiece which can then be removed.

A layout generally shows the stroke of the ram, the stroke of the retriever slide, and the dimensions of the machine, from which the fixture designer can specify the dimensions of the fixture components and the length and profile of the broach holder and of the broach bar. Broach-holder dimensions must allow the broach holder to clear the workpiece at the upper and lower extremes of the stroke. The broach dimensions must permit the pilot to be centered before cutting starts.

For some applications, the broach is made in one piece instead of two pieces, and it may be piloted by the rough workpiece without a pilot.

Master Push Broaching Fixture. Figure 12-51 illustrates a master fixture which, with interchangeable locating blocks, can position a wide variety of workpieces for push-broaching operations. These locators align the workpiece with the broach center line and allow clearance so that the workpiece is free to center itself on the broach.

The locating blocks (1) are keyed to the fixture base (2) and can be set at various distances from the broach center line to accommodate the OD of various workpieces. The hardened wear plate (3) is subjected to abrasion from the workpiece sliding over it when being loaded and unloaded. Alternate rest bushings (4) accommodate workpieces of different ID.

A locating ring (5) attached to the fixture base mates to and nests in the machine table. A wear bushing (6) between the locating ring and the rest bushing completes the thrust column. The rest bushing is held in place by two standard drill-bushing lock screws (7).

Self-contained Broaching Unit. Figure 12-52 illustrates a fixture for broaching four surfaces, two per part, of two workpieces. The fixture is a self-contained broaching machine requiring only an external source of reciprocating motion and pressure.

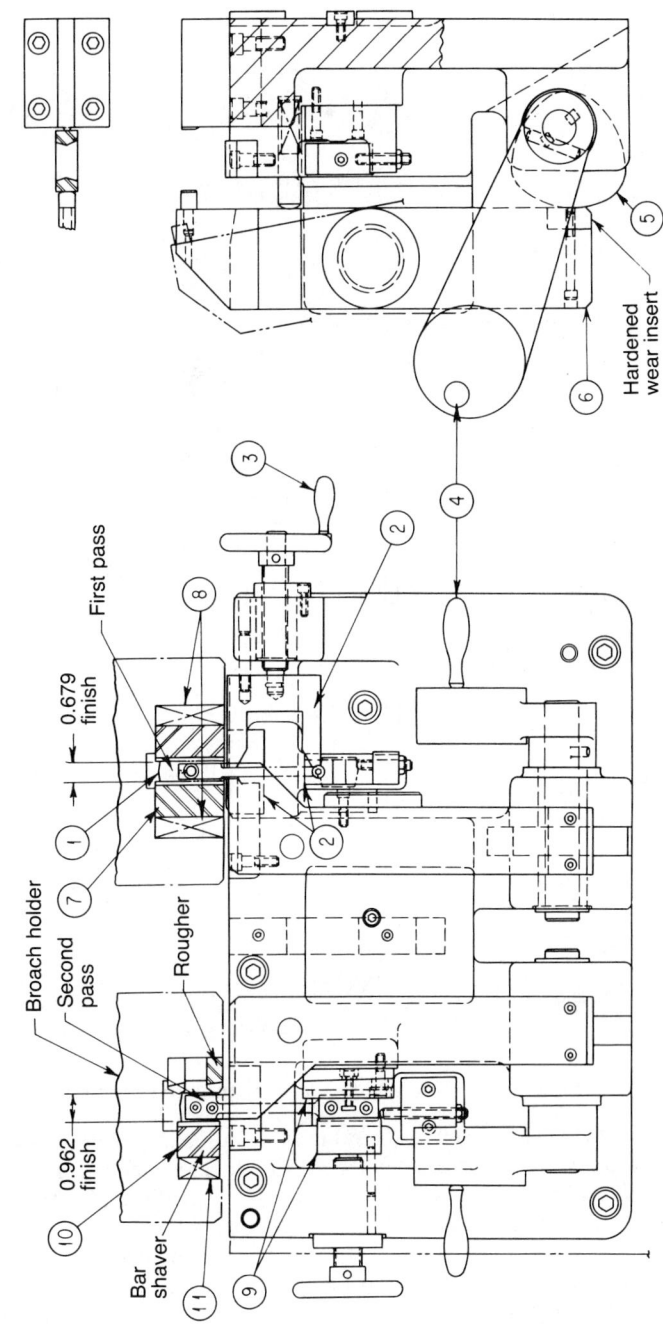

Fig. 12-49 Two-station fixture for straddle broaching crank and pin bosses of a connecting rod. *(Courtesy Detroit Broach and Machine Co.)*

Hardened
wear insert

First pass

0.679
finish

Broach holder

Second
pass

Rougher

0.962
finish

Bar
shaver

12-51

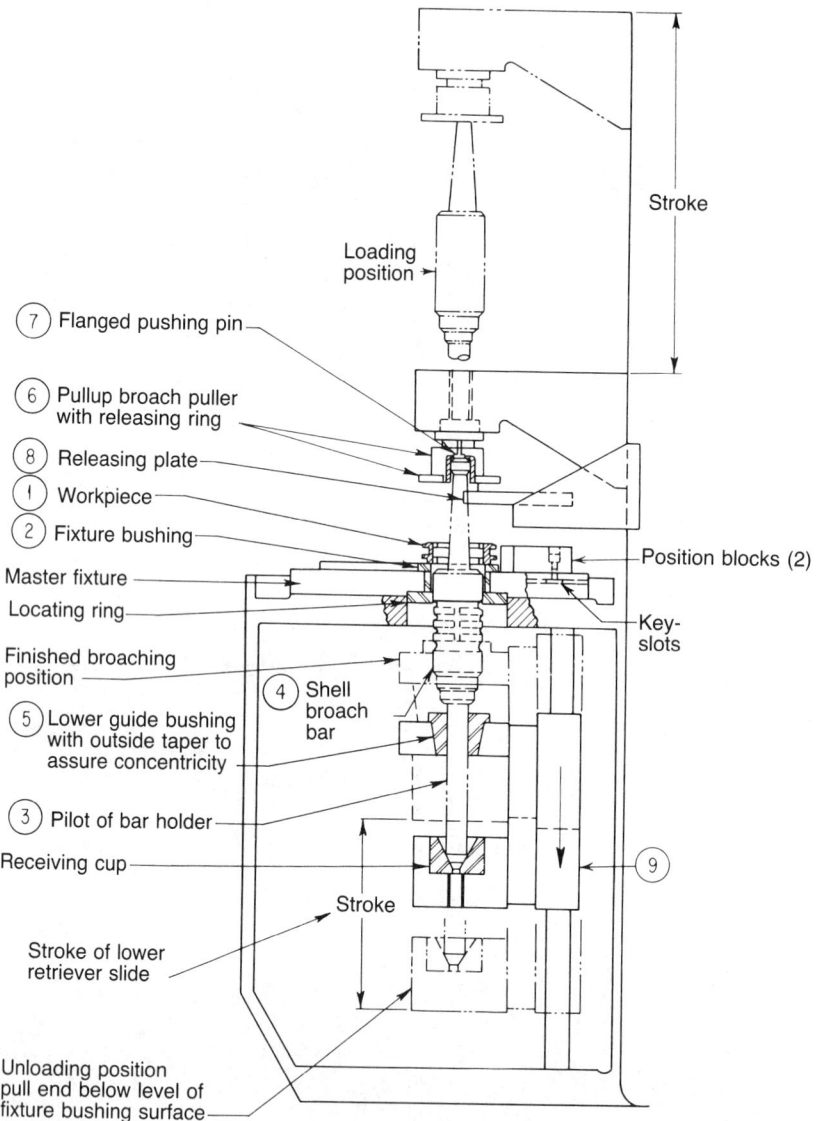

Fig. 12-50 Push broach layout of fixture and pilot-guided broach bar.

The fixture may be set between the ram and bolster plate of a conventional hydraulic press, with the ram adapter (1) aligned with the press ram. The base of the fixture is then keyed (2) and bolted to the bolster. Ram travel is adjusted so that the broach-bar inserts (3) clear the workpiece at the bottom of the stroke.

Two workpieces are placed between the pair of plates (4). The shuttle cylinder (5) moves the transfer table (6) from the loading position shown to the work position. The clamp bar (7) locks the workpieces in location as the table moves to the work position. The press ram descends, supplying power for the broaching operation, remaining at this lower position while the transfer table retracts to the load position; then the ram returns to its top position. The transfer table travels on hardened ways (8). Travel is limited by an adjustable stop block (9). Each broach holder can be adjusted for position by an

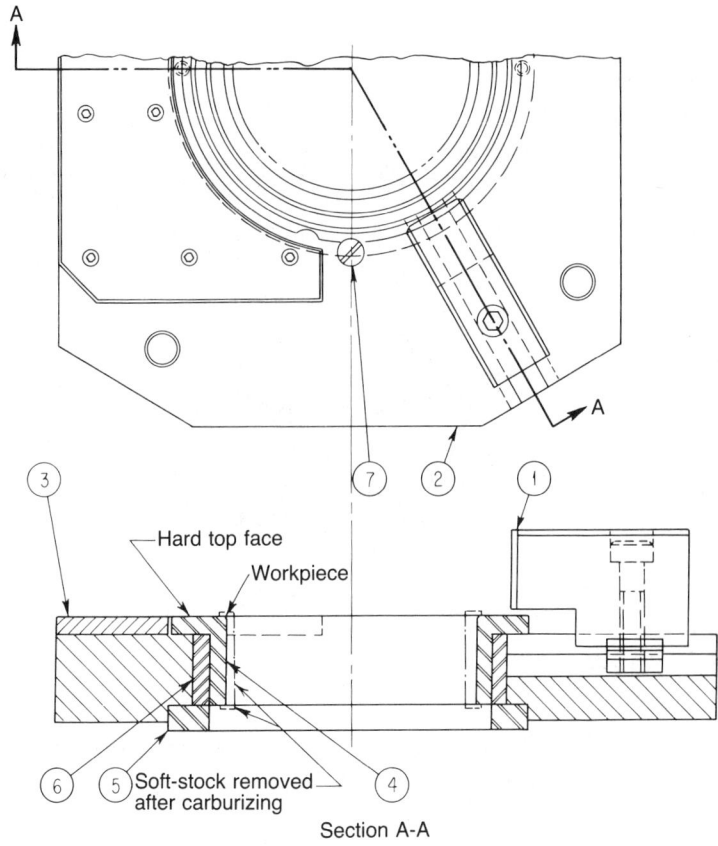

Hard top face

Workpiece

Soft-stock removed
after carburizing

Section A-A

Fig. 12-51 Master push broaching fixture with rest bushing.

individual wedge-and-bar keeper assembly (10) and individual key plates and push blocks (11).

Pull Up Broaching Layout. Figure 12-53 is a layout for pull-up broaching. The broach is shown in the loading position and at the beginning of the cutting stroke. In the loading position, the broach (1) rests in a cup (2) while being held upright and in alignment by a bushing (3) attached to the lower fixture plate (4).

The workpiece (5) is placed on the exposed leading end of the broach. The cycle begins with hydraulic elevation of the broach, cup, fixture plate, and workpiece until the broach engages the puller (6). The workpiece is held up against the thrust plate (7) by the upward motion of the broach. At the end of the stroke, the workpiece drops to the incline (8) and slides off. The broach puller returns the broach to its original position in the cup and bushing and trips the releasing keys (9). The free broach and lower elements descend to the lower loading position.

The internal surface of the thrust plate (7) and bushing (3) are soft to prevent damage to the broach. Ample clearance is provided between the thrust plate ID and the broach. Adequate coolant should be introduced as close to the point of work as possible, preferably through the thrust plate. Broach length must permit the workpiece to clear the ends of the broach at both upward and lower extremes of its travel.

Fixture for Round Bar Stock. An automatic loading and unloading surface-broaching fixture for round bar stock is illustrated in Fig. 12-54. A gravity loading chute (1) feeds

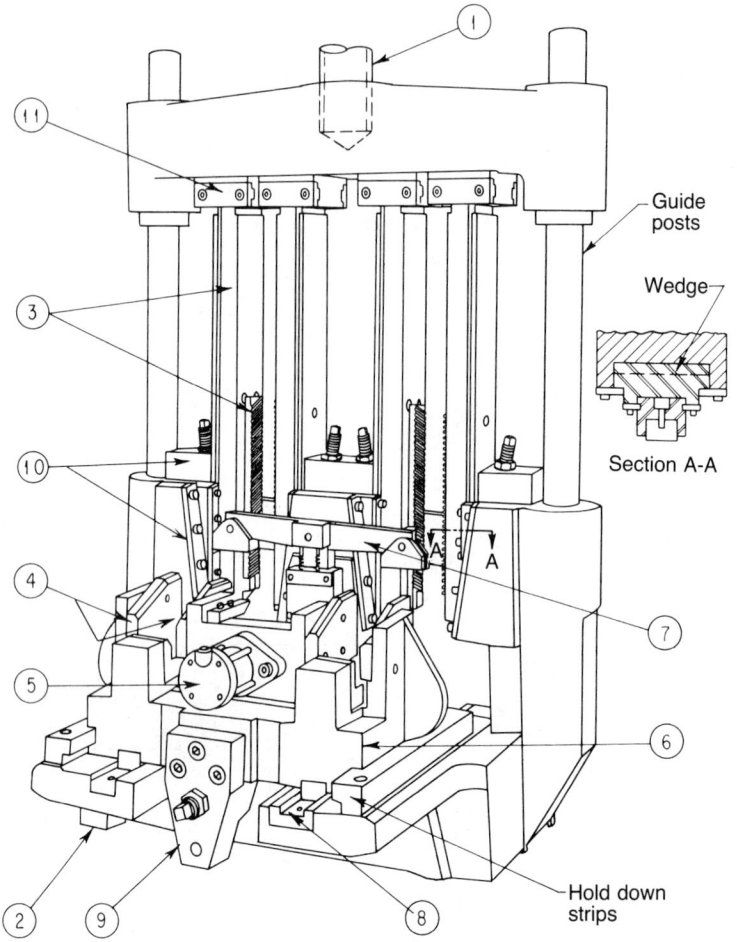

Fig. 12-52 Self-contained broaching fixture. *(Courtesy Continental Tool Works, Div. of Ex-Cell-O Corp.)*

the workpieces into a space between the clamping block (2) and the transfer block (3). The workpiece is moved from the loading position under the chute by the hydraulic cylinder (4) to the broaching position shown. Upon reaching the stop (5), the forward motion of the fixture ceases while continued motion of the cylinder piston clamps the workpiece through the push rod (6).

The descending broaches cut two grooves in the two workpieces and finish them to length. On the upward stroke of the broach holder (see Fig. 12-55), two spring-loaded hooks lift the workpieces from the fixture and carry them upward to the unloading hook (7).

Working faces of the hydraulic piston rod, the push rod, and the clamping block are of hardened and ground tool steel. The fixture base (8) and the transfer-block support and retainers are of hot-rolled steel. The loading and unloading chutes are weldments.

The broach holder, shown as in Fig. 12-55, has two keyways which position the inserts (1) for cutting the two grooves in the workpieces. Another insert (2) cuts the part to length. Back-up blocks (3) help hold the broach inserts in place. Attached to the side of the holder are cam blocks which actuate the fixture controls. At the top are two unloading hooks (4) for removing the part from the fixture.

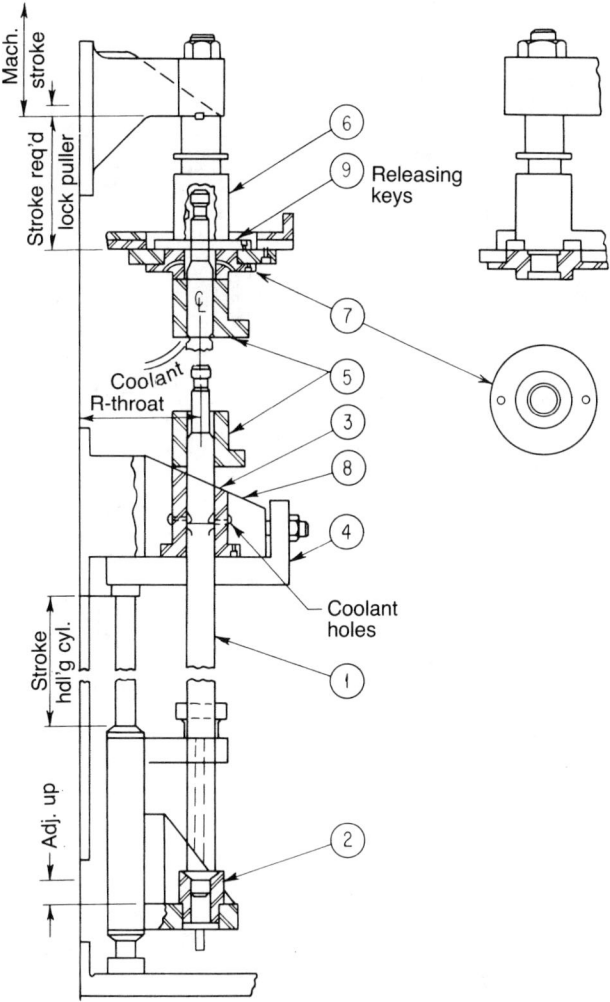

Fig. 12-53 Pull-up broach layout.

Equalizing Fixtures. When it is not possible to properly align a bearing surface for the workpiece, as when broaching a cored hole in a casting or a forging, an equalizing fixture may be employed. Such a fixture usually consists of a hemispherical bushing which rests in a hemispherical cavity. Pressure of the broach against the workpiece is sufficient to move the bushing to the position where the axis of the hole coincides with the axis of the broach.

Shown in Fig. 12-56 are concave and convex hemispherical equalizing fixtures. Figure 12-56a and b suggest the extent and center lines of spherical bearing surfaces. Figure 12-56c and d show representative hemispherical equalizing fixtures. If the broaching operation is in a horizontal or pull-down position, a suitable chip shield should be provided to prevent chips from falling onto the spherical surfaces.

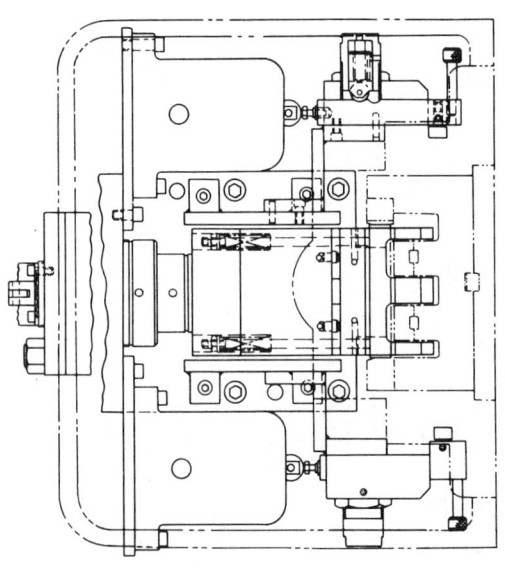

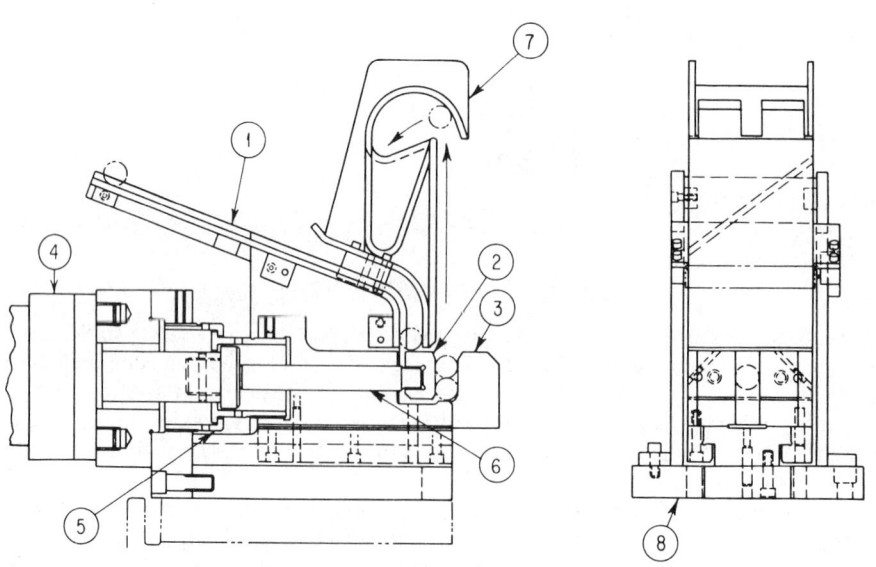

Fig. 12-54 Automatic loading and unloading surface-broaching fixture.

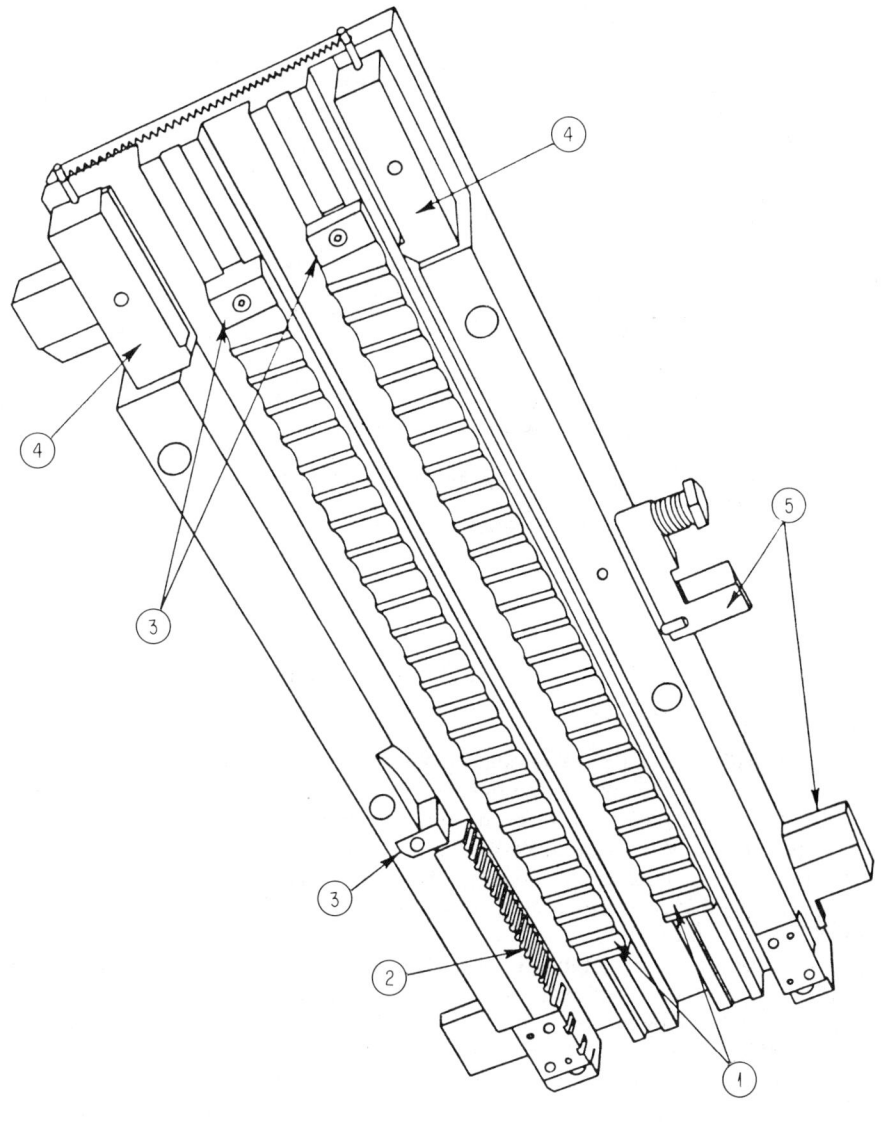

Fig. 12-55 Broach holder for use with Fig. 12-54.

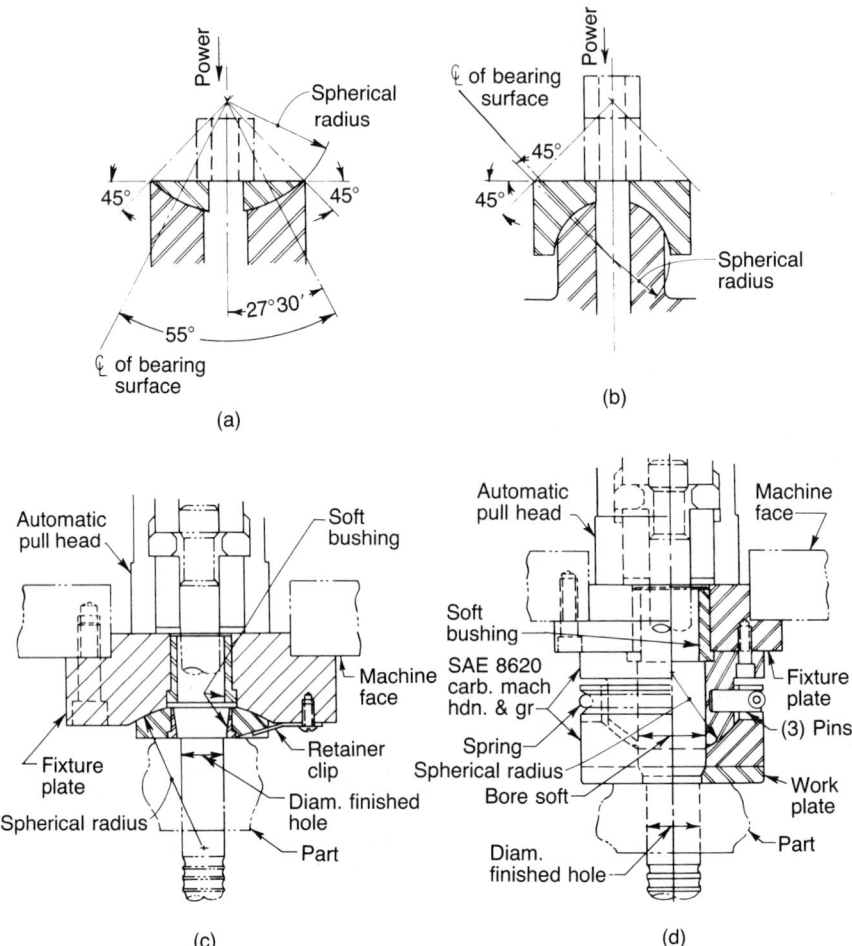

Fig. 12-56 Equalizing fixtures.

BROACH HOLDERS

A knowledge of broach-holder and broach-insert design and function is invaluable to the fixture designer in coordinating fixture design with these and other machine elements.

It is general practice in surface broaching to design simple broach inserts which are easily produced and easily replaced in case of damage or wear. These inserts are then assembled in broach holders to produce the desired shape in the finished part. Holders are not of universal design but are constructed to suit the particular workpiece and the assembled broach for it.

The broach-holder assembly usually fills the throat of the machine to minimize overhang of the fixture and workpiece.

The holder can be made of ordinary machine steel, high-strength cast iron, or a heat-treatable steel, such as SAE 1045 or SAE 8645 hardened and drawn to Rockwell C 28-36. This hardness permits machining after heat-treating with a minimum of finish grinding. The material selected depends upon the use and amount of handling to which the holder is subjected.

The method of holding the inserts in the holder usually permits their removal, replacement, and adjustment without removing the holder from the machine. However, the assembly may be removed to the toolroom for resharpening of the inserts and resetting to the proper dimensions.

Since the position of the roughing inserts is not critical, they can be brought to the required dimension by using shims between them and the holder. The broach inserts containing the finishing teeth are often set to close tolerances by using an adjusting wedge similar to that shown in Fig. 12-34.

Figures 12-57 and 12-58 show various methods of securing inserts in the holders. The choice of holding method depends upon the accuracy required in the broaching operation, the amount of space and clearance available for the broach-holder assembly, and the frequency with which the inserts must be replaced.

View *a* of Fig. 12-57 shows an insert with a right-angle groove at 30° to the side of the insert. Holes tapped in the holder are spaced at approximately 2½ in. (63.5 mm) for 1/4- or 5/16-in.-diam. dog-point setscrews. The angle of inclination may be increased to 45° max, thus increasing the stock at *B*. Dimension *A* is 1/8 in. (3.18 mm) min. This method of holding is adaptable to inserts up to 1½ in. (38.1 mm) wide.

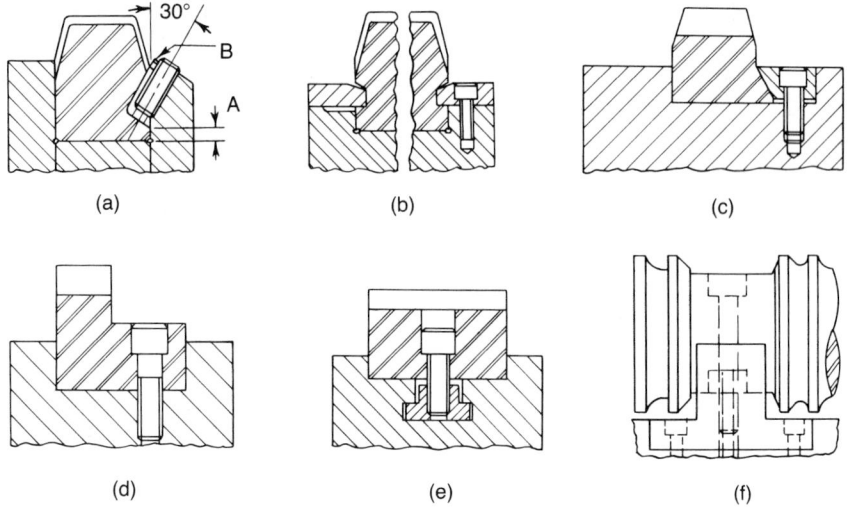

(a) (b) (c)

(d) (e) (f)

Fig. 12-57 Broach-insert holding methods.

In Fig. 12-57*b*, the insert is held in place by clamping strips along each side. By loosening the strips, the inserts may be removed from the bottom of the holder. This type of holder should be used when the location of the form is not very critical or the surfaces are relatively straight. A more accurate method of retaining the insert is shown in view *c*. One side of the slot in the holder is accurately machined to position, and the form on the insert is accurately machined. The tapered wedge and insert push the insert to accurate location, as well as clamping it in the holder.

A method of holding an insert for a narrow broached surface is shown in Fig. 12-57*d*. Holes are drilled and counterbored in the insert and tapped in the holder. Inserts with teeth the full width of the face may also be retained by this method. The use of a T-slot is illustrated in view *e*.

The mounting of a round insert used to surface-broach parts such as bearing caps is shown in Fig. 12-57*f*. A groove is machined into the holder in which support blocks are mounted. Holes are drilled through the insert and counterbored for socket-head cap screws which attach the insert to the support blocks. When one side is dull, the bar is rotated 180°, and another pass is made with the second side before resharpening. The support-block diameters must be held to +0.000 in., −0.0002 in. tolerance, and spaced

3 to 6 in. apart, depending upon the bar-diameter and broaching pressures. The support blocks are separate parts so that the height can be adjusted by grinding or shimming.

Figure 12-58a shows the broach insert mounted on a subholder instead of being mounted directly on the main holder. Each insert has an individual subholder which is slightly shorter than the insert. An advantage of this arrangement is that the machine operator only has to remove the dull insert in its subholder and replace it with a sharp set which has been set to dimensions A and B in the tool-grinding department. Shims are placed between the insert and subholder for proper dimensions. This broach insert has soft-steel inserts which are tapped for the mounting screws.

The wedge and spacers shown in Fig. 12-58b and c provide a means of adjusting broach finishing teeth to the required dimension A . The adjusting wedges usually have a

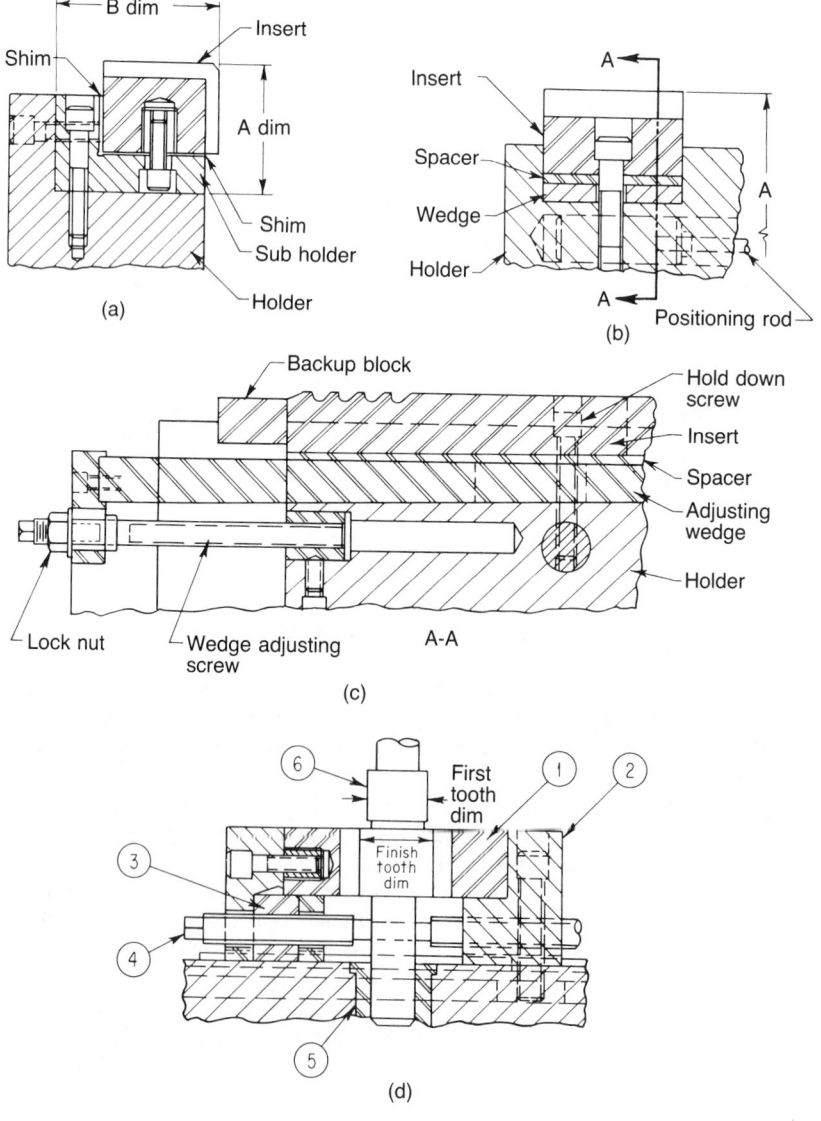

Fig. 12-58 Broach-insert holding methods.

taper of 0.156 in. per ft (13 mm per meter) with a movement of 3½ to 4 in. (89 to 102 mm), giving the insert an adjustment of 0.0045 to 0.052 in. (1.1 to 1.32 mm). The original spacer used with a new insert may be 0.125 in. (3.18 mm) thick. After the wedge reaches its full adjustment, it is returned to its original position and a thicker spacer replaces the original. Spacers are provided to compensate for the amount ground off the insert during its useful life.

Also illustrated in view *b* is a tapped plug fitted in a reamed hole to receive the hold-down screw. The positioning rod is removed after the insert hold-down screw has been started.

Figure 12-58*c* is Section *A—A* of view *b* showing the wedge adjusting screw.

An adjustable straddle-broach holder with setting gages is shown in Fig. 12-58*d*. The inserts (1) are held in a subholder (2) having a close-fitting plug (3) which is tapped for the adjusting screw (4). The end of the plug extends into a T-slot to control the movement of the broaches. The adjusting screw has right- and left-hand threads so that each subholder moves the same amount.

Bushings (5) are press-fitted into the holder opposite the first and last teeth of the broach inserts. Using the setting gage (6), the inserts may be easily set to the proper width for the part being broached. With this arrangement one holder and one set of broach inserts can be used for several similar parts requiring only a setting gage for each part.

CONTINUOUS BROACHING

Fixture for Continuous Broaching. Figure 12-59 illustrates a high-production fixture for a chain-driven broaching machine. The fixture is guided by two channels (1) that move on the slideways of the machine. Drivepins (2) are engaged by a chain to pull the fixture through a fixed broaching station.

The workpiece is placed in a nest (3). Forward travel of the fixture on the slideways actuates cam bars (4 and 5). The forward cam bar (4) moves the front slide (6) against the workpiece. The rear cam bar (5) moves the rear slide (7) forward to engage the vertically positioned workpiece keyway with a locating key (8). The workpiece may be rotated manually to permit engagement of the key. With the key engaged, a safety pin (9) is seated in a cam flat. If, owing to mislocation of the workpiece, the locating key cannot engage the workpiece, the safety pin protrudes to trip a limit switch stopping the machine. The rear slide (7) bears on and supports the nest during broaching.

After the fixtured workpiece is drawn through the fixed broach holders (10) and bars (11), the cam bars are again actuated by being drawn past lugs fixed to the slideways. The forward and rear slides return to their at rest positions, and the finished workpiece falls into an unloading chute.

Continuous Broaching of Connecting Rods. Figure 12-60 illustrates a broaching fixture for a connecting rod. The part is placed against two rough locators (1) with its small end against a work rest (2) and against a back-up block (3) on the bearing end of the part.

The small end of the part is held against the work rest by bevel pins (4). The bearing end of the part is supported by a thrust and locating block (5). A cam on the machine drives the cam bar (6) inwardly. A locking angle (7) on the cam bar assists in holding the clamp (8) securely against the part. After the part is broached, a cam on the opposite side of the machine returns the cam bar, loosening the clamp and releasing the part.

Wear strips (9) bear against the ways of the machine. A number of these fixtures are used on a machine and are pulled through and spaced by a motor-driven chain drive. Four chain-drive pins (10) are fastened to each fixture.

The broach holder is in an inverted position in the top of the machine. It roughs and finishes the outside, cap, and bearing surfaces of the connecting rod in one pass. Figure 12-61 illustrates a section through each stage of the broaching operation.

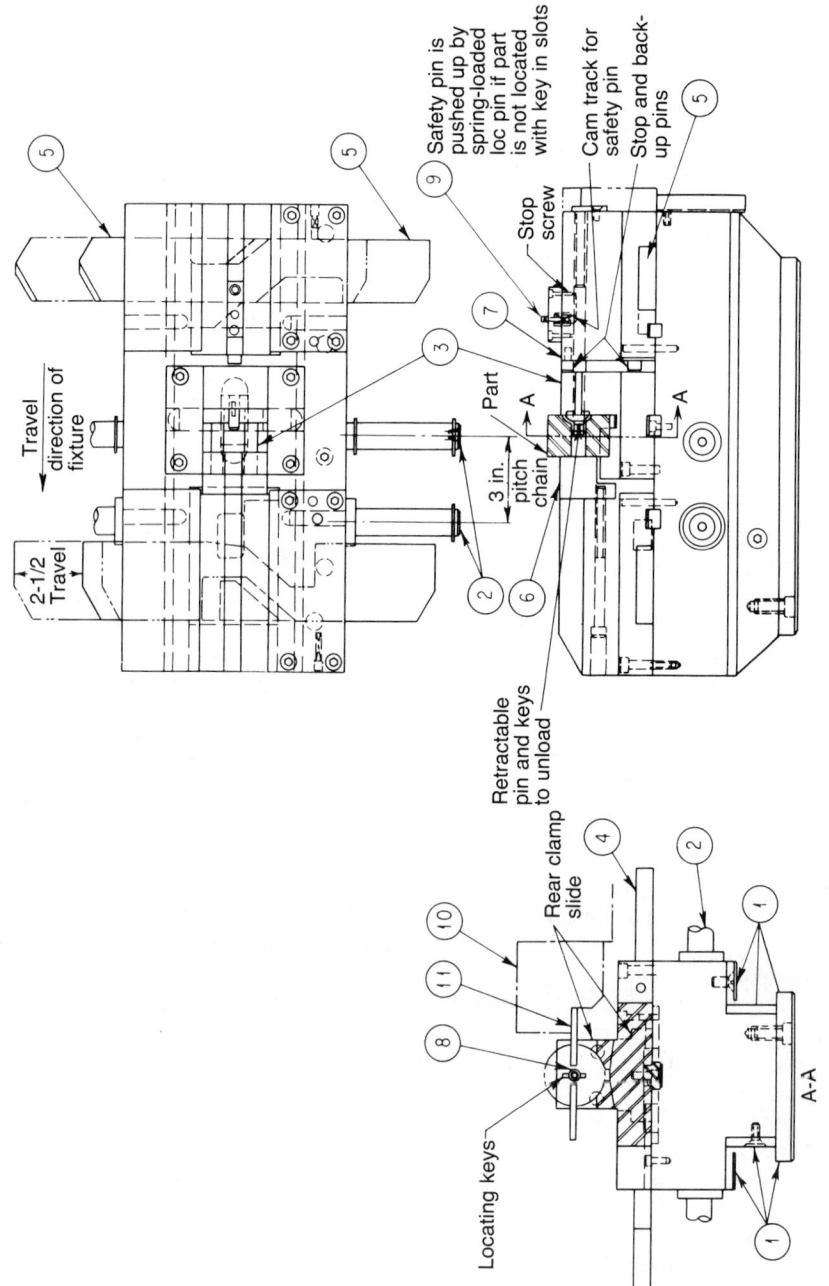

Travel direction of fixture

2-1/2 Travel

Safety pin is pushed up by spring-loaded loc pin if part is not located with key in slots

Cam track for safety pin

Stop and back-up pins

Stop screw

Part

3 in. pitch chain

Retractable pin and keys to unload

Rear clamp slide

Locating keys

A-A

Fig. 12-59 Fixture for chain broaching of two slots in a circular workpiece. *(Courtesy Detroit Broach and Machine Co.)*

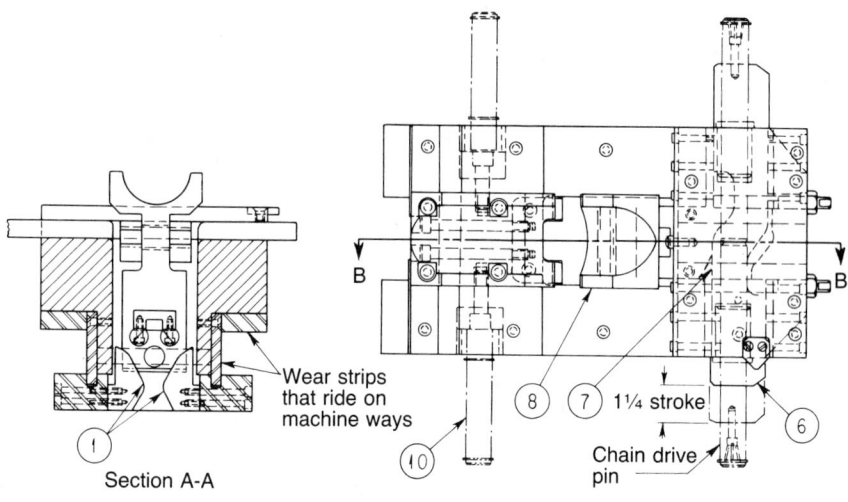

Section A-A

Wear strips that ride on machine ways

① ⑧ ⑦ 1¼ stroke ⑥

⑩

Chain drive pin

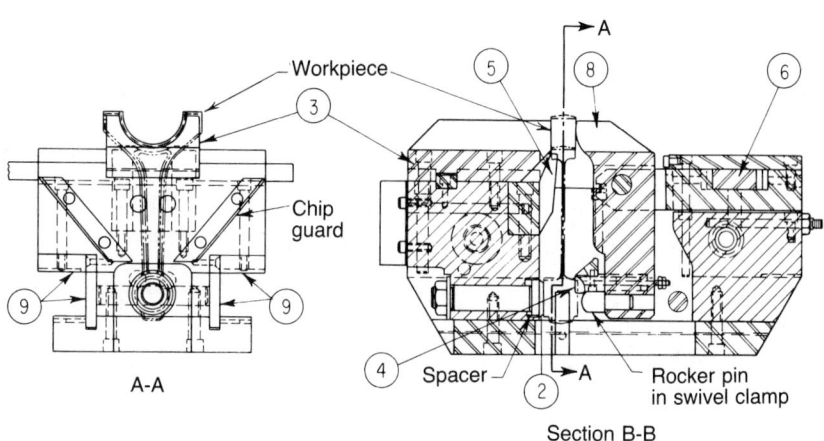

Workpiece

③

Chip guard

⑨ ⑨

A-A

⑤ ⑧ ⑥

④ Spacer ② Rocker pin in swivel clamp

Section B-B

Fig. 12-60 Fixture for continuous broaching of connecting rods. *(Courtesy The LaPointe Machine Tool Co.)*

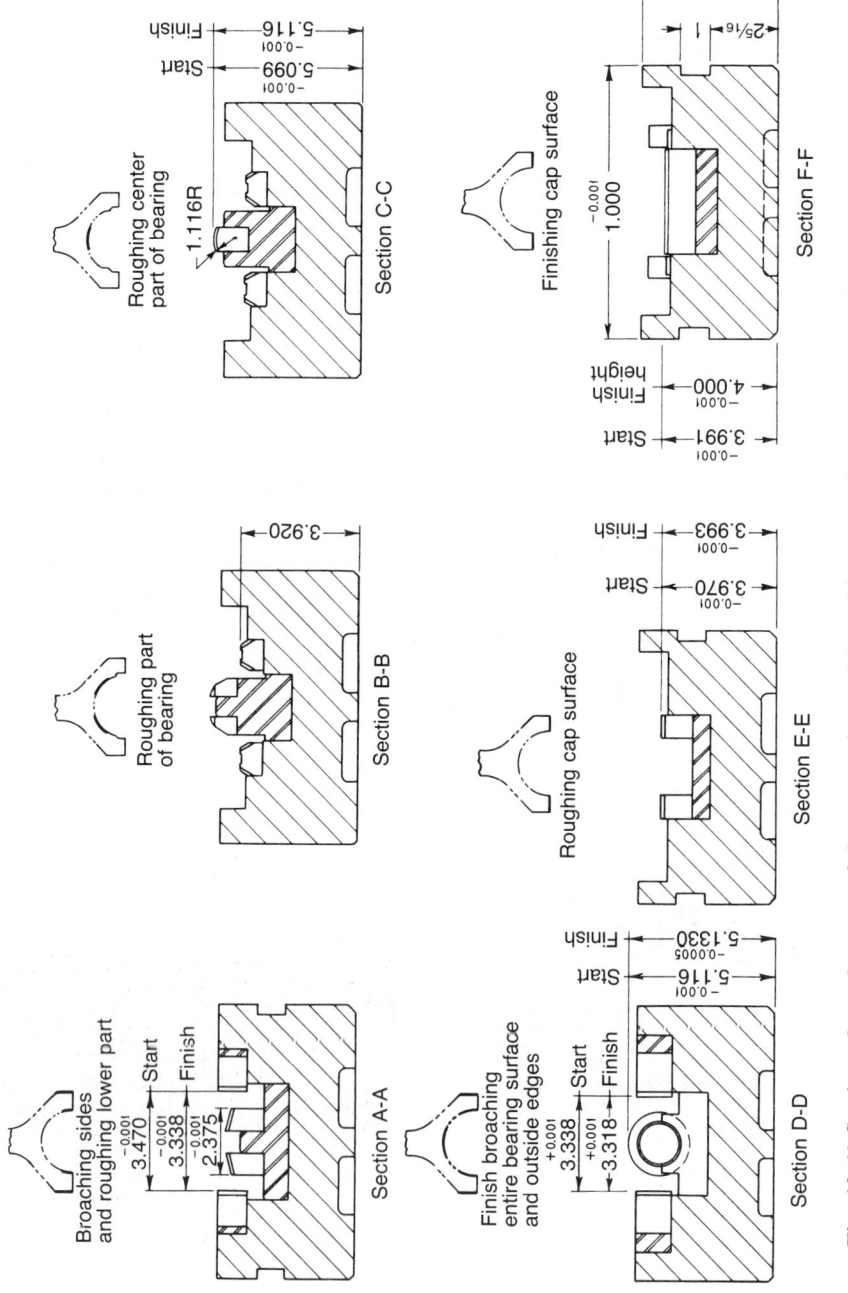

Fig. 12-61 Sections through stages of the connecting-rod broaching operation. *(Courtesy The LaPointe Machine Tool Co.)*

12-64

BROACHING SPLINES AND GEARS[4]

Many splines and gears are produced by broaching. Broaching is the fastest of all gear machining methods. The process, however, is generally limited to high-production application because machine and tooling costs are high. With sufficient production requirements, cost per part produced is low.

Spline Broaching. Before splined holes are broached, it should first be determined what portion of the spline fits its mating member. Most involute-spline fits are on the sides (pitch diameter) of the teeth, but others may locate on the major or minor diameters of the spline teeth. If the spline in the gear is a side-bearing fit with its mating part and the part is processed from the ID, the spline inside diameter must be broached or otherwise machined concentric with the sides of the teeth. If it is a major-diameter fit and the part is processed from the ID, the spline minor diameter must be machined concentric with the major diameter and the sides of the teeth.

Nibbling-type spline broaches with alternate round and spline finishing sections are generally used to provide the required minor-diameter concentricity. Such tools tend to drift off center, however, and do not always provide the required concentricity conditions. Reasons for this include back taper in the broach, relief on the sides of the teeth and breakdown of the cutting corners, machine misalignment, and improper face-grinding techniques.

These problems can be corrected by using concentricity broaches having a floating full-form finishing shell on the end of a conventional nibbling-type broach section. The finishing shell has alternate round and full-form finishing teeth that produce accurate concentric spline teeth with smooth surface finishes. Simultaneous cutting action on the critical surfaces ensures that the concentricity of the broached spline tooth dimensions is equal to the accuracy ground in the tool itself, which is generally less than 0.0005 in.

Broaching Internal Gears. Internal spur and helical gears are being economically and accurately produced in high production by a single pass of a full-form finishing broaching-tool assembly. Such assemblies consist of a one-operation, two-piece broach comprising a roughing section and a finish broaching tool. The roughing section is of the nibbling type that produces the desired involute form by a generating process as it moves through the work. Each tooth is of increasing height. This roughing section is followed by a floating, side-shaving shell which removes stock along the entire tooth thickness. The amount of stock removed by the full-form finishing shell is usually about 0.010 in. (0.25 mm) on the tooth thickness, 0.005 in. (0.13 mm) per surface on helical parts, and half that amount on spur applications.

Internal helical gears are usually broached on vertical broaching machines. Accurate leads are produced by the action of a precision lead bar, follower nut, and associated gearing, which rotate the broaching tool as it is pulled through the blank. Some broaching machines have a direct-drive lead bar to the broach, with no gearing required.

In one application, two fully automated, full-form finishing broaching machines are producing internal helical gears for automotive transmissions at a rate of 180 pieces per hour. The internal gear has 72 teeth, with a 15.5 diametral pitch, 17½° pressure angle, and a 22°, 11 minute, 30 second right-hand helix angle. Gear blanks, made from SAE 4028 steel seamless tubing, are 6 in. diam. x 1⁹⁄₁₆ in. (40 mm) wide and have a hardness of 179-217 Bhn. The broaching tools are 82 in. (2080 mm) long and have a chip load of 0.0036 in. (0.091 mm) per tooth. These gears were originally shaped and shaved. It took 3 minutes to shaper-cut the teeth and 1¼ minutes to shave each gear. This method required 28 gear-shaper spindles and six rotary gear shavers. Now, each of the two broaching machines makes a finished gear every 40 seconds. Life of each broaching tool is about 100,000 gears.

Large internal spur gears for automotive differentials, with 5/7 diametral pitch teeth up to 9.400 in. pitch diameter, are being produced with nibbling-type broaching tools.

12-65

Broaching External Gears. External gears, splines, and parts with specially formed teeth can be produced rapidly and economically in medium and high-production lots by pot broaching, utilizing tools having internal cutting teeth. External helical gears are produced by using special pot-broaching machines equipped with lead bars, but this process is limited by gear size, helix angle, and material.

Another process called push-up pot broaching uses a machine in which the part is pushed upward through a fixed pot-broaching tool of either stick, ring, or combination design to produce external teeth. Ring-type broaching tools are used where tooth form and spacing are critical, and the lower cost stick type is used where accuracy permits and where the length of the cut is very short. Machines have the pot broach securely mounted in a stationary position on the front, directly above a hydraulic cylinder with a nonrotating piston rod. The rod has a splined push plate which forces the workpiece up through the pot broach. This method ensures quick and complete chip removal from the broach teeth, with coolant being flushed into the tool area. Smooth finishes and precise tooth form, size, and spacing can be obtained. Tool life varies from 500,000 parts on steel applications to 1,250,000 on cast-iron and pearlitic malleable parts.

The process is ideally adapted to full automation. Finished parts can be ejected at the top of the pot broach, where gravity can help move them to the next operation. One such setup is illustrated in Fig. 12-62. Incoming parts from a roller conveyor are fed into a loading chute through a gage that prevents oversized parts from entering. A pivoting-arm moves each part from this chute to a position above the nosepiece on the end of the push-up cylinder rod. An unloader above the pot broach holder is a mechanical, spring-loaded linkage that pushes the finished part into a gravity chute. As the part slides down this chute, it trips a switch that permits the cylinder rod to retract for the next broaching sequence.

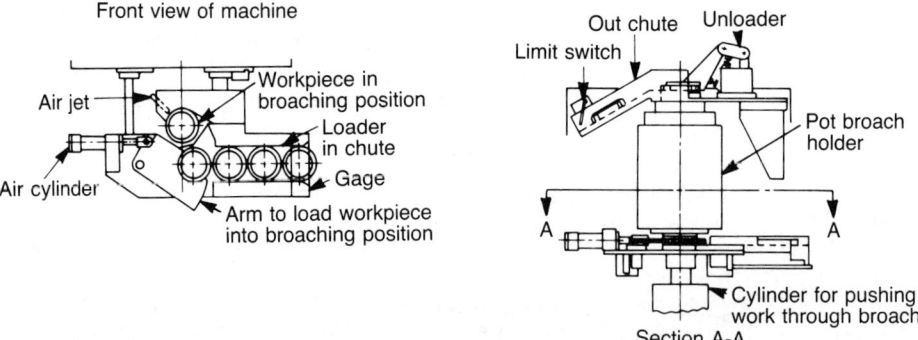

Fig. 12-62 Automatic loading and unloading arrangement for pot-broaching gears.
(Courtesy National Broach & Machine Co.)

References

1. Thomas J. Drozda and Charles Wick, eds., "Broaching, Planning, Shaping and Slotting," *Tool and Manufacturing Engineers Handbook*, Vol. 1, 4th ed. (Dearborn, MI: Society of Manufacturing Engineers, 1983), pp. 7-1 to 7-33.
2. *Ibid.*
3. Leonard J. Smith, *Modular Broach Tooling* (Westchester, IL: Ty Miles, Inc.).
4. Thomas J. Drozda and Charles Wick, eds., "Gear and Spline Production," *Tool and Manufacturing Engineers Handbook*, Vol. 1, 4th ed. (Dearborn, MI: Society of Manufacturing Engineers, 1983), pp. 13-33 to 13-34.

CHAPTER 13
PLANING, SHAPING AND SLOTTING FIXTURES

PLANING[1]

Planing is a material-removal method for producing flat surfaces that may be horizontal, vertical, or at an angle. With special equipment, planing machines, called planers, can form curved or irregular shapes. Simplicity of operation, cutting tool design, and application make planers versatile machine tools. They are used primarily for medium-to-large size workpieces. Productivity, however, is comparatively low; most of the work previously done on planers is now performed on planer-type milling machines and surface grinders.

THE PLANING PROCESS

In operations performed on planers, the workpiece is reciprocated and a single-point cutting tool is fed into the workpiece. The feed in planing is intermittent and represents the width of the cut. Planers are made with mechanical or hydraulic drives. The mechanical drive consists of a variable speed, reversing drive motor; gear train to the table; and control equipment. The table of a planer with a hydraulic drive is reciprocated by one or more hydraulic cylinders secured to the bed, the piston rods being secured to the table. The speed at which a mechanical-drive planer operates depends on the speed of the driving motor and on the gear ratio. In hydraulic planers, the speed of the table is determined by the effective area of the piston and by the volume of oil pumped against this area in a given time.

While many jobs formerly handled on planers are now being performed on other machine tools, applications still remain for which planing is economical. Workpieces of certain size and shape, and long, narrow, and angular surfaces are often easier to machine on a planer. Planing is often preferred for flat bearing surfaces that have to be hand scraped because, with planing, work hardening of the surfaces is minimized.

Tooling costs are less for planing than milling, which may be important when production quantities are limited. Tool setting and regrinding are easier with single-point planing tools.

Types of Planers. Several types of planers are available; double-housing and open-side planers are the basic types. The heads on the crossrail of some planers are constructed rigidly enough to permit planing across the table.

Double-housing Planers. This type of planer has two housings supporting the crossrail, as shown in Fig. 13-1. It is usually equipped with four heads, two on the crossrail and one sidehead on each housing.

Open-side Planer. The open-side type shown in Fig. 13-2 has a column on one side of the machine only. The width of the work that can be handled is not limited as it is on a double-housing planer. The work can extend far beyond the left side of the table and may

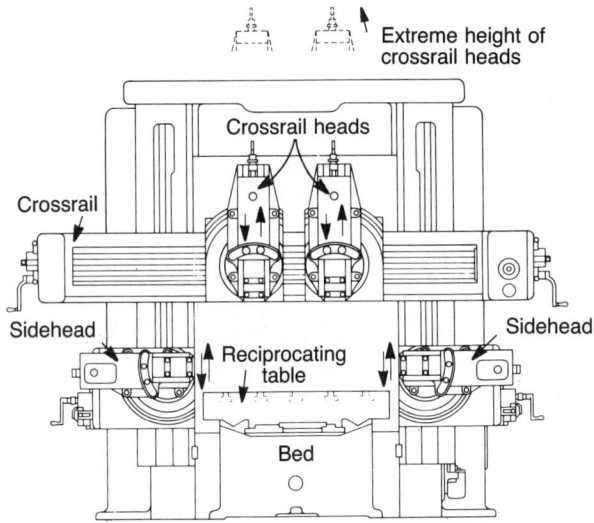

Fig. 13-1 Double-housing planer having two heads on the crossrail and one sidehead on each housing.

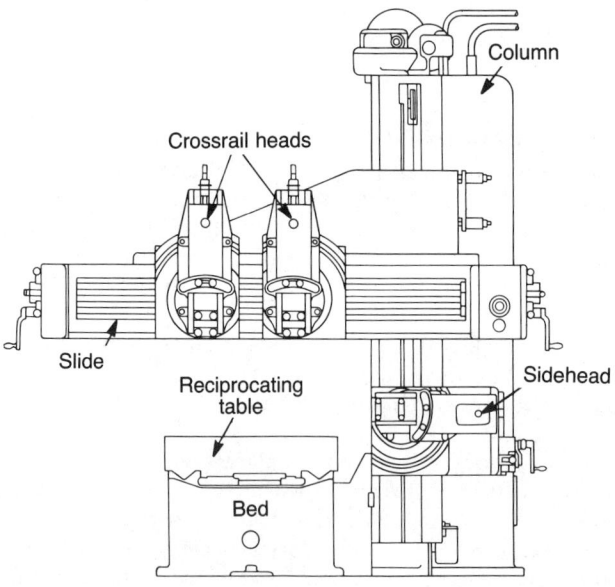

Fig. 13-2 Open-side planer which permits handling work of unlimited width. Work supports can be placed at left of machine if needed.

have an additional support on an auxiliary rolling table placed to the left of the planer and extending parallel to the bed.

Convertible Open-side Planers. The convertible open-side planer is an adaptation of the open-side type of planer with a removable housing fastened to the left hand side of the bed and supporting the outer end of the rail. A sidehead may be mounted on this housing.

Adjustable Convertible Open-side Planers. This type of planer is provided with a removable left-hand housing mounted on a runway perpendicular to the table travel, allowing this housing's position to be adjusted to suit the particular job. The adjustment permits positioning of the left-hand sidehead to the greatest advantage.

Milling Planers. These machines are made with various combinations of planing, milling, boring, and drilling heads. They are principally suited for work which requires various types of operations and which can be done to advantage in the same fixturing of the work. In this way, greater accuracy results from eliminating resetting of the work and work handling is minimized. These machines have found favor for large jig and fixture work. They are made in double-housing, open-side, and convertible types.

Double-cut Planers. This type of planer is designed by some manufacturers to incorporate the ability to cut on both the forward and reverse strokes of the table. The head on the planer has a limited rotation spindle, oscillated by a small air cylinder that engages one bit of a double-bit toolholder with the work on the forward stroke of the table and then the other on the table's reverse stroke. This planer is available in both the double-housing and open-side design.

SPECIAL PLANER APPLICATIONS

Special planer applications include planing radii, helical grooves, and contoured surfaces. A number of methods can be used in these applications.

Planing Radii. Surfaces with large radii can be planed on plates or similar workpieces with the method illustrated in Fig. 13-3. A radius rod is attached to a plate that is free to oscillate with respect to a second plate attached to the planer table. The workpiece is fastened to the plate carrying the radius rod, and as the planer table reciprocates, a surface of the required radius is planed on the workpiece.

Another method of planing surfaces to required radii is shown in Fig. 13-4. The planer head is arranged to be swiveled by means of a gear sector and rack. The saddle on which the swiveling head is mounted is clamped in position on the rail and is rotated by feeding the adjacent head on the rail, the latter head having the rack attached to it. The radius planed is determined by the distance of the tool point from the center of the swivel, and this distance can be changed by adjusting the slide on the swivel member.

Planing Helical Grooves. A special application is planing helical grooves in rolls, accomplished with the method illustrated in Fig. 13-5. The roll is mounted in V-blocks and is end-stopped against an angle plate. An arm attached to the roll neck and having a roller follower that is guided by an inclined plate fastened to the bed of the machine causes the roll to oscillate through a predetermined arc as the planer table reciprocates.

Planing Contoured Surfaces. One method of planing contoured surfaces is shown in Fig. 13-6. In this setup, vertical movements of the planer-head slides are controlled by a cam mounted above the rail on the machine.

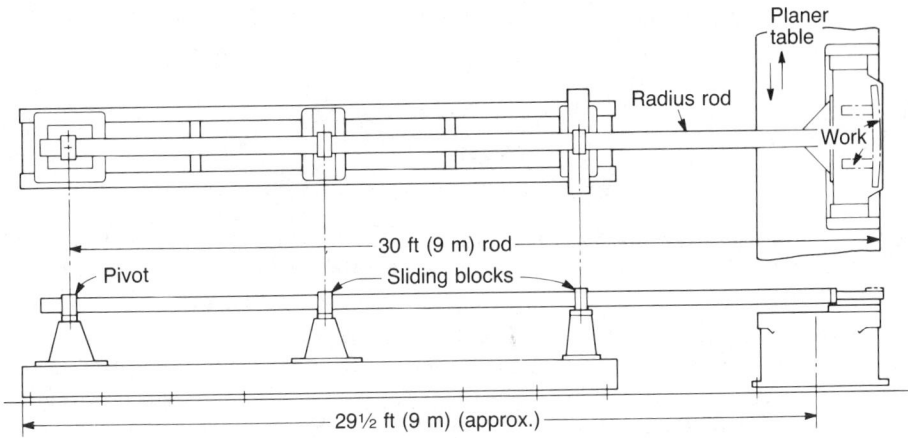

Fig. 13-3 Pivoted radius rod which is used to plane surfaces having large radii.

13-3

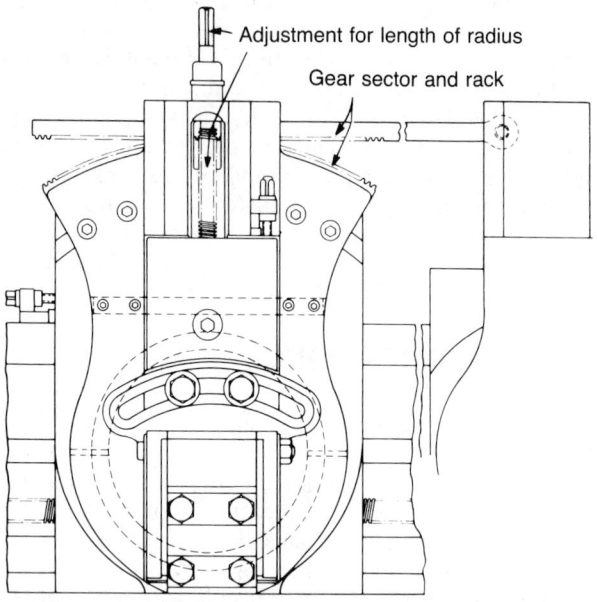

Adjustment for length of radius

Gear sector and rack

Fig. 13-4 Method of swiveling planer head by means of gear sector and rack to produce surfaces having different radii.

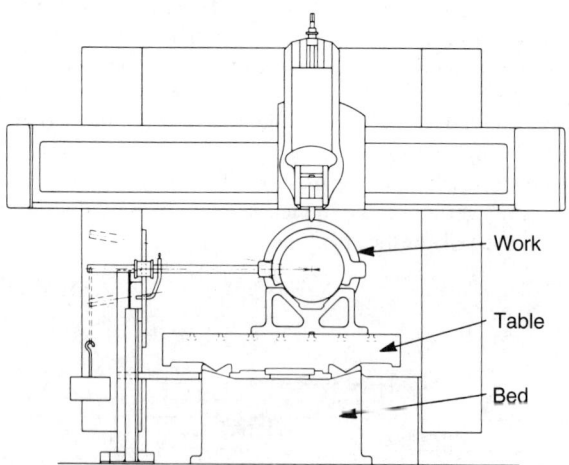

Work

Table

Bed

Fig. 13-5 Arrangement for planing helical grooves in rolls. Helical grooves are planed in rolls by oscillating the workpiece with an arm having a roller follower in contact with an inclined plate.

Hydraulic tracer controls shown in Fig. 13-7 are also used on planers for machining certain three-dimensional contours. In the application illustrated, a propeller blade is being planed. As the table reciprocates, the planer tool is moved up and down by the tracer in contact with the master pattern. The plane tool also moves through an arc as the plane head is fed crosswise on the master pattern.

NC and CNC can also be used for contour planning.

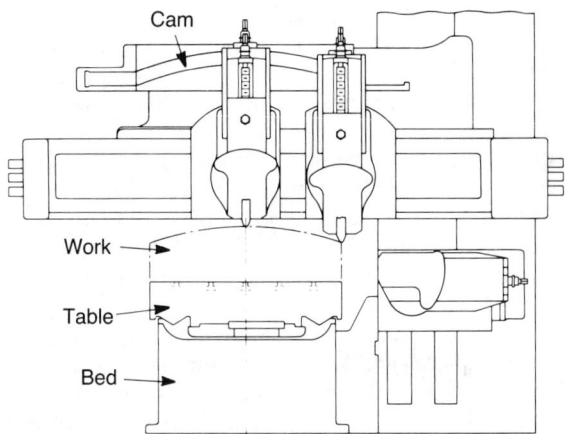

Fig. 13-6 Cam which is mounted above the rail and controls vertical movements of the planer-head slides to machine contoured surface.

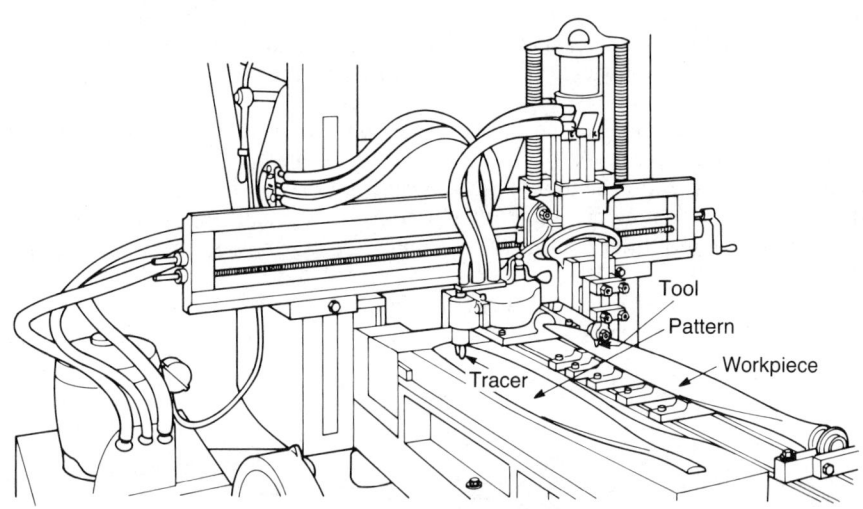

Fig. 13-7 Hydraulic tracer control mounted on a planer to machine propeller blades.

SHAPING AND SLOTTING[2]

Shaping and slotting are material-removal processes in which a single-point cutting tool is reciprocated across or through a stationary workpiece to produce plane or formed surfaces. This mode of operation differentiates shaping from planing. In shaping and slotting, the work is stationary and the tool reciprocates: In planing, the work is reciprocated while the tool is stationary.

Simplicity of operation, flexibility of setup, low-cost tooling, and good accuracy and finish capabilities make shapers and slotting machines desirable for toolroom and die-shop needs and for limited production requirements. The machines, however, are seldom used for medium or high-production applications because of their comparatively low productivity. Possible operations are also limited by the maximum lengths of the ram strokes on these machines.

TYPES OF SHAPERS AND SLOTTING MACHINES

Several types of shapers and slotting machines are available. Cutting tools used can be of different configurations and can be set at various angles to profile, notch, cut angled slots and grooves, and produce flat surfaces. Both the workpiece and the cutting tool are firmly held in preselected positions, and the toolholder head is reciprocated by a powered ram.

Horizontal Shapers. The most common shaper is the horizontal crank-operated push-cut type (see Fig. 13-8) with ram movement in the horizontal plane. These shapers range in maximum cutting stroke from 7 or 8 in. (178 or 203 mm) in bench models to 36 in. (914 mm) in heavy-duty models. They are built with either a mechanical or hydraulic drive and with a plain box table or universal table permitting angular tilt in addition to horizontal and vertical adjustments.

A cutting tool is mounted on a shaper head that is attached to the ram, which reciprocates the tool. Workpieces are held in a vise on the shaper table or directly on the table. Power or hand feeding of the table is provided parallel to the table top and perpendicular to the stroke of the ram. The tool cuts on the forward stroke of the ram, and the table feeds the workpiece in a direction perpendicular to the ram motion, for the next cut, on the return stroke of the ram. Many shapers have a rapid traverse for moving the table to various positions along a crossrail fitted to the front of the machine column.

On shapers powered by an electric motors through a V-belt drive, a quick-change gear box provides different speeds (strokes per minute) for the ram. On hydraulically-powered shapers, the ram speeds are infinitely variable. Stroke lengths are varied by changing the relative positions of components on the crank mechanisms or adjusting the positions of two dogs.

A shaper head is clamped to the end of the ram and has a slide actuated by a feedscrew to adjust the depth of cut. A clapper box and block are fastened to the front of the shaper-head slide to allow the tool to pivot away from the workpiece on the return stroke of the ram, thus preventing dragging of the tool over the machined surface. Most shapers have an automatic tool lifter that pivots the clapper box. A post for the toolholder is held in the clapper block.

Special horizontal shapers are available in a variety of designs to suit specific applications. One example is a hydraulic shaper with two toolheads and two holding

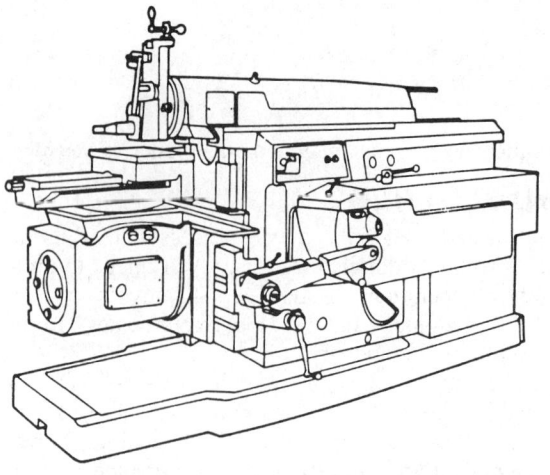

Fig. 13-8 Typical horizontal crank-operated push cut shaper.

fixtures for increased production. Draw-cut shapers have also been built with special fixtures for mounting and feeding the workpieces.

Vertical Shapers or Slotters. Vertical shapers, also called slotting machines, operate somewhat like horizontal shapers except that the ram reciprocates vertically rather than horizontally. A typical vertical slotting machine is shown in Fig. 13-9. Most machines of this type have provisions for adjustable inclination of their rams, and rotary tables are practically standard equipment. Standard machines are available with ram strokes ranging from 6 to 36 in. (152 to 914 mm), with hydraulic or mechanical drives.

Vertical slotting machines are available with five axes—longitudinal and transverse travel of the workpiece in the X and Y axes, vertical movement of the ram in the Z-axis, swiveling of the ram in the B axis, and rotating the workpiece in the C-axis—to permit a wide variety of operations. Such machines are available for manual operation, numerical control or tracer control.

Keyseaters are a specialized form of vertical shapers designed specifically for machining internal keyways. They use a tool mounted on a cutter bar above the ram, and it is pulled rather than pushed through the workpiece.

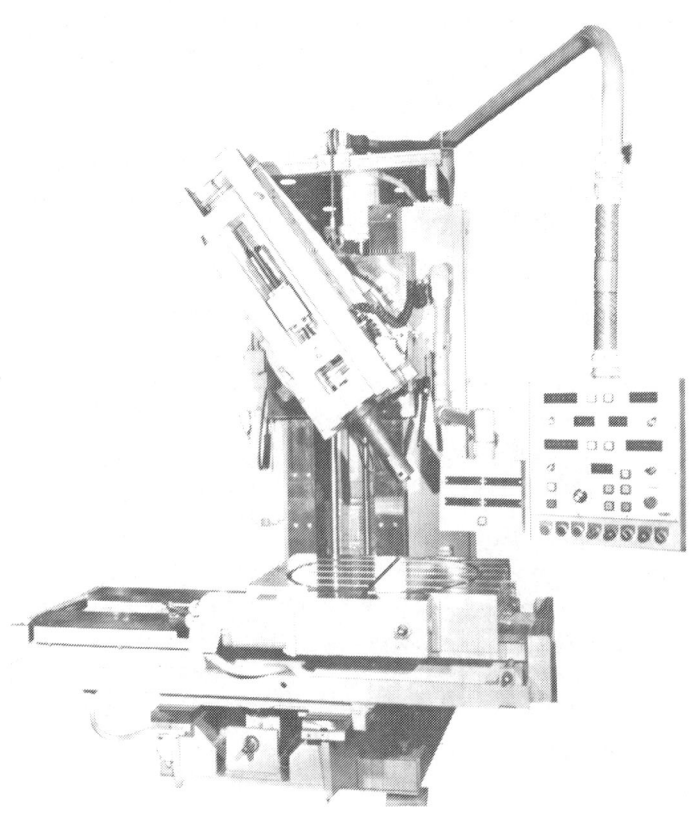

Fig. 13-9 Five-axis shaper/slotter. (*Courtesy Morey Machinery, Inc.*)

SHAPING AND SLOTTING OPERATIONS

Shaping of flat surfaces is performed primarily with the workpieces held in vises. Some common methods of holding the workpieces are illustrated in Fig. 13-10. For shaping rough castings, emery cloth is often placed between the castings and the vise jaws, as shown in view *a*. For shaping parallel surfaces, soft metal is sometimes placed between the workpiece and vise jaws, and parallels are sometimes placed under the workpiece, as illustrated in view *b*. For right-angle shaping, a wedge, parallels, and shims are used, as shown in view *c*. A setup for shaping a workpiece having a tapered face is shown in view *d*.

Standard vises commonly employed for shaping include single-screw types, which permit rapid clamping, and double-screw types, which develop higher pressure and have swivel jaws for workpieces having tapered surfaces. Other types include moldmaker vises, popular in manufacturing glass and plastic molds; overhung vises, convenient for shaping the ends of bars; and on-end vises for special operations. Air and hydraulically operated vises are also used in some applications.

Workpieces are also frequently fastened directly to the shaper table. A typical setup is illustrated in Fig. 13-11. With proper support on the outboard ends by auxiliary standards, long, heavy workpieces can be machined on shapers.

While keyways, slots, and other similar surfaces can be machined on horizontal shapers, they are commonly cut on slotting machines (vertical shapers) or keyseaters. The setup shown in Fig. 13-12, with the workpiece mounted on the rotary table of a vertical slotting machine, is used to cut four internal slots, several bosses, and outside surfaces simultaneously. Automatic power downfeed to the head, with automatic depth stop, is useful for slotting on horizontal shapers.

Contouring Operations. Contouring operations can be performed efficiently on both horizontal and vertical shapers. A front-mounted control for table crossfeed on horizontal shapers facilitates dual operation with the head slide. By manipulating both the head slide and table feed, contours scribed on the workpiece can be shaped easily. Another method of shaping contours is to fasten a template to the base of the machine and a follower to

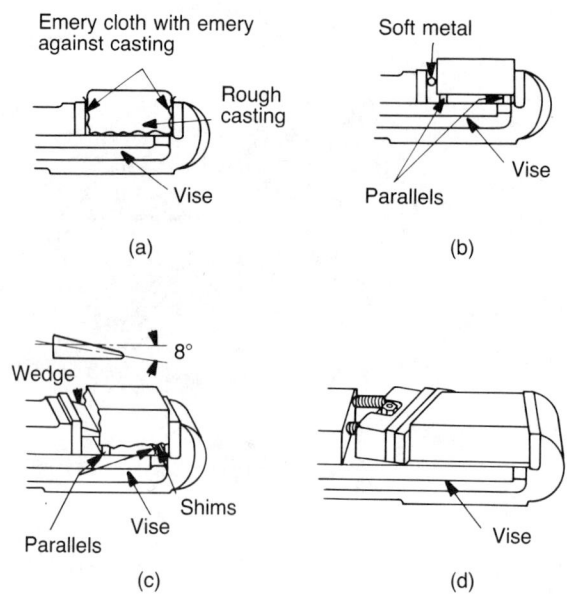

Fig. 13-10 Common methods of holding workpieces in vises on horizontal shapers.

13-8

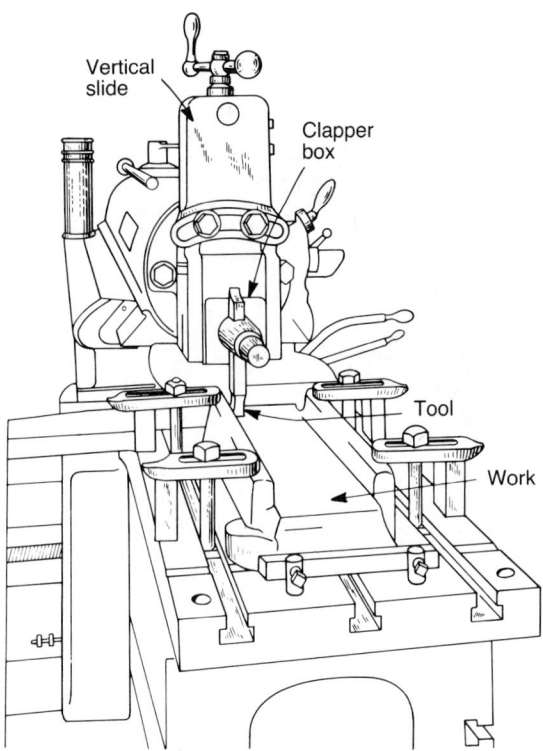

Vertical slide

Clapper box

Tool

Work

Fig. 13-11 Typical setup on a horizontal shaper with workpiece fastened to table.

the underside of the table, as illustrated in Fig. 13-13. Automatic duplicating equipment, such as the hydraulic tracing device shown in Fig. 13-14, is available for producing more complex shapes from templates.

Rotary feeding heads and similar devices are also used on horizontal shapers to produce irregular contours. Vertical shapers accomplish similar work when equipped with rotary tables. A master cam and special form tool are used in the setup on a horizontal shaper, as illustrated in Fig. 13-15, to produce a helical impeller.

Cutting Gears and Splines. One-of-a-kind or limited quantities of splined shafts and gears are occasionally cut on horizontal shapers by using an indexing head on the outer end of the table to support the workpieces.

Five-axis vertical slotting machines can be equipped to cut gears and splines with rack or rotary shaper cutters, the workpieces being mounted on a rotary table. When a rack cutter is used, the traverse axis is coordinated with the rotary axis to roll the cutter past the workpiece and the tool is repositioned between passes. Tool relief and infeed are controlled by the longitudinal axis.

When rotary shaper cutters are used, a rotating head mechanism can be placed in the ram toolholder. Rotary motion of the head is synchronized with the rotary table. The longitudinal axis is used for variable infeed.

With suitable profiled tools, chain wheels, ratchets, splines, and other profiles can be produced. Racks can be produced by rack or single-tool cutters, using a slotting process. Internal gears can be made by using a rotating head mechanism. Crowning of gears can be done by using a small copying attachment, but templates must be made for each contour.

13-9

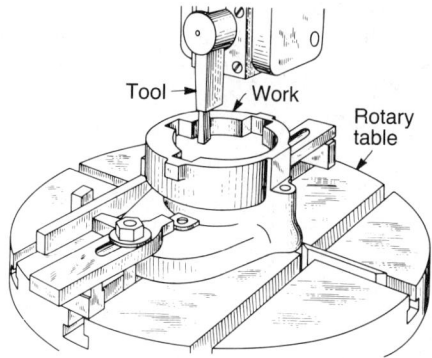

Fig. 13-12 Four internal slots, several bosses, and outside surfaces are machined simultaneously in this one setup on the rotary table of a vertical shaper.

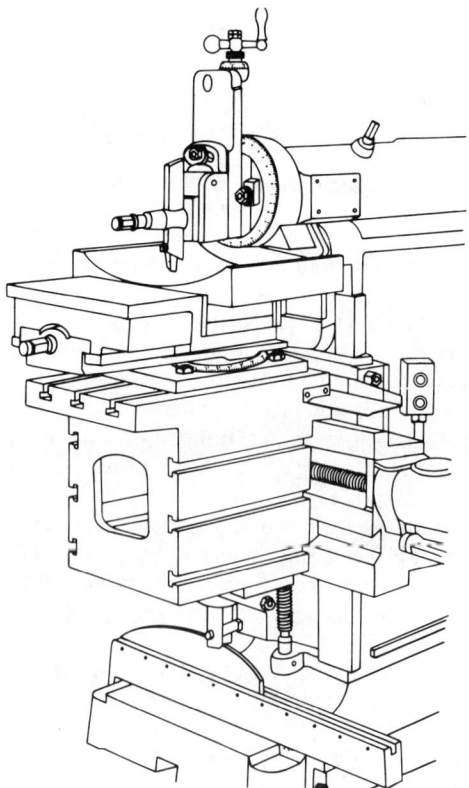

Fig. 13-13 A template on the machine base and a follower under the table can be used to shape simple contours.

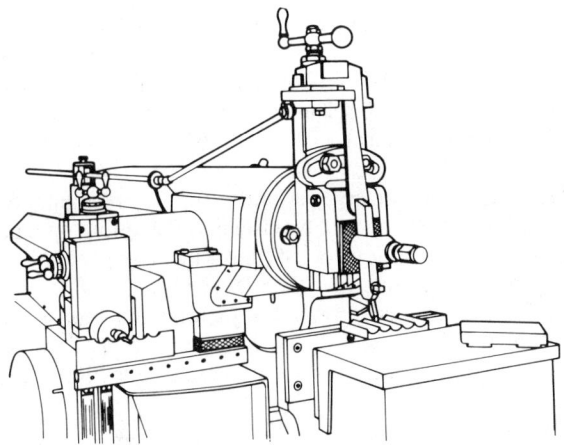

Fig. 13-14 Shaper equipped with a hydraulic tracer used to automatically duplicate a shape from a template.

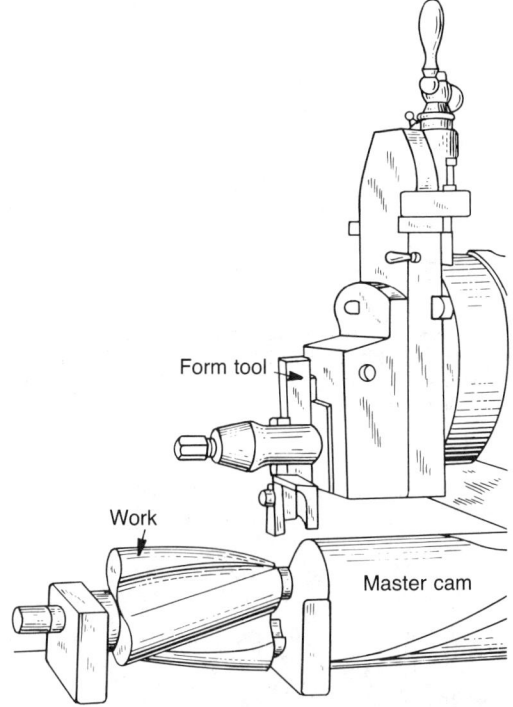

Form tool

Work

Master cam

Fig. 13-15 Horizontal shaper with a master cam and special form tool used to cut a helical impeller.

WORKHOLDING FOR PLANING, SHAPING AND SLOTTING[3]

Due to the similarity of these operations, the following section can be applied jointly, as applicable, to planing, shaping, and slotting operations.

Setting up work is probably the most important aspect for increasing the output of the planer, shaper, or slotter since setup on these machines is more difficult than on other types of machine tools. This is particularly true when a number of small or medium-sized pieces of irregular shape are to be planed simultaneously. The reason for this is that the work is subjected to the intermittent cutting pressures of the several tools as well as the inertia forces developed during reversal. Also, when finish cuts are taken, proper shimming must be done to avoid bending or warping strains due to clamping because such strains would distort the piece upon release of the clamping pressure. Paper is commonly used under the clamp point of surfaces to be finished in order to increase friction and protect the table.

Setup and Clamping Accessories. A plentiful supply of clamps, bolts, stop pins, etc., such as are shown in Fig. 13-16, should be provided for setting up and clamping the work on the planer table. Clamping devices of this kind are generally used when several different kinds of jobs are machined on the planer.

An end view of the workpiece setup for planing the top and the right-hand side simultaneously is shown in Fig. 13-17. The work is end-stopped by stop pins and an angle bracket. Side stop pins prevent the work from moving to the left. A jackscrew is used to

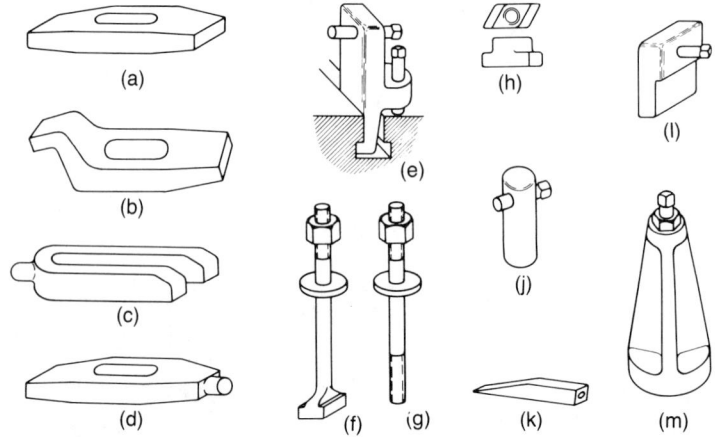

Fig. 13-16 Common accessories for work setup and clamping on planers: (*a*) plain clamp, (*b*) offset clamp, (*c*) U-clamp with pin end, (*d*) pin clamp, (*e*) T-slot stop bracket, (*f*) T-slot bolt, (*g*) stud, (*h*) T-slot removable nut, (*j*) stop pin or planer stop, (*k*) chisel point, (*l*) T-slot stop block, and (*m*) jackscrew.

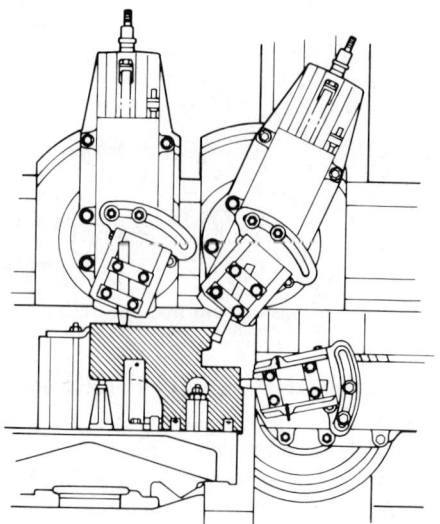

Fig. 13-17 Setup for simultaneously planing the top and right-hand side of a workpiece.

support the overhanging part of the workpiece, and offset clamps on the left side and pin clamps hold the work to the table. The clamp studs screw into T-slot nuts.

Removable T-slot nuts, illustrated in view *h* of Fig. 13-16 are more convenient and require less time to use than the ordinary T-slot bolt. The nuts can be placed into the slot from the top, turned clockwise about one-sixth of a turn, and then lifted out. Their use eliminates cleaning the chips out of the T-slots over the whole length, which is necessary when standard T-slot bolts are used.

Chucks and Vises. Magnetic chucks are used in some instances for holding thin plates made of cast iron or steel. If the cutting pressure is not too great, these chucks provide a simple, quick, and convenient means for holding the work. Positive stops are usually incorporated in the chuck to help carry the cutting pressure. Taper gibs are commonly planed on such chucks. A wedge-shaped plate is placed between the chuck body and the planer table to produce the proper taper on the gib. Workholding vises are sometimes used to good advantage, particularly when the pieces are small or when only a few pieces of a kind are to be planed.

Duplex Table. When a number of pieces are planed at one time (gang planing), the setup time may be greater than the actual cutting time. The work must be placed on the table, clamped in place, and after being planed, must be removed from the table; the table must be cleaned off in preparation for the next load. While all this is being done, the planer is cutting no metal. On planers with divided or duplex tables, work can be planed on one half of the table while the other half is being unloaded and reloaded. A quick-acting coupling connects the two halves of the table, bringing one half into the position for planing and placing the other half at the end of the bed for setting up work. Automatic valves in the ends of the tables control the flow and pressure of the lubricating oil to the table ways. The tables can also remain permanently connected for planing long workpieces.

Setup Plates. Setup plates are sometimes used to reduce the time in which the machine is not used for actual cutting. Such plates have T-slots and holes for end and side stop pins. The plates have a key at each end that fits into the center T-slot on the planer table for aligning the plate parallel to the table. Lugs are provided on the ends of the plate for bolting it down on the table. The plate butts against an end stop secured on the front end of the machine table to prevent the plate from sliding on the table because of the cutting pressure. Lifting loops are provided on the plate for attaching chain or cable slings.

While the parts on one setup plate on the machine are machined, finished parts are removed and rough parts are set up on another plate positioned near the machine. The time required to remove one plate from the machine and to install the other is small compared with the total setup time.

Setup Fixtures. For some types of work, setup fixtures are used to good advantage to reduce the setup time. If the fixture is carefully designed, the part can be clamped in place rapidly. The strains due to clamping must be considered to avoid springing the work. Usually the fixture can be so designed that the chips will fall clear of the surfaces on which the part registers, so that the cleaning time is minimized.

When the quantity of parts being made does not warrant the cost of setup fixtures, the parts must be held in the usual way with clamps, end and side stops, etc. Such jobs do not often repeat at frequent intervals, and the operator may forget the arrangement used the last time or another operator may get the job. To save time and faulty work in such setups, a sketch should be made in the tool engineering department showing the various clamps, jackscrews, end stops, etc., all in proper relation to the job.

Work Layout. In nearly all planing jobs, the planer work is the first operation on the piece, and in subsequent operations, measurements or locations are taken from the planed surfaces. In cases when a setup fixture is not used and the piece is more or less complex in form, it is necessary that lines representing the approximate locations of the finished surfaces be scribed on the piece. This is done to ensure correct relationship between the finished surfaces and the cored holes (to be bored later) and to get correct wall thickness, etc. Accurate surfaces must be located by gage blocks or similar means. Laying out the surfaces to be planed on a piece should be done on a layout plate before the pieces are brought to the planer. In this way the operator requires much less time to set up the pieces, and the one who lays out the pieces becomes more skilled in this phase of the work.

Tool Setting. Tool-setting gages are used for roughing and semifinishing operations. A gage or template is secured to the top of the table at the rear end in correct relation to the work to be planed. The tools are then set to the gage by pulling a paper strip between the tool point and the gage, or by the use of a feeler gage. By this method, much time is saved and the chance of error in dimensions is greatly reduced. The gages are usually made of cast iron; sometimes they have hardened steel inserts at the points at which the tool positions are gaged. When setup fixtures are used, the points of the tool-setting gage are sometimes incorporated in the fixture.

SETUP METHODS

The double-screw shaper vise (see Fig. 13-18) has a tongue that engages one of the grooves in the plate to accommodate work of various sizes. The rear (movable) jaw can be pivoted to hold work with a slight taper. The vise can be rotated and locked down by hold-down bolts in the base at any angle preset on the scale.

Parallels (see Figs. 13-10*b*, *c*, and 13-19) are supports which are placed underneath the work to raise it for necessary clearances or to simplify the shaping or planing operation. The angular types are for raising or otherwise bolstering or leveling workpieces having nonparallel and/or irregular surfaces, or for presenting a workpiece surface to the tool at an angle other than 90°.

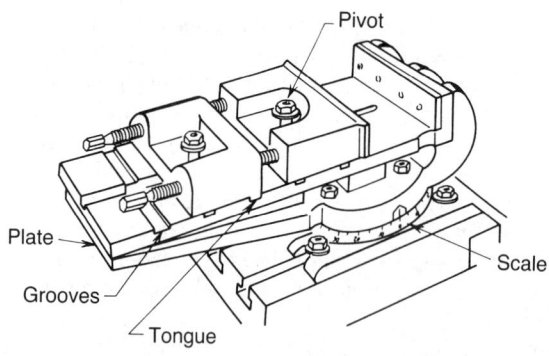

Fig. 13-18 A double-screw shaper vise. (*Courtesy The Cincinnati Shaper Co.*)

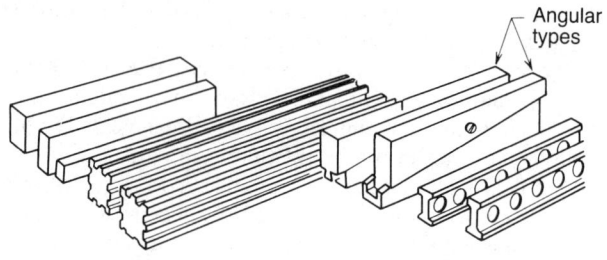

Fig. 13-19 Parallels.

13-14

Hold-downs, which are thin strips of an approximately triangular cross section, apply a downward force to the work in the vise (see Fig. 13-20) in addition to the clamping pressure of the vise jaws.

Workpieces may be clamped directly to the table with T-slot bolts and a wide variety of clamps (see Chapter 3). The plain clamp of Fig. 13-21a may be made adjustable with the addition of a setscrew, as shown.

Figure 13-22 shows typical clamping of a workpiece to a shaper table, as well as two end stops for holding the workpiece against the thrust of the tool.

Stop pins and blocks are placed at the ends or sides of the workpiece to prevent its movement on the table. Plain stops (see Fig. 13-23a) are round or square pieces of steel to fit T-slots or holes in the table; or they are blocks, shown at b, held in slots or held by

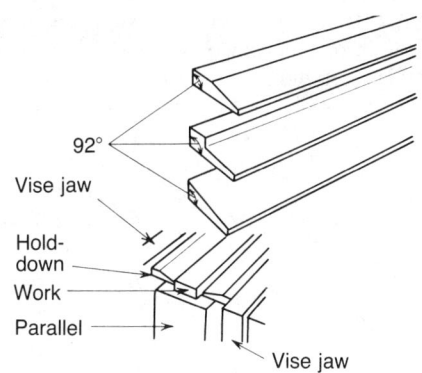

Fig. 13-20 Hold-downs.

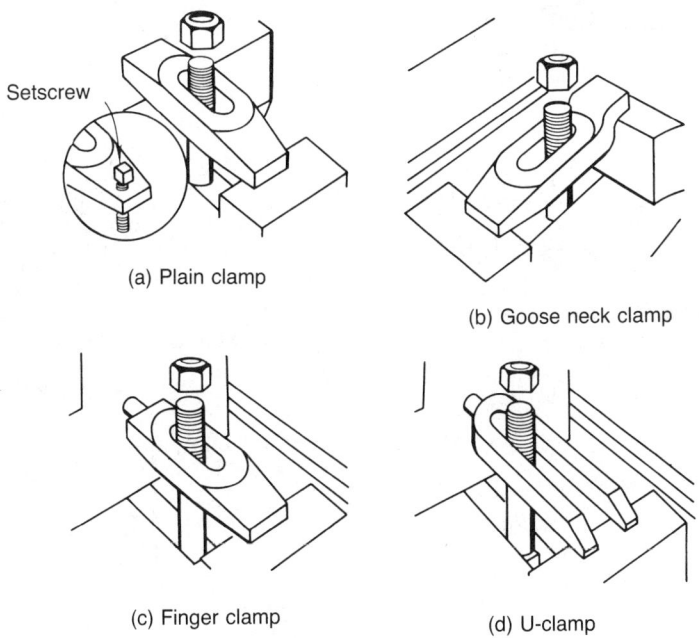

(a) Plain clamp

(b) Goose neck clamp

(c) Finger clamp

(d) U-clamp

Fig. 13-21 Strap clamps.

13-15

bolts. The stops illustrated at c, d, and e fit in T-slots and incorporate setscrews which can be tightened against the workpiece.

Clamping of a thin, flat workpiece by means of toe dogs is shown in Fig. 13-24. Generally, enough holding pressure will be obtained by setting the toe dogs at an angle of from 8 to 12° from the horizontal.

Aligning strips shown in Fig. 13-25a, b, c, and d are bolted to the machine table for setting the work on the table, as well as to function as stops. Those shown at c, d, and e incorporate tongues to fit the table T-slots. The angular alignment strip, shown at e, can be used in clamping cylindrical workpieces.

Shafting and similar cylindrical workpieces are clamped in V-blocks (see Fig. 13-26) which are bolted to the machine table.

Workpieces which must be held at a right angle to a finished surface may be secured to an angle plate (see Fig. 13-27) with C-clamps or other suitable clamps.

Jacks (see Fig. 13-28) are frequently useful in supporting overhanging workpiece sections or in leveling the stock or workpiece. After they are adjusted, jacks should be bolted or clamped to the machine table.

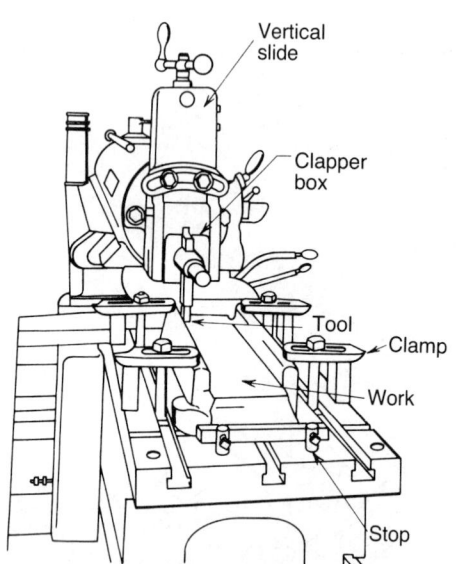

Fig. 13-22 Shaper workpiece fastened directly to the table.

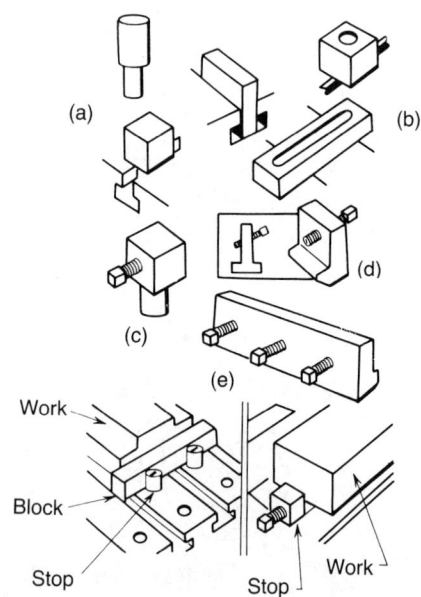

Fig. 13-23 Stop pins and blocks.

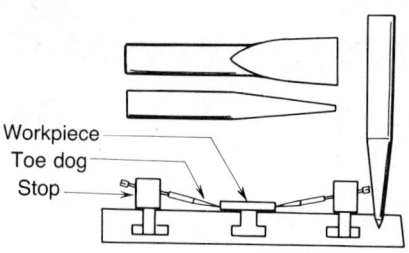

Fig. 13-24 Toe dogs.

13-16

Vises are rarely used with the vertical shaper, but rotary tables are commonly used; various clamps, jacks, etc., are mounted to position and hold the workpiece on the table.

Flat and tilting as well as supplementary or extension tables are commercially available for the fixturing of workpieces larger than the machine table or for workpieces that are to be set at an angle to it.

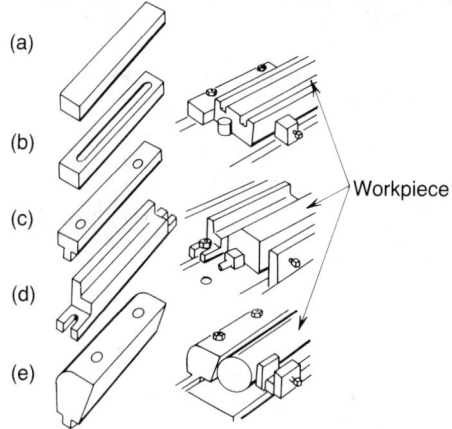

Fig. 13-25 Aligning strips.

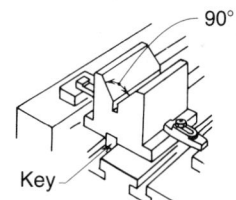 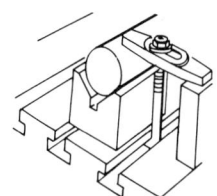 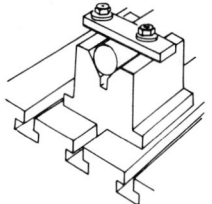

Fig. 13-26 V-blocks.

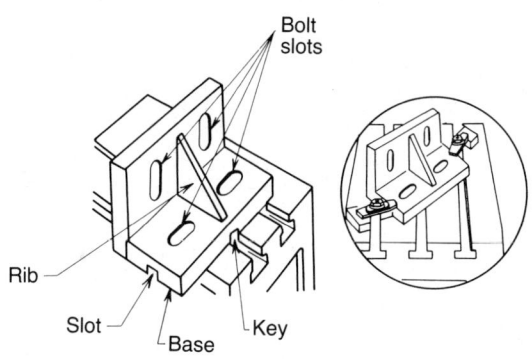

Fig. 13-27 An angle plate.

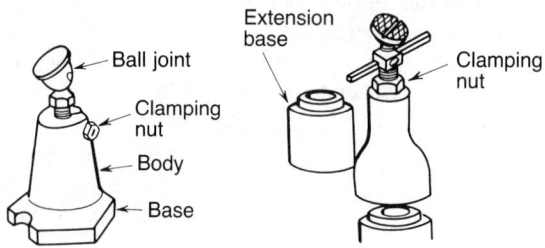

Fig. 13-28 Jacks.

References

1. Thomas J. Drozda and Charles Wick, eds., "Breaching, Planing, Shaping and Slotting," *Tool and Manufacturing Engineers Handbook*, 4th ed., Vol. 1 (Dearborn, Mi: Society of Manufacturing Engineers, 1983), pg. 7-38 to 7- 47.
2. *Ibid*, pg. 7-49 to 7-54.
3. *Ibid*, pg. 7-42 to 7-43.

Additional
"Shaper Work," New York State Dept. of Education.
"Vertical Shaper," The Pratt & Whitney Co.
"Shaper Setups," The Cincinnati Shaper Co.

CHAPTER 14

TOOLING FOR FLEXIBLE MANUFACTURING SYSTEMS

A flexible manufacturing system or flexible machining system (FMS) is an automated production system for the manufacture of families of workpieces at midvolume output rates.[1] The acronym FMS is often used generically to describe a wide range of systems that are generally similar in concept. As shown in Fig. 14-1, a typical FMS consists of a number of machine tools tied together by a workpiece handling system and controlled by a central computer.

Although the acronym FMS is considered to be somewhat generic, many other terms and acronyms are used to describe this general class of manufacturing equipment—Computer Integrated Manufacturing System (CIMS), Computer Managed Parts Manufacturing (CMPM), Variable Mission Manufacturing (VMM), for example. In countries other than the United States, terms such as Flexible Automation, Flexible Manufacturing System Complex (FMC), and Computer Integrated and Automated Manufacturing System (CIAM) are used.

Machine tools employed in an FMS usually are CNC machining centers or headchangers, but may also be other production equipment such as CNC lathes, automated testing or assembly stations, or even forming or finishing equipment. The uniqueness of the FMS concept of manufacturing is characterized by the ability to bring together in an integrated fashion, work stations, automated material handling, and computer control.

An FMS is capable of producing similar workpieces (one or more families of parts) randomly and simultaneously. Some systems require batching of workpiece families, while other systems accept workpieces from various families of parts in random order. Workpieces are transported to and from member machine tools via automated fixture carts or conveyors, although robots may be employed in special applications.

FMS ELEMENTS

As mentioned previously, there are three major building blocks of an FMS—work stations, material handling or material transport, and control systems. Often, the form each element takes can vary significantly among FMSs, depending upon such things as system configurations, processing requirements, economics, operating environment, level of system configuration, etc.

The work stations of an FMS are employed to execute the many manufacturing processes required for the production of parts. To date, the stations employed most often for metal-cutting operations have been three, four, or five-axis machining centers. Except for a few modifications, such machining centers are standard. Modifications that are often required include provisions in the machine control for accepting DNC-mode downloading of NC part programs from the central computer (normal FMS operation

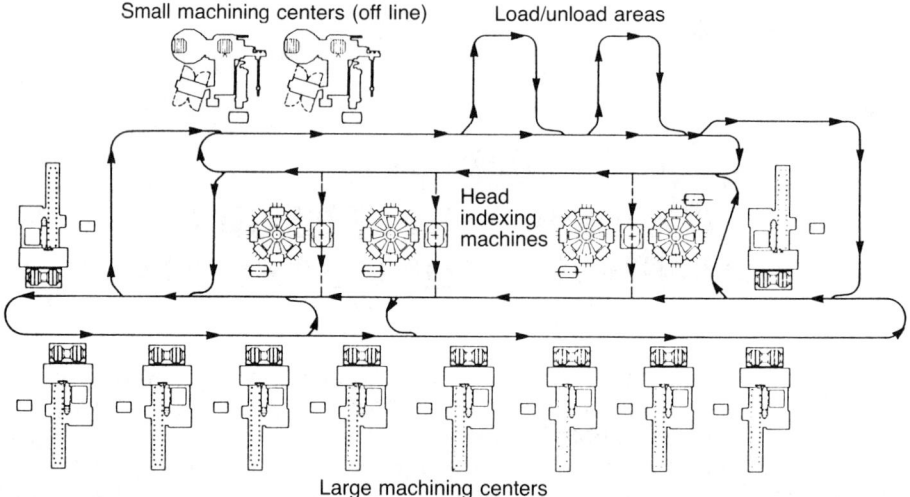

Small machining centers (off line)   Load/unload areas

Head indexing machines

Large machining centers

Fig. 14-1 Plan view of typical flexible machining system (FMS). Large machining centers and head-indexing machines are linked via automated fixture cart transportation system under computer control. NC part programs are downloaded to CNC machining centers from memory of the central computer. (*Courtesy Kearney & Trecker Corp.*)

does not require the use of a tape reader); the addition of a special shuttle mechanism for accepting fixture carts from the workpiece handling system; and special modifications for cutting fluid handling and chip removal. In some cases, machining centers have been specially modified for rough milling or drilling operations; thus, the particular machining center is transformed into a "roughing station" for general use in the production of a family of workpieces.

TYPES OF MACHINING CENTERS

Machining centers are available in a wide variety of types, configurations, capabilities, sizes, and costs. Machines with manual toolchanging are still available and being used, but most users do not consider such machines to be machining centers. Machining centers with automatic toolchangers are much more popular. Most machining centers can be categorized as horizontal or vertical-spindle types and traveling-table or column types.

Numerically controlled, turret-type machines are considered by some builders and users to be machining centers. They differ from conventional machining centers, however, in that their spindles are locked in a turret head and equipped with tools that are permanently retained throughout the cycle. The spindles are successively indexed into machining position, rather than the tools being automatically inserted and removed from a single spindle. This design limits the number of tools that can be provided on a single machine, but it is often adequate for many applications.

Headchanging machines are also considered by some builders and users to be machining centers or systems. They differ, however, from conventional machining centers in that entire heads (including multispindle units), rather than spindles or tools, are transferred in proper sequence to a single work station to perform the required series of operations. The distinction between machining centers and headchanging machines is becoming less clear because multi-spindle cluster heads are now being used on machining centers.

The two major types of machining centers are vertical and horizontal-spindle models. Some are available with two spindles (one horizontal and the other vertical), others have more than two spindles, and another has a single spindle that can be swiveled to either a horizontal or a vertical position. One model has a full contouring head with a 150° sweep from 30° above the horizontal to 30° beyond the vertical.

Selection of a specific type of machining center depends primarily upon the application—the size, complexity, and variety of the workpieces to be machined; production requirements; the number and types of tools needed; tolerances that have to be maintained; and other factors. Group technology, the classification of workpieces into families on the basis of commonality of size, shape, and/or part features, aids in selecting the proper type and size of machine, required tooling, and desirable options.

Vertical-spindle Models. Machining centers with vertical spindles (see Fig. 14-2) provide clear work areas for easy setup and loading/unloading. They are usually preferred for plate-type workpieces if the X-axis travel is sufficient to clear the spindle from over the table. A wide variety of work positioning and indexing equipment available for processing small, multisided parts increases the versatility of these machines. Figure 14-3 illustrates a dual setup on a vertical machining center for performing operations on large diesel engine blocks and heads.

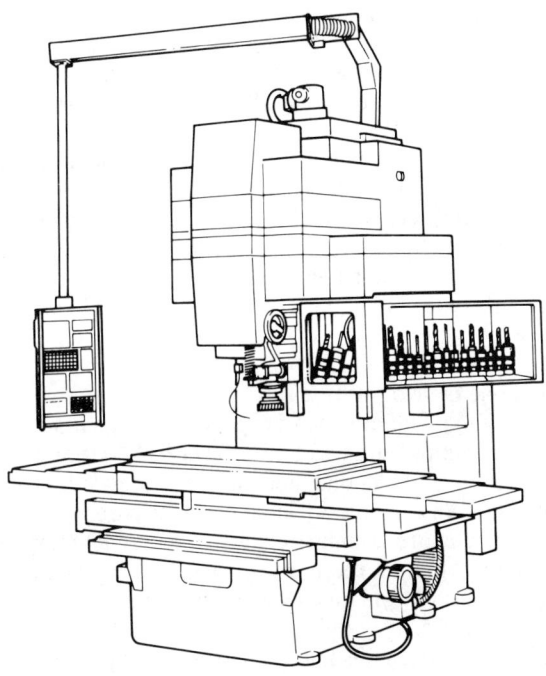

Fig. 14-2 Vertical-spindle machining center with pendant CNC. (*Courtesy Monarch Cortland*)

Many vertical-spindle machining centers provide X- and Y-axis motions with a traveling table and saddle. Machines are also available with traveling columns for X-axis dle larger workpieces, and sliding heads or rail types for Y-axis motions. Z-axis movements are provided by quill-type spindles, sliding heads, or knees under the machine tables.

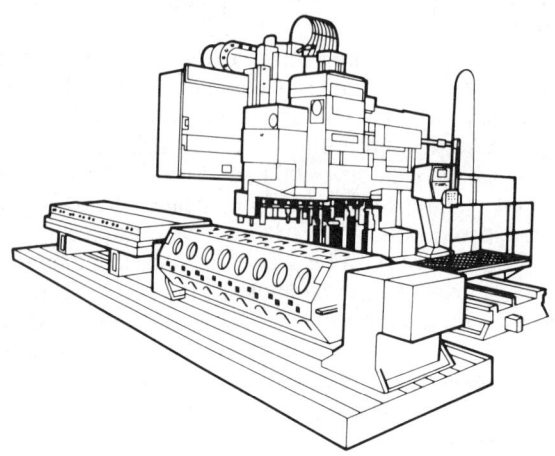

Fig. 14-3 Dual setup for diesel engine blocks and heads on a vertical-spindle machining center (*Courtesy Giddings & Lewis Machine Tool Co.*)

Vertical machining centers of the table type, with adjustable or fixed rail construction, are a direct descendant of rail-type milling machines. The addition of a right-angle head, automatically loaded and unloaded, which can be indexed in at least 90° increments, provides a universal machine with large workpiece capacity. Operations on top surfaces of the workpieces are done with the vertical spindle, and the indexing right-angle attachment is used for operations on all sides of the workpieces. Tilting right-angle heads are also available.

Horizontal-spindle Models. Machining centers with horizontal spindles are generally more flexible than vertical-spindle models and are available in a wider range of sizes. Horizontal-spindle machining centers with numerical control of three, four, and five axes are shown in Fig. 14-4. These machines are usually preferred for large, multisided parts because they have no restrictions on workpiece height.

Horizontal-spindle bar-type machining centers (see Fig. 14-5) are direct descendants of horizontal bar-type boring mills. The addition of automatic toolchangers, numerical control, and pallet loading has resulted in accurate, large-capacity machining centers having four linear and one or two rotary axes.

Many horizontal-spindle machining centers provide X-axis motions with a traveling table, sometimes in combination with a saddle to furnish W-axis movements. Motions in the Y-axis on some traveling-table machines are provided by a vertical column or spindle carrier mounted on a ram, both located on a rear base.

Traveling-column designs are popular for larger size machining centers. With the column traveling to the workpiece, the need for pallet changers can usually be eliminated. Dual tables are common on traveling-column machines, with the workpieces being changed on the idle table. This style of machining center, however, requires more travel in the X-axis. Movements in the Y-axis are provided by a spindle carrier mounted on the vertical column or by mounting the machine table on a knee. Traveling-column machining centers provide selection of X-axis travel ranges and workholding modules (see Fig. 14-6). The most popular configurations have two work-holding modules (view b) that carry 72- or 360-position rotary index tables or full contouring tables.

Machine tool builders commonly offer a few standard versions of a particular machine type with various options. The modular machining center shown in Fig. 14-7 is available in 88 different combinations to suit specific requirements.

Five-axis machining centers, used for contouring complex workpieces, are available

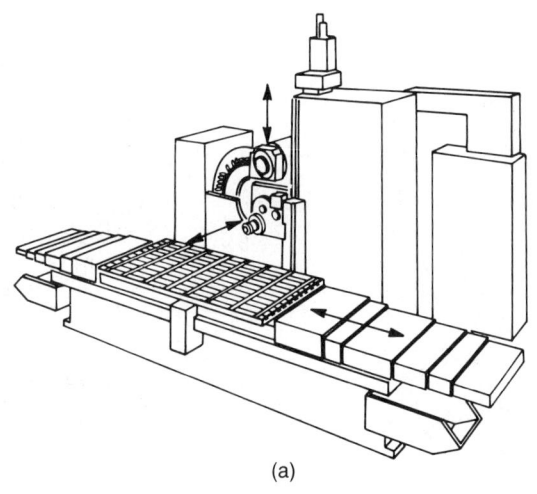

(a)

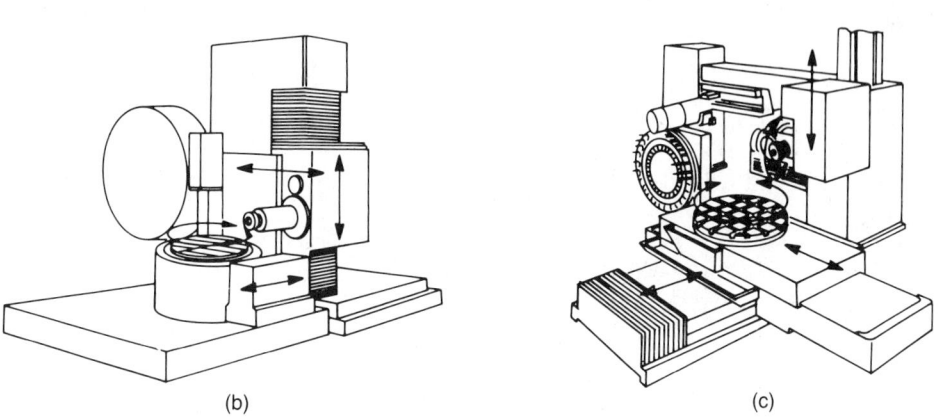

(b)   (c)

Fig. 14-4 Horizontal-spindle machining centers with numerical control of: (*a*) **three axes,** (*b*) **four axes, and** (*c*) **five axes.**

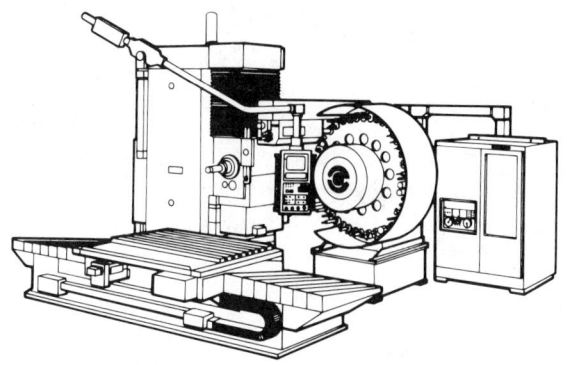

Fig. 14-5 Horizontal-spindle bar-type machining center. (*Courtesy DeVlieg Machine Co.*)

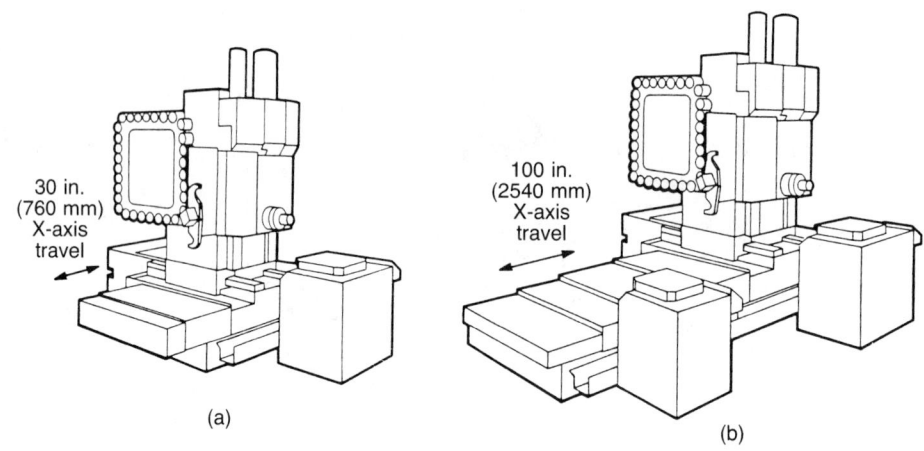

Fig. 14-6 Traveling-column machining center with: (*a*) one work module and (*b*) two work modules. (*Courtesy Cincinnati Milacron*)

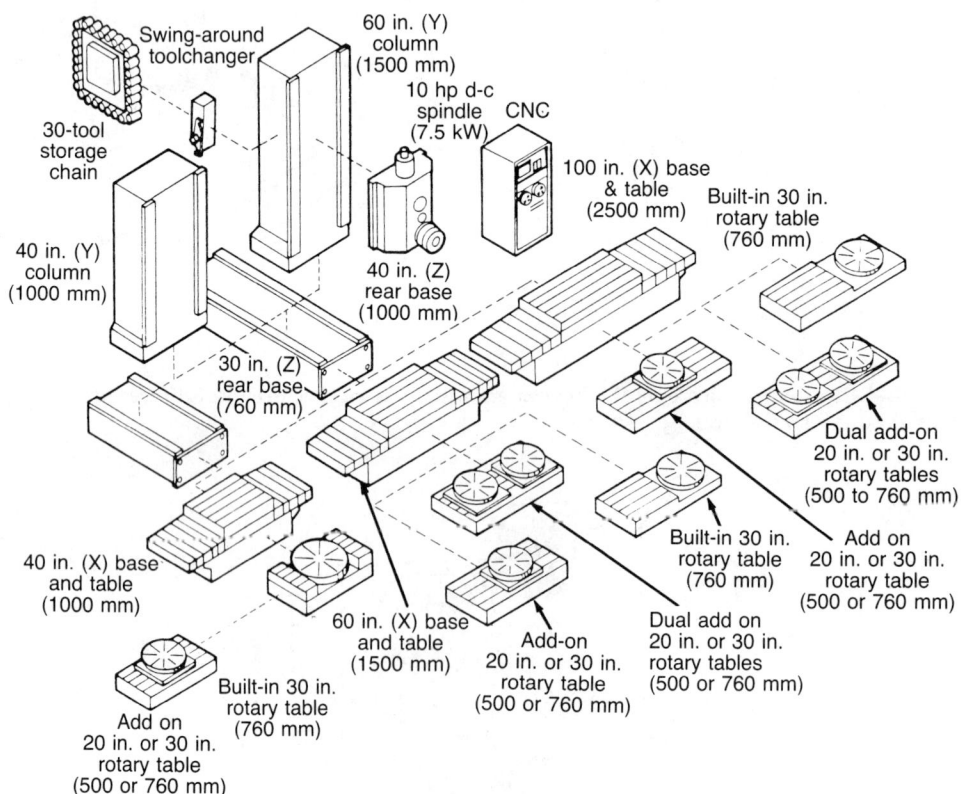

Fig. 14-7 Modular machining center available in 88 different combinations. (*Courtesy Cincinnati Milacron*)

in several designs. One design uses a contouring rotary table as the fourth B-axis and a vertical, contouring rotary table (mounted on the B-axis table) as the fifth A-axis. When the vertical table is removed, the machine can be used for four-axis work. In another design, the contouring B-axis is combined with an A-axis that automatically tilts the B-axis through a limited range. A third design combines the B-axis contouring rotary table with an A-axis spindle carrier designed with a programmable tilting spindle.

CONTROLS FOR MACHINING CENTERS

Most builders now offer more compact, solid-state electronic CNC units with increased reliability built into or mounted on their machining centers for increased convenience and reduced floor space requirements.

Features generally desirable on controls for machining centers include the following:

- Sufficient memory storage for multiple part programs.
- Canned cycles and subroutines that reduce programming times.
- Program editing capability at the machine.
- Display, readout, or cathode ray tube (CRT) for position and block data.
- Linear and circular interpolation.
- Direct spindle speed and feed rate programming.
- Speed and feed overrides.

Other features (standard or optional) that can be useful include tool and fixture offsets, inch/metric switching, and cutter diameter, tool length, and backlash compensation. Manual data input (MDI) is essential for program editing at the machine, and an alphanumeric keyboard is desirable for this purpose.

Adaptive control systems to make automatic adjustments of spindle speeds and/or feed rates to compensate for changing workpiece/tool conditions are offered by some builders. Computer-based, analytic diagnostic systems are also available to quickly detect and isolate faults, problems, or malfunctions, thus reducing downtime.

WORK HANDLING

Many methods are available for holding and positioning workpieces on machining centers. Their purpose is to permit the greatest number of operations to be performed in one setup, thus increasing productivity. Workpiece transfer and handling equipment is being incorporated in some machining centers.

Plain machine tables with single-station fixtures are the simplest method, requiring no optional equipment. Small workpieces can often be set up in multiples on the tables. Multipart fixtures can be used for small workpieces. With duplicate fixtures, one fixture can be unloaded and reloaded while workpieces on the other fixture are being machined. Two-station fixtures are often used when two settings are required to machine various surfaces on the workpieces.

On vertical machining centers, tailstocks or other outboard supports are used for long slender parts. A fourth-axis indexer is also used on these machines to rotate box-like workpieces in a vertical plane to bring multiple surfaces under the tools. A column riser may be necessary for some applications to provide more distance from the spindle nose to the table top for indexing clearance. Trunnion-type indexers are also available for multisided machining with a single fixturing (as an alternative to using a horizontal-spindle machine with an indexing table).

Multiposition dial index tables, some with bidirectional rotation; pallet shuttle systems (see Fig. 14-8); and automatic pallet changers (see Fig. 14-9) are used on many machining centers. (Duplicate pallets permit the operator to unload and reload (or set up the next job) while another workpiece is being machined. One builder offers two rotary tables, each with an independent drive, for its horizontal-spindle machining

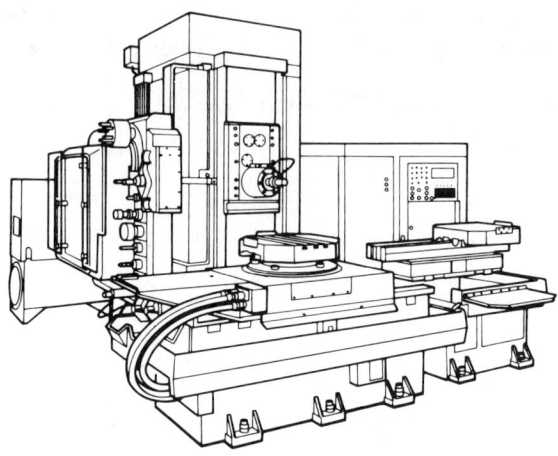

Fig. 14-8 Pallet shuttle system on a horizontal-spindle machining center. (*Courtesy Kearney & Trecker Corp.*)

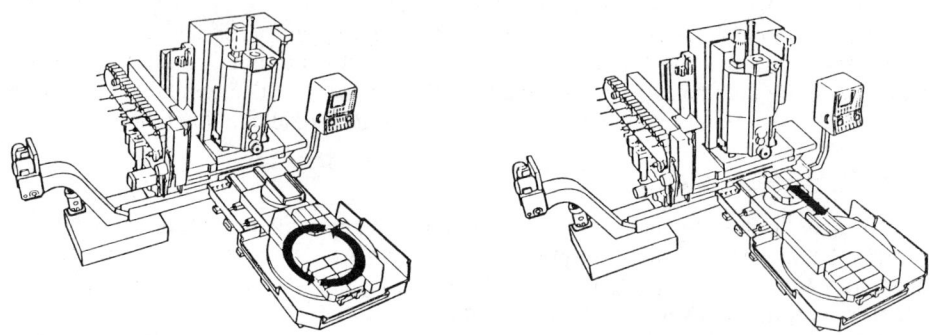

Fig. 14-9 Workpiece transfer is accomplished in under 26 seconds with this automatic pallet changer. (*Courtesy Cincinnati Milacron*)

centers. This permits one table to remain stationary for loading, unloading, or setup, while a workpiece on the other table is being machined.

Traveling-column, horizontal machining centers permit using two post-type work modules at the front of the machine, with the spindle-carrying column traversing from one to the other. The posts can be equipped with rotary indexing tables or other workholding arrangements to suit specific requirements. These two basic work areas are suitable for most needs, but long parts can be bridged across the posts.

Loading and unloading of machining centers is being done with industrial robots for some applications.

HEADCHANGING MACHINES

Headchanging machines, like machining centers discussed in the preceding section of this chapter, are also a relatively new class of multifunction, numerically controlled machine tools. They differ from machining centers in that single or multiple-spindle heads, rather than tools, are transferred to a single work station in proper sequence to perform the required series of operations. The single work station is equipped with a spindle drive and slide feed unit; the workpiece remains in a fixed or indexable position. Additional work stations can be added on some machines if required.

On the machine shown in Fig. 14-10, standard size, cubical machining heads, with single or multiple preset tools, are stored on a multilevel carousel alongside the traveling-column machine. On command of the machine controller, the proper head is automatically transferred, positioned, and clamped on the machine spindle. Multitooth couplings ensure accurate registration of toolheads and work pallets. The shuttle pallets on the machine table permit loading and unloading one workpiece while another is being machined. Programs and tooling can be stored in this system for a variety of workpieces. Some toolheads can be dedicated to operations performed on a specific workpiece, while others can be used for one or more operations common to several workpieces.

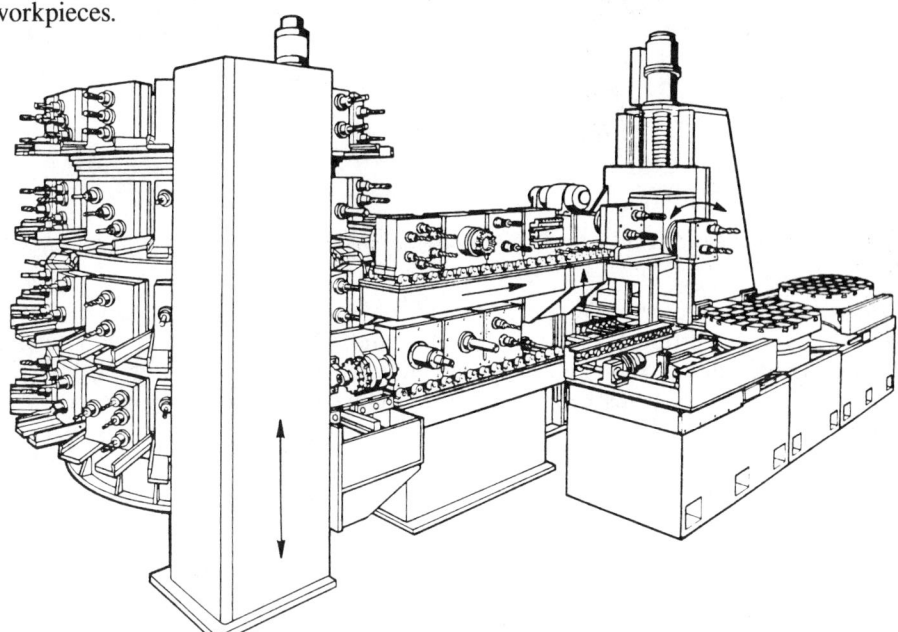

Fig. 14-10 Machining heads, stored on a multilevel carousel, are automatically transferred to spindle of traveling-column machine. (*Courtesy Cincinnati Milacron*)

A CNC headchanging machine made by another builder (see Fig. 14-11) is equipped with four multiple-spindle heads in an overhead indexing unit that rotates in either direction. With a workpiece loaded in the fixture, the required head is automatically indexed over the feed unit, lowered into position on ways on the column face, and located and clamped. The drive quill in the feed unit then automatically advances and engages the driver in the multispindle head.

When machining is completed, the feed unit returns, the head is raised, the index unit brings the next head into position, and the process is repeated. The complete headchanging sequence is accomplished in 25 seconds. The machine can be equipped with T-slot mounted fixtures, indexing fixtures, or shuttle fixtures.

Programs can be loaded into the CNC unit by punched tape, magnetic tape cassette, or manual data input (MDI). With MDI, the control can be programmed by the operator when the first workpiece is being machined or during dry-run cycling. Programming normally only involves the Z-axis with cutting tools preset to the required length in each head.

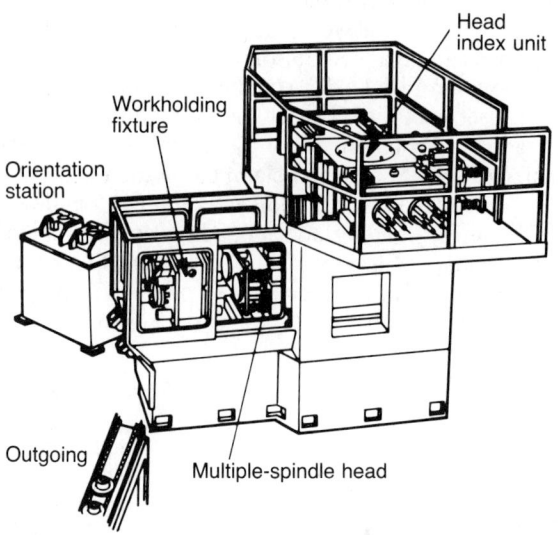

Fig. 14-11 Headchanging machine with four multiple-spindle heads in an overhead indexing unit. (*Courtesy Olofsson Corp.*)

Headchanging machines offered by other builders are similar to rotary dial-type machines. A major difference is that multiple-spindle heads (instead of workholding fixtures) are mounted at each index position on the main rotary dial (see Fig. 14-12). From 4 to 20 geared heads can be used depending upon workpiece size and dial diameter.

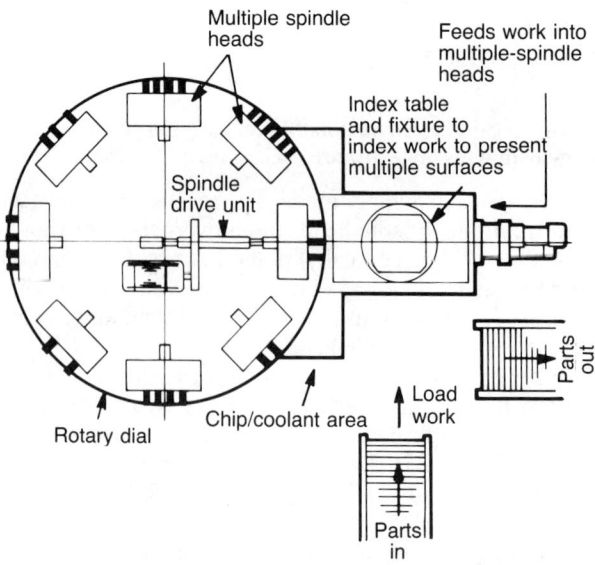

Fig. 14-12 Headchanging machine with multiple-spindle heads mounted on rotary indexing dial. (*Courtesy Kingsbury Machine Tool Corp.*)

One workholding fixture, which can be equipped with a multiple-position indexing table, is mounted on a separate feed unit to move the workpiece into the tooling. A spindle drive unit is mounted inside the dial to provide power to each head as it is indexed to the machining station. Different operations can be performed in any sequential order, with a programmable controller establishing and controlling the indexing sequence of the heads, as well as all functions of the feed slide and drive spindle.

Automatic machining of large tractor transmission housings is being done with two headchanging systems, one of which is illustrated schematically in Fig. 14-13. Each system has a single work station and a number of interchangeable machining heads. Switching from the production of one housing casting to another design requires changing only 13 tools on one machine and 55 on the other. For this application, many stand-alone machines, requiring a substantially greater capital investment, would have been needed to perform the same operations as the two headchanging machines.

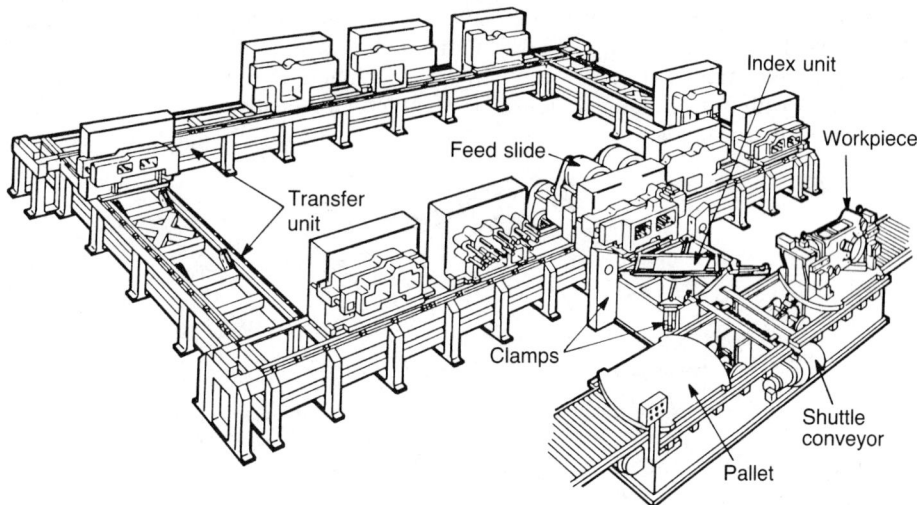

Fig. 14-13 Headchanger system has two palletized work fixtures, a load/unload pallet shuttle, a four-position index unit, a single work station, and a transfer unit for positioning multitool machining heads. (*Courtesy Ingersoll Milling Machine Co.*)

Each machine consists of two palletized work fixtures, a load/unload pallet shuttle, a four-position index unit, a feed slide, and a recirculating head transfer mechanism. The feed slide has dual spindle drives—one for boring and drilling operations, and the other for tapping. Each transfer mechanism is equipped with a number of interchangeable machining heads. The heads move on skid rails, driven by hydraulically actuated transfer bars. Each head contains one driveshaft which engages the driveshaft on the feed slide when the head is in position on the slide.

While one casting is being machined, the operator loads and clamps another on the second pallet. Transfer of the pallets to and from the four-position index table is done with a chain shuttle conveyor. Four 90° movements of the index table allow each workpiece to be machined on all four sides.

As each machining head is transferred onto the slide at the work station, it engages either the drilling drive coupling or the tapping drive coupling and is clamped. Headchanging requires about 20 seconds. One motor on the spindle drive unit is for drilling, boring, and reaming operations, and the other is for tapping. The feed slide is moved by a ballscrew with two motors: a 3 hp (2.2 kW) a-c motor for rapid traverse at 300 ipm (7620 mm/min) and a 1 hp (0.7 kW) d-c motor for the required feed rates.

Control of the headchanging and other functions is accomplished with a programmable limit switch which uses a special-purpose computer. A digital encoder on the end of the slide ballscrew, connected to the computer, replaces scores of cam-operated mechanical limit switches. Each machining head automatically selects its own preprogrammed rapid-advance cycle, feed rate, dwell, and rapid-return cycle as it moves into place on the slide. The heads identify themselves by carrying dogs that engage limit switches.

With a system offered by another machine tool builder, modular and interchangeable, geared toolheads are stored and transported on an overhead monorail, power-and-free type of conveyor. A single work station with one slide unit is provided to selectively hold and feed the heads, and a workholding fixture is mounted on a fixed base unit.

Options available with this system include rotary indexing capability for the fixture, extension of the table base to allow horizontal (X-axis) movement of the fixture with respect to the main slide (Z-axis), an automatic pallet changer for loading/unloading one workpiece while another is being machined, and additional storage loops for handling more heads per machine. Two or more such machines can be used together by connecting the main conveyor loops on the machines. Figure 14-14 illustrates an installation with 3 machining stations and 88 machining heads. Some of the heads are equipped with 23 spindles.

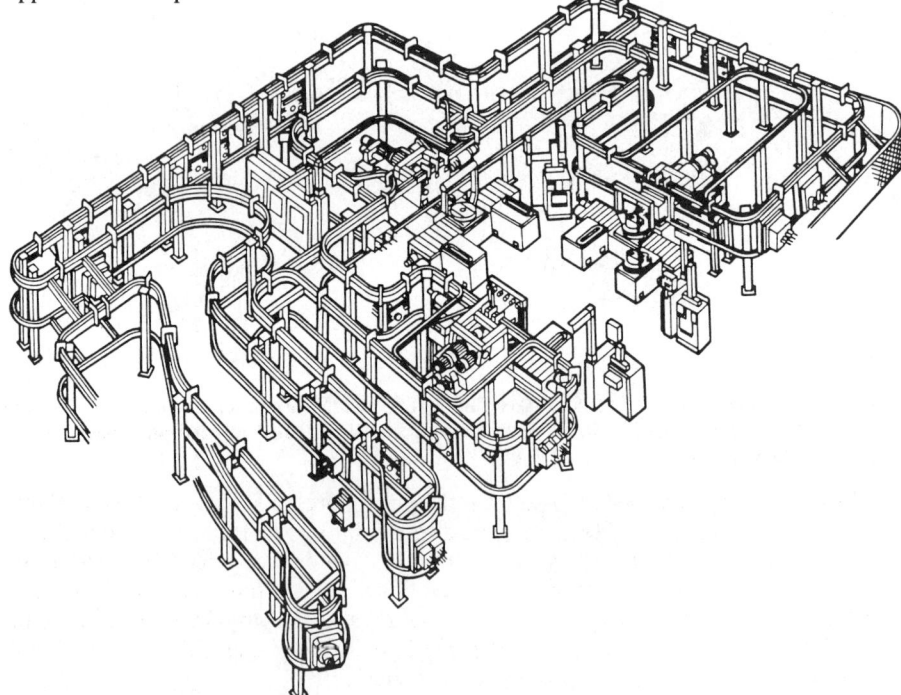

Fig. 14-14 Multiple-spindle heads are stored and transported on an overhead conveyor in this headchanging system with three machining stations. (*Courtesy The Cross Co.*)

Toolhead selection is sequential, but any head not required for a specific workpiece can be quickly bypassed. Headchanging is accomplished by rotation of an overhead, reciprocating transfer bar, which causes drive dogs to engage yokes in the backing plates on the heads during transfer. Conical locator clamps hold the head backing plates to the slide unit. Total sequence time from cut to cut is about 10 seconds, with only 2¼ seconds needed for actual headchanging and the rest of the time required for clamping/unclamping and rapid advance and retraction.

The overhead conveyors for these machines run continuously, but most of the heads remain stationary until required. This permits maintenance, adjustments, and tool-changing to be performed while the heads are stationary, thus minimizing downtime. A CNC unit controls transfer of the heads; rapid advance, feed, and rapid retraction of the main slide; cross slide movement of the workholding fixture; and rotary indexing of the fixture. A CRT is provided on the control console for program optimization and diagnostic troubleshooting.

WORKPIECE HANDLING SYSTEMS

Material Transport Systems. Various types of material transport systems are in current use or have been proposed for use in future FMS installations. Of the types in the following list, the tow-line, powered cart, and roller conveyor types of transportation systems are the most commonly employed today. Robotic systems are increasing in use. Systems which employ robots as the transportation media are sometimes referred to as flexible transfer lines or robotic work cells.

- Tow-line systems—Workpieces are transported by individual cart-like carriers that are towed by chains under the floor. Such fixture carts are guided by slots in the floor.
- Powered cart systems—Following rails or electronically defined pathways (in-floor wiring), powered cart transportation systems are self-propelled either with an on-board energy source or with power pick-up.
- Roller conveyor systems—Fixture pallets are propelled along floor-mounted, powered roller conveyors.
- Air-film conveyor systems—Fixture pallets float on films of air along conveyor-like pathways, driven by linear motors.
- Overhead conveyor systems—Workpieces are held in fixtures suspended from the ceiling, following specific pathways.
- Stacker crane systems—Stacker cranes serve as workpiece transportation devices, interfacing with work stations and storage matrixes.
- Robot systems—Programmable robots move workpieces to and from work stations.

The function of the material transport system of an FMS is to move workpieces to and from member work stations. Under control by the central computer, the movement of workpieces through the system is usually automatic. The material transport system of an FMS interfaces with work stations and serves as a banking medium for temporary storage of workpieces. In addition, short operations such as manual loading and unloading of workpieces, cleaning, deburring, etc., may be performed at designated positions along the material transport system.

In general, the main objective of a material transport system of an FMS is to help achieve maximum work station utilization through efficient workpiece movement. Capacity, speed, and random delivery capabilities must be considered in the design of such systems. Extremely important is the ability of the transport system to effectively handle congestion in the system caused by work station downtime, system surges, or other irregularities.

Flexibility in transport system design is also important. Potential changes in production mix or other operating characteristics of the FMS must be considered in the design phase of the transport system to ensure efficient operation as changes occur.

Reliability is also important as the transport system is the central unit upon which all work stations depend. The most productive transportation systems are simple, durable, and easy to repair. Provisions should be designed into the system to bypass any section that is inoperative due to system failure until another modular transport section can be installed in the failed section. Manual operation should be a built-in capability in case of failure of automatic control.

Many other considerations must be given to the material transport system of an FMS. For example, maintenance of workpiece integrity is of prime concern. The transport system must be designed to ensure that the workpiece is not damaged in any way or that location of the workpiece in the fixture cart is not altered as a result of movement through the FMS. Shocks and bumps should be avoided.

Expandability is one of the most significant advantages of the FMS concept and must be considered in the design phases of the system. With careful planning, modular growth at various levels of automation can significantly enhance the effectiveness of an FMS.

Shuttle mechanisms, integral components of an FMS transportation system, are employed to interface the individual work stations with the main transportation network. Shuttles remove workpieces from the main transportation system, store workpieces until the work station is ready to accept it, move workpieces into the station, remove workpieces from the station, store the workpiece until the transportation system is ready to accept it, and move workpieces into the main transportation network.

Shuttle mechanisms can take many different forms, depending upon the type of FMS. In-line shuttles with two-position banking before and two-position banking after the work station have been used extensively by one FMS manufacturer. Rotating and side-ways slicing shuttle devices have also been used effectively. Such devices feature two banking positions which are shared for both before and after work station functions.

In some cases, manual loading/unloading, small assembly jobs, or inspection operations are performed on the fixture cart or are performed on small tables adjacent to the work handling system of the FMS.

Coordinate inspection, stock allowance checks, and workpiece and fixture cleaning are additional operations that have been incorporated in existing FMS installation. Future systems may include stations for such operations as grinding, hobbing, forming, heat treatment, or even painting.

Control Systems. Flexible manufacturing systems typically feature hierarchical control. The first level of control is the intelligence built in at the CNC units of the machine tools themselves. The second level of control is provided by the central computer which operates in a DNC mode, downloading NC part programs to member machine tools. Also supplied by the central computer is the third level of control which directs the flow of workpieces through the system, maintains production scheduling information, and produces management reports. The following is a summary of the various functions of an FMS control system:

- Control of workpiece and fixture location.
- Material transportation system control.
- Work station control.
- Records maintenance.
- NC part program control and maintenance.
- Tool control and tool life control and maintenance.
- Generation of performance reports.
- Visual display of status.
- Communication with systems operator(s).
- Provide information for production planning.

The control system is comprised of both software and hardware elements. Sometimes, two minicomputers are used simultaneously to provide required control; in such cases, one computer is employed for DNC data transmission and related tasks, and the second computer is employed for overall control of the system. Additional computers are sometimes employed as backup.

Usually, minicomputers, associated memory, power supply, and interface boards make up the heart of an FMS control system. Mass data storage is usually in the form of disc or drum. Communication terminals in various forms are provided for human intervention; CRT terminals may also be available for NC part program editing. A line printer is usually part of the control system for efficient generation of reports and listing of NC part programs.

Communications hardware is an important component of any FMS control system. Such hardware, which may include digital multiplexing, is employed to transmit and receive signals from the material transport system and member work stations. Peripherals, including punched tape reader and tape punch (for program generation and loading) and magnetic tape drives (for quick system backup and update), may also be part of the control system.

Work stations usually are equipped with data input/output devices for human interaction with the control system. Interface modules may be required for data input to NC machines via DNC. Software for the control system usually includes modules written by the computer manufacturer, including real time operating systems. It also includes modules written by the FMS supplier, some of which will be standard and some tailored to the requirements of the particular FMS.

FMS OPERATION

The operations of a typical FMS are relatively simple. Typically, an FMS is programmed to operate according to predefined objectives; for example, the optimization of material flow or the maximizing of station utilization. The central computer selects a specific workpiece to be machined according to production schedules stored in computer memory. An appropriate fixture cart is sent via the workpiece handling system to the load/unload station. The load/unload station operator receives instructions (via teletype or CRT) from the computer as to which workpiece to position in the fixture cart. When the operator has loaded the workpiece, he signals the computer to move the fixture cart to the first operation.

Stored in the central computer is an ordered listing of processing steps for each workpiece. This listing is used by the computer to select an appropriate station (machine tool) for the first processing step. Upon command by the computer, the fixture cart is directed to an appropriate station to begin processing. An optimum route through the system is selected as calculated by the control system. At the first processing station, the workpiece may be required to wait; when the station is clear, the workpiece is shuttled into it to begin processing. When the first operation is complete, the workpiece is automatically moved to the next appropriate station as defined by the ordered list of processing steps stored in computer memory. Thus, workpieces simultaneously travel through the system in random order stopping only at selected stations. When processing is complete, the workpieces are sent to the load/unload station for removal by the operator. At this stage, the workpiece may be complete or may require further processing using a different fixture cart; in the latter case, an appropriate fixture cart is automatically sent to the load/unload station for loading by the operator, and a new sequence of processing steps through the FMS is initiated by the computer.

Loading and unloading of workpieces in fixture carts is the only manual function required in the operation of an FMS (except, of course, normal tool setup, monitoring, and maintenance); every other function is completely automatic in most cases.

An FMS installation is capable of accommodating changes in part volumes and/or product mix, design changes, etc., with fewer problems than conventional equipment. Because FMS equipment is flexible with respect to part design, the useful life of the equipment is considered to be longer than specially tooled conventional equipment;

thus, increased flexibility can eliminate the need for some future capital outlays for new equipment.

Because an FMS can process a wide variety of workpieces at random, downtime associated with traditional changeover techniques is eliminated. Computer control allows more flexibility in part routing to minimize production time.

FLEXIBLE MANUFACTURING CELLS

The flexible manufacturing cell (FMC) is a modest version of the full-blown flexible manufacturing system shown in Fig. 14-1.

Definitions of what constitutes a flexible manufacturing cell vary. In the SME Manufacturing Insights Videotape "Flexible Manufacturing Cells", Dr. Michael C. Burnstein describes an FMC as "an automated machine for manufacturing, which includes some automated material handling, and typically some automated tool changing capability, so that it is capable by itself of unattended operation, at least for some limited time."

Figure 14-15 illustrates a typical cell that is tended by a robot which sequentially loads and unloads three machine tools—a vertical milling machine, a broach, and a drill. Operation is as follows:

Starting at the end of one-production sequence and working from there, the process is as follows:

1. Gripping the OD, the robot removes a workpiece from an index-type drilling machine and deposits it on the outgoing conveyor.
2. Gripping the OD, the robot extracts a workpiece from the broach and loads it into the drill.
3. The robot returns to the intermediate rest stand, picks up a workpiece (gripping the OD), turns it over, and loads the broach.
4. The robot approaches the milling machine, unloads a workpiece (gripping the ID), and places it in the rest stand.
5. The robot returns to the input conveyor, grips a part on the ID, and leads it into the milling machine.
6. The robot returns to the drilling machine and repeats the process.

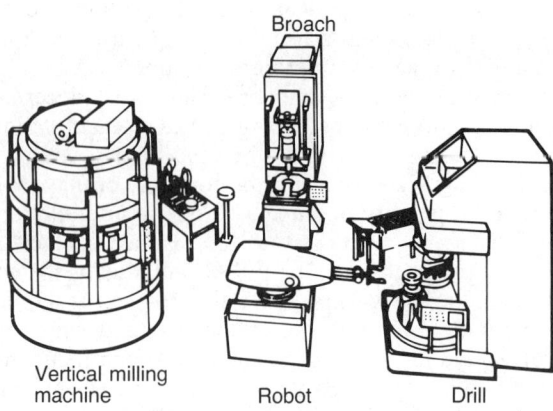

Broach

Vertical milling machine   Robot   Drill

Fig. 14-15 Robot-driven work cell-vertical milling machine, broach, and drill loaded and unloaded with a robot.

Both the mill and drill are index-type machines with load/unload stations. The milling and drilling cycle times relative to the broach and robot cycle times are such that idle time is minimized. Throughout the process, a series of limit switches in each machine are interfaced to the robot, indicating that the machining cycle is complete and that safe conditions exist for workpiece unloading and loading. Similarly, the robot provides output signals to start the machine tools once a part has been properly loaded. A relatively short input conveyor is manually supplied with a bank of raw forgings by an operator who oversees this and other operations in the area.

While most metalcutting applications employ two-part end effectors to maximize machine tool utilization, the application described in Fig. 14-15 precludes this approach because of limited access to the machines. Also, in part of the sequence, the workpiece must be gripped on the ID for loading into the machine chucks; otherwise, it must be gripped on the OD. Thus, the rest table is required for regripping.

Prior to the introduction of the robot, these three operations were performed in different plant locations, each machine tool being manned by one operator per shift, substantial savings are realized by reducing in-process inventory, material handling, and transporting and process interruptions.

WORKHOLDING FOR FLEXIBLE MANUFACTURING SYSTEMS

The basic requirements of an adequate workholding system for use with a flexible manufacturing system are:

- The ability to precisely and repeatedly position the workpiece to the axes of all machines in the system.
- The flexibility to handle the various configurations of the parts of the family that it is designed to hold.
- The ability to resist the cutting forces of the various operations.
- The elimination of the need for on-line setups or adjustments that would prevent round-the-clock unattended machining.
- To provide for automatic chuck changing and pallet systems that permit off-line fixturing and chucking.

QUICK CHANGE SYSTEMS

The Q-axis. One manufacturer of workholding equipment has labelled the systematic means by which workpieces can be aligned and clamped in alignment with the machine tool axes as "Registration and Lock-Up Technology—the Q-axis". The manufacturer has gone on to develop a complete system that positions the workpiece in exact relationship to all axes on all machines and permits interactive accuracy, repeatability, quick change speed, and high holding force between various machine technologies. It allows metalcutting, inspection, and assembly operations to be performed with extreme accuracy.

The system consists of a receiver (see Fig. 14-16) at every work station, and a high speed mating carrier (see Fig. 14-17) to which a chuck, expanding mandrel, collet chuck, end driver, face plate or just about any other special fixture has been attached to hold the workpiece. The receiver is the non-mobile element of the system. It contains a precision Hirth-tooth coupling ring; the double toggle, preloaded Bellville washer design clamping mechanism with locking forces ranging between 8,000 to 24,000 lbf (35.6 to 106.8 kN); and an orient mechanism for easy loading and for the precise, controlled engagement of the carrier.

The receiver is permanently fixed to the spindle or table of the machine tool. This allows a part to be moved from machine to machine without additional setup and permits parts to be set-up on the carrier away from the machine while other parts are

 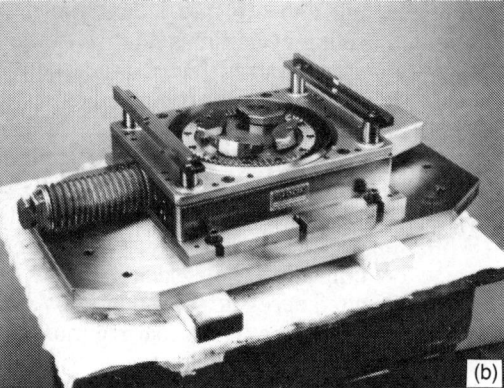

Fig. 14-16 Quick change locating and lockup system: (*a*) **rotary receiver,** (*b*) **fixed receiver.** (*Polymax® system, courtesy Taft Peirce Manufacturing Co.*)

(a)   (b)

Fig. 14-17 Quick change system carriers: (*a*) **rotary carrier,** (*b*) **fixed carrier.** (*Polymax® system, courtesy Taft Peirce Manufacturing Co.*)

being machined. Once a machine is set-up with the system, it is always set up.

From cubical (prismatic) machining to cylindrical (turning) machining, to precision measurement, the alignment and lockup process takes but a few seconds and provides repeatable centrality to 0.00005 in., angularity to ±1 arc sec., and height to 0.000125 in. The system is available in five standard sizes to fit all types of new or existing machine tools such as lathes, milling machines, machining centers, etc. In most cases existing fixturing can be retrofitted to the system.

Figure 14-18 shows the sequence of operations in machining a part using the system. Operations are as follows:

(*a*) Workpiece is set up on the carrier away from the machine.
(*b*) Workpiece and carrier loaded on lathe for first turning operation.
(*c*) Carrier and workpiece transferred to vertical machining center for drilling and tapping bolt circle.
(*d*) Workpiece removed and reversed off-line for second series of operations.
(*e*) Carrier/chuck/workpiece reloaded on lathe for second series of turning operations.
(*f*) Carrier and workpiece transferred to horizontal machining center for machining of vanes.

Spindle mounted receivers can be actuated by draw bar, manually or internal pneu-

(a)   (b)   (c)

(d)   (e)   (f)

Fig. 14-18 Machining using the quick change system. (*Polymax® system, courtesy Taft Peirce Manufacturing Co.*)

matic actuation. Table mounted receivers are cam bar actuated, usually hydraulically.

The Multiple Chuck Approach. Putting a chuck within a chuck to permit off-machine part fixturing or robotic changeover is one manufacturer's approach to minimize downtime for difficult-to-handle parts. By utilizing multiple chucks that permit the operator or setup man to set up the part off-line, the machine can be cutting one workpiece while another workpiece is being mounted or checked. Part setup time is not part of the machining time and changeover time is limited to the amount of time that it takes to remove one chuck/workpiece combination from the machine and replace it with another.

The multiple chucking approach is based on a master chuck (see Fig. 14-19) that is permanently mounted on the machine spindle: The type of chuck varies depending on the application. For example, both universal Ball-Lok chucks and diaphragm chucks are being employed in applications.

The workholding chuck is typically a mandrel, a pin chuck, a collet chuck, or a special tool.

During changeover, the master chuck is released and the workholding chuck is removed. The operation can be performed manually or robotically. Since the master chuck is exposed to the machining environment, it should be flushed or air blasted to remove any chips or contaminants. Then the chuck holding the next part (see Fig. 14-20), can be loaded into the jaws of the master chuck as shown in Fig. 14-21.

One application of this multiple chuck arrangement has been on an unmanned cell for grinding two different parts. The grinding machine has been equipped with a hydraulically-actuated diaphragm chuck. There are two different parts and a workhold-

Fig. 14-19 Master chuck. (*Courtesy ITW Woodworth*)

Fig. 14-20 Workpiece mounted in chuck. (*Courtesy ITW Woodworth*)

Fig. 14-21 Arbor is loaded into the diaphragm. (*Courtesy ITW Woodworth*)

ing device appropriate for each. The diaphragm chuck grips either a Roto-Lok arbor or a centering fixture.

The robot is programmed to insert the arbor in the diaphragm chuck. Air sensors in the chuck indicate when the arbor is correctly positioned for chuck actuation. When the second part/fixture combination must be loaded, the robot automatically switches end-of-arm tooling and makes the change.

The Tru-Change System. This system (see Fig. 14-22) is based on a precision coupling utilizing a spiroid gear form. One half of the coupling is ground to fit the spindle pilot and bolted to the spindle permanently. The other half is attached to the back plate of the workholder. When the two are mated at the precision gear form, the workpiece is automatically located within 0.0003 in. FIM, both axially and radially.

A dual drawbar system is employed. Each drawbar is actuated by a piston. Once the two halves are mated, one of the drawbars is used to secure the two with from 8,000 to 10,000 pounds (35.6 to 44.4 kN) of force. The second drawbar performs chuck actuation. There are no mounting screws involved, nor is it necessary to use a master part for

Fig. 14-22 The try-change system. (*Courtesy ITW Woodworth*)

centering. Sensors can be installed to signal control that the change has been made. All setup work is done off-machine in a staging area.

A leading automaker is using this system as a fundamental building block of three unmanned cells to produce front-wheel-drive steering components. Five different parts and several different machining operations are involved. Each cell consists of two horizontal-spindle CNC lathes and a robot loader. A single coordinate measuring machine (CMM) serves the three cells. Twenty-one chucks are used: Seven pin arbor chucks, seven power chucks and seven universal Ball-Lok chucks. There are 18 chucks for the machining operations and three chucks for the CMM.

Each of the machines is equipped with one-half of the coupling. As required by the operation, the robot changes chucks on command from the cell controller.

Drawtube-operated Chuck Changing System. The system illustrated in Fig. 14-23 was designed for quickly changing chucks without the need for bolted connections. The chuck piston ring and actuator drawtube are linked together so that when the drawtube pulls the chuck onto the tapered surface of the spindle nose, it is secured in place by a hydraulically-operated locking mechanism. Chuck changing can become completely automatic when the gantry or overhead crane for handling the workpiece is replaced

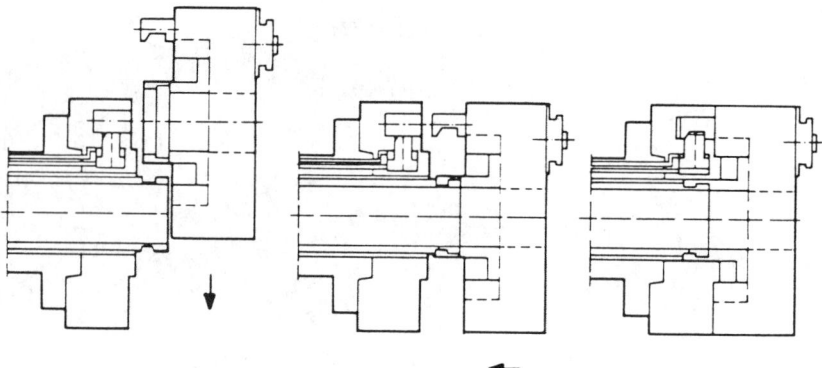

Fig. 14-23 Drawtube-operated chuck changing system. (*Courtesy Forkardt, Inc.*)

with a programmable manipulator or robot.

Chuck Changing System with Hydraulic Clamping Head. Figure 14-24 shows an alternative to some of the existing systems. A hydraulically-operated clamping head mounted on a lathe spindle actuates the chuck proper, while a special vane-type cylinder with appropriate safety devices mounted at the spindle end operates the clamping head, and thus the chuck.

Fig. 14-24 Quick-acting chuck changing system with hydraulic clamping head. (*Courtesy Rohm Products of America*)

The clamping head has a short taper nose, and is screwed to the spindle just like any conventional chuck, except that it stays there permanently. Integrated into the clamping head are six radially movable pins with rearward-acting clamping bevels. The chuck to be used in conjunction with this clamping head has a matching adapter which envelopes the clamping head. In the adapter is an annular groove into which six pins move to pull it axially against the taper nose. The chuck proper features a bayonet-type piston connection which is latched in by a push-pull linkage operated by the vane in the actuating cylinder. At the same time, the six pins are locked in clamping position, and the chuck is ready for use.

An Automatic Chuck Change System. The automatic chuck change system (the Gamet® CAM System) shown in Fig. 14-25 was designed for use with flexible turning centers to permit automatic changing of chucks or other workpiece gripping devices by a robot or an integrated loading system. When several machines are fitted with the system, each gripping device can be used on any machine without adjustment. Operation of the system is illustrated in Fig. 14-26.

Fig. 14-25 Automatic quick chuck change system. (*Gamet® system, courtesy Powerhold, Inc.*)

Pallet Changer System.[2] The system shown in Fig. 14-27 was designed mainly to improve and enhance the productivity of vertical turning lathes (VTLs). However, it can also be applied to vertical and horizontal machining centers and other machines such as gear hobbing machines, parts washing machines, induction heat treat machines, CMMs, AGVs and others. In a complete FMS it is possible to have many types of machines or operations using the same pallet system.

All of the aforementioned machines can be designed to accept this type of fully automatic power chucking system so that all of the pallets will be able to move through all of the machines.

This system is easier to interface with the design of a new piece of equipment, but it can be used with an existing piece of equipment. The spindle, as discussed earlier, must

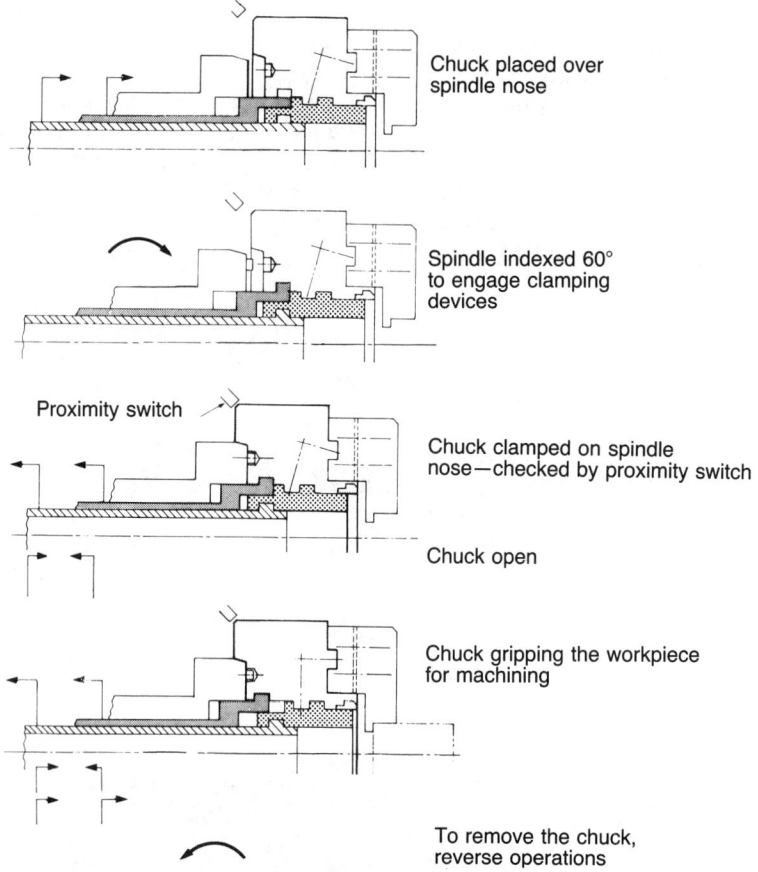

Chuck placed over spindle nose

Spindle indexed 60° to engage clamping devices

Proximity switch

Chuck clamped on spindle nose—checked by proximity switch

Chuck open

Chuck gripping the workpiece for machining

To remove the chuck, reverse operations

Fig. 14-26 Operation of automatic quick chuck change system. (*Gamet® system, courtesy Powerhold, Inc.*)

be strong enough to accept the extra weight and have a through hole big enough to accept at least a tube bundle for the delivery of hydraulic fluid plus an air line.

Since this rework could be quite expensive, a complete investigation should be made beforehand to determine if the cost would be justified.

The pallet system is made up of six (6) components. They are:

- The pallet holder/receiver
- The pallet
- The transfer station
- The stand-by station
- The load/unload station
- The control unit

A typical pallet system is shown with a VTL in Fig. 14-28. This system has 3-jaw, self-centering power chucks for pallets.

The pallet holder/receiver is the heart of the system. This device locates the pallet on the machine spindle, clamps the pallet in place, and, in the case of powered pallets, directs hydraulic pressure to the pallet, holding the part in place while it is being machined. The machine spindle is made to accept the receiver, including a through hole in the spindle, a machined flange with pilot diameters, and bearings designed to accept the weight of the receiver, pallet, part, and load during machining operations. A pallet holder for powered pallets is shown in Fig. 14-29.

Fig. 14-27 Pallet changer system. (*Courtesy The S-P Manufacturing Corp. and Rotomors SPA*)

The pallets are drawn down onto the receiver by means of two (2) T-shaped rails which are controlled by hydraulic cylinders built inside the receiver. The pallets are located on the receiver with eight (8) opposed pads. They are adjustable and cross placed as far from the center as possible. These locating pads simulate the function and obtain the advantages of a large crown coupling. Each pad is equipped with a nozzle for compressed air to assure pad cleaning and, through a pressure switch, verifies the exact seating of the pallet on the receiver.

The size and diameter of the pallet and pallet holder are determined by the parts which are going to be machined, the same way in which the size of the machine is determined. The parts also determine what type of pallets are to be used. There are

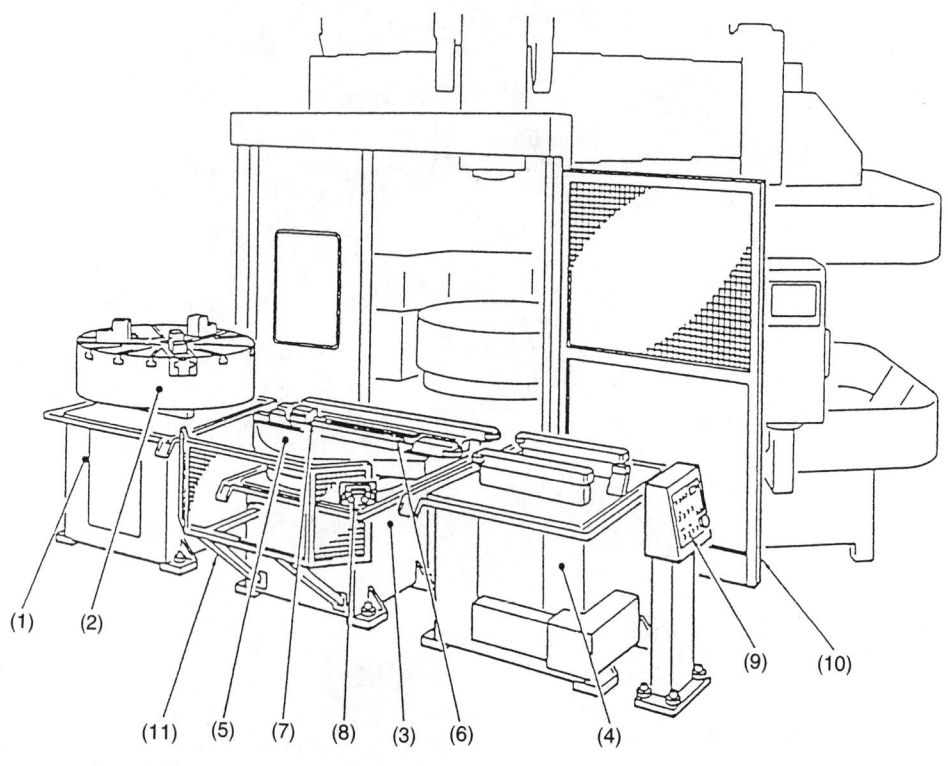

(1) Stand-by Station (FB)	(6) Slide Plate (TC)
(2) Pallet (Chuck)	(7) Hook
(3) Rotating Station (RTB)	(8) Index Pin
(4) Loading Station (FBS)	(9) Operation Panel
(5) Rotation Table	(10) (11) Safety Fence

Fig. 14-28 Pallet changer system with a VTL. (*Courtesy The S-P Manufacturing Corp. and Rotomors SPA*)

many different types of pallets available. The following is a sample of the types available:

- Plain type pallets, round, square or rectangular. Different configurations of T-slots and tapped holes can be incorporated in the top of the pallet.
- Plain chuck pallets with 4-jaw configuration serrated with moving jaws for different positions. The jaws are equipped with adjustable clamps to hold the part.
- Three or four independent, manually-operated jaw chuck pallets.
- Manual, self-centering scroll chuck pallets with two, three, or four jaws. Each jaw is manually adjustable.
- Powered self-centering chuck pallets with two or three jaws, or 2-jaw/3-jaw type.
- Many other types of powered chucks.

Fig. 14-29 Pallet holder/receiver. (*Courtesy The S-P Manufacturing Corp. and Rotomors SPA*)

In short, any type of plain pallet or chuck now being used in a lathe type machine could be incorporated into a pallet to fit this system. The pallet must be machined on the bottom to fit the pallet holder. It must have T-slots to fit the rails that draw down the pallet. It also must have the eight (8) locating pads like the receiver. In additional there are (8) roller bearing assemblies for the pallets to ride on while transferring through the system.

In Fig. 14-30, the pallet is shown in place on the pallet holder. The pallet is operated by hydraulic pressure transmitted into the pallet through injectors mounted in the receiver. There is a cylinder internal to the pallet which, when pressurized, operates the draw cam mechanism to open or close the jaws. By adjusting the pallets to the pallet holder, flatness and concentricity is guaranteed to be one thousandths (0.001) of an inch or better from pallet to pallet. An added advantage of this type of powered chuck is that it is able to perform Hi-Lo chucking operations because of the lever/spool type of internal chuck operating mechanism. Hi-Lo chucking is cutting first operation under high gripping forces, then being able to switch to low chucking forces for final turning operations.

The pallets are shuttled to and from the machine and stations by the intermediate rotating transfer station, as shown in Figs. 14-28 and 14-31. This station is equipped with a hydraulically controlled double chain pay-out mechanism for the transferring of pallets. It can be automatically rotated 360° in either direction by means of a hydraulic motor. There are four (4) angular stop positions at 90°.

After the part is finished it must be removed and a new part installed on the pallet. This operation is done on the load/unload station, as shown in Figs. 14-28 and 14-31. This station is equipped with an automatic lift mechanism, which carries locating pins

Fig. 14-30 Pallet mounted on a pallet holder. (*Courtesy The S-P Manufacturing Corp. and Rotomors SPA*)

and injectors that transmit hydraulic pressure to the pallet. This allows the built-in cylinder in the pallet to operate the jaws. After the part is loaded, the lift mechanism retracts. The clamping force is maintained in the pallet by means of special sealed check valves located within the pallet.

When the pallet is removed from the machine, it must be stored in a location so that the next pallet can be loaded into the machine. This station is called the stand-by station. It is a station that serves only as a holding area as shown in Fig. 14-28.

The last component in the pallet system is the control unit. The system is capable of automatic as well as manual control. Hydraulic power is controlled by means of proximity switches, pressure switches, solenoid valves, relays, programmable controllers, and the machine computer control. In a system such as this, the time from stop of machine spindle to start is approximately two minutes.

Fig. 14-31 Intermediate rotating transfer station. (*Courtesy The S-P Manufacturing Corp. and Rotomors SPA*)

FLEXIBLE FIXTURING SYSTEMS FOR FMC AND FMS

Flexible fixturing systems should possess the ability to accommodate parts of various shapes and sizes when subjected to a wide variety of force-fields and torques associated with various manufacturing operations such as assembly tasks, inspection, metal cutting and cleaning.[3] Moreover, these fixturing systems should have various dimensions of flexibility such as:

- Mix flexibility, which relates to the processing of a mix of different parts loosely related to one another.
- Parts flexibility, which relates the addition of parts to, or removal from, the parts set.

- Routing flexibility, which relates to the dynamic assessment of parts to machines to maintain workload balance.
- Design-change flexibility, which relates to the potential of faster implementation of design changes to a part or parts.
- Volume flexibility, which relates to the ability to accommodate changes in production volume for various parts.
- Response-to-failure flexibility, which relates the capability to re-route parts when a machine or line segment is out of service.

These flexible fixturing systems, if available, would have several distinct advantages over the current generation of dedicated fixtures employed in CIM environments. First, the lead-time and the effort required to design, engineer, and fabricate special-purpose fixtures would be substantially reduced. Secondly, the storage and retrieval of a multiplicity of dedicated fixtures required to effect rapid change-overs between manufacturing operations and to accommodate changing parts mixes would be eliminated. These advantages would not only result in substantial improvements in machine utilization, but also permit a more cost-effective and time-efficient CIM environment to be developed.

With the market for CIM system projected to achieve an annual expenditure of more than $1.8 billion by the year 1990,[4] and the typical cost of dedicated fixtures amounting to 10-20 percent of the total costs,[5] the technological and economic impact of flexible fixturing technologies will clearly be of major significance.

A number of systems to provide this flexibility are currently being developed. They include the following:

- Fluidized-bed fixturing (pseudo phase change).
- Temperature-induced phase change fixturing (authentic phase change).
- Computer-controlled reconfigurable vises.
- A system approach to the total tooling and fixturing package.

Fluidized-bed Fixturing Systems. Fluidized-bed fixturing systems and modular fixturing systems have recently emerged as one of the significant solutions to the insatiable demand for viable flexible-fixturing systems for incorporation in modern computer-integrated manufacturing environments.

A schematic diagram of a class of particulate fluidized-bed fixtures[6,7,8] is presented in Fig. 14-32 which shows a container filled with particles and incorporating a porous floor through which an air system passes at a carefully controlled rate. When the air supply is activated, the particulate bed acts as a fluid permitting the part to be introduced into the fixture with minimal resistance. If the air supply is then switched off, the particles will then compact under gravitational loading to form a solid mass which holds the part fixed. The part can then be subjected to the desired sequence of manufacturing operations and upon completion of these tasks, the part can then be removed from the fixture by initiating the air flow in order to create the fluid phase again.

Particulate fluidized-bed fixtures can be usefully employed to fixture parts in the configuration schematically presented in Fig. 14-33 for applications involving low-force fields. High-force field applications can be accommodated by subjecting the free surface of the compacted bed to surface tractions (normal loads), which further compact the bed and thereby increase the forces imposed on the workpiece. This is accomplished in practice, by activating a hydraulic clamp arm, which exerts a controlled force on the compaction plate. By this means, parts have been fixtured in a prototype device on a state-of-the-art machining center while being subjected to end-milling and drilling operations.[9] The ability to tailor the compliance characteristics of the fixture to suit the specific fixturing task can be usefully exploited in a large variety of manufacturing tasks, such as in robotic assembly operations.

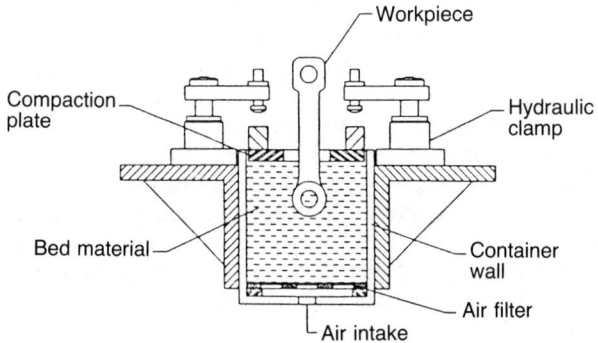

Fig. 14-32 Schematic of particulate fluidized-bed fixture.

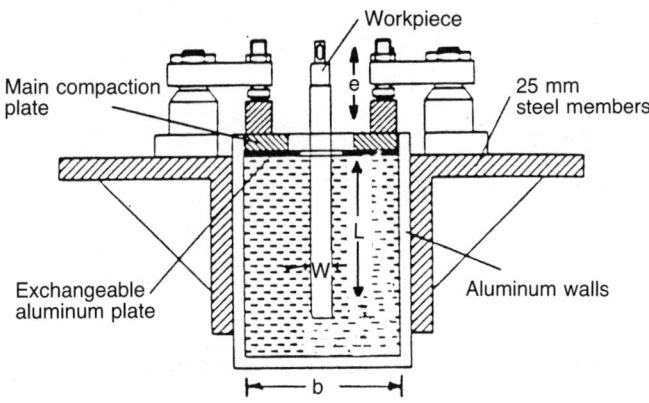

Fig. 14-33 Particulate fluidized-bed fixture showing characteristic dimensions.

Temperature-induced Phase Change Fixturing (TPF). Temperature induced phase-change fixturing (TPF) has traditionally been employed in encapsulation for special purpose precision machining, such as the milling of turbine blades. But TPF can be prohibitively expensive in high precision applications which use complicated machinery. In general-purpose fixturing, though, the workpiece has to be merely grasped. Therefore, the stringent constraints of encapsulation can be relaxed, making TPF a viable approach. Low melting point bismuth alloys (such as Cerrobend®) are currently on the market as an encapsulating medium. These are ideal candidate materials for TPF.

Though still at an experimental stage, authentic phase-change fixturing appears to be promising. Prototypes based on this concept are currently being developed. Since most authentic phase-change fixtures involve temperature changes, computer-based predictive capabilities for induced thermal stresses and/or relief of residual stresses are being developed simultaneously. The development of these capabilities is needed because of the intrinsic integration of CAD and CAM in a truly flexible manufacturing system.

Computer-controlled Reconfigurable Vises.[10] The basic unit in any fixturing system is a clamping mechanism, of which the most common is a machine vise. Making vises more flexible usually involves modifications to the jaws[11,12] which must also be done by the machine operator. An alternative to replacing the jaws is predrilling holes in each jaw face.[13] A part can then be located on pins that are inserted in selected holes. However, this method is not easily computer-controlled, nor fully flexible.

A fixturing system for use in a flexible manufacturing environment must be computer controlled and reconfigurable. The fixture should be able to be tended by a robot and be able to hold a part in a known orientation and position with respect to the machine.

Design Theory of a Computer-Controlled Flexible Fixturing System. To define the position of an object in space, six degrees of freedom must be specified. Figure 14-34 shows a sketch of the proposed system, where a robot loads a prismatic part into a computer-controlled vise which positions and clamps the part with respect to a machine tool. The fixed anvil acts as one reference plane, servo-controlled levelling bars act as a second orthogonal reference plane, and controllable discrete stops act as a third reference axis. For purposes of clarity, the fixed and moving jaws will be referred to as anvils, in order to distinguish them from the replaceable jaws discussed subsequently.

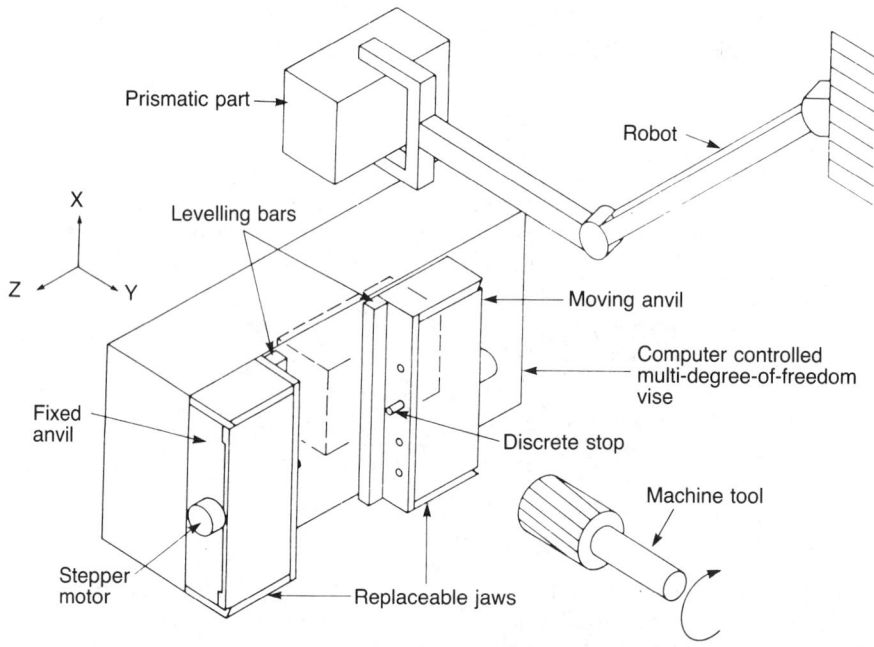

Fig. 14-34 Flexible automated fixturing system.

For nonprismatic parts, and some special prismatic parts such as thin plates, the anvils need to have removable surfaces, that can be changed by a robot, to act as the interface between the part and the anvils as shown in Figure 14-35. Before placing a part in the vise, the contour of the part can be machined into the face of the replaceable jaws in order to properly align and clamp the part. Therefore, a large inventory of fixturing is not necessary because the fixturing can be machined prior to the machining of the part, and either stored or discarded after the part is machined.

Mechanical Configuration of the Prototype Fixturing System. The general construction of the prototype fixturing system (vise) is shown in Figure 14-36. This particular configuration was designed to be mounted on a shuttle pallet on a horizontal machining center in the Automated Manufacturing Research Facility (AMRF) at the National Bureau of Standards[14] and is shown in Figure 14-37. The vise had to be short enough in length to allow the pallet to rotate, and since the vise projects up from the pallet, it had to provide stiffness to resist clamping moments. These constraints resulted in a short, box-type design.

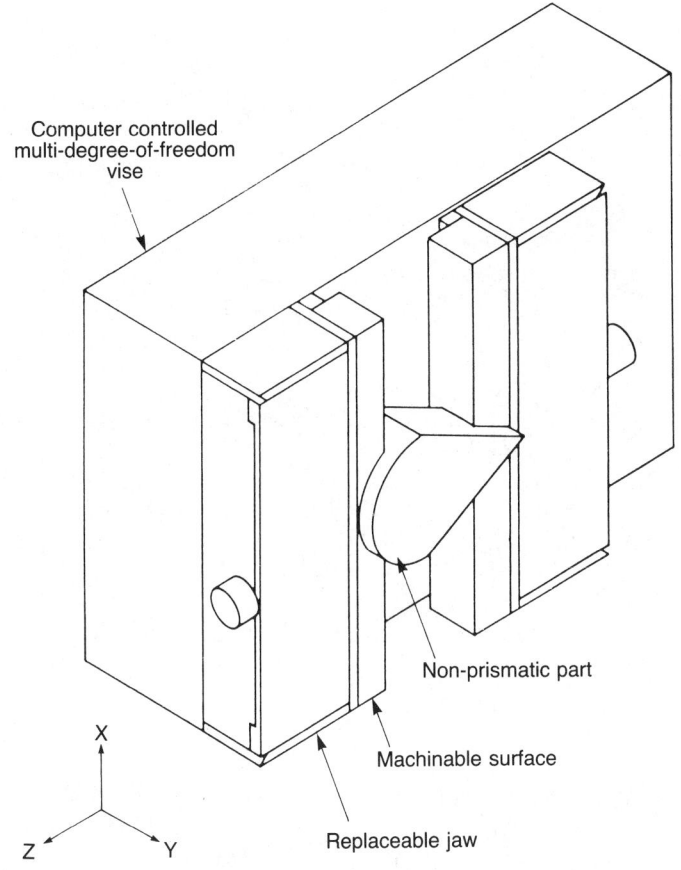

Computer controlled
multi-degree-of-freedom
vise

Non-prismatic part

Machinable surface

Replaceable jaw

X

Z

Y

Fig. 14-35 Method for fixturing non-prismatic parts.

The functional requirements for the vise were:

1.) Holding force of 100 to 10,000 lbf (450 to 45,000 N) controllable in 100 lbf (450 N) increments.
2.) Jaw opening to 8 in. (200 mm), position controllable to within 0.02 in. (0.5 mm).
3.) Levelling bars position accurate to within 0.001 in. (0.02 mm).
4.) Discrete stops on anvils located every 2 in. (50 mm).
5.) Maximum static deflection less than 0.002 in. (0.05 mm).
6.) Anvil jaws replaceable by a robot.
7.) Self contained microprocessor control with RS-232 serial interface.

The vise has one fixed anvil and one moving anvil, which establish the Z-position and Y-rotation of a part. In addition, the anvils contain robot changeable jaws. For ease of machining and for reduction in weight, the main body of the vise is made of aluminum. The moving anvil is cast integral with the ductile iron carriage which is moved by a ballscrew. The ballscrew is chain driven by a hydraulic geroler motor. Clamping forces are transferred through the ballscrew to a thrust nut/washer assembly and into the end bulkhead of the structure. The carriage is fully constrained about five axes by specially designed bearings. The bearing preload is insensitive to uniform temperature changes. Two leveling bars establish the Y-position and Z-rotation of a part. The position of the leveling bars is established by servo-controlled hydraulic

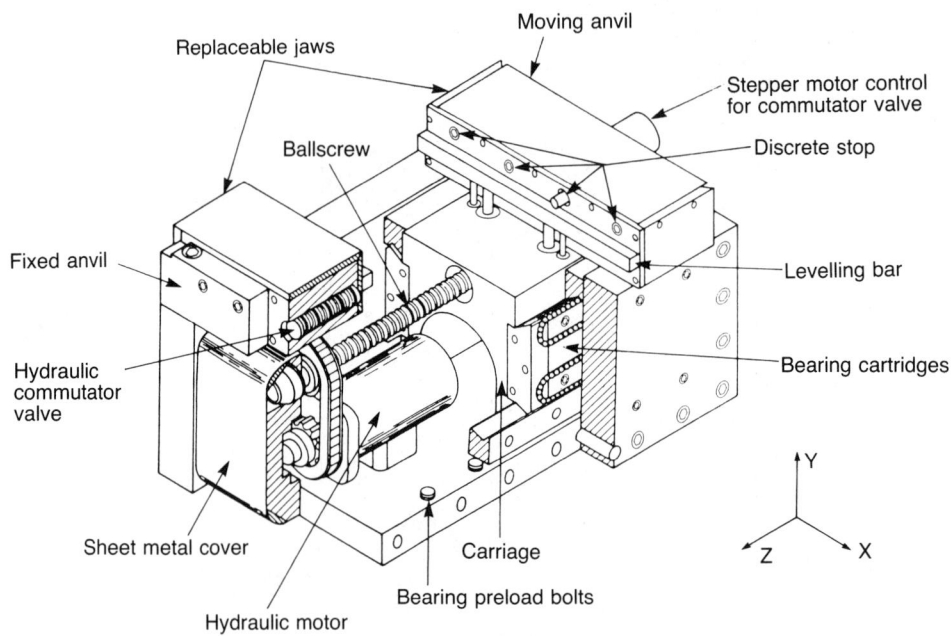

Fixed anvil

Hydraulic
commutator
valve

Sheet metal cover

Hydraulic motor

Replaceable jaws

Ballscrew

Moving anvil

Stepper motor control
for commutator valve

Discrete stop

Levelling bar

Bearing cartridges

Carriage

Bearing preload bolts

Y

Z   X

Fig. 14-36 Section view of computer controlled multi-degree-of-freedom vise.

pistons. Four hydraulic pistons in each anvil form discrete stops which are used to establish the X-position of the part between the jaws. A specially designed stepper motor-actuated rotary hydraulic valve controls the discrete stops in each anvil. Overall size of the fixture is $11 \times 11 \times 20$ in. ($280 \times 280 \times 500$ mm). It weighs 250 lb (110 kg) and has a maximum clamping force of 10,000 lbf (45 kN). The maximum jaw opening is 8 in. (200 mm).

In order to achieve a relatively compact system, all the hydraulic mechanisms were designed integral with the structure. To avoid increasing the overall length of the structure by the use of telescoping metal covers or bellows, a new covering method was devised. The cover is comprised of a thin stainless steel band that wraps around the structure and connects to each end of the carriage. The band moves back and forth with the carriage and prevents any chips and coolant from contaminating the ballscrew or bearings.

Levelling Bars for Y-Axis Part Positioning. The levelling bars provide reference surfaces for positioning a part in the Y-direction and can be used as sine bars to orient the part about the Z-axis. Each bar is actuated by two 0.5 in. (12.7 mm) hydraulic pistons actuated at 2,000 lbf/in.[2] (13.8 MPa) which provide a net force of 674 lbf (3 kN) on each levelling bar. The pistons can be positioned with a resolution of 0.0005 in. (0.013 mm) over a range of 1.75 in. (44.5 mm). Linearized LVDTs[15] are used to provide position feedback, instead of linear potentiometers, because the LVDTs are smaller and more compatible with the hostile environment. Other enhancing characteristics of LVDTs are infinite resolution and excellent repeatability. The configuration of the actuation system is shown in Fig. 14-38.

Hydraulic pistons were chosen as actuators because of their high force to size ratio,

Fig. 14-37 Subassembly of computer controlled multi-degree-of-freedom vise.

although in some applications a ballscrew/motor system may be useful. Each levelling bar can also be used as a sine bar by extending one piston relative to the other. Thus, the orientation of a part about the Z-axis can be adjusted.

Discrete Stops for X-Axis Part Location. Part position with respect to the X-axis is determined by selectively actuated stops that are positioned at discrete increments. The stops are sets of double-acting hydraulic pistons as shown in Fig. 14-39. In order to reduce radial play in each piston, a bushing is used as a piston guide with a tight sliding fit. If a continuous X-axis position resolution is desired, a piston/transducer mechanism may be utilized.

Replaceable Jaw Design. In order for the replaceable jaw concept to fully function in an automated machine environment, a mechanism must be provided that allows a robot to remove and replace jaws easily. The jaws must be securely locked in a known fixed position in a manner that does not allow chips and coolant to contaminate the alignment surfaces. This is accomplished as shown in Fig. 14-40. The replaceable jaw is composed of four surfaces: two side plates, a top plate, and a faceplate. The leading edges of the replaceable jaws have large bevels to aid the robot in guiding the jaws over the anvils. Once roughly in place, tapered pistons are actuated to pull the jaw down and back so it is firmly seated against the front and top of the anvil.

Rotary Hydraulic Valve Design.[16]   To provide a small compact valve system for actuating the discrete stops and tapered pistons, a stepper motor-controlled rotary hydraulic commutator valve was developed. Rotary valves are not generally used because of their inherent leakage problems. However, this design, channels any leakage to the reservoir instead of letting pressure build up on the low pressure side of a piston. Each

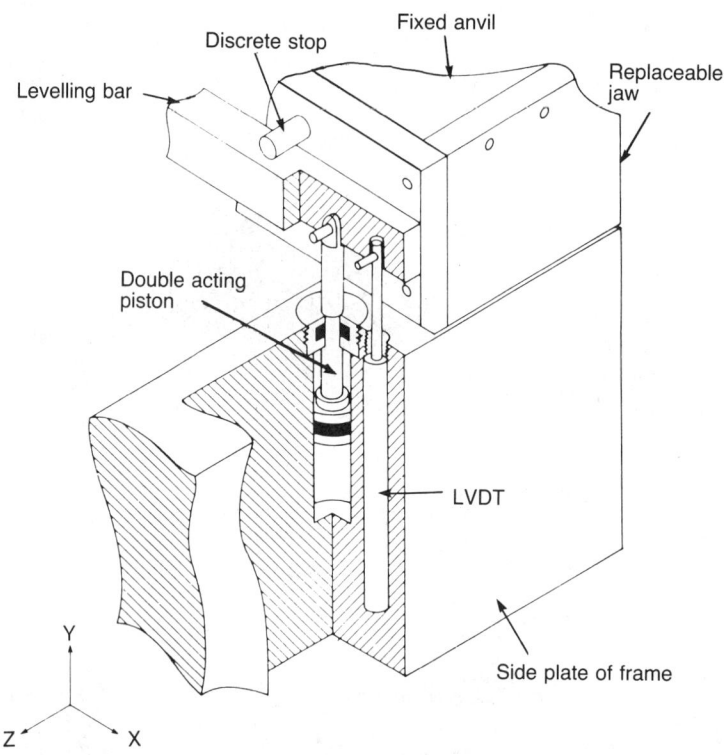

Fig. 14-38 Levelling bar actuation system.

valve is capable of actuating any one of the four discrete stops while simultaneously actuating both tapered pistons.

Linear Bearing Design. The bearing system, shown in Fig. 14-41, consists of fixed top rails and adjustable bottom rails. The top rails are bolted and dowel-pinned to the side plates, and the bottom rails are supported by set screws, which allow the bearings to be preloaded. Once preloaded, the bottom rails are bolted to the side plates. Four tracks of recirculating roller bearings ride in hardened steel blocks and contact their respective bearing rails at an angle which was chosen on the basis of two criteria: The first is to provide the proper stiffness about the axes, and the second is to maintain the bearing preload despite structural expansion and contraction due to temperature fluctuations. The angled contact surfaces are also positioned so as to resist spreading of the side plates.

Digital Control System Design.[17] The function of the vise controller is to execute control algorithms for positioning the moving anvil, closing the jaws with a specified amount of force, positioning the levelling bars, and actuating the discrete stops. The vise controller receives commands from a higher level fixturing controller in an automated mode, or from a CRT terminal in a manual mode.

A SYSTEM APPROACH TO THE TOTAL TOOLING AND FIXTURING PACKAGE[18]

The job shop environment with its large numbers of part types and low production quantities has been unable to share in the world of automation until now. Using the principles of automation, Flexible Manufacturing Systems (FMS) and Flexible Machining Cells (FMC) provide this segment of American industry the opportunity to further

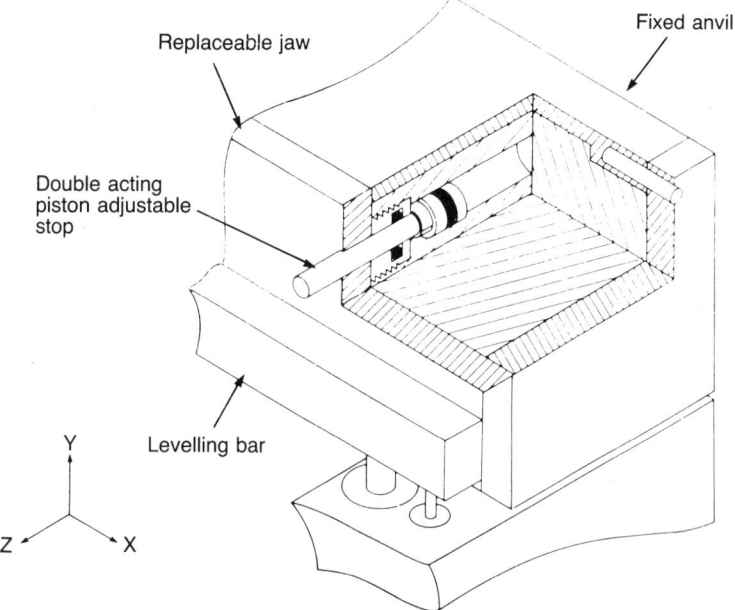

Fig. 14-39 Discrete stop mechanism.

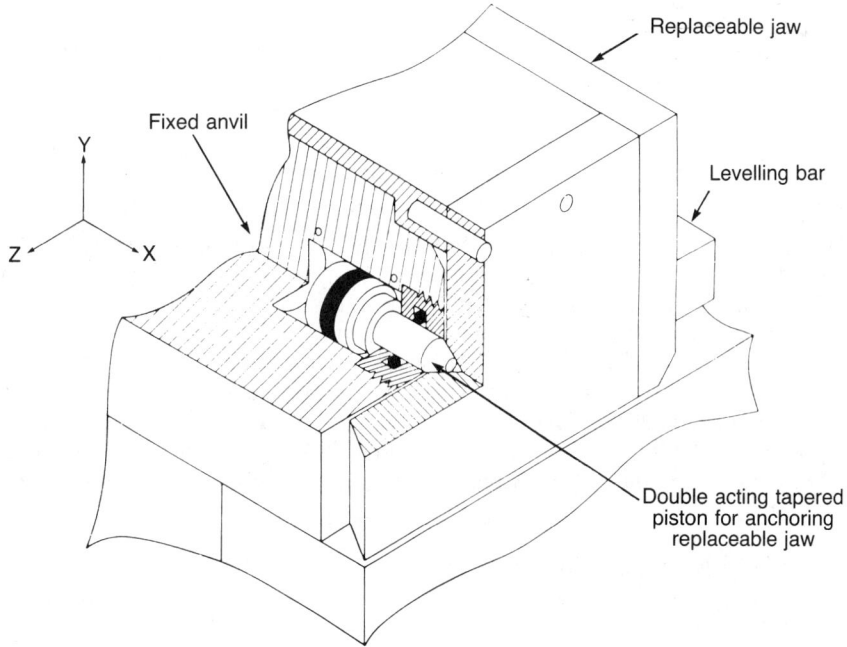

Fig. 14-40 Tapered piston actuator for anchoring replaceable jaw.

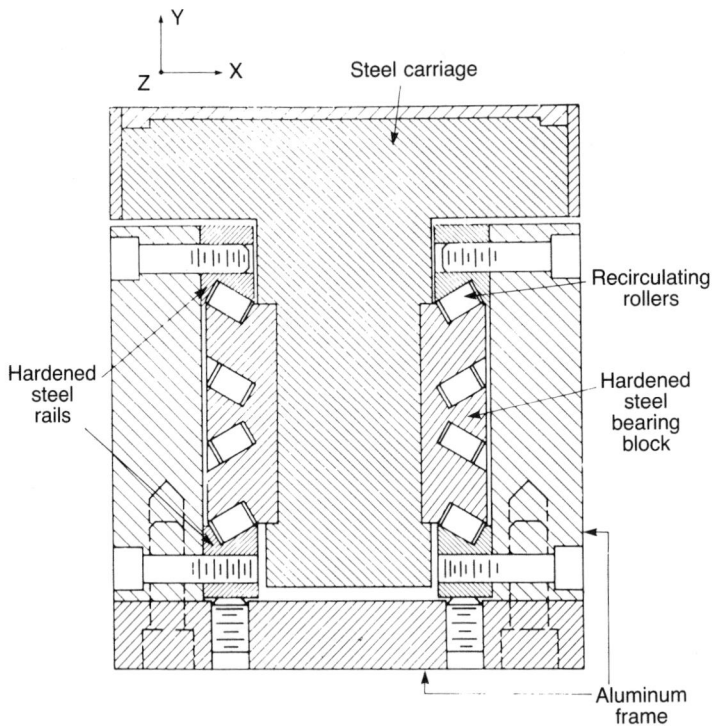

Fig. 14-41 Fully constrained, multi-material bearing system that is unaffected by uniform temperature changes.

reduce manufacturing cycle times, work-in-process inventories, and labor costs, as well as to improve product quality. Although the implementation of an FMS or FMC is hard work, it represents a unique challenge to the manufacturing engineer. The manufacturing engineer must design the processes, fixturing, and tooling as a system with the built-in flexibility that assures this system is capable of meeting any future demands on the FMS or FMC. The following tooling and fixturing package discussed in this paper has been designed as a flexible system by following the objectives listed below:

- The part and fixture is moved as a unit from machine to machine in the FMC until all machining and inspection possible is completed for that pass of the part through the cell. A common interface allows the part-and-fixture unit to mount to any machine tool or inspection machine within the FMC.
- Fixturing must be designed to minimize the total number of fixture types in the FMC. The accepted convention is three-jaw chucks and arbor fixtures for the first and second passes through the FMC. This provides a common processing approach that limits the numbers of fixtures. Although special fixtures are used when the chuck and arbor fixture approach is unable to manufacture a quality part, the system is flexible enough to accommodate these.
- The number of tools in the lathe and machining center tool packages must be minimized. Additions to the tool packages must be justified.
- Standard tool holding devices are preferred over the use of special tool holding devices.
- Chips must be controlled.
- Machining in the FMC must be unattended.

System Description. In the fall of 1983, a team of five engineers and a manager at the Electro-Mechanical Division (EMD) of Westinghouse Electric Corporation were assigned the task of selecting a vendor for a Small Parts Flexible Manufacturing System (SP/FMS). The SP/FMS was to be a mini-factory-within-a-factory capable of manufacturing the nuclear pump seals and the hydro-dynamic bearings from the raw material to finished product. This integrated manufacturing system will consist of an Automated Storage and Retrieval System (ASRS), an FMC, manual machining operations, assembly operations, seal testing inspection, packaging, receiving and shipping under the control of a VAX 785 computer. Figure 14-42 shows a layout of the SP/FMS.

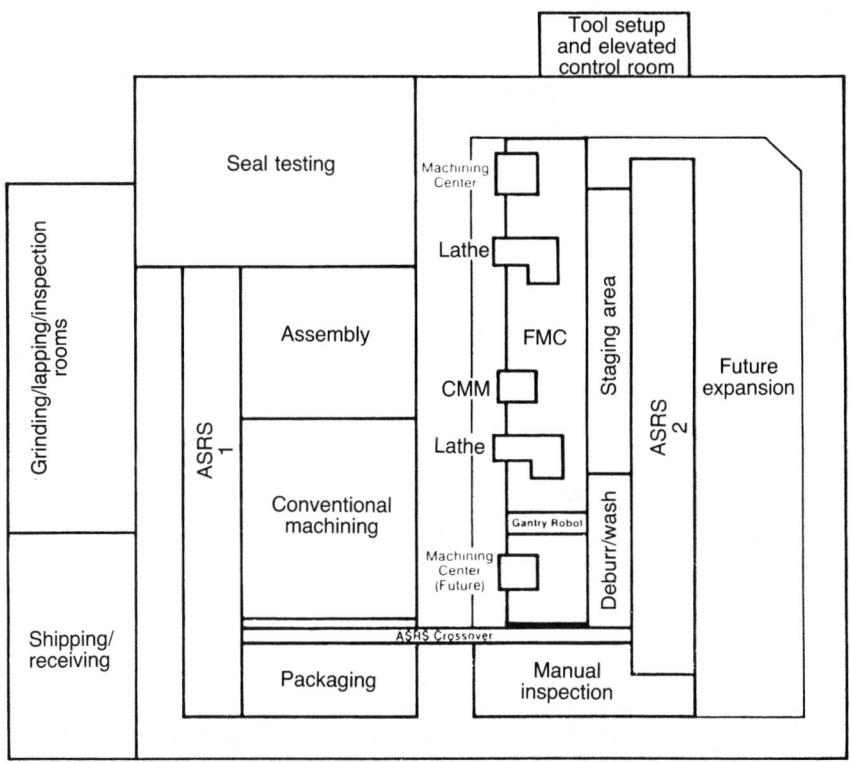

Fig. 14-42 Westinghouse EMD flexible manufacturing system layout.

The FMC is the central parts processing area for the SP/FMS, although all grinding and lapping processes, selected inspections, and the machining of characteristics that do not fit the unattended environment of the FMC are completed in the manual areas. The final FMC design consists of eight load/unload stations, a GCA gantry robot, two Bullard 6000 CNC lathes, one White-Sundstrand OM2A five-axis machining center, a Brown and Sharpe coordinate measuring machine (CMM), and a wash/deburr station.

The area between the ASRS and the gantry robot is utilized for the buildup of fixtures, loading, and unloading of parts onto the fixtures, and washing/deburring of parts in preparation for the CMM. Parts are delivered to an FMC operator by the ASRS under the control of the VAX 785. A CRT displays instructions that designate the ASRS port to which the part has been delivered, the part number and serial number of that part, the fixture to which that part is mounted for processing, and any special instructions.

Once the part is loaded onto the appropriate fixture, the gantry robot picks up the part and its fixture and either buffers it until the system is ready for it or mounts it onto an awaiting lathe. The FMC is sized to accommodate rotating parts 18 inches in diameter by 18 inches (457.2 mm) long and up to 250 pounds (113.4 kg). Figure 14-43 shows some typical FMC parts.

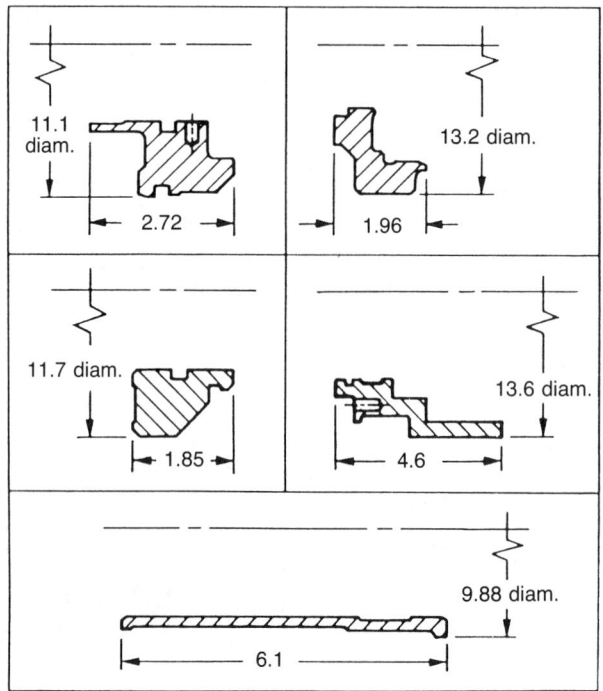

Fig. 14-43 Typical part shapes.

The FMC Fixtures. A part pallet (see Fig. 14-44) conceived and designed by White Consolidated Industries has an A11 nose machined on one face and a curvic coupling attached onto the other face to provide a common interface between the machine tools and the fixtures. The fixtures center on the A11 nose. The curvic coupling of the part pallet mates with the curvic coupling on each machine tool and the CMM. This part pallet allows a fixture to be mounted onto the lathes, the machining center, and the CMM so all machining and inspection can be accomplished through the FMC on that fixture in a single pass. The general single-pass processing for a part in the FMC is:

1. Load a part onto the proper fixture.
2. Perform a lathe operation.
3. Perform a machining center operation.
4. Wash and deburr the part.
5. Perform a CMM inspection.
6. Unload the part.

For the first-pass machining of parts in the FMC, a fixture assembly consists of the part pallet, a 15 inch or 18 inch low-profile three-jaw chuck, and special jaws, auxiliary stand-offs and clamping tailored to a specific part (see Fig. 14-45). An arbor fixture assembly for the second-pass machining consists of the part pallet, a fixture plate with

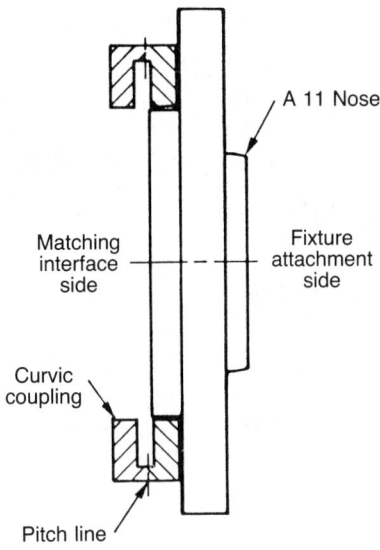

Fig. 14-44 Part pallet interface.

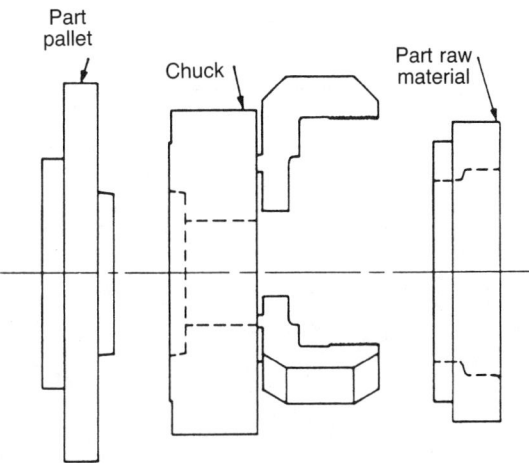

Fig. 14-45 15 in. diameter three-jaw chuck fixture first operation.

assembly for the second-pass machining consists of the part pallet, a fixture plate with one of two sizes of arbors mounted to it, and auxiliary standoffs, clamping and collets designed for an individual part (see Fig. 14-46). To minimize the number of fixtures and provide the greatest flexibility to the fixturing package, the three-jaw chucks and the arbor fixtures are the preferred fixturing devices. Special fixtures and chuck sizes or types may be integrated, but one of a kind of any fixture or chuck reduces the flexibility of the fixturing system. Two single-purpose fixtures, each designed for one specific part, were used. For one part the three-jaw chuck was unable to produce a quality part (see Fig. 47). The other part required one of the standard arbors to be mounted on a pedestal

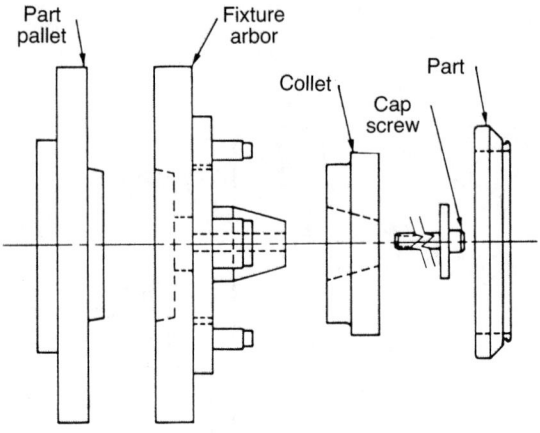

Fig. 14-46 Arbor fixture assembly second operation.

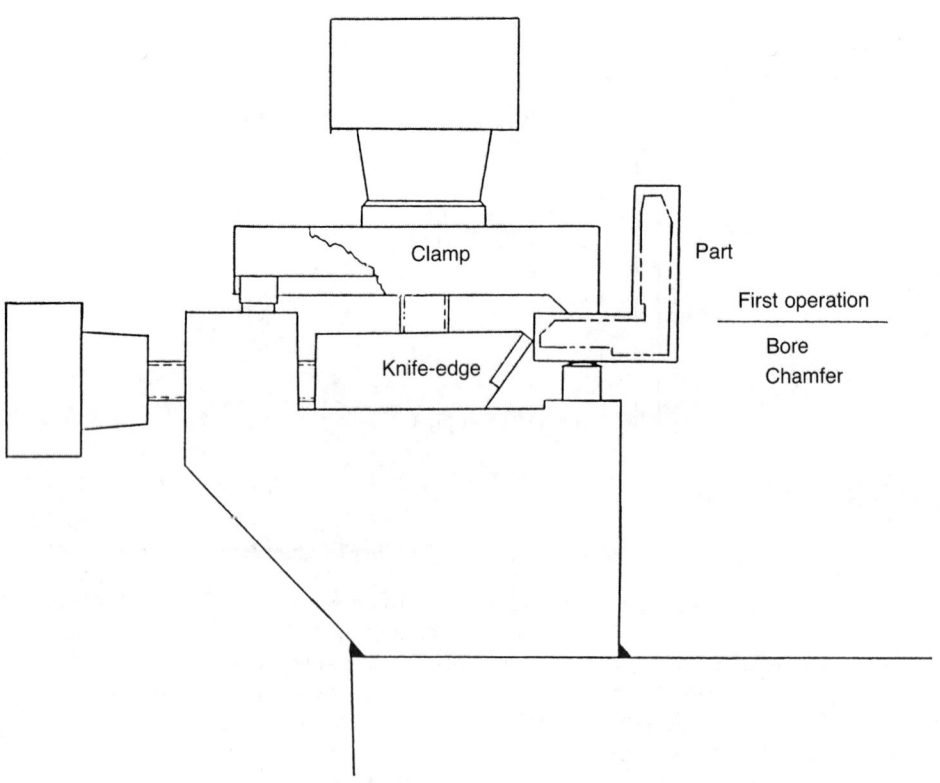

Fig. 14-47 Special fixture.

(see Fig. 14-48). Another exception is a special jaw that mounts on a 15 inch three-jaw chuck to provide both internal and external holding of a part (see Fig. 14-49). This approach affects the flexibility of the fixturing package by competing for a first-pass fixture assembly with a 15 inch three-jaw chuck. Three other parts of the first thirty parts to be processed in the FMC will fall into this last category.

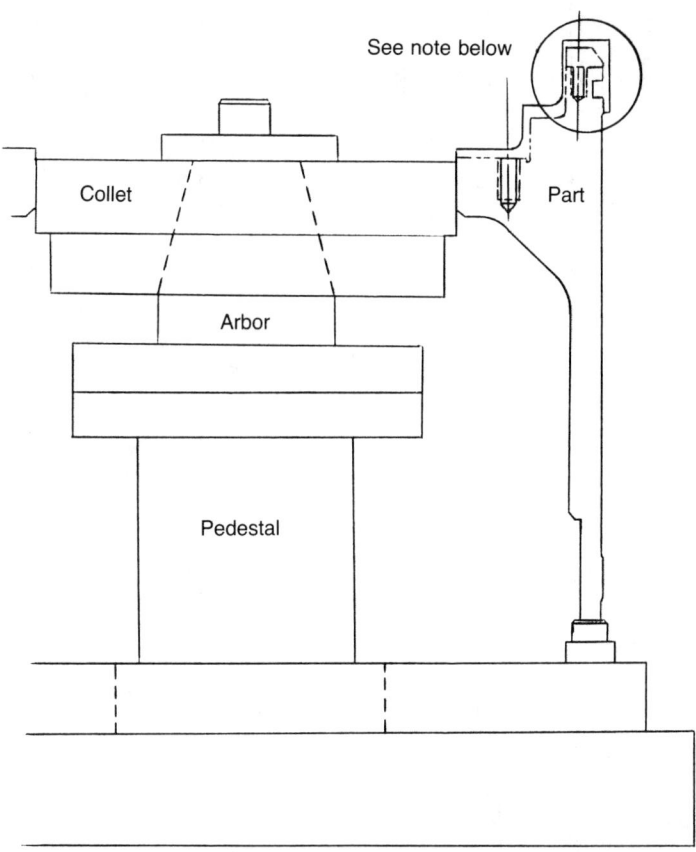

Note: Circled area is where O-ring groove distorted
during the drilling and tapping operation.

Fig. 14-48 Special fixture with arbor on pedestal.

Another feature of this fixturing concept is a design that utilizes a three-jaw chuck to obtain the benefits of a six-jaw chuck (see Fig. 14-50). Special knife-edge clamps are mounted onto the three-jaw chucks for six-jaw action on those parts requiring better distribution of the clamping forces than the three-jaw chuck itself gives. This technique uses the self-centering capabilities of the three-jaw chuck to establish three points quickly, yet provides six-jaw advantage with the addition of the three independent knife-edge clamps that are easily removed. This was an adaptation of the special fixtures originally proposed by the Jack Haines Company. It provided flexibility to the fixturing package by utilizing the three-jaw chucks already in the package.

A two-pass machining sequence utilizing a three-jaw chuck during the first pass and an arbor fixture during the second pass can machine 80 percent of the parts selected. Being limited to twenty active pallets in the FMC for machining, this approach reduces

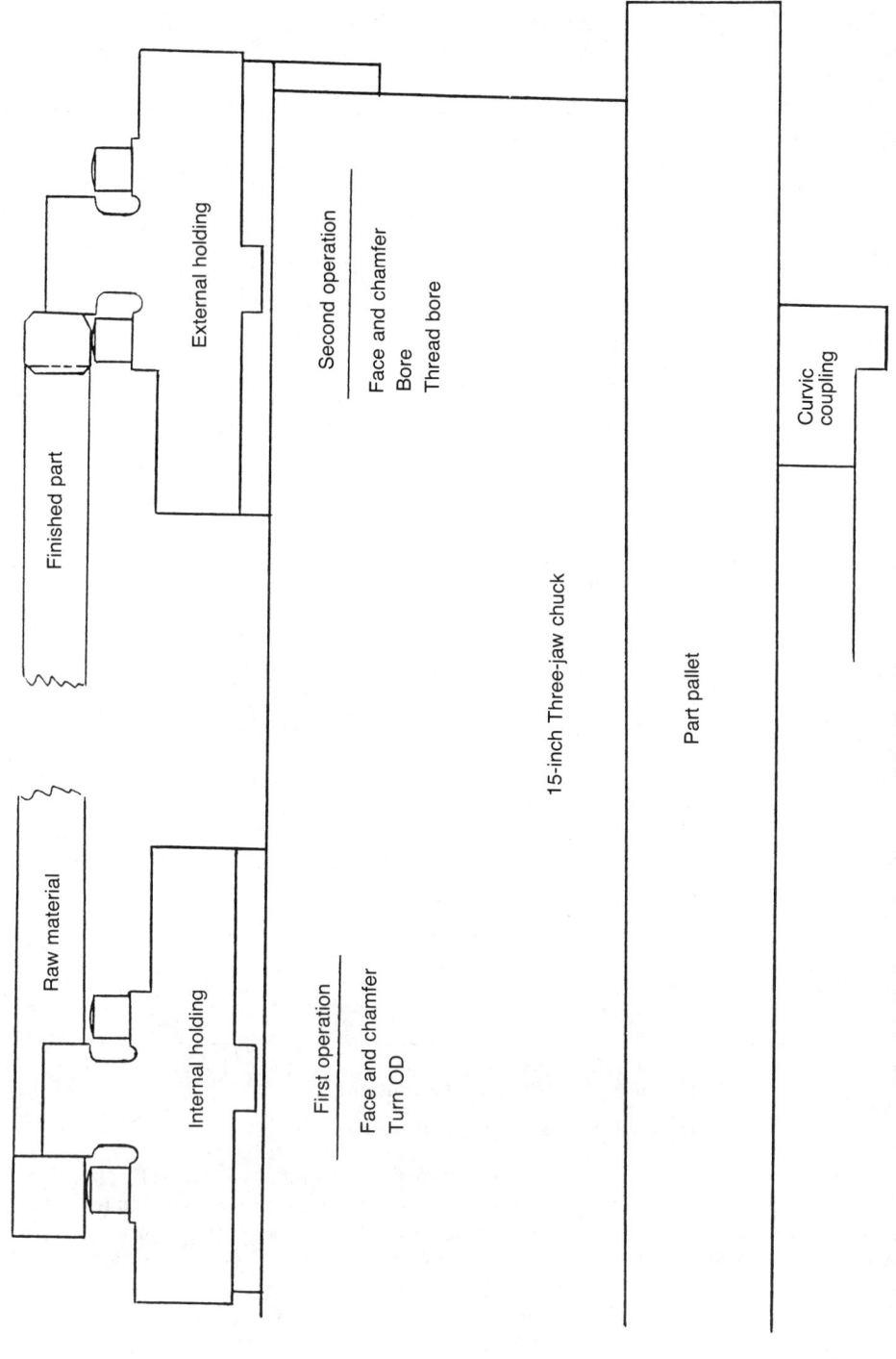

Fig. 14-49 Internal and external holding of a part using same jaw.

Raw material

Internal holding

First operation

Face and chamfer
Turn OD

Finished part

External holding

Second operation

Face and chamfer
Bore
Thread bore

15-inch Three-jaw chuck

Part pallet

Curvic coupling

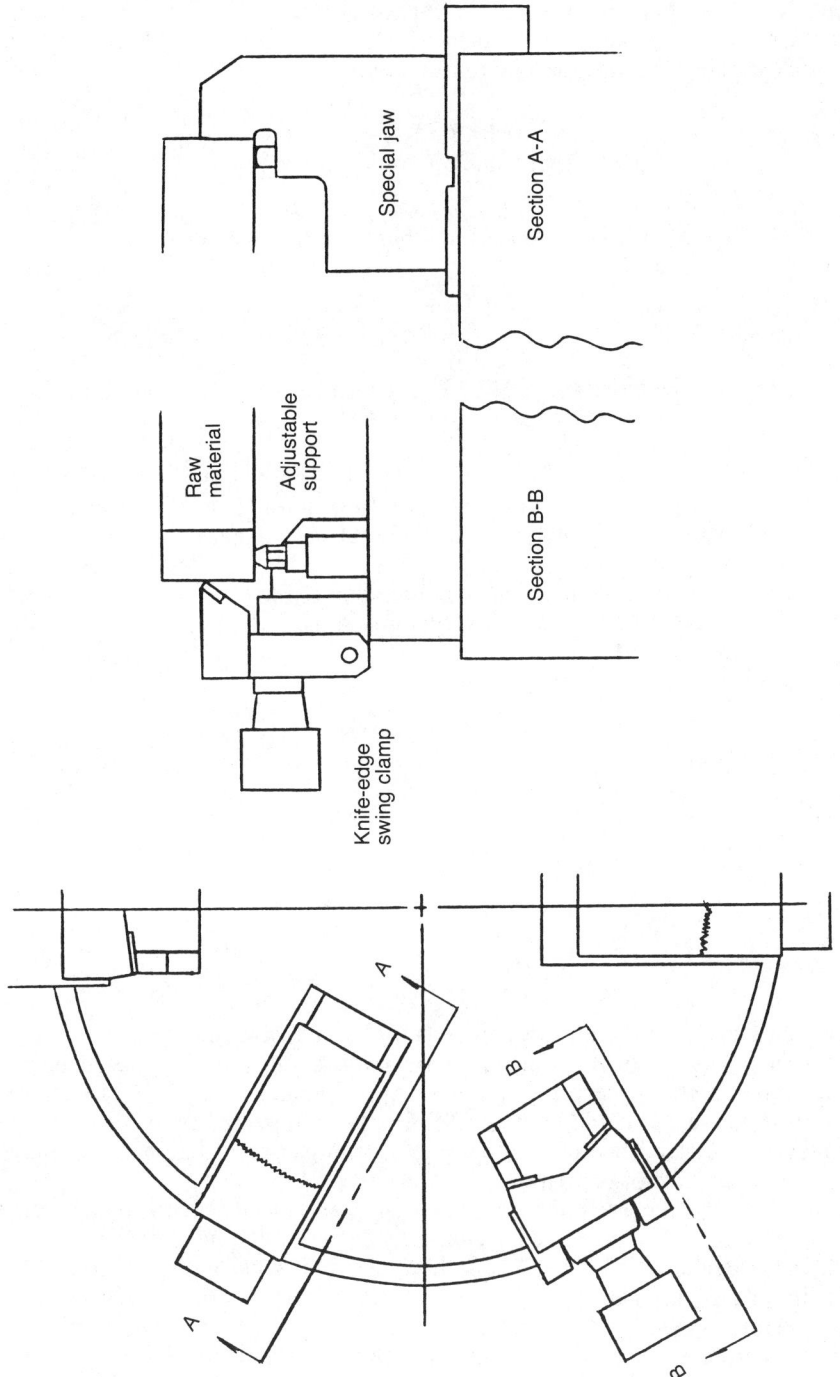

Special jaw

Section A-A

Raw material

Adjustable support

Section B-B

Knife-edge swing clamp

A

A

B

B

Fig. 14-50 Three-jaw chuck utilizing six-jaw capability.

14-45

the number of fixture types—and the associated costs—as well as maintaining a flexible FMC fixturing package. Table 14-1 shows the six fixture types and the quantity of each fixture type purchased to process the first thirty parts designated for the FMC. Table 14-2 displays the distribution of the first thirty parts across the six fixture types. Third-pass and fourth-pass fixturing is ignored to simplify the table. No additional fixture types are contemplated for the third and fourth passes.

TABLE 14-1
Fixture Types and Quantities in FMC

Special Fixture	15 in. Chuck	18 in. Chuck	6M Arbor	4½M Arbor	4¼M on Pedestal
1	6	3	1	4	1

TABLE 14-2
Distribution of First Thirty Parts Across
Six Fixture Types in FMC

	Second-Pass Fixtures				
First-Pass Fixtures	6M Arbor	4½M Arbor	4½M Pedestal	15 in. Chuck	Number of Parts Across First-Pass Fixtures
	No. of Parts Across Combination of First-Pass and Second-Pass Fixtures in the FMC				
Special		1			1
15 in. Chuck	1	14		4	19
18 in. Chuck	4	5	1		10
No. of Pts Across 2nd Pass Fixtures	5	20	1	4	30

The two-pass machining sequence demands that all possible first-pass characteristics are finished during that pass and the remaining features are completed on the second pass. This machining sequence is not always acceptable. Fragile parts and parts with very close tolerances could require a third pass or more passes to complete the features that were not finished on the first and second passes, or be finish machined outside the FMC as some of our parts are.

Additional benefits are derived for features such as tapped holes with tight true position requirements. The measurement of such tapped holes are problematic on a CMM and the inspection results open to question. The processing approach used allows the flexibility of drilling, reaming, and/or boring these holes and inspecting them for true position prior to the tapping operation; then, returning to the machining center for the completion of the tapping cycle. An example of such a machining cycle—although not a tapping cycle—was found during an investigation of the manufacturing process for one of the FMC parts (see Fig. 14-48). The O-ring groove machined on the OD of this part distorted during the drilling and tapping operation. An additional setup and operation was needed to remachine this feature after the drilling and tapping cycle. The FMC with the processing and fixturing approach selected is capable of including such a step in the machining sequence without removing the part from the fixture and with little penalty for the time spent in the FMC.

Another consideration for this fixturing system was the adaptation to the FMC of any product line in which the parts fall within the guidelines established—any part 18 inches in diameter by 18 inches (457.2 mm) long and no heavier than 250 pounds (113.4 kg). The three-jaw chuck fixtures and arbor fixtures are expected to accommodate most new parts added to the system in the future. The part pallet with the curvic coupling interface provides the added flexibility to start from scratch by stripping the chucks and arbor fixtures from the part pallets if this should be required. The FMC is always available for a new or redesigned product line.

No matter how flexible the fixturing system is, though, if chips load up the fixture, unattended machining is virtually impossible. Each fixture has been reviewed for chip removal. Parts have been set up on buttons and plenty of open area has been provided for clearing chips. After the fixtures have been built, and prior to system and NC program proveout, each fixture will be tested and evaluated for chip problems along with the fixture's capability to hold the part during machining without distorting the part. These alone will not eliminate chip problems; the chips must be small enough to pass through the openings provided. For this reason, a chip control program was implemented.

Information on the chip control program and cutting tools used with the system can be found in the SME Technical Paper MR 86-128, "A FMS Tooling and Fixturing Package that Provides Flexibility."

FLEXIBLE FIXTURES FOR FMS AND FMC

The fact that flexible manufacturing systems and flexible manufacturing cells are mainly dedicated to producing families of parts requires that the design of the supporting fixtures be flexible to the point that an individual fixture be able to handle as many of the family parts as possible with very little or no changeover between parts. When changeover is necessary, it must be fast so that duplicate fixtures are kept to the minimum number possible without causing downtime in the system.

Some examples of fixtures of this type are shown in Figs. 14-51 thru 14-58. They include:

A Modular Fixturing System for Valves. The system shown in Fig. 14-51 was designed to expand and contract to suit the largest and smallest parts by re-arranging the basic location of clamping components, thereby reducing the number of dedicated fixtures required for a family of valves. The fixture shown employs a 31½ in. (800 mm) T-slot base that mounts directly on a machine tool pallet and is used on a machining center to perform operations on the flange ends and stem of the valve. The fixture includes self-centering Vees mounted on the adjustable rail with individual adjustments in all axes. In the adjustable rail, a cross T-slot is provided to hold the chain anchor and chain clamp which are mounted directly in the cross T-slots in the adjustable rail to exert tension on the workpiece without effecting the V-locating supports. When chains are securely anchored, the valve becomes an integral part of the fixture adding rigidity to the fixture permitting very heavy machining.

Chains can be released quickly by backing up the jack bolt in the chain and folding it under the cam clamp. The machined valve can then be replaced with an unmachined one, the chain clamp reengaged, and the jack bolt pulled up thereby securing the new part for machining. Figure 14-52 shows the serrated positioning pin (removed for clarity) that establishes the exact position of the rail. The nest is expanded or retracted by means of Acme serrations on a common right and left hand operating screw, as

14-47

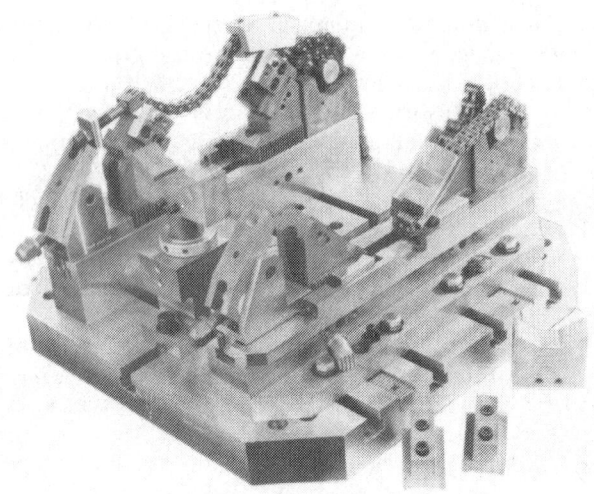

Fig. 14-51 Modular fixture with workpiece. (*Courtesy Royal Machine & Tool Corp.*)

Fig. 14-52 Modular fixture shown in Fig. 14-51 without workpiece. (*Courtesy Royal Machine & Tool Corp.*)

shown by the arrows. This system can be applied equally well to hold a wide variety of other family type workpieces such as pump and transmission housings, pillow blocks, and most other parts having configurations similar to the single and double flange parts shown in Fig. 14-53.

Dual Vertical Combination Chuck (DVC). The DVC chuck shown in Fig. 14-54 provides a unique solution for holding up to four or more parts for precision machining on a horizontal machining center. It mounts directly on the machine indexing pallet. The chuck permits virtually continuous spindle use, drastically decreases tool changes,

Fig. 14-53 Modular fixturing showing use of yoke support on single flange part and standard clamping of double flange part. (*Courtesy Royal Machine & Tool Corp.*)

(a)

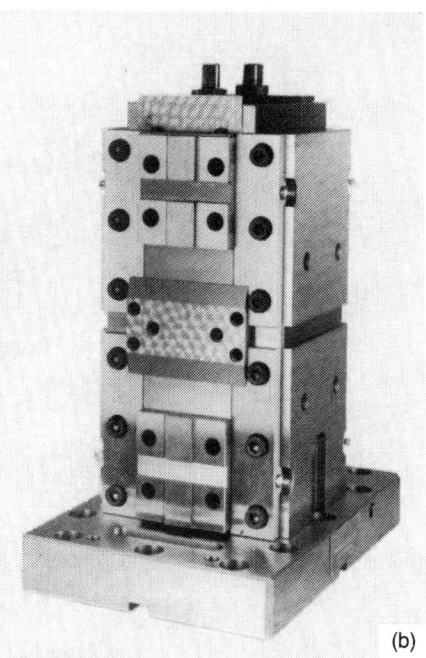

(b)

Fig. 14-54 Dual vertical combination chuck. (*a*) mixed setup showing single part and dual part gripping. (*b*) bare chuck. (*Courtesy Royal Machine & Tool Corp.*)

and practically eliminates downtime for workpiece changing. When two workpieces are to be gripped on each side, the DVC is set in compensating mode and a fixed center jaw is used to locate the workpieces. Swivel or compensating jaws, and a broad range of standard jaw components (see Fig. 14-55) are available.

Hydraulic fixtures, such as that shown in Fig. 14-56*a*, can accommodate up to 16 identical or different workpieces for first or second operations on horizontal or vertical machining centers. The fixture shown was designed for use on a horizontal machining center. Eight pieces are visible and an additional eight identical pieces are stacked on the rear of the fixture. Locating plates holding workpieces are movable in a vertical plane on ball bushing guideways to maintain part location and attitude. Two vertically opposed hydraulic pistons clamp the workpieces securely against a fixed center bracket. An internal hydraulic accumulator maintains a constant pressure throughout the machining cycle and in excess of 24 hours. Hydraulic manifold construction is used throughout whenever possible to reduce chip traps. In Fig. 14-56*b*, the fixture is shown without workpieces to show the diamond and plain pins used to locate the workpieces. Both the hydraulic pressure and air hoses have quick disconnects. Air is used to quickly exhaust oil from the system in the loading/unloading sequence.

Another hydraulic fixture is shown in Fig. 14-57. The fixture holds 12 parts, six for the first operation and six for the secondary operations. The design has 100% hydraulic manifold construction with the hydraulic accumulator located inside the center column.

Standard hydraulic manifold tooling blocks (see Fig. 14-58) are available in a range of sizes for customer-designed fixtures. They can be used with a wide variety of chucks, collet chucks and expanding mandrels to hold a wide variety of workpieces.

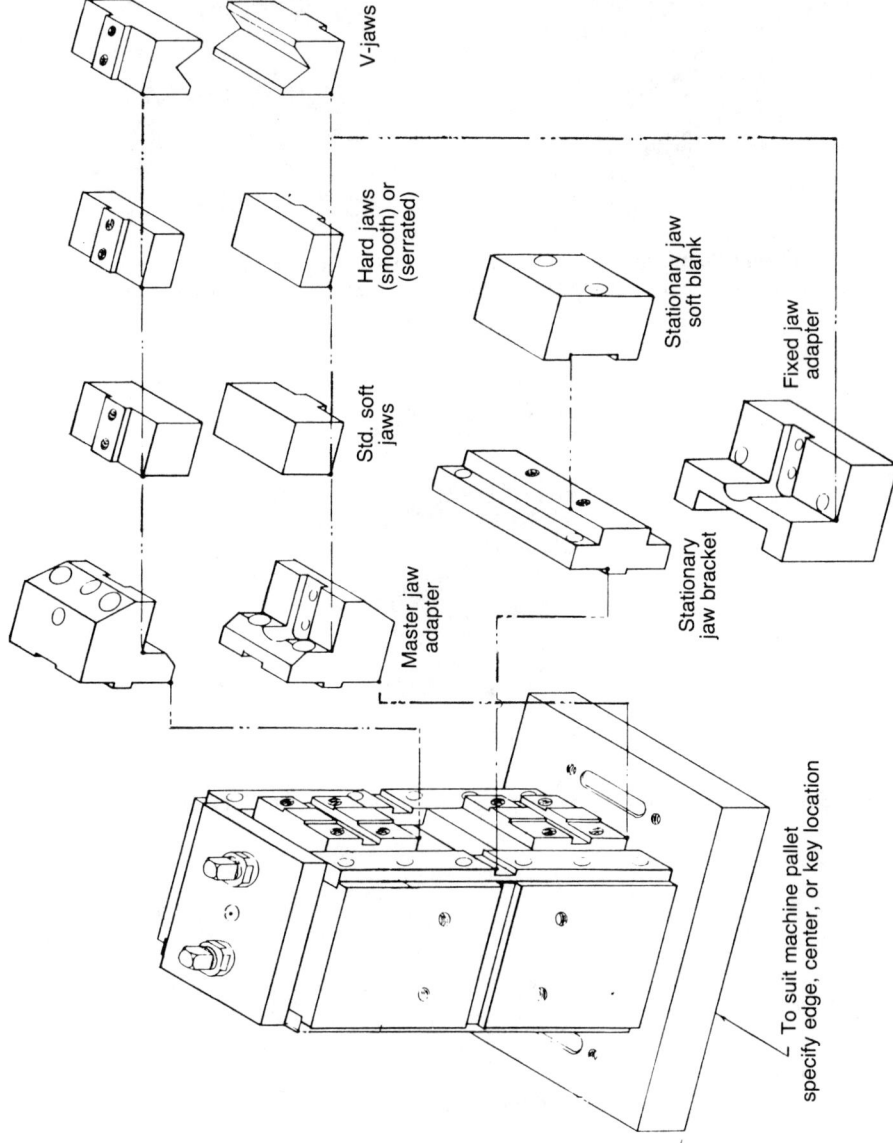

V-jaws

Hard jaws
(smooth) or
(serrated)

Std. soft
jaws

Master jaw
adapter

Stationary jaw
soft blank

Fixed jaw
adapter

Stationary
jaw bracket

To suit machine pallet
specify edge, center, or key location

Fig. 14-55 Jaw components. (*Courtesy Royal Machine & Tool Corp.*)

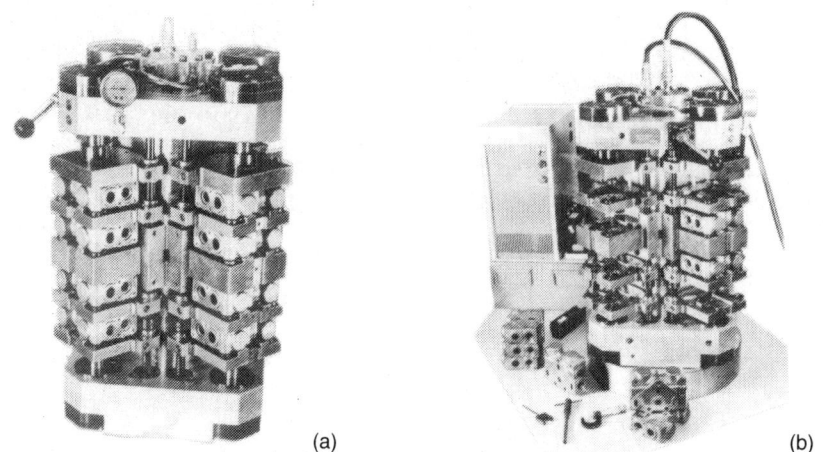

(a)   (b)

Fig. 14-56 Hydraulic fixturing system. (*a*) **setup for machining 16 identical workpieces.** (*b*) **fixture with workpieces removed to show locating pins.** (*Courtesy Royal Machine & Tool Corp.*)

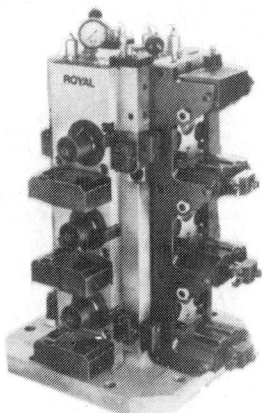

Fig. 14-57 Hydraulic fixture for 12 parts. A and B position. (*Courtesy Royal Machine & Tool Corp.*)

Fig. 14-58 Hydraulic manifold tooling block. (*Courtesy Royal Machine & Tool Corp.*)

References

1. Thomas J. Drozda and Charles Wick, eds., "Multifunction Machines," *Tool and Manufacturing Engineers Handbook*, Vol. 1, 4th ed. (Dearborn, MI: Society of Manufacturing Engineers, 1983), pp. 15-88 to 15-91 and 15-64 to 15-74.
2. James F. Farrell, *-Pallet Systems—How to Increase Productivity*, (Cleveland, OH: S-P Manufacturing Co.).
3. M.V. Gandhi and B.S. Thompson, "Flexible Fixturing Systems for CIM Environments," Shyam K. Samanta, ed., *Manufacturing Processes, Systems and Machines*, 14th Conference on Production Research and Technology, Oct. 6-9, 1987 (Ann Arbor, MI: University of Michigan, College of Engineering, 1987), pp. 399-408.
4. *Ibid.*
5. *Ibid.*
6. *Ibid.*
7. *Ibid.*
8. *Ibid.*
9. *Ibid.*
10. Alexander H. Slocum, Alkan Doumez, James Peris, "Development of a Flexible Automated Fixturing System," SME Technical Paper MR 86-126 (Dearborn, MI: Society of Manufacturing Engineers, 1986).
11. P. Chiappetti, "Vise With Interchangeable Jaw Members" (U.S. Patent #4,437,654, March 1984.).
12. C.L. Bowling, "Vise" (U.S. patent #4,251,066, February 1984).
13. E.T. Hennessey, "Workpiece Positioning Device for Machine Tool Vises" (U.S. patent #3,463,479, August 1969).
14. J.A. Simpson, R.J. Hocken, and J.S. Albus, "The Automated Manufacturing Research Facility at the National Bureau of Standards," *Journal of Manufacturing Systems*, Vol. 1, no. 1, pp. 17-31 (April 1982).
15. J.V. Moskaitis, D.S. Blomquist, "A Microprocessor Based Techniques for Transducer Linearization," *Precision Engineering*, Vol. 5, no. 1, pp. 5-8 (January 1983).
16. Dr. Alexander H. Slocum, and James Peris, "A Stepper Motor Controlled Multi-port Hydraulic Valve."
17. Dr. Alexander H. Slocum, "Design to Limit Thermal Effects on Linear Motion Bearing Performance."
18. Harold Cable, "A FMS Tooling and Fixturing Package that Provides Flexibility," SME Technical Paper MR 86-128, (Dearborn, MI: Society of Manufacturing Engineers, 1986).

CHAPTER 15

FIXTURES FOR ASSEMBLY AND JOINING OPERATIONS

Fixtures described in this chapter, and broadly classified as assembly and joining fixtures, are of two general types:

- Mechanical assembly and joining fixtures for operations performed at ordinary (room) temperatures with mechanical means.
- Fixtures for hot-joining methods for assembly work using energy in the form of heat as an intrinsic major process factor.

MECHANICAL ASSEMBLY FIXTURES

There never has been any standard or unique classification of these types of assembly fixtures. The figures in this chapter have been classified according to the operation or process performed with the fixture. The various categories follow:

1. *Riveting fixtures* hold two or more parts together in predetermined positions while the parts are riveted as specified by the part print.
2. *Drilling and pinning jigs* hold two or more parts to the part-print dimensions while the parts are drilled and pinned to assembly specifications. Drilling is normally done through bushings. This application can also apply to several pinning operations in one jig. Sometimes a means for staking or setting the pin in place is also provided.
3. *Staking fixtures* are designed to hold and position an assembly while a pin or other detail is staked by hand or machine to prevent its loosening during use.
4. *Crimping and swaging fixtures* are used in the assembly of two parts by crimping a portion of one part over another.
5. *Pressing fixtures* are of two types:
   a. Holding fixtures hold parts together while an adhesive dries. A means for applying pressure during the drying cycle is provided when necessary. Whenever possible such a fixture holds a multiple quantity of assemblies.
   b. Other pressing fixtures hold two parts while one is pressed into another. Usually an arbor press or hydraulic press is used for this purpose. When necessary, various means can be provided in a press-fitting fixture for sizing a part after it is pressed into another. Ball sizing and sizing arbors are most commonly used.
6. *Tab-bending fixtures* are designed for holding parts together, positioning them, and forcing tabs of one part over the other.
7. *Wire-stitching fixtures* hold parts in position for fastening with wire stitches.
8. *Wire-stapling fixtures* hold parts together and position them for fastening with wire staples.

9. *Special holding fixtures* are designed for holding and positioning parts for unique assembly applications, such as assembling a detent ball in a deep hole or locating screws through deep holes.
   a. Trunnion holding fixtures hold a part or assembly while other parts not in the same plane are assembled to it.
   b. Cradle holding fixtures are for the purpose of holding or nesting a part having an irregular contour in a comfortable working position while other parts are assembled on or in it.
   c. Plastic holding fixtures, for assemblies, are usually cradles that fit the irregular contours of a part or assembly and hold or nest them in working position while other parts are assembled on or in it.
   d. Support legs are another simple means for holding a part or assembly having an irregular contour in position while other parts are assembled on or in it.
   e. Harness boards are heavy boards into which pegs are driven at predetermined locations as an aid in winding and assembling cables and harnesses.
   f. Potting or encapsulating holding fixtures hold connectors with cables or harnesses in a cavity while a melted potting compound is poured into the cavity and solidifies.
10. *Masking fixtures* are of several types:
   a. Some types are designed for keeping paint or other coatings, such as anodizing compounds, from certain surfaces of the workpiece.
   b. Other masking fixtures, for the convenience of the assembler, identify different terminal locations on a terminal-board assembly with a template having various color codes around its holes.

RIVETING EQUIPMENT

Rivets can be deformed or set in many ways. Pressure may be applied continuously or by a series of hammer blows. The rivets may be manually or automatically inserted. The holes may be drilled prior to or during the riveting sequence. The tool used to apply the deformation pressure may be a common hammer, a pneumatic hammer (riveter or rivet gun), a portable squeezing yoke, or a stationary machine.

The final shape of the rivet becomes that of the tool (die) used to apply the deformation pressure. The shape may be flat (reflecting the contour of a hammer or a conventional bucking bar) or may be curved as shown in Figs. 15-1 and 15-2. The rivet die may be a simple bucking bar, and interchangeable rivet set placed in the nozzle of an air hammer, or a complete forming die placed in a standard hydraulic or mechanical press.

Workholders or fixtures used to hold and locate workpieces being assembled by riveting are generally of three types: stationary, portable, and self-contained (riveting die fixture).

Pneumatic Hammer. Conventional riveting is performed by placing the rivet in a predrilled hole, holding a pneumatic hammer against the head of the rivet, holding a bucking bar against the end of the rivet, and then cycling or activating the hammer. The initiating pressure is exerted by the hammer while the formation pressure is exerted by the bucking bar. Pneumatic hammers (rivet guns) are commercially available in a wide range of types and sizes. The nozzle of the rivet gun receives and retains the rivet set or die. Rivet sets are commercially available in a wide variety of shapes to mate with the many types of rivets commonly used.

Portable Yoke Type. This type of riveting equipment is commonly used for squeezing large rivets ranging from 3/16 to 1 in. diameter, and consists of a yoke with a cylinder (air or oil) to provide the squeezing action. Equipment size can be minimized by using high pressure hydraulic cylinders. Equipment weight is minimized by using special high-strength heat-treated steel. The cylinder advances an anvil to the rivet with a primary

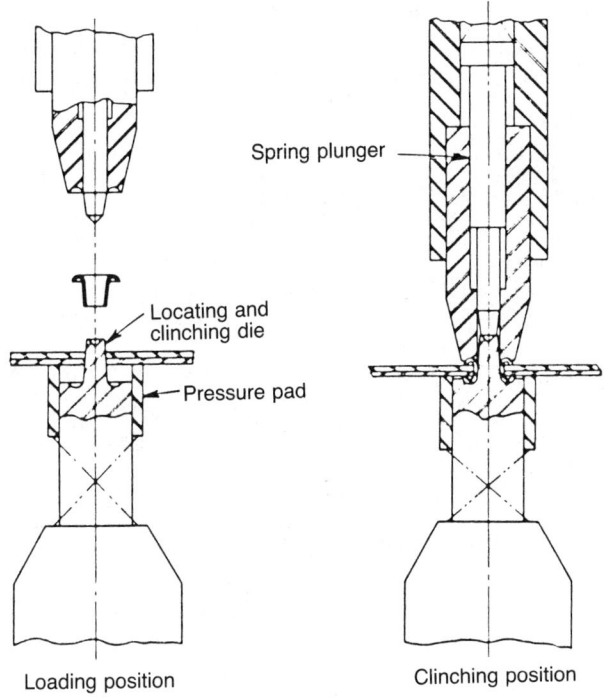

Spring plunger

Locating and
clinching die

Pressure pad

Loading position   Clinching position

Fig. 15-1 Eyelet curling.

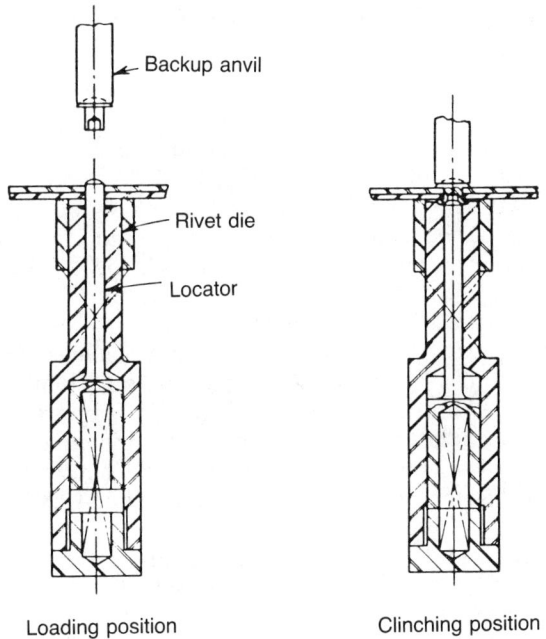

Backup anvil

Rivet die

Locator

Loading position   Clinching position

Fig. 15-2 Tubular riveting.

15-3

pressure of approximately 1000 lbf/in.² (6.9 MPa). When resistance is encountered, the pressure increases to 5,000 lbf/in.² (34.5 MPa) for the rivet upsetting portion of the action. Figure 15-3 shows a hydraulic riveting yoke.

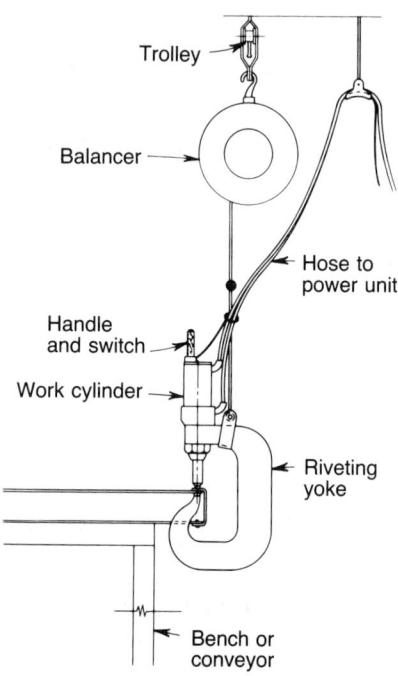

Fig. 15-3 Workpiece simply supported for riveting with a riveting yoke.

Stationary Machines. Stationary machines are often used for riveting. The workpieces being assembled are located with reference to each other (mated) and are placed between the upper and lower elements of the machine. Small stationary machines have a spring-loaded pin locator in the rivet die. Predrilled holes through the mated workpieces engage the pin locator as shown in Fig. 15-4. The upper riveting die (backup anvil) pushes the rivet into the holes, depresses the spring pin, and upsets the driven head on the lower anvil. The rivets are fed from a hopper to a feed track. The lower end of the feed track locates the rivet directly above the pin locator. The end of the track is split to allow the upper die to pick off the rivet for insertion.

Large stationary machines often combine both riveting and hole piercing. Figure 15-5 illustrates the sequence of operations for such a machine. The workpieces need not be predrilled, but must be located with reference to each other. The locating and holding fixture may be part of the machine. Extremely large stationary machines can hold and precisely locate large aircraft sections while thousands of holes are pierced and rivets are driven. The entire production sequence is automatic, with the machine movements governed by tape control or CNC. Closed-circuit TV is used to monitor the operation.

Automatic Drilling and Riveting Machines. Similar machines that drill and countersink the hole instead of punching it are also used extensively in the aircraft and appliance industries (see Fig. 15-6).

Tooling.[1] The basic tooling for a machine is illustrated in Fig. 15-7. With the workpieces to be joined firmly clamped in the machine, a drilling unit moves into place to

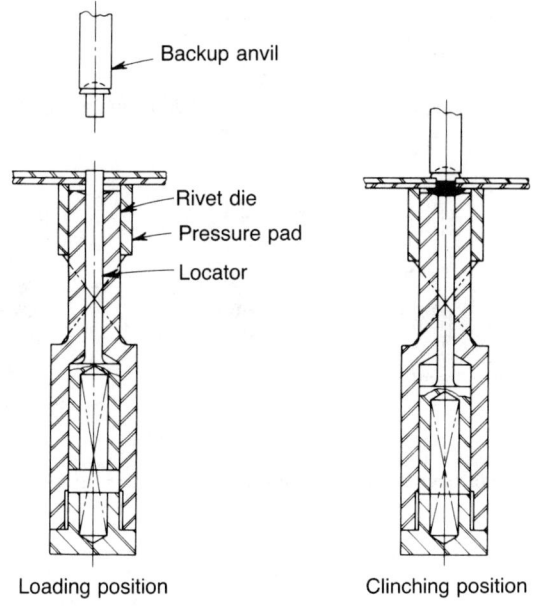

Fig. 15-4 Stationary riveting machine operation.

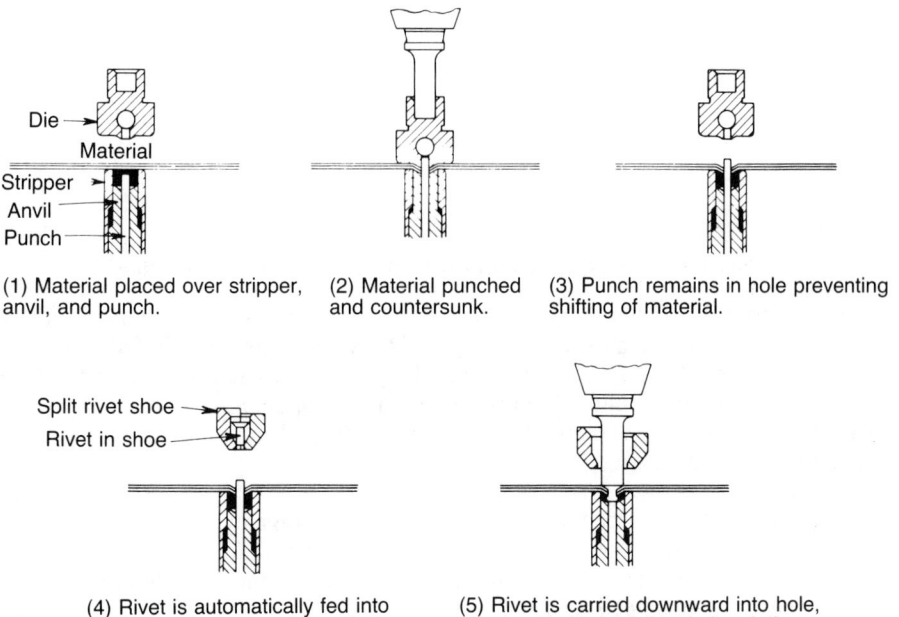

(1) Material placed over stripper, anvil, and punch.

(2) Material punched and countersunk.

(3) Punch remains in hole preventing shifting of material.

(4) Rivet is automatically fed into rivet shoe during punching stroke.

(5) Rivet is carried downward into hole, punch recedes and rivet is headed.

Fig. 15-5 Sequence of punching and riveting operations.

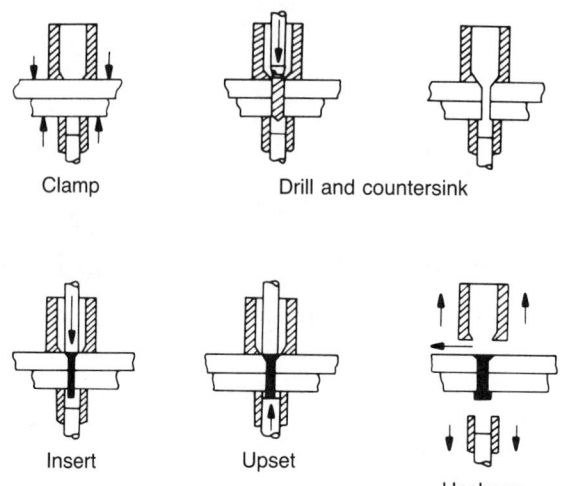

Clamp   Drill and countersink

Insert   Upset

Unclamp

Fig. 15-6 Sequence of operations for automatic riveting. (*Courtesy GEMCOR Drivmatic Div.*)

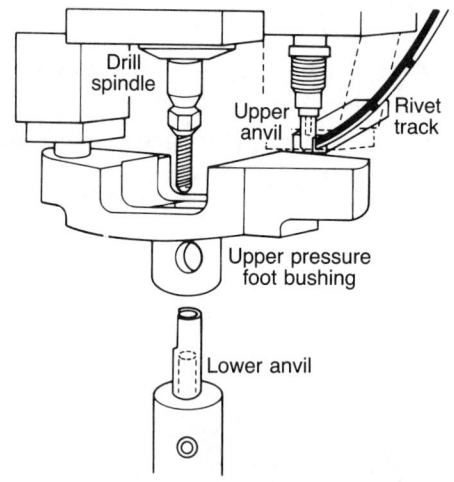

Drill
spindle

Upper
anvil

Rivet
track

Upper pressure
foot bushing

Lower anvil

Fig. 15-7 Tooling components for automatic drilling and riveting.

produce the hole. The drilling unit is then moved aside and, with the clamping force still applied, a riveting unit is moved into position. A rivet is automatically fed from one or more hoppers, down a track, and into feed fingers that insert it into the hole. In this position, the rivet is hydraulically squeezed against the upper anvil to form the required head. Clamping pressure is then released, and the assembly is removed or repositioned for additional fastening.

The machines exert as much as 6,000 lbf (27 kN) of clamping force and up to 50,000 lbf (222 kN) of force for heading the rivets. Average cycle time is 3½ seconds, and production rates of more than 24 rivets per minute are attained. When required, the formed rivet heads are shaved flush on the same automatic machine. For hot dimpling, a three-position tooling head is used. Tooling at the first position has a built-in cartridge heater and produces a male dimple profile. Drilling is performed at the second position and upsetting at the third.

Hole-location Methods. Several methods are used to locate the holes for automatic drilling and riveting. In one method, a masking template containing the desired rivet hole pattern is placed on the assembly, sprayed, and then removed, leaving dots on the assembly. One of the dots is then positioned in alignment with a fiber-optic or laser light system and the machine cycle is initiated. Then the procedure is repeated. Another method of hole location is to provide a pilot pin in the lower anvil that enters predrilled pilot holes in the assembly.

Accessory Equipment. Various accessories are available for use with automatic drilling and riveting machines. One is a closed-loop servosystem for controlling drilling speed and feed. Speeds are variable from 100 to 6,000 rpm and feed rates from 1 to 96 ipm (25 to 2438 mm/min). Another accessory is a system to automatically select the proper length rivet. With this system, the thickness of the assembly stack is measured, and encoders send signals to a programmable controller that selects a proper rivet from a number of vibratory feeder bowls.

ORBITAL RIVETING

Orbital riveting (see Fig. 15-8) is a low-pressure, line-of contact (*T*), cold forming process. The riveting tool, mounted in a rotating spindle, is inclined at a slight angle (3 to 6°) so that the tool axis intersects the centerline, *P*, of the spindle at the working end of the tool. As the orbiting tool is fed toward the work, material at the end of the rivet shank is incrementally displaced to form the required head. Machines are available for pneumatic or hydraulic operation and in bench, floor, and opposed-head models. Modular heads that fit most machines are also available with one or more spindles. Multi-spindle systems with center distances ranging from 3/16 to 20 in. (5 to 508 mm) and multilevel assembly systems are being used.

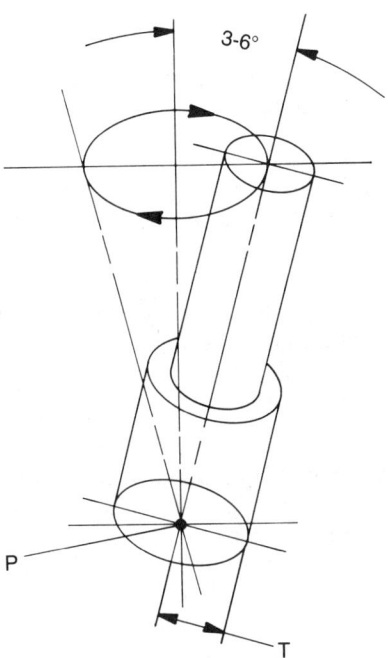

Fig. 15-8 Orbital riveting. (*Courtesy VSI Automation Assembly*)

An important advantage of orbital riveting is the consistently high-quality results attained, with close tolerances and smooth finishes. Because there is no impact between the tooling and the workpiece, the process is quiet. Versatility is another advantage; a wide range of metals and plastics can be formed in this way, and many other forming operations, in addition to riveting, can be done on these machines. The process requires less power and force than most other riveting methods. Typical head shapes and forming peens are illustrated in Fig. 15-9.

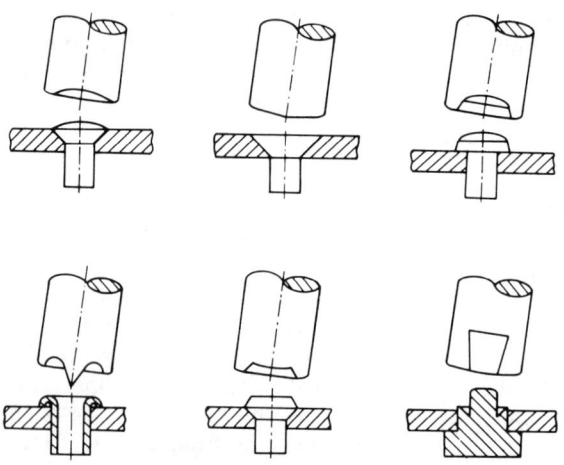

Fig. 15-9 Typical forming peens used in orbital riveting and heads produced. (*Courtesy Weber Automatic Screwdrivers & Assembly Systems*)

RADIAL RIVETING

Radial riveting is similar to orbital riveting except that the tools move in a planetary or rosette motion instead of being mounted in rotating spindles. In the rosette forming pattern, R, shown in Fig. 15-10, each loop of the rosette path is guided through center, Z. The longitudinal axis of the riveting tool always overlaps the center of rivet point, N. A cycloidal movement guides the tool through the rosette pattern. The rivet material is spread radially outward and inward, with some tangential overlapping, to form the required head.

Advantages of radial riveting are the same as those just discussed for orbital riveting. However, radial riveting is said to impart improved conductivity to the materials because of the kneading action. As a result, it is used extensively in the production of electrical contact points.

RIVETING FIXTURES

Air-clamping Riveting Fixtures. Production from standard riveting machines can be considerably increased for such components as levers with riveted studs by use of the simple holding fixture illustrated in Fig. 15-11.

The 0.094-in.-square stud is held securely in the clamp jaws (1) when the air-clamp assembly (2) is actuated, thereby moving a plunger (3) forward. The tapered plunger end causes a scissors action of the jaws which then exert clamping force on the stud. The lever, positioned on the clamped stud and on the pin locator (4), is ready to be riveted by the machine. Retraction of the plunger releases the clamped stud and allows the completed assembly to be removed.

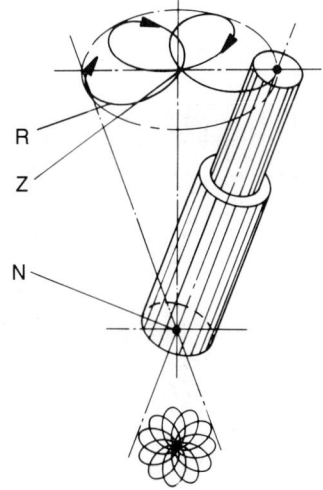

Fig. 15-10 Radial riveting. (*Courtesy Bracker Corp.*)

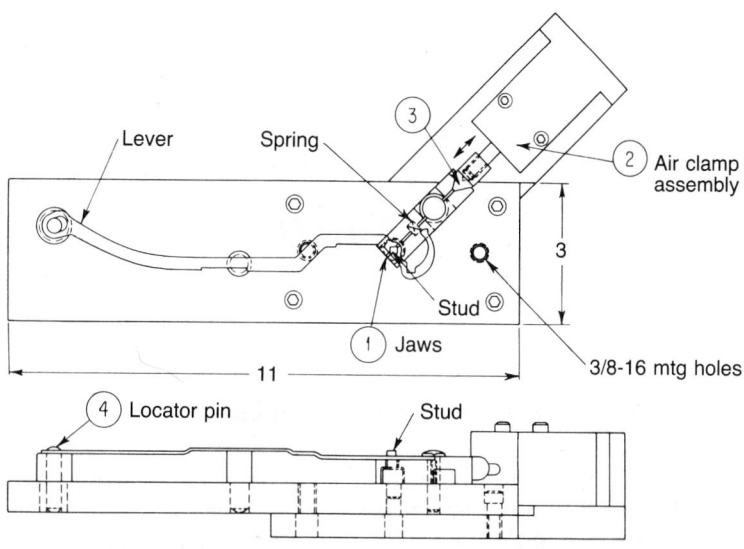

Fig. 15-11 Riveting fixture with air clamping. (*Courtesy Burroughs Corp.*)

Fixtures for Riveting Both Ends of a Shaft Simultaneously. Upsetting both ends of a shaft simultaneously with a single-head riveting machine can be performed in the fixture depicted in Fig. 15-12.

The parts, two levers and a shaft with flatted ends, are located by pins (1) and blocks (2) on a holder plate (3) which is free to float up and down on an upright (4). A lower anvil (5) (not attached to the machine) is slip-fit in a collar (6) and spring-loaded from the fixture base.

When the rivet hammer engages the top end of the shaft, the resultant pressure forces the floating holder plate down, making the lower end of the shaft contact the lower anvil. The anvil is then rotated by hand with a screw handle (7). Thus, the hammer force

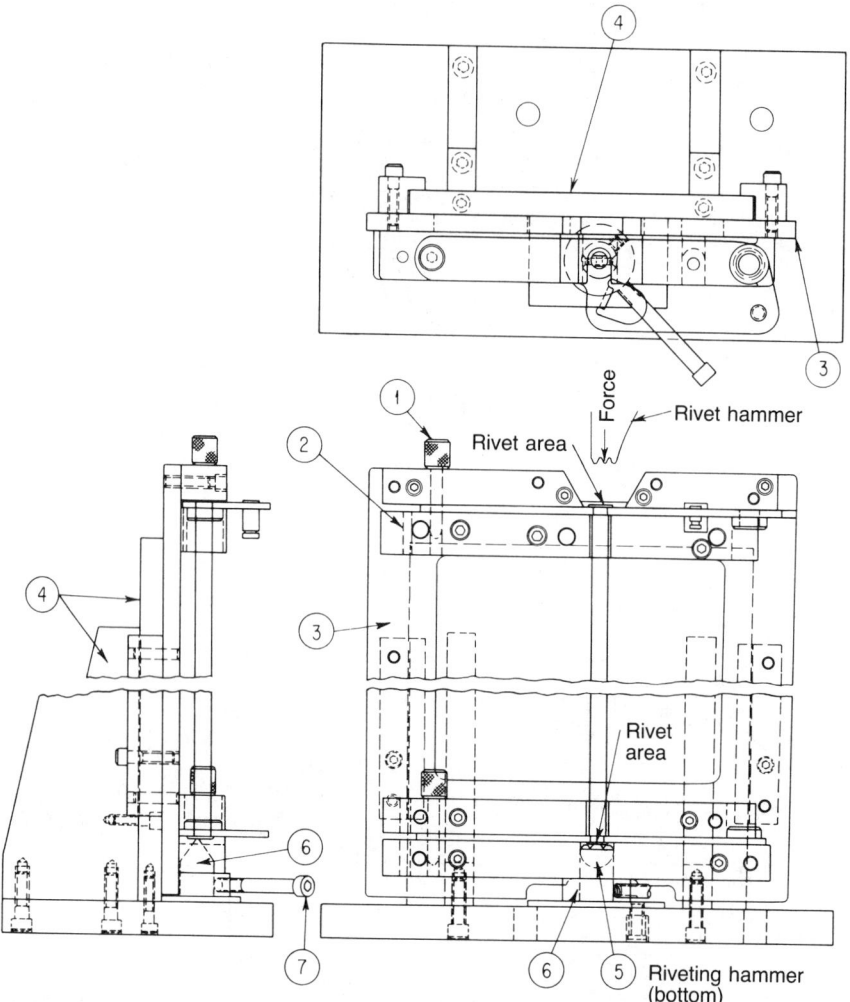

Fig. 15-12 Fixture for riveting both ends of a shaft simultaneously. (*Courtesy Speed-O-Print Corp.*)

exerted upon the upper end is used to simultaneously rivet over the opposite shaft end.

A Riveting Fixture with Spring-loaded Adjustable Center Punch. Cold riveting of gold-alloy contacts into electrical-contact assemblies can be performed by an inexpensive riveting fixture which features a standard, purchased, toolmaker's spring-loaded adjustable center punch, illustrated in Fig. 15-13.

Powered by a small air cylinder (1) which compresses the center punch (2), the contact is riveted to the phosphor-bronze spring by a specially ground tip (3). An anvil (4) machined to receive the working end of the contact is interchangeable for other contact shapes and sizes. Two springs (5) return the center punch and carrier slide to starting position when the cylinder is released.

A Stationary Riveting Fixture. In the aircraft industry and other applications involving the assembly of several components, a free-standing fixture of the type illustrated in Fig. 15-14 is often used. Components are usually aligned and clamped or pinned in place with a sheet holder for riveting with portable equipment. Clamps shown in the figure are hand-operated toggle clamps. For high production, air-operated clamps of

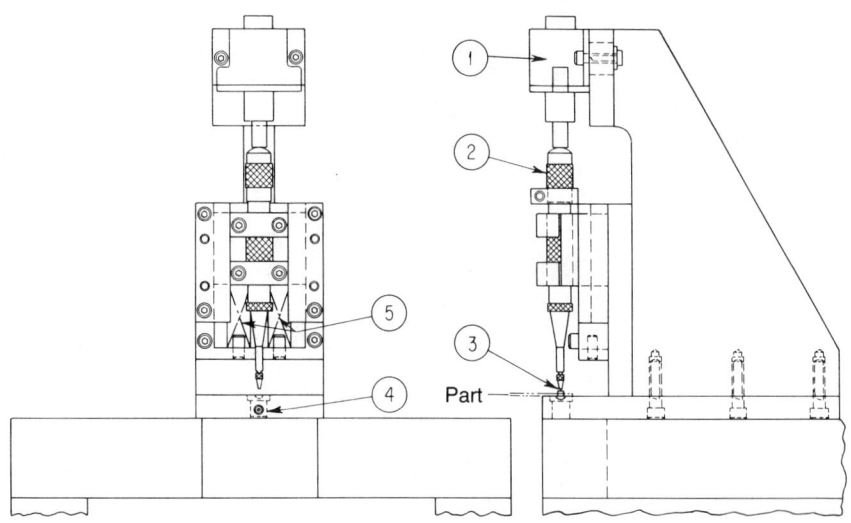

Fig. 15-13 Riveting fixture with a spring-loaded adjustable center punch. (*Courtesy Link Aviation, Inc.*)

Fig. 15-14 Stationary riveting fixture.

the same type can be used. Large fixtures of this type are often built with tilting or turnover features to provide easy access for riveting tools.

Riveting Dies. The riveting of many assemblies can be performed in a punch press with a riveting die similar to that of Fig. 15-15.

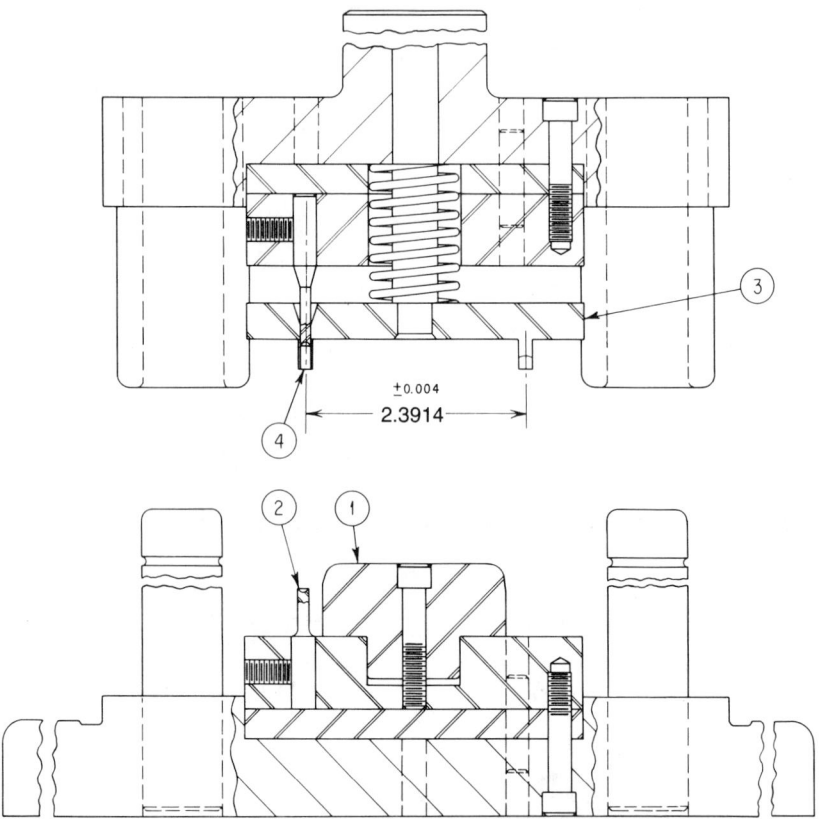

Fig. 15-15 Riveting die. (*Courtesy Marlin-Rockwell Corp.*)

The riveting die swages the rivets which secure the upper and lower ball separators, making the ball bearing a completed and permanent assembly. Components for the bearing assembly consist of bearing balls, an inner race, an outer race, an upper ball separator (with rivet holes only), and a lower ball separator (with rivets attached); these are assembled by hand prior to insertion into the die and swaging of the rivet heads.

The die section contains a tapered locator (1) for positioning the inner bearing race. Sixteen punches (2) spaced around the locator support and locate the lower ball separator, which contains the previously staked-in rivets. Swaging is accomplished by the punch section which compresses a spring-loaded pressure pad (3); through the pressure pad, sixteen upper punches (4) descend and swage over the protruding rivet ends, joining the separator halves and making the ball bearing a permanent assembly.

A feature of this tool is the consistent pressure which it applies on all rivets in one particular assembly.

Positioning Systems.[2] Methods of moving assemblies for automatic drilling and riveting vary from simple manual means to sophisticated electronic controls. Manual positioning is used extensively for smaller and lighter assemblies, as well as those with

15-12

access problems. These systems are generally equipped with bearings and/or rollers to minimize friction, and chains or straps and a sling arrangement are often used for vertical movements.

Semiautomatic positioning systems are generally equipped with hydraulic and/or pneumatic cylinders, and electric motors to jog the assemblies into position. In positioning with computer numerical control (CNC), a preprogrammed microprocessor automatically energizes servo-motors to accurately control positioning.

EYELETS

Eyelets are thin-walled tubular fasteners having a flange or formed head on one end. Most are formed from metal strip, but some are machined, and are set during assembly by forcing their small diameter ends against dies that curl or funnel the edges and clinch the eyelets against the workpieces. The assembly of eyelets, called setting or eyeleting, requires access to both sides of the parts to be assembled.

Eyelets differ from rivets in that their bores extend completely through the fasteners. Grommets, not discussed in this section, are large eyelet-type fasteners designed for securing by curling their tubular ends over formed washers to provide strength in holes through resilient materials.

Applications. Eyeleting is used extensively in the metalworking industry as a fastening method for the assembly of many different types of light-gage parts. Typical applications include the assembly of automotive components, electrical and electronic components (including use as terminals), hardware, toys, paper products, shoes, textiles, and garments.

Eyeleting Machines. The basic operation of eyeleting machines is similar to that of riveting machines. Hand-fed machines are available in bench and floor models, with hand, foot, electric, or pneumatic power. Setting tools used on the machines are made special specifically for the particular eyelets to be used. Semiautomatic and automatic machines are available with special positioning and feeding devices for single or multiple settings. Automatic clamping devices eliminate the need for punching material from the workpieces.

On a typical semiautomatic machine, eyelets are placed in a hopper that contains a rotating hopper brush for orienting the eyelets to be fed into a raceway. Feeding is done through a slot in the hopper, specially designed to allow each eyelet to enter the raceway in one position. The eyelet then sits at the bottom of the raceway, held in position by spring-loaded fingers. The raceway is held in an outboard position by a cam affixed to the main driveshaft. When the machine is actuated, the main shaft rotates. This causes the raceway, by virtue of the cam design, to position the eyelet at the centerline of the spindle. At the same time, the spindle has begun to move downward, picking the eyelet from the raceway and completing the clinching action. Many machines use a vibrating bowl to achieve orientation before the eyelets enter the raceway.

Programmable and microprocessor controls and mechanical positioners are used to locate assemblies for setting. Several eyelets, as well as different length eyelets, can be set on a single machine, and different style eyelets can be set with a change of the tooling.

Eyelet Setting. Setting (clinching) of eyelets is done by tooling that upsets or curls the barrel ends of the eyelets (see Fig. 15-16). Hardness of material from which the assembly component is made is a critical consideration in eyelet setting. When setting an eyelet in an assembly consisting of both a hard and a soft material, the clinch should be made on the harder material whenever possible. Figure 15-17 illustrates the following setting dies for producing various clinch configurations:

- Roll form die (view *a*). A medium-roll setting die is most common and is consi-

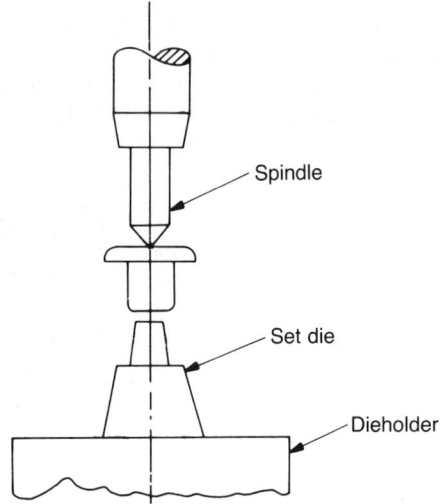

Fig. 15-16 Tooling for setting eyelets.

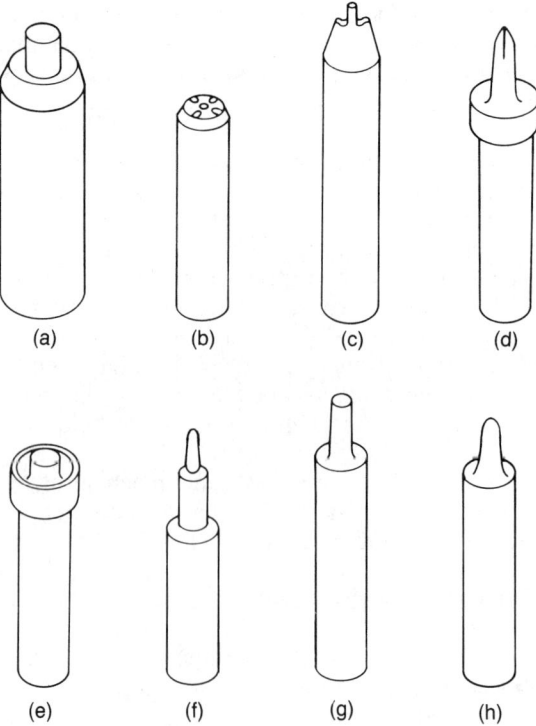

Fig. 15-17 Various setting dies for producing different clinch configurations. (*Courtesy PCI Group, Inc.*)

dered a standard. The anvil form of this die is designed to provide a maximum roll diameter without splitting the eyelet. Close-roll dies provide rolls of smaller diameter and are used when space is a limiting factor. Wide-roll dies produce wider rolls but there is a greater tendency for the eyelets to split.

- Corrugated die (view *b*). This type of setting die has serrations machined into the anvil. The result is a scored setting with the eyelet barrel cut into equal segments. Corrugated setting provides greater holding power in some type of fabrics.
- Bifurcating die (view *c*). This setting die segments the eyelet barrel to provide one or two posts for wire wrapping.
- Spear-point die (view *d*). This setting die has three sharp cutting edges to pierce materials such as closely woven fabrics, plastics, and rubber-like materials.
- Hood die (view *e*). This setting die acts in conjunctions with the eyelet to punch through plastics, paper, and other thin materials.
- Receding-pilot die (view *f*). A spring-loaded pilot in this die has a portion of the setting form machined into it. It is used to align holes and lead eyelets through the holes.
- Prepunch die (view *g*). This type die is used on double-stroke setting machines. On the first stroke, the die punches a hole in soft materials, and on the second stroke it receives and sets an eyelet.
- Needle-point die (view *h*). This setting die has a sharp point that is used to separate loosely woven fabrics.

DRILL AND PIN FIXTURES

A Drill and Pin Fixture for Gear and Motor Shaft. When parts have to be drilled and pinned together at assembly, a fixture, such as that shown in Fig. 15-18, can be used. In this application, an aluminum gear is to be pinned to a stainless steel motor shaft to a predetermined dimension. After the gear and motor are correctly positioned, they are securely held together by means of a screw through a tapped hole in the gear hub.

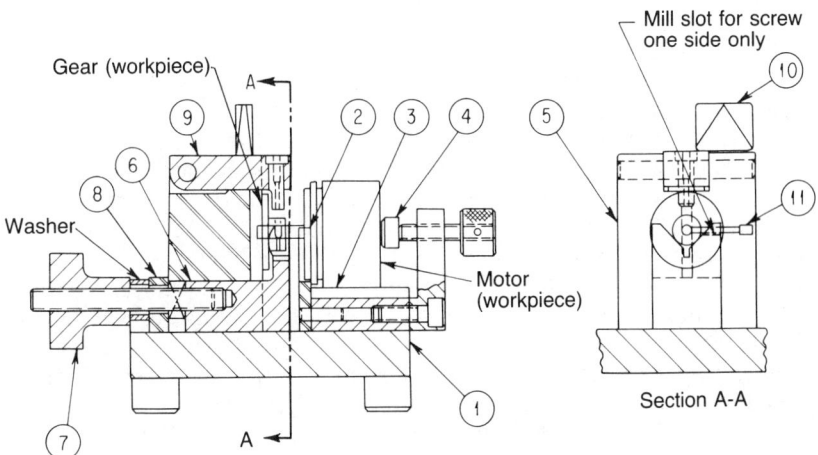

Fig. 15-18 Drill and pin fixture for gear and motor shaft. (*Courtesy General Electric Co.*)

The fixture consists of a base (1) on which is mounted a hardened locating plate (2) that is ground to fit the mounting hub of the motor. A soft pad (3) supports the motor, and a thumbscrew (4) with a swivel foot pushes it against the locating plate. A block (5) is also mounted on the base. A locating surface for the gear is ground on the block, and a clearance slot for the motor shaft is also machined in it. The gear is clamped against the locating surface of the block by a sliding V-clamp (6) fitted in the block and moved with a stud and hand knob (7) which is threaded through another block (8) mounted on the base. A bushing leaf (9) is also fastened to the block. It is clamped securely with a quarter-turn screw (10). A clearance slot for the motor shaft is also machined in the large block. On one side of the sliding V-clamp is a clearance slot for the screw (11) which holds the gear and motor together for drilling through a tapped hole in the gear hub.

To operate, a motor on whose shaft a gear has been loosely assembled is placed on the locating plate while the bushing leaf is open. The motor is then pushed against the locating plate with the thumbscrew. The gear is then pulled against the locating surface by the sliding V-clamp. Now the gear can be secured to the motor shaft with the screw (11), and the workpieces are ready for drilling. The bushing leaf is closed and locked by the quarter-turn screw. After the parts are drilled, the bushing leaf is raised and the pin driven in place while the parts are still held securely. Then the clamps are loosened and the assembled workpiece can be removed.

A Drill and Pin Fixture that Controls Concentricity. Specifications for a workpiece, a frame assembly, require holes in the bottom plate and holes in the top plate to be concentric within 0.001 in. FIM so that electrical components can be mounted accurately. The fixture illustrated in Fig. 15-19 positions the workpiece for this purpose and holds it securely for drilling and pinning.

The end plate (1) is removed from the fixture. The frame assembly, which has been loosely assembled with the screws, is slid onto the locating plates (2 and 3). An error-proof pin (9) prevents faulty positioning of the workpiece. The end plate is then replaced and secured with a C-washer (4) and a knurled nut (5) at each end.

A round locating pin (6) and a diamond locating pin (7) slide into bushings (10) and align the holes in the bottom plate and the holes in the top plate of the workpiece. They are locked in place by means of knurled-head screws (8) to allow tumbling of the fixture, because the frame assembly must be drilled and pinned from both sides.

No drill bushings are required, because the dowel-pin holes are predrilled undersize in the top and bottom plates of the assembly.

After the dowel-pin holes are drilled, the grease-coated dowels are driven in place. Then the end plate is removed and the workpiece taken out of the fixture.

A Drill Fixture to Drill, Ream, and Pin a Geneva Drive Assembly. It is often necessary to assemble parts to predetermined, close-toleranced locations and then pin them together. The Geneva drive assembly, illustrated in Fig. 15-20, requires such a procedure. It consists of a gear, drive cam, and bail cam that are pinned to a shaft.

To drill, ream, and pin this assembly, the two cams and the gear are preassembled on the shaft and placed in the fixture, which is illustrated in Fig. 15-21. V-blocks (1 and 2) position the shaft on the center line. It is held in the V-blocks with a strap clamp (3). Since all dimensions are taken from the groove in the cam shaft, the surface is positioned in the locator block (4). A spring-loaded pusher (5) ensures that the shaft is held firmly against this locating surface. The angular relationship for the bail and drive cams is set by engaging a locating pin (6) in a hole in the bail cam and by a locator slide (7) on the button of the drive cam. The two cams and the gear are also clamped against their locating surfaces by two clamps (8 and 9). A hinged leaf (10) is closed and locked into position with a quarter-turn screw (11). Since limited space prohibits the use of drill bushings, the leaf is hardened and the drill holes (*A, B,* and *C*) in it are ground and lapped. The assembly is now ready for drilling.

After drilling, the bushing leaf is released and swung out of the way. The assembly is now ready for reaming.

While parts are still securely clamped in the fixture, it is advisable to drive and stake

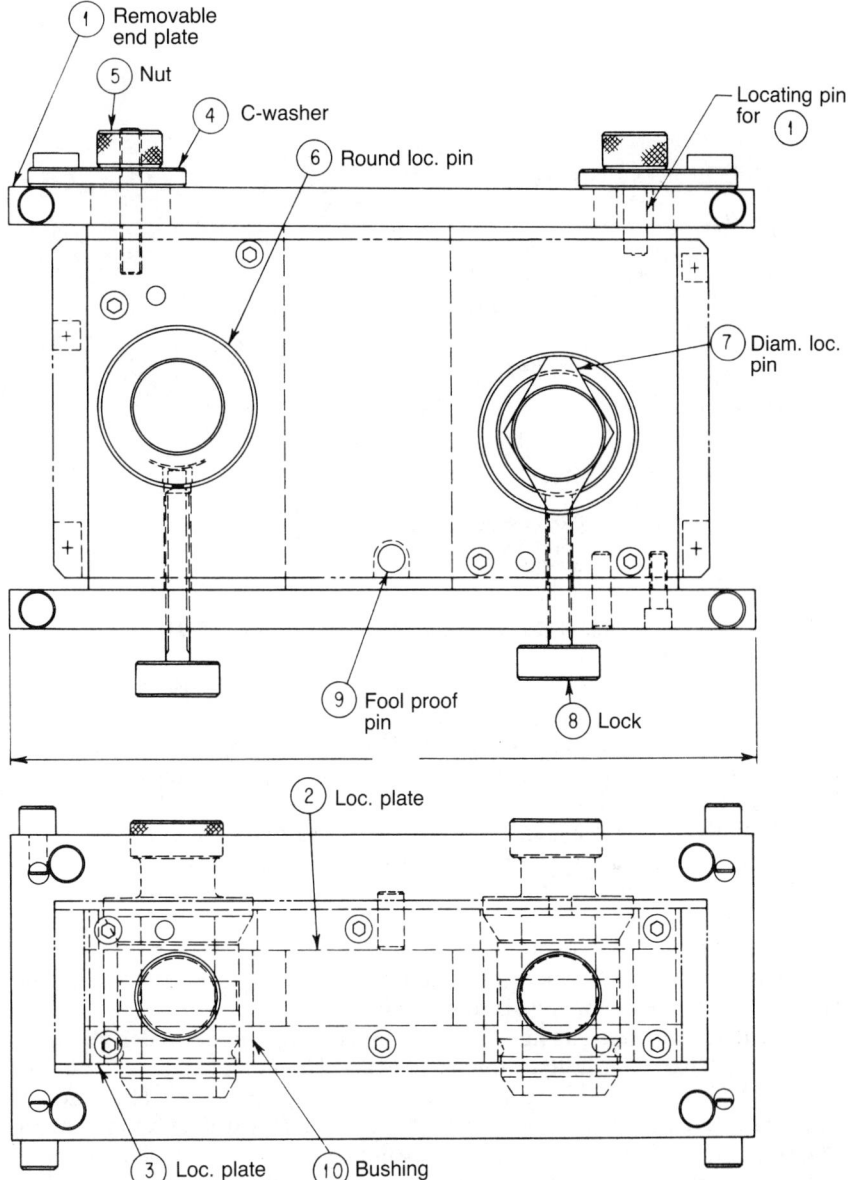

Fig. 15-19 Drill and pin fixture for concentric holes. *(Courtesy General Electric Co.)*

the three taper pins to assemble the unit. Then the assembly can be removed from the fixture and stored as one unit.

A Jig for Drilling Rivet Holes. The rivet holes in the parts of an aluminum frame were drilled in the jig of Fig. 15-22. A master block (1) is machined to fit the inside of the assembly and to position the gussets. The gussets are held in place against the block with two strap clamps (2) and knurled nuts (3). Two pins (4) allow movement of the clamps in one direction only. One edge of the bracket rests on a locating button (5), and a locating pin (6) vertically positions the bracket. A knurled-head screw (7) clamps the

15-17

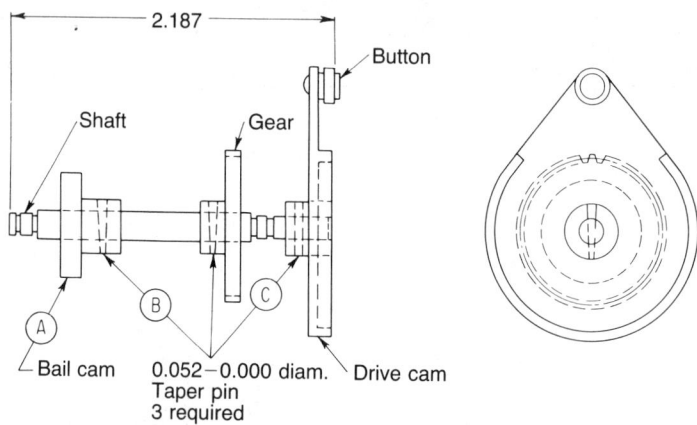

Fig. 15-20 Workpiece for fixture of Fig. 15-21.

bracket and incorporates a fiber plug (8) to prevent marring. Bushing blocks (9, 10, 11, and 12) incorporate bushings for guiding the drills. Knurled-head screws (13) provide additional clamping pressure against the bracket and gussets. Locating pins (14) vertically position the support. The jig is supported by pins (15) and a support block (16). The parts are removed from the jig for later riveting.

A Drill, Ream, and Pin Jig. Two cams and two arms are slip-fit on the shaft (see Fig. 15-23) before the shaft is held by V-locators (1, 2, and 3) incorporated in the jig of Fig. 15-24. A pin (4) positions the two cams by engaging the 0.3145-in. (7.988 mm) slot and by engaging square busings (5), 0.314 × 0324 in. (7.98 × 8.23 mm) and is held by a clamp (6). The arms are clamped in position as shown in sections *A-A* and *B-B*.

After the holes are drilled and reamed, four pins are inserted and driven lightly before the assembly is removed from the jig.

A Drill and Pin Jig. The jig of Fig. 15-25, although simple in design, can accommodate various shaft lengths to be pinned to gears. The slotted holders (2) allow the center distance between the V-blocks (1) to be set up with gage blocks. The gears to be pinned to a shaft 3.583 in. (91.01 mm) long have been spot-drilled before they have been placed in the V-blocks of the jig. Two clamping screws (3) which hold the shaft in the vees are of brass to prevent marring the stainless steel shaft.

STAKING

In staking, two or more parts are joined permanently by forcing the metal edge of one member to flow either inward or outward around the other parts. Staking is an economical method of fastening parts. The operation is completed with a single stroke of an arbor press, kick press, punch press, air, or hydraulic press. Figure 15-26 illustrates locking a ring to a shaft with center punch staking. Figure 15-27 illustrates joing together a bushing, a bracket, and a shell with a ring-staking punch. Figure 15-28 illustrates the principles of inward staking by forcing metal of a ring against the knurled portion of a shaft. To provide added rigidity and torque in assembly, spot staking may

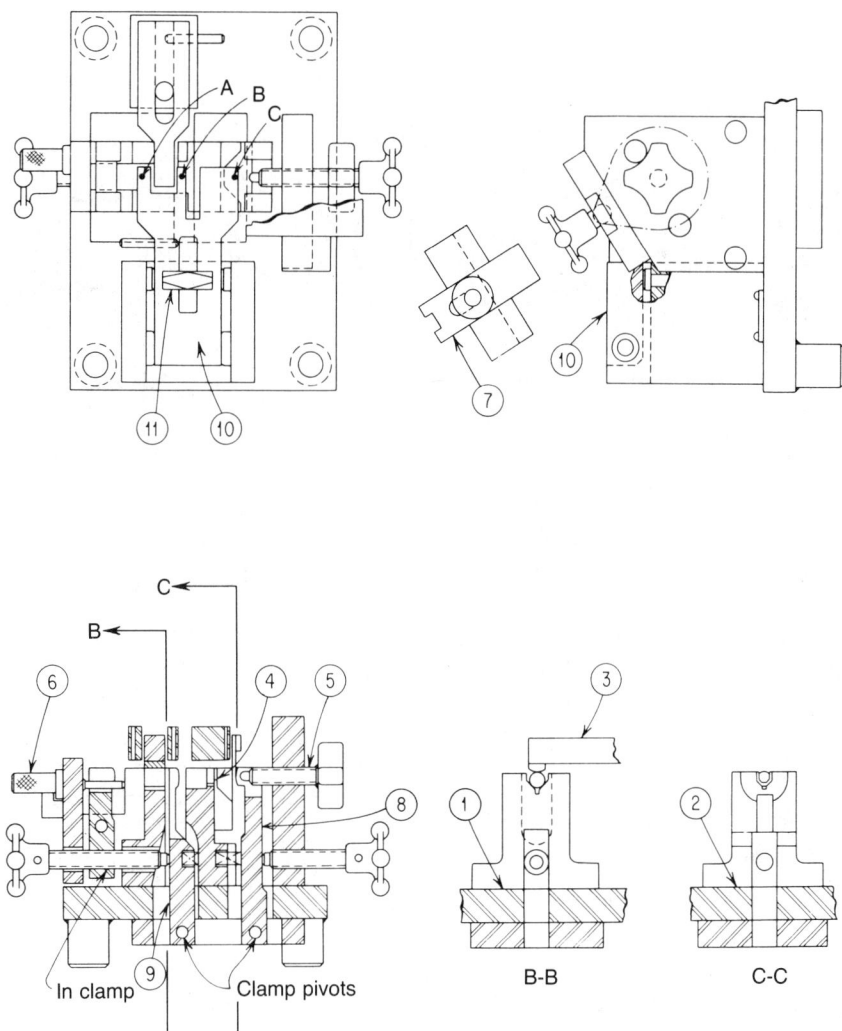

Fig. 15-21 Drill, ream, and pin fixture for Geneva Drive Assembly. (*Courtesy IBM*)

staking may be used. Spot staking is essentially the same as ring staking except that three or more equally spaced chisel edges of the staking punch force metal into splined portions of the parts to be assembled. Figure 15-29 illustrates a typical splined design and spot-staking punch to force metal into this spline. In some cases, it is desirable to use a combined spot- and ring-staking punch, as is shown in Fig. 15-30.

To facilitate efficient metal flow, the tips of punches must be free of nicks and circular grooves, and, after hardening, these surfaces should be highly polished. Polishing the punch tips in the direction of metal flow, instead of circular polishing, is desirable.

A Standard Assembly and Staking Fixture for a Hydraulic Press. Figure 15-31 shows a gear that is being pressed onto a shaft and staked prior to copper brazing. The shank of the adapter (1) is made to fit in the ram of a commercial hydraulic press. The

16
9
7
5
15
11
13
3
2
4
8
1
10
6
14
12
Bracket
Gussets
Support
Assembly parts

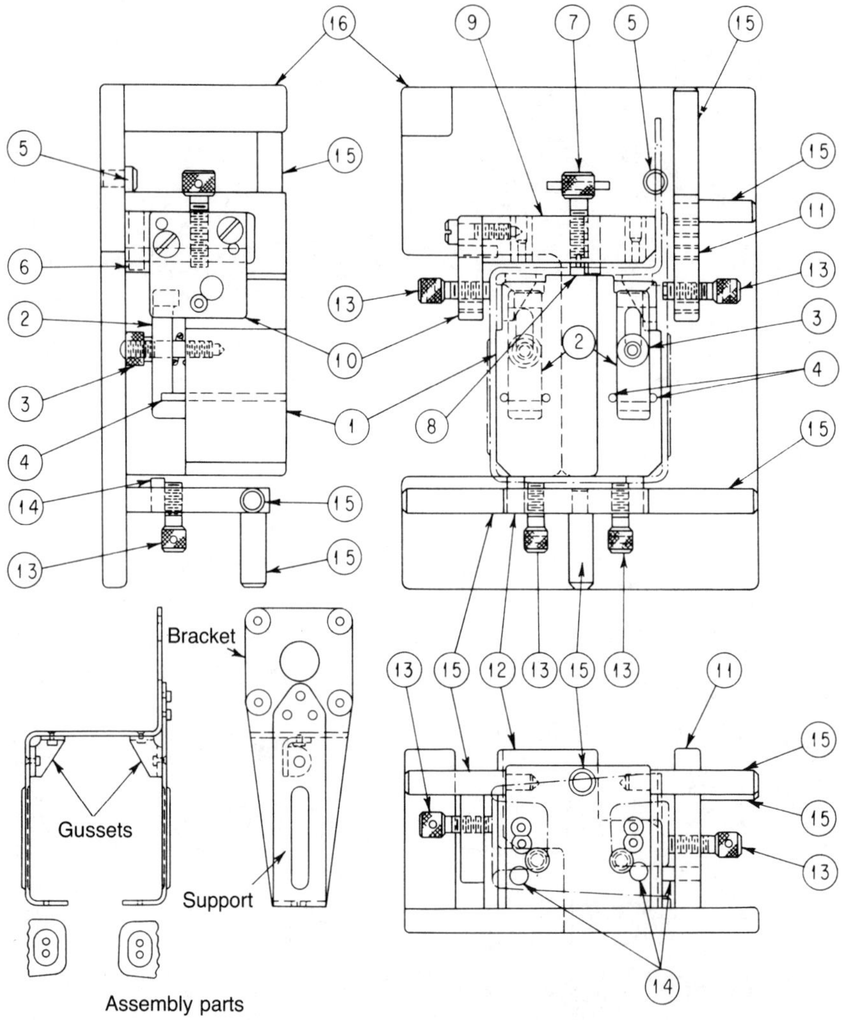

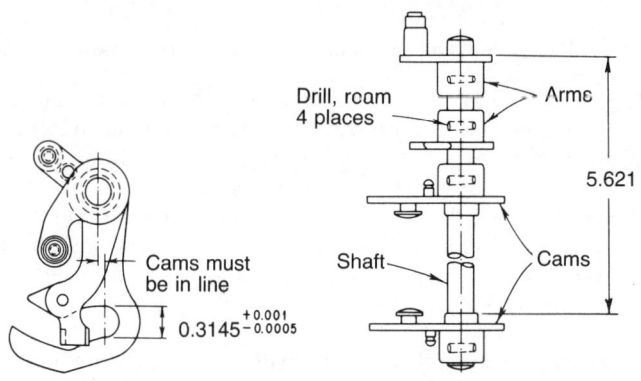

Fig. 15-22 Jig for drilling subassemblies.[3]

Drill, ream
4 places
Arms
5.621
Shaft
Cams
Cams must
be in line
0.3145 +0.001 −0.0005

Fig. 15-23 Workpieces for the jig of Fig. 15-24.

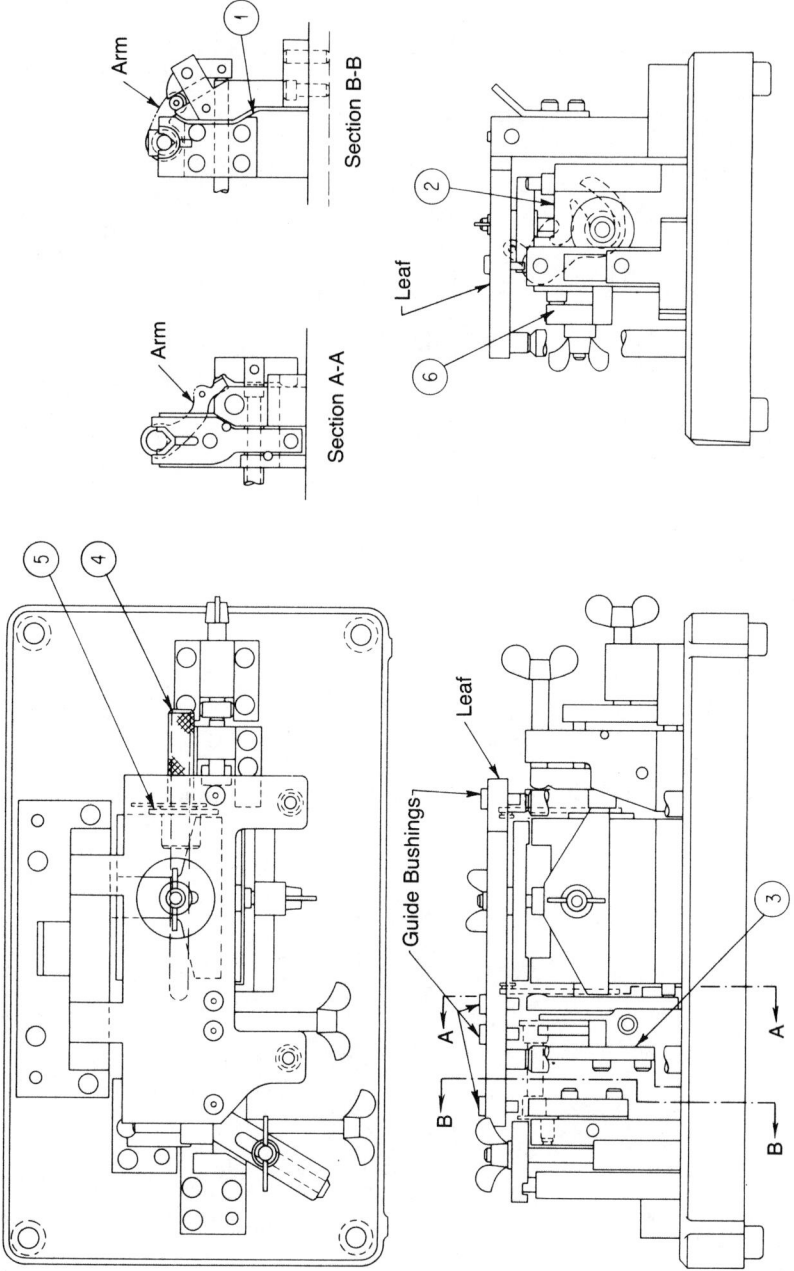

Section B-B

Arm

Section A-A

Arm

Leaf

Guide Bushings

Leaf

Fig. 15-24 Jig for drilling, reaming, and pinning. (*Courtesy Burroughs Adding Machine Co.*)

15-21

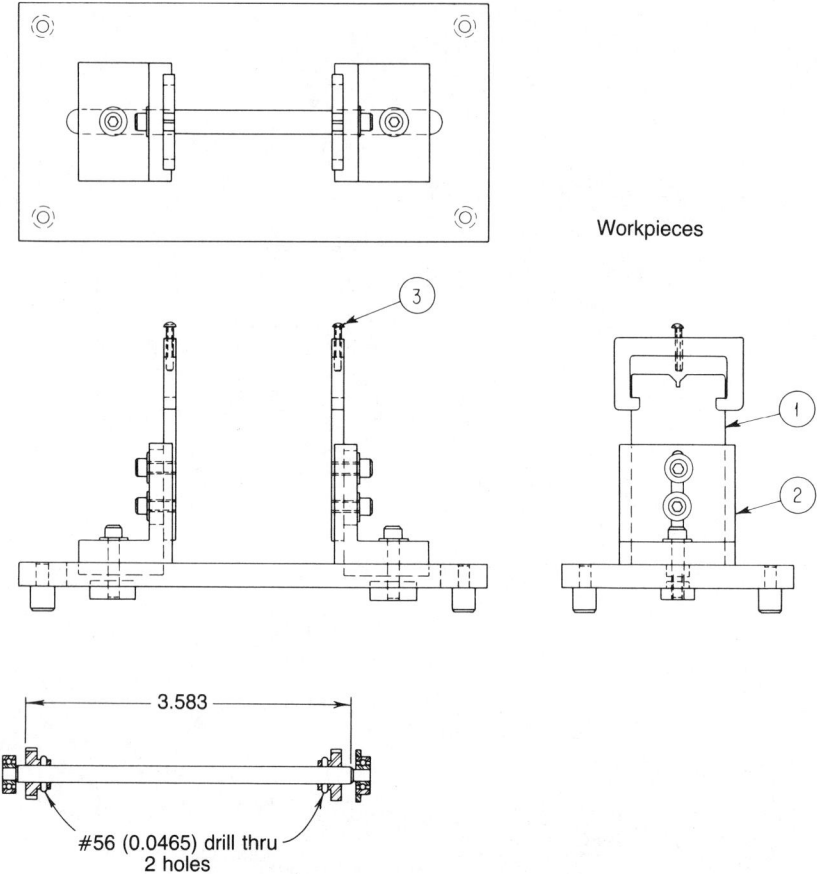

Workpieces

Fig. 15-25 Drill-and-pin jig for shafts and gears. (*Courtesy Norden Instruments, Inc.*)

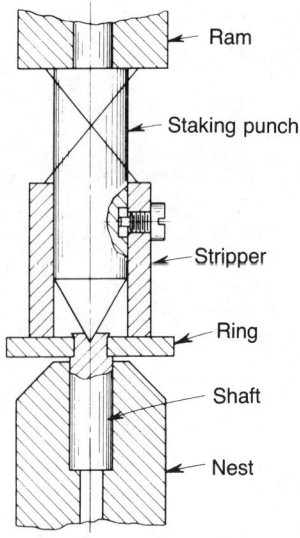

Fig. 15-26 Staking by center punch.

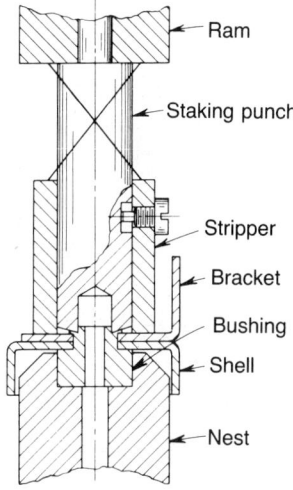

Fig. 15-27 Staking by ring punch.

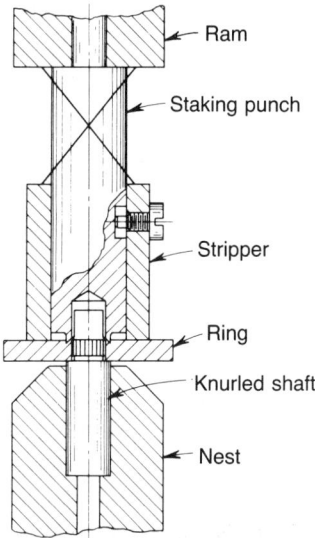

Fig. 15-28 Inward staking by ring punch.

punch holder (2) is a slip in fit in the adapter and holds the staking punches (5).

The lower adapter (3) is a slip fit in the base of the press, and the adapter ID is a slip fit for the shaft (workpiece).

When assembling, the shaft is placed in the adapter, and the gear is placed upon the shaft. Spring-tempered fingers (4) are adjusted to hold the gear perpendicular to the shaft. When the press ram is lowered, the staking punches contact the gear and press it onto the shaft until seated against the shoulder. The four staking punches stake the gear to the shaft in four places by the continued pressure of the ram.

Similar gear and shaft assemblies can be staked in this manner by changing the following three items as required: the adapter to hold the shaft, the punch holder (2), and the staking punches (5).

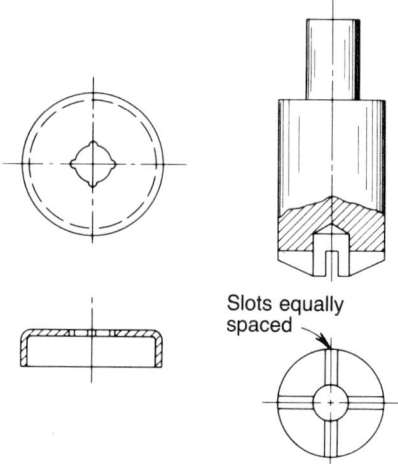

Fig. 15-29 Spot-staking punch and workpiece with splined hole.

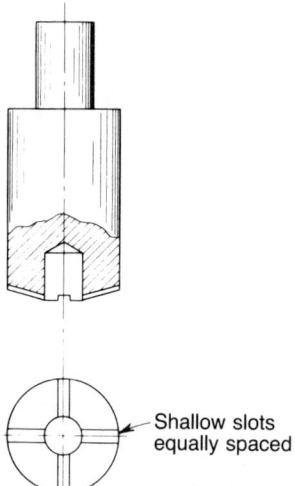

Fig. 15-30 Combined spot-and-ring-staking punch.

An Assembly and Staking Fixture. In the assembly shown in Fig. 15-32, it is necessary to press a hub into a lever and stake the two parts together before brazing in an atmospheric furnace.

The fixture, also shown in Fig. 15-32, is used in a standard hydraulic press, which has an adapter for a 1.750-in. diam. and a pressure pad in the bottom to push a pad (2) upward to eject the completed assembly.

To operate, the lever is placed with its locating diameter on the pad (2) and against a locating pin (6) which prevents the lever from twisting. The hub is then placed with its locating diameter on the pad. By this method the hub is aligned with the hole in the lever.

Pressure is applied to the top of the hub by a flat punch (8) mounted in the press ram. When the ram descends, the hub is pressed through the hole in the lever; the pad is forced down, and the four staking punches (3) stake the lever to the hub in four places.

15-24

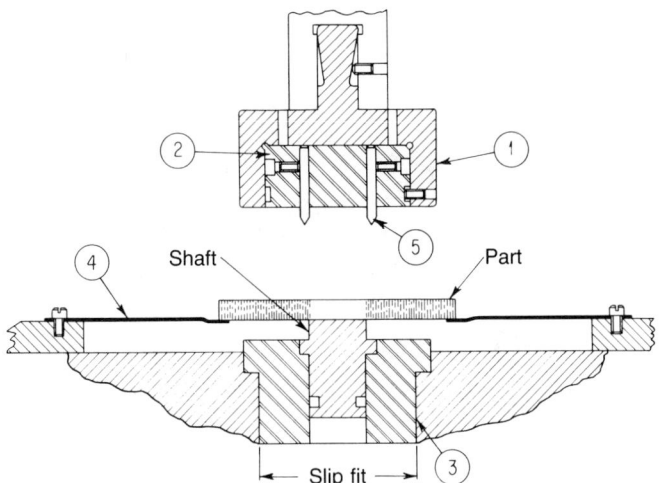

Fig. 15-31 Standard assembly and assembly fixture for hydraulic press. (*Courtesy IBM*)

When the press ram is raised, the pad is returned to its normal position by a pressure pad mounted in the press bed, and the completed assembly can be removed.

The staking punches can be adjusted for different staking depths by one setscrew (7) and held in alignment by another setscrew (4).

Movement of the pad is restricted by a dog-point setscrew (5) mounted in a base (1).

A Multiple Staking and Assembly Fixture. Shown in Fig. 15-33 is a standard die set used in a knuckle-action air press. Interchangeable punches and anvils are provided for staking and assembling different parts. To reduce the number of staking punches required, the staking diameter could be standardized with product design.

Two 0.500-in.-diam holes are bored in alignment in the upper and lower shoes of the die set (1). A dowel (9) is press-fitted into the bottom portion with sufficient length left exposed for locating the adapter (3) in alignment with the staking punch (7). The staking punch is a slip fit for the 0.500-in.-diam hole in the upper shoe of the die set. It is clamped by a thumbscrew (8).

The anvil (2) is a slip fit in a hole in the adapter (3). It is clamped by means of the thumbscrew (15). The locating plate (4) is a slip fit over the anvil. It is clamped by a headless setscrew (12). The spring-loaded pressure pad (5) slides on the staking punch (7). Its movement is restricted by the dowel (11), which is press-fit in the staking punch (7) and slides into a slot in the pressure pad.

The lower shoe of the die set is fastened to an adapter plate mounted on the airpress base with fillister head screws (10). The upper shoe of the die set is attached to the press ram with a floating adapter assembly (13 and 14).

To operate, the head of a rivet is placed in the recess of the anvil (2), and a lever is placed over the rivet and on the locating plate (4). When the air press is actuated, the ram descends and the pressure pad contacts the lever and holds it firmly against the rivet. Continuation of the press-ram stroke depresses the punch (7) to stake the rivet to the lever, and then the ram returns to the raised or normal position.

A Fixture to Crimp a Latch to a Handle Bracket. The fixture shown in Fig. 15-34 hangs from a retractor so that the parts can be crimped on an assembly line. The workpieces, a latch and handle bracket, are crimped together as shown in the illustration.

The fixture consists of a punch (1) machined to a slip fit for the OD of a shaft (6) and

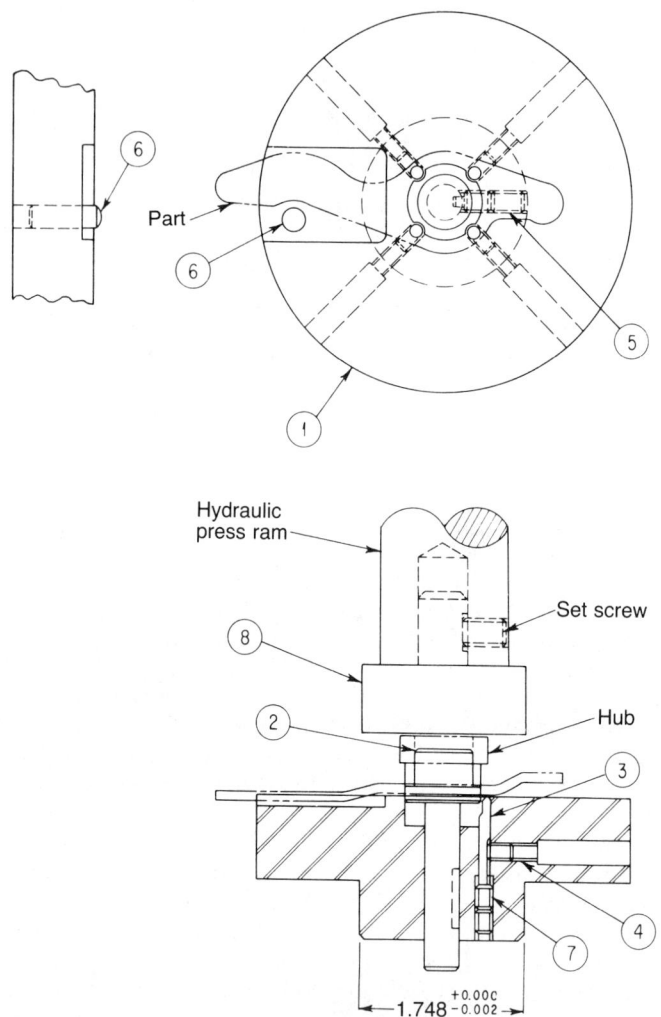

Fig. 15-32 Assembly and staking fixture. (*Courtesy IBM*)

a slip fit in an anvil (3). The shaft and anvil are assembled inside of the punch and held together by a ½-13 thread. A retainer (2) provides guiding surfaces for the punch (1). Plates (4 and 5) serve as nests for the workpieces.

To operate, the latch and handle bracket are nested together on the anvil and between the two nest plates. When an air cylinder is actuated, the punch and retainer are forced downward. The anvil, which is fastened to the shaft, remains stationary, thus crimping the latch around the handle-bracket flange. When the air cylinder is reversed, the punch moves up. The assembled workpiece can be removed and another latch and handle bracket positioned for crimping.

A Swaging Fixture for Electrical Plug Connectors. Assembling electrical plug connectors to a chassis, previously assembled with other electronic components, requires special treatment such as that performed by a swaging fixture (see Fig. 15-35).

The chassis has printed circuits, resistors, capacitors, transistors, potentiometers, etc., assembled in a drawn-steel container having a flanged opening for the electrical plug

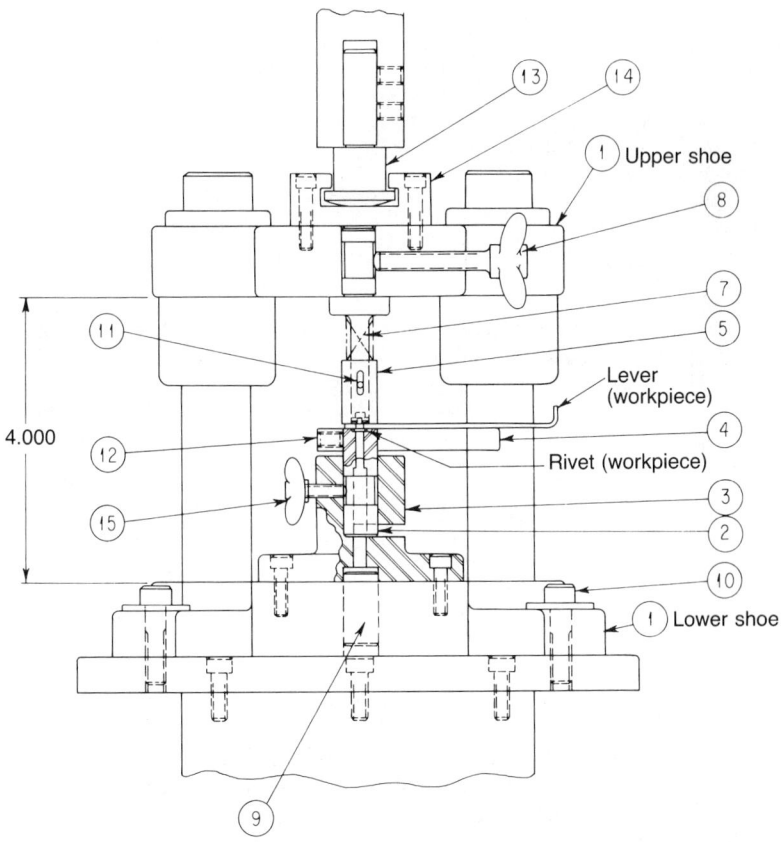

Fig. 15-33 Multiple staking and assembly fixture. (*Courtesy Argus Cameras, Inc.*)

connector shown in the same figure. The plastic electrical plug connector is hand-placed over the wires protruding from the container and into the flanged hole which receives and seats it. Portions of the hole flange are swaged into the four slots of the plug connector to prevent its removal by a swage punch (1). The swage punch descends and partially lances four segments of the flange and forces them into the slots of the plastic plug. The cutting and swaging angles of the four prongs of the punch must be carefully developed and their surfaces maintained in a sharp condition.

The plastic plug connector is oriented by a retracting locator (2). The assembled chassis is supported by locator pins (3) in a stationary block (4) and locator pins (5) in a movable clamping block (6). Power for operation of the punch can be supplied by any small assembly press, either air, electrical, or hand operated. A stop collar on the upper end of the punch limits travel, preventing damage to chassis components.

PRESSING FIXTURES

A Pressing Fixture for Adhesive Joining. Eight workpieces are clamped during the adhesive-drying cycle in the fixture illustrated in Fig. 15-36. The adhesive is applied to each hub of the gears and to each hole in the clutch plates. The C-washer (1) permits fast loading and unloading. Four stop pins (2) together with two locating pins (3) position the upper plate (4) in correct relation to the lower plate (5).

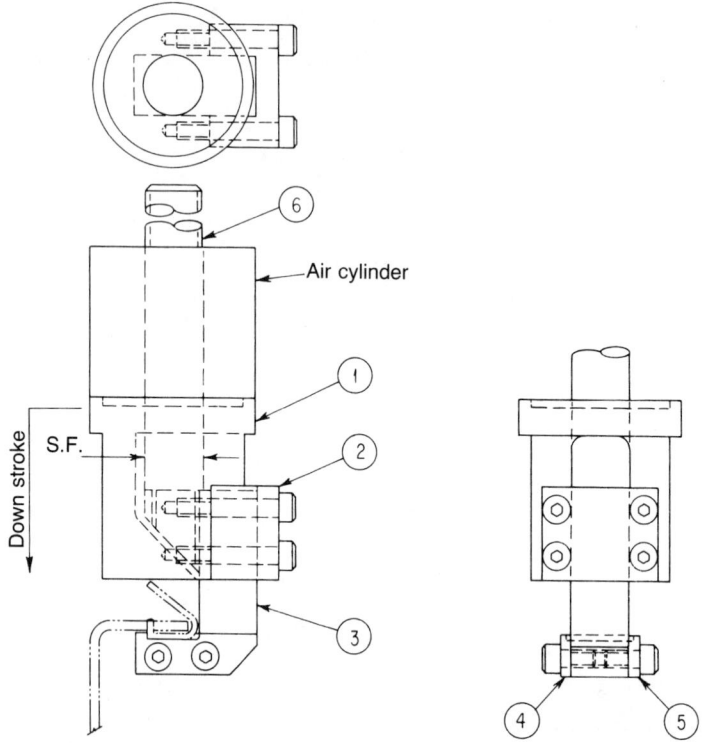

Fig. 15-34 Crimping fixture. (*Courtesy Lawn-Boy*)

An Assembly Fixture for Cementing and Baking. One way to hold or clamp parts for cementing, baking, or curing is to use weights. Nine workpieces, each consisting of a rectangular plate and a square plate, are held by weights in the fixture shown in Fig. 15-37 while they are cemented and baked.

The fixture consists of a base plate (1) on which are mounted two guide rails (2) for positioning the rectangular workpieces and two guide rails (3 and 7) for positioning the square workpieces, in which nine 0.031-in. locating holes are drilled. Hubs on the ends of the nine weights (5) are turned to a 1.238-in. diam and to a length of 0.045 in. (1.14 mm) to fit into the rectangular workpiece. Locating pins (4) pressed into the weights pass through the center holes in the square workpieces and into the locating holes in the fixture base. Knurled handles on the weights and handles on the fixture base are provided for the convenience of the operator.

The number of pieces that can be held in this type of fixture is limited only by part size, loaded-fixture weight, and baking-oven dimensions.

A Cementing Fixture. Figure 15-38 illustrates a fixture designed to hold delicate instrument-pointer components until cured rubber cement has bonded the three components into an integral assembly (see Fig. 15-39a).

The tool, which is inexpensively designed for a short-run production, uses clamps (1) to secure the V-shaped lever arm which locates in a stepped V-groove of the block (2). Pins (3) locate the L-shaped pointer on the base (4) while other pins (5) locate a gear-sector assembly. Another clamp (6) maintains it in the proper position.

The sequence of operations is as follows: Cement is applied to the three component parts at the required areas; then the pointer is placed into position between pins (3) and held by a spring (7). Next, the lever arm is placed in the V-groove and secured by the clamps. Then the gear-sector assembly is positioned by the pins and secured by a top

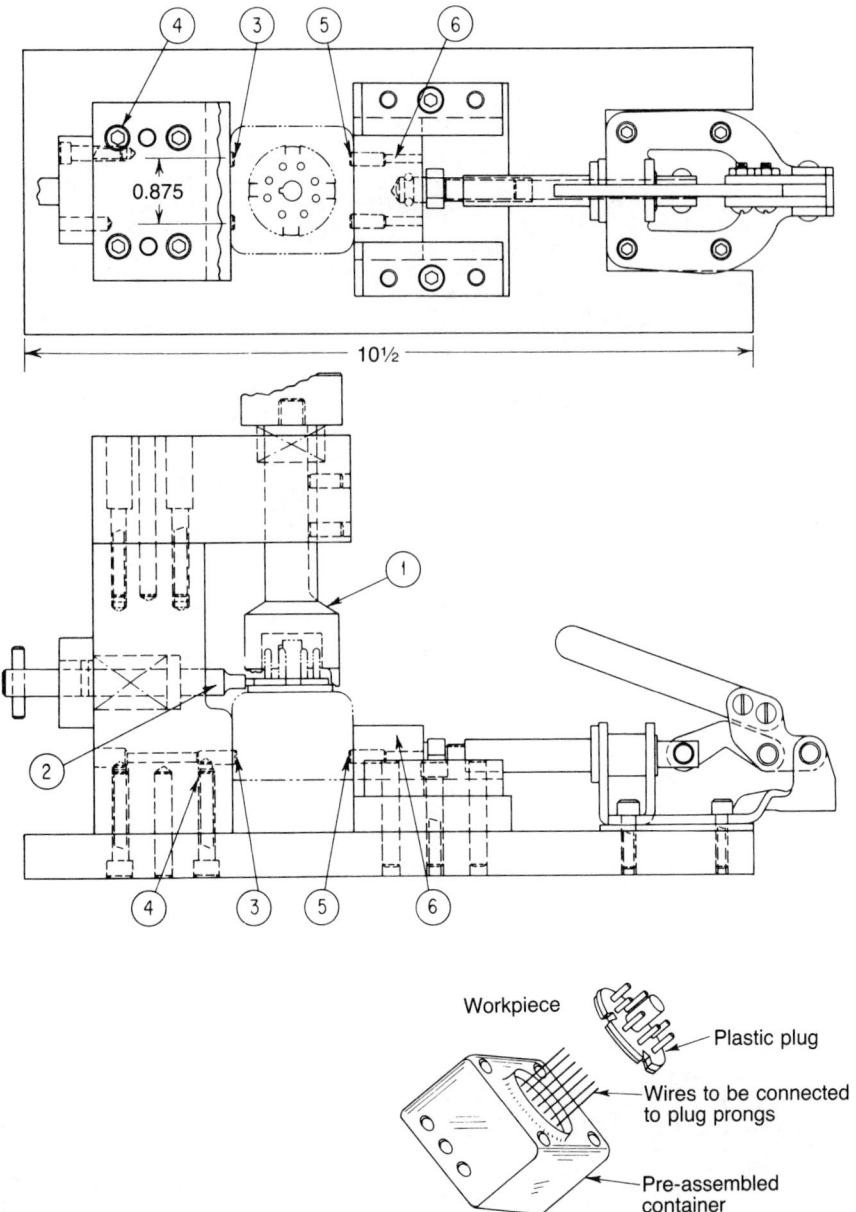

Fig. 15-35 Swaging fixture for electrical connectors. (*Courtesy Link Aviation, Inc.*)

clamp. Parts make contact with each other at the cemented areas. The fixture is then placed in an oven at 280° F for 2½ hr to cure the cement. The fixture parts and body are fabricated from CRS.

A Fixture to Assemble and Align a Drive Pulley Shaft in a Disc Assembly. In Fig. 15-39b is shown a disc and pulley-shaft assembly. The cam follower has been riveted to the disc in a previous operation. As shown, the keyway in the drive pulley shaft has a linear relationship to the cam follower of the disc assembly. The hydropress fixture shown in Fig. 15-40 maintains this relationship during the assembly of the two workpieces.

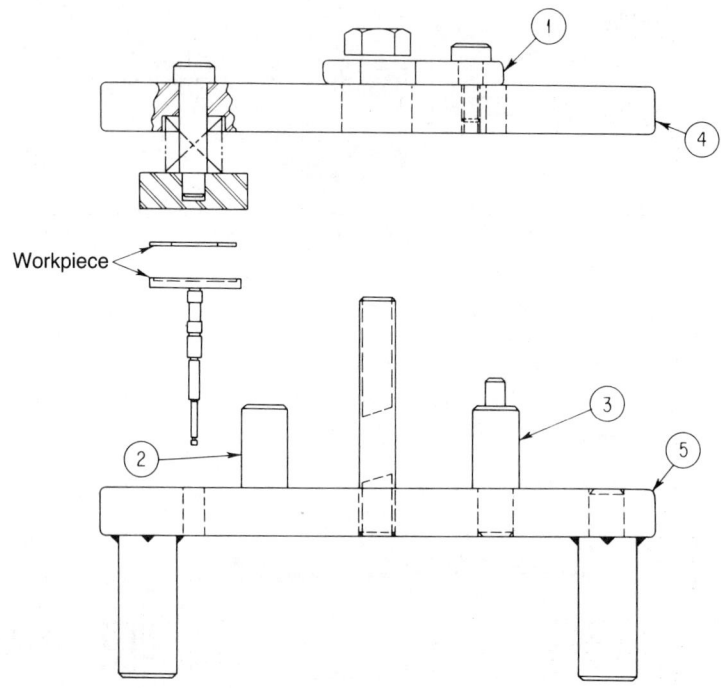

Workpiece

Fig. 15-36 Pressing fixture. (*Courtesy IBM*)

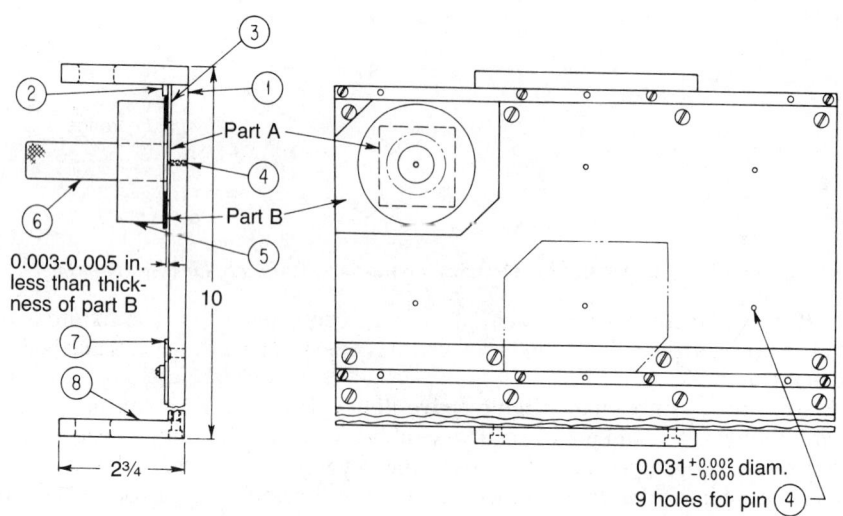

Part A

Part B

0.003-0.005 in.
less than thick-
ness of part B

10

2¾

0.031$^{+0.002}_{-0.000}$ diam.
9 holes for pin ④

Fig. 15-37 Cementing fixture. (*Courtesy General Electric Co.*)

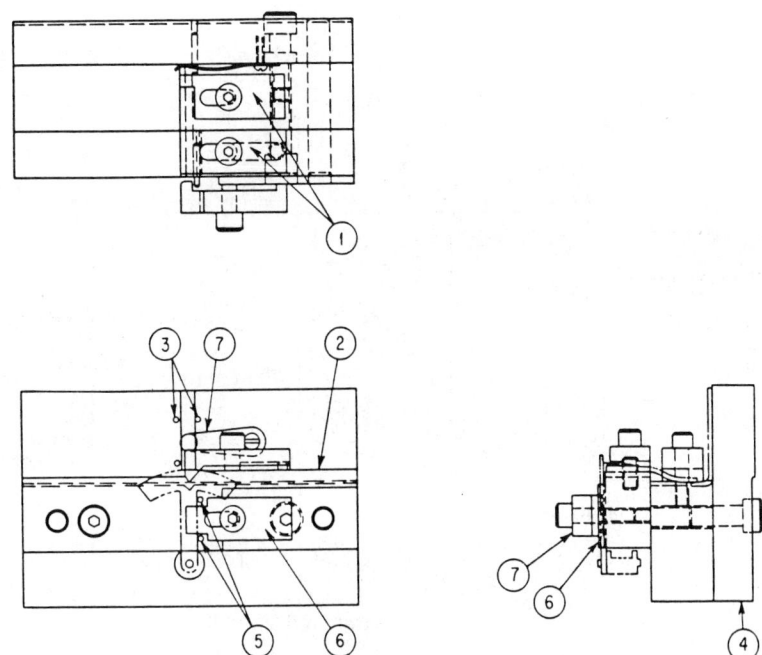

Fig. 15-38 Cementing fixture. (*Courtesy Link Aviation, Inc.*)

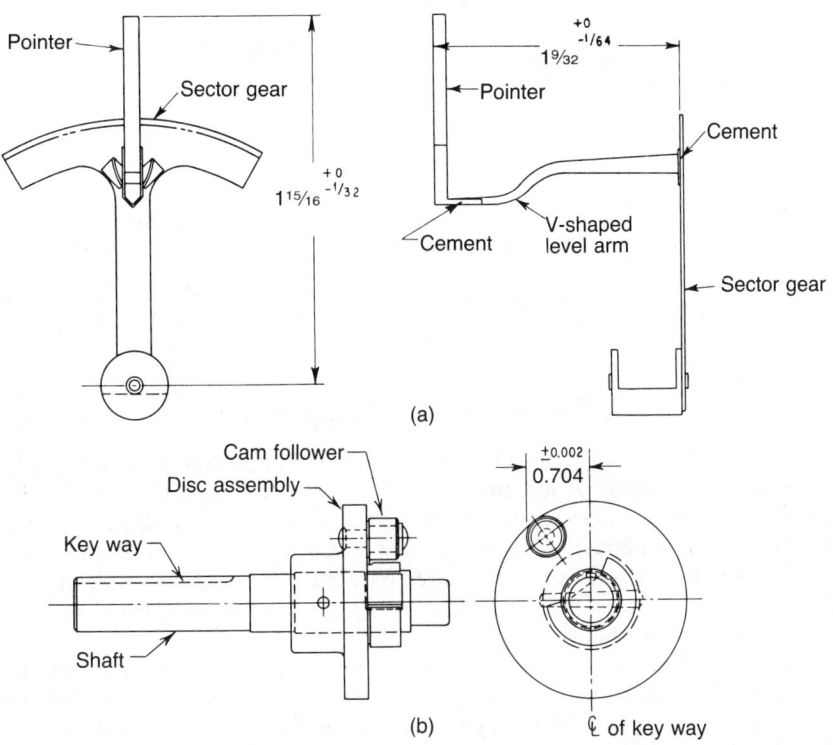

Fig. 15-39 (*a*) **Workpiece for fixture in Fig. 15-28;** (*b*) **workpiece for fixture in Fig 15-40.**

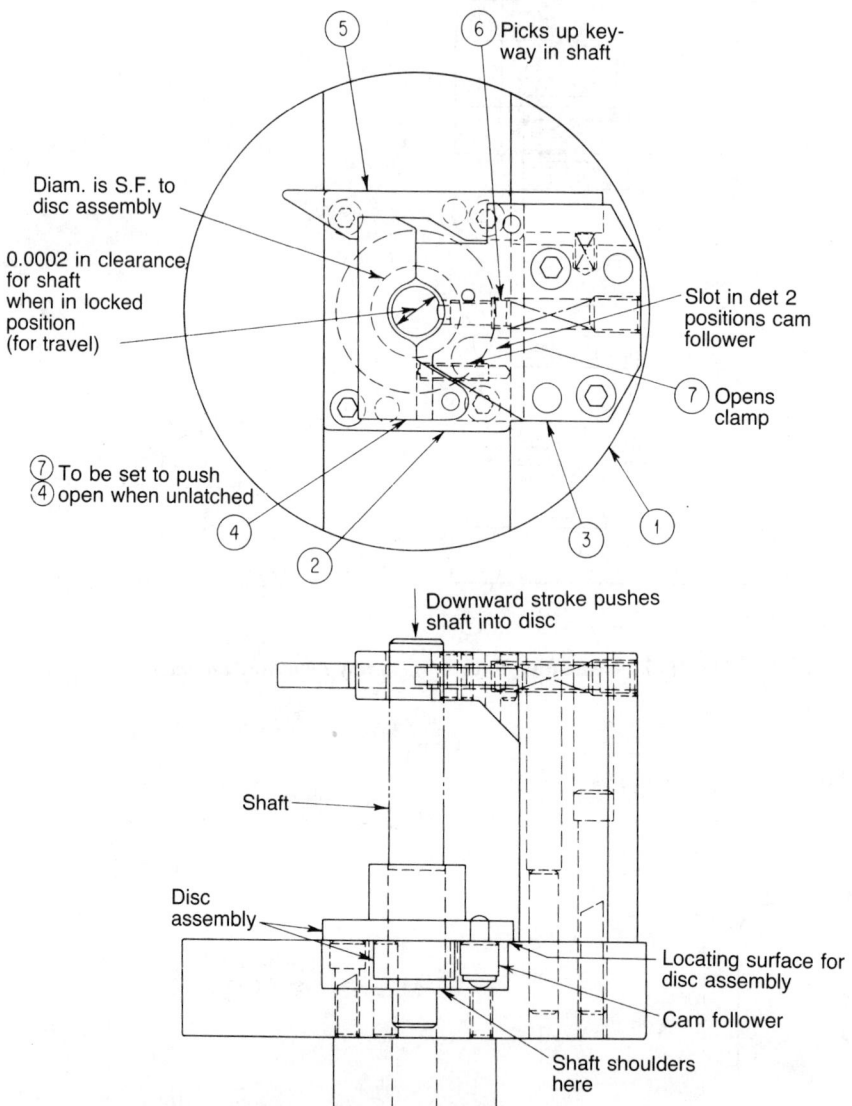

Fig. 15-40 Hydropress fixture. (*Courtesy IBM*)

The fixture consists of a base (1) on which is turned a hub that fits a center hole in the ram of a hydraulic press. A locating block (2) to position the disc and cam follower assembly is mounted on the base. Also mounted on the base is a block (3). A locating hole in this block and one in the clamp (4) are ground to allow 0.0002 in. clearance for the shaft when they are clamped and locked by a latch (5). A spring-loaded pin (6), also contained in the block, positions the keyway in the correct relationship with the cam follower of the disc assembly.

To operate, a disc assembly is placed on the locating block with the cam follower in the slot provided. While the clamp is open, a drive pulley shaft is placed in the locating hole with the locating pin in the keyway. Then the clamp is closed and locked by the latch. When the press is actuated, the downward stroke of the ram presses the shaft into the disc until its shoulder rests on the bottom of the step in the base. The length of the locating block controls the relationship of the shaft and the disc assembly. When the latch is opened, a spring plunger (7) forces the clamp open, which facilitates the removal of the completed assembly.

Air-operated Fixtures for Assembly Operations. Air-operated fixtures sometimes improve assembly operations by applying a desired amount of pressure at a predetermined rate with a simple and inexpensive fixture. Air-operated fixtures can also reduce a tedious, time-consuming assembly operation to an easy part-loading task.

The assembly fixture illustrated in Fig. 15-41 is used to insert bearing sleeves into each end of the workpieces shown and to burnish the bearing holes to the finished dimension after assembly.[4] The workpiece is located on two V-blocks which hold it in alignment with two square plungers. The plungers slide in guide blocks and are moved by actuating double-acting cylinders on both ends of the fixture. The piston travel and pressure applied by the air cylinders can be preset or adjusted to prevent damage to the workpiece.

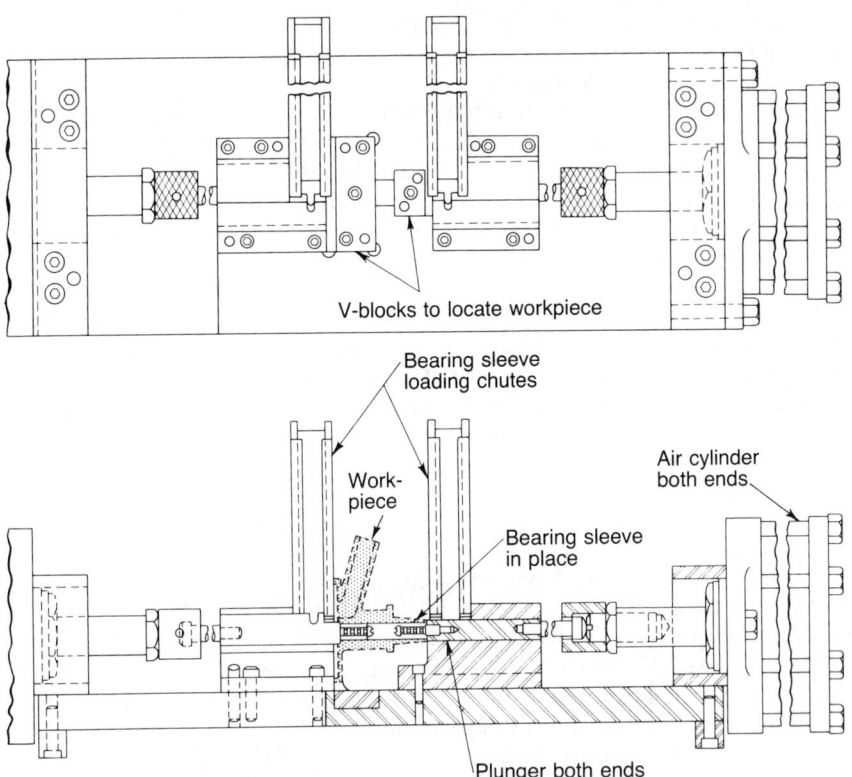

Fig. 15-41 Air-operated fixture for bearing sleeve insertion.[4]

A burnishing tool is mounted on the end of each plunger. It serves as a pilot for the bearing sleeve during insertion into the workpiece and finishes the bore in the sleeve during the completion of the air-cylinder piston's forward stroke.

The bearing sleeves are fed through two chutes, each of which drops a bearing into position in front of the plunger when it is retracted.

To operate, the two chutes are loaded with bearing sleeves. A workpiece is positioned on the two V-blocks. Two bearing sleeves are now in position in the path of the plungers. The burnishing tools on the ends of plungers pick up the bearings and insert them into the workpiece simultaneously from both ends when the air cylinders are actuated. As the plungers continue moving through the full stroke of the air cylinder, the burnishing ends are forced into the bearings which finish the bores to the proper size and alignment. When the plunger retracts completely, two more bearing sleeves drop into position. The workpiece can then be removed and another positioned on the V-blocks for another assembly cycle.

An Air-operated Jewel-setting Press. "Miniaturization," the design and manufacture of extremely small parts, is fast gaining widespread use outside of the watchmaking industry. Aircraft, missile, and space-vehicle weight and space limitations require the packaging of smaller and smaller electronic units for bombing and navigational instrument controls.

The jewel-setting press illustrated in Fig. 15-42 is an example of assembly tooling for miniature work. Five jewel bearings are pressed into a watch-pillar plate to exact depths at one and the same operation. The jewels must not be canted in the holes. Although they can be set individually by hand, it would be impossible to achieve the required depth precision by doing so.radial orientation of the pillar. Five feeding tubes (3) are vertically arranged in the base to coincide with the holes in the pillar. Inside each tube is a push rod (4) located below the end of the tube to form a pocket or nest into which a cylindrical jewel is manually inserted.

The depth to which the jewels are lowered is controlled by the position of the push rod. Each of the five push rods is individually adjusted for height by an adjustment screw (6) and a jam-lock mechanism (7). Any play or flexing of the pillar at the instant of jewel insertion would result in loss of control of seating depth. To prevent this, the upper die element mates perfectly to the pillar and has five support rods (8) which press on the pillar at the jewel-setting points. The support rods are also individually adjusted by cam rods (9) for control of penetration.

In operation, five jewels are placed in the feeding tubes, the pillar is carefully positioned, and a spring-loaded hand cam (10) is moved to close the die and lock all components in place. An air cylinder (11) in the base of the press bears against and raises a plate (12) to which the lower ends of the five push rods are fastened. The upward motion of the plate and push rods simultaneously seats the five jewels in the pillar.

A cam-type ejector (13) is provided to free the workpiece after the operation. Turning the handle forces the cam plate (14) to raise three ejector rods (15) which push the workpiece out of the next.

An Arbor Press Fixture. A bushing is to be press-fitted into a casting at a location shown in Fig. 15-43. The fixture consists of a sizing plug (1) which is mounted in the ram of an arbor press (not shown). Two strippers (5) are mounted to a plate (2) which is fastened to the base (7) by studs (8). A block (6) is pressed into this base on the center line of the ram and plug. The top of this block is a positive stop for the bushing when it is pressed into the casting. The casting is positioned on the base by around pin (3) and a diamond pin (4) for peripheral location.

The sizing plug has two functional diameters and a quill end used for mounting it in the arbor press. Diameter A is ground to a slip fit for the bushing and chamfered on the end for easy loading of the workpiece. Diameter B is ground to the ID of the bushing. When the bushing is seated on top of the block, it will be sized as diameter B is forced through it by the downward stroke of the press.

To operate, a casting is positioned on the base. A bushing is also loaded on the sizing plug with its lower end above the stripper plate while the press is at top of its stroke. During the downward stroke of the press, the bushing is seated on top of the block and sized by diameter B of the plug. On the return stroke of the press, the completed workpiece is lifted from the locating pins and stripped from the plug by the stripper block.

TAB BENDING FIXTURE

After internal components are assembled inside a sheet-metal can (see Fig. 15-44), four tabs on its end must be bent over to retain them. With the simple fixture illustrated in Fig. 15-45, the assembly can be held and the tabs bent.

It consists of a base (5) on which is mounted a block (1). A bushing (2) is a sliding fit in the loading hole in the block and serves as a stop for the workpiece. A clearance hole is provided in the bushing for wires that protrude from the assembly.

By means of four levers (3) and an anvil assembly (6), the tabs are bent over.

A lever mechanism (4) provided in the base raises the bushing to eject the part.

To operate, the four levers must be in the horizontal or loading position. The can assembly is loaded into the hole in the block until it rests on the top of the bushing. When the levers are raised to the vertical or bending position, the angular faces of the anvils bend and crimp the tabs on the workpiece to approximately a 90° setting. The operation of each lever crimps one tab.

The completed assembly is easily removed from the fixture when the handle of the ejector assembly is depressed. This forces the bushing and the workpiece to rise so that the end of the workpiece is above the top of the block.

STITCHING AND STAPLING[5]

Stitching and stapling are similar processes in that they both use U-shaped fasteners for product assembly. They differ, however, in how the fasteners are made and applied. Stitches are formed on machines that also apply them, while staples are individually preformed and applied from strips, generally with portable pneumatic tools.

Wire Stitching. Wire stitching is a fastening method in which U-shaped stitches are formed from a coil of steel wire by a machine that also applies the stitch to the materials being joined together. When the method is used to fasten together two or more pieces of metal, or to fasten one or more pieces of metal to nonmetallic materials, it is referred to as metal stitching.

Stitching Machines. There are many models of stitching machines available, two of which are shown in Fig. 15-46. View *a* is a machine with a straight, solid arm; the machine in view *b* has a deep throat (distance from the stitching point to the vertical frame of the machine). Machines are made with different throat depths and have straight, overhung, gooseneck, or other style arms to suit specific requirements. Compact stitching machines for bench or portable operation are also available.

All stitching machines feed accurate lengths of wire directly from a coil, cut and form the wire into U-shaped stitches, and then drive the stitches through the materials to be joined. The operating speeds range up to 300 stitches per minute.

A mandrel or anvil having a spring-actuated gripper holds the wire during cutoff and positions the cutoff lengths under formers. The formers bend each wire length over the mandrel to produce a U-shaped stitch and guide and support the stitch as it is driven into the work material. A driver, mounted between the formers, exerts pressure on the crown of the stitch to force it through the work material. Air jets are generally provided to eject slugs of material pushed out by the legs of the stitch.

Assembly components to be joined are placed over a clincher, mounted on an arm or bracket under the formers. The clincher turns the legs of the stitch back against the assembly after they have penetrated the work material.

An Indexing Fixture for Stitching. The indexing fixture for stitching shown in Fig. 15-47 presses ten wire terminals through both sides of a terminal strip and bends them to form the terminal shown in Fig. 15-48. This fixture is used on a double-headed stitcher.

It consists of a plate (29) upon which are mounted two holder plates (1 and 2) for the flat terminal strip. A clamp plate (1) pivots on a pin (27) and is held open for loading by

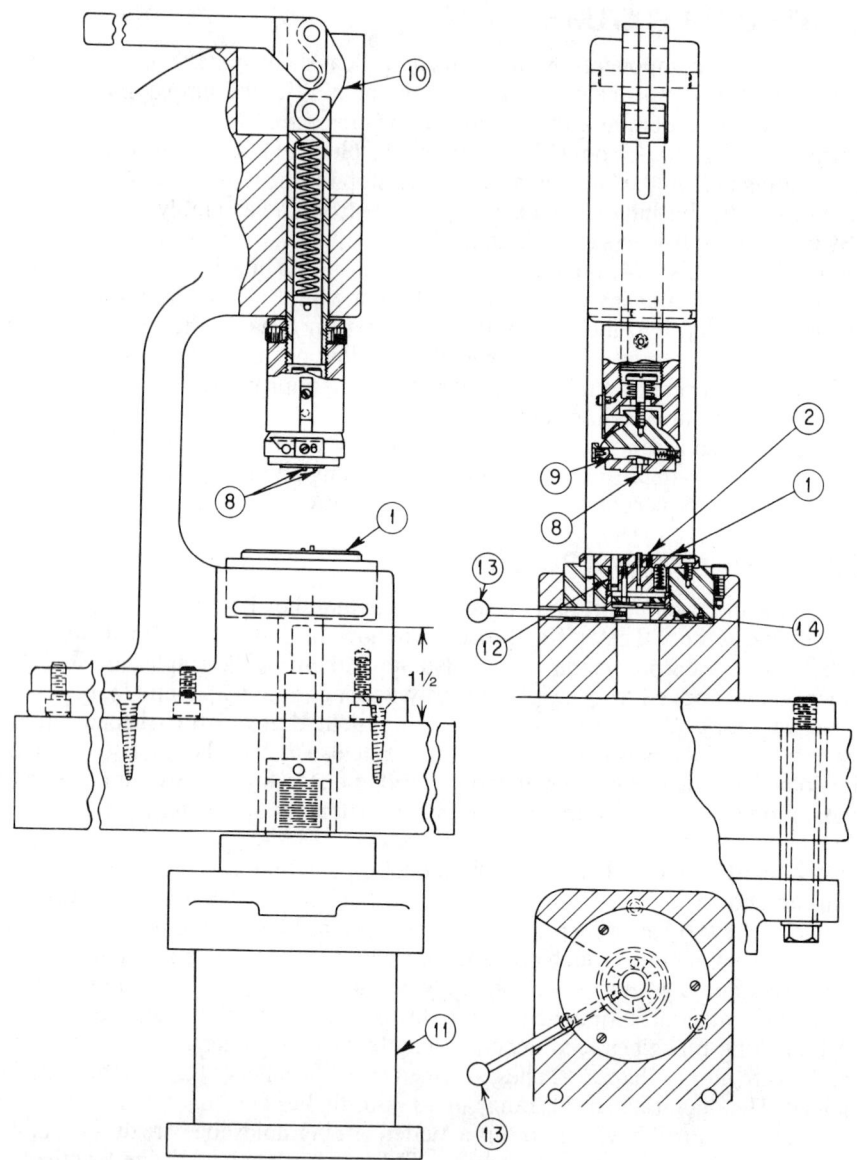

Fig. 15-42 Jewel setting press. (*Courtesy Hamilton Watch Co., U.S. patent no. 2,602,986*)

a spring plunger (28). A plate (2) slides between guide blocks (21 and 22) and is connected to the indexing mechanism by a bracket (20). The workpiece is centered against an adjustable stop (3). A handle (4) containing a starting switch (7) pivots on a pin (5) to clamp the workpiece between the plates. The handle is held in the clamping position by a spring (6). The indexing mechanism consists of a rack (14) and two pawls (12 and 13) which are moved by two solenoids (10 and 11) through a toggle pivot (15). A double-acting air cylinder (8) powers the indexing mechanism through connecting linkage (9). An upper limit switch (17) tripped by an adjustable setscrew (16), which is attached to the rack (14), starts the forward cycle of the operation. A lower limit switch (19) opened by an adjustable setscrew (18), also attached to the rack, stops its movement and ends the cycle. The fixture can be aligned with adjusting and locking screws

15-36

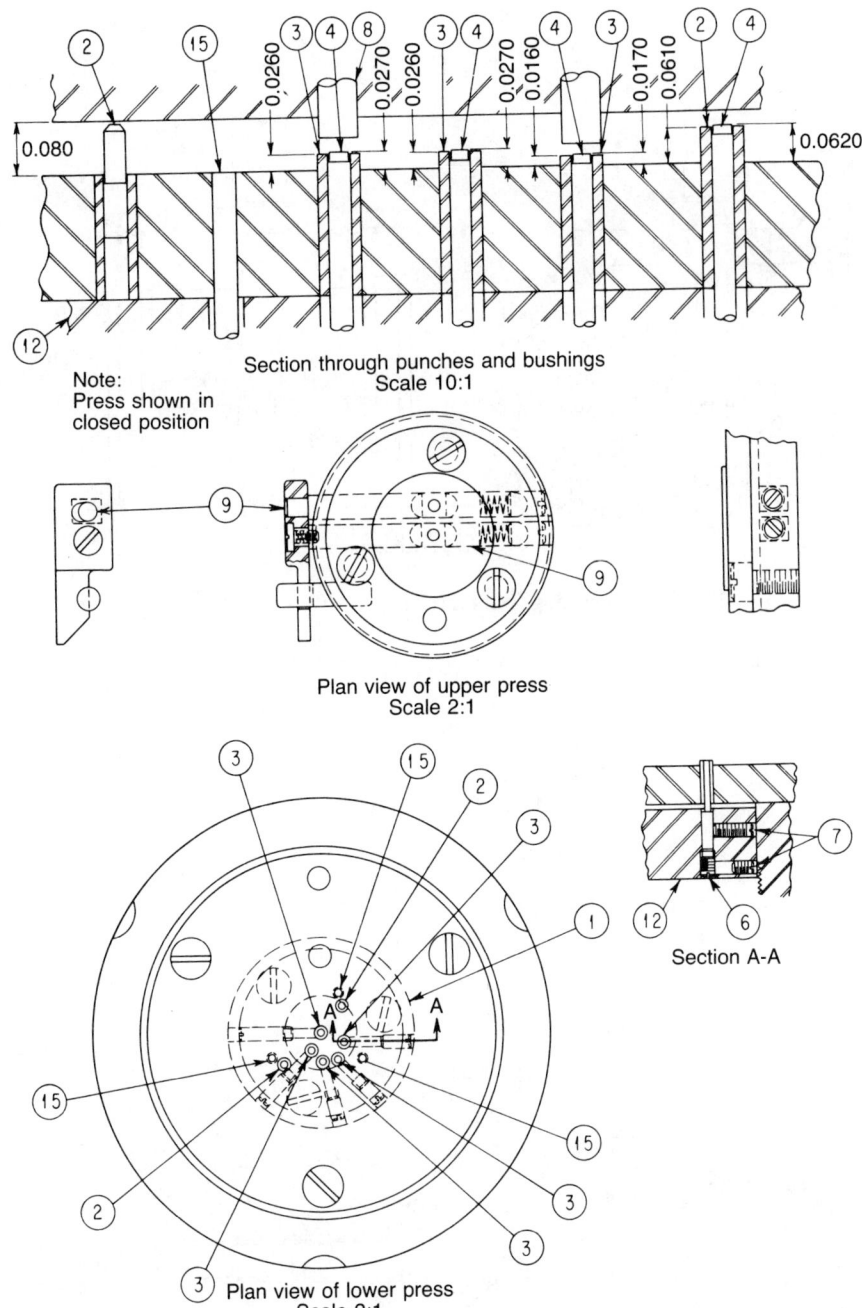

Section through punches and bushings
Scale 10:1

Note:
Press shown in
closed position

Plan view of upper press
Scale 2:1

Section A-A

Plan view of lower press
Scale 2:1

Fig. 15-42 (continued)

(23 and 24). It is clamped to the stitching machine by a block (26) and an arm (25). The two open areas in the fixture plate, *A* and *B* (29), provide clearances for the movement of the stitching anvils when the terminal wires are being assembled.

To operate, a flat terminal strip (workpiece) is inserted between the two holder plates (1 and 2). The clamp plate (1) is held open for loading by raising the handle (4). After

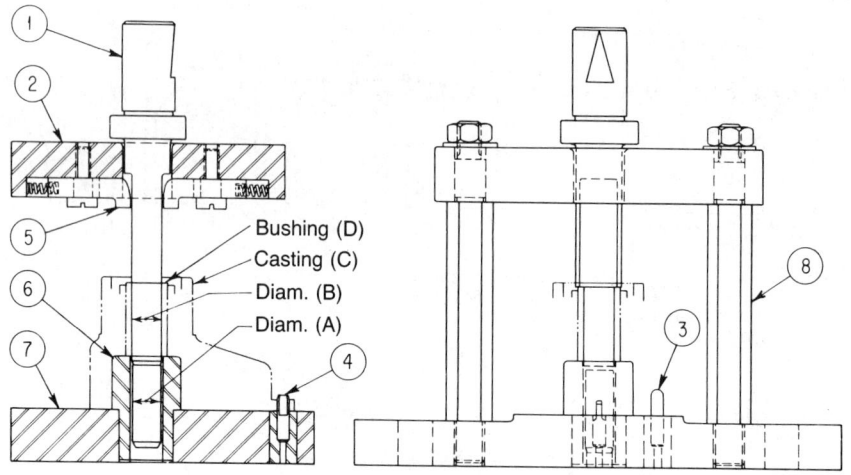

Fig. 15-43 Pressing fixture. (*Courtesy Millers Falls Co.*)

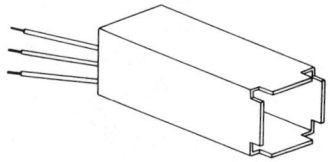

Fig. 15-44 Workpiece for fixture of Fig. 15-45.

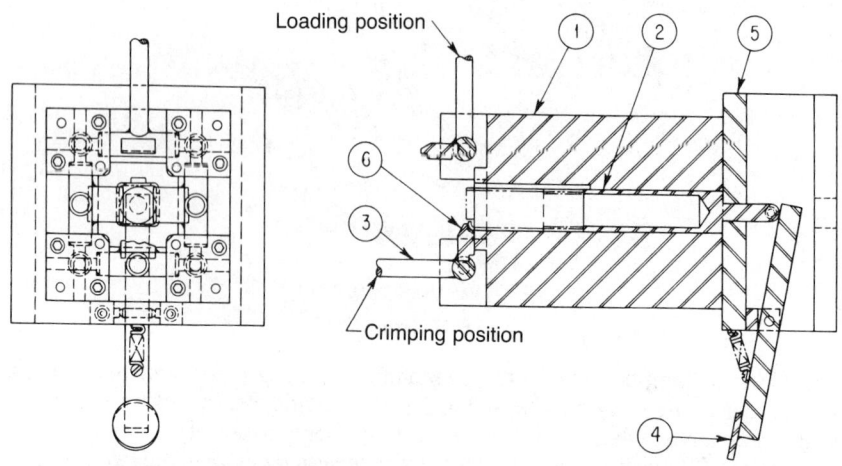

Fig. 15-45 Tab-crimping fixture. (*Courtesy IBM*)

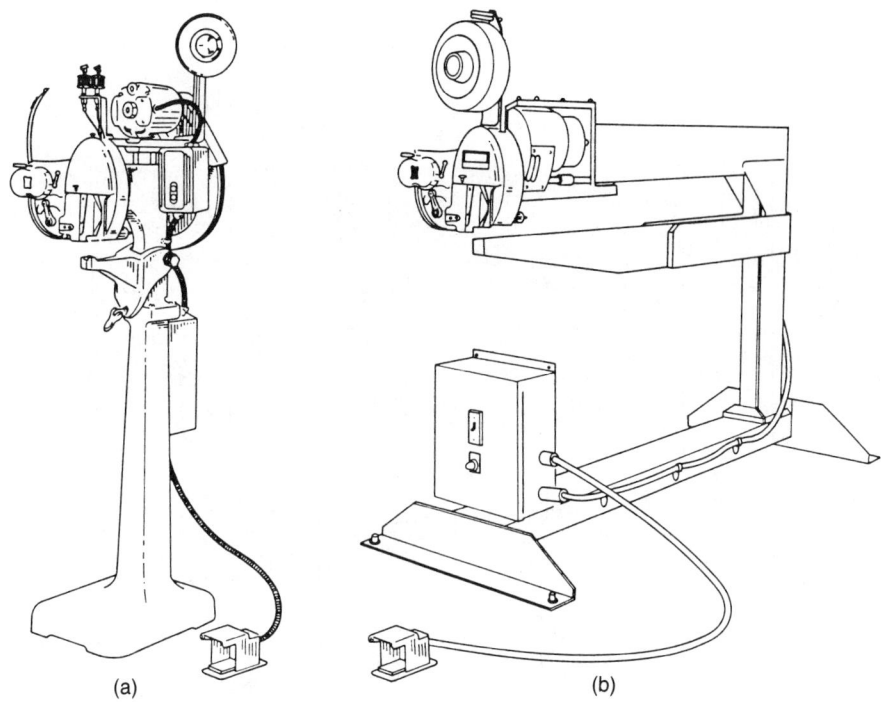

Fig. 15-46 Two types of stitching machines: (*a*) with straight, solid arm and (*b*) with deep throat.

the workpiece is centered against the adjustable stop, it is clamped by releasing the handle and allowing pressure to be exerted against it by the spring. When the starting-switch button is pressed, the air cylinder which exerts continuous pressure during the forward cycle retracts the plate (2) to the starting position. As soon as the setscrew (16) on the indexing rack (14) contacts the upper limit switch, the forward cycle begins. Two pawls (12 and 13), alternately moved by the two solenoids, engage the first notch, second notch, etc., in the indexing rack. At the completion of the cycle, a setscrew (18), also on the indexing rack, contacts the lower limit switch and shuts off the machine's motor. Then the handle is raised and the terminal assembly removed.

TOOLING FOR STAPLING

Staples used by industry for fastening applications are normally applied with pneumatic portable tools. The size of the tool is proportional to the size of the staple to be driven.

Because stapling tools are relatively small in size, they are easy to work with and easy to mount side by side in a fixtured arrangement.

A Wire-stapling Fixture for a Plastic Cover. A plastic cover is to be assembled on a switch and held in place by a formed wire staple (see Fig. 15-49). The staple is fitted in grooves over the cover and through holes in the switch body; finally, it is crimped under the body.

The staple is formed into a U-shape by the stapling machine before it is inserted in the parts.

The fixture illustrated in Fig. 15-50 has a workholding anvil (1) which locates workpieces. This anvil has two crimping grooves (2) which crimp the staple under the switch body. The anvil is mounted on a slide (3) which rides in a track (4). Two

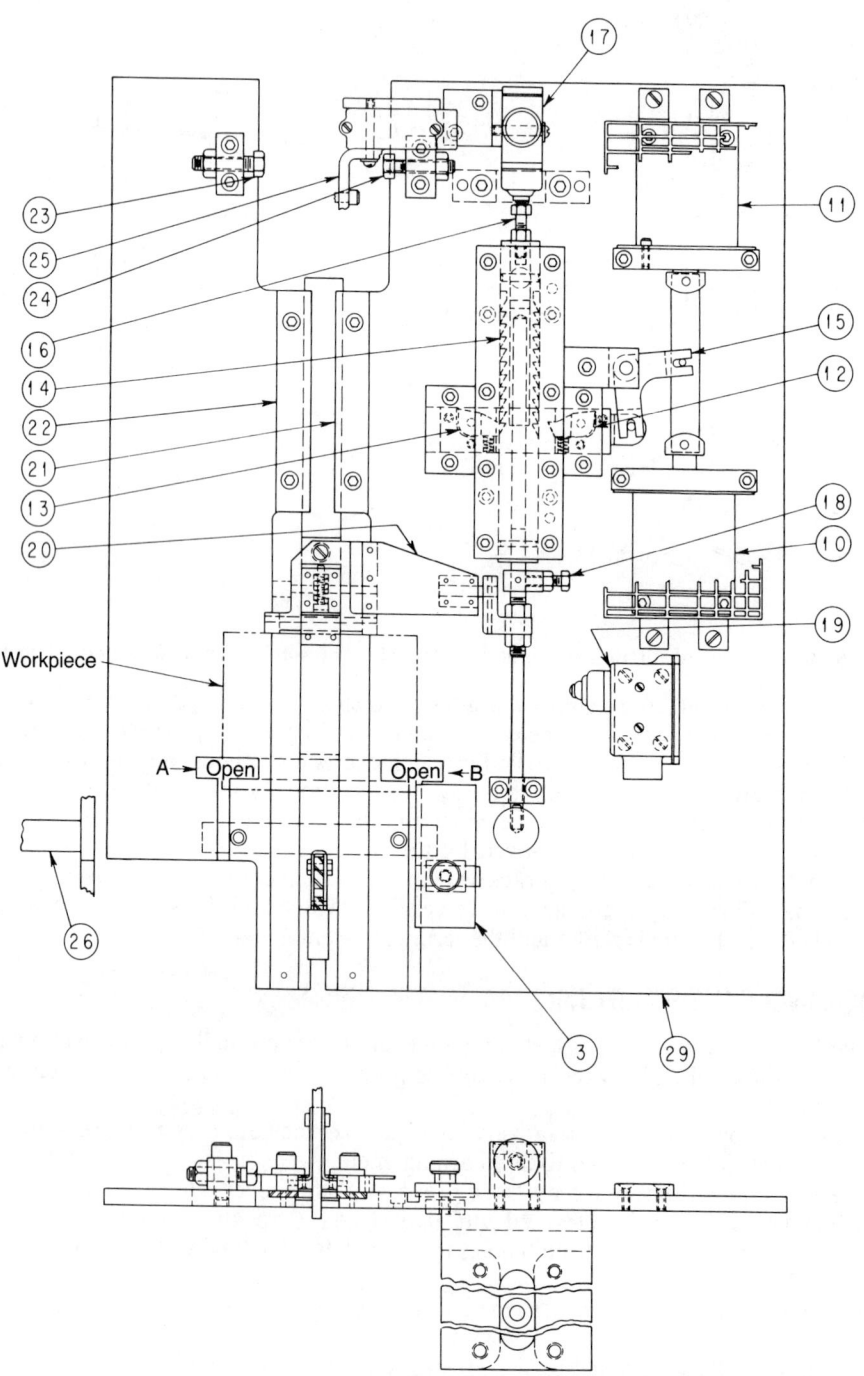

Workpiece

A → Open   Open ← B

Fig. 15-47 Indexing stitching fixture. (*Courtesy Western Electric Co., Inc.*)

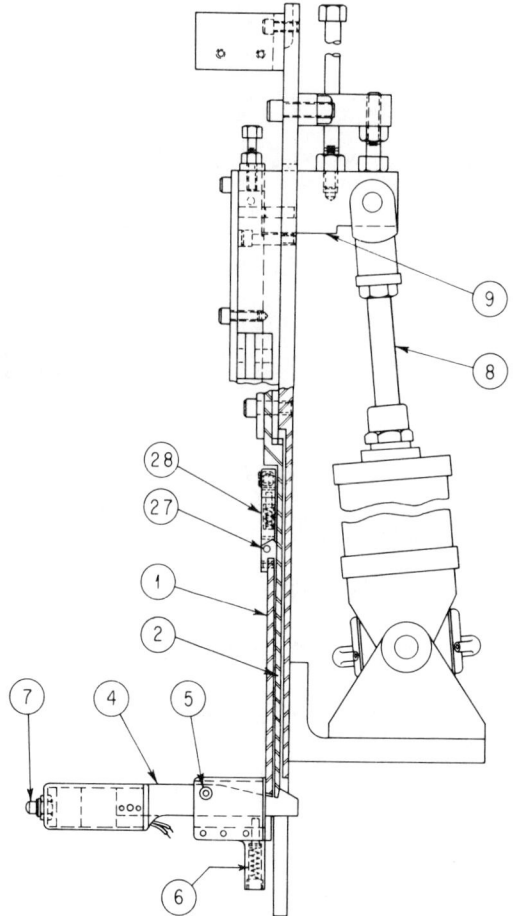

Fig. 15-47 (continued)

spring-loaded plungers (5) are located on the anvil assembly on the center line of the crimping grooves. These plungers guide the formed staple into the parts. Two cam plates (6) are mounted on either side of the track and, when the slide is pushed in, engage the plungers and push them toward the center of the anvil. A socket-head cap screw (8) and check nut, mounted on the back of the track, are adjusted to stop the slide when it is under the head of the stapling machine. The fixture is mounted on the table of the stapling machine by the mounting block (7).

To operate, the plastic cover is prepositioned on the switch body. This preassembly is then positioned on the anvil with the slide pulled out toward the operator in the loading position. When the slide is pushed in, the plungers engage the cam plates which force them in toward the anvil. When the slide contacts a stop screw (8), a limit switch (not shown) in the stapling-machine circuit is closed and the stapling head with the formed staple descends. The staple fits between the grooves in the cover and the guides on the plungers and through the holes in the switch body; it is crimped by the crimping grooves on the anvil. When the stapling head retracts, the slide can be pulled back for convenient unloading of the completed assembly and the loading of another cover and switch body.

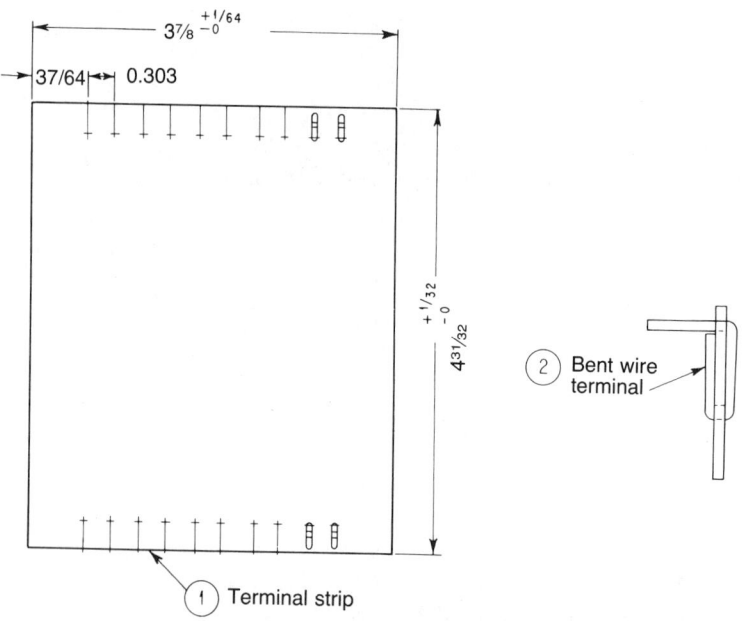

Fig. 15-48 Workpiece for fixture of Fig. 15-47.

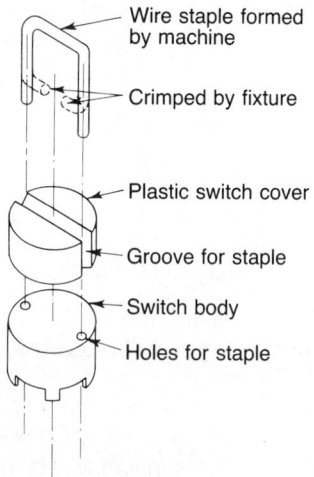

Fig. 15-49 Workpieces for fixture of Fig. 15-50.

Stapling Fixture to Hold a Fiber Terminal Strip. The fixture illustrated in Fig. 15-51 holds a fiber terminal strip (see Fig. 15-48) in a coiled position so that a steel end cap may be inserted into each end and then wire-stapled in three positions (120° apart), thus securing the caps and maintaining a cylindrical part.

The assembly illustrated in Fig. 15-52 is a case for loading coils for telephone circuits. The body of the stapling fixture holds the eyelet, end cap, and coiled terminal strip under pressure exerted by a toggle clamp (1). The opposite and unclamped end of this assembly has an end cap inserted by hand which is then presented to the wire-

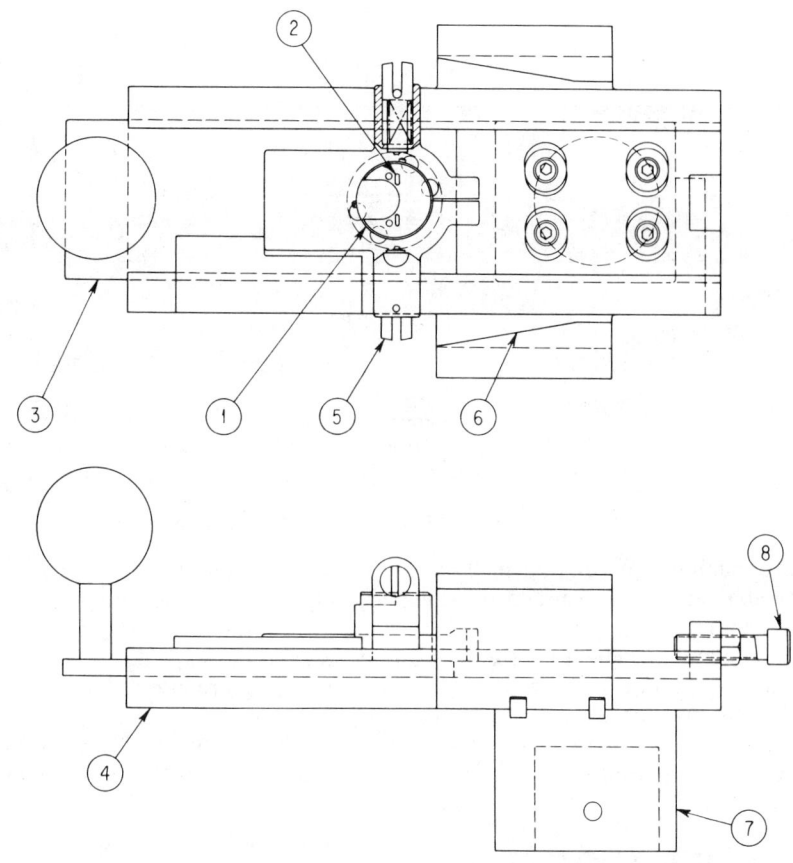

Fig. 15-50 Wire-stapling fixture. (*Courtesy International Resistance Co.*)

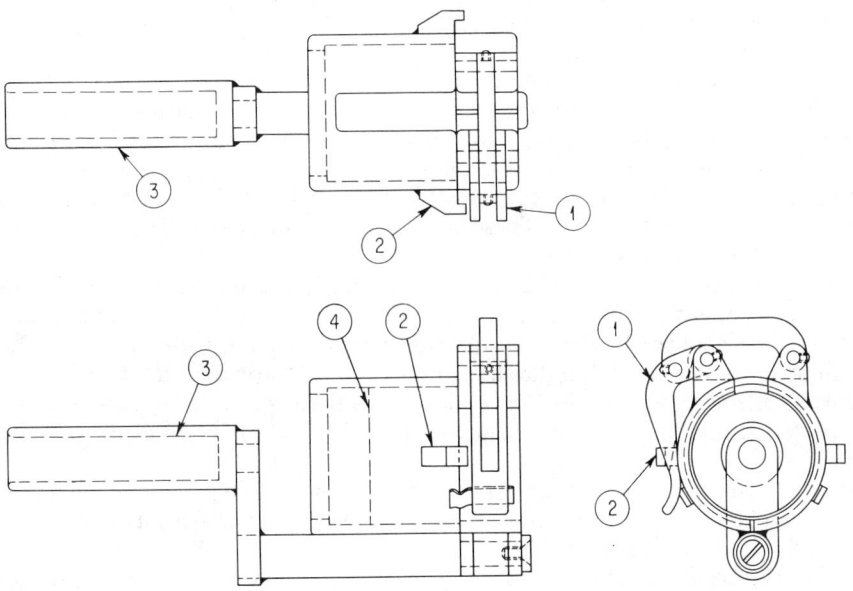

Fig. 15-51 Stapling fixture to hold a fiber terminal strip. (*Courtesy Western Electric Co., Inc.*)

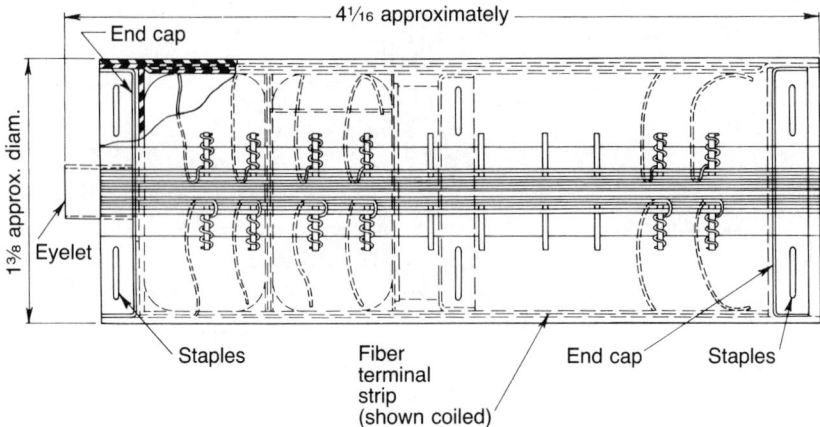

Fig. 15-52 Workpiece for fixture of Fig. 15-51.

stitching machine for stapling in three places. Orientation of the staple positions is facilitated by two keys (2) attached to the body of the fixture, which are presented to the machine with a handle (3).

After stapling one end, the assembly is released, and the stapled end is inserted into the fixture and clamped. The required coils and insulators are inserted into the tubelike case; then the end cap is inserted and similarly stapled in three places.

Spacers (4) placed in the body of the fixture permit locational adjustment for different length eyelets. End caps can also be stapled and positioned at any point within the case.

SPECIAL HOLDING FIXTURES

Assembly Fixtures Using Ball-and-Socket Arms. Figures 15-53 through 15-55 show fixtures for holding various parts during assembly. These fixtures securely hold a main component of an assembly at a convenient angle in order that other parts can be assembled to it. With the main component held securely, the assembly operator has the use of both hands in performing the assembly operations. An adjustable arm or work positioner, commercially available, is used with all three of these fixtures. The arm has a simple ball-and-socket joint which is clamped by friction locking force. When the locking pressure is released, the ball can move freely in three planes and can be locked at any desired angle and position. These arms can be obtained in different sizes that will hold up to 1,000 lb (454 kg).

Adjustable Assembly Holding Fixture. The fixture shown in Fig. 15-53 is adjustable for different sizes of assemblies, since the arms (1 and 2) can be adjusted to different widths on the slide bar (3). The arms are then clamped in place with screws (4). Hooks (5) can be moved in and out in the slots of the arms for parts of different lengths. The slide bar is attached to the positioner (6). It can be raised or lowered to different heights on a post (7) and clamped with a handwheel (8). The post is assembled to a suitable base.

Assembly Holding Fixture With 360° Rotation. The holding fixture shown in Fig. 15-54, in addition to the movements provided by the positioner, permits 360 ° rotation of the workpiece about a vertical axis.

The workpiece is located on locating pins (1 and 2) and then secured with clamps (3). The rotary-table base (4) can turn 360° through a post (5) and a bushing (6). The base is then clamped in the desired position by a clamp arm (7).

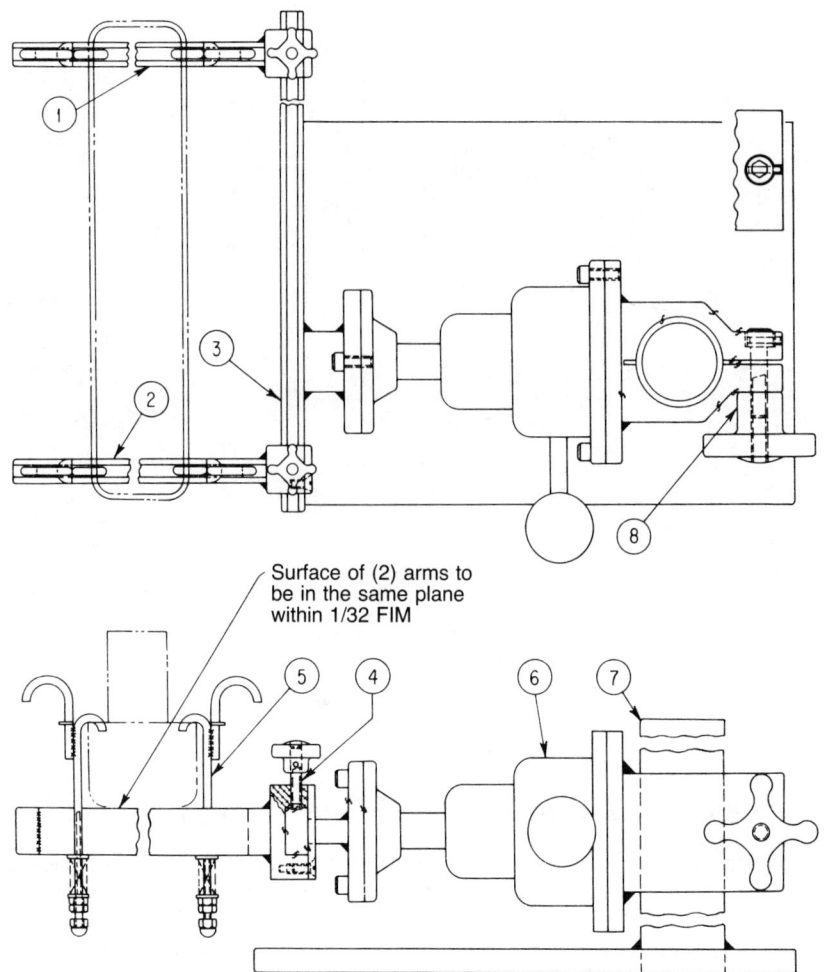

Fig. 15-53 **Adjustable assembly holding fixture.** (*Courtesy IBM*)

Assembly Holding Fixture For Electronic Parts. The fixture shown in Fig. 15-55 holds a connector and electronic assembly while wires are being soldered into the connector. The connector is inserted into the holder (1), and the electronic assembly is held above the connector by pins (2 and 3). These pins go through the mounting holes, raising the assembly above the normal mounting height from the connector. This provides clearance to solder the wires into the connector pins.

Modular Vises. Figure 15-56 illustrates how the standard components of one commercially available modular vise system can be combined to provide quick solutions to many assembly workholding problems.

A (Ball Detent) Assembly Fixture. When a ball detent is to be assembled in a blind hole between an inner housing and an outer housing, the ball is spring-loaded from the outer housing to a spherical seat in the inner housing.

The inserting tool shown in Fig. 15-57 is an arbor (3) whose pilot diameter *B* is a slip fit for the bore of the outer housing. The diameter *A* is a slip fit for the smaller bore of the inner housing. A slot in the arbor holds a pivoted lever (2). A magnet (1) is press-fit into a hole in this lever.

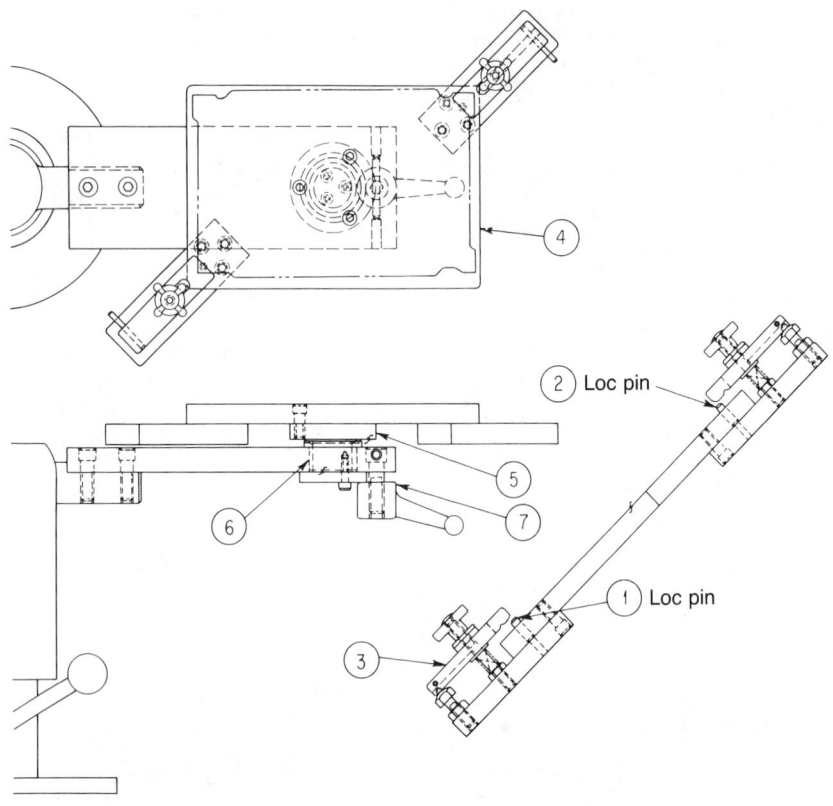

Fig. 15-54 Assembly-holding fixture with 360° rotation. (*Courtesy IBM*)

To operate, the steel ball is placed on the cupped end of the magnet in the lever. The outer housing is slipped on the arbor, locating on the *B* diameter, and stopped against the shoulder *F*. The ball is now correctly positioned from the end of the outer housing. The lever is pressed, and the housing is rotated until the ball contacts the blind hole. Pressing on the lever holds the ball in the hole against the spring tension. The inner housing is next guided into the outer housing by the *A* diameter of the arbor. After the inner housing contacts the surface *C*, it is pushed from the opposite end of the outer housing. The ball is held in the blind hole by the OD of the inner housing. When the inner housing is seated in the counterbore of the outer housing, it is rotated until the ball rests in the spherical seat. The assembly is now complete.

An Internal Retaining-ring Assembly Fixture. A snap ring is compressed, inserted into a length of tubing, and seated in a groove inside the tube with the fixture illustrated in Fig. 15-58. It consists of two spring-loaded slides (1) which have a circular groove for the snap ring (workpiece). The outer edges of the slides are tapered.

The base (2) of the fixture, which is mounted on a small arbor press, locates the tubing under the ram inserting tool (3).

The inserting tool, which is mounted in the arbor press, mates with the outer edges of the slides and has a pilot that is a slip fit in the ID of the tubing.

The tubing is placed down into the base and against the locating surfaces (5 and 4). The snap ring is then positioned by hand between the slides and located in the circular groove. When the ram is brought down, the inserting tool engages the slides, forcing them in and squeezing the snap ring into a diameter small enough to fit inside the tubing. As the inserting tool continues down, it pushes the snap ring out of the slides and

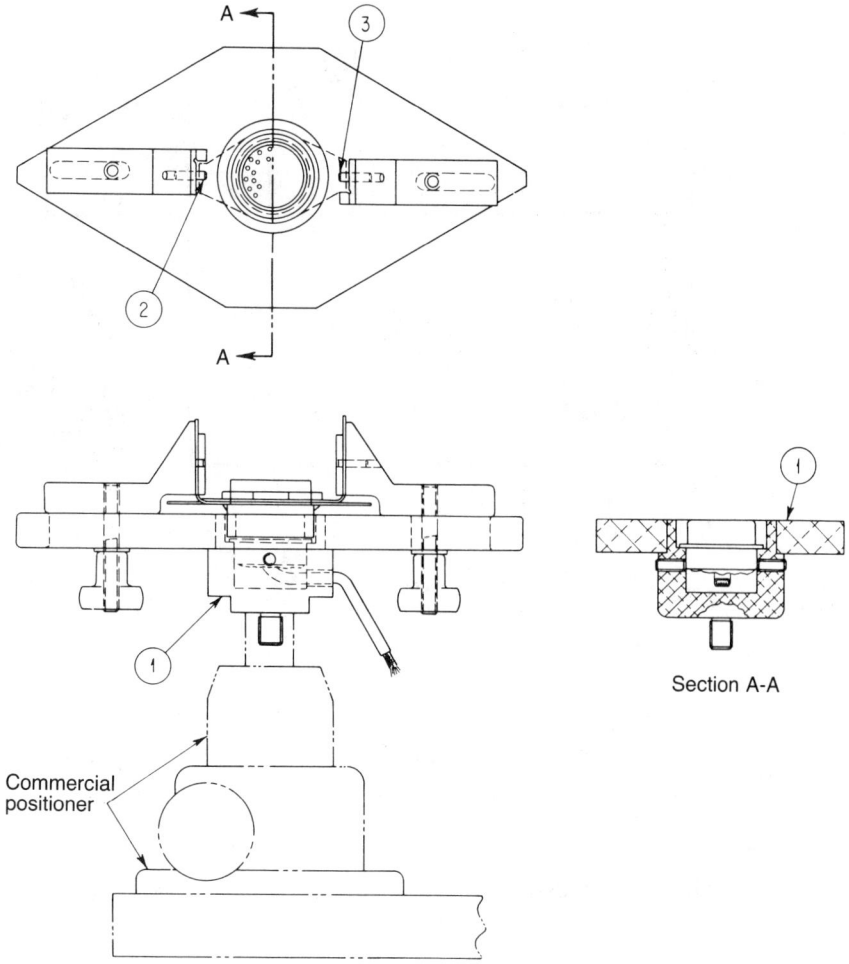

Fig. 15-55 Assembly-holding fixture for electronic parts. (*Courtesy IBM*)

Section A-A

Commercial
positioner

down into the tubing until it snaps into place in the groove inside the tubing.

The tool is then retracted and the slides move out to loading position for insertion of another snap ring. The assembled tube and ring can then be removed from the base of the fixture.

A Setscrew-loading Fixture. A socket setscrew (1), illustrated in Fig. 15-59, is to be inserted and partially threaded into the recessed hub of a workpiece. The tapped hole in the hub is too deep in the recess for convenient loading of the setscrew by hand.

The fixture consists of a drum (2) fastened to a right-angle plate which can be secured to a stand or bench. The OD of the drum is a slip fit for the inside of the workpiece. A spring-loaded plunger (3) is mounted in a hole in the drum that is a slip fit for the hub (4) on the workpiece. The plunger is retained with a pinned collar (5). Also in the drum are a hole for loading the setscrew and a slot by means of which the workpiece, with its setscrew protruding from the hub, can be removed from the fixture.

To operate, a setscrew is dropped into the hole in the drum. The spring plunger, in released position, covers this hole and prevents the screw from falling through. Then the workpiece is loaded onto the drum. When the workpiece is seated against the end of the

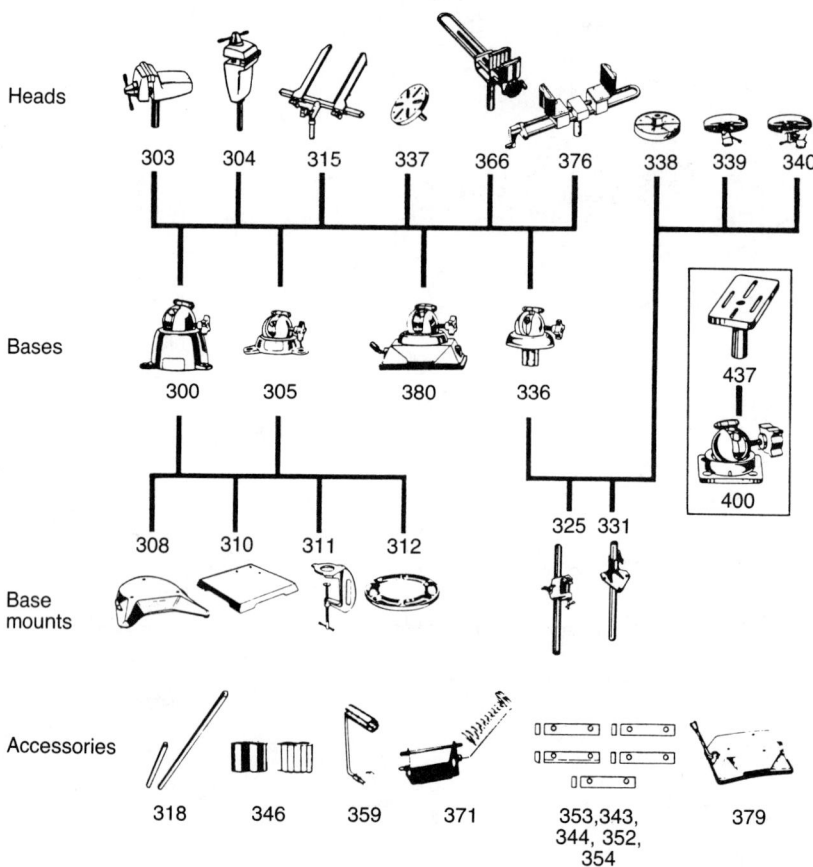

Fig. 15-56 Modular vises. (*Courtesy Panavise Products, Inc.*)

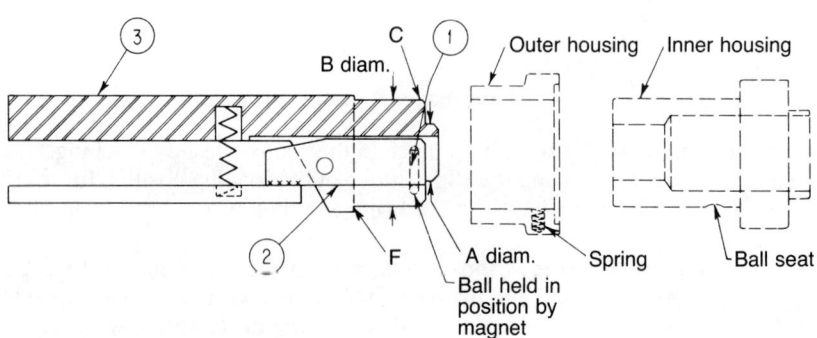

Fig. 15-57 Ball-detent assembly fixture. (*Courtesy SME Denver Chapter 77*)

drum, the hub retains the setscrew. It may be necessary to rotate the part until the setscrew drops into the tapped hole. A hex wrench can then be inserted through a clearance hole in the part and through the loading hole in the drum to turn the setscrew. When the screw is partially set, the part can be removed. The slot in the drum allows the setscrew to pass without being turned all the way into the part.

Assembly Fixtures for Screw Fastening. The simple design of the fixture of

15-48

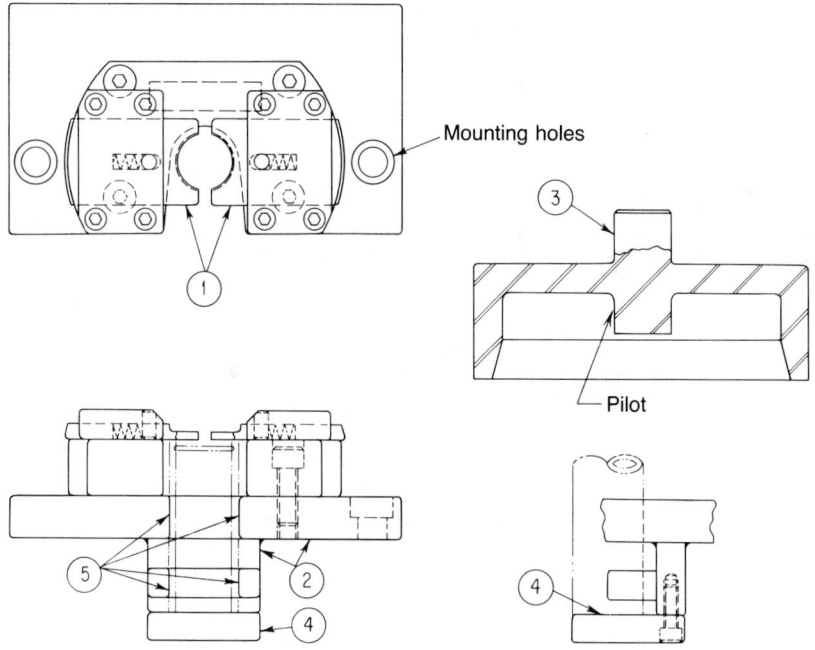

Fig. 15-58 Internal retaining-ring assembly fixture. (*Courtesy SME Denver Chapter 77*)

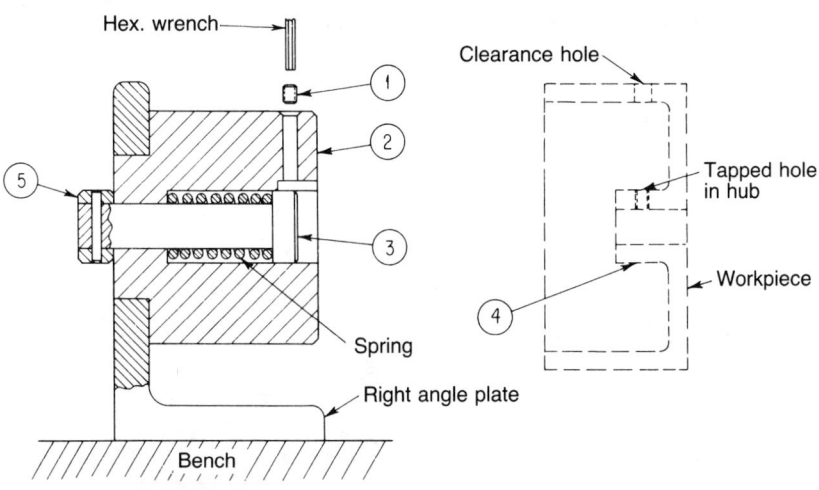

Fig. 15-59 Setscrew-loading fixture. (*Courtesy Torrington Co.*)

Fig. 15-60 can be adapted for the assembly of various types of parts held together by screws or bolts. The bench assembly of parts by unskilled labor using air-operated or manual nut spinners or screwdrivers can be easily and speedily accomplished with modifications of this fixture design. The base incorporates nests for hexagon head screws and locators for the two plates that correctly align the plates while the nuts are tightened. The completed assembly is lifted off the locators, and the fixture is again loaded with screws and plates.

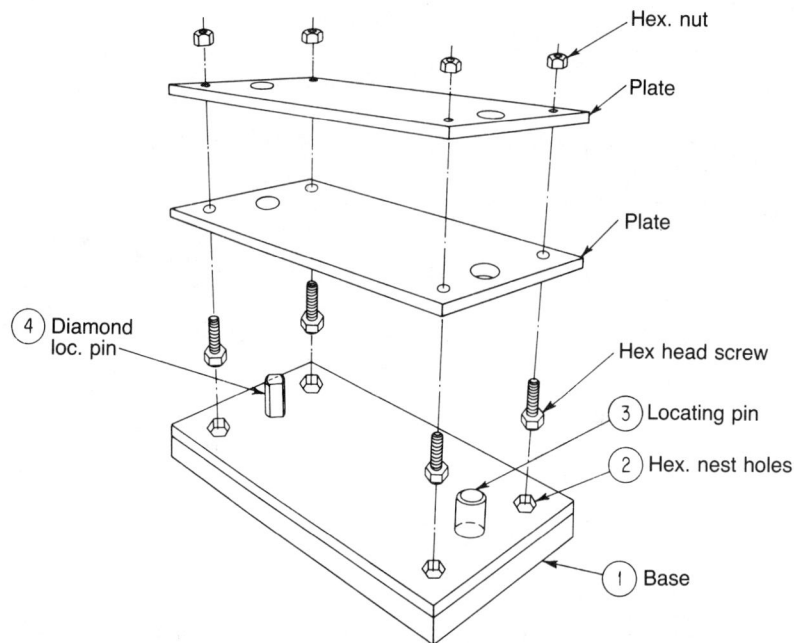

Fig. 15-60 Fixture for screwed assembly. (*Courtesy IBM*)

The fixture shown in Fig. 15-61 is used when two or more parts are to be fastened together with standard head screws. The parts must also be held in correct relation to each other. Parts *A*, *B*, and *C* are to be fastened together in this manner.

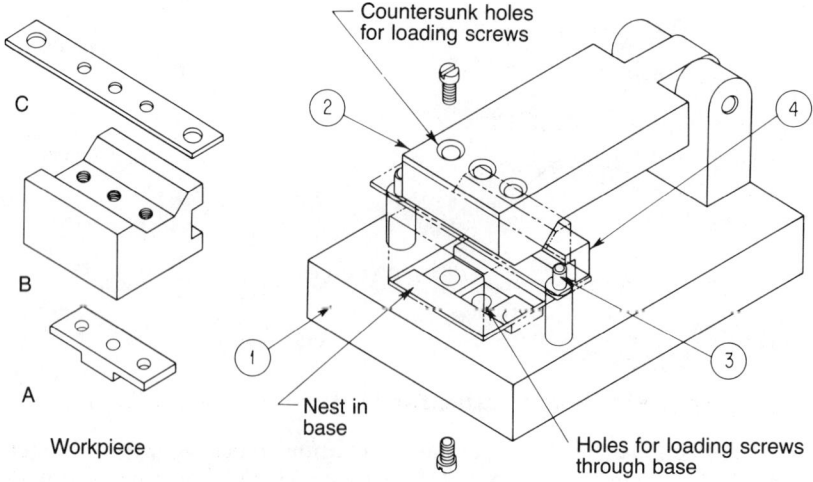

Fig. 15-61 Fixture for screwed assembly. (*Courtesy South Bend Controller Co.*)

The fixture consists of a base (1) machined to nest parts *A* and *B*. Three holes are located in the base for loading screws. Two locating pins (3) are positioned on the base to locate part *C*. An error-proof block (4) correctly orients part *B*. A hinged leaf (2) has three holes for loading screws and is machined to hold the three parts together. The leaf also serves as a rest surface when screws are being loaded through the base.

To operate, the jig is set on the base with the leaf open. The parts are positioned, and the leaf is closed. The leaf now holds the parts together. Three screws are dropped into the holes in the leaf and driven with a power screwdriver. The jig is turned over, and three screws are driven through the base in the same manner. The leaf is opened, and the assembly is removed.

A Deep-hole Multiple O-ring Inserter. The problem of inserting O-rings into internal grooves in internal bores increases as the depth of the bore increases in proportion to the ID.

An assembly calling for six O-rings to be more or less equally spaced along the inside of a ⅞-in. bore that is over 7 in. (177.8 mm) in length is shown in Fig. 15-62. As this is part of a production-valve assembly, a fast means of inserting the O-rings was devised to assure complete seating of all six O-rings.

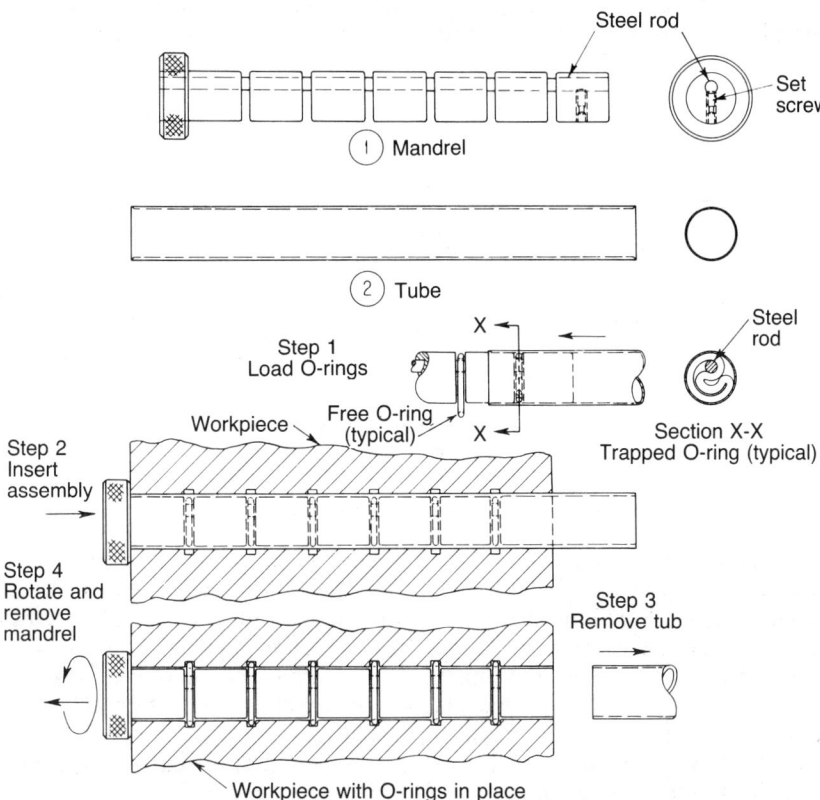

Fig. 15-62 O-ring insertion fixture. (*Courtesy Sunstrand, Denver*)

A mandrel (1) is made up of nylon sections equally spaced and eccentrically located along the length of a steel rod and attached by setscrews. For ease of handling, the mandrel has a knurled head. The length of the nylon sections corresponds to the O-ring seat spacing in the valve body (workpiece), and the OD of the nylon sections is slightly less than the ID of the O-rings. The OD of the thin-walled steel tube (2) is made a sliding fit for the valve-body bore, and the ID is made a sliding fit over the nylon sections of the mandrel.

15-51

To operate, six lubricated O-rings are loaded onto the mandrel, each hanging loosely in its slot. The steel tube is then started over the end of the mandrel. As shown in section X-X, each O-ring is doubled back into its slot and trapped as the tube slides over it until the tube stops against the mandrel knob.

The assembled mandrel and tube are then inserted into the bore of the valve body (workpiece) until the knurled head of the mandrel is against the end of the workpiece. The tube is then pulled out of the far end of the bore. The released O-rings pop into their respective grooves. The mandrel is then removed, and the assembly is complete.

Should any of the O-rings not be fully seated, the mandrel cannot be removed. Rotation of the mandrel by its knurled knob will force the off-center steel rod to remove any kinks in the O-rings, allowing the mandrel to be easily removed and indicating 100 per cent seating of the O-rings.

A Plastic Holding Fixture. Figure 15-63 shows a holding fixture made from layers of plastic casting resins and glass cloth. It nests a casting having irregular contours in a comfortable working position while another part is assembled to it. The molding of plastic fixtures around a part is often inexpensive compared with the required machining of fixtures to hold some irregular contours. The best sequence to follow when making plastic tooling is to build the tool and then draw the design according to the existing tool.

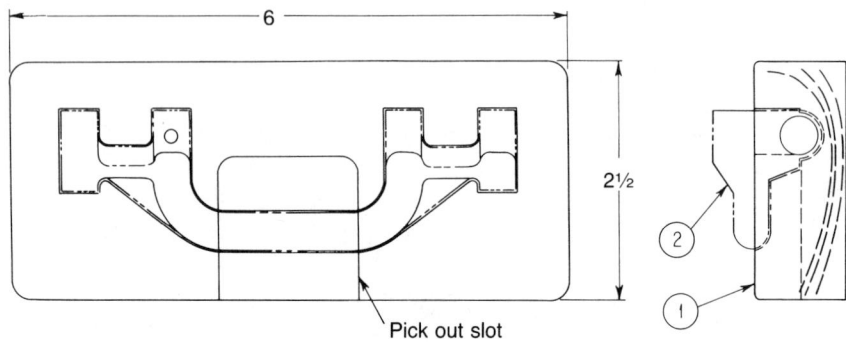

Fig. 15-63 Plastic holding fixture. (*Courtesy IBM*)

A form or mold is made from cardboard to the outside contour of the fixture (1). The mold and the part (2) are coated with wax. After the casting resin is mixed according to the manufacturer's directions, it is poured into the bottom of the mold, together with three or four alternate layers of glass cloth, to the required depth. The parting line of the part should be approximately 1/32 in. (0.79 mm) above the top of the fixture. Then a part is pressed into the plastic and glass-cloth mixture and leveled. The plastic is allowed to cure. After curing is completed, the plastic fixture is removed from the mold. The base of the fixture is machined parallel with the top of the part. A pick-out slot is also machined in the fixture, which completes its fabrication.

Support Legs. When components must be assembled to both sides of a panel, three sets of simple leg assemblies, such as those shown in Fig. 15-64, can hold the assembly securely. The assembly can then be turned over easily for working from the opposite side. These legs can be left on until this subassembly is assembled into the final unit, as it provides a way for the assembly to be stored on a shelf without damage.

Top and bottom legs (1 and 2) are made from aluminum bars. A stud (4) is a slip fit in each leg and pinned in place by a pin (3), or it may be brazed in place. The extended portion of each stud is threaded into each top leg. A flanged nut (5) secures each leg to the assembly (workpiece).

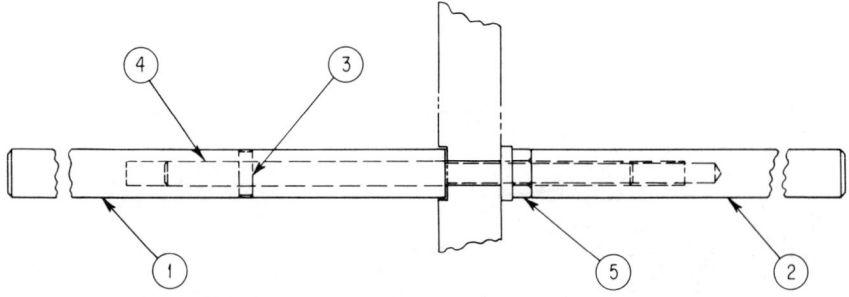

Fig. 15-64 Support legs as fixture. (*Courtesy IBM*)

Wire Harness Boards. The assembly of single wires into a completed harness or cable is facilitated by a wire harness board. Figure 15-65*a* illustrates such a tool, which is composed of three sheets of ¾-in. (19.1 mm)-thick plywood, each 4 × 8 ft (1.22 × 2.44 m). Nails or special pins with grooves are driven into the board at terminal and bend positions. The paths of the wires are painted on the boards.

Riser blocks with pins at areas 851, 870, and 882 provide for special terminal and contouring considerations in another plane. Wire code number applied to the layout and a wiring list at *A* complete the tool. The assembled wires are laced and taped before removal from the tool.

Smaller harness layouts, Fig. 15-65*b* and *c*, on smaller plywood boards are made with an actual-size print of the part drawing glued to the base. Varnish or shellac is applied to the surface to reduce wear. Nails or special pins are driven into the base at the terminal and bend positions through the attached part print.

Harness areas or terminal sections in which variations are required from one part to another can be facilitated by modules. These are removable and replaceable board sections which can be accurately relocated to provide the harness with such variations as a terminal fan of 6, 12, or 20 wires.

Potting or Encapsulating Fixtures. In the electronics industry, many types of electrical connectors are potted. Potting is the process of enclosing soldered connections, as in a connector, with a protective material, such as plastic, rubber, or similar material.

The potting fixture shown in Fig, 15-66 is actually a holding fixture for a cable with six connectors on it (one of which is shown).

The connectors are placed in the holes in the holding block and retained by the thumbscrews along the sides. The potting compound can then be poured into the connectors while they are held rigidly in place. The holes in this type of fixture can be varied to suit any combination or position of connectors on a cable.

A Lens and Holder Assembly Fixture. The fixture of Fig. 15-68 is used with an operation to twist and crimp four ears to hold a lens on a holder plate, as shown in Fig. 15-67.

A loose lens is positioned on a spring-loaded plunger (1). A mounting plate with four vertical tabs is inverted and nested between three pins (2) and a pusher spring (3). The four tabs to be twisted and crimped are in line with slots in four anvils (4). Each anvil serves as a shaft within a spur gear (5) which is meshed with a ring gear (6).

After a platen (7) is brought down lightly by a foot-treadle assembly, an air cylinder (8) is actuated and an end pad (9) contacts an arm (10). This motion rotates the ring gear, forcing the anvils to revolve. Thus, the tabs are twisted to a preset position which can be varied by the adjustable stops (11).

After the tabs are twisted, platen pressure can give additional crimping action if required.

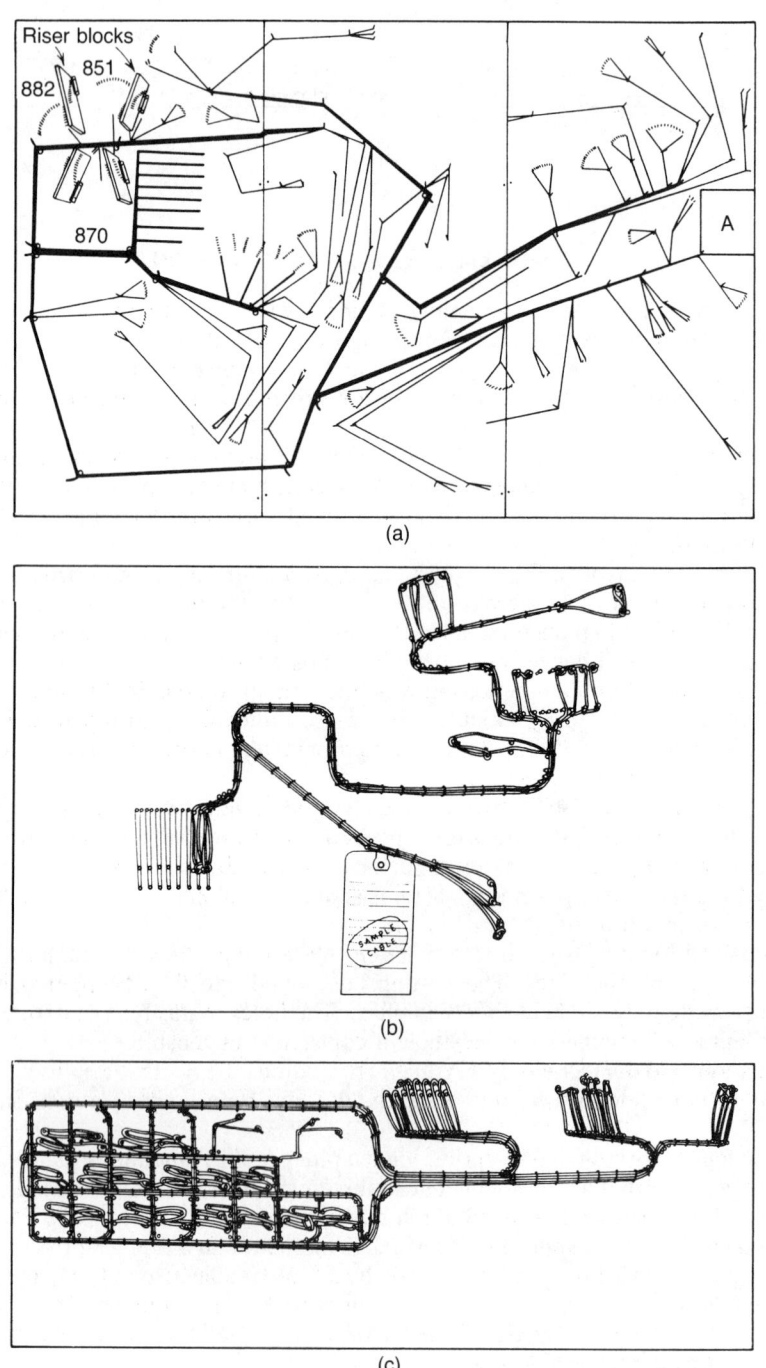

Fig. 15-65 Wire harness boards. (*Courtesy Link Aviation, Inc.*)

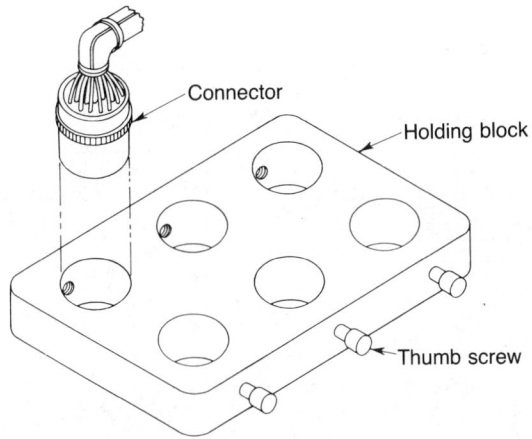

Fig. 15-66 Potting fixture. (*Courtesy IBM*)

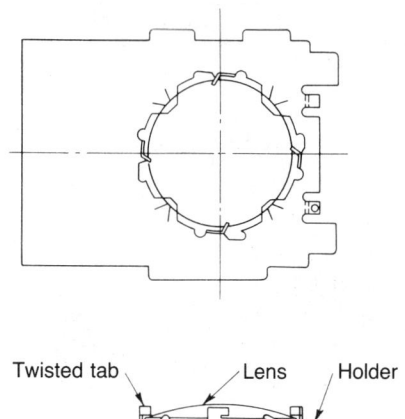

Twisted tab   Lens   Holder

Fig. 15-67 Workpieces for fixture of Fig. 15-68.

Trunnion Holding Fixture for Rotating a Large Assembly. A trunnion holding fixture, such as the one illustrated in Fig. 15-69, is designed to hold a large part or assembly in several different planes while other parts are assembled to it.

The fixture shown consists of a body or framework (1) which is made from square tubing of welded construction.

On one end of the fixture, a mounting plate (4) is fastened to a shaft (5) that is rotated by a worm gear (2) and a work pinion (3). With a worm-gear drive, an assembly can be rotated 360° without operator fatigue. Heavy unbalanced parts or assemblies can be easily turned and will not slip past a stop. A handle (6) may be placed on either end of the worm for right- or left-hand operation of the fixture.

The workpiece is positioned and clamped to the mounting plate with two screws (7) which are threaded into tapped holes in the mounting plate through two locating holes in the workpiece.

The support block (8), mounted on the opposite end of the fixture, is machined to fit a hub on the end of the workpiece. A very long or extra-heavy part or assembly needs support at both ends. The block may be replaced with a free-turning mounting-plate assembly to be clamped to a workpiece.

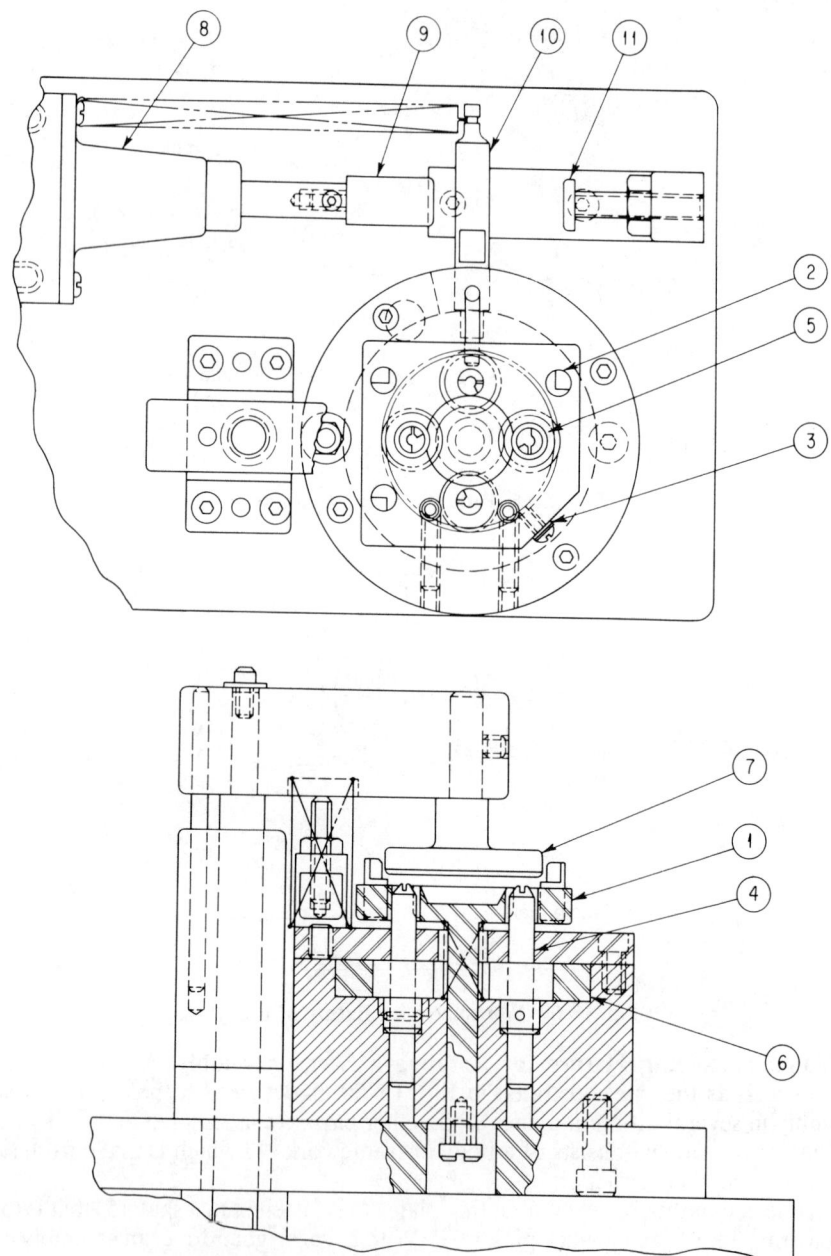

Fig. 15-68 Lens and holder assembly fixture. (*Argus Cameras, Inc.*)

Chassis Mounts. Smaller versions of the trunnion fixture are shown in Figs. 15-70 and 15-71. These chassis mounts are commercial items that can be used to mount standard and odd-shaped chassis weighing up to 100 lb (45.4 kg.) for rotating during assembly.

WELDING

Welding is a materials joining process in which localized coalescence (joining) is

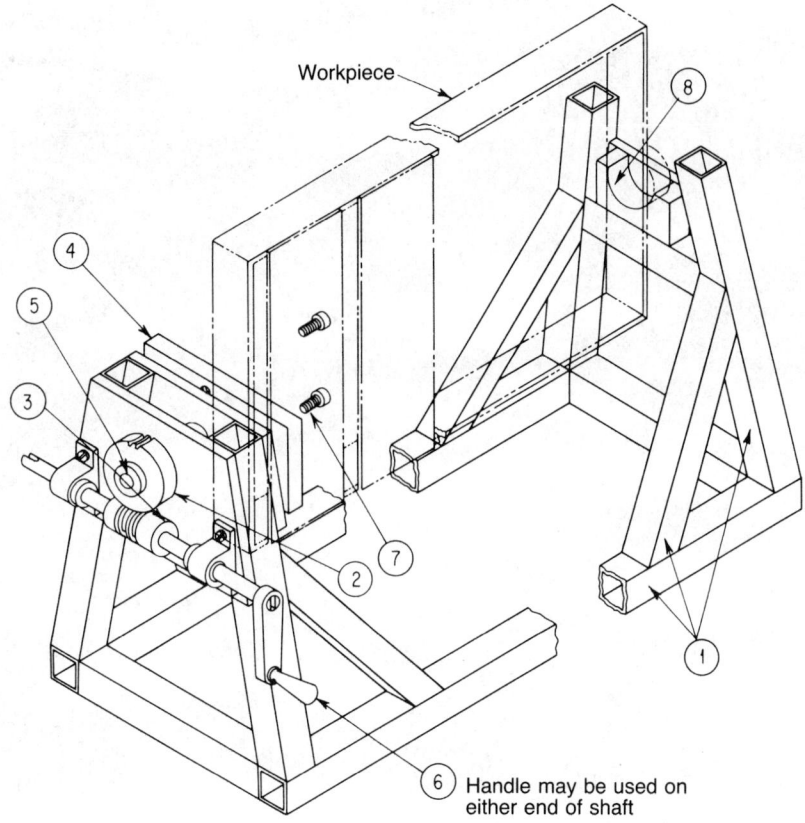

Workpiece

Fig. 15-69 Trunnion fixture.

produced along the faying surfaces of the workpieces. Coalescence is produced either by heating the materials to suitable temperatures, with or without the application of pressure, or it is produced by the application of pressure alone.

With some welding processes, filler material is added during welding.

There are more than 50 different welding processes. Welding processes can be classified as either fusion or solid-state (nonfusion) methods.

Fusion welding processes, in which the workpieces are melted together at their faying surfaces, are the most commonly used processes. Arc, resistance, and oxyfuel gas welding are the predominant fusion processes. Filler metals often used with the arc and oxyfuel gas welding methods have melting points about the same as or just below those of the metals being joined.

In solid-state welding, the workpieces are joined by the application of heat and usually pressure, or by the application of pressure only. However with these processes, the welding temperature is essentially below the melting point of the materials being joined or if any liquid metal is present it is squeezed out of the joint. No filler metal is added during welding.

The major welding processes include the following:

- Oxyfuel gas welding (OFW).
- Arc welding (AW).
- Resistance welding (RW).

Fig. 15-70 Chassis mount with scissor clamps. (*Courtesy Panavise Products, Inc.*)

- Electron beam welding (EBW).
- Laser beam welding (LBW).
- Solid state welding.

The primary function of a welding fixture is to hold the components to be welded in the proper relationship, both before and after welding. A fixture will often maintain the proper relationship between the components of an assembly during the welding process, but allow the assembly to distort when removed from the fixture.

Except for electrode pressures, fixtures need not be designed to withstand the torque and other forces of cutters, drills, and other tools.

Stresses resulting from thermal expansion of workpieces and/or fixtures must be considered in the design of clamps and locators and in the proper positioning of the workpieces before and during assembly, depending upon the necessary distribution of heat to the work and fixture. Fixtures for some operations must absorb considerable heat and provide clamping pressure to prevent excessive thermal expansion of the work and of fixture elements.

The thermal conductivity and coefficient of expansion of some metals will result in cracking adjacent to the weld when tightly clamped. This difficulty may be overcome with a fixture for tack welding or through final welding performed without a fixture. Under the same condition, the distortion of other metals may be difficult or impossible to control and must be corrected by a subsequent operation to produce uniform workpieces.

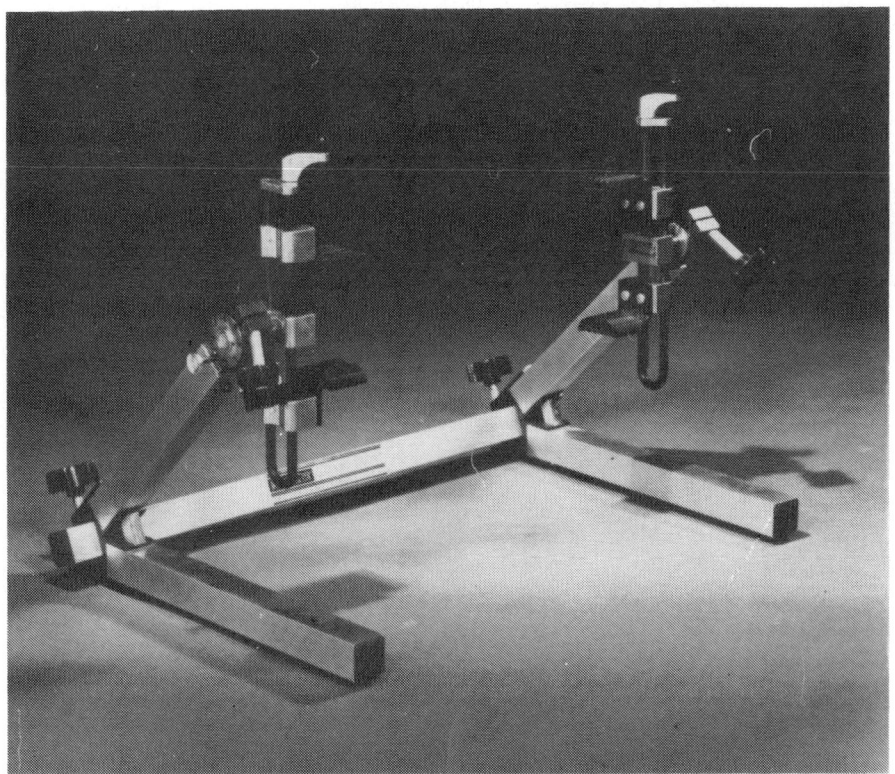

Fig. 15-71 **Chassis mount with self-centering heads.** (*Courtesy Panavise Products, Inc.*)

WELDING JIGS AND FIXTURES

In general, welding fixtures and jigs are grouped in three classifications: tacking jigs, welding fixtures, and holding fixtures.

Tacking Jigs. A tacking jig locates the components of a weldment in their correct relationship with proper fit-up, while a tack welder tacks them together prior to their final welding. The workpiece is usually then removed from the tacking jig and transferred to a separate fixture for completion of the welding. A tacking jig need not be exceptionally strong or of heavy construction, since heat of the few short tacking welds induces only slight thermal stresses in it.

Welding Fixtures. A welding fixture properly locates and holds workpieces for a complete welding operation. It simplifies and/or eliminates handling and moving of the workpieces and of associated tooling, but it necessitates construction to withstand thermal pressures and stresses within the weldment. It is often impractical or even impossible to design satisfactory welding fixtures for intricate, complex assemblies and heavy, bulky weldments; hence in general practice, the parts are initially tacked together in a tacking jig and then the workpiece is transferred to a holding fixture, usually used in conjunction with a welding positioner, for completion of the work.

Holding Fixtures. A holding fixture is a device specifically designed to hold previously tacked assemblies in place on a positioner. The fixture itself can often be adapted for positioning by the addition of an economical trunnion stand with index plate and plunger of suitable design. Counterweights may be used to make positioning easy, and if necessary, dolly mounting will make the entire unit more readily portable. Like the welding jig, the holding fixture must be strongly and rigidly constructed to withstand the cumulative stresses generated within the workpiece in the process of welding.

A simple, economical positioning device, such as that shown in Fig. 15-72, incorporates a circular plate to which a workpiece or a fixture can be attached. The table can be rotated in three planes and locked in any position by hand screws.

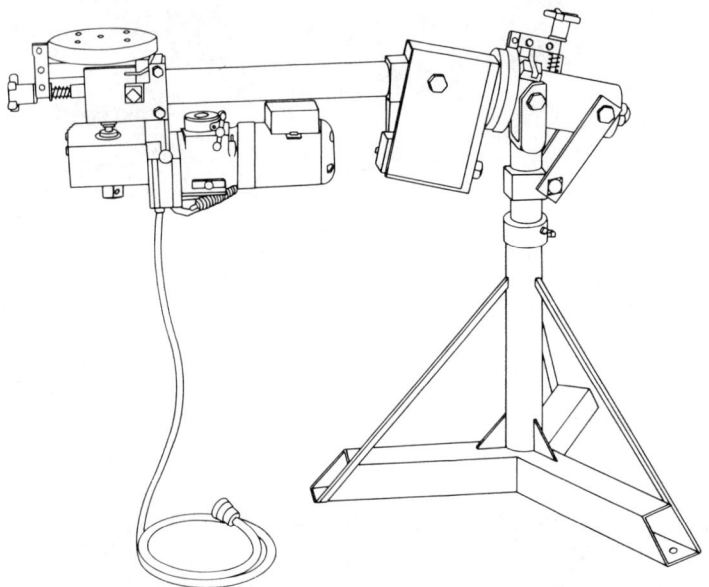

Fig. 15-72 Welding positioner. (*Courtesy Aronson Machine Co.*)

GENERAL DESIGN CONSIDERATIONS

Jigs and fixtures for welding may incorporate standard clamps, locating buttons, pins, and blocks employed in machining and assembly fixtures. Clamping and locating devices should be basically simple and strong. Simple, nonbinding locators are essential.

Figure 15-73 illustrates standard strap clamps for clamping tack-welded workpieces in a holding fixture. The holding fixture can be mounted on a standard revolving positioner.

Interference Considerations. Clamps and locators required to position and secure components must be carefully placed to preclude interference with the welding tool. Provision must be made to prevent its fusion to the fixture or burn-through by including slots, relief areas, or back-up bars. Burn- and fusion-resistant materials may be used.

Unloading Workpieces. Unlike machining fixtures, where the size and shape of the workpiece remain essentially the same at loading and unloading, workpieces for welding fixtures generally are separately loaded, individually located, welded together, and finally removed as a single and often an unwieldy, unyielding unit. Unless the locators have been properly placed for easy removal of the finished workpiece, it can be difficult, or even impossible, to remove the weldment from the fixture.

Workpiece Expansion. Expansion, contraction, and distortion from welding may further complicate workpiece removal by tightly forcing the workpiece against locating devices, or the fixture frame, and thereby binding the finished weldment. Fixed locators may locate on one and the same side of all components in the weldment, and removable or retractable locators and clamps may locate on the other sides whenever it is expedient or necessary to locate a workpiece from several sides to maintain accuracy and critical dimensions. The threaded shoulder pin, of suitable length and design, is a simple

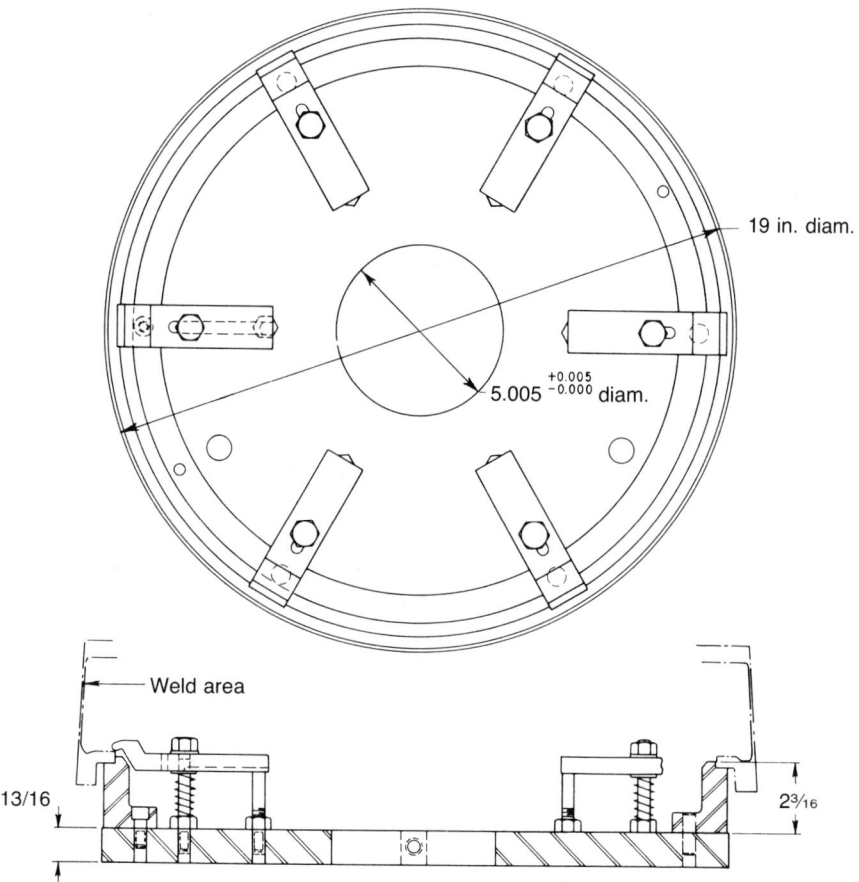

19 in. diam.

5.005 $^{+0.005}_{-0.000}$ diam.

Weld area

13/16

2³/₁₆

Fig. 15-73   Fusion-welding fixture for tack-welded workpieces. (*Courtesy Pratt & Whitney Aircraft*)

and economical retractable locator, readily adaptable, and often utilized for such applications; but it must be designed and positioned to adequately protect its threaded portions during tacking and welding operations against damage from weld spatter. Distortion and expansion from welding that can force the workpiece against such threaded locators or pins, or other removable and retractable locators, thereby making their removal difficult, must be anticipated.

Figure 15-74 illustrates a fixture to maintain critical internal dimensions and parallel relationship of the sides of a box type of machine-base weldment. The fixture can quickly be disassembled for easy removal from the welded structure. The threaded members are at a distance adequate to prevent damage from weld spatter. The fixture design affords rigidity and strength to withstand the strains generated in the welding.

Cylindrical Workpieces. Expanding or collapsible mandrels may be adaptable for weldments incorporating cylindrical and tubular sections of relatively small diameter. Trunnion devices are readily adaptable for locating, revolving, and positioning large, unwieldy cylinders.

Figure 15-75 shows a simple air-operated expanding fixture which incorporates a bicycle tube as an economical and trouble-free expanding member.

Figure 15-76 shows a positioner for large cylindrical workpieces.

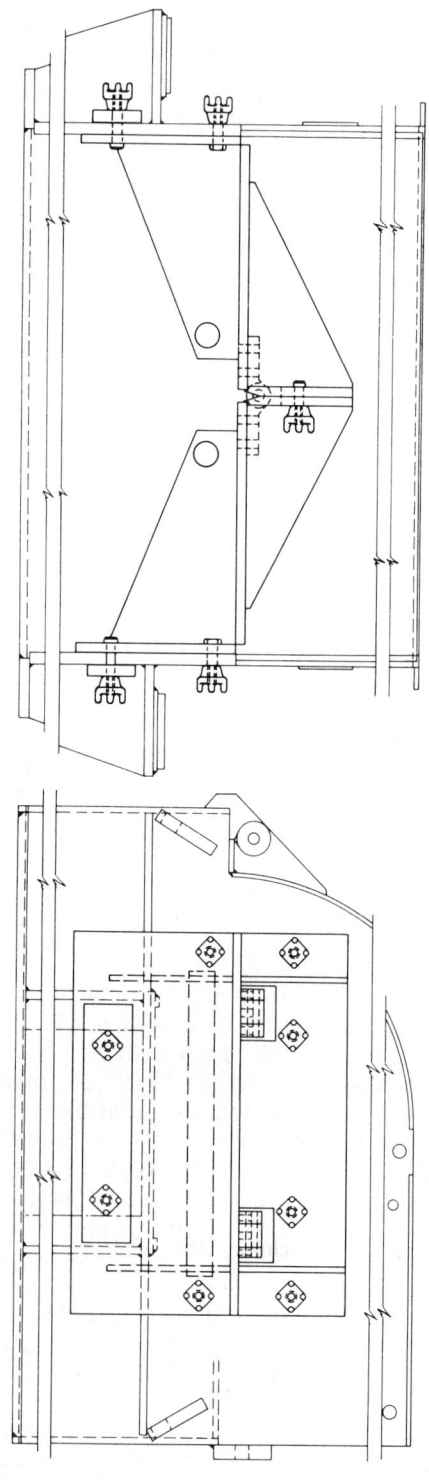

Fig. 15-74 A welding fixture designed for disassembly. (*Courtesy Universal Engineering Corp.*)

15-62

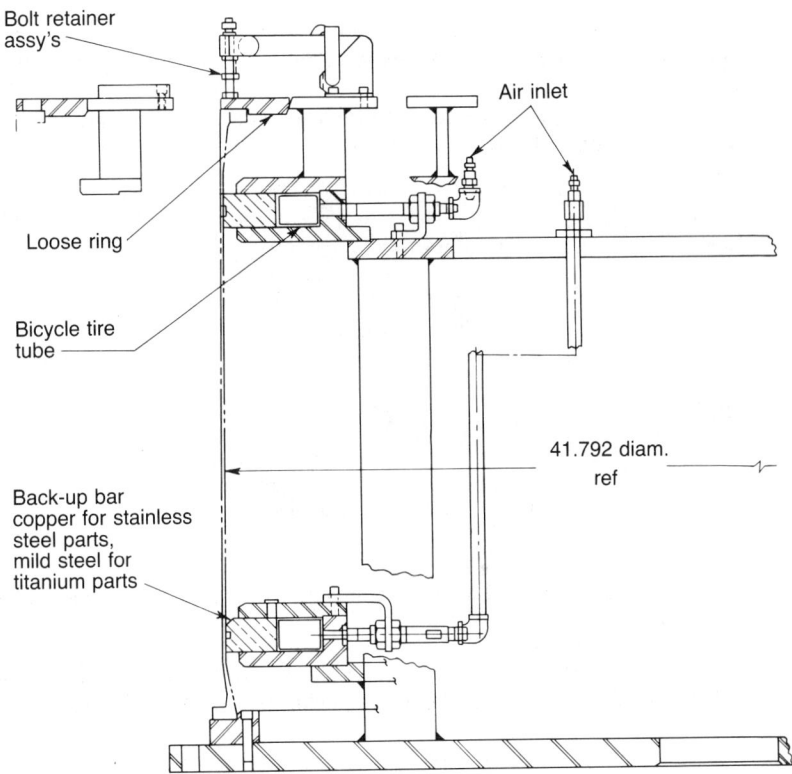

Fig. 15-75 Air-operated expansion-type welding fixture. (*Courtesy Pratt & Whitney Aircraft.*)

Bolt retainer assy's

Air inlet

Loose ring

Bicycle tire tube

41.792 diam. ref

Back-up bar copper for stainless steel parts, mild steel for titanium parts

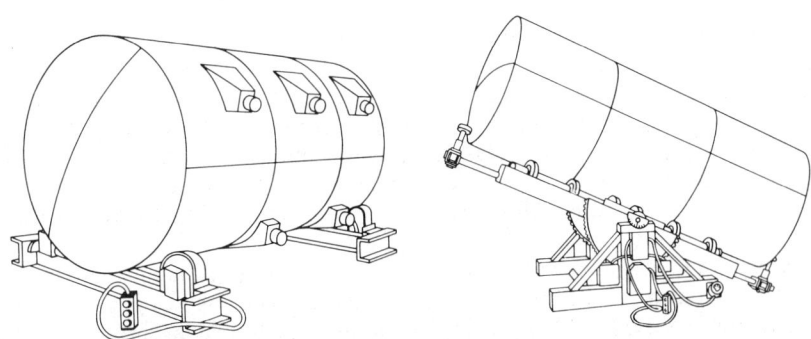

Fig. 15-76 Positioner for welding large workpieces. (*Courtesy Aronson Machine Co.*)

Clamping Considerations. Quick-acting and cam-actuated clamps offer secure and positive initial pressure, rapid release, adequate clearance, and low susceptibility to damage from weld spatter. A wide variety of mechanical clamping devices are advantageously adapted to welding fixtures, including screw, strap, cam, toggle, hydraulic, air, and many other clamps, the choice depending upon application, pressure requirements, etc. Screw clamps, which are relatively simple, can exert great pressure but should be avoided unless the threads can be adequately protected from weld spatter. Heavy toggle clamps are well suited to welding fixtures. Air and hydraulic clamps are fast-acting, positive, and readily obtainable in pressure ratings to suit most requirements. Clamp handles and knobs should be large enough and long enough to allow easy manipulation by the welder's gloved hands.

Figure 15-77 shows a simple clamping and locating wedge which can be instantly closed or opened by a hammer blow.

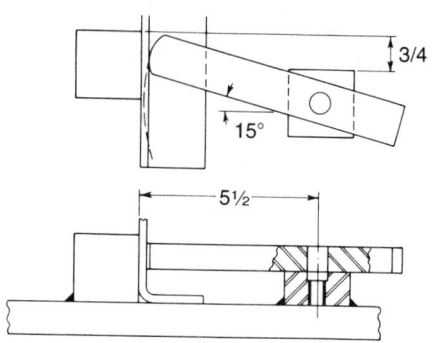

Fig. 15-77 Cam clamping and locking fixture. (*Courtesy Universal Engineering Corp.*)

Magnetic Retention. Magnetic holding devices, both electromagnets and permanent magnets, are adaptable, economical, and timesaving. Fixtures incorporating magnets and fabricated from nonferrous metals or plastics permit the magnetic holding forces to be directed to ferrous-metal workpieces.

Figure 15-78 shows a magnetic welding fixture in which aluminum is used wherever possible, since the magnets should not be in contact with ferrous metals other than the workpiece. If it is impractical to construct the entire fixture of aluminum, the magnets may be inserted in aluminum blocks or bushings attached to the fixture. Magnets may be retained in the aluminum blocks by setscrews or cap screws.

Plastic Fixtures. Welding fixtures made of cast epoxy or phenolic tooling resins may also be used with conventional locating and clamping devices, but the inherent close nesting of the workpiece often makes other locating and clamping means unnecessary. Plastic welding fixtures can also afford a substantial cost advantage over metal fixtures. Design time and problems are minimized; fabrication time is substantially reduced; and positive nesting of the assembly in the cast fixture ensures dimensional accuracy sometimes not obtained in fabricated metal construction and even permits use of the fixture as an initial inspection device. Epoxy and phenolic resins retain dimensional stability, have minimum deterioration, will not support combustion, and will shatter rather than permit distortion in the workpiece.

Flexibility. If feasible, all locating devices should permit some adjustment for changing locating dimensions necessitated by design changes and engineering revisions or to compensate for expected weld distortion. Locating areas should be carefully correlated with any subsequent machine operations, since welding and machining must often index and originate from the same locating points.

Utility. All jigs and fixtures must be strong enough to withstand the abuses of loading and unloading and the built-up stresses from welding within the workpiece. They should be simply designed to permit easy accessibility for part positioning and permit the welder to work from the most advantageous angle, generally downhand, with no part of the fixture located to interfere with the electrode or torch.

Jigs and fixtures should be readily operated by welders of varying skill and should incorporate error-proof pins or elements to prevent inverted or reversed loading of workpieces or other welders' errors.

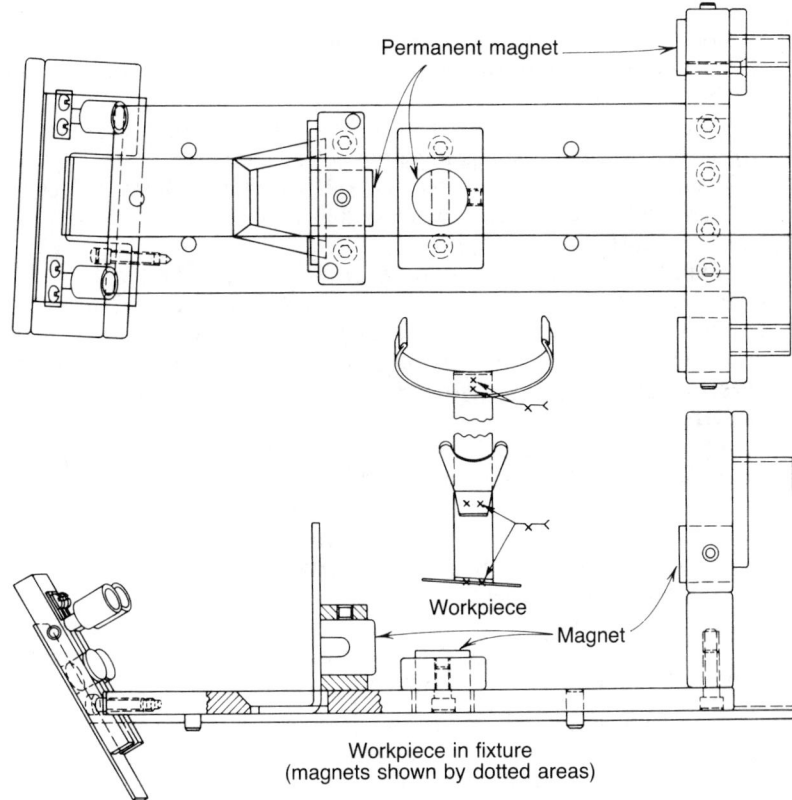

Permanent magnet

Workpiece

Magnet

Workpiece in fixture
(magnets shown by dotted areas)

Fig. 15-78 Magnetic welding fixture. (*Courtesy The Tool Engineer*)

Large fixtures may be made in sections for ease of handling and construction, for replacement of worn sections, for change of sections to accommodate product revision, or for the interchange of sections with several weldments of similar basic design.

Duplicate Fixtures. Duplicate jigs and fixtures are often economically justified, since they can substantially increase the output of a work station by allowing a helper to fit up the next assembly and load and unload it in one fixture, while the welder devotes a major portion of his productive time and ability to actually welding the assembly in the other fixture.

BASIC DESIGN PRINCIPLES

Some design principles listed by the Canadian Welding Bureau are:

1. Whenever possible, a fixture should be a positioner; that is, a fixture should enable all welds to be brought to a convenient welding position. Indexing positioners are accurate and convenient for the welder.
2. A fixture should be easily and quickly positioned (by one hand if possible); balancing may be necessary to enable this to be done. The use of light alloys will reduce the weight of moving parts. Air motors or electric motors can be used for revolving heavy, cumbersome fixtures, and air or hydraulic rams or racks can be used for tilting them.
3. Design must be simple and inexpensive; accuracy and elaboration must be no greater than required. Welded construction is best; toolroom work should be avoided, and machining should be kept to a minimum.

4. A fixture should be built around the workpiece and should locate and clamp it in a position for assembly, tacking, and welding.
5. The tool designer should attempt to control only essential workpiece dimensions in a fixture.
6. A fixture should permit freedom of workpiece movement in one direction to avoid locked-in stresses. A floating anchorage is recommended.
7. Joints must be readily accessible for welding. Slots, cutouts, or openings in the fixture should readily present to the welding tool any seams, spots, etc., located on the reverse side of the workpiece.
8. To compensate for thermal distortion, the parts may be bent in the welding fixture before welding, or they may be bent or sprung in a separate fixture.
9. Heat distortion should release rather than bind the workpiece in the fixture. Rams or bumpers may assist in unloading parts that are heat-bound in the fixture.
10. For safe handling, fixtures should be kept cool with air, water, fins, or insulated handles.
11. Convenient positioning of the operator with ladders, trestles, cradles, or trolleys is sometimes advisable for efficient operation.
12. If necessary, the fixture may be mounted on a separate positioner, form, or cradle.
13. To facilitate the flow of weldments, fixtures or positioners may be mounted on wheels or used with floor-mounted or overhead conveyors.
14. Use either integral or separate copper backing bars for poor-fitting or light-plate workpieces to prevent blowout of molten filler metal and ensure proper fusion.
15. Revolving the fixture is preferable to removing and turning the workpiece.
16. Vertical or overhead welding should be avoided.

Economics can be effected by designing the fixture to accommodate several identical small weldments, permitting the welder to progressively weld them with a single loading and unloading sequence. This practice becomes even more productive when duplicate fixtures are utilized.

There is no universal jig entirely satisfactory for the welding of a number of diverse parts. Each workpiece requires and merits individual consideration and presents unique problems.

GAS WELDING FIXTURES

The general design of a gas welding fixture must take into consideration the heating and cooling conditions. A minimum of heat loss from the welding area is required. If the heat loss is too rapid, the weld may develop cracks. Heat loss by materials, particularly aluminum and copper, must be carefully controlled. To accomplish this, large fixture masses should not be placed close to the weld line; however, the part may distort. The contact area and clamps should therefore be of the minimum size consistent with the load transmitted through the contact point. In welding copper and aluminum, the minimum contact surface often permits excessive heat loss, and prevents good fixture welds. This necessitates tack welding the fixtured parts at points most distant from the fixture contact points, with the rest of the welding being done out of the fixture. However, with this method, excessive distortion may result, and subsequent stress relieving of the part may be required.

One of the simplest fixtures for gas welding is a gravity-type fixture shown in Fig. 15-79. This design eliminates excess fixture material from the weld area to minimize heat loss, while providing sufficient support and locating points. The design also permits making welds in a horizontal position, which is generally advantageous.

Figure 15-80 shows another simple form of gas welding fixture which holds two flat sheets for joining. C-clamps hold the workpieces to steel support bars. Alignment is done visually or with a straight edge. A heat barrier of alumina-ceramic fiber is placed

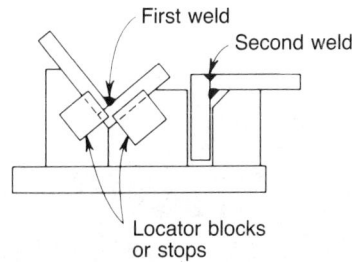

Fig. 15-79 Simple welding fixture using gravity to help locate parts.

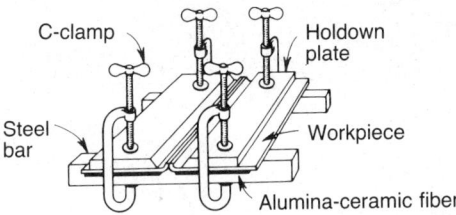

Fig. 15-80 Workpieces with simple fixturing for gas welding operations.

between the workpieces and the steel bars. Holddown plates are used to keep the workpieces flat and to prevent distortion. If the parts to be welded have curved surfaces, the supporting bars and holddown plates may be machined to match the part.

Simple parts may be properly located or positioned in a fixture visually. As the workpiece shape becomes complex, or the production rate increases, positive location is desirable. The same locating methods used in workholder design can readily be adapted for the design of welding fixtures.

The selection of material for gas welding fixtures is governed by these factors: (1) part print tolerances; (2) material heat resistance; (3) heat transfer qualities, and (4) the fixture rigidity required to assure workpiece alignment accuracy. The fixture material should not be affected in the weld zone and should prevent rapid heat dissipation from the weld area. Some of the fixture materials commonly used are cast iron, carbon steel, and stainless steel.

ARC WELDING FIXTURES

Arc welding concentrates more heat at the weld line than gas welding. The fixtures for this process must provide support, alignment, and restraint on the parts, and also must permit heat dissipation.

Some of the more important design considerations for arc welding fixtures are as follows: (1) the fixture must exert enough force to prevent the parts from moving out of alignment during the welding process, and this force must be applied at the proper point by a clamp supported by a backing bar; (2) backing bars should be parallel to the weld lines; (3) backing bars should promote heat dissipation from the weld lines; and (4) backing bars should support the molten weld, govern the weld contour, and protect the root of the weld from the atmosphere.

Backing bars are usually made from solid metal or ceramics. A simple backup could be a rectangular bar with a small groove directly under the weld. This would allow complete penetration without pickup material by the molten metal. In use, the backup would be clamped against the part to make the weld root as airtight as possible. Some common shapes are shown in Fig. 15-81. Figure 15-82 shows a backing bar in position against a fixed workpiece.

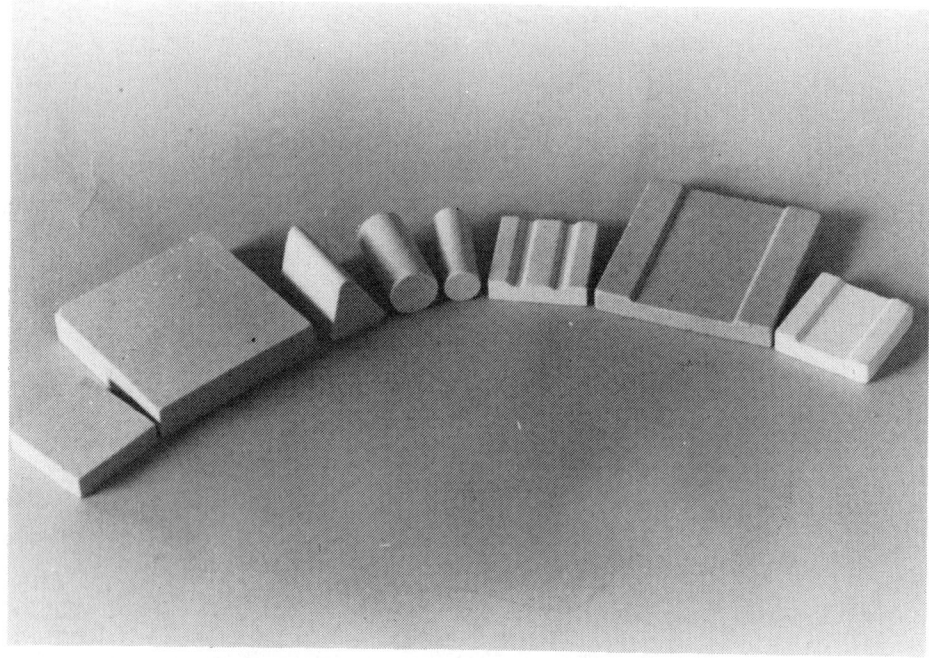

Fig. 15-81 Typical backing bars. (*Courtesy Alloy Rods Corp.*)

Fig. 15-82 Workpiece with simple fixturing for arc welding operations. (*Courtesy Alloy Rods Corp.*)

The size of the backup is dependent upon the metal thickness and the material to be welded. A thin weldment requires larger backup to promote heat transfer from the weld. A material with greater heat-conducting ability requires less backup than that required for a comparable thickness of a poor conductor.

Figure 15-83 shows backing bars designed for use with gas, which may be used to blast the weld are (A), flood the weld area (B), or may be concentrated in the weld area (C). Backup bars may be made of copper, stainless steel (used for tungsten inert gas), titanium ceramic, or a combination of several metals (sandwich construction).

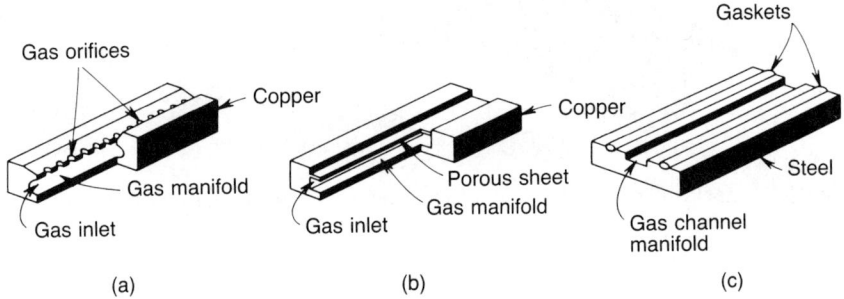

Fig. 15-83 Backing bars with provisions for (*a*) directed gas flow, (*b*) diffused gas flow, and (*c*) pressurized gas.

For either manual or automatic arc welding techniques, some tooling is usually necessary in the form of jigs, fixtures, clamps, dies, or gages. These tools frequently are inexpensive, and small-lot production lends itself to temporary tooling. The tooling itself is almost invariably of welded construction, which helps minimize cost and makes for versatility and flexibility.

The primary function of welding jigs and fixtures is to bring parts into accurate alignment and to present the assembled components in the best position for welding, which is downhand wherever possible, requiring joints to be in flat or near-flat position. In welding parlance, jigs are considered stationary while fixtures rotate, usually on trunnions, about a vertical or horizontal axis, either by hand operation or through motor and reduction-gear drive. Many standard types of welding positioners and tables, such as shown in Figs. 15-84 thru 15-86, can be purchased or built. They are readily adaptable to a wide variety of work, at lower cost than with more intricate and special single-purpose devices.

Fabrication of jigs and fixtures by arc welding is generally advisable. In most cases, standard steel shapes can be used, and the cost of patterns for castings avoided. Furthermore, welded construction permits easy modification. If a jig or fixture does not function exactly as anticipated the first time, economical alterations may be made by torch cutting and rewelding. Lightweight, high strength, portability, and easy storage are other advantages. If wear is involved, surfaces may be hardfaced with special high-alloy welding electrodes. As with any form of tooling, precision is needed in the construction of welding jigs, and stress relieving is seldom required.

Old or discarded machine equipment may sometimes be modified to serve as welding jigs, at a considerable savings over building an entirely new unit. A radial drill or perhaps an outmoded lathe might be adapted conveniently, with the addition of some air or toggle clamps to position the elements of a weldment.

For assembly of both large and small weldments, it is sometimes practical to provide two jigs, the first for assembly and positioning of the various components before they are manually tack welded. The tack-welded assembly is then transferred to a second jig, or simply to the floor, for completion of the welds either manually or automatically. In

Fig. 15-84 Rocker-type positioner of 8-ton capacity with power driven variable speed table.

Fig. 15-85 Variable speed range positioner with vertical adjustment of table.

Fig. 15-86 Special-purpose rotating frame jig for welding of mineral wagons.

this way, distortion is held to a minimum, and accurate alignments are better assured.

For large weldments, especially when only two or three are being made, jigs and fixtures can be eliminated. Parts can be aligned for welding with the aid of a scale and square and then clamped for welding with C-clamps, wedges, or other holding devices such as magnetic clamps.

Many other expedients have been devised to minimize distortion and warpage. The problem of warpage is critical in welding thin material and can be overcome by using jigs or clamps of copper to which water-cooling tubes have been soldered. Another method compensating for warpage is to shape jigs or fixtures with suitable curvature or camber so that when the weldment is completed it will allow for distortion to the desired final contour.

General Fixture Design Considerations. Simple fixtures may have the part located visually with scribed lines as a guide. This is quite similar to locating parts for gas welding. For higher production, a quicker locating method is needed. A locating land may be incorporated in the fixture to accurately establish the edge position of the part to be welded (see Fig. 15-87). In some cases, setup blocks may be used in place of a locating land (see Fig. 15-88).

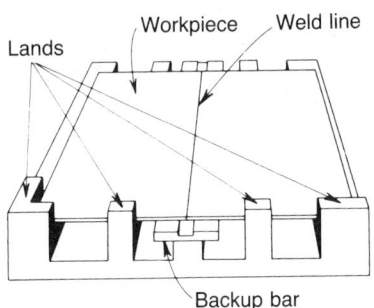

Fig. 15-87 Locating lands.

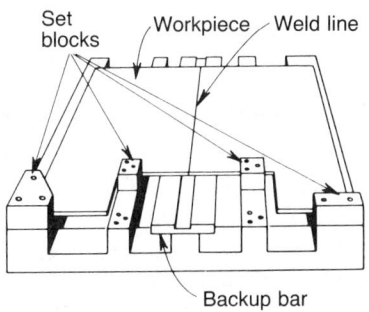

Fig. 15-88 Set block locators.

When welding a variety of similar parts with different dimensions, setup blocks have a distinct advantage over the land method of locating. With proper design, setup blocks can be interchangeable to accommodate varying workpieces. Dowel pins may be used as locators (see Fig. 15-89).

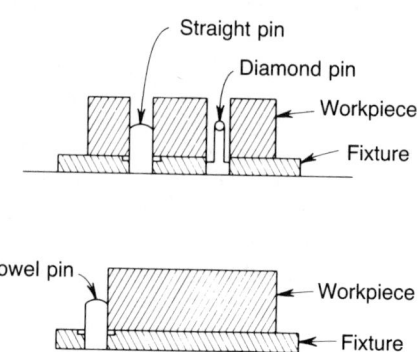

Fig. 15-89 Dowel pin locators.

Other means of locating are V-blocks, adjustable clamps, rest buttons and pads, spring plungers, and magnets where applicable.

Clamping Design Considerations. Clamps used in welding fixtures must hold the parts in the proper position and prevent their movement due to alternate heating and cooling. Clamping pressure should not deform the parts to be joined. Clamps must be supported underneath the workpiece (see Fig. 15-90). Owing to the heat involved, deflection by clamping force could remain in the part.

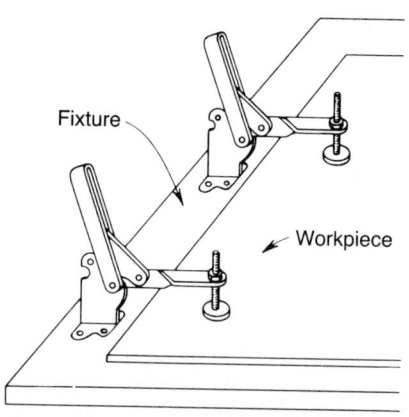

Fig. 15-90 Typical clamp installation with the fixture supporting the workpiece directly beneath the clamps.

Quick-acting and power-operated clamps are recommended to achieve fast loading and unloading. C-clamps may be used for low production volume. Power clamping systems may be direct acting or work through lever systems (see Fig. 15-91).

In heavier plate applications, urethane tip or spring-loaded clamp spindles are recommended to compensate for plate thickness variations.

Elimination of Welding and Bending Jigs. The installation shown in Fig. 15-92 was designed to eliminate the need for special welding and bending jigs. An installation consists of one or more platens, such as shown in Fig. 15-93, which can be used along with the accessories shown in Fig. 15-94. The platens are solid semisteel castings, 6 in. (152.4 mm) thick with holes machined out of the casting so that it resembles a waffle. The working surfaces are machined to within 0.005 in. flatness. The sides are machined

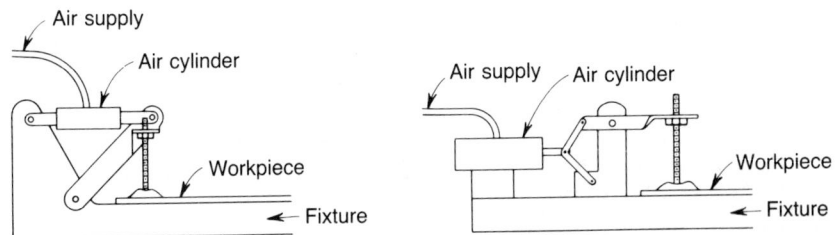

Fig. 15-91 Air-actuated clamping methods.

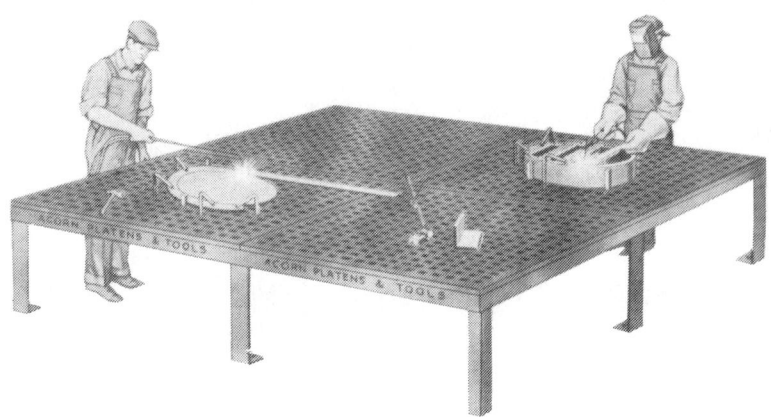

Fig. 15-92 Typical four-platen installation. (*Courtesy Acorn Iron & Supply Company*)

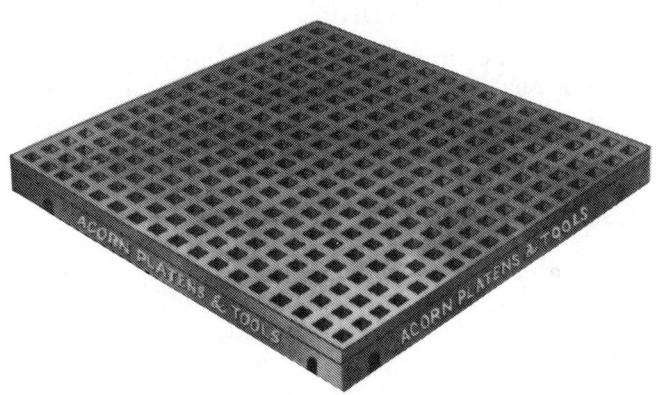

Fig. 15-93 Platen. (*Courtesy Acorn Iron & Supply Company*)

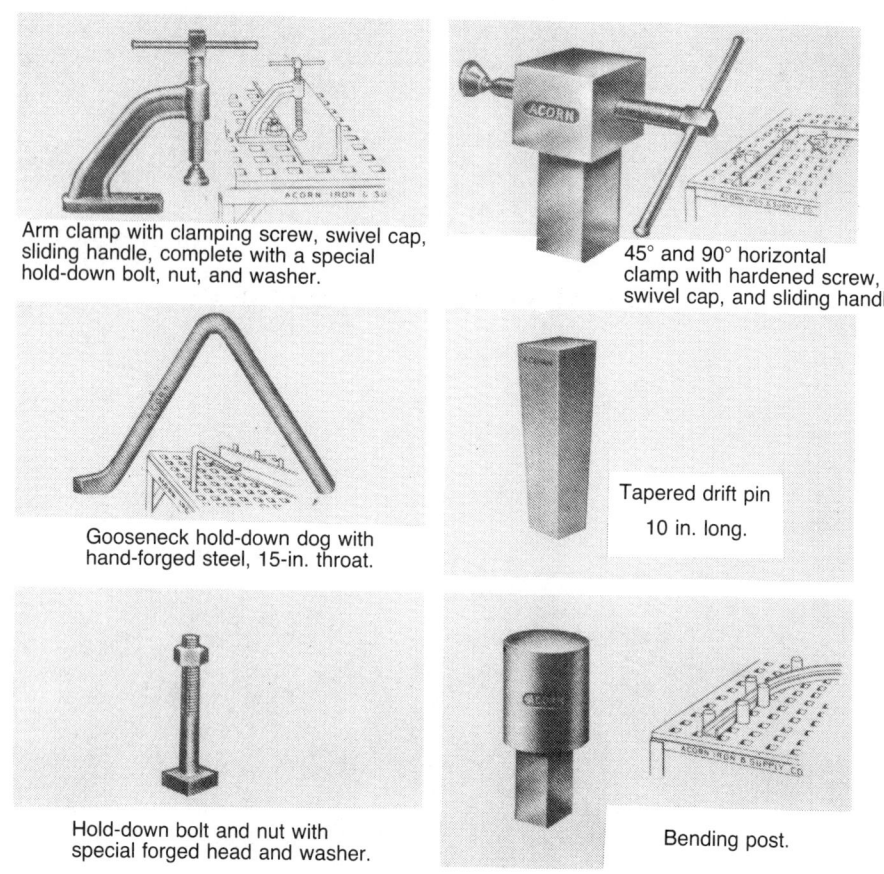

Arm clamp with clamping screw, swivel cap, sliding handle, complete with a special hold-down bolt, nut, and washer.

45° and 90° horizontal clamp with hardened screw, swivel cap, and sliding handle.

Gooseneck hold-down dog with hand-forged steel, 15-in. throat.

Tapered drift pin 10 in. long.

Hold-down bolt and nut with special forged head and washer.

Bending post.

Fig. 15-94 Accessories and their uses. (*Courtesy Acorn Iron & Supply Company*)

square to the top to permit connecting of two or more together. Six sizes are available, from widths as narrow as 2.5 ft (.076 m) to lengths as long as 8 ft (2.44 m). Special stands which are designed to stand alone or be bolted to the floor are available to accommodate the heavy weight of the platens.

RESISTANCE WELDING FIXTURES

During the resistance-welding process, an electric current flows through the parts to be welded and meets resistance which heats and softens the parts. Then the mechanical power presses the soft parts together to make the weld. The current that melts the parts should not melt the jig. The jig can be prevented from melting in four basic ways:

1. By ensuring that current-carrying parts of the jig are of low electrical resistance.
   Copper is the most-used metal. Rolled copper (which will carry 1,800 amp per sq in.) in flats, rounds, and copper tubing is almost indispensable. Also, based on a 50 percent duty cycle, cast copper will carry 1,500 amp per sq in. Water cooling will approximately double allowable current flow. Tubing is especially valuable, since it can be connected to the welder's water supply and the generated heat removed by the water.
   Aluminum bronze and similar copper-base alloys can be used when higher strength is desired for bases, arms, clamping devices, and stops. They should not

be annealed during fabrication of the fixture and thus lose their higher strengths.

Aluminum and its alloys can be used to conserve weight but not for actual current-carrying parts, because oxidation will develop at the joints or clamps.

Nonmagnetic cast iron (nickel iron) is sometimes used as a cheap, strong material for a portion of the jig that is in or around the magnetic field of the machine. Magnetic materials cut down the flow of current, reduce machine efficiency, and become hot owing to induced currents.

The resistance of some metals can be reduced by silver-plating them. This is especially helpful at joints.

2. By water-cooling the jig.

Water flowing through copper tubing is an excellent coolant. A system in which water floods into a drain pan is very efficient, particularly for seam welding.

3. By keeping materials out of the throat area of the machine.

The magnetic field of the machine will heat any metal in this area, but metals of high electrical conductivity will not become as hot as magnetic materials.

4. By keeping the number of joints to a minimum.

When connections have to be made, their clamped surfaces must be at least twice the area of the cross section carrying the current. It is a good practice to bridge the connections with flexible members, such as braided copper wire.

TOOLING FOR SPOT WELDING

Spot-welding Electrodes. In spot welding, the parts are positioned between electrodes which exert heavy pressure, conduct the current into the materials to be welded, and dissipate the heat from the outer surface of the materials being welded. Holders and adapters are mounted in the machines so that the position of the electrode can be adjusted to suit a particular workpiece. Wherever possible, the electrode tips should be water cooled. Fig. 15-95 illustrates typical electrode tips and their application. The design of welding electrodes and the material from which they are made are of great importance. For increased life, the design must provide sufficient strength with adequate heat conduction and cooling.

Spot-welding Fixtures. Some workpieces can be spot-welded without fixtures. They can be manually oriented and placed between the machine electrodes. When the two assembled workpieces have a common straight edge, a block may be mounted adjacent to the electrodes against which the workpieces can be held during joining.

Figure 15-96 shows a mainspring-and-brace assembly for a watch. The two workpieces are held in alignment while being joined by a single spot weld. Figure 15-97 shows the fixture in which the two workpieces are placed in a common nest.

Figure 15-98 shows a small portable fixture for spot welding two small stampings. This simple fixture incorporates two handles removed from purchased hacksaws and a proprietary toggle clamp. The stampings are designed and formed to nest within each other. They are positioned and clamped in the fixture, which is placed between the electrodes.

Figure 15-99 illustrates a fixture for holding a circular, dome-shaped workpiece while brackets are welded to its outer perimeter at four places. The fixture has an aluminum base plate (1) with two locating dowels (2) which radially locate the workpiece (3). At three points on the base-plate circumference, screw clamps (4) hold the workpiece. Attached to the base plate is an aluminum locating ring (5) which locates in the ID of the workpiece. A micarta guide (6) has eight cutouts which are in turn placed against the lower electrode for location during welding. The fixture is placed over the horn of the spot welder with the micarta cutout against the lower electrode. The bracket is located, and the two workpieces are spot-welded. The sequence is repeated for two spots in each of four brackets.

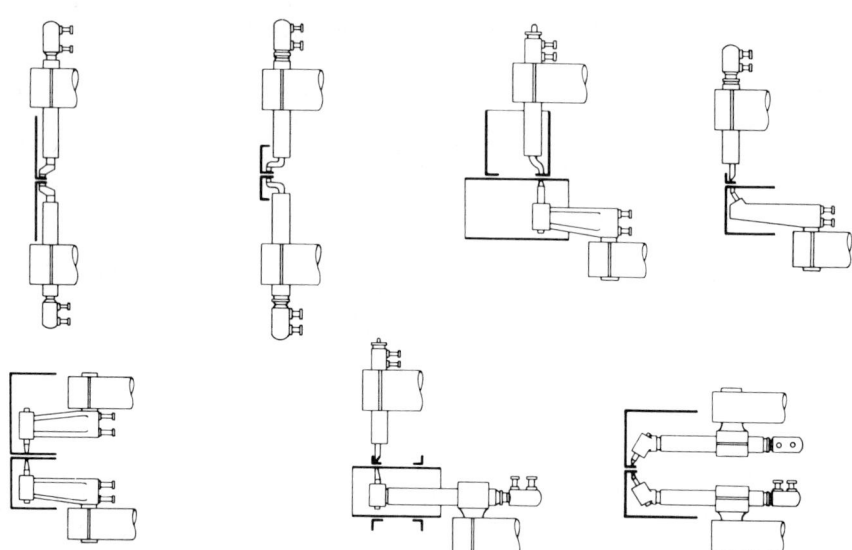

Fig. 15-95 Typical standard electrode tips and operations.

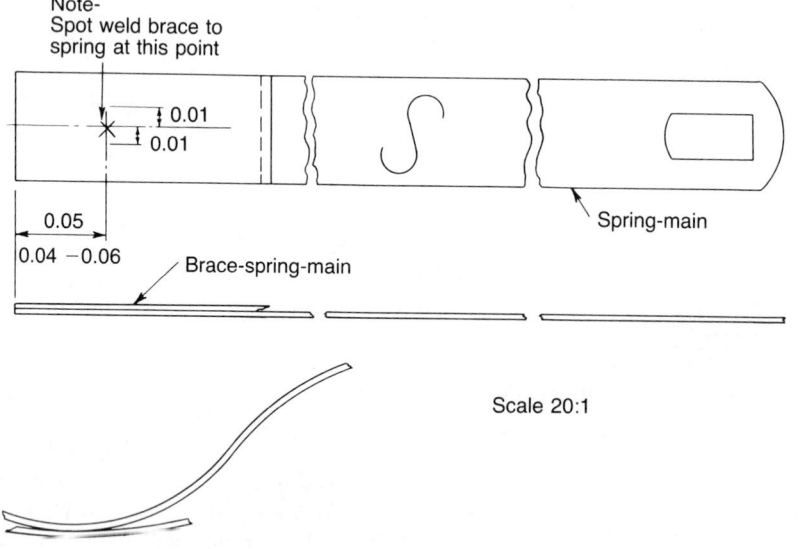

Note-
Spot weld brace to
spring at this point

0.01
0.01

0.05
0.04 −0.06

Brace-spring-main

Spring-main

Scale 20:1

Fig. 15-96 Workpieces for the fixture of Fig. 15-97.

Figure 15-100 shows a sizing and spot-welding fixture for a receptacle-cover assembly. The four stampings are placed in the fixture, and four cam clamps (1) press against them to bring the assembly to its required size and alignment. The fixture (2) is removed from its base (3) and is manually positioned to accomplish the welding. The fixture is replaced on its base, the clamps are released, and the fixture is pressed down on its spring-loaded mounting against ejector pins (4) which push the finished workpiece out of the fixture.

Figure 15-101 shows a spot-welding jig consisting of a slotted plate with two locating pins. Symmetrical right- and left-hand parts are placed on the pins as shown,

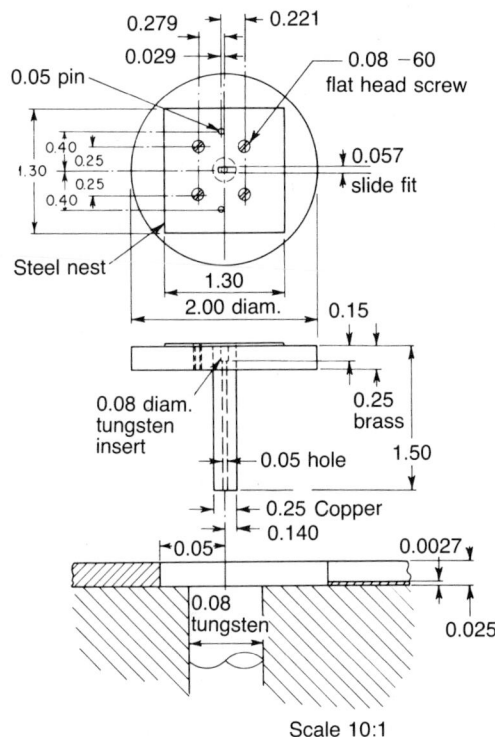

0.279 — 0.221
0.029
0.08 −60 flat head screw
0.05 pin
0.40
0.25
1.30
0.25
0.40
0.057
slide fit
Steel nest
1.30
2.00 diam.
0.15
0.08 diam. tungsten insert
0.25 brass
0.05 hole
1.50
0.25 Copper
0.140
0.05
0.0027
0.08 tungsten
0.025

Scale 10:1

Fig. 15-97 Fixture for welding watch parts. (*Courtesy Elgin National Watch Co.*)

and the jig is placed between the electrodes for spot welding. The slot in the plate permits the lower electrode to contact the workpiece.

Figure 15-102 illustrates a special electrode which fits a small space between two toroidal workpieces. A solenoid-actuated clamp (1) holds a small workpiece (2) in position against the lower-electrode button (3). The larger workpiece (4) is placed over the lower electrode, and the machine is cycled to spot weld the two workpieces. The magnetic clamp is attached to, but insulated from, the lower electrode.

Figure 15-103 illustrates a method of equalizing the pressure of several spot-welding tips simultaneously pressing on workpieces of varying thickness.

If a workpiece heavier than the rest is inserted, it will force the electrode and its wedge block down, displacing the other wedges until the pressure at all electrodes is equal.

The fixture of Fig. 15-104 holds an open box for spot welding it to a top plate in six places. Top, front, and side locators align the box and top plate and, with the box inverted, align it with the bottom plate for again spot welding it in six places. Water-cooling passages are machined in the heavy current-carrying members of the fixture, which are insulated from the other metallic parts with heat-resistant vulcanized fiber.

Spot Welding Jig for Making Six Spot Welds. The workholder shown in Fig. 15-105 shows a typical spot-welding jig to hold the workpiece for spot welding. It also aids loading and unloading the machine.

Fixturing Large Assemblies for Spot welding. In those cases where large assemblies are spot welded together using portable spot-welding equipment, fixtures similar to the stationary fixture for riveting large assemblies (see Fig. 15-14) can be designed. However, special provision will have to be made to provide access for maneuvering the electrodes.

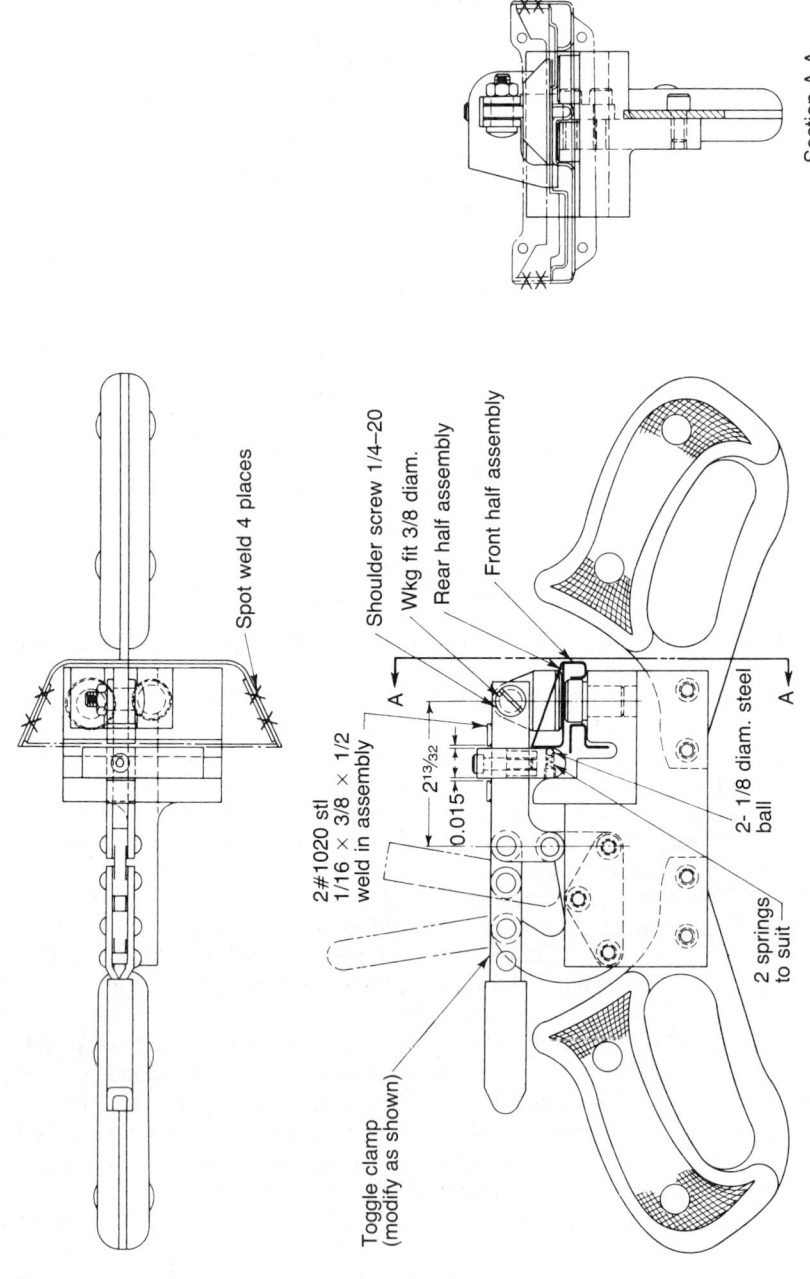

Spot weld 4 places

Shoulder screw 1/4–20

Wkg fit 3/8 diam.

Rear half assembly

Front half assembly

2#1020 stl
1/16 × 3/8 × 1/2
weld in assembly

$2^{13}/_{32}$

0.015

2- 1/8 diam. steel
ball

2 springs
to suit

Toggle clamp
(modify as shown)

Section A-A

Fig. 15-98 A manual spot-welding fixture. (*Courtesy Western Electric Co., Inc.*)

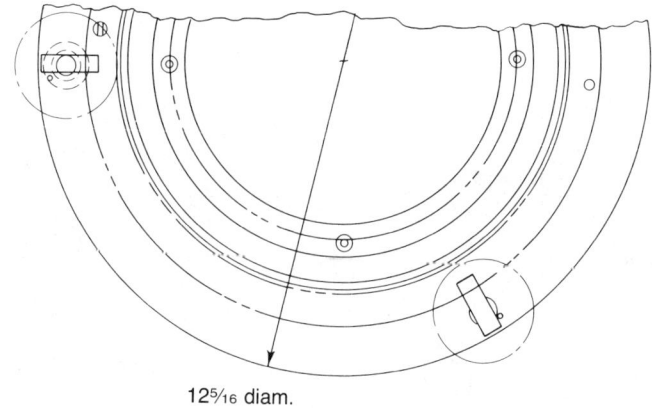

12⁵⁄₁₆ diam.

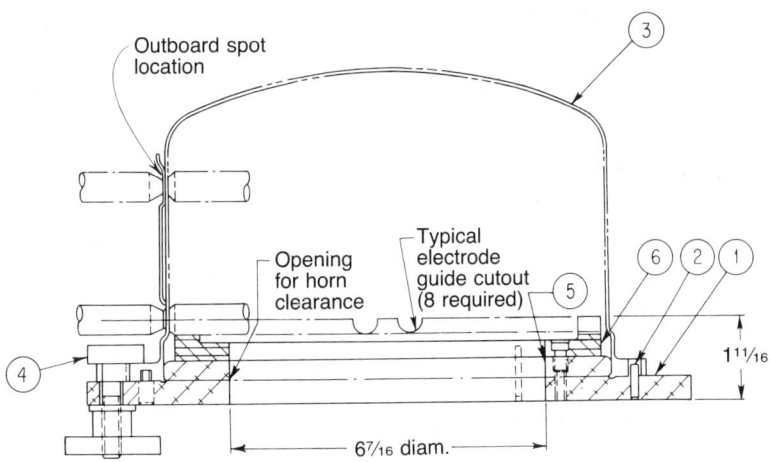

Outboard spot location

Opening for horn clearance

Typical electrode guide cutout (8 required)

1¹¹⁄₁₆

6⁷⁄₁₆ diam.

Fig. 15-99 Fixture for spot-welding circular workpieces. (*Courtesy Pratt & Whitney Aircraft*)

Projection-welding Fixtures. Essentially, a projection-welding fixture is that part of the die exclusive of the electrodes. For all practical purposes, the die and fixture may be considered to be the same. A die is a device, usually shaped to the work contour, which clamps the parts being welded and conducts the welding current from the machine platens to the workpiece. The lower die consists of the necessary work-locating and clamping devices and will either contain or comprise the lower electrode, depending upon the nature of the parts being welded.

Assembly fixtures and electrodes for projection welding differ in several respects from those designed for conventional spot welding. For projection welding, the fixtures usually become a part of the welding dies, which are mounted on the machine platens; for spot welding, it is necessary to move the fixture and work when more than one weld must be made. Projection-welding dies are designed to allow multiple welds to be made in one cycle of the machine. The stationary fixture locates and holds the work during the welding cycle, after which the completed work is removed. Since a portion of the projection-welding fixture forms part of the secondary-current path during the welding cycle, its current-carrying components must be insulated from the rest of the die. Figure 15-106 shows a projection-welding die for welding a dowel-pin assembly. The die was designed for mounting into the horns of a combination press-type welding machine,

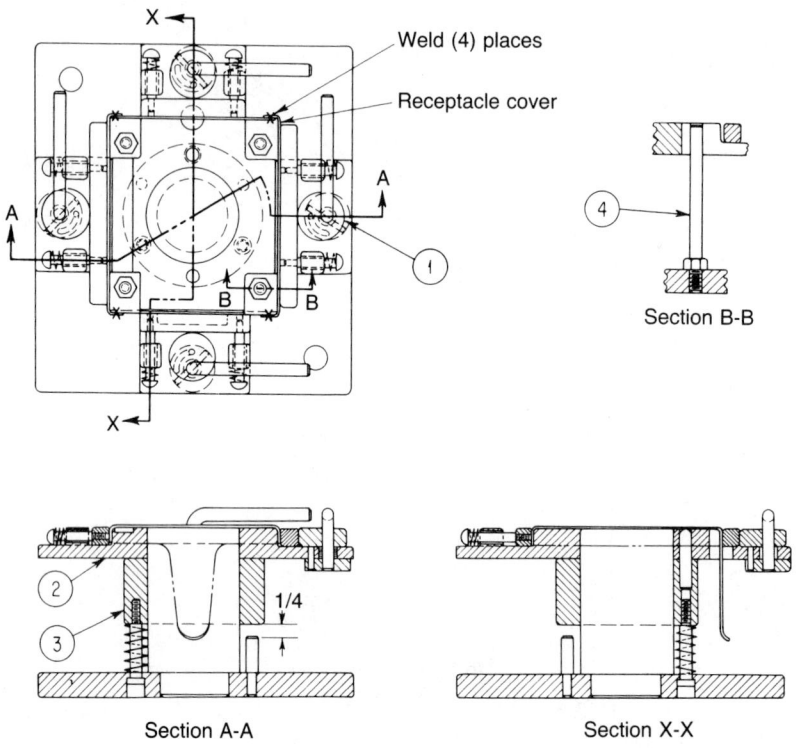

Weld (4) places

Receptacle cover

Section B-B

Section A-A

Section X-X

Fig. 15-100 Sizing and spot-welding fixture. (*Courtesy Western Electric Co., Inc.*)

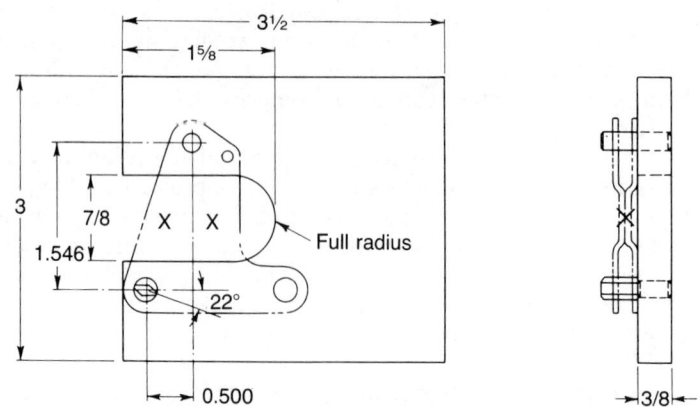

Full radius

Fig. 15-101 Simple spot welding jig. (*Courtesy The Vendo Co.*)

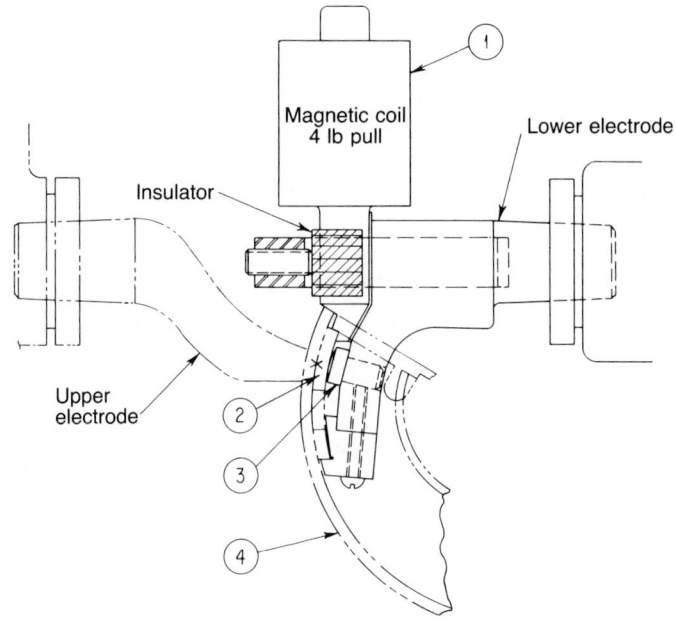

Fig. 15-102 Special spot-welding electrode assembly. (*Courtesy Detroit Transmission Div., General Motors Corp.*)

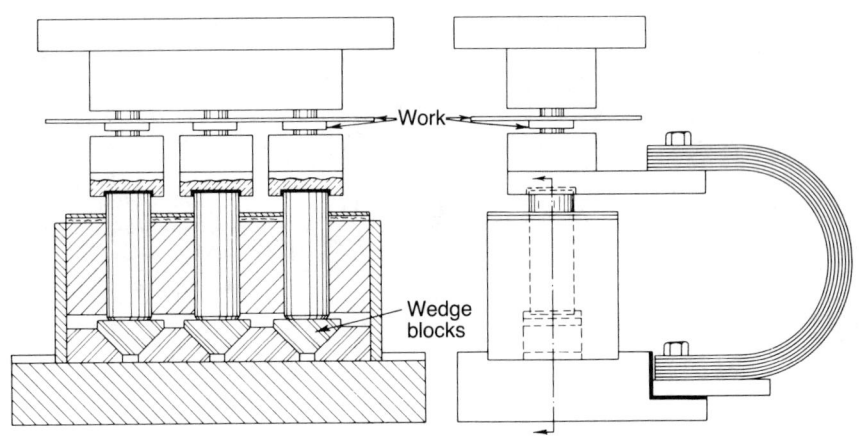

Fig. 15-103 Welding fixture with equalized electrode pressures.

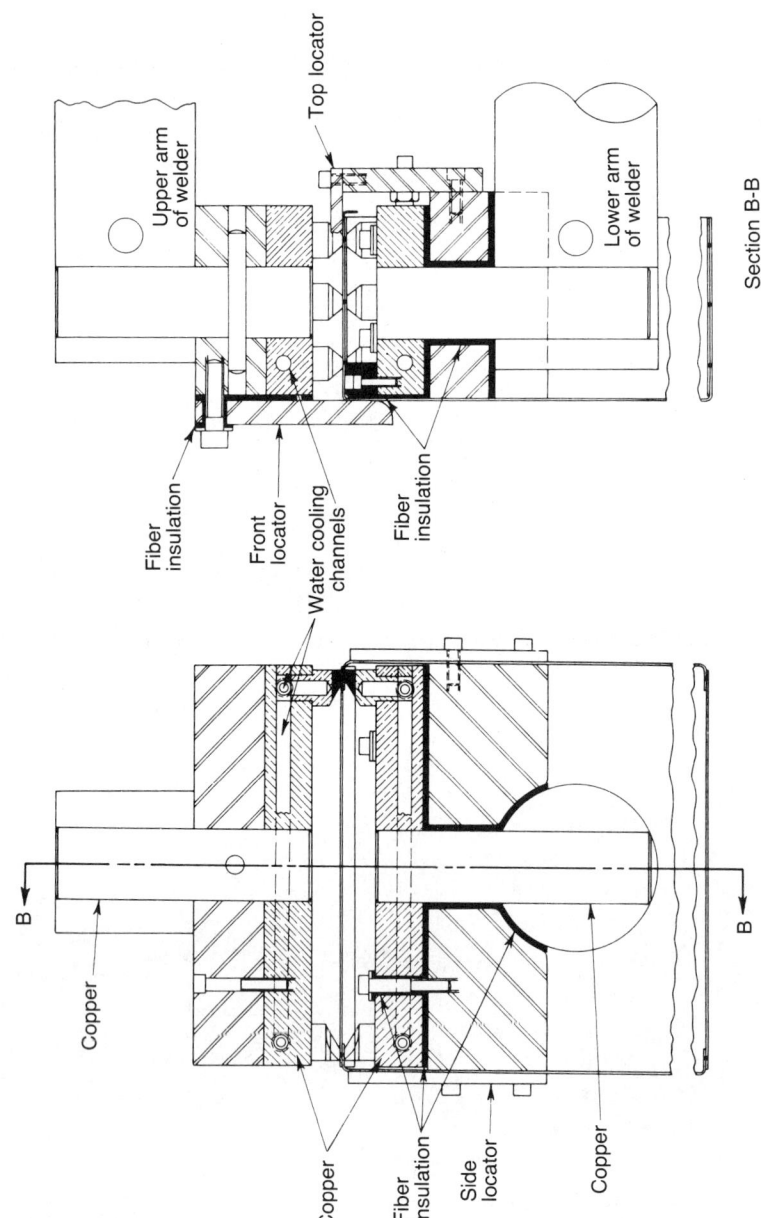

Fig. 15-104 Fixture for spot-welding a rectangular box. (*Courtesy Craft Mfg. Co.*)

Upper arm of welder

Top locator

Lower arm of welder

Section B-B

Fiber insulation

Front locator

Water cooling channels

Fiber insulation

Copper

B

B

Copper

Fiber insulation

Side locator

Copper

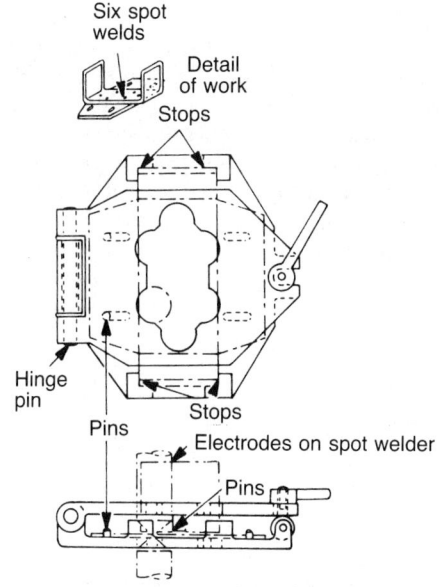

Fig. 15-105 Spot-welding jig for making six spot welds.

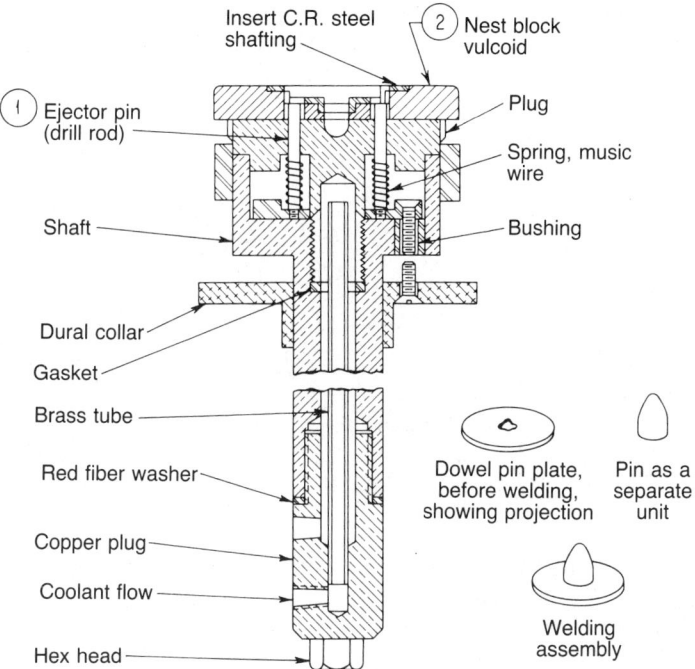

Fig. 15-106 Projection welding die.[6]

rather than directly to the machine platens.

It is necessary to use a welding machine with as small a throat as possible, as well as to keep the height of the fixture to a minimum, for maximum welder efficiency resulting from the minimum of metal mass in the magnetic field of the throat.

All gage pins, clamps, locators, index pins, etc., should be insulated from current-carrying components. Figure 15-107 shows a locating pin pressed into an insulating sleeve, which in turn is pressed into the lower die. Fabricating these parts out of insulating materials, such as fiber, micarta, vulcoid, Bakelite, etc., will eliminate the insulating of metal-fixture parts. If abrasion resistance is important or if long production runs are encountered, an insulated metal part may be required. If a locating pin contacts both workpieces, as shown in Fig. 15-107, current shunted across the pin will pit and burn it; therefore, it should be easily replaceable. Pin life can be prolonged in such cases by chromium-plating the pins.

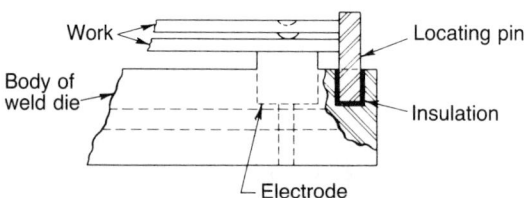

Fig. 15-107 Welding die with a knockout hole for replacing electrodes.[6]

Electrode contact faces are subject to considerable wear, and when worn, they will fail to maintain a constant pressure contact with the work. It then becomes necessary to adjust them by raising the lower arm or fixture or to replace them with refaced or new electrodes. Figure 15-108 shows the component (1) of Fig. 15-106 and illustrates a recessed electrode for refacing when worn. The plug allows 1/16-in. (1.59 mm) wear and can be refaced four times before complete replacement is necessary. The die shown in Fig. 15-107 has a knockout hole to drive out the worn electrode.

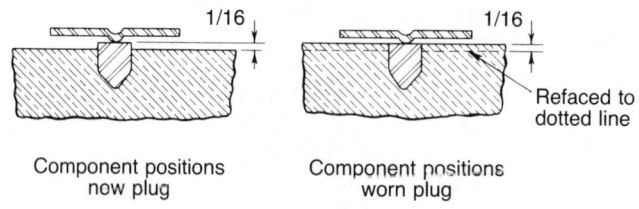

Fig. 15-108 Refaceable plug design.[6]

In addition to electrode or die wear, consideration must be given to stops, gage points, and pins to assure their proper functioning at both new and worn electrode heights.

Internal cooling of the electrodes is necessary to avoid overheating and wear during the welding cycle. Water at 70° F, introduced at a rate of 1 to 5 gal per min (3.8 to 18.9 liters per min), will provide proper cooling. Figure 15-106 illustrates a method to cool projection-welding dies in which water is fed through a tube to the electrode faces. When coolant must pass through a cast copper die or electrode, cast copper tubing or stainless-steel or seamless-steel high-strength annealed tubing cast in the die or electrode is preferred to drilling holes in the cast metal, because holes drilled in cast copper may permit difficult-to-stop water leakage. Electrode design should be kept as simple as possible, since the more complicated electrodes usually require more intricate water-cooling passages. On high-production jobs involving high-duty cycles (speed of operation of the welding machine), separate cooling lines should be run to upper and lower electrodes. When dial feeds are used, welding under water with a suitable container built onto the table has been used to simplify the water-line circuits.

Current-carrying fixture components should be as close to the electrodes as possible.

The high-amperage, low-voltage welding currents in projection welding necessitate sizes of current-carrying fixture components having electrical properties conforming to the welding current required. When sizing such conductors, whether they be one of the copper-base alloys or other nonferrous materials, the current-carrying capacity of the metal is available from electrode manufacturers. The electrode contact on parts welded should extend a minimum of five times the diameter of the projection in all directions from the weld to assure uniform heat distribution.

There should be no alternative path for the welding current. Non-current-carrying fixture components must be insulated from those carrying current to ensure that all of the current goes through the welds. The die of Fig. 15-106 utilizes an insulating nest block (2) so that the current follows a path from the dowel-pin plate directly through the projection into the dowel pin. All die components are insulated from the current-carrying copper alloy.

All moving slides, bearings, index pins, adjusting screws, and any accurate locating devices should be protected against flash. Some flashing is inevitable and the current can arc across insulated pins, creating a short circuit.

The fixture components must accurately locate the parts to be welded, since the simultaneous formation of multiple welds requires that all projections be in uniform contact with the mating material. The upper and lower dies must be parallel and must register accurately in a manner similar to punch-press dies. Proper registration prevents slippage and ensures good electrical contact and is one of the reasons that press-type machines are used for multiple-projection welding.

The effect of welding pressure on the machine, the part, and the fixture components and their resistance to deflection are fixture-design considerations. One part can be accurately positioned to another by punching holes in one part and matching them to semipunchings in the other, thus avoiding the necessity of having the fixture control the location of both parts.

Ease of loading and unloading the fixtures and the safety of the operator are particularly important with hand-loaded dies to protect the operator's hands. Air jets or ejector pins, operated through a lever coupled with air knockouts or mechanical strippers, lower unloading time and contribute to operator safety, especially when the work tends to stick to the electrode faces. The upper electrode may be designed to pick up the part from the lower die. In the die of Fig. 15-106, rapid unloading of the welded assembly is accomplished by means of the spring-loaded ejector pins (1).

Electrical shock is a remote hazard to the operator during loading and unloading of the fixture. To protect the operator, the machine base should be insulated from the secondary circuit on one side only, at either the upper electrode or the fixture base. Additional protection can be provided by guards for hand-loaded dies and by dual push buttons requiring both hands to control the machine.

Workpiece Considerations for Fixture Design. Some parts to be welded may be nested in a recessed electrode without auxiliary clamping, over a pilot pin pressed into the electrode, or into an insulating sleeve mounted on the electrode. Parts produced on screw machines, having the projection formed as a radiused projection, an annular ring, or a beveled, annular edge, are frequently fused to a flat sheet or stamping. Specialized parts of fasteners are in the form of weld bolts, weld nuts and pads, weld pins, and weld brackets, and are normally commercially available forged products designed to be components of a welded fastener assembly.

A smaller fastener part can be held in a recessed lower electrode with the larger part on top. To locate the smaller part on top, additional holding devices may be required. For example, parts may be nested into the upper electrode and held by spring clips assembled on either the inside or outside of the electrode. A spring-loaded ball or plunger bearing on the part through a hole drilled in the electrode may hold small parts. Vacuum may also be used to hold small parts in the upper electrode. Examples of electrode design for welding this type of part are shown in Fig. 15-109. Such parts are readily adaptable to hopper or magazine feeds which feed the parts automatically into the upper or lower electrode; the mating part is manually added.

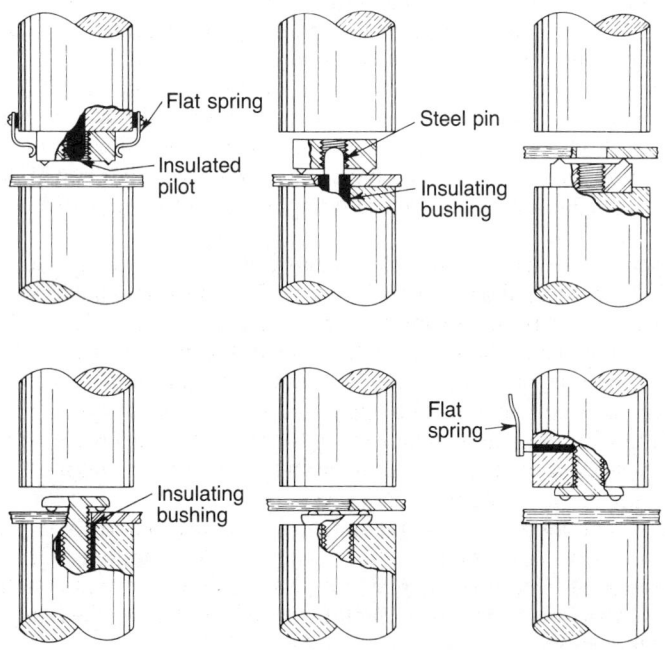

Fig. 15-109 Electrode designs. (*Courtesy The Tool Engineer*)

Figure 15-110 shows a fixture for welding two stamped sheet-metal parts. The channel-shaped workpiece is placed on the lower platen in a nest formed by a plate (1), the locating dowels (2), and the lower electrodes (3). The rectangular workpiece, having projections at the weld areas, is positioned by a locating block (4) ensuring contact of the projections with the other workpiece. Upper and lower electrodes are pressed into machined copper bars (5 and 6) which are cross-drilled for water circulation. The bars are mounted directly to copper base plates (7 and 8) which are fastened to the machine table and ram.

A steel plate (1) and locating block (4) are insulated from contact with the copper base (7) by micarta inserts (9). Attaching bolts are insulated by micarta sleeves (10) and washers (11). The outboard fixture elements for location of the channel-shaped workpiece are now shown.

TOOLING FOR SEAM WELDING[7]

Electrodes. The electrodes used for seam welding must be of the proper material and

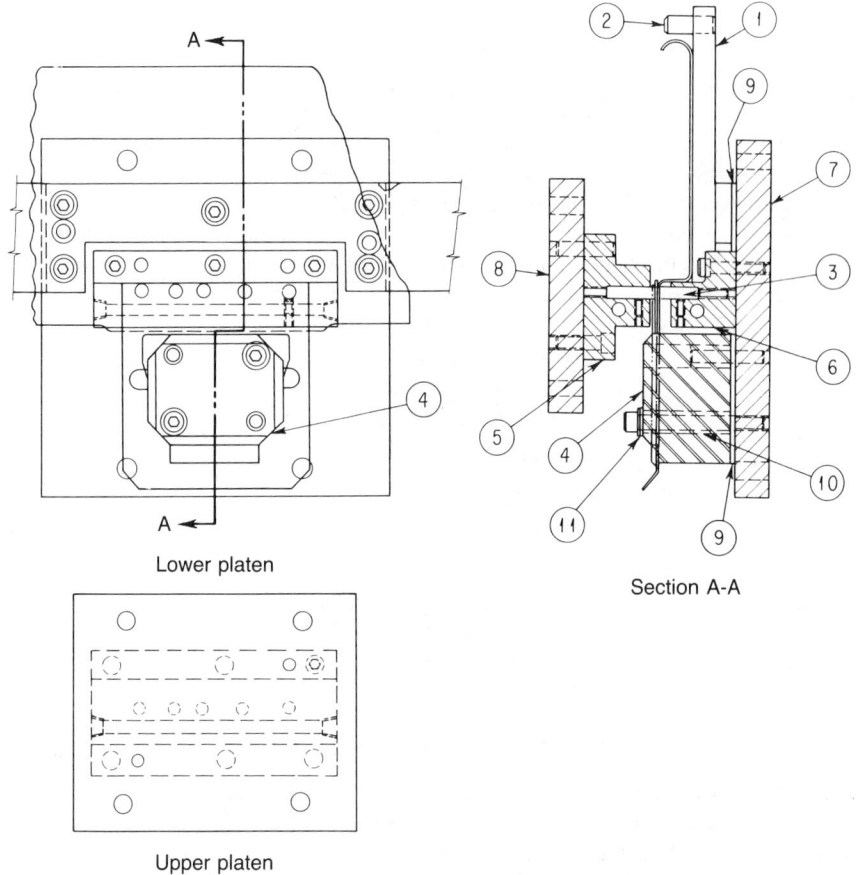

A

A

Lower platen

Upper platen

Section A-A

Fig. 15-110 Welding two stampings. (*Courtesy American Metal Products Co.*)

shape, and adequate cooling is mandatory. Cooling is generally done by flooding, usually with water jets directed to locations immediately before and after the electrode wheels. In some case, internally cooled electrodes are used.

Size and Shape. The size and general shape of the electrode will usually be determined by the shape of the parts to be welded, by the location of the welds, and by the need of a driving mechanism to keep the electrodes rotating. If welds are to be made on flanges, one end of the electrode face is often made practically flush with the side of the electrode, allowing the face to weld the flange with the minimum degree of clearance.

Workholding Fixtures. Well-designed workholding fixtures are essential for resistance seam welding to ensure accurate position and minimize distortion. A typical two-station fixture for seam welding a cylindrical tank is shown in Fig. 15-111.

TOOLING FOR FLASH WELDING

In flash welding, the portions of the clamps that grip the workpieces are the current-carrying electrodes. For some workpieces, workholding fixtures are required in addition to the dies. For some applications, water cooling of the dies and/or fixtures is necessary.

The tolerance of overall length of the parts after welding is influenced by the tolerance before welding. If pieces are located in the welder by touching the edges to be welded, tolerances after welding will equal the sum of the tolerances before welding. Misalignment also results in reduction of material thickness (see Fig. 15-112). If

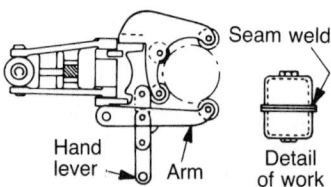

Fig. 15-111 Two-station seam welding fixture.

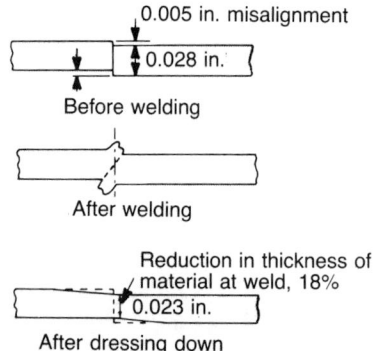

Fig. 15-112 Misalignment of workpieces results in reduction in material thickness.

backup locators are used, the tolerance after welding can normally be reduced to less than that of one part. The influence of tolerance (see Fig. 15-113) shows the importance of proper alignment design of the dies in the production of accurate work.

Flash butt welding is shown in Fig. 15-114.

BRAZING AND SOLDERING

Brazing and soldering are joining processes that use heat and filler metals to produce metallurgical bonds. Unlike most of the fusion welding processes discussed earlier, brazing and soldering do not involve any melting of the base metals being joined. As a result, the mechanical and physical properties of the base metals are not generally duplicated at the joints. However, diffusion brazing can produce a strength equal to the base metal.

While both brazing and soldering use filler metals, the processes differ with respect to temperature and bonding action. In brazing, the filler metals have liquidus temperatures *above* 840° F (450° C), but below those of the base metals, and the filler metals are distributed between the mating surfaces of the joints by capillary action. In soldering, the filler metals have liquidus temperatures *below* 840° F (450° C). Filler metals are distributed by both capillary action and wetting between the surfaces of the components that are being soldered, using the surface energies of the materials that are being joined.

Brazing Processes. There are many brazing processes currently being used. They are generally classified by the method used to heat the assembly. In some applications, however, several methods of heating are used to produce brazed joints. Selection of a process depends primarily on the parts to be brazed, equipment available, and costs. Some brazing filler metals and base metals can be brazed by only one of the heating methods.

Relieved area in clamp faces allow clamps to follow up to compensate for die wear to a greater extent than at (b).

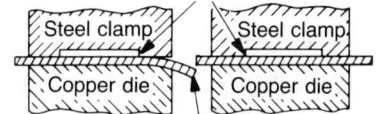

Lack of alignment at weld zone due to wear, resulting in skidding of components during welding.

(a)

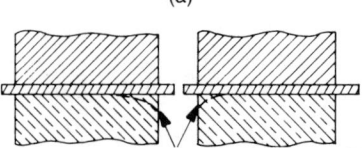

Wear occurs here, allowing flexing of components. Clamps not able to follow up to compensate for die wear.

(b) Poor arrangement

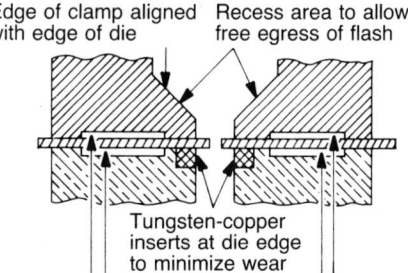

(c) Recommended arrangement

Fig. 15-113 Effect of die design and alignment on weld quality.

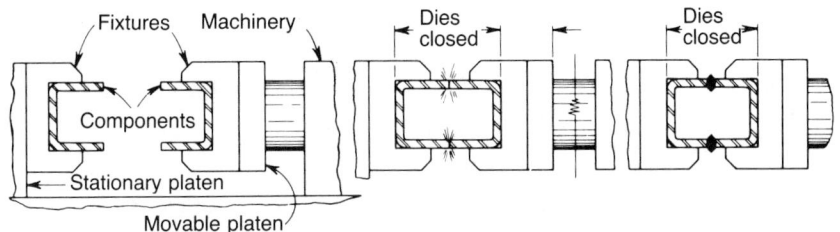

Fig. 15-114 Flash butt welding.

The most common brazing processes are torch, induction, dip, infrared, and furnace brazing. Other processes used less commonly include arc, diffusion, electron beam, exothermic, laser beam, resistance, block, blanket, and flow brazing.

Furnace Brazing. Furnace brazing is the process most suited to mass-production brazing and for critical applications. This is particularly true in brazing small- to medium-sized components of up to 3 to 4 lb (1.4 to 1.8 kg) each. This process probably accounts for the largest share of brazed hardware in the United States today. The following features distinguish furnace brazing:

1. The filler metal must be preplaced so that it will flow into the joints with no

operator assistance after the parts have reached brazing temperatures.

2. Fixturing of the parts must be kept at a minimum and best design makes the brazement self-fixturing. Large quantities of fixtures increase process cost and lower furnace productivity by adding deadweight.

3. An atmosphere protects the parts from oxidation at brazing temperatures, reduces trace oxides, and aids in the wetting of the filler metal on the parent metal.

Furnace Types. Furnace brazing may be performed as either a batch or a continuous operation. Batch operations use retorts or cold-wall vacuum furnaces in which the load is stacked in rows on trays of nickel-chromium alloy. The entire load is then brought to brazing temperature, and all the parts braze at the same time. Vacuum furnaces are hermetically sealed, and the air is pumped out to produce a protective atmosphere. Semicontinuous vacuum furnaces are used for brazing aluminum automotive components such as radiators and air-conditioner heat exchangers. Continuous furnace brazing uses a conveyor mechanism that carries the parts through the heat zone and into a cooling zone on a mesh belt or on rolls driven by a chain and sprocket arrangement. The latter design is known as a roller-hearth furnace.

SOLDERING METHODS

Soldering methods are generally classified by the method of heat application. Typical methods are conduction, convection, radiation, resistance, and induction. Ultrasonic energy may also be used as an aid to soldering. Selection of a heating method depends primarily on the cost and efficiency of the method, production requirements, and the sensitivity of the assembly to heat.

FIXTURES FOR BRAZING AND SOLDERING

Requirements for workholding fixtures to be used in brazing and soldering vary with the specific application. Self-locating components generally do not require fixtures. When fixtures are necessary, the following general rules usually apply:

- Fixture rigidity is essential, especially in area of high stress.
- Workpiece supports must provide precise alignment and should be located as far from the joint to be soldered as possible to minimize the heat-sink effect.
- The fixture should hold components in inclined positions for easier flux and filler metal location. Use gravity to assist capillary action whenever possible.
- Ample access should be provided to the joint area to facilitate the application of flux, filler metal, heat, and the cooling medium.
- When workpiece hold-down is required, quick-acting mechanical clamps or counterweights are preferable to springs, which lose their resiliency.
- The baseplates of fixtures should be secured to the machine to ensure proper alignment.
- The fixture must permit easy insertion of components and easy removal of the completed assembly.
- Direct the heat source around the entire joint area so that the heat pattern designed into the system can flow the alloy throughout the joint.
- In the case of soldering, the fixture must maintain alignment and dimensional stability of the components until the solder solidifies.

When families of similar parts are to be brazed or soldered, the use of a common fixture with interchangeable inserts can reduce cost. Providing nests on the machines for rapid changeover of fixtures can also cut costs. Fixtures components are often made of Type 300 series stainless steels to resist corrosion during repeated heating and cooling cycles.

A Simple Nesting Fixture. If the shape of the workpiece is such that it will not support itself in an upright or convenient position, a simple nesting fixture may be required. Figure 15-115 shows a simple nesting fixture in which two workpieces and a brazing ring have been placed. The fixture can be mounted on a table while an operator applies heat with a hand torch. The same fixture could be mounted on a powered rotating base in the flame path of a fixed torch, while a feed mechanism would introduce wire solder at a predetermined rate (see Fig. 15-116). The same fixture could be attached in quantity to the belt of a tunnel furnace. A number of the fixtures could be attached to a rack for processing in a batch furnace.

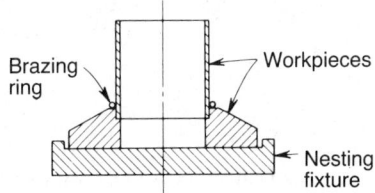

Fig. 15-115 Simple nesting fixture with work in place.

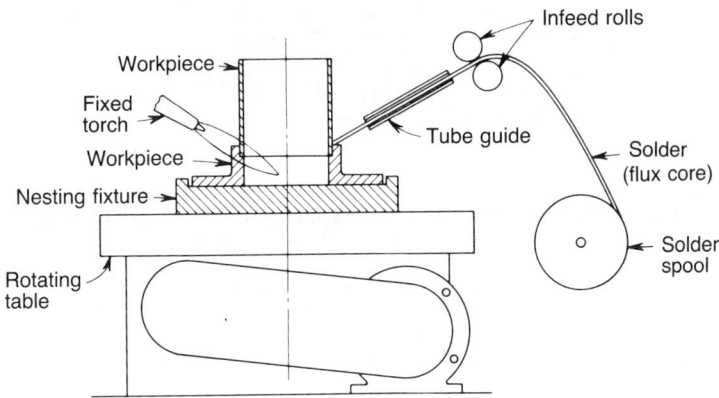

Fig. 15-116 Soldering machine using simple nesting fixture.

Nesting Fixture for Brazing with an External Inductor. Figure 15-117 shows a nest-type fixture to hold mating workpieces within the field of an induction work coil. Figure 15-118 shows the same fixture as altered to permit use of an internal induction heating coil. If the external coil is used, the fixture designer must provide some method of moving the fixture or coil while workpieces are loaded and unloaded.

Induction coils (inductors) provide a convenient and precise way of quickly and efficiently heating any selected area of an electrically conductive part or assembly of such parts to any required depth to provide a specified brazed joint. Correct selection must be made of frequency, power density, heating time, and inductor design.

Fixture for Brazing Tungsten Carbide Discs. Tungsten discs to be copper-brazed to steel shanks are placed in the holes in the graphite base of the fixture of Fig. 15-119. A slight clearance between the holes and the shanks allows gravity, as the copper shims melt, to move them downward against the tungsten discs. Thin sheets of asbestos paper between steel parts and graphite fixture blocks generally prevent carbon diffusion into the parts and their possible melting.

Fixture for Furnace Brazing. Figure 15-120 shows steel and tungsten carbide components held by clamps made of heat-resisting alloy bolts and bar stock. The mica insert prevents the tungsten carbide component from being brazed to the alloy bar.

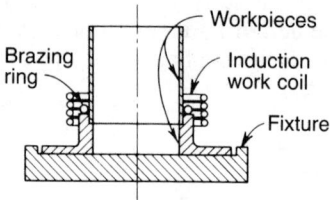

Fig. 15-117 Nesting fixture for brazing with an external inductor.

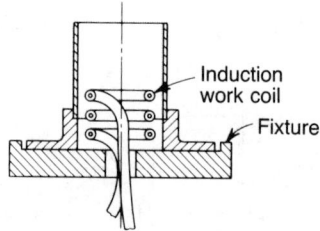

Fig. 15-118 Nesting fixture for brazing with an internal inductor.

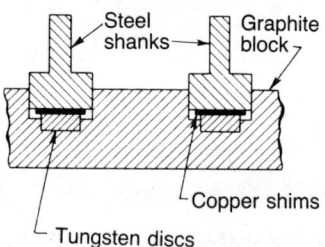

Fig. 15-119 Fixture for brazing tungsten carbide discs.[8]

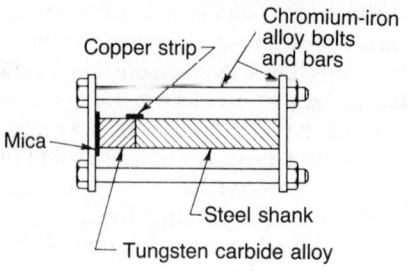

Fig. 15-120 Fixture for furnace brazing.[8]

Figure 15-121 shows a fixture for the acetylene-torch brazing of a siphon-tube and washer assembly. This simple fixture consists of a base (1), a block (2), and two screws (3). The fixture holds the tube and washer in the position required for the operation.

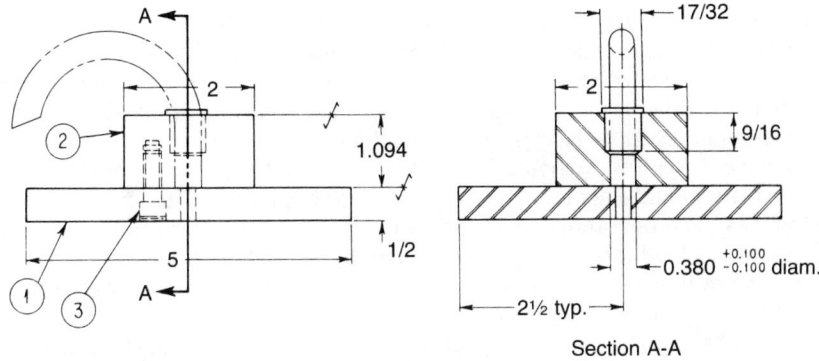

Fig. 15-121 **Fixture for acetylene torch brazing.** (*Courtesy The Vendo Co.*)

AUTOMATED ASSEMBLY[9]

Before automated assembly is adopted, several factors should be considered. These include practicality of the process for automation, simulation for economic considerations and justification, management involvement, and labor relations.

Practicality of Automation. Determining the practicality of automated assembly requires careful evaluation of the following:

- The number of parts in the assembly.
- Design of the parts with respect to producibility, assemblability, automatic handling, and testability (materials, forms, sizes, dimensional tolerances, and weights).
- Quality of parts to be assembled. Out-of-tolerance or defective parts can cause production losses and increased costs because of stoppages.
- Availability of qualified, technically competent personnel to be responsible for equipment operation.
- Total production and production-rate requirements.
- Product variations and frequency of design changes.
- Joining methods required.
- Assembly times and costs.
- Assembly line or system configuration, using simulation, including material handling.

The best candidates for successful and economical automated assembly are generally simple, small products having a fairly stable design life. Such products are usually required in relatively large volumes and have a high labor content and/or a high reject rate because of their manual assembly. However, the development of flexible, programmable, and robotic assembly systems (discussed subsequently in this chapter) can decrease production and products-life requirements.

Labor Relations. Whether assembly is done manually, semiautomatically, or automatically, people playing the proper roles are essential to success. Properly trained and motivated personnel are especially important in automation to ensure the effective use of human resources. Education is necessary to demonstrate to everyone involved that automation is not a threat to their livelihood. Rather, automation is a vital means of survival for companies by increasing quality and productivity, and reducing costs. It also improves the work environment with respect to safety and health.

Management Involvement. Involvement and support by all levels of management are essential to the success of automated assembly. Capital investment for the necessary equipment must be justified for automated manufacturing. Top management must be sold on the importance of the concept and support the belief that the financial investment will improve product quality, increase productivity, reduce costs, and result in increased profits. Realistic expectations must be established for equipment performance and its effect on both short and long-term planning for the company. Top management must also motivate other levels of management and all employees affected and encourage participation in decision making and goalsetting.

Cost-effective Assembly Systems. Cost-effective assembly for some products often lies between manual and fully automated systems. Both the feasibility and cost of each proposed mechanized operation should be compared to manual assembly. It is sometimes preferable to load large components manually, as well as those with smooth or decorative surface finishes. In other cases, it is better to fabricate the components (for example, coil spring winding) on the assembly machine.

For complex products having many parts, it is generally preferable to divide the assembly operations among two or more machines. Combining too many parts and assembly functions on one machine can be inefficient, result in excessive downtime, or even cause failure of the entire system. While the initial cost of using more than one machine is higher, the increased efficiency and reduced downtime resulting from fewer stations on each machine generally provide more economical operation. The machines can be connected by conveyors and each machine operated individually. Accumulating banks for temporary storage and repair stations can be provided between machines.

ASSEMBLY MACHINES AND SYSTEMS

A broad variety of machines and systems is available for automated assembly. A general outline of some of the concepts is shown in Fig. 15-122.[10] In addition, combinations of these basic systems and flexible, robotic, and electronic assembly systems are discussed subsequently in this section.

Selection Factors. Selection of the optimum assembly system often depends on careful consideration of many factors, including the following:[11]

1. Production rate requirements.
2. Size and weight of parts to be assembled.
3. Manual operations required, if any.
4. Number of automated operations.
5. Complexity of the operations performed.
6. Material handling and supply logistics.

The possibility of product and/or component design changes is another important factor to be considered.

Production Rate Requirements. Approximate production rates for various assembly system arrangements having single tooling are shown in Fig. 15-123. Higher production rates can be realized with systems having multiple tooling. Physical size and weight of the parts to be assembled and the complexity and number of operations must be considered in determining the most efficient system.

Size and Weight of Parts. The size and weight of the parts to be assembled can present several problems, including difficulty with positioning accuracy and equipment necessary to physically move the parts if the parts are large. Single-station machines are generally best for precision location where few operations are required. Synchronous and nonsynchronous systems are used for more operations and/or when manual operations are necessary.

Manual Operations. Although it is generally desirable to eliminate all manual operations, this is not always possible. Dial-type (rotary) assembly machines are usually limited to one or two manual operations, in-line machines have space for a number of operators, and carousel systems allow even more manual operations. A number of

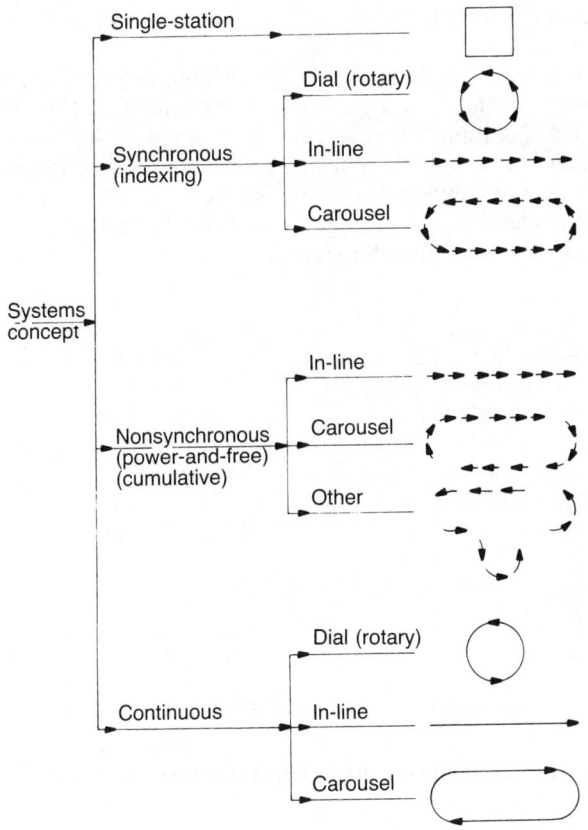

Fig. 15-122 Basic concepts for automated assembly systems.

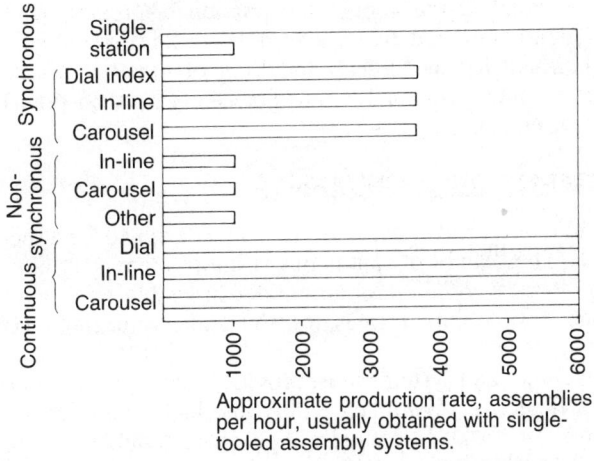

Approximate production rate, assemblies per hour, usually obtained with single-tooled assembly systems.

Fig. 15-123 Approximate production rates with single-tooled assembly.

manual operations can also be performed on synchronous and nonsynchronous systems. Continuous systems are generally almost fully automatic for the high-speed production of small assemblies and usually have many or all manual operations for the low-volume production of large assemblies.

Number of Automated Operations. The suggested number of automated operations for various assembly machine configurations is presented in Fig. 15-124. As the number of automated operations increases, the efficiency of the individual stations must be higher to maintain an acceptable machine efficiency because the overall machine efficiency is the product of individual station efficiencies. Combining too many assembly operations in one machine or system can sometimes be inefficient: it may be better to divide the operations among several machines.

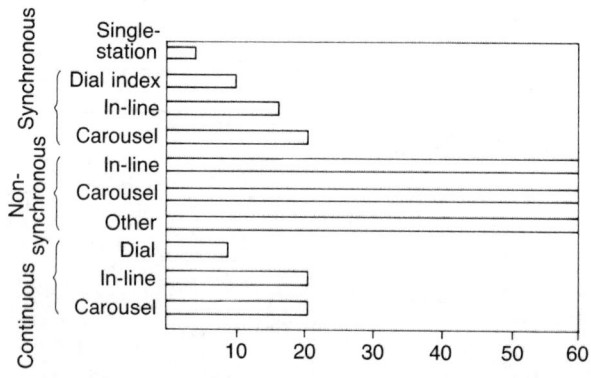

Approximate number of automatic operations performed

Fig. 15-124 Approximate number of automated operations that can be performed with various assembly systems.

Complexity of Operations. The complexity of the individual operations to be performed must be carefully considered along with the efficiencies of the various assembly configurations possible in determining which type of automation arrangement is most suitable for the assembly task.

Material Handling and Supply Logistics. Floor space and additional equipment required for material handling and storage may possibly be greater than that needed for assembly itself. Synchronous and nonsynchronous in-line assembly systems permit spreading out equipment for the orderly handling of material and assessibility for operators and maintenance personnel. Concepts such as just-in-time inventory help minimize space requirements.

BASIC EQUIPMENT REQUIREMENTS

Most assembly machines and systems are specially designed for a special product or a family of products. They can be of continuous or intermittent operation, with intermittent transfer being the most common for automated assembly. Basic assembly machine components include workholding devices, transfer and/or indexing mechanisms, parts feeding and orienting devices.

All assembly machines and systems must provide means for easy and rapid removal of jammed parts or defective assemblies. Safety interlocks, noise control devices, and environmental protection are also essential. Ample space should be provided around the system for material handling and storage as well as for access by maintenance and repair personnel. A good structural foundation and suitable lighting are also essential.

Workholding. Although some product housings or frames (to which parts are to be assembled) can be conveyed individually, it is more common to load them on pallets (special reusable fixtures) that are conveyed through the system. The pallets are generally loaded and unloaded manually, but this can be done automatically by dedicated automation, pick-and-place units, or robotic systems.

On indexing machines, the pallets are generally locked by clamps at each station to permit positive location for assembly. For some applications, it is advantageous to code the pallets mechanically, optically, or magnetically for proper placement. Pallets are often made from cast iron, but aluminum or plastics are sometimes used to reduce their mass. Ample space should be provided to facilitate loading and unloading and, when required, orienting.

Transfer and Index Mechanism. Transfer and index mechanisms are required to move pallets or assembly components from one workstation to another. Mechanical feeds are most common with conveyors and slide motions, but air, hydraulic, and electric actuators are sometimes used. Cam and turret systems, Geneva motions, walking beams, roll-bar transfers, and rack-and-pinion units are also commonplace.

Modular Components and Machines. Many elements of assembly equipment can be purchased as standard items that can sometimes be used directly for specific requirements. Standard modules include machine bases, conveyors, dial index tables, drives, part transfer units, slide units, powered heads, parts feeders, tracks, chutes, tooling, and controls. Integral assembly machines use standard modules including a basic chassis that combines indexing and actuation of all tooling from a single power unit rather than having individually powered units.

Advantages of using modular components and machines include lower design and hardware costs, shorter development time, improved reliability, easier maintenance, and greater reusability to accommodate product design changes. In many cases, most standard modules can be adapted to new or different assembly operations by replacing certain tooling such as gripper jaws and orienting devices.

One type of standardized, interchangeable, cam-actuated station-movement unit that can be mounted anywhere along an assembly machine is shown schematically in Fig. 15-125. Each basic unit contains a slide mechanism (to which the required tooling is attached) that can be mounted horizontally, vertically, or at any angle in between. Movement is imparted to the slide mechanism by a chain or lever linkage that is actuated by a follower arm in contact with a cam. The piston rod of an air-counterweight cylinder maintains constant loading on the chain linkage and moves in and out of the cylinder as the cam imparts motion to the follower arm. In case of jamming, which would prevent movement of the slide mechanism, the 2:1 mechanical advantage of the chain linkage is overcome, and the cylinder itself is pulled downward away from its stop. This provides 100% overtravel protection and prevents damage.

Check switches are provided for both forward and return travel of the slide mechanism. If these switches are not actuated at the proper time during the cycle, the machine will stop and an individual light will pinpoint the location of the jam that prevented full travel or return.

A small lockout cylinder, with a pawl mounted on its piston rod, is also provided. when it is desired to lock out movement of the slide (by a selector switch or the machine's checking and memory system), the pawl is raised. As a result, the air-counterweight cylinder is merely pulled away from its stop, just as in the case of a jam. When the pawl is retracted, the slide is again free to move in response to cam actuation.

A single camshaft (extending the full length of the machine) actuates all transfer and slide motions, ensuring positive interlocking and synchronization for fast, accurate assembly. Double-movement units are available so that two independent motions can be provided at each station. To change the operations performed at any station, it is only

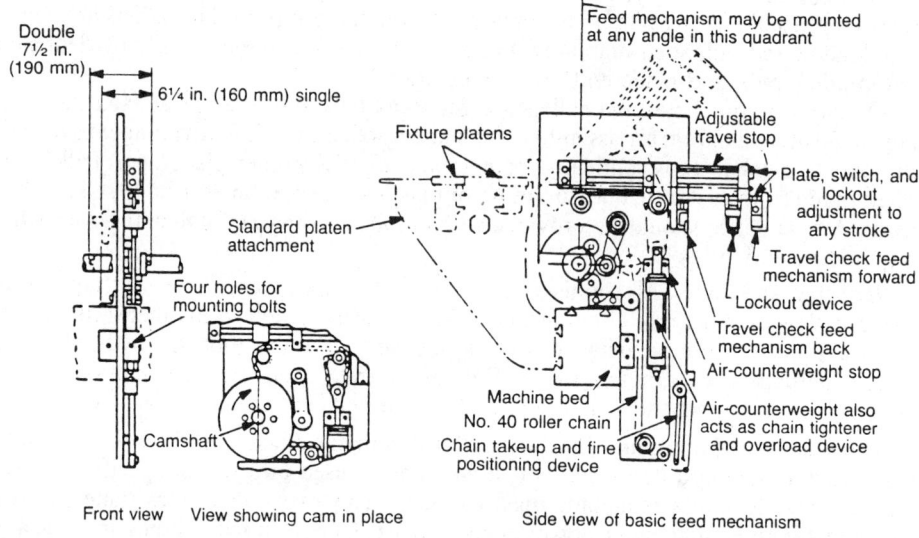

Double
7½ in.
(190 mm)

6¼ in. (160 mm) single

Feed mechanism may be mounted
at any angle in this quadrant

Fixture platens

Standard platen
attachment

Four holes for
mounting bolts

Camshaft

Adjustable
travel stop

Plate, switch, and
lockout
adjustment to
any stroke

Travel check feed
mechanism forward

Lockout device

Travel check feed
mechanism back

Air-counterweight stop

Air-counterweight also
acts as chain tightener
and overload device

Machine bed

No. 40 roller chain

Chain takeup and fine
positioning device

Front view   View showing cam in place   Side view of basic feed mechanism

Fig. 15-125 Interchangeable station-movement unit contains slide mechanism that can be mounted at any angle between horizontal and vertical. (*Courtesy Gilman Engineering & Manufacturing Co.*)

necessary to retool the slide mounting block, change the plate cam, and adjust the feed mechanism.

Platens (and the possible workholding fixtures attached to them) can be of the free-floating type, being entirely unattached to any moving mechanism. They are transferred from station to station by means of fingers that, during each cycle, engage the platens, carry them to the next station position, and then retract. Side-acting shotpins enter bushings in the platens during each dwell period for precise location. Should any repairs be required, the platens can be lifted from the tracks and spares substituted. Also, platens can be left out of the system, and the memory-control circuit will automatically prevent the loading of parts onto the vacant spaces.

SINGLE-STATION ASSEMBLY

Machines having a single workstation are used most extensively when a specific operation has to be performed many times on one or a few parts. Assembling many parts into a single unit, like inserting blades or buckets into turbine or compressor wheels, is a common application. These machines may also be used when a number of different operations have to be performed, if the required tooling is not too complicated. These machines are also incorporated into multistation assembly systems.

SYNCHRONOUS ASSEMBLY SYSTEMS

Synchronous (indexing) assembly systems are available in dial (rotary), in-line, and carousel varieties. With these systems, all pallets or workpieces are moved at the same time and for the same distance. Because indexing intervals are determined by the slowest operation to be performed at any of the stations, operation time is the determining factor affecting production rate. Operators cannot vary the production rate, and a breakdown at any station causes the whole line to stop. By proper consideration to line balancing and parallel assembly operations, such downtime problems can be minimized.

The number of automatic operations that can be performed with synchronous systems is generally limited to a maximum of 20 for in-line machines and less for dial (rotary) systems. However, because the cycle times at the individual stations are generally low (3 seconds or less), production rates are high—3,600 assemblies per hour or more. Double or triple tooling provides higher production rates.

Synchronous systems are used primarily for high-speed and high-volume applications on small, lightweight assemblies where the various operations are required have relatively equal cycle times. They are also generally used for fully or substantially automated operations because manual operations are not usually compatible with these systems. However, manual stations, both semiautomatic and completely manual, can be used on synchronous lines. Stations can also be bypassed and operators inserted if idle stations have been initially designed into the system. Dual palm buttons should be provided at manual stations to prevent transfer until operators are finished with their tasks.

The inefficiency of synchronous systems can be increased by providing surge (buffer or banking) and repair loops. With some systems, certain operations are performed off-line to ensure that good subassemblies in the required amounts are presented to the final assembly system.

NONSYNCHRONOUS ASSEMBLY SYSTEMS

Nonsynchronous transfer (accumulative or power-and-free type) assembly systems, with free or floating pallets or workpieces and independently operated individual stations, are being widely used where the times required to perform different operations vary greatly and for larger products having many components. Such machines have slower cycle rates than synchronous machines, but slower stations can be double or triple tooled to boost production. One major advantage of these so-called power-and-free systems is increased versatility. The individually actuated, independent stations operate only when a pallet supplied on demand, is present and when manual and automatic operations can easily be combined. Different methods can be used to meet line balancing needs. For example, multiple loading, joining, or testing stations can be banked or sent down multiple tracks for longer operations, while shorter operations are done on a one-at-a-time basis. Nonsynchronous machines often have a lower initial cost, but require more controls (a set at each station) and generally require more space.

With nonsynchronous systems, the workpieces or pallets can be stopped individually at any station for work to be done or can be queued at manual stations to allow for variations in operator speed. When one or more stations are down for any reason, other stations can continue to operate from their floats of partial assemblies, minimizing production interruptions. Such systems have been described as a series of single-station machines with an integrated, automatic part transfer and in-process buffering system. Practically any number of operations can be linked together, and standby stations and repair loops can be provided. A limitation with nonsynchronous system is that they operate at slower speeds—generally at a maximum production rate of about 1,400 assemblies per hour.

CONTINUOUS-MOTION SYSTEMS

With continuous-motion systems, assembly operations are performed while the workpieces or pallets move at a constant speed and the workheads reciprocate. High production rates are possible because indexing time is eliminated. However, the cost and complexity of these systems are high because the workheads have to synchronize and move with the product being assembled. Applications for continuous-motion automated assembly are limited except for high-production uses in the packaging and bottling industries. The systems are, however, used for the manual assembly of large and heavy products, such as automobiles and refrigerators, with the operators moving with the products while performing their functions.

DIAL (ROTARY) ASSEMBLY

Dial or rotary index machines of synchronous design, one of the first types used for assembly, are still used for many applications. Workstations and tooling can be mounted on a central column or around the periphery of the indexing table. These machines are generally limited to small and medium-sized lightweight assemblies requiring a relatively low number of operations that are not too complex; as the table diameter increases, its mass and complexity can become impractical. Another possible disadvantage is limited accessibility to the workheads and tooling. Also, servicing the indexing table and mechanism, as well as the controls, is difficult with center-column designs.

Typical Application. A good example of a successful application of a 20-station dial index machine with two operators is the assembly of a furnace fan limit control that contains 11 parts, as shown in Fig. 15-126. A block diagram of the machine is seen in Fig. 15-127. At Station 1, the first operator drives a setscrew into the post of each cam assembly and places the post in an inclined track. A pickup mechanism at the bottom of the track automatically transfers the post into a nest on the index table. Stations 2, 4, 6, 8, 10, 12, 14, and 16 are all checking stations to ensure that each part has been placed into the nests correctly.

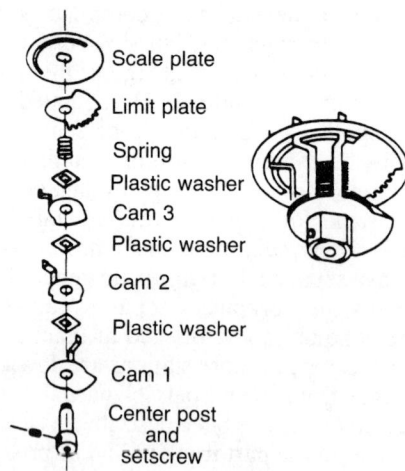

Scale plate

Limit plate

Spring

Plastic washer

Cam 3

Plastic washer

Cam 2

Plastic washer

Cam 1

Center post
and
setscrew

Fig. 15-126 Components and assembly of a furnace fan limit control produced on machine shown in Fig. 15-127.

At Stations 3, 7, and 11, preplated coil stock is fed through a progressive die mounted in a punch press located at the side of the assembly machine. Here required cams are made in chain form and are fed to the assembly machine, where the chain is cut apart and the cams are automatically picked up and placed in the nest.

At Stations 5, 9, and 13, coiled plastic stock is fed through a two-stage progressive die. A hole is punched into the strip at the first stage, and the washer is cut off and pushed into the nest at the second stage. A spring winder at Station 15 produces one complete spring for each machine cycle. As the spring is cut off, it is blown through a

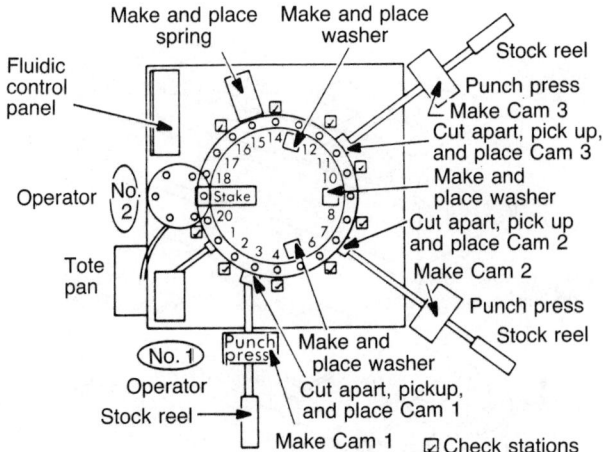

Fig. 15-127 Block diagram of a 20-station dial index machine used to assemble parts shown in Fig. 15-126.

plastic tube into the nest.

Stations 17 and 18 are open to allow for possible design changes in the cam assembly. At Station 19, a second operator manually places a limit plate and a scale plate into a nest on a small auxiliary index table. This table indexes the parts over the nest of the main table. The small table has a floating nest that allows a staking tool to push the two parts down on top of the post and stake the assembly together. As the staking tool is raised, the floating nest picks up the completed assembly, indexes it, and deposits it on an inclined track leading to a tote pan. A gage at Station 20 ensures that the nest is empty.

Advantages and Limitations. Advantages of dial machines include minimum floor space requirements because of their compact designs, high production rates—up to 3,600 or more assemblies per hour, and the ease with which standard modules and tooling can be used. Cycle time, however, is limited by the slowest operation required. Dial machines are often tied together with transfer devices to other machines and systems. Limitations include practical physical size and space available for loading, unloading, tooling, maintenance, and repairs.

Versatility. Tables for rotary indexing machines are available in various sizes, with a maximum practical diameter of about 200 in. (5,080 mm). Fixtures or nests are equally spaced around the tables, and standard tables usually have from 4 to 32 stations. The stations can be single or double tooled, depending on production requirements.

Double indexing is possible when it is desired to have a workpiece pass a manual operating station twice during assembly. Lift-and-carry devices can be provided to transport parts from station to station where they must be placed down into nests or fixtures.

IN-LINE SYSTEMS

In-line assembly machines are used in synchronous (indexing), nonsynchronous (accumulative or power-and-free), and continuous designs. In-line indexing assembly machines can be of the wraparound (circumferential) or over-and-under type (see Fig. 15-128) or of the conventional transfer-machine type. In the over-and-under type, workholding pallets or platens move horizontally in a straight path and when empty return to the loading station on a conveyor under the machine. In the wrap-around type, the work moves around the periphery of the machine in an oval, rectangular, or square path.

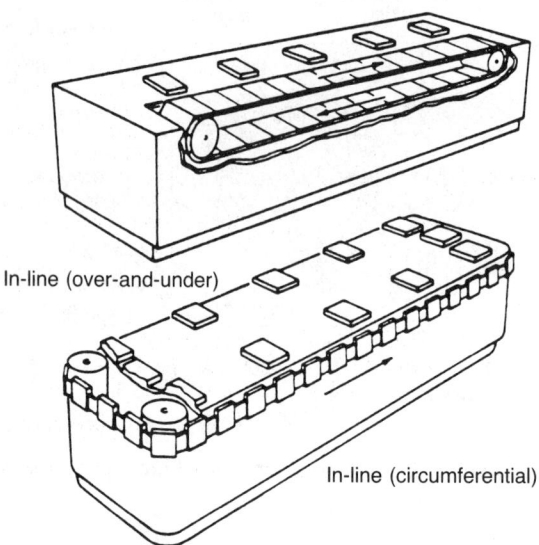

In-line (over-and-under)

In-line (circumferential)

Fig. 15-128 In-line indexing assembly machine bases of the over-and-under and circumferential (wraparound) types.

Various methods of moving the workpieces from station to station are used on different assembly machines. On one over-and-under type, the platens are rolled over in two 90° rotations when they reach the end of the machine and are returned on a lower track to the starting end. In another type, for assembling smaller components, the platens are indexed along two sets of parallel tracks, with automatic operations performed as the platens are transferred along the back row and manual operations (if required) performed as the platens return along the front row. On one-in-line wraparound type, a single indexing unit is provided at one end of the machine, with a flexible steel band that is driven by a drum wheel and rides around the edge of a built-up table to support the pallets for moving from station to station. The workholder pallets are attached to and indexed by the steel-band drive, with locator pins preventing shifting of the band on the drive drum. Another type of assembly machine is equipped with self-propelled pallets.

Typical Applications. A cam-operated nonsynchronous assembly system for producing rear drum-brake backing plates (12 in. (305 mm) diam. and weighting 6 ½ lb. (3 kg)) at the rate of 900 per hour is illustrated in Fig. 15-129. Operations performed include piercing, welding, shaving, hot upsetting, and hollow milling, with automatic loading, assembling, and unloading on the one machine. Although this system operates on a 4-second cycle, several stations are capable of operating faster if needed because each station has its own drum cam. The drum cams are powered by continuously running electric motors and are driven through one revolution each cycle by alternately engaged air-operated clutch and brake units.

Workpieces are transported around the rectangular system on friction-driven pallet carriers by a power-and-free conveyor. The pallets are supported by an oil film on hardened-steel plates fastened to the roller-chain conveyor. With this floating transport system, pallets can be accumulated ahead of any of the independent stations if required.

Sensors at the independent stations actuate flags on the pallets if the required operations are not performed. The flags cause the pallets to bypass subsequent stations and thus prevent further work from being done on the assemblies. At the unloading station, incomplete assemblies are automatically rejected.

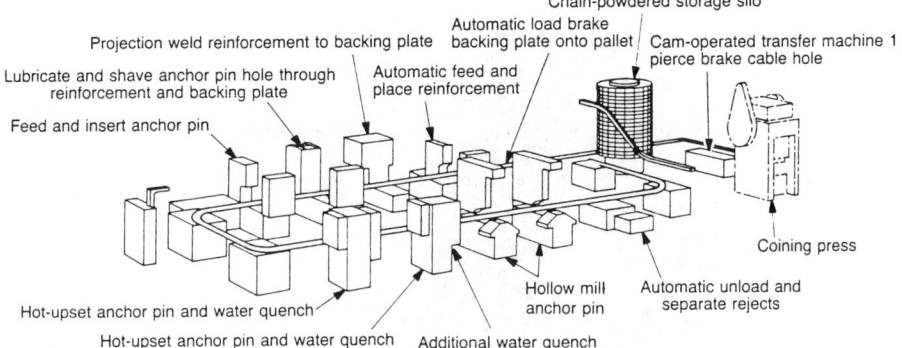

Chain-powdered storage silo

Automatic load brake
Projection weld reinforcement to backing plate   backing plate onto pallet / Cam-operated transfer machine 1
                                                                        pierce brake cable hole

Lubricate and shave anchor pin hole through   Automatic feed and
   reinforcement and backing plate   place reinforcement

Feed and insert anchor pin

                                                                              Coining press

                                                         Hollow mill   Automatic unload and
Hot-upset anchor pin and water quench   anchor pin   separate rejects

   Hot-upset anchor pin and water quench   Additional water quench

Fig. 15-129 Nonsynchronous system automatically assembles and machines 900 brake backing plates per hour.

Hot upsetting requires more than 4 seconds. To compensate for this, two duplicate stations have been provided side by side in the system. Production is shared by these two stations by means of signal flags on the pallets and counting units at each station.

Blank plates enter the system from a coining press. A cam-operated walking-beam transfer unit unloads the press and carries the parts through a station that pierces either a right or left-hand emergency brake cable hole in each blank. These parts are stored in a 600-piece capacity chain-powered silo ahead of the 10-station machine.

Brake backing plates are automatically loaded onto pallets at the first station. A reinforcement plate is automatically fed and placed on each part at the next station. These plates (as well as anchor pins added later) are fed from bowls by horizontal vibratory tracks. Vibratory presorting bowls ahead of the feeder bowls reject any misformed parts and stray material that might interfere with proper feeding.

Reinforcements are projection welded to the backing plates and anchor pin holes are shaved through both plates at the next two stations. Anchor pins are inserted and then hot-upset on either of two standard resistance welders. The final two working stations are used for hollow milling the anchor pins. Cycle time for this operation is only 4 seconds (including pallet indexing and clamping, rapid advance, machining, rapid return, and unclamping). As a result, one station can handle the full production of 900 parts per hour while cutting tools are being changed at the other station. An air cylinder in the cam-drive system lifts the milling unit for tool changes, allowing pallets to pass without interrupting production.

A machine for producing disc brake caliper assemblies at the rate of 1,200 per hour is shown schematically in Fig. 15-130. It handles both left and right-hand assemblies for three different models or six different assemblies in all. The machine, monitored and partially controlled by a computer system, consists essentially of 24 individual automatic machines and three manual stations spaced around an elongated, oval-shaped power-and-free conveyor. The conveyor transports the workpiece around the system in pallet carriers, with a right and left-hand pair in each pallet. Automatic operations performed include loading, installing and torquing bleeder screws, placing rubber piston seals, cleaning the bores, pressing pistons into the bores, air-leak testing, installing rubber boots, torquing plugs, placing O-rings, probing, placing spacers, crimping flanges, inserting mounting bolts, stamping, and unloading. The only manual operation required are positioning outer brake shoes in the calipher assemblies, adding a retainer spring and inserting a plastic spacer.

Advantages. In-line indexing systems allow more operations and provide more accessibility than dial machines. They can also be used for heavier and more complex

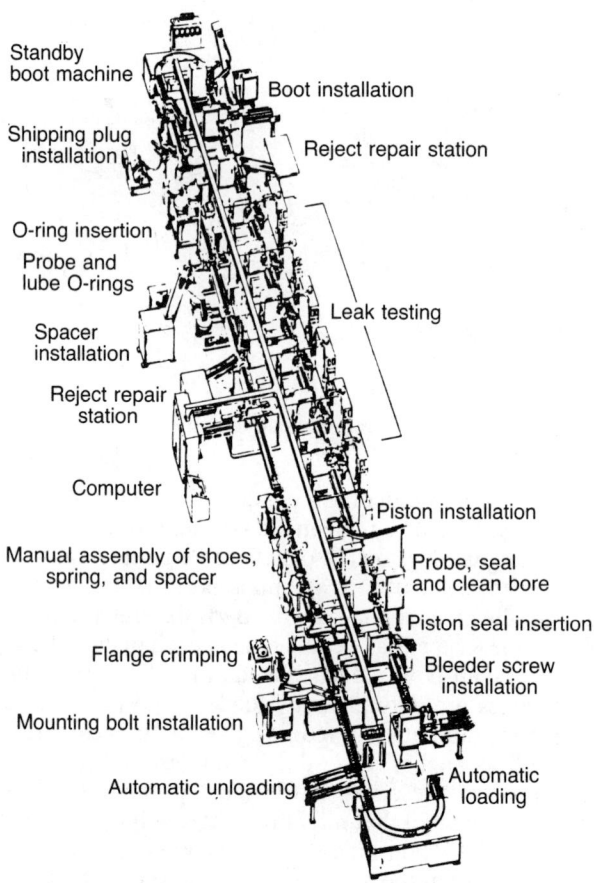

Fig. 15-130 System consists of 24 individual automatic machines and three manual stations spaced around a power-and-free conveyor for producing disc brake caliper assemblies at a rate of 1200 per hour. (*Courtesy The Cross Co.*)

assemblies. Manual operations and automatic stations can be added anywhere along the line, and repair and storage loops can be provided as required. Virtually any number of operations can be tied together, subject only to mechanical limitations. Modular construction is possible because of the availability of standard transfer mechanism, workstations, tooling, and other components.

Limitations. The inefficiency of in-line assembly systems becomes increasingly cumulative as additional stations are added. The slowest operation limits the production rate, but the use of multiple tooling increases the output. Nonsynchronous systems are more costly and have lower production rates than dial machines and synchronous systems and require more floor space.

CAROUSEL MACHINES

Similar to the synchronous in-line assembly systems just discussed, carousel machines consist of a series of fixtures or holding devices attached to a roller chain, precision chain, or steel belts and moved by fingers from one workstation to another. However, the carousel machine moves the work in a horizontal plane through a rectangular path, or some variation of the same, returning the pallets to their starting point. All parts are indexed at the same time for the same distance on either a timed or an on-demand basis.

Advantages of the carousel include utilization of all the fixtures in the system because none are returned below, possibility of more operations in the same space, operations can be performed on all sides of the machine, and workpieces are returned to the starting point.

FLEXIBLE ASSEMBLY SYSTEMS

Greater flexibility from automated assembly systems is essential because of continuing increases in product differences resulting from market demands and reductions in product life-cycles. Requirements for high-volume, long-running production are decreasing.

Considerable development work has been done and is continuing with respect to more flexible assembly systems for handling smaller lot sizes and a wider variety of products. The objectives of such systems include increased cost effectiveness and reduced obsolescence of capital equipment expeditures.

One developing concept is the use of automatic guided vehicles (AGVs), which are currently being applied to low-volume large assemblies such as automotive and appliance products. The vehicles are usually self-powered electrically or by compressed air. They electrically follow cables buried in the floor and are computer controlled for any required paths to various assembly stations. The cost of AGVs and their control systems limit their application to large assemblies required in low volumes. Combining AGVs with programmable workstations offers considerable flexibility.

Two major classifications of flexible assembly systems are programmable and adaptable. Programmable and adaptable systems include those using industrial robots, which are discussed next in this section.

Dedicated, special-purpose assembly systems are designed to assemble specific products with few or no modifications. They generally require high-volume production for economic justification. Flexible assembly systems are capable of assembling more than one product model or models. Truly flexible systems can assemble on demand from an ensemble of different but similar products without tooling changeover. Other systems may require only extra fixtures or different pallets, changes in tooling, and, for some applications, extra stations. These systems can be economically justified with lower production requirements.

Adaptable systems that are totally automated and capable of assembling any variety of products are difficult to implement and are rare today, but they are expected to become more common in the future. They require both passive controls for programming and active controls (sensors) capable of decision and control tasks. A mixture of manual, dedicated, and flexible methods seems to be one promising solution for adaptable assembly systems.

ROBOTIC ASSEMBLY SYSTEMS

Robotic assembly (the use of industrial robots for assembly) is being increasingly applied. One major robot manufacturer has estimated that by 1990 more than 16,000 robots will be used in assembly systems. About 30% of these units will be dedicated to mechanical assembly applications, while the remaining 70% will be used in the electronics industry.

Industrial robots are programmable manipulators that perform a variety of tasks. An effective robotic assembly system requires careful consideration of the delivery of components to the workstations, component feeding and orienting, robot end effectors, sensing requirements, and system controls.

Typical Applications. Most current applications of robotic assembly systems involve small products in medium volume requirements, families of products, and products or production mixes that are likely to change significantly. Predominant users of such systems include the automotive, electronic, electromechanical, and precision mechanical industries. Electronic applications are discussed later in this chapter.

Robotic systems are being used to assemble numerous automotive components. The assembly of universal joints involves the insertion of needles in bearings. Systems for engine cylinder heads (see Fig. 15-131) include the assembly of valves, tappets, and covers. Spot welding guns are positioned automatically by means of robots in the assembly of automobile bodies (see Fig. 15-132).

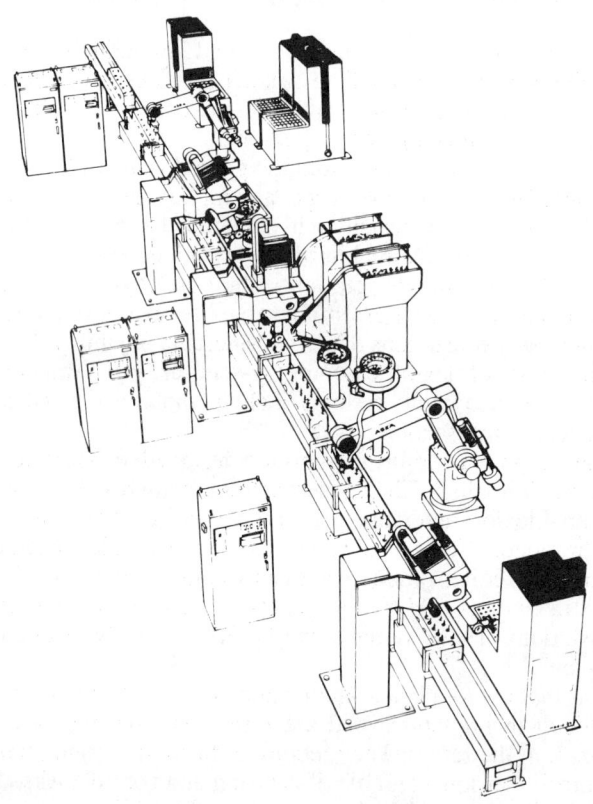

Fig. 15-131 Robotic assembly system for automotive engine cylinder heads. (*Courtesy ABB Robotics, Inc.*)

A vision-guided robot carrying pneumatic wrenches (see Fig. 15-133) is being used to tighten bolts on car underbodies being transported down a moving conveyor line at the Oldsmobile Div. of General Motors Corp. The robot is mounted on a carriage that is temporarily clamped to the car and travels with it. Solid-state cameras view the underbody and report the location of gage holes to the robot system, which then locates the position of the bolts. Cycle time is 53 seconds to find and torque the 12 fasteners on each body and return to the starting position.

A robotic assembly system at the Fisher Body Div. of General Motors Corp. is being used to assemble 12 different door trim panels at a rate of more than 400 assemblies per hour. The system consists of a 37-station nonsynchronous conveyor with 13 robots. Three optical sensors at one station determine which car line and style of trim panels

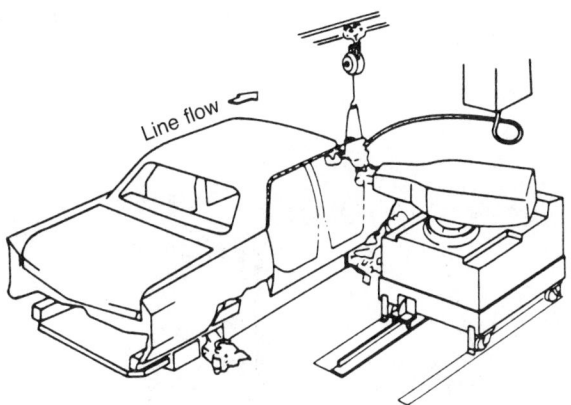

Fig. 15-132 Spot welding guns are positioned accurately and automatically by means of robots in assembly of automobile bodies.

are to be assembled. Data are relayed to a master programmable controller that controls subsequent operations. A vision system with two cameras at another station scans the trim panels to determine locations of the studs. If the studs are improperly located, the vision system alters the robot program for proper location. The various robots install stamped nuts and plastic fasteners supplied from overhead hopper bowls and spray adhesive onto the panels. A communications network system provides diagnostic information and production data.

Manipulator Configurations. The manipulator configuration to be used for a specific assembly application will usually be determined by one or more of the following requirements:

- The work envelope needed. The envelope is the three-dimensional volume of spatial points in which the end of the robot arm can be moved.
- The weight (payload) of the components to be assembled.
- Cycle time, repeatability, and accuracy requirements.

The most popular manipulator configurations for robotic assembly systems include Cartesian coordinate, cylindrical coordinate, articulated arm, SCARA (Selective Compliance Assembly Robot Arm), and gantry.

End Effectors. End effectors (end-of-arm tooling) consist of grippers, hands, holders, and other tools for handling components to be assembled. They are not generally integral parts of robots and commonly have to be designed and built for specific applications. They should be designed to handle as many different components as possible. For example, multiple sets of jaws can possibly be used with a single end effector to handle several types of components. The end effectors can be provided with or without mechanical compliance or sensory devices and vision systems for more precise location.

Machine Vision Systems. Machine vision systems involve the use of cameras and processing computers to analyze images and make interpretations so that some action may be initiated. One approach is to use an array of photosensitive elements (photodiodes or pixels) arranged in a matrix where each element reacts to light rays reflected or emitted from a part, producing a two-dimensional digital pattern of the part. For correlation systems, recognition is achieved by comparing this pattern with one in the computer memory.

Machine vision systems are being increasingly applied for object recognition, guidance, and inspection operations. Advantages of these systems include reduced tooling (gripper) and fixture costs, increased flexibility because of their reprogrammability, reduced scrap and/or rework of assemblies, and improved product quality.

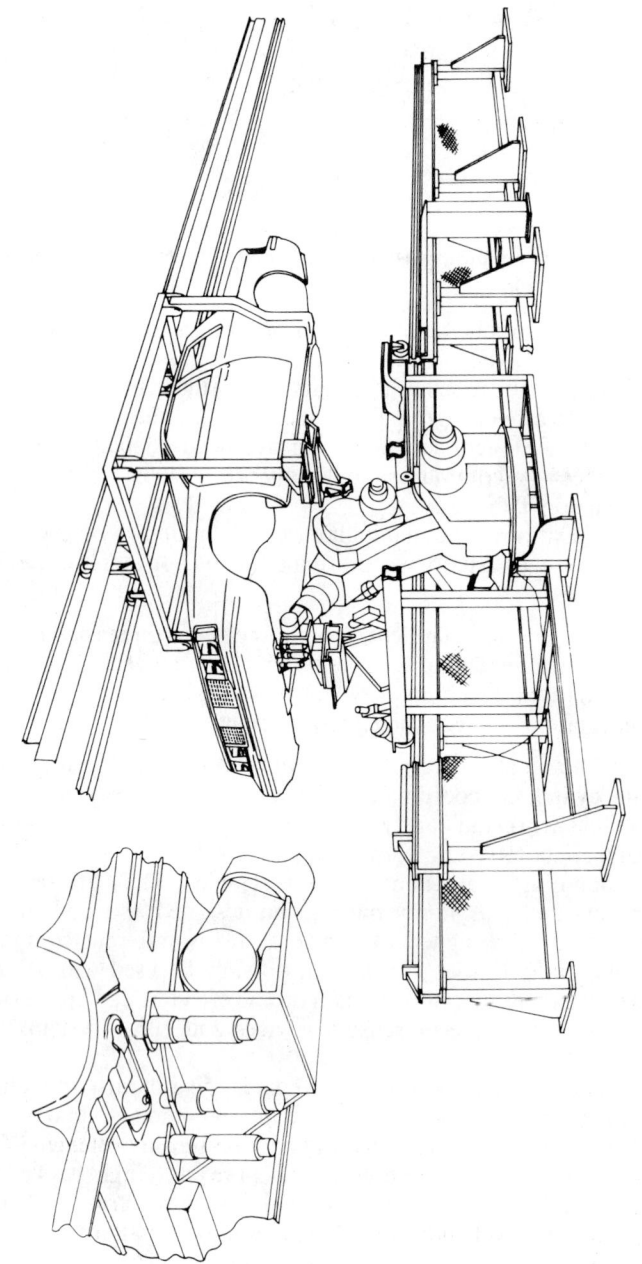

Fig. 15-133 Underbody bolt securing using a vision-guided robot.

AUTOMATED ELECTRONIC ASSEMBLY

Most electronic assemblies consist of inserting components into or placing them onto printed circuit boards (PCBs) or substrates.

Automation of printed circuit board assemblies has progressed from manually formed component leads, with blueprint-guided insertion, to fully automatic insertion machines and robotic systems. All types of components are now being sequentially inserted through a continuous array of in-line machines or through groups of machines bridged by material handling equipment. Today's electronic manufacturing facility is also equipped with a wide range of automated test equipment, controlled by computers.

Commercial equipment covers automated board handling and surface-mount pick-and-place or robotic systems. Figure 15-134 illustrates how both leaded and surface-mount components can be placed by a robot. Some systems incorporate optical registration capabilities to correct board misalignment or pattern displacement automatically. Of today's automatic component insertion systems, a broad mix of equipment is available to satisfy both small and large-volume manufacturers. The goal of most equipment suppliers is to offer automation capable of suiting the widest range of companies and applications.

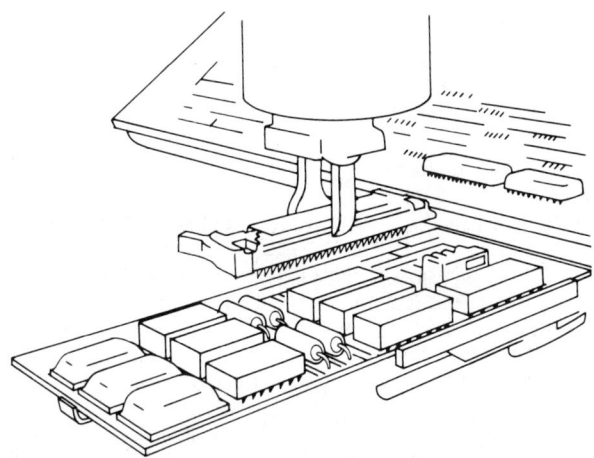

Fig. 15-134 Connectors and odd-shaped components, both leaded and surface-mount, can be placed by robots.

FACTORY AUTOMATION

The major factory automation strategies involving component insertion and printed circuit board assembly are in-line systems and flexible assembly systems.

In-line Systems. These systems use the production line concept, where individual machines are physically connected together to form a sequential process. Surface-mounted technology offers an opportunity to use this approach to combine several processes. There is a balancing dilemma with the in-line approach; the wide range of placement equipment insertion rates, board designs, and component configurations make system balancing difficult.

Flexible Assembly Systems. These systems utilize separate islands or cells of automation where the destination of output from each cell can be programmed. The material transportation system can consist of power roller conveyor systems, automated guided vehicles, and automated storage and retrieval systems (AS/RS) for moving magazines containing printed circuit boards. Figure 15-135 diagrams the material flow

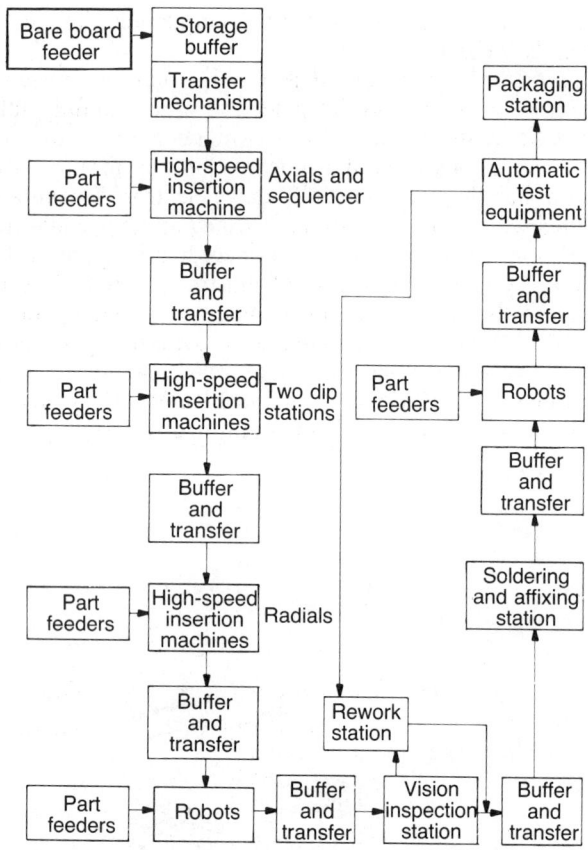

Fig. 15-135 Flexible automated electronic assembly flowchart. Printed circuit boards can be stuffed, tested, and packaged without any human contact. (*Courtesy CERRIS International, Inc.*)

in a flexible assembly system made possible by software programmed to take bad boards out and send them to repair stations.

A printed circuit board manufacturer with a high volume of a single type of board having a low component mix might best use a dedicated in-line production arrangement. However, a company that makes many types of boards using many components will be most efficiently served with a flexible assembly line.

Whether to include dedicated machines in flexible automated assembly is determined by the volume of components and the mix of axial and radial leads, dual in-line packages of integrated circuits (DIPs), surface-mounted devices (SMDs), number of pins, and sizes. A robot-only flexible system is proper for a highly mixed, low-volume (thousands of boards per month) operation. An assembly line setup with robots may be quickly reconfigured with an existing program to handle several different product mixes.

AUTOMATED ARC WELDING

Automated arc welding is welding with equipment that performs the entire operation without human observation or adjustment of controls. The process was developed to meet increasing demands for improved productivity and higher quality welds. It makes use of microprocessor memories, sensing devices, and programmable and adaptive controls. Sensing devices may continuously monitor the operation and feed back information to the control system, which modifies welding parameters or motion patterns to provide necessary changes. Quality welds are produced even when the weldment conditions are less than optimum, such as poorly fitted joints. Programs for automated welding can be recorded, stored, and reused when required.

The automated arc welding process produces more consistent, higher quality welds than automatic welding. While automatic welding can be programmed to produce quality welds, the results obtained depend on preparation of the components for welding. This preparation is usually not consistent. For example, springback can vary with different heats of metals to be joined, bend lines can differ and change joint fitup, flame-cut parts can vary because of torch tips, cutting dies can also wear, and workpiece warpage during welding can affect results. All of these variations are accommodated with automated welding.

TOOLING FOR AUTOMATED ARC WELDING

Tooling problems in automatic arc welding are so dependent on the nature of the job to be done that few basic principles for guidance can be detailed. Each job must be studied and the solution worked out for it. Engineers employed by the manufacturers of automatic welding equipment are available for consultation and help in designing tooling.

Because arc blow, when using direct current, can be a problem common to different types of jobs, several basic principles apply to designing fixtures to minimize arc blow, including the following:

1. Make the clamping fingers and as much of the fixture as possible of nonmagnetic material.
2. Keep all steel parts far enough from the work and the arc so that very little detrimental magnetic-flux path will cross the gap to be welded or be in the way of the arc. A 1 in. (25 mm) minimum distance between steel parts and the work is recommended, with the top members 2 in. (50 mm) away from the arc.
3. Always ground at the start end. Try to have the actual point of contact between ground and work at the start end of the seam. Try the ground on the following locations before deciding which is best: (a) start end of top clamping fingers and (b) start end of work.
4. Weld toward the closed end of the fixture or close both ends so that there is a bridge for the magnetic flux at both ends; most of the flux will circulate in the frame rather than across the gap to be welded.
5. Eliminate tack welds, if possible, except at the very end of the seam. Tabs at the finish end are usually helpful. They provide an easy path for the flux that would otherwise crowd across the gap at the end of the weld.
6. If necessary, reduce travel speed.

In automated welding, the work is usually stationary and the welding head or arc moves. In these cases, the workholding devices may merely be a welding table with hold-down clamps. As the production rate increases, the complexity of various fixtures required to hold the individual pieces in specific locations generally increases. Such fixtures may involve tunnel clamps or even clamps powered with air or hydraulic cylinders.

For more complicated weldments, workholding fixtures may be mounted on universal positioners. Fixtures of this type have a tilt function from vertical to horizontal and may have a rotation function of 360°. This means that there are two axes of motion on the work-motion device. The level of control determines whether they are coordinated or not.

The accuracy of motion devices is extremely important and, as the weldment becomes more complex or thinner materials or specific procedures are used, the accuracy must be improved. The highest degree of accuracy utilizes feedback sensing devices that monitor the location and provide signals to the controller of the exact location on a continuous basis.

Other work-motion devices can be rotating fixtures or rings, or headstock/tailstock units. Many special types of workmotion devices are available, and many of these are standardized and based on specific sizes and weight capacities. It is important to select devices having the weight capacity required. Weight capacity involves off-center loading, both from the vertical and rotational axes. As the off-center loading increases, the capacity of the machines must be reduced. It is also important to determine the accuracy required for the particular job because accuracy requirements increase the cost of this equipment.

The workholding device is usually custom-made for the particular weldment. Many such devices are used for tacking purposes only, while others may be used for the complete welding operation. Design of these fixtures is extremely important because torch accessibility must be provided for. Workholding fixtures must also be built sufficiently robust to counteract warpage forces involved in making the weldment; in addition, they must be easy to load and unload and must be protected against weld spatter and other possible abuses.

Robotic Arc Welding. Industrial robots are increasingly being applied to arc welding applications, primarily because of their versatility. High-volume production is not required for economical robotic arc welding. The versatility of robots makes them economically justifiable for low to medium production requirements. They are well suited for handling a variety of welding operations, small lot sizes, and parts having a variety of welds requiring different approach angles. Design changes are easily accommodated, and different parts are handled by changing the program and end-of-arm tooling.

Robots, however, are not applicable to all arc welding applications. Assemblies requiring welds that are difficult or awkward to reach and that necessitate long reaches are not generally suitable for robotic welding. Also, unlike a skilled operator, robots made with the present state of the art do not have the ability to sense what is happening during welding nor do they have the dexterity of an operator. Rapid advances in improved sensors and software capabilities, however, are narrowing the differences between robots and skilled welders.

Workcells or systems being used for robotic arc welding consist of five principal components: robot manipulator, controller, positioner, processing package, and tooling.

TOOLING FOR ROBOTIC ARC WELDING

Unlike a skilled welder, a robot does not recognize and does not correct for deficiencies in the tooling. If the tool does not position the part correctly, the robot may weld the part in the wrong location. If the tool controls the part position by rigidly fixturing the part prior to welding, the distortion from welding can cause the part to bind in the fixture and be difficult to remove. For a tool to be successful, the stackup of tolerances must be controlled, the part must be accurately positioned, and the part must not bind in the fixture after welding. After meeting all these requirements, the fixture must be capable of being quickly loaded and unloaded so that operation of the fixture does not cause the robot to be idle an excessive amount of time.

Tooling may restrict accessibility to the part. The motion of the torch and the robot around the part must be investigated to ensure adequate accessibility. In some cases, part of the fixture can be removed by an air cylinder midway through the weld cycle to improve access. The operation of the air cylinder could be part of the controller program. In other cases, manually tacking the part in a fixture and then robotically welding the tacked part in a simple fixture is the best solution to the accessibility problem. Fixtures for robotic arc welding are generally custom designed for specific parts, the major requirement being to accurately locate the parts to be joined in their best positions.

Robotic Spot Welding. Spot welding of metal components in the automotive industry represents the largest use of industrial robots. Robotics have also been successfully integrated into the manufacturing process for welding appliances, cabinets, truck assemblies, and other sheet metal assemblies. Major reasons for these applications are the increased flexibility and cost savings obtained. Even though a robotic system is expensive, it is not susceptible to obsolescence. Another important advantage is improved product quality. Robotic systems ensure uniform weld placement, accuracy in following welding procedures, and, if required, a feedback printout of every weld produced.

Typical Applications. Robotic spot welding is done by two different methods. In one method, the robot holds the workpiece and passes it through a stationary welding gun. In the second method, which is more prevalent, the welding gun is attached to the robot and moves to the component to be spot welded.

In the automotive sector of robotic spot welding, there are two major categories of applications: respot line welding and subassembly buildup. In respot line welding, the body or subassembly is passed through special framing fixtures to locate the parts to one another and tack weld them together with stationary welding guns. The component is then passed down stream via a conveyor system or transfer bars to an area where the robots add the additional structural load-carrying spot welds. Typical component buildups that are done in this fashion are final body framing, front structure, underbody, and body sides. A typical assembly line for right and left-hand body sides is shown schematically in Fig. 15-136.

The other area of subassembly buildup generally uses smaller off-line groups of automation employing indexing lines, turntables, and stationary fixtures for part presentation. Typical components built up with this method are inner rails and package tray subassemblies, instrument panels, torque boxes, front apron assemblies, and bumper buildups. Figure 15-137 depicts an installation for the assembly of instrument panels.

BRAZING AUTOMATION

Brazing is being done automatically with various heating methods, including torches, furnaces (controlled atmosphere, including vacuum), resistance, induction, dip, and infrared methods. Accurate control of temperature and time at temperature is essential for any automated process. Filler metals are either preplaced at the joints during assembly of the components or, in some processes, are automatically fed into the joints at the brazing temperature.

Automatic applicators for paste alloys (mixtures of powdered filler metal and flux in a paste binder) have expanded the use of automatic brazing and soldering systems. Such systems include rotary index, in-line, fixed station, and shuttle machines.

Various degrees of automation are being used. Completely automated systems can include automatic fluxing (if paste alloys are not used), in-line inspection and cleaning, simultaneous brazing of multiple joints, and continuous brazing operations. The cost of automating is generally justified by increased productivity and, in many cases, by the material and energy savings.

Automated Soldering Systems. Most automated systems for soldering are custom built for specific applications. With most systems, an operator loads and unloads components, and the application of solder, heat, and cooling is done automatically.

Rotary Index Machines. On these machine (see Fig. 15-138), an index table conveys

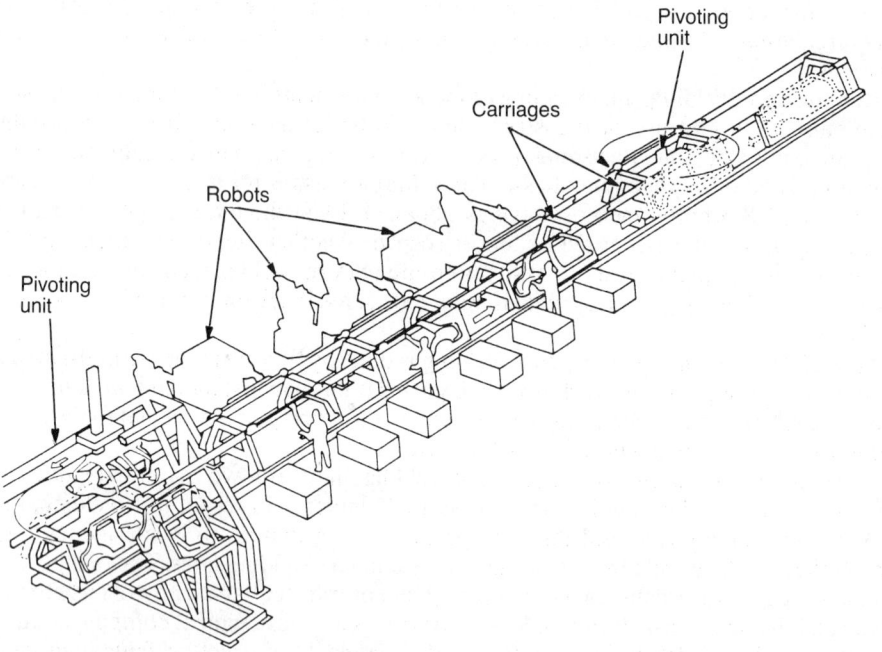

Fig. 15-136 Assembly line for robotic spot welding of right and left-hand automotive body sides. (*Courtesy Ferranti-Skiaky, Inc.*)

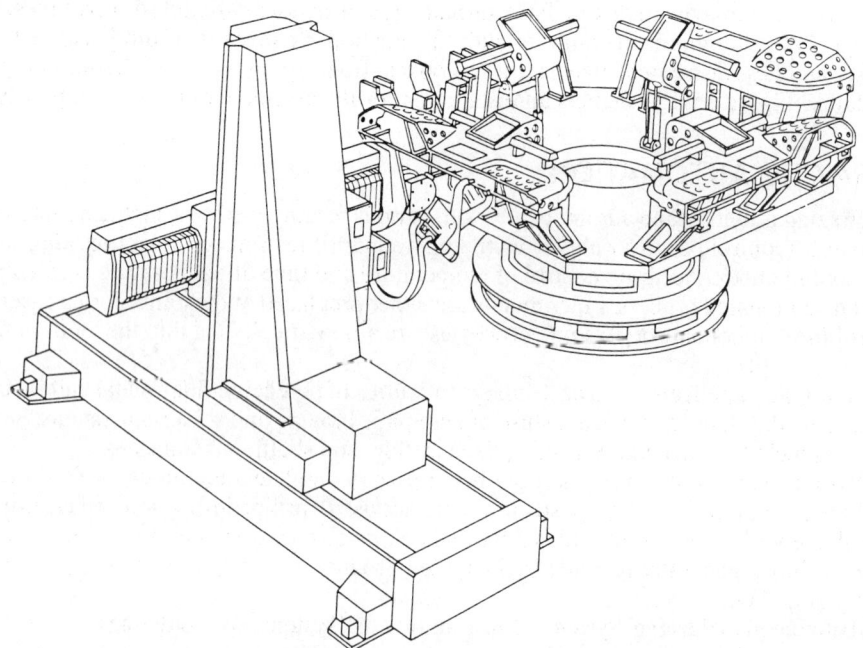

Fig. 15-137 Installation for robotic spot welding of instrument panels. (*Courtesy Ferranti-Skiaky, Inc.*)

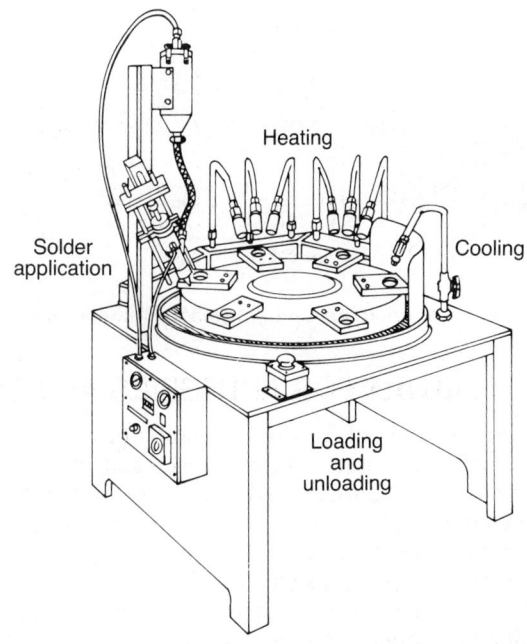

Fig. 15-138 Rotary index machine for automatic soldering. (*Courtesy Fusion Inc.*)

fixtured parts through a timed sequence of operations, resulting in production rates to 1,000 assemblies per hour. Fixtures at each station on the table facilitate loading and unloading and hold the components in proper alignment for soldering. The number of stations on a table depends on production requirements and the operator's ability to unload and reload each fixture during the index cycle. The loading and unloading can also be automated with vibratory feeders, pick-and-place units, robots, or other means. Unloading of soldered assemblies can also be done with ejection devices.

The application of solder and flux or paste is generally done at the first station adjacent to the loading and unloading position. Automatic applicators are frequently used for paste solders, with one or more guns mounted on a slide or slides. Heating is usually performed at several stations to progressively bring the parts to soldering temperature. Open-flame burners supplied with a natural gas and air mixture are a common means of heating, but radiant, induction, resistance, and oven heating are also used. Cooling is often done with compressed air jets or a water wash.

In-line Systems. These systems, such as the one shown in Fig. 15-139, are generally desirable for high production rates and for soldering certain assembly configurations, such as long and narrow parts. They are generally designed for continuous operation with chain-driven fixtures that return to the operator or a mesh belt to carry self-locating parts. Methods of heating include gas-fired burners, heating chambers (gas or electric), or controlled atmospheres. Vacuum furnaces can be used for low vapor pressure metals.

Fixed-station Machines. These machines, for soldering one assembly at a time, are often used for large assemblies and when production requirements are moderate.

Shuttle Machines. These machines are generally designed to solder two assemblies simultaneously, with the parts being moved from the loading and unloading station to the heating station. They are suitable for low to moderate production requirements, with maximum production rates of about 200 assemblies per hour.

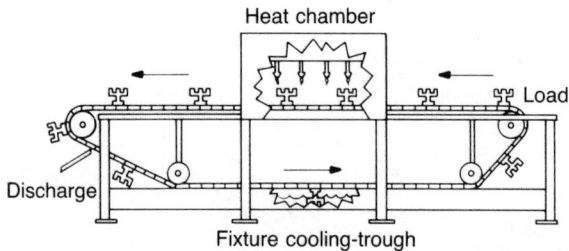

Fig. 15-139 In-line system for automatic soldering with chain-driven fixtures. (*Courtesy Fusion Inc.*)

ROBOTIC APPLICATORS FOR ADHESIVES AND SEALANTS

Industrial robots are being used for the application of adhesives and sealants. The robots are generally used to manipulate the dispensing gun, but occasionally the parts to be joined are manipulated by the robots. Advantages of using robots for such applications include reduced labor requirements and costs, faster production, consistently high quality, and reduced adhesive usage. Adhesives can be applied to a number of parts simultaneously by using multiple guns on a single robot. A possible limitation is that high volumes are generally necessary for cost-effectiveness. However, the flexibility of robots permits handling a variety of different parts in small batches.

The selection of a robot for adhesive or sealant application depends on the specific application. For light-duty applications with small parts having flat or slightly contoured surfaces, robots having low payload, reach, and positioning capacity are often satisfactory. Speeds below 600 ipm (15.2 m/min) are common for such applications. However, variable speed capability with fast, smooth-acceleration and deceleration is generally desirable for most applications to increase flexibility. For heavy-duty applications and faster production, robots with increased capacity, often specially engineered for the specific application, are usually necessary.

Five-axis robots are generally adequate for most applications, but a sixth axis may be necessary for nonsymmetrical nozzles. Electric servocontrolled robots having a high degree of accuracy and repeatability are usually preferable to hydraulic units because of smoother motions and better repeatability. Dispensing speeds to 3,000 ipm (76.2 m/min) have been used for straight-line applications, but 1,200 to 1,800 ipm (30.5 to 45.7 m/min) are more typical speeds, depending on bead-path complexity. Programming can be accomplished with a teach pendant, a programmable controller, or off-line CNC.

One robot dispensing system being used by automotive manufacturers is of gantry design to allow the system to straddle production lines. Figure 15-140 illustrates a car-door assembly system. A programmable interface integrates the unit with the parts handling system.

A ROBOTIC ASSEMBLY SYSTEM

Westinghouse Electric Corp., with funding from the National Science Foundation, developed a programmable assembly system for the low-volume or batch production of small, fractional-horsepower electric motors having a number of variations. Called APAS (adaptable-programmable assembly system), the system consists of six computer-controlled workstations, robots at four of the six stations, part presentation equipment, fixtures and tools, transfer conveyors, and sensory devices in a complete assembly line (see Fig. 15-141).

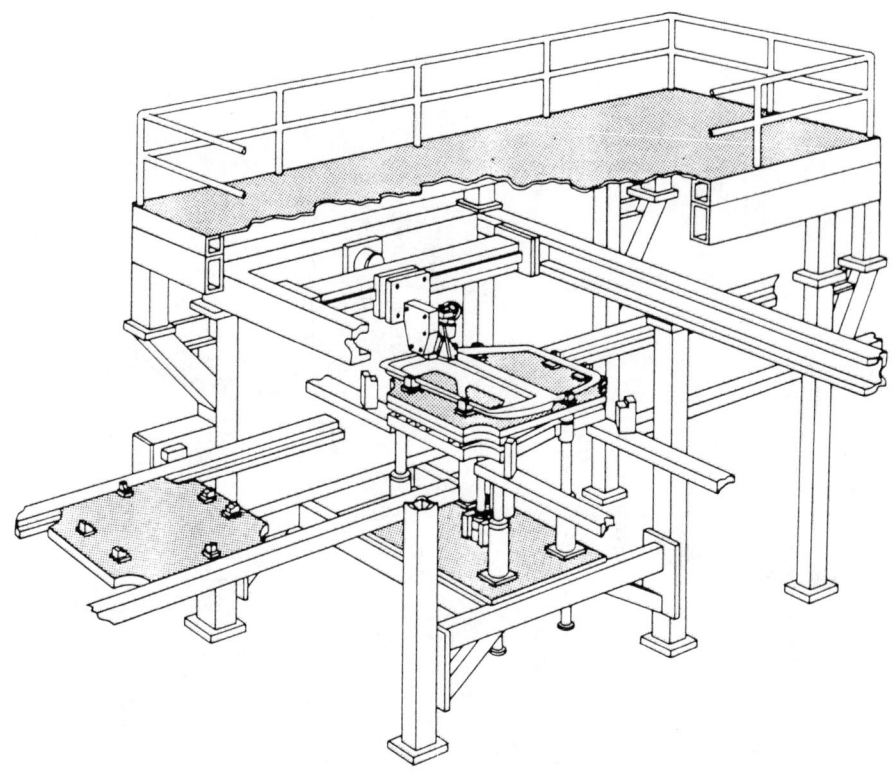

Fig. 15-140 Robotic door assembly system.

FIXTURELESS ASSEMBLY MANUFACTURING[12]

Fixtureless assembly manufacturing (FLAM) is the ability to process and assemble parts without the use of fixtures or part-orientation devices that are totally dedicated to —while not part of—a product. Items targeted for elimination include any tool, fixture, part-presentation/orientation device, or piece of processing equipment that would need to be changed or discarded if the product changes.

The industrial robot is a good example of short-sighted thinking with regard to flexibility. In a typical scenario, the user buys a flexible $100,000 robot that can perform many different types of tasks. Then, without recognizing the dichotomy, the user spends an additional $200,000 - $400,000 and thousands of engineering hours on dedicated fixtures and support equipment for the robot's workstation. If the product changes, the robot can be moved or reprogrammed, but many additional engineering hours and dollars are required to change or adapt the fixtures and equipment. Clearly, dedicated equipment quickly takes the flexibility out of a system.

A key, and sometimes overlooked, rule of manufacturing is to locate and orient the part at the beginning of the manufacturing/assembly process and not lose that orientation until the finished product is shipped out the door. Without the use of dedicated fixtures, one or more other processes must be used to achieve and maintain part location and orientation. These include the use of the following:

- Vision and tactile-array systems to determine location and orientation.
- Industrial robots and programmable arms as reprogrammable fixtures.
- Part and product features that enable self-location within universal fixtures.
- Packaging dunnage as the fixture.

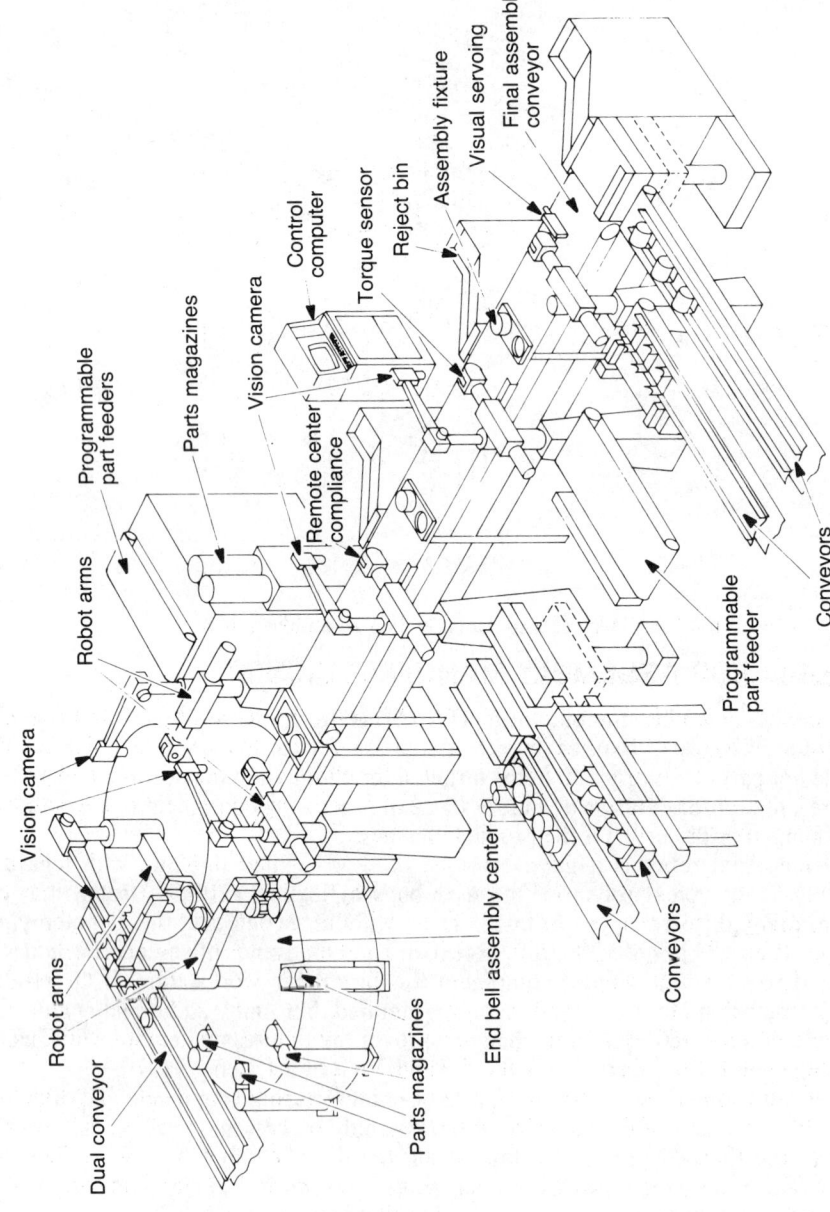

Vision camera

Robot arms

Dual conveyor

Robot arms

Parts magazines

End bell assembly center

Conveyors

Programmable
part feeders

Parts magazines

Vision camera

Remote center
compliance

Control
computer

Vision camera

Torque sensor

Reject bin

Assembly fixture

Visual servoing

Final assembly
conveyor

Programmable
part feeder

Conveyors

Fig. 15-141 Robotic assembly system for small electric motors.

Sensing the Location and Orientation of Unfixtured Parts. Sensing systems now available make it possible to determine the location and orientation of randomly presented parts and locate insertion positions during assembly. Both globally mounted and robot-maneuvered vision systems are now used as part recognition sensors. Gray-scale and dense vision/range images are processed for such tasks as part identification, part location and orientation, and selection of an acquisition method. Although vision system capabilities have increased dramatically over the last few years, processing time can be a drawback. For that reason, the following guidelines should be followed:

- Limit the number of parts that must be viewed at one time.
- Limit the number of objects that must be recognized.
- Lay part to be viewed on a single plane.
- If possible, limit the number of positions a part may have. This can be done by incorporating special part features and controlling the part's center of gravity.
- Design parts to have high-contrast features.
- If possible, make certain that parts do not touch or overlap unless the contrast feature used for location identification are internal to the part.

The use of wrist force sensors and tactile-array sensors is also increasing. Tactile-array sensing systems consist of contact or pressure-sensing elements whose signals are processed to produce a pressure pattern, or "footprint", that can be used to identify part or insertion location.

One company has demonstrated an assembly operation in which parts, presented randomly in a bin, are picked up, properly oriented, and inserted into a subassembly. In this application, a bin of metal brackets is presented to the workstation, where a robot uses magnetic gripping to obtain a part. A wrist sensor (see Fig. 15-142) calculates the part's center of gravity and uses this information to guide the robot to place the part in the center of a tactile-array pad. The part's footprint is recognized by the system's software, its location and orientation are calculated, and the robot is directed to a precise part pickup position.

The Industrial Robot as a Reprogrammable Fixture. Once part location and orientation have been determined, they must be maintained as the part moves through the process. Robots or pick-and-place mechanisms can perform this function by moving parts from one staging or assembly area to another. Also, two or more robots can work together to perform an assembly task. As one robot arm accurately positions the base of an assembly/subassembly, another robot arm can insert parts. In using robots as programmable fixtures, part location and alignment should be monitored and verified through sensing.

Designing the Part to Self-locate. Features can also be incorporated into the base of an assembly to enable the base to self-locate in a universal fixturing device. If parts are properly designed, a single flexible holding device can accommodate many different types of bases. As with the use of robots, this technique requires verification of part position through sensing.

Packaging Dunnage as a Value-added Fixture. Many products are shipped with packaging dunnage that is shaped to fit the product contours exactly. Currently, this dunnage is designed strictly for protection and is not fitted onto the product until after production. If the dunnage and product base are properly designed, however, the dunnage can be used to fixture the part during assembly.

Implementation. Achieving FLAM is not an easy task. Most companies feel they are far too busy handling day-to-day challenges to consider the major change in manufacturing approach required for fixtureless assembly. Most of the technologies required for FLAM, however, are being developed and refined in industry and academia.

One program that is yielding some exciting results using vision and force sensing is the Intelligent Task Automation (ITA) program. ITA is funded by the Air Force and

Fig. 15-142 A robot equipped with a wrist sensor places a part on a tactile-array pad, which produces a pressure pattern that can be used to determine part location and orientation.

sponsored by the Defense Advanced Research Projects Agency and Air Force Wright Aeronautical Laboratory. Also working on the program is a team representing the Honeywell Corporate Systems Development Div., Adept Technology, SRI International, and Stanford University. The ultimate goal is to develop an assembly workcell that illustrates programmable, sensory-controlled manipulation in an unstructured environment. The objective is to stretch current knowledge and technologies to demonstrate the use of sensing and intelligent control as a viable means of locating, acquiring, and assembling parts.

The ITA system, although impractical for most current assembly applications, is expected to have a high payoff in the future, especially for unfixtured assembly.

Fixtureless assembly systems are not like a robot that can be purchased from a catalog. They require complex strategies that affect, and are affected by, all phases of the manufacturing process.

Concept of a FLAM SYSTEM. The robotic workcell illustrated in Fig. 15-143 is expected to demonstrate the feasibility of fixtureless assembly. Major elements of the workcell include a five-axis SCARA robot (A) with a force-sensing wrist, a servoable gripper, and an integrally mounted vision system; a six-axis, jointed-arm robot (B) to position a verification and inspection vision system; and a stationary vision system mounted overhead. The workcell operates as follows:

1. Product presentation equipment positions a parts tray beneath the overhead vision system. The parts may be touching, overlapping, or occluded.

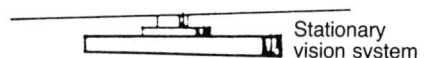

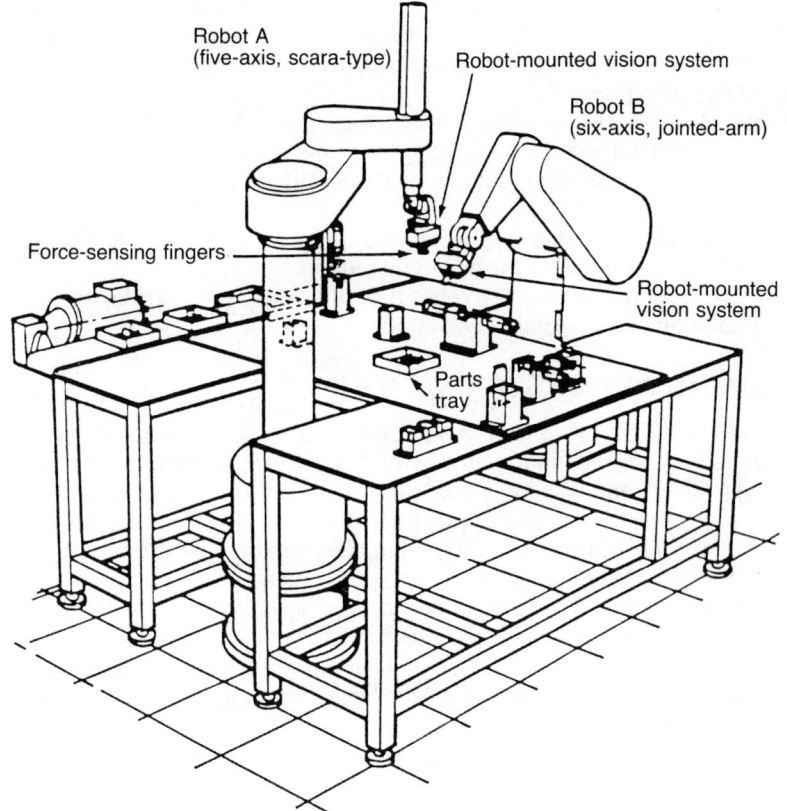

Fig. 15-143 Concept of a FLAM system.

2. Robot A uses force sensing to seat the tray against registration stops.
3. The overhead vision system uses edge-detection techniques to acquire gray-scale and dense-range (terrain map) images to locate and recognize a specified part. (Geometric models derived from CAD descriptions of the parts and work space are used as the basis for generating databases to drive both control and sensory processing functions).
4. The overhead vision system may tag some of the difficult to recognize parts it has found for verification by the robot-mounted vision system. When robot A is not performing an assembly operation, it positions its vision system over the part to gather vision/range data and provide appropriate feedback. If this vision system rejects an identification by the overhead vision system, the system controller directs the overhead system to locate another part.
5. After part recognition, the system analyzes the relative positions of other objects to determine the overall configuration of parts. It then selects a grasping position.
6. When directed to pick up a part, robot A acquires quickchange fingers and grasps the part. It uses a force-controlled, guarded move to check for collisions while placing its force-sensing fingers around the part, closes the griper with force appropriate for the part, verifies that its finger opening matches the part dimensions, and removes the part from the tray.

7. Simultaneously, robot B poses its vision system at the appropriate fixture/subassembly for the upcoming part-assembly operation.
8. Robot A blindly brings the two parts to be assembled into the appropriate position necessary for mating. The vision system held by robot B measures the relative misalignment between the parts and provides feedback to the robot. When the parts are aligned, the vision system verifies that conditions are correct for the assembly to proceed.
9. Robot A mates the two parts, using high-speed force servoing for compliant, delicate micromanipulation. Mating conditions terminate when position and/or force limits are reached; data from the termination are interpreted for contact verification.
10. Robot A returns to the tray to acquire the next part that the overhead vision system has found during the assembly sequence.
11. With robot A out of the way, robot B positions its vision system wherever necessary to verify post-assembly conditions.

JOINING AND FASTENING METHODS

As previously mentioned in this chapter, it is desirable to design or redesign products to facilitate automated assembly, reduce the number of components to be assembled, and when possible, eliminate or minimize the need for joining and fastening operations. Although snap and press fits can often be made as part of the normal machine functions, many assemblies require the use of joining and fastening processes. When required, joining and fastening operations should generally be performed at separate stations, preceded by devices that automatically check the presence and position of the components.

Practically every known method of joining and fastening is being performed on assembly machines. Details of most of these processes have been covered earlier in the chapter.

Selection of a particular joining or fastening method for a specific application depends on several factors, including the following:

- The materials to be joined.
- Size, weight, and geometry of the components to be assembled.
- Joint designs and accessibility.
- Functional requirements of the assembled product, including strength, reliability, environment, appearance, and whether it has to be dismantled for maintenance or repair.
- Production requirements (rate and total).
- Edge and surface preparations necessary.
- Adaptability and compatibility of the joining method to automation, and effects on joint properties.
- Available equipment.
- Tooling requirements.
- Costs.
- Safety considerations.

References

1. Charles Wick and Raymond F. Veilleux, eds., "Mechanical Fastening," *Tool and Manufacturing Engineers Handbook*, Vol. 4, 4th ed. (Dearborn, MI: Society of Manufacturing Engineers, 1987), pp. 8-53 to 8-54.
2. *Ibid.*, pp. 8-53, 8-61 to 8-63.
3. R.W. Newton, "Jig Designed to Drill Sub-assemblies," *Machinery* (July 1951).
4. G.W. Lessman, "Air Power Saves Assembly Time," *American Machinist*, p. 89 (August 7, 1950).
5. Wick and Veilleux, pp. 8-83, 8-86.
6. M.L. Ochieans, "Design of Fixtures for Projection Welding," *Iron Age*, p. 55 (May 2, 1946).

7. Wick and Veilleux, pp. 9-118, 9-124 to 9-125, 10-1 to 10-9.

8. H.M. Webber, "Holding and Supporting Assemblies in Electric Furnace Brazing," *Iron Age* (September 15, 22, 1938).

9. Wick and Veilleux, pp. 12-1 to 12-72.

10. Jack D. Lane, *Automated Assembly*, 2nd ed. (Dearborn, MI: Society of Manufacturing Engineers, 1986), p. 127.

11. *Ibid.*, pp. 157-174.

12. David R. Hoska, "FLAM: What It Is—How To Achieve It," *Manufacturing Engineering* (April 1988).

CHAPTER 16
INSPECTION FIXTURES AND GAGES

An inspection (qualifying, gaging) operation is any examination of a workpiece that determines whether or not it meets standards of quality (conformance to specifications).

Standards of quality considered in this section are all permissible linear and angular dimensions and relations, including specified tolerances, as defined or implied by the engineering or manufacturing drawings and specifications. Other standards of quality such as surface technology, defect detection, mechanical testing, hardness, etc., are not considered.

As noted in the Introduction, whenever it is necessary to place the workpiece into a gaging device to permit inspection of the workpiece, the gaging device is usually referred to as an inspection fixture, whereas the term gage is reserved for those gaging devices that are placed onto or into the workpiece to inspect the workpiece.

BASIC PRINCIPLES OF GAGING

Gage Tolerances. Since it is not possible to produce many parts with exactly the same dimensions, working tolerances are necessary. For the same reason, gage tolerances are necessary. Gage tolerance is generally determined from the amount of workpiece tolerance. A 10% rule is generally used for determining the amount of gage tolerance for fixed, limit-type working gages. When no gage tolerance is specified, the gagemaker will use 10% of the working tolerance as the gage tolerance for a working gage. Working gages are those used by production workers during manufacture.

The amount of tolerance on inspection gages—those used by the inspection department—is generally 5% of the work tolerance. Tolerance on master gages—those used for checking the accuracy of other gages—is generally 10% of the gage tolerance. Where tolerances are large, gages used by the inspection department are not different from the working gages.

Four classes of gagemakers' tolerances have been established by the American Gage Design Committee and are in general use. These four classes establish maximum variations for any desired gage size. The degree of accuracy needed determines the class of gage to be used. Figure 16-1 shows these four classes of gagemakers' tolerances.

Class *XX* gages are precision smoothed (lapped) to the very closest tolerances practicable. They are used primarily as master gages and for final close tolerance inspection.

Class *X* gages are precision lapped to close tolerances. They are used for some types of master gage work, and as close tolerance inspection and working gages.

Class *Y* gages are precision lapped to slightly larger tolerances than Class *X* gages. They are used as inspection and working gages.

Class *Z* gages are precision lapped. They are used as working gages where part tolerances are large and the number of pieces to be gaged is small.

Above	To and including	Class			
		XX	X	Y	Z
0.010 in.	0.825 in.	0.00002 in.	0.00004 in.	0.00007 in.	0.00010 in.
0.825 in.	1.510 in.	0.00003 in.	0.00006 in.	0.00009 in.	0.00012 in.
1.510 in.	2.510 in.	0.00004 in.	0.00008 in.	0.00012 in.	0.00016 in.
2.510 in.	4.510 in.	0.00005 in.	0.00010 in.	0.00015 in.	0.00020 in.
4.510 in.	6.510 in.	0.000065in.	0.00013 in.	0.00019 in.	0.00025 in.
6.510 in.	9.010 in.	0.00008 in.	0.00016 in.	0.00024 in.	0.00032 in.
9.010 in.	12.010 in.	0.00010 in.	0.00020 in.	0.00030 in.	0.00040 in.

Fig. 16-1 Standard gagemaker's tolerances.

Going from Class *XX* to Class *Z*, tolerances become increasingly greater, and the gages are used for inspecting parts having increasingly larger work tolerances.

To show the use of the 10% rule in connection with Fig. 16-1, assume a gagemaker is to choose the correct tolerance class for a working plug gage that is to be used on a 1.0000 in. diam hole having a working tolerance of 0.0012 in. One-tenth of the work tolerance would indicate a gage tolerance of 0.00012 in., or as noted in the table, a class *Z* gage. If the work tolerance were only 0.0006 in. on the 1.0000 in. diam. hole, then a class *X* gage would be indicated, with a tolerance of 0.00006 in. If the work tolerance, however, were 0.015 in., then the gage tolerance indicated by the 10% rule would be 0.0015 in. As this is larger than the maximum tolerance class, a class *Z* gage would be needed, and the gage tolerance would be 0.00012 in.

The smaller degree to which a gage tolerance must be held, the more expensive the gage becomes. Just as the production cost rises sharply as working tolerances are reduced, the cost of buying or manufacturing a gage is much higher if close tolerances are specified. Gage tolerances should be realistically applied from the work to be gaged.

ALLOCATION OF GAGE TOLERANCES

After deciding the tolerance for a specific gage, the direction, plus or minus, of that allowance must be decided. Two basic systems, and many versions of them, are used in making this decision.

THE BILATERAL SYSTEM

In the bilateral system, the GO and NOT GO gage tolerance zones are divided into two parts by the high and low limits of the workpiece tolerance zone. The division is illustrated by Fig. 16-2a, which shows the black rectangles representing the gage tolerance zones are half plus and half minus in relation to the high or low limit of the work tolerance zone.

Referring to Fig. 16-1, assume that the diameter of the hole to be gaged is 1.2500 ±0.0006 in. The total work tolerance in this case is 0.0012 in., since the hole size may vary from 1.2506 to 1.2494 in. Using 10% of the total work tolerance as the gage tolerance, the gage tolerance is then 0.00012 in. From Fig. 16-1, this diameter would require a Class *Z* gage tolerance. The diameter on the go-plug gage for this example would be 1.2494 ±0.00006 in., and the diameter of the no-go gage would be 1.2506 ±0.00006 in.

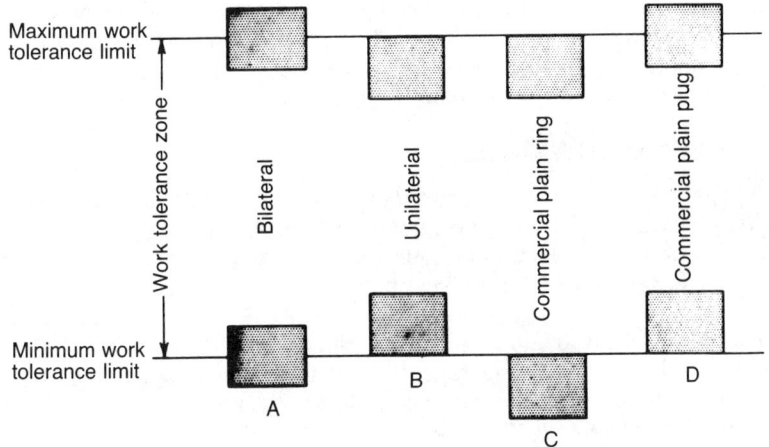

Fig. 16-2 Different systems of gage tolerance allocation.

One disadvantage of this system is that parts that are not within the working limits can pass inspection. Using the above example, if the hole to be gaged is reamed to the low limit (1.2494 in.) and if the GO-plug gage is at the low limit (1.24934 in.), then the GO-plug gage will enter the hole and the part will pass inspection, even though the diameter of the hole is outside the working tolerance zone. A part passed under these conditions would be very close to the working limit, and the tolerance on the mating part should not be such as to prevent assembly. Plug gages using the bilateral system could also pass parts in which the holes were too large. A common misconception is that gages accept good parts and reject bad. With the bilateral system, however, parts can also be rejected as being outside the working limits when they are not.

THE UNILATERAL SYSTEM

In the unilateral system (see Fig. 16-2b), the work tolerance zone entirely includes the gage tolerance zone. This makes the work tolerance smaller by the sum of the gage tolerance, but guarantees that every part passed by such a gage, regardless of the amount of the gage size variation, will be within the work tolerance zone.

If the diameter of the hole is 1.2500 ±0.0006 in., and again using 10% of the working tolerance as the gage tolerance, the GO gage diameter would be 1.24940 +0.00012 in., and the NOT GO gage diameter 1.25060—0.00012 in.

This system of applying gage tolerance, like the bilateral system, may reject parts as being outside the working limits when they are not, but all parts passed using the unilateral system will be within the working limits. The unilateral system has found wider use in industry than the bilateral system for plain plug and ring gages.

One partial solution to the problem of gages rejecting parts that are within working limits is to use working gages with the largest unilateral gage tolerance practical, and inspection gages with the smallest unilateral gage tolerance practical. Thus, no piece can pass inspection that is outside tolerance, and the possibility of the inspection gage turning down acceptance work is reduced because of its small tolerance.

Figure 16-2c shows the commercial practice of allocating the plain ring gage tolerances negatively with reference to both the maximum and minimum limits of the workpiece tolerance. In another practice Fig. 16-2d, the NOT GO gage tolerance is divided by the maximum limit of the workpiece tolerance, and the GO gage tolerance is held within the minimum limit of the workpiece tolerance.

The final results of these allocation systems will differ greatly. The choice of the system to be used, modified, or unmodified, must be determined by the product and the facilities for producing it. The objectives in choosing an allowance system should be the economic production of as near 100% usable parts as possible, and the acceptance of the good pieces and rejection of the bad.

GAGE WEAR ALLOWANCE

Perfect gages cannot be made. If one did exist, it no longer would be perfect after just one checking operation. Although the amount of gage wear during just one operation is difficult to determine, it is easy to measure the total wear of several checking operations. A gage can wear beyond usefulness unless some allowance for wear is built into the gage.

The wear allowance is an amount added to the nominal diameter of a GO-plug and subtracted from that of a GO-ring gage. It is used up during the gage life by wearing away of the gage metal. Wear allowance is applied to the nominal gage diameter before gage tolerance is applied.

The amount of wear allowance does not have to be decided in relation to the amount of work tolerance, although a small work tolerance can restrict wear allowances. When specifying a wear allowance, the material from which the gage and work are made, the quantity of the work, and the type of gaging operation to be performed must be taken into consideration. It is important to establish a specific amount of wear allowance. When the gage has worn the established amount, it should be removed from service without question. This avoids any controversy as to whether a gage is still accurate.

One method, which uses a percentage of the working tolerance as the wear tolerance, can be explained with the following example: For a 1.500 ±0.0006 in. diameter hole, the working tolerance is 0.0012 in. The basic diameter of the GO-plug gage would be 1.49940 in. Using 5% of the working tolerance (0.00006 in.) as the wear allowance, and adding this to the basic diameter, the new basic diameter would then be 1.49946 in. The gagemaker's tolerance of 10% of the working tolerance (0.00012 in.) would then be applied in a plus direction as allowed by the unilateral system, with a resultant GO plug diameter of 1.49946 +0.00012. Figure 16-3 shows the wear allow-
-0.00
ances and gage tolerances used by the manufacturers of U.S. weapons.

Other manufacturing companies do not build a wear allowance into their gages, but set up a standard to determine when a gage has worn beyond its usefulness. The gage is allowed to wear a certain percentage above or below its basic size before being taken out of service. Gages should be inspected regularly for wear. No set policy for wear allowance or gage inspection is practical for all industries. In operations where an extremely high degree of accuracy must be maintained, the amount of allowable wear is smaller, and inspection must be more frequent than in operations where tolerances are greater.

A gagemaker normally makes the gage to provide maximum wear even if no wear allowance is designed into the gage. That is, he or she makes the GO end of a plug gage to its high limit, and the GO component of a ring gage to its low limit.

The NOT GO gage will slip in or over very few pieces and so wear very little, and as any wear on a NOT GO gage puts that gage farther within the product limits, no wear allowance is applied. When the NOT GO gage begins to reject work actually well within acceptable limits, it must be retired.

GAGE MATERIALS

For medium production runs, hardened alloy steel is used for wear surfaces of gages. For higher-volume production runs, gage wear surfaces are usually chromium-plated.

Component Total tolerance	Wear allowance	Gage Tolerance	
		GO	NOT GO
0.0005	0.00000	0.00005	0.00005
0.001	0.0001	0.00005	0.00005
0.002	0.0001	0.0001	0.0001
0.003	0.0001	0.0002	0.0001
0.004	0.0002	0.0002	0.0002
0.005	0.0003	0.0002	0.0002
0.006	0.0004	0.0002	0.0002
0.007	0.0004	0.0003	0.0002
0.008	0.0005	0.0003	0.0002
0.009	0.0005	0.0004	0.0002
0.010	0.0005	0.0005	0.0003
0.012	0.0006	0.0006	0.0003
0.014	0.0006	0.0008	0.0004
0.015	0.0006	0.0009	0.0005
0.016	0.0006	0.0010	0.0005
0.018	0.0006	0.0010	0.0006
0.020	0.0006	0.0010	0.0007
0.022	0.0006	0.0010	0.0008
0.024	0.0006	0.0010	0.0009
0.025 and up	0.0006	0.0010	0.0010

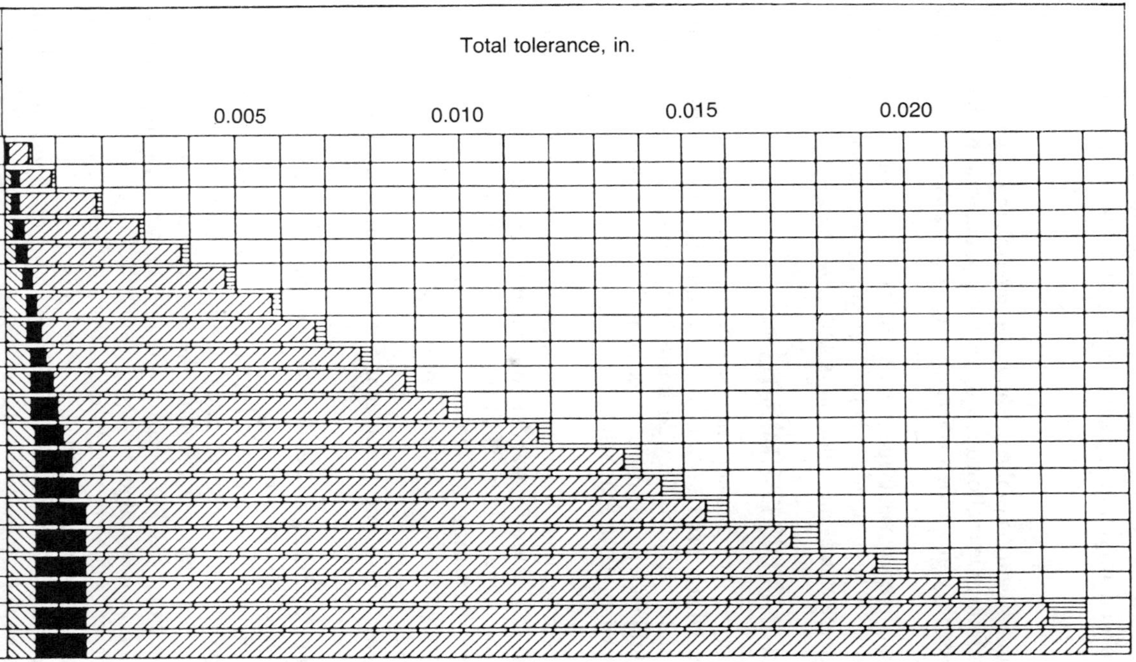

Total tolerance, in.

Gage maker's tolerance, flush pin, and adjustable snap gage

0.0005	0.00005	0.00005
0.001	0.00005	0.00005
0.002	0.0001	0.0001
0.003	0.0001	0.0001
0.004	0.0002	0.0002
0.010	0.0003	0.0003
0.015	0.0004	0.0004
0.020 and up	0.0005	0.0005

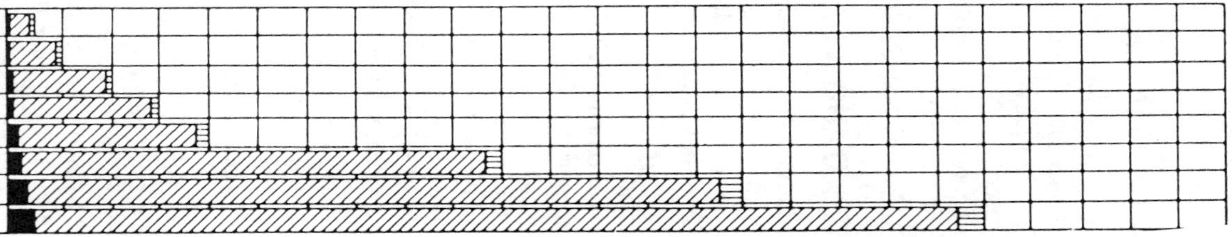

Fig. 16-3 Wear allowances and tolerances used as standard practice by plants in U.S. Ordnance production.

16-5

When a high degree of accuracy is needed, the production run is long, and wear is excessive, tungsten carbide contacts are often used on gages. Worn gaging surfaces can be ground down, chrome-plated, reground, lapped to size, and put back into service.

GAGING POLICY

Gaging policy is the standardization of the methods for determining gage tolerances and their allocation, and of fixing wear allowance. It is a guide to determine when gages are required, when and how they are to be inspected, and what types of gages should be used.

There is no one policy in universal use. Gage users should have their own policy—the one best suited to their work. A gage policy is helpful in eliminating controversy over the method of gaging, gage tolerances and allocation, and gage wear.

STANDARD MEASURING INSTRUMENTS

Standard off-the-shelf gages such as micrometers and vernier instruments, and also indicating type gages, are widely used in limited production because of their wide measurement capabilities and versatility. They do, however, require a certain amount of skill to make accurate and repeatable measurements. Some of their uses, measurement ranges, and discrimination (smallest scale division), are covered in the following section.

Micrometer Instruments. Micrometer instruments (see Fig. 16-4) are available for a wide variety of applications. For example, standard outside micrometer calipers generally have a one-in. measuring range, read to 0.001 in., or, with a vernier scale to 0.0001 in., and are available in sizes measuring to 24 in. Direct reading electronic versions are available with 0.0001 in. resolution and a zeroing feature. They are used for measuring ODs and lengths.

In addition to the micrometer instruments shown in Fig. 16-4, other types are available for many purposes. They include:

- Hub micrometer calipers which can be inserted through small holes to measure hub thicknesses and other related uses.
- Sheet metal micrometer, sometimes called deep throat micrometers which are used to reach over the edge of a sheet to take measurements away from the edge toward the center, and for other jobs requiring the deep throat.
- Tube micrometers which are used to measure wall thicknesses of tubing and also for measuring from a hole to an edge.
- Blade or groove type micrometers which are used to measure the diameter of narrow grooves or for checking close shoulder diameters.
- Flange or disc micrometers which are used for checking the thickness of lands or sections bounded by narrow grooves or slots.
- Groove width micrometers which are used to measure groove widths from 0.050 to 1.050 in. (1.27 to 26.67 mm) and land widths from 0 to 1 in. (0 to 25.4 mm).
- Multi-anvil micrometers which can handle a wide variety of measurements impossible to obtain with regular micrometers.
- Internal groove micrometers which are used to measure all types of internal grooves as narrow as 0.030 in. (0.76 mm).
- Internal micrometers which permit precision 3-point measurement of internal diameters.
- Internal and external taper micrometers which permit measuring tapers of work-pieces without removing them from the machine.

Vernier Instruments. To a lesser degree, vernier instruments, such as those shown in Fig. 16-5, can also be used for a variety of applications. They include:

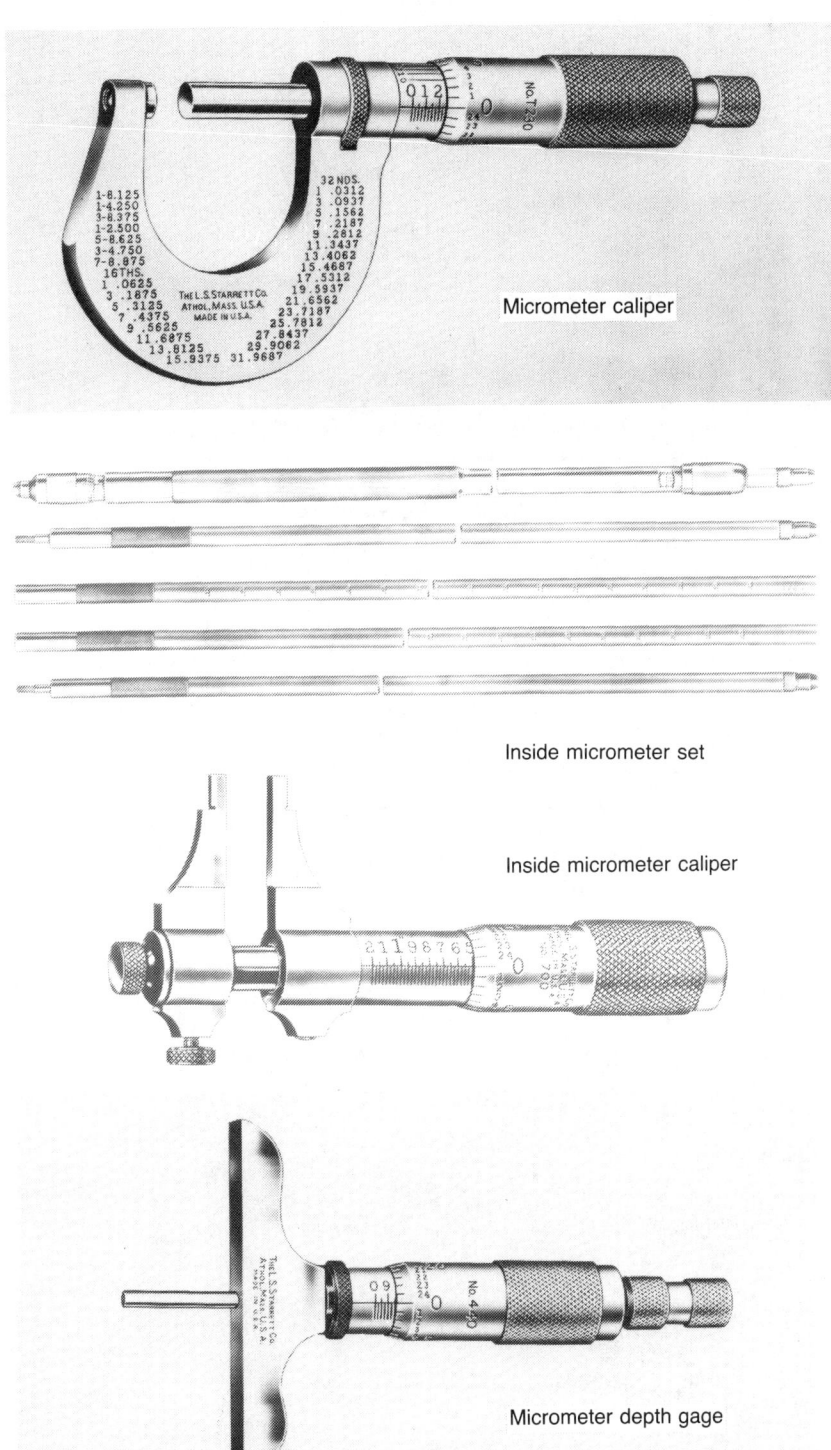

Micrometer caliper

Inside micrometer set

Inside micrometer caliper

Micrometer depth gage

Fig. 16-4 Micrometer instruments. (*Courtesy The L.S. Starrett Company*)

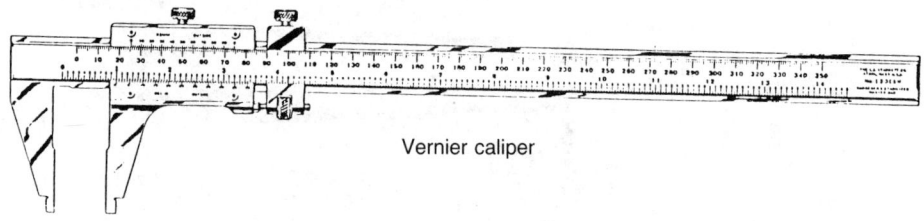

Vernier caliper

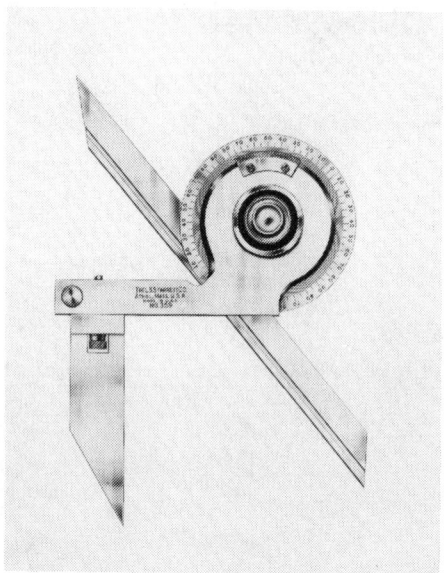

Universal bevel protractor

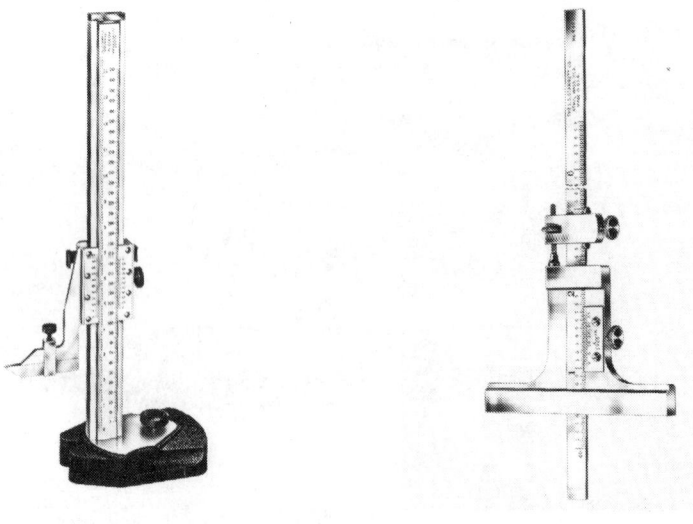

Vernier height gage   Vernier depth gage

Fig. 16-5 Vernier instruments. (*Courtesy The L.S. Starrett Company*)

- Vernier calipers which are used primarily for making inside and outside measurements.
- Vernier height gages which are generally used with a surface plate. With scribers they are used for layout work, and with dial test indicators, they are used for inspection work.
- Vernier depth gages which are designed to measure the depths of holes, slots, and recesses.

Graduations on most vernier instruments are 0.001 in. or 0.02 mm. They are also available with direct digital readout.

Another useful vernier instrument is the universal bevel protractor, which permits the measurement of angles up to 360° to an accuracy of 5 min.

Dial Indicators. The dial indicator (see Fig. 16-6) is perhaps the most widely used instrument for precise measurement. Basically, it consists of a probe, rack, pinion, pointer, dial, and case. The probe, which is attached to the end of the rack, is placed on the workpiece. A change in workpiece size changes the position of the probe, which in turn moves the rack. The rack movement turns the pinion, which through a gear train causes the dial pointer to move. The graduated dial is calibrated for direct reading of variation from the nominal dimension. Several amplification factors are involved.

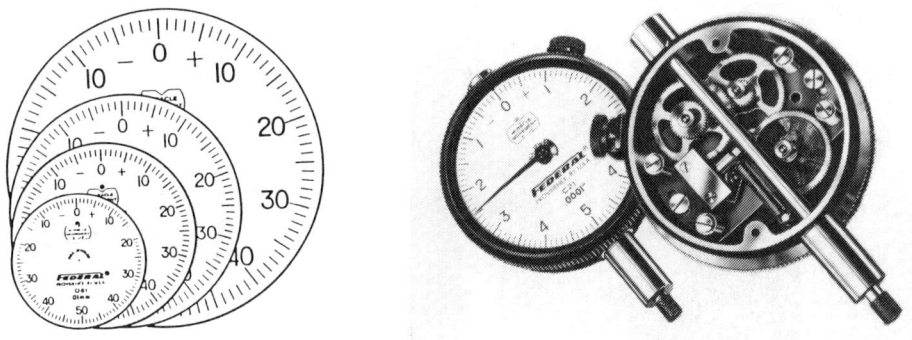

Fig. 16-6 Dial indicators. (*Courtesy Federal Products Corp.*)

Dial indicators are commercially available from many sources. Standard models vary greatly in size, amplification ratio, mounting facilities, and precision.

An indicator gage has one primary advantage over a fixed gage: It shows how much a workpiece is oversize or undersize. When using an indicator as part of a gaging device, a master block built to the nominal dimension to be checked must be used to preset the indicator to zero. Then, in applying the gaging device, the variation from zero, the nominal dimension, is read from the dial scale. The use of dial indicators with surface plates, parallels, V-blocks and height stands was discussed in Chapter 6.

Mechanical Indicating Gages. Also called dial gages, indicating gages are available for checking almost any dimension imaginable. Some of the more common ones are shown in Fig. 16-7. Their primary functions are usually expressed by their names.

Other types of indicating gages not shown include indicating plug gages (Comtor gages), internal and external indicating thread gages, and internal and external indicating spline gages.

One of the drawbacks to using indicating type gages is the fact that most of them must be set and constantly compared (mastered) with a calibrated master gage such as a setting ring, setting disc, or depth master. Master gages can be relatively expensive for larger diameters and also have long lead times which should be taken into account

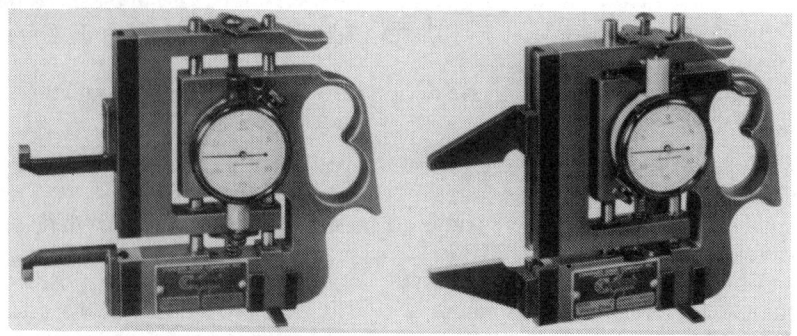

Typical setup for ID gaging   Easily convertible for OD gaging

Indicating groove diameter gages

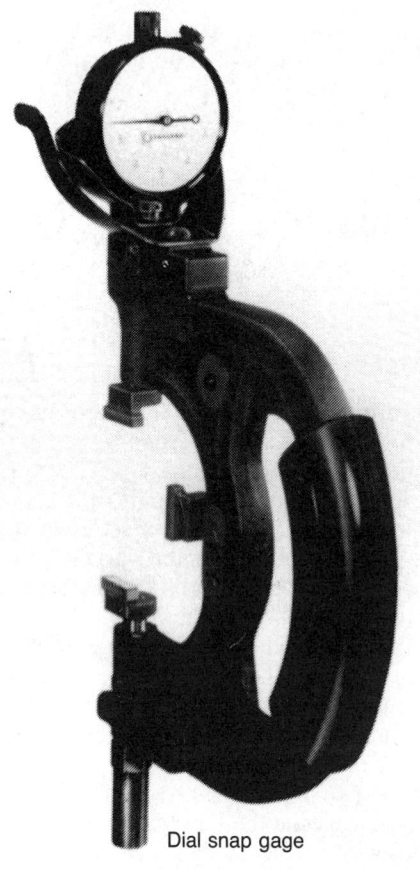

Dial snap gage

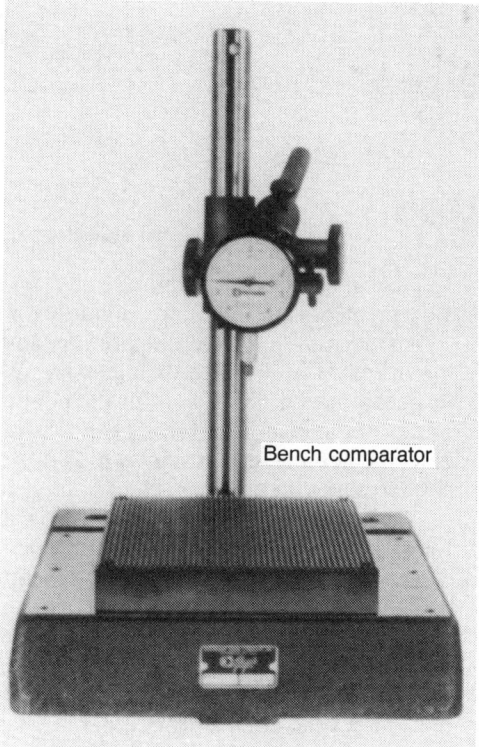

Bench comparator

Fig. 16-7 Mechanical indicating gages. (*Courtesy Standard Gage Company, Inc.*)

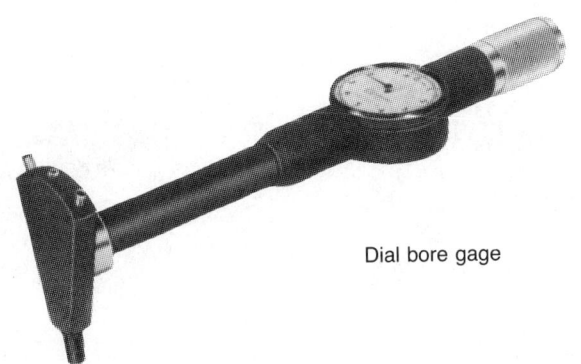

Dial bore gage

Q-type set up for OD gaging

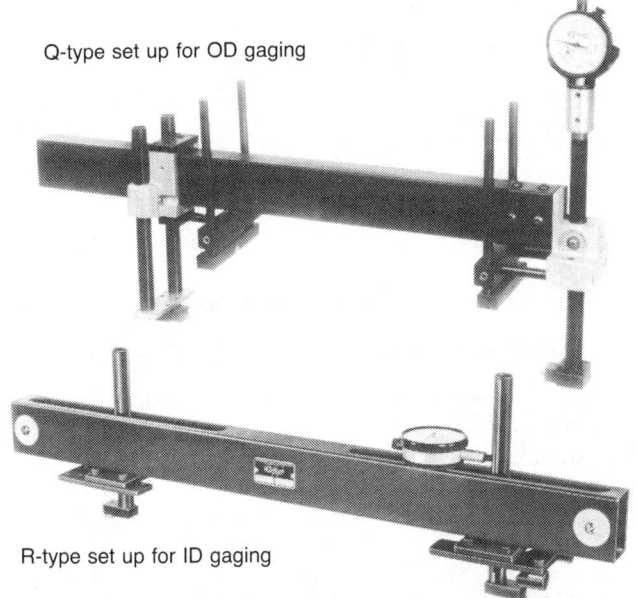

R-type set up for ID gaging

Shallow diameter gages

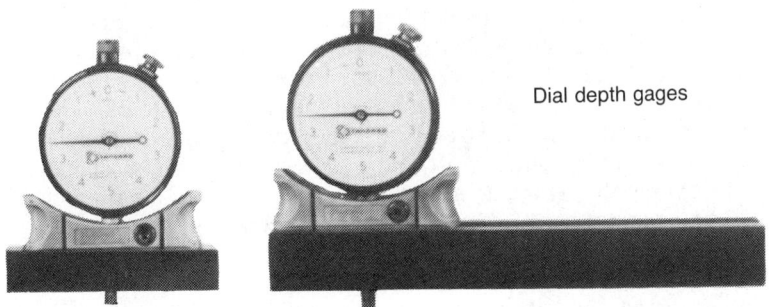

Dial depth gages

Fig. 16-7 (*Continued*)

when planning for limited production. There are, however, universal type masters which are practical for short runs. Some major ones are shown in Fig. 16-8.

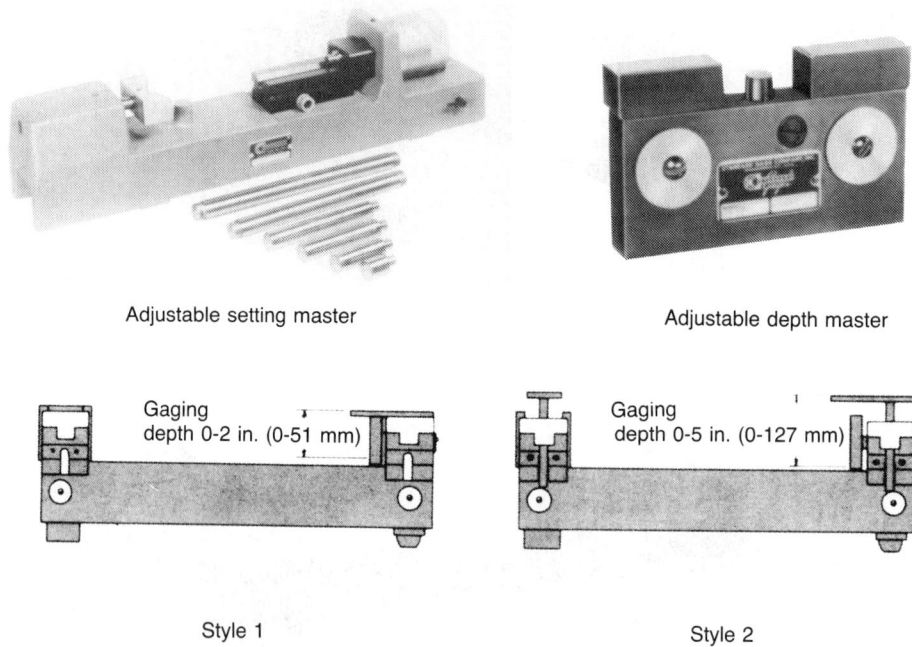

Adjustable setting master

Adjustable depth master

Gaging depth 0-2 in. (0-51 mm)

Gaging depth 0-5 in. (0-127 mm)

Style 1

Style 2

Shallow diameter reference masters

Fig. 16-8 Adjustable masters. (*Courtesy Standard Gage Company, Inc.*)

The adjustable setting master shown along with a complete set of measuring rods, can be used to accurately set and master dial bore gages from 2 to 8 in.

Caution should be taken when using this type of master. The contacts must be constantly examined for wear, since the dial bore gage is being set to a dimension between two flat surfaces and used to check between curved surfaces. Consequently, any flattening of the contact points will result in measurement errors. Also, this type of master, unlike a fixed master, can be tampered with, thereby causing part errors.

Dial snap gages and dial comparators of all types can usually be set and mastered with gage blocks. Note with caution that the same type of conditions can cause measurement errors with these gages, except that concave wear in the anvils or platens is the culprit.

For noncritical internal groove diameters, internal groove diameter gages can be set and mastered with a micrometer. For tight tolerances, a setting ring is recommended.

Adjustable depth masters, such as that shown in Fig. 16-8, can be used to accurately set and master dial depth gages in the range of 0 to 1.00 in. (0 to 25.4 mm).

The preferred method of setting and mastering shallow diameter gages, whether for short run or for high production, is with an adjustable shallow diameter reference master as shown in the figure, as it provides a wide range of adjustment for different diameters and gaging depths. Most shallow diameter gage users set the gage to a standard length measurement device, such as a set of gage blocks, and then use the gage to set the reference master.

Indicating thread and spline indicating gages are set with master plugs and rings which are ground to the correct size and configuration.

Fixed Gages. Fixed gages, such as those in Fig. 16-9, offer a viable alternative requiring less skill to use. Fixed gages are usually designed to measure a single dimension such as a hole diameter (ID) or a shaft diameter (OD).

For example, to check a 1.000 to 1.004 in. ID, a cylindrical plug gage, *a*, consisting of a 1.000 in. diameter GO member, a 1.004 in. diameter NOT GO member, and a handle for convenience would be used.

In the case of a 1.000 to 1.004 in. OD, separate 1.004 in. GO and 1.000 in. NOT GO ring gages, *b*, would be used. Adjustable snap gages, *c*, set to these dimensions could also be used.

GO members of gages like the thread gages, *d* and *e*, or spline gages, *f* and *g*, are composite gages which check the composite maximum material condition (MMC), while individual least material conditions (LMC) are checked with separate NOT GO gages.

Thread gages and spline gages are a must, even with limited production, since without them it is virtually impossible to know whether or not a threaded workpiece or a spline will assemble with its mating part. Only if one is fortunate enough to be making both of the mating parts, can the tool engineer consider production without them.

If lead time is critical, ring gages, spline gages, and other composite gages can sometimes be a problem. It may be necessary to make up soft gages to get the job started. On the other hand, plug gages and thread gages can usually be procured in a relatively short time; and, snap gages, both standard and groove type, can be stocked and set up as necessary.

Templates. A template represents a specified profile, or it may be a guide to the location of workpiece features with reference to a single plane. A straightedge may be used as a template to check flatness. To control or gage special shapes or contours in manufacturing, special templates are used for comparison by eye to insure uniformity of individual parts. These templates are made from thin, easily machinable materials, some of which may be hardened later if production requirements demand longer use. Figure 16-10 shows an application of the contour template to inspect a turned surface. Templates of this type are also used widely in the sheet metal industry and where production is limited. Templates are satisfactory when the part tolerance will permit this type of inspection.

Flush-Pin Gages. The flush-pin gage is a simple mechanical device used to measure linear dimensions. The important parts of the gage are the body and a sliding pin or plunger. The indicating device is a step, ground either on the plunger or on the flush-pin body, equal to the total tolerance of the dimension. When the gage is mounted on the workpiece, the position of the plunger can be checked visually or by fingernail touch.

Figure 16-11 shows a slotted workpiece being checked with a flush-pin gage. Also shown are the relative positions of the plunger at the high and low limits of the depth. The flush-pin principle applied in this way is simple in operation, is rugged and foolproof, does not require a master for presetting, and is economical when compared to micrometer or dial gaging methods. The dimension could also be checked with a depth micrometer. However, the depth micrometer requires a greater degree of operator skill, and there is the possibility of misreading the instrument.

Figure 16-12 shows an inspection fixture containing two flush-pin gages. Also shown is the workpiece being checked. The first dimension being checked (X) is the distance from the center of the spherical radius to a flat surface. The dimension (Y) is between the center of the same spherical radius and over the outside of a roll (wire). A standard tooling ball in the base of the fixture locates the radius of the workpiece and provides the origin for both dimensions.

PNEUMATIC INDICATING GAGES[1]

Air Gage Systems. Air gage systems are usually divided and classified according to

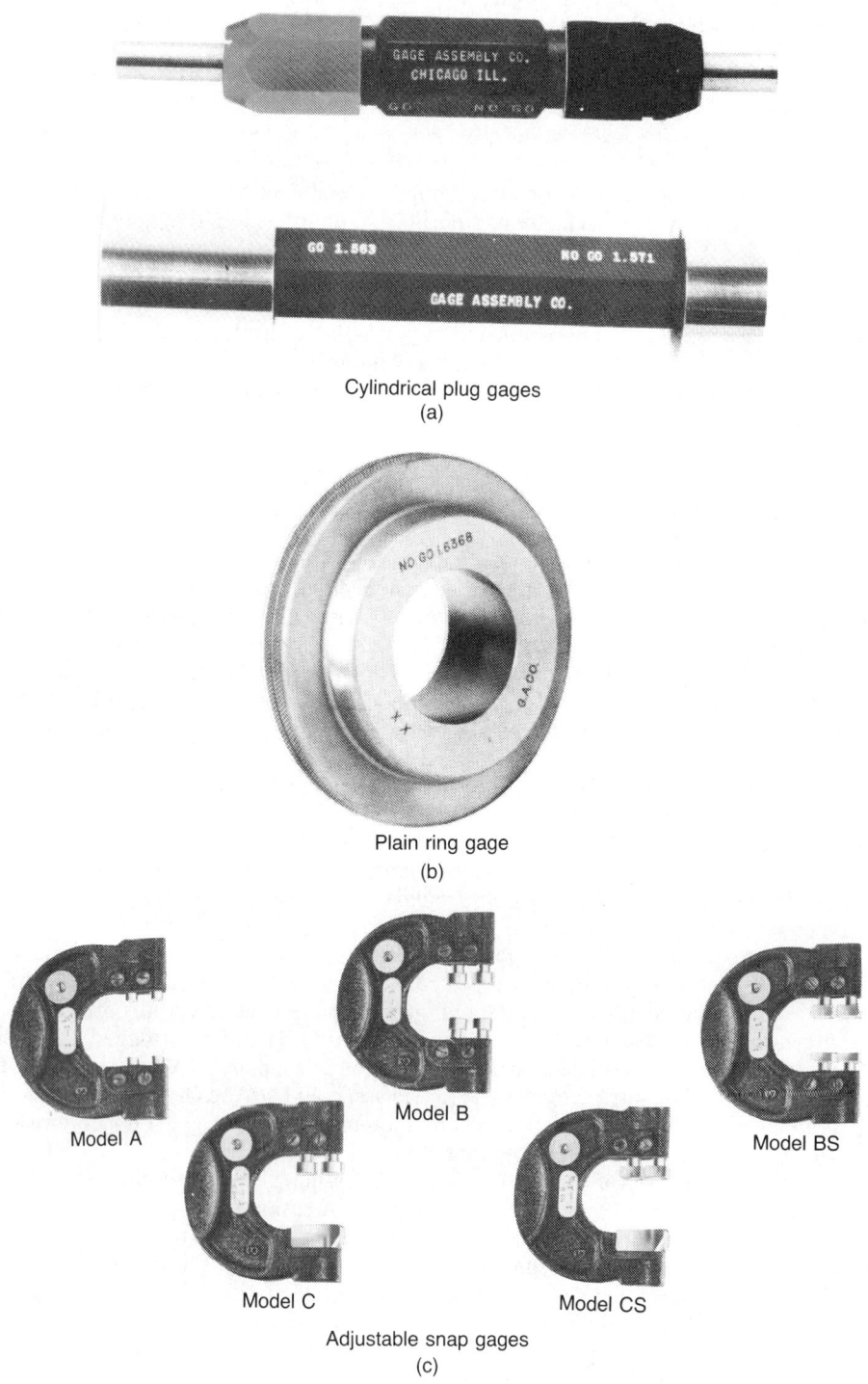

Cylindrical plug gages
(a)

Plain ring gage
(b)

Model A

Model B

Model BS

Model C

Model CS

Adjustable snap gages
(c)

Fig. 16-9 Fixed gages. (*Courtesy (a) thru (d) Gage Assembly Co., (g) Standard Gage Co., Inc.*)

16-14

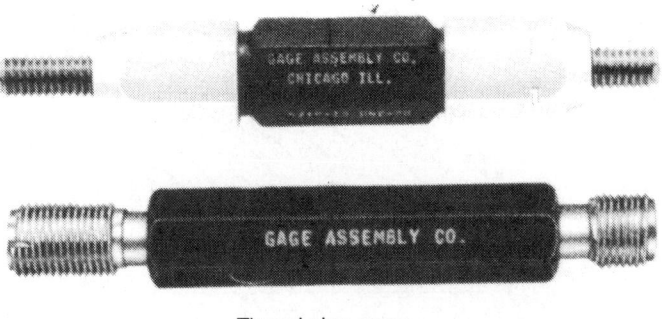

Thread plug gages
(d)

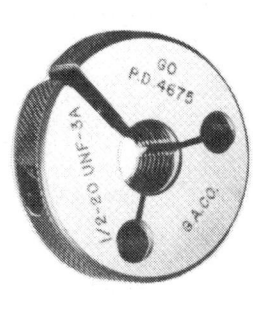

Thread ring gage
(e)

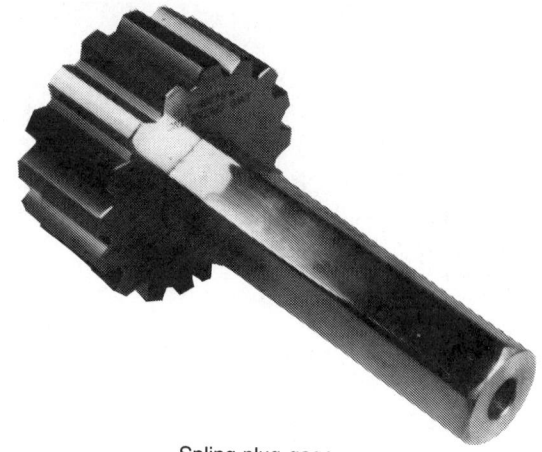

Spling plug gage
(f)

Spline ring gage
(g)

Fig. 16-9 (*Continued*)

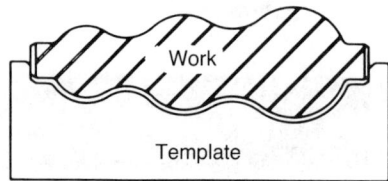

Fig. 16-10 Gaging the profile of a workpiece with a template.

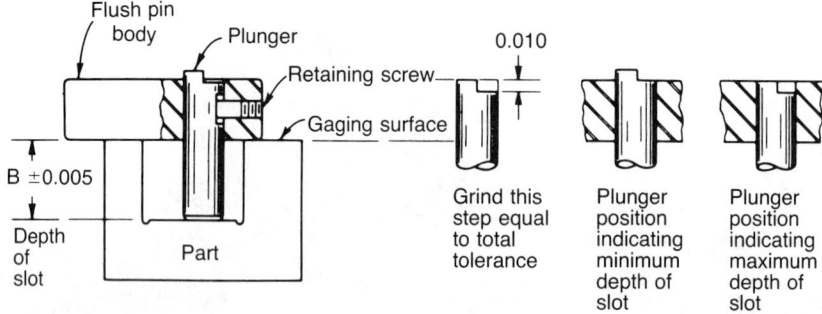

Fig. 16-11 Basic application of flush pin gage indicating various positions of plunger.

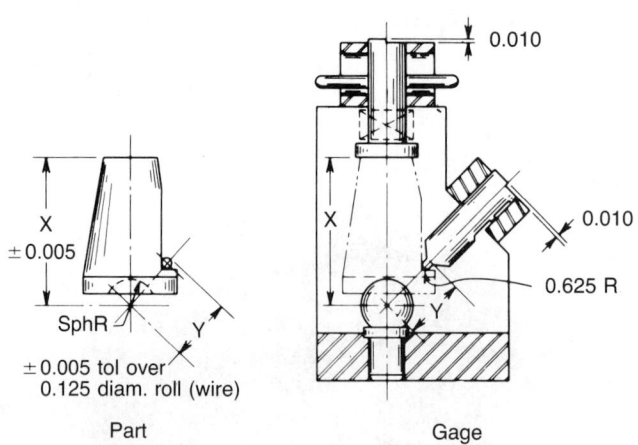

Fig. 16-12 Workpiece with flush pin-type inspection fixture.

their operating principles. The two general types of circuits used are flow and back pressure. Each type of circuit has individual advantages and areas of performance. Back-pressure gaging is used with an air-to-electronic converter to generate electrical signals for control and analysis.

Flow Gage System. The flow gage system is characterized by freedom from restricting orifices and mechanical wearing elements. In principle, air under constant pressure enters the bottom of an internally tapered glass column and flows to the gaging element or tooling (see Fig. 16-13*a*). A lightweight float moves up or down in direct ratio to the flow of air between the tooling and the workpiece.

A limitation to this type of system is that the float and tapered glass column tend to

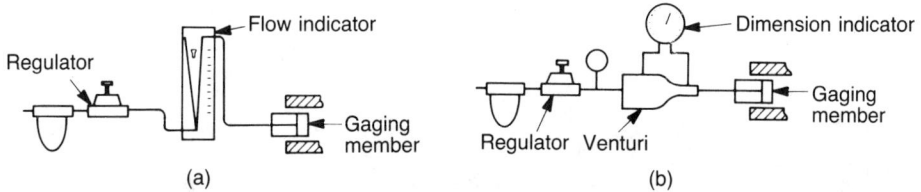

Fig. 16-13 Diagram of basic types of airflow gage systems: (*a*) **airflow gage with rotameter tube and** (*b*) **velocity-type air gage with venturi chamber.**

get loaded down with the oil in the shop-supplied air. This requires scheduled cleaning of the flow monitoring system.

A modification of the basic flow gage system is shown in Fig. 16-13*b*. In operation, air under constant pressure passes through a venturi tube into the gaging element or tooling. Each chamber of the venturi has a pressure tube connected to the opposite sides of a bellows or diaphragm. A difference in pressure existing between the two sections of the venturi tube actuates this bellows, which in turn operates a mechanical amplifier. Variations of air escaping between the tooling and workpiece effect a change in pressure differential in the venturi.

Back-pressure Gage System. Several different types of back-pressure gage systems have been developed. In its basic form, the back-pressure gage system consists of air under constant pressure passing through a controlling orifice of predetermined or adjustable size and into the gaging element or tooling (see Fig. 16-14*a*). A suitable pressure-indicating device inserted in the system between the controlling orifice and the tooling indicates changes in pressure resulting from the air escaping between the tooling and workpiece.

The water-column gage system was first developed to determine the size of carburetor jets (see Fig. 16-14*b*). This system uses the self-balancing properties of connected vessels, the constant pressure being maintained by the height of the water column. The level of the liquid in the graduated tube indicates the amount of obstruction that is facing the escaping jets in the gage head.

Another modification of the basic back-pressure circuit is the differential air gage system, which employs a parallel circuit as shown in Fig. 16-14*c*. In this system, air under constant pressure enters two separate channels and passes into opposite sections of a bellows cavity and housing. Air in one of the channels is allowed to escape through the gaging plug. In the other channel, air is allowed to escape through the zero setting valve. In operation, the difference between air escaping between the tooling jets and the workpiece as compared to the amount escaping when the master is in place causes a pressure differential at the bellows. The pressure differential is registered by a dial-type indicator or converted to an electrical signal using a pressure transducer.

Air Gage Tooling. The tooling used in air gaging is classified as either noncontact or contact.

Noncontact. Noncontact tooling, also referred to as open-jet tooling, uses the direct flow of air from the air escapement orifice to contact the part. The rate of flow depends on the diameter of the nozzle hole and the clearance between the jet and the part. Because the freeflowing air helps to blow away oil or foreign material, noncontact tooling is commonly used in automatic gaging machines if the cycle time permits. The speed of the air circuit must be considered in many applications.

A noncontact gage head may have single jets, dual jets, or multiple jets. Single-jet tooling permits simplicity in design, a minimizing of many pneumatic problems, and practical handling by a nonspecialist. Because single-jet tooling is inherently sensitive to gage position, it is not used for inside and outside diameter applications. Figure 16-15

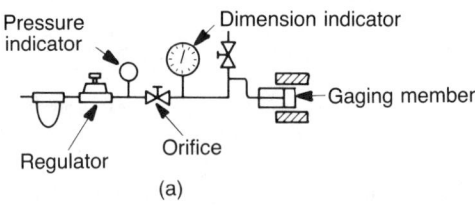

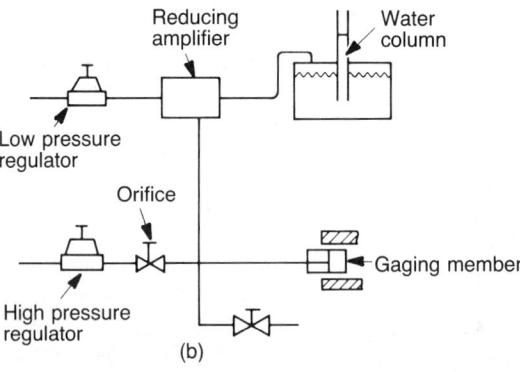

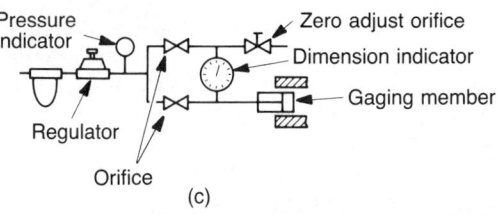

Fig. 16-14 Diagram of basic types of back-pressure gage systems: (a) air gage with variable amplification, (b) water-column gage system, and (c) differential-type air gage with fixed amplification. (*Courtesy Western Gage Corp.*)

illustrates some of the many ways that single-jet tooling can be used.

Dual-jet tooling is used in air probes for internal diameter inspection and in air snap and air ring gages for outside diameter measurements. This type of tooling eliminates the need for precise placement of the workpiece and the use of semiskilled help. Figure 16-16 illustrates some dual-jet tooling applications.

A dual-jet probe can measure true diameter because it has diametrically opposed jets. By traversing and rotating the probe as the hole is gaged, two-point out-of-round, bellmouth, hourglass, and barrel-shape conditions can be determined.

Dual-jet ring and air snap gages are the most widely used noncontact tooling for external diameter measurement. They inspect the true and average outside diameter of a cylindrical part and reveal conditions of taper and out-of-roundness. They are manufactured in many different types, shapes, and sizes, and may be designed for presenting the part to the gage or the gage to the part. Air rings and snap gages with three jets are used for diameter, taper, and cloverleaf (three-lobe) conditions.

Contact. Contact tooling has a mechanical member between the air escapement

16-18

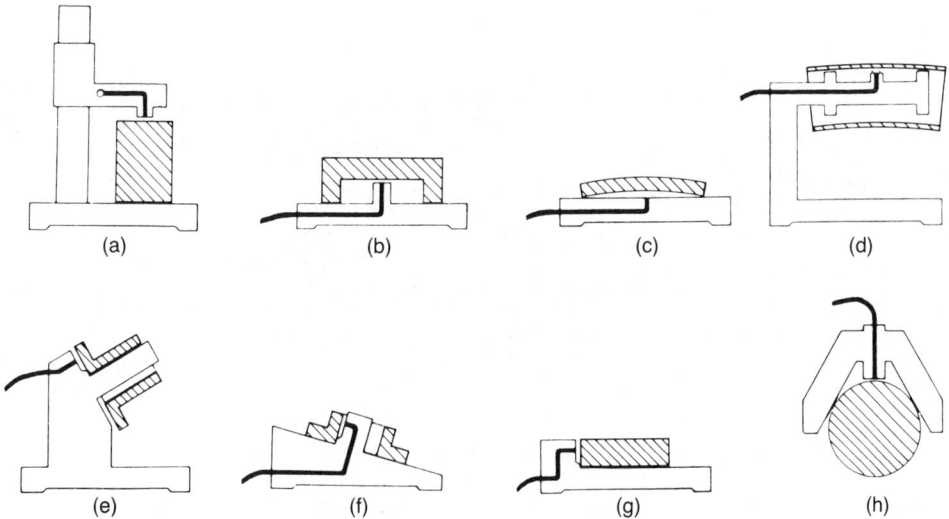

Fig. 16-15 Examples of single-jet tooling: (*a*) height gage; (*b*) depth gage; (*c*) flatness measurement; (*d*) chamber of banana-shape measurement; (*e*), (*f*), and (*g*) squareness; and (*h*) outside diameter snap gage. (*Courtesy Sheffield Measurement, A Cross & Trecker Company*)

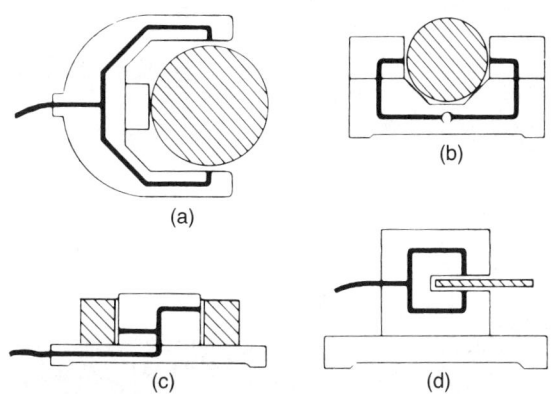

Fig. 16-16 Examples of dual-jet tooling: (*a*) outside diameter snap gage, (*b*) outside diameter V-block gage, (*c*) perpendicularity measurement, and (*d*) thickness measurement.

orifice and the part. This mechanical member can be freely rotating balls, a plunger, or levers. The movement of the mechanical member may be in an axial or a radial direction. Contact-type tooling is generally used for the measurement of rough and porous surfaces or to extend the linear measuring range of the air nozzle.

A typical air cartridge is shown in Fig. 16-17. It consists of a plunger that moves in a radial direction and a poppet-type air valve. Any change in the plunger position changes the airflow and the reading on the pneumatic comparator. Because the tapered plunger moves in and out of the air nozzle, the escape area of the air nozzle changes more gradually with the position of the measured surface. This allows for a linear measuring range of up to 0.080 in. (2.03 mm). Some typical air cartridge applications are shown in Fig. 16-18. Air cartridges must be fixed securely on the measuring fixture before measurements are made.

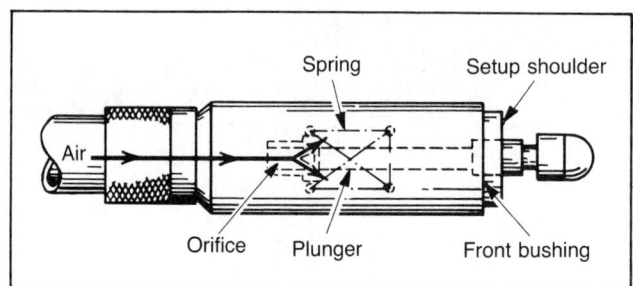

Fig. 16-17 Basic parts of an air cartridge.

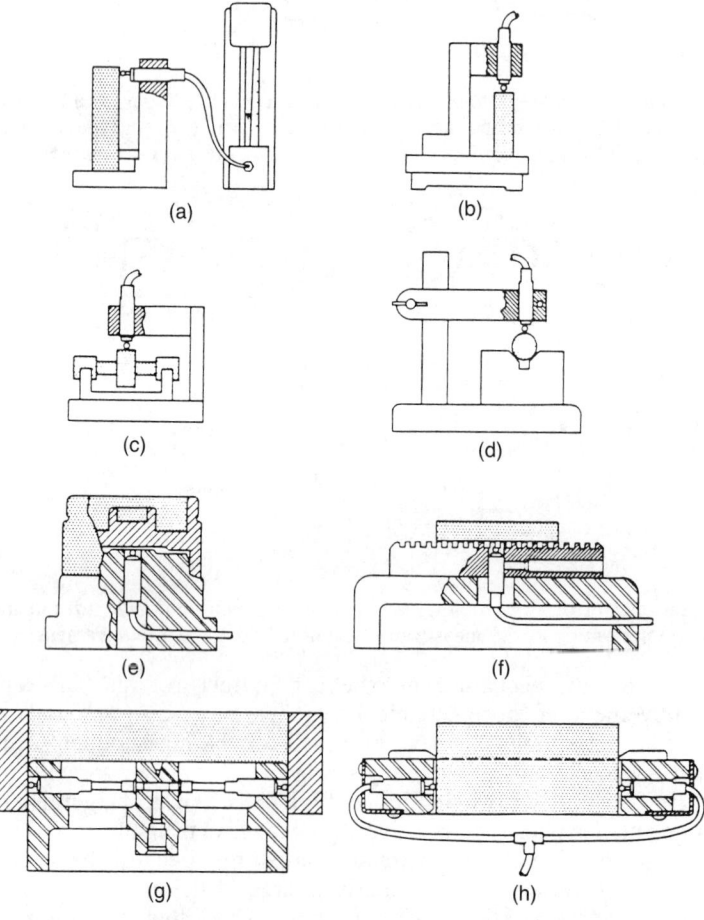

Fig. 16-18 Simple air-cartridge applications: (*a*) **squareness,** (*b*) **height,** (*c*) **concentricity,** (*d*) **three-point outside diameter,** (*e*) **depth,** (*f*) **flatness,** (*g*) **inside diameter, and** (*h*) **outside diameter** (*Courtesy Sheffield Measurement, A Cross & Trecker Company*)

Figure 16-19 shows a special air-electric gage designed for 100% inspection.

Fig. 16-19 Thirty seven dimensions on camshafts are checked simultaneously by this gage which utilizes the Federal air-electric measuring system. A green master light at the top of the panel lights to show when all dimensions are good. Lights on individual modular units signal out of tolerance dimensions and show whether they are "scrap" or "salvage". (*Courtesy Federal Products Corp.*)

Machine Control. Air gaging can be used on external grinders, surface grinders, and centerless grinding machines to locate parts precisely, indicate grinding wheel position if needed, measure wheel wear, and measure and control part size. Figure 16-20 shows an air cartridge mounted to the infeed slide of an external grinder. The cartridge indicates against a fixed adjustable stop attached to the stationary part of the machine. As the part is ground, infeed slide movement is shown by the falling float in the air column. When the float reaches a preset position in the column, the operator knows that the part is at final size.

In setting up the operation, the first part is ground and then gaged on a comparator or air snap gage. The stop is adjusted to position the float correctly in the column. The infeed slide wheel is next manipulated until the float is at "zero" in the tube, indicating the correct diameter size. All succeeding parts are ground till "zero" float position is reached in the column gage.

Another method of continuous grinding control is to use an air cartridge in a caliper sizing gage. This enables the operator to control stock removal accurately by watching the float action against the scale.

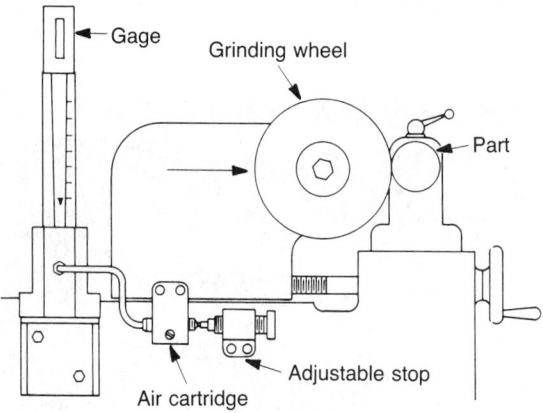

Fig. 16-20 Schematic of air gage machine control. (*Courtesy Sheffield Measurement, A Cross & Trecker Company*)

ELECTRONIC INDICATING GAGES

The three characteristics most responsible for the ever-widening use of electronic gaging equipment are its ability to sense size differences as small as 1 μin. (0.025 μm), its ability to amplify these small measurements as much as 100,000 times, and its ability to generate an electronic signal that can be computer processed. Systems measuring dimensions having very tight tolerances (10 μin.) are best put to use in laboratory measuring instruments, such as gage block comparators, and in comparators and height gages for shop applications. Electronic gages also find their way into automatic sizing and automatic gaging and sorting systems. These applications will be discussed subsequently in the section on automatic gaging and process control.

When using an electronic comparator, the gage is first calibrated by a master to the master dimension. The workpieces are then compared with this dimension, and the variation is displayed on an indicator.

Equipment. As was previously mentioned, the most common types of electronic gaging equipment are the electronic comparator and the height gage. An electronic comparator usually consists of the gaging head(s), the stand or support to which the head is attached, the indicator, and the amplifier. The basic difference between the comparator and the height gage is that the comparator has a built-in work support or reference surface. Height gages require a surface plate or some other reference base to support the workpiece and the stand.

Gaging Heads. Gaging heads transform a displacement of a measuring tip into a proportional electrical signal. They come in a variety of sizes and configurations and are built around different types of transducers.

The three most common head configurations are the lever type, cartridge type, and frictionless type[2] (see Fig. 16-21). The lever-type head, probably the most versatile, features an angularly adjustable, clutch-mounted contact finger. This allows the head to be set at the most convenient gaging angle and protects it against accidental blows. A reversing mechanism allows most of these heads to be used for measuring from above or below without turning the head upside down. Lever-type heads are most often used in height-gage setups.

The cartridge head is generally used in production gaging fixtures, snap gages, and in jobs involving space and mounting restrictions. Many of them are designed to fit into clamps normally used to hold dial indicators.

The "frictionless" head is the most accurate of these gaging heads and is used mainly

16-22

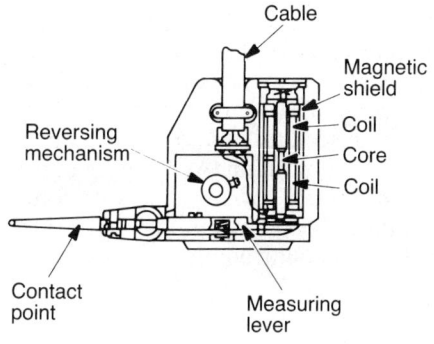

(a)

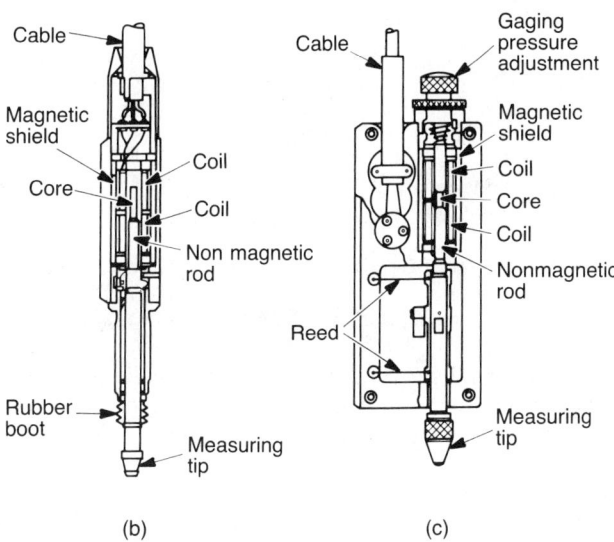

(b)   (c)

Fig. 16-21 Common gage heads used in electronic gaging: (*a*) lever type, (*b*) cartridge type, and (*c*) frictionless type.

in comparator setups. The spindle is suspended from two reeds, assuring virtually frictionless operation.

Of the many types of transducers used in electronic gaging heads—inductance bridge, differential transformer, strain gages, variable capacitors, piezoelectric crystals, and others—the inductance bridge, differential transformer, and strain gage are the most widely used. Both the linear variable differential transformer (LVDT) and the inductance bridge can sense small displacements over a limited range.

The gage head used in connection with an inductance bridge consists of two coils with a small iron core centered between them. When this core is in the center position, both coils have the same inductance, but when the core is displaced (as the tip contacts a workpiece), the inductance of one coil increases and that of the other decreases. This changes the current through the coils, and the change, within certain limits, is proportional to the core displacement.

The LVDT produces an electrical output proportional to the displacement of a separate movable core. It consists of three coils equally spaced on a cylindrical coil form (see Fig. 16-22). A rod-shaped magnetic core positioned axially inside this coil assembly provides a path for magnetic flux linking the coils. The secondary coils are connected in series opposition so that the two voltages in the secondary circuit are opposite in phase; the net output of the transformer is the difference of these voltages. When the magnetic core is in the central position, the output voltage is 0. This position is called the balance point or null position. As the core moves from this position, the voltage induced in the secondary coil toward which the core is moved increases. The voltage in the other secondary coil decreases. If the gage head is properly designed, this produces a differential voltage output from the transformer that varies linearly with a change in core-position.

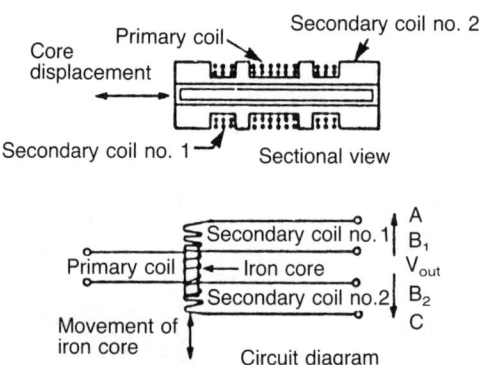

Fig. 16-22 Linear variable differential transformer (LVDT).

Both the inductance bridge and the LVDT depend on magnetic fields, so it is important that they be adequately shielded from external magnetic fields that would influence measurement. This is especially true in shops where many different sources of magnetic fields are present—machines, power lines, and magnetic chucks, to name just a few.

Strain gages are also used as transducers in gaging heads. The strain gage principle involves the stretching of a wire. Any strain on the wire changes its length and diameter, thereby changing its resistance in proportion to the strain.

Another type of transducer used in gage heads is the capacitive transducer. Gaging heads with capacitive transducers have two steel plates separated by an air gap (see Fig. 16-23). When the gage tip moves, the gap between the plates vary, thereby changing the capacitance. The change in capacitance is a measure of tip displacement.

Linear encoders can also be used to measure dimensions on different parts. The main advantage to using linear encoders is that measurements can be taken over a very long range up to 24 in. (610 mm) with an accuracy of ± 20 μin. (0.5 μm). Different applications include camshaft lobe profile, single-flank gear lead, and length checks.

Stand. With the interest in transducers, gage head mechanisms, and the workings of electronic amplifiers, it is easy to overlook the stand, which is a very important part of the electronic gaging system. Several manufacturers have devised special stands for certain applications such as thread measurement, squareness, and ID measurement. However, most electronic gaging is done either on a comparator or with a height gage. In designing a comparator stand, the goal is maximum stability and rigidity; in designing a height gage stand, stability and rigidity are kept in mind, but the aim is range and versatility.

Amplifier. The sturdiest stand and the finest gage head are practically useless unless they are teamed up with a quality amplifier. The stability, accuracy, and drift of a gaging system depend directly on amplifier quality.

The recent growth of electronic gaging owes much to the development of the transis-

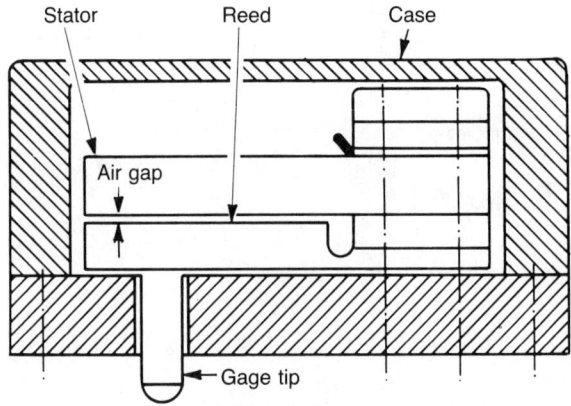

Fig. 16-23 Capacitive-type gage head.

torized amplifier. Utilizing transistors instead of vacuum tubes and printed circuits instead of hand-wired ones, the modern electronic gaging amplifier is smaller, lighter, and more troublefree than its predecessors. Also, the operating temperature of such an amplifier is so close to room temperature that it can be used in the proximity of the comparator or height gage without affecting gage accuracy.

Power for portable amplifiers can usually be furnished by mercury cell battery packs, rechargeable batteries, or direct line power.

Applications. Most electronic gages of the comparator type are used in a manner similar to dial indicators. The major difference is that the electronic gage can read much smaller deviations because the signal is digitized.

Because electronic instruments are highly stable, they can be used as absolute measuring devices. Thin parts, up to the maximum range of the instrument, can be measured directly without the use of a master. The accuracy depends on the type of probe and gaging system. For the best accuracy, at least one master is always required.

Differential measurements are also commonly made with electronic gages. Two gages are connected to one amplifier, and the difference or sum of the gage head outputs is measured. This technique can be used for checking roundness, thickness, parallelism, and taper. Because two gaging operations are combined in one, time savings are considerable.

Squareness, or lack of it, can be detected to 10 μin (0.25 μm). through use of electronic gage heads and simple fixtures.

STANDARD GAGE COMPONENTS

Standard gage components, available from many gage supply houses, provide a relatively inexpensive and fast way to make special gages. For example, the gage blanks shown in Fig. 16-24 can be used to fabricate a bar type flush pin gage in a relatively short period of time, since they are finish ground with the exception of the ends of the gage pin. To order, it is only necessary to specify the bar length, pin location, gage pin length, and the minimum and maximum gaging dimensions. Interchangeability of the component parts means that they can be used and reused from job to job.

These bar type flush pin gages can be converted to dial indicator type gages by the addition of a dial indicator housing as presented in Fig. 16-25. As with most indicator type gages, a depth master is required. Off-the-shelf masters shown in Fig. 16-26, along with pertinent dimensions, can be supplied by specifying the overall length dimension, the tolerance code, and the mean set dimension.

16-25

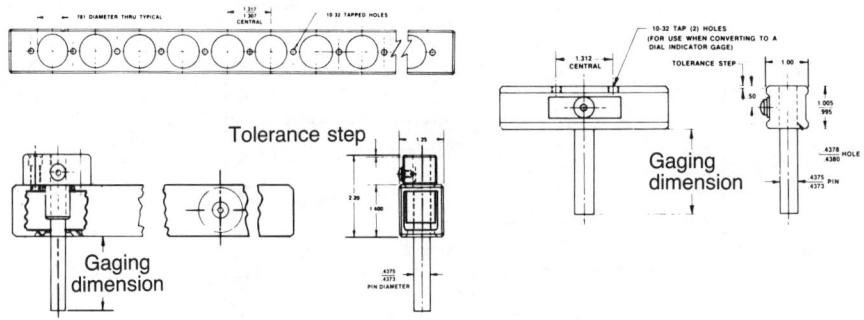

W Series Bar

BF series bar

Tolerance step

Gaging dimension

Gaging dimension

Fig. 16-24 Bar-type flush pin gages. (*Courtesy A. G. Davis Gage & Engineering Company*)

No modification to the flush pin gage is required if the tolerance step is on the gage body. Where the tolerance step is on the gage pin (and does not exceed 0.050) the end of the gage pin can be ground flat and adjustment in the Model "V" housing will permit its reuse.

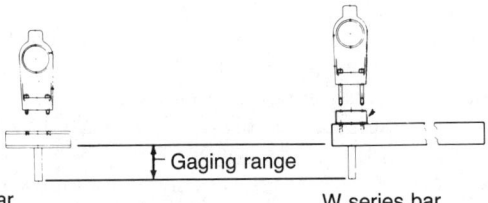

Gaging range

BF series bar   W series bar

Fig. 16-25 Converting bar-type flush pin gages to indicator gages. (*Courtesy A. G. Davis Gage & Engineering Company*)

Models DM-3.5 through DM-10

Model DM-18 only

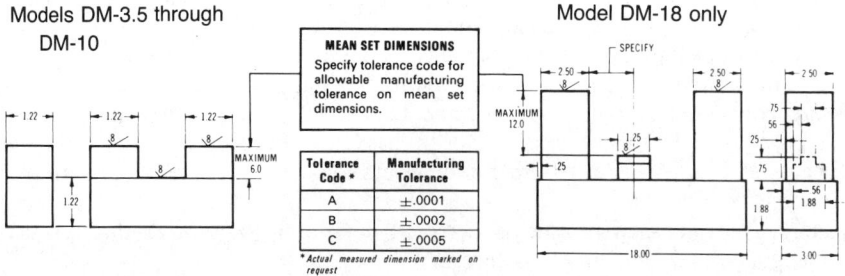

Tolerance Code *	Manufacturing Tolerance
A	±.0001
B	±.0002
C	±.0005

*Actual measured dimension marked on request

MEAN SET DIMENSIONS
Specify tolerance code for allowable manufacturing tolerance on mean set dimensions.

Fig. 16-26 Off-the-shelf depth masters. (*Courtesy A. G. Davis Gage & Engineering Company*)

Barrel type flush pin gages can also be made up in the same manner as the bar type using the gage blanks shown in Fig. 16-27. These gages can also be converted to indicator type gages as shown in Fig. 16-28. Specifications for the gages and off-the-shelf masters shown in Figs. 16-24 to 16-28 can be found in company product literature.

Transfer units are also available to adapt the dial indicator housing just mentioned. These units are shown in Fig. 16-29 along with some typical applications.

Another versatile off-the-shelf unit that can be quickly adapted to special needs is the Omni-gage (see Fig. 16-30), along with specifications and ordering information. Typical applications are illustrated in Fig. 16-31.

Most indicator gages discussed in this chapter can be easily converted for use with

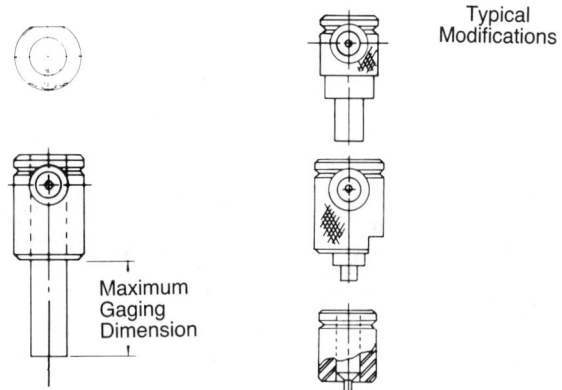

Typical
Modifications

Maximum
Gaging
Dimension

Fig. 16-27 Barrel-type flush pin gage blanks. (*Courtesy A. G. Davis Gage & Engineering Company*)

No modification to the gage pin is required if the tolerance step is on the gage body. Where the tolerance step is on the gage pin (and does not exceed 0.050) the end of the gage pin can be ground flat and adjustment in the Model CHR. 1 housing will permit its reuse. Gage body alterations are required as per drawing.

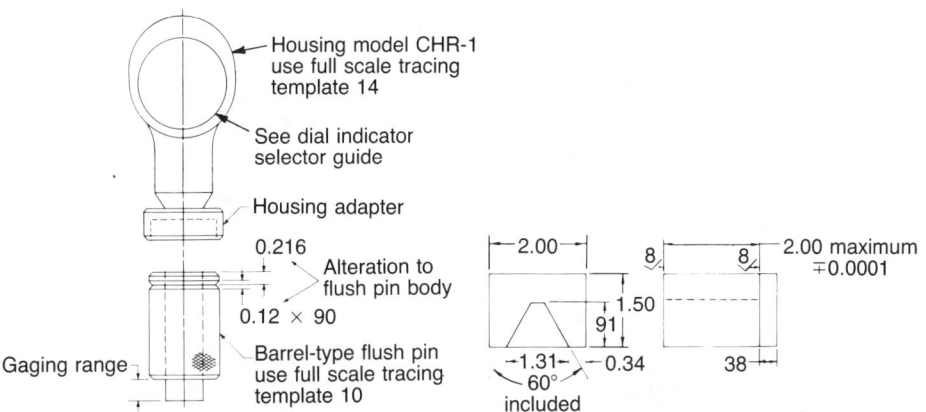

Housing model CHR-1
use full scale tracing
template 14

See dial indicator
selector guide

Housing adapter

0.216

Alteration to
flush pin body

0.12 × 90

Gaging range

Barrel-type flush pin
use full scale tracing
template 10

2.00

8

8

2.00 maximum
∓0.0001

1.50

91

1.31
60°
included

0.34

38

Fig. 16-28 Converting barrel-type flush pin gages to indicator gages. (*Courtesy A. G. Davis Gage & Engineering Company*)

air or electronic (analog and digital) readout equipment, since the stem mounting diameters on the dial indicators are the same as the mounting diameters of air probes and electronic transducers.

Many gage builders provide a complete line of interchangeable components such as mounting tables and bases, backstops, riser blocks, gage head mounting brackets and posts, motion transfer mechanisms (see Fig. 16-32), contacts, etc., which can be assembled in various configurations and combined with standard American Gage Design (AGD) type dial indicators, test indicators, air probes, and electronic gage heads to provide a precision inspection fixture. Some examples of fixtures built using these devices are shown in Figs. 16-33 and 16-34.

The fixture in Fig. 16-33 was designed to check the concentricity of the pitch diameters of two sets of teeth and concentricity of end holes to the body OD using standard AGD dial indicators.

Model	Features	Typical application
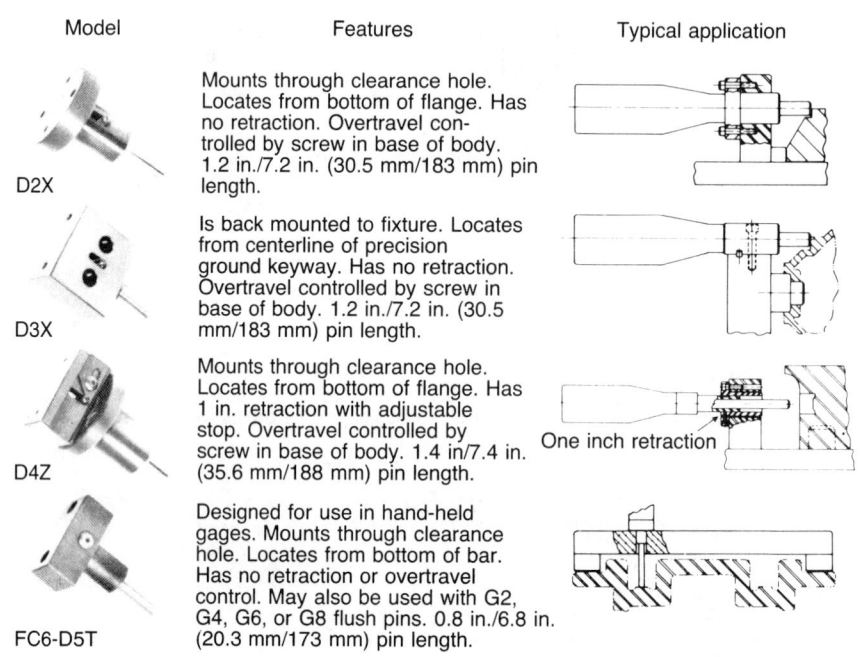 D2X	Mounts through clearance hole. Locates from bottom of flange. Has no retraction. Overtravel controlled by screw in base of body. 1.2 in./7.2 in. (30.5 mm/183 mm) pin length.	
D3X	Is back mounted to fixture. Locates from centerline of precision ground keyway. Has no retraction. Overtravel controlled by screw in base of body. 1.2 in./7.2 in. (30.5 mm/183 mm) pin length.	
D4Z	Mounts through clearance hole. Locates from bottom of flange. Has 1 in. retraction with adjustable stop. Overtravel controlled by screw in base of body. 1.4 in/7.4 in. (35.6 mm/188 mm) pin length.	One inch retraction
FC6-D5T	Designed for use in hand-held gages. Mounts through clearance hole. Locates from bottom of bar. Has no retraction or overtravel control. May also be used with G2, G4, G6, or G8 flush pins. 0.8 in./6.8 in. (20.3 mm/173 mm) pin length.	

Fig. 16-29 Transfer units and applications. (*Courtesy A. G. Davis Gage & Engineering Company*)

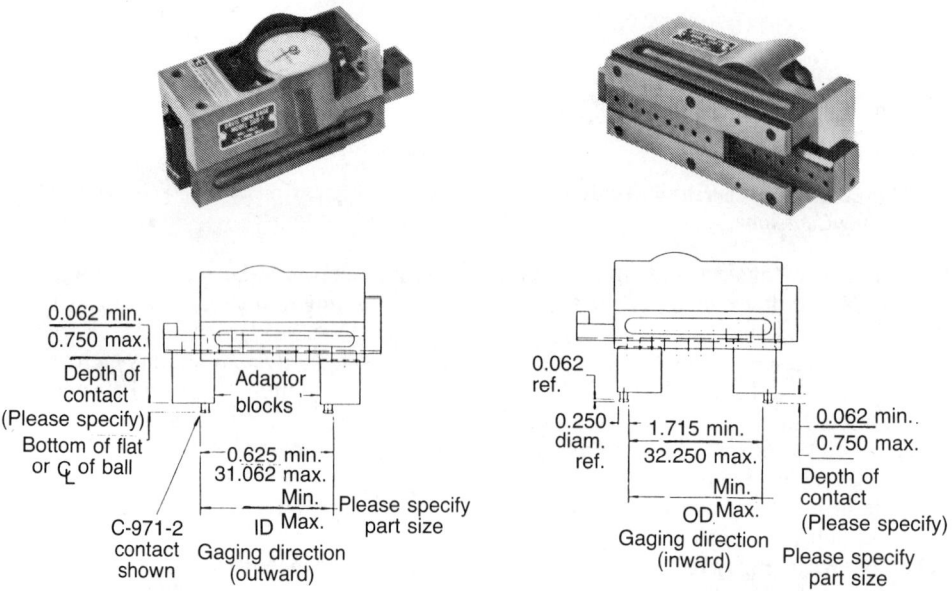

0.062 min.
0.750 max.
Depth of contact
(Please specify)
Bottom of flat or ℄ of ball

Adaptor blocks

0.625 min.
31.062 max.
Min.
Max.
ID
Please specify part size

C-971-2 contact shown

Gaging direction (outward)

0.062 ref.
0.250 diam. ref.

1.715 min.
32.250 max.
Min.
Max.
OD

0.062 min.
0.750 max.
Depth of contact
(Please specify)
Please specify part size

Gaging direction (inward)

Fig. 16-30 Omni-gage. (*Courtesy A. G. Davis Gage & Engineering Company*)

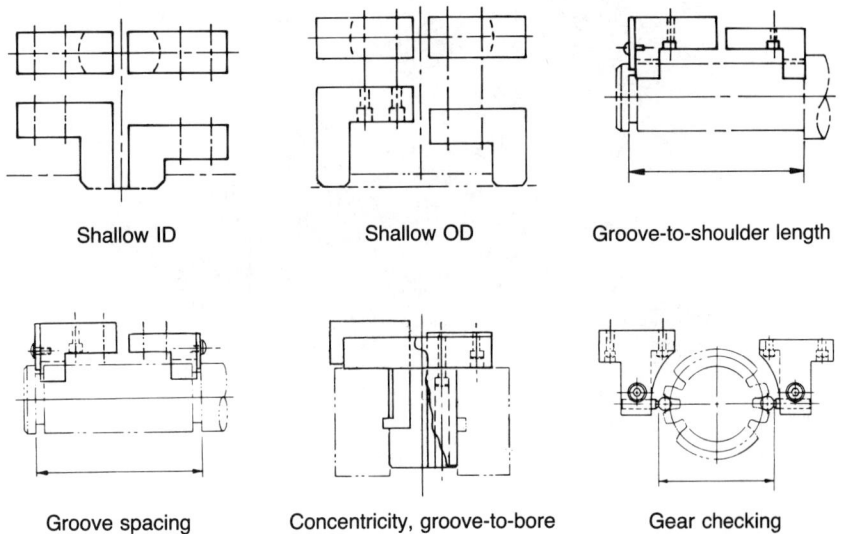

Shallow ID   Shallow OD   Groove-to-shoulder length

Groove spacing   Concentricity, groove-to-bore   Gear checking

Fig. 16-31 Omni-gage applications. (*Courtesy A. G. Davis Gage & Engineering Company*)

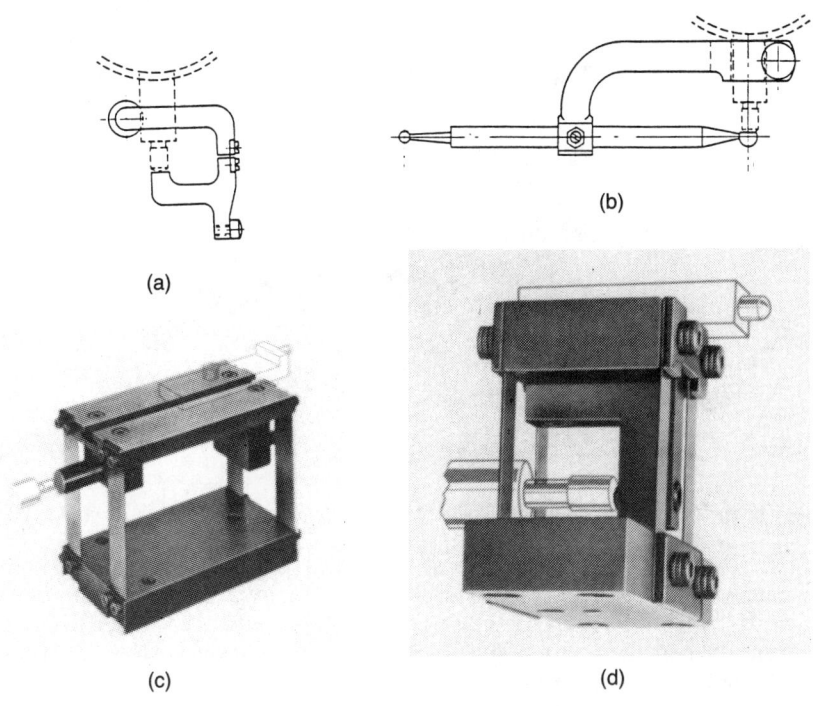

Fig. 16-32 Motion transfer mechanisms: (*a*) **right angle attachment,** (*b*) **hole attachment,** (*c*) **and** (*d*) **reed spring units (pantograph).** (*Courtesy Federal Products Corp.*)

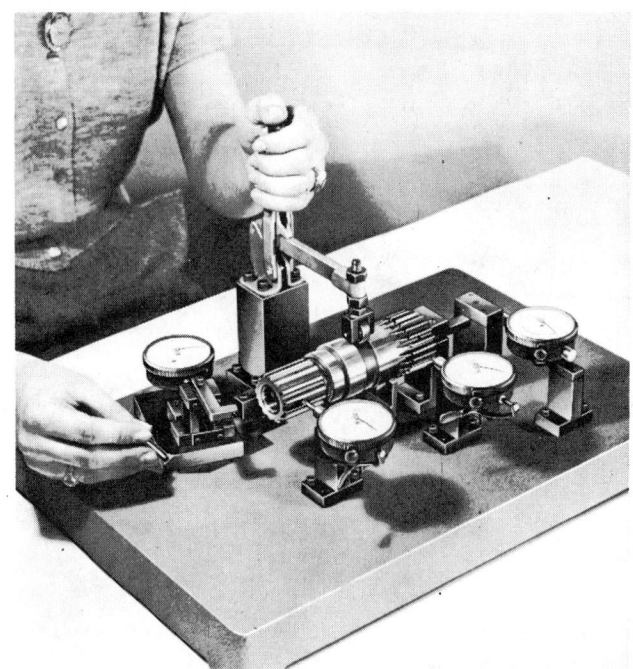

Fig. 16-33 Concentricity gage. (*Courtesy Federal Products Corp.*)

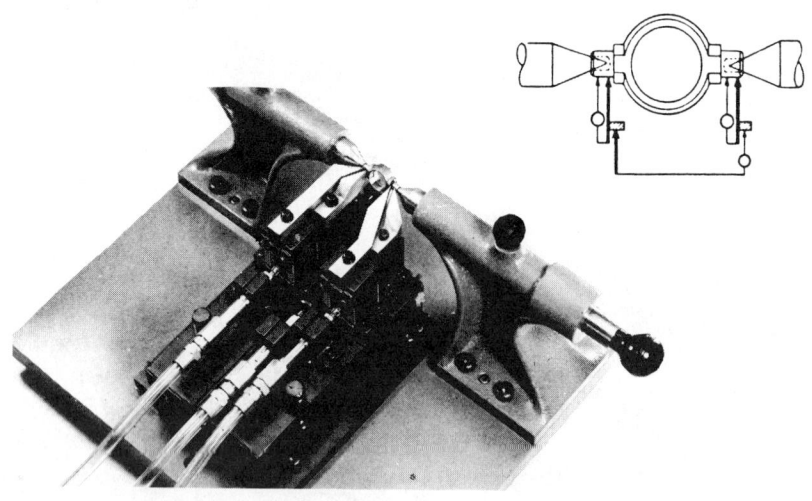

Fig. 16-34 Alignment and concentricity gage. (*Courtesy Federal Products Corp.*)

The fixture in Fig. 16-34 is connected to a triple unit air gage to check pivot alignment on a guidance gimbal plus the concentricity of one pivot with the other. The upper platform of the fixture is split so that reference contacts change positions relative to each other to show any lack of concentricity (see inset). The part is located in a V-block to establish the OD as reference. As the part is rotated, an axially located single jet air plug sweeps the ID. Any lack of concentricity will cause movement of the meter hand from the zero position.

Fixtures of this type can be used with dial indicators, air probes, or LVDT cartridges.

INSPECTION FIXTURES

Inspection fixtures need not be designed to withstand forces, such as shock and vibration, associated with machining or with some other fabricating and assembly processes, such as riveting, staking, and stitching. Inspection fixtures are not required to resist temperatures present in welding, brazing, soldering, and heat-treating. Clamping forces in an inspection fixture are generally too small to affect its design, but they should not distort the workpiece.

The accuracy of the construction of an inspection fixture and the design of gaging devices and any linkage associated with them are dependent upon the standards of quality specified for the workpiece.

Problems coupled with chips and coolants, with hazards of cutting tools, hot electrodes, and electric currents, or with rapid fixture loading need not usually be considered in the design of inspection fixtures.

Hole Relation Checking Fixtures. This type of fixture is an important tool used in the production of interchangeable parts and assemblies to check the location of bored, drilled, reamed, or tapped holes.

When the part is placed in position on the fixture, the pins that do not enter the hole give an indication of which holes are out of location, and the part is rejected.

In designing this type of fixture, the mean dimension of the workpiece is used for the fixture dimension with 10% of the workpiece tolerance as the fixture dimension tolerance. The pin diameters may depend directly on the minimum hole size and hole spacing.

Figure 16-35 shows a simple workpiece and its hole-location fixture. If the workpiece has four holes within the diameter tolerance, this fixture will indicate their location in relation to the center hole and to each other within 0.001 in. (0.03 m). The fixture cannot differentiate between oversize, undersize, tapered, or elongated holes.

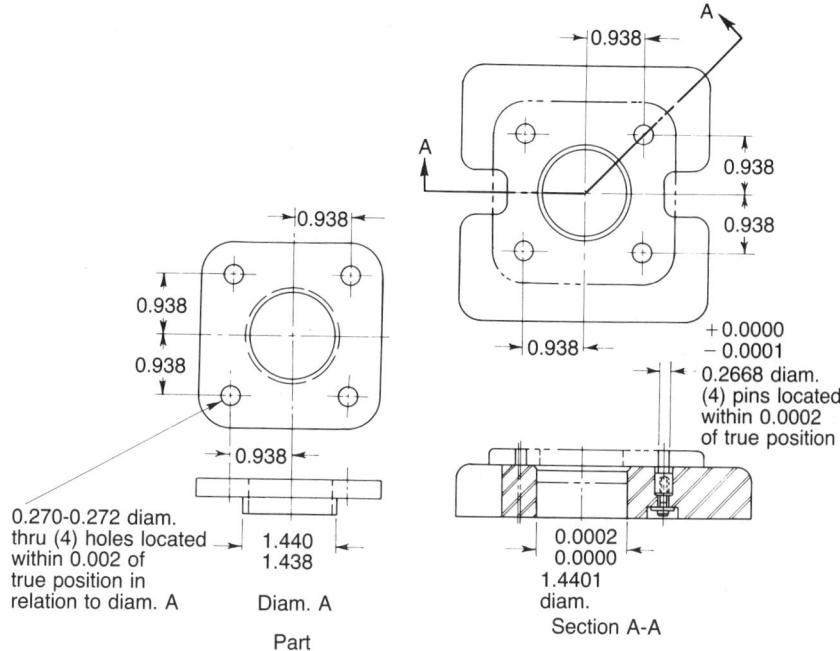

Fig. 16-35 Hole-location fixture. (*Courtesy Pratt & Whitney Aircraft*)

Figure 16-36 shows a more sophisticated and precise fixture for checking hole and bore locations on a bell housing for a heavy-duty truck. With fixtures of this type, the nominal hole and bore locations are precisely located in the fixture. A sweep gage is then inserted through the bushing in the fixture into the workpiece bore where it is rotated 360° (swept) to determine the deviation (direction and amount) of the workpiece bore from the nominal dimensions.

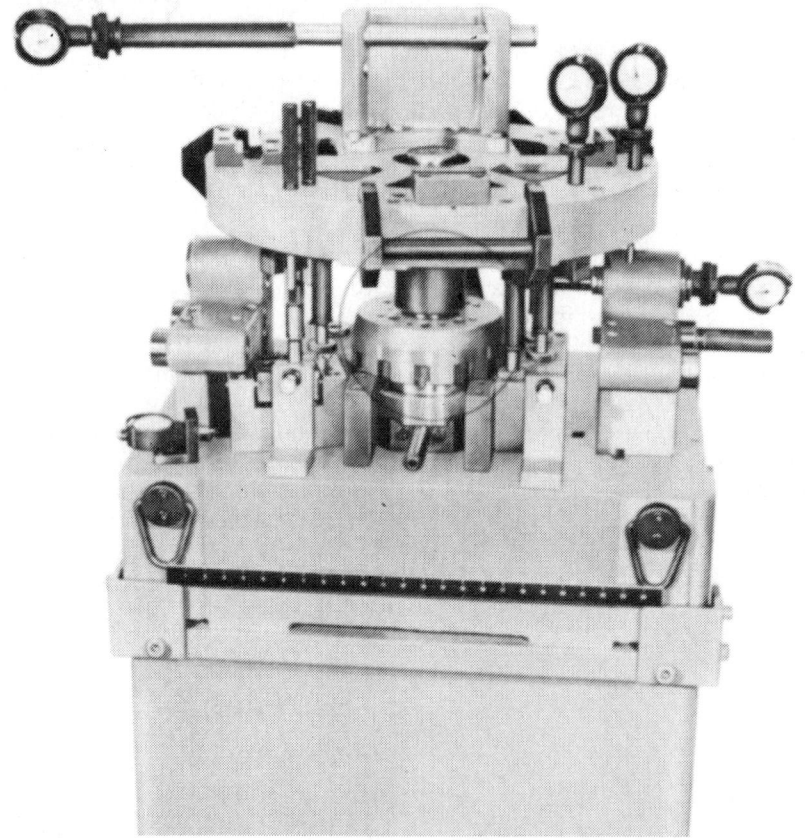

Fig. 16-36 Inspection fixture with sweep gages. (*Courtesy A. G. Davis Gage & Engineering Company*)

In use, the top of the fixture is lifted off, the bell housing is placed over an expanding arbor with the transmission mounting face vertically located on locating blocks. The housing is radially located by another expanding plug. When correctly in place the arbor and plug are expanded to establish the datum surfaces from which all checks are made.

The top portion, which is indexed to the bottom section is then replaced and the bores are swept with various sweep gages.

Typical design variations and applications of sweep gages are shown in Fig. 16-37. They include the following:

1. This unit, *a*, is equipped with two contact points utilizing a single indicator. With a spacer between the head of the bushing and the sweep unit, the bore is gaged for location. With the spacer removed, the face is gaged for squareness.

2. This unit, *b*, is mounted in an expanding or ball type arbor. It is used to locate in one bore and check its relationship to a second bore.
3. This unit, *c*, utilizes an eccentrically mounted sweep unit. It checks the hole location of a larger bore after entering through a smaller bore.
4. This unit, *d*, is mounted in a Con-Ax thread locator. The Con-Ax unit establishes a functional thread axis and the sweep gage checks the bore relationship to the thread axis.

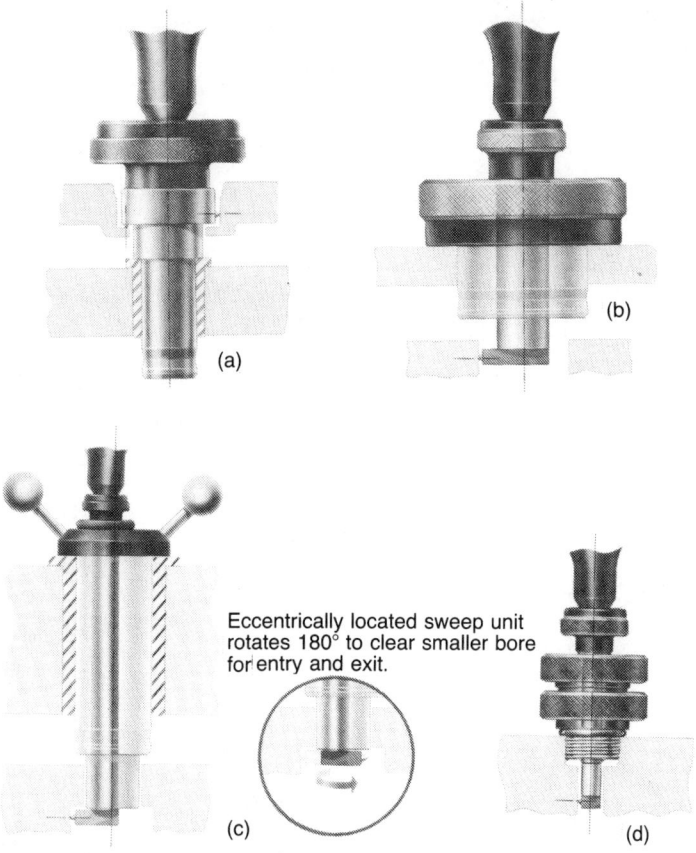

Fig. 16-37 Typical design variations and applications of sweep gages. (*Courtesy A. G. Davis Gage & Engineering Company*)

Typical contact point variations are shown in Fig. 16-38.

The fixture of Fig. 16-39 checks the size of the flange and hole locations on an automobile parking light casting.

A die casting having an oversize flange will not fit between the six locating blocks (1, 2, 3, and 4) of the fixture. Two pins (5) inserted through headless bushings (6) and into the three tapped holes of the casting inspect their locations with respect to each other and to the flange.

The distances from six mounting holes to the outside flange surfaces of a sheet aluminum chassis, as well as interhole distances, are checked in the fixture of Fig. 16-40. The chassis is loaded with the edges down between seven gage blocks (1), and hole location is checked by six pins (2). An oversize chassis will not fit between the gage blocks, while an undersize chassis permits the insertion of a 0.030-in. (0.76-mm) feeler gage between the blocks and the flange surfaces.

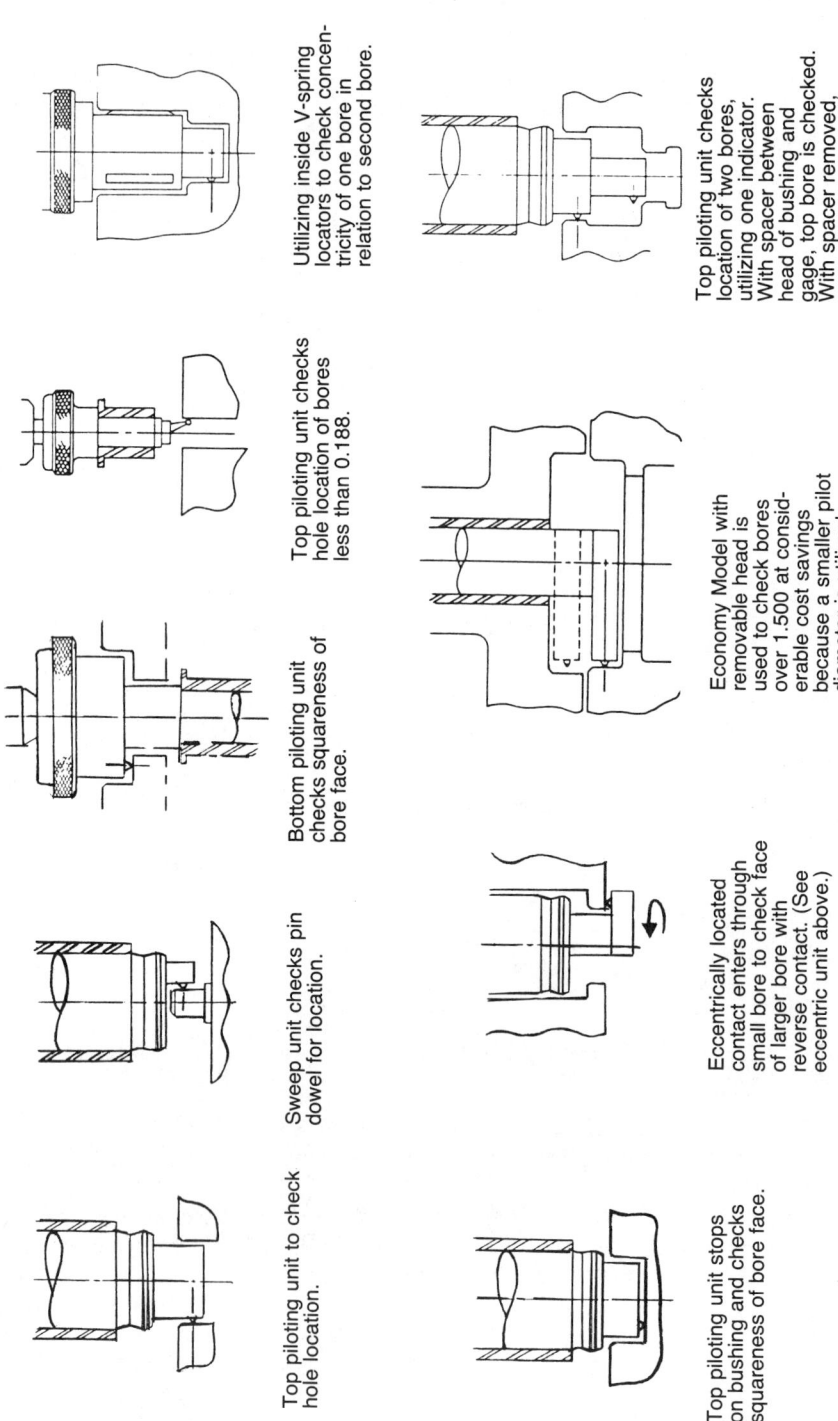

Utilizing inside V-spring locators to check concentricity of one bore in relation to second bore.

Top piloting unit checks location of two bores, utilizing one indicator. With spacer between head of bushing and gage, top bore is checked. With spacer removed, unit checks bottom bore.

Top piloting unit checks hole location of bores less than 0.188.

Bottom piloting unit checks squareness of bore face.

Economy Model with removable head is used to check bores over 1.500 at considerable cost savings because a smaller pilot diameter is utilized.

Sweep unit checks pin dowel for location.

Eccentrically located contact enters through small bore to check face of larger bore with reverse contact. (See eccentric unit above.)

Top piloting unit to check hole location.

Top piloting unit stops on bushing and checks squareness of bore face.

Fig. 16-38 Typical contact point variations. (*Courtesy A. G. Davis Gage & Engineering Company*)

16-34

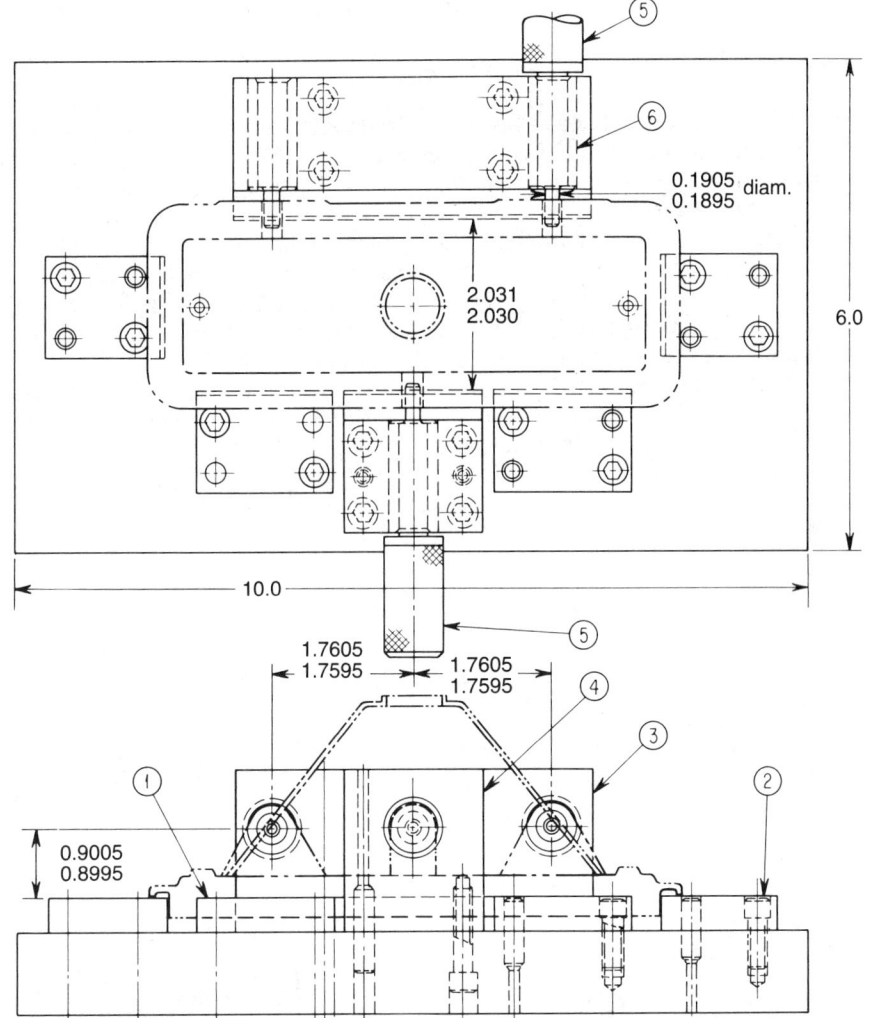

Fig. 16-39 Fixture for checking flange dimensions and hole location. (*Courtesy Ford Motor Co.*)

Dimensions of a stamped part (see Fig. 16-41) are inspected in the fixture shown in Figure 16-42 together with a conventional dial indicator and stand. Base *A* of the fixture is placed on a surface plate and all GO pins are retracted. The sliding gage (1) is opened by pushing on the fixture surface marked "push here to load and unload." The part is placed on pin locators (2) with part surface *V* parallel to the fixture base *A*. The inspection procedure consists of the following major steps:

1. The sliding gage (1) is released, and the entry of the pin (3) into the 0.134-in. (3.40-mm) notch is checked.
2. With the gage (1) on part surface *W*, the insertion of the go pins (4) checks the 0.166-in. (4.22-mm) dimension.
3. With the GO pins (4) inserted, the flush-gage surfaces check the 1.103-in. (28.02-mm) dimension between the locating holes and holes in which pins (4) are inserted.

4. The insertion of GO pins (5) checks the 1.187- and 0.593-in. (30.15- and 15.06-mm) dimensions for the two holes in the tabs opposite the locating holes.
5. The 0.265-in. (6.73-mm) notch width is checked by the insertion of the sliding gage (6).
6. The insertion off the four GO pins (7) checks the location of the four 6-32 tapped holes.
7. The tip of a dial indicator is passed over the part surface *X* to check its flatness.
8. The insertion of another GO pin (8) checks the 0.468-in. (11.89-mm) dimension locating the 0.190-in.-diam. hole in the end of the stamping.
9. The fixture is turned to rest on its base *B*. The dial indicator is set to zero with its probe on top of the indicating pins (9); then the indicator probe is passed over the part surface *Y* to check the 1.192-in. (30.28-mm) dimension.
10. The fixture is turned to rest on its base *C*. The indicator is set to zero with its probe on the indicating surface (10) of the fixture. The part surface *V* is held against the fixture while the part width, 0.937 in. (23.80-mm), is checked.
11. With the fixture resting on its base *D*, the indicator is brought to zero with its probe on top of the lower indicating pin (9). Surface *Z* of the bent tabs is indicated to check the 1.000-in. (25.4-mm) spacing dimension. This procedure is repeated with the fixture resting on base *E*.

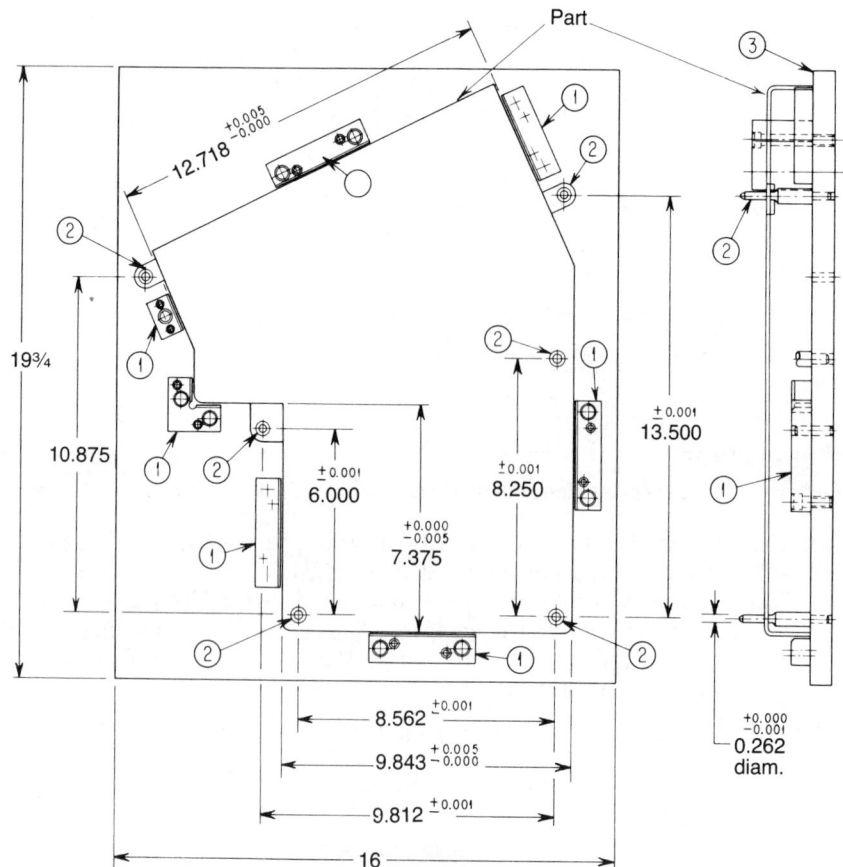

Fig. 16-40 Chassis-inspection fixture. (*Courtesy Western Electric Co., Inc.*)

16-36

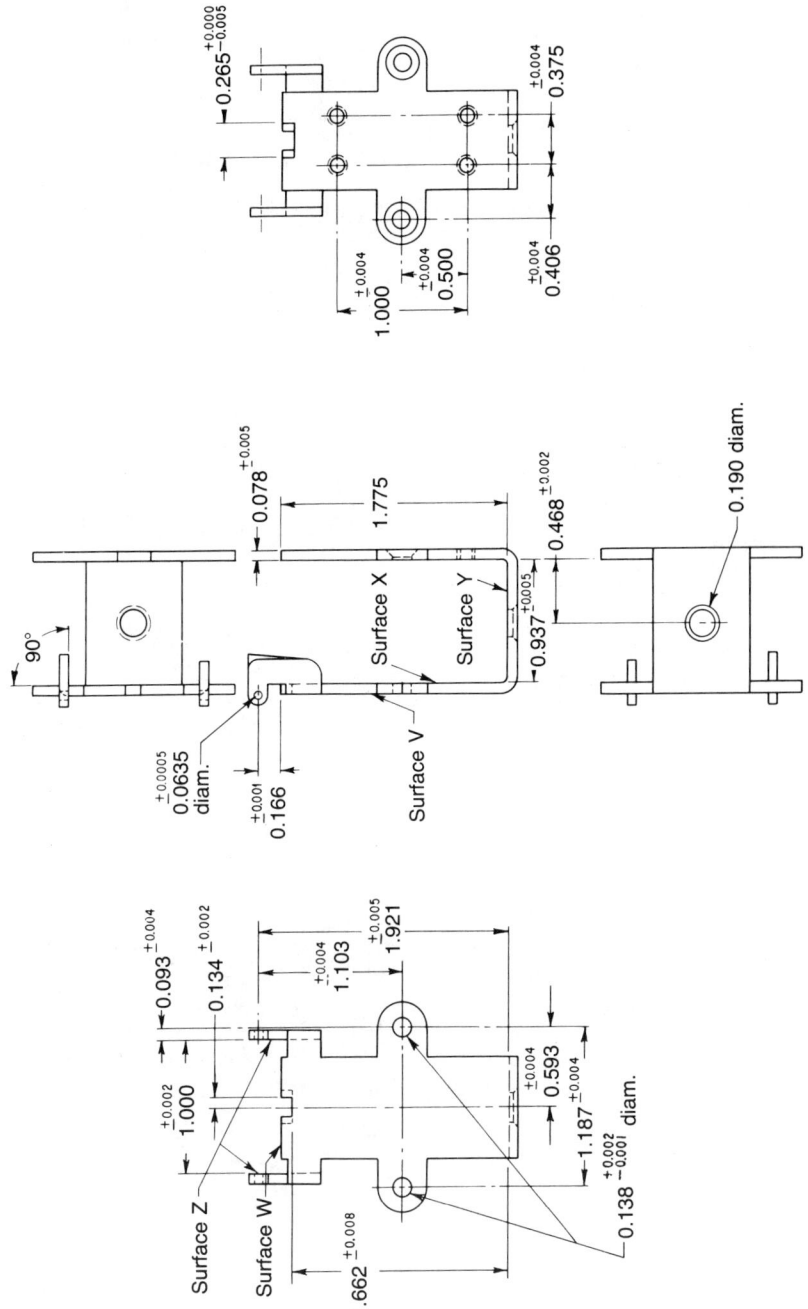

Fig. 16-41 Stamping which is inspected in fixture of Fig. 16-42.

16-37

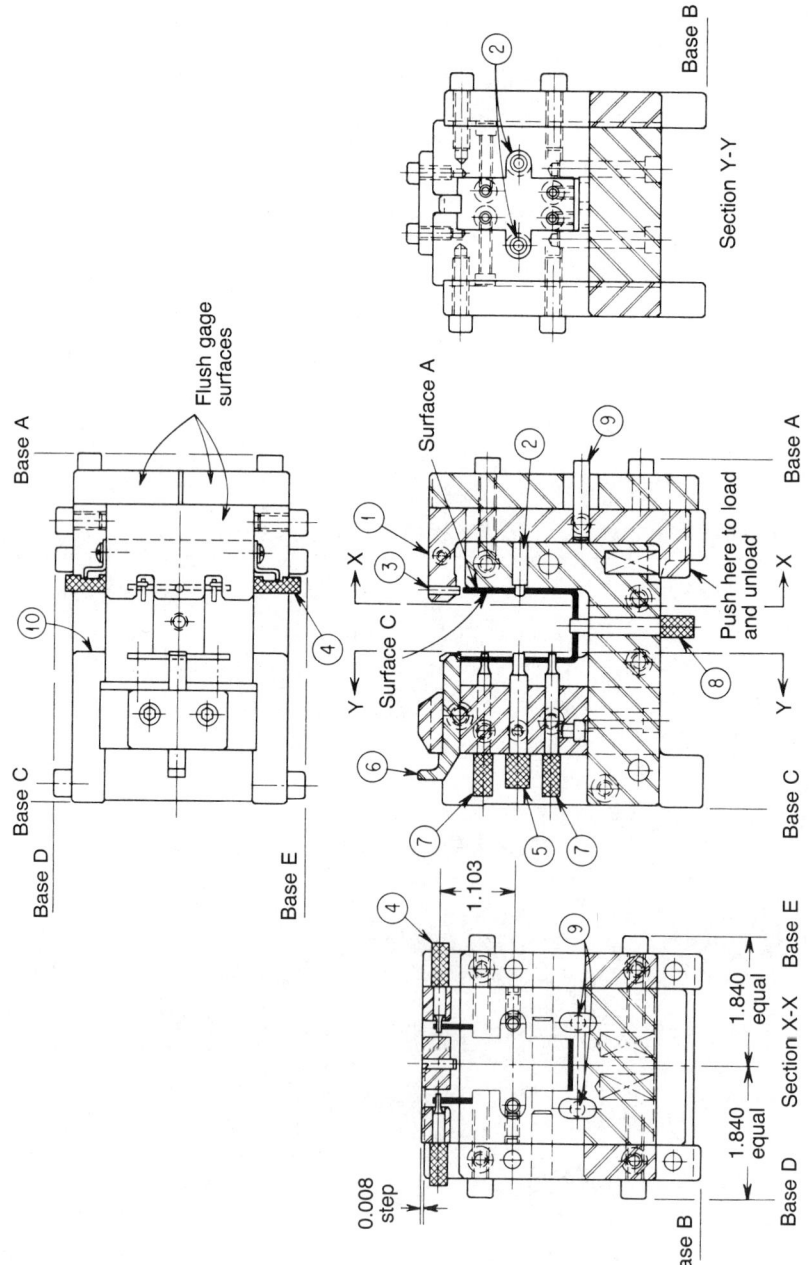

Flush gage surfaces

Base A

Base C

Base D

Base E

10

4

Section Y-Y

Base B

2

Surface A

Surface C

X

Y

X

Y

1

3

2

9

Push here to load and unload

8

Base A

6

7

5

7

Base C

0.008 step

1.103

4

9

1.840 equal

1.840 equal

Section X-X

Base E

Base D

Base B

Fig. 16-42 Fixture for inspecting a stamped part. (*Courtesy Harig Mfg. Corp.*)

During the inspection procedure, the checking pins are held in place by spring detents or screws bearing on flatted surfaces of the pins. Each base has hardened and ground rest buttons to support the fixture.

The hole-relation gage of Fig. 16-43 is used to check the distance from the center line of the two large holes to the shoulder of the inside bore in the neck. Also, it is used to check the distance from the outside face of the larger hole (left hand) to the center line of the bores in the neck.

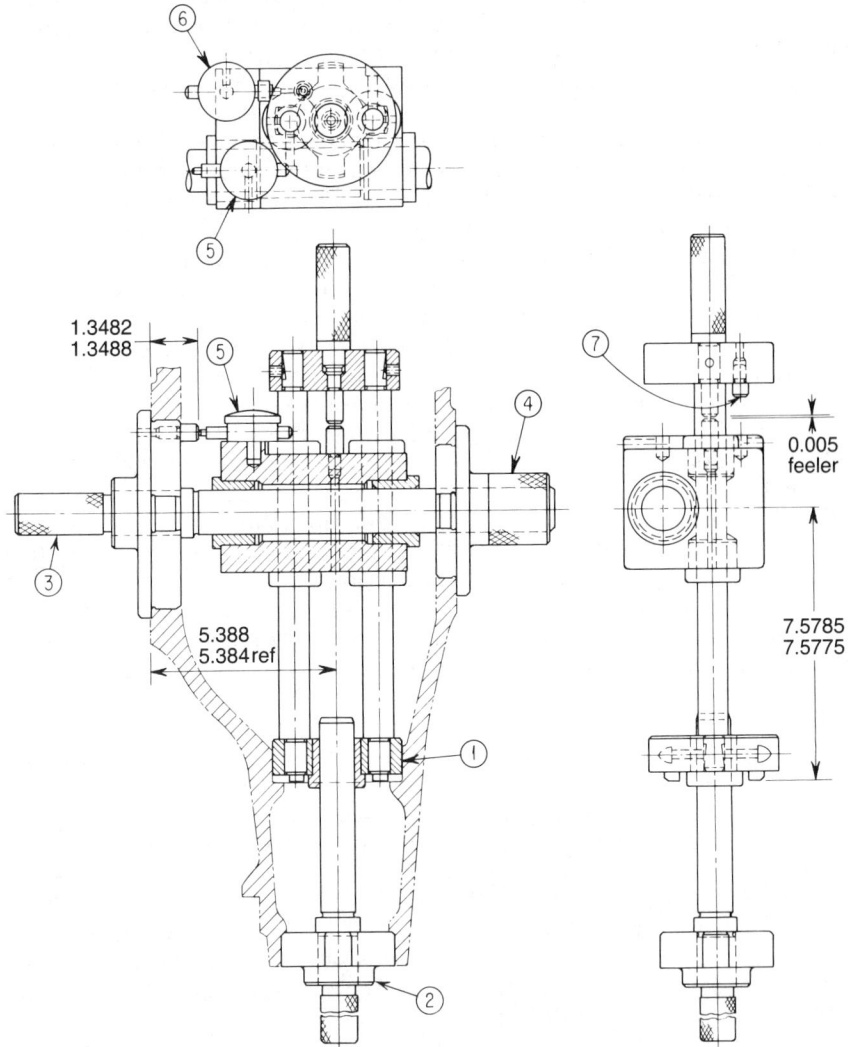

Fig. 16-43 Hole-relation gage for gearbox. (*Courtesy New Holland Machine Div., Sperry Rand Corp.*)

The central portion of the gage is inserted into the workpiece with the plug (1) in the bore of the neck bearing on the shoulder. The pin assembly (2) is inserted in the outer bore of the neck and through the plug (1). A second pin assembly (3) is placed in the cross bore through the bushings in the central portion of the gage. A locator plug (4) supports the end of the pin.

The indicator gage (5) is used to determine the distance from the center line of the neck bores to the outside face of the large bore. A second dial indicator (6), acting through linkage bearing on a pin (7), checks the distance from the center line of the two large bores to the shoulder of the inside bore in the neck.

All of the locating plugs are relieved to have a four-point bearing on their locating surfaces.

Surface Relationship Fixture. The inspection fixture of Fig. 16-44 establishes dimensional tolerances and relations of four surfaces of a stamping.

The stamping is located on pins (1) which are 0.0002 in. under the low limit of the 0.1895-in. holes. The 0.115-in. (2.92-mm) dimension is maintained by a spring-loaded clamp (3) which holds the stamping against a pin (2).

Variations in the surfaces to be inspected are reflected in the movement of the pointer-type indicators (4). These indicators are levers with ratios of 15 to 1.

The fixture is calibrated with a master part, and the tolerances for production parts are scribed in white plastic inserts (5) located under the indicator points.

Flush-pin Fixtures. This type of fixture checks workpiece surface relations.

Figure 16-45 shows a typical fixture to check hole and face location on elbow and T-shaped workpieces. The workpiece is placed on the base locator (1); then two movable locators (flush-pin gages) (2) are pushed into the workpiece. When they are fully inserted, the ground faces of the mounting blocks (3) must be coincident with or between the steps ground on the locators (4), or the workpiece is rejected.

Figure 16-46 shows a flush-pin fixture in which a workpiece diameter is checked by inspection of the radius. The acceptable diameter range is 33.552 to 33.570 in., or a total tolerance of 0.018 in. The radius range must then be 16.776 to 16.785 in., or a total tolerance of 0.009 in. The fixture-construction tolerance of 0.0005 in. results in a net acceptable tolerance of 0.0085 in. The 0.008-in. step of the gage pin (2) establishes workpiece acceptability if either step of the gage pin or any part of it between the steps is aligned with the outer ground face of the gaging surface. As tolerances decrease, the flush-pin method must be changed to one of amplification. A typical dial-indicator assembly (1) is mounted to the fixture. Using either a master part or a precise linear measurement, the indicator is brought to zero at the mean radius. Workpiece acceptability is then determined by indicator deviation from the mean in accordance with design tolerance.

The fixture shown in Fig. 16-47 incorporates a dial indicator (1) which slides in a slot (2) in the base to gage various shoulder lengths. Separate adapters and masters are provided for different workpieces. The master is inserted into the adapter, and the indicator reading is noted. Production workpieces then inserted must duplicate the indicator reading within the prescribed tolerance. A tapped hole in the adapter provides storage for the master.

The inspection fixture of Fig. 16-48 incorporates a flush pin (3) to check the contour of a parabolic (dish) shaped radar reflector which is mounted on a swinging arm (1).

The parabolic surface of the workpiece is checked by placing the stepped flush pin in a hole in each step of the gaging member (2). The part is rotated, and the relation of the step in the pin to the gaging surface is noted.

The dial indicator (5) is placed on the dead center of the workpiece by rotating the handwheel (6) which controls lateral movement of the gaging member. The dial indicator is set to zero by turning a lower handwheel (7) which controls vertical movement of the workpiece. The dial indicator (4) checks the position of the mounting screws in relation to the part center.

Figure 16-49 illustrates the entire fixture.

Squareness Checking Fixtures. Workpieces are often placed in fixtures to check the squareness of surfaces or parallelism of holes to surfaces.

The fixture shown in Fig. 16-50 is placed on a surface plate together with a dial indicator and its stand. The workpiece (1), an aluminum die casting, is placed on two

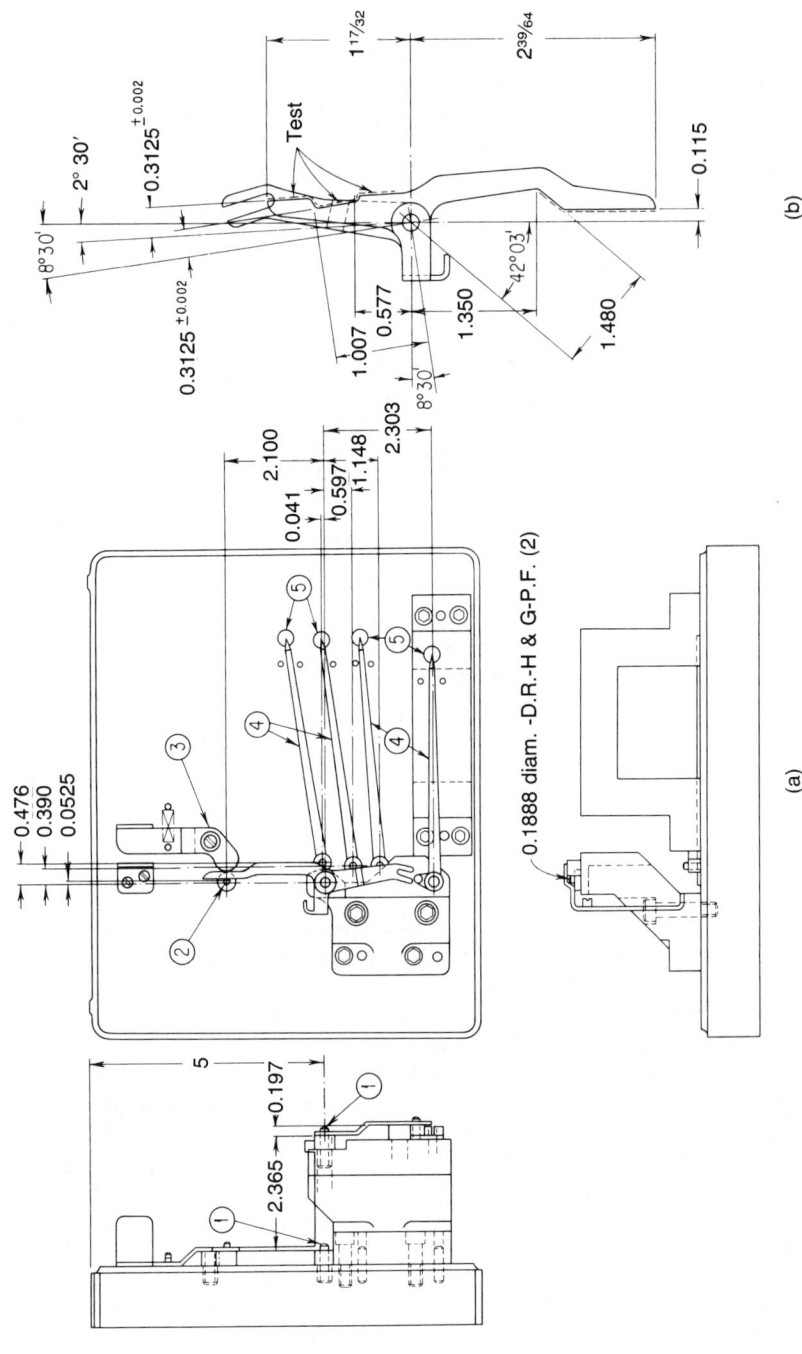

Test

2° 30′

0.3125 ±0.002

8° 30′

0.3125 ±0.002

1.007

0.577

8° 30′

1.350

1.480

42° 03′

1 17/32

2 39/64

0.115

(b)

0.476
0.390
0.0525

2.100

0.041

0.597

1.148

2.303

0.1888 diam. -D.R.-H & G.P.F. (2)

(a)

5

0.197

2.365

Fig. 16-44 (*a*) **Fixture for checking dimensional tolerances and relations of four surfaces of a stamping;** (*b*) **the stamping.** (*Courtesy Unisys*)

16-41

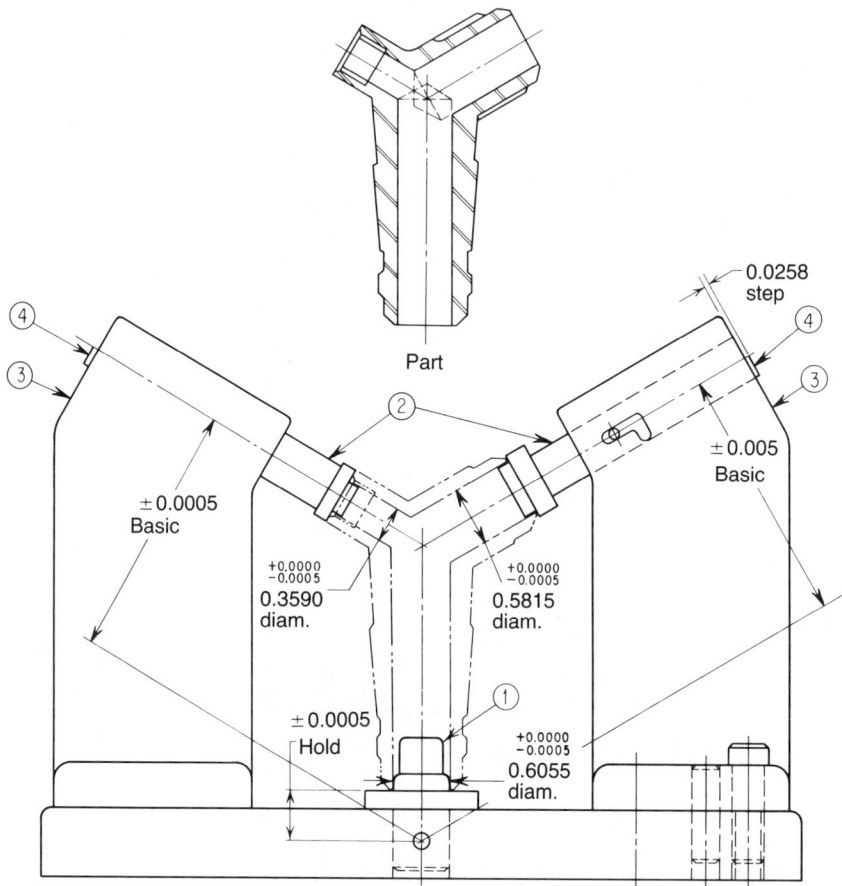

Fig. 16-45 Flush-pin fixture for inspecting elbows and T-shaped workpieces. (*Courtesy Pratt & Whitney Aircraft*)

pin locators (2) and held in position by a spring plunger (3). A ground plug (4) is inserted in the casting to project the center line of the bored hole.

An indicator reading shows whether or not the plug center line is parallel to the base and consequently to the locator center lines and the two holes in the workpiece within the required tolerance of 0.0005 in. per inch.

Figure 16-51 shows a fixture to check the squareness of an OD with the face of the workpiece. The fixture consists of a ground plate (1), two locators (2), and a dial indicator (3). A setting master is provided to zero the indicator. The workpiece is placed face down on the plate against the two locators and manually rotated. Indicator deflection must not exceed 0.001 in. FIM.

The workpiece of Fig. 16-52 is a rectangular pipe formed in a U-shape. Its flanges are parallel but have an axial twist of 90°.

The fixture for this workpiece (see Fig. 16-53) has a fixed rectangular locator (1) that fits in one flange while the other flange determines the position of the other rotatable locator assembly (2). The fixture base has ground side rails (3) and a movable indicator assembly (4). A dowel pin (5), serving as an indicator setting gage, permits the operator to zero the indicator by passing it between the rail and the dowel. Measuring the distance from the rear locator assembly to the two side rails checks the 3.624

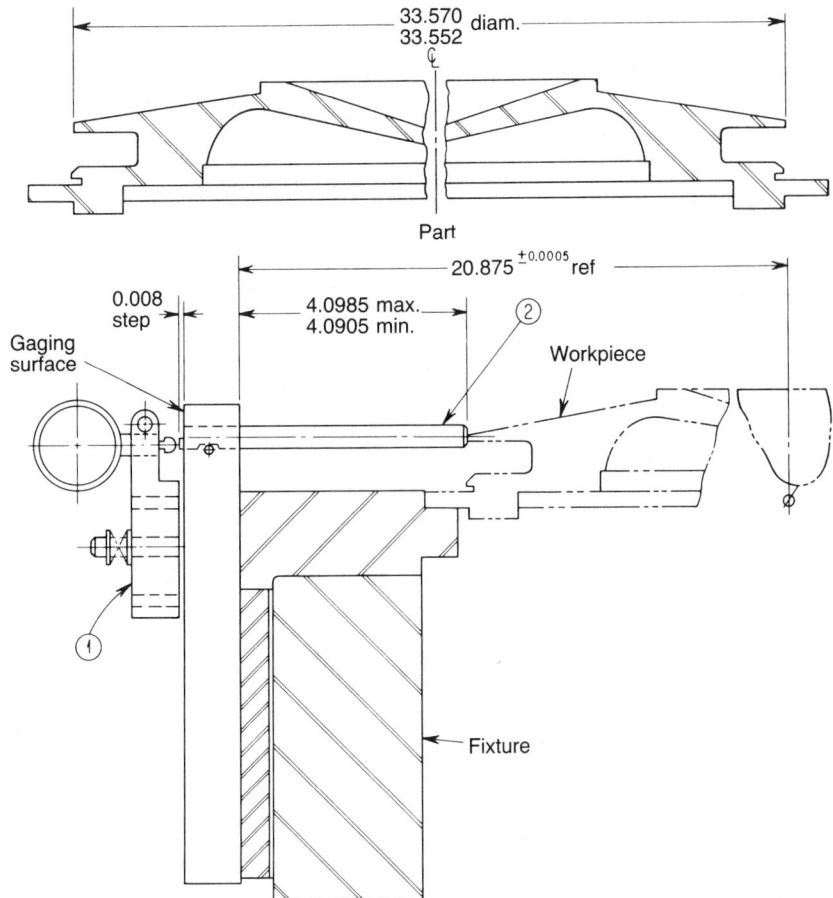

Fig. 16-46 Fixture for inspecting diameters. (*Courtesy Pratt & Whitney Aircraft*)

±0.015 and 2.450 ±0.015 part dimensions. The axis of a pin (6) is coincident with the center line of the rear locator.

Measuring the distance between the pin and a fixed bar locator (7) checks the 90° angle between the rectangular openings of the workpiece.

The bases of the rectangular locators are parallel but differ in elevation by 0.285 in. (7.24 mm). A workpiece with flanges closer together than that distance cannot be clamped in position. If a positioned workpiece has its flanges more than 0.291 in. (7.39 mm) apart, a 0.007 in. (0.178 mm) feeler gage can be inserted between the flange and the locator base.

To assure the tight fitting of the locators in the flanges, the locators are tapered and spring-loaded along the long side. For endwise location, screw-actuated pins are provided.

Concentricity and Squareness Checking Fixtures. The extent of the concentricity of bores, bearing surfaces, etc., and the squareness of these surfaces to shoulders or mounting surfaces are quite commonly specified. The checking of these characteristics can be done with a dial indicator and a means of holding or rotating the workpiece.

The fixture shown in Fig. 16-54 incorporates a ground V-locator in which the workpiece is placed and manually rotated. A dial indicator (1) with its probe bearing on an ID checks concentricity between the ID and the OD of the workpiece. A second dial

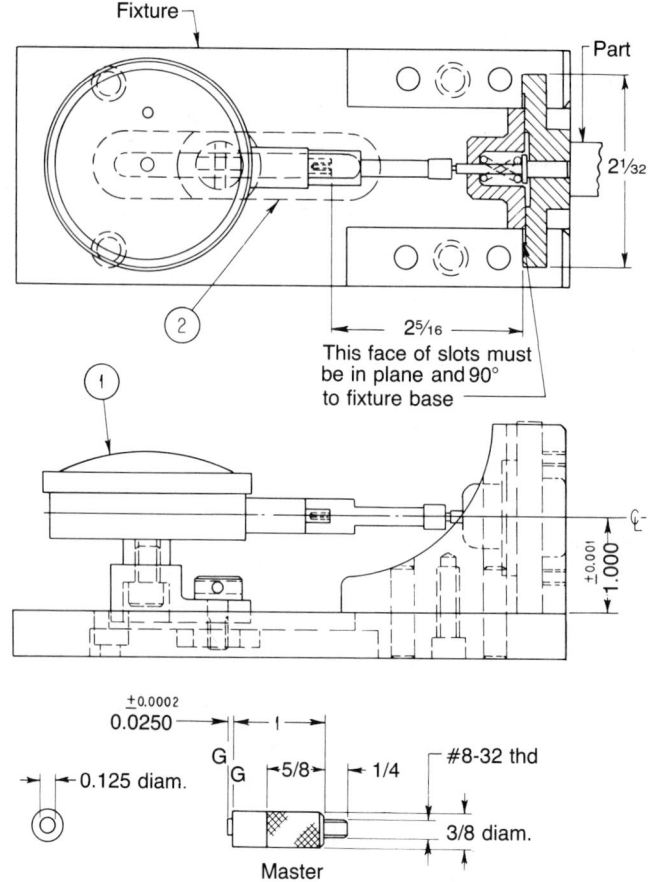

Fig. 16-47 Flush-pin fixture for inspection of shoulder lengths. (*Courtesy Argus Cameras, Inc.*)

indicator (2), mounted on a slide, allows its probe to contact the internal face which shows squareness of the face. Concentricity of the ID is checked by placing the probe on the surface to be checked and rotating the workpiece.

Figure 16-55 shows a typical bushing having an ID and an OD which must be concentric within 0.001 in. Both diameters have a tolerance of 0.0005 in., and both bushing faces must be square to the center line of the bushing within 0.0005 in. FIM. Any two points on either face can each vary up to 0.0005 in. in squareness with a full indicator movement of no more than 0.001 in.

The fixture consists of a relieved mandrel (1) on which the workpiece is manually rotated while seated against a second locator (2) which bears on the face being inspected. A dial-indicator probe (3) contacting the OD of the rotating part allows any difference in wall thickness to be registered directly on it. The probe (4) of a second indicator bears on the workpiece face to detect lack of squareness during rotation.

The workpiece of Fig. 16-56 is a hollow cylinder. The fixture here utilizes an expanding and centering mandrel (1) with its allowable runout held within 0.001 in. FIM. The workpiece is mounted on the mandrel and manually rotated while a dial-indicator probe (2) bearing on the OD detects concentricity variation. A second dial-indicator probe, bearing on the face of the workpiece through a linkage (3), checks its squareness.

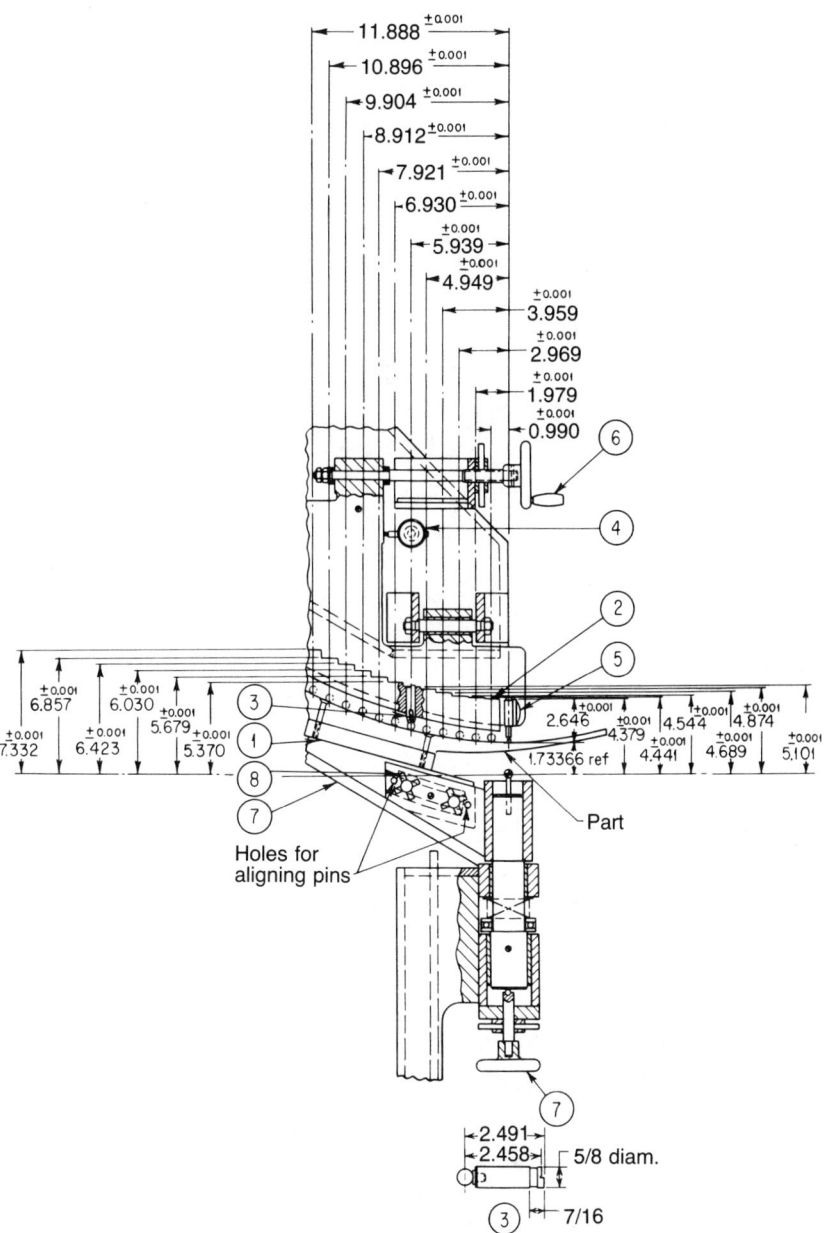

11.888 ±0.001
10.896 ±0.001
9.904 ±0.001
8.912 ±0.001
7.921 ±0.001
6.930 ±0.001
5.939 ±0.001
4.949 ±0.001
3.959 ±0.001
2.969 ±0.001
1.979 ±0.001
0.990 ±0.001

⑥
④
②
⑤
③
①
⑧
⑦

7.332 ±0.001
6.857 ±0.001
6.423 ±0.001
6.030 ±0.001
5.679 ±0.001
5.370 ±0.001

2.646 ±0.001
1.73366 ref
4.379 ±0.001
4.441 ±0.001
4.544 ±0.001
4.689 ±0.001
4.874 ±0.001
5.101 ±0.001

Part

Holes for
aligning pins

⑦

2.491
2.458
5/8 diam.
③ 7/16

Fig. 16-48 View of operating mechanism for inspection fixture of Fig. 16-49. (*Courtesy The Emerson Electric Mfg. Co.*)

The centering mandrel is a standard proprietary item designed to allow rotation of the workpiece about the best average bore center line. If the bore of a workpiece is slightly out of round, this type of mandrel will allow correct gaging, while a solid type will not.

Two internal diameters, Y and Z, of an aluminum casting must be concentric within 0.002 in. FIM and must be square with the X surfaces within 0.002 in. FIM.

The inspection fixture (see Fig. 16-57) for the casting has a ground plate (1) against

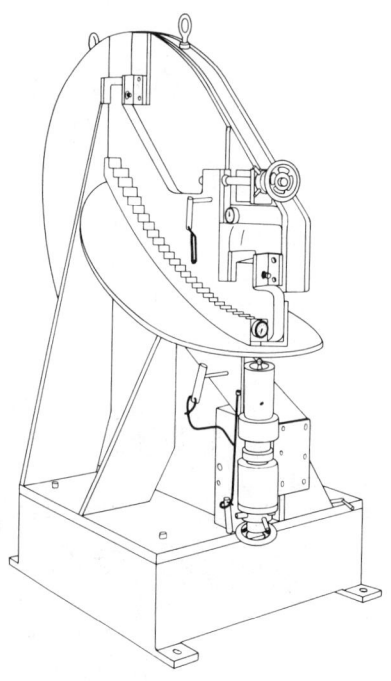

Fig. 16-49 Fixture for checking contour of a parabolic-shaped workpiece. (*Courtesy The Emerson Electric Mfg. Co.*)

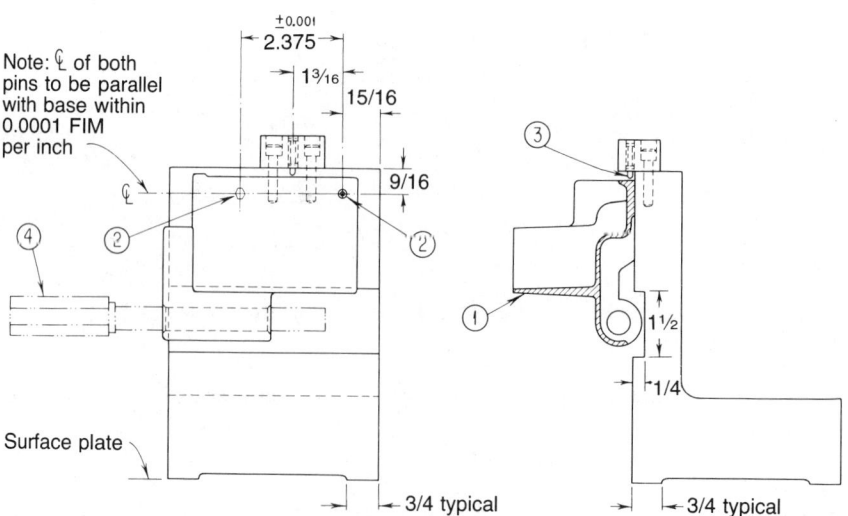

Fig. 16-50 Inspection for parallelism of holes in an aluminum casting. (*Courtesy Universal Winding Co.*)

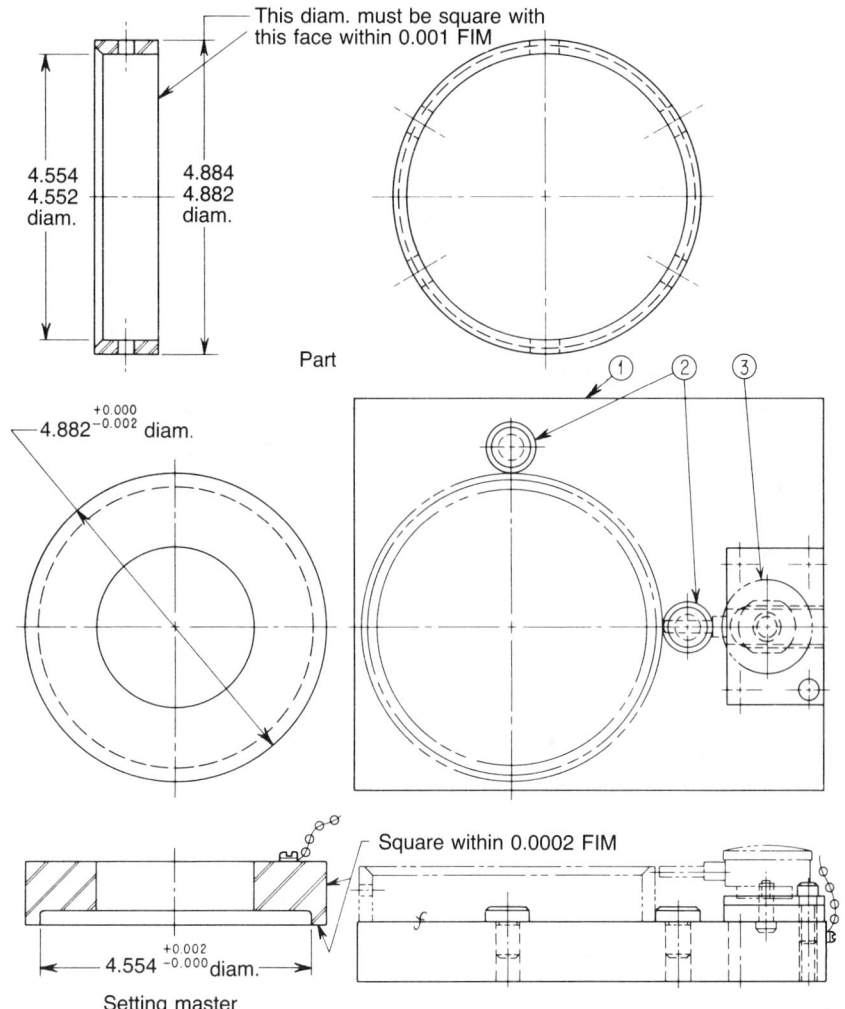

This diam. must be square with this face within 0.001 FIM

4.554
4.552
diam.

4.884
4.882
diam.

Part

$4.882^{+0.000}_{-0.002}$ diam.

Square within 0.0002 FIM

$4.554^{+0.002}_{-0.000}$ diam.

Setting master

Fig. 16-51 Fixture for inspecting squareness. (*Courtesy Pratt & Whitney Aircraft*)

which the workpiece base is held by a clamp (4). A dial-indicator probe (2) is moved against each ID. Revolving the workpiece in the V-locator (3) permits checking the concentricity of the two diameters and their squareness to the X surfaces by moving the indicator mounted on a slide (5).

An aluminum casting is checked for the proper relationship between its bore and its outside surface contacted by the indicator probe. The part is placed on the tapered spring-loaded locator (1) and clamped against a fixed locator (2) with the strap clamp (3). A jig leaf (4) carrying a dial indicator (5) is closed and locked with a quarter-turn screw. The indicator assembly is rotated in its bushing (6) which revolves the indicator probe around the external surface of the part, thereby measuring any runout. A construction hole in the base is used by the tool inspector to check the position of the locator and indicator assembly (see Fig. 16-58).

A part consisting of a curved aluminum cylinder, a flared sleeve with a counter balance, and a thick ring is inspected in the fixture of Fig. 16-59. After assembly, the OD of the ring should not run out more than 0.010 in. in relation to the center line of the

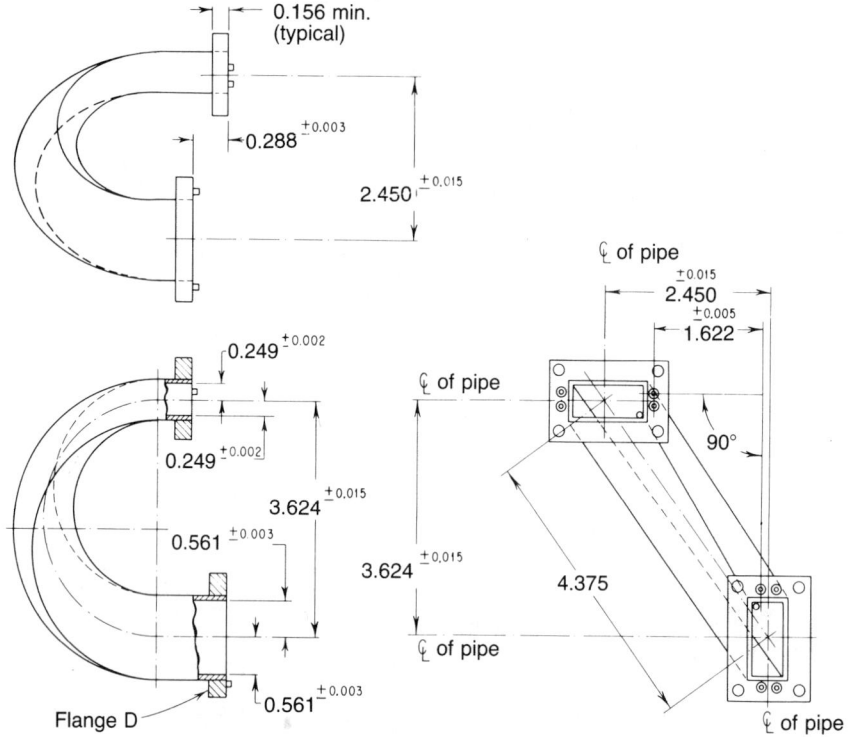

Fig. 16-52 Workpiece for fixture of Fig. 16-53.

sleeve. The distance from the base of the sleeve to the outer edge of the ring must be 7.282 ±0.005 in.

The inspection fixture includes a hollow mandrel (1) in which the assembly is mounted. The mandrel is rotated in a V-locator (2), and runout of the ring is shown by the indicator (4). The distance between one end of the cylinder and the inner surface of the sleeve's flange is checked with a flush pin (3).

The workpiece inspected in the fixture of Fig. 16-60 is a ball-bearing assembly which is checked for width of inner race, runout, and position of grooves in outer race. Five dial indicators are used to check the part dimensions.

A master setup ring is placed on the spring-loaded locating mandrel (1), and the indicators are set to zero. An air cylinder supplies clamping pressure to the bearing's inner race equal to its average-application preload rating of 6.5 to 7.5 lbf (28.9 to 33.4 N).

After the bearing has been placed on the mandrel and the clamping pressure applied, the variation in the width of the inner race is measured by the indicator (2) as it bears against the indicator arm. The inspector rotates the outer bearing race manually and checks the concentricity of the bore of the bearing within 0.0015 in. FIM by watching indicators (3 and 4). As the workpiece is rotated, any variation in the location of the grooves moves the checking rolls (7) longitudinally. This movement is registered on two dial indicators (5 and 6).

The spindles of the checking rolls are mounted on miniature ball bearings (8) in a spring-loaded sleeve (11) which permits axial (longitudinal) movement. The checking-roll units are mounted on ball slides (9) permitting lateral movement. Cone-point setscrews (10) are used to adjust and align the ball slides.

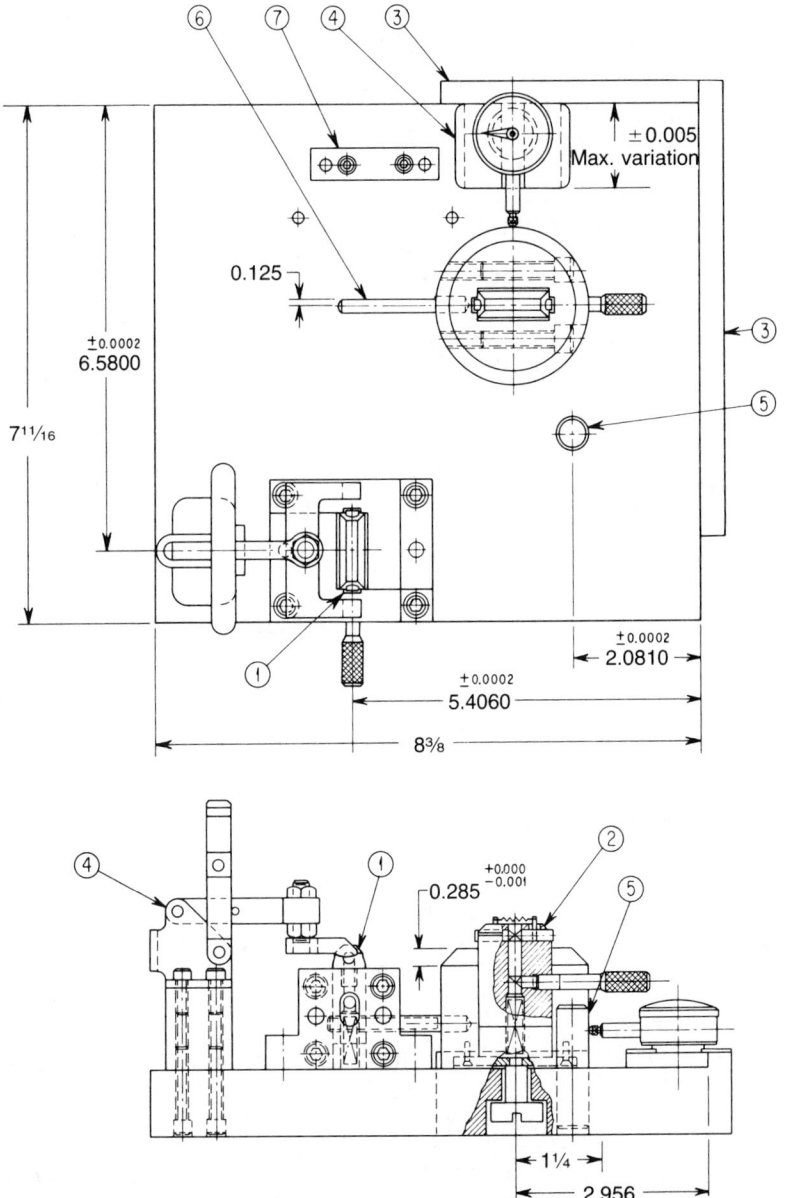

Fig. 16-53 Inspection fixture for a rectangular pipe. (*Courtesy Western Electric Co., Inc.*)

Contour Checking Fixture. The fixture of Fig. 16-61 has a master cam for checking the contour of a workpiece which is located directly above the master cam.

A dial indicator (1), a master-cam tracer (2), and a workpiece tracer (3) are mounted on a guidepost (4). The workpiece is held in the fixture by a strap clamp (5) and a swiveling two-point contact clamp (6). Two dog-point setscrews (7) serve as part locators.

Manual rotation of the guidepost simultaneously causes the master-cam tracer to follow the surface of the master cam (8) and the workpiece tracer to follow the corres-

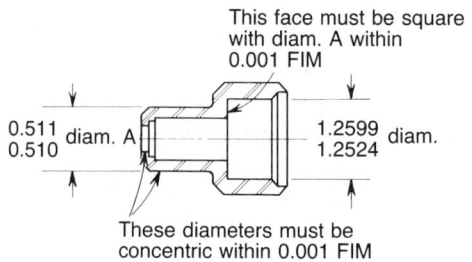

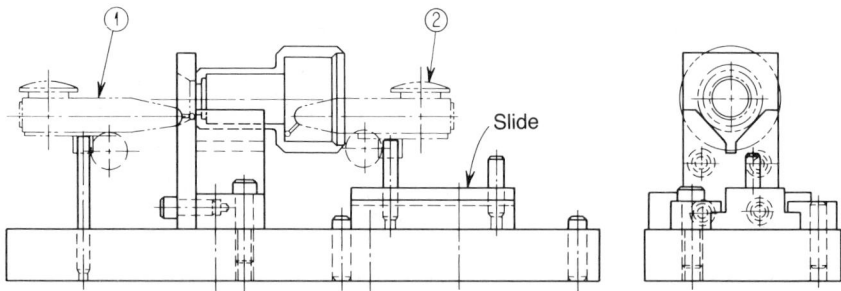

Fig. 16-54 Fixture for checking concentricity and squareness. (*Courtesy Pratt & Whitney Aircraft*)

ponding surface on the workpiece. The workpiece tracer is spring-loaded and bears against the contact tip of the dial indicator; therefore, any deviations between the master- and workpiece-cam contours are shown on the indicator dial.

During loading and unloading of the workpiece, the guidepost is raised and turned to the left, allowing the lower tracer arm to rest on the support (9). During storage the tracer arm is held by a safety clamp (10).

The tracers incorporate ½-in.-diam. fixture-construction balls. The master cam is made of tool steel, hardened and ground.

Staging Fixtures. When using optical instruments for inspecting workpieces, the surfaces to be checked are positioned in the light beam with work holders known as staging fixtures. Fixtures having centers hold shafts and other cylindrical parts containing machined centers.

Most fixtures designed specially for holding individual parts can be classified as single-position, step-shift, multiple-position, interposer, and tracer fixtures.

The single-position fixture is loaded to present a workpiece to a light beam for the inspection of certain outlines with only one positioning.

A step-shift fixture is advantageous when it is desirable to see all dimensioned outlines of a workpiece, although the workpiece may be larger than the lens field area can cover.

The work-holding components of the multiple-position fixture are mounted on a sliding base. Controlled movement is obtained against end stops if two positions are needed or against various indexing stops if three or more positions are needed.

When views of a part from more than one direction are needed, workpiece loading blocks can be designed to present various faces of the work effectively to the light beam.

Auxiliary interposers may be used to inspect indirectly the position of a remote surface. For example, a pin of known length may be placed in a hole with the end of the pin extending into the light beam. Thus the distance the pin extends above the surface

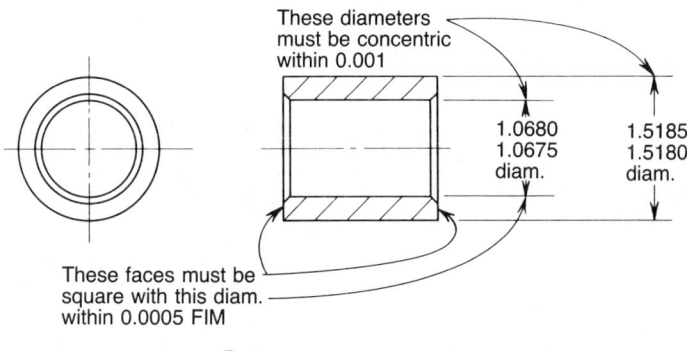

These diameters
must be concentric
within 0.001

1.0680
1.0675
diam.

1.5185
1.5180
diam.

These faces must be
square with this diam.
within 0.0005 FIM

Part

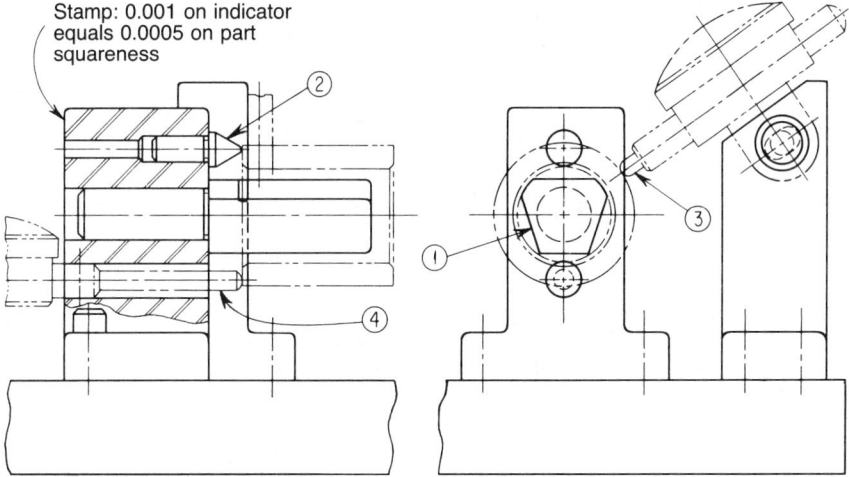

Stamp: 0.001 on indicator
equals 0.0005 on part
squareness

②

③

①

④

Fig. 16-55 Fixture for inspecting a bushing. (*Courtesy Pratt & Whitney Aircraft*)

around the hole, or any other reference surface, may be used to inspect the hole depth.

Large or hidden contours may be inspected by means of a tracer fixture. By using accurate floating heads capable of coordinate movements in two perpendicular directions, a contour staged at some distance from the projector light beam can be reproduced on the screen for study of its magnified movement and shape.

The fixture of Fig. 16-62 is held on an optical comparator table by a clamping screw (1) and its hand knob (2). A chuck (3) holding a small part is rotated to project the form of the workpiece on the screen of the comparator. Rapid and accurate inspection of small, complex parts is practical with similar staging fixtures mounted on a comparator table.

The inspection fixture of Fig. 16-63 comprises a carriage (1) which moves on bearing balls (2) in V-shaped ways that are parallel to the base within 0.0002 in. The fixture is mounted on a comparator.

Two locating pins (10) incorporated in a mounting plate (8) engage two 0.159-in. (4.04-mm) slots in the workpiece (see Fig. 16-64). The mounting plate is positioned with its 9/32-in. (7.14-mm) slot over a locating dowel (3) in the carriage. The lower edge of the mounting plate is held in the carriage by a clamp assembly (4).

A notched spacing bar (9) is located on the carriage by two locating pins (5).

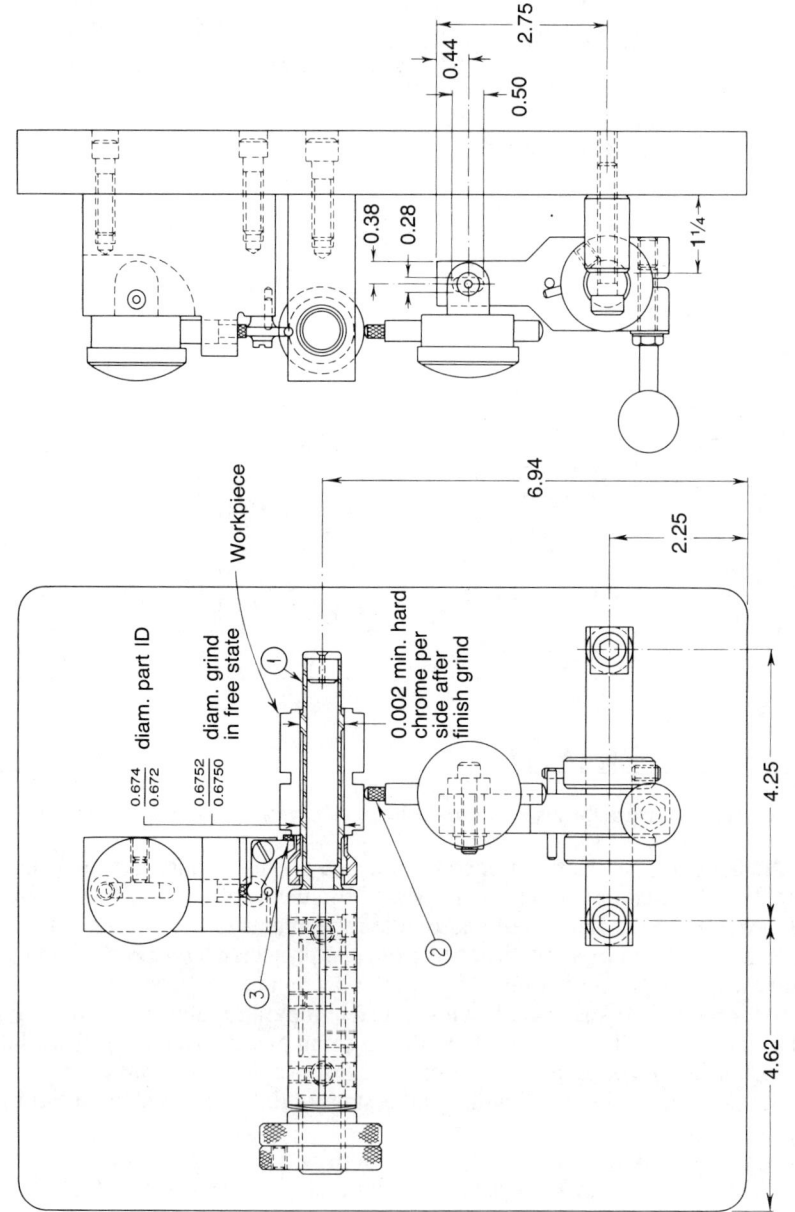

Fig. 16-56 Concentricity-inspection fixture with a centering mandrel. (*Courtesy N.A. Woodworth Co.*)

2.75

0.44

0.50

0.38

0.28

1¼

Workpiece

diam. part ID

0.674
0.672

diam. grind
in free state

0.6752
0.6750

0.002 min. hard
chrome per
side after
finish grind

6.94

2.25

4.25

4.62

16-52

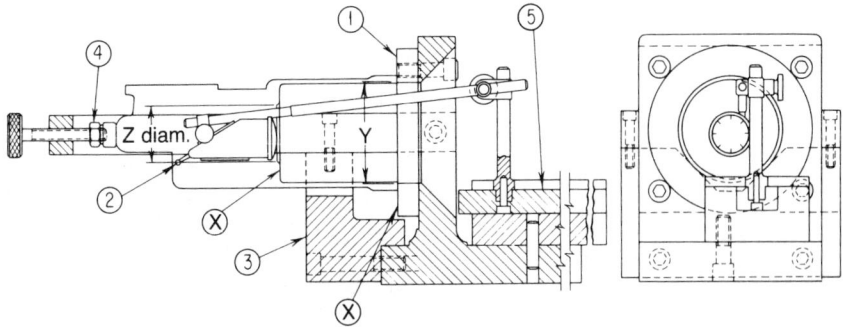

Fig. 16-57 Squareness- and concentricity-checking fixture. (*Courtesy Thompson Products, Inc.*)

Positioning of the bar and carriage is controlled by an indexing detent (7) which engages notches in the bar corresponding to the inspection positions for each of the workpiece teeth. Detent contact with and retraction from the notches is manually controlled by a lever (6).

The detent, the spacing bar, and the mounting plate can be modified to accommodate racks and similar workpieces having teeth or other contours along their edges.

A workpiece may have dimensional or other tolerances so small that magnification is required for inspection. The location of the features to be inspected may not permit projection of their shadows with an optical comparator, but a shop microscope can be used.

The fixture shown in Fig. 16-65 features a microscope (1) mounted on a carriage (2). A dial indicator with a wheel-type probe (3) is mounted on the carriage with its probe bearing on the ground edge of a worktable (4). As the carriage is moved along the table, the indicator shows the position of the microscope with reference to the table edge. The workpiece, a printed-circuit board, is clamped down in position against a locating block (5). The entire workpiece edge is visually inspected through the microscope eyepiece (6).

The fixture of Fig. 16-66a has a binocular microscope incorporating reticles with engraved lines (see Fig. 16-66b) that agree with the specified skew angles (3-½° and 7°) for the slots of small armatures (in this case, 0.760 in. diam) under inspection. Other lines on the reticle are spaced at distances equal to commutator widths.

A commercial table (1), with suitable slides and an indexing plate, provides movement of the centers (2) which engage the shaft ends of the armature. A bracket (3) has a chrome-plated hole (0.204 +0.001, -0.000 in. diam) in which a shaft diameter (0.2030 in.) is held.

Plastic Contour Checking Fixtures. Compared with all-metal fixtures, plastic types are light and, therefore, easier to handle and transport. Construction costs are generally lower, and plastic compounds may cost less than some metals. Although many plastics are wear-resistant, metal wear plates and bushings can be cast in or attached to a plastic fixture. Elements of a fixture which must duplicate a surface of a workpiece can be cast against or built up to such a surface.

Shown in Fig. 16-67 is part of a fixture for checking the door-line contour of an automotive fender. This fixture, approximately 34 in. (863.6 mm) long and weighing less than 12 lb (5.4 kg), can easily be moved into checking position. Allowable deviations are checked by inserting feeler gages at the points shown.

Figure 16-68 shows a large checking fixture of epoxy resin and fiberglass for checking the contour of a stamping and also the size and location of cutouts in it. The bed and frame members are of 2-in.-OD thin (⅛ in.) wall tubing. The fixture provides a locator (2) for the workpiece and provides a contour bar (1) located alongside the positioned

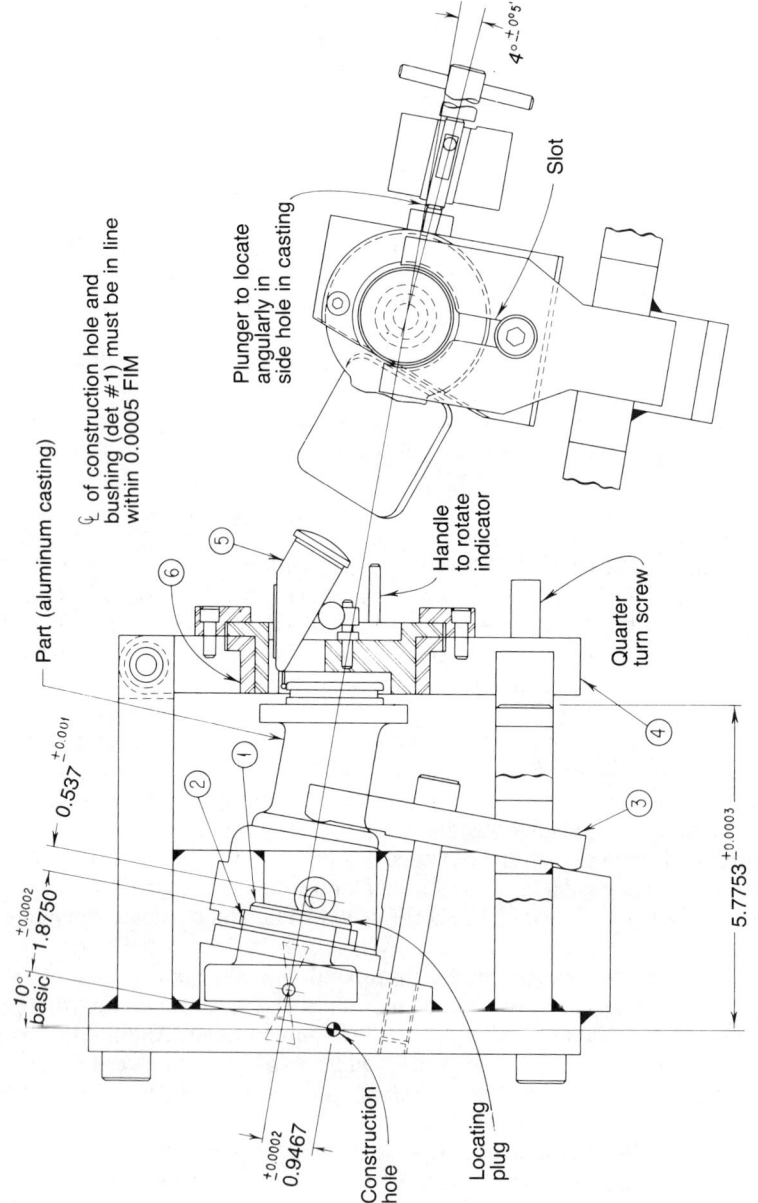

Part (aluminum casting)

℄ of construction hole and bushing (det #1) must be in line within 0.0005 FIM

Plunger to locate angularly in side hole in casting

Slot

$4°^{+0°5'}_{-}$

Handle to rotate indicator

Quarter turn screw

$0.537^{+0.011}_{-}$

$10°$ basic

$1.8750^{+0.0002}_{-}$

$0.9467^{+0.0002}_{-}$

Construction hole

Locating plug

$5.7753^{+0.0003}_{-}$

Fig. 16-58 Runout-inspection fixture. (*Courtesy Thompson Products, Inc.*)

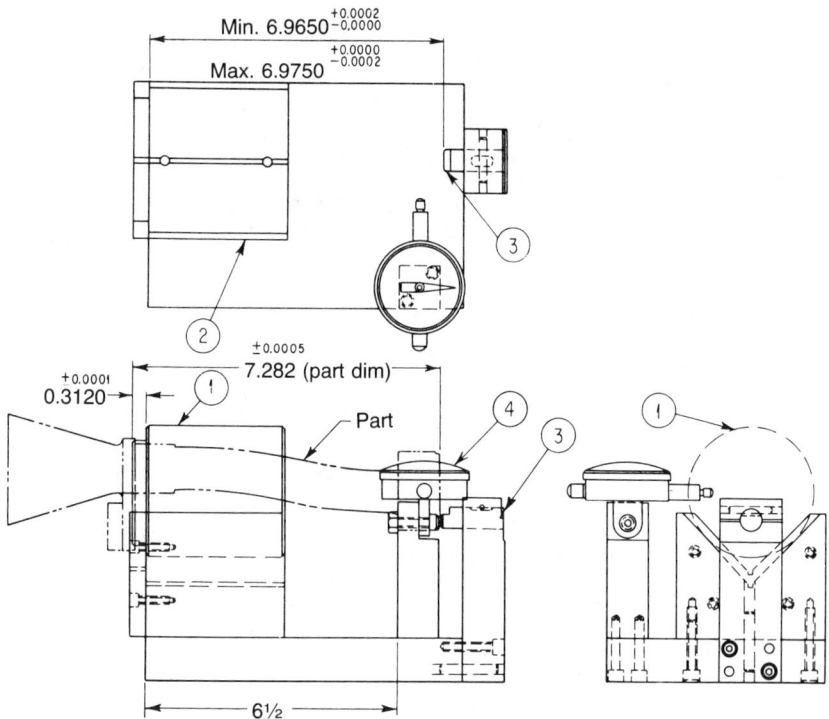

Fig. 16-59 Inspection fixture for a flared pipe. (*Courtesy Western Electric Co., Inc.*)

workpiece. A 0.120-in. (3.05-mm) feeler is used to check required clearance between the contour bar and the workpiece.

Figure 16-69 shows a portion of a fixture of laminated fiberglass and epoxy resin by which the contour of a head-lamp area of an automotive front fender is checked. The fixture is made in both the right-hand version (shown) and one of the opposite hand. Bullet-nose metal locating pins and metal pads are incorporated at wear points. When the fixture is placed in its gaging position, its edges coincide with the contour of the workpiece. Clearance between the workpiece and fixture at locations shown is checked by a 0.062-in. (1.57-mm) feeler gage.

Figure 16-70 shows a portion of a large contour- and hole-location-checking fixture of epoxy resin and fiberglass construction. It is approximately 40 in. (1,016 mm) long, 13 in. (330.2 mm) wide, and 10 in. (254 mm) high but weighs only 26 lb (11.8 kg).

The bed and frame members are lengths of fiberglass tubing. Metal hardware is added at contact surfaces and hole locations. Contours are checked by inserting feeler gages between the workpiece and fixture. Hole locations are checked by their alignment with bushing-guided metal plug gages.

Checking Rotors and Impellers. The fixture of Fig. 16-71 incorporates a flat circular-index plate (3) that carries four rest buttons (2) upon which the workpiece is clamped. The central hole of the workpiece (a 22-blade forged-aluminum impeller) is placed on a locating plug (4) in the center of the fixture. The outer edge of the reference blade of the impeller is located by a sliding V-locator (5).

The impeller is held down on the rest buttons by a clamp plate (7) and a knurled socket-head cap screw (8). Twenty-two bushings (9) equally spaced around the circular-index plate, an indexing pin (10), and a handle (11) comprise the indexing mechanism (see section *C-C*).

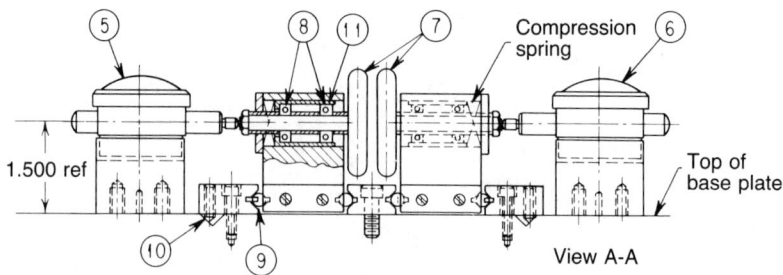

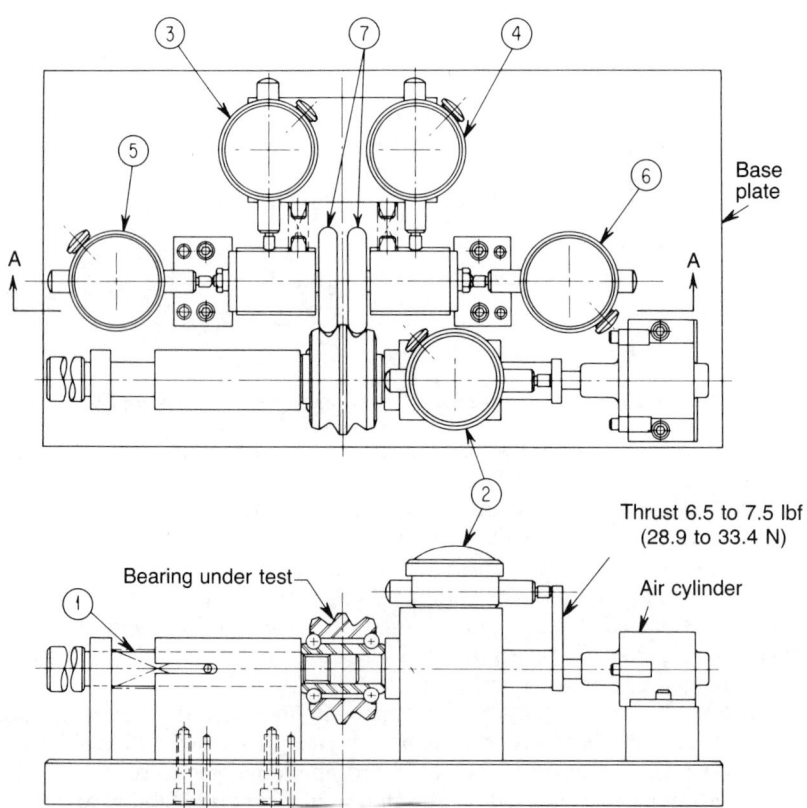

Fig. 16-60 Fixture for inspecting ball bearings. (*Courtesy Marlin-Rockwell Corp.*)

Each of the 22 X holes between blades is successively checked within 0.005 in. of its specified position by an indicator (12) (see section A-A). An indicator arm (13) mounted to the cast fixture base holds an indicator mounting slide (14) which can be retracted and revolved in a slide bushing (20).

A spring plunger (15) engages a groove in the indicator slide to hold it up during rotation of the index plate and during loading and unloading of the fixture.

Shown in section B-B is another spring plunger (16) which similarly holds a second slide (17) that carries a dial indicator (1).

Each of the 22 Y holes adjacent to an X hole is checked by this indicator as the index plate is rotated to an index station for each pair of holes.

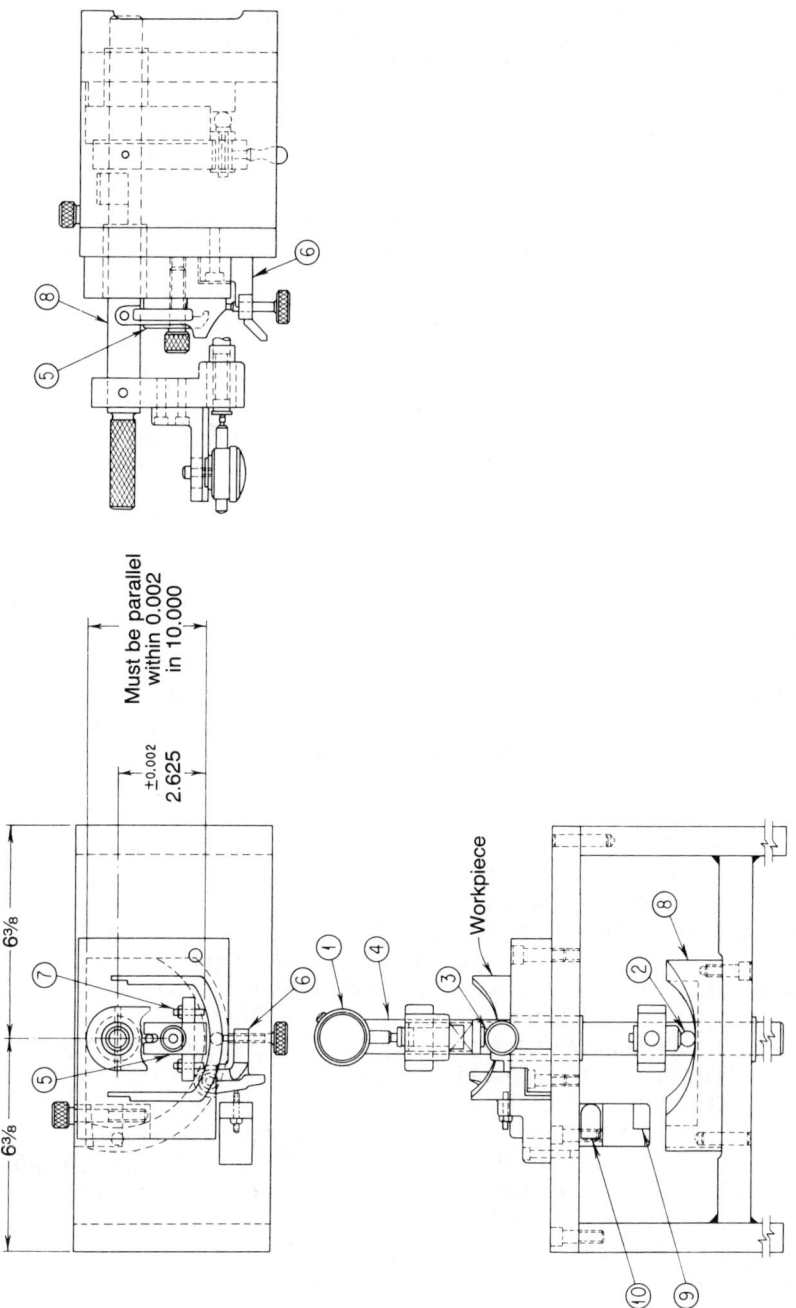

Fig. 16-61 Cam-inspection fixture. (*Courtesy The Emerson Electric Mfg. Co.*)

16-57

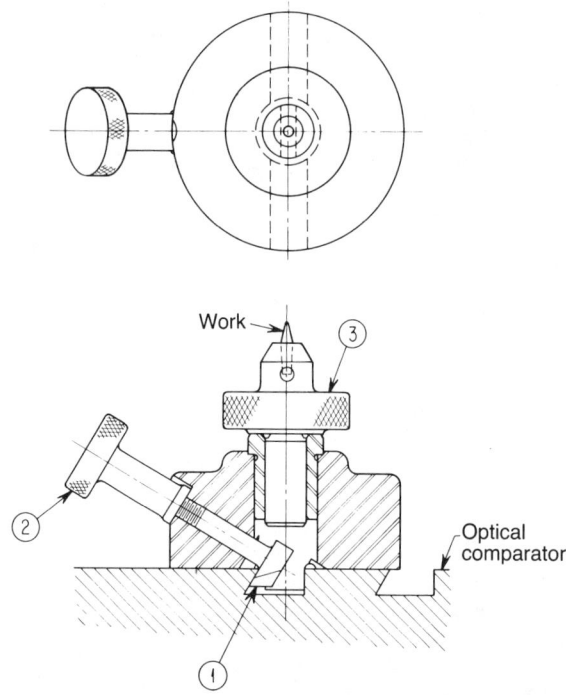

Fig. 16-62 Staging fixture for optical inspection of a small part. (*Courtesy SME Northern Massachusetts Chapter 100*)

The indicator assembly has an indicator lever (18) which pivots around a dowel (19). The two indicator assemblies are mounted 180° apart on the circular base of the fixture. The indexing assembly and the sliding V-locator are also mounted on the circular base 180° apart but exactly between the indicator assemblies.

The design of this fixture can be modified to check the location of holes (or teeth, bosses, etc.) circularly spaced at various radial distances from a central point on workpieces which are not necessarily of circular outline.

In the fixture of Fig. 16-72, each of the 16 blades or vanes of a forged-aluminum rotor is checked for correct spacing and thickness. A setting master is used to set the indicator dials to zero. The rotor is placed on an expanding slotted collet (11) and is located by a pin (12). Outward clamping pressure on the center hole of the workpiece is provided by rotation of the knurled end of an expander (5).

When the lever handle (8) is depressed, it pulls an index pin (6) out of one of 16 index bushings (7) circularly spaced around an index plate (2) and pushes a bullet-nosed pin (9) into an indexing notch (10).

The handle is swung to bring the notch in alignment with the next index station. Release of the lever allows the index pin to be pushed upward by a flat spring (not shown) and into the index bushing, which locates the plate and workpiece vane in the inspection position below six dial indicators (3). At the inspection position, each of the 16 blades is checked for correct spacing and thickness.

Two indicator latches, or mounting arms (4), each carrying three dial indicators, are swung upward to allow rotation of the index plate and to allow for loading and unloading of the workpiece.

The workpiece (see Fig. 16-73) to be inspected in the fixture of Fig. 16-74 is a 16-bladed aluminum rotor. It is clamped on a locator (2) and against a ring (9) by a

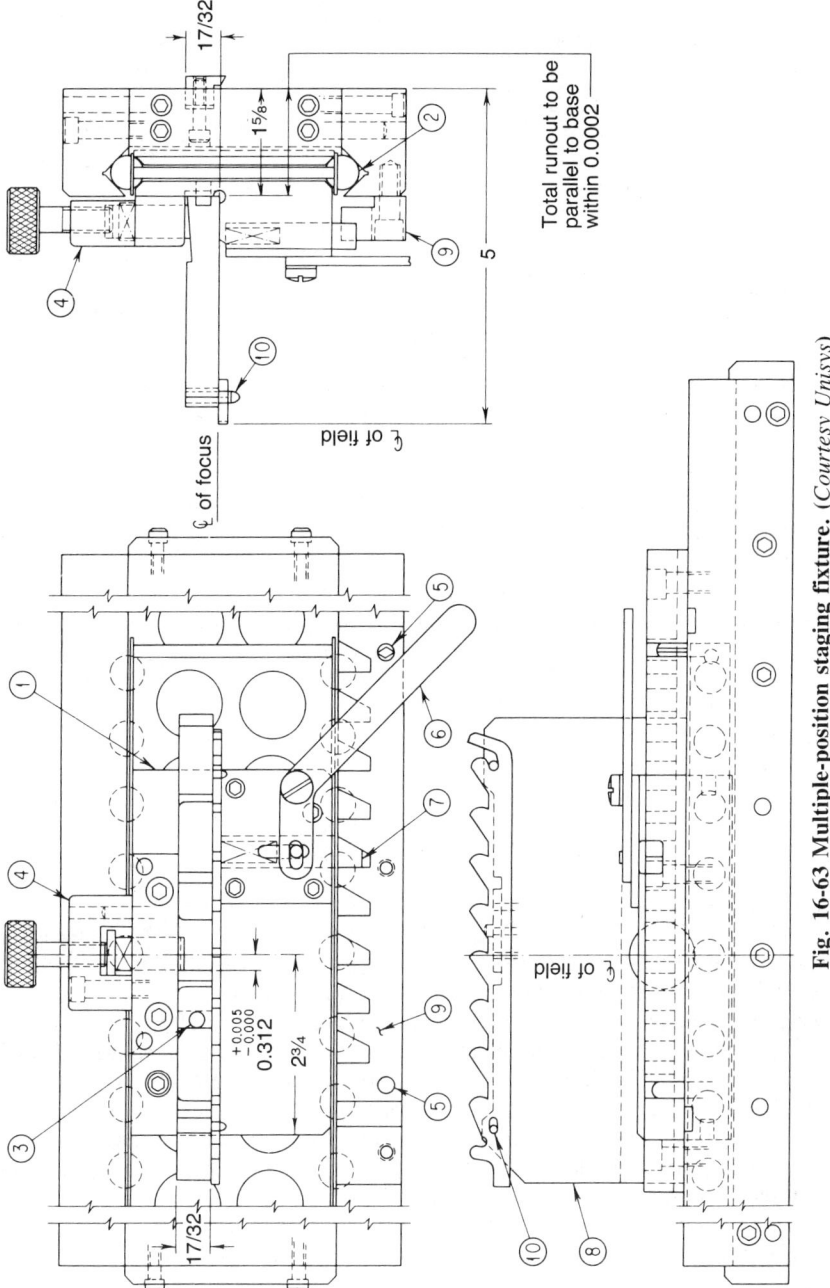

Fig. 16-63 Multiple-position staging fixture. (*Courtesy Unisys*)

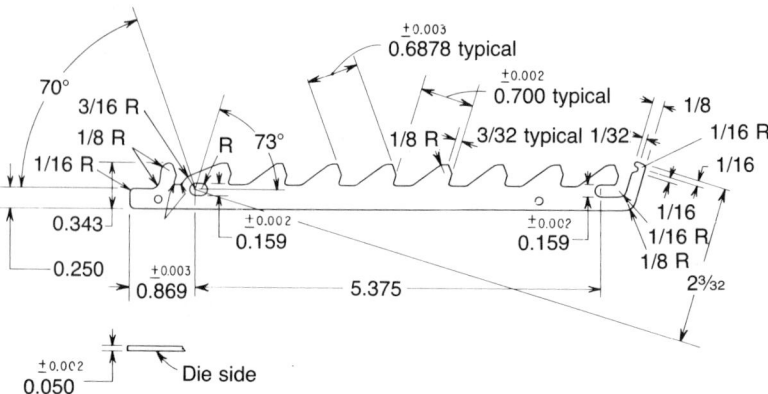

Fig. 16-64 Part for inspection in fixture of Fig. 16-63.

C-clamp (3) and a knurled nut (4). A roller follower assembly (6) is lowered into a spiral-cam track (5). The follower is held by an arm (10) welded to the fixture base (not shown).

The diamond point of the locating stylus (7) mounted on one end of the indicator arm (8) rests on the first of three inspection points on the surface of a rotor blade.

As the operator turns the knurled end of the shaft (1), the shaft and the workpiece move in a spiral path about the shaft center line. Rotation of the shaft also guides the stylus along the initial inspection surface of the rotor blade.

Deviations from the specified contour of the blade result in vertical movements of the indicator arm which actuate a dial indicator (15). If the blade contour is within the specifications, there will be little or no movement of the stylus point, since its travel is synchronized with that of the roller cam follower in the spiral-cam track.

For inspection of two other blade surfaces, two other separate spiral-cam tracks are ground in the cam ring (11). The slide (12) on which the indicator assembly is mounted is shifted to any one of the corresponding inspection positions. The slide is located by a plug (14) which is pushed into the correct locating bushing (13) and clamped in that position by the knurled screw (16).

OVERLAY TEMPLATES[3]

Overlay templates are transparent plates that are often used in the inspection of flat parts made of paper, rubber, plastic, fabric, and metal as well as other materials. They are also used to check out processes such as the registration of printing on paper and plastic, the legibility and quality of text coming off of computer printout devices, and the size and positioning of test images in photographic processes.

Overlay templates are made of a transparent material onto which is engraved or scribed the min-max profile of the part or feature to be inspected. Incorporated into the overlay may be fixturing devices such as stops, dowel pins, or other machined features to promote precise positioning of the overlay and the part being inspected.

Materials used for direct-contact overlays are usually plastic, although glass is sometimes used when extra dimensional stability is needed. Commonly used plastics include polycarbonates, acrylics, and sometimes vinyls or polyesters. When glass is used, it is usually not fitted with fixturing pins, and it is usually either tempered or laminated safety plate to protect the user from injury in case of breakage. Dimensional stability of glass is comparable to that of steel, while dimensional stability of the plastic materials is an order of magnitude less than that of steel (as measured by the thermal coefficients of

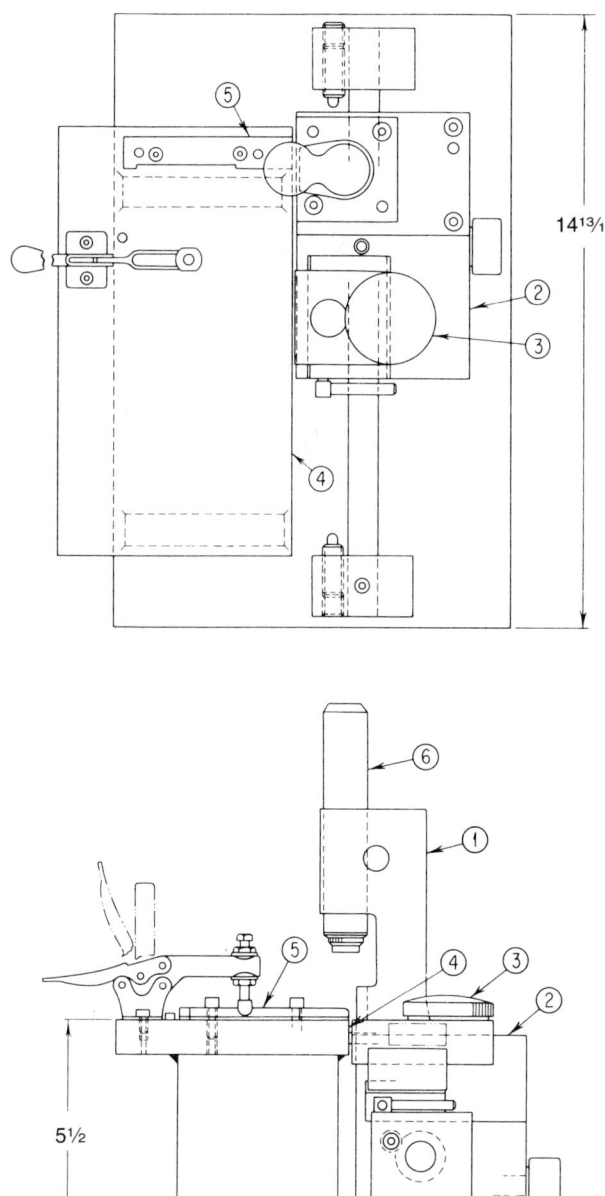

Fig. 16-65 Fixture for inspection of printed-circuit boards. (*Courtesy The Emerson Electric Mfg. Co.*)

expansion), while remaining high enough to suit most practical gaging operations.

Line work for the overlay templates is either photoengraved from scribed artwork masters or directly scribed or chemically etched into the surface of the template. For contrast against dark parts, line colors such as red may be used instead of the standard black. Line widths, unless otherwise specified, are usually approximately 0.004 to 0.006 in. (0.10 to 0.15 mm) in width, but can be made wider for special inspection requirements. Although the most accurate overlays are usually drawn up using computer-

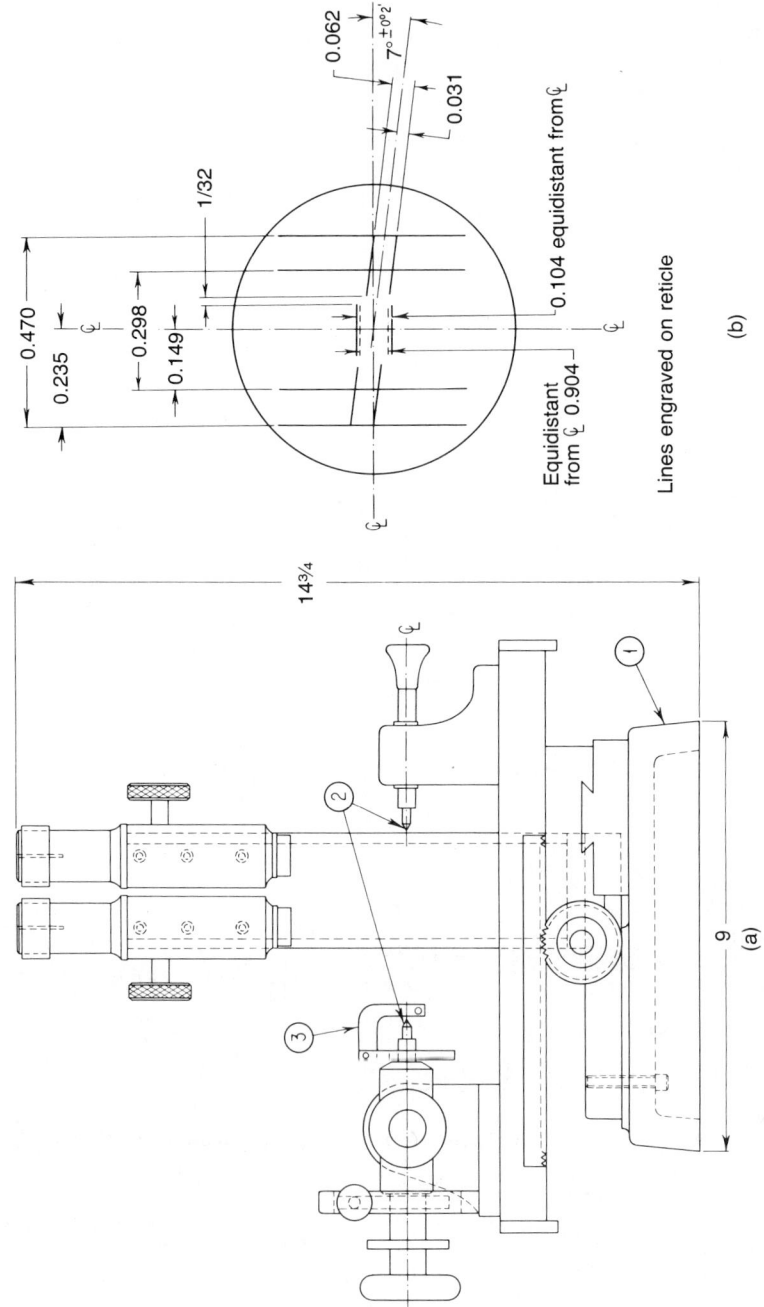

0.062

7°±0°2'

0.031

1/32

0.470

0.235

0.298

0.149

0.104 equidistant from ₵

Equidistant
from ₵ 0.904

Lines engraved on reticle

(b)

14³⁄₄

2

3

1

6

(a)

Fig. 16-66 (*a*) Fixture for armature inspection; (*b*) engraving on reticle. (*Courtesy Western Electric Co., Inc.*)

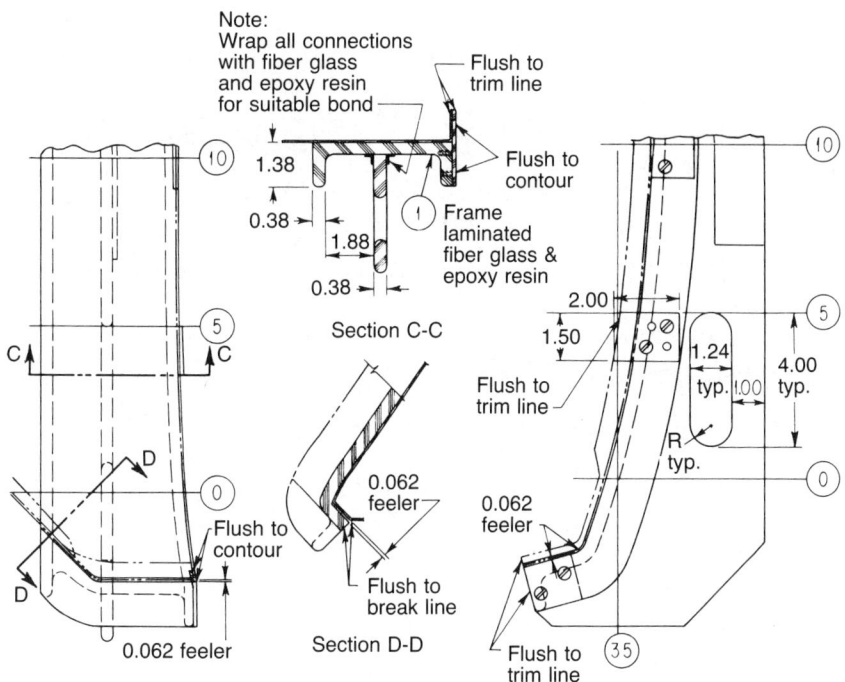

Fig. 16-67 Fixture for inspection of automotive fender. (*Courtesy Ford Motor Co.*)

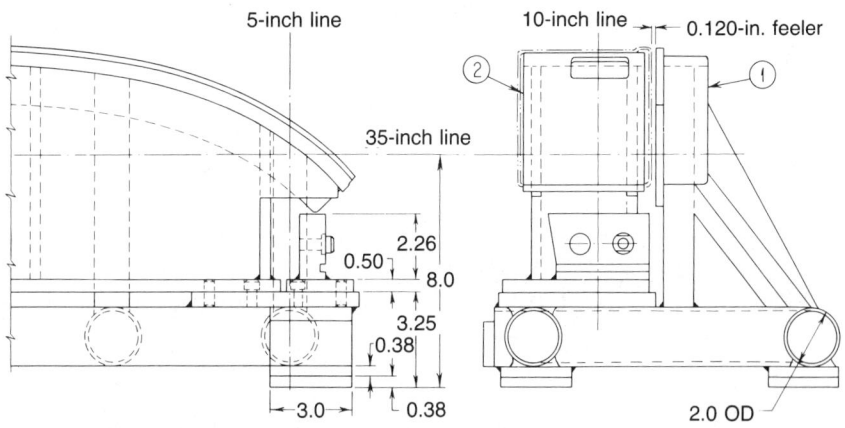

Fig. 16-68 Plastic inspection fixture for an automotive stamping. (*Courtesy Cadillac Motor Car Div., General Motors Corp.*)

controlled CNC engraving or photo plotting machines, it is possible to draw up overlays by hand using manual drafting materials. The accuracy and durability of these overlays needs to be carefully monitored, however, because drafting vellum expands and contracts rapidly with humidity, and the characteristics of the line produced from a pencil or handheld pen can vary widely in width and position.

The finest determination that an inspector can make using an overlay without magnification is about ±0.010 in. (±0.25 mm)—a tolerance band 0.020 in. (0.50 mm) wide. For finer tolerances, it is recommended that the inspection process make use of magni-

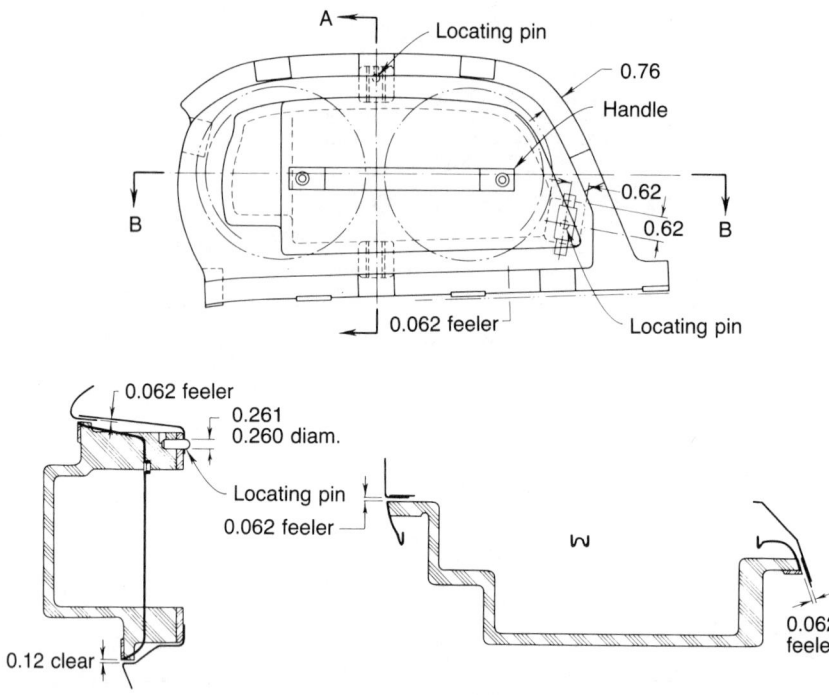

Fig. 16-69 Plastic fixture for inspection of head-lamp area. (*Courtesy Ford Motor Co.*)

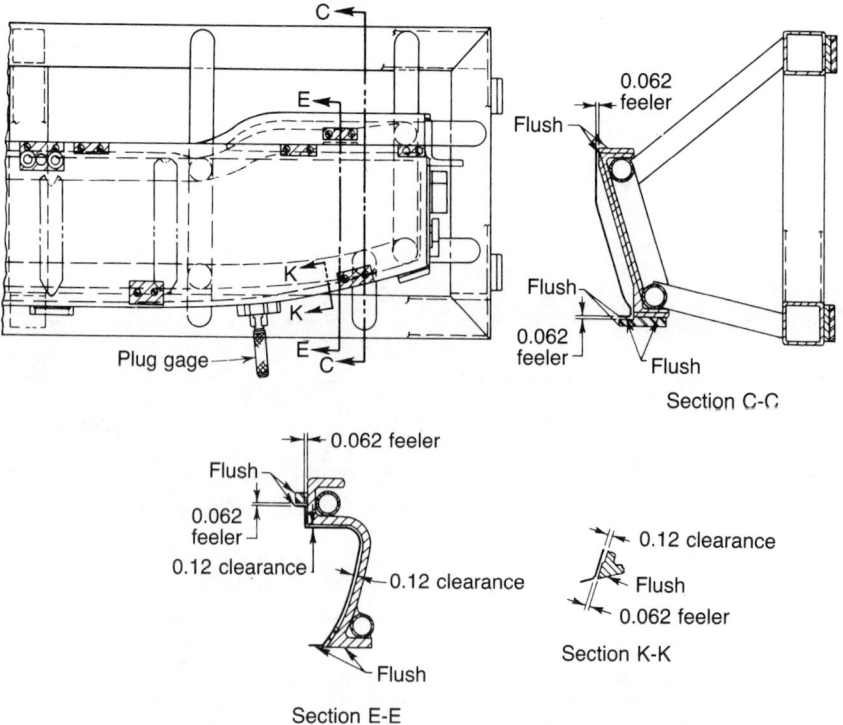

Fig. 16-70 Contour and hole-location fixture. (*Courtesy Ford Motor Co.*)

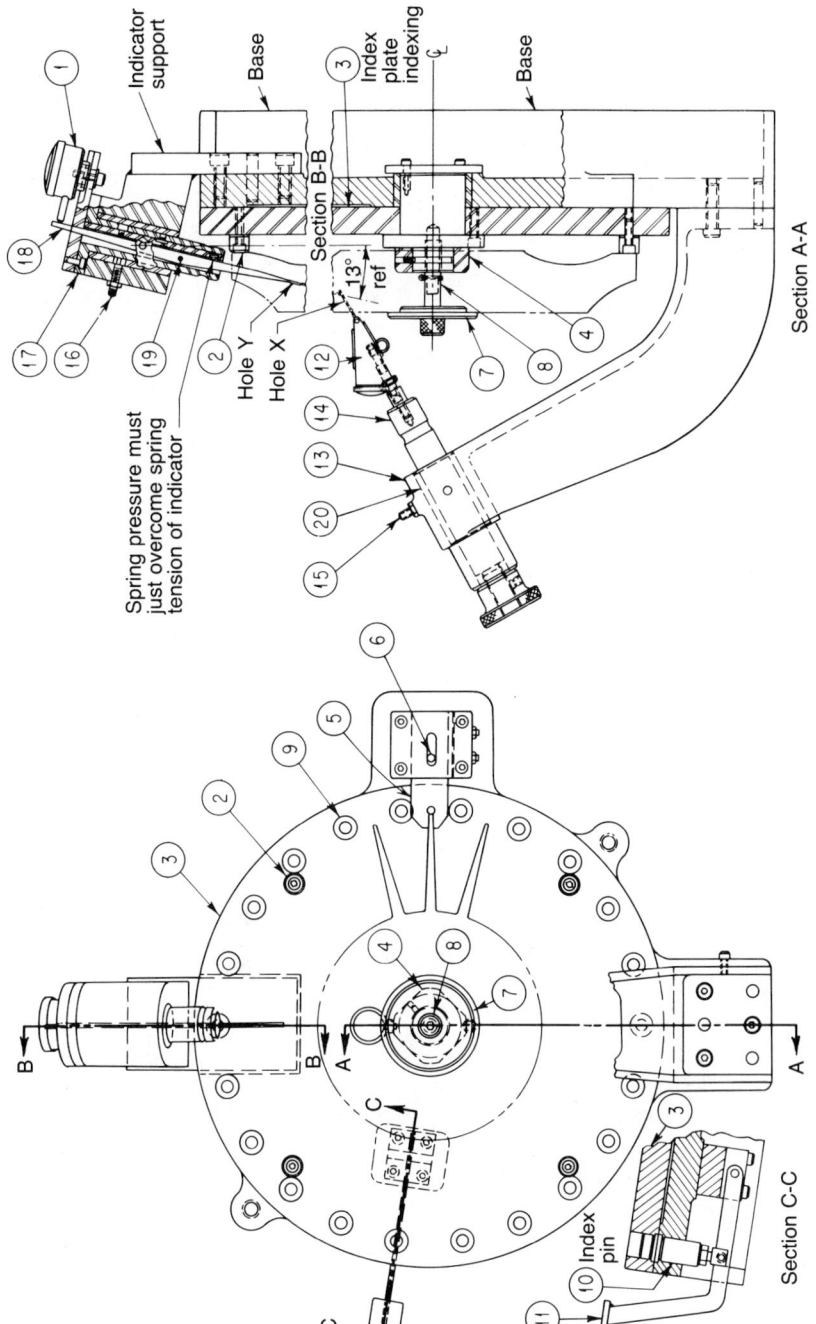

Fig. 16-71 Inspection for location of 44 holes in an impeller. (*Courtesy Thompson Products, Inc.*)

16-65

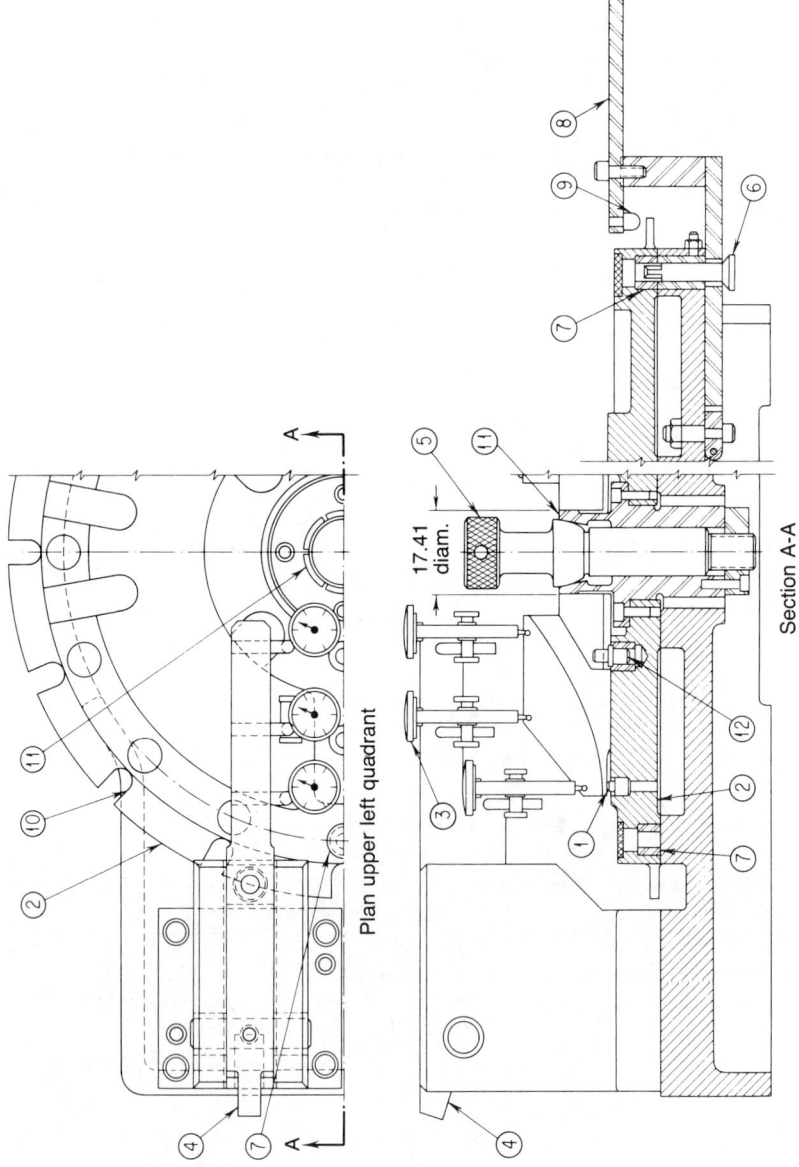

Plan upper left quadrant

Section A-A

Fig. 16-72 Inspection fixture for rotor-blade spacing and thickness. (*Courtesy Thompson Products, Inc.*)

17.41 diam.

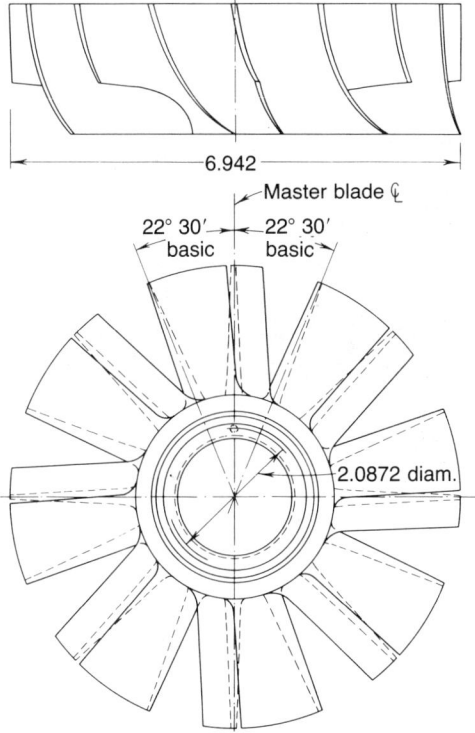

Fig. 16-73 Rotor for inspection in fixture of Fig. 16-74.

fication either through use of a loupe, a bench magnifier, or an optical comparator.

Major advantages of overlay templates, in addition to those for all visual reference gaging, are low cost, ready acceptance by operators and inspectors, and physical toughness, except for those made of glass. The physical toughness characteristic permits overlay templates to be used on the shop floor without extra precautions.

An example of an overlay template for final inspection of a floppy disk jacket assembly used on many personal computers is shown in Fig. 16-75. The overlay image is engraved on the back side of a ¼ in. (6 mm) thick clear plastic plate. The image is engraved on the back side of the template so that it can be in contact with the part inspected, thereby eliminating parallax. Dowel pins are incorporated as stops on the left side of the gage. During inspection, the part is pushed lightly against these pins to locate it for checking. The allowable positioning of the features of the jacket, such as holes, notches, and edges, are incorporated into the min-max lines. The dimensions that the gage measures and measurement instructions are also incorporated on the template. In use, the part is held behind the overlay, and conformance to dimensions is judged by reference to the part outline shown.

It is important to note that the min-max outline given for this part checks only the positioning of the features of the part and not feature sizes themselves. As in other gaging processes, position and size must be checked separately. In this case, feature size could be checked by another overlay showing the min-max feature sizes without regard to position, or they could be checked using functional gaging such as plug gages. Because the product is made of vinyl plastic or paper, the use of contact measuring probes such as calipers might distort the part while measurement was being attempted.

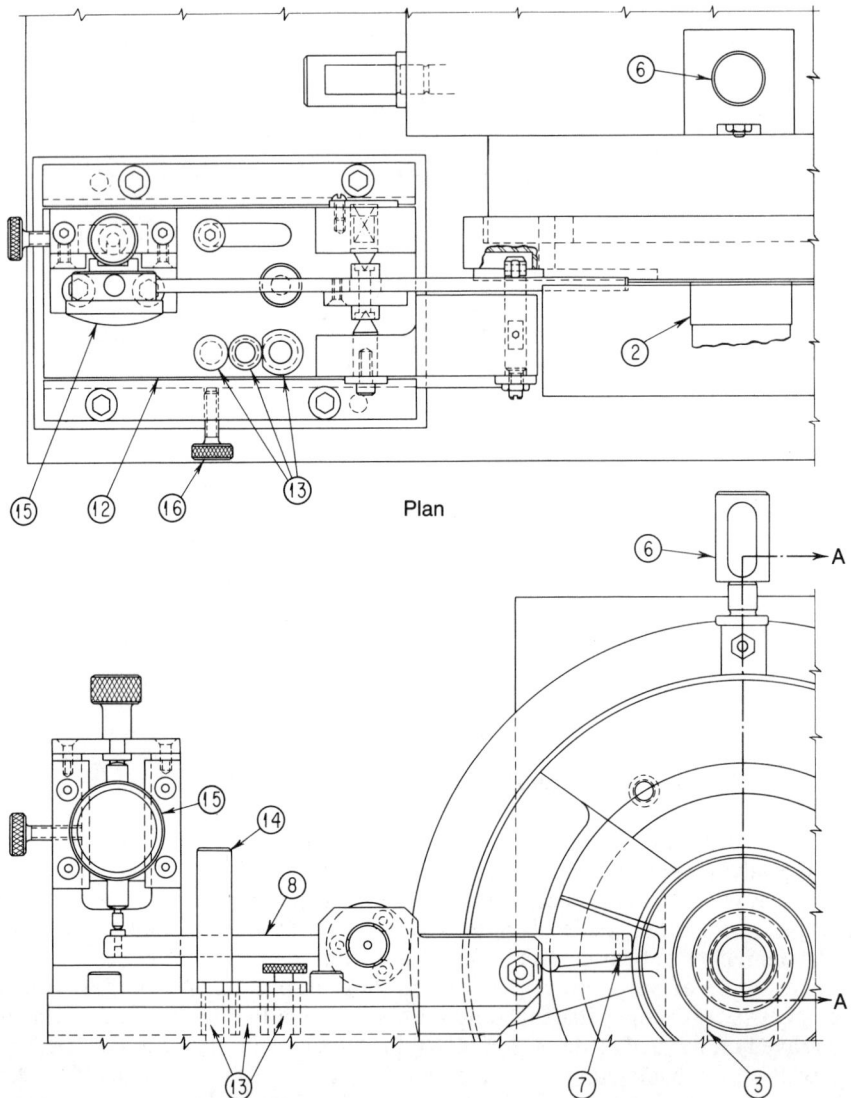

Fig. 16-74 Contour-inspection fixture for rotor blades. (*Courtesy Thompson Products, Inc.*)

TOOLMAKER'S MICROSCOPES

The toolmaker's microscope consists of a microscope mounted to a base that carries an adjustable stage, a stage transport mechanism, and optional supplementary lighting for the objects mounted on the stage. Micrometer barrels are often incorporated into the stage transport mechanism to permit precisely controlled movements, and digital readouts of stage positioning are becoming increasingly available. Various objective lenses provide magnifications range from 10 to 200X.

Engraved glass reticles, mounted in a reticle holder in the eyepiece of the microscope, can be used to measure parts or to inspect parts on a GO/NOT GO basis just as overlay templates are used. In some microscope setups, other types of reticles can more easily be introduced into the optical path of the microscope by light-splitting arrange-

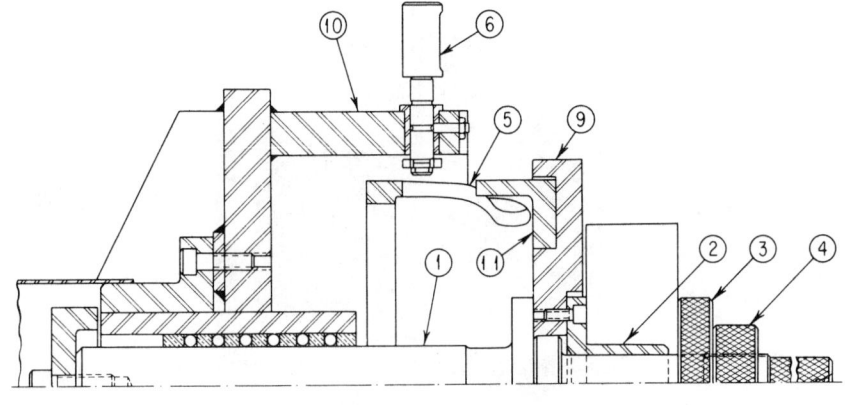

Section A-A

Fig. 16-74 (*Continued*)

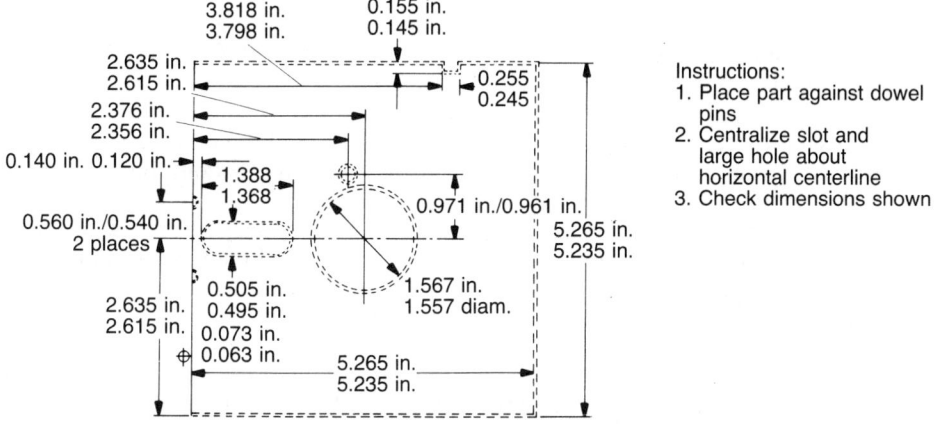

Instructions:
1. Place part against dowel pins
2. Centralize slot and large hole about horizontal centerline
3. Check dimensions shown

Fig. 16-75 Sight gaging for a floppy disk envelope. (*Courtesy Visual Inspection Products*)

ment that lets the reticle be mounted outside the microscope barrel. Here, film or engraved plastic reticles may also be used to check parts.

Accessories available to users of microscopes include a full range of general-purpose fixturing devices such as vises, centers, and rotating tables. In addition, special work-holding fixtures may be designed and built to speed up inspection or to make it more reliable.

Optical zooming features are incorporated in some microscopes. Although this can be a useful feature, it usually prevents the calibration of the instrument for accurate measuring work using reticles mounted in the eyepiece.

OPTICAL MEASUREMENT INSPECTION SYSTEMS

The optical measurement inspection system (OMIS) shown in Fig. 16-76 utilizes fundamental optical measuring techniques to combine the features of an optical comparator, toolmaker's microscope, and coordinate measuring machine in a solid-state video based system.

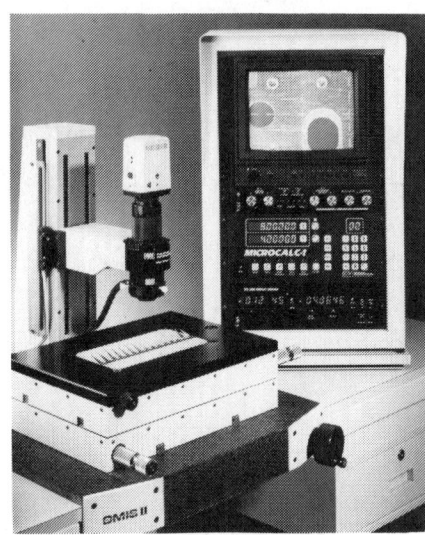

Fig. 16-76 Optical measurement inspection system. (*Courtesy Ram Optical Instrumentation, Inc.*)

High resolution images are delivered to the color video monitor via direct viewing microscope optics. Parfocal zoom magnification (20X—250X) permits control of the view without the need to change lenses, rotate turrets, or refocus.

Fully adjustable crosshairs are superimposed on the video image which eliminates the need for screen overlays and eyepiece reticles. A fixed center line switch calibrated with the zoom optics guarantees an on-axis reference throughout the entire range of magnification.

The OMIS is combined with a computerized 2-axis digital microprocessor to permit geometric function computing capabilities giving the OMIS measurement power similar to a traditional coordinate measuring machine. Radius, diameter, angle, polar/cartesian, skew alignment, and datum reference computations are made through dedicated keyboard command sequences. The system can be equipped with Z-axis measuring capability to provide a 3-axis non-contact optical measuring system for small parts. Z-axis measurements are accomplished by depth of focus with 0.0001 in. repeatability under ideal conditions (lighting, surface quality, flatness, etc.). A rotary table provides 4-axis measurement ability.

Optional right angle panoranic probes can be attached to the zoom optics assembly to permit internal viewing of bores and sidewalls. This accessibility makes inspection and measurement of internal small features possible without sectioning and destroying the part. Many of the features of this system can be retrofitted to most current optical measurement systems such as the toolmaker's microscopes previously discussed.

Optical Projection Gaging. Optical projection is a method of measurement and gaging using a precision instrument known as an optical projector, contour projector, or optical comparator (see Fig. 16-77). Optical gaging is gaging by sight rather than feel or pressure. The measurement or gaging is performed by placing a workpiece in the path of a beam of light and in front of a magnifying-lens system, thereby projecting an enlarged silhouette shadow of the object upon a translucent screen as illustrated in Fig. 16-78.

Measurement of a workpiece normally requires a chart gage with reference lines in two planes. In gaging applications, a precisely scaled layout of the contour of the part to be gaged, usually with tolerance limits, is drawn on the chart. Figure 16-79 shows a workpiece with the chart gage used for its inspection.

Fig. 16-77 Contour projector with vidiprobe. (*Courtesy Optical Gaging Products.*)

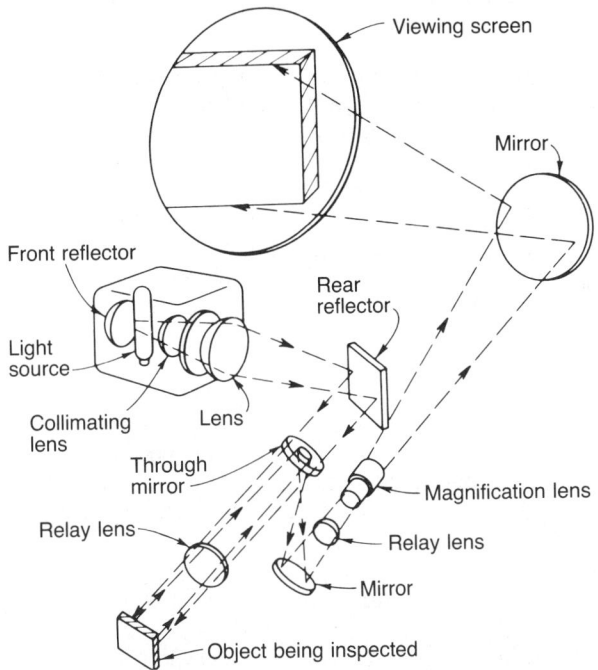

Fig. 16-78 Optical projection gaging principle.

Optical gages are almost unaffected by wear. There is no wear to a light beam, and any fixture wear can be compensated for by repositioning to the setting point. Little operator skill is required; no touching skill or sensitivity is required. Dimensions can be changed on the screen easily and quickly. The chart provides exact duplication. Several dimensions can be checked at the same time, eliminating too much handling of the part.

There are often two lighting systems in an optical comparator. One permits silhouette viewing of an outside profile of a part.[4] A second surface illuminator permits viewing of the area within the silhouette outline. The silhouette image is formed on the

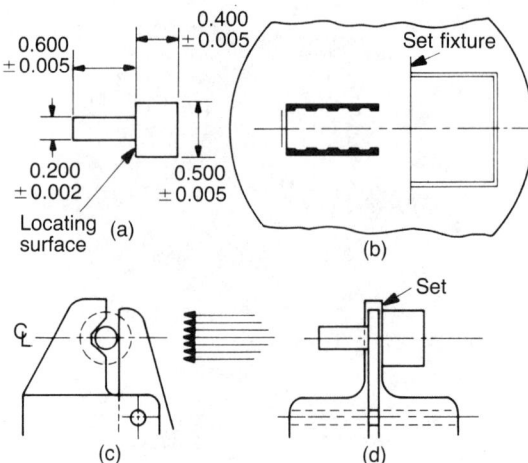

Fig. 16-79 Example of optical gaging: (*a*) part to be gaged, (*b*) chart with bridge line for clear visibility, (*c*) end view of workpiece located in a vee, and (*d*) front view of fixture with workpiece shouldered against set (reference) surface.

screen by placing the sample part between the light source and the objective lens. Surface illumination requires that light be projected onto the part either through the objective lens using a ½ reflecting mirror or from a supplementary oblique lighting system. With sufficient illumination, the objective lens can "see" the surface features of the part. The surface features can then be measured on the screen. Both types of illumination can be used simultaneously, but care should be taken to prevent the part from being subject to high temperatures when high wattage mercury or zenon illuminators are used. Special filters are usually provided to eliminate much of this heat.

The objective lens, together with the other optical components of the comparator, controls the magnification of the image presented to the operator. The operator sees an image enlarged precisely by the magnification factor, as long as the optical system of the machine is in calibration. Overlay charts, drawn at this magnification, can then be placed over the screen image to quickly judge the conformance of the part to the requirements. Alternatively, if part measurements are necessary, a general-purpose cross line may be placed on the screen and the stage positioning mechanisms used to measure the part to high precision. Still a third method is to have an overlay drawn of the part at its nominal contour, without any tolerance allowances, and to check the part using the stage positioners to "bring in" the part to its correct contour, noting the correcting adjustments as this is done. Specific part overlays are illustrated in Fig. 16-80.

Each of these measuring methods has its own inspection tooling cost, data output, and inspection process time tradeoffs. A fully tolerated chart is more expensive to develop, but it permits rapid GO/NOT GO inspection by unskilled operators. This type of chart is often used for checking thread pitch and other simple contour measurements. Use of the general-purpose measuring grid is simple but relatively much slower, and it requires a more skilled individual. The nominal profile chart falls somewhere between these two approaches in both development cost and inspection process time.

Most optical projectors have standard magnification of 10 power up to 100 power.

To establish the effective specimen area that can be projected onto the comparator screen, the screen diameter is divided by the magnification of the lens system being used. For example, a 30 in. (760 mm) comparator working at a magnification of 50X

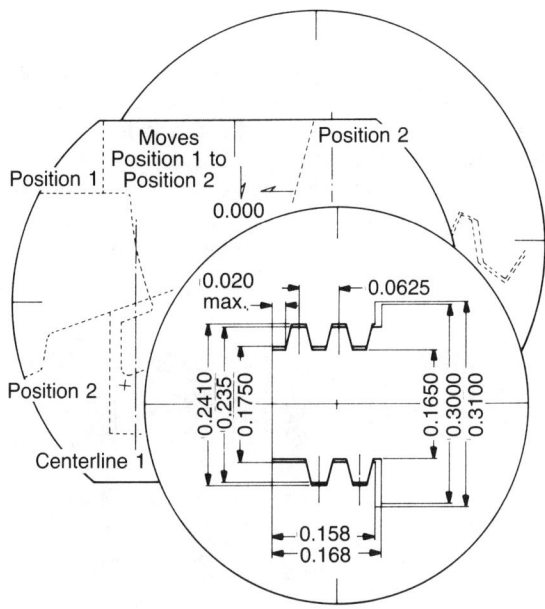

Fig. 16-80 Typical part overlay for use with an optical comparator. (*Courtesy Visual Inspection Products*)

presents a viewing field of 0.600 in. (15.24 mm), and a 20 in. (510 mm) comparator working at a magnification of 10X shows an image field of 2.000 in. (50.8 mm). These fields of view, however, need not be limitations on overall part or feature size because parts may be stepped into the viewing field by means of the stage transport mechanism. Most old-style stage transports use a micrometer barrel; measurements must be read off the barrel vernier. Many stage transports have provisions for inserting gage blocks as a way of offsetting the stage a precise amount, thereby bringing a new field into view and permitting the controlled stepping of dimensions too long to measure with the motion permitted by the barrel micrometer. Electronic readout linear encoder stages are becoming more common because they eliminate operator error and increase the speed of the measuring process. These stages are able to accurately measure distances of several inches without the use of gage blocks.

OPTICAL COMPARATOR CHARTS

The comparator chart for inspecting a specific workpiece is a very accurately scribed, magnified outline drawing of the workpiece to be gaged containing all the contours, dimensions, and tolerance limits necessary for the purpose and mounted in an appropriate way on the viewing screen. Chart gages may be made on glass, certain types of plastics, paper, or vellum and laid out by hand drafting methods, special scribing, or chart layout devices. The material and method of layout are such that the chart gage will not significantly add to or detract from manufacturing tolerances. Glass offers the greatest dimensional stability; paper or vellum is suitable only for temporary use.

Chart layout lines should be dense black, sharply defined, and about 0.006 to 0.010 in. (0.15 to 0.25 mm) wide for best legibility. Dimensions are normally to the center of the lines. When maximum and minimum tolerance lines are used, the magnification should be high enough to maintain a minimum of 0.020 in. (0.51 mm) spacing between

16-73

the lines of the chart gage. For closer tolerance checking, special lines or "bridge" arrangements based on gaging to the edge of the lines are often used.

For contrast reasons, the dimensional lines are purposely broadened and normally appear on the chart gage as a dense black opaque line when the shadow of the part is projected on the chart screen. The operator's only concern is that some light appear between the edge of the workpiece shadow and a dimension line for GO tolerance that it not be seen for NOT GO tolerance (see Fig. 16-81).

When bridge liners are used on the chart page, the dimension line must be widened sufficiently to produce sharp definition between the shadow of the part and the chart line itself. In Fig. 16-81b, the distance from edge A to B represents the prescribed tolerance.

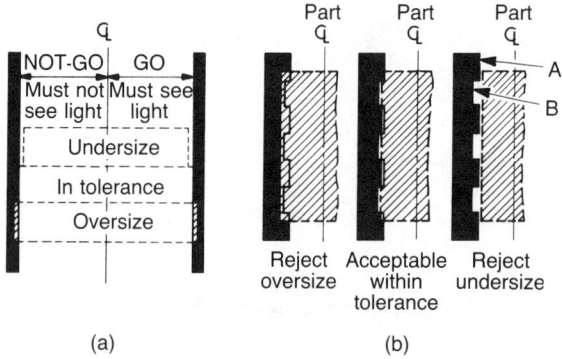

(a)   (b)

Fig. 16-81 Optical gaging for tolerance.

For inspection of individual geometric elements, standard chart gages with grids, protractors, and radii are frequently used (see Fig. 16-82). They are also sometimes employed in conjunction with the horizontal and vertical measuring attachments of the comparator.

For some applications, precision reticles may be used on the comparator stage in place of the magnified chart gage screen. Reticles are 1:1 scale precision master outlines on glass, usually made from larger layouts photographically reduced. The reticle is mounted into a special floating fixture that enables the workpiece to control the motion of the reticle so as to compare the magnified deviation between the workpiece and the projected master outline on the viewing screen. Such fixtures ordinarily explore the part by tracing or probing. By the use of such methods, parts may be checked that when magnified would be many times the screen area. Contours that normally could not be seen by direct projection can also be checked in this manner.

When the magnified layout is too large to be contained within the available screen area, one or more section of it may be superimposed and the part shifted accordingly. When employing staging fixtures with special chart gages, set lines for coordinating the chart gage and fixture should be incorporated on the chart layout.

MEASUREMENT BY TRANSLATION

Many parts can be successfully gaged on optical comparators even though the part configuration cannot be projected by the light beam. Parts having recessed contours such as actuator cam tracks, ball sockets, and the internal grooves of ball nuts can all be gaged by means of tracer techniques. A tracer, as the term is used in projection gaging, is a one-to-one pantograph. On one arm of the pantograph is a stylus that freely traces over the part contour in a given plane. The other arm carries a follower, visible in the

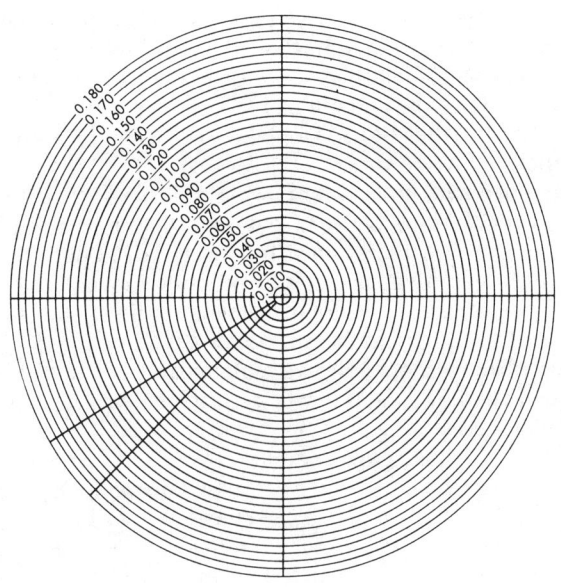

Fig. 16-82 Standard chart gage.

light path that is projected by the light beam as it moves. Three types of followers are used (see Fig. 16-83):

1. Probe follower, *a*—an exact duplicate of the stylus tracer in size and shape.
2. Dot follower, *b*—a glass reticle having an opaque dot of the same diameter as the stylus racer.
3. Reticle-gage follower, *c*—a glass reticle having an exact one-to-one actual-size reproduction of the part profile.

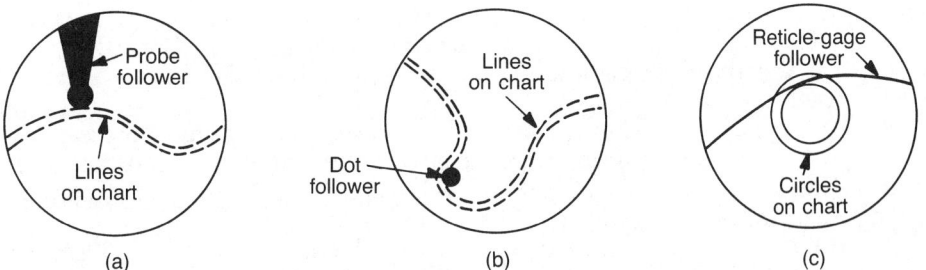

Fig. 16-83 Projector tracer followers: (*a*) probe type, (*b*) dot type, and (*c*) recticle-gage type.

The choice of follower for a given gaging problem depends on the size of the path and the magnification to be used. In general, the probe or dot is used if the size of the part is less than the field of view of the projector at the given magnification. In some cases, larger parts are gaged by using two followers suitably spaced to correlate with a special type of chart in which one section of the contour is superimposed on another section. For some purposes, the dot follower is preferred to the probe because it provides a complete circle shadow unrestricted by the shadow of the supporting stem.

16-75

The reticle gage follower is more versatile in its application because if is not restricted by part size or magnification. Large parts can be gaged with reticle gages using high magnification. The reticle gages must be of a very high order of accuracy because any error in them shows up directly as an error in the part. To achieve the necessary accuracy, the contours should be laid out on precision scribing machines at a magnified size. Precision cameras can then be used to reduce them photographically to the one-to-one size for the reticle.

Tracer units equipped with either probe or dot followers are used with chart gages having a contour layout of the part. The layout may be a single-line profile or it may be a double-line profile showing the permissible limits of the part. As the stylus traces across the part, the projected image of the follower moves across the screen. If a single-line chart is being used, the follower shadow must stay tangent to the line throughout the transit for a part to be without error. Using the double-line chart, the edge of the follower shadow should always remain between the two lines.

A different type of chart gage is used when tracing with a reticle gage follower. This chart has a circle on it representing the diameter of the stylus tracer at the magnification being used. The projected reticle gage contour moves past this fixed circle as the part is traced and, if the part is perfect, will always remain tangent to it. If the tolerance limits on the part are uniform throughout, it is convenient to put two circles on the screen to represent the tolerance spread. The projected reticle contour then should fall between these circles as it passes across the screen. If the part tolerance varies from point to point along the contour, the tolerance lines can be put on the reticle follower and projected to a single circle on the screen.

Standard tracer units are available as accessory equipment and can be used on many projectors. Their coordinate slides operate on precision preloaded balls to provide uniform motion without play or backlash. They can be fitted with special stylus arms for specific purposes such as the tracing of internal contours and checking for concentricity. Some tracers are designed to be used with horizontal light beams and others are for use with vertical beam. The standard units can provide coordinate movements up to 4 × 9 in. (101.6 × 228.6 mm), but special tracers of considerably greater travel have been built.

Contour Projector Video Measurement System. The contour projector shown in Fig. 16-77 is equipped with a video measurement system. When centerline and chart gage measurements are required, it functions as a contour projector to provide erect and unreversed images at all magnifications. When fast, high accuracy, repetitive measurements are needed, it works as a complete video measurement system. Coincident video and optical centerlines prevent loss of accuracy where video and chart gage measurements are intermixed.

While the optical system forms a distortion free image of part features on the optical viewing screen, it also forms an image directly on the surface of a solid state video camera. This image is shown on the video monitor and it is analyzed by a microprocessor system to determine the size, form, and location of features.

To measure an image, each field of view is separated into over 65,000 picture elements (pixels). Each pixel can have one of 256 different values of grey assigned to it depending on the brightness of the light from the image.

The image analysis method used by the system allows edges to be measured to within one tenth the size of a pixel, resulting in high resolution over a large field of view. This type of image analysis, called Grey Scale Processing, is insensitive to changes in brightness of the image and can even measure an out-of-focus edge.

A unique feature of the systems camera is its ability to enhance low contrast images by adding video frames together. This technique, coupled with image processing technology, allows measurement of part that could not be measured optically before due to insufficient surface reflectivity.

The system measures part features within a large viewing "window" centered on the screen of the contour projector. The field of view and resolution at the part depend on the contour projector magnification in use. The system shown can measure approximately one X-Y location per second. Video measurements are resolved to 0.0005 in. (0.013 mm) at 10X magnification and 0.00005 in. (0.0013 mm) at 100X magnification. Linear measurements are made by finding the "edges" seen by the optical system. For systems equipped with optional Z-axis measurement, height and depth measurements are made using autofocus techniques.

The inspection report generated by the system contains nominal and actual values, upper and lower tolerances, deviations from nominals and out of tolerance values. Inspection reports can be viewed on the computer's screen, printed in their entirety, or printed on a feature by feature basis. Operators can create their own report formats and include program headings, messages to be printed at the end of the report, or messages to be printed on a feature by feature basis.

This advanced software can store data on diskettes for reference, or additional analysis, select values for printing, step and repeat program sequences, adjust video parameters, control a 4th (rotary) axis, print messages, and interact with the operator.

2D Optical Measuring Machine. Figure 16-84 shows a general purpose CNC optical measuring machine designed to measure cylindrical components, analyze the results, and then feed back correction data to the production process. Unlike many other non-contact devices, this system is a complete quality management package, consisting of a flexible gaging system; with fully integrated data acquisition, storage, and analysis facilities. The standard software includes analysis procedures for statistical process control and machine tool capability studies.

The gaging sequence and component data—nominal sizes, tolerances, etc.—is preprogrammed using the stow-away computer keyboard, and is stored by component type or part number. In the gaging mode, the part to be checked is simply selected from a displayed directory using the built-in keypad. The measurement then proceeds automatically and upon completion the measurements are displayed along with the deviations from nominal sizes. The operator can select numeric or graphic display and out of tolerance features are highlighted. Measurements are stored by component type or part number automatically unless cancelled by the operator.

Standard software allows for collection of measurement data from up to 10 production machines at random. Stored data can be displayed, printed out, and transmitted to other data processing equipment if desired. The stored data can be analyzed in the following ways:

- Individual Measurement Chart—A trend plot of the last 100 component measurements with reference to process control limits.
- Individual Measurement Report—A numeric listing of measurements with indicated X and R values for each subgroup.
- Control Chart—A plot of X and R for the last 25 subgroups with respect to process control limits.
- Capability Report—A histogram of distribution of measurement with respect to specification tolerances.

LASER INSPECTION DEVICES[5]

The work "laser" is an acronym that stands for "Light Amplification by Stimulated Emission of Radiation." Laser light differs from ordinary light by being extremely intense highly directional, strongly monochromatic, and coherent to a high degree. Unlike light emitted from an ordinary source, the waves of laser light are coordinated in time and space (they are coherent) and have essentially the same wavelength (they are monochromatic). Directionality results largely from the geometry of the device and the

Fig. 16-84 2D optical measuring machine. (*Courtesy Brown & Sharpe Mfg. Co.*)

coherence of light. The intensity of the laser beam is the result of the light energy at a single wavelength in a particular direction.

There are a number of different types of lasers available. The type of laser used depends on the specific application. Manufacturing operations such as welding metals or drilling and cutting tough steels, ceramics, and diamonds employ high-energy, solid-state lasers such as pulsating ruby lasers or high-power, molecular carbon dioxide lasers. For metrology, low-power lasers, usually of a continuous-wave output type, are employed; these are generally gas lasers.

The uses of the laser in metrology arise from the characteristics of laser light that differentiate it from ordinary light. Those characteristics are the extreme intensity, the highly directional, small, collimated beam, the monochromaticity, and the coherent nature of the light.

One of the largest uses of lasers is by contractors for alignment and surveying. Here the intensity and directionality properties make the laser a natural.

These same properties are fundamental for the high-speed measuring devices that employ a scanning laser beam. The transmitter section of the gage emits a moving beam of light that scans at a regular speed. The object being measured interrupts the beam, and the detector determines the time that the beam took to traverse the part. The electronic controller converts the data into discrete dimensional readings for end use. The inherent stability of these devices have led to their being used in harsh industrial environments such as steel bar mills.

Again, the intensity and directional properties are fundamental to high-speed contour gages that measure by optical triangulation. These gages direct a small, intense beam of light onto the workpiece. A lens system and photodetector are located at a known angle with respect to the incident beam axis. As the part is moved in the Y direction, the gage determines the change in location of the spot in the X direction. To avoid the problems involved in having the image of the spot move across the detector, the gage moves the part in the X direction to the original location using a null-seeking system. The resulting data are a series of X-Y locations that can be plotted or compared to master data by the gage's computer.

The laser is used in the measurement of straightness deviation, such as in the inspection of surface plates and for machine tool alignment. Before the availability of the laser, it was necessary to use a measuring autocollimator, which requires a high degree of skill on the part of the operator. The laser autocollimator unit is much simpler and easier to use. It directs a collimated laser beam to a flat target mirror that can be at varying distances from the light source.

If the surface being examined is perfect, the reflected beam would be returned superimposed on the projected beam. Imperfections in the surface cause misalignment of the mirror and an angular offset of the return beam. The autocollimator detector array senses the offset in two axes simultaneously.

There are many applications of lasers in metrology based on the coherence of laser light.

LASER SCANNING INSTRUMENTS

For the accurate measurement of the diameter of soft, delicate, hot, or moving objects, noncontacting sensors must be used. Devices of this character include capacitive gages, eddy-current gages, air gages, and optical sensors.

Optical sensors have advantages over these other gages because of the nature of light itself. The principal advantages are the following:

1. They do not require direct mechanical contact between the sensor and the object to be measured.
2. The distance from the sensor to the object to be measured can be large.
3. The response time is limited only to that of the photodetector and its electronics.
4. Light variations or interruptions are directly converted to electrical signals.

Optical sensors used for the dimensional gaging of part profiles employ various techniques, such as shadow projection, diffraction phenomena, diode arrays, and scanning light beams. If the object to be measured is small or does not move about more than a small fraction of an inch, a dimensional gage based on diffraction phenomena or diode arrays can be used. However, if the object to be measured has a dimension of more than a small fraction of an inch, diffraction techniques and diode arrays become impractical.

A scanning laser beam is particularly suited to this latter type of measurement. The concept of using a scanning light beam for noncontacting dimensional gaging is certainly not new and predates the laser. Instruments using scanning laser beams in a variety of ways have been designed and manufactured. These instruments are increasingly utilizing the potential of this technique when precision performance is required.

System Components and Operation. A typical laser scanning instrument consists of a transmitter module, a receiver module, and processor electronics (see Fig. 16-85). The transmitter contains a low-power HeNe gas laser, a power supply, a collimating lens, a multifaceted reflector prism, a synchronizing pulse photodetector, and a protective window. In operation, the transmitter module produces a collimated, parallel, scanning laser beam moving at a high, constant, linear speed. The scanning beam appears as a line of red light and sweeps across its measurement field. When a part is placed in the

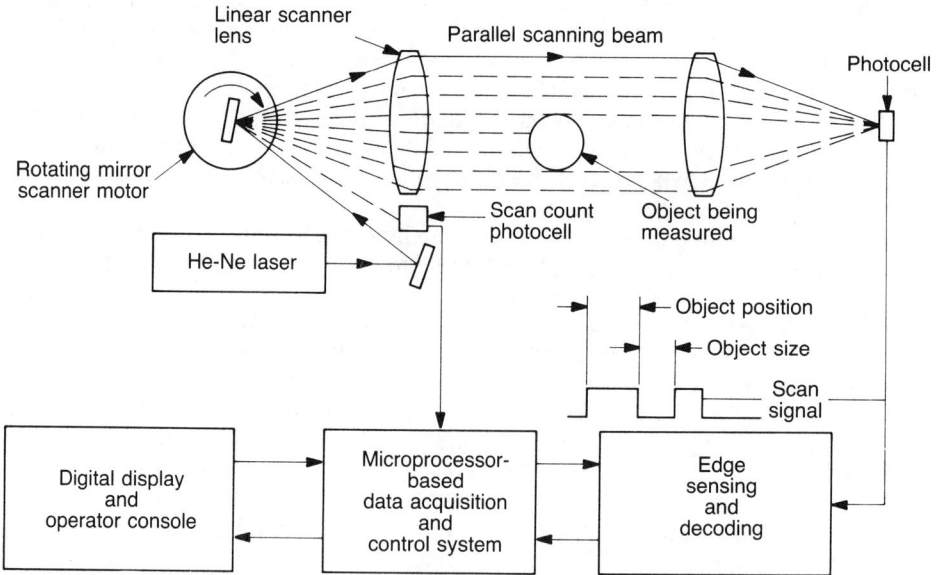

Fig. 16-85 Schematic of laser scanning instrument. (*Courtesy Lasermike Inc., A Bunzl Instrumentation Co.*)

field, it interrupts the beam. The receiver module collects and photoelectrically senses the laser light transmitted past the part being measured. The processor electronics process the receiver signals, converting them to a convenient form and then displaying the dimension being measured.

Applications. Laser scanning instruments can be used in a broad range of manufacturing operations and a variety of industries. Some of the potential areas of application are wire manufacturing, centerless grinding, plastic extrusion, metal product fabrication, and nuclear reactor metrology.

By modifying the techniques by which the detector output is digitized and interpreted by the processor unit, measurements can be made on translucent material such as fiber-optic cables or transparent material such as glass tubing. In addition to simple diameter measurement, product position, gap size, and multiple dimensions, measurements are possible by examining the detector output in different ways. More elaborate scanner geometries can be used to achieve dual-axis inspection. In these applications, the laser beam is alternately swept across the measurement field in two axes 90° apart. By stacking individual scanners back to back or detecting only the edge of a product and relating it to the position of a reference edge, products much larger than the range of an individual scanner can be measured. Extra-high-speed scanners, which measure at four to six times the normal rate, allow detection of smaller defects, such as lumps or neckdowns, in moving product applications.

LASER TRIANGULATION

A variety of noncontact techniques can be used for proximity or range-type measurements. these include time-of-flight techniques such as laser radars, ultrasonic and acoustic radar ranging, and a variety of optical techniques. Ultrasonic and acoustic systems have the advantage of large range, but in general are only capable of providing medium resolutions of proximity. Also, they use relatively large spot sizes or footprints on the part being measured. The large spot size is a disadvantage when the part to be measured is small or of a nonflat geometry. Laser radar devices tend to be only moderately precise and relatively expensive.

Of the many optical techniques, several procedures have been utilized. These include measurement of the width of a spot with a conical or tapered beam, measurement of spacing between two projected spots with the input angles being selected for sensitivity, and single-spot laser triangulation. Of these three, laser triangulation is the preferred method for high-accuracy measurements. The simplicity of this method allows the development of a highly rugged, reliable, and for the most part accurate device as part of the mechanical and optical hardware design.

It is important to note that there are a number of techniques that fit under the general title of laser triangulation. These include structured light, light stripe, and single-spot techniques. This discussion is limited to single-spot laser triangulation techniques.

Operating Principle. The principle of single-spot laser triangulation is illustrated in Fig. 16-86. The sensors use a small, low-powered laser. A beam of laser light from the source is projected and focused by optics to the surface of the object. This creates a spot of light on the object surface similar to shining a flashlight on a wall. At some angle relative to the axis of the projected laser light, an image of the spot falls on the detector. As shown in Fig. 16-86, the location of the centroid of the imaged spot is directly related to the standoff distance from the sensor to the object surface. A change in standoff distance results in a lateral shift of the spot centroid along the sensor array; calculation of the optical triangles, hence the name optical triangulation, is carried out by the sensor processor. The sensor processor is frequently remotely mounted from the sensor head itself. The microprocessor-controlled processor typically provides a readout of the surface standoff distance relative to the sensor or of the standoff distance variation relative to a programmable nominal.

A variety of single-spot laser triangulation sensors are available at various specifications. Typically, the nominal standoff distance of such as sensor is 2 to 6 in. (50 to 150 mm). The measurement range is from ±0.02 to ±0.50 in. Accuracies, proportionally, are in the region of 50 μin. to 0.003 in. Data rates from single-spot laser triangulation sensors are typically 100 to 300 readings per second, with some suppliers offering sampling rates of more than 30,000 readings per second. Surfaces that are oriented at an angle to the input beam of up to 20° or larger can be measured depending on the texture and reflectivity characteristics of the surface.

For many measurement applications, particularly where flexibility is required, the sensor must be equipped with a form of adaptive gain control to compensate for varying surface reflectivities. This is particularly important in a programmable system when a variety of surfaces must be inspected. Sensors are generally equipped with an automated gain control that operates by varying the sensor sensitivity depending on the light level reflected. Typical gain control ranges from 500 to 1 in reflectivity ratio for a simple sensor to a 100,000 to 1 ratio for a complex sensor designed for a variety of surface applications. It is desirable that this gain control function be carried out automatically and not require operator intervention to set up the sensor.

Sensors. A single-spot laser triangulation sensor is sealed to withstand the heat and/or dust conditions of the industrial environment. Frequently a crash detector or contact plate is fitted to the front of the sensor to provide an indication to a measuring system controller in case the sensor contacts the part being measured. A contact plate is required if the sensor chosen for a given application has a small standoff distance and measuring angle. It is also particularly useful in flexible programmable measuring systems because it is used to stop machine motions before damage to the sensor or machine occurs. Selecting a sensor with a longer standoff distance or measuring range may negate the need for a crash alarm device.

Applications. Single-spot laser triangulation sensors have found a wide number of applications in the industrial environment. One such area is in dimensional gaging of

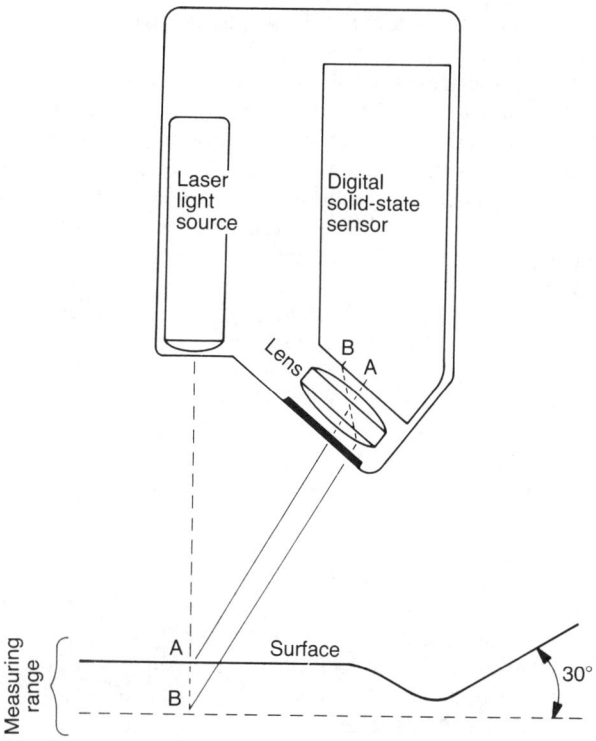

Fig. 16-86 Principle of laser triangulation operation. (*Courtesy Diffracto, Ltd.*)

components where the sensor provides a direct replacement for a contact (LVDT) or noncontact (air or capacitance) probe. The advantage of such sensors over LVDTs include remote measurement without contact and a high data rate. Relative to air and capacitance gaging techniques, laser triangulation permits longer standoff distances, higher response, and greater resolution.

The disadvantage of a single-spot laser triangulation sensor as a direct replacement for other forms of gaging probes is that the triangulation sensor cost is currently higher than that of more traditional measuring probes. However, in many applications, the speed of the measurement, the greater resolution, and the facts that there are no contact and no moving parts in the sensor provide ready justification for their use.

Laser triangulation sensors can be used as a replacement for the touch trigger probes typically used on coordinate measuring machines. In this application, the sensor determines surface features and surface locations utilizing an edge-finding feature. However, the sensors cannot be used for probing down the depth of a bore to determine size or location. When utilized for surface measurement applications, the advantage of the use of the laser triangulation sensor on the coordinate measuring machine is a significant increase in speed of measurement.

Typically this increase over touch trigger probe is on the order of 4 to 10 times.

This advantage stems from several factors. First, the sensor does not have to be indexed toward the surface to determine the null point. Instead, the sensor provides an active measurement of the plus or minus deviation of surface location from the nominal position used to drive the machine. Second, when indexing from measurement point to measurement point, the sensor does not need to be retracted to avoid crashing into the surface because the standoff distance provides adequate clearance for movement between measurement points. In addition, the noncontact nature of the laser triangulation sensor eliminates the potential for deformation of flexible surfaces and damage to soft or other delicate surfaces.

Laser triangulation sensors can also be used with industrial robots. The sensor provides a feedback signal to the robot controller indicating the range or proximity to an object. This can be used to assist the robot in acquiring the location of the component and to provide a vision capability for gripping of the part. In addition, such a sensor mounted on a robot can be used to create a measurement robot. The limitation in this case, however, is that the accuracy of the overall system is limited by the positioning accuracy of the robot, which generally is not adequate for measurement applications requiring total accuracies of +0.004 in. or better.

LASER MEASUREMENT SYSTEMS

The laser measurement system set up to check the flatness of a surface plate in Fig. 16-87 can also be provided with the optical components and mounting accessories necessary to check linear distance/velocity, angle, straightness/parallelism, and squareness.

Fig. 16-87 Checking flatness of a surface plate. (*Courtesy Hewlett Packard*)

The system uses the wavelength of light from a low-power, helium-neon laser as a length standard. This specially designed laser also uses a two-frequency laser technique that virtually eliminates the problems resulting from beam intensity changes common to other laser systems, thereby permitting unusually high resolutions and excellent accuracies over large distances in shop environments. The system consists of a laser head, a measuring display, and a variety of optical components and mounting accessories.

One setup of the laser head (usually mounted on a tripod) permits linear distance, angle, and straightness measurements, by just changing the optical components. Typical setups are shown in Fig. 16-88. Included are the following:

1. Optical setup, *a*, for *X*-axis linear positioning measurement with fixed interferometer and moving retroflector. When taking measurements, the change in distance between the interferometer and retroflector is measured. Thus, prior to any movement, any point can be defined as a measurement starting point and be designated as zero or other useful value using the "preset" key.
2. *Y*-axis linear measurement setup, *b*, using the right angle feature of the interferometer.

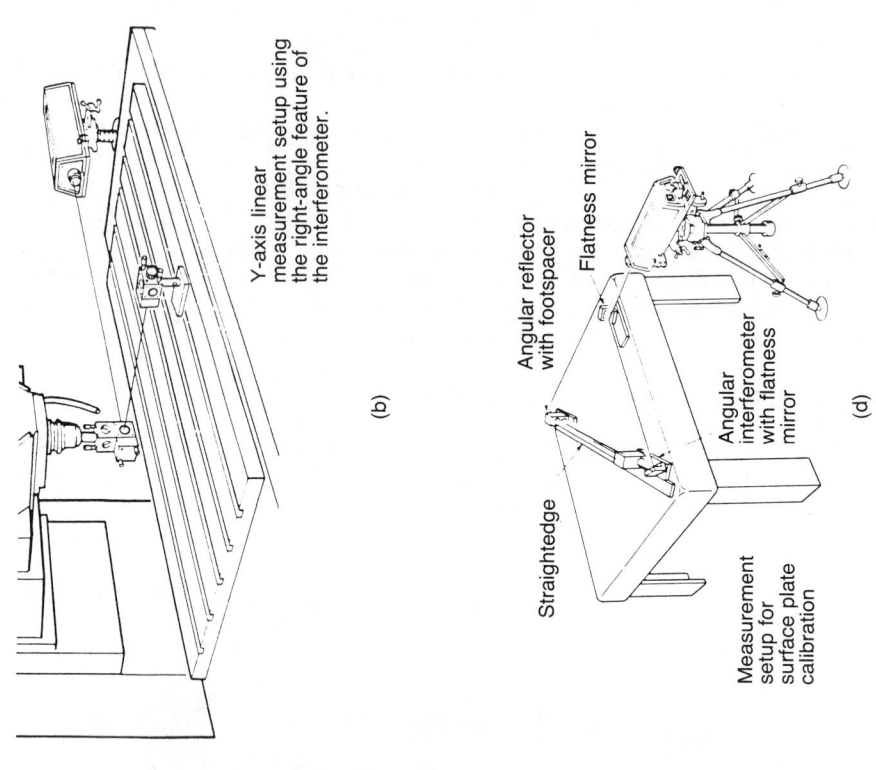

(b)

Y-axis linear
measurement setup using
the right-angle feature of
the interferometer.

Flatness mirror

Angular reflector
with footspacer

Straightedge

Angular
interferometer
with flatness
mirror

(d)

Measurement
setup for
surface plate
calibration

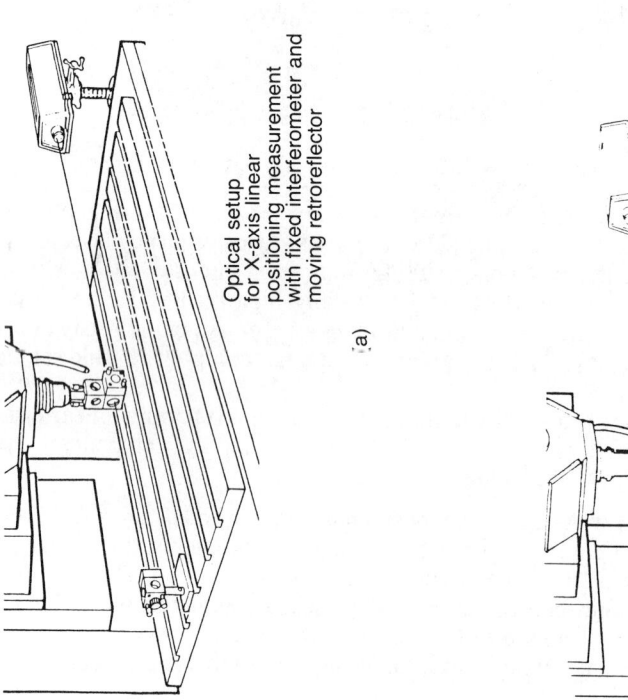

Optical setup
for X-axis linear
positioning measurement
with fixed interferometer and
moving retroreflector

(a)

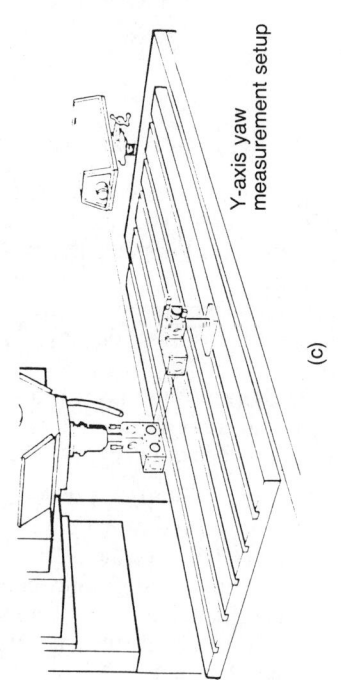

Y-axis yaw
measurement setup

(c)

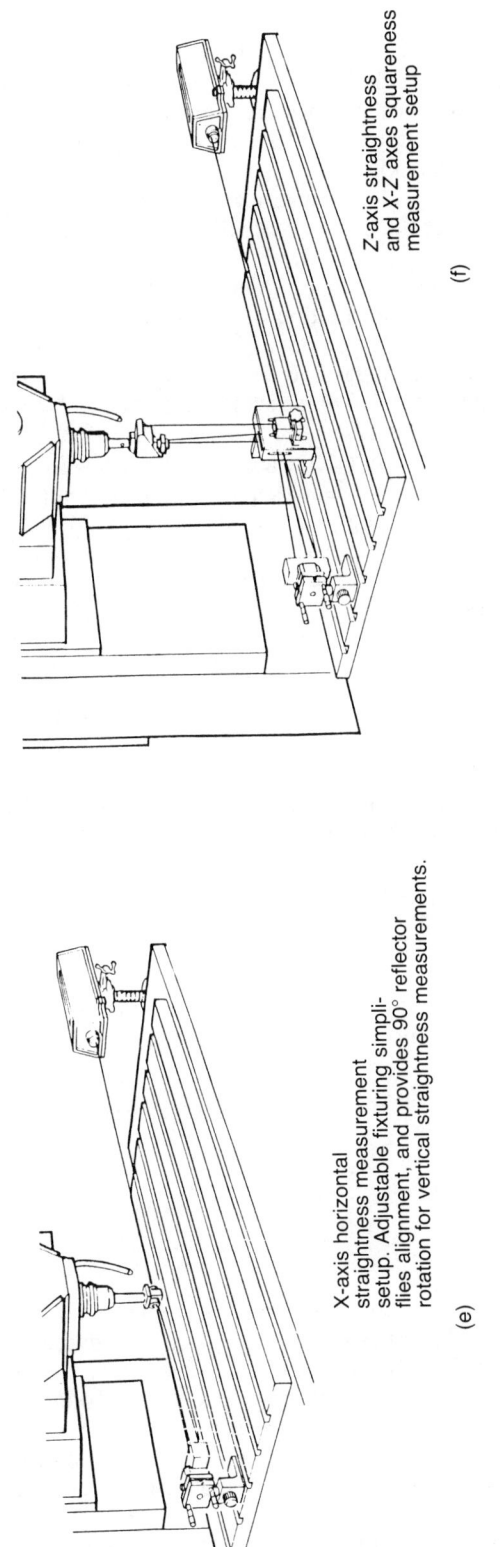

X-axis horizontal
straightness measurement
setup. Adjustable fixturing simpli-
fies alignment, and provides 90° reflector
rotation for vertical straightness measurements.

(e)

Z-axis straightness
and X-Z axes squareness
measurement setup

(f)

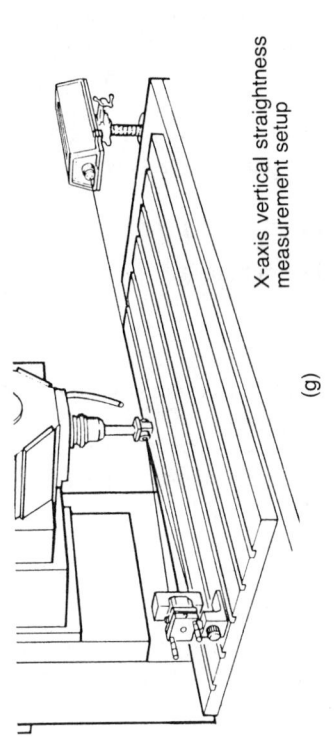

X-axis vertical straightness
measurement setup

(g)

Fig. 16-88 Typical setups with a laser measurement system. (*Courtesy Hewlett Packard*)

16-85

3. *Y*-axis yaw measurement, *c*, setup using an angular reflector and angular interfe-rometer. The setup to perform angular measurements is very simple once a linear distance setup has been completed. The linear optics are removed and replaced with angular optics on the same height adjusters. Interchangeable optics with a common optical centerline makes this possible.
4. Measurement setup, *d*, for surface plate calibration using the angular optics, a flatness mirror, and a footspacer to move the angular reflector along the straight-edge in equally spaced steps.
5. *X*-axis horizontal straightness measurement setup, *e*. Adjustable fixturing simpli-fies alignment, and provides 90° reflector rotation for vertical straightness measurements.
6. *Z*-axis straightness and *X*-*Z* axes squareness measurement setup, *f*. In the example shown, *X*-axis out-of-straightness in the vertical plane is measured first as shown in *g*. Then the optical square is positioned under the spindle axis to bend the optical straightedge 90° and the straightness interferometer and retroreflector are mounted on the spindle. The turning mirror is mounted on the square to complete the beam path to the laser head. Out-of-straightness in the same plane in the *Z*-axis is then measured. A comparison of the two straightness measurements with respect to the 90° reference established by the optical square yields out-of-squareness between the *Y* and *Z* axes.

AUTOCOLLIMATORS[6]

The popularity of autocollimators rests on their ability to sense remotely, with high accuracy, the angular rotation of a flat mirror around axes that are in the plane of the mirror. With sensitivities approaching 1/10 arc second, or even less under special conditions, it has become common practice to use autocollimators not only to monitor angular tilts as such, but to convert linear displacements into angular ones so that they can be monitored with this versatile instrument.

Optically, an autocollimator is simply a special form of a telescope. It consists basically of an illuminated target pattern or reticle located in the focal plane of the telescope objective. A plane mirror perpendicular to the optical axis in front of this telescope will reflect an image of the pattern back on itself in the same plane and in focus. A rotation of the mirror by an angle about its perpendicular position causes the return image to be displaced by a specific amount. The amount of displacement can be calculated using the equation:

$$d = 2f\theta \tag{1}$$

where:

d = displacement, in. (mm)

f = focal length of the autocollimator objective, in. (mm)

θ = angular rotation of the mirror

A viewing system is required to observe the relative position of the image, which can be in the form of an illuminated slit or cross line or cross hair in an illuminated field. A simple eyepiece may serve or a compound microscope can be used as shown in Fig. 16-89. The fiducial index should be designed for maximum precision in zeroing the image; for example, a double line to frame a single line. Measurement is made by moving either the image or the index under micrometer control. Although most autocol-limators measure around one axis only, a suitable target pattern and a two-axial index micrometer system are all that is required to make readings about two axes.

Mirror Characteristics. Because the reflecting mirror is part of the overall system, mirror properties such as size, flatness, and distance from the objective play a role in

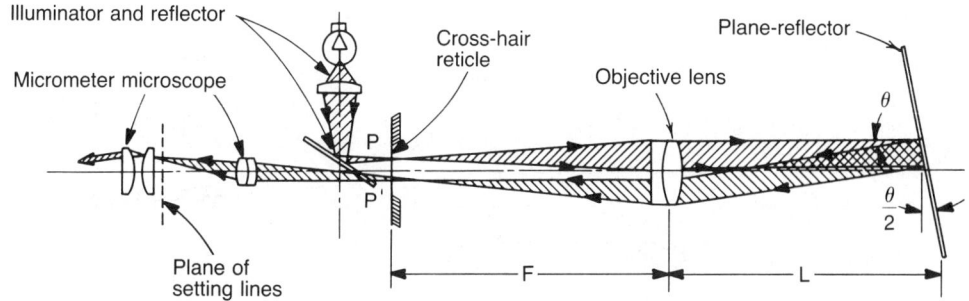

Illuminator and reflector

Cross-hair reticle

Plane-reflector

Micrometer microscope

Objective lens

θ

P

P'

$\frac{\theta}{2}$

Plane of setting lines

F

L

Fig. 16-89 Principle of autocollimation.

making measurements. A mirror smaller than the objective will send rays back through different portion of the objective, depending on where its center is located with respect to the optical axis. This causes readings to vary unless the objective is free of all aberrations, which is most unlikely. One test for quality of an autocollimator is to move a ⅛ in. (3 mm) wide slit in front of the objective with the reflector mirror fixed while observing whether the image shifts noticeably.

If the mirror is not flat, it will not focus the returning image and present an undefined reference plane. Hence high-quality autocollimator mirrors are held to flatness tolerance of ¼ fringe or better. At first glance it might seem that there should be no limit to the distance between an autocollimator and the reflecting mirror because they are separated by light that is collimated (has parallel rays). In practice, however, limitations arise from several sources. One source is that the light is never perfectly collimated. Another more direct limit is set by simple geometry. Assume a mirror is centered on an axis a distance L away from the objective of diameter C (see Fig. 16-90). When $L = C/\theta$, no light whatsoever is returned to the autocollimator. For a 2 in. diam. objective, a mirror tilt of 10 arc second leads to $L_{max} = 700$ in. (18 m). In practice, however, the mirror could not be farther away than a fraction of this amount.

It is important to remember that the air path between the mirror and the autocollimator is a real part of the optical system. Measurements to 1 arc second over distances up to 5 feet (1.5 m) in a reasonably quiet environment seldom cause trouble. However, when higher resolution or longer distances, or both, are required, close attention must be paid to adequate shielding of the air path from drafts and especially temperature gradients. Even a simple cardboard tube can be helpful for shielding.

Photoelectric Autocollimators. Autocollimators that replace the judgement of the human eye with appropriate photoelectric systems have some important advantages that can outweigh their increased cost and complexity. Setting accuracy is improved and no longer differs between observers. Readings can be made remotely and monitored continuously when required. Such autocollimators come in sizes from 1 in. (with null-setting sensitivity better than 0.1 arc second) to very large instruments with 10 in. objectives. Some provide merely a photoelectric null setting without measuring capability, while others have analog or digital readout with ranges from 10 seconds to a full degree or more.

In the system shown in Fig. 16-91, the illuminated target reticle slit is imaged back in its own plane through the autocollimator objective and reflecting mirror, but displaced radially for convenience. It is then reimaged onto a vibrating slit by means of a relay lens. Behind the slit is a photocell whose output is now modulated by the vibrating slit, which makes possible the phase discrimination required to make the amplified output sensitive to the direction as well as the amount of mirror rotation from a central null position. Such a system can be used to read mirror tilt in analog fashion on the meter. If

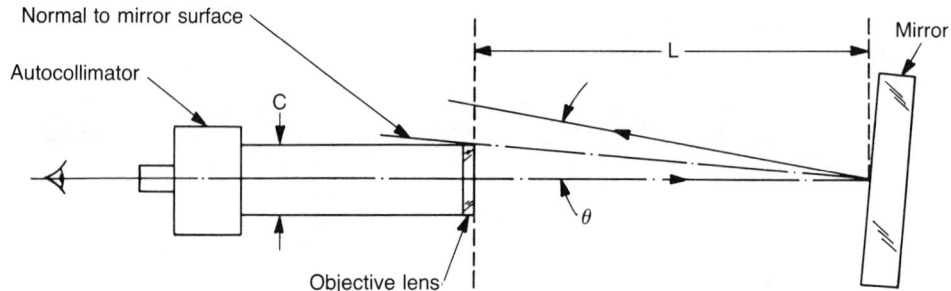

Fig. 16-90 No light is reflected back into the autocollimator when $L(\theta) \geqq C$.

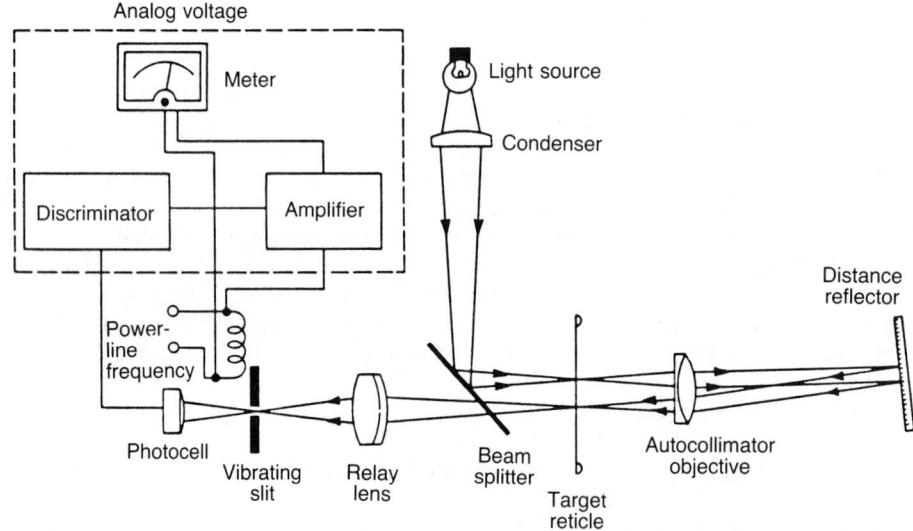

Fig. 16-91 Schematic of photoelectric autocollimator.

the vibrating slit assembly is moved with a precision micrometer, a reading is obtained with the meter acting merely as a null indicator. In the latter case, the electronics need no longer behave linearly and may be simplified. A sensitivity of 0.1 arc second is readily obtainable.

A different type of system is shown in Fig. 16-92. Here an entire grid pattern is imaged back on itself by the autocollimator optics. As a result, what a photodetector sees when the mirror tilts are periodic changes in intensity; the period is a function of grid spacing and the focal length of the objective and can vary from 10 arc seconds to 10 minutes of arc. Corresponding ranges vary from 1 to 3°. Keeping track of these periods is equivalent to digitizing the angle of tilt and may be all that is required. For highest sensitivity, the analog position between periods can also be recorded. An important advantage of this approach is that a much larger part of the field is optically active, so that the systems can be made relatively compact even in applications where high sensitivity is combined with a long angular range. The illumination is much more effectively utilized resulting in excellent signal-to-noise ratio.

Calibration. The only effective method for calibrating autocollimators is to monitor output or readings as the reference mirror is tilted through accurately controlled angles.

The problem of how to generate small angles accurate to 1 arc second or better has been solved by designing special sine-bar fixtures with a precisely defined axis at one end, while at the other end a well-defined cylinder is raised or lowered with a special micrometer or with gage blocks. A fixed wedge can also be used to calibrate an autocollimator, however, a fixed wedge only gives a specific angle whereas a sine bar can give an infinite number of angles.

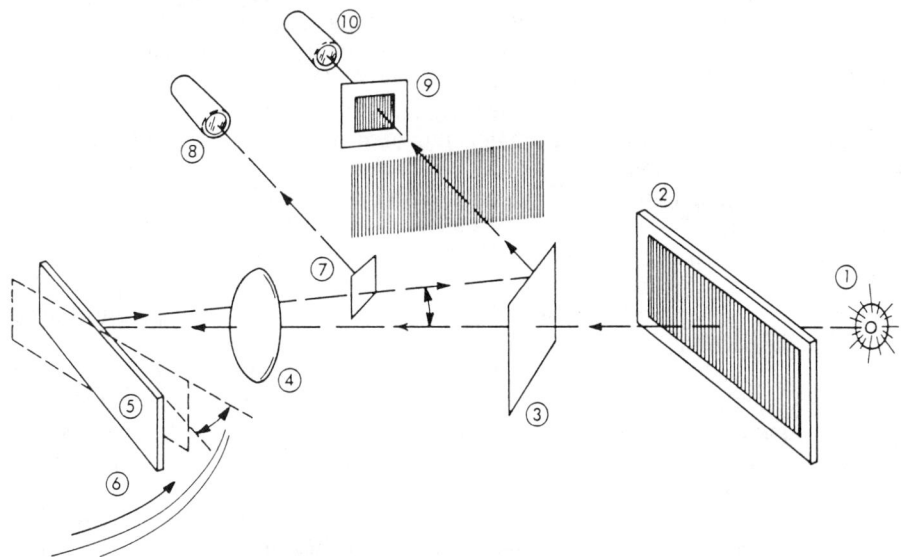

Fig. 16-92 Continuous photoelectric autocollimator. Light from a monochromatic source (1) passes through a grid (2), a beam splitter (3), a collimating lens (4), and strikes a mirror (5) mounted on the rotating specimen being tested (6). The image is reflected back into the autocollimator, where it is directed by a beam splitter (7) to the stability reference photosensor (8). The image is also reflected by beam splitter (3) through a second grid (9) to the control photosensor (10), which generates a periodic signal as mirror (5) is rotated.

Checking Way Straightness. In designing for applications of an autocollimator, the central thought must be that these instruments are sensitive to angular tilts only, not to translations. In this respect, they differ from alignment telescopes. A series of measurements cannot be better than the angular stability of the surface on which the autocollimator rests. This tends to show up in such applications as the checking of a machine bed when the instrument is mounted on no more than a floor-supported tripod. A platform fastened directly to the casting involved is likely to be much more stable.

Checking the straightness and flatness of a way or equivalent surface is one of the most frequent applications of an autocollimator. The first objective is to convert deviation from straightness stepwise into successive tilts of a mirror carriage as it is moved along a straight line in increments just equal to the distance between locating pads. At each point, readings are taken from a rigidly mounted autocollimator. These readings are then converted back to a profile curve. Note that such a test says nothing about the geometry between the contact points of the mirror carriage; this requires some other type of assurance or traverses with a carriage of shorter base length. It may seem odd to go through such a double conversion to angles and back when all that is wanted is to measure straightness or flatness; manual recording of readings and subsequent graphing can be tedious and time consuming.

The photoelectric autocollimator can be interfaced to a computer that enables the time for straightness checks and calibration of surface plates for flatness to be considerably reduced. The computer with an interactive program permits three X, three Y, and two diagonal generator lines to be used with a printout of results including a straightness graph and an isometric plot of the surface plate.

COORDINATE MEASURING MACHINES

With the advent of numerically controlled machine tools, the demand has grown for a means to support this equipment with faster first-piece inspection and, in many cases, 100% dimensional inspection. To fill this need, coordinate measuring machines (CMMs) were developed in the early 1960s. A few CMMs can even be used as layout machines before machining and for checking feature locations after machining. Thus the CMM plays a vital role in the mechanization of the inspection process because it is a universal measuring machine.

Currently, coordinate measuring machines are being used in one of three ways in a manufacturing firm. The simplest approach is to place the CMM at the end of the production line or in an inspection area. With this approach, the CMM is used to inspect the first part of a production run to verify the machine setup. Once the setup is verified, it then measures parts on a random basis. For many applications, this permits the best approach to inspection.

Another approach is to incorporate the coordinate measuring machine between two workcenters and then measure 100% of the parts produced at the first center before any secondary operations are performed at the second workcenter. This approach is possible because CMMs are capable of measuring three-dimensional geometry and making many different measurements within a short period of time. When this approach is used, the CMM indirectly controls the production process. In this setting, however, the CMM must be "hardened" to perform in the shop environment or it must be completely enclosed to provide an optimum environment for part inspection.

A third approach integrates the CMM into the production line. This permits the CMM to directly control the production process. In operation, an integrated system would measure the workpiece, compare the measurements with required dimensions, and if necessary, automatically adjust the machine controls so that the part is manufactured within the required specifications.

A basic coordinate measuring machine consists of four elements: (1) the machine structure, which basically is an X-Y-Z positioning device; (2) the probing system used to collect raw data on the part and provide input to the control system; (3) machine control and computer hardware; and (4) the software for three-dimensional geometry analysis. The measuring envelope is defined by the X, Y, and Z travel of the machine. A diagram of a coordinate measuring system is shown in Fig. 16-93.

Although a variety of machine designs and configurations exist all designs incorporate the same fundamental concept of three coordinate axes. Each axis is square in its own relationship to the reference plane created by the other two axes. Each axis is also fitted with a linear measurement transducer for positional feedback. This allows position displays within the envelope to be independent of any fixed reference point.

The most common reference systems in use are stainless steel and glass scales. Both systems utilize noncontact, electro-optical reader heads for determining the exact position of the machine. Stainless steel reference systems are widely used in shop environments because the difference in the coefficient of expansion between the stainless steel scale and workpiece is minimal. Glass scale reference systems are generally used in controlled environments because of the difference in the coefficient of expansion between glass and the metal workpiece. Although glass scales can be more accurate than stainless steel scales, the advent of computer compensation all but eliminates any performance differences.

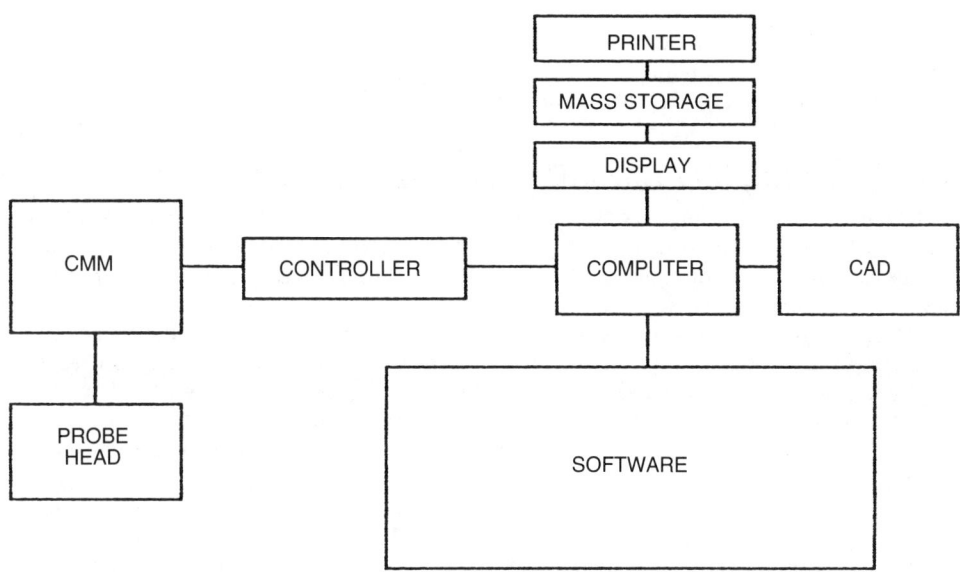

Fig. 16-93 Diagram of a coordinate measuring system. (*Courtesy Multi-Metrics, Inc.*)

The worktable of the machine generally contains tapped holes to facilitate the clamping and locating of parts. It may be made from granite because of its stability in various environments. Electronic or solid probes are inserted in to the probe arm, which is supported by cantilever, bridge, gantry, or column members. Probe arm movement is guided by means of frictionless air bearings or mechanical bearings.

Coordinate measuring is a two or three-dimensional process that determines the position of holes, surfaces, centerlines, and slopes. Up to six sides of a cube-shaped part may be inspected without repositioning.

In a typical operation, the part is placed on the table of the CMM at a random location; generally this is approximately central to the machine axes to access all the part surfaces to be inspected with the probe. Depending on the size of the part and the type of probes used, the part may need to be clamped to the machine table. If multiple inspections of similar parts are required, a reference location point may be established with a reference precision cube or sphere. The probe is then moved, manually or by machine control, until contact is made with desired part features. Reader heads, traveling on each axis along built-in axis measuring scales, transfer the instantaneous machine position through the digital display to the computer interface. The dimensional and geometric elements may then be calculated, compared, and evaluated, or stored, or printed out as required.

Advantages. Some of the advantages of using CMMs over conventional gaging techniques are flexibility, reduced setup time, improved accuracy, reduced operator influence, and improved productivity.[7]

Flexibility. Coordinate measuring machines are essentially universal measuring machines and do not need to be dedicated to any single or particular measuring task. They can measure practically any dimensional characteristic of virtually any part configuration, including cams, gears, and contoured surfaces. No special fixtures or gages are required; because electronic probe contact is light, most parts can be inspected without being clamped to a surface plate.

Reduced Setup Time. Establishing part alignment and appropriate reference points are very time consuming with conventional surface-plate inspection techniques. These procedures are greatly simplified or virtually eliminated through software available on computer-assisted or computer-controlled CMMs.

Such software allows the operator to define the part's orientation on the CMM and all coordinate data are subsequently automatically corrected for any misalignment between the part reference system and the machine coordinates. A CMM with sophisticated software can inspect parts in a single setup without the need to orient the part for access to all features even when a fourth axis (rotary table) is employed.

Improved Accuracy. All measurements on a CMM are taken from a common geometrically fixed measuring system, eliminating the introduction and accumulation of errors that can result with hardgage inspection methods and transfer techniques. Moreover, measuring all significant features of a part in one setup prevents the introduction of errors due to setup changes.

Reduced Operator Influence. The use of digital readouts eliminates the subjective interpretation of readings common with dial or vernier-type measuring devices. Operator "feel" is virtually eliminated with modern electronic probe systems. All CMMs have canned software routines for typical part features, such as bores or center distances. In the part-program-assisted mode, the operator positions the machine; once the intial position has been set, the machine is under the control of a program that eliminates operator choice. In the computer numerically controlled (CNC) mode, motor-driven machines run totally unattended by operators. Also, automatic data recording, available on most machines, prevents errors in transcribing readings to the inspection report. This all adds up to the fact that less skilled operators can be readily instructed to perform relatively complex inspection procedures.

Improved Productivity. All the factors previously mentioned help to make CMMs more productive than conventional inspection techniques. Further dramatic productivity improvements are realized through the computational and analytical capabilities of associated data handling systems, including calculators and all levels of computers.

Machine Configurations. A variety of machine configurations is available from the manufacturers of CMMs. Each configuration has advantages that make it suitable for particular applications. A total of 11 different machine configurations exist; however, some of these configurations are modifications of one of the five primary configurations: cantilever, bridge, column, gantry, and horizontal arm.

Cantilever. Cantilever-type coordinate measuring machines employ three movable components moving along mutually perpendicular guideways. The probe is attached to the first component, which moves vertically (Z direction) relative to the second. The second component moves horizontally (Y direction) relative to the third. The third component is supported at one end only, cantilever fashion, and moves horizontally (X direction) relative to the machine base. The workpiece is supported on the worktable. A typical machine of this configuration is shown in Fig. 16-94a. A modification of the fixed-table cantilever configuration is the moving-table cantilever CMM (see Fig. 16-94b).

Cantilever-type CMMs are usually the smallest in size and lowest in cost and occupy a minimum of floor space. This configuration permits a completely unobstructed work area, allowing full access to load, inspect, and unload parts that may be larger than the table. It also provides convenient, close grouping of machine controls. The single overhanging beam support for the probe head may limit accuracy if a special compensation is not built into the cantilever arm. The movement of the probe from one inspection point to another is usually performed manually by the machine operator; however, joystick and CNC machines are available.

Bridge. Bridge-type coordinate measuring machines employ three movable components moving along mutually perpendicular guideways. The probe is attached to the first component, which moves vertically (Z direction) relative to the second. The second component moves horizontally (Y direction) relative to the third. The third component is supported on two legs that reach down to opposite sides of the machine base and

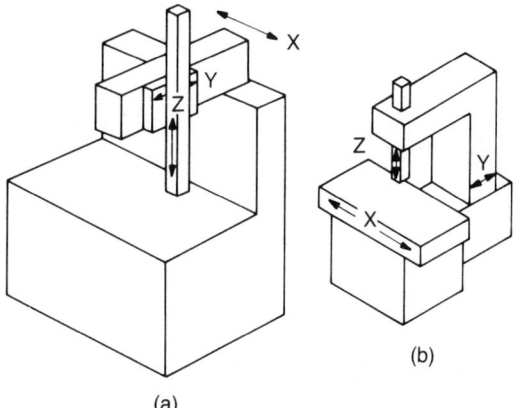

Fig. 16-94 Cantilever-type coordinate measuring machines: (a) fixed table and (b) moving table. (*Courtesy The American Society of Mechanical Engineers*)

moves horizontally (X direction) relative to the base. The workpiece is supported on the base. A typical machine of this configuration is shown in Fig. 16-95a. This type of configuration is often referred to as a moving-bridge or a traveling-bridge CMM.

One modification of the moving-bridge configuration has each end of the bridge structure fixed to the machine base (see Fig. 16-95b). The workpiece is mounted on a separate table that moves horizontally (X direction) relative to the base. The configuration is referred to as a fixed-bridge CMM.

Another modification of the bridge configuration has two bridge-shaped components (see Fig. 16-95c). One of these bridges is fixed at each end to the machine base. The other bridge, which is an inverted L-shape, moves horizontally (X direction) on guideways in the fixed bridge and machine base.

A third modification of moving-bridge configuration is the central-bridge drive (see Fig. 16-95d). The drive forces are applied to the center of mass of the bridge assembly. This eliminates pitching and yawing moments on the bridge assembly allowing higher acceleration and deceleration rates.

The bridge-type CMM is the most popular configuration. The double-sided support of this CMM provides more support for large and medium-sized machines. The bridge can slide back on the base to give complete accessibility to the working area for safe, easy loading and unloading of parts.

Traveling-bridge CMMs have longer Y strokes for less cost than do cantilever-type CMMs. However, because of the weight of the extra support, the inertia of the moving mass is greater than in the cantilever configuration. In addition, the parts being measured with this type of CMM cannot be wider than the clearance between the two sides of the bridge.

Column. Column-type CMMs are similar in construction to accurate jig boring machines (see Fig. 16-96). The column moves in a vertical (Z) direction only, and a two-axis saddle permits movement in the horizontal (X and Y) direction.

Column-type CMMs are often referred to as universal measuring machines rather than CMMs by manufacturers and are considered gage room instruments rather than production floor machines.

Gantry. Gantry-type CMMs employ three movable components moving along mutually perpendicular guideways (see Fig. 16-97). The probe is attached to the probe quill, which moves vertically (Z direction) relative to cross beam. The probe quill is mounted in a carriage that moves horizontally (Y direction) along the cross beam. The

16-93

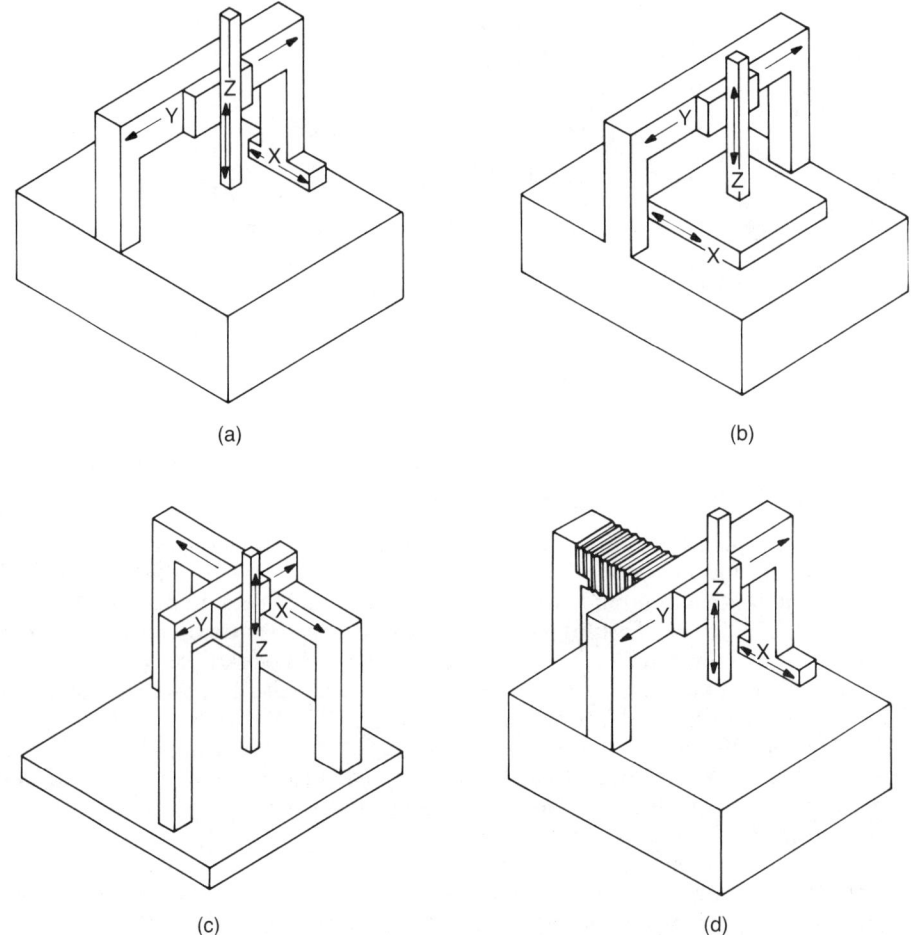

Fig. 16-95 Bridge-type coordinate measuring machines: (*a*) moving bridge, (*b*) fixed bridge, (*c*) L-shaped bridge, and (*d*) central-drive bridge. (*Courtesy The American Society of Mechanical Engineers*)

cross beam is supported and moves in the X direction along two elevated rails, which are supported by columns attached to the floor.

The gantry-type configuration was initially introduced in the early 1960s to inspect large parts such as airplane fuselages, automobile bodies, ship propellers, and diesel engine blocks. The open design permits the operator to remain close to the part being inspected while minimizing the inertia of the moving machine parts and maintaining structural stiffness.

Horizontal Arm. Several different types of horizontal arm CMMs are available (see Fig. 16-98). As is typical of all CMMs, the horizontal arm configuration employs three movable components moving along mutually perpendicular guideways. In the moving-ram design, the probe is attached to the horizontal arm, which moves in a horizontal Y direction (see view *a*). The ram is encased in a carriage that moves in a vertical (Z) direction and is supported on a column that moves horizontally (X direction) relative to the base.

In the moving-table design, the probe is attached to the horizontal arm, which is permanently attached at one end only to a carriage that moves in a vertical (Z) direction

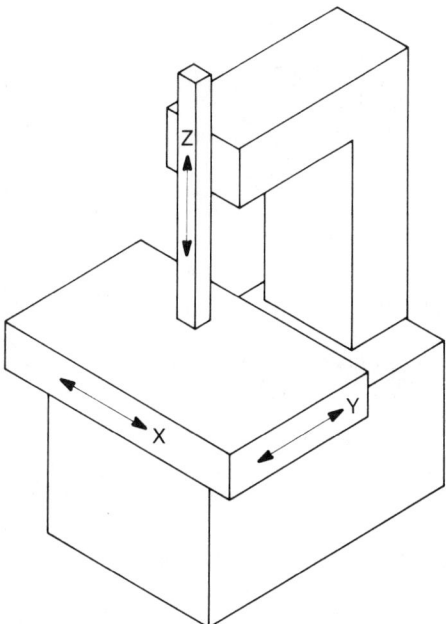

Fig. 16-96 Column-type coordinate measuring machines. (*Courtesy The American Society of Mechanical Engineers*)

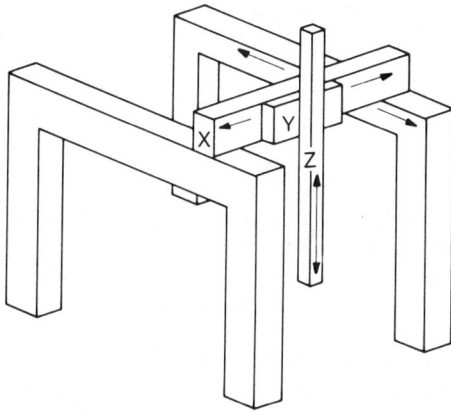

Fig. 16-97 Gantry-type coordinate measuring machines. (*Courtesy The American Society of Mechanical Engineers*)

(see view *b*) on the column. The arm support and table move horizontally (X and Y directions) relative to the machine base.

In the fixed-table design, the probe is attached to the horizontal arm, which is supported cantilever style at the arm support and moves in a vertical (Z) direction (see view *c*). The arm support moves horizontally (X and Y directions) relative to the machine base. Parts to be inspected are mounted on the machine base. Horizontal arm CMMs are used to inspect the dimensional and geometric accuracy of a broad spectrum of machined or fabricated workpieces. Utilizing an electronic probe, these machines

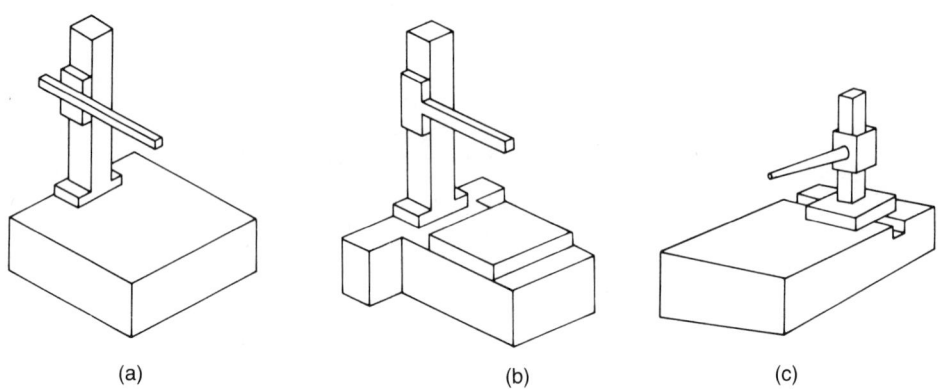

Fig. 16-98 Horizontal arm coordinate measuring machines: (a) moving ram, (b) moving table, and (c) fixed table. (*Courtesy The American Society of Mechanical Engineers*)

check parts in a mode similar to the way they are machined on horizontal machine tools. They are especially suited for measuring large gearcases and engine blocks, where high-precision bore alignment and geometry measurements are required. By incorporating a rotary table, four-axis capability is obtainable.

Probes. The utility of a coordinate measuring machine depends largely on the nature of the probing devices. Three types of probes are commonly used: (1) hard, (2) electronic, and (3) noncontact. A probe is selected according to the dimensional and geometrical requirements of the inspection process.

Hard Probes. Hard probes (see Fig. 16-99) consist of a shaft and probe tip mounted in various ways to the probe arm. A variety of probe tip shapes and sizes are available; the shape of the probe determines its application. Concial probes are used for locating holes; ball probes for establishing surface locations; cylindrical probes for checking slots and holes in sheet metal parts; and edge-finder probes are used for part alignment and measurement of flat surfaces or edges of part. Hard probes can only be used in small, manually operated CMMs when inspecting simple parts of a short production run.

Electronic Probes. Electronic probes are commonly classified into one of three categories: (1) switching, (2) proportional, and (3) nulling probes. Switching probes (see Fig. 16-100) are the most popular probes in use. This electronic probe, also called a touch probe, is an omnidirectional triggering device consisting of a probe body and a stylus; multiple stylus arrangements are also available. When the stylus is brought into contact with the workpiece, a signal is sent to the computer interface, indicating the instantaneous three-dimensional location of the stylus. All probe designs allow stylus overtravel, some by as much as 0.04 in. (1.0 mm) normal to probe axis and 0.08 in. (2.0 mm) perpendicular to the probe axis. When the deflection force is removed, the stylus returns to its initial position. Switching-type probes suffer from lobing due to stylus bending. This lobing effect is exacerbated by high trigger forces and long stylus extensions. Electronic touch probes are used on all CMMs.

Figure 16-101 shows an integrated probe system for CMMs. Fully automatic, and featuring a patented autochange joint, this motorized system exchanges probes and accessories onto probe heads. The rack locks and unlocks the joints, and stores alternate probe setups within the machines working envelope. The autojoint repositions the probe tip to within 40 μin. (1 μm) after a probe exchange.

Because of their design, proportional-type probes are used exclusively on CMMs that are controlled by direct computer control (DCC). This type of probe is designed for automatic scanning of profiles contained in section planes passing through the probe axis. The probe consists of transducer and a motorpowered, servocontrolled axis and

Fig. 16-99 Hard probes. (*Courtesy Sheffield Measurement, A Cross & Trecker Company*)

carries on its tip a servo-assisted feeler that is kept in contact with the surface to be inspected. The feeler generates an error signal, proportional to the pressure exerted on the surface, for the control of the probe motor. During the scanning operation, the probe applies a very light contact pressure to the part and reacts with its motor to profile variations whose amplitudes are smaller than the probe axis working stroke. Longer profile variations are in turn followed by the CMM axes that are coupled to the probe axis position through the control system. A typical proportional probe stroke is ±0.5 in. (±12.5 mm) from the center of probe axis stroke. Other probes with simultaneous radial and axial scanning capabilities are designed with the above concept.

Nulling probes are basically the same as the proportional probe with two major differences. First of all, it is more accurate than the proportional probe because the control system indicates the three-dimensional location of the stylus when the probe is at null condition (machine axis at rest). The second major difference is that the probe must leave the surface to proceed to the next inspection location whereas the proportional probe does not.

Noncontact Probes. Noncontact probes are used when fast, accurate measurements are required with no physical contact with the part. Several types of noncontact probes are used.

Optical probes are used when inspecting drawings, printed circuit boards, and small, fragile workpieces. When these probes are used, the basic measuring programs can still be used.

The two types of optical probes used on manual CMMs are a projection microscope and a centering microscope. On the projection microscope, the image under inspection is displayed on the screen. Part feature locations are obtained by moving the CMM to align the screen reticle to the feature. With the centering microscope, part feature

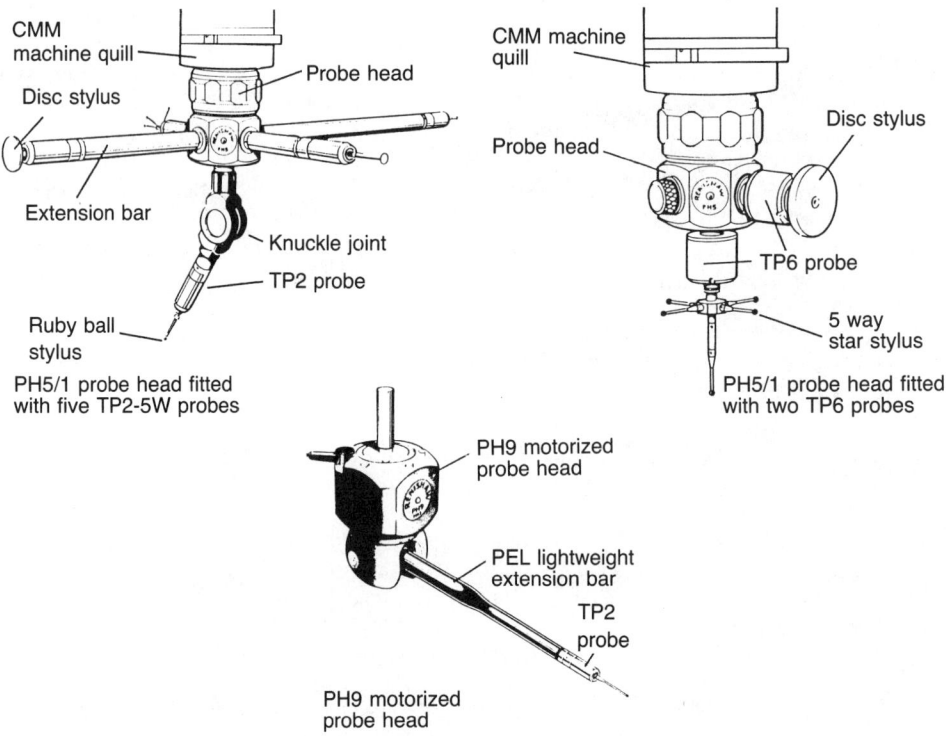

CMM machine quill

Probe head

Disc stylus

Extension bar

Knuckle joint

TP2 probe

Ruby ball stylus

PH5/1 probe head fitted with five TP2-5W probes

CMM machine quill

Probe head

Disc stylus

TP6 probe

5 way star stylus

PH5/1 probe head fitted with two TP6 probes

PH9 motorized probe head

PEL lightweight extension bar

TP2 probe

PH9 motorized probe head

Fig. 16-100 Probe system components. (*Courtesy Renishaw, Inc.*)

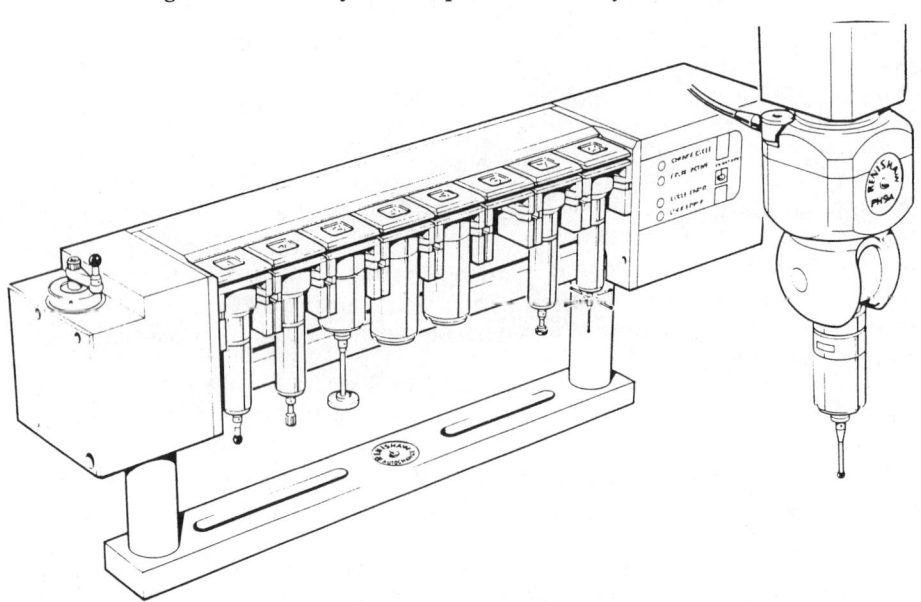

Fig. 16-101 Integrated probe change system for CMMs. (*Courtesy Renishaw, Inc.*)

locations are obtained in the same way as the projection microscope as the user looks through the eyepiece.

Another manufacturer has developed an acoustical probe that senses contact with the workpiece by the sound wave generated by the touch rather than by any physical displacement of the probe. At contact, vibration travels up the probe and is picked up by a sensitive acoustic microphone inside the head.

A third type of noncontact probe contains a laser light source that projects a small diameter spot on the part surface. A digital, solid-state sensor detects the position of this spot and computes part surface location by optical triangulation.

Accessories. Various accessories used in conjunction with the probes enhance the capability coordinate measuring machines.

Indexable Probe Heads. Indexable probe heads permit orienting the measuring probe in horizontal and vertical planes to keep the probe normal to the plane desired. This feature gives the CMM the capability to reach and inspect geometrical elements that are not aligned to the machine axes. In addition, the use of indexable head is generally required when inspecting and scanning complex surfaces. Indexable probe heads, however, tend to shrink CMM measuring volume.

A microprocessor control system is usually supplied with indexable heads to operate as a power drive and intelligent interface between machine control and indexing heads. Head plane wobble during rotation is compensated for through a special software program that runs on the control system computer.

Rotary Tables. Rotary tables are especially useful when inspecting complex, multi-faced parts or workpieces with a rotation axis such as cams, gears, and rotors. A variety of sizes are available to accommodate different size workpieces. Rotary tables expand CMM measuring volume.

Rotary tables can be controlled manually or automatically. When automatically controlled tables are used, special software programs interact with the machine controls to control table movement and provide misalignment compensation.

Machine Control. Besides their physical configurations, coordinate measuring machines can also be classified according to their mode of operation: manual, manual computer-assisted, motorized computer-assisted, and direct computer controlled.[8] Manual machines have a free-floating, solid probe that the operator moves along the machine's coordinate axes to establish each measurement. Digital readouts, associated with each axis, provide the measurement values that the operator notes and records manually. In some instances, a simple digital printout device may be used to record the readings.

Manual computer-assisted CMMs use a data processing system to manipulate the measurements, which are still made by manually moving the probe through a series of measurement locations. Solid or electronic probes may be used on this type of machine. The data processing may be accomplished by a special microprocessor-based digital readout, a programmable calculator, or a full-fledged computer.

Depending on the sophistication of the data processing system and associated software, computer-assisted CMMs perform functions ranging from simple inch/millimeter conversion to automatic three-dimensional compensation for misalignment and a host of geometric and analytical measuring tasks. Storing of predetermined program sequences and operator prompting are also available to create part programs.

In effect, the computer system can carry out all the calculations and analyses required to arrive at dimensional and tolerance evaluations and can lead the operator through a prescribed series of positioning and measuring moves. Data recording is usually included with computer-assisted CMMs.

A motorized computer-assisted CMM has all the features of a computer-assisted CMM, but uses power-operated motions under the control of the operator, who uses a joystick. The part program is generated and stored in the computer, which determines the inspection sequence and compares measured results with nominal values and tolerances for automatic GO/NOT GO decision making. Most motorized CMMs also provide means for disengaging the power drive to permit manual manipulation of the machine motions. Some machines use direct-current servomotors and pneumatically operated friction clutches to reduce the effect of collisons, and all permit drive disengagement for manual movements.

Direct computer controlled (DCC) CMMs are equivalent to CNC machine tools. A computer controls all the motions of a motorized CMM. In addition, the computer also performs all the data processing functions of the most sophisticated computer-assisted CMM. Both control and measuring cycles are under program control. Most DCC machines offer various programming options, including program storage and, in some instances, off-line programming capability.

Software. Beyond the microprocessor-based digital readouts, which were initially developed to provide basic measurement data processing capabilities for manual coordinate measuring machines, there is also a need to solve sophisticated measuring problems involving three-dimensional geometry and to provide more flexible general-purpose programming capabilities to solve special measuring problems.[9] Many CMM manufacturers offer a series of data processing equipment for such purposes, including full DCC capability.

The key to the productivity of all forms of computer-assisted CMMs lies in the sophistication and ease of use of the associated software. Software is the most important element in any coordinate measuring system because its power determines how many part features can be measured, and its ease of use determines the extent to which the machine is used.

The functional capabilities of CMM software depend on the number and type of application programs available. Virtually all CMMs offer some means of compensation for misalignment between the part reference system and the machine coordinates by probing selected points; some are limited to alignment in one plane, while most machines provide full three-dimensional alignment. Once the designated points have been taken, the program calculates the misalignment and applies the appropriate correction to all subsequent measurement readings.

Conversion between Cartesian, polar, and, in some instances, spherical coordinate systems is also commonly handled. Most systems also calculate the deviation of measurements from nominal dimensions of the part stored in memory and flag out-of-tolerance conditions.

Geometric functions handled by CMM software define geometric elements—such as points, lines, planes, circles, cylinders, spheres, and cones—from a series of point measurements and solve measurement problems dealing with the interaction of such geometric elements. Such software can determine, for example, the intersection of two circles established on the basis of a selected number of measurements or it can establish the angle of intersection of two surfaces.

Many software packages also provide a means for evaluating geometric tolerance conditions by determining various types of form and positional relationships (such as flatness, straightness, circularity, parallelism, or squareness) for single features and related groups of features.

Best-fit programs can identify the location of a part finished to size within a rough part from which it is to be made, to optimize the machining-allowance distribution; maximum material condition (MMC) programs evaluate features dimensioned according to MMC principles.

Other application programs include automatic part scanning for digitizing profiles and a variety of special programs to handle the inspection of special shapes such as gears and cams. Statistical analysis software available provides for graphic data display, including histograms.

The accuracy of some CMMs is enhanced beyond the mechanical rigidity and stability of the machine with the aid of software geometry error compensation. A typical compensation package automatically interpolates the probe position throughout the measurement envelope. It corrects each axis for inaccuracies in pitch, yaw, scale errors, straightness, and squareness to the other axes. This software package is usually an integral part of the system software provided with the machine.

Universal CMM with Laser Interferometer. Figure 16-102, shows a CNC universal CMM with laser interferometer position feedback. The machine is a single fixed-column design with up to five servo-controlled programmable axes—three linear (X-, Y-, and Z-axes) and two rotary (C-axis "normalcy" and optional rotary table A-axis). A laser measuring system is used for the three linear axes, with optical encoders for the two rotary axes. Positioning accuracy in the X-, Y-, or Z-axes is 0.000024 in. Linear axis repeatability is ±0.000006 in. Resolution when used in the inch mode is as follows;

X—0.000001 in.
Y—0.000001 in.
Z—0.000001 in.
C—0.00001 revolution
A—0.00001 revolution

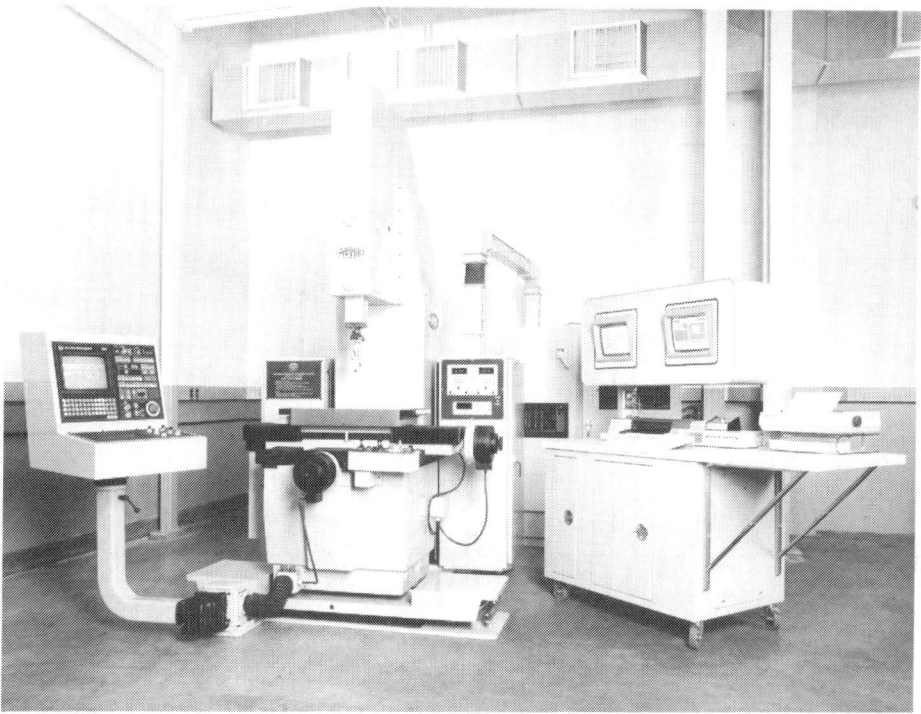

Fig. 16-102 CNC universal coordinate measuring machine with laser interferometer position feedback. (*Courtesy Moore Special Tool Co., Inc.*)

The spindle is CNC controlled to maintain "normalcy" of the probe to the part being measured, thereby estimating the need for mapping probe tip geometry.

CNC Control. A separate CNC machine-tool control station is mounted near the machine. Some of the advantages of this type of control are:

- Allows programming in standard, widely understood machine-tool language, using G-functions, departure commands, and M-functions.

- The same part program used to manufacture the part can be used to measure deviation from the programmed path.
- Proven communications interfaces.
- Programs written to manufacture the part, usually in a form like APT, can be post-processed.
- There is compatibility with local area network

Probes. A variety of analog-type, LVDT probes are available. These probes provide accuracy and repeatability, high resolution, and low gaging forces, measuring only the deviation from the programmed path or position.

Software. The metrology software system Fig. 16-103 is a versatile inspection and analysis package conforming to definitions specified in ANSI Y14.5.

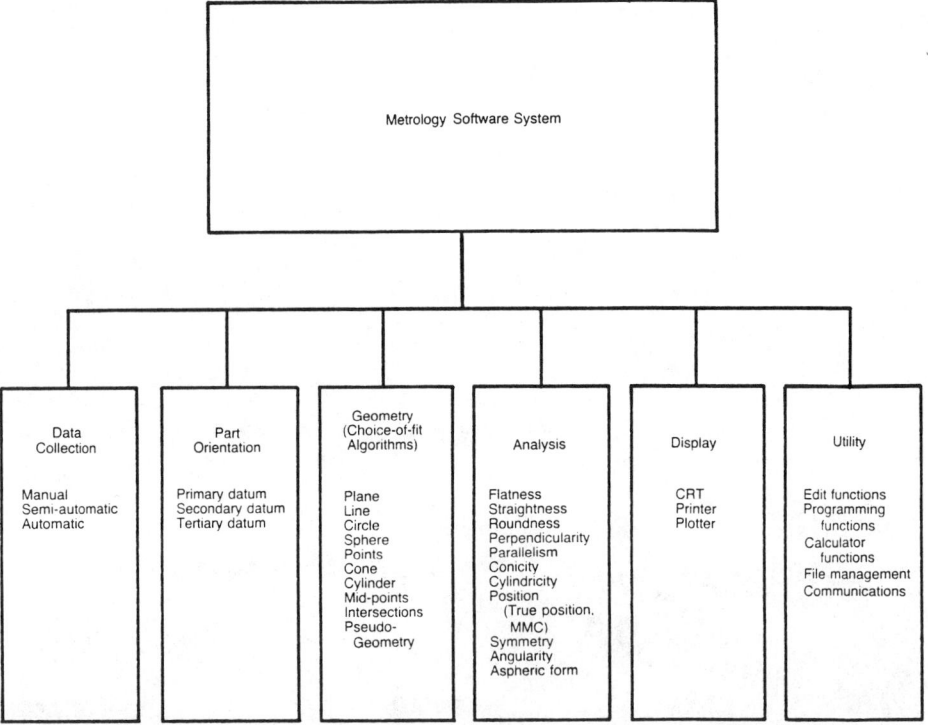

Fig. 16-103 Metrology software system. (*Courtesy Moore Special Tool Co., Inc.*)

By offering menu-driven functions and choice-of-fit algorithms (unique mathematical options), this unique system provides the operator with the needed power and flexibility to handle today's high-precision inspection requirements.

The data-collection process can be point-to-point or continuous path, extending flexibility. Other functions provide for part skew, a flexible geometry construction package, and an analysis module for both graphic and numeric results.

Software design conforms to U.S. MIL Standard 2169 quality assurance.

Five-axis Automatic Inspection Center. The five-axis automatic inspection center shown in Fig. 16-104 was designed to provide a high speed, environmentally enclosed measuring system directly on the manufacturing line. It can be used as a stand alone cell, as a station in a traditional manufacturing line, or as the AGV-linked inspection component in a flexible manufacturing system. The workpiece to be inspected is merely placed on a coded pallet located on the shuttle which carries the palletized workpiece to

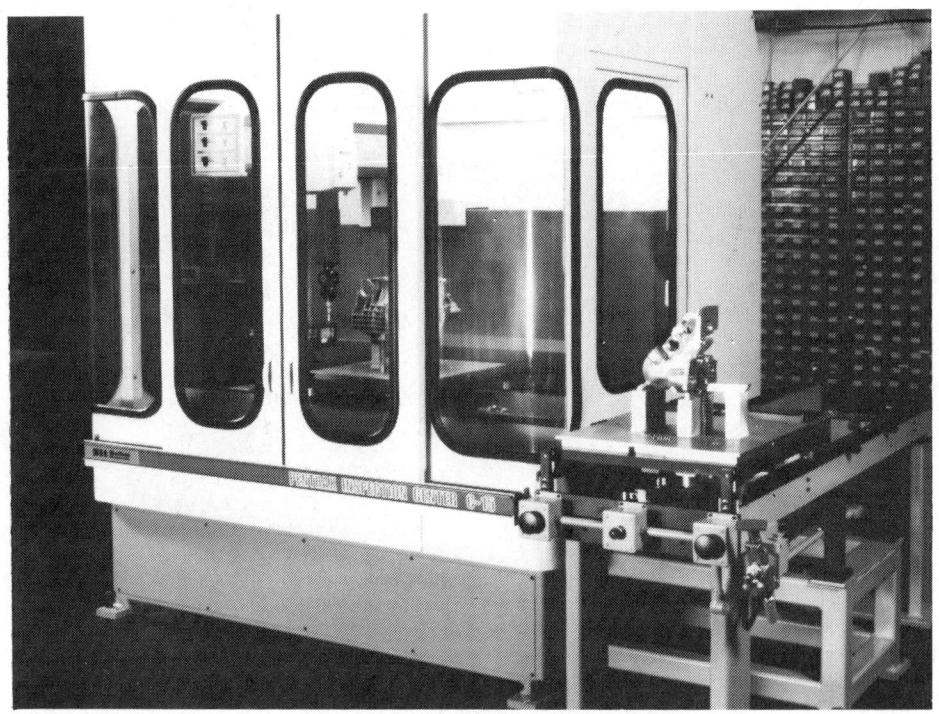

Fig. 16-104 Five-axis automatic inspection center. (*Courtesy Sheffield Measurement, A Cross & Trecker Company*)

the measuring position where the inspection begins automatically. An eight-station automated probe changer (16 stations optional) requires only one calibration for each probe tip. Up to 100 tip locators are stored in the systems controller, so there is no need for operator recalibration if probe configurations are not altered.

The system will measure hole and shaft diameters, distances, concentricities between hole and shaft axes, distances between parallel planes, the angle between two planes, and angles between axes of holes and shafts. It also automatically calculates geometric relationships among the various elements. An automatic skewed-axis compensating feature eliminates the need for precise workpiece positioning.

The host computer's multi-tasking capability allows off-line programming, editing and automatic statistical analysis while measuring the workpiece. For a statistical summary report for a feature of any part, the programmer simply defines the characteristic to be monitored, the type of analysis to be run for that characteristic, and the lot size. As soon as the system reads the pallet and identifies the part programs, it begins retrieving past measurements for the specified features from its data base. Then, as each of those features is being measured, it automatically compares current measurements with past data, performs the defined statistical analyses, and reports variances to the operator or an off-line terminal.

Vacuum Workholding Fixture for CMMs. The fixture (the Rayco Universal fixture system, patent no. 4,805,887) shown in Fig. 16-105 is a unique new system that uses suction cups and magnets in a universal-design vacuum plate to hold articles for measurement on coordinate measuring machines. The major components of the system include a universal vacuum plate, vacuum pump, manifold and a full complement of vacuum cup and magnetic holders and standoffs. Plates are available that range in size up to 30 in. (760 mm) square to fit major brand CMMs. The plate is made of ½ in.

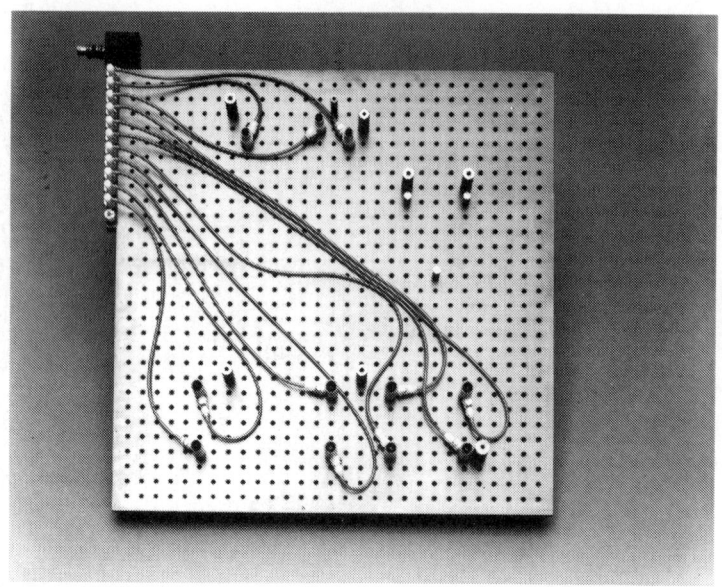

Fig. 16-105 R & R fixture. (*Courtesy Rayco Mfg., Inc.*)

(12.7 mm) thick anodized aluminum and has multiple pre-drilled mounting holes arranged in a precise matrix pattern so that exact distances between holes can be determined and recorded. The holes are labeled for easy identification and mapping, either manually or by computer program. In a typical application, one or more article holders are mounted on a fixture vacuum plate in the desired clamping position for the part being measured (see Fig. 16-106). Clamp positions are identified from the grid coordinates on the plate and recorded for future re-establishment.

When the part(s) has been properly staged, vacuum pressure can be applied in variable increments to secure the part for measurement by the CMM probe. The power, normally from the CMM, is converted to vacuum by the system's pump and transferred via manifold to the plate, and in turn to the suction cups.

After measurements have been taken, the inspected article can then be easily removed, and additional like parts mounted and measured immediately. Or, the holders can be quickly relocated, added, to or deleted for securing parts having a different size or shape.

Most CMM programs include the ability to add text statements for placing the hold down cups or magnets and for locating the standoffs for repeatable part programs.

The system is not limited to CMMs. It can be used wherever variable fixturing is needed.

MACHINE VISION SYSTEMS[10]

Many individuals within the industrial and research communities consider machine vision to be a subset of the larger field of artificial intelligence. Others view machine vision as a separate topic based on a number of other fields such as image processing, pattern recognition, and scene analysis. In either case, machine vision represents a relatively complex subject drawing on many technical disciplines.

To be classified as machine vision, the system must be capable of performing four primary functions.[11] The first function is image formation. In image formation, incoming light is received from an object or scene and then converted into electrical signals. In the next step, the signals are organized in a form compatible with computer processing capabilities. The third function is to analyze and measure various features or character-

Fig. 16-106 Parts mounted on an R & R fixture for inspection. (*Courtesy Rayco Mfg., Inc.*)

istics of these signals that represent the image. Finally, a machine vision system interprets the data so that some useful decisions can be made about the object or scene being studied.

This description of machine vision makes a clear distinction between several broad categories of optical sensing equipment currently used in manufacturing applications. For example, optical comparators, which are used to project silhouettes of a workpiece on a viewing screen, would not fall under this classification because they do not possess the image analysis and interpretation capability normally associated with a machine vision system. Similarly excluded would be equipment such as photocells and other light-beam equipment for measuring presence or dimensions and closed-circuit television systems where the monitors are observed by human operators for off-line inspection applications.

Applications. Machine vision as applied to manufacturing extracts information from visual sensors to enable machines to make intelligent decisions. Such decisions are needed in quality control (detection of defects), process monitoring (prevention of defects), product routing (parts acquisition and sorting), and statistical reporting (performance evaluation).

The three main industrial application categories are inspection, identification, and machine guidance. Among the inspection tasks are the following:

- *Gaging.* Checking to make sure that dimensions fall within acceptable tolerance bands.
- *Verification.* Checking to make sure that a product is present, complete, or the right one in the proper orientation.
- *Flaw detection.* Checking for unwanted features of unknown shape anywhere on the observed portion of the product.

Among the identification tasks are the following:

- *Symbol recognition.* Deciding which one of many possible symbols is present in a given location. Examples of this application are reading serial numbers or bar codes.
- *Object recognition.* Deciding which of many possible objects is present by examining features of the object under test.

Among the guidance functions performed by machine vision are the following:

- *Object location.* Two or three-dimensional determination of position and orientation for purposes of part acquisition, transfer, and assembly.
- *Tracking.* Continuously updating the position of a feature relative to a tool to control continuous processes such as gluing or welding.

System Operation. The machine vision process consists of four basic steps (see Fig. 16-107).[12] In the first step, an image of the scene is formed. The formed image is usually transformed into digital data that can be used by the computer. In the third step, the characteristics of the image are enhanced and analyzed. Finally, the image is interpreted, conclusions are drawn, and a decision is made so that some action can be taken.

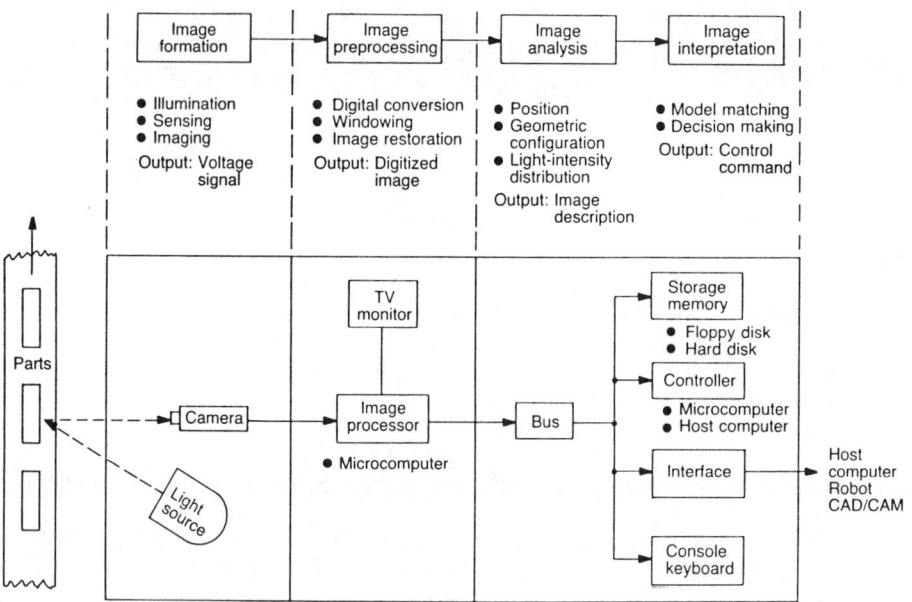

Fig. 16-107 Typical machine vision process. (*Courtesy Tech Tran Consultants*)

Image Interpretation. When the system has completed the process of analyzing image features some conclusion must be made about the findings, such as the verification that a part is or is not present, the identification of any object based on recognition of its image, or the establishment that certain parameters of the object fall within acceptable limits. Based on these conclusions, certain decisions can then be made about the object or the production process. These conclusions are formed by comparing the results of the analysis with a prestored set of standard criteria. These standard criteria describe the expected characteristics of the image and are developed either through a programmed model of the image or by building an average profile of previously examined objects. the two most commonly used methods of image interpretation are feature weighting and template matching.

- Feature weighting. In cases in which image features must be measured to interpret an image, a simple factor weighting method may be used to consider the relative contribution of each feature to the analysis. For example, when identifying a valve stem from among a group of stems of several sizes the image area may not be sufficient by itself to ensure a positive identification. The measurement of height may add some additional information, as may the determination of the centroid of the image. Each feature would be compared with a standard for a goodness-of-fit measurement. Features that are known to be the most likely indicators of match would be weighted more than others. A weighted total goodness-of-fit score could then be determined to indicate the likelihood that the object has been correctly identified.

- Template matching. In template matching, a mask is electronically generated to match a standard image of an object. When the system inspects other objects in an attempt to recognize them, it aligns the image of each object with that of the standard object. In the case of a perfect match, all pixels would align perfectly. If the objects are not precisely the same, some pixels will fall outside of the standard image. The percentage of pixels in the two images that match is a measure of the goodness of fit. A threshold value can then be assigned to test for "pass" (positive match) or "reject" (no match). A probability factor, which presents the degree of confidence that a correct interpretation has been made, is normally calculated along with the GO/NOT GO conclusion.

Interfacing. A machine vision system is rarely used without some form of interaction with other factory equipment, such as CAD/CAM devices, robots, or host computers. This interaction is the final element of the machine vision process, in which conclusions about the image are translated into actions. In some case, the final action may take the form of cumulative storage of information in a host computer, such as counting the number of parts in various categories for inventory control. In other situations, a final action may be a specific motion such as the transfer of parts into different conveyors, depending on their characteristics. The use of vision systems for control purposes is increasingly being performed through the combination of vision systems and robots. In this case, the vision system acts to greatly expand the flexibility of the robot.

AUTOMATIC GAGING AND PROCESS CONTROL[13]

Automatic control over forming, machining, inspection, and assembly ensures greater productivity and lower costs, higher quality, and maximum use of machine capability. Control units must be accurate, have high-speed response, and be unaffected by vibration, oil, dirt, and coolant.

Practically all dimensions, conditions, or spatial relationships can be automatically inspected, including internal and external diameters, length, depth, taper, out of round, and geometrical conditions such as squareness, parallelism, concentricity, and center distance. Advances in electronic circuitry permit almost all configuration of workpieces to be inspected during all stages of the manufacturing process. Parts with large interruptions can be moved or rotated through gage fingers and measured to an accuracy of 20 μin. (0.5 μm) by damping, filtering, or by electronically detecting the interruptions and disregarding the resulting size change.

Automatic gage systems often include statistical process control features to ensure that corrections are made to the process only when the corrections are warranted. For example, if one workpiece in 100 measures oversize because of some periodic malfunction in the process, statistical controls will cause the system to disregard the measurement and not provide a correction to the workpiece.

Gaging Feasibility. Among the variables to be considered in automatic gaging are part size and shape, material and finish, production rate, tolerances, part handling, cleanliness of part, type of gage element, and inspection rate. Interchangeable and adjustable tooling enable a gage to handle different parts, sizes, and tolerances. To accommodate slightly misaligned holes or locations, automatic gages are sometimes designed with floating-type gaging elements. If a part's size or shape prevents it from being gaged in one operation, it is better to inspect the close tolerances first. This prevents wasting the expense of checking the broader tolerances first only to have the part rejected later.

Usually, locating surfaces for the gaging operation should be the same as those used in the machining operation. However, for final or assembly inspection they may be based on the function or end use of the part. A large variety of part transfer devices are used in automatic gages, such as walking beam devices, endless belts, gravity feeds, or robots.

With the advent of the computer, it has become practical to design automatic gages that can separate size tolerances from location tolerances at one gaging station. To obtain increased (faster) speed, this type of gage may employ laser gaging or vision (video) gaging. These gages do not rely on a fixed location of the part, but will determine the location of the datum surfaces and inspect in relation to them. Although air, air-electric, or electronic automatic gages require interchangeable or adjustable gage heads or tooling to handle different part sizes or tolerances, video systems need only to be programmed to inspect a wide variety of parts. With tutorial, menu-driven (software), user friendly programming, video automatic systems are easy to change from one part to another. Once the program is written, it is only a matter of calling up the new program from the system memory. Flexible, programmable gaging systems using CNC logic and LVDT transducers are also available. These systems can provide higher accuracy than optical systems or coordinate measuring machines and are designed to operate in a harsh shop environment. In addition to providing totally automatic parts measurement, these systems can directly control one or more machining processes by sending statistically based compensation commands directly to the machine tool.

The computer has blurred the dividing line between manual and automatic gages. For instance, the coordinate measuring machine (CMM) was always known as a manual device because it depended on an operator to position the probe in relation to the surfaces being gaged. However, the use of the sensing or touch probe and the computer to direct the motions of the probe holder have made a semiautomatic system out of the CMM. With automatic loading, the CMM would be completely automatic in operation.

The following questions are presented as a guide to assist the manufacturing engineer in deciding on the exact type of process control to use. The questions highlight some of the distinctions used in defining the connections between the product measurement and the process correction.

1. What part variability is to be processed?
   a. Dedicated to single part.
   b. For family of parts.
   c. For batches of unrelated parts.
2. What type of machine tool is to be used?
   a. Single-purpose.
   b. Machining center.
   c. CNC lathe.
   d. Dial machine.
   e. Linear transfer line.

f. Manufacturing cell.

g. FMS.

3. How is part to be transferred?

a. Into the machine tool.

b. Into the gage.

c. Out of the system.

4. What are the objectives of gaging and process control?

5. How timely is the correction to the process?

a. Corrections are made on the very piece.

b. Corrections are made on the very next piece.

c. Corrections are made several pieces later.

d. Corrections are made on a statistical basis.

6. When is the measuring done?

a. While cutting the workpiece.

b. While not cutting.

7. Where is the measuring done?

a. On the machine tool.

b. Off the machine tool.

8. What is the environment?

a. Shop floor—"in-process."

b. Clean room/QC area.

9. What is the measuring capability?

a. Dedicated gaging—specialized for a given part.

b. Flexible gaging—suited for a family of parts.

c. General-purpose—suited for almost any part produced on the machine tool

10. How good does the gage have to be?

a. Repeatability.

b. Accuracy.

11. How much processing is performed on the measured data?

a. Makes a single measurement and displays it.

b. Makes measurements of different product features and calculates their relationships.

c. Makes many measurements and stores the readings.

d. Measures, stores, and processes many data points statistically.

12. How is gaging information linked to the process control?

a. Measurements are taken for historical purposes only.

b. Measurements are taken and QC tells operations about the results.

c. Measurements are taken by manufacturing personnel and they make corrections.

d. Measurements are taken and automatically fed into the machine tool for correction.

Types of Systems. Automatic gaging devices are usually referred to by function or position in the manufacturing process: as preprocess gages (inspection before machining), in-process gages (inspection during machining), postprocess gages (inspection after machining), final inspection gages, and assembly gages. Combinations of various types of gaging can provide fully automatic control over dimensional size from the moment the part enters the manufacturing process through assembly.

Preprocess Gaging. In preprocess gaging, the part is inspected before being loaded into the machine tool to ensure proper conditions of stock and location of machining area. Preprocess gaging helps to avoid damage to the machine and/or tooling, eliminates the expense of machining parts with insufficient stock, and extends tool life by ensuring that only correct parts are fed to the manufacturing process.

In-Process Gaging. With in-process gaging, the gage measures the part during metal removal and stops the process when the correct size is reached. With the advent of the flexible machining system concept there is more demand for in-process gaging to control the indexing and/or changing of the tooling.

Part shape and tolerances, type of machining, method of chucking, and the ability of the machine to utilize the gaging signal determine the type of in-process gaging employed. Earlier applications tended to be air or air-electric gaging. More recently, the flexibility of electronic gaging has led to it being the most commonly used system. The noncontact capabilities of electro-optical gaging and the ease with which it may be interfaced to computers and control systems have sparked interest in that approach.

Postprocess Gaging. Postprocess gaging has been the most common type of automatic gaging, with the part being gaged after the manufacturing operation is completed. Feedback signals can be sent to the producing machine to warn, adjust, or shut down the machine if faulty parts are being produced. Frequently, automatic classification and segregation of parts by dimensional size is performed by postprocess gages. The postprocess gage may also function as the preprocess gage for a subsequent operation.

Many earlier postprocess automatic gages employed air gaging or air-electric gaging; some even used fluidic logic systems. Air-electronic systems are used primarily when there are internal dimensions to be checked and high speed is required. The dominant system used today is the solid-state electronic gage, which is fast in operation, highly accurate, and readily interfaced with microprocessors and computers.

Final Inspection Gages. Final inspection gages are usually high-speed gages that inspect 100% of the output of a line of manufacturing machines. They may inspect as many as 25,000 parts per hour, but more commonly will inspect at a rate of several thousand parts per hour. Frequently they may categorize the parts by size and segregate salvageable parts from the rejects. Data may be kept relating to total throughput and individual categories.

Assembly Gaging. An automatic assembly gage may be used for preassembly gaging, selective fit assembly, or postassembly inspection. Electronic gaging circuits are normally used in automatic assembly for both pre and postassembly inspection. Parts are inspected for dimensional correctness and selective assembly.

The automatic assembly of a taper-rolling bearing illustrates how this system works. In operation, a preassembly gage checks the diameter and flange thickness of the inner race to determine the correct roller size to be assembled within a given ring. Then the gage feeds a signal to one of six preselected-size storage hoppers to release 18 rollers to the assembly station where race, rollers, and cage are assembled into a bearing of predetermined tolerance. The bearing is then inspected under a revolving-load condition for torque, noise level, and standout, the latter usually being checked with a linear displacement transducer of the LVDT type. Standout is the distance that the back face of the cone extends from the cup. Bearings are segregated as acceptable or into reject classes based on noise, torque, or standout.

Process Control. Gaging systems used for machine size control are most often used on external grinders, ID grinders, centerless grinders, and double disc grinders to precisely locate parts, indicate wheel infeed, measure wheel wear, and measure and control part size.

They are also used extensively in automatic transfer lines to monitor each station and correct for size variations or to halt the process in the event that catastrophies caused by tool breakage occur.

There are two types of process control systems in use: inprocess and postprocess. In-process gages are used to measure the workpiece during grinding and control the grinder wheel slide to produce workpieces within the desired tolerance limits. Postprocess gages measure the workpiece after it has been ground and provide a size offset that will apply a correction to the next workpiece to be ground.

An increasing number of gaging systems are also being used for turning applications and for automatic assembly equipment. In turning, the gage is often used to measure the location of the cutting tool in reference to the workpiece and correct for variations that occur. It is also used in postprocess applications to measure the workpiece after it has been turned, then provide any necessary correction to the cutting tool that will apply to the subsequent workpiece. Additional information on automatic gaging systems can be found in Chapter 10, Grinding Fixtures.

Figure 16-108a, shows a typical application of a gaging system mounted on a plunge grinder. The gage measures the workpiece while it is being ground, and the size of the workpiece is displayed continuously on the amplifier meter.

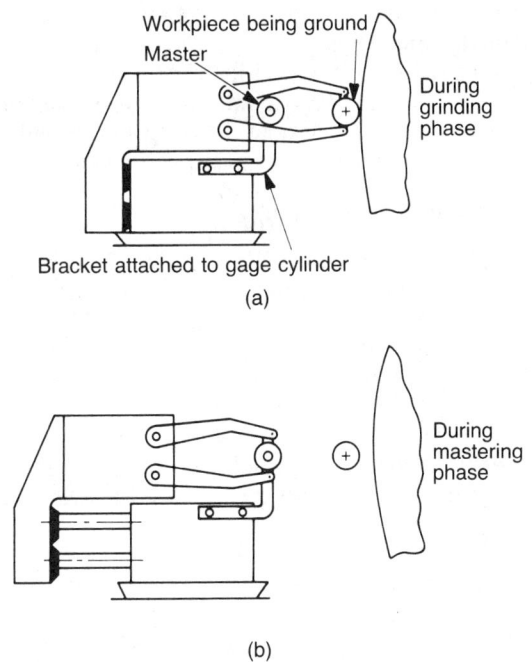

Fig. 16-108 Typical application of a gaging system mounted on a plunge grinder. (*Courtesy Control Gaging, Inc.*)

In setting up the system, either a master workpiece is used for setup or a workpiece is ground manually and then gaged with bench-type gaging equipment. The gage amplifier is then set to the correct reading on the meter while the gage fingers are positioned on the ground workpiece.

In operation, with the gage fingers measuring the diameter of the workpiece, the grinding proceeds at a fast rate until the workpiece nears final size, at which time a preset control in the gage system causes the infeed rate of the wheel slide to decrease to a slower rate. When the workpiece is within 0.001 in. (0.025 mm) or less from the desired size, a second gage preset control point causes an additional decrease in the infeed rate. This allows the desired size to be approached at a slow rate, which improves the finish and roundness and causes the final size to be held to a closer tolerance. When the gage system measures final size, the gage causes the wheel slide to retract to the rear position.

In production grinding, economic considerations dictate that metal should be removed as rapidly as possible. This can result in a large force buildup (workforce pressure) between the grinding wheel and the workpiece. As this force continues to exist even when the infeed movement of the wheel is stopped, it is sometimes necessary to allow the workpiece pressure to dissipate before final size is reached. This is known as "sparkout" or "dwell" and is accomplished by stopping the wheel slide when the workpiece is approximately 0.0005 to 0.001 in. (0.013 to 0.025 mm) above final size and then allowing the pressure buildup of the workpiece against the grinding wheel to cause grinding to proceed until either the final size is reached or the pressure is dissipated. The grinding rate at this time is a function of the magnitude of the workpiece pressure and the sharpness of the grinding wheel. In the event that the pressure is dissipated during dwell before final workpiece size is reached, it is necessary to restart the wheel slide infeed movement to attain final size and terminate the grinding cycle.

Figure 16-108b, shows a self-mastering system included in the gage that is used to maintain size of the workpiece by compensating for temperature changes, wear of the gage tips, or accidental bumping of the gage fingers. Whenever the gage is in the retracted position, the gage fingers are positioned on a master, and the gage amplifier detects and automatically resets the gage to the size of the master prior to each grinding cycle. This arrangement provides a system, generally used with automatic machine loading, that will operate unattended for extended periods of time.

ROBOTIC INSPECTION SYSTEMS[14]

Gaging systems can be broadly classified into fixed inspection and flexible inspection systems. Fixed inspection utilizes multiple contacting or noncontacting sensors mounted in a test fixture that holds the part to be inspected. This approach lends itself to the inspection of parts at high throughput rates. However, to switch from one part to another requires changing the test and inspection fixture. Flexible inspection utilizes sensors that are moved along a programmed path trajectory of the part being inspected. This approach lends itself to processing at moderate throughput rates. Changing from one part to another can be accomplished quickly by downloading a new path trajectory program to the machine controller. There are also systems available that move the part on an X-Y slide.

With the recent introduction of sophisticated machine vision systems into the workplace, it is now possible to expand the role of robots in flexible inspection.[15, 16] Recent advances in CAD/CAM technology now make possible the integration of CAD/CAM into robotic systems.[17] This marriage of CAD/CAM with robotics significantly improves the productivity and economies of robot inspection systems.

The application areas for robotic inspection systems can be generalized as follows:

• Moderate throughput rates.
• Frequent part or model changes or model mix.
• Off-line part inspection requiring a large number of measurements.
• Large parts with complex geometry such as cavities.

Advantages and Limitations. Robot-based inspection systems can provide the maximum in flexibility. A variety of sensors can be mounted on the robot wrist. Robots with articulated arms can reach inside of parts with cavities, such as car bodies and appliances. Robots can be programmed to measure reference datum points and planes on a part. Algorithms, using these reference point measurements, can calibrate the part coordinate system, which allows the CAD/CAM database to be integrated into the robotic measuring system. This integration eliminates the need for precision part fixturing, allows real-time adaptive robot path trajectory control, and provides off-line programming of robot path trajectories.

Inspection robots have a number of limitations. As previously pointed out, they can inspect parts only at moderate throughput rates; about 100 parts per hour would be a nominal rate. They are, therefore, not well suited for very high speed production lines where 1000 parts per hour are common. Gaging accuracy is another concern. At the present time, robot gaging systems rely on the repeatability of the robot for the gaging tolerance. Positioning repeatabilities of commercially available robots suitable for inspection applications range from ±0.001 to ±0.008 in. The sensors are typically accurate to one part in 500 to one part in 1000 of the total field of view, which is usually 2 in.

System Components. The main components in a robotic inspection system are the robot, sensors, part presentation device, computer/control system, and software.

Selection. In selecting a robot-based inspection system for a particular application, the following factors must be considered:

- Robot size, repeatability, resolution, and reach.
- Sensor selection.
- Accuracy requirements.
- Process inspection times.

Robot size and geometry are established by the inspection volume specified for a given application. It is important to consider design trends in the parts to be inspected so as to allow for future increases in part size and/or geometry. Sensor selection is largely dependent on the geometrical characteristics of the part features to be inspected.

Inspection accuracies that the system must provide are determined by the product specifications. In selecting equipment, it is important to consider the effects that aging and wear will have on inspection system accuracies. Process inspection times are principally governed by the number of inspection locations, length of robot path trajectories, and robot settling times. Other delays, such as vision image processing times, can be handled in parallel with other system functions using distributed data processing.

The Robot. For inspection applications, the Cartesian-style robot appears most appropriate. Because of its geometric design, the Cartesian robot can provide higher repeatable positioning accuracy than other articulated arm robot styles. Experience has shown that a five-axis robot is adequate for most inspection work. This is because coordinate transformation algorithms can be used to correct sensor limitations imposed by a five-degree-of-freedom robot.

Robot positioning accuracy is determined by the ability to match its actual position in three-dimensional space to the command position called for by the program's position instruction. The error between actual and command positions is caused by a number of factors, including servocomponent design, structural natural frequencies, bearing friction, gear backlash, and load torques. This error is a summation of static and dynamic error components. Bearing friction and steady-state load torques produce static position errors. Structural natural frequencies, inertia load torques, gear backlash, and closed-loop servo gain contribute to dynamic errors. As the robot approaches its command position, it searches for its position by dithering about the position until it stops. This is called settling time. The inspection system must wait for the robot to settle before it can make its measurement.

Robot settling time is a very important performance consideration because it causes a direct tradeoff between measurement accuracy and process inspection time. This tradeoff is shown by the data in Fig. 16-109 which compares robot positioning error distributions for two different settling times. These data were obtained with the robot executing an inspection path program representative of a typical process inspection cycle for a production application. Increasing the settling time by 117% reduced the variability in robot position by 36%; however, process inspection cycle time increased by 19%.

Vision Sensors. There are three type of sensors typically used in gaging systems: (1) one-dimensional sensors, (2) contour sensors, and (3) array sensors. One-dimensional sensors give the range of distance from the sensor to a point on the object. These sensors

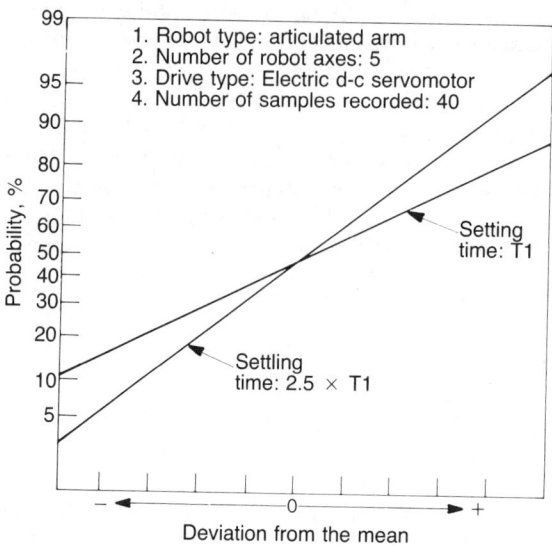

Fig. 16-109 Comparison of robot position repeatability for two different settling times.

use triangulation techniques, where the light source is usually a single-point laser diode set at a known angle from the pickup sensor. The pickup sensor is a one-dimensional linear device, either digital (solid-state line scan) or analog (lateral effect photodiode). The range can be calculated from the position of the reflected light on the linear sensor.

A contour sensor analyzes a line of light across an object: the light is usually from a laser. The laser in the visible range (red) is a gas tube device containing the helium and neon. More recently these are being replaced by solid-state lasers that operate in the near-infrared range. The laser light source provides a point source of light that is converted to a line by using a cylindrical lens or by scanning the light with an oscillating or rotating mirror. It is placed at a known angle to the pickup sensor, which is usually a solid-state array camera. Subpixel techniques are used to obtain the X, Y, and Z values of the line of light across the part to better than one part in 1,000 of the total field of view in the X and Z coordinates. The measurement resolution in the Y coordinate is the scanning resolution, which is typically 240 lines. Triangulation methods are used to locate and measure surfaces, contours, and edges.

An array sensor can be used to take area images of the part for locating features such as holes. This two-dimensional information can be further enhanced by adding a range sensor to obtain Z-axis information, effectively creating a simple but limited three-dimensional device.

One-dimensional sensors can take several thousand measurements per second, while the structured light and area sensors are limited to 60 frames per second; each frame contains several hundred points. The system throughput is slowed down by the postprocessing of the data, not by the data acquisition of the sensor.

Sensor selection is determined by the geometry of the part. Range sensors can be used for point information only and cannot be used to analyze edges, holes, or contours. Structured light sensors are used for edges and contours, but are not well suited for holes. Area sensors work well on holes, but need additional information for use on surfaces and contours. Depending on the part geometry of the application, one or more sensors (either different types or different focal lengths) are mounted on the robot arm to make the measurements.

Computer/Control Systems. A robotic inspection system may be composed of two to four small computers that are required to perform different distributed processing functions. These computers are interconnected by a data communication and control network. This configuration allows a host computer to coordinate and control the robot and sensor(s). For example, a robot vision inspection system could be composed of a host computer or cell controller interconnected to a robot controller and a vision controller. Communications between the vision controller and the robot controller can be direct or through the host computer, with the former most common and preferred.

The communication and control links can be either parallel or serial. Parallel links provide handshaking signals for synchronizing control activities and to handle high-speed transfer of measurement data. Serial data links provide two-way communications to allow the host computer to carry on a dialog with other processors in the system. This capability provides many advantages, and it makes possible many of the advanced control features discussed in the section on system software.

System Software. The host computer required by the robotic inspection system can range from a small microcomputer or programmable controller to a powerful minicomputer, depending on the degree of flexibility desired and level of data processing and storage required. Consequently, the system software can range from a 64K-byte package for a small microcomputer to several million bytes for a large minicomputer. Even the smallest software package should provide, as a minimum, the following functions:

- Initiate and coordinate the process inspection cycle.
- Read in and store sensor measurements data during inspection cycle execution.
- Transform measured data points into real-world coordinates and compare to desired measurement.
- Output process data results in some acceptable report format.
- Provide a limited operator interface to handle calibration and diagnostic requirements.
- Output warning and diagnostic messages to indicate system malfunction and type of error(s).

An example of the flexibility and increased system functions that can be provided by a large software package, running on a powerful minicomputer, is illustrated by the software functional diagram in Fig. 16-110. This configuration is used to operate a robot vision inspection system. In addition to the functions previously described, the software operating system provides the following functions:

- Uploading/downloading of robot path program.
- Robot off-line programming.
- Vision off-line programming.
- Real-time robot program debugging through the computer terminal.
- Integration of the CAD/CAM database into the measuring system.
- Adaptive vision image processing.
- Adaptive real-time robot path trajectory control.
- Measurement of three-dimensional part features using a two-dimensional vision sensor.

The application-specific software can, depending on application requirements, be quite extensive. This software coordinates and controls the robot and sensor(s) to run reference point programs (required for setting up the CAD/CAM coordinate transformation system) and to run process inspection programs. Another function that it usually provides is acting as the database manager for storing processed inspection data. This manager can then retrieve selected portions of this data for outputting, in the proper report format, to a CRT terminal or hard-copy printer.

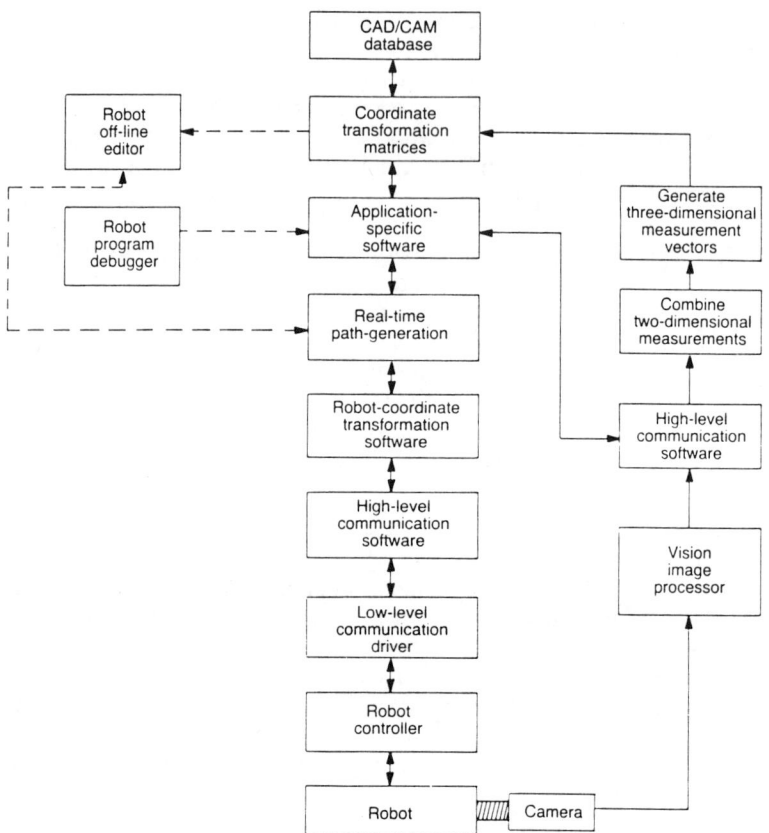

Fig. 16-110 Functional diagram of the software package needed to operate a robot inspection system using vision sensors.

References

1. Charles Wick and Raymond F. Veilleux, eds., "Inspection Equipment and Techniques," *Tool and Manufacturing Engineers Handbook*, Vol. 4, 4th ed. (Dearborn, MI: Society of Manufacturing Engineers, 1987), pp. 3-11 to 3-16.
2. William M. Stocker, Jr., and Diane Heiberg, *Tools of Our Metalworking Trade* (New York: McGraw Hill, Inc., 1982), p. 96.
3. Wick and Veilleux, pp. 3-24 to 3-25.
4. *Ibid.*, pp. 3-25 to 3-28.
5. *Ibid.*, pp. 3-33 to 3-36.
6. *Ibid.*, pp. 3-36 to 3-39, 3-48 to 3-54.
7. George Schaffer, "Taking the Measure of CMMs," *American Machinist* (October 1982), pp. 146-147.
8. *Ibid.*, p. 153.
9. *Ibid.*, p. 158.
10. Wick and Veilleux, pp. 3-54 to 3-59.
11. *Machine Vision Systems: A Summary and Forecast*, 2nd ed. (Lake Geneva, WI: Tech Tran Consultants, 1985), p 1.
12. *Ibid.*, pp. 29-66.
13. Wick and Veilleux, pp. 3-44 to 3-48.
14. *Ibid.*, pp. 3-59 to 3-62.
15. P. Villers, *Recent Proliferation of Industrial Artificial Vision Applications*, SME Technical Paper MS 83-311 (Dearborn, MI: Society of Manufacturing Engineers, 1983).
16. T. Pryor, and W. Pastorius, *Applications of Machine Vision to Parts Inspection and Machine Control in the Piece Part Manufacturing Industries*, SME Technical Paper MS 83-312 (Dearborn, MI: Society of Manufacturing Engineers, 1983).
17. R.L. Simon, "The Marriage Between CAD/CAM System and Robotics" (Bedford, MA: Computer-Vision Corp.).

INDEX

Porous ceramic plates, 3-62
Portable, machines, 9-100
Position, 6-41, 6-44
Positionally toleranced parts, 6-46
Positioning system components, 5-21
Positioning systems, 5-21, 15-12
Post-process gaging, 10-51, 16-110
Pot broaching machines, 12-6
Potting fixtures, 16-55
Pot-type internal-broaching fixtures, 12-37
Pour method, 4-36
Powdered metal parts, 9-37
Power chucks, 9-43, 9-75
Power hacksawing, 11-3
Power stroking, 10-66
Power workholding, 3-75, 7-65
Practical wedge angles, 3-33
Precision air chucks, 9-67
Precision boring, 9-93, 9-95, 9-97, 9-108
Precision boring machines, 9-93, 9-95, 9-97
Precision center assemblies, 4-25
Precision expanding mandrels, 9-17
Precision sine vises, 10-17
Precision vises, 10-17
Predesign analysis, 1-1–1-58
Predesign checklists, 1-3
Premachined section forms, 1-40
Preprocess gaging, 10-50, 16-109
Pressing fixtures, 15-1, 15-27–15-35, 15-38
Pressure methods, 4-36
Pressure plates, 9-76
Pressure rings, 1-11
Printed circuit boards, 16-61
Probes, 16-96, 16-98, 16-102
Probe system components, 16-98
Process control, 16-107–16-112
Processed wood, 4-8
Product analysis, 1-2
Product data, 1-12
Production rates, 8-12, 15-94
Production-type centerless grinders, 10-6
Production-type horizontal spindle-internal grinders, 10-8
Productive capacity, 2-3
Product quality, 1-2
Profile control tolerances, 6-24–6-28
Profile milling, 7-2, 7-41, 7-49, 7-50
Programmers, 5-10, 5-14
Program zero, 4-1, 5-64
Progressive milling, 7-1
Projection welding dies, 15-83
Projection welding fixtures, 15-79
Projector tracer followers, 16-75
Propellers, 7-50
Prototypes, 4-32
Pull action toggle clamps, 3-38
Pull bars, 10-42
Pull dowels, 5-19

Pull-down broaching, 12-3, 12-41, 12-44
Pull-up broaching, 12-3
Pull-up broach layouts, 12-53, 12-55
Pump jigs, 4-16, 4-17, 8-23
Punching, 12-1, 15-5
Push-down broaching, 12-2
Push-out collets, 9-26, 9-27, 9-28

Q

Quick-acting cams, 8-19
Quick-acting chuck changing systems, 14-22
Quick-acting screw clamps, 3-19
Quick change pallets, 5-71
Quick change systems, 14-17–14-29
Quick changing jaws, 9-68

R

Rabbet and dado joints, 4-29
Rack-and-pinion clamps, 3-44
Radial drilling machines, 8-2
Radial indexing, 2-49
Radial locating, 2-4, 2-8, 2-16
Radial riveting, 15-8, 15-9
Raised workpiece supports, 2-50
Rake angles, 9-8
Ram head machines, 7-2
Ram strokes, 13-5
Raw material dimensional variances, 2-3
Reaming, 8-1, 8-45, 8-51, 8-69, 8-78, 15-21
Reciprocal milling, 7-1, 7-37
Reciprocating in-feed tables, 12-14
Rectangular chucks, 3-62
Rectangular tooling plates, 5-40
Reinforcement, 4-34
Remote control valves, 3-85
Replaceable jaw design, 14-35
Reprogrammable fixtures, 15-119
Resistance to shock, 4-7
Resistance to splitting, 4-7
Resistance welding, 16-57
Rest buttons, 2-10, 2-12, 2-21, 5-48, 5-54
Rest pads, 2-19
Rest pins, 10-26
Retainer assemblies, 4-24
Retractable jaw chucks, 9-65, 10-1
Retractable spring-loaded plungers, 3-19
Retracting clamps, 7-74
Reusability, 5-13
Reversible clamps, 9-89
Right-angle faceplate fixtures, 9-85, 10-58
Right-angle lathes, 5-26, 9-4
Rigidity, 1-3, 5-3, 5-4
Ring punches, 15-23
Rings, 9-22
Riser blocks, 5-14, 7-62, 7-66
Riser plates, 5-41